J.K. LASSER'S™

YOUR INCOME TAX 2011

PROFESSIONAL EDITION

Prepared by the

J.K. LASSER INSTITUTE™

John Wiley & Sons, Inc.

New York • Chichester • Weinheim • Brisbane • Singapore • Toronto

Staff for This Book

J.K. Lasser Editorial

Elliott Eiss, Member of the New York Bar, Senior Editor
Barbara Weltman, Member of the New York Bar, Contributing Editor
Angelo C. Jack, Senior Production Editor
Carolyn Francis, Copyediting and Proofreading
Helen Chin, Indexing
William Hamill, Production Assistant
Kimberly Q. Purnell, Production Assistant

John Wiley & Sons, Inc.

John Wiley & Sons, Inc.
111 River Street
Hoboken, NJ 07030

Published by John Wiley & Sons, Inc., Hoboken, New Jersey
Published simultaneously in Canada

For general information on our other products and services or for technical support, please contact our Customer Care Department within the United States at (800) 762-2974, outside the United States at (317) 572-3993, or fax (317) 572-4002.

Wiley also publishes its books in a variety of electronic formats. Some content that appears in print may not be available in electronic books. For more information about Wiley products, visit our web site at www.wiley.com.

ISBN 978-0470-59721-7

ISBN 978-0132-59921-4

Printed in the United States of America

10 9 8 7 6 5 4 3 2 1

Seventy-Fourth Edition

How To Use the Professional Edition of *Your Income Tax 2011*

Tax alert symbols. Throughout the text of *Your Income Tax*, these special symbols alert you to advisory tips about filing your federal tax return and tax planning opportunities:

Filing Tip or Filing Instruction............... A **Filing Tip** or **Filing Instruction** helps you prepare your 2010 return.

Planning Reminder.......................... A **Planning Reminder** highlights year-end tax strategies for 2010 or planning opportunities for 2011 and later years.

Caution .... A **Caution** points out potential pitfalls to avoid and areas where IRS opposition may be expected.

Law Alert................................ A **Law Alert** indicates recent changes in the tax law and pending legislation before Congress.

Court Decision............................ A **Court Decision** highlights key rulings from the Tax Court and other federal courts.

IRS Alert................................ An **IRS Alert** highlights key rulings and announcements from the IRS.

The PROFESSIONAL EDITION of *Your Income Tax* is divided into two volumes.

Volume I includes the complete 2011 edition of *Your Income Tax*, which for over 73 years has helped subscribers solve their tax problems and has proven to be a solid reference work for tax professionals.

Volume II expands the usefulness of *Your Income Tax* for tax professionals by providing citations of tax authorities and sections devoted to practice before the IRS.

VOLUME I: YOUR INCOME TAX

This volume includes the 2011 edition of *Your Income Tax* (*see* the contents starting on page v). The index begins on page 961.

VOLUME II: PROFESSIONAL TAX PRACTICE

This volume includes the following technical tax information:

TAX LAW AUTHORITIES (Part 9). Here is an explanation of tax authorities—legislative, administrative, and judicial—and their relative importance in the practice of tax law. Part 9 begins on page 793.

CITATIONS OF AUTHORITY (Part 10). Here are key authorities for the text of *Your Income Tax* that can save you time and effort in researching income tax problems. The authorities cited are the Internal Revenue Code, IRS regulations and rulings, and court decisions. Law review and professional tax journal articles also are cited as an additional aid. Part 10 begins on page 799.

PRACTICE BEFORE THE IRS (Part 11). This section discusses how to handle tax audits and negotiate with the IRS. Part 11 begins on page 919.

Contents Chapter by Chapter

Special Tax Rules for Senior Citizens 575

Members of the Armed Forces 585

How To Treat Foreign Earned Income 593

What's New for 2010

For an update on tax developments and a free download of the *e-Supplement* to this book, visit us online at *www.jklasser.com.*

Tax News for 2010

Item—	***Highlight—***
"Extenders" package for expired benefits pending	When this book went to press, Congress had not yet passed a bill extending to 2010 numerous provisions that expired at the end of 2009. These include the deductions for state and local general sales taxes *(16.3)*, tuition and fees *(33.13)*, and educator expenses *(12.2)*, the additional standard deductions for real estate taxes and net disaster losses *(13.3)*, and higher deduction limits for charitable donations of qualified conservation contributions *(14.10, 14.17)*. An extension is needed to exclude from 2010 income direct transfers from IRAs to charity *(8.8)*. A "patch" is needed for the 2010 AMT exemption to prevent the exemption from dropping drastically *(23.1)*. An extension is needed to allow all nonrefundable personal credits to be claimed against the AMT *(23.5, 25.1)*. *See* the *e-Supplement at jklasser.com* for an update on the legislation.
Small business tax relief enacted	The Small Business Jobs Act of 2010 (signed into law 9/27/10) enacts mostly temporary tax relief provisions. Under the new law, net earnings are reduced by the deduction for health insurance premiums in figuring self-employment tax for 2010 *(45.1)*. The first-year expensing limit *(42.3)* for 2010 and 2011 is doubled to $500,000; this limit is reduced if investments in qualifying property during the year exceed $2 million. Expensing is allowed for 2010 and 2011 investments of up to $250,000 in qualified leasehold, restaurant, and retail improvements *(42.15)*. First-year bonus depreciation equal to 50% of basis has been extended to 2010 investments in eligible property *(42.21)*. The bonus increases the depreciation limit for cars, trucks, and vans purchased new in 2010 by $8,000 if used over 50% for business *(43.4)*. For 2010 only, the deduction for business start-up ex-penses *(40.11)* is doubled to $10,000, with the limit reduced by the amount of start-up costs exceeding $60,000. Cell phones are removed from the "listed property" category starting in 2010, thereby eliminating the strict substantiation rules and restrictions on cell phone expensing or depreciation *(42.10)*. For 2010 only, the carryback period for general business credits is extended to five years for businesses with average gross receipts up to $50 million *(40.26)*. A 100% exclusion will be allowed for gain on the sale of small business C corporation stock held over five years, but only for stock acquired after September 27, 2010 and before January 1, 2011 *(5.7)*. *See* the *e-Supplement at jklasser.com* for details on the new law provisions.
Fate of Bush tax cuts	The fate of the Bush Administration tax cuts enacted in 2001 and 2003, which are scheduled to expire at the end of 2010, was not yet settled when this book went to press, although support appeared to be growing for a temporary extension, possibly 1-2 years, for all the Bush tax cuts, including those that benefit high-income taxpayers. Failure to enact an extension would result in the loss of numerous tax benefits, such as: the 10% bracket would disappear, the top two rates would increase to 36% and 39.6%, the maximum capital gain rate would increase to 20%, dividends would be taxed as ordinary income, marriage penalty relief would be eliminated, tax credits such as the child tax credit and dependent care credit would be scaled back. *See* the *e-Supplement* at *jklasser.com* for an update.
Small business health tax credit	Employers that pay at least half of the health insurance premiums for their employees in 2010 may be able to claim a 35% credit on Form 8941, but stringent eligibility rules apply *(41.14)*.

Tax News for 2010

Item—	*Highlight—*
Estate tax repealed for 2010; basis rules for heirs	The scheduled repeal of the estate tax for estates of individuals dying in 2010 was allowed to take effect *(39.7)*. Some heirs of large 2010 estates may not receive a full step-up in basis to fair market value for the inherited assets. The executor may designate up to $1.3 million of property as eligible for a basis step-up, plus an additional $3 million for property passing to a surviving spouse. For amounts over these limits, the heir's basis is the decedent's basis (carryover basis) in the property *(39.7)*. The basis rules may be changed by the estate tax legislation that Congress is considering for years after 2010. *See* the *e-Supplement* at *jklasser.com* for estate tax developments.
Alternative minimum tax (AMT) exemption for 2010	The legislative "patch" needed to prevent a drastic reduction in the AMT exemptions *(23.1)* for 2010 was part of the "extenders" package being considered by Congress when this book went to press; *see* the *e-Supplement* at *jklasser.com* for the exemption amounts.
First-time homebuyer credit	The homebuyer credit *(25.23)* is allowed to eligible "first-time homebuyers" and "long-time residents" who purchased their home through April 30, 2010. Those who entered into a binding contract by April 30, 2010 to close by June 30, 2010, and who otherwise qualify, can claim the credit if title was acquired by September 30, 2010. These deadlines are extended into 2011 if you or your spouse were a member of the U.S. uniformed services or Foreign Service, or an employee of the intelligence community on qualified official extended duty outside the United States for at least 90 days between January 1, 2009 and April 30, 2010. If you claimed a credit for a 2008 home purchase, you must begin to repay it in 15 installments starting with your 2010 return, but you may have to repay the entire credit claimed for 2008 or 2009 if in 2010 you sold the residence or stopped using it as your principal residence *(25.23)*.
Self-employment tax for 2010	Net self-employment earnings of up to $106,800 (no change from 2009) are subject to the 12.4% Social Security rate for 2010 *(45.3)*. As noted above, the newly enacted Small Business Jobs Act of 2010 allows a self-employed taxpayer to reduce net earnings by deductible health insurance premiums when figuring self-employment tax liability for 2010. *See 45.3–45.4* for details on how the IRS will implement the reduction on the 2010 tax forms.
IRA and Roth IRA contributions; special deferral rule for 2010 conversions to Roth IRA	For 2010, the contribution limit for traditional IRAs *(8.2)* and Roth IRAs *(8.20)* remains $5,000, or $6,000 for those age 50 or older. The deduction limit for 2010 contributions to a traditional IRA is phased out *(8.4)* for active plan participants with modified AGI (MAGI) of over $56,000 and under $66,000 for a single person or head of household, or over $89,000 and under $109,000 for married persons filing jointly. The phaseout range is MAGI of over $167,000 and under $177,000 for a spouse who is not an active plan participant and files jointly with a spouse who is an active plan participant. The 2010 Roth IRA contribution limit is phased out *(8.20)* for a single person or head of household with MAGI over $105,000 and under $120,000, and for married persons filing jointly with MAGI over $167,000 and under $177,000. A conversion to a Roth IRA in 2010 is allowed regardless of income and filing status *(8.21)*. A rollover is taxable (unless attributable to after-tax contributions), but the taxable amount for a conversion made during 2010 may be deferred to 2011 and 2012, half in each year, unless an election is made to report the entire amount as income for 2010 *(8.21)*.
Required minimum distributions reinstated for 2010	The law that waived required minimum distributions for 2009 was not extended to 2010. A required minimum distribution for 2010 must be received by individuals age 70½ and older from their traditional IRA *(8.13)* or employer's defined contribution retirement plan *(7.13)*, as well as by beneficiaries *(8.14, 7.13)*.

Tax News for 2010

Item—	*Highlight—*
Unemployment compensation fully taxed	Recipients of unemployment compensation in 2010 are fully taxed on the benefits *(2.5)*. The exclusion that was allowed for the first $2,400 of benefits in 2009 was not extended to 2010.
Health coverage exclusion extended to children under age 27	The exclusions for employer-paid health coverage *(3.2)* and employer reimbursements of medical expenses *(3.3)* apply to an employee's children who are under age 27 at the end of the year, regardless of whether they can be claimed as dependents by the employee.
Restriction on health FSA reimbursement of over-the-counter medications after 2010	Starting in 2011, a health flexible spending arrangement cannot make a tax-free reimbursement of an over-the-counter medication unless it has been prescribed by a physician or it is insulin *(3.16)*.
Personal casualty and theft losses	The "extenders" package (*see* first item above) will determine the 2010 floor for each casualty or theft loss of personal-use property. The $500 floor that applied for 2009 is likely to be extended for 2010; otherwise, the floor drops to $100 *(18.12)*. The rule that exempted 2009 personal-use property losses due to federally declared disasters from the 10% AGI floor is also likely to be extended to 2010 *(18.12)*. *See* the *e-Supplement at jklasser.com* for an update.
Rollover from qualified plan by nonspouse beneficiaries	In plan years starting after 2009, nonspouse beneficiaries of deceased employees must be allowed to roll over a distribution in a trustee-to-trustee transfer to an IRA that is treated as an inherited IRA subject to required minimum distribution rules *(7.8, 7.14)*.
IRS mileage rates	For 2010, the IRS standard business mileage rate *(43.1)* is 50 cents per mile. For medical *(17.9)* and moving expenses *(12.3)*, the rate is 16.5 cents per mile and the rate for charitable volunteers *(14.4)* is 14 cents per mile.
Vehicle depreciation limits	The maximum depreciation deduction (including expensing) for a car placed in service in 2010 is $11,060 if bonus depreciation applies, otherwise $3,060. For a light truck or van, the maximum deduction is $11,160 with bonus depreciation, or $3,160 without the special allowance *(43.4)*.
Additional child tax credit	The child tax credit is refundable for 2010 to the extent of 15% of earned income in excess of $3,000, the same as for 2009 *(25.3)*.
Annual exclusion for gifts	For gift tax purposes, the per-donee exclusion for gifts of present interests in 2010 is $13,000, the same as for 2009 *(39.2)*.
Advanced earned income credit	2010 is the last year for which advance payments of the earned income credit can be made *(25.13)*.
Foreign earned income and housing exclusions	The maximum foreign earned income exclusion for 2010 is $91,500 *(36.3)*. The maximum housing exclusion is generally $12,810, but the IRS may increase the exclusion for high cost localities *(36.4)*.

Key Tax Numbers for 2010

Exemptions

Each allowable exemption *(21.1)*	$ 3,650
No Phaseout for 2010 *(21.12)*	
Joint return/Qualifying widow(er)	$ 250,200 / $ 372,700
Head of Household	$ 208,500 / $ 331,000
Single	$ 166,800 / $ 289,300
Married filing separately	$ 125,100 / $ 186,350

Standard Deduction *(13.1)*

Joint return/Qualifying widow(er)	$ 11,400
Head of Household	$ 8,400
Single	$ 5,700
Married filing separately	$ 5,700
Dependents-minimum deduction *(13.5)*	$ 950
Additional deduction if age 65 or older, or blind *(13.4)*	
Married-per spouse, filing jointly or separately	$ 1,100 ($2,200 for age and blindness)
Qualifying widow(er)	$ 1,100 ($2,200 for age and blindness)
Single or head of household	$ 1,400 ($2,800 for age and blindness)

Long-term Care Premiums *(17.15)*

Limit on premium allowed as medical expense	
Age 40 or under	$ 330
Over 40 but not over 50	$ 620
Over 50 but not over 60	$ 1,230
Over 60 but not over 70	$ 3,290
Over 70	$ 3,110

IRA Contributions

Traditional IRA contribution limit *(8.2)*	$ 5,000
Additional contribution if age 50 or older	$ 1,000
Deduction phaseout for active plan participant *(8.4)*	
Single or head of household	$ 56,000 – $ 66,000
Married filing jointly, two participants	$ 89,000 – $ 109,000
Married filing jointly, one participant	
Participant spouse	$ 89,000 – $ 109,000
Non-participant spouse	$ 167,000 – $ 177,000
Married filing separately, live together, either participates	$ 0 – $ 10,000
Married filing separately, live apart all year	
Participant spouse	$ 56,000 – $ 66,000
Non-participant spouse	no phaseout
Roth IRA contribution limit *(8.20)*	$ 5,000
Additional contribution if age 50 or older	$ 1,000
Contribution limit phaseout range	
Single, head of household	$ 105,000 – $ 120,000
Married filing separately, live apart all year	$ 105,000 – $ 120,000
Married filing jointly, or qualifying widow(er)	$ 167,000 – $ 177,000
Married filing separately, live together at any time	$ 0 – $ 10,000

Elective deferral limits

401(k), 403(b), 457 plans *(7.18)*	$ 16,500
Salary-reduction SEP *(8.16)*	$ 16,500
SIMPLE IRA *(8.17)*	$ 11,500
Additional contribution if age 50 or older	
401(k), 403(b), governmental 457 and SEP plans *(7.18, 8.16)*	$ 5,500
SIMPLE IRA *(8.17)*	$ 2,500

Education

American Opportunity credit limit *(33.8)*	$2,500
Lifetime Learning credit limit *(33.9)*	$2,000
Phaseout of Hope/American Opportunity credit*(33.10)*	
Married filing jointly	$ 160,000–$ 180,000
Single, head of household, or qualifying widow(er)	$80,000–$ 90,000
Phaseout of Lifetime Learning credit *(33.10)*	
Married filing jointly	$ 100,000–$ 120,000
Single, head of household, or qualifying widow(er)	$ 50,000–$ 60,000
Student loan interest deduction limit *(33.14)*	$2,500
Phaseout of deduction limit	
Married filing jointly	$120,000–$150,000
Single, head of household, or qualifying widow(er)	$60,000–$75,000
Coverdell ESA limit *(33.11)*	$2,000
Phaseout of limit	
Married filing jointly	$190,000–$220,000
All others	$95,000–$110,000
Tuition and fees deduction (assuming deduction is extended by Congress *(33.13)*)	
Tuition and fees deduction-tier 1 limit	$4,000
Income cut-off	
• Married filing jointly	$130,000
• Single, head of household, or qualifying widow(er)	$65,000
Tuition and fees deduction limit-tier 2 limit	$2,000
Income cut-off	
• Married filing jointly	$160,000
• Single, head of household, or qualifying widow(er)	$80,000

Capital gain rates-assets held over one year *(5.3)*

If otherwise subject to 10% or 15% rate	0%
If otherwise subject to rate over 15%	15%
Collectibles gain-maximum rate	28%
Unrecaptured Section 1250 gain on depreciated real estate-maximum rate	25%

Qualified dividends tax rate *(4.1)*

If otherwise subject to 10% or 15% rate	0%
If otherwise subject to rate over 15%	15%

IRS mileage rates

Business *(43.1)*	50 cents
Medical *(17.9)* and Moving *(12.3)*	16.5 cents
Charitable volunteers *(14.4)*	14 cents

Exclusion for employer provided transportation *(3.8)*

Transit passes and commuter vehicle transport	$230/month
Qualified parking	$230/month
Qualified bicycle commuting	$ 20/ month

PART 1

Filing Basics

In this part, you will learn these income tax basics:

- Whether you must file a return
- When and where to file your return
- Which tax form to file
- What filing status you qualify for
- When filing separately is an advantage for married persons
- How to qualify as head of household
- How filing rules for resident aliens and nonresident aliens differ
- How to claim personal exemption deductions for yourself, your spouse, and your dependents.

Do You Have to File a 2010 Tax Return?

If you are—	*You must file if gross income is at least*
Single	
Under age 65	$ 9,350
Age 65 or older on or before January 1, 2010	10,750
Married and living together at the end of 2010	
Filing a joint return—both spouses under age 65	18,700
Filing a joint return—one spouse age 65 or older	19,800
Filing a joint return—both spouses age 65 or older	20,900
Filing a separate return (any age)	3,650
Married and living apart at the end of 2010	
Filing a joint or separate return	3,650
Head of a household maintained for a child or other relative *(1.12)*	
Under age 65	12,050
Age 65 or older on or before January 1, 2010	13,450
Widowed in 2009 or 2008 and have a dependent child *(1.11)*	
Under age 65	15,050
Age 65 or older on or before January 1, 2011	16,150

Marital status. For federal tax purposes, only a man and woman in a legal union as husband and wife are considered married. For 2010 returns, marital status is generally determined as of December 31, 2010. Thus, if you were divorced or legally separated during 2010, you are not considered married for 2010 tax purposes, and you must use the filing threshold for single persons unless you qualify as a head of household *(1.12)*, or you remarried in 2010 and are filing a joint return with your new spouse.

If your spouse died in 2010 and you were living together on the date of death, use the filing threshold shown for married persons living together at the end of 2010. If you were not living together on the date of death, the $3,650 filing threshold applies, unless you remarried during 2010 and are filing jointly with your new spouse.

Age 65. Whether you are age 65 or older is generally determined as of the end of the year, but if your 65th birthday is on January 1, 2011, you are treated as being age 65 at the end of 2010.

Gross income. Gross income is generally all the income that you received in 2010, except for items specifically exempt from tax.

Include wages and tips *(Chapter 2)*, self-employment income *(Chapter 45)*, taxable scholarships *(Chapter 33)*, taxable interest and dividends *(Chapter 4)*, capital gains *(Chapter 5)*, taxable pensions and annuities *(Chapter 7)*, rents *(Chapter 9)*, and trust distributions *(Chapter 11)*. Home sale proceeds that are tax free *(Chapter 29)* and tax-free foreign earned income *(Chapter 36) are* considered gross income for purposes of the filing test.

Exclude tax-exempt interest *(Chapter 4)*, tax-free fringe benefits *(Chapter 3)*, qualifying scholarships *(Chapter 33)*, and life insurance *(Chapter 11)*. Also exclude Social Security benefits *unless* (1) you are married filing separately and you lived with your spouse at any time during 2010, or (2) 50% of net Social Security benefits plus other gross income and any tax-exempt interest exceeds $25,000 ($32,000 if married filing jointly). If 1 or 2 applies, the taxable part of Social Security benefits as determined in *34.3* is included in your gross income.

Other situations when you must file. Even if you are not required to file under the gross income tests, you must file a 2010 return if:

- You are self-employed and you owe self-employment tax because your net self-employment earnings for 2010 are $400 or more *(Chapter 45), or*
- You are entitled to a refund of taxes withheld from your wages *(Chapter 26)* or a refund based on any of these credits: the earned income credit for working families; the Making Work Pay credit, the government retiree credit, the additional child tax credit *(Chapter 25), or* the American Opportunity credit *(Chapter 38)*.
- You received any earned income credit payments in advance from your employer *(Chapter 25), or*

- You owe any special tax such as alternative minimum tax *(Chapter 23)*, IRA penalty *(Chapter 8)*, household employment taxes *(Chapter 38)*, and FICA on tips *(Chapter 26)*, *or*
- You are a nonresident alien with a U.S. business or have tax liability not covered by withholding; *see* Form 1040NR.

Filing Tests for Dependents: 2010 Returns

The income threshold for filing a tax return is generally lower for an individual who may be claimed as a dependent than for a nondependent. You are a "dependent" if you are the qualifying child or qualifying relative of another taxpayer, and the other tests for dependents at *21.1* are met.

If, under the tests at *21.1*, you may be claimed as a dependent by someone else, use the chart on this page to determine if you must file a 2010 return. Include as unearned income taxable interest and dividends, capital gains, pensions, annuities, and distributions of unearned income from a trust. Earned income includes wages, tips, self-employment income, and taxable scholarships or fellowships *(Chapter 33)*. Gross income is the total of unearned and earned income.

For married dependents, the filing requirements in the chart assume that the dependent is filing a separate return and not a joint return *(Chapter 1)*. Generally, a married person who files a joint return may not be claimed as a dependent by a third party who provides support.

If you are the parent of a dependent child who had only investment income subject to the "kiddie tax" *(24.3)*, you may elect to report the child's income on your own return for 2010 instead of filing a separate return for the child; *see 24.5* for the election rules.

For purposes of the following chart, a person is treated as being age 65 (or older) if his or her 65th birthday is on or before January 1, 2011. Blindness is determined as of December 31, 2010.

Filing Instruction

File for Refund of Withholdings

Even if you are not required to file a return under the income tests on this page, you should file to obtain a refund of federal tax withholdings.

File a Return for 2010 If You Are a—

Single dependent. Were you **either** age 65 or older **or** blind?

☐ **No.** You must file a return if **any** of the following apply.
- Your unearned income was over $950.
- Your earned income was over $5,700.
- Your gross income was more than the **larger** of—
  - $950, or
  - Your earned income (up to $5,400) plus $300.

☐ **Yes.** You must file a return if **any** of the following apply.
- Your unearned income was over $2,350 ($3,750 if 65 or older **and** blind).
- Your earned income was over $7,100 ($8,500 if 65 or older **and** blind).
- Your gross income was more than the **larger** of—
  - $2,350 ($3,750 if 65 or older **and** blind), or
  - Your earned income (up to $5,400) plus $1,700 ($3,100 if 65 or older **and** blind).

Married dependent. Were you **either** age 65 or older **or** blind?

☐ **No.** You must file a return if **any** of the following apply.
- Your unearned income was over $950.
- Your earned income was over $5,700.
- Your gross income was at least $5 and your spouse files a separate return and itemizes deductions.
- Your gross income was more than the **larger** of—
  - $950, or
  - Your earned income (up to $5,400) plus $300.

☐ **Yes.** You must file a return if **any** of the following apply.
- Your unearned income was over $2,050 ($3,150 if 65 or older **and** blind).
- Your earned income was over $6,800 ($7,900 if 65 or older **and** blind).
- Your gross income was at least $5 and your spouse files a separate return and itemizes deductions.
- Your gross income was more than the **larger** of—
  - $2,050 ($3,150 if 65 or older **and** blind), or
  - Your earned income (up to $5,400) plus $1,400 ($2,500 if 65 or older **and** blind).

Where to File

If you received an IRS packet of forms with a pre-addressed envelope, use it unless you moved. If your return includes numerous attachments, make sure that you purchase sufficient postage.

If you do not have an IRS envelope or you moved during the year, and you are filing Form 1040, mail your return to the applicable address shown in the table below. If you are filing Form 1040A or 1040EZ, the Service Centers are the same as shown in the table below, but the last four digits of the zip code are different; *see* the note at the bottom of the table.

Where Do You File Form 1040?

	THEN use this address if you:	
If you live in—	***Are not enclosing a check or money order—***	***Are enclosing a check or money order—***
Florida, Georgia, North Carolina, South Carolina	Department of the Treasury Internal Revenue Service Center Atlanta, GA 39901-0002	Department of the Treasury Internal Revenue Service Center Atlanta, GA 39901-0102
Arkansas, Connecticut, Delaware, District of Columbia, Maine, Maryland, Massachusetts, Missouri, New Hampshire, New Jersey, New York, Ohio, Pennsylvania, Rhode Island, Vermont, Virginia, West Virginia	Department of the Treasury Internal Revenue Service Center Kansas City, MO 64999-0002	Department of the Treasury Internal Revenue Service Center Kansas City, MO 64999-0102
Alabama, Kentucky, Louisiana, Mississippi, Tennessee, Texas	Department of the Treasury Internal Revenue Service Center Austin, TX 73301-0002	Department of the Treasury Internal Revenue Service Center Austin, TX 73301-0102
Alaska, Arizona, California, Colorado, Hawaii, Idaho, Illinois, Indiana, Iowa, Kansas, Michigan, Minnesota, Montana, Nebraska, Nevada, New Mexico, North Dakota, Oklahoma, Oregon, South Dakota, Utah, Washington, Wisconsin, Wyoming	Department of the Treasury Internal Revenue Service Center Fresno, CA 93888-0002	Department of the Treasury Internal Revenue Service Center Fresno, CA 93888-0102
A foreign country, American Samoa, or Puerto Rico (or are excluding income under Internal Revenue Code section 933), or use an APO or FPO address, or file Form 2555, 2555-EZ, or 4563, or are a dual-status alien or nonpermanent resident of Guam or the Virgin Islands*	Department of the Treasury Internal Revenue Service Center Austin, TX 73301-0215 USA	Department of the Treasury Internal Revenue Service Center Austin, TX 73301-0215 USA

*Permanent residents of Guam should use: Department of Revenue and Taxation, Government of Guam, P.O. Box 23607, GMF, GU 96921; permanent residents of the Virgin Islands should use: V.I. Bureau of Internal Revenue, 9601 Estate Thomas, Charlotte Amalie, St. Thomas, VI 00802.

***Filing Form 1040A or 1040EZ:** *If you are filing Form 1040A, the last four digits of the zip codes for the IRS Service Centers are 0015 (no payment) or 0115 (payment). For Form 1040EZ the last four digits are 0014 (no payment) or 0114 (payment). Check your tax form instructions and the e-Supplement at jklasser.com for any late changes to the addresses or zip codes on this page.*

Filing Deadlines (on or Before)

January 18, 2011— Pay the balance of your 2010 estimated tax. If you do not meet this date, you may avoid an estimated tax penalty for the last quarter by filing your 2010 return and paying the balance due by February 1, 2011.

Farmers and fishermen: File your single 2010 estimated tax payment by this date. If you do not, you may still avoid an estimated tax penalty by filing a final tax return and paying the full tax by March 1, 2011.

January 31, 2010— Make sure you have received a Form W-2 from each employer for whom you worked in 2010.

April 15, 2011— File your 2010 tax return and pay the balance of your tax. If you cannot meet the April 15 deadline, you may obtain an automatic six-month filing extension by filing Form 4868 (on paper or electronically). However, even if you get an extension, interest will still be charged for taxes not paid by April 15, and late payment penalties will be imposed unless at least 90% of your tax liability is paid by this date or you otherwise show reasonable cause. If you cannot pay the full amount of tax you owe when you file your return, you can file Form 9465 to request an installment payment arrangement.

If on this date you are a U.S. citizen or resident living and working abroad or in military service outside the U.S. or Puerto Rico, you have an automatic two-month filing extension until June 15, 2011.

Pay the first installment of your 2011 estimated tax by this date.

June 15, 2011— Pay the second installment of your 2011 estimated tax. You may amend your estimate at this time.

If on April 15 you were a U.S. citizen or resident living and working abroad or in military service outside the U.S. or Puerto Rico, file your 2010 return and pay the balance due. You may obtain an additional four-month filing extension until October 17, 2011, by filing Form 4868.

If you are a nonresident alien who did not have tax withheld from your wages, file Form 1040NR by this date and pay the balance due.

September 15, 2011— Pay the third installment of your 2011 estimated tax. You may amend your estimate at this time.

October 17, 2011— File your 2010 return if you received an automatic six-month filing extension using Form 4868. Also file your 2010 return and pay the balance due if on April 15 you were a U.S. citizen or resident living and working abroad or in military service outside the U.S. or Puerto Rico, and by June 15 you qualified for an additional four-month extension by filing Form 4868.

December 31, 2011— If self-employed, this is the last day to set up a Keogh plan for 2011.

January 17, 2012— Pay the balance of your 2011 estimated tax.

April 17, 2012— File your 2011 return and pay the balance of your tax. Pay the first installment of your 2012 estimated tax by this date.

15th day of the 4th month after the fiscal year ends— File your fiscal year return and pay the balance of the tax due. If you cannot meet the filing deadline, apply for an automatic four-month filing extension on Form 4868.

2011

JANUARY

S	M	T	W	T	F	S
						1
2	3	4	5	6	7	8
9	10	11	12	13	14	15
16	17	18	19	20	21	22
23	24	25	26	27	28	29
30	31					

FEBRUARY

S	M	T	W	T	F	S
		1	2	3	4	5
6	7	8	9	10	11	12
13	14	15	16	17	18	19
20	21	22	23	24	25	26
27	28					

MARCH

S	M	T	W	T	F	S
		1	2	3	4	5
6	7	8	9	10	11	12
13	14	15	16	17	18	19
20	21	22	23	24	25	26
27	28	29	30	31		

APRIL

S	M	T	W	T	F	S
					1	2
3	4	5	6	7	8	9
10	11	12	13	14	15	16
17	18	19	20	21	22	23
24	25	26	27	28	29	30

MAY

S	M	T	W	T	F	S
1	2	3	4	5	6	7
8	9	10	11	12	13	14
15	16	17	18	19	20	21
22	23	24	25	26	27	28
29	30	31				

JUNE

S	M	T	W	T	F	S
			1	2	3	4
5	6	7	8	9	10	11
12	13	14	15	16	17	18
19	20	21	22	23	24	25
26	27	28	29	30		

JULY

S	M	T	W	T	F	S
					1	2
3	4	5	6	7	8	9
10	11	12	13	14	15	16
17	18	19	20	21	22	23
24	25	26	27	28	29	30
31						

AUGUST

S	M	T	W	T	F	S
	1	2	3	4	5	6
7	8	9	10	11	12	13
14	15	16	17	18	19	20
21	22	23	24	25	26	27
28	29	30	31			

SEPTEMBER

S	M	T	W	T	F	S
				1	2	3
4	5	6	7	8	9	10
11	12	13	14	15	16	17
18	19	20	21	22	23	24
25	26	27	28	29	30	

OCTOBER

S	M	T	W	T	F	S
						1
2	3	4	5	6	7	8
9	10	11	12	13	14	15
16	17	18	19	20	21	22
23	24	25	26	27	28	29
30	31					

NOVEMBER

S	M	T	W	T	F	S
		1	2	3	4	5
6	7	8	9	10	11	12
13	14	15	16	17	18	19
20	21	22	23	24	25	26
27	28	29	30			

DECEMBER

S	M	T	W	T	F	S
				1	2	3
4	5	6	7	8	9	10
11	12	13	14	15	16	17
18	19	20	21	22	23	24
25	26	27	28	29	30	31

2012

JANUARY

S	M	T	W	T	F	S
1	2	3	4	5	6	7
8	9	10	11	12	13	14
15	16	17	18	19	20	21
22	23	24	25	26	27	28
29	30	31				

FEBRUARY

S	M	T	W	T	F	S
			1	2	3	4
5	6	7	8	9	10	11
12	13	14	15	16	17	18
19	20	21	22	23	24	25
26	27	28	29			

MARCH

S	M	T	W	T	F	S
				1	2	3
4	5	6	7	8	9	10
11	12	13	14	15	16	17
18	19	20	21	22	23	24
25	26	27	28	29	30	31

APRIL

S	M	T	W	T	F	S
1	2	3	4	5	6	7
8	9	10	11	12	13	14
15	16	17	18	19	20	21
22	23	24	25	26	27	28
29	30					

MAY

S	M	T	W	T	F	S
		1	2	3	4	5
6	7	8	9	10	11	12
13	14	15	16	17	18	19
20	21	22	23	24	25	26
27	28	29	30	31		

JUNE

S	M	T	W	T	F	S
					1	2
3	4	5	6	7	8	9
10	11	12	13	14	15	16
17	18	19	20	21	22	23
24	25	26	27	28	29	30

JULY

S	M	T	W	T	F	S
1	2	3	4	5	6	7
8	9	10	11	12	13	14
15	16	17	18	19	20	21
22	23	24	25	26	27	28
29	30	31				

AUGUST

S	M	T	W	T	F	S
			1	2	3	4
5	6	7	8	9	10	11
12	13	14	15	16	17	18
19	20	21	22	23	24	25
26	27	28	29	30	31	

SEPTEMBER

S	M	T	W	T	F	S
						1
2	3	4	5	6	7	8
9	10	11	12	13	14	15
16	17	18	19	20	21	22
23	24	25	26	27	28	29
30						

OCTOBER

S	M	T	W	T	F	S
	1	2	3	4	5	6
7	8	9	10	11	12	13
14	15	16	17	18	19	20
21	22	23	24	25	26	27
28	29	30	31			

NOVEMBER

S	M	T	W	T	F	S
				1	2	3
4	5	6	7	8	9	10
11	12	13	14	15	16	17
18	19	20	21	22	23	24
25	26	27	28	29	30	

DECEMBER

S	M	T	W	T	F	S
						1
2	3	4	5	6	7	8
9	10	11	12	13	14	15
16	17	18	19	20	21	22
23	24	25	26	27	28	29
30	31					

Choosing Which Tax Form to File

There are three individual tax forms: Form 1040, Form 1040A, and Form 1040EZ. Use the simplified Form 1040EZ or Form 1040A only if you find the return will save you time and not cause you to give up tax-saving deductions or credits that are only available if you file Form 1040. To help you make your selection, fill in the following chart.

By checking the box that indicates your tax status, income, expenses, and credit items, you will be guided in choosing which form to use.

Item—	*Form 1040EZ—*	*Form 1040A—*	*Form 1040—*
Single	X[1, 2]	X[1]	X
Head of household		X[1]	X
Married filing jointly	X[1, 2]	X[1]	X
Married filing separately		X[1]	X
Widow or widower		X[1]	X
Exemption for dependents		X	X
Wages, salary	X	X	X
Interest	X[3]	X	X
Ordinary dividends		X	X
Qualified dividends taxed as long-term capital gains		X[5]	X
Unemployment compensation	X	X	X
Self-employment income			X
Pension-annuity		X	X
IRA distributions		X	X
Rents and royalties			X
Gains and losses from property sales			X
Capital gain distributions from mutual funds		X[5]	X
Alimony			X
State tax refunds			X
Social Security benefits		X	X
IRA deduction		X	X
Alimony paid			X
Student loan interest		X	X
Tuition and fees deduction *(33.13)*		X	X
Educator expenses *(12.2)*		X	X
Moving expenses			X
Self-employed health insurance			X
50% of self-employment tax			X
Archer MSA deduction			X
Penalty for early withdrawal of savings			X
Deduction for Keogh, SEP, and SIMPLE plans			X
Employee business expenses			X
State and local taxes			X
Real estate taxes			X
Home mortgage interest, investment and business interest			X
Charitable contributions			X
Medical and dental expenses			X
Casualty and theft losses			X
Miscellaneous deductions (investment expenses, tax preparation)			X
Credit for child and dependent care		X	X
Earned income credit	X[4]	X	X
Credit for elderly and disabled		X	X
Child tax credit or additional child tax credit		X	X
Adoption credit		X	X
Retirement savings contributions credit		X	X
Education credits		X	X
All other credits			X
Estimated tax payments and estimated tax penalty		X	X
Advance earned income credit (EIC) payments		X	X
Self-employment tax			X
Roth conversion IRA			X
Penalty tax on an IRA			X
Alternative minimum tax			X
Social Security tax on tips not reported to your employer			X
Uncollected Social Security tax on tips shown on your Form W-2			X
"Kiddie" tax on child's return		X	X
"Kiddie" tax on parent's return			X
Household employee taxes			X
All other taxes or penalties			X

[1] *Taxable income less than $100,000.*

[2] *Under age 65 and not blind on January 1, 2011.*

[3] *Up to $1,500.*

[4] *If you did not receive any advance earned income credit payments.*

[5] *If you do not need Schedule D of Form 1040 for any other transaction.*

Chapter 1

Filing Status

The filing status you use when you file your return determines the tax rates that will apply *(1.2)* to your taxable income. Filing status also determines the standard deduction you may claim *(13.1)* if you do not itemize deductions and your ability to claim certain other deductions, credits, and exclusions.

This chapter explains the five different filing statuses: single, married filing jointly, married filing separately, head of household, and qualifying widow(er). If you are married, filing a joint return is generally advantageous, but there are exceptions discussed in *1.3*. If you are unmarried and are supporting a child who lives with you, you may qualify as a head of household *(1.12)*, which will enable you to use more favorable tax rates than those allowed for single taxpayers. If you were widowed in either 2009 or 2008 and in 2010 a dependent child lived with you, you may be able to file as a qualifying widow(er) for 2010, which allows you to use joint return rates *(1.11)*.

Special filing situations, such as for children, nonresident aliens, and deceased individuals, are also discussed in this chapter.

Your personal or family status also determines the number of personal exemptions you may claim on your return. For 2010, each personal exemption you claim is the equivalent of a $3,650 deduction *(21.1)*.

1.1 Which Filing Status Should You Use?

Your filing status generally depends on whether you are married at the end of the year, and, if unmarried, whether you maintain a household for a qualifying dependent. The five filing statuses are: single, married filing jointly, married filing separately, head of household, and qualifying widow or widower.

If you are *married at the end of the year,* you may file jointly *(1.4)* or separately *(1.3)*. If you lived apart from your spouse for the last half of 2010 and your child lived with you, you may qualify as an "unmarried" head of household *(1.12)*, which allows you to apply more favorable tax rates than you could as a married person filing separately.

If you are *unmarried at the end of the year,* your filing status is single unless you meet the tests for a head of household or qualifying widow(er). Generally, you are a head of household *(1.12)* if you pay more than 50% of the household costs for a dependent child or relative who lives with you, or for a dependent parent, whether or not he or she lives with you. You generally are a qualifying widow(er) *(1.11)* if you were widowed in 2008 or 2009 and in 2010 you pay more than 50% of the household costs for you and your dependent child. The tax rates for heads of household and for qualifying widow(er)s are more favorable than those for single taxpayers *(1.2)*.

The filing status you use determines the tax rates that apply to your taxable income *(1.2)*, as well as the standard deduction you may claim *(13.1)* if you do not itemize deductions. Certain other deductions, credits, or exclusions are also affected by filing status. For example, if you are married, certain tax benefits are only allowed if you file jointly, but more deductions overall may be allowed in certain cases if you file separately *(1.3)*.

Planning Reminder

Getting Married Can Raise Your Taxes

The so-called marriage penalty is faced by couples whose joint return tax liability exceeds the combined tax they would pay if single. This is generally the case where each spouse earns a substantial share of the total income. On the other hand, if one spouse has little or no income, there generally is a marriage bonus or singles penalty, as the couple's tax on a joint return is less than the sum of the tax liabilities that would be owed if they were single.

Tax legislation has reduced the marriage penalty by increasing the standard deduction *(13.1)* for married couples filing jointly to double the amount allowed to a single person, and also making the 15% bracket *(1.2)* twice as wide. However, these benefits may not be extended beyond 2010; *see* the *e-Supplement at jklasser.com* for an update.

Marital status determined at the end of the year. For federal tax purposes, a marriage means only a legal union between a man and a woman as husband and wife.

If you are divorced during the year under a final decree of divorce or separate maintenance, you are treated as unmarried for that whole year, assuming you have not remarried before the end of the year. For the year of the divorce, file as a single person unless you care for a child or parent and qualify as a head of household *(1.12)*.

If at the end of the year you are living apart from your spouse, or you are separated under a provisional decree that has not yet been finalized, you are not considered divorced. If you care for a child and meet the other head of household tests *(1.12)*, you may file as an unmarried head of household. Otherwise, you must file a joint return or as a married person filing separately.

If at the end of the year you live together in a common law marriage that is recognized by the law of the state in which you live or the state where the marriage began, you are treated as married.

If your spouse dies during the year, you are treated as married for that entire year and may file a joint return for you and your deceased spouse, assuming you have not remarried before year's end *(1.10)*.

1.2 Tax Rates Based on Filing Status

The most favorable tax brackets apply to married persons filing jointly and qualifying widow(er)s *(1.11)*, who also use the joint return rates. The least favorable brackets are those for married persons filing separately, but filing separately is still advisable for married couples in certain situations *(1.3)*. *See Table 1-1* for a comparison of the 2010 tax rate brackets.

If you have children and are unmarried at the end of the year, do not assume that your filing status is single. If your child lives with you in a home you maintain, you generally may file as a head of household *(1.12)*, which allows you to use more favorable tax rates than a single person. If you were widowed in either of the two prior years and maintain a household for your dependent child, you generally may file as a qualified widow(er), which allows you to use favorable joint return rates *(1.11)*.

If you are married at the end of the year but for the second half of the year you lived with your child apart from your spouse, and you and your spouse agree not to file jointly, you may use head of household tax rates, which are more favorable than those for married persons filing separately.

What is your top tax bracket and effective tax rate? For 2010, your top marginal tax rate can be either 10%, 15%, 25%, 28%, 33%, or 35%, depending on your taxable income *(22.1)*. The rate brackets for 2010 are shown in *Table 1-1*. If your top bracket is 25%, for example, this means that each additional dollar of *ordinary* income (such as salary or interest income) will be taxed at 25% for regular income tax purposes. However, because the rate brackets are graduated, your effective tax rate may be significantly lower than your top (marginal) rate. For example, if in

2010 you are single with taxable income of $35,150, all of which is ordinary income, your marginal rate is 25%, but the first $8,375 is taxed at 10%, the next $25,625 ($34,000 – $8,375) is taxed at 15%, and only the last $1,150 ($35,150 – $34,000) is taxed at 25%. The total tax is $4,969, which represents an "effective rate" of 14.14% ($4,969/$35,150 taxable income), reflecting the fact that most of your taxable income is taxed in the 10% and (especially) the 15% brackets.

Looking ahead to 2011. Without new legislation, the 10% bracket will expire at the end of 2010 and the top two brackets of 33% and 35% will revert to their pre-2001 levels of 36% and 39.6% as the top two brackets. However, this was still uncertain when this book went to press. *See* the *e-Supplement at jklasser.com* for the 2011 brackets.

The tax rate on qualified dividends *(4.2)* **and net capital gains** *(5.3)* **for 2010 is generally lower than your top bracket rate on ordinary income.** Qualified dividends and net capital gains are generally subject to a maximum 15% tax rate, but for taxpayers whose top rate bracket for 2010 *(Table 1-1)* is 10% or 15%, there is no tax; the rate on qualified dividends and net capital gains is zero (0%). For 28% rate gains or unrecaptured Section 1250 gains *(5.3)*, the zero and 15% rates do not apply, but the rate cannot exceed 25% for unrecaptured Section 1250 gains or 28% for 28% rate gains.

To actually compute your 2010 regular income tax, you will either look up your tax in the Tax Table, use the Tax Computation Worksheet, or, if you have net capital gains or qualified dividends, use the Qualified Dividends and Capital Gain Tax Worksheet or Schedule D Tax Worksheet. *Chapter 22* explains these alternatives.

AMT. If you are subject to alternative minimum tax (AMT) on Form 6251, you generally apply either a 26% or 28% rate to your AMT taxable income (as reduced by the applicable AMT exemption), but the favorable regular tax rates for net capital gains and qualified dividends also apply for AMT purposes *(23.1)*.

Table 1-1 Taxable Income Brackets for 2010

	10% bracket applies to taxable income up to—	*15% bracket applies to taxable income up to—*	*25% bracket applies to taxable income up to—*	*28% bracket applies to taxable income up to—*	*33% bracket applies to taxable income up to—*	*35% bracket applies to taxable income over—*
Married filing separately	$ 8,375	$ 34,000	$ 68,650	$ 104,625	$ 186,825	$ 186,825
Single	8,375	34,000	82,400	171,850	373,650	373,650
Head of household	11,950	45,550	117,650	190,550	373,650	373,650
Married filing jointly or Qualifying widow(er)	16,750	68,000	137,300	209,250	37,650	373,650

1.3 Filing Separately Instead of Jointly

Filing a joint return saves taxes for a married couple where one spouse earns all, or substantially all, of the taxable income. If both you and your spouse earn taxable income, you should figure your tax on joint and separate returns to determine which method provides the lower tax.

Although your tax rate *(1.2)* will generally be higher on a separate return, filing separately may provide an overall tax savings (for both of you together) where filing separately allows you to claim more deductions. On separate returns, larger amounts of medical expenses, casualty losses, or miscellaneous deductions may be deductible because lower adjusted gross income floors apply. Unless one spouse earns substantially more than the other, separate and joint tax rates are likely to be the same, regardless of the type of returns filed. The Example on page 12 illustrates how filing separately can save you taxes.

Suspicious of your spouse's tax reporting? If you suspect that your spouse is evading taxes and may be liable on a joint return, you may want to file a separate return. By filing separately, you avoid liability for unpaid taxes due on a joint return, plus interest and penalties.

If you do file jointly and the IRS tries to collect tax due on the joint return from you personally, you may be able to avoid liability under the innocent spouse rules *(1.7)*. If you are no longer married to or are separated from the person with whom you jointly filed, you may be able to elect separate liability treatment *(1.8)*.

Planning Reminder

Switching From Separate to Joint Return

If you and your spouse file separate returns, you have three years from the due date (without extensions) to change to a joint return. If a joint return is filed, you may not change to separate returns once the due date has passed. The filing of separate or joint estimated tax installments *(27.4)* does not commit you to a similar tax return.

Standard deduction restriction on separate returns. Keep in mind that if you and your spouse file separately, both must either itemize or claim the standard deduction, which is $5,700 in 2010 for married persons filing separately *(13.3)*. Thus, if your spouse itemizes deductions on Schedule A of Form 1040, your standard deduction is zero; you do not have the option of claiming the $5,700 standard deduction and must itemize your deductions even if they are much less than $5,700.

EXAMPLE

Mike Palmer's 2010 adjusted gross income (AGI) is $84,775, and Fran, his wife, has AGI of $60,000. Neither of them has dependents. Mike has unreimbursed medical expenses of $7,984 *(17.2)* before taking into account the 7.5% of AGI floor *(17.1)*; Fran's unreimbursed expenses are $1,000. A tornado damaged property owned by Mike in his own name, and he has a casualty loss of $20,078 prior to taking into account the $500 floor and the 10% of AGI floor *(18.13)*. Mike has unreimbursed miscellaneous expenses of $2,996 and Fran has $500 prior to taking into account the 2% of AGI floor *(19.1)*. Mike has deductible mortgage interest expenses of $5,000 and Fran has $2,000. Mike's deductible state and local taxes are $2,499; Fran's are $1,000. If they file separately and Mike itemizes deductions, Fran must also itemize even though the standard deduction would give her a larger deduction *(13.3)*.

As the example worksheet below shows, filing separate returns saves Mike and Fran an overall $2,082, because they can deduct more on separate returns. If they filed jointly, their deductible casualty loss would be substantially lower and they would receive no deduction for medical expenses because it would be eliminated by the adjusted gross income floor.

Item		*Mike (Separately)*	*Fran (Separately)*	*Joint Return*
1.	**AGI**	**$ 84,775**	**$ 60,000**	**$ 144,775**
2.	Medical expenses	7,984	1,000	8,984
	Less 7½% of AGI	6,358	4,500	10,858
	Allowable medical	1,626	0	0
3.	Taxes	2,499	1,000	3,499
4.	Mortgage interest	5,000	2,000	7,000
5.	Casualty loss	20,078	0	20,078
	Less $500 and 10% of AGI *(18.12)*	8,978		14,978
	Allowable casualty	11,100		5,100
6.	Miscellaneous expenses	2,996	500	3,496
	Less 2% of AGI	1,696	1,200	2,896
	Allowable miscellaneous	1,300	0	600
7.	**Total itemized *(Lines 2–6)***	**21,525**	**3,000**	**16,199**
8.	Personal exemptions	3,650	3,650	7,300
9.	**Itemized plus exemptions**	**25,175**	**6,650**	**23,499**
10.	**Taxable income** *(Line 1 minus Line 9)*	59,600	53,350	121,276
11.	***Tax liability***	**11,081**	**9,519**	**22,682**
	Total tax filing separately			20,600
	Savings from filing separately			***2,082***

Joint return required for certain benefits. Also be aware that certain tax benefits may be claimed by married persons only if they file jointly.

If you want to take advantage of the $25,000 rental loss allowance *(10.2)* or the credit for the elderly and disabled *(Chapter 34)*, you must file jointly unless you live apart for the whole year. You must file jointly to claim an IRA deduction for a nonworking spouse *(8.3)*. Roth IRA contributions generally may not be made by a married person filing separately because of an extremely low phase-out range *(8.20)*. You must file jointly to convert a traditional IRA to a Roth IRA *(8.21)*. A joint return is required to claim the Hope credit or lifetime learning credit *(33.7)*, the tuition and fees deduction *(33.13)*, or the deduction for student loan interest *(33.14)*. You must file jointly to claim the dependent care credit or the earned income credit *(Chapter 25)*, unless you live apart for the last six months of the year.

Other restrictions may increase your tax if you file a separate return. In figuring whether you are subject to alternative minimum tax (AMT), your exemption amount is half that allowed to a joint return filer *(23.1)*. Furthermore, if you receive Social Security benefits, 85% of your benefits are generally subject to tax on a separate return; *see Chapter 34*.

1.4 Filing a Joint Return

If you are married at the end of the year, you may file a joint return with your spouse. For federal tax purposes, a marriage means only a legal union between a man and woman as husband and wife. Filing jointly saves taxes for many married couples, but if you and your spouse both earn taxable income, in some cases overall tax liability is reduced by filing separately *(1.3)*.

You may not file a 2010 joint return if you were divorced under a decree of divorce or separate maintenance that is *final* by the end of the year. You may file jointly if you separated during 2010 under an interlocutory (temporary or provisional) decree or order, so long as a final divorce decree was not entered by the end of the year. If during the period that a divorce decree is interlocutory you are permitted to remarry in another state, the IRS recognizes the new marriage and allows a joint return to be filed with the new spouse. However, courts have refused to allow a joint return where a new marriage took place in Mexico during the interlocutory period in violation of California law.

Both spouses generally liable on joint return but "innocent" spouse may be relieved of liability. When you and your spouse file jointly, each of you may generally be held individually liable for the entire tax due, plus interest and any penalties. The IRS may try to collect the entire amount due from you even if your spouse earned all of the income reported on the joint return, or even if you have divorced under an agreement that holds your former spouse responsible for the taxes on the joint returns you filed together. However, there are exceptions to this joint liability rule for "innocent" spouses and for divorced or separated persons.

You may be able to obtain *innocent spouse* relief where tax on your joint return was understated without your knowledge because your spouse omitted income or claimed erroneous deductions or tax credits. In such a case, you may make an innocent spouse election within two years from the time the IRS begins a collection effort from you for taxes due on the return *(1.7)*.

Furthermore, if you are divorced, legally separated, living apart or the spouse with whom you filed jointly has died, you may be able to avoid tax on the portion of a joint return deficiency that is allocable to your ex-spouse by making a separate liability election *(1.8)* within two years of the time the IRS begins collection efforts against you. You may make the separate liability election even if you apply for innocent spouse relief. In some cases, it may be easier to qualify for relief under the separate liability rules than under the innocent spouse rules because innocent spouse relief may be denied if you had "reason to know" that tax was understated on the joint return, whereas the IRS must show that you had "actual knowledge" of the omitted income or erroneous deductions or credits to deny a separate liability election.

Signing the joint return. Both you and your spouse must sign the joint return. Under the following rules, if your spouse is unable to sign, you may sign for him or her.

If, because of illness, your spouse is physically unable to sign the joint return, you may, with the oral consent of your spouse, sign his or her name on the return followed by the words "By ______, Husband (or Wife)." You then sign the return again in your own right and attach a signed and dated statement with the following information: (1) the type of form being filed, (2) the tax year, (3) the reason for the inability of the sick spouse to sign, and (4) that the sick spouse has consented to your signing.

To sign for your spouse in other situations, you need authorization in the form of a power of attorney, which must be attached to the return. IRS Form 2848 may be used.

If your spouse does not file, you may be able to prove you filed a joint return even if your spouse did not sign and you did not sign as your spouse's agent where:

- You intended it to be a joint return—your spouse's income was included (or the spouse had no income).
- Your spouse agreed to have you handle tax matters and you filed a joint return.
- Your answers to the questions on the tax return indicate you intended to file a joint return.
- Your spouse's failure to sign can be explained.

Filing Tip

Spouse in Combat Zone

If your spouse is in a combat zone or a qualified hazardous duty area *(35.4)*, you can sign a joint return for your spouse. Attach a signed explanation to the return.

Filing Tip

Election To File a Joint Return

Where a U.S. citizen or resident is married to a nonresident alien, the couple may file a joint return if both elect to be taxed on their worldwide income. The requirement that one spouse be a U.S. citizen or resident need be met only at the close of the year. Joint returns may be filed in the year of the election and all later years until the election is terminated.

Filing Tip

Nonresident Alien Becomes Resident

Where one spouse is a U.S. citizen or resident and the other is a nonresident alien who becomes a resident during the tax year, the couple may make a special election to file a joint return for that year and be taxed on their worldwide income. Thereafter, neither spouse may make the election again even if married to a new spouse. *See* the tests for determining status as a resident or nonresident alien *(1.18)*.

EXAMPLE

The Hills generally filed joint returns. In one year, Mr. Hill claimed joint return filing status and reported his wife's income as well as his own; in place of her signature on the return, he indicated that she was out of town caring for her sick mother. She did not file a separate return. The IRS refused to treat the return as joint. The Tax Court disagreed. Since Mrs. Hill testified that she would have signed had she been available, her failure to do so does not bar joint return status. The couple intended to make a joint return at the time of filing.

1.5 Nonresident Alien Spouse

If either you or your spouse was a nonresident alien *(1.16)* during any part of the year, a joint return may be filed only if both of you make a special election to be taxed on your worldwide income. Thus, if you are a U.S. citizen and your spouse is a nonresident alien at the beginning of the year who becomes a resident during the year, the special election to file jointly must be made.

If the election is not made, you may be able to claim your nonresident alien spouse as an exemption on a return filed as married filing separately, but only if the spouse had no income and could not be claimed as a dependent by another taxpayer *(21.2)*. If the alien spouse becomes a resident before the beginning of the next tax year, you may file jointly for that year.

A couple who make the election must keep books and records of their worldwide income and give the IRS access to such books and records. If either spouse does not provide the necessary information to the IRS, the election is terminated. Furthermore, the election is terminated if either spouse revokes it or dies; revocation before the due date of the return is effective for that return. The election automatically terminates in the year following the year of the death of either spouse. However, if the survivor is a U.S. citizen or resident and has a qualifying child, he or she may be able to use joint return rates as a qualifying widow or widower *(1.11)* in the two years following the year of the spouse's death. The election to file jointly also terminates if the couple is legally separated under a decree of divorce or separate maintenance. Termination is effective as of the beginning of the taxable year of the legal separation. If neither spouse is a citizen or resident for any part of the taxable year, an election may not be made and an existing election is suspended. If an election is suspended it may again become effective if either spouse becomes a U.S. citizen or resident. Once the election is terminated, neither spouse may ever again make the election to file jointly.

Electing to file a joint return does not terminate the special withholding on the nonresident alien's income.

1.6 Community Property Rules

If you live in Arizona, California, Idaho, Louisiana, Nevada, New Mexico, Texas, Washington, or Wisconsin, the income and property you and your spouse acquire during the marriage is generally regarded as community property. Community property means that each of you owns half of the community income and community property, even if legal title is held by only one spouse. But note that there are some instances in which community property rules are disregarded for tax purposes; these instances are clearly highlighted in the pertinent sections of this book.

If the community property rules apply for tax purposes and you and your spouse file separate returns instead of filing jointly, then on your separate returns each of you must report half of your combined community income and deductions in addition to your separate income and deductions.

Separate property may still be owned. Property owned before marriage generally remains separate property; it does not become community property when you marry. Property received during the marriage by one spouse as a gift or an inheritance from a third party is generally separate property. In some states, if the nature of ownership cannot be fixed, the property is presumed to be community property.

In some states, income from separate property may be treated as community property income. In other states, income from separate property remains the separate property of the individual owner.

Divorce or separation. If you and your spouse divorce, your community property automatically becomes separate property. A separation agreement or a decree of legal separation or of separate maintenance may or may not end the marital community, depending on state law.

Community income rules may not apply to separated couples. If a husband and wife in a community property state file separate returns, each spouse must generally report one-half of the community income. However, a spouse may be able to avoid reporting income earned by his or her spouse if they live apart during the entire calendar year and do not file a joint return.

To qualify, one or both spouses must have earned income for the year and none of that earned income may be transferred, directly or indirectly, between the spouses during the year. One spouse's payment to the other spouse solely to support the couple's dependent children is not a disqualifying transfer. If the separated couple qualifies under these tests, community income is allocated as follows:

- Earned income (excluding business or partnership income) is taxed to the spouse who performed the personal services.
- Business income (other than partnership income) is treated as the income of the spouse carrying on the business.
- Partnership income is taxed to the spouse entitled to a distributive share of partnership profits.

Innocent spouse rules apply to community property. As discussed above, community property rules may not apply to earned income where spouses live apart for the entire year and file separate returns. In addition, a spouse who files a separate return may be relieved of tax liability on community income that is attributable to the other spouse if he or she does not know (or have reason to know) about the income and if it would be inequitable under the circumstances for him or her to be taxed on such income. Even if you fail to qualify for such relief because you knew (or had reason to know) about the income, the IRS may relieve you of liability if it would be inequitable to hold you liable.

The IRS may disregard community property rules and tax income to a spouse who treats such income as if it were solely his or hers and who fails to notify the other spouse of the income before the due date of the return (including extensions).

Relief from liability on joint return. If you file jointly, you may elect to avoid liability under the innocent spouse rules *(1.7)* and the separate liability rules *(1.8)*. In applying those rules, items that would otherwise be allocable solely to your spouse will not be partly allocated to you merely because of the community property laws.

Death of spouse. The death of a spouse dissolves the community property relationship, but income earned and accrued from community property before death is community income.

Moving from a community property to a common law (separate property) state. Most common law states (those which do not have community property laws) recognize that both spouses have an interest in property accumulated while residing in a community property state. If the property is not sold or reinvested, it may continue to be treated as community property. If you and your spouse sell community property after moving to a common law state and reinvest the proceeds, the reinvested proceeds are generally separate property, which you may hold as joint tenants or in another form of ownership recognized by common law states.

Moving from a common law to a community property state. Separate property brought into a community property state generally retains its character as separately owned property. However, property acquired by a couple after moving to a community property state is generally owned as community property. In at least one state (California), personal property that qualifies as community property is treated as such, even though it was acquired when the couple lived in a common law state.

Supporting a dependent with separate rather than community income. Filing a Form 2120 multiple support agreement is not necessary where either parent can prove that he or she has income that is considered separate income rather than community income; that parent may be able to satisfy the more-than-50% support test. In certain community property states, the law may provide that income of a husband and wife living apart is considered separate income rather than community income.

IRS Alert

California Registered Domestic Partners Must Split Income

Since January 1, 2007, California has treated the earned income of a California registered domestic partner as community property for state income tax purposes unless the partners opt out of community property treatment. In a late response to the California law change, the IRS announced in a 2010 legal memorandum that California registered domestic partners are subject to the federal income tax community property rules. Each California registered domestic partner must report half of the community property income on his or her federal tax return, whether from earnings for personal services or income from property, and this applies retroactively to 2007. Each domestic partner must file as a single taxpayer. Federal law continues to prohibit joint return status, or married filing separately status, except in traditional marriages between husbands and wives.

Prior to 2007, the earned income of a registered domestic partner was treated as community property for California property law purposes but not for state income tax purposes. The IRS concluded in a 2006 legal memorandum that under the pre-2007 California law, each registered domestic partner had to report all of his or her own earned income and could not report half of the combined earnings on a separate federal return.

If a California registered domestic partner included all of his or her earned income on a federal return for 2007–2009, in accordance with the 2006 IRS legal memorandum, the partners may file amended returns (they do not have to) and follow the new community property rule for those years if that would provide a tax savings.

1.7 Innocent Spouse Rules

Unless you qualify for relief, you are personally liable for any tax due on a joint return you have filed, whether you are still married to the spouse with whom you filed the joint return or you have since divorced or separated.

Caution

Knowledge May Bar Innocent Spouse Relief

The IRS may try to defeat your claim for innocent spouse relief on the grounds that you knew, or should have known, that tax was understated on the joint return.

Law Alert

IRS Must Notify Non-Electing Spouse

After the filing of Form 8857, the IRS is required to notify the non-electing spouse (or former spouse) of an electing spouse's request for relief and allow the non-electing spouse an opportunity to participate in the determination. If the IRS makes a preliminary determination granting full or partial relief to the electing spouse, the non-electing spouse may file a written protest and obtain an Appeals Office conference.

If you are still married and living with the same spouse, the only way to avoid personal liability on the joint return is to qualify as an innocent spouse under the rules in this section, or to apply for equitable relief from the IRS *(1.9)*.

If you are divorced, legally separated, living apart, or your spouse has died, you may either seek relief under the innocent spouse rules below or you may be able to elect separate liability treatment *(1.8)* or seek equitable relief *(1.9)* from the IRS.

Qualifying tests for innocent spouse election. You must satisfy all of the following conditions to qualify for innocent spouse relief:

1. The tax shown on the joint return was understated due to the omission of income by your spouse, or erroneous deductions or credits claimed by your spouse. This means that your actual tax liability is more than the amount shown on the joint return. Innocent spouse relief is not available if the right amount of tax was reported on the return but it was not paid. However, where tax was underpaid, you may request equitable relief *(1.9)*.
2. When signing the joint return, you did not know and had no reason to know that tax on the return was understated.

   In considering whether you had "reason to know" of the tax understatement, the IRS and Tax Court will ask whether a reasonable person in similar circumstances would have known of it. All facts and circumstances will be taken into account including your education level, business experience, involvement in the activity that gave rise to the understatement, and whether you failed to ask about items on the joint return or about omissions from the return that a reasonable person would have questioned.

   Although the "knowledge" test continues to be a significant hurdle, partial relief may be available. If you knew or had reason to know that there was "some" tax understatement on the return but were unaware of the extent of the understatement, innocent spouse relief is available for the liability attributable to the portion of the understatement that you did not know about or have reason to know about.
3. Taking all the circumstances into account, it would be inequitable to hold you liable for the tax. The IRS and courts will consider the extent to which you benefitted from the tax underpayment, beyond receiving normal support. Thus, it is possible to be held liable for a tax understatement that you did not know about or have reason to know about, on the grounds that you benefitted from the underpayment in the form of a high standard of living. The IRS will also consider whether you later divorced or were deserted by your spouse.
4. You file an innocent spouse election with the IRS on Form 8857.

Election must be filed on Form 8857 to obtain relief. You must file an election on Form 8857 to claim innocent spouse relief. You do this by attaching a statement explaining why you qualify; follow the Form 8857 instructions. The election must be made no later than two years from the date that the IRS first begins collection activity (such as IRS garnishment of your wages) against you for tax due on the joint return. If the election is not made by the end of that two-year period, you will not be granted innocent spouse relief even if you meet the above qualification tests.

Tax Court appeal. If the IRS denies your election for innocent spouse relief, you have 90 days to petition the Tax Court for review. If you petition the Tax Court, the non-electing spouse has the right to intervene in the proceeding.

1.8 Separate Liability Election for Former Spouses

If the IRS attempts to collect the taxes due on a joint return from you and you have since divorced or separated, you may be able to avoid or at least limit your liability by filing a separate liability election on Form 8857. If you qualify, you will be liable only for the part of the tax liability (plus interest and any penalties) that is allocable to you. If you make the election and a tax deficiency is entirely allocable to your former spouse under the rules discussed below, you will not have to pay any part of it. However, you may not avoid liability for any part of a tax deficiency allocable to the other spouse if you had actual knowledge of the income or expense item that gave rise to the tax deficiency that the IRS is trying to collect. *See* below for details of the knowledge test.

Furthermore, you may not avoid liability to the extent that certain disqualified property transfers were made between you and the other spouse. An election may be completely denied for both spouses if transfers were made as part of a fraudulent scheme.

As with innocent spouse relief *(1.7)*, the separate liability election applies only to tax understatements where the proper tax liability was *not* shown on the joint return. If the proper liability was shown but not paid, equitable relief *(1.9)* may be requested.

Are you eligible for the separate liability election? You may make the separate liability election on Form 8857 if at the time of the election:

1. You are divorced or legally separated from the spouse with whom you filed the joint return, *or*
2. You have not lived with your spouse (with whom you filed the return) at any time in the 12-month period ending on the date you file the election, *or*
3. The spouse with whom you filed the joint return has died.

   If you qualify under any of the above, you may make the separate liability election on Form 8857 by attaching a statement that identifies which items giving rise to the tax understatement are allocable to you and which are allocable to the other spouse. You do not have to actually compute your separate liability, however. You may make the separate liability election in addition to the innocent spouse election *(1.7)*.

Caution

Actual Knowledge Bars Relief

The separate liability election generally allows you to avoid liability for the portion of a tax deficiency that is allocable to the other spouse. Such relief is unavailable, however, to the extent that you had actual knowledge of the omitted income or deducted item that gave rise to the tax deficiency.

Timing of the election. The separate liability election must be filed with the IRS on Form 8857 no later than two years after the IRS begins collection activities against you.

Actual knowledge of the item allocable to the other spouse bars relief. If you elect separate liability treatment and the IRS shows that at the time you signed the joint return you had actual knowledge of an erroneous item (omitted income or improper deduction or credit) that would otherwise be allocated to the other spouse, you may not avoid liability for the portion of a deficiency attributable to that item. However, if you signed the return under duress, separate liability is not barred despite your knowledge.

The actual knowledge test is intended by Congress to be more favorable to the taxpayer than the "had reason to know" test under the innocent spouse rules *(1.7)*. Congressional committee reports state that the IRS is required to prove that an electing spouse had actual knowledge of an erroneous item and may not infer such knowledge. According to the Tax Court, the IRS must prove actual knowledge by a "preponderance of the evidence." If the IRS proves actual knowledge of an erroneous item, that item is treated as allocable to both spouses, so the IRS can collect that portion of the deficiency from either spouse.

Where income attributable to your spouse was omitted from your joint return, you will be considered to have "actual knowledge" of it, and separate liability relief will not be allowed, if you knew your spouse received the income, even if you did not know whether the correct taxable amount was reported on the return; *see* Example 1 below.

In the case of a disallowed deduction, the Tax Court requires the IRS to prove that you had actual knowledge of the "factual circumstances" that made the item nondeductible in order for relief to be denied. In one case, the Tax Court denied relief to a spouse who prepared the joint returns on which unsubstantiated Schedule C deductions attributable to her former husband's business were claimed. She had "actual knowledge" because she had access to the business records and knew the extent of the substantiation available for the deductions when she prepared the returns.

In cases involving limited partnership tax-shelter deductions, the IRS may be unable to prove that the spouse claiming relief had disqualifying knowledge, but relief may still be partially denied if he or she received a tax benefit from the deductions; *see* Example 3 below.

EXAMPLES

1. Cheshire knew that her husband had received an early retirement distribution. She knew that the distribution had been deposited into their joint account and used to pay off a mortgage, buy a truck, pay other family expenses and provide start-up capital for the husband's business. Cheshire's husband falsely told her that a CPA had determined that most of his retirement distribution was not taxable. After they divorced, Cheshire made a separate liability election to avoid tax on the unreported income. She claimed that she was entitled to relief because she did not know that the taxable amount of the retirement distribution had been misstated on their joint return. The Tax Court held that she could not obtain relief because she knew about the retirement distribution. It is immaterial that she did not know that the reporting of the distribution on the tax return was incorrect. The Court of Appeals for the Fifth Circuit affirmed. The District of Columbia Circuit has also denied a wife's claim for relief because she had actual knowledge of her husband's retirement income.

2. You file a joint return on which you report wages of $150,000 and your husband reports $30,000 of self-employment income. The IRS examines your return and determines that your husband failed to report $20,000 of income, resulting in a $9,000 deficiency. You file a separate liability election with the IRS after obtaining a divorce.

   Assume that the IRS proves that you had actual knowledge of $5,000 of the unreported income but not the other $15,000. You are liable for 25% of the deficiency, or $2,250, allocable to the $5,000 of income that you knew about ($2,250 = $5,000 × $20,000 × $9,000). Your former spouse is liable for the entire deficiency since the unreported income was his. The IRS can collect the entire deficiency from him, or can collect $2,250 from you and the balance from him.

3. Mora's husband arranged an investment in a cattle-breeding tax shelter partnership. He put the partnership in both of their names, although Mora did not sign any of the partnership papers. On their joint returns, they claimed partnership losses which turned out to be inflated; deductions were based on overvalued cattle. After their divorce, the IRS disallowed the partnership losses and Mora elected separate liability relief. The IRS refused, claiming that she participated in making the investment so the claimed losses were allocable to her as well as her husband. The Tax Court held that Mora was not involved in making the investment and so the partnership losses are allocable to the husband unless Mora knew the factual basis for the denial of the deductions or she received a tax benefit from the deductions. She did not know about the overvaluation of the cattle, which was the factual basis for the IRS's denial of the deductions. In fact, the IRS conceded that neither spouse understood the nature of their investment or the basis of the deductions. This may often be the case where passive investors claim deductions passed through to them by a limited partnership. For this reason, the IRS argued that the "knowledge of the factual basis" test makes it too easy for limited partnership investors to obtain relief. The Tax Court responded that the law does not distinguish between passive and active investments and there is no policy reason for the courts to create a distinction. Furthermore, although the husband also lacked knowledge of the factual basis for the disallowance of the losses, he cannot avoid liability for the deficiency since the erroneous deductions would be allocable to him on a separate return.

   Despite Mora's "win" on the actual knowledge issue, she remained partially liable for the deficiency because she received a tax benefit from the erroneous deductions. Under the tax benefit rule discussed below, the deductions first offset the income that would have been reported by the husband had he filed a separate return. The balance of the deductions benefitted Mora by reducing her separate return income. If she benefitted from 25% of the deductions, she would remain liable for 25% of the deficiency.

Allocating tax liability between spouses. Generally, if you make a separate liability election, you are liable only for the portion of the tax due on the joint return that is allocable to you, determined as if you had filed a separate return. If erroneous items (omitted income or improper deductions or credits) are allocable to the other spouse but you had actual knowledge of the items as discussed above, you cannot avoid liability and the IRS remains able to collect the tax due from either of you. Where deductions are allocable to the other spouse and you are not barred from relief by the actual knowledge test, you can still be held partially liable if you received a tax benefit from the deductions; *see* the discussion of the tax benefit rule below.

In general, the allocation of a tax deficiency depends on which spouse's "items" gave rise to the deficiency. The items may be omitted income or disallowed deductions or credits. Items are generally allocated to the spouse who would have reported them on a separate return. If a deficiency is based on unreported income, the deficiency is allocated to the spouse who earned the income. Income from a jointly owned business is allocated equally unless you provide evidence that more should be allocated to the other spouse. Similarly, if a deficiency is based on the denial of personal deductions, the deficiency is allocated equally between you unless you show that a different allocation is appropriate. A deficiency based on the denial of business deductions is allocated according to your respective ownership shares in the business. If the IRS can show fraud, it can reallocate joint return items.

On Form 8857, you do *not* have to figure the portion of the deficiency for which you are liable. The IRS will figure your separate liability (and any related interest and penalties). However, you can use a worksheet in IRS Publication 971 to figure your separate liability.

Planning Reminder

Unpaid Tax on Correct Return

The separate liability election is not available where the proper amount of tax was reported on a joint return but your spouse did not pay the tax. However, equitable relief *(1.9)* may be available in this type of tax underpayment situation.

EXAMPLES

1. After you obtain a divorce, the IRS examines a joint return you filed with your former husband and assesses a tax deficiency attributable to income he failed to report. If you did not know about the omitted income and timely elect separate liability treatment, you are not liable for any part of the tax deficiency, which is entirely allocable to your former husband who earned the income. You are not liable even if the IRS is unable to collect the tax from your former husband and you have substantial assets from which the tax could be paid.
2. The IRS assesses a joint return deficiency attributable to $35,000 of income that your former spouse failed to report and $15,000 of disallowed deductions that you claimed. Both of you may make the separate liability election and limit your respective liabilities.

   If you make the election, your liability will be limited to 30% of the deficiency, as your disallowed deductions of $15,000 are 30% of the $50,000 of items causing the deficiency. If your former husband makes the election, he will be liable for the remaining 70% of the deficiency (his $35,000 of unreported income is 70% of the $50,000 of items causing the deficiency).

   If either of you does not make the election, the non-electing person could be held liable for 100% of the deficiency unless innocent spouse relief is available or the IRS grants equitable relief.

Tax benefit rule limits relief based on erroneous deductions or credits. The tax benefit limitation is an exception to the general rule that allocates items between the spouses as if separate returns had been filed. If you received a tax benefit from an erroneous deduction or credit that is allocable to the other spouse, you remain liable for the proportionate part of the deficiency. You are treated as having received a tax benefit if the disallowed deduction exceeded the income that would have been reported by the other spouse on a hypothetical separate return.

EXAMPLE

On a joint return, you report wages of $100,000 and your husband reports $15,000 of self-employment income. You divorce the following year. The IRS examines the return and disallows a $20,000 business expense deduction claimed by your former husband, resulting in a $5,600 tax deficiency. You elect separate liability relief. Of the $20,000 deduction, $15,000 is allocable to your former husband as that amount offset his entire income. The $5,000 balance offset your separate income and thereby gave you a tax benefit. Your former husband will be liable for 75% of the deficiency ($4,200) and you will be liable for the 25% balance ($1,400).

If your former husband had reported income of $30,000 instead of $15,000, you would not be liable for any part of the deficiency under the tax benefit rule. The deduction is attributed entirely to his income, so the entire deficiency is allocated to him.

These allocations assume that the IRS does not show that you had "actual knowledge" (*see* above) of the deductions attributable to your former husband. To the extent you had such knowledge, the deductions are allocable to both of you, so both of you remain liable for that part of the deficiency.

Transfers intended to avoid tax. You may be held liable for more than your allocable share of a deficiency if a disqualified asset transfer was made to you by your spouse with a principal purpose of avoiding tax. Transfers made to you within the one-year period preceding the date on which the IRS sends the first letter of proposed deficiency are presumed to have a tax avoidance purpose unless they are pursuant to a divorce decree or decree of separate maintenance. You may rebut the presumption by showing that tax avoidance was not the principal purpose of the transfer. If the tax avoidance presumption is not rebutted, the transfer is considered a disqualified transfer and the value of the transferred asset adds to your share of the liability as otherwise determined under the above election rules.

If the IRS proves that you and your former spouse transferred assets between you as part of a fraudulent scheme, neither of you will be allowed to make the separate liability election; both of you will remain individually liable for the entire joint return deficiency.

Appeal to Tax Court. You may petition the Tax Court if the IRS disputes your election or your allocation of liability. The petition must be filed within 90 days of the date on which the IRS mails a determination to you by registered or certified mail if the IRS mailing is within six months of the filing of the election. If an IRS notice is not mailed within the six-month period, a Tax Court petition may be filed without waiting for an IRS response or, if you do wait, you have until 90 days after the date the IRS mails the notice to file the petition.

The IRS may not take any collection action against you during the 90-day period and if the Tax Court petition is filed, the suspension lasts until a final court decision is made.

1.9 Equitable Relief

The IRS may grant equitable relief for liability on a joint return where innocent spouse relief *(1.7)* and separate liability *(1.8)* are not available. For example, the separate liability election and innocent spouse relief are not available where the proper amount of tax was reported on a joint return but your spouse failed to pay the tax owed. If you signed a correct return on which tax was owed and, without your knowledge, your spouse used the funds intended for payment of the tax for other purposes, the IRS may grant you equitable relief. A request for equitable relief is made on Form 8857. The IRS may also grant equitable relief in cases where the proper amount of tax was understated on the joint return if it would be inequitable to hold you liable.

Threshold conditions you must meet for relief. Each of the following conditions must be met before the IRS will even consider granting you equitable relief:

1. You filed a joint return for the year that relief is sought.
2. Relief is not available under the innocent spouse *(1.7)* or separate liability election *(1.8)* rules.
3. No assets were transferred between you and your spouse as part of a fraudulent scheme.
4. Your spouse did not transfer assets to you for the purpose of tax avoidance. If there was such a transfer, relief can be granted only to the extent income tax liability exceeds the value of these assets.
5. You did not file or fail to file the return with fraudulent intent.
6. The income tax liability for which you are seeking relief is attributable to the other spouse (with whom the joint return was filed). There are exceptions to this requirement if community property law applies, you have nominal ownership of property subject to a deficiency, the other spouse misappropriated funds intended for payment of the tax without your knowledge, or you did not challenge the treatment of items on the joint return because of prior abuse that made you fear retaliation by the other spouse.

The IRS also requires as a threshold condition that the request for equitable relief be made within two years of the first IRS collection activity. The Tax Court in 2009 struck down the two-year limitation on the grounds that the equitable relief statute did not explicitly require it, but the Seventh Circuit reversed the Tax Court in a 2010 decision, upholding the IRS's two-year deadline.

Safe harbor for tax liability reported on return but unpaid. The IRS will ordinarily grant you equitable relief for unpaid tax liability if when you filed for relief you were divorced, legally separated, or living apart from the other spouse for the 12-month period before your request, and both of the following tests are also met: (1) you would face economic hardship if forced to pay the tax, meaning that you would be unable to meet reasonable basic living expenses, and (2) you can show that at the time the joint return was filed, it was reasonable for you to believe that the other spouse would pay the tax liability.

Factors the IRS will consider. If the threshold conditions are satisfied and you do not qualify for relief under the safe harbor discussed in the preceding paragraph, you must convince the IRS that equitable relief is appropriate. The IRS will consider all the facts and circumstances.

The following is a nonexclusive list of factors that the IRS will take into account in determining whether to grant equitable relief: whether you are separated or divorced from the other spouse, whether you would suffer economic hardship (*i.e.*, be unable to meet basic living expenses), whether the other spouse was legally obligated to pay the outstanding liability, whether you received any significant benefit from the unpaid tax or item giving rise to the deficiency (beyond normal support), whether you have made a good faith effort to comply with the tax laws in later years. The case for relief is strengthened if there was a history of abuse by the other spouse or you were in poor health (physical or mental) at the time the return was filed.

The IRS will also consider whether you had knowledge or constructive knowledge (reason to know) that should bar relief. If the tax was properly reported but not paid, the IRS will look at whether you knew or had reason to know that it would not be paid by the other spouse. If the liability results from an IRS deficiency notice, the issue is whether you knew or had reason to know of the item (omitted income or erroneous deduction or credit) giving rise to the deficiency. Actual knowledge strongly weighs against relief, although relief may still be granted in limited cases where there are compelling grounds. If you had constructive knowledge—reason to know—of the item giving rise to the deficiency, this is considered a factor weighing against relief but it is not weighed more heavily than other factors. In determining constructive knowledge, the IRS will look at your level of education, your involvement in family finances and business matters, whether the other spouse deceived you, and whether there was an increase in lavish or unusual expenditures.

Appeal to Tax Court. If the IRS denies your request for equitable relief, you may petition the Tax Court for review of the IRS decision. The petition must be filed with the Tax Court no later than the 90th day after the date that the IRS mails its final determination notice to you.

1.10 Death of Your Spouse in 2010

If your spouse died in 2010, you are considered married for the whole year. If you did not remarry in 2010, you may file a 2010 joint return for you and your deceased spouse. Generally, you file a joint return with the executor or administrator. But you alone may file a joint return if you are otherwise entitled to file jointly and:

1. The deceased did not file a separate return, and
2. Someone other than yourself has not been appointed as executor or administrator before the due date for filing the return. An executor or administrator appointed after the joint return is filed may revoke the joint return within the one-year period following the due date.

If you do file jointly, you include on the return all of your income and deductions for the full year and your deceased spouse's income and deductions *up to the date of death (1.14)*.

For 2011 and 2012, you may be able to file as a qualifying widow(er) if a dependent child lives with you *(1.11)*.

Filing Instruction

Reporting Income of Deceased Spouse

If your spouse died during the year and you are filing a joint return, include his or her income earned through the date of death.

Joint return barred. As a surviving spouse, you may not file a joint return for you and your deceased spouse if:

1. You remarry before the end of the year of your spouse's death. In this case you may file jointly with your new spouse. A final return for the deceased spouse must be filed by the executor or administrator using the filing status of married filing separately.
2. You or your deceased spouse has a short year because of a change in annual accounting period.
3. Either of you was a nonresident alien at any time during the tax year; but *see 1.5*.

Executor or administrator may revoke joint return. If an executor or administrator is later appointed, he or she may revoke a joint return that you alone have filed by filing a separate return for the decedent. Even if you have properly filed a joint return for you and the deceased spouse (as just discussed), the executor or administrator is given the right to revoke the joint return. But a state court held that a co-executrix could not refuse to sign a joint return where it would save the estate money.

To revoke the joint return, the executor must file a separate return within one year of the due date (including extensions). The executor's separate return is treated as a late return; interest charges and a late filing penalty apply. The joint return that you filed is deemed to be your separate return. Tax on that return is recalculated by excluding items belonging to your deceased spouse.

Planning Reminder

Possible Estate Insolvency

If you will be appointed executor or administrator and are concerned about estate insolvency, it may be advisable to hedge as follows: (1) File separate returns. If it is later seen that a joint return is preferable, you have three years to change to a joint return. (2) File jointly but postpone being appointed executor or administrator until after the due date of the joint return. In this way, the joint return may be disaffirmed if the estate cannot cover its share of the taxes.

Signing the return. A joint return reporting your deceased spouse's income should list both of your names. Where there is an executor or administrator, the return is signed by you as the surviving spouse and the executor or administrator in his or her official capacity. If you are the executor or administrator, sign once as surviving spouse and again as the executor or administrator. Where there is no executor or administrator, you sign the return, followed by the words "filing as surviving spouse."

Surviving spouse's liability. If a joint return is filed and the estate cannot pay its share of the joint income tax liability, you, as the surviving spouse, may be liable for the full amount. Once the return is filed and the filing date passes, you can no longer change the joint return election and file a separate return unless an administrator or executor is appointed after the due date of the return. In that case, as previously discussed, the executor may disaffirm the joint return.

1.11 Qualifying Widow(er) Status If Your Spouse Died in 2009 or 2008

If your spouse died in either 2009 or 2008 and you meet the following three requirements, your 2010 filing status is *qualifying widow or widower*, which allows you to use joint return rates on an individual return.

1. You did not remarry before 2011 (if you did remarry, you may file a 2010 joint return with your new spouse).
2. You may claim as your dependent *(21.1)* in 2010 a child, stepchild, or adopted child who lived with you during 2010 and you paid over half the cost of maintaining your home. The child must live with you for the entire year, not counting temporary absences such as to attend school or take a vacation. A foster child is not considered your child for purposes of these rules.
3. You were entitled to file jointly in the year of your spouse's death, even if you did not do so.

If you meet all these tests and do not itemize deductions (Schedule A, Form 1040), use the standard deduction for married couples filing jointly *(13.1)*. To figure your regular income tax liability, you generally use the IRS Tax Table or Tax Computation Worksheet *(22.2)* for qualifying widows or widowers, the same one used by married couples filing jointly.

Spouse's death before 2008. If your spouse died before 2008 and you did not remarry before 2011, you may be able to use head of household rates for 2010 if you qualify under the rules discussed in *1.12*.

Filing Tip

Advantages of Head of Household Status

Tax rates are lower for a head of household than for those filing as single. The standard deduction is also higher. For a married person who lived apart from his or her spouse during the last half of the year, qualifying as a head of household allows use of tax rates that are more favorable than those for married persons filing separately.

1.12 Qualifying as Head of Household

You can file as "head of household" for 2010 if you are unmarried at the end of 2010 and you maintained a household for your child, parent, or other qualifying relative. You must be a U.S. citizen or resident *(18.1)* for the entire year. Tax rates are lower for a head of household than for a person filing as single *(1.2)* and the standard deduction is higher *(Chapter 13)*. If you are married but for the last half of 2010 you lived apart from your spouse, you may be treated as unmarried and able to qualify for head of household tax rates and standard deduction, which are more favorable than those for a married person filing separately; *see* Test 1 below.

Head of household tests. You must meet both of these tests to qualify as a head of household:

1. You were unmarried at the end of the year or treated as unmarried.
2. You paid more than half of the year's maintenance costs for the home of a qualifying person. A qualifying person other than your parent must live with you in that same house for over half the year, disregarding temporary absences. A qualifying parent does not have to live with you.

Details of the tests are in the following paragraphs.

Test 1: Are you unmarried? You are "unmarried" for 2010 head of household purposes if you are any one of the following:

- *Single as of the end of 2010.*
- *A widow or widower and your spouse died before 2010.* If a dependent child lives with you, *see 1.11* to determine if you may use the even more advantageous filing status of qualifying widow(er). If your spouse died in 2010, you are treated as married for the entire year and *cannot* qualify as a 2010 head of household, but a joint return may be filed *(1.10)*.
- *Legally separated or divorced under a final court decree as of the end of 2010.* A custody and support order does not qualify as a legal separation. A provisional decree (not final), such as a support order *pendente lite* (while action is pending) or a temporary order, has no effect for tax purposes until the decree is made final.

- *Married but living apart from your spouse.* You are considered unmarried for 2010 head of household purposes if your spouse was not a member of your household during the last six months of 2010, you file separate returns, and you maintain a household for more than half the year for a dependent child, stepchild, or adopted child. You are not considered to be "living apart" if you and your spouse lived under the same roof during the last six months of the year. A foster child qualifies if he or she was placed with you by an authorized placement agency, or by a court judgment, decree, or order. You must be able to claim the child as a dependent unless your spouse (the noncustodial parent) has the right to the exemption *(21.7)*.
- *Married to an individual who was a nonresident alien during any part of 2010 and you do not elect to file a joint return reporting your joint worldwide income (1.5).*

Note: Same-sex marriages are *not* recognized as marriages under the federal tax law.

Test 2: Did you maintain a home for a qualifying person? You must pay more than half the costs of maintaining a home for a qualifying person.

Qualifying person. A child or relative can be your qualifying person for head of household purposes only if he or she is a qualifying child or relative under the exemption rules for dependents *(21.1)*. However, you may be eligible for head of household status even if you are unable to actually claim the person as your dependent. For example, an unmarried child who meets the definition of a qualifying child *(21.1)* but who cannot be claimed as your dependent because of one of the additional tests *(21.1)* is nonetheless a qualifying person for head of household purposes. If, under the special rules for divorced or separated parents *(21.7)*, you are the custodial parent and you waive your right to the exemption for your child in favor of the other parent, you may claim head of household status; the other parent may not.

A married child must be your dependent to be a qualifying person for head of household purposes unless the only reason you cannot claim the dependency exemption for the child is that you are the dependent of another taxpayer *(21.1)*.

Your parent or any other qualifying relative can be your qualifying person for head of household purposes only if you can claim an exemption for him or her as your dependent *(21.1)*. However, even if you can claim the exemption, you are not eligible for head of household status if the relative is your dependent only because (1) you have a multiple support agreement granting you the right to the exemption *(21.6)* or (2) he or she is your qualifying relative under the member-of-household test *(21.4)*.

Planning Reminder

Special Separate Household Rule for Parent

If your dependent parent is the qualifying person, you may claim head of household status even if he or she does not live with you. You must pay over half of your parent's household expenses, whether your parent lives alone, with someone else, or in a senior citizens' residence.

Maintaining a household. For a qualifying person other than your parent, the home that you maintain must be the principal residence for both of you for more than half the year, disregarding temporary absences; *see* Example 2 below. If the qualifying person is your parent, it does not matter where he or she lives, so long as you pay more than half of the household costs.

You must pay for more than half of the rent, property taxes, mortgage interest, utilities, repairs, property insurance, domestic help, and food eaten in the home. Do not consider the rental value of the lodgings provided to the qualifying person or the cost of clothing, medical expenses, education, vacation costs, life insurance, or transportation you provide, or the value of your work around the house.

Temporary absences disregarded. In determining whether you and a qualifying person lived in the same home for more than half the year, temporary absences are ignored if the absence is due to illness, or being away at school, on a business trip, on vacation, serving in the military, or staying with a parent under a child custody agreement. The IRS requires that it be reasonable to expect your qualifying child or relative to return to your household after such a temporary absence, and that you continue to maintain the household during the temporary absence. Under this rule, you would lose the right to file as head of household if your qualifying person moved into his or her own permanent residence before the end of the year.

EXAMPLES

1. Your mother lived with your sister in your sister's apartment, which cost $12,000 to maintain in 2010. Of this amount, you contributed $7,000 and your sister $5,000. Your mother's only income is from Social Security and she did not contribute any funds to the household. You qualify as head of household for 2010 because you paid over half the cost of maintaining the home for your mother, who qualifies as your dependent *(21.1)*. A child or dependent relative other than your parent would have to live with you to enable you to file as head of household.

2. Doctors advised McDonald that her mentally ill son might become self-sufficient if he lived in a separate residence, but one nearby enough for her to provide supervision. She took the advice and kept up a separate home for her son that was about a mile from her own home. She frequently spent nights at his home and he at hers. The Tax Court agreed with the IRS that McDonald could not file as head of household since her principal residence was not the same as her son's.

1.13 Filing for Your Child

The income of your minor child is *not* included on your return unless you make a special election to report a child's investment income *(24.4)*. A minor is considered a taxpayer in his or her own right. If the child is required to file a return but is unable to do so because of age or for any other reason, the parent or guardian is responsible for filing the return.

A tax return must be filed for a dependent child who had more than $950 of investment income and no earned income (for personal services) for 2010. If your child had only earned income (for personal services) and no investment income, a tax return must be filed if the earned income exceeded $5,700. *See* page 4 for further filing threshold rules.

If the child is unable to sign the return, the parent or guardian should sign the child's name in the proper place, followed by the words, "by [signature], parent [or guardian] for minor child." A parent is liable for tax due on pay earned by the child for services, but not on investment income.

A child who is not required to file a return should still do so for a refund of taxes withheld.

Caution

Kiddie Tax May Apply to Investment Income

If your child has 2010 investment income exceeding $1,900, his or her tax liability generally must be figured on Form 8615, and under the "kiddie tax" rules, the excess over $1,900 will be taxed at your top tax rate rather than at your child's rate. The kiddie tax applies to children under age 18, and also to children who at the end of the year are either age 18 or full-time students under age 24 if their earned income is no more than 50% of their total support for the year *(24.2)*.

Social Security numbers. A parent or guardian must obtain a Social Security number for a child before filing the child's first income tax return. The child's Social Security number must also be provided to banks, brokers, and other payers of interest and dividends to avoid penalties and backup withholding *(26.12)*. To obtain a Social Security number, file Form SS-5 with your local Social Security office. If you have applied for a Social Security number but not yet received it by the filing due date, write "applied for" on the tax return in the space provided for the number.

Whether or not you are filing a return for a child, you must obtain and report on your return a Social Security number for a child whom you are claiming as a dependent *(21.1)*.

Wages you pay your children. You may deduct wages paid to your children in your business. Keep records showing that their activities are of a business rather than personal nature.

Withholding for children. Children with wages are generally subject to withholding and should file Form W-4 with their employer. An exemption from withholding may be claimed only in limited cases. The child must certify on Form W-4 that he or she had no federal tax liability in the prior year and expects no liability in the current year for which the withholding exemption is sought. For example, on Form W-4 for 2010, a child with investment income exceeding $300 who expected to be claimed as another taxpayer's dependent could claim an exemption from withholding only if the expected amount of investment income plus wages was $950 or less (this amount may change annually).

Wages you pay to your own children under age 18 for working in your business are not subject to FICA taxes (Social Security and Medicare) *(26.9)*.

1.14 Return for Deceased

When a person dies, another tax-paying entity is created—the decedent's estate. Until the estate is fully distributed, it will generally earn income for which a return must be filed. For example, Carlos Perez dies on June 30, 2010. The wages and bank interest he earned through June 30 are reported on his final income tax return, Form 1040, which is due by April 15, 2011. Interest earned on his bank account after June 30 is attributed to the estate, or to the account beneficiary if the right to the account passes by law directly to the account beneficiary. Income received by the estate is reported on Form 1041, the income tax return for the estate, if the estate has gross income of $600 or more. If Carlos was married, his surviving spouse could file a joint return *(1.10)* for 2010 and include all of Carlos's earnings through June 30. If she jointly owned the bank account with Carlos, the interest after as well as before June 30 could be reported on their joint return.

Planning Reminder

Promptly Closing the Estate

To expedite the closing of the decedent's estate, an executor or other personal representative of the decedent may file Form 4810 for a prompt assessment. Once filed, the IRS has 18 months to assess additional taxes. The request does not extend the assessment period beyond the regular limit, which is three years from the date the return was filed. Form 4810 must be filed separately from the final return.

What income tax returns must be filed on behalf of the deceased? If the individual died after the close of the taxable year but before the income tax return was filed, the following must be filed:

1. Income tax return for the prior year;
2. Final income tax return, covering earnings in the period from the beginning of the taxable year to the date of death; *and*
3. Estate income tax return, covering earnings in the period after the decedent's death.

If the individual died after filing a return for the prior tax year, then only 2 and 3 are filed.

EXAMPLE

Steven Jones died on January 31, 2011, before he could file his 2010 tax return. His 2010 income tax return must be filed by April 15, 2011, unless an extension is obtained. A final income tax return to report earnings from January 1, 2011, through January 31, 2011, will have to be filed by April 17, 2012. Jones's estate will have to file an income tax return on Form 1041 to report earnings and other income that were not earned by Jones before February 1, 2011, unless the gross income of the estate is under $600.

Who is responsible for filing? The executor, administrator, or other legal representative is responsible for filing all returns. For purposes of determining whether a final income tax return for the decedent is due, the annual gross income test at page 3 is considered in full. You do not prorate it according to the part of the year the decedent lived. A surviving spouse may assume responsibility for filing a joint return for the year of death if no executor or administrator has been appointed and other tests are met *(1.10)*. However, if a legal representative has been appointed, he or she must give the surviving spouse consent to file a joint return for the year of the decedent's death. In one case, a state court held that a co-executrix could not refuse consent and was required to sign a joint return where it would save the estate money.

How do you report the decedent's income and deductions? You follow the method used by the decedent during his or her life, either the cash method or the accrual method, to account for the income up to the date of death. The income does not have to be put on an annual basis. Each item is taxed in the same manner as it would have been taxed had the decedent lived for the entire year.

If the decedent owned U.S. Savings Bonds, *see 4.29*.

When one spouse dies in a community property state *(1.6)*, how should the income from the community property be reported during the administration of the estate? The IRS says that half the income is the estate's and the other half belongs to the surviving spouse.

Deductible expenses paid (or accrued under the accrual method) by the decedent before death are claimed on the final return.

Medical expenses of the decedent. If the estate pays the decedent's personal medical expenses (not those for the decedent's dependents) within one year of the date of death, the expenses can be deducted on the decedent's final return, subject to the regular 7.5% of adjusted gross income floor *(17.8)*. However, the expenses are not deductible for income tax purposes if they are deducted for estate tax purposes. To deduct such medical expenses on the decedent's final return, a statement must be attached to the final return affirming that no estate tax deduction has been taken and that the rights to the deduction have been waived.

Partnership income. The death of a partner closes the partnership tax year for that partner. The final return for the partner must include his or her distributive share of partnership income and deductions for the part of the partnership's tax year ending on the date of death. Thus, if a partner dies on July 26, 2010, and the partnership's taxable year ends December 31, 2010, the partner's final 2010 return must include partnership items for January 1, 2010 through July 26, 2010. Partnership items for the balance of 2010 must be reported by the partner's executor or other successor in interest on the estate's income tax return.

Exemptions allowed on a final return. These are generally the same exemptions the decedent would have had if he or she had not died *(21.1)*. You do not reduce the exemptions because of the shorter taxable year.

1040 *Filing Instruction*

IRD Not Included on Decedent's Final Return

Do not report on the decedent's final return income that is received after his or her death, or accrues after or because of death if the decedent used the accrual method. This income is considered "income in respect of a decedent," or IRD *(11.16)*. IRD is taxed to the estate or beneficiary receiving the income in the year of the receipt. On the decedent's final return, only deductible expenses paid up to and including the date of death may be claimed. If the decedent reported on the accrual basis, those deductions accruable up to and including the date of death are deductible. If a check for payment of a deductible item was delivered or mailed before the date of the decedent's death, a deduction is allowable on the decedent's last return, even though the check was not cashed or deposited until after the decedent's death. If the check was not honored by the bank, the item is not deductible.

Estimated taxes. No estimated tax need be paid by the executor after the death of an unmarried individual; the entire tax is paid when filing the final tax return. But where the deceased and a surviving spouse paid estimated tax jointly, the rule is different. The surviving spouse is still liable for the balance of the estimated tax unless an amended estimated tax voucher is filed. Further, if the surviving spouse plans to file a joint return *(1.10)* that includes the decedent's income, estimated tax payments may be required; *see Chapter 27.*

Where the estate has gross income, estimated tax installments are not required on Form 1041-ES for the first two years after the decedent's death.

Signing the return. An executor or administrator of the estate signs the return. If it is a joint return, *see 1.10.*

When a refund is due on a final return. The decedent's final return may also be used as a claim for a refund of an overpayment of withheld or estimated taxes. Form 1310 may be used to get the refund, but the form is not required if you are a surviving spouse filing a joint return for the year your spouse died. If you are an executor or administrator of the estate and you are filing Form 1040, 1040A, or 1040EZ for the decedent, you do not need Form 1310, but you must attach to the return a copy of the court certificate showing your appointment as personal representative.

Itemized deduction for IRD subject to estate tax. Items of gross income that the decedent had a right to receive but did not receive before death (or accrue if under the accrual method) are subject to income tax when received by the estate or beneficiary. This "income in respect of a decedent," or IRD, is also included in the decedent's estate for estate tax purposes. If estate tax is paid, an individual beneficiary may claim an itemized deduction for an allocable share of the estate tax paid on IRD items; *see 11.17* for deduction details.

1.15 Return for an Incompetent Person

A legal guardian of an incompetent person files Form 1040 for an incompetent whose gross income meets the filing tests on page 3. Where a spouse becomes incompetent, the IRS says the other spouse may file a return for the incompetent without a power of attorney, if no legal guardian has been appointed. For example, during the period an individual was in a mental hospital, and before he was adjudged legally incompetent, his wife continued to operate his business. She filed an income tax return for him and signed it for him although she had no power of attorney. The IRS accepted the return as properly filed. Until a legal guardian was appointed, she was charged with the care of her husband and his property.

The IRS has accepted a joint return filed by a wife in her capacity as legal guardian for her missing husband. However, the Tax Court has held that where one spouse is mentally incompetent, a joint return may not be filed because the incompetent spouse was unable to consent to a joint return; an appeals court agreed.

1.16 How a Nonresident Alien Is Taxed

A nonresident alien is generally taxed only on income from U.S. sources. A nonresident alien's income that is effectively connected with a U.S. business and capital gains from the sale of U.S. real property interests are subject to tax at regular U.S. rates. Other capital gains are not taxed unless a nonresident alien has a U.S. business or is in the U.S. for 183 days during the year. Generally, investment income of a nonresident alien from U.S. sources that is not effectively connected with a U.S. business is subject to a 30% tax rate (or lower rate if provided by treaty).

Nonresident aliens who are required to file must do so on Form 1040NR. If you are a nonresident alien, get a copy of IRS Publication 519, U.S. Tax Guide for Aliens. It explains how nonresident aliens pay U.S. tax.

Caution

Who Is a Resident?

An alien's mere presence in the U.S. does not make him or her a "resident." An alien is generally treated as a "resident" only if he or she is a lawful permanent resident who has a "green card" or meets a substantial presence test *(1.18)*.

Dual status. In the year a person arrives in or departs from the U.S., both resident and nonresident status may apply.

EXAMPLE

On May 1, 2010, Leon Marchand arrived on a non-immigrant visa and was present in the U.S. for the rest of the year. From January 1 to April 30, 2010, he is a nonresident; from May 1 to the end of the year, he is a resident, under the 183-day test *(1.18)*. Despite "dual status," he does not file two returns. Since he is a U.S. resident on the last day of the year, he files Form 1040 and reports income on the basis of his status for each part of the year. He writes "Dual-Status Return" across the top of the Form 1040. The income for the nonresident portion of the year should be shown on Form 1040NR (or, if eligible, Form 1040NR-EZ) and "Dual-Status Statement" marked across the top.

Certain restrictions apply to dual status taxpayers. For example, a joint return may not be filed, unless you and your spouse agree to be taxed as U.S. residents for the entire year.

For details on filing a return for a dual status year, *see* IRS Publication 519 and the instructions to Form 1040NR.

1.17 How a Resident Alien Is Taxed

A resident alien *(1.18)* is taxed on worldwide income from all sources, just like a U.S. citizen. The exclusion for foreign earned income may be claimed if the foreign physical presence test is satisfied or if the bona fide residence test is met by an individual residing in a treaty country *(36.5)*. A resident alien may generally claim a foreign tax credit *(36.14)*. A resident alien's pension from a foreign government is subject to regular U.S. tax. A resident alien working in the United States for a foreign government is not taxed on the wages if the foreign government allows a similar exemption to U.S. citizens.

1.18 Who Is a Resident Alien?

The following tests determine whether an alien is taxed as a U.S. resident. Intent to remain in the U.S. is not considered.

You are treated as a resident alien and taxed as a U.S. resident for 2010 tax purposes if you meet either of the following tests:

1. You have been issued a "green card," which grants you the status of lawful permanent resident. If you were outside the U.S. for part of 2010 and then became a lawful permanent resident, *see* the rules below for dual tax status.
2. You meet a 183-day substantial presence test. Under this test, you are treated as a U.S. resident if you were in the U.S. for at least 31 days during the calendar year and have been in the U.S. for at least 183 days within the last three years (the current year and the two preceding calendar years). The 183-day test is complicated and there are several exceptions.

To determine if you meet the 183-day test for 2010, the following cumulative times are totaled. Each day in the U.S. during 2010 is counted as a full day. Each day in 2009 counts as $1/3$ of a day; each day in 2008 counts as $1/6$ of a day. Note that you must be physically present in the U.S. for at least 31 days in the current year. If you are not, the 183-day test does not apply.

Other exceptions to the substantial presence test are: commuting from Canada or Mexico; keeping a tax home and close contacts or connections in a foreign country; having a diplomat, teacher, trainee, or student status; being a professional athlete temporarily in the U.S. to compete in a charitable sports event; or being confined in the U.S. for certain medical reasons. These exceptions are explained in the following paragraphs.

Commute from Mexico or Canada. If you regularly commute to work in the U.S. from Mexico or Canada, commuting days do not count as days of physical presence for the 183-day test.

Tax home/closer connection exception. If you are in the United States for less than 183 days during 2010, show that you had a closer connection with a foreign country than with the U.S., and keep a tax home there for the year, you generally will not be subject to tax as a U.S. resident even if you meet the substantial presence test. Under this exception, it is possible to have a U.S. abode and a tax home in a foreign country. A tax home is usually where a person has his or her principal place of business; if there is no principal place of business, it is the place of regular abode. Proving a tax home alone is not sufficient; the closer connection relationship must also be shown.

To claim the closer connection exception, you must file Form 8840 explaining the basis of your claim. The tax home/closer connection exception does not apply to an alien who is present for 183 days or more during a year or who has applied for a "green card." A relative's application is not considered as the alien's application.

Exempt-person exception. Days of presence in the U.S. are not counted under the 183-day test if you are considered an exempt person such as a teacher, trainee, student, foreign-government-related person, or professional athlete temporarily in the U.S. to compete in a charitable sports event.

Planning Reminder

Is 2010 Your First Year of Residency?

If you were not a resident during 2009 but in 2010 you satisfy both the lawful resident (green card) test and the 183-day presence test, your residence begins on the earlier of the first day you are in the U.S. while a lawful permanent resident and the first day of physical presence.

To exclude days of presence as a teacher, trainee, student, or professional athlete, you must file Form 8843 with the IRS.

A foreign-government-related person is any individual temporarily present in the U.S. who (1) has diplomatic status or a visa that the Secretary of the Treasury (after consultation with the Secretary of State) determined represents full-time diplomatic or consular status; or (2) is a full-time employee of an international organization; or (3) is a member of the immediate family of a diplomat or international organization employee.

A teacher or trainee is any individual other than a student who is temporarily present in the U.S. under a "J" or "Q" visa and who substantially complies with the requirements for being so present.

A student is any individual who is temporarily present in the U.S. under either an "F," "J," "M," or "Q" visa and who substantially complies with the requirements for being so present.

The exception generally does not apply to a teacher or trainee who has been exempt as a teacher, trainee, or student for any part of two of the six preceding calendar years. However, if during the period you are temporarily present in the U.S. under an "F," "J," "M," or "Q" visa and all of your compensation is received from outside the U.S., you may qualify for the exception if you were exempt as a teacher, trainee, or student for less than four years in the six preceding calendar years. The exception also does not apply to a student who has been exempt as a teacher, trainee, or student for more than five calendar years, unless you show that you do not intend to reside permanently in the U.S. and that you have substantially complied with the requirements of the student visa providing for temporary presence in the U.S.

Medical exception. If you plan to leave but cannot physically leave the U.S. because of a medical condition that arose in the U.S., you may be treated as a nonresident, even if present here for more than 183 days during the year. You must file Form 8843 to claim the medical exception.

Tax treaty exceptions. The lawful permanent residence test and the substantial physical presence test do not override tax treaty definitions of residence. Thus, you may be protected by a tax treaty from being treated as a U.S. resident even if you would be treated as a resident under either test.

Dual tax status in first year of residency. If you first became a lawful permanent resident of the U.S. (received a green card) during 2010 and were not a U.S. resident during 2009, your period of U.S. residency begins with the first day in 2010 that you are present in the U.S. with the status of lawful permanent resident. Before that date, you are a nonresident alien. This means that if you become a lawful permanent resident during 2010 and remain a resident at the end of the year, you have a dual status tax year. On Form 1040, you attach a separate statement showing the income for the part of the year you are a nonresident. Form 1040NR (or 1040NR-EZ) may be used as the statement. Write "Dual-Status Return" or "Dual-Status Statement" across the top, as applicable.

To figure tax for a dual status year, *see* IRS Publication 519 and the instructions to Form 1040NR.

You also may have a dual status year if you were not a U.S. resident in 2009, and in 2010 you are a U.S. resident under the 183-day presence test. Your period of U.S. residency starts on the first day in 2010 for which you were physically present; before that date you are treated as a nonresident alien. However, if you meet the 183-day presence test (but not the green card test) and also spent 10 or fewer days in the U.S. during a period in which you had a closer connection to a foreign country than to the U.S., you may disregard the 10-day period. The purpose of this exception is to allow a brief presence in the U.S. for business trips or house hunting before the U.S. residency period starts.

If you are married at the end of the year to a U.S. citizen or resident alien, you and your spouse may elect to be treated as U.S. residents for the entire year by reporting your worldwide income on a joint return. You must attach to the joint return a statement signed by both of you that you are choosing to be treated as full-year U.S. residents.

EXAMPLES

1. Manuel Riveras, who has never before been a U.S. resident, lives in Spain until May 15, 2010. He moves to the U.S. and remains in the U.S. through the end of the year, thereby satisfying the physical presence test. On May 15, he is a U.S. resident. However, for the period before May 15, he is taxed as a nonresident.

2. Same facts as in Example 1, but Riveras attends a meeting in the U.S. on February 2 through 8. On May 15, he moves to the U.S.; May 15, not February 2, is the starting date of the residency. During February, he had closer connection to Spain than to the U.S. Thus, his short stay in February is an exempt period.

First-year choice. If you do not meet either the green card test or the 183-day substantial presence test for the year of your arrival in the U.S. or for the immediately preceding year, but you do meet the substantial presence test for the year immediately following the year of your arrival, you may elect to be treated as a U.S. resident for part of the year of your arrival. To do this, you must (1) be present in the U.S. for at least 31 consecutive days in the year of your arrival; and (2) be present in the U.S. for at least 75% of the number of days beginning with the first day of the 31-consecutive-day period and ending with the last day of the year of arrival. For purposes of this 75% requirement, you may treat up to five days of absence from the U.S. as days of presence within the U.S.

Do not count as days of presence in the U.S. days for which you are an *exempt individual* as discussed earlier.

You make the first-year election to be treated as a U.S. resident by attaching a statement to Form 1040 for the year of your arrival. A first-year election, once made, may not be revoked without the consent of the IRS.

If you make the election, your residence starting date for the year of your arrival is the first day of the earliest 31-consecutive-day period of presence that you use to qualify for the choice. You are treated as a U.S. resident for the remainder of the year.

Last year of residence. You are no longer treated as a U.S. resident as of your residency termination date. If you do not have a green card but are a U.S. resident for the year under the 183-day presence test, and you leave the U.S. during that year, your residency termination date is the last day you are present in the U.S., provided that: (1) after leaving the U.S. you had a closer connection to a foreign country than to the U.S. and had your tax home in that foreign country for the rest of the year, and (2) you are not treated as a U.S. resident for any part of the next calendar year.

If during the year you give up your green card (lawful permanent resident status) and meet tests (1) and (2), your residency termination date is the first day that you are no longer a lawful permanent resident. If during the year you meet both the green card test and the 183-day presence test and meet tests (1) and (2), your residency termination date is the *later* of the last day of U.S. presence or the first day you are no longer a lawful permanent resident. If tests (1) and (2) are not met, the residency termination date is the last day of the calendar year. In the year of your residency termination date, the filing rules for dual status taxpayers in this section apply.

For the year you give up your residence in the United States, you must file Form 1040NR (or Form 1040NR-EZ if eligible) and write "Dual-Status Return" across the top. Attach Form 1040 (or other statement) to show the income for the part of the year you are a resident; across the top write "Dual-Status Statement." *See* the instructions to Form 1040NR and IRS Publication 519 for filing the dual status return.

1.19 When an Alien Leaves the United States

Current law generally requires an alien who leaves the U.S., regardless of how long the trip is, to obtain a "sailing" or "departure" permit, technically known as a "certificate of compliance." The permit states that you have fulfilled your income tax obligations to the U.S. Without it, unless you are excused from obtaining one, you will be required at your point of departure to file a tax return and pay any tax due or post a bond. Diplomats, employees of international organizations or foreign governments, and students are generally exempt from the permit requirement. If a permit is required, Form 1040-C or in some cases a shorter Form 2063 must be filed with the IRS. *See* Publication 519 for further details.

Planning Reminder

Departure Permit

An alien planning to leave the U.S. should obtain a copy of Form 1040-C from the IRS to review his or her tax reporting obligations.

1.20 Expatriation Tax

U.S. citizens who have renounced their citizenship and long-term U.S. residents who end their residency are considered expatriates subject to special tax rules. You are considered a long-term resident for purposes of these rules if you give up lawful permanent residency ("green card") after holding it for at least eight of the prior 15 years. Form 8854 must be filed if the expatriation date was on or after June 4, 2004. Individuals who expatriated after June 3, 2004 and before June 17, 2008 are subject to different tax consequences than individuals who expatriate after June 16, 2008.

Expatriation after June 16, 2008. If you expatriated after June 16, 2008, you are subject to a "mark-to-market" tax if any of the following is true: (1) your average annual net income tax liability for the five years ending before the date of expatriation exceeds an annual ceiling, which for 2010 is $145,000, or (2) your net worth on the date of expatriation was $2 million or more, or (3) you fail to certify on Form 8854 under penalty of perjury that you complied with all U.S. federal tax obligations for the five years preceding the expatriation date.

Under the "mark-to market" tax, you are treated as if you had sold all of your assets for their fair market value on the day before the expatriation date, and any net gain on the deemed sale is taxable for the year of the deemed sale to the extent it exceeds an annual floor, which is $627,000 for expatriations in 2010. Losses are taken into account and the wash sale rules do not apply. An election can be made to deter the tax on the deemed sales until asset is sold (or death, if sooner) provided a bond or other security is provided to the IRS. Deferred compensation items and interests in nongrantor trusts are not subject to the mark-to-market tax, but are generally subject to a withholding tax of 30% when distributed to you. IRAs and certain other tax-deferred accounts are treated as if they were completely distributed on the day before the expatriation date, but early distribution penalties do not apply. *See* the Form 8854 instructions for further details.

Expatriation after June 3, 2004 and before June 17, 2008. If you expatriated after June 3, 2004 but before June 17, 2008 and any of the following apply, you are subject to tax on U.S. source income for the following 10 years: (1) your average annual net income tax liability for the five years ending before the date of expatriation exceeds $139,000 if you expatriated in 2008, $136,000 if you expatriated in 2007, $131,000 if you expatriated in 2006, $127,000 if you expatriated in 2005, or $124,000 if you expatriated in 2004, or (2) your net worth on the date of expatriation was $2 million or more, or (3) you fail to certify on Form 8854 under penalty of perjury that you complied with all U.S. federal tax obligations for the five years preceding the expatriation date.

U.S. source income and gains are subject to regular individual tax rates unless the tax would be higher under the 30% tax on investment income not connected with a U.S. business. Form 8854 must be filed for the 10-year period. *See* the Form 8854 instructions and Publication 519 for further details.

Reporting Your Income

In this part, you will learn what income is taxable, what income is tax free, and how to report income on your tax return.

Pay special attention to—

- Form W-2, which shows your taxable wages and provides other important information on fringe benefits received *(Chapter 2)*.
- Tax-free fringe benefit plans available from your employer *(Chapter 3)*.
- Reporting rules for interest and dividend income *(Chapter 4)*.
- Reporting gains and losses from sales of property *(Chapter 5)*.
- Rules for tax-free exchanges of like-kind property *(Chapter 6)*.
- Planning for retirement distributions. Lump-sum distributions from employer plans may qualify for special averaging or tax-free rollover *(Chapter 7)*.
- IRA contributions and distributions. Penalties for distributions before age 59½ and after age 70½ may be avoided by advance planning *(Chapter 8)*.
- Restrictions on rental losses where a rented residence is used personally by you or by family members during the year *(Chapter 9)*.
- Passive activity restrictions. Losses from rentals or passive business operations are generally not allowed, but certain real estate professionals are exempt from the loss restrictions, and for others, a special rental loss allowance of up to $25,000 may be available *(Chapter 10)*.
- Reporting refunds of state and local taxes. A refund of previously deducted taxes is generally taxable unless you had no benefit from the deduction *(Chapter 11)*.
- Cancellation of debts. When your creditor cancels debts you owe, you generally have taxable income, but there are exceptions for debts discharged while you are bankrupt or insolvent *(Chapter 11)*.
- Damages received in court proceedings. Learn when these are tax free and when taxable *(Chapter 11)*.
- How life insurance proceeds are taxed *(Chapter 11)*.

Chapter 2

Wages, Salary, and Other Compensation

Except for tax-free fringe benefits *(Chapter 3)*, tax-free foreign earned income *(Chapter 36)* and tax-free armed forces and veterans' benefits *(Chapter 35)*, practically everything you receive for your work or services is taxed, whether paid in cash, property, or services. Your employer will generally report your taxable compensation on Form W-2 and other information returns, such as Form 1099-R for certain retirement payments. Do not reduce the amount you report on your return by withholdings for income taxes, Social Security taxes, union dues, or U.S. Savings Bond purchases. Your Form W-2 does not include in taxable pay your qualifying salary-reduction contributions to a retirement plan, although the amount may be shown on the form.

Attach Copy B of Form W-2 to your return; do not attach Forms 1099 unless there are withholdings.

Unemployment benefits received in 2010 are fully taxable. The benefits are reported to the IRS on Form 1099-G. You do not have to attach your copy of Form 1099-G to your return.

Income and expenses from self-employment are discussed in *Chapter 40*.

Table 2-1 Understanding Your Form W-2 for 2010 Wages and Tips

Amount in—	*What You Should Know—*
Box 1	***Taxable wages and tips.*** Your taxable wages, tips, and other forms of taxable compensation *(2.1)* are listed in Box 1. Taxable fringe benefits will also be included in Box 1 and may be shown in Box 14.
Box 2	***Federal tax withholdings.*** This is the amount of federal income tax withheld from your pay. Enter the amount on Line 61 of Form 1040, Line 38 of Form 1040A, or on Line 7 of Form 1040EZ.
Boxes 3, 4, and 7	Social Security withholdings. Wages subject to Social Security withholding are shown in Box 3. Tips you reported to your employer are shown separately in Box 7. The total of Boxes 3 and 7 should not exceed $106,800, the maximum Social Security wage base for 2010. Social Security taxes withheld from wages and tips are shown in Box 4 and should not exceed the maximum 2010 tax of $6,621.60 ($106,800 x 6.2% rate). If you worked for more than one employer in 2010 and total Social Security tax withholdings exceeded $6,621.60, you claim the excess as a tax payment on your tax return; *see 26.9.* Elective salary deferrals to a 401(k), SIMPLE, salary-reduction SEP, or 403(b) plan, as well as employer payments of qualified adoption expenses, are included in Box 3 even though these amounts are not includible in Box 1 taxable wages. Amounts deferred under a nonqualified plan or a 457 plan are included in Box 3 in the year that the deferred amounts are no longer subject to a substantial risk of forfeiture.
Boxes 5–6	***Medicare tax withholdings.*** Wages, tips, elective salary deferrals, and other compensation subject to Social Security tax (Boxes 3 and 7) are also subject to a 1.45% Medicare tax, except that there is no wage base limit for Medicare tax. Thus, the Medicare wages shown in Box 5 are not limited to the $106,800 maximum for Boxes 3 and 7. In Box 6, total Medicare withholdings are reported.
Box 8	***Allocated tips.*** If you worked in a restaurant employing at least 10 people, your employer will report in Box 8 your share of 8% of gross receipts unless you reported tips at least equal to that share *(26.7)*. The amount shown here is not included in Boxes 1, 3, 5, or 7, but you must add it to wages on Line 7 of Form 1040; you cannot file Form 1040A or 1040EZ.
Box 9	***Advance earned income payment.*** If you filed a Form W-5 asking for a part of the credit to be added to your wages, the amount of the advance is shown in Box 9. You report the advance as a tax liability when you file Form 1040 or 1040A; *see Chapter 25.*
Box 10	***Dependent care benefits.*** Reimbursements from your employer for dependent care expenses and the value of employer-provided care services under a qualifying plan *(3.5)* are included in Box 10. Amounts in excess of $5,000 are also included as taxable wages in Boxes 1, 3, and 5. Generally, amounts up to $5,000 are tax free, but you must determine the amount of the exclusion on Form 2441. The tax-free amount reduces expenses eligible for the dependent care credit; *see Chapter 25.*
Box 11	***Nonqualified plan distributions.*** Distributions shown in Box 11 are from a nonqualified deferred compensation plan, or a nongovernmental Section 457 plan *(7.21)*. Do not report these distributions separately since they have already been included as taxable wages in Box 1.
Box 12	***Elective deferrals to retirement plans.*** Elective salary deferrals to a 401(k) plan or SIMPLE 401(k) (including any excess over the annual deferral limit; *see 7.18)* are shown in Box 12 with Code D. For example, if you made elective pre-tax salary deferrals of $4,500 to a 401(k) plan, your employer would enter D 4500.00 in Box 12. Designated Roth contributions *(7.20)* to a 401(k) plan are reported in Box 12 with Code AA. Code E is used for deferrals to a 403(b) tax-sheltered annuity plan *(7.20)*, Code F for deferrals to a salary-reduction simplified employee pension *(8.16)*, Code G for deferrals (including non-elective as well as elective) to a Section 457 plan *(7.21)*, Code H for elective deferrals to a pension plan created before June 25, 1959, and funded only by employee contributions, and Code S for salary-reduction deferrals to a SIMPLE IRA *(8.18)*. ***Travel allowance reimbursements.*** If you received a flat mileage allowance from your employer for business trips *(20.33)*; or a *per diem* travel allowance to cover meals, lodging, and incidentals *(20.32)*; and the allowance exceeded the IRS rate, the amount up to the IRS rate (the nontaxable portion) is shown in Box 12 using Code L. The excess is included as taxable wages in Box 1. ***Group-term life insurance over $50,000.*** The cost of taxable coverage over $50,000 is shown in Box 12 using Code C. It is also included in Box 1 wages, Box 3 Social Security wages, and Box 5 Medicare wages and tips. If you are a retiree or other former employee who received group-term coverage over $50,000, any uncollected Social Security tax is shown using Code M and uncollected Medicare tax using Code N. The uncollected amount must be reported on Line 60 of Form 1040 (total tax); write "UT" next to it. ***Nontaxable sick pay.*** If you contributed to a sick pay plan, an allocable portion of benefits received is tax free and is shown using Code J.

Table 2-1 (continued)

Box 12	***Uncollected Social Security and Medicare taxes on tips.*** If your employer could not withhold sufficient Social Security on tips, the uncollected amount is shown using Code A. For uncollected Medicare tax, Code B is used. This amount must be reported on Line 60 of Form 1040 (total tax); write "UT" next to it. ***Excess golden parachute payments.*** If you received an "excess parachute payment as wages," Code K identifies the 20% penalty tax on the excess payment that was withheld by the employer. This withheld amount is included in Box 2, but you also must add it as an additional tax on Line 60 (total tax) of Form 1040. ***Moving expense reimbursements.*** Tax-free employer reimbursements to you for deductible moving expenses *(12.8)* are shown with Code P. ***Employer contributions to health savings account (HSA) or Archer MSA.*** Total employer contributions to an HSA are shown with Code W. Total employer contributions to an MSA are shown with Code R. Contributions exceeding the excludable limit *(Chapter 3)* are included as taxable wages in Boxes 1, 3, and 5. ***Employer-financed adoption benefits.*** Total qualified adoption expenses paid or reimbursed by your employer *(3.6)* plus *any* pre-tax contributions you made to an adoption plan account under a cafeteria plan *(3.13)* are shown with Code T. ***Nonstatutory stock option exercised.*** If you exercised a nonstatutory stock option, Code V shows the taxable "spread" (excess of fair market value of stock over exercise price). The income should be included in Boxes 1, 3 (up to the $106,800 Social Security wage ceiling), and 5. ***Deferrals and income under Section 409A nonqualified deferred compensation plan.*** Current year deferrals plus all earnings under a 409A plan may be shown (its optional) with Code Y. Code Z shows amounts included as income in Box 1; this income is subject to a penalty plus interest on Form 1040 *(2.7)*.
Box 13	***Statutory employee.*** If this box is checked you report your wage income and deductible job expenses on Schedule C *(40.6)*. Your earnings are not subject to income tax withholding, but are subject to Social Security and Medicare taxes. ***Retirement plan.*** This box is checked if you were an active participant in an employer plan at some point during the year. As an active participant, you are subject to the phase-out rules for IRA deductions) *(8.4)*.
Box 14	***Taxable fringe benefits and miscellaneous payments.*** Your employer may use Box 14 to report fringe benefits or deductions from your pay, such as state disability insurance taxes, union dues, educational assistance, health insurance premiums, or voluntary after-tax contributions to profit-sharing or pension plans. If your employer included in Box 1 the lease value of a car *(3.7)* provided to you, this value must also be shown in Box 14 or on a separate statement.
Boxes 17 and 19	***State and local taxes.*** If you itemize, deduct on Schedule A state and local tax withholdings shown in Boxes 17 and 19, unless you elect to deduct state and local general sales taxes *(16.3)*.

a Employee's social security number	OMB No. 1545-0008	Safe, accurate, FAST! Use IRS e-file	Visit the IRS website at www.irs.gov/efile
08-X1X0X1X			

b Employer identification number (EIN)	1 Wages, tips, other compensation 57,800.00	2 Federal income tax withheld 10,000.00
c Employer's name, address, and ZIP code Finkle Construction Company 5532 Glasgow Plaza City, State XX111	3 Social security wages 63,580.00	4 Social security tax withheld 3,941.96
	5 Medicare wages and tips 63,580.00	6 Medicare tax withheld 921.91
	7 Social security tips	8 Allocated tips
d Control number 0X1 - XX - 1X00	9 Advance EIC payment	10 Dependent care benefits
e Employee's first name and initial Last name Suff. Mary Moll 176 Garden Road City, State 1XXX1 f Employee's address and ZIP code	11 Nonqualified plans	12a See instructions for box 12 5,780.00
	13 Statutory employee ☐ Retirement plan ☐ Third-party sick pay ☐	12b
	14 Other	12c
		12d

15 State	Employer's state ID number	16 State wages, tips, etc.	17 State income tax	18 Local wages, tips, etc.	19 Local income tax	20 Locality name
State	11-X1X0X1X	57,800.00	2,980.00	57,800.00	1,734.00	City

Form **W-2** **Wage and Tax Statement** 2010

Department of the Treasury—Internal Revenue Service

Copy B—To Be Filed With Employee's FEDERAL Tax Return.
This information is being furnished to the Internal Revenue Service.

2.1 Salary and Wage Income

The key to reporting your pay is Form W-2, sent to you by your employer. It lists your taxable wages, which may include not only your regular pay, but also other taxable items, such as taxable fringe benefits. *Table 2-1* explains how employee pay benefits and tax withholdings are reported on Form W-2.

Your employer reports your taxable pay under a simple rule. Unless the item is specifically exempt from tax, you are taxed on practically everything you receive for your work whether paid in cash, property, or services. Benefits that the law specifically excludes from tax are discussed in *Chapter 3*. The most common tax-free benefits are employer-paid premiums for health and accident plans, medical expense reimbursements, and group-term life insurance coverage up to $50,000.

Your employer will include in Box 1 of your Form W-2 the total wages, tips, and other compensation, before payroll deductions, that were paid to you during the year. Box 1 may include, in addition to regular wages and tips, the following types of taxable compensation:

- Bonuses (including signing bonuses)
- Taxable fringe benefits *(Chapter 3)*
- *Per diem* or mileage allowances exceeding the IRS rate *(20.32–20.33)*
- Expense allowances or business expense reimbursements under a non-accountable plan *(20.34)*
- Awards or prizes not exempt under *3.11*
- Cost of group-term life insurance over $50,000 *(3.4)*
- Cost of accident and health insurance premiums paid by an S corporation for 2%-or-more shareholder-employees
- Deferred income that is currently taxable under a Section 409A nonqualified deferred compensation plan *(2.7)*

Compensation reported in Box 1 must be reported as wages on Line 7 of Form 1040 or 1040A, or Line 1 of Form 1040EZ. Other types of income must also be reported as wages on your return although they are not included in Box 1 of Form W-2, such as non-excludable dependent care *(3.5)* or adoption *(3.6)* benefits, tips not reported to your employer or allocated tips *(26.8)*, disability pension shown on Form 1099-R if you are under your employer's minimum retirement age, or excess salary deferrals to an employer retirement plan *(7.18)*.

Withholdings for retirement plans. Amounts withheld from wages as your contribution to your pension or profit-sharing account are generally taxable as compensation unless they are tax-deferred elective deferrals under the limits allowed for Section 401(k) plans *(7.18)*, simplified employee pension plans *(8.16)*, SIMPLE IRAs *(8.18)*, or tax-sheltered annuity plans *(7.20)*. Elective deferrals are reported in Box 12 of Form W-2.

Wages withheld for compulsory forfeitable contributions to a nonqualified pension plan are not taxable if these conditions exist:

1. The contribution is forfeited if employment is terminated prior to death or retirement.
2. The plan does not provide for a refund of employee contributions and, in the administration of the plan, no refund will be made. Where only part of the contribution is subject to forfeiture, the amount of withheld contribution not subject to forfeiture is taxable income.

You should check with your employer to determine the status of your contributions.

Assigning your pay. You may not avoid tax on income you earned by assigning the right to payment to another person. For example, you must report earnings that you donate to charity, even if they are paid directly by your employer to a charity. If you claim itemized deductions, you may claim a contribution deduction for the donation; *see Chapter 14*. Assignments of income-generating intellectual property are held taxable to the assignee. However, if the assignor retained power or control of the property, the assignor could be held liable for the tax according to the 8th Circuit.

The IRS allowed an exception for doctors working in a clinic. The doctors were not taxed on fees for treating patients with limited income (teaching cases) where they were required to assign the fees to a foundation.

Caution

Severance Pay Taxable

You must pay tax on severance pay received upon losing a job. The severance pay is taxable even if you signed a waiver releasing your former employer from potential future damage claims. The waiver does not change the nature of the payments from taxable pay to tax-free personal injury damages *(11.7)*.

Filing Instruction

Tips Must Be Reported

Tips you receive are taxable income. You must report tips to your employer so your employer can withhold FICA and income tax from your regular pay to cover the tips *(26.8)*.

Court Decision

Tax on Assigned Contingent Fee

An attorney who took a medical malpractice case on a contingent fee basis agreed to split the net fee with his ex-wife pursuant to their divorce agreement. After a favorable settlement, the attorney's take was approximately $40,000 after expenses, half of which went to his ex-wife. Each paid tax on his or her share. The attorney argued that his partial assignment of the fee could shift the tax liability because collection was contingent on the outcome of the lawsuit. However, the IRS and the Tax Court held that the attorney was liable for the tax on the entire contingent fee, and an appeals court agreed. The attorney transferred only the right to receive income. Although his fee was contingent upon the successful outcome of the case, once the fee materialized, it was indisputably compensation for his personal services.

Gifts from employers. A payment may be called a gift but still be taxable income. Any payment made in recognition of past services or in anticipation of future services or benefits is taxable as wages even if the employer is not obligated to make the payment. However, there are exceptions for employee achievement awards *(3.11)*.

To prove a gift is tax free, you must show that the employer acted with pure and unselfish motives of affection, admiration, or charity. This is difficult to do, given the employer-employee relationship. A gift of stock by majority stockholders to key employees has been held to be taxable.

Employee leave-sharing plan. Some companies allow employees to contribute their unused leave into a "leave fund" for use by other employees who have suffered medical emergencies. If you use up your regular leave and benefit from additional leave that has been donated to the plan, the benefit is taxable and will be reported as wages on Form W-2.

"Golden parachute" payments. Golden parachute arrangements are agreements to pay key employees additional compensation upon a change in company control. If you receive such a payment, part of it may be deemed to be an "excess payment" under a complex formula in the law. You must pay a 20% penalty tax on the "excess" amount in addition to regular income tax on the total. The 20% penalty should be identified on Form W-2 with Code K in Box 12; *see Table 2-1*.

If the golden parachute payment is made to a non-employee, the company will report it in Box 7 (non-employee compensation) of Form 1099-MISC. If you are self-employed, report the total compensation on Schedule C *(40.6)* and compute self-employment tax on Schedule SE *(45.3)*. Any "excess parachute payment" should be separately labeled in Box 13 of Form 1099-MISC. Multiply the Box 13 amount by 20% and report it on Line 60 (total tax) of Form 1040; label it "EPP."

2.2 Constructive Receipt of Year-End Paychecks

As an employee, you use the cash-basis method of accounting. This means that you report all income items in the year they are actually received and deduct expenses in the year you pay them.

You are also subject to the "constructive receipt rule," which requires you to report income not actually received but which has been credited to your account, subject to your control, or put aside for you. Thus, if you received a paycheck at the end of 2010 , you must report the pay on your 2010 return, even though you do not cash or deposit it to your account until 2011. This is true even if you receive the check after banking hours on the last business day of the year and cannot cash or deposit it until the next year. The Tax Court has also ruled that receipt by an agent (*e.g.*, an attorney) is constructive receipt by the principal. In one case, a woman argued that alimony received by her in 1991 was taxable in 1991. Because the funds were given to her attorney on December 27, 1990, the Tax Court held that she was in constructive receipt of the funds and that they were taxable in 1990.

If your employer does not have funds in the bank and asks you to hold the check before depositing it, you do not have taxable income until the check is cashed. If services rendered in 2010 are paid for by check dated for 2011, the pay is taxable in 2011.

The IRS has ruled that an employee who is not at home on December 31 to take delivery of a check sent by certified mail must still report the check in that year. However, where an employee was not at home to take certified mail delivery of a year-end check that she did not expect to receive until the next year, the Tax Court held that the funds were taxable when received in the following year.

2.3 Pay Received in Property Is Taxed

Your employer may pay you with property instead of cash. You report the fair market value of the property as wages.

EXAMPLE

For consulting services rendered, Kate Chong receives a check for $10,000 and property with a fair market value of $5,000. She reports $15,000 as wages.

If you receive your unrestricted company stock as payment for your services, you include the value of the stock as pay in the year you receive it. However, if the stock is nontransferable or subject to substantial risk of forfeiture, you do not have to include its value as pay until the restrictions no longer apply *(2.18)*. You must report dividends on the restricted stock in the year you receive the income.

If you receive your employer's note that has a fair market value, you are taxed on the value of the note less what it would cost you to discount it. If the note bears interest, report the full face value. But do not report income if the note has no fair market value. Report income on the note only when payments are made on it.

A debt cancelled by an employer is taxable income.

Salespeople employed by a dealer have taxable income on receipt of "prize points" redeemable for merchandise from a distributor.

2.4 Commissions Taxable When Credited

Earned commissions are taxable in the year they are credited to your account and subject to your drawing, whether or not you actually draw them.

On your 2010 tax return, you do not report commissions that were earned in 2010 but cannot be computed or collected until a later year.

Caution

Earned Commissions Credited to Your Account

You may not postpone tax on earned commissions credited to your account in 2010 by not drawing them until 2011 or a later year. However, where a portion of earned commissions is not withdrawn because your employer is holding it to cover future expenses, you are not taxed on the amount withheld.

EXAMPLE

Arno Jeffers earns commissions based on a percentage of the profits from realty sales. In 2010 he draws $10,000 from his account. However, at the end of 2010 the full amount of his commissions is unknown because profits for the year have not been figured. In January 2011, his 2010 commissions are computed to be $15,000, and the $5,000 balance is paid to him. The $5,000 is taxable in 2011 even though earned in 2010.

Advances against unearned commissions. Under standard insurance industry practice, an agent who sells a policy does not earn commissions until premiums are received by the insurance company. However, the company may issue a cash advance on the commissions before the premiums are received. Agents have claimed that they may defer reporting the income until the year the premiums are earned. The IRS, recognizing that in practice companies rarely demand repayment, requires that advances be included in income in the year received if the agent has full control over the advanced funds. A repayment of unearned commissions in a later year *(2.8)* is deducted on Schedule A.

Salespeople have been taxed on commissions received on property bought for their personal use. In one case, an insurance agent was taxed on commissions paid to him on his purchase of an insurance policy. In another case, a real estate agent was taxed on commissions he received on his purchase of land. A salesman was also taxed for commissions waived on policies he sold to friends, relatives, and employees.

Kickback of commissions. An insurance agent's kickback of his or her commission is taxable where agents may not under local law give rebates or kickbacks of premiums to their clients. The commissions are income and may not be offset with a business expense deduction; illegal kickbacks may not be deducted.

However, in one case, a federal appeals court allowed an insurance broker to avoid tax when he did not charge clients the basic first-year commission. The clients paid the broker the net premium (gross premium less the commission), which he remitted to the insurance company. The IRS and Tax Court held that the commissions were taxable despite the broker's voluntary waiver of his right to them. He could not deduct them because his discount scheme violated state anti-rebate law (Oklahoma). On appeal, the broker won. The Tenth Circuit Court of Appeals held that since the broker never had any right to commissions under the terms of the contracts he structured with his clients, he was not taxed on the commissions. The court cautioned that if the broker had remitted the full premium (including commission) to the insurance company and then reimbursed the client after having received the commission from the company, the commission probably would have been taxable.

2.5 Unemployment Benefits

All unemployment benefits received in 2010 are taxable. You should receive Form 1099-G, showing the amount of the payments. Report the payments on Line 19 of Form 1040, Line 13 of Form 1040A, or Line 3 of Form 1040EZ.

Supplemental unemployment benefits paid from company-financed funds are taxable as wages and not reported as unemployment compensation. Such benefits are usually paid under guaranteed annual wage plans made between unions and employers.

Unemployment benefits from a private or union fund to which you voluntarily contribute dues are taxable as "other" income on Form 1040, but only to the extent the benefits exceed your contributions to the fund. Your contributions to the fund are not deductible.

Worker's compensation payments *(2.13)* are not taxable.

Taxable unemployment benefits include federal trade readjustment allowances (1974 Trade Act), airline deregulation benefits (1978 Airline Deregulation Act), and disaster unemployment assistance (1974 Disaster Relief Act).

Repaid supplemental unemployment benefits. If you had to repay supplemental unemployment benefits to receive trade readjustment allowances (1974 Trade Act), taxable unemployment benefits are reduced by repayments made in the same year. If you repay the benefits in a later year, the benefits are taxed in the year of receipt and a deduction may be claimed in the later year. If the repayment is $3,000 or less, the deduction is added to your other adjustments to income on Line 36 of Form 1040; label it "sub-pay TRA." If the repayment exceeds $3,000, a deduction or a credit may be *(2.8)*.

2.6 Strike Pay Benefits and Penalties

Strike and lockout benefits paid out of regular union dues are taxable as wages unless the payment qualifies as a gift, as discussed below. However, if you have made voluntary contributions to a strike fund, benefits you receive from the fund are tax free up to the amount of your contributions and are taxable to the extent they exceed your contributions.

Strike benefits as tax-free gifts. Here are factors indicating that benefits are gifts: Payments are based on individual need; they are paid to both union and non-union members; and no conditions are imposed on the strikers who receive benefits.

If you receive benefits under conditions by which you are to participate in the strike and the payments are tied to your scale of wages, the benefits are taxable.

EXAMPLE

A striking union pilot claimed that strike benefits were tax-free gifts because they were funded by assessments paid by other union pilots who were not on strike. The IRS and Tax Court held that the benefits were taxable. They were not gifts because they were not motivated by a "detached and disinterested generosity." The union was promoting its own self-interest by giving pilots an incentive to support the strike. The non-striking pilots contributed to the strike fund as an obligation of union membership. The strikers were eligible for benefits only if they agreed to perform any strike activities requested by the union, did not fly for airlines in dispute with the union, and did not take actions that could adversely affect the outcome of the dispute.

Strike pay penalties. Pay penalties charged to striking teachers are not deductible. State law may prohibit public school teachers from striking and charge a penalty equal to one day's pay for each day spent on strike. For example, when striking teachers returned to work after a one-week strike, a penalty of one week's salary was deducted from their pay. Although they did not actually receive pay for the week they worked after the strike, they earned taxable wages. Furthermore, the penalty is not deductible. No deduction is allowed for a fine or penalty paid to a government for the violation of a law.

Caution

Law Violation Not Deductible

No deduction is allowed for a fine or penalty paid to a government for the violation of a law.

2.7 Nonqualified Deferred Compensation

The rules for determining whether tax may be deferred under a nonqualified deferred compensation plan are governed by Code Section 409A. Section 409A applies generally to amounts deferred after 2004. Amounts deferred before 2005 are "grandfathered," and thus generally exempt, but they become subject to Section 409A (unless excluded under IRS rules) if the plan is materially modified after October 3, 2004.

Caution

Penalty and Interest on Nonqualified Deferred Compensation

If deferred pay is currently taxable under the rules of Code Section 409A, you must also pay a 20% penalty and interest at a rate 1% higher than the regular underpayment rate.

Plans subject to and excluded from Section 409A. Unless an exception applies, Code Section 409A applies to all plans, including arrangements between an independent contractor and a service recipient, and a partner and partnership, under which the service provider has a legally binding right during a year to compensation that is not actually or constructively received, and which is payable in a later year. The law does *not* apply to qualified retirement plans (such as 401(k) plans), Section 403(b) tax-deferred annuities, SIMPLE accounts, simplified employee pensions, and Section 457 plans; these are excluded from the definition of "nonqualified deferred compensation plans." Also excluded are welfare benefit plans such as vacation, sick leave, and disability programs.

The IRS has allowed exceptions for short-term deferrals, incentive stock options, employee stock purchase plan options, and certain stock appreciation rights, tax equalization payments, separation payments, reimbursement arrangements, and fringe benefits. For details, *see* the IRS final regulations (T.D. 9321, 2007-19 IRB 1123).

Section 409A requirements. Plans subject to Section 409A must meet detailed requirements pertaining to the timing of deferral elections and the availability of distributions. For example, a deferral election generally must be made prior to the beginning of the year during which the services will be provided, but special rules apply to short-term deferrals and deferrals with respect to forfeitable rights. Distributions before separation from service are generally allowed only if the participant is disabled or has an unforeseeable emergency, the distribution is used to satisfy a domestic relations order, the distribution is on a specific date or under a fixed schedule specified in the plan, or there has been a change in the ownership or effective control of the corporation or in the ownership of a substantial portion of the assets.

If the Section 409A requirements are *not* met at any time during a taxable year, all amounts deferred under the plan for all years are currently includible in a participant's gross income to the extent that the amounts are not subject to a substantial risk of forfeiture and were not previously included in gross income.

Reporting of Section 409A plan deferrals and earnings on your tax return. Your employer may include 2010 plan deferrals in Box 12 of your Form W-2 using Code Y. Code Y may also be used to show earnings in 2010 on all deferrals, whether for 2010 or prior years. If any amounts are taxable because the Section 409A requirements have not been met, the taxable amount is reported as taxable wages in Box 1 of Form W-2, and also is shown in Box 12 using Code Z.

Current year Section 409A deferrals of at least $600 and earnings on deferrals for all years may be reported in Box 15a of Form 1099-MISC. If any amounts are taxable because the Section 409A requirements have not been met, the taxable amount is reported in Box 15b and also included as non-employee compensation in Box 7 of Form 1099-MISC; this amount is generally subject to self-employment tax.

If there is a taxable amount, a penalty also must be paid equal to 20% of the includible compensation, plus interest at a rate that is 1% higher than the regular underpayment rate. The penalty and interest must be added to the line for "total tax" on Form 1040.

Financial health triggers and offshore rabbi trusts. Section 409A blocks the benefit of two funding arrangements that set aside assets to secure the payment of promised deferred compensation. If a nonqualified deferred compensation plan provides that assets will be restricted to payment of deferrals if the employer's financial condition deteriorates, the setting aside of the assets will be considered a transfer of restricted property to the participants, taxable under the Section 83 rules *(2.17)*. This is so even if the assets nominally remain available to satisfy the claims of the employer's general creditors.

Also, a Section 83 transfer *(2.17)* is generally deemed to occur when assets to pay nonqualified deferred compensation are set aside in an offshore rabbi trust. Section 409A treats the funding of an offshore trust as a transfer of property to the participants, taxable under the Section 83 rules *(2.17)*, unless substantially all of the services relating to the deferred compensation were performed in the foreign jurisdiction where the assets are held. A Section 83 transfer is deemed to occur whether or not the offshore assets are nominally available to satisfy the claims of the employer's general creditors.

If deferrals are includible in a participant's income because of the financial health trigger or offshore trust provisions, there is an additional 20% penalty plus interest at 1% more than the regular rate.

Rabbi trusts. If IRS tests are met, employer contributions to a domestic "rabbi trust" are not taxed until distributions from the trust are received or made available. The trust must be irrevocable and the trust assets must be subject to the claims of the employer's creditors in the event of insolvency or bankruptcy. Employees and their beneficiaries must have no preferred claim on the trust assets.

Offshore rabbi trusts are subject to Section 409A, as discussed above.

2.8 Did You Return Wages Received in a Prior Year?

Did you return income in 2010 such as salary or commissions that you reported in a prior taxable year because it appeared you had an unrestricted right to them in the earlier year? If so, you may deduct the repayment as a miscellaneous itemized deduction. If the repayment of wages exceeds $3,000, the deduction is claimed on Line 28 of Schedule A and is *not* subject to the 2% adjusted gross income (AGI) floor *(19.1)*. However, if the repayment is $3,000 or less, the deduction must be claimed on Line 23 ("Other Expenses") of Schedule A, where it *is* subject to the 2% floor.

Filing Instruction

Repayments Exceeding $3,000

If a repayment of wages in 2010 exceeds $3,000, a special law (Code Section 1341) gives this alternative: Instead of claiming an itemized deduction from 2010 income, you may recompute your tax for the prior year as if the wages had not been reported. The difference between the actual tax paid in the prior year and the recomputed tax may be claimed as a credit on your 2010 return. The credit is claimed on Line 69 of Form 1040; write next to the line "IRC 1341." If you claim the repayment as a miscellaneous itemized deduction, enter it on Line 28 of Schedule A, where it is not subject to the 2% floor. Choose either the credit or the itemized deduction, whichever gives you the larger tax reduction.

Option of tax credit or deduction for repayments over $3,000. If your repayment of wages exceeded $3,000, you may claim the repayment as an itemized deduction, *or* you may claim a tax credit, based upon a recomputation of the prior year's tax; *see* the Filing Instruction on this page.

Repayment of supplemental unemployment benefits. Where repayment is required to qualify for trade readjustment allowances, you may deduct the repayment from gross income. Claim the deduction on Line 36 of Form 1040, and to the left of the line write "sub-pay TRA." The deduction is allowed even if you do not itemize. If repayment exceeds $3,000, you have the choice of a deduction or claiming a tax credit based on a recomputation of your tax for the year supplemental unemployment benefits were received, as explained in the Filing Instruction on this page.

Repayment of disallowed travel and entertainment expenses. If a "hedge" agreement between you and your company requires you to repay salary or travel and entertainment ("T & E") expenses if they are disallowed to the company by the IRS, you may claim a deduction in the year of repayment. According to the IRS, you may not recalculate your tax for the prior year and claim a tax credit under the rules of Section 1341. However, an appeals court rejected the position taken by the IRS and allowed a tax recomputation under Section 1341 to an executive who returned part of a disallowed salary under the terms of a corporate by-law.

2.9 Waiver of Executor's and Trustee's Commissions

Commissions received by an executor for services performed are taxable as compensation. An executor may waive commissions without income or gift tax consequences by giving a principal legatee or devisee a formal waiver of the executor's right to commissions within six months after the initial appointment or by not claiming commissions at the time of filing the usual accountings.

The waiver may not be recognized if the executor takes any action that is inconsistent with the waiver. An example of an inconsistent action would be the claiming of an executor's fee as a deduction on an estate, inheritance, or income tax return.

A *bequest* received by an executor from an estate is tax free if it is not compensation for services.

2.10 Life Insurance Benefits

Company-financed insurance gives employees benefits at low or no tax cost.

Group life insurance. Group insurance plans may furnish not only life insurance protection but also accident and health benefits. Premium costs are low and tax deductible to the company while tax free to you unless you have nonforfeitable rights to permanent life insurance, or, in the case of group-term life insurance, your coverage exceeds $50,000 *(3.4)*. Even where your coverage exceeds $50,000, the tax incurred on your employer's premium payment is generally less than what you would have to pay privately for similar insurance.

It may be possible to avoid estate tax on the group policy proceeds if you assign all of your ownership rights in the policy, including the right to convert the policy, and if the beneficiary is other than your estate. Where the policy allows assignment of the conversion right, in addition to all other rights, and state law does not bar the assignment, you are considered to have made a complete assignment of the group insurance for estate tax purposes.

The IRS has ruled that where an employee assigns a group life policy and the value of the employee's interest in the policy cannot be ascertained, there is no taxable gift. This is so where the employer could simply have stopped making payments. However, there is a gift by the employee to the assignee to the extent of premiums paid by the employer. The gift may be a present interest qualifying for the annual gift tax exclusion *(39.2)*.

Caution

Charitable Split-Dollar Insurance

In a charitable split-dollar insurance plan, you give money to a charity, which invests in a life insurance policy and splits the proceeds with your beneficiaries. Taxpayers have attempted to deduct the initial "donations," but the tax law was changed to disallow the deduction.

Split-dollar insurance. Where you want more insurance than is provided by a group plan, your company may be able to help you get additional protection through a split-dollar insurance plan. Under the basic split-dollar plan, your employer purchases permanent cash value life insurance on your life and pays all or part of the annual premium. At your death, your employer is entitled to part of the proceeds equal to the premiums he or she paid. You have the right to name a beneficiary to receive the remaining proceeds which, under most policies, are substantial compared with the employer's share. Equity split-dollar arrangements allow employees to retain the right to the cash surrender value in excess of the premiums paid by the employer.

In final regulations applicable to split-dollar arrangements entered into or materially modified after September 17, 2003, the IRS has provided two sets of rules, depending on whether the employee or the employer owns the insurance policy (T.D. 9092, 2003-46 IRB 1055). If the employee is the owner, the employer's premium payments will be treated as loans and the imputed interest will be taxed to the employee. If the employer owns the policy, the employee will be taxed on the value of the life insurance protection, the policy cash value that the employee has access to, and the value of any other economic benefits received from the policy.

In addition, the Section 409A rules for nonqualified deferred compensation plans *(2.7)* may also apply to certain types of split-dollar arrangements. Notice 2007-34 contains IRS guidance on applying the Section 409A rules and explaining the effect of modifications to a split-dollar arrangement.

2.11 Educational Benefits for Employees' Children

Private foundations. The IRS has published guidelines for determining whether educational grants made by a private foundation established by an employer to children of employees constitute scholarships. An objective, nondiscriminatory program must be adopted. If the guidelines are satisfied, employees are not taxed on the benefits provided to their children. Advance approval of the grant program must be obtained from the IRS.

IRS guidelines require that:

- Grant recipients must be selected by a scholarship committee that is independent of the employer and the foundation. Former employees of the employer or the foundation are not considered independent.
- Eligibility for the grants may be restricted to children of employees who have been employed for a minimum of up to three years, but eligibility may not be related to the employee's position, services, or duties.
- Once awarded, a grant may not be terminated if the parent leaves his job with the employer, regardless of the reason for the termination of employment. If a one-year grant is awarded or a multi-year grant is awarded subject to renewal, a child who reapplies for a later grant may not be considered ineligible because his parent no longer works for the employer.
- Grant decisions must be based solely upon objective standards unrelated to the employer's business and the parent's employment such as prior academic performance, aptitude tests, recommendations from instructors, financial needs, and conclusions drawn from personal interviews.
- Recipients must be free to use the grants for courses that are not of particular benefit to the employer or the foundation.
- The grant program must not be used by the foundation or employer to recruit employees or induce employees to continue employment.
- There must be no requirement or suggestion that the child or parent is expected to render future employment services.
- A percentage test generally must be met. The number of grants awarded in a given year to children of employees must not exceed (1) 25% of the number of employees' children who were eligible, applied for the grants, and were considered by the selection committee in that year; or (2) 10% of the number of employees' children who were eligible during that year, whether or not they applied. Renewals of grants are not considered in determining the number of grants awarded.

If all of the above tests *other than* the percentage test are met, the educational grant program can still qualify if the facts and circumstances indicate that the primary purpose of the program is to provide educational benefits rather than to compensate the employees.

Caution

Primary Purpose Determination

If all guidelines other than the percentage test are satisfied, the IRS will determine whether the primary purpose of the program is to educate the children. If it is, the grants will be considered scholarships or fellowships; if it is not, the grants are taxed to the parent-employees as extra compensation.

Educational benefit trusts and other plans. A medical professional corporation set up an educational benefit plan to pay college costs for the children of "key" employees. Children enrolled in a degree program within two years of graduating from high school could participate in the plan. If an eligible employee quit for reasons other than death or permanent disability, his or her children could not longer receive benefits except for expenses actually incurred before termination. The company made annual contributions to a trust administered by a bank. According to the IRS, amounts contributed to the trust were a form of pay to qualified employees, because the contributions were made on the basis of the parents' employment and earnings records, not on the children's need, merit, or motivation. However, the employees could not be taxed when the funds were deposited because the children's right to receive benefits was conditioned upon each employee's future performance of services and was subject to a substantial risk of forfeiture. Tax is not incurred until a person has a vested right to receive benefits; here, vesting did not occur until a child became a degree candidate and incurred educational expenses while his or her parent was employed by the corporation. Once the child's right to receive a distribution from the plan became vested, the parent of the child could be taxed on the amount of the distribution. The company could deduct the same amount.

The Tax Court and appeals court have upheld the IRS position in similar cases.

2.12 Sick Pay Is Taxable

Sick pay received from an employer is generally taxable as wages unless it qualifies as workers' compensation *(2.13)*. Payments received under accident or health plans are generally tax free *(3.3)*, unless they constitute excess reimbursements *(17.4)*. Payments from your employer's plan for certain serious permanent injuries are tax free *(3.3)*.

Disability pensions are discussed in *2.14*.

Sick pay received from your employer is subject to income tax withholding as if it were wages. Sick pay from a third party such as an insurance company is not subject to withholdings unless you request it on Form W-4S.

2.13 Workers' Compensation Is Tax Free

You do not pay tax on workers' compensation payments for job-related injuries or illness. However, your employer might continue paying your regular salary but require you to turn over your workers' compensation payments. Then you are taxed on the difference between what was paid to you and what you returned.

EXAMPLE

John Wright was injured while at work and was out of work for two months. His company continues to pay his weekly salary of $775. He also receives workers' compensation of $200 a week from the state, which is tax free. He gives the $200 back to his employer. The balance of $575 a week is considered taxable wages.

To qualify as tax-free workers' compensation, the payments must be made under the authority of a *law* (or regulation having the force of a law) that provides compensation for on-the-job injury or illness. Payments made under a labor agreement do *not* qualify as tax-free workers' compensation.

A retirement pension or annuity does *not* qualify for tax-free treatment if benefits are based on age, length of service, or prior plan contributions. Such benefits are taxable even if retirement was triggered by a work-related injury or sickness.

State law may impose a penalty for unreasonable delay in paying a worker's compensation award. If the penalty is considered to have the remedial purpose of facilitating the injured employee's return to work, the IRS may treat the penalty as part of the original tax-free compensation award.

EXAMPLES

1. Kane, a federal district judge, suffered from sleep apnea, a condition characterized by a cessation of breathing during sleep, which was aggravated by the stress of his judicial work. He received a retirement disability payment of $65,135.

   A federal appeals court held that the payment was taxable because it was paid under a statute which did not specifically require that the payments be for work-related injuries. Here, the federal law under which the judge received his payments provided benefits for all permanent disabilities, whether or not job related.

Caution

Job-Related Injury or Illness

Not all payments for job-related illness or injury qualify as tax-free workers' compensation. Unless the statute or regulation authorizing your disability payment restricts awards to on-the-job injury or illness, your payment is taxable. Even if your payments are in fact based upon job-related injury or illness, they are taxed if other individuals can receive payments from the plan for disabilities that are not work related; *see* Example 1 *(2.13)*.

Court Decision

Is Sick Leave Tax-Free Workers' Compensation?

According to the Tax Court, sick leave may qualify as tax-free workers' compensation if it is paid under a specific workers' compensation statute or similar government regulation that authorizes the sick leave payment for job-related injuries or illness; *see* Examples 2, 3, and 4 *(2.13)*.

2. A teacher, injured while working, received full salary during a two-year sick leave. She argued that the payments, made under board of education regulations, were similar to workers' compensation and thus tax free. The IRS disagreed; the regulations were not the same as a workers' compensation statute. The Tax Court supported the teacher. The payments were made because of job-related injuries and were authorized by regulations having the force of law.

3. The IRS, relying on the court decision in Example 2, claimed that a police officer in Lynbrook, N.Y., was subject to tax on line-of-duty disability pay because the payment was under a labor agreement with the Police Benevolent Association (PBA). The Tax Court supported the police officer's claim that the payments were authorized by a specific New York State law requiring full salary for job-related police injuries. The PBA agreement did not affect the officer's rights to those state law payments. Lynbrook treated the case as a workers' compensation claim and in fact received reimbursement from the state workers' compensation board for the payments made to the officer.

4. A Los Angeles sheriff injured on the job retired on disability and, under the Los Angeles workers' compensation law, was allowed to elect sick pay in lieu of the regular workers' compensation amount because the sick pay was larger. The IRS argued that the sheriff had merely received taxable sick pay because he would have received the same amount as sick pay if his injuries had been suffered in a personal accident. However, the Tax Court allowed tax-free treatment. The sick leave was paid under a workers' compensation law that applied solely to work-related injuries. The fact that sick leave may also have been available to other employees under other laws does not mean that it may not be included as an option under a workers' compensation statute.

   The IRS announced that it does not agree with the Tax Court's decision allowing full tax-free treatment. According to the IRS, benefits up to the regular workers' compensation amount should be tax free but excess amounts should be taxed.

Effect of workers' compensation on Social Security. In figuring whether Social Security benefits are taxable *(34.2)*, workers' compensation that reduces Social Security or equivalent Railroad Retirement benefits is treated as a Social Security (or Railroad Retirement) benefit received during the year. Thus, the workers' compensation may be indirectly subject to tax *(34.2)*.

2.14 Disability Pensions

Disability pensions financed by your employer are taxable wages unless they are for severe permanent physical injuries that qualify for tax-free treatment *(3.3)*, they are tax-free workers' compensation *(2.13)*, or they are tax-free government payments as discussed in this section.

Taxable disability pensions are reported as wages until you reach the minimum retirement age under the employer's plan. After reaching minimum retirement age, payments are reported as a pension *(7.25)*.

If you receive little or no Social Security and your other income is below a specified threshold, you may be eligible to claim a tax credit for disability payments received while you are under the age of 65 and permanently and totally disabled *(34.7)*.

Injury or sickness resulting from active military service. Disability pensions for personal injuries or sickness resulting from active service in the armed forces are taxable if you joined the service after September 24, 1975.

Military disability payments are tax free if before September 25, 1975, you were entitled to military disability benefits or if on that date you were a member of the armed forces (or reserve unit) of the U.S. or any other country or were under a binding written commitment to become a member. A similar tax-free rule applies to disability pensions from the following government agencies if you were entitled to the payments before September 25, 1975, or were a member of the service (or committed to joining) on that date: The Foreign Service, Public Health Service, or National Oceanic and Atmospheric Administration. The exclusion for pre–September 25, 1975, service applies to disability pensions based upon percentage of disability. However, if a disability pension was based upon years of service, you do not pay tax on the amount that would be received based upon percentage of disability.

Law Alert

Refund After Retroactive Military Disability Determination

If you pay tax on retirement benefits from the military and then receive a retroactive disability determination from the Department of Veterans Affairs, you may file a refund claim for the tax paid on the retroactively excluded benefits. The Heroes Earnings Assistance and Relief Tax Act of 2008 extends the deadline for filing the refund claim beyond the normal three-year period *(47.2)*. For disability determinations after June 17, 2008, a refund claim for tax years beginning within five years prior to the determination date can be filed until one year after the date of the determination if that is later than the regular refund deadline.

Veterans Administration pensions. Disability pensions from the Veterans Administration (now called the Department of Veterans Affairs) are tax free. If you retire from the military and are later given a retroactive award of VA disability benefits, retirement pay during the retroactive period is tax free (other than a lump-sum readjustment payment upon retirement) to the extent of the VA benefit (*see* the first Law Alert in this section).

If a veteran receives a VA pension for a military service disability, and also disability benefits from the Social Security Administration, the VA benefits are tax free but the Social Security payments may be taxable *(34.2)*.

Pension based on combat-related injuries. Tax-free treatment applies to payments for combat-related injury or sickness that is incurred as a result of any one of the following activities: (1) as a direct result of armed conflict; (2) while engaged in extra-hazardous service, even if not directly engaged in combat; (3) under conditions simulating war, including maneuvers or training; or (4) that is caused by an instrumentality of war, such as weapons.

Social Security disability benefits. Disability benefits from the Social Security Administration (SSA) are treated as regular Social Security retirement benefits that may be taxable *(34.2)*.

In one case, a veteran who received disability benefits from the SSA as well as a disability pension from the Department of Veterans Affairs (VA) for cancer caused by exposure to Agent Orange during the Vietnam War tried to exclude both benefits from income. The IRS did not dispute the exclusion for the VA payments, but it held that the SSA disability benefits were subject to tax as if they were Social Security retirement benefits. The Tax Court and the Second Circuit Court of Appeals rejected the taxpayer's argument that his SSA disability benefits were excludable as amounts received for personal injuries/sickness resulting from active military service. The Second Circuit held that the military service exclusion is not applicable for SSA disability payments because they are a wage-replacement benefit based on the number of quarters of Social Security coverage, and are payable whether or not the disability arose from military service.

Terrorist attacks or United States military actions. Tax-free treatment applies to disability payments received by any individual for injuries incurred as the direct result of a terrorist attack against the United States or its allies. The exclusion also applies to disability income received as a direct result of a military action involving U.S. Armed Forces in response to aggression against the United States or its allies.

Law Alert

Terrorist Attacks

Tax-free treatment applies to disability payments resulting from terrorist attacks inside as well as outside the United States.

2.15 Stock Appreciation Rights (SARs)

Stock appreciation rights, or SARs, enable employees to receive the benefit of an increase in value of the employer's stock between the date the SARs are granted and the date they are exercised. When the SARs are exercised, cash or stock may be delivered as payment for the post-grant appreciation. For example, when your employer's stock is worth $30 a share, you get 100 SARs exercisable within five years. Two years later, when the stock price has increased to $50 a share, you exercise the SARs and receive $2,000.

If IRS tests are satisfied, the employee is taxed when the post-grant appreciation is received. The situation has been complicated by the enactment of Code Section 409A *(2.7)*, which restricts deferrals of income under nonqualified deferred compensation plans. However, the IRS has provided an exception to the Section 409A rules for SARs issued with an exercise price equal to the stock's fair market value when the rights are granted.

2.16 Stock Options

Employees receiving statutory stock options do not incur regular income tax liability either at the time the option is granted or when the option is exercised. However, the option spread is generally subject to AMT *(23.2)*. Statutory options include incentive stock options (ISOs) and options under an employee stock purchase plan (ESPP). Receipt of a nonstatutory (nonqualified) stock option generally results in an immediate tax.

Incentive stock options (ISOs). A corporation may provide its employees with incentive stock options to acquire its stock (or the stock of its parent or subsidiaries). For regular income tax purposes, ISOs meeting tax law tests are not taxed when granted or exercised. Income or loss is not reported until you sell the stock acquired from exercising the ISO. The option must be exercisable within 10 years of the date it is granted and the option price must be at least equal to the fair market

Caution

Possible AMT Liability for ISO

If you exercise an incentive stock option and your rights in the acquired stock are transferable and not subject to a substantial risk of forfeiture, then on your tax return for the year of exercise you must treat the "bargain element" as an adjustment for alternative minimum tax purposes *(23.2)* unless you sell the stock by the end of that year. The bargain element is the excess of the fair-market value of the stock when the option was exercised over the option price. You must report an AMT adjustment based on the value of the stock when the option was exercised, even if the value later declines substantially. You avoid the AMT adjustment if you sell the stock in the same year the option was exercised. If your rights in the stock are restricted in the year you exercise the option, the AMT adjustment applies for the year the restrictions are lifted. *See 23.2* for further details.

value of the stock when the option is granted. If the fair market value of stock for which ISOs may first be exercised in a particular year by an employee exceeds $100,000 (valued at date of grant), the excess is not considered a qualifying ISO. An ISO may be exercised by a former employee within three months of the termination of employment; if exercised after three months, income is realized under the rules for nonqualified options, discussed later in this section.

AMT consequences of exercising ISO. Although you do not realize taxable income for regular tax purposes when you exercise an ISO, you may incur a substantial liability for alternative minimum tax (AMT) *(23.2)*. *See* the Caution on this page.

Gain or loss on sale of ISO stock. If the stock acquired by the exercise of the ISO is held for more than one year after acquisition and more than two years after the ISO was granted, you have long-term capital gain or loss *(5.3)* on the sale, equal to the difference between the selling price of the stock and the option price you paid when you exercised the ISO.

If you sell *before* meeting the one-year and two-year holding period tests, a gain on the sale is generally treated as ordinary wage income to the extent of the option spread—the excess of the value of the stock when you exercised the ISO over the option price. Any gain in excess of the spread is reported as capital gain. In figuring the capital gain, cost basis for the stock is increased by the amount treated as wages. If the fair market value of the stock declines between the date the option was exercised and the date the stock is sold, the amount that must be treated as wages is generally reduced. The ordinary income (wages) is limited to the actual gain on the stock sale where the gain is less than the option spread at exercise. However, the reduction to ordinary income does *not* apply on a sale of the stock to a related person or if replacement shares are purchased within the wash-sale period *(30.6)* because the reduction applies only if a loss "would be" recognized if sustained (actual loss is not required for limitation to apply so long as a loss "would be" recognized).

If you have a loss on the sale of stock acquired by exercising an ISO, it is a capital loss and there is no ordinary wage income to report.

EXAMPLE

You were granted an incentive stock option (ISO) on March 7, 2008, to buy 1,000 shares of your employer company's stock at its then fair market value of $10 a share. You exercised the option on January 9, 2009, when the market price for the stock was $15 a share. You sold the stock on January 22, 2010, for $20 a share. Although you held the stock for more than one year, you did not sell more than two years after the date the option was granted. Therefore, part of your gain on the sale in 2010 is ordinary wage income. You have ordinary wage income of $5,000, equal to the option spread ($15,000 value on January 9, 2009, minus $10,000 option price) and $5,000 of long-term capital gain.

Selling price ($20 x 1,000 shares)	$20,000
Less: Cost of stock ($10 exercise price x 1,000 shares)	10,000
Gain	10,000
Less: Ordinary wage income ($15,000 value – $10,000 option price)	$5,000
Capital gain ($20,000 sales price – basis of $15,000 ($10,000 cost + $5,000 treated as wages))	$5,000

Employee stock purchase plans (ESPPs). These plans allow employees to buy their company's stock, usually at a discount. The plan must be nondiscriminatory and meet tax law tests on option terms. Options granted under qualified plans are not taxed until you sell the shares acquired from exercising the option.

If you sell the stock more than one year after exercising the option and also more than two years after the option was granted, gain on the sale is capital gain unless the option was granted at a discount. If at the time the option was granted the fair market value of the stock exceeded the option price, then when you sell the stock, gain is ordinary wage income to the extent of that discount. Any excess gain is long-term capital gain. A loss on the sale is long-term capital loss.

If you sell the acquired stock before meeting the one-year and two-year holding period tests, you must report as ordinary wage income the option spread—the excess of the value of the stock when you exercised the option over the option price. This amount must be reported as ordinary income even if it exceeds the gain on the sale (which would occur if the sale price were lower than the exercise price). Add the ordinary income amount to your cost basis for the stock. If the increased basis is less than the selling price, the difference is capital gain. You have a capital loss if the increased basis exceeds the selling price.

EXAMPLES

1. You are granted an option to buy 1,000 shares from your employer's ESPP for $20 a share at a time when the market price is $22 a share. You exercise the option 14 months later when the value of the stock is $23 a share. You sell the stock for $30 a share 18 months after exercising the option. You meet the one-year and two-year holding period tests but because the option was granted at a discount, part of the gain on the sale is treated as ordinary income.

Selling price ($30 x 1,000 shares)	$30,000
Less: Cost of stock ($20 x 1,000 shares)	20,000
Gain	10,000
Less: Ordinary wage income	2,000
($22,000 value at grant – $20,000 option price)	
Capital gain ($30,000 sales price – basis of $22,000	$8,000
($20,000 cost + $2,000 treated as wages))	

2. Same facts as in Example 1, except that you sold the stock only six months after you exercised the ESPP option. Since the one-year holding period test was not met, $3,000 of your $10,000 gain is taxed as ordinary wage income. The $3,000 ordinary income equals the option spread between the $23,000 value of the stock when you exercised the option and the $20,000 option price. You also have a $7,000 short-term capital gain: $30,000 sales price – $23,000 basis ($20,000 cost + $3,000 treated as wages).

Nonstatutory (nonqualified) stock options. A nonstatutory stock option (also called a nonqualified option) can in some cases be considered nonqualified deferred compensation subject to the requirements of Code Section 409A *(2.7)*. Under IRS regulations, the Section 409A rules apply if the exercise price can be less than the value of the underlying stock when the option is granted or the option permits any other deferral feature.

If the Section 409A rules do *not* apply, the amount of income to include and the time to include it depends on whether the option has a readily ascertainable fair market value when the option is granted. It is very rare for a nonstatutory option to be actively traded on an established securities market or to meet the other tests in IRS regulations for having a readily ascertainable fair market value.

In the usual case where there is no readily ascertainable fair market value for the option at the time it is granted, no income is realized on the receipt of the option. Income will not be realized until the year the option is exercised, assuming you are vested in the stock in the year you receive it. If the stock is *not* vested when you exercise the option, income is deferred until the vesting year under the restricted property rules *(2.17)*. In the year that you become vested in the stock, you must report as ordinary wage income the value of the stock (as of the vesting date), minus the amount you paid. If you receive vested stock when the option is exercised, you are taxed on the difference between the fair market value of the stock when you exercise the option and the option price. For example, in 2010, you exercise a nonstatutory stock option to buy 1,000 shares of your employer's stock at $10 a share when the stock has a value of $30 a share. Your rights to the stock are vested when you buy it. When you exercise the option you are treated as receiving wages of $20,000, equal to the option spread ($30,000 value – $10,000 cost). This income is subject to withholding taxes that you will have to pay out-of-pocket at the time of exercise unless the withholding can be taken from regular cash wages. The taxable spread will be reported as wages on Form W-2 and will be separately identified in Box 12, using Code V. Your cost basis for the shares is increased by the ordinary income reported for exercising the option. If you hold the shares for more than one year after exercising the option and then sell them for $35,000 ($35 a share × 1,000 shares), you will have a $5,000 long-term capital gain ($35,000 – $30,000 increased basis).

Caution

Tax Due on Option Exercise

Determine the amount of cash you will need to make the purchases and meet your tax liability before you exercise a nonqualified option and receive vested stock. If you receive vested stock when you exercise the option, you will realize wage income equal to the excess of the value of the stock over the option price. In addition to the cash to buy the stock, you will need cash to pay the tax on the wage income. The tax is due even if you plan to hold onto the stock before selling.

If in a rare case a nonstatutory stock option has an ascertainable fair market value, the value of the option less any amount you paid is taxable under the restricted property rules *(2.17)* as ordinary wage income in the first year that your right to the option is freely transferable or not subject to a substantial risk of forfeiture. However, a Section 83(b) election *(2.17)* may *not* be made for the nonstatutory option. For other details and requirements, *see* IRS Regulation Section 1.83-7.

Nonstatutory stock options may be granted in addition to or in place of incentive stock options. There are no restrictions on the amount of nonstatutory stock options that may be granted.

2.17 Restricted Stock

If in return for performing services you buy or receive company stock (or other property) subject to restrictions, special tax rules apply. Unless you make the Section 83(b) election discussed below, you do not have to pay tax on the stock until the first year in which it is substantially vested, which means that it is either transferable or not subject to a substantial risk of forfeiture. A risk of forfeiture exists where your rights are conditioned upon the future performance of substantial services. In the year the property becomes substantially vested, you must report as compensation (wages) the difference between the amount, if any, that you paid for the stock and its value at the time the risk of forfeiture is removed. The valuation at the time the forfeiture restrictions lapse is not reduced because of restrictions imposed on the right to sell the property. However, restrictions that will never lapse do affect valuation.

SEC restrictions on insider trading are considered a substantial risk of forfeiture, so that there is no tax on the receipt of stock subject to such restrictions. However, the SEC permits insiders to immediately resell stock acquired through exercise of an option granted at least six months earlier. As the stock acquired through such options is not subject to SEC restrictions, the executive is subject to immediate tax upon exercise of an option held for at least six months.

If the stock is subject to a restriction on transfer to comply with SEC pooling-of-interests accounting rules, the stock is considered to be subject to a substantial restriction.

Non-employees. The tax rules for restricted property are not limited to employees. They also apply to independent contractors who are compensated for services with restricted stock or other property.

Sale of property that is not substantially vested. If you sell restricted property in an arm's-length transaction before it has become substantially vested and you did not make the Section 83(b) election discussed below, gain on the sale (amount realized minus what you paid) must be reported as compensation income for the year of the sale. If the sale is to a related person or is otherwise not at arm's length, compensation must be reported not only for the year of sale but also for the year the original property becomes substantially vested, as if you still held it. In the later year, the compensation income equals the fair market value of the stock minus the total of the amount you paid for it and the compensation reported on the earlier sale.

Planning Reminder

Electing Immediate Tax on Restricted Stock

If you expect restricted stock to appreciate, consider making an election (Section 83(b) election) to be immediately taxed on the value of the restricted stock, minus your cost. If you make the election, any appreciation in value that has accrued since the election was made will not be taxable when the stock becomes substantially vested. Tax on appreciation will not be due until the stock is sold.

Election to include value of restricted stock in income when received (Section 83(b) election). Although restricted stock is generally not taxable until the year in which it is substantially vested, you may elect to be taxed in the year you receive it on the unrestricted value (as of the date the stock is received), less any payment you made. This election, called a Section 83(b) election, must be made by filing a statement with the IRS no later than 30 days after the date the stock is transferred to you. The election may not be revoked without the consent of the IRS.

If you make the election, you are treated as an investor and later appreciation in value is not taxed as pay when your rights to the stock become vested. To figure capital gain or loss when you sell the stock, your cost basis for the stock is increased by the amount of income you reported as pay under the election. If you forfeit the stock after the election is made, a capital loss *(5.4)* is allowed for your cost minus any amount realized on the forfeiture.

EXAMPLES

1. In 2010, when your employer's stock has a market value of $100 a share, your employer allows you to buy 100 shares at $10 a share, or $1,000. Under the terms of your purchase, you must resell the stock to your employer at $10 a share if you leave your job within five years. Because your rights to the stock are subject to a substantial risk of forfeiture, you do not have to include any amount as income in 2010 when you buy it. Assume that in 2015, when the restrictions are lifted, the stock is selling for $200 a share. In 2015, you will have to report $19,000 as ordinary wage income ($20,000 unrestricted value – $1,000 you paid).
2. Same facts as in Example 1, except that within 30 days after you receive the stock, you file a Section 83(b) election with the IRS. With the election, you have wage income for 2010 of $9,000, the value of the stock when you received it ($10,000 for 100 shares) minus your cost ($1,000).

   A signed election statement must be filed with the IRS Service Center where you file your return no later than 30 days after the date you received the stock. The statement must include the following: your name, address, Social Security number, the year for which you are making the election, a description of the stock and the restrictions on the stock, the date you received the stock, the fair market value of the stock at receipt (ignoring restrictions unless they never lapse), your cost, if any, for the stock, and a statement that you have provided a copy of the statement to your employer.

   You will not have to report any wage income when the stock vests in 2015. If after vesting you sell the shares for $20,000, you will have a long-term capital gain of $10,000 ($20,000 – $10,000 increased basis ($1,000 cost plus $9,000 wage income from election)).

Chapter 3

Fringe Benefits

Employer-furnished fringe benefits are exempt from tax if the tests discussed in this chapter are met.

The most common tax-free benefits are accident and health plan coverage, including employer contributions to health savings accounts (HSAs), group-term life insurance plans, dependent care plans, education assistance plans, tuition reduction plans, adoption benefit plans, cafeteria plans, and plans providing employees with discounts, no-additional-cost services, or employer-subsidized meal facilities.

Highly compensated individuals may be taxed on certain benefits from such plans if nondiscrimination rules are not met.

Table 3-1 Are Your Fringe Benefits Tax Free?

Fringe benefit—	*Tax Pointer—*
Adoption benefits	Employer payments to a third party or reimbursements to you in 2010 for qualified adoption expenses are generally tax free up to a limit of $13,170. The exclusion is phased out if modified adjusted gross income is between $182,520 and $222,520 *(3.6)*.
Athletic facilities	The fair market value of athletic facilities, such as gyms, swimming pools, golf courses, and tennis courts, is tax free if the facilities are on property owned or leased by the employer (not necessarily the main business premises) and substantially all of the use of the facilities is by employees, their spouses, and dependent children. Such facilities must be open to all employees on a nondiscriminatory basis in order for the company to deduct related expenses.
Child or dependent care plans	The value of day-care services provided or reimbursed by an employer under a written, nondiscriminatory plan is tax free up to a limit of $5,000, or $2,500 for married persons filing separately. Expenses are excludable if they would qualify for the dependent care credit; *see Chapter 25*. On your tax return, you must report employer-provided benefits to figure the tax-free exclusion. Tax-free employer benefits reduce eligibility for the dependent care tax credit *(3.5)*.
De minimis *(minor)* fringe benefits	These are small benefits that are administratively impractical to tax, such as occasional supper money and taxi fares for overtime work, company parties or picnics, and occasional theater or sporting event tickets *(3.10)*.
Discounts on company products and services	Services from your employer that are usually sold to customers are tax free if your employer does not incur additional costs in providing them to you *(3.16)*. Merchandise discounts and other discounted services are also eligible for a tax-free exclusion *(3.17)*.
Education plans	An up-to-$5,250 exclusion applies to employer-financed undergraduate and graduate courses *(3.7)*.
Employee achievement awards	Achievement awards are taxable unless they qualify under special rules for length of service or safety achievement *(3.12)*.
Group-term life insurance	Premiums paid by employers are not taxed if policy coverage is $50,000 or less *(3.4)*.
Health and accident plans including HSAs	Premiums paid by an employer are tax free. For 2010, employer contributions to a health savings account, or HSA, on behalf of an eligible employee are generally not taxed up to $3,050 for self-only coverage or $6,150 for family coverage *(3.2)*. Benefits under an employer plan are also generally tax free *(3.1–3.4)*.
Interest-free or low-interest loans	Interest-free loans received from your employer may be taxed *(4.31)*.
Retirement planning advice	Employer-provided retirement income planning advice and information are tax free to employees (and their spouses) so long as the employer maintains a qualified retirement plan. The exclusion does not apply to tax preparation, accounting, legal, or brokerage services.
Transportation benefits	Within limits, employer-provided parking benefits, transit passes, and bicycle commuting reimbursements are tax free; *see 3.8.*
Tuition reductions	Tuition reductions for courses below the graduate level are generally tax free. Graduate students who are teaching or research assistants are not taxed on tuition reduction unless the reduction is compensation for teaching services *(3.7)*.
Working condition benefits	Benefits provided by your employer that would be deductible if you paid the expenses yourself are a tax-free working condition fringe benefit. *See* the discussion of company cars *(3.8)* and other working condition benefits *(3.9)*.
Volunteer firefighter and emergency medical responder benefits	Volunteer firefighters and emergency medical responders are not taxed on property tax rebates or reductions or on up to $30 per month received from a state or local government for their services; *see 3.19.*

3.1 Tax-Free Health and Accident Coverage Under Employer Plans

You are not taxed on *contributions* or *insurance premiums* your employer makes to a health, hospitalization, or accident plan to cover you, your spouse, your dependents, and your children under age 27 whether or not they can be claimed as your dependents. If you obtain coverage by making *pre-tax* salary-reduction contributions under your employer's cafeteria plan *(3.14)*, the salary reductions are treated as employer contributions that are tax free to you. If you are temporarily laid off and continue to receive health coverage, the employer's contributions during this layoff period are tax free. If you are retired, you do not pay tax on insurance paid by your former employer. Medical coverage provided to the family of a deceased employee is tax free since it is treated as a continuation of the employee's fringe-benefit package.

If your employer provides health and accident coverage to your live-in companion who is not recognized as your "spouse" under state law or as your "dependent" (even if support and household membership tests in *Chapter 21* are met) because the relationship violates local law, you are taxed on the value of the coverage in excess of what you paid (on an after-tax basis) for it. Furthermore, under the 1996 Defense of Marriage Act, a gay or lesbian partner is not treated as a spouse for federal tax purposes.

If you are age 65 or older, Medicare premiums paid by your employer are not taxed. If you retire and have the option of receiving continued coverage under the medical plan or a lump-sum payment covering unused accumulated sick leave instead of coverage, the lump-sum amount is reported as income at the time you have the option to receive it. If you elect continued coverage, the amount reported as income may be deductible as medical insurance if you itemize deductions *(17.5)*.

Disability coverage. If your employer pays the premiums for your disability coverage (short term or long term) and does not report the payment as compensation income on your Form W-2, or if you pay the premiums with pre-tax salary-reduction contributions, your coverage is tax free but any benefits you subsequently receive from the plan upon becoming disabled will be includible in your gross income *(3.3)*. If you pay the premiums with after-tax contributions or your employer makes contributions that are included on your Form W-2, any disability benefits you receive from the plan will not be taxable to you.

Health Reimbursement Arrangements (HRAs). Employer contributions to health reimbursement arrangements (HRAs) are not taxed to the employees. The contributions must be paid by the employer and not provided by salary reduction. HRA contributions can be used to reimburse the medical costs of employees, their spouses, and their dependents, and unused expenses may be carried forward to later years *(3.3)*.

Long-term care coverage. An employee is not taxed on employer-provided long-term care coverage that pays benefits in the event the employee becomes *chronically ill (17.15)*. However, long-term care coverage may not be offered to employees through a cafeteria plan *(3.15)* and reimbursements of long-term care expenses may not be made through a flexible spending arrangement *(3.16)*.

Access and Portability Rules for Group Health Plans

Generally, a group health plan may not bar eligibility to an employee and his or her dependents because of health status or medical history. A plan may exclude coverage for specified conditions or procedures, or limit such coverage, but only if there is no discrimination among similarly situated employees based on health-related factors. Employers are subject to daily penalties if they do not comply with the rules, but small employers with an average of no more than 50 employees in the preceding year are not subject to the penalties, except for those relating to the hospital-length-of-stay requirements for mothers and newborns.

Pre-existing conditions can bar coverage only in limited circumstances. Coverage may be denied for a condition that was diagnosed or treated within six months before enrollment. However, the exclusion cannot last more than 12 months, or 18 months for those who enroll late, and the 12- or 18-month period must be reduced by creditable coverage the employee had before enrollment in the new plan if there was no break in the prior coverage of more than 62 days. Coverage may not be denied to women pregnant on the enrollment date. Newborn children who are enrolled within 30 days of birth must be covered and if the parent changes jobs and enrolls in a new plan without a break in coverage of more than 62 days, the new plan may not exclude the child. A similar protective rule applies to adopted children under age 18 who are enrolled within 30 days of the adoption.

Continuing coverage for group health plans (COBRA coverage). Employers are subject to daily penalties unless they offer continuing group health and accident coverage to employees who leave the company and to spouses and dependent children who would lose coverage in the case of divorce or the death of the employee. Federal COBRA continuing coverage rules apply to employers with 20 or more employees but smaller employees may be required under state law to provide comparable continuing coverage under "mini-COBRA" laws.

Generally, an employer may charge for continuing coverage a premium that is as much as 102% of the regular plan premium for the applicable (family or individual) coverage. However, a special law temporarily reduced premiums for individuals who became eligible for COBRA coverage because of their own or a family member's involuntary termination from employment occurring from September 1, 2008 through May 31, 2010.

Temporary premium reduction after involuntary termination. Workers who were involuntarily terminated from employment *on or after September 1, 2008, and before June 1, 2010*, and their families, are entitled to a reduced COBRA premium if they were enrolled in the health plan at the time of the involuntary termination and elected continuing coverage. Eligible workers and family members only have to pay 35% of the regular COBRA premium for up to 15 months. A termination for cause qualifies for the premium reduction, but not a termination for gross misconduct. The remaining 65% of the premiums are reimbursed to the employer (or if applicable the multiemployer health plan or insurance company) through a payroll tax credit.

The premium reduction applies to coverage under the federal COBRA rules as well as for comparable coverage under state continuation coverage laws. The subsidy is available only for 15 months and ends sooner if the individual becomes eligible for coverage under a new group health plan or for Medicare benefits. Individuals receiving reduced COBRA premiums must notify their plans if they obtain new coverage or a tax penalty may be imposed.

Higher income individuals are subject to a recapture provision. Any premium reduction is subject to recapture as an increase in income tax liability if the individual has modified adjusted gross income (MAGI) over $125,000, or $250,000 if married filing jointly; recapture is complete once MAGI reaches $145,000, or $290,000 on a joint return. Individuals who expect to be subject to the recapture rule may waive their right to the premium reduction. In addition, an individual who receives the premium reduction for a month may not claim the health coverage credit *(25.18)* for that month.

Employers must explain the premium subsidy rules to all qualified individuals.

Court Decision

COBRA Required Despite Other Coverage

The Supreme Court has held that an employer may not deny continuing care coverage to a former employee who on the date of election has coverage under his or her spouse's group health plan.

How COBRA is triggered. Federal COBRA is triggered in these situations:

1. An employee with coverage who voluntarily or involuntarily leaves the company—unless termination is for gross misconduct. Employees who would lose coverage because of a reduction in hours must also be offered continuing coverage. Continuing coverage must also be offered for the employee's spouse and dependent children who were covered before the employee's termination or reduction in hours. If accepted, the coverage must last for at least 18 months. Within this period, an employee who elects continuing coverage is protected against the possibility of a coverage gap if he or she joins a new company that limits group health coverage for pre-existing conditions; the old employer's continuing coverage must remain available.

   Extended coverage may apply to disabled individuals. The coverage period is extended from 18 months to 29 months for individuals who notify the plan administrator within 60 days of a determination under Title II or XVI of the Social Security Act that they are disabled. The coverage extension applies if the disability exists at any time during the first 60 days of continuing coverage.
2. On the death of a covered employee, continuing coverage must be offered to the surviving spouse and dependent children who are beneficiaries under the plan on the day before the death. Coverage must be for at least 36 months.
3. If a covered employee obtains a divorce or legal separation, continuing coverage must be offered to the spouse and dependent children for at least 36 months.

Law Alert

COBRA Premium Reduction for Laid-Off Workers

Individuals who were involuntarily terminated from employment on or after September 1, 2008, and before June 1, 2010, and their family members, only have to pay 35% of the regular COBRA premium for up to 15 months. High-income individuals who receive the premium reduction may have to repay it when they file their tax returns.

If a covered employee drops the coverage for his or her spouse in anticipation of a divorce or legal separation, the spouse must be offered continuing coverage for at least 36 months beginning with the date of divorce or separation. However, the plan does not have to make COBRA coverage available for the period between the date the spouse is dropped from the plan and the date of divorce or separation.

4. If a covered employee becomes eligible for Medicare benefits, continuing coverage under the employer's plan must be offered to the employee's spouse and dependent children for at least 36 months.
5. If a dependent child becomes ineligible under the plan upon reaching a certain age, continuing coverage must be offered for at least 36 months.
6. If an employee with health coverage takes unpaid leave under the Family and Medical Leave Act of 1993 (FMLA) upon the birth or adoption of a child or to deal with a serious family illness, and the employee does not return to work following the leave, continuing coverage must be offered as of the last day of the leave. Continuing coverage must also be offered to the employee's spouse and dependent children if they would otherwise lose coverage.

Employers must provide written notice of the continuing coverage option. If one of the previously discussed qualifying events occurs, the eligible employees, spouses, and/or dependent children generally have 60 days to elect continuing coverage.

3.2 Health Savings Accounts (HSAs) and Archer MSAs

If you are covered by a qualifying high-deductible health plan (HDHP), your employer may make tax-free contributions to a health savings account (HSA) on your behalf. Earnings accumulate tax free within an HSA and distributions are tax free if used to pay your qualified medical expenses, or those of your spouse or dependents. If your employer does not make the maximum tax-free contribution to your HSA, you can make a deductible contribution, so long as the total does not exceed the annual contribution limit (*see* below).

Archer MSAs are an older type of medical savings plan that HSAs are intended to replace. If your employer set up an Archer MSA on your behalf before 2008, or you became eligible to participate after 2007 in a pre-2008 plan, your employer may continue to contribute to the account. If you work for an eligible small employer with a high-deductible plan, your employer may make tax-free contributions to an Archer MSA on your behalf. A rollover can be made from an Archer MSA to a new health savings account (HSA) that accepts rollovers. If the Archer MSA is retained, withdrawals will be tax free if used to pay qualified medical expenses for you, your spouse, or your dependents.

Filing Tip

Above-the-Line Deduction for HSA Contributions

If you are an eligible employee, contributions you make to your HSA are reported on Form 8889 and deducted on Line 25 of Form 1040; *see 3.2* for contribution limits. The deduction is "above the line," so it is allowed even if you claim the standard deduction.

If you are self-employed, you may claim the "above-the-line" HSA deduction subject to the same limits; *see Chapter 41* for further details.

Health Savings Account (HSA)

You may set up an HSA only if you are covered by a qualifying high-deductible health plan (HDHP, *see* details below), you are not enrolled in Medicare, and you are not the dependent of another taxpayer. Generally, you must have no coverage other than HDHP coverage, but there are exceptions. You are allowed to have separate coverage for vision, dental, or long-term care, accidents, disability, *per diem* insurance while hospitalized, insurance for a specific disease or illness, car insurance (or similar insurance for owning or using property), or insurance for workers' compensation or tort liabilities. Preventive care is also exempt from the deductible requirement.

As an eligible employee, you, your employer, or both may contribute to your HSA. The same maximum annual contribution limit applies (*see* below) regardless of the number of contributors. Your employer may allow you to make pre-tax salary-reduction contributions to an HDHP and HSA as an option under a "cafeteria" plan *(3.13)*.

High-deductible health plan (HDHP). An HDHP must have a minimum annual deductible and an annual out-of-pocket maximum. For 2010 self-only coverage, an HDHP must have an annual deductible of at least $1,200 and an annual out-of-pocket maximum of $5,950 for co-payments, deductibles, and other payments excluding premiums. The annual deductible for 2010 family coverage must be at least $2,400 and there is an $11,900 limit on out-of-pocket expenses (excluding premiums). Given the lack of inflation, the same deductibles and out-of-pocket limits will apply for 2011.

In the case of family coverage, the terms of the HDHP must deny payments to all family members until the family as a unit incurs annual covered expenses in excess of the minimum annual deductible ($2,400 for 2010 and 2011). Thus, if a plan for 2010 or 2011 allowed payment of an individual family member's medical expenses exceeding $1,200 even if the family as a whole did not have expenses over $2,400, the plan would not be a qualified HDHP.

However, the minimum annual HDHP deductible does not apply to preventive care benefits. The plan can qualify as an HDHP even if it pays for preventive care without a deductible or after a small deductible (below the regular HDHP minimum). The IRS has provided a safe harbor list of preventive care benefits, including annual physicals, routine prenatal and well-child care, immunizations, tobacco cessation and obesity programs, and screening services for a broad range of conditions including cancer (such as breast, cervical, prostate, ovarian, and colorectal cancer) and cardiovascular disease. Prescription drugs qualify for the preventive care safe harbor if taken by asymptomatic patients with risk factors for a disease, or by recovering patients to prevent the recurrence of a disease.

By law, prescription drug coverage, other than coverage meeting the preventive care safe harbor, is not a permitted exception to the high-deductible requirement. This is a problem for employees whose employers offer separate prescription drug plans that provide first-dollar drug coverage with either a flat dollar or percentage co-payment. HSA contributions cannot be made for individuals with an HDHP and such a prescription drug plan because the prescription drug benefits are not subject to the HDHP minimum annual deductible.

Maximum annual HSA contribution for employees. For 2010, the maximum HSA contribution for an employee with self-only coverage is $3,050, and for an employee with family coverage, the maximum contribution for 2010 is $6,150. For employees who are age 55 or older in 2010, an additional "catch-up" contribution of $1,000 may be made. The applicable limit must be reduced by any contributions to an Archer MSA. The same HSA contribution limits will apply for 2011; there is no increase given the lack of inflation.

If you become eligible under an HDHP, contributions are allowed for the months prior to your enrollment in the HDHP, provided you are eligible in December of that year. However, the contributions for the months prior to your enrollment will be included in your income and subject to a 10% penalty if you do not remain eligible for the 12 months following the end of the first eligibility year, unless you are disabled (or die).

All employer contributions must be reported on Form 8889, which you attach to your Form 1040. Contributions by your employer up to the above limit are tax free and are not subject to withholding for income tax or FICA (Social Security and Medicare) purposes. All employer contributions to an HSA are reported in Box 12 of Form W-2 with Code W. Contributions exceeding the excludable limit are also reported in Box 1 of Form W-2 as taxable wages. If you do not remove an excess contribution (and any net income) by the due date for your return (including extensions), the excess is subject to a 6% penalty; *see* the instructions to Forms 8889 and 5329.

If your employer contributes less than the limit, you may contribute to your HSA but the same overall limit applies to the aggregate contributions. Contributions you make are reported on Form 8889 and deductible "above the line" from gross income on Line 25 of Form 1040. You must attach Form 8889 to your Form 1040.

Planning Reminder

One-Time Transfer From IRA to HSA

You can make a one-time tax-free transfer from your IRA or Roth IRA to your HSA. A qualifying transfer is not taxable or subject to the 10% penalty for distributions before age 59½. Generally, only one IRA/Roth IRA transfer to an HSA is allowed during your lifetime, but if a transfer is made to a self-only HDHP, and later in the same year you obtain family HDHP coverage, a second transfer from an IRA or Roth IRA may be made in that year. The transfer (or transfers) count towards the annual HSA contribution limit for that year, so if the transfer exceeds the annual HSA contribution limit, the excess is taxable (and possibly subject to the pre-59½ penalty). If you want to transfer amounts from more than one IRA or Roth IRA to an HSA, you have to first roll the funds into a single IRA/Roth IRA and then make the transfer from that account.

To be tax free, the transfer must be directly to the HSA trustee or custodian. Furthermore, you must remain HSA-eligible (have qualifying HDHP coverage) for 12 months following the date of the distribution; otherwise, the distribution is taxable (and possibly subject to the pre-59½ penalty) in the year that you cease to be eligible. Changing from family-HDHP coverage to a self-only HDHP during the 12-month testing period is not considered a cessation of HSA eligibility.

Archer MSAs

Archer MSAs (medical savings accounts) are in the process of being replaced by HSAs. However, an Archer MSA that is not rolled over to a new HSA may continue to be funded.

To contribute, you must have coverage under a high-deductible health plan and must work for a "small employer," one that had an average of 50 or fewer employees during either of the two preceding years. For 2010, a high-deductible health plan for self-only coverage must have a deductible of at least $2,000 and no more than $3,000. For family coverage, the deductible must be at least $4,050 and no more than $6,050. The high-deductible plan must limit out-of-pocket expenses (other than premiums) for 2010 to $4,050 for self-only coverage and $7,400 for family coverage.

Generally, you are not eligible for an Archer MSA if you have any other health insurance in addition to the high-deductible plan coverage, except for policies covering only disability, vision or dental care, long-term care, or accidental injuries, or plans that pay a flat amount during hospitalization.

Employer contribution limits. Your employer's contributions to your Archer MSA are tax free up to an annual limit of 65% of the plan deductible if you have individual coverage and 75% of the deductible for family coverage. The limit is reduced on a monthly basis if you are not covered for the entire year. For example, if for all of 2010 you were covered by a qualifying family coverage high-deductible plan with a $6,050 annual deductible, the maximum tax-free contribution is $4,538 (75% of $6,050). If you had coverage for only 10 months, the limit would be $3,782 ($^{10}/_{12}$ × $4,538). All employer contributions to your Archer MSA are reported in Box 12 of Form W-2 (Code R). If the contributions exceed the tax-free limit, the excess is reported in Box 1 of Form W-2 as taxable wages. You must report all employer contributions on Form 8853, which you attach to your Form 1040.

If your employer makes any contributions to your account, you may not make any contributions for that year. In addition, if you and your spouse have family coverage under a high-deductible plan and your spouse's employer contributes to his or her Archer MSA, you cannot contribute to your Archer MSA. If your employer (or spouse's employer) does not contribute, you may make deductible contributions up to the above employer contribution limits. You report your contributions on Form 8853 and claim your deduction on Line 23 of Form 1040. Contributions exceeding the annual limit are subject to a 6% penalty.

3.3 Reimbursements and Other Tax-Free Payments From Employer Health and Accident Plans

Several types of payments from a health or accident plan are not taxable even if your employer paid the entire cost of your coverage:

1. Reimbursements of your medical expenses; *see* below.
2. Payments for permanent physical injuries; *see* below.
3. Distributions from a health savings account (HSA) or Archer MSA if they are used to pay for qualified medical expenses; *see* below.
4. Payments to a chronically ill individual from a qualifying long-term-care insurance contract, but if payments are made on a *per diem* or other periodic basis the exclusion may be limited. For 2010, payments of up to $290 per day are tax free regardless of actual expenses. If the payments exceed $290 per day, you are only taxed to the extent that the payments exceed your qualifying long-term-care expenses. *See 17.15* for further details.

Payments that are not within the above tax-free categories, such as disability benefits, are not taxable to you if you paid all of the premiums with after-tax contributions. If your contributions were made on a pre-tax basis, benefits received from the plan are taxable. For example, benefits are taxable if you paid premiums paid under a cafeteria plan *(3.14)* with pre-tax contributions that were excluded from your income. If your employer paid all the premiums and you were not taxed on your employer's payment, any benefits you receive from the plan are fully taxable. If both you (with after-tax contributions) and your employer contributed to the plan, only the amount received that is attributable to your employer's payments is taxable.

Caution

Reimbursed Cosmetic Surgery

An employer's reimbursement of expenses for cosmetic surgery is taxable unless the employee had surgery to correct disfigurement from an accident, disease, or congenital deformity.

Tax-Free Reimbursements for Medical Expenses

Reimbursements of medical expenses *(17.2)* that you paid for yourself, your spouse, or any dependents and your children under age 27 are tax free, provided you incurred the expenses after the plan was established. Payment does not have to come directly to you to be tax free; it may go directly to your medical care providers. Reimbursements made under a qualifying health reimbursement arrangement (HRA) qualify for tax-free treatment; *see* below.

Tax-free treatment applies only for reimbursed expenses, not amounts you would have received anyway, such as sick leave that is not dependent on actual medical expenses. If your employer reimburses you for premiums you paid, the reimbursement is tax free so long as your payment was from after-tax funds. If you paid premiums with pre-tax salary reductions, a "reimbursement" from the employer will be taxable to you because the salary reductions are treated as your employer's payment, not yours.

Reimbursements for cosmetic surgery do *not* qualify for tax-free treatment, unless the surgery is for disfigurement related to congenital deformity, disease, or accidental injury.

Reimbursements for your *dependents'* medical expenses are tax free. This exclusion applies not only to reimbursed expenses of persons claimed as dependents *(21.1)* on your return, but also to expenses of qualifying children or relatives who *cannot* be claimed as your dependents because: (1) they are claimed by the other parent under the special rules for divorced/separated parents *(21.7)*, (2) their gross income exceeds the limit for qualifying relatives ($3,650 for 2010), (3) they file a joint return with their spouse, or (4) you are the dependent of another taxpayer and thus are barred from claiming any dependents on your return.

A qualifying dependent does *not* include a live-in mate where the relationship violates local law.

If the reimbursement is for medical expenses you deducted in a previous year, the reimbursement may be taxable. *See 17.4* for the rules on reimbursements of deducted medical expenses.

If you receive payments from more than one policy and the total exceeds your actual medical expenses, the excess is taxable if your employer paid the entire premium; *see* the Examples in *17.4*.

Health Reimbursement Arrangements (HRAs). Employers can set up health reimbursement arrangements (HRAs) to reimburse out-of-pocket medical expenses of employees, their spouses, children under age 27 and their dependents. Former employees including retired employees, and spouses and dependents of deceased employees can be covered. Self-employed individuals are not eligible. An HRA must be funded solely by employer contributions and not by salary reductions or after-tax contributions from employees.

Employees are not taxed on HRA reimbursements for medical expenses that may be claimed as itemized deductions *(17.2)*, including premiums. Before 2011, over-the-counter medicines also qualify, but starting in 2011 a drug qualifies for tax-free reimbursement only if a physician prescribes it or it is insulin. For contributions and reimbursements *(3.1)* to be tax free, employees must not receive cash or any benefit (taxable or nontaxable) from an HRA other than reimbursement for medical expenses. If the reimbursement limit is not fully used up by the end of a coverage year, the unused limit can be carried forward to a subsequent year. Nondiscrimination rules apply to self-insured HRAs.

Planning Reminder

Direct Transfer From HRA to HSA

Your employer can make a one-time direct transfer of your HRA balance to your HSA. The direct transfer must be made before 2012 and it cannot exceed the HRA balance as of September 21, 2006, where that is less than the date-of-transfer balance. Following the transfer, you must remain eligible for an HSA by being covered by a high-deductible health plan (HDHP) *(3.2)* for at least 12 months. Otherwise, the transferred funds will become taxable and also subject to a 10% penalty.

Self-employed health plan that includes spouse. If a self-employed person hires his or her spouse and provides family coverage under a health plan purchased in the name of the business, the employee-spouse may be reimbursed tax-free for medical expenses incurred by both spouses and their dependent children.

Executives taxed in discriminatory self-insured medical reimbursement plans. Although reimbursements from an employer plan for medical expenses of an employee and his or her spouse and dependents are generally tax free, this exclusion does not apply to certain highly compensated employees and stockholders if the plan is self-insured and it discriminates on their behalf. A plan is self-insured if reimbursement is not provided by an unrelated insurance company. If coverage is provided by an unrelated insurer, these discrimination rules do not apply. If a self-insured plan is deemed discriminatory, rank-and-file employees are not affected; only highly compensated employees are subject to tax.

Highly compensated participants subject to these rules include employees owning more than 10% of the employer's stock, the highest paid 25% of all employees (other than employees who do not have to be covered under the law), and the five highest paid officers.

If highly compensated employees are entitled to reimbursement for expenses not available to other plan participants, any such reimbursements are taxable to them. For example, if only the five highest paid officers are entitled to dental benefits, any dental reimbursements they receive are taxable. However, routine physical exams may be provided to highly compensated employees (but not their dependents) on a discriminatory basis. This exception does not apply to testing for, or treatment of, a specific complaint.

If highly compensated participants are entitled to a higher reimbursement limit than other participants, any excess reimbursement over the lower limit is taxable to the highly compensated participant. For example, if highly compensated employees are entitled to reimbursements up to $5,000 while all others have a $1,000 limit, a highly compensated employee who receives a $4,000 reimbursement must report $3,000 ($4,000 received minus the $1,000 lower limit) as income.

A separate nondiscrimination test applies to plan *eligibility*. The eligibility test requires that the plan benefit: (1) 70% or more of all employees or (2) 80% or more of employees eligible to participate, provided that at least 70% of all employees are eligible. A plan not meeting either test is considered discriminatory unless proven otherwise. In applying these tests, employees may be excluded if they have less than three years of service, are under age 25, do part-time or seasonal work, or are covered by a union collective bargaining agreement. A fraction of the benefits received by a highly compensated individual from a nonqualifying plan is taxable. The fraction equals the total reimbursements to highly compensated participants divided by total plan reimbursements; benefits available only to highly compensated employees are disregarded. For example, assume that a plan failing the eligibility tests pays total reimbursements of $50,000, of which $30,000 is to highly compensated participants. A highly compensated executive who is reimbursed $4,500 for medical expenses must include $2,700 in income:

$$\frac{30{,}000}{50{,}000} \times 4{,}500 = 2{,}700$$

Filing Tip

Permanent Physical Injuries

An employer's payment for permanent disfigurement or permanent loss of bodily function is tax free if the payment is based solely on the nature of the injury. Whether or not you qualify for this exclusion, you may deduct as an itemized deduction any unreimbursed medical expense you have in connection with these injuries subject to the 7.5% adjusted gross income floor *(17.1)*.

Taxable reimbursements are reported in the year during which the applicable plan year ends. For example, in early 2011 you are reimbursed for a 2010 expense from a calendar-year plan. If under plan provisions the expenses are allocated to the 2010 plan year, the taxable amount should be reported as 2010 income. If the plan does not specify the plan year to which the reimbursement relates, the reimbursement is attributed to the plan year in which payment is made.

Tax-Free Payments for Permanent Physical Injuries

Payments from an employer plan are tax free if they are for the permanent loss of part of the body, permanent loss of use of part of the body, or for permanent disfigurement of yourself, your spouse, your children under age 27, or your dependent. An appeals court held that severe hypertension does not involve loss of a bodily part or function and thus does not qualify for the exclusion.

To be tax free, the payments must be based on the kind of injury and have no relation to the length of time you are out of work or prior years of service. If the employer's plan does not specifically allocate benefits according to the nature of the injury, the benefits are taxable even if an employee is in fact permanently disabled.

EXAMPLE

After he loses a foot in an accident, Marc Jones receives $50,000 as specified in his employer's plan. The payment is tax free as it does not depend on how long Jones is out from work.

Disability payments from profit-sharing plan. The Tax Court has held that a profit-sharing plan may provide benefits that qualify for the exclusion for permanent disfigurement or permanent loss of bodily function. The plan must clearly state that its purpose is to provide qualifying tax-free benefits, and a specific payment schedule must be provided for different types of injuries. Without such provisions, payments from the plan are treated as taxable retirement distributions.

HSA or Archer MSA Payments

Tax-free distributions from a health savings account (HSA). Distributions from an HSA *(3.2)* are tax free if used to pay qualified medical expenses for you, your spouse, or your dependents. Qualified medical expenses are unreimbursed costs eligible for the itemized deduction *(17.2)* on Schedule A of Form 1040. In addition, over-the-counter medicines qualify for HSA purposes before 2011 even though they do not (except for insulin) qualify for a medical expenses deduction. However, starting in 2011, only medicines that are actually prescribed by a physician and insulin will qualify. Medical expenses are "qualified" only if incurred *after* the HSA has been established. A distribution is taxable to the extent it is not used to pay qualified medical expenses. A taxable distribution in 2010 is also subject to a 10% penalty unless you are disabled or are age 65 or older. Distributions will be reported to you on Form 1099-SA and you must report them on Form 8889, which you attach to Form 1040. On Form 8889, you determine if any part of the distribution is taxable and, if it is, that amount must be included as "Other income" on Line 21 of Form 1040. The 10% penalty from Form 8889, if any, is entered on Form 1040, Line 60 (total tax). On the dotted lines next to Lines 21 and 60, enter "HSA" and the amount on the dotted line. The penalty doubles to 20% for distributions after 2010.

A non-spouse beneficiary who inherits an HSA after the death of the account owner generally must include in income the fair market value of the assets as of the date of death. However, the beneficiary is not subject to the 10% penalty for taxable distributions. If the beneficiary is the account owner's spouse, he or she becomes the owner of the HSA and will be taxed only on distributions that are not used for qualified medical expenses.

Tax-free distributions from Archer MSA. If you work for a small-business employer and have a qualifying Archer MSA *(3.2)*, earnings accumulate in the account tax free. Withdrawals are tax free if used to pay deductible medical costs for you, your spouse, or dependents. Withdrawals used for a non-qualifying purpose are taxable and a taxable distribution before age 65 or becoming disabled is also subject to a 15% penalty (20% for distributions after 2010). *See 12.12* for further details.

3.4 Group-Term Life Insurance Premiums

You are not taxed on your employer's payments of premiums on a policy of up to $50,000 on your life. You are taxed only on the cost of premiums for coverage of over $50,000 as determined by the IRS rates shown in the table below. On Form W-2 your employer should include the taxable amount as wages in Box 1 and separately label the amount in Box 12 with Code C. You may not avoid tax by assigning the policy to another person.

If two or more employers provide you with group-term insurance coverage, you get only one $50,000 exclusion. You must figure the taxable cost for coverage over $50,000 by using the IRS rates below.

Regardless of the amount of the policy, you are not taxed if, for your entire tax year, the beneficiary of the policy is a tax-exempt charitable organization or your employer.

Filing Instruction

Uncollected Social Security and Medicare of Former Employees

If you receive coverage as a former employee, you must pay with Form 1040 on the line for "total tax" your share of Social Security and Medicare taxes on group-term life insurance over $50,000. The taxable amounts are shown in Box 12 of Form W-2, with Codes M and N.

Your payments reduce taxable amount. If you pay part of the cost of the insurance, your payment reduces dollar for dollar the amount includible as pay on Form W-2.

Retirees. If you retired before 1984 at normal retirement age or on disability and are still covered by a company group-term life insurance policy, you are not taxed on premium payments made by your employer even if coverage is over $50,000. If you retired after 1983 because of disability and remain covered by your company's plan, you are not taxed even if coverage exceeds $50,000. Furthermore, if you retired after 1983 and are not disabled, you may qualify for tax-free coverage over $50,000 if the following tests are met:

1. The insurance is provided under a plan existing on January 1, 1984, or under a comparable successor plan;
2. You were employed during 1983 by the company having the plan, or a predecessor employer; and
3. You were age 55 or over on January 1, 1984.

However, even if the three tests are met, you may be taxed under the rule below for discriminatory plans if you retired after 1986 and were a key employee.

Key employees taxed under discriminatory plans. The $50,000 exclusion is not available to key employees unless the group plan meets nondiscrimination tests for eligibility and benefits. For 2010, key employees include those who during the year were: (1) more-than-5% owners; (2) more-than-1% owners earning over $150,000; and (3) officers with compensation over $160,000. If the plan discriminates, a key employee's taxable benefit is based on the larger of (1) the actual cost of coverage or (2) the amount for coverage using the IRS rate table below.

The nondiscrimination rules also apply to former employees who were key employees when they separated from service. The discrimination tests are applied separately with respect to active and former employees.

Group-term life insurance for dependents. Employer-paid coverage for your spouse or dependents is a tax-free *de minimis* fringe benefit *(3.10)* if the policy is $2,000 or less. For coverage over $2,000, you are taxed on the excess of the cost (determined under the IRS table below) over your after-tax payments for the insurance, if any.

Table 3-2 Taxable Premiums for Group-Term Insurance Coverage Over $50,000

*Age—**	*Monthly cost for each $1,000 of coverage over $50,000—*
Under 25	$0.05
25–29	0.06
30–34	0.08
35–39	0.09
40–44	0.10
45–49	0.15
50–54	0.23
55–59	0.43
60–64	0.66
65–69	1.27
70 and over	2.06

**Age is determined at end of year.*

EXAMPLE

Lynda Jackson, a 52-year-old executive (not a "key" employee), is provided $200,000 of group-term life insurance in 2010. The taxable value of the coverage is based on the $150,000 coverage in excess of the $50,000 exclusion. As shown in the rate table above, the premium used to determine the taxable coverage is $0.23 for every $1,000 of coverage over $50,000. The taxable amount for the year is $414 ($0.23 x 12 months x 150).

If Lynda had paid $120 towards the coverage, the taxable amount would be reduced to $294 ($414 – $120).

Permanent life insurance. If your employer pays premiums on your behalf for permanent nonforfeitable life insurance, you report as taxable wages the cost of the benefit, less any amount you paid. A permanent benefit is an economic value that extends beyond one year and includes paid-up insurance or cash surrender value, but does not include, for example, the right to convert or continue life insurance coverage after group coverage is terminated. Where permanent benefits are combined with term insurance, the permanent benefits are taxed under formulas found in IRS regulations.

Caution

Tax-Free Exclusion for Employer-Provided Dependent Care

You cannot assume that your employer-provided dependent care benefit is completely tax free merely because your employer has not included any part of it in Box 1 of Form W-2 as taxable wages. Although up to $5,000 of benefits are generally tax free, the tax-free amount is reduced where you or your spouse earn less than $5,000 or where you file separately from your spouse. You must show the amount of your qualifying dependent care expenses and figure the tax-free exclusion on Form 2441.

3.5 Dependent Care Assistance

The value of qualifying day-care services provided by your employer under a written, nondiscriminatory plan is generally not taxable up to a limit of $5,000, or $2,500 if you are filing separately. The same tax-free limits apply if you make pre-tax salary deferrals to a flexible spending account for reimbursing dependent care expenses *(3.15)*. However, you may not exclude from income more than your earned income. If you are married and your spouse earns less than you do, your tax-free benefit is limited to his or her earned income. If your spouse does not work, all of your benefits are taxable unless he or she is a full-time student or is disabled. If a full-time student or disabled, your spouse is treated as earning $250 a month if your dependent care expenses are for one dependent, or $500 a month if the expenses are for two or more dependents.

Expenses are excludable from income only if they would qualify for the dependent care credit; *see Chapter 25*. If you are being reimbursed by your employer, the exclusion is not allowed if dependent care is provided by a relative who is your dependent (or your spouse's dependent) or by your child under the age of 19. You must give your employer a record of the care provider's name, address, and tax identification number. The identifying information also must be listed on your return.

Reporting employer benefits on your return. Your employer will show the total amount of your dependent care benefits in Box 10 of your Form W-2. Any benefits over $5,000 will also be included as taxable wages in Box 1 of Form W-2 and as Social Security wages (Box 3) and Medicare wages (Box 5).

You must report the benefits on Part III of Form 2441, where you determine both the tax-free and taxable (if any) portions of the employer-provided benefits. If any part is taxable, that amount must be included on Line 7 of your return as wages and labeled "DCB."

Follow IRS instructions for identifying the care provider (employer, babysitter, etc.) on Part I of Form 2441.

The tax-free portion of employer benefits reduces eligibility for the dependent care credit (Chapter 25).

3.6 Adoption Benefits

If your employer pays or reimburses you in 2010 for qualifying adoption expenses under a written, nondiscriminatory plan, up to $13,170 per qualifying child may be tax free. The limit may be increased for 2011 by an inflation adjustment. Employer-provided adoption assistance may be for any child under age 18, or a person physically or mentally incapable of self-care. The exclusion applies to adoption fees, attorney fees, court costs, travel expenses, and other expenses directly related to a legal adoption. Expenses for adopting your spouse's child and the costs of a surrogate-parenting arrangement do *not* qualify. If you have other qualifying adoption expenses, you may also be able to claim a tax credit up to a separate $13,170 limit; both the exclusion and the credit may be claimed for the same adoption if they are not for the same expenses. The exclusion and the credit are subject to similar limitations, including a phaseout based on income. *See Chapter 25* for a full discussion of the credit.

The full $13,170 exclusion limit is available for the adoption of a "special needs" child even if actual adoption expenses are less than $13,170. A "special needs" designation is made when a state determines that adoption assistance is required to place a child (U.S. citizen or resident) with adoptive parents because of special factors, such as the child's physical condition or ethnicity.

If you are adopting a child who is not a U.S. citizen or resident when the adoption effort begins, the exclusion is available only in the year the adoption becomes final. For example, if in 2010 your employer pays for expenses of adopting a foreign child but the adoption has not become final by the end of the year, you must report the employer's payment as wage income for 2010. You will claim the exclusion on Form 8839 in the year the adoption is final.

Filing Tip

Claiming Credit and Exclusion

If you paid adoption expenses in 2010 that were not reimbursed by your employer, and the adoption was final in 2010, you may be able to claim the adoption credit; *see Chapter 25*.

Reporting employer benefits and claiming the exclusion on your 2010 return. You must file Form 8839 to report your employer's payments and to figure the tax-free and taxable portions of the benefits. The employer's payments will be included in Box 12 of Form W-2 (Code T). This total includes pre-tax salary reduction contributions that you made to a cafeteria plan *(3.14)* to cover such expenses.

If you are married, you generally must file a joint return to exclude the benefits as income. However, if you are legally separated or if you lived apart from your spouse for the last six months of the year, the exclusion may be available on a separate return; *see* Form 8839 for details.

On 2010 tax returns, the allowable exclusion is phased out if your modified adjusted gross income (MAGI) is between $182,520 and $222,520 (including the employer's adoption assistance and adding back certain tax-free income from foreign sources). Figure the tax-free amount on Form 8839. If your modified adjusted income for 2010 is $222,520 or more, employer-paid adoption expenses are fully taxable.

3.7 Education Assistance Plans

If your employer pays for job-related courses, the payment is tax free to you provided that the courses do not satisfy the employer's minimum education standards and do not qualify you for a new profession. If these tests are met, the employer's education assistance is a tax-free working condition fringe benefit *(3.9)*.

Even if not job related, your employer's payment for courses is tax free up to $5,250, provided the assistance is under a qualifying Section 127 plan meeting nondiscriminatory tests. Graduate courses qualify for the exclusion as well as undergraduate courses. The Section 127 exclusion covers tuition, fees, books, and equipment, plus supplies that you cannot keep at the end of the course. Lodging, meals, and transportation are not covered by the exclusion. Sports or hobby-type courses qualify only if the courses are related to your business or are required as part of a degree program.

Planning Reminder

Graduate Courses

Your employer's payment of graduate school expenses qualifies for the up-to-$5,250 exclusion.

Tuition reductions. Employees and retired employees of educational institutions, their spouses, and their dependent children are not taxed on tuition reductions for *undergraduate* courses provided the reduction is not payment for teaching or other services. However, an exclusion is allowed for tuition reductions under the National Health Services Corps Scholarship Program and the Armed Forces Health Professions Scholarship Program despite the recipient's service obligation. Widows or widowers of deceased employees or of former employees also qualify. Officers and highly paid employees may claim the exclusion only if the employer plan does not discriminate on their behalf. The exclusion applies to tuition for undergraduate education at any educational institution, not only the employer's school.

Graduate students who are teaching or research assistants at an educational institution are not taxed on tuition reductions for courses at that school if the tuition reduction is in addition to regular pay for the teaching or research services or the reduction is provided under the National Health Services Corps Scholarship Program or the Armed Forces Health Professions Scholarship Program. The graduate student exclusion for tuition reductions applies only to teaching and research assistants, and not to faculty or other staff members (or their spouses and dependents) who take graduate courses and also do research for or teach at the school. However, if the graduate courses are work related, a tuition reduction for faculty and staff may qualify as a tax-free working condition fringe benefit *(3.9)*.

3.8 Company Cars, Parking, and Transit Passes

The costs of commuting to a regular job site are not deductible *(20.2)*, but employees who receive transit passes or travel to work on an employer-financed van get a tax break by not having to pay tax on some or all of such benefits. Where a company car is provided, the value of personal use is generally taxable, as discussed below.

Planning Reminder

Year-End Benefits

Your employer may decide to treat fringe benefits provided during the last two months of the calendar year as if they were paid during the following year. For example, if your employer makes this election for a company car provided to you in November or December of 2010, only the value of personal use from January through October is taxable to you in 2010; personal use in November and December is taxable in 2011. If your employer elects this special year-end rule, you should be notified near the end of the year or when you receive Form W-2.

Company cars. The use of a company car is tax free under the working condition fringe benefit rule *(3.9)* to the extent you use the car for business. If you use the car for personal driving, your company has the responsibility of calculating taxable income, which generally is based on IRS tables that specify the annual lease value of various priced cars. You are also required to keep for your employer a mileage log or similar record to substantiate your business use. Your employer should tell you what type of records are required.

Regardless of personal use, you are not subject to tax for a company vehicle that the IRS considers to be of limited personal value. These are ambulances or hearses; flatbed trucks; dump, garbage, or refrigerated trucks; one-passenger delivery trucks (including trucks with folding jump seats); tractors, combines, and other farm equipment; or forklifts. Also not taxable is personal use of school buses, passenger buses (seating at least 20), and moving vans where such personal use is restricted. Exclusions are also allowed for commuting use of a clearly marked police, fire, or public safety officer vehicle by officers required to be on call at all times, and for officially authorized uses of unmarked vehicles by law enforcement officers.

Demonstration cars. The value of a demonstration car used by a full-time auto salesperson is tax free as a working condition fringe benefit if the use of the car facilitates job performance and if there are substantial personal-use restrictions, including a prohibition on use by family members and for vacation trips. Furthermore, mileage outside of normal working hours must be limited and personal driving must generally be restricted to a 75-mile radius around the dealer's sales office.

Chauffeur services. If chauffeur services are provided for both business and personal purposes, you must report as income the value of the personal services. For example, if the full value of the chauffeur services is $30,000 and 30% of the chauffeur's workday is spent driving on personal trips, then $9,000 is taxable (30% of $30,000) and $21,000 is tax free.

If an employer provides a bodyguard-chauffeur for business security reasons, the entire value of the chauffeur services is considered a tax-free working condition fringe benefit if: (1) the automobile is specially equipped for security and (2) the bodyguard is trained in evasive driving techniques and is provided as part of an overall 24-hour-a-day security program. If the value of the bodyguard-chauffeur services is tax free, the employee is still taxable on the value of using the vehicle for commuting or other personal travel.

How your employer reports taxable automobile benefits. Social Security and Medicare tax must be withheld. Income tax withholding is not required, but your employer may choose to withhold income tax. If income tax is not withheld, you must be notified of this fact so that you may consider the taxable benefits when determining whether to make estimated tax installments; *see Chapter 27*. Whether or not withholdings are taken, the taxable value of the benefits is entered on your Form W-2 in Box 14 or on a separate Form W-2 for fringe benefits.

A special IRS rule allows your employer to include 100% of the lease value of using the car on Form W-2, even if you used the car primarily for business. Your employer must specifically indicate on Form W-2 (Box 14) or on a separate statement if 100% of the lease value has been included as income on your Form W-2. If it has, you should compute a deduction on Form 2106 for the business-use value of the car. However, this deduction, plus any unreimbursed car operating expenses, may be claimed only as a miscellaneous itemized deduction on Schedule A subject to the 2% AGI floor *(19.1)*.

Company planes. Under rules similar to those for company cars, employees who use a company airplane for personal trips are taxable on the value of the flights, as determined by the employer using IRS tables.

Qualified Transportation Benefits

Your employer may provide you with transportation benefits that are tax free within certain limits. There are three categories of qualified benefits: (1) transit passes and commuter transportation in a van, bus, or similar highway vehicle are considered together, (2) parking, and (3) bicycle commuting reimbursements.

You may receive benefits from each category so long as the applicable monthly limit (*see* below) is not exceeded. If the benefits exceed the monthly limit, the excess is treated as wages subject to income tax, Social Security, and Medicare tax.

Transit pass/commuter transportation benefits and parking benefits may be provided through a salary-reduction arrangement. An irrevocable salary-reduction election may be made prospectively for a monthly amount of benefits. The salary reduction for any month may not exceed the total limit for both categories. Unused salary reductions may be carried over to later months and from year to year. However, if you leave the company before using the carryover, the unused amount is forfeited; you cannot get a refund.

Employer-provided transit passes and van/bus transportation. The combined value of employer-provided transit passes plus commuting in an employer's van or bus is tax free in 2010 up to $230 per month. If the value of benefits for any month does not equal the exclusion limit, the unused amount is lost and may not be carried over to other months. For 2011, the $230 monthly limit may be increased for inflation.

Qualifying transit passes include tokens, fare cards, or vouchers for mass transit or private transportation businesses using highway vehicles seating at least six passengers. A cash reimbursement for a transit pass is taxable if vouchers (or similar items) are readily available to the employer for distribution to employees. "Ready availability" is determined under tests in IRS regulations. Cash advances are taxable.

Qualifying van or bus pool vehicles must seat at least six passengers and be used at least 80% of the time for employee commuting; on average, the number of employees must be at least half the seating capacity.

The exclusion applies only to regular employees. For partners, more than 2% S corporation shareholders, and independent contractors who are provided transit passes, the IRS allows up to $21 per month as a tax-free *de minimis* benefit. If the monthly value exceeds $21, the full value is taxable and not just the excess over $21.

Parking provided by employer. For regular employees, the value of employer-provided parking spots or subsidized parking is tax free in 2010 up to a limit of $230 per month. Parking must be on or near the employer's premises, at a mass transit facility such as a train station or car pooling center. The value of parking benefits exceeding $230 per month is taxable in 2010. For 2011, the $230 monthly cap may be adjusted for inflation.

According to the IRS, parking benefits are to be valued according to the regular commercial price for parking at the same or nearby locations. For example, if an employer in a rural or suburban location provides free parking for employees and there are no commercial parking lots in the area, the employee parking is tax free. Where free parking is available to both business customers and employees, the employee parking is considered to have "zero" value unless the employee has a reserved parking space that is closer to the business entrance than the spaces allotted to customers.

Planning Reminder

Transportation Benefits

If your employer offers you the choice of receiving parking, transit pass, or van pooling benefits instead of cash salary as part of a "cafeteria" plan *(3.13)* and you elect the benefits rather than the cash, you are not taxed, provided the value does not exceed the monthly tax-free limit.

If the value of the right of access to a parking space for a month in 2010 exceeds $230, an employee will be taxed on the excess even if he or she actually uses the space for only a few days during the month.

If the employee pays a reduced monthly price for parking in 2010, there is a taxable benefit for that month only if the price paid plus the $230 exclusion is less than the value of the parking.

Commuter parking benefits for self-employed partners, independent contractors, or more than 2% S corporation shareholders do not qualify for the $230 exclusion but may qualify as a tax-free *de minimis* benefit *(3.10)*.

Employer-reimbursed bicycle costs. A limited exclusion is allowed for employer reimbursements of qualified bicycle commuting costs of employees. Reimbursements for the cost of a bicycle used for commuting, and for storing, repairing and improving the bicycle, are tax free up to $20 per qualifying month. A qualifying reimbursement may be made until March 31 of the following year.

However, qualifying month restrictions may block the bicycle benefit. The $20 monthly exclusion is allowed only for months in which the employee (1) regularly uses the bicycle for a substantial portion of the commute from home to the place of employment, and (2) does not receive either transit pass/commuter vehicle benefits or parking benefits.

Because of the second condition, an employee who bicycles from home to a train or bus station and continues his or her commute from there cannot get the $20 a month bicycle benefit for any month for which he or she takes advantage of the transit pass/commuter vehicle benefit.

3.9 Working Condition Fringe Benefits

An employer-provided benefit that would be deductible by you if you paid for it yourself *(19.3)* is a tax-free working condition fringe benefit. Under IRS regulations, such benefits include:

Company car or plane. The value of a company car or plane is tax free to the extent that you use it for business; *see 3.8* for more on company cars.

Employer-paid business subscriptions or reimbursed membership dues in professional associations.

Product testing. This is a limited exclusion for employees who test and evaluate company manufactured goods away from company premises.

Employer-provided education assistance. Employer-paid undergraduate and graduate courses may be a tax-free working condition fringe benefit if the courses maintain or improve job skills but are not needed to meet your employer's minimum educational requirements and do not prepare you for a new profession.

Job-placement assistance. According to the IRS, job placement services are tax free so long as they are geared to helping the employees find jobs in the same line of work and the employees do not have an option to take cash instead of the benefits. The employer must also have a business purpose for providing such assistance, such as maintaining employee morale.

For tax-free treatment, there is no nondiscrimination requirement; different types of job placement assistance may be offered, or no assistance at all, in the case of discharged employees with readily transferable skills. Tax-free benefits include the value of counseling on interviewing skills and resume preparation. Executives may be given secretarial support and the use of a private office during the job search.

Job placement benefits received as part of a severance pay arrangement are taxable to the extent that cash could have been elected. An offsetting deduction can be claimed only as a miscellaneous itemized deduction subject to the 2% of adjusted gross income floor *(19.3)*.

3.10 *De Minimis* Fringe Benefits

Small benefits that would be administratively impractical to tax are considered tax-free *de minimis* (minor) fringe benefits. Examples are occasional meal money or local transportation fares given to employees working overtime, employer-provided coffee, doughnuts, or soft drinks, personal use of company copying machines, company parties, or tickets for the theater or sporting events. Other *de minimis* benefits include:

Company eating facility. The value of meals received by employees on workdays at a subsidized eating facility is a tax-free *de minimis* fringe benefit if the facility is located on or near the business premises and the annual revenue from meal charges equals or exceeds the facility's direct operating costs. Revenue is treated as equal to operating costs for meals that are tax-free to employees under the employer convenience test *(3.13)*.

Highly compensated employees or owners with special access to executive dining rooms may not exclude the value of their meals as a *de minimis* fringe benefit; however, the meals may be tax free if meals must be taken on company premises for business reasons *(3.13)*.

Commuting under unsafe circumstances. If you are asked to work outside your normal working hours and due to unsafe conditions your employer provides transportation such as taxi fare, the first $1.50 per one-way commute is taxable but the excess over $1.50 is a tax-free *de minimis* benefit. This exclusion is not available to certain highly compensated employees and officers, corporate directors, or owners of 1% or more of the company.

Even when working their regular shift, hourly employees who are not considered highly compensated are taxed on only $1.50 per one-way commute if their employer pays for car service or taxi fare because walking or taking public transportation to or from work would be unsafe. The excess value of the transportation over $1.50 is tax free. These rules can apply to day-shift employees who work overtime as well as night-shift employees working regular hours so long as transportation is provided because of unsafe conditions.

Planning Reminder

Occasional Overtime Meal Money or Cab Fare

If you work overtime and occasionally receive meal money or cab fare home, the amount is tax free. The IRS has not provided a numerical standard for determining when payments are "occasional."

3.11 Employer-Provided Retirement Advice

If your employer maintains a qualified retirement plan, the value of retirement planning information and advice provided to you by the employer is not taxable. The exclusion is not limited to information pertaining to the employer's particular retirement plan. It applies to information for you and your spouse on general retirement income planning, as well as information on how the employer's plan fits within your overall plan.

Highly compensated employees qualify for the exclusion if similar services are provided to all employees who normally receive information updates on the employer's retirement plan.

The exclusion does not apply to related services that may be provided by the employer, such as brokerage services, tax preparation, accounting, or legal services; the value of such services is taxable.

3.12 Employee Achievement Awards

Achievement awards are taxable unless they meet special rules for awards of tangible personal property (such as a watch, television, or golf clubs) given to you in recognition of length of service or safety achievement. Cash awards, gift certificates, and similar items are taxable.

As a general rule, if your employer is allowed to deduct the cost of a tangible personal property award, you are not taxed. The employer's deduction limit, and therefore the excludable limit for you, is $400 for awards from nonqualified plans and $1,600 for awards from qualified plans or from a combination of qualified and nonqualified plans. If your employer's deduction is less than the item's cost, you are taxed on the greater of: (1) the difference between the cost and your employer's deduction, but no more than the award's fair market value; or (2) the excess of the item's fair market value over your employer's deduction. Deduction tests for achievement awards are discussed in *20.25*. Your employer must tell you if the award qualifies for full or partial tax-free treatment.

An award will not be treated as a tax-free safety achievement award if employee safety achievement awards (other than those of *de minimis* value) during the year have already been granted to more than 10% of employees (not counting managers, administrators, clerical employees, or other professional employees). An award made to a manager, administrator, clerical employee, or other professional employee for safety achievement does not qualify for tax-free treatment.

Tax-free treatment also does not apply when you receive an award for length of service during the first five years of employment or when you previously received such awards during the last five years, unless the prior award qualified as a *de minimis* fringe benefit.

Caution

Underpriced Award Items

If the value of an achievement award item is disproportionately high compared to the employer's cost, the IRS may conclude that the award is disguised compensation, in which case the entire value would be taxable.

Court Decision

House One Block Away

Two federal courts held that a school superintendent received tax-free lodging where the home was one block away from the school and separated by a row of other houses. This met the business premises test. The IRS announced that it would continue to litigate similar cases arising outside the Eighth Circuit in which the case arose. The Eighth Circuit includes the states of Arkansas, Iowa, Minnesota, Missouri, Nebraska, and North and South Dakota.

3.13 Employer-Furnished Meals or Lodging

The value of employer-furnished *meals* is not taxable if furnished on your employer's business premises for the employer's convenience. The value of *lodging* is not taxable if, as a condition of your employment, you must accept the lodging on the employer's business premises for the employer's convenience.

Business premises test. The IRS generally defines business premises as the place of employment, such as a company cafeteria in a factory for a cook or an employer's home for a household employee. The Tax Court has a more liberal view, extending the area of business premises beyond the actual place of business in such cases as these:

- A house provided a hotel manager, although located across the street from the hotel. The IRS has agreed to the decision.
- A house provided a motel manager, two blocks from the motel. However, a court of appeals reversed the decision and held in the IRS's favor.
- A rented hotel suite that is used daily by executives for a luncheon conference.

Remote camp in foreign country. Lodging in certain foreign "camps" is considered to be furnished on the business premises of the employer. To qualify, lodging must be provided to employees working in remote foreign areas where satisfactory housing is not available on the open market, it must be located as near as practicable to where they work, and it must be in a common area or enclave that is not available to the public and which normally accommodates at least 10 employees.

Convenience of employer test. The employer convenience test requires proof that an employer provides the free meals or lodging for a business purpose other than providing extra pay. In the case of meals, the employer convenience test is deemed to be satisfied for *all* meals provided on employer premises if a qualifying business purpose is shown for more than 50% of the meals. If meals and lodging are described in a contract or state statute as extra pay, this does not bar tax-free treatment provided they are *also* furnished for other substantial, noncompensatory business reasons; for example, you are required to be on call 24 hours a day, or there are inadequate eating facilities near the business premises.

Meal charges. Your company may charge for meals on company premises and give you an option to accept or decline the meals. However, by law, the IRS must disregard the charge and option factors in determining whether meals that you buy are furnished for noncompensatory business reasons. If such business reasons exist, the convenience-of-employer test is satisfied. If such reasons do not exist, the value of the meals may be tax free as a *de minimis* benefit *(3.10)*; otherwise, the value of the meal subsidy provided by the employer is taxable.

Where your employer provides meals on business premises at a fixed charge that is subtracted from your pay whether you accept the meals or not, the amount of the charge is excluded from your taxable pay. If the meal is provided for the employer's convenience, as in the previous Examples, the value of the meals received is also tax free. If it is not provided for the employer's convenience, the value is taxable whether it exceeds or is less than the amount charged.

Planning Reminder

Meal Exclusion

You may be able to avoid tax on meals that you receive on your employer's premises even if your meals do not satisfy the employer convenience test. If more than half of the employees to whom meals are furnished on the employer's business premises are furnished the meals for the employer's convenience, all of the on-premises meals are treated as being furnished for the employer's convenience.

EXAMPLES

1. A Las Vegas casino operator provided free cafeteria meals to employees, who were required to remain on casino premises during their entire shift. A federal appeals court (Ninth Circuit) held that the casino's "stay-on-premises" requirement constituted a legitimate business reason for the meals and thus all of the employee meals were tax free under the employer convenience test. The court refused to second guess the casino's business decision that a "stay-on-premises" policy was necessary for security and logistics reasons. Once that policy was adopted, the casino employees had no choice but to eat on the premises. The IRS responded to the decision by announcing that it would not challenge "employer convenience" treatment in similar cases where employees are precluded from obtaining a meal off-premises within a normal meal period.
2. A waitress who works from 7 a.m. to 4 p.m. is furnished two meals a day without charge. Her employer encourages her to have her breakfast at the restaurant before working, but she is required to have her lunch there. The value of her breakfast and lunch is not taxable under IRS regulations because it is furnished during her work period or immediately before or after the period. But say she is also allowed to have free meals on her days off and a free supper on the days she works. The value of these meals is taxable; they are not furnished during or immediately before or after her work period.
3. A hospital maintains a cafeteria on its premises where all of its employees may eat during their working hours. No charge is made for these meals. The hospital furnishes meals to have the employees available for emergencies. The employees

are not required to eat there. Since the hospital furnishes the meals in order to have employees available for emergency call during meal periods, the meals are not income to any of the hospital employees who obtain their meals at the hospital cafeteria.

4. To assure bank teller service during the busy lunch period, a bank limits tellers to 30 minutes for lunch and provides them with free meals in a cafeteria on the premises so they can eat within this time period. The value of the meals is tax free.

Lodging must be condition of employment. This test requires evidence that the lodging is necessary for you to perform your job properly, as where you are required to be available for duty at all times. The IRS may question the claim that you are required to be on 24-hour duty. For example, at one college, rent-free lodgings were provided to teaching and administrative staff members, maintenance workers, dormitory parents who supervised and resided with students, and an evening nurse. The IRS ruled that only the lodgings provided to the dorm parents and the nurse met the tax-free lodging tests because for the convenience of the college, they had to be available after regular school hours to respond to emergencies.

If you are given the choice of free lodging at your place of employment or a cash allowance, the lodging is not considered to be a condition of employment, and its value is taxable.

If the lodging qualifies as tax free, so does the value of employer-paid utilities such as heat, electricity, gas, water, sewerage, and other utilities. Where these services are furnished by the employer and their value is deducted from your salary, the amount deducted is excluded from taxable wages on Form W-2. But if you pay for the utilities yourself, you may not exclude their cost from your income.

Caution

Housing as Job Requirement

If housing is provided to some employees with a certain job and not others, the IRS may hold that the lodging is not a condition of employment. For example, the IRS taxed medical residents on the value of hospital lodging where other residents lived in their own apartments.

EXAMPLE

Tyrone Jones is employed at a construction project at a remote job site. His pay is $1,500 a week. Because there are no accessible places near the site for food and lodging, the employer furnishes meals and lodging for which it charges $400 a week, which is taken out of Jones's pay. Jones reports only the net amount he receives—$1,100 a week. The value of the meals and lodging is a tax-free benefit.

Groceries. An employer may furnish unprepared food, such as groceries, rather than prepared meals. Courts are divided on whether the value of the groceries is excludable from income. One court allowed an exclusion for the value of nonfood items, such as napkins and soap—as well as for groceries—furnished to a doctor who ate at his home on the hospital grounds so that he would be available for emergencies.

Cash allowances. A cash allowance for meals and lodging is taxable.

Faculty lodging. Teachers and other employees (and their spouses and dependents) of an educational institution, including a state university system or academic health center, do not have to pay tax on the value of school-provided lodging if they pay a minimal rent. The lodging must be on or near the campus. The minimal required rent is the smaller of: (1) 5% of the appraised value of the lodging; or (2) the average rental paid for comparable school housing by persons who are neither employees nor students. Appraised value must be determined by an independent appraiser and the appraisal must be reviewed annually.

For purposes of the 5% minimum rent rule, academic health centers include medical teaching hospitals and medical research organizations with regular faculties and curricula in basic and clinical medical science and research.

EXAMPLE

Carol Eng, a professor, pays annual rent of $6,000 for university housing appraised at $100,000. The average rent for comparable university housing paid by non-employees and non-students is $7,000. She does not have to pay any tax on the housing since her rental payments are at least 5% of the appraised housing value (5% of $100,000, or $5,000). If her rent was $4,000, she would have to report income of $1,000 ($5,000 minimum required rent – $4,000).

Peace Corps and VISTA volunteers. Peace Corps volunteers working overseas may exclude subsistence allowances from income under a specific code provision. The law does not provide a similar exclusion for the small living expense allowances received by VISTA volunteers.

Caution

Partners Are Not Employees

The IRS does not consider partners or self-employed persons as employees and so does not allow them to exclude the value of partnership-provided meals and lodging.

Table 3-3 Are Your Board and Lodging Tax Free?

Yes—	*No—*
Hotel executives, managers, housekeepers, and auditors who are required to live at the hotel. Domestics, farm laborers, fishermen, canners, seamen, servicemen, building superintendents, and hospital and sanitarium employees who are required to have meals and lodging on employer premises. Restaurant and other food service employees who have meals furnished during or immediately before or after working hours. Employees who must be available during meal periods for emergencies. Employees who, because of the nature of the business, must be given short meal periods. Workers who must use company-supplied facilities in remote areas. Park employees who voluntarily live in rent-free apartments provided by a park department in order to protect the park from vandalism.	Your employer gives you a cash allowance for your meals or lodgings. You have a choice of accepting cash or getting the meals or lodging. For example, under a union contract you get meals, but you may refuse to take them and get an automatic pay increase. A state hospital employee is given a choice. He or she may live at the institution rent free or live elsewhere and get extra pay each month. Whether he or she stays at the institution or lives outside, the extra pay is included in his or her income. A waitress, on her days off, is allowed to eat free meals at the restaurant where she works.

Filing Tip

Mortgage Interest and Taxes

If you itemize deductions on Schedule A (Form 1040), deduct payments for qualifying home mortgage interest *(15.1)* and real estate taxes *(16.6)* on your home even if you use a tax-free housing allowance to finance the payments.

3.14 Minister's Rental or Housing Allowance

A duly ordained minister pays no tax on the rental value of a home provided as part of his or her pay. If a minister is provided with an allowance rather than a home itself, the allowance is generally tax free if used to pay rent, to make a down payment to buy a house, to pay mortgage installments, or for utilities, interest, tax, and repair expenses of the house. However, the exclusion for an allowance is limited to the fair rental value of the home, including furnishings and appurtenances such as a garage, *plus* the cost of utilities. A rabbi or cantor is treated the same as a minister for purposes of the allowance or in-kind housing exclusion.

The church or local congregation must officially designate the part of the minister's compensation that is a rental or housing allowance. To qualify for tax-free treatment, the designation must be made in advance of the payments. Official action may be shown by an employment contract, minutes, a resolution, or a budget allowance.

Who qualifies for tax-free allowance? Tax-free treatment is allowed to ordained ministers, rabbis, and cantors who receive housing allowances as part of their compensation for ministerial duties. Retired ministers qualify if their allowance is furnished in recognition of past services.

The IRS has allowed the tax-free exclusion to ministers working as teachers or administrators for a parochial school, college, or theological seminary which is an integral part of a church organization. A traveling evangelist was allowed to exclude rental allowances from out-of-town churches to maintain his permanent home. Church officers who are not ordained, such as a "minister" of music (music director) or "minister" of education (Sunday School director), do not qualify.

The IRS has generally barred an exclusion to ordained ministers working as executives of non-religious organizations even where services or religious functions are performed as part of the job. The Tax Court has focused on the duties performed. A minister employed as a chaplain by a municipal police department under church supervision was allowed a housing exclusion, but the exclusion was denied to a minister-administrator of an old-age home that was not under the authority of a church and a rabbi who worked for a religious organization as director of inter-religious affairs.

Caution

Lawsuit Challenges Constitutionality of Minister's Tax-Free Benefits

When this book went to press, a federal district court was considering a challenge to the constitutionality of the housing exclusion for ministers. The Freedom From Religion Foundation (FFRF), a nonprofit group that advocates for the separation of church and state, claimed that the exclusion for housing or a housing allowance violates the Establishment Clause of the First Amendment by providing a subsidy that advances religion. The district court denied the IRS's motion to dismiss and held that a trial was necessary to decide the constitutional issues because the FFRF had alleged facts that leave open the possibility that an objective observer would conclude that the tax law goes too far in aiding and subsidizing religion by providing ministers and churches with tangible financial benefits not allowed secular employers and employees.

Allowance subject to self-employment tax. Although parsonage allowances are not taxable income, they are reported by self-employed ministers, rabbis, and cantors as self-employment income for Social Security purposes; *see Chapter 45*. If you do not receive a cash allowance, report the rental value of the parsonage as self-employment income. Rental value is usually equal to what you would pay for similar quarters in your locality. Also include as self-employment income the value of house furnishings, utilities, appurtenances supplied—such as a garage—and the value of meals furnished that meet the rules in *3.13*.

Business expenses allocable to tax-free allowance are not deductible. A minister may deduct business expenses allocable to taxable compensation, but not expenses allocable to a tax-free housing allowance. If part of a minister's salary is designated as a housing allowance, and the minister also has self-employment earnings from the exercise of his ministry, a double allocation is required, first between salary income and self-employment income, and then between the taxable and tax free parts of salary.

For example, in one case a minister had self-employment income comprising 21.56% of his annual income. Of the rest, 53.85% was a tax-free housing allowance and 46.15% was taxable salary. The Tax Court agreed with the double allocation required by the IRS. Since the minister did not provide evidence as to which expenses were generated by which type of income, the Court allocated expenses on a pro rata basis, applying the ratio of salary and self-employment income to total income. Since the self-employment income was 21.56% of total income (including the allowance), 21.56% of the expenses were deductible on Schedule C. The remaining expenses were treated as job-related costs deductible, if at all, as miscellaneous itemized expenses on Schedule A. However, because 53.85% of the minister's salary was a tax-free housing allowance, 53.85% of the expenses were nondeductible. The balance (46.15% of the expenses) could be claimed on Schedule A as a miscellaneous itemized deduction subject to the 2% of adjusted gross income floor *(19.3)*.

3.15 Cafeteria Plans Provide Choice of Benefits

"Cafeteria plans" is a nickname for plans that give an employee a choice of selecting either cash or at least one qualifying nontaxable benefit. You are not taxed when you elect qualifying nontaxable benefits, although cash could have been chosen instead. A cafeteria plan may offer tax-free benefits such as group health insurance or life insurance coverage, long-term disability coverage, dependent care or adoption assistance, medical expense reimbursements, or group legal services. Long-term care insurance may *not* be offered through a cafeteria plan under current law.

Employees may be offered a premium-only plan (POP), which allows them to purchase group health insurance coverage or life insurance on a pre-tax basis using salary-reduction contributions.

Health savings accounts (HSAs) and their related high-deductible health plans (HDHPs) may be offered as options by a cafeteria plan *(3.2)*. If so, employees may elect to have contributions made to an HSA and an HDHP on a pre-tax salary-reduction basis.

A cafeteria plan may also offer benefits that are nontaxable because they are attributable to after-tax employee contributions. For example, employees may be offered the opportunity to purchase disability benefits (short term or long term) with after-tax contributions. If a covered employee subsequently receives disability benefits that are attributable to after-tax contributions, the benefits will be tax free. On the other hand, the plan may allow employees to elect paying for disability coverage on a pre-tax basis and, in this case, any benefits from the plan attributable to the pre-tax contributions will be taxable when received.

Under a flexible spending arrangement (FSA), employees may be allowed to make tax-free salary-reduction contributions to a medical or dependent care reimbursement plan *(3.16)*.

A qualified cafeteria plan must be written and not discriminate in favor of highly compensated employees and stockholders. If the plan provides for health benefits, a special rule applies to determine whether the plan is discriminatory. If a plan is held to be discriminatory, the highly compensated participants are taxed to the extent they could have elected cash. Furthermore, if key employees *(3.4)* receive more than 25% of the "tax-free" benefits under the plan, they are taxed on the benefits.

3.16 Flexible Spending Arrangements

A flexible spending arrangement (FSA) allows employees to get reimbursed for medical or dependent care expenses from an account they set up with pre-tax dollars. Under a typical FSA, you agree to a salary reduction that is deducted from each paycheck and deposited in a separate account. The

Law Alert

Direct Transfer From Health FSA to HSA

Your employer can make a one-time direct transfer of the balance in your health FSA to your HSA. The direct transfer must be made before 2012 and it cannot exceed the health FSA balance as of September 21, 2006, where that is less than the date-of-transfer balance. Following the transfer, you must remain eligible for an HSA by being covered by a high-deductible health plan (HDHP) *(3.2)* for at least 12 months. Otherwise, the transferred funds will become taxable and also subject to a 10% penalty.

Planning Reminder

2½-Month Grace Period Eases Use-It-or-Lose-It Deadline

The IRS has given employers an opportunity to relax the use-it-or-lose-it deadline for health-care and dependent care FSAs. Employers have the option of amending their plans to allow employees an additional 2½ months to use the money in their FSAs. If the grace period is adopted, FSA funds that are unused at the end of a plan year can be applied to expenses incurred within the first 2½ months of the following year.

salary-reduction contributions are not included in your taxable wages reported on Form W-2. As expenses are incurred, you are reimbursed from the account. Reimbursements used to pay qualified medical expenses are excluded from income.

The tax advantage of an FSA is that your salary-reduction contributions are not subject to federal income tax or Social Security taxes, allowing your medical or dependent care expenses to be paid with pre-tax rather than after-tax income. The salary deferrals are also exempt from most state and local taxes; check with the administrator of your employer's plan.

In the case of a health FSA, paying medical expenses with pre-tax dollars allows you to avoid the 7.5% adjusted gross income (AGI) floor *(17.1)* that limits itemized deductions for medical costs.

However, to get these tax advantages, you must assume some risk. Under a "use-it-or-lose-it" rule, if your out-of-pocket expenses for the year are less than your contributions, the balance is generally forfeited although your employer can give you an additional 2½ months to spend the funds, as discussed below.

FSA election to contribute generally irrevocable. The IRS has imposed restrictions on FSAs that make them unattractive for many employees. An election to set up an FSA for a given year must be made before the start of that year. You elect how much you want to contribute during the coming year and that amount will be withheld from your pay in monthly installments.

Once the election for a particular year takes effect, you may not discontinue contributions to your account or increase or decrease a coverage election unless there is a change in family or work status that qualifies under IRS regulations.

Use-it-or-lose-it deadline may be extended 2½ months by employer. The use-it-or-lose-it rule in IRS regulations generally prevents employees from using salary-reduction contributions made in one year to pay expenses incurred after the end of that year. Any unused account balance as of the end of the year must be forfeited to the employer.

The use-it-or-lose-it rule was criticized for discouraging participation in FSAs and encouraging participants to incur unnecessary expenses at the end of the year to avoid forfeiture of unused contributions. In response to pressure from Congress, the IRS relaxed the rule by permitting unused amounts from a health-care FSA or dependent care FSA to pay or reimburse expenses incurred within a 2½-month (two months and 15 days) grace period following the end of each plan year. The grace period is allowed only if the employer amends the cafeteria plan document (which includes the FSA option) to allow it.

For the grace period to apply to the current plan year, the employer must amend the plan before the end of the plan year. For example, if a calendar year plan is amended before the end of 2010, employees with unused health FSA funds at the end of 2010 may use them to reimburse qualified medical expenses incurred during the grace period beginning January 1 and ending March 15, 2011. If the expenses incurred by March 15, 2011, did not cover the unused amount from 2010, the balance would be forfeited to the employer. The end-of-year balance of health FSA funds may only be applied to health expenses incurred during the grace period and not to dependent care or other expenses. Similarly, unused dependent care FSA amounts may be used only for dependent care expenses incurred during the grace period. During the grace period, unused amounts may not be cashed out or converted to any other benefit (taxable or nontaxable). The employer may allow additional time following the end of the grace period to submit reimbursement claims for qualified expenses paid during the plan year and the grace period.

Health-care FSA. The IRS does not impose a dollar limit on contributions to health FSAs, but employers limit employee salary-reduction contributions. However, a provision of the 2010 health-care reform legislation will limit the maximum salary-reduction contribution for 2013 to $2,500, with possible inflation adjustments for years after 2013.

Funds from a health FSA may generally be used to reimburse you for expenses that you could claim as a medical expense deduction *(17.2)* such as the annual deductible under your employer's regular health plan, co-payments you must make to physicians or for prescriptions, and any other expenses that your health plan does not cover. These may include eye examinations, eyeglasses, routine physicals, and orthodontia work for you and your dependents. The IRS has also allowed FSAs to reimburse over-the-counter medications such as cold remedies, pain relievers, and allergy medications even though they are not deductible as medical expenses *(17.12)*. However, this will change starting in 2011. Expenses incurred after 2010 for over-the-counter medications can be reimbursed tax free from an FSA only if a physician provides a prescription for the medication, or it is insulin.

In addition, a health FSA may not be used to reimburse you for premiums paid for other health plan coverage, including premiums for coverage under a plan of your spouse or dependent. Also, expenses for long-term care services cannot be reimbursed under a health FSA. You may not receive tax-free reimbursements for cosmetic surgery expenses unless the surgery is necessary to correct a deformity existing since birth or resulting from a disease or from injury caused by an accident. Nonqualifying reimbursements are taxable.

At any time during the year, you may receive reimbursements up to your designated limit, even though your payments into the FSA account up to that point may add up to less. For example, if you elect to make salary-reduction contributions of $100 per month to a health-care FSA and you incur $500 of qualifying medical expenses in January, you may get the full $500 reimbursement even though you have paid only $100 into the plan. Your employer may not require you to accelerate contributions to match reimbursement claims.

Law Alert

Restriction on Reimbursement of Over-the-Counter Medications After 2010

For 2010, over-the-counter medications are considered qualified medical expenses that can be reimbursed by a health FSA. However, under a provision in the 2010 healthcare reform legislation, an over-the-counter medication is a qualified expense for 2011 and later years only if it has been prescribed by a physician or it is insulin.

Employees on medical or family leave. Employees who take unpaid leave under the Family and Medical Leave Act (FMLA) to deal with medical emergencies or care for a newborn child may either continue or revoke their coverage during FMLA leave. If the coverage continues, the maximum reimbursement selected by such an employee must be available at all times during the leave period. If the coverage is terminated, the employee must be reinstated under the FSA after returning from the leave, but no reimbursement claims may be made for expenses incurred during the leave.

Law Alert

$2,500 Limit on Health FSA Contributions in 2013

Employee salary-reduction contributions to a health FSA in 2013 will be limited to $2,500 under a provision in the 2010 healthcare reform legislation. For 2014 and later years, inflation adjustments may increase the $2,500 limit.

Dependent care FSA. You may contribute to a dependent care FSA if you expect to have expenses qualifying for the dependent care tax credit discussed in Chapter 25, but if you contribute to a dependent care FSA, *any tax-free reimbursement from the account reduces the expenses eligible for the credit* (25.7). If you are married, both you and your spouse must work in order for you to receive tax-free reimbursements from an FSA, unless your spouse is disabled or a full-time student (3.5).

The maximum tax-free reimbursement under the FSA is $5,000, but if either you or your spouse earns less than $5,000, the tax-free limit is the lesser earnings. If your spouse's employer offers a dependent care FSA, total tax-free reimbursements for both of you are limited to $5,000. Furthermore, if you are considered a highly compensated employee, your employer may have to lower your contribution ceiling below $5,000 to comply with nondiscrimination rules.

You must use Part III of Form 2441 to figure how much of your reimbursement is tax free and how much must be included in your income. Unlike health FSAs, an employer may limit reimbursements from a dependent care FSA to your account balance. For example, if you contribute $400 a month to the FSA and in January you pay $1,500 to a day-care center for your child, your employer may choose to reimburse you $400 a month as contributions are made to your account.

Filing Instruction

Dependent Care Reimbursements Affect Credit

Reimbursements received tax free from your dependent care FSA reduce the expense base for figuring the dependent care credit; *see* Chapter 25.

3.17 Company Services Provided at No Additional Cost

Employees are not taxed on the receipt of services usually sold by their employer to customers where the employer does not incur additional costs in providing them to the employees. Examples are free or low-cost flights provided by an airline to its employees; free or discount lodging for employees of a hotel; and telephone service provided to employees of telephone companies. These tax-free fringes also may be provided to the employee's spouse and dependent children; retired employees, including employees retired on disability; and widows or widowers of deceased or retired employees. Tax-free treatment also applies to free or discount flights provided to parents of airline employees. Benefits provided by another company under a reciprocal arrangement, such as standby tickets on another airline, may also qualify as tax free.

The employer must have excess service capacity to provide the service and not forego potential revenue from regular customers. For example, airline employees who receive free reserved seating on company planes must pay tax on the benefit because the airline is foregoing potential revenue by reserving seating that could otherwise be sold.

Caution

Highly Compensated Employees

Highly compensated employees can receive tax-free company services only if the same benefits are available to other employees on a nondiscriminatory basis. For 2010, highly compensated employees include employees owning more than a 5% interest in 2010 or 2009, and employees who in 2009 had compensation over $110,000. Employers have the option of including only the top-paid 20% in the over-$110,000 category. The $110,000 compensation threshold may be increased for 2011.

Line of business limitations. If a company has two lines of business, such as an airline and a hotel, an employee of the airline may not receive tax-free benefits provided by the hotel. However, there are exceptions. An employee who provides services to both business lines may receive benefits from both business lines. Benefits from more than one line in existence before 1984 may also be available under a special election made by the company for 1985 and later years. Your employer should notify you of this tax benefit.

Caution

Line of Business Rule

The line of business limitation discussed at *3.17* for no-additional-cost services also applies to qualified employee discounts. Thus, if a company operates an airline and a hotel, employees who work for the airline may generally not receive tax-free hotel room discounts. However, if a special election was made by the company, employees may receive tax-free benefits from any line of business in existence before 1984.

3.18 Discounts on Company Products or Services

The value of discounts on company products is a tax-free benefit if the discount does not exceed the employer's gross profit percentage. For example, if a company's profit percentage is 40%, the maximum tax-free employee discount for merchandise is 40% of the regular selling price. If you received a 50% discount, then 10% of the price charged customers would be taxable income. The employer has a choice of methods for figuring profit percentage.

Discounts on services that are not tax free under *3.17* for no-additional-cost services qualify for an exclusion, limited to 20% of the selling price charged customers. Discounts above 20% are taxable. An insurance policy is treated as a service. Thus, insurance company employees are not taxed on a discount of up to 20% of the policy's price.

Some company products do not qualify for the exclusion. Discounts on real estate and investment property such as securities, commodities, currency, or bullion are taxable. Interest-free or low-interest loans given by banks or other financial institutions to employees are not excludable. Such loans are subject to tax under the rules discussed at *4.31*.

Highly compensated employees are subject to nondiscrimination rules *(3.17)* for no-additional-cost services.

3.19 Volunteer Firefighter and Emergency Medical Responder Benefits

Volunteer firefighters and volunteer emergency medical responders do not have to include in income certain benefits provided by a state or local government, provided that their firefighting or emergency medical services response organization furnishes such services under written agreement with the state or local government.

Rebate or reduction of property taxes or income taxes. A volunteer firefighter or emergency medical responder is not taxed on a rebate or reduction of state or local property or income taxes. If itemized deductions are claimed, the otherwise deductible amount for such taxes is reduced by the tax rebate or reduction.

Payments for volunteer services. If a state or local government provides payments or expense reimbursements to volunteer firefighters or emergency medical responders, up to $30 for each month of volunteer services is tax free.

Chapter 4

Dividend and Interest Income

Dividends and interest that are paid to you in 2010 are reported by the payer to the IRS on Forms 1099.

You will receive copies of:

- Forms 1099-DIV, for dividends
- Forms 1099-INT, for interest
- Forms 1099-OID, for original issue discount

Dividends paid by most domestic corporations and many foreign corporations are subject to the same preferential tax rates as net long-term capital gains *(4.2)*.

Report the amounts shown on the Forms 1099 on your tax return. The IRS uses the Forms 1099 to check the income you report. If you fail to report income reported on Forms 1099, you will receive a statement asking for an explanation and a bill for the tax deficiency. If you receive a Form 1099 that you believe is incorrect, contact the payer for a corrected form.

Do not attach your copies of Forms 1099 to your return. Keep them with a copy of your tax return.

4.1 Reporting Dividends and Mutual-Fund Distributions

Dividends paid to you out of a corporation's earnings and profits are taxable as ordinary income. The corporation will report dividends on Form 1099-DIV (or equivalent statement). Mutual-fund dividends and distributions are also reported on Form 1099-DIV (or similar form). Corporate dividends and mutual-fund distributions are reported on Form 1099-DIV (or equivalent) whether you receive them in cash or they have been reinvested at your request.

Form 1099-DIV. Form 1099-DIV for 2010 gives you a breakdown of the dividends and distributions paid to you during the year. A mutual-fund or real estate investment trust (REIT) dividend paid to you in January 2011 will also be reported to you on the 2010 Form 1099-DIV if it was declared and was payable in October, November, or December of 2010. The company or fund may send a statement that is similar to Form 1099-DIV. You do not have to attach the Form 1099-DIV (or similar statement) to your tax return.

Box 1a. Ordinary dividends taxed to you are shown in Box 1. These are the most common type of distribution, payable out of a corporation's earnings and profits. Your share of a mutual fund's ordinary dividends is also shown on Form 1099-DIV; short-term capital gain distributions are included in the Box 1a total.

Box 1b. Part of the Box 1a amount may be qualified dividends. Qualified dividends reported in Box 1b are generally taxed at the same favorable rates (zero or 15%) as net capital gains. *See 4.2* for further details on qualified dividends.

Boxes 2a–2d. Capital gain distributions (long term) from a mutual fund (or real estate investment trust) are shown in Box 2a. Box 2b shows the portion of the Box 2a amount, if any, that is unrecaptured Section 1250 gain from the sale of depreciable real estate. Box 2c shows the part of Box 2a that is Section 1202 gain from small business stock eligible for a 50% or 60% exclusion. Box 2d shows the amount from Box 2a that is 28% rate gain from the sale of collectibles. If any amount is reported in Box 2b, 2c, or 2d, you must file Schedule D with Form 1040 *(5.3)*.

Box 3. Nontaxable distributions that are a return of your investment are shown in Box 3; *see* "Return of capital distributions" below.

Box 4. If you did not give your taxpayer identification number to the payer, backup withholding at a 28% rate *(26.11)* is shown in Box 4.

Box 5. Your share of expenses from a non–publicly offered mutual fund is shown in Box 5 and may be deductible as a miscellaneous itemized deduction subject to the 2% floor *(19.15)*. This amount is included in Box 1a.

Boxes 6 and 7. The foreign tax shown in Box 6 (imposed by the country shown in Box 7) may be claimed as a tax credit on Form 1116 or as an itemized deduction on Schedule A *(36.14)*.

Boxes 8 and 9. Cash and noncash liquidation distributions are shown in these boxes.

Filing Instruction

So-Called Dividends That Are Really Interest

Distributions from the following financial institutions are called "dividends," but are actually interest reported on Form 1099-INT: dividends from credit unions, cooperative banks, savings and loan associations, building and loan associations, and mutual savings banks.

Nominee distribution—joint accounts. If you receive dividends on stock held as a nominee for someone else, or you receive a Form 1099-DIV that includes dividends belonging to another person, such as a joint owner of the account, you are considered to be a "nominee recipient." If the other owner is someone other than your spouse, you should file a separate Form 1099-DIV showing you as the payer and the other owner as the recipient of the allocable income. Give the owner a copy of Form 1099-DIV by January 31, 2011, so the dividends can be reported on his or her 2010 return. File the Form 1099-DIV, together with a Form 1096 ("Transmittal of Information Return"), with the IRS by February 28, 2011; the deadline is March 31, 2011, if filing electronically.

On your Schedule B (Form 1040) or Schedule 1 (Form 1040A), you list on Line 5 the ordinary dividends reported to you on Form 1099-DIV. Several lines above Line 6, subtract the nominee distribution (the amount allocable to the other owner) from the total dividends. Thus, the nominee distribution is not included in the taxable dividends shown on Line 6 of Schedule B or Schedule 1.

Planning Reminder

Dividends on Life Insurance Policies

Dividends on a life insurance policy (other than a modified endowment contract) are actually a refund of your premiums and are not taxed until they exceed the total premiums paid.

Return of capital distributions. A distribution that is not paid out of earnings is a nontaxable return of capital, that is, a partial payback of your investment. The company will report the distribution in Box 3 of Form 1099-DIV as a nontaxable distribution. You must reduce the cost basis of your stock by the nontaxable distribution. If your basis is reduced to zero by a return of capital distributions, any further distributions are taxable as capital gains, which you report on Schedule D of Form 1040. Form 1040A or Form 1040EZ may not be used.

☐ CORRECTED (if checked)

PAYER'S name, street address, city, state, ZIP code, and telephone no.		1a Total ordinary dividends	OMB No. 1545-0110	Dividends and Distributions
Very Mutual Fund 155 East 38th Street City, State 010X0		$ 500 1b Qualified dividends $ 435	2010 Form 1099-DIV	
		2a Total capital gain distr. $ 375	2b Unrecap. Sec. 1250 gain $	Copy B For Recipient
PAYER'S federal identification number X1-01X0110	RECIPIENT'S identification number 00X-1X-0X00	2c Section 1202 gain $	2d Collectibles (28%) gain $	
RECIPIENT'S name Noelle Ballesteros		3 Nondividend distributions $	4 Federal income tax withheld $	This is important tax information and is being furnished to the Internal Revenue Service. If you are required to file a return, a negligence penalty or other sanction may be imposed on you if this income is taxable and the IRS determines that it has not been reported.
			5 Investment expenses $	
Street address (including apt. no.) 21 Chauncy Street		6 Foreign tax paid $	7 Foreign country or U.S. possession	
City, state, and ZIP code City, State 111X0		8 Cash liquidation distributions $	9 Noncash liquidation distributions $	
Account number (see instructions)				

Form **1099-DIV** (keep for your records) Department of the Treasury - Internal Revenue Service

4.2 Qualified Corporate Dividends Taxed at Favorable Capital Gain Rates

Dividends paid out of current or accumulated earnings of a corporation are taxable *(4.5)*. Stock dividends on common stock *(4.6)* are generally not taxable, but other types of stock dividends are taxed *(4.8)*.

Dividends from most domestic corporations and many foreign corporations are treated as "qualified dividends," which are subject to the same favorable rates as net capital gain (the excess of net long-term capital gains over net short-term losses *(5.3)*). For 2010, the rate is either 15% or zero, depending on the rate that would otherwise apply to the dividends. The benefit of the zero or 15% reduced rate is obtained as part of the computation of tax liability on the "Qualified Dividends and Capital Gain Tax Worksheet" in the instructions for Form 1040 or Form 1040A, or, if required, on the Schedule D Tax Worksheet *(5.3)*. On the Qualified Dividends and Capital Gain Tax Worksheet (or Schedule D Tax Worksheet, if applicable), the 15% rate is applied to qualified dividends and net capital gain that does not escape tax under the zero rate.

Generally, the zero rate applies to taxpayers whose top bracket is 10% or 15%. Such taxpayers are not taxed at all on their qualified dividends and net capital gain. However, the zero rate is generally not available for qualified dividends (or net capital gain) earned by children and students under age 24 who are subject to the "kiddie tax" rules *(24.2)*; their dividends and gains are taxed as if earned by their parents, who likely are subject to the 15% (rather than zero) rate on dividends/gains. Although the zero rate is intended to benefit taxpayers with modest incomes, taxpayers with substantial dividends/gains whose top bracket would be 25% or higher if there were no capital gain rates may pay no tax (zero rate) on a portion of their qualified dividends/net capital gains, provided their ordinary income (such as salary and interest) is low.

On Form 1099-DIV for 2010, the amount of qualified dividends eligible for the zero or 15% rate will be shown in Box 1b. Certain dividend distributions are not eligible. The reduced rate does not apply unless the dividend is received on stock you held at least 61 days during the 121-day period beginning 60 days before the ex-dividend date. The ex-dividend date is the first date following the declaration of a dividend on which the purchaser of the stock is *not entitled* to receive the dividend *(4.9)*. You cannot count towards the 61-day test any days on which your position in the securities was hedged, thereby diminishing your risk of loss.

Filing Tip

Dividends Eligible for Reduced 2010 Rates

In Box 1b of Form 1099-DIV for 2010, payers of dividends will report the amount eligible for the zero rate (if the 10% or 15% bracket would otherwise apply) or 15% rate (if the rate would otherwise be 25% or higher). You must enter the qualified dividends on the "Qualified Dividends and Capital Gain Tax Worksheet" in the IRS instructions for Form 1040 or Form 1040A to obtain the benefit of the preferential rate, unless you need the "Schedule D Tax Worksheet" to report other transactions *(5.3)*.

Law Alert

Taxation of Dividends in 2011

Unless Congress acts, the law that allows qualified dividends to be taxed at the same rates as long-term capital gains will not apply after 2010 and so all dividends in 2011 will be taxed as ordinary income. However, there is pressure on Congress to retain capital gain treatment for dividends. *See* the *e-Supplement at jklasser.com* for a legislation update.

Some dividends from a mutual fund or exchange-traded fund (ETF) may be reported as qualified distributions on Form 1099 although they are not actually qualified distributions and cannot be reported as such on your return. Both you and the fund must hold the underlying security for the required 61-day period. The fund may report a dividend as qualifying without taking into account whether you purchased or sold your shares during the year, so you must determine whether you have met the 61-day holding period test for the shares on which the dividends were paid. When counting the number of days you held the shares, include the day you disposed of the shares but not the day you acquired them.

Generally, distributions on preferred stock instruments do not qualify for qualified dividend treatment because the instruments are hybrid securities that are treated as debt and not stock. Payments on such hybrid instruments are considered interest rather than dividends and thus are not eligible for the reduced tax rate. If the preferred instrument is treated as stock, the reduced rate does not apply to dividends attributable to periods totaling less than 367 days unless the 61-day holding period (discussed above) is met. If the dividends are attributable to periods of more than 366 days, the stock must be held at least 91 days in the 181-day period starting 90 days before the ex-dividend date.

Some dividends are actually interest. Distributions that are called dividends but are actually interest income, such as payments from credit unions and mutual savings banks, are not eligible for the reduced dividend rate. Similarly, certain dividends from exchange-traded funds (ETFs) and from mutual funds represent interest earnings and are not eligible for the reduced rate. Dividends paid by a real estate investment trust (REIT) generally are not eligible, but the reduced rate does apply to REIT distributions that are attributable to corporate tax at the REIT level or which represent qualified dividends received by the REIT and passed through to shareholders.

Dividends from foreign corporations qualify for the reduced rate if the corporation is traded on an established U.S. securities market, incorporated in a U.S. possession, or certain treaty requirements are met.

If your broker loans out your shares as part of a short sale, substitute payments in lieu of dividends may be received on your behalf while the short sale is open. Such substitute payments are not considered dividends and should be included in Box 8 of Form 1099-MISC and reported by you as "Other income" on Line 21 of Form 1040.

Tax-deferred retirement accounts such as traditional IRAs and 401(k) plans do not benefit from the reduced dividend rate. Distributions from such retirement plans are taxable as ordinary income even if the distribution is attributable to dividends.

4.3 Dividends From a Partnership, S Corporation, Estate, or Trust

Dividends you receive as a member of a partnership, stockholder in an S corporation, or as a beneficiary of an estate or trust may be qualified dividends eligible for the reduced tax rate of zero or 15% *(4.2)*.

A distribution from a partnership or S corporation is reported as a dividend only if it is portfolio income derived from nonbusiness activities. Your allowable share of the dividend will be shown on the Schedule K-1 you receive from the partnership or S corporation.

4.4 Real Estate Investment Trust (REIT) Dividends

Dividends from a real estate investment trust (REIT) are shown on Form 1099-DIV. Ordinary dividends reported in Box 1a are taxable at ordinary income rates except for the portion, if any, shown in Box 1b that qualifies for the zero or 15% capital gain rate. Dividends designated by the trust as capital gain distributions in Box 2a are reported by you as long-term capital gains regardless of how long you have held your trust shares. A loss on the sale of REIT shares held for six months or less is treated as a long-term capital loss to the extent of any capital gain distribution received before the sale plus any undistributed capital gains. However, this long-term loss rule does not apply to sales under periodic redemption plans.

4.5 Taxable Dividends of Earnings and Profits

You pay tax on dividends only when the corporation distributing the dividends has earnings and profits. Publicly held corporations will tell you whether their distributions are taxable. If you hold stock in a close corporation, you may have to determine the tax status of its distribution. You need to know earnings and profits at two different periods:

1. Current earnings and profits as of the *end of the current taxable year*. A dividend is considered to have been made from earnings most recently accumulated.
2. Accumulated earnings and profits as of the *beginning of the current year*. However, when current earnings and profits are large enough to meet the dividend, you do not have to make this computation. It is only when the dividends exceed current earnings (or there are no current earnings) that you match accumulated earnings against the dividend.

The tax term "accumulated earnings and profits" is similar in meaning to the accounting term "retained earnings." Both stand for the net profits of the company after deducting distributions to stockholders. However, "tax" earnings may differ from "retained earnings" for the following reason: Reserve accounts, the additions to which are not deductible for income tax purposes, are ordinarily included as tax earnings.

EXAMPLES

1. During 2010, Corporation A paid dividends of $25,000. At the beginning of 2010 it had accumulated earnings of $50,000. It lost $25,000 during 2010. You are taxed on your dividend income in 2010 because the corporation's net accumulated earnings and profits exceed its dividends.
2. At the end of 2009, Corporation B had a deficit of $200,000. Earnings for 2010 were $100,000. In 2010, it paid stockholders $25,000. The dividends are taxed in 2010; earnings exceeded the dividends.

Planning Reminder

Dividend Reinvestment in Company Stock

Your company may allow you either to take cash dividends or automatically reinvest the dividends in company stock. If you elect the stock plan, and pay fair market value for the stock, the full cash dividend is taxable.

If the plan lets you buy the stock at a discount, the amount of the taxable dividend is the fair market value of the stock on the dividend payment date plus any service fee charged for the acquisition. The basis of the stock is also the fair market value at the dividend payment date. The service charge may be claimed as an itemized deduction subject to the 2% adjusted gross income floor *(19.1)*. If at the same time you also have the option to buy additional stock at a discount and you exercise the option, you have additional dividend income for the difference between the fair market value of the optional shares and the discounted amount you paid for the shares.

4.6 Stock Dividends on Common Stock

If you own common stock in a company and receive additional shares of the same company as a dividend, the dividend is generally not taxable *(see Chapter 30)* for the method of computing cost basis of stock dividends *(30.3)* and rights and sales of such stock *(30.4)*.

Exceptions to tax-free rule. A stock dividend on common stock is taxable *(4.8)* when (1) you may elect to take either stock or cash; (2) there are different classes of common stock, one class receiving cash dividends and another class receiving stock; or (3) the dividend is of convertible preferred stock.

Fractional shares. If a stock dividend is declared and you are only entitled to a fractional share, you may be given cash instead. To save the trouble and expense of issuing fractional shares, many companies directly issue cash in lieu of fractional shares or they set up a plan, with shareholder approval, for the fractional shares to be sold and the cash proceeds distributed to the shareholders. Your company should tell you how to report the cash payment. According to the IRS, you are generally treated as receiving a tax-free dividend of fractional shares, followed by a taxable redemption of the shares by the company. You report on Schedule D capital gain or loss equal to the excess of the cash over the basis of the fractional share; long- or short-term treatment depends on the holding period of the original stock. In certain cases, a cash distribution may be taxed as an ordinary dividend and not as a sale reported on Schedule D; your company should tell you if this is the case.

Stock rights. The rules that apply to stock dividends also apply to distributions of stock rights. If you, as a common stockholder, receive rights to subscribe to additional common stock, the receipt of the rights is not taxable provided the terms of the distribution do not fall within the taxable distribution rules *(4.8)*.

Filing Tip

Stock Splits Are Not Taxed

The receipt of stock under a stock split is not taxable. Stock splits resemble the receipt of stock dividends, but they are not dividends. They do not represent a distribution of surplus as in the case of stock dividends. Although you own more shares, your ownership percentage has not changed. The purpose of a stock split is generally to reduce the price of individual shares in order to increase their marketability. The basis of the old holding is divided among all the shares in order to find the basis for the new shares *(30.2)*.

4.7 Dividends Paid in Property

A dividend may be paid in property such as securities of another corporation or merchandise. You report as income the fair market value of the property. A dividend paid in property is sometimes called a *dividend in kind*.

EXAMPLE

You receive one share of X corporation stock as a dividend from the G company of which you are a stockholder. You received the X stock when it had a market value of $25; you report $25, the value of the property received. The $25 value is also your basis for the stock.

Corporate benefit may be treated as constructive dividend. On an audit, the IRS may charge that a benefit given to a shareholder-employee should be taxed as a constructive dividend. For example, the Tax Court agreed with the IRS that a corporation's payment for a license that gave the sole shareholder the right to buy season tickets to Houston Texans football games was a constructive dividend.

4.8 Taxable Stock Dividends

The most frequent type of stock dividend is not taxable: the receipt by a common stockholder of a corporation's own common stock as a dividend *(4.6)*.

Taxable stock dividends. The following stock dividends are taxable:

- Stock dividends paid to holders of preferred stock. However, no taxable income is realized where the conversion ratio of convertible preferred stock is increased only to take account of a stock dividend or split involving the stock into which the convertible stock is convertible.
- Stock dividends elected by a shareholder of common stock who had the choice of taking stock, property, or cash. A distribution of stock that was immediately redeemable for cash at the stockholder's option was treated as a taxable dividend.
- Stock dividends paid in a distribution where some shareholders receive property or cash and other shareholders' proportionate interests in the assets or earnings and profits of the corporation are increased.
- Distributions of preferred stock to some common shareholders and common stock to other common shareholders.
- Distributions of convertible preferred stock to holders of common stock, unless it can be shown that the distribution will not result in the creation of disproportionate stock interests.

Constructive stock dividends. You may not actually receive a stock dividend, but under certain circumstances, the IRS may treat you as having received a taxable distribution. This may happen when a company increases the ratio of convertible preferred stock.

4.9 Who Reports the Dividends

Stock held by broker in street name. If your broker holds stock for you in a street name, dividends earned on this stock are received by the broker and credited to your account. You report all dividends credited to your account in 2010. The broker is required to file an information return on Form 1099 (or similar form) showing all such dividends.

If your statement shows only a gross amount of dividends, check with your broker if any of the dividends represented nontaxable returns of capital.

Dividends on stock sold or bought between ex-dividend date and record date. Record date is the date set by a company on which you must be listed as a stockholder on its records to receive the dividend. However, in the case of publicly traded stock, an ex-dividend date, which usually precedes the record date by several business days, is fixed by the exchange to determine who is entitled to the dividend.

If you buy stock before the ex-dividend date, the dividend belongs to you and is reported by you. If you buy on or after the ex-dividend date, the dividend belongs to the seller.

If you sell stock before the ex-dividend date, you do not have a right to the dividend. If you sell on or after the ex-dividend date, you receive the dividend and report it as income.

The dividend declaration date and date of payment do not determine who receives the dividend.

Nominees or joint owners. If you receive ordinary dividends on stock held as a nominee for another person, other than your spouse, give that owner a Form 1099-DIV and file a copy of that return with the IRS, along with a Form 1096 ("Transmittal of U.S. Information Return"). The actual owner then reports the income. List the nominee dividends on Schedule B of Form 1040 (or Schedule 1, Form 1040A) along with your other dividends, and then subtract the nominee dividends from the total.

EXAMPLE

You receive Form 1099-DIV showing dividends of $960 including a $200 nominee distribution. You prepare a Form 1099-DIV for the actual owner showing the $200 distribution, and file a copy of the form with the IRS, plus Form 1096. When you file your return, report the nominee distribution along with other ordinary dividends on Schedule B of Form 1040 and then subtract it from the total.

Dividend Income	***Amount***
Mutual Fund	$ 310
Computer Inc.	450
Utility Inc.	200
Subtotal	$ 960
Less: Nominee distribution	(200)
Net dividends	$ 760

Follow the same procedure if you receive a Form 1099-DIV for an account owned jointly with someone other than your spouse. Give the other owner a Form 1099-DIV, and file a copy with the IRS, along with a Form 1096. The other owner then reports his or her share of the joint income. On your return, you list the total dividends shown on Forms 1099-DIV and avoid tax by subtracting from the total the nominee dividends reported to the other owner.

4.10 Year Dividends Are Reported

Dividends are generally reported on the tax return for the year in which the dividend is credited to your account or when you receive the dividend check.

Dividends received from a corporation in a year after the one in which they were declared, when you held the stock on the record date, are taxed in the year they are received; *see* Example 4 below.

EXAMPLES

1. A corporation declares a dividend payable on December 30, 2010. It follows a practice of paying dividends by checks that are mailed so that stockholders do not receive them until January 2011. You report this dividend on your 2011 return.
2. On December 30, 2010, a dividend is declared by a mutual fund. You receive it in January 2011. The dividend is taxable in 2010, when declared, and not 2011, when received under the special rule for dividends declared and payable by a mutual fund in the last three months of the year.
3. On December 30, 2010, a dividend is credited by a corporation to a stockholder's account and made immediately available. The dividend is taxable in 2010 as the crediting is considered constructive receipt in 2010, even though the dividend is not received until 2011 or a later year.
4. You own stock in a corporation. In April 2010, the corporation declared a dividend, but it provided that the dividend will be paid when it gets the cash. It finally pays the dividend in September 2011; the dividend is taxable in 2011.

Caution

Year-End Dividend From Mutual Fund

A dividend declared and payable in October through December by a mutual fund or REIT is taxable in the year it is declared, even if it is not paid until January of the following year.

4.11 Distribution Not Out of Earnings: Return of Capital

A return of capital or "nontaxable distribution" reduces the cost basis of the stock. If your shares were purchased at different times, reduce the basis of the oldest shares first. When the cost basis is reduced to zero, further returns of capital are taxed as capital gains on Schedule D. Whether the gain is short term or long term depends on the length of time you have held the stock. The company paying the dividend will usually inform you of the tax treatment of the payment.

Filing Tip

Insurance Premium Refund

Dividends on insurance policies are actually returns of premiums you previously paid. They are not subject to tax until they exceed the net premiums paid for the contract.

Life insurance dividends. Dividends on insurance policies are not true dividends. They are returns of premiums you previously paid. They reduce the cost of the policy and are not subject to tax until they exceed the net premiums paid for the contract. Interest paid or credited on dividends left with the insurance company is taxable. Dividends on VA insurance are tax free, as is interest on dividends left with the VA.

Where insurance premiums were deducted as a business expense in prior years, receipts of insurance dividends are included as business income. Dividends on capital stock of an insurance company are taxable.

4.12 Reporting Interest on Your Tax Return

You must report all taxable interest. Forms 1099-INT, sent by payers of interest income, give you the amount of interest to enter on your tax return. Although they are generally correct, you should check for mistakes, notify payers of any error, and request a new form marked "corrected." If tax was withheld *(26.12)*, claim this tax as a payment on your tax return. The IRS will check interest reported on your return against the Forms 1099-INT sent by banks and other payers. If you earn over $1,500 of taxable interest, you list the payers of interest on Part I of Schedule B if you file Form 1040, or on Part I of Schedule 1 if you file Form 1040A. Form 1040EZ may not be used if your taxable interest exceeds $1,500. You must also list tax-exempt interest on your return even though it is not taxable.

You must report interest that has been shown on a Form 1099-INT in your name although it may not be taxable to you. For example, you may have received interest as a nominee or as accrued interest on bonds bought between interest dates. In these cases, list the amounts reported on Form 1099 along with your other interest income on Schedule B if you file Form 1040, or Schedule 1 if you file Form 1040A. On a separate line, label the amount as "Nominee distribution," or "Accrued interest" *(4.15)*, and subtract it from the total interest shown. Accrued interest is discussed below. Nominee distributions are discussed below under "Joint Accounts."

If you received interest on a frozen account *(4.13)*, include the interest from Form 1099 on Schedule B if you file Form 1040, or on Schedule 1 if you use Form 1040A. On a separate line, write "frozen deposits" and subtract the amount from the total interest reported.

You generally do not have to list the payers of interest if your interest receipts are $1,500 or less. However, complete Part I of Schedule B if you have to reduce the interest shown on Form 1099 by nontaxable amounts such as accrued interest, tax-exempt interest, nominee distributions, frozen deposit interest, amortized bond premium, or excludable interest on savings bonds used for tuition.

Joint accounts. Form 1099-INT will be sent to the joint owner whose name and Social Security number was reported to the bank (or other payer) on Form W-9 when the account was opened. If you receive a Form 1099-INT for interest on an account you own with someone other than your spouse, you should file a nominee Form 1099-INT with the IRS to indicate that person's share of the interest, together with Form 1096 ("Transmittal of Information Return"). Give a copy of the Form 1099-INT to the other person. When you file your own return, you report the total interest shown on Form 1099-INT and then subtract the other person's share so you are taxed only on your portion of the interest; *see* the Example below.

Do not follow this procedure if you contributed all of the funds and set up the joint account merely as a "convenience" account to allow the other person to automatically inherit the account when you die. In this case, you report all of the interest income.

Filing Instruction

Tax-Exempt Interest

Tax-exempt interest, such as from municipal bonds, must be reported on your return although it is not subject to regular income tax. Tax-exempt interest is shown in Box 8 of Form 1099-INT and any portion that is subject to AMT *(23.3)* is shown in Box 9. Report the Box 8 amount on Line 8b of Form 1040 or Form 1040A. On Part I of Schedule B of Form 1040 or Schedule 1 of Form 1040A, report the tax-exempt interest on Line 1 but then subtract it from a subtotal of the total interest so that it is not included in the amount shown on Line 2 of the schedule.

EXAMPLE

Your Social Security number is listed on a bank account owned jointly with your sister. You each invested 50% of the account principal and have agreed to share the interest income. You receive a Form 1099-INT for 2010 reporting total interest of $1,700 on the account. By January 31, 2011, prepare and give to your sister another Form 1099-INT that identifies you as the payer and her as the recipient of her share, or $850 interest. Send a copy of the Form 1099-INT and a Form 1096 to the IRS no later than February 28, 2011 (March 31, if filing electronically). Your sister will report the $850 interest on her return. On your Form 1040, report the full $1,700 interest on Line 1 of Schedule B, along with your other interest income. Above Line 2, subtract the $850 belonging to your sister to avoid being taxed on that amount; label the subtraction "Nominee distribution."

Savings certificates, deferred interest. The interest element on certificates of deposit and similar plans of more than one year is treated as *deferred interest* original issue discount (OID) and is taxable on an annual basis. The bank notifies you of the taxable OID amount on Form 1099-OID. If you discontinue a savings plan before maturity, you may have a loss deduction for forfeited interest, which is listed on Form 1099-INT or Form 1099-OID *(4.16)*.

Tax on interest can be deferred on a savings certificate with a term of one year or less. Interest is taxable in the year it is available for withdrawal without substantial penalty. Where you invest in a six-month certificate before July 1, the entire amount of interest is paid six months later and is taxable in the year of payment. However, when you invest in a six-month certificate after June 30, only interest actually paid or made available for withdrawal before the end of the year without substantial penalty is taxable in the year of issuance. The balance is taxable in the year of maturity. You can defer interest to the following year by investing in a six-month certificate after June 30, provided the payment of interest is specifically deferred to the year of maturity by the terms of the certificate. Similarly, interest may be deferred to the following year by investing in longer term certificates of up to one year, provided that the crediting of interest is specifically deferred until the year of maturity.

Accrued interest on a bond bought between interest payment dates. Interest accrued between interest payment dates is part of the purchase price of the bond. This amount is taxable to the seller as explained in *4.15*. If you purchased a bond and received a Form 1099-INT that includes accrued interest on a bond, include the interest on Line 1 of Schedule B, Form 1040, and then on a separate line above Line 2 subtract the accrued interest from the Line 1 total.

Custodian account of a minor (Uniform Transfers to Minors Act). The interest is taxable to the child if his or her name and Social Security number were provided to the payer on Form W-9. However, if the child has net investment income for 2010 over $1,900, the "kiddie tax" *(24.2)* probably applies, in which case the excess over $1,900 is subject to tax at the parent's top tax rate.

4.13 Interest on Frozen Accounts Not Taxed

If you have funds in a bankrupt or insolvent financial institution that freezes your account by limiting withdrawals, you do not pay tax on interest allocable to the frozen deposits. The interest is taxable when withdrawals are permitted. Officers and owners of at least a 1% interest in the financial institution, or their relatives, may not take advantage of this rule and must still report interest on frozen deposits.

On Part I of Schedule B of Form 1040 or on Schedule 1 of Form 1040A, report the full amount shown on Form 1099-INT, even if the interest is on a "frozen" deposit. Then, on a separate line, subtract the amount allocable to the frozen deposit from the total interest shown on the Schedule; label the subtraction "frozen deposits." Thus, the interest on the frozen deposit is not included on the line of your return showing taxable interest.

Refund opportunity. If you reported interest on a frozen deposit on a tax return for a prior year, you generally have three years to file a refund claim for the tax paid on the interest *(47.2)*.

4.14 Interest Income on Debts Owed to You

You report interest earned on money that you loan to another person. If you are on the cash basis, you report interest in the year you actually receive it or when it is considered received under the "constructive receipt rule." If you are on the accrual basis, you report interest when it is earned, whether or not you have received it.

See 4.31 for minimum interest rates required for loans and *4.18* when OID rules apply.

Where partial payment is being made on a debt, or when a debt is being compromised, the parties may agree in advance which part of the payment covers interest and which covers principal. If a payment is not identified as either principal or interest, the payment is first applied against interest due and reported as interest income to the extent of the interest due.

Interest income is not realized when a debtor gives you a new note for an old note where the new note includes the interest due on the old note.

If you give away a debtor's note, you report as income the collectible interest due at the date of the gift. To avoid tax on the interest, the note must be transferred before interest becomes due.

Filing Tip

Lost Deposits

If you lose funds because of a financial institution's bankruptcy or insolvency, and you can reasonably estimate such a loss, you may deduct the loss as a nonbusiness bad debt, as a casualty loss, or as a miscellaneous itemized deduction *(18.5)*.

4.15 Reporting Interest on Bonds Bought or Sold

When you buy or sell bonds between interest dates, interest is included in the price of the bonds. If you are the buyer, you do not report as income the interest that accrued before your date of purchase. The seller reports the accrued interest. Reduce the basis of the bond by the accrued interest reported by the seller. The following Examples illustrate these rules.

Filing Tip

Accrued Interest

When you buy bonds between interest payment dates and pay accrued interest to the seller, this interest is taxable to the seller. The accrued interest is included on the Form 1099-INT you receive, but you should subtract it from your taxable interest; *see* Example 1 in *4.15*.

EXAMPLES

1. *Purchase.* On April 30, you buy for $5,200 a $5,000 corporate bond bearing interest at 5% per year, payable January 1 and July 1. The purchase price of the bond included accrued interest of $88.33 for the period January 1–April 30.

Interest received on 7/1	$125.00
Less: Accrued interest	83.33
Taxable interest	$ 41.67

Form 1099 sent to you includes the $83.33 of accrued interest. On Schedule B of Form 1040, you report the total interest of $125 received on July 1 and then on a separate line subtract the accrued interest of $83.33. Write "Accrued Interest" on the line where you show the subtraction.

Your basis for the bond is $5,117 ($5,200 – $83.33) for purposes of figuring gain or loss on a later sale of the bond.

2. *Sale.* On April 30, you sell for $5,200 a $5,000 5% bond with interest payable January 1 and July 1. The sales price included interest of $83.33 accrued from January 1–April 30. Your cost for the bond was $5,000. On your return, you report interest of $83.33 and capital gain of $117.

You receive	$ 5,200.00
Less: Accrued interest	83.33
Sales proceeds	$ 5,116.67
Less: Your cost	5,000.00
Capital gain	$ 116.67, or $117

Redemptions, bankruptcy, reorganizations. On a redemption, interest received in excess of the amount due at that time is not treated as interest income but as capital gain.

EXAMPLE

You hold a $5,000 9% bond with interest payable January 1 and July 1. The company can call the bonds for redemption on any interest date. In May, the company announces it will redeem the bonds on July 1. But you may present the bond for redemption beginning with June 1 and it will be redeemed with interest to July 1. On June 1 you present the bond and receive $5,225 – $5,000 principal, $187.50 interest to June 1, and $37.50 extra interest to July 1. The $37.50 is treated as a capital gain; the $187.50 is interest.

Taxable interest may continue on bonds after the issuer becomes bankrupt, if a guarantor continues to pay the interest when due. The loss on the bonds will occur only when they mature and are not redeemed or when they are sold below your cost. In the meantime, the interest received from the guarantor is taxed.

Bondholders exchanging their bonds for stock, securities, or other property in a tax-free reorganization, including a reorganization in bankruptcy, have interest income to the extent the property received is attributable to accrued but unpaid interest; *see* Internal Revenue Code Section 354(a)(2)(B).

Bonds selling at a flat price. When you buy bonds with defaulted interest at a "flat" price, a later payment of the defaulted interest is not taxed. It is a tax-free return of capital that reduces your cost of the bond. This rule applies only to interest in default at the time the bond is purchased. Interest that accrues after the date of your purchase is taxed as ordinary income.

4.16 Forfeiture of Interest on Premature Withdrawals

Banks usually impose an interest penalty if you withdraw funds from a savings certificate before the specified maturity date. You may lose interest if you prematurely withdraw funds in order to switch to higher paying investments, or if you need the funds for personal use. In some cases, the penalty may exceed the interest earned so that principal is also forfeited to make up the difference.

If you are penalized, you must still report the full amount of interest credited to your account. However, on Form 1040, you may deduct the full amount of the penalty-forfeited principal as well as interest. The deductible penalty/forfeited amount is shown in Box 2 of Form 1099-INT sent to you. You may claim the deduction even if you do not itemize deductions. On Form 1040, enter the deduction on Line 30, marked "Penalty on early withdrawal of savings."

Caution

CD Early Withdrawal

If you are penalized for making an early withdrawal from a certificate of deposit, you may lose part of your interest or principal. You must report the full amount of interest credited to your account, but you may deduct the full amount of the penalty/forfeited principal as well as interest on Line 30 of Form 1040.

Loss on redemption before maturity of a savings certificate. If you redeem a long-term (more than one year) savings certificate for a price less than the stated redemption price at maturity, you are allowed a loss deduction for the amount of original issue discount (OID) reported as income but not received. The deductible amount is shown in Box 3 of Form 1099-OID. Claim the deduction on Line 30 of Form 1040. The basis of the obligation is reduced by the amount of the deductible loss.

Do not include in the computation any amount based on a fixed rate of simple or compound interest that is actually payable or is treated as constructively received at fixed periodic intervals of one year or less.

4.17 Amortization of Bond Premium

Bond premium is the extra amount paid for a bond in excess of its principal or face amount when the value of the bond has increased due to falling interest rates. Investors may elect to amortize the premium on a taxable bond by deducting it over the life of the bond. Amortizing the premium annually is usually advantageous because it gives an annual deduction to offset the interest income from the bond. Basis of the bond is reduced by the amortized premium. If you claim amortization deductions and hold the bond to maturity, basis is reduced by the entire amortized premium and you have neither gain nor loss at redemption.

You may not claim a deduction for a premium paid on a *tax-exempt* bond; however, you must still decrease your basis by the premium.

Dealers in bonds may not deduct amortization but must include the premium as part of cost.

Planning Reminder

Amortized Premium Reduces Basis

You reduce the cost basis of the bond by the amount of the premium taken as a deduction.

If you hold the bond to maturity, the entire premium is amortized and you have neither gain nor loss on redemption of the bond. If before maturity you sell the bond at a gain (selling price exceeds your basis for the bond), you realize long-term capital gain if you held the bond long term. A sale of the bond for less than its adjusted basis gives a capital loss.

Capital loss alternative to amortizing premium. If you do not elect to amortize the premium on a taxable bond, you will realize a capital loss when the bond is redeemed at par or you sell it for less than you paid for it. For example, you bought a $1,000 corporate bond for $1,300 and did not amortize the $300 premium; you will realize a $300 capital loss when the bond is redeemed at par: $1,000 proceeds less $1,300 cost basis ($1,000 face value plus $300 premium). You could realize a capital gain if you sell the bond for more than the premium price you paid.

Determining the amortizable amount for the year. The annual amortizable premium is based on the constant yield method if the bond was issued after September 27, 1985. This method is the same as the optional constant yield method for reporting market discount *(4.20)*. *See* IRS Publication 1212 or consult a tax professional for making the complex computations.

For taxable bonds subject to a call before maturity, the amortization computation is based on the earlier call date if that results in a smaller amortization deduction.

Amortization election allowed in or after the year you acquire a bond. An election to amortize premium on a taxable bond does not have to be made in the year you acquire the bond. Attach a statement to the tax return for the first year to which you want the election to apply. If the election is made after the year of acquisition, the premium allocable to the years prior to the year of election is not amortizable; the unamortized amount is included in your cost basis for the bond and will result in a capital loss when the bond is redeemed at par or sold prior to maturity for less than basis.

How to deduct amortized premium on taxable bonds. The premium amortization for such bonds offsets your interest income from the bonds; *see* the Filing Tip on page 84. Any excess of the allocable premium over interest income may be fully deducted as a miscellaneous deduction (not subject to the 2% floor) on Line 28 of Schedule A (Form 1040). However, the miscellaneous deduction is limited to the excess of total interest inclusions on the bonds in prior years over total bond premium deductions in the prior years.

1040 *Filing Tip*

How To Deduct Amortized Premium

If you paid a premium on a taxable bond during 2010, you offset interest income on the bond by the amortized premium. You must file Form 1040 and show the reduction on Schedule B. Report the full interest from the bond on Line 1 of Schedule B, along with the rest of your interest income. On a separate line, subtract the amortized premium from a subtotal of the other interest. Label the subtraction "ABP Adjustment."

Effect of amortization election on other taxable bonds you acquire. If you elect to amortize the premium for one bond, you must also amortize the premium on all similar bonds owned by you at the beginning of the tax year, and also to all similar bonds acquired thereafter. An election to amortize may not be revoked without IRS permission. If you file your return without claiming the deduction, you may not change your mind and make the election for that year by filing an amended return or refund claim.

Callable bonds. On taxable bonds, amortization is based either on the maturity or earlier call date, depending on which date gives a smaller yearly deduction. This rule applies regardless of the issue date of the bond. If the bond is called before maturity, you may deduct as an ordinary loss the unamortized bond premium in the year the bond is redeemed.

Convertible bonds. A premium paid for a convertible bond that is allocated to the conversion feature may not be amortized; the value of the conversion option reduces basis in the bond.

Premium on tax-exempt bonds. You may not take a deduction for the amortization of a premium paid on a tax-exempt bond. However, you must still figure the amortization for each year and reduce your basis in the bond by the amortized amount. When you dispose of the bond, you amortize the premium for the period you held the bond and reduce the basis of the bond by the amortized amount. If the bond has call dates, the IRS may require the premium to be amortized to the earliest call date.

4.18 Discount on Bonds

There are two types of bond discounts: original issue discount and market discount.

Market discount. Market discount arises when the price of a bond declines because its interest rate is less than the current interest rate. For example, a bond originally issued at its face amount of $1,000 declines in value to $900 because the interest payable on the bond is less than the current interest rate. The difference of $100 is called market discount. The tax treatment of market discount is explained in *4.20*.

Original issue discount (OID). OID arises when a bond is issued for a price less than its face or principal amount. OID is the difference between the principal amount (redemption price at maturity) and the issue price. For publicly offered obligations, the issue price is the initial offering price to the public at which a substantial amount of such obligations were sold. All obligations that pay no interest before maturity, such as zero coupon bonds, are considered to be issued at a discount. For example, a bond with a face amount of $1,000 is issued at an offering price of $900. The $100 difference is OID.

Generally, part of the OID must be reported as interest income each year you hold the bond, whether or not you receive any payment from the bond issuer. This is also true for certificates of deposit (CDs), time deposits, and similar savings arrangements with a term of more than one year, provided payment of interest is deferred until maturity. OID is reported to you by the issuer (or by your broker if you bought the obligation on a secondary market) on Form 1099-OID *(4.19)*.

1040 *Filing Tip*

When OID May Be Ignored

You may disregard OID that is less than one-fourth of one percent (.0025) of the principal amount multiplied by the number of full years from the date of original issue to maturity. On most long-term bonds, the OID will exceed this amount and must be reported.

Exceptions to OID. OID rules do *not* apply to: (1) obligations with a term of one year or less held by *cash-basis taxpayers (4.21)*; (2) tax-exempt obligations, except for certain stripped tax-exempts *(4.26)*; (3) U.S. Savings Bonds; (4) an obligation issued by an individual before March 2, 1984; and (5) loans of $10,000 or less from individuals who are not professional money lenders, provided the loans do not have a tax avoidance motivation.

EXAMPLES

1. A 10-year bond with a face amount of $1,000 is issued at $980. One-fourth of one percent (.0025) of $1,000 times 10 is $25. As the $20 OID is less than $25, it may be ignored for tax purposes.
2. Same facts as in Example 1, except that the bond is issued at $950. As OID of $50 is more than the $25, OID must be reported under the rules explained at *4.19*.

Bond bought at premium or acquisition premium. You do not report OID as ordinary income if you buy a bond at a premium. You buy at a premium where you pay more than the total amount payable on the bond after your purchase, not including qualified stated interest. When you dispose of a bond bought at a premium, the difference between the sale or redemption price and your basis is a capital gain or loss *(4.17)*.

If you do not pay more than the total due at maturity, you do not have a premium, but there is "acquisition premium" if you pay more than the adjusted issue price. This is the issue price plus previously accrued OID but minus previous payments on the bond other than qualified stated interest. The acquisition premium reduces the amount of OID you must report as income. The rules for computing the reduction to OID are in IRS Publication 1212.

4.19 Reporting Original Issue Discount on Your Return

The issuer of the bond (or your broker) will make the Original Issue Discount (OID) computation and report in Box 1 of Form 1099-OID the OID for the actual dates of your ownership during the calendar year. In most cases, the entire OID must be reported as interest income on your return. However, the amount shown in Box 1 of Form 1099-OID must be adjusted if you bought the bond at a premium or acquisition premium, the bond is indexed for inflation, the obligation is a stripped bond or stripped coupon (including zero coupon instruments backed by U.S. Treasury securities), or if you received Form 1099-OID as a nominee for someone else. Your basis in the bond is increased by the OID included in income.

If you did not receive a Form 1099-OID, contact the issuer or check IRS Publication 1212 for OID amounts.

Treasury inflation-indexed securities. You must report as OID any increase in the inflation-adjusted principal amount of a Treasury inflation-indexed security that occurs while you held the bond during the tax year. This amount should be reported to you in Box 6 of Form 1099-OID, but this amount must be adjusted if during the year you bought the bond after original issue or sold it. The adjusted amount of OID must be computed using the coupon bond method discussed in IRS Publication 1212.

Periodic interest (non-OID) paid to you during the year on a Treasury inflation-indexed security may be reported to you either in Box 2 of Form 1099-OID or in Box 3 of Form 1099-INT.

Premium. If you paid a premium *(4.18)* for a bond originally issued at discount, you do not have to report any OID as income. Report the amount shown on Form 1099-OID and then subtract it as discussed in the Filing Tip in this section.

Acquisition premium. The amount that is shown in Box 1 of Form 1099-OID is not correct if you pay an acquisition premium *(4.18)* because such premium reduces the amount of OID you must report as income. *See* IRS Publication 1212 to recompute OID. On your return, report the amount shown on Form 1099-OID and then reduce it, as discussed in the Filing Tip in this section.

Stripped bonds or coupons. The amount that is shown in Box 1 of Form 1099-OID may not be correct for a stripped bond or coupon *(4.22)*. If it is incorrect, adjust it following the rules in Publication 1212 and report the proper amount, as discussed in the Filing Tip in this section.

Nominee. If you receive a Form 1099-OID for an obligation owned by someone else, other than your spouse, you must file another Form 1099-OID for that owner. The OID computation rules shown in IRS Publication 1212 should be used to compute the other owner's share of OID. You file the other owner's Form 1099-OID and a transmittal Form 1096 with the IRS, and give the other owner a copy of the Form 1099-OID. On your own tax return, report the amount shown on the Form 1099-OID you received and then reduce it, as discussed in the Filing Tip in this section.

Periodic interest reported on Form 1099-OID. If in addition to OID there is regular interest payable on the bond, such interest will be reported in Box 2 of Form 1099-OID. However, for a Treasury inflation-indexed security, the interest may be reported in Box 3 of Form 1099-INT. Report the full amount as interest income if you held the bond for the entire year. If you acquired the bond or disposed of it during the year, figure the interest allocable to your ownership period *(4.15)*.

REMICS. If you are a regular interest holder in a REMIC (real estate mortgage investment conduit), Box 1 of Form 1099-OID shows the amount of OID you must report on your return and Box 2 includes periodic interest other than OID. If you bought the regular interest at a premium or acquisi-

Filing Tip

Reporting OID and Recomputed OID

If you are reporting the full amount of OID from Box 1 of Form 1099-OID include the amount as interest on your Form 1040, 1040A, or 1040EZ. However, if you are reporting less OID than the amount shown in Box 1 of Form 1099-OID, you must file Form 1040 and fill out Schedule B *(4.19)*. Include the full amount shown in Box 1 of Form 1099-OID on Line 1 of Schedule B, along with other interest income. Make a subtotal of the Line 1 amounts and subtract from it the OID you are not required to report. Write "OID Adjustment" on the line where you show the subtraction, or "Nominee distribution," if that is the reason for the reduction. If you are reporting more OID than the amount shown in Box 1 of Form 1099-OID, add the additional amount to the subtotal of the interest on Line 1 of Schedule B, and label it "OID Adjustment."

Your basis for the obligation is increased by the taxable OID for purposes of figuring gain on a sale or redemption *(4.23)*.

tion, the OID shown on Form 1099-OID must be adjusted as discussed above. If you are a regular interest holder in a single-class REMIC, Box 2 also includes your share of the REMIC's investment expenses. These expenses should be listed in a separate statement and are deductible on Schedule A as a miscellaneous itemized deduction subject to the 2% adjusted gross income floor *(19.1)*.

4.20 Reporting Income on Market Discount Bonds

Market discount arises where the price of a bond declines below its face amount because it carries an interest rate that is below the current rate of interest.

When you realize a profit on the sale of a market discount bond, the portion of the profit equal to the accrued discount must be reported as ordinary interest income rather than as capital gain. Alternatively, an election may be made to report the accrued market discount annually instead of in the year of disposition.

Planning Reminder

Older Tax-Exempts

Tax-exempt bonds bought before May 1, 1993, are *not* subject to the market discount interest income rule; all the gain at disposition is capital gain.

These rules apply to taxable as well as tax-exempt bonds bought after April 30, 1993. However, there are these exceptions: (1) bonds with a maturity date of up to one year from date of issuance; (2) certain installment obligations; and (3) U.S. Savings Bonds. Furthermore, you may treat as zero any market discount that is less than one-fourth of one percent (.0025) of the redemption price multiplied by the number of full years after you acquire the bond to maturity. Such minimal discount will not affect capital gain on a sale.

Bonds bought before May 1, 1993. A *tax-exempt* bond bought before May 1, 1993, is not subject to the market discount rules. For *taxable* bonds bought before May 1, 1993, application of the market discount rules depends on the issue date.

If you bought a *taxable* bond before May 1, 1993, the market discount interest income rule applies if the bond was issued *after* July 18, 1984. If the bond was issued before July 19, 1984, the market discount interest income rule does *not* apply. However, if you borrowed money to purchase or carry a market discount bond acquired after July 18, 1984 and before May 1, 1993, the interest deduction deferral rules discussed in the next paragraph apply, and in the year you sell the bond, gain is treated as interest income to the extent of the deferred interest that is deductible in the year of disposition.

Deferral of interest deduction and ordinary income at disposition if you borrow to buy or carry market discount bonds. If you took a loan to buy or carry a market discount bond, and your interest expense exceeds the income earned on the bond (including OID income, if any), the excess may not be currently deducted to the extent of the market discount allocated to the days you held the bond during the year. The allocation of market discount is based on either the ratable accrual method or constant yield method; *see* below.

You can avoid this interest deduction limitation if you elect to report the market discount annually as interest income; *see* below for "How to figure accrued market discount."

In the year you dispose of the bond, you may deduct the interest expenses that were disallowed in prior years because of the above limitations.

You may choose to deduct disallowed interest in a year before the year of disposition if you have net interest income from the bond. Net interest income is interest income for the year (including OID) less the interest expense incurred during the year to purchase or carry the bond. This election lets you deduct any disallowed interest expense to the extent it does not exceed the net interest income of that year. The balance of the disallowed interest expense is deductible in the year of disposition.

How to figure accrued market discount. Where the market discount rules apply, gain is taxed as ordinary interest income to the extent of the market discount accrued to the date of sale. There are two methods for figuring the accrued market discount. The basic method, called the *ratable accrual method,* is figured by dividing market discount by the number of days in the period from the date you bought the bond until the date of maturity. This daily amount is then multiplied by the number of days you held the bond to determine your accrued market discount; *see* Example 1 below.

Instead of using the ratable accrual method to compute accrual of market discount you may elect to figure the accrued discount for any bond under an optional *constant yield* (economic accrual) method. If you make the election, you may not change it. The constant yield method initially provides a smaller accrual of market discount than the ratable method, but it is more complicated to figure. It is generally the same as the constant yield method used in IRS Publication 1212 to compute taxable OID *(4.19)*. For accruing market discount, treat your acquisition date as the original issue date and your basis for the market discount bond (immediately after you acquire it) as the issue price when applying the formula in Publication 1212.

Reporting discount annually. Rather than report market discount in the year you sell the bond, you may elect, in the year you acquire the bond, to report market discount currently as interest income. You may use either the ratable accrual method, as in Example 3 below, or the elective constant yield method discussed earlier. Your election to report annually applies to all market discount bonds subject to the interest income rule that you later acquire. You may not revoke the election without IRS consent. If the election is made, the interest deduction deferral rule discussed earlier does not apply. Furthermore, the election could provide a tax advantage if you sell the bond at a profit and you can benefit from lower tax rates applied to net long-term capital gains.

Filing Instruction

Discount Bonds Held to Maturity

If you do not report the discount annually and hold a bond until maturity, the discount is reported as interest income in the year of redemption. However, you have the option of reporting the market discount annually instead of at sale.

EXAMPLES

1. You buy a taxable bond at a market discount of $200. There are 1,000 days between the date of your purchase and the maturity date. The daily accrual rate is 20 cents. You hold the bond for 600 days before selling it for a price exceeding what you paid for the bond. Under the ratable accrual method, up to $120 of your profit is market discount taxable as interest income (600 x $0.20).
2. You paid $9,100 for a $10,000 bond maturing in 2010. If you hold the bond to maturity, you will receive $10,000, giving you a gain of $900, equal to the market discount. The entire $900 market discount will be taxable as interest income in 2010 when the bond is redeemed.
3. In 2010, you buy at a $200 discount a bond that was issued after July 18, 1984. There are 1,000 days between the date of your purchase and the maturity date, so that daily accrual is 20 cents. You elect to report the market discount currently using the ratable accrual method. If you held the bond for 112 days in 2010, on your 2010 return you report $22 as interest income (112 x $0.20).

Partial principal payments on bonds acquired after October 22, 1986. If the issuer of a bond (acquired by you after October 22, 1986) makes a partial payment of the principal (face amount) and you did not elect to report the discount annually, you must include the payment as ordinary interest income to the extent it does not exceed the accrued market discount on the bond. *See* IRS Publication 550 for options on determining accrued market discount. A taxable partial principal payment reduces the amount of remaining accrued market discount when figuring your tax on a later sale or receipt of another partial principal payment.

Market discount on a bond originally issued at a discount. A bond issued at original issue discount may later be acquired at a market discount because of an increase in interest rates. If you acquire at market discount an OID bond issued after July 18, 1984, the market discount is the excess of: (1) the issue price of the bond plus the total original issue discount includible in the gross income of all prior holders of the bond over (2) what you paid for the bond.

Exchanging a market discount bond in corporate mergers or reorganizations. If you hold a market discount bond and exchange it for another bond as part of a merger or other reorganization, the new bond is subject to the market discount rules when you sell it. However, under an exception, market discount rules will not apply to the new bond if the old market discount bond was issued before July 19, 1984, and the terms and interest rates of both bonds are identical.

4.21 Discount on Short-Term Obligations

Short-term obligations (maturity of a year or less from date of issue) may be purchased at a discount from face value. If you are on the cash basis, you report the discount as interest income in the year the obligation is paid. The interest is reported on Form 1099-INT.

EXAMPLE

In May 2009, you paid $970 for a short-term note with a face amount of $1,000. In January 2010, you receive payment of $1,000 on the note. On your 2010 tax return, you report $30 as interest.

Discount must be currently reported by dealers and accrual-basis taxpayers. Discount allocable to the current year must be reported as income by accrual-basis taxpayers, dealers who sell short-term obligations in the course of business, banks, regulated investment companies, common trust funds, certain pass-through entities, and for obligations identified as part of a hedging transaction. Current reporting also applies to persons who separate or strip interest coupons from a bond and then retain the stripped bond or stripped coupon; the accrual rule applies to the retained obligation.

For short-term nongovernmental obligations, OID is generally taken into account instead of acquisition discount, but an election may be made to report the accrued acquisition discount. *See* IRS Publication 550 for details.

Basis in the obligation is increased by the amount of acquisition discount (or OID for nongovernmental obligations) that is currently reported as income.

Filing Tip

Discount on Short-Term Government Obligations

For short-term governmental obligations (other than tax-exempts), the acquisition discount is accrued in daily installments under the ratable method, unless an election is made to use the constant yield method.

Interest deduction limitation for cash-basis investors. A cash-basis investor who borrows funds to buy a short-term discount obligation may not fully deduct interest on the loan unless an election is made to report the accrued acquisition discount as income. If the election is not made, a complicated formula limits deductible interest to the excess of the interest expense for the year over the taxable interest from the bond during the year less (1) the portion of the discount allocated to the days you held the bond during the year, and (2) the portion of interest not taxable for the year under your method of accounting. Any interest expense disallowed under this limitation is deductible in the year in which the obligation is disposed.

The interest deduction limitation does *not* apply if you elect to include in income the accruable discount under the ratable accrual method or constant yield method *(4.20)*. The election applies to all short-term obligations acquired during the year and also in all later years.

Gain or loss on disposition of short-term obligations for cash-basis investors. If you have a gain on the sale or exchange of a discounted short-term governmental obligation (other than tax-exempt local obligations), the gain is ordinary income to the extent of the ratable share of the acquisition discount received when you bought the obligation. Follow the computation shown in the discussion of Treasury bills *(4.27)* to figure this ordinary income portion. Any gain over this ordinary income portion is short-term capital gain; a loss would be a short-term capital loss.

Gain on short-term *nongovernmental* obligations is treated as ordinary income up to the ratable share of OID. The formula for figuring this ordinary income portion is similar to the formula for short-term governmental obligations *(4.27)*, except that the denominator of the fraction is days from original issue to maturity, rather than days from acquisition. A constant yield method may also be elected to figure the ordinary income portion. Gain above the computed ordinary income amount is short-term capital gain *(Chapter 5)*. For more information, *see* IRS Publication 550.

4.22 Stripped Coupon Bonds and Stock

Brokers holding coupon bonds may separate or strip the coupons from the bonds and sell the bonds or coupons to investors. Examples include zero-coupon instruments sold by brokerage houses that are backed by U.S. Treasury bonds (such as CATS and TIGRS).

The U.S. Treasury also offers its version of zero coupon instruments, with the name STRIPS, which are available from brokers and banks.

Brokers holding preferred stock may strip the dividend rights from the stock and sell the stripped stock to investors.

Caution

Recomputing Form 1099-OID Amount

Do not report the amount shown in Box 1 of Form 1099-OID for a stripped bond or coupon; that amount must be recomputed under complicated rules described in IRS Publication 1212. *See 4.19* for reporting the recomputed OID on your return.

If you buy a stripped bond or coupon, the spread between the cost of the bond or coupon and its higher face amount is treated as original issue discount (OID). This means that you annually report a part of the spread as interest income. For a stripped bond, the amount of the original issue discount is the difference between the stated redemption price of the bond at maturity and the cost of the bond. For a stripped coupon, the amount of the discount is the difference between the amount payable on the due date of the coupon and the cost of the coupon. The rules for figuring the amount of OID *(4.19)* to be reported annually are in IRS Publication 1212.

If you strip a coupon bond, interest accrual and allocation rules prevent you from creating a tax loss on a sale of the bond or coupons. You are required to report interest accrued up to the date of the sale and also add the amount to the basis of the bond. If you acquired the obligation after October 22, 1986, you must also include in income any market discount that accrued before the date you sold the stripped bond or coupons. The method of accrual depends on the date you bought the obligation; *see* IRS Publication 1212. The accrued market discount is also added to the basis of the bond. You then allocate this basis between the bond and the coupons. The allocation is based on the relative fair market values of the bond and coupons at the date of sale. Gain or loss on the sale is the difference between the sales price of the stripped item (bond or coupons) and its allocated basis. Furthermore, the original issue discount rules apply to the stripped item which you keep (bond or coupon). Original issue discount for this purpose is the difference between the basis allocated to the retained item and the redemption price of the bond (if retained) or the amount payable on the coupons (if retained). You must annually report a ratable portion of the discount.

4.23 Sale or Retirement of Bonds and Notes

Gain or loss on the sale, redemption, or retirement of debt obligations issued by a government or corporation is generally capital gain or loss.

A redemption or retirement of a bond at maturity must be reported as a sale on Schedule D of Form 1040 *(5.8)* although there may be no gain or loss realized.

Corporate bonds with OID issued after 1954 and before May 28, 1969, and government bonds with OID issued after 1954 and before July 2, 1982. If the bonds were originally issued at a discount (OID), you report your ratable monthly share of the OID element as ordinary income when the bonds are sold or redeemed; any gain exceeding OID is reported as capital gain. However, if there was an intention to call before maturity, gain is ordinary income to the full extent of the OID. A loss is a capital loss.

Corporate bonds with OID issued after May 27, 1969, and government bonds with OID issued after July 1, 1982. The accrued amount of OID is reported annually as interest income *(4.19)* and added to basis; this includes the accrued OID for the year the bond is sold. If the bonds are sold or redeemed before maturity, you realize capital gain for the proceeds over the adjusted basis (as increased by accrued OID) of the bond, provided there was no intention to call the bond before maturity. If at the time of original issue there was an intention to call the obligation before maturity, the entire OID that has not yet been included in your income is taxable as ordinary income; the balance is capital gain. IRS Publication 1212 has examples for figuring the amount taxable as ordinary income.

Market discount on bonds is taxable under the rules in *4.20.*

Tax-exempts. *See 4.26* for discount on tax-exempt bonds.

Obligations issued by individuals. If you hold an individual's note issued after March 1, 1984, for over $10,000, accrued OID must be reported annually *(4.19)* and added to basis. Gain on your sale of the note is subject to the rules discussed above for corporate and government OID bonds.

If the note is $10,000 or less (when combined with other prior outstanding loans from the same individual), OID is not reported annually provided you are not a professional lender and tax avoidance was not a principal purpose of the loan. On a sale of the note at a gain, your ratable share of the OID is taxed as ordinary income; any balance is capital gain. A loss is a capital loss.

Caution

Reporting Zero Coupon Bond Discount

Zero coupon bond discount is reported annually as interest over the life of the bond, even though interest is not received. This tax cost tends to make zero coupon bonds unattractive to investors, unless the bonds can be bought for IRA and other retirement plans that defer tax on income until distributions are made.

Zero coupon bonds also may be a means of financing a child's education. A parent buys the bond for the child. The child must report the income annually, and if the income is not subject to the parent's marginal tax bracket under the "kiddie tax" *(Chapter 24)*, the income subject to tax may be minimal.

The value of zero coupon bonds fluctuates sharply with interest rate changes. This fact should be considered before investing in long-term zero coupon bonds. If you sell zero coupon bonds before the maturity term at a time when interest rates rise, you may lose part of your investment.

4.24 State and City Interest Generally Tax Exempt

Generally, you pay no tax on interest on bonds or notes of states, cities, counties, the District of Columbia, or a possession of the United States. This includes bonds or notes of port authorities, toll road commissions, utility services activities, community redevelopment agencies, and similar bodies created for public purposes. Bonds issued after June 30, 1983, must be in registered form for the interest to be tax exempt. Interest on federally guaranteed obligations is generally taxable, but *see* exceptions in *4.25.*

Check with the issuer of the bond to verify the tax-exempt status of the interest.

Reporting on Schedule B or Schedule 1. On your 2010 return, you must list the amount of tax-exempt interest received during the year although it is not taxable. On Form 1040, you list the tax-exempt interest on Line 8b. On Form 1040A, you list the amount on Line 8b. On Form 1040EZ, you write "TEI" and then the amount of tax-exempt interest to the right of the last word on Line 2, but do not include it in the taxable interest shown on Line 2.

Private activity bonds. Interest on so-called private activity bonds is generally taxable *(4.25)*, but there are certain exceptions. For example, interest on the following "qualified bonds" is tax exempt even if the bond may technically be in the category of private activity bonds: qualified student loan bonds; exempt facility bonds, including New York Liberty bonds, Gulf Opportunity

Law Alert

AMT Exception for 2009 or 2010 Private Activity Bonds

The American Recovery and Reinvestment Act of 2009 provides an exception to the law that subjects interest on certain private activity bonds to alternative minimum tax (AMT). Interest on qualified private activity bonds issued in 2009 or 2010 is exempt from the AMT.

Zone bonds, Midwestern disaster and Hurricane Ike area bonds, and enterprise zone facility bonds; qualified small issue bonds; qualified mortgage bonds and qualified veterans' mortgage bonds; qualified redevelopment bonds; and qualified 501(c)(3) bonds issued by charitable organizations and hospitals. Check with the issuer for the tax status of a private activity bond.

AMT treatment. Tax-exempt interest on qualified private activity bonds issued after August 7, 1986 and before 2009 is generally treated as a tax preference item subject to alternative minimum tax (AMT, *23.2*), but there are exceptions. The AMT does not apply to interest on qualified 501(c)(3) bonds, New York Liberty bonds, Gulf Opportunity Zone bonds, Midwestern disaster and Hurricane Ike disaster area bonds, and exempt facility, qualified mortgage, and qualified veterans' bonds issued after July 30, 2008.

In addition, under the American Recovery and Reinvestment Act of 2009, the interest on any qualified bond issued in 2009 or 2010 is not subject to AMT.

4.25 Taxable State and City Interest

Interest on certain state and city obligations is taxable. These taxable obligations include federally guaranteed obligations, mortgage subsidy bonds, private activity bonds, and arbitrage bonds.

Federally guaranteed obligations. Interest on state and local obligations issued after April 14, 1983, is generally taxable if the obligation is federally guaranteed, but there are exceptions allowing tax exemptions for obligations guaranteed by the Federal Housing Administration, Department of Veterans Affairs, Bonneville Power Authority, Federal Home Loan Mortgage Corporation, Federal National Mortgage Association, Government National Mortgage Corporation, Resolution Funding Corporation, and Student Loan Marketing Association.

Mortgage subsidy bonds. Interest on bonds issued by a state or local government after April 24, 1979, may not be tax exempt if funds raised by the bonds are used for home mortgages. There are exceptions for certain qualified mortgage bonds and veterans' bonds. Check on the tax-exempt status of mortgage bonds with the issuing authority.

Private activity bonds. Generally, a private activity bond is any bond where more than 10% of the issue's proceeds are used by a private business whose property secures the issue, or if at least 5% of the proceeds (or $5 million if less) are used for loans to parties other than governmental units. Interest on such bonds is generally taxable, but there are exceptions *(4.24)*. Check on the tax status of the bonds with the issuing authority.

4.26 Tax-Exempt Bonds Bought at a Discount

Original issue discount (OID) on tax-exempt obligations is not taxable, and on a sale or redemption, gain attributed to OID is tax exempt. Gain attributed to market discount is capital gain or ordinary income depending on whether the bond was purchased before May 1, 1993, or on or after that date *(4.20)*. Amortization of premiums is discussed in *4.17*.

Original issue discount tax-exempt bond. This arises when a bond is issued for a price less than the face amount of the bond. The discount is considered tax-exempt interest. Thus, if you are the original buyer and hold the bond to maturity, the entire amount of the discount is tax free. On a disposition of a tax-exempt bond issued after September 3, 1982, and acquired after March 1, 1984, you must add to basis accrued OID before determining gain or loss. OID must generally be accrued using a constant yield method; *see* IRS Publication 1212.

When bonds issued after June 8, 1980, are redeemed before maturity, the portion of the original issue discount earned to the date of redemption is tax-free interest; the balance of the OID, the "unearned" part is capital gain. Bonds issued with an intention to redeem before maturity are not subject to this rule; all interest is tax exempt.

Market discount tax-exempts. A market discount arises when a bond originally issued at not less than par is bought at below par because its market value has declined. If *before* May 1, 1993, you bought at a market discount a tax-exempt bond which you sell for a price exceeding your purchase price, the excess is capital gain. If the bond was held long term, the gain is long term. A redemption of the bond at a price exceeding your purchase price is similarly treated.

However, for market discount tax-exempt bonds purchased *after* April 30, 1993, the ordinary income rules *(4.20)* apply.

Stripped tax-exempt obligations. OID is not currently taxed on a stripped tax-exempt bond or stripped coupon from the bond if you bought it before June 11, 1987. However, for any stripped bond or coupon you bought or sold after October 22, 1986, OID must be accrued and added to basis for purposes of figuring gain or loss on a disposition. Furthermore, if you bought the stripped bond or coupon after June 10, 1987, part of the OID may be taxable; *see* Publication 1212 for figuring the tax-free portion.

4.27 Treasury Bills, Notes, and Bonds

Interest on securities issued by the federal government is fully taxable on your federal return. However, interest on federal obligations is not subject to state or local income taxes. Interest on Treasury bills, notes, and bonds is reported on Form 1099-INT.

Treasury bonds and notes. Treasury notes have maturities of two, five, or 10 years. Treasury bonds have maturities of over 10 years. You report the fixed or coupon interest as interest income in the year the coupon becomes due and payable. Treasury bonds and notes are capital assets; gain or loss on their sale, exchange, or redemption is reported as capital gain or loss on Schedule D *(Chapter 5)*. If you purchased a federal obligation below par (at a discount) after July 1, 1982, *see* *4.19* for the rules on reporting original issue discount. If you purchased a Treasury bond or note above par (at a premium), you may elect to amortize the premium *(4.17)*. If you do not elect to amortize and you hold the bond or note to maturity, you have a capital loss.

Treasury inflation-indexed bonds. These pay interest semiannually at a fixed rate on a principal amount that is adjusted to take into account inflation or deflation. The interest is taxable when received and any increase in the inflation-adjusted principal amount while you hold the bond must be reported as original issue discount (OID) *(4.19)*. Your basis in the bond is increased by the OID included in income. On a sale or redemption before maturity, any gain is generally capital gain, but if there was an intention to call before maturity, gain is ordinary income to the extent of the previously unreported OID; *see* "Corporate bonds with OID issued after May 27, 1969, and government bonds with OID issued after July 1, 1982" *(4.23)*.

Planning Reminder

Tax Deferral: T-Bill Maturing Next Year

If you are a cash-basis taxpayer, you may postpone the tax on Treasury bill interest by selecting a Treasury bill maturing next year. Income is not recognized until the date on which the Treasury bill is paid at maturity, unless it has been sold or otherwise disposed of earlier.

Treasury bills. These are short-term U.S. obligations with maturities of four weeks, 13 weeks, 26 weeks, or 52 weeks. On a bill held to maturity, you report as interest income the difference between the discounted price and the amount you receive on a redemption of the bills at maturity.

Treasury bills are capital assets and a loss on a disposition before maturity is taxed as a capital loss. If you are a cash-basis taxpayer and have a gain on a sale or exchange, ordinary income is realized up to the amount of the ratable share of the discount received when you bought the obligation. This amount is treated as interest income and is figured as follows:

$$\frac{\text{Days T-bill was held}}{\text{Days from acquisition to maturity}} \times \text{Acquisition discount (redemption value at maturity } \textit{minus} \text{ your cost)}$$

Any gain over this amount is capital gain; *see* the Example below. Instead of using the above fractional computation for figuring the ordinary income portion of the gain, an election may be made to apply the constant yield method. This method follows the OID computation rules shown in IRS Publication 1212 for obligations issued after 1984, except that the acquisition cost of the Treasury bill would be treated as the issue price in applying the Publication 1212 formula.

EXAMPLE

You buy at original issue a 26-week $10,000Treasury bill (182-day maturity) for $9,800. You sell it 95 days later for $9,900. Your entire $100 gain ($9,900 – $9,800) is taxed as interest income as it is less than the $104 treated as interest income under the ratable daily formula:

$$\frac{\text{95 days held}}{\text{182 days from acquisition to maturity}} \times \$\ 200 \text{ discount} = \$104$$

Accrual-basis taxpayers and dealers who are required to currently report the acquisition discount element of Treasury bills using either the ratable accrual method or the constant yield method *(4.20)* do not apply the above formula on a sale before maturity. In figuring gain or loss, the discount included as income is added to basis.

Interest deduction limitation. Interest incurred on loans used to buy Treasury bills is deductible by a cash-basis investor only to the extent that interest expenses exceed the following: (1) the portion of the acquisition discount allocated to the days you held the bond during the year; and (2) the portion of interest not taxable for the year under your method of accounting. The deferred interest expense is deductible in the year the bill is disposed of. If an election is made to report the acquisition discount as current income under the rules for governmental obligations *(4.21)*, the interest expense may also be deducted currently. The election applies to all future acquisitions.

4.28 Interest on United States Savings Bonds

Savings Bond Tables: The e-Supplement at www.jklasser.com will contain redemption tables showing the 2010 year-end values of Series E bonds, Series EE bonds, and Series I bonds.

EE Bonds. Series EE bonds may be cashed for what you paid for them plus an increase in their value over their 30-year maturity period. *See* the discussion of the interest accrual and redemption rules for U.S. Savings Bonds *(30.14)*.

The increase in redemption value is taxable as interest, but you do not have to report the increase in value each year on your federal return. You may defer *(4.29)* the interest income until the year in which you cash the bond or the year in which the bond finally matures, whichever is earlier. But if you want, you may report the annual increase by merely including it on your tax return. If you use the accrual method of reporting, you must include the interest each year as it accrues. Savings bond interest is not subject to state or local taxes.

If you initially choose to defer the reporting of interest and later want to switch to annual reporting, you may do so. You may also change from the annual reporting method to the deferral method. *See 4.29* for rules on changing reporting methods.

Series I bonds. "I bonds" are inflation-indexed bonds issued at face amount *(30.15)*. As with EE bonds, you may defer the interest income (the increase in redemption value each year is interest) until the year in which the bond is redeemed or matures in 30 years, whichever is earlier *(4.29)*.

Education funding. If you buy EE or I bonds to pay for educational expenses and you defer the reporting of interest *(4.29)*, you may be able to exclude the accumulated interest from income when you redeem the bonds *(33.4)*.

Planning Reminder

Election for Children Not Subject to Kiddie Tax

If your child has net investment income under the annual threshold ($1,900 for 2010) for the kiddie tax *(24.2)*, making the election to report the interest annually may be advisable. For example, a dependent child is not allowed to claim a personal exemption, but he or she may claim a standard deduction for 2010 of at least $950 *(13.5)*. If the election to report the savings bond interest currently was made for 2010, up to $950 of the interest would be offset by the standard deduction, assuming the child had no other income.

Bonds registered in name of child. Interest on U.S. savings bonds bought for and registered in the name of a child will be taxed to the child, even if the parent paid for the bonds and is named as beneficiary. Unless an election is made to report the increases in redemption value annually, the accumulated interest will be taxable to the child in the year he or she redeems the bond, or if earlier, when the bond finally matures. The kiddie tax *(24.2)* may apply to a portion of the annually reported interest or to interest on redeemed bonds. For example, if a child under age 18 has 2010 investment income over $1,900, the excess is taxed at the parent's top tax rate on the child's 2010 return *(24.2)*. To avoid kiddie tax, savings bond interest may be deferred *(4.29)*.

Bonds must be reissued to make gift. Assume you have bought I or EE bonds and had them registered in joint names of yourself and your daughter. The law of your state provides that jointly owned property may be transferred to a co-owner by delivery or possession. You deliver the bonds to your daughter and tell her they now belong to her alone. According to Treasury regulations, this is not a valid gift of the bonds. The bonds must be surrendered and reissued in your daughter's name. For the year of reissue, you must include in your income all of the interest earned on the bonds other than interest you previously reported.

If you do not have the bonds reissued and you die, the bonds are taxable to your estate. Ownership of the bonds is a matter of contract between the United States and the bond purchaser. The bonds are nontransferable. A valid gift cannot be accomplished by manual delivery to a donee unless the bonds also are surrendered and registered in the donee's name in accordance with Treasury regulations.

Series E bonds. The last Series E bonds were issued in June 1980. By June 2010, all E bonds reached final maturity, 30 years from the date of issue.

Series HH. These bonds were available after 1979 and before September 1, 2004, in exchange for E or EE bonds, or for Freedom Shares. They were issued at face value and pay semiannual interest that is taxable when received. They mature in 20 years.

Series H. These bonds were available before 1980 and they reached final maturity 30 years later. If you obtained Series H bonds in an exchange for Series E bonds, and you did not report the E bond interest annually, the accumulated interest on the E bonds became taxable when the H bonds were redeemed or, if earlier, when the H bonds reached final maturity 30 years from issue.

4.29 Deferring United States Savings Bond Interest

You do not have to make a special election on your tax return in order to defer the interest on Series EE or I savings bonds. You may simply postpone reporting the interest until the year you redeem the bond or the year in which it reaches final maturity, whichever is earlier. If you choose to defer the interest, you may decide in a later year to begin reporting the increase in redemption value each year as interest. You may also switch from annual reporting to the deferral method. These options are discussed in this section.

Changing from deferral to annual reporting. If you have deferred reporting of interest (the annual increases in redemption value) and want to change to annual reporting starting with your 2010 return, you must report on your 2010 return all interest accrued through 2010 on all your EE and I bonds. Then, starting in 2011, you report the interest accruing each year on all of your bonds, including bonds you acquired after the 2010 election. Suppose you do not change from the deferral method to the annual method on your 2010 return and later wish you had. If the due date of the return has passed, it is too late to make the election. You may not file an amended return for 2010 to report the accrued interest. You have to wait until next year's return to make the election.

Changing from annual reporting to deferral. If you have been reporting annual increases in redemption value as interest income, you may change your method and elect to defer interest reporting until the bonds mature or are redeemed. You make the election by attaching a statement to your federal income tax return for the year of the change; *see* IRS Publication 550 for details.

Co-Owners. How to report interest on a Series EE or I bond depends on how it was bought or issued:

1. You paid for the entire bond: Either you or the co-owner may redeem it. You are taxed on all the interest, even though the co-owner cashes the bond and you receive no proceeds. If the other co-owner does cash in the bond, he or she will receive a Form 1099-INT reporting the accumulated interest. However, since that interest is taxable to you, the co-owner should give you a nominee Form 1099-INT, as explained in the rules for joint accounts in *4.12*.
2. You paid for only part of the bond: Either of you may redeem it. You are taxed on that part of the interest which is in proportion to your share of the purchase price. This is so even though you do not receive the proceeds.
3. You paid for part of the bond, and then had it reissued in another's name. You pay tax only on the interest accrued while you held the bond. The new co-owner picks up his or her share of the interest accruing afterwards.

Changing the form of registration. Changing the form of registration of an I or EE bond may result in tax. Assume you use your own funds to purchase a bond issued in your name, payable on your death to your son. Later, at your request, a new bond is issued in your son's name only. The increased value of the original bond up to the date it was redeemed and reissued in your son's name is taxed to you as interest income.

As shown in the Examples below, certain changes in registration do not result in an immediate tax.

EXAMPLES

1. Jones buys an EE bond and has it registered in his name and in the name of his son as co-owner. Jones has the bonds reissued solely in his own name; he is not required to report the accumulated interest at that time.
2. You and your spouse each contributed an equal amount toward the purchase of a $1,000 EE bond, which was issued to you as co-owners. You later have the bond reissued as two $500 bonds, one in your name and one in your spouse's name. Neither of you has to report the interest earned to the date of reissue. But if you bought the $1,000 bond entirely with your own funds, you report half the interest earned to the date of reissue.

Filing Tip

Form 1099-INT When Savings Bond Is Cashed

When you cash in an E, EE, or I bond, you receive Form 1099-INT that lists as interest the difference between the amount received and the amount paid for the bond. The form may show more taxable interest than you are required to report because you have regularly reported the interest or a prior owner reported the interest. Report the full amount shown on Form 1099-INT on Schedule B if you file Form 1040, or on Part I of Schedule 1 if you file Form 1040A, along with your other interest income. Enter a subtotal of the total interest and then, on a separate line, reduce the subtotal by the savings bond interest that was previously reported and identify the reduction as "Previously Reported U.S. Savings Bond Interest." The interest is exempt from state and local taxes.

Caution

E Bonds No Longer Earn Interest

All E bonds have reached final maturity and no longer earn interest. E bonds issued during 1979 ceased earning interest in 2009, 30 years from the date of issuance. E bonds issued in 1980 through June 1980 (the last issue date for E bonds) ceased earning interest in 2010, 30 years from their issue date *(30.14)*. All deferred interest is taxable in the year of final maturity.

3. You add another person's name as co-owner to facilitate a transfer of the bond on death. The change in registration does not result in a tax.

Filing Tip

Deduction for Estate Tax Paid on Interest

Where an estate tax has been paid on bond interest accrued during the owner's lifetime, the new bondholder may claim the estate tax as a miscellaneous itemized deduction in the year that he or she pays tax on the accumulated interest. The deduction is not subject to the 2% adjusted gross income floor *(11.17)*.

Transfer to a spouse. If you have been deferring interest on U.S. Savings Bonds, and then you transfer them to your spouse or ex-spouse as part of a divorce-related property settlement, you will be taxed on the interest deferred before the transfer date *(6.7)*.

Transfer to a trust. If you transfer U.S. Savings Bonds to a trust giving up all rights of ownership, you are taxed on the accumulated interest to date of transfer. If, however, you are considered to be the owner of the trust and the interest earned before and after the transfer is taxable to you, you may continue to defer reporting the interest.

Transfer to a charity. Tax on the accumulated interest is not avoided by having the bonds reissued to a philanthropy. The IRS held that by having the bonds reissued in the philanthropy's name, the owner realized taxable income on the accumulated bond interest.

Transfer of savings bond at death. If an owner does not report the bond interest annually and dies before redeeming the bond, the income tax liability on the interest accumulated during the deceased's lifetime becomes the liability of the person who acquires the bond, unless an election is made to report the accrued interest in the decedent's final income tax return *(1.14)*. If the election is not made on the decedent's final return, the new owner may choose to report the accumulated interest annually, or defer reporting it until the bond is redeemed or reaches final maturity, whichever is earlier. If the election is made on the decedent's final return, the new owner is taxable only on interest earned after the date of death.

4.30 Minimum Interest Rules

The law requires a minimum rate of interest to be charged on loan transactions unless a specific exception covers the transaction. Where minimum interest is not charged, the law imputes interest as if the parties agreed to the charge.

The rules are complicated and have been subject to several revisions. There are different minimum interest rates and reporting rules depending on the nature of the transaction. The following discussion provides the important details for understanding the rules. For specific cases and computations, we suggest that you consult IRS regulations for details not covered in this book.

There are two broad classes of transactions:

Filing Instruction

Tax Return Statement Requirements

A lender reporting imputed interest income or a borrower claiming an interest deduction must attach statements to their income tax returns reporting the interest, how it was calculated, and the names of the parties and their tax identification numbers.

Loans. These are generally covered by Internal Revenue Code Section 7872. Below-market or low-rate interest loans are discussed in *4.31*.

Seller-financed sales of property. These are covered by either Internal Revenue Code Section 1274 or Section 483. Seller-financed sales are discussed in *4.32*. If parties fail to charge the minimum required interest rate, the same minimum rate is imputed by law.

4.31 Interest-Free or Below-Market-Interest Loans

For many years, the IRS tried to tax interest-free or below-market-interest loans. However, court decisions supported taxpayers who argued that such loans did not result in taxable income or gifts. To reverse these decisions, the IRS convinced Congress to pass a law imposing tax on interest-free or low-interest loans made by individuals and businesses. You may not make interest-free or low-interest loans to a relative who uses the loan for personal or investment purposes without adverse income tax consequences, unless the exception discussed in this section for $10,000 or $100,000 loans applies.

Caution

Get Professional Advice To Draft Loan Agreement

Given the complexity of the imputed interest rules and exceptions, you and your tax advisor should carefully review regulations to the Internal Revenue Code Section 7872 when drafting a loan agreement.

How the imputed interest rules work. If interest at least equal to the applicable federal rate set by the IRS is not charged, the law generally treats a below-market-interest loan as two transactions:

1. The law assumes that the lender has transferred to the borrower an amount equal to the "foregone" interest element of the loan. In the case of a loan between individuals, such as a parent and child, the lender is subject to gift tax on this element; in the case of a stockholder borrowing from a company, the element is a taxable dividend; in the case of a loan made to an employee, it is taxable pay.

Note: For *gift tax* purposes *(39.2)*, a term loan is treated as if the lender gave the borrower the excess of the amount of the loan over the present value of payments due during the loan term. Demand loans are treated as if the lender gave the borrower annually the amount of the foregone interest.

2. The law assumes that imputed interest equal to the applicable federal rate is paid by the borrower to the lender. The borrower may be able to claim a deduction for the interest if the loan is used to buy a home and the loan is secured by the residence *(15.1)*, or the loan is used to buy investment property *(15.10)*.

In applying the imputed interest rules, all loans to or from a husband are combined with all loans to or from his wife; they are treated as one person.

With gift loans between individuals, interest computed during the borrower's taxable year is treated for both the lender and the borrower as transferred on the last day of the borrower's taxable year. Treasury regulations to Section 7872 provide rules for figuring "foregone" interest. Where a demand loan is in effect for the entire calendar year, a "blended annual rate" issued by the IRS to simplify reporting may be used to compute the imputed interest. The blended annual rate is announced by the IRS each July. For 2010, the blended rate is only 0.59%. The blended rate is not available if the loan was not outstanding for the entire year or if the loan balance fluctuated; computations provided by Treasury regulations must be used.

Charging the applicable federal rate avoids the imputed interest rules. Gift loans qualifying for the $10,000 and $100,000 exceptions are not subject to imputed interest rules. For other loans, the rules imputing income to you as the lender may be avoided by charging interest at least equal to the applicable federal rate. Applicable federal rates are set by the IRS monthly and published in the Internal Revenue Bulletin; you can also get the rates from your local IRS office. For a term loan, the applicable rate is the one in effect as of the day on which the loan is made, compounded semiannually. The short-term rate applies to loans of three years or less; the mid-term rate to loans over three and up to nine years; the long-term rate applies to loans over nine years. For a demand loan, the applicable federal rate is the short-term rate in effect at the start of each semiannual period (January and July).

Different computations for different types of loans. There are two general classes of loans: (1) Gift loans, whether term or demand, and nongift demand loans, and (2) nongift term loans.

The distinction is important for figuring and reporting imputed interest. For example, in the case of nongift term loans, the imputed interest element is treated as original issue discount *(4.19)*.

Gift loans and nongift loans payable on demand. As a lender, you are taxable on the "foregone interest," that is, the interest that you would have received had you charged interest at the applicable federal rate over any interest actually charged. The borrower may be able to claim an interest deduction if the funds are used to buy investment property *(15.10)*.

Nongift term loans. A term loan is any loan not payable on demand. As a lender of a nongift term loan, you are taxable on any excess of the loan principal over the present value of all payments due under the loan. The excess is treated as original issue (OID) which you report annually as interest income *(4.19)*.

Reporting imputed interest. Imputed interest is generally treated as transferred by the lender to the borrower and retransferred by the borrower to the lender on December 31 in the calendar year of imputation and is reported under the regular accounting method of the borrower and lender.

EXAMPLE

On January 1, 2010, Jones Company makes a $200,000 interest-free demand loan to Frank, an executive. The loan remains outstanding for the entire 2010 calendar year. Jones Company has a taxable year ending September 30. Frank is a calendar year taxpayer. For 2010 the imputed compensation payment and the imputed interest payment are treated as made on December 31, 2010.

Certain Loans Are Exempt From Imputed Interest Rules

Planning Reminder

Gift Loans up to $100,000

If you give a child or other individual an interest-free or below-market-interest loan, such as to buy a home or start a business, imputed interest is limited or completely avoided provided (1) the total outstanding loan balance owed to you by the borrower at all times during the year does not exceed $100,000, and (2) avoidance of federal tax is not a principal purpose of the interest arrangement.

If the above tests are met, imputed interest is limited to the borrower's net investment income where that income exceeds $1,000. If the borrower's net investment income is $1,000 or less, it is treated as zero, so no interest is imputed.

The $10,000 gift loan exception. In the case of a gift loan to an individual, no interest is imputed to any day on which the aggregate outstanding amount of all loans between the parties is not over $10,000, provided the loan is not attributed to the purchase or carrying of income-producing assets. If the exception applies, there are no income tax or gift tax consequences to the loan.

The $100,000 gift loan exception. No interest is imputed on an interest-free or low-interest loan to an individual of up to $100,000 if the borrower's net investment income is $1,000 or less; *see* the following Examples.

EXAMPLE

On January 1, 2010, you make a $100,000 interest-free loan to your son, payable on demand, which he uses for a down payment on a home. This is the only outstanding loan between you and your son. Your son's net investment income for 2010 is $650. Since the loan does not exceed $100,000, and your son's net investment income does not exceed $1,000, you do not have to report the "foregone interest" as interest income. Imputed interest is limited to the borrower's net investment income and net investment income of $1,000 or less is treated as zero.

For gift tax purposes, the foregone interest is a taxable gift. Using the IRS blended annual rate for 2010 of 0.59%, the foregone interest of $590 ($100,000 × 0.59%) is a taxable gift, but if this was your only gift to your son in 2010, there would be no gift tax, and a gift tax return would not have to be filed because of the annual gift tax exclusion of $13,000 per donee *(39.2)*.

Exceptions for compensation-related loans. For compensation-related and corporate-shareholder loans, the imputed interest rules do not apply to any day on which the total amount of outstanding loans between the parties is $10,000 or less, provided the principal purpose of the loan is not tax avoidance. Certain low-interest loans given to employees by employers to buy a new residence in a new job location are exempt from the imputed interest requirements.

Loans to continuing care facilities. Senior citizens moving into a community with a continuing care facility are required to pay a fee to the facility. The fee may be treated as a "loan" subject to the imputed interest rules but loans to qualified continuing care facilities are completely exempt *(34.11)*.

4.32 Minimum Interest on Seller-Financed Sales

The law requires minimum interest charges for seller-financed sales. If the minimum rate is not charged, the IRS imputes interest at the minimum applicable rate requiring both buyer and seller to treat part of the purchase price as interest even though it is not called interest in the sales contract. Generally, interest at the applicable federal rate (AFR) must be charged; *see* the chart at the end of this section for minimum required rates. For example, investment property is sold on the installment basis for $100,000 and the parties fail to charge adequate interest. Assume the IRS imputes interest of $5,000. For tax purposes, $95,000 is allocated to the sale of the property and the principal amount of the debt; the balance is imputed interest of $5,000, taxable to the seller and deductible by the buyer if allowed under the rules of *Chapter 15*.

Two statute classes. The minimum or imputed interest rules are covered by two Internal Revenue Code statutes: Sections 1274 and 483. Under both, the same minimum interest rates apply but the timing of interest reporting is different, as discussed below.

Section 483 applies to any payment due more than six months after the date of sale under a contract which calls for some or all payments more than one year after the date of sale. If the sales price cannot exceed $3,000, Section 483 does not apply. Transactions within Section 483 are sales or exchanges of: (1) principal residences; (2) any property if total payments, including interest and any other consideration to be received by the seller, cannot exceed $250,000; (3) farms if the total price is $1 million or less; and (4) sales of land between family members to the extent the aggregate sales price of all sales between the same parties in the same year is $500,000 or less.

If the selling price exceeds the respective $250,000, $1 million, or $500,000 amount listed in (2) through (4) above, the sale is subject to Section 1274 reporting rules provided some or all payments are due more than six months after the date of sale. Section 1274 also applies to all other transactions where neither the debt instrument nor the property being sold is publicly traded as long as some payments are deferred more than six months.

Caution

Buyer's Personal-Use Property

If adequate interest is not charged on an installment sale of personal-use property, such as a residence to be used by the buyer, imputed interest rules do not apply to the buyer. Thus, the buyer may not deduct the imputed interest. The buyer's deduction is limited to the payment of interest stated in the contract if a deduction is allowed under the home mortgage interest rules in *Chapter 15*.

Timing of interest reporting. One important practical difference between the two statutes covering minimum interest involves the timing of the reporting and deducting of interest.

Under Section 483, a seller and lender use their regular reporting method for imputed interest. For a cash-basis seller, interest is taxed when received; a cash-basis buyer deducts interest when paid if a deduction is allowable. However, if too much interest is allocated to a payment period, the excess interest is treated as prepaid interest, and the deduction is postponed to the year or years interest is earned. Section 483 also describes imputed interest as unstated interest.

Under Section 1274, the interest element is generally reported by both buyer and seller according to the OID accrual rules, even if they otherwise report on the cash basis. Where the seller financing is below an annual threshold ($3,653,600 for 2010 sales), the parties can elect the cash method to report the interest regardless of the OID and accrual rules if: (1) the seller-lender is on a cash-basis method and is not a dealer of the property sold and (2) the seller and buyer jointly elect to use the cash method. The cash-basis election binds any cash-basis successor of the buyer or seller. If the lender transfers his interest to an accrual-basis taxpayer, the election no longer applies; interest is thereafter taxed under the accrual-method rules. The OID rules also do not apply to a cash-basis buyer of personal-use property; here, the cash-basis debtor deducts only payments of interest required by the contract, assuming a deduction is allowed under the home mortgage rules discussed in *Chapter 15*.

Figuring applicable federal rate (AFR). There is no imputed interest if the sales contract provides for interest that is at least equal to the AFR. *See Table 4-1* below for determining the AFR.

Assumptions of loans. The imputed interest rules of Sections 1274 and 483 do not generally apply to debt instruments assumed as part of a sale or exchange, or if the property is taken subject to the debt, provided that neither the terms of the debt instrument nor the nature of the transactions are changed.

Important: *In planning deferred or installment sales, review Treasury regulations to the Internal Revenue Code Sections 483 and 1274 for further examples and details.*

Table 4-1 Minimum Interest Rate for Seller Financing

Type—	*Description—*
Applicable federal rates	The IRS determines the AFR rates which are published at the beginning of each month in the Internal Revenue Bulletin. There are three AFR rates depending on the length of the contract: *Short-term AFR*—A term of three years or less. *Mid-term AFR*—A term of over three years but not over nine years. *Long-term AFR*—A term of over nine years. The imputed interest rules do not apply if the interest rate provided for in the sales contract is at least the lesser of (1) the lowest AFR in effect during the three-month period ending with the month in which a binding written sales contract is entered into, or (2) the lowest AFR in effect during the three-month period ending with the month of sale. If insufficient interest is charged, the total unstated interest is allocated to payments under an OID computation.
9% safe harbor rate	If seller financing in 2010 is $5,115,100 or less, the minimum required interest is the lower of 9% compounded semiannually and the applicable federal rate (AFR). The amount of seller financing is the stated principal amount under the contract. If the seller-financed amount exceeds $5,115,100, the minimum interest rate is 100% of the AFR. The threshold for the 9% safe harbor is indexed annually for inflation. The 9% safe harbor provides a benefit only if it is less than the AFR, but in recent years the AFR has been much lower than 9%. Thus, until prevailing interest rates substantially increase, charging interest at the AFR will be sufficient to avoid application of the minimum interest rules. IRS regulations allow the parties to use an interest rate lower than the AFR if it is shown that the borrower could obtain a loan on an arm's-length basis at lower interest.
Seller-financed sale-leaseback transactions	Interest equal to 110% of AFR must be charged.
Sales of land between family members	To the extent that the sales price does not exceed $500,000 during a calendar year, the minimum required interest rate is 6%, compounded semiannually. To prevent multiple sales from being used to avoid the $500,000 limit, the $500,000 ceiling applies to all land sales between family members during the same year. To the extent that the $500,000 sales price limit is exceeded, the general 9% or 100% of AFR rules apply.

Chapter 5

Reporting Property Sales

Long-term capital gains are generally taxed at lower rates than those imposed on ordinary income. Some or all of your long-term capital gains for 2010 may qualify for a 0% rate and thus completely avoid tax *(5.3)*. If the 0% rate does not apply, your long-term gains are subject to maximum rates of 15%, 25%, or 28%, depending on what the gains are from *(5.3)*, but regular tax rates apply if they result in a lower tax than the maximum rate.

If in 2010 you sold property and will be receiving payments in a later year, you may report the sale as an installment sale on Form 6252 and spread the tax on your gain over the installment period *(5.21)*.

Sales of business assets and depreciable rental property are reported on Form 4797. Most assets used in a business are considered Section 1231 assets, and capital gain or ordinary loss treatment may apply depending upon the result of a netting computation made on Form 4797 for all such assets sold during the year *(44.8)*.

Special types of sale situations are detailed in other chapters.

See Chapter 29 for the exclusion of gain on the sale of a principal residence.

See Chapter 32 for figuring gain or loss on the sale of mutual-fund shares.

See Chapter 6 for tax-free exchanges of property.

See Chapter 30 for sales of stock dividends, stock rights, wash sales, short sales, and sales by traders in securities.

5.1 General Tax Rules for Property Sales

1. Property is classified according to its nature and your purpose for holding it; *see 5.2, Table 5-1*, and holding period rules at *5.3* and *5.9–5.12*.
2. If you sell property at a gain, the applicable tax rate depends on the classification of the property (*see Table 5-1*) and, in the case of capital assets, the period you held the property before sale. Short-term capital gains are subject to regular income tax rates. A capital gain is long term if you held the asset for more than one year. A capital gain rate is applied to long-term capital gain if the rate is less than the top regular income tax rate applied to your taxable income. Depending on your taxable income and the amount and source of your long-term gains, gains realized in 2010 may be completely tax free under the 0% rate or subject to a maximum rate of 15%, 25%, or 28% where that maximum rate is less than the otherwise applicable regular tax rate *(5.3)*.

   Sales of capital assets must generally be reported on Schedule D of Form 1040, and the lower capital gain rates are applied on the Qualified Dividends and Capital Gains Tax Worksheet in the Form 1040 instructions, where you compute your tax liability taking into account the favorable capital gain rates. If you have either 28% gain or unrecaptured Section 1250 gain, use the Schedule D Tax Worksheet in the Schedule D instructions to compute your tax liability. Filing Schedule D may not be necessary if your only capital gains are from a mutual fund or REIT *(32.8)*.
3. Loss deductions are allowed on the sale of investment and business property but not personal assets; *see Table 5-1*. Capital loss deductions in excess of capital gains are limited to $3,000 annually, $1,500 if married filing separately; *see* the details on the capital loss limitations later in this Chapter *(5.4 – 5.5)*.

Caution

Loss on Personal-Use Assets

You may not deduct a capital loss on the sale of property held for personal use, such as a car or vacation home. The loss is not deductible.

Losses on the sale of property held for investment, such as stock or mutual-fund shares, are fully deductible against capital gains but any excess loss is subject to the $3,000 limit *(5.4)*.

5.2 How Property Sales Are Classified and Taxed

The tax treatment of gains and losses is not the same for all types of property sales. Tax reporting generally depends on your purpose in holding the property, as shown in *Table 5-1*.

When capital gain or loss treatment does not apply. Certain sales do not qualify for capital gain or loss treatment. Business inventory and property held for sale to customers are not capital assets. Depreciable business and rental property are not capital assets, but you may still realize capital gain after following a netting computation for Section 1231 assets *(44.8)*.

Although assets held for *personal* use, such as a car or home, are technically capital assets, you may not deduct a capital loss on their sale.

Certain other assets held for investment or personal use are excluded by law from the capital asset category. These include copyrights, literary or musical compositions, letters, memoranda, or similar property that: (1) you created by your personal efforts or (2) you acquired as a gift from the person who created the property or for whom the property was prepared or produced.

Although musical compositions and copyrights in musical works that you personally created (or you acquired as a gift from the creator) are generally excluded from the capital asset category, you can make an election on a timely filed (including extensions) Schedule D for the year the musical composition or copyright is sold to treat the sale as a sale of a capital asset.

Also excluded from the capital asset category are letters, memoranda, or similar property prepared or produced for you by someone else. Finally, U.S. government publications obtained from the government for free or for less than the normal sales price do not qualify as capital assets.

Stock is generally treated as a capital asset, but losses on *Section 1244 stock* of qualifying small businesses may be claimed as ordinary losses on Form 4797, rather than on Schedule D as capital losses subject to the $3,000 deduction limit ($1,500 if married filing separately) *(30.13)*.

Traders in securities may elect to report their sales as ordinary income or loss rather than as capital gain or loss *(30.16)*.

Small business stock deferral. Taxable gains from the sale of publicly traded securities may be postponed if you roll over the proceeds to stock or a partnership interest in an SSBIC (specialized small business investment company) *(5.7)*. Furthermore, gains from the sale of qualifying small business stock may be deferred by making a tax-free rollover to other small business stock.

Filing Tip

Holding Periods

The time you own a capital asset determines short-term or long-term treatment. The short-term holding period is a year or less, the long-term period more than one year *(5.9–5.12)*.

Small business/empowerment zone business stock exclusion. Gains on the 2010 sale of qualifying small business stock held for more than five years qualify for a 50% exclusion. The exclusion is 60% for gains on the sale of qualifying empowerment zone business stock *(5.7)*.

Like-kind exchanges of business or investment property. Exchanges of *like-kind* business or investment property are subject to special rules that allow gain to be deferred, generally until you sell the property received in the exchange *(6.1)*. When property received in a tax-free exchange is held until death, the unrecognized gain escapes income tax forever because the basis of property in the hands of an heir is generally the fair market value of the property at the date of death *(5.17)*. A loss on a like-kind exchange is not deductible.

Stock redemption allocation to covenant not to compete. If you sell company stock back to your employer and you are subject to a covenant not to compete with the company for a period of time, any portion of the purchase price for the stock that is allocated to the covenant in the contract is taxed to you as ordinary income and not capital gain.

5.3 Capital Gains Rates and Holding Periods

Sales of capital assets during 2010 should be separated into short-term and long-term categories. Assets held for one year or less are in the short-term category and assets held for more than one year are in the long-term category. Follow the line-by-line computation on Schedule D (Form 1040) to report your sales and obtain the benefit of the lower rates on qualifying long-term gains.

A sample Schedule D *(5.8)* illustrates the reporting of capital asset sales. The computation of tax liability using the favorable long-term capital gain rates is not made directly on Schedule D, but on worksheets in the IRS instructions. Mutual-fund and REIT investors may be able to apply the favorable rates on the "Qualified Dividends and Capital Gain Tax Worksheet" included in the Form 1040 or Form 1040A instructions, without having to file Schedule D *(32.8)*.

Held for a year or less. Gains and losses realized on sales of capital assets held for a year or less are short term and reported in Part I of Schedule D. Short-term gains and losses are netted in this part. A net gain is subject to regular tax rates. A net short-term loss offsets a net long-term gain, if any, from Part II of Schedule D. A net short-term loss in excess of net long-term gain is deductible up to the $3,000 capital loss limit *(5.4)*.

Held for more than a year. Gains and losses on sales of capital assets held for more than a year are long term. They are generally reported in Part II of Schedule D, where long-term gains and losses are netted. A net long-term loss offsets a net short-term gain, if any, from Part I of Schedule D. If you have a net long-term gain and also a net short-term loss from Part I of Schedule D, the short-term loss offsets the net long-term gain. If the net short-term loss exceeds the net long-term gain, the excess short-term loss is deductible up to the $3,000 capital loss limit *(5.4)*. If you have a net long-term gain in excess of net short-term capital loss (if any), the excess is called *net capital gain* and it is this amount to which the favorable capital gain rates may apply, as discussed below.

Reduced Rates on Net Capital Gain for 2010

Tax liability must be computed on IRS worksheets to benefit from capital gain rates. Net capital gain (net long-term capital gain in excess of net short-term capital loss) is subject to maximum tax rates that are generally lower than the rates applied to ordinary income. Qualified dividends *(4.1)* are subject to the same favorable rates as net capital gain.

If you have a net capital gain that does *not* include a 28% rate gain or unrecaptured Section 1250 gain (*see* below), you should compute your 2010 regular tax liability on the "Qualified Dividends and Capital Gain Tax Worksheet" in the IRS instructions for Line 44 of Form 1040. On the Worksheet, you figure your regular tax liability for 2010, taking into account the favorable capital gain rates, as applicable, and the regular tax rates on the rest of your taxable income. The Worksheet must be used instead of the regular IRS Tax Table or Tax Computation Worksheet to benefit from the maximum capital gain rates. The tax liability from the Worksheet is entered on Line 44 of Form 1040.

If you have a net capital gain that includes either a net 28% rate gain or unrecaptured Section 1250 gain, you must compute your tax liability on the "Schedule D Tax Worksheet" in the Schedule D instructions to benefit from the maximum capital gain rates. The tax liability from the Worksheet is entered on Line 44 of Form 1040.

Law Alert

0% Rate May Apply to 2010 Gains

For taxpayers with a top 2010 bracket of 10% or 15%, the 0% rate applies to eligible long-term capital gains and qualified dividends, making them tax free. Even taxpayers with a top bracket exceeding 15% may be able to benefit from the 0% rate, depending on their filing status, taxable income, and amount of eligible long-term gains and qualified dividends. To the extent that the 0% rate is not applicable, the 15% maximum rate on long-term gains applies except for 28% rate gains or unrecaptured Section 1250 gains. Net capital gain of a child subject to the "kiddie tax" *(24.2)* is taxed at his or her parent's capital gain rate if that is higher than the child's rate.

Table 5-1 Capital or Ordinary Gains and Losses From Sales and Exchanges of Property

If you sell—	*Your gain is—*	*Your loss is—*	*Reported on—*
Stocks, mutual funds, bonds, land, art, gems, stamps, and coins held for investment are capital assets.	*Capital gain.* Holding period determines short-term or long-term gain treatment *(5.3)*. Security traders may report ordinary income and loss under a mark-to-market election *(30.17)*.	*Capital loss.* Capital losses are deductible from capital gains with only $3,000 of any excess deductible from ordinary income, $1,500 if married filing separately *(5.4)*.	Schedule D. However, if the only amounts you have to report on Schedule D are mutual-fund capital gain distributions, then you may report the distributions directly on Form 1040A or Form 1040 *(32.8)*. Form 4797 for gains and losses of a trader in securities who makes the mark-to-market election *(30.17)*.
Business inventory held for sale to customers. Also, accounts or notes receivable acquired in the ordinary course of business or from the sale of inventory or property held for sale to customers, or acquired for services as an employee.	*Ordinary income.* Such property is excluded by law from the definition of capital assets.	*Ordinary loss.* Ordinary loss is not subject to the $3,000 deduction limit imposed on capital losses. However, passive loss restrictions, discussed in *Chapter 10*, may defer the time when certain ordinary losses are deductible.	Schedule C if self-employed; Schedule F if a farmer; Form 1065 for a business operated as a partnership; Form 1120 or 1120-S for an incorporated business.
Depreciable residential rental property or trucks, autos, computers, machinery, fixtures, or equipment used in your business.	*Capital gain or ordinary income.* Section 1231 determines whether gain is taxable as ordinary income or capital gain *(44.8)*. *Where an asset such as an auto or residence is used partly for personal purposes and partly for business or rental purposes, the asset is treated as two separate assets for purposes of figuring gain or loss (44.9).*	*Ordinary loss if there is a net Section 1231 loss (44.8).* However, if you are considered to be an investor in a passive activity, *see 10.12* and *10.13*.	Form 4797 for Section 1231 transactions.
Personal residence, car, jewelry, furniture, art objects, and coin or stamp collection held for personal use.	*Capital gain. See* the holding period rules that determine short-term or long-term gain treatment and the preferential tax rates applied to net long-term capital gains *(5.3)*. Where an asset such as an auto or residence is used partly for personal purposes and partly for business or rental purposes, the asset is treated as two separate assets for purposes of figuring gain or loss *(44.9)*. *Tax on all or part of a profit from a sale of a principal residence may be avoided; see Chapter 29.*	*Not deductible.* Losses on assets held for personal use are not deductible although profits are taxable.	Schedule D

On both the Qualified Dividends and Capital Gain Tax Worksheet and the Schedule D Tax Worksheet, net capital gain eligible for the maximum capital gain rates is reduced by any gains that you elect to treat as investment income on Form 4952 to increase your itemized deduction for investment interest *(15.10)*.

The 0% and 15% rates. Qualified dividends *(4.1)* and net capital gain (net long-term gains in excess of short-term losses) for 2010 are generally subject to the 0% or 15% capital gain rate. However, the 0% and 15% rates do *not* apply to any portion of net capital gain that is 28% rate gain (from collectibles and Section 1202 exclusion) or unrecaptured Section 1250 gain; these are subject, respectively, to maximum rates of 28% and 25% as discussed below. ***When this book went to press, the fate of the 0% and 15% rates for years after 2010 had not been decided; see the e-Supplement for the 2011 rules.***

You qualify for the 0% rate if your top tax bracket for 2010 is 10% or 15%. This means that if your taxable income for 2010 is within the 10% and 15% brackets, and all of your net capital gain is eligible for the 0%/15% rates (gains are not 28% rate gains or unrecaptured Section 1250 gains), then all of your gains and qualified dividends are tax free under the 0% rate. On 2010 returns, the top of the 15% bracket is taxable income of $34,000 for single taxpayers and married persons filing separately, $45,550 for heads of household, and $68,000 for married persons filing jointly. Thus, if your 2010 taxable income is no more than the applicable amount for your filing status, none of your qualified dividends or gains are taxable.

Perhaps surprisingly, high-income individuals with a top bracket higher than 15% may also be able to benefit from the 0% rate. The extent to which higher-bracket taxpayers can benefit from the 0% rate depends on their taxable income, their filing status, which determines the top of their 15% bracket, and the amount of their qualified dividends and net capital gain. On the IRS worksheets used to figure tax liability (the "Qualified Dividends and Capital Gain Tax Worksheet," or the "Schedule D Tax Worksheet," as applicable), your taxable income is reduced by your qualified dividends and net capital gain (other than 28% rate gain and unrecaptured Section 1250 gain). The resulting amount is treated as ordinary income and if it is less than the top of your 15% bracket, your qualified dividends and capital gains (other than 28% rate gain and unrecaptured Section 1250 gain) are tax free under the 0% rate to the extent that they "fill up" the rest of the 15% bracket. For example, if you are single and for 2010 you have taxable income of $36,000 and $7,000 of eligible net capital gain, your ordinary income for purposes of the worksheet computation is $29,000 ($36,000 – $7,000), and since the top of the 15% bracket for single taxpayers is taxable income of $34,000, the 0% rate applies to $5,000 of your gains ($34,000 – $29,000) and the $2,000 balance ($7,000 – $5,000) is taxed at 15%.

If the ordinary income is equal to or more than the top of your 15% bracket ($34,000, $45,550, or $68,000, as applicable), the 0% rate will not apply to any of your qualified dividends and eligible gains. The Examples below further illustrate the application of the 0% and 15% rates. Also *see* the Example in *5.8*, which includes a filled-in Schedule D and Qualified Dividends and Capital Gain Tax Worksheet.

Caution: Children subject to the kiddie tax. If your child is subject to the kiddie tax *(24.2)* and has net investment income exceeding $1,900, the excess is treated as your own income and subject to your tax rate. If the excess includes net capital gains and qualified dividends, your maximum capital gain rate will apply if it is higher than your child's rate. Even if the 0% rate would apply to your child's 2010 gains and dividends based on his or her taxable income, the 0% rate will not be available unless your rate is also 0% when you make the kiddie tax computation on Form 8615.

Law Alert

Capital Gain Rates After 2010

The capital gain rates for 2011 were not yet settled when this book went to press. Unless Congress enacts legislation, the zero and 15% rates will be replaced by 10% and 20% rates, respectively, but it appears that the zero and 15% rates will be retained for many if not all taxpayers. The Administration wants low- and middle-income taxpayers to have the benefit of the zero and 15% rates, but to apply the 20% rate to high -income taxpayers. *See* the *e-Supplement at jklasser.com* for an update on the 2011 rates.

EXAMPLES

1. Arlen and Alice Able file a joint return for 2010 and report taxable income of $64,328. This includes qualified dividends of $3,298 and a long-term gain of $6,702 from the sale of stock. The 0% rate applies to the qualified dividends and long-term gain to the extent that they fit within the 15% bracket after taking into account the Ables' "ordinary" income. Their ordinary income is considered to be $54,328 ($64,328 taxable income – $10,000 ($3,298 qualified dividends + $6,702 long-term gain). Since the top, or end-point, of the 15% bracket for 2010 joint returns is taxable income of $68,000, the 0% rate can apply to dividends/gains of up to $13,672 ($68,000 – $54,328 ordinary income) and as $13,672 exceeds the Ables' $10,000 of qualified dividends and long-term gain, the entire $10,000 is tax free under the 0% rate.

2. Same facts as in Example 1, except Arlen and Alice have taxable income of $70,128. Ordinary income is $60,128 ($70,128 – $10,000 qualified dividends and long-term gain). The 0% rate applies to $7,872 of the dividends/gain ($68,000 top of the 15% bracket – $60,128 ordinary income). The $2,128 balance of dividends/gain ($10,000 – $7,872) is taxed at 15%.
3. Same facts as in Example 1, except Arlen and Alice's taxable income is $80,000. Since the ordinary income of $70,000 ($80,000 – $10,000 qualified dividends and long-term gain) exceeds the $68,000 top of the 15% bracket, none of the dividends/gains are eligible for the 0% rate. The entire $10,000 is taxed at 15%.

28% rate gains from sales of collectibles and small business or empowerment zone business stock eligible for exclusion. Long-term gains on the sale of collectibles such as art, antiques, precious metals, gems, stamps, and coins are considered "28% rate gains." If you sell qualified small business stock eligible for the 50% exclusion or empowerment zone business stock eligible for the 60% exclusion (Section 1202 exclusion *(5.7)*), the taxable 50% or 40% portion of the gain is also treated as a 28% rate gain. The 28% rate gains are reported first in Part II (long-term capital gains and losses) of Schedule D, and then transferred to the "28% Rate Gain Worksheet" in the Schedule D instructions. On the Worksheet, 28% rate gains are reduced by any long-term collectibles losses and net short-term capital loss for the current year, and any long-term capital loss carryover from the previous year.

A net 28% rate gain from the 28% Rate Gain Worksheet is entered on Line 18 of Schedule D and then on the "Schedule D Tax Worksheet" in the Schedule D instructions. The Schedule D Tax Worksheet is used to figure the regular tax on all of your taxable income (not just on your net capital gain and qualified dividends). The effect of the worksheet computation is to tax 28% rate gain at either the 28% rate or at the regular rates on ordinary income, whichever results in the lower tax.

The tax figured on the "Schedule D Tax Worksheet" is entered on Line 44 of Form 1040.

Unrecaptured Section 1250 gain on sale of real estate. Long-term gain in 2010 that is attributable to real estate depreciation is not eligible for the 0% or 15% capital gain rate. Gain attributable to pre-1987 depreciation may be recaptured as ordinary income *(44.2)*. To the extent of depreciation that is not recaptured, gain is considered "unrecaptured Section 1250 gain." Unrecaptured Section 1250 gain is figured on the "Unrecaptured Section 1250 Gain Worksheet" in the Schedule D instructions. The computation reduces unrecaptured Section 1250 gain by a net loss, if any, from the 28% rate group.

The net unrecaptured Section 1250 gain from the worksheet is entered on Line 19 of Schedule D and then on the Schedule D Tax Worksheet, where tax liability on all of your taxable income is computed. The effect of the computation on the Schedule D Tax Worksheet is to tax unrecaptured Section 1250 gain at either a 25% rate or at the regular rates on ordinary income, whichever results in the lower tax. The tax figured on the Schedule D Tax Worksheet is entered on Line 44 of Form 1040.

Capital gain distributions from mutual funds. Your fund will report long-term capital gain distributions on Form 1099-DIV. *See Chapter 32* for details on how to report the distributions.

Capital gain from Schedule K-1. Net capital gain or loss from a pass-through entity such as a partnership, S corporation, estate, or trust is reported to you on a Schedule K-1. Report net short-term gain or loss in Part I of Schedule D and net long-term gain or loss in Part II of Schedule D.

Filing Tip

Keep Records of Loss Carryovers

If you have capital losses for 2010 in excess of the deductible limit, keep a copy of your 2010 Form 1040 and Schedule D to figure your loss carryover when you file your 2011 Schedule D. The 2011 Schedule D instructions will have a worksheet you can use to figure your loss carryovers from 2010 to 2011.

5.4 Capital Losses and Carryovers

Capital losses are fully deductible against capital gains on Schedule D, and if losses exceed gains, you may deduct the excess from up to $3,000 of ordinary income on Form 1040. Net losses over $3,000 are carried over to future years. On a joint return, the $3,000 limit applies to the combined losses of both spouses *(5.5)*. The $3,000 limit is reduced to $1,500 for married persons filing separately.

Although qualified dividends *(4.1)* are subject to the same rates as net capital gains, such dividends are not reported as long-term gains on Part II of Schedule D and thus are *not* offset by capital losses in determining whether you have net capital gain or loss.

In preparing your 2010 Schedule D, remember to include any capital loss carryovers from your 2009 return. Short-term carryover losses are entered on Line 6 of Part I and long-term carryover losses are entered on Line 14, Part II. Use the carryover worksheet in the 2010 Schedule D instructions for figuring your short-term and long-term loss carryovers from 2009 to 2010.

Losses from wash sales not deductible. You cannot deduct a loss from a wash sale of stock or securities unless you are a dealer in those securities. A wash sale occurs if within 30 days before or after your sale at a loss, you acquire substantially identical securities or purchase an option to acquire such securities *(30.6)*.

Report a wash sale on Schedule D on Line 1 (short-term) or Line 8 (long-term) capital gains and losses, and directly below the entry, identify the transaction as a "wash sale" in column (a) and in column (f) enter the disallowed loss as a positive amount.

Death of taxpayer cuts off carryover. If an individual dies and on his or her final income tax return net capital losses, including prior year carryovers, exceed the $3,000 or $1,500 limit, the excess may not be deducted by the individual's estate. If the deceased individual was married, his or her unused individual losses may not be carried over by the surviving spouse *(5.5)*.

5.5 Capital Losses of Married Couples

On a joint return, the capital asset transactions of both spouses are combined and reported on one Schedule D. A carryover loss of one spouse may offset capital gains of the other spouse on a jointly filed Schedule D. Where you and your spouse separately incur net capital losses, $3,000 is the maximum capital loss deduction that may be claimed for the combined losses on your joint return. This limitation may not be avoided by filing separate returns. If you file separately, the deduction limit for each return is $1,500. Neither of you may deduct any of the other's losses on a separate return.

EXAMPLE

In 2010, you individually incurred net long-term capital losses of $5,000 and your spouse incurred net long-term losses of $4,000. If you file separate returns, the maximum amount deductible from ordinary income on each return is $1,500. The balance must be carried forward to 2011.

If you had net losses below the $1,500 limit, you could not claim any part of your spouse's losses on your separate return.

Filing Tip

Carryovers From Joint or Separate Returns

If you or your spouse has a capital loss carryover from a year in which separate returns were filed, and you are now filing a joint return, the carryovers from the separate returns may be combined on the joint return. If you previously filed jointly and are now filing separately, any loss carryover from the joint return may be claimed only on the separate return of the spouse who originally incurred the loss *(5.5)*.

Death of a spouse. The IRS holds that if a capital loss is incurred by a spouse on his or her own property and that spouse dies, the loss may be deducted only on the final return for the spouse (which may be a joint return). The surviving spouse may not claim any unused loss carryover on a separate return and the decedent's estate may not deduct the unused carryover.

EXAMPLE

In 2007, Alex Smith realized a substantial net long-term capital loss on separately owned property, which was reported on a 2007 joint return filed with his wife, Anne. Part of the excess loss (over the $3,000 limit) was carried over to the couple's 2008 joint return. In 2009, before the carryover loss was used up, Alex died. Anne could claim the unused carryover, up to the $3,000 limit, on a joint return filed for 2009, the year of Alex's death. However, any remaining loss carryover to 2010 or later years is lost. Although the loss was originally reported on a joint return, Anne may claim only her allocable share of the loss on her individual returns for years after 2009, the year of Alex's death. However, since the loss property was owned solely by Alex, no part of the loss is allocable to Anne.

5.6 Losses May Be Disallowed on Sales to Related Persons

A loss on a sale to certain related taxpayers may not be deductible, even though you make the sale at an arm's-length price, the sale is involuntary (for example, a member of your family forecloses a mortgage on your property), or you sell through a public stock exchange and related persons buy the equivalent property; *see* Examples 1 and 2 in this section.

Related parties. Losses are not allowed on sales between you and your brothers or sisters (whether by the whole or half blood), parents, grandparents, great-grandparents, children, grandchildren, or great-grandchildren. Furthermore, no loss may be claimed on a sale to your spouse; the tax-free exchange rules discussed in *Chapter 6* apply *(6.7)*.

A loss is disallowed where the sale is made to your sister-in-law, as nominee of your brother. This sale is deemed to be between you and your brother. But you may deduct the loss on sales to your spouse's relative (for example, your brother-in-law or spouse's step-parent) even if you and your spouse file a joint return.

The Tax Court has allowed a loss on a direct sale to a son-in-law. In a private ruling, the IRS allowed a loss on a sale of a business to a son-in-law where it was shown that his wife (the seller's daughter) did not own an interest in the company. Losses have been disallowed upon withdrawal from a joint venture and from a partnership conducted by members of a family. Family members have argued that losses should be allowed where the sales were motivated by family hostility. The Tax Court ruled that family hostility may not be considered; losses between proscribed family members are disallowed in all cases.

Losses are barred on sales between an individual and a controlled partnership or controlled corporation (where that individual owns more than 50% in value of the outstanding stock or capital interests). In calculating the stock owned, not only must the stock held in your own name be taken into account, but also that owned by your family. You also add (1) the proportionate share of any stock held by a corporation, estate, trust, or partnership in which you have an interest as a shareholder, beneficiary, or partner; and (2) any other stock owned individually by your partner.

Losses may also be disallowed in sales between controlled companies, a trust and its creator, a trust and a beneficiary, a partnership and a corporation controlled by the same person (more than 50% ownership), or a tax-exempt organization and its founder. An estate and a beneficiary of that estate are also treated as related parties, except where a sale is in satisfaction of a pecuniary bequest. Check with your tax counselor whenever you plan to sell property at a loss to a buyer who may fit one of these descriptions.

Related buyer's resale at profit. Sometimes, the disallowed loss may be saved. When you sell to a related party who resells the property at a profit, he or she gets the benefit of your disallowed loss. Your purchaser's gain up to the amount of your disallowed loss is not taxed; *see* Example 4 below.

EXAMPLES

1. You sell 100 shares of A Co. stock to your brother for $1,000. They cost you $5,000. You may not deduct your $4,000 loss.
2. The stock investments of a mother and son were managed by the same investment counselor. But neither the son nor mother had any right or control over the other's securities. The counselor followed separate and independent policies for each. Without the son's or his mother's prior approval, the counselor carried out the following transactions: (1) on the same day, he sold at a loss the son's stock in four companies and bought the same stock for the mother's account; and (2) he sold at a loss the son's stock in a copper company, and 28 days later bought the same stock for his mother. The losses of the first sale were disallowed, but not the losses of the copper stock sale because of the time break of 28 days. However, the court did not say how much of a minimum time break is needed to remove a sale-purchase transaction from the rule disallowing losses between related parties.
3. You own 30% of the stock of a company. A trust in which you have a one-half beneficial interest owns 30%. Your partner owns 10% of the stock of the same company. You are deemed the owner of 55% of the stock of that company (30%, plus one-half of 30%, plus 10%) and may not deduct a loss on the sale of property to that company since your deemed ownership exceeds 50%.
4. Smith bought securities in 2004 that cost $10,000. In 2007, he sold them to his sister for $8,000. The $2,000 loss was not deductible by Smith. His sister's basis for the securities is $8,000. In 2010, she sells them for $9,000. The $1,000 gain is not taxed because it is washed out by part of the brother's disallowed loss. If she sold the securities for $11,000, then only $1,000 of the $3,000 gain would be taxed.

5.7 Deferring or Excluding Gain on Small Business Stock Investment

To encourage investments in certain "small" businesses, the tax law provides special tax benefits.

Rollover of gain from sale of qualified small business stock (QSB stock). Gain on the sale of qualifying small business stock (QSB stock) held for more than six months may be rolled over tax free to other QSB stock. The rollover must be made within 60 days of the sale. To qualify as QSB stock, the stock must be stock in a C corporation (not S corporation) that was originally issued after August 10, 1993. The gross assets of the corporation must have been no more than $50 million at all times after August 9, 1993, and before issuance of the stock, as well as immediately after issuance of the stock. An active business requirement must also be met. You must have acquired the stock at its original issue, as a gift or inheritance from a qualifying transferor, or in a conversion of other qualified stock. See the Schedule D instructions and IRS Publication 550 for further QSB requirements.

If the sale proceeds exceed the cost of the replacement stock, your gain is taxed to the extent of the difference. The basis of the replacement stock is reduced by the deferred gain.

To elect deferral, you must report the entire gain on Part I (short-term gain) or Part II (long-term gain) of Schedule D. Then, directly below that entry, write "Section 1045 Rollover" and report the rolled-over amount as a loss in column (f). Generally, the election to defer gain must be made by the due date or extended due date for your return. If you timely file your original return without the election, the election may be made on an amended return filed no more than six months after the original due date.

Exclusion of gain on small business stock (Section 1202 exclusion). You only have to pay tax on 50% of a gain from the sale of qualified small business stock (QSB stock, as defined above) issued after August 10, 1993, *provided* you hold the stock for more than five years before the sale. If you qualify for the exclusion, report the entire gain as a long-term gain on Line 8 of Schedule D and then, below it, enter the allowable exclusion as a loss, labelling it "Section 1202 exclusion." If you have a net capital gain (net long-term gain in excess of net short-term loss, if any), the amount of the exclusion is included on the 28% Rate Gain Worksheet in the Schedule D instructions *(5.3)*.

The amount of the Section 1202 exclusion increases to 60% if the gain is on the sale of stock that you acquired after December 21, 2000 and which you held for more than five years in a corporation that qualified as an empowerment zone business. The gain and exclusion are reported as described above for the 50% QSB exclusion.

There is an annual and lifetime limit on the Section 1202 exclusion for QSB stock or empowerment zone business stock from any one issuer. For 2010, the amount of gain from any one issuer that is eligible for the 50% or 60% exclusion is limited to the greater of (1) 10 times your basis in the qualified stock that you disposed of during 2010, or (2) $10 million ($5 million if married filing separately) minus any gain on stock from the same issuer that you excluded in prior years.

Rollover from publicly traded securities to SSBIC. You may be able to defer taxable gain on the sale of publicly traded securities provided the sale proceeds are rolled over within 60 days into common stock or a partnership interest in a "specialized small business investment company," or SSBIC. Subject to the deferrable limit, the entire gain is deferrable if the cost of your SSBIC stock or partnership interest is at least equal to the sale proceeds. If the SSBIC investment is less than the sale proceeds, your gain is taxed to the extent of the difference.

There is an annual and lifetime limit on the deferrable gain. The deferrable limit each year is limited to the smaller of (1) $50,000, or $25,000 if you are married filing separately, or (2) $500,000, or $250,000 if married filing separately, minus any gains deferred for all prior years.

To elect deferral, you must report the sale on Schedule D and attach an explanation of your SSBIC investment. After reporting the entire gain on Line 1 or Line 8 of Schedule D, immediately below that line enter the amount of the deferred gain as a loss and label it "SSBIC Rollover"; *see* IRS Publication 550 for further details. The deferred gain reduces the basis of your SSBIC stock or partnership interest.

An SSBIC is a small business (partnership or corporation) licensed by the Small Business Administration to invest in small businesses that are owned by socially or economically disadvantaged individuals.

Law Alert

Increased Section 1202 Exclusion

The exclusion will increase to 75% (from 50% or 60%) if qualified small business stock acquired after February 17, 2009 and before September 28, 2010 is sold at a gain after being held more than five years.

Under the Small Business Jobs Act of 2010 (signed into law on September 27, 2010), a full 100% exclusion will be allowed, but only for qualified stock bought after September 27, 2010 and before January 1, 2011, and held over five years.

Planning Reminder

Rollover of Gain From Sale of Empowerment Zone Assets

You may be able to defer capital gain on the sale of qualified empowerment zone assets that you acquired after December 21, 2000, and held for more than one year. You must purchase replacement assets in the same empowerment zone during the 60-day period beginning on the date of the sale. *See* IRS Publications 550 and 954 for details.

Caution

Selling Price Reported to IRS

If you sold stocks, bonds, or other investment property through a broker, the sale is reported to the IRS on Form 1099-B. You are sent Copy B of Form 1099-B or a substitute statement. On your statement, the broker must indicate whether gross proceeds or gross proceeds minus commissions and option premiums were reported to the IRS. If the gross proceeds were reported, enter that amount as the sales price in column (d) of Schedule D and add any commissions or option premiums to cost basis in column (e). If only the net proceeds were reported, enter that amount as the sales price in column (d) of Schedule D and do not include commissions or option premiums in column (e).

5.8 Sample Entries of Capital Asset Sales on Schedule D

You report many different types of transactions on Schedule D of Form 1040: sales of securities, redemptions of mutual-fund shares, worthless personal loans, sales of stock rights and warrants, sales of land held for investment, and sales of personal residences where part of the gain does not qualify for the home sale exclusion *(29.1)*. Although capital gain distributions from mutual funds and REITs are generally reported as long-term capital gains on Line 13 of Schedule D, investors who receive such distributions but have no other capital gains or losses to report may generally report the distributions directly on Form 1040 or 1040A without having to file Schedule D; *see 32.8* for details.

The favorable maximum capital gain rates *(5.3)* apply to net capital gain (net long-term capital gain in excess of net short-term capital loss) from Schedule D, and also to qualified dividends *(4.1)*. Although qualified dividends are subject to the same favorable maximum rates as net capital gain, they are not entered as long-term gains in Part II of Schedule D. The favorable rates are applied to qualified dividends when tax liability is computed on either the Qualified Dividends and Capital Gain Tax Worksheet or the Schedule D Tax Worksheet. The Schedule D Tax Worksheet in the Schedule D instructions is used only if you have a net 28% rate gain or unrecaptured Section 1250 gain *(5.3)*. If you do not have a net 28% rate gain or unrecaptured Section 1250 gain, use the Qualified Dividends and Capital Gain Tax Worksheet in the Form 1040 instructions. The applicable Worksheet must be used to obtain the benefit of the favorable maximum capital gain rates for your net capital gain and qualified dividends.

EXAMPLE

For 2010, John and Karen Taylor report three short-term transactions in Part I of Schedule D and four long-term transactions and a long-term loss carryover in Part II of Schedule D, as listed below and shown on the sample Schedule D. For each stock sale, broker's commissions and state and local transfer taxes, if any, have been added to the cost of the stock in column (e) of Schedule D.

1. ***Sale of stock (short-term gain)***—The Taylors bought 200 shares of Bio-X-Cell Research, Inc. stock on July 20, 2010, for $1,400. On October 15, 2010, they sold the 200 shares for $1,600.
2. ***Sale of stock received as a gift (short-term loss)***—Karen's father gave the Taylors a gift of 100 shares of Ajax Auto stock on November 5, 2010, which he had bought on February 15, 1990, for $4,000. The value of the stock at the time of the gift was $3,000. The couple sold the stock on November 23, 2010, for $2,000. Since the value of the stock at the time of the gift was less than the father's basis, the Taylors' basis for loss purposes is the $3,000 date-of-gift value *(5.17)* and the holding period begins on the day after the date of the gift *(5.12)*.
3. ***Sale of mutual-fund shares (short-term gain)***—The Taylors bought 200 shares of the XYZ Mutual Fund on February 9, 2010, for $4,000. On August 11, they bought another 200 shares for $6,480. They sell 200 of the shares on September 28, 2010, for $6,000. They decide to use the average basis method (single-category method) to figure the basis of the sold shares. Their average basis is $26.20 per share, the total cost basis of $10,480 divided by 400 shares. Thus, their basis for the 200 sold shares is $5,240 (200 × $26.20). In column (a) of Line 1 on Schedule D, they enter "AVGB" to indicate that they are using an average basis. *See Chapter 32* for further details on determining basis of mutual-fund shares *(32.10)*.
4. ***Sale of stock (long-term gain)***—The Taylors bought 100 shares of Acme Steel stock on October 1, 1991, for $6,000. On April 26, 2010, they sold the 100 shares for $13,000.
5. ***Sale of stock (long-term loss)***—The Taylors bought 200 shares of Zero Computer Co. stock for $5,000 on July 10, 1997. On March 12, 2010, they sold the shares for $2,000.
6. ***Sale of mutual-fund shares (long-term gain)***—The Taylors bought 1,435 shares of the ABC Mutual Fund between 1996 and 2001, including reinvested dividends. On July 16, 2010, they sold 500 of the shares for $21,500. The statement from the ABC Fund shows that their average basis (single-category method) is $24.50 per share. Thus, their basis for the 500 sold shares is $12,250 (500 × $24.50). In column (a) of Line 8, Schedule D, they enter "AVGB" to indicate that they are using the average basis method *(32.10)* for further details.

7. ***Worthless bond***—On August 10, 1998, the Taylors bought a $5,000 bond of Tech Co. at par. The bond became completely worthless during 2010 *(5.32)*.
8. ***Capital gain distributions***—The Taylors received capital gain distributions of $1,050 in December 2010 from mutual funds *(32.4, 32.8)*.
9. ***Long-term capital loss carryover***—The Taylors had a long-term capital loss carryover of $950 from their 2009 return.

Because the Taylors do not have a net 28% rate gain or unrecaptured Section 1250 gain, they use the Qualified Dividends and Capital Gain Tax Worksheet in the Form 1040 instructions to compute their regular income tax liability for 2010; *see* the sample worksheet below. If they did have a net 28% rate gain or unrecaptured Section 1250 gain, the Taylors would use the Schedule D Tax Worksheet in the Schedule D instructions to figure their tax.

For purposes of the tax computation on the Qualified Dividends and Capital Gain Tax Worksheet, we have assumed that John and Karen file a joint return and have taxable income of $78,000 for 2010. In addition to the long-term gains reported in Part II of Schedule D, the Taylors have $400 of qualified dividends *(4.1)* that are eligible for the maximum capital gain rates. The qualified dividends are reported on Line 2 of the Qualified Dividends and Capital Gain Tax Worksheet.

Under this set of facts, the Taylors have total tax liability of $10,988, as shown on Line 19 of the Qualified Dividends and Capital Gain Tax Worksheet. This is $881 less than the $11,869 liability that would apply (Line 18 of the Worksheet) if there were no favorable rates for net capital gain and qualified dividends. Note that on Line 15 of the Worksheet, the 15% capital gain rate applies to all $8,710 of qualifying dividends and long-term gain. The 0% rate on Line 11 does not apply because the Taylors' "ordinary" income of $69,290 ($78,000 taxable income – $8,710 dividends/gains) exceeds $68,000, the top of the 15% bracket for married persons filing jointly. The Taylors enter their $10,988 liability from the Worksheet on Line 44 of their Form 1040. This is their regular tax for 2010.

SCHEDULE D (Form 1040)

Department of the Treasury
Internal Revenue Service (99)

Capital Gains and Losses

► Attach to Form 1040 or Form 1040NR. ► See Instructions for Schedule D (Form 1040).
► Use Schedule D-1 to list additional transactions for lines 1 and 8.

OMB No. 1545-0074
2010
Attachment Sequence No. 12

Name(s) shown on return: John and Karen Taylor — Your social security number: X11-01-11X0

Part I **Short-Term Capital Gains and Losses—Assets Held One Year or Less**

	(a) Description of property (Example: 100 sh. XYZ Co.)	(b) Date acquired (Mo., day, yr.)	(c) Date sold (Mo., day, yr.)	(d) Sales price (see page D-7 of the instructions)	(e) Cost or other basis (see page D-7 of the instructions)	(f) Gain or (loss) Subtract (e) from (d)
1	200 Shares - Bio-X-Cell Research	7/20/2010	10/15/2010	7,600	1,400	200
	100 Shares - Ajax Auto	11/5/2010	11/23/2010	2,000	3,000	(1,000)
	200 Shares - XYZ Mutual Fund: "AVGB"	Various	9/28/2010	6,000	5,240	760
2	Enter your short-term totals, if any, from Schedule D-1, line 2		2			
3	**Total short-term sales price amounts.** Add lines 1 and 2 in column (d)		3	9,600		

4	Short-term gain from Form 6252 and short-term gain or (loss) from Forms 4684, 6781, and 8824	4	
5	Net short-term gain or (loss) from partnerships, S corporations, estates, and trusts from Schedule(s) K-1	5	
6	Short-term capital loss carryover. Enter the amount, if any, from line 10 of your **Capital Loss Carryover Worksheet** on page D-7 of the instructions	6	( )
7	**Net short-term capital gain or (loss).** Combine lines 1 through 6 in column (f)	7	(40)

For Paperwork Reduction Act Notice, see your tax return instructions. Cat. No. 11338H **Schedule D (Form 1040) 2010**

Part II **Long-Term Capital Gains and Losses—Assets Held More Than One Year**

(a) Description of property (Example: 100 sh. XYZ Co.)	(b) Date acquired (Mo., day, yr.)	(c) Date sold (Mo., day, yr.)	(d) Sales price (see page D-7 of the instructions)	(e) Cost or other basis (see page D-7 of the instructions)	(f) Gain or (loss) Subtract (e) from (d)
8 100 Shares - Acme Steel	10/1/1991	4/26/2010	13,000	6,000	7,000
200 Shares - Zero Computer Company	7/10/1997	3/12/2010	2,000	5,000	(3,000)
500 Shares - ABC Mutual Fund - "AVGB"	Various	7/16/2010	21,500	12,250	9,250
Tech. Co. Bond	8/10/1998	Worthless	Worthless	5,000	(5,000)

9	Enter your long-term totals, if any, from Schedule D-1, line 9	
10	**Total long-term sales price amounts.** Add lines 8 and 9 in column (d).	
11	Gain from Form 4797, Part I; long-term gain from Forms 2439 and 6252; and long-term gain or (loss) from Forms 4684, 6781, and 8824	
12	Net long-term gain or (loss) from partnerships, S corporations, estates, and trusts from Schedule(s) K-1	
13	Capital gain distributions. See page D-2 of the instructions	1,050
14	Long-term capital loss carryover. Enter the amount, if any, from line 15 of your **Capital Loss Carryover Worksheet** on page D-7 of the instructions	(950)
15	**Net long-term capital gain or (loss).** Combine lines 8 through 14 in column (f). Then go to Part III on the back	8,350

For Paperwork Reduction Act Notice, see your tax return instructions. Cat. No. 11338H **Schedule D (Form 1040) 2010**

Schedule D (Form 1040) 2010 Page **2**

Part III **Summary**

16 Combine lines 7 and 15 and enter the result . . . **16** 8,310

- If line 16 is a **gain**, enter the amount from line 16 on Form 1040, line 13, or Form 1040NR, line 14. Then go to line 17 below.
- If line 16 is a **loss**, skip lines 17 through 20 below. Then go to line 21. Also be sure to complete line 22.
- If line 16 is **zero**, skip lines 17 through 21 below and enter -0- on Form 1040, line 13, or Form 1040NR, line 14. Then go to line 22.

17 Are lines 15 and 16 **both** gains?

☑ **Yes.** Go to line 18.

☐ **No.** Skip lines 18 through 21, and go to line 22.

18 Enter the amount, if any, from line 7 of the **28% Rate Gain Worksheet** on page D-8 of the instructions . . . ▶ **18**

19 Enter the amount, if any, from line 18 of the **Unrecaptured Section 1250 Gain Worksheet** on page D-9 of the instructions . . . ▶ **19**

20 Are lines 18 and 19 **both** zero or blank?

☑ **Yes.** Complete Form 1040 through line 43, or Form 1040NR through line 41. Then complete the **Qualified Dividends and Capital Gain Tax Worksheet** on page 39 of the Instructions for Form 1040 (or in the Instructions for Form 1040NR). **Do not** complete lines 21 and 22 below.

☐ **No.** Complete Form 1040 through line 43, or Form 1040NR through line 41. Then complete the **Schedule D Tax Worksheet** on page D-10 of the instructions. **Do not** complete lines 21 and 22 below.

21 If line 16 is a loss, enter here and on Form 1040, line 13, or Form 1040NR, line 14, the **smaller** of:

- The loss on line 16 or
- ($3,000), or if married filing separately, ($1,500)

21 ( )

Note. When figuring which amount is smaller, treat both amounts as positive numbers.

22 Do you have qualified dividends on Form 1040, line 9b, or Form 1040NR, line 10b?

☐ **Yes.** Complete Form 1040 through line 43, or Form 1040NR through line 41. Then complete the **Qualified Dividends and Capital Gain Tax Worksheet** on page 39 of the Instructions for Form 1040 (or in the Instructions for Form 1040NR).

☐ **No.** Complete the rest of Form 1040 or Form 1040NR.

Schedule D (Form 1040) 2010

Sample worksheet for John and Karen Taylor (see the Example on pages 108–109)

Qualified Dividends and Capital Gain Worksheet—Line-44

Before you begin:
√ See the instructions for line 44 on page 35 to see if you can use this worksheet to figure your tax.
√ If you do not have to file Schedule D and you received capital gain distributions, be sure you checked the box on line 13 of Form 1040.

Line	Description		Amount	Amount
1.	Enter the amount from Form 1040, line 43. However, if you are filing Form 2555 or 2555-EZ (relating to foreign earned income), enter the amount from line 3 of the worksheet on page 36	1.	78,000	
2.	Enter the amount from Form 1040, line 9b*	2. 400		
3.	Are you filing Schedule D?* [X] **Yes.** Enter the **smaller** of line 15 or 16 of Schedule D. If either line 15 or line 16 is a loss, enter -0- [ ] **No.** Enter the amount from Form 1040, line 13	3. 8,310		
4.	Add lines 2 and 3	4. 8,710		
5.	If filing Form 4952 (used to figure investment interest expense deduction), enter any amount from line 4g of that form. Otherwise, enter -0-	5. - 0 -		
6.	Subtract line 5 from line 4. If zero or less, enter -0-	6.	8,710	
7.	Subtract line 6 from line 1. If zero or less, enter -0-	7.	69,290	
8.	Enter: $34,000 if single or married filing separately, $68,000 if married filing jointly or qualifying widow(er), $45,550 if head of household.	8.	68,000	
9.	Enter the smaller of line 1 or line 8	9.	68,000	
10.	Enter the smaller of line 7 or line 9	10.	68,000	
11.	Subtract line 10 from line 9. This amount is taxed at 0%	11.	- 0 -	
12.	Enter the smaller of line 1 or line 6	12.	8,710	
13.	Enter the amount from line 11	13.	- 0 -	
14.	Subtract line 13 from line 12	14.	8,710	
15.	Multiply line 14 by 15% (.15)	15.		1,307
16.	Figure the tax on the amount on line 7. If the amount on line 7 is less than $100,000, use the Tax Table to figure this tax. If the amount on line 7 is $100,000 or more, use the Tax Computation Worksheet	16.		9,681
17.	Add lines 15 and 16	17.		10,988
18.	Figure the tax on the amount on line 1. If the amount on line 1 is less than $100,000, use the Tax Table to figure this tax. If the amount on line 1 is $100,000 or more, use the Tax Computation Worksheet	18.		11,869
19.	**Tax on all taxable income.** Enter the **smaller** of line 17 or line 18. Also include this amount on Form 1040, line 44. If you are filing Form 2555 or 2555-EZ, do not enter this amount on Form 1040, line 44. Instead, enter it on line 4 of the worksheet on page 36	19.		10,988

**If you are filing Form 2555 or 2555-EZ, see the footnote in the worksheet on page 36 before completing this line.*

5.9 Counting the Months in Your Holding Period

The period of time you own a capital asset before its sale or exchange determines whether capital gain or loss is short term or long term.

These are the rules for counting the holding period:

1. A holding period is figured in months and fractions of months.
2. The beginning date of a holding month is generally the day after the asset was acquired. The same numerical date of each following month starts a new holding month regardless of the number of days in the preceding month.
3. The last day of the holding period is the day on which the asset is sold.

As a rule of thumb, use the numerical date on which you acquired the asset as the numerical date ending a holding month in each following month. However, if you acquire an asset on the last day of a month, a holding month ends on the last day of a following calendar month, regardless of the number of days in each month.

EXAMPLES

1. On September 15, 2010, you buy stock. The holding months begin on September 16, October 16, November 16, and December 16, and end on October 15, November 15, December 15, etc. A sale on or after September 16, 2011, would result in long-term gain or loss.
2. You buy stock on November 30. A holding month ends on December 31, January 31, February 28 (or 29 in a leap year), etc.

5.10 Holding Period for Securities

Rules for counting your holding period for various securities transactions are as follows:

Stock sold on a public exchange. The holding period starts on the day after your purchase order is executed (trade date). The day your sale order is executed (trade date) is the last day of the holding period, even if delivery and payment are not made until several days after the actual sale (settlement date).

Planning Reminder

Long-Term Holding Period of More Than a Year

To obtain the benefit of favorable long-term capital gains rates *(5.3)*, you must hold an asset more than a year before selling it.

EXAMPLES

1. On June 3, you sell a stock at a profit. Your holding period ends on June 3, although proceeds are not received until June 6.
2. You sell stock at a gain on a public exchange on December 31, 2010. The gain must be reported in 2010 even though the proceeds are received in 2011. The installment sale rule does not apply; *see 5.21*.

Stock subscriptions. If you are bound by your subscription but the corporation is not, the holding period begins the day after the date on which the stock is issued. If both you and the company are bound, the date the subscription is accepted by the corporation is the date of acquisition, and your holding period begins the day after.

Tax-free stock rights. When you exercise rights to acquire corporate stock from the issuing corporation, your holding period for the stock begins on the day of exercise, not on the day after. You are deemed to exercise stock rights when you assent to the terms of the rights in the manner requested or authorized by the corporation. An option to acquire stock is not a stock right.

Stock sold from different lots. If you purchased shares of the same stock on different dates and cannot determine which shares you are selling, the shares purchased at the earliest time are considered the stock sold first; this is called the FIFO (first-in, first-out) method *(30.2)*.

Commodities. If you acquired a commodity futures contract, the holding period of a commodity accepted in satisfaction of the contract includes your holding period of the contract, unless you are a dealer in commodities.

Employee stock options. When an employee exercises a stock option, the holding period of the acquired stock begins on the day after the option is exercised. If an employee option plan allows the exercise of an option by giving notes, the terms of the plan should be reviewed to determine when ownership rights to the stock are transferred. The terms may affect the start of the holding period for the stock.

Wash sales. After a wash sale, the holding period of the new stock includes the holding period of the old stock for which a loss has been disallowed *(30.6)*.

Other references. For the holding period of stock dividends, *see 30.3*; for short sales, *see 30.5*; and for convertible securities, *see 30.7*.

EXAMPLE

You purchased 100 shares of ABC stock on May 3, 1995, 100 shares of ABC stock on May 1, 1997, and 300 shares of ABC stock on September 2, 1998. In 2010, you sell 250 shares of ABC stock, and are unable to determine when those particular shares were bought. Using the "first-in, first-out" method, 100 shares are from May 3, 1995, 100 shares from May 1, 1997, and 50 shares are from September 2, 1998 *(30.2)*.

5.11 Holding Period for Real Estate

The holding period starts the day after the date of acquisition, which is the earlier of: (1) the date title passes to you or (2) the date you take possession and you assume the burdens and privileges of ownership. In disputes involving the starting and closing dates of a holding period, you may refer to the state law that applies to your sale or purchase agreement. State law determines when title to property passes.

If you convert a residence to rental property and later sell the home, the holding period includes the time you held the home for personal purposes.

Year-end sale. The date of sale is the last day of your holding period even if you do not receive the sale proceeds until the following year. For example, you sell land at a gain on December 31, 2010, receiving payment in January 2011. The holding period ends on December 31, although the sale is reported in 2011 when the proceeds are received. Note that the December 31 gain transaction can be reported in 2010 by making an election to "elect out" of installment reporting *(5.23)*. A sale at a loss is reported in 2010.

Planning Reminder

Year-End Sales

Tax reporting for year-end sales of real estate is different from that for publicly traded securities. Gain on a sale of realty at the end of 2010 may be deferred under the installment sale rules *(5.22)* if payments will be received in 2011 or later years. Gain on a sale of publicly traded securities at the end of 2010 must be reported on your 2010 return although you receive payment in 2011.

5.12 Holding Period: Gifts, Inheritances, and Other Property

Gift property. If, in figuring a gain or loss, your basis for the property under *5.17* is the same as the donor's basis, you add the donor's holding period to the period you held the property. If you sell the property at a loss using as your basis the fair market value at the date of the gift *(5.17)*, your holding period begins on the day after the date of the gift.

Inherited property. The law gives an automatic holding period of more than one year for inherited property. Report the transaction on Line 8 of Schedule D and enter "INHERITED" in column (b) as the date of acquisition.

Where property is purchased by the executor or trustee and distributed to you, your holding period begins the day after the date on which the property was purchased.

Partnership property. When you receive property as a distribution in kind from your partnership, the period your partnership held the property is added to your holding period. But there is no adding on of holding periods if the partnership property distributed was inventory and was sold by you within five years of distribution.

Involuntary conversions. When you have an involuntary conversion and elect to defer tax on gain, the holding period for the qualified replacement property generally includes the period you held the converted property. A new holding period begins for new property if you do not make an election to defer tax.

Filing Tip

Selling Inherited Property

When you sell property that you inherited, report the sale as long-term gain or loss on Schedule D even if you actually held the property for less than one year. The law automatically treats inherited property as if it were held for more than one year.

Planning Reminder

Records for Rental Property Improvements

Keep records of permanent improvements and legal fees for rental property. These increase your basis and lower any potential gain when you sell the property.

5.13 Calculating Gain or Loss

In most cases, you know if you have realized an *economic* profit or loss on the sale or exchange of property. You know your cost and selling price. The difference between the two is your profit or loss. The computation of gain or loss for tax purposes is similarly figured, except that the basis adjustment rules may require you to increase or decrease your cost or selling price and the amount-realized rules may require you to increase the selling price. As a result, your gain or loss for tax purposes may differ from your initial calculation.

Worksheet 5-A Figuring Gain or Loss on Schedule D

1.	Amount realized or total selling price *(5.14)*.		$_____
2.	Cost or other unadjusted basis *(5.16)*.	$_____	
3.	*Plus:* Improvements; certain legal fees *(5.20)*.	$_____	
4.	*Minus:* Depreciation, casualty losses *(5.20)*.	$_____	
5.	Adjusted basis: 2 *plus* 3 *minus* 4 *(5.20)*.	$_____	
6.	Add selling expenses to 5. This is the total cost shown on Schedule D.	$_____	$_____
7.	Gain or loss: Subtract 6 from 1.		$_____

EXAMPLE

You sell rental property to a buyer who pays you cash of $50,000 and assumes your $35,000 mortgage. You bought the property for $55,000 and made $12,000 of permanent improvements. You deducted depreciation of $7,250. Selling expenses were $2,000. Your gain on the sale is $23,250, figured as follows:

1.	Amount realized *(5.14)*	
	Cash	$50,000
	Mortgage assumed by buyer	35,000
		$85,000
2.	Original cost	55,000
3.	*Plus* improvements	12,000
		$67,000
4.	*Minus* depreciation	7,250
5.	Adjusted basis	59,750
6.	*Plus* selling expenses*	2,000
7.	Total cost: Combined result of Lines 2–6	61,750
8.	Gain: Subtract Line 7 from Line 1	$23,250

***Selling expenses on Schedule D.** When reporting a sale on Schedule D, IRS instructions require you to include *selling expenses* (Step 6) in the column for *cost*, rather than as a reduction to the sales price. The only exception is where a broker has reported *net* sale proceeds (gross proceeds *less* selling expenses) on Form 1099-B; you would then report the net amount as the sales price. Where a broker has reported the gross sales price on Form 1099-B, the IRS wants you to treat sales commissions as an addition to cost (rather than a reduction to selling price) so that it can compare the gross amount shown on Form 1099-B with the sales price reported on your return.

Using the facts in the previous Example, you report the gross selling price of $85,000 in column (d) of Schedule D. In column (e), enter the adjusted basis of $59,750 *plus* the selling expenses of $2,000 for a total of $61,750. The final result, a gain of $23,250 ($85,000 – $61,750), is the same as if the selling price were reduced by the selling expenses.

5.14 Amount Realized Is the Total Selling Price

Amount realized is the tax term for the total selling price. It includes cash, the fair market value of additional property received, and any of your liabilities that the buyer agrees to pay. The buyer's note is included in the selling price at fair market value. This is generally the discounted amount that a bank or other party will pay for the note.

Sale of mortgaged property. The selling price includes the amount of the unpaid mortgage. This is true whether or not you are personally liable on the debt, and whether or not the buyer assumes the mortgage or merely takes the property subject to the mortgage. The full amount of the unpaid mortgage is included, even where the value of the property is less than the unpaid mortgage. Computing amount realized on foreclosure sales is discussed in *Chapter 31 (31.9)*.

If, at the time of the sale, the buyer pays off the existing mortgage or your other liabilities, you include the payment as part of the sales proceeds.

Caution

Mortgaged Property

When you sell mortgaged property, you must include the unpaid balance of the mortgage as part of the sales price received, in addition to any cash.

EXAMPLES

1. You sell property subject to a mortgage of $60,000. The seller pays you cash of $30,000 and takes the property subject to the mortgage. The sales price or "amount realized" is $90,000.
2. A partnership receives a nonrecourse mortgage of $1,851,500 from a bank to build an apartment project. Several years later, the partnership sells the project for the buyer's agreement to assume the unpaid mortgage. At the time, the value of the project is $1,400,000 and the partnership basis in the project is $1,455,740. The partnership figures a loss of $55,740, the difference between basis and the value of the project. The IRS figures a gain of $395,760, the difference between the unpaid mortgage and basis. The partnership claims the selling price is limited to the lower fair market value and is supported by an appeals court. The Supreme Court reverses, supporting the IRS position. That the value of property is less than the amount of the mortgage has no effect on the rule requiring the unpaid mortgage to be part of the selling price. A mortgagor realizes value to the extent that his or her obligation to repay is relieved by a third party's assumption of the mortgage debt.

5.15 Finding Your Cost

In figuring gain or loss, you need to know the "unadjusted basis" of the property sold. This term refers to the original cost of your property if you purchased it. The general rules for determining your unadjusted basis are in *5.16*. Basis for property received by gift or inheritance is in *5.17*; rules for surviving joint tenants are in *5.18*. Keep in mind that you have to adjust this figure for improvements to the property, depreciation, or losses *(5.20)*.

5.16 Unadjusted Basis of Your Property

To determine your tax cost for property, first find in the following section the unadjusted basis of the property, and then increase or decrease that basis *(5.20)*.

Property you bought. Unadjusted basis is your cash cost plus the value of any property you gave to the seller. If you assumed a mortgage or bought property subject to a mortgage, the amount of the mortgage is part of your unadjusted basis.

Purchase expenses are included in your cost, such as commissions, title insurance, recording fees, survey costs, and transfer taxes.

If you buy real estate and reimburse the seller for property taxes he or she paid that cover the period after you took title, and you include the payment in your itemized deduction for real estate taxes *(16.4)*, do not add the reimbursement to your basis. However, if you did not reimburse the seller, you must reduce your basis by the seller's payment.

If at the closing you also paid property taxes attributable to the time the seller held the property, you add such taxes to basis.

Filing Tip

Basis of Mutual-Fund Shares

To figure gain or loss on the sale of mutual-fund shares where purchases are made at various times, you may use an averaging method to determine the cost basis of the shares sold *(32.10)*.

EXAMPLE

You bought a building for $120,000 in cash and a purchase money mortgage of $60,000. The unadjusted basis of the building is $180,000.

Property obtained for services. If you paid for the property by providing services, the value of the property, which is taxable compensation, is also your adjusted basis.

Property received in taxable exchange. Technically, your unadjusted basis for the new property is the fair market value of the surrendered property at the time of exchange. In practice, however, the basis usually is equal to the fair market value of the property received. *See* below for tax-free exchanges.

EXAMPLE

You acquire real estate for $35,000. When the property has a fair market value of $40,000, you exchange it for machinery also worth $40,000. You have a gain of $5,000 and the basis of the machinery is $40,000.

Property received in a tax-free exchange. The computation of basis is made on Form 8824. If the exchange is completely tax free *(6.1)*, your basis for the new property will be your basis for the property you gave up in the exchange, plus any additional cash and exchange expenses you paid. If the exchange is partly nontaxable and partly taxable because you received "boot" *(6.3)*, your basis for the new property will be your basis for the property given up in the exchange, decreased by any cash received and by any liabilities on the property you gave up, and increased by any cash and exchange expenses you paid, liabilities on the property you received, and gain taxed to you on the exchange. Gain is taxed to the extent you receive "boot," in the form of cash or a transfer of liabilities that exceeds the liabilities assumed in the exchange; *see 6.3* for a discussion on taxable boot. *The Example in 6.3 illustrates the basis computation.*

Planning Reminder

Carryover Basis From Spouse or Ex-Spouse

If you receive a gift of property from your spouse or you receive property from a former spouse in a divorce settlement, your basis for the property is generally the same as the spouse's basis *(6.7)*.

Property received from a spouse or former spouse. Tax-free exchange rules apply to property transfers after July 18, 1984, to a spouse, or to a former spouse where the transfer is incident to a divorce *(6.7)*. The spouse receiving the property takes a basis equal to that of the transferor. Certain adjustments may be required where a transfer of mortgaged property is made in trust.

If you received property before July 19, 1984, under a prenuptial agreement in exchange for your release of your dower and marital rights, your basis is the fair market value at the time you received it.

EXAMPLES

1. You exchange investment real estate, which cost you $20,000, for other investment real estate. Both properties have a fair market value of $35,000 and neither property is mortgaged. You pay no tax on the exchange. The unadjusted basis of the new property received in the exchange is $20,000.
2. Same facts as in Example 1, but you receive real estate worth $30,000 and cash of $5,000. On this transaction, you realize gain of $15,000 (amount realized of $35,000 less your basis of $20,000), but only $5,000 of the gain is taxable, equal to the cash "boot" received. Your basis for the new property is $20,000, figured this way:

Basis of old property	$20,000
Less: Cash received	5,000
	15,000
Plus: Gain recognized	5,000
Basis of new property	$20,000

New residence purchased under tax deferral rule of prior law. If you sold your old principal residence and bought a qualifying replacement under the prior law deferral rules, your basis for the new house is what you paid for it, less any gain that was not taxed on the sale of the old residence.

Property received as a trust beneficiary. Generally, you take the same basis the trust had for the property. But if the distribution is made to settle a claim you had against the trust, your basis for the property is the amount of the settled claim.

If you received a distribution in kind for your share of trust income before June 2, 1984, the basis of the distribution is generally the value of the property to the extent allocated to distributable net income. For distributions in kind after June 1, 1984, in taxable years ending after June 1,

1984, your basis is the basis of the property in the hands of the trust. If the trust elects to treat the distribution as a taxable sale, your basis is generally fair market value.

Property acquired with involuntary conversion proceeds. If you acquire replacement property with insurance proceeds from destroyed property, or a government payment for condemned property, basis is the cost of the new property decreased by deferred gain *(18.23)*. If the replacement property consists of more than one piece of property, basis is allocated to each piece in proportion to its respective cost.

EXAMPLE

A building with an adjusted basis of $100,000 is destroyed by fire. The owner receives an insurance award of $200,000, realizing a gain of $100,000. He buys a building as a replacement for $150,000. Of the $100,000 gain, $50,000 is taxable, while the remaining $50,000 is deferred. Taxable gain is limited to the portion of the insurance award not used to buy replacement property ($200,000 – $150,000). The basis of the new building is $100,000:

Cost of the new building	$150,000
Less: deferred gain	50,000
Basis	$100,000

5.17 Basis of Property You Inherited or Received as a Gift

Special basis rules apply to property you received as a gift or that you inherited. Gifts from a spouse are subject to the rules discussed in *6.7*. If you are a surviving joint tenant who received full title to property upon the death of the other joint tenant, *see 5.18*.

Basis of Property Received as Gift

If the fair market value of the property *equalled or exceeded* the donor's adjusted basis *(5.20)* at the time you received the gift, your basis for figuring gain or loss when you sell it is the donor's adjusted basis plus all or part of any gift tax paid; *see* the gift tax rule below. Additional basis adjustments may be required for the period you held the property *(5.20)*.

If on the date of the gift the fair market value was less than the donor's adjusted basis, your basis for purposes of figuring gain is the donor's adjusted basis, and your basis for figuring loss is the fair market value on the date of the gift. Additional basis adjustments may be required for the period you held the property *(5.20)*.

Caution

Basis for Gift

The basis of gift property you receive generally depends on the donor's basis. Make sure you get this information from the donor.

Did the donor pay gift tax? If the donor paid a gift tax *(39.2)* on the gift to you, your basis for the property is increased under these rules:

1. For property received after December 31, 1976, the basis is increased by an amount that bears the same ratio to the amount of gift tax paid by the donor as the net appreciation in the value of the gift bears to the amount of the gift after taking into account the annual gift tax exclusion *(39.2)* that applied in the year of the gift. The increase may not exceed the tax paid. Net appreciation in the value of any gift is the amount by which the fair market value of the gift exceeds the donor's adjusted basis immediately before the gift. *See* Example 3 below.
2. For property received after September 1, 1958, but before 1977, basis is increased by the gift tax paid on the property but not above the fair market value of the property at the time of the gift.

Depreciation on property received as a gift. If the property is depreciable *(Chapter 42)*, your basis for computing depreciation deductions is the donor's adjusted basis *(5.20)*, plus all or part of the gift tax paid by the donors as previously discussed.

To figure gain or loss when you sell the property, you must adjust basis for depreciation you claimed and make other adjustments required for the period you hold the property *(5.20)*. If accelerated depreciation is claimed and you sell at a gain, you are subject to the ordinary income recapture rules *(44.1)*.

EXAMPLE

1. Assume that in 1998 you received a gift of stock from your father that you sold in 2010. His adjusted basis was $1,000.

   The basis you use to determine gain or loss depends on whether the fair market value of the stock on the date of the gift equalled or exceeded your father's $1,000 adjusted basis. If it did, your basis is your father's $1,000 basis and you will realize a gain if your selling price exceeds $1,000, as on Line 1 below, or a loss if the selling price is below $1,000, as on Line 4.

   If the value of the stock on the date of the gift was less than $1,000 (father's basis) then you have: a gain if you sell for more than $1,000, as on Line 5; a loss if you sell for less than the date-of-gift value, as on Line 2; or neither gain nor loss if you sell for more than the date-of-gift value but no more than $1,000 (father's basis), as on Line 3.

	If value of the gift at receipt was—	*And you sold it for—*	*Your basis is—*	*Your gain is—*	*Your loss is—*
1.	$ 3,000	$ 2,000	$ 1,000	$ 1,000	none
2.	700	500	700	none	$ 200
3.	300	500	*	none	none
4.	1,500	500	1,000	none	500
5.	500	1,200	1,000	200	none

*On Line 3 of the Example, where you sell for more than the date-of-gift value but for no more than the donor's basis, there is neither gain nor loss. To *see* if you have a gain, you use the donor's $1,000 basis as your basis, but on a sale for $500, you have a loss ($500) and not a gain. To *see* if you have a loss, you use the $300 date-of-gift value of the stock as your basis, but on a sale for $500, you have a gain ($200) and not a loss. Thus, you have neither gain nor loss under the basis rules, which require you to use the donor's basis for determining if you have a gain and the date-of-gift value for determining if you have a loss.

Filing Tip

No Gain or Loss

When you sell property received as a gift, it is possible that you may realize neither gain nor loss. You have neither gain nor losses if you sell for more than the date-of-gift value but not more than the donor's adjusted basis.

2. In 1975, your father gave you rental property with a fair market value of $78,000. The basis of the property in his hands was $60,000. He paid a gift tax of $15,000 on the gift. The basis of the property in your hands is $75,000 ($60,000 + $15,000).

3. In 2001, your father gave you rental property with a fair market value of $178,000. His basis in the property was $160,000. He paid a gift tax of $44,560 on a taxable gift of $168,000, after claiming the $10,000 annual exclusion. The basis of the property in your hands is your father's basis increased by the gift tax attributable to the appreciation. Gift tax attributable to the appreciation is:

$$\frac{\text{Appreciation}}{\text{Gift } \textit{minus} \text{ annual exclusion}} \times \text{Gift tax paid}$$

$$\frac{\$18{,}000}{\$168{,}000} \times \$44{,}560 = \$\,4{,}774$$

   Your basis for figuring gain or loss or depreciation is $164,774 ($4,774 + $160,000 father's basis).

Basis of Inherited Property

Your basis for inherited property is generally "stepped up" to the fair market value of the property on the date of the decedent's death. If the executor of the decedent's estate elected to use an *alternate valuation date* after the death, your basis is the alternate value at that date. Since your basis for inherited property is the value at the decedent's death or alternate valuation date, income tax is completely avoided on the appreciation in value that occurred while the decedent owned the property.

If you owned the property jointly with the deceased, *see 5.18*.

If you inherit appreciated property that you (or your spouse) gave to the deceased person within one year of his or her death, your basis is the decedent's basis immediately before death, not its fair market value.

If the inherited property is subject to a mortgage, your basis is the value of the property, and not its equity at the date of death. If the property is subject to a lease under which no income is to be received for years, the basis is the value of the property—not the equity.

You might be given the right to buy the deceased person's property under his or her will. This is not the same as inheriting that property. Your basis is what you pay—not what the property is worth on the date of the deceased's death.

If property was inherited from an individual who died after 1976 and before November 7, 1978, and the executor elected to apply a carryover basis to all estate property, your basis is figured with reference to the decedent's basis. The executor must inform you of the basis of such property.

Special rules for property inherited from individuals dying in 2010. Congress allowed the scheduled repeal of the estate tax to take effect for 2010 and along with repeal a modified carryover basis rule took effect for assets inherited from individuals dying in 2010. Under the modified carryover basis rule, stepped-up basis still applies for up to $1.3 million of assets selected by the executor of the estate, plus an additional $3 million inherited by a surviving spouse. For larger amounts, the heir's basis is the decedent's basis for the asset.

When this book went to press, the IRS had not yet provided any guidelines on the modified carryover basis rules.

In addition, when this book went to press, Congress was considering estate tax reform legislation for 2011 and later years that would modify the rules that were in effect for 2009 by phasing in an increase to the $3.5 million exemption as well as a reduction to the 45% top rate, while retaining stepped-up basis. A provision in the legislation would allow estates of individuals dying in 2010 to follow the 2010 rules so no estate tax would apply but the heirs would be subject to the modified carryover basis rules, or the estate could elect to file an estate tax return for 2010 and pay estate tax under the new rules taking effect in 2011, thereby allowing a stepped-up basis for the heirs. *See* the *e-Supplement at jklasser.com* for an update on the proposed legislation and on the modified carryover basis rules.

Community property. Upon the death of a spouse in a community property state, one-half of the fair market value of the community property is generally included in the deceased spouse's estate for estate tax purposes. The surviving spouse's basis for his or her half of the property is 50% of the total fair market value. For the other half, the surviving spouse, if he/she receives the asset, or the other heirs of the deceased spouse have a basis equal to 50% of the fair market value.

Law Alert

Modified Carryover Basis for 2010 Estates

When Congress allowed the scheduled repeal of the estate tax to take effect for 2010, it kept in place a modified carryover basis rule for assets inherited from individuals dying in 2010. Under the modified carryover basis rule, stepped-up basis still applies for up to $1.3 million of assets selected by the executor of the estate, plus an additional $3 million inherited by a surviving spouse. For larger amounts, the heir's basis is the decedent's basis for the asset. When this book went to press, the IRS had not yet provided any guidelines on the modified carryover basis rules. It is possible that Congress will enact estate tax reform legislation that includes an election for estates of individuals dying in 2010 to avoid the modified carryover basis rules. *See* the *e-Supplement at jklasser.com* for an update on the proposed legislation and on the modified carryover basis rules.

5.18 Joint Tenancy Basis Rules for Surviving Tenants

If you are a surviving joint tenant, your basis for the property depends on how much of the value was includible in the deceased tenant's gross estate, and this depends on whether the joint tenant was your spouse or someone other than your spouse.

Qualified joint interest rule for survivor of spouse who died after 1981. A "qualified joint interest" rule applies to a joint tenancy with right of survivorship where the spouses are the only joint tenants, and to a tenancy by the entirety between a husband and wife. Where the surviving spouse is a U.S. citizen, one-half of the fair market value of the property is includible in the decedent's gross estate. This is true regardless of how much each spouse contributed to the purchase price. Fair market value is fixed at the date of death, or six months later if an estate tax return is filed and the optional alternate valuation date is elected. These rules do not apply if the surviving spouse is not a U.S. citizen on the due date of the estate tax return. In this case, the basis rule is generally the same as the rule discussed below for unmarried joint tenants.

The surviving spouse's basis equals 50% of the date-of-death fair market value (the amount included in the decedent's gross estate), plus one-half of the original cost basis for the property; *see* Example 1 below. If no estate tax return was due because the value of the estate was below the filing threshold, the surviving spouse's basis is one-half of the fair market value of the property at the date of death (alternate valuation is not available) plus one-half of the original cost basis. If depreciation deductions for the property were claimed before the date of death, the surviving spouse must reduce basis by his or her share (under local law) of the depreciation; *see* Example 2 below.

Planning Reminder

Spousal Joint Tenancies Created Before 1977

If spouses jointly own property and one spouse dies, the surviving spouse generally receives a stepped-up basis of 50% of the date-of-death value. The IRS at one time took the position that the 50% stepped-up basis rule applied to pre-1997 spousal joint tenancies. However, after the Tax Court and two federal appeals courts allowed a surviving spouse a 100% stepped-up basis if the spousal joint tenancy was created before 1977 (*see* Example 3 in *5.18*), the IRS decided to follow the Tax Court decision and will no longer litigate the issue.

EXAMPLES

1. John and Jennifer Jones jointly bought a house for $50,000 in 1979. John paid $45,000 of the purchase price and Jennifer $5,000. In 2009, John died when the house was worth $200,000. One-half, or $100,000, was included in his estate although he contributed 90% of the purchase price. For income tax purposes, Jennifer's basis for the house is $125,000.

One-half of cost basis	$25,000
Inherited portion	100,000
Jennifer's basis	$125,000

2. Same facts as in Example 1 except that the home was rental property for which $20,000 of depreciation deductions had been allowed before John's death. Under local law, Jennifer had a right to 50% of the income from the property and, thus, a right to 50% of the depreciation. Her basis for the property is $115,000: $125,000 as shown in Example 1, reduced by $10,000, her share of the depreciation.

3. The Gallensteins purchased farm property in 1955 as joint tenants; Mr. Gallenstein provided all the funds. When he died in 1987, Mrs. Gallenstein claimed that 100% of the property was includible in her husband's gross estate and she had a stepped-up basis for that full amount. The IRS argued that under the rules for estates of spouses dying after 1981, she received a stepped-up basis for only 50% of the date-of-death value. The federal appeals court for the Sixth Circuit (Kentucky, Michigan, Ohio, and Tennessee) agreed with Mrs. Gallenstein. The appeals court held that pre-1977 spousal joint tenancies were not affected when the law was changed to provide a 50% estate tax inclusion and 50% stepped-up basis for spousal deaths after 1981. For pre-1977 spousal joint tenancies, the prior law rule continues to apply: 100% of the date-of-death value of jointly held property is included in the estate of the first spouse to die unless it is shown that the survivor contributed towards the purchase. In this case, where Mrs. Gallenstein's deceased husband had paid the entire purchase price, her basis was 100% of the value of the property and she realized no taxable gain when she sold the property at a price equal to that stepped-up basis.

   The Tax Court and the Fourth Circuit Appeals Court (Maryland, North Carolina, South Carolina, Virginia, and West Virginia) agreed with the Sixth Circuit's approach of allowing a 100% stepped-up basis for a pre-1977 spousal joint interest where the deceased spouse had paid the entire purchase price. In October 2001, the IRS acquiesced to the Tax Court decision and will no longer litigate the issue.

   If the statute of limitations has not expired, a surviving spouse who reported gain on a sale of property using the 50% basis rule should consult with his or her tax adviser about filing a refund claim based upon the 100% basis rule.

Planning Reminder

Joint Property Held With Non-Spouse

If you own property with someone other than your spouse, then at the other owner's death your basis for the property equals your original contribution to the purchase plus the portion of the property's value that was includible in the gross estate of the deceased owner.

Unmarried joint tenants. If you are a surviving joint tenant who owned property with someone other than your spouse, your basis for the entire property is your basis for your share before the joint owner died plus the fair market value of the decedent's share at death (or on the alternate valuation date if the estate uses the alternate date). Even if the estate is too small to require the filing of an estate tax return, you may still include the decedent's share of the date-of-death value in your basis. However, if no estate tax return is required, you may not use the alternate valuation date basis.

EXAMPLE

You and your sister bought a home in 1990 for $120,000. She paid $72,000, and you paid $48,000. Title to the house was held by both of you as joint tenants. In 2009, when she died, the house was worth $250,000. Since she paid 60% of the cost of the house, 60% of the value at her death, $150,000, is included in her estate tax return (or would be included if an estate tax return was due). Your basis for the house is now $198,000—the $48,000 you originally paid plus the $150,000 fair market value of your sister's 60% share at her death.

Exception for pre-1954 deaths. Where property was held in joint tenancy and one of the tenants died before January 1, 1954, no part of the interest of the surviving tenant is treated, for purposes of determining the basis of the property, as property transmitted at death. The survivor's basis is the original cost of the property.

Survivor of spouse who died before 1982. The basis rule for a surviving spouse who held property jointly (or as tenancy by the entirety) with a spouse who died before 1982 is generally the same as the above rule for unmarried joint tenants. However, special rules applied to qualified joint interests and eligible joint interests are discussed below.

EXAMPLE

A husband and wife owned rental property as tenants by the entirety that they purchased for $30,000. The husband furnished two-thirds of the purchase price ($20,000) and the wife furnished one-third ($10,000). Depreciation deductions taken before the husband's death were $12,000. On the date of his death in 1979, the property had a fair market value of $60,000. Under the law of the state in which the property is located, as tenants by the entirety, each had a half interest in the property. The wife's basis in the property at the date of her husband's death was $44,000, computed as follows:

Interest acquired with her own funds	$ 10,000
Interest acquired from husband ($^2/_3$ of $60,000)	40,000
	$50,000
Less: Depreciation of $^1/_2$ interest not acquired by reason of death ($^1/_2$ of $12,000)	6,000
Wife's basis at date of husband's death	$ 44,000

If she had not contributed any part of the purchase price, her basis at the date of her husband's death would be $54,000 ($60,000 fair market value less $6,000 depreciation). This basis would be increased by any additions or improvements made to the property by the wife since the husband's death, and reduced by any depreciation *(5.20)*.

Qualified joint interest and eligible joint interest where spouse died before 1982. Where, after 1976, a spouse dying before 1982 elected to treat realty as a "qualified joint interest" subject to gift tax, such joint property was treated as owned 50–50 by each spouse, and 50% of the value was included in the decedent's estate. Thus, for income tax purposes, the survivor's basis for the inherited 50% half of the property is the estate tax value; the basis for the other half is determined under the gift rules *(5.17)*. Personal property is treated as a "qualified joint interest" only if it was created or deemed to have been created after 1976 by a husband and wife and was subject to gift tax.

Where death occurred before 1982 and a surviving spouse materially participated in the operation of a farm or other business, the estate could have elected to treat the farm or business property as an "eligible joint interest," which means that part of the investment in the property was attributed to the surviving spouse's services and that part was not included in the deceased spouse's estate. Where such an election was made, the survivor's basis for income tax purposes includes the estate tax value of property included in the decedent's estate.

5.19 Allocating Cost Among Several Assets

Allocation of basis is generally required in these cases: when the property includes land and building; the land is to be divided into lots; securities or mutual-fund shares are purchased at different times; stock splits; and in the purchase of a business.

Purchase of land and building. To figure depreciation on the building, part of the purchase price must be allocated to the building. The allocation is made according to the fair market values of the building and land. The amount allocated to land is not depreciated.

Purchase of land to be divided into lots. The purchase price of the tract is allocated to each lot, so that the gain or loss from the sale of each lot may be reported in the year of its sale. Allocation is not made ratably, that is, with an equal share to each lot or parcel. It is based on the relative value of each piece of property. Comparable sales, competent appraisals, or assessed values may be used as guides.

Securities. See 30.2 for details on methods of identifying securities bought at different dates. *See* 30.3 for allocating basis of stock dividends and stock splits and 30.4 for allocating the basis of stock rights.

Mutual-fund shares. See 32.10 for determining the basis of mutual-fund shares where purchases were made at different times.

Purchase price of a business. See 44.9 for allocation rule.

5.20 How To Find Adjusted Basis

After determining the *unadjusted* cost basis for property (5.16–5.19), you may have to increase it or decrease it to find your *adjusted basis*, which is the amount used to figure your gain or loss on a sale (5.13).

Court Decision

Improvements Covered by Note

In an unusual case, the owner of office condominiums financed substantial improvements to the units by giving promissory notes to a contracting company that he controlled. Before paying off the notes he sold the units. He included the cost of the improvements in basis to figure his gain on the sale, but the IRS, with the approval of a federal district court, held that this was improper. The court held that as a cash-basis taxpayer, he could not include the face amount of the notes in the basis of the condominiums until the notes were paid.

1. **Additions to basis.** You add to unadjusted basis the cost of these items:
   - ***All permanent improvements and additions to the property and other capital costs.*** Increase basis for capital improvements such as adding a room or a fence, putting in new plumbing or wiring, and paving a driveway. Also include capital costs such as the cost of extending utility service lines, assessments for local improvements such as streets, sidewalks, or water connections, and repairing your property after a casualty (for example, repair costs after a fire or storm).
   - ***Legal fees.*** Increase basis by legal fees incurred for defending or perfecting title, or for obtaining a reduction of an assessment levied against property to pay for local benefits.
   - ***Sale of unharvested land.*** If you sell land with unharvested crops, add the cost of producing the crops to the basis of the property sold.

2. **Decreases to basis.** You reduce cost basis for these items:
   - ***Return of capital,*** such as dividends on stock paid out of capital or out of a depletion reserve when the company has no available earnings or surplus (4.11).
   - ***Losses from casualties and thefts,*** including insurance awards and payments in settlement of damages to your property, and deductible casualty/theft losses not covered by insurance.
   - ***Depletion allowances*** (9.15).
   - ***Depreciation, first-year expensing deduction, ACRS deductions, amortization, and obsolescence on property used in business or for the production of income.*** In some years, you may have taken more or less depreciation than was allowable.

     If you claim less than what was allowable, you must deduct from basis the allowable amount rather than what was actually claimed. You may be able to file an amended return to claim the full allowable depreciation for a year. If IRS rules do not allow the correction on an amended return, you can change your accounting method in order to claim the correct amount of depreciation; *see* IRS Publication 946 for details.

     If you took more depreciation than was allowable, you may have to make the following adjustments: If you have deducted more than what was allowable and you received a tax benefit from the deduction, you deduct from basis the full amount of the depreciation. But if the excess depreciation did not give you a tax benefit, because income was eliminated by other deductions, the excess is not deducted from basis.
   - ***Amortized bond premium*** (4.17).
   - ***Cancelled debt excluded from income.*** If you did not pay tax on certain cancellations of debt because of bankruptcy or insolvency, or on qualifying farm debt or business real property, you reduce basis of your property for the amount forgiven (11.8).
   - ***Investment credit.*** Where the full investment credit was claimed in 1983 or later years, basis is reduced by one-half the credit.

EXAMPLE

Your vacation home, which cost $75,000, is damaged by fire. You deducted the uninsured loss of $10,000 and spent $11,000 to repair the property. Several years later, you sell the house for $90,000. To figure your profit, increase the original cost of the house by the $11,000 of repairs and then reduce basis by the $10,000 casualty loss to get an adjusted basis of $76,000 ($75,000 + $11,000 – $10,000). Your gain on the sale is $14,000 ($90,000 – $76,000).

5.21 Tax Advantage of Installment Sales

If you sell property at a *gain* in 2010 and you will receive one or more payments in a later year or years, you may use the installment method to defer tax unless the property is publicly traded securities or you are a dealer of the property sold. If you report the sale as an installment sale on Form 6252, your profit is taxed as installments are received. You may elect not to use the installment method if you want to report the entire profit in the year of sale; *see* Example 1 below and *5.23*.

Losses may not be deferred under the installment method.

How the installment method works. For each year you receive installment payments, report the allocable gain for that year on Form 6252. Installment income from the sale of a capital asset is then transferred to Schedule D. If your gain in the year of sale is long-term capital gain, gain in later years is also long term; short-term treatment in the year of sale applies also to later years. Interest payments you receive on the deferred sale installments are reported with your other interest income on Form 1040, not on Form 6252.

Filing Instruction

Payments from Prior Installment Sales

If you reported a pre-2010 sale on the installment method, use Form 6252 to report any 2010 payments on the sale.

EXAMPLES

1. In October 2010, you sell vacant land for $100,000 that you bought in 1999 for $44,000. Selling expenses were $6,000. You are to receive $20,000 in 2010, 2011, 2012, and 2013, plus interest of 5% compounded semiannually. Your gross profit is $50,000 ($100,000 contract price less $44,000 cost and $6,000 selling expenses). For installment sale purposes, your gross profit percentage, which is the percentage of each payment that you must report, is 50% ($50,000 profit ÷ $100,000 contract price). When the buyer makes the installment note payments, you report the following:

In	***You report***	
	Payment of:	*Income of:*
2010	$20,000	$10,000
2011	20,000	10,000
2012	20,000	10,000
2013	40,000	20,000
Total	$100,000	$50,000

In 2010, you file Form 6252 to figure your gross profit and gross profit percentage. You report only $10,000 as profit on Line 11, column (f), of Schedule D; *see* the sample Schedule D at *5.8*. If you do not want to use the installment method, you make an election by reporting the entire gain of $50,000 on Schedule D *(5.23)*.

The buyer's interest payments are separately reported as interest income on Form 1040.

2. On December 17, 2010, you sell a building for $150,000, realizing a profit of $25,000. You take a note payable in January 2011. You report the gain on Form 6252 with your 2011 return. Receiving a lump-sum payment in a taxable year after the year of sale is considered an installment sale.

Installment income from the sale of business or rental property is figured on Form 6252 and then entered on Form 4797. If you make an installment sale of depreciable property, any *depreciation recapture (44.1)* is reported as income in the year of disposition. The recaptured amount is first figured on Form 4797 and then entered on Form 6252. On Form 6252, recaptured income is added to basis of the property for purposes of figuring the gross profit ratio for the balance of gain to be reported, if any, over the installment period (44.6).

Installment sales of business or rental property for over $150,000 may be subject to a special tax if deferred payments exceed $5 million (5.31).

Year-end sales of publicly traded stock or securities. You have no choice about when to report the gain from a sale of publicly traded stock or securities made at the end of 2010. Any gain must be reported in 2009, even if the proceeds are not received until early 2011. The sale is not considered an installment sale.

Farm property. A farmer may use the installment method to report gain from the sale of property that does not have to be inventoried under his method of accounting. This is true even though such property is held for regular sale.

Dealer sales. Generally, dealers must report gain in the year of sale for personal property regularly sold on an installment plan or real estate held for resale to customers. However, the installment method may be used by dealers of certain time shares (generally time shares of up to six weeks per year) and residential lots, but only if an election is made to pay interest on the tax deferred by using the installment method. For further details, *see* the instructions to Line 1 of Schedule C (Form 1040).

Caution

Year-End Sales of Securities

You cannot defer to 2011 reporting of gain on a 2010 year-end sale of publicly traded securities, even if you do not receive payment until early January 2011.

5.22 Figuring the Taxable Part of Installment Payments

On the installment method, a portion of each payment other than interest represents part of your gain and is taxable. This taxable gain amount is based on the gross profit percentage or ratio, which is figured by dividing gross profit by the selling price or the contract price. The contract price is the same as the selling price unless an adjustment is made for an existing mortgage assumed or "taken subject to" by the buyer. The term *contract price* is used in the computation to describe only payments that the seller receives or is considered to have received. Thus, it does not include the buyer's assumption of an existing mortgage; *see* below for the mortgage adjustment to contract price. By following the line-by-line instructions to Form 6252, you get the gross profit percentage. Selling price, gross profit, and contract price are explained in the following paragraphs.

Interest equal to the *lesser* of 100% of the applicable federal rate and 9% compounded semiannually must generally be charged on a deferred payment sale. Otherwise, the IRS treats part of the sale price as interest (4.32).

EXAMPLE

On December 14, 2010, you sell real estate for $100,000. The property had an adjusted basis of $56,000. Selling expenses are $4,000. You are to receive installment payments of $25,000 in 2010, 2011, 2012, and 2013 plus interest at 5%, compounded semiannually. The gross profit percentage of 40% is figured as follows:

Selling price (contract price)	$100,000
Less: Adjusted basis and selling expenses	60,000
Gross profit	$ 40,000

$$\frac{\text{Gross profit}}{\text{Contract price}} = \frac{\$\,40{,}000}{\$\,100{,}000} = 40\%\ \text{(gross profit percentage)}$$

In 2010, you report a profit of $10,000 (40% of $25,000) on Form 6252. Interest received is separately reported as income on your Form 1040. Similarly, in each of the following three years, a profit of $10,000 is reported so that by the end of four years, the entire $40,000 profit will have been reported.

Caution

Foreclosures

If your property is foreclosed, the amount of the mortgage is treated as sales proceeds even if you do not receive anything on the sale.

Selling price. Include cash, fair market value of property received from the buyer, the buyer's notes (at face value), and any outstanding mortgage on the property that the buyer assumes or takes subject to. If, under the contract of sale, the buyer pays off an existing mortgage or assumes liability for any other liens on the property, such as taxes you owe, or pays the sales commissions, such payments are also included in the selling price.

Interest, including minimum interest imputed under the rules in *4.32*, is not included in the selling price.

Notes of a third party given to you by the buyer are valued at fair market value.

Gross profit and gross profit percentage. Gross profit is the selling price less what the IRS calls installment sale basis, which is the total of adjusted basis of the property *(5.20)*, selling expenses, such as brokers' commissions and legal fees, and recaptured depreciation income, if any *(44.1)*.

Divide the gross profit by the contract price to get the gross profit percentage. Each year, you multiply this percentage by your payments to determine the taxable amount under the installment method.

Contract price where the buyer takes subject to or assumes an existing mortgage. To figure the gross profit percentage first reduce the selling price by the amount of your existing mortgages that the buyer assumes or takes the property subject to. The reduced amount is the *contract price*. You then divide your gross profit by the contract price to get the gross profit percentage.

If the mortgage exceeds your installment sale basis (total of adjusted basis of the property, selling expenses, and depreciation recapture), you are required to report the excess as a payment received in the year of sale and also increase the *contract price* by that excess amount. Where the mortgage equals or exceeds your installment sale basis, the gross profit percentage will be 100%; *see* Example 3 below.

Caution

Recapture of Depreciation or First-Year Expensing Deduction

The entire recaptured amount *(44.1–44.3)* is reported in the year of sale on Form 4797, even though you report the sale on the installment basis. An installment sale does not defer the reporting of the recaptured deduction. You also add the recaptured amount to the basis of the sold asset on Line 12 of Form 6252 to compute the amount of the remaining gain to be reported on each installment. *See* the instructions to Form 6252.

EXAMPLES

1. You sell a building for $300,000. The building was secured by an existing mortgage of $50,000 that you pay off at the sale closing from the buyer's initial payment. The contract price is $300,000.
2. Same facts as in Example 1, but the buyer assumes the mortgage of $50,000. The contract price is $250,000 ($300,000 – $50,000).
3. You sell a building for $90,000. The buyer will pay you $10,000 annually for three years and assume an existing mortgage of $60,000. The adjusted basis of the property is $45,000. Selling expenses are $5,000. The total installment sale basis is $50,000 ($45,000 plus $5,000). The mortgage exceeds this basis by $10,000 ($60,000 – $50,000). This $10,000 excess is included in the contract price and treated as a payment made in the year of sale. The contract price is $40,000:

Selling price	$90,000
Less: Mortgage	60,000
	$30,000
Add: Excess of mortgage ($60,000) over installment sale basis ($50,000)	10,000
Contract price	$40,000
Selling price	$90,000
Less: Installment sale basis	50,000
Gross profit	$40,000
Gross profit percentage ($40,000 gross profit ÷ $40,000 contract price)	100%

4. Abel sells real property worth $2 million, encumbered by a mortgage of $900,000. Installment sale basis (adjusted basis plus selling costs) is $700,000. The buyer pays $200,000 cash and gives an interest-bearing wraparound mortgage note for $1.8 million. Abel remains obligated to pay off the $900,000 mortgage. The gross profit ratio is 65% ($1,300,000 gross profit ÷ $2,000,000 contract price). In the year of sale, Abel reports the $200,000 cash of which 65% of $200,000, or $130,000, is taxable income.

In a wraparound mortgage transaction, the buyer does not assume the seller's mortgage or take the property subject to it, but instead makes payments that cover the seller's outstanding mortgage liability. At one time, the IRS treated a wraparound mortgage transaction as an assumption of a mortgage by the buyer and required a reduction of the selling price by the mortgage to compute the contract price. The Tax Court rejected the IRS position, and the IRS acquiesced in the decision. Currently, the IRS does not require a reduction of selling price for a wraparound mortgage in the Form 6252 instructions or in Publication 537; *see* Example 4 above.

Change of selling price. If the selling price is changed during the period payments are outstanding, the gross profit percentage is refigured on the new selling price. The adjusted profit ratio is then applied to payments received after the adjustment.

EXAMPLE

Jones sold real estate in 2007 for $100,000. His basis, including selling expenses, was $40,000, so his gross profit was $60,000. The buyer agreed to pay, starting in 2008, five annual installments of $20,000 plus 10% interest. As the gross profit percentage was 60% ($60,000 ÷ $100,000), Jones reported profit of $12,000 (60% of $20,000) on the installments received in 2008 and 2009.

In 2010, the parties renegotiated the sales price, reducing it from $100,000 to $85,000, and reducing payments for 2010, 2011, and 2012 to $15,000. Jones's original profit of $60,000 is reduced to $45,000 ($85,000 revised sales price less $40,000 basis). Of the $45,000 profit, $12,000 was reported in 2008 and an additional $12,000 in 2009. To get the revised profit percentage, Jones must divide the $21,000 of profit not yet received by the remaining sales price of $45,000 ($85,000 less $40,000 in total installments in 2008 and 2009). The revised profit percentage is 46.67% ($21,000 ÷ $45,000). In 2010, 2011, and 2012, Jones reports profit of $7,000 on each $15,000 installment (46.67% of $15,000).

Payments received. Payments include cash, the fair market value of property, and payments on the buyer's notes. Payments do not include receipt of the buyer's notes or other evidence of indebtedness, unless payable on demand or readily tradable. "Readily tradable" means registered bonds, bonds with coupons attached, debentures, and other evidences of indebtedness of the buyer that are readily tradable in an established securities market. This rule is directed mainly at corporate acquisitions. A third-party guarantee (including a standby letter of credit) is not treated as a payment received on an installment obligation.

If the buyer has assumed or taken property subject to a mortgage that exceeds your installment sale basis (adjusted basis plus selling expenses plus depreciation recapture, if any), you include as a payment in the year of the sale the excess of the mortgage over the installment basis; *see* the Johnson Example below.

EXAMPLE

Johnson sells a building for $160,000, subject to a mortgage of $60,000. Installments plus interest are to be paid over five years. His adjusted basis in the building was $30,000 and his selling expenses were $10,000, so his installment sale basis is $40,000 and his gross profit is $120,000 ($160,000 – $40,000). The contract price is also $120,000, the selling price of $160,000 less $40,000, the part of the mortgage that did not exceed the installment sale basis.

The $20,000 difference between the $60,000 mortgage and the installment sale basis of $40,000 is part of the contract price and is also treated as a payment received in the year of sale. Since the mortgage exceeds Johnson's installment sale basis, he is treated as having recovered his entire basis in the year of sale, and all installment payments will be taxable, as his gross profit ratio is 100%: gross profit of $120,000 ÷ contract price of $120,000. In the year of sale, Johnson must report as taxable gain 100% of the installment payment received, plus the $20,000 difference between the mortgage and his installment sale basis.

Caution

Extension of Pledge Rule

If a loan arrangement gives you the right to repay the debt by transferring an installment obligation, you are treated as if you had directly pledged the obligation as security for the debt. As a result, the loan proceeds are treated as a payment on the installment obligation, which will increase installment income for the year of the "deemed pledge."

Pledging installment obligation as security. If, as security for a loan, you pledge an installment obligation from a sale of property of more than $150,000 (excluding farm property, personal-use property and timeshares and residential lots), the net loan proceeds must be treated as a payment on the installment obligation. The net loan proceeds are treated as received on the later of the date the loan is secured and the date you receive the loan proceeds. These pledging rules do not apply if the debt refinances a debt that was outstanding on December 17, 1987, and secured by the installment obligation until the refinancing. If the refinancing exceeds the loan principal owed immediately before the refinancing, the excess is treated as a payment on the installment obligation. *See* the Form 6252 instructions.

5.23 Electing Not To Report on the Installment Method

If any sale proceeds are to be received after the year of sale, you must file Form 6252 and use the installment method unless you "elect out" by making a timely election to report the entire gain in the year of sale. If you want to report the entire gain in the year of sale, include it on Schedule D or Form 4797 by the due date for filing your return (plus extensions) for the year of sale. Do not use Form 6252. For example, if you sold property in 2010, with payments due over five years, and you are concerned that the maximum capital gain rates may be raised by Congress, you might consider electing out of the installment method and report the entire gain on your 2010 return to ensure a tax based on the 2010 capital gain rates *(5.3)*.

Switching from full reporting to installment method. If you "elect out" of the installment method by reporting the entire gain in the year of sale, you may change to the installment method on an amended return only with the consent of the IRS. In private rulings, the IRS has granted permission to revoke an election out that was inadvertent, such as where the taxpayer's accountant was instructed to use the installment method but the accountant mistakenly reported the entire gain in the year of sale. If the IRS is not convinced that the election out was inadvertent, it will likely refuse permission to retroactively allow the change to the installment method, on the grounds that a revocation of the election would involve hindsight and result in tax avoidance.

In one case, a seller "elected out" in a year in which he planned to deduct a net operating loss carryforward from an installment sale gain. In a later year, the IRS substantially reduced the loss. The seller then asked the IRS to allow him to revoke the "election out" so he could use the installment method. The IRS refused in a private ruling, claiming that the seller asked for the revocation to avoid tax. The installment sale would defer gain to a later year, which is a tax avoidance purpose.

Filing Tip

"Electing Out" of Installment Reporting

When you have losses to offset your gain in the year of sale, installment sale reporting may not be advantageous. In such a case, you may want to report the full gain in the year of sale so the gain may be offset by the losses. However, there is a risk. If the losses are later disallowed by an IRS audit, you may not be given a second chance to use the installment method to spread the gain over the payment period. The IRS *may* not allow you to revoke your "election out" on the grounds that to do so would result in tax avoidance.

5.24 Restriction on Installment Sales to Relatives

The installment sale method is not allowed where you sell depreciable property to a controlled business, or to a trust in which you or your spouse is a beneficiary. All payments to be received over the installment period are considered received in the year of sale.

Further, if you sell property to a relative on the installment basis, and the relative later resells the property, you could lose the benefit of installment reporting. Generally, you are taxed on your relative's sale if it is within two years of the original sale.

Caution

Installment Sale to Relative

If you sell property on the installment basis to a relative who later resells the property, you could lose the benefit of installment reporting.

EXAMPLE

In 2010, Jones sells land to his son for $250,000, realizing a profit of $100,000. The son agrees to pay in five annual installments of $50,000 plus interest, starting in 2011. Later in 2010, the son sells the land to a third party for $260,000. Jones Sr. reports his profit of $100,000 in 2010, even though he received no payment that year. Payments other than interest received by Jones Sr. after 2010 are tax free because he reported the entire profit in 2010.

Two-year resale rule for property. If you make an installment sale of property to a related party, you are taxed on a second sale by the related party only if it occurs within two years of the initial installment sale and before all payments from the first installment sale are made. However, the two-year limitation does not apply if the property is marketable securities.

Related parties include a spouse, child, grandchild, parent, grandparent, brother or sister, controlled corporation (50% or more direct or indirect ownership), any S corporation in which you own stock or partnership in which you are a partner, a trust in which you are a beneficiary, or a grantor trust of which you are treated as the owner. You are treated as owning stock held by your spouse, brothers, sisters, children, grandchildren, parents, and grandparents.

You must report as additional installment sale income: (1) the proceeds from the related party's sale or the contract price from the initial installment sale, whichever is less, *minus* (2) installment payments received from the related party as of the end of the year. The computation is made in Part III of Form 6252.

Caution

IRS Notice of Related Party Transfer

Where you transfer property to a related party, the IRS has two years from the date you notify it that there has been a second disposition to assess a deficiency with respect to your transfer.

The two-year period is extended during any period in which the buyer's risk is lessened by a put on the property, an option by another person to acquire the property, or a short sale or other transaction lessening the risk of loss.

Exceptions to related-party rule. There are exceptions to the related-party rule. Second dispositions resulting from an involuntary conversion of the property will not be subject to the related-party rule so long as the first disposition occurred before the threat or imminence of conversion. Similarly, transfers after the death of the person making the first disposition or the death of the person acquiring the property in the first disposition are not treated as second dispositions. Also, a sale or exchange of stock to the issuing corporation is not treated as a first disposition. Finally, you may avoid tax on a related party's second sale by satisfying the IRS that neither the initial nor the second sale was made for tax avoidance purposes.

Sales of depreciable property to related party. Installment reporting is not allowed for sales of depreciable property made to a controlled corporation or partnership (50% control by seller) and between such controlled corporations and partnerships. In figuring control of a corporation, you are considered to own stock held by your spouse, children, grandchildren, brothers or sisters, parents, and grandparents. Installment reporting is also disallowed on a sale to a trust in which you or a spouse is a beneficiary unless your interest is considered a remote contingent interest whose actuarial value is 5% or less of the trust property's value. On these related-party sales, the entire gain is reported in the year of sale, unless the seller convinces the IRS that the transfer was not motivated by tax avoidance purposes.

On a sale of depreciable property to a related party, if the amounts of payments are contingent (for example, payments are tied to profits), the seller must make a special calculation. He or she must treat as received in the year of sale all noncontingent payments plus the fair market value of the contingent payments if such value may be reasonably ascertained. If the fair market value of the contingent payments may not be reasonably calculated, the seller recovers basis ratably. The purchaser's basis for the acquired property includes only amounts that the seller has included in income under the basis recovery rule. Thus, the purchaser's basis is increased annually as the seller recovers basis.

5.25 Contingent Payment Sales

Where the final selling price or payment period of an installment sale is not fixed at the end of the taxable year of sale, you are considered to have transacted a "contingent payment sale." Special rules apply where a maximum selling price may be figured under the terms of the agreement or there is no fixed price but there is a fixed payment period, or there is neither a fixed price nor a fixed payment period.

Stated maximum selling price. Under IRS regulations, a stated maximum selling price may be determined by assuming that all of the contingencies contemplated under the agreement are met. When the maximum amount is later reduced, the gross profit ratio is recomputed.

EXAMPLE

Smith sells stock in Acme Co. for a down payment of $100,000 plus an amount equal to 5% of the net profits of Acme for the next nine years. The contract provides that the maximum amount payable, including the $100,000 down payment but exclusive of interest, is $2,000,000. Smith's basis for the stock is $200,000; $2,000,000 is the selling price and contract price. Gross profit is $1,800,000. The gross profit ratio is 90% ($1,800,000 ÷ $2,000,000). Thus, $90,000 of the first payment is reportable as gain and $10,000 as a recovery of basis.

Fixed period. When a stated maximum selling price is not determinable but the maximum payment period is fixed, basis—including selling expenses—is allocated equally to the taxable years in which payment may be received under the agreement. If, in any year, no payment is received or the amount of payment received is less than the basis allocated to that taxable year, no loss is allowed unless the taxable year is the final payment year or the agreement has become worthless. When no loss is allowed in a year, the basis allocated to the taxable year is carried forward to the next succeeding taxable year.

EXAMPLE

Brown sells property for 10% of the property's gross rents over a five-year period. Brown's basis is $5,000,000. The sales price is indefinite and the maximum selling price is not fixed under the terms of the contract; basis is recovered ratably over the five-year period.

Year	*Payment*	*Basis recovered*	*Gain*
First	$ 1,300,000	$ 1,000,000	$ 300,000
Second	1,500,000	1,000,000	500,000
Third	1,400,000	1,000,000	400,000
Fourth	1,800,000	1,000,000	800,000
Fifth	2,100,000	1,000,000	1,100,000

No stated maximum selling price or fixed period. If the agreement fails to specify a maximum selling price and payment period, the IRS may view the agreement as a rent or royalty income agreement. However, if the arrangement qualifies as a sale, basis (including selling expenses) is recovered in equal annual increments over a 15-year period commencing with the date of sale. If in any taxable year no payment is received or the amount of payment received (exclusive of interest) is less than basis allocated to the year, no loss is allowed unless the agreement has become worthless. Excess basis not recovered in one year is reallocated in level amounts over the balance of the 15-year term. Any basis not recovered at the end of the 15th year is carried forward to the next succeeding year, and to the extent unrecovered, carried forward from year to year until basis has been recovered or the agreement is determined to be worthless. The rule requiring initial level allocation of basis over 15 years may not apply if you prove to the IRS that a 15-year general rule will substantially and inappropriately defer recovery of basis.

In some cases, basis recovery under an income forecast type of method may also be allowed.

Caution

Contingent Sales

An example of a contingent sale in which the selling price cannot be determined by the end of the year of the sale is a sale of your business where the selling price includes a percentage of future profits. You and your tax advisor should consult the technical rules in IRS regulation 15A.453-1(c) for details on reporting such sales.

5.26 Using Escrow and Other Security Arrangements

You sell property and the sales proceeds are placed in escrow pending the possible occurrence of an event such as the approval of title or your performance of certain contractual conditions. The IRS may argue that installment reporting is not allowed unless there are escrow restrictions preventing immediate payment.

EXAMPLES

1. Anderson sold stock and mining property for almost $5 million. He agreed to place $500,000 in escrow to protect the buyer against his possible breaches of warranty and to provide security for certain liabilities. The escrow agreement called for Anderson to direct the investments of the escrow fund and receive income from the fund in excess of $500,000.

   The IRS claimed that in the year of sale Anderson was taxable on the $500,000 held in escrow on the ground that Anderson's control of the fund rendered the fund taxable immediately. Anderson argued he was only taxable as the funds were released to him, and the Tax Court agreed. The fund.was not under his unqualified control. He might never get the fund if the liabilities materialized. Although Anderson had a free hand with investment of the money, he still lacked ultimate ownership.
2. Rhodes sold a tract to a buyer who was willing to pay at once the entire purchase price of $157,000. But Rhodes wanted to report the sale on the installment basis over a period of years. The buyer refused to execute a purchase money mortgage on the property to allow the installment sale election (required under prior law) because he wanted clear and unencumbered title to the tract. As a solution, Rhodes asked the buyer to turn over the purchase price to a bank, as escrow agent, which would pay the sum over a five-year period.

   The escrow arrangement failed to support an installment sale. Rhodes was fully taxable on the entire price in the year of the sale. The buyer's payment was unconditional and irrevocable. The escrow arrangement involved no genuine conditions that could defeat Rhodes's right to payment, as the buyer could not revoke, alter, or end the arrangement.

3. In January, an investor sold real estate for $100,000. He received $10,000 as a down payment and six notes, each for $15,000, secured by a deed of trust on the property. The notes, together with interest, were due annually over the next six years. In July, the buyer deposited the remainder of the purchase price with an escrow agent and got the seller to cancel the deed of trust.

   The agreement provides that the escrow agent will pay off the buyer's notes as they fall due. The buyer remains liable for the installment payments. The escrow deposit is irrevocable, and the payment schedule may not be accelerated by any party under any circumstances. According to the IRS, the sale, which initially qualified as an installment sale, is disqualified by the escrow account.

Filing Tip

Installment Reporting on Escrow Allowable

If an escrow arrangement imposes a substantial restriction, the IRS may allow installment reporting. An example of a substantial restriction: Payment of the escrow is tied to the condition that the seller refrain from entering a competing business for a period of five years. If, at any time during the escrow period, he or she engages in a competing business, all rights to the amount then held in escrow would be forfeited.

If the terms of the escrow involve no genuine conditions that prevent you from demanding immediate payment, there will be immediate tax. Substitution of an escrow account for unpaid notes or deeds of trust disqualifies installment reporting.

5.27 Minimum Interest on Deferred Payment Sales

The tax law requires a minimum amount of interest to be charged on deferred payment sales. The rules for imputing interest on sales are discussed in *4.32*. Imputed interest is included in the taxable income of the seller. Imputed interest is deductible by the buyer if the property is business or investment property, but not if it is used substantially all the time for personal purposes.

Caution

Charging Minimum Interest

If you do not charge a minimum interest rate, the IRS may do so. This would require you and the buyer to treat part of the purchase price as interest.

5.28 Dispositions of Installment Notes

A sale, a gift, an exchange or other transfer or cancellation of mortgage notes or other obligations received in an installment sale has tax consequences. If you sell or exchange the notes or if you accept less than face value in satisfaction of the obligation, gain or loss results to the extent of the difference between the basis of the notes and the amount realized. For example, if in satisfaction of an installment note, the buyer gives you other property worth less than the face value of the note, you have gain (or loss) to the extent your amount realized exceeds (or is less than) your basis in the installment note. The basis of an installment note or obligation is the face value of the note less the income that would be reported if the obligation were paid in full; *see* Example 2 below.

EXAMPLES

1. You sell a lot for $200,000 that cost you $100,000. In the year of the sale, you received $50,000 in cash and the purchaser's notes for the remainder of the selling price, or $150,000. A year later, before the buyer makes a payment on the notes, you sell them for $130,000 cash:

Selling price of property	$200,000
Cost of property	100,000
Total profit	$100,000
Profit percentage, or proportion of each payment returnable as income, is 50% ($100,000 total profit ÷ $200,000 contract price)	
Unpaid balance of notes	$150,000
Amount of income reportable if notes were paid in full (50% of $150,000)	75,000
Adjusted basis of the notes	$75,000

   Your profit on the sale is $55,000 ($130,000 – $75,000). It is capital gain if the sale of the lot was taxable as capital gain.

2. You sell a lot on the installment basis for $200,000 that cost you $120,000. In the year of sale, you received $20,000 in cash and the buyer's note for $180,000. Your gross profit percentage is 40% ($80,000 total profit ÷ $200,000 contract price).

   Two years later, the buyer is facing financial difficulties and is unable to make payments on the $180,000 note. In satisfaction of the installment note, the buyer agrees to give you two other parcels of real estate, each worth $50,000. By accepting less than the $180,000 face value of the note in satisfaction of the obligation, you realize an $8,000 capital loss; the difference between the amount you realize and your basis in the installment obligation is figured as follows:

Amount realized ($50,000 for each parcel)	$100,000
Face value of note	180,000
Less: Amount of income reportable if note was paid in full given 40% profit percentage (40% of $180,000 = $72,000)	72,000
Basis in installment note	$108,000

The difference between the $100,000 amount realized and $108,000 basis gives you an $8,000 loss. Assuming your profit on the original sale was long-term capital gain, the loss would be deducted as a long-term capital loss.

Gain or loss is long term if the original sale was entitled to long-term capital gain treatment. This is true even if the notes were held short term. If the original sale resulted in short-term gain or ordinary income, the sale of the notes gives short-term gain or ordinary income, regardless of the holding period of the notes.

Suppose you make an installment sale of your real estate, taking back a land contract. Later a mortgage is substituted for the unpaid balance of the land contract. The IRS has ruled that the substitution is not the same as a disposition of the unpaid installment obligations. There is no tax on the substitution.

Filing Tip

Installment Notes in Marital Transfer

A transfer of installment obligations to your spouse or a transfer to a former spouse that is incident to a divorce is treated as a tax-free exchange *(6.7)* unless the transfer is in trust.

Gift of installment obligation. If the installment obligations are disposed of other than by sale or exchange, such as when you make a gift of the installment obligations to someone else, gain or loss is the difference between the basis of the obligations and their fair market value at the time of the disposition. If an installment obligation is cancelled or otherwise becomes unenforceable, the same rule for determining gain or loss applies. However, no gain or loss is recognized on a gift to a spouse *(6.7)*.

A gift of installment obligations to a person other than a spouse or to a charitable organization is treated as a taxable disposition. Gain or loss is the difference between the basis of the obligations and their fair market value at the time of the gift. If the notes are donated to a qualified charity, you may claim a contribution deduction for the fair market value of the obligations at the time of the gift.

Transfer at death. A transfer of installment obligations at the death of the holder of the obligation is not taxed as a disposition. As the notes are paid, the estate or beneficiaries report income in the same proportion as the decedent would have, had he or she lived. A transfer of installment obligations to a revocable trust is also not taxed. However, the estate is subject to tax if the obligation is cancelled, becomes unenforceable, or is transferred to the buyer because of the death of the obligation holder.

5.29 Repossession of Personal Property Sold on Installment

When a buyer defaults and you repossess personal property, either by a voluntary surrender or a foreclosure, you may realize gain or loss. The method of calculating gain or loss is similar to the method used for disposition of installment notes *(5.28)*. Gain or loss is the difference between the fair market value of the repossessed property and your basis for the installment obligations satisfied by the repossession. This rule is followed whether or not title was kept by you or transferred to the buyer. The amount realized is reduced by costs incurred during the repossession. The basis of the obligation is face value less unreported profit.

If the property repossessed is bid in at a lawful public auction or judicial sale, the fair market value of the property is presumed to be the purchase or bid price, in the absence of proof to the contrary.

Gain or loss in the repossession is reported in the year of the repossession.

EXAMPLE

In December 2009, you sell furniture for $1,500—$300 down and $100 a month plus 6% interest beginning January 2010. You reported the installment sale on your 2009 tax return. The buyer defaulted after making three monthly payments. You foreclosed and repossessed the property; the fair market value was $1,400. The legal costs of foreclosure were $100. The gain on the repossession in 2010 is computed as follows:

Fair market value of property repossessed		$ 1,400
Basis of the buyer's notes at time of repossession:		
Selling price	$ 1,500	
Less: Payments made	600	
Unpaid balance of notes at repossession	$ 900	
Less: Unrealized profit (assume gross profit percentage of $33^{1}/_{3}$ × $900)	$ 300	
Basis of obligation		600
Gain on repossession		$ 800
Less: Repossession costs		100
Taxable gain on repossession		$ 700

Repossession gain or loss keeps the same character as the gain or loss realized on the original sale. If the sale originally resulted in a capital gain, the repossession gain is also a capital gain. Your basis in the repossessed property is its fair market value at the time of repossession.

Real property. Repossessions of real property are discussed in *Chapter 31 (31.12)*.

Planning Reminder

Taxable Boot Received in Exchange

If you make an exchange of like-kind property and also receive cash or other property that is payable in one or more future years, you may report the gain using the installment method.

5.30 Boot in Like-Kind Exchange Payable in Installments

An exchange of like-kind property is tax free unless boot is received. "Boot" may be cash or notes. If you transfer property subject to a mortgage and the amount of the mortgage you give up exceeds the mortgage you assume on the property received, that excess is boot *(6.3)*. Boot is taxable, and if payable in installments, the following rules apply. Contract price is reduced by the fair market value of like-kind property received. Gross profit is reduced by gain not recognized. "Payment" does not include like-kind property.

The same treatment applies to certain tax-free reorganizations that are not treated as dividends, to exchanges of certain insurance policies, exchanges of the stock of the same corporation, and exchanges of United States obligations.

EXAMPLE

In 2010, property with an installment sale basis (basis plus selling expenses) of $400,000 is exchanged for like-kind property worth $200,000, plus installment obligations of $800,000, of which $100,000 is payable in 2011, plus interest. The balance of $700,000 plus interest will be paid in 2012. The contract price is $800,000 ($1 million selling price less $200,000 like-kind property received). The gross profit is $600,000 ($1 million less $400,000 installment sale basis). The gross profit ratio is 75% (gross profit of $600,000 ÷ contract price of $800,000). Like-kind property is not treated as a payment received in the year of sale, so no gain is reported in 2010. In 2011, gain of $75,000 will have to be reported (75% gross profit ratio × $100,000 payment), and in 2012 there will be a gain of $525,000 (75% of $700,000 payment).

5.31 "Interest" Tax on Sales Over $150,000 Plus $5 Million Debt

If deferred payments from installment sales of over $150,000 exceed $5 million, an interest charge is imposed on the tax-deferred amount. The special tax applies to non-dealer sales of business or rental property (real estate or personal property) for over $150,000.

Farm property and personal-use property, such as a residence, are exempt from the tax.

How to report interest tax. The interest charge is an additional tax. The method of computing the interest tax is complicated; the rules are in Internal Revenue Code Section 453A. In general, you compute the ratio of the face amount of outstanding installment obligations in excess of $5 million to the face amount of all outstanding installment obligations. This ratio is multiplied by the year-end unrecognized gain on the obligation, your top tax rate (ordinary income or capital gain) for the year, and also by the IRS interest rate for the last month of the year.

The interest tax is reported on Line 60 of Form 1040, the line for total tax. The tax is considered personal interest, and is not deductible; *see Chapter 15.*

Dealer sale of time shares and residential lots. The above interest tax and pledging rules do not apply to installment obligations from the sale of certain time-share rights (generally time shares of up to six weeks per year) or residential lots. However, under a separate rule, the seller must pay interest on tax deferred under the installment method; *see* the instructions to Line 1 of Schedule C (Form 1040) for reporting the interest charge as an additional tax.

5.32 Worthless Securities

As an investor (not a securities dealer), you may deduct as a capital loss on Schedule D for 2010 the cost basis of a security (stock or bond) that became totally worthless in 2010, subject to the deduction limit of $3,000 in excess of capital gains *(5.4)*. Capital loss treatment applies unless ordinary loss treatment is available for worthless Section 1244 stock *(30.13)*.

A loss of worthless securities is deductible only in the year the securities become completely worthless. If you abandon the securities, the securities are treated as completely worthless under an IRS regulation; *see* below. The loss may not be deducted in any other year. You may not claim a loss for a partially worthless security. However, if there is a market for it, sell the security and deduct the capital loss on Schedule D.

Filing Tip

Refund Deadline for Worthless Stock

You can take advantage of a special seven-year statute of limitations to claim a refund due to a worthless security or bad debt. An amended return for the year the security or debt became worthless can be filed within seven years from the date your original return for that year had to be filed, or, if later, within two years from the date you paid the tax.

For example, if you have held securities that you learn became worthless in 2003, you still have until April 15, 2011, to file for a refund of 2003 taxes by claiming a deduction for the worthless securities on an amended return (Form 1040X) for 2002.

Because it is sometimes difficult to determine the year in which a security becomes completely worthless, the law allows you to file a refund claim within seven years from the due date of the return for the proper year (the year the security actually became completely worthless), or if later, within two years from the date you paid the tax for that year.

To support a deduction for 2010, you must show:

1. The security had some value in 2009. That is, you must be ready to show that the stock did not become worthless in a year prior to 2010. If you learn that the security did become worthless in a prior year, file an amended return for that year; *see* the Filing Tip on this page.
2. The security became totally worthless in 2010. You must be able to present facts fixing the time of loss during this year. For example, the company went bankrupt, stopped doing business, and is insolvent. Despite evidence of worthlessness, such as insolvency, the stock may be considered to have some value if the company continues to do business, or there are plans to reorganize the company. No deduction may be claimed for a partially worthless corporate bond.

If you are making payments on a negotiable note you used to buy the stock that became worthless and you are on the cash-basis method, your payments are deductible losses in the years the payments are made, rather than in the year the stock became worthless.

If the security is a bond, note, certificate, or other evidence of a debt incurred by a corporation, the loss is deducted as a capital loss, provided the obligation is in registered form or has attached interest coupons. A loss on a worthless corporate obligation is always deemed to have been sustained on the last day of the year, regardless of when the company failed during the year.

If the obligation is not issued with interest coupons or in registered form, or if it is issued by an individual, the loss is treated as a bad debt. If you received the obligation in a business transaction, the loss is fully deductible. You may also make a claim for a partially worthless business bad debt. If it is a nonbusiness debt, the loss is a capital loss and no claim may be made for partial worthlessness *(5.33)*.

When to deduct worthless stock. If at the end of 2010 a company is in financial trouble but you are not sure whether its condition is hopeless, it is advisable to claim the deduction for 2010 to protect your claim. This advice was given by a court: "The taxpayer is at times in a very difficult position in determining in what year to claim a loss. The only safe practice, we think, is to claim a loss for the earliest year when it may possibly be allowed and to renew the claim in subsequent years if there is a reasonable chance of its being applicable for those years."

Planning Reminder

Selling Before the Security Becomes Worthless

To claim a deduction for worthless stock or bonds, you must be able to prove that the stock became completely worthless in the year for which you are claiming the deduction. Sometimes you can avoid the problem of proving worthlessness by selling while there is still a market for the security. For example, a company is on the verge of bankruptcy, but in 2011 there is some doubt about the complete worthlessness of its securities. You might sell the securities for whatever you can get for them and claim the loss on the sale. However, if the security became worthless in a prior year, say in 2010, a sale for a nominal sum in 2011 will not give you a deduction in 2011.

If you claim the deduction for 2010 and it turns out that complete worthlessness did not occur until a later year, claim the deduction for the proper year and then file an amended return for 2010 to eliminate the deduction.

Another option in fixing the timing of your loss deduction is to abandon the securities, as discussed below.

Abandoned securities treated as worthless. An IRS final regulation treats abandoned securities as totally worthless, effective for abandonments after March 12, 2008. To abandon a security, you must permanently surrender and relinquish all rights in the security and receive no payment in exchange for the security. The IRS will determine whether these tests have been met based on all the facts and circumstances. Under the general timing rule for worthless securities, the loss on abandonment is treated as resulting from a sale of a capital asset on the last day of the year in which the abandonment occurs.

Reporting long-term or short-term loss on Schedule D. If securities became worthless during 2010, they are treated as if they were sold on the last day of the year, regardless of when worthlessness actually occurred.

EXAMPLE

You bought 100 shares of Z Co. stock on July 1, 1999. On March 22, 2010, the stock is considered wholly worthless. The loss is deemed to have been incurred on December 31, 2010. The loss is deducted as a long-term capital loss; the holding period is from July 2, 1999, to December 31, 2010.

Ordinary loss on Small Business Investment Company (SBIC) stock. On Form 4797, investors may take ordinary loss deductions for losses on the worthlessness or sale of SBIC stock. The loss may also be treated as a business loss for net operating loss purposes. However, a loss realized on a short sale of SBIC stock is deductible as a capital loss. A Small Business Investment Company is a company authorized to provide small businesses with equity capital. Do not confuse investments in these companies with investments in small business stock (Section 1244 stock) *(30.13)*.

S corporation stock. If an S corporation's stock becomes worthless during the taxable year, the basis in the stock is adjusted for the stockholder's share of corporate items of income, loss, and deductions before a deduction for worthlessness is claimed.

Bank deposit loss. If you lose funds in a bank that becomes insolvent, you may claim the loss as a nonbusiness bad debt *(5.33)*, a casualty loss *(18.5)*, or in some cases, an investment expense *(19.15)*. These options are discussed in *Chapter 18 (18.5)*.

5.33 Tax Consequences of Bad Debts

When you lend money or sell on credit and your debtor does not repay, you may deduct your loss. The type of deduction depends on whether the debt was incurred in a business or personal transaction. This distinction is important because business bad debts receive favored tax treatment.

Business bad debt. A business bad debt is fully deductible from gross income on Schedule C if you are self-employed, or on Schedule F if your business is farming. You may deduct partially worthless business debts; *see* IRS Publication 535 for details.

Nonbusiness bad debt. A nonbusiness bad debt is deducted as a short-term capital loss on Schedule D. This is a limited deduction. For 2010, you deduct it from capital gains, if any, and $3,000 of ordinary income ($1,500 if married filing seperately). Any excess is deductible as a capital loss carryover to 2011 and later years *(5.4)*. You may not deduct partially worthless nonbusiness bad debts. The debt must be totally worthless.

Examples of nonbusiness bad debts:

- You enter into a deal for profit that is not connected with your business; for example, debts arising from investments are nonbusiness bad debts.
- You make a personal loan to a family member or friend with a reasonable hope of recovery and you are not in the business of making loans. You must be able to show that this is a bona fide loan and not a gift. Put the loan in writing and spell out repayment terms.
- You are assigned a debt that arose in the assignor's business. The fact that he or she could have deducted it as a business bad debt does not make it your business debt. A business debt must arise in your business.

Caution

Accounts and Notes Receivable

You may claim a bad debt deduction for accounts and notes receivable on unpaid goods or services only if you have included the amount due as gross income. Thus, if a client or customer fails to pay a bill for services rendered, you do not have a deductible bad debt where you have not reported the amount as income *(40.6)*.

- You pay liens filed against your property by mechanics or suppliers who have not been paid by your builder or contractor. Your payment is considered a deductible bad debt when there is no possibility of recovering reimbursement from the contractor and a judgment obtained against him or her is uncollectible.
- You lose a deposit on a house when the contractor becomes insolvent.
- You loan money to a corporation in which you are a shareholder, and your primary motivation is to protect your investment rather than your job; *see* below.
- You had an uninsured savings account in a financial institution that went into default. Instead of claiming the bank deposit loss as a nonbusiness bad debt, the loss may be claimed as a casualty loss, or in some cases, as an investment loss *(18.5)*.
- You are held secondarily liable on a mortgage debt assumed but not paid by a buyer of your home. Your payment to the bank or other holder of the mortgage is deductible as a bad debt if you cannot collect it from the buyer of the home.

Filing Instruction

Nonbusiness Bad Debt

If a nonbusiness bad debt became totally worthless in 2010, claim it as a short-term capital loss in Part I of Schedule D. Attach a statement describing the loan, your relationship to the debtor, how you tried to collect it, and why you decided it was worthless.

Guarantor or endorsement losses as bad debts. If you guarantee a loan and must pay it off after the principal debtor defaults, your payment is deductible as a business bad debt if you had a business reason for the guarantee. For example, to protect a business relationship with a major client, you guarantee the client's loan. Your payment on the guarantee qualifies as a business bad debt. If, as a result of your payment, you have a legal right to recover the amount from the client (right of subrogation or similar right), you may not claim a bad debt deduction unless that right is partially or totally worthless.

A loss on a guarantee may be a nonbusiness bad debt if you made the guarantee to protect an investment, such as where you are a main shareholder of a corporation and guarantee a bank loan to the company. No deduction is allowed if you guaranteed the loan as a favor to a relative or friend. Bank deposit losses are discussed in *Chapter 18 (18.5)*.

Loans by shareholders. It is a common practice for stockholders to make loans to their corporations or to guarantee loans made to the company by banks or other lenders. If the corporation fails and the stockholder is not repaid or has to make good on the guarantee, tax treatment of the bad debt depends on whether the stockholder is an employee who made the loan to protect his or her job. If the dominant motivation for the loan was to maintain employment, the bad debt is an employee business expense deductible only as a miscellaneous itemized deduction subject to the 2% of adjusted gross income floor *(19.1)*. If the dominant motivation for the loan was to protect the stockholder's investment in the company and not his or her job, the bad debt is generally a nonbusiness bad debt deductible on Schedule D as a short-term capital loss.

If the stockholder is in the business of lending money and the loan was made in that capacity, the bad debt would be a business bad debt, deductible on Schedule C by a sole proprietor.

5.34 Four Rules To Prove a Bad Debt Deduction

To determine whether you have a bad debt deduction in 2010, read the four rules explained below. Pay close attention to the fourth rule, which requires proof that the debt became worthless in the year the deduction is claimed. Your belief that your debt is bad, or the mere refusal of the debtor to pay, is not sufficient evidence. There must be an event, such as the debtor's bankruptcy, to fix the debt as worthless.

Planning Reminder

Debt Worthless Before Due

You do not have to wait until the debt is due in order to deduct a bad debt. Claim the deduction for the year that you can prove worthlessness occurred.

Rule 1. You must have a valid debt. You have no loss if your right to repayment is not fixed or depends upon some event that may not happen. Thus, advances to a corporation already insolvent are not valid debts. Nor are advances that are to be repaid only if the corporation has a profit. Voluntary payment of another's debt is also nondeductible. If usurious interest was charged on a worthless debt, and under state law the debt was void or voidable, the debt is not deductible as a bad debt. However, where the lender was in the business of lending money, a court allowed him to deduct the unpaid amounts as business losses.

If advances are made to a company that has lost outside borrowing sources and is thinly capitalized, with heavy debt-to-equity ratio, this indicates that the advances are actually capital contributions and not loans.

Rule 2. A debtor-creditor relationship must exist at the time the debt arose. You have a loss if there was a promise to repay at the time the debt was created and you had the right to enforce it. If the advance was a gift and you did not expect to be repaid, you may not take a deduction.

Rule 3. The funds providing the loan or credit were previously reported as income or part of your capital. If you are on the cash basis, you may not deduct unpaid salary, rent, or fees. On the cash basis, you do not include these items in income until you are paid.

Rule 4. You must show that the debt became worthless during 2010. To prove the debt became worthless in 2010, you must show:

First, that the debt had some value at the end of the previous year (2009), and that there was a reasonable hope and expectation of recovering something on the debt. Your personal belief unsupported by other facts is not enough.

Second, that an identifiable event occurred in 2010—such as a bankruptcy proceeding—that caused you to conclude the debt was worthless. In the case of a business debt that has become partially worthless, you need evidence that the debt has declined in value. Additionally, reasonable collection steps must have been undertaken. That you cancel a debt does not make it worthless. You must still show that the debt was worthless when you cancelled it. You do not have to go to court to try to collect the debt if you can show that a court judgment would be uncollectible.

Third, that there is no reasonable hope the debt may have some value in a later year. You are not required to prove that there is no possibility of ever receiving some payment on your debt.

Effect of statute of limitations. A debt is not deductible merely because a statute of limitations has run against the debt. Although the debtor has a legal defense against your demand for payment, he or she may still recognize the obligation to pay. A debt is deductible only in the year it becomes worthless. This event—for example, the debtor's insolvency—may have occurred even before the statute became effective. What if your debtor recognized his or her moral obligation to pay in spite of the expiration of the statute of limitations, but dies before paying? Your claim would be defeated if the executor raises the statute of limitations. You have a bad debt deduction in the year you made the claim against the estate.

5.35 Family Bad Debts

The IRS views loans to relatives, especially to children and parents, as gifts, so that it is rather difficult to deduct family bad debts.

To overcome the presumption of a gift when you advance money to a relative, take the same steps you would in making a business loan. Take a note, set a definite payment date, and require interest and collateral. If the relative fails to pay, make an attempt to collect. Failure to enforce collection of a family debt is viewed by the courts as evidence of a gift, despite the taking of notes and the receipt of interest.

Caution

Formalize Loan With Relative

To protect against a possible IRS claim that your loan was a gift and not a loan, put the loan in writing with repayment terms as if the debtor were a third party.

Husband's default on child support—a basis for wife's deductible bad debt? A wife who supports her children when her husband defaults on court-ordered support payments may consider claiming her expenses as a nonbusiness bad debt deduction, arguing that her position is similar to a guarantor who pays a creditor when the principal debtor defaults. The IRS does not agree with the grounds of such a claim and will disallow the deduction; its position is supported by the Tax Court.

The federal appeals court for the Ninth Circuit left open the possibility that such a claim may have merit if a wife can show: (1) what she spent on the children; and (2) that her husband's obligation to support was worthless in the year the deduction is claimed.

The Tax Court has subsequently reiterated its position that defaulted child support payments are not a basis for a bad debt deduction. Following these Tax Court decisions, the IRS also announced its continuing opposition to the Ninth Circuit's suggestion that a deduction may be possible. The IRS holds that since the support obligation of the defaulting spouse is imposed directly by the divorce court, the other parent who pays support to make up for the arrearage has no "basis" to support a bad debt deduction.

Periodically, legislation has been proposed to allow a bad debt deduction for unpaid child support, but none of the proposals have been enacted into law.

Chapter 6

Tax-Free Exchanges of Property

You may exchange property without incurring a tax in the year of exchange if you meet the rules detailed in this chapter. Gain may be taxed upon a later disposition of the property because the basis of the property received in the exchange is usually the same as the basis of the property surrendered in the exchange. Thus, if you exchange property with a tax basis of $10,000 for property worth $50,000, the basis of the property received in exchange is fixed at $10,000, even though its fair market value is $50,000. The gain of $40,000 ($50,000 – $10,000), which is not taxed, is technically called "unrecognized gain." If you later sell the property for $50,000, you will realize a taxable gain of $40,000 ($50,000 – $10,000).

Where property received in a tax-free exchange is held until death, the unrecognized gain escapes income tax forever because basis of the property in the hands of an heir is generally the value of the property at the date of death. If the exchange involves the transfer of boot, such as cash or other property, gain on the exchange is taxable to the extent of the value of boot.

You may not exchange U.S. real estate for foreign real estate tax free.

Tax-free exchanges between related parties may become taxable if either party disposes of the exchanged property within a two-year period.

6.1 Trades of Like-Kind Property

You may not have to pay tax on gain realized on the "like-kind" exchange of business or investment property. By making a qualifying exchange, you can defer the gain. On the other hand, a loss is not deductible unless you give up "unlike" property (not like-kind); *see* below. For tax-free gain treatment, you must trade property held for business use or investment for like-kind business or investment property. If the properties are not simultaneously exchanged, the time limits for deferred exchanges *(6.4)* must be satisfied. The entire gain is deferred only if you do not receive any "boot"; gain is taxed to the extent of boot received *(6.3)*. Where gain on a qualifying exchange is deferred and not immediately taxed, it may be taxable in a later year when you sell the property because your basis for the new property is generally the same as the basis for the property you traded *(5.16 – 5.20)*.

If you make a qualifying like-kind exchange with certain related parties, tax-free treatment may be lost unless both of you keep the exchanged properties for at least two years *(6.6)*.

The term *like-kind* refers to the nature or character of the property, that is, whether real estate is traded for real estate. It does not refer to grade or quality, that is, whether the properties traded are new or used, improved or unimproved. In the case of real estate, land may be traded for a building, farm land for city lots, or a leasehold interest of 30 years or more for an outright ownership in realty. Trades of personal property are discussed in *6.2*.

Filing Instruction

Depreciation of Property Received in Exchange

If you make a like-kind exchange of depreciable MACRS property *(42.4)* for other MACRS property, your basis for the new property is the same as the basis of the traded property. You depreciate that basis over the remaining recovery period, and using the same rate and convention *(42.5)* as for the traded property.

If you also paid cash as part of the exchange, you have an additional basis attributable to that investment that is depreciable as new MACRS property subject to a new recovery period.

EXAMPLES

1. Jones, a real estate investor, purchased Parcel A for investment in 1986 for $5,000. In 2004, he exchanged it for another parcel, Parcel B, which had a fair market value of $50,000. The gain of $45,000 was not taxed in 2004.
2. Same facts as above, except that in 2010 Jones sells Parcel B for $50,000. His taxable gain in 2010 is $45,000. The "tax-free" exchange rules have the effect of deferring tax on appreciation until the property received in the exchange is sold.
3. Same facts as in 1 above, but the value of Parcel B was $3,000 in 2004. Jones could not deduct the loss in 2004. The basis of the parcel is $5,000, the same as the basis of Parcel A. If Jones sells Parcel B in 2010 for $3,000, he may deduct a loss of $2,000.

Personal use safe harbor for rental residence. The IRS has provided a safe harbor (Revenue Procedure 2008-16) that allows rental real estate used occasionally as a vacation home to be treated as investment property so that tax-deferred treatment on an exchange is not endangered. The safe harbor applies to exchanges occurring on or after March 10, 2008.

To qualify, the residence has to be owned for at least 24 months immediately before the exchange, and, in each of the two 12-month periods immediately preceding the exchange, the residence must be rented at a fair rental for at least 14 days and personal use by the owner and his or her relatives cannot exceed the greater of 14 days or 10% of the days for which the residence is rented at a fair rental in the 12-month period.

Parallel requirements apply to the residence received (replacement residence) in the exchange. The replacement residence must be owned for at least 24 months after the exchange and, within each of the two 12-month periods following the exchange, it must be rented at a fair rental for 14 days or more and the taxpayer's personal use (including use by relatives) cannot exceed the greater of 14 days or 10% of the fair rental days during the 12-month period.

If a taxpayer expects to meet the fair rental and personal use tests for the replacement residence and based on that expectation reports the exchange on his or her return as a tax-deferred exchange, but it turns out that the tests are not met, an amended return must be filed to report the exchange as a taxable sale.

Caution

Exchanging Depreciable Realty Subject to Depreciation Recapture

Recapture provisions supersede tax-free exchange rules. Thus, if you exchange a depreciable building placed in service before 1987, depreciation recapture may apply, so check the consequences of any "recapture" element. For example, if you exchange the building for land, the recaptured amount is fully taxable as ordinary income; *see 44.2.*

Losses. If a loss is incurred on a like-kind exchange, the loss is not deductible, whether you receive only like-kind property or "unlike" property together with like-kind property. However, a deductible loss may be incurred if you give up unlike property as part of the exchange; the loss equals any excess of the adjusted basis of the unlike property over its fair market value.

Reporting an exchange. You must file Form 8824 to report an exchange of like-kind property. If you figure a recognized gain or loss on Form 8824, you also must report the exchange on Schedule D (investment property) or Form 4797 (business property).

See below for reporting an exchange with a related party *(6.6)*.

Property not within the tax-free trade rules:

Property used for personal purposes (but exchanges of principal residences may qualify as tax free under different rules; *see Chapter 29*)
Foreign real estate
Property held for sale
Inventory or stock-in-trade
Securities
Notes
Partnership interest; *see* below

See also 31.3 for tax-free exchanges of realty and *6.12* for tax-free exchanges of insurance policies.

Exchange of partnership interests. Exchanges of partnership interests in different partnerships are not within the tax-free exchange rules. Under IRS regulations, tax-free exchange treatment is denied regardless of whether the interests are in the same or different partnerships.

If you made an election to exclude a partnership interest from the application of partnership rules, your interest is treated as interest in each partnership asset, not as an interest in the partnership.

Real estate or personal property in foreign countries. You may not make a tax-free exchange of U.S. real estate for foreign real estate; by law they are not considered like-kind property. However, if your real estate is condemned, foreign and U.S. real estate are treated as like-kind property for purposes of making a tax-free reinvestment *(18.23)*.

You may not make tax-free exchanges of personal property used predominantly in the U.S. for personal property used predominantly outside the U.S.

6.2 Personal Property Held for Business or Investment

Gain on an exchange of depreciable tangible personal property held for productive business or investment use is not taxed if the properties meet either the general like-kind test *(6.1)* or a more specific "like-class" test created by IRS regulations. The assumption of liabilities is treated as "boot" *(6.3)*. Where each party assumes a liability of the other party, the respective liabilities are offset against each other to figure boot, if any.

Under the like-class test, there are two types of "like" classes: (1) General Asset Classes and (2) Product Classes. The like-class test is satisfied if the exchanged properties are both within the same General Asset Class or the same Product Class. A specific asset may be classified within only one class. Thus, if an asset is within an Asset Class, it is not within a Product Class. The Asset Class or Product Class is determined as of the date of the exchange. This limitation may disqualify an exchange when exchanged assets do not fit within the same Asset Class and are not allowed to qualify within the Product Class; *see* the Brown Example below.

Planning Reminder

The "Like-Class" Test

Gain on an exchange is not taxed if the exchanged properties are either "like kind" or "like class." The like-class test is satisfied if the exchanged properties are both within the same General Asset Class or the same Product Class; *see 6.2*. The Asset Class or Product Class is determined at the time of transfer.

General Asset Classes. There are 13 classes of depreciable tangible business property. Here are some of the asset classifications: office furniture, fixtures, and equipment (class 00.11); information systems: computers and peripheral equipment (class 00.12); data handling equipment, except computers (class 00.13); airplanes and helicopters, except for airplanes used to carry passengers or freight (class 00.21); automobiles and taxis (class 00.22); light trucks (class 00.241); heavy trucks (class 00.242); and over-the-road tractor units (class 00.26). For example, trades of trucks in class 00.241 would be of like class.

Even if exchanged properties are in different General Asset Classes (and thus are not of "like class"), they can be of like kind, so that gain on the exchange is not immediately taxed under the like-kind exchange rules *(6.1)*. For example, the IRS in a private ruling held that although an SUV and an automobile are in different asset classes, the differences between them are merely in grade or quality and do not rise to the level of a difference in nature or character. They are therefore of like kind and gain on the exchange is not taxed.

Product Classes. The IRS uses the North American Industry Classification System (NAICS) for determining product classes of depreciable tangible personal property. A product class is assigned a six-digit NAICS code.

EXAMPLES

1. Baker exchanges a personal computer used in his business for a printer. Both assets are productively used in business and are in the same General Asset Class of 00.12; the exchange meets the like-class test.
2. Brown exchanges an airplane (asset class 00.21) used in her business for a heavy truck (asset class 00.242). The exchanged properties are not of a like class. Furthermore, since each property is within a specific General Asset Class, the Product Class test may not be applied to qualify the exchange. Brown must report any gain realized on the exchange because the properties also do not meet the general like-kind test.

Intangible personal property and goodwill. Exchanges of intangible personal property (such as a patent or copyright) or nondepreciable personal property must meet the general like-kind test to qualify for tax-free treatment; the like-class tests do not apply. However, regulations close the door for qualifying exchanges of goodwill in an exchange of going businesses. According to the regulations, goodwill or going concern value of one business can never be of a like kind to goodwill or going concern value of another business.

Exchanges of multiple properties. Generally, exchanges of assets are considered on a one-to-one basis. Regulations provide an exception for exchanges of multiple properties, such as an exchange of businesses. Transferred assets are separated into exchange groups. An exchange group consists of all properties transferred and received in the exchange that are of a like kind or like class. All properties within the same General Asset Class or same Product Class are in the same exchange group. For example, automobiles and computers are exchanged for other automobiles and computers; two exchange groups are set up—one for the automobiles and the other for the computers. If the aggregate fair market values of the properties transferred and received in each exchange group are not equal, the regulations provide calculations for setting up a residual group for purposes of calculating taxable gain, if any.

All liabilities of which a taxpayer is relieved in the exchange are offset against all liabilities assumed by the taxpayer in the exchange, regardless of whether the liabilities are recourse, nonrecourse, or are secured by the specific property transferred or received. If excess liabilities are assumed by the taxpayer as part of the exchange, regulations provide rules for allocating the excess among the properties.

6.3 Receipt of Cash and Other Property—"Boot"

If, in addition to like-kind *(6.1)* property, you receive cash or other property (unlike kind), gain is taxable up to the amount of the cash and the fair market value of any *unlike* property received. The additional cash or unlike property is called "boot." If a loss was incurred on the exchange, the receipt of boot does not permit you to deduct the loss unless it is attributable to *unlike*-kind property you gave up in the exchange.

If you transfer mortgaged property, the amount of the mortgage is part of your boot. If both you and the other party transfer and receive mortgaged property, the party giving up the larger debt treats the excess as taxable boot. The party giving up the smaller debt does not have boot; *see* also *31.3*. If you pay cash to the other party, add this to the mortgage you receive in figuring which party has given up the larger debt.

Caution

Deducting a Loss

You may deduct a loss incurred on an exchange if it is attributable to unlike property *transferred* in the exchange. The loss is recognized to the extent that the basis of the unlike property (other than cash) transferred exceeds its fair market value. However, a loss is not recognized if the unlike property is *received* together with the like-kind property in the exchange. Such a loss is *not* deductible.

Form 8824. The computation of boot, gain (or loss), and basis of the property received is made on Form 8824. Form 8824 must be filed for the year in which you transfer like-kind property. If the other party to the exchange is related to you, Form 8824 must also be filed for each of the two years following your transfer *(6.6)*.

EXAMPLE

Jones owns an apartment house with a fair market value of $220,000, subject to an $80,000 mortgage. His adjusted basis is $100,000. Jones exchanges his building for Smith's apartment building, which has a value of $250,000, subject to a $150,000 mortgage. Jones also receives $40,000 in cash. Smith's adjusted basis for the building he trades is $175,000. Smith and Jones each pay $5,000 in exchange expenses.

Sample Form 8824 for Jones (see the Example beginning on the preceding page)

Form 8824 (2010) Page **2**

Name(s) shown on tax return. Do not enter name and social security number if shown on other side.
John Jones

Your social security number **X00-01-XX11**

Part III **Realized Gain or (Loss), Recognized Gain, and Basis of Like-Kind Property Received**

Caution: *If you transferred* **and** *received* **(a)** *more than one group of like-kind properties or* **(b)** *cash or other (not like-kind) property, see* **Reporting of multi-asset exchanges** *in the instructions.*

Note: *Complete lines 12 through 14* **only** *if you gave up property that was not like-kind. Otherwise, go to line 15.*

Line	Description		Amount
12	Fair market value (FMV) of other property given up	12	
13	Adjusted basis of other property given up	13	
14	Gain or (loss) recognized on other property given up. Subtract line 13 from line 12. Report the gain or (loss) in the same manner as if the exchange had been a sale	14	
	Caution: *If the property given up was used previously or partly as a home, see* **Property used as home** *in the instructions.*		
15	Cash received, FMV of other property received, plus net liabilities assumed by other party, reduced (but not below zero) by any exchange expenses you incurred (see instructions)	15	40,000
16	FMV of like-kind property you received	16	250,000
17	Add lines 15 and 16	17	250,000
18	Adjusted basis of like-kind property you gave up, net amounts paid to other party, plus any exchange expenses **not** used on line 15 (see instructions)	18	175,000
19	**Realized gain or (loss).** Subtract line 18 from line 17	19	115,000
20	Enter the smaller of line 15 or line 19, but not less than zero	20	40,000
21	Ordinary income under recapture rules. Enter here and on Form 4797, line 16 (see instructions)	21	-0-
22	Subtract line 21 from line 20. If zero or less, enter -0-. If more than zero, enter here and on Schedule D or Form 4797, unless the installment method applies (see instructions)	22	40,000
23	**Recognized gain.** Add lines 21 and 22	23	40,000
24	Deferred gain or (loss). Subtract line 23 from line 19. If a related party exchange, see instructions	24	75,000
25	**Basis of like-kind property received.** Subtract line 15 from the sum of lines 18 and 23	25	175,000

Form **8824** (2010)

Sample Form 8824 for Smith (see the Example beginning on the preceding page)

Form 8824 (2010) Page **2**

Name(s) shown on tax return. Do not enter name and social security number if shown on other side.
Al Smith

Your social security number **11X-10-X00X**

Part III **Realized Gain or (Loss), Recognized Gain, and Basis of Like-Kind Property Received**

Caution: *If you transferred* **and** *received* **(a)** *more than one group of like-kind properties or* **(b)** *cash or other (not like-kind) property, see* **Reporting of multi-asset exchanges** *in the instructions.*

Note: *Complete lines 12 through 14* **only** *if you gave up property that was not like-kind. Otherwise, go to line 15.*

Line	Description		Amount
12	Fair market value (FMV) of other property given up	12	
13	Adjusted basis of other property given up	13	
14	Gain or (loss) recognized on other property given up. Subtract line 13 from line 12. Report the gain or (loss) in the same manner as if the exchange had been a sale	14	
	Caution: *If the property given up was used previously or partly as a home, see* **Property used as home** *in the instructions.*		
15	Cash received, FMV of other property received, plus net liabilities assumed by other party, reduced (but not below zero) by any exchange expenses you incurred (see instructions)	15	30,000
16	FMV of like-kind property you received	16	220,000
17	Add lines 15 and 16	17	250,000
18	Adjusted basis of like-kind property you gave up, net amounts paid to other party, plus any exchange expenses **not** used on line 15 (see instructions)	18	180,000
19	**Realized gain or (loss).** Subtract line 18 from line 17	19	70,000
20	Enter the smaller of line 15 or line 19, but not less than zero	20	30,000
21	Ordinary income under recapture rules. Enter here and on Form 4797, line 16 (see instructions)	21	-0-
22	Subtract line 21 from line 20. If zero or less, enter -0-. If more than zero, enter here and on Schedule D or Form 4797, unless the installment method applies (see instructions)	22	30,000
23	**Recognized gain.** Add lines 21 and 22	23	30,000
24	Deferred gain or (loss). Subtract line 23 from line 19. If a related party exchange, see instructions	24	40,000
25	**Basis of like-kind property received.** Subtract line 15 from the sum of lines 18 and 23	25	180,000

Form **8824** (2010)

The sample Forms 8824 for Jones and Smith show how they report the exchange. On Line 15, they show the boot received; their taxable below gain is limited to this boot. For Jones, boot is the $40,000 in cash received. The $80,000 in liabilities transferred to Smith is not included because it does not exceed the $150,000 of liabilities Jones assumed.

For Smith, the Line 15 boot is $30,000:

Mortgage transferred	$150,000
Less: Mortgage assumed	(80,000)
Less: Cash paid	(40,000)
Boot received by Smith	$30,000

On Line 18, Jones and Smith increase their basis for the buildings they traded by exchange expenses and the net amounts paid to the other party. For Jones, the Line 18 total of $175,000 includes:

Adjusted basis of building traded		$100,000
Plus: Exchange expenses		5,000
Plus: Net mortgage assumed:		
Mortgage assumed	$150,000	
Less: Mortgage transferred	80,000	70,000
	70,000	$175,000

For Smith, the Line 18 total of $180,000 includes:

Adjusted basis of building traded		$175,000
Plus: Exchange expenses		5,000
Plus: Net amount paid:		
Mortgage assumed	$80,000	
Plus: Cash paid	40,000	
Less: Mortgage transferred	(150,000)	0
	(30,000)	$180,000

The liabilities Smith assumed and the cash he paid are not included on Line 18 because their total does not exceed the $150,000 of liabilities he transferred to Jones. Line 25 shows the basis of the buildings Jones and Smith received in the exchange.

6.4 Time Limits for Deferred Exchanges

Assume you own property that has appreciated in value. You want to sell it and reinvest the proceeds in other property, but you would like to avoid having to pay tax on the appreciation. You can defer the tax on the gain if you are able to arrange an exchange for like-kind *(6.1)* property.

The problem is that it may be difficult to find a buyer who has property you want in exchange, and the time for closing the exchange is restricted. If IRS tests are met, intermediaries and security arrangements may be used without running afoul of constructive receipt rules that could trigger an immediate tax.

Deferred exchange distinguished from a reverse exchange. A *deferred* exchange is one in which you first transfer investment or business property and then later receive like-kind investment or business property *(6.1)*. If before you receive the replacement property you actually or constructively receive money or unlike property as full payment for the property you have transferred, the transaction will be treated as a sale rather than a deferred exchange. In that case, you must recognize gain (or loss) on the transaction even if you later receive like-kind replacement property. In determining whether you have received money or unlike property, you may take advantage of certain safe harbor security arrangements that allow you to ensure that the replacement property will be provided to you without jeopardizing like-kind exchange treatment; *see* below for the safe harbor security tests.

A *reverse* exchange is one in which you acquire replacement property before you transfer the relinquished property. The like-kind exchange rules generally do not apply to reverse exchanges.

However, the IRS has provided safe harbor rules that allow like-kind exchange treatment to be obtained if either the replacement property or the relinquished property is held in a *qualified exchange accommodation arrangement (QEAA)* *(6.5)*.

Time limits for completing deferred exchanges. You generally have up to 180 days to complete an exchange, but the period may be shorter. Specifically, property will not be treated as like-kind property if received (1) more than 180 days after the date you transferred the property you are relinquishing or (2) after the due date of your return (including extensions) for the year in which you made the transfer, whichever is earlier. Furthermore, the property to be received must be identified within 45 days after the date on which you transferred property.

If the transaction involves more than one property, the 45-day identification period and the 180-day exchange period are determined by the earliest date on which any property is transferred. When the identification or exchange period ends on a Saturday, Sunday, or legal holiday, the deadline is not advanced to the next business day (as it is when the deadline for filing a tax return is on a weekend or holiday).

Caution

Strict Time Limits

No extensions of time are allowed if the 45-day or 180-day statutory deadline for a deferred exchange cannot be met. If extra time is needed for finding suitable replacement property, it is advisable to delay the date of your property transfer because the transfer date starts the 45-day identification period.

How to identify replacement property. You must identify replacement property in a written document signed by you and either hand delivered, mailed, telecopied, or otherwise sent before the end of the 45-day identification period to a person involved in the exchange other than yourself or a related party. The identification may also be made in a written agreement. The property must be unambiguously described by a legal description or street address.

You may identify more than one property as replacement property. However, the maximum number of replacement properties that you may identify without regard to the fair market value is three properties. You may identify any number of properties provided the aggregate fair market value at the end of the 45-day identification period does not exceed 200% of the aggregate fair market value of all the relinquished properties as of the date you transferred them. If, as of the end of the identification period, you have identified more than the allowable number of properties, you are generally treated as if no replacement property has been identified.

If property is valued at no more than 15% of the total value of a larger item of property that it is transferred with, the smaller property is considered "incidental" and does not have to be separately identified.

Receipt of security. In a deferred exchange, you want financial security for the buyer's performance and compensation for delay in receiving property. To avoid immediate tax, you must not make a security arrangement that gives you an unrestricted right to funds before the deal is closed.

EXAMPLE

You and Jones agree to enter a deferred exchange under the following terms and conditions. On May 14, 2010, you transfer to Jones real estate that has been held for investment; it is unencumbered and has a fair market value of $100,000. On or before June 28, 2010 (the end of the 45-day identification period), you must identify like-kind replacement property. On or before November 10, 2010 (the end of the 180-day exchange period), Jones is required to buy the property and transfer it to you. At any time after May 14, 2010, and before Jones has purchased the replacement property, you have the right, upon notice, to demand that he pay you $100,000 instead of acquiring and transferring the replacement property. However, you identify replacement property, and Jones purchases and transfers it to you. According to the regulations, you have an unrestricted right to demand the payment of $100,000 as of May 14, 2010. You are therefore in constructive receipt of $100,000 on that date. Thus, the transaction is treated as a taxable sale, and the transfer of the real property does not qualify as a tax-free exchange. You are treated as if you received the $100,000 for the sale of your property and then purchased replacement property.

Safe harbor tests for deferred exchange security arrangements. If one of the following safe harbors applies to your security arrangement, you are not taxed as if a sale were made and like-kind exchange treatment may be obtained.

The first two "safe harbors" cover transfers dealing directly with the buyer. The third allows the use of professional intermediaries who, for a fee, arrange the details of the deferred exchange. The fourth allows you to earn interest on an escrow account. The safe harbors generally prohibit you from receiving money or other non-like-kind property before replacement property is received. The terms of the agreement govern whether your right to receive the funds is limited as required by the safe harbor rules; possible state law complications are disregarded.

1. The transferee may give you a mortgage, deed of trust, or other security interest in property (other than cash or a cash equivalent), or a third-party guarantee. A standby letter of credit may be given if you are not allowed to draw on such standby letter except upon a default of the transferee's obligation to transfer like-kind replacement property.

2. The transferee may put cash or a cash equivalent in a qualified escrow account or a qualified trust. The escrow holder or trustee must not be related to you. Your rights to receive, pledge, borrow, or otherwise obtain the cash must be limited. For example, you may obtain the cash after all of the replacement property to which you are entitled is received. After you identify replacement property, you may obtain the cash after the later of (1) the end of the identification period and (2) the occurrence of a contingency beyond your control that you have specified in writing. You may receive the funds after the end of the identification period if within that period you do not identify replacement property. In other cases, there can be no right to the funds until the exchange period ends.

3. You may use a *qualified intermediary* if your right to receive money or other property is limited (as discussed in safe harbor rule 2, above). A qualified intermediary (QI) is an unrelated party who, for a fee, acts to facilitate a deferred exchange by entering into an agreement with you for the exchange of properties pursuant to which the intermediary acquires your property from you, acquires the replacement property, and transfers the replacement property to you. Typically, the QI transfers your property to the buyer in exchange for cash and uses the cash to purchase the replacement property that will be transferred to you.

   There are restrictions on who may act as an intermediary. You may not employ any person as an intermediary who is your employee or is related to you or your agent or has generally acted as your professional adviser, such as an attorney, accountant, investment broker, real estate agent, or banker, in a two-year period preceding the exchange. Related parties include family members and controlled businesses or trusts *(5.6)*, except that for purposes of control, a 10% interest is sufficient under the intermediary rule. The performance of routine financial, escrow, trust, or title insurance services by a financial institution or title company within the two-year period is not taken into account. State laws that may be interpreted as fixing an agency relationship between the transferor and transferee or fixing the transferor's right to security funds are ignored.

   In a simultaneous exchange, the intermediary is not considered the transferor's agent.

4. You are permitted to receive interest or a "growth factor" on escrowed funds if your right to receive the amount is limited as discussed under safe harbor rule 2.

IRS Alert

Safe Harbor If Exchange Fails Due to Qualified Intermediary's Default

The IRS has provided relief if you hire a qualified intermediary (QI) to facilitate an exchange but are unable to meet the deadlines for relinquishing or receiving replacement property solely because the QI defaults on its obligations due to bankruptcy or receivership proceedings. By meeting the requirements of Revenue Procedure 2010-14, you can use a safe harbor that allows you to avoid having to report gain from the failed exchange until payments attributable to the relinquished property are received. A safe harbor gross profits ratio method is provided for reporting the gain. The safe harbor applies to exchanges that fail because of QI defaults occurring after 2008. If an exchange failed because of a QI's default before 2009, safe harbor relief can be claimed on an original or amended return that is filed within the regular three-year period for filing a refund claim *(47.2)*. *See* Revenue Procedure 2010-14 for further details including examples on applying the safe harbor.

Escrow account earnings are generally exempt from imputed interest rules. Under final IRS regulations, it is possible for a taxpayer who has an escrow arrangement with a qualified intermediary to be taxed on imputed interest, but there is a $2 million exemption that is expected to apply to the majority of exchange arrangements with small business exchange facilitators. Under the regulations, when a qualified intermediary holds exchange funds (cash, cash equivalents, or relinquished property) in escrow for a taxpayer under a deferred exchange agreement prior to the acquisition of replacement property, the exchange funds are treated as a loan from the taxpayer to the qualified intermediary unless the agreement provides that all of the earnings (such as bank interest) on the exchange funds will be paid to the taxpayer.

However, even when the intermediary retains the escrow earnings, as is typically the case with small nonbank exchange facilitators, the imputed interest rules do not apply if the deemed loan does not exceed $2 million and the loan does not extend beyond six months. If the loan exceeds $2 million or lasts more than six months, the taxpayer must report imputed interest. For example, a taxpayer transfers property to a qualified intermediary who transfers it to a purchaser in exchange for $2.1 million cash, which the intermediary deposits in a money market account for three months until the intermediary withdraws the funds and purchases replacement property identified by the taxpayer. Assuming that the taxpayer is not entitled to the earnings under the exchange agreement, the taxpayer is treated as having made a $2.1 million loan to the intermediary. The amount of the imputed interest taxable to the taxpayer is based on the lower of (1) the short-term applicable federal rate in effect on the day the deemed loan was made, compounded semiannually, or (2) the rate on a 91-day Treasury bill issued on or before the date of the deemed loan. The IRS could increase the $2 million exempt amount in future guidance.

The final regulations apply to transfers of relinquished property and exchange facilitator loans issued on or after October 8, 2008. For transfers before October 8, 2008, the IRS will accept any reasonable, consistently applied method for taxing the earnings.

6.5 Qualified Exchange Accommodation Arrangements (QEAAs) for Reverse Exchanges

The like-kind exchange rules *(6.1)* generally do not apply to a so-called reverse exchange in which you acquire replacement property *before* you transfer relinquished property. However, if you use a qualified exchange accommodation arrangement (QEAA), the transfer may qualify as a like-kind exchange.

Under a QEAA, either the replacement property or the relinquished property is transferred to an exchange accommodation titleholder (EAT) who is treated as the beneficial owner of the property for federal income tax purposes. If the property is held in a QEAA, the IRS will accept the qualification of property as either replacement property or relinquished property, and the treatment of an EAT as the beneficial owner of the property for federal income tax purposes.

The QEAA rules allow taxpayers to structure "parking transactions" in which the replacement property is acquired by the EAT before the transfer of the relinquished property. However, the QEAA safe harbor does not apply if the taxpayer transfers property to an EAT and receives that same property back as replacement property for other property of the taxpayer.

The IRS has set numerous technical requirements for QEAAs. Property is held in a QEAA only if you have a written agreement with the EAT, the time limits for identifying and transferring the property are met, and the qualified indicia of ownership of property are transferred to the EAT.

The EAT must meet all the following requirements: (1) Hold qualified indicia of ownership (*see* below) at all times from the date of acquisition of the property until the property is transferred within the 180-day period (*see* below); (2) be someone other than you, your agent, or a person related to you or your agent; (3) be subject to federal income tax. If the EAT is treated as a partnership or S corporation, more than 90% of its interests or stock must be owned by partners or shareholders who are subject to federal income tax.

The IRS defines qualified indicia of ownership as either legal title to the property, other indicia of ownership of the property that are treated as beneficial ownership of the property under principles of commercial law (for example, a contract for deed), or interests in an entity that is disregarded as an entity separate from its owner for federal income tax purposes (for example, a single member limited liability company) and that holds either legal title to the property or other indicia of ownership.

There are time limits for identifying and transferring property under a QEAA. No later than 45 days after the transfer of qualified indicia of ownership of the replacement property to the EAT, you must identify the relinquished property in a manner consistent with the principles for deferred exchanges *(6.4)*. If qualified indicia of ownership in replacement property have been transferred to the EAT, then no later than 180 days after that transfer, the replacement property must be transferred to you either directly or indirectly through a qualified intermediary *(6.4)*. If the EAT receives qualified indicia of ownership in the relinquished property, then no later than 180 days after that transfer, the relinquished property must be transferred to a person other than you, your agent at the time of the transaction, or a person who is related to you or your agent.

Note: For further details on the IRS's guidelines for QEAAs, *see* IRS Publication 544 and Revenue Procedure 2000-37, as modified by Revenue Procedure 2004-51 (parking transactions).

Caution

Parking Transactions

Property transferred to you by the exchange accommodation titleholder (EAT) cannot be treated as property received in an exchange if you previously owned it within 180 days of its transfer to the EAT.

6.6 Exchanges Between Related Parties

Tax-free treatment of like-kind exchanges between related persons may be lost if either party disposes of property received in the exchange within two years after the date of the last transfer that was part of the exchange. Any gain not recognized on the original exchange is taxable as of the date of the later disposition of the original like-kind property by either party within the two-year period. If a loss was not recognized, the loss becomes deductible if allowed under the rules in *5.6*.

Indirect dispositions of the property within the two-year period, such as transfer of stock of a corporation or interests in a partnership that owns the property, may also be treated as taxable dispositions.

Related parties. Related persons falling within the two-year rule include your children, grandchildren, parent, brother, or sister, controlled corporations or partnerships (more than 50% ownership), and a trust in which you are a beneficiary. A transfer to a spouse is not subject to the two-year rule unless he or she is a nonresident alien.

Filing Instruction

Filing Form 8824

The IRS requires related parties who exchange property to file Form 8824 for the year of the exchange and also for the two years following the exchange. If either party disposes of the property received in the original exchange in any of these years, the deferred gain must be reported in the year of disposition as if the property had been sold.

The two-year period is suspended for a holder of exchanged property who has substantially diminished his or her risk of loss, such as by use of a put or short sale.

Plan to avoid two-year rule. If you set up a prearranged plan under which you first transfer property to an unrelated party who within two years makes an exchange with a party related to you, the related party will not qualify for tax-free treatment on that exchange.

Exceptions. No tax will be incurred on a disposition made because of death; in an involuntary conversion provided the original exchange occurred before the threat of the conversion; or if you can prove that neither the exchange nor the later disposition was for a tax avoidance purpose.

6.7 Property Transfers Between Spouses and Ex-Spouses

Under Section 1041, all transfers of property between spouses are treated as tax-free exchanges, *other* than transfers to a nonresident alien spouse, certain trust transfers of mortgaged property, and transfers of U.S. Savings Bonds; these exceptions are discussed below. Section 1041 applies to transfers during marriage as well as to property settlements incident to a divorce. In a Section 1041 transfer, there is no taxable gain or deductible loss to the transferor spouse. The transferee-spouse takes the transferor's basis in the property, and so appreciation in value will be taxed to the recipient on a later sale. These rules apply to all property received after July 18, 1984, under divorce or separation instruments in effect after that date.

A transfer is "incident to a divorce" if it occurs either within one year after the date the marriage ceases or, if later, is related to the cessation of the marriage, such as a transfer authorized by a divorce decree. Under temporary regulations, any transfer pursuant to a divorce or separation agreement occurring within six years of the end of the marriage is considered "incident to a divorce." Later transfers qualify only if a transfer within the six-year period was hampered by legal or business disputes such as a fight over the property value.

EXAMPLES

1. In a property settlement accompanying a divorce, a husband plans to transfer to his wife stock worth $250,000 that cost him $50,000. In deciding whether to agree to the transfer, the wife should be aware that her basis for the stock will be $50,000; if she sells the stock, she will have to pay tax on the $200,000 gain. This tax cost should be accounted for in arriving at the settlement.
2. Basis of the property in the hands of the transferee-spouse is not increased even if cash is paid as part of the transfer. For example, a husband received a house originally owned by the wife as part of a marital settlement. Her basis for the house was $32,200. He paid her $18,000 cash as part of the settlement and when he later sold the house for $64,000, he argued that his basis for purposes of computing profit was $50,200—the wife's $32,200 basis plus his $18,000 cash payment. The IRS refused to consider the cash payment as part of basis, and the Tax Court agreed that the carryover basis rule applies.

Planning Reminder

Recipient Spouse Bears Tax Consequences of Transferred Property

Under the tax-free exchange rules, there is no taxable gain or deductible loss on the transfer of property, even if cash is received for the property or the other spouse (or former spouse) assumes liabilities or gives up marital rights as part of a property settlement. The spouse who receives property may incur tax on a later sale because his or her basis in the property is the same as the transferor-spouse's basis; *see* the Examples in *6.7*. Because the transferee bears the tax consequences of a later sale, he or she should consider the potential tax on the appreciation in negotiating a marital settlement. In a marital settlement, the transferee spouse can lessen the tax burden by negotiating for assets that have little or no unrealized appreciation.

Nonresident alien. The tax-free exchange rule does not apply to transfers to a nonresident alien spouse or former spouse.

Transfers of U.S. Savings Bonds. The IRS has ruled that the tax-free exchange rules do not apply to transfers of U.S. Savings Bonds. For example, if a husband has deferred the reporting of interest on E or EE bonds and transfers the bonds to his ex-wife as part of a divorce settlement, the deferred interest is taxed to him on the transfer. The wife's basis for the bonds is the husband's basis plus the income he realizes on the transfer. When she redeems the bonds, she will be taxed on the interest accrued from the date of the transfer to the redemption date.

Payment for release of community property interest in retirement pay. The Tax Court allowed tax-free treatment for a payment made to a wife for releasing her community property claim to her husband's military retirement pay. The IRS had argued that the tax-free exchange rules discussed in this section did not apply to the release of rights to retirement pay that would otherwise be subject to ordinary income tax. The Tax Court disagreed, holding that the tax-free exchange rule applies whether the transfer is for relinquishment of marital rights, cash, or other property.

Transfers in trust. The tax-free exchange rules generally apply to transfers in trust for the benefit of a spouse or a former spouse if incident to a divorce. However, gain cannot be avoided on a trust transfer of heavily mortgaged property. If the trust property is mortgaged, the transferor spouse must report a taxable gain to the extent that the liabilities assumed by the transferee spouse plus the liabilities to which the property is subject (even if not assumed) exceed the transferor's adjusted basis for the property. If the transferor realizes a taxable gain under this rule, the transferee's basis for the property is increased by the gain.

Sole proprietorship sale to spouse. Tax-free exchange rules may apply to a sale of business property by a sole proprietor to a spouse. The buyer spouse assumes a carryover basis even if fair market value is paid. The transferor is not required to recapture previously claimed depreciation deductions or investment credits. However, the transferee is subject to the recapture rules on premature dispositions or if the property ceases to be used for business purposes.

Transfer of nonstatutory options or nonqualified deferred compensation. According to the IRS, if a vested interest in nonstatutory (nonqualified) stock options or nonqualified deferred compensation is transferred to a former spouse as part of a property settlement, the transferor-spouse (the employee) does not have to report any income; the Section 1041 tax-free exchange rules apply. When the transferee-spouse later exercises the options or receives the deferred compensation, he or she will be taxed on the option spread *(2.17)* or the deferred compensation as if he or she was the employee. Income tax withholding and FICA tax withholding (Social Security and Medicare taxes) is generally required from the payments made to the transferee-spouse.

Divorce-related redemptions of stock in closely held corporation. When a married couple own all (or most) of the stock in a closely held corporation, the corporation may redeem the stock of one of the spouses as part of an overall divorce settlement. Does the transferring spouse avoid tax on the redemption under the Section 1041 tax-free exchange rules?

If the redemption of one of the spouses' stock is treated as a transfer to a third party *on behalf of* the other spouse, Section 1041 applies and the transferor-spouse would escape tax on the redemption. However, there has been much confusion and litigation as to the standards for determining whether a redemption is "on behalf of" the non-transferor spouse, and whether different tests should apply for determining the tax treatment of each spouse. Court decisions have generally supported tax-free treatment for a spouse whose stock is redeemed under the terms of the couple's divorce or separation instrument, or where the other (non-transferring) spouse requests or consents to the redemption. However, the courts are divided on the issue of whether the non-transferor spouse, who is left in control of the corporation, has realized a constructive dividend as a result of the redemption. *See* Example 2 below for the disputed positions taken by Tax Court judges in the *Read* case.

In response to the inconsistent standards used by the courts (*see* the Examples below), the IRS amended its regulations to provide a specific rule for determining which spouse will be taxed on the redemption. The regulation allows tax-free exchange treatment under Section 1041 to the transferor spouse (whose stock was redeemed) only if under applicable law the redemption is treated as resulting in a constructive dividend to the non-transferor spouse. If constructive dividend treatment does not apply to the non-transferor spouse, the form of the redemption transaction is followed and the transferor-spouse taxed on the redemption. The IRS regulation adopts the position of some of the dissenting judges in the *Read* case; *see* Example 2 below. The spouses are allowed to provide in a divorce or separation agreement that the redemption will be taxable to the non-transferor spouse even if the redemption would not result in a constructive dividend to that spouse under applicable law. Alternatively, they can provide that the transferor will be taxed on the redemption although the redemption would otherwise be treated as a constructive dividend to the nontransferor spouse.

Court Decision

Interest on Marital Property Settlements

Parties may agree to pay interest on property transfers relating to divorce settlements when payments are to be made over time. The actual property transfer is generally a tax-free exchange. According to the Tax Court, the interest is separate and apart from the property transferred. The deductibility of the interest paid depends on the nature of the property transferred. Interest allocated to residential property, for instance, is deductible as residential mortgage interest; interest allocated to investment property is deductible as investment interest subject to the net investment income limit. *See Chapter 15.*

Planning Reminder

Transfers to Third Parties

If you transfer property to a third party on behalf of your spouse or former spouse where the transfer is required by a divorce or separation instrument, or if you have your spouse's or former spouse's written request or consent for the transfer, the transfer is tax free to you under Section 1041. The transfer is treated as if made to your spouse or former spouse, who then retransfers the property to the third party. A written request or consent must specifically state that the tax-free exchange rules of Code Section 1041 are intended, and you must receive it before filing the tax return for the year of the transfer. As discussed in the Examples on this page, a divorce-related stock redemption may qualify for Section 1041 treatment as a transfer "on behalf of" the other spouse.

EXAMPLES

1. A federal district court and the Ninth Circuit Court of Appeals held that, under Section 1041, a wife was not taxable on the redemption of her stock by the couple's closely held corporation where the redemption was pursuant to their divorce agreement and incorporated into the divorce decree. The Ninth Circuit viewed the transfer as if the husband had received the stock directly from the wife and then transferred it to the company.

   After the Ninth Circuit held that the redemption was not taxable to the wife, the IRS argued in a separate case against the nonredeeming husband that he received a taxable constructive dividend. However, the Tax Court disagreed, holding that there was no dividend to the husband because under state law he was merely a guarantor; he was not primarily and unconditionally obligated to buy the stock. The IRS did not appeal the Tax Court decision.

In this unusual situation, the IRS is in the position of being unable to collect tax on the redemption proceeds from either the transferor or transferee spouse.

2. After William and Carol Read divorced, William, pursuant to their divorce decree, elected to have their controlled corporation purchase all of Carol's stock. A Tax Court majority held that her transfer was on behalf of William and qualified for Section 1041 non-recognition treatment.

   The Tax Court majority also held that William realized a constructive dividend on the corporation's redemption of Carol's stock. However, the majority relied on a concession by William and did not specify a legal standard for determining whether he should be taxed. Concurring judges suggested that constructive dividend treatment for William followed automatically from the holding that Carol's stock transfer was on his behalf and thus within Section 1041. There were four dissenting opinions, all of which held that under traditional law for constructive dividends, there is no constructive dividend unless William had a "primary and unconditional obligation" to buy the shares, an obligation the corporation satisfied by making the redemption. Most of the dissenters argued that William did not have such an obligation and should not be taxed. They further argued that if William was not obligated to buy the shares, Section 1041 does not apply and thus Carol realized capital gain on the redemption of her shares. Other dissenting judges held that a spouse can never avoid taxable gain under Section 1041 on a redemption incident to divorce.

3. The Eleventh Circuit Court of Appeals allowed tax-free treatment to a redemption of a wife's stock, following the Tax Court majority in *Read* (Example 2 above). The redemption was on behalf of her ex-husband. The redemption was required by their divorce decree and it left him in control of 98% of the corporation's stock. He had guaranteed the corporation's 10-year promissory note to her, and the terms of the note specifically said that the guarantee was in his interests.

   Furthermore, although the corporation's note did not provide for interest, interest income was not imputed to the wife. Imputed interest does not apply where the underlying transfer is not taxable under Section 1041.

Basis of property received before July 19, 1984, or under instruments in effect before that date. The tax-free exchange rules do not apply to property received before July 19, 1984, from your spouse (or former spouse if the transfer was incident to divorce). Your basis for determining gain or loss when you sell such property is its fair market value when you received it. The same fair market value basis rule applies to property received after June 18, 1984, under an instrument in effect on or before that date unless a Section 1041 election was made to have the tax-free exchange rules apply. For property subject to such an election, your basis is the same as the transferor-spouse's adjusted basis.

6.8 Tax-Free Exchanges of Stock in Same Corporation

Gain on the exchange of common stock for other common stock of the same corporation is not taxable. The same rule generally applies to an exchange of preferred stock of the same corporation, but not if "nonqualified" preferred with special redemption rights or a varying dividend rate is received. Loss realized on a qualifying exchange is not deductible. The exchange may take place between the stockholder and the company or between two stockholders.

An exchange of preferred stock for common, or common for preferred, in the same company is generally not tax free, unless the exchange is part of a tax-free recapitalization. In such exchanges, the company should inform you of the tax consequences.

Convertible securities. Conversion of securities under a conversion privilege is tax free *(30.7)*.

6.9 Joint Ownership Interests

The change to a tenancy in common from a joint tenancy is tax free. You may convert a joint tenancy in corporate stock to a tenancy in common without income-tax consequences. The transfer is tax free even though survivorship rights are eliminated. Similarly, a partition and issuance of separate certificates in the names of each joint tenant is also tax free.

A joint tenancy and a tenancy in common differ in this respect. On the death of a joint tenant, ownership passes to the surviving joint tenant or tenants. But on the death of a tenant holding property in common, ownership passes to his or her heirs, not to the other tenant or tenants with whom the property was held.

A tenancy by the entirety is a form of joint ownership recognized in some states and can be only between a husband and wife.

Dividing properties held in common. A division of properties held as tenants in common may qualify as tax-free exchanges.

For example, three men owned three pieces of real estate as tenants in common. Each man wanted to be the sole owner of one of the pieces of property. They disentangled themselves by exchanging interests in a three-way exchange. No money or property other than the three pieces of real estate changed hands, and none of the men assumed the others' liability. The transactions qualified as tax-free exchanges and no gain or loss was recognized.

Receipt of boot. Exchanges of jointly owned property are tax free as long as no "boot," such as cash or other property, passes between the parties *(6.3)*.

6.10 Setting up Closely Held Corporations

Tax-free exchange rules facilitate the organization of a corporation. When you transfer property to a corporation that you control solely in exchange for corporate stock in that corporation (but not nonqualified preferred stock), no gain or loss is recognized on the transfer. For control, you alone or together with other transferors (such as partners, where a partnership is being incorporated) must own at least 80% of the combined voting power of the corporation and 80% of all other classes of stock immediately after the transfer to the corporation. If you receive securities in addition to stock, the securities are treated as taxable "boot." The corporation takes your basis in the property, and your basis in the stock received in the exchange is the same as your basis in the property. Gain not recognized on the organization of the corporation may be taxed when you sell your stock, or the corporation disposes of the property.

Caution

Consider Taxable Transfer

Before making a property transfer to a closely held corporation, consult an accountant or an attorney on the tax consequences. There may be instances when you have potential losses or you desire the corporation to take a stepped-up basis that would make tax-free treatment undesirable.

EXAMPLE

You transfer a building worth $100,000, which cost you $20,000, to your newly organized corporation in exchange for all of its outstanding stock. You realize an $80,000 gain ($100,000 – $20,000) that is not recognized. Your basis in the stock is $20,000; the corporation's basis in the building is $20,000. The following year, you sell all your stock to a third party for $100,000. The $80,000 gain is now recognized.

Transfer of liabilities. When assets subject to liabilities are transferred to the corporation, the liability assumed by the corporation is not treated as taxable "boot," but your stock basis is reduced by the amount of liability. The transfer of liabilities may be taxable when the transfer is part of a tax avoidance scheme, or the liabilities exceed the basis of the property transferred to the corporation.

6.11 Exchanges of Coins and Bullion

An exchange of "gold for gold" coins or "silver for silver" coins may qualify as a tax-free exchange of like-kind investment property. An exchange is tax free if both coins represent the same type of underlying investment. An exchange of bullion-type coins for bullion-type coins is a tax-free like-kind exchange. For example, the exchange of Mexican pesos for Austrian coronas has been held to be a tax-free exchange as both are bullion-type coins.

However, an exchange of silver bullion for gold bullion is not tax free. Silver and gold bullion represent different types of property. Silver is an industrial commodity, whereas gold is primarily an investment in itself. Similarly, an exchange of U.S. gold collector's coins for South African Krugerrands is taxable. Krugerrands are bullion-type coins whose value is determined solely by metal content, whereas the U.S. gold coins are numismatic coins whose value depends on age, condition, number minted, and artistic merit, as well as metal content. Although both coins appear to be similar in gold content, each represents a different type of investment.

Planning Reminder

Financially Troubled Insurer

If your annuity contract or insurance policy is with an insurance company that is in a rehabilitation, conservatorship, insolvency, or a similar state proceeding, you may surrender the policy and make a tax-free reinvestment of the proceeds in a new policy with a different insurance company. The transfer must be completed within 60 days. If a government agency does not allow you to withdraw your entire balance from the troubled insurance company, you must assign all rights to any future distributions to the issuer of the new contract or policy. *See* IRS Revenue Procedure 92-44.

6.12 Tax-Free Exchanges of Insurance Policies

These exchanges of insurance policies are considered tax free:

- Life insurance policy for another life insurance policy, endowment policy, or an annuity contract.
- Endowment policy for another endowment policy that provides for regular payments beginning no later than the date payments would have started under the old policy, or in exchange for an annuity contract.
- Annuity contract for another annuity contract with identical annuitants.

These exchanges are not tax free:

- Endowment policy for a life insurance policy, or for another endowment policy that provides for payments beginning at a date later than payments would have started under the old policy.
- Annuity contract for a life insurance or endowment policy.
- Transfers of life insurance contracts where the insured is not the same person in both contracts. The IRS held that a company could not make a tax-free exchange of a key executive policy where the company could change insured executives as they leave or join the firm.

Endorsement of annuity check for another annuity is taxable. Cashing out a commercial annuity or nonqualified employee contract and investing it in another annuity does not qualify as a tax-free exchange. The IRS denied tax-free exchange treatment to a taxpayer who tried to complete a direct exchange of a non-qualified annuity contract but was foiled by the insurance company holding the contract. The taxpayer had asked the insurance company to issue a check directly to another insurer as consideration for a new annuity contract, intending the transaction to be treated as a tax-free exchange under Section 1035. The insurer refused and instead issued a check to the taxpayer. The taxpayer did not deposit the check, but instead endorsed it to the second insurance company to obtain the new annuity contract.

The IRS ruled that endorsing the check over to the second insurance company as consideration for the new contract was not a tax-free exchange. Instead, the taxpayer had to include in gross income the portion of the check that was allocable to income on the contract. If this had been a tax-sheltered 403(b) annuity or a qualifed employee annuity, a distribution from the policy could have been rolled over tax-free to another such annuity, or even to another eligible retirement plan such as an IRA or qualified employer trust. However, in the case of a non-qualified annuity, there is no rollover provision for amounts distributed from the contract.

IRS scrutiny of partial exchanges of annuity contracts. The IRS has been concerned that a direct transfer of a portion of the cash surrender value of an existing annuity contract for another annuity contract, followed by a withdrawal from or surrender of either the surviving annuity contract or the new contract, could be used to reduce the tax on earnings that would otherwise be due on a non-annuity distribution. In Revenue Procedure 2008-24, the IRS issued guidelines for determining whether the direct transfer of a portion of the cash surrender value of an existing annuity contract to another contract is a tax-free exchange. The rules apply whether or not the two contracts are issued by the same or different companies. If tax-free treatment is allowed under these rules, the two annuity contracts will be treated separately and not aggregated, even if the same company issued both. A transfer that does not qualify under the guidelines will be treated as a distribution that is taxable to the extent of the earnings in the contract, followed by a payment for the second annuity contract.

Under the guidelines, the direct transfer will be treated as a tax-free exchange if there is no withdrawal from or amount received in surrender of either contract in the 12 months beginning with the date of transfer. Tax-free exchange treatment will also be allowed if between the partial exchange and the surrender or distribution, one of the penalty exceptions for pre-59½ annuity distributions *(7.23)* is met, such as the taxpayer becoming disabled, or if another similar life event such as divorce or unemployment occurs. However, this favorable rule does not apply to the penalty exceptions for distributions that are part of a series of substantially equal payments or are under an "immediate" annuity.

Chapter 7

Retirement and Annuity Income

For employees, coverage in a qualified employer retirement plan is a valuable fringe benefit, as employer contributions are tax free within specified limits. Certain salary-reduction plans allow you to make elective deferrals of salary that are not subject to income tax. An advantage of all qualified retirement plans is that earnings accumulate tax free until withdrawal.

Along with tax savings opportunities come technical restrictions and pitfalls. For example, retirement plan distributions eligible for rollover are subject to a mandatory 20% withholding tax if you receive the distribution rather than asking your employer to make a direct trustee-to-trustee transfer of the distribution to an IRA or another qualified employer plan.

This chapter discusses tax treatment of annuities and employer plan distributions, including how to avoid tax penalties, such as for distributions before age 59½. IRAs are discussed in *Chapter 8*. Retirement plans for self-employed individuals are discussed further in *Chapter 41*.

A tax credit is available to low-to-moderate income taxpayers who make traditional or Roth IRA contributions, electives deferrals to a 401(k) or other employer plan, and voluntary after-tax contributions to a qualified plan. The credit is discussed in *Chapter 25*.

Table 7-1 Key to Tax-Favored Retirement Plans

Type—	*General Tax Considerations—*	*Tax Treatment of Distributions—*
Company qualified plan	A company qualified pension or profit-sharing plan offers these benefits: (1) You do not realize current income on your employer's contributions to the plan on your behalf. (2) Income earned on funds contributed to your account compounds tax free. (3) Your employer may allow you to make voluntary after-tax contributions. Although these contributions may not be deducted, income earned on the voluntary contributions is not taxed until withdrawn.	If you were born before January 2, 1936, and receive a lump sum, tax on employer contributions and plan earnings may be reduced by a special averaging rule *(7.4)*. If you receive a lump-sum distribution including company securities, unrealized appreciation on those securities is not taxed until you finally sell the stock *(7.10)*. Distributions before age 59½ are generally subject to penalties, but there are exceptions *(7.15)*. Rather than pay an immediate tax, you may elect to roll over a lump-sum payment to an IRA account *(7.7)*. If you collect your retirement benefits as an annuity over a period of years, *see 7.27*.
Plans for self-employed	You may set up a self-employed retirement plan called a Keogh plan if you earn self-employment income through your performance of personal services. You may deduct contributions up to limits discussed in *Chapter 41*; income earned on assets held by the plan is not taxed. You must include employees in your Keogh under rules explained in *Chapter 41*. Other retirement plan options, such as a SEP or SIMPLE plan, are also discussed in *Chapter 41*.	You may not withdraw Keogh plan funds until age 59½ unless you are disabled or meet other exceptions at *7.15*. Qualified distributions to self-employed persons or to beneficiaries at death may qualify for favored lump-sum treatment *(7.2)*. Distributions from a SEP are subject to traditional IRA rules *(8.8)*. Distributions from a SIMPLE-IRA also are subject to traditional IRA rules, but a 25% penalty (instead of 10%) applies to pre-age-59½ distributions in the first two years *(8.18)*.
IRA and Roth IRA	Anyone who has earned income may contribute to a traditional IRA, but the contribution is deductible only if certain requirements are met. Your status as a participant in an employer retirement plan and your income determine whether you may claim a deduction up to the annual contribution limit ($5,000 for 2010, $6,000 if age 50 or older), a partial deduction, or no deduction at all. *See Chapter 8* for these deduction limitations. Income earned on IRA accounts is not taxed until the funds are withdrawn. This tax-free buildup of earnings also applies where you make nondeductible contributions to a Roth IRA under the rules in *Chapter 8*.	Traditional IRA distributions are fully taxable unless you have previously made nondeductible contributions *(8.9)*. A taxable withdrawal before age 59½ is subject to a 10% penalty, but there are exceptions if you are disabled, have substantial medical expenses, pay medical premiums while unemployed, or receive payments in a series of substantially equal installments; *see* the details on these and other exceptions *(8.12)*. Starting at age 70½, you must receive minimum annual distributions to avoid a 50% penalty *(8.13)*. Distributions from a Roth IRA of contributions are tax free. Distributions of earnings are taxable unless you are over age 59½ and have held the account for at least five years *(8.23)*.
SEP	A simplified employee pension plan set up by your employer allows the employer to contribute to an IRA more than you can under regular IRA rules *(8.15)*. Employer contributions to your account of up to 25% of your compensation (but no more than $49,000 for 2010) are not taxable to you. Elective deferrals of salary may be made to qualifying plans set up before 1997 *(8.16)*.	Withdrawals from a SEP are taxable under the rules explained above for IRAs.
Deferred salary or 401(k) plans	If your company has a profit-sharing or stock bonus plan, the tax law allows the company to add a cash or deferred pay plan that can operate in one of two ways: (1) Your employer contributes an amount for your benefit to your trust account. You are not taxed on your employer's contribution. (2) You agree to take a salary reduction or to forego a salary increase. The reduction is placed in a trust account for your benefit. The reduction is treated as your employer's contribution *(7.18)*. Income earned on the trust account accumulates tax free until it is withdrawn.	Withdrawals are penalized unless you have reached age 59½, become disabled, or meet other exceptions *(7.15)*. If you were born before January 2, 1936, and receive a qualifying lump sum, tax on the lump sum may be computed according to the rules in *7.2*.

7.1 Retirement Distributions on Form 1099-R

On Form 1099-R, payments from pensions, annuities, IRAs, Roth IRAs, SIMPLE IRAs, insurance contracts, profit-sharing, and other employer plans are reported to you and the IRS. Social Security benefits are reported on Form SSA-1099; *see Chapter 34* for the special rules to apply in determining the taxable portion of Social Security benefits.

Here is a guide to the information reported on Form 1099-R. A sample form is on the next page.

Box 1. The total amount received from the payer is shown here without taking any withholdings into account. If you file Form 1040, report the Box 1 total on Line 15a if the payment is from an IRA, or on Line 16a if from a pension or an annuity. However, if the amount is a qualifying lump-sum distribution for which you are claiming averaging, use Form 4972 *(7.4)*.

If you file Form 1040A, report the Box 1 total on Line 11a if from an IRA or on Line 12a if from a pension or an annuity.

If an exchange of insurance contracts was made, the value of the contract will be shown in Box 1, but if the exchange qualified as tax free, a zero taxable amount will be shown in Box 2a and Code 6 will be entered in Box 7.

Boxes 2a and 2b. The taxable portion of distributions from employer plans and insurance contracts may be shown in Box 2a. The taxable portion does not include your after-tax contributions to an employer plan or insurance premium payments.

If the payer cannot figure the taxable portion, the first box in 2b should be checked; Box 2a should be blank. You will then have to figure the taxable amount yourself. A payment from a pension or an annuity is only partially taxed if you contributed to the cost and you did not recover your entire cost investment before 2010. *See* the discussion of commercial annuities *(7.23)* or employee annuities *(7.27)* for details on computing the taxable portion if you have an unrecovered investment.

The payer of a traditional IRA distribution will probably not compute the taxable portion, and in this case, the total distribution from Box 1 will be entered as the taxable portion in Box 2a. This amount is fully taxable unless you have made nondeductible contributions, in which case Form 8606 is used to figure the taxable portion of the distribution *(8.9)*. Form 8606 is also used to figure the taxable part, if any, of a Roth IRA distribution *(8.23)*.

If the payment is from an employer plan and the "total distribution" box has been checked in 2b, *see* the discussion of possible rollover and special averaging options *(7.2)*. The taxable amount in Box 2a should not include net unrealized appreciation (NUA *(7.10)*) in any employer securities included in the lump sum or the value of an annuity contract included in the distribution.

Box 3. If the payment is a lump-sum distribution, you were born before January 2, 1936, and you participated in the plan before 1974, the amount shown here may be treated as capital gain *(7.5)*.

Box 4. Any federal income tax withheld is shown here. Do not forget to include it on Line 61 of Form 1040 or Line 38 of Form 1040A. If Box 4 shows any withholdings, attach Copy B of Form 1099-R to your return.

Box 5. If you made after-tax contributions to your employer's plan, or paid premiums for a commercial annuity or insurance contract, your contribution is shown here, less any such contributions previously distributed. IRA or SEP contributions *(see Chapter 8)* are not shown here.

Box 6. If you received a qualifying lump-sum distribution that includes securities of your employer's company, the total net unrealized appreciation (NUA) is shown here. Unless you elect to pay tax on it currently *(7.10)*, this amount is not taxed until you sell the securities. If you did not receive a qualifying lump sum, the amount shown here is the net unrealized appreciation attributable to your after-tax employee contributions, which are also not taxed until you sell the securities *(7.10)*.

Box 7. In Box 7, the payer will indicate if the distribution is from a traditional IRA, SEP, or SIMPLE and enter codes that are used by the IRS to check whether you have reported the distribution correctly, including the penalty for distributions before age 59½.

Code 2 will be entered in Box 7 if you are under age 59½ and the payer knows that you qualify for an exception to the 10% early distribution penalty *(7.15)*, such as the exception for separation of service after age 55 for an employer-plan distribution or for a distribution that is part of a series

Filing Instruction

Conversion of Traditional IRA to Roth IRA

If you converted a traditional IRA to a Roth IRA in 2010, the converted amount will be included in Box 1 and Box 2a of Form 1099-R, but in Box 2b, the "Taxable amount not determined" box will be checked. Because of the special rule for 2010 conversions *(8.21)*, none of the taxable amount has to be reported on your 2010 return. Half will be taxable on your 2011 return and half on your 2012 return unless you make an election on Form 8606 to report the entire amount as 2010 income.

of substantially equal payments. Code 3 will be used if the disability exception applies. Code 4 is the exception for distributions paid to beneficiaries. If Code 1 is entered, this indicates that you were under age 59½ at the time of the distribution and, as far as the payer knows, no penalty exception applies. However, although Code 1 is entered, you may not be subject to a penalty. For example, you may qualify for the medical expense exception *(7.15)* or you may have made a tax-free rollover instead of having your employer make a direct rollover *(7.7)*.

If the employer made a direct rollover, Code G will be entered.

If you are at least age 59½, Code 7 should be entered.

If you are the beneficiary of a deceased employee, Code 4 should be entered. The 10% early distribution penalty does not apply.

If you contribute to a 401(k) plan and are a highly compensated employee, your employer may have to make a corrective distribution to you of contributions (and allocable income) that exceed allowable nondiscrimination ceilings. In this case, the employer will enter Code 8 if the corrective distribution is taxable in 2010, Code P if taxable in 2009, or Code D if taxable in 2008.

If you receive a lump-sum distribution that qualifies for special averaging, Code A will be entered. *See* the sample Form 1099-R below and the discussion of the special averaging rules *(7.4)*.

Filing Tip

Lump-Sum Distribution

If you are paid a distribution that qualifies for lump-sum averaging *(7.4)*, Code A will be entered in Box 7 of Form 1099-R.

Box 8. If the value of an annuity contract was included as part of a lump sum you received, the value of the contract is shown here. It is not taxable when you receive it and should not be included in Boxes 1 and 2a. For purposes of computing averaging on Form 4972, this amount is added to the ordinary income portion of the distribution *(7.4)*.

Box 9. If several beneficiaries are receiving payment from an employer plan total distribution, the amount shown in Box 9a is your share of the distribution. Box 9b may show your after-tax contributions to your employer's plan.

Boxes 10–15. The payer may make entries in these boxes to show state or local income tax withholdings.

See the Andrew Kellogg Example (7.4).

☐ CORRECTED (if checked)

PAYER'S name, street address, city, state, and ZIP code		1 Gross distribution	OMB No. 1545-0119	Distributions From Pensions, Annuities, Retirement or Profit-Sharing Plans, IRAs, Insurance Contracts, etc.
StarShine Systems, Inc. Retirement Plan **1220 Silver Lake Drive** **City, State 1X001**		$ **182,438**	**2010**	
		2a Taxable amount $ **182,438**	Form **1099-R**	
		2b Taxable amount not determined ☐	Total distribution ☐	**Copy B Report this income on your federal tax return. If this form shows federal income tax withheld in box 4, attach this copy to your return.**
PAYER'S federal identification number **X0-1101X01**	RECIPIENT'S identification number **010-XX-10XX**	3 Capital gain (included in box 2a) $ **8,620**	4 Federal income tax withheld $ **36,488**	
RECIPIENT'S name **Andrew Kellogg**		5 Employee contributions /Designated Roth contributions or insurance premiums $	6 Net unrealized appreciation in employer's securities $	
Street address (including apt. no.) **44 Hampton Lane**		7 Distribution code(s) **7A** IRA/SEP/SIMPLE ☐	8 Other $ %	This information is being furnished to the Internal Revenue Service.
City, state, and ZIP code **City, State 1X011**		9a Your percentage of total distribution %	9b Total employee contributions $	
	1st year of desig. Roth contrib.	10 State tax withheld $ $	11 State/Payer's state no.	12 State distribution $ $
Account number (see instructions)		13 Local tax withheld $ $	14 Name of locality	15 Local distribution $ $

Form **1099-R**   Department of the Treasury - Internal Revenue Service

7.2 Lump-Sum Distributions

If you are entitled to a lump-sum distribution from a qualified company retirement plan or self-employed Keogh plan, you may avoid current tax by asking your employer to make a direct rollover of your account to an IRA or another qualified employer plan. If the distribution is made to you, 20% will be withheld, but it is still possible to make a tax-free rollover within 60 days *(7.7)*.

If you receive a lump sum and do *not* make a rollover, the taxable part of the distribution (shown in Box 2a of Form 1099-R) must be reported as ordinary pension income on your return unless you were born before January 2, 1936, and qualify for special averaging, as discussed below. Your after-tax contributions and any net unrealized appreciation (NUA *(7.10)*) in employer securities that are included in the lump sum are recovered tax free; they are not part of the taxable distribution.

A taxable distribution before age 59½ is subject to a 10% penalty in addition to regular income tax, unless you qualify for an exception *(7.15)*.

Lump-sum distribution defined. A lump-sum distribution is the payment within a single taxable year of a plan participant's entire balance from an employer's qualified plan. If the employer has more than one qualified plan of the same kind (profit-sharing, pension, stock bonus), you must receive the balance from all of them within the same year. A series of payments may qualify as a lump-sum distribution provided you receive them within the same tax year. The account balance does not include deductible voluntary contributions you made after 1981 and before 1987; these are not eligible for lump-sum distribution treatment.

Requirements for 10-year averaging or capital gain election. If you were born before January 2, 1936, and receive a qualified lump-sum distribution (defined above), you generally may elect to figure your tax on the distribution using the 10-year averaging method. The law technically requires that you be born before 1936, but a favorable IRS rule treats you as born before 1936 if you were born *on* January 1, 1936. If you participated in the plan before 1974, you may elect to apply a 20% rate to the pre-1974 part of the lump-sum distribution if 20% is lower than the averaging rate.

However, averaging and capital gain treatment are *not allowed* for a lump-sum distribution if any of the following are true: (1) you rolled over any part of the lump-sum distribution to an IRA or an employer qualified plan, (2) you received the distribution during the first five years that you participated in the plan, (3) you previously received a distribution from the same plan and you rolled it over tax free to an IRA or another qualified employer plan, (4) you elected 10-year or five-year averaging or capital gain treatment for any other lump-sum distribution after 1986, (5) after 2001 you rolled over to the same plan a distribution from a traditional IRA (other than a conduit IRA *(7.3)*), a 403(b) plan *(7.21)*, or a governmental 457 plan *(7.22)*, or (6) after 2001 you rolled over to the same plan a distribution that you received as a surviving spouse from the qualified plan of your deceased spouse.

Caution

Prior Rollover Bars Averaging

You may not claim averaging for a lump-sum distribution if you previously received a distribution from the same plan that was rolled over tax free *(7.7)* to an IRA or to another qualified employer plan.

See the details on electing averaging *(7.4)* and the 20% capital gain rate *(7.5)*.

If you are the beneficiary of a deceased plan participant, the participant's age, not yours, determines your right to claim averaging, and the five-year participation rule does not apply; *see 7.6*.

Spousal consent to lump-sum distribution. If you are married, you may have to obtain your spouse's consent to elect a lump-sum distribution *(7.11)*.

Withholding tax. An employer must withhold a 20% tax from a lump-sum distribution that is paid to you and not rolled over directly by the employer *(7.7)*.

Beneficiaries. A surviving spouse can roll over a lump-sum distribution to another qualified employer plan or to his or her own IRA. A nonspouse beneficiary of a lump-sum distribution may instruct the plan to make a direct trustee-to-trustee transfer to an IRA that must be treated as an inherited IRA *(7.8)*.

If the deceased employee was born before January 2, 1936, any beneficiary may elect special averaging or capital gain treatment for a lump-sum distribution of the account, unless the distribution is disqualified as discussed above under "Requirements for 10-year averaging or capital gain election" *(7.6)*.

Court ordered lump-sum distribution to a spouse or former spouse. A distribution received by a spouse or former spouse of an employee under a qualified domestic relations order (QDRO) may be eligible for tax-free rollover or, in some cases, special averaging treatment *(7.12)*.

Planning Reminder

Once in a Lifetime Election

You are allowed to elect averaging only once as a plan participant after 1986. If you were born before January 2, 1936, have not previously elected averaging, and elect averaging for a distribution received in 2010, you will not be able to claim averaging again if you join another company and receive a lump-sum distribution from the new employer.

Even if you are barred from electing averaging for a lump sum from your own plan, you can make the election as a beneficiary of a deceased plan participant born before January 2, 1936.

7.3 Lump-Sum Options If You Were Born Before January 2, 1936

Plan ahead if you expect to receive a lump-sum distribution eligible for averaging *(7.2)*. You must decide whether to pay tax currently using the averaging method (and possibly the 20% capital gain method for pre-1974 participation), or to defer tax by making a tax-free rollover *(7.7)*. If you receive more than one lump sum during the year, you must make the same choice for all of them; you may not roll over one lump sum and claim averaging for another.

If you do not instruct the payer to make a direct rollover *(7.8)*, 80% of the taxable distribution will be paid to you; a 20% tax will be withheld. If you later decide to make a rollover, you have 60 days from the time of receiving the distribution to do so *(7.8)*. However, to avoid tax on the entire distribution, you will have to include in the rollover an amount equal to the withheld tax. Withholding is discussed further at *7.8* and *26.11*. Ordinary income tax rates apply to the amount not rolled over, unless you are eligible for averaging or the 20% capital gain method.

Conduit IRA preserves averaging option. If you are changing jobs, a direct rollover or personal rollover may be made to a traditional IRA or a qualified plan of your new employer. However, if the distribution is rolled over to a traditional IRA, you lose the right to claim averaging in the future for those assets unless the IRA is a "conduit IRA" that serves as a holding account until a later rollover may be made to another employer's plan. As long as the distribution and earnings on the distribution are the only assets in the conduit IRA, a rollover may later be made from the conduit IRA to a new employer's plan, from which a lump-sum distribution eligible for averaging may later be received. Distributions from a traditional IRA are taxable as ordinary income.

If you plan to continue working and expect to receive another lump sum in the future, you may not claim averaging for the current lump sum and also for the later distribution. Averaging may be claimed only once as a plan participant after 1986.

An IRA rollover cannot be revoked to claim averaging. If you make a rollover to an IRA, you cannot change your mind and cancel the IRA account in order to apply special averaging. The rollover election is irrevocable, according to an IRS regulation that has been upheld by the Tax Court. If an IRA rollover account is revoked, the entire distribution is taxable as ordinary income, and a 10% penalty may be imposed if the recipient is under age 59½ *(7.15)*.

Disqualification of retirement plan. If you receive a lump-sum distribution from a plan that loses its exempt status, the IRS may argue that the distribution does not qualify for lump-sum treatment. Under the IRS position, you may not roll over the distribution to an IRA or elect special averaging. The Tax Court previously took the position that if the plan qualified when contributions were made, an allocable portion of the distribution was a qualified lump sum. However, the majority of appeals courts that reviewed Tax Court decisions on this issue supported the IRS position. In response, the Tax Court reversed its position and adopted the harsher IRS approach: no part of the distribution qualifies for rollover or averaging if the plan loses its exempt status.

Caution

Averaging Not Allowed for Those Born After January 1, 1936

If you were born after January 1, 1936, a lump-sum distribution from your plan is not eligible for averaging.

7.4 Averaging on Form 4972

If you were born before January 2, 1936, and the other averaging tests *(7.2)* are satisfied, you may elect on Form 4972 to compute the tax on a lump-sum distribution received using a 10-year averaging method based on 1986 tax rates for single persons.

If you were born after January 1, 1936, you may not elect averaging for a lump-sum distribution of your account balance. However, you may elect averaging as the beneficiary of a deceased plan participant who was born before January 2, 1936 *(7.6)*.

Averaging on 2010 returns. If you qualify for averaging *(7.2)*, follow IRS instructions to Form 4972 for applying the 10-year averaging method. If you received more than one qualified lump sum, you may elect averaging for one of the distributions only if you elect averaging for all.

The amount eligible for averaging is the taxable portion of the distribution shown in Box 2a of Form 1099-R. You may also elect to add to the Box 2a amount any net unrealized appreciation in employer securities (shown in Box 6) included in the lump sum. If you are receiving the distribution as a beneficiary of a plan participant who died before August 21, 1996, follow the instructions to Form 4972 for claiming a death benefit exclusion that reduces the Box 2a taxable portion.

If the distribution includes capital gain (Box 3 of Form 1099-R) and you want to apply the special 20% capital gain rate *(7.5)*, you should subtract the capital gain in Box 3 from the taxable amount in Box 2a and apply averaging to the balance of ordinary income.

Form **4972**

Department of the Treasury
Internal Revenue Service (99)

Tax on Lump-Sum Distributions

(From Qualified Plans of Participants Born Before January 2, 1936)

▶ **Attach to Form 1040, Form 1040NR, or Form 1041.**

OMB No. 1545-0193

2010

Attachment Sequence No. **28**

Name of recipient of distribution	**Identifying number**

Part I **Complete this part to see if you can use Form 4972**

			Yes	No
1	Was this a distribution of a plan participant's entire balance (excluding deductible voluntary employee contributions and certain forfeited amounts) from all of an employer's qualified plans of one kind (pension, profit-sharing, or stock bonus)? If "No," **do not** use this form . . .	1	✓	
2	Did you roll over any part of the distribution? If "Yes," **do not** use this form . . .	2		✓
3	Was this distribution paid to you as a beneficiary of a plan participant who was born before January 2, 1936?	3		✓
4	Were you **(a)** a plan participant who received this distribution, **(b)** born before January 2, 1936, **and (c)** a participant in the plan for at least 5 years before the year of the distribution? . . .	4	✓	
	If you answered "No" to both questions 3 **and** 4, **do not** use this form.			
5a	Did you use Form 4972 after 1986 for a previous distribution from your own plan? If "Yes," **do not** use this form for a 2010 distribution from your own plan . . .	5a		✓
b	If you are receiving this distribution as a beneficiary of a plan participant who died, did you use Form 4972 for a previous distribution received for that participant after 1986? If "Yes," **do not** use the form for this distribution . . .	5b		

Part II **Complete this part to choose the 20% capital gain election** (see instructions)

6	Capital gain part from Form 1099-R, box 3 . . .	6	8,620
7	Multiply line 6 by 20% (.20) . . . ▶	7	1,724
	If you also choose to use Part III, go to line 8. Otherwise, include the amount from line 7 in the total on Form 1040, line 44, Form 1040NR, line 42, or Form 1041, Schedule G, line 1b, whichever applies. . .		

Part III **Complete this part to choose the 10-year tax option** (see instructions)

8	Ordinary income from Form 1099-R, box 2a minus box 3. If you did not complete Part II, enter the taxable amount from Form 1099-R, box 2a . . .			8	173,818
9	Death benefit exclusion for a beneficiary of a plan participant who died before August 21, 1996 .			9	-0-
10	Total taxable amount. Subtract line 9 from line 8 . . .			10	173,818
11	Current actuarial value of annuity from Form 1099-R, box 8. If none, enter -0- . . .			11	-0-
12	Adjusted total taxable amount. Add lines 10 and 11. If this amount is $70,000 or more, **skip** lines 13 through 16, enter this amount on line 17, and go to line 18 . . .			12	173,818
13	Multiply line 12 by 50% (.50), but **do not** enter more than $10,000 . .	13			
14	Subtract $20,000 from line 12. If line 12 is $20,000 or less, enter -0- . . .	14			
15	Multiply line 14 by 20% (.20) . . .	15			
16	Minimum distribution allowance. Subtract line 15 from line 13 . . .			16	
17	Subtract line 16 from line 12 . . .			17	173,818
18	Federal estate tax attributable to lump-sum distribution . . .			18	-0-
19	Subtract line 18 from line 17. If line 11 is zero, **skip** lines 20 through 22 and go to line 23 . . .			19	173,818
20	Divide line 11 by line 12 and enter the result as a decimal (rounded to at least three places) . . .	20	.		
21	Multiply line 16 by the decimal on line 20 . . .	21			
22	Subtract line 21 from line 11 . . .	22			
23	Multiply line 19 by 10% (.10) . . .			23	17,382
24	Tax on amount on line 23. Use the Tax Rate Schedule in the instructions . . .			24	3,012
25	Multiply line 24 by ten (10). If line 11 is zero, **skip** lines 26 through 28, enter this amount on line 29, and go to line 30 . . .			25	30,120
26	Multiply line 22 by 10% (.10) . . .	26			
27	Tax on amount on line 26. Use the Tax Rate Schedule in the instructions . . .	27			
28	Multiply line 27 by ten (10) . . .			28	
29	Subtract line 28 from line 25. Multiple recipients, see instructions . . . ▶			29	30,120
30	**Tax on lump-sum distribution.** Add lines 7 and 29. Also include this amount in the total on Form 1040, line 44, Form 1040NR, line 42, or Form 1041, Schedule G, line 1b, whichever applies . . ▶			30	31,844

For Paperwork Reduction Act Notice, see instructions. Cat. No. 13187U Form **4972** (2010)

The tax computed on Form 4972 is reported on Form 1040, Line 44, as an additional tax. It is completely separate from the tax computed on your other income reported on Form 1040.

See the following Example and the Sample Form 4972 above.

EXAMPLE

Andrew Kellogg was born in 1935. In 2010, he retired from StarShine Systems, Inc., and received a lump-sum distribution of $182,438, before withholdings. The Form 1099-R provided by the company (*see* page 154) shows in Box 3 the capital gain portion of $8,620, attributable to pre-1974 participation.

On Form 4972, Andrew applies the special 20% rate to the capital gain portion for a tax of $1,724. He then figures the tax on the $173,818 ordinary income part of the distribution under the 10-year averaging method. As shown on the sample Form 4972 on page 157, Andrew's total tax on the distribution is $31,844, the sum of the $30,120 tax under 10-year averaging and the $1,724 tax on the capital gain portion. In Andrew's case, the special 20% capital gains rate is advantageous because it results in a lower tax than if the capital gain were treated as ordinary income subject to the averaging computation. The tax would be $32,360 if the special capital gain rate was not elected.

Community property. Only the spouse who has earned the lump sum may use averaging. Community property laws are disregarded for this purpose. If a couple files separate returns and one spouse elects averaging, the other spouse is not taxed on the amount subject to the computation.

EXAMPLE

A husband in a community property state receives a lump-sum distribution of which the ordinary income portion is $10,000. He and his wife file separate returns. If averaging is not elected, $5,000, or one-half, is taxable on the husband's return and the other $5,000 on his wife's return. However, if he elects the averaging method, only he reports the $10,000 on Form 4972.

7.5 Capital Gain Treatment for Pre-1974 Participation

The portion of a qualifying lump-sum distribution attributable to pre-1974 participation is eligible for a 20% capital gain rate if you were born before January 2, 1936, and the other tests *(7.2)* are met.

On Form 1099-R, the company paying the lump-sum distribution shows the capital gain portion in Box 3. The ordinary income portion is Box 2a (taxable amount) *minus* Box 3. If you elect to treat the pre-1974 portion as capital gain subject to a flat rate of 20% on Form 4972, the tax on the balance of the distribution may be figured under the averaging method *(7.4)*. The 20% rate for the capital gain portion is fixed by law, and applies regardless of the tax rate imposed on your other capital gains. Alternatively, you may elect to treat the capital gain portion as ordinary income eligible for averaging on Form 4972. You may not elect to report any portion of the pre-1974 portion of the lump-sum distribution as long-term capital gain on Schedule D.

Under the one-time election rule, if you elect to apply the averaging and/or 20% capital gain rule for a 2010 distribution, you may not elect averaging or capital gain treatment for any later distribution.

Filing Tip

Pre-1974 Capital Gain Portion of Distribution

If you were born before January 2, 1936, and a portion of your lump-sum distribution is attributable to plan participation before 1974 *(7.5)*, you may treat it as ordinary income eligible for averaging, or you may elect to treat it as capital gain taxable at a flat 20% rate; choose the method on Form 4972 that gives the lower overall tax.

Capital gain treatment not allowed for individuals born after January 1, 1936. If you were born after January 1, 1936, you may *not* treat any portion of a lump-sum distribution as capital gain. You may not apply the flat 20% rate to the pre-1974 portion of the lump-sum distribution on Form 4972, or include any part of it as capital gain on Schedule D.

7.6 Lump-Sum Payments Received by Beneficiary

A beneficiary of a deceased employee or self-employed plan participant may elect 10-year averaging on Form 4972 for a qualifying lump-sum distribution *(7.2)* because of the participant's death, provided the participant was born before January 2, 1936. The age of the beneficiary is irrelevant. A beneficiary may elect averaging even though the deceased employee was in the plan for less than five years. If the participant was born before January 2, 1936, and had participated in the plan before 1974, a 20% capital gain election may be made for that portion of the distribution *(7.5)*, and the averaging method applied to the balance.

Form 4972 is used to compute tax under the averaging method or to make the 20% capital gain election *(7.5)*. Follow the Form 4972 instructions to claim the up-to-$5,000 death benefit exclusion where the plan participant died before August 21, 1996. Any federal estate tax attributable to the distribution reduces the taxable amount on Form 4972. Any election that you make as a beneficiary does not affect your right to elect lump-sum treatment for a distribution from your own plan.

A lump sum paid because of an employee's death may qualify for capital gain and averaging treatment, although the employee received annuity payments before death.

An election may be made on Form 4972 only once as the beneficiary of a particular plan participant. A beneficiary who receives more than one lump-sum distribution for the same participant in the same year must treat them all the same way. Averaging must be elected for all of the distributions on a single Form 4972 or for none of them.

Payment received by a second beneficiary (after the death of the first beneficiary) is not entitled to lump-sum treatment or the death benefit exclusion.

Beneficiaries of plan participants born after January 1, 1936. A beneficiary may *not* claim averaging or capital gain treatment for a lump-sum distribution if the plan participant was born after January 1, 1936.

Distribution to trust or estate. If a qualifying lump sum is paid to a trust or an estate, the employee, or, if deceased, his or her personal representative, may elect averaging.

EXAMPLE

Gunnison's father was covered by a company benefit plan. The father died, as did Gunnison's mother, before benefits were fully paid out. Gunnison received a substantial lump sum. He argued that he collected on account of his father's death. The IRS disagreed.

The Tax Court and an appeals court sided with the IRS. Gunnison was entitled to the payment following his mother's death, not his father's death. For special lump-sum treatment, the payout must arise solely on account of the death of the covered employee.

Filing Tip

Lump Sums to Multiple Beneficiaries

A lump-sum distribution to two or more beneficiaries may qualify for averaging and capital gain treatment, so long as the plan participant was born before January 2, 1936. Each beneficiary may separately elect the averaging method for the ordinary income portion, even though other beneficiaries do not so elect. Follow the Form 4972 instructions for multiple recipients.

7.7 Tax-Free Rollovers From Qualified Plans

A rollover allows you to make a tax-free transfer of a distribution from a qualified employer retirement plan to another qualified plan, a traditional IRA, a 403(b) plan *(7.21)*, or a state or local government 457 plan *(7.22)* that accepts rollovers. If a rollover is made to a traditional IRA, later distributions are subject to the IRA rules *(8.8)* and will not qualify for special averaging *(7.4)*. ***Caution***: If the distribution is for part of your account balance and you roll it over, a later lump-sum distribution from the same plan will not qualify for averaging even if you were born before January 2, 1936 *(7.4)*.

Eligible rollover distributions. Almost all taxable distributions received from a qualified corporate or self-employed pension, profit-sharing, stock bonus, or annuity plan are eligible for tax-free rollover. Exceptions include substantially equal periodic payments over your lifetime or over a period of at least 10 years, hardship distributions, and minimum distributions *(7.13)* required after age 70½; *see* below for the list of ineligible distributions.

Rollover of after-tax contributions. After-tax contributions may be rolled over to a traditional IRA. A trustee-to-trustee transfer of after-tax contributions may also be made to a qualified defined contribution plan, a defined benefit plan, or a 403(b) tax-sheltered annuity that separately accounts for the after-tax amount.

Rollover options. If you want to make a tax-free rollover of an eligible rollover distribution, you should instruct your employer to directly roll over the funds to a traditional IRA you designate or to the plan of your new employer. You could also choose to have the distribution paid to you, and within 60 days you could make a tax-free rollover yourself. *However, to avoid the 20% mandatory withholding tax, you must elect to have the plan make a direct rollover. If an eligible rollover distribution is paid to you, the 20% withholding tax applies. Before a distribution is made, your employer must provide you with written notice concerning the rollover options and the withholding tax rules.* See *7.8 for further details on the direct rollover and personal rollover alternatives.*

Planning Reminder

Direct Rollover to Roth IRA

A distribution from a qualified employer plan, 403(b) plan, or governmental 457 plan can be rolled over to a Roth IRA, but the rollover is a taxable distribution except to the extent it is allocable to after-tax contributions. If the rollover was made in 2010, half of the taxable amount will be treated as income for 2011 and half will be treated as income for 2012 unless you make an election on Form 8606 to report the entire amount as 2010 income *(8.21)*.

Rollover from employer plan to IRA after age 70½. Starting with the year you reach age 70½, you may no longer make contributions to a traditional IRA. However, if you are over age 70½ and you receive an eligible rollover distribution from your employer's plan, you may instruct your employer to make a direct rollover of the distribution to a traditional IRA *(7.8)*. If you receive the distribution from the employer, a 20% tax will be withheld. You may then make a tax-free rollover within 60 days of the distribution; *see* the discussion of "personal rollovers" *(7.8)*. In the year of the rollover, you must receive a minimum distribution from the IRA *(8.13)*.

Beneficiaries. See the discussion of rollover options open to beneficiaries *(7.8)*.

Distributions that may not be rolled over. Any lump-sum or partial distribution from your account is eligible for rollover *except for the following*:

- Hardship distributions from a 401(k) plan or 403(b) plan *(7.19)*.
- Payments that are part of a series of substantially equal payments made at least annually over a period of 10 years or more or over your life or life expectancy (or the joint lives or joint life and last survivor expectancies of you and your designated beneficiary).
- Minimum required distributions after attaining age 70½ or retiring *(7.13)*.
- Corrective distributions of excess 401(k) plan contributions and deferrals.
- Dividends on employer stock.
- Life insurance coverage costs.
- Loans that are deemed to be taxable distributions because they exceed the limits discussed in *7.16*.

For all of the above taxable distributions that are *ineligible* for rollover, you may elect to completely avoid withholding on Form W-4P.

7.8 Direct Rollover or Personal Rollover

If you receive an eligible rollover distribution *(7.7)* from a qualified plan, you may choose a direct rollover, or if you actually receive the distribution you may make a personal rollover. To avoid withholding, choose a direct rollover. You must receive a written explanation of your rollover rights from your employer before an eligible rollover distribution is made.

Rollover to Roth IRA. An eligible rollover distribution from a qualified employer plan, 403(b) plan, or governmental 457 plan may be rolled over to a Roth IRA. A rollover to a Roth IRA, like a conversion from a traditional IRA, is a taxable distribution except to the extent it is allocable to after-tax contributions *(8.21)*. However, under the special conversion rules for 2010, half of the taxable amount will be treated as income for 2011 and half will be treated as income for 2012 unless you make an election on Form 8606 to report the entire amount as 2010 income *(8.21)*.

Planning Reminder

IRA Conduit Between Employer Plans

If you roll over a distribution from an employer plan to a traditional IRA, you may later roll over a distribution from the IRA to a new employer's plan. You can make the subsequent rollover from the IRA even if the funds from the first employer were mixed with regular IRA contributions and earnings.

However, if you were born before January 2, 1936, expect to join another employer's qualified plan, and want to preserve the possibility of claiming averaging for a lump-sum distribution *(7.2)* from the new employer's plan, a rollover from the first employer plan should be to a segregated "conduit IRA." A conduit IRA contains only the assets distributed from the first qualified plan plus the earnings on those assets. If you then join a company with a plan that accepts rollovers and make the rollover from the conduit IRA into that plan, a subsequent lump-sum distribution from the new employer plan will qualify for 10-year averaging (and possibly 20% capital gain treatment for pre-1974 participation), assuming the distribution otherwise qualifies *(7.2)*.

Direct Rollover From Employer Plan

If you choose to have your employer make a direct rollover of an eligible rollover distribution to a traditional IRA or another eligible employer plan *(7.7)*, you avoid tax on the payment and no tax will be withheld. If you are changing jobs and want a direct rollover to the plan of the new employer, make sure that the plan accepts rollovers; if it does not, choose a direct rollover to a traditional IRA.

When you select the direct rollover option, your employer may transfer the funds directly by check or wire to the new plan, or you may be given a check payable to the new plan that you deliver.

In choosing a direct rollover to a traditional IRA, the terms of the payer-employer's plan will determine whether you may divide the distribution among several IRAs or whether you will be restricted to one IRA. For example, you may want to split up your distribution into several traditional IRAs, but the employer may force you to select only one. After the direct rollover is made, you may then diversify your holdings by making tax-free trustee-to-trustee transfers to other traditional IRAs.

You may elect to make a direct rollover of part of your distribution and to receive the balance. The portion paid to you will be subject to 20% withholding and is not eligible for special averaging. Withholding is generally not required on distributions of less than $200.

A direct rollover will be reported by the payer plan to the IRS and to you on Form 1099-R, although the transfer is not taxable. The direct rollover will be reported in Box 1 of Form 1099-R, but zero will be entered as the taxable amount in Box 2a. In Box 7, Code G should be entered.

Personal Rollover After Receiving a Distribution

If you do not tell your employer to make a direct rollover of an eligible rollover distribution, and you instead receive the distribution yourself, you will receive only 80% of the taxable portion (generally the entire distribution unless you made after-tax contributions); 20% will be withheld. Withholding does not apply to the portion of the distribution consisting of net unrealized appreciation from employer securities that is tax-free *(7.10)*.

Although you receive only 80% of the taxable eligible rollover distribution, the full amount before withholding will be reported as the gross distribution in Box 1 of Form 1099-R. To avoid tax you must roll over the full amount within 60 days to a traditional IRA or another eligible employer plan. However, to roll over 100% of the distribution you will have to use other funds to replace the 20% withheld. If you roll over only the 80% received, the 20% balance will be taxable; *see* the John Anderson Example below. For the taxable part that is not rolled over, you may not use special averaging or capital gain treatment even if you meet the age test *(7.4)*. In addition, if the distribution was made to you before you reached age 59½, the taxable amount will be subject to a 10% penalty unless you are disabled, separating from service after reaching age 55, or have substantial medical expenses; *see* the full list of exceptions below *(7.15)*.

Planning Reminder

Pre-Age-$59^1/_2$ Distributions

If you are under age $59^1/_2$ and do not roll over an eligible distribution, you will generally be subject to a 10% penalty in addition to regular income tax. However, penalty exceptions apply if you separate from service and are age 55 or older, you are disabled, or you pay substantial medical expenses; *see* the full list of penalty exceptions in this Chapter *(7.15)*.

If a distribution includes your voluntary after-tax contributions to the qualified plan, they are tax free to you when you receive them. However, after-tax contributions may be rolled over to a qualified plan or a 403(b) plan that separately accounts for the after-tax amounts.

A rollover *may* include salary deferral contributions that were excludable from income when made, such as qualifying deferrals to a 401(k) plan. The rollover may also include accumulated deductible employee contributions (and allocable income) made after 1981 and before 1987. Your employer's retirement plan may invest in a limited amount of life insurance which is then distributed to you as part of a lump-sum retirement distribution. You may be able to roll over the life insurance contract to the qualified plan of your new employer but not to a traditional IRA. The law bars investment of IRA funds in life insurance contracts.

You may not claim a deduction for your rollover.

Multiple rollover accounts allowed. You may wish to diversify a distribution in different investments. There is no limit on the number of rollover accounts you may have. A lump-sum distribution from a qualified plan may be rolled over to several traditional IRAs.

Caution

IRA Rollover Election Is Irrevocable

A rollover from an employer plan to a traditional IRA is irrevocable, according to the IRS. At the time of the rollover, you must elect in writing to irrevocably treat the contribution as a rollover. If a qualifying lump-sum distribution is made to you and you roll it over, you may not later change your mind in order to claim averaging even though you were born before January 2, 1936, and the other tests for averaging are met *(7.4)*. Before making a rollover, figure what the current tax would be on the lump-sum distribution under the special averaging method. Compare it with an estimate of the regular tax that will be payable on a later distribution of the rolled-over account from the IRA.

EXAMPLE

In June 2011, John Anderson retires at age 52. He is due a lump-sum distribution of $100,000 from a qualified plan of his company. If he instructs his employer to make a direct rollover of the amount to a traditional IRA or eligible employer plan, there is no tax withholding, and the $100,000 is transferred tax free.

Now assume that John decides not to choose a direct rollover because he is planning to use the funds to invest in a business. The plan will pay him $80,000 and withhold a tax of $20,000 that John will apply to his tax liability when he files his 2011 return. But, say, a month later John changes his mind about the investment and now wants to roll over his benefits to a traditional IRA. He must make the rollover within 30 days because 30 days of the 60-day rollover period have already passed. Furthermore, to avoid tax on the entire distribution, he must deposit $100,000 in the traditional IRA, even though $20,000 tax has been withheld. If he does not have the $20,000, he must borrow the $20,000 and deposit it in the IRA. If he rolls over only $80,000, he must report $20,000 as a taxable distribution on his 2011 return and since John is under age 59½, the 10% penalty for early withdrawals will apply; based on these facts, John does not qualify for a penalty exception *(7.15)*.

Reporting a personal rollover on your return. When you receive a distribution that could have been rolled over, the payer will report on Form 1099-R the full taxable amount before withholding, although 20% has been withheld. However, if you make a rollover yourself within the 60-day period, the rollover reduces the taxable amount on your tax return. For example, if in 2009 you were entitled to a $100,000 lump-sum distribution and received $80,000 after mandatory 20% withholding and then you rolled over the full $100,000 into a traditional IRA, report $100,000 on Line 16a of Form 1040 or Line 12a of Form 1040A, but enter zero as the taxable amount on Line 16b or Line 12b and write "Rollover" next to the line. If you roll over only part of the distribution, the amount of the lump sum *not* rolled over is entered as the taxable amount. Remember to include the 20% withholding on the line for federal income tax withheld.

IRS may waive 60-day deadline for personal rollover on equitable grounds. Generally, a personal rollover must be completed by the 60th day following the day on which you receive a distribution from the employer plan. However, the IRS has discretion to waive the 60-day deadline and permit more time for a rollover where failure to complete a timely rollover was due to events beyond your reasonable control, and failure to waive the deadline would be "against equity or good conscience."

The same waiver rule applies to rollovers from traditional IRAs. *See* the IRS guidelines on granting a waiver *(8.10)*.

Extension of 60-day rollover period for frozen deposits. If you receive a qualifying distribution from a retirement plan and deposit the funds in a financial institution that becomes bankrupt or insolvent, you may be prevented from withdrawing the funds in time to complete a rollover within 60 days. If this happens, the 60-day period is extended while your account is "frozen." The 60-day rollover period does not include days on which your account is frozen. Further, you have a minimum of 10 days after the release of the funds to complete the rollover.

Rollover by Beneficiary

Surviving spouse. If you are your deceased spouse's beneficiary, you may roll over your interest in his or her qualified plan account. You may choose to have the plan make a direct rollover to your own traditional IRA. The advantage of choosing the direct rollover is to avoid a 20% withholding. If the distribution is paid to you, 20% will be withheld. You may make a rollover within 60 days, but to completely avoid tax, you must include in the rollover the withheld amount, as illustrated in the John Anderson Example above. If you receive the distribution but do not make the rollover, you will be taxed on the distribution, but if your spouse was born before January 2, 1936, you may be able to use special averaging *(7.4)* to compute the tax. You are *not* subject to the 10% penalty for premature distributions *(7.15)* even if you are under age 59½.

You can roll over the distribution to a Roth IRA but the rollover is taxable under the rules for conversions from traditional IRAs. A special rule for 2010 treats half of the taxable amount as income for 2011 and half as income for 2012 unless you make an election on Form 8606 to report the entire amount as 2010 income *(8.21)*.

You may also roll over a distribution from your deceased spouse's account to your own qualified plan, 403(a) qualified annuity, 403(b) tax-sheltered annuity, or governmental section 457 plan. However, if you were born before January 2, 1936, and want to preserve the option of electing averaging *(7.4)* or capital gain treatment (for pre-1974 participation, *see 7.5*) for a later distribution from your employer's qualified plan, you should *not* roll over your deceased spouse's account to your employer's qualified plan. If the rollover is made to your employer's qualified plan, a lump-sum distribution from the plan will not be eligible for averaging or capital gains treatment.

Law Alert

Nonspouse Beneficiary Rollover to Inherited IRA

Starting in 2010, employer plans must allow a nonspouse beneficiary to make a trustee-to-trustee transfer to an IRA that is treated as an inherited IRA.

Rollover of distribution received under a divorce or support proceeding. In a qualified domestic relations order (QDRO) meeting special tax law tests, a state court may give you the right to receive all or part of your spouse's or former spouse's retirement benefits. You can choose to have the payment made to you or you can instruct the plan to make a direct rollover to a traditional IRA or to your employer's qualified plan if it accepts rollovers. Alternatively, if the distribution is paid to you, 20% withholding will apply. You may complete a rollover within 60 days under the rules for personal rollovers discussed earlier. If you do not make the rollover, the distribution you receive is taxable, but you may be able to elect special averaging if averaging would have been allowed had it been received by your spouse or former spouse *(7.3)*. If only part of the distribution is rolled over, the balance is taxed as ordinary income in the year of receipt. In figuring your tax, you are allowed a prorated share of your former spouse's cost investment, if any. You are not subject to the 10% penalty for premature distributions even if under age 59½.

Nonspouse beneficiaries. Starting with plan years beginning after 2009, a nonspouse beneficiary must be allowed to roll over a distribution from a qualified plan, 403(b) plan, or governmental 457 plan to an IRA in a trustee-to-trustee transfer. The IRA must be treated as an inherited IRA subject to the required minimum distribution rules for nonspouse beneficiaries *(8.14)*.

For distributions after 2006 and before 2010, employer plans had the option of allowing rollovers by nonspouse beneficiaries, but this was not a plan requirement.

7.9 Rollover of Proceeds From Sale of Property

A lump-sum distribution from a qualified plan may include property, such as non-employer stock; *see 7.10* for employer securities. If you plan to roll over the distribution, you may find that a bank or other plan trustee does not want to take the property. You cannot get tax-free rollover treatment by keeping the property and rolling over cash to the new plan. If you sell the property, you may roll over the sale proceeds to a traditional IRA as long as the sale and rollover occur within 60 days of receipt of the distribution. If you roll over all of the proceeds, you do not recognize a gain or loss from the sale; the proceeds are treated as part of the distribution. If you make a partial rollover of sale proceeds, you must report as capital gain the portion of the gain that is allocable to the retained sale proceeds.

If you receive cash and property, and you sell the property but only make a partial rollover, you must designate how much of the rolled-over cash is from the employer distribution and how much from the sale proceeds. The designation must be made by the time for filing your return (plus any extensions) and is irrevocable. If you do not make a timely designation, the IRS will allocate the rollover between cash and sales proceeds on a ratable basis; the allocation will determine tax on the retained amount.

Court Decision

Stock Purchased With Cash Withdrawal Cannot Be Rolled Over

A taxpayer withdrew cash from his Keogh accounts and used most of the net distribution (after withholdings) to buy stock, which was then transferred to an IRA within 60 days of the withdrawal. He treated the entire distribution as a tax-free rollover but the IRS and Tax Court held it was taxable. The transfer of stock to the IRA was not a tax-free rollover; only the cash distribution itself could be rolled over. A negligence penalty was also imposed.

A direct rollover from the Keogh accounts to an IRA would have been tax free; the stock could then have been purchased through the new IRA.

7.10 Distribution of Employer Stock or Other Securities

If you are entitled to a distribution from an employer plan that includes employer stock (or other employer securities), you may be able to take advantage of a special exclusion rule. If you withdraw the stock from the plan as part of a lump-sum distribution and invest the stock in a taxable brokerage account instead of rolling it over to a traditional IRA, tax on the "net unrealized appreciation," or NUA, may be deferred until you sell the stock. To defer tax on the full NUA, the employer stock must be received in a lump-sum distribution, as discussed below. If the distribution is not a lump sum, a less favorable NUA exclusion is available, but only if you made after-tax contributions to buy the shares; *see* below.

Planning Reminder

Deferring Tax on NUA

If you receive a lump-sum distribution that includes appreciated employer securities, you may defer the tax on the net unrealized appreciation (NUA) in the securities.

Lump-sum distribution. If you receive appreciated stock or securities as part of a lump-sum distribution, net unrealized appreciation (increase in value since purchase of securities) is not subject to tax at the time of distribution unless you elect to treat it as taxable.

For purposes of the NUA exclusion, a lump-sum distribution is the payment within a single year of the plan participant's entire balance from all of the employer's qualified plans of the same kind (all of the employer's profit-sharing plans, or all pension or stock bonus plans). The distribution must be paid to: (1) a participant after reaching age 59½, (2) an employee-participant who separates from service (by retiring, resigning, changing employers, or being fired), (3) a self-employed participant who becomes totally and permanently disabled, or (4) a beneficiary of a deceased plan participant. If there is any plan balance at the end of the year, there is no lump sum and the NUA exclusion is not available.

Assuming you do not waive the NUA exclusion, you are taxed (at ordinary income rates) only on the original cost of the stock when contributed to the plan. Tax on the appreciation is delayed until the shares are later sold by you at a price exceeding cost basis and the gain attributable to the NUA will be taxed at long-term capital gain rates *(5.3)*.

The NUA in employer's securities is shown in Box 6 of the Form 1099-R received from the payer. It is *not* included in the taxable amount in Box 2a.

If, when distributed, the shares are valued at below the cost contribution to the plan, the fair market value of the shares is subject to tax. If you contributed to the purchase of the shares and their value is less than your contribution, you do not realize a loss deduction on the distribution. You realize a loss only when the stock is sold for less than your cost or becomes worthless *(5.32)* at a later date. If a plan distributes worthless stock, you may deduct your contributions to the stock as a miscellaneous itemized deduction subject to the 2% of adjusted gross income floor.

EXAMPLES

1. *Shares valued below your cost contribution.* You contributed $500 and your employer contributed $300 to buy 10 shares of company stock having at the time a fair market value of $80 per share. When you retire, the fair market value of the stock is $40 per share, or a total of $400. You do not realize income on the distribution, and you do not have a deductible loss for the difference between your cost contribution

and the lower fair market value. Your contribution to the stock is its basis. This is $50 per share. If you sell the stock for $40 per share, you have a capital loss of $10 per share. However, if you sell the stock for $60 per share, you have gain of $10 per share.

2. *Appreciated shares.* You receive 10 shares of company stock that was purchased entirely with the employer's funds. Your employer's cost was $50 a share. At the time of a lump-sum distribution, the shares are valued at $80 a share. Your employer's contribution of $50 a share, or $500, is included as part of your taxable distribution. The appreciation of $300 is not included, assuming you do not elect to be taxed currently on the appreciation. The cost basis of the shares in your hands is $500 (the amount currently taxable to you). The holding period of the stock starts from the date of distribution. However, if you sell the shares for any amount exceeding $500 and up to $800, your profit is long-term capital gain regardless of how long you held the shares. If you sell for more than $800, the gain exceeding the original unrealized appreciation of $300 is subject to long-term capital gain treatment only if the sale is long term from the date of distribution. Thus, if within a month of the distribution you sold the shares for $900, $300 would be long-term gain; $100 would be short-term gain.

Election to waive tax-free treatment. You may elect to include the NUA in employer stock or securities as income. You might consider making this election when the NUA is not substantial or you want to accelerate income to the current year by taking into account the entire lump-sum distribution. If you were born before January 2, 1936, and are claiming averaging or capital gain treatment on Form 4972 *(7.4)*, follow the form instructions for adding the unrealized appreciation to the taxable distribution. If you are not filing Form 4972, the election to include the unrealized appreciation as ordinary income is made by reporting it on Line 16b (taxable pensions and annuities) of Form 1040 or Line 12b of Form 1040A.

Distribution not a lump sum. If you receive appreciated employer securities in a distribution that does not meet the lump-sum tests above, you report as ordinary income the amount of the employer's contribution to the purchase of the shares and the appreciation allocated to the employer's cost contribution. You do not report the amount of appreciation allocated to your own after-tax contribution to the purchase. In other words, tax is deferred only on the NUA attributable to your after-tax employee contributions. Net unrealized appreciation is shown in Box 6 of Form 1099-R. Cost contributions must be supplied by the company distributing the stock.

EXAMPLE

A qualified plan distributes 10 shares of company stock with an average cost of $100, of which the employee contributed $60 and the employer, $40. At the date of distribution, the stock had a fair market value of $180. The portion of the unrealized appreciation attributable to the employee's contribution is $48 (60% of $80); the employer's is $32 (40% of $80). The employee reports $72 as income: the employer's cost of $40 and the employer's share of appreciation, which is $32. For purposes of determining gain or loss on a later sale, the employee's basis for each share is $132, which includes the employee contribution of $60 and the $72 reported as taxable income.

7.11 Survivor Annuity for Spouse

If you have been married for at least a year as of the annuity starting date, the law generally requires that payments to you of vested benefits be in a specific annuity form to protect your surviving spouse. All defined benefit and money purchase pension plans must provide benefits in the form of a *qualified joint and survivor annuity (QJSA)* unless you, with the written consent of your spouse, elect a different form of benefit. A qualified joint and survivor annuity must also be provided by profit-sharing or stock bonus plans if you elect a life annuity payout or the plan does not provide that your nonforfeitable benefit is payable in full upon your death to your surviving spouse, or to another beneficiary if the spouse consents or there is no surviving spouse.

Under a QJSA, you receive an annuity for your life and your surviving spouse receives an annuity for his or her life that is no less than 50% of the amount payable during your joint lives. You may waive the QJSA only with your spouse's consent. Without the consent, you may not take a lump-sum distribution or a single life annuity ending when you die. A single life annuity pays higher monthly benefits during your lifetime than the qualified joint and survivor annuity. If benefits begin under a QJSA and you divorce the spouse to whom you were married as of the annuity starting date, that former spouse will be entitled to the QJSA survivor benefits if you die unless there is a contrary provision in a QDRO *(7.12)*.

The law also requires that a qualified pre-retirement survivor annuity (QPSA) be paid to your surviving spouse if you die before the date vested benefits first become payable or if you die after the earliest payment date but before retiring. The QPSA is automatic unless you, with your spouse's consent, agree to a different benefit.

Your plan should provide you with a written explanation of these annuity rules within a reasonable period before the annuity starting date, as well as the rules for electing to waive the joint and survivor annuity benefit and the pre-retirement survivor annuity.

Planning Reminder

Spouse Must Consent in Writing to Your Waiver

Your spouse must consent in writing to your waiver of a required annuity and the selection of a different type of distribution. A spouse's consent must be witnessed by a plan representative or notary public. An election to waive the qualified joint and survivor annuity may be made during the 90-day period ending on the annuity starting date. An election to waive the qualified pre-retirement survivor annuity may be made any time after the first day of the plan year in which you reach age 35. A waiver is revocable during the time permitted to make the election.

Plan may provide exception for marriages of less than one year. The terms of a plan may provide that a QJSA or QPSA will not be provided to a spouse of the plan participant if the couple has been married for less than one year as of the participant's annuity starting date (QJSA) or, if earlier, the date of the participant's death (QPSA).

Cash out of annuity. If the present value of the QJSA is $5,000 or less, your employer may "cash out" your interest without your consent or your spouse's consent by making a lump-sum distribution of the present value of the annuity before the annuity starting date. After the annuity starting date, you and your spouse must consent to a cash-out. Written consent is required for a cash-out if the present value of the annuity exceeds $5,000. Similar cash-out rules apply to a QPSA.

7.12 Court Distributions to Former Spouse Under a QDRO

As a part of a divorce-related property settlement, or to cover alimony or support obligations, a state domestic relations court can require that all or part of a plan participant's retirement benefits be paid to a spouse, former spouse, child, or other dependent. Administrators of pension, profit-sharing, or stock bonus plans are required to honor a qualified domestic relations order (QDRO) that meets specific tax law tests. For example, the QDRO generally may not alter the amount or form of benefits provided by the plan, but it may authorize payments after the participant reaches the earliest retirement age, even if he or she continues working. A QDRO may provide that the recipient spouse is entitled to all, some, or none of the spousal survivor benefits payable under the plan.

QDRO distributions to spouse or former spouse. If you are the spouse or former spouse of an employee and you receive a distribution pursuant to a QDRO, the distribution is generally taxable to you. However, you may make a tax-free rollover to an IRA or to an eligible employer plan *(7.7)*. If you do not make a rollover, and your spouse or former spouse (the plan participant) was born *before* 1936, a distribution to you of your entire share of the benefits may be eligible for special averaging, provided the distribution, if received by your spouse (or former spouse), would satisfy the lump-sum distribution tests *(7.2)*. If the distribution qualifies, you may use Form 4972 to claim 10-year averaging, and possibly the 20% capital gain election *(7.4)*. If your spouse (or former spouse) was born after 1935, you may *not* elect averaging or 20% capital gain treatment for the distribution. Transfers from a governmental or church plan pursuant to a qualifying domestic relations order are also eligible for special averaging or rollover treatment.

To create a valid QDRO, the court order must contain specific language. The recipient spouse (or former spouse) must be assigned rights to the plan participant's retirement benefits plan, and must be referred to as an "alternate payee" in the court decree. The decree must identify the retirement plan and indicate the amount and number of payments subject to the QDRO. Both spouses must be identified by name and address.

If the above information is not clearly provided in the decree, QDRO treatment may be denied and the plan participant taxed on the retirement plan distributions, rather than the spouse who actually receives payments.

Distributions to a child or other dependent. Payments from a QDRO are taxed to the plan participant, not to the dependent who actually receives them, where the recipient is not a spouse or former spouse.

Law Alert

RMDs Were Waived for 2009 But Not for 2010

In response to the economic crisis, Congress waived required minimum distributions (RMDs) but the waiver applied only to RMDs for 2009. For plan participants and beneficiaries who were receiving RMDs for 2008 or earlier years, the waiver applied to the RMD that otherwise would have been required for 2009, and for those who turned age 70½ in 2009, the waiver applied to the first RMD that otherwise would have been due by their required beginning date of April 1, 2010. The waiver did not apply to the RMD for 2008, even for individuals who turned age 70½ and chose to take their first RMD by April 1, 2009.

Congress did not extend the waiver law, so the RMD for 2010 (and later years) must be received or a penalty could be imposed. If you reached age 70½ in 2009, your first RMD must be received by December 31, 2010.

7.13 When Retirement Benefits Must Begin

The longer you can delay taking retirement distributions from your company plan or self-employed Keogh plan, the greater will be the tax-deferred buildup of your retirement fund. To cut off this tax deferral, the law requires minimum distributions to begin no later than a specified date in order to avoid an IRS penalty. The required beginning date rules apply to distributions from all qualified corporate and self-employed Keogh plans, qualified annuity plans, and Section 457 plans of tax-exempt organizations and state and local government employers. The rules also apply to distributions from tax-sheltered annuities *(7.21)* but only for benefits accrued after 1986; there is no mandatory beginning date for tax-sheltered annuity benefits accrued before 1987.

You do not have to figure your required minimum distributions (RMDs). If you are not receiving an annuity, your plan administrator will determine the minimum amount that must be distributed each year from your account balance, based upon IRS regulations. The rules are similar to the traditional IRA rules *(8.13)*.

If you do not receive your RMD for a year, a penalty tax applies, unless the IRS waives it, equal to 50% of the difference between what was received and what should have been received.

A temporary law waived the RMD that otherwise would have been due for 2009, but the law expired at the end of 2009, so the RMD due for 2010 must be received.

Required beginning date. Unless you are a more-than-5% owner for the plan year ending in the calendar year in which you reach age 70½, your required beginning date is generally the later of these dates: (1) April 1 following the year in which you reach age 70½ *or* (2) April 1 following the year in which you retire. For example, if you retired in 2009 and reached age 70½ in March 2010, you must receive your first RMD (the RMD for 2010) from the plan by April 1, 2011. You must receive the RMD for 2011 by December 31, 2011.

If you reach age 70½ in 2010, are not a more-than-5% owner in 2010, and do not retire until 2012, your first RMD from the plan does not have to be received until April 1, 2013, the year after the year of retirement, assuming the plan does not require all employees to take the first RMD by April 1 of the year after the year of reaching age 70½.

If you turned age 70½ in 2009, you did not have to receive your first RMD by your required beginning date of April 1, 2010 because of the special waiver law for 2009 RMDs (*see* the Law Alert on this page). Your first RMD is the distribution for 2010, which must be received by December 31, 2010.

If you are a more-than-5% owner for the plan year ending in the calendar year in which you reach age 70½, your required beginning date is April 1 of the year following the year in which you reach age 70½, even if you are still working. Being a more-than-5% owner means that you own over 5% of the capital or profits interest in the business.

However, an IRS regulation permits a plan to require all employees, and not just more-than-5% owners, to begin required minimum distributions no later than April 1 of the year after the year in which age 70½ is attained, even if they are still working.

7.14 Payouts to Beneficiaries

As the beneficiary of an employee's qualified plan account, 403(b) tax-sheltered annuity, or Section 457 plan, your distribution options depend on the terms of the plan. You may prefer the option of receiving payments over your life expectancy but the plan may require that you receive a lump-sum distribution or allow installment payments over only a limited number of years.

Although IRS final regulations generally allow beneficiaries to use a life expectancy distribution method, the IRS rules represent the longest permissible payment period. Employer plans are allowed to require a shorter period and most do.

If you receive a lump-sum distribution, you generally may claim special averaging if the plan participant was born before January 2, 1936 *(7.6)*.

As discussed in *7.13*, the requirement to take a minimum distribution for 2009 was waived. Since the law providing for the waiver was not extended, beneficiaries will have to receive the RMD for 2010 by December 31, 2010.

Surviving spouse. If you are a surviving spouse and receive a lump-sum distribution, you may make a tax-free rollover to another plan *(7.7)* whether or not special averaging is allowed for the distribution.

If the plan gives you the option of taking distributions over your life expectancy as allowed by the IRS rules, you may be able to delay the commencement of distributions for several years. If your spouse died before the year in which he or she attained age 70½, and you are the sole designated beneficiary of the account as of September 30 of the year following the year of death, you do not have to begin receiving distributions until the end of the year in which your spouse would have attained age 70½. This is an exception to the general rule that requires distributions under the life expectancy method to begin by the end of the year following the year in which the employee died.

Nonspouse beneficiary. If you are the designated beneficiary of a deceased employee, you are allowed to roll over a distribution, by means of a direct trustee-to-trustee transfer, to an IRA that is set up as an inherited IRA *(7.8)*.

7.15 Penalty for Distributions Before Age 59½

A 10% penalty generally applies to taxable distributions made to you before you reach age 59½ from a qualified corporate or Keogh plan, qualified annuity plan, and tax-sheltered annuity plan, but there are several exceptions. For example, the penalty does not apply to distributions made to you after separation from service if the separation occurs during or after the year in which you reach age 55. A full list of exceptions is shown below.

If no exception applies, the penalty is 10% of the taxable distribution. If you make a tax-free rollover *(7.7)*, the distribution is not taxable and not subject to the penalty. If a partial rollover is made, the part not rolled over is taxable and subject to the penalty.

A similar 10% penalty applies to IRA distributions before age 59½ *(8.12)*. The penalty is 25% if a distribution before age 59½ is made from a SIMPLE IRA in the first two years of plan participation *(8.18)*. There is a penalty for pre–age 59½ distributions from deferred annuities *(7.23)*. The penalty generally does *not* apply to Section 457 plans of tax-exempt employers or state or local governments. However, if a rollover is made to a governmental Section 457 plan from a qualified plan, 403(b) annuity, or IRA, a later distribution from the Section 457 plan is subject to the penalty to the extent of the rollover.

Exceptions to the penalty. The following distributions are exempt from the 10% penalty, even if made to you before age 59½. If your employer knows that an exception applies, a code for the exception will be entered in Box 7 of Form 1099-R on which the distribution is reported.

- ***Rollovers.*** Distributions that you roll over tax free under the "direct rollover" or "personal rollover" rules *(7.8) are not subject to the early distribution penalty.*
- ***Disability.*** Distributions made on account of your total disability do not subject you to the early distribution penalty.
- ***Separation from service if age 55 or older.*** The early distribution penalty does not apply to distributions after separation from service if you are age 55 or over in the year you retire or leave the company.
- ***Medical costs.*** Distributions are not subject to the early distribution penalty to the extent that you pay deductible medical expenses exceeding 7.5% of your adjusted gross income (whether or not an itemized deduction for medical expenses is claimed).
- ***Substantially equal payments.*** The early distribution penalty does not apply to distributions received after your separation from service that are part of a series of substantially equal payments (at least annually) over your life expectancy, or over the joint life expectancy of yourself and your designated beneficiary. If you claim the exception and begin to receive such a series of payments but then before age 59½ you receive a lump sum or change the distribution method and you are not totally disabled, a recapture penalty tax will generally apply. The recapture tax also applies to payments received before age 59½ if substantially equal payments are not received for at least five years. The recapture tax applies the 10% penalty to all amounts received before age 59½, as if the exception had never been allowed, plus interest for that period. However, the IRS allows taxpayers who have been receiving substantially equal payments under the fixed amortization or fixed annuitization method to switch without penalty to the required minimum distribution method; *see* Revenue Ruling 2002-62 for details. In private rulings, the IRS has allowed the annual distribution amount to be reduced without penalty after the account is divided in a divorce settlement.
- ***Beneficiaries.*** If you are the beneficiary of a deceased plan participant, you are not subject to the 10% penalty, regardless of your age or the participant's age.
- ***Qualified reservist distribution.*** If you are a member of the reserves called to active

Caution

Penalty Exception for Substantially Equal Payments

The substantially equal payments exception to the 10% early distribution penalty is generally revoked if qualifying payments are not received for at least five years. For example, you separate from service when you are age 57 and you begin to receive a series of qualifying substantially equal payments. When you are age 61, you stop the payments or modify the payment schedule so that it no longer qualifies. Unless the IRS permits an exception, the 10% penalty applies to the payments received before age 59½ because the five-year test was not met.

military duty for over 179 days, or indefinitely, distributions received during the active duty period that are attributable to elective deferrals (401(k) or 403(b) plan) are not subject to the early distribution penalty. Furthermore, a qualified reservist distribution may be recontributed to the plan within two years after the end of the active duty period.

- ***Public safety employees separated from service.*** The early distribution penalty does not apply to a distribution from a state or local defined benefit pension plan to a public safety officer (police, fire, emergency medical) who has separated from service in or after the year of reaching age 50.
- ***IRS levy.*** Involuntary distributions that result from an IRS levy on your plan account are not subject to the early distribution penalty.
- ***QDRO.*** Distributions paid to an alternate payee pursuant to a qualified domestic relations court order (QDRO) are not subject to the early distribution penalty.
- ***TEFRA designations.*** Distributions made before 1984 pursuant to a designation under the 1982 Tax Act (TEFRA).
- ***Separation from service before March 2, 1986.*** Distributions to an employee who separated from service by March 1, 1986, are not subject to the early distribution penalty, provided that accrued benefits were in pay status as of that date under a written election specifying the payout schedule.

Filing Instruction

Reporting the Early Distribution Penalty

If you received a distribution before age 59½, do not qualify for a penalty exception, and Code 1 is shown in Box 7 of your Form 1099-R, multiply the taxable distribution by 10% and enter that amount as the penalty on Line 58 of Form 1040; write "no" next to Line 58 to indicate that Form 5329 does not have to be filed. If you are subject to the penalty and Code 1 is not entered in Box 7 of Form 1099-R, you must file Form 5329.

You may also have to file Form 5329 to claim a penalty exception. However, filing the form is not required if you qualify for the rollover exception or you qualify for another exception that is correctly coded in Box 7 of Form 1099-R.

Financial hardship distributions or distributions used for college or home-buying costs are subject to the penalty. The 10% penalty applies to a hardship distribution that you receive before age 59½ from a 401(k) plan *(7.19)* or 403(b) tax-sheltered annuity plan *(7.21)*. Even where it is used to pay tuition costs or to buy a principal residence, there is no penalty exception, although a penalty exception generally applies for IRA distributions used for such purposes *(8.12)*.

A hardship distribution used to pay medical costs may qualify for an exception; *see* above.

Corrective distributions from 401(k) plans. If you are considered a highly compensated employee and excess elective deferrals or excess contributions are made on your behalf, a distribution of the excess to you is not subject to the penalty.

Filing Form 5329 for exceptions. If your employer correctly entered a penalty exception code in Box 7 of Form 1099-R, you do not have to file Form 5329 to claim the exception. You also do not have to file Form 5329 if you made a tax-free rollover of the entire taxable distribution. You must file Form 5329 if you qualify for an exception, other than the rollover exception, that is not indicated in Box 7 of Form 1099-R.

Caution

Unpaid Loan Taxable If You Leave Job Unless Rolled Over

If you leave your company before your loan is paid off, the company will reduce your vested account balance by the outstanding debt and report the defaulted amount as a taxable distribution on Form 1099-R.

For example, if your vested account balance is $100,000, and the outstanding loan is $20,000, your account balance is reduced to $80,000. If you elect to receive the balance, rather than choosing a direct rollover, $20,000 will be withheld (20% of the full $100,000) and you will receive only $60,000 *(7.8)*. However, the full $100,000 is treated as a taxable distribution. If you do not roll over *(7.8)* the entire $100,000 within 60 days, you will be taxed on the portion not rolled over, and possibly be subject to a 10% penalty if you were under age 59½ at the time of the distribution *(7.15)*.

In other words, tax on the defaulted loan balance can be avoided by depositing that amount into a rollover IRA within 60 days of the date that the balance was treated as being in default.

7.16 Restrictions on Loans From Company Plans

Within limits, you may receive a loan from a qualified company plan, annuity plan, 403(b) plan, or government plan without triggering tax consequences. The maximum loan you can receive without tax is the lesser of 50% of your vested account balance or $50,000, but the $50,000 limit is subject to reductions where there are other loans outstanding; *see* below. Loans must be repayable within five years, unless they are used for buying your principal residence. Loans that do not meet these guidelines are treated as taxable distributions from the plan. If the plan treats a loan as a taxable distribution, you should receive a Form 1099-R with Code L marked in Box 7.

If your vested accrued benefit is $20,000 or less, you are not taxed if the loan, when added to other outstanding loans from all plans of the employer, is $10,000 or less. However, as a practical matter, your maximum loan may not exceed 50% of your vested account balance because of a Labor Department rule that allows only up to 50% of the vested balance to be used as loan security. Loans in excess of the 50% cap are allowed only if additional collateral is provided.

If your vested accrued benefit exceeds $20,000, then the maximum tax-free loan depends on whether you borrowed from any employer plan within the one-year period ending on the day before the date of the new loan. If you did not borrow within the year, you are not taxed on a loan that does not exceed the lesser of $50,000 or 50% of the vested benefit.

If there were loans within the one-year period, the $50,000 limit must be further reduced. The loan, when added to the outstanding loan balance, may not exceed $50,000 less the excess of (1) the highest outstanding loan balance during the one-year period (ending the day before the new loan) over (2) the outstanding balance on the date of the new loan. This reduced $50,000 limit applies where it is less than 50% of the vested benefit; if 50% of the vested benefit was the smaller amount, that would be the maximum tax-free loan.

EXAMPLE

Your vested plan benefit is $200,000. Assume that in December 2010 you borrow $30,000 from the plan. On November 1, 2011, when the outstanding balance on the first loan is $20,000, you want to take another loan without incurring tax.

You may borrow an additional $20,000 without incurring tax: The $50,000 limit is first reduced by the outstanding loan balance of $20,000—leaving $30,000. The reduced $30,000 limit is in turn reduced by $10,000, the excess of $30,000 (the highest loan balance within one year of the new loan) over $20,000 (the loan balance as of November 1).

Repayment period. Generally, loans within the previously discussed limits must be repayable within five years to avoid being treated as a taxable distribution. However, if you use the loan to purchase a principal residence for yourself, the repayment period may be longer than five years; any reasonable period is allowed. This exception does not apply if the plan loan is used to improve your existing principal residence, to buy a second home, or to finance the purchase of a home or home improvements for other family members; such loans are subject to the five-year repayment rule.

Level loan amortization required. To avoid tax consequences on a plan loan, you must be required to repay using a level amortization schedule, with payments at least quarterly. According to Congressional committee reports, you may accelerate repayment, and the employer may use a variable interest rate and require full repayment if you leave the company.

Giving a demand note does not satisfy the repayment requirements. The IRS and Tax Court held the entire amount of an employee's loan to be a taxable distribution since his demand loan did not require level amortization of principal and interest with at least quarterly payments. It did not matter that the employee had paid interest quarterly and actually repaid the loan within five years.

If required installments are not made, the entire loan balance must be treated as a "deemed distribution" from the plan under IRS proposed regulations. However, the IRS allows the plan administrator to permit a grace period of up to one calendar quarter. If the missed installment is not paid by the end of the grace period, there is at that time a deemed distribution in the amount of the outstanding loan balance.

Under IRS regulations, loan repayments may be suspended for up to one year (or longer if you are in the uniformed services) if you take a leave of absence during which you are paid less than the installments due. However, the installments after the leave must at least equal the original required amount and the loan must be repaid by the end of the allowable repayment period (five years if not used to buy a principal residence). For example, on July 1, 2008, when his vested account balance is $80,000, Joe Smith takes out a $40,000 non–principal residence loan, to be repaid with interest in level monthly installments of $825 over five years. He makes nine payments and then takes a year of unpaid leave. When he returns to work he can either increase his monthly payment to make up for the missed payments or resume paying $825 a month and on June 30, 2013, repay the entire balance owed in a lump sum.

If loan payments are suspended while you are serving in the uniformed services, the loan payments must resume upon returning to work and the loan repayment period (five years from the date of the loan unless the loan was used to buy your principal residence) is extended by the period of suspension.

Spousal consent generally required to get a loan. All plans subject to the joint and survivor rules *(7.11)* must require spousal consent in order to use your account balance as security for the loan in case you default. Check with your plan administrator for consent requirements.

Interest deduction limitations. If you want to borrow from your account to buy a first or second residence and you are not a "key" employee *(3.4)*, you can generally obtain a full interest deduction by using the residence as collateral for the loan *(15.2)*. Your account balance may not be used to secure the loan. Key employees are not allowed any interest deduction for plan loans.

If you use a plan loan for investment purposes and are not a key employee, and the loan is not secured by your elective deferrals (or allocable income) to a 401(k) plan or tax-sheltered annuity, the loan account interest is deductible up to investment income *(15.10)*. Interest on loans used for personal purposes is not deductible, unless your residence is the security for the loan.

7.17 Tax Benefits of 401(k) Plans

If your company has a profit-sharing or stock bonus plan, it has the opportunity of giving you additional tax-sheltered pay. The tax law allows the company to add a cash or deferred pay plan, called a 401(k) plan.

Your company may offer to contribute to a 401(k) plan trust account on your behalf if you forego a salary increase, but in most plans, contributions take the form of salary-reduction deferrals. Under a salary-reduction agreement, you elect to contribute a specified percentage of your wages to the 401(k) plan instead of receiving it as regular salary. In addition, your company may match a portion of your contribution. A salary-reduction deferral is treated as a contribution by your employer that is not taxable to you if the annual contribution limits are not exceeded.

Employers have the option of amending their 401(k) plans to allow employees to designate part or all of their elective contributions as Roth contributions *(7.20)*.

Law Alert

Automatic 401(k) Plan Coverage

Employers are encouraged to automatically enroll employees in a 401(k) plan. Unless employees affirmatively opt out, a specified percentage of their pay is contributed to the plan. Even though the employees do not make affirmative elections to contribute, such plans are qualified provided that the employees are given advance notice of their right either to receive cash or have the designated amount contributed by the employer to the plan.

Employers are granted protection from nondiscrimination restrictions if they have automatic enrollment plans that include mandatory matching or non-elective employer contributions.

Salary-reduction deferrals. Making elective salary deferrals allows you to defer tax on salary and get a tax-free buildup of earnings within your 401(k) plan account until withdrawals are made.

The tax law sets a maximum annual limit on salary deferrals to a 401(k) plan, and the same limit applies to 403(b) annuities *(7.21)*, 457 plans *(7.22)* and salary-reduction SEPs *(8.16)*. However, the terms of your employer's plan may limit your maximum deferral to a percentage of your compensation, so you may be unable to defer the maximum allowed by the law.

For 2010, the maximum deferral was $16,500, plus an additional $5,500 for plan participants age 50 or older if the plan permitted the extra "catch-up" contribution. It is not clear if these limits will be increased for 2011 because inflation has been very low; *see* the *e-Supplement at jklasser.com* for the 2011 limits. The maximum deferral is lower for employees of "small" employers who adopt a SIMPLE 401(k); *see* below.

Elective deferrals within the annual limit are *pre-tax* contributions, so they are not subject to income tax withholding. However, the contributions are subject to Social Security and Medicare withholdings.

Your employer may not require you to make elective deferrals in order to obtain any other benefits, apart from matching contributions. For example, benefits provided under health plans or other compensation plans may not be conditioned on your making salary deferrals to a 401(k) plan.

Distributions. Withdrawals from a 401(k) plan before age 59½ are restricted *(7.19)*. For those born before January 2, 1936, a lump-sum distribution may be eligible for averaging *(7.4)*. Mandatory 20% withholding applies to a lump sum as well as other distributions that are eligible for averaging; however, there are exceptions *(7.7)*.

Nondiscrimination rules. The law imposes strict contribution percentage tests to prevent discrimination in favor of employees who are highly compensated. If these tests are violated, the employer is subject to penalties and the plan could be disqualified unless the excess contributions (plus allocable income) are distributed back to the highly compensated employees within specified time limits.

Caution

Reduced Deferral Limit for Highly Compensated Employees

To avoid discrimination problems an employer may set a lower limit for elective salary deferrals by highly compensated employees than the generally applicable ceiling.

If, after contributions are made, the plan fails to meet the nondiscrimination tests, the excess contributions will either be returned to the highly compensated employees or kept in the plan but recharacterized as after-tax contributions. In either case, the excess contribution is taxable. Form 1099-R will indicate the excess contribution.

SIMPLE 401(k). Nondiscrimination tests are eased for employers who adopt a 401(k) plan with SIMPLE contribution provisions. A SIMPLE 401(k) may be set up only by employers who in the preceding year had no more than 100 employees with compensation of at least $5,000. An employer who contributes to a SIMPLE 401(k) must report on a calendar-year basis and may not maintain another qualified plan for employees eligible to participate in the SIMPLE plan.

If the SIMPLE contribution requirements are met, the plan is considered to meet 401(k) nondiscrimination requirements. Employee elective deferrals may not exceed an annual limitation, which was $11,500 for 2010. The plan may also allow additional contributions by participants who are age 50 or older by the end of the year. The limit on the additional contribution was $2,500 for 2010. Given the low level of inflation, it is not clear if the $11,500 and $2,500 limits will be increased for 2011; *see* the *e-Supplement at jklasser.com* for an update.

The employer must either match the employee deferral, up to 3% of compensation, or contribute 2% of compensation for all eligible employees, whether or not they make elective deferrals. All contributions are nonforfeitable. No other type of contribution is allowed. In figuring the 3% or 2% employer contribution, compensation is subject to an annual compensation ceiling; for 2010, the compensation limit is $245,000.

Partnership plans. Partnership plans that allow partners to vary annual contributions are treated as 401(k) plans by the IRS. Thus, elective deferrals are subject to the annual limit *(7.18)* and the special 401(k) plan nondiscrimination rules apply.

7.18 Limit on Salary-Reduction Deferrals

Elective deferrals to a 401(k) plan must not exceed the annual tax-free ceiling; otherwise, the plan could be disqualified. If you also participate in a 403(b) tax-sheltered annuity plan *(7.21)* or simplified employee pension plan established before 1997 *(8.16)*, the limit applies to the total salary reductions for all the plans and any excess deferral should be withdrawn as discussed below. Because of percentage-of-compensation limitations in your employer's plan, you may be unable to make deferrals up to the annual tax-free ceiling. Also, certain highly compensated employees may be unable to take advantage of the maximum annual tax-free ceiling because of restrictions imposed by nondiscrimination tests.

Both the regular annual deferral limit ($16,500 for 2010) and the "catch-up" contribution limit for those age 50 or older ($5,500 for 2011) are subject to cost-of-living increases, but there may not be an increase for 2011 because of low inflation; *see* the *e-Supplement at jklasser.com* for an update.

To avoid the strict nondiscrimination tests for employee elective deferrals and employer matching contributions, an employer may make contributions to a SIMPLE 401(k) *(7.17)*.

An employer may make matching or other contributions, provided the total contribution for the year, including the employee's pre-tax salary deferral and any employee after-tax contributions, does not exceed the annual limit for defined contribution plans, which for 2010 was the *lesser* of 100% of compensation or $49,000.

Withdrawing excess deferrals. A single plan must apply the annual limit on salary deferrals to maintain qualified status. If your deferrals to the plan for a year exceed the annual limit, the excess, plus allocable earnings, must be distributed to you or the plan risks disqualification. If you participated in more than one plan and the deferrals to all of the plans exceeded the limit, you should withdraw the excess, plus the allocable income, from any of the plans, by April 15 of the year following the year of the excess deferral.

Whether the excess deferrals were made to one or several plans, you must report the excess as wages for the year of the deferral on Line 7 of Form 1040. If you withdraw the excess by April 15 of the following year, it is not taxable again when you receive it. However, if the withdrawal of the excess is not received by the April 15 date, the excess is taxed again when received. The withdrawal of allocable earnings is always taxable in the year of the distribution. If a withdrawal of an excess deferral to a salary-reduction SEP (set up before 1997 *(8.16)*) is not withdrawn by the April 15 date, it is treated as a regular IRA contribution that could be subject to the penalty for excess IRA contributions *(8.7)*.

Excess deferrals (and earnings) distributed by the April 15 date are not subject to the 10% penalty for premature distributions *(7.15)* even if you are under age 59½ .

For the year in which the excess deferral and allocable earnings are distributed to you, the plan will send you a Form 1099-R. Box 7 will include a code designating the year for which the excess is taxable.

7.19 Withdrawals From 401(k) Plans Restricted

By law, you may not withdraw funds attributable to elective salary-reduction contributions to a 401(k) plan unless (1) you no longer work for the employer maintaining the plan; (2) you have reached age 59½; (3) you have become totally disabled; (4) you can show financial hardship; (5) you are eligible for a qualified reservist distribution *(7.15)*; (6) you are the beneficiary of a deceased employee; or (7) the plan is terminated and no successor defined contribution plan (other than an employee stock ownership plan) is maintained by the employer. If a distribution is allowed and all of your plan contributions were pre-tax elective salary deferrals, the entire distribution is taxable unless it is rolled over to an eligible plan *(7.7)*.

Under IRS rules, it is difficult to qualify for hardship withdrawals; *see* below. If you do qualify, the withdrawal is taxable, and if you are under age 59½ , it is subject to the 10% early distribution penalty unless you meet a penalty exception *(7.15)*.

The hardship provision and age 59½ withdrawal allowance do not apply to certain "pre-ERISA" money purchase pension plans (in existence June 27, 1974).

An "involuntary" distribution resulting from an IRS levy on a 401(k) plan account is taxable to the employee (assuming only "pre-tax" contributions) but is not subject to the 10% penalty on pre-age 59½ distributions *(7.15)*.

Planning Remindert

Hardship Distribution Not Subject to Withholding

A hardship distribution from a 401(k) plan is not eligible for rollover *(7.7)* to an IRA or an eligible employer plan. Your employer will not apply 20% withholding to the distribution, as mandatory withholding applies only to rollover-eligible distributions *(7.7)*.

Withdrawals before age 59½. Withdrawals for medical disability, financial hardship, or separation from service are subject to the 10% penalty for premature withdrawals unless you meet one of the exceptions *(7.15)*.

Loans. If you are allowed to borrow from the plan, loan restrictions *(7.16)* apply.

Qualifying for hardship withdrawals. IRS regulations restrict hardship withdrawals of pre-tax salary deferrals. If you qualify under the following restrictive rules you may withdraw your elective deferrals. Income allocable to elective deferrals may be withdrawn as part of a hardship distribution only in limited circumstances. If the plan so provides, income may be withdrawn if it was credited to your account by a cut-off date that is *no later* than the end of the last plan year ending before July 1, 1989.

The IRS requires you to show an immediate and heavy financial need that cannot be met with other resources.

Financial need includes the following expenses (this list may be expanded by the IRS in rulings):

- Purchase of a principal residence for yourself (but not mortgage payments);
- Tuition, related fees and room and board for the next 12 months of post-secondary education for yourself, your spouse, children, or other dependents;
- Medical expenses previously incurred for yourself, your spouse, or dependents or expenses incurred to obtain medical care for such persons;
- Preventing your eviction or mortgage foreclosure; and
- Paying funeral expenses for a family member.

Even if you can show financial need, you may not make a hardship withdrawal if you have other resources to pay the expenses. You do not have to provide your employer with a detailed financial statement, but you must state to your employer that you cannot pay the expenses with: compensation, insurance, or reimbursements; liquidation of your assets without causing yourself hardship by virtue of the liquidation; stopping your contributions, including salary deferrals, to the plan; other distributions or nontaxable loans from plans of any employer; or borrowing from a commercial lender. Your spouse's assets, as well as those of your minor children, are considered to be yours unless you show that they are not available to you. For example, property held in trust for a child or under the Uniform Transfers (or Gifts) to Minors Act is not treated as your property.

Under a special rule, you are considered to lack other resources if you have taken all available distributions from all plans of the employer, including nontaxable loans, and you suspend making any contributions to any of the employer's qualified and nonqualified deferred compensation plans for at least six months after receipt of the hardship distribution. Furthermore, all of the employer's plans must provide that for the year after the year of the hardship distribution, elective contributions must be limited to the excess of the annual salary deferral limitation over the elective contributions made for the year of the hardship distribution.

Law Alert

Conversion from 401(k) to Roth 401(k)

Under the Small Business Jobs Act of 2010 (9/27/10), 401(k) plans that have a designated Roth account component may (but are not required to) allow employees to roll over distributions to a designated Roth account, effective for distributions after the September 27 date of enactment. A rollover distribution is taxable (unless attributable to after-tax contributions), but a rollover made by the end of 2010 qualifies for the same two-year deferral option allowed for 2010 conversions of traditional IRAs to Roth IRAs: half is taxable in 2011 and half in 2012 unless an election is made to report the entire amount as income for 2010 *(8.21)*.

7.20 Designated Roth Contributions to 401(k) Plans

Employers with 401(k) plans may allow employees to irrevocably designate all or part of their pre-tax elective salary deferrals (and catch-up contributions if age 50 or older) as after-tax Roth contributions. The plan must be amended to allow Roth contributions. The Roth contributions, being after-tax, are treated as taxable wages subject to withholding.

The major incentive for employees to designate 401(k) plan contributions as Roth contributions is to obtain tax-free treatment for distributions under the qualified distribution rules applicable to Roth IRAs. That is, distributions of designated Roth contributions plus accrued earnings would be totally tax free if received after age 59½ and a five-year holding period *(8.23)*.

Roth 401(k) contributions are available to individuals who might otherwise be unable to make annual contributions to a Roth IRA. Subject to 401(k) nondiscrimination tests, there are no income limitations on the right to make Roth 401(k) contributions, whereas contributions to a Roth IRA are barred if adjusted gross income exceeds an annual threshold *(8.20)*.

Plans must segregate designated Roth contributions from regular 401(k) elective deferrals and maintain separate accounts for employees with both types of contributions. Gains, losses, and other credits or charges, as well as contribution and withdrawals, must be allocated between the accounts on a reasonable and consistent basis. Designated Roth contributions are subject to the 401(k) nonforfeitability and distribution restrictions and also to the nondiscrimination tests for pre-tax elective contributions.

403(b) plans. Under similar rules, designated Roth contributions may be made available under 403(b) plans *(7.21)* sponsored by public schools and tax-exempt organizations.

7.21 Annuities for Employees of Tax-Exempts and Schools (403(b) Plans)

If you are employed by a state or local government public school, or by a tax-exempt religious, charitable, scientific, or educational organization, or are on the civilian staff or faculty of the Uniformed Services University of the Health Sciences (Department of Defense), you may be able to arrange for the purchase of a nonforfeitable tax-sheltered annuity. Tax-sheltered annuities may also be purchased by self-employed ministers and by non-tax-exempt employers of ordained or licensed ministers or chaplains. Another name for a tax-sheltered annuity is a 403(b) plan. A 403(b) plan may invest funds for employees in mutual-fund shares as well as in annuity contracts.

The purchase of the annuity or mutual-fund shares is generally made through pre-tax salary-reduction contributions. Your plan may allow you to make after-tax contributions, and the employer may make non-elective contributions.

Caution: As the following contribution rules for tax-sheltered annuities have been stated in general terms, we suggest that you also consult your employer or the issuer of the contract. IRS Publication 571 has detailed examples.

Limit on tax-free contributions. Tax-free salary reductions are limited to the annual ceiling for elective deferrals, and the plan may permit additional deferrals for participants who are age 50 or older *(7.18)*.

If, in addition to a tax-sheltered annuity, you make salary deferrals to a 401(k) plan, SIMPLE plan, or simplified employee pension plan, the annual salary-reduction limit applies to the total deferrals *(7.18)*. If you defer more than the annual limit, the excess is taxable. Further, if a salary-reduction deferral in excess of the annual limit is made and the excess is not distributed to you by April 15 of the following year, the excess will be taxed twice—not only in the year of deferral but again in the year it is actually distributed. To avoid the double tax, any excess deferral plus the income attributable to such excess should be distributed no later than April 15 of the year following the year in which the excess deferral is made *(7.18)*.

The annual salary-reduction ceiling is generally increased by $3,000 for employees of educational organizations, hospitals, churches, home health service agencies, and health and welfare service agencies who have completed 15 years of service. However, the extra $3,000 annual deferral may not be claimed indefinitely. There is a lifetime limit of $15,000 on the amount of extra deferrals allowed. Furthermore, the extra deferrals may not be claimed after lifetime elective deferrals to the plan exceed $5,000 multiplied by your years of service. Publication 571 has a worksheet for figuring the extra deferral.

The employee's salary reduction plus any after-tax contributions and any non-elective contributions made by the employer for the year are tax free only if they do not exceed the annual limit on contributions to a defined contribution plan, which for 2010 is the lesser of 100% of compensation or $49,000.

Distributions from tax-sheltered annuities. Distributions attributable to salary-reduction contributions to a 403(b) tax-sheltered annuity are allowed only when an employee reaches age 59½, has experienced a severance from employment, becomes disabled, suffers financial hardship, becomes eligible for a qualified reservist distribution *(7.15)*, or dies. The hardship distribution rules are the same as for 401(k) plans *(7.19)*. Annuity payments are taxed under the general rules for employees *(7.26)*. Payments are fully taxable if the only contributions to the plan were salary-reduction contributions excluded from income (pre-tax contributions) under the annual limits discussed earlier in this section.

Non-annuity distributions from a tax-sheltered annuity do not qualify for special averaging *(7.4)*, but a tax-free rollover of a distribution may be made to another tax-sheltered annuity or traditional IRA unless the distribution is not eligible under the rollover rules *(7.7)*. An eligible rollover distribution *(7.7)* from a 403(b) plan may also be rolled over to a qualified plan or governmental Section 527 plan. However, if a rollover from a 403(b) plan to a qualified plan is made, a subsequent lump-sum distribution from the qualified plan will not be eligible for special averaging *(7.4)* or capital gain treatment *(7.5)* even if you were born before January 2, 1936, and those provisions would otherwise be available. If you do not choose to have the payer of the distribution make a direct rollover, mandatory 20% withholding will be applied. You may then personally make a rollover within 60 days, but you would have to include the withheld amount in the rolled-over amount to avoid tax on the entire distribution. *See 7.8* for further rollover and withholding details.

Benefits accruing after 1986 are subject to the required beginning date rules and a penalty may be imposed for failure to take minimum required distributions *(7.13)*. Benefits accrued before 1987 are not subject to the required minimum distribution rules until the year you reach age 75.

7.22 Government and Exempt Organization Deferred Pay Plans

Federal government civilian employees may make tax-deferred salary-reduction contributions to the Federal Thrift Savings Plan. Employees of state and local governments and of tax-exempt organizations may be able to make tax-free salary-reduction contributions to a Section 457 deferred compensation plan.

Federal Thrift Savings Plan. Federal employees may elect to make salary-reduction deferrals to the Thrift Savings Plan up to the elective deferral limit for 401(k) plans *(7.17)*. Deferrals are not taxed until distributed from the plan. The deferred amount is counted as wages for purposes of computing Social Security taxes and benefits.

Distributions from the Thrift Savings Plan are generally fully taxable. However, lump-sum distributions are eligible for special averaging *(7.4)* or tax-free rollover treatment *(7.7)*. If you separate from service before the year in which you reach age 55, you are subject to the 10% penalty for premature distributions unless you are disabled or qualify for a medical exception *(7.15)*.

Section 457 plans. State and local governments and tax-exempt organizations other than churches may set up Section 457 deferred compensation plans. Employees may annually defer compensation up to the 401(k) elective deferrable limit *(7.17)*. Employees in state and local government 457 plans who are 50 or older may be permitted by the plan to make additional contributions *(7.17)*. In addition, a limited "catch-up" provision may allow employees in the last three years before reaching normal retirement age to defer even larger amounts. The "catch-up" rule allows up to double the regular limit to be deferred, provided that the full deferrable limit has not been used in prior years. For state and local government plan participants, the deferral limit under the three-year rule will never be less than the regular deferral limit for the year plus the additional contribution limit for participants age 50 or older.

Deferred compensation (and allocable income) under a Section 457 plan of a tax-exempt employer (non-governmental) is not taxed until paid or otherwise made available. Amounts deferred (and earnings) under state or local government 457 plans are taxed only when paid.

Distributions to employees or beneficiaries generally may not be made before the year the employee turns age 70½, has a severance from employment, or faces an "unforeseeable" emergency, assuming the plan allows payment in cases of emergency. Under IRS regulations, an unforeseeable emergency generally means severe financial hardship resulting from a sudden illness or accident of the employee or a dependent, or loss of property due to a casualty. If the employee can obtain funds by ceasing deferrals to the plan or by liquidating assets without causing himself or herself severe financial hardship, payment from the plan is not allowed. The regulations specifically prohibit payments from the plan to purchase a home or pay for a child's college tuition.

Eligible rollover distributions *(7.7)* from a governmental 457 plan (but not a nongovernmental plan) may be rolled over tax free to a traditional IRA, another governmental 457 plan, a qualified plan, or a 403(b) plan. An eligible distribution from a governmental 457 plan may also be rolled over to a Roth IRA, subject to the conditions for a taxable conversion *(7.8)*. If a rollover from a governmental 457 plan is made to a qualified plan, special averaging *(7.4)* and capital gain treatment *(7.5)* will *not* be allowed for a lump-sum distribution from the qualified plan even if such treatment

Caution

Unforeseen Emergency Distributions

If you can show severe financial hardship arising from a sudden illness or accident, or loss of property due to events beyond your control, and you are unable to obtain funds elsewhere, you may make a withdrawal from your employer's Section 457 plan. However, the need to buy a home or pay college expenses does not qualify as an unforeseeable emergency.

would otherwise be available. Rollovers of eligible distributions may also be made *to* governmental 457 plans.

See 7.13 for required distribution starting dates after age 70½ and minimum payout rules.

Note: Check with your employer for other details on Section 457 contributions and distribution rules.

7.23 Figuring the Taxable Part of Your Annuity

Tax treatment of a distribution depends on whether you receive it before or after the annuity starting date, and on the amount of your investment. A cash withdrawal before age 59½ from an annuity contract is generally subject to a 10% penalty, but there are exceptions; the penalty is discussed at the end of this section. If your annuity is from an employer plan, *see 7.26.*

The *annuity starting date* is either the first day of the first period for which you receive a payment or the date on which the obligation under the contract becomes fixed, whichever is later. If your right to an annuity was fixed on January 1, 2010, and your monthly payments started on July 1, 2010, for the period starting June 1, 2010, June 1, 2010 is your annuity starting date.

Payments before the annuity starting date. If your commercial annuity contract was purchased *after* August 13, 1982, withdrawals before the annuity starting date are taxable to the extent that the cash value of the contract (ignoring any surrender charge), immediately before the distribution, exceeds your investment in the contract at that time. Loans under the contract or pledges are treated as cash withdrawals.

If the contract was purchased before August 14, 1982, withdrawals *before* the annuity starting date are taxable only to the extent they exceed your investment. Loans are tax free and are not treated as withdrawals subject to this rule. Where additional investments were made after August 13, 1982, cash withdrawals are first considered to be tax-free distributions of the investment before August 14, 1982. If the withdrawal exceeds this investment, the balance is fully taxable to the extent of earnings on the contract, with any excess withdrawals treated as a tax-free recovery of the investment made after August 13, 1982.

Filing Tip

Surrender of Contract

Payments on a complete surrender of the annuity contract or at maturity are taxable only to the extent they exceed your investment.

Payments on or after the annuity starting date. If the withdrawal is a regular (not variable) annuity payment, the part of the annuity payment that is allocated to your cost investment is treated as a nontaxable return of the cost; the balance is taxable income earned on the investment. You may find the taxable part of your annuity payment by following the six steps listed below under "Taxable Portion of Commercial Annuity Payments." If you have a variable annuity, the computation of the tax-free portion is discussed following Step 6.

Payments on or after the annuity starting date that are not part of the annuity, such as dividends, are generally taxable, but there are exceptions. If the contract is a life insurance or endowment contract, withdrawals of earnings are tax free to the extent of your investment, unless the contract is a modified endowment contract.

Taxable Portion of Commercial Annuity Payments

If the payer of the contract does not provide the taxable amount in Box 2a of Form 1099-R, you can compute the taxable amount of your commercial annuity using the following steps.

Step 1: Figure your investment in the annuity contract. If you have no investment in the contract, annuity income is fully taxable; therefore, ignore Steps 2 through 6.

If your annuity is—	*Your cost is—*
Single premium annuity contract	The single premium paid.
Deferred annuity contract	The total premiums paid.
A gift	Your donor's cost.
An employee annuity	The total of your after-tax contributions to the plan plus your employer's contributions that you were required to report as income *(7.26)*.
With a refund feature	The value of the refund feature.

From cost, you subtract the following items:

- Any premiums refunded, and rebates or dividends received on or before the annuity starting date.
- Additional premiums for double indemnity or disability benefits.
- Amounts received under the contract before the annuity starting date to the extent these amounts were not taxed; *see* above.
- Value of a refund feature; *see* below.

Value of refund feature. Your investment in the contract is reduced by the value, if any, of the refund feature.

Your annuity has a refund feature when these three requirements are present: (1) the refund under the contract depends, even in part, on the life expectancy of at least one person; (2) the contract provides for payments to a beneficiary or the annuitant's estate after the annuitant's death; and (3) the payments to the estate or beneficiary are a refund of the amount paid for the annuity.

The value of the refund feature is figured by using a life expectancy multiple that may be found in Treasury Table III or Table VII, depending on the date of your investment; the tables are in IRS Publication 939.

Where an employer paid part of the cost, the refund is figured on only the part paid by the employee.

The refund feature is considered to be zero if (1) for a joint and survivor annuity, both annuitants are age 74 or younger, the payments are guaranteed for less than 2½ years, and the survivor's annuity is at least 50% of the first annuitant's (retiree's) annuity or (2) for a single-life annuity without survivor benefits, the payments are guaranteed for less than 2½ years and you are age 57 or younger if using the new (unisex) annuity tables, age 42 or younger if male and using the old annuity tables, or age 47 or younger if female and using the old annuity tables.

Also subtract from cost any tax-free recovery of your investment received *before* the annuity starting date, as previously discussed.

Planning Reminder

Life Expectancy Tables

The life expectancy tables for figuring your expected return are in IRS Publication 939.

Step 2: Find your expected return. This is the total of all the payments you are to receive. If the payments are to be made to you for life, your expected return is figured by multiplying the amount of the annual payment by your life expectancy as of the nearest birthday to the annuity starting date. The annuity starting date is the first day of the first period for which an annuity payment is received. For example, on January 1 you complete payment under an annuity contract providing for monthly payments starting on July 1 for the period beginning June 1. The annuity starting date is June 1. Use that date in computing your investment in the contract under Step 1 and your expected return.

If payments are for life, you find your life expectancy in IRS tables included in IRS Publication 939. If you have a single life annuity for which you made any investment after June 30, 1986, use IRS Table V from Publication 939, shown in *Table 7-2* below. *Table 7-2* also shows IRS Table I, which generally is used if the entire investment was before July 1, 1986, but you may elect to use Table V *(7.24)*. When using the single life table, your age is the age at the birthday nearest the annuity starting date. If you have a joint and survivor annuity and after your death the same payments are to be made to a second annuitant, the expected return is based on your joint life expectancy. Use Table II in IRS Publication 939 to get joint life expectancy if the entire investment was before July 1, 1986. Use Table VI if any investment was made after June 30, 1986. If your joint and survivor annuity provides for a different payment amount to the survivor, you must separately compute the expected return for each annuitant; this method is explained in Publication 939. Adjustments to the life expectancy multiple are required when your annuity is payable quarterly, semiannually, or annually *(7.24)*.

If the payments are for a fixed number of years or for life, whichever is shorter, find your expected return by multiplying your annual payments by a life expectancy multiple found in Table IV if your entire investment was before July 1, 1986, or Table VIII if any investment was made after June 30, 1986.

If payments are for a fixed number of years (as in an endowment contract) without regard to your life expectancy, find your expected return by multiplying your annual payment by the number of years.

Note: There is more information on the life expectancy tables in the following section *(7.24)*.

Table 7-2 Life Expectancy Tables from IRS Publication 939

TABLE I Investments Before July 1, 1986

Ages			Ages			Ages		
Male	*Female*	*Multiples*	*Male*	*Female*	*Multiples*	*Male*	*Female*	*Multiples*
6	11	65.0	41	46	33.0	76	81	9.1
7	12	64.1	42	47	32.1	77	82	8.7
8	13	63.2	43	48	31.2	78	83	8.3
9	14	62.3	44	49	30.4	79	84	7.8
10	15	61.4	45	50	29.6	80	85	7.5
11	16	60.4	46	51	28.7	81	86	7.1
12	17	59.5	47	52	27.9	82	87	6.7
13	18	58.6	48	53	27.1	83	88	6.3
14	19	57.7	49	54	26.3	84	89	6.0
15	20	56.7	50	55	25.5	85	90	5.7
16	21	55.8	51	56	24.7	86	91	5.4
17	22	54.9	52	57	24.0	87	92	5.1
18	23	53.9	53	58	23.2	88	93	4.8
19	24	53.0	54	59	22.4	89	94	4.5
20	25	52.1	55	60	21.7	90	95	4.2
21	26	51.1	56	61	21.0	91	96	4.0
22	27	50.2	57	62	20.3	92	97	3.7
23	28	49.3	58	63	19.6	93	98	3.5
24	29	48.3	59	64	18.9	94	99	3.3
25	30	47.4	60	65	18.2	95	100	3.1
26	31	46.5	61	66	17.5	96	101	2.9
27	32	45.6	62	67	16.9	97	102	2.7
28	33	44.6	63	68	16.2	98	103	2.5
29	34	43.7	64	69	15.6	99	104	2.3
30	35	42.8	65	70	15.0	100	105	2.1
31	36	41.9	66	71	14.4	101	106	1.9
32	37	41.0	67	72	13.8	102	107	1.7
33	38	40.0	68	73	13.2	103	108	1.5
34	39	39.1	69	74	12.6	104	109	1.3
35	40	38.2	70	75	12.1	105	110	1.2
36	41	37.3	71	76	11.6	106	111	1.0
37	42	36.5	72	77	11.0	107	112	0.8
38	43	35.6	73	78	10.5	108	113	0.7
39	44	34.7	74	79	10.1	109	114	0.6
40	45	33.8	75	80	9.6	110	115	0.5
						111	116	0.0

TABLE V Investments After June 30, 1986

Age	*Multiple*	*Age*	*Multiple*	*Age*	*Multiple*
5	76.6	42	40.6	79	10.0
6	75.6	43	39.6	80	9.5
7	74.7	44	38.7	81	8.9
8	73.7	45	37.7	82	8.4
9	72.7	46	36.8	83	7.9
10	71.7	47	35.9	84	7.4
11	70.7	48	34.9	85	6.9
12	69.7	49	34.0	86	6.5
13	68.8	50	33.1	87	6.1
14	67.8	51	32.2	88	5.7
15	66.8	52	31.3	89	5.3
16	65.8	53	30.4	90	5.0
17	64.8	54	29.5	91	4.7
18	63.9	55	28.6	92	4.4
19	62.9	56	27.7	93	4.1
20	61.9	57	26.8	94	3.9
21	60.9	58	25.9	95	3.7
22	59.9	59	25.0	96	3.4
23	59.0	60	24.2	97	3.2
24	58.0	61	23.3	98	3.0
25	57.0	62	22.5	99	2.8
26	56.0	63	21.6	100	2.7
27	55.1	64	20.8	101	2.5
28	54.1	65	20.0	102	2.3
29	53.1	66	19.2	103	2.1
30	52.2	67	18.4	104	1.9
31	51.2	68	17.6	105	1.8
32	50.2	69	16.8	106	1.6
33	49.3	70	16.0	107	1.4
34	48.3	71	15.3	108	1.3
35	47.3	72	14.6	109	1.1
36	46.4	73	13.9	110	1.0
37	45.4	74	13.2	111	0.9
38	44.4	75	12.5	112	0.8
39	43.5	76	11.9	113	0.7
40	42.5	77	11.2	114	0.6
41	41.5	78	10.6	115	0.5

Table 7-3 Multiple Adjustment Table

If the number of whole months from the annuity starting date to the first payment date is—	*0–1*	*2*	*3*	*4*	*5*	*6*	*7*	*8*	*9*	*10*	*11*	*12*
And payments under the contract are to be made:												
Annually	+0.5	+0.4	+0.3	+0.2	+0.1	0.0	0.0	−0.1	−0.2	−0.3	−0.4	−0.5
Semiannually	+0.2	+0.1	0.0	0.0	−0.1	−0.2						
Quarterly	+0.1	0.0	−0.1									

Step 3: Divide the investment in the contract (Step 1) by the expected return (Step 2). This will give you the tax-free percentage of your yearly annuity payments. The tax-free percentage remains the same for the remaining years of the annuity, even if payments increase due to a cost-of-living adjustment. A different computation of the tax-free percentage applies to variable annuities; *see* below.

If your annuity started before 1987, and you live longer than your projected life expectancy (shown in the IRS table), you may continue to apply the same tax-free percentage to each payment you receive. Thus, you may exclude from income more than you paid. However, if your annuity starting date is after 1986, your lifetime exclusion may not exceed your net cost, generally your unrecovered investment as of the annuity starting date, without reduction for any refund feature. Once you have recovered your net cost, further payments are fully taxable.

If your annuity starting date is after July 1, 1986, and you die before recovering your net cost, a deduction is allowed on your final tax return for the unrecovered cost. If a refund of the investment is made under the contract to a beneficiary, the beneficiary is allowed the deduction. The deduction is claimed as a miscellaneous itemized deduction that is *not* subject to the 2% adjusted gross income floor; *see Chapter 19*.

Step 4: Find your total annuity payments for the year. For example, you received 10 monthly payments of $1,000 as your annuity began in March. Your total payments are $10,000, the monthly payment multiplied by 10.

Step 5: Nontaxable portion—multiply the percentage in Step 3 by the total in Step 4. The result is the nontaxable portion (or excludable amount) of your annuity payments.

Step 6: Taxable portion—subtract the amount in Step 5 from the amount in Step 4. This is the part of your annuity for the year that is subject to tax.

Note: There is an example of figuring the taxable and nontaxable portions for a single life annuity in the following section *(7.24)*.

Variable annuities. If you have a variable annuity that pays different benefits depending on cost-of-living indexes, profits earned by the annuity fund, or similar fluctuating standards, the tax-free portion of each payment is computed by dividing your investment in the contract (Step 1 above) by the total number of payments you expect to receive. If the annuity is for a definite period, the total number of payments equals the number of payments to be made each year multiplied by the number of years you will receive payments. If the annuity is for life, you divide the amount you invested in the contract by a multiple obtained from the appropriate life expectancy table; *see* Step 2. The result is the tax-free amount of annual annuity income.

If you receive a payment that is less than the nontaxable amount, you may elect when you receive the next payment to recalculate the nontaxable portion. The amount by which the prior nontaxable portion exceeded the payment you received is divided by the number of payments you expect as of the time of the next payment. The result is added to the previously calculated nontaxable portion, and the sum is the amount of each future payment to be excluded from tax. A statement must be attached to your return explaining the recomputation.

EXAMPLES

1. Andrew Taylor's total investment of $12,000 for a variable annuity was made after June 30, 1986. The annuity starting date was June 1, 2010. The annuity payments began July 1, 2010, in varying annual installments for life. Andrew's age (nearest birthday) on the June 1 starting date was 65. To figure the tax-free part of each payment, he uses a life expectancy multiple of 20.0, the amount shown in Table V (*see Table 7-2* above) for a person age 65. The amount of each payment excluded from tax is:

Investment in the contract	$12,000
Multiple (from Table V)	20.0
Amount of each payment excluded from tax ($12,000 ÷ 20)	$600

If the first payment is $920, then 320 ($920 – $600) will be included in Andrew's 2010 income.

2. Assume that, after receiving the 2010 payment of $920 in Example 1, Andrew receives $500 in 2011 and $1,200 in 2012. None of the 2011 payment is taxed, as $600 is excludable from each annual payment. Andrew may also elect to recompute his annual exclusion starting with the 2012 payment. The exclusion is recomputed as follows:

Amount excludable in 2011	$600
Amount received in 2011	500
Difference	$100
Multiple as of 1/1/2012 (*see* Table V in *Table 7-2* for age 67)	18.4
Amount added to previously determined annual exclusion ($100 ÷ 18.4)	$5.43
Revised annual exclusion for 2012 and later years ($600 + $5.43)	$605.43
Amount taxable in 2012 ($1,200 – $605.43)	$594.57

Penalty on Premature Withdrawals From Deferred Annuities

Withdrawals before the annuity starting date may be taxable or tax free, depending on whether investments were made before or after August 13, 1982 *(7.23)*.

Withdrawals before age 59½ are also generally subject to a penalty of 10% of the amount includable in income. A withdrawal from an annuity contract is penalized unless:

1. You have reached age 59½ or have become totally disabled.
2. The distribution is part of a series of substantially equal payments, made at least annually over your life expectancy or over the joint life expectancies of you and a beneficiary. If you can avoid the penalty under this exception and you change to a nonqualifying distribution method within five years or before age 59½, such as where you receive a lump sum, a recapture tax will apply to the payments received before age 59½.
3. The payment is received by a beneficiary or estate after the policyholder's death.
4. Payment is from a qualified retirement plan, tax-sheltered annuity, or IRA; in this case the penalty rules for qualified plans *(7.15)* or IRAs *(8.8)* apply.
5. Payment is allocable to investments made before August 14, 1982.
6. Payment is from an annuity contract under a qualified personal injury settlement.
7. Payment is from a single-premium annuity where the starting date is no more than one year from the date of purchase (an "immediate" annuity).
8. Payment is from an annuity purchased by an employer upon the termination of a qualified retirement plan and held until you separated from service.

Filing Tip

Form 5329

If no exception to the early withdrawal penalty applies, you compute the 10% penalty in Part I of Form 5329. The penalty is 5% instead of 10% if as of March 1, 1986, you were receiving payments under a specific schedule pursuant to your written election. Attach an explanation to Form 5329 if you are applying the 5% rate.

7.24 Life Expectancy Tables

IRS unisex actuarial tables must be used if you made any investment in a commercial annuity contract after June 30, 1986. Generally, life expectancies are longer under the unisex tables than under the prior male-female tables. The unisex life expectancy table for single life annuities is IRS Table V from Publication 939, shown above in *Table 7-2*. The unisex table for ordinary joint life and last survivor annuities is Table VI, in IRS Publication 939.

If your *entire* investment was before July 1, 1986, you use the older male/female tables. The tables, IRS Tables I through IV, are in Publication 939. Table I, shown above, is for single life expectancies. Table II, for ordinary joint life and last survivor annuities, is in Publication 939.

You may make an irrevocable election to use the unisex tables for all payments received under the contract, even if you did not make an investment after June 30, 1986.

If you invested in the contract both before July 1, 1986, and after June 30, 1986, and you are the first person to receive annuity payments under the contract, you may make a special election to use the prior tables for the pre–July 1986 investment and the unisex tables for the post–June 1986 investment. *See* IRS Publication 939 for further information. Treasury Regulation 1.72-6(d) has examples showing how to figure the post–June 1986 and pre–July 1986 investments.

Birthday nearest annuity starting date. In looking up single life or joint life expectancy in the applicable table, use your age (and the age of a joint annuitant) at the birthday nearest to the annuity starting date. The number in the table next to this age is the life expectancy multiple used to figure the tax-free and taxable portions of a monthly annuity; *see* the following Examples.

Adjustments for nonmonthly payments. An adjustment is required when your annuity payments are received quarterly, semiannually, or annually; *see* Example 3 below.

EXAMPLES

1. Bill Jones was 66 years old on April 14, 2010. On May 1, 2010, he received his first monthly annuity check of $1,000. This covered his annuity payment for April. Bill's annuity starting date was April 1, 2010, and his entire investment was before July 1, 1986.

   Looking at Table I in *Table 7-2* under "Male" at age 66 (age on birthday nearest April starting date), Bill finds the multiple 14.4. (He does not have to adjust that multiple because the payments are monthly.) Bill multiplies the 14.4 by $12,000 ($1,000 a month for a year) to find his expected return of $172,800. Assume there is no refund feature and Bill's net investment (Step 1 at *7.23*) is $129,600. He divides his expected return into the net cost and gets his exclusion percentage of 75%. Until Bill recovers his net cost, he receives tax free 75% of his annuity payments and is taxable on 25%. In 2010, Bill receives $8,000 ($1,000 in May through December) and reports $2,000 as the taxable amount:

Amount received	$8,000
Amount excludable (75%)	6,000
Taxable portion	$2,000

   For 2011, Bill will receive annuity payments for the full year. The amount received will be $12,000; amount excludable, $9,000; and taxable portion, $3,000. The excludable and taxable portions will remain the same in later years until Bill has excluded his net cost of $129,600. After that, the annuity payments will be fully taxable.

2. Same facts as in Example 1 except there was an investment after June 30, 1986, and Table V is used. Looking at Table V (in *Table 7-2*) under age 66, Bill finds the multiple 19.2. The same multiple applies to males and females. Multiplying the 19.2 by $12,000 gives an expected return of $230,400. Using a net investment of $129,600, the exclusion percentage is 56.25% ($129,600 ÷ $230,400). For 2010, Bill reports annuity income as follows:

Amount received	$8,000
Amount excludable (56.25%)	4,500
Taxable portion	$3,500

   For 2011, $12,000 is received. The amount excludable will be $6,750 (56.25% × $12,000), and the taxable portion, $5,250. The same treatment will apply in later years until Bill has excluded his net cost of $129,600. Thereafter, all payments will be fully taxable.

3. You receive quarterly annuity payments. Your first payment comes on January 15, covering the first quarter of the year. Since the period between the starting date of January 1 and the payment date of January 15 is less than one month, you adjust the life expectancy multiple as shown in *Table 7-3* above by adding 0.1. If the life expectancy multiple from the IRS table was 14.4, the adjusted multiple is 14.5.

7.25 When You Convert Your Endowment Policy

When an endowment policy matures, you may elect to receive a lump sum, an annuity, an interest option, or a paid-up life insurance policy. If you elect—

A lump sum. You report the difference between your cost (premium payments less dividends) and what you receive.

An annuity before the policy matures or within 60 days after maturity. You report income in the years you receive your annuity *(7.23)*. Use as your investment in the annuity contract the cost of the endowment policy less premiums paid for other benefits such as double indemnity or disability income. If you elect the annuity option more than 60 days after maturity, you report income on the matured policy as if you received the lump sum; *see* above rule. The lump sum is treated as the cost investment in the annuity contract.

An interest option before the policy matures. You report only the interest as it is received, provided you do not have the right to withdraw the policy proceeds. If you have the right to withdraw the proceeds, you are treated as in constructive receipt; the difference between your cost and what you receive would be taxed as if you had received a lump sum.

Paid-up insurance. You report the difference between the present value of the paid-up life insurance policy and the premium paid for the endowment policy. In figuring the value of the insurance policy, you do not use its cash surrender value, but the amount you would have to pay for a similar policy with the company at the date of exchange. Your insurance company can give you this figure. The difference is taxed at ordinary income tax rates.

Tax-free exchange rules apply to the policy exchanges listed in *6.12*.

Sales of endowment, annuity, or life insurance policies are taxable as ordinary income, not as capital gains.

The proceeds of a veteran's endowment policy paid before the veteran's death are not taxable.

7.26 Reporting Employee Annuities

Tax treatment of employee annuity payments from a qualified employee plan, qualified employee annuity, or tax-sheltered annuity *(7.21)* depends on the amount of your contributions and your annuity starting date. These rules are discussed in *7.26 – 7.29*. If payments are from a nonqualified employee plan, you must use the rules for commercial annuities *(7.23)*.

Fully taxable payments if you have no investment in the plan. If you did not contribute to the cost of a pension or employee annuity, and you did not report as income your employer's contributions, you are fully taxed on payments after the annuity starting date. On your 2010 return, you report fully taxable payments on Line 16b of Form 1040 or Line 12b of Form 1040A.

An employee is taxed on the full value of a nonforfeitable annuity contract that the employer buys him or her if the employer does not have a qualified pension plan. Tax is imposed in the year the policy is purchased. A qualified plan is one approved by the IRS for special tax benefits.

Disability pension before minimum retirement age. Disability payments received before you reach the minimum retirement age (at which you would be entitled to a regular retirement annuity) are fully taxable as wages. After minimum retirement age, payments are treated as an annuity *(7.27)*.

Partially taxable payments if you have an investment in the plan. If you and your employer both contributed to the cost of your annuity, the part of each payment allocable to your investment is tax free and the balance is taxable. You generally must use the simplified method to figure the tax-free portion allocable to your investment *(7.27)*. For withdrawals before the annuity starting date, *see 7.29*.

Filing Tip

Deducting Repaid Pension Overpayment

If you pay tax on a pension distribution and in the next year the plan determines that there was an overpayment, which you repay, the repayment may be deductible. If the repayment is $3,000 or less, it is deductible as a miscellaneous itemized deduction subject to the 2% floor *(19.1)*, which may limit or eliminate the deduction. If the repayment exceeds $3,000, you may claim either a miscellaneous deduction *not* subject to the 2% floor, or if it would provide a lower tax for the year of repayment, a tax credit based on a recomputation of the prior year's tax *(2.9)*.

7.27 Simplified Method for Calculating Taxable Employee Annuity

If you have an investment in the plan and your annuity starting date was in 2010, you must use the simplified method explained below to figure the tax-free portion of your annuity payments from a qualified employer plan, qualified employee annuity, or 403(b) tax-sheltered annuity. The only exception is for an annuitant who is age 75 or older at the time payments begin and has payments guaranteed for at least five years; he or she must use the six-step method *(7.23)* for commercial annuities rather than the simplified method.

A beneficiary receiving a survivor annuity may use the simplified method.

If your annuity started before 2010 and you have been using the simplified method to report your annuity payments, continue to do so, using the applicable number of expected monthly payments from either Table I or Table II, as discussed below.

Figuring taxable and tax-free payments under the simplified method. Under the simplified method, a level tax-free portion is determined for each monthly payment with the following steps:

Filing Instruction

Simplified Method Mandatory

If your annuity starting date was in 2010, you must use the simplified method *(7.27)* to figure the taxable part of your 2010 payments, unless on the annuity starting date you were age 75 or older and your payments are guaranteed for at least five years.

Step 1. Figure your investment in the contract as of the annuity starting date. Include premiums you paid and any after-tax contributions you made to the employer's pension plan *(7.28)*. If you are the beneficiary of an employee (or former employee) who died before August 21, 1996, also include the death benefit exclusion of up to $5,000 as part of the investment in the contract.

Step 2. Divide the investment from Step 1 by the number of expected monthly payments shown in Table I or Table II below, using your age on the annuity starting date. The result is the tax-free recovery portion of each monthly payment. However, multiply this amount by three (3 months) to get the tax-free portion if payments are made quarterly rather than monthly. The tax-free portion remains the same if a spouse or other beneficiary receives payments under a joint and survivor annuity after the employee's death.

Use either Table I or Table II, described below. Table II is used for annuities based on more than one life if the annuity starting date is after December 31, 1997.

Table I: Use this table if the annuity starting date was after July 1, 1986, and before January 1, 1998, whether the annuity is based on your life only or is a joint and survivor annuity.

Also use Table I if the annuity starting date was after December 31, 1997, and the annuity is based on your life only.

Table II: Use this table if the annuity starting date is after December 31, 1997, and benefits are based on the life of *more than* one annuitant. For example, use this table if you started to receive payments in 2010 under a joint and survivor annuity. If there is *more than* one survivor annuitant, the primary annuitant's age plus the youngest survivor annuitant's age is the combined age used for Table II. If there is no primary annuitant and the annuity is payable to several survivor annuitants, the ages of the oldest and youngest are combined. Disregard a survivor annuitant whose entitlement to payment is contingent on something other than the primary annuitant's death.

Table I

Age of primary annuitant at starting date	Number of expected monthly payments	
	Annuity starting date before November 19, 1996	*Annuity starting date after November 18, 1996*
55 and under	300	360
56–60	260	310
61–65	240	260
66–70	170	210
71 and over	120	160

Table II

Combined ages of annuitants at starting date	Number of expected monthly payments
110 and under	410
111–120	360
121–130	310
131–140	260
141 and over	210

Step 3. Multiply the Step 2 result by the number of monthly payments received during the year; this is the total tax-free payment for the current year. However, if your annuity starting date was after 1986, your total tax-free recovery under the simplified method for all years is limited to your cost in the plan from Step 1. Thus, you need to keep track of your annual tax-free cost recoveries. The tax-free amount for any year under the Step 3 computation cannot exceed the excess of your investment from Step 1 over the prior year cost recoveries.

Step 4. Subtract the Step 3 tax-free payment from the total pension received this year; this is the taxable pension you must report on Form 1040 or Form 1040A. If the payer of the annuity shows a higher taxable amount on Form 1099-R, use the amount figured here.

EXAMPLE

Fred Smith, age 57, retires and beginning August 1, 2010, he receives payments under a joint and 50% survivor annuity with his wife Betty, also age 57. Fred receives an annuity of $1,500 per month and Betty will receive a survivor annuity of $750 per month after Fred's death. Fred's investment in the plan was $29,000. To figure the tax-free portion of each payment, Fred divides his $29,000 investment by 360, the number of expected monthly payments shown in Table II for two annuitants with a combined age of 114 years. The result, or $80.56, is the tax-free portion of each $1,500 payment. The balance of each payment , or $1,419.44 ($1,500 – $80.56), is taxable. On his 2010 return, Fred reports $7,097.20 (5 payments x $1,419.44) as taxable annuity payments.

If Fred dies before the receipt of 360 payments, Betty will also exclude $80.56 from each of her payments of $750 until a total of 360 payments (hers and Fred's) have been recovered. After 360 payments are received, all subsequent payments will be fully taxable. If Betty dies before the 360th payment, a deduction for the unrecovered investment is allowed on her final income tax return; the deduction is a miscellaneous itemized deduction not subject to the 2% AGI floor.

7.28 Employee's Cost in Annuity

For purposes of figuring the tax-free recovery of your investment under the general rules *(7.23)* or the simplified method *(7.27)*, include the following items paid as of the annuity starting date as your cost in an employee annuity:

- Premiums paid by you or by after-tax withholdings from your pay.
- Payments made by your employer and reported as additional pay.

Reduce the total by any refunded premiums that you received by the annuity starting date, or, if later, the date of your first payment.

7.29 Withdrawals Before Annuity Starting Date

You generally may not make tax-free withdrawals from your employer's qualified retirement plan, qualified employee annuity plan, or 403(b) plan before the annuity starting date, even if your withdrawals are less than your investment. On a withdrawal before the annuity starting date, you must pay tax on a portion of the withdrawal unless the exceptions below apply. The portion of the withdrawal allocable to your investment is recovered tax free; the portion allocable to employer contributions and income earned on the contract is taxed. To compute the tax-free recovery, multiply the withdrawal by this fraction:

$$\frac{\text{Your total investment}}{\text{Your vested account balance or accrued benefit}}$$

Your investment and vested benefit are determined as of the date of distribution.

Exceptions. More favorable investment recovery rules are allowed in the following cases:

1. ***Employer plans in effect on May 5, 1986.*** If on May 5, 1986, your employer's plan allowed distributions of employee contributions before separation from service, the above pro-rata recovery rule applies only to the extent that the withdrawal exceeds the total investment in the contract on December 31, 1986.

   For example, assume that as of December 31, 1986, you had an account balance of $9,750, which included $4,000 of your own contributions. If the plan on May 5, 1986, allowed pre-retirement distributions of employee contributions, you may receive withdrawals up to your $4,000 investment without incurring tax.
2. ***Separate accounts for employee contributions.*** A defined contribution plan (such as a profit-sharing plan) is allowed to account for after-tax employee contributions (and earnings on the contributions) separately from employer contributions. If separate accounting is maintained, withdrawals of employee contributions from the separate account may be made tax free. A defined benefit pension plan may also maintain employee contributions (and earnings) in a separate account to which actual earnings and losses are allocated.

Caution

Favorable Recovery Rules

Both of the favorable cost recovery rules discussed under "Exceptions" in this section *(7.29)* are complicated and you should consult your plan administrator to determine if the exceptions apply and how to make the required calculations.

Chapter 8

IRAs

There are several types of IRAs: Traditional IRAs, Roth IRAs, SIMPLE IRAs, and SEPs. You may personally set up a traditional or Roth IRA with your bank or broker. SIMPLE IRAs *(8.18)* and SEPs *(8.15)* are available only if your employer offers such plans. For 2010, the contribution limit for both traditional *(8.2)* and Roth IRAs *(8.20)* is $5,000, or $6,000 for individuals who are age 50 or older. Traditional IRA contributions may be fully deductible, partly deductible, or not deductible at all, depending on whether you (and your spouse) have retirement coverage where you work and if so, whether your income subjects you to the deduction phaseout rules *(8.4)*.

Traditional IRA distributions are generally fully taxable and if made before age 59½, subject to a penalty; *see 8.12* for penalty exceptions. Minimum distributions from a traditional IRA must begin after you reach age 70½ *(8.13)*.

Although contributions are not deductible, the major tax advantage of the Roth IRA is that tax-free withdrawals of earnings may be made after a five-year waiting period if you are over age 59½ *(8.23)*. Tax-free withdrawals of contributions may be made at any time. A traditional IRA may also be converted to a Roth IRA. After a conversion, a Roth IRA may be recharacterized back to a traditional IRA, and subsequently reconverted to a Roth IRA. *See* the discussion of annual contributions *(8.20)*, conversions *(8.21)*, and recharacterizations and reconversions *(8.22)*.

Low-to-moderate-income taxpayers may be able to claim a tax credit on Form 8880 for contributions to a traditional IRA, Roth IRA, SIMPLE IRA, or salary-reduction SEP *(25.16)*.

Also Refer to:

8.1 Starting a Traditional IRA

If you have earnings, you may contribute to a traditional IRA up to an annual limit *(8.2)*. The contribution may be deductible *(8.4)* or nondeductible *(8.6)*. You also may set up a traditional IRA by rolling over a distribution received from a qualified employer plan or from another IRA. IRA accounts provide tax-free accumulation of earnings until withdrawals are made. On a rollover, you can avoid immediate tax when you receive a lump-sum payment upon retirement, changing jobs, or disability *(7.8)*.

Your employer can set up a "deemed IRA" as a separate account under a qualified retirement plan. As long as the separate account otherwise meets IRA requirements, you can make voluntary employee contributions that will be treated as IRA contributions subject to the regular IRA rules. The separate account can be treated as a traditional IRA or Roth IRA *(8.19)*.

Roth IRAs. Annual contributions to a Roth IRA and conversions of traditional IRAs to Roth IRAs are discussed at *8.19–8.21*.

Restrictions on traditional IRAs. You may not freely withdraw IRA funds until the year you reach age 59½ or become disabled. If you take money out before that time, you are subject to a penalty *(8.12)*. Pledging the account as collateral is treated as a taxable distribution from the account *(8.8)*. In the year you reach age 70½, you may no longer make traditional IRA contributions, and you must start to withdraw *(8.13)* from the account. All IRA withdrawals are fully taxable except for amounts allocable to nondeductible contributions *(8.8– 8.9)*. Special averaging for lump-sum distributions does not apply. Excess contributions *(8.7)* are penalized.

If your IRA loses value because of poor investments, you may not deduct the loss. A loss is allowed only if you make nondeductible contributions that you have not recovered when the account is depleted *(8.9)*.

Types of traditional IRAs. You may set up an IRA as:

1. An individual retirement account with a bank, savings and loan association, federally insured credit union, or other qualified person as trustee or custodian. An individual retirement account is technically a trust or custodial account. Your contribution may be invested in vehicles such as certificates of deposit, mutual funds, and certain limited partnerships.
2. An individual retirement annuity by purchasing an annuity contract (including a joint and survivor contract for the benefit of you and your spouse) issued by an insurance company; no trustee or custodian is required. The contract, endorsed to meet the terms of an IRA, is all that is required. Contracts issued after November 6, 1978, must provide for flexible premiums up to the annual contribution limit, so that if your compensation changes, your payment may also change. As borrowing or pledging of the contract is not allowed under an IRA, the contracts will not contain loan provisions. Endowment contracts issued after November 6, 1978, that provide life insurance protection may not be used as individual retirement annuities.

You may set up one type of IRA one year and choose another form the next year. You also may split your contribution between two or more investment vehicles. For example, you are eligible to contribute $5,000 for 2010 if under age 50. You may choose to put $2,500 into an investment retirement annuity and $2,500 into an individual retirement account with a bank, mutual fund, or brokerage firm.

You do not have to file any forms with your tax return when you set up or make contributions to a deductible IRA. Form 8606 must be attached to Form 1040 or Form 1040A if you make nondeductible IRA contributions *(8.6)*. The trustee or issuer of your IRA will report your contribution to the IRS on Form 5498, and you should receive a copy.

Self-directed IRA. If you wish to take a more active role in managing your IRA investments, you may set up a "self-directed" IRA using an IRS model form. The model trust (Form 5305) and the model custodial account agreement (Form 5305-A) meet the requirements of an exempt individual retirement account and so do not require a ruling or determination letter approving the exemption of the account and the deductibility of contributions made to the account. If you use this method, you still have to find a bank or other institution or trustee to handle your account or investment. Investments in a self-directed IRA are subject to restrictions; *see* the Caution in *8.1*.

Filing Tip

IRA Fees and Brokerage Commissions

Fees paid to set up or manage an IRA, and annual account maintenance fees, are not considered IRA contributions provided they are separately billed. They are investment expenses that may be deducted as a miscellaneous itemized deduction subject to the 2% of adjusted gross income floor *(19.1)*. However, broker's commissions that are paid when you make investments for your IRA are not separately deductible, according to the IRS. They are considered IRA contributions subject to the $5,000 contribution limit ($6,000 if age 50 or older) for 2010.

Caution

Restrictions on Collectibles Investments

If you have a self-directed traditional IRA and you invest in collectibles, such as art works, gems, stamps, antiques, rugs, metals, guns, or certain coins, you will have to pay a tax on your investment. The investment is treated as a taxable distribution to you in the year you make it. Coins are treated as collectibles, except for state-issued coins or certain U.S. minted gold, silver, and platinum coins. There is also an exception for gold, silver, platinum, or palladium bullion held by the IRA trustee, provided the fineness of the metal meets commodity market standards. If bullion is stored with a company other than the IRA trustee, the investment is subject to the deemed distribution rule for collectibles.

SIMPLE IRA. If you work for a company with 100 or fewer workers, your employer may set up a SIMPLE IRA to which you may make salary-reduction contributions *(8.17)*.

Contributions allowed up until filing due date. You have until April 15, 2011 (the regular filing due date for your 2010 return) to make deductible or nondeductible IRA contributions for 2010. You must make your contribution by April 15, 2011, even if you get an extension to file your return. If you are short of cash, you may borrow the funds to make the contribution without jeopardizing the deduction. If an IRA deduction entitles you to a refund, you can file your return early, claim the IRA deduction, and if you receive the refund in time, apply it towards an IRA contribution before the due date.

8.2 Traditional IRA Contributions Must Be Based on Earnings

You may make contributions to a traditional IRA for 2010 of up to $5,000, $6,000 if you are age 50 or older in 2010, provided you have wage, salary, or net self-employment earnings and that you have not reached age 70½ by the end of the year. If your earned income is less than $5,000 ($6,000 if age 50 or older), the contribution limit is 100% of your pay or net earned income if self-employed. If you have more than one traditional IRA, the limit applies to total contributions to all of the IRAs for the year. Contributions for 2010 may be made up to the filing deadline of April 15, 2011, for 2010 returns; this is the deadline even if you obtain a filing extension for your 2010 return.

If you are married filing jointly, you may each contribute up to $5,000 (or $6,000 if age 50 or older) to an IRA for 2010, as long as your combined compensation covers the contributions *(8.3)*.

Planning Reminder

IRA Contribution Based on Tax-Free Combat Pay

Members of the armed services serving in a combat zone *(35.4)* can contribute to either a traditional IRA or a Roth IRA *(8.20)* based on their tax-free combat pay. Without this law, members of the military who did not have any earnings apart from the combat zone pay could not make IRA contributions, which must be based on taxable compensation.

Deductibility. Contributions up to the $5,000 or $6,000 limit are *fully deductible* on your 2010 return if neither you nor your spouse is an active participant in an employer or self-employed retirement plan. Deductions for active plan participants are phased out for single persons with 2010 modified adjusted gross income over $56,000. The phaseout threshold on a joint return is generally $89,000 for 2010 *(8.3)*, but a more favorable $167,000 phaseout threshold applies to a jointly filing spouse who is not a plan participant *(8.4)*.

Contribution limit increased by $1,000 if age 50 or older. If you are age 50 or older by the end of 2010, an additional contribution of up to $1,000 may be made for 2010, increasing your contribution limit to the lesser of $6,000 (up from the general limit of $5,000) or your taxable compensation. If you are an active participant in an employer retirement plan, the $6,000 limit is subject to the phaseout rule *(8.4)*.

Taxable compensation. Traditional IRA contributions, whether deductible or nondeductible, must be based on taxable compensation received for rendering personal services, such as salary, wages, commissions, tips, fees, bonuses, jury fees, or net earnings from self-employment (less Keogh plan contributions on behalf of the self-employed). An IRA contribution (deductible or nondeductible) may not be based upon:

1. Investment income such as interest, dividends, or profits from sales of property;
2. Deferred compensation, pensions, or annuities; or
3. Income earned abroad for which the foreign earned income exclusion is claimed.

EXAMPLE

A trader whose sole income was derived from stock dividends and gains in buying and selling stocks contributed to an IRA. The IRS disallowed the deduction on the grounds that his income was not earned income.

If you live in a community property state, the fact that one-half of your spouse's income is considered your income does not entitle you to make contributions to an IRA. The contributions must be based on pay earned through your services.

Working for spouse. If you work for your spouse, you may make an IRA contribution provided you actually perform services and receive an actual payment of wages. A wife who worked as a receptionist and assistant to her husband, a veterinarian, failed to meet the second test. Her husband did not pay her a salary. Instead, he deposited all income from his business into a joint bank account held with his wife. In addition, no federal income tax was withheld from her wages.

In a ruling, the IRS held that the wife could not set up her own IRA, even though she performed services; she failed to receive actual payment. Depositing business income into a joint account is neither actual nor constructive payment of the wife's salary. Furthermore, any deduction claimed for the wife's wages was disallowed.

Self-employed may make IRA contributions. IRA contributions may be based on net self-employment earnings *(45.1)*, after taking into account deductible Keogh or SEP retirement plan contributions *(41.5)* and the deduction for one-half of self-employment tax liability *(45.3)*. If you have a net loss for the year, you may not make an IRA contribution unless you also have wages.

If you have more than one self-employed activity, you must aggregate profits and losses from all of your self-employed businesses to determine if you have net income on which to base an IRA contribution. For example, if one self-employed business produces a net profit of $15,000 but another a net loss of $20,000, you may not make an IRA contribution based on the net profit of $15,000 since you have an overall loss. This netting rule does not apply to salary or wage income. If you are an employee who also has an unprofitable business, you may make an IRA contribution based on your salary.

If you have a self-employed retirement plan from your business, you are considered an active participant in a retirement plan for purposes of the adjusted gross income phaseout rules *(8.4)*.

Taxable alimony treated as compensation. A divorced spouse with little or no earnings may treat taxable alimony as compensation, giving a basis for deductible IRA contributions. If you are divorced, you generally may make an IRA contribution for 2010 equal to 100% of taxable alimony up to the $5,000 limit ($6,000 if age 50 or older). However, if you are an active participant in an employer plan and your adjusted gross income exceeds the $56,000 threshold for unmarried individuals, *see 8.4* for the phaseout of the deduction limit. Taxable alimony is alimony paid under a decree of divorce or legal separation, or a written agreement incident to such a decree; *see Chapter 37*. It does not include alimony payments made under a written agreement that is not incident to such a decree.

No contributions to traditional IRA allowed for those age 70½. Even if you still have earnings, you may not make contributions to a traditional IRA for the year in which you reach age 70½, or any later year. For example, if you were born in the last six months of 1939 or the first six months of 1940, you will reach age 70½ in 2010 and may not make any traditional IRA contributions for 2010 or later years.

If you have a nonworking spouse under age 70½, you may contribute to his or her IRA, even though no contribution may be made to your own traditional IRA because you have reached age 70½ *(8.3)*.

Qualified reservist repayments. If you were called to active duty as a member of the reserves for over 179 days, or indefinitely, and took a distribution from your IRA during your active duty period, the distribution may be repaid to an IRA within the two-year period beginning on the day after the end of the active duty period. The repayment is allowed regardless of the regular IRA contribution limit for the year of repayment. The repaid amount is not deductible. The qualified reservist repayment must be reported as a nondeductible IRA contribution *(8.6)* on Line 1 of Form 8606.

8.3 Contributions to a Traditional IRA If You Are Married

If both you and your spouse earned compensation in 2010 of at least $5,000 and are under age 50 at the end of the year, each of you may make a contribution of up to $5,000 to a traditional IRA for 2010 by April 15, 2011. Under the spousal IRA rule, the $5,000 per spouse contribution limit applies even if only one of you works, provided you file jointly and your combined compensation is at least $10,000. An additional contribution of up to $1,000 can be made for each spouse who is age 50 or older by the end of the year so long as there is compensation to cover it.

Contributions for 2010 are fully deductible up to the $5,000 limit ($6,000, if applicable) if neither you nor your spouse was covered by an employer retirement plan during the year. If either of you was an active plan participant, you are both considered active participants, and a deduction may be limited or disallowed depending on your modified adjusted gross income (MAGI). However, if you file jointly and only one of you was an active plan participant, a more favorable MAGI phaseout rule applies to the nonparticipant spouse, so that the spouse without coverage may be able to claim a deduction even if the participant spouse may not. The deduction phaseout rules are discussed below.

Planning Reminder

Roth IRA Contributions after Age 70½

Contributions to a traditional IRA may not be made after age 70½, but contributions to a Roth IRA may be made even if you are over age 70½, provided you have compensation *(8.2)* to support the contribution and your income is within the limit allowed under the Roth IRA contribution rules *(8.20)*.

Spousal IRA contribution on joint return for nonworking or low-earning spouse. On a joint return for 2010, the contribution limit is $5,000 for each spouse as long as the combined compensation of both spouses is at least $10,000. If both spouses were age 50 or older by the end of 2010, the limit for each is raised to $6,000, so long as the combined compensation of both spouses is at least $12,000. This spousal IRA rule allows a spouse with minimal earnings to "borrow" compensation from his or her spouse in order to reach the maximum contribution limit. In figuring their combined compensation for purposes of the "borrowing" rule, the higher earning spouse's compensation is reduced by his or her deductible IRA contribution and by any regular contributions made by the higher earning spouse to a Roth IRA for the year.

EXAMPLE

Rhonda and Elliot Richards file a joint return for 2010. Both are under age 50 in 2010. Rhonda had salary income of $56,000 in 2010. Elliot was a full-time student and had no compensation. Rhonda may contribute up to $5,000 to a traditional IRA for 2010. Even though Elliot did not work in 2010, he also may contribute up to $5,000 to a traditional IRA for 2010. Since Rhonda's earnings exceeded $10,000, $5,000 of her earnings may be credited to Elliot for contribution purposes.

If Rhonda and Elliot's modified adjusted gross income (MAGI) *(8.4)* for 2010 does not exceed $89,000, contributions for each of them up to the $5,000 limit are fully deductible. If MAGI on their 2010 joint return exceeded $89,000 and if Rhonda were an active participant in her employer's retirement plan during 2010, her deduction would be phased out over a MAGI range of $89,000–$109,000. Elliot would be allowed a full $5,000 deduction so long as the joint return MAGI was $167,000 or less. *See* the phaseout rule below.

Deduction phaseout rule for spouses filing jointly for 2010. If either you or your spouse was an active participant in an employer retirement plan during 2010, the phaseout rule may limit or completely disallow an IRA deduction. However, even if one or both of you were active participants in an employer plan, the phaseout rule does not apply and you may each deduct contributions up to the $5,000 limit ($6,000 if age 50 or older) if your 2010 joint return modified adjusted gross income (MAGI) *(8.4)* is $89,000 or less.

If both of you were active plan participants for 2010, the deduction limit is phased out if your joint return MAGI is more than $89,000 but less than $109,000. No deduction is allowed for either of you if your 2010 joint return MAGI is $109,000 or more.

If you were not an active plan participant in 2010 but your spouse was, a different phaseout rule applies to each of you. Your spouse, as an active plan participant, is subject to the deduction phaseout if MAGI on the joint return is between $89,000 and $109,000; no deduction is allowed if MAGI is $109,000 or more. However, as the nonparticipant spouse, your deduction limit is not subject to phaseout unless MAGI on the joint return is over $167,000. Your deduction is phased out if joint MAGI is between $167,000 and $177,000, and no deduction is allowed if MAGI is $177,000 or more.

Planning Reminder

Phaseout Rule for Nonparticipant Spouses

If you are not covered by an employer retirement plan but your spouse is, and you file a joint return for 2010, your individual deduction limit is not subject to the phaseout rule unless modified adjusted gross income (MAGI) on the joint return is between $167,000 and $177,000. Your spouse, who is covered by an employer plan, is subject to the deduction phaseout for 2010 if modified adjusted gross income on the joint return is between $89,000 and $109,000.

See 8.4 for an example of how the reduced deduction limit is figured if MAGI is within the above phaseout ranges.

Deduction phaseout rule for married persons filing separately for 2010. If you are married, live together at any time during 2010, file separately, and either of you is an active participant in an employer plan, the other spouse is also considered an active participant. Both of you are subject to the $0 to $10,000 MAGI deduction phaseout *(8.4)*.

If you live apart for all of 2010, you each figure IRA deductions as if single. Thus, the more favorable deduction phaseout range of $56,000 to $66,000 applies if you are covered by an employer retirement plan *(8.4)*. If you are not covered, you may claim a full deduction on your separate return.

Contribution for nonworking spouse under age 70½. If in 2010 you were age 70½ or over and had taxable compensation, you may contribute to a spousal IRA for 2010 if your spouse is nonworking and is under age 70½ at the end of the year. The entire contribution must be allocated to the nonworking spouse. No contribution may be made to your own traditional IRA for the year in which you reach age 70½, or any later year. However, you may contribute to a Roth IRA even if you are over age 70½, provided your compensation is within the Roth IRA limits *(8.20)*.

8.4 IRA Deduction Restrictions for Active Participants in Employer Plan

If you are covered by an employer retirement plan, including a self-employed plan, you may be unable to make deductible IRA contributions to a traditional IRA. When you have coverage, your right to claim a full deduction, a limited deduction, or no deduction at all depends on your modified adjusted gross income (MAGI). If you are married, and your spouse has employer plan coverage for 2010 you are also considered to have coverage in most cases. However, if you file jointly and do not individually have employer plan coverage, a special MAGI phaseout rule may allow you to deduct IRA contributions even if a deduction for your spouse is limited or barred.

If you are unmarried and do not have employer plan coverage, or if you are married and neither of you has coverage, an IRA deduction of up to $5,000 ($6,000 if age 50 or older) for 2010 is allowed as long as you have compensation of $5,000 ($6,000 if age 50 or older) or more. The deduction phaseout rules do not apply, regardless of your income.

Are you an active plan participant? Generally, you are considered to be "covered" by a retirement plan if you are an active participant in the plan for any part of the plan year ending within your taxable year. If you are an employee, your Form W-2 for 2010 should indicate whether you are covered for the year; if you are, the "Retirement plan" box within Box 13 of Form W-2 should be checked. Active participation *(8.5)* in a self-employed Keogh plan or SEP *(Chapter 41)* is treated as employer plan coverage for purposes of the IRA deduction phaseout rules.

EXAMPLE

Sara Wartes, a college teacher, quit her job in 1988 and withdrew all of the contributions she had made to her employee pension plan. The Tax Court held that Sara could not claim an IRA deduction in that year. Sara was an active participant in the college plan during 1988 and under the phaseout rules based upon adjusted gross income, no IRA deduction was allowed. The court noted that the active participation test is not made at the end of the year. Participation in a company plan at any time during the year triggers the deduction phaseout rules. This is true even where a person has forfeitable benefits.

You are not an active plan participant but your spouse is. Even if you were not an active participant in an employer retirement plan at any time in 2010, your IRA deduction limit for 2010 may be phased out because of your spouse's coverage. However, if you file jointly, your own deduction is not limited unless modified adjusted gross income (MAGI) on the 2010 joint return exceeds $167,000. For your spouse who has employer plan coverage, the rule is different: the phaseout threshold for his or her 2010 deduction is joint MAGI of $89,000, assuming you file jointly.

As a nonparticipant, you are not allowed any deduction if MAGI on your joint return is $177,000 or more. A deduction for your spouse as an active participant is completely phased out if joint return MAGI for 2010 is $109,000 or more.

Stricter phaseout rules apply to married persons filing separately if they live together at any time during the year. If you lived with your spouse at any time during 2010 and either of you was an active plan participant in 2010, you are both subject to the $0 – $10,000 MAGI phaseout range on separate returns. Neither of you may claim an IRA deduction if the MAGI on your separate return is $10,000 or more.

If you are married filing separately and you lived apart for all of 2010, your spouse's plan participation does not affect your IRA deduction. Take into account only your own participation, if any, and if you are an active participant, your IRA deduction under the phaseout rules is figured as if you were single. If you are not an active participant, you may claim the full $5,000 deduction limit for 2010 ($6,000 if age 50 or older).

Modified adjusted gross income (MAGI) determines your deduction limit if you or your spouse is an active plan participant. If either you or your spouse is an active plan participant, you still may be allowed a full or limited deduction, but this will depend on whether your 2010 modified adjusted gross income (MAGI) is within the phaseout range that applies to you as shown below.

For purposes of figuring your IRA deduction limit, MAGI may be higher than the actual AGI reported on your return because certain deductions and exclusions are not taken into account. To get MAGI, you ignore IRA contributions and must add back to AGI any deduction claimed for student loan interest *(33.14)*, qualified college tuition and fees *(33.13)*, or domestic production activities income *(40.23)*. If you are claiming an exclusion for employer-provided adoption assistance *(3.6)* or an exclusion for interest on U.S. Savings Bonds used for tuition *(33.4)*, you must add back that excluded amount to adjusted gross income to get MAGI. If you worked abroad and are claiming the foreign earned income exclusion *(36.1)*, or a foreign housing exclusion or deduction *(36.4)*, these amounts also must be added back to adjusted gross income to get MAGI.

Figuring Your 2010 IRA Deduction Under the Phaseout Rules

If you are an active plan participant for 2010, or you file a joint return for 2010 and your spouse was an active participant, the full $5,000 (or $6,000 if age 50 or older) deduction limit is available to you only if your modified adjusted gross income (MAGI) is below a phaseout threshold shown below. Your deduction limit is phased out over the first $10,000 of MAGI exceeding the threshold, or $20,000 if you are married filing jointly or a qualifying widow(er) and you are an active plan participant.

Phaseout threshold for 2010 returns. On 2010 returns, the $5,000 (or $6,000 if age 50 or older) deduction limit is subject to phaseout if modified adjusted gross income exceeds:

- $56,000 if you are single or head of household;
- $56,000 if you are married filing separately, you lived apart from your spouse for all of 2010, and you were an active plan participant during 2010. If you lived apart the entire year and you were not an active participant, you qualify for the full deduction limit; the phaseout rule is inapplicable to you even if your spouse was an active plan participant.
- $89,000 if you are married filing jointly and both you and your spouse were active plan participants during 2010, or you are a qualifying widow or widower and were an active plan participant during 2010;
- $89,000 if you are married filing jointly and you are an active plan participant during 2010 but your spouse was not. You use the $89,000 threshold; your spouse uses the $167,000 threshold;
- $167,000 if you are married filing jointly and you were not an active plan participant at any time during 2010 but your spouse was. You use the $167,000 threshold; your spouse uses the $89,000 threshold; and
- $0 if you are married filing separately, you lived with your spouse at any time in 2010, and either you or your spouse was an active plan participant during 2010. You and your spouse are both subject to the "0" threshold on 2010 returns so long as you lived together at any time in 2010 and either of you was an active plan participant during the year.

Table 8-1 Phaseout Range for Deduction Limit on 2010 Returns

If your phaseout threshold (see above) is—	*Deduction limit is phased out if MAGI is—*	*No deduction if MAGI is—*
$56,000	Over $56,000 and under $66,000	$66,000 or more
$89,000	Over $89,000 and under $109,000	$109,000 or more
$167,000	Over $167,000 and under $177,000	$177,000 or more
$0	$0–$9,999	$10,000 or more

Compute the deduction limit under the phaseout rule. If your MAGI is within the phaseout range shown in the middle column of *Table 8-1,* you are allowed a portion of the deduction limit. You can figure the limit in your case by applying the following four steps. If you are married and both you and your spouse are contributing to traditional IRAs for 2010, you should separately figure your deduction limits, as each spouse may have a different phaseout threshold. The Examples below illustrate the computation.

1. Enter excess of your MAGI over your phaseout threshold. If married filing jointly, use the combined MAGI for both of you. ________

2. Multiply Step 1 by 50%, or by 60% if you were age 50 or older at the end of 2010. However, if you are married filing jointly or a qualifying widow or widower and you are an active plan participant, multiply Step 1 by 25% if you were under age 50 at the end of 2010, or by 30% if you were age 50 or older at the end of 2010. ________

3. Subtract Step 2 from $5,000, or from $6,000 if you were age 50 or older at the end of 2010. ________

4. If Step 3 is not a multiple of $10, round it up to the next highest multiple of $10. If the result is under $200, increase it to $200. This is your deductible limit for 2010. ________

EXAMPLES

1. Rob Porter is single and under age 50 at the end of 2010. He is an active participant in an employer retirement plan. His salary for 2010 is $56,865 and his MAGI for 2010 is $57,343. His MAGI exceeds the $56,000 phaseout floor for single persons by $1,343. Rob figures a deduction limit for 2010 of $4,330.00 as follows:

1. Excess of MAGI over phaseout threshold for single persons ($57,343 – $56,000)	$1,343.00
2. 50% of Step 1	671.50
3. $5,000 minus Step 2	$4,328.50
4. Round Step 3 to the next highest multiple of $10. This is Rob's deductible limit.	4,330

2. Ted and Lynn Baker are both under age 50 at the end of 2010 and they file a 2010 joint return. They report wages of $44,000 for Ted and $45,000 for Lynn. Their modified adjusted gross income (MAGI) is $92,020. Ted and Lynn are both active participants in employer retirement plans in 2010 and so they are both subject to the $89,000 phaseout threshold. They each figure a deduction of $4,250 as follows:

1. Excess of MAGI over phaseout threshold for married couples filing jointly ($92,020 – $89,000)	$3,020.00
2. 25% of Step 1	755.00
3. $5,000 minus Step 2	$4,245.00
4. Round Step 3 to the next highest multiple of $10. This is the deductible limit for Ted and also for Lynn. On their joint return, they can each deduct IRA contributions of up to $4,250, for a total maximum deduction of $8,500.	$4,250

3. Assume the same facts as in Example 2 except that only Lynn was an active participant in an employer plan. Ted and Lynn must figure their deduction limitations separately using different phaseout thresholds

   For Lynn, the same $4,250 deduction limit applies as in Example 2. The $89,000 phaseout threshold applies, her excess MAGI is $3,020 ($92,020 MAGI on joint return – $89,000 threshold), and her deduction limit as shown in Example 2 is $4,250.

   For Ted, the special $167,000 threshold for nonparticipant spouses applies. Since joint return MAGI is well below the $167,000 threshold, he is not affected by the phaseout rules and may deduct IRA contributions up to the $5,000 ceiling for 2010.

Nondeductible contributions. Any contributions exceeding the amount allowed under the above rules may be treated as nondeductible IRA contributions *(8.6)*. Alternatively, the excess may be contributed to a Roth IRA if allowed under the Roth IRA rules *(8.20)*.

Planning Reminder

Roth IRA vs. Deductible IRA

Even if you qualify for a full IRA deduction, you may want to consider making a nondeductible contribution to a Roth IRA *(8.20)*. For example, you may be willing to give up the current tax deduction in order to create a Roth IRA from which distributions will be completely tax free after age 59½ and a five-year waiting period has passed. If you choose to make a deductible contribution to a traditional IRA, distributions from the traditional IRA will be taxable. You may also prefer the Roth-IRA advantage of not having to take minimum distributions starting at age 70½, as is required with traditional IRAs.

Figuring your IRA deduction if you receive Social Security benefits. If you or your spouse *(8.3)* is an active participant in an employer plan and either of you receives Social Security benefits, you need to make an extra computation before you can figure whether an IRA deduction is allowed. Follow the rules discussed in *34.3* to determine if part of your Social Security benefits would be subject to tax, assuming no IRA deduction were claimed. If none of your benefits would be taxable, you follow the regular rules above for determining IRA deductions. If part of your Social Security benefits would be taxable, MAGI for IRA purposes is increased by the taxable benefits. The allowable IRA deduction is then taken into account to determine the actual amount of taxable Social Security. IRS Publication 590 has worksheets for making these computations.

8.5 Active Participation in Employer Plan

Active participants in an employer retirement plan are subject to the phaseout rules for deducting contributions *(8.4)*. When a married couple files jointly and only one of the spouses was an active plan participant for the taxable year, a more favorable phaseout range applies to the non-participant spouse than to the spouse who was an active participant *(8.4)*.

An employer retirement plan means:

1. A qualified pension, profit-sharing, or stock bonus plan, including a qualified self-employed Keogh plan, SIMPLE IRA, or simplified employee pension (SEP) plan;
2. A qualified annuity plan;
3. A tax-sheltered annuity; and
4. A plan established for its employees by the United States, by a state or political subdivision, or by any agency or instrumentality of the United States or a state or political subdivision, but not eligible state Section 457 plans.

Caution

Active Participant Status

You are treated as an active participant in a 401(k) plan, profit-sharing plan, stock bonus plan, or money-purchase pension plan if contributions are made or allocated to your account for the plan year that ends within your tax year. Under this rule, you may be considered an active participant for a year during which no contributions by you or your employer are made to your account; *see* the Examples in this section.

Form W-2. If your employer checks the "Retirement plan" box within Box 13 of your 2010 Form W-2, this indicates that you were an active participant in your employer's retirement plan during the year. If you want to make a contribution before you receive your Form W-2, check the following guidelines and consult your plan administrator for your status.

Type of plan. Under any type of plan, if you are considered an active participant for any part of the plan year ending with or within your taxable year, you are treated as an active participant for the entire taxable year. Because of this plan year rule, you may be treated as an active participant even if you worked for the employer only part of the year. Under IRS guidelines, it is possible to be treated as an active participant in the year of retirement and even in the year after retirement if your employer maintains a fiscal year plan.

The plan year rule works differently for defined benefit pension plans than for defined contribution plans such as profit-sharing plans, 401(k) plans, money purchase pension plans, and stock bonus plans. These rules are discussed below.

If you are married, and either you or your spouse is treated as an active participant for 2010, *see* 8.3 for the effect on the other spouse.

EXAMPLES

1. Pat O'Neil joins a company in February 2010 that has a 401(k) plan (a type of defined contribution plan) with a plan year starting July 1 and ending the following June 30. He is not eligible to participate in the plan year ending June 30, 2010. After he becomes eligible to participate in the second half of 2010, he elects to defer 6% of his 2010 salary to the 401(k) plan for the plan year ending June 30, 2011. Although he makes elective deferrals to the plan during 2010, he is not considered an active participant for 2010 because his contributions were made for the plan year ending in 2011. He will be considered an active participant in 2011 even if he decides not to defer any part of his 2011 salary for the plan year ending June 30, 2012.
2. Clarise Jones's employer has a defined benefit pension plan with a plan year starting July 1 and ending the following June 30. She is not excluded from participating. If she retired during September 2010, she is considered an active participant for 2010 because she was eligible to participate during the plan year ending June 30, 2010. She will also be considered an active participant for 2011. Although she will retire before the end of the plan year starting July 1, 2010, and ending June 30, 2011, she will still be eligible to participate during part of that plan year (July 1, 2010, until retirement in September 2010), and since the 2010–2011 plan year ends within her 2011 tax year, she will be considered an active participant for 2011.

Defined benefit pension plans. You are treated as an active participant in a defined benefit pension plan if, for the plan year ending with or within your taxable year, you are eligible to participate in the plan. Under this rule, as long as you are eligible, you are treated as an active participant, even if you decline participation in the plan or you fail to make a mandatory contribution specified in the plan. Furthermore, you are treated as an active participant even if your rights to benefits are not vested.

Defined contribution plan. For a defined contribution plan, you are generally considered an active participant if "with respect to" the plan year ending with or within your taxable year (1) you make elective deferrals to the plan; (2) your employer contributes to your account; or (3) forfeitures are allocated to your account. If any of these events occur, you are treated as an active participant for that taxable year, even if you do not have a vested right to receive benefits from your account.

8.6 Nondeductible Contributions to Traditional IRAs

If you are not allowed to deduct any IRA contributions for 2010 because of the phaseout rule *(8.4)*, you may make *nondeductible* contributions of up to $5,000 ($6,000 if age 50 or over at the end of 2010) where you have compensation of at least that much. If the deduction limit is reduced under the phaseout rules *(8.4)*, you may make a nondeductible contribution to the extent the maximum contribution limit of $5,000 (or $6,000) exceeds the deductible limit *(8.4)*.

If you make contributions to a traditional IRA during the year, you may not know whether your active participation status *(8.5)* and modified adjusted gross income (MAGI) will permit you to claim a deduction under the phaseout rules in 8.4. You can make your contribution and wait until you file your return to determine if you are eligible for a deduction. Assume that you make a contribution and after the end of the year you determine that you are eligible for only a portion of the deductible amount under the phaseout rule *(8.4)*. In that case, you can leave the nondeductible portion in a nondeductible traditional IRA (reporting it on Form 8606), or you may recharacterize *(8.22)* the nondeductible contribution as a Roth IRA contribution assuming you qualify to contribute to a Roth IRA *(8.20)*. On the other hand, you may decide to withdraw the nondeductible contribution as discussed below.

Roth IRA alternative. If you are not barred from making Roth IRA contributions *(8.20)* because of your income level, the Roth IRA has advantages over the nondeductible traditional IRA. Although both types of plans allow earnings to accumulate tax free until withdrawal, the Roth IRA has advantages at withdrawal. After a five-year period, completely tax-free withdrawals of earnings as well as contributions may be made from a Roth IRA if you are age 59½ or older, you are disabled, or you withdraw no more than $10,000 for first-time home-buyer expenses. Even within the first five-year period, contributions may be withdrawn tax free from a Roth IRA. On the other hand, withdrawals from a nondeductible traditional IRA are partially taxed if any deductible contributions to any traditional IRA were previously made. Even if only nondeductible contributions had been made, earnings from traditional IRAs are taxed at withdrawal. Furthermore, contributions after age 70½ may be made only to a Roth IRA, and mandatory required minimum distributions are not required from a Roth IRA, as they are from a traditional IRA. *See* the discussion of Roth IRAs in this chapter *(8.19–8.24)*.

Form 8606. If you made a nondeductible contribution to a traditional IRA for 2009, you must report it on Form 8606 unless you withdraw the contribution as discussed below. You must list on Form 8606 the value of all of your IRAs as of the end of the year, including amounts based on deductible contributions. If you are married and you and your spouse both make nondeductible contributions, you must each file a separate Form 8606. A $50 penalty may be imposed for not filing Form 8606 unless there is reasonable cause. Furthermore, if you overstate the amount of designated nondeductible contributions made for any taxable year, you are subject to a $100 penalty for each such overstatement unless you can demonstrate that the overstatement was due to reasonable cause. You may file an amended return for a taxable year and change the designation of IRA contributions from deductible to nondeductible or nondeductible to deductible.

Withdrawing nondeductible contributions. If you make an IRA contribution for 2010 and later realize it is not deductible, you may make a tax-free withdrawal of the contribution by the filing due date (plus extensions), instead of designating the contribution as nondeductible on Form 8606. To do this, you must also withdraw the earnings allocable to the withdrawn contribution and include the earnings as income on your 2010 return. You might want to make the withdrawal if

Planning Reminder

Roth IRA Alternative

A Roth IRA is a nondeductible IRA that offers significant tax and retirement planning advantages. Contributions up to the annual limit for a Roth IRA may be made if modified adjusted gross income is below the annual phaseout threshold *(8.20)*. In general, after the five-year period beginning with the first taxable year for which a Roth IRA contribution was made, tax-free withdrawals may be made if you are age 59½ or older, you are disabled or you have qualifying first-time home-buyer expenses. If you have a traditional IRA, you can also obtain the advantages of a Roth IRA by making a conversion to a Roth IRA. The conversion is taxable except to the extent that it is attributable to nondeductible contributions; a special two-year deferral rule is allowed for conversions in 2010 *(8.21)*.

Planning Reminder

Form 8606 for Traditional IRA Distributions

Keep a copy of each Form 8606 filed showing nondeductible contributions and keep a separate record of deductible contributions. When you make withdrawals from a traditional IRA, the portion of each withdrawal allocable to nondeductible contributions is not taxed. You may not completely avoid tax even if you withdraw an amount equal to your nondeductible contributions. The tax-free portion of the withdrawal is figured on Form 8606. *See* the rules for figuring tax on withdrawals *(8.9)*.

you incorrectly determined that a contribution would be deductible and you do not want to leave nondeductible contributions in your account. However, making the withdrawal could subject you to bank penalties for premature withdrawals, or other withdrawal penalties imposed by the IRA trustee. Furthermore, if you are under age 59½, the 10% premature withdrawal penalty applies to the withdrawn earnings unless one of the exceptions *(8.12)* is available.

8.7 Penalty for Excess Contributions to Traditional IRAs

If you contribute more than the allowable amount to a traditional IRA, whether deductible or nondeductible, the excess contribution may be subject to a penalty tax of 6%. The penalty tax is cumulative. That is, unless you correct the excess, you will be subject to another penalty on the excess contribution in the following year. The penalty tax is not deductible. The penalty is figured in Part III of Form 5329, which must be attached to Form 1040.

The 6% penalty may be avoided by withdrawing the excess contribution by the due date for your return, including extensions, plus any income earned on it. The withdrawn excess contribution is not taxable provided no deduction was allowed for it. The withdrawn earnings must be reported as income on your return for the year in which the excess contribution was made. The earnings should be reported to you as a taxable distribution on Form 1099-R. If you are under age 59½ (and not disabled) when you receive the income, the 10% premature withdrawal penalty applies to the income. Similar rules apply to withdrawals of excess employer contributions to a simplified employee pension plan *(8.15)* made by the due date for your return.

If an excess contribution for 2010 is not withdrawn by the due date (plus extensions) for your 2010 return, but you filed by the due date (with extensions), the IRS allows the withdrawal to be made no later than October 17, 2011 (six months after the original due date without extensions), provided the related earnings are reported on an amended return that explains the withdrawal; *see* the Form 5329 instructions for details. If the withdrawal is not made, the 6% penalty will apply to your 2010 return but it may be avoided for 2011 by withdrawing the excess by the end of 2011. Instead of withdrawing the excess contribution during 2011, you may also avoid a penalty for 2011 by reducing your allowable 2011 IRA contribution by the 2010 excess. *See* IRS Publication 590 and Form 5329 for details.

If you deducted an excess contribution in an earlier year for which total contributions were no more than the maximum deductible amount for that year, you may make a tax-free withdrawal of the excess by filing an amended return by the deadline *(47.2)* to correct the excess deduction. However, the 6% penalty tax applies for each year that the excess was still in the account at the end of the year.

See IRS Publication 590 for further information on correcting excess contributions made in a prior year.

Roth IRAs. A similar 6% penalty applies on Form 5329 to excess contributions to a Roth IRA; *see* Form 5329 and IRS Publication 590 for further details.

8.8 Taxable Distributions From Traditional IRAs

If all of your IRA contributions were deductible, any traditional IRA distribution you receive that you do not roll over or redeposit within 60 days *(8.10)* will be taxable. Not only are distributions taxable, but the timing and amount of IRA payments is subject to these restrictions:

- Distributions before age 59½ are subject to a 10% tax penalty, unless you are totally disabled, meet exceptions for paying medical costs, receive annual payments under an annuity-type schedule or you qualify for another exception *(8.12)*.
- After you reach age 70½, you must start to receive annual distributions under a life-expectancy calculation. The required starting date is the April 1 of the year after the year in which you reach age 70½. For example, if you reach age 70½ during 2010, you must start taking IRA distributions by April 1, 2011. Failure to take the annual required minimum distribution could result in penalties *(8.13)*.

How to report IRA distributions on your 2010 return. All IRA distributions are reported to you and to the IRS on Form 1099-R *(7.1)*. Form 1099-R must be attached to your return only if federal tax has been withheld. You can avoid withholding by instructing the payer not to withhold using Form W-4P or a substitute form *(26.11)*.

If you have never made nondeductible contributions, your IRA withdrawals are fully taxable and should be reported on Line 15b of Form 1040 or Line 11b of Form 1040A. If you have made deductible and nondeductible contributions, complete Form 8606 to figure the nontaxable and taxable portions *(8.9)*. Then you report the total IRA withdrawal on Line 15a of Form 1040 or Line 11a of Form 1040A and enter only the taxable portion on Line 15b or Line 11b, respectively.

If you have an individual retirement annuity, your investment in the contract is treated as zero so all payments are fully taxable. Distributions from an endowment policy due to death are taxed as ordinary income to the extent allocable to retirement savings; to the extent allocable to life insurance, they are considered insurance proceeds.

Proceeds from U.S. retirement bonds (which were issued by the Treasury before May 1982) are taxable in the year the bonds are redeemed. However, you must report the full proceeds in the year you reach age 70½ even if you do not redeem the bonds.

Conversion to Roth IRA. A conversion of a traditional IRA to a Roth IRA is generally treated as a taxable distribution from the traditional IRA *(8.21)*.

Distribution of IRA to charity—Exclusion not extended to 2010 when this book went to press. At the time this book went to press, Congress had not extended to 2010 the law that since 2006 has allowed individuals age 70½ and older to exclude from income up to $100,000 of IRA distributions transferred directly to charitable organizations. An extension of the law is expected and the following discussion assumes that the exclusion will be allowed for 2010 transfers. However, check the *e-Supplement at jklasser.com* for an update.

If the exclusion is extended and in 2010 you had the trustee of your traditional IRA make a direct transfer to charity, up to $100,000 of the distribution is tax free, provided you were at least age 70½ at the time of the distribution. The transfer must be made directly by the IRA trustee to a qualifying charity other than a "supporting organization" or donor advised fund. If your spouse also directed the trustee of his or her IRA to make a qualifying direct transfer in 2010, and you file jointly, you can each claim the up-to-$100,000 exclusion.

A charitable deduction cannot be claimed for the amount of the excludable distribution. A qualifying charitable distribution counts towards the required minimum distributions *(8.13)* that you must otherwise receive.

If you made any nondeductible contributions to any of your traditional IRAs, the direct transfer to charity is partly allocable to nondeductible IRA contributions and partly allocable to deductible contributions plus earnings. The transfer to charity is deemed to come first out of the otherwise taxable part of the distribution—that is, the deductible contributions plus earnings. The part of the distribution equal to the deductible contributions plus earnings is the excludable amount, up to the $100,000 limit. Any balance of the transfer is deemed to be a transfer of nondeductible contributions that must be reported on Form 8606 *(8.9)* and which reduces your remaining basis in your IRAs; this amount is nontaxable.

The total transfer to charity must be reported on Line 15a, Form 1040 (IRA distributions), and if any part is excludable, you should enter "QCD" (for qualified charitable distribution) next to Line 15b (taxable amount). If the entire transfer is a QCD, enter "0" on Line 15b. Any part of the distribution allocable to deductible contributions plus earnings that is not excludable is entered as taxable on Line 15b. Any part of the distribution allocable to nondeductible contributions reported on Form 8606 is not taxable and is not entered on Line 15b.

If you itemize deductions, the portion of the transfer allocable to nondeductible contributions, if any, can be claimed as a charitable contribution on Schedule A *(14.1)*. No charitable deduction is allowed for the excludable portion (deductible contributions plus earnings).

The exclusion is not allowed unless the entire distribution would be deductible as a charitable contribution (had you received the distribution and contributed the proceeds), without regard to the annual percentage-of-income ceilings *(14.17)*.

Since a qualifying transfer is not included in adjusted gross income, you may be able to preserve eligibility for the $25,000 loss allowance under the passive loss rules *(10.2)*. The exclusion may also help limit the amount of Social Security benefits subject to tax *(34.3)*.

Loan treated as distribution. If you borrow from your IRA account or use it as security for a loan, you generally are considered to have received your entire interest. Borrowing will subject the account or the fair market value of the contract to tax at ordinary income rates as of the first day of the taxable year of the borrowing. Your IRA account loses its tax-exempt status. If you use

Law Alert

Tax-Free Transfers From IRA to Charity

The exclusion from income for up-to-$100,000 in IRA distributions transferred directly to charity applied to 2009 transfers but will not apply to 2010 transfers unless Congress extends the law allowing the exclusion, which had not yet occurred when this book went to press; *see* the *e-Supplement at jklasser.com.*

Court Decision

Penalty on Garnished IRA

The Tax Court held that an IRA owner received a taxable distribution when a bank enforced a court's garnishment award for past-due child support by transferring his IRA to his ex-wife. The Tax Court found that the distribution to the owner's former wife was a discharge of indebtedness to her and was constructively received by him. Whether the transfer of funds was voluntary or in settlement of a legal obligation was held to be of no consequence. The 10% tax penalty for distributions before age 59½ also applied.

the account or part of it as security for a loan, the portion that is pledged is treated as a distribution. However, under the rollover rules, a short-term loan may be made by withdrawing IRA funds and redepositing them in an IRA within 60 days, subject to the once-a-year rollover rule *(8.10)*.

IRS seizure of IRA treated as distribution. The Tax Court has held that an IRS levy of an IRA to cover back taxes is a taxable distribution to the account owner, even though the funds are transferred directly from the account to the IRS and not actually received by the owner. Where the owner is under age 59½, the 10% penalty for early withdrawals *(8.12)* does *not* apply to involuntary distributions attributable to an IRS levy.

8.9 Partially Tax-Free Traditional IRA Distributions Allocable to Nondeductible Contributions

If you ever made a nondeductible contribution to a traditional IRA, you must file Form 8606 to report a 2010 distribution from any of your traditional IRAs, even if the distribution is from an IRA to which only nondeductible contributions were made. All of your traditional IRAs are treated as one contract. If you receive distributions from more than one IRA in the same year, they are combined for reporting purposes on Form 8606. When you withdraw an amount from any traditional IRA during a taxable year and you previously made both deductible and nondeductible IRA contributions, the part of your withdrawal that is allocable to your nondeductible contributions is tax-free; any balance is taxable. You may not claim that you are withdrawing only your tax-free contributions, even if your withdrawal is less than your nondeductible contributions. The six steps below reflect the IRS method used on Form 8606 to figure the nontaxable and taxable portions of the IRA distributions.

The rule requiring you to combine nondeductible and deductible IRAs when making IRA withdrawals does not apply to withdrawals from a Roth IRA. A Roth IRA is treated separately. After a five-year period, withdrawals after age 59½ from a Roth IRA are completely tax-free *(8.23)*.

A bank or other payer of a distribution from a traditional IRA will not indicate on Form 1099-R whether any part of a distribution is a tax-free return of basis allocable to nondeductible contributions. It is up to you to keep records that show the nondeductible contributions you have made. IRS instructions require you to keep copies of all Forms 8606 on which nondeductible contributions have been designated, as well as copies of (1) your tax returns for years you made nondeductible contributions to traditional IRAs; (2) Forms 5498 showing all IRA contributions and showing the value of your IRAs for each year you received a distribution; and (3) Form 1099-R and Form W-2P showing IRA distributions. According to the IRS, you should keep such records until you have withdrawn all IRA funds.

Figuring the taxable portion of a traditional IRA distribution. If you received a distribution from a traditional IRA in 2010 and have ever made nondeductible contributions to any of your traditional IRAs, follow Steps 1–6 to determine the tax-free and taxable portions of the 2010 distribution. These steps assume that you did not convert a traditional IRA to a Roth IRA during 2010. If you did convert a traditional IRA to a Roth IRA, follow the instructions to Form 8606.

Step 1. Total IRA withdrawals during 2010.

Step 2. Total nondeductible contributions to all IRAs made by the end of 2010. Tax-free withdrawals of nondeductible contributions in prior years reduce the total. If you made any contributions to traditional IRAs for 2010 (including a contribution made between January 1 and April 15, 2011) that may be partly nondeductible because your modified adjusted gross income is within the deduction phaseout range shown in *8.4* for active plan participants, you should include the contributions in the Step 2 total.

Step 3. Add Step 1 to the value of all your IRAs (include SIMPLE IRAs and SEP IRAs) as of the end of 2010. If you received an IRA distribution within the last 60 days of 2010 that was rolled over to another IRA within the 60-day rollover period *(8.10)* *but* not until 2011, add the 2011 rollover to the year-end balance.

Step 4. Divide Step 2 by Step 3. This is the tax-free percentage of your IRA withdrawal.

Step 5. Multiply the Step 4 percentage by Step 1. This amount is tax free.

Step 6. Subtract Step 5 from Step 1. This amount is fully taxable.

EXAMPLE

In 2010, Nick James withdraws $5,000 from his traditional IRA, having made deductible IRA contributions of $8,000 and nondeductible contributions of $6,000 as follows:

Year	*Deductible*	*Nondeductible*
1991	$2,000	0
1992	2,000	0
1993	2,000	0
1994	1,000	$1,000
1995	1,000	1,000
1996	0	2,000
1997	0	2,000
	$8,000	$6,000

Assume that at the end of 2010, Nick's total IRA account balance, including earnings, is $27,500, and that this is his first IRA withdrawal. On Form 8606 for 2010, Nick figures that $923 of the $5,000 IRA withdrawal is tax free and $4,077 is taxable.

Step 1.	IRA withdrawal	$5,000
Step 2.	Nondeductible contributions	6,000
Step 3.	IRA balance at end of the year ($27,500) *plus* Step 1	32,500
Step 4.	Tax-free percentage: $6,000 ÷ $32,500	18.46%
Step 5.	Tax-free withdrawal: 18.46% × $5,000	923
Step 6.	Taxable withdrawal: $5,000 – $923	$4,077

The total $5,000 withdrawal should be reported on Line 15a of Form 1040 or on Line 11a of Form 1040A, and the taxable $4,077 portion should be entered on Line 15b (Form 1040) or on Line 11b (Form 1040A).

Planning Reminder

Deducting Loss

A loss on an IRA investment is deductible only if your basis in nondeductible contributions has not been received after the entire account has been distributed.

Deductible IRA loss based on unrecovered nondeductible contributions. According to the IRS, a loss is allowed if all IRA funds have been distributed and you have not recovered your basis in nondeductible contributions. However, the loss must be claimed as a miscellaneous itemized deduction subject to the 2%-of-adjusted-gross-income floor on Schedule A, Form 1040.

EXAMPLE

Paula Brown made nondeductible IRA contributions of $10,000 from 1994–1998. In 2009, she withdrew $6,000. The 2009 year-end balance was $8,000. The tax-free portion of the withdrawal was $4,286 ($10,000 nondeductible contributions ÷ $14,000 total of withdrawal plus year-end balance × $6,000 withdrawal).

After the 2009 withdrawal, her basis is $5,714 ($10,000 – $4,286). If because of stock market losses in 2010 the value of the IRA falls to $3,000 by the end of 2010 and she withdraws the entire $3,000 balance, she can claim a $2,714 loss ($5,714 basis – $3,000 distribution) for 2010 but only as a miscellaneous itemized deduction subject to the 2% floor *(19.1)* on Schedule A of Form 1040. Depending on her adjusted gross income and other miscellaneous itemized deductions, Paula may be unable to claim the loss on her IRA because of the 2% floor. If the loss is allowed on Schedule A, it must be added back to income for purposes of figuring whether Paula is subject to alternative minimum tax *(23.2)*.

8.10 Tax-Free Rollovers and Direct Transfers to Traditional IRAs

There are two types of tax-free rollovers that you can make to a traditional IRA. You may roll over funds to a traditional IRA from a qualified company or self-employed retirement plan, 403(b) plan, or governmental 457 plan *(7.8)*. You may also use a rollover to switch funds from one traditional IRA to another, although another option, a direct transfer, is a more advantageous way of changing IRA investments.

Direct transfer from one IRA to another. A *direct transfer* is made by instructing the trustee of a traditional IRA to transfer all or part of your account to another IRA trustee. Direct transfers are tax free because you do not receive the funds. With a direct transfer, there is no risk of missing the 60-day deadline for rolling over a withdrawal into a new IRA. The tax law does not require a waiting period between direct transfers, whereas rollovers are subject to a once-a-year limitation, as discussed below.

For example, assume you have a traditional IRA at Bank "A" and decide to switch your account to Mutual Fund "ABC." The mutual fund will provide you with transfer request forms that you complete and return to the fund, which will then forward the forms to the bank to complete the direct transfer. The transfer from the bank to the mutual fund is tax free. Because the IRA funds were not paid to you, the transfer is not considered a rollover subject to the once-a-year rollover limitation. This means that if within one year you become unhappy with the performance of Mutual Fund "ABC," you may make another tax-free direct transfer of your IRA to Fund "XYZ" or to Bank "B."

Planning Reminder

60-Day Loan From IRA

You can take advantage of the rollover rule to borrow funds from your IRA if you need a short-term loan to pay your taxes or other expenses. As long as you redeposit the amount in an IRA within 60 days you are not taxed on the withdrawal; the redeposit is considered a tax-free rollover. You may roll over the funds to a different IRA from the one from which the withdrawal was made. A second withdrawal from the same IRA within one year would be taxable *(8.10)*.

Rollover within 60 days. If you withdraw funds from a traditional IRA, you have 60 days to make a tax-free rollover to another traditional IRA. The amount you receive from your old IRA must be transferred to the new plan by the 60th day after the day you received it. Amounts not rolled over within the 60-day period must be treated as a taxable distribution for the year you received the distribution (not the year in which the 60-day period expired, if that is later) and the 10% penalty for a distribution before age 59½ applies unless an exception *(8.12)* is available.

The IRS may waive the 60-day rollover deadline on equitable grounds if a distribution cannot be rolled over on time because of events beyond your reasonable control, such as illness, natural disaster, or a financial institution's error; *see* the IRS waiver guidlines below. An extension to the 60-day deadline is also allowed if your distribution is "frozen" and cannot be withdrawn from an insolvent or bankrupt financial institution; *see* below. The deadline is extended to 120 days if a distribution is taken to buy or build a qualifying "first home" and the deal falls through; *see* below.

Once you complete a rollover between traditional IRAs, you must wait one year before you can roll over the same funds; *see* below.

IRS may waive 60-day rollover deadline on equitable grounds. The IRS has discretion to waive the 60-day deadline for completing a rollover if failure to do so was due to events beyond your reasonable control and failure to waive the deadline would be against "equity or good conscience."

The IRS will automatically waive the deadline if: (1) you deposit the rollover funds with a financial institution within the 60-day period, (2) you follow all of the institution's rollover procedures but the rollover account is not established on time solely because of the institution's error, and (3) the funds are actually deposited in a valid rollover account within one year of the start of the 60-day period.

In other hardship situations not eligible for the automatic waiver, you must apply to the IRS for a waiver by requesting a private letter ruling and paying the required user fee. You must show that failure to meet the 60-day deadline was beyond your reasonable control, such as where you were disabled, hospitalized, or there was a natural disaster, postal error, or error by the financial institution other than one qualifying for an automatic waiver. The IRS will take into account the length of the delay and whether you cashed a distribution paid to you by check.

For example, the IRS issued a private ruling allowing a waiver to a taxpayer whose IRA funds were stolen by his investment advisor. Without a rollover, the advisor's withdrawals would be treated as taxable distributions to the taxpayer. Since the taxpayer did not learn of the misappropriation until after the 60-day rollover period expired, a waiver was requested. The IRS agreed that not granting a waiver would be inequitable and it gave the taxpayer 30 days from the date of the ruling to make a cash rollover of the misappropriated amount.

However, the IRS has denied waivers to taxpayers who use an IRA distribution as a short-term loan to pay personal expenses but are unable to put back the funds into an IRA within 60 days. For example, an unemployed taxpayer withdrew money from his IRA to pay his mortgage and avoid a threatened foreclosure of the home. After he was turned down for loans by numerous mortgage companies, his mother borrowed against her home and loaned him the funds, which he redeposited into his IRA, but 102 days had passed since he received the distribution. The IRS in a private ruling denied his request for a waiver of the 60-day rollover deadline.

The once-a-year rollover rule applies separately to each of your IRAs. A tax-free rollover may occur only once in a one-year period starting on the date you receive the first distribution. If within that one-year period you receive a distribution from the previously rolled over IRA, the distribution is taxable and if you are under age 59½, could be subject to the 10% penalty for premature distributions *(8.12)*. However, this rule applies separately to each of your traditional IRAs. For example, you have one traditional IRA invested in a bank and another invested in a mutual fund. Within the same one-year period, you may roll over the bank IRA to a different traditional IRA and you may also roll over the mutual-fund IRA to a different traditional IRA. However, neither of the new IRAs may be rolled over again within the one-year period starting on the date that you received the distribution from the original traditional IRA.

There is an exception to the one-year waiting period between rollovers if the second distribution is made from an insolvent financial institution by the FDIC (Federal Deposit Insurance Corporation) acting as receiver. The exception applies only if the receiver makes the distribution to you because it is unable to find a buyer for the insolvent institution.

Note: A *direct transfer* may be used as discussed above if you want to invest in another IRA within the one-year period.

Deposits in insolvent financial institutions. The 60-day limit for completing a rollover is extended if the funds are "frozen" and may not be withdrawn from a bankrupt or insolvent financial institution. The 60-day period is extended while the account is frozen and you have a minimum of 10 days after the release of the funds to complete the rollover.

If a government agency takes control of an insolvent bank, you might receive an "involuntary" distribution of your IRA account from the agency. According to the IRS and Tax Court, such a payment is subject to the regular IRA distribution rules. For example, a couple received payment for their $11,000 IRA balance from the Maryland Deposit Insurance Fund after the bank in which the funds were invested became insolvent. The Tax Court held that the payment was taxable, even though the distribution was from a state insurance fund and not from the bank itself. Furthermore, since they were under age 59½, the 10% penalty for early distributions *(8.12)* was imposed, even though the distribution was involuntary. The tax and penalty could have been avoided by making a rollover of the distribution within 60 days, but this was not done.

120-day rollover period after failure to acquire "first-time" home. A "first-time" homebuyer may be able to limit or avoid a 10% penalty for a distribution before age 59½ by using the funds within 120 days to help buy, build, or rebuild a principal residence *(8.12)*. If the requirements of the exception cannot be met because the planned purchase or construction of the home falls through, the law allows the taxpayer to return the distribution to an IRA within 120 days after receiving the distribution. The extension of the tax-free rollover period from 60 days to 120 days is automatic if the requirements are met; a waiver of the 60-day deadline (as discussed above) from the IRS is not required. For example, a taxpayer withdrew IRA funds to buy a home and would have qualified as a "first-time" homebuyer, but his offer was rejected by the seller and approximately 72 days after the IRA withdrawal he put the amount of the distribution back into his IRA. The IRS in a private ruling held that the recontribution to the IRA was timely under the special 120-day rollover rule.

Filing Tip

Reporting a Rollover on Your 2010 Return

If in 2010 you rolled over a qualifying distribution from an employer plan to a traditional IRA *(7.8)*, report the total distribution on Line 16a of Form 1040 or Line 12a of Form 1040A. Enter zero as the taxable amount on Line 16b or Line 12b if the entire amount was rolled over. If only part of the distribution was rolled over, enter the portion not rolled over on Line 16b or Line 12b. Write "Rollover" next to the line.

If you rolled over funds from one traditional IRA to another, the total distribution should be reported on Line 15a of Form 1040 or Line 11a of Form 1040A. If the entire distribution was rolled over, enter zero as the taxable amount on Line 15b or Line 11b. Otherwise, enter the amount not rolled over on Line 15b or Line 11b. Write "Rollover" next to the line.

If you made a tax-free direct transfer from one IRA to another, you do not have to report it on your return.

8.11 Transfer of Traditional IRA to Spouse at Divorce or Death

If you receive your former spouse's IRA pursuant to a divorce decree or written instrument incident to the decree, the transfer is not taxable to either of you. From the date of transfer the account is treated as your IRA. If you are legally separated, a transfer of your spouse's IRA to you is tax free if made under a decree of separate maintenance or written instrument incident to the decree. The transferred account is then treated as your IRA.

How to make a divorce-related transfer. If you are required to transfer IRA assets to your spouse or former spouse by a decree of divorce or separate maintenance, or a written instrument incident to such a decree, use one of these transfer methods to avoid being taxed on the transfer: (1) change the name on the IRA from your name to the name of your spouse or former spouse, or (2) direct your IRA trustee to transfer the IRA assets directly to the trustee of a new or existing IRA in the name of your spouse or former spouse.

If you simply withdraw money from your IRA and pay it to your spouse, you will be treated as having received a taxable distribution from your IRA. If you are under age 59½, you will be subject to the 10% early distribution penalty as well as regular tax on the withdrawal.

QDRO transfer of employer plan benefits to your IRA. If you receive your share of your spouse's or former spouse's benefits from an employer plan under a qualified domestic relations order (QDRO), the distribution is taxable to you unless you roll it over to a traditional IRA or another eligible retirement plan *(7.12)*. If you roll over only part of a qualifying QDRO distribution, you figure the tax on the retained portion by taking into account a prorated share of your former spouse's cost investment.

Surviving spouse. If you inherit your spouse's IRA when he or she dies, you may elect to treat the IRA as your own, or you may receive distributions from the account as a beneficiary. *See 8.14* for a discussion of these options.

8.12 Penalty for Traditional IRA Withdrawals Before Age 59½

You have to pay a 10% penalty if you receive a distribution from a traditional IRA before you are age 59½, unless (1) you make a qualifying rollover to another IRA *(8.10)*, (2) you are totally disabled, (3) you pay medical expenses exceeding 7.5% of adjusted gross income, (4) you receive unemployment compensation for at least 12 consecutive weeks and pay medical insurance premiums, (5) you pay qualified higher education expenses, (6) the distribution is $10,000 or less and used for qualified first-time home-buyer expenses, (7) you receive a qualified reservist distribution, (8) the distribution is one of a series of payments being made under one of several annuity-type methods, (9) you are a beneficiary receiving IRA distributions following the death of the owner, or (10) the distribution was due to an IRS levy on your IRA.

The penalty is 10% of the taxable IRA distribution. For example, if before age 59½ you withdraw $3,000 from your traditional IRA, you must include the $3,000 as part of your taxable income and, in addition, pay a $300 penalty tax. If part of a premature distribution is tax free because it is allocable to nondeductible contributions *(8.9)* or rolled over to another IRA *(8.10)*, the 10% penalty applies only to the taxable portion of the distribution.

If you are subject to the 10% early distribution penalty for 2010 but not the excess contribution penalty *(8.7)*, the penalty is entered directly on Form 1040, Line 58.

If you do not owe the penalty because you qualify for an exception, you may have to file Form 5329 with Form 1040, depending on whether the payer of the distribution correctly marked the exception in Box 7 of Form 1099-R. If you qualify for the annuity-method exception and the payer correctly indicated that exception by marking Code 2 in Box 7, you do not have to file Form 5329. Similarly, if you are the beneficiary of a deceased IRA owner and the payer has correctly noted that with Code 4 in Box 7, you do not have to file Form 5329 to claim the exception.

If you qualify for the disability exception (*see* below), it is unlikely that the payer will know of that fact and thus Code 3 (for the disability exception) will probably not be marked in Box 7 of Form 1099-R. In that case, you must file Form 5329 to claim the exception. You also must file Form 5329 if the annuity method or beneficiary exception applies but it is not coded in Box 7 of Form 1099-R.

If you rolled over your entire distribution within 60 days to another IRA *(8.10)*, the penalty does not apply and Form 5329 does not have to be filed.

Beneficiaries. Beneficiaries are exempt from the pre–age 59½ penalty. If the IRA owner was not your spouse and you liquidate the account and receive the proceeds, or if you receive annual payments as a beneficiary under the inherited IRA rules *(8.14)*, any distributions you receive before age 59½ are not subject to the early distribution penalty.

If you inherit an IRA from your deceased spouse and elect to treat it as your own IRA as discussed in *8.14*, you are not eligible for the beneficiary exception; distributions from the account before you reach age 59½ will be subject to the penalty unless another exception applies. The beneficiary exception applies if the account is maintained in the name of your deceased spouse and you are receiving the distribution according to the rules for a spousal beneficiary *(8.14)*.

Disability exception. To qualify for the disability exception, you must be able to show that you have a physical or mental condition that can be expected to last indefinitely or result in death and that prevents you from engaging in "substantial gainful activity" similar to the type of work you were doing before the condition arose.

In one case, a 53-year-old stockbroker claimed that his IRA withdrawal of over $200,000 should be exempt from the 10% penalty because he suffered from mental depression. However, the Tax Court upheld the IRS imposition of the penalty because he continued to work as a stockbroker.

Medical expense exception. If you withdraw IRA funds in a year in which you pay substantial medical costs, part of the distribution may avoid the pre–age 59½ penalty. If your unreimbursed medical expenses in the year of the distribution exceed 7.5% of your adjusted gross income (AGI), the distribution, to the extent of the excess, is not subject to the penalty. The taxable part of the IRA distribution is included in AGI for purposes of applying the 7.5% test. The medical costs must be eligible for the itemized medical deduction *(17.2)*, but the IRA penalty exception applies whether you itemize or claim the standard deduction.

Unemployed person's medical insurance exceptions. There is no general penalty exception for being unemployed. However, if you are unemployed and received unemployment benefits under Federal or state law for at least 12 consecutive weeks, you may make penalty-free IRA withdrawals to the extent of medical insurance premiums paid during the year for you, your spouse, and your dependents. The withdrawals may be made in the year the 12-week unemployment test is met, or in the following year. However, the penalty exception does not apply to distributions made more than 60 days after you return to the work force.

Self-employed persons who are ineligible by law for unemployment benefits may be treated as meeting the 12-week test, and thus eligible for the exception, under regulations to be issued by the IRS.

Higher education expenses exception. A penalty exception is allowed for IRA distributions that do not exceed higher education expenses, including graduate school costs, for you, your spouse, your or your spouse's children, or your or your spouse's grandchildren that you paid during the year of the IRA distribution. Eligible expenses include tuition, fees, books, supplies, and equipment that are required for enrollment or attendance, plus room and board for a person who is at least a half-time student.

The penalty exception applies only if the withdrawal from the IRA and the payment of the qualified higher education expenses occur within the same year. For example, in one case, a taxpayer under age 59½ took IRA distributions in 2001 to pay credit card debt incurred in 1999 and 2000 to pay qualified higher education expenses for those years. Another taxpayer under age 59½ took IRA distributions in 2002 and used them to pay qualified expenses incurred in 2003 and 2004. In both cases, the Tax Court agreed with the IRS that the penalty exception was not available because the IRA withdrawals were not made in the same year that the qualified higher education expenses were incurred.

First-time home-buyer expense exception. A penalty exception is allowed for up to $10,000 of qualifying "first-time" home-buyer expenses. You are a qualifying first-time home-buyer if you did not have a present ownership interest in a principal residence in the two-year period ending on the acquisition date of the new home. If you are married, your spouse also must have had no such ownership interest within the two-year period. The penalty does not apply to IRA distributions that are used within 120 days to buy, construct, or reconstruct a principal residence for you, your spouse, child, grandchild, or ancestor of you or your spouse. Qualifying home acquisition costs include reasonable settlement, financing, or other closing costs. If you qualify, the exception applies only for $10,000 of home-buyer expenses. This is a lifetime cap per IRA owner and not an annual limit.

If you take a distribution, intending to use it for home acquisition costs that would qualify for the first-time buyer exception, but the transaction falls through, you have 120 days from the date you receive the distribution to roll it back to an IRA *(8.10)*.

IRS levy. The 10% penalty does not apply to an "involuntary" distribution due to an IRS levy on your IRA.

Caution

Medical Expenses Exception

The medical expense exception to the 10% penalty applies only to the extent that in the year you receive the distribution, you pay deductible medical costs *(17.2)* in excess of 7.5% of your adjusted gross income. If the deductible medical expenses are not paid in the year the distribution is received, the exception is not available.

Planning Reminder

Annuity-Schedule Penalty Exceptions

If you are planning a series of payments to avoid the 10% early-distribution penalty, keep in mind that payments under this exception must continue for at least five years, or until you reach age 59½, whichever is the longer period.

Caution

Timing Problem for Higher Education Costs

Qualified higher education expenses must be paid in the same year that the distribution is received for the penalty exception to apply. This timing rule turns the penalty exception into a tax trap when a tuition payment made at the end of the year is "reimbursed" by an IRA withdrawal at the beginning of the following year, or an IRA distribution is taken at the end of the year to cover a tuition payment due at the start of the next year.

Qualified reservist distribution. If you are a member of the reserves called to active military duty for over 179 days, or indefinitely, distributions received during the active duty period are not subject to the early distribution penalty. Furthermore, a qualified reservist distribution may be recontributed to the plan within two years after the end of your active duty period without regard to the regular limits on IRA contributions *(8.2)*. A recontribution is not deductible.

Annuity Schedule Payments Avoid 10% Penalty

You may avoid the penalty if you are willing to receive annual distributions under one of the three IRS-approved annuity-type methods discussed in this section. Before arranging an annuity-type schedule, consider these points: all of the payments will be taxable (unless allocable to nondeductible contributions *(8.9)*), and if you do not continue the payments for a minimum number of years, the IRS will impose the 10% penalty for all taxable payments received before age 59½, plus interest charges. The minimum payout period rules do not apply to totally disabled individuals or to beneficiaries of deceased IRA owners.

The payments must continue for at least five years, or until you reach age 59½, whichever period is longer. Thus, if you are in your 40s, you would have to continue the scheduled payments until you are age 59½. If you are in your mid-50s, the minimum payout period is not as serious a burden, as you only need to continue the scheduled payments for at least five years, starting with the date of the first distribution, provided that the period ends after you reach age 59½.

During this minimum period, the arranged annuity-type schedule generally may not be changed unless you become disabled. For example, taking a lump-sum distribution of your account balance before the end of the minimum payout period would trigger the retroactive penalty, plus interest charges. The penalty is triggered even if the change in distribution methods is made after you reach age 59½. However, the IRS may allow a reduction in payments during the minimum period, such as where part of an IRA has been transferred to an ex-spouse following a divorce. Also, as discussed below, the IRS allows a one-time irrevocable switch from the fixed amortization method or fixed annuitization method to the required minimum distribution method. After the minimum payout period, you can discontinue the payments or change the method without penalty.

IRS Alert

Division of IRA in Divorce

The IRS in private rulings has allowed a reduction in the scheduled payments from an IRA if part of the IRA is transferred to an ex-spouse as part of a divorce settlement. The reduction is not treated by the IRS as a "modification" that triggers the penalty.

Three approved payment methods. If you would like to take advantage of this penalty exception, you may apply one of the following three payout methods that have been approved by the IRS. With each method, you must receive at least one distribution annually. Under Method 1, the payment changes annually based on the value of the account. Under Methods 2 and 3 the annual payment is generally fixed when the payments begin, but in private rulings the IRS has approved payment schedules that from inception recalculate the amount to be withdrawn each year. Methods 2 and 3 require the assistance of a tax professional and financial advisor to plan the series of payments. The IRS allows taxpayers receiving payments under Method 2 or 3 to reduce the required annual amount without penalty by switching to Method 1.

1. *Required minimum distribution method.* This is the easiest method to figure but provides smaller annual payments than the other methods. Figure the annual withdrawal by dividing your account balance by your life expectancy or by the joint life and last survivor expectancy of you and your beneficiary.

For example, assume that you are age 50 in 2011 and have an IRA of $100,000 at the beginning of the year. If you use your single life expectancy, you may take a penalty-free payment of $2,924 in 2011 ($100,000 account balance ÷ 34.2 life expectancy). Single life expectancy is shown in *Table 8.5*, Beneficiary's Single-Life Expectancy Table *(8.14)*.

If instead of using your single life expectancy you used the joint life and last survivor expectancy of you and your beneficiary, the annual penalty-free amount would be smaller given the longer joint life expectancy. For example, if your beneficiary was age 45, your joint life and last survivor life expectancy would be 43.2 years (using ages 50 and 45), and the penalty-free withdrawal $2,315 ($100,000 account balance ÷ 43.2). *See Table 8-2* for a sample section of the IRS joint life and last survivor life expectancy table. The full IRS table showing joint life and last survivor life expectancy is in IRS Publication 590 and can also be obtained from your IRA trustee.

IRS Alert

IRS Allows Switch to Required Minimum Distribution Method

Because of stock market declines, taxpayers who began a series of payments under the fixed amortization or annuitization factor method may have experienced a much more rapid decrease in their account balances than anticipated when the payments began. To avoid a premature depletion of the accounts, the IRS allows a one-time irrevocable switch without penalty to the required minimum distribution method. *See* Revenue Ruling 2002-62 for further details.

2. *Fixed amortization method.* Under this method, you amortize your IRA account balance like a mortgage, using the same life expectancy as under Method 1 (your single life expectancy or the joint life and last survivor expectancy of you and your beneficiary). The interest rate used must be no more than 120% of the federal mid-term rate for either of the two months immediately preceding the month in which distributions begin. In private rulings, the IRS has approved proposed payment schedules that annually recalculate the payments to be received under the fixed amortization method.

Table 8-2 Joint Life and Last Survivor Life Expectancy
(see *"Required minimum distribution method" above*)

Ages	30	31	32	33	34	35	36	37	38	39	40	41	42	43	44	45	46	47	48	49	50	51	52	53	54	55	56	57	58	59
30	60.2	59.7	59.2	58.8	58.4	58.0	57.6	57.3	57.0	56.7	56.4	56.1	55.9	55.7	55.5	55.3	55.1	55.0	54.8	54.7	54.6	54.5	54.4	54.3	54.2	54.1	54.0	54.0	53.9	53.8
31	59.7	59.2	58.7	58.2	57.8	57.4	57.0	56.6	56.3	56.0	55.7	55.4	55.2	54.9	54.7	54.5	54.3	54.1	54.0	53.8	53.7	53.6	53.5	53.4	53.3	53.2	53.1	53.0	53.0	52.9
32	59.2	58.7	58.2	57.7	57.2	56.8	56.4	56.0	55.6	55.3	55.0	54.7	54.4	54.2	53.9	53.7	53.5	53.3	53.2	53.0	52.9	52.7	52.6	52.5	52.4	52.3	52.2	52.1	52.1	52.0
33	58.8	58.2	57.7	57.2	56.7	56.2	55.8	55.4	55.0	54.7	54.3	54.0	53.7	53.4	53.2	52.9	52.7	52.5	52.3	52.2	52.0	51.9	51.7	51.6	51.5	51.4	51.3	51.2	51.2	51.1
34	58.4	57.8	57.2	56.7	56.2	55.7	55.3	54.8	54.4	54.0	53.7	53.3	53.0	52.7	52.4	52.2	52.0	51.7	51.5	51.4	51.2	51.0	50.9	50.8	50.6	50.5	50.4	50.3	50.3	50.2
35	58.0	57.4	56.8	56.2	55.7	55.2	54.7	54.3	53.8	53.4	53.0	52.7	52.3	52.0	51.7	51.5	51.2	51.0	50.8	50.6	50.4	50.2	50.0	49.9	49.8	49.7	49.5	49.4	49.4	49.3
36	57.6	57.0	56.4	55.8	55.3	54.7	54.2	53.7	53.3	52.8	52.4	52.0	51.7	51.3	51.0	50.7	50.5	50.2	50.0	49.8	49.6	49.4	49.2	49.1	48.9	48.8	48.7	48.6	48.5	48.4
37	57.3	56.6	56.0	55.4	54.8	54.3	53.7	53.2	52.7	52.3	51.8	51.4	51.1	50.7	50.4	50.0	49.8	49.5	49.2	49.0	48.8	48.6	48.4	48.2	48.1	47.9	47.8	47.7	47.6	47.5
38	57.0	56.3	55.6	55.0	54.4	53.8	53.3	52.7	52.2	51.7	51.3	50.9	50.4	50.1	49.7	49.4	49.1	48.8	48.5	48.2	48.0	47.8	47.6	47.4	47.2	47.1	47.0	46.8	46.7	46.6
39	56.7	56.0	55.3	54.7	54.0	53.4	52.8	52.3	51.7	51.2	50.8	50.3	49.9	49.5	49.1	48.7	48.4	48.1	47.8	47.5	47.3	47.0	46.8	46.6	46.4	46.3	46.1	46.0	45.8	45.7
40	56.4	55.7	55.0	54.3	53.7	53.0	52.4	51.8	51.3	50.8	50.2	49.8	49.3	48.9	48.5	48.1	47.7	47.4	47.1	46.8	46.5	46.3	46.0	45.8	45.6	45.5	45.3	45.1	45.0	44.9
41	56.1	55.4	54.7	54.0	53.3	52.7	52.0	51.4	50.9	50.3	49.8	49.3	48.8	48.3	47.9	47.5	47.1	46.7	46.4	46.1	45.8	45.5	45.3	45.1	44.8	44.7	44.5	44.3	44.2	44.0
42	55.9	55.2	54.4	53.7	53.0	52.3	51.7	51.1	50.4	49.9	49.3	48.8	48.3	47.8	47.3	46.9	46.5	46.1	45.8	45.4	45.1	44.8	44.6	44.3	44.1	43.9	43.7	43.5	43.3	43.2
43	55.7	54.9	54.2	53.4	52.7	52.0	51.3	50.7	50.1	49.5	48.9	48.3	47.8	47.3	46.8	46.3	45.9	45.5	45.1	44.8	44.4	44.1	43.8	43.6	43.3	43.1	42.9	42.7	42.5	42.4
44	55.5	54.7	53.9	53.2	52.4	51.7	51.0	50.4	49.7	49.1	48.5	47.9	47.3	46.8	46.3	45.8	45.4	44.9	44.5	44.2	43.8	43.5	43.2	42.9	42.6	42.4	42.1	41.9	41.7	41.5
45	55.3	54.5	53.7	52.9	52.2	51.5	50.7	50.0	49.4	48.7	48.1	47.5	46.9	46.3	45.8	45.3	44.8	44.4	44.0	43.6	43.2	42.8	42.5	42.2	41.9	41.6	41.4	41.2	40.9	40.7
46	55.1	54.3	53.5	52.7	52.0	51.2	50.5	49.8	49.1	48.4	47.7	47.1	46.5	45.9	45.4	44.8	44.3	43.9	43.4	43.0	42.6	42.2	41.8	41.5	41.2	40.9	40.7	40.4	40.2	40.0
47	55.0	54.1	53.3	52.5	51.7	51.0	50.2	49.5	48.8	48.1	47.4	46.7	46.1	45.5	44.9	44.4	43.9	43.4	42.9	42.4	42.0	41.6	41.2	40.9	40.5	40.2	40.0	39.7	39.4	39.2
48	54.8	54.0	53.2	52.3	51.5	50.8	50.0	49.2	48.5	47.8	47.1	46.4	45.8	45.1	44.5	44.0	43.4	42.9	42.4	41.9	41.5	41.0	40.6	40.3	39.9	39.6	39.3	39.0	38.7	38.5
49	54.7	53.8	53.0	52.2	51.4	50.6	49.8	49.0	48.2	47.5	46.8	46.1	45.4	44.8	44.2	43.6	43.0	42.4	41.9	41.4	40.9	40.5	40.1	39.7	39.3	38.9	38.6	38.3	38.0	37.8
50	54.6	53.7	52.9	52.0	51.2	50.4	49.6	48.8	48.0	47.3	46.5	45.8	45.1	44.4	43.8	43.2	42.6	42.0	41.5	40.9	40.4	40.0	39.5	39.1	38.7	38.3	38.0	37.6	37.3	37.1
51	54.5	53.6	52.7	51.9	51.0	50.2	49.4	48.6	47.8	47.0	46.3	45.5	44.8	44.1	43.5	42.8	42.2	41.6	41.0	40.5	40.0	39.5	39.0	38.5	38.1	37.7	37.4	37.0	36.7	36.4
52	54.4	53.5	52.6	51.7	50.9	50.0	49.2	48.4	47.6	46.8	46.0	45.3	44.6	43.8	43.2	42.5	41.8	41.2	40.6	40.1	39.5	39.0	38.5	38.0	37.6	37.2	36.8	36.4	36.0	35.7
53	54.3	53.4	52.5	51.6	50.8	49.9	49.1	48.2	47.4	46.6	45.8	45.1	44.3	43.6	42.9	42.2	41.5	40.9	40.3	39.7	39.1	38.5	38.0	37.5	37.1	36.6	36.2	35.8	35.4	35.1
54	54.2	53.3	52.4	51.5	50.6	49.8	48.9	48.1	47.2	46.4	45.6	44.8	44.1	43.3	42.6	41.9	41.2	40.5	39.9	39.3	38.7	38.1	37.6	37.1	36.6	36.1	35.7	35.2	34.8	34.5
55	54.1	53.2	52.3	51.4	50.5	49.7	48.8	47.9	47.1	46.3	45.5	44.7	43.9	43.1	42.4	41.6	40.9	40.2	39.6	38.9	38.3	37.7	37.2	36.6	36.1	35.6	35.1	34.7	34.3	33.9
56	54.0	53.1	52.2	51.3	50.4	49.5	48.7	47.8	47.0	46.1	45.3	44.5	43.7	42.9	42.1	41.4	40.7	40.0	39.3	38.6	38.0	37.4	36.8	36.2	35.7	35.1	34.7	34.2	33.7	33.3
57	54.0	53.0	52.1	51.2	50.3	49.4	48.6	47.7	46.8	46.0	45.1	44.3	43.5	42.7	41.9	41.2	40.4	39.7	39.0	38.3	37.6	37.0	36.4	35.8	35.2	34.7	34.2	33.7	33.2	32.8
58	53.9	53.0	52.1	51.2	50.3	49.4	48.5	47.6	46.7	45.8	45.0	44.2	43.3	42.5	41.7	40.9	40.2	39.4	38.7	38.0	37.3	36.7	36.0	35.4	34.8	34.3	33.7	33.2	32.8	32.3
59	53.8	52.9	52.0	51.1	50.2	49.3	48.4	47.5	46.6	45.7	44.9	44.0	43.2	42.4	41.5	40.7	40.0	39.2	38.5	37.8	37.1	36.4	35.7	35.1	34.5	33.9	33.3	32.8	32.3	31.8

3. ***Fixed annuitization method.*** This method is similar to the fixed amortization method, but an annuity factor from a mortality table is used. Revenue Ruling 2002-62 provides the mortality table to be used. The maximum interest rate used cannot exceed 120% of the federal mid-term rate for either of the two months immediately preceding the month in which distributions begin. In private rulings, the IRS has approved proposed payment schedules that annually recalculate the payments to be received under the fixed annuitization method.

8.13 Mandatory Distributions From a Traditional IRA After Age 70½

The tax law requires that by April 1 of the year following the year in which you reach age 70½, you have to start receiving annual distributions from your traditional IRAs under a schedule that meets IRS tests. If you do not receive the required minimum amount, a penalty tax of 50% applies (unless the IRS waives it) to the difference between the amount that should have been received and the amount you did receive. For example, if you reach age 70½ in 2010, you must receive your first required minimum distribution (RMD) by April 1, 2011; this is your "required beginning date." Assume that, under the rules discussed below, your RMD for 2010 is $3,818, but you received only $3,000. Unless the IRS waives the penalty, you would have to pay a penalty of $409, 50% of the $818 shortfall.

If you are subject to a penalty, you should figure it on Form 5329, which must be attached to Form 1040. You can request a waiver of the penalty on Form 5329; follow the form instructions.

For 2009, RMDs were waived in response to the severe recession, but the waiver applied only to the RMD for 2009; *see* the Law Alert in this section.

The RMD rules for account owners of traditional IRAs are discussed in this section. Beneficiaries of traditional IRAs also must receive annual RMDs unless their share of the account is received by the end of the year after the year of the owner's death *(8.14)*. Roth IRA owners *(8.19)* are not subject to RMD rules, but beneficiaries of Roth IRAs are *(8.24)*.

Deadline for receiving your first required minimum distribution (RMD). If you reached age 70½ in 2009, and under the waiver law for 2009 decided not to receive your first RMD by April 1, 2010, you must take your first RMD, which will be the RMD for 2010, by December 31, 2010.

If you reach age 70½ in 2010, you can take your first RMD (the RMD for 2010) any time in 2010, or delay it until April 1, 2011, your required beginning date. Your RMD for 2011 will have to be received by December 31, 2011, so if you delay your first RMD until early 2011 (but no later than April 1), you will have to take two distributions in 2011, one by April 1 and the other by December 31. This could substantially increase your 2011 taxable income. The RMD for 2012 and later years must be received by December 31 of that year.

Law Alert

RMDs Were Waived for 2009 But Not for 2010

In response to the economic crisis, Congress passed a law waiving required minimum distributions (RMDs) for 2009. This meant that IRA owners over age 70½ could voluntarily take the RMD for 2009 but failure to take it was not subject to a penalty.

For IRA owners who were receiving RMDs before 2009, the waiver applied to the RMD that otherwise would have been required for 2009, and for those who turned age 70½ in 2009, the waiver applied to the first RMD that otherwise would have been due by their required beginning date of April 1, 2010. The waiver did *not* apply to the RMD for 2008, even for individuals who turned age 70½ and chose to take their first RMD by April 1, 2009.

The waiver applied only to RMDs for 2009. Congress did not extend the waiver law, so the RMD for 2010 (and later years) must be received by December 31, 2010, or a penalty could be imposed. If you reached age 70½ in 2009 and because of the waiver law decided not to take your first RMD by April 1, 2010, you must take your first RMD, which will be the RMD for 2010, by December 31, 2010. If you reach age 70½ in 2010, you can take your first RMD (the RMD for 2010) any time in 2010, or delay it until April 1, 2011, your required beginning date.

Figuring Your Required Minimum Distribution (RMD)

The trustee or custodian of your traditional IRA must calculate the amount of your required minimum distribution or offer to do so. If you are required to receive a required minimum distribution (RMD) for 2010, the trustee or custodian should have reported the amount to you by February 1, 2010, or offered to calculate it upon your request. The calculation is based on final IRS regulations.

If you are required to receive an RMD for 2011, the IRA trustee or custodian must tell you by January 31, 2011 what your RMD is, or offer to calculate it for you upon your request.

To calculate the RMD for yourself, you can use Steps 1–3 below, which are based on the final IRS regulations.

If the IRA trustee or custodian calculates the RMD, the calculation may be based on the Uniform Lifetime Table (*Table 8-3* below), which assumes that your beneficiary is 10 years younger than you are. However, if your sole beneficiary is your spouse who is more than 10 years younger than you, your RMD can be reduced by using the Joint Life and Last Survivor Expectancy Table (*see Table 8-4*). If this more-than-10-years-younger spousal exception applies and your IRA trustee or custodian does not use the Joint Life and Last Survivor Expectancy Table in calculating your RMD, you can do so yourself by calculating the RMD under Steps 1–3 below.

Steps for figuring your required minimum distribution (RMD). For each of your traditional IRAs, figure the required minimum distribution (RMD) you must receive using the following steps. Keep in mind that once you have separately determined the RMD for each IRA, the IRS allows you to withdraw the total RMD for the year from any of the accounts in any combination you choose.

Step 1: Find the account balance of your IRA as of the previous December 31. If you reach age 70½ during 2010, the account balance to be used for figuring your first required minimum distribution (RMD) is the account balance for December 31, 2009, even if the actual distribution for 2010 is not made until the first quarter of 2011 (January 1–April 1).

The year-end account balance must be adjusted if toward the end of the year there is an outstanding rollover. For example, if in December of 2009 you withdrew funds from your IRA and you rolled the funds back to the same IRA or a different one within 60 days but not until early in 2010, the rollover amount must be included as part of the December 31, 2009 account balance of the receiving IRA, even though it was not actually in any account on that date.

Step 2: Divide the account balance (Step 1) by the applicable life expectancy. Your life expectancy under the IRS rules is taken from the Uniform Lifetime Table unless your sole beneficiary is your spouse who is more than 10 years younger than you are. The Uniform Lifetime Table *(Table 8-3)* provides a joint life expectancy for you and a "deemed" beneficiary who is exactly 10 years younger than you are. Your beneficiary's actual age does not matter. The life expectancy period from the uniform table applies even if you have not named a beneficiary as of your required beginning date (April 1 of the year after the year you reach age 70½). Furthermore, you continue to use the Uniform Lifetime Table even if you change your beneficiary or beneficiaries after starting to receive RMDs, unless the change results in the naming of your spouse as sole beneficiary for the entire year and you qualify to use the Joint Life and Last Survivor Expectancy Table *(Table 8-4)* because your spouse is more than 10 years younger than you are.

Filing Tip

Uniform Lifetime Table

To figure your required minimum distribution (RMD) for the year you become age 70½ and later years, use the Uniform Lifetime Table unless the exception for younger spouses applies.

Your "deemed" life expectancy from the Uniform Lifetime Table is the number of years listed next to your age on your birthday in the year for which you are making the computation. For example, if you are figuring your RMD for 2010, and you are age 71 on your birthday in 2010, your life expectancy from the table, based on age 71, is 26.5 years. For 2011, your life expectancy from the table, using age 72, will be 25.6 years.

Exception for younger spouses. If the sole beneficiary of your IRA is your spouse and he or she is more than 10 years younger than you are, do not use the Uniform Lifetime Table to get your life expectancy for Step 2. Use the actual joint life expectancy of you and your spouse, which will allow you to spread out RMDs over an even longer period. *See Table 8-4*, which has a sample section of the Joint Life and Last Survivor Expectancy Table from IRS Publication 590.

This rule applies only if your spouse meets the age test and is the sole beneficiary of your entire interest in the IRA at all times during the calendar year for which the RMD is being figured. If your spouse is named beneficiary during the year or he or she is one of several beneficiaries on the account, the Uniform Lifetime Table must be used for that year. Your spouse would not meet the sole beneficiary test. However, if you are married on January 1 of a year and during the year you divorce or your spouse dies, you are considered married for the entire year and may use the spousal exception to figure that year's RMD using the joint life table.

If the exception for spousal beneficiaries applies, find your joint life expectancy from the IRS table corresponding to both of your ages on your birthdays for the year of the computation. For example, if you are age 71 on your birthday in 2010 and your spouse on his or her birthday is age 58, use a joint life expectancy of 28.6 years *(see Table 8-4)* to figure your RMD for 2010. This is longer than the 26.5-year distribution period provided by the Uniform Lifetime Table for a 71-year-old, which means that your RMD will be somewhat lower.

Step 3: If you have more than one IRA, total the required minimum distributions (RMDs) for all the accounts. After separately figuring the required minimum distribution (RMD) for each of your IRAs under Step 2, total the amounts. This is the minimum you must receive for the year; you are, of course, free to withdraw more than that. Although you must calculate the RMD separately for each account, you do not have to make withdrawals from each of them. The total RMD from all accounts may be taken from any one account, or more than one account if you prefer. For example, if you have five bank IRAs, you may take the entire RMD from the bank where you have the largest balance, or from any other combination of banks; *see* Example 3 below. The entire distribution is taxable unless part is allocable to nondeductible IRA contributions *(8.9)*.

EXAMPLES

1. Joe Blake reaches age 70½ in March 2010. A minimum distribution for 2010 must be received from his traditional IRA by April 1, 2011. As of December 31, 2009, Joe's IRA balance was $200,000. The 2009 year-end balance is used in the computation even if the distribution for 2010 is made in the first quarter of 2011 (by the April 1 deadline). Joe's beneficiary is his wife, who is age 63 on her birthday in 2010. On his birthday in September 2010, Joe is age 71. Here is how Joe figures his required minimum distribution (RMD) for 2010:

   Step 1. Account balance of $200,000 as of December 31, 2009.

   Step 2. Based on Joe's age of 71 (as of his birthday in 2010), the life expectancy from the Uniform Lifetime Table *(Table 8-3)* is 26.5 years. The table assumes that Joe has a beneficiary who is age 61 (10 years younger than he is). The fact that his wife is age 63 does not matter.

   Step 3. Divide Step 1 by Step 2.

   $200,000 ÷ 26.5 = $7,547. This is the RMD for 2010 that Joe must receive by April 1, 2011.

2. Same facts as Example 1, except that Joe's wife is age 56 on her birthday in 2010. Because Joe's wife is more than 10 years younger than Joe, he uses the joint life and last survivor expectancy table. Based on their ages of 71 and 56 (on their birthdays in 2010), the joint life expectancy from the table *(see Table 8-4)* is 30.1 years. Joe's RMD for 2010 is $6,645 ($200,000 ÷ 30.1), which he must receive by April 1, 2011.

3. Cynthia Lowell has two traditional IRAs. She reaches age 70½ on January 15, 2010, and thus must receive her first RMD by April 1, 2011. The beneficiary of IRA-1 is her brother, who is age 61 on his birthday in 2010; the account balance of IRA-1 as of December 31, 2009, is $100,000. The beneficiary of IRA-2 is her husband, who is age 74 on his birthday in 2010; the account balance of IRA-2 at the end of 2009 is $10,000.

   To figure her RMD for 2010, Cynthia uses the IRS's Uniform Lifetime Table *(Table 8-3)* shown below. The ages of her beneficiaries do not affect the computation.

   IRA-1: The RMD is $3,774. This is the account balance of $100,000 divided by 26.5, the life expectancy from the Uniform Lifetime Table for a person age 71 (Cynthia's age on her birthday in 2010).

   IRA-2: The RMD is $377, the account balance of $10,000 divided by 26.5, the life expectancy from the Uniform Lifetime Table, using age 71.

   The total RMD of $4,151 for 2010 from both IRAs must be received by April 1, 2011. Cynthia may withdraw the money from either one or both of the IRAs.

Table 8-3 Uniform Lifetime Table*

IRA Owner's Age	*Distribution Period*	*IRA Owner's Age*	*Distribution Period*	*IRA Owner's Age*	*Distribution Period*
70	27.4	85	14.8	100	6.3
71	26.5	86	14.1	101	5.9
72	25.6	87	13.4	102	5.5
73	24.7	88	12.7	103	5.2
74	23.8	89	12.0	104	4.9
75	22.9	90	11.4	105	4.5
76	22.0	91	10.8	106	4.2
77	21.2	92	10.2	107	3.9
78	20.3	93	9.6	108	3.7
79	19.5	94	9.1	109	3.4
80	18.7	95	8.6	110	3.1
81	17.9	96	8.1	111	2.9
82	17.1	97	7.6	112	2.6
83	16.3	98	7.1	113	2.4
84	15.5	99	6.7	114	2.1
				115 and over	1.9

**Use this table unless your spouse is your sole IRA beneficiary and he or she is more than 10 years younger than you are. If the spousal beneficiary exception applies, use the IRS's joint life and last survivor expectancy table with the actual ages of both spouses (see Table 8-4, which will provide a longer life expectancy distribution period than the above table provides).*

Law Alert

RMDs Were Waived for 2009 But Not for 2010

If you are a beneficiary of a deceased owner's traditional IRA, you did not have to receive a required minimum distribution (RMD) for 2009 because of the special law that waived 2009 RMDs. However, the waiver applied only for 2009. If you are required to receive an RMD for 2010 under the beneficiary rules in *8.14*, you must receive it by December 31, 2010 or a penalty could be imposed.

8.14 Inherited Traditional IRAs

Although inheritances are generally tax free *(11.4)*, distributions that you receive as a beneficiary of a traditional IRA are taxable. However, if the account owner made nondeductible contributions to the account, distributions allocable to those contributions on Form 8606 are tax free under the rules at *8.6*. Taxable distributions received as a beneficiary are not subject to the 10% penalty for distributions received before age 59½ *(8.12)*.

Surviving spouses. A surviving spouse who is the sole beneficiary of a deceased spouse's IRA may elect to treat the account as his or her own IRA or roll it over to his or her own IRA. By becoming the IRA owner, the surviving spouse determines his or her required minimum distributions (RMDs) under the regular owner rules *(8.13)*, rather than under the beneficiary rules discussed in this section.

Nonspouse beneficiaries. A nonspouse beneficiary may *not* elect to be treated as the owner or make a rollover. However, the IRS allows a nonspouse beneficiary to make a trustee-to-trustee transfer of the IRA to another financial institution as long as the IRA into which the funds are moved is set up and maintained in the name of the deceased IRA owner for the benefit of the nonspouse beneficiary. Whether or not the account is transferred, a nonspouse beneficiary must receive required minimum distributions (RMDs) under the beneficiary rules below. The financial institution holding the account will change the Social Security number on the account from the deceased owner's number to the number of the beneficiary for purposes of tracking RMDs. However, a nonspouse beneficiary must make sure that the deceased owner's name remains on the account. Putting the account in the nonspouse beneficiary's name would be treated by the IRS as a prohibited rollover, resulting in a taxable distribution, as if the beneficiary had received a total distribution of his or her share of the IRA. For example, if Jane Smith dies in November 2010 and her brother John is her IRA beneficiary, the account should indicate that the IRA is held for the benefit of (FBO) John as beneficiary, with wording such as this: "Jane Smith IRA, deceased November 16, 2010, FBO John Smith, beneficiary."

Caution

Estate as Beneficiary

If you name your estate as beneficiary of your IRA and you die before your required beginning date, the entire account must be withdrawn by the end of the fifth year following the year of your death. If you die on or after the required beginning date, the account can be distributed over the balance of your single life expectancy, determined by your age in the year of death. *See Table 8-5*, "Beneficiary's Single Life Expectancy Table."

Beneficiaries must receive required minimum distributions (RMDs). Beneficiaries of a traditional IRA must receive a required minimum distribution (RMD) from the inherited account for each year after the year of the IRA owner's death. This includes a surviving spouse who elects to receive distributions from an inherited traditional IRA as a beneficiary rather than treating the IRA as her or his own.

If you are the "designated beneficiary" as determined under the final IRS regulations discussed below, RMDs may be spread over your life expectancy (*see Table 8-5*). You must receive the first RMD by the end of the year following the year of the IRA owner's death. The RMD for each subsequent year must be received by December 31 of that year. If the RMD for a year is not received, you are subject to a penalty tax of 50% on the difference between the required minimum amount and the amount actually received. Of course, you are not limited to the RMD. You may withdraw more than the annual RMD amount or even withdraw your entire interest in the account should you want the funds. Keep in mind that whatever you receive will be taxable except to the extent that it is allocable to nondeductible contributions made by the deceased account owner.

The waiver of RMDs that applied for 2009 was for one year only. The obligation to receive RMDS begins again in 2010.

EXAMPLE—

Todd Taxpayer died in 2007 at age 73 after receiving the 2007 required minimum distribution (RMD) from his traditional IRA. Todd's IRA beneficiary was his son, Fred, who was age 47 on his birthday in 2008. Fred's life expectancy in 2008, shown in *Table 8-5*, was 37 years (for a 47-year-old). Using the rules discussed below for owner deaths after the required beginning date, Fred figured his RMD for 2008 by dividing the account balance at the end of 2007, which was $100,000, by his 37-year life expectancy, to get a required minimum distribution of $2,703.

For 2009, Fred did not have to receive an RMD because of the law that waived 2009 RMDs, and he chose not to take the RMD. Fred's next required distribution, the distribution for 2010, is figured by dividing the account balance at the end of 2009 by his remaining life expectancy. Fred must reduce the initial 37-year life expectancy by one for each year that has passed since 2008 when the life expectancy was determined. Thus, Fred will use a life expectancy of 35 years (37 – 2) to figure the required distribution for 2010. If the account balance at the end of 2009 was $105,000, Fred's required minimum distribution for 2010 is $3,000 ($105,000 ÷ 35). Fred must receive the $3,000 distribution by December 31, 2010.

Who Is the Designated Beneficiary?

The maximum life expectancy period over which required minimum distributions (RMDs) may be extended generally depends on the identity of the "designated beneficiary" as of September 30 of the year following the year of the owner's death. Any individual who is a beneficiary as of the date of the owner's death can be a "designated" beneficiary, whether he or she is selected as beneficiary by the IRA owner or is selected under the terms of the plan, but for purposes of determining the maximum period over which RMDs can be paid, there can be only one "designated beneficiary" for each inherited traditional IRA.

Table 8-4 Joint Life and Last Survivor Expectancy Table (for use by owners whose spouses are more than 10 years younger)*

Age	70	71	72	73	74	75	76	77	78	79	80	81	82	83	84	85	86	87	88	89	90
35	48.7	48.7	48.7	48.6	48.6	48.6	48.6	48.6	48.6	48.6	48.5	48.5	48.5	48.5	48.5	48.5	48.5	48.5	48.5	48.5	48.5
36	47.8	47.7	47.7	47.7	47.7	47.7	47.6	47.6	47.6	47.6	47.6	47.6	47.6	47.6	47.6	47.5	47.5	47.5	47.5	47.5	47.5
37	46.8	46.8	46.8	46.7	46.7	46.7	46.7	46.7	46.6	46.6	46.6	46.6	46.6	46.6	46.6	46.6	46.6	46.6	46.6	46.6	46.6
38	45.9	45.9	45.8	45.8	45.8	45.7	45.7	45.7	45.7	45.7	45.7	45.7	45.6	45.6	45.6	45.6	45.6	45.6	45.6	45.6	45.6
39	44.9	44.9	44.9	44.8	44.8	44.8	44.8	44.8	44.7	44.7	44.7	44.7	44.7	44.7	44.7	44.7	44.6	44.6	44.6	44.6	44.6
40	44.0	44.0	43.9	43.9	43.9	43.8	43.8	43.8	43.8	43.8	43.7	43.7	43.7	43.7	43.7	43.7	43.7	43.7	43.7	43.7	43.7
41	43.1	43.0	43.0	43.0	42.9	42.9	42.9	42.9	42.8	42.8	42.8	42.8	42.8	42.8	42.7	42.7	42.7	42.7	42.7	42.7	42.7
42	42.2	42.1	42.1	42.0	42.0	42.0	41.9	41.9	41.9	41.9	41.8	41.8	41.8	41.8	41.8	41.8	41.8	41.8	41.8	41.7	41.7
43	41.3	41.2	41.1	41.1	41.1	41.0	41.0	41.0	40.9	40.9	40.9	40.9	40.9	40.9	40.8	40.8	40.8	40.8	40.8	40.8	40.8
44	40.3	40.3	40.2	40.2	40.1	40.1	40.1	40.0	40.0	40.0	40.0	39.9	39.9	39.9	39.9	39.9	39.9	39.9	39.9	39.8	39.8
45	39.4	39.4	39.3	39.3	39.2	39.2	39.1	39.1	39.1	39.1	39.0	39.0	39.0	39.0	39.0	38.9	38.9	38.9	38.9	38.9	38.9
46	38.6	38.5	38.4	38.4	38.3	38.3	38.2	38.2	38.2	38.1	38.1	38.1	38.1	38.0	38.0	38.0	38.0	38.0	38.0	38.0	38.0
47	37.7	37.6	37.5	37.5	37.4	37.4	37.3	37.3	37.2	37.2	37.2	37.2	37.1	37.1	37.1	37.1	37.1	37.0	37.0	37.0	37.0
48	36.8	36.7	36.6	36.6	36.5	36.5	36.4	36.4	36.3	36.3	36.3	36.2	36.2	36.2	36.2	36.2	36.1	36.1	36.1	36.1	36.1
49	35.9	35.9	35.8	35.7	35.6	35.6	35.5	35.5	35.4	35.4	35.4	35.3	35.3	35.3	35.3	35.2	35.2	35.2	35.2	35.2	35.2
50	35.1	35.0	34.9	34.8	34.8	34.7	34.6	34.6	34.5	34.5	34.5	34.4	34.4	34.4	34.3	34.3	34.3	34.3	34.3	34.3	34.2
51	34.3	34.2	34.1	34.0	33.9	33.8	33.8	33.7	33.6	33.6	33.6	33.5	33.5	33.5	33.4	33.4	33.4	33.4	33.4	33.3	33.3
52	33.4	33.3	33.2	33.1	33.0	33.0	32.9	32.8	32.8	32.7	32.7	32.6	32.6	32.6	32.5	32.5	32.5	32.5	32.5	32.4	32.4
53	32.6	32.5	32.4	32.3	32.2	32.1	32.0	32.0	31.9	31.8	31.8	31.8	31.7	31.7	31.7	31.6	31.6	31.6	31.6	31.5	31.5
54	31.8	31.7	31.6	31.5	31.4	31.3	31.2	31.1	31.0	31.0	30.9	30.9	30.8	30.8	30.8	30.7	30.7	30.7	30.7	30.7	30.6
55	31.1	30.9	30.8	30.6	30.5	30.4	30.3	30.3	30.2	30.1	30.1	30.0	30.0	29.9	29.9	29.9	29.8	29.8	29.8	29.8	29.8
56	30.3	30.1	30.0	29.8	29.7	29.6	29.5	29.4	29.3	29.3	29.2	29.2	29.1	29.1	29.0	29.0	29.0	28.9	28.9	28.9	28.9
57	29.5	29.4	29.2	29.1	28.9	28.8	28.7	28.6	28.5	28.4	28.4	28.3	28.3	28.2	28.2	28.1	28.1	28.1	28.0	28.0	28.0
58	28.8	28.6	28.4	28.3	28.1	28.0	27.9	27.8	27.7	27.6	27.5	27.5	27.4	27.4	27.3	27.3	27.2	27.2	27.2	27.2	27.1
59	28.1	27.9	27.7	27.5	27.4	27.2	27.1	27.0	26.9	26.8	26.7	26.6	26.6	26.5	26.5	26.4	26.4	26.4	26.3	26.3	26.3
60		27.2	27.0	26.8	26.6	26.5	26.3	26.2	26.1	26.0	25.9	25.8	25.8	25.7	25.6	25.6	25.5	25.5	25.5	25.4	25.4
61			26.3	26.1	25.9	25.7	25.6	25.4	25.3	25.2	25.1	25.0	24.9	24.9	24.8	24.8	24.7	24.7	24.6	24.6	24.6
62				25.4	25.2	25.0	24.8	24.7	24.6	24.4	24.3	24.2	24.1	24.1	24.0	23.9	23.9	23.8	23.8	23.8	23.7
63					24.5	24.3	24.1	23.9	23.8	23.7	23.6	23.4	23.4	23.3	23.2	23.1	23.1	23.0	23.0	22.9	22.9
64						23.6	23.4	23.2	23.1	22.9	22.8	22.7	22.6	22.5	22.4	22.3	22.3	22.2	22.2	22.1	22.1
65							22.7	22.5	22.4	22.2	22.1	21.9	21.8	21.7	21.6	21.6	21.5	21.4	21.4	21.3	21.3
66								21.8	21.7	21.5	21.3	21.2	21.1	21.0	20.9	20.8	20.7	20.7	20.6	20.5	20.5
67									21.0	20.8	20.6	20.5	20.4	20.2	20.1	20.1	20.0	19.9	19.8	19.8	19.7
68										20.1	20.0	19.8	19.7	19.5	19.4	19.3	19.2	19.2	19.1	19.0	19.0
69											19.3	19.1	19.0	18.8	18.7	18.6	18.5	18.4	18.3	18.3	18.2
70												18.5	18.3	18.2	18.0	17.9	17.8	17.7	17.6	17.6	17.5
71													17.7	17.5	17.4	17.3	17.1	17.0	16.9	16.9	16.8
72														16.9	16.7	16.6	16.5	16.4	16.3	16.2	16.1
73															16.1	16.0	15.8	15.7	15.6	15.5	15.4
74																15.4	15.2	15.1	15.0	14.9	14.8
75																	14.6	14.5	14.4	14.3	14.2
76																		13.9	13.8	13.7	13.6
77																			13.2	13.1	13.0
78																				12.6	12.4
79																					11.9

** This is a sample of the Joint Life and Last Survivor Expectancy Table shown in IRS Publication 590. Use this table to figure your required minimum distribution only if your spouse is your sole beneficiary and he or she is more than 10 years younger than you are; see "Exception for younger spouses" on page 205. Find your age (as of your birthday for the year you are making the computation) on the horizontal line and your spousal beneficiary's age in the vertical column. For example, if you are age 74 and your spousal beneficiary is 63, the life expectancy factor is 24.5 years. If your age or your spouse's age is not shown here, refer to IRS Publication 590.*

Under the final IRS regulations, the determination of the designated beneficiary is not made until September 30 of the year following the year of the IRA owner's death. However, despite the September 30 rule, an exception allows multiple individual beneficiaries to separate their accounts and use their individual life expectancies to figure their RMDs, provided the separate accounts are established by December 31 of the year following the year of the owner's death; *see* the discussion of the separate account rule below.

A beneficiary named through an estate, either under the owner's will or by state law, cannot be a designated beneficiary for RMD purposes. An estate or a charity cannot be a designated beneficiary. Trust beneficiaries may qualify if certain tests are met, as discussed below.

The delay in determining the designated beneficiary does not mean that new beneficiaries can be added after the owner's death. However, after the account owner's death and prior to the September 30 determination date, a beneficiary named as of the date of death can be eliminated by means of the beneficiary's qualified disclaimer or distribution of the beneficiary's benefit. A beneficiary's interest can be cashed out by the September 30 determination date, leaving the balance to other co-beneficiaries named by the owner. For example, if a charity and an individual are named as co-beneficiaries, and the charity's interest is cashed out by the September 30 determination date, the remaining beneficiary can use his or her life expectancy to figure RMDs.

Qualified disclaimer. A qualified written disclaimer made no later than nine months after the IRA owner's death can be used by an older primary beneficiary to pass all or part of an IRA to a younger contingent beneficiary. The disclaimer, made by the September 30 determination date, leaves the younger beneficiary as the designated beneficiary, thereby allowing required minimum distributions to be spread out over his or her longer life expectancy. Of course, a younger primary beneficiary may also disclaim in favor of an older contingent beneficiary. An estate may *not* disclaim its interest in order to create a designated beneficiary.

One of the requirements for a qualified disclaimer is that the person making the disclaimer must not have accepted the property prior to the disclaimer. The IRS in Revenue Ruling 2005-36 held that this rule does not prevent a beneficiary from making a disclaimer after taking the RMD for the year of the death (where the owner dies before receiving it). The act of taking the RMD is treated as an acceptance of that portion of the property, plus the income attributable to the distribution. However, after receiving the RMD, the beneficiary may make a qualified disclaimer (by the nine-month deadline) of all or part of the balance of the account, except for the income allocable to the RMD. The disclaimed amount and the income allocable to the disclaimed amount must either be paid outright to the successor beneficiary entitled to receive it following the disclaimer or be segregated in a separate IRA for the benefit of that beneficiary. *See* Revenue Ruling 2005-36 for further details.

Multiple individual beneficiaries can split IRA into separate accounts. If a traditional IRA has several beneficiaries as of the September 30 determination date, all of whom are individuals, the general rule under the regulations is that the oldest beneficiary with the shortest life expectancy is considered to be the designated beneficiary, and that life expectancy is the period over which all the beneficiaries must receive required minimum distributions (RMDs). This result can be avoided by splitting the IRA into separate IRAs, one for each beneficiary. Each beneficiary can then spread distributions over his or her individual life expectancy.

If the IRA account owner did not split the account into separate IRAs, the regulations allow the beneficiaries to do so by December 31 of the year after the year of the owner's death. If the account is split in the year following the year of the owner's death by the December 31 date, each beneficiary may compute the RMD for that year using his or her own life expectancy as determined by their ages in that year. That life expectancy is reduced by one year for each subsequent-year RMD.

Individual and non-individual beneficiary for same account. If as of the September 30 determination date there is a *non-individual* beneficiary other than a qualifying trust, as well as one or more individual beneficiaries, the owner is treated as *not* having a designated beneficiary. If the owner's death was on or after his or her required beginning date (April 1 of the year after the year age 70½ is reached), the regulations require RMDs to be made over the owner's remaining life expectancy. Use the owner's life expectancy as of his or her birthday in the year of death and reduce it by one year for each subsequent year.

If the owner died before the required beginning date without a designated beneficiary, the entire account must be distributed by the end of the fifth year following the year of death. No distribution has to be received before that fifth year. If the interest of the non-individual beneficiary is distributed from the plan and separate accounts are established for the individual beneficiaries by the September 30 deadline, the individual beneficiaries can base required minimum distributions on their own life expectancies.

If the IRA owner died before 2009 and the five-year rule applies, the distribution period is extended to six years if no RMD was taken for 2009 under the law waiving 2009 RMDs. For example, the five-year rule applies if an IRA owner died in 2007 at age 68 (before his required beginning date), having named a charity and a nephew as his IRA beneficiaries. If the RMD for 2009 was waived, the IRA must be completely distributed by the end of 2013 (the sixth year following the year of death) rather than by the end of 2012.

Trust as beneficiary. If a trust is named the beneficiary of the account, the trust beneficiaries may be treated as designated beneficiaries if certain tests are met. The trust must be irrevocable or become irrevocable upon the account owner's death. Documentation of the trust beneficiaries must be provided to the IRA trustee or plan administrator. The deadline under the regulations for providing the documentation is October 31 of the year following the year of the owner's death. However, the regulations do not allow separate accounts to be created for the trust beneficiaries. All of the trust beneficiaries must receive RMDs over the life expectancy of the oldest beneficiary.

Beneficiary's death before September 30 determination date. If an individual named as a beneficiary by the account owner dies after the owner but before the September 30 date for determining the designated beneficiary, that individual continues to be treated as a designated beneficiary under the final regulations. This rule allows his or her life expectancy to be used by a successor beneficiary named by the original beneficiary or who inherits the account through the estate of the original beneficiary.

Did IRA Owner Die On or After His/Her Required Beginning Date?

The distribution period for beneficiaries may depend on whether the IRA owner died before his or her required beginning date, or on or after the required beginning date, which is April 1 of the year that the owner reached or would have reached age 70½ *(8.13)*.

Owner's death on or after required beginning date. If an owner dies on or after the required beginning date (April 1 of the year after the year the owner reaches age 70½), and there is a designated beneficiary, required minimum distributions (RMDs) are generally payable over the beneficiary's life expectancy. However, if on the date of the owner's death the designated beneficiary is older than the owner, the final regulations allow the beneficiary to receive RMDs over the owner's remaining life expectancy rather than over the beneficiary's shorter life expectancy. If there is no "designated" beneficiary, as when the owner's estate is named as the beneficiary, RMDs are based upon the deceased owner's remaining life expectancy.

If the owner did not receive his or her RMD for the year of death, the beneficiary must receive that amount in the year of death or as soon as possible in the next year.

The first RMD to a designated beneficiary must be received in the year following the year of the owner's death. The RMD is figured by dividing the year-end account balance for the year of death by the designated beneficiary's life expectancy in the year following the year of death, taken from the Beneficiary's Single Life Expectancy Table *(Table 8-5)*.

To figure the RMDs for later years, the designated beneficiary reduces the initial life expectancy by one for each succeeding year. The Example at the beginning of *8.14* (Todd and Fred Taxpayer) illustrates how the computation is made.

If the designated beneficiary dies before receiving the balance of the IRA, his or her successor beneficiary must continue to use the remaining life expectancy of the designated beneficiary, reducing the initial life expectancy by one each year until the IRA is completely distributed or the declining life expectancy is used up.

Owner's death before required beginning date. If an owner dies before the required beginning date and there is an individual designated beneficiary, the period for receiving required minimum distributions (RMDs) is generally the life expectancy of the designated beneficiary. The computation of required minimum distributions under the life expectancy method is explained above under "Owner's death on or after required beginning date." The life expectancy method is the "default" rule under the final regulations, but the plan may require application of the five-year rule, although this is unlikely, or the plan may allow the account owner or beneficiary to elect the five-year rule.

Under the five-year rule, the entire account must be distributed by the end of the fifth year after the year of the owner's death; no distribution is required for any year prior to that fifth year. The five-year rule always applies if the owner dies before the required beginning date and there is no designated beneficiary.

The RMD for 2009 could be waived and, if it was, the distribution period under the five-year rule for an IRA of an owner who died before 2009 is effectively increased to six years. For example, if an IRA owner died before his required beginning date in 2007 and named his estate as the IRA beneficiary, the five-year rule applies and the entire account would ordinarily have to be distributed by the end of 2012. However, if the RMD for 2009 was waived, the entire account does not have to be distributed until the end of 2013.

Table 8-5 Beneficiary's Single Life Expectancy Table

Age	Life expectancy	Age	Life expectancy
0	82.4	56	28.7
1	81.6	57	27.9
2	80.6	58	27.0
3	79.7	59	26.1
4	78.7	60	25.2
5	77.7	61	24.4
6	76.7	62	23.5
7	75.8	63	22.7
8	74.8	64	21.8
9	73.8	65	21.0
10	72.8	66	20.2
11	71.8	67	19.4
12	70.8	68	18.6
13	69.9	69	17.8
14	68.9	70	17.0
15	67.9	71	16.3
16	66.9	72	15.5
17	66.0	73	14.8
18	65.0	74	14.1
19	64.0	75	13.4
20	63.0	76	12.7
21	62.1	77	12.1
22	61.1	78	11.4
23	60.1	79	10.8
24	59.1	80	10.2
25	58.2	81	9.7
26	57.2	82	9.1
27	56.2	83	8.6
28	55.3	84	8.1
29	54.3	85	7.6
30	53.3	86	7.1
31	52.4	87	6.7
32	51.4	88	6.3
33	50.4	89	5.9
34	49.4	90	5.5
35	48.5	91	5.2
36	47.5	92	4.9
37	46.5	93	4.6
38	45.6	94	4.3
39	44.6	95	4.1
40	43.6	96	3.8
41	42.7	97	3.6
42	41.7	98	3.4
43	40.7	99	3.1
44	39.8	100	2.9
45	38.8	101	2.7
46	37.9	102	2.5
47	37.0	103	2.3
48	36.0	104	2.1
49	35.1	105	1.9
50	34.2	106	1.7
51	33.3	107	1.5
52	32.3	108	1.4
53	31.4	109	1.2
54	30.5	110	1.1
55	29.6	111+	1.0

Special Rules for Surviving Spouses

A surviving spouse may take advantage of rules not available to nonspouse beneficiaries.

Surviving spouse's rollover or election to treat IRA as his or her own. A surviving spouse who is the sole beneficiary of an IRA with unlimited withdrawal rights may elect to treat the IRA as his or her own by retitling the IRA in his or her name. If the surviving spouse contributes to the IRA or does not receive a timely RMD under the beneficiary rules, the surviving spouse is deemed to have made the election. The final regulations confirm that to make the election, the surviving spouse must take the RMD for the year of the owner's death (if any) to the extent that it was not received by the owner.

A surviving-spouse beneficiary may also make a spousal rollover by authorizing a direct transfer (trustee-to-trustee) of the IRA, or rolling over a distribution within 60 days of receiving it, to his or her own IRA. However, if the deceased IRA owner did not receive the RMD for the year of death, the surviving spouse must receive and pay tax on that RMD; that amount cannot be rolled over (or directly transferred).

If the surviving spouse elects to treat the inherited IRA as his or her own or makes a spousal rollover, the surviving spouse is then subject to the same rules as any IRA owner. The surviving spouse should immediately name a new beneficiary for the IRA. The regular distribution rules apply, including the 10% penalty for taxable distributions received before age 59½ *(8.8)*. If the surviving spouse is under age 70½, RMDs may be delayed until April 1 of the year following the year in which he or she reaches age 70½, at which time distributions will be based on the Uniform Lifetime Table for owners *(8.13)*.

Planning Reminder

Surviving Spouse Under Age 70½

If you inherit your spouse's traditional IRA and you are under age 70½, you may delay the start of required minimum distributions by treating the IRA as your own.

Surviving spouse as sole beneficiary. If the surviving spouse does not elect to treat an inherited IRA as his or her own, and does not make a spousal rollover, the surviving spouse must receive required minimum distributions (RMDs) as a beneficiary. A surviving spouse who is under age 59½ and needs the funds from the IRA may prefer this option because withdrawals, although taxable (unless allocable to nondeductible contributions made by the deceased spouse), are not subject to the 10% penalty for pre-59½ distributions *(8.12)*.

If the surviving spouse is the sole designated beneficiary, RMDs are based on his or her life expectancy from the Beneficiary's Single Life Expectancy Table *(Table 8-5)*. Each year, life expectancy is recalculated using the spouse's attained age during the year. A spousal beneficiary is the only beneficiary who may recalculate life expectancy. Others must reduce their life expectancy from *Table 8-5* for the year after the year of the owner's death by one year in each succeeding year.

If a surviving spouse is the sole designated beneficiary and the deceased spouse died before the year in which he or she would have reached age 70½, the surviving spouse does not have to begin receiving RMDs until the year that the deceased spouse would have reached age 70½.

Even if a surviving spouse begins receiving RMDs under the beneficiary rules, the surviving spouse may at any time make a spousal rollover to his or her own IRA, excluding the RMD for the year, which must be received and reported as income as it is not eligible for rollover.

8.15 SEP Basics

A simplified employee pension plan (SEP) set up by an employer allows the employer to contribute to an employee's IRA account more money than is allowed under regular IRA rules. For 2010, your employer generally could contribute and deduct up to 25% of your compensation or $49,000, whichever is less. Your employer's SEP contributions are excluded from your pay and are not included on Form W-2 unless they exceed the limit. If contributions exceed the limit, the excess is included in your gross income and a 6% penalty tax may be imposed unless the excess (plus allocable income) is withdrawn by the due date of the return, plus extensions *(8.7)*. If you are under age 59½, the 10% early distribution penalty may apply to the withdrawal of income earned on the excess contributions *(8.12)*.

Caution

Employees over Age 70½

An employee over age 70½ may still participate in an employer SEP plan. Minimum distributions from the plan must begin as discussed in *7.13*.

Self-employed plans. Self-employed individuals may set up a SEP as an alternative to a Keogh plan; *see Chapter 41*.

Eligibility. A SEP must cover all employees who are at least age 21, earn over $550 (this amount may be adjusted for years after 2010 for inflation), and who have worked for the employer at any time during at least three of the past five years. Union employees covered by union agreements may generally be excluded.

SEP salary-reduction arrangements. If a qualifying small employer set up a salary-reduction SEP before 1997, employees may contribute a portion of their pay to the plan instead of receiving it in cash *(8.16)*.

SEP distributions. Distributions from a SEP, including salary-reduction SEPs established before 1997, are subject to the regular distribution rules for traditional IRAs *(8.8)*.

8.16 Salary-Reduction SEP Set Up Before 1997

Qualifying small employers may offer employees the option of deferring a portion of their salary to an IRA. There are two types of salary-reduction IRAs, with different eligibility and contribution rules: (1) salary-reduction SEPs established before 1997 and (2) "SIMPLE" IRA accounts established after 1996.

After 1996, an employer may establish a SIMPLE plan but not a salary-reduction SEP. Rules for SIMPLE IRAs established after 1996 are at *8.17–8.18*. A salary-reduction SEP that was established before 1997 may continue to receive contributions under the prior law rules discussed below, and employees hired after 1996 may participate in the plan, subject to those rules.

Salary-reduction SEPs established before 1997. Salary reductions are allowed for a year only if the employer had no more than 25 employees eligible to participate in the SEP at any time during the prior taxable year. Furthermore, at least 50% of the eligible employees must elect the salary-reduction option, and the deferral percentage for highly compensated employees may not exceed 125% of the average contribution of regular employees.

If salary reductions are allowed, the maximum salary-reduction contribution under the law for 2010 was $16,500 ($22,000 for participants age 50 or older if the plan permitted the extra deferral), although a lower limit may be imposed by the plan terms. These are the same limits as for 401(k) plans *(7.18)*. Deferrals over $16,500 ($22,000 if extra deferral for participants age 50 or older was allowed) are taxable, and if not timely distributed to the employee, can be taxed again when distributed from the plan. The deferral limits for 2011 will be in the *e-Supplement* at *jklasser.com*.

If an employee contributes to both a SEP and a 401(k) plan, the annual limit applies to the total salary reductions from both plans. If an employee makes salary-reduction contributions to a SEP and also to a tax-sheltered annuity plan *(7.21)*, the annual limit generally applies to the total salary reductions to both plans. In some cases, employees with at least 15 years of service may be able to defer an additional $3,000 to the tax-sheltered annuity plan *(7.21)*.

8.17 Who Is Eligible for a SIMPLE IRA?

A SIMPLE IRA is a salary-reduction retirement plan that qualifying small employers may offer their employees. For 2010, the maximum salary-reduction contribution was $11,500, or $14,000 for participants age 50 or older (by the end of 2010) if the plan allowed the additional contributions. *See* the *e-Supplement* at *jklasser.com* for the 2011 limits. Employers are required to make matching contributions or a flat contribution *(8.18)*.

Qualifying employers. A SIMPLE IRA may be maintained only by an employer that (1) in the previous calendar year had no more than 100 employees who earned compensation of $5,000 or more and (2) does not maintain any other retirement plan (unless the other plan is for collective bargaining employees). A self-employed individual who meets these tests may set up a SIMPLE IRA, as discussed in *Chapter 41*. A simple IRA must be maintained on a calendar-year basis.

In determining whether the 100-employee test is met for the prior year, all employees under the common control of the employer must be counted. For example, Joe Smith owned two businesses in 2010—a computer rental company with 80 employees and a computer repair company with 60 employees. If they all earned at least $5,000, they all count towards the 100 limit, so if Joe decides in 2011 to set up a retirement plan for his businesses, a different type of plan must be used. He may not establish a SIMPLE IRA for either business under the 100-employee limit.

If a SIMPLE IRA is established but the employer in a later year grows beyond the 100-employee limit, the employer generally has a two-year "grace period" during which contributions may continue to be made.

Planning Reminder

401(k) SIMPLE Plans

An employer with a 401(k) plan that reports on the calendar year may avoid the regular 401(k) nondiscrimination tests by following the contribution rules for SIMPLE IRAs *(7.17)*.

Eligible employees. In general, an employee must be allowed to contribute to a SIMPLE IRA for a year in which he or she is reasonably expected to earn $5,000 or more, provided at least $5,000 of compensation was received in any two prior years, whether or not consecutive. If the employer owns more than one business (under common control rules) and sets up a SIMPLE IRA for one of them, employees of the other business must also be allowed to participate if they meet the $5,000 compensation tests. Employees who are covered by a collective bargaining agreement may be excluded if retirement benefits were the subject of good-faith negotiations.

The employer may lower or eliminate the $5,000 compensation requirement in order to broaden participation in the plan. No other conditions on eligibility, such as age or hours of work, are permitted.

Deadline for setting up a SIMPLE IRA. An employer generally may establish a SIMPLE IRA effective on any date between January 1 and October 1 of a year. If the employer (or a predecessor employer) previously maintained a SIMPLE IRA, a new SIMPLE IRA may be effective only on January 1 of a year. A new employer that comes into existence after October 1 of a year may establish a SIMPLE IRA for that year if the plan is established as soon as administratively feasible after the start of the business.

The employer may use a model SIMPLE IRA approved by the IRS to set up a SIMPLE IRA. Form 5304-SIMPLE allows employees to select a financial institution to which the contributions will be made. With Form 5305-SIMPLE, the employer selects the financial institution to which contributions are initially deposited, but employees have the right to subsequently transfer their account balances without cost or penalty to another SIMPLE-IRA at a financial institution of their own choosing. Use of the IRS model forms is optional; other documents satisfying the statutory requirements for a SIMPLE IRA may be used.

SIMPLE IRA contributions and distributions. Contributions and distributions to SIMPLE IRAs are subject to limitations *(8.18)*.

8.18 SIMPLE IRA Contributions and Distributions

The only contributions that may be made to a SIMPLE IRA are elective salary-reduction contributions by employees and matching or non-elective contributions by employers. All contributions are fully vested and nonforfeitable when made.

Regardless of compensation, eligible employees *(8.17)* may elect each year to make salary-reduction contributions to the plan up to the annual SIMPLE IRA limit *(8.17)*. Salary-reduction contributions are excluded from the employee's taxable pay on Form W-2 and not subject to federal tax withholding. They are subject to FICA withholding for Social Security and Medicare tax.

Eligible employees must be given notice by the employer of their right to elect salary-reduction contributions and at least 60 days to make the election. After the first year of eligibility, the election to defer for the upcoming year is made during the last 60 days (at minimum) of the prior calendar year. If the employer uses model IRS Form 5304-SIMPLE or 5305-SIMPLE, a notification document is included.

Planning Reminder

Employer's Intended Contributions

The IRS model notification included with Form 5304-SIMPLE or 5305-SIMPLE requires the employer to tell employees how much the employer will be contributing for the upcoming year.

If an employee contributes to a SIMPLE IRA and also to a 401(k) plan, 403(b) or salary-reduction SEP of another employer for the same year, the salary-reduction contributions to the SIMPLE IRA count toward the overall annual limit on tax-free salary-reduction deferrals *(7.17)*. Deferrals over the annual limit are taxable and must be removed to avoid being taxed again when distributed from the plan *(7.18)*.

Employer contributions. Each year, the employer must make either a matching contribution or a fixed "non-elective" contribution. If the employer chooses matching contributions, the employee's elective salary-reduction contribution generally must be matched, up to a limit of 3% of the employee's compensation. For up to two years in any five-year period, the 3% matching limit may be reduced to as low as 1% for each eligible employee.

Instead of making either the 3% or reduced (between 1% and 3%) limit matching contribution, the employer may make a "non-elective" contribution equal to 2% of each eligible employee's compensation. If this option is chosen, the 2% contribution must be made for eligible employees whether or not they elect to make salary-reduction contributions for the year. The 2% contribution is subject to an annual compensation limit, which for 2010 was $245,000. Thus, for 2010, the maximum 2% non-elective contribution was $4,900 (2% of $245,000) even if an employee earned more than $245,000. The 3% matching contribution is not subject to the annual compensation limit, but only to the annual salary-reduction limit *(8.17)*. The employer must notify eligible employees of the type of contribution it will be making for the upcoming year prior to the employees' 60-day election period for making elective salary-reduction contributions. The employer must make the matching or non-elective contributions by the due date for filing the employer's tax return (plus extensions) for the year.

Caution

Increased Pre–Age 59½ Penalty

In the first two years of SIMPLE IRA participation, the penalty for distributions before age 59½ is increased from 10% to 25%. Proposals to eliminate the higher 25% penalty have not been approved by Congress.

Distributions from a SIMPLE IRA. A distribution from a SIMPLE IRA is fully taxable unless a tax-free rollover or trustee-to-trustee transfer is made. The penalty for distributions before age 59½ *(8.12)* is increased to 25% from 10%, assuming no penalty exception applies, if the distribution is received during the two-year period starting with the employee's initial participation in the plan. After the first two years, the regular 10% penalty applies.

In the initial two-year period, a tax-free rollover or direct trustee-to-trustee transfer *(8.10)* of a SIMPLE IRA may be made to another SIMPLE IRA. After two years of participation, a tax-free rollover or direct transfer may be made to a traditional IRA, qualified plan, 403(b) plan, or state or local government 457 plan, as well as to a SIMPLE IRA. The mandatory distribution rules that apply to regular IRAs after age 70½ also apply to SIMPLE IRAs *(8.13)*.

8.19 Roth IRA Advantages

As with traditional IRAs, earnings accumulate within a Roth IRA tax free until distributions are made. The key benefit of the Roth IRA is that tax-free withdrawals of contributions may be made at any time and earnings may be withdrawn tax free after a five-year holding period by an individual who is age 59½ or older, is disabled, or who pays qualifying first-time home-buyer expenses.

A Roth IRA can provide attractive retirement planning and estate planning opportunities. Although annual contributions to a traditional IRA are barred once you reach age 70½ *(8.2)*, contributions to a Roth IRA are allowed after age 70½, provided you have taxable compensation for the year and your modified adjusted gross income does not exceed the annual limitation *(8.20)*. Also, the minimum required distribution rules that apply to traditional IRAs after age 70½ *(8.13)* do not apply to Roth IRAs. Thus, a Roth IRA can remain intact after age 70½ and continue to grow tax free. The balance of the account not withdrawn during the owner's lifetime generally may be paid out to the beneficiaries tax free over their life expectancies, thereby providing a substantial tax-deferred buildup within the plan over an extended period *(8.24)*.

Caution

Roth IRA Contribution Deadline

The deadline for making Roth IRA contributions for 2010 is April 15, 2011, the regular due date for your 2010 return. This is the contribution deadline even if you obtain a filing extension for your 2010 return.

In addition to making annual nondeductible contributions (subject to the income phaseout rule at *8.20*), a Roth IRA can be funded by converting a traditional IRA, SEP or SIMPLE IRA, or rolling over a distribution from an employer plan, but the conversion or rollover to the Roth IRA is treated as a taxable transfer, as discussed at *8.21*.

Your employer can set up a "deemed Roth IRA" as a separate account under a qualified retirement plan. As long as the separate account otherwise meets the Roth IRA rules, you can make voluntary employee contributions that will be subject only to the Roth IRA rules. A deemed IRA can also be set up as a traditional IRA *(8.1)*.

8.20 Annual Contributions to a Roth IRA

You may make a nondeductible Roth IRA contribution for 2010 if you have taxable compensation for personal services and your modified adjusted gross income (MAGI) does not exceed the upper end of the phaseout range. For 2010, the phaseout range does not begin until MAGI reaches $105,000 if you are unmarried (single or head of household), or $167,000 if you are married filing jointly or a qualifying widow(er). If your 2010 MAGI is under that phaseout threshold, you may contribute up to the 2010 contribution ceiling, which is $5,000 if you are under age 50 or $6,000 if you are age 50 or older by the end of the year, assuming you have taxable compensation of at least that much (the contribution cannot exceed the compensation).

If your 2010 MAGI exceeds the applicable $105,000/$167,000 phaseout threshold, the phaseout rule applies and your contribution limit is either partially or fully phased out. The $5,000/$6,000 contribution limit is phased out for unmarried taxpayers with MAGI of over $105,000 and under $120,000 and for married joint filers with MAGI of over $167,000 and under $177,000. If MAGI equals or exceeds the $120,000 or $177,000 limit, you cannot contribute to a Roth IRA for 2010; the contribution limit is completely phased out.

A stricter phaseout rule applies to a married person filing separately who lives with his or her spouse at any time during the year. In that case, the contribution limit is phased out over the first $10,000 of MAGI. No contribution is allowed if MAGI is $10,000 or more. However, a married person who lives apart from his or her spouse for the entire year is treated as unmarried, subject to the same phaseout range as single persons and heads of household.

Individuals who qualify for deductible IRA contributions *(8.4)* as well as the Roth IRA should consider whether the tax value of deductible contributions outweighs the advantage of future tax-free distributions from the Roth IRA; distributions from traditional deductible IRAs are taxable. *See* the discussion of Roth IRA distribution rules *(8.23)*.

The Roth IRA rules do not replace the traditional IRA nondeductible contribution rules *(8.6)*. For an individual who is unable to contribute to a Roth IRA because the contribution limit is phased out, and is unable to make deductible IRA contributions because of the phaseout rules for active plan participants *(8.4)*, nondeductible contributions may still be made to a traditional IRA *(8.6)*.

Spousal contribution on joint return for nonworking or low-earning spouse. If you are married filing jointly, you generally may contribute up to the annual limit (*see* above) for each spouse to a Roth IRA so long as the total compensation of both spouses is at least double the limit. This is the same spousal contribution rule as for traditional IRAs *(8.3)*; the lower-earning spouse is allowed to "borrow" compensation of the higher-earning spouse for contribution purposes. However, the Roth IRA contribution limit may be reduced because of the MAGI phaseout rules, discussed below.

MAGI phaseout of 2010 Roth IRA contribution limit. The $5,000 or $6,000 Roth IRA contribution limit for 2010 (*see* above) is phased out if your 2010 modified adjusted gross income (MAGI) is between:

- $167,000 and $177,000, if you are married filing jointly, or a qualifying widow(er);
- $105,000 and $120,000, if you are single, head of household, or married filing separately and you lived apart for the entire year;
- $0 and $10,000, if you are married filing separately and you lived with your spouse at any time during the year.

If MAGI equals or exceeds the applicable $177,000, $120,000, or $10,000 limit, no contribution for 2010 is allowed.

For 2011, the $105,000 and $167,000 phaseout thresholds may be subject to inflation indexing.

For purposes of the phaseout rule, MAGI is figured in the same way as under the traditional IRA deduction phaseout rules *(8.4)*, except that a taxable conversion *(8.21)* from a traditional IRA to a Roth IRA is disregarded. The MAGI phaseout rule applies to Roth IRA contributions regardless of whether you are covered by an employer retirement plan, unlike the deductible traditional IRA phaseout rules *(8.4)*, which apply only to active plan participants.

The MAGI formula reduces the contribution limit by an amount that bears the same ratio to the limit as your "excess MAGI" (MAGI over phaseout threshold) bears to the phaseout range (which is either $10,000 or $15,000, depending on your filing status as shown above). *See* the Example below for the way the phaseout limit is computed. If the phaseout formula results in a reduced contribution limit that is not a multiple of $10, round it up to the next highest $10. If the reduced limit is between $0 and $200, you are allowed a $200 contribution limit.

Law Alert

Roth IRA Contribution Based on Tax-Free Combat Pay

Members of the armed services serving in a combat zone *(35.4)* can contribute to either a Roth IRA or a traditional IRA *(8.2)* based on their tax-free combat pay. Without this law, members of the military who did not have any earnings apart from the combat zone pay could not make IRA contributions, which must be based on taxable compensation.

EXAMPLE

In 2010, Mark is under age 50 and single. His 2010 salary is $90,000 and modified adjusted gross income (MAGI) is $108,000, $3,000 more than the $105,000 phaseout threshold for a single person's Roth IRA contributions. Under the MAGI phaseout rule, Mark's Roth IRA contribution limit for 2010 is reduced by $1,000, from $5,000 to $4,000. The $1,000 reduction equals the $5,000 limit multiplied by the phaseout percentage of 20% ($3,000 MAGI over the phaseout threshold ($108,000 – $105,000) ÷ $15,000 phaseout range for single persons).

If Mark was age 50 or over in 2010, the $6,000 contribution limit would be reduced by $1,200 to $4,800 (20% phaseout percentage × $6,000 limit = $1,200 reduction).

Contributing to Roth IRA and traditional IRA for the same year. If you contribute to both a traditional IRA and Roth IRA for the same year, total contributions for the year to all the accounts are limited to the annual limit, or your compensation if that is less. The annual limit is applied first to the traditional IRA contributions and then to the Roth IRA contributions. Thus, the maximum contribution limit for 2010 to a Roth IRA is the lesser of (1) $5,000, or $6,000 if age 50 or older, or (2) taxable compensation, minus deductible *(8.4)* or nondeductible *(8.6)* contributions to traditional IRAs.

However, if you are subject to the MAGI phaseout for Roth IRA contributions, as discussed above, the maximum Roth IRA contribution limit is the lesser of these two amounts: (1) the annual contribution limit (*see* above) or, if less, compensation, minus contributions for the year to traditional IRAs, or (2) the contribution limit figured under the MAGI phaseout rule.

Excess contributions. If Roth IRA contributions exceed the allowable limit, the excess contribution is subject to a 6% penalty tax unless you withdraw the excess, plus any earnings on the excess contribution, by the filing due date including extensions. The earnings must be reported as income for the year the contribution was made. If you timely file your 2010 return without withdrawing an excess contribution made in 2010, the IRS will give you until six months from the orginal due date (April 15 with no extensions) to make the withdrawal, or until October 17, 2011, and an amended return must be filed for 2010 to report the earnings on the withdrawn contributions; *see* the instructions to Form 5329.

Contribution deadline. Contributions to a Roth IRA for a year may be made by the filing due date, without extensions. For 2010 contributions, the deadline is April 15, 2011.

8.21 Converting a Traditional IRA to a Roth IRA

There is no longer an income limitation for converting a traditional IRA to a Roth IRA. Before 2010, a taxpayer could not make a conversion if his or her modified adjusted gross income (MAGI) for the year of the transfer exceeded $100,000, but the income limit has been eliminated for conversions made in 2010 and later years. In addition, married persons filing separately were ineligible for a conversion but this restriction also has been lifted starting in 2010.

A conversion is a taxable transfer. Unless after-tax contributions were made to the traditional IRA being converted, the entire transfer must be reported as taxable income (*see* "How to report a conversion," below). In all years other than 2010, the income from a conversion must be reported on the tax return for the year of the conversion.

A special deferral rule applies to a 2010 conversion of a traditional IRA to a Roth IRA. None of the income from a 2010 conversion has to be reported as 2010 income. Half of the income can be reported on your 2011 return and the other half on your 2012 return. If you do not want the deferral rule to apply, you can make an election on Form 8606 to report the entire taxable amount on your 2010 return.

A conversion may be made by directing the trustee of your traditional IRA to make a trustee-to-trustee transfer of your IRA to a new Roth IRA trustee, or by keeping the account with the same trustee but instructing the trustee to change the registration of the account from a traditional IRA to a Roth IRA. You may also make a conversion by receiving a distribution from your traditional IRA and rolling it over to a Roth IRA; the rollover must be completed within 60 days from the time you receive the distribution.

Conversion from SEP or SIMPLE IRA. You may also convert a SEP *(8.15)* to a Roth IRA. A SIMPLE IRA *(8.18)* may be converted to a Roth IRA if more than two years have passed since you began participation in the SIMPLE IRA.

Required minimum distributions (RMDs) may not be converted to a Roth IRA. If you are age 70½ or older, you may not convert to a Roth IRA amounts that represent the required minimum distribution (RMD) from a traditional IRA *(8.13)*. Similarly, the RMD from an employer plan *(7.13)* may not be rolled over to a Roth IRA. Only the amount exceeding the RMD is eligible for conversion or rollover.

How to report a conversion. A conversion of a traditional IRA to a Roth IRA is a taxable distribution, except to the extent that it is allocable to after-tax contributions in *all* of your traditional IRAs. If you made any after-tax contributions and you are converting only part of your traditional IRAs, a *pro-rata* calculation based on the year-end value of all the IRAs must be made on Part 1 of Form 8606 to determine the nontaxable portion of the transfer that is allocable to the after-tax contributions. The 10% penalty for pre-age-59½ distributions *(8.12)* does not apply to the taxable part of the conversion.

Planning Reminder

Contributions After Age 70½

That you are over 70½ years of age is no bar to setting up and contributing to a Roth IRA. For an annual contribution, you must have taxable compensation and not be subject to the MAGI phaseout.

Law Alert

Income From 2010 Conversion Deferrable to 2011 and 2012

The taxable income from a conversion made in 2010 may be deferred to 2011 and 2012. You can report half of the conversion income on your 2011 return and half on your 2012 return. If you do not want to defer the income, you can check a box on Form 8606 and elect to report the entire taxable amount on your 2010 return.

For high tax bracket taxpayers, it is possible that the tax advantage of deferring the income from a 2010 conversion to 2011 and 2012 might be offset by an increase in the top rates. When this book went to press, Congress had not yet decided on whether to raise the top two rates of 33% and 35% to 36% and 39.6% starting in 2011, as favored by the Administration; *see* the *e-Supplement at jklasser.com*.

Law Alert

Conversions Allowed Regardless of Income and Marital Filing Status

Before 2010, taxpayers with modified adjusted gross income over $100,000 could not convert a traditional IRA to a Roth IRA. Married persons filing separately also were ineligible for a conversion. Starting in 2010 these restrictions no longer apply.

A one-time only deferral opportunity applies to conversions made in 2010. On Part II of Form 8606, you can elect to report half of the taxable income from the conversion on your 2011 return and half on your 2012 return, or you can elect to report all of the income on your 2010 return. If you made more than one conversion in 2010, you must report them all the same way; they are aggregated on Form 8606. For example, if in 2010 you made conversions from two traditional IRAs, you cannot choose to report the income from one of the conversions on your 2010 return and defer the income from the other to 2011 and 2012.

If you withdrew funds from a traditional IRA towards the end of 2010 and complete a rollover to a traditional Roth IRA in early 2011 within 60 days of the withdrawal, this is treated as a 2010 conversion, subject to the 2010 deferral option.

Keep in mind that if you made a conversion in 2010 and timely file your 2010 return, you have until October 17, 2011, to "undo" the conversion by recharacterizing the conversion back to a traditional IRA *(8.22)*.

A conversion made in 2011 or later, like a conversion before 2010, will not qualify for the deferral break. The conversion income will be taxable for the year of the conversion.

Law Alert

Rollover From Employer Plan

A distribution from a qualified employer plan, a 403(b) plan, or a governmental 457 plan may be rolled over to a Roth IRA under the same rules as for converting a traditional IRA to a Roth IRA *(8.21)*. This means that a rollover is treated as a taxable distribution except to the extent it is allocable to after-tax contributions.

Rollover from employer plan to Roth IRA. The tax treatment of a rollover to a Roth IRA from a 401(k) plan or other qualified employer plan, 403(b) plan, or governmental 457 plan is similar to that of a conversion from a traditional IRA. That is, the rollover is a taxable distribution except to the extent that it is a return of your after-tax contributions, if any.

The income from a 2010 rollover to a Roth IRA qualifies for the two-year deferral rule. The rollover is reported on Part III of Form 8606, where you elect either to report the entire taxable income on your 2010 return or to defer half of the income to 2011 and the other half to 2012.

8.22 Recharacterizations and Reconversions

When you convert a traditional IRA to a Roth IRA *(8.21)*, you have an opportunity to reconsider the move. You can in effect "undo" the conversion by recharacterizing all or part of it. If you timely file your return for the year of the conversion, you have until October 15 of the following year to complete a recharacterization; *see* below for deadline details.

You may want to recharacterize because the value of the Roth IRA has dropped substantially since the conversion, and you do not want to pay the tax that would be due on the higher value at conversion, or you may simply be unable to pay the tax due on the conversion *(8.21)*. In a declining stock market, a recharacterization may be the first step in a plan to reconvert back to a Roth IRA when the taxable conversion value is lower, subject to the waiting period for reconversions (*see* below).

You make an election to recharacterize the conversion by making a trustee-to-trustee transfer of the Roth IRA contribution (part or all) to a traditional IRA; it does not have to be the same traditional IRA from which the conversion was made. You can also recharacterize by keeping the account with the same trustee and notifying the trustee to transfer the account to a traditional IRA. The transfer must include any net income allocable to the contribution being recharacterized. If there has been a loss in value since the conversion, the allocable negative net income reduces the amount that must be recharacterized to a traditional IRA. The Roth IRA trustee generally figures the net income or loss allocable to the recharacterized contribution; IRS Publication 590 has a worksheet for calculating the amount.

You must notify both trustees (if different) of your intent to recharacterize by specifically identifying the original contribution that is being recharacterized and the amount being recharacterized and you must direct the transferor trustee to make the transfer, including any allocable income.

The effect of the recharacterization is to disregard the conversion to the Roth IRA and to treat the contribution as if it had been contributed to the transferee traditional IRA (to which recharacterization was made) on the date of the conversion. The recharacterized contribution is not treated as a rollover for purposes of the one-rollover-per-year rule *(8.10)*.

Other types of recharacterizations. You may recharacterize an annual Roth IRA contribution *(8.20)* as a traditional IRA contribution, where this might enable you to obtain a deduction for the traditional IRA contribution *(8.4)*. If you initially contribute to a traditional IRA, you may be able to recharacterize the contribution as an annual Roth IRA contribution. *See* the Planning Reminder in this section.

Deadline for recharacterizing a conversion. IRS regulations generally require that a recharacterization election and the actual transfer be made on or before the due date, including extensions, for filing the tax return for the year of the conversion. However, the IRS allows timely filers an automatic extension of six months from the original filing due date, excluding extensions. To recharacterize a conversion made in 2010, you have until October 17, 2011 (October 15 is a Saturday), provided that you timely filed your 2010 return, including any extension. *See* the instructions to Form 8606 for how to report the conversion and the recharacterization. If you file a timely 2010 return and pay tax on the converted amount, and then recharacterize by the October 17 deadline, you must file an amended return. For example, by April 15, 2011, you file your 2010 return, which includes a taxable conversion made in 2010, and then by October 17, 2011, you recharacterize the converted amount back to a traditional IRA. You must file an amended 2010 return to report the recharacterization and claim a refund for the tax paid on the conversion. The amended return must be filed, within the regular amendment period, generally three years *(47.1)*. On the amended return, write "Filed pursuant to Section 301.9100-2."

What if you miss the IRS recharacterization deadlines? A regulation gives the IRS authority to grant an extension if an "innocent" mistake was made and you act in good faith by promptly asking the IRS for the additional time after discovering the error (Reg. Sec. 301.9100-3). In several private rulings, the IRS has allowed the extra extension to taxpayers who missed the deadline and who requested recharacterization relief before the IRS discovered that they did not qualify for the conversion under the pre-2010 $100,000 MAGI limit *(8.21)*, or that the attempted recharacterization had not been timely made. At the time of each request, the statute of limitations had not yet passed; if it had, the IRS would almost surely have denied the requests. In one private ruling, the IRS allowed extra time to recharacterize a Roth IRA back to a traditional IRA after an IRS audit uncovered additional income that pushed a taxpayer over the $100,000 MAGI limit. The taxpayer, according to the IRS, had acted reasonably and was not aware of the excess income.

Reconverting to a Roth IRA after a recharacterization. As discussed above, a traditional IRA that has been converted to a Roth IRA may be transferred back to a traditional IRA in a recharacterization. That amount may subsequently be reconverted back to a Roth IRA. This recharacterization/reconversion rule may allow an IRA owner to lower the tax due on a conversion to a Roth IRA. For example, if you convert a traditional IRA to a Roth IRA and the value of the account drops as a result of a stock market decline, you may be able to reduce the taxable conversion amount value by recharacterizing the account as a traditional IRA and then reconverting to a Roth IRA at a time when the value of the account is lower. The amount that you must include in income from the conversion is based on the value of the account as of the date of the reconversion.

However, the IRS has imposed a waiting period before a reconversion may be made. You may not convert to a Roth IRA, recharacterize back to a traditional IRA, and reconvert the same funds to a Roth IRA in the same calendar year. If you converted a traditional IRA to a Roth IRA and also recharacterized that amount back to a traditional IRA during 2010, you may not reconvert those same funds to a Roth IRA until January 1, 2011. If the recharacterization was made in the last 30 days of 2010, you must wait until the 30th day following the date of the recharacterization before a valid reconversion may be made in early 2011.

The 30-day waiting period also applies if in 2011 you recharacterize a conversion made in 2010; *see* the Joe Smith Example below. A reconversion after the 2011 recharacterization is treated as a new conversion in 2011.

The effect of the waiting period is to make it impossible to take immediate advantage of a stock market decline that lowers the value of a Roth IRA. If you want to recharacterize back to a traditional IRA and then reconvert to a Roth IRA in order to lower the taxable conversion amount, you will have to wait a minimum of 30 days before reconverting. By that time, the value of the reconverted account may be as high, or higher, than it was at the time of the recharacterization.

If a reconversion is attempted before the end of the waiting period, the attempt will be treated as a "failed" conversion. A failed conversion is treated as a taxable distribution from the traditional IRA followed by a regular contribution to a Roth IRA. The pre–age 59½ early distribution penalty could apply to the taxable distribution *(8.12)* and the excess of the deemed regular contribution to the Roth IRA over the annual limit would be subject to the 6% excess contribution penalty *(8.7)*. A failed conversion may be remedied by making a timely recharacterization to a traditional IRA.

Planning Reminder

Recharacterization of Roth IRA to Traditional IRA and Vice Versa

The recharacterization rule is not limited to reversing a conversion to a Roth IRA. A regular Roth IRA contribution (up to the annual limit) may be recharacterized as a contribution to a traditional IRA if, for example, doing so would allow you to claim an IRA deduction under the rules discussed at *8.4*. Similarly, if you contribute to a traditional IRA and decide that you would like to switch to a Roth IRA, you may recharacterize the contribution by transferring the contribution plus allocable income to a Roth IRA, assuming the contribution is not barred by the MAGI phaseout *(8.20)*. A recharacterization must be made by the filing due date, *plus* extensions. If you recharacterize a traditional IRA contribution to a Roth IRA, the transfer is treated as if it were made to the Roth IRA on January 1 of the year in which the original traditional IRA contribution was made, regardless of when the recharacterization occurred. This may be an advantage for purposes of establishing the beginning of the five-year holding period for tax-free distributions of Roth IRA earnings *(8.23)*.

Caution

Delay on Reconversion to Roth IRA

After converting a traditional IRA to a Roth IRA, you may undo the conversion by recharacterizing the account as a traditional IRA. If you want to reconvert to a Roth IRA, you must stay within the IRS guidelines. A reconversion may not be made until the year following the year of the original conversion, or, if later, 30 days after the day on which the recharacterization took place *(8.22)*.

EXAMPLE

In 2010, Joe Smith converts a traditional IRA worth $150,000 to a Roth IRA. In early 2011, Joe loses his job. The tax on the income from the conversion would be substantial and even though the income could be deferred to 2011 and 2012 under the special rule for 2010 conversions *(8.21)*, Joe decides to recharacterize the entire conversion. He recharacterizes the Roth IRA as a traditional IRA on January 26, 2011. Joe may not reconvert that amount to a Roth IRA until February 25, 2011. This is the first day after the 30-day period that begins on January 26, 2011, the date of the recharacterization, and ends on February 24, 2011.

If Joe attempts to reconvert before February 25, 2011, the transfer will be treated as a "failed" conversion. Unless the failed conversion amount is recharacterized back to a traditional IRA, it will be treated as a taxable distribution from the traditional IRA; the 10% penalty for pre–age 59½ distributions could also apply. It will also be treated as a regular contribution to a Roth IRA and the amount over the annual limit *(8.20)* would be subject to the 6% excess contribution penalty tax. To avoid these tax consequences, Joe may recharacterize the failed conversion back to a traditional IRA and later reconvert it to a Roth IRA at any time after the 30-day waiting period. Assume that Joe reconverts to a Roth IRA on March 3, 2011. If Joe recharacterizes the March 3 conversion amount back to a traditional IRA during 2011, he must wait until 2012 before he may reconvert that amount again.

8.23 Distributions From a Roth IRA

A distribution from a Roth IRA is tax free if it is a *qualified* distribution, as discussed below. Even if a distribution is not a qualified distribution, it is tax free to the extent it does not exceed your regular Roth IRA contributions *(8.20)* and conversion contributions *(8.21)*. The part of a non-qualified distribution allocable to earnings is taxable, but distributions are considered to be from contributions first and then from earnings; *see* the ordering rule below for the allocation between contributions and earnings.

You may make a tax-free direct transfer from one Roth IRA to another. A tax-free rollover of a Roth IRA distribution may be made to another Roth IRA if you complete the rollover within 60 days.

You do not have to receive minimum required distributions from a Roth IRA after you reach age 70½ as you would from a traditional IRA *(8.13)*. No Roth IRA distributions at all are required during your lifetime. After your death, your beneficiaries will be subject to a minimum distribution requirement *(8.24)*.

Qualified Roth IRA distributions are tax free. Two tests must be met for a Roth IRA distribution to be "qualified," and thus completely tax free: (1) the distribution must be made after the end of the five-year period beginning with the first day of the first taxable year for which any Roth IRA contribution was made and (2) one of the following conditions must be met:

- you are age 59½ or older when the distribution is made,
- you are disabled,
- you use the distribution to pay up to $10,000 of qualifying first-time home-buyer expenses as discussed below, *or*
- you are a beneficiary receiving distributions following the death of the account owner.

Filing Instruction

Form 8606

IRS Form 8606 must be filed to report Roth IRA distributions. It is also used to report a conversion to a Roth IRA. If you recharacterized part of the converted amount, you must report the non-recharacterized amount on Form 8606. The recharacterized portion is not reported on Form 8606, but an explanation must be attached to your return; follow the Form 8606 instructions.

Five-year holding period. Even if you are age 59½ or older or meet one of the other tests for qualified distributions, you must also satisfy the five-year holding period test in order to make tax-free withdrawals of earnings from a Roth IRA. The five-year holding period begins with January 1 (assuming you are a calendar-year taxpayer) of the first year for which any Roth IRA contribution is made.

You have only one five-year period regardless of the number of Roth IRAs you have. Once you satisfy the five-year test for one Roth IRA, you also meet it for all subsequently established Roth IRAs. For example, if you converted a traditional IRA to a Roth IRA during 1998 (the first year Roth IRA contributions were allowed), or made a regular Roth IRA contribution for 1998 at any time between January 1, 1998, and April 15, 1999, your five-year holding period began January 1, 1998. If in a later year you converted *(8.21)* a traditional IRA to a Roth IRA, or made a regular

Roth IRA contribution (8.20), that did not begin a new five-year holding period for that Roth IRA. In this case, the five-year period for all your Roth IRAs began January 1, 1998, and ended December 31, 2002. If your first Roth IRA contribution was a regular contribution for 2006 (by April 17, 2007) or a conversion made during 2006, your five-year period for all your Roth IRAs ends December 31, 2010.

If you receive a Roth IRA distribution *after* the end of your five-year holding period, and you also meet one of the other qualified distribution requirements such as being age 59½ or older, the distribution is completely tax free. If you receive a distribution before satisfying both the five-year holding period requirement and one of the other qualified distribution requirements, and the withdrawal exceeds your contributions, the excess (i.e., earnings) is taxable and possibly subject to the 10% penalty for pre–age 59½ distributions (8.12). Under the ordering rules discussed below, Roth IRA distributions are treated as being made first from contributions and then from earnings.

Ordering rules for distributions. Even if a distribution is not fully tax free as a qualified distribution, it is not taxable to the extent of your Roth IRA contributions. All of your Roth IRAs are treated as one account for purposes of determining if contributions or earnings have been withdrawn. If a distribution does not exceed total contributions to all of your Roth IRAs, it is not taxable.

Where you have made regular annual contributions and also conversion contributions from a traditional IRA or rollover contributions from an employer plan to a Roth IRA, the regular contributions are considered to be withdrawn first. Then, conversion contributions and rollover contributions are considered to be withdrawn in the order in which they were made. If part of a conversion or rollover contribution was not treated as a taxable distribution (because it was allocable to nondeductible or after-tax contributions in the converted or rolled-over account), the taxable part of the conversion or rollover is deemed withdrawn before the nontaxable part. Taking into account the taxable part of a conversion or rollover contribution before the nontaxable part (if any) of the contribution may be important for purposes of determining whether the 10% early distribution penalty applies to the withdrawal of a conversion or rollover contribution within five years of the conversion (*see* below).

Earnings on Roth IRA contributions are considered to be withdrawn last, after all contributions are taken into account. If the distribution is not a qualified distribution, the withdrawn earnings are subject to tax and if you are under age 59½, to the 10% early distribution penalty, although there are exceptions (8.12).

Penalty on withdrawals before age 59½ and within five years of conversion or rollover to Roth IRAs. The regular 10% early withdrawal penalty (8.12) applies if withdrawals from a Roth IRA are made by taxpayers under age 59½ before January 1 of the fifth year after the year of a conversion from a traditional IRA or rollover from an employer plan. Unless a penalty exception is available, the 10% penalty applies to the extent that a withdrawal within the five-year period is allocable under the ordering rule (*see* above) to the taxable part of the conversion or rollover. Under the ordering rule for Roth IRA distributions, the entire withdrawal may be tax free because it does not exceed regular Roth IRA contributions, plus conversion or rollover contributions, but the 10% penalty still applies if a taxable conversion or rollover amount is deemed to be withdrawn before the end of the five-year period. The five-year period for purposes of this penalty rule is figured separately for each conversion or rollover contribution. If you made a conversion in 2006, the five-year holding period for avoiding the early distribution penalty on a withdrawal from that Roth IRA ends December 31, 2010.

Distribution used for up to $10,000 of first-time home-buyer expenses. Tax-free treatment will apply to a Roth IRA distribution received after the first five-year period and used for up to $10,000 of qualifying "first-time" home-buyer expenses. The $10,000 limit is a lifetime cap per IRA owner, not an annual limitation. Expenses qualify if they are used within 120 days of the distribution to pay the acquisition costs of a principal residence for you, your spouse, your child, or your grandchild, or an ancestor of you or your spouse. The residence does not have to be the homeowner's "first" home. A qualifying first-time home-buyer is considered to be someone who did not have a present ownership interest in a principal residence in the two-year period ending on the acquisition date of the new home. If the home-buyer is married, both spouses must satisfy the two-year test. Eligible acquisition costs include buying, constructing, or reconstructing the principal residence, including reasonable settlement, financing, and closing costs.

Planning Reminder

Meeting the Five-Year Holding Test

For a withdrawal of earnings from a Roth IRA to be tax free, the five-year holding period test must be met and the taxpayer must be at least age 59½ or meet one of the other conditions for a qualified distribution. For example, a taxpayer whose first Roth IRA contribution was for 2006 satisfies the five-year test at the end of 2010 so a distribution received after age 59½ in 2011 (or later) will be a tax-free qualified distribution.

IRS Alert

Loss on Liquidation of Roth IRA

You may have a loss on your Roth IRA investment because of declines in the stock market. If you liquidate all of your Roth IRA accounts, and the total distribution is less than your contributions to all of the Roth IRAs, you may be able to claim the difference as a deductible loss. However, the deduction is allowed only as a miscellaneous itemized deduction subject to the 2%-of-adjusted-gross-income floor (19.1) on Schedule A and if allowed, it must be added back to income to determine liability for the alternative minimum tax (23.2).

Caution

Early Withdrawal From Conversion IRA

The 10% penalty (8.12) for pre–age 59½ distributions may apply if within five years of making a conversion to a Roth IRA, a distribution from that Roth IRA is received. The penalty applies to the portion of the withdrawal allocable to the conversion amount that was taxable in the year of the conversion. This is so even if the withdrawal is tax free under the ordering rule for Roth IRA distributions.

8.24 Distributions to Roth IRA Beneficiaries

Caution

Some Distributions Partly Taxable to Beneficiary

Tax treatment of a distribution you receive as the beneficiary of a Roth IRA depends on whether it would have been a qualified distribution had the owner been alive to receive it on the distribution date. If you receive the distribution before the end of the owner's five-year holding period *(8.23)*, and part of the distribution is allocable to earnings under the ordering rules *(8.23)*, you must include that amount in your taxable income. However, even if you receive a taxable distribution and are under age 59½, you are not subject to the 10% early distribution penalty.

If you are the surviving spouse of the Roth IRA owner and you are the owner's sole Roth IRA beneficiary, you may elect to treat the inherited account as your own Roth IRA. If you treat the account as your own, you do not have to take distributions from the account at any time, since a Roth IRA owner is not subject to minimum distribution requirements. If you take some distributions, you are not locked into a specific distribution schedule unless you agree to that schedule.

Surviving spouses who do not elect to treat an inherited Roth IRA as their own, and beneficiaries other than surviving spouses, must receive required minimum distributions (RMDs). If there is an individual designated beneficiary under the final IRS regulations as of September 30 of the year following the year of the Roth IRA owner's death *(8.14)*, RMDs are generally payable over the life expectancy of the designated beneficiary; *see* the Single Life Expectancy table *(Table 8-5) (8.14)*. If there is more than one individual beneficiary, they may split the inherited account into separate accounts by December 31 of the year following the year of the Roth IRA owner's death, allowing each beneficiary to use his or her own life expectancy in figuring RMDs *(8.14)*. Although it is unlikely, the plan document may require distributions under the five-year rule, which requires that the entire account be distributed by December 31 of the fifth year following the year of the owner's death but does not require any distributions prior to that date. The plan may allow a choice between the life expectancy rule and the five-year rule. Of course, a beneficiary who is receiving RMDs under the life-expectancy method may choose to receive more than the minimum amount required under the life expectancy rule.

If 2009 RMD was waived. Any RMD that was otherwise due for 2009 did not have to be received; the distribution for 2009 could be waived. If you are a beneficiary receiving distributions under the five-year rule and you waived the RMD for 2009, the distribution period is extended to six years.

When distributions to beneficiary must start under life expectancy rule. For a nonspouse beneficiary, RMDs must begin by the end of the year following the year of the Roth IRA owner's death. This is also the starting date for a surviving spouse who is a co-beneficiary of the account along with other individuals.

If you are the surviving spouse and are sole beneficiary of the Roth IRA, you may elect to treat the Roth IRA as your own and if you do, you do not have to receive any RMDs. If you do not treat it as your own, you may delay the start of RMDs until whichever is later: December 31 of the year your spouse would have reached age 70½, or December 31 of the year following the year of your spouse's death.

If there is no designated beneficiary under the IRS rules, such as where the Roth IRA owner's estate is the beneficiary *(8.14)*, the entire account must be paid out by the end of the fifth year following the year of the owner's death.

Five-year holding period for tax-free treatment. The same five-year holding period for receiving fully tax-free distributions that applied to the account owner *(8.23)* also applies to you as the beneficiary. The five-year holding period began on January 1 of the year for which the owner's first Roth IRA contribution was made. If you receive distributions before the end of the five-year holding period, the distributions will be tax free to the extent that they are a recovery of the owner's Roth IRA contributions and taxable to the extent they are earnings. Distributions you receive after the end of the five-year holding period are completely tax free.

Chapter 9

Income From Rents and Royalties

Use Schedule E of Form 1040 to report real estate rental income and expenses. You must also file Form 4562 to claim depreciation deductions for buildings you placed in service in 2010.

Use Schedule C instead of Schedule E if you provide additional services for the convenience of the tenants, such as maid service. That is, Schedule C is used to report payments received for the use and occupancy of rooms or other areas in a hotel, motel, boarding house, apartment, tourist home, or trailer court where services are provided primarily for the occupant.

If you rent out an apartment or room in the same building in which you live, you report the rent income less expenses allocated to the rental property *(9.4)*.

The law prevents most homeowners from deducting losses (expenses in excess of income) on the rental of a personal vacation home or personal residence if the owner or close relatives personally use the premises during the year. Tests based on days of personal and rental use determine whether you may deduct losses *(9.7)*.

Rental losses may also be limited by the passive activity rules discussed in *Chapter 10*. Real estate professionals may avoid the passive restrictions on rental income. An investor who actively manages property may deduct rental losses of up to $25,000 under an exception to the passive activity loss restrictions.

Use Schedule E to report royalties, but if you are a self-employed author, artist, or inventor, report royalty income and expenses on Schedule C.

Business rentals of equipment, vehicles, or similar personal property are reported on Schedule C, not Schedule E.

Filing Tip

Husband-Wife Owners Can File Schedule C for Qualified Joint Venture

If you and your spouse are sole owners of a rental real estate business that you both materially participate in, and you file jointly, you can elect to be treated as a qualified joint venture rather than a partnership by reporting the rental income and expenses as sole proprietors on Schedule C (or in some cases C-EZ; *see 40.6*) instead of Schedule E. Each of you files a separate Schedule C on which you report your respective share of the income and expenses. On Line 1 of Schedule C, you check a box that indicates you ae reporting only rental real estate income that is not subject to self-employment tax. The rule that exempts rental income from self-employment tax *(45.1)* is not affected by the fact that the income is reported on Schedule C rather than Schedule E.

Caution

Security Deposits

Distinguish advance rentals, which are income, from security deposits, which are not. Security deposits are amounts deposited with you solely as security for the tenant's performance of the terms of the lease, and as such are usually not taxed, particularly where local law treats security deposits as trust funds. If the tenant breaches the lease, you are entitled to apply the sum as rent, at which time you report it as income. If both you and your tenant agree that a security deposit is to be used as a final rent payment, it is advance rent. Include it in your income when you receive it.

9.1 Reporting Rental Income and Expenses

On the cash basis, you report rent income on your tax return for the year in which you receive payment or in which you "constructively" receive it, such as where payment is credited to your bank account.

On the accrual basis, you report income on your tax return for the year in which you are entitled to receive payment, even if it is not actually paid. However, you do not report accrued income if the financial condition of the tenant makes collection doubtful. If you sue for payment, you do not report income until you win a collectible judgment.

Advance rentals. Advance rentals or bonuses are reported in the year received, whether you are on the cash or accrual basis.

Tenant's payment of landlord's expenses. The tenant's payment of your taxes, interest, insurance, mortgage amortization (even if you are not personally liable on the mortgage), repairs, or other expenses is considered additional rental income to you. If your tenant pays your utility bills or your emergency repairs and deducts the amount from the rent payment, you must include as rental income the full rental amount, not the actual net payment. However, you can claim an offsetting deduction for expenses, such as repairs, that would have been deductible had you paid them.

Tenant's payment to cancel lease. A tenant's payment for cancelling a lease or modifying its terms is considered rental income in the year you receive it regardless of your method of accounting. You may deduct expenses incurred because of the cancellation or modification and any unamortized balance of expenses paid in negotiating the lease.

Insurance. Insurance proceeds for loss of rental income because of fire or other casualty are rental income.

Improvements by tenants. You do not realize taxable income when your tenant improves the leased premises, provided the improvements are not substitute rent payments. Furthermore, when you take possession of the improvements at the time the lease ends, you do not realize income. However, you may not depreciate the value of the improvements as the basis to you is considered zero.

Property or services. If you receive property or services instead of money, include the fair market value of such property or services as rental income.

If you agree upon a specified price for services rendered, that price is generally treated as the fair market value.

Rental losses. Rental income may be offset by deductions claimed for depreciation, mortgage interest, and repair and maintenance costs. However, if these expenses exceed rental income, the resulting loss is subject to the passive activity loss restrictions. If you do not qualify as a real estate professional *(10.3)*, you generally may not deduct rental losses from other income (such as salary, interest, and dividends). Rental losses may offset only other rental and passive activity income. However, if you perform some management role, you may deduct from other income *real estate* rental losses of up to $25,000, provided your adjusted gross income does not exceed $100,000 *(10.2)*. The passive activity restrictions have the positive effect of making rental income attractive. Consider purchasing rental property if you have passive tax losses that may be used to offset the rental income. *See Chapter 10 for details on the passive loss restrictions.*

Application of the passive activity loss rules and exceptions assumes that the property is not considered a residence under the personal-use rules *(9.7)*. If it is, rental expenses are deductible from rental income *(9.9)* but a loss is not allowed for that property.

9.2 Checklist of Rental Deductions

The expenses in this section are deductible from rental income on Schedule E of Form 1040 in determining your profit.

Real estate taxes. However, special assessments for paving, sewer systems, or other local improvements are not deductible; they are added to the cost of the land. *See 16.4* through *16.7* for real estate tax deductions.

Construction period interest and taxes. These expenses generally have to be capitalized and depreciated *(16.4)*.

Depreciation of a rental building. You may start claiming depreciation in the month the building is ready for tenants. For example, you bought a house in May 2010 and spent June and July making repairs. The house is ready to rent in August and you advertise for tenants. You begin depreciation as of August, even if a tenant does not move in until September or some later month. The month the building is ready for tenants is the month that determines the first-year depreciation write-off under the mid-month convention. *See 9.5* for the monthly depreciation rates for residential rental property. Rates for nonresidential buildings are at *42.13*.

Depreciation for furniture and appliances. Furniture, carpeting, and appliances such as stoves and refrigerators used in residential rental property are considered five-year property for MACRS depreciation purposes. Furniture used in office buildings is considered seven-year property. *See 42.5* for MACRS rates.

Management expenses, such as a fee paid to a company for collecting the rent.

Maintenance expenses, such as heating, repairs, lighting, water, electricity, gas, telephone, coal, and other service costs *(9.3)*.

Salaries and wages, paid to superintendents, janitors, elevator operators, and service and maintenance personnel.

Traveling expenses to look after the properties. If you travel "away from home" to inspect or repair rental property, be prepared to show that this was the primary purpose of your trip, rather than vacationing or other personal purposes. Otherwise, the IRS may disallow deductions for round-trip travel costs.

Legal expenses for dispossessing tenants. But expenses of long-term leases are capital expenditures deductible over the term of the lease.

Interest on mortgages and other indebtedness. But deductible interest does not include expenses paid to obtain a mortgage such as mortgage commissions and abstract or recording fees. Such costs are capital expenses that can be amortized over the life of the mortgage. For a mortgage obtained in 2010, amortization is claimed on Form 4562 (Depreciation and Amortization) and amortization for expenses of pre-2010 mortgages is claimed on Schedule E as an "Other expense."

Commissions paid to collect rentals. But commissions paid to secure long-term rentals must be deducted over the life of the lease. Commissions paid to acquire the property are capitalized as an addition to basis.

Premiums for fire, liability, and plate glass insurance. If payment is made in one year for insurance covering a period longer than one year, you amortize and deduct the premium over the life of the policy, even though you are on a cash basis.

Tax return preparation. You may deduct as a rental expense the part of a tax preparation fee allocable to Part 1 of Schedule E (income or loss from rentals or royalties). You may also deduct, as a rental expense, a fee paid to a tax consultant to resolve a tax underpayment related to your rental activities.

Charging below fair market rent. If you rent your property to a friend or relative for less than the fair rental value, you may deduct expenses and depreciation only to the extent of the rental income *(9.8)*.

Co-tenants. One of two tenants-in-common may deduct only half of the maintenance expenses even if he or she pays the entire bill. A tenant-in-common who pays all of the expenses of the common property is entitled to reimbursement from the other co-tenant, so one-half of the bill is not his or her ordinary and necessary expense. Each co-tenant owns a separate property interest in the common property that produces separate income for each. Each tenant's deductible expense is that portion of the entire expense that each separate interest bears to the whole, and no more.

Costs of cancelling lease. A landlord may pay a tenant to cancel an unfavorable lease. The way the landlord treats the payment depends on the reason for the cancellation. If the purpose of the cancellation is to enable the landlord to construct a new building in place of the old, the cancellation payment is added to the basis of the new building. If the purpose is to sell the property, the payment is added to the cost of the property. If the landlord wants the premises for his or her own use, the payment is deducted over the remaining term of the old lease. If the landlord gets a new tenant to replace the old one, the cancellation payment is also generally deductible over the remaining term of the old lease.

Court Decision

Co-Tenant's Deduction for Real Estate Taxes

The Tax Court may allow a co-tenant to deduct more than his or her proportionate share of real estate taxes. According to the court, the deduction test for real estate taxes is whether the payment satisfies a personal liability or protects a beneficial interest in the property. In the case of co-tenants, nonpayment of taxes by the other co-tenants could result in the property being lost or foreclosed. To prevent this, a co-tenant who pays the tax is protecting his or her beneficial interest and, therefore, is entitled to deduct the payment of the full tax, provided the payment is from his or her own funds. In several cases, the Tax Court limited the taxpayer's deduction to his or her proportionate share, despite payment of the entire amount of taxes, because the taxpayer could not prove that the payment came from his own separate funds.

EXAMPLE

Handlery Hotels, Inc., had to pay its *lessee* $85,000 to terminate a lease on a building three years before the lease term expired. Handlery entered into a new 20-year lease on more favorable terms with another lessee. Handlery amortized the $85,000 cancellation payment over the three-year unexpired term of the old lease. The IRS claimed that the payment had to be amortized over the 20-year term of the new lease because it was part of the cost of obtaining the new lease. A federal district court agreed with the IRS, but an appeals court sided with Handlery. Since the unexpired lease term is the major factor in determining the amount of the cancellation payment, the cost of cancellation should be amortized over that unexpired term.

9.3 Distinguishing Between a Repair and an Improvement

Maintenance and repair expenses are not treated in the same way as expenses for improvements and replacements. Only maintenance and incidental repair costs are deductible against rental income. Improvements that add to the value or prolong the life of the property or adapt it to new uses are capital improvements. Capital improvements may not be deducted currently but may be depreciated according to certain rules *(42.13)*. If you make improvements to property before renting it out, add the cost of the improvements to your basis in the property.

A repair keeps your property in good operating condition. For example, repairs include painting, fixing gutters or floors, fixing leaks, plastering, and replacing broken windows. However, putting a recreation room in an unfinished basement, paneling a den, putting up a fence, putting in new plumbing or wiring, and paving a driveway are all examples of depreciable capital improvements *(42.13)*. Putting on a new roof is generally a depreciable capital improvement; however, the Tax Court has allowed current deductions for roof replacements intended to prevent leaks; *see* Example 2 below.

Repairs may not be separated from capital expenditures when both are part of an improvement program; *see* Example 3 below.

Planning Reminder

Repairs and Improvements

What if repairs and improvements are unconnected and not part of an overall improvement program? Assume you repair the floors of one story and improve another story by cutting new windows. You probably may deduct the cost of repairing the floors provided you have separate bills for the jobs. To safeguard the deduction, schedule the work at separate times so that the two jobs are not lumped together as an overall improvement program.

EXAMPLES

1. The cost of painting the outside of a building used for business purposes and the cost of papering and painting the inside are repair costs and may be deducted. A change in the plumbing system is a capital expenditure that must be depreciated under MACRS *(42.13)*.
2. Campbell owned a one-story house that she rented to a tenant. She paid $8,000 to repair the roof after the tenant complained of leaks. The contractor she employed removed the existing layers of roof and replaced them with fiberglass and asphalt; no structural changes were made. The Tax Court allowed Campbell to deduct the full amount of the payment to the contractor as an ordinary and necessary repair because the roof replacement merely restored the property to a leak-free condition and did not add to the value of the home.

   The Tax Court also allowed an owner of a commercial building with a leaky roof to fully deduct the $52,000 cost of stripping the roof layers, replacing them, and spraying the new ones with foam to prevent future leaks. These were repairs intended to keep the property in working condition and did not extend the life of the building.
3. You buy a dilapidated business building and has it renovated and repaired. The total cost comes to about $130,000, of which $17,800 is allocable to the repairs. The cost of the repairs is not deductible because the entire project is a capital expenditure. When a general improvement program is undertaken, you may not separate repairs from improvements. Both become an integral part of the overall betterment and are a capital investment, although a portion could be characterized as repairs when viewed independently.

Normal maintenance or major improvement? Normal maintenance expenses were distinguished from major improvement costs in a case involving a major hotel where improvements and maintenance were generally done at the same time. The operators of the hotel capitalized the cost of the improvements but claimed expense deductions for the cost of painting and repapering rooms. The IRS disallowed the deductions, claiming they were part of the improvement program. The operators claimed that the papering and painting were normal and usual maintenance work required to keep the hotel in first-class condition. The Tax Court disagreed and sided with the IRS. However, on appeal, the appeals court allowed the deduction. The "rehabilitation doctrine" does not apply where it can be shown that repairs are part of a normal range of ongoing maintenance. Here, the painting and papering only served to maintain the first-class status of the hotel. The fact that the work was done under a general improvement plan did not defeat the deduction. Any commercial enterprise, such as a hotel, that annually spends large sums of money on replacements and repairs must do so under a detailed plan and budget.

9.4 Reporting Rents From a Multi-Unit Residence

If you rent out an apartment or room in a multi-unit residence in which you also live, you report rent receipts and deduct expenses allocated to the rented part of the property on Schedule E of Form 1040 whether or not you itemize deductions. You deduct interest and taxes on your personal share of the property as itemized deductions on Schedule A of Form 1040 if you itemize deductions. If you or close relatives personally use the rented portion during the year and expenses exceed income, loss deductions may be barred under the personal-use rules *(9.7)*.

Even if a loss is not barred by the personal-use rules *(9.7)*, a loss shown on Schedule E is subject to the passive loss restrictions discussed in *Chapter 10*. The loss, if it comes within the $25,000 allowance *(10.2)* or the exception for real estate professionals *(10.3)*, may be deducted from any type of income. If your only passive activity losses are rental losses of $25,000 or less from actively managed rental real estate and your modified adjusted gross income is $100,000 or less, you do not have to use Form 8582 to deduct losses under the $25,000 allowance *(10.12)*. If you are not a qualifying real estate professional and cannot claim the allowance, the loss may be deducted only from passive activity income.

EXAMPLE

You buy a three-family house in March 2010. You occupy one floor as your personal residence and starting in June 2010 you rent out the other two floors. The house cost you $300,000 ($270,000 for the building and $30,000 for the land). Two-thirds of the basis of the building is subject to depreciation, or $180,000 ($^2/_3$ of $270,000). For a building placed in service in June, the depreciation rate is 1.970%, as shown in Table 9-1, so your depreciation deduction is $3,546 (1.970% $180,000). Assuming you paid property taxes of $6,000, mortgage interest of $3,900, and repairs of $3,000, this is how you deduct expenses for 2010:

	Total	*Deduct itemized deductions*	*Deduct on Schedule E*	*Not deductible*
Taxes	$ 6,000	$ 2,000	$ 4,000	
Interest	3,900	1,300	2,600	
Repairs	3,000		2,000	$ 1,000
Depreciation	3,546		3,546	
	$ 16,446	$ 3,300	$ 12,146	$ 1,000

The taxes and interest allocated to personal use are deductible on Schedule A of Form 1040 if you itemize deductions. Repairs allocated to your apartment are nondeductible personal expenses.

Court Decision

Rented Rooms That Are Not Separate Dwelling Units

A rental loss was denied to an owner of a two-story, four-bedroom house when he rented out two bedrooms to separate tenants after he lost his job. Although individual locks were placed on the doors of the rented bedrooms, the tenants and the owner shared access to the kitchen, bathroom, and other parts of the house. The Tax Court held that the rented rooms were not separate and distinct from the rest of the house that the owner used. The house was a single dwelling unit shared by the owner and tenants and under the personal-use rules *(9.7)*, the owner could not claim a rental loss.

9.5 Depreciation on Converting a Home to Rental Property

When you convert your residence to rental property, you may depreciate the building. You figure depreciation on the *lower* of:

- Fair market value of the building at the time you convert it to rental property; *or*
- Adjusted basis. This is your original cost for the building, exclusive of land, *plus* permanent improvements and other capital costs, and *minus* items that represent a return of your cost, such as casualty or theft loss deductions claimed on prior tax returns.

Table 9-1 Depreciation: Use the Row for the Month the Residence Is Ready for Rental in the First Rental Year

Year	Month property placed in service											
	1	2	3	4	5	6	7	8	9	10	11	12
1	3.485%	3.182%	2.879%	2.576%	2.273%	1.970%	1.667%	1.364%	1.061%	0.758%	0.455%	0.152%
2–9	3.636	3.636	3.636	3.636	3.636	3.636	3.636	3.636	3.636	3.636	3.636	3.636
10	3.637	3.637	3.637	3.637	3.637	3.637	3.636	3.636	3.636	3.636	3.636	3.636
11	3.636	3.636	3.636	3.636	3.636	3.636	3.637	3.637	3.637	3.637	3.637	3.637
12	3.637	3.637	3.637	3.637	3.637	3.637	3.636	3.636	3.636	3.636	3.636	3.636
13	3.636	3.636	3.636	3.636	3.636	3.636	3.637	3.637	3.637	3.637	3.637	3.637
14	3.637	3.637	3.637	3.637	3.637	3.637	3.636	3.636	3.636	3.636	3.636	3.636
15	3.636	3.636	3.636	3.636	3.636	3.636	3.637	3.637	3.637	3.637	3.637	3.637
16	3.637	3.637	3.637	3.637	3.637	3.637	3.636	3.636	3.636	3.636	3.636	3.636
17	3.636	3.636	3.636	3.636	3.636	3.636	3.637	3.637	3.637	3.637	3.637	3.637
18	3.637	3.637	3.637	3.637	3.637	3.637	3.636	3.636	3.636	3.636	3.636	3.636
19	3.636	3.636	3.636	3.636	3.636	3.636	3.637	3.637	3.637	3.637	3.637	3.637
20	3.637	3.637	3.637	3.637	3.637	3.637	3.636	3.636	3.636	3.636	3.636	3.636
21	3.636	3.636	3.636	3.636	3.636	3.636	3.637	3.637	3.637	3.637	3.637	3.637
22	3.637	3.637	3.637	3.637	3.637	3.637	3.636	3.636	3.636	3.636	3.636	3.636
23	3.636	3.636	3.636	3.636	3.636	3.636	3.637	3.637	3.637	3.637	3.637	3.637
24	3.637	3.637	3.637	3.637	3.637	3.637	3.636	3.636	3.636	3.636	3.636	3.636
25	3.636	3.636	3.636	3.636	3.636	3.636	3.637	3.637	3.637	3.637	3.637	3.637
26	3.637	3.637	3.637	3.637	3.637	3.637	3.636	3.636	3.636	3.636	3.636	3.636
27	3.636	3.636	3.636	3.636	3.636	3.636	3.637	3.637	3.637	3.637	3.637	3.637
28	1.97	2.273	2.576	2.879	3.182	3.485	3.636	3.636	3.636	3.636	3.636	3.636
29							0.152	0.455	0.758	1.061	1.364	1.667

You claim MACRS depreciation based on a 27½-year recovery period, which extends to 28 or 29 years due to the mid-month convention. The specific rate for the year of conversion is the rate for the month in which the property is ready for tenants. For example, you move out of your home in May and make some minor repairs. You advertise the house for rent in June. Depreciation starts in June because that is when the home is ready for rental, even if you do not actually obtain a tenant until a later month. Under a mid-month convention, the house is treated as placed in service during the middle of the month. This means that one-half of a full month's depreciation is allowed for that month. In *Table 9-1*, the monthly depreciation rates for the year the property is placed in service and later years are shown. The table incorporates the mid-month convention.

Planning Reminder

Obtain Appraisal

Have an appraiser estimate the fair market value of the house when it is rented. The appraisal will help support your basis for depreciation or a loss deduction on a sale if your return is examined.

EXAMPLE

In 2001, you bought a house for $125,000, of which $100,000 is allocated to the house; the $25,000 balance is allocated to the land. In June 2010, you move out of the house and rent it. At that time, the fair market value of the house exclusive of the land is $150,000. The depreciable basis of the house is the lower adjusted basis of $100,000. The depreciation rate for placing the house in service in June is 1.970%, as shown in *Table 9-1*. Thus, your 2010 depreciation deduction is $1,970 ($100,000 × 1.970%). Your 2011 depreciation deduction is $3,636 ($100,000 × 3.636%).

Depreciating a rented cooperative apartment. If you rent out a co-op apartment, you may deduct your share of the total depreciation claimed by the cooperative corporation. The method for computing your share depends on whether you bought your co-op shares as part of the first offering. If you did, follow these steps: (1) Ask the co-op corporation officials for the total real estate depreciation deduction of the corporation, not counting depreciation for office space that cannot be lived in by tenant-shareholders. (2) Multiply Step 1 by the following fraction: number of your co-op shares divided by total shares outstanding. The result is your share of the co-op's depreciation, but you may not deduct more than your adjusted basis.

The computation is more complicated if you bought your co-op shares after the first offering. You must compute your depreciable basis as follows: Increase your cost for the co-op shares by your share of the co-op's total mortgage. Reduce this amount by your share of the value of the co-op's land and your share of the commercial space not available for occupancy by tenant-stockholders. Your "share" of the co-op's mortgage, land value, or commercial space is the co-op's total amount for such items multiplied by the fraction in Step 2 above, that is, the number of your shares divided by the total shares outstanding. After computing your depreciable basis, multiply that basis by the depreciation percentage for the month your apartment is ready for rental.

Basis to use when you sell a rented residence. For purposes of figuring gain, you use adjusted basis at the time of the conversion, plus subsequent capital improvements, and minus depreciation and casualty loss deductions. For purposes of figuring loss, you use the lower of adjusted basis and fair market value at the time of the conversion, plus subsequent improvements and minus depreciation and casualty losses. You may have neither gain nor loss to report; this would happen if you figure a loss when using the above basis rule for gains and you figure a gain when using the basis rule for losses.

Depreciation on a vacant residence. If you move from your house before it is sold, you generally may not deduct depreciation on the vacant residence while it is held for sale. The IRS will not allow the deduction, and, according to the Tax Court, a deduction is possible only if you can show that you held the house expecting to make a profit on an increase in value over and above the value of the house when you moved from it. That is, you held the house for sale on the expectation of profiting on a future increase in value after abandoning the house as a residence.

9.6 Renting a Residence to a Relative

The tax law distinguishes between a rental of a unit used by a close relative as a principal residence and a rental of a unit that is not the relative's principal residence, such as a second home or vacation home. It is easier to deduct a rental loss on the principal residence rental.

On a fair market rental of a unit used by the close relative as a principal residence, your relative's use is *not* considered personal use by you that could bar a loss under the personal-use test *(9.7)*. A relative's use of the unit as a second or vacation home *is* attributed to you in applying the personal-use test *(9.7)*, even if you receive a fair market value rent.

Close relatives who come within these rules are: brothers and sisters, half-brothers and half-sisters, spouses, parents, grandparents, children, and grandchildren.

Fair market rental is the amount a person who is not related to you would be willing to pay. The most direct way to determine fair market rental is to ask a real estate agent in your neighborhood for comparative rentals.

EXAMPLE

Barranti inherited a residence from her grandmother. The house was in a state of disrepair. A real estate agent estimated the fair market rental rate for the house to be between $700 and $750 per month. Barranti rented the house to her brother for $500 a month while he repaired the structure. After a year, he moved out and Barranti sold the house and claimed a rental loss and a loss on the sale. The Tax Court disallowed both losses. The below-market rental to Barranti's brother was treated as her own personal use of the house, preventing the rental loss deduction. The below-market rental was also treated as evidence that Barranti held the property for personal purposes and therefore she could not deduct the loss on the sale either.

9.7 Personal Use and Rental of a Residence During the Year

The number of personal-use days and fair-market-rental days for your residential unit determines how you must report rental income and expenses. If rental use exceeds 15 days and your personal use of the unit exceeds the 14 day/10% limit described below, the unit is treated as a residence rather than rental property. If it is treated as a residence, some of your rental expenses are deductible only to the extent of the rental income from the property *(9.9)*.

List your days of use in 2010:
Fair market rental days:_____________
Personal-use days:_______________

Personal-use days may also include rental days to family members listed at *9.6* and use days under co-ownership agreements. *See 9.8* for details on personal-use days.

The daily-use tests apply to any "dwelling unit" you rent out that is also used as a residence during the year by yourself or other family members. A dwelling unit may be a house, apartment, condominium, cooperative, house trailer, mini motor home, boat, or similar property with basic living accommodations, including any appurtenant structure such as a garage. A dwelling unit does not include property used exclusively as a hotel, motel, inn, or similar establishment.

The hotel/motel/inn exception applies only to property that is used exclusively in such a business. The exception does not apply to the dual-use portion of a hotel, inn, or bed and breakfast. In one case, the Tax Court agreed with the IRS that the owners of a three-floor bed-and-breakfast could not claim business expense deductions for depreciation or interest on the areas that were used both in the B&B business as well as by them personally. The lobby, registration area, office, kitchen, and laundry room were used 75% of the time for the business and 25% of the time for personal purposes. Because these areas were not used solely for operating the B&B, they could not qualify for the hotel exception. The dual-use areas were treated as part of the owners' dwelling unit for purposes of the 14-day/10% personal-use test.

Rented less than 15 days during the taxable year. If you rent the unit for fewer than 15 days in the taxable year, you do not report the rental income and the only deductions allowed are those you would be allowed anyway as a homeowner. That is, if you itemize deductions on Schedule A, you deduct mortgage interest, real estate taxes, and casualty losses, if any. No other rental expenses such as depreciation and maintenance expenses are deductible. Interest is generally fully deductible if the home qualifies as a first or second home under the mortgage interest rules discussed in *Chapter 15*.

14-day/10% personal-use test applies if unit rented 15 days or more in the taxable year. A daily-use test determines whether your use of the unit during the taxable year is treated as residential use that requires you to limit your deductions to the rental income under the rules governing the allocation of expenses of a residence to rental days *(9.9)*. You are considered to have used the unit as a residence if your personal-use days during the year, determined according to the rules for counting personal-use and rental days *(9.8)*, exceeded 14 days, or, if greater, 10% of the days on which the unit was rented to others at a fair market rental price.

When the unit is treated as a residence, rental expenses are deductible on Schedule E only to the extent of rental income, following the allocation rules *(9.9)*. Expenses not deductible in the current year under this limitation may be carried forward and will be deductible up to rental income in the following year. The deduction limit is irrelevant if your rental income exceeds expenses. You report the rental income and claim the deductible expenses on Schedule E.

If your personal-use days do not exceed 14 days or 10% of the fair market rental days, whichever is more, your rental deductions on Schedule E (Form 1040) are not limited to rental income by the personal-use test. However, a loss deduction is subject to the passive activity loss restrictions *(10.1)*. Furthermore, you lose part of the mortgage interest deduction because the unit is not a qualified second home for mortgage interest purposes if personal use does not exceed the greater of 14 days or 10% of the fair market rental days. The interest allocable to the rental use *(9.9)* is deductible against rental income on Schedule E, but the balance is nondeductible personal interest.

EXAMPLES

1. In 2010, you rented out a condominium unit in Florida at a fair market rental for 260 days. If you used the unit personally for 27 or more days, the condominium is considered a residence subject to the deduction limitation rules *(9.9)* because your personal use exceeds 26 days, 10% of the fair market rental days. If you used the unit for 26 days or less, you may treat the unit for the taxable year as rental property and you may deduct a loss, if any, subject to the passive activity rules *(10.1)*. *However, if personal use did not exceed 26 days, the mortgage interest allocable to the personal-use days would be nondeductible personal interest.*
2. Assume the same unit as in Example 1 but you rented the unit for 130 days. If you used the unit personally for 14 days or less, you may treat the unit as a rental property. To treat it as a residence, your personal use would have to exceed 14 days, since 14 days is greater than 10% of the rental days.

9.8 Counting Personal-Use Days and Rental Days for a Residence

In applying the 14-day/10% personal-use test *(9.7)*, personal-use days are:

- Days you used the residence for personal purposes other than days primarily spent making repairs or getting the property ready for tenants. If you use a residence for personal purposes on a day you rent it at fair market value, count that day as a personal day, not a rental day, in applying the 14-day/10% test.
- Days on which the residence is used by your spouse, children, grandchildren, parents, brothers, sisters, or grandparents. However, if such a relative pays you a fair rental value to use the home as a principal residence, the relative's use is not considered personal use by you. If you rent a vacation home to such relatives, their use is considered personal use by you even if they pay a fair rental value amount; *see* Example 1 below.

The same rules apply to days of use by a relative of a co-owner of the property.

- Days on which the residence is used by any person under a reciprocal arrangement that allows you to use some other dwelling during the year.
- Days on which you rent the residence to any person for less than fair market value.
- Days that a co-owner of the property uses the residence, unless the co-owner's use is under a shared-equity financing agreement discussed later in this section.

An owner is not considered to have personally used a home that is used by an employee if the value of such use is tax-free lodging required as a condition of employment *(3.13)*.

Shared-equity financing agreements for co-owners. Use by a co-owner is not considered personal use by you if you have a shared-equity financing agreement under which: (1) the co-owner pays you a fair rent for using the home as his or her principal residence; and (2) you and your co-owner each have undivided interests for more than 50 years in the entire home and in any appurtenant land acquired with the residence.

Any use by a co-owner that does not meet these two tests is considered personal use by you if, for any part of the day, the home is used by a co-owner or a holder of any interest in the home (other than a security interest or an interest under a lease for fair rental) for personal purposes. For this purpose, any other ownership interest existing at the time you have an interest in the home is counted, even if there are no immediate rights to possession and enjoyment of the home under such other interest. For example, you have a life estate in the home and your friend owns the remainder interest. Use by either of you is personal use.

Rental of principal residence prior to sale. You are not considered to have made any personal use of a principal residence that you rent or try to rent at a fair rental for (1) a consecutive period of 12 months or more *or* (2) a period of less than 12 months that ends with the sale or exchange of the residence. For example, you move out of your principal residence on May 31, 2010, offering it for rental as of June 1. You rent it from June 15 until mid-November, when you sell the house. Under the special rental period rule, your use of the house from January 1 until May 31, 2010, is *not* counted as personal use. This means that deductions for the rental period are *not* subject to the rental income limitation *(9.9)*.

EXAMPLES

1. A son rented a condominium in Florida to his parents, who split their time between the Florida apartment and the home they owned in Illinois. Although the parents paid a fair amount for the Florida condo, the son's rental deductions were limited by the IRS and the Tax Court to interest and real estate taxes that did not exceed the rental income. The parents' rental days were attributed to the son under the 14 day/10% rental day limit since the home in Illinois, and not the Florida apartment, was their principal residence.

2. You and your neighbor Joe are co-owners of a vacation condominium. You rent the unit out whenever possible; Joe uses the unit for two weeks every year. As Joe owns an interest in the unit, both of you are considered to have used the unit for personal purposes during those weeks.

Planning Reminder

Shared-Equity Financing Agreements

As an investor, you can help finance the purchase of a principal residence for a family member or other individual. The rental income you receive for your ownership share in the property may be offset by deductions for your share of the mortgage interest, taxes, and operating expenses you pay under the terms of the agreement, as well as depreciation deductions for your percentage share. Rental losses are subject to the passive loss restrictions in *Chapter 10*.

The other co-owner living in the house may claim itemized deductions for payment of his or her share of the mortgage interest and taxes.

3. You and your neighbor Tom are co-owners of a house under a shared-equity financing agreement. Tom lives in the house and pays you a fair rental price. Even though Tom has an interest in the house, the days he lives there are not counted as days of personal use by you because Tom rents the house as a main home under a shared-equity financing agreement.
4. You rent a beach house to Jane. Jane rents her house in the mountains to you. You each pay a fair rental price. You are using your house for personal purposes on the days that Jane uses it because your house is used by Jane under an arrangement that allows you to use her house.

Caution

Rental Pool Arrangements

Pool arrangements have been devised to avoid the loss restriction by attempting to increase the days the home is held for a fair rental value. They have not been successful. Courts have ruled that only days on which a home is actually rented count as fair rental days, not days of availability through the rental pool.

Rental pool arrangements. The IRS holds that a rental pool is not a basis for counting fair rental days. However, the proposed regulations permit rental pool participants to elect to average the actual rental of their units. Unanimous consent is required to elect the averaging rule. If the election is made, the number of rental days for a unit is determined by multiplying the aggregate number of days that all units in the rental pool were rented at fair rental during the pool season by a fraction. The numerator of the fraction is the number of participation days of a particular unit; the denominator is the aggregate number of participation days of all the units.

The IRS may apply the rental pool rule to a rental guarantee option. The Tax Court supported the IRS position, but an appeals court did not, in the following Example.

EXAMPLE

Razavi owned a condo in Florida and elected to take a rental guarantee option from the resort operator over a three-year period. The annual guaranteed rent was $21,000 plus 40% of rentals over $52,500. In 1987, the resort actually received gross rentals of $48,300 for the unit, but Razavi received $21,000 under the guarantee and claimed a rental loss deduction. The IRS disallowed the loss because it claimed that Razavi personally used the unit for 27 days, exceeding 10% of the 200 days the unit had actually been rented.

Razavi claimed that the 27 days were less than 10% of the 338 days covered by a rental guarantee. That is, the guarantee covered 365 days less 27 days of personal use. The Tax Court disagreed on the grounds that the guarantee was based on a rental period of between 142 days and 179 days and this was far below the 270 rental days needed to support his 27 personal-use days.

The Sixth Circuit allowed the loss. The $21,000 guarantee was a fair rental for the entire year based on rentals of comparable units. Although Razavi probably could have earned more than $21,000 with daily or weekly rentals, such short-term rentals also would have carried added risks and responsibilities that he was able to avoid by choosing the rent guarantee.

9.9 Allocating Expenses of a Residence to Rental Days

When you rent out your home or other dwelling unit *(9.7)* for part of the year at fair market value and also use it personally on some days during the taxable year, expenses are allocated between personal and rental use. By law, deductible rental expenses are limited by this fraction:

$$\frac{\text{Days of fair market rental}}{\text{Total days of rental and personal use}}$$

The days a unit is held out for rent but not actually rented are not counted as rental days. Any day for which the unit is rented at a fair rental price is counted as a rental day for allocation purposes even if in fact you use it for personal purposes on that day.

Mortgage interest and real estate taxes. There is a conflict of opinion between the IRS and some courts over the issue of whether the above fractional formula applies also to interest and taxes. According to the IRS, it does. According to the Tax Court and two federal appeals courts, interest and taxes are allocated on a daily basis. Thus, if a house is rented for 61 days in 2010, 16.71% ($^{61}/_{365}$) of the deductible interest and taxes is deducted first from the rental income. This rule allows a larger amount of other expenses to be deducted from rental income than is allowed under the IRS application of the formula; *see* Example 2 below.

Claiming expenses on Schedule E if personal use limits a loss deduction. If your personal use of a residence exceeds the 14-day /10% test *(9.7)*, the residence was rented for at least 15 days during the year, and the allocable rental expenses (including depreciation) exceed rental income, you cannot deduct the net loss from other income. Some of the expenses will not be currently deductible. The allocable rental expenses are deducted from rental income in a specific order:

Step 1. The rental portion of the following expenses is fully deductible on Schedule E of Form 1040, even if the total exceeds rental income: deductible home mortgage interest *(15.1)*, real estate taxes, deductible casualty and theft losses *(Chapter 18)*, and directly related rental expenses. Directly related rental expenses are rental expenses not related to the use or maintenance of the residence itself, such as office supplies, rental agency fees, advertising, and depreciation on office equipment used in the rental activity.

Step 2. If there is any rental income remaining after the income is reduced by the expenses in Step 1, the balance is next offset by the rental portion of operating expenses for the residence itself, such as utilities, repairs, and insurance. Do not include depreciation on the rental part of the home in this group.

Step 3. If any rental income remains after Step 2, depreciation on the rental portion of the residence may be deducted from the balance.

Step 1 expenses, as well as the expenses from Steps 2 and 3 that offset rental income, are deducted on the applicable lines of Schedule E. Operating expenses from Step 2 and depreciation from Step 3 that exceed the balance of rental income are carried forward to the next year as rental expenses for the same property. In the next year, the carried-over expenses are deductible only to the extent of rental income from the property for that year, following Steps 1–3, whether or not your personal use of the residence exceeds the 14-day/10% test *(9.7)* for that year.

If you itemize deductions, you claim the *personal-use* portion of deductible mortgage interest, real estate taxes, and casualty and theft losses on Schedule A of Form 1040.

Filing Tip

Carryover of Disallowed Expenses

If your deductions for operating expenses and depreciation are limited by the personal-use rules, the disallowed amounts may be carried over to the following year.

Interest expenses. If you personally use a rental vacation home for more than the greater of 14 days or 10% of the fair market rental days *(9.7)*, the residence may be treated as a qualifying second residence under the mortgage interest rules *(15.1)*. The interest on a qualifying second home is generally fully deductible and is not subject to disallowance under the passive activity restrictions in *Chapter 10*. As shown in Step 1 above, the portion of the deductible mortgage interest allocable to the rental portion is deducted from rental income (along with taxes) before other expenses.

EXAMPLES

1. You rent out your vacation home for June and July of 2010 (61 days), receiving rent of $2,000. You also use the home yourself for 61 days during the year. You may deduct expenses only up to the amount of rental income because your personal use exceeds the 14-day/10% rental test *(9.7)*. Your expenses are mortgage interest of $1,600, real estate taxes of $800, and maintenance and utility costs of $1,200. Depreciation (based on 100% rental use) is $1,500. Assume the vacation home is a qualifying second home *(15.1)*, so that all the interest is deductible under the mortgage interest rules. Under the IRS method, one-half of all the expenses (61 rental days divided by 122 total days of use), including the interest and taxes, are deducted in this order:

Rent income		$ 2,000
Less: Interest (½ of $1,600)	$ 800	
Taxes (½ of $800)	400	1,200
		$ 800
Less: Maintenance (½ of $1,200)		600
Less: Depreciation (½ of $1,500, or $750,		$ 200
limited to $200 balance of rental income)		$ 200

Under the Tax Court's method of allocating interest and taxes, 16.71% ($^{61}/_{365}$) of the interest and taxes would be deducted from rental income, rather than one-half as under the IRS method. The balance of interest and taxes is deductible as itemized deductions provided you claim itemized deductions on Schedule A of Form 1040.

Depreciation not deductible because of the rental income limitation may be carried forward to the following year.

If the vacation home were not a qualifying second residence as discussed in 15.1, the interest would not be deducted with taxes from the \$2,000 of rental income, but would be treated as an operating expense and deducted along with the maintenance expenses.

Court Decision

Allocation of Taxes and Interest

The IRS position on allocating mortgage interest and real estate taxes to rental income is not as favorable as the position adopted by the Tax Court and several appeals courts.

2. The Boltons paid interest and property taxes totaling \$3,475 on their vacation home. Maintenance expenses (not including depreciation) totaled \$2,693. The Boltons stayed at the home 30 days and rented it for 91 days, receiving rents of \$2,700. Because the personal use for 30 days exceeded the 14-day limit, the Boltons could deduct rental expenses only up to the gross rental income of \$2,700, reduced by interest and taxes allocable to rental. In figuring the amount of interest and taxes deductible from rents, they divided the number of rental days, or 91, by 365, the number of days in the year. This gave them an allocation of 25%. After subtracting \$869 for interest and taxes (25% of \$3,475) from rental income, they deducted \$1,831 (\$2,700 – \$869) of maintenance expenses from rental income.

   The IRS argued that 75% of the Boltons' interest and tax payments had to be allocated to the rental income. The IRS used an allocation base of 121 days of personal and rental use. Thus, the IRS allocated 75% ($^{91}/_{121}$) of the interest and taxes, or \$2,606, to gross rental income of \$2,700. This allocation allowed only \$94 maintenance expenses to be deducted (\$2,700 – \$2,606).

   The Tax Court sided with the Boltons and an appeals court (the Ninth Circuit) agreed. The IRS method of allocating interest and taxes to rental use is bizarre. Interest and taxes are expenses that accrue ratably over the year and are deductible even if a vacation home is not rented for a single day. Thus, the allocation to rental use should be based on a ratable portion of the annual expense by dividing the number of rental days by the number of days in a year.

   The Tenth Circuit appeals court also supports the Tax Court allocation method.

9.10 Rentals Lacking Profit Motive

If you rent a residential unit for 15 days or more and a loss is not barred under the personal-use limitation *(9.7)*, the IRS may attempt to disallow a loss by claiming that you had no profit motive in placing the unit up for rent. If the IRS makes such an argument, you must try to prove a profit motive *(40.10)*. Any loss disallowed on these grounds may not be carried over to a later year.

Planning Reminder

Profit Motive

A profit motive is presumed if you can show a profit for at least three of the last five years you engaged in rental activities. The IRS, however, may *rebut* this presumption, but there are ways to fight this rebuttal *(40.10)*.

EXAMPLES

1. *(Loss allowed.)* In 1973, Clancy purchased a house and land in a coastal resort area of California. Prior to the purchase, Clancy was told by a renting agent that he could expect reasonable income and considerable appreciation from the property. Previously, he had sold similar property in the same development at a profit. After the purchase, Clancy spent \$5,000 to prepare the house for rental, and gave a rental agency the exclusive right to offer the property for rent. The house was available for rent 95% of the time in 1973, and 100% of the time in 1974. However, rentals proved disappointing, totaling only \$280 in 1973 and \$1,244 in 1974, despite the active efforts of the agency to rent the property. However, the house did appreciate in value and was eventually sold at a profit of \$14,000. In 1973 and 1974, Clancy deducted rental expenses of approximately \$21,000, which the IRS disallowed. The IRS claimed that the house was not rental property used in a business. Furthermore, as Clancy knew that he could not make a profit from the rentals, he could not be considered to hold the property for the production of income.

   The Tax Court agreed that the expenses were not deductible business expenses. But this did not mean they were not deductible as expenses of income production. Although the rental income from the property was minimal, Clancy acquired and held the property expecting to make a profit on a sale. He had previously sold similar property at a profit and was told to expect considerable rental income as well as appreciation from the new house. Where an owner holds property, as Clancy did here, because he or she believes that it may appreciate in value, such property is held for the production of income. Further evidence that Clancy held the property to make a profit: He rarely used it for personal purposes and an agent actively sought to rent it.

2. *(Loss allowed.)* Nelson bought a condominium, hired a rental agent, and even advertised in the *Wall Street Journal* and *Indianapolis Star.* He also listed the unit for sale. During 1974, he was unable to rent the apartment but deducted expenses and depreciation of over $6,100, which the IRS disallowed. The IRS argued that he did not buy the unit to make a profit but to shelter substantial income from tax. The Tax Court disagreed. Although his efforts to rent were not successful in 1974, he was successful in later years in renting the unit. He rarely visited the apartment other than to initially furnish it. When he went on vacation, he went abroad or to other vacation spots.
3. *(Loss disallowed.)* The Lindows purchased a condominium that they rented out during the prime winter rental season. However, over an eight-year period their expenses consistently exceeded rental income. The Tax Court agreed with the IRS that expenses in excess of rental income were not deductible. Substantial, repeated losses, even after the initial years of operation, indicated that the operation was not primarily profit-oriented. The rental return during the prime rental season could not return a profit. Even if the condominium were fully rented for the entire prime rental season, annual claimed expenses would exceed rent income. The couple also used the unit for several months and intended to live there on retirement. They did not consider putting the unit up for sale with an agent. Finally, that they had detailed records of income and expenses did not prove a business venture. Records, regardless of how detailed, are insufficient to permit the deduction of what are essentially personal expenses.

IRS may challenge losses claimed on temporary rental before sale. If you are unable to sell your home and must move, it may be advisable to put it up for rent. This way you may be able to deduct maintenance expenses and depreciation on the unit even if it remains vacant. However, the IRS has disallowed loss deductions for rentals preceding a sale on the ground that there was no "profit motive" for the rental *(40.10)*. Courts have allowed loss deductions in certain cases.

EXAMPLES

1. The IRS and Tax Court disallowed a loss deduction for rental expenses under the "profit-motive rules" *(40.10)* where a principal residence was rented for 10 months until it could be sold. According to the Tax Court, the temporary rental did not convert the residence to rental property. Since the sales effort was primary, there was no profit motive for the rental. Thus, no loss could be claimed; rental expenses were deductible only to the extent of rental income. The favorable side of the Tax Court position: Since the residence was not converted to rental property, the owners could under prior law rules defer tax on the gain from the sale by buying a new home. An appeals court reversed the Tax Court and allowed both tax deferral and a loss deduction. The rental loss was allowed since the old home was actually rented for a fair rental price. Furthermore, the owners had moved and could not return to the old home, which was rented almost continuously until sold.
2. In 1976, a couple bought a condo apartment in Pompano Beach, Florida. In 1983, they decided to move and listed the unit for either sale or rent with a local real estate broker. Sale of the unit was difficult because of the saturation of the Florida real estate market. Rental of the unit was also difficult because the condominium association's rules barred the rental of condominium units on a seasonal basis. The unit remained unrented until it was sold in 1986 for a substantial gain. In 1984, the couple deducted a $9,576 rental loss ($7,596 for maintenance expenses and $1,980 for depreciation). The IRS disallowed the deduction as not incurred in a bona fide rental activity. The Tax Court allowed the deduction. The couple made an honest and reasonable effort to rent the condominium. Lack of rental income was caused by a slack rental market and the condominium association rules prohibiting short-term rentals.

9.11 Reporting Royalty Income

Royalties are payment for use of patents or copyrights or for the use and exhaustion of mineral properties. Royalties are taxable as ordinary income and are reported on Schedule E (Form 1040). Depletion deductions relating to the royalties are also reported on Schedule E. If you own an operating oil, gas, or mineral interest, or are a self-employed writer, investor, or artist, you report royalty income, expenses, and depletion on Schedule C.

Examples of Royalty Income

License fees received for use, manufacture, or sale of a patented article.

Renting fees received from patents, copyrights, and depletable assets (such as oil wells).

Authors' royalties including advance royalties if not a loan.

Royalties for musical compositions, works of art, etc.

Proceeds of sale of part of your rights in an artistic composition or book, for example, sale of motion picture or television rights.

Royalties from oil, gas, or other similar interests *(9.16)*. To have a royalty, you must retain an economic interest in the minerals deposited in the land you have leased to the producer. You usually have a royalty when payments are based on the amount of minerals produced. However, if you are paid regardless of the minerals produced, you have a sale that is taxed as capital gain if the proceeds exceed the basis of the transferred property interest. Bonuses and advance royalties that are paid to you before the production of minerals are taxable as royalty income and are entitled to an allowance for depletion. However, bonuses and advance royalties for gas and oil wells and geothermal deposits are not treated as gross income for purposes of calculating percentage depletion. If the lease is terminated without production and you received a bonus or advance royalty, you report as income previously claimed depletion deductions. You increase the basis of your property by the restored depletion deductions.

Planning Reminder

Passive Income Exception

Certain working oil and gas interests are exempt from the passive activity loss restrictions *(10.10)*.

9.12 Production Costs of Books and Creative Properties

Freelance authors, artists, and photographers may deduct their costs of producing original works in the years that the expenses are paid or incurred. The uniform capitalization rules that generally apply to property that you produce *(40.3)* do not apply.

You qualify for current expense deductions if you are self-employed and you *personally create* literary manuscripts, musical or dance scores, paintings, pictures, sculptures, drawings, cartoons, graphic designs, original print editions, photographs, or photographic negatives or transparencies. However, the exception to the uniform capitalization rules does not apply to, and thus current deductions are not allowed for, expenses relating to motion picture films, videotapes, printing, photographic plates, or similar items.

If you conduct business as an owner-employee of a personal service corporation and you are a qualifying author, artist, or photographer, the corporation may claim current deductions related to your expenses in producing books or other eligible creative works. Substantially all of the corporation's stock must be owned by you and your relatives.

Caution

Hobby Loss Restrictions

Authors and artists with expenses exceeding income may be barred by the IRS from claiming loss deductions *(40.10)*.

9.13 Deducting the Cost of Patents or Copyrights

If you create an artistic work or invention for which you get a government patent or copyright, you may depreciate your costs over the life of the patent or copyright. Basis for depreciation includes all expenses that you are required to capitalize in connection with creating the work, such as the cost of drawings, experimental models, stationery, and supplies; travel expenses to obtain material for a book; fees to counsel; government charges for patent or copyright; and litigation costs in protecting or perfecting title.

If you purchased the patent or artistic creation, depreciate your cost over the remaining life of the patent or copyright. If your cost for a patent is payable annually as a fixed percentage of the revenue derived from use of the patent, the depreciation deduction equals the royalty paid or incurred for that year. However, if a copyright or patent is acquired in connection with the acquisition of a business, the cost is amortizable over a 15-year period as a Section 197 intangible *(42.18)*.

If you inherited the patent or rights to an artistic creation, your cost is the fair market value either at the time of death of the person from whom you inherited it *(5.17)* or the alternate valuation date if elected by the executor. You get this cost basis even if the decedent paid nothing for it. Figure your depreciation by dividing the fair market value by the number of years of remaining life.

If your patent or copyright becomes valueless, you may deduct your unrecovered cost or other basis in the year it became worthless.

9.14 Intangible Drilling Costs

Intangible drilling and development costs (IDCs) refer to drilling and development costs of items with no salvage value, including wages, fuel, repairs, hauling, and supplies incident to and necessary for the preparation and drilling of wells for the production of oil or gas, and geothermal wells. For wells you are developing in the United States, you can elect to deduct the costs currently as business expenses or treat them as capital expenses subject to depreciation or depletion.

Electing current business deduction. The election to deduct IDCs as a current business expense must be made on your income tax return for the first tax year in which you pay or incur the costs. As a sole proprietor, you deduct the IDCs as "other expenses" on Schedule C (Form 1040).

Prepayments. Tax-shelter investors may deduct prepayments of drilling expenses only if the well is "spudded" within 90 days after the close of the taxable year in which the prepayment is made. The prepayment must also have a business purpose, not be a deposit, and not materially distort income. The investor's deduction is limited to his or her cash investment in the tax shelter. For purposes of this limitation, an investor's cash investment includes loans that are not secured by his or her shelter interest or the shelter's assets and loans that are not arranged by the organizer or promoter. If the above tests are not met, a deduction may be claimed only as actual drilling services are provided.

Amortizing intangible drilling costs. If you do not elect to deduct IDCs as current business expenses, you may amortize them on Form 4562 (Depreciation and Amortization) over a 60-month period, beginning with the month they were paid or incurred.

Caution

Drilling Expense Prepayments

Prepayments of drilling expenses are deductible by tax-shelter investors only if the well is "spudded" within 90 days after the close of the taxable year in which the prepayment was made, and the deduction is limited to the original amount of the investment.

Recapture of intangible drilling costs for oil, gas, geothermal, or mineral property. Upon the disposition of oil, gas, geothermal, or other mineral property placed in service after 1986, ordinary income treatment applies to previously claimed deductions for intangible drilling and development costs for oil, gas, and geothermal wells, and to mineral development and exploration costs. Depletion deductions *(9.15)* are also generally subject to this ordinary income treatment upon disposition of the property.

AMT and intangible drilling costs. If you are an independent producer or royalty owner, you may qualify for an exception to the AMT preference rules for IDCs, but the exception is limited. If your IDC preference (figured under the regular AMT rules) exceeds 40% of your alternative minimum taxable income, figured without regard to the AMT net operating loss deduction, the excess over 40% must be included as a preference item; *see* the instructions on Form 6251.

9.15 Depletion Deduction

Properties subject to depletion deductions are mines, oil and gas wells, timber, and exhaustible natural deposits.

Two methods of computing depletion are: (1) cost depletion and (2) percentage depletion. If you are allowed to compute under either method, you must use the one that produces the *larger* deduction. In most cases, this will be percentage depletion. For timber, you must use cost depletion.

Cost depletion. The cost depletion of minerals is computed as follows: (1) divide the total number of units (such as tons or barrels) remaining in the deposit to be mined into the adjusted basis of the property; and (2) multiply the unit rate found in Step 1 by the number of units for which payment is received during the taxable year if you are on the cash basis, or by the number of units sold if you are on the accrual basis.

Adjusted basis is the original cost of the property, less depletion allowed, whether computed under the percentage or cost depletion method. It does not include nonmineral property such as mining equipment. Adjusted basis may not be less than zero.

Timber depletion is based on the cost of timber (or other basis in the owner's hands) and does not include any part of the cost of land. Depletion takes place when standing timber is cut. Depletion must be computed by the cost method, not by the percentage method. However, instead of claiming the cost depletion method, you may elect to treat the cutting of timber as a sale subject to capital gain or loss treatment. For further details, *see* IRS Publication 535.

Percentage depletion. Percentage depletion is based on a certain percentage rate applied to annual gross income derived from the resource. In determining gross income for percentage depletion, do not include any lease bonuses, advance royalties, or any other amount payable without regard to production. A deduction for percentage depletion is allowed even if the basis of the property is already fully recovered by prior depletion deductions. The percentage to be applied depends upon the mineral involved; the range is from 5% up to 22%. For example, the maximum 22% depletion deduction applies to sulphur, uranium, and U.S. deposits of lead, zinc, nickel, mica, and asbestos. A 15% depletion percentage applies to U.S. deposits of gold, silver, copper, iron ore, and shale.

Taxable income limit. For properties other than oil and gas, the percentage depletion deduction *may not exceed* 50% of taxable income from the property computed without the depletion deduction. In computing the 50% limitation, a net operating loss deduction is not deducted from gross income. A 100% taxable income limit applies to oil and gas properties *(9.16)*.

Oil and gas property. Percentage depletion for oil and gas wells was repealed as of January 1, 1975, except for the following exemptions: (1) small independent producers and royalty owners and (2) for gas well production *(9.16)*.

9.16 Oil and Gas Percentage Depletion

Small independent producers and royalty owners generally are allowed to deduct percentage depletion at a 15% rate for domestic oil and gas production. The deduction is subject to a taxable income limit.

The 15% rate applies to a small producer exemption that equals the gross income from a maximum daily average of 1,000 barrels of oil or 6 million cubic feet of natural gas, or a combination of both. Gross income from the property does not include advance royalties or lease bonuses that are payable without regard to the actual production.

The depletable natural gas quantity depends on an election made annually by independent producers or royalty owners to apply part of their 1,000-barrel-per-day oil limitation to natural gas. The depletable quantity of natural gas is 6,000 cubic feet times the barrels of depletable oil for which an election has been made. The election is made on an original or amended return or on a claim for credit or refund. For example, if your average daily production is 1,200 barrels of oil and 6.2 million cubic feet of natural gas, your maximum depletable limit is 1,000 barrels of oil, which you may split between the oil and gas. You could claim depletion for 500 barrels of oil per day and for 3 million cubic feet of gas per day: 3 million cubic feet of gas is the equivalent of the remaining 500 barrels of oil limit (500 barrels × 6,000 cubic feet depletable gas quantity equals 3 million cubic feet of gas).

Transferees receiving "proven" properties after 1974 and before October 12, 1990, are not allowed percentage depletion unless the transfer was made because of the death of the prior owner, a tax-free transfer to a controlled corporation, a transfer between commonly controlled corporations, or changes in beneficiaries of a trust where the changes are due to births, adoptions, or deaths within a single family.

Ineligible retailers and refiners. The small producer exemption is not allowed to any producer who owns or controls a retail outlet for the sale of oil, natural gas, or petroleum products. A taxpayer is not treated as a retailer where gross sales of oil and gas products are less than $5 million in any one year or if all sales of oil or natural gas products occur outside the United States, and none of the taxpayer's domestic production is exported. Bulk sales of oil or natural gas to industrial or utility customers are not to be treated as retail sales.

The small producer exemption is not allowed to a refiner who refines (directly or through a related person) more than 75,000 barrels of crude oil on any day during the year. The limit is based on average (rather than actual) daily refinery runs for the tax year.

Figuring average daily domestic production. Average daily production is figured by dividing your aggregate production during the taxable year by the number of days in the taxable year. If you hold a partial interest in the production (including a partnership interest), production rate is found by multiplying total production of such property by your income percentage participation in such property.

The production over the entire year is averaged regardless of when production actually occurred. If average daily production for the year exceeds the 1,000-barrel or 6-million-cubic-feet limit, the exemption must be allocated among all the properties in which you have an interest.

Taxable income limits on percentage depletion. The percentage depletion deduction for a small producer or royalty owner may not exceed the *lesser* of (1) 100% of the taxable income from the property before the depletion allowance or (2) 65% of your taxable income from all sources computed without regard to the depletion deduction allowed under the small producer's exemption, any net operating loss carryback, and any capital loss carryback.

The above 100% limit was suspended for production from marginal production properties for taxable years starting after 1997 and before 2008, and for taxable years beginning in 2009. The legislation extending the suspension to 2009 did not include 2008. At the time this book went to press, the suspension of the 100% limit had not been extended beyond 2009; *see* the *e-Supplement at jklasser.com* for a legislation update.

Limitations where family members or related businesses own interests. The daily exemption rate is allocated among members of the same family in proportion to their respective production of oil. Similar allocation is required where business entities are under common control. This affects interests owned by you, your spouse, and minor children; by corporations, estates, and trusts in which 50% of the beneficial interest is owned by the same or related persons; and by a corporation that is a member of the same controlled group.

Depletion for marginal production. For independent producers and royalty owners with production from "marginal" wells, the 15% depletion rate is increased by 1% for each whole dollar that the "reference price" (the average annual wellhead price as estimated by the IRS) of domestic crude oil for the previous year was below $20 per barrel. However, since the reference price in recent years has been substantially over $20 per barrel, the basic 15% rate has applied for marginal production and this is likely to remain the case for the foreseeable future given high crude oil prices.

Chapter 10

Loss Restrictions: Passive Activities and At-Risk Limits

The passive activity laws were intended to discourage tax-shelter investments, but their reach goes beyond tax shelters to cover all real estate investors and persons who invest in businesses as "silent partners" or who are not involved full time in the business. The passive activity rules prevent an investor from deducting what the law defines as a passive loss from salary, self-employment income, interest, dividends, sales of investment property, or retirement income. Such losses are deductible only from income from other passive activities. Losses disallowed by the passive activity rules are suspended and carried forward to later taxable years and become deductible only when passive income is realized or substantially all of the activity is sold.

Casualty and theft losses are not passive losses unless they are of the type usually occurring in a business, such as shoplifting theft losses.

On your tax return, passive income items and allowable deductible items are reported as regular income and deductions. For example, rental income and allowable deductions are reported on Schedule E. However, before you make these entries, you may have to prepare Form 8582, which identifies your passive income and losses and helps you to determine whether passive loss items are deductible.

At-risk rules generally limit losses for an activity to your cash investment and loans for which you are personally liable, as well as certain nonrecourse financing for real estate investments. *See 10.17.*

10.1 Rental Activities

Rental activities (real estate or personal property) are *automatically* treated as passive unless you qualify as a real estate professional *(10.3)* or the rentals are considered by law to be business activity as discussed below. If "automatic" passive activity treatment applies, you may not deduct a rental loss against nonpassive income such as salary or investment income unless you can take advantage of the up-to-$25,000 allowance that applies to rental real estate losses *(10.2)*. Even where rental income or loss is not automatically treated as passive because you qualify as a real estate professional or because the activity is excluded from the rental category and treated as a business (*see* the list below), income or loss will still be "passive" unless you materially participate *(10.6)* in the business activity.

What is a rental activity? Except for activities specifically excluded from the rental category (*see* the list of rentals treated as businesses below), rentals include all activities in which a customer pays for the use of tangible property (real estate or personal property). Such activities include rentals of apartments and commercial office space (whether long- or short-term); long-term rentals of office equipment, automobiles, and/or a vessel under a bareboat charter or a plane under a dry lease (no pilot or captain and no fuel); and net-leased property. A property is under a net lease if the deductions (other than rents and reimbursed amounts) are less than 15% of rental income or where the lessor is guaranteed a specific return or is guaranteed against loss of income.

Rentals treated as business activity. Although rental activities are generally treated as "passive," the following six activities are excluded from the category of rental activity and thus losses from the activities are not deductible under the $25,000 rental real estate loss allowance *(10.2)*. The fact that these activities are not treated as rentals does not mean that the passive activity rules are inapplicable. Income or loss from these activities will still be treated as passive income or loss if you fail to meet one of the business material participation tests *(10.6)*.

1. **The average period of customer use of the property is seven days or less.** Short-term rentals of vacation units, autos, videocassettes, tuxedos, and hotel and motel rooms are *not* considered rental activities if the average period of customer use is seven days or less. You figure the average period of customer use for the year by dividing the aggregate number of days in all rental periods that end during the tax year by the number of rentals. Each period during which a customer has a continuous or recurring right to use the property is treated as a separate rental.

   A loss from a seven-day-or-less real estate rental activity is *not* eligible for the up-to-$25,000 loss allowance *(10.2)*. Since it is not treated as a real estate rental activity, it may not be included in the election to aggregate rental real estate activities under the real estate professional rules *(10.3)*.

Planning Reminder

Vacation Home Rentals

If you rent out a vacation unit for an average rental period of seven days or less at a loss, the loss is treated as a business loss deductible from nonpassive income if you meet the material participation tests *(10.6)*. If you do not materially participate, the loss is treated as a passive loss, deductible only from passive income. The loss does not qualify for the up-to-$25,000 rental loss allowance *(10.2)* because the property is not treated as rental property.

EXAMPLE

The Toups purchased a cottage in Callaway Gardens, a vacation resort south of Atlanta, Georgia. The unit was rented for short-term periods of seven days or less during the year to resort guests. The resort's operator was the sole managing and rental agent. Over a three-year period, they deducted net losses of $46,848. Under the seven-days-or-less rule, the activity was not a rental activity, but the IRS disallowed their losses as passive activity losses because they were passive investors who did not materially participate in the activity. The Toups argued that they materially participated, spending more than 300 hours each year preparing an annual budget and cash flow analysis and meeting with other owners to set rental fees and inspect the grounds.

The Tax Court sided with the IRS. The losses were passive because the Toups did not materially participate in the resort operation. They had nothing to do with running the resort on a day-to-day basis. Their activity was merely that of investors.

2. **The average period of customer use of the property is more than seven days but is 30 days or less, and you provide significant personal services.** Personal services include only services performed by individuals and do not include (a) services necessary to permit the lawful use of the property; (b) construction or repair services that extend the useful life of the property for a period substantially longer than the average period of customer use; and (c) services that are provided

with long-term rentals of high-grade commercial or residential real property such as cleaning and maintenance of common areas, routine repairs, trash collection, elevator service, and security guards.

Note: For purposes of Exceptions 1 and 2, if more than one class of property is rented as part of the same activity, average period of customer use is figured separately for each class. The average period of customer use (as explained in Exception 2) is multiplied by the ratio of gross rental income from that class to the total rental income from the activity; *see* the Form 8582 instructions.

3. **Regardless of the average period of customer use, extraordinary personal services are provided so that rental is incidental.** In a rare case, it may be possible to avoid the passive loss disallowance rule by showing that "extraordinary personal services" were provided to tenants who rented the space primarily to obtain these services. IRS regulations give as examples the use by patients of a hospital's room and board facilities, which is incidental to the medical services provided, and the use by students of school dormitories, which is incidental to the teaching services provided.

   In one case, an attorney and her husband, a medical doctor, convinced the Tax Court that they met the "personal services" exception by providing legal support services to law firms who leased office space from their LLC. The attorney supervised three clerical employees in providing legal support services to the tenant firms, which included client intake, answering phones and taking messages, conducting legal research, typing briefs and memoranda, binding briefs, photocopying, taking dictation, express mailing, process serving, filing documents at the courthouse and state capital, maintaining a file room, law library, and conference facilities, and providing coffee service. Her husband provided consulting services to the attorneys, reviewing medical malpractice cases, serving as an expert medical witness, helping the attorneys prepare for accreditation reviews of health-care organizations, and providing quality assurance trainings.

   Before the Tax Court, the tenant firms testified that these support services, particularly the legal research, were unique and that they would not have moved into the LLC's building without them. The Tax Court held that the LLC's leasing activity was not a rental activity under the extraordinary services exception, but the taxpayers still had to prove that they "materially participated" in the leasing/support activities to avoid passive loss disallowance for the rental losses. They did so by showing that at least 500 hours were spent working on the activity *(10.6)*.

4. **Rental is incidental to a nonrental activity.** A rental of property is excluded from the rental activity category if the property is held mainly for investment or for use in a business. A rental is considered incidental to an investment activity if the principal purpose of holding the property is to realize gain from its appreciation and the gross rental income from the property for the year is less than 2% of the unadjusted basis or fair market value of the property, whichever is less.

   A rental is incidental to a business activity if (1) you own an interest in the business during the year, (2) the rented property was predominately used in that business during the current year or during at least two of the immediately preceding five tax years, and (3) gross rental income from the property is less than 2% of the lower of the unadjusted basis of the property or its fair market value. Under test (2), a rental may qualify for the exception although it is not rented to the related business in the current year, so long as it was used in the business in two or more of the preceding five years.

EXAMPLE

Kyle Gail owns unimproved land with a fair market value of $400,000 and an unadjusted basis of $300,000. He holds it for the principal purpose of realizing gain from its appreciation. To help reduce the cost of holding the land, he leases it to a rancher for grazing purposes at an annual rental of $3,500. The gross rental income of $3,500 is less than 2% of the lower of the fair market value or the unadjusted basis of the land. The rental of the land is not a rental activity.

5. **Providing property to a partnership or S corporation that is not engaged in rentals.** If you own an interest in a partnership or S corporation and you contributed property to it as an owner, the contributed property is not considered a rental activity. For example, if as a partner you contribute property to a partnership, your distributive share of partnership income will not be considered as income from a rental activity. However, this exception will not apply if the partnership is engaged in a rental activity.

6. **The property is generally allowed for the non-exclusive use of customers during fixed business hours, such as operating a golf course.** The customers are treated as licensees, not lessees.

Grouping rental and nonrental business activities. Where you conduct rental as well as nonrental business activities, you may not group a rental activity with a nonrental activity, unless they form an appropriate economic unit and one of the activities is considered insubstantial in relation to the other. No guidelines are provided for determining what is "substantial" or "insubstantial."

Under an exception, a rental of property to a business may be grouped together with the business, although one activity is not insubstantial to the other, provided each business owner has the same proportionate ownership in the rental activity and the activities are an appropriate economic unit.

Real property rentals and personal property rentals. An activity involving the rental of realty and one involving the rental of personal property may not be treated as a single activity, unless the personal property is provided in connection with the real property or the realty is provided in connection with the personal property.

Planning Reminder

Rental of Personal Residence

Renting a personal residence is not treated as a passive rental activity if you personally use the home for more than the greater of (1) 14 days or (2) 10% of the days the home is rented for a fair market rental amount *(9.7)*. On Schedule E, you may claim a full deduction for the rental portion of real estate taxes and mortgage interest, assuming the home is a principal residence or qualifying second home under the mortgage interest rules *(15.1)*.

See 9.9 for limitations on deductions of other rental expenses.

10.2 Rental Real Estate Loss Allowance of up to $25,000

If you are not a real estate professional *(10.3)* but you actively participate by performing some management role in a real estate rental venture, you may deduct up to $25,000 of a real estate rental loss against your regular, nonpassive income such as wages. The allowance is phased out if your modified adjusted gross income (MAGI) is between $100,000 and $150,000. You generally take the allowance into account on Schedule E but Form 8582 is sometimes required *(10.12)*. If you are married filing separately, you are not eligible for the special loss allowance unless you lived apart for the entire year, and in that case, the allowance is limited to $12,500; *see* below.

The allowance applies only to real estate rentals not excluded from the rental category by the rules at *10.1*. For example, short-term vacation home rentals averaging seven days or less do not qualify for the allowance. The allowance applies only to real estate rentals, not to any rentals of equipment or other personal property.

A trust may not qualify for the $25,000 allowance. Thus, you may not circumvent the $25,000 ceiling or multiply the number of $25,000 allowances by transferring rental real properties to one or more trusts. However, an estate may qualify for the allowance if the decedent actively participated in the operation. The estate is treated as an active participant for two years following the death of the owner.

Married filing separately. If you file separately and at any time during the taxable year live with your spouse, you are not allowed to claim any allowance. If you are married but live apart from your spouse for the entire year and file a separate return, the $25,000 allowance and the adjusted gross income phase-out range are reduced by 50%. Thus, the maximum allowance on your separate return is $12,500 and this amount is phased out by 50% of MAGI over $50,000. Therefore, if your MAGI exceeds $75,000, no allowance is allowed.

Active participation test must be met. To qualify for the allowance, you must meet an *active participation* test. Having an agent manage your property does not prevent you from meeting the test, but you must show that you or your spouse participates in management decisions, such as selecting tenants, setting rental terms, and reviewing expenses. The IRS may not recognize your activity as meeting the test if you merely ratify your manager's decisions. You (together with your spouse) must also have at least a 10% interest in the property. Limited partners are not considered active participants and do not qualify for the allowance.

If a decedent actively participated in property held by an estate, the estate is deemed to actively participate for the two years following the death of the taxpayer.

Planning Reminder

Proving Management Activities

To take advantage of the $25,000 loan allowance, make sure you have proof of active management, such as approving leases and repairs.

EXAMPLES

1. You live in New York and own a condominium in Florida that you rent through an agent. You set the rental terms and give final approval to any rental arrangement. You also have final approval over any repairs ordered by the agent. You are an active participant and may claim the $25,000 rental allowance.
2. A married couple who owned a time-share interest in an ocean-front condominium rented the condo during their allotted period to vacationers. They claimed a rental loss that the IRS held did not qualify for the up-to-$25,000 allowance. Since the average rental period for their unit was seven days or less, the rentals were excluded from the category of rental activity; *see 10.1*.

Figuring the $25,000 allowance. First match income and loss from all of your passive rental real estate activities in which you actively participate. A net loss from these activities is then applied to net passive income (if any) from other activities to determine the $25,000 allowance. Keep in mind that rental income or loss from renting a personal residence is disregarded in figuring the $25,000 allowance if the rental is not a passive activity, which it is not if your personal use of the home during the year exceeds the greater of 14 days or 10% of the days the home is rented at a fair market rental amount *(9.7)*. The allowance may not be used against carryover losses from prior taxable years when you were not an active participant.

EXAMPLE

David Chung is single and for 2010 has a $90,000 salary, $15,000 income from a limited partnership, and a $26,000 loss from rental real estate in which he actively participated. The $26,000 loss is first reduced by the $15,000 of passive income from the partnership. Since he actively participated in the rental real estate activities, the remaining balance of the $11,000 rental loss can be deducted from his nonpassive salary income. David's loss allowance is not subject to phaseout (*see* below) because his modified adjusted gross income (MAGI) is under $100,000. The partnership income and rental loss, which are passive, are disregarded in figuring MAGI.

Phaseout of the allowance. The maximum loss allowance of $25,000 ($12,500 if married filing separately and living apart for the entire year) is reduced by 50 cents for every dollar of modified adjusted gross income (MAGI) over $100,000 (or $50,000 if married filing separately).

Modified adjusted gross income (MAGI). For purposes of the allowance phaseout, MAGI is adjusted gross income shown on your return, but you should disregard:

- Any passive activity income or loss.
- Any loss allowed for real estate professionals *(10.3)*.
- Taxable Social Security and railroad retirement payments *(34.3)*. For example, if your adjusted gross income on Form 1040 is $90,000, and that includes $5,000 of taxable Social Security benefits, your modified adjusted gross income is $85,000.
- Deductible IRA contributions *(Chapter 8)*.
- Deductible tuition and fees *(33.13)*.
- The deduction on Form 1040 for one-half of self-employment tax liability *(45.3)*.
- Deductible student loan interest *(33.13)*.
- Overall loss from a publicly traded partnership (*see* instructions to Form 8582).
- Excluded interest on U.S. savings bonds used for paying tuition in the year the bonds are redeemed. If you are allowed to exclude the interest from income for regular tax purposes *(33.4)*, the interest must still be included for purposes of the allowance phaseout.
- Employer-provided adoption assistance that is a tax-free fringe benefit *(Chapter 3)*. The assistance must be included in MAGI for purposes of applying the allowance phaseout rule.
- The domestic production activities deduction *(40.23)*.

A rental loss that is carried over because it exceeds the allowance may be deductible in a later year if you continue to meet the active participation rule.

Filing Tip

Rental Allowance Based on Income

If you are single or married filing jointly, the rental loss allowance is phased out when your modified adjusted gross income is over $100,000. For every dollar of income over $100,000, the loss allowance is reduced by 50 cents. When your modified adjusted gross income reaches $150,000, the allowance is completely phased out.

If modified AGI is–	Loss allowance is–
Up to $100,000	$25,000
110,000	20,000
120,000	15,000
130,000	10,000
140,000	5,000
150,000 or more	0

EXAMPLES

1. In 2010, Liz Blake had $120,000 in salary, $5,000 of partnership income from a limited partnership, and a $31,000 loss from a rental building in which she actively participates. She may deduct only $15,000 of the rental loss.The remaining $11,000 must be carried over to 2011.The $5,000 limited partnership income and the $31,000 rental loss are disregarded in figuring MAGI because they are passive. Her deduction and carryover are computed as follows:

Modified adjusted gross income	$ 120,000
Less: amount not subject to phaseout	$ 100,000
Amount subject to phaseout	$ 20,000
Phaseout percentage	50%
Portion of allowance phased out	$ 10,000
Maximum rental allowance offset	$ 25,000
Less: Amount phased out	$ 10,000
Deductible rental loss allowance in 2010	$ 15,000

Passive loss from rental real estate	$ 31,000
Less: Passive income from partnership	$ 5,000
Passive activity loss	$ 26,000
Less: Deductible rental loss allowance in 2010	$15,000
Carryover loss to 2011	$ 11,000

2. In 2011, Liz's modified adjusted gross income is below the phase-out range and she continues to actively participate in the rental building, which incurred a loss of $5,000. Under the allowance, she may deduct a rental loss of $16,000 (the current loss plus the carryover loss).

Real estate allowance for tax credits. On Form 8582-CR, a deduction equivalent of up to $25,000 may allow a credit that otherwise would be disallowed. You must meet the active participation test in the year the credit arose. The $25,000 allowance is generally subject to the regular MAGI phaseout rule.

To claim low-income housing and rehabilitation credits, you need not meet the active participation test. Furthermore, for rehabilitation credits and credits for low-income housing property placed in service before 1990, the phaseout for the $25,000 allowance starts at MAGI of $200,000 ($100,000 if married filing separately and living apart the entire year); thus, the deduction equivalent is completely disallowed when MAGI reaches $250,000 ($100,000 if married filing separately). The phaseout is figured on Form 8582-CR. There is no MAGI phaseout for low-income housing property placed in service after 1989, unless you have a pass-through interest in a partnership or S corporation that you acquired before 1990.

The *deduction equivalent* of a credit is the amount which, if allowed as a deduction, would reduce your tax by an amount equal to the credit. For example, a tax credit of $1,000 for a taxpayer in the 25% bracket equals a deduction of $4,000 and would come within the $25,000 allowance provided you actively participated. In the 25% bracket, the equivalent of a $25,000 deduction is a tax credit of $6,250 ($25,000 × 25%). Thus, if you have a rehabilitation credit of $7,000 and you are in the 25% bracket, the $25,000 allowance may allow you to claim $6,250 of the credit, while the balance of the credit would be carried forward to the following year.

If in one year you have both losses and tax credits, the $25,000 allowance applies first to the losses, then to tax credits from rental real estate with active participation, then to tax credits for rehabilitation or low-income housing placed in service before 1990, and finally to tax credits for low-income housing placed in service after 1989.

The allowance and net operating losses. If losses are allowed by the $25,000 allowance but your nonpassive income and other income are less than the loss, the balance of the loss may be treated as a net operating loss and may be carried back and forward; *see 40.18* for further details.

Planning Reminder

Tax Break for Real Estate Professionals

Proving professional status and material participation allows you to avoid passive loss limitations. You may improve your ability to meet the material participation tests in *10.6* by aggregating your rental real estate activities. However, you may not want to aggregate activities if you have passive losses from non–real estate activities and have rental income from an operation that, if treated as passive income, could be offset by the losses.

Also be aware that if you elect to group all of your rental real estate activities as one activity and later sell one of the rental properties, you will probably be unable to deduct suspended losses from that property because of the rule that requires "substantially all" of your interest in an activity (here, the combined activity) to be disposed of in order to deduct suspended losses *(10.13)*.

Caution

Consistent Treatment Required

Once you treat activities separately or group them together as a single activity, the IRS generally requires you to continue the same treatment in later taxable years. You can regroup activities only if the original treatment was "clearly inappropriate" or has become clearly inappropriate because of a material change in circumstances.

10.3 Real Estate Professionals

Real estate rental activities are automatically passive *(10.1)* for all taxpayers except qualifying real estate professionals. You qualify as a real estate professional if you meet both parts of Test 1 below. If you qualify, any rental real estate activity in which you materially participate (Test 2) is *not* a passive activity. Income or loss from the rental real estate is reported as nonpassive on Schedule E (Form 1040).

Test 1: Qualifying as a real estate professional. You must meet both of the following two activity tests for the tax year:

1. More than 50% of your personal services in all of your businesses must be performed in real property businesses in which you materially participate *(10.6)*. For this purpose, a real property business means any real property development, redevelopment, construction, reconstruction, acquisition, conversion, rental operation, management, leasing, or brokerage trade or business. Real estate financing is not included. Personal services performed as an employee are *not* treated as performed in a real estate business unless you are considered a "more than 5% owner" in the employer. That is, you must own more than 5% of the outstanding stock or more than 5% of total combined voting powers of all stock issued by the corporation. In a noncorporate employer such as a partnership, you must own more than a 5% capital or profit interest.
2. More than 750 hours of your services are in real property businesses in which you materially participate *(10.6)*.

For purposes of determining hours of material participation under (1) and (2) above, each interest in rental real estate property is treated as a separate activity unless you elect to treat all of your interests as one rental activity as discussed below. If, under the rules in *10.1*, you group a rental real estate activity with a business activity, that rental activity is not treated as rental real estate for purposes of the real estate professional rules.

Attorneys who specialize in real estate practice while participating in a rental business may not treat the legal practice as material participation for purposes of qualifying as real estate professionals.

For a married couple filing jointly, both the "50% of services test" and the "750 hours test" must be met by one of the spouses individually, without regard to the other spouse's services.

A closely held C corporation qualifies under the real estate professional rules if in a taxable year more than 50% of the gross receipts of the corporation are from a real property business in which the corporation materially participates *(10.15)*.

Test 2: Rental real estate activity material participation. If you qualify as a real estate professional under Test 1 above, you must still show that you materially participate *(10.6)* in your rental real estate activity(ies) to avoid passive activity treatment. If you have more than one rental real estate activity and elect to aggregate (*see* below), total participation in all of the activities is combined in applying the material participation tests in *10.6*. If an election to aggregate has not been made, material participation must be determined separately for each rental property.

Election to aggregate rental real estate activities. You may elect to aggregate all of your rental real estate activities for any year you qualify as a real estate professional by attaching a statement to your original tax return for that year. If you file your original return without the election, the IRS may allow an extension if the failure to include the election was inadvertent. For example, when a married couple qualified as real estate professionals but their tax preparer inadvertently failed to attach the required election statement to their joint return, the IRS in a private ruling gave them 60 days from the date of the ruling to file an amended return with the required statement.

The required election statement must contain a declaration that you are a qualifying real estate professional and are treating all of your rental real estate activities as a single activity under Internal Revenue Code Section 469(c)(7)(A). The election is binding for all future years in which you qualify as a real estate professional, even if there are intervening years in which you do not qualify. In the nonqualifying years, the election has no effect. You may not revoke the election in a later year unless there has been a material change in circumstances that you explain in a statement attached to your original return for the year of revocation. That the election no longer gives you a tax advantage is not a basis for a revocation.

EXAMPLE

Kosonen owned seven rental properties. In 1994, he worked on all his properties a total of 877 hours, which qualified him as a real estate professional. But he could not meet the material participation test for each of the individual properties. If he could aggregate the activities, the material participation test would be met for the combined activity, which would be treated as nonpassive, allowing him to deduct his net rental losses against nonpassive income.

On his 1994 return, he reported the losses from all the activities as an aggregate deduction and treated it as nonpassive. The IRS disallowed the deduction because he had not made a specific election to aggregate. Kosonen argued that by claiming on his return the total of his losses, he had put the IRS on notice that he was aggregating his rental activities.

The Tax Court disagreed. A specific election is required to put the IRS on notice that a taxpayer is a qualifying real estate professional making the election to aggregate rental activities. Reporting the net losses on his return as an aggregate active (nonpassive) loss was not enough because Kosonen could also have reported his net losses as active if he had materially participated in each of the seven activities and had not elected to aggregate.

If the election to aggregate is made and there is net income for the aggregated activity, the income may be offset by prior year suspended losses from any of the aggregated rental real estate activities regardless of which of the rental activities produced the income.

Rental loss allowance may apply to nonqualifying rental activity. A real estate professional may also be able to claim all or part of the $25,000 rental loss allowance *(10.2)*. For example, you are a real estate professional and meet the material participation test for one rental real estate activity but not for another and do not elect to aggregate. Losses from the nonqualifying activity can qualify for the rental allowance. Furthermore, suspended prior year losses from the qualifying activity may also be deductible under the rental loss allowance, as illustrated in the following Example.

EXAMPLE

Jane Morton owns a rental building in Manhattan and a rental building in Newark. In 2010, she qualifies as a real estate professional. She does not elect to treat the two buildings as one activity. She materially participates in the operations of the Manhattan building, which has $100,000 of disallowed passive losses from prior years and a $20,000 loss for 2010. She does not materially participate in the operation of the Newark building, which has $40,000 of rental income for 2010. Jane also has $50,000 of 2010 income from other nonpassive sources.

Because Jane materially participates in operating the Manhattan building, the $20,000 loss from the building for 2010 is treated as nonpassive and offsets $20,000 of the $50,000 nonpassive income from other sources.

Jane can also use $40,000 of the $100,000 prior year suspended losses from the Manhattan building to offset the $40,000 of passive rental income from the Newark building in 2009. Of the $60,000 remaining suspended loss, $25,000 may be deducted under the rental loss allowance provided Jane's MAGI is under $100,000, the phase-out threshold for the allowance *(10.2)*.

The rental loss allowance is deducted from the $30,000 of remaining nonpassive income ($50,000 – $20,000), leaving Jane with $5,000 of nonpassive income for 2010. The balance of suspended losses of $35,000 ($60,000 – $25,000 rental allowance) may be used in 2011 to offset income from the Newark building or passive income from other sources.

Interests in S corporations and partnerships. Your interest in rental real estate held by a partnership or an S corporation is treated as a single interest in rental real estate if the entity grouped its rental real estate as one rental activity. If not, each rental real estate activity of the entity is treated as a separate interest in rental real estate. However, you may elect to treat all interests in rental real estate, including the rental real estate interests held by an S corporation or partnership, as a single rental real estate activity.

If you hold a 50% or greater interest in the capital, income, gain, loss, deduction, or credit in a partnership or S corporation for the taxable year, each interest in rental real estate held by the entity is treated as a separate interest in rental real estate, regardless of the entity's grouping of activities. However, you may elect to treat all interests in rental real estate, including your share of the rental real estate interests held by the entities, as a single rental real estate activity.

Limited partners. Generally, a person who has a limited partnership interest in rental real estate must establish material participation by participating for more than 500 hours during the year (Test 1 in *10.6*) or meeting Test 5 or Test 6 in *10.6*. These material participation tests also generally apply if an election is made to aggregate limited partnership interests in rental real estate with other rental real estate interests. However, under a *de minimis* exception, these more stringent rules may be avoided if the election to aggregate is made and less than 10% of the gross rental income for the taxable year from all rental real estate activities is attributed to limited partnership interests. In such a case, you may make the election to aggregate all rental real estate activities and determine material participation for the aggregated activity under any of the seven material participation tests *(10.6)*.

10.4 Participation May Avoid Passive Loss Restrictions

To avoid passive activity treatment of income and loss from a business investment, you must show material participation in that activity. The word "activity" does not necessarily relate to one specific business. If you invest in several businesses, you may be able to treat all or some of those activities as one activity or treat each separately.

Determining aggregate or separate treatment for your activities is discussed in *10.5* and material participation tests are discussed in *10.6*.

For a rental activity, material participation tests apply only if you are trying to qualify for the passive activity exception for real estate professionals *(10.3)*. For other rental real estate operators or investors, an "active" participation test that requires only certain management duties may allow you to deduct rental losses of up to $25,000 *(10.2)*.

10.5 Classifying Business Activities as One or Several

If you are in more than one activity, determining aggregate or separate treatment is important for:

Deducting suspended losses when you dispose of an activity. If the activity is considered separate from the others, you may deduct a suspended loss incurred from that activity when you dispose of it. If it is not separate from the others, the suspended loss is deductible only if you dispose of substantially all of your investment *(10.13)*.

Applying the material participation rules *(10.6)*. If activities are separate and apart from each other, the material participation tests are applied to each activity separately. If the activities are aggregated as one activity, material participation in one activity applies to all.

Determining if you meet the 10% interest requirement for active participation *(10.2)*.

Grouping activities together. You may use any reasonable method under the facts and circumstances of your situation to determine if several business activities should be grouped together or treated separately. To be grouped together, the IRS says that the activities should be "an appropriate economic unit" for measuring gain or loss. For making this determination, the IRS sets these general guidelines: (1) similarities and differences in types of business; (2) the extent of common control; (3) geographic location; (4) the extent of common ownership; and (5) interdependencies among the activities. Interdependency is measured by the extent to which several business activities buy or sell among themselves, use the same products or services, have the same customers and employees, or use a single set of books and records.

The IRS will not require that all five factors be present for grouping for multiple activities.

Rental activities. Rental activities may not be grouped with business activities unless one of the exceptions discussed in *10.1* applies.

EXAMPLE

Lance Jones has a significant interest in a bakery and a movie theater at a shopping mall in Baltimore and in a bakery and a movie theater in Philadelphia. The IRS does not explain what constitutes a significant interest. In grouping his activities into appropriate economic units based on the relevant facts and circumstances, Jones could: (1) group the theaters and bakeries into a single activity; (2) place the two theaters into one group and the bakeries into a second group; (3) put his Baltimore businesses into one group and his Philadelphia businesses in another group; or (4) treat the two bakeries and two movie theaters as four separate activities.

Once he chooses a grouping, he must consistently use that grouping for all future years unless a material change makes the grouping inappropriate. His decision is also subject to IRS review and, if questioned, he must show the factual basis for his grouping.

IRS may regroup activities. The IRS may regroup your activities if your grouping does not reflect one or more appropriate economic units and a primary purpose of the grouping is to circumvent the passive loss rules.

EXAMPLE

Five doctors operate separate medical practices and also invest in tax shelters that generate passive losses. They form a partnership to operate X-ray equipment. In exchange for the equipment contributed to the partnership, each doctor receives limited partnership interests. The partnership is managed by a general partner selected by the doctors. Partnership services are provided to the doctors in proportion to their interests in the partnership and service fees are set at a level to offset the income generated by the partnership against individual passive losses. Under these facts, the IRS will not allow the medical practices and the partnership to be treated as separate activities as this would circumvent the passive loss limitations by generating passive income from the partnership to offset the tax-shelter losses. The IRS will require each doctor to treat his or her medical practice and interests in the partnership as a single activity.

Partnerships and S corporations. A partnership or S corporation must group its activities under the facts and circumstances test. Once a partnership or S corporation determines its activities, the partners or shareholders are bound by that decision and may not regroup them. The partners and shareholders then apply the facts and circumstances test to combine the partnership or S corporation activities with, or separate them from, their other activities.

Special rule for certain limited partners and limited entrepreneurs. A limited entrepreneur is a person with an ownership interest who does not actively participate in management. A limited entrepreneur or limited partner in films, videotapes, farming, oil and gas, or the renting of depreciable property generally may combine each such activity only with another of such activities in the same type of business, and only if he or she is a limited entrepreneur or partner in both. Grouping of such activities with other activities in the same type of business in which he or she is not a limited partner or entrepreneur is allowed if the grouping is appropriate under the general facts and circumstances test.

10.6 Material Participation Tests for Business

The IRS has seven tests for determining material participation in a business. Some tests require only a minimum amount of work, such as 500 hours a year, and others only 100 hours. You need to meet only one of the seven tests to qualify as a material participant. If you do, then the income and loss from that business is treated as *nonpassive*.

The tests apply whether you do business as a sole proprietor or in an S corporation or partnership. Losses and credits passed through S corporations and partnerships are subject to passive activity rules.

If you are a limited partner, the law presumes that you are not a material participant in the activities of the limited partnership, but IRS regulations provide a limited opportunity to show that you materially participate. Only three of the seven material participation tests are available to you; *see 10.11*.

Caution

Overcoming Investor Status

The IRS will not recognize time spent as an investor as "participation" unless you can show you are involved in daily operations or management of the activity. According to the IRS, this requires you to be at the business site on a regular basis. Even if you do appear daily, the IRS may ignore such evidence if there is an on-site manager or you have full-time business obligations at another site. Activity of an investor includes the studying and reviewing of financial reports for your own use that are considered unrelated to management decisions. If you invest in a business that is out of state or a distance from your home, you may also find it difficult to prove material participation.

Your tax position towards the IRS participation rules will depend on whether the particular activity produces income or loss. If you have passive activity losses from other activities, you may prefer to have a profitable business activity treated as a passive activity in order to offset the income by the losses from passive activities. On the other hand, if the business activity operates at a loss and you do not have passive income from other sources, you may want to meet the material participation test for that business activity in order to claim current loss deductions. IRS strategy in reviewing your activities would be the opposite. If your return were under audit, an agent would attempt to prevent you from treating income from a business activity as passive. For example, the IRS, by applying Tests 5 and 6, can prevent a retired person from treating post-retirement income from a prior business or profession as passive income to offset passive losses from another activity. If you realize a loss in one passive activity, Test 4 may prevent you from generating passive income by merely reducing your participation in another activity.

Planning Reminder

Proof of Material Participation

Material participation must be determined on an annual basis. Show proof of your participation by keeping an appointment book, calendar, or log of the days and time spent in the operation. If you want to treat contacts by phone as material activity, keep a log of phone calls showing the time and purpose of the calls.

Material participation results in nonpassive treatment. There are two key terms: material participation and significant participation. If you materially participate by meeting one of the seven IRS tests, your activity is not a passive activity. For example, under Test 1, work for more than 500 hours in an activity is considered material participation. Under Test 4, significant participation is work for more than 100 hours but less than 500 hours at an activity in which you do not otherwise materially participate. The IRS applies a significant participation rule to convert passive activity income into nonpassive income and to convert several significant participation activities into material participation if the total participation in those activities exceeds 500 hours; *see* Test 4.

IRS Tests for Material Participation

If you meet one of the following tests for the year in question, you are considered to have materially participated in that activity, and therefore the activity is considered *nonpassive* for that year. Tests 5 and 6 prevent retired individuals from treating post-retirement income as passive income.

Rules for limited partners and members of LLCs and LLPs are at *10.11*. For participation rules for personal service and closely held corporations, *see 10.15*.

Work by you or your spouse that counts as participation. Apart from the exceptions listed below, any work you do in a business in which you have an ownership interest is treated as "participation." If you are married, work by your spouse in the activity during the tax year is generally treated as participation by you. This is true even if your spouse does not own an interest in the business or if you file separately. However, this favorable spousal participation rule does *not* apply if you and your spouse elect to treat your jointly owned business as a qualified joint venture, thereby requiring each of you to file a separate Schedule C on which your respective shares of the business income, deductions, credits, gains, and losses are reported; *see* the Schedule C instructions.

Do not count the following types of work as participation:

1. Work that is not of a type customarily done by an owner of an activity, if one of the principal reasons for the performance of the work is to avoid the passive loss rules (*see* the Example below).
2. An investor's review of financial statements or analysis that is unrelated to day-to-day management or operation of the activity.

EXAMPLE

An attorney owns an interest in a professional football team for which he performs no services. He anticipates a net loss from the football activity and to qualify as a material participant, he hires his wife to work 15 hours a week as an office receptionist for the team. Although a spouse's participation in an activity generally qualifies as participation by both spouses, the receptionist work here does not qualify as participation because (1) it is not the type of work customarily done by an owner of a football team and (2) the attorney hired his spouse to avoid disallowance of a passive loss.

Test 1. You participate in the activity for more than 500 hours during the tax year.

Test 2. Your participation in the activity for the tax year constitutes substantially all of the participation in the activity of all individuals including non-owners for the year.

Test 3. You participate in the activity for more than 100 hours during the tax year, and your participation is at least as great as that of any other person including non-owners for that year.

EXAMPLE

Joan Brown and Pat Collins are partners in a moving van business that they conduct entirely on weekends with the help of two employees. They both work for eight hours each weekend. Although neither partner participates for more than 500 hours (Test 1) and do not meet Test 2, they are both treated as material participants under Test 3 because they each participate for more than 100 hours and no one else participates more.

Test 4. You are active in several enterprises but each activity does not in itself qualify as material participation. However, if you spend more than 100 hours in each activity and the total hours of these more-than-100-hour activities exceeds 500, you are treated as a material participant in each of these activities. This test is referred to as the "significant participation" test.

EXAMPLES

1. Mike Smith is a full-time accountant with ownership interests in a restaurant and shoe store. He works 150 hours in the shoe store and 360 hours in the restaurant. Under the significant participation test (Test 4), Smith is considered a material participant in both activities, as the total hours of both exceed 500.
2. Carl Young invests in five businesses. In activity (a) he works 110 hours; in activity (b), 100 hours; in activity (c), 125 hours; in activity (d), 120 hours; and in activity (e), 140 hours. He does not qualify under the significant participation test (Test 4). Although his total hours in the five activities exceed 500, activity (b) is ignored in the total count because the hours did not exceed 100. The total of the four other activities is 495.
3. Assume that Young worked one hour more for activity (b). It and all of the other activities would be considered as meeting the significant material participation test. The total hours are 596. Assuming that activity (a) totaled 125 hours and activity (b) remained at 100 hours or less, he would meet the test for all of the activities except for activity (b), which did not exceed 100 hours. The total of the four qualified activities is 510 hours.

Caution

Retired Farmers

Retired or disabled farmers are treated as materially participating in a farming activity if they materially participated for five of the eight years preceding their retirement or disability. A surviving spouse is also treated as materially participating in a farming activity if the real property used in the activity meets the estate tax rules for special valuation of farm property passed from a qualified decedent and the surviving spouse actively manages the farm.

Test 5. You materially participated in the activity for any five tax years during the 10 tax years preceding the tax year in question. The five tax years do not have to be consecutive. Thus, if you are retired but meet the five-out-of-10-year participation test, you are currently considered a material participant, with the result that net income is treated as nonpassive, rather than passive. If you retired from a personal service profession, an even stricter rule applies; *see* Test 6.

Test 6. In a personal service activity, you materially participated for any three tax years preceding the tax year in question. The three years do not have to be consecutive. Examples of personal services within this test are the professions of health, law, engineering, architecture, accounting, actuarial science, the performing arts, consulting, or any other trade or business in which capital is not a material income-producing factor.

Test 7. Under the facts and circumstances test, you participate in the activity on a regular, continuous, and substantial basis. *According to the IRS, you do not come within this test if you participate less than 100 hours in the activity.*

10.7 Tax Credits of Passive Activities Limited

You may generally not claim a tax credit from a passive activity unless you report and pay taxes on income from a passive activity. Furthermore, the tax allocated to that income must be at least as much as the credit. If the tax credit exceeds your tax liability on income allocable to passive activities, the excess credit is not allowed. Use Form 8582-CR to figure the allowable credit. Suspended credits are not allowed when property is disposed of. The credits may be used only when passive income is earned.

EXAMPLE

Ben Wall has a $1,000 credit from a passive activity. He does not report income from any passive activity. He may not claim the credit because no part of his tax is attributed to passive activity income. The credit is suspended until he has income from a passive activity and he incurs tax on that income. All or part of the credit may then be claimed to offset the tax. If he disposed of his interest before using a suspended credit, the credit may no longer be claimed but the election to reduce basis, discussed below, could be made.

Credits for real estate activities. More favorable tax credit rules apply to real estate activities *(10.2)*.

Basis adjustment for suspended credits. If the basis of property was reduced by tax credits, you may elect on Form 8582-CR to add back a suspended credit to the basis when your entire interest in an activity is disposed of. If the property is disposed of in a transaction that is not treated as a fully taxable disposition *(10.13)*, then no basis adjustment is allowed.

EXAMPLE

Mark places in service rehabilitation credit property and claims an allowable credit of $50, which also reduces basis by $50. However, under the passive loss rule, he is prevented from claiming the credit. In a later year, he disposes of his entire interest in the activity, including the property whose basis was reduced. He may elect to increase basis of the property by the amount of the original basis adjustment.

10.8 Determining Passive or Nonpassive Income and Loss

The purpose of the passive loss rules is to prevent you from deducting passive losses from nonpassive income. Passive losses are losses from business activities in which you do not materially participate *(10.6)* or losses from rental activities that are not deductible under the $25,000 allowance *(10.2)* or which do not qualify you as a real estate professional *(10.3)*. In some cases passive income may be recharacterized as nonpassive income *(10.9)*.

Where you do not materially participate in a business activity, passive income or loss is determined by matching income and expenses of that activity. Portfolio income (*see* below) earned by the activity or any pay that you earn is not included to determine passive income or loss.

1040 *Filing Tip*

Portfolio Income Accounting

You cannot deduct passive losses from portfolio income. The tax law broadly defines "portfolio income" to include nonbusiness types of income including interest, dividends, and profits on the sale of investment property.

Portfolio income. Portfolio income is nonpassive income and broadly defined as income that is not derived in the ordinary course of business of the activity. Portfolio income includes interest, dividends, annuities, and royalties from property held for investment. However, interest income on loans and investments made in the business of lending money or received on business accounts receivable is generally not treated as portfolio income; *see 10.9* for special recharacterization rules. Similarly, royalties derived from a business of licensing property are not portfolio income to the person who created the property or performed substantial services or incurred substantial costs.

Portfolio income also includes gains from the sale of properties that produce portfolio income or are held for investment.

Expenses allocable to portfolio income, including interest expenses, do not enter into the computation of passive income or loss.

Sale of property used in activity. Gain realized on the sale of property used in the activity is generally treated as passive activity income if at the time of disposition the activity was passive. Under this rule, if you transact an installment sale, the treatment of installment payments depends on your status at the time of the initial sale. If you were not a material participant in the year of sale, installment payments in a later year are treated as passive income, even if you become a material participant in the later year. However, an exception to the year-of-sale status rule applies to certain sales of property formerly used in a passive activity *(10.16)*.

Installment payments from a pre-1987 installment sale are treated as passive income if the activity would have been considered passive had the passive activity rules been in effect before 1987.

Although gain on the sale of property is generally passive income if the activity is passive at the time of sale, there is an exception that could recharacterize the gain as nonpassive income if the property was formerly used in a nonpassive activity *(10.16)*.

Compensation for personal services is not passive activity income. The term "compensation for personal services" includes only (1) earned income, including certain payments made by a partnership to a partner and representing compensation for the services of the partner; (2) amounts included in gross income involving the transfer of property in exchange for the performance of services; (3) amounts distributed under qualified plans; (4) amounts distributed under retirement, pension, and other arrangements for deferred compensation of services; and (5) Social Security benefits includible in gross income.

Passive activity gross income also does not include (1) income from patent, copyright, or literary, musical, or artistic compositions, if your personal efforts significantly contributed to the creation of the property; (2) income from a qualified low-income housing project; (3) income tax refunds; and (4) payments on a covenant not to compete.

Passive activity deductions. Deductible expenses that offset passive income of an activity must be related to the passive activity, such as real property taxes. The following are not considered passive activity deductions:

Casualty and theft losses if similar losses do not recur regularly in the activity.

Charitable deductions.

Miscellaneous itemized deductions subject to the 2% AGI floor.

State, local, and foreign income taxes.

Carryovers of net operating losses or capital losses.

Expenses clearly and directly allocable to portfolio income.

Loss on the sale of property producing portfolio income.

Loss on the sale of your entire interest in a passive activity to an unrelated party. The loss is allowed in full *(10.13)*.

Interest deductions. Interest expenses attributable to passive activities are treated as passive activity deductions and are not subject to the investment interest limitations. For example, if you have net passive loss of $100, $40 of which is of interest expense, the entire $100 is a passive loss. $40 of the loss is not subject to the investment interest limitation *(15.10)*. Similarly, income and loss from passive activities generally are not treated as investment income or loss in figuring the investment interest limitation.

EXAMPLE

As an employee of his S corporation, Hillman provided real estate management services to rental real estate partnerships in which he had invested. On his personal return, he reported the management fees as passed-through S corporation income and deducted his allocable share of the fee payments by the partnership. The IRS disallowed the deduction: Since Hillman materially participated in the S corporation but not the partnerships, the fee payments by the partnerships were passive activity expenses that could not be deducted against the S corporation's nonpassive fee income. The fact that IRS regulations allow a deduction for self-charged interest does not mean that other self-charged passive expenses should also be deductible.

The Tax Court agreed with Hillman that there is no difference between interest and other self-charged expenses. The legislative history indicates a Congressional intent to allow deductions for self-charged expenses because they do not result in a net accretion to the taxpayer's wealth.

However, the Fourth Circuit, while sympathetic to Hillman's situation, reversed the Tax Court. Nothing in the tax law allows self-charged expenses to be deducted against nonpassive income. Although there is no reason why management fees should be distinguished from interest, the legislative history on self-charged expenses specifically mentioned only interest as an exception to the general statutory rule. The Congressional Committee reports that gave the IRS discretion to provide a deduction for other self-charged expenses did not limit that discretion. Unless the IRS changes its regulations, relief must come from Congress. The Fourth Circuit noted that while the denial of a deduction in this situation appears harsh, the deduction is not completely lost; the fee payments may be carried forward to later years as a passive expense.

After the Fourth Circuit ruled against him, Hillman went back to the Tax Court and tried an alternative argument in an attempt to deduct the management fees paid by the partnerships. He argued that the fees were nonpassive deductions that could offset the nonpassive income from the S corporation because the payment of the fees, by itself, constituted a separate business distinguishable from the passive rental activities of the partnerships. The Tax Court disagreed. The management fees were incurred in connection with the rental activities and thus were passive deductions. The Tax Court again acknowledged the unfairness of denying a deduction for the "self-charged" fees. Hillman's plight is lamentable, but as the Fourth Circuit ruled, relief can only come from Congress if the IRS does not liberalize its regulation on self-charged expenses.

If you rent out a vacation home that you personally use for more than the greater of 14 days or 10% of the fair market rental days *(9.7)*, you may treat the residence as a qualified second residence under the mortgage interest rules *(15.1)*. Interest on such a qualifying second home is generally fully deductible, and the deductible interest *(15.1)* is not treated as a passive activity deduction. The rental portion of the interest is deducted on Schedule E of Form 1040 and the personal-use portion on Schedule A if itemized deductions are claimed *(9.9)*.

Self-charged management fees or interest. For an individual with interests in several business entities, the payment of management fees by one of the entities to another is in effect a payment by the owner to himself. However, if the taxpayer materially participates in the entity providing the management services but not in the entity that pays the fees, the passive loss rules prevent the "self-charged" expense from offsetting the nonpassive fee income. IRS final regulations allow a netting deduction *only* for self-charged interest but not for any other self-charged expense.

10.9 Passive Income Recharacterized as Nonpassive Income

There is an advantage in treating income as passive income when you have passive losses that may offset the income. However, the law may prevent you from treating certain income as passive income. The conversion of passive income to nonpassive income is technically called "recharacterization." This may occur when you do not materially participate in the business activity, but are sufficiently active for the IRS to consider your participation as significant. Recharacterization may also occur when you rent property to a business in which you materially participate, rent nondepreciable property, or sell development rental property.

Caution

"Recharacterization" of Passive Income

Gain on the sale of property used in a passive activity may be recharacterized as nonpassive income if the property was formerly used in a nonpassive activity *(10.16)*.

Significant participation. The IRS compares income and losses from all of your activities in which you work more than 100 hours but less than 500 and that are not considered material participation under the law. If you show a net aggregate gain, part of your gain is treated as nonpassive income according to the computation illustrated in the following Example.

EXAMPLE

Carol Warren invests in three business activities—A, B, and C. She does not materially participate in any of the activities during the year but participates in Activity A for 105 hours, in Activity B for 160 hours, and in Activity C for 125 hours. Her net passive income or loss from the three activities is:

	A	B	C	Total
Passive activity gross income	$600	$700	$900	$2,200
Passive activity deductions	(200)	(1,000)	(300)	(1,500)
Net passive activity income	$400	($300)	$600	$700

Carol's passive activity gross income from significant participation passive activities of $2,200 exceeds passive activity deductions of $1,500. A ratable portion of her gross income from significant participation activities with net passive income for the tax year (Activities A and C) is treated as gross income that is not from a passive activity. The ratable portion is figured by dividing:

1. The excess of her passive activity gross income from significant participation over passive activity deductions from such activities (here $700) by
2. The net passive income of only the significant participation passive activities having net passive income (here $1,000). The ratable portion is 70%.

Thus, $280 of gross income from Activity A ($400 x 70%) and $420 of gross income from Activity C ($600 x 70%) is treated as nonpassive gross income. This adjustment prevents $700 from being offset by passive losses from another activity.

Net interest income from passive equity-financed lending. Gross income from "equity-financed lending activity" is treated as nonpassive income to the extent of the lesser of the equity-financed interest income or net passive income. An activity is an "equity-financed lending activity" for a tax year if (1) the activity involves a trade or business of lending money and (2) the average outstanding balance of the liabilities incurred in the activity for the tax year does not exceed 80% of the average outstanding balance of the interest-bearing assets held in the activity.

Incidental rental of property by development activity. Where gains on the sale of rental property are attributable to recent development, passive income treatment may be lost if the sale comes within the following tests: (1) the rental started less than 12 months before the date of disposition; and (2) you materially participated or significantly participated in the performance of services enhancing the value of the property. The 12-month period starts at the completion of the development services that increased the property's value.

Self-rental rule: Renting to your business. If you rent a building to your business, the rental income, normally treated as passive income, may be recharacterized by the IRS as nonpassive income where you also have losses from other rentals. Recharacterization prevents you from deducting the rental losses against the net rental income. Although not specifically written into the law, the recharacterization rules are incorporated in IRS regulations. For the recharacterization rule to apply, you must "materially participate" in the business renting the property; *see* the following Examples. The Tax Court and several federal appeals courts have upheld the IRS recharacterization rule.

Caution

Property Rented to Nonpassive Activity (Self-Rental Property)

You may not generate passive income by renting property to a business in which you materially participate. *See* "Self-rental rule: Renting to your business" in this section.

EXAMPLES

1. Krukowski, an attorney who operated two businesses through wholly owned C corporations, claimed that the IRS's recharacterization regulations were arbitrary and capricious. He rented personally owned buildings to the corporations, one of which ran a health club and the other the attorney's law firm. He reported net income of $175,149 from the rental to the law firm and a $69,100 net loss from the rental to the health club. He deducted the loss from the income and reported net rental income of $106,049. The IRS disallowed the loss offset by recharacterizing the rental income from the law firm as nonpassive income. Recharacterization could be applied under the regulations because the time spent by the attorney in the law firm was material participation. The attorney had to report rental income of $175,149; the health club rental loss was treated as a "suspended" passive loss.

   Before the Tax Court, the attorney claimed that the recharacterization rule was arbitrary and contrary to the passive loss statute. The Court disagreed. The law authorizes the IRS to write regulations interpreting the law. Further, Congressional committee reports contemplate that the IRS would define nonpassive income in such a way as to prevent a taxpayer from offsetting active business income with passive business losses.

   The Seventh Circuit Court of Appeals affirmed the Tax Court. The IRS was given authority by Congress to enact the self-rental rule as a way of eliminating tax shelters. Three other appeals courts, the First, Fifth, and Ninth Circuits, have also upheld the IRS regulation.

2. Carlos argued that he could avoid the IRS's self-rental rule by grouping together *(10.5)* as a single rental activity two rental properties. He operated a steel company and a restaurant through wholly owned S corporations. He leased one of his personally owned buildings to the steel company and another to the restaurant. He had substantial rental income from the steel company lease but a loss on the restaurant lease because the restaurant did not pay the agreed upon rent. On his tax returns for 1999 and 2000, Carlos grouped both properties together as a single activity and on Schedule E netted the loss from the restaurant rental against the net income from the steel company rental.

   Applying the self-rental rule, the IRS required the income from the steel company rental to be reported, while disallowing the losses from the restaurant rental. The income from the steel company rental that would otherwise be treated as passive was recharacterized as nonpassive income since Carlos materially participated in the steel company. After the recharacterization, there was no passive income to be offset by the passive losses from the restaurant rental. The passive losses can be carried forward.

   The Tax Court rejected Carlos's argument that his grouping of passive income and loss within a single activity precluded application of the self-rental recharacterization rule. To allow netting in this situation would defeat Congressional intent that a taxpayer not be able to use self-rentals as a means of sheltering nonpassive income from an active business with passive losses.

Rental of property with an insubstantial depreciable basis. This rule prevents you from generating passive rental income with vacant land or land on which a unit is constructed that has a value substantially less than the land. If less than 30% of the unadjusted basis *(5.16)* of rental property is depreciable, and you have net passive income from rentals (taking into account carried-over passive losses from prior years), the net passive income is treated as nonpassive income.

EXAMPLES

1. A limited partnership buys vacant land for $300,000, constructs improvements on the land at a cost of $100,000, and leases the entire property. After the rental period, the partnership sells the property for $600,000, realizing a gain. The unadjusted basis of the depreciable improvements of $100,000 is only 25% of the basis of the property of $400,000. The rent and the gain allocated to the improvements are treated as nonpassive income.
2. Shirley offset a passive rental loss from an investment in a limited partnership, LP, which was a substantial owner of a general partnership, GP, against rental income from an investment in a joint venture, JV. JV had leased to GP land on which GP constructed a shopping center. The IRS held that the rental income from JV was nonpassive rental income within the 30% test and could not be offset by the passive rental loss. The Tax Court agreed and also rejected Shirley's attempt to aggregate her investment activities in JV and LP as one activity. The operations of each group, JV, LP, and GP, were separate and not owned by the same person. She was not the direct owner of any of the units. Further, the aggregation rule does not apply to property falling within the 30% test.

Licensing of intangible property. Your share of royalty income in a partnership, S corporation, estate, or trust is treated as nonpassive income if you invested after the organization created the intangible property, performed substantial services, or incurred substantial costs in the development or marketing of it. *See* Publication 925 for further details.

10.10 Working Interests in Oil and Gas Wells

Planning Reminder

Limited Liability for Oil or Gas Well

A working interest in an oil or gas well is exempt from the passive activity restrictions if your liability is unlimited. The following forms of loss protection are disregarded and, thus, are not treated as limiting your liability: protection against loss by an indemnification agreement; a stop-loss agreement; insurance; or any similar arrangement or combination of agreements.

Working interests are not treated as passive activities provided your liability is not limited. This is true whether you hold your interest directly or through an entity. As long as you have unlimited liability, the working interest is not a passive activity even if you do not materially participate in the activity. A working interest is one burdened with the financial risk of developing and operating the property, such as a share in tort liability (for example, uninsured losses from a fire); some responsibility to share in additional costs; responsibility for authorizing expenses; receiving periodic reports about drilling, completion, and expected production; and the possession of voting rights and rights to continue operations if the present operator steps out.

Limited liability. If you hold a working interest through any of the following entities, the entity is considered to limit your liability and you are subject to the passive loss rules: (1) a limited partnership interest in a partnership in which you are not a general partner; (2) stock in a corporation; or (3) an interest in any entity other than a limited partnership or corporation that, under applicable state law, limits the liability of a holder of such interest for all obligations of the entity to a determinable fixed amount.

Working interests are considered on a well-by-well basis. Rights to overriding royalties or production payments, and contract rights to extract or share in oil and gas profits without liability for a share of production costs, are not working interests.

Planning Reminder

Publicly Traded Partnerships (PTPs)

A PTP is a partnership whose interests are traded on established securities exchanges or are readily tradable in secondary markets. PTPs that are not treated as corporations for tax purposes are subject to special rules that allow losses to be used only to offset income from the same PTP. *See* the instructions to Form 8582.

10.11 Partners and Members of LLCs and LLPs

As a general partner, your share of partnership income or loss during the partnership year ending within your tax year is passive or nonpassive, depending on whether you materially participated *(10.6)* in the partnership activities during the year. Generally, limited partners are subject to passive activity treatment, but there are some exceptions. On Schedule K-1 of Form 1065, the partnership will identify each activity it conducts and specify the income, loss, deductions, and credits from each activity.

> ***EXAMPLE***
>
> Don Bailey is a general partner of a fiscal year partnership that ends on March 31, 2010. During that fiscal year he was inactive. Since he did not materially participate, his share of partnership income or loss reported in 2010 is passive activity income or loss, even if he becomes active from April 1, 2010, to the end of 2010.

Not treated as passive income are payments for services and certain guaranteed payments made in liquidation of a retiring or deceased partner's interest unless attributed to unrealized receivables and goodwill at a time the partner was passive.

Gain or loss on the disposition of a partnership interest may be attributed to different trade, investment, or rental activities of the partnership. The allocation is made according to a complicated formula included in IRS regulations.

Payments to a retired partner. Gain or loss is treated as passive only to the extent that it would be treated as such at the start of the liquidation of the partner's interest.

Limited partners. Under IRS regulations, a limited partner has only a limited opportunity to establish material participation. A limited partner may use only three of the seven tests to establish material participation and thereby avoid passive treatment for the partnership income or loss:

1. The limited partner participates for more than 500 hours during the tax year; *see* Test 1 *(10.6)*, or
2. The limited partner materially participated in the partnership during prior years under either Test 5 or Test 6 *(10.6)*.

The IRS regulations also provide a general partner exception. If the limited partner is also a general partner at all times during the partnership year that ends with or within the partner's taxable year, the restricted material participation rules for limited partners do not apply, and material participation may be established under any of the seven material participation tests at *10.6*.

To determine material participation in rental real estate activities under the special rules for real estate professionals, Test 1, Test 5, or Test 6 *(10.6)* must generally be met, but *see* the *de minimis* exception at *10.3*.

A limited partner is not considered to be an "active participant" and thus does not qualify for the $25,000 rental loss allowance *(10.2)*.

LLC and LLP members. The Tax Court and the Court of Federal Claims rejected IRS attempts to apply its limited partner regulation to LLC and LLP members. The IRS argued that since LLC and LLP members have limited liability under state law, they, like limited partners, could only demonstrate material participation under Test 1, 5, or 6. Both the Tax Court and Court of Federal Claims disagreed, holding that the presumption in the law (Code Section 469(h)(2)) that limited partners do not materially participate should not apply to LLC and LLP members, as they are not barred (as limited partners are) from participating in the management and operations of the business. According to both courts, the LLC or LLP member's participation is a question of fact that should be determined under the IRS's seven general tests for material participation.

The IRS acquiesced to the result in the Court of Federal Claims case and announced that it would no longer litigate similar cases. It also announced that it was considering revisions to its material participation regulations to cover LLC and LLP members; *see* the *e-Supplement at jklasser.com* for future developments.

10.12 Form 8582

The purpose of Form 8582 is to assemble in one place items of income and expenses from passive activities in order to determine the effect of the passive loss rules on these items. After this determination, income and allowable deductions are reported as regular income and deductions in appropriate schedules attached to your tax return. For example, net profits of a self-employed person who is not active in the business are reported on Schedule C, sales of capital assets of a passive activity are reported on Schedule D, your share of partnership income and allowable deductions is reported on Schedule E, and rental income and allowable deductions are reported on Schedule E.

Schedule D or Form 4797. Gains or losses from the sale of assets from a passive activity or from the sale of a partial interest that is less than "substantially all" of your entire interest in a passive activity are reported on Schedule D or on Form 4797 (sale of business property). The gain is also entered on Form 8582. Losses must first be entered on Form 8582 to *see* how much, if any, is allowable under the passive loss restrictions before an amount can be entered as a loss on Schedule D or Form 4797.

A disposition of an insubstantial part of your interest in the activity does not allow a deduction of suspended passive losses from prior years. When you dispose of your entire interest in a passive activity to a nonrelated party in a fully taxable transaction, your losses for the year plus prior year suspended losses from the activity are fully deductible. The same rule applies to a partial disposition only if you are disposing of *substantially all* of the activity and you have proof of the current year and prior year suspended losses allocable to the disposed-of portion. You net the gain or loss from the disposition with the net income or loss from current year operations and any prior year suspended passive losses. If the netting gives you an overall gain, you need to file Form 8582 only if you have other passive activities. If you have an overall loss after the netting, you do not file Form 8582.

Schedule E. If you have a net profit from rental property or other passive activity reported on Schedule E and you also have losses from other passive activities, the income reported on Schedule E is also entered on Form 8582. A net loss from rental activities generally must be entered on Form 8582 but Form 8582 is not needed if you qualify for the full $25,000 allowance *(10.2)* for rental real estate losses and meet these tests:

Your only passive activities are rental real estate activities and you have no suspended prior year passive losses from such activities;

You have no credits related to passive activities;

You actively participated in the rental real estate operations;

Your overall net loss from the rental real estate activities is $25,000 or less ($12,500 or less if married filing separately and you lived apart from your spouse all year);

Your modified adjusted gross income is $100,000 or less ($50,000 or less if married filing separately and you lived apart from your spouse all year); and

You do not own any interest in a rental real estate activity as a limited partner or beneficiary of a trust or estate.

If you have a loss from a passive interest in a partnership, trust, estate, or S corporation, you first determine on Form 8582 whether the loss is deductible on Schedule E.

Schedule F. A passive activity farm loss is entered on Form 8582 to determine the deductible loss. If only part of the loss is allowed, only that portion is claimed on Schedule F. A net profit from passive farm activities is also entered on Form 8582 to offset losses from other passive activities.

Other tax forms. Other forms tied to Form 8582 are Form 4797 (sale of business assets or equipment), Form 4835 (farm rental income), and Form 4952 (investment interest deductions). For further details *see* Form 8582; also *see* IRS Publication 925 for filled-in sample forms.

10.13 Suspended Losses Allowed on Disposition of Your Interest

Losses and credits that may not be claimed in one year because of the passive activity limitations are suspended and carried forward to later years. The carryover lasts indefinitely, until you have passive income against which to claim the losses and credits. No carryback is allowed. What if you have suspended losses and later materially participate in the business in which the loss was realized? The losses remain passive losses but since you now materially participate, the suspended losses may offset nonpassive income of that activity.

Caution

$3,000 Capital Loss Limit

Capital losses incurred on a disposition of a passive interest are also subject to the general $3,000 loss limitation ($1,500 if married filing separately) *(5.4)*.

EXAMPLE

In 2009, Nick Milo was not a material participant in a business activity and his share of losses was $10,000, which was suspended because he had no passive income. In 2010, he becomes a material participant in the business and his share of income is $1,000. The $1,000 is treated as nonpassive income, and he may apply $1,000 of the suspended loss to offset that income.

Allocation of suspended loss. If your suspended loss is incurred from several activities, you allocate the loss among the activities using the worksheets accompanying Form 8582. The loss is allocated among the activities in proportion to the total loss. If you have net income from significant participation activities (*see* Test 4 *(10.6)*), such activities may be treated as one single activity in making the allocation; *see* the instructions to Form 8582.

EXAMPLES

1. Jill Stein has a 5% interest in a limited partnership with an adjusted basis of $42,000. In 2010, she sells her interest in the partnership to an unrelated person for $50,000. For 2010, she has a current year loss from the partnership (shown on Schedule K-1) of $3,000. She also has $2,000 of suspended passive losses from prior years that have been carried forward to 2010. Jill's $8,000 gain from the sale of her interest is combined on Form 8582 with the current year loss and suspended losses giving her an overall gain of $3,000, figured as follows:

Sales price	$50,000	
Less: Adjusted basis	$42,000	
Gain	$8,000	
Less: Current year loss	$3,000	
Suspended losses	$2,000	$5,000
Overall gain		$3,000

If Jill has other passive activities, the $8,000 gain would be reported as current year income on Form 8582. The $3,000 current year loss and $2,000 suspended losses would also be entered on Form 8582.

If this was Jill's *only* passive activity, she does not have to file Form 8582. The gain from the sale is reported on Schedule D and the current year and suspended losses are reported as nonpassive losses on Schedule E.

2. Assume that Jill's suspended losses from prior years were $10,000 instead of $2,000. She has an overall loss of $5,000 after combining the gain from the sale of $8,000, the current year loss of $3,000, and the suspended losses of $10,000.

Since there is an overall loss after combining the gain and losses, Jill does not file Form 8582. The current year loss plus the suspended losses are reported as nonpassive losses on Schedule E and the gain from the disposition on Schedule D.

3. Assume in Example 1 that Jill sold her interest for $30,000 instead of $50,000. She would have a $12,000 loss on the sale ($42,000 adjusted basis less $30,000 sales price). Combining the loss with the current year loss of $3,000 and the $2,000 of suspended losses, she has an overall loss of $17,000.
Since there is an overall loss, Jill does not file Form 8582. The current year loss plus the suspended losses are reported as nonpassive losses on Schedule E. The $12,000 loss on the sale is reported on Schedule D as a capital loss. Under the regular rules for capital losses, the loss will offset capital gains for 2010 and any excess will be deductible only up to $3,000 *(5.4)*. Assuming the $3,000 limit applies, Jill has a $9,000 capital loss carryover to 2010.

Disposition of a passive interest. A fully taxable sale of your entire interest to a nonrelated person will allow you to claim suspended deductions from the activity. Worthlessness of a security in a passive activity is treated as a disposition. An abandonment also releases suspended losses.

On a disposition, the suspended losses plus any current year income or loss from the activity are combined with the gain or loss from the disposition; *see* the Examples below and follow the instructions to Form 8582 for reporting the net gain or loss.

Partial disposition. You may for the taxable year in which there is a disposition of *substantially all* of an activity treat the part disposed of as a separate activity. You must show: (1) the amount of prior year suspended deductions and credits allocable to that part of the activity for the taxable year, and (2) the amount of gross income and any other deductions and credits allocable to that part of the activity for the taxable year.

Caution

Partial Disposition

To deduct suspended passive losses on a disposition of part of an activity, the part disposed of must constitute substantially all of the activity *(10.13)*.

Gifts. When a passive activity interest is given away, you may not deduct suspended passive losses. The donee's basis in the property is increased by the suspended loss if he or she sells the property at a gain. If a loss is realized by the donee on a sale of the interest, the donee's basis may not exceed fair market value of the gift at the time of the donation.

Death. On the death of an investor in a passive interest, suspended losses are deductible on the decedent's final tax return, to the extent the suspended loss exceeds the amount by which the basis of the interest in the hands of the heir is increased.

EXAMPLE

An owner dies holding an interest in a passive activity with a suspended loss of $8,000. After the owner's death, the heir's stepped-up basis for the property (equal to fair market value) is $6,000 greater than the decedent's basis. On the decedent's final return, $2,000 of the loss is deductible ($8,000 – $6,000).

Filing Tip

Installment Sale of Your Interest

If you sell your passive activity interest at a profit and have suspended losses, you may deduct a percentage of the losses each year during the installment period *(10.13)*.

Installment sales. If you sell your entire interest in a passive activity at a profit on the installment basis, suspended losses are deducted over the installment period in the same ratio as the gain recognized each year bears to the gain remaining to be recognized as of the start of the year. For example, if you realize a gain of $10,000 and report $2,000 of gain each year for five years, in the year of sale you report 20% of your total gain under the installment method, and 20% of your suspended losses are also allowed. In the second year, you report $2,000 of the remaining $8,000 gain and 25% of the remaining losses ($2,000 ÷ $8,000) are allowed.

10.14 Suspended Tax Credits

If you have tax credits that were barred under the passive activity rules, they may be claimed only in future years when you have tax liability attributable to passive income. However, in the year you dispose of your interest, a special election may be available to decrease your gain by the amount of your suspended credit; *see* below.

Basis election for suspended credits. If you qualify for an investment credit (under transition rules) or a rehabilitation credit, you are required to reduce the basis of the property even if you are unable to claim the credit because of the passive activity rules. If this occurs and you later dispose of your entire interest in the passive activity, including the property whose basis was reduced, your gain will be increased by virtue of the basis reduction although you never benefitted from the credit. To prevent this, you may reduce the taxable gain by electing to increase the pre-transfer basis of the property by the amount of the unused credit. The election is made on Form 8582-CR.

EXAMPLE

Dan Brown places in service rehabilitated credit property qualifying for a $50 credit, but the credit is not allowed under the passive loss rules. However, his basis is still reduced by $50. In a later year, Brown makes a taxable disposition of his entire interest in the activity and in the rehabilitation property. Assuming that no part of the suspended $50 credit has been used, Brown may elect on Form 8582-CR to increase his basis in the property by the unused $50 credit.

10.15 Personal Service and Closely Held Corporations

To prevent avoidance of the passive activity rules through use of corporations, the law imposes restrictions on income and loss offsets in closely held C corporations and personal service corporations.

Unless the material participation tests discussed in this section are met, the activities of a personal service corporation or a closely held corporation are considered passive activities, subject to the restrictions on loss deductions and tax credits. For purposes of these passive activity rules, a closely held C corporation is a corporation in which more than 50% in value of the stock is owned by five or fewer persons during the last half of the tax year.

A personal service corporation is a C corporation the principal activity of which is the performance of personal services by the employee-owners. Personal services are services in the fields of health, law, engineering, architecture, accounting, actuarial sciences, performing arts, or consulting. An employee-owner is any employee who on any day in the tax year owns any stock in the corporation. If an individual owns any stock in a corporation which in turn owns stock in another corporation, the individual is deemed to own a proportionate part of the stock in the other corporation. Further, more than 10% of the corporation's stock by value must be owned by owner- employees for the corporation to be a personal service corporation.

Form 8810 must be used. Personal service corporations and closely held corporations use Form 8810 to figure the amount of the passive activity loss or credit that is allowed on the corporation's tax return for the year.

Material participation. A personal service corporation or closely held corporation is treated as materially participating in an activity during a tax year *only if* either:

1. One or more stockholders are treated as materially participating in the activity and they directly or indirectly hold in the aggregate more than 50% of the value of the corporation's outstanding shares; *or*
2. The corporation is a closely held corporation and in the 12-month period ending on the last day of the tax year, the corporation had at least one full-time manager, three full-time employees, none of whom own more than 5% of the stock, and business deductions exceeded 15% of gross income from the activity.

A stockholder is treated as materially participating or significantly participating in the activity of a corporation if he or she satisfies one of the seven tests for material participation *(10.6)*. For purposes of applying the significant participation test (Test 4), an activity of a personal service or closely held corporation will be treated as a significant participation activity for a tax year *only if*:

1. The corporation is not treated as materially participating in the activity for the tax year; and
2. One or more individuals, each of whom is treated as significantly participating in the activity directly or indirectly, hold in the aggregate more than 50% of the value of the outstanding stock of the corporation. Furthermore, in applying the seven participation tests, all activities of the corporation are treated as activities in which the individual holds an interest in determining whether the individual participates in an activity of the corporation; and the individual's participation in all activities other than activities of the corporation is disregarded in determining whether his or her participation in an activity of the corporation is treated as material participation under the significant participation test (Test 4).

Closely held corporation's computation of passive loss. Even if a closely held corporation does not meet the material participation tests above, it still qualifies for a slight break from the passive loss restrictions. On Form 8810, a closely held corporation may use passive activity deductions to offset not only passive activity gross income but also *net active income*. Generally, net active income is taxable income from business operations, disregarding passive activity income and expenses, and also disregarding portfolio income and expenses *(10.8)*. Passive activity losses cannot offset portfolio income.

If a corporation stops being closely held, its passive losses and credits from prior years are not allowable against portfolio income but continue to be allowable only against passive income and net active income.

Tax liability on net active income may be offset by passive activity credits.

10.16 Sales of Property and of Passive Activity Interests

Gain on the sale or disposition of property is generally passive or nonpassive, depending on whether your activity is passive or nonpassive in the year of sale or disposition. Thus, gain on the sale of property used in a rental activity is generally treated as passive income, as is the gain on property used in a nonrental business if you did not materially participate in the business in the year of sale. On the other hand, gain on the sale of property is generally nonpassive if the property was used in a business that you materially participated in during the year of sale. However, exceptions described below may change this treatment.

Where you transact an installment sale, treatment of gain in later years depends on your status in the year of sale. For example, if you were considered a material participant in a business, all gain is treated as nonpassive income, including gain for later installments. If you were in a rental activity or were not a material participant in a nonrental business, the gain is treated as passive income, unless the exceptions in this section apply.

Gain on substantially appreciated property formerly used in nonpassive activity. Even if an activity is passive in the year that you sell substantially appreciated property, gain on the sale is treated as nonpassive unless the property was used in a passive activity for either 20% of its holding period or the entire 24-month period ending on the date of the disposition. Property is substantially appreciated if fair market value exceeds 120% of its adjusted basis.

EXAMPLE

In December 1991, Andy Jones buys a building for use in a business in which he materially participates until March 31, 2009. On April 1, 2009, he rents out the building. On December 31, 2010, he sells the building for more than 120% of its adjusted basis. Gain from the sale is treated as nonpassive although the building was used in a passive rental activity in the year of the sale. The building was used in a passive rental activity for 21 months before disposition (April 1, 2009, through December 31, 2010). Thus, it was not used in a passive activity for the entire 24-month period ending on the date of the sale. Further, the 21-month period during which the building was used in a passive activity is less than 20% of Jones's holding period of 19 years.

Property used in more than one activity in a 12-month period preceding disposition. You are required to allocate the amount realized on the disposition and the adjusted basis of the property among the activities in which the property was used during a 12-month period preceding the disposition. For purposes of this rule, the term "activity" includes personal use and holding for investment. The allocation may be based on the period for which the property is used in each activity during the 12-month period. However, if during the 12-month period the value of the property does not exceed the lesser of $10,000 or 10% of the value of all property used in the activity at the time of disposition, gain may be allocated to the predominant use.

EXAMPLE

Joe Smith sells a personal computer for $8,000. During the 12-month period that ended on the date of the sale, 70% of Smith's use of the computer was in a passive activity. Immediately before the sale, the fair market value of all property used in the passive activity, including the personal computer, was $200,000. The computer was predominantly used in the passive activity during the 12-month period ending on the date of the sale. The value of the computer, $8,000, did not exceed the lesser of $10,000 or 10% of the $200,000 value of all property used in the activity immediately before the sale. Thus, the amount realized and the adjusted basis are allocated to the passive activity.

Disposition of partnership and S corporation interests. Gain or loss from the disposition of an interest in a partnership and S corporation is generally allocated among the entity's activities in proportion to the amount that the entity would have allocated to the partner or shareholder for each of its activities if the entity had sold its interest in the activities on the "applicable valuation date" chosen by the entity, either the date of the disposition or the beginning of the entity's taxable year in which the disposition occurs.

Gain is allocated only to appreciated activities. Loss is allocated only to depreciated activities. The entity may select either the beginning of its tax year in which the holder's disposition occurs or the date of the disposition as the applicable valuation date.

Claiming suspended loss on disposition of interest in passive activity. A fully taxable sale of your entire interest or of substantially all of your interest to a nonrelated person will allow you to claim suspended loss deductions from the activity *(10.13)*.

Dealer's sale of property similar to property sold in the ordinary course of business. IRS regulations set down complex tests that determine whether the result of the sale is treated as passive or nonpassive income or loss.

10.17 At-Risk Limits

The at-risk rules prevent investors from claiming losses in excess of their actual tax investment by barring them from including nonrecourse liabilities as part of the tax basis for their interest. Almost all ventures are subject to the at-risk limits. Real estate placed in service after 1986 is subject to the at-risk rules as well, but most real estate nonrecourse financing can qualify for an exception *(10.18)*.

> **EXAMPLE**
>
> Crystal Parker invests cash of $1,000 in a venture and signs a nonrecourse note for $8,000. In 2010, her share of the venture's loss is $1,200. The at-risk rules limit her deduction to $1,000, the amount of her cash investment; as she is not personally liable on the note, the amount of the liability is not included as part of her basis for loss purposes.

Losses disallowed under the at-risk rules are carried over to the following year *(10.21)*.

Caution

At-Risk Rules Limit Loss Deductions

The purpose of at-risk rules is to keep you from deducting losses from investments in which you have little cash invested and no personal liability for debts.

Form 6198. If you have amounts that are not at risk, you must file Form 6198 to figure your deductible loss. A separate form must be filed for each activity. However, if you have an interest in a partnership or S corporation that has more than one investment in any of the following four categories, the IRS currently allows you to aggregate all of the partnership or S corporation activities within each category. For example, all partnership or S corporation films and videotapes may be treated as one activity in determining amounts at risk. The aggregation rules may be changed by the IRS; *see* the instructions to Form 6198.

1. Holding, producing, or distributing motion picture films or videotapes;
2. Exploring for or exploiting oil or gas properties;
3. Exploring for, or exploiting, geothermal deposits (for wells commenced on or after October 1, 1978); *and*
4. Farming. For this purpose, farming is defined as the cultivation of land and the raising or harvesting of any agricultural or horticultural commodity—including raising, shearing, breeding, caring for, or management of animals. Forestry and timber activities are not included, but orchards bearing fruits and nuts are within the definition of farming. Certain activities carried on within the physical boundaries of the farm may not necessarily be treated as farming.

Filing Tip

Form 6198

If you have invested an amount for which you are not at risk, such as a nonrecourse loan, you generally must file Form 6198 to figure a deductible loss. However, nonrecourse financing for real estate that secures the loan is treated as an at-risk investment in most cases *(10.18)*.

In addition to the previous categories, the law treats as a single activity all leased depreciable business equipment (Section 1245 property) that is placed in service during any year by a partnership or S corporation.

Exempt from the at-risk rules are C corporations which meet active business tests and are not in the equipment leasing business or any business involving master sound recording, films, videotapes, or other artistic, literary, or musical property. For details on the active business tests, as well as a special at-risk exception for equipment leasing activities of closely held corporations, *see* IRS Publication 925.

The at-risk limitation applies only to tax losses produced by expense deductions that are not disallowed by reason of another provision of the law. For example, if a prepaid interest expense is deferred under the prepaid interest limitation *(15.14)*, the interest will not be included in the loss subject to the risk limitation. When the interest accrues and becomes deductible, the expense may be considered within the at-risk provision. Similarly, if a deduction is deferred because of farming syndicate rules, that deduction will enter into the computation of the tax loss subject to the risk limitation only when it becomes deductible under the farming syndicate rules.

Effect of passive loss rules. Where a loss is also subject to the at-risk rules, you apply the at-risk rules first. If the loss is deductible under the at-risk rules, the passive activity rules then apply. On Form 6198 (at risk), you figure the deductible loss allowed as at risk and then carry the loss over to Form 8582 to determine the passive activity loss.

10.18 What Is At Risk?

The following amounts are considered at risk in determining your tax position in a business or investment:

Cash;

Adjusted basis of property that you contribute; and

Borrowed funds for which you are personally liable for repayment.

Personal liability alone does not assure that the borrowed funds are considered at risk. The lender generally must have no interest in the venture other than as a creditor and must not be related to a person (other than the borrower) with an interest in the activity other than that of a creditor. Under final IRS regulations, a lender or person related to the lender is considered to have an interest other than that of a creditor only if the person has a capital interest in the activity or an interest in the net profits of the activity. However, even if the lender has such an interest, a loan after May 3, 2004, for which you are personally liable is treated as at risk if: (1) the loan is secured by real estate used in the activity and (2) the loan, were it nonrecourse, would be qualified nonrecourse financing, as discussed below.

At-risk basis is figured as of the end of the year. Any loss allowed for a year reduces the at-risk amount as of the start of the next year. Therefore, if a loss exceeds your at-risk investment, the excess loss will not be deductible in later years unless you increase your at-risk investment; *see* the Example below and *10.21*.

EXAMPLE

Julie Kahn, an investor, pays a promoter of a book purchase plan $45,000 for a limited partnership interest. The promoter is the general partner. Kahn pays $30,000 cash and gives a note for $15,000 on which she is personally liable. Her amount at risk is $30,000; the $15,000 personal liability note is not counted because it is owed to the general partner.

Qualified nonrecourse financing for real estate considered at risk. Generally, you are not considered at risk for nonrecourse financing, that is, loans for which you are not personally liable, unless the loan is secured by property not used in the activity. However, you are considered to be at risk for qualified nonrecourse financing. This is financing from an unrelated commercial lender or government agency for which no one is personally liable and which is secured by real estate used in the activity. The debt obligation must not be convertible to an ownership interest. In determining whether the financing is secured only by real property used in the activity, you can ignore security that is property valued at less than 10% of the total value of all property securing the financing, as well as property that is incidental to the activity of holding real property. Loans from the seller or promoter do not qualify. Third-party nonrecourse debt from a related lender, other than the seller or promoter, may also be treated as at risk, providing the terms of the loan are commercially reasonable and on substantially the same terms as loans involving unrelated persons.

Pledges of other property. If you pledge personally owned real estate used outside the activity to secure a nonrecourse debt and invest the proceeds in an at-risk activity, the proceeds may be considered part of your at-risk investment. The proceeds included in basis are limited by the fair market value of the property used as collateral (determined as of the date the property is pledged as security) less any prior (or superior) claims to which the collateral is subject.

Partners. A partner is treated as at-risk to the extent that basis in the partnership is increased by the share of partnership income. That partnership income is then used to reduce the partnership's nonrecourse indebtedness will have no effect on a partner's amount at risk. If the partnership makes actual distributions of the income in the taxable year, the amount distributed reduces the partner's amount at risk. A buy-sell agreement, effective at a partner's death or retirement, is not considered for at-risk purposes.

10.19 Amounts Not At Risk

The following may not be treated as part of basis for at-risk purposes in determining your tax position in a business or investment:

- Liabilities for which you have no personal liability, except in the case of certain real estate financing *(10.18)*.
- Liabilities for which you have personal liability, but the lender also has a capital or profit-sharing interest in the venture; but *see* the exception in *10.18*.
- Recourse liabilities convertible to a nonrecourse basis.
- Money borrowed from a relative listed in *5.6* who has an interest in the venture, other than as a creditor, or from a partnership in which you own more than a 10% interest.
- Funds borrowed from a person whose recourse is solely your interest in the activity or property used in the activity.
- Amounts for which your economic loss is limited by a nonrecourse financing guarantee, stop-loss agreement, or other similar arrangement.

Caution

Lender Has Interest

Even if you are personally liable for a debt, you may not be considered at risk if the lender has an interest in the activity other than as a creditor *(10.18)*.

Investments protected by insurance or loss reimbursement agreement between you and another person. If you are personally liable on a mortgage but you separately obtain insurance to compensate you for any mortgage payments, you are at risk only to the extent of the uninsured portion of the personal liability. You may, however, include as at risk any amount of premium paid from your personal assets. Taking out casualty insurance or insurance protecting you against tort liability is not considered within the at-risk provisions, and such insurance does not affect your investment basis.

EXAMPLES

1. Some commercial feedlots in livestock feeding operations may reimburse investors against any loss sustained on sales of the livestock above a stated dollar amount per head. Under such "stop-loss" orders, an investor is at risk only to the extent of the portion of his or her capital against which he or she is not entitled to reimbursement. Where a limited partnership makes an agreement with a limited partner that, at the partner's election, his or her partnership interest will be bought at a stated minimum dollar amount (usually less than the investor's original capital contribution), the partner is considered at risk only to the extent of his or her investment exceeding the guaranteed repurchase price.
2. A TV film promoter sold half-hour TV series programs to individual investors. Each investor gave a cash down payment and a note for which he or she was personally liable for the balance. Each investor's note, which was identical in face amount, terms, and maturity date, was payable out of the distribution proceeds from the film. Each investor also bought from the promoter the right to the unpaid balance on another investor's note. The promoter arranged the distribution of the films as a unit and was to apportion the sales proceeds equally among the investors.

   The IRS held that each investor is not at risk on the investment evidenced by the note. Upon maturity, each may receive a payment from another investor equal to the one that he or she owes.
3. A gold mine investment offered tax write-offs of four times the cash invested. For $10,000 cash, an investor bought from a foreign mining company a seven-year mineral claim lease to a gold reserve. Under the lease, he could develop and extract all of the gold in the reserve. At the same time, he agreed to spend $40,000 to develop the lease before the end of the year. To fund this commitment, the investor authorized the promoter to sell an option for $30,000 to a third party who was to buy all the gold to be extracted. The $30,000 along with the $10,000 down payment was to be used to develop the reserve. The promoter advised the investor that he could claim a $40,000 deduction for certain development costs.

   The IRS ruled that $30,000 was not deductible because the amount was not "risk capital." The investor got $30,000 by selling an option that could be exercised only if gold were found. If no gold were found, he would be under no obligation to the option holder. The investor's risk position for the $30,000 was substantially the same as if he had borrowed from the option holder on a nonrecourse basis repayable only from his interest in the activity.

   The Tax Court struck down a similar plan on different grounds. Without deciding the question of what was at risk, the court held that the option was only a right of first refusal. Thus, $30,000 was taxable income to the investor in the year of the arranged sale.
4. David Krepp, an investor, purchases cattle from a rancher for $10,000 cash and a $30,000 note payable to the rancher. Krepp is personally liable on the note. In a separate agreement, the rancher agrees to care for the cattle for 6% of Krepp's net profits from the cattle activity. Krepp is considered at risk for $10,000; he may not increase the amount at risk by the $30,000 borrowed from the rancher.

Limited partner's potential cash call. Under the terms of a partnership agreement, limited partners may be required to make additional capital contributions under specified circumstances. Whether such a potential cash call increases the limited partner's at-risk amount has been a matter of dispute.

In one case, the IRS and Tax Court held that a limited partner was not at risk with respect to a partnership note where, under the terms of the partnership agreement, he could be required to make additional capital contributions if the general partners did not pay off the note at maturity. The possibility of such a potential cash call was too uncertain; the partnership might earn profits to pay off the note and even if there were losses, the general partners might not demand additional contributions from the limited partners.

However, a federal appeals court reversed, holding that the limited partner was at risk because his obligation was mandatory and "economic reality" insured that the general partners would insure their rights by requiring the additional capital contribution.

In another case, limited partners relied upon the earlier favorable federal appeals court decision to argue that they were at risk where they could be required by the general partners to make additional cash contributions, but only in order to cover liabilities or expenses that could not be paid out of partnership assets. So long as the partnership was solvent, the limited partners could "elect out" of the call provision. Because of this election, the Tax Court held that the limited partners' obligation was contingent, rather than unavoidable as in the earlier federal appeals court case. Thus, the cash call provision did not increase their at-risk amount.

10.20 At-Risk Investment in Several Activities

If you invest in several activities, each is generally treated separately when applying the at-risk limitation on Form 6198. You generally may not aggregate basis, gains, and losses from the activities for purposes of at-risk limitations. Thus, income from one activity may not be offset by losses from another; the income from one must be reported while the losses from the other may be nondeductible because of at-risk limitations.

However, you may aggregate activities that are part of a business you actively manage. Activities of a business carried on by a partnership or S corporation qualify if 65% or more of losses for the year are allocable to persons who actively participate in management.

The law allows partnerships and S corporations to treat as a single activity all depreciable equipment (Section 1245 property) that is leased or held for lease and placed in service in any tax year. Furthermore, you may aggregate all partnership or S corporation activities within the four categories of films and videotapes, oil and gas properties, geothermal properties, and farms *(10.17)*.

10.21 Carryover of Disallowed Losses

Filing Tip

Carryover Losses

Losses disallowed by at-risk rules are carried over and may be deductible in a later year.

A loss disallowed in a current year by the at-risk limitation may be carried over and deducted in the next taxable year, provided it does not fall within the at-risk limits or the passive loss limits in that year. The loss is subject to an unlimited carryover period until there is an at-risk basis to support the deduction. This may occur when additional contributions are made to the business or when the activity has income which has not been distributed.

Gain from the disposition of property used in an at-risk activity is treated as income from the activity. In general, the reporting of gain will allow a deduction for losses disallowed in previous years to be claimed in the year of disposition.

10.22 Recapture of Losses Where At Risk Is Less Than Zero

To prevent manipulation of at-risk basis after a loss is claimed, there is a special recapture rule. If the amount at risk in an activity is reduced to below zero because of a distribution or a change in the status of an indebtedness from recourse to nonrecourse, income may be realized to the extent of the negative at-risk amount. The taxable amount may not exceed the amount of losses previously deducted.

The recaptured amount is not treated as income from the activity for purposes of determining whether current or suspended losses are allowable. Instead, the recaptured amount is treated as a deduction allocable to that activity in the following year. *See* IRS Publication 925 for further details.

Chapter 11

Other Income

This chapter discusses various types of payments you may receive; some are taxable and others are not taxable. Examples of taxable items include:

- Taxable state tax refunds, which are reported on Line 10 of Form 1040.
- Prizes, gambling winnings, and awards, which are reported on Line 21 of Form 1040. There are several exceptions, including the new exclusion for debts discharged in a mortgage restructuring or foreclosure *(11.8)*.
- Cancellations of debt, which are reported on Line 21 of Form 1040.
- Your share of partnership, S corporation, trust, or estate income or loss, which is reported in Schedule E according to Schedule K-1 statements provided you by the entity, and then transferred to Line 17 of Form 1040.

Further reporting details are discussed in this chapter.

11.1 Prizes and Awards

Prizes and awards are taxable income except for an award or prize that meets *all* these four tests:

1. It is primarily in recognition of religious, charitable, scientific, educational, artistic, literary, or civic achievement.
2. You were selected without any action on your part.
3. You do not have to perform services.
4. You assign the prize or award to a government unit or tax-exempt charitable organization. You must make the assignment before you use or benefit from the award. You may not claim a charitable deduction for the assignment.

Prize taxed at fair market value. A prize of merchandise is taxable at fair market value. For example, where a prize of first-class steamship tickets was exchanged for tourist-class tickets for a winner's family, the taxable value of the prize was the price of the tourist tickets. What is the taxable fair market value of an automobile won as a prize? In one case, the Tax Court held that the taxable value was what the recipient could realize on an immediate resale of the car.

Employee achievement awards. The above restrictions on tax-free treatment do not apply to awards from employers for length of service or safety achievement. The rules for such employee awards are in *Chapter 3 (3.11)* and *Chapter 20 (20.25)*.

11.2 Lottery and Sweepstake Winnings

Sweepstake, lottery, and raffle winnings are taxable as "other income" on Line 21 of Form 1040. The cost of tickets is deductible only to the extent you report winnings, and only if you itemize deductions. The deduction is claimed on Schedule A as a miscellaneous deduction that is *not* subject to the 2% adjusted gross income (AGI) floor *(Chapter 19)*. For example, if you buy state lottery tickets and win a 2010 drawing, you may deduct the cost of your losing tickets in 2010 up to the amount of your winnings.

When a minor wins a state lottery and the prize is held by his or her parents as custodians under the Uniform Transfers to Minors Act, the prize is taxed to the minor in the year the prize is won.

Court Decision

Assignment of Future Lottery Payments

Courts have agreed with the IRS that a lump sum received for assigning the rights to future state lottery payments is taxed as ordinary income, not capital gain. The right to receive annual lottery payments is not a capital asset.

Installment payments. If lottery or sweepstakes winnings or casino jackpots are payable in installments, you pay tax only as installments are received. If within 60 days of winning a prize you have an option to choose a discounted lump-sum payment instead of an annuity, and you elect the annuity, you are taxed as the annuity payments are received. Merely having the cash option does not make the present value of the annuity taxable in the year the prize is won.

11.3 Gambling Winnings and Losses

Gambling winnings are taxable. Losses from gambling are deductible only up to the gains from gambling. You may not deduct a net gambling loss even though a particular state says gambling is legal. Nor does it matter that your business is gambling. You may not deduct the loss even if you are a professional gambler.

If you are not a professional gambler, gambling income is included on Form 1040 as "other income" on Line 21. Gambling losses (*not* exceeding the amount of the gains) are deductible as "miscellaneous deductions" on Schedule A. The losses are not subject to the 2% AGI floor *(Chapter 19)*. According to the IRS, professional gamblers who bet only for their own account are not in a business and must deduct losses (up to gains) as miscellaneous itemized deductions. However, the Supreme Court has held that full-time gamblers may deduct losses as business expenses even if they place wagers only for themselves. According to the Supreme Court, in order to be considered engaged in a business, a gambler must prove that he or she gambles full time to earn a livelihood and not merely as a hobby. A professional gambler reports winnings and losses (lost wagers and gambling transaction expenses) on Schedule C; the losses are deductible only to extent of the winnings.

To prove your losses in the event your return is questioned, you must retain evidence of loss.

Filing Tip

Winnings Paid in Installments

Gambling losses are deductible as miscellaneous deductions up to the amount of your gambling winnings. Lottery winnings paid in installments qualify as such gambling winnings. If you receive lottery installments in 2010, for instance, you may deduct any gambling losses incurred in 2010 up to the amount of that installment. Lottery winnings paid in installments do not lose their characteristic as gambling winnings.

Casual slot machine players. A 2008 memo from IRS Chief Counsel sets out the IRS method of determining how casual slot machine players realize gambling gains and losses. Under the memo, a casual slot machine player on a day trip to a casino determines gain or loss at the end of slot play, disregarding the winning and losing bets along the way. The gains on the winnings days must be reported as gross income and the losses on the losing days are deductible only if the taxpayer itemizes deductions and only to the extent of the reported winnings (claimed as miscellaneous deductions not subject to the 2% floor). The Tax Court has repeatedly rejected attempts by casual gamblers to net gambling gains and losses realized at different times. In a 2010 decision, the Tax Court applied the 2008 IRS memo on the way casual slot machine players should report gambling gains and losses. *See* Example 1.

EXAMPLES

1. The Shollenbergers withdrew $500 from their checking account to take to the casino on March 29, 2005. They hit a $2,000 jackpot on a dollar slot machine that apparently was reported to the IRS on a Form W-2G. The IRS initially determined in its notice of deficiency that the full $2,000 jackpot on the dollar slot machine should have been reported as gambling income. However, after the Tax Court found as a fact that the Shollenbergers entered the casino with and bet $500 and left the casino with $1,600, the IRS conceded that $1,100 was the amount of winnings that should have been reported. Once the $500 and $1,600 amounts were determined, the IRS's own methodology in Chief Counsel Advice 2008-011 required that the reportable amount be $1,100 and not $2,000 since the Chief Counsel Advice uses an "enters with/leaves with" approach, and not a bet-by-bet approach. The Tax Court accepted the method in the Chief Counsel Advice and held that the "net win" for the day of $1,100 was taxable gambling winnings.

   Since the Shollenbergers claimed the standard deduction for 2005 rather than itemizing deductions, they could not offset the $1,100 of gambling income with gambling losses from other casino trips. They claimed to have incurred $2,264 of losses throughout 2005. They argued in the Tax Court that it was unfair not to allow them to net their 2005 slot machine gains and losses. The Court held that permitting a casual gambler to net all wagering gains or losses throughout the year would render superfluous the Code requirement that non-professional gamblers may claim gambling losses, if at all, only as a miscellaneous itemized deduction (not subject to the 2% floor for itemized deductions) and subject to the limitation (applicable to professional and nonprofessional gamblers alike) that the losses cannot exceed gambling income.

2. Tschetschot, a professional gambler, argued that her losses from poker tournaments should not be limited to her winnings because tournament poker, unlike traditional poker is not "gambling," but a sports and entertainment activity like a golf or tennis tournament. Her tournaments were distinguishable from "wagering activities," she argued, because tournament players have a limited monetary stake in the form of a buy-in entrance fee, they receive the same number of chips, and the highest place finishers receive cash prizes in predetermined amounts. The Tax Court, however, held that despite the differences between tournament play and other types of poker, the basic nature of the game remains a wagering activity, as bets are still played on each hand and each betting round has consequences. The Court also held that it is not unconstitutional to treat gambling losses differently from losses in sports tournaments, but it implied that Congress might want to reconsider the restriction on gambling losses given the increased acceptance of gambling in our society and improvements in the IRS's ability to accurately track winnings and losses.

3. To appear on *Wheel of Fortune,* Whitten traveled from Chicago to Los Angeles, spending $1,820 for transportation, meals, and lodging. When he won cash prizes of $14,850 plus an automobile, he tried to offset his winnings by the travel costs, claiming they were gambling losses on Schedule A not subject to the 2% AGI floor. The IRS and Tax Court disagreed; travel costs are not like wager or bet losses.

4. Trump Casino in Atlantic City gave Libutti, a high roller at its gaming tables, over $2.5 million in "comps" during a three-year period in which he lost over $8 million. The comps included 10 expensive automobiles, jewelry, European vacations, and tickets to sporting events. Libutti reported the comps as income and then claimed a matching miscellaneous deduction for gambling losses not subject to the 2% floor. The IRS disallowed the deduction, claiming that the comps were not gambling income because they were perks given to stimulate his desire to gamble at Trump's, and not winnings from the success of his wagers.

Court Decision

Gambler Not Taxed on Cancelled Gambling Debt

The federal appeals court for the Third Circuit (New Jersey, Pennsylvania, and Delaware) held that the settlement by an Atlantic City casino of a gambler's $3.4 million debt for $500,000 was not taxable. The debt was not enforceable under New Jersey law because the casino did not comply with state regulations on issuance of credit. Furthermore, the gambling chips were not "property" securing the debt; they had no economic value outside the casino.

The Tax Court disagreed. Libutti would not have received the comps unless he gambled at high stakes in Trump's casino. Although the comps did not directly hinge on the success or failure of his wagers, the comps were sufficiently related to his gambling losses to allow the deduction.

11.4 Gifts and Inheritances

Gifts and inheritances you *receive* are not taxable. However, distributions taken from an inherited traditional IRA *(8.14)*, and distributions from inherited qualified plan accounts such as 401(k) and profit-sharing plan accounts, are taxable, except for amounts attributable to nondeductible contributions made by the deceased account owner.

Income earned from gift or inherited property after you receive it is taxable.

Describing a payment as a gift or inheritance will not necessarily shield it from tax if it is, in fact, a payment for your services. Treatment of gifts to employees is covered in *Chapter 2 (2.4)*.

A sale of an expected inheritance from a living person is taxable as ordinary income.

EXAMPLES

1. An employee is promised by his employer that he will be remembered in his will if he continues to work for him. The employer dies but fails to mention the employee in his will. The employee sues the estate, which settles his claim. The settlement is taxable.
2. A nephew left his uncle a bequest of $200,000. In another clause of the will, the uncle was appointed executor, and the bequest of the $200,000 was described as being made in lieu of all commissions to which he would otherwise be entitled as executor. The bequest is considered tax-free income. It was not conditioned upon the uncle performing as executor. If the will had made the bequest contingent upon the uncle's acting as executor, the $200,000 would have been taxed.
3. An attorney performed services for a friend without expectation of pay. The friend died and in his will left the attorney a bequest in appreciation for his services. The payment was considered a tax-free bequest. The amount was not bargained for.
4. A lawyer agreed to handle a client's legal affairs without charge; she promised to leave him securities. Twenty years later, under her will, the lawyer inherited the securities. The IRS taxed the bequest as pay. Both he and the client expected that he would be paid for legal services. If the client meant to make a bequest from their agreement, she should have said so in her will.

Planning Reminder

Gifts You Make

You may have to file a gift tax return if your gifts to an individual within the year exceed the annual gift tax exclusion, which for 2010 was $13,000 *(39.2)*.

11.5 Refunds of State and Local Income Tax Deductions

A refund of state or local income tax is not taxable if you did not previously claim the tax as an itemized deduction in a prior year. For example, if you claimed the standard deduction on your 2009 return and in 2010 you received a refund for state tax withheld from your 2009 wages, the refund is not taxable on your 2010 return.

Refund of deduction for state/local income taxes or state/local general sales taxes. If in 2010 you received a refund for state or local income tax that you claimed as an itemized deduction, the taxable portion of the refund depends on the amount of the state/local general sales tax that you could have deducted in lieu of the state/local income tax *(16.3)*. In general, the full amount of the refund is taxable for 2010 if it is less than the excess of the state/local income tax claimed as a deduction in the prior year over the state/local general sales tax that you could have but did not deduct. If the refund is more than the excess, the amount subject to tax is limited to the excess. For example, on your 2009 return, you claimed an itemized deduction for $11,000 in state/local income taxes, as this exceeded your payment of $10,000 in state/local general sales taxes. If in 2010 you received a $750 refund of 2009 state income tax, the entire refund would be taxable, since it is less than the $1,000 excess of the state/local income taxes over the state/local general sales taxes for 2009. However, if the refund had been $2,500 instead of $750, only $1,000 of the refund would be includible in 2010 income ($11,000 deduction minus $10,000 in state sales tax that could have been deducted).

Planning Reminder

Refund of State and Local Tax

A state and local tax refund received in 2010 is taxable only if you claimed the tax as an itemized deduction, and only to the extent that your itemized deductions in that year exceeded the standard deduction you could have claimed.

To help you figure the taxable portion of 2009 itemized deductions recovered in 2010, 2009 standard deduction amounts are shown in *Table 11-1*.

Similarly, if in 2009 you deducted state/local general sales taxes in lieu of state/local income taxes, and you received a sales tax refund in 2010, the IRS generally requires you to include the entire sales tax refund in your income if it is less than the excess of your sales tax deduction over the income tax deduction that could have been deducted.

The amount subject to tax could be further reduced because of the standard deduction limit discussed below.

Note: If your itemized deductions in the earlier year were subject to the overall reduction *(13.7)*, follow the IRS method in Publication 525 for determining the taxable portion of a refund.

If AMT applied in year of deduction. If the refunded state tax was claimed as an itemized deduction but you were subject to the alternative minimum tax (AMT) for that year, the deduction was not allowable for AMT purposes *(23.2)*. The refund is taxable only if the deduction gave you a tax benefit in the prior year. To determine if there was a tax benefit, you must recompute regular tax liability and AMT for the prior year after increasing your income by the refunded amount. If the recomputation does not increase your total tax, there was no tax benefit and the refund is not taxable. If your total tax increases by any amount, the deduction gave you a tax benefit and the refund is taxable to the extent that the deduction reduced your tax in the prior year.

Standard deduction limit. The taxable portion of a refunded state tax cannot exceed the standard deduction limit. You include in income the lesser of the refund or the excess of your itemized deductions for the prior year over the standard deduction that could have been claimed.

The standard deduction limit applies to your total recoveries where you had other recoveries in addition to a refund of state tax *(11.6)*.

EXAMPLE

On your 2008 return, you filed as a single taxpayer. You claimed itemized deductions of $5,950, of which $3,850 was for state and local income taxes, $1,500 was for mortgage interest, and $600 was for charitable contributions. Your deductions exceeded by $250 the $5,700 standard deduction you could have claimed. The deductions were not subject to the reduction *(13.1)* and you were not subject to alternative minimum tax.

In 2010, you received from the state a $750 refund for 2009 state income tax. The $3,850 deduction for state and local income tax exceeded your 2009 state and local general sales taxes by more than $750. You must report $250 of the refund as income on your 2010 Form 1040. The taxable recovery is limited to the $250 difference between the claimed itemized deductions of $5,950 and the $5,700 standard deduction for 2009.

If you had a negative taxable income in 2009, the taxable recovery figured under the above rule is reduced by the negative amount. If you had a negative taxable income of $100 in 2009, only $150 of the refund would be taxable.

Filing Instruction

Negative Taxable Income

If your taxable income was a negative amount in the year in which the recovered item was deducted, you reduce the recovery includible in income by the negative amount. For example, if the taxable recovery would be $1,700 but you had a negative taxable income of $500 for the year the deduction was claimed, only $1,200 is taxable.

Allocating a refund recovery. If in 2010 you received a refund of state or local income taxes and also a recovery of other deductions, and only part of the total recovery is taxable, you allocate the taxable amount of the recovery according to the ratio between the state income tax refund and the other recovery. You do this by first dividing the state income tax refund by the total of all itemized deductions recovered. The resulting percentage is then applied to the taxable recovery to find the amount to report as the unrefunded state income tax on Line 10 of Form 1040; other taxable recoveries are reported on Line 21.

EXAMPLE

In 2010, you received a refund of state income taxes of $500 and a recovery of other itemized expenses of $2,000 deducted for 2009. You figure that only $1,500 of the recovery is taxable because your total 2009 itemized deductions were $1,500 more than the standard deduction you could have claimed. As a state income tax refund is reported separately from other recoveries, you must find how much of the taxable recovery is attributed to the refund. By dividing the state income tax refund by the amount of the total recovery, you find that 20% is attributed to the refund ($500/$2,500). Thus, 20% of the taxable recovery, or $300 (20% of $1,500), is reported as a state income tax refund on Line 10, Form 1040, and the balance of $1,200 on Line 21, Form 1040. Also attach a statement showing that the allocation of recoveries required the reporting on Line 10, Form 1040, of an amount less than the actual state income tax refund shown on Form 1099-G.

Table 11-1 2009 Standard Deduction
(For Determining Whether Recovery in 2010 of 2009 Itemized Deductions Is Taxable for 2010)

If you were—	*2009 standard deduction was—*
Married filing jointly	$ 11,400
Single	5,700
Head of household	8,350
Married filing separately	5,700
Qualifying widow or widower	11,400
Single age 65 or over	7,100
Single and blind	7,100
Single age 65 or over and also blind	8,500
Married filing jointly with:	
One spouse age 65 or over	12,500
Both spouses age 65 or over	13,600
One spouse blind under age 65	12,500
Both spouses blind under age 65	13,600
One spouse age 65 or over and also blind	13,600
One spouse age 65 or over and other spouse blind and under age 65	13,600
One spouse age 65 or over and also blind; other spouse blind and under age 65	14,700
Both spouses age 65 or over and also blind	15,800
Qualifying widow or widower age 65 or over	12,500
Qualifying widow or widower and blind	12,500
Qualifying widow or widower age 65 or over and also blind	13,600
Head of household age 65 or over	9,750
Head of household and blind	9,750
Head of household age 65 or over and also blind	11,150
Married filing separately age 65 or over*	6,800
Married filing separately and blind*	6,800
Married filing separately age 65 or over and also blind*	7,900

**If on your 2009 return you claimed your spouse as an exemption (21.2), add $1,100 if he or she was either blind or age 65 or older; add $2,200 if he or she was both blind and age 65 or older.*

Refund of state tax paid in installments over two tax years. If you pay estimated state or local income taxes, your last tax installment may be in the year you receive a refund. In this case, you allocate the refund between the two years; *see* the following Example.

EXAMPLE

Your estimated state income tax for 2009 was $4,000, which you paid in four equal installments. You made your fourth payment in January 2010. No state income tax was withheld during 2009. In 2010, you received a state income tax refund of $400 for 2009. You claimed itemized deductions on your 2009 federal return. You allocate the $400 refund between 2009 and 2010. As you paid 75% ($3,000 ÷ $4,000) of the estimated tax in 2009, 75% of the $400 refund, or $300, is treated as a recovery of taxes paid in 2009. On your 2010 return, you include $300 as income on Line 10, Form 1040. You also attach a statement explaining that the amount on Line 10 is less than the $400 refund shown on the Form 1099-G received from the state in 2010 because of the allocation required for the estimated tax installment made in January 2010.

When you figure your 2010 deduction for state income taxes, you reduce the $1,000 paid in January by $100, the portion of the refund attributed to your January 2010 payment of estimated state income tax. Your 2010 deduction for state income taxes will include the January net amount of $900 plus any estimated state income taxes paid in 2010 for 2010, any state income tax withheld during 2010, and any state income tax for 2009 that you paid when you filed your 2009 state return in 2010.

Note: If the $300 refund allocated to 2009 in the previous Example was more than the excess of your 2009 itemized deductions over the 2009 standard deduction you could have claimed, you report only that excess as income on your 2010 return.

11.6 Other Recovered Deductions

The rules in the preceding section *(11.5)* for determining whether a refund of state sales tax is taxable also apply to the recovery of other items for which you claimed a tax deduction, such as a refund of real estate taxes *(16.1)* adjustable rate mortgage interest *(15.1)*, reimbursement of a deducted medical expense *(17.4)*, a reimbursed casualty loss *(18.2)*, a return of donated property that was claimed as a charitable deduction *(14.1)*, and a payment of debt previously claimed as a bad debt *(5.33)*.

EXAMPLE

You filed a joint return for 2009 and claimed itemized deductions of $12,400, which exceeded your standard deduction of $11,400. You were not subject to the reduction to itemized deductions or to the alternative minimum tax. In 2010, you received the following recoveries for amounts deducted for 2009:

Medical expenses	$ 200
State income tax refund	400
Interest expense	325
Total	$ 925

The $400 state income tax refund was less than the difference between the state income tax you deducted and your state general sales taxes. The total recovery of $925 is taxable on your 2010 return. It is less than $1,000, the excess of your 2009 itemized deductions over the allowable standard deduction ($12,400 – 11,400). You report the state and local income tax refund of $400 on Line 7, Form 1040, and the balance of $525 on Line 21, Form 1040.

If the total recovery had been $2,500 instead of $925, $1,000 would be taxable (the excess of $12,400 in itemized deductions over the $11,400 standard deduction). The $1,500 balance would be tax free.

Unused tax credit in prior year. If you recover an item deducted in a prior year in which tax credits exceeded your tax, you refigure the prior year tax to determine if the recovery is taxable. Add the amount of the recovery to taxable income of the prior year and refigure the earlier year tax based on the increased taxable income. If the recomputed tax, after application of the tax credits, exceeds the actual tax for the earlier year, include the recovery in income to the extent the recovery reduced your tax in the prior year. The recovery may reduce an available credit carryforward to the current year.

Alternative minimum tax in the prior year. If you were subject to the alternative minimum tax (AMT) in the year the recovered deduction was claimed, recompute your regular and AMT tax for the prior year based on the taxable income you reported plus the recovered amount. If inclusion of the recovery does not change your total tax, you do not include the recovery in income. If your total tax increases by any amount, the recovered deduction gave you a tax benefit and you must include the recovery in income to the extent the deduction reduced your tax in the prior year. The recovery may reduce a carryforward of a tax credit based on prior year AMT.

Recovery of previously deducted items used to figure carryover. A deductible expense may not reduce your tax because you have an overall loss. If in a later year the expense is repaid or the obligation giving rise to the expense is cancelled, the deduction of that expense will be treated as having produced a tax reduction if it increased a carryover that has not expired by the beginning of the taxable year in which the forgiveness occurs. For example, you are on the accrual basis and deducted but did not pay rent in 2009. The rent obligation is forgiven in 2010. The 2009 rent deduction is treated as having produced a reduction in tax, even if it resulted in no tax savings in 2009, if it figured in the calculation of a net operating loss that has not expired or been used by the beginning of 2010, the year of forgiveness. The same rule applies to other carryovers such as the investment credit carryover.

11.7 How Legal Damages Are Taxed

By statute, compensatory damages for physical injury or physical sickness are tax free, whether fixed by a court or in a negotiated settlement. Damages for *nonphysical* personal injuries, such as for discrimination, back pay, or injury to reputation, are taxable; a limited exception for certain emotional distress damages may be available as discussed below. Damages for lost profits, breach of contract, or interference with business operations are taxable. Interest added to an award is taxable, even if the award is tax-free damages for physical injury.

Caution

Deducting Legal Fees

You may not deduct legal fees incurred in obtaining tax-free damages for physical injury or physical sickness. If you recover taxable damages, you may be able to deduct legal fees, as discussed in this section *(11.7)*.

Emotional distress. By statute, damages for emotional distress are tax free if attributable to a physical injury or sickness. If emotional distress damages are due to an injury other than a physical injury or sickness, as in a discrimination action, the damages are taxable with one exception: Damages up to the amount of actual medical care expenses attributable to emotional distress are tax free. Apart from the medical expenses exception, damages for emotional distress are taxable when received for a personal injury other than a physical injury or sickness. This is true even where the emotional distress damages cover physical symptoms such as insomnia, headaches, and stomach disorders. The emotional distress by itself is not treated as a physical injury or sickness.

According to the National Taxpayer Advocate, allowing tax-free treatment for emotional distress damages that are attributable to physical injury or sickness, but not non-physical injuries such as employer discrimination, is confusing and unfair. In her 2009 annual report, the Taxpayer Advocate asked Congress to change the law and allow tax-free treatment for all emotional distress, mental anguish, and pain and suffering awards.

EXAMPLE

A wrongful death recovery clearly is attributable to a physical injury. The IRS in several private rulings held that where a claim for intentional infliction of emotional distress is part of a wrongful death action, any recovery of compensatory damages is excludable from gross income. In these rulings, the estates of individuals killed in an accident initially brought claims for wrongful death and intentional infliction of emotional distress and a court awarded compensatory damages, prejudgment interest and punitive damages. The exact nature of the accident was not disclosed in the rulings, but it was apparently severe enough that local legislators passed a law to provide compensation to claimants for all their wrongful death and physical injury claims, including emotional distress. The law voided all prior court proceedings. The original defendant paid into a government fund from which damages to the claimants were paid.

The IRS ruled that all recoveries of compensatory damages from the government fund were for wrongful death, including amounts for emotional distress, and thus excludable as being received on account of a personal physical injury. The only exception is for amounts equal to medical expenses incurred to treat emotional distress that were previously deducted in prior years. Any damages reimbursing the previously deducted expenses are taxable.

Damages for wrongful termination. If damages are received from a former employer for wrongful termination, the damages are usually taxable as compensation, but any amount for a workplace-related physical injury or illness are excludable from income. Unless the terms of a settlement or verdict specifically allocate damages to a physical illness or injury, it may be difficult to show that you are entitled to the exclusion. But the Tax Court was convinced in the following case.

Domeny was working as a fundraiser for nonprofit organizations when she was diagnosed with multiple sclerosis (MS) in 1996. She managed her symptoms without medication but in 2000 she took a job with an autism center where she could spend less time on her feet. The position involved fundraising, grant writing and community development. Domeny had a strained relationship with her supervisor, who restricted her duties. The stress caused her MS symptoms to flare up. In November 2004 she discovered that her supervisor was embezzling funds and she reported this to the center's board of directors, who promised her that they would take action but did not. She felt uncomfortable about having to raise funds from parents while knowing that that her supervisor was embezzling funds. This situation continued for months, during which time her distress increased and her MS symptoms intensified. In March 2005, she went to her physician, complaining of vertigo, leg pain, numbness in both feet, burning behind her eyes and extreme fatigue. Her physician told her to stay home from work for two weeks but when Domeny notified the center, she was fired.

Domeny sued the center, alleging numerous discrimination and civil rights violations. The center agreed to settle and paid her a total of $33,308 of which $8,187.50 was treated as Form W-2 wages and $8,187.50 as attorney fees. The $16,933 balance was reported on Form 1099-MISC as nonemployee compensation. Domeny did not include the $16,933 on her 2005 return on the grounds that it was to compensate her for the worsening of her physical condition caused by working in a hostile work environment, and the fact that her condition prevented her from returning to work until more than a year after her termination.

The Tax Court agreed that the $16,933 payment was excludable from Domeny's income. Even though the settlement agreement did not specify why the payment was made, the inference was clear that the center was recognizing Domeny's complaint that a hostile and stressful work environment aggravated her physical illness. The fact that the settlement was segregated into three portions suggested that the center knew that part of the settlement was to compensate for physical illness. The center knew about Domeny's illness before her termination, and her only claim was that she was fired after her work environment had caused the flareup in her MS symptoms.

Punitive damages. Punitive damages are taxable, even if they relate to a physical injury or sickness. An exception in the law allows an exclusion from income for punitive damages awarded under a state wrongful death statute if the punitive damages are the only damages that may be awarded.

Holocaust restitution payments. There is a broad exclusion from gross income for Holocaust restitution payments. Tax-free treatment applies to payments received by persons persecuted by Nazi Germany or any Nazi-controlled or allied country, as well as to payments received by heirs or estates of such persecuted persons. Persecution on the basis of race, religion, physical or mental disability, or sexual orientation is covered.

Excludable restitution includes compensation for assets that were stolen or lost before, during, or immediately after World War II and to life insurance issued by European insurers immediately before and during the war. Tax-free treatment also applies to interest earned on escrow accounts and funds established in settlement of Holocaust victim claims against European banks or corporations.

Legal fees. If your damages are tax free, you may not deduct your litigation costs. If your damages are taxable, including the contingency fee portion of a taxable recovery (*see* below) you may be able to deduct your legal fees. A business expense deduction may be claimed on Schedule C for legal fees to recover taxable business income. An above-the-line deduction (directly from gross income) is allowed for legal fees in employment discrimination suits, certain other unlawful discrimination cases, and federal False Claims Act cases paid after October 22, 2004, with respect to settlements or judgments occurring after that date. The deduction cannot exceed the amount of the judgment or settlement you are including for the year. The above-the-line deduction is claimed on Line 36 of Form 1040 *(12.2)*.

Legal fees not eligible for the above-the-line deduction or Schedule C deduction may be claimed only as miscellaneous itemized deductions on Schedule A subject to the 2% adjusted gross income floor and the limitation on itemized deductions for higher-income taxpayers. The miscellaneous itemized deduction is not allowed at all for alternative minimum tax (AMT) purposes.

Attorney's contingent fee paid from taxable award. If you receive taxable damages, such as back pay in an employment dispute, and a percentage goes directly to your attorney under a contingent fee agreement, can you exclude from your income the contingent fee payment, so that you are only taxed on the net amount you receive?

The answer from the Supreme Court is no. The Supreme Court held in its 2005 *Banks* decision that the contingency-fee portion of a taxable damages award or settlement generally must be included in the litigant's gross income. The Court's decision did not resolve whether attorney fees paid pursuant to a statutory fee-shifting provision must be included in income, but it suggested that such statutory fees might in some cases be excludable. However, a subsequent Tax Court decision held that the attorney-fee portion of a taxable settlement was includible in the litigant's income where attorney fees were awarded under a California fee-shifting statute. Since the Supreme Court had not decided that issue, the Tax Court relied on its own prior decisions and precedent of the Ninth Circuit (where appeal would lie), which required inclusion of the fee portion of a settlement where a contingency-fee obligation was satisfied by a fee-shifting statute.

Note: If the contingency-fee portion of a taxable award in an unlawful employment discrimination case must be included in gross income under the Supreme Court decision, you may be able to offset the inclusion of the fees by an above-the-line deduction, as discussed above.

11.8 Cancellation of Debts You Owe

If a debt is cancelled or forgiven other than as a gift or a bequest the debtor generally must include the cancelled amount in gross income for tax purposes. Exclusions are allowed for discharges of farm or business real estate debt and debts of insolvent and bankrupt persons. If qualified principal residence indebtedness is discharged as part of a mortgage restructuring or foreclosure, the discharge is excluded from income. This exclusion is allowed for debt discharges in 2007 through 2012 of up to $2 million of debt that was incurred in acquiring, constructing, or substantially improving your principal residence and which is secured by your principal residence. Details on this as well as the other exclusions are provided below.

If you qualify for one of the exclusions, you generally must reduce certain "tax attributes" (such as the basis of property) by the amount excluded. The reduction of tax attributes is made on Form 982.

Form 1099-C. You should receive Form 1099-C from a federal government agency, credit union, or bank that cancels or forgives a debt you owe of $600 or more. The IRS receives a copy of the form. Generally, the amount of cancelled debt shown in Box 2 of Form 1099-C must be reported as "other income" on Line 21 of Form 1040, unless one of the exclusions discussed below applies.

Caution

Cancellation of Credit Card Debt

If debt on your personal (non-business) credit card was cancelled, you must report the cancelled amount as income unless you were insolvent immediately before the cancellation or the cancellation occurred in a Title 11 bankruptcy case.

Mortgage loan "workouts" and repayment discounts. If your lender agrees to a "workout" that restructures your loan and reduces the principal balance of your debt, or you are allowed a discount for paying off your loan early, the debt reduction or discount is generally considered cancellation of debt income that you must report on Line 21 of Form 1040, but you may be able to exclude the debt from income under the exclusion for qualified principal residence indebtedness or one of the other exclusions discussed below.

Foreclosure, repossession, or voluntary conveyance. If a lender forecloses on a loan secured by your property (such as your home mortgage) or repossesses the property secured by the loan (such as your car), or you voluntarily convey the property to the lender, the transaction is treated as a sale on which you realize gain or loss, as explained in *31.9*.

In addition, if you are personally liable on the loan (recourse debt) and the amount of the debt cancelled by the lender exceeds the fair market value of the property, you have cancellation of debt income that must be reported as ordinary income unless one of the exclusions discussed below applies. The lender will report fair market value of the property in Box 7 Form 1099-C.

Law Alert

Exclusion for Cancellation of Health Professional's Student Loan

The 2010 healthcare reform law expanded the exclusion for student loan debt forgiveness that benefits health professionals who have their student loans forgiven or repaid to them under state programs because they work in underserved communities. The new law applies retroactively to 2009 debt forgiveness; *see 11.8.*

Cancellation of student loans. The cancellation of a student loan results in taxable income unless one of the following exceptions applies.

If a loan by a government agency, by a government-funded loan program of an education organization, or by a qualified hospital organization is cancelled because you worked for a period of time in certain geographical areas in certain professions, such as practicing medicine in rural areas or teaching in inner-city schools, then the cancelled amount is not taxable. The IRS has ruled that the exception also applies to law school graduates who have student loan indebtedness forgiven under the Loan Repayment Assistance program if they work for a specified period of time in law-related public service positions in government or with tax-exempt charitable organizations. If a loan from an educational organization is cancelled because you work for that organization, the exclusion from gross income does not apply.

There is also a special exclusion for healthcare professionals who have student loans forgiven or repaid to them because they work in underserved communities. The 2010 healthcare reform law expanded the exclusion to include loans forgiven or repaid under any state program that is intended to increase the availability of healthcare services in underserved areas. Previously, the exclusion for health professionals was limited to debt forgiven or repaid under the National Health Services

Corps Loan Repayment Program or under state loan repayment programs eligible for funding under the Public Health Service Act. The expansion of this exclusion is retroactive to 2009. If you are a health professional and reported debt forgiveness income on your 2009 return, you should check with your state loan program office to determine if you qualify for the new law exclusion. If you do, you should file an amended return on Form 1040X to claim a refund for 2009. If the debt relief was reported as income on Form W-2, you can ask the payer to give you a corrected Form W-2c that omits the income and attach it to your Form 1040X, but you do not have to; you can file the Form 1040X without it. In Part II of the Form 1040X (on page 2), where you explain the changes made to your original return, you should write: "Excluded student loan amount under 2010 Health Care Act." If Social Security and Medicare (FICA) taxes were withheld on a loan repayment covered by the new exclusion, ask the payer to refund the withholdings to you.

Exclusion for discharge of qualified principal residence indebtedness. You are allowed to exclude cancelled debt from gross income if it is qualified principal residence indebtedness. The debt cancellation can be in the course of a mortgage loan modification ("workout") or a foreclosure. Qualified principal residence indebtedness is debt incurred in acquiring, constructing, or substantially improving your principal residence and which is secured by your principal residence. It also includes debt secured by your principal residence that refinances debt incurred to acquire, construct, or substantially improve your principal residence, but only to the extent of such refinanced debt. If part of the cancelled debt is not qualified principal residence indebtedness, such as refinancing used to pay personal expenses, that part must be included in income, unless another exception applies, such as the insolvency exclusion; *see* the Nancy Oak example below.

The exclusion applies to a cancellation of qualified principal residence indebtedness that occurs in 2007 through 2012. The limit on qualifying debt for all six years is $2 million, or $1 million if filing separately.

You claim the exclusion for cancelled qualified principal residence indebtedness on Form 982 by checking the box on Line 1e and entering the excluded amount on Line 2. If you continue to own the residence after the cancellation of debt, then on Line 10b of Form 982 you must reduce your basis in the residence by the excluded amount. However, if the qualified principal residence indebtedness is cancelled in a Title 11 bankruptcy case, the bankruptcy exclusion (*see* below) must be applied and not the exclusion for discharge of qualified principal residence indebtedness. Check the box on Line 1a of Form 982 (discharge in Title 11 case) rather than the box on Line 1(e).

If your cancelled debt is qualified principal residence indebtedness and you also were insolvent immediately before the debt cancellation because your liabilities exceeded the fair market value of your assets, you can elect to apply the insolvency exclusion (*see* below) instead of the exclusion for qualified principal residence indebtedness. If only part of the cancelled debt is qualified principal residence indebtedness, you can claim the qualified principal residence indebtedness exclusion for the qualifying portion and, to the extent of your insolvency, the insolvency exception can be applied to the nonqualified debt.

The following example illustrates application of the exclusion for discharges of qualified principal residence indebtedness. It is based on an example from IRS Publication 4681 (Canceled Debts, Foreclosures, Repossessions, and Abandonments), which also has other detailed examples on the exclusion for qualified principal residence indebtedness.

Law Alert

Exclusion for Qualified Principal Residence Indebtedness

If debt on your principal residence is cancelled in a mortgage restructuring or foreclosure, you may avoid cancellation of debt income on a qualifying debt discharge that occurs in 2007 through 2012. The cancelled debt must have been secured by your principal residence and incurred in the acquisition, construction, or substantial improvements of the principal residence. The maximum amount of qualified principal residence indebtedness for all six years is $2 million.

EXAMPLE

Nancy Oak purchased her principal residence in 2003 for $435,000, making a down payment of $15,000 and taking out a $420,000 mortgage loan on which she was personally liable (recourse debt) and which was secured by the residence. In 2004, Nancy took out a second recourse loan of $30,000 to remodel her kitchen and in 2007, when the value of her home was $500,000 and the outstanding principal amount on both mortgages was $440,000, she refinanced both loans, obtaining a recourse mortgage of $475,000. Nancy used the additional $35,000 (in excess of the refinanced $440,000 of outstanding loan principal) to pay off credit card debts and her son's college tuition.

By 2010, Nancy could no longer pay her mortgage loan installments. In August 2010, when the balance due on the mortgage was still $475,000, and the value of the home had fallen to $425,000, her bank agreed to a loan modification ("workout"). Under the workout, the principal balance of Nancy's loan was reduced by $40,000. Nancy was not insolvent nor in bankruptcy at that time.

Nancy receives a 2010 Form 1099-C from the bank showing cancelled debt of $40,000 in Box 2. Only $5,000 of the cancelled debt may be excluded from Nancy's gross income as qualified principal residence indebtedness. This is because the $35,000 of her loan used to pay off credit cards and college tuition does not qualify. The exclusion applies only to the extent that the cancelled debt of $40,000 exceeds the $35,000 of debt that was not (immediately before the cancellation) qualified principal residence indebtedness.

As Nancy does not qualify for any other exclusion, her exclusion on Form 982 is limited to $5,000. She must check the box on Line 1e and enter the $5,000 exclusion for qualified principal residence indebtedness on Line 2. On Line 10b, the excluded $5,000 must be entered as a reduction to her basis in the residence. Her basis is now $460,000: $435,000 purchase price plus $30,000 for improving the kitchen minus the $5,000 exclusion.

Nancy must report $35,000 as ordinary income on Line 21 of Form 1040 ("Other income").

Debts cancelled in bankruptcy. Debt cancelled in a Title 11 bankruptcy case is not included in your gross income if the cancellation is granted by the court or under a plan approved by the court. Instead, certain losses, credits, and basis of property must be reduced by the amount excluded from income. These losses, credits, and basis of property are called "tax attributes." The amount of cancelled debt is used to reduce the tax attributes in the order listed below:

1. Net operating losses and carryovers—dollar for dollar of debt discharge;
2. Carryovers of the general business credit—33⅓ cents for each dollar of debt discharge;
3. AMT minimum tax credit as of the beginning of the year immediately after the taxable year of the discharge—33⅓ cents for each dollar of debt discharge;
4. Net capital losses and carryovers—dollar for dollar of debt discharge;
5. Basis of depreciable and nondepreciable assets—dollar for dollar of debt discharge (but not below the amount of your total undischarged liabilities). Basis of property held at the beginning of the year is reduced in a specific order and within each category, in proportion to adjusted basis. *See* Publication 4681 for details.
6. Passive activity loss and credit carryovers—dollar for dollar of debt discharge for passive losses; 33⅓ cents for each dollar of debt discharge in the case of passive credits; and
7. Foreign tax credit carryovers—33⅓ cents for each dollar of debt discharge.

After these reductions, any remaining balance of the debt discharge is disregarded. On Form 982, you may make a special election to first reduce the basis of any depreciable assets before reducing other tax attributes in the order above. Realty held for sale to customers may be treated as depreciable assets for purposes of the election. The election allows you to preserve your current deductions, such as a net operating loss carryover or capital loss carryover, for use in the following year. The election also will have the effect of reducing your depreciation deductions for years following the year of debt cancellation. If you later sell the depreciable property at a gain, the gain attributable to the basis reduction will be taxable as ordinary income under the depreciation recapture rules *(44.1)*.

Court Decision

Credit Card Insurance Payments Taxable

Insurance can be purchased to cover a portion of credit card debt in the event you become unemployed or disabled, or you die. The Tax Court held that insurance payments of an unemployed credit card holder's debt were a taxable cancellation of debt to the extent the payments exceeded the premiums paid.

Debts discharged while you are insolvent. If your debt is cancelled outside of bankruptcy while you are insolvent, the cancellation does not result in taxable income to the extent of the insolvency. Insolvency means that liabilities exceed the fair market value of your assets immediately before the discharge of the debt. IRS Publication 4681 has a worksheet you can use to determine whether you were insolvent immediately before the debt discharge and the extent of the insolvency. The IRS and Tax Court hold that in determining whether liabilities exceed the value of assets at the time of a debt discharge, a taxpayer must include assets that are shielded from creditors under state law. This is true even though for federal bankruptcy purposes creditor-exempt assets do not have to be counted in determining whether an individual seeking bankruptcy protection is insolvent.

If liabilities do exceed the value of assets, the discharged debt is not taxed to the extent of your insolvency and is applied to the reduction of tax attributes on Form 982 in the same manner as to a bankrupt individual. If the cancelled debt exceeds the insolvency, any remaining balance is treated as if it were a debt cancellation of a solvent person and, thus, it is taxable unless another exclusion is available as discussed in this section.

See the Example below for the IRS approach to figuring insolvency upon a debt cancellation.

EXAMPLE

In 2009, Jones borrowed $1,000,000 from Chester and signed a note payable for that amount. Jones was not personally liable on the note, which was secured by an office building valued at $1,000,000 that he bought from Baker with the proceeds of Chester's loan. In 2010, when the value of the building declined to $800,000, Chester agreed to reduce the principal of the loan to $825,000. At the time, Jones held other assets valued at $100,000 and owed another person $50,000.

To determine the extent of Jones's insolvency, the IRS compares the value of Jones's assets and liabilities immediately before the discharge. According to the IRS, his assets total $900,000: the building valued at $800,000 plus other assets of $100,000. His liabilities total $1,025,000: the other debt of $50,000 plus the liability on the note, which the IRS considered to be $975,000, equal to the $800,000 value of the building and the discharged debt of $175,000. Jones is insolvent by $125,000 ($1,025,000 in liabilities less $900,000 in assets). As $175,000 was the amount of the discharged debt and Jones was insolvent to the extent of $125,000, only $50,000 is treated as taxable income in 2010.

Jones claims the insolvency exception on Form 982 by checking the box on Line 1b and entering the excludable $125,000 on Line 2. In Part II of Form 982, Jones must reduce his "tax attributes," as discussed above under the bankruptcy rules. The $50,000 debt cancellation that is not excludable under the insolvency rule must be reported as ordinary income on Line 21 of Form 1040 ("Other income").

Partnership debts. When a partnership's debt is discharged because of bankruptcy, insolvency, or if it is qualified farm debt or business real estate debt that is cancelled, the discharged amount is allocated among the partners. Bankruptcy or insolvency is tested not at the partnership level, but separately for each partner. Thus, a bankrupt or insolvent partner applies the allocated amount to reduce the specified tax attributes as previously discussed. A solvent partner may not take advantage of the rules applied to insolvent or bankrupt partners, even if the partnership is insolvent or bankrupt.

S corporation debts. The tax consequences of a debt discharge are determined at the corporate level. A debt discharge that is excludable from the S corporation's income because of insolvency or bankruptcy does not pass through to the shareholders and thus does not increase the shareholders' basis.

Purchase price adjustment for solvent debtors. If you buy property on credit and the seller reduces or cancels the debt arising out of the purchase, the reduction is generally treated as a purchase price adjustment (reducing your basis in the property). Since the reduction is not treated as a debt cancellation, you do not realize taxable income on the price adjustment. This favorable price adjustment rule applies only if you are solvent and not in bankruptcy, you have not transferred the property to a third party, and the seller has not transferred the debt to a third party, such as with the sale of your installment contract to a collection company.

Qualified farm debt. A solvent farmer may avoid tax from a discharge of indebtedness by an unrelated lender, including any federal, state, or local government agency, if the debt was incurred in operating a farm business. This relief is available only if 50% or more of your total gross receipts for the preceding three taxable years was derived from farming. The excluded amount first reduces tax attributes such as net operating loss carryovers and business tax credits, next reduces basis in all property other than farmland, and then reduces the basis in land used in the farming business. *See* IRS Publication 4681 for details.

1040 *Filing Instruction*

Price Adjustments Not Taxed

If you bought property on credit and the seller cancels or reduces your purchase-related debt, this is a price adjustment, not a taxable cancellation of debt.

Business real estate debt. A solvent taxpayer may elect on Form 982 to avoid tax on a discharge of qualifying real property business debt. Such a discharge may occur where the fair market value of the property securing the debt has fallen in value. The debt must have been incurred or assumed in connection with business real property and must be secured by such property. A debt incurred or assumed after 1992 must be incurred or assumed to buy, construct, or substantially improve real property used in a business, or to refinance such acquisition debt (up to the refinanced amount). Debt incurred after 1992 to refinance a pre-1993 business real property debt (up to the refinanced amount) also qualifies. The debt must be secured by the property. Discharges of farm indebtedness do not qualify but may be tax free under the separate rules discussed earlier.

The maximum amount that can be excluded from income is the excess of the outstanding loan principal (immediately before the discharge) over the fair market value (immediately before the discharge) of the real property securing the debt, less any other outstanding qualifying real property business debts secured by the property. The excludable amount also may not exceed the taxpayer's adjusted basis for all depreciable real property held before the discharge. On Line 4 of Form 982, you reduce your basis in all your depreciable real property by the excluded amount.

Effect of basis reduction on later disposition of property. A reduction of basis is treated as a depreciation deduction so that a profitable sale of the property at a later date may be subject to the rules of recapture of depreciation *(44.1)*.

11.9 Schedule K-1

Although partnerships, S corporations, trusts, and estates are different types of tax entities, they share a common tax-reporting characteristic. The entity itself generally does not pay income taxes. As a partner, shareholder, or beneficiary, you report your share of the entity's income or loss. The entity files a Schedule K-1 with the IRS that indicates your share of the income, deductions, and credits passed through from the entity. You will receive a copy of the Schedule K-1, which you should keep for your records; it does not have to be attached to your tax return.

To ensure that Schedule K-1 income is being reported, IRS computers match the information shown on the schedules with the tax returns of partners, S corporation shareholders, and beneficiaries.

11.10 How Partners Report Partnership Profit and Loss

A partnership files Form 1065, which informs the IRS of partnership profit or loss and each partner's share on Schedule K-1. The partnership pays no tax on partnership income; each partner reports his or her share of partnership net profit or loss and special deductions and credits, whether or not distributions are received from the partnership, as shown on Schedule K-1. Income that is not distributed or withdrawn increases the basis of a partner's partnership interest.

Your share reported to you on Schedule K-1 (Form 1065) is generally based on your proportionate capital interest in the partnership, unless the partnership agreement provides for another allocation.

Your partnership must give you a copy of Schedule K-1 (Form 1065), which lists your share of income, loss, deduction, and credit items, and where to report them on your return. For example, your share of income or loss from a business or real estate activity is reported on Schedule E and is subject to passive activity adjustments, if any. Interest and dividends are reported on Schedule B, royalties on Schedule E, and capital gains and losses on Schedule D. Your share of charitable donations is claimed on Schedule A if you itemize deductions. Tax preference items for alternative minimum tax purposes are also listed.

Filing Instruction

Partnership Elections

The partnership, not the individual partners, makes elections affecting the computation of partnership income such as the election to defer involuntary conversion gains, to amortize organization and start-up costs, and to choose depreciation methods, including first-year expensing. An election to claim a foreign tax credit is made by the partners.

Health insurance premiums. A partnership that pays premiums for health insurance for partners has a choice. It may treat the premium as a reduction in distributions to the partners. Alternatively, it may deduct the premium as an expense and charge each partner's share as a guaranteed salary payment taxable to the partner. The partner reports the guaranteed payment shown on Schedule K-1 as nonpassive income on Schedule E and may deduct 100% of the premium on Line 29, Form 1040, as an above-the-line deduction from gross income *(12.2)*.

Guaranteed salary and interest. A guaranteed salary that is fixed without regard to partnership income is taxable as ordinary wages and not as partnership earnings. If you receive a percentage of the partnership income with a stipulated minimum payment, the guaranteed payment is the amount by which the minimum guarantee exceeds your share of the partnership income before taking into account the minimum guarantee.

Interest on capital is reported as interest income.

Self-employment tax. As a general partner, you pay self-employment tax on your net partnership income, including guaranteed salary and other guaranteed payments. The self-employment tax is explained in *Chapter 45*. Limited partners do not pay self-employment tax, unless guaranteed payments are received *(45.2)*.

Special allocations. Partners may agree to special allocations of gain, income, loss, deductions, or credits disproportionate to their capital contributions. The allocation should have a substantial economic effect to avoid an IRS disallowance. The IRS will not issue an advance ruling on whether an allocation has a substantial economic effect. If the allocation is rejected, a partner's share is determined by his or her partnership interest.

To have substantial economic effect, a special allocation must be reflected by adjustments to the partners' capital accounts; liquidation proceeds must be distributed in accordance with the partners' capital accounts, and following a liquidating distribution, the partners must be liable to the partnership to restore any deficit in their capital.

If there is a change of partnership interests during the year, items are allocated to a partner for that part of the year he or she is a member of the partnership. Thus, a partner who acquires an interest late in the year is barred from deducting partnership expenses incurred prior to his entry into the partnership. If the partners agree to give an incoming partner a disproportionate share of partnership losses for the period after he or she becomes a member, the allocation must meet the substantial economic effect test to avoid IRS disallowance.

See IRS regulations to Code Section 704 and Form 1065 instructions for further details.

Reporting transfers of interest to IRS. If you transfer a partnership interest that includes an interest in partnership receivables and appreciated inventory, you must report the disposition to the partnership within 30 days, or, if earlier, by January 15 of the calendar year after the year of the transfer. The partnership in turn files a report with the IRS on Form 8308. You must also attach a statement to your income tax return describing the transaction and allocating basis to the receivables and inventory items. The IRS wants to keep track of such dispositions because partners have to pay ordinary income tax on the portion of profit attributable to the receivables and inventory.

Within 30 days of your transfer, provide the partnership with a statement that includes the date of the exchange and identifies the transferee (include Social Security number if known). You can be penalized for failure to notify the partnership. You and your transferee should receive a copy of the Form 8308 that the partnership will send to the IRS along with its Form 1065.

11.11 When a Partner Reports Income or Loss

You report your share of the partnership gain or loss for the partnership year that ends in your tax reporting year. If you and the partnership are on a calendar-year basis, you report your share of the 2010 partnership income on your 2010 income tax return. If the partnership is on a fiscal year ending March 31, for example, and you report on a calendar year, you report on your 2010 return your share of the partnership income for the whole fiscal year ending March 31, 2010—that is, partnership income for the fiscal year April 1, 2009, through March 31, 2010.

If a Section 444 election of a fiscal year is made on Form 8716, a special tax payment must be computed for each fiscal year and if the computed payment exceeds $500, it must be paid to the IRS. The tax payment is figured and reported on Form 8752. The tax does not apply to the first tax year of a partnership's existence but Form 8752 must still be filed. In later years, a refund of prior payments is available to the extent the prior payments exceed the payment required for the current fiscal year. For example, if the required payment was $12,000 for the fiscal year July 1, 2010–June 30, 2011, and the required payment for the fiscal year starting July 1, 2011, is $10,000, a $2,000 refund may be claimed on Form 8752. Refunds of prior year payments also are available if the fiscal-year election is terminated and a calendar year adopted or if the partnership liquidates.

11.12 Partnership Loss Limitations

Your share of partnership losses may not exceed the adjusted basis of your partnership interest. If the loss exceeds basis, the excess loss may not be deducted until you have partnership earnings to cover the loss or contribute capital to cover the loss. The basis of your partnership interest is generally the amount paid for the interest (either through contribution or purchase) less withdrawals plus accumulated taxed earnings that have not been withdrawn. You also have a basis in loans to the partnership for which you are personally liable.

A partner's basis is not increased by accrued but unpaid expenses such as interest costs and accounts payable unless the partnership uses the accrual accounting method. However, basis is increased by capitalized items allocable to future periods such as organization and construction period expenses.

Partners are subject to the "at-risk" loss limitation rules. These rules limit the amount of loss that may be deducted to the amount each partner personally has at stake in the partnership, such as contributions of property and loans for which the partner is personally liable. *See* the discussion of the "at-risk" rules in *Chapter 10 (10.17)*. Furthermore, if the IRS determines that a tax-shelter partnership is not operated to make a profit, deductions may be disallowed even where there is an "at-risk" investment. Finally, any loss not barred by these limitations may be disallowed under the passive activity rules discussed in *Chapter 10*.

Court Decision

Settlements Need Not Be Consistent

Neither the IRS nor the Department of Justice is required to offer consistent settlements to audited partners so long as they do not discriminate for arbitrary reasons.

11.13 Unified Tax Audits of Partnerships

Tax audits of both a partnership of more than 10 partners and its partners must be at the partnership level. To challenge the partnership treatment of an item, the IRS must generally audit the partnership, not the individual partner. To avoid a personal audit of a partnership item, a partner should report partnership items as shown on the partnership return or identify any inconsistent treatment on his or her return. Otherwise, the IRS may assess a deficiency without auditing the partnership.

For a partnership-level audit, the partnership names a "tax matters partner" (TMP) to receive notice of the audit. If one is not named, the IRS will treat as a TMP the general partner having the largest interest in partnership profits at the end of the taxable year involved in the audit. Notice of the audit must also be given to the other partners. All partners may participate in the partnership audit. If the IRS settles with some partners, it is not required to offer consistent settlement terms. However, the IRS is required to apply the tax law consistently.

Within 90 days after the IRS mails its final determination, the TMP may appeal to the Tax Court; individual partners have an additional 60 days to file a court petition if the TMP does not do so. An appeal may also be filed in a federal district court or the claims court if the petitioning partner first deposits with the IRS an amount equal to the tax that would be owed if the IRS determination were sustained. A Tax Court petition takes precedence over petitions filed in other courts. The first Tax Court petition filed is heard; if other partners have also filed petitions, their cases will be dismissed. If no Tax Court petitions are filed, the first petition filed in federal district court or the claims court takes precedence. Regardless of which petition takes precedence, all partners who hold an interest during the taxable year involved will be bound by the decision (unless the statute of limitations with respect to that partner has run out).

Exception for 10 or fewer partners. The unified audit rules do not apply if there are 10 or fewer partners. The exception applies if all the partners are individuals (but not nonresident aliens), estates of deceased partners, or C corporations. A husband and wife (and their estates) are treated as one partner.

11.14 Stockholder Reporting of S Corporation Income and Loss

S corporations are subject to tax reporting rules similar to those applied to partnerships. However, shareholders who work for the corporation are treated as employees for payroll tax purposes. The IRS and the courts require that S corporation shareholders receive reasonable compensation on which Social Security and Medicare taxes (FICA) must be paid. Self-employment tax does not apply to a shareholder's salary or similar receipts from the S corporation.

Your company must give you a copy of Schedule K-1 (Form 1120-S), which lists your share of income or loss, deductions, and credits that must be reported on your return. For example, your share of business income or loss is reported on Schedule E and is subject to passive activity adjustments, if any. Interest and dividends from other corporations are reported on Schedule B, capital gains and losses on Schedule D, Section 1231 gains or losses on Form 4797, and charitable donations on Schedule A. Tax preference items for alternative minimum tax purposes are also listed.

Health insurance premimums paid by an S corporation for more-than-2% stockholders are treated as wages, deductible on Form 1120-S by the corporation and reported to the stockholder on Form W-2. A more-than-2% shareholder who reports premiums as wages may deduct the premiums on Line 29 of Form 1040 as an adjustment to income.

Allocation to shareholders. The following items are allocated to and pass through to the shareholders based on the proportion of stock held in the corporation:

- Gains and losses from the sale and exchange of capital assets and Section 1231 property, as well as interest and dividends on corporate investments and losses. Investment interest expenses subject to the rules discussed in *Chapter 15 (15.10)* also pass through.

- Tax-exempt interest. Tax-exempt interest remains tax free in the hands of the stockholders but increases the basis of their stock. Dividends from other companies may qualify for the exclusion.
- First-year expense deduction (Section 179 deduction).
- Charitable contributions made by the corporation.
- Foreign income or loss.
- Foreign taxes paid by the corporation. Each stockholder elects whether to claim these as a credit or deduction.
- Tax preference items.
- Recovery of bad debts and prior taxes.

If your interest changed during the year, your pro rata share must reflect the time you held the stock.

Passive activity rules limit loss deductions. Losses allocated to you may be disallowed under the passive activity rules discussed in *Chapter 10*.

Planning Reminder

Basis Limits Loss Deductions

Deductible losses may not exceed your basis in S corporation stock and loans to the corporation. If losses exceed basis, the excess loss is carried over and becomes deductible when you invest or lend an equivalent amount of money to the corporation. This rule may allow for timing a loss deduction. In a year in which you want to deduct the loss, you may contribute capital or make an additional loan to the corporation. If a carryover loss exists when an S election terminates, a limited loss deduction may be allowed.

EXAMPLES

1. A calendar-year corporation incurs a loss of $10,000. Smith and Jones each own 50% of the stock. On May 1, Smith sells all of his stock to Harris. For the year, Smith was a shareholder for 120 days, Jones for 365 days, and Harris for 245 days. The loss is allocated on a daily basis; the daily basis of the loss is $27.3973 ($10,000 divided by 365 days). The allocation is as follows:

   Smith: $1,644 ($27.3973 × 120 days × 50% interest)
   Jones: $5,000 ($27.3973 × 365 days × 50% interest)
   Harris: $3,356 ($27.3973 × 245 days × 50% interest)

2. Same facts as in Example 1, except that on May 1, Smith sells only 50% of his stock to Harris. The allocation for Smith accounts for his 50% interest for 120 days and his 25% interest for the remainder of the year.

   Smith: $3,322 ($27.3973 × 120 days × 50% plus $27.3973 × 245 days × 25%)
   Jones: $5,000 (as above)
   Harris: $1,678 ($27.3973 × 245 days × 25%)

$$\frac{\$1{,}000}{\$1{,}500} \times \$390 = \$260$$

Basis adjustments. Because of the nature of S corporation reporting, the basis of each shareholder's stock is subject to change. Basis is increased by the pass-through of income items and by loans to the S corporation for which the shareholder is personally liable, and basis is reduced by the pass-through of loss items and the receipt of certain distributions. Because income and loss items pass through to stockholders, an S corporation has no current earnings and profits. An income item will not increase basis, unless you actually report the amount on your tax return. The specific details and order of basis adjustments are listed in the instructions to Schedule K-1 of Form 1120S.

11.15 How Beneficiaries Report Estate or Trust Income

Trust or estate income is treated as if you had received the income directly from the original source instead of from the estate or trust. This means capital gain remains capital gain, ordinary income is fully taxed, and tax-exempt income remains tax free. Tax preference items of a trust or estate are apportioned between the estate or trust and beneficiaries, according to allocation of income.

Your share of the trust or estate income, deductions and credits is reported by the fiduciary on Schedule K-1 of Form 1041. You do not file Schedule K-1 with your return; keep it for your records. The instructions to Schedule K-1 indicate where to report the trust or estate items on Form 1040. For example, capital gains are reported on Schedule D, as are other capital gains. Income or loss from real estate or business activities shown on Schedule K-1 is reported by you on Schedule E, subject to the passive activity restrictions discussed in *Chapter 10*.

Filing Instruction

Consistent Reporting by Beneficiaries

Beneficiaries of trusts and estates must report items consistently with the Schedule K-1 provided by the trust or estate. If an item is treated inconsistently and a statement identifying the inconsistency is not attached to the return, the IRS may make a summary assessment for additional tax without issuing a deficiency notice.

Reporting rule for revocable grantor trusts. A grantor who sets up a revocable trust or keeps certain powers over trust income or corpus must report all of the trust income, deductions, and credits. This rule applies if a grantor retains a reversionary interest in the trust that is valued at more than 5% of the trust (valued at the time the trust is set up) *(39.6)*. If a grantor is also a trustee of a revocable trust and all the trust assets are in the United States, filing Form 1041 is not necessary. The grantor simply reports the trust income, deductions, and credits on Form 1040. *See* the Form 1041 instructions for reporting requirements.

11.16 Reporting Income in Respect of a Decedent (IRD)

If you receive income that was earned by but not paid to a decedent before death, such as wages, IRA and qualified plan distributions, lottery prize winnings, or installment sale proceeds, you are said to have "income in respect of a decedent," or IRD. You report the IRD on your return. Where the purchaser of a deferred annuity contract dies before the annuity starting date, payments to a beneficiary in excess of the purchaser's investment are IRD, whether payable in a lump sum or as periodic payments.

If the decedent's estate paid federal estate tax that was attributable to the IRD you received, you may claim an itemized deduction for the estate tax paid on that income *(11.17)*.

11.17 Deduction for Estate Tax Attributable to IRD

A beneficiary can claim an itemized deduction for the amount, if any, of federal estate tax paid on income in respect of a decedent (IRD). The deduction is allowed to the IRD recipient only for the year in which the recipient reports the IRD income. No deduction is allowed for state death taxes paid on IRD. If you receive IRD, ask the executor of the decedent's estate for the amount of federal estate tax paid and the portion of the estate that the IRD represented to help you compute the deduction.

The itemized deduction is a miscellaneous deduction claimed on Line 28 of Schedule A. The Line 28 deduction is not subject to the 2% AGI floor that applies to most miscellaneous itemized deductions.

EXAMPLE

When Jim Bennett's uncle died, he was owed a fee of $1,000. He also had not collected accrued bond interest of $500. Bennett, as the sole heir, will collect both items and pay income tax on them. These items are called "income in respect of a decedent." Assume that an estate tax of $390 was paid on the $1,500. Bennett collects the $1,000, which he reports on his income tax return. If he itemizes deductions, he may deduct $260, computed as follows:

$$\frac{\$1{,}000}{\$1{,}500} \times \$390 = \$260$$

When he collects the $500, he will deduct the balance, or $130 ($390 – $260).

However, if the IRD you receive is long-term capital gain, such as an installment payment on a sale transacted before a decedent's death, the estate tax attributed to the capital gain item is not claimed as a miscellaneous deduction. The deduction is treated as if it were an expense of sale and, thus, reduces the amount of gain, but not below zero.

11.18 How Life Insurance Proceeds Are Taxed to a Beneficiary

Life insurance proceeds received upon the death of the insured are generally tax free. However, insurance proceeds may be subject to estate tax so that the beneficiary actually receives a reduced amount *(39.8)*. Interest paid on proceeds left with the insurer is taxable.

Read the following checklist to find how your insurance receipts are taxed—

A lump-sum payment of the full face value of a life insurance policy: The proceeds are generally tax free. The tax-free exclusion also covers death benefit payments made under endowment contracts, workers' compensation insurance contracts, employers' group insurance plans, or accident and health insurance contracts.

Insurance proceeds may be taxable where the policy was transferred for valuable consideration. Exceptions to this rule are made for transfers among partners and corporations and their stockholders and officers.

Installment payments spread over your life under a policy that could have been paid in a lump sum: Part of each installment attributed to interest may be taxed. Divide the face amount of the policy by the number of years the installments are to be paid. The result is the amount that is received tax free each year.

If the policy guarantees payments to a secondary beneficiary if you should die before receiving a specified number of payments, the tax-free amount is reduced by the present value of the secondary beneficiary's interest in the policy. The insurance company can give you this figure.

Installment payments for a fixed number of years under a policy that could have been paid in a lump sum. Divide the full face amount of the policy by the number of years you are to receive the installments. The result is the amount that is received tax free each year.

Planning Reminder

Accelerated Death Benefits

A person who is terminally ill may withdraw without tax life insurance proceeds to pay medical bills and other living expenses. For policies lacking an accelerated benefits clause, it is possible to sell a life insurance policy without incurring tax to a viatical settlement company *(17.16)*.

EXAMPLE

Fran is the beneficiary of her husband's $100,000 life insurance policy. She elects to take installment payments for 10 years. Each year she may receive tax-free principal of $10,000 ($100,000 ÷ 10).

Installment payments when there is no lump-sum option in the policy: You must find the discounted value of the policy at the date of the insured's death and use that as the principal amount. The insurance company can give you that figure. After you find the discounted value, you divide it by the number of years you are to receive installments. The result is the amount that is tax free. The remainder is taxed.

EXAMPLE

The insured died in 2010. Under an insurance policy, his surviving spouse is entitled to $5,000 a year for life. Her life expectancy is 20 years. There is no lump sum stated in the policy. Say the discounted value of the wife's rights is $60,000. The principal amount spread to each year for the wife is $3,000 ($60,000 ÷ 20). Subtracting $3,000 from each annual $5,000 payment gives her taxable income of $2,000.

Payments to you along with other beneficiaries under the same policy, by lump-sum or varying installments. *See* the following Example for the way multiple beneficiaries may be taxed.

EXAMPLE

Under a life insurance policy of an insured man who died in 2010, a surviving wife, daughter, and nephew are all beneficiaries. The wife is entitled to a lump sum of $60,000. The daughter and nephew are each entitled to a lump sum of $35,000. Under the installment options, the wife chooses to receive $5,000 a year for the rest of her life. (She has a 20-year life expectancy.) The daughter and the nephew each choose a yearly payment of $5,000 for 10 years. This is how each yearly installment is taxed:

Wife: The principal amount spread to each year is $3,000 ($60,000 ÷ 20-year life expectancy). Subtracting $3,000 from the yearly $5,000 payment gives the wife taxable income of $2,000.

Daughter and Nephew: Both are taxed the same way. The principal amount spread to each of the 10 years is $3,500 ($35,000 ÷ 10-year installment period). Subtracting this $3,500 from the yearly $5,000 installment gives the daughter and the nephew taxable income of $1,500 each.

Caution

Surrender of Policy for Cash

If the cash received on the surrender of a policy exceeds the premiums paid less dividends received, the excess is taxed as ordinary income (not capital gain). If you take, instead, a paid-up policy, you may avoid tax *(6.12)*. You get no deduction if there is a loss on the surrender of a policy.

Tax may be avoided by a terminally ill individual on the surrender of a policy under an accelerated death benefit clause or on a sale of the policy to a viatical settlement company *(17.16)*.

11.19 A Policy With a Family Income Rider

Payments received under a family income rider are taxed under a special rule. A family income rider provides additional term insurance coverage for a fixed number of years from the date of the basic policy. Under the terms of a rider, if the insured dies at any time during the term period, the beneficiary receives monthly payments during the balance of the term period, and then at the end of the term period, receives the lump-sum proceeds of the basic policy. If the insured dies after the end of the term period, the beneficiary receives only the lump sum from the basic policy.

When the insured dies during the term period, part of each monthly payment received during the term period includes interest on the lump-sum proceeds of the basic policy (which is held by the company until the end of the term period). That interest is fully taxed. The balance of the monthly payment consists of an installment (principal plus interest) of the proceeds from the term insurance purchased under the family income rider. You may exclude from this balance a prorated portion of the present value of the lump sum under the basic policy. The lump sum under the basic policy is tax free when you eventually receive it.

The rules here also apply to an integrated family income policy and to family maintenance policies, whether integrated or with an attached rider.

In figuring your taxable portions, ask the insurance company for its interest rate and the present value of term payments.

11.20 Selling or Surrendering Life Insurance Policy

Surrendering or selling a life insurance policy results in ordinary income, long-term gain, or a combination of both, depending on the type of policy and type of transaction. In Revenue Ruling 2009-13, the IRS presents three situations that illustrate the tax consequences of selling or surrendering a whole life or term insurance contract.

Situation 1 - surrender of whole life insurance contract. On January 1 of Year 1, Tom Taxpayer bought a whole life insurance policy on his life, with the proceeds payable to a family member. Tom retained the right to change the beneficiary, take out a policy loan, or surrender the contract for its cash surrender value.

After 89 ½ months, on June 15 of Year 8, Tom surrenders the contract for its cash surrender value of $78,000. As of the surrender date, Tom had paid total premiums of $64,000, $10,000 of which was the cost of the insurance protection received as of that date. The $78,000 cash surrender value reflected the subtraction of the $10,000 insurance cost.

On the surrender, Tom recognizes income of $14,000, the $78,000 received minus the total premiums paid of $64,000.

The Tax Code does not specify whether income recognized upon the surrender of a life insurance contract, as opposed to a sale, is treated as ordinary income or as capital gain. However, relying on a 1964 ruling (Revenue Ruling 64-51), the IRS holds that the proceeds received by an insured upon the surrender of a life insurance policy constitute ordinary income to the extent such proceeds exceed the cost of the policy. Thus here the $14,000 of income recognized on the surrender of the insurance contract is ordinary income and not capital gain.

Situation 2 - sale of whole life insurance contract. Same facts as in Situation 1 except that Tom sold the contract for $80,000 to an unrelated person. To figure gain on the sale, the $80,000 amount realized must be reduced by the insured's adjusted basis in the insurance contract. To figure basis, the $64,000 of total premiums paid must be reduced by the $10,000 cost of insurance provided before the sale. Therefore, adjusted basis is $54,000, and the gain on the sale is $26,000 ($80,000 proceeds minus $54,000 basis).

Part of the $26,000 gain is ordinary income and part is capital gain. The Supreme Court has held that under the "substitute for ordinary income" doctrine, income that has been earned but not yet recognized by a taxpayer cannot be converted into capital gain by a sale or exchange. In the case of a sale of a life insurance policy, the portion of the gain that would have been ordinary income if the policy had been surrendered (i.e., the inside buildup under the contract) is ordinary income. However, any income over that amount can qualify for capital gain treatment.

Here, $14,000 of the $26,000 gain is ordinary income representing the inside buildup under the contract ($78,000 cash surrender value minus $64,000 total premiums paid). The remaining $12,000 of income is long-term capital gain.

Situation 3 - sale of term life insurance contract. Assume that Tom had entered into a 15-year level premium term contract with no cash surrender value, rather than the whole life contract in Situation 2. Monthly premiums were $500 and total premiums paid were $45,000 when the policy was sold after 89.5 months to an unrelated party for $20,000.

In this case, as in Situation 2, the adjusted basis of the contract for purposes of determining gain or loss is the total premiums paid minus charges for the provision of insurance before the sale. The cost of insurance protection in this case amounted to $44,750 ($500 × 89.5 months), so Tom's adjusted basis is $250 ($45,000 total premiums minus $44,750).

Tom's gain on the sale is $19,750 ($20,000 sale proceeds minus $250 basis). Because the term insurance contract had no cash surrender value, and thus no inside buildup to which ordinary income treatment could apply, the entire $19,750 is long-term capital gain.

PART 3

Claiming Deductions

In this part, you will learn how to reduce your tax liability by claiming deductions from gross income, and either the standard deduction or itemized deductions. Pay special attention to—

- Deductions you may claim directly from gross income in arriving at adjusted gross income. These are allowed even if you claim the standard deduction. *See Chapter 12.*
- The standard deduction. Although the standard deduction *(Chapter 13)* may provide an automatic tax reduction, read the chapters on itemized deductions to see that you have not overlooked itemized deductions for charitable donations, interest expenses, state and local taxes, medical expenses, casualty and theft losses, miscellaneous expenses for job costs, and investment expenses. For 2010, there is no reduction to overall itemized deductions for high-income taxpayers, as there has been in prior years. The reduction is scheduled to resume in 2011.
- Personal exemptions. Each personal exemption claimed on your 2010 return—for yourself, your spouse, your children, and other dependents, is the equivalent of a $3,650 deduction. For 2010, the deduction for personal exemptions is not phased out, regardless of income. The phaseout is scheduled to resume in 2011. *See Chapter 22* for the rules on personal exemptions.
- Other deductions are discussed in the following chapters:

Chapter 40	Business expenses
Chapter 9	Rental expenses
Chapter 43	Automobile expenses

Chapter 12

Deductions Allowed in Figuring Adjusted Gross Income

Adjusted gross income (AGI) is the amount used in figuring the 7.5% floor for medical expense deductions *(17.1)*, the 10% floor for personal casualty and theft losses *(18.11)*, the 2% floor for miscellaneous itemized deductions *(19.1)*, and the charitable contribution percentage limitations *(14.17)*.

If you follow the instructions and order of the tax return, you will arrive at adjusted gross income automatically. But if you are planning the tax consequences of a transaction in advance of preparing your return, *see* the explanation of how to figure adjusted gross income (AGI) *(12.1)*.

There is an advantage in being able to claim deductions directly from gross income in arriving at adjusted gross income, since such deductions are allowed even if you claim the standard deduction and do not itemize deductions on Schedule A of Form 1040. Another advantage of such deductions is that they also reduce state income tax for taxpayers residing in states that compute tax based on federal adjusted gross income. This chapter will explain the deductions that qualify for the direct deduction from gross income.

12.1 Figuring Adjusted Gross Income (AGI)

Adjusted gross income is the difference between gross income in Step 1 and the deductions listed in Step 2. Most of the Step 2 deductions can be claimed only on Form 1040 *(12.2)*.

Step 1. Figure gross income. This is all income received by you from any source, such as wages, salary, tips, gross business income, income from sales and exchanges of property, interest and dividends, rents, royalties, annuities, pensions, etc. But because of exclusions allowed by the tax law, gross income does not include such items as tax-free interest from state or local bonds *(4.24)*, tax-free parsonage allowance *(3.13)*, tax-free insurance proceeds *(11.8–11.20)*, gifts and inheritances *(11.4)*, certain home sale gains *(29.1)*, Social Security benefits that are not subject to tax *(34.3)*, tax-free scholarship grants *(33.1)*, tax-free board and lodging *(3.12)*, and other tax-free fringe benefits *(Chapter 3)*.

Step 2. Deduct from your 2010 gross income only the following items:

Repayment of supplemental unemployment benefits required because of receipt of trade readjustment allowances *(2.9)*
Forfeiture-of-interest penalties because of premature withdrawals *(4.16)*
Capital loss deduction up to $3,000 *(5.4)*
IRA contributions *(8.4)*
Rent and royalty expenses *(9.2)*
Educator expenses *(12.2)*. *See* the note below.
Tuition and fees *(12.2)*. *See* the note below.
50% of self-employment tax liability *(12.2)*
Health savings account (HSA) contributions *(12.2)*
Health insurance premiums if self-employed *(12.2)*
Jury duty pay turned over to your employer *(12.2)*
Performing artist's qualifying expenses *(12.2)*
Reforestation expenses *(12.2)*
Reservists' travel costs *(12.2)*
State and local official expenses *(12.2)*
Moving expenses *(12.3)*
Student loan interest *(33.6)*
Alimony payments *(37.1)*
Domestic production activities deduction *(40.23)*
Business expenses *(40.7)*
Net operating losses *(40.19)*
Keogh or SEP retirement plan contributions for yourself *(41.5)*
Archer MSA contributions *(41.13)*

Note: Educator expenses and tuition and fees. The laws authorizing these deductions expired at the end of 2009 and Congress had not extended them to 2010 when this book went to press. An extension is expected, and in *12.2* we have assumed that the deductions will be available on 2010 returns.

Step 3. The difference between Steps 1 and 2 is adjusted gross income.

12.2 Claiming Deductions From Gross Income

Many deductions taken directly from gross income in arriving at adjusted gross income are deducted on Form 1040 schedules devoted to a specific activity, such as business deductions claimed on Schedule C *(Chapter 40)*, capital losses claimed on Schedule D *(Chapter 5)*, and real estate rental expenses claimed on Schedule E *(Chapter 9)*.

Other expenses are claimed directly from gross income on page 1 of Form 1040 or Form 1040A in figuring adjusted gross income. On Form 1040, these deductions, claimed on Lines 23–36, are referred to as "above-the-line" deductions, as they reduce total (gross) income shown on Line 22 regardless of whether itemized deductions are claimed. On Form 1040A, only a few deductions are allowed in figuring adjusted gross income: traditional IRA deductions, student loan interest, educator expenses, and tuition and fees.

Deductions for educator expenses and tuition/fees—not yet extended to 2010 when this book went to press. Although Congress had not yet extended the laws authorizing the deductions for educator expenses and tuition/fees for 2010 when this book went to press, the extension is expected. On the assumption that the deductions will be available on 2010 returns, the following rules apply.

Educator expenses. If you were a teacher, instructor, counselor, principal, or aide in a private or public elementary or secondary school (kindergarten through grade 12) for at least 900 hours during the school year in 2010, you generally may deduct up to $250 of out-of-pocket costs for books and classroom supplies. Eligible expenses include computer equipment, including related software and services, other equipment, and supplementary materials used in the classroom. For courses in health or physical education, supplies must be related to athletics to qualify. Home schooling expenses do not qualify. If you are married filing jointly and you and your spouse both qualify as educators, each of you may deduct up to $250 of your qualified costs, for a $500 maximum on your joint return.

If eligible expenses exceed the $250 limit, the excess may be deductible as a miscellaneous itemized expense on Schedule A of Form 1040 *(19.1)*.

The $250 deduction limit may have to be reduced or eliminated completely if certain tax-free amounts are received during the year. The deduction is reduced by tax-free interest on savings bonds used for tuition *(33.4)* and tax-free distributions from qualified tuition programs *(33.5)* and Coverdell education savings accounts *(33.12)*.

Tuition and fees. Up to $4,000 of college tuition and fees paid in 2010 may be deducted on Form 8917 if MAGI does not exceed $65,000 for single and head of household filers and $130,000 for joint returns. A deduction of up to $2,000 is allowed for single and head of household filers with MAGI exceeding $65,000 but not $80,000 and for joint filers with MAGI exceeding $130,000 but not $160,000 *(33.13)*.

Overnight travel costs of Reservists and National Guard members. Armed Forces Reservists and National Guard members who travel over 100 miles and stay overnight to attend Reserve and Guard meetings may deduct their travel expenses as an above-the-line-deduction to the extent of the Federal Government *per diem* rate for that locality *(35.8)*.

Expenses of performing artists. If you are a performing artist, you may be able to deduct job expenses from gross income, but only if your income is extremely low. You must have:

1. Two or more employers in the performing arts during 2010 with at least $200 of earnings from at least two of them.
2. Expenses from acting or other services in the performing arts that exceed 10% of gross income from such work; and
3. Adjusted gross income (before deducting these expenses) that does not exceed $16,000.

If you are married, a joint return must be filed to claim the deduction, unless you lived apart from your spouse during the whole year. The $16,000 adjusted gross income limitation applies to your combined incomes. If both spouses are performing artists, the $16,000 adjusted income limit applies to the combined incomes, but each spouse must separately meet the two-employer test and 10% expense test for his or her job expenses to be deductible on the joint return.

You report the performing artist expenses on Form 2106 (or Form 2106-EZ where eligible) and enter the total on Line 24 of Form 1040, instead of on Schedule A. If you do not meet the tests, the expenses are deducted on Schedule A subject to the 2% AGI floor *(19.1)*.

State and local officials. State and local officials paid on a fee basis may deduct from gross income unreimbursed business expenses.

Health savings account (HSA) deduction. If you are self-employed and have coverage under a high-deductible health plan, are not entitled to Medicare benefits, and are not the dependent of another taxpayer, you generally can deduct contributions to an HSA within the limits discussed in *41.10*. If you are an employee, and your employer has contributed less than the applicable limit to an HSA on your behalf, you may contribute the balance and deduct it from gross income *(3.2)*.

Moving expenses. Deductible moving expenses are discussed in this chapter *(12.3–12.8)*.

50% of self-employment tax. After you figure your self-employment tax liability on Schedule SE, you deduct 50% of it as an above-the-line deduction. *See Chapter 45* for the calculation of self-employment tax *(45.3–45.4)*.

Keogh plan contributions and self-employed SEP or SIMPLE deductions. *See Chapter 41* for further details.

Law Alert

Self-Employed Deduction for Health Insurance Premiums

When this book went to press, Congress was close to passing legislation that would allow a self-employed person's income tax deduction for health insurance premiums *(12.2)* to be taken into account as a reduction to net earnings in figuring the self-employment tax due for 2010 *(45.3)*. Assuming the provision becomes law, the IRS could change its tax forms and treat the deduction as a business expense to be claimed on Schedule C *(40.6)* rather than as an above-the-line deduction claimed on page 1 of Form 1040. *See* the *e-Supplement at jklasser.com* for an update on where to claim the 2010 deduction for health insurance premiums. .

Self-employed health insurance deduction. If you were self-employed in 2010, you may deduct from gross income 100% of premiums paid in 2010 for medical and dental insurance, and qualified (*see* below) long-term-care insurance, for yourself, your spouse, your dependents, and your children under age 27 as of the end of the year. The deduction is also allowed if you are a general partner in a partnership, a limited partner receiving guaranteed payments, or you received wages from an S corporation in which you were a more-than-2% shareholder. As a sole proprietor, you may claim the 100% above-the-line deduction whether the policy is purchased in your own name or the name of the business. If you are a more than 2% shareholder-employee of an S corporation, the IRS position is that the S corporation must "establish" the health plan, but the plan can be considered "established" by the S corporation even if you obtain the policy in your own name, so long as (1) the corporation makes the premium payments to the insurance company or the corporation reimburses you for premiums you pay, and (2) the premiums are reported as wages on your Form W-2 and on your tax return. Similarly, if you are a partner, a health plan in your name is considered "established" by the partnership if (1) the partnership pays the premiums or you pay them and are reimbursed by the partnership, and (2) the partnership reports the premiums as guaranteed payments on Schedule K-1 (Form 1065) and you include the payments as income on your tax return.

If you have a qualified long-term-care policy, part of the premium is deductible depending on your age *(17.15)* and this amount is included in the above-the-line deduction.

The 100% deduction may not exceed your net profit from the business under which the health premiums are paid, less deductions claimed for 50% of self-employment tax and Keogh, SEP, or SIMPLE retirement plan contributions.

The 100% health insurance deduction may not be claimed for any month during 2010 that you were eligible to participate in an employer's subsidized health plan, including a plan of your spouse's employer. If the deduction would be barred for any month because of such eligibility and you have long-term-care coverage that is not employer subsidized, you may claim the 100% deduction for the portion of the long-term-care premiums that is deductible for your age *(17.15)*.

The instructions to Form 1040 and IRS Publication 535 (Business Expenses) have worksheets for figuring the self-employed health insurance deduction.

Penalty on early savings withdrawals *(4.16)*.

Alimony paid. *See Chapter 37*.

Traditional IRA contribution. The deductible limits, including the phaseout rules for individuals covered by employer retirement plans, are explained in *8.3–8.4*.

Student loan interest. Within limits, you may deduct interest you pay on a qualified student loan *(33.14)*.

Domestic production activities deduction *(40.23–40.25)*.

Attorney fees in employment discrimination cases. Attorney fees and court costs in actions involving unlawful discrimination claims are deductible on Line 36 of Form 1040 if they were paid with respect to settlements or judgments occurring after October 22, 2004. The deduction may not exceed the amount included in income as a result of the judgment or settlement *(11.7)*.

Archer MSA contribution. If you are self-employed or employed by a qualifying small business and have high-deductible health coverage, a deduction for contributions to an Archer MSA account may be deductible. The deduction is figured on Form 8853 and then entered on Form 1040 *(41.13)*.

Jury duty pay turned over to employer. If you receive your regular pay while on jury duty and turn over your jury duty fees to your employer, report the fees as other income on Line 21, Form 1040 and claim an offsetting deduction.

Repayment of supplemental unemployment benefits. You may claim a deduction from gross income for the repayment or in some cases a tax credit *(2.9)*. Claim the deduction on Line 36 of Form 1040 and on the adjacent dotted line write the amount and label it "subpay TRA" (trade readjustment allowances).

Reforestation amortization. If you do not have to file Schedule C or F to report income from a timber activity, an amortization deduction for qualifying reforestation expenses may be claimed over an 84-month period; *see* Code Section 194 for details. On Line 36 of Form 1040, the amortization deduction should be labeled "RFST."

Costs incurred in obtaining whistleblower award from the IRS. You may claim an above-the-line deduction for costs you incurred, including attorneys' fees, in connection with obtaining a whistleblower award from the IRS as an informant, up to the amount of the award reported as income. Label the deduction on Line 36 of Form 1040 as "WBF."

12.3 What Moving Costs Are Deductible?

You may deduct unreimbursed expenses of moving your household goods and traveling to a new job location, provided you meet

- A 50-mile distance test *(12.4)*, and
- A 39-week or 78-week work test for remaining in the new location *(12.5–12.6)*. A deduction may be claimed even if the work test has not been met by the filing due date *(12.7)*.

You may be able to deduct moving costs if you move to take your first full-time job or if you are returning to full-time work after a long period of working part-time or being unemployed; *see 12.4*.

Members of the Armed Forces do not have to meet the distance and time tests if their move is to a permanent change of station; *see* the instructions to Form 3903.

You claim the moving expense deduction as an adjustment to gross income on Form 1040, Line 26, whether you claim the standard deduction or itemized deductions.

If your expenses are reimbursed, you do not have to report the reimbursement, provided your employer reimburses you under an accountable plan *(20.31, 12.8)*.

If the tests are met, you may deduct on your 2010 return the following unreimbursed moving expenses incurred during 2010:

1. ***Traveling costs of yourself and members of your household en route from your old to the new locality.*** Here, you include the costs of transportation and lodging for yourself and household members while traveling to your new residence. Lodging before departure for one day after the old residence is unusable and lodging for the day of arrival at the new locality are included. If you use your own car, you may either deduct your actual costs of gas, oil, and repairs (but not depreciation) during the trip or take a deduction based on the IRS standard mileage rate. For 2010, the IRS standard mileage rate for moving expenses is 16.5 cents per mile. Also add parking fees and tolls. Meal expenses are not a deductible moving expense.
2. ***The actual cost of moving your personal effects and household goods.*** This includes the cost of packing, crating, and transporting furniture and household belongings, in-transit storage up to 30 consecutive days, insurance costs for the goods, and the cost of moving a pet or shipping an automobile to your new residence. You may also deduct expenses of moving your personal effects from a place other than your former home, but only up to the estimated cost of such a move from your former home. Also deduct the cost of connecting or disconnecting utilities when moving household appliances. The cost of connecting a telephone in your new home is not deductible.

In one case, a moving expense deduction was allowed for the cost of shipping a sailboat. The IRS had disallowed the deduction, claiming the sailboat was not a "personal effect." The Tax Court, however, allowed the deduction based on these facts: the couple were active sailors and frequently used the boat; they lived on the sailboat for two weeks immediately before they moved and also for nine weeks after they arrived in the new location; and they kept on board personal effects such as a refrigerator, kitchen utensils, and chairs. According to the court, the boat was so "intimately related" to their lifestyle that it should be considered a deductible personal effect.

Filing Tip

Family Move

It is not necessary for you and members of your household to travel together, or at the same time, to claim a deduction for the expenses incurred by each family member.

Delay in moving to new job location. You may delay moving to the area of a new job location. A delay of up to one year does not jeopardize a deduction for moving expenses. Furthermore, if you move to the new job area within one year, your family may stay in the old residence for a longer period. Their later moving expenses will generally be deductible, even though incurred after one year. For example, the IRS allowed a moving expense deduction to a husband who immediately moved to a new job location, although his wife and children did not join him until 30 months after he began the new job. They delayed so that the children could complete their education. The IRS held that since part of the moving expenses were incurred within one year, the moving expenses incurred later were also deductible.

Nondeductible expenses. You may not deduct the cost of travel incurred for a maid, nurse, chauffeur, or similar domestic help (unless the person is also your dependent), expenses of refitting rugs and drapes, forfeited tuition, car tags or driver's license for the state you move to, losses on disposing of memberships in clubs, mortgage penalties, expenses for trips to sell your old house, or loss on the sale of the house. Furthermore, when your employer reimburses you for such costs, you realize taxable income equal to the amount of the reimbursement.

You may not deduct the cost of transporting furniture that you purchased en route from your old home.

You may not deduct the cost of pre-move house-hunting trips, temporary living expenses, or expenses of selling, purchasing, or leasing the old or new residence, such as attorneys' fees, real estate fees, or costs of settling an unexpired lease. Meal expenses while traveling to your new residence are not deductible.

Filing Tip

Meeting the Mileage Test

Use the following worksheet to *see* if your move satisfies the 50-mile test. Find the shortest of the most commonly traveled routes in measuring the distances.

Distance between	*In miles*
1. Old residence and new job location	_______
2. Old residence and old job location	_______
3. Excess of Line 1 over Line 2 must be at least 50 miles	_______

12.4 The Distance Test

The distance between your new job location and your former home must be at least 50 miles more than the distance between your old job location and your former home. For this purpose, your home may be a house, apartment, trailer, or even a houseboat, but not a seasonal residence such as a summer cottage. Self-employed individuals are also subject to the mileage test.

In applying the distance test, take into account the shortest of the most commonly traveled routes in measuring the distance between your old home and the new and old job locations. The location of your new home is not considered in applying the test; only the location of your old home is taken into account.

Your job location is where you spend most of your working time. If you work at various locations, the job location is where you report to work. If you work for several employers on a short-term basis and get jobs through a union hall system, the union hall is considered your job location.

First job or returning to full-time work. If you had no previous job or are returning to full-time work after a long period of unemployment or part-time work, your new job location must be at least 50 miles from your former home to meet the distance test.

Moving overseas. A member of the Armed Forces may deduct the cost of moving his or her family to an overseas post.

If you take a new job overseas and qualify for the foreign earned income exclusion, moving expenses allocable to the excluded income are not deductible *(36.6)*.

Alien moving to the U.S. The deduction is not limited to U.S. citizens and residents. An alien may deduct the cost of travel here to work at a full-time position.

EXAMPLES

1. Your company's office is in the center of a metropolitan area. You live 18 miles from your office. You are transferred to a new office and buy a new house. To deduct moving costs, you must show that the new office is at least 68 miles from your previous residence.
2. Your old job was four miles from your former residence and your new job is 55 miles from your former residence. You move to a house that is less than 50 miles from your old house. Nevertheless, you have met the 50-mile test since your new job is 51 miles further from your former home than your old job was.

12.5 The 39-Week Test for Employees

In addition to meeting the distance test *(12.4)*, you must work in the locality of the new job as a full-time employee for at least 39 weeks during the 12-month period immediately following your arrival at the new job location. You do not need to have a job prior to your arrival at the new location. Your family does not have to arrive with you. The 39 weeks of work need not be consecutive or with the same employer. You may change jobs provided you remain in the same general commuting area for 39 weeks. The 39-week test does not apply to employees who become disabled and lose their jobs, or who die.

If you are temporarily absent from work through no fault of your own, due to illness, strikes, shutouts, layoffs, or natural disasters, your temporary absence counts toward the 39-week requirement as full-time employment.

Planning Reminder

Loss of Job

If you lose your job for reasons other than your willful misconduct, the 39-week requirement is waived. Should you resign or lose your job for willful misconduct, a part-time job will not satisfy the 39-week test. The time test is not waived because you reach mandatory retirement age first where this retirement was anticipated.

EXAMPLE

You accept a position with a company 600 miles from your former position. You move to the new location. After you have worked in the new position 14 weeks, you resign and take another job with a nearby company. You may add the 14 weeks of work with the first company to 25 weeks with the second company to meet the 39-week requirement.

Job transfers. The 39-week period is also waived if you are transferred from your new job for your employer's benefit. However, it must be shown that you could have satisfied the 39-week test except for the transfer.

What if *you* initiate the transfer? The IRS held in a ruling that the 39-week test is not waived if an employee initiates the transfer, even if the employer approves. An individual was not allowed to deduct the costs of moving across the country to take a government position when, within 39 weeks of taking the position, he applied for and took another government job in another area. The IRS disallowed the deduction, although the government reimbursed part of the employee's moving expenses to the new job post, thereby indicating that it considered the transfer to be in the government's interest. According to the IRS, the waiver of the 39-week test applies to transfers initiated by employers, not by employees.

Filing Tip

Job Status

For purposes of the 39-week test, full-time status is determined by the customary practices of your occupation in the area. If work is seasonal, off-season weeks count as work weeks if the off-season period is less than six months and you have an employment agreement covering the off-season.

Joint returns. On a joint return, either spouse may meet the time test. But the work time of one spouse may not be added to the time of the other spouse.

EXAMPLE

Smith moves from New York to a new job in Denver. After working full time for 30 weeks, he resigns from his job and cannot find another position during the rest of the 12-month period. He may not deduct his moving expenses. But assume that Mrs. Smith also finds a job in Denver at the same time as her husband and continues to work for at least 39 weeks. Since she has met the 39-week test, the moving expenses from New York to Denver paid by her husband are deductible, provided they file a joint return. However, if Mrs. Smith had worked for only nine weeks, her work period could not be added to her husband's to meet the 39-week test.

12.6 The 78-Week Test for the Self-Employed and Partners

In addition to meeting the distance test *(12.4)*, you must work full time in the area of the new business for at least 78 weeks during the 24 months immediately following your arrival, of which at least 39 weeks occur in the first 12 months. The full-time work requirement may prevent semi-retired hobbyists, students, or others who work only a few hours a week in self-employed trades or occupations from claiming the deduction.

You are considered to have obtained employment at a new principal place of work when you have made substantial arrangements to begin such work.

The time test is waived if disability or death prevents compliance.

Change of employee or self-employed status. If you start work at a new location as an employee and then become self-employed before meeting the 39-week employee time test, you must meet the 78-week test. Time spent as an employee is counted along with the time spent self-employed in meeting the test.

If, during the first 12 months, you change from working as a self-employed person to working as an employee, you may qualify under the 39-week employee time test, provided you have 39 weeks of work as an *employee.* If you do not have 39 weeks as an employee in the first 12 months, you must meet the 78-week test.

Joint returns. Where you file a joint return, you deduct moving expenses if either you or your spouse can satisfy the time test based on individual work records.

12.7 Claiming Deductible Moving Expenses

Qualifying unreimbursed moving expenses *(12.3)* are deductible on your return whether you claim the standard deduction or itemize deductions. Report your expenses and nontaxable employer reimbursements on Form 3903. Qualifying unreimbursed moving expenses from Form 3903 are then deducted on Form 1040, Line 26, as an adjustment to gross income.

Claiming the deduction before meeting the time test. If the due date for filing your tax return arrives before you can satisfy the 39-week *(12.5)* or 78-week *(12.6)* work test, you may, nevertheless, deduct unreimbursed moving expenses. If you subsequently fail to complete the work requirement, you have to file an amended return or report income; *see* the Example below. If you file your return without taking the deduction, you may file an amended return after meeting the time test to claim the deduction.

Caution

Reimbursement for Loss on Sale of a Home

To encourage or facilitate an employee's move, an employer may reimburse the employee for a loss incurred on the sale of his or her home. The IRS taxes such reimbursements as pay.

EXAMPLE

You move to a new location on November 1, 2009. At the end of the year, you have worked in your new position only nine weeks. You deduct your moving expenses on your 2009 tax return even though you did not complete the 39- or 78-week period of work. But if, after you file the 2009 return, you move from the location before completing the applicable 39-week or 78-week work period, you must report the 2009 deduction as income on the return for the year you move from the location. Alternatively, you may file an amended 2009 return on which you eliminate the deduction.

12.8 Reimbursements of Moving Expenses

If your employer reimburses you for deductible moving expenses *(12.3)* under an accountable plan, the reimbursement should not be reported as salary or wage income on Form W-2. The requirements for an accountable plan are similar to those for business travel expenses *(20.31)*.

Qualified moving expenses an employer pays to a third party, such as to a moving company, are not reported on Form W-2.

A reimbursement for expenses that do *not* qualify for a deduction, such as pre-move house-hunting costs, temporary living expenses, meal costs, or real estate expenses, is reported as compensation on your Form W-2.

On Form 3903, you report your deductible expenses in excess of nontaxable reimbursements, and enter the deductible amount on Form 1040, Line 26, as an adjustment to gross income.

If in 2009 you had deductible moving expenses that you claimed on your 2009 return and you receive a reimbursement for the expenses in 2010, you report your employer's reimbursement as compensation in 2010. Alternatively, you may delay the deduction until 2010, the year of the reimbursement. You may deduct on your 2010 return the excess of your 2009 expenses over the nontaxable reimbursement received in 2010.

Chapter 13

Claiming the Standard Deduction or Itemized Deductions

Claim the standard deduction only if it exceeds your allowable itemized deductions for mortgage interest, property taxes, medical costs, charitable donations, casualty losses, and miscellaneous deductions for job costs and investment expenses. Generally, a single person may claim a 2010 standard deduction of $5,700; a head of household, $8,400; a married couple filing jointly or a qualifying widow(er), $11,400; and a married person filing separately, $5,700. Larger standard deductions are allowed to individuals who (1) are age 65 or older or blind, (2) pay state or local real estate taxes, or (3) have a net disaster loss from a federally declared disaster. Lower standard deductions are allowed to dependents with only investment income.

Before deciding whether to itemize or claim the standard deduction, read Chapters 14 through 20 to *see* that you have not overlooked any itemized deductions. To itemize, you must file Form 1040 and report your deductions on Schedule A.

Table 13-1 Itemized Deductions and the Standard Deduction for 2010

Item—	*Explanation—*	*Limitations and Examples—*
Standard deduction	The basic standard deduction is fixed by law according to your filing status and age. The standard deduction in 2010 is: $11,400 if you are married filing jointly or a qualifying widow or widower. $5,700 if you are single. $8,400 if you are a head of household. $5,700 if you are married filing separately. Additional standard deductions are allowed for real estate taxes, net disaster losses *(13.3)*, and for being age 65 or older or blind *(13.4)*.	A married person filing separately may not use the standard deduction if his or her spouse itemizes deductions *(13.2)*. The standard deduction may not be claimed by a nonresident or dual-status alien or on a return filed for a short taxable year caused by a change in accounting period. A lower standard deduction of $950 is allowed to dependents with only unearned income *(13.5)*.
Itemized deductions	You should itemize deductions on Schedule A of Form 1040 if your deductions exceed the standard deduction for your filing status. Itemized deductions include charitable contributions, interest expenses, local and state taxes, medical and dental costs, casualty and theft losses, job and investment expenses, and educational costs.	For 2010, higher-income taxpayers are *not* subject to an overall limitation on itemized deductions based on adjusted gross income, as they were for 2009 and earlier years *(13.7)*. Thus, after applying the individual limitations for each itemized deduction (such as the income-based floors for medical, casualty, and miscellaneous deductions), compare the total of your allowable deductions to the standard deduction allowed for your filing status in 2010. For example, you are single and so may claim the standard deduction of $5,700 for 2010. However, your allowable itemized deductions are $5,784. You can claim $5,784 on Schedule A of Form 1040.
Charitable contributions	If you itemize, you may deduct donations to religious, charitable, educational, and other philanthropic organizations that have been approved to receive deductible contributions *(14.1)*.	The contribution deduction is generally limited to 50% of adjusted gross income *(14.17)*. Lower ceilings apply to most property donations and contributions to foundations. The deductible amount is included in the reduction explained above. *See Chapter 14* for details on charitable contributions.
Interest expenses	If you itemize, you may deduct interest on qualified home mortgages, points, home equity loans, and interest on loans to carry investments.	Interest on investment loans is deductible only to the extent of net investment income *(15.10)*. Interest on personal and consumer loans is not deductible. Interest on home mortgages is deductible if certain tests are met *(15.1)*. Deductions for home mortgage interest and points are included in the reduction explained above. *See Chapter 15* for details on interest deductions.
Taxes	If you claim the standard deduction, you may be able to increase the deduction by up to S500 for state and local real estate taxes paid in 2010, or $1,000 if you are married filing jointly *(13.3)*. If you itemize, you can deduct state and local income taxes, or in lieu of the income taxes, you may be able to elect to deduct general sales taxes *(16.3)*. You claim your deduction for real estate taxes on the tax return of the year in which you paid the taxes, unless you report on the accrual basis *(16.6)*.	*See Chapter 16* for details on deductible taxes.
Medical expenses	You may deduct payments of medical expenses for yourself, your spouse, and your dependents *(17.1)*. A checklist of deductible medical items is provided in *(17.2)*. With the exception of insulin, drugs are deductible *only* if they require a prescription by a physician.	Only expenses in excess of 7.5% of adjusted gross income are deductible. *See Chapter 17* for details.

Table 13-1 Itemized Deductions and the Standard Deduction for 2010 (continued)

Casualty and theft losses	You may deduct personal property losses caused by storms, fires, and other natural events and as the result of theft *(18.1)*.	Each individual casualty loss must exceed $500 and the total of all losses other than net disaster losses during the year must exceed 10% of adjusted gross income *(18.12)*. *See Chapter 18* for casualty and theft loss details.
Job expenses	You may deduct unreimbursed costs of union dues, job educational courses, work clothes, entertainment, travel, and looking for a new job.	Included as miscellaneous expenses of which only the excess over 2% of adjusted gross income is deductible *(19.1)*. The 2% floor does not apply to performing artists *(12.2)*, handicapped employees, or job-related moving expenses *(12.3)*. The deductible amount is included in the reduction explained above. *See Chapter 19* for details.
Investment expenses and tax preparation costs	You may deduct investment expenses and other expenses of producing and collecting income, expenses of maintaining income-producing property, expenses of preparing your tax return or refund claims, and IRS audits.	Included as miscellaneous expenses of which only the excess over 2% of adjusted gross income is deductible *(19.1)*. The deductible amount is included in the reduction explained above. *See Chapter 19* for details.

13.1 Claiming the Standard Deduction

On your 2010 Form 1040, 1040A, or 1040EZ, you are allowed a standard deduction, which is an "automatic" deduction you may claim regardless of your actual expenses. The standard deduction reduces adjusted gross income (AGI).

If you file Form 1040, choose the standard deduction if it exceeds the itemized deductions that could be claimed on Schedule A. Claim the standard deduction only if it exceeds your allowable itemized deductions for charitable donations, certain local taxes, interest, allowable casualty losses, miscellaneous expenses, and medical expenses. If your deductions exceed your standard deduction, you elect to itemize by claiming the deductions on Schedule A of Form 1040. However, if you are married filing separately and your spouse itemizes deductions, you also must itemize, even if the standard deduction exceeds your itemized deductions *(13.3)*.

Basic standard deduction. The basic standard deduction is allowed if you are under age 65 and not blind. The amount is adjusted each year to reflect inflation. For 2010, the basic standard deduction is:

$11,400 if married filing jointly or a qualifying widow(er);
$8,400 if filing as a head of household;
$5,700 if single; and
$5,700 if married filing separately.

A married person filing separately must itemize deductions and may not claim any standard deduction if his or her spouse itemizes on a separate return *(13.2)*.

Additional standard deduction if age 65 or older or blind. For taxpayers age 65 or over, or taxpayers of any age who are blind, the basic standard deduction is increased by an additional amount *(13.4)*.

Additional standard deduction for property taxes and net disaster loss were not yet extended to 2010 when this book went to press. At the time this book went to press, Congress had not yet extended to 2010 the additional standard deduction for state and local real estate taxes, or the additional standard deduction for a net disaster loss, both of which were allowed in 2008 and 2009. An extension to 2010 is expected and in *13.3* we have assumed that the additional deductions will be part of the 2010 standard deduction. However, check the *e-Supplement at jklasser.com* for an update.

Law Alert

Additional Standard Deductions for Real Estate Taxes and Net Disaster Loss

Congress was expected to pass legislation extending to 2010 the additional standard deduction for state and local real estate taxes and the additional standard deduction for a net disaster loss, but it had not yet done so when this book went to press *(13.3)*. *See* the *e-Supplement at jklasser.com* for a legislation update.

Dependents. Individuals who may be claimed as dependents by other taxpayers are generally limited to a $950 standard deduction for 2010, unless they have earned income *(13.5)*.

Dual-status alien. You are generally not entitled to any standard deduction if for part of the year you are a nonresident and part of the year a resident alien. However, a standard deduction may be claimed on a joint return if your spouse is a U.S. citizen or resident and you elect to be taxed on your worldwide income *(1.5)*.

EXAMPLES

1. Ellen Bates is single and her 2010 adjusted gross income is $48,000. Her itemized deductions total $5,926. As the $5,700 standard deduction is less than her itemized deductions, she claims itemized deductions of $5,926 on Schedule A.
2. Ben Green is age 25 and single. In 2010, he has salary income of $47,225 and receives interest income *(32.4)* of $148. He makes a tax deductible contribution of $5,000 to a traditional IRA. Ben reduces his adjusted gross income of $42,373 by the $5,700 standard deduction because it exceeds his allowable itemized deductions for the year.

Gross income:		
Salary	$47,225	
Interest income	148	$47,373
Deduction from gross income:		
IRA *(8.4)*		5,000
Adjusted gross income		$42,373
Less: Standard deduction		5,700
		$36,673
Less: Exemption *(21.1)*		3,650
Taxable income		$33,023

Filing Instruction

Changing an Election

If you filed your return using the standard deduction and want to change to itemized deductions, or you itemized and want to change to the standard deduction, you may do so within the three-year period allowed for amending your return. If you are married and filing separately, each of you must consent to and make the same change; you both must either itemize or claim the standard deduction.

13.2 Husbands and Wives Filing Separate Returns

If you and your spouse file separate returns *(1.3)* for 2010, and neither of you is a qualifying head of household *(1.12)*, you must both claim itemized deductions or limit yourselves to a standard deduction of $5,700 each. You must both make the same election; when one of you itemizes the other is not entitled to any standard deduction. That is, if your spouse has itemized deductions exceeding $5,700 and elects to itemize, you must also itemize, even if your itemized deductions are less than $5,700.

On a separate return, each spouse may deduct only those itemized expenses for which he or she is liable and pays. This is true even if one spouse pays expenses for the other. For example, if a wife owns property, then the interest and taxes imposed on the property are her deductions, not her husband's. If he pays them, neither one may deduct them on separate returns. The husband may not because they were not his liability. The wife may not because she did not pay them. This is true also of casualty or theft losses.

No restrictions if divorced or legally separated. Following a divorce or legal separation under a decree of divorce or separate maintenance, you and your former spouse are free to compute your tax as you each see fit, without reference to the way the other files. Both of you are treated as single. If you have itemized deductions, you may elect to claim them, and your former spouse is not required to itemize. Head of household tax rates may be available if certain requirements are met *(1.12)*.

Head of household possibility if you live apart from your spouse. If you are separated but do not have a decree of divorce or separate maintenance, both of you must either itemize or claim the standard deduction of $5,700 for 2010. However, you may file your 2010 return as a head of household *(1.12)* and may choose between an $8,400 standard deduction and itemizing deductions if you are married and live apart from your spouse and meet the following conditions:

- Your spouse was not a member of your household during the last six months of 2010.
- You paid over half of the costs of maintaining a home that for more than half of 2010 was the principal residence for you and a qualifying child or qualifying relative whom you may claim as your dependent. *See* Test 2 *(1.12)* for details.

As a head of household, you may elect to itemize whether your spouse itemizes or not. If you elect not to itemize, your 2010 standard deduction as a head of household is $8,400 if you are under age 65 and not blind. If you are age 65 or over or blind, your standard deduction is increased by $1,400 *(13.4)*. The filing status of your spouse remains married filing separately. He or she must itemize deductions if you itemize. If you claim the $8,400 standard deduction for a head of household (or $9,800 if age 65 or older, or blind), he or she can itemize or claim the $5,700 standard deduction for married persons filing separately. The $8,400, $9,800, or $5,700 deduction amounts may be increased if the additional deductions discussed in *13.3* are available.

13.3 Additional Standard Deduction for Real Estate Taxes, Motor Vehicle Taxes and Net Disaster Loss

Caution: ***The additional standard deduction for state and local real estate taxes expired at the end of 2009 and the additional deduction for a net disaster loss expired for disasters occurring after 2009. Although an extension of these deductions to 2010 is expected, Congress had not yet passed the extension legislation when this book went to press. The following discussion and examples assume that the extensions will be enacted and that the real estate and net disaster loss deductions will be part of the 2010 standard deduction. However, check the e-Supplement at jklasser.com for a legislation update.***

If the additional standard deductions for real estate taxes and net disaster losses are allowed for 2010 (*see* above), they are in addition to the basic standard deduction *(13.1)* and any additional standard deduction for being at least age 65 or blind *(13.4)*.

Schedule L. You must use Schedule L (Form 1040 or Form 1040A) to figure your total standard deduction for 2010 if you are claiming the additional standard deduction for real estate taxes, motor vehicle taxes, or a net disaster loss. To claim a net disaster loss, you must file Form 1040.

Additional standard deduction for property taxes. You can claim an additional standard deduction for state and local real estate taxes paid during 2010 on personal-use property. The additional standard deduction is the lower of (1) the actual taxes paid in 2010 or (2) $500, $1,000 if you are married filing jointly. It is allowed regardless of your income. Taxes paid on business or rental property, and on foreign real estate, do *not* qualify for the additional standard deduction. The additional deduction for real estate taxes is claimed on Lines 7 through 9 of Schedule L.

Additional standard deduction for net disaster loss. If you have a 2010 net disaster loss from a federally declared disaster, you may increase your standard deduction by that amount. A net disaster loss is the excess of personal casualty losses (taking into account the $500 reduction per personal casualty) attributable to federally declared disasters over personal casualty gains *(18.12)*. Your 2010 net disaster loss may include a loss that was incurred in a 2008 or 2009 disaster that did not become deductible until 2010 when you became certain that the loss would not be reimbursed. Even though you are not itemizing deductions, you must complete Form 4684 (Casualty and Theft Losses) to figure the net disaster loss, which is then entered on Schedule L. You must file Form 1040 to claim the net disaster loss as part of your standard deduction.

Additional standard deduction for sales or excise taxes on new vehicle purchased in 2009. On 2009 returns, an additional standard deduction was allowed for state and local sales taxes or excise taxes paid on a motor vehicle that was purchased new from February 17, 2009 through December 31, 2009. You may claim the additional standard deduction for 2010 if you paid the taxes in 2010 for a vehicle purchased during the February 17–December 31, 2009 period.

If the vehicle cost over $49,500, only the taxes on the first $49,000 of the purchase price are deductible, and the deduction is subject to a phaseout. If your modified adjusted gross income exceeds $125,000, or $250,000 if married filing jointly, the additional standard deduction is phased out over the next $10,000. The computation of the deduction is made on Schedule L.

EXAMPLES-

1. You are single and 48 years old. In 2010 you paid real estate taxes of $3,600 on your home. On your 2010 return, you claim the standard deduction as it exceeds your itemized deductions. You can claim a total standard deduction for 2010 of $6,200, which equals the $5,700 basic standard deduction, plus an additional standard deduction for real estate taxes of $500, the maximum additional deduction for a single taxpayer.
2. You file a joint return for 2010. You and your husband are both over age 65. In 2010, you paid $3,000 of real estate taxes on your home. You also had a $7,750 net disaster loss from a federally declared disaster. You figure the net disaster loss on Form 4684, which you attach to your 2010 Form 1040. You claim the standard deduction as it exceeds your itemized deductions for 2010. You can claim a total standard deduction for 2010 of $22,350, which equals the $11,400 basic standard deduction on a joint return, plus $2,200, the additional standard deduction on a joint return ($1,100 x 2) where both spouses are age 65 or older *(13.4)*, plus the $7,750 net disaster loss, plus $1,000, the maximum additional standard deduction for real estate taxes on a joint return.

Filing Instruction

Total or Partial Blindness

An additional standard deduction for 2010 is allowed to a person who is completely blind as of December 31, 2010. You may claim an additional deduction if you are partially blind and attach a letter certified by your doctor stating that you cannot see better than 20/200 in your better eye with lenses or that your field of vision is 20 degrees or less. Keep a copy of this letter. If the certification states that your vision will never improve beyond these limits, you will not have to file a new certification in later years; you will only have to attach a statement referring to the earlier certification.

13.4 Standard Deduction If 65 or Older or Blind

A larger standard deduction is provided for persons who are age 65 or over or who are blind. The larger deduction for blindness is allowed regardless of age.

For purposes of the 2010 standard deduction, blindness and age are determined as of December 31, 2010. However, if your 65th birthday is January 1, 2011, the IRS treats you as reaching age 65 on the last day of 2010, allowing you to claim on your 2010 return the additional standard deduction for those age 65 or older.

If you are age 65 or older or blind for 2010, you may claim an additional standard deduction of $1,400 if you file as a single person or head of household, or $1,100 if your filing status is married filing jointly, married filing separately, or qualifying widow(er). Keep in mind that if you are married filing separately, you are allowed to claim any standard deduction only if your spouse also claims the standard deduction on his or her own return *(13.2)*.

You may be able to increase your standard deduction further if you paid real estate taxes in 2010, or you had a net disaster loss for 2010 *(13.3)*.

You can use *Worksheet 13-1* to figure your standard deduction for 2010.

Worksheet 13-1 Standard Deduction if 65 or Older or Blind*

Check applicable boxes

	65 or older	*Blind*
Yourself	☐	☐
Your spouse if you file a joint return	☐	☐
Your spouse if you file separately and can claim an exemption for your spouse *(21.2)*	☐	☐
Total checks____		

1.	Enter your basic standard deduction: Married filing jointly or qualifying widow(er)—$11,400 Head of household—$8,400 Single or married filing separately—$5,700	$ ______
2.	Multiply the number of checks above by: $1,400 if you are single or head of household $1,100 if you are married filing jointly, married filing separately, or a qualifying widow(er)	______
3.	Add Lines 1 and 2. This is your standard deduction for 2010.*	______

* *Worksheet 13-1* does *not* include the additional standard deduction amounts allowed for real estate taxes, sales/excise taxes on qualified motor vehicles, and net disaster losses. These additional deductions are discussed at *13.3.*

13.5 Standard Deduction for Dependents

If someone can claim you as a dependent for 2010 under the tests at *21.1*, your standard deduction is determined under the following rules. You may elect to itemize deductions if these exceed the allowable standard deduction. If you are married and your spouse itemizes on a separate return, you *must* itemize *(13.2)*.

Caution

Determine Dependency Status First

The reduced standard deduction rules apply to you if you *may* be claimed as a dependent on another tax return, such as by your parents. If you can be claimed as a dependent under the rules at *21.1*, it does not matter if you are actually claimed as a dependent.

Dependent under age 65 and not blind. Your standard deduction is generally the greater of $950 ***or*** your earned income plus $300, but no more than the basic standard deduction for your filing status *(13.1)*. However, you can increase your standard deduction if you paid state or local real estate tax in 2010 or had a net a disaster loss for 2010; *see Worksheet 13-2*.

EXAMPLES

1. Susan, age 17, is claimed as a dependent by her parents. For 2010, she has earned income of $595 and interest income of $40. Her standard deduction is $950, the greater of $950 or $895, the total of her earned income ($595) and $300.
2. Assume that Susan's earned income is $2,000 rather than $595. Her standard deduction for 2010 is $2,300, the greater of $950 or $2,300, the total of her earned income ($2,000) and $300.

Dependents age 65 or older or blind. Your standard deduction consists of at least two parts. First, you can deduct the greater of $950 ***or*** your earned income plus $300, but no more than the basic standard deduction for your filing status *(13.1)*. You then add $1,100 if you are married filing jointly or married filing separately, or $1,400 if single or head of household. Double the $1,100 or $1,400 amount if you are age 65 or older and also blind.

In addition, you may be able to increase your standard deduction if you paid state or local real estate tax in 2010 or had a net disaster loss for 2010; *see 13.3*.

EXAMPLE

Jane Dell claims her widowed mother, Beth, who is age 67, as her dependent for 2010. For 2010, Beth has interest income of $400, wages of $2,000, and Social Security benefits of $10,000 that are exempt from tax under the rules discussed at *34.3*. Beth's standard deduction is $3,700: $2,300 (the greater of $950 or her wage income of $2,000 plus $300) plus $1,400, the additional deduction for a single person over age 65. Beth's taxable income is zero. Although her gross income of $2,400 is below the filing threshold (*see* filing tests for dependents on page 4), she should file a tax return to obtain a refund of income tax withheld from her wages.

Worksheet 13-2 Standard Deduction for Dependents in 2010

1.	Enter the larger of: $950, or Your earned income* in 2010 plus $300	$ ______
2.	Enter your basic standard deduction: Married filing jointly or qualifying widow(er)—$11,400 Head of household—$8,400 Single or married filing separately—$5,700	______
3.	Enter the smaller of Line 1 or 2	______
4.	If you are age 65 or older or blind *(13.4)*, enter: $1,400 if you are single or head of household $1,100 if you are married filing jointly or separately If both age 65 or older and blind, the $1,400 or $1,100 amount is doubled to $2,800 or $2,200, respectively.	______
5.	Add Lines 3 and 4. This is your standard deduction for 2010.**	______

***Earned income.** *Include pay for services and taxable scholarships (33.1). Include net earnings from self-employment and then subtract 50% of self-employment tax liability (45.3) when figuring earned income. However, if your gross income (earned and unearned) is $3,650 or more, you may be claimed as a dependent only if you are the qualifying child of another taxpayer (21.1).*

*** Worksheet 13-2 does not include the additional standard deduction amounts allowed for real estate taxes, net disaster losses, and sales/excise taxes on qualified motor vehicles. These additional deductions are discussed at 13.3.*

Planning Reminder

Prepaying Deductible Expenses May Allow You To Itemize

As the end of the year approaches, check your records for payments of deductible itemized expenses. If these payments are slightly less than the allowable standard deduction for the year, making a year-end payment of a deductible expense that you would otherwise pay in the following year could allow you to itemize.

13.6 Prepaying or Postponing Itemized Expenses

Before the end of the year, check your records for payments of deductible itemized expenses. If you find that your payments up to that time are slightly less than the allowable standard deduction for that year, accelerating payment of an expense that you would otherwise pay in the following year could allow you to itemize. For example, at the end of 2010, you may make an additional charitable contribution, or pay a state or local tax bill not due until 2011, or extend by one year professional association dues or job-related subscriptions. However, do not prepay state or local taxes if you are either subject to AMT or the deduction will make you subject to AMT *(23.2)*. You cannot deduct prepayments of interest, insurance premiums, or rent on investment property.

On the other hand, making the year-end payment might still not increase your deductions enough to itemize. In that case, you would get no tax benefit from the payment. By postponing the payment until the next year, you may make it easier to itemize on that year's return.

If your year-to-year payments of itemized expenses have consistently been below the standard deduction, a prepayment or postponement strategy may allow you to itemize in at least one of two consecutive years, enabling you to reduce your taxes over the two-year period without increasing your overall expenditures.

Law Alert

Phaseout Eliminated for 2010

Regardless of how high your adjusted gross income for 2010 is, you will not lose part of your overall itemized deductions. The law authorizing the reduction expired at the end of 2009, but for one year only. The phaseout is scheduled to return in 2011; *see* the *e-Supplement at jklasser.com* for the 2011 rules.

13.7 No Phaseout of Itemized Deductions for 2010

For 2010, there is no phaseout of itemized deductions. In prior years, a portion of the overall itemized deductions claimed by taxpayers with adjusted gross income over an annual threshold was disallowed, but the phaseout was gradually eliminated from 2006 through 2009. After figuring your 2010 itemized deductions under the regular limitations for each deduction (*see* Chapters 14 through 20), the total is allowed on Schedule A with no reduction.

However, the phaseout is scheduled to return in 2011. The rules for applying the phaseout for 2011 had not yet been determined when this book went to press; *see* the *e-Supplement at jklasser.com* for details.

Chapter 14

Charitable Contribution Deductions

By making deductible donations, you help your favorite philanthropy and at the same time receive a tax benefit. For example, if you are in the 25% tax bracket, a donation of $1,000 reduces your taxes by $250.

For cash donations of any amount, your deduction will be disallowed if you do not have a cancelled check or account statement, or a written receipt from the charity, to substantiate your contribution.

For donations of $250 or more, you must receive a written acknowledgement from the organization that indicates whether you received goods or services in return for your donation. A cancelled check is not sufficient evidence for a cash donation of $250 or more *(14.14)*.

If you claim deductions for property valued at more than $500, you also must attach Form 8283 to Form 1040. If the value you claimed exceeds $5,000, you also may have to obtain a written appraisal *(14.15)*.

If you donated a car (or other vehicle) valued at over $500, you also must attach Copy B of Form 1098-C to your return. Your deduction is generally limited to the gross sales proceeds received by the charity on a sale of the vehicle, even if you could substantiate a higher fair market value *(14.7)*.

There are deduction ceilings depending on the type of donation and the nature of the charity, and an annual ceiling based on adjusted gross income *(14.17)*.

14.1 Deductible Contributions

Charitable contributions are deductible only as itemized deductions on Schedule A of Form 1040. You may deduct donations to religious, charitable, educational, and other philanthropic organizations approved by the IRS to receive deductible contributions; *see* the listing later in this section. If you are unsure of the tax status of a philanthropy, ask the organization about its status, or check the IRS list of tax-exempt organizations (IRS Publication 78). Donations to the federal, state, and local government are also deductible.

Substantiating your 2010 donations. Keep a cancelled check or receipt from the charity as proof of your donations. For donations of $250 or more, you need to obtain a written acknowledgment that notes any benefits or goods that you received in exchange *(14.14)*.

For a donated car, other motor vehicle, boat, or airplane valued at over $500, you must obtain an acknowledgment on Form 1098-C (or equivalent substitute) that you must attach to your return *(14.7)*.

Year-end donations. You deduct donations on the tax return filed for the year in which you paid them in cash or property. A contribution by check is deductible in the year you give the check, even if it is cashed in the following year. A check mailed and dated on the last day of 2010 is deductible in 2010. A postdated check with a 2011 date is not deductible until 2011. A pledge or a note is not deductible until paid. Donations made through a credit card are deductible in the year the charge is made. Donations made through a pay-by-phone bank account are not deductible until the payment date shown on the bank statement.

Law Alert

Direct Transfer From IRA to Charity

The law allowing IRA owners age 70½ to make a tax-free direct transfer of up to $100,000 from an IRA to a charity *(8.8)* expired at the end of 2009. Although Congress is expected to extend the law to 2010, it had not yet done so when this book went to press. If the exclusion is extended to 2010, a charitable deduction cannot be claimed for the tax-free transfer. *See 8.8* and the *e-Supplement at jklasser.com* for further details.

Delivering securities. If you are planning to donate appreciated securities near the end of the year, make sure that you consider these delivery rules in timing the donation. If you unconditionally deliver or mail a properly endorsed stock certificate to the donee or its agent, the gift is considered completed on the date of delivery or mailing, provided it is received in the ordinary course of the mails. If you deliver the certificate to your bank or broker as your agent, or to the issuing corporation or its agent, your gift is not complete until the stock is transferred to the donee's name on the corporation's books. This transfer may take several weeks, so, if possible, make the delivery at least three weeks before the end of the year to assure a current deduction. If you plan to donate mutual fund shares to a charity towards the end of the year, contact the fund company to ensure that the transfer of shares to the name of the charity can be completed by the end of the year.

Debts. You may assign to a charity a debt payable to you. A deductible contribution may be claimed in the year your debtor pays the charity.

Limits on deduction. Depending on the nature of the organization and the donated property, a deduction ceiling of 50%, 30%, or 20% of adjusted gross income applies. In general, the deduction ceiling is 50% for cash contributions and 30% for contributions of appreciated property held long term *(14.17)*. Where donations in one year exceed the percentage limits, a five-year carryover of the excess may be allowed *(14.18)*.

A deduction may also be limited under the rules for reduction of itemized deductions *(13.7)*.

Organizations Qualifying for Deductible Donations

The following types of organizations may qualify to receive deductible contributions:

A domestic nonprofit organization, trust, community chest, fund, or foundation that is operated exclusively for one of the following purposes:

Religious. Payments for pew rents, assessments, and dues to churches and synagogues are deductible.

Charitable. In this class are organizations such as Boy Scouts, Girl Scouts, American Red Cross, Community Funds, Cancer Societies, CARE, Salvation Army, Y.M.C.A., and Y.W.C.A.

Scientific, literary, and educational. Included in this group are hospitals, research organizations, colleges, universities, and other schools that do not maintain racially discriminatory policies; and leagues or associations set up for education or to combat crime, improve public morals, and aid public welfare.

Prevention of cruelty to children or animals.

Fostering amateur sports competition. However, the organization's activities may not provide athletic facilities or equipment.

Domestic nonprofit veterans' organizations or auxiliary units.

A domestic fraternal group operating under the lodge system. The contributions must be used exclusively for religious, charitable, scientific, literary, or educational purposes; or for the prevention of cruelty to children or animals.

Nonprofit cemetery and burial companies, where the voluntary contribution benefits the whole cemetery, not only your plot.

Legal services corporations established under the Legal Services Corporation Act. Such corporations provide legal assistance to financially needy people in noncriminal proceedings.

The United States, a U.S. possession, Puerto Rico, a state, city, or town or Indian tribal government. The gift must be for public purposes. The gift may be directed to a government unit, or it may be to a government agency such as a state university, a fire department, a civil defense group, or a committee to raise funds to develop land into a public park. Donations may be made to the Social Security system (Federal Old Age and Survivors Insurance Trust Fund). Donations may be made to the federal government to help reduce the national debt; checks should be made payable to "Bureau of the Public Debt."

14.2 Nondeductible Contributions

The following types of contributions are not deductible:

1. Donations to or on behalf of specific individuals, even if needy or worthy. Generally, scholarships for specific students, or gifts to organizations to benefit only certain groups. However, the IRS in private rulings has allowed deductions for scholarship funds that are limited to members of a particular religion, so long as that religion is open to all on a racially nondiscriminatory basis, and to scholarship funds open only to male students.
2. Payments to political campaign committees or political action committees.
3. Payments to an organization that devotes a substantial part of its activities to lobbying, trying to influence legislation, or carrying on propaganda or whose lobbying activities exceed certain limits set by the law, causing the organization to lose its tax-exempt status. The IRS has disallowed contributions to a civic group opposing saloons, nightclubs, and gambling places, although the group also aided libraries, churches, and other public programs.
4. Gifts to organizations such as:

   Fraternal groups—except when they set up special organizations exclusively devoted to charitable, educational, or other approved purposes.

   Professional groups such as those organized by accountants, lawyers, and physicians—except when they are specially created for exclusive charitable, educational, or other philanthropic purposes. The IRS will disallow unrestricted gifts made to state bar associations, although such organizations may have some public purposes. Some courts have allowed deductions for donations to bar associations on the ground that their activities benefit the general public. However, an appeals court disallowed deductible donations to a bar association that rates candidates for judicial office.

   Clubs for social purposes—fraternities and sororities are generally in this class. Unless an organization is exclusively operated for a charitable, religious, or other approved purpose, you may not deduct your contribution, even though your funds are used for a charitable or religious purpose.
5. Donations to civic leagues, communist or communist-front organizations, chambers of commerce, business leagues, or labor unions.
6. Contributions to a hospital or school operated for profit.
7. Purchase price of church building bond. To claim a deduction, you must donate the bond to the church. The amount of the deduction is the fair market value of the bond when you make the donation. Interest on the bond is income each year, under the original issue discount rules *(4.19)*, where no interest will be paid until the bond matures.
8. Donations of blood to the Red Cross or other blood banks.
9. Contributions to foreign charitable organizations or directly to foreign governments. Thus, a contribution to the State of Israel was disallowed.

Donation of services. You may not deduct the value of volunteer work you perform for charities. But you can deduct unreimbursed expenses incurred during such work *(14.4)*.

Law Alert

Contributions to Donor-Advised Funds

No deduction can be claimed for a contribution to a donor-advised fund if the sponsoring organization is a war veteran's organization, fraternal society, veteran's organization, or a non-functionally integrated Type III supporting organization.

Caution

Foreign Charities

You may deduct donations to domestic organizations that distribute funds to charities in foreign countries, as long as the U.S. organization controls the distribution of the funds overseas. An outright contribution to a foreign charitable organization is not deductible. Some exceptions to this ban are provided by international treaties. For example, if you have income from Canadian, Mexican, or Israeli sources, contributions to certain organizations in those countries are deductible subject to limitations. For details, *see* IRS Publication 526.

Free use of property. You may not deduct the rental value of property you allow a charity to use without charge. That is, if you allow a charity rent-free use of an office in your building, you may not deduct the fair rental value. You also have no deduction when you lend money to a charity without charging interest.

To raise money for a charity, supporters of the organization may donate rental time for their vacation home, to be auctioned off to the public. No deduction is allowed for donating the rental time *(14.10)*.

Parents' support payments of children serving as Mormon missionaries. According to the Supreme Court, support payments made by parents directly to their children who serve as missionaries are not deductible because the church does not control the funds.

14.3 Contributions That Provide You With Benefits

A contribution to a qualifying organization *(14.1)* is generally deductible only to the extent that you intend to give more than the value of benefits you receive and actually do so.

If you contribute $75 or less and receive benefits, the organization may tell you the value of the benefits. If your contribution exceeds $75, the organization by law *must* give you a written statement that estimates the value of the benefits provided to you and instructs you to deduct only the portion of your contribution that *exceeds* the benefits. However, the disclosure statement does not have to be provided to you if you receive only token benefits, or if you receive from a religious organization only "intangible religious benefits."

Caution

Tuition or Other Benefits Received

Except for certain token benefits and memberships that are disregarded for tax purposes, you may not deduct a contribution to a qualified charity to the extent that you receive goods, services, or financial benefits in exchange *(14.3)*.

The Tax Court and Ninth Circuit Court of Appeals agree with the IRS that you may not deduct tuition payments to a religious school for the education of your children if secular courses that lead to a recognized degree are provided, unless the payments exceed the usual tuition charged for a secular education in your area.

Fees paid to a tax-exempt rest home in which you live, or to a hospital for the care of a particular patient, are not deductible if any benefit is received from the contribution. A gift to a retirement home, over and above monthly fees, is not deductible if your accommodations are dependent on the size of your gift.

EXAMPLES

1. You contribute $200 to a philanthropy and receive a book that you have seen on sale for prices ranging between $18 and $25. The charity estimates the value at $20. As the estimate is between the typical retail prices, it is acceptable to the IRS. Although the book sold at a price as high as $25, you may treat the $20 estimate as fair market value and claim a deduction of $180.
2. A charitable organization sponsors an art auction and provides a catalogue that lists the items being auctioned and estimates of fair market value. The catalogue lists the value of a vase at $100. At the auction, you bid and pay $500 for the vase. Because you were aware of the estimate before the auction and paid more for the vase, you may deduct $400.

Dues. Dues paid to a qualified tax-exempt organization are deductible to the extent they exceed the value of benefits from the organization, such as monthly journals, use of a library, or the right to attend luncheons and lectures. As discussed above, you generally must be provided with an estimate of any benefits you received if your donation exceeds $75.

If dues are paid to a social club with the understanding that a specified part goes to a qualifying charity *(14.1)*, you may claim a charitable deduction for dues earmarked for the charity. If the treasurer of your club is actually the agent of the charity, you take the deduction in the year you give him or her the money. If the treasurer is merely your agent, you may take the deduction only in the year the money is remitted to the charity.

Caution

Bingo and Lotteries

You may not deduct the cost of raffle tickets, bingo games, or tickets for other types of lotteries organized by charities.

Benefit tickets. Tickets to theater events, tours, concerts, and other entertainments are often sold by charitable organizations at prices higher than the regular admission charge. The difference between the regular admission and the higher amount you pay is deductible as a charitable contribution. If you decline to accept the ticket or return it to the charity for resale, your deduction is the price you paid.

The charity should explain to you how much is deductible. The charity must provide an explanation if you paid more than $75; *see* the discussion above.

If the ticket is at or below its normal cost, no deduction is allowed unless you decline the ticket or return it to the charity.

If tickets were purchased for a charity-sponsored series of events and the average cost of a single event is equal to or less than the cost of an individual performance, then a deduction for a returned ticket is based upon the time the ticket was held. Generally, you may deduct only your cost. However, if you have held the ticket for more than a year, you may deduct the price the charity will charge on resale of the ticket.

EXAMPLE

A couple claimed a full deduction for regular-price tickets to a high-school fund-raising event that they did not attend. They argued that they were entitled to the deduction because they received no benefit from their ticket purchase. The IRS disallowed the deduction and the Tax Court agreed, holding that a donor receives a benefit by merely having the right to attend the event. To claim a deduction for the price of the tickets the couple should have returned them to the charity.

Donation for the right to buy athletic stadium tickets. If you contribute to a public or nonprofit college or university and receive the right to buy preferential seating at the school's athletic complexes, you may deduct 80% of the contribution to the school. The 80% deduction also applies where your contribution gives you the right to buy seating in stadium skyboxes, suites, or special viewing areas. The cost of any tickets you buy is not deductible. The deduction is allowed only to the extent that you receive the right to buy tickets rather than the tickets themselves. For example, if in exchange for a substantial donation you receive a season ticket worth $200, your payment is reduced by $200 before applying the 80% deductible percentage.

Token Items and Membership Benefits That Do Not Reduce Your Deduction

Token items. Popular fund-raising campaigns, such as those for museums, zoos, and public TV, offer token items such as calendars, tote bags, tee shirts, and other items carrying the organization's logo. You are allowed a full deduction for your contribution if the item is considered to be of insubstantial value under IRS guidelines.

The charity must tell you how much of your contribution is deductible in the solicitation that offers the token item. If the items are insubstantial in value, the charity should tell you that your payment is fully deductible. For example, if in 2010 you contributed at least $48, and the offered items cost the charity no more than $9.60, the value of the benefits is ignored and a full 2010 deduction is allowed. A full deduction for 2010 is also allowed if the items were worth no more than 2% of the contribution or $96, whichever is less. The $48, $9.60, and $96 amounts change annually for inflation.

Newsletters or program guides that are not of commercial quality are treated as token items having no fair market value or cost if their primary purpose is to inform members about the organization's activities, and they are not available to nonmembers by paid subscription or through newsstand sales.

Publications with articles written for compensation and advertising are treated as commercial-quality publications for which the organization must figure value to determine if a full deduction is allowed under the "insubstantial value" test. Professional journals, whether or not they have such articles and advertising, will generally be treated as commercial-quality publications that must be valued.

Filing Tip

Estimated Value of Benefits

You may rely on a written estimate from the organization of the value of any benefits given to you unless it seems unreasonable. Although the value of benefits received generally reduces your deductible contribution, certain token items and membership benefits do not reduce the amount of your deduction.

Membership benefits. If you contribute $75 or less for an annual membership in a qualified charity *(14.1)* and you receive only the following benefits, the benefits can be disregarded and you may deduct your entire payment:

1. Privileges that can be exercised frequently, such as free or discounted parking or admission, or discounts on gift shop or mail order merchandise, *or*
2. Admission to events that are open only to members and the organization's reasonably projected cost per person for each event excluding overhead (as of the time the membership package is offered) is no more than the annual limit for "low cost articles." For 2009, the "low cost article" limit is $9.50.

14.4 Unreimbursed Expenses of Volunteer Workers

If you work without pay for an organization listed at *14.1*, you may deduct as charitable contributions your unreimbursed expenses in providing the services. This includes commuting expenses to and from its place of operations, and meals and lodging on a trip away from home *(20.6)* for the organization.

To qualify for the deduction, the expenses must be incurred for a domestic organization that authorizes you to travel. You may not deduct the value of your donated services.

If you are claiming a deduction for under $250 in unreimbursed expenses, IRS proposed regulations waive the substantiation requirement, generally applicable to all cash or other monetary gifts, that a bank record or written receipt be obtained *(14.15)*, but it is advisable for you to keep records of your expenses in case your deduction is questioned. To deduct an unreimbursed expense of $250 or more, such as for a plane ticket or a luncheon you hosted on behalf of the organization, obtain for each such expense a statement from the charitable organization that acknowledges the services you provided. The acknowledgment must describe the services, and state whether you were provided any goods or services by the charity. If so, an estimate of their value must be given unless the benefits are "intangible religious benefits." The acknowledgment must be obtained by the date you file your return, but if you file after the due date (or extended due date if you get an extension), the acknowledgment must be obtained by the due date of your return, including extensions. For 2010 returns, the due date is April 15, 2011, unless you get an extension.

Car expenses. If you used your car (or other motor vehicle) during 2010 to provide volunteer services for a charity, you may deduct either the actual vehicle operating costs (such as gas and oil) that are directly related to your volunteer services, or you may claim a flat mileage rate of 14 cents per mile. The 14-cents-per-mile rate was set by Congress in 1997 and although there have been numerous proposals to increase the rate, none have yet been enacted into law; *see* the *e-Supplement at jklasser.com* for any update.

Parking fees and tolls are deductible whether you claim actual expenses or the flat mileage rate.

EXAMPLE

In the course of doing volunteer work for a charity in 2010, Jill Patton drove her car 1,000 miles. She may claim a contribution deduction of $140 (14 cents a mile), plus tolls and parking.

Planning Reminder

Foster Parent Expenses

If you receive payments from a state agency to reimburse you for the costs of caring for a foster child in your home, and you can show that your costs of caring for the child exceed the reimbursements, the excess is deductible as a charitable contribution. Keep detailed records to substantiate your support payments.

Also deductible as charitable contributions are:

- Uniform costs required in serving the organization
- Cost of telephone calls, and cost of materials and supplies you furnished such as stamps or stationery
- Travel expenses, including meals and lodging on overnight trips away from home as an official delegate to a convention of a church, charitable, veteran, or other similar organization. If you are a member but not a delegate, you may not deduct travel costs, but you may deduct expenses paid for the benefit of your organization at the convention.
- All related expenses in hosting a fund-raiser are deductible, from the invitations to the food and drink.

The IRS does not allow a deduction for "babysitting" expenses of charity volunteer workers. Although incurred to make the volunteer work possible, babysitting costs are a nondeductible personal expense. Furthermore, the expense is not a dependent care cost; it is not related to a paying job.

Recreational purposes may bar travel expense deduction. To claim a charitable deduction for travel expenses of a research project for a charitable organization, you must show the trip had no significant element of personal pleasure, recreation, or vacation.

EXAMPLES

1. Al Jones sails from one Caribbean island to another and spends eight hours a day counting whales and other forms of marine life as part of a project sponsored by a charitable organization. According to the IRS, he may not claim a charitable deduction for the cost of the trip.
2. Sara Smith works on an archaeological excavation sponsored by a charitable organization for several hours each morning, with the rest of the day free for recreation and sightseeing. According to the IRS, she may not deduct the cost of the trip.
3. Myra Scott, a member of a chapter of a local charitable organization, travels to New York City and spends the entire day at the required regional meeting. According to the IRS, she may deduct her travel expenses as a charitable donation, even if she attends a theater in the evening.

14.5 Support of a Student in Your Home

A limited charitable deduction is allowed for support of an elementary or high-school student in your home under an educational program arranged by a charitable organization. If the student is not a relative or your dependent, you may deduct as a charitable contribution your support payments up to $50 for each month the student stays in your home. For this purpose, 15 days or more of a calendar month is considered a full month. You may not deduct any payments received from the charitable organization if any reimbursements are received for the student's maintenance. The only exception is that if you prepay a "one-time" expense such as a hospital bill or vacation for the child at the request of the child's parents or the sponsoring charity, and you are later reimbursed for part of your payment, you may deduct your unreimbursed expenses.

To support the deduction, be prepared to show a written agreement between you and the organization relating to the support arrangement. Keep records of amounts spent for such items as food, clothing, medical and dental care, tuition, books, and recreation in order to substantiate your deduction. No deduction is allowed for depreciation on your house.

14.6 What Kind of Property Are You Donating?

Generally, a deduction for the fair market value of donated property may be claimed, but the tax law does not treat all donations of appreciated property in the same way. Whether the full amount of the fair market value of the property is deductible depends on the type of property donated, your holding period, the nature of the philanthropy, and the use to which the property is put by the philanthropy. For donations of motor vehicles, boats, or airplanes valued at over $500, special deduction restrictions and substantiation restrictions apply *(14.7)*.

Save records to support the market value and cost of donated property. Get a receipt or letter from the charitable organization acknowledging and describing the gift. You *must* get a receipt for donations of property valued at $250 or more *(14.14)*. Lack of substantiation may disqualify an otherwise valid deduction. Furthermore, if the total claimed value of your 2010 property donations exceeds $500, you must report the donation on Form 8283, which you attach to Schedule A, Form 1040. *See also 14.15* for when you need an appraisal of the value of the property.

Filing Instruction

Long-Term Holding Period

In this chapter, property held "long term" is property held more than one year by the donor.

Figuring value. When donating securities listed on a public exchange, fair market value is readily ascertainable from newspaper listings of stock prices. It is the average of the high and low sales price on the date of the donation.

To value other property, such as real estate or works of art, you will need the services of an experienced appraiser. Fees paid to an appraiser are not deductible as a charitable contribution, but rather as a miscellaneous itemized deduction *(19.1)* subject to the 2% adjusted gross income floor on Schedule A.

Caution

Appraisal Fees

A fee paid for an appraisal of donated real estate or art is not deductible as a charitable contribution. It may be claimed only as a miscellaneous itemized deduction subject to the 2% floor *(19.1)*.

Fair market value deductible for appreciated intangible personal property (such as securities) and real estate held long term. Fair market value is deductible where you have held such property long term (longer than one year) and you give it to a publicly supported charity or to a private foundation that qualifies as a 50% limit organization, but you may not deduct more than 30% of adjusted gross income *(14.17)*. A five-year carryover for the excess is allowed *(14.18)*. If the donation exceeds the 30% ceiling, you may consider a special election that allows you to apply the 50% ceiling *(14.19)*.

A contribution of appreciated securities or real estate held long term has two tax advantages that reduce the real cost of making the contribution:

1. Your taxes are reduced by the deduction of the fair market value of the property. For example, you donate appreciated stock that is selling at $1,000. You are in the 25% tax bracket. The deduction for the donation reduces your taxes by $250.
2. You avoid the tax you would have paid on a sale of the stock. Assume that your cost for the stock was $400 and that your regular top bracket is 25%. On a sale at $1,000, you would pay tax of $90 (15% capital gain rate on $600 profit). By donating the stock, you save that $90 plus $250 from the $1,000 deduction, for a total tax savings of $340. Your "cost" for donating the $1,000 asset is $660 ($1,000 – $340).

The IRS ruled that you may not claim a deduction on donated stock if you retain the voting rights, even though the charity has the right to receive dividends and sell the stock. The right to vote is considered a substantial interest and is crucial in protecting a stockholder's investment.

If you are planning a year-end donation of securities, keep in mind that the gift is generally not considered complete until the properly endorsed securities are mailed or delivered to the charity or its agent *(14.1)*.

Caution

Tangible Personal Property

When you donate appreciated collectibles and artwork held long term, you get a full deduction for the fair market value of the property if the items are used in connection with the charity's main activity or tax-exempt purpose. However, a deduction for fair market value is not available for certain contributions of taxidermy property; *see* IRS Publication 526.

If the charity sells your property, your deduction is limited to your basis in the property (what you paid for it, rather than its appreciated value). Protect a deduction for fair market value by obtaining a letter from the charity stating that it intends to use your gift in connection with its tax-exempt purposes.

Deduction limited to cost for appreciated property not held long term and ordinary income property. This is property that, if sold by you at its fair market value, would not result in long-term capital gain. The deduction for donations of this kind is restricted to your cost for the property. Examples include: stock and other capital assets held by you for one year or less, inventory items donated by business, farm crops, Section 306 stock (preferred stock received as a tax-free stock dividend, usually in a closely held corporation), and works of art *(14.9)*, books, letters, and memoranda donated by the person who prepared or created them. For example, a former Congressman claimed a charitable deduction for the donation of his papers. His deduction was disallowed. His papers were ordinary income property, and since his cost basis in the papers was zero, he could claim no deduction. Depreciable business property is considered ordinary income property to the extent that depreciation would be recaptured as ordinary income on a sale *(44.1–44.3)*. If the cost of the property was fully deducted under first-year expensing *(42.3)*, you have no cost basis and you may not claim a deduction.

EXAMPLE

Bob James holds stock that cost him $1,000. It is now worth $1,500. If he holds it for one year or less and donates it to a philanthropy, his deduction would be limited to $1,000. He would get no tax benefit for the appreciation of $500. On the other hand, if the stock were held over a year, he could claim a deduction for the full market value of the stock on its donation.

Law Alert

Recapture of Deduction for Property Sold Within Three Years

If you donate appreciated tangible personal property held long term, for which you claim a deduction exceeding $5,000, and it is sold by the charity by the end of the year of the contribution, the deduction is limited to your cost basis (and not fair market value) unless the charity makes a qualifying written certification to the IRS and gives you a copy.

If you deduct more than your basis for the property and the charity sells the property after the year of the contribution but within three years of the contribution, and the charity does not provide the required certification, you must recapture part of the previously claimed deduction.

Use of property by charity determines whether fair market value or cost is deductible for appreciated tangible personal property held long term. If you donate appreciated tangible personal property held long term, such as works of art *(14.9)*, jewelry, furniture, books, equipment, fixtures (severed from realty), and antique cars, the deduction limit depends on how the charitable organization uses the property. If the property is used by the organization for purposes related to its tax-exempt purpose or function, you may deduct the fair market value.

If the organization puts the property to a use that is unrelated to its tax-exempt purpose or function, the deduction is limited to your cost basis because the fair market value must be reduced by the amount of long-term capital gain that would have been realized if the property had been sold at fair market value. If the charity sells your gift to obtain cash for its exempt purposes, your donation is treated as being put to a nonrelated use by the charity, and your deduction must be reduced by the long-term gain element unless on the date of the donation you could reasonably anticipate that the property would not be sold (or put to another nonrelated use). A certification of exempt use from the charity is required if you claim a deduction exceeding $5,000 and the charity sells the property within three years; *see* below.

If the donation of tangible personal property is to a 50% deduction limit organization such as a church or college, and you must reduce the deduction as a *nonrelated* gift, the reduced gift is then subject to the 50% annual deduction ceiling discussed in *14.17*. If the organization's use of the property is *related* to its tax-exempt charitable purposes, and it is a 50% limit organization, you may deduct the property's fair market value subject to the 30% of adjusted gross income deduction ceiling *(14.17)*. Alternatively, you may elect to deduct up to 50% of adjusted gross income by reducing the deduction by the long-term gain *(14.19)*.

Deductions of appreciated tangible personal property exceeding $5,000 may be reduced or recaptured on sale by charity within three years. Special certification rules apply to donations of appreciated tangible personal property for which you claim a deduction of more than $5,000:

(1) If the charity sells or otherwise disposes of the property during the year that you donated it, your deduction is limited to your cost basis unless the charity provides a written certification of exempt use to the IRS on Form 8282, and gives you a copy. The certification, signed by an officer under penalty of perjury, must either state that the charity's use of the property was substantial and furthered its tax-exempt purpose or function, or state that a related and substantial use of the property was intended at the time of the donation but it became impossible or unfeasible to implement such intent.

(2) If you deduct more than your basis in the property and the charity sells it (or otherwise disposes of it) after the year of contribution but within three years of the contribution, and the charity does not provide the IRS and you with the required certification described in (1) above, you must recapture part of your original deduction. In the year of the sale, you must report as ordinary income the excess of the deduction claimed over your cost basis for the property at the time of the donation. Report the recaptured amount as "other income" on Line 21 of Form 1040.

EXAMPLE

On October 15, 2010, you contribute to a college a painting worth $7,500 that you held long term. The college displays it in a library where art students may study it. The college's use of the painting is related to its tax-exempt educational purposes and you may deduct fair market value.

However, assume that the charity sells the painting in 2011 and uses the proceeds for educational purposes. Because the deduction exceeded $5,000, the charity must report the sale to the IRS on Form 8282 and give you a copy. There is no effect on your deduction if the charity on Form 8282 certifies its exempt use or its intended exempt use. Without the required certification, the recapture rule would apply (rule 2 above) and you would have to report the excess of your $7,500 deduction over your cost basis for the paintings as income for 2011. The same result would apply if the charity disposed of the painting in 2012 or in 2013 by October 14, 2013, the end of the three-year recapture period.

Donating mortgaged property. A donation of mortgaged property may be taxable. Before you give mortgaged property to a charity, have an attorney review the transaction. You may deduct the excess of fair market value over the amount of the outstanding mortgage. However, you may realize a taxable gain. The IRS and Tax Court treat the transferred mortgage debt as cash received in a part-gift, part-sale subject to the rules for bargain sales of appreciated property *(14.8)*. You will realize a taxable gain if the transferred mortgage exceeds the portion of basis allocated to the sale part of the transaction. This is true even if the charity does not assume the mortgage.

EXAMPLE

Bob Hill donates to a college land held over a year that is worth $250,000 and subject to a $100,000 mortgage. His basis is $150,000. Hill's charitable contribution deduction is $150,000 ($250,000 – $100,000). He also is considered to have made a bargain sale for $100,000 (transferred mortgage debt) on which he realized $40,000 long-term capital gain. 40% of the transaction is treated as a bargain sale:

$$\frac{\$100{,}000 \text{ (amount of mortgage)}}{\$250{,}000 \text{ (fair market value)}} = 40\%$$

Basis allocated to sale: 40% of $150,000, or $60,000

Amount realized	$100,000
Allocated basis	60,000
Gain	$ 40,000

Donating capital gain property to private non-operating foundations. You generally may not deduct the full fair market value of gifts of capital gain property to private non-operating foundations that are subject to the 20% deduction ceiling for non–50% limit organizations *(14.17)*. (Capital gain property is property that, if sold by you at fair market value, would result in long-term capital gain.) The deduction must be reduced by the long-term gain that would have been realized if the property had been sold at fair market value. In other words, your deduction is limited to your cost basis.

An exception is available for certain contributions of stock to a private non-operating foundation; *see* below.

Stock donation to private non-operating foundation. A deduction for fair market value is allowed on a donation to a non-operating private foundation of appreciated publicly traded stock held long term. To qualify, there must be readily available market quotations on an established securities market for the stock on the date of the contribution. If you or family members donated more than 10% of a corporation's stock, the fair market value deduction is allowed only for the first 10%. Under the family aggregation rule, your contributions of stock in a particular publicly traded corporation are aggregated with those of your spouse, brothers, sisters, parents and grandparents, children, grandchildren, and great-grandchildren to all private non-operating foundations, whether the foundations are related or not. If the 10% limit is exceeded, the excess contributions are subject to the cost basis deduction limitation.

The IRS has ruled that for purposes of applying the 10% limit, you must take into account previous stock contributions that the private foundation sold before the new contributions were made. Once publicly traded stock is donated to a private foundation, it must be counted toward the 10% limit, even if it is later disposed of. Furthermore, the value of each contribution at the time it is made is the value taken into account for applying the 10% limitation; prior contributions are not revalued each time there is a new contribution.

Patents and other intellectual property. If you donate patents or other intellectual property to charity, such as trademarks, trade names, trade secrets, know-how, and certain copyrights and software, you can claim an initial charitable contribution deduction for your cost basis in the property (assuming that is less than its fair market value). Additional deductions may be claimed in the year of the donation and in later years, based on a percentage of the income that the charity realizes from the property.

The additional deductions are allowed on a sliding scale percentage basis for the 10-year period beginning on the date of the contribution. In order to obtain the additional deductions, you must accompany the donation with a written statement to the charity that includes your name, address, and taxpayer identification number, a description of the intellectual property, and the date of the contribution. The statement must specify that you intend to treat the contribution as a qualified intellectual property contribution and will claim additional deductions for the allowable annual percentage of the charity's income from the property.

For each year that the charity realizes net income from the property in the 10-year period beginning on the date of the contribution, the charity must report the income to the IRS on Form 8899. A copy of Form 8899 is sent to you and the income shown may be used as the basis for claiming an additional contribution deduction.

For further details, *see* the instructions to Form 8899 and IRS Publication 526.

U.S. Saving Bonds. You may not donate U.S. Saving Bonds, such as EE bonds, because you may not transfer them. They are nonnegotiable. You must first cash the bonds and then give the proceeds to the charity, or surrender the bonds and have new ones registered in the donee's name. When you do this, you have to report the accrued interest on your tax return. Of course, you will get a charitable deduction for the cash gift.

Gift of installment obligations. You may deduct your donation of installment notes to a qualified philanthropy. However, if you received them on your sale of property that you reported on the installment basis, you may realize gain or loss on the gift of the notes *(5.28)*. The amount of the contribution is the fair market value of the obligation, not the face amount of the notes.

14.7 Cars, Clothing, and Other Property Valued Below Cost

If you donate property whose value has declined below your cost, your deduction generally is limited to the fair market value. However, the rules for cars, trucks, boats, and airplanes are more complicated. Strict substantiation requirements apply to prevent donors from claiming inflated deductions for donated vehicles where the charity actually received much less on a sale to raise cash; *see* below.

If you are planning a donation of stock or other investment or business property worth less than your basis *(5.20)*, consider selling the property and then donating the proceeds. If you donate the property, your deduction is limited to the fair market value and you cannot deduct a loss. If you first sell the property, you can claim a loss on the sale and then claim a charitable contribution on your donation of the sale proceeds; *see* the Example below.

EXAMPLE

Betty Dunn owns securities that cost $20,000 several years ago but have declined in value to $5,000. A donation of these securities gives a charitable contribution deduction of $5,000. If Betty sold the securities for $5,000, she could claim a long-term capital loss of $15,000. She could then donate the sales proceeds and claim a $5,000 charitable deduction for the cash contribution.

Clothing or household items. You can claim a deduction for used clothing or household items only if they are in good used condition or better. Household items include furniture or furnishings, linens, appliances or electronics, but not antiques, art, collections, or jewelry. Your deduction for "good condition" clothing or household items is limited to their fair market value, which is usually much less than your orginal cost. Prices paid in thrift shops for similar items are an indication of fair market value. If you have photographs of the donated items, or a statement describing them from the charity, this would help support your valuation should the IRS later question your deduction. If an item is valued at over $500 in a qualified appraisal that you attach to your return, a deduction is allowed even if the item is not in good used condition or better.

Cars, other motor vehicles, boats, and airplanes. You must obtain a timely written acknowledgment from the charity to substantiate a deduction for a car or other motor vehicle, boat, or airplane with a *claimed value of over $500.* The required acknowledgment must be on Form 1098-C or an equivalent statement from the charity. Copy B of the Form 1098-C (or equivalent acknowledgment) must be attached to your return; if you do not attach the form to your return, the IRS will disallow your deduction. If you e-file your return, you must attach Copy B of Form 1098-C to Form 8453 and mail the forms to the IRS. You also must attach Form 8283 if your total deduction for all property donations exceeds $500 *(14.15).* Vehicles held primarily for sale, such as dealer inventory, are not subject to the acknowledgment rules or the deduction restrictions in the following paragraphs *(14.12).*

If the charity sells the vehicle for more than $500 to a buyer other than a needy individual (*see* below) without having put it to a significant intervening use, or without materially improving it, your deduction is limited to the gross sales proceeds. You must be sent the Form 1098-C (or equivalent substitute) within 30 days of the sale. The charity must certify in Box 4a that the sale was made in an arm's-length transaction to an unrelated party. The amount of the gross proceeds (not reduced by expenses or fees) will be shown in Box 4c.

If the charity intends to significantly use the vehicle in furtherance of its regularly conducted activities or to materially improve it before selling it, Form 1098-C (or other acknowledgment) must be provided to you within 30 days of the donation. In Box 5a, the charity must certify its intent and in Box 5c it must certify a detailed description of the planned use or improvement, including the intended duration of such use or improvement. If Box 5a is checked, you may take a deduction equal to the fair market value of the vehicle on the date of contribution.

Fair market value is also deductible if the charity checks Box 5b to certify that the donated vehicle will be given to a needy individual, or sold to such to an individual for significantly less than fair market value, in furtherance of the organization's charitable purpose. You must be given Form 1098-C (or equivalent acknowledgment) with Box 5b checked within 30 days of the donation.

Copy B of Form 1098-C states that the deduction may not exceed the gross sales proceeds unless Box 5a or 5b is checked. If fair market value is deductible because Box 5a or 5b is checked, value may be based on an established used-vehicle-pricing guide, provided the amount is for a comparable model in similar condition and sold in the same area.

In Boxes 6a–6c of Form 1098-C, the charity indicates whether any goods or services were provided to the donor and, if so, they are described and a good faith estimate of their fair market value is shown. The deduction must be reduced by the value of the goods/services provided, with one exception. If the only benefits provided to the donor are intangible religious benefits (such as admission to a religious ceremony), Box 6c will be checked and the deduction does not have to be reduced by such benefits.

If the claimed value of the vehicle is at least $250 but not over $500. If the claimed value of a car, other motor vehicle, boat, or airplane (but not dealer property) is at least $250 but not over $500, the contribution is not acknowledged on Form 1098-C (or equivalent), but you must obtain a written acknowledgment meeting the general substantiation rules *(14.14)* by the due date for filing.

If the charity sells the donated vehicle (other than a sale to a needy person in furtherance of charitable purposes) without a significant intervening use or material improvement, and the gross sale proceeds are $500 or less, IRS guidelines allow a deduction to be claimed for fair market value if that exceeds the proceeds, but no more than $500 can be deducted. For example, if the gross sale proceeds are $400 but the donor can substantiate a fair market value of $450, a deduction of $450 would be allowed, provided a qualified acknowledgment *(14.14)* is obtained. If the donor could substantiate a fair market value exceeding $500, the deduction would be limited to $500.

14.8 Bargain Sales of Appreciated Property

A sale of appreciated property to a philanthropy for less than fair market value allows you to claim a charitable deduction while receiving proceeds from the sale. However, you must pay a tax on part of the gain attributed to the sale. That is, the transaction is broken down into two parts: the sale and the gift.

To compute gain on the sale, you allocate the adjusted basis of the property between the sale and the gift following these steps:

Step 1. Divide the sales proceeds by the fair market value of the property. If the property is mortgaged, include the outstanding debt as sale proceeds.

Step 2. Apply the Step 1 percentage to the adjusted basis of the property. This is the portion of basis allocated to the sale.

Step 3. Deduct the resulting basis of Step 2 from the sales proceeds to find the gain.

You may deduct the donated appreciation if full market value would be deductible on a straight donation (no sale) under the rules in *14.6*. Thus, the donated appreciation is deductible if the property is securities or real estate held long term or long-term tangible personal property related to the charity's exempt function; *see* Example 1 below. However, if a deduction for the property (assuming no sale) would be reduced to cost basis as discussed in *14.6*, your charitable deduction on the sale is also reduced; *see* Example 2 below. This reduction affects sales of capital gain property held short term; ordinary income property; tangible personal property not related to the charity's exempt function; depreciable personal property subject to recapture; and sales of capital gain property to private non-operating foundations.

EXAMPLES

1. Lana Briggs sells to a university for $12,000 stock she held over a year. The adjusted basis of the stock is $12,000, and the fair market value is $20,000. On the sale, she recouped her investment and donated the appreciation of $8,000, but, at the same time, she realized taxable gain of $4,800 computed as follows: The percentage of basis applied to the sale is 60% ($12,000 sale proceeds ÷ $20,000 fair market value). Thus, 60% of the $12,000 basis, or $7,200, is allocated to the sale. Gain on the sale equals the $12,000 sale proceeds less the $7,200 allocated basis, or $4,800.
2. Joel Marx sells to his church stock held short term for his basis of $4,000. The stock is worth $10,000. Using the allocation method in Example 1, 40% ($4,000 sale proceeds ÷ $10,000 fair market value) of his $4,000 basis, or $1,600, is allocated to the sale. Thus, he has a short-term capital gain of $2,400 ($4,000 sale proceeds – $1,600 allocated basis). Furthermore, his deductible charitable contribution is also $2,400, equal to the 60% of basis allocated to the gift (60% of $4,000 = $2,400).

Basis allocation applies even if a deduction is barred by the annual ceiling. The basis allocation rules for determining gain on a bargain sale apply even if the annual deduction ceilings *(14.17)* bar a deduction in the year of the donation and in the five-year carryover period.

EXAMPLE

The Hodgdons contributed real estate valued at $3.9 million but subject to mortgage debt of $2.6 million. The IRS treated the mortgage debt as sales proceeds and figured gain based on the difference between the debt and the portion of basis allocated to the sale element. The Hodgdons claimed that the basis allocation rule, which increased the amount of their gain, should not apply. Earlier in the year, they had made another donation that used up their charitable deduction ceiling for that year as well as for the following five-year carryover period. The Tax Court held that the basis allocation rule applied because a charitable deduction was "allowable," even if the contribution did not actually result in a deduction in the carryover period.

14.9 Art Objects

You may claim a charitable deduction for a painting or other art object donated to a charity. The amount of the deduction depends on (1) whether you are the artist; (2) if you are not the artist, how long you owned it; and (3) the type of organization receiving the gift.

If you owned the art work short term, your deduction is limited to cost, under the rules applying to donations of ordinary income property *(14.6)*.

If you owned the art work long term *(14.6)*, your deduction depends on the way the charity uses the property. If the charity uses it for its exempt purposes, you may deduct the fair market value. However, if the charity uses it for unrelated purposes, your deduction is reduced by 100% of the appreciation. A donation of art work to a general fund-raising agency would be reduced because the agency would have no direct use for it. It would have to sell the art work and use the cash for its exempt purposes.

Deductions of over $5,000 for art donations (as well as other types of appreciated tangible personal property) may be limited or recaptured if the charity disposes of the property within three years *(14.6)*.

Caution

Donations of Personal Creative Works

If you are the artist, your deduction is limited to cost regardless of how long you held the art work or to what use the charity puts it. In the case of a painting, the deduction would be the lower of the cost for canvas and paints and the fair market value.

EXAMPLES

1. You give your college a painting that you have owned for many years. Its cost was $1,000 but it is now worth $10,000. The school displays the painting in its library for study by students. This use is related to the school's educational purposes. Your donation is deductible at fair market value. If, however, the school told you it was going to sell the painting and use the proceeds for general education purposes, its use would not be considered related. Your deduction would be reduced by the $9,000 appreciation to $1,000.

   If a deduction for fair market value is allowed, sale by the charity within three years of the donation will trigger a recapture of a deduction, unless the charity makes a qualifying certification *(14.6)*.
2. You donate to the Community Fund a collection of first edition books held for many years and worth $5,000. Your cost is $1,000. Since the charity is a general fund-raising organization, its use of your gift is not related. Your deduction would be $1,000 ($5,000 less $4,000).
3. You contribute to a charity antique furnishings you owned for years. The antiques cost you $500 and are now worth $5,000. The charity uses the furnishings in its office in the course of carrying on its functions. This is a related use. Your contribution deduction is $5,000.

Appraisals. Be prepared to support your deduction with detailed proof of cost, the date of acquisition, and how value was appraised. The appraisal fee is treated as a "miscellaneous" itemized deduction subject to the 2% adjusted gross income floor *(19.1)*. *See* the discussion of appraisal requirements later in this chapter *(14.15)*.

The IRS has its own art advisory panel to assess whether the fair market value claimed for donated art works is reasonable.

Filing Instruction

Appraisal Required

If you claim a deduction for art of $20,000 or more, you must attach a copy of a signed qualifying appraisal to Form 8283 and file it with your return *(14.15)*.

Requesting advance valuation of art from the IRS. To avoid a later dispute, you may ask the IRS for an advance valuation of art that you have had appraised at $50,000 or more. A request for an IRS Statement of Value (SOV) may be submitted for income tax, gift tax, or estate tax purposes. The IRS has the discretion to value items appraised at less than $50,000 if the SOV request includes at least one item appraised at $50,000 or more, and the IRS determines that the valuation is in the best interest of efficient tax administration.

A request for an SOV must be submitted to the IRS before filing the tax return reporting the donation. The request must include a copy of an appraisal for the item of art and a $2,500 fee, which pays for an SOV for up to three items of art. There is an additional charge of $250 for each item of art over three. It takes the IRS between six and 12 months to issue an SOV.

If the IRS agrees with the value reported on the appraisal, the IRS will issue an SOV approving the appraisal. If the IRS disagrees, the IRS will issue an SOV indicating its own valuation and stating the reasons it disagrees with the appraised amount. Regardless of whether you agree with the IRS appraisal, the SOV must be attached to and filed with the return reporting the donation. If you file the return before the SOV is issued, a copy of your request for the SOV must be attached to your return and on receipt of the SOV, an amended return must be filed with the SOV attached. For further SOV details, *see* IRS Publication 561 and Revenue Procedure 96-15.

Law Alert

Recapture of Deductions for Certain Fractional Interests

If a fractional interest in art or other tangible personal property *(14.6)* is donated after August 17, 2006, and the charity does not receive complete ownership of the item within 10 years of the initial contribution, or, if earlier, the death of the donor, all prior charitable deductions for the property will have to be recaptured, and interest charges plus a 10% penalty will be imposed.

Donating a fractional interest in an art collection. You may deduct the value of a donated partial interest in an art collection, such as where you give a museum the right to exhibit the works for a specific period during the year. The deduction is allowed even if the museum does not take possession of the art works, provided it has the right to take possession. However, if you made a fractional donation after August 17, 2006, and later donate an additional fractional interest in the same property, the deduction for the later contribution is based on the fair market value of the property at the time of the initial fractional contribution where that is less than the value at the time of the later contribution. Furthermore, if you do not transfer your entire remaining interest to the same charity within 10 years of the initial fractional donation, or, if earlier, the date of your death, your charitable contributions will have to be recaptured, plus interest, and a penalty equal to 10% of the recaptured amount will be imposed. *See* Publication 526 for further details.

Keeping a reversionary interest. The IRS may challenge a charitable deduction where you retain some control over the donated property. However, if the possibility of the property reverting back to you is considered to be remote, a deduction may be allowed. For example, a taxpayer who donated her art collection to a museum was allowed to claim a charitable deduction even though she retained the right to decide where and how the art would be displayed. Disputes concerning art displays would be settled by a mutually acceptable museum curator. If the museum breached a condition, it had a period of time to cure the violation. If the violation was not cured, the ownership would revert back to the donor. The IRS allowed the deduction; the retained rights were fiduciary in nature and the possibility of the art reverting to the donor was so remote as to be negligible.

14.10 Interests in Real Estate

No deduction is allowed for the rental value of property you allow a charity to use free of charge. This is the case even if the property is used directly in furtherance of the organization's charitable purpose; *see* the Example below.

If you donate an undivided fractional part of your entire interest, a deduction will be allowed for the fair market value of the proportionate interest donated.

A donation of an option is not deductible until the year the option to buy the property is exercised.

Caution

Donating Vacation Home Use Not Advisable

To raise funds, a charitable organization may ask contributors who own vacation homes to donate use of the property, which the charity then auctions off to the public. Be warned that if you offer your home in this way you will not only be denied a charitable deduction for your generosity, but you may jeopardize your deduction for rental expenses. A deduction is not allowed for giving a charity the free use of your property.

EXAMPLE

To help a charity raise money, one owner allowed the charity to auction off a week's stay in his vacation home, and the highest bidder paid the charity a fair rental. The IRS ruled that not only was the owner's donation not deductible, but the one week stay by the bidder was considered personal use by the owner for purposes of figuring deductions for rental expenses. True, if the owner had directly rented the property to the bidder, the bidder's payment of a fair rental value would have been counted as a rental day and not a personal use day. However, the donation for charitable use is not a business rental, and the bidder's rental payment to the charity is not considered a payment to the owner.

Furthermore, the bidder's use of the home pushed the owner over the personal-use ceiling, which in turn prevented him from deducting a rental loss. A rental loss may not be claimed if personal use of a home exceeds the greater of 14 days and 10% of the number of days the home is rented at fair rental value *(9.7)*. Here, the owner personally used the home for 14 days and rented the home for 80 days. The rental expenses exceeded rental income. If the bidder's use of the home was not considered his personal use, the owner could have deducted the loss because his personal use did not exceed the 14-day limit (which was more than 10% of the 80 rental days). However, by adding the bidder's seven days of use to the owner's 14 days, the resulting 21 days of personal use exceeded the 14-day ceiling.

Remainder interest in home or farm. You may claim a charitable deduction for a gift of the remainder value of a residence or farm donated to a charity, even though you reserve the use of the property for yourself and your spouse for a term of years or life. Remainder gifts generally must be made in trust. However, where a residence or farm is donated, the remainder interest must be conveyed outright, not in trust. A remainder interest in a vacation home or in a "hobby" farm is also deductible. There is no requirement that the home be your principal residence or that the farm be profitable.

Contribution of real property for conservation purposes. A deduction may be claimed for the contribution of certain partial interests in real property to government agencies or publicly supported charities for exclusively conservational purposes. Qualified conservation contributions include: (1) your entire interest in real property other than retained rights to subsurface oil, gas, or other minerals; (2) a remainder interest; or (3) an easement, restrictive covenant, or similar property restriction granted in perpetuity. The contribution must be in perpetuity and further at least one of the following "conservation purposes"—preservation of land areas for outdoor recreation, education, or scenic enjoyment; preservation of historically important land areas or structures; or the protection of plant, fish, and wildlife habitats or similar natural ecosystems.

To obtain the deduction, there must be legally enforceable restrictions that prevent you from using your retained interest in the property in a way contrary to the intended conservation purpose. The donee organization must be prohibited from transferring the contributed interest except to other organizations that will hold the property for exclusively conservational purposes. If you retain an interest in subsurface oil, gas, or minerals, surface mining must generally be specifically prohibited. However, where the mineral rights and surface interests are separately owned, a deduction will be allowed if the probability of surface mining is so remote as to be considered negligible. The exception does not apply if you are related to the owner of the surface interest or if you received the mineral interest (directly or indirectly) from the surface owner.

Law Alert

Deduction Limit for Conservation Contributions

Qualified conservation contributions for 2006–2009 could be deducted up to 50% of adjusted gross income (AGI), or up to 100% for farmers and ranchers, instead of the usual 30% of AGI limit *(14.17)*, but the law allowing the higher limits expired at the end of 2009. However, the 50%/100% limits may be extended to 2010; *see* the *e-Supplement at jklasser.com* for a legislation update.

Historic building facade easements. A donation of a façade easement with respect to a certified historic structure in a registered historic district, other than one listed in the National Register, is allowed only if the easement preserves the entire exterior, including the space above as well as the front, rear, and sides of the building. The easement must bar exterior changes inconsistent with the historical character of the building. A written agreement between the donor and the donee must certify that the donee is a qualifying historic preservation organization with the resources and commitment to enforce the easement.

The donor must attach to his or her tax return a qualified appraisal of the easement, photographs of the building exterior, and a description of all zoning laws and similar restrictions on development.

If a deduction of over $10,000 is claimed for a façade easement, a $500 fee must be paid or no deduction will be allowed. The fee may be paid electronically or sent to the IRS with Form 8283-V.

Reduction for prior rehabilitation credit. The deduction for a historic building easement must be reduced if a rehabilitation tax credit *(31.8)* was claimed for the building in the five years preceding the donation.

14.11 Life Insurance

You may deduct the value of a life insurance policy if the charity is irrevocably named as beneficiary and you make both a legal assignment and a complete delivery of the policy. A deduction may be disallowed where you reserve the right to change the beneficiary.

The amount of your deduction generally depends on the type of policy donated. Your insurance company can furnish you with the information necessary to calculate your deduction. In addition, you may deduct premiums you pay after you assign the policy.

Caution

Split-Dollar Insurance Arrangements

No deduction is allowed for giving a charitable organization money with the understanding that it will be used to pay premiums on life insurance, annuities, or endowment contracts for your benefit or that of a beneficiary designated by you.

Deducting premium payments on donated policy. If you assign a life insurance policy to a charity and continue to pay the premiums, you generally may deduct the premiums. However, in states where charities do not have an "insurable interest" in the donor's life, the IRS may challenge income tax and gift tax deductions for the premium payments. The IRS took this position in a private ruling interpreting New York law. In response, New York amended its insurance code to allow individuals to buy a life insurance policy and immediately transfer it to a charity. The IRS then revoked the earlier ruling but it did not announce a change in its position. Thus, the IRS may challenge premium deductions of donors in other states where a charity's insurable interest is not clearly provided by state law.

14.12 Business Inventory

Self-employed business owners generally may not deduct more than cost for donations of inventory. If a charitable deduction is claimed, costs incurred in a year prior to the year of donation must be removed from opening inventory and excluded from the cost of goods sold when figuring business gross profit for the year of the contribution.

No contribution deduction is allowed for a gift of merchandise that was produced or acquired in the year donated. Instead, the cost is added to the cost of goods sold to figure gross profit for the year of the contribution. Business deductions are not subject to the percentage limitation applied to donations.

14.13 Donations Through Trusts

Outright gifts are not the only way to make deductible gifts to charities. You may transfer property to a charitable lead trust or a charitable remainder trust to provide funds for charity.

A charitable lead trust involves your transfer of property to a trust directed to pay income to a charity you name, for the term of the trust, and then to return the property to you or to someone else. A charitable remainder trust is one that provides income for you or another beneficiary for life, after which the property passes to a charity.

Trust arrangements require the services of an experienced attorney who will draft the trust in appropriate form and advise you of the tax consequences.

Planning Reminder

Life Income Plans

A philanthropy may offer a life income plan (pooled income fund) to which you transfer property or money in return for a guaranteed income for life. After your death, the philanthropy has full control over the property. If you enter such a plan, ask the philanthropy for the amount of the deduction that you may claim for the value of your gift.

Deductions for gifts of income interests in trust. Current law is designed to prevent a donor from claiming an immediate deduction for the present value of trust income payable to a charity for a term of years. In limited situations, you may claim a deduction if either: (1) You give away all of your interests in the property to qualifying *(14.1)* organizations. For example, you put your property in trust, giving an income interest for 20 years to a church and the remainder to a college. A deduction is allowed for the value of the property. Or (2) you create a unitrust or annuity trust, and are taxed on the income. A unitrust for this purpose provides that a fixed percentage of trust assets is payable to the charitable income beneficiary each year. An annuity trust provides for payment of a guaranteed dollar amount to the charitable income beneficiary each year. A deduction is allowed for the present value of the unitrust or annuity trust interest.

Because income remains taxable to the grantor, alternative (2) will probably not be chosen, unless the income of the trust is from tax-exempt securities. If such a trust is created, a tax may be due if the donor dies before the trust ends or is no longer the taxable owner of trust income. The law provides for recapture of part of the tax deduction, even where the income was tax exempt.

Charitable remainder trusts. A charitable deduction is allowable for transfers of property to charitable remainder trusts only if the trust meets these requirements: The income payable for a noncharitable income beneficiary's life or a term of up to 20 years must be guaranteed under a unitrust or annuity trust. If a donor gives all of his or her interests in the property to the charities, the annuity or unitrust requirements need not be satisfied. The value of the charitable deduction allowable for a gift in trust is determined by IRS tables.

14.14 Records Needed To Substantiate Your Contributions

The type of records you must keep to substantiate your donations generally depends on their amount and whether you are contributing cash or property.

Caution

All Cash Contributions Need Bank Record or Receipt

All charitable contributions of money regardless of the amount, must be substantiated by a cancelled check, bank or credit card statement, or receipt from the charity showing the name of the organization and the date and amount of the contribution. Other written records do not qualify.

Cash contributions. A deduction is not allowed for a cash contribution, regardless of amount, unless you have a receipt or bank record to substantiate it. This includes donations made by check, credit card, electronic fund transfer, or gift card redeemable for cash. You need a canceled check, bank copy of both sides of a canceled check, electronic fund transfer receipt, monthly account statement, credit card statement, or written receipt (including e-mail) that shows the name of the organization and the date and amount of the contribution. Maintaining a diary or log is not sufficient substantiation. However, the IRS provides two exceptions to the bank record/receipt substantiation requirement. The IRS waives the sustantiation requirement for a deduction of under $250 for out-of-pocket expenses by a volunteer for charity *(14.4)*. The substantiation rule also does not apply for transfers to charitable remainder trusts.

For a contribution of $250 or more, you need, in addition to a record of the name of the organization and the date and amount of the contribution, a written acknowledgment from the charity, as described below.

For a contribution made by payroll deduction, you need to keep a pay stub, Form W-2, or other employer-furnished document showing the amount withheld as a donation, along with a pledge card or similar document from the charity. If the amount withheld from a single paycheck is $250 or more, the pledge card must include a statement to the effect that no goods or services were provided in return for the contribution.

Noncash contributions under $250. As proof of your donation, you need a dated receipt from the organization that provides a reasonably detailed description of the property. However, if it is impractical to obtain a receipt, as where you deposit canned food at a charity's drop site, you can satisfy the recordkeeping requirement with a contemporaneous notation that documents the contribution.

You need a written acknowledgment from the charity for contributions of $250 or more. A written acknowledgment is necessary to prove cash or noncash contributions of $250 or more; *see* below for content details. The acknowledgment requirement does not apply if the donation is less than $250, but if the contribution exceeds $75, you must be given a disclosure statement from the charity estimating the value of any benefits you received in return for the donation.

The IRS exempts from the acknowledgment requirement grantors of a charitable lead trust, charitable remainder annuity trust, or charitable remainder unitrust. Since a specific charity does not have to be designated as beneficiary at the time the trust transfer is made, there may be no organization available to provide an acknowledgment.

A special acknowledgment rule applies if you are deducting over $500 for a motor vehicle, boat, or airplane. You must attach Copy B of Form 1098-C to your return *(14.7)*.

Content of acknowledgment. An acknowledgment for a donation of $250 or more may be a letter, e-mail, computer-generated form, or postcard. If you gave cash, the amount of the donation must be shown. If you gave property, the property must be described in the acknowledgment, but the charity does not have to value it. If the acknowledgment does not show the date of the contribution, you need a dated bank record or receipt.

The acknowledgment must state whether or not you have received any goods or services from the charity in exchange for the contribution. If you have, the receipt must include a statement describing such benefits and estimating their value. However, "token" items and certain membership benefits, as described in *14.3*, do not have to be described or valued. There is also an exception if the contribution is to a religious organization and the *only* benefits received are "intangible" religious benefits, such as admission to religious ceremonies; these do not have to be described or valued, but the statement must indicate that they are the sole benefits provided.

Payments throughout the year. For purposes of the $250 threshold for an acknowledgment, each contribution is generally considered separate. Thus, for small donations made during the year, you do not have to obtain an acknowledgment even if they total $250 or more.

If contributions are made by payroll deductions from your wages, the amount withheld from each paycheck is treated separately. An acknowledgment is not required unless withholding on a single paycheck is at least $250. A pay stub or Form W-2 from the employer indicating the amount of a single withholding over $249 is considered a valid "acknowledgment"; a pledge card or other document from the charity must state that you have not received benefits in exchange for the payroll deduction contribution.

Deadline for 2010 donation acknowledgments. For a 2010 contribution, the deadline for obtaining an acknowledgment is the date you file your 2010 return but no later than the April 15, 2011, filing due date, or if you obtain a filing extension, the extended due date.

A charity must provide a disclosure statement if you contribute more than $75 and receive benefits. If you contribute more than $75 but less than $250 to a charity, the charity is required to give you a "disclosure" statement that estimates the value of any benefits you received, such as concert tickets or books. The statement will tell you to deduct only the excess of your contribution over the value of the benefits. Certain "token" items and membership benefits, and "intangible" religious benefits, can be disregarded; *see Table 14-1*. If a required disclosure statement is not provided when contributions are solicited, it must be provided when you make a contribution exceeding $75.

Filing Tip

Right To Buy Athletic Stadium Tickets

The IRS considers 20% of the amount paid for the right to buy college or university athletic seating to be the fair market value of the right. You may deduct 80% *(14.3)*. When your payment is $312.50 or more, you are considered to have made a contribution of at least $250 ($250 = 80% of $312.50), requiring a written acknowledgment from the charity.

Table 14-1 What You Need To Substantiate Your Donations

For each individual contribution of—	*You need—*
Cash	Regardless of amount, you need a canceled check, bank copy of a canceled check, account statement, electronic fund transfer receipt, credit card statement, or written receipt from the charity showing the name of the organization and the date and amount of the contribution. The only exceptions are for contributions to a charitable remainder trust and unreimbursed expenses of under $250 incurred by volunteer workers for charity. In addition, for a donation of $250 or more, you need a written acknowledgment as described below.
Less than $250	For a cash donation, you need a bank record or receipt as described above. For a noncash donation, you need a receipt from the charity unless it is impractical to obtain one, as when you have deposited canned food in an organization's drop site. The receipt must show the name of the organization and the date and amount of the contribution and provide a reasonably detailed description of the property, which for securities includes their type and whether they are publicly traded. In addition, if you contributed over $75 and received benefits, the charity is required to give you a "disclosure" statement that estimates the value of any benefits you received, such as concert tickets or books. The statement will tell you to deduct only the excess of your contribution over the value of the benefits. If a required disclosure statement is not provided when contributions are solicited, it must be provided when you make a contribution exceeding $75. The disclosure statement is not required if the only benefits you receive are "token items" or membership benefits that can be disregarded *(14.3)*. Nor is it required where you contribute to a religious organization and the only benefits you receive are "intangible religious benefits." An example of an intangible religious benefit would be admission to religious ceremonies. A Congressional committee report also suggests that tuition for wholly religious education that does not lead to a recognized degree would qualify.
$250 or more	A written acknowledgment from the charity. You may not rely on a canceled check or credit card statement to document a cash contribution of $250 or more. A written acknowledgment is also required for a donation of property if you are claiming a deduction of $250 or more, but the charity does not have to value the property, just describe it. If you received any goods or services from the charity in exchange for the contribution, the acknowledgment must estimate their value unless you receive only "token" items or "intangible religious benefits" as discussed in the preceding paragraph. The deadline for obtaining acknowledgments is the date you file your return. If you file after the filing due date or extended due date, get the acknowledgment by the due date or extended due date. Keep the acknowledgment from the charity with your tax records; do not attach it to your tax return. If your total deduction for all property donations exceeds $500, you must report each of the contributions on Form 8283 (not just those valued over $500). If you are not allowed to deduct fair market value for a property donation under the rules at *14.6*, you must attach a statement to Form 8283 explaining the reduction for the appreciation. For property deductions exceeding $5,000, you need a written appraisal *(14.12)*.
More than $500 in the case of a donated car, other motor vehicle, boat, or airplane	Special acknowledgment rules apply where the claimed value of the vehicle exceeds $500 *(14.7)*.

14.15 Form 8283 and Written Appraisal Requirements

Attach Form 8283 to your Form 1040 for 2010 if the total deduction claimed for all of your donations of property exceeds $500. The IRS may disallow your deduction if you fail to attach Form 8283.

If you are claiming a deduction exceeding $5,000 for an item, or for a group of similar items (such as paintings, buildings, coins, stamps, or books), you generally need a written appraisal from a qualified appraiser. The appraiser must sign a declaration in Part III of Section B of Form 8283 that he or she is unrelated to you and meets the other requirements for qualified appraisers. The appraisal must be made no earlier than 60 days before your donation, and you must receive it by the due date (including extensions) of the return on which you claim the deduction.

You do not need an appraisal for a car, boat, or airplane if your deduction is limited to the gross proceeds from its sale *(14.17)*, or for publicly traded securities, non-publicly-traded securities of $10,000 or less, intellectual property *(14.6)*, or business inventory.

Whether or not a written appraisal is required, you must describe the property, value it, and provide your cost and other acquisition details in Section B, Part 1 of Form 8283.

The appraisal itself should be kept with your records and does not have to be attached to your return except in two situations: If you are claiming a deduction of $20,000 or more for art, you must attach a complete copy of the appraisal to Form 8283 and you may be asked by the IRS to submit a color photograph (8" × 10") or a slide (4" × 5") of the art. If the claimed deduction exceeds $500,000, the qualified appraisal must be attached to your return (assuming no exception to the appraisal requirement). *See* the Form 8283 instructions for further details on the appraisal requirements.

Donee acknowledgment. For property donations exceeding $5,000, the donee organization must acknowledge the receipt of the property in Section B, Part IV of Form 8283. If the organization sells or otherwise disposes of the property within three years of the donation, it must file Form 8282 with the IRS and give you a copy.

Penalty for overvaluation. You may be penalized for a substantial overvaluation of donated property *(14.16)*.

Appraisal fees. A fee paid to an appraiser is not considered a charitable deduction but is deductible as a "miscellaneous" expense subject to the 2% adjusted gross income floor *(19.1)*.

14.16 Penalty for Substantial Overvaluation of Property

If the IRS disallows a portion of your claimed deduction for appreciated property on the grounds that you have overvalued it, you may be subject to a penalty as well as additional tax. Depending on the extent of the overvaluation, a 20% or 40% penalty may apply. No penalty is imposed unless the overvaluation results in a tax underpayment exceeding $5,000.

20% penalty. If the claimed value of donated property is 150% or more of the correct value, the penalty is 20% of the tax underpayment resulting from the overvaluation, provided the underpayment exceeds $5,000.

40% penalty. If the claimed value of donated property is 200% or more of the correct value, the penalty is 40% of the tax underpayment resulting from the overvaluation, provided the underpayment exceeds $5,000.

Reasonable cause exception for relying on appraisal. The 20% penalty (but not the 40%) may be avoided under a reasonable cause exception if you relied on a qualified appraisal prepared by a qualified appraiser and, in addition, you made a good faith investigation of the value of the property.

14.17 Ceiling on Charitable Contributions

Unless you make donations that are very substantial in relation to your adjusted gross income (Line 38, Form 1040), you do not have to be concerned with the deduction ceilings discussed in this section. For cash contributions, the deduction ceiling is generally 50% of adjusted gross income, but in some cases a 30% limit applies. For property donations, the deduction limit is generally 30% of adjusted gross income, although it sometimes is 50% or even 20%. As detailed below, the specific limit for each donation depends on whether it is made to a "50% limit organization" and whether it is capital gain property. Where you have made contributions subject to different ceilings, the ceilings are applied in a specific order and are subject to an overall ceiling of 50% of adjusted gross income. If your deduction is limited by any of the ceilings, a five-year carryover is allowed for the excess *(14.18)*.

Volunteer expenses. The deduction ceiling for unreimbursed expenses you incur doing volunteer work for a charity *(14.4)* is 50% of adjusted gross income if your services were for a 50% limit organization such as a church or college (*see* the list below), or 30% of adjusted gross income if the services were on behalf of an organization other than a 50% limit organization.

Caution

Charity Reports Transfer Within Three Years

If you reported a property donation exceeding $5,000 on Form 8283 and the charity sells or otherwise disposes of the property within three years after your gift, it must notify the IRS on Form 8282 and send you a copy. The sale might trigger the recapture of a deduction claimed for a contribution made after September 1, 2006 *(14.6)*. Reporting on Form 8282 is not required by the charity for a particular item if in Part II, Section B of Form 8283 you indicated that the appraised value of that item was not more than $500. Similar items such as a collection of books by the same author, stereo components, or place settings of silverware may be treated as one item. Reporting is also not required on Form 8282 for donated property that the organization uses or distributes without consideration, if this use furthers the organization's tax-exempt function or purpose.

Planning Reminder

Advance Valuation of Art From IRS

To protect against the possibility of a valuation dispute that could lead to a penalty where you are claiming a deduction of at least $50,000 for a work of art, you may request a valuation from the IRS prior to the time you file. *See* the guidelines for obtaining the IRS valuation *(14.9)*.

Law Alert

Deduction Limit for Conservation Contributions

For 2006 through 2009, qualified conservation contributions *(14.10)* could be deducted up to 50% of adjusted gross income (AGI), or up to 100% for farmers and ranchers, instead of the usual 30% of AGI limit for capital gain property *(14.17)*. The law allowing the 50%/100% deduction limits expired at the end of 2009, but the higher limits may be extended to 2010; *see* the *e-Supplement at jklasser.com* for a legislation update.

30% limit for contributions for the use of an organization. If a donation is treated as for the use of, rather than directly to, any organization, it is deductible under the 30% ceiling described below for contributions to organizations that are not 50% limit organizations.

This 30% ceiling applies to a charitable unitrust or annuity trust income interest that is deductible under the rules for donations through trusts *(14.13)*. A charitable remainder trust transfer is also subject to the 30% limit if the trust provides that after the death of the income beneficiary, the property is to be held in the trust for the benefit of the charity, rather than distributed to the charity.

Deductible expenses for supporting a student in your home *(14.5)* are considered to be for the use of a charitable organization and thus subject to the 30% ceiling for contributions to organizations that are *not* 50% limit organizations.

Contributions to 50% Limit Organizations

Organizations in the 50% limit category include churches, schools, publicly supported charities, and private foundations in the list below. Cash contributions to such organizations are deductible up to 50% of adjusted gross income and contributions of capital gain property held long term generally are deductible up to 30% of adjusted gross income.

The 50% deduction ceiling also applies to donations to the United States, Puerto Rico, a U.S. possession, a state, a political subdivision of a state or U.S. possession, or an Indian tribal government.

Filing Tip

Cash Gifts

A donation of cash to a church, college, or publicly supported charity is deductible up to 50% of your adjusted gross income; *see* the list of 50% limit organizations *(14.17)*.

50% ceiling. Contributions of cash, ordinary income property, and capital gain property held short term are deductible up to 50% of adjusted gross income if made to the following types of charitable organizations:

- Churches, synagogues, mosques, and other religious organizations.
- Schools, colleges, and other educational organizations that normally have regular faculties and student bodies in attendance on site.
- Hospitals and medical research organizations associated with hospitals.
- Government-supported or publicly supported foundations for state and municipal universities and colleges.
- Religious, charitable, educational, scientific, or literary organizations that receive a substantial part of their financial support from the general public or a government unit. Libraries, museums, drama, opera, ballet and orchestral societies, community funds, the American Red Cross, the Heart Fund, and the United Way are in this category. Also included are organizations to prevent cruelty to children or animals, or to foster amateur sports (provided they do not provide athletic facilities or equipment).
- Private operating foundations.
- Private non-operating foundations that distribute their contributions annually to qualified charities within 2 months after the end of their taxable year.
- Private non-operating foundations that pool donations and allow donors to designate the charities to receive their gifts, if the foundation pays out all income within 2 months after the end of the tax year.
- Organizations that normally receive more than one-third of their support from the general public or governmental units.

Filing Instruction

Appreciated Securities and Real Estate

When you contribute appreciated securities or real estate that you have held for more than a year to a church, college, or other organization treated as a 50% limit organization, your deduction for the property donation is limited to 30% of your adjusted gross income unless you elect the 50% ceiling *(14.19)*.

30% ceiling for capital gain property held long term. The deduction ceiling is generally 30% (not 50%) of adjusted gross income where you donate to a 50% limit organization property that would have resulted in long-term capital gain had you sold it at fair market value.

The 30% ceiling applies where the fair market value of the property is deductible under the rules discussed in *14.6*. This includes donations of appreciated securities and real estate held long term. It also includes donations of appreciated tangible personal property (such as furniture or art) held long term where the organization's use of your gift is directly related to its tax-exempt charitable purposes.

However, you may elect to apply the 50% ceiling instead of the 30% ceiling to such property donations if you reduce the fair market value of the property by the appreciation *(14.19)*.

If you donate tangible personal property held long term that is not used by the organization for its tax-exempt charitable purposes, so that your deduction must be reduced for the appreciation *(14.6)*, the reduced amount is deductible under the 50% ceiling.

Contributions to Non–50% Limit Organizations

If a contribution is made to a qualifying organization that is *not* in the above list of 50% limit organizations, a 30% or 20% deduction ceiling applies. Organizations in this category include veterans' organizations, fraternal societies, nonprofit cemeteries and private non-operating foundations that do not meet the payout requirements for 50% limit status.

The 30% limit applies to contributions of cash, ordinary income property, and capital gain property held short term. The 20% limit applies to contributions of capital gain property held long term (more than one year). However, the actual ceiling may be less than 30% or 20% of adjusted gross income where in the same year you have made contributions to 50% limit organizations. In that case, follow Steps 2 and 4 below in applying the deduction ceilings.

Applying the Deduction Ceilings

The various deduction ceilings are applied in a specific order, with the total deduction for the year limited to 50% of adjusted gross income. Check above for the ceilings that apply to your donations and then apply the ceilings in the following order. *See* the discussion of carryover rules *(14.18)* if a portion of your deduction is barred by the deduction ceilings.

1. 50% of adjusted gross income ceiling for contributions to 50% limit organizations.
2. 30% of adjusted gross income ceiling for contributions to organizations that are *not* 50% limit organizations, except for contributions of capital gain property subject to the 20% ceiling under Step 4 below.

   If any contributions to 50% limit organizations were made, including donations of capital gain property that are subject to the 30% ceiling under Step 3 below, this Step 2 ceiling is the lesser of (1) 30% of adjusted gross income or (2) 50% of adjusted gross income minus the contributions to the 50% limit organizations.
3. 30% of adjusted gross income ceiling for contributions of capital gain property to 50% limit organizations.

   If contributions qualifying for the 50% ceiling (Step 1) were made, your deduction for these 30% limit contributions is the lesser of (1) 30% of adjusted gross income or (2) 50% of adjusted gross income minus the contributions qualifying for the 50% ceiling.
4. 20% of adjusted gross income ceiling for contributions of capital gain property to organizations that are not 50% limit organizations.

   If contributions are deductible under any of the other ceilings (Steps 1–3), you may deduct contributions subject to the 20% ceiling only to the extent that there is any adjusted gross income remaining under the overall 50% adjusted gross limit.

Filing Instruction

Carryover for Excess Contributions

If you contribute cash and property in the same year, your deductions may be subject to different limits, such as 50% of adjusted gross income for the cash and 30% for the property. Follow the steps and Examples in this section *(14.17)* for applying the ceilings.

If your donation exceeds the limits, you may carry over the excess for five years.

EXAMPLES

1. Linda Jones in 2010 contributes to a church $22,000 in cash and land held long term valued at $35,000. Her adjusted gross income is $100,000, so the total deduction for the year may not exceed $50,000 under the 50% overall limit. Since the $22,000 cash contribution subject to the 50% ceiling is considered first, the deduction for the land (subject to the 30% ceiling under Step 3 above) is limited to $28,000, the difference between the $50,000 overall limit and the $22,000 cash gift. Jones may carry over the unused $7,000 donation attributable to the land.
2. Earl Smith in 2010 has an adjusted gross income of $100,000. He contributes land worth $40,000 to a college, deductible under the 30% ceiling of Step 3 above. He also contributes $30,000 in cash to a non-operating private foundation subject to the 30% ceiling discussed in Step 2 above. The 30% limitation for cash gifts to non-operating private foundations is applied before the 30% limitation applicable to gifts of capital gain property to public charities. The deduction for the cash gift is reduced under Step 2 above to $10,000 (50% of $100,000 adjusted gross income, or $50,000, minus $40,000 gift to college). The deduction for the land is limited to $30,000 (30% of $100,000). Accordingly, Smith's charitable contribution deduction for 2010 is $40,000 ($10,000 + $30,000).

   Smith is allowed to carry over *(14.18)* the amounts disallowed by the ceilings: $20,000 ($30,000 – $10,000) for the cash gift and $10,000 ($40,000– $30,000) for the land.

Planning Reminder

Project Your Income

When planning substantial donations that may exceed the annual ceiling, make a projection of your income for at least five years. Although the carryover period of five years will probably absorb most excess donations, it is possible that the excess may be so large that it will not be completely absorbed during the year of the contribution and the five-year carryover period. It is also possible that your income may drop in the future so that you cannot adequately take advantage of the excess. For qualified conservation contributions *(14.17)*, these concerns are reduced since the carryover period is increased to 15 years.

14.18 Carryover for Excess Donations

If you make donations that are not deductible because they exceed the 50%, 30%, or 20% of adjusted gross income ceilings *(14.17)*, you may carry the excess over the next five years. There is a special 15-year carryforward for donations of qualified conservation contributions *(Law Alert 14.17)*. In each carryover year, the original percentage ceiling applies. For example, where contributions of appreciated long-term intangible personal property or real estate (or tangible personal property put to a related use by the charity) exceed the 30% ceiling for capital gain property *(14.17)*, the excess remains subject to the 30% ceiling in the carryover years.

In any carryover year, you must first figure your deduction for contributions in the current year under the applicable 50%, 30%, or 20% ceilings. For each category of property carried over, the carryover contributions are deductible only after the deduction for current year donations is figured. The total deduction in the carryover year, for both current year and carryover contributions, cannot exceed 50% of adjusted gross income for the carryover year.

EXAMPLE

In 2010, you contribute to a university stock held over a year with a fair market value of $19,000. The contribution is subject to the 30% ceiling for capital gain property *(14.17)*. You also have a $2,000 carryover from 2009 for a cash gift to your church subject to the 50% ceiling. Your 2010 adjusted gross income is $40,000. Under the 30% ceiling, the deduction for the contribution of stock is limited to $12,000 (30% of $40,000 adjusted gross income). Since the overall deduction limit is $20,000 (50% of $40,000 adjusted gross income), the $2,000 carryover from 2009 is fully deductible. The total deduction on your 2010 return is $14,000 ($12,000 plus $2,000 carryover). You carry over to 2011 the $7,000 balance from the gift of stock that was subject to the 30% ceiling.

14.19 Election To Reduce Fair Market Value by Appreciation

Although the 30% ceiling generally applies to long-term intangible property (such as securities) and real estate contributed to 50% limit organizations *(14.17)*, you may elect the 50% ceiling, provided you reduce the fair market value of the property by 100% of the appreciation on all such donations during the year. The reduction also applies to donations of tangible personal property related in use to the organization's charitable function. In most cases, this election should be made only where the amount of appreciation is negligible. Where there is substantial appreciation, the increase in the deduction may not make up or exceed the required 100% reduction, which allows you to claim a deduction only for your cost basis in the property. If the election is made in a year in which there are carryovers of capital gain property subject to the 30% ceiling, the carryovers are subject to reduction; *see* IRS Publication 526.

The election of the 50% ceiling is made by attaching a statement to your original return or amended return filed by the original due date. Even where no formal electing statement is made, claiming a deduction without the appreciation in order to come within the 50% ceiling is treated as an election. A formal or "informal" election is not revocable unless a material mistake is shown. A revocation based on a reconsideration of tax consequences is not considered sufficient grounds.

Chapter 15

Itemized Deduction for Interest Expenses

On Schedule A of Form 1040, you may deduct three types of interest charges:

- Home mortgage interest, which includes interest on qualifying home acquisition loans *(15.2)* and home equity loans *(15.3)*
- Points *(15.8)*
- Investment interest *(15.10)*, but only up to the amount of net investment income *(15.10)*.

In addition, qualified mortgage insurance premiums *(15.6)* are deductible as interest for 2010.

Interest on personal loans (such as loans to buy autos and other personal items and credit card finance charges) is not deductible with the exception of qualifying student loan interest; *see Chapter 33*.

Interest on loans for business purposes is fully deductible on Schedule C. Interest on loans related to rental property is fully deductible from rental income on Schedule E. Whether interest is a business, investment, or a personal expense generally depends upon the use made of the money borrowed, not on the kind of property used to secure the loan. However, interest on a loan secured by a first or second home may be deductible as home equity mortgage interest regardless of the way you use the loan.

Interest on a loan used to finance an investment in a passive activity is subject to the limitations discussed in *Chapter 10*. However, if you rent out a second home that qualifies as a second residence, the portion of mortgage interest allocable to rental use is deductible as qualified mortgage interest and is not treated as a passive activity expense.

15.1 Home Mortgage Interest

You generally may deduct on Schedule A (Form 1040) qualifying mortgage interest on up to two residences (*see* two-residence limit, below). Premiums paid for mortgage insurance on a principal or second residence may be deductible mortgage interest *(15.6)*.

Mortgage loan obtained after October 13, 1987. Whether you can take a full mortgage interest deduction for a loan taken out after October 13, 1987, depends on the amount of the mortgage debt and how you use the proceeds. Loans used to buy, construct, or improve a first or second home are called *home acquisition loans*, and up to $1 million of such debt qualifies for a mortgage interest deduction, $500,000 if married filing separately *(15.2)*. Loans used for any other purpose are called *home equity loans* by the tax law, and up to $100,000 of such debt may qualify for an interest deduction; the home equity limit is $50,000 for married persons filing separately *(15.3)*.

Loan must be secured by residence. To deduct interest on a home acquisition or home equity loan, the loan must be secured by your main home or a second home. For the loan to be "secured," it must be recorded or satisfy similar requirements under state law. For example, if a relative gives you a loan to help you purchase a home, the relative must take the legal steps required to record the loan with local authorities; otherwise, you may not deduct interest that you pay on the loan. The IRS, in a private ruling, held that interest paid by a homeowners' association on a loan to rebuild the common area is not deductible by the individual homeowners where their residences are not pledged as collateral.

Home acquisition loans are further discussed in *15.2*. *Home equity loans* are discussed in *15.3*.

Mortgage loan obtained before October 14, 1987. You may deduct all of the interest on a loan secured by a first or second home if the loan was obtained before October 14, 1987. Technically, such loans are considered home acquisition debt, but they are treated as "grandfathered debt," exempt from the $1 million loan limit ($500,000 for married persons filing separately).

However, the amount of your pre–October 14, 1987, loan reduces the $1 million (or $500,000) limit on home acquisition debt after October 13, 1987 *(15.2)*. It also reduces the fair market value limit for home equity debt *(15.3)*. If you refinance your loan, *see 15.7*.

Two-residence limit for qualifying mortgage debt. The rules for deducting interest on qualifying acquisition debt or home equity debt apply to loans secured by your principal residence and one other residence. A residence may be a condominium or cooperative unit, houseboat, mobile home, or house trailer that has sleeping, cooking, and toilet facilities. If you own more than two houses, you decide which residence will be considered your second residence. Interest debt secured by the second residence is deductible under the rules for acquisition debt *(15.2)* or home equity debt *(15.3)*.

A residence that you rent out for any part of the year may be treated as a second residence only if you use it for personal nonrental purposes for more than the greater of 14 days or 10% of the rental days. In counting rental days, include days that the home is held out for rental or listed for resale. In counting days of personal use, use by close relatives generally qualifies as your personal use *(9.6)*.

Interest on debt secured by a residence other than your principal or second home may still be deductible, but only if you use the proceeds for investment or business purposes *(15.12)*.

EXAMPLE

You pay $5,000 interest for a mortgage issued under a qualifying mortgage credit certificate. Under its terms, you are allowed a tax credit of $750. You may claim the balance of your mortgage interest, or $4,250 ($5,000 – $750), as an itemized deduction. If the allowable credit exceeds tax liability, a three-year carryover is allowed for the excess credit.

Interest on mortgage credit certificates. Under special state and local programs, you may obtain a "mortgage credit certificate" to finance the purchase of a principal residence or to borrow funds for certain home improvements. A tax credit for interest paid on the mortgage may be claimed. The credit is computed on Form 8396 and claimed on Line 53 of Form 1040 ("Other credits"). The credit equals the interest paid multiplied by the certificate rate set by the governmental authority, but the maximum annual credit is $2,000. If you claim the credit, your home mortgage interest

Caution

Mortgage Interest Reported on Form 1098

Banks and other lending institutions report mortgage interest payments of $600 or more to the IRS on Form 1098. You should receive a copy of Form 1098 or a similar statement by January 31, 2011, showing your mortgage payments in 2011. Deductible points *(15.8)* paid on the purchase of a principal home are included on Form 1098.

Planning Reminder

Home Acquisition Loan Limits

Interest is deductible on up to $1 million of home acquisition loans taken out after October 13, 1987 ($500,000 limit if married filing separately). Mortgage loans taken out before October 14, 1987, are not subject to the $1,000,000 (or $500,000) limit. However, outstanding loans from before October 14, 1987, reduce the $1 million (or $500,000) ceiling for post–October 13, 1987, loans.

Planning Reminder

Mortgage Interest on a Third Home

Interest on debt secured by a residence *other than* your principal or second home may still be deductible, if you use the proceeds for investment or business purposes *(15.12)*.

deduction is reduced by the amount of the current year credit claimed on Form 8396. If you buy a home using a qualifying mortgage credit certificate and sell that home within nine years, you may have to recapture part of the tax credit on Form 8828.

15.2 Home Acquisition Loans

A qualifying "home acquisition loan" is a loan used to buy, build, or substantially improve your principal residence or second home, provided the debt is secured by that same residence. Interest paid on such home acquisition loans is fully deductible if the total debt does not exceed $1,000,000, or $500,000 if you are married filing separately. The $1,000,000 (or $500,000) limit applies to acquisition loans taken out after October 13, 1987.

If your mortgages taken after October 13, 1987, exceed the $1,000,000 (or $500,000) limit, you must use IRS worksheets included in Publication 936 to figure the amount of your deductible interest. Furthermore, if you incurred substantial loans before October 14, 1987, and later purchase a new home, your deduction for the mortgage for the new home may be limited. The $1 million limit for acquisition debt after October 13, 1987, is reduced by the amount of outstanding pre–October 14, 1987, debt.

Although interest on a pre–October 14, 1987, debt is generally fully deductible regardless of the size of the loan, refinancing a pre–October 14, 1987, debt for more than the existing balance subjects the excess to the $1 million ceiling *(15.7)*.

Generally, a debt qualifies as being incurred in buying, constructing, or improving a residence if you satisfy IRS tracing rules *(15.12)* that prove the use of the loan proceeds for such residential purposes. Even if you cannot prove under the tracing rules that a loan was used to buy a residence, a loan will be treated by the IRS as incurred for buying a home to the extent you can show acquisition expenses within 90 days before or 90 days after incurring the loan. Special construction loan and improvement loan rules are discussed in *15.4* and *15.5*.

Interest on a mortgage to buy or build a home other than your principal residence or qualifying second home is treated as nondeductible personal interest. If a nonqualifying home is rented out, the part of the mortgage interest that is allocable to the rental activity is treated as passive activity interest subject to the limitations discussed in *Chapter 10*; the interest allocable to your personal use is nondeductible personal interest.

A married couple filing jointly may designate as a second residence a home owned or used by either spouse.

If a married couple files separately, each spouse may generally deduct interest on debt secured by one residence. However, both spouses may agree in writing to allow one of them to deduct the interest on a principal residence plus a designated second residence.

Cooperatives. In the case of housing cooperatives, debt secured by stock as a tenant-stockholder is treated as secured by a residence. The cooperative should provide you with the proper amount of your deductible interest. If the stock cannot be used to secure the debt because of restrictions under local law or the cooperative agreement, the debt is still considered to be secured by the stock if the loan was used to buy the stock. For further details on allocation rules, *see* IRS Publication 936.

Line-of-credit mortgages. If you had a line-of-credit mortgage on your home on October 13, 1987, and you borrowed additional amounts on this line of credit after that date, the additional borrowed amounts are treated as a mortgage taken out after October 13, 1987. If the newly borrowed amounts are used to buy, build, or improve your first or second home, they are treated as home acquisition debt subject to the $1 million or $500,000 limit. If used for any other purpose, the amounts are subject to the home equity debt rules *(15.3)*.

Mortgage interest paid after house destroyed. If your principal residence or second home *(15.1)* is destroyed and the land is sold within a reasonable period of time following the destruction, the IRS treats the property as a residence for purposes of deducting interest payments on the mortgage during the period between the destruction of the residence and the sale of the land. In one case, the IRS allowed the interest deduction where a sale of land took place 26 months after the destruction of a home by a tornado.

If the destroyed residence is reconstructed and reoccupied within a reasonable period of time following the destruction, the property will continue to be treated as a residence during that period, and the interest payments on the mortgage on the property will be deductible. The IRS allowed an interest deduction where reconstruction began 18 months after, and was completed 34 months after, destruction of the home.

Caution

Unmarried Owners Must Allocate $1 Million Limit Between Them

IRS Chief Counsel has held that the $1 million debt limit applies to the total acquisition debt secured by a principal residence or second home, regardless of the number of debtors. Where unmarried taxpayers jointly acquire a home with a mortgage exceeding $1 million, they must split the $1 million limit between them. Each co-owner is able to deduct only a pro rata share of the interest he or she pays. Each must multiply the interest paid by a fraction, the numerator of which is the $1 million limit and the denominator of which is the average outstanding mortgage balance. Where payments towards mortgage principal are made, several methods can be used to figure the average mortgage balance, as explained in IRS Publication 936. Where only interest payments are made on the mortgage, the denominator of the fraction is the amount of the mortgage.

Court Decision

Family Financing of Residence

The Tax Court allowed a taxpayer to deduct mortgage interest payments on a loan that his brother obtained when the taxpayer's poor credit rating prevented him from obtaining a mortgage loan. The taxpayer's brother bought the house but allowed the taxpayer and his wife to live there on the condition that they make the mortgage payments directly to the bank.

The IRS disallowed the taxpayer's deduction for the mortgage interest on the grounds that he was not liable for the mortgage debt; his brother was. However, the Tax Court allowed the deduction, holding that the taxpayer was the equitable owner of the home and that he was legally obligated to his brother to pay off the mortgage.

Planning Reminder

Home Equity Loan To Pay Consumer Debts

Interest on consumer loans is not deductible but, within limits, you can deduct interest on a home equity line-of-credit mortgage to pay off existing consumer debts and finance future consumer expenses. Interest on a home equity loan is fully deductible for regular tax purposes if within the $100,000 limit, but the interest is not deductible for purposes of alternative minimum tax, unless the loan proceeds were used to improve your first or second home *(23.2)*.

15.3 Home Equity Loans

Interest you pay on home equity debt is deductible within limits. You may deduct interest on debt that is secured by your first or second home *(15.1)* where the amount of debt does not exceed the lesser of:

1. $100,000, or $50,000 if married filing separately, *or*
2. The fair market value of your principal residence and second home *(15.1)*, reduced by the amount of acquisition debt *(15.2)* and by any "grandfathered" pre–October 14, 1987, mortgages *(15.1)*. According to the IRS, fair market value, acquisition debt, and grandfathered debt are determined on the date that the last debt was secured by the home.

If you have a second home as well as a principal residence, the above limitation under (1) and (2) applies to the total debt for both homes. Interest on a qualifying home equity loan is deductible regardless of the way you spend the proceeds, unless it is used to buy tax-exempt obligations *(15.11)*.

On loans exceeding the home equity debt limit, interest may be deductible if the proceeds are used for investment or business purposes. Otherwise, interest on the excess is nondeductible personal interest.

EXAMPLES

1. You bought your house for $200,000 subject to a mortgage of $150,000. When the mortgage principal is $120,000 and the fair market value of the house is $210,000, you take out a home equity loan. Interest on a home equity loan of up to $90,000 is fully deductible. Qualifying home equity debt may not exceed the difference between the fair market value of the house ($210,000) and the current acquisition debt ($120,000). If the value of the house exceeded $220,000, you could have borrowed up to the $100,000 limit as a qualifying home equity loan.
2. The fair market value of your house is $200,000 and the current mortgage is $160,000. You may deduct interest on a home equity loan of up to $40,000 ($200,000 – $160,000).

A loan may qualify partially as acquisition debt and partially as home equity debt where part of it is used to refinance an existing acquisition debt. The refinanced amount is still considered acquisition debt. Debt in excess of the refinanced amount is either home equity debt subject to the $100,000 ceiling or home acquisition debt subject to the $1 million ceiling, depending on the way the proceeds are used *(15.7)*.

15.4 Home Construction Loans

Interest on a home construction loan may be fully deductible from the time construction begins for a period of up to 24 months while construction takes place. Within the 24-month period, the loan is considered acquisition debt subject to the $1 million ceiling *(15.2)*, provided that the home is a principal residence or second home when it is actually ready for occupancy. Furthermore, the loan proceeds must be directly traceable to home construction expenses, including the purchase of a lot, and the loan must be secured by the lot to be treated as acquisition debt. According to the IRS, if construction begins before a loan is incurred, the loan is treated as acquisition debt to the extent of construction expenses within the 24-month period *before* the loan. In determining when a loan is "incurred" for purposes of this 24-month rule, you can treat the date of a written loan application as the date the loan was "incurred," provided you receive the loan within 30 days after loan approval.

Interest incurred on the loan before construction begins is treated as nondeductible personal interest (*see* Example 1 in this section). If construction lasts more than 24 months, interest after the 24-month period also is treated as nondeductible personal interest.

Interest on loans taken out within 90 days *after* construction is completed may qualify for a full deduction. The loan is treated as acquisition debt to the extent of construction expenses within the last 24 months before the residence was completed, plus expenses through the date of the loan (see Example 2 below). For purposes of the 90-day rule, the loan proceeds generally are treated as received on the loan closing date. However, a debt may be considered "incurred" on the date a written loan application is made, provided the loan proceeds are actually received within 30 days after loan approval. If a loan application is made within the 90-day period and it is rejected, and a new application with another lender is made within a reasonable time after the rejection, a loan from the second lender will be considered timely even if more than 90 days have passed since the end of construction.

EXAMPLES

1. On January 12, 2009, you borrow $100,000 to buy a residential lot. The loan is secured by the lot. You begin construction of a principal residence on January 1, 2010, and use $250,000 of your own funds for construction expenses. The residence is completed December 31, 2011.

   The interest paid in 2009 is nondeductible personal interest. It was paid before the 24-month qualifying construction period that started January 1, 2010, and ended December 31, 2011.

   Interest paid in 2010 and 2011 is fully deductible as the $100,000 loan is treated as acquisition debt for the 24-month construction period. 2. Same facts as in Example 1, but on March 12, 2012, you take out a $300,000 mortgage on the completed house to raise funds. You use $100,000 of the loan proceeds to pay off the $100,000 loan on the lot and keep the balance.

   All of the interest on the $300,000 loan is fully deductible because the loan qualifies as acquisition debt; $100,000 of the debt is treated as acquisition debt used for construction, since it was used to refinance the original 2009 debt to purchase the lot. The $200,000 balance is also treated as a construction loan under the 90-day rule. It was borrowed within 90 days after the residence was completed (December 31, 2011), and it reimbursed construction expenses of at least $200,000 incurred within 24 months before the completion date.

2. On January 12, 2010, you purchased a residential lot and began building a home on the lot using $45,000 of your personal funds. The home was completed on October 31, 2010. On November 24, 2010, you received a loan of $36,000 that was secured by the home. The debt may be treated as taken out to build the home as it was taken out no later than 90 days after the home was completed, and expenditures of at least $36,000 were made within the period of 24 months before the home was completed.

15.5 Home Improvement Loans

Loans used for substantial home improvements are treated as acquisition debt subject to the $1 million ceiling for loans after October 13, 1987 *(15.2)*. Include only the cost of home improvements that must be added to the basis of the property because they add to the value of the home or prolong useful life. Repair costs are not considered.

EXAMPLE

Your current acquisition mortgage is $100,000. You borrow $20,000 to build a new room. Your qualifying acquisition debt is now $120,000.

If substantial improvements to a home are begun but not completed before a loan is incurred, the loan will be treated as acquisition debt (assuming the debt is secured by the home) to the extent of improvement expenses made within 24 months before the loan. If the loan is incurred within 90 days after an improvement is completed, the loan is treated as acquisition debt (assuming the debt is secured by the home) to the extent of improvement expenses made within the period starting 24 months before completion of the improvement and ending on the date of the loan.

15.6 Mortgage Insurance Premiums and Other Payment Rules

Payments to the bank or lending institution holding your mortgage may include interest, principal payments, taxes, and insurance premiums. You may deduct eligible home mortgage interest *(15.2, 15.3)*, taxes *(16.4)*, and mortgage insurance premiums.

Law Alert

Deduction for Mortgage Insurance Premiums Through 2010

The deduction for mortgage insurance premiums has been extended through 2010. At the time this book went to press, it was not clear if the deduction would be extended to 2011. *See* the *e-Supplement at jklasser.com* for an update.

Caution

Mortgage Fees Not Deductible

You may not deduct expenses incurred in obtaining a mortgage loan, such as loan assumption fees or costs of an appraisal or credit report.

Filing Tip

Joint Liability on Mortgage

If you do not personally receive a Form 1098 but a person (other than your spouse with whom you file a joint return) who is also liable for and paid interest on the mortgage received a Form 1098, you deduct your share of the interest and attach a statement to your Schedule A showing the name and address of the person who received the form. If you are the payer of record on a mortgage on which there are other borrowers entitled to a deduction for the interest shown on the Form 1098 you received, provide them with information on their share of the deductible amount.

The Tax Court has allowed a joint obligor to deduct his or her payment of another obligor's share of the mortgage interest if the payment is made to avoid the loss of the property, and payment is made with his or her separate funds.

In the year you sell your home, check your settlement papers for interest charged up to the date of sale; this amount is deductible.

Mortgage insurance premiums. If you paid premiums in 2010 on qualified mortgage insurance, and the deduction is not disallowed by the income phaseout, the premiums are deductible as interest on Line 13 of Schedule A (Form 1040). Under the phaseout, the deductible amount is reduced by 10% for every $1,000 or part of $1,000 ($500 or part of $500 if married filing separately) of adjusted gross income exceeding $100,000 ($50,000 if married filing separately). The deduction is completely phased out if adjusted gross income exceeds $109,000, or $54,500 if married filing separately.

Qualified mortgage insurance means mortgage insurance under a contract issued after 2006 by the Department of Veterans Affairs, the Federal Housing Administration, the Rural Housing Service, or private mortgage insurance as defined by section 2 of the Homeowners Protection Act as in effect on December 20, 2006.

Prepayments. Mortgage insurance premiums paid in 2010 to the Department of Veterans Affairs or the Rural Housing Service are deductible on your 2010 return even if the payment is allocable to periods after 2010. A prepayment of premiums on mortgage insurance from other providers cannot be fully deducted in the year paid. The IRS allows the prepaid premiums to be allocated over the shorter of the mortgage term or 84 months, starting with the month the insurance is obtained. Unless the mortgage insurance is provided by the Department of Veterans Affairs or the Rural Housing Service, no deduction is allowed for the unamortized balance if the mortgage is satisfied before its term.

Mortgage credit. If you qualify for the special tax credit for interest on qualified home mortgage certificates, you only deduct interest in excess of the allowable credit *(15.1)*.

Prepayment penalty. A penalty for prepayment of a home mortgage is deductible as home mortgage interest provided the penalty is not for specific services provided by the mortgage holder.

Mortgage assistance payments. You may not deduct interest paid on your behalf under Section 235 of the National Housing Act.

Delinquency charges for late payment. According to the IRS, a late payment charge is deductible as mortgage interest if it was not for a specific service provided by the mortgage holder. In one case, the Tax Court agreed with the IRS that delinquency charges imposed by a bank were not interest where they were a flat percentage of the installment due, regardless of how late payment was. The late charges were primarily imposed by the bank to recoup costs related to collection efforts, such as telephone calls, letters, and supervisory reviews. They were also intended to discourage untimely payments by imposing a penalty.

Graduated payment mortgages. Monthly payments are initially smaller than under the standard mortgage on the same amount of principal, but payments increase each year over the first five- or 10-year period and continue at the increased monthly amount for the balance of the mortgage term. As a cash-basis taxpayer, you deduct the amount of interest actually paid even though, during the early years of the mortgage, payments are less than the interest owed on the loan. The unpaid interest is added to the loan principal, and future interest is figured on the increased unpaid mortgage loan balance. The bank, in a year-end statement, will identify the amount of interest actually paid. (An accrual-basis taxpayer may deduct the accrued interest each year.)

Reverse mortgage loan. Homeowners who own their homes outright may in certain states cash in on their equity by taking a "reverse mortgage loan." Typically, 80% of the value of the home is paid by a bank to a homeowner in a lump sum or in installments. Principal is due when the home is sold or when the homeowner dies; interest is added to the loan and is payable when the principal is paid. The IRS has ruled that an interest deduction may be claimed by a cash-basis home-owner only when the interest is paid, not when the interest is added to the outstanding loan balance. A deduction is subject to the limits for interest on home equity loans *(15.3)*.

Shared appreciation mortgage. Under a shared appreciation mortgage (SAM) for a personal residence, the lender agrees to charge a fixed rate of interest that is lower than the prevailing market rate. In return, the homeowner promises to pay a percentage of the appreciation on the property at a later date to make up the difference. The fixed-rate interest is deductible when paid and the percentage of appreciation is also treated as interest that you can deduct in the year of payment, subject to the limits discussed in *15.2*. For example, you agree to pay interest of 5% plus 40% of the appreciation in the value of the property within 10 years or earlier if you sell the home or pay off the mortgage. If, at the end of 10 years, the residence is not sold or the loan repaid, you may refinance at the prevailing rate the outstanding balance plus the interest based on the appreciation. If you refinance with the same lender, you may not claim an immediate deduction for the extra interest. The execution of a note is not considered payment. The amount covering the extra interest is deducted ratably over the period of the new loan. If you refinance with another lender and use the funds to pay off the old loan plus the extra interest, the extra interest is deductible in the year of payment, subject to the deduction limits *(15.2)*.

Redeemable ground rents. In a ground rent arrangement, you lease rather than buy the land on which your home is located. Ground rent is deductible as mortgage interest if: (1) the land you lease is for a term exceeding 15 years (including renewal periods) and is freely assignable; (2) you have a present or future right to end the lease and buy the entire interest; and (3) the lessor's interest in the land is primarily a security interest. Payments to end the lease and buy the lessor's interest are not deductible ground rents.

15.7 Interest on Refinanced Loans

When you refinance a mortgage on a first or second home *(15.1)* for the same amount as the remaining principal balance on the old loan, there is no change in the tax treatment of interest. In other words, if interest was fully deductible on the old loan, then it is fully deductible on the new loan.

If you refinance a home mortgage for more than the existing balance, the deductibility of interest on the excess amount depends upon how you use the funds and the amount of refinancing. If the excess amount is used to buy, build, or substantially improve your first or second home, then it is considered home acquisition debt *(15.2)*. If the excess plus all other home acquisition loans does not exceed $1 million ($500,000 if married filing separately), the interest is fully deductible. If the excess is used for any other purpose, such as to pay off credit card debt or to finance a child's education, the excess is considered home equity debt *(15.3)*. If the excess plus all other home equity loans does not exceed $100,000 ($50,000 if married filing separately), the interest is fully deductible. If the refinanced loan is partly home acquisition debt and partly home equity debt, the overall limit of $1.1 million applies ($1 million home acquisition debt and $100,000 home equity debt) or, if married filing separately, $550,000 ($500,000 home acquisition debt and $50,000 home equity debt).

Interest paid on loans in excess of home acquisition and home equity debt ceilings is generally treated as nondeductible personal interest unless the proceeds are used for business or investment purposes *(15.12)*.

EXAMPLE

In 2002, Robert and Michelle Stein purchased a home for $250,000. They put $50,000 down and obtained a $200,000, 30-year mortgage secured by the home. In 2010, when their house is worth $300,000 and there is a $175,000 principal balance on the mortgage, they refinance to take advantage of lower interest rates. The refinanced mortgage is for $225,000, payable over 20 years. The Steins use $175,000 to pay off the old mortgage, $30,000 to purchase a car and to pay off credit card debt, and the remaining $20,000 to build a new deck on their home.

The interest on up to $175,000 of the debt incurred to pay off the old mortgage is fully deductible; the amount equals the outstanding balance before refinancing and also falls within the $1 million home acquisition debt ceiling. The $20,000 used to remodel the house is also treated as home acquisition debt. Interest on this amount is fully deductible; the amount falls within the $1 million ceiling when added to the $175,000.

The $30,000 used to buy a car and pay off credit cards is treated as home equity debt. Interest on this amount is fully deductible; the amount falls within the $100,000 ceiling.

Pre–October 14, 1987 loans. Refinanced pre–October 14, 1987 loans are not subject to the $1 million home acquisition and $100,000 home equity debt ceilings during the period of the original loan term. However, after the end of the loan term, the ceilings apply to the refinanced

Court Decision

Current Deduction for Points on Refinancing

Huntsman replaced a three-year loan used to purchase his principal residence with a 30-year mortgage. He deducted $4,400 of points paid on the new mortgage. The IRS and the Tax Court held that the points had to be deducted over the 30-year loan term.

The Federal Appeals Court for the Eighth Circuit disagreed and allowed a full deduction in the year the points were paid. The first loan was temporary and merely a step in obtaining permanent financing for the purchase of the principal residence.

The IRS has announced that in areas outside of the Eighth Circuit, it will continue to disallow full deductions in the year of payment for points paid on refinancings. The Eighth Circuit includes only these states: Minnesota, Iowa, North and South Dakota, Nebraska, Missouri, and Arkansas. In these states, the IRS will not challenge deductions for points on refinancing agreements similar to Huntsman's that replace short-term financing with long-term permanent financing.

In a later case, the Tax Court held that the *Huntsman* exception does not apply where a borrower refinances a long-term mortgage to take advantage of lower interest rates; the points must be deducted over the term of the new mortgage.

amount as explained above. Furthermore, where a refinanced pre–October 14, 1987 debt exceeds the remaining principal balance, the excess is also subject to the $1 million home acquisition and $100,000 home equity debt ceilings.

Points Paid on Refinancing

The IRS does not allow a current deduction for points on a refinanced mortgage. According to the IRS, the points must be deducted ratably over the loan period, unless part of the new loan is used for home improvements. Thus, if you pay points of $2,400 when refinancing a 20-year loan on your principal residence, the IRS allows you to deduct only $10 a month, or $120 each full year.

A federal appeals court rejected the IRS allocation rule where points are paid on a long-term mortgage that replaces a short-term loan; see the Court Decision in this section *(15.7)*.

If part of a refinancing is used for home improvements to a principal residence, the IRS allows a deduction for a portion of the points allocable to the home improvements.

EXAMPLE

In June 2010, Craig Smith refinances his home mortgage, which has a principal of $80,000 outstanding. The new loan is for $100,000, payable over 15 years starting in July 2010. He uses $80,000 to pay off the old $80,000 balance and the remaining $20,000 is used for home improvements. Assume that at the closing of the new loan, Smith pays points of $2,000 from his separate funds. In the year of payment he may deduct $400 allocable to the 20% of the loan used for home improvements. He may also deduct the ratable portion of the $1,600 balance of the points, which must be deducted over the period of the new loan. The ratable portion is $53 ($1,600 ÷ 180-month loan term x 6 months in 2010). Thus, Craig's total deduction for points in 2010 is $453 ($400 + $53).

Mortgage ends early. If you are ratably deducting points on a refinanced loan and you refinance again with a different lender, or the mortgage ends early because you prepay it or the lender forecloses, you can deduct the remaining points in the year the mortgage ends *(15.8)*.

Caution

Service Fees Are Not Deductible Points

You may not deduct as points amounts that are for specific lender services. To be deductible, points on the purchase of a principal residence must be prepaid interest for the use of the loan money.

Filing Tip

Amortize Points Starting in Second Year

A married couple purchased a principal residence and paid points late in the year. For the year of the purchase, their standard deduction exceeded their itemized deductions. The IRS ruled that claiming the standard deduction for the year the points are paid would not entirely forfeit the deduction for points. The points may be amortized starting in the second year. Assuming that they itemize deductions starting in the second year, the allocable portion of the points may be deducted each year over the remaining loan term.

15.8 "Points"

Lenders sometimes charge "points" in addition to the stated interest rate. The points increase the lender's upfront fees, but in return borrowers generally are charged a lower interest rate over the loan term. Points are either treated as a type of prepaid interest *(15.14)* or as a nondeductible service fee, depending on what the charge covers. If the points qualify as interest, they are deductible over the term of the loan unless they are paid on the purchase or improvement of your principal residence, in which case they are deductible in the year they are paid, as discussed below. If you pay points on a loan to purchase or improve a second home, you must deduct the points ratably over the term of the loan.

Points are treated as interest if your payment is solely for your use of the money and is not for specific services performed by the lender that are separately charged. Whether a payment is called "points" or a "loan origination fee" does not affect its deductibility if it is actually a charge for the use of money. The purpose of the charge—that is, for the use of the money or the services rendered—will be controlling. For example, you may not deduct points that are fees for services, such as appraisal fees, preparation of a mortgage note or deed of trust, settlement fees, notary fees, abstract fees, commissions, and recording fees.

If you are *selling* property and you assume the buyer's liability for points, do not deduct the payment as interest but include it as a selling expense that reduces the amount realized on the sale.

Deduction for Points on Purchase or Improvement of Principal Residence

Points are generally treated as prepaid interest *(15.14)* that must be deducted over the period of the loan. However, there is an exception for points you pay on a loan to buy, build, or improve your principal residence. The points on such loans are deductible in the year paid if these tests are met: (1) the loan is secured by your principal residence; (2) the charging of points is an established business practice in the geographic area in which the loan is made; (3) the points charged do not exceed the points generally charged in the area; (4) the amount of points is computed as a percentage of the loan and specifically earmarked on the loan closing statement as "points," "loan origination fees," or "loan discount"; and (5) you pay the points directly to the lender; *see* "Points withheld from the principal," below.

Points paid by seller are deductible by buyer. The seller's payment is treated as an adjustment to the purchase price that the seller gives to you as the buyer and that you then turn over to the lender to pay off the points. You may fully deduct the points in the year paid if you meet the tests in the preceding paragraph. Otherwise, deduct them over the term of the loan. You must reduce your cost basis for the home by the seller-paid points.

Points withheld from the principal. Points withheld from the principal of a loan used to buy, build, or improve your principal residence are deductible as if you paid them directly to the lender if, at or before closing, you have made a down payment, escrow deposit, or earnest money payment that is at least equal to the amount of points withheld. These payments must have been from your own funds and not from funds that have been borrowed from the lender as part of the overall transaction.

Points on second home. If you pay points on a mortgage secured by a second home or a vacation home, the points are not fully deductible in the year of payment; you must claim the deduction ratably over the loan term.

Points paid on refinancing. The IRS does not allow a current deduction for points on a refinanced mortgage *(15.7)*.

Deduct balance of points if mortgage ends early. If you are deducting points over the term of the loan because a full first-year deduction is not allowed, you are allowed to deduct the balance in the year the mortgage ends, such as when you prepay the loan, or the lender forecloses. If the mortgage ends early because you refinance the mortgage with a different lender, you may deduct the balance of the points. For example, if you refinanced your mortgage in 2000 and paid points, those points had to be amortized over the loan term *(15.7)*. If in 2010 you refinance again with a different lender and pay points again, the balance of the points from the 2000 loan are deductible on your 2010 return, and the points on the new loan must be amortized over the loan term. If you refinanced with the same lender, the balance of the points from the 2000 loan must be deducted over the term of the new loan.

Caution

Points Reported to the IRS

Points you paid in 2010 on the purchase of your principal residence will be reported to the IRS by the lender on Form 1098 if they meet the five tests for a deduction listed in *15.8*. Seller-paid points are also included on Form 1098. Form 1098 is used by the IRS to check on the deduction you claim for points on Line 10 of Schedule A. Points paid on an improvement loan for your principal residence are deductible on Line 12 of Schedule A if they meet the tests; they are not shown on Form 1098.

15.9 Cooperative and Condominium Apartments

Cooperative apartments. If you are a tenant-stockholder of a cooperative apartment, you may deduct your portion of:

- Interest paid by the cooperative on its debts, provided you do not pay interest on more than two residences *(15.1)*. This includes your pro rata share of the permanent financing expenses (points) of the cooperative on its mortgage covering the housing project.
- Taxes paid by the cooperative *(16.6)*. However, if the cooperative does not own the land and building but merely leases them and is required to pay real estate taxes under the terms of the lease, you may not deduct your share of the tax payment.

In some localities, such as New York City, rent control rules allow tenants of a building converted to a cooperative to remain in their apartments even if they do not buy into the co-op. A holdover tenant may prevent some co-op purchasers from occupying an apartment. The IRS ruled that the fact that a holdover tenant stays in the apartment will not bar the owner from deducting his or her share of the co-op's interest and taxes.

Condominiums. If you own an apartment in a condominium, you have a direct ownership interest in the property and are treated, for tax purposes, just as any other property owner. You may deduct your payments of real estate taxes and mortgage interest. You may also deduct taxes and interest paid on the mortgage debt of the project allocable to your share of the property. The deduction of interest from condominium ownership is also subject to the two-residence limit *(15.1)*. If your condominium is used part of the time for rental purposes, you may deduct expenses of maintenance and repairs and claim depreciation deductions subject to certain limitations *(9.7)*.

Caution

Interest on Loans To Buy Market Discount Bonds and Treasury Bills

Limits apply to the deduction for interest on loans used to buy or carry market discount bonds *(4.20)* and Treasury bills *(4.27)*.

15.10 Investment Interest Limitations

Interest paid on margin accounts and debts to buy or carry other investments is deductible on Schedule A up to the amount of net investment income. If you do not have investment income such as interest, you may not deduct investment interest. Investment income for purposes of the deduction generally does not include net capital gains or qualified dividends, but you may elect to include them in order to increase your investment interest deduction. If you make the election, the elected amount will not be eligible for the favorable capital gain rates; *see* "Computing the Deduction" below. Investment interest in excess of net investment income may be carried forward and deducted from next year's net investment income.

You compute the deduction for investment interest on Form 4952, which must be attached along with Schedule A to Form 1040.

What is investment interest? It is all interest paid or accrued on debts incurred or continued to buy or carry investment property such as interest on securities in a margin account. However, interest on loans to buy tax-exempt securities is not deductible *(15.11)*.

Investment interest does not include interest on qualifying home acquisition debt *(15.2)* or home equity debt *(15.3)*, production period interest that is capitalized *(16.4)*, or interest related to a passive activity *(10.8)*.

Investment property includes property producing portfolio income (interest, dividends, or royalties not realized in the ordinary course of business) under the passive activity rules discussed in *Chapter 10*, and property in activities that are not treated as passive activities, even if you do not materially participate, such as working interests in oil and gas wells.

Passive activity interest is not investment interest. Interest expenses incurred in a passive activity such as rental real estate *(10.1)*, or a limited partnership or S corporation in which you do not materially participate *(10.6)*, are taken into account on Form 8582 when figuring net passive income or loss. This includes interest incurred on loans used to finance your investment in a passive activity. Do not treat passive activity interest as investment interest on Form 4952.

However, interest expenses allocable to *portfolio* income (non–business activity interest, dividends, or royalties) from a limited partnership or S corporation are investment interest and not passive interest. The investment interest will be listed separately on Schedule K-1 received from the partnership or corporation.

Computing the Deduction

Deductible investment interest is limited to net investment income. Net investment income is the excess of investment income over investment expenses. The key terms *investment income* and *investment expenses* are defined below.

Investment income. Investment income is generally gross income from property held for investment, such as interest, dividends, other than qualified dividends, annuities, and royalties. Income or expenses considered in figuring profit or loss of a passive activity *(10.8)* is not considered investment income or expenses. Property subject to a net lease is not treated as investment property, as it is within the passive activity rules.

If you have net capital gains (net long-term capital gains exceeding net short-term losses) from the sale of investment property such as stocks or mutual-fund shares, or capital gain distributions from mutual funds, such gains and distributions are not treated as investment income unless you specifically elect to include them in investment income on Form 4952. You may elect to include all or part of them. The same election rule applies to qualified dividends *(4.1)* that are subject to net capital gain tax rates. An election must be made on Form 4952 to include qualified dividends in investment income. If you make this election, you may not apply preferential capital gain rates *(5.3)* to the amount of the net capital gains (and capital gain distributions) or qualified dividends treated as investment interest on Form 4952. If you make the election on Form 4952, the elected amount is subtracted from net capital gains when applying the capital gain tax rates on the IRS worksheets *(5.3)*.

Investment expenses. There are expenses, other than interest, directly connected with the production of investment income. However, for purposes of determining net investment income, only those investment expenses (other than interest) allowable after figuring the 2% floor for miscellaneous itemized deductions *(19.1)* are taken into account. The 2% floor will bar a deduction for some of the miscellaneous itemized deductions. For purposes of this net investment income computation, assume that miscellaneous itemized deductions other than investment expenses are disallowed first.

Net investment income. Reducing investment income by investment expenses gives you net investment income. Your deduction for investment interest expenses is limited to this amount; any excess interest expense for 2010 may be carried over to 2011, as discussed below.

Where to enter the deduction on your return. The deduction figured on Form 4952 is generally entered on Line 14 of Schedule A as investment interest. However, if the interest is attributable to royalties, you may have to enter the interest on Schedule E; follow the Form 4952 instructions. Furthermore, there is an additional complication if you have investment interest for an activity for which you are not "at risk" *(10.18)*. After figuring the investment interest deduction on Form 4952, you must enter the portion of the interest that is attributable to the at-risk activity on Form 6198. The amount carried over to Form 6198 is subtracted from the investment interest deduction claimed on Form 4952.

Carryover to 2011 and future years. Investment interest in excess of net investment income for 2010 may be carried forward to 2011 and is deductible in 2011 to the extent that when added to 2011 investment interest expenses it does not exceed net investment income. If not used in 2011, the carryforward extends indefinitely to 2012 and future years.

EXAMPLE

For 2010, Larry Jones has $10,000 of interest income. He has investment expenses, other than interest, of $3,200, after taking into account the 2% floor on miscellaneous itemized deductions. His investment interest expense from securities margin account loans is $8,000. Jones also has income of $2,000 from a passive partnership investment.

Jones's net investment income is $6,800: $10,000 of interest income less $3,200 of non-interest investment expenses. The passive activity income from the partnership is not included in investment income.

Jones's investment interest deduction for 2010 is limited to the $6,800 of net investment income. The $1,200 of investment interest in excess of net investment income ($8,000 – $6,800) is carried forward to 2011.

Caution

Electing To Treat Long-Term Gains or Dividends as Investment Income

If you elect on Form 4952 to treat net capital gains or qualified dividends as investment income in order to increase your 2010 investment interest deduction, that amount is not eligible to be taxed at favorable capital gain rates *(5.3)*.

15.11 Debts To Carry Tax-Exempt Obligations

When you borrow money in order to buy or carry tax-exempt bonds, you may not deduct any interest paid on your loan. Application of this disallowance rule is clear where there is actual evidence that loan proceeds were used to buy tax-exempts or that tax-exempts were used as collateral. But sometimes the relationship between a loan and the purchase of tax-exempts is less obvious, as where you hold tax-exempts and borrow to carry other securities or investments. IRS guidelines explain when a direct relationship between the debt and an investment in tax-exempts will be inferred so that no interest deduction is allowed. The IRS will *not* infer a direct relationship between a debt and an investment in tax-exempts in these cases:

1. The investment in tax-exempts is not substantial. That is, it is not more than 2% of the adjusted basis of the investment portfolio and any assets held in an actively conducted business.
2. The debt is incurred for a personal purpose. For example, an investor may take out a home mortgage instead of selling his tax-exempts and using the proceeds to finance the home purchase. Interest on the mortgage is deductible subject to certain limitations *(15.1)*.
3. The debt is incurred in connection with the active conduct of a business and does not exceed business needs. But if a person reasonably could have foreseen when the tax-exempts were purchased that he or she would have to borrow funds to meet ordinary and recurrent business needs, the interest expenses are not deductible.

The guidelines infer a direct relationship between the debt and an investment in tax-exempts in this type of case: An investor in tax-exempts has outstanding debts not directly related to personal expenses or to his or her business. The interest will be disallowed even if the debt appears to have

Caution

Tax-Exempt Income From Mutual Fund

You may not deduct interest on loans used to buy or carry tax-exempt securities. If you receive exempt-interest dividends from a mutual fund during the year, you may deduct interest on a loan used to buy or carry the mutual-fund shares only to the extent that the proceeds can be allocated to taxable dividends you also receive.

been incurred to purchase other portfolio investments. Portfolio investments include transactions entered into for profit, including investments in real estate, that are not connected with the active conduct of a business; *see* the Example below.

EXAMPLE

An investor owning $360,000 in tax-exempt bonds purchased real estate in a joint venture, giving a purchase money mortgage and cash for the price. He deducted interest on the mortgage. The IRS disallowed the deduction, claiming the debt was incurred to carry tax-exempts. A court allowed the deduction. A mortgage is the customary manner of financing such a purchase. Furthermore, since the purchase was part of a joint venture, the other parties' desires in the manner of financing had to be considered.

15.12 Earmarking Use of Loan Proceeds

The IRS has set down complex record keeping and allocation rules for claiming interest deductions on loans used for business or investment purposes, or for passive activities. The rules deal primarily with the *use* of loan proceeds for more than one purpose and the commingling of loan proceeds in an account with unborrowed funds. The thrust of the rules is to base deductibility of interest on the use of the borrowed funds. The allocation rules do not affect mortgage interest deductions on loans secured by a qualifying first or second home *(15.1)*.

Keep separate accounts for business, personal, and investment borrowing. For example, if you borrow for investment purposes, keep the proceeds of the loan in a separate account and use the proceeds only for investment purposes. Do not use the funds to pay for personal expenses; interest is not deductible on personal loans other than qualifying student loans *(Chapter 33)*. Furthermore, do not deposit loan proceeds in an account funded with unborrowed money, unless you intend to use the proceeds within 30 days of the deposit. By following these directions, you can identify your use of the proceeds with a specific expenditure, such as for investment, personal, or business purposes, and the interest on the loan may be treated as incurred for that purpose. The 30-day rule is discussed below.

The IRS treats undisbursed loan proceeds deposited in an account as investment property, even though the account does not bear interest. When proceeds are disbursed from the account, the use of the proceeds determines how interest is treated; *see* Examples 1 and 2 below.

Planning Reminder

Keep Loans Separate

To safeguard your investment and business interest deductions, you must earmark and keep a record of your loans. You should avoid using loan proceeds to fund different types of expenditures.

30-day disbursement rule. If you deposit borrowed funds in an account with unborrowed funds, a special 30-day rule allows you to treat payments from the account as made from the loan proceeds. Where you make more than one disbursement from such an account, you may treat any expenses paid within 30 days before or after deposit of the loan proceeds as if made from the loan proceeds. Thus, you may allocate interest on the loan to that disbursement, even if earlier payments from the account have been made; *see* Example 3 below. If you make the disbursement after 30 days, the IRS requires you to allocate interest on the loan to the first disbursement; *see* Example 4 below. Furthermore, if an account includes only loan proceeds and interest earned on the proceeds, disbursements may be allocated first to the interest income and then to the loan proceeds.

Allocation period. Interest is allocated to an expenditure for the period *beginning* on the date the loan proceeds are used or treated as used and *ending* on the earlier of either the date the debt is repaid or the date it is reallocated.

Accrued interest is treated as a debt until it is paid, and any interest accruing on unpaid interest is allocated in the same manner as the unpaid interest is allocated. Compound interest accruing on such debt, other than compound interest accruing on interest that accrued before the beginning of the year, may be allocated between the original expenditure and any new expenditure from the same account on a straight-line basis. That is done by allocating an equal amount of such interest expense to each day during the taxable year. In addition, you may treat a year as *twelve 30-day months* for purposes of allocating interest on a straight-line basis.

Planning Reminder

Using Borrowed Funds To Pay Interest

To get an interest deduction you must pay the interest; you may not claim a deduction by having the creditor add the interest to the debt. If you do not have funds to pay the interest, you may borrow money to pay the interest. The borrowed funds must be from a different creditor. The IRS disallows deductions where a debtor borrows from the same creditor to make interest payments on an earlier loan. The second loan is considered a device for getting an interest expense deduction without actually making payments. The Tax Court and several federal appeals courts have sided with the IRS.

Payments from a checking account. A disbursement from a checking account is treated as made at the time the check is written on the account, provided the check is delivered or mailed to the payee within a reasonable period after the writing of the check. You may treat checks written on the same day as written in any order. A check is presumed to be written on the date appearing on the check and to be delivered or mailed to the payee within a reasonable period thereafter. However, the presumption may not apply if the check does not clear within a reasonable period after the date appearing on the check.

Change in use of property. You must reallocate interest if you convert debt-financed property to a different use; for example, when you buy a business auto with an installment loan, interest paid on the auto is business interest, but if during the year you convert the auto to personal use, interest paid after the conversion is personal interest.

Order of repayment. If you used loan proceeds to repay several different kinds of debt, the debts being repaid are assumed to be repaid in the following order: (1) personal debt; (2) investment debt and passive activity debt other than active real estate debt; (3) debt from a real estate activity in which you actively participate; (4) former passive activity debt; and (5) business debt. *See* Example 5 below. Payments made on the same day may be treated as made in any order.

EXAMPLES

1. On January 1, you borrow $10,000 and deposit the proceeds in a non–interest-bearing checking account. No other amounts are deposited in the account during the year and no part of the loan is repaid during the year. On April 1, you invest $2,000 of the proceeds in a real estate venture. On September 1, you use $4,000 to buy furniture.

   From January 1 through March 31, interest on the entire undisbursed $10,000 is treated as investment interest. From April 1 through August 31, interest on $2,000 of the debt is treated as passive activity interest and interest on $8,000 of the debt is treated as investment interest. From September 1 through December 31, interest on $4,000 of the debt is treated as personal interest; interest on $2,000 is treated as passive activity interest; and interest on $4,000 is treated as investment interest.
2. On September 1, you borrow money for business purposes and deposit it in a checking account. On October 15, you disburse the proceeds for business purposes. Interest incurred on the loan before the disbursement of the funds is treated as investment interest expense. Interest starting on October 15 is treated as business interest. However, you may elect to treat the starting date for business interest as of the first of the month in which the disbursement was made—that is, October 1—provided all other disbursements from the account during the same month are similarly treated.
3. On September 1, you borrow $5,000 to invest in stock and deposit the proceeds in your regular checking account. On September 10, you buy a TV and stereo for $2,500 and on September 11 invest $5,000 in stock, using funds from the account. As the stock investment was made within 30 days of depositing the loan proceeds in the account, interest on the entire loan is treated as incurred for investment purposes.
4. Same facts as in Example 3, but the TV and stereo were bought on October 1 and the stock on October 31. As the stock investment was not made within 30 days, the IRS requires you to treat the purchase of the TV and the stereo for $2,500 as the first purchase made with the loan proceeds of $5,000. Thus, the 50% of loan interest that is allocated to the stereo purchase is nondeductible.
5. On July 12, Smith borrows $100,000 and immediately deposits the proceeds in an account. He uses the proceeds as follows:

August 31	$40,000 for passive activity
October 5	$20,000 for rental activity
December 24	$40,000 for personal use

   On January 19 of the following year, Smith repays $90,000. Of the repayment, $40,000 is allocated as a repayment of the personal expenditure, $40,000 of the passive activity, and $10,000 of the rental activity. The outstanding $10,000 is treated as debt incurred in a rental activity.

15.13 Year To Claim an Interest Deduction

As a cash-basis taxpayer, you deduct interest in the year of payment except for prepayments of interest *(15.14)*. Giving a promissory note is not considered payment. Increasing the amount of a loan by interest owed, as with insurance loans, is also not considered payment and will not support a deduction. If a person pays your interest obligation with the understanding you will repay him or her, you take the deduction in the year the interest is paid, not when you repay him or her. However, an accrual-basis taxpayer generally deducts interest in the year the interest accrues *(40.3)*.

Here is how a cash-basis taxpayer treats interest in the following situations:

On a life insurance loan, where proceeds are used for a deductible (nonpersonal) purpose, you claim a deduction in the year in which the interest is paid. You may not claim a deduction when the insurance company adds the interest to your debt. You may not deduct your payment of interest on an insurance loan after you assign the policy.

On a margin account with a broker, interest is deductible in the year in which it is paid or your account is credited after the interest has been charged. But an interest charge to your account is not payment if you do not pay it in cash or the broker has not collected dividends, interest, or security sales proceeds that may be applied against the interest due. Note that the interest deduction on margin accounts is subject to investment interest limitations *(15.10)*.

For partial payment of a loan used for a deductible (nonpersonal) purpose, interest is deductible in the year the payment is credited against interest due. When a loan has no provision for allocating payments between principal and income, the law presumes that a partial payment is applied first to interest and then to principal, unless you agree otherwise. Where the payment is in full settlement of the debt, the payment is applied first to principal, unless you agree otherwise. Where there is an involuntary payment, such as that following a foreclosure sale of collateral, sales proceeds are applied first to principal, unless you agree to the contrary. *See also* 15.12 for the effect of payments on the allocation of debt proceeds.

Note renewed. You may not deduct interest by merely giving a new note. You claim a deduction in the year the renewed note is paid. The giving of a new note or increasing the amount due is not payment. The same is true when past due interest is deducted from the proceeds of a new loan; this is not a payment of the interest.

Planning Reminder

Business or Investment Loans

If you prepay business or investment loan interest, you must spread the interest deduction over the period of the loan. In the year of payment, you may deduct only the interest allocable to that year.

15.14 Prepaid Interest

If you prepay interest on a loan used for *investment* or *business* purposes you may not deduct interest allocable to any period falling in a later taxable year. The prepaid interest must be deducted over the period of the loan, whether you are a cash-basis or accrual-basis taxpayer.

Points paid on the purchase of a *principal residence* are generally fully deductible in the year paid *(15.8)*. Points paid on refinancing generally are not deductible *(15.7)*.

Treatment of interest included in a level payment schedule. Where payments of principal and interest are equal, a large amount of interest allocated to the payments made in early years of a loan will generally not be considered prepaid interest. However, if the loan calls for a variable interest rate, the IRS may treat interest payments as consisting partly of interest, computed under an average level effective rate, and partly of prepaid interest allocable to later years of the loan. An interest rate that varies with the "prime rate" does not necessarily indicate a prepaid interest element.

When you borrow money for a deductible purpose and give a note to the lender, the amount of your loan proceeds may be less than the face value of the note. The difference between the proceeds and the face amount is interest discount. For loans that do not fall within the OID rules *(4.18)*, such as loans of a year or less, interest is deductible in the year of payment if you are on the cash basis. If you use the accrual basis, the interest is deductible as it accrues. For loans that fall within OID rules, your lender should provide a statement showing the interest element and the tax treatment of the interest.

EXAMPLE

In February 2010, you borrow $1,000 for an investment and receive $900 in return for your $1,000 one-year note. You repay the full loan in January 2011. You are on the cash basis. You do not deduct the interest of $100 when the note is given. The $100 interest is treated as investment interest *(15.10)* when the loan is paid in 2011.

Chapter 16

Deductions for Taxes

If you itemize deductions on Schedule A, you may deduct your 2010 payments of state, local, and foreign income taxes and real property taxes, as well as state and local personal property taxes. *See 16.3* for state and local general sales taxes.

To increase your deduction for state and local taxes, consider making a year-end prepayment of estimated tax liability. You also may be able to increase withholdings from your pay to increase your deduction. If you pay transfer taxes on the sale of securities or investment real estate, the taxes are not deductible. However, they increase your cost basis when figuring your profit or loss.

Taxes paid in operating a business are generally deductible, except for sales taxes, which are added to the cost of the property.

16.1 Deductible Taxes

If you itemize deductions for 2010 on Schedule A (Form 1040), you may deduct your 2010 payments of:

- State, local, and foreign income taxes
- State, local, and foreign real property taxes
- State and local personal property taxes

Filing Tip

State Income Tax Paid in 2009

In figuring your 2010 itemized deduction for state and local income taxes paid, remember to include tax that you paid in 2010 when you filed your 2009 state and local tax returns.

In lieu of state and local income taxes, you may be able to elect to deduct state and local general sales taxes *(16.3)*.

In figuring deductible state or local income taxes, include the amount of state or local income tax withheld from your 2010 pay, any state or local estimated tax you paid in 2010, and any part of a prior year refund that you credited to your 2010 state or local tax. Also, do not forget to include tax that you paid in 2010 when you filed your 2009 state and local tax returns.

Taxes incurred in your business are generally deductible on Schedule C *(16.9)*.

Claim the deduction for deductible taxes on the tax return for the year in which you paid the taxes, unless you report on the accrual basis *(16.7)*.

Table 16-1 Checklist of Taxes

Type of tax—	*Deductible as itemized deduction—*
Admission	No
Alcoholic beverage	No
Assessments for local benefits	No
Automobile license fees not qualifying as personal property tax	No
Cigarette	No
Customs duties	No
Driver's license	No
Estate—federal or state	No*
Excise—federal or state, for example, on telephone service	No
Gasoline—federal	No
Gasoline and other motor fuel—state and local	No
Gift taxes—federal and state	No
Income—federal (including alternative minimum tax)	No
Income—state, local, or foreign	Yes
Inheritance tax	No
Mortgage tax	No
Personal property—state or local	Yes
Poll	No
Real estate (state, local, or foreign)	Yes
Regulatory license fees (dog licenses, parking meter fees, hunting and fishing licenses)	No
Social Security	No
Tolls	No
Transfer taxes on securities and real estate	No

* But *see* the exception for miscellaneous itemized deduction for estate tax paid on "income in respect of a decedent" *(11.17)*.

16.2 Nondeductible Taxes

Sales tax. Sales taxes on personal property are generally not deductible. However, an election may be available to deduct general state and local sales taxes in lieu of state and local income taxes *(16.3)*.

Transfer taxes. Transfer taxes paid on the sale of securities or investment real estate are not separately deductible, but you may increase your cost basis by the transfer tax in figuring profit or loss on Schedule D; *see Chapter 5*.

A transfer tax (which may be called an excise tax in some states) on the sale of a personal residence is not deductible as a real estate tax; it is imposed on the transaction and not on the value of the property. Transfer taxes are added to cost basis by the buyer or treated as an expense of sale by the seller.

Gasoline taxes. State and local taxes on gasoline used for personal purposes are not deductible. If you travel for business, the taxes are deductible as part of your gasoline expenses.

Law Alert

State and Local Sales Tax Option Needs Extension to 2010

The law authorizing the option to deduct state and local general sales taxes in lieu of state and local income taxes expired at the end of 2009. Without an extension, state and local sales taxes will not be deductible on 2010 returns. However, an extension is likely; *see* the *e-Supplement at jklasser.com* for an update.

16.3 State and Local Income Taxes or General Sales Taxes

The option to deduct state and local general sales taxes in lieu of state and local income taxes expired at the end of 2009 and although an extension of the sales tax option to 2010 is expected, Congress had not yet enacted the extension legislation when this book went to press. Assuming that the extension legislation is enacted, the election to deduct state and local general sales taxes for 2010 will be made by checking a box on Line 5 of Schedule A (Form 1040). Check the e-Supplement at jklasser.com for a legislation update.

State and local income taxes. You may deduct on your 2010 return state and local income taxes withheld from your pay and estimated state and local taxes paid in 2010. Also deduct the balance of your 2009 state and local taxes you paid during 2010. If in 2011 you pay additional state income tax on your 2010 income, you deduct the payment on your 2011 tax return.

State income taxes may be claimed only as itemized deductions, even if attributed solely to business income. That is, state income taxes may not be deducted as business expenses from gross income.

To increase your itemized deductions on your 2010 return, consider prepaying state income taxes before the end of 2010. The prepayment is deductible provided the state tax authority accepts prepayments and state law recognizes them as tax payments. The IRS has ruled, however, that prepayments are not deductible if you do not reasonably believe that you owe additional state tax. Do not make prepayments if you expect to be subject to alternative minimum tax, since state and local taxes are not deductible for AMT purposes *(23.2)*.

If you report on the accrual basis and you contest a tax liability, claim the deduction in the year of payment.

You may deduct on your federal return state and local income taxes allocable to interest income that is exempt from federal tax but not state and local income tax. However, state and local taxes that are allocated to other federal exempt income are not deductible. For example, state income tax allocated to a cost-of-living allowance exempt from federal income tax is not deductible as a state tax.

The IRS has held that mandatory employee contributions to state disability or worker's compensation funds in California, New Jersey, New York, Rhode Island and Washington, and mandatory contributions to the Alaska, New Jersey, and Pennsylvania state unemployment funds, are deductible as state income taxes.

However, employee contributions to a private or voluntary disability plan in California, New Jersey, or New York have been held by the IRS to be nondeductible.

Note: A refund of state income taxes claimed as an itemized deduction may have to be reported as income *(11.5)*.

State and local general sales taxes. The following paragraphs assume that the option to elect a deduction of state and local general sales taxes in lieu of state and local income taxes will be extended to 2010 returns, as discussed below.

Deductible state and local general sales taxes can be figured using your credit card receipts and other records of non-business purchases during 2010. Alternatively, you can use the IRS's optional tables and worksheet in the Schedule A instructions or the Sales Tax Deduction Calculator at IRS.gov.

Filing Tip

Refund Credited to State Estimated Tax

If you were entitled to a refund on your 2009 state tax return and you credited the overpayment towards your 2010 estimated state tax, do not forget to include the credited amount with other 2010 payments of state and local income tax on your 2010 Schedule A.

Law Alert

Deduction for Sales/Excise Tax Paid in 2010 on Motor Vehicle Purchased New in 2009

On 2009 returns, a deduction was allowed on Schedule A, subject to an income phaseout, for state and local sales tax or excise taxes paid on a motor vehicle purchased new from February 17, 2009 through December 31, 2009. This deduction was allowed in addition to a deduction for state and local income taxes.

This special deduction is not allowed for a 2010 vehicle purchase. Sales tax on a vehicle bought in 2010 will be deductible only as part of the election to deduct state and local general sales taxes in lieu of state and local income taxes, assuming that option is made available by Congress as discussed in *16.3*.

However, if you purchased the vehicle from February 17, 2009 through December 31, 2009, but did not pay the sales tax or excise tax until 2010, you may claim a 2010 deduction. Figure your allowable deduction on the worksheet on page 2 of your 2010 Schedule A.

Sales taxes paid on the purchase of a motor vehicle may be included whether you use the IRS tables or your actual expenses, but if more than the general sales tax rate was paid on the vehicle, you may only include up to the general sales tax rate. Sales taxes paid at the general sales tax rate on the purchase of a home (or on a major home renovation), a boat, or aircraft may also be included; follow the Schedule A instructions.

Sales or excise taxes paid in 2010 on vehicle purchased in 2009. If you purchased a qualifying vehicle new during the period from February 17, 2009 through December 31, 2009, but did not pay the sales tax or excise tax until 2010, you may be able to claim a 2010 deduction for the sales or excise tax. The deduction is in addition to the deduction for state and local income taxes. If the cost of the vehicle exceeded $49,500, only the tax on the first $49,500 of the purchase price can be deducted. The deduction begins to phase out if your 2010 modified adjusted gross income (MAGI) exceeds $125,000, or $250,000 if married filing jointly, and no deduction is allowed if MAGI is at least $135,000, or $260,000 if filing jointly. Use the worksheet on page 2 of Schedule A to figure your allowable 2010 deduction.

Table 16-2 Who Claims the Deduction for Real Estate Taxes?

If the tax is paid by—	*Then it is deductible by—*
You, for your spouse	Neither, if your spouse has title to the property, and you each file a separate return. This is true even if the mortgage requires you to pay the taxes. The tax is deductible on a joint return.
You, as owner of a condominium	You deduct real estate tax paid on your separate unit. You also deduct your share of the tax paid on the common property.
Your cooperative apartment or corporation	You deduct your share of real estate tax paid on the property; *see 15.9*. But if the organization leases the land and building and pays the tax under the terms of the lease, you may not deduct your share.
A life tenant	A court allowed the deduction to a widow required to pay the taxes under a will for the privilege of occupying the house during her life.
A tenant	The tenant of a business lease may deduct the payment of tax as additional rent, not tax. The tenant of a personal residence may not deduct the payment as either a tax or rent expense, unless placed on the real estate assessment rolls so that the tax is assessed directly against him or her; *see 16.6*.
You, as a local benefit tax to maintain, repair, or meet interest costs arising from local benefits	You deduct only that part of the tax that you can show is for maintenance, repair, or interest. If you cannot make the allocation, no deduction is allowed. If the benefit increases the value of the property, you add the non-deductible assessment to the basis of the property.
You, where your property was foreclosed for failure to pay taxes	You may not deduct the taxes paid out of the proceeds of the foreclosure sale if your interest in the property ended with the foreclosure.
Tenant by the entirety or joint tenant	A tenant who is jointly and severally liable for the tax may deduct it if it is paid with his or her separate funds. If a husband and wife own real estate as joint tenants or as tenants by the entirety, taxes paid by either of them may be deducted on their joint return, or if they file separately, by the spouse who pays the tax from his or her own funds.
Tenant in common	When property is owned as a tenancy in common, under an IRS rule, a tenant may deduct only his or her share of the tax, even if the entire tax was paid. However, the Tax Court may allow a co-tenant to deduct the full amount if it is paid from his or her separate funds and the payment protects against the possibility of foreclosure in the event the other co-tenants failed to pay their share of the taxes *(9.2)*.
A mortgagee	No deduction. If tax is paid before the foreclosure, it is added to the loan. If paid after the foreclosure, it is added to the cost of property.

16.4 Deducting Real Estate Taxes

Your payments of state, local, or foreign real estate taxes on your non-business property are deductible on Schedule A (Form 1040). The tax must be based on the assessed value of the property and the assessment must be based on a uniform rate imposed for public purposes. *See 16.5* for deductible and nondeductible assessments for local benefits.

The monthly mortgage payment to a bank or other mortgage holder generally includes amounts allocated to real estate taxes, which are paid to the taxing authority on their due date. Mortgage payments allocated to real estate taxes are deductible in the year you make the payments only if the mortgage holder actually pays the taxes to the tax authority by the end of that year. Typically, banks will furnish you with a year-end statement of disbursements to taxing authorities, indicating dates of payment.

See 16.5–16.7 for further details on real estate taxes.

Who may deduct real property taxes. A person who pays a property tax must have an ownership interest in the property to deduct the payment. The following table summarizes who may deduct payments of real property taxes.

16.5 Assessments

Assessments by homeowner's association not deductible as taxes. Assessments paid to a local homeowner's association for the purpose of maintaining the common areas of the residential project and for promoting the recreation, health, and safety of the residents are not deductible as real property taxes.

Assessments for government services. If property is used solely as your residence, you may not deduct charges for municipal water bills (even if described as a "tax"), sewer assessments, assessments for sanitation service, or title registration fees. A permit fee to build or improve a personal residence is added to the cost basis of the house.

Assessments for local benefits are deductible if they cover maintenance or repairs of streets, sidewalks, or water or sewer systems, or interest costs on such maintenance. However, assessments for construction of streets, sidewalks, or other local improvements that tend to increase the value of your property are not deductible as real estate taxes. You add such assessments to your cost basis for the property.

If you are billed a single amount, you may deduct the portion allocable to assessments for maintenance or repairs. The burden is on you to support the allocation.

Filing Tip

Cooperative Apartments

Tenant-stockholders of a cooperative housing corporation may deduct their share of the real estate taxes paid by the corporation. However, no deduction is allowed if the corporation does not own the land and building but merely leases them and pays taxes under the lease agreement *(15.9)*.

16.6 Tenants' Payment of Taxes

You generally may not deduct a portion of your rent as property taxes. This is so even where state or local law identifies a portion of the rent as being tied to tax increases.

Tenants have been allowed a deduction for property taxes in the following areas: In Hawaii tenants with leases of 15 years or more may deduct the portion of the rent representing taxes. In California, tenants who have their names placed on the tax rolls and who pay the taxes directly to the taxing authority may claim a deduction.

In New York, liability for tax is placed directly on the tenant and the landlord is a collecting agent for paying over the tax to the taxing authorities; the landlord also remains liable for the tax. The IRS ruled that it will not permit tenants to deduct a portion of rent as a payment of taxes.

EXAMPLE

A municipal rent control ordinance allowed landlords to charge real property tax increases to the tenants as a monthly "tax surcharge." The ordinance stated that the surcharge was not to be considered rent for purposes of computing cost-of-living rental increases. The IRS ruled that the tenant may not deduct the "tax surcharge" as a property tax. The tax is imposed on the landlord, not on the tenant. The city ordinance, which permitted the landlord to pass on the tax increases to a tenant, did not shift liability for the property taxes from the landlord to the tenant. For federal tax purposes, the surcharge is merely an additional rental payment by the tenant. Similarly, "rates tax" or "renters' tax" imposed on tenants was ruled to be nondeductible because the tax is imposed on the person using the property rather than the property itself.

16.7 Allocating Taxes When You Sell or Buy Realty

When property is sold, the buyer and seller apportion the real estate taxes imposed on the property during the "real property year." A "real property year" is the period that a real estate tax covers. This allocation is provided for you in a settlement statement at the time of closing. If you want to figure your own allocations, your local tax authority can give you the "real property year" of the taxes you plan to apportion. If you are the ***seller***, you deduct that portion of the tax covering the beginning of the real property year through the day before the sale. If you are the ***buyer***, you deduct the part of the tax covering the date of the sale through the end of the real property year.

EXAMPLE

The real property year in East County starts April 1 and ends March 31. On July 2, 2010, you sell realty located in East County to Jones. Assume the real estate tax for the real property year ending March 31, 2011, is $1,000. You deduct $252 ($^{92}/_{365}$ of $1,000, since there are 92 days in the period beginning April 1, 2010 and ending July 1, 2010). Jones deducts $748 ($^{273}/_{365}$ of $1,000), since there are 273 days in the period beginning July 2, 2010, and ending March 31, 2011).

The allocation of taxes between the buyer and seller is mandatory whether or not your contract provides for an allocation. However, you do not allocate taxes of a real property year when property is sold before the real property year. This rule prevents the seller from deducting any part of the tax for that year, even though it became a personal liability or lien while he or she owned the property. The buyer gets the deduction because he or she owns the property for the entire real property year. You also do not allocate taxes when property is sold after the real property year. This rule prevents the buyer from deducting the tax for that year even though it becomes a personal liability or lien after he or she takes possession of the property. The seller gets the deduction because the tax covers the property year in which the seller owns the property. The allocation is limited to a tax covering a property year during which both the seller and the buyer own the property.

IRS Alert

Form 1099-S for Sale of Principal Residence

The lender or real estate agent responsible for the closing does not have to report the sale of your principal residence on Form 1099-S if (1) the sales price is $250,000 or less, or $500,000 or less if you are married filing jointly, and (2) you certify in writing under penalty of perjury that you have met the tests for excluding from income the full gain on the sale *(29.1)*.

Form 1099-S. If Form 1099-S is filed by the mortgage lender or real estate broker responsible for the closing, Box 5 will show the buyer's share of the real estate tax paid in advance by the seller. For example, Smith sells her house in Green County, where the real estate tax is paid annually in advance. In the year of sale she paid $1,200 in real estate taxes. Assuming that the home is sold at the end of the ninth month of the real property tax year, the amount of the real estate tax allocable to the buyer is $300 ($100 per month × 3 months). This amount, which is shown as paid by the seller in advance on an HUD-1 (Uniform Settlement Statement) form provided at the closing, is reported as the buyer's share of the real estate tax in Box 5 of Form 1099-S.

When to deduct allocated taxes. After you have made the allocation based on the "real property year," you then must fix the year in which you deduct your share of the allocated tax. Here you consider your method of reporting your income—cash or accrual basis—and the date on which either you or the other party became liable for the tax or paid the tax. If neither you nor the other party is liable for the tax under local law, then the party who holds the property at the time the tax became a lien on the property is considered liable. Check the following rules to determine when you deduct the apportioned tax:

Seller on the cash basis—If the buyer is liable for the tax under local law, the seller may deduct his or her share of the allocated tax either in the year of the sale or a later year when the tax is actually paid. If the seller is liable for the tax under local law, and the tax is not payable until after the sale date, the seller may deduct the tax either in the year of sale or in the year he or she pays the tax.

Buyer on the cash basis—If the seller is liable for the tax under local law, the buyer may deduct the tax either in the year of sale or when the tax is actually paid. If the buyer is liable for the tax, he or she deducts the tax in the year the tax is paid.

Seller on the accrual basis—The seller accrues his or her share of the tax on the date of the sale, unless taxes have been accrued ratably over the years. If this is so, the last accrual is the sale date.

Buyer on the accrual basis—If the seller is liable for the tax, the buyer accrues his or her share of the tax on the date of the sale, unless taxes are accrued ratably. If taxes are accrued ratably, the accrual begins with the date of sale. If the buyer is liable for the tax, he or she deducts the tax in the return for the year the tax accrues unless an election is made to accrue ratably from the date of sale.

Seller's deduction in excess of the allocated amount is taxed. If, in the year before the sale, the seller deducts an amount for taxes in excess of the allocated amount, the excess must be reported as income in the year of the sale. This may happen when the seller is on the cash basis and pays the tax in the year before the sale.

> ***EXAMPLE***
>
> A real property tax of $1,000 is due and payable on November 30 for the following calendar year. On November 30, 2009, Keith Jones, who uses the cash basis and reports on a calendar year, pays the 2010 tax. On June 30, 2010, he sells the real property. Under the apportionment rule, Jones is allowed to deduct only $493 ($^{180}/_{365}$ of $1,000, since there are 180 days in the period from January 1 to June 29, 2010) of the tax for the 2010 real property tax year. But Jones has already deducted the full amount in the 2009 return. Therefore, he reports as income that part of the tax deduction that he was not entitled to under the apportionment.

Buyer may not deduct payment of seller's back taxes. The back taxes paid are added to the cost of the newly purchased property. The amount realized by the seller is increased by the buyer's payment of back taxes.

Seller's payment upon buyer's failure to pay. If a buyer is obligated to pay taxes under a land contract but fails to pay, the owner who pays the tax may deduct the payment if the tax is assessed to him or her.

Buyer of foreclosed property. If you buy realty at a tax sale and you do not receive immediate title to the property under state law until after a redemption period, you may not be able to deduct payment of realty taxes for several years.

Filing Instruction

Buyer's Share of Real Estate Tax

If you sold a house in 2010 and received Form 1099-S, check Box 5 for the amount of real estate tax that you paid in advance and that is allocable to the buyer. The buyer may deduct this amount. You subtract it from the amount you paid when claiming your 2010 itemized deduction for real estate taxes.

16.8 Automobile License Fees

You may not deduct an auto license fee based on weight, model, year, or horsepower. But you may deduct a fee based on the value of the car as a state personal property tax if these three tests are met: (1) the fee is an *ad valorem* tax, based on a percentage of value of the property; (2) it is imposed on an annual basis, even though it is collected more or less frequently; and (3) it is imposed on personal property. This third test is met even though the tax is imposed on the exercise of a privilege of registering a car or for using a car on the road.

The majority of state motor vehicle registration fees are not *ad valorem* taxes and do not qualify for the deduction. Various states and localities impose *ad valorem* or personal property taxes on motor vehicles that may qualify for the deduction. Contact a state or local authority to determine whether a license fee qualifies.

Filing Tip

Value Portion of Auto License Fee

If an automobile license fee is based partly on value and partly on weight or other tests, the tax attributed to the value is deductible as an *ad valorem* tax and is deductible as a personal property tax on Schedule A.

16.9 Taxes Deductible as Business Expenses

That a tax is not deductible as an itemized deduction does not mean you may not deduct it elsewhere on your return. For example, you may generally deduct property taxes incurred as a cost of doing business on Schedule C. Here are some other examples:

If you pay excise taxes on merchandise you sell in your business, you deduct the tax as a business expense. If you pay Social Security taxes (FICA) on your employees' wages, you deduct the tax as a business expense on Schedule C. If you pay sales tax on business property, you add the tax to the cost of the property for depreciation purposes. If the tax is paid on nondepreciable property, the tax is included in the currently deductible cost. If you pay sales tax on a deductible business meal, the tax is deductible as part of the meal costs, subject to the cost limit *(20.24)*.

50% self-employment tax deduction. One-half of the self-employment tax figured on Schedule SE is deductible from gross income on Line 27 of Form 1040, rather than on Schedule C *(45.3)*.

Note: If you are not a material participant in the business, your Schedule C expenses are subject to passive activity limitations; *see Chapter 10*.

16.10 Foreign Taxes

You may deduct your payment of foreign real property taxes and income and excess profits taxes as itemized deductions. Where you pay foreign income or excess profits tax, you have an election of either claiming the tax as a deduction or a credit. Claiming the credit may provide a larger tax savings *(36.14)*.

Chapter 17

Medical and Dental Expense Deductions

Tax deductions for the high cost of unreimbursed medical care are limited. Medical expenses are deductible only if you itemize and only if you have expenses exceeding 7.5% of your adjusted gross income. Expenses up to 7.5% of AGI are not deductible. There is an exception for health insurance premiums paid by self-employed individuals. The self-employed do not have to itemize any premiums; 100% of their premiums is an above-the-line deduction that can be claimed directly from gross income *(12.2)*.

Carefully review the list of deductible expenses in this chapter so that you do not overlook any deductible expenses. Include payments of doctors' fees, health-care premiums, prescription medicines, travel costs for obtaining medical care, and eligible home improvements.

If you are married, both you and your spouse work, and one of you has substantial medical expenses, filing separate returns may result in a lower overall tax.

Qualifying long-term-care expenses may be treated as medical expenses subject to the 7.5% of AGI floor, including a specified deductible amount of premiums paid for a qualifying long-term-care contract *(17.15)*.

Deductible contributions to health savings accounts (HSAs) and Archer MSAs may be available to individuals covered by high deductible health plans; *see Chapters 12* and *41*.

Workers displaced from jobs by import competition may claim a refundable tax credit for health insurance premiums. The credit is claimed on Form 8885 *(25.18)*.

Also see

17.1 Medical Expenses Must Exceed 7.5% of AGI

The tax law provides only a limited opportunity to deduct medical costs for you, your spouse, and your dependents *(17.7)*. Although a wide range of expenses are potentially deductible *(Table 17-1)* if you itemize expenses on Schedule A of Form 1040, your deduction may be completely disallowed or severely limited because only expenses in excess of 7.5% of your adjusted gross income may be claimed *(12.1)*. Adjusted gross income is shown on Line 37 and Line 38 of Form 1040.

Married persons filing joint returns apply the 7.5% floor to their combined adjusted gross income.

On your 2010 return, you may deduct expenses paid in 2010 by cash or check (unless the check is postdated to 2011) for yourself, your spouse *(17.6)*, or dependents *(17.7)*. If you borrow to pay medical or dental expenses, you claim the deduction in the year you use the loan proceeds to pay the bill, not in the later year when you repay the loan. If you paid medical or dental expenses by credit card in 2010, the deduction is allowed in 2010, although you do not pay the charge bill until 2011.

Caution

Only Unreimbursed Expenses Are Deductible

You may not deduct medical expenses for which you have been reimbursed by insurance or other awards *(17.4)*. Furthermore, reimbursement of medical expenses deducted in prior tax years may be taxable income *(11.6)*.

EXAMPLES

1. Frank Ryan's adjusted gross income (AGI) *(12.1)* is $40,000 for 2010. His unreimbursed medical expenses were $2,000 for doctor and dentist visits, $420 for prescribed drugs and medicines, and $1,250 for medical insurance premiums. If he itemizes deductions on Schedule A, he may deduct medical expenses of $670, figured this way:

Unreimbursed expenses	$ 2,000
Premiums	1,250
Drugs	420
Total	$ 3,670
Less: 7.5% of adjusted gross income (7.5% of $40,000)	3,000
Medical expense deduction	$670

2. Same as facts as in Example 1 except that Frank's AGI is $50,000, not $40,000. Here, Frank may not claim any medical deduction because his expenses of $3,670 do not exceed $3,750, 7.5% of his AGI.

Law Alert

Deduction Threshold Increasing After 2012

Under the 2010 healthcare reform legislation, the 7.5% floor for deducting medical expenses will generally increase to 10% starting in 2013, but if the taxpayer or the taxpayer's spouse is age 65 or over by the end of the year, the 7.5% floor will continue to apply through 2016.

17.2 Allowable Medical Care Costs

In determining whether you have paid deductible medical expenses exceeding the 7.5% AGI floor *(17.1)*, include the cost of diagnosis, cure, mitigation, treatment, or prevention of disease or any treatment that affects a part or function of your body *(Table 17-1)*. Also include qualifying costs you paid for your spouse *(17.6)* and your dependents *(17.7)*.

Expenses that are *solely* for cosmetic reasons are not deductible. Also, expenses incurred to benefit your general health are not deductible even if recommended by a physician *(17.3)*.

Medicine and drugs. To be deductible, medicines and drugs other than insulin must be obtainable solely through a prescription by a doctor. Insulin is deductible even though a prescription may not be required. You may not deduct the cost of over-the-counter medicines and drugs, such as aspirin and other cold remedies, even if you have a doctor's prescription.

Marijuana is not deductible even if prescribed by a doctor in a state allowing the prescription.

A prescribed drug brought in or shipped into the U.S. from another country is not deductible unless the FDA (Food and Drug Administration) allows that drug to be legally imported by individuals.

Caution

Over-the-Counter Drugs

OTC drugs, even if prescribed by a doctor, are not deductible, with the exception of insulin.

Diagnostic tests. The IRS treats unreimbursed diagnostic procedures as deductible medical expenses (subject to the 7.5% of AGI floor), even if you had no symptoms of illness and you underwent the test without a physician's recommendation. For example, the cost of an annual physical performed by a doctor and related laboratory tests is a medical expense, whether or not you were feeling ill. Similarly, a full body scan is a deductible diagnostic procedure, whether or not a physician recommended it. Where a procedure does not have a nonmedical function, a physician's recommendation is not necessary. It also does not matter if a less expensive alternative to the full body scan is available. Finally, a home pregnancy test qualifies as a medical expense even though its purpose is not to detect disease but to test for the healthy functioning of the body.

Vitamins and nutritional or herbal supplements. The IRS does not allow a deduction for the cost of vitamins, nutritional or herbal supplements, or "natural" medicines unless a medical practitioner recommends them as treatment for a specific medical condition diagnosed by a physician. Otherwise, they are considered to be for maintaining your general health rather than for medical care.

Stop-smoking programs. The cost of smoking cessation programs is a deductible medical expense, as well as nicotine withdrawal drugs that require a physician's prescription. Over-the-counter nicotine patches and gums are not deductible.

IRS Alert

Weight-Loss Program for Obesity

The IRS allows a deduction for the costs of joining a weight-loss program and fees for follow-up meetings if a physician has made a diagnosis of obesity.

Exercise and weight-reduction programs. If you incur costs for such programs to improve your *general* health, the costs are not deductible even if your doctor has recommended them. However, if your doctor has recommended a program as treatment for a *specific* condition, such as heart disease or hypertension, the IRS allows a deduction for the cost.

The IRS considers obesity a disease. If a physician has made a diagnosis of obesity, the costs of joining a weight-loss program and additional fees for meetings are eligible medical expenses. However, reduced-calorie diet foods that are substitutes for foods normally consumed are not deductible even if they are part of the program; *see* "Special foods" below.

Caution

Deducting Costs of Health Improvement Programs

Exercise and weight-reduction programs are deductible as treatments for specific conditions, but not as ways to improve your general health, even if your doctor has recommended them *(17.2)*.

Special foods. According to the IRS, the cost of special foods or beverages is not a deductible medical expense if the food or beverages substitute for those normally consumed.

EXAMPLE

To alleviate an ulcer, your doctor puts you on a special diet. According to the IRS, the cost of your food and beverages is not deductible. The special diet replaces the food you normally eat.

Applying this "nutritional needs" test, the IRS in a private ruling denied a mother's deduction for the cost of infant formula for her healthy child. Although the mother had a medical reason for buying the formula—she was unable to breastfeed her baby following a double mastectomy—the formula was food satisfying the child's ordinary nutritional needs, and therefore was a nondeductible personal expense.

The Tax Court has set its own standard for deducting the extra cost of special foods as medical costs. The test is to show a medical need for taking the special food and the extra cost of the health food over ordinary food. Only the extra cost is deductible.

EXAMPLES

1. Anna Von Kalb suffered from hypoglycemia and her physician prescribed a special high protein diet, which required her to consume twice as much protein as an average person and exclude all processed foods and carbohydrates. She spent $3,483 for food, and deducted 30%, or $1,045, as the extra cost of her high protein diet. The IRS disallowed the deduction, claiming that the protein supplements were a substitute for foods normally consumed. The Tax Court disagreed. The high protein food did not substitute for her usual diet but helped alleviate her hypoglycemia. Thus, she may deduct its additional expense.
2. The Bechers suffered from allergies and were advised by a physician to eat organically grown food to avoid the chemicals in commercial food. The Bechers claimed a medical expense deduction of $2,255, the extra cost of buying organic food.
   The IRS disallowed the deduction and the Tax Court agreed. They did not present evidence that their allergies could be cured by limiting their diet to organic food. That the food was beneficial to their general health and was prescribed by a doctor is not sufficient for a deduction.

Filing Tip

Childbirth Classes

A mother-to-be may deduct the cost of classes instructing her in Lamaze breathing and relaxation techniques, stages of labor, and delivery procedures. If her husband or other childbirth "coach" also attends the classes, the portion of the fee allocable to the coach is not deductible. Costs of classes on early pregnancy, fetal development, or caring for newborns also are not deductible.

Portion of monthly service fees paid to retirement community. The portion of the monthly fees that is allocable to medical care is a deductible medical expense *(34.10)*.

Table 17-1 Deductible Medical Expenses

Professional Services

- Chiropodist
- Chiropractor
- Christian Science practitioner
- Dermatologist
- Dentist
- Gynecologist
- Neurologist
- Obstetrician
- Ophthalmologist
- Optician
- Optometrist
- Orthopedist
- Osteopath
- Pediatrician
- Physician
- Physiotherapist
- Plastic surgeon; but *see 17.3.*
- Podiatrist
- Practical or other nonprofessional nurse for medical services only, not for care of a healthy person or a child who is not ill. Costs for medical care of elderly person unable to get about or person subject to spells are deductible *(17.12).*
- Psychiatrist
- Psychoanalyst
- Psychologist
- Registered nurse
- Surgeon
- Unlicensed practitioner services are deductible if the type and quality of the services are not illegal.

Dental Services

- Artificial teeth
- Cleaning teeth
- Dental X-rays
- Extracting teeth
- Filling teeth
- Gum treatment
- Oral surgery
- Straightening teeth

Equipment and Supplies

- Abdominal supports
- Air conditioner where necessary for relief from an allergy or for relieving difficulty in breathing *(17.13).*
- Ambulance hire
- Arches
- Artificial eyes, limbs
- Autoette (auto device for handicapped person)
- Back supports
- Braces
- Contact lenses and solutions
- Cost of installing stair-seat elevator for person with heart condition *(17.13).*
- Crutches
- Elastic hosiery
- Eyeglasses
- Fluoridation unit in home
- Hearing aids
- Heating devices
- Invalid chair
- Iron lung
- Orthopedic shoes—excess cost over cost of regular shoes
- Oxygen or oxygen equipment to relieve breathing problems caused by a medical condition
- Reclining chair if prescribed by doctor
- Repair of special telephone equipment for the deaf
- Sacroiliac belt
- Special mattress and plywood bed boards for relief of arthritis or spine
- Splints
- Truss
- Wheelchair
- Wig advised by doctor as essential to mental health of person who lost all hair from disease

Medical Treatments

- Abortion
- Acupuncture
- Blood transfusion
- Childbirth delivery
- Diathermy
- Electric shock treatments
- Hearing services
- Hydrotherapy (water treatments)
- Injections
- Insulin treatments
- Laser eye surgery or radial keratotomy to improve vision
- Navajo healing ceremonies ("sings")
- Nursing
- Organ transplant
- Prenatal and postnatal treatments
- Psychotherapy
- Sterilization
- Radial keratotomy
- Radium therapy
- Ultraviolet ray treatments
- Vasectomy
- Whirlpool baths
- X-ray treatments

Medicines and Drugs

- Cost of prescriptions only; over-the-counter medicine is not deductible.

Laboratory Examinations and Tests

- Blood tests
- Cardiographs
- Metabolism tests
- Spinal fluid tests
- Sputum tests
- Stool examinations
- Urine analyses
- X-ray examinations

Hospital Services

- Anesthetist
- Hospital bills
- Oxygen mask, tent
- Use of operating room
- Vaccines
- X-ray technician

Premiums for Medical Care Policies *(17.5)*

- Blue Cross and Blue Shield
- Contact lens replacement insurance
- Medicare A (if not covered by Social Security), Medicare B supplemental insurance, and Medicare D prescription drug coverage
- Health insurance covering hospital, surgical, and other medical expenses
- Membership in medical service cooperative

Miscellaneous

- Alcoholic inpatient care costs
- Birth control pills or other birth control items prescribed by your doctor
- Braille books—excess cost of Braille works over cost of regular editions
- Childbirth classes for expectant mother
- Clarinet lessons advised by dentist for treatment of tooth defects
- Convalescent home—for medical treatment only
- Drug treatment center—inpatient care costs
- Fees paid to health institute where the exercises, rubdowns, etc., taken there are prescribed by a physician as treatments necessary to alleviate a physical or mental defect or illness
- Kidney donor's or possible kidney donor's expenses
- Lead-based paint removal to prevent a child who has had lead poisoning from eating the paint. Repainting the scraped area is not deductible.
- Legal fees for guardianship of mentally ill spouse where commitment was necessary for medical treatment
- Lifetime care—advance payments made either monthly or as a lump sum under an agreement with a retirement home *(34.10).*
- Long-term care costs for chronically ill *(17.15).*
- Nurse's board and wages, including Social Security taxes paid on wages
- Pregnancy test kit
- Remedial reading for child suffering from dyslexia
- School—payments to a special school for a mentally or physically impaired person if the main reason for using the school is its resources for relieving the disability *(17.10).*
- "Seeing-eye" dog and its maintenance
- Smoking cessation programs
- Special school costs for physically and mentally handicapped children *(17.10).*
- Telephone-teletype costs and television adapter for closed caption service for deaf person
- Travel to obtain medical care *(17.9).*
- Wages of guide for a blind person
- Weight-loss program to treat obesity or other specific disease *(17.2).*

Table 17-2 Nondeductible Medical Expenses

Antiseptic diaper service
Athletic club expenses
Babysitting fees to enable you to make doctor's visits
Boarding school fees paid for healthy child while parent is recuperating from illness
Bottled water bought to avoid drinking fluoridated city water
Cost of divorce recommended by a psychiatrist
Cost of hotel room suggested for sex therapy
Cost of moving away from airport noise by person suffering a nervous breakdown
Cost of trips prescribed by a doctor for a "change of environment" to boost an ailing person's morale
Dance lessons advised by a doctor as general physical and mental therapy
Divorced spouse's medical bills
Domestic help; but *see 17.12* if nursing duties are performed.
Ear piercing
Funeral, cremation, burial, cemetery plot, monument, or mausoleum
Health programs offered by resort hotels, health clubs, and gyms
Illegal operations and drugs
Marijuana, even if prescribed by a physician in a state permitting the prescription
Marriage counseling fees
Massages recommended by physician for general stress reduction
Maternity clothes
Premiums on policies guaranteeing you a specified amount of money each week in the event hospitalization
Scientology fees
Special food or beverage substitutes; but *see 17.2.*
Tattooing
Teeth whitening to reverse age-related discoloration
Toothpaste
Transportation costs of a disabled person to and from work
Travel costs to favorable climate when you can live there permanently
Travel costs to look for a new place to live—on a doctor's advice
Tuition and travel expenses to send a problem child to a particular school for a beneficial change in environment *(17.10).*
Weight-loss program to improve general health *(17.2).*

Table 17-3 How Your Medical Expense Deduction Is Reduced by the 7.5% Floor

	Your medical expenses are													
	$1,000	*$1,500*	*$2,000*	*$2,500*	*$3,000*	*$3,500*	*$4,000*	*$4,500*	*$5,000*	*$5,500*	*$6,000*	*$6,500*	*$7,000*	*$7,500*
If your adjusted gross income is	***You may deduct***													
$15,000	0	375	875	1,375	1,875	2,375	2,875	3,375	3,875	4,375	4,875	5,375	5,875	6,375
$20,000	0	0	500	1,000	1,500	2,000	2,500	3,000	3,500	4,000	4,500	5,000	5,500	6,000
$25,000	0	0	125	625	1,125	1,625	2,125	2,625	3,125	3,625	4,125	4,625	5,125	5,625
$30,000	0	0	0	250	750	1,250	1,750	2,250	2,750	3,250	3,750	4,250	4,750	5,250
$35,000	0	0	0	0	375	875	1,375	1,875	2,375	2,875	3,375	3,875	4,375	4,875
$40,000	0	0	0	0	0	500	1,000	1,500	2,000	2,500	3,000	3,500	4,000	4,500
$45,000	0	0	0	0	0	125	625	1,125	1,625	2,125	2,625	3,125	3,625	4,125
$50,000	0	0	0	0	0	0	250	750	1,250	1,750	2,250	2,750	3,250	3,750
$55,000	0	0	0	0	0	0	0	375	875	1,375	1,875	2,375	2,875	3,375
$60,000	0	0	0	0	0	0	0	0	500	1,000	1,500	2,000	2,500	3,000
$65,000	0	0	0	0	0	0	0	0	125	625	1,125	1,625	2,125	2,625
$70,000	0	0	0	0	0	0	0	0	0	250	750	1,250	1,750	2,250
$75,000	0	0	0	0	0	0	0	0	0	0	375	875	1,375	1,875
$80,000	0	0	0	0	0	0	0	0	0	0	0	500	1,000	1,500
$85,000	0	0	0	0	0	0	0	0	0	0	0	125	625	1,125
$90,000	0	0	0	0	0	0	0	0	0	0	0	0	250	750
$95,000	0	0	0	0	0	0	0	0	0	0	0	0	0	375
$100,000	0	0	0	0	0	0	0	0	0	0	0	0	0	0

Advance payment for lifetime care in retirement community. The portion of a life-care fee or "founder's fee" that you pay in a lump sum or monthly to a retirement community for lifetime care may be included as a current medical expense to the extent that it is allocable to future medical care *(34.10)*.

Advance payments for lifetime care of disabled dependent. You can treat as a current medical expense a nonrefundable advance payment to a private institution for the lifetime care and treatment of your physically or mentally impaired child upon your death or when you become unable to provide care. The nonrefundable payment must be a condition for the institution's future acceptance of your child.

EXAMPLE

Parents contracted with an institution to care for their handicapped child after their death. The contract provided for payments as follows: 20% on signing, 10% within 12 months, 10% within 24 months, and the balance when the child enters. Payment of specified amounts at specified intervals was a condition imposed by the institution for its agreement to accept the child for lifetime care. Since the obligation to pay was incurred at the time payments were made, the IRS held that they were deductible as medical expenses, although the medical services were not to be performed until a future time, if at all.

17.3 Nondeductible Medical Expenses

The most common nondeductible medical expense is the cost of over-the-counter medicines and drugs, such as aspirin and other cold remedies. A deduction for over-the-counter medicines is disallowed even if you have a doctor's prescription *(17.2)*. Expenses incurred to improve your general health, such as exercise programs not related to a specific condition, are not deductible. Also *see Table 17-2*.

Cosmetic procedures. A medical expense deduction is allowed for cosmetic surgery if it is necessary to improve a disfigurement related to a congenital abnormality, disfiguring disease, or an accidental injury.

You may not deduct the cost of cosmetic surgery or other procedures that do not have a medical purpose. Thus, face lifts, hair transplants, electrolysis, teeth-whitening procedures, and liposuction intended to improve appearance are generally not deductible. However, in one case, the Tax Court allowed an exotic dancer to claim a depreciation deduction for breast implants essential for her business *(19.8)*.

Future medical care. Generally, you cannot include as a current medical expense payment for medical care that is to be provided substantially beyond the end of the year. However, advance payments for the care of a disabled dependent or the portion of a life-care fee or "founder's fee" to a retirement community that is allocable to future medical care is a currently deductible expense *(17.2)*.

17.4 Reimbursements Reduce Deductible Expenses

Insurance or other reimbursements of your medical costs reduce your potential medical deduction. Reimbursements for loss of earnings or damages for personal injuries and mental suffering do not have to be taken into account. A reimbursement first reduces the medical expense for which it is paid. The excess is then applied to your other deductible medical costs. *See* Example 1 below.

Personal injury settlements or awards. Generally, a cash settlement recovered in a personal injury suit does not reduce your medical expense deduction. The settlement is not treated as reimbursement of your medical bills. But when part of the settlement is specifically earmarked by a court or by law for payment of hospital bills, the medical expense deduction is reduced.

If you receive a settlement for a personal injury that is partly allocable to future medical expenses, you reduce medical expenses for these injuries by the allocated amount until it is used up.

Fake claims. Medical reimbursements for fake injury claims are treated as taxable income; *see* Example 2 below.

Court Decision

Sex Reassignment Surgery Is Deductible Expense

In a 2006 legal memorandum, IRS Chief Counsel determined that sex reassignment surgery (SRS) was nondeductible cosmetic surgery, as it does not fit the narrow definition of allowable cosmetic procedures intended to correct a disfigurement arising from congenital abnormality, disease or accident. Chief Counsel declined to rule that SRS is "treatment" for a mental illness or disease, which would exclude SRS from the definition of cosmetic surgery. Given the lack of tax authority for that conclusion and the controversy over the issue, Chief Counsel held that Congress must amend the law if SRS procedures are to be deductible.

A majority of a sharply divided Tax Court disagreed in a 2010 decision, holding that Gender Identity Disorder (GID) is a disease for medical deduction purposes. A taxpayer's expenses for cross-gender hormone therapy and SRS were held to be deductible as treatment for that disease. Expert testimony confirmed that the taxpayer suffered from severe GID, and hormone therapy and SRS are essential elements of a widely accepted treatment protocol for that condition. The cost of breast augmentation surgery was potentially deductible, but under the facts of the case the Tax Court majority denied a deduction because the accepted protocol justifies such surgery only if it is documented, as it was not here, that after 18 months of hormone therapy there was insufficient breast enlargement. Five judges would have disallowed a deduction for all of the taxpayer's expenses; the procedures were not "treatment" and did not meet the other exceptions to the definition of cosmetic surgery.

EXAMPLES

1. Gail Hurz paid $2,400 in medical insurance premiums. She paid doctor and hospital bills totaling $1,200 and purchased prescription drugs costing $750. Group hospitalization insurance reimbursed $800 for doctors and hospital bills and $375 for medicines and drugs. Her adjusted gross income is $32,100. If Gail itemizes, she can claim a medical expense deduction of $767, computed as follows:

Prescription drugs	$750
Medical care expenses	1,200
Premiums	2,400
Total	$4,350
Less reimbursement	1,175
	$3,175
Less: 7.5% of $32,100	2,408
Medical expense deduction	$767

2. Dodge, with the aid of a "friendly" doctor, arranged to be hospitalized for alleged back injuries and realized over $200,000 from HIP policies. The IRS charged that the insurance proceeds were taxable income. Dodge argued they were tax-free reimbursements of medical costs.

   The Tax Court sided with the IRS. The tax-free rules cover the payment of legitimate medical costs. Here there were no legitimate medical costs of actual injuries. Dodge took out the policies in a scam arrangement with the doctor.

Caution

Reimbursements Exceeding Expenses

If you have more than one policy and receive reimbursements that exceed your total medical expenses for the year, you must pay tax on all or part of the reimbursement where your employer paid premiums on the policies; *see* Examples 1–4 in this section.

Reimbursements in excess of your medical expenses. If you paid the entire premium for health insurance, you are not taxed on payments from the plan even if they exceed your medical expenses for the year. If you and your employer each contributed to the policy, you generally have to include in income that part of the excess reimbursement that is attributable to employer premium contributions not included in your gross income; *see* Examples 2–4 below. The taxable excess reimbursement must be reported as "Other income" on Line 21 of Form 1040.

However, you do not have to report any excess reimbursements that are tax-free payments for permanent disfigurement or loss of bodily functions *(3.2)*.

If your employer paid the total cost of the policy and the contributions were not taxed to you, you report as income all of your excess reimbursement, unless it covers payment for permanent injury or disfigurement *(3.2)*.

For the treatment of insurance reimbursements of long-term care costs, *see 17.15*.

EXAMPLES

1. Henry Knight pays premiums of $240 and $120 for two personal health insurance policies. His total medical expenses are $900. He receives $700 from one insurance company and $500 from the other. The excess reimbursement of $300 ($1,200 – $900) is not taxable because he paid the entire premium on the policy.

2. Lionel Guest's employer paid premiums of $1,800 for two employee health insurance policies covering medical expenses. Guest's medical expenses in one year are $900. He receives $1,200 from the two companies. The entire $300 excess is taxable because Guest's employer paid the total cost of the policy and the contributions were not taxed to him.

3. Kay Brown's employer paid a premium of $1,000 for a group health policy covering Brown, and Brown herself paid $300 for a personal health policy. Her medical expenses are $900. She receives reimbursements of $1,200, $700 under her employer's policy and $500 under her own policy. Brown's reimbursements exceed expenses by $300, but the taxable portion attributed to her employer's premium contribution is $175, computed this way:

Reimbursement allocated to Brown's policy ($500 ÷ $1,200) × $900	$375
Reimbursement allocated to employer's policy ($700 ÷ $1,200) × S900	$525
Taxable excess allocated to employer's policy ($700 – $525)	$175

4. Mike Green's employer paid $1,200 for a health insurance policy but contributed only $450 and deducted $750 from Green's wages. Green also paid $300 for a personal health insurance policy. His medical expenses are $900. He recovered $700 from the employer's policy and $500 from his personal policy. The excess attributable to the employer's policy is $175 (computed as in Example 3 above). However, the taxable portion is only $65.63. Both Green and his employer contributed to the cost of the employer's policy and a further allocation is necessary:

Green's contribution	$750
Employer's contribution	450
Total cost of policy	$1,200
Ratio of employer's contribution to annual cost of policy (450 ÷ 1,200, or 37.50%)	
Taxable portion: 37.50% of excess reimbursement of $175	$65.63

Reimbursement in a later year may be taxed. If you took a medical expense deduction in one year and are reimbursed for all or part of the expense in a later year, the reimbursement may be taxed in the year received. The reimbursement is generally taxable income to the extent the deduction reduced your tax in the prior year. *See* the details for figuring taxable income on a recovery of a prior deduction in *Chapter 11 (11.6)*.

EXAMPLES

1. In 2009, Anna Gurchani had adjusted gross income of $32,000. She claimed itemized deductions that exceeded her allowable standard deduction by $1,000; on her Schedule A, Gurchani listed medical expenses of $3,800. She deducted $1,400 for 2009, computed as follows:

Medical expenses	$3,800
Less: 7.5% of $32,000	2,400
Allowable deduction	$1,400

In 2010 she collects $300 from insurance, reimbursing part of her 2009 medical expenses. If she had collected that amount in 2009, her medical expense deduction would have been $1,100. The entire reimbursement of $300 is subject to tax in 2010. It is the amount by which the 2009 deduction of $1,400 exceeds the deduction of $1,100 that would have been allowed if the reimbursement had been received in 2009.

2. Same facts as in Example 1 above, but Anna did not deduct medical expenses in 2009 because she did not itemize deductions. The reimbursement in 2010 is not taxable.

17.5 Premiums of Medical Care Policies

Unless you are self-employed and qualify for the 100% above-the-line deduction (discussed below), health insurance premiums are deductible only as an itemized medical expense on Schedule A (Form 1040), subject to the overall 7.5% AGI floor. Include premiums you paid for health insurance that covers hospital, surgical, drug costs, and other medical expenses for you, your spouse *(17.6)*, and your dependents *(17.7)*. Also deductible are premiums paid for contact lens replacement insurance. Include premiums for Medicare Part B supplemental insurance and Medicare Part D prescription drug insurance. Payment for voluntary coverage under Medicare (Part A) is deductible by those over age 65 who are not covered by Social Security. Deductions may be claimed for membership payments in associations furnishing cooperative or free-choice medical services, group hospitalization, or clinical care policies, including HMOs (health maintenance organizations) and medical care premiums paid to colleges as part of a tuition bill, if the amount is separately stated in the bill.

Premiums paid before you reach age 65 for medical care insurance for protection after you reach age 65 are deductible in the year paid if they are payable on a level payment basis under the contract (1) for a period of 10 years or more or (2) until the year you reach age 65 (but in no case for a period of less than five years).

Premiums for qualifying long-term care policies are deductible subject to limitations *(17.15)*.

Filing Instruction

Long-Term Care Premiums

The amount of deductible premiums for a qualifying long-term care policy depends on your age *(17.15)*.

Nondeductible premiums. You may not deduct premiums for a policy guaranteeing you a specified amount each week (not to exceed a specified number of weeks) in the event you are hospitalized. Also, no deduction may be claimed for premiums paid for a policy that compensates you for loss of earnings while ill or injured, or for loss of life, limb, or sight. If your policy covers both medical care and loss of income or loss of life, limb, or sight, no part of the premium is deductible unless (1) the contract or separate statement from the insurance company states what part of the premium is allocated to medical care and (2) the premium allocated to medical care is reasonable.

You may not deduct part of the car insurance premiums for medical insurance coverage for persons injured by or in your car where the premium covering you, your spouse *(17.6)*, or your dependents *(17.7)* is not stated separately from the premium covering medical care for others.

Law Alert

Deduction for Health Insurance Premiums

When this book went to press, Congress was close to passing legislation that would reduce 2010 net earnings from self-employment by the income tax deduction for health insurance premiums paid by a self-employed individual. *See* the *e-Supplement at jklasser.com* for an update.

Self-employed deduction. If you were self-employed in 2010, you may claim a special deduction on Form 1040, Line 29, for 100% of health insurance premiums you paid for yourself, your spouse, and your dependents. The deduction is also allowed if you received wages from an S corporation in which you were more than a 2% shareholder, you were a general partner, or were a limited partner who received guaranteed payments.

The above-the-line deduction *(12.2)* may not be claimed for any month during 2010 that you were eligible for coverage under an employer's subsidized health plan, including a plan of your spouse's employer. Also, the deduction may not exceed your net earnings from the business under which the health premiums are paid.

Any balance of premiums not deductible because you had coverage under a subsidized employer health plan may be claimed as an itemized medical expense subject to the 7.5% income floor *(17.1)*.

17.6 Expenses of Your Spouse

Subject to the 7.5% floor, you may deduct as medical expenses your payments of medical bills for your spouse if you were married either at the time the expenses were incurred or at the time the bills were paid. That is, you may deduct your payment of your spouse's medical bills even though you are divorced or widowed, if, at the time the expenses were incurred, you were married. Furthermore, if your spouse incurred medical expenses before you married and you pay the bills after you marry, you may deduct the expense.

Filing Tip

Should Spouses File Separately?

If you are married and both you and your spouse have separate incomes, and one of you has substantial medical expenses, consider filing separate returns. This way the 7.5% floor will apply separately to your individual incomes, not to the higher joint income. To make sure which option to take—filing jointly or separately—you compute your tax on both types of returns and choose the one giving the lower overall tax *(1.3)*.

EXAMPLES

1. Your spouse has doctor bills covering an operation performed in 2009, before you were married. You married in 2010. You pay those bills in 2010. You may claim a 2010 medical expense deduction for your payment.
2. In October 2009, your spouse had dental work done. In February 2010, you are divorced; in April 2010, you pay your former spouse's dental bills. You may deduct the payment on your 2010 tax return.
3. In 2010, you pay medical expenses for your spouse who died in 2009. You remarry in 2010. On a 2010 joint return filed with your new spouse, you may deduct your payment of your deceased spouse's medical expenses.

Filing separately in community property states. If you and your spouse file separately and live in a community property state, any medical expenses paid out of community funds are treated as paid 50% by each of you. Medical expenses paid out of separate funds of one spouse can be deducted only by that spouse.

17.7 Expenses of Your Dependents

You may deduct your payment of medical bills for your children or other dependents, subject to the 7.5% floor *(17.1)*. You may deduct the expenses of a person who was your dependent either at the time the medical services were provided or at the time you paid the expenses. In determining dependent status for medical expense purposes, some of the regular exemption tests for dependents *(21.1)* can be disregarded. You may deduct the medical costs of qualifying children or relatives even if you cannot claim exemptions for them because: (1) they are claimed by the other parent under the special rules *(21.7)* for divorced/separated parents; *see* below, (2) their gross income exceeds the limit for qualifying relatives ($3,650 for 2010), (3) they file a joint return with their spouse, or (4) you are the dependent of another taxpayer and thus are barred from claiming any dependents on your return. The qualifying child or relative must be a U.S. citizen or national, or a resident of the United States, Canada, or Mexico, unless he or she is an adopted child who lives with you. *See* Examples 1–3 below. A child may not deduct medical expenses paid with his or her parent's welfare payments; *see* Example 4 below.

Divorced and separated parents. You may be able to deduct your payment of your child's medical costs, even though your ex-spouse is entitled to claim the child as a dependent *(21.7)*. For purposes of a 2010 medical deduction, the child is considered to be the dependent of *both* parents if (1) they are divorced or legally separated under a court agreement, separated under a written agreement, or married but living apart during the last six months of 2010; (2) the child was in the custody of one or both parents for more than half of 2010; and (3) more than half of the child's 2010 support was provided by both parents.

EXAMPLES

1. You contribute more than half of your married son's support, including a payment of a medical expense of $800. Because he filed a joint return with his wife, you may not claim him as a dependent *(21.1)*. But you still may include your payment of the $800 medical expense with your other qualifying medical expenses since you contributed more than half of his support.
2. Your mother, a U.S. citizen, underwent an operation in November 2009. You paid for the operation in February 2010. You may deduct the cost of the operation in 2010 if you furnished more than one-half of your mother's support in either 2009 or 2010.
3. Same facts as Example 2, except your mother is a citizen and resident of Italy. You may not deduct the cost of the operation. She is not a U.S. citizen or a resident of the United States, Canada, or Mexico and thus does not qualify as a dependent for exemption purposes *(21.8)* or for medical deduction purposes.
4. A son is the legal guardian of his mother who is mentally incompetent. As guardian, he received his mother's state welfare and Social Security benefits, which he deposited in his personal bank account and used to pay part of his mother's medical expenses. On his tax return, he claimed a deduction for the total medical expenses paid on behalf of his mother. The court held that he could deduct only medical expenses in excess of the amounts received as welfare and Social Security payments. The benefits, to the extent used to pay medical expenses, represented the mother's payments in her own behalf.

Adopted children. You may deduct medical expenses of an adopted child if you may claim the child as a dependent either when the medical services are rendered or when you pay the expenses. An adopted child is treated as your child for dependent purposes when a court has approved the adoption or the child is lawfully placed with you for legal adoption.

If you reimburse an adoption agency for medical expenses it paid under an agreement with you, you are considered to have paid the expenses. But reimbursement of expenses incurred and paid before adoption negotiations began does not qualify them as your medical expenses and you may not deduct them.

You may not deduct medical expenses for services rendered to the natural mother of the child you adopt.

Multiple support agreements. If you may claim a person as your dependent under a multiple support agreement *(21.6)*, your unreimbursed payments of that person's medical expenses are deductible. Even if you may not claim the dependent exception for 2010 because the person has a gross income of $3,650 or more, you may still deduct your payment of medical expenses provided the other multiple support agreement tests are met.

Filing Instruction

Multiple Support Agreement

If you may claim a person as your dependent under a multiple support agreement, include with your medical expenses only the amount you actually pay for the dependent's medical expenses. If you are reimbursed by others who signed the multiple support agreement, you must reduce your deduction by the amount of reimbursement.

EXAMPLE

Ingrid Fromm and her brother and sister share equally in the support of their mother. Part of their mother's support includes medical expenses. Should the three of them share in the payment of the bills or should only one of them pay the bills?The answer: Payment should be made by the person who may claim the mother as a dependent under a multiple support agreement. Only that person may deduct the payment. If Ingrid is going to claim her as an exemption, she should pay the bill. She may deduct the payment although she did not contribute more than half of her mother's support. If her brother and sister reimburse her for part of the bill, she may include only the unreimbursed portion in her medical expenses. Neither Ingrid's brother nor her sister may deduct this share.Thus, a deduction is lost for these amounts.

17.8 Decedent's Medical Expenses

If you pay the medical expenses of your deceased spouse or dependent *(17.7)*, you may claim the payment as a medical expense in the year you pay the expenses, whether that is before or after the person's death.

If the executor or administrator of the estate pays the decedent's medical expenses within one year after the date of death, an election may be made to treat the expenses as if the deceased had paid them in the year the medical services were provided. The executor or administrator may file an amended return for the year the services were provided and claim them as a medical deduction for that year, assuming the period for filing the amended return *(47.2)* has not passed.

If the election is made by the executor to claim the expenses as an income tax deduction, they may not be claimed as a deduction on the estate tax return. The executor must file a statement with the decedent's income tax return that the expenses have not been deducted on the estate tax return and the estate waives its right to deduct them for estate tax purposes.

If medical expenses are claimed as an income tax deduction, the portion of the expenses that are below the 7.5% floor, and, therefore, not deductible, may not be deducted on the estate tax return. Although the expenses were not actually deducted, the IRS considers them to be part of the overall income tax deduction.

EXAMPLE

Oscar Reyes incurred medical expenses of $5,000 in 2009 and $3,000 in 2010. He died June 1, 2010, without having paid these expenses. He had already filed his 2009 return before the due date. In August 2010, his executor pays the $8,000 in medical expenses. The executor may file an amended return for 2009, claim a medical expense deduction for the $5,000, and get a refund for the increased deductions. The executor may claim the remaining $3,000 as a medical expense deduction on Reyes's final return for 2010.

17.9 Travel Costs May Be Medical Deductions

Travel costs to a doctor's office, hospital, or clinic where you, your spouse, or your dependents receive medical care are deductible medical expenses, subject to the 7.5% AGI floor. Commuting to work is not a medical expense, even if your condition requires you to make special travel arrangements.

Deductible travel includes fares for buses, taxis or trains, and the costs of hiring a car service or ambulance to obtain medical care. Plane fares to another city are allowed by the IRS so long as obtaining medical care is the primary purpose of the trip; *see* below for lodging expense rule.

If you used your automobile in 2010 to obtain medical care, you may deduct a flat IRS rate of 16.5 cents a mile. In addition, you may deduct parking fees and tolls. If, however, auto expenses exceed this standard mileage rate, you may deduct your actual out-of-pocket costs for gas, oil, repairs, tolls, and parking fees. Do not include depreciation, general maintenance, or car insurance. The cost, as well as the operating and repair costs, of a wheelchair, autoette, or special auto device for a handicapped person is deductible if not used mainly for commuting.

Filing Tip

Deductible Travel Costs

The costs of trips to receive medical treatment are deductible as medical expenses subject to the 7.5% AGI floor. The costs of a trip to a conference to learn about medical treatment may be deductible if recommended by a doctor.

EXAMPLE

In 2010, you drove your car to a doctor's office for treatment 40 times. Each round trip was 25 miles. If you use the IRS's flat mileage rate to compute your medical expense deduction for 2010, you include $165 (1,000 miles x 16.5 cents) with your other medical expenses to figure your deduction for 2010. If you incurred tolls or parking fees during the trips, add these expenses to the mileage costs.

Medical conferences. Travel costs and admission fees to a medical conference are deductible medical expenses if an illness suffered by you, your spouse, or your dependents is the subject of the conference. For example, the IRS allowed a parent to deduct the registration fees and cost of traveling to a medical conference dealing with treatment options for a disease suffered by her dependent child. The child's doctor had recommended the conference. During the conference, most of the parent's time was spent attending sessions on her child's condition. Any recreational activities were secondary. If the parent had attended the conference because of her own condition the same deductions would have been allowed.

Lodging and meals while attending the conference are not deductible; these are allowed only if treatment is received at a licensed hospital or similar facility, as discussed below.

Lodging expenses. If you are receiving inpatient care at a hospital or similar facility, your expenses, including lodging and meals, are deductible. If you are not an inpatient, lodging expenses while away from home are deductible as medical expenses if the trip is primarily to receive treatment from a doctor in a licensed hospital, hospital-related outpatient facility, or a facility equivalent to a hospital. Meal expenses are not deductible unless they are paid as part of inpatient care.

The deduction for lodging while receiving treatment as an outpatient at a licensed hospital, clinic, or hospital-equivalent facility is limited to $50 per night per person. For example, the limit is $100 if a parent travels with a sick child. The IRS ruled that the $50 allowance could be claimed by a parent for a six-week hotel stay while her eight-year-old daughter was treated in a nearby hospital for serious injuries received in an automobile accident. The mother's presence was necessary so that she could sign release forms.

Caution

Meal Costs of Medical Trip

While transportation to receive medical care is a deductible medical expense subject to the 7.5% AGI floor, meals while on a trip for medical treatment are not deductible. They simply replace the meals you normally would eat. However, if you are hospitalized, the cost of meals while an inpatient is a deductible expense.

EXAMPLE

Polyak spent the winter in Florida on the advice of her doctor to alleviate a chronic heart and lung condition. While in Florida, she stayed in a rented trailer that cost $1,426. She saw a physician for treatment of an infection and to renew medications. She deducted the trailer costs as a medical deduction, which the IRS and Tax Court disallowed. Although her Florida trip was primarily for mitigating her condition, she did not travel to receive medical care from a physician in a licensed hospital or related outpatient facility. The medical care was routine and incidental to her travel to Florida. Her deduction for transportation costs to Florida was not contested by the IRS, which conceded that the trip was primarily for and essential to her health.

Deductible Transportation Costs

Examples of travel costs that have been treated as medical expenses by IRS rulings or court decisions are:

- Nurse's fare if nurse is required on trip
- Parent's fare if parent is needed to accompany child who requires medical care
- Parent's fare to visit his child at an institution where the visits are prescribed by a doctor
- Trip to visit specialist in another city
- Airplane fare to a distant city in which a patient used to live to have a checkup by a family doctor living there. That he could have received the same examination in the city in which he presently lived did not bar his deduction.
- Trip to escape a climate that is bad for a specific condition. For example, the cost of a trip from a northern state to Florida during the winter on the advice of a doctor to relieve a chronic heart condition is deductible. The cost of a trip made solely to improve a post-operative condition by a person recovering from a throat operation was ruled deductible.

- Travel to an Alcoholics Anonymous club meeting if membership in the group has been advised by a doctor
- Disabled veteran's commuting expenses where a doctor prescribed work and driving as therapy
- Wife's trip to provide nursing care for an ailing husband in a distant city. The trip was ordered by her husband's doctor as a necessity.
- Driving prescribed as therapy
- Travel costs of kidney transplant donor or prospective donor

Nondeductible Transportation Costs

- Commuting to work
- Trip for the general improvement of your health
- Traveling to areas of favorable climates during the year for general health reasons, rather than living permanently in a locality suitable for your health
- Meals while on a trip for outpatient medical treatment—even if cost of transportation is a valid medical cost. However, a court has allowed the deduction of the extra cost of specially prepared food.
- Trip to get "spiritual" rather than medical aid. For example, the cost of a trip to the Shrine of Our Lady of Lourdes is not deductible.
- Moving a family to a climate more suitable to an ill mother's condition. Only the mother's travel costs are deductible.
- Moving household furnishings to area advised by physician
- Operating an auto or special vehicle to go to work because of a disability
- Convalescence cruise advised by a doctor for a patient recovering from pneumonia
- Loss on sale of car bought for medical travel
- Medical seminar cruise taken by patient whose condition was reviewed by physicians taking the cruise

17.10 Schooling for the Mentally or Physically Disabled

You may include as medical expenses subject to the 7.5% floor the costs of sending on a doctor's recommendation a mentally or physically disabled dependent to a school or institution with special programs to overcome or alleviate his or her disability. Such costs may cover:

- Teaching of Braille or lip reading
- Training, caring for, supervising, and treating a mentally retarded person
- Training for a child with dyslexia
- Cost of meals and lodgings, if boarding is required at the school
- Costs of regular education courses also taught at the school, provided they are incidental to the special courses and services provided to overcome the disability

Caution

Counseling at a Private School

The parent of a child with psychological problems may deduct only that part of a private school fee directly related to psychological aid given to the child.

The school must have professional staff competent to design and supervise a program for helping your dependent overcome his or her disability. The fact that a particular school or camp is recommended for an emotionally disturbed child by a psychiatrist will not qualify the tuition as a deduction if the school or camp has no special program geared to the child's specific personal problem. The IRS allows a deduction for the costs of maintaining a mentally handicapped person in a home specially selected to meet the standards set by a psychiatrist to aid in an adjustment from life in a mental hospital to community living.

Payment for future medical care expenses is deductible if immediate payment is required by contract.

EXAMPLES

1. An emotionally disturbed child was sent to a private school maintaining a staff of three psychologists. His father deducted the school fee of $6,270 as a medical expense. The IRS disallowed the amount, claiming that the child, who was neither mentally impaired nor handicapped, was sent to school primarily for an education. The Tax Court allowed the father to deduct $3,000 covering the psychological treatment.

2. A mentally handicapped boy had been excluded from several schools for the mentally handicapped because he needed close attention. The director of a military academy had extensive experience in training young boys. Although it was not the usual practice of the academy to enroll mentally handicapped children, the director accepted the boy on a day-to-day basis as a personal challenge. The Tax Court held that the cost of both tuition and transportation to bring the boy to and from the school were deductible medical expenses. The primary purpose of the training given the boy was not ordinary education but remedial training designed to overcome his handicap. But note that, in other cases, a deduction for tuition of a military school to which a child was sent in order to remove him from a tense family environment, and the cost of a blind boy's attendance at a regular private school that made a special effort to accommodate his Braille equipment, were disallowed.

17.11 Nursing Homes

A payment for medical services, meals, and lodging to a nursing home, convalescent home, home for the aged, or sanitarium is treated as a medical expense subject to the 7.5% floor if you, your spouse, or dependent is confined for medical treatment.

If obtaining medical care is not the main reason for admission, but you can show the part of the cost covering actual medical and nursing care, that amount is deductible, but not the cost of meals and lodging.

Establishing medical purpose. The following facts are helpful in establishing the full deductibility of payments to a nursing home, convalescent home, home for the aged, or sanitarium:

- The patient entered the institution on the direction or suggestion of a doctor.
- Attendance or treatment at the institution had a direct therapeutic effect on the condition suffered by the patient.
- The attendance at the institution was for a specific ailment rather than for a "general" health condition. Simply showing that the patient suffers from an ailment is not sufficient proof that he or she is in the home for treatment.

In an unusual case, a court allowed a medical expense deduction for apartment rent of an aged parent; *see* the following Example.

Filing Tip

Meal Costs at a Nursing Home

If the patient entered a nursing home to receive medical care, a deduction may be taken for meals and lodging while there, in addition to medical care costs.

EXAMPLE

A doctor recommended to Ungar that his 90-year-old mother, convalescing from a brain hemorrhage, could receive better care at less expense in accommodations away from a hospital. A two-room apartment was rented, hospital equipment installed, and nurses engaged for seven months. The rent totaled $1,400. Ungar's sister, who worked in her husband's shoe store, nursed her mother for six weeks. Ungar paid the wages of a clerk who was hired to substitute for his sister in the store. Ungar deducted both the rent and wages as medical expenses. The IRS disallowed them; a Tax Court reversed the IRS's decision. The apartment rent was no less a medical expense than the cost of a hospital room. As for the clerk's wages, they too were deductible medical costs. The clerk was hired specifically to allow the daughter to nurse her mother, thereby avoiding the larger, though more direct, medical expense of hiring a nurse.

17.12 Nurses' Wages

Wages or fees paid for nursing services are medical expenses subject to the 7.5% floor. Include any Social Security or Medicare (FICA) tax, federal unemployment (FUTA) and state unemployment tax that you pay for the nurse. A nurse does not have to be registered or licensed so long as he or she provides you with nursing services. Nursing services include giving medications, changing dressings, and bathing and grooming the patient. If the nurse also performs personal or household services, you generally can deduct only that part of the pay attributable to nursing services for the patient. However, if the patient is considered chronically ill, certain maintenance or personal care services are deductible as long-term care services *(17.15)*.

The cost of an attendant's meals is included in your medical expenses. Divide total food costs among the household members to determine the attendant's share.

Caution

Nurse's Services

The cost of a nurse's services is a deductible medical expense, even if the nurse is not licensed or registered, so long as he or she provides the patient with nursing services. If household services are also provided, only the portion of the nurse's pay attributable to the provision of nursing services qualifies.

Costs eligible for tax credit. If, in order to work, you pay a nurse to look after a physically or mentally disabled dependent, you may be able to claim a credit for all or part of the nurse's wages as a dependent care expense *(25.4)*. You may not, however, claim both a credit and a medical expense deduction. First, you claim the nurse's wages as a dependent care cost. If not all of the wages are allowed as dependent care costs because of the expense limits *(25.5)*, the remaining balance is deductible as a medical expense.

The salary of a clerk hired specifically to relieve a wife from working in her husband's store in order to care for her ill mother was allowed as a medical expense; *see* the Ungar Example *(17.11)*.

EXAMPLE

Dodge's wife was arthritic. He was advised by her doctor to have someone take care of her to prevent her from falling. He moved her to his daughter's home and paid the daughter to care for her mother. He deducted the payments to his daughter. The IRS disallowed the deduction, claiming that the daughter was not a trained nurse. The Tax Court allowed that part of the deduction specifically attributed to nursing aid. Whether a medical service has been rendered depends on the nature of the services rendered, not on the qualifications or title of the person who renders them. Here, the daughter's services, following the doctor's advice, qualify as medical care.

Caution

Does Equipment Increase Value of Home?

When special equipment is installed in your home to alleviate a disease or ailment, you must determine if it increases the value of your home. You generally may claim a medical deduction only to the extent that the cost of the equipment exceeds the increase in value. However, if you install a ramp or railing, widen doorways or hallways, or add similar improvements to cope with a disability, these are usually treated by the IRS as not adding to the value of the home.

17.13 Home Improvements as Medical Expenses

A disease or ailment may require the construction or installation of special equipment or facilities in a home: A heart patient may need an elevator to carry him or her upstairs; a polio patient, a pool; and an asthmatic patient, an air cleaning system.

Subject to the 7.5% floor, you may deduct the full cost of minor equipment installed for a medical reason if it does not increase the value of your property, as, for example, the cost of a detachable window air conditioner. Where equipment or home improvement increases the value of your property, only the cost in excess of the increase in value to the home may be treated as a medical expense. This increased-value test does not apply to certain structural changes to a residence made to accommodate a disabling condition, as discussed below. If the equipment does not increase the value of the property, its entire cost is deductible, even though it is permanently fixed to the property.

The expense of maintaining and operating equipment installed for medical reasons may be claimed as a medical expense. This is true even if some or all of the cost does not qualify for a deduction because it must be reduced by the increase in value to your home. For example, if a heart patient installs an elevator in his home on the advice of his doctor, but an appraisal shows that the elevator increased the value of the home by more than the cost of the elevator, the cost would not be a medical expense. However, the cost of electricity to operate it and any maintenance costs are medical expenses as long as the medical reason for the elevator continues.

EXAMPLE

Mike Gerard's daughter suffered from cystic fibrosis. While there is no known cure for the disease, doctors attempt to prolong life by preventing pulmonary infection. One approach is to maintain a constant temperature and high humidity. A doctor recommended that Gerard install a central air-conditioning unit in his home for his daughter. It cost $1,300 and increased the value of his home by $800. The $500 balance was a deductible medical expense.

Certain structural improvements to accommodate disability fully taken into account. The increased-value test does not apply to structural changes made to a residence to accommodate your disabled condition, or the condition of your spouse or dependents who live with you. Eligible expenses include adding ramps, modifying doorways and stairways, installing railings and support bars, and altering cabinets, outlets, fixtures, and warning systems. Such improvements are treated for medical deduction purposes as not increasing the value of the home. Lifts, but not elevators, also are in this category. The full cost of such improvements is added to other deductible expenses and the total is deductible to the extent that it exceeds the 7.5% AGI floor.

Prepaid home construction costs. Zipkin suffered from multiple chemical sensitivity syndrome and built a house with special filtering and ventilation systems. The cost of the special features exceeded the fair market value of the home by $645,000. She claimed a deduction for the full amount when the house was completed. The IRS disallowed the deduction for the construction costs incurred in the years before the home was completed. Zipkin successfully argued before a federal district court that the construction costs should be treated as prepaid medical expenses that are deductible in the year medical benefits are received. The federal court allowed Zipkin to deduct the full amount in the year the home became habitable.

Deducting the cost of a swimming pool. If swimming is prescribed as physical therapy, the cost of constructing a home swimming pool may be partly deductible as a medical expense but only to the extent the cost exceeds the increase in value to the house. However, the IRS is likely to question any deduction because of the possibility that the pool may be used for recreation. If you can show that the pool is specially equipped to alleviate your condition and is not generally suited for recreation, the IRS will allow the deduction unless the expense is considered to be "lavish or extravagant." For example, the IRS allowed a deduction for a pool constructed by an osteoarthritis patient. His physician prescribed swimming several times a day as treatment. He built an indoor lap pool with specially designed stairs and a hydrotherapy device. Given these features, the IRS concluded that the pool was specially designed to provide medical treatment.

In one case the IRS tried to limit the cost of a luxury indoor pool built for therapeutic reasons to the least expensive construction. The Tax Court rejected the IRS position, holding that a medical expense is not to be limited to the cheapest form of treatment; on appeal, the IRS position was adopted.

If, instead of building a pool, you buy a home with a pool, can you deduct the part of the purchase price allocated to the pool? The Tax Court said no. The purchase price of the house includes the fair market value of the pool. Therefore, there is no extra cost above the increase in the home's value that would support a medical expense deduction.

The operating costs of an indoor pool were allowed by the Tax Court as a deduction to an emphysema sufferer.

A deduction is barred where the primary purpose of the improvement is for personal convenience rather than medical necessity.

EXAMPLES

1. Ken Cherry was advised by his doctor to swim to relieve his severe emphysema and bronchitis. He could not swim at local health spas; they did not open early enough or stay open late enough to allow him to swim before or after work. His home was too small for a pool. He bought a lot and built a new house with an indoor pool. He used the pool several times a day, and swimming improved his condition; if he did not swim, his symptoms returned. Cherry deducted pool operating costs of $4,000 for fuel, electricity, insurance, and repairs. The IRS disallowed the deductions, claiming that the pool was used for personal recreation. Besides, it did not have special medical equipment. The Tax Court allowed the deduction. Cherry built the pool to swim in order to exercise his lungs. That there was no special equipment is irrelevant; Cherry did not need special ramps, railings, a shallow floor, or whirlpool. Finally, his family rarely used the pool.
2. Doug Haines broke his leg in a skiing accident and underwent various forms of physical therapy, including swimming. To aid his recovery, his physician recommended that he install a swimming pool at his home. The Tax Court agreed with the IRS that the cost of the pool was not deductible. Although swimming was beneficial to his condition, he needed special therapy only for a limited period of time, and he could have gotten it at less cost at a nearby public pool. Finally, because of weather conditions, the pool could not be used for about half of the year.

17.14 Costs Deductible as Business Expenses

In some cases, expenses may be deductible as business expenses rather than as medical expenses. Claiming a business deduction is preferable because the deduction is not subject to the 7.5% adjusted gross income floor. However, the cost of a checkup required by your employer is a miscellaneous job expense subject to the 2% of adjusted gross income floor *(19.3)*.

Filing Tip

Disability-Related Job Costs

If you are disabled and incur costs to enable you to work, the payments may be treated as a deductible business expense rather than as a medical expense.

EXAMPLE

An airline pilot is required by his company to take a semi-annual physical exam at his own expense. If he fails to produce a resultant certificate of good health, he is subject to discharge. The cost of such checkups certifying physical fitness for a job is an ordinary and necessary business expense but the deduction is subject to the 2% floor for miscellaneous itemized deductions *(19.3)*. If the doctor prescribes a treatment or further examinations to maintain the pilot's physical condition, the cost of these subsequent treatments or examinations may be deducted only as medical expenses, even though they are needed to maintain the physical standards required by the job. Thus, a professional singer who consults a throat specialist may not deduct the fee as a business expense. The fee is a medical expense subject to the 7.5% AGI floor.

The Tax Court allowed a licensed social worker working as a therapist to deduct psychoanalysis costs as an education expense; *see 33.15*.

Impairment-related work expenses. Some expenses incurred by a physically or mentally disabled person may be deductible as business expenses rather than as medical expenses. A business expense deduction may be allowed if the expense is necessary for you to satisfactorily perform your job and is not required or used, except incidentally, for personal purposes.

If you are self-employed, claim the deduction on Schedule C *(40.6)*.

If you are an employee, the expenses are listed on Form 2106 and if not reimbursed, entered on Schedule A; *see 19.4*. The expenses are a fully deductible miscellaneous itemized deduction; the 2% AGI floor does not apply.

EXAMPLES

1. A professor is paralyzed from the waist down and confined to a wheelchair. When he attends out-of-town business meetings, he has his wife, a friend, or a colleague accompany him to help him with baggage, stairs, narrow doors, and to sit with him on airplanes when airlines will not allow wheelchair passengers without an attendant. While he does not pay them a salary, he does pay their travel costs. He may deduct these costs as business expenses. They are incurred solely because of his occupation.
2. An attorney uses prostheses due to bilateral amputation of his legs and takes medication several times a day for other ailments. On both personal and business trips, his wife or a neighbor accompanies him to help him travel and receive medication. He may deduct the out-of-town expenses paid for his neighbor only as a medical expense. The neighbor's services are not business expenses because assistance in personal activities is regularly provided. When his wife accompanies him, he may deduct her transportation costs as a medical expense; her food and lodging are nondeductible ordinary living expenses.

17.15 Long-Term Care Premiums and Services

You may include as medical expenses (subject to the 7.5% adjusted gross income floor) premiums paid for qualified long-term-care policies; the amount depends on your age. You also can include unreimbursed expenses for qualifying long-term care services that you require because you are "chronically ill" or because your spouse or dependent is chronically ill.

Qualifying long-term-care services for a chronically ill individual. A chronically ill person is someone who has been certified by a licensed health-care practitioner within the preceding 12 months as being unable to perform for a period of at least 90 days at least two of the following activities without substantial assistance: eating, toileting, dressing, bathing, continence, or transferring. Also qualifying as chronically ill is someone who requires substantial supervision because of severe cognitive impairment, such as from Alzheimer's disease.

Qualifying long-term-care services for a chronically ill individual are broadly defined as necessary diagnostic, preventive, therapeutic, curing, treating, mitigation, and rehabilitative services, and also maintenance or personal care services. The services must be provided under a plan of care prescribed by a licensed health-care practitioner, who may be a physician, a registered nurse, a licensed social worker, or other individual meeting Treasury requirements. Services provided by a spouse or relative are deductible only if that person is a licensed professional; services provided by a related corporation or partnership do not qualify.

Deductible premium costs of long-term-care policies. Depending on your age, all or part of your premium payments for a qualified long-term-care policy may be included as deductible medical expenses, subject to the 7.5% adjusted gross income floor. To qualify, the policy must provide for long-term-care services for the chronically ill (*see* above). The amount of the deductible premium depends on your age at the end of the year. For 2010, the maximum deductible premium amount for *each* person covered under the policy is: $330 if you are age 40 or younger at the end of 2010; $620 for those age 41 through 50; $1,230 for those age 51 through 60; $3,290 for those age 61 through 70; and $4,110 for those over age 70. These limits will likely be increased for 2011 by an inflation factor; *see the e-Supplement at jklasser.com*.

If you are considering purchase of a long-term-care insurance policy, make sure that it qualifies for the tax treatment explained in this section. A qualified contract must provide only for coverage of qualified long-term-care services and be guaranteed renewable; it may not provide for a cash surrender value or money that can be assigned, pledged, or borrowed; it may not reimburse expenses covered by Medicare except where Medicare is a secondary payer or the contract makes per diem payments without regard to expenses.

Filing Tip

Long-Term Care Insurance

Unreimbursed expenses for long-term care services to care for a chronically ill patient are deductible medical expenses subject to the 7.5% AGI floor. Premiums paid for a qualifying policy are includible in your medical expenses subject to a limit based on your age.

Benefits paid by qualified long-term-care policies. Benefits from a qualified long-term-care insurance contract (other than dividends) are generally excludable from income. If payments are made on a *per diem* or other periodic basis, meaning that they are made without regard to actual expenses incurred, there is an annual limitation on the amount that can be excluded. For 2010, *per diem* payments of up to $290 per day are tax free. If *per diem* payments exceed the $290 limit, the excess is tax free only to the extent of unreimbursed expenses for qualified long-term-care services. The *per diem* limit must be allocated among all policyholders who own qualified long-term-care insurance contracts for the same insured.

You should receive a Form 1099-LTC showing any payments to you from a long-term-care insurance contract. Box 3 of Form 1099-LTC should indicate whether the payments were made on a *per diem* basis or were reimbursements of actual long-term-care expenses. *Per diem* payments and reimbursements must be reported on Form 8853 to determine if any of the *per diem* payments are taxable.

Filing Instruction

Form 8853

If you received payments in 2009 from a qualified long-term care policy, you must figure the amount of taxable payments, if any, on Form 8853.

17.16 Life Insurance Used by Chronically ill or Terminally ill Persons

A person who is terminally ill may be forced to cash in a life insurance policy to pay medical bills and other living expenses. Insurance companies have developed life insurance policies with accelerated death benefit clauses to help terminally ill patients meet the high cost of medical care. Where a policy lacks an accelerated payment clause, it is also possible to sell a life insurance policy to a viatical settlement company that specializes in buying policies from ill persons who require funds to pay expenses.

Accelerated death benefits and viatical settlement proceeds received by terminally ill individuals are *not taxed*.

Payment of long-term care costs. A chronically ill *(17.15)* individual may sell a life insurance policy to a viatical settlement company to pay for long-term-care costs. However, tax-free treatment is determined under the tax rules applied to long-term-care policies *(17.15)*. Thus, if the proceeds exceed the $290 *per diem* limit for 2010 and also exceed actual long-term care costs, the excess is taxable on Form 8853. Accelerated life insurance proceeds paid under a long-term-care rider are also subject to these rules *(17.15)*.

Chapter 18

Casualty and Theft Losses and Involuntary Conversions

All casualty and theft losses are claimed on Form 4684. The tax treatment of an unreimbursed casualty or theft loss depends on the purpose for which you held the damaged, destroyed, or stolen property. A loss of property held for:

- ***Personal purposes*** is subject to the sudden events test *(18.1)* and a dollar floor *(18.12)* that reduces the deduction. In addition, net losses other than losses attributable to federally declared disasters are reduced by 10% of your adjusted gross income on Form 4684 *(18.12)*. Because of the 10% floor, you may be unable to deduct a casualty or theft loss unless the loss is quite substantial.
- ***Income-producing purposes,*** such as negotiable securities, should be claimed on Form 4684 and then entered on Line 28 of Schedule A as an "other miscellaneous deduction" not subject to the 2% AGI floor *(19.1)*.
- ***Business or rental purposes*** is claimed on Form 4684 and then as a loss on Form 4797. It is not subject to any floor or the sudden event test. Follow the instructions to Form 4684.

If you have realized a gain, you may defer tax by replacing or repairing the property *(18.19)*.

Appraisal fees and other incidental costs, such as taking photos to establish the amount of the loss, are claimed as a miscellaneous itemized deduction subject to the 2% AGI floor on Line 23 of Schedule A, Form 1040.

18.1 Sudden Event Test for Casualty Losses

To be a deductible casualty loss, property must be damaged or destroyed as the result of a sudden, unexpected, or unusual event. A sudden event is one that is swift, not gradual or progressive. An unexpected event is one that is ordinarily unanticipated and unintended. An unusual event is one that is not a day-to-day occurrence and that is not typical of the activity in which you were engaged. Chance or a natural phenomenon must be present. Examples include earthquakes, hurricanes, tornadoes, floods, severe storms, landslides, and fires. Loss due to vandalism during riots or civil disorders also is treated as a casualty loss. Damage to your car from an accident is generally deductible *(18.7)*. Courts have allowed deductions for other types of accidents; *see* Example 2 below. The requirement of suddenness is designed to bar deductions for damage caused by a natural action such as erosion, corrosion, and termite infestation occurring over a period of time.

The IRS and the courts have generally disallowed casualty deductions based on a loss in property value due to permanent buyer resistance rather than actual physical damage; *see* Examples 4 and 5 below.

EXAMPLES

1. A homeowner claimed a loss for water damage to wallpaper and plaster. The water entered through the window frame. The loss was disallowed. He gave no evidence that the damage came from a sudden or destructive force, such as a storm. The damage may have been caused by progressive deterioration.
2. Mr. White accidentally slammed the car door on his wife's hand. In pain, she shook her hand vigorously. A diamond flew out of her ring's setting, which was loosened by the impact. The diamond was never found. The IRS disallowed the deduction, contending that a casualty loss requires a cataclysmic event. The Tax Court disagreed. A deductible casualty loss occurs whenever an accidental force is exerted against property, and its owner is powerless to prevent the damage because of the suddenness. The IRS has accepted the decision.
3. A boat, which was in a poor state of repair, was equipped with a pump that automatically began operating when the water in the hull rose above a certain level. One day, the dockside power source failed, and the boat sank at its mooring within four hours. The IRS claimed that no deductible casualty occurred because the leakage was a chronic problem. The Tax Court allowed the deduction. The sinking was not a direct result of the boat's leaking hull, but of the failure of the on-board water pump.
4. A Brentwood couple, whose home was near the O.J. Simpson house, filed for a refund in federal district court to claim a $400,000 casualty loss deduction. The couple claimed that the double murder and the media frenzy surrounding the Simpson trial caused permanent buyer resistance in their neighborhood, lowering the value of their home by at least $400,000. The district court denied the refund. The couple relied on a 1986 case in which the Eleventh Circuit appeals court allowed Finkbohner a casualty loss deduction based on permanent buyer resistance when 12 nearby homes were razed by local authorities following severe floods and the lots were required to be kept as open space. However, the Brentwood couple's case was appealable to the Ninth Circuit, and the Ninth Circuit requires that a casualty loss be based on actual physical damage caused by a fire, storm, or other sudden unusual event and not merely buyer resistance. Therefore, the claim for a casualty loss deduction for the Brentwood home was denied.

   In a similar case, the Tax Court denied a casualty loss deduction to O.J. Simpson's next-door neighbors, who claimed they had suffered a permanent devaluation of their home's value due to the trial publicity. The Tax Court holds that actual physical damage is required for a deduction.
5. A 1983 avalanche caused $9,000 of physical damage to the Lunds' vacation home in Sundance, Utah, but they claimed a $221,000 deduction. They argued that there was a permanent loss in property value due to the avalanche risk in the area. Local authorities blocked road access during heavy snowfalls and some neighbors had decided not to rebuild destroyed homes. A federal district court agreed with the IRS that their loss could not exceed the actual physical damage. There may have been temporary buyer resistance following the avalanche, but not a permanent change in the area itself as there was in the Eleventh Circuit Finkbohner case mentioned above in Example 4.

Is drought damage deductible? The IRS does not generally allow deductions for drought damage. An agent may argue that the loss resulted from progressive deterioration, which does not fit the legal definition of a personal casualty loss. Courts have allowed deductions for severe drought where the damages occur in the same year as the drought.

If the damage becomes noticeable a year later, a court will view this as evidence of progressive deterioration that does not qualify as a deductible casualty. Where there are drought conditions, inspect your property for damage before the end of the year and claim a deduction for the damage in that year to negate an IRS argument that damage was caused by progressive deterioration.

Damage to surrounding property. Loss due to buyer resistance because of damage to surrounding property is generally not deductible. However, the Eleventh Circuit allowed a deduction. *See* Example 4 above.

Caution

Loss Prevention Measures

The cost of preventive measures, such as burglar alarms or smoke detectors, or the cost of boarding up property against a storm, is not deductible.

Damage to trees. The destruction of trees by southern pine beetles over a period of 5 to 10 days was held by the IRS to be a casualty. One court decided similarly where the destruction occurred over a 30-day period. For figuring the casualty deduction for tree and shrub damage *(18.6)*.

Deduction despite faulty construction. A plumber stepped on a pipe that was improperly installed. Resulting underground flooding caused damage of over $20,000. The IRS argued that this was caused by a construction fault and thus was not a casualty loss. The Tax Court disagreed. The plumber caused the damage. Improper construction was only an element in the causative chain.

Foreseeable events and preventable accidents. The IRS may disallow a deduction by claiming that the loss was foreseeable and therefore not a deductible casualty loss; *see* the following Examples.

EXAMPLES

1. Heyn owned a hillside lot on which he contracted for the building of a home. A soil test showed a high proportion of fine-grain dense sandstone, which is unstable. His construction contract called for appropriate shoring up and support. But, because of the contractor's negligence, a landslide occurred. The IRS disallowed the loss on the ground that it was not a "casualty" because the danger was known before Heyn undertook the project and because of the negligence involved. The Tax Court disagreed. The contractor's negligence is not a decisive factor in determining whether there was a casualty. For example, an automobile collision is considered a casualty, even if caused by negligent driving (but not willful misconduct). Foreseeability is also not a conclusive factor. A weather report may warn property owners to take protective steps against an approaching hurricane, but losses caused by the hurricane are deductible. The IRS has agreed to accept the decision.
2. Mrs. Kane placed her dirty ring in a glass of ammonia. Not knowing the contents of the glass, her husband emptied it into the sink and started the automatic garbage disposal, crushing the ring. The court allowed a full deduction for the loss, which it said resulted from a destructive force. That Mr. Kane was negligent has no bearing on whether the event was a casualty.
3. At Christmastime in 1982, Hananel left his 1974 Plymouth Valiant in Chicago in an area in which the city was towing away cars to make room for construction work. When he returned a week later, he found that his car was missing and reported it stolen. A month later, he learned that the city pound had towed the car away and then crushed it because its ownership could not be determined. He claimed a casualty loss for the car. The IRS disallowed the deduction, claiming that the towing and crushing were not an unforeseeable event, and thus did not qualify as a casualty.

   The Tax Court agreed that Hananel could have foreseen that leaving the car on the street subjected it to being towed. He was negligent. However, the penalty for this is a towing charge. He could not have foreseen its destruction. Therefore, the destruction occurred from an unusual and unexpected event, and he was allowed to claim a casualty loss deduction.
4. Destruction of a lawn through the careless use of weed killer was held by the Tax Court to be a casualty.

Caution

Loss From Termites

Termite damage is generally nondeductible since it often results from long periods of termite infestation. Proving a sudden action in the sense of fixing the approximate moment of the termite invasion is difficult. Some courts have allowed a deduction, but the IRS will bar deductions for termite damage under any conditions based on a study that found that serious termite damage results only after an infestation of three to eight years. *See* examples of other nondeductible casualty losses later in this chapter *(18.11)*.

18.2 When To Deduct a Casualty Loss

Generally, you deduct a casualty loss in the year the casualty occurs, regardless of when you repair or replace damaged or destroyed property. However, for a qualifying disaster area loss *(18.3)*, you have the option of claiming the loss on your return for the year immediately preceding the year in which the disaster occurred. If a casualty occurs in one year and you do not discover the damage until a later year, or you know damage has been inflicted, but you do not know the full extent of the loss because you expect reimbursement in a later year, here is what to do:

If you reasonably expect reimbursement in a later year. You should deduct in the year the casualty occurred only that part of your loss, after applying the personal property floors *(18.12)* for which you do not expect reimbursement. For example, if you expect a full insurance recovery in 2011 for a 2010 loss, you would take no deduction on your 2010 return.

If you do not expect any reimbursement and deduct a loss in 2010, but you receive insurance or other reimbursement in 2011, the reimbursement is taxable in 2011 to the extent that the 2010 deduction gave you a tax benefit by reducing your 2010 taxable income *(11.6)*. You may not amend your 2010 tax return.

You must file a timely insurance claim if your property is covered by insurance. Otherwise, the amount covered by the insurance cannot be taken into account when figuring your deductible casualty loss; *see 18.13* and *18.16*.

Caution

Deducting Loss in Proper Year

Read the rules on this page to insure that you deduct your casualty loss in the correct year.

EXAMPLE

In 1969, Hurricane Camille destroyed oceanfront real estate owned jointly by two brothers. The buildings were insured under two policies that included wind damage but not losses resulting from floods, tidal waves, or water. The insurers, claiming the tidal wave had caused the destruction, denied their claim. The brothers consulted an attorney about the possibility of suit against the insurance companies, but there seemed to be little likelihood of recovery, so the brothers deducted their shares of the casualty loss in 1969. However, in January 1970, the adjusters of both companies changed their decisions, reimbursing the brothers for more than two-thirds of their loss. One of the brothers filed an amended 1969 tax return, reducing the previously reported casualty loss.

The IRS claimed that the insurance recovery was taxable in the year of receipt, 1970, to the extent that the prior deduction reduced 1969 income. The brother claimed that he made an error in claiming the deduction in 1969 because he had a reasonable prospect of reimbursement. Thus it was proper to reduce the deduction by the reimbursement on an amended return.

The Tax Court disagreed. Tax liability is based on facts as they exist at the end of each year. A recovery in a later tax year does not prove that a reasonable prospect of recovery existed in the earlier year. Amendments to previously filed tax returns may be made only to correct mathematical errors or miscalculations, not to rearrange facts and readjust income for two years.

If your reimbursement is less or more than you expected. Assume you took no loss deduction in 2009 because you expected to recover your entire loss in 2010—but the insurance company refuses to pay your claim. When do you deduct your loss? You deduct your loss in the year you find that you have no reasonable prospect of recovery. For example, you sue the insurance company in 2010, with a reasonable prospect of winning your claim. However, in 2011, a court rules against you. You deduct your loss in 2011, subject to the personal property floors *(18.12)*. If you, as lessee, are liable to the lessor for damage to property, you may deduct the loss in the year you pay the lessor.

If you claim a loss and in a later year receive a larger reimbursement than you expected when you figured your deduction, you have to include the reimbursement in income for the year you receive it to the extent the deduction gave you a tax benefit *(11.6)*. For example, if you claimed a loss on your 2009 return and in 2010 you receive a larger insurance reimbursement than expected, you must include the recovery as 2010 income to the extent the deduction reduced your 2009 taxable income *(11.6)*.

If you do not discover the loss until a later year. In this case, IRS regulations do not specifically allow a deduction for the loss in the year it is discovered, but court decisions have. In one case, an unseasonable blizzard damaged a windbreak planted to protect a house, buildings, and livestock. The damage to the evergreens did not become apparent until the next year, when about half of the trees died and the others were of little value. The court held that the loss occurred in the later year. In another case, hurricane damage did not become apparent for two years. The Tax Court allowed the deduction in the later year. A deduction may be allowed where drought damage occurs *(18.1)*.

If your loss is in a federal disaster area. If your property is damaged in an area eligible for federal disaster assistance, you have a choice of years for which the loss may be claimed *(18.3)*.

If reimbursements exceed your adjusted basis for the property. Receiving reimbursements in excess of adjusted basis results in a gain that you must report on your return unless you acquire qualifying replacement property and elect to defer the gain *(18.19)*. If a loss is claimed in one year and in a later year you receive reimbursements that exceed your adjusted basis, the gain is included in income for the later year to the extent the original deduction reduced your taxable income *(11.6)*. The remainder of the gain is taxable unless you buy replacement property that enables you to defer the gain *(18.19)*.

Filing Tip

Accelerating a Tax Refund With Disaster Loss

Disaster loss rules give you a chance to deduct a loss earlier than under general rules. This may result in a tax refund for the prior year. You may make an election to claim the loss for the prior year in a signed statement attached to an amended return for that year if the original return has already been filed. List the date of the disaster and where the property was located (city, town, county, and state). To amend a filed return for the prior year, use Form 1040X. Consider making the election if the deduction on the return of the prior year gives a greater tax reduction than if claimed on the return for the year in which the loss occurred, or if you need the refund for the prior year tax and do not want to wait until you file your return for the year of the disaster to claim the loss.

18.3 Disaster Losses

If you suffer a loss from a disaster in an area declared by the President as warranting federal assistance, you may deduct the loss either on the return for the year of the loss or on the return of the prior tax year *(18.13)*.

You may elect to claim the deduction on a tax return for the previous year any time on or before the *later* of (1) the due date (without extensions) of the return for the year of the disaster *or* (2) the due date considering any extension for filing the return for the prior tax year. For a 2010 disaster loss, you generally have until April 15, 2011, to amend a 2009 tax return to claim the 2010 loss for 2009. In the case of a 2011 disaster loss, you generally have until April 17, 2012, to amend a 2010 tax return to claim the 2011 loss for 2010.

Revoking prior year election. You have 90 days in which to revoke an election to deduct a disaster loss for the previous year. After the 90-day period, the election becomes irrevocable. However, where an early election is made, you have until the due date for filing your return for the year of the disaster to change your election. Your revocation of an election is not effective unless you repay any credit or refund resulting from the election within the revocation period. A revocation made before you receive a refund will not be effective unless you repay the refund within 30 days after you receive it.

Homeowners forced to relocate. If you were forced to relocate or demolish your home in a disaster area, you may be able to claim a loss even though the damage, such as from erosion, does not meet the sudden event test *(18.1)*. For example, after a severe storm, there is danger to a group of homes from nearby mudslides. State officials order homeowners to evacuate and relocate their homes. Disaster loss treatment is allowed provided: (1) the President has determined that the area warrants federal disaster relief; (2) within 120 days of the President's order, you are ordered by the state or local government to demolish or relocate your residence; and (3) the home was rendered unsafe by the erosion or other disaster. The law applies to vacation homes and rental properties, as well as to principal residences.

If these tests are met, the loss in value to your home is treated as a disaster loss so that you may elect to deduct the loss either in the year the demolition or relocation order is made or in the prior taxable year.

Law Alert

Tax-Free Disaster Relief Payments to Individuals

You are not taxed on disaster relief payments from any source that reimburses or pays you for unreimbursed costs of repairing or rehabilitating your personal residence, or replacing its contents, as a result of a federally declared disaster.

You are not taxed on payments, regardless of the source, that cover reasonable and necessary personal, family, living, or funeral expenses as a result of a federally declared disaster, so long as they are not otherwise paid by insurance or other reimbursement. The exclusion also applies to payments made by the federal, state, or local government to individuals affected by a Presidentially declared disaster in order to promote the general welfare.

Fiscal year. If you are on a fiscal year, an election may be made for disaster losses occurring after the close of a fiscal year on the return for that year. For example, if your fiscal year ends June 30, and you suffer a disaster loss at any time between July 1, 2009, and June 30, 2010, you may elect to deduct it on your return for the fiscal year ending June 30, 2009.

Disaster relief grants and loans. Cancellation of part of a federal disaster loan under the Robert T. Stafford Disaster Relief and Emergency Assistance Act is treated as a reimbursement that reduces your loss *(18.16)*. If you receive a post-disaster grant under the Disaster Relief Act to help you meet medical, dental, housing, transportation, personal property, or funeral expenses, the grant is excludable from income. However, to the extent the grant specifically reimburses a casualty loss or medical expense *(17.2)*, that expense is not deductible. Unemployment assistance payments under the Disaster Relief Act are taxable unemployment benefits *(2.6)*.

Disaster grants for business property losses. Payments by the federal government or a state or local government to a business for property losses may not be excluded from business gross income. The IRS has ruled that the disaster relief exclusion that applies to government payments made to individuals to promote the general welfare does not apply to business property losses. The business realizes a taxable gain to the extent the grant exceeds the adjusted basis in the damaged or destroyed property, but that gain can be deferred under the involuntary conversion rules *(18.19)* by making a timely reinvestment of the payments in qualified replacement property. The replacement period for damaged or destroyed business property is two years *(18.22)*.

IRS interest abatement. For declared disasters, the IRS will abate interest on taxes due for the period covered by an extension to file tax returns and pay taxes.

Insurance Proceeds for Damaged or Destroyed Residence

Destruction of principal residence and contents. Generally, you have a taxable gain if you receive insurance proceeds in excess of your adjusted basis for damaged or destroyed property *(18.19)*. However, where your principal residence is destroyed, any gain from the receipt of insurance proceeds may generally be excluded from gross income under the $250,000 ($500,000 if married filing jointly) home sale exclusion *(29.1)*. According to the IRS, a principal residence must be completely destroyed to qualify for the home sale exclusion; a partial destruction does not qualify. If a residence is damaged to the extent that the remaining structure must be deconstructed in order to rebuild, or the costs of repair substantially exceed the pre-disaster value of the home, the home is considered to have been completely destroyed, allowing the gain to be excluded from income subject to the $250,000/$500,000 exclusion limit. If the home sale exclusion is not available to you or if the gain exceeds your exclusion, the nonexcludable gain may be deferred under the involuntary conversion rules if you buy a replacement residence *(18.19)*.

Where your principal residence is damaged or destroyed in a federally declared disaster, favorable involuntary conversion rules eliminate tax on some of the gain and make it easier to defer the balance. These rules apply to renters as well as home owners.

1. You do not have to pay tax on gain from insurance proceeds received for "unscheduled" personal property in your principal residence (rented or owned). Personal property is unscheduled if it is not separately listed on a schedule or rider to the basic insurance policy.
2. Insurance proceeds received for the home itself or for *scheduled* property are treated as received for a single item of property. Gain on this combined insurance pool may be deferred by reinvesting in replacement property that is similar or related in service or use to either the damaged residence or its contents. If the cost of a new principal residence and/or contents equals or exceeds the combined insurance pool, you may elect to defer any gain attributable to the insurance recovery *(18.21)* for making the election. The deferred gain reduces your basis in the replacement property. The period for purchasing replacement property generally ends four years after the end of the first tax year in which any part of your gain is realized. However, the replacement period is extended from four years to five years if your principal residence was located in the Hurricane Katrina disaster area, Kansas disaster area, or Midwestern disaster area, provided that the replacement residence is in or the home contents are used in the respective disaster area. If the cost of the replacement property is less than the combined insurance pool, your gain is taxed to the extent of the unspent reimbursement.

EXAMPLE

You rent an apartment as your principal residence. Your apartment and its contents were completely destroyed by a hurricane in 2010; the county in which your apartment was located was in a federally declared disaster area. You received insurance proceeds of $17,000 for unscheduled personal property in your apartment. The proceeds are not taxable.

Sale of land underlying destroyed principal residence or second home. If your principal residence is destroyed in a federally declared disaster, and you decide to relocate elsewhere and sell the underlying land, the IRS treats the sale and the destruction as a single involuntary conversion. If you have a gain that is not excludable under the home sale exclusion rules *(Chapter 29)*,

Planning Reminder

IRS Interest Abatement

If the IRS extends the due date to file tax returns and pay taxes for a person in an area declared to be a disaster area by the President, the IRS will abate interest on past-due taxes for the period covered by the extension.

Filing Tip

Nontaxable Disaster Mitigation Payments

Property owners are not taxed on qualified disaster mitigation payments from FEMA (Federal Emergency Management Agency) to elevate or relocate flood-prone homes and businesses or build hurricane shelters.

the land sale proceeds are combined with your insurance recovery for purposes of figuring deferrable gain under the involuntary conversion replacement rules *(18.19)*. All of the gain resulting from the insurance recovery may be deferred if a new principal residence is purchased within the four-year replacement period and it costs at least as much as the combined insurance and sales proceeds. The replacement period ends four years after the close of the first year in which any part of your gain is realized. The replacement period is extended from four years to five years if the destroyed principal residence was located in the Hurricane Katrina disaster area, Kansas disaster area, or Midwestern disaster area, provided that the replacement residence is in the respective disaster area.

The above "single conversion" rule also applies if a second residence such as a vacation home that qualifies for a mortgage interest deduction *(15.1)* is destroyed, but in that case the replacement period *(18.22)* is two years (instead of four years), unless the five-year replacement period for residences in the Hurricane Katrina disaster area, Kansas disaster area, or Midwestern disaster area applies.

Note: The IRS treats the sale of land and destruction of a residence as a single involuntary conversion even if the destruction was not in a federally declared disaster area. In this case, a two-year (rather than four-year) replacement period applies.

18.4 Who May Deduct a Casualty Loss

A casualty loss deduction may be claimed only by the owner of the property. For example, a husband filing a separate return may not deduct damage to a car belonging to his wife; only she may deduct it on her separate return.

On jointly owned property, the loss is divided among the owners. If you and your spouse own the property jointly, you deduct the entire loss on a joint return. If you file separately, each owner deducts his or her share of the loss on each separate return.

If you have a legal life estate in the property, the loss is apportioned between yourself and those who will get the property after your death. The apportionment may be based on actuarial tables that consider your life expectancy.

You may claim a casualty loss for property lost or destroyed by your dependent if you own the property. You may not claim a loss deduction for destroyed property that belongs to your child who has reached majority, even though he or she is still your dependent.

Caution

Damage to Nearby Property

The casualty must have caused damage to your property. Damage to a nearby area that lowered the value of your property does not give you a loss deduction.

Lessee. A person leasing property may be allowed to deduct payments to a lessor that are required under the lease to compensate for a casualty loss. A tenant was allowed to deduct as a casualty loss payment of a judgment obtained by the landlord for fire damage to the rented premises that had to be returned in the same condition as at the start of the lease. However, the Tax Court does not allow a deduction for the cost of repairing a rented car, as the lessee has no basis in the car.

EXAMPLE

You buy or lease a lot on which to build a cottage. Along with your purchase or lease, you have the privilege of using a nearby lake. The lake is later destroyed by a storm and the value of your property drops. You may not deduct the loss. The lake is not your property. You only had a privilege to use it, and this is not an ownership right that supports a casualty loss deduction.

18.5 Bank Deposit Losses

If a bank or other financial institution in which you deposit funds fails and your loss is not covered by insurance, generally you may claim your loss either as a bad debt deduction or casualty loss. Alternatively, if none of the deposits were federally insured, an investment loss may be claimed. A casualty loss deduction may not be claimed for lost deposits in foreign financial institutions that are not organized and supervised under federal or state law. Neither the casualty loss nor the investment loss option is available to stockholders of the bank with more than a 1% interest, officers of the bank, or relatives of shareholders or officers.

Filing Tip

Lost Bank Deposit

If you have other miscellaneous deductions that exceed 2% of adjusted gross income, claiming investment loss treatment may be preferable to treating the loss as a casualty subject to the 10% floor or a bad debt subject to the $3,000 limit. However, investment loss treatment is not advisible if you are subject to alternative minimum tax (AMT), as miscellaneous deductions are not allowed for AMT purposes *(23.2)*.

Bad debt. You may claim a bad debt deduction for a loss of a bank deposit in the year there is no reasonable prospect of recovery from the insolvent or bankrupt bank. You claim the loss as a short-term capital loss on Schedule D (Form 1040) unless the deposit was made in your business. A nonbusiness bad debt deduction is deductible from capital gains. If you do not have capital gains or the bad debt loss exceeds capital gains, only $3,000 of the loss may offset other income. The remaining loss is carried over. A lost deposit of business funds is claimed as a business bad debt *(5.33)*.

Casualty loss. You may elect to take a casualty loss deduction for the year in which the loss can be reasonably estimated. A loss of personal funds is subject to the $500/10% AGI floors for personal-use property losses *(18.12)*. Once the casualty loss election is made, it is irrevocable and will apply to all other losses on deposits in the same financial institution.

The casualty loss election may allow you to claim the loss in an earlier year because you do not have to wait until the year there is no prospect of recovery as required in the case of bad debts. The casualty loss election may also be advisable if other casualty losses may absorb all or part of the 10% AGI floor.

Investment loss. If *none* of your deposits were federally insured and you reasonably estimate that you will not recover the funds, up to $20,000 ($10,000 if married filing separately) may be claimed on Schedule A (Form 1040) as an investment loss subject to the 2% adjusted gross income floor for miscellaneous itemized deductions *(19.1)*. The $20,000 limit (or $10,000) applies to total losses from any one financial institution, regardless of the number of accounts you have. A separate $20,000 deduction limit applies to each financial institution. The $20,000 (or $10,000) limit is reduced by any insurance proceeds authorized by state law that you reasonably expect to receive. If you claimed a bad debt deduction for a lost deposit in a prior year and you qualify for the investment loss, you may file an amended return to claim the investment loss if the statute of limitations has not passed.

Reasonable estimate of casualty or investment loss. Generally, the trustees of the troubled bank will provide depositors with an estimate of the expected recovery and loss. In the year of that determination, you may claim the estimated loss deduction. If you deduct an estimated loss that is less than you are entitled to, you may claim the additional loss in the year of the final determination as a bad debt. If you deduct more than the actual loss, the excess loss must be reported as income in the year of the final determination. Failure to claim the loss in the year in which the loss can first be reasonably estimated does not bar a deduction in a later year.

For any particular year, only one election may be made for losses in the same bank. If you elect the up-to-$20,000 investment loss for losses in one bank and your loss exceeds the limit, the balance may not be claimed as a casualty deduction. Similarly, if you elect casualty loss treatment, the amount that is not deductible because of the $500 and 10% of adjusted gross income floors *(18.12)* is not deductible under the $20,000 investment loss rule.

18.6 Damage to Trees and Shrubs

Not all damage to trees and shrubs qualifies as a casualty loss. The damage must be occasioned by a sudden event *(18.1)*. Destruction of trees over a period of 5–10 days by southern pine beetles is deductible. One court allowed a deduction for similar destruction over a 30-day period. However, damage by Dutch Elm disease or lethal yellowing disease has been held to be gradual destruction not qualifying as a casualty loss. The Tax Court has allowed a deduction for the cost of removing infested trees, but denied a deduction for the loss of trees after a horse ate the bark.

If shrubbery and trees on *personal-use property* are damaged by a sudden casualty, you figure the loss on the value of the entire property before and after the casualty. You treat the buildings, land, and shrubs as one complete unit; *see* Example 2 below.

In fixing the loss on *business or income-producing property*, however, shrubs and trees are valued separately from the building; *see* Example 1 below.

EXAMPLES

1. Wayne Smith bought an office building for $90,000. The purchase price was allocated between the land ($18,000) and the building ($72,000). Smith planted trees and ornamental shrubs on the grounds surrounding the building at a cost of $1,200. When the basis of the building had been depreciated to $66,000, a hurricane caused extensive property damage in 2010. The fair market value of the land and building immediately before the hurricane was $18,000 and $80,000; immediately afterwards it was $18,000 and $52,000. The fair market value of the trees and shrubs immediately before the casualty was $2,000 and immediately afterwards, $400. Insurance of $15,000 is received to cover damage to the building. Deductible losses

are figured separately for the building and the trees and shrubs. The deduction for the building is $13,000, computed as follows:

Value of building immediately before casualty	$80,000
Less: Value immediately after casualty	52,000
Loss in value	$28,000
Less: Insurance received	15,000
Deduction allowed	$13,000

The deduction for the trees and shrubs is $1,200:

Value immediately before casualty	$2,000
Less: Value of trees immediately after casualty	400
Loss in value	$1,600*

**However, the deductible loss cannot exceed the adjusted basis of the property, $1,200.*

2. Same facts as in Example 1, except that Smith purchases a personal residence instead of an office building. Smith's 2010 adjusted gross income is $75,000, and this is his only loss. No allocation of the purchase price is necessary for the land and house because the property is not depreciable. Likewise, no individual evaluation of the fair market values of the land, house, trees, and shrubs is necessary. The amount of the deduction in 2010 for the land, house, trees, and shrubs is $6,600, computed as follows:

Value of property immediately before casualty		$100,000
Less: Value of property immediately after casualty		70,400
Loss in value		$29,600
Less: Insurance received	$15,000	
10% floor ($7,500) and $500 floor *(18.12)*	8,000	23,000
Deduction allowed		$6,600

18.7 Deducting Damage to Your Car

Damage to your car in an accident may be a deductible casualty loss unless caused by your willful conduct, such as drunken driving.

You may not deduct legal fees and costs of a court action for damages or money paid for damages to another's property because of your negligence while driving for commuting or other personal purposes. But if at the time of the accident you were using your car on business, you may deduct as a business loss a payment of damages to the other party's car. For purposes of a business loss deduction, driving between two locations of the same business is considered business driving but driving between locations of two separate businesses is considered personal driving. Therefore, the payment of damages arising from an accident while driving between two separate businesses is not deductible as a business expense.

Filing Tip

Auto Damage

Unreimbursed accident damage may be a deductible casualty loss.

A court has allowed casualty deductions for damage resulting from a child starting a car and from flying stones while driving over a temporary road. In a private letter ruling, the IRS disallowed a loss for damage to a race car by an amateur racer on the ground that in races, crashes are not an unusual event and so do not constitute a casualty.

If the deduction is questioned, be prepared to show the amount, if any, of your insurance recovery. A deduction is allowed only for uninsured losses. Not only must the loss be proved, but also that it was not compensated by insurance.

Towing costs are not included as part of the casualty loss.

A parent may not claim a casualty loss deduction for damage to a car registered in a child's name, although the parent provided funds for the purchase of the car.

Expenses of personal injuries arising from a car accident are not a deductible casualty loss.

Automobile used partly for business. When you use an automobile partly for personal use and partly for business, your loss is computed as though two separate pieces of property were damaged—one business and the other personal. The $500 and 10% floors *(18.12)* reduce only the loss on the part used for personal purposes.

Court Decision

Failure To Winterize Car

The Tax Court held that the loss of an engine because of a failure to use antifreeze is not deductible as a casualty loss since the damage is not the result of a destructive force or accident but of personal neglect.

18.8 Proving a Casualty Loss

If your return is audited, you will have to prove that the casualty occurred and the amount of the loss. The time to collect your evidence is as soon after the casualty as possible. Table 18-1, Proving a Casualty Loss, indicates the information that you will need when computing your loss *(18.13)*.

Table 18-1 Proving a Casualty Loss

To prove—	*You need this information—*
That a casualty actually occurred	With a well-known casualty, like regional floods, you will have no difficulty proving the casualty occurred, but you must prove it affected your property. Photographs of the area, before and after, and newspaper stories placing the damage in your neighborhood are helpful. If only your property is damaged, there may be a newspaper item on it. Some papers list all the fire alarms answered the previous day. Police, fire, and other municipal departments may have reports on the casualty.
The cost of repairing the property	Cost of repairs is allowed as a measure of loss of repairing the value if it is not excessive and the repair merely restored your property to its condition immediately before the casualty. Save cancelled checks, bills, receipts, and vouchers for expenses of clearing debris and restoring the property to its condition before the casualty.
The value immediately before and after the casualty	Appraisals by a competent expert are important. Get them in writing—in the form of an affidavit, deposition, estimate, appraisal, etc. The expert—an appraiser, engineer, or architect—should be qualified to judge local values. Any records of offers to buy your property, either before or after the casualty, are helpful. Automobile "blue books" may be used as guides in fixing the value of a car. But an amount offered for your car as a trade-in on a new car is not usually an acceptable measure of value.
Cost or other basis of your property—the deductible loss cannot be more than that	A deed, contract, bill of sale, or other document probably shows your original cost. Bills, receipts, and cancelled checks probably show the cost of improvements. One court refused to allow a deduction because an owner failed to prove the original cost of a destroyed house and its value before the fire. In another case, estimates were allowed where a fire destroyed records of cost. A court held that the homeowner could not be expected to prove cost by documents lost in the fire that destroyed her property. She made inventories after the fire and again at a later date. Her reliance on memory to establish cost, even though inflated, was no bar to the deduction.The court estimated the market value based on her inventories. If you acquired the property by gift or inheritance, you must establish an adjusted basis in the property from records of the donor or the executor of the estate; *see* 5.17 and 5.18.

18.9 Theft Losses

You can deduct a theft loss in the year you discover that your property was stolen. The taking of property must be illegal under state law to support a theft loss deduction. That property is missing is not sufficient evidence to sustain a theft deduction. It may have been lost or misplaced. So if all you can prove is that an article is missing or lost, your deduction may be disallowed. Sometimes, of course, the facts surrounding the disappearance of an article indicate that it is reasonable to assume that a theft took place. A deduction has been allowed for the theft of trees.

If you expect to be reimbursed by insurance, you must subtract the expected reimbursement when you figure your deductible loss *(18.13)*.

A legal fee paid to recover stolen property has been held to be deductible as part of the theft loss. To figure the amount of a theft loss deduction, *see 18.13*.

Filing Instruction

If Stolen Property Is Recovered

If you claim a theft loss and in a later year the property is returned to you, you must refigure your loss deduction. If the refigured deduction is lower than the amount you claimed, the difference must be reported as income in the year of the recovery. To recalculate the loss, follow the steps for figuring deductible losses *(18.13)*, but in Step 1, compute the loss in fair market value from the time the property was stolen until you recovered it. The lower of this loss in value, if any, or your adjusted basis for the property is then reduced by insurance reimbursements and the personal-use floors *(18.12)* to get the recalculated loss.

Fraud by building contractors. A deduction was allowed when a building contractor ran away with a payment he received to build a residence. The would-be homeowner was allowed a theft loss deduction for the difference between the money he advanced to the contractor and the value of the partially completed house. In another case, a theft deduction was allowed for payments to subcontractors. The main contractor had fraudulently claimed that he had paid them before he went bankrupt.

The Tax Court rejected a theft loss claim that a contractor who failed to meet the construction plan specifications for a home had committed fraud under New Mexico law. The job was completed and repairmen were sent by the contractor to fix defects even after the one-year warranty period had expired. The contractor may have acted negligently or committed breach of contract, but poor workmanship is not fraud.

Embezzlement losses are deductible as theft losses in the year the theft is discovered. However, if you report on a cash basis, you may not take a deduction for the embezzlement of income you have not reported. For example, an agent embezzled royalties of $46,000 due an author. The author's theft deduction was disallowed. The author had not previously reported the royalties as income; therefore, she could not get the deduction.

Madoff Ponzi scheme and similar fraudulent schemes. The IRS released a revenue ruling (Revenue Ruling 2009-9) allowing a theft loss deduction and a net operating loss carryback to be claimed by investors who fell victim to the Ponzi scheme perpetrated by Bernard Madoff and similar fraudulent schemes. These losses are deductible as theft losses of income-producing property (so the loss is figured in Section B of Form 4684 and the floors for personal-use property in *18.12* do not apply) on your tax return for the year the loss was discovered.

The IRS also provided in Revenue Procedure 2009-20 an optional safe harbor method for computing and reporting losses for 2008 and later years, which, if available, eliminates uncertainty about the timing of a possible deduction and avoids having to prove how much income reported in prior years was fictitious or a return of capital. However, eligibility for the safe harbor is limited to investors who had a taxable investment account in the fraudulent arrangement and the investment must have been made directly, not through a fund, partnership, or other entity. Losses in IRAs or other tax-deferred retirement plans invested with the scheme do not qualify for the safe harbor.

For qualifying investors, a loss is deemed to be the result of theft and therefore eligible for safe harbor relief if (1) the "lead figure" in the scheme was charged under federal or state law (by way of indictment or information) with fraud, embezzlement, or a similar crime, or (2) in response to a federal or state complaint, the lead figure admitted guilt or a receiver or trustee was appointed to freeze the assets. The theft loss is deductible for the taxable year in which the theft was discovered (the "discovery year"). This is the year in which the indictment, information, or complaint against the lead figure was filed. In the case of the Madoff scheme, the discovery year is 2008. In the case of the SEC's fraud complaint against Robert Allen Stanford, it is 2009. The safe harbor does not apply to losses for which the discovery year was a taxable year beginning before 2008.

The safe harbor allows a deduction for 95% of the "qualified investment" if the investor is not pursuing any third-party recovery, or 75% if the investor is pursuing or intends to pursue a third-party recovery. The "qualified investment" is the sum of cash and the basis of property invested in the arrangement over the years, plus the income from the arrangement, including any fictitious income (so-called phantom income), credited to the investor's account, that the investor included on his or her federal tax returns for years before the discovery year, minus any cash or property (whether income or principal) withdrawn by the investor from the arrangement. After applying the 95%/75% percentage, the deductible amount is then reduced by any actual recovery and all potential recovery claims under insurance policies, loss protection arrangements, or claims against the Securities Investor Protection Corporation (SIPC).

See the instructions to Form 4684 for further details on claiming Ponzi scheme theft losses, including the safe-harbor relief.

Fraudulent sales offers. Worthless stock purchases made on the representation of false and fraudulent sales offers are deductible as theft losses in the year there is no reasonable prospect of recovery. However, the illegal sale of unregistered stock does not support a theft loss deduction. In addition, buying stock from a bad tip and losing money is not deductible.

Kidnapping ransom. Payment of ransom to a kidnapper is generally a deductible theft loss. However, the expense of trying to find an abducted child is not a theft loss.

Fortune tellers. The Tax Court allowed a theft loss deduction in New York, where fortune telling is by law a theft-related offense. The law assumes that telling fortunes or promising to control occult forces is a form of fraud. An exception is made for fortune telling at shows for the purpose of entertaining or amusement. That a person voluntarily asks for advice does not bar the deduction. According to the court, a gullible person who gives money to fortune tellers in the belief that he or she will be helped is still defrauded or swindled. Theft is a broad term and includes theft by swindling, false pretenses, and any other form of guile. In this case, the taxpayer, who was suffering from depression, had become attached to two fortune tellers whom he claimed took him for over $19,000.

Riot losses. Losses caused by fire, theft, and vandalism occurring during riots and civil disorders are deductible. To support your claim of a riot loss, keep evidence of the damage suffered and the cost of repairs. Photographs taken prior to repairs or replacement, lists of damaged or missing property, and police reports would help to establish and uphold your loss deduction.

Foreign government confiscations. The IRS and courts have disallowed casualty deductions for confiscations of personal property by foreign governments. This includes deposits in foreign banks; the loss is limited to a short-term capital loss.

Swindled by friend. A theft loss deduction was allowed to a widow who gave her old beau over $2 million to acquire stock for her in his bank. He used the money to pay his personal debts. The IRS barred the theft loss, arguing that the widow failed to prove fraud. A district court disagreed and allowed the deduction. Under Oklahoma state law, a person who makes a promise in return for cash has committed larceny by fraud if he never intended to return the funds or make good on the promise. Here, that the widow gave him the money voluntarily does not bar a theft loss deduction. She parted with the funds based upon his false claim that he would invest the money for her when he had no intention of doing so, but planned all along to pay off his debts with the funds.

Caution

Stock Devaluation Due to Corporate Misconduct

The IRS has warned shareholders who suffer a loss in the value of their stock due to the fraud, misappropriation, or other misconduct of corporate officers or directors that their loss is not a deductible theft loss. A decline in stock value is not a theft if the stock was purchased on the open market rather than directly from the corporate officials accused of misconduct. The loss is deductible only as a capital loss when the stock is sold or becomes worthless *(5.4)*.

The Tax Court took the same approach in holding that a taxpayer who bought stock on the open market could not support a theft loss under California law because there was no "privity" relationship between the taxpayer and the corporate officers accused of wrongdoing, and so it could not be shown that there was intent to obtain the taxpayer's property.

18.10 Proving a Theft Loss

Get statements from witnesses who saw the theft or police records documenting a break-in to your house or car. A newspaper account of the crime might also help.

When you suspect a theft, make a report to the police. Even though your reporting does not prove that a theft was committed, it may be inferred from your failure to report that you were not sure that your property was stolen. But a theft loss was allowed where the loss of a ring was not reported to the police or an attempt made to demand its return from the suspect, a domestic employee. The owner feared being charged with false arrest.

18.11 Nondeductible Losses

Review the rules *(18.1, 18.9)* to make sure you have a deductible casualty or theft. Certain losses, though "casualties" for you, may not be deducted if they are not due to theft, fire, or from some other sudden natural phenomenon. The following have been held to be nondeductible losses:

- Termite damage *(18.1)*
- Carpet beetle damage
- Dry rot damage
- Damages for personal injuries or property damage to others caused by your negligence
- Legal expenses in defending a suit for your negligent operation of your personal automobile
- Legal expenses to recover personal property wrongfully seized by the police
- Expenses of moving to and rental of temporary quarters
- Loss of personal property while in storage or in transit
- Loss of passenger's luggage put aboard a ship. The passenger missed the boat and the luggage could not be traced.
- Accidental loss of a ring from your finger
- Injuries resulting from tripping over a wire
- Loss by husband of joint property taken by his wife when she left him
- Loss of a valuable dog (or family pet) that strayed and was not found

- Steady weakening of a building due to normal wind and weather conditions
- Damage to a crop caused by plant diseases, insects, or fungi
- Damage to property from drought in an area where a dry spell is normal and usual
- Damage to property caused by excavations on adjoining property
- Damage from rust or corroding of understructure of house
- Moth damage
- Dry well
- Losses occasioned by water pockets, erosion, inundation at still water levels, and other natural phenomena (there was no sudden destruction.)
- Death of a saddle horse after eating a silk hat
- A watch or spectacles dropped on the ground
- Sudden drop in the value of securities
- Loss of contingent interest in property due to the unexpected death of a child
- Improper police seizure of private liquor stock
- Chinaware broken by a family pet
- Temporary fluctuation of property value
- Damage to property from local government construction project
- Fire purposely set by owner
- Engine damage due to failure to use antifreeze

Note: Some of the above items may be allowed as business expenses.

Law Alert

Floors for 2010 Personal-Use Property Losses

For 2009, the floor for each casualty or theft loss of personal-use property was $500 and Congress was expected to extend the $500 floor to 2010, but had not yet done so when this book went to press. If Congress does not act, the floor for 2010 will revert back to $100, which was the floor before 2009. Congress also had not yet determined whether 2010 losses on personal-use property that are attributable to federally declared disasters are exempt from the 10% of adjusted gross income floor. *See* the *e-Supplement at jklasser.com* for an update.

18.12 Floors for Personal-Use Property Losses

Casualty and theft losses attributable to personal-use property are subject to "floors" that will reduce, and in some cases eliminate, your deduction on Form 4684. After the amount of your casualty or theft loss is figured (Steps 1–4 at *18.13*), a dollar floor reduces the loss. For 2009, the dollar floor was raised from $100 to $500 and Congress was expected to extend the $500 floor to 2010 personal-use losses, but had not yet done so when this book went to press. If the extension legislation is not enacted, the floor will drop to $100, the more favorable pre-2009 floor. In addition, after the dollar floor ($500 or $100 as just discussed) reduces each separate casualty or theft loss, net personal casualty and theft losses for the year are further reduced by 10% of your adjusted gross income. However, for 2008 and 2009, losses attributable to federally declared disasters were exempt from the 10% floor and Congress was expected to extend the disaster loss exemption to 2010 losses, but had not yet done so when this book went to press. *See* the *e-Supplement at jklasser.com* for an update on legislation affecting the dollar floor and net disaster losses for 2010.

Dollar floor for each loss. Each casualty or theft loss of property used for personal purposes is reduced by a specific amount, the dollar floor. If the loss does not exceed the floor, no amount is deductible. As discussed above, it is expected that the $500 floor that applied for 2009 will be extended to 2010 and the following paragraphs assume that the applicable floor for 2010 will be $500 rather than the $100 floor that would apply without the extension. However, *see* the *e-Supplement* at *jklasser.com* for developments in Congress.

Assuming the floor for 2010 is $500, each casualty and theft loss of property used for personal purposes will be reduced by $500; *see* Step 5 at *18.13*.

The $500 floor does not apply to losses of business property or property held for the production of income such as securities. If property used both in business and personal activities is damaged, the $500 offset applies only to the loss allocated to personal use.

For each casualty or theft in 2010, a separate $500 reduction applies. For example, if you are involved in five different casualties during the year, there will be a $500 offset applied to each of the five losses. But when two or more items of property are destroyed in one event, only one $500 offset is applied to the total loss. For example, a storm damages your residence and also your car parked in the driveway. You figure the loss on the residence and car separately on Form 4684, but only one $500 offset applies to the total loss.

The $500 floor is applied after taking into account insurance proceeds received and insurance you expect to receive in a later year.

The $500 floor applies separately to the loss of each individual whose property has been damaged by a single casualty, even where the damaged property is owned by two or more individuals. The only exception is for a married couple filing jointly who apply only one $500 floor to their losses from a single casualty.

EXAMPLES

1. Two sisters own and occupy a house that in 2010 is damaged in a storm. Each sister applies the $500 floor to figure her separate deduction.
2. Your house is partially damaged in 2009 by a fire that also damages the personal property of a houseguest. You are subject to one $500 floor and the houseguest is subject to a separate $500 floor.

10% AGI floor. The 10% adjusted gross income (AGI) floor reduces your deduction for net casualty and theft losses realized during the year on personal-use property. If you have gains as well as losses from casualties and thefts on personal-use property, and the total loss (after the $500 floor reduces each casualty/theft loss) exceeds the total gain, the net loss is generally reduced by 10% of your AGI. The Example below illustrates the application of the $500 floor to each separate casualty event and the 10% AGI floor to the total losses.

Note: It is likely that Congress will exempt losses attributable to federally declared disasters from the 10% floor, thereby extending to 2010 the rules applicable to 2008 and 2009 disaster losses. However, Congress had not yet enacted the extension legislation when this book went to press. *See* the *e-Supplement at jklasser.com* for an update.

EXAMPLE

In January 2010, you have an uninsured jewelry theft loss of $1,400, and in July 2010 uninsured damage of $5,400 to your personal car. Your adjusted gross income is $45,000. If you itemize deductions for 2010, you may claim a deductible loss on Form 4684. Assuming that the dollar floor for each 2010 casualty is $500 (*see* the discussion above), your deductible loss is $1,300, figured as follows:

Theft loss	$1,400	
Less $500 floor	500	$ 900
Car damage	5,400	
Less $500 floor	500	4,900
Total loss		5,800
Less 10% of $45,000		4,500
Deductible loss		$1,300

18.13 Figuring Your Loss on Form 4684

Form 4684 is used to report casualties or thefts of personal-use property, business property, or income-producing property. The deductible loss for 2010 is usually the difference between the fair market value of the property before and after the casualty or theft *less* (1) reimbursements received for the loss and (2) if the property was used for personal purposes, by the dollar floor for 2010, which is expected to be $500 *(18.12)*. However, the loss may not exceed your adjusted basis *(5.20)* for the property, which for many items will be your cost. If your adjusted basis is less than the loss in value, your deduction is limited to basis, less reimbursements and the $500 floor for personal-use assets. After figuring all allowable casualty and theft losses and gains for personal-use property, the net loss (losses in excess of gains if any) is deductible only to the extent it exceeds the 10% adjusted gross income floor *(18.12)*.

Caution—expected legislation: As discussed in *18.12*, Congress is expected to pass legislation that will extend both the $500 dollar floor and the exemption of net disaster losses from the 10% AGI floor to 2010 losses of personal-use property, and we have assumed in *18.12* and in this section *(18.13)* that such legislation will be enacted. If the legislation is not enacted, the dollar floor for 2010 will be reduced to $100, but disaster losses will be subject to the 10% AGI floor. Check the *e-Supplement at jklasser.com* for an update on the legislation.

Steps for calculating your deductible loss for 2010. The following five steps reflect the procedure on Form 4684 for computing a casualty or theft loss. If your loss is to business inventory, you do not have to use Form 4684, but may take the loss into account when figuring the cost of goods sold; *see* "Inventory losses" later in this section.

Filing Instruction

Reporting on Form 4684

If you are claiming a loss for personal-use property, use Section A on page 1 of Form 4684. If you suffered more than one casualty or theft during the year, use a separate Form 4684 for each one. For 2010, the total deductible casualty or theft loss from Section A of Form 4684 is then entered on Line 20, Schedule A of Form 1040.

To figure your deductible loss, follow these five steps:

Step 1. Compute the loss in fair market value of the property. This is the difference between the fair market value immediately before and immediately after the casualty. You do not have to compute the loss in fair market value for business or income-producing property (such as a rental property) that has been *completely* destroyed or stolen; go to Step 2.

You will need written appraisals to support your claim for loss of value. You may *not* claim sentimental or aesthetic values or a fluctuation in property values caused by a casualty; you must deal with cost or market values of what has been lost. If the value of your property has been lowered because of damage to a nearby area, you do not have a deductible loss since your own property has not been damaged. No deduction may be claimed for estimated decline in value based on buyer resistance in an area subject to landslides.

For household items, the Tax Court has allowed losses based on cost less depreciation, rather than on the decrease in fair market value.

Step 2. Compute your adjusted basis *(5.20)* for the property. This is usually the cost of the property plus the cost of improvements, less previous casualty loss deductions and depreciation if the property is used in business or for income-producing purposes. Unadjusted basis of property acquired other than by purchase is explained at *5.16*.

Step 3. Take the lower amount of Step 1 or 2. For business or income-producing property that was stolen or completely destroyed, reduce adjusted basis from Step 2 by any salvage value.

Step 4 Reduce the loss in Step 3 by the insurance proceeds or other compensation for the loss (18.16). This is your deductible loss for business or income-producing property. If the loss was on property used for personal purposes, apply the reductions in Step 5.

If the insurance or other compensation exceeds your adjusted basis for the property, you have a taxable gain rather than a deductible loss. You may be able to defer the gain by buying replacement property *(18.19)*.

Step 5. If you had only one 2010 casualty or theft loss and the property was used for personal purposes, the loss from Step 4 must be reduced by the dollar floor and any balance is deductible only to the extent it exceeds 10% of your adjusted gross income. If you have more than one personal casualty or theft loss, you must reduce each loss by the dollar floor and the net loss (total losses exceeding total gains if there any gains) is deductible only to the extent it exceeds the 10% AGI floor.

As noted above, the dollar floor for a personal-use loss will be $500 if Congress, as expected, passes legislation extending the $500 floor to 2010 losses but the floor will be $100 if the legislation is not passed. In addition, if the legislation is enacted, it is likely to exempt 2010 losses attributable to federally declared disasters from the 10% AGI floor. *See* the *e-Supplement at jklasser.com* for an update on the status of the legislation.

Filing Tip

Appraisals for Disaster Relief

The IRS may accept an appraisal that is used to obtain federal loans or loan guarantees following a federally declared disaster as proof of the amount of a casualty loss.

Caution

Incidental Expenses

Expenses that are incidental to a casualty or theft, such as medical treatment for personal injury, temporary housing, fuel, moving, or rentals for temporary living quarters, are not deductible as casualty losses.

EXAMPLES

1. Your home, which cost $76,000 in 1979, was damaged by a fire in 2010. The value of the house before the fire was $217,500, but afterwards $202,500. Furniture that cost $5,000 in 1990 and was valued at $2,500 before the fire was totally destroyed. The insurance company reimbursed you $10,000 for your house damage and $1,000 for your furnishings. This was the only casualty for the year. Your adjusted gross income is $48,000. You figure your loss for the furniture separately from the loss on the house but apply only one dollar floor because the damage was from a single casualty. The dollar floor in Step 5 is assumed to be $500, although this is dependent on Congressional legislation as discussed above.

1. Decrease in home's fair market value:

Value of house before fire	$217,500
Value of house after fire	202,500
Decrease in value	$15,000

2. Adjusted basis:	$76,000
3. Loss sustained (lower of 1 or 2)	$15,000
Less: Insurance	10,000
Loss on house	$5,000
4. Loss on furnishings (decreased value)*	$2,500
Less: Insurance	1,000
Loss on furnishings	$1,500
5. Total loss ($5,000 and $1,500)	$6,500
Less: $500 floor	500
Casualty loss (subject to 10% floor)	$6,000
6. 10% AGI floor (10% of $48,000 AGI)	$4,800
7. Casualty loss ($6,000 – $4,800)	$1,200

**The loss for the furnishings on Line 4 is $2,500, the decrease in fair market value, as this is lower than the $5,000 basis.*

2. Depreciable business property with a fair market value of $1,500 and an adjusted basis of $2,000 is totally destroyed. Because property used in your business was totally destroyed (see Step 3 *(18.13)*), your loss is measured by your adjusted basis of $2,000, which is larger than the $1,500 loss in fair market value. Salvage value, if any, reduces your deduction, but you disregard the $500 floor applied to casualty losses on personal property. If the property was used for personal purposes, the loss would have been limited to the $1,500 loss in market value less $500, leaving a loss of $1,000 subject to the 10% adjusted gross income floor.

Business losses. Losses from business property are generally netted against gains from casualties or thefts on Form 4684 and the net gain or loss is entered on Form 4797. Follow the instructions to Form 4684.

Inventory losses. A casualty or theft loss of inventory is automatically reflected on Schedule C in the cost of goods sold, which includes the lost items as part of your opening inventory. Any insurance or other reimbursement received for the loss must be included as sales income.

You may separately claim the inventory loss as a casualty or theft loss on Form 4684 instead of automatically claiming it as part of the cost of goods sold. If you do this, you must eliminate the items from inventory by lowering either opening inventory or purchases when figuring the cost of goods sold.

Cost less depreciation method for household items. The Tax Court has allowed casualty loss deductions based on cost less depreciation, rather than on the difference in fair market value immediately before and after the casualty. *See* the following Example.

Filing Tip

Business or Income-Producing Property

If you are claiming a loss for property used in your business or income-producing activity, use Section B on page 2 of Form 4684. For 2010, losses from income-producing property are entered on Line 28 of Schedule A as "other miscellaneous deductions" and are not subject to the 2% adjusted gross income floor.

EXAMPLE

Basing a deduction on the difference between the value of furnishings immediately before and immediately after a casualty may limit your deduction to the going price for secondhand furnishings. A homeowner whose furniture was destroyed by fire claimed that the fair market value immediately before the fire should be original cost less depreciation. He based his figures on an inventory prepared by certified public adjusters describing each item, its cost and age. The deduction figured this way came to approximately $27,500 ($55,000 cost, less $13,000 depreciation, a $14,400 insurance recovery, and the then-$100 floor).

The IRS estimated that the furniture was worth $15,304 before the fire and limited the deduction to $804 after accounting for the insurance and the then-$100 floor. The Tax Court disagreed. The householder's method of valuing his furniture is consistent with methods used by insurance adjusters who have an interest in keeping values low. He is not limited to the amount his property would bring if "hawked off by a secondhand dealer or at a forced sale." However, in another case, the court refused to allow the cost less depreciation formula where the homeowner's inventory list was based on memory.

18.14 Personal and Business Use of Property

For property held partly for personal use and partly for business or income-producing purposes, a casualty or theft loss deduction is computed as if two separate pieces of property were damaged, destroyed, or stolen. Follow the steps for figuring the allowable loss *(18.13)*, but apply the $500 and 10% of adjusted gross income floors only to the personal part of the loss.

EXAMPLE

A building with two apartments, one used by the owner as his home and the other rented to a tenant, is damaged by a fire. The fair market value of the building before the fire was $169,000 and it was $136,000 after the fire, which damaged both apartments equally. Cost basis of the building was $120,000. Depreciation taken before the fire was $14,000. The insurance company paid $20,000. The owner has adjusted gross income of $40,000. This is his only loss this year. He has a business casualty loss of $6,500 and a deductible personal casualty loss of $2,000 figured as follows:

	Business	***Personal***
1. Decrease in value of building:		
Value before fire ($169,000)	$84,500	$84,500
Value after fire ($136,000)	(68,000)	(68,000)
Decrease in value	$16,500	$16,500
2. Adjusted basis of building:	$60,000	$60,000
Less: Depreciation	(14,000)	
Adjusted basis	$46,000	$60,000
3. Loss sustained (lower of 1 or 2)	$16,500	$16,500
Less: Insurance (total $20,000)	($10,000)	($10,000)
4. Loss	$6,500	$6,500
Less: $500 floor and 10% of adjusted gross income	–	(4,500)
Deductible casualty loss	$6,500	$2,000

18.15 Repairs May Be a "Measure of Loss"

The cost of repairs may be treated as evidence of the loss of value (Step 1 *(18.13)*), if the amount is not excessive and the repairs do nothing more than restore the property to its condition before the casualty. An estimate for repairs will not suffice; only actual repairs may be used as a measure of loss. However, where you measure your loss by comparing appraisals of value for before and after the casualty, repairs may be considered in arriving at a post-casualty value even though no actual repairs are made.

Planning Reminder

Keep Records of Deductible Losses

If your property is damaged, you must reduce the basis of the damaged property by the casualty loss deduction and compensation received for the loss *(5.20)*. When you later sell the property, gain or loss is the difference between the selling price and the reduced basis.

Deduction not limited to repairs. A casualty loss deduction is not limited to repair expenses where the decline in market value is greater, according to a federal appeals court; *see* the following Example.

EXAMPLE

Connor claimed that the market value of his house dropped $93,000 after it was damaged by fire. His $52,000 cash outlay in repairing the house was reimbursed by insurance. He claimed a casualty loss of approximately $40,000, the uncompensated drop in market value. The IRS barred the deduction. The house was restored to pre-casualty condition. The cost of the repairs is a realistic measure of the loss, and, as the expense was fully compensated by insurance, Connor suffered no loss. A federal appeals court disagreed. The house dropped $70,000 in market value, of which $20,000 was uncompensated by insurance. The deduction is measured by the uncompensated difference in value before and after the casualty. It is not limited to the cost of repairs, even where the repair expense is less than the difference in fair market values. Had the repairs cost more than this difference, the IRS would not have allowed a larger deduction.

18.16 Insurance Reimbursements

You reduce the amount of your loss *(18.13)* by insurance proceeds, voluntary payments received from your employer for damage to your property, and cash or property received from the Red Cross. Also reduce your loss by reimbursements you expect to receive in a later year *(18.2)*. However, cash gifts from friends and relatives to help defray the cost of repairs do not reduce the loss where there are no conditions on the use of the gift. Also, gifts of food, clothing, medical supplies, and other forms of subsistence do not reduce the loss deduction nor are they taxable income.

Cancellation of part of a disaster loan under the Disaster Relief Act is treated as a partial reimbursement of the loss and reduces the amount of the loss. Payments from an urban renewal agency to acquire your damaged property under the Federal Relocation Act of 1970 are considered reimbursements reducing the loss.

Insurance payments for the cost of added living expenses because of damage to a home do not reduce a casualty loss. The payments are treated as separate and apart from payments for property damage. Payments for excess living costs are generally not taxable *(18.17)*.

Caution

Failure To Make an Insurance Claim

If you are insured for your full loss and do not file a claim because you do not want to risk cancellation of liability coverage, you may not claim a deduction. If you do not file an insurance claim but your loss exceeds the coverage, the noncovered loss may be deductible. For example, if you have a $2,500 deductible on your personal automobile insurance policy, a loss of up to $2,500 would be reduced by the $500 floor and the balance would be deductible only to the extent the 10% of adjusted gross income floor was exceeded; *see* Step 5 *(18.13)*.

Passive activity property loss reimbursements. A reimbursement of a casualty or theft loss deduction is not considered passive activity income if the original loss was not treated as a passive deduction *(10.1)*. The reimbursement may be taxed *(11.6)*.

Realizing a gain from insurance. If you receive insurance proceeds in excess of your adjusted basis for the property, you generally realize a gain, which you may be able to defer by buying replacement property *(18.19)*.

18.17 Excess Living Costs Paid by Insurance Are Not Taxable

Your insurance contract may reimburse you for excess living costs when a casualty or a threat of casualty forces you to vacate your house. The payment is tax free if these tests are met:

1. Your principal residence is damaged or destroyed by fire, storm, or other casualty or you are denied use of it by a governmental order because of the occurrence or threat of the casualty.
2. You are paid under an insurance contract for living expenses resulting from the loss of occupancy or use of the residence.

Whether you have a taxable or tax-free reimbursement is figured at the end of the period you were unable to use your residence. Thus, if the dislocation covers more than one taxable year, the taxable income, if any, will be reported in the taxable year in which the dislocation ended.

The tax-free amount includes only excess living costs paid by the insurance company. The excess is the difference between (1) the actual living expenses incurred during the time you could not use or occupy your house and (2) the normal living expenses that you would have incurred for yourself and members of your household during the period. Living expenses during the period may include the cost of renting suitable housing and extraordinary expenses for transportation, food, utilities, and miscellaneous services. The expenses must be incurred for items and services (such as laundry) needed to maintain your standard of living that you enjoyed before the loss and must be covered by the policy.

Where a lump-sum settlement does not identify the amount covering living expenses, an allocation is required to determine the tax-free portion. In the case of uncontested claims, the tax-free portion is that part of the settlement that bears the same ratio to total recovery as increased living expense bears to total loss and expense. If your claim is contested, you must show the amount reasonably allocable to increased living expenses consistent with the terms of the insurance contract, but not in excess of coverage limitations specified in the contract.

The exclusion from income does not cover insurance reimbursements for loss of rental income or for loss of or damage to real or personal property; such reimbursements for property damage reduce your casualty loss *(18.16)*.

If your home is used for both residential and business purposes, the exclusion does not apply to insurance proceeds and expenses attributable to the nonresidential portion of the house. There is no exclusion for insurance recovered for expenses resulting from governmental condemnation or order unrelated to a casualty or threat of casualty.

The insurance reimbursement may cover part of your normal living expenses as well as the excess expenses due to the casualty. The part covering normal expenses is income; it does not reduce your casualty loss.

EXAMPLES

1. On March 1, your home was damaged by fire. While it was being repaired, you and your spouse lived at a motel and ate meals at restaurants. Costs are $1,200 at the motel, $1,000 for meals, and $75 for laundry services. You make the required March payment of $790 on your home mortgage. Your customary $40 commuting expense is $20 less for the month because the motel is closer to your work. Your usual commuting expense is therefore treated as not being incurred to the extent of the $20 decrease. Furthermore, you do not incur your customary $700 food expense for meals at home, $75 for utilities, and $60 for laundry at home. Your insurance company pays you $1,700 for expenses. The tax-free exclusion for insurance payments is limited to $1,420, computed in the third column below. On Line 21 of Form 1040 ("Other income") you must report as income $280 ($1,700 – $1,420).

	Expenses from casualty	*Expenses not incurred*	*Increase (Decrease)*
Housing	$1,200		$1,200
Utilities		$75	(75)
Meals	1,000	700	300
Transportation		20	(20)
Laundry	75	60	15
Total	$2,275	$855	$1,420

2. Same facts as in Example 1 except that you rented the residence for $400 per month and the risk of loss was to the landlord. You did not pay the March rent. The excludable amount is $1,020 ($1,420 less $400 normal rent not incurred). You would have to report as income the excess of the insurance received over the $1,020 exclusion.

18.18 Do Your Casualty or Theft Losses Exceed Your Income?

If your 2010 casualty or theft losses exceed your income, you pay no tax in 2010. Under the net operating loss (NOL) rules *(40.18)*, you may carry back the excess casualty or theft loss three years and forward 20 years. Thus, an excess casualty or theft loss for 2010 can be carried back three years to 2007 and you can claim a refund for that year. Any balance of the 2010 loss (not applied to 2007) can be carried back to 2008 and 2009 and then forward 20 years to 2011 through 2030.

The $500 or $100 floor *(18.12)* and the 10% of adjusted gross income floor *(18.12)* for personal casualty or theft losses apply only in the year of the loss; you do not again reduce your loss in the carryback or carryforward years.

18.19 Defer Gain by Replacing Property

If your property is destroyed, damaged, stolen, or seized or condemned by a government authority, this is considered to be an *involuntary conversion* for tax purposes. If upon an involuntary conversion you receive insurance or other compensation that exceeds the adjusted basis of the property, you realize a gain that is taxable unless you may defer gain *(18.20–18.24)* or, in the case of a principal residence, you may exclude gain under the rules in *Chapter 29*.

You may elect to postpone tax on the full gain provided you invest the proceeds in replacement property the cost of which is equal to or exceeds the net proceeds from the conversion. Buying a replacement from a related party generally qualifies only if your gains from involuntary conversions are $100,000 or less *(18.23)*. Gain realized on a destroyed or condemned principal residence that exceeds the allowable exclusion under the rules in *Chapter 29* may be postponed by reinvesting at least the conversion proceeds minus the excluded gain *(18.20–18.24)*. The replacement period for

Filing Tip

Involuntary Conversion of Personal Residence

Gain on the conversion of a principal residence may escape tax under the rules discussed in *Chapter 29*. If not, tax may be deferred under the involuntary conversion replacement rules.

personal-use property is two years; for business and investment property it is two or three years depending on the type of involuntary conversion; for a residence and its contents involuntarily converted due to a federally declared disaster *(18.3)* it is four years. The replacement period is extended from four years to five years if the involuntarily converted property was located in the Hurricane Katrina disaster area, Kansas disaster area, or Midwestern disaster area, provided that substantially all of the use of the replacement property is in the respective disaster area. *See 18.22* for further replacement period details.

Basis in replacement property. Your basis in the replacement property is its replacement cost, minus any postponed gain. If you find that you cannot buy a replacement by the end of the period, ask the IRS for an extension of time *(18.22)*.

18.20 Involuntary Conversions Qualifying for Tax Deferral

For purposes of an election to defer tax on gains, "involuntary conversion" is more broadly defined than "casualty loss." You have an involuntary conversion when your property is:

Damaged or destroyed by some outside force.

Stolen, seized, requisitioned, or condemned by a governmental authority. If you voluntarily sell land made useless to you by the condemnation of your adjacent land, the sale may also qualify as a conversion. Condemnation of property as unfit for human habitation does not qualify. Condemnation, as used by the tax law, refers to the taking of private property for public use, not to the condemnation of property for noncompliance with housing and health regulations. Similarly, a tax sale to pay delinquent taxes is not an involuntary conversion.

Sold under a threat of seizure, condemnation, or requisition. The threat must be made by an authority qualified to take property for public use. A sale following a threat of condemnation made by a government employee is a conversion if you reasonably believe he or she speaks with authority and could and would carry out the threat to have your property condemned. If you learn of the plan of an imminent condemnation from a newspaper or other news media, the IRS requires you to confirm the report from a government official before you act on the news.

Farmers. Farmers also have involuntary conversions when:

Land is sold within an irrigation project to meet federal acreage limitations ;

Cattle are destroyed by disease or sold because of disease; *or*

Draft, breeding, or dairy livestock is sold because of drought. The election to treat the sale as a conversion is limited to livestock sold over the number that would have been sold but for the drought.

In some cases, livestock may be replaced with other farm property where there has been soil or other environmental contamination.

Should you elect to postpone gain? An election gives an immediate advantage: tax on gain is postponed and the funds that would have been spent to pay the tax may be used for other investments.

However, as a condition of deferring tax, the basis of the replacement property is generally fixed at the same adjusted basis as the converted property. If your reinvestment exceeds the insurance proceeds, the excess increases the basis of the replacement property. As long as the value of the replacement property does not decline, tax on the original gain is finally incurred when the property is sold.

If your home was destroyed in a federally declared disaster area, and you have a gain that is not excludable under the home exclusion rules (Chapter 29), the gain may be excludable or deferrable under the special rules discussed in *18.3* under the heading "Insurance Proceeds for Damaged or Destroyed Residence."

EXAMPLE

Assume a rental building is destroyed by fire and a proper replacement is made. Assume that gain on the receipt of the insurance proceeds is taxable as capital gain. An election is generally not advisable if you have capital losses to offset the gain. However, even if you have no capital losses, you may still decide not to make the election and pay tax in order to fix, for purposes of depreciation, the basis of the new prop-

Filing Tip

Sale of Property Under Hazard Mitigation Program

A sale or other transfer of vulnerable property to federal, state, or local authorities (or Indian tribal governments) under a hazard mitigation program is treated as an involuntary conversion, thereby allowing a gain to be deferred if a qualifying replacement *(18.19)* is made.

erty at its purchase price, if the future depreciation deductions will offset income taxable at a higher rate than the current tax. If there is little or no difference between the two rates so that a net after-tax benefit from the depreciation would not arise, an election might be made solely to postpone the payment of tax.

Planning Reminder

Basis Reduction

Consider whether postponement of gain at the expense of a reduced basis for property is advisable, compared to the tax consequences of reporting the gain in the year it is realized.

18.21 How To Elect To Defer Tax

To defer tax on your gain, do not report the gain as income for the year it is realized. Attach to your return a statement giving details of the transaction, including computation of the gain and your intention to buy a replacement if you have not yet done so. *See* the discussion of replacement periods and IRS notification requirements *(18.22)*.

If your property is condemned and you are given similar property, no election is necessary. Postponement of tax on the gain is required. For example, the city condemns a store building and gives you another store building the value of which exceeds the cost basis of the old one; gain is not taxed.

Partnerships. The election to defer gain must be made at the partnership level. Individual partners may not make separate elections unless the partnership has terminated, with all partnership affairs wound up. Dissolution under state law is not a termination for tax purposes.

18.22 Time Period for Buying Replacement Property

To defer tax, you generally must buy property similar or related in use *(18.23)* to the converted property within a fixed time period. The replacement period is either two, three, four years or five:

1. A two-year replacement period applies for destroyed, damaged, or stolen property, whether used for business, investment, or personal purposes, but there is a four-year period for principal residences in federally declared disaster areas *(18.3)*. The two-year period for damaged, destroyed, and stolen property *starts* on the date the property was destroyed, damaged, or stolen, and *ends* two years after the end of the first year in which any part of your gain is realized. A two-year period also applies to a condemned residence.
2. A three-year replacement period applies for condemned business or investment real estate, excluding inventory. However, the two-year and not the three-year period applies if the condemned business or investment real estate is replaced by your acquiring control of a corporation that owns the replacement property.
3. A four-year replacement period applies for a principal residence or its contents involuntarily converted as a result of a federally declared disaster *(18.3)*. The four-year replacement period *starts* on the date the residence is involuntarily converted and *ends* four years after the end of the first taxable year in which any part of the gain is realized.
4. A five-year replacement period applies for property damaged or destroyed by Hurricane Katrina or in the 2007 Kansas disaster area or the 2008 Midwestern disaster area, but only if substantially all of the use of the replacement property is in the applicable disaster area. The five-year period *ends* five years after the end of the first taxable year in which any part of your gain is realized.

Planning Reminder

Extension of Time To Replace

Within the time limits, you must buy replacement property rather than merely contracting to do so. If you cannot replace property within the time required, ask your local IRS area director for additional time. Apply for an extension before the end of the period. If you apply for an extension within a reasonable time after the statutory period has run out, you must have a reasonable cause for the delay in asking for the extension.

Replacing condemned property. For condemnations, the replacement period starts on the earlier of (1) the date you receive notification of the condemnation threat or (2) the date you dispose of the condemned property. Depending on the replacement period (*see* above), the period ends two, three, four, or five years after the end of the first year in which any part of the gain on the condemnation is realized. You may make a replacement after a threat of condemnation. If you buy property before the actual threat, it will not qualify as a replacement even though you still own it at the time of the actual condemnation.

EXAMPLES

1. On January 12, 2010, a parcel of investment real estate is condemned; the parcel cost $15,000. On March 16, 2010, you received a check for $23,500 from the state. You may defer the tax on the gain of $8,500 if you invest at least $23,500 in other real estate not later than December 31, 2013, the end of the three-year replacement period.

2. Business property was contaminated by dangerous chemicals, and after the Environmental Protection Agency ordered businesses and residents to relocate, the property was sold to the local government under a threat of condemnation. The owner was paid the full pre-contamination fair market value for the property. The owner wanted to defer gain under the three-year replacement rule for condemnations. However, the IRS said that part of the gain was deferrable under the two-year rule and part under the three-year rule. There were two conversions: (1) the contamination, subject to the two-year replacement rule; and (2) the later condemnation, subject to the three-year rule.

   To determine the amount eligible for deferral for each period, an allocation must be made between the proceeds allocable to the destruction of the property and the proceeds allocable to the condemnation.

   According to the IRS, the burden for making the allocation between the two conversions rests with the owner. The government's payments are allocable to the condemnation and, therefore, eligible for the three-year replacement rule, only to the extent of the post-contamination value. Practically speaking, it may be advisable to make the replacement within the two-year period, as it may be difficult to show the contaminated land had any value after the contamination.

Advance payment of award. Gain is realized in the year compensation for the converted property exceeds the basis of the converted property. An advance payment of an award that exceeds the adjusted basis of the property starts the running of the replacement period.

An award is treated as received in the year that it is made available to you without restrictions, even if you contest the amount.

Replacement by an estate. A person whose property was involuntarily converted may die before he or she makes a replacement. According to the IRS, his or her estate may not reinvest the proceeds within the allowed time and postpone tax on the gain. The Tax Court rejects the IRS position and has allowed tax deferral where the replacement was made by the deceased owner's estate. However, the Tax Court agreed with the IRS that a surviving spouse's investment in land did not defer tax on gain realized by her deceased husband on an involuntary conversion of his land. She had received his property as survivor of joint tenancy and could not, in making the investment, be considered as acting for his estate.

Giving IRS notice of replacement. If you have not bought replacement property by the time you file your return for the year of the involuntary conversion but you intend to do so, attach a statement to your return describing the conversion and the computation of gain, and state that you intend to make a timely replacement. Then, on the return for the year of replacement, attach a statement giving the details of your replacement property. This notice starts the running of the period of limitations for any tax on the gain. Failure to give notice keeps the period open. Similarly, a failure to give notice of an intention not to replace also keeps the period open. When you do not buy replacement property after making an election to postpone tax on the gain, file an amended return for the year in which gain was realized and pay the tax (if any) on the gain.

Assume you have a gain from an involuntary conversion and do not expect to reinvest the proceeds. You report the gain and pay the tax. In a later year, but within the prescribed time limits, you buy similar property. You may make an election to defer tax on the gain and file a claim for tax refund.

Caution

Nullifying Deferral Election on Amended Return

If you elect to defer tax on a gain, intending to buy replacement property, but you fail to make a replacement within the time limit, you must file an amended return for the year of the gain and pay the tax that you had elected to defer. You also must file an amended return and report the gain not eligible for deferral if you invest in property that does not qualify as a replacement, or which costs less than the amount realized from the involuntary conversion.

However, if you elect to defer and make a timely qualifying replacement, you may not change your mind and pay tax on the gain in order to obtain a higher basis *(18.20)* for the replacement property. The Tax Court has agreed with the IRS that the election to defer is irrevocable once a qualified replacement is made within the time limits. Similarly, once you report to the IRS *(18.22)* that a qualified replacement has been made, you may not substitute other replacement property, even if the replacement period has not yet expired.

18.23 Types of Qualifying Replacement Property

Although exact duplication is not required, the replacement generally must be *similar* or *related in service or use* to the property that was involuntarily converted in order to defer tax. Where *real property* held for productive use in a business or for investment is converted through a *condemnation* or threat of condemnation, the replacement test is more liberal. A replacement merely has to be of a *like kind* to the converted property.

Under the *like-kind* test for condemned real estate, a replacement with other real estate qualifies. Improved real property may be replaced by unimproved real property *(6.1)*. Foreign and U.S. real property are considered to be of like kind for purposes of this replacement test, even though under the like-kind exchange rules *(6.1)*, U.S. real estate and foreign real estate are not considered like-kind property.

Under the *related-service/use* test, the replacement of unimproved land for improved land does not qualify. A replacement generally must be closely related in function to the destroyed property. For example, a condemned personal residence must be replaced with another personal residence. The replacement of a house rented to a tenant with a house used as a personal residence does not qualify for tax deferral; the new house is not being used for the same purpose as the condemned one. This functional test, however, is not strictly applied to conversions of rental property. Here, the role of the owner toward the properties, rather than the functional use of the buildings, is reviewed. If an owner held both properties as investments and offered similar services and took similar business risks in both, the replacement may qualify.

You may own several parcels of property, one of which is condemned. You may want to use the condemnation award to make improvements on the other land such as drainage and grading. The IRS generally will not accept the improvements as a qualified replacement. However, an appeals court has rejected the IRS approach in one case.

If it is not feasible to reinvest the proceeds from the conversion of livestock because of soil contamination or other environmental contamination, then other property (including real property) used for farming purposes is treated as similar or related and qualifies as replacement property.

Caution

Buying Replacement From Relative

Buying a replacement from a relative or related business organization will not defer gain unless total gains from involuntary conversions for the year are $100,000 or less.

Deferral may be barred when buying a replacement from a relative. The gain deferral rules do not apply if you buy a replacement from a close relative or a related business organization unless the total gain you realized for the year on all involuntary conversions on which there are realized gains is $100,000 or less. In determining whether gains exceed $100,000, gains are not offset by losses. Affected related parties are the same as defined for loss transactions discussed in *5.6*.

Buying controlling interest in a corporation. The replacement test may be satisfied by purchasing a controlling interest (80%) in a corporation owning property that is similar or related in service to the converted property.

Business and investment property in a disaster area. The similar or related-use tests do not have to be met when replacing business or investment property damaged or destroyed in a federally declared disaster area. You may make a qualified replacement by buying any tangible property held for business use.

18.24 Cost of Replacement Property Determines Postponed Gain

To fully defer tax on the replacement of involuntarily converted property *(18.20)*, the cost of the replacement property must be equal to or exceed the net proceeds from the conversion. If replacement cost is no more than the adjusted basis of the converted property, you report the entire gain. If replacement cost is less than the amount realized on the conversion but more than the basis of the converted property, the difference between the amount realized and the cost of the replacement is reported as gain; you may elect to postpone tax on the balance of the gain. *See* Examples 1–3 below.

Condemnation award. The award received from a state authority may be reduced by expenses of getting the award such as legal, engineering, and appraisal fees. The treatment of special assessments and severance damages received when part of your property is condemned is explained below *(18.25)*. Payments made directly by the authority to your mortgagee may not be deducted from the gross award.

Do not include as part of the award interest paid on the award for delay in its payment; you report the interest as interest income. The IRS may treat as interest part of an award paid late, even though the award does not make any allocation for interest.

Relocation payments are not considered part of the condemnation award and are not treated as taxable income to the extent that they are spent for purposes of relocation; they increase basis of the newly acquired property.

Distinguish between insurance proceeds compensating you for loss of profits because of business interruption and those compensating you for the loss of property. Business interruption proceeds are fully taxed as ordinary income and may not be treated as proceeds of an involuntary conversion.

A single standard fire insurance policy may cover several assets. Assume a fire occurs, and in a settlement the proceeds are allocated to each destroyed item according to its fair market value before the fire. In comparing the allocated proceeds to the tax basis of each item, you find that on some items, you have realized a gain; that is, the proceeds exceed basis. On the other items, you have a loss; the proceeds are less than basis. According to the IRS, you may elect to defer tax on the gain items by buying replacement property. You do not treat the proceeds paid under the single policy as a unit, but as separate payments made for each covered item.

EXAMPLES

1. The cost basis of your four-family apartment house is $175,000. It is condemned to make way for a thruway. After expenses, the net award from the state is $200,000. Your gain is $25,000. If you buy a similar apartment house for $175,000 or less, you report the entire $25,000 gain.
2. Same facts as in Example 1, except that you buy an apartment house for $185,000. Of the gain of $25,000, you report $15,000 as taxable gain ($200,000 – $185,000). You may elect to postpone the tax on the balance of the gain, or $10,000. If you elect deferral, your basis for the new building is $175,000 ($185,000 – $10,000 postponed gain).
3. Same facts as in Example 1, but you buy an apartment house for $200,000 or more. You may elect to postpone tax on the entire gain because you have invested all of the award in replacement property.

18.25 Special Assessments and Severance Damages

When only part of a property parcel is *condemned* for a public improvement, the condemning authority may:

1. Levy a special assessment against the remaining property, claiming that it is benefitted by the improvement. The authority usually deducts the assessment from the condemnation award.
2. Grant an award for severance damages if the condemnation of part of your property causes a loss in value or damage to the remaining property that you keep.

Special assessments reduce the amount of the gross condemnation award. If they exceed the award, the excess is added to the basis of the property. An assessment levied after the award is made may not be deducted from the award.

EXAMPLE

Two acres of a 10-acre tract are condemned for a new highway. The adjusted basis of the land is $30,000, or $3,000 per acre. The condemnation award is $10,000; the special assessment against the remaining eight acres is $2,500. The net gain on the condemnation is $1,500:

Condemnation award		$10,000
Less:		
Basis of two condemned acres	$6,000	
Special assessment	2,500	8,500
Net gain		$1,500

When both the condemnation award and severance damages are received, the condemnation is treated as two separate involuntary conversions: (1) A conversion of the condemned land. Here, the condemnation award is applied against the basis of the condemned land to determine gain or loss on its conversion; and (2) a conversion of part of the remaining land in the sense that its utility has been reduced by condemnation, for which severance damages are paid.

Net severance damages reduce the basis of the retained property. Net severance damages are the total severance damages, reduced by expenses in obtaining the damages and by any special assessment withheld from the condemnation award. If the damages exceed basis, gain is realized.

Tax may be deferred on the gain through the purchase of replacement property under the "similar or related in service or use" test *(18.23)*, such as adjacent land or restoration of the property to its original condition.

Allocating the proceeds between the condemnation award and severance damages will either reduce the gain or increase the loss realized on the condemned land. The IRS will allow such a division only when the condemnation authority specifically identifies part of the award as severance damage in the contract or in an itemized statement or closing sheet. The Tax Court, however, has allowed an allocation in the absence of earmarking where the state considered severance damages, and the value of the condemned land was small in comparison to the damages suffered by the remaining property. To avoid a dispute with the IRS, make sure the authority makes this breakdown. Without such identification, the IRS will treat the entire proceeds as consideration for the condemned property.

Filing Instruction

Business and Income-Producing Property

Follow the instructions to Form 4684 for reporting gains or losses from casualties and thefts of property used in a business or held for the production of income.

18.26 Reporting Gains From Casualties

If an involuntary conversion was the result of a *theft or casualty*, you have to prepare Form 4684. To report net gains, Form 4684 will direct you to Form 1040, Schedule D, or Form 4797, depending on the type of property involved. Generally, use of Form 4797 reflects the netting requirements for involuntary conversions of business, rental, or royalty property under Section 1231 *(44.8)*.

If the conversion occurred because of a *condemnation*, you use Form 4797 for business or investment property and Schedule D for personal-use property.

Chapter 19

Deducting Job Costs and Other Miscellaneous Expenses

On Schedule A (Form 1040), you may be able to deduct a portion of miscellaneous expenses covering a wide and varied range of items, such as employee travel and entertainment expenses, work clothes expenses, union and employee professional dues, investment expenses, legal expenses, tax preparation expenses, and educational expenses. They share a significant limitation: the 2% of adjusted gross income (AGI) floor. If your expenses do not exceed this floor, you may not deduct them. If the expenses exceed the floor, only the excess is deductible on Schedule A *(19.1)*. However, the deduction (after the 2% floor) must be added back to income in determining if you are subject to AMT *(23.2)* and if you are, the benefit of the Schedule A deduction is effectively lost. Some miscellaneous expenses, such as gambling losses and impairment-related work expenses, are not subject to the 2% AGI floor.

In addition to the 2% AGI floor, employees who incur unreimbursed meal and entertainment costs face this further restriction: Only 50% of meal and entertainment costs are deductible.

Caution

AMT Disallowance

Even if you are able to deduct for regular tax purposes a portion of miscellaneous expenses because they exceed the 2% AGI floor, you will lose the benefit of that deduction if you are subject to alternative minimum tax (AMT). The deduction from Schedule A for miscellaneous expenses (after the 2% floor) must be added back to income in determining whether you are liable for AMT *(23.2)*.

19.1 2% AGI Floor Reduces Most Miscellaneous Expenses

A floor of 2% of adjusted gross income (AGI) applies to the total of most miscellaneous deductions that are claimed on Schedule A of Form 1040. AGI is the amount on Lines 37 and 38 of Form 1040. The purpose of the floor is to reduce or eliminate such deductions. Only expenses above the floor are deductible.

Miscellaneous expenses subject to the 2% AGI floor include:

- Unreimbursed travel, meals, and entertainment expenses of employees on trips away from home *(20.1* and *20.30)*
- Taxable reimbursements of job expenses or taxable expense allowances under non-accountable plans *(20.34)*
- Unreimbursed local transportation costs of visiting clients or customers *(19.8)*
- Union dues *(19.5)*
- Professional and business association dues *(19.5)*
- Work clothes expenses *(19.6)*
- Cost of looking for a new job *(19.7)*
- Job agency fees *(19.7)*
- Tax advice and preparation fees *(19.16)*
- Appraisal fees related to casualty losses and charitable property contributions *(19.16)*
- Investment costs, e.g, IRA custodial fees, safe-deposit rentals, and fees to investment counselors *(19.15)*
- Employee home office expenses *(19.13)*
- Legal fees for recovering taxable job-related or personal damages *(19.17)*
- Work-related education costs *(33.15)*
- Business bad debt on a loan made to your employer to protect your job *(5.33)*

Miscellaneous expenses not subject to the 2% AGI floor include:

- Casualty and theft losses from income-producing property *(18.13)*
- Impairment-related work expenses for disabled employees *(19.4)*
- Gambling losses up to gambling income *(11.3)*
- Estate tax attributable to income in respect of a decedent *(11.16)*
- The deduction for repayment of amounts held under a claim of right *(2.8)*
- Amortizable bond premium on bonds purchased before October 23, 1986 *(4.17)*
- Unrecovered investments in pension on deceased retiree's final return *(7.22)*

EXAMPLES

1. You pay union dues of $380, work clothes costs of $400, and $150 for the preparation of your tax return. Your adjusted gross income (AGI) is $35,000. Your miscellaneous deduction on Schedule A after applying the 2% floor is $230:

Union dues	$380
Work clothes	400
Tax preparation	150
	$930
Less: 2% of $35,000	700
Deductible amount	$230

2. Your adjusted gross income (AGI) is $90,000. You pay the following deductible miscellaneous expenses:

Professional dues	$100
Investment counsel fee	300
Safe-deposit box	50
Tax preparation fee	500
Unreimbursed travel expenses	800
	$1,750

Since the 2% floor of $1,800 (2% x $90,000) exceeds your miscellaneous expenses, none of the expenses are deductible.

19.2 Effect of 2% AGI Floor on Deductions

The table below shows the effect of the 2% AGI floor on miscellaneous deductible expenses. A higher bracket taxpayer may also be subject to the reduction to itemized deductions *(13.7)*.

If your adjusted gross income (AGI) is—	*Only miscellaneous expenses exceeding this amount are deductible—*
$10,000	$200
20,000	400
30,000	600
40,000	800
50,000	1,000
60,000	1,200
70,000	1,400
80,000	1,600
90,000	1,800
100,000	2,000
200,000	4,000

19.3 Checklist of Job Expenses Subject to the 2% AGI Floor

The following expenses that are job related—ranging from professional dues and subscriptions to employment agency fees—are subject to the 2% AGI floor and so you may be unable to deduct them *(19.2)*. Generally, you must file Form 2106 to claim job-related expenses that were not reimbursed by your employer. For 2010, you enter your expenses and any reimbursements on Form 2106, and the allowable amount is then transferred to Line 21 of Schedule A (unreimbursed employee expenses), where it is subject to the 2% AGI floor along with other miscellaneous deductions *(19.1)*. If you are using the standard mileage rate *(43.1)* for 2010 vehicle expenses, and you were not reimbursed by your employer for any job expenses, you may file Form 2106-EZ to report your auto and other job expenses.

You may enter your unreimbursed expenses directly on Line 21 of Schedule A without having to complete Form 2106 or Form 2106-EZ if you are not claiming any job-related travel, local transportation, meal, or entertainment expenses and you received no employer reimbursement at all for any of your other job costs (such as education expenses, union dues, or uniforms).

Filing Instruction

Form 2106 or 2106-EZ

You generally must report your job-related expenses, and any employer reimbursements, on Form 2106. Form 2106-EZ is a shorter form that you may use if none of your job expenses are reimbursed and you deduct car expenses, if any, using the IRS flat mileage allowance.

Airfares *(20.5)*
Auto club membership *(43.2)*
Auto expenses *(19.4, 43.1)*
Books used on the job *(19.5)*
Bond costs *(19.15)*
Business bad debt for loan to employer *(5.33)*
Car insurance premiums *(43.2)*
Cleaning costs *(19.6)*
Commerce association dues *(19.5)*
Commuting costs *(20.2)*
Computers *(19.10)*
Convention trips *(20.12, 20.14)*
Correspondence course *(19.16)*
Depreciation *(42.1)*
Dues *(19.5)*
Educational expenses *(33.13)*
Employment agency fees *(19.7)*
Entertainment expenses *(20.15–20.29)*
Equipment *(19.10–19.12)*
Foreign travel costs *(20.11, 20.14)*
Furniture *(19.13)*
Garage rent *(43.2)*
Gasoline *(43.2)*
Gasoline taxes *(43.2)*
Gifts *(20.25)*
Home office expenses *(19.13)*
Hotel costs *(20.5)*
Job-hunting costs *(19.7)*
Labor union dues *(19.5)*
Laundry *(19.6)*
Legal expenses *(19.17)*
Local transportation and travel away from home *(20.1)*
Lodging *(20.5)*
Magazines *(19.5)*
Malpractice liability premiums *(40.6)*
Meals *(20.3, 20.4)*
Medical examinations *(17.2)*
Membership dues and fees *(19.5)*
Motel charges *(20.5)*
Moving expenses *(12.7)*
Parking fees *(43.2)*
Passport fees for business travel *(20.11)*
Pay turned over to employer *(2.9)*
Periodicals *(19.5)*
Protective clothing *(19.6)*
Rail fares *(20.5)*
Reimbursed expenses *(20.30–20.34)*
Safety helmets *(19.6)*
Safety shoes *(19.6)*
Secretarial convention *(20.12)*
Subscriptions *(19.5)*
Taxi fares *(20.5)*
Telephone calls *(19.14)*
Toll charges *(43.2)*
Tools *(19.12)*
Trade association dues *(19.5)*
Tuition *(33.13)*
Typewriter *(19.11)*
Uniforms *(19.6)*
Union dues *(19.5)*
Work clothes *(19.6)*

19.4 Job Expenses Not Subject to the 2% AGI Floor

Expenses of teachers, instructors, counselors, principals, or aides. Legislation that was expected to extend the "educator" deduction to 2010 had not yet been enacted when this book went to press. If the extension occurs, eligible costs up to the $250 limit may be claimed as an "above-the-line" deduction as discussed in *12.2*. Expenses not allowed under the above-the-line deduction must be claimed as miscellaneous itemized deductions subject to the 2% AGI floor *(19.3)*. *See* the *e-Supplement at jklasser.com* for an update on the extension legislation.

Filing Tip

Life Insurance Agents and Food Deliverers

Statutory employees, such as full-time life insurance salespersons, may deduct expenses on Schedule C and so avoid the 2% AGI floor *(40.6)*.

Impairment-related work expenses. Unreimbursed impairment-related work expenses are reported on Form 2106 (or Form 2106-EZ where eligible) and then the unreimbursed portion is entered on Line 28 of Schedule A as a miscellaneous itemized deduction that is *not* subject to the 2% AGI floor. You have to show:

1. You are physically or mentally disabled. The physical or mental disability must result in a functional limitation of employment that substantially limits one or more major life activities. Generally, showing blindness or deafness will meet this test, but other disabilities that impair your ability to walk, speak, breathe, or perform manual tasks also may qualify if they limit the ability to work.
2. You incur the expenses in order to work. The expenses must be ordinary and necessary to allow you to work. Attendant care services at a place of employment that are necessary for you to work are also deductible.

Expenses of performing artists. As a performing artist, you may deduct job expenses from gross income, whether or not itemized deductions are claimed *(12.2)*.

You report the performing artist expenses on Form 2106 (or Form 2106-EZ where eligible) and enter the total on Line 24 of Form 1040, instead of on Schedule A. If you do not meet the tests, the expenses are deducted on Schedule A subject to the 2% AGI floor.

Moving expenses. Moving expenses to a new job location, although job related, are deducted directly from gross income on Form 1040, Line 26, and not as an itemized deduction on Schedule A.

19.5 Dues and Subscriptions

You may deduct as miscellaneous itemized deductions, subject to the 2% AGI floor on Schedule A, dues paid to a:

- Professional society if you are a salaried lawyer, accountant, teacher, physician, or other professional
- Trade association when conducted for the purpose of furthering the business interests of its members
- Stock exchange if you are a securities dealer
- Community "booster" club conducted to attract tourists and settlers to the locality where the members do business
- Chamber of Commerce if it is conducted to advance the business interests of its members

Union costs. Union members may deduct as "miscellaneous" itemized deductions union dues and initiation fees. Similarly, non-union employees may deduct monthly service charges to a union. An assessment paid for unemployment benefits is deductible if payment is required as a condition of remaining in the union and holding a union job. Voluntary payments to a union unemployment benefit or strike fund are not deductible.

No deduction is allowed for mandatory contributions to a union pension fund applied toward the purchase of a retirement annuity; the contributions are treated as the cost of the annuity. Furthermore, to the extent that an assessment covers sick, accident, or death benefits payable to you or your family, it is not deductible. Similarly, an assessment for a construction fund to build union recreation centers was disallowed by the Tax Court, even though the payment was required for keeping the job.

Campaign costs for running for union office are not deductible.

Subscriptions. Subject to the 2% AGI floor, you may claim as miscellaneous itemized deductions unreimbursed payments for job-related subscriptions to professional journals and trade magazines.

19.6 Uniforms and Work Clothes

The unreimbursed cost of uniforms and other apparel, including their cleaning, laundering, and repair, is deductible as an employee job expenses only if the clothes are:

1. Required to keep your job, and
2. Not suitable for wear when not working.

The deduction is claimed on Form 2106 (or Form 2106-EZ) and then entered on Line 21 of Schedule A, where it is subject to the 2% AGI floor *(19.1)*.

Special work clothes. Courts have held that the cost of special work clothes that protect you from injury is deductible even if you are not required to wear them to keep your job. However, you may not deduct the cost of special clothing, such as aprons and overalls, that protect your regular street clothing. Nor may you deduct the cost of ordinary clothes used as work clothes on the grounds that: (1) they get harder use than customary garments receive; (2) they are soiled after a day's work and cannot be worn socially; or (3) they were purchased for your convenience to save wear and tear on your better clothes. For example, a sanitation inspector, a machinist's helper, a carpenter, and a telephone repairman were not allowed to deduct the cost of their work clothes.

Employer allowance. An allowance paid by your employer for work clothes or a uniform is not reported as income, unless you do not substantiate the expenses to your employer. If you do substantiate the expenses, those exceeding the reimbursement are reported on Form 2106, and the deduction is subject to the 2% AGI floor *(20.30)*.

High-fashion work clothes. That your job requires you to wear expensive clothing is not a basis for deducting the cost of the clothes if the clothing is suitable for wear off the job.

Deductions allowed. Deductions for costs of uniforms and work clothes have been allowed to:

- Airline pilot
- Bakery salesperson—for a uniform with a company label
- Baseball player
- Bus driver
- Cement finisher for gloves, overshoes, and rubber boots
- Civilian faculty members of a military school
- Commercial fisherman for protective clothing, such as oil cloths, gloves, and boots
- Dairy worker for rubber boots, white shirts, trousers, and cap worn only while inside the dairy
- Entertainer for theatrical clothing used solely for performances
- Exotic dancer for breast implants used as a "stage prop" essential to her business; *see* Example 7 below *(19.9)*
- Factory foreman for white coat bearing the word "foreman" and the name of the company
- Factory worker for safety shoes
- Firefighter
- Hospital attendant for work clothes; he came in contact with patients having contagious diseases
- Jockey
- Letter carrier
- Meat cutter for special white shoes
- Musician for formal wear
- Paint machine operator for high top shoes and long leather gloves
- Plumber for special shoes and gloves
- Police officer
- Railroad conductor
- Railroad firefighter for boots, leather gloves, raincoat, caps, and work gloves

EXAMPLES

1. A painter may not deduct the cost of work clothing consisting of a white cap, a white shirt, white bib overalls, and standard work shoes. The clothing is not distinctive in character as a uniform would be. That his union requires him to wear such clothing does not make it a deductible expense.
2. A tennis pro who taught at private clubs was not allowed to deduct the cost of tennis outfits or shoes required for his job. He did not wear them outside of work and argued that he replaced the shoes every few weeks to reduce the chances of injury. However, the Tax Court upheld the IRS's disallowance of his deductions because the clothes and shoes are suitable for everyday wear; warm-up suits and tennis clothes are fashionable and frequently worn as casual wear. Furthermore, there was no evidence that his tennis shoes reduced chances of injury.

Filing Tip

Uniform Required

Your claim of a work clothes deduction is helped if your employer requires you to wear a uniform. Uniform costs of reservists and service persons, in excess of any uniform allowance, are deductible if you are prohibited from wearing the uniform off duty.

Filing Tip

Cleaning and Laundering

If you are allowed to deduct the cost of work clothes and uniforms, you also may deduct the cost of cleaning and laundering them. Also, courts have allowed the cost of cleaning and laundering to be deducted in situations where:

- The clothes could only be worn one day at a time because they became too dirty.
- Dirty clothes were a hazard; they became baggy and might have gotten caught in machinery.
- Clothes were worn only at work and a place for changing clothes was provided by the employer.
- A meat cutter had to wear clean work clothes at all times.

19.7 Expenses of Looking for a New Job

Subject to the 2% AGI floor, you may deduct expenses of looking for a new job in the *same line of work,* whether or not a new job is found. If you are unemployed when seeking a new job, and the period of unemployment has been substantial, the IRS may disallow the deduction.

EXAMPLE

The IRS disallowed the driving expenses of an unemployed secretary on the ground that she was not currently employed. The Tax Court disagreed and held that for purposes of deducting job-hunting expenses, she could still be considered in the business of being a secretary. She had worked as an administrative secretary with Toyota in San Francisco. The firm relocated, resulting in a 100-mile-per-day commute. She quit her job at the end of January 1984. From February to November 1984, she drove her Cadillac El Dorado over 4,600 miles looking for a new job. The Tax Court allowed her a depreciation deduction of $2,880 and $981 for car operating costs.

Caution

First Job

You may not deduct the expenses of seeking your first job.

Expenses of seeking your *first job* are not deductible, even if a job is obtained. Also, expenses of looking for a job in a different line of work are not deductible, even if you get the job.

The IRS may also dispute the deduction of search expenses of a previously employed professional who forms a partnership.

EXAMPLE

A CPA working for a firm decided to go out on his own. After a period of investigation, he formed a partnership with another CPA. The IRS disallowed his deduction of search expenses, claiming his expenses were incurred in a new business. As an employee he was in a different business from that of a self-employed practitioner. Thus, the expenses should be capitalized as a cost of setting up or organizing the partnership. The Tax Court disagreed, allowing the deduction. The travel expenses were incurred to seek work as a CPA, whether as a self-employed or employed CPA.

Travel expenses. If you travel to find a new job in the same line of work, such as an interview in a distant city, you may deduct travel expenses, including meals and lodging. If, during the trip, you also do personal visiting, you may deduct the transportation expenses to and from the area if the trip was primarily related to your job search. Time spent on personal activity is compared with time spent looking for a job to determine the primary purpose of the trip. If the transportation expenses to and from the destination are not deductible because the trip was primarily personal, you may still deduct the expenses of seeking a new job while you are away.

Filing Tip

Employment Agency Fee

If your new employer pays the fee under an agreement with an agency, you may disregard the payment for tax purposes. However, if you pay the fee and deduct it as a job search expense and in a later year you are reimbursed by your employer, you must report the reimbursement as taxable income to the extent you received a tax benefit from the earlier deduction *(11.6)*.

A company interested in your services may invite you to a job interview and agree to pay all of the trip expenses to its office, even if you are not hired. The company payment is tax free up to your actual expenses.

Are you between jobs? If you are between jobs and you continue to *see* and entertain your former customers, the IRS holds that you may not deduct the cost of entertainment and other business expenses during this period on the ground that you are not in business and earning income. However, the Tax Court in the following case allowed the deduction.

EXAMPLE

Haft was a successful jewelry salesman earning as much as $60,000 a year. In the fall of one year, he left his employer and started to look for a new connection. During the following year, he continued to maintain contacts with his former customers by entertaining buyers and their representatives. He deducted the expenses of entertaining and other business costs. The IRS disallowed the deduction, claiming he was not in business. The Tax Court disagreed. His lack of business income was temporary and resulted from a period of transition that lasted a reasonable time.

19.8 Local Transportation Costs

Unreimbursed local transportation costs to *see* your employer's clients or customers, such as taxi, bus, or train fares, are miscellaneous itemized deductions (19.1) subject to the 2% AGI floor. Transportation from your regular job to a second job on the same day is also deductible. You may not deduct the cost of commuting from home to a regular job or second job, but commuting to a temporary work location *(20.2)* is deductible.

If you use your own car for job-related travel, you may deduct unreimbursed out-of-pocket costs for gasoline, tolls, and parking. The IRS mileage allowance *(43.1)* is available for the occasional business use of your personal car if you elected the allowance for the first year you used the car for business purposes; *see* the instructions to Form 2106 or Form 2106-EZ.

19.9 Unusual Job Expenses

The following are not typical deductible expenses. However, deductions in the following cases have been allowed.

EXAMPLES

1. *Shoeshine expense of a pilot.* Company rules required a commercial airline pilot to look neat, keep his hair cut, and wear conservative black shoes, properly shined. The pilot deducted as a business expense $100 for his haircuts and $25 for his shoe shines. The IRS disallowed the deductions, but the Tax Court allowed the cost of the shoe shines. The shoes were of a military type which he wore only with his pilot's uniform. The cost of keeping up a uniform is deductible. The haircuts were merely nondeductible personal expenses.

2. *Depreciation on furnishings bought by executive for his company office.* Following a quarrel with an interior decorator, a sales manager bought his own office furniture when his firm moved to new quarters. Rather than complain or ask for reimbursement, he footed the bill and deducted depreciation. The IRS disallowed the deduction, claiming the expense was that of his company. The Tax Court allowed the deduction. The manager's action was unusual, but prudent. He did not want to cause difficulties, and at the same time had to maintain his image as a successful manager. His expenses for furniture were appropriate and helpful.

3. *Salesman's cost of operating a private plane.* Sherman flew his own plane to visit clients in six southern states and deducted $18,000 as operating costs of the plane. The IRS disallowed the deduction, claiming there was no business reason for the plane. He could have taken commercial flights or used a company car to reach his clients. Furthermore, his company did not reimburse him for the private airplane costs, although it would cover costs of his car and commercial air travel. Finally, the amount of airplane expenses was unreasonable compared to his salary of $25,000. Sherman convinced the Tax Court that use of a private airplane was the only reasonable way he could cover his six-state sales area. He showed that most of his clients were not near commercial airports. Although the airplane costs were large in relation to his salary, they were still reasonable and, therefore, deductible.

4. *Executive's purchase of blazers for sales force.* Jetty, the president of an oil equipment manufacturing firm, thought that he could generate goodwill for the company if employees who attended industrial trade shows wore a blazer and vest set in the company colors. He personally paid and deducted $6,725 for 27 blazers and vests. The IRS disallowed the deduction on the grounds that it was a company expense and that Jetty should have sought reimbursement from the company.

   The Tax Court allowed the deduction. Paying for the clothes was a legitimate business expense for Jetty since he depended on bonuses for a large portion of his pay, and, as company president, he had responsibility for seeing to it that there were profits to share in. Furthermore, the outlay was not the type of expense covered by the company's manual on expense reimbursements.

5. *Repayment of layoff benefits to restore pension credit.* When he was laid off, an employee received a lump-sum payment from his company based on his salary and years of service. When he was rehired a year later, he repaid the lump sum in order to restore his pension credits and other benefit rights. The IRS ruled that he may deduct the repayment as a condition of being rehired; the repayment was required to restore employee benefits.

6. *Politician's expenses.* Elected officials may incur out-of-pocket expenses in excess of the allowances received from the government. They may deduct as miscellaneous deductions their payment of office expenses such as salaries, office rent, and supplies. Part-time officials may claim the deduction. The expenses are deductible even if they exceed the official's income.

7. *Depreciation for exotic dancer's breast implants.* Hess, an exotic dancer, enlarged her breasts to the abnormal size of 56N and claimed a $2,088 depreciation deduction for their cost. The IRS disallowed the deduction, claiming that cosmetic surgery is a personal expense. The Tax Court disagreed. Hess's expenses were incurred solely in furtherance of her business and not for her own personal benefit. The breast implants were not of the kind that women usually get to enhance their appearance. Rather, Hess enlarged her breasts to a "freakish" size to substantially increase her annual income, which she did. The court also compared the implants to special work clothes *(19.6)*, required for a job and not for personal wear. As an exotic dancer, Hess's large breasts are like a "costume" needed to keep her job. Although she could not remove them daily, she would have, if possible, because they caused her serious medical problems.

19.10 Computers Bought for Work

Computers (and peripherals) are treated as "listed property" subject to deduction restrictions: To get a first-year expensing deduction *(42.3)* or to claim any type of depreciation, the computer must be used for the convenience of your employer, which means your use of the computer satisfies a substantial business need of your employer. The computer must also be required as a condition of your job, which means that you cannot properly do your job without it. The IRS strictly interprets these requirements.

Court Decision

Tax Court Allows Computer Deduction

The Tax Court allowed a first-year expensing deduction to a working couple who used the same home computer given these facts: The husband, a professor, used it to store historical data; the wife, a state transportation planner, used it to do extensive number crunching. What apparently won the decision for the couple was evidence that (1) the husband did not have access to a computer at the university, and (2) the state office in which the wife worked did not have funds to buy a computer. The court held that the use of the computer was necessary for them to properly do their jobs, and as the purchase of a computer spared their employers from having to provide them with computers, the purchase was for the employers' convenience.

In a later case, a telemarketing sales manager was allowed a first-year expensing deduction for a home computer and printer used to prepare reports. The key to winning the deduction was her supervisor's testimony that as a mid-level manager, she could not enter the office after regular hours to use a company computer, and that she was able to keep up with the volume of sales reports she was required to submit by using her home computer and accessing information via modem.

Computer. A letter from your employer stating that a computer is needed for your position does not by itself satisfy the deduction tests. Even where your employer encourages use of a personal computer that is used for basic job requirements, the IRS requires proof that you need your own computer to do your job because your employer does not provide one, or because the computer supplied by your employer is not adequate for your job. In the following Examples, the IRS disallowed depreciation writeoffs.

EXAMPLES

1. An electric company offered to help pay for its engineers' personal computers where this would improve productivity. Qualifying engineers received extra pay and had to buy a computer meeting company specifications, take approved computer courses, and agree to restrictions on resale of the computer. An engineer bought a computer and used it 95% of the time for writing business memos and reports, and studying business flow charts. He did not use the computer for entertainment.

   The IRS held that although the engineer's computer was work related and benefitted his employer, buying a computer was not required for his job; it was not "inextricably related" to proper job performance. Further, his participation in the employer's computer program was optional, not mandatory.

2. A professor of nursing, trying to keep her temporary position, bought a personal computer, needing a word processor for independent research papers and to document her qualifications for research grants. The research and external grant support were implied university requirements for faculty appointments. She did not have access to university word-processing equipment during regular work hours; and because of her classroom responsibilities, her research and grant development work had to be done on her own time. To help her pursue outside grants, the university bought her a "modem" that allowed a phone hook-up with its computer at night. Her computer was used 100% for research and grant work.

   As in Example 1, the IRS held that use of the computer was not "inextricably related" to proper job performance and did not qualify for a depreciation writeoff. Furthermore, there was no evidence that employees who did not use computers were professionally disadvantaged.

3. The IRS held that an insurance agent could not deduct depreciation for a laptop computer he used to help develop insurance plans for clients. The insurance company encouraged its agents to buy the computer because office computers were not generally accessible. According to the IRS, it is not enough that the agent's productivity increased or that he used the computer solely for business. Purchasing the computer was optional, not a mandatory job requirement. Employees who did not purchase computers were not professionally disadvantaged.

4. The IRS barred a third-grade teacher from deducting the cost of a Macintosh computer because it was not required for her job. She bought the computer using an interest-free loan from the school after the school decided that report cards and student evaluations would have to be prepared on a Macintosh instead of being written. The Tax Court and an appeals court sided with the IRS. It may have been convenient for the teacher to use a home computer but it was not required. Other teachers were able to timely complete their duties using school computers.

Claiming a deduction. If you can meet the "convenience of the employer" and "job condition" tests for a computer phone that you purchased in 2010, and you have records to prove that the unit is used more than 50% of the time for your job, you may write off the cost using first-year expensing *(42.3)*, bonus depreciation *(42.20)*, or accelerated MACRS depreciation rates *(42.5)*. If business use of the unit is 50% or less, you may not use first-year expensing, bonus depreciation, or accelerated MACRS but you may claim straight-line depreciation *(42.9)*.

First-year expensing or depreciation is claimed on Form 4562 and then entered on Form 2106 or Form 2106-EZ along with other job-related costs. The deduction from Form 2106 or Form 2106-EZ is subject to the 2% AGI floor for miscellaneous deductions on Schedule A *(19.1)*. If you use first-year expensing, bonus depreciation, or accelerated MACRS and business use in a later year falls to 50% or less, the deductions are subject to recapture *(42.10)*.

Cell phones no longer treated as listed property. For 2009 and prior years, cell phones were treated, like computers, as "listed property." However, for 2010 and later years, cell phones have been removed from the listed property category by the Small Business Jobs Act of 2010.

Law Alert

Cell Phones Removed From List of "Listed" Property

The Small Business Jobs Act of 2010 (9/27/10) removes cell phones from the category of "listed property" effective for 2010 and later years.

19.11 Calculators, Copiers, Fax Machines, and Typewriters

The listed property requirements applied to computers and cell phones *(19.9)* do not apply to calculators, copiers, fax machines, adding machines, and typewriters. This means that the restrictive convenience of the employer and job condition rules do not apply. However, to depreciate the cost of such equipment, you should be ready to prove that you need the equipment for your job, and keep a record of the time it is used for business. To claim first-year expensing *(42.3)*, rather than regular depreciation, you must use the equipment *more* than 50% of the time for business.

19.12 Small Tools

If you furnished your own small tools used on your job, you may deduct their cost if they are not expected to last beyond a year. The deduction is subject to the 2% AGI floor. The cost of tools with a useful life of more than a year must be recovered through depreciation or first-year expensing *(42.3)*. Be prepared to substantiate your deduction with receipts showing the cost and type of tools purchased, and the business necessity for them.

Filing Instruction

Office for Sideline Business

If you are an employee and also have a sideline business for which you use a home office, the office expenses are deductible if the office is used regularly and exclusively as your principal place of business or a meeting place with clients, customers, or patients. If the tests are met, you claim your home office expenses as a self-employed person on Form 8829, which you attach to Schedule C. The deduction may not exceed your income from the sideline business. *See* a sample Form 8829 and other deduction details in *40.15*.

19.13 Employee Home Office Deductions

The tax law has been drafted to prevent most employees from deducting the expenses of an office at a home. Even if an employee should meet one of the tests for deducting home office expenses *(40.12)*, such as doing administrative work at home, the employee must also show that the home office was required for the "convenience of his or her employer" in order to claim the deduction. Telecommuters who are required to work at home satisfy the employer convenience test but if an employee requests telecommuting and the employer has on-premises office space available, the IRS is likely to argue, barring unusual facts, that the home office is for the employee's convenience and not for the employer's convenience. The IRS has not provided specific guidelines for telecommuters.

Even if the deduction tests can be met, the allowable office expenses (other than mortgage interest and taxes) are subject to the 2% AGI floor on Schedule A; *see* IRS Publication 587 for reporting instructions.

Caution

Deducting Telephone Costs

To support your deduction, keep a record of business calls made at home or anywhere outside your employer's office.

Filing Tip

Deduction for Credit Card Fees To Pay Tax

Companies authorized by the IRS to process credit card or debit card payments of taxes charge a convenience fee. A deduction for the convenience fee may be claimed on Line 23 of Schedule A as an "other" expense subject to the 2% floor, along with investment management costs *(19.15)*. The convenience fee should not be included with tax preparation fees *(19.16)*.

Planning Reminder

Travel to Check Investments

Travel costs of a trip away from home *(20.6)* to look after investments, or to confer with your attorney, accountant, trustee, or investment counsel about the production of income, may be deducted as miscellaneous itemized deductions subject to the 2% of adjusted gross income floor. If you have investment property in a resort area, keep proof that the trip was taken primarily to check your investment property, not to vacation.

EXAMPLE

Charlie, a teacher, has a small office at school where he can grade papers and tests, work on lesson plans, and meet with parents and students. The school does not require him to work at home, but he prefers to use the office he has set up in his home, and does not use the office the school provides. Although Charlie's home office is used for the administrative duties of teaching, Charlie may not deduct his home office expenses because he does not meet the convenience of the employer test. His employer provides him with an office at school and does not require him to work at home.

19.14 Telephone Costs

For business calls made outside of your employer's office or at home, keep a record or diary of business calls to support your deduction. To avoid the problem of allocating the costs of a single phone for both business and personal use, consider a separate phone for business use only.

Deduction barred for basic charge of first phone line. You may not claim as a deductible home office expense any part of the standard monthly charge for the first telephone line into your home. This disallowance rule only applies to the first telephone line. If you have more than one telephone line and use additional lines in a home office, costs for these lines remain deductible, subject to restrictions *(19.13)*. The restriction does not affect deductibility of long-distance calls, phone rentals, or optional services such as call waiting, call forwarding, three-way calling, or extra directory listings.

19.15 Checklist of Deductible Investment Expenses

The following investment expenses are deductible as miscellaneous expenses on Schedule A subject to the 2% adjusted gross income (AGI) floor.

- Accounting fees for keeping records of investment income.
- Bank deposit loss if not federally insured *(18.5)*.
- Casualty or theft losses of income-producing property such as stock certificates, but not rental or royalty property; the deduction is figured on Form 4684 *(18.13)* and entered on Schedule A.
- Fees for collecting interest and dividends. Also deductible are fees paid to a bank that acts as dividend agent in an automatic dividend reinvestment plan of a publicly owned corporation. Costs of collecting tax-exempt interest are not deductible; expenses deducted on an estate tax return are also not deductible. Fees paid to a broker to acquire securities are not deductible but are added to the cost of the securities. Commissions and fees paid by an investor on the sale of securities reduce the selling price; a dealer, however, may deduct selling commissions as business expenses.
- Fees to set up or administer an IRA. The fees must be billed and paid separately from the regular IRA contribution.
- Guardian fees or fees of committee for a ward or minor incurred in producing or collecting income belonging to the ward or minor or in managing income-producing property of the ward or minor.
- Investment management or investment planner's fees. However, fees allocated to advice dealing with tax-exempt obligations are not deductible.
- Investment fees from non–publicly offered mutual fund, shown in Box 5 of Form 1099-DIV.
- Legal costs *(19.17)*.
- Premiums and expenses on indemnity bonds for the replacement of missing securities. If part of the expenses are refunded in the year the expenses are paid, only the excess expense is deductible. A refund in a later year is taxable income to the extent the expenses were deducted and reduced your tax *(11.6)*.
- Proxy fight expenses where the dispute involves legitimate corporate policy issues, not a frivolous desire to gain membership on the board.
- Safe-deposit box rental fee or home safe to hold your securities, unless used to hold personal effects or tax-exempt securities.
- Salary of a secretary, bookkeeper, or other employee hired to keep track of your investment income.
- Subscriptions to investment services.

Computer used to manage investments. Subject to the 2% floor, depreciation may be claimed *(42.10)*.

Managing investment property. Expenses incurred in managing property held for income are deductible, even if the property does not currently produce income. Expenses incurred to maintain or conserve the property are also deductible.

Rental or royalty expenses. Expenses of earning royalty or rental income are deducted directly from the income, rather than as itemized deductions subject to the 2% AGI floor.

EXAMPLE

You pay deductible investment management fees of $1,500, a tax preparation fee of $500, and a safe-deposit box fee of $40. Your other miscellaneous expense deductions subject to the 2% floor are $500 for unreimbursed job expenses. Your adjusted gross income is $80,000. Your deduction after applying the 2% AGI floor is $940, figured as follows:

Investment management fees	$1,500
Tax preparation fee	500
Safe-deposit box fee	40
Other miscellaneous expenses	500
	$2,540
Less: 2% of $80,000	1,600
Total deductible	$ 940

Caution

Investment Seminars

You may not deduct the cost of an investment or financial planning seminar or similar meeting.

Nondeductible travel costs. Investors may not deduct the costs of these types of trips:

- Trips to investigate prospective rental property.
- Trips to attend a convention, seminar, or similar meeting that deals with investment, financial planning, or the production or collection of income. Convention costs are deductible only in the case of a business activity *(20.12)*.
- Trips to attend stockholder meetings. However, in a private letter ruling, one stockholder was allowed a deduction. He owned substantial stockholdings that had lost value because his corporation had been issuing stock to the public at prices below book value. He went to the annual shareholders' meeting to present a resolution requesting management to stop the practice; the resolution passed. Under such circumstances, the IRS held that the trip was directly related to his stockholdings and allowed him the deduction. The IRS distinguished his case from a ruling that bars most stockholders from deducting the cost of travel to an annual meeting. Here the stockholder's purpose in getting the resolution passed was more closely related to his investment activities than if he had attended the meeting, as most stockholders do, to pick up data for future investment moves.

Hobby expenses. Deductions for hobby expenses are subject to limitations *(40.10)*.

Home office of an investor. An investor may not deduct the costs of an office at home unless investing constitutes a business. For example, you get no deduction for use of a home office in your residence where you manage your investments and read financial periodicals and reports. These activities are not considered a business.

EXAMPLE

In his home office, Moller spent 40 hours a week managing four stock portfolios worth over $13 million. However, an appeals court held he could not deduct home office expenses despite the time spent there managing his investment. To deduct home office expenses, Moller had to show he was a trader. A trader is in a business; an investor is not. A trader buys and sells frequently to catch daily market swings. An investor buys securities for capital appreciation and income without regard to daily market developments. Here, Moller was an investor. He was primarily interested in the long-term growth potential of stock. He did not earn his income from the short-term stock turnovers. He had no significant trading profits.

19.16 Costs of Tax Return Preparation and Audits

You may deduct on Schedule A your payment of fees charged for the services listed below, subject to the 2% AGI floor.

- Preparing your tax return or refund claim involving any tax;
- Preparing and obtaining a private IRS ruling, including IRS filing fees; *and*
- Representing you before any examination, trial, or other type of hearing involving any tax.

Tax preparation fees include the cost of tax publications and tax preparation software programs. Deductible tax preparation expenses also include fees paid to electronically file your return. The term "any tax" covers not only income taxes but also gift, property, estate, or any other tax, whether the taxing authority be federal, state, or municipal.

Tax practitioner's fees. Deductible fees for services of tax practitioners are claimed on Schedule A as miscellaneous itemized deductions (subject to the 2% AGI floor) on the tax return for the year in which the fee was paid. For example, if in March 2010 you paid an accountant to prepare your 2009 return, the fee is deductible on your 2010 return.

You deduct fees related to preparing Schedule C or F (and related business Schedules) on the Schedule C or F, thereby avoiding the 2% AGI floor on Schedule A. In one case, the Tax Court allowed a Schedule C deduction for a $55 tax preparation fee claimed by a self-employed lumberjack, although nonbusiness income was also reported on his return. Any allocation to the nonbusiness income would have been minimal. The Court noted that the IRS's position in disallowing the deduction reflected misguided zeal and was not only petty but impractical.

If you report rental or royalty income or loss on Schedule E, you deduct the allocated tax preparation fee on Schedule E.

An accountant's fee for arranging the purchase of real estate was deductible where the purchase was part of a plan to cut taxes; *see* the Collins Example below.

Personal checking account fees. These are nondeductible, even though the checks are used for tax records. Similarly, the per-check fee on an interest-bearing NOW account is nondeductible. However, fees charged on a bank money-market account may be deductible if check writing is severely limited and writing excess checks forfeits the status of the account as a money-market account.

Appraisal fees. Appraisals for determining a casualty loss or charitable donation are miscellaneous expenses.

EXAMPLES

1. Stockholders of a closely held corporation negotiated with a publicly held company for a tax-free exchange of their stock. An accounting firm asked the IRS for a ruling to determine whether the exchange would be taxable or tax free. The accounting fee was $8,602. Of this, $7,602 was for the ruling and $1,000 was for fixing the basis of the new stock. The stockholders deducted the full fee, which the IRS disallowed because the fee was not charged for the preparation of a tax return nor for representation at a contest of a tax liability.

   The Tax Court disagreed in part. The fee paid for the ruling was deductible; it was connected with determining the extent of the stockholders' liability, if any, in the proposed exchange. But a deduction could not be allowed for the $1,000 charged to determine the basis of the new stock. This was computed for the stockholders' information, not for determining tax liability. The disallowed fee could be added to the cost basis of the stock.

2. Collins paid an accountant $4,511 for tax advice to reduce his tax on a sweepstakes winning. He was advised to buy an apartment house under a contract obligation to make a large prepayment of interest (which was deductible under prior law). The accountant helped prepare contracts, escrow agreements, and other documents to implement the plan. Collins's deduction of his accountant's fee was disallowed. The IRS held that the fee was a capital expense in acquiring the property. The Tax Court disagreed. The accountant was hired to minimize Collins's income tax through the purchase of the building and the terms of the purchase. Therefore, his fee was deductible.

Filing Tip

Tax Advice and Tax Return Preparation

Subject to the 2% AGI floor, you may deduct on your 2010 return fees paid in 2010 for preparing your 2009 return or a refund claim for 2009 or an earlier year. You also may deduct 2010 payments of fees to practitioners for representing you at an examination, trial, or hearing involving any tax. Legal fees incurred in defending against a tax imposed by a foreign country are also deductible. However, legal fees incurred in reducing an assessment on property to pay for local benefits are not deductible; the fees are capital expenses which are added to basis.

Planning Reminder

Allocate Fees for Tax Advice

There have been disputes over the deductibility of fees charged for general tax advice unconnected to the preparation of a return or a tax controversy. A deduction for fees charged for general tax advice not within these areas may be disallowed, unless the fee can be related to the production of business or investment income or the management of income-producing property *(19.16)*.

Filing Tip

Deducting the Cost of This Book

The purchase of *J.K. Lasser's Your Income Tax* in 2010 may be claimed as a miscellaneous expense deduction on your 2010 return. The cost, when included with other miscellaneous expenses, is subject to the 2% AGI floor. If you purchase the book in 2011, include the cost with your other miscellaneous expenses on your 2011 return.

19.17 Deducting Legal Costs

A legal expense is generally deductible if the dispute or issue arose in the course of your business or employment or involves income-producing property. Legal expenses for personal lawsuits are not deductible unless you recover taxable damages. Legal fees incurred in obtaining an award of tax-free damages, such as for physical injuries *(11.7)*, are not deductible.

If you are self-employed, your deduction for legal fees arising from a business-related dispute is claimed on Schedule C. Legal expenses related to your job as an employee or to investment activities are claimed as miscellaneous itemized deductions subject to the 2% AGI floor, except for fees relating to employment discrimination claims, which may qualify for an above-the-line deduction *(19.18)*. The IRS may disallow the deduction on the ground that the legal dispute does not directly arise from the business or income activity. Thus, for example, the cost of contesting the suspension of a driver's license for drunken driving is not deductible despite a business need for the license; the suspension arose out of a personal rather than a business-related activity. A deduction may also be disallowed where the dispute involves title to property.

Legal fees incurred in organizing a new business may be deductible *(40.11)*.

Planning Reminder

Lawyer's Bill Should Be Itemized

Your lawyer should bill you separately or itemize fees for services connected with deductible items (collection of taxable alimony or separate maintenance payments; or preparation of tax returns, tax audits, and tax litigation) and nondeductible capital items (expenses incurred in purchase of property or dispute over title).

Employment suits. The following Examples illustrate when legal costs for job-related matters may be deductible.

EXAMPLES

1. An Army officer was allowed to deduct the cost of successfully contesting a court martial based on charges of misrepresentations in official statements and reports. He would have lost his position had he been convicted.
2. Tellier, a securities dealer, was convicted of mail fraud and securities fraud. He was allowed to deduct legal fees as business expenses related to his securities business. That he was found guilty of the criminal charge does not affect the deductibility of the expense. The deduction of legal expenses is not disallowed on public policy grounds since a defendant has a constitutional right to an attorney.
3. In an alimony action, Gilmore was successful in preventing his wife from securing stock and taking control of corporations from which he earned practically all his income. He was not allowed to deduct his legal costs. The dispute did not arise from an income-producing activity; the fact that an adverse determination of the dispute might affect his income did not make the legal expenses deductible.
4. A doctor who attempted to bribe a judge to suspend his sentence for tax evasion was convicted of the bribe attempt and lost his license to practice medicine. He could not deduct his defense costs. His practice of medicine did not give rise to his need for an attorney. The fact that the conviction affected his ability to earn income was merely a consequence of personal litigation.
5. Siket, a police officer, was not allowed to deduct expenses of successfully defending a criminal charge of assault while off duty. The origin of the claim was personal, even though a conviction might have been detrimental to his position as a police officer. The arrest did not occur within the performance of his duties; he was off duty and in a different municipality at the time of the arrest.
6. A resort company instructed its staff to stop serving drinks to intoxicated patrons and to encourage the patrons to either take a taxi home or to stay on the premises at a reduced rate. One of the company's executives attempted to deduct legal defense fees when he was charged with criminal sexual assault, arguing that the assault allegation arose from his business duty to procure a room for three intoxicated guests. The IRS and the Tax Court denied the deduction on the grounds that the allegation arose from the executive's second visit to the guests' room, not from the time he placed them in the room. Even if the alleged assault had occurred during the first visit, the executive personally violated company policy by not stopping the guests from drinking when they were already drunk.

Will contests and wrongful death actions. Legal costs of a will contest are generally not deductible because an inheritance is not taxable income. Similarly, legal fees incurred to collect a wrongful death award (which is tax-free income) are not deductible.

EXAMPLE

Parker, an heir who was left out of his grandmother's estate, sued to recover his inheritance. In a settlement, he received his share of his grandmother's property plus income earned on that property. The allocable portion of legal fees attributed to the income, which was taxable, was deductible; the balance of the fees was not deductible.

Title issues or disputes. Legal costs related to the acquisition of property or to the determination of title to property, whether such property is business or personal, are nondeductible capital expenditures. They are added to the basis of the property. For example, litigation costs to fix the value of shares of dissident shareholders are not deductible because they are related to the purchase of the stock and are part of the cost of acquisition.

Legal fees incurred to acquire title to stock are also nondeductible.

Where a dispute over property does not involve title, such as in a recovery of income-producing securities loaned as collateral, the Tax Court holds that legal fees are deductible.

Personal injury actions. Where you recover taxable damages, the legal fees *(19.18)* are deductible above the line (from gross income) in unlawful discrimination cases or as a miscellaneous itemized deduction subject to the 2% floor in other cases *(12.2)*. If the damages are not taxable, legal fees are not deductible *(11.7)*.

Legal expenses incurred in marital actions *(37.8)*.

Collecting Social Security. If you hire an attorney to press a claim for disputed benefits, such as disability benefits, you may deduct the legal fees only to the extent that your benefits are taxable *(34.3)*. For example, if 50% of your Social Security benefits are taxable, 50% of your legal fees are treated as miscellaneous expenses subject to the 2% AGI floor.

Estate tax planning fee. All or part of an attorney's fee for estate tax planning services may be deductible subject to the 2% AGI floor. Estate tax planning usually involves tax and non-tax matters. To the extent that the services do not cover tax advice or income-producing property, the fee is not deductible. A bill allocating a fee between deductible and nondeductible services may help support a deduction claimed for the deductible portion of the fee.

Recovery of attorneys' fees from government. *See Chapter 47.*

19.18 Contingent Fees Paid Out of Taxable Awards

Contingent attorney fees paid to recover taxable damages have been held by the Supreme Court to be includible in the litigant's income *(11.7)*. An offsetting deduction for the fees may be available. An above-the-line deduction (directly from gross income) is allowed for attorneys' fees and court costs in employment discrimination suits, certain other unlawful discrimination actions, and Federal False Claims Act cases. The deduction, claimed on Line 36 of Form 1040 *(12.2)*, is limited to the amount of the judgment or settlement reported as taxable income for the year.

If the above-the-line deduction does *not* apply, fees for recovering taxable personal damages or job-related damages *(19.17)* are allowed only as a miscellaneous itemized deduction subject to the 2% AGI floor *(19.1)*. If the alternative minimum tax (AMT) applies, fees claimed as a miscellaneous itemized deduction for regular tax purposes must be added back to income in calculating AMT *(23.2)*, so the benefit of the deduction is lost.

Fees incurred in recovering lost business income *(19.17)* are deductible on Schedule C.

Chapter 20

Travel and Entertainment Expense Deductions

Unreimbursed employee travel expenses are deductible but are subject to the 2% of adjusted gross income (AGI) floor on Schedule A. If you are self-employed, the 2% floor does not apply to travel expenses claimed on Schedule C. The types of deductible travel expenses are highlighted in *Table 20-1*. Generally, you must be away from home to deduct travel expenses on business trips. Meals and entertainment costs are subject to restrictions, including a 50% deduction limit *(20.15)* that applies to employees prior to the 2% floor *(20.29)*. On one-day business trips within the general area of your employment, only transportation costs may be deducted; meals may not.

To support your travel expense deductions, keep records that comply with IRS rules *(20.26)*. To avoid the 2% AGI floor, consider an "accountable" reimbursement arrangement of your travel expenses with your employer *(20.31)*.

You report unreimbursed employee transportation and travel expenses on Form 2106 or on short form 2106-EZ if you are not reimbursed by your company and you do not claim depreciation on a car used for business.

Unreimbursed expenses from Form 2106 or 2106-EZ are entered on Schedule A, where they are subject to the 2% AGI floor.

An expense allowance for travel costs is not reported as income on Form W-2 if you substantiated the expenses to your employer and returned any unsubstantiated portion of the allowance *(20.31)*.

If you are self-employed, you deduct travel costs on Schedule C. The 2% AGI floor does not apply, but only 50% of meal and entertainment expenses are deductible.

20.1 Deduction Guide for Travel and Transportation Expenses

Table 20-1 summarizes the rules for deducting local business transportation costs and travel expenses while "away from home" *(20.6)* on business trips. Generally, commuting expenses from your home to your place of business when you are not away from home are not deductible *(20.2)*. However, you may be able to claim a deduction for daily transportation expenses incurred in commuting *(20.2)* to a temporary job location; *see Table 20-1*.

See 20.28 for how to report deductible expenses if you are self-employed, and *20.29* if you are an employee.

20.2 Commuting Expenses

The cost of travel between your home and place of work is generally not deductible, even if the work location is in a remote area not serviced by public transportation. Nor can you justify the deduction by showing you need a car for faster trips to work or for emergency trips. Travel from a union hall to an assigned job is also considered commuting. If you join a car pool, you may not deduct expenses of gasoline, repairs, or other costs of driving you and your passengers to work.

According to the IRS, if you use your cell phone to make calls to clients or business associates while driving to your office, you are still commuting and your expenses are not deductible. Similarly, the deduction is not allowed if you drive passengers to work and discuss business.

Court Decision

Self-Employed Person's Office at Home

If you are self-employed and your regular office is outside your home, you may not deduct the cost of commuting to the office or from that office to your home even if you work at home at a second job. However, if your home office is your principal place of business *(40.12)*, you can deduct travel costs between the home office and the offices or worksites of your clients or customers.

Deductible commuting expenses. The IRS allows these exceptions to its blanket ban on commuting expense deductions.

If you are on a business trip out of town, you may deduct taxi fares or other transportation costs from your hotel to the first business call of the day and all other transportation costs between business calls.

If you use your car to carry tools to work, you may deduct transportation costs where you can prove that they were incurred in addition to the ordinary, nondeductible commuting expenses. The deduction will be allowed even if you would use a car in any event to commute; *see* the Examples below.

EXAMPLES

1. Jones commuted to and from work by public transportation before he had to carry tools. Public transportation cost $2 per day to commute to and from work. When he had to use the car to carry the tools, the cost of driving was $3 a day and $5 a day to rent a trailer to carry the tools. Jones may deduct only the cost of renting the trailer. The IRS does not allow a deduction for the additional $1 a day cost of operating the car. It is not considered related to the carrying of the tools. It is treated as part of the cost of commuting, which is not deductible.
2. Same facts as above, but Jones does not rent a trailer. He uses the car trunk to store his tools. He may not claim a deduction because he incurs no additional cost for carrying the tools.
3. Smith uses his car regardless of the need to transport tools. He rents a trailer for $5 a day to carry tools. He may deduct $5 a day under the "additional-cost" rule.

Commuting to a temporary place of work. Whether you can deduct commuting expenses to a temporary place of work may depend on the location of the temporary assignment and whether you have a regular place of business or a home office that is your principal place of business. According to the IRS, if you have a *regular* place of work outside of your home, or you have a home office that is your principal place of business, you may deduct the cost of commuting between your home and a temporary (*see* below) work location, regardless of where the temporary location is. If you do not have a regular place of work but normally work at several locations in the metropolitan area where you live, you may deduct the costs of commuting to a temporary location that is outside that metropolitan area, but not to a temporary location within the metropolitan area.

If you do not have a regular place of work and all of your jobs are outside the metropolitan area where you live, none of your commuting costs are deductible under the IRS rule. In one case, a commuting cost deduction was denied to an iron worker who lived in Yuba City, California, and who obtained temporary work assignments at a union hall in Sacramento, 40 miles from her home. All of the temporary jobs were in or near Sacramento. The Tax Court agreed with the IRS that none of her commuting costs to the temporary locations were deductible because she did not work in the Yuba City area where she lived. Since all of her assignments were in other cities, her decision to live in Yuba City was for personal, not business, reasons.

Caution

IRS Definition of "Temporary"

The IRS considers a work location temporary if the period of employment is realistically expected to last, and actually does last, one year or less. If you take an assignment expected to last more than a year but it actually lasts less than a year, your assignment is *not* considered temporary and commuting costs are not deductible.

What is a temporary place of work? A temporary work location is one at which your employment is realistically expected to last, and actually does last, for one year or less. If at first you realistically expect an assignment to last for no more than one year but that expectation changes, the IRS will generally treat the employment as temporary until the date that it became realistic to expect that the work would exceed one year.

Accountants, architects, engineers, and other professionals often have to travel to job sites of their clients. If such work at the site is temporary and they can show they also have a regular work office, they may deduct commuting expenses from their homes to their work sites.

EXAMPLE

The IRS ruled that a professional who spent 25–27% of his time at his employer's field office satisfied the regular place of business test. His remaining time was spent at client locations. These were considered temporary because he went to each client location only once every two years for two to three weeks at a time. He was allowed to deduct his unreimbursed costs of driving between his home and the client locations.

20.3 Overnight-Sleep Test Limits Deduction of Meal Costs

The overnight-sleep rule prevents the deduction of meal costs on one-day business trips. To be deductible, meal costs must be incurred while "away from home" and this test requires that they be on a business trip that lasts longer than a regular working day (but not necessarily 24 hours) and requires time off to sleep (not just to eat or rest) before returning home. Meal costs while away from home are subject to the 50% deduction limit *(20.15)*. Taking a nap in a parked car off the road does not meet the overnight-sleep test.

EXAMPLES

1. A New Yorker flies to Washington, D.C., which is about 250 miles away, to *see* a client. He arrives at noon, eats lunch, and then visits the client. He flies back to New York that evening. He may deduct the cost of the plane fare, but not the cost of the lunch. He was not away overnight nor was he required to take time out to sleep before returning home.
2. Same facts as above except he sleeps overnight in a Washington hotel. He eats breakfast there, and then sees another client and returns home to New York in the afternoon. He may deduct not only the cost of the plane fare but also the cost of the meals while on the trip and the cost of the hotel, since he was away overnight.
3. A trucker's run is from Seattle to Portland and back. He leaves at about 2:00 a.m. and returns to Seattle the same day, getting in at about 6:00 p.m. While in Portland, he is released from duty for about four hours layover time to get necessary sleep before returning to Seattle. He may deduct the cost of meals because he is released at a layover location to obtain necessary sleep. Official release from duty, however, is not a prerequisite for satisfying the sleep or rest test.

Several courts held that the IRS rule was unreasonable and outdated in the world of supersonic travel, and they would have allowed the New Yorker on the one-day trip to Washington, D.C., to deduct the cost of his lunch. The Supreme Court disagreed and upheld the IRS rule as a fair administrative approach.

Meal costs during overtime. Such costs are not deductible if you are not away from your place of business. Thus, for example, a resident physician could not deduct the cost of meals and sleeping quarters at the hospital during overnight or weekend duty.

Table 20-1 Deductible Travel and Transportation Expenses

Your Travel Status—	*Tax Rule—*
Local trips to see customers and client	You may deduct your transportation expenses but not the cost of personal meals on one-day business trips within the general area of your tax home.
Local lodging necessary to participate in employer meeting.	Lodging costs are generally deductible only on business trips "away from home" *(20.6)*. However, the IRS will allow an employee to deduct local lodging costs (not away from home) if the lodging is necessary on a temporary basis for the employee to participate in a bona fide business meeting or function of the employer.
Two job locations for one employer in the same area **EXAMPLE:** Your employer has two business locations in the city in which you live. You work about half of the time in each place—at one location in the morning and at the other in the afternoon.	You deduct transportation expenses from one location to the other. However, if, for personal reasons, such as the choice of a place for eating lunch, you do not go directly from one location to the other, you may deduct your transportation expenses only to the extent that they do not exceed the cost of going directly from the first location to the second. But say your employer has several locations in the same city, but you do not move from one location to another in the same day. You spend the entire day at one place. You may not deduct transportation expenses between your home and the various locations, even if you report to a different location each day.
Two different jobs in the same area **EXAMPLE:** You work for two different employers in the city in which you live. Most of the time you work a full work shift at your principal place of employment. Then you work a part-time shift for your second employer some distance away.	You may deduct the transportation expenses from one job to another within the same working day. But you may not claim the deduction if you return home after the first job and then, after supper, go to your second job.
Permanent job in an area other than where you have your residence **EXAMPLE:** You live with your family in Chicago, but work in Milwaukee. During the week, you stay in a hotel in Milwaukee and eat meals in a restaurant. You return to your family in Chicago every weekend.	Milwaukee is your "home" for tax purposes; *see 20.6*. Thus, your expenses for traveling to Milwaukee and your meals and lodging there are personal, nondeductible expenses.
Temporary assignment in an area other than where you have your residence **EXAMPLE:** You live in Kansas City, where you work. You have been assigned to duty in Omaha for 60 days. Occasionally, you return to Kansas City on your days off, but most of the time you stay in Omaha.	You may deduct the necessary expenses for traveling from Kansas City to Omaha and returning to Kansas City after your temporary assignment is completed. You may also deduct expenses for meals and lodging (even for your days off) while you are in Omaha. As discussed at *20.9*, deductions are not allowed on temporary assignments that are *expected* to last more than one year.
Weekend trip home from temporary assignment **EXAMPLE:** Same facts as in the Example above except that you return home to Kansas City during the weekend.	You are not "away from home" while you are in Kansas City on your days off and your meals and lodging while you are there are not deductible. However, you may deduct your traveling expenses (including meals and lodging, if any) from Omaha to Kansas City and back if they are no more than the amount it would have cost you for your meals and lodging if you had stayed in Omaha. If they are more, your deduction is limited to the amount you would have spent in Omaha. If you retain your room in Omaha while in Kansas City, your expenses of returning to Kansas City on days off are deductible only to the extent of the amount you would have spent for your meals had you stayed in Omaha.
Temporary job location away from home where there are no living accommodations **EXAMPLE:** You live and work in Chicago. You have been assigned for three months to a construction job located 20 miles outside Nashville. There are no living facilities near the job site and you have to stay at a hotel in Nashville.	Under these circumstances, your necessary expenses in getting to and from your temporary job are business expenses and not commuting expenses. If you were employed at the site for an indefinite period *(20.9)*, then the costs of commuting would be nondeductible, regardless of the distance *(20.2)*.

Table 20-1 Deductible Travel and Transportation Expenses (continued)

Your Travel Status—	*Tax Rule—*
Taxi trips between customers' locations	The cab fares are deductible *(20.2)*.
Seasonal jobs in different areas **EXAMPLE:** You live in Cincinnati, where you work for eight months each year. You earn the greater share of your annual income from that job. For the remaining four months of the year, you work in Miami. When in Miami, you eat and sleep in a hotel. You have been working on both of these jobs for several years and expect to continue to do so.	You have two recurring seasonal places of employment. Cincinnati is your principal place of employment. You may deduct the costs of your traveling expenses while away from Cincinnati working at your minor place of employment in Miami, including meals and lodging in Miami.
Trailer home moved to different job sites **EXAMPLE:** You are a construction welder. You live in a trailer that you move from city to city, where you work on construction projects. You have no other established home	You may not deduct your expenses for meals and lodging. Each place where you locate becomes your principal place of business and, therefore, you are not "away from home."
Travel to school after work to take job-related courses	You may deduct travel costs if you meet the rules discusse at *33.17*.
Finding a new job in the same line of work **EXAMPLE:** You live in New York. You travel to Chicago for an interview for a new position.	You may deduct the cost of the trip and living expenses in Chicago *(19.7)*.
Convention trip	You may deduct costs of travel to a business convention under the rules in *20.12*. If you are a delegate to a charitable or veterans' convention, you may claim a charitable deduction for the travel costs *(14.4)*.
Trip to out-of-town college for educational courses	You deduct the cost of the trip if you meet the rules at *33.17*.
Trip for health reasons	You may deduct the cost of the trip as a medical expense if you meet the rules at *17.9*.

20.4 IRS Meal Allowance

If you find it difficult to keep records of meal costs while away from home *(20.3)* on business trips, you may prefer to claim an IRS meal allowance. In government tables, the allowance is referred to as the "M&IE" rate (meals and incidental expenses). In addition to meals and tips for food servers, the allowance (M&IE rate) includes a limited number of "incidental" expenses such as fees and tips for porters, baggage carriers, hotel maids, or room stewards. Self-employed individuals may claim the M&IE allowance as well as employees who are not reimbursed for meals under an "accountable" plan *(20.31)*. However, the meal allowance may not be used if your employer is your brother, sister, spouse, parent, child, grandparent, or grandchild, or if you own more than 10% of the employer's outstanding stock.

Meal allowance on 2010 tax returns. For travel within the continental U.S. (referred to as CONUS locations), the standard meal allowance (M&IE) for 2010 is usually $46 per day, but higher rates apply in certain high-cost areas designated by the government. The high-cost-areas are generally major metropolitan cities or resort areas. The basic and high-cost-area meal rates are determined by the federal government's General Services Administration (GSA) and the IRS allows taxpayers to use the applicable rates in figuring their meal allowance deduction.

You must keep a record of the time, place, and business purpose of the trips. As long as you have this proof, you may claim the allowance even if your actual costs are less than the allowance.

The IRS provides the CONUS M&IE rates in Publication 1542, available online at www.irs.gov/formspubs/index.html. Publication 1542 is available only online; print copies can no longer be ordered. Publication 1542 shows the CONUS M&IE rates in tables that coincide with the start of

IRS Alert

Incidental Expenses

The IRS standard meal allowance (M&IE rate) does not include laundry, cleaning, and pressing of clothing. If you have receipts to substantiate laundry and cleaning costs, you may deduct them separately from the M&IE allowance, which includes as incidental expenses fees and tips for porters, baggage carriers, hotel maids, and room stewards.

If you do *not* pay or incur any meal expenses for a particular day on a trip away from home but you do have qualifying incidental expenses on that day, you have the option of deducting the actual costs or an allowance of $3 per day for the incidental expenses. The $3-per-day allowance must be prorated for the first and last days of the trip.

a new fiscal year for the federal government each October. For example, Table 4 of the April 2010 revision of Publication 1542 shows the rates applicable for business trips from October 1, 2009 through September 30, 2010 (Table 3 shows the rates for the prior one-year period). When the GSA changes the nationwide rates for the fiscal year starting October 1, 2010, the IRS will revise Publication 1542 and the rates for October 1, 2010 through September 30, 2011, will be shown in a new Table 4 and the rates for the first nine months of 2010 will be in Table 3. The IRS will post other online revisions to Publication 1542 throughout the year following GSA rate changes for particular localities.

The CONUS rates can also be obtained from the GSA website at www.gsa.gov; click on "Per Diem Rates."

In computing your meal allowance (M&IE) deduction for 2010 business trips, you can apply the rates that were in effect for the first nine months of the year to business trips in the last three months. You may use the first set of rates for the first nine months and the updated rates for the last three months. For trips within the last three months, you must consistently use either the rates in effect for the first nine months or the revised rates that took effect on October 1; you cannot switch between the sets of rates on a trip-by-trip basis. If you travel to more than one city on the same day, use the meal allowance for the area where you stay overnight.

Travel outside the continental United States. Different rates apply for travel in Alaska, Hawaii, Puerto Rico, and U.S. possessions, as well as for travel to foreign countries. These rates (OCONUS) can be obtained by using links from the GSA website at www.gsa.gov.

Transportation industry workers. Employees or self-employed persons in the transportation industry may elect to claim a special M&IE rate. For the first nine months of 2010, the rate is $59 per day for any CONUS location and $65 per day for any OCONUS location. The rates may change effective October 1, 2010; *see* the *e-Supplement at jklasser.com* for an update. The special rate avoids the need to apply the CONUS or OCONUS rates on a locality-by-locality basis. You cannot combine the two methods. If the special rate is used for one trip, it must be used for all trips during the same year.

Allowance must be reduced. The allowance is prorated for the first and last day of a trip. You may claim 75% of the allowance for the days you depart and return. Alternatively, you may claim 100% of the allowance if you are away for a regular "9-to-5" business day.

If you are an employee and claim a deduction based on the allowance, you must reduce the deduction by 50% on Form 2106 or Form 2106-EZ and the balance, when added to your other miscellaneous deductions, is subject to the 2% AGI floor on Schedule A *(20.29)*. If you are self-employed, the allowance is claimed on Schedule C, where it is subject only to the 50% reduction *(20.28)*.

A higher deduction percentage is allowed to interstate truck drivers, pilots, railroad operators, and other transportation industry employees subject to Department of Transportation hours of service limits, who are allowed to deduct 80% of meal costs.

20.5 Business Trip Deductions

The following expenses of a business trip *away from home (20.6)* are deductible if not reimbursed by your employer:

- Plane, railroad, taxi, and other transportation fares between your home and your business destination
- Hotel and other lodging expenses. You need receipts or similar evidence for lodging expenses; there is no IRS standard lodging allowance as there is for meals *(20.4)*. Although lodging costs are generally deductible only on business trips "away from home" *(20.6)*, the IRS will allow an employee to deduct local lodging costs (not away from home) if the lodging is necessary on a temporary basis for the employee to participate in a bona fide business meeting or function of the employer.
- Meal costs. You may claim your actual meal costs if you maintain records, or you may use the standard meal allowance *(20.4)*. Whichever method you use, only 50% of the unreimbursed meal costs are deductible *(20.15)*.
- Tips, telephone, and telegraph costs
- Laundry and cleaning expenses

- Baggage charges (including insurance)
- Cab fares or other costs of transportation to and from the airport or station and your hotel. Also deductible are cab fares or other transportation costs, beginning with your first business call of the day, of getting from one customer to another, or from one place of business to another.
- Travel costs to find a new job are deductible *(19.7)*.
- Entertainment expenses incurred while traveling away from home are deductible subject to restrictions, including the 50% deduction limit *(20.15)*.

Cruise ship. If you travel by cruise ship on a business trip, your deductible cruise costs are limited to twice the highest federal *per diem* rate for travel in the United States on that date multiplied by the number of days in transit.

EXAMPLE

You sail to Europe on business. While you are away, the highest *per diem* federal rate is $389 and the trip lasts six days. The maximum deduction for the cost of the trip is $4,668 (2 x $389 x 6). The double *per diem* rule applies without regard to the 50% limit on meal costs if meals are not separately stated in your bill. If a separate amount for meals or entertainment is included, such amount must be reduced by 50%.

The double *per diem* rule does not apply to cruise ship convention costs that are deductible up to $2,000 a year if all the ports of call are in the U.S. or U.S. possessions and if the ship is registered in the United States *(20.14)*.

Important: Record-keeping requirements. *See* the section for record-keeping rules to support a deduction for unreimbursed travel expenses or to avoid being taxed on employer reimbursements *(20.26)*.

20.6 When Are You Away From Home?

You have to meet the "away from home" test to deduct the cost of meals (only 50% deductible) and lodging while traveling. You have to be away from your tax home and satisfy the overnight-sleep rule *(20.3)* to be "away from home." In general, your tax home is the city or general area in which your regular place of business or post of duty is located, regardless of where your family is.

EXAMPLES

1. Your residence is in a suburb within commuting distance of New York City where you work full time. Your personal home and tax home are the same, that is, within the metropolitan area of New York City. You are away from home when you leave this area, say for Philadelphia. Meals and lodging are deductible only if you meet the overnight-sleep test *(20.3)*.
2. Your residence is in New York City, but you work in Baltimore. Your tax home is Baltimore; you may not deduct living expenses there. But you may deduct travel expenses on a temporary assignment to New York City even while living at your home there.
3. A construction worker works for a utility company on construction sites in a 12-state area. Assignments are sent from his employer's regional office; he is not required to report to the office. The IRS ruled that his residence, which is in a city in the 12-state area, is his tax home.

Are you constantly on the road? If you move from job to job and do not work within any particular locality, an IRS agent may disallow your travel deductions on the grounds that your tax home is wherever you work; thus, you are never "away from home." You are considered a transient worker.

If your deduction is questioned because you have no regular or main place of business, you may be able to show that your tax home is the area of your residence. If you meet the following three tests, the IRS will treat your residence as your tax home: (1) you do some work in the vicinity of your residence, house, apartment, or room and live there while performing services in the area; (2) you have mortgage expenses or pay rent for the residence while away on the road; and (3) the residence is in an area where you were raised or lived for a long time, or a member of your immediate family such as your parent or child lives in the residence, or you frequently return there.

Law Alert

Tax Home Defined

For travel expense purposes, your home is your place of business, employment, or post of duty, regardless of where you maintain your family residence. This tax home includes the entire city or general area of your business premises or place of employment. The area of your residence may be your tax home if your job requires you to work at widely scattered locations, you have no fixed place of work, and your residence is in a location economically suited to your work.

According to the IRS, if you meet only two of these three tests, it will decide on a case-by-case basis if your residence is your tax home. If you meet less than two of the tests, the IRS will not allow a deduction; each of your work locations is treated as your tax home.

If you live in a trailer at each job assignment and have no other home, each job location is your principal place of business and you are not "away from home."

Permanent duty station of service members. The Supreme Court held that a member of the Armed Forces is not away from home when he or she is at a permanent duty station. This is true even if the service member has to maintain a separate home for family members who are not permitted to live at the duty station.

20.7 Fixing a Tax Home If You Work in Different Locations

If you regularly work in two or more separate areas, your tax home is the area of your principal place of business or employment. You are away from home when you are away from the area of your principal place of business or employment. Therefore, you may deduct your transportation costs to and from your minor place of business and your living costs there.

Professional sports players, coaches, and managers. When the only business of such persons is the professional sport, their home is the "club town." But if they are in another business in addition to their professional playing, how much time is spent and how much is earned at each place determines whether their club's hometown or the place of their off-season business is their tax home. If it is the club's hometown, they deduct travel and living expenses while away from that town—including the time they are where the second business is. (If the second place is where their families also live, they may not deduct the families' expenses there.) If the town where the other business is located is the tax home, then expenses in the club's hometown may be deducted.

Airline pilots. It is important for airline pilots who fly in and out of various locations to determine a tax home for income and deduction purposes. Generally, the IRS considers an airline pilot's tax home to be the airport at which the pilot is regularly based. For example, in one case the IRS barred a pilot from claiming the foreign earned income exclusion *(36.1)* because his tax home was deemed to be his base in New York, rather than in London, where he and his wife actually lived.

Planning Reminder

Determining Your Principal Place of Business

If you have more than one regular place of business, your tax home is your principal place of business. Your principal place of business or employment is determined by comparing: (1) the time ordinarily spent working in each area; (2) the degree of your business activity in each area; (3) the amount of your income from each area; (4) the taxpayer's permanent residence; and (5) whether employment at one location is temporary or indefinite.

No single factor is determinative. The relative importance of each factor will vary depending on the facts of a particular case. For example, where there are no substantial differences between incomes earned in two places of employment, your tax home is probably the area in which you spend more of your time. Where there are substantial income differences, your tax home is probably the area in which you earn more of your income.

EXAMPLES

1. Sherman lived in Worcester, Mass., where he managed a factory. He opened his own sales agency in New York. He continued to manage the factory and spent considerable time in Worcester. The larger part of his income came from the New York business. However, he was allowed to treat New York as his minor place of business and to deduct his travel expenses to New York and his living expenses there because he spent most of his time in Worcester and his income there was substantial.
2. Benson, a consulting engineer, maintained a combination residence-business office in a home he owned in New York. He also taught four days a week at a Technological Institute in West Virginia under a temporary nine-month appointment. He spent three-day weekends, holidays, and part of the summer at his New York address. At the Institute, he rented a room in the student union building. The IRS disallowed transportation expenses between New York and West Virginia and meals and lodging there as not incurred while away from home. The Tax Court disagreed. A taxpayer may have more than one occupation in more than one city. When his occupations require him to spend a substantial amount of time in each place, he may deduct his travel expenses, including meals and lodging, at the place away from his permanent residence. That Benson's teaching salary happened to exceed his income from his private practice does not change the result.

20.8 Tax Home of Married Couple Working in Different Cities

When a husband and wife work and live in different cities during the week, one of them may seek to deduct travel expenses away from home. Such deductions have generally been disallowed, but courts have allowed some exceptions. Although for common law purposes the domicile of the husband may be the domicile of the wife, for tax purposes when each spouse works in a different city, each may have a separate tax home.

EXAMPLES

1. Robert worked in Wilmington, Delaware; his wife, Margaret, worked in New York City. During the weekend, she traveled to Wilmington and deducted, as travel expenses away from home, her living costs in New York and weekend travel expenses to Wilmington. She argued that because she and her husband filed a joint return, they were a single taxable unit, and the tax home of this unit was Wilmington where her husband lived. The deduction was disallowed. That a couple can file a joint return does not give them deductions that are not otherwise available to them as individuals. Margaret's tax home was New York, where she worked. Therefore, her expenses there are not deductible. And, as the weekend trips to Wilmington had no relationship to her job, they, too, were not deductible.
2. Hundt and his wife lived in Arlington, Va., but he wrote and directed films in various parts of the country. He wrote screenplays either at his Arlington home or on location, but most of his business came from New York City, where he lived in hotels. One year, he spent 175 days in New York City on business and rented an apartment for $1,200 because it was cheaper than a hotel. He deducted half the annual rent for the New York apartment, the costs of traveling between Arlington and New York, and the cost of meals in New York. The IRS disallowed the expenses, finding New York to be his tax home. The Tax Court disagreed. Arlington was Hundt's tax home because (1) part of his income came from his creative writing in Arlington; and (2) his travel to other parts of the country was temporary. The fact that most of his income came from New York did not make New York his tax home.

20.9 Deducting Living Costs on Temporary Assignment

A business trip or job assignment away from home *(20.6)* at a single location may last a few days, weeks, or months. If your assignment is considered *temporary*, you may deduct travel costs (*see* below) while there because your tax home has not changed. An assignment is considered temporary by the IRS if you realistically expect it to last for one year or less and it actually does last no more than one year. If an assignment is realistically expected to last more than a year it is considered *indefinite*, and you cannot deduct your living costs at the area of the assignment because that location becomes your tax home. This is true even if the assignment actually lasts only a year or less. That is, you can be away for a year or less and still be barred from claiming a deduction if at the time you started the assignment you realistically expected it to last for more than a year. Likewise, employment that is initially temporary may become indefinite due to changed circumstances; *see* the Examples below.

Planning Reminder

Federal Crime Investigations

Federal employees such as FBI agents and prosecutors who are certified by the Attorney General as traveling on behalf of the federal government in a temporary duty status to investigate, prosecute, or provide support services for the investigation or prosecution of a federal crime are not subject to the one-year limitation on deductibility of expenses while away from home on temporary assignments.

EXAMPLES

1. You are on a job assignment away from home in a single location that is expected to last (and it does in fact last) for one year or less. The IRS will treat the employment as temporary, unless facts and circumstances indicate otherwise. Expenses are deductible.
2. You are sent on a job assignment away from home at a *single* location. You expected that the job would last 18 months. However, due to financial difficulties you were transferred home after 11 months. Even though your assignment actually lasted for less than one year the IRS treats the employment as indefinite because you realistically expected it to last more than one year. Thus, your travel and living expenses while away from home are not deductible.
3. You are sent on a job assignment away from home at a *single* location. You expected that the job would last only nine months. However, due to changed circumstances occurring after eight months, you were asked to remain on the assignment for six more months. The IRS treats the assignment as temporary for eight months, and indefinite for the remaining time you are away from home. Thus, travel and living expenses you paid or incurred during the first eight months are deductible; expenses paid or incurred thereafter are not.

Deductible travel costs on temporary trip. While on a temporary job assignment expected to last a year or less, you may deduct the cost of meals and lodging there, even for your days off. If you return home, say for weekends, your living expenses at home are not deductible. You may deduct travel expenses, meals, and lodging en route between your home and your job assignment provided they do not exceed your living expenses had you stayed at the temporary job location. If you keep a hotel room at the temporary location while you return home, you may deduct your round-trip expenses for the trip home only up to the amount you would have spent for meals had you stayed at the temporary workplace.

Caution

Taking Your Family With You

If you take your family with you to a temporary job site, an IRS agent may argue that this is evidence that you considered the assignment to be indefinite. In the Michaels Example in this section, however, such a move was not considered detrimental to a deduction of living expenses at the job location.

EXAMPLE

Michaels, a cost analyst for Boeing, lived in Seattle. He traveled for Boeing, but was generally not away from home for more than five weeks. Michaels agreed to go to Los Angeles for a year to service Boeing's suppliers in that area. He rented his Seattle house and brought his family with him to Los Angeles. Ten months later, Boeing opened a permanent office in Los Angeles and asked Michaels to remain there permanently. Michaels argued that his expenses for food and lodging during the 10-month period were deductible as "away from home" expenses. The IRS contended that the Los Angeles assignment was for an indefinite period.

The Tax Court sided with Michaels. He was told that the stay was for a year only. He leased his Seattle house to a tenant for one year, planning to return to it. He regarded his work in Los Angeles as temporary until Boeing changed its plans. The one-year period justified his taking the family but did not alter the temporary nature of the assignment.

Separate assignments over a period over a year. Where over a period of years you work on several separate assignments for one client, the IRS may attempt to treat the separate assignments as amounting to a permanent assignment and disallow living costs away from home, as in Mitchell's situation, below.

EXAMPLE

Mitchell, a publishing consultant who lived and worked out of his home in Illinois, advised a publisher of a magazine with offices in California. Over a five-year period, from 1991 to 1995, he worked on short job assignments that averaged 130 days a year for the magazine. Some assignments arose because of unforeseen events, such as the abrupt firing of a novice editor, the hiring of a new editor, and the editor's later absence because of cancer and her death. In 1994 and 1995, when working in California, he rented an apartment because it was cheaper than a hotel. He claimed lodging and meal expenses in California that the IRS disallowed on the grounds that his employment in California was not temporary; it lasted more than one year.

The Tax Court disagrees. Just because an independent contractor returns to the same general location in more than one year does not mean that he is employed there on an indefinite basis. Mitchell's work followed an on again, off again pattern. Each job assignment that lasted less than a year ended with no expectation of future employment. Throughout the five-year period, his consultancy services were required by unexpected events.

No regular job where you live. That you do not have regular employment where you live may prevent a deduction of living costs at a temporary job in another city. The IRS may disallow the deduction on the grounds that the expenses are not incurred while you are away from home; the temporary job site is the tax home.

20.10 Business-Vacation Trips Within the United States

Caution

Primary Business Purpose

If your return is examined, proving the business purpose of your trip depends on presenting evidence to convince an examining agent that the trip, despite your vacationing, was planned primarily to transact business. Keep a log or diary to substantiate business activities.

On a business trip to a resort area, you may also spend time vacationing. If the *primary purpose* of the trip is to transact business and the area is within the United States (50 states and the District of Columbia) you may deduct all of the costs of your transportation to and from the area, lodging, and 50% of meal expenses, even if you do spend time vacationing. If the main purpose of the trip is personal, you may not deduct any part of your travel costs to and from the area. The amount of time spent on business as opposed to sightseeing or personal visits is the most important issue in determining your primary purpose. Regardless of the primary purpose of your trip, you are allowed to deduct expenses related to the business you transacted while in the area.

No deductions will be allowed if you attend a convention or seminar where you are given videotapes to view at your own convenience and no other business-related activities or lectures occur during the convention. The trip is considered a vacation.

If your trip is primarily for business, and while at the business destination you extend your stay for a few days for nonbusiness reasons, such as to visit relatives, you deduct travel expenses to and from the business destination.

> ***EXAMPLE***
>
> You work in Atlanta and make a business trip to New Orleans. You stay in New Orleans for six days and your total costs, including round-trip transportation to and from New Orleans, meals, and lodging, is $1,600, which you may deduct subject to the 50% limit for meals. If, on your way home, you spend three days in Mobile visiting relatives and incur an additional $400 in travel costs, your deduction is limited to the $1,600 (less 50% of meals) you would have spent had you gone home directly from New Orleans.

Reimbursement for weekend travel. If your employer extends your business trip over a weekend to take advantage of discount airfares that require a Saturday night stayover, you may deduct the cost of meals, lodging, and other incidental expenses incurred for the additional night. The reason for the stayover has a business purpose: to cut travel costs. If your employer pays for the expenses directly or if you are reimbursed under an accountable plan *(20.31)*, the payment is not taxable to you.

20.11 Business-Vacation Trips Outside the United States

On a business trip abroad, you may deduct your travel expenses (the 50% limit applies for meals), even though you take time out to vacation, provided you can prove: (1) the primary purpose of the trip was business and (2) you did not have control over the assignment of the trip.

Fixing the date of the trip does not mean that you had control over the assignment. IRS regulations assume that when you travel for your company under a reimbursement or allowance arrangement, you do not control the trip arrangements, provided also that you are not: (1) a managing executive of the company; (2) related to your employer *(20.4)*; or (3) have more than a 10% stock interest in the company. You are considered a managing executive if you are authorized without effective veto procedures to decide on the necessity of the trip. You are related to your employer if the employer is your spouse, parent, child, brother, sister, grandparent, or grandchild.

Caution

Vacation Areas

If the IRS determines that you were primarily on vacation, it will disallow all travel costs except for costs directly related to your business in the area such as registration fees at a foreign business convention *(20.14)*.

Rule for managing executives and self-employed persons. If you are a managing executive, self-employed, related to your employer, or have a more-than-10% stock interest, your deduction for transportation costs to and from your business destination may be limited. However, a full deduction for transportation costs is allowed if:

1. The trip outside the United States took a week or less, not counting the day you left the U.S. but counting the day you returned,
2. If the trip abroad lasted more than a week, you spent less than 25% of your time, counting the days your trip began and ended, on vacation or other personal activities, *or*
3. In planning the trip you did not place a major emphasis on taking a vacation.

If the vacationing and other personal activities took up 25% or more of your time on a trip lasting more than one week, and you cannot prove that the vacation was a minor consideration in planning the trip, you must allocate travel expenses between the time spent on business and that spent on personal affairs. The part allocated to business is deductible; the balance is not. To allocate, count the number of days spent on the trip outside the United States, including the day you leave the U.S. and the day you return. Then divide this total into the number of days on which you had business activities; include days of travel to and from a business destination.

If you vacation at, near, or beyond the city in which you do business, the expense subject to allocation is the cost of travel from the place of departure to the business destination and back. For example, you travel from New York to London on business and then vacation in Paris before returning to New York. The expense subject to allocation is the cost of traveling from New York to London and back; *see* Example 2 below. However, if from London you vacationed in Dublin before returning to New York, you would allocate the round-trip fare between New York and Dublin and also deduct the difference between that round-trip fare and the fare between New York and London; *see* Example 3 below.

EXAMPLES

1. You fly from New York to Paris to attend a business meeting for one day. You spend the next two days sightseeing and then fly back to New York. The entire trip, including two days for travel en route, took five days. The plane fare is deductible. The trip did not exceed one week.
2. You fly from Chicago to New York, where you spend six days on business. You then fly to London, where you conduct business for two days. You then fly to Paris for a five-day vacation after which you fly back to Chicago. You would not have made the trip except for the business that you had to transact in London. The nine days of travel outside the United States away from home, including two days for travel en route, exceeded a week, and the five days devoted to vacationing were not less than 25% of the total travel time outside the U.S. The two days spent traveling between Chicago and New York, and the six days spent in New York, are not counted in determining whether the travel outside the United States exceeded a week and whether the time devoted to personal activities was less than 25%.

   Assume you are unable to prove either that you did not have substantial control over the arrangements of the trip or that an opportunity for taking a personal vacation was not a major consideration in your decision to take the trip. Thus, $^5/_9$ (five nonbusiness days out of nine days outside the U.S.) of the plane fare from New York to London and from London to New York is not deductible. You may deduct $^4/_9$ of the New-York-to-London round-trip fare, plus lodging, 50% of meals, and other allowable travel costs while in London. No deduction is allowed for any part of the costs of the trip from London to Paris.
3. Same facts as in Example 2, except that the vacation is in Dublin, which is closer to the U.S. than London. The allocation is based on the round-trip fare between New York and Dublin. Thus, $^4/_9$ of the New York to Dublin fare is deductible and $^5/_9$ is not deductible. Further, the IRS allows a deduction for the excess of the New-York-to-London fare over the New-York-to-Dublin fare.

Filing Tip

Weekend Expenses

If your business trip is extended over a weekend to take advantage of reduced airfares, the additional cost of meals, lodging, and other incidental expenses is deductible.

Weekends, holidays, and business standby days. If you have business meetings scheduled before and after a weekend or holiday, the days in between the meetings are treated as days spent on business for purposes of the 25% business test just discussed. This is true although you spend the days for sightseeing or other personal travel. A similar rule applies if you have business meetings on Friday and the next scheduled meeting is the following Tuesday; Saturday through Monday are treated as business days. If your trip is extended over a weekend to take advantage of reduced airfares, the additional expense of meals, lodging, and other incidental expenses is deductible *(20.10)*.

20.12 Deducting Expenses of Business Conventions

Conventions and seminars at resort areas usually combine business with pleasure. Therefore, the IRS scrutinizes deductions claimed for attending a business convention where opportunities exist for vacationing. Especially questioned are trips where you are accompanied by your spouse and other members of your family. Deducting expenses of foreign conventions is subject to restrictions *(20.14)*.

Generally, you may not deduct expenses of attending investment conventions and seminars *(19.15)*. You also may not deduct the costs of business conventions or seminars where you merely receive a videotape of business lectures to be viewed at your convenience and no other business-related activities occur during the event.

In claiming a deduction for convention expenses, be prepared to show that your attendance at the convention benefitted your business. Cases and IRS rulings have upheld deductions for doctors, lawyers, and dentists attending professional conventions. One case allowed a deduction to a legal secretary for her costs at a secretaries' convention. If you are a delegate to a business convention, make sure you prove you attended to serve primarily your own business interests, not those of the association. However, it is not necessary for you to show that the convention dealt specifically with your job. It is sufficient that attendance at the convention may advance or benefit your position. If you fail to prove business purpose, the IRS will allocate your expenses between the time spent on your business and the time spent as a delegate. You then deduct only the expenses attributed to your business activities.

EXAMPLES

1. An attorney with a general law practice was interested in international law and relations. He was appointed a delegate to represent the American branch of the International Law Association at a convention in Paris. The attorney deducted the cost of the trip and convention as business expenses which the IRS and a court disallowed. He failed to prove that attending the conference on international law helped his general practice. He did not get any business referrals as a result of his attendance at the convention. Nor did he prove the chance of getting any potential business from the conference.
2. An insurance agent doing business in Texas attended his company's convention in New York. One morning of the six-day convention was devoted to a business meeting and luncheon; the rest of the time was spent in sightseeing and entertainment. The company paid for the cost of the trip. The IRS added the reimbursement to the agent's pay and would not let him deduct the amount. The convention in New York served no business purpose. It was merely a method of entertaining company personnel. If there was any valid business to be transacted, the company could have called a meeting in Texas, the area of his home office.
3. A plywood company could not deduct the costs of entertaining 116 customers and employees at a New Orleans hotel during a Superbowl weekend. The company did not reserve conference rooms or make any other arrangements for organized business meetings. The IRS and two federal courts held that although business discussions may have occurred on a random basis, these were secondary to entertainment.

Caution

Substantiate Convention Business

Keep a copy of the convention program and a record of the business sessions you attend. If the convention provides a sign-in book, sign it. In addition, keep a record of all of your business expenses *(20.26)*.

What expenses are deductible? If the convention trip is primarily for business, you may deduct travel costs both to and from the convention, food costs, tips, display expenses (such as sample room costs), and hotel bills. If you entertain business clients or customers, you may deduct these amounts too.

Food and beverage costs are subject to the 50% cost limitation rule *(20.24)*.

EXAMPLE

You attend a business convention held in a coastal resort city primarily for business reasons. During the convention period, you do some local sightseeing, social entertaining, and visiting—all unrelated to your business. You may deduct your traveling expenses to and from the resort, your living expenses at the resort, and other expenses such as business entertaining, sample displays, etc. But you may not deduct the cost of sightseeing, personal entertaining, and social visiting.

Keep records of your payments identifying expenses directly connected with your business dealings at the convention and those that are part of your personal activity, such as sightseeing, social visiting, and entertaining. Recreation costs are not deductible even though a part of your overall convention costs.

Fraternal organizations. You may not deduct expenses at conventions held by fraternal organizations, such as the American Legion, Shriners, etc., even though incidental business was carried on. However, delegates to fraternal conventions may in some instances deduct expenses as charitable contributions *(14.4)*.

20.13 Travel Expenses of a Spouse or Dependents

Travel costs of a spouse, dependent, or any other individual who is not a business associate and who accompanies you on a business trip are not deductible unless that person is also your employee and has a bona fide business reason for taking the trip that would justify claiming a deduction if the person took the trip on his or her own.

Even though the travel costs of a non-employee spouse or other person are not deductible, you may deduct the cost of such person's participation in the entertainment of business clients at conventions or business trips if the trip or entertainment meets certain tests *(20.21)*. Generally, you may deduct the cost of goodwill entertaining of associates immediately before or after convention business meetings. A convention meeting qualifies as a bona fide business meeting.

Filing Tip

How Much To Deduct for Spouse

If your spouse accompanied you on a business trip, your bills will probably show costs for both of you. These usually are less than twice the cost for a single person. To find what you may deduct where your spouse's presence is for personal and not qualifying business reasons, do not divide the bill in half. Figure what accommodations and transportation would have cost you alone and deduct that. The excess over the single person's costs is not deductible.

EXAMPLES

1. You and your spouse travel by car to a convention. You pay $200 a day for a double room. A single room would have cost $150 a day. Your spouse's presence at the convention was for social reasons. You may deduct the total cost of operating your car to and from the convention city. You may deduct $150 a day for your room. If you traveled by plane or railroad, you would deduct only your own fare.
2. Connie worked with her husband operating a home improvement contracting business. With him, she attended trade shows and conventions, where they ran a display booth. There, she talked about their company's services and solicited new business. The IRS disallowed the company's deduction of her travel expenses as having no business purpose. The Tax Court disagreed. Both Connie and her husband were officers and employees of the company. They attended the conferences together. As the IRS allowed her husband's expenses, it should have also allowed expenses attributed to her participation, especially as they were incurred together as employees.

20.14 Restrictions on Foreign Conventions and Cruises

You may not deduct expenses at a foreign convention outside the North American area unless you satisfy the deduction rules *(20.11)* and also can show the convention is directly related to your business and it was as reasonable for the meeting to be held outside the North American area as within it.

Apart from the United States, the North American area includes Mexico, Canada, Puerto Rico, U.S. Virgin Islands, American Samoa, Northern Mariana Islands, Guam, Marshall Islands, Micronesia, Palau and U.S. island possessions.

Conventions may also be held in eligible Caribbean countries that agree to exchange certain data with the U.S. and do not discriminate against conventions held in the United States. Antigua and Barbuda, Aruba, Bahamas, Barbados, Bermuda, Costa Rica, Dominica, Dominican Republic, Grenada, Guyana, Honduras, Jamaica, Netherlands Antilles, and Trinidad and Tobago have qualified and are considered to be within the North American area.

Check with the convention operator about whether the country in which your convention is being held has qualified.

Limited cruise ship deduction. Up to $2,000 a year is allowed for attending cruise ship conventions if all the ports of call are in the U.S. or U.S. possessions and if the ship is registered in the United States. A deduction is allowed only if you attach to your return statements signed by you and by an officer of the convention sponsor that detail the daily schedule of business activities, the number of hours you attended these activities, and the total days of the trip. Do not confuse the $2,000 limitation with the *per diem* limitation for cruise ship costs *(20.5)*. The *per diem* limitation does not apply to cruises that meet the tests for the up-to-$2,000 deduction.

20.15 50% Deduction Limit

To be deductible at all, dining and entertainment costs for clients, customers, or employees must meet one of two restrictive tests *(20.16)*. Even if the expenses qualify under one of the tests, only 50% of unreimbursed expenses are generally deductible and this 50% balance is reduced by the 2% AGI floor if you are an employee. Furthermore, all entertainment costs, including meals, must be backed up with records. If you do not keep adequate records, your deductions will be disallowed. *See* the discussion of the 50% deduction limit and exceptions to the limit *(20.24)*.

20.16 The Restrictive Tests for Meals and Entertainment

Meal and entertainment costs are deductible, subject to the 50% limit *(20.24)*, if they are ordinary and necessary to your business, and also are either:

1. Directly related to the active conduct of your business *(20.17)*, *or*
2. Directly preceding or following a substantial and bona fide business discussion on a subject associated with the active conduct of your business. This test applies to dining and entertainment in which you seek new business or to goodwill entertainment to encourage the

continuation of an existing business relationship. Under this test, you may entertain business associates in nonbusiness settings such as restaurants, theaters, sports arenas, and nightclubs, provided the entertainment directly precedes or follows the business discussion. Business associates are: established or prospective customers, clients, suppliers, employees, agents, partners, or professional advisers, whether established or prospective *(20.18)*.

Ordinary and necessary expenses are those considered helpful and common practice in your business or profession; they do not have to be indispensable to your business.

20.17 Directly Related Dining and Entertainment

The directly related test limits the deduction of dining and entertainment costs at restaurants, nightclubs, on yachts, at sporting events, on hunting trips, and during social events.

The directly related test for dining and entertainment costs may be met in one of three ways: (1) under the generally related test; (2) as expenses incurred in a clear business setting; or (3) as expenses incurred for services performed. If dining or entertainment fails to meet the directly related tests, it may qualify under the goodwill entertainment rules *(20.18)*, which require the holding of a business discussion before or after the entertainment.

Generally related test. Under this test, you must show a business motive for the dining or entertainment and business activity during the entertainment. You must show that you had more than a general expectation of getting future income or other specific business benefit (other than goodwill). Although you do not have to prove that income or other business benefit actually resulted from the expense, such evidence will help support your claim. What type of business activity will an IRS agent look for? The agent will seek proof that a business meeting, negotiation, or discussion took place during the period of dining or entertainment. It is not necessary that more time be devoted to business than to entertainment. What if you did not talk business? You must prove that you would have done so except for reasons beyond your control.

Clear business setting test. Expenses incurred in a clear business setting meet the directly related test provided also that you had no significant motive for incurring the expenses other than to further your business. Entertainment of people with whom you have no personal or social relationship is usually considered to have occurred in a clear business setting. For example, entertainment of business representatives and civic leaders at the opening of a new hotel or theatrical production to obtain business publicity rather than goodwill is considered to be entertainment in a clear business setting. Also, entertainment that involves a price rebate is considered to have occurred in a clear business setting, as, for example, when a hotel owner provides occasional free dinners at the hotel for a customer who patronizes the hotel.

The cost of a hospitality room displaying company products at a convention is also a directly related expense.

Entertainment occurring under the following circumstances or in the following places is generally *not* considered as directly related:

- You are not present during the entertainment.
- The distractions are substantial, as at nightclubs, sporting events, or during a social gathering such as a cocktail party.
- You meet with a group that includes persons other than business associates at cocktail lounges, country clubs, golf and athletic clubs, or at vacation resorts.

Services performed test. An expense is directly related if it was directly or indirectly made for the benefit of an individual (other than an employee) either as taxable compensation for services he or she rendered or as a taxable prize or award.

EXAMPLE

A manufacturer provides a vacation trip for retailers whose sales of his products exceed quotas. The value of the vacation is a taxable prize to the retailers. The vacation cost is a directly related entertainment expense for the manufacturer.

Planning Reminder

Scheduling Entertainment and Business Discussions

A business discussion generally must take place the same day as the dining or entertainment. If not, and your deduction is questioned, you must give an acceptable reason for the interval between the discussion and the dining or entertainment. IRS regulations recognize that a day may separate a business meeting and the entertainment of an out-of-town customer. He or she may come to your office to discuss business one day and you provide entertainment the next day, or you provide the entertainment on the first day and discuss business the day after.

The IRS does not estimate how long a business discussion should last. But it does warn that a meeting must involve a discussion or negotiation to obtain income or business benefits. It does not require that more time be devoted to the meeting than to the entertainment.

Caution

Hunting or Fishing Trips

The IRS presumes that entertainment during a hunting or fishing trip or on a yacht is not conducive to business discussion or activity. You must prove otherwise.

In one case, a printing-press-parts manufacturer convinced a federal appeals court (Eighth Circuit) that there was a business purpose for the annual fishing trips it held for factory workers and sales personnel following its sales conference. Specific company business was discussed during the trips. Salespersons gave feedback to factory employees concerning manufacturing problems that increased the need for repairs, parts distribution issues were discussed, and plans made to counter competitors.

20.18 Goodwill Entertainment

Goodwill entertaining may qualify as deductible entertainment. Dining and entertainment costs may be deductible if a substantial and *bona fide* business discussion directly preceded or followed the dining or entertainment.

An officially scheduled meeting at a convention is generally considered a bona fide business discussion.

EXAMPLES

1. During the day, you negotiate with a group of business associates. In the evening, you entertain the group and their spouses at a theater and nightclub. The cost of the entertainment is deductible, even though arranged to promote goodwill.
2. In the evening after a business meeting at a convention, you entertain associates or prospective customers and their spouses. You may deduct the entertainment costs.

20.19 Home Entertaining

The cost of entertaining business customers or clients at home is deductible provided a business discussion occurs before, during, or after the meal. When you claim such a deduction, be ready to prove that your motive for dining with them was business rather than social. Have a record of the entertainment costs, names of the guests, and their business affiliations.

Filing Tip

Allocating Payment Covering Lodging and Meals

A hotel may include meals in a room charge. In such cases, the room charge must be allocated between the meals/entertainment and lodging. The amount allocated to meals and entertainment is subject to the 50% cost limitation. If you receive a *per diem* allowance from your employer covering both lodging and meals under an accountable reimbursement plan, you may have to allocate part of the reimbursement to meals in order to deduct expenses in excess of the reimbursement (20.31).

20.20 Your Personal Share of Entertainment Costs

If the entertaining occurred while on a business trip away from home, you deduct your own meal costs as travel expenses away from home (20.6). If the entertaining occurred within the locality of your regular place of business. The IRS will generally not disallow your deduction of your own part of the meal cost unless you are claiming a substantial amount that includes personal living expenses. In such a case, which generally is limited to situations where personal meals are regularly claimed as part of an "abusive" pattern, the IRS will follow the stricter Tax Court rule (sometimes referred to as the "Sutter" rule) and allow only that part of the meal cost that exceeds what you would usually spend on yourself when alone.

20.21 Entertainment Costs of Spouses

A deduction is allowed for the spouses' share of the entertainment costs if they were present during entertainment that qualified as directly related entertainment (20.17). For goodwill entertainment, the cost of entertainment of the spouses is deductible if your share and the business associate's share of the entertainment is deductible. The IRS recognizes that when an out-of-town customer is accompanied by his or her spouse, it may be impracticable to entertain the customer without the spouse. Under such circumstances, the cost of the spouse's entertainment is deductible if the customer's entertainment costs are also deductible. Furthermore, if your spouse joined the party because the customer's spouse was present, the expenses of your spouse are also deductible.

20.22 Entertainment Facilities and Club Dues

You may not deduct the expenses of maintaining and operating facilities used to entertain clients and customers. By law, entertainment facilities are not considered business assets. Examples of entertainment facilities are yachts, hunting lodges, fishing camps, swimming pools, tennis courts, automobiles, airplanes, apartments, hotel suites, or homes in a vacation area. A season box seat or pass at a sporting event or theater is *not* considered an entertainment facility; *see* the special rule for skybox rentals (20.24).

The disallowance rule applies to operating expenses such as rent, utilities, and security, and also to depreciation, but not to such expenses as interest, taxes, and casualty losses that are deductible without having to show business purpose.

Exceptions. A deduction may be allowed for expenses such as the cost of food and drinks incurred at an entertainment facility, if they meet certain rules (20.16–20.21).

Club dues. You may not deduct dues for country clubs, golf and athletic clubs, airline clubs, hotel clubs, business luncheon clubs, and other clubs organized for business, pleasure, recreation, or other social purposes. However, IRS regulations generally allow a deduction for dues paid to (1) civic or public service organizations such as Kiwanis, Lions, and Rotary clubs; (2) professional organizations such as medical or bar associations; and (3) chambers of commerce, trade associations, business leagues, real estate boards, and boards of trade. The deduction for dues is allowed provided that the organization in (1)–(3) does not have a principal purpose of providing entertainment for members or their guests.

20.23 Restrictive Test Exception for Reimbursements

As an employer, you can deduct expense allowances or other reimbursements of employee expenses that you treat as compensation and from which you withhold federal tax. You are not subject to the 50% deduction limit for meals and entertainment; the employee is, when claiming the meals on Form 2106.

A similar rule applies to meal allowances or reimbursements that you give to an independent contractor and that you report as compensation on Form 1099-MISC where the contractor does not adequately account for the expenses.

The restrictive tests *(20.16)* do not apply to such reimbursements. They are deductible if they are "ordinary and necessary" business expenses, and you have records to back up the deduction.

20.24 50% Cost Limitation on Meals and Entertainment

You generally may not deduct the full amount of your deductible expenses for business meals and entertainment expenses, such as tickets to sports events. Unless one of the exceptions below applies, only 50% of the otherwise allowable amount for food, beverages, and entertainment is deductible. However, the deductible percentage for workers subject to the Department of Transportation's "hours of service" limits is 80% rather than 50%.

Taxes and tips are considered part of the cost subject to the 50% limit. If your employer reimburses your expenses, the 50% limit applies to the employer.

The 50% limit applies to both employees and the self-employed. It applies to the IRS meal allowance deduction *(20.4)*. For employee expenses the limit is taken into account on Form 2106 or 2106-EZ (if you are not reimbursed by your employer and do not claim depreciation for a business car), and on Schedule C for self-employment expenses.

EXAMPLES

1. You pay meal and entertainment costs of $5,000. Only $2,500 ($5,000 × 50%) is considered deductible.
2. Same facts as above, but your employer reimburses your costs after you account for the expenses. The employer's deduction is limited to $2,500. You have no deduction.

Tickets. The deductible amount for a ticket treated as an entertainment expense is generally restricted to the face value of the ticket. Amounts in excess of face value paid to ticket agencies or scalpers are not deductible. Also *see* the special rule for skybox rental costs below. The deductible cost of tickets is also generally subject to the 50% limitation. However, a full deduction is allowed for tickets to qualifying charitable sporting events; *see* Exception 7 below.

EXAMPLE

You buy from a ticket broker five tickets to entertain clients. The face value of the five tickets is $500. You paid $600 for them. The deductible amount is $250 (50% × $500).

Exceptions to 50% cost limitation. In the following cases, you may claim a full deduction for meals and entertainment; the 50% limitation does not apply:

1. As an employer, you pay for an employee's meals and entertainment that are treated as taxable compensation to the employee and as wages for purposes of withholding of income tax.

2. You reimburse an independent contractor for meal and entertainment expenses he or she incurs on your behalf and the contractor does not adequately account for the expenses. You should report and deduct the reimbursements as compensation to the contractor, assuming the reimbursements are ordinary and necessary business expenses.
3. As an employer, you incur expenses for recreational, social, or similar activities (including facilities) primarily for the benefit of employees who are not highly compensated employees. For example, the expenses of food, beverages, and entertainment for a company-wide summer party are not subject to the 50% limit.
4. Expenses for meals and entertainment, including the use of facilities made available to the general public, such as a free concert, for advertising or goodwill purposes. For example, the IRS allowed a real-estate broker to fully deduct the cost of free dinners it provided to potential investors who attended its sales presentations. The 50% deduction limitation for meals does not apply to promotional activities that are made available to the general public. The IRS relied on the following example in a 1986 Congressional committee report for purposes of allowing a 100% deduction: A wine merchant provides customers with wine and food to demonstrate the suitability of the wine with certain types of meals. The committee report indicated that the cost of the wine, food, and other costs associated with the wine-tasting function would be fully deductible.
5. Expenses for meals and entertainment sold to the public in your business, such as meal expenses if you run a restaurant, or the cost of providing entertainment if you run a nightclub. These expenses are fully deductible.
6. Food or beverage provided to your employees as a tax-free *de minimis* fringe benefit *(3.10)*. This would include expenses of a cafeteria on your premises for employees where meal charges cover the direct operating cost of the cafeteria. The *de minimis* benefit exception allows a full deduction for all meals provided to employees on employer premises if more than half of the employees who are provided meals are furnished them for the employer's convenience (substantial noncompensatory business purpose). If the more-than-half test is met, the meals are tax free to all the employees *(3.12)*.
7. The price of tickets to charitable sports events (including amounts in excess of face value) provided the ticket package includes admission to the event. To qualify, a charitable sports event must: (1) be organized for the primary purpose of benefitting a tax-exempt organization; (2) contribute 100% of its net proceeds to such organization; and (3) use volunteers for substantially all work performed in carrying out the event. According to Congressional committee reports, a golf tournament that donates all its proceeds to charity is eligible to qualify under this exception, even if it offers prize money to the golfers who participate or uses paid concessionaires or security personnel. However, tickets to a college football game or similar scholastic events generally do not qualify because they do not satisfy the requirement that substantially all work be performed by volunteers.

Filing Tip

Meals Provided to Employees

An employer who provides meals to employees on employer premises is allowed a full deduction for all the meals provided that more than half of the employees who are provided meals are furnished them for substantial noncompensatory business reasons.

Law Alert

Transportation Industry Workers

Individuals subject to Department of Transportation limitations on hours of service, such as interstate truck and bus drivers, pilots and other air transportation workers, and train crews, may claim a higher deductible percentage of food and beverage costs when working away from home. The deductible amount is 80% rather than 50%.

Skybox rental costs. A skybox is a private luxury seating area at a sports arena. Skybox seats are generally rented for the season or for a series of games such as the World Series. The deductible amount for a rental covering more than one game or performance may not exceed the sum of the face values of non-luxury box seat tickets for the number of seats in the box. The allowable amount is also subject to the 50% cost limitation. Separately stated charges for food or beverages at the skybox are deductible as entertainment expenses and are subject to the 50% cost rule. For example, assume that for two games, you paid $2,500 for a skybox containing 10 seats—$1,250 per game. The cost of 10 non-luxury box seat tickets for each game was $250, or $500 total. You may deduct 50% of the $500 non-luxury face value, or $250. If you had rented the skybox for one game, you could deduct $625 (50% of $1,250) for that skybox because the special limitation applies only where the rental is for more than one game or other performance.

20.25 Business Gift Deductions Are Limited

Deductions for gifts to business customers and clients are restricted. Your deduction for gifts is limited to $25 a person. You and your spouse are treated as one person in figuring this limitation even if you do not file a joint return and even if you have separate business connections with the recipient. The $25 limitation also applies to partnerships; thus a gift by the partnership to one person may not exceed $25, regardless of the number of partners.

In figuring the $25 limitation to each business associate, do not include the following items:

1. A gift of a specialty advertising item that costs $4 or less on which your name is clearly and permanently imprinted. This exception saves you the trouble of having to keep records of such items as pens, desk sets, plastic bags, and cases on which you have your name imprinted for business promotion.
2. Signs, displays, racks, or other promotional material that is used on business premises by the person to whom you gave the material.
3. Incidental costs of wrapping, insuring, mailing, or delivering the gift. However, the cost of an ornamental basket or container must be included if it has a substantial value in relation to the goods it contains.

If you made a gift to the spouse of a business associate, it is considered as made to the associate. If the spouse has an independent bona fide business connection with you, the gift is not considered as made to the associate unless it is intended for the associate's eventual use.

If you made a gift to a corporation or other business group intended for the personal use of an employee, stockholder, or other owner of the corporation, the gift generally is considered as made to that individual.

Packaged food or drink given to a business associate is a gift if it is to be consumed at a later time. Theater or sporting event tickets given to business associates are entertainment, not gift, expenses if you accompany them. If you do not accompany them, you may elect to treat the tickets either as gifts, which are subject to the $25 limitation, or as entertainment expenses subject to the entertainment expense rules, such as the requirement to show a business conference before or after the entertainment and the 50% cost limitation.

Gifts not coming within the $25 limit are: (1) scholarships that are tax free under the rules in *Chapter 33*; (2) prizes and awards that are tax free under the rules in *11.1*; and (3) awards to employees, discussed below.

Caution

Employee Bonuses

Employee bonuses should not be labeled as gifts. An IRS agent examining your records may, with this description, limit the deduction to $25 unless you can prove the excess over $25 was compensation. By describing the payment as a gift, you are inviting an IRS disallowance of the excess over $25. This was the experience of an attorney who gave his secretary $200 at Christmas. The IRS disallowed $175 of his deduction. The Tax Court refused to reverse the IRS. The attorney could not prove that the payment was for services.

Awards to employees. There is an exception to the $25 gift deduction limitation for achievement awards of tangible personal property given to your employees in recognition of length of service or safety achievement. Special deduction limits apply to such achievement awards provided they are given as part of a presentation under circumstances indicating that they are not a form of disguised compensation. For example, awards will not qualify if given at the time of annual salary adjustments, or as a substitute for a prior program of cash bonuses, or if awards discriminate on behalf of highly compensated employees.

The amount of your deduction depends on whether the achievement award is considered a qualified plan award. You may deduct up to $1,600 for all qualified plan awards (safety and length of service) given to the same employee during the taxable year. If the award is not a qualified plan award, the annual deduction ceiling for each employee is $400. The $1,600 overall limit applies if the same employee receives some qualified plan awards and some non-qualified awards during the same year.

To be a qualified plan award, the award for length of service or safety achievement must be given under an established written plan or program that does not discriminate in favor of highly compensated employees. The average cost of all awards under the plan for the year (to all employees) must not exceed $400. In determining this $400 average cost, awards of nominal value are not to be taken into account. In case of a partnership, the deduction limitation applies to the partnership as well as to each partner.

Safety and length of service. A length of service award does not qualify as an employee achievement award if it is given during the employee's first five years. Furthermore, only one length of service award every five years is considered an employee achievement award.

Safety awards granted to managers, administrators, clerical employees, or professional employees are not considered employee achievement awards. Furthermore, if during the year more than 10% of other employees (not counting managers, administrators, clerical employees, or professional employees) previously received safety awards, none of the later awards are subject to the employee achievement award rules.

Employee's tax. The employer's deductible amount for an employee achievement award is tax free to the employee *(3.12)*. For example, you give a qualified plan award costing $1,800 to an employee. You may deduct only $1,600. The employee is not taxed on the award up to $1,600; the $200 balance is taxable.

20.26 Record-Keeping Requirements

Your testimony—even if accepted by an IRS agent or a judge as truthful—is not sufficient to support a deduction of travel and entertainment expenses. By law, your personal claim must be supported by other evidence such as records or witnesses. The most direct and acceptable way is to have records that meet IRS rules discussed below. Failure to have adequate records will generally result in an examination of your return and in a disallowance of your travel and entertainment expense deductions. Only in unusual circumstances will evidence other than records provide all of the required details of proof. If your expenses are reimbursed by your company, you must keep records to support the reimbursement arrangement with your company *(20.30)*.

20.27 Proving Travel and Entertainment Expenses

To satisfy the IRS requirements and to substantiate your expense deductions in the event of an audit, you need two types of records:

1. A computer log, diary, account book, or similar record to list the time, place, and business purpose of your travel and entertainment expenses; and
2. Receipts, itemized paid bills, or similar statements for lodging regardless of the amount, and for other expenses of $75 or more. But note these exceptions:
   - A receipt for transportation expenses of $75 or more is required only when it is readily obtainable. For example, for air travel a receipt or a boarding pass is usually provided.
   - A cancelled check by itself is not an acceptable voucher. If you cannot produce a bill or voucher, you may have to present other evidence such as a statement in writing from witnesses to prove business purpose of the expense.

Planning Reminder

Credit Cards

Credit card charge statements for traveling and entertainment expenses meet the IRS tests, provided the business purpose of the expense is also shown. Credit card statements provide space for inserting the names of people entertained, their business relationship, the business purpose of the expense, and the portion of the expense to be allocated to business and personal purposes. These statements generally meet the IRS requirements of accounting to your employer for reimbursed expenses *(20.31)*, provided a responsible company official reviews them. The IRS will not accept a credit card statement as substantiation of a lodging expense.

A receipted bill or voucher must show (1) the amount of the expense; (2) the date the expense was incurred; (3) where the expense was incurred; and (4) the nature of the expense.

A hotel bill must show the name, location, date, and separate amounts for charges such as lodgings, meals, and telephone calls. A receipt for lodging is not needed if its cost is covered by a *per diem* allowance *(20.32)*. The IRS will not allow a credit card statement to substitute for a lodging receipt. The IRS wants detailed receipts to catch personal items such as personal phone calls or the purchase of gifts.

A restaurant bill must show the restaurant's name and location, the date and amount of the expense, and, when a charge is made for items other than meals or beverages, a description of the charge.

Account book or computer entries. Your records do not have to duplicate data recorded on a receipt, provided that a notation in your record is connected to the receipt. You are also not required to record amounts your company pays directly for any ticket or fare. Credit card charges should be recorded.

Your records for entertainment costs must also show (1) the names of those you entertained; (2) the business purpose served by the entertainment; (3) the business relationship between you and your guests; and (4) the place of entertainment. Inattention to these details of substantiation can cost you the deduction. For example, an executive's company treasurer verified that the executive was required to incur entertainment expenses beyond reimbursed amounts. He also kept a cash diary in which he made contemporaneous notes of the amounts he spent. But he failed to note place, purpose, and business relationship. Consequently, there was no record that tied the expenses to his employment and the deduction was disallowed.

Planning Reminder

Sampling Can Support Deduction

If an adequate record of expenses is kept for part of a tax year, and that period is representative of the whole year, the IRS will accept those records as proof of expenses for the entire year. For example, if you keep records for the first week of each month that show that 75% of the use of your car is for business purposes, and your invoices and bills show the same business pattern for the rest of each month, the IRS will treat your partial record as proof of 75% business use for the whole year.

Excuses for Inadequate Records

Substantial compliance. If you have made a "good faith" effort to comply with the IRS rules, you will not be penalized if your records do not satisfy every requirement. For example, you would not automatically be denied a deduction merely because you did not keep a receipt.

Accidental destruction of records. If receipts or records are lost through circumstances beyond your control, you may substantiate deductions by reasonable reconstruction of your expenditures.

Exceptional circumstances. If, by reason of the "inherent nature of the situation," you are unable to keep adequate records, you may substantially comply by presenting the next best evidence.

A supporting memorandum from your files and a statement from the persons entertained may be an adequate substitute. IRS regulations do not explain the meaning of "inherent nature of the situation."

EXAMPLES

1. Bryan's 1966 records were lost by a moving company. He claimed a T&E deduction of $15,301.87. The IRS estimated his T&E and other business expenses as $8,669 on the basis of his 1971 expense records. The Tax Court affirmed the IRS's approach. True, Bryan's loss of records made his burden of proof difficult, but he had to provide a reasonable reconstruction of his records to support his claimed deduction. His testimony of what he incurred in 1966 was not sufficient. A more accurate method was the IRS's use of his 1971 records and receipts.
2. Jackson claimed the IRS lost his records. He left his records with the IRS when he was audited, and the records were never returned. The Tax Court held that to be a good excuse for not producing his records and allowed a deduction on the basis of reconstructed records. Evidence that the IRS lost them: The IRS discovered Jackson's worksheet a year after the audit interview.
3. Murray claimed he lost his records when he was evicted from his apartment for failure to pay rent for a month. The Tax Court accepted his excuse on proof that he had kept records before they were lost. The eviction was beyond his control. However, if the records had been lost during a voluntary move, the loss would not have been excused, as in Example 1.

20.28 Reporting T&E Expenses If You Are Self-Employed

You must keep travel and entertainment (T&E) records in accordance with IRS rules *(20.27)*. You may claim the meal allowance *(20.4)* on overnight business trips. The reimbursement rules *(20.30)* do not apply to you.

In preparing your tax return, you report your expenses on the appropriate lines of Schedule C or Schedule C-EZ *(40.6)*. You do not use Form 2106. An advantage of reporting on Schedule C (or C-EZ) is that your travel and entertainment expenses (T&E) are not subject to the 2% adjusted gross income (AGI) floor. Only 50% of meals and entertainment costs are deductible, but there are exceptions *(20.24)*.

20.29 Employee Reporting of Unreimbursed T&E Expenses

If you are paid a salary with the understanding that you will pay your own expenses and you pay all of your travel and entertainment (T&E) expenses *without* reimbursement, you report all of your salary or commission income as shown on Form W-2. You report your expenses on Form 2106 or Form 2106-EZ *(19.3)*. Meals and entertainment are only 50% deductible. You must also keep records *(20.27)* to support your deduction. The deductible amount from Form 2106 or Form 2106-EZ is entered on Schedule A as a miscellaneous expense subject to the 2% AGI floor *(19.1)*. If your total miscellaneous expenses, including the unreimbursed T&E costs, do not exceed 2% of adjusted gross income, none of the miscellaneous expenses will be deductible.

If your employer has a reimbursement plan but the rules for accountable plans are *not* met, reimbursements are treated as part of your taxable pay *(20.34)*.

20.30 Tax Treatment of Reimbursements

Compliance rules are imposed on employees and employers for reporting reimbursed travel and entertainment expenses in order to prevent reimbursement arrangements from being used to avoid the 2% of adjusted gross income (AGI) floor for employee miscellaneous expenses. Plans that allow reimbursements that *do not* comply with the IRS rules are called *non-accountable plans*. All reimbursements under a non-accountable plan are reported as salary or wage income on Form W-2. You then deduct your expenses as miscellaneous deductions subject to the 2% AGI floor *(20.34)*.

If a plan meets the IRS rules, the plan is called an *accountable plan* and reimbursements made by the plan are not reported on Form W-2 as taxable wages. You also do not have to deduct expenses, assuming the reimbursement equals your expenses. In other words, there is a bookkeeping "wash" in which the full amount of expenses offsets the reimbursement without being reduced by the 2%

Court Decision

Ask for Reimbursement

If you are entitled to reimbursement from your employer, make sure you ask for reimbursement. Failure to be reimbursed may prevent you from deducting your out-of-pocket expenses. A supervisor whose responsibility was to maintain good relations with his district and store managers entertained them and their families and also distributed gifts among them. His cost was $2,500, for which he could have been reimbursed by his company, but he made no claim. Consequently, the Tax Court disallowed the cost as a deduction on his return. The expense was the company's; any goodwill he created benefitted it. But because he failed to seek reimbursement, he was not allowed to convert company expenses into his own.

Planning Reminder

Importance of Adequate Accounting

If you adequately report expenses to your employer and return excess reimbursements, you are treated as being reimbursed under an accountable plan and generally do not have to report any reimbursement on your return *(20.31)*.

AGI floor, and in the case of meal and entertainment costs, by the 50% reduction. Even though the employer may only deduct 50% of qualifying meal and entertainment expenses, you are not taxed on any part of a reimbursement of such costs if the accountable plan rules are met.

To qualify a plan as accountable, your employer must *see* to it that you submit adequate proof of your expenditures, and that you return any excess advances *(20.31)*. To reduce record-keeping for actual costs, the company may reimburse you according to certain fixed *per diem* allowance rates *(20.32)*. Your company must also determine how much of the advance or reimbursement, if any, is to be reported on your Form W-2.

EXAMPLE

Your adjusted gross income is $85,000, and you incur T&E expenses of $1,600 that are reimbursed by your company. If the reimbursement arrangement does not meet the IRS rules, the $1,600 reimbursement is reported as wage income on your Form W-2. You may report the expenses on Form 2106 and after reducing meal and entertainment costs by 50%, enter the balance as a deduction on Schedule A as a miscellaneous expense subject to the 2% AGI floor. However, if these are your only miscellaneous expenses, you will not get the benefit of a deduction because they do not exceed 2% of $86,600 ($85,000 + $1,600), or $1,732. The $1,600 is fully taxable although spent for T&E.

If your reimbursement arrangement qualified as an accountable plan, and you made an adequate reporting to your employer, the $1,600 would not be reported as income on your Form W-2, and you would not have to be concerned with the 2% floor for miscellaneous itemized deductions. There is a bookkeeping "wash." In other words, you receive a full deduction by substantiating the expenses to your employer.

Reimbursements of club dues or spousal travel costs. If you are reimbursed for nondeductible club dues *(20.22)* or nondeductible travel costs of a spouse or other person *(20.13)*, the reimbursement may be treated by your employer as taxable wages. If it is, you are not allowed an offsetting deduction. If the reimbursement is not treated as taxable wages by your employer, and you substantiate a business purpose for the club dues or for a travel companion's presence, the reimbursement is considered to be a tax-free working condition fringe benefit *(3.9)*.

EXAMPLE

A company pays for the country club dues of an executive. It reimbursed dues of $20,000, and the executive used the club for business purposes 40% of the time. If the company does not treat the reimbursement as taxable wages but as a fringe benefit, $8,000 of the reimbursement is tax free to the executive; the $12,000 allocated to personal use is taxable.

20.31 What Is an Accountable Plan?

A reimbursement or allowance arrangement is an accountable plan *(20.30)* if you must:

- Adequately account to your employer for your expenses; *and*
- Return to your employer any excess reimbursement or allowance that you do not show was spent for ordinary and necessary business expenses.

If these terms are met and your expenses are fully reimbursed, you do not report the expenses or the reimbursement on your return. If the reimbursement is less than your payment of expenses, you use Form 2106 and Schedule A to claim a deduction for the unreimbursed expenses. The unreimbursed expenses are subject to the 2% AGI floor on Schedule A *(19.3)*.

What is an adequate accounting? You adequately account to your employer by submitting receipts and an account book, diary, or similar record in which you entered each expense at or near the time you had it. You must account to your employer for all amounts received as advances, reimbursements, or allowances, including amounts charged on a company credit card. Your records and supporting information must meet IRS rules *(20.27)*. You must also pay back reimbursements or allowances that exceed the expenses that you adequately accounted for, or the nonreturned excess will be taxable under the rules for non-accountable plans *(20.34)*.

The accounting requirements are eased if you are reimbursed under a *per diem* arrangement covering meals, lodging, and incidental expenses *(20.32)* or you receive a flat mileage allowance *(20.33)*.

Time limits for receiving advances, substantiating expenses, and returning excess payments. The general rule is that these events must occur within a reasonable time. Under an IRS "safe harbor," the following payments are considered to be within a reasonable time:

- Advance payments—if given to you within 30 days before you reasonably anticipate to pay or incur expenses;
- Substantiation of expenses—if provided to your employer within 60 days after the expense is paid or incurred; and
- Return of excess—if done within 120 days after you pay or incur expense.

An employer may set up a "periodic statement method" to meet IRS rules. Here, an employer gives each employee periodic statements (at least quarterly) that list the amounts paid in excess of expenses substantiated by the employee and request substantiation of the additional amounts paid, or a return of the excess, within 120 days of the date of the statement. Substantiation or return within the 120-day period satisfies the reasonable time test.

Allocating reimbursements to meals and entertainment. Only 50% of meals and entertainment expenses are deductible. Therefore, if you adequately account for your expenses, and receive a flat reimbursement that is partly for meals and entertainment, and partly for other expenses, you must allocate part of the reimbursement to meals and entertainment if the employer has not provided an item-by-item breakdown. You must make this allocation if you want to deduct expenses exceeding reimbursements because on Form 2106, you must separately list meals and entertainment costs and reimbursements for meals and entertainment. The Form 2106 instructions have a worksheet for allocating the reimbursement based on the percentage that your meal costs bear to the total T&E expenses.

EXAMPLE

You receive an allowance of $1,000 for travel expenses and have total expenses of $1,500, including $300 for meals. The percentage of your meals to total expenses is 20% (300 ÷ 1,500). On Form 2106, you show 20% of the allowance, or $200, as the allocable reimbursement for meals and $800 as the allocable reimbursement to the non-meal expenses. The balance of the non-meal expenses, or $400 ($1,200 – $800), is deductible. The unreimbursed $100 balance for meals ($300 – $200) must be reduced to $50 by the 50% reduction for meals. The total deductible amount of $450 ($50 for meals and $400 for other expenses) is transferred from Form 2106 to Schedule A, where it is deductible as a miscellaneous itemized expense subject to the 2% AGI floor.

Filing Tip

Failure To Timely Return Excess

If you fail to return excess payments within a reasonable time but you meet all of the other tests applied to an accountable plan, such as providing proof of the expenses, only the retained excess is taxed to you as if paid outside of an accountable plan.

20.32 *Per Diem* Travel Allowance Under Accountable Plans

Instead of providing a straight reimbursement for substantiated out-of-pocket travel expenses, an employer may use a *per diem* allowance to cover meals, lodging, and incidental *(20.4)* expenses of employees on business trips away from home. If you are not related to the employer, you do not have to give your employer proof of your actual expenses if you receive a *per diem* allowance or reimbursement that is equal to or less than the federal travel rate for the particular area. You do have to account for the time, place, and business purpose of your travel. If you do not provide such an accounting for some travel days, you must be required to return the *per diem* allowance received for such days in order for the employer's plan to qualify. If these tests are met, the allowance satisfies the accountable plan *(20.31)* requirements and it does not have to be reported as income on your Form W-2.

Tables published by the government show the federal travel rate for areas within the continental U.S. (called CONUS locations) and for areas outside the continental U.S., including Hawaii and Alaska (called OCONUS locations). New CONUS tables are released every October, effective for the government's October 1–September 30 fiscal year *(20.24)*. The best way to obtain the CONUS *per diem* rates is from IRS Publication 1542, available online at www.irs.gov/formspubs. The rates are also available from the General Services Administration website at www.gsa.gov. The OCONUS rates can also be accessed from the GSA website.

High-low rate. For business trips within the continental United States (CONUS), employers may use the IRS's "high-low" method to reimburse employees for lodging, meals, and incidental expenses instead of using the locality-by-locality *per diem* CONUS rates set by the General Services Administration (GSA) for federal government workers. For each employee, either the federal *per diem* rates or the high-low method must be used for the entire year.

Planning Reminder

High-Low Method

An employer that uses the high-low method to reimburse an employee for the first nine months of the year must continue to do so for the rest of the year. Although the rates and high-cost localities list may change on October 1, the pre-October rates and high-cost localities may be used for the rest of the year as long as this is done consistently for all employees.

For the first nine months of 2010, the rate for most areas was $163 per day and the rate for designated high-cost areas was $258 per day. For employer deduction purposes, $65 of the $258 high-cost-area rate, and $52 of the $163 rate for other localities, must be allocated to meals. Only 50% of the allocated meals portion is generally deductible *(20.24)*. The meal deduction percentage is 80% for meal costs of transportation workers such as pilots and interstate truck/bus drivers who are subject to Department of Transportation limits on service hours.

The $163 and $258 rates and the areas treated as high-cost areas are scheduled to change, effective October 1, 2010. After the IRS announces the changes, it will revise Publication 1542, which is available only online at www.irs.gov/forms/pubs. The revised Publication will have tables showing the high-cost areas for the period before October 1 and the period beginning October 1. An employer that used the high-low method before October 1, 2010, to reimburse an employee must continue to do so for the rest of 2010. However, the pre-October rates and high-cost localities list may be used for the rest of the year as long as this is done consistently for all employees. Employers that did not use the high-low method for an employee before October 1 may not do so until 2011.

Planning Reminder

Online Revisions to IRS Publication 1542

As changes to *per diem* rates are announced by the General Services Administration (GSA), the IRS will revise Publication 1542 at www.irs.gov/formspubs.

Employees related to the employer. The IRS *per diem* rules that allow you to avoid accounting for actual expenses do not apply if you work for a brother, sister, spouse, parent, child, grandparent, or grandchild. They also do not apply if you are an employee-stockholder who owns more than 10% of the company's stock.

Reporting a *per diem* allowance. If the allowance does not exceed the federal travel rate or IRS high-low rate, the reimbursement is not reported on Form W-2. If your expenses do not exceed the reimbursement, you do not have to report the expenses or the reimbursement on your tax return; *see* Example 1 below. If your expenses exceed the allowance, you may deduct the excess by reporting the expenses and reimbursement on Form 2106. The net amount from Form 2106, after applying the 50% reduction for meals, is claimed on Schedule A as a miscellaneous expense subject to the 2% AGI floor; *see* Example 2 below.

If the allowance exceeds the federal rate, the allowance up to the federal rate is reported by the employer in Box 12 of your Form W-2, using Code L. This amount is not taxable. However, the excess allowance will be included as wages in Box 1 of your Form W-2; *see* Example 3 below.

Caution

Excess *Per Diem* Allowances

If a *per diem* allowance exceeds the federal travel rate or the IRS high-low rate, the excess will be reported as income on your Form W-2, unless you return the excess. The excess reportable on Form W-2 is also subject to income tax and FICA tax withholding.

EXAMPLES

1. You take a three-day business trip to a locality at a time when the federal travel rate for the area is $106 per day. You account for the date, place, and business purpose of the trip. Your employer reimburses you at the federal rate of $106 a day for lodging, meals, and incidental expenses, for a total of $318. Your actual expenses do not exceed this amount. Your employer does not report the reimbursement on your Form W-2. You do not have to report the reimbursement or deduct any expenses on your return.
2. Same facts as in Example 1, except that the reimbursement is less than your actual expenses of $450, for which you have records. On Form 2106, you report the $318 reimbursement and your $450 of expenses and also must allocate part of the allowance to meals and entertainment to apply the 50% deduction limit *(20.24)*. The instructions to Form 2106 have a worksheet for making the allocation. The net amount from Form 2106 is deductible on Schedule A as a miscellaneous expense subject to the 2% AGI limit.
3. Same facts as in Example 1, except that you receive a per diem allowance of $114 per day—$8 per day more than the federal travel rate. If you do not return the excess of $24 ($8 × 3 days) within a reasonable time *(20.31)*, your employer must report the $24 as income in Box 1 of your Form W-2. The amount up to the federal travel rate, or $318, will be reported in Box 12 of Form W-2 with Code L, but not included as income.

Meal allowance only. If your employer gives you a *per diem* allowance covering only meals and incidental expenses, it is not taxable to you if you are not related to the employer and the allowance does not exceed the IRS meal allowance rates discussed at *20.4*.

20.33 Automobile Mileage Allowance

If your employer paid you a fixed mileage allowance of up to 50 cents per mile for business miles driven during 2010, the amount of your driving costs is treated as substantiated under the accountable plan rules *(20.31)*, provided you show the time, place, and business purpose of your travel. If the allowance is in the form of an advance, it must be given within a reasonable period before the anticipated travel and you must also be required to return within a reasonable period *(20.31)* any portion of the allowance that covers mileage that you have not substantiated.

If these tests are met, the allowance will not be reported as income on Form W-2, and you will not have to report the allowance or expenses on your return; *see* Example 1 below. If you do not prove to your employer the time, place, and purpose of your travel, the entire reimbursement is treated as paid from a non-accountable plan and will be reported as income on Form W-2.

Your employer may reimburse you for any parking fees and tolls in addition to the mileage allowance.

EXAMPLES

1. In 2010 you drove 12,000 miles for business. You accounted to your employer for the time, place, and business purpose of each trip. Your employer reimbursed you at the IRS rate of 50 cents per mile. None of the reimbursements will be reported as income on your 2010 Form W-2, and you do not have to report the reimbursements or any expenses on your return if you do not have substantiated expenses exceeding 50 cents per mile.
2. Same facts as in Example 1, except that you were reimbursed at a rate of 58 cents per mile. The amount using the IRS rate, or $6,000 (.50 x 12,000), is $960 less than the reimbursement of $6,960 (.58 x 12,000). The $960 excess over the IRS rate will be reported as wages on your 2010 Form W-2.

   If you had records substantiating expenses over the IRS rate of .50 cents per mile, you could claim them on Form 2106 if you itemize deductions. The excess of your expenses over the IRS rate would be reported on Form 2106 and that excess would be entered on Schedule A (Form 1040) as an unreimbursed employee expense, but the deduction is subject to the 2% AGI floor for miscellaneous itemized deductions *(19.1)*.
3. Same facts as in Example 1, except that you were reimbursed only 45 cents per mile for all your business driving. The reimbursements will not be reported as income on your Form W-2. You may be able to deduct expenses up to the IRS rate by reporting the expenses and the reimbursements on Form 2106. The amount using the IRS rates is $6,000 (.50 x 12,000 miles). This is $600 more than the reimbursement of $5,400 (.45 x 12,000). If you itemize deductions, you can report the $600 excess on Form 2106 and then enter it on Schedule A (Form 1040) as an unreimbursed employee expense, but the deduction is subject to the 2% AGI floor for miscellaneous itemized deductions *(19.1)*.

Fixed and variable rate allowance (FAVR). In lieu of setting the allowance at the IRS standard mileage rate, an employer may use a fixed and variable rate allowance, called a FAVR, that gives employees a cents-per-mile rate to cover gas and other operating costs, plus a flat amount to cover fixed costs such as depreciation or lease payments, insurance, and registration. A FAVR allowance must reflect local driving costs and allows employers to set reimbursements at a rate that more closely approximates employee expenses. If your employer sets up a qualifying FAVR under IRS guidelines, you will be required to provide records substantiating your mileage and certain car ownership information. Expenses up to the FAVR limits are deemed substantiated and will not be reported as wages on your Form W-2.

20.34 Reimbursements Under Non-Accountable Plans

A non-accountable plan is one that either does not require you to adequately account for your expenses or allows you to keep any excess reimbursement or allowances over the expenses for which you did adequately account.

Your employer reports allowances or reimbursements for a non-accountable plan as part of your salary income in Box 1 of your Form W-2. The allowance or reimbursement is also subject to income tax and FICA tax (Social Security) withholding. To claim deductions, you must use Form 2106 and itemize your deductions on Schedule A, subject to the 2% AGI floor *(19.1)*. Because of the 2% floor, you may be unable to offset the taxable reimbursement (allowance) included on your Form W-2.

Chapter 21

Personal Exemptions

Each personal exemption you claim on your 2010 return is the equivalent of a $3,650 deduction. Exemptions for children, parents, and other dependents are allowed if the tests in this chapter are met.

Taxpayers with high adjusted gross income receive a break for 2010. There is no phaseout of exemptions *(21.12)*.

Number of Exemptions	*Deduction Allowed*
1	$ 3,650
2	7,300
3	10,950
4	14,600
5	18,250
6	21,900

21.1 How Many Exemptions May You Claim?

On your 2010 return, you may claim a $3,650 exemption for each of the following:

- **Yourself.** You claim an exemption for yourself unless you are the dependent of another taxpayer. If someone else can claim you as a dependent for 2010, you may not claim a personal exemption for yourself on your own return; this is true even if the other person does not actually claim you as a dependent. Similarly, your child or other dependent may not claim an exemption on his or her own return if you can claim an exemption for that child or other dependent.
- **Your spouse.** You claim your spouse as an exemption when you file a joint return. If you file a separate return, you claim your spouse as an exemption if he or she has no income and is not a dependent of another person *(21.2)*.
- **Your dependents.** A dependent must be either your qualifying child or your qualifying relative. In addition to meeting the tests for a qualifying child or relative, the child/relative must meet a citizen or resident test and if married, generally must file separately (*see* below for exceptions). Regardless of whether these tests are met, you are not entitled to claim any exemptions if you, or your spouse if filing jointly, could be claimed as a dependent by another taxpayer.

Qualifying children. In addition to your biological children, "qualifying children" for exemption purposes can include your stepchildren, foster children, siblings or stepsiblings, and the descendants of any of these, such as your grandchildren, nieces or nephews, provided all of the following tests are met:

1. The child had the same principal place of abode (residence) as you did for more than half of 2010. Temporary absences are disregarded.
2. The child is under age 19 at the end of 2010, or under age 24 at the end of 2010 if a full-time student for at least five months during the year. In addition, the child must be younger than you are, or younger than your spouse if you file jointly. However, if the child is permanently and totally disabled at any time during the year, these age requirements do not apply.
3. The child did not provide more than half of his or her own support for 2010.
4. If married, the child does not file a joint return for 2010, unless the return is only a claim for a refund.

See 21.3 for further details on the qualifying child rules, including the tie-breaker rules that determine who can claim the child when the child is a qualifying child of more than one person.

Qualifying relatives. An individual is your qualified relative for 2010 if the following tests are met:

1. The individual is your relative or member of your household *(21.4)*, but you cannot claim a person as a qualifying relative if he or she is your qualifying child or the qualifying child of any other taxpayer.
2. The individual had gross income for 2010 of under $3,650.
3. You contributed over half of the individual's support for 2010 or more than 10% of his or her support under the multiple support test *(21.6)*.

See 21.4 for further details on the qualifying relative rules.

Additional tests for claiming dependents. *Even if a person is your qualifying child or relative, you cannot claim that person as your dependent if any of the following apply:*

1. You, or your spouse if filing jointly, could be claimed as a dependent by another taxpayer for the taxable year.
2. The child/relative is not a U.S. citizen or national, or a resident of the U.S., Canada, or Mexico for at least some part of the year; there is an exception for certain adopted children *(21.8)*.
3. If married, the child/relative files a joint return, unless the return is only a claim for refund and neither spouse would owe tax on a separate return *(21.9)*.

1040 *Filing Instruction*

You Must Report I.D. Numbers for Dependents

You must obtain and report on your return the Social Security number of each dependent claimed. Nonresident and resident aliens not eligible for Social Security numbers must have an individual taxpayer identification number *(21.11)*.

Special rules for divorced or separated parents. *See* the rules for determining which parent may claim the exemption for their children *(21.7)*.

Death of dependent during the year. If a dependent who otherwise met the tests for a qualifying child or relative died during the year, you can claim an exemption for that dependent.

Social Security numbers checked by IRS. The IRS verifies the Social Security numbers for both spouses on a joint return *(21.10)* and for all claimed dependents *(21.11)*.

21.2 Your Spouse as an Exemption

Your spouse is not your dependent for tax purposes. An exemption for a spouse is based on the marital relationship, not support. On a joint return, each spouse receives an exemption as a taxpayer. The name and Social Security number of each spouse listed on a joint return will be matched by the IRS against computer records of the Social Security Administration. If there is a mismatch, the exemption for that spouse will be disallowed *(21.10)*.

On a separate return (as married filing separately or as head of household), you may claim your spouse as an exemption if he or she has no gross income and cannot be claimed as a dependent by another taxpayer. You may not claim an exemption for your spouse who has income, *unless you file a joint return that includes that income*. For example, if a wife files a separate return, her husband may not claim her as an exemption, even if she filed the return merely for a refund of taxes withheld on her wages.

If your spouse is a nonresident alien, has no income from U.S. sources, and is not a dependent of another person, you may claim an exemption for your spouse on a separate return.

Caution

Spouses' Social Security Numbers and Names

Make sure that the names used when you and your spouse file your joint return match the names you have provided to the Social Security Administration. If there is a mismatch between a name and Social Security number, the IRS will disallow the exemption and then send you a notice that allows you to explain the discrepancy and restore the deduction *(21.10)*.

If divorced or legally separated during the year. You may not claim your former spouse as an exemption if you are divorced or legally separated under a *final* decree of divorce or separate maintenance, even if you provided his or her entire support. However, an interlocutory (not final) decree does not bar you from claiming your spouse as an exemption.

EXAMPLE

An interlocutory (not final) decree of divorce is entered in 2010, and a final decree in 2011. For 2010, the couple may file a joint return on which exemptions for both are claimed. A marriage is not dissolved until a final decree is entered, which in this case is in 2011.

Your spouse died during the year. If you did not remarry and your deceased spouse had gross income, you may claim an exemption for your spouse only if you file a joint return that includes his or her income. You may claim the exemption on a separate return only if your spouse had no gross income and was not a dependent of another taxpayer.

EXAMPLE

Sylvia Smith dies on June 27, 2010. Her husband, Steve Smith, may file a joint return for 2010 and claim Sylvia as an exemption. They were married as of the date of Sylvia's death. The joint return must include all of Steve's income for 2010, but only that part of Sylvia's income earned up to June 27 *(1.10)*.

If you remarry before the end of the year in which your spouse died, you may not claim an exemption for your deceased spouse. If you file a joint return with your new spouse, you may be claimed as an exemption on that return. If you had *no* income for the year, you may be claimed as an exemption on both your deceased spouse's separate return and on a separate return filed by your new spouse, provided no one else may claim you as a dependent.

21.3 Qualifying Children

You may claim an exemption for your qualifying children provided you (and your spouse if you file jointly) cannot be claimed as a dependent by someone else and the citizenship or resident *(21.8)* and joint return *(21.9)* tests applicable to all dependents also are met.

Qualifying children include your children, siblings, and their descendants (see the relationship test below) if a residence test and age or student test are also met. If the relationship, residence, and age/student tests are met, you do not have to show that you provided more than half of the child's support, as is required for a qualifying relative *(21.4)*. However, a child is not a qualifying child if he or she provides over half of his or her own support. A married child who files a joint return also cannot be your qualifying child, unless the joint return is filed solely to obtain a refund. For a qualifying child, there is *no* gross income test; he or she may earn any amount and still be claimed as your dependent. Even if a child is not a qualifying child, as where the age/student test or place of abode test is not met, you may still be able to claim an exemption for a child with little or no income as a "qualifying relative" *(21.4)*.

Planning Reminder

Qualifying Children

If a child or sibling (or his or her descendant) is your qualifying child under *21.3,* his or her gross income does not matter. You also do not have to provide over half of the child's support. You may claim the exemption if the other tests for an exemption are met *(21.3)*.

Relationship test. Your children, stepchildren, and their descendants (your grandchildren and great-grandchildren), and your siblings, including step- and half-brothers and -sisters and their descendants (your nieces and nephews), meet the relationship test. A legally adopted child or a child lawfully placed with you for adoption is treated as your child, as is a foster child placed with you by a court order or by an authorized placement agency.

Residence test (abode test). The qualifying child must have the same principal place of abode as you for more than half the year. You do not have to own the home or pay the maintenance costs, but the child must live with you for over half the year.

Temporary absences disregarded. In applying the residence test, your child is considered to be living with you while either of you is temporarily absent (or you both are) due to special circumstances. This includes temporary absences while away at school or on business, while obtaining medical treatment, taking vacations, or serving in the military.

Kidnapped child. The principal place of abode test is considered met for a child under age 18 who met the test prior to being kidnapped by a non–family member.

Birth or death of child during the year. You may claim a full exemption for a child born during the year ($3,650 for 2010) if the child lived with you after birth, apart from required hospital stays; the principal place of abode test is considered met for the year. An exemption is allowed for a child born alive even if he or she lived only for a moment. No exemption is allowed for a stillborn child.

The principal place of abode test is considered met for a child who died during the year if the child lived with you while alive.

Age or student test. A qualifying child must be under age 19 at the end of the year, a full-time student under age 24 at the end of the year, or permanently and totally disabled, regardless of age.

In addition, a child who is not permanently and totally disabled must be younger than you. If you are married and file jointly, the child must be younger than you or your spouse. For example, you are age 21 and you file jointly with your 25-year-old spouse. Your 23-year-old brother, a non-disabled full-time student, lives with you and your spouse. On your joint return, you can claim your brother as a qualifying child because he is younger than your spouse although older than you.

Qualifying as a full-time student. A full-time student is one who attends school full time during at least five calendar months in the tax year. For example: attendance from February through some part of June—or from February through May and then at least one month from September through December—qualifies. The five months do not have to run consecutively. Attendance at a vocational, trade, or technical school for the five-month period qualifies, but not correspondence schools or on-the-job training courses. Your child who attends school at night is considered a full-time student only if he or she is enrolled for the number of hours or classes that is considered full-time attendance.

Tie-breaker rules. The law provides tie-breaker rules to determine who can treat a child as a qualifying child when the qualifying child tests are met by more than one taxpayer.

If only one of the taxpayers is the parent of the child, the child is treated as the qualifying child of that parent. This situation could arise, for example, where a parent and infant child live with the child's grandparent for more than half the year. Both the child's parent and grandparent would meet the principal place of abode test and relationship test with respect to the child, but under the tie-breaker rule, the child is treated as the qualifying child of the parent. However, the parent can choose not to claim the child, and allow the grandparent to claim the exemption, provided the grandparent's adjusted gross income (AGI) exceeds his or her own AGI. If the parent's AGI equals or is higher than the grandparent's AGI, the grandparent cannot claim the exemption; only the parent can.

If the parents file separate returns and both meet the tests for treating the child as a qualifying child, they may be unable to agree on which of them should claim the child. If they each claim the child on a separate return, the IRS will first determine if the noncustodial parent is entitled to the exemption under the special rule for divorced or separated parents *(21.7)*. If the special rule applies, the tie-breaker rules do not apply. If the special rule does not apply and the child is a qualifying child of both parents under the above tests, the tie-breaker rule deems the child to be the qualifying child of the parent with whom the child has resided for the longer period during the year. If the residency period with both parents is the same, the parent with the higher adjusted gross income is entitled to treat the child as a qualifying child.

If no parent meets the tests for claiming the child and more than one non-parent meets the tests, the non-parent with the highest adjusted gross income is entitled to claim the child as a qualifying child.

21.4 Qualifying Relatives

On your 2010 return, you may claim an exemption for a qualifying relative who is not your qualifying child *(21.3)* and is not the qualifying child of any other taxpayer for 2010, provided you cannot be claimed as a dependent (nor your spouse if you file jointly) by another taxpayer and the citizenship/resident test *(21.8)* and joint return test *(21.9)* are also met. If the member-of-household test described below is met, it may be possible to claim an individual as your qualifying relative even if he or she is "technically" the qualifying child of another taxpayer.

Assuming a person meets the relationship test, you must provide over 50% of his or her support and his or her gross income must be under the exemption amount ($3,650 for 2010) for you to claim that person as a qualifying relative.

Filing Tip

Nephew, Niece, Uncle, and Aunt

Nephews, nieces, uncles, and aunts must be your blood relatives to qualify under the relationship test. For example, the brother or sister of your father or mother qualifies as your relative; their spouses do not. You may not claim your spouse's nephews, nieces, uncles, or aunts as your qualifying relatives unless you file a joint return.

Relationship test. Relatives listed below meet the relationship test; they do not have to live with you. Unrelated or distantly related persons not on this list meet the relationship test if they live with you as discussed below under the member-of-household test.

Children, grandchildren, and great-grandchildren who are not qualifying children. Your children, grandchildren, and great-grandchildren can meet the relationship test for a qualifying relative only if they are not your qualifying children or the qualifying children of any other taxpayer under the rules for qualifying children *(21.3)*. For example, if your child is not your qualifying child for 2010 because he or she does not meet the age/student test or the principal place of abode test *(21.3)*, you may still be able to claim an exemption for the child as your qualifying relative, but only if he or she has gross income under the $3,650 limit and you provide over 50% of his or her support for the year.

Brothers, sisters, and their children. The same considerations discussed above for children, grandchildren, and great-grandchildren apply for your siblings (including half- or step-siblings) and their children. They can be your qualifying relatives only if they are not your qualifying children *(21.3)* or the qualifying children of anyone else.

Parents, grandparents, and other relatives. The following individuals also meet the relationship test: your parent, grandparent, great-grandparent, step-parent, son- or daughter-in-law, father- or mother-in-law, and brother- or sister-in-law. If related by blood, aunts and uncles also qualify.

Stepchild's husband or wife or child. Your stepchild's spouse does not meet the relationship test. Nor may you claim an exemption for a step-grandchild if you file a separate return. But you may claim them on a joint return as qualifying relatives if the other exemption tests are met. On a joint return, it is not necessary that the close relationship exist between the dependent and the spouse who furnishes the chief support. It is sufficient that the relationship exists with either spouse.

EXAMPLE

You contribute more than half of the support of the sister of your wife's mother (your wife's aunt). If you and your wife file a joint return, her aunt meets the relationship test. But your wife's aunt's husband is not related by blood to you or your wife. You cannot claim an exemption for him, even on a joint return, unless he is a member of your household under the rules discussed below and other exemption tests are met.

In-laws. Brother-in-law, sister-in-law, father-in-law, mother-in-law, son-in-law, and daughter-in-law are relatives by marriage. They meet the relationship test and you may claim them as exemptions if the other tests for qualifying relatives are satisfied.

An in-law who was related to you by marriage and whom you continue to support after divorce or the death of your spouse meets the relationship test.

EXAMPLE

For many years, Allen has contributed all the support of his father-in-law, Jerry, who has no gross income. Allen's wife died in 2009. Allen continued to be Jerry's sole source of support in 2010. Allen may claim Jerry as a qualifying relative for 2010.

Death during the year. If a relative died during 2010 but was supported by you while alive, and the other tests for an exemption are met, you may claim an exemption for the relative.

EXAMPLE

On January 21, 2010, your father died. Until that date, you contributed all of his support. He had no gross income for 2010. You may claim him as an exemption for 2010. The full deduction is taken; exemptions are not prorated.

Member-of-household test for unrelated or distantly related dependents living with you. A relative not listed above, such as a cousin, meets the relationship test if he or she lives with you all year as a member of your household, except for temporary absences due to schooling, vacationing, being away on business, serving in the military, or being confined to a hospital. A friend or mate living with you can also qualify, but not if the relationship violates local law. For example, if you live with a person married to someone else and the relationship violates the law of the state where you live, you cannot claim an exemption for that person.

Under the tax law, one spouse is not considered a dependent of the other *(21.2)*. If you are divorced or legally separated during the year, your former spouse cannot be your qualifying relative even if he or she is a member of your household for the whole year.

Special exception for child of unmarried cohabitant. If a taxpayer lives with and supports a mate and the mate's child, an exemption for the child may or may not be allowed to the taxpayer under the member-of-household test. For example, if a taxpayer supports his girlfriend and her child as members of his household, he "technically" cannot claim the child as his qualifying relative because the child is the mother's qualifying child *(21.3)* and a qualifying child cannot be the qualifying relative of someone else. However, the IRS allows a limited exception. The exemption for the child can be claimed if the child's mother (for whom the child is a qualifying child) is not required to file a tax return because of low income, and she does not file a return or files *solely* to get a refund of withheld income taxes. If the mother files a return to claim the earned income credit as well as to obtain a refund for withheld income taxes, the exception does not apply and the taxpayer cannot treat the child as his qualifying relative.

The mother can also be the qualifying relative of the taxpayer under the member-of-household test, provided that their relationship is not illegal under local law.

Caution

Students Age 24 or Older

The gross income test does not apply to qualifying children *(21.3)*, including full-time students who are under age 24 as of the end of the year. However, if your child was age 24 or older at the end of 2010 and had gross income of $3,650 or more, you may not claim him or her as a dependent for 2010.

Gross income limit. A person meeting the above relationship test cannot be claimed as your qualifying relative if he or she had gross income for 2010 of $3,650 or more. This is true even if you provide most or all of that person's support. The $3,650 limit, equal to the exemption amount, changes annually as the exemption amount is adjusted for inflation.

Keep in mind that the gross income test does *not* apply to children who meet the tests for a qualifying child *(21.3)*. However, if a child does not meet the age/student test or principal place of abode test, and thus is not a qualifying child *(21.3)*, he or she must have gross income under the annual limit ($3,650 for 2010) to be claimed as a dependent under the qualifying relative rules.

Gross income here means taxable income items includible in the dependent's tax return. It does not include nontaxable items such as gifts and tax-exempt bond interest. Gross income for a service-type business is gross receipts without deductions of expenses and for a manufacturing or merchandising business is total sales less cost of goods sold. A partner's share of partnership gross income, not the share of net income, is treated as gross income.

Social Security benefits are treated as gross income only to the extent they are taxable *(34.3)*.

Exception for disabled student working at sheltered workshop. For purposes of the gross income test gross income does not include income earned by a totally and permanently disabled individual at a school operated by a government agency or tax-exempt organization, if the school provides special instruction for alleviating the disability and the income is incidental to medical care received.

Support test. A person cannot be your qualifying relative unless you provide over half of his or her total support for the year. The support test applies to a child who does not meet the tests for a qualifying child *(21.3)*. *See 21.5* for how to count total support and your contribution to the total.

21.5 Meeting the Support Test for a Qualifying Relative

To claim an exemption for a dependent as a qualifying relative *(21.4)*, you must contribute more than 50% of the dependent's total support for the year. The support test does not apply for children who meet the tests for a qualifying child *(21.3)*.

Meeting the support test. Follow these steps to figure support: (1) Total the value of the support contributed by you, by the dependent, and by others for the dependent. Use the checklists later in this section for determining what to include in total support and what to exclude. (2) Determine your share of the total. If your share is more than 50% of the dependent's total support, you meet the support test. It does not matter how many months or days you provided the support; only the total cost of the support is considered. You may not take the exemption if the dependent contributed 50% or more of his or her own support or 50% or more was contributed by others, including government sources.

Multiple support agreement. If the dependent or someone else did not contribute 50% or more of the support, and you contributed more than 10% of the total support, you may be able to claim the exemption under a multiple support agreement *(21.6)*.

Divorced or separated parents contributing to support of their children should follow a special rule *(21.7)*.

EXAMPLE

Eric Hill receives Social Security benefits of $6,000 and also $300 in bank interest in 2010. He has no other income. Eric spends $4,400 on food, clothes, transportation, and recreation. The $4,400 spent is his contribution to his own support. Eric's rent, utilities, unreimbursed medical expenses, and other necessities are paid by his son, Mike. If Mike's payments exceed $4,400, and no one else contributes to Eric's support, Mike may claim Eric as a dependent.

Checklist of Support Items

- Food and lodging; *see* below.
- Clothing
- Medical and dental expenses, including premiums paid for health insurance policies and supplementary Medicare
- Education expenses such as tuition, books, and supplies. If your child receives a student loan and is the primary obligor, the loan proceeds are considered his or her own support contribution. This is true even if you are a guarantor of the loan. Scholarships received by full-time students are not treated as support; *see* the checklist of nonsupport items in this section.
- Cars and transportation expenses. Include the cost of a car bought for a dependent as support. If you buy a car but register it in your own name, the cost of the car is not support provided by you, but any out-of-pocket expenses you have for operating the car are part of your support contribution.
- Recreation and entertainment. A computer or TV set bought for your child or other dependent is support. Also include costs of summer camp, singing and dancing lessons, and musical instruments, as well as wedding expenses.

Planning Reminder

Savings and Investments as Support

Income that is invested is not treated as support. However, personal savings are treated as support if they are used for food, clothing, lodging, or other support items.

Dependent's income and personal savings may be support. In figuring a person's total support, include his or her taxable and tax-exempt income and personal savings if actually used for support items such as food, lodging, or clothing. Also include support items that are financed by loans. Income that is invested and not actually spent for support is not included in the earner's total support.

Social Security. Social Security benefits (whether taxable or tax-exempt) received by your dependent are included in his or her total support only if they are actually spent on support items and not invested.

Social Security benefits paid to children of deceased workers that are used for their support are treated as the children's contribution to their own support. Follow this rule even though benefits are paid to you as the child's parent or custodian. If the Social Security benefits used for a child's support are more than half of the child's total support, no one may claim the child as a dependent.

Where husband and wife are paid Social Security benefits in one check made out in their joint names, 50% is considered to be used by each spouse unless shown otherwise.

Government benefits. In figuring whether you have provided more than 50% of the dependent's support, you have to consider certain government benefits as support provided by a third party to the dependent. For example, welfare, food stamps, or housing payments based on need are support payments from the government if they are used for support of the dependent. G.I. Bill education assistance is support provided by the government.

Foster care payments by a child placement agency to parents are support provided by the agency and not by the parents. The value of board, lodging, and education provided to a child in a state juvenile home is treated as support provided by the state.

When a person joins the Armed Forces, the value of board, lodging, and clothing he or she receives is treated as the government's support contribution. However, if you are in the Armed Forces, dependency allotments withheld from your pay and used to support your dependents are included in your support contributions for them. Also included in your support contribution is a military quarters allowance covering a dependent.

Planning Reminder

Dependents in the Armed Forces

If your dependent joins the military, the value of food, lodging, clothing, and educational assistance provided by the government constitutes government support.

Lodging and food as support. The dependent's total support includes the *fair rental value* of a room, apartment, or house in which the dependent lives. In your estimate of fair retail value, include a reasonable allowance for the rental value of furnishings and appliances, and for heat and other utilities. You do *not* add payments of rent, taxes, interest, depreciation, paint, insurance, and utilities. These are presumed to be accounted for in the fair rental estimate. The fair rental value of lodging you furnish a dependent is the amount you could reasonably expect to receive from a stranger for the lodging.

Does dependent live in his or her own home? If a dependent listed in *21.4* lives in his or her own home, treat the total fair rental value as his or her own contribution to support. However, if you help maintain the home by giving cash, or you directly pay such expenses as the mortgage, real estate taxes, fire insurance premiums, and repairs, you reduce the total fair rental value of the home by the amount you contributed when figuring his or her own support contributions; *see* the Example below.

If you lived with your dependent rent-free in his or her home, the fair rental value of lodging furnished to you must be offset against the amounts you spent for your dependent in determining the net amount of your contribution to the dependent's support.

Planning Reminder

Lump-Sum Payment to Care Facilities

A lump-sum contribution covering a relative's stay in a long-term care facility is prorated over the relative's life expectancy to determine your current support contribution.

EXAMPLE

You contribute $7,000 as support to your father who lives in his own home, which has a fair rental value of $8,000 a year. He uses $4,600 of the money you give him to pay real estate taxes and $2,400 for food. He spends $3,000 of his Social Security for recreation and invests the rest. He has no gross income *(21.4)* and receives no other support. Your father's contribution to his own support is $6,400:

Fair rental value of house	
($8,000 less $4,600 you gave for taxes)	3,400
Social Security spent	3,000
Father's contribution to his own support	$6,400

You may claim your father as a dependent because your contribution of $7,000 exceeds half of his total support of $13,400 (your $7,000 contribution and his $6,400 contribution).

Food and other similar household expenses. If the dependent lives with you, you divide your total food expenses equally among all the members of your household, unless you have records showing the exact amount spent on the dependent; *see* the Examples at the end of this section. If he or she does not live with you, you count the actual amount of food expenses spent by or for that dependent.

Do you pay for a relative's care in a health facility? If you pay part of a relative's expenses for care in a nursing home or other facility, your payment is a support contribution. If you make a lump-sum contribution covering a relative's stay in an old-age home or other care facility, you prorate your payment over the relative's life expectancy to determine the current support contribution.

Checklist of Items Not Counted as Support of Dependent

- Federal, state, and local income taxes and Social Security taxes paid by the dependent from his or her own income
- Funeral expenses
- Life insurance premiums
- Medicare Part A (basic Medicare) and Part B (Supplementary Medicare benefits). In one case the IRS argued that Medicaid benefits were includible in total support but the Tax Court disagreed, holding that Medicaid is similar to excludable Medicare benefits.
- Medical insurance benefits received by the dependent
- Scholarships received by your child, stepchild, or legally adopted child who is a full-time student for at least five calendar months during the year. Scholarship aid is counted as support contributed by the child if he or she is not a full-time student for at least five months. Naval R.O.T.C. payments and payments made under the War Orphans Educational Assistance Act are scholarships that are not counted as support. State aid to a disabled child for education or training, including room and board, is a scholarship.

Allocating Support

The Examples below illustrate how you should allocate various support items when your contributions benefit more than one person or when your dependent provides part of his or her own support.

Earmarking support to one dependent. If you are contributing funds to a household consisting of several persons and the amount you contribute does not exceed 50% of the total household support, you may be able to claim an exemption for at least one dependent by earmarking your support to his or her use. Your earmarked contributions must exceed 50% of this dependent's support costs. Mark your checks for the benefit of the dependent, or provide the dependents with a written statement of your support arrangement at the time you start your payments. If you do not designate for whom you are providing support, your contribution is allocated equally among all members of a household.

Filing Tip

Households with Several Dependents

If your contribution does not exceed 50% of total household support, earmark contributions to at least one of the dependents. This will allow you to claim at least one exemption. Without proper records, however, the IRS treats your contributions as divided among the members of the household.

EXAMPLES

1. Your father lives in your home with you, your spouse, and your three children. He receives Social Security benefits of $9,800, which are not subject to tax *(34.3)* and half of which ($4,900) he spends for his own clothing, travel, and recreation. You spend $6,600 for food during the year. You also paid his dental bill of $500. You estimate the annual fair rental value of the room furnished him as $3,600. Your father's total support is:

Social Security used for support	$4,900
Share of food costs ($^1/_6$ of $6,600)	1,100
Dental bill paid by you	500
Rental value of room	3,600
	$10,100

   You meet the support test. You contributed more than half his total support, or $5,200 ($3,600 for lodging, $500 for the dental bill, and $1,100 for food).

2. Your parents live with you, your spouse, and your two children in a house you rent. The annual fair rental value of their room is $3,000. Your father receives a tax-free government pension of $5,200, all of which he spent equally for your mother and himself for clothing and recreation. Your parents' only other income was $500 of tax-exempt interest. They did not make any other contributions toward their own support. Your total expense in providing food for the household is $6,000. You pay heat and utility bills of $1,200. You paid your mother's medical expenses of $600. Your father's total

support from all sources is $5,100 and your mother's is $5,700, figured as follows:

	Father	*Mother*
Fair rental value of room	$1,500	$1,500
Pension used for their support	2,600	2,600
Share of food costs ($^1/_6$ of $6,000)	1,000	1,000
Medical expenses for mother		600
	$5,100	$5,700

In figuring your parents' total support, you do not include the cost of heat and utilities, because these are presumed to be included in the fair rental value of the room ($3,000). The support you furnish your father, $2,500 (lodging, $1,500; food, $1,000), is not over half of his total support of $5,100. The support you furnish your mother, $3,100 (lodging, $1,500; food, $1,000; medical, $600), is over half of her total support of $5,700. You meet the support test for your mother but not your father. Since she did not have taxable income, the gross income test (21.4) is satisfied.

21.6 Multiple Support Agreements

Are you and others sharing the support of one person, but with no one individual providing more than 50% (21.5) of his or her total support? You are treated as meeting the support test for a qualifying relative (21.4) if:

1. You gave more than 10% of the support;
2. The amount contributed by you and others to the dependent's support equals more than half the support;
3. Each contributor could have claimed the exemption—except that he or she gave less than half the support; and
4. Each contributor who gave more than 10% agrees to let you take the exemption. Each signs a Form 2120, "Multiple Support Declaration." You then attach the forms to your return.

Filing Instruction

Multiple Support Agreement

If you contribute more than 10% of a person's support and all other more-than-10% contributors agree to let you claim the exemption, each of them should sign a consent on separate Forms 2120 that you attach to your return.

EXAMPLES

1. You and your two brothers contribute $2,000 each toward the support of your mother. She contributes $1,000 of her own to support herself. Your two sisters contribute $500 each. Thus, the total support comes to $8,000. Of this, you and your brothers each gave 25% ($2,000 ÷ $8,000), for a total of 75%. Each sister gave 6¼% ($500 ÷ $8,000). You or one of your brothers may claim the exemption, assuming the other tests for a qualifying relative (21.4) are met. Since each of you contributed more than 10% and the total of your contributions is more than half of your mother's support, you may decide among yourselves which of the three of you will claim the exemption. If you claim the exemption, your brothers must sign Forms 2120, which you attach to your return. If one of your brothers claims the exemption, you sign a Form 2120, which is attached to the return of the brother who claims the exemption. Since neither of your sisters furnished more than 10%, neither can claim the exemption; they need not sign Forms 2120.

2. Your mother's support totals $10,000; you contribute $3,000; your brother, $2,000; your father, $1,600; and your mother from her savings contributes $3,400. Assume your father does not file a tax return claiming your mother as an exemption. You and your brother cannot use your father's contribution to meet the more than 50% test required by Rule 2 above. Your father may not join in a multiple support agreement because your mother is not his dependent for tax purposes, although an exemption may be claimed for a wife on the basis of the marital relationship (21.2).

21.7 Special Rule for Divorced or Separated Parents

A special rule for divorced or separated parents allows the parent with whom the child lives for the greater part of the year (the custodial parent) to waive the exemption in favor of the other parent (the noncustodial parent). The special rule applies only if the following threshold conditions are met: (1) the child receives over one-half of his or her total support for the year from one or both parents, (2) the parents are divorced or legally separated under a decree of divorce or separate maintenance, separated under a written separation agreement, or live apart at all times during the last six months of the year (this includes parents who were never married to each other), and (3) the child is in the custody of one or both parents for more than half the year.

The first condition is not met, and the special rule does not apply, if a parent and other individuals contributing more than 10% of the child's support enter into a multiple support agreement *(21.6)* authorizing the parent to claim the exemption.

Planning Reminder

Form 8332 Waiver Applies to Child Tax Credit

If a custodial parent releases the right to claim a dependency exemption for his or her child on Form 8332 (or substitute statement), the release also gives the noncustodial parent the right to claim the child tax credit and the additional child tax credit, assuming the credits are not phased out; *see* 25.2.

Custodial parent and noncustodial parent. For purposes of the special rule, the custodial parent is the parent with whom the child resides for the greater number of nights during the year. The other parent is the noncustodial parent. A child who is temporarily absent is treated as residing with the parent with whom the child would otherwise have resided on that night. If during the year the child resides with both parents for an equal number of nights, the parent with the higher adjusted gross income is treated as the custodial parent.

How the special rule works. The noncustodial parent is entitled to the exemption for the child if the above threshold conditions are met and the custodial parent provides a written waiver on Form 8332 (or similar statement) releasing the exemption for the taxable year to the noncustodial parent, and the noncustodial parent attaches the waiver to his or her return. If a pre-1985 divorce decree or written separation agreement gives the exemption for 2010 to the noncustodial parent, that provision has not been changed after 1984, at least $600 of the child's support for the year is provided by the noncustodial parent, and the child is totally disabled, the noncustodial parent may claim an exemption for the child for 2010.

A waiver on Form 8332 (or similar written release) by the custodial parent must specify the year or years for which it is effective. The waiver cannot be conditioned on the payment of support, or the meeting of some other obligation, by the noncustodial parent.

Caution

Custodial Parent's Revocation of Waiver Not Immediately Effective

A custodial parent can use Part III of Form 8332 to revoke a previous waiver of the right to an exemption for a child. The revocation takes effect for the year following the year in which a copy of the revocation is provided to the noncustodial parent. Thus, if you made a revocation on Form 8332 and you gave a copy to the noncustodial parent in 2009, the revocation can take effect with your 2010 return. If the copy is provided in 2010, the revocation cannot apply until 2011.

If a post-1984 decree or agreement executed before 2009 states that the noncustodial parent has the unconditional right to claim the exemption for the child, and that the custodial parent is waiving the exemption for a specified year or years, the noncustodial parent can attach to his or her return the relevant pages from the decree or agreement instead of attaching Form 8332. The attachment must include the page that gives the noncustodial parent the unconditional right to the exemption, the page showing the custodial parent's waiver, the cover page, on which the custodial parent's Social Security number should be written, and the signature page showing the custodial parent's signature and date of the agreement.

Starting with 2009 returns, the option to attach pages from a decree or agreement is not available if the decree/agreement was executed after 2008. The noncustodial parent may claim the exemption only by obtaining the custodial parent's waiver on Form 8332 (or similar written release) and attaching that to his or her return.

Custodial parent may revoke waiver. A custodial parent who has waived the exemption in favor of the noncustodial parent can revoke the waiver. The revocation can be made in Part III of Form 8332.

However, a revocation has a delayed effect. It does not apply until the year after the year in which you give a copy of it to the noncustodial parent or make a reasonable attempt to do so. For example, if you waived your right to the exemption for the years 2007 through 2012 and then in 2009 made a revocation on Form 8332 and gave a copy of it to the noncustodial parent, you can claim the exemption for the child on your 2010 return, but if a copy of the revocation was not given to the noncustodial parent until 2010, the revocation is not effective until 2011. You must attach a copy of the revocation to your return for each year that you claim the exemption.

21.8 The Dependent Must Meet a Citizen or Resident Test

To claim a 2010 exemption for a dependent, the dependent must have at some time during 2010 qualified as a:

- Citizen or resident of the United States;
- United States national (one who owes permanent allegiance to the U.S.; principally, a person born in American Samoa or the Northern Mariana Islands who has not become a naturalized American citizen); *or*
- Resident of Canada or Mexico.

Child born abroad. A child born in a foreign country, one of whose parents is a nonresident alien and whose other parent is a U.S. citizen, qualifies as a U.S. citizen and thus as a dependent if the other tests are met.

If you are a U.S. citizen or national who has legally adopted a child who is not a U.S. citizen or resident, or the child was lawfully placed with you for adoption, and the child lived with you as a member of your household for the entire year, the child is treated as a U.S. citizen or resident and thus can be claimed as your dependent if the other exemption tests are satisfied.

21.9 The Dependent Does Not File a Joint Return

You may not claim an exemption for a dependent who files a joint return. For example, if you meet the other tests entitling you to an exemption for your married daughter as your dependent *(21.1)*, but she files a joint return with her husband, you may not claim her as your dependent on your tax return.

Exception. Even if your dependent files a joint return, you may claim the exemption where the income of each spouse is under the income limit required for filing a return and the couple files a joint return merely to obtain a refund of withheld taxes. Under these circumstances, the dependent's return is considered a refund claim, and you may claim the dependency exemption.

The exception would not apply if the couple had low earnings but no withheld taxes, did not owe any tax, and did not have to file a return, but filed anyway in order to claim the Making Work Pay credit *(25.24)*. Here, the joint return is not filed solely as a refund claim, and you may not claim an exemption for your dependent.

Caution

Should Married Dependents File Separately?

When a married dependent files a joint return, the parent cannot claim an exemption. The loss of the exemption may cost a parent more than the joint return saves the couple. In such a case, it may be advisable for the couple to file separate returns so that the parent may benefit from the larger tax saving.

If the couple decides to revoke their election to file jointly and then file separately in order to preserve the exemption for a parent, they must do so before the filing date for the return. Once a joint return is filed, the couple may not, after the filing deadline, file separate returns for the same year.

21.10 Spouses' Names and Social Security Numbers on Joint Return

The IRS checks the Social Security number (SSN) of each spouse on a joint return. If the SSN and name on the return do not match IRS/Social Security Administration records, the IRS will disallow the exemption for that spouse.

The most common reason for a mismatch is when, after marriage, one spouse takes the other spouse's last name, or a hyphenated name is used. An updated Social Security card should be obtained using Form SS-5, available from the Social Security Administration website at www.ssa.gov, or calling 1-800-772-1213.

If a new name is used on the return but Social Security Administration records have not been updated, the IRS will disallow that spouse's exemption unless the new name is shown on an enclosed Form W-2 or the name change is explained and documented, such as by enclosing a copy of a new driver's license or marriage certificate.

If a spouse's exemption is disallowed, the IRS will mail the taxpayers an explanatory notice. By contacting the IRS and verifying a name change, the exemption can be restored.

21.11 Reporting Social Security Numbers of Dependents

On your return, you must list the Social Security number (SSN) of each dependent you claim. Include the SSNs of parents or other adults you claim as dependents, as well as those of children.

An SSN may be obtained from the Social Security Administration for U.S. citizens and aliens who have been lawfully admitted for permanent residence or employment. If a dependent is a resident alien or nonresident alien ineligible to obtain an SSN, an individual taxpayer identification number (ITIN) must be obtained from the IRS by filing Form W-7.

If you are in the process of legally adopting a U.S. citizen or resident child who has been placed in your home by an authorized placement agency, and you cannot obtain a Social Security number for the child in time to file your tax return, you may use Form W-7A to apply to the IRS for a temporary adoption taxpayer identification number (ATIN).

If you fail to include a correct SSN or ITIN for a dependent claimed on your return, the IRS may disallow the exemption, although it may contact you and give you an opportunity to provide the number. If an exemption is disallowed, the IRS may assess the extra tax using a summary assessment procedure if you fail to request abatement of the assessment within 60 days of receiving notice; this procedure does not require issuance of a deficiency notice, so there is no appeal to the Tax Court.

Planning Reminder

Filing for SSN or ITIN

If you are planning to claim an exemption for a dependent who as of the end of 2010 does not have the required Social Security number or individual taxpayer identification number, either you or that person should file Form SS-5 with the Social Security Administration or Form W-7 with the IRS (for an ITIN) as soon as possible so the number may be obtained before the April 15, 2011, filing deadline for your 2010 return. If you do not have the SSN by the filing due date, you should file Form 4868 for an automatic extension to file *(46.3)*.

To obtain a Social Security number for a dependent child, file Form SS-5 with your local Social Security Administration office. Parents of newborn children may request a number when filling out hospital birth-registration records.

Religious beliefs. Religious beliefs against applying for and using SSN numbers for their children do not excuse taxpayers from the obligation to provide them. That's what the Tax Court told the Millers, who had refused to use SSN numbers for claiming their two children as exemptions. They argued that SSNs are universal numerical identifiers equal to the "mark of the Beast," as described in the New Testament. However, they were willing to use Individual Taxpayer Identification Numbers (ITINs).

The Court held that the IRS properly refused to issue ITINs in this case because ITINs are issued only to taxpayers who are ineligible to receive SSNs, which are issued by the Social Security Administration. The couple had argued that the requirement to use SSNs "substantially burdened" their First Amendment right to free exercise of religion, which entitled them to relief under the Religious Freedom Restoration Act of 1993. The Court held that it did not have to decide the "burden" issue because the IRS was able to show that the SSN requirement furthers a compelling governmental interest and is the least restrictive means of achieving this interest. Here, the Government has a compelling interest in effectively tracking claimed dependency exemptions and administering the tax system in a uniform and mandatory way. Moreover, the requirement to supply SSNs for dependent children has significantly reduced the improper claiming of dependents. Allowing the use of ITINs would be a less effective means of detecting fraud than requiring SSNs. If an individual entitled to an SSN was issued an ITIN, an SSN could later be obtained, allowing duplicate exemption claims to be made.

21.12 Personal Exemptions Not Subject to Phaseout for 2010

For 2010, you may claim the full $3,650 deduction for each personal exemption regardless of income. There is no phaseout. For years before 2010, a portion of the deduction was phased out for taxpayers with adjusted gross income exceeding an annual threshold. The disallowed amount was gradually decreased for 2006–2009 and for 2010 there is no phaseout at all.

However, the phaseout is scheduled to return in 2011. The phaseout formula for 2011 (and later years) had not yet been determined when this book went to press; *see* the *e-Supplement at jklasser.com* for details.

Part 4

Personal Tax Computations

In this part, you will learn how to:

- ***Figure your regular tax.*** After claiming the standard deduction or itemized deductions *(13.1)* and deducting your allowable personal exemptions *(21.1)*, you figure your 2010 regular tax by looking up the tax in the Tax Table or by figuring the tax using the Tax Computation Worksheet or special capital gain worksheets *(22.1)*.
- ***Apply the alternative minimum tax.*** If you have reduced your taxable income by certain deductions and tax benefits, you may be subject to the AMT *(23.1)*.
- ***Reduce your tax liability with tax credits.*** You may be entitled to tax credits *(22.7)* that lower your regular tax as well as any AMT.
- ***Figure estimated tax payments.*** If you have investment and self-employment income, you generally have to pay quarterly estimated tax *(27.1)*.
- ***Compute the "kiddie tax."*** If your child under age 18 has investment income for 2010 exceeding $1,900, you must compute tax on that income as if it were your own. The "kiddie tax" rules also apply if at the end of 2010 your child is age 18 or a full-time student under age 24, unless the child's earned income for 2010 exceeds 50% of his or her total support for the year *(24.2)*.

Chapter 22

Figuring Your Regular Income Tax Liability

There are two types of income tax rates: (1) regular rates, which apply to all taxpayers, and (2) alternative minimum tax (AMT) rates, which apply only if certain tax benefits, when added back to your income, result in an AMT tax that exceeds your regular tax. Most taxpayers do not have to compute the regular tax. They find the tax for their income and filing status in the IRS Tax Table if their taxable income is less than $100,000 *(22.2)*. The Tax Computation Worksheet must be used to figure your regular income tax if taxable income is $100,000 or more *(22.3)*. However, if you have net capital gain or qualified dividends, do not use the Tax Table or the Tax Computation Worksheet. Instead, figure your regular tax liability on the applicable capital gains worksheet in the IRS instructions *(22.4)*. Use the Foreign Earned Income Tax Worksheet to figure your regular tax if you are claiming the foreign earned income exclusion or foreign housing exclusion *(22.5)*.

Computation of the alternative minimum tax *(23.1)* is more complicated and requires the preparation of Form 6251.

22.1 Taxable Income and Regular Income Tax Liability

The way you determine your regular tax liability depends on the amount of your taxable income and in some cases the type of income you have. If your taxable income is less than $100,000, you generally must use the IRS Tax Table to look up your tax *(22.2)*. If your taxable income is $100,000 or more, you use the Tax Computation Worksheet to determine the tax *(22.3)*. However, if you have net capital gain or qualified dividends, you generally figure your tax on the Qualified Dividends and Capital Gain Tax Worksheet in the IRS instructions for Form 1040 *(22.4)*. Tax is figured on the Foreign Earned Income Tax Worksheet if you claim the foreign earned income or housing exclusion, or on Form 8615 if the "kiddie tax" computation *(24.4)* must be made.

Taxable income is your adjusted gross income *(12.1)* minus the following: (1) your standard deduction or itemized deductions, whichever you claim, and (2) deductions for personal exemptions *(21.1)*. On Form 1040 for 2010, taxable income is entered on Line 43. On Form 1040A and Form 1040EZ, the computation of taxable income generally takes fewer steps because only limited types of income and deductions may be reported. Itemized deductions may not be claimed. Personal exemptions for dependents may be claimed on Form 1040A but not on Form 1040EZ. *See* the table on page 7 for the types of income and deductions that may not be reported on these forms.

On Form 1040A for 2010, taxable income is entered on Line 27; on Form 1040EZ, it is on Line 6.

Caution: regardless of how your regular tax liability is determined, you may also be liable for alternative minimum tax (AMT), which is figured on Form 6251 *(23.1)*.

22.2 Using the Tax Table

If you file Form 1040EZ or Form 1040A, the Tax Table in Part 8 is generally used to look up your regular income tax liability. If you file Form 1040, you also use the Tax Table if your taxable income is *less* than $100,000; if your taxable income is $100,000 or more, you use the Tax Computation Worksheet *(22.3)*. However, use the special capital gain worksheets discussed in *22.4* if you have net capital gain or qualified dividends. Use the Foreign Earned Income Tax Worksheet *(22.5)* if you claim the foreign earned income or housing exclusion.

If you use the Tax Table, you do not have to compute your tax mathematically. To use the Table you first figure your taxable income *(22.1)*, then turn to your income bracket and look for the tax liability listed in the column for your filing status. Filing status (single, married filing jointly, head of household, married filing separately, and qualifying widow(er)) is discussed in *Chapter 1*.

Filing Instruction

Taxable Income Under $100,000

If you do not have net capital gains on Schedule D *(22.4)*, do not claim foreign income or housing exclusions *(22.5)*, and are not using Form 8615 to compute the "kiddie tax" for a child *(24.4)*, the IRS requires you to use the Tax Table to determine the regular tax on your taxable income if it is less than $100,000.

EXAMPLES

1. You are single and have adjusted gross income for 2010 of $36,995, consisting solely of salary and interest income. You claim one personal exemption and the standard deduction.

Adjusted gross income		$36,995
Less: Standard deduction	$5,700	
Exemption	3,650	9,350
Taxable income		$27,645

Your tax liability from the Tax Table is $3,725. The tax is shown in the column for single persons with taxable income of at least $27,600 but less than $27,650.

2. You are married filing jointly and have 2010 adjusted gross income of $53,440, consisting solely of salary and interest. You claim itemized deductions of $12,900, and three exemptions.

Adjusted gross income		$53,440
Less: Itemized deductions	$12,900	
Exemptions (3 × $3,650)	10,950	23,850
Taxable income		$29,590

Your tax liability from the Tax Table is $3,599.

Table 22-1 Sample Section From 2010 Tax Computation Worksheet

Section B—Use if your filing status is **Married filing jointly** or **Qualifying widow(er).** Complete the row below that applies to you.

Taxable income. If line 43 is—	**(a)** Enter the amount from line 43	**(b)** Multiplication amount	**(c)** Multiply (a) by (b)	**(d)** Subtraction amount	**Tax.** Subtract (d) from (c). Enter the result here and on Form 1040, line 44
At least $100,000 but not over $137,300	$	× 25% (.25)	$	$ 7,637.50	$
Over $137,300 but not over $209,250	$ 142,274	× 28% (.28)	$ 39,836.72	$ 11,756.50	$ 28,080.22
Over $209,250 but not over $373,650	$	× 33% (.33)	$	$ 22,219.00	$
Over $373,650	$	× 35% (.35)	$	$ 29,692.00	$

Note: The complete Tax Computation Worksheet is in *Part 8*.

22.3 Tax Computation Worksheet

If your taxable income is $100,000 or more and you do not have net capital gain or qualified dividends *(22.4)*, or claim the foreign earned income or housing exclusion *(22.5)*, you must figure your 2010 regular tax liability on the Tax Computation Worksheet shown in *Part 8*. The Tax Computation Worksheet has replaced the tax rate schedules but provides the same result.

There are six tax rate brackets for 2010: 10%, 15%, 25%, 28%, 33%, and 35%. At the top of page 11, we show the amount of taxable income subject to each tax bracket for each filing status in 2010. However, since the Tax Computation Worksheet applies only to taxable incomes of $100,000 and more, it only shows the brackets that a taxpayer with taxable income of at least $100,000 can be subject to. These brackets vary with each filing status.

To figure regular income tax liability using the Tax Computation Worksheet, follow the column-by-column instructions. First go to the section corresponding to your filing status and find the (horizontal) row that includes your taxable income from Line 43 of Form 1040. In column (a) of that row, enter your taxable income. Multiply your taxable income by your top tax rate shown in column (b), enter the result in column (c), and then reduce it by the subtraction amount shown in column (d) to obtain the regular tax liability that you enter on Form 1040. The Example below and *Table 22-1* illustrate the computation for a married couple filing jointly.

EXAMPLE

You and your spouse file a joint return reporting taxable income of $142,274 for 2010. You do not have capital gains or losses or qualified dividends. To figure your regular tax liability, you follow the line-by-line instructions for Section B of the Tax Computation Worksheet, shown in *Table 22-1*, and get a liability of $28,080.22:

$142,274 x 28% rate from column (b)	$39,836.72
Less subtraction amount from column (d)	11,756.50
Tax	$ 28,080.22

22.4 Tax Calculation If You Have Net Capital Gain or Qualified Dividends

If a portion of your taxable income consists of net capital gain (net long-term capital gain in excess of net short-term capital loss *(5.3)*) or qualified dividends *(4.1)*, you should figure your regular tax liability on the Qualified Dividends and Capital Gain Tax Worksheet in the IRS instruction booklet. On the Worksheet, you can apply the favorable capital gain rates *(5.3)* to your net gain and qualified dividends. An example of how to report transactions on Schedule D (Form 1040) and a filled-in sample of the Qualified Dividends and Capital Gain Tax Worksheet is shown in *5.8*. You may be able to figure your liability on the Qualified Dividends and Capital Gain Tax Worksheet without having to file Schedule D if you have capital gain distributions from Box 2a of Form 1099-DIV *(32.8)* and/or qualified dividends from Box 1b of Form 1099-DIV and no other capital gains or losses.

However, you use a different worksheet if you report any 28% rate gains or unrecaptured Section 1250 gain on Schedule D. In this case, you must use the Schedule D Tax Worksheet *(5.3)* in the Schedule D instructions to figure tax liability.

22.5 Foreign Earned Income Tax Worksheet

If you claim the foreign earned income exclusion on Form 2555 or Form 2555-EZ, or the foreign housing exclusion on Form 2555, you must figure your regular tax liability using the Foreign Earned Income Tax Worksheet in the Form 1040 instructions. The worksheet computation must be used because of the rule requiring non-excluded income to be "stacked" on top of the excluded income, so that the non-excluded income is subject to the same tax rate or rates that would have applied had the foreign exclusions not been elected.

22.6 Income Averaging for Farmers and Fishermen

A farmer or fisherman may elect to average 2010 farm or fishing income over three years on Schedule J of Form 1040. On Schedule J, one-third of elected farm or fishing income is allocated to each of 2007, 2008, and 2009. The tax for 2010 equals the tax liability figured without elected farm or fishing income plus increases in tax liability for the three prior years by including allocated elected farm or fishing income. Income averaging is available only to individual farmers or fishermen and may not be elected by estates or trusts engaged in the farming or fishing business.

Elected farm or fishing income is taxable income attributable to a farming or fishing business. A farming business is generally any business that involves cultivating land or raising or harvesting agricultural or horticultural commodities. A fishing business is generally any business involving the actual or attempted catching, taking, or harvesting of fish. *See* the Schedule J instructions.

A previous election to average farm income may by revoked or the elected farm income may be changed by filing an amended return within the period of limitations for a refund claim *(47.2)*.

AMT relief for averaging. When computing AMT on Form 6251, regular tax liability is determined without regard to averaging. Since AMT liability is based on the excess of tentative AMT over regular tax, ignoring the reduction to the regular tax from averaging limits or eliminates the AMT.

22.7 Tax Credits

After applying the Tax Table or Tax Computation Worksheet to get your 2010 regular tax liability, you may be able to reduce that liability as well as AMT liability *(23.1)* by claiming tax credits. The first-time homebuyer credit, child tax credit, the dependent care credit, alternative motor vehicle credit, earned income credit, adoption credit, credit for retirement savings contributions, health insurance credit, mortgage interest credit, and the District of Columbia First-Time Homebuyer Credit are discussed in *Chapter 25*. Also discussed in *Chapter 25* is the special Making Work Pay Credit that applies for 2010 if you had earned income. The education tax credits are discussed in *Chapter 33*. The credit for the elderly is discussed in *Chapter 34* and the foreign tax credit in *Chapter 36*. The business tax credits are discussed in *Chapter 40*. The credit for prior year AMT liability is discussed at *23.5*.

If you worked for more than one employer in 2010 and Social Security taxes of more than $6,621.60 were withheld from your wages, the excess may be claimed as a credit on Line 69 in the "Payments" section of Form 1040 *(26.10)*.

Chapter 23

Alternative Minimum Tax (AMT)

The purpose of AMT is to effectively take back some of the tax breaks allowed for regular tax purposes. The AMT is an additional tax that you may owe if for regular tax purposes you claimed:

- Itemized deductions, such as taxes, interest on home equity loans used for nonresidential purposes, medical expenses, and miscellaneous job and investment expenses.
- Certain tax-exempt interest, accelerated depreciation, and incentive stock option benefits.
- A substantial number of exemptions for dependents.

There are no specific tests to determine whether or not you are liable for AMT. You must first figure your regular income tax and then *see* whether tax benefit items must be added back to taxable income to figure alternative minimum taxable income, on which the AMT is figured. If after claiming the AMT exemption and applying the AMT rates of 26% and 28% the tentative alternative minimum tax exceeds your regular income tax, the excess is your AMT liability, which is added to the regular tax on your return. In other words, your tax liability for the year will be the greater of your regular tax or your AMT.

AMT liability is figured on Form 6251 and is attached to Form 1040. If you file Form 1040A, AMT liability, if any, is figured on a worksheet and the AMT is entered on the line for total tax on Form 1040A.

Table 23-1 Key to AMT Rules for 2010

Item—	*AMT Rule—*
Tax rate	A 26% rate applies to AMT taxable income of $175,000 or less (after the AMT exemption), $87,500 or less if married filing separately. A 28% rate applies to AMT income exceeding the $175,000 or $87,500 threshold.
AMT taxable income	Regular taxable income without personal exemptions, increased or decreased by adjustments and increased by preferences.
AMT exemption	The AMT exemption amounts for 2010 were unsettled when this book went to press *(23.1)*.
AMT adjustments	Itemized deductions for taxes, certain interest, and most miscellaneous deductions are not allowed. Personal exemptions and the standard deduction are not allowed. MACRS depreciation is figured under the alternative MACRS system for real estate using 40-year straight-line recovery, and, for personal property, the 150% declining balance method. For incentive stock options; *see 23.2*. Mining exploration and development costs are allowable costs amortized over 10 years. For long-term contracts entered into after February 28, 1986, income is figured under the percentage-of-completion method. Pollution control facilities amortization is figured under alternate MACRS. Alternative tax net operating loss is allowed with adjustments. Circulation expenditures must be amortized ratably over three years. Research and experimental expenditures must be amortized ratably over 10 years. Passive activity losses are recomputed; certain tax-shelter farm losses may not be allowed.
AMT preference items	Tax-exempt interest from certain private activity bonds. Accelerated depreciation on real property and leased personal property placed in service before 1987—excess depreciation or amortization taken over straight-line deduction. If you sell qualified small business stock that qualifies for an exclusion *(5.7)*, 7% of the exclusion is a preference item.
Adjusted gross income	In making AMT computations involving adjusted gross income limitations, use adjusted gross income as computed for regular tax purposes.
Partnership AMT	If you are a partner, include for AMT your distributive share of the partnership's adjustments and tax preference items. These are reported on Schedule K-1 (Form 1065). The partnership itself does not pay alternative minimum tax.
Trust or estate AMT	If you are a beneficiary of an estate or trust, consider for AMT your share of distributable net alternative minimum taxable income shown on Schedule K-1 (Form 1041). The estate or trust must pay tax on any remaining alternative minimum taxable income.
S corporation stockholder	If you are a shareholder, consider for AMT your share of the adjustments and tax preference items reported on Schedule K-1 (Form 1120-S).
Children subject to "kiddie tax"	Children under age 24 who are subject to the "kiddie tax" *(24.3)* for 2010 may have to compute AMT liability on Form 6251. The 2010 AMT exemption for a child subject to the "kiddie tax" generally equals the child's earned income plus $6,700.

23.1 Computing Alternative Minimum Tax on Form 6251

After you determine your regular income tax liability, you use Form 6251 to compute AMT liability, if any. The checklist below gives an indication as to when you may have to use Form 6251. The checklist items are discussed at *23.2–23.5*.

If you check any of the items on the list, you should complete Form 6251 to determine if you are liable for AMT. These items are AMT adjustments and preferences and generally are added back to regular taxable income to calculate alternative minimum taxable income (AMTI). The items that most commonly get added back to income when calculating AMTI are state and local taxes and miscellaneous itemized deductions.

Items subject to AMT:		***Check: √***
1.	Personal exemptions	❑
2.	Standard deduction	❑
3.	Itemized deductions for taxes, miscellaneous expenses, and medical expenses	❑
4.	Interest on home equity debt used for nonresidential purposes	❑
5.	Accelerated depreciation in excess of straight line	❑
6.	Income from the exercise of incentive stock options	❑
7.	Tax-exempt interest from private activity bonds	❑
8.	Intangible drilling costs	❑
9.	Depletion	❑
10.	Circulation expenses	❑
11.	Mining exploration and development costs	❑
12.	Research and experimental costs	❑
13.	Pollution control facility amortization	❑
14.	Tax-shelter farm income or loss	❑
15.	Passive income or loss	❑
16.	Certain installment sale income	❑
17.	Income from long-term contracts computed under percentage-of-income method	❑
18.	Net operating loss deduction	❑
19.	Foreign tax credit	❑
20.	Investment expenses	❑
21.	Gain on small business stock qualifying for exclusion	❑

AMT exemption amounts for 2010 unsettled when this book went to press. Because AMT exemptions are not indexed for inflation, Congress has been forced to enact annual "patches" to increase the exemptions in order to prevent millions of taxpayers from becoming subject to the AMT. Without the patches, the AMT exemptions would have fallen back to what they were before 2001: $45,000 for married persons filing jointly and qualifying widow(er)s, $33,750 for single persons and heads of households, and $22,500 for married persons filing jointly. For 2009, a one-year patch increased the exemptions to: $70,950 for married persons filing jointly and qualifying widow(er)s, $46,700 for single persons and heads of households, and $35,475 for married persons filing separately.

However, when this book went to press, Congress had not yet passed an exemption patch for 2010. A patch could extend the above 2009 exemption amounts to 2010 or more likely slightly increase them. Given the outcry that would result if the exemptions were allowed to fall back to the pre-2001 amounts ($45,000, $33,750, and $22,500), it is extremely likely that an exemption patch will eventually be enacted for 2010. The Congressional response will be reported in the *e-Supplement* at *jklasser.com*.

Phaseout. The exemptions are subject to a phaseout rule: 25% of the exemption amount is phased out for each $1 of AMTI exceeding $150,000 for joint filers and qualifying widow(er)s, $112,500 for single taxpayers and heads of household, and $75,000 for married persons filing separately. A married person filing separately whose exemption is completely phased out must increase his or her AMTI by an additional amount.

AMT calculation. After reducing AMTI by the allowable exemption, a 26% AMT rate generally applies to the first $175,000 of AMT income ($87,500 if married filing separately), and a 28% rate applies to any balance of the AMT income. However, if you had net capital gains that qualify for reduced capital gains rates *(5.3)*, you apply the same capital gains rate for AMT purposes as for regular income tax purposes.

The resulting tax, less any AMT foreign tax credit, is the tentative AMT, which applies only to the extent it *exceeds* your regular income tax. For this purpose, regular income tax is the tax on Line 44 of Form 1040, with no reduction for tax credits other than the foreign tax credit, *minus* any special averaging tax on a lump-sum distribution. The excess of tentative AMT over this regular tax, if any, is the AMT liability that you must report as an additional tax on Line 45 of Form 1040.

Follow the line-by-line instructions to Form 6251 to figure your AMT liability, if any.

23.2 Adjustments for AMT

If you itemize deductions on Schedule A, the starting point for figuring alternative minimum taxable income (AMTI) on Form 6251 is your adjusted gross income reduced by the itemized deductions and if you claim the standard deduction, the AMT starting point is your adjusted gross income. In either case, you can reduce adjusted gross income by any special exemption claimed on Form 8914 *(21.1)* for providing housing to a person displaced by storms in the Midwestern disaster area. Other exemptions claimed for regular tax purposes are not allowed for AMT purposes.

You generally must increase this starting point amount by adjustments and preferences, although sometimes a negative adjustment reduces AMTI.

Caution

Standard Deduction and Exemptions Disallowed for AMT

Exemptions for yourself and your dependents are not allowed for AMT purposes. If you claimed the standard deduction instead of itemizing deductions on Form 1040, the standard deduction is not allowed as an AMT deduction, but it is possible that net disaster losses may be allowed as an additional standard deduction (*see* the *e-Supplement at jklasser.com*), and if they are, the deductible amount would be allowed when figuring AMT.

Standard deduction and personal exemptions. Personal exemptions can provide a substantial deduction for regular tax purposes, but for AMT purposes, exemptions are not allowable. If you claim the standard deduction for regular tax purposes, the deduction is not allowed when figuring AMTI. However, *if* an additional standard deduction is allowed for a net disaster loss, which will depend on Congress's passing legislation that extends the deduction to 2010, the net disaster amount will be allowed as a negative adjustment on Form 6251; *see* the *e-Supplement at jklasser.com* for an update on legislation affecting net disaster losses.

Certain itemized deductions disallowed for AMT purposes. Some key itemized deductions claimed on Schedule A are disallowed or reduced when figuring alternative minimum taxable income (AMTI) on Form 6251. For example, no AMT deduction is allowed for state and local income (or, if elected, sales) taxes, real property taxes, or personal property taxes, or for foreign income or real property taxes. Also not allowed for AMT purposes are miscellaneous itemized deductions that were allowed on Schedule A after application of the 2% AGI floor. A smaller deduction for medical expenses is allowed for AMT than for regular tax purposes. The deduction for interest on home equity mortgage loans may have to be reduced. Investment interest may have to be refigured for AMT.

The required AMT adjustments for these deductions are discussed in the following paragraphs.

Court Decision

10 Children Subject Parents to AMT

A married couple found themselves paying AMT tax when their regular tax deduction of 12 personal exemptions for themselves and their 10 children was disregarded for AMT purposes. In the Tax Court, they argued that AMT was not intended to apply to taxpayers merely because they had large families. The Tax Court disagreed. Congress specifically wrote the law considering the effect of personal exemptions on AMT tax liability. The Tenth Circuit appeals court, although more sympathetic to the couple, agreed with the Tax Court that their situation fit within the AMT rules.

Mortgage interest. Less interest may be deductible for AMT purposes than for regular tax purposes. If an interest deduction is claimed on Schedule A for debt that does not qualify under the AMT rules, that interest is added back as an adjustment on Form 6251.

No AMT adjustment is required for home mortgage interest paid on a debt incurred to buy, construct, or substantially rehabilitate your principal residence or qualifying second residence. The residence may be a house, apartment, cooperative apartment, condominium, or mobile home not used on a transient basis. Nor is an adjustment required for interest on a debt incurred before July 1, 1982, provided that the mortgage was secured at the time it was taken out by your principal residence or any other home used by you or a family member.

An adjustment is required for home mortgage interest on a loan used for any purpose other than to buy, build, or substantially improve your principal residence or second residence. If your Schedule A deduction includes interest on a refinanced loan (including a second or later refinancing), you must treat as an AMT adjustment any interest on the new mortgage balance that exceeded the balance of the prior debt immediately before the refinancing (whether it was the balance of the original debt or balance of a prior refinancing).

The instructions to Form 6251 have a worksheet for figuring the home mortgage interest adjustment.

Taxes. State, local, and foreign taxes deducted on Schedule A must be added back to income in figuring AMT. If you received in 2010 a refund of taxes deducted in a prior year and the refund is reported as income on your 2010 Form 1040 *(11.5–11.6)*, you enter the refund on Form 6251 as a negative adjustment in figuring alternative minimum taxable income.

Medical expenses. If medical expenses in excess of the 7.5% AGI floor are deducted for regular tax purposes, you must add back to income on Form 6251 the smaller of the allowable medical deduction from Schedule A or 2.5% of adjusted gross income. The effect of this adjustment is to allow medical expenses as an AMT deduction only to the extent that they exceed 10% of AGI.

Miscellaneous deductions. In figuring alternative minimum taxable income (AMTI), you may not deduct miscellaneous itemized deductions in excess of 2% of adjusted gross income that you claim on Schedule A. These include unreimbursed job expenses *(19.3)*, tax preparation fees *(19.16)*, and contingent legal fees paid to recover taxable damages in employment or personal legal actions *(19.18)*.

Investment interest. If for regular tax purposes you claimed an itemized deduction (Schedule A) for investment interest on Form 4952, you must complete a second Form 4952 to determine if your allowable deduction for AMT is more or less than the itemized deduction, taking into account AMT adjustments and preferences. The difference between the regular tax deduction and the allowable AMT deduction is entered on Form 6251 as a positive adjustment if the regular tax deduction is more, or as a negative adjustment if the AMT amount is more. For example, if you paid interest on a home equity loan whose proceeds were invested in stocks or bonds, that interest is not treated as investment interest on Form 4952 when figuring the itemized deduction for regular tax purposes, but it is included as investment interest on the second Form 4952 used to figure the allowable AMT amount.

MACRS depreciation. Depreciation allowed for AMT may differ from that allowed for regular tax purposes. For tangible personal property (such as cars or furniture) placed in service before 1999, the AMT depreciation rate is the 150% declining balance method over the alternative depreciation system recovery period (ADS; *see 42.9*), switching to the straight-line method once it provides a larger deduction than the 150% method. For tangible personal property placed in service after 1998, the AMT deduction is figured using the 150% declining balance rate (switching to straight line when it gives a larger deduction) over the general depreciation system (GDS) recovery periods of three, five, seven, or 10 years *(42.4)*. Real property acquired after 1986 is depreciated for AMT over a 40-year period using the straight-line method. Depreciation deductions for films, videotapes, and sound recordings under the unit-of-production method or other method not based on a term of years are not adjusted under AMT.

If, for regular tax purposes, you use the regular 200% declining balance method to depreciate business equipment with a recovery period of three, five, seven, or 10 years, the difference between the regular depreciation and the 150% rate for AMT is generally an adjustment, but there is an exception for property eligible for bonus depreciation *(42.21)*; *see* the Form 6251 instructions. For real estate, the adjustment is the difference between the straight-line depreciation claimed for regular tax purposes using the recovery period discussed in *42.13* and the straight-line recovery over the AMT 40-year recovery period.

The adjustment for MACRS may result in providing more depreciation for AMT purposes where the AMT depreciation computation towards the latter part of the useful life of the property provides larger deductions than the regular MACRS deduction. If the AMT deduction exceeds the regular tax deduction, the difference is entered as a negative adjustment that reduces alternative minimum taxable income.

Basis adjustment affects AMT gain or loss. When post-1986 depreciable assets are sold, gain for AMT purposes is figured on the basis of the property as adjusted by depreciation claimed for AMT purposes. This gain or loss will be different from the gain or loss figured for regular tax purposes where regular MACRS depreciation was used.

Planning Reminder

Selling ISO Stock to Avoid AMT Adjustment

If you exercise an incentive stock option and your rights in the acquired stock are transferable and not subject to a substantial risk of forfeiture, you have to treat as an AMT adjustment the excess of the fair-market value of the stock when the option was exercised over the option price. Unless you sell the stock by the end of that same year, you must report an AMT adjustment based on the value of the stock when the option was exercised, *even if* the value later declines substantially. You avoid the AMT adjustment if you sell the stock in the same year the option was exercised.

Caution

Gain on Sale of Incentive Stock Option Stock

Your AMT basis in stock acquired through the exercise of an ISO is increased by the amount of the required AMT adjustment. Keep basis records for both AMT and regular tax purposes, since in the year the stock is sold, the higher AMT basis will reduce (or even eliminate in some cases) the gain reportable for AMT purposes.

Incentive stock option (ISO). For regular tax purposes, you are not taxed when you exercise an incentive stock option (ISO) *(2.16)*. If you acquire stock by exercising an ISO and you dispose of that stock in the *same* year, the tax treatment under the regular tax and the AMT is the same. No AMT adjustment is required. However, if you do not sell the stock in the same year that the option is exercised, the exercise of an ISO can result in a substantial AMT liability. You generally must increase AMT income by including on Form 6251 the excess, if any, of:

1. The fair market value of the stock acquired through exercise of the option (determined without regard to any lapse restriction) when your rights in the acquired stock first become transferable or when these rights are no longer subject to a substantial risk of forfeiture, over
2. The amount you paid for the stock, including any amount you paid for the ISO used to acquire the stock.

If your rights in the acquired ISO stock are not transferable and are subject to a substantial risk of forfeiture in the year you exercise the ISO, you do not report the AMT adjustment until the year your rights become transferable or are no longer forfeitable. However, within 30 days of the transfer to you of the stock acquired through exercise of the ISO, you may elect to include in AMT income for that year the excess of the stock's fair market value (determined without regard to any lapse restriction) over the exercise price; *see* the discussion of the Section 83(b) election at *2.17*.

If you report an AMT adjustment for stock acquired through the exercise of an ISO, increase the AMT basis of the stock by the amount of the adjustment. Since the AMT basis in stock acquired through an ISO is likely to be significantly higher than your regular tax basis, you may have a larger gain for regular tax purposes and a larger loss for AMT purposes in the year you sell the stock. This would produce a negative adjustment for AMT. Follow the instructions to Line 18 ("Disposition of Property") of Form 6251.

Liability for older ISO-related AMT has been eliminated. The 2008 Emergency Economic Stabilization Act abated AMT for 2007 and earlier years that was attributable to the ISO adjustment and still owed as of October 3, 2008, as well as interest and penalties on such AMT. In other words, these amounts were in effect "forgiven" by Congress.

Mining exploration and development costs. The deduction allowed for regular tax purposes for mining exploration and development costs is amortized ratably over a 10-year period for AMT purposes. The difference between the regular tax deduction and AMT deduction is entered on Form 6251 as an adjustment (positive or negative).

If a mine is abandoned as worthless, all mining exploration and development costs that have not been written off are deductible in the year of abandonment.

Circulation costs. Circulation costs deducted in full for regular tax purposes must be amortized over three years for the AMT. The difference between the two allowable deductions must be reported as an adjustment on Form 6251.

Long-term contracts. The use of the completed contract method of accounting or certain other methods of accounting for long-term contracts is generally not allowable. For AMT, the percentage of completion method must be used. However, there is an exception for home construction contracts.

Research and experimental expenditures. Costs must be amortized over 10 years for AMT purposes if incurred in a business in which you are not a material participant. The difference between the regular tax and AMT deductions must be entered as an adjustment (positive or negative)on Form 6251.

Passive tax-shelter farm losses. Generally, no AMT loss is deductible for any tax-shelter farm activity. A tax-shelter farm activity is any farming syndicate or any farming activity in which you do not materially participate. You may be treated as a material participant if a member of your family materially participates or you meet certain retirement or disability tests discussed at *10.6*.

Gains and losses reported for regular tax purposes from tax-shelter farm activities must be refigured by taking into account any AMT adjustments and preferences. However, a refigured loss is not allowed for AMT purposes except to the extent that you are insolvent at the end of the year. This means that you deduct the loss to the extent of your insolvency. Insolvency is the excess of liabilities over fair market value of assets. Any AMT-disallowed loss is carried forward to later years in which there is gain from that same activity, or until you dispose of the activity.

Passive losses from nonfarming activities. These are adjusted for preference or adjustment items not allowed for AMT purposes. For example, an adjustment for MACRS depreciation is made directly against the passive loss and is not treated as a separate AMT adjustment item. The loss allowed for AMT purposes is increased by the amount by which you are insolvent at the end of the year. *See* the instructions to Form 6251, which suggest that the AMT adjustment of passive losses be figured on a separate Form 8582 that you do not file.

23.3 Tax Preference Items

The following are tax preference items that increase the amount of 2010 AMT taxable income.

Tax-exempt interest on private activity bonds. You generally must increase alternative minimum taxable income (AMTI) by tax-exempt interest on private activity bonds issued after August 7,1986 and before 2009, but this does not include qualified 501(3) bonds, New York Liberty bonds, Gulf Opportunity Zone bonds, and Midwestern disaster area bonds. Also, if issued after July 30, 2008, qualified mortgage bonds, veterans' mortgage bonds, and exempt-facility bonds that have at least 95% of the net proceeds going to fund qualified residential rental projects are not treated as private activity bonds for AMT purposes.

Any bonds issued in 2009 and 2010 that would otherwise be treated as private activity bonds are not considered private activity bonds, so the interest on the 2009/2010 bonds is not a tax preference item.

Filing Instruction

Private Activity Bond Interest

Private activity bond interest that is subject to AMT is reported in Box 9 of Form 1099-INT.

Exclusion on qualifying small business stock. If you sold small business stock qualifying for the 50% or 60% exclusion *(5.7)*, 7% of the excluded gain is treated as an AMT preference item.

Oil and gas preference items. Independent oil and gas producers and royalty owners do not have to compute preference items for excess percentage depletion deductions. Excess intangible drilling costs (IDC) are generally not treated as a preference item unless they exceed 40% of AMT income; *see* the instructions to Form 6251.

23.4 Net Operating Losses

A net operating loss (NOL) claimed for regular tax purposes must be recomputed for AMT after all other AMT adjustments and preference items are taken into account. The alternative tax net operating loss deduction allowed for AMT purposes is generally the amount of the regular net operating loss except that in figuring the nonbusiness deduction adjustment *(40.19)* only AMT itemized deductions are taken into account. Thus, state and local taxes and other itemized deductions that are not allowable AMT deductions *(23.2)* do not reduce nonbusiness income in figuring the alternative tax net operating loss deduction.

The AMT net operating loss may be limited to 90% of alternative minimum taxable income; follow the instructions to Form 6251 for further details on computing the alternative tax net operating loss deduction.

23.5 Tax Credits Allowed Against AMT

The only tax credit allowed in computing tentative alternative minimum tax liability on Form 6251 is a revised version of the foreign tax credit allowed for regular tax purposes. The allowable credit is generally based on foreign source AMT income. The AMT foreign tax credit reduces the tentative AMT figured on Form 6251 before comparing it to the regular tax liability (actual AMT is the excess if any, of tentative AMT over the regular tax). If the AMT foreign tax credit exceeds the limits detailed in the Form 6251 instructions, the unused amount generally may be carried back or forward; follow the Form 6251 instructions.

If there is an AMT liability on Form 6251, that AMT is added to regular tax liability on Form 1040. The child tax credit and the retirement savings credit are allowed against the AMT as well as against the regular income tax. It was not clear when this book went to press if other nonrefundable credits (such as the dependent care credit and the education credits) will also be allowed to offset AMT for 2010; *see* the *e-Supplement* at *jklasser.com*.

23.6 AMT Tax Credit From Regular Tax

You may be able to reduce your regular 2010 tax by a tax credit based on AMT incurred in prior years. The prior-year AMT had to be attributable to "deferral items" such as the ISO adjustment or depreciation that provide only a temporary reduction to taxable income. Furthermore, the credit, which is computed on Form 8801, is generally allowed only to the extent that your regular tax liability (as reduced by allowable tax credits) exceeds tentative alternative minimum tax liability computed on Form 6251.

However, a refundable credit may be allowed on Form 8801 if you have long-term unused minimum tax credits from prior years. The refundable credit primarily benefits taxpayers who incurred substantial AMT liability by exercising incentive stock options (ISOs).

23.7 Avoiding AMT

If you are within the range of the AMT tax, review periodically your income and expenses to determine whether to postpone or accelerate income, defer the payment of expenses, and/or make certain tax elections.

There are elections, such as the election of alternative straight-line MACRS depreciation, that may avoid AMT adjustments. However, such elections will increase your regular tax. Similarly, adjustment treatment for mining exploration and development costs, circulation expenses, and research expenses can be avoided by elections to amortize *(23.2)*.

If you are on the verge of becoming subject to the AMT, or are already subject to the AMT, and the 26% or 28% AMT rate exceeds your top rate for regular tax purposes you might want to consider the following steps:

- Postpone capital gains or business income that could trigger AMT by pushing your income over the AMT exemption. On a sale of property, an installment sale *(5.21)* can spread gain over a number of years.
- Do not prepay state or local income taxes or property taxes, as these are not deductible under the AMT.
- Spread out the exercise of incentive stock options (ISOs) over more than one year to limit the AMT adjustment for the bargain element (the difference between the option price and the fair market value of the stock on the date of exercise). If you exercise an ISO and hold the acquired stock beyond the end of the year, the bargain element is subject to AMT *(23.2)*. You may find yourself with an unexpected tax liability and if the stock has depreciated in value since the date of exercise, you may find yourself short of funds to pay the liability even after selling the stock. To limit the AMT adjustment, you can stagger the exercise of options over more than one year. You can avoid the adjustment completely by selling the stock in the same year that the option was exercised, but if you do, any gain on the sale will be taxed as ordinary income and not at the favorable rate for long-term capital gains.

Accelerating income. If you find that you will be subject to AMT in a current year, you may want to subject additional income in that year to the 26% or 28% AMT tax rate. In such a case, consider accelerating the receipt of income to that year. If you are in business, you might ask for earlier payments from customers or clients. If you control a small corporation, you might prepay salary or pay larger bonuses. But here be careful not to run afoul of reasonable compensation rules. You might also consider paying dividends.

Chapter 24

Computing the "Kiddie Tax" on Your Child's Investment Income

If the "kiddie tax" applies to your child, your child's 2010 investment income in excess of $1,900 is taxed at your tax rate. The kiddie tax applies not only to children under age 18, but also to children who are age 18 or full-time students age 19–23 who do not have earned income exceeding half of their support. Only investment income of a child over $1,900 is subject to the kiddie tax, not wages or self-employment earnings.

The kiddie tax is generally figured on Form 8615 as part of the computation of the child's regular tax liability for the year. The liability from Form 8615 is then entered on the child's own tax return, and Form 8615 is attached. The Form 8615 computation has no effect on the treatment of items on your own return or on your tax computation. Instead of completing Form 8615, you may elect on Form 8814 to report the child's investment income on your own return, provided the child received only interest and dividend income. If you elect on Form 8814 to report the child's investment income on your own return, your adjusted gross income will increase and this could adversely affect your right to claim various deductions *(24.4)*.

If you are married but file separately, the parent with the larger amount of taxable income is responsible for the kiddie tax computation. If parents are divorced, separated, unmarried, or living apart for the last six months of the year, the parent who has custody of the child for the greater part of 2010 computes the tax. If a child cannot get tax information directly from a parent, the legal representative of the child may ask the IRS for the necessary information.

24.1 Filing Your Child's Return

To discourage substantial income splitting of investment income between parents and minor children, the tax law has complicated income reporting for parents and children by—

1. Imposing a "kiddie tax" that taxes a child's investment income over an annual floor ($1,900 for 2010) at the parent's tax bracket. The kiddie tax applies not only to children under age 18, but also to most 18-year-olds and students under age 24 *(24.2)*.
2. Barring a dependent child *(21.1)* from claiming a personal exemption on his or her own tax return.
3. Limiting the standard deduction for a dependent child who has only investment income. For 2010 the deduction is $950 *(13.5)*.

Does your child have to file? For a child who can be claimed as a dependent either as a qualifying child or a qualifying relative *(21.1)*, the income filing threshold is generally $950. If your dependent child has gross income (earned and investment income) of $950 or less for 2010, he or she is not subject to tax and does not have to file a tax return.

A 2010 return must be filed for a dependent child with investment income exceeding $300 and gross income of more than $950. If a dependent child has salary or other earned income but no investment income, a return does not have to be filed unless such earned income exceeds $5,700 in 2010. If your child's only income is from interest and dividends, you may be able to make an election to report the income on your own return *(24.4)*.

Although a dependent child may not claim a personal exemption on his or her 2010 tax return, the child is allowed to claim at least a $950 standard deduction. A dependent child with earned income over $950 may claim a standard deduction up to those earnings plus an additional $300, but no more than the basic standard deduction, which is generally $5,700 *(13.1)*.

How to file a 2010 return for your child. If your child is not subject to the "kiddie tax" under the rules at *24.2*, follow the regular filing rules and use Form 1040EZ, 1040A, or Form 1040 to report the child's income and deductions. Since the "kiddie tax" computation does not apply, all of the child's income will be taxed at his or her own tax rate. If your child is unable to sign his or her tax return, you must do so *(1.13)*.

If the kiddie tax computation applies *(24.2)*, Form 8615 must be filed to compute the kiddie tax unless your child's only income is interest and dividends and you elect to report your child's investment earnings on your own return *(24.4)*. On Form 8615 you must provide your Social Security number and taxable income. Form 8615 is attached to the child's tax return *(24.3)*.

Child's AMT liability. A child who has substantial tax-exempt interest, tax preferences, or tax adjustments subject to the alternative minimum tax must compute tentative AMT liability on Form 6251; *see Chapter 23*.

EXAMPLES

1. Your 14-year-old daughter, whom you claim as your dependent, has interest and dividend income of $480 and no other income for 2010. She has no income tax liability and does not have to file a return.

Interest and dividend income	$480
Less: standard deduction *(13.5)*	950
Tax liability	0

2. In 2010, your 17-year-old daughter, whom you claim as your dependent, has interest income of $700 and qualified dividends *(4.2)* of $450. Her taxable income is $200.

Interest income	$700
Qualified dividends	450
	$1,150
Less: standard deduction	950
Taxable income	$200

You must file a Form 1040A or 1040 for your daughter because she has taxable income, but the kiddie tax computation does not apply because her investment income does not exceed $1,900. On the Qualified Dividends and Capital Gain Tax

Worksheet in the Form 1040 instructions, the $200 of taxable income will be attributed to the interest income and subject to your daughter's 10% tax rate and the qualified dividends will not be taxed at all because the 0% rate for qualified dividends and capital gains applies *(4.2)*.

24.2 Children Subject to "Kiddie Tax" for 2010

The "kiddie tax" may subject a portion of your child's investment income to tax at your tax rate, where your child's tax rate is lower than yours. For 2010 tax returns, the kiddie tax applies if all of the following are true:

- Your child either (1) was under age 18 at the end of 2010, (2) was age 18 at the end of 2010 and did not have earned income exceeding half of his or her support for the year, or (3) was a full-time student during 2010 who at the end of the year was age 19 through 23 and did not have earned income exceeding half of his or her support for the year.

  For children born on January 1, the IRS treats the child's birthday as being on the last day of the prior year. Thus, a child who attains age 24 on January 1, 2011 is considered to be age 24, not 23, on December 31, 2010, and so the kiddie tax does not apply to the child's 2010 investment income.

  The dependency exemption rules for determining full-time student status *(21.3)* and support *(21.5)* apply for determining if the kiddie tax age test applies.
- Your child had more than $1,900 of investment income. The $1,900 floor is increased, as discussed below, if the child has itemized deductions exceeding $950 that are directly connected to the production of investment income.
- If married, your child filed separately from his or her spouse.

If both of a child's parents were deceased at the end of 2010, the kiddie tax computation does not apply, and the child's tax is figured under the regular rules.

Exceptions for children filing jointly and distributions from qualified disability trusts. The kiddie tax does not apply to a child who is married and files a joint return for the tax year. The exception does not apply if the child is married filing separately.

If a child is a beneficiary of a qualified disability trust, distributions of investment income from the trust are treated as earned income and thus not subject to the kiddie tax rules.

Figuring kiddie tax on child's or parent's return. The kiddie tax computation is generally made on Form 8615, which must be attached to your child's return. However, if the only income of your child who is under age 18 is interest and dividends and other tests are met, you may elect on Form 8814 to include your child's investment income on your own tax return, instead of computing the kiddie tax on Form 8615 *(24.4)*.

Kiddie tax on Form 8615 applies to investment income exceeding $1,900 floor. If your child files his or her own 2010 return, the "kiddie tax" computation on Form 8615 applies to the child's *net investment income*. For purposes of this rule, *net investment income* equals gross investment income minus $1,900 if your child does not itemize deductions on Schedule A. Thus, if your child does not itemize, the first $1,900 of investment income is exempt from the kiddie tax. Investment income exceeding $1,900 is considered net investment income subject to the kiddie tax; *see* Example 1 in this section.

Investment income includes all taxable income that is not earned income (compensation for personal services). Include taxable interest income (but not tax-exempt interest), dividends, capital gain distributions and capital gains on the sale of property, royalties, rents, and taxable pension payments. Payments from a trust are generally included to the extent of distributable net income, but, as noted earlier, there is an exception for distributions from qualified disability trusts, which are treated as earned income and thus not subject to the kiddie tax. Income in custodial accounts is treated as the child's income and is subject to the kiddie tax computation. Capital losses first offset capital gains, and any excess loss offsets up to $3,000 of other investment income.

Investment income on all of your child's property must be considered, even if the property was a gift from you or someone else, or if the property was produced from your child's wages, such as a bank account into which the wages were deposited. The wages themselves, or self-employment earnings, are not considered.

If your child does itemize deductions, and has more than $950 of deductions that are directly connected to the production of investment income, the $1,900 floor is increased. The floor is $950 plus the directly connected deductions. If the directly connected deductions are $950 or less, the regular $1,900 kiddie tax exemption applies, as in Example 2 below. Directly connected itemized deductions are expenses paid to produce or collect income or to manage, conserve, or maintain income-producing property. Only the part of the total expenses exceeding the 2% AGI floor may be deducted. These expenses include custodian fees and service charges, service fees to collect interest and dividends, and investment counsel fees. If, after you subtract the itemized deductions, your child's net investment income exceeds his or her taxable income, you apply the tax to the lower taxable income, rather than to the net investment income.

EXAMPLES

In the following Examples, assume the child is your dependent for 2010 and is subject to the kiddie tax under the age test described above.

1. For 2010, your son has dividend income of $2,050. After taking into account a standard deduction of $950, taxable income is $1,100, of which $150 is subject to the kiddie tax computation on Form 8615.

Figuring taxable income:	
Dividend income	$2,050
Less: standard deduction	950
Taxable income	$1,100
Income subject to tax at your rate:	
Investment income	$2,050
Less: $1,900 subject to kiddie tax	$1,900
	$150

2. Your daughter has $500 of wages and $2,035 of dividends and mutual-fund capital gain distributions for 2010. On Schedule A, your daughter claims itemized deductions of $400 related to investment income after the 2% AGI floor. She also has $800 of other itemized deductions. Itemized deductions of $1,200 are claimed; they exceed the $950 standard deduction. Your daughter's taxable income is $1,335, of which $135 is subject to your tax rate under the kiddie tax computation on Form 8615.

Figuring taxable income:	
Gross income	$2,535
Less: itemized deductions	1,200
Taxable income	$1,335
Income subject to tax at parent's rate:	
Investment income	$2,035
Less: greater of (1) $1,900 or (2) the sum of	
$950 and directly related expenses of $400	1,900
Subject to kiddie tax	$135

24.3 Computing "Kiddie Tax" on Child's Return

If your child is subject to the "kiddie tax" *(24.2)* for 2010, your child's regular income tax liability is computed on Form 8615, which is attached to his or her return, unless you make the parent's election to report the child's dividends and interest income on your own return *(24.4)*. Before your child's Form 8615 can be completed, your own taxable income and regular income tax must be determined. When you make the computation on Form 8615 for your child, you add your taxable income to your child's net investment income in excess of $1,900. You figure the tax on the combined amount based on your filing status, using the Qualified Dividends and Capital Gain Tax Worksheet (or, if applicable, the Schedule D Tax Worksheet) if the combined amount includes net capital gain or qualified dividends (5.3). The excess of the resulting tax over your own separately figured tax liability is generally the kiddie tax on the child's investment income exceeding $1,900. That tax, plus the tax on the portion of the child's taxable income not subject to the kiddie tax, is reported as the child's regular tax liability on his or her Form 1040 or 1040A.

As parents, the kiddie tax computation on Form 8615 does not affect your tax liability or the way you compute any limitation on deductions or credits. For example, the addition of the child's net investment income to your taxable income on Form 8615 does *not* affect the adjusted gross income floors for purposes of figuring your deduction for IRA contributions, medical expenses, or miscellaneous expenses.

Planning Reminder

Prepare Your Return First

Before your child can complete Form 8615, or you prepare it for the child, your own taxable income and regular income tax liability must be determined.

Which parent's return to use. If the parents file a *joint return*, their joint taxable income is entered on Form 8615, along with the net investment income (24.2) of all their children subject to the kiddie tax. If the parents file *separate returns*, the larger of the parents' separate taxable incomes is used on the child's Form 8615.

Where parents are legally separated or divorced and custody of the child is shared, Form 8615 should be completed using the taxable income of the parent who has custody for the greater part of the year. If parents are married but living apart, and the custodial parent qualifies as unmarried under the Head of Household rules (Test 1, *1.12*), the custodial parent's taxable income is used on Form 8615. If the custodial parent is not considered unmarried, the income of the parent with the larger taxable income is used. If the custodial parent has remarried and files a joint return with a new spouse, their joint return taxable income is used on the child's Form 8615. If the parents were never married but they live together with the child, the income of the parent with the larger taxable income is used; if the parents live apart, the income of the parent with custody for most of the year is used on Form 8615.

More than one child subject to kiddie tax. You file a separate Form 8615 for each child and on each form net investment income of all the children subject to the tax is included. The computed tax is allocated to each of your children, according to his or her share of their combined net investment income. This computation is incorporated in the steps of Form 8615 and by following the order of the form, you will make the proper allocation.

Planning Reminder

Estimating Tax on Form 8615

If you are unable to file your 2010 return by April 15, 2011, but your child's return is filed by the April 15 deadline, the child's Form 8615 may be based on an estimate of your tax liability. When you have the completed income information, file an amended return.

Estimating the kiddie tax in case of filing delay. If you are unable to file your 2010 return by April 15, 2011, the child's tax on Form 8615 may be based on an estimate. You may make a reasonable estimate of your taxable income on Form 8615 or may estimate the net investment income of children under age 18 if that information is not yet available. When you have the complete income details, file an amended return on Form 1040X.

A reasonable estimate may be based on your 2009 taxable income and the 2009 investment income of the child. If a refund is due, the IRS will pay interest from April 15, 2011, or, if the return was filed late, from the filing date. If additional tax is due on the amended return, interest will be charged from April 15, but no penalty will be imposed.

Instead of estimating the kiddie tax, you may file Form 4868 to get a six-month extension (46.3) for your return on which the kiddie tax is included. However, interest will be charged on any tax due that was not paid by the original filing date, and late payment penalties may also apply (46.3).

24.4 Parent's Election To Report Child's Dividends and Interest

Instead of filing a separate return for your child (24.3) whose income is subject to the "kiddie tax," you may elect on Form 8814 to compute the kiddie tax on your 2010 return if all of the following tests are met:

- The child's only 2010 income is from interest and dividends (including mutual-fund capital gain distributions and Alaska Permanent Fund dividends);
- The total interest and dividends are over $950 but less than $9,500;
- Estimated tax payments were not made in the child's name and Social Security number for 2010, and there was no overpayment from the child's 2009 return applied to his or her 2010 estimated tax; *and*
- The child was not subject to 2010 backup withholding.

On Form 8814, you determine the portion of the child's qualified dividends and capital gain distributions that you report on your own return, where they are eligible for the preferential rates (5.3) for qualified dividends/net capital gains. You report the balance of the child's investment income over $1,900 as "other income" on Line 21 of your Form 1040. You also figure an additional tax equal to the smaller of $95 or 10% of your child's income over $950, which is included in the regular income tax liability you enter on Line 44 of your Form 1040.

If the parents are married filing separately, or are divorced, separated, unmarried, or living apart for the last six months of the year, the parent whose taxable income would be taken into account on Form 8615 *(24.3)* is the parent who may elect to report the income on his or her own return.

In figuring whether you owe alternative minimum tax (AMT), you must include as a tax preference item interest income your child receives from specified private activity bonds *(23.3)*; *see* the Form 6251 instructions.

Should you make the election? The only advantage in making the election is to skip the paperwork involved in preparing a return in the child's name or returns in your children's names. This could save you money in the form of reduced tax preparation costs. However, there is a distinct disadvantage to the election if your child's investment income consists of qualified dividends or capital gain distributions. With the election, there is a 10% tax on the child's income between $950 and $1,900 (the income not subject to kiddie tax), whereas if a separate election is filed for the child, it is highly likely that the qualified dividends and capital gain distributions will escape tax entirely under the zero rate applicable in 2010 *(5.3)*.

In addition, including the child's income as your own increases your AGI, which may create these disadvantages:

- Make it more difficult to deduct job expenses and other miscellaneous itemized deductions, which are subject to a 2% AGI floor *(19.1)*, and medical deductions, subject to a 7.5% AGI floor *(17.1)*.
- Limit a deduction for IRA contributions under the phaseout rules *(8.4)*.
- Limit your ability to claim the special $25,000 rental loss allowance under the passive activity rules *(10.2)*.
- Increase local and state tax liability.

Finally, if you elect to report the child's income on your own return, you may not claim any deductions that your child would have been able to claim on his or her return such as investment expenses or a penalty on premature withdrawals from a savings account. On the other hand, reporting your child's interest or dividends increases your net investment income, which may allow you to claim a larger deduction for investment interest *(15.10)*. Also, your ceiling for charitable donations may be increased. If you plan to report your child's income on your 2011 return, provide for the tax in your estimated tax payments or withholdings during 2011.

Caution

Reporting Child's Income on Your Return

Including the child's income on your return could be disadvantageous not only by subjecting the income to a higher tax rate (than on the child's own return), but also by making it more difficult for you to claim certain deductions and raising your state and local taxes.

Chapter 25

Personal Tax Credits Reduce Your Tax Liability

In this chapter you will find discussions of the Making Work Pay credit, the credit for first-time homebuyers, the child tax credit, dependent care credit, earned income credit (EIC), adoption credit, retirement savings credit, health coverage credit, mortgage interest credit, and the credits for hybrid and plug-in electric vehicles. Education tax credits are discussed in *Chapter 33*.

The child tax credit is $1,000 for each qualifying dependent child under age 17. To claim the credit, you must follow the steps on the "Child Tax Credit Worksheet." There is a phaseout of the credit *(25.3)*. If the credit exceeds your tax liability, you may be entitled to a refundable credit called the "additional child credit" on Form 8812.

The dependent care credit is for working people who pay care costs that allow them the freedom to work. Depending on your income, the credit is 20% to 35% of up to $3,000 of care expenses for one dependent and up to $6,000 of expenses for two or more dependents. If your adjusted gross income exceeds $43,000, the maximum credit is $600 for one dependent and $1,200 for two or more dependents.

The earned income credit (EIC) is provided to low-income workers who support children, and a limited credit is allowed to certain workers without qualifying children *(25.10)*.

An adoption credit of up to $13,170 may be claimed in 2010 for costs of adopting a child under the age of 18 or a disabled person incapable of self-care.

25.1 Overview of Personal Tax Credits

After you determine your regular tax liability using the tax table *(22.2)*, Tax Computation Worksheet *(22.3)*, or capital gain worksheets *(22.4)*, and your AMT liability if any *(23.1)*, you may be able to reduce that liability by claiming one or more tax credits. For 2010, some personal credits, such as the child tax credit, adoption credit, retirement savings credit, and American Opportunity credit, are allowed to the full extent of regular tax liability as well as alternative minimum tax (AMT) liability. *See* the *e-Supplement at jklasser.com* for an update on extenders legislation that would allow all personal credits to offset AMT.

The additional child tax credit, earned income credit, adoption credit, and the health coverage credit are refundable for 2010, meaning that if the credit exceeds your tax liability you will receive a refund for the excess.

Eligibility rules and credit limitations for many of the personal credits are discussed in this chapter, while some are discussed in other chapters as shown below. Business tax credits are in *Chapter 40*.

Child tax credit and additional child tax credit *(25.2–25.3)*.
Child and dependent care credit *(25.4–25.9)*.
Earned income credit *(25.10–25.13)*.
Adoption credit *(25.14–25.15)*.
Qualified retirement savings contributions credit *(25.16–25.17)*.
Health coverage credit *(25.18)*.
Mortgage interest credit *(25.19)*.
District of Columbia first-time homebuyer credit *(25.20)*.
Education credits (American Opportunity and Lifetime Learning credits) *(33.7–33.10)*.
Credit for elderly or disabled *(34.7–34.9)*.
Foreign tax credit *(36.14)*.
Prior-year AMT credit *(23.6)*.
Residential energy tax credits *(25.21)*.
Hybrid and alternative vehicle credit *(25.22)*.
First-time homebuyer credit *(25.23)*.
Making Work Pay and government retiree credits *(25.24)*.
Credit for excess Social Security or Railroad Retirement withholdings *(26.10)*.
Credit for tax on mutual-fund undistributed capital gain *(32.8)*.

Law Alert

Credit for Interest on Build America Bond

If the issuer of a Build America bond does not elect to keep the credit, the bondholders may claim a credit on Form 8912 for 35% of the interest payable on the bond. A bondholder must report the amount of the credit as interest income; *see* the Form 8912 instructions.

25.2 Child Tax Credit for Children Under Age 17

For 2010, you may be able to claim a tax credit of $1,000 for each qualifying child who is under age 17 at the end of 2010. To figure the exact amount of your credit, however, you must complete the "Child Tax Credit Worksheet" in the IRS instructions to Form 1040 or 1040A. On the IRS worksheet, you determine if the potential credit ($1,000 × number of qualifying children) is limited by the phaseout rule and if it is, whether the reduced credit is limited by your tax liability (regular tax plus AMT minus specified credits).

The potential credit is phased out by 5% of your adjusted gross income in excess of the phaseout threshold, shown below. If the credit, after application of the phaseout rule, is more than your tax liability *(25.3)*, your credit is limited to the liability. However, even if the credit does exceed your tax liability, part or all of the credit may be refundable as an additional credit on Form 8812 if your earned income for 2010 exceeds $3,000 or you have three or more children *(25.3)*.

Qualifying child. The credit may be claimed for a child who is under age 17 at the end of 2009 if the child is your "qualifying child" under the dependency exemption rules in *21.3* and you are otherwise entitled to the exemption for the child. A qualifying child may be your child, stepchild, grandchild, great-grandchild, brother, sister, stepbrother, stepsister, half-brother or -sister, or the descendant of any of these. An adopted child qualifies if placed with you by an authorized agency for legal adoption, even if the adoption is not final by the end of 2010. A foster child placed with you by a court or an authorized agency qualifies. A qualifying child must live with you for over half the year and not provide over half of his or her own support *(21.3)*. The child also must be a U.S. citizen, resident, or national, or an adopted child who lived with you all year, in order for you to claim the credit for him or her.

Law Alert

Child Tax Credit After 2010

The $1,000 maximum child tax credit per qualifying child applies through 2010. The amount of the child tax credit for years after 2010 had not yet been set by Congress when this book went to press; *see* the *e-Supplement at jklasser.com*.

Phaseout of credit. The credit is limited or eliminated if your adjusted gross income is above a threshold amount for your filing status. In applying the phaseout, AGI is increased by any foreign earned income exclusion, foreign housing exclusion or deduction, or possession exclusion for American Samoa residents. If your income exceeds the following threshold for your filing status, *see 25.3*.

Filing status	*Phaseout applies if MAGI exceeds*
Married filing jointly	$110,000
Head of household	75,000
Single	75,000
Qualifying widow(er)	75,000
Married filing separately	55,000

Changing your withholding. If you can claim the child tax credit, you may have too much tax withheld from your wages during the year. If so, you can claim more withholding allowances. File the new Form W-4 with your employer so that less income tax will be withheld.

25.3 Figuring the Child Tax Credit

You use the Child Tax Credit Worksheet in the IRS instruction booklet or in Publication 972 to figure the credit. You do not attach the worksheet to your return.

Phaseout formula. If your income exceeds the phaseout threshold shown in *25.2*, the maximum credit of $1,000 per qualifying child is reduced by $50 for each $1,000 (or fraction of $1,000) that your AGI exceeds the phaseout threshold *(25.2)* for your filing status. The computation is made on the worksheet in the IRS instructions. *See* Example 2 below.

Liability limitation. The IRS worksheet limits the child tax credit to your tax liability (regular tax plus alternative minimum tax, if any). If you are subject to the phaseout rule, the amount of the credit allowed after the phaseout computation is subject to the liability limitation. Tax liability is reduced if you claim the child and dependent care credit, education credits, retirement savings credit, residential energy credits, alternative motor vehicle credit, plug-in electric vehicle credit, foreign tax credit, or credit for the elderly or disabled. If your credit exceeds your liability, the credit is limited to the liability but you can probably claim the "additional child tax credit" on Form 8812 to receive a refund; *see* below.

Refundable portion of credit claimed as additional child tax credit. If the full amount of the credit cannot be claimed on the Child Tax Credit Worksheet because of the tax liability limitation, you may be able to obtain a refund for the balance on Form 8812, Additional Child Tax Credit. The credit for 2010 is refundable to the extent of 15% of your taxable earned income plus tax-free combat pay *(35.4)* in excess of $3,000. If your earned income is *not* over $3,000, a refundable credit may still be available if you have three or more qualifying children and you paid Social Security taxes that exceed your earned income credit *(25.13)*, if any. Follow the instructions to Form 8812. Any portion of the credit that is phased out as discussed above is "lost" and is not eligible for the additional credit on Form 8812.

Law Alert

Refundable Credit

The refundable portion of the child tax credit for 2010 is 15% of taxable earned income in excess of $3,000. Combat pay that is otherwise excluded from income *(35.4)* is treated as taxable earned income for purposes of figuring the refundable amount.

EXAMPLES

1. Carl and Abby's only children, twin daughters, were born in 2010. Carl and Abby file a joint return for 2010, report AGI of $44,000, and claim the standard deduction. Their AGI is well below the $110,000 phaseout threshold *(25.2)*. They may claim the full child tax credit of $2,000 ($1,000 per child), as it does not exceed their tax liability.
2. Jane is single and has two dependent children, ages six and three. She files her 2010 return as head of household. Her 2010 AGI is $77,500. Because her AGI exceeds the $75,000 phaseout threshold for a head of household, her credit for 2010 is reduced. Jane's credit limit of $2,000 is reduced by $50 for each $1,000 or fraction of $1,000 of excess AGI. The excess income of $2,500 is rounded up to $3,000 (next multiple of $1,000) and multiplied by the phaseout percentage of 5%, resulting in a credit reduction of $150 ($3,000 × 5%). Jane may claim a child tax credit of $1,850 ($2,000 – $150) on her 2010 return. She is not subject to the liability limitation as her liability exceeds the $1,850 credit.

25.4 Qualifying for Child and Dependent Care Credit

Did you hire someone to care for your children or other dependents while you work? If so, you may qualify for a tax credit for the expenses. You may claim the credit even if you work part time. You may claim the credit if you work from home and pay someone to care for your child while you are there. The credit is generally available to the extent you have earnings from employment. Your employer may have a plan qualifying for tax-free child care and, if you are covered, you may be unable to claim a tax credit *(25.8)*.

Caution

Nonrefundable Credit

The dependent care credit is limited to your tax liability. In other words, if the credit amount exceeds the tax that you owe, you will not be given a refund of the difference.

Where to claim the credit. The credit is claimed on Form 2441 if you file Form 1040 or Form 1040A. The size of the credit depends on the amount of your care expenses, number of dependents, and income. Depending on your adjusted gross income, the credit for 2010 is 20% to 35% of up to $3,000 of care expenses for one dependent and up to $6,000 of expenses for two or more dependents. The minimum credit percentage of 20% applies if your adjusted gross income exceeds $43,000. *See Table 25-1 (25.5).*

Credit requirements. To qualify for the credit on your 2010 return, you must:

1. Incur expenses to care for a qualifying person *(25.7)* in order to earn income. In the case of a married couple, this requires both spouses to work either at full- or part-time positions. An exception to the earned income rule is made for a spouse who is a full-time student or incapacitated *(25.6)*. Qualifying care expenses are discussed in *25.8*. Limits on the amount of qualifying costs are discussed in *25.5*.
2. File jointly if you are married, unless you are separated under the rules discussed in *25.9*.
3. Hire a care provider *other than* your child who is under age 19 at the end of the year, your spouse, or a person you can claim as a dependent *(25.8)*.
4. Have qualifying expenses *(25.8)* in excess of tax-free reimbursements received from your employer.
5. Report on your tax return the name, address, and taxpayer identification number (Social Security number for individuals) of the child-care provider; *see* below.

Identifying care provider on your return. You must list the name, address, and taxpayer identification number of the person you paid to care for your dependent on Form 2441. You do not need the taxpayer identification number if a tax-exempt charity provides the dependent care services. Failure to list the correct name, address, and number may result in a disallowance of the credit. To avoid this possibility, ask the provider to fill out Form W-10 or get the identifying information from a Social Security card, driver's license, or business letterhead or invoice. If a household employee has filled out Form W-4 for you, this may act as a backup record.

Withholding tax for a housekeeper. Where you employ help to care for your dependent in your home, you may be liable for FICA (Social Security) and FUTA (unemployment) taxes *(38.3)*.

Filing Tip

Employer Reimbursements Reduce Credit

Expenses qualifying for the dependent care credit are reduced by any tax-free reimbursements under a qualified employer dependent care program. That is, the reimbursements reduce the $3,000 expense limit for one dependent, or the $6,000 expense limit for two or more qualifying dependents *(25.8)*. Your employer will report reimbursements in Box 10 of your Form W-2. You figure the tax-free portion of the reimbursement, and any reduction to the credit expense base, on Form 2441.

25.5 Limits on the Dependent Care Credit

The credit is a percentage of expenses paid for the care of a qualifying person *(25.7)* to allow you to work and earn income. Qualifying expenses are discussed at *25.8*. The credit percentage depends on your income.

Limit on expenses. In figuring the credit for 2010, you take into account qualifying expenses *(25.8)* up to a limit of $3,000 for one dependent, or $6,000 for two or more dependents. The $3,000 or $6,000 limit applies even if your actual expenses are much greater. Further, the $3,000 or $6,000 limit must be reduced by tax-free benefits received from an employer's dependent care plan. Finally, if your earned income is less than the $3,000 or $6,000 limit, your credit is figured on the lower income amount.

Take into account only payments in 2010 for 2010 services. Your credit for 2010 must be based on payments made in 2010 for care services provided in 2010. If you paid for 2009 services in 2010, you may be able to claim an additional credit on your 2010 return, but only in limited circumstances, as discussed at the end of this section. If in 2010 you prepay for 2011 services, you must allocate your payment. Only payments for 2010 services should be counted toward the $3,000 or $6,000 limit when figuring your 2010 credit.

Credit percentage. Depending on your income, a credit percentage of 20% to 35% applies to your expenses up to the $3,000 (one dependent) or $6,000 (two or more dependents) limit. The maximum credit is 35% for families with adjusted gross income of $15,000 or less. For adjusted gross income over $15,000, the 35% credit is reduced by 1% for each $2,000 of adjusted gross income or fraction of $2,000 over $15,000, but not below 20%. The 20% credit applies to adjusted gross incomes exceeding $43,000.

The dependent care credit is nonrefundable. It is limited to your tax liability; follow the IRS instructions.

Table 25-1 Allowable Credit*

Adjusted gross income	*Credit percentage*	*Maximum credit for one dependent**	*Maximum credit for two or more dependents**
$15,000 or less	35%	$1,050	$2,100
15,001–17,000	34	1,020	2,040
17,001–19,000	33	990	1,980
19,001–21,000	32	960	1,920
21,001–23,000	31	930	1,860
23,001–25,000	30	900	1,800
25,001–27,000	29	870	1,740
27,001–29,000	28	840	1,680
29,001–31,000	27	810	1,620
31,001–33,000	26	780	1,560
33,001–35,000	25	750	1,500
35,001–37,000	24	720	1,440
37,001–39,000	23	690	1,380
39,001–41,000	22	660	1,320
41,001–43,000	21	630	1,260
43,001 and over	20	600	1,200

**Maximum credit assumes qualifying expenses are at least $3,000 for one dependent, or $6,000 for two or more dependents. If qualifying expenses are less than the $3,000/$6,000 maximum, your credit is the credit percentage multiplied by the expenses.*

EXAMPLES

1. You pay $6,500 in 2010 to a neighbor to care for your two children while you work. Your adjusted gross income is $34,824. The credit percentage of 25% is applied to the maximum expense limit of $6,000, giving you a credit of $1,500.
2. Same as above, except you receive a tax-free reimbursement of $2,500 from your employer's plan. The reimbursement reduces the $6,000 expense limit *(25.8)* to $3,500 ($6,000 – $2,500). Your credit is $875 (25% of $3,500). If the tax-free reimbursement were $5,000 or more (the maximum allowable exclusion), the credit would be $250 (25% × $1,000 ($6,000 – $5,000)).

Additional credit for 2010 payment of 2009 dependent care expenses. Payments made in 2010 for 2009 services may be eligible for an additional credit on your 2010 return but only if you did not use up the $3,000 or $6,000 expense limit that applied for the 2009 credit. Follow the instructions for Form 2441 to figure the additional credit.

25.6 Earned Income Test for Dependent Care Credit

To claim the credit, you must earn wage, salary, or self-employment income figured without regard to community property laws. Expenses for dependent care incurred while looking for a job may be included. However, you must have earnings during the year to claim the credit.

Filing Tip

No Credit if Neither Spouse Works

If both husband and wife are full-time students and neither works, they may not claim the credit for dependent care costs. While one student-spouse is considered to have earned income of $250 ($500 if more than one qualified person is cared for) each month, the other spouse's earned income is zero. Care costs eligible for the credit are limited to the lesser amount of earned income, which in this case is zero.

Earned income rule for married couples. Generally, both spouses must work at least part time, unless one is incapable of self-care or is a full-time student. If either you or your spouse earns less than the maximum $3,000 or $6,000 credit base *(25.5)*, the base is limited to the smaller income.

EXAMPLE

John and Mary are married. In 2010, John earns $5,300. Mary earns $33,000. They incur care costs of $6,200 for their two children, ages 5 and 7. Their adjusted gross income including interest earnings is $38,575; their credit percentage is 23%. The maximum $6,000 credit base (for two or more dependents) is limited to John's lower income of $5,300. They may claim a credit of $1,219 ($5,300 × 23%).

Spouses who are students or disabled. An incapacitated spouse or a spouse who is a full-time student is considered to have earned income of $250 a month if expenses are incurred for one dependent, or $500 a month for two or more dependents.

A full-time student is one who attends school full time during each of five calendar months during the year.

EXAMPLE

Same facts as in the Example above, except John was a full-time student for nine months and earned no income for the year. The credit base is limited to $4,500 ($500 × 9).

25.7 Credit Allowed for Care of Qualifying Persons

To claim a credit for 2010, you must incur employment-related expenses *(25.8)* for at least one of the following qualifying persons who lives with you more than half the year:

1. A dependent *under the age of 13* who is a "qualifying child" under *21.3*. If you are divorced or separated, and you resided with the child for a longer time during the year than the other parent, you may be able to claim the credit even if the other parent is entitled to claim the child as a dependent *(25.9)*.
2. Your spouse, if physically or mentally incapable of caring for him- or herself.
3. A dependent, regardless of age, who is physically or mentally incapable of caring for himself or herself. For example, he or she needs help to dress or to take care of personal hygiene or nutritional needs, or requires constant attention to avoid hurting him- or herself or others. Generally, you must be able to claim the person as a dependent, either as a qualifying child *(21.3)* or qualifying relative *(21.4)*, but even if the person cannot be claimed as your qualifying relative because he or she has gross income of $3,650 or more for 2010, you may still claim a credit for his or her care costs. Also, if you cannot claim an exemption for the person because you (or your spouse if you file jointly) can be claimed as a dependent by another taxpayer, a credit can still be claimed for the person's care costs.

EXAMPLE

You live with your mother, who is physically incapable of caring for herself. You hire a practical nurse to care for her in the home while you are at work. Payments to the nurse qualify as care costs. However, if you placed her in a nursing home, the cost of the nursing home would not qualify as a dependent care cost, but a medical expense deduction may be available *(17.11)*.

If your child becomes age 13 during the year. Take into account expenses incurred for his or her care prior to the 13th birthday. However, you do not prorate the $3,000 limitation. For example, if your child becomes age 13 on May 1, 2010, and you incurred $3,000 or more in care expenses between January 1 and April 30, the entire $3,000 qualifies for the 2010 credit.

25.8 Expenses Qualifying for the Dependent Care Credit

If you do not receive tax-free dependent care benefits from an employer's plan, you may take into account up to $3,000 of the following types of expenses paid in 2010 when figuring the credit for one dependent, or up to $6,000 for two or more dependents. If you receive employer-financed dependent care, tax-free reimbursements reduce the $3,000 or $6,000 base.

1. Costs of caring for your qualifying child under age 13, incapacitated spouse, or incapacitated dependent (of any age) in your home *(25.7)*. If you pay FICA or FUTA taxes on your housekeeper's wages *(38.3)*, you may include your share of the tax (employer) as part of the wages when entering your qualifying expenses. Also include your housekeeper's share of FICA tax if you pay it. Note that these taxes may more than offset your allowable credit.

   The manner of care need not be the least expensive alternative. For example, where a grandparent resides with you and may provide adequate care for your child to enable you to work, the cost of hiring someone to care for the child is still eligible for the credit.
2. Ordinary domestic services in your home, such as laundry, cleaning, and cooking (but not payments to a gardener or chauffeur) that are partly for the care of the qualifying person. Expenses for the dependent's food, clothing, or entertainment do not qualify. Food costs for a housekeeper who eats in your home may be added to qualifying expenses. Extra expenses for a housekeeper's lodging (extra rent or utilities) also qualify.
3. Outside-the-home care costs for a child under age 13, as in a day-care center, day camp (including a specialty camp such as a computer or soccer camp), nursery school, or in the home of a babysitter. Outside-the-home care costs also qualify if incurred for a handicapped dependent, regardless of age, provided he or she regularly spends at least eight hours per day in your home. However, the cost of schooling in kindergarten or higher does not qualify for the credit. Costs for sleep-away camp also do not qualify for the credit.

   You may not take into account your transportation costs in taking your qualifying person to and from a care center, or your payment of a care provider's transportation to and from your home.

Filing Tip

Day-Care Center or Nursery School

The amount you pay to a day-care center or nursery school for a dependent child under age 13 is eligible for the credit, even if it covers such incidental benefits as lunch. However, tuition for a child in kindergarten or higher is not taken into account. If the dependent is not your child, costs for care outside the home qualify only if the dependent regularly spends at least eight hours per day in your home. Up to $3,000 a year of outside-the-home care expenses may be taken into account in figuring the credit for one dependent, and up to $6,000 for two or more.

Payments to relatives or dependents. No credit may be claimed for payments made to persons you may claim as your dependents *(21.1)*. Thus, if you pay your mother to care for your child and you cannot claim your mother as a dependent, such payments qualify for the credit.

No credit may be claimed for payments to your child who is under 19 years of age at the close of the tax year, whether or not you may claim the child as a dependent.

Allocating expenses when employed less than an entire year. If your dependent care expenses covered a period in which you worked or looked for work only part of the time, you must allocate the expenses on a daily basis to determine the work-related portion. However, if you were away on vacation or missed work due to illness for a short period (generally two weeks or less according the IRS), this is treated as a temporary absence from work and the expenses incurred during the absence qualify for the credit.

EXAMPLE

You are employed or look for work for only two months and 10 days. Monthly care expenses are $300. Eligible care expenses amount to $700 ($300 × 2 months, plus $^1/_3$ of $300).

Employer-financed dependent care reduces credit base. Tax-free reimbursements under an employer's dependent care program reduce the $3,000 or $6,000 credit base. For example, if you have one child and you receive a $1,500 reimbursement of child-care costs from your company's plan, the amount eligible for the tax credit is reduced to $1,500 ($3,000 – $1,500). A reimbursement of $3,000 or more would bar any credit. The $6,000 credit expense limit for two or more dependents is similarly reduced by dependent care benefits from your employer. On your Form W-2, your employer will report the amount of tax-free reimbursement *(3.4)*.

If your employer's plan allows you to fund a reimbursement account with salary-reduction contributions that are excluded from taxable pay *(3.14)*, reimbursements from the account are considered employer-financed payments that reduce the $3,000 or $6,000 credit base. In deciding whether to make salary-reduction contributions, you should determine whether the tax-free reduction will provide a larger tax savings than that provided by the credit. You may find that the salary reduction provides the larger tax savings, taking into consideration not only the decrease in federal income tax, but also the Social Security tax and state and local taxes avoided by using the salary reduction. Further, by lowering your adjusted gross income, a salary reduction may enable you to claim a larger IRA deduction if you are subject to the deduction phase-out rule *(8.4)*, or a larger deduction for miscellaneous itemized deductions subject to the 2% floor *(19.1)*.

Filing Tip

Care Costs Qualifying as Medical Expenses

Care costs, such as a nurse's wages, may also qualify as medical expenses, but you may not claim both the dependent care credit and the medical expense deduction. If you use the expenses to figure the credit and your care costs exceed the amount allowed as dependent care costs, the excess, to the extent it qualifies as a medical expense, may be added to other deductible medical costs.

Allocation if expenses cover noncare services. If a portion of expenses is for other than dependent care or household services, only the portion allocable to dependent care or household services qualifies. No allocation is required if the non–dependent care services are minimal.

EXAMPLES

1. A person accepts a full-time position and sends his 12-year-old child to boarding school. The expenses paid to the school must be allocated. The part representing care of the child qualifies; the part representing tuition does not.
2. A full-time housekeeper is hired to care for two children, ages 9 and 12. The housekeeper also drives the mother to and from work each day. The driving takes no longer than 30 minutes. No allocation is required because the non–dependent care services of chauffeuring are minimal.

25.9 Dependent Care Credit Rules for Separated Couples

A married person generally must file a joint return to claim the dependent care credit *(25.4)*, but if you are living apart from your spouse you may claim the credit on a separate return if you meet the following tests:

1. You maintain as your home a household that a qualifying person *(25.7)* lives in for more than half the year;
2. You furnish over half the cost of maintaining the household for the entire year; *and*
3. Your spouse was not a member of the household during the *last six months* of the year.

If you satisfy these tests, you are treated as unmarried and may claim the credit on a separate return. You do not have to take your spouse's income into account or show that he or she is employed in order to claim a credit.

Your child may be your qualifying person for purposes of a 2010 credit even if you cannot claim the child as your dependent under the rules at *21.7*. This favorable rule applies if: you are legally divorced or separated, separated under a written agreement, or you lived apart from your spouse during the last six months of 2010; you or you and the other parent had custody of the child for more than half the year and provided more than half of the child's support; and you are the *custodial parent* (lived with the child longer than the other parent). If these tests are met, you may claim the credit for care of a dependent child who is under age 13 or physically or mentally incapable of caring for himself or herself even though the noncustodial parent has the right to the exemption under *21.7*. The noncustodial parent may not claim the credit even if he or she is allowed the exemption.

25.10 Qualifying Tests for EIC

The earned income credit (EIC) may be claimed not only by workers with qualifying children who meet the tests below, but also, in limited cases, by childless workers. For 2010, the maximum earned income credit is $3,050 if you have one qualifying child, $5,036 if you have two qualifying children, $5,666 if you have three or more qualifying children, and $457 if you do not have a qualifying child. There is a phaseout of the credit *(25.11)*. You look up the credit amount in IRS tables included in the tax form instructions. The EIC is "refundable"; you will receive a refund from the IRS if the credit exceeds your tax liability.

Law Alert

Higher EIC for Some Families

A higher credit rate for 2010 is allowed to taxpayers with three or more qualifying children. Also, a more favorable phaseout range is allowed for married couples filing jointly.

Claiming the EIC for 2010 With Qualifying Children

You may claim the EIC on a 2010 return if you:

- Have earned income, such as wages and self-employment earnings, and also adjusted gross income, under the following amount: $35,535 ($40,545 if married filing jointly) if you have one qualifying child, $40,363 ($45,373 if married filing jointly) if you have two qualifying children, or $43,352 ($48,362 if married filing jointly) if you have three or more qualifying children. However, the maximum credit begins to phase out at much lower income levels *(25.11)*.
- Have a qualifying child who lived with you in your main home in the U.S. for more than six months in 2010; *see* below.
- File a joint return if married. Married persons filing separately may not claim the EIC. If you lived apart from your spouse for the last half of the year, you may be able to claim the credit as a head of household.
- File Schedule EIC with your Form 1040 or Form 1040A. On Schedule EIC, you identify and provide information about a qualifying child. Your child's Social Security number must be entered on Schedule EIC.
- Are not a qualifying child of another person.
- Include on your return your Social Security number and, if married, that of your spouse.

Caution

Recertification Required if EIC Denied

If the IRS denies an EIC by issuing a deficiency notice, the credit may not be claimed in a future tax year unless you show on Form 8862 that you are eligible to take the credit. If the IRS recertifies eligibility, Form 8862 does not have to be filed again in subsequent tax years unless the IRS again denies the EIC in a deficiency proceeding.

A qualifying child. A qualifying child is your son, daughter, adopted child, grandchild, stepchild, or descendents of any of these who at the end of 2010 is under age 19 or under age 24 and a full-time student (enrolled full time during any five months), or any age if permanently and totally disabled. The qualifying person must live with you for over half the year. Your brother, sister, step- or half-brother or step- or half-sister, or their descendents, who meet the age 19 or 24 test and live with you more than half the year also qualify if they are younger than you (or your spouse if you file jointly) or are permanently and totally disabled. A foster child who lives with you for more than half the year qualifies if the child was placed with you by a court order or by an authorized placement agency.

Household requirement. The qualifying child must have lived with you in your main home in the U.S. for more than six months. Temporary absences for school, vacation, medical care, or detention in a juvenile facility count as time lived at home.

A person in the U.S. Armed Forces who is stationed outside the U.S. on extended active duty is treated as maintaining a main residence within the U.S.

If you are married, you must file a joint return with your spouse to claim the credit. However, if your spouse did not live in your household for the last six months of the year, and you maintained a home for a child who lived with you for more than half of the year, you may claim the credit as a head of household *(1.12)*.

Caution

Denial of Future Credits for Recklessness or Fraud

A taxpayer who negligently or fraudulently claims the EIC is prohibited from claiming future credits over a period of several years. The credit is disallowed for two years from the tax year for which it is determined that the EIC claim was claimed recklessly or in disregard of the rules. The period increases to 10 years from the most recent tax year for which it is found that the EIC was claimed fraudulently.

Permanently and totally disabled. A person is permanently and totally disabled if: (1) he or she cannot engage in any substantial gainful activity because of a physical or mental condition and (2) a physician determines that the condition has lasted or is expected to last for at least a year or lead to death.

Qualifying child of two or more people. "Tie-breaking" rules determine who can take the EIC if a child is a qualifying child of more than one person.

If both parents are eligible to claim the credit for the same qualifying child and they do not file a 2010 joint return, the parent with whom the child resided for the longer period during the year may claim the child. If the child lived with each parent for the same amount of time, the child will be treated as the qualifying child of the parent who had the higher adjusted gross income (AGI) for 2010.

If a parent and one or more nonparents are otherwise entitled to claim the child as a qualifying child, only the parent may claim the credit for the child. If none of the persons otherwise entitled to treat the child as a qualifying child are the child's parent, the child will be treated as the qualifying child of the person who had the highest AGI for 2010.

Married child. If your child was married at the end of 2010, he or she is your qualifying child only if you can claim an exemption for the child under the rules at *21.3*, or you would be so entitled except that the noncustodial parent is given the exemption under the rules at *21.7*. However, if your child files a joint return, he or she is not your qualifying child unless the joint return is filed only as a refund claim.

Nonresident aliens. An individual who is a nonresident alien for any part of the year is not eligible for the credit unless he or she is married and an election is made by the couple to have all of their worldwide income subject to U.S. tax.

Claiming the Credit for 2010 Without Qualifying Children

If you do not have a qualifying child, you may claim the EIC on a 2010 return if you:

- Have earned income, such as wages and self-employment earnings and also adjusted gross income under $13,460 ($18,470 if married filing jointly). However, the credit phaseout rule may apply *(25.11)*.
- Have your main home in the U.S. for more than six months in 2010.
- Are at least 25 but under age 65 at the end of 2010. If filing a joint return, either you or your spouse must satisfy this age test.
- File a joint return if married, unless you lived apart for the last six months and qualify to file as a head of household.
- Are not a dependent of another taxpayer. If filing jointly, your spouse also must not be another taxpayer's dependent.
- Are not a qualifying child of another taxpayer. If filing jointly, your spouse also must not be another taxpayer's qualifying child.
- Include your Social Security number on your return, and, if married, that of your spouse.

25.11 Income Tests for Earned Income Credit (EIC)

For purposes of the credit, earned income includes wages, salary, tips, commissions, jury duty pay, union strike benefits, certain disability pensions, and net earnings from self-employment. An election may be made to include combat pay that is otherwise excluded from income *(35.4)* as earned income for EIC purposes. Apart from such combat pay, nontaxable employee compensation, such as salary deferrals, or excludable dependent care benefits, is not considered when computing the credit.

Disqualifying income. For 2010, an individual is not eligible for the earned income credit if he or she has "disqualified income" exceeding $3,100. Disqualified income includes interest (taxable and tax-exempt), dividends, net rent and royalty income, net capital gain income, and net passive income that is not self-employment income.

Credit phases out with income. There are different phaseout ranges for married couples filing jointly than for taxpayers filing as single, head of household, or qualifying widow(er).

Filing Tip

Definition of Earned Income for EIC Purposes

Earned income includes tax free combat pay *(35.4)*, but does *not* include other nontaxable employee compensation such as salary deferrals and reductions, excludable dependent care benefits, and excludable education assistance.

If your filing status is single, head of household, or qualifying widow(er), and you have qualifying children, your 2010 credit begins to phase out in the EIC Table if either earned income or adjusted gross income is at least $16,450, regardless of the number of children. The phaseout endpoint depends on the number of children. The credit is completely phased out if earned income or adjusted gross income is at least $35,535 for one child, $40,363 for two children, and $43,352 for three or more children.

If you are married filing jointly and have qualifying children, the 2010 credit begins to phase out in the EIC Table if either earned income or adjusted gross income is at least $21,500, regardless of the number of children. The phaseout endpoint depends on the number of children. The credit is completely phased out if earned income or adjusted gross income is at least $40,545 for one child, $45,373 for two children, and $48,632 for three or more children.

If you do not have any qualifying children, the phaseout of the credit begins when either earned income or AGI is at least $7,500 ($12,500 if married filing jointly), and the credit is completely phased out if either amount is $13,460 or more ($18,470 or more if married filing jointly).

Self-employed. If you were self-employed in 2010, your earned income for credit purposes is the net earnings shown on Schedule SE, *less* the income tax deduction for 50% of self-employment tax claimed on Line 27 of Form 1040. If your net earnings were less than $400, the net amount is your earned income for purposes of the credit. If you had a net loss, the loss is subtracted from any wages or other employee earned income. If you are a statutory employee, the income reported on Schedule C qualifies for the credit.

Foreign earned income. If you work abroad and claim the foreign income exclusion, you may *not* take the credit.

25.12 Look up EIC in Government Tables

After completing a worksheet in the IRS instructions that determines whether your earned income credit (EIC) is based on your earned income or adjusted gross income *(25.11)*, you then look up the amount of your credit in the EIC Table, which will be shown in the *e-Supplement at jklasser.com*.

> ***EXAMPLE***
>
> Jane is divorced. Her only income in 2010 is wages of $26,574. She supports her eight-year-old daughter, who lives with her for the entire year.
>
> To find her credit, Jane turns to the 2010 EICTable. In the table, the credit shown for her income bracket is $1,432.

25.13 Advance Payment of Earned Income Credit

If you filed Form W-5 and received advance payments of the earned income credit from your employer during 2010, you must report them on Form 1040 or Form 1040A. Your employer will show the amount in Box 9 of your Form W-2. If you received advance payments in excess of the credit you are entitled to, the excess is treated as a tax you owe when you file your return. If the credit you are entitled to exceeds the advance payments, the excess credit reduces any other tax you owe. If the credit exceeds your liability, the difference is refunded to you.

2010 was the last year for which advance payments of the credit could be received. The opportunity to receive advance payments was eliminated for years after 2010 by the Education Jobs and Medicaid Assistance Act of 2010. Thus, starting in 2011, workers who have been receiving advance payments will have to wait until they file their tax return to claim the earned income credit.

25.14 Qualifying for the Adoption Credit

A tax credit of up to $13,170 may be available on your 2010 return for the qualifying costs of adopting a child under age 18, or a person who is physically and mentally incapable of self-care. The credit is phased out ratably for those with modified adjusted gross income between $182,520 and $222,520.

The credit is claimed on Form 8839. If you paid qualifying adoption costs in 2010 but the adoption was not final at the end of the year, the credit may *not* be claimed on your 2010 return *(25.15)*.

If you are married, you generally must file a joint return to take the adoption credit or exclusion. You may take the credit or exclusion on a separate return if you are legally separated under a decree of divorce or separate maintenance, or if you lived apart from your spouse for the last six months of the tax year and (1) your home is the eligible child's home for more than half the year and (2) you pay more than half the cost of keeping up your home for the year.

Employer plans. As discussed in *3.6*, an exclusion from income is also available to employees if adoption expenses are paid through a qualifying employer program, subject to rules similar to that of the credit. If you receive employer adoption benefits that are less than your qualifying adoption expenses, you may be able to claim the credit on Form 8839.

Law Alert

Adoption Credit Increased and Made Refundable

The 2010 health care reform law increased the maximum adoption credit for 2010 by $1,000 to $13,170. The credit has also been made refundable, so if the credit exceeds your 2010 tax liability, you will be refunded the excess.

25.15 Claiming the Adoption Credit on Form 8839

The fact that you paid qualified adoption expenses during 2010 does not mean that you can claim a credit for those costs on your 2010 return. A 2010 credit is not allowed for 2010 expenses unless the adoption was finalized by the end of the year. Under the credit timing rules discussed below, you may claim a 2010 credit for expenses incurred in 2009 if the eligible child was a U.S. citizen or resident when the adoption effort began. If the child was not a U.S. citizen or resident when the adoption effort began, a credit is not allowed until the year the adoption is finalized even if you incurred expenses in one or more previous years.

If a credit is allowed for 2010, figure it on Form 8839 and attach the form to your Form 1040. You must enter an identification number for the child on Form 8839. Generally this is a Social Security number (SSN), but if you are in the process of adopting a child who is U.S. citizen or resident and you cannot get an SSN for the child before you file your return, you should apply for an adoption taxpayer identification number (ATIN) on IRS Form W-7A. If the child is not eligible for an SSN, apply for an individual identification number (ITIN) on Form W-7.

A new law makes the credit refundable for 2010, so it is allowed in full even if it exceeds your tax liability. Claim the credit on Line 71 of Form 1040, in the "Payments" section of the form.

Credit limitations. The maximum adoption credit on a 2010 return is $13,170 per child, but the limit is subject to a phaseout based on modified adjusted gross income. For 2011, the $13,170 credit limit may be increased for inflation.

The $13,170 credit limit is per child, not per taxpayer. If unmarried parents each paid expenses to adopt the same child and the expenses are allowed in 2010 under the credit timing rules, the parents must divide the $13,170 limit between them.

If under the credit timing rules you are claiming adoption expenses for a child on Form 8839 for 2010, but you claimed expenses for the same child in an earlier year, the earlier expenses reduce the $13,170 maximum credit for 2010. If under the credit timing rules you are allowed a 2010 credit for more than one child, a separate $13,170 limit applies for each. However, if an adoption of a child with special needs is finalized in 2010, the maximum $13,170 credit is allowed even if this amount exceeds your qualified adoption expenses; *see* below. For years after 2010, an inflation adjustment may raise the $13,170 maximum credit.

Phaseout. The credit may be reduced or eliminated by a phaseout rule based on modified adjusted gross income (MAGI). For 2010, the phaseout applies if MAGI is over $182,520, and the credit is completely phased out if MAGI is $222,520 or more. For years after 2010, the phaseout range may be adjusted for inflation.

Qualified adoption expenses. Qualifying adoption expenses are reasonable and necessary adoption fees, court costs, attorney fees, travel expenses away from home, and other expenses directly related to, and whose principal purpose is for, the legal adoption of an eligible child *(25.14)*. Do not include expenses paid or reimbursed by your employer or any other person or organization. You may not claim a credit for the costs of a surrogate parenting arrangement or for adopting your spouse's child.

When to claim the adoption credit for a child who is a U.S. citizen or resident. If at the time the adoption effort begins the child is a U.S. citizen or resident and you pay qualifying expenses in any year before the year the adoption becomes final, the credit is delayed one year. The credit is allowed in the year after the year of the payment, whether or not the adoption is final in that year. If you pay qualifying expenses in the year the adoption becomes final, the credit for those expenses is claimed in that year. If qualifying expenses are paid in any year after the year in which the adoption becomes final, the credit is claimed in the year of payment.

When to claim the adoption credit for a foreign child. If you adopt a child who is not a U.S. citizen or resident at the time the adoption effort begins, a credit may not be claimed until the year the adoption becomes final. If adoption expenses are paid after the tax year in which the adoption became finalized, a credit for such expenses is allowed for the tax year of payment.

The IRS has released safe harbors for determining the finality of an adoption of a foreign-born child and thereby the timing of a credit. These safe harbors apply only to adoptions of foreign-born children who receive an "immediate relative" (IR) visa from the State Department. IR visas are issued to a foreign-born child entering the U.S. after a foreign court or government agency (with authority over child welfare) has granted an adoption or guardianship decree.

Adoptive parents who bring a foreign-born child into the U.S. with an IR-2 visa, an IR-3 visa, or an IR-4 (if a "simple" adoption) visa may treat the adoption as final in either the taxable year in which the foreign court or agency enters the adoption decree or in the taxable year in which a court in the parents' home state enters a decree of "re-adoption" or the home state otherwise recognizes the foreign adoption decree, provided this occurs in one of the two years after the year in which the foreign court or agency enters its decree. If the child receives an IR-4 visa under a guardianship or legal custody arrangement, the adoption may not be treated as final for tax purposes until the year in which a court in the parents' home state enters a decree of adoption.

Special needs adoption. An adoption is considered a "special needs" adoption if the child is a U.S. citizen or resident when the adoption process begins, and a state (or District of Columbia) determines that the child cannot or should not be returned to his or her parents and that because of special factors, assistance is required to place the child with adoptive parents.

A special rule allows qualifying expenses to be grossed up to the maximum credit in the year the adoption is finalized where the aggregate of qualifying expenses for that year and all prior years is under the maximum. For example, if a special needs adoption is initiated in 2009 and finalized in 2010 and actual qualifying expenses for both years are $9,020, a $13,170 credit may be claimed for 2010. Total expenses are deemed to be the $13,170 maximum, so the credit for 2010 includes not only the $9,020 of actual expenses, but also an additional $4,150, the excess of $13,170 over the actual expenses. This special rule applies only to finalized special needs adoptions.

25.16 Eligibility for the Saver's Credit

You may be able to claim the retirement savings contributions credit (saver's credit) on your 2010 return if you made contributions *(25.17)* to a retirement plan for 2010. This includes a contribution made to a traditional IRA or Roth IRA for 2010 by April 15, 2011.

Eligibility for the credit is restricted. You cannot claim the saver's credit if your 2010 adjusted gross income exceeds $55,500 if you are married filing jointly, $41,625 if you are a head of household, or $27,750 if you are single, married filing separately, or a qualifying widow (er). Adjusted gross income is increased by any exclusion for foreign earned income or income from Puerto Rico or American Samoa, or the foreign housing exclusion or deduction. If your adjusted gross income is under the applicable $55,500, $41,625, or $27,750 limit, a credit percentage of 50%, 20%, or 10% *(Table 25-2)* applies to the first $2,000 of your contributions *(25.17)*. However, regardless of your income, you cannot claim the credit if you were born after January 1, 1993, are claimed as a dependent on another taxpayer's 2010 return, or you were a full-time student during five or more months in 2010.

Other limitations apply. In computing the credit on Form 8880, you must reduce contributions by recent retirement plan withdrawals *(25.17)*. In addition, the credit is not refundable; it is limited to your tax liability *(25.17)*.

Any allowable credit is in addition to other tax breaks you receive for making the contribution, such as the exclusion for elective salary deferrals to a 401(k) plan, or a deduction for a traditional IRA contribution.

Table 25-2 Credit Based on Adjusted Gross Income for 2010

Credit Rate	*Married Filing Jointly*	*Head of Household*	*Single, Married Filing Separately, or Qualifying Widow(er)*
50%	up to $33,500	up to $25,125	up to $16,750
20%	$ 33,501–$36,000	$25,126–$27,000	$16,751–$18,000
10%	$ 36,001–$55,500	$27,001–$41,625	$18,001–$27,750
0%	over $55,500	over $41,625	over $27,750

For 2011, the income limits may be increased by an inflation adjustment; *see* the *e-Supplement at jklasser.com* for an update.

25.17 Figuring the Saver's Credit

You figure your saver's credit on Form 8880. The maximum credit equals the applicable income-dependent rate shown in *Table 25-2* (50%, 20%, or 10%) multiplied by the first $2,000 of eligible retirement contributions made for 2010. If you are married filing jointly, you and your spouse may each take into account up to $2,000 of eligible contributions. Eligible contributions include: (1) traditional IRA or Roth IRA contributions, (2) salary-reduction contributions to a 401(k) plan (including a SIMPLE 401(k)), 403(b) plan, SIMPLE IRA, governmental Section 457 plan, or salary-reduction SEP, or (3) voluntary after-tax contributions to a qualified plan or 403(b) plan.

Withdrawals can eliminate the credit. A credit can be lost because you have withdrawn money from a retirement plan. In figuring a credit for 2010, your eligible contributions for 2010 must be reduced by the total of distributions you received (and also your spouse if filing jointly) after 2007 and *before* the due date of your 2010 return (including extensions) from traditional IRAs and Roth IRAs, 401(k) plans, SEPs, SIMPLE plans, 403(b) plans, and other qualified retirement plans. Do not count tax-free rollovers, direct transfers (trustee-to-trustee), conversions of a traditional IRA to a Roth IRA, distributions of excess contributions or deferrals, or returned contributions; *see* the instructions to Form 8880.

Tax liability limit. The credit is not refundable. It is limited to your tax liability (regular tax plus AMT, if any), reduced by certain other nonrefundable credits such as the child tax credit, the dependent care credit or the American Opportunity or Lifetime Learning credits.

25.18 Health Coverage Credit

A health insurance credit on Form 8885 may be available to displaced workers who have lost jobs due to foreign competition and are receiving Trade Adjustment Assistance (TAA) benefits, older workers receiving wage subsidies under an alternative trade adjustment assistance (ATAA) program established by the Department of Labor, and Pension Benefit Guaranty Corporation (PBGC) pension beneficiaries age 55 or older. The credit is 80% of eligible premiums paid in 2010.

Premiums must be for unsubsidized COBRA continuing coverage, coverage under certain state-sponsored plans or coverage under a spouse's employer-sponsored plan that meets certain tests. Premiums for individual health insurance may also qualify if the eligible individual was enrolled in the plan for at last 30 days before becoming unemployed and becoming eligible for TAA, ATAA or PBGC benefits.

Credit eligibility is determined on a month-by-month basis on Form 8885. The credit from Form 8885 is entered on Form 1040, Line 71; box d should be checked. The credit is a refundable credit not limited by tax liability.

Claim the credit in advance. Your state workforce agency or the PBGC can provide instructions for enrolling in the advanced tax credit plan. Once your eligibility and health coverage are confirmed, you only have to pay 20% of the premium and the Treasury Department will then pay it plus the other 80% to your insurer. Advance payments made on your behalf will be reported to you on Form 1099-H. The advance payments reduce the amount of the credit that can be claimed on Form 8885.

25.19 Mortgage Interest Credit

Under special state and local programs, you may obtain a "mortgage credit certificate" to finance the purchase of a principal residence or to borrow funds for certain home improvements. Generally, a qualifying principal residence may not cost more than 90% of the average area purchase price, 110% in certain targeted areas. A tax credit for interest paid on the mortgage may be claimed. The credit is computed on Form 8396 and claimed on Line 52 (check box a) of Form 1040. The credit equals the interest paid multiplied by the certificate rate set by the governmental authority, but if the credit rate is over 20%, the credit is limited to $2,000.

Caution

Recapture of Mortgage Subsidy

If within nine years of receiving a mortgage credit certificate you sell or dispose of your home at a gain, the mortgage subsidy you received generally must be recaptured as income. *See* Form 8828 for details.

Liability limit and carryover. The mortgage interest credit is subject to a tax liability limit and any excess is nonrefundable. The tax liability limitation is figured on Form 8396. However, if your allowable credit exceeds the liability limitation, the unused credit can be carried forward for up to three years.

Mortgage interest deduction must be reduced. If you itemize deductions, you must reduce your home mortgage interest deduction *(15.1)* by the current year mortgage interest credit claimed on Line 3 of Form 8396 (certificate credit rate multiplied by interest paid, subject to the $2,000 limit). The reduction to the mortgage interest deduction applies even if part of the Line 3 credit is carried forward to the next tax year.

25.20 District of Columbia First-Time Homebuyer Credit

When this book went to press, Congress had not yet extended the credit for first-time D.C. homebuyers to 2010 purchases, but an extension is still possible. *See* the *e-Supplement at jklasser.com* for an update.

Even if you bought a home in the District in 2010 and the D.C. homebuyer credit is extended to purchases in 2010, you cannot take it if you qualify for the refundable first-time homebuyer credit on Form 5405. If a credit is not allowed on Form 5405, and the D.C. credit is extended, *see* the instructions to Form 8859 to determine if you qualify.

If you claimed the D.C. homebuyer credit on your 2009 return and part of the credit was disallowed because of the tax liability limitation, you can carry forward the unused credit to 2010 on Form 8859.

If the D.C. homebuyers credit is extended and you bought a home in 2010 and you qualify for the first-time homebuyer credit on Form 5405 *(25.23)*, you cannot claim the District of Columbia first-time homebuyer credit. However, if you are not eligible for the credit on Form 5405, you may be able to claim a credit on Form 8859 for a home purchased in the District of Columbia in 2010, provided neither you nor your spouse owned a principal residence in the District in the one-year period preceding the 2010 purchase.

On Form 8859, the credit of up to $5,000 ($2,500 if married filing separately) is phased out if modified adjusted gross income is between $110,000 and $130,000 if married filing jointly and between $70,000 and $90,000 for other taxpayers.

The credit is limited to regular tax plus AMT liability reduced by other personal credits. A carryforward is allowed for any portion of the credit that may not be claimed because of the tax liability limitation; *see* Form 8859.

25.21 Residential Energy Credits

There are two types of home energy credits available for 2010 on Form 5695:

(1) The nonbusiness energy property credit in Part I, which covers improvements such as energy efficient insulation, storm windows, heaters, and air conditioners, and

(2) The residential energy efficient property credit in Part II, which covers qualifying solar, wind, geothermal and fuel cell costs.

The credits from both parts of Form 5695 are combined and entered on Line 52 of Form 1040.

Nonbusiness energy property. The credit for nonbusiness energy property is allowed only for improvements to a principal residence located in the United States. The credit is 30% of the cost of qualified improvements with an overall limit of $1,500. The $1,500 limit is a two-year combined limit on total expenses in 2009 and 2010, so if you claimed a 2009 credit for qualified improvements on your 2009 return, the $1,500 limit is reduced by that amount and a 2010 credit is allowed only to the extent of any excess. Qualified improvements include insulation, exterior windows including skylights, exterior doors, certain metal or asphalt roofs designed to reduce heat gain, and energy-efficient heat pumps, water heaters, furnaces, water boilers and central air conditioners. These improvements must meet specified energy-efficiency standards to qualify for the credit. The IRS has provided manufacturers with guidelines for certifying that their products meet these standards. You may rely on a manufacturer's written certification that a product qualifies for the credit. You do *not* have to attach the certification to your return. Retain the certification as part of your tax records.

Residential energy efficient property. A 30% credit is allowed for the cost of qualified residential solar panels, solar water heating equipment, wind turbines, and geothermal heat pumps. This includes the cost of labor for onsite preparation, assembly and installation. There is no dollar limit on the 30% credit; prior law limits have been repealed. The residence does not have to be your principal residence. However, no credit is allowed for costs allocable to heating a swimming pool or hot tub.

There is also a 30% credit for qualified fuel cell property. This property must be installed in a principal residence located in the United States. The 30% credit is subject to a limit based on kilowatt capacity. The fuel cell property must have a capacity of at least one-half kilowatt of electricity and the credit cannot exceed $500 for each half-kilowatt of electric capacity generated.

25.22 Credits for Hybrid and Other Alternative Fuel Vehicles and Plug-in Electric Vehicles

The alternative motor vehicle credit on Form 8910 potentially includes credits for five distinct categories of vehicles: hybrid vehicles, advanced lean burn technology vehicles, alternative fuel vehicles, fuel cell vehicles, and vehicles converted to qualified plug-in electric drive motor vehicles. Almost all vehicles qualifying for the alternative motor vehicle credit are hybrid and advanced lean burn technology vehicles, but these are subject to a manufacturer phaseout rule (*see* below), which prevents a 2010 credit from being claimed for the most popular models.

The IRS acknowledges certifications made by vehicle manufacturers that certain models qualify for a credit. The IRS acknowledgment allows the manufacturers to certify to consumers that these models qualify for a credit equal to the certified amount. You may generally rely on the manufacturer's certification that the specified credit amount is allowable. The instructions to Form 8910 will have a list of qualifying models and the allowable credit amounts for 2010, which may include a reduction because of the phaseout rule discussed below.

Law Alert

Hybrid and Advanced Lean Burn Credits Set to Expire at End of 2010

The law authorizing a tax credit for hybrid and advanced lean burn technology vehicles expires at the end of 2010. It is not clear if the credits will be extended to years after 2010. *See* the *e-Supplement at jklasser.com* for an update.

Qualifying for the credit on Form 8910. You must be the original purchaser of a new qualifying vehicle to claim the credit. A credit is not allowed for a used vehicle. If you lease a qualifying vehicle, only the leasing company (and not you) may claim the credit. The vehicle must be used predominantly within the United States.

Hybrid and advanced lean burn technology vehicle credits are subject to phaseout on a manufacturer-by-manufacturer basis. Once a manufacturer sells its 60,000th hybrid vehicle after 2005 (all models), the tax credit for any of that manufacturer's certified hybrids is reduced as follows: For the second and third calendar quarters after the quarter in which the 60,000th qualifying vehicle is sold, you may claim 50% of the credit. For the fourth and fifth calendar quarters, you may claim 25% of the credit; no credit is allowed after the fifth quarter. If a manufacturer sells any advanced lean burn vehicles, these are added to the total of hybrid vehicle sales in applying the 60,000-vehicle limit.

Because of the phaseout rule, no credit is allowed for a 2010 purchase of any Toyota or Lexus hybrid or advanced lean burn technology vehicle or for any Honda hybrid or advanced lean burn technology vehicle. The phaseout period for Toyota and Lexus ended in 2007 and the phaseout period for Honda ended at the end of 2008. No credit is allowed for a Ford or Mercury vehicle purchased after March 31, 2010. The credit for certified Volkswagen and Audi models (which Volkswagen manufactures) is reduced by 50% for vehicles purchased from July 1 through December 31, 2010.

Note: Without a law change, no credit for any hybrid or advanced lean burn technology vehicle, regardless of manufacturer, will be allowed for a purchase after 2010. This is not due to the phaseout rule, but to the fact that the law authorizing the credits expires at the end of 2010. *See* the *e-Supplement at jklasser.com* for an update.

Tax liability limit for personal use of alternative motor vehicle. The credit for personal use of a vehicle qualifying for the alternative motor vehicle credit, including the new plug-in conversion credit, is subject to a tax liability limit on Form 8910. The credit is limited to your regular tax plus AMT liability, minus various nonrefundable personal credits. The allowable credit for personal use is entered on Line 53 of Form 1040.

If the vehicle is used for business, the credit for business use figured on Form 8910 is entered on Form 3800 as part of the general business credit *(40.26)*.

Credits for plug-in electric vehicles. There are two new credits for plug-in electric vehicles. The credit on Form 8834 is generally for smaller vehicles with a lower electric battery capacity than the credit on Form 8936.

Qualified plug-in electric vehicle credit on Form 8834. On Form 8834, a credit is allowed for qualifying two-wheel or three-wheel rechargeable electric vehicles and for four-wheel "low-speed" rechargeable electric vehicles. The credit is 10% of the cost, up to a maximum of $2,500. Only the original purchaser may claim the credit.

The credit applies to vehicles that are propelled to a significant extent by a rechargeable battery that has a capacity of at least 2.5 kilowatt-hours in the case of a two- or three-wheel vehicle, or at least 4 kilowatt hours in the case of a four-wheel low-speed vehicle. The vehicle must be manufactured primarily for use on public streets, roads, and highways. Vehicles manufactured primarily for off-road use, such as a golf course, do not qualify for the credit. To qualify as a low-speed vehicle, the vehicle must have a gross weight under 3,000 pounds and a sustainable speed of no more than 25 miles per hour.

The personal use portion of the credit on Form 8834 is limited to tax liability (regular tax plus AMT) reduced by various nonrefundable personal credits. The allowable credit for personal use is entered on Line 53 of Form 1040. If the vehicle is used for business, the credit for business use figured on Form 8834 is entered on Form 3800 as part of the general business credit *(40.26)*.

Qualified plug-in electric drive motor vehicle credit on Form 8936. A qualifying vehicle placed in service in 2010 must have at least 4 wheels and be propelled to a significant extent by a rechargeable battery that has a capacity of at least 4 kilowatt hours. The minimum credit is $2,500, and the maximum credit is $7,500.

The personal use portion of the credit on Form 8936 is limited to tax liability (regular tax plus AMT) reduced by various nonrefundable personal credits. The allowable credit for personal use is entered on Line 53 of Form 1040. If the vehicle is used for business, the credit for business use figured on Form 8936 is entered on Form 3800 as part of the general business credit *(40.26)*.

Note: More restrictive credit rules apply to qualified plug-in electric drive motor vehicles acquired in 2010 than in 2009. Only vehicles with a gross vehicle weight rating of less than 14,000 pounds qualify for the 2010 credit, and the maximum credit is $7,500 regardless of weight and battery capacity.

25.23 First-Time Homebuyer Credit

If you purchased a principal residence in the United States in 2010 before May 1, 2010, you may claim a refundable tax credit on Form 5405 if you qualify as a "first-time homebuyer" or "long-time resident" as described below. If you had entered into a binding contract by April 30, 2010 to close by June 30, 2010, and the transaction was actually closed by September 30, 2010, the purchase was timely and the credit may be claimed if you otherwise qualify.

A further extension is allowed if you, or your spouse, were a member of the U.S. uniformed services or Foreign Service, or an employee of the intelligence community on qualified official extended duty outside the United States for at least 90 days between January 1, 2009 and April 30, 2010. Your deadline to purchase a home eligible for the credit is April 30, 2011, and if by that date you enter into a binding contract to close by June 30, 2011, you have until June 30, 2011 to complete the purchase. Being on qualified official extended duty means serving at a duty station that is at least 50 miles from your principal residence, or living in government-furnished quarters under government orders.

First-time homebuyers and long-time residents. For a first-time homebuyer, the credit is $8,000 ($4,000 if married filing separately), or, if lower, 10% of the purchase price of the new home, but the credit may be reduced or eliminated by the phaseout rule. For a long-time resident, the credit, subject to the phaseout, is $6,250 ($3,250 if married filing separately), or 10% of the purchase price if lower. You are a first-time homebuyer if you, and your spouse if married on the purchase date, did not own another principal residence in the three years ending on the purchase date of the new home. You are a long-time resident if you, and your spouse if married on the purchase date, had owned and used the same home as your principal residence for any five-consecutive-year period during the eight years ending on the purchase date of the new home.

As discussed next, the credit is not allowed in certain cases even if you qualify as a first-time homebuyer or long-time resident, such as when you bought the home from your parent or other specified relative.

Credit denied to certain homebuyers. Whether or not you meet the tests for a first-time homebuyer or long-time resident, a credit cannot be claimed in certain cases. No credit can be claimed if the purchase price of the home exceeds $800,000. You cannot claim the credit if you can be claimed as a dependent by another taxpayer. If you were under age 18 on the date of purchase, you cannot claim the credit unless you were married on that date and your spouse was at least age 18. You cannot claim the credit for a home acquired by gift or inheritance.

You cannot claim the credit for a home purchased from a "related person." This includes your spouse, parents, grandparents, children, and grandchildren, or your spouse's parents, grandparents, children, and grandchildren. A corporation or partnership in which you or your spouse own over a 50% interest is also considered a related person. If you are a beneficiary of an estate and you buy the decedent's residence from the executor of the estate, the IRS considers this to be a disqualified related party sale unless the sale satisfies a pecuniary bequest from the decedent to the beneficiary.

Phaseout. On Form 5405, the credit is subject to phaseout based on your modified adjusted gross income (MAGI). The phaseout threshold is $125,000, or $225,000 if married filing jointly. The phaseout range is only $20,000, so the credit is completely phased out when MAGI equals or exceeds $145,000, or $245,000 for joint filers.

Documentation must be attached to your return. When you claim a credit on Form 5405, whether on an original or amended return, you must attach documentation of your home purchase. Attach a copy of a properly executed HUD-1 settlement statement or other settlement statement showing the date of purchase, contract sales price, address of the home, and the names and signatures of all parties. If you purchased a mobile home and do not have a settlement statement,

Filing Instruction

Repayment of 2008 or 2009 Credit On 2010 Return

If you claimed a credit for a 2008 home purchase, you must begin to repay it in 15 installments starting with your 2010 return. Report the installment for 2010 on Part IV of Form 5405 and add it to your 2010 tax on Line 59 of Form 1040.

However, if in 2010 you sold or stopped using as your principal residence the home on which the 2008 credit was claimed, or you sold or stopped using the home for which you claimed a 2009 credit, you may have to repay the entire 2008 or 2009 credit, depending on the circumstances. You must report the disposition or change in use on Part III of Form 5405. Any repayment of the 2008 or 2009 credit is reported on Part IV of Form 5405 and added to your 2010 tax on Line 59 of Form 1040.

Filing Tip

2009 Amended Return Option for 2010 Home Purchase

If you qualify for the first-time homebuyer credit for a purchase in 2010 you may claim the credit on an amended return for 2009 instead of on your 2010 return if that would provide a larger benefit. If you are electing to claim the credit on an amended return for 2009, you report the purchase on Form 5405 filed with your 2010 return and check the box on Line F.

attach a copy of your executed sales contract showing the parties' names and signatures, address of the home, contract date, and purchase price. For a newly constructed house, attach a dated copy of your certificate of occupancy showing your name and the address of the home.

If you qualify for the credit because you had a binding contract on April 30, 2010 to close by September 30, 2010, and did so, the Form 5405 instructions recommend that to avoid processing delays, you should attach to your return the pages from your contract showing the names and signatures of all parties, the contract date, purchase price, and address of the home.

If you are claiming a credit as a long-time resident, you can avoid processing delays (according to the Form 5405 instructions) by attaching home ownership records for the required five-consecutive-year period. You should include either Form 1098 (or substitute statements) showing your mortgage interest payments for the five years, property tax records, or homeowner's insurance records.

Allocation of credit between unmarried buyers. If unmarried individuals purchase a principal residence as tenants in common or as joint tenants, the IRS requires the purchasers to allocate the credit limit between them on their separate returns. They may allocate the credit however they choose, so long as an allocation is not made to a co-owner who is not eligible for that part of the credit. No allocation can be made to a purchaser who is not an eligible "first-time" homebuyer or who has bought his or her interest from a disqualifying relative. If one of the purchasers is subject to a partial or complete MAGI phaseout, his or her allocation must be reduced accordingly.

What if a parent co-signs a mortgage loan for a child? A parent may co-sign a loan for an unmarried child to enable the child to obtain a mortgage for a first home. Where the parent does not qualify as a first-time homebuyer and the child does qualify as a first-time homebuyer and has income under the phaseout threshold, the child may claim the entire credit.

Credit for home bought in 2008 must be repaid starting in 2010. The 2008 credit for a home purchased after April 8, 2008 (Form 5405 for 2008) generally must be repaid over 15 years in 15 equal installments, starting in 2010. No interest is charged. For example, if you bought a qualifying home in September 2008 and you claimed the full $7,500 credit on your 2008 return, $500 (1/15 of $7,500) must be included on your 2010 return as an additional tax and the same $500 amount must be included on each return through 2024. Report the 2010 installment on Line 16 of Form 5405 and add it to your 2010 tax liability on Line 59 of Form 1040.

This 15-year repayment rule assumes that you still owned the home and used it for all of 2010 as your principal residence. If you disposed of the home or changed your use of it in 2010, you generally have to repay the entire 2008 credit (not just 1/15) with your 2010 return; *see* the accelerated repayment requirements below.

Accelerated repayment may be required for 2008 or 2009 credit on 2010 return. If in 2010 you sold the home for which a 2008 credit or 2009 was claimed, or you stopped using it as your principal residence, the entire 2008 or 2009 credit generally must be reported as income for 2010. The disposition or cessation of use must be reported on Part III of Form 5405 and the repayment is reported in Part IV.

However, if a 2010 sale was to an unrelated party and there is a gain on the sale, the repayment amount is limited to the gain. If there was a loss on a sale to an unrelated party, no repayment of the 2008 or 2009 credit is required. Sales subject to these rules include foreclosure or repossession sales and in figuring gain or loss, basis of the residence is reduced by the 2008 or 2009 credit.

There are other exceptions to the accelerated repayment requirements. If the home for which a 2008 credit was claimed was destroyed or condemned in 2010 and you acquired a new home or intend to within two years *(18.19)*, repayment of the 2008 credit is made under the general 15-year repayment rule starting with your 2010 return. If a 2009 credit was claimed for the destroyed or condemned residence, there is no repayment requirement if a replacement home is purchased within two years; *see* the Form 5405 instructions.

If, as part of a divorce settlement, you transferred your home in 2010 to your ex-spouse (under the tax-free exchange rules in *6.7*), your ex-spouse becomes responsible for repaying a 2008 credit over the 15-year period or subject to the disposition rules for repayment of any 2009 credit.

You do not have to repay any part of the 2008 or 2009 credit if you or your spouse were a member of the U.S. uniformed services or Foreign Service, or an employee of the intelligence community on qualified official extended duty outside the United States, and you had to sell your home or stop using it as your principal residence in 2010 because you received orders to serve on qualified official extended duty. Qualified official extended duty means that you or your spouse was ordered to active duty for more than 90 days or for an indefinite period at a duty station that is at least 50 miles from the residence or is in government-furnished quarters.

If you are filing a final return for a taxpayer who claimed a 2008 or 2009 credit and died in 2010, *see* the instructions to Part III of Form 5405.

No repayment of credit for home bought in 2009 or 2010 and held for 36 months. You will not have to repay a credit claimed for a home bought in 2009 or 2010 if you continue to own it and use it as your principal residence for at least 36 months starting with the date of purchase. If within the 36-month period you sell the home, stop using it as your principal residence, or convert the entire home to rental or business property, repayment of the entire credit will be required, unless one of the exceptions discussed in the preceding section ("Accelerated repayment may be required for 2008 or 2009 credit on 2010 return") applies for the year in which the sale or cessation of residential use occurs.

25.24 Making Work Pay and Government Retiree Credits

If you have earned income for 2010, you may be entitled to the "Making Work Pay" credit of up to $400, $800 on a joint return. You must figure the credit on Schedule M and attach it to your Form 1040 or 1040A to get the benefit of the credit. If you file Form 1040EZ, the Making Work Pay Credit can be figured on an attached worksheet and you do not need to file Schedule M. You are not allowed any Making Work Pay credit if you may be claimed as a dependent by another taxpayer. If your modified adjusted gross income (same as adjusted gross income unless you are claiming exclusions for foreign income or housing) equals or exceeds $95,000, or $190,000 if married filing jointly, the credit is completely phased out. Nonresident aliens are not entitled to the credit.

Although federal income tax withholdings from your wages may have been reduced during 2010 to reflect the credit, this did not give you a tax benefit; it merely reduced your withholdings. You must claim the credit on your return to get the tax benefit of the credit, assuming you are eligible. If you are entitled to a credit on Schedule M (or Form 1040EZ worksheet), it is treated as a refundable credit that is reported on your return in the "Payments" section. In effect, the credit is treated as additional withholding that can increase your refund or lower the tax you must pay with your return.

The credit is 6.2% of your earned income in 2010, but the maximum credit is $400, $800 if filing jointly. The $400/$800 credit maximum is reached when earned income exceeds $6,451, or $12,903 on a joint return.

Under the phaseout rule, the credit is reduced or eliminated on Schedule M (or Form 1040EZ worksheet) if your modified adjusted gross income (MAGI) exceeds $75,000, or $150,000 on a joint return. The credit is reduced by 2% of your MAGI exceeding the $75,000 or $150,000 phaseout. For example, if the MAGI on your 2010 joint return is $162,000 and you are otherwise entitled to an $800 credit, the credit is reduced by $240 (.02 × $12,000 ($162,000 – $150,000) to $560. The credit is completely phased out when MAGI is $95,000 or more, or if filing jointly, $190,000 or more.

$250 economic recovery payment reduces Making Work Pay credit. You may have received a $250 economic recovery payment in 2010 if you were getting Social Security, SSI, railroad retirement or veterans' disability compensation in the last two months of 2008 or in January 2009, but did not receive your economic recovery payment during 2009. If you received the payment in 2010, it reduces the 2010 Making Work Pay credit that you are otherwise entitled to. If your spouse also received a $250 payment in 2010 and you are filing jointly, his or her payment also reduces the credit.

Chapter 26

Tax Withholdings

Withholding taxes gives the Government part of your income before you have a chance to use it. Withholding tax is imposed on salary and wage income, tip income, certain gambling winnings, pensions, and retirement distributions, but you may avoid withholding on retirement payments *(26.10)*. Withholding is also imposed on interest and dividends if you do not give your taxpayer identification number to a payer of interest or dividend income.

You may increase or decrease withholdings on your wages by submitting a new Form W-4 to your employer. Withholdings may be reduced by claiming allowances based on tax deductions and credits.

Make sure that tax withholdings meet or help you meet the estimated tax rules that require withholdings plus estimated tax payments to equal 90% of your current year liability or the required percentage of the prior year's liability; *see Chapter 27*.

A 20% withholding rate applies to eligible rollover distributions from an employer retirement plan. You may avoid the withholding by instructing your employer to directly transfer the funds to an IRA or the plan of your new employer *(26.10)*.

26.1 Withholdings Should Cover Estimated Tax

In fixing the rate of withholding on your wages, pay attention to the tests for determining whether sufficient income taxes have been withheld from your pay. A penalty will apply if your wage withholdings plus estimated tax payments (including prior year overpayments credited to current estimated tax) do not equal the lesser of 90% of your current tax liability or the required percentage of the prior year's tax *(27.1)*.

Taxes are withheld from payments made to you for services that you perform as an employee, subject to certain exceptions *(26.2)*. By filing Form W-4, you claim allowances for yourself, your spouse, and dependents. The number of allowances claimed will either decrease or increase the amount of withholding. On Form W-4, you also may claim withholding allowances for itemized deductions and credits such as the child tax credit, child and dependent care credit, education tax credits, adoption credit, retirement savings credit, prior-year AMT credit, credit for the elderly and disabled, the foreign tax credit, credit for home mortgage interest, the general business credit, and earned income credit (if you have not filed for an advance payment of the credit on Form W-5).

If you need to increase your withholding, such as to cover investment or self-employment income, you can choose not to claim all of the allowances allowed on Form W-4. You can also direct your employer on Form W-4 to withhold an additional flat amount from each paycheck.

You can change your withholdings, either increasing or decreasing them, if your financial or family situation changes *(26.5)*.

Caution

Making Work Pay Credit Reduces Withholding

If you earn wages, your employer has probably reduced your federal income tax withholdings to reflect the Making Work Pay tax credit *(25.24)*. However, in some cases, the withholding reduction may be more than the actual MWP credit that you will be entitled to when you file your federal tax return. This could be true if you have more than one job, or your spouse works. You are not allowed the MWP credit if you can be claimed as a dependent by another taxpayer. If your MWP credit will be limited, your refund could be less than you expect or the tax owed could be higher unless you increase your federal withholdings. You can estimate if your withholdings will be high enough by using the IRS Withholding Calculator at irs.gov, and if you want to increase your withholdings, you can submit a new Form W-4 to your employer.

26.2 Income Taxes Withheld on Wages

The amount of income tax withheld for your wage bracket depends on your marital status and the number of allowances you claim. You file a withholding certificate, Form W-4, with your employer, indicating your status and allowances. Without a Form W-4, your employer must withhold tax as if you are a single person with no exemptions.

Cash payments or the cash value of benefits paid to an employee by an employer are subject to withholding, unless the payments are specifically excluded.

Income Taxes Are Withheld on:

- Payments to employees as salaries, wages, fees, commissions, pensions, retirement pay, vacation allowances, dismissal pay, etc. (whether paid in cash or goods). If bonuses, commissions, overtime pay accumulated, leave, or taxable expense allowances (under nonaccountable plans) are separately identified from regular wages, an employer may withhold at a flat rate of 25% instead of using the regular withholding tables. *See* the discussion of withholding on pensions and annuities *(26.10)*.
- Sick pay paid by your employer. If a third party pays you sick pay on a plan funded by your employer, you may request withholding by filing Form W-4S.
- Taxable group insurance coverage over $50,000.
- Reimbursements of expenses that do not meet qualifying rules of accountable plans discussed in *20.31*. Also, reimbursements from accountable plans that exceed federal rates if the employee does not return the reimbursement or show that it is substantiated by proof of expenses.
- Pay to members of the U.S. Armed Forces. Differential wages paid by an employer to a former employee while on active military duty are subject to withholding.
- Prize awarded to a salesperson in a contest run by his or her employer.
- Retroactive pay and overtime under the Fair Labor Standards Act.
- Taxable supplemental unemployment compensation benefits.

Law Alert

Differential Wages Paid to Workers Joining Military

Employees who enlist or are called up to active military service may receive "differential wages" from their former employer to cover the difference between their military pay and the wages that were being received prior to joining the military. Income tax must be withheld from the differential wages, but not FICA tax (Social Security and Medicare).

Income Taxes Are Not Withheld on:

- Payments to household workers. However, although income tax withholding is not required, the worker and the employer may make a voluntary withholding agreement; *see Chapter 38*.
- Payments to agricultural workers, college domestics, ministers of the gospel (except chaplains in the Armed Forces), casual workers, nonresident aliens, public officials who receive fees directly from the public, notaries, jurors, witnesses, precinct workers, etc.
- Pay for newspaper home delivery by children under age 18.

Planning Reminder

Adjust Withholdings

If you do not expect withholdings to meet your final tax liability, ask your employer to withhold a greater amount of tax; *(26.1)*. On the other hand, if the withholding rate applied to your wages results in overwithholding, you may claim extra withholding allowances to reduce withholding during the year *(26.4–26.5)*.

- Advances for traveling expenses if the employee substantiates expenses to the employer and if the employee returns any unsubstantiated amount *(20.31)*.
- Value of tax-free board and lodging furnished by an employer.
- Fringe benefits not subject to tax.
- Substantiated reimbursements for deductible moving expenses or medical care benefits under a self-insured medical reimbursement plan.
- Death benefit payments to beneficiary of employee; wages due but unpaid at employee's death and paid to estate or beneficiary.
- Pay for U.S. citizen working abroad or in U.S. possessions to the extent that the pay is tax free *(36.1)*.
- Earnings of self-employed persons; they may pay estimated tax installments throughout the year.

Form W-2. By January 31, 2011, your employer must give you duplicate copies of your 2010 Form W-2, which is a record of your pay and the withheld income tax, Social Security and Medicare taxes. If you leave your job or your employment is terminated during 2010 and you request a Form W-2 from the employer, you should receive it within 30 days of the request or, if later, within 30 days of your final wage payment.

Planning Reminder

When To Change Withholdings

Adjust the withholdings that were in effect during 2010 if you expect there to be a significant change in the tax you owe for 2011. For example, if you expect to have lower income or a larger number of dependents, you can reduce your withholdings to increase your take home pay. On the other hand, a withholding increase may be advisable if previously claimed deductions or credits will not be available to you, or if you expect an increase in nonwage income such as capital gains. Check the instructions to Forms W-4 and 1040-ES for 2011 to help you adjust your withholdings.

26.3 Low Earners May Be Exempt From Withholding

If you had no income tax liability in 2010 and expect none for 2011, you may be exempt from income tax withholdings on your 2011 wages. If eligible, students working for the summer, retired persons, and other part-time workers do not have to wait for a refund of withheld taxes they do not owe. The exemption applies only to income tax withholding, not to withholdings for Social Security and Medicare *(26.9)*. However, if you can be claimed as a dependent on another person's tax return, the exemption from withholding is not allowed if your expected total income (wages and investments) and investment income exceeds annual limits. For 2010, the total income limit was $950 and the investment income limit was $300. These amounts may be increased by an inflation adjustment for 2011, and if so, the revised amounts will be on the Form W-4 for 2011.

If you cannot be claimed as a dependent by another person, you can claim the exemption from withholding if your total income is expected to be no more than the sum of your personal exemption and the standard deduction for your filing status.

To claim an exemption for 2011, you must file a withholding exemption certificate, Form W-4, with your employer. If you will file a joint return for 2011, do not claim an exemption on Form W-4 if the joint return will show a tax liability. An exemption claimed during 2010 will expire February 16, 2011.

Planning Reminder

Part-Year Employees May Avoid Overwithholding

Starting a new job in the middle of a year presents a withholding problem. The amount of tax withheld from your paycheck is figured by taking your weekly pay and multiplying this by a 52-week pay period. For example, if as a recent graduate you start a job on July 1 and your weekly pay is $1,000 for 26 weeks (July 1–December 31), your withholding will be based on an annual income of $52,000 ($1,000 × 52 weeks) and not the $26,000 you will actually earn that year. This will result in overwithholding. To alleviate this problem, you may ask your employer to calculate withholdings on what is known as the "part year" method if your work days during the year are expected to be 245 or fewer. This formula calculates withholding based on actual earnings rather than expected earnings over a full year of employment. As an alternative, you may elect to claim extra exemptions on Form W-4, which has the same effect of reducing the amount withheld each week from your paycheck.

26.4 Are You Withholding the Right Amount?

You do not want to withhold too little from your pay and you do not want to withhold too much. You may need to withhold more to avoid a large tax payment or an estimated tax penalty *(26.1)* when you file your return, especially if you have substantial income from investments or a business. You may also want to increase withholding if you have received a withholding reduction that reflects a Making Work Pay tax credit *(25.24)* that you will not be able to claim when you file your tax return; *see* the Caution in *26.1* above.

On the other hand, if you have been receiving large refunds from the IRS, you may want to consider reducing your Form W-4 allowances to avoid over-withholding. Balance the loss of the use of your earnings during the year against the value of receiving a substantial refund check from the IRS after you file your return.

If you are starting a new job or if you have not changed your withholding allowances in several years, review the Form W-4 worksheets to help you determine if you are withholding the right amount.

Working couples filing jointly should figure withholding allowances on their combined wage income, deductions, adjustments, and credits, but can divide the total number of allowances between them in any way they wish. On separate returns, the allowances must be figured separately.

If you work for only one employer and are unmarried, you may claim an additional withholding allowance. If you are married, you may claim the additional allowance if you work for only one employer and your spouse does not work, or your wages from a second job or your spouse's wages are $1,500 or less. This special allowance is only for withholding purposes. You may not claim it on your tax return.

If you work for two or more employers at the same time, you figure your withholding allowances based on the total income, and then split the allowances between the two jobs in any way you wish. Do not claim the same allowances with more than one employer at the same time.

File a new Form W-4 each year for withholding allowances based on your anticipated deductions and credits. Furthermore, you may have to file a new form to increase your withholding if withholding allowances you had been claiming are no longer allowed *(26.5)*.

IRS review of Form W-4. Employers are not required to submit Forms W-4 to the IRS for review unless the IRS sends written notice directing the employer to provide the W-4 forms of specified employees. The IRS uses the information on Form W-2 wage statements to spot employees who are not withholding enough federal income tax from their income. If the IRS determines that too many withholding allowances are being claimed, the IRS can issue a "lock-in letter" requiring your employer to limit the number of allowances to a specified maximum. You will receive a copy of the "lock-in letter" and be given an opportunity to dispute the IRS determination before your employer adjusts your withholding.

The IRS may impose a $500 civil penalty if you did not have a reasonable basis for claiming allowances that reduced your withholding on Form W-4. There is also a criminal penalty of up to $1,000 plus a jail sentence upon conviction for willfully supplying false information.

26.5 When To File a New Form W-4

You should file a new Form W-4 any time the number of your exemptions or withholding allowances increases or decreases, such as when a child is born or adopted, you marry, you get a divorce, or your deductible expenses change.

Your employer may make the new Form W-4 effective with the next payment of wages. However, an employer may postpone the new withholding rate until the start of the first payroll period ending on or after the 30th day from the day you submit the revised form.

You must file a new Form W-4 within 10 days if the number of allowances previously claimed by you decreases, such as where you divorce or legally separate, or a person who has been claimed as your dependent no longer qualifies.

The death of a spouse or a dependent in a current year does not affect your withholding until the next year but requires the filing of a new certificate, if possible, by the first business day in December, or within 10 days if the death is in December. However, a widow or widower entitled to joint return rates in the next two years as a qualifying widow or widower with a dependent child *(1.11)* need not file a new withholding certificate.

When you file on or before December 1, your employer must reduce your withholding as of January 1 of the next year.

26.6 Voluntary Withholding on Government Payments

You can choose to have income tax withheld from Social Security benefits (and equivalent tier 1 Railroad Retirement benefits), unemployment compensation, crop damage payments, and Commodity Credit Corporation loans. The withholding request is made on Form W-4V. Electing to have tax withheld may eliminate the need to make estimated tax installments *(27.2)*.

For unemployment compensation you may choose a withholding rate of 10%. For the other government payments, you may select a withholding rate of 7%, 10%, 15%, or 25%.

26.7 When Tips Are Subject to Withholding

Tips are subject to income tax and FICA (Social Security and Medicare) withholdings. If you receive cash tips amounting to $20 or more in a month, you must report the total amount of tips received during the month to your employer on Form 4070 (or a similar written report). Include cash tips paid to you in your own behalf. If you "split" or share tips with others, you include in your report only your share. You do not include tips received in the form of merchandise or your share of service charges turned over to you by your employer. Make the report on or before the 10th day after the end of the month in which the tips are received. (If the 10th day is a Saturday, Sunday, or legal holiday, you must submit the report by the next business day.) For example, tips amounting to $20 or more that are received during January 2011 are reported by February 10, 2011. Your employer may require more frequent reporting.

You are considered to have income from tips when you receive the tips, even if they are not reported to the employer.

Your employer withholds the Social Security, Medicare, and income tax due on the tips from your wages or from funds you give him or her for withholding purposes. If the taxes due cannot be collected on the tips, either from your wages or from voluntary contributions, by the 10th day after the end of the month in which tips are reported, you have to pay the tax when you file your income tax return.

Penalty for failure to report tips. Failure to report tip income of $20 or more received during the month to your employer may subject you to a penalty of 50% of the Social Security and Medicare tax due on the unreported tips, unless your failure was due to reasonable cause rather than to willful neglect.

Tips of less than $20 per month are taxable but not subject to withholding.

Filing Instruction

Tip Reporting

If you have not reported tips of $20 or more in any month, or tips are allocated to you under the special tip allocation rules, you must compute Social Security and Medicare tax on that amount on Form 4137 and enter it as a tax due on Line 57 of Form 1040; attach Form 4137 to Form 1040. The unreported tips must be included as wages on Line 7 of Form 1040.

Tip allocation reporting by large restaurants. To help the IRS audit the reporting of tip income, restaurants employing at least 10 people must make a special report of income and allocate tips based on gross receipts. For purposes of the allocation, the law assumes tip income of at least 8%. If you voluntarily report tips equal to your allocable share of 8% of the restaurant's gross receipts, no allocation will be made to you. However, if the total tips reported by all employees is less than 8% of gross receipts and you do not report your share of the 8%, your employer must make an allocation based on the difference between the amount you reported and your share of the 8% amount. The allocated amount is shown on Form W-2. However, taxes are not withheld on the allocated amount. Taxes are withheld only on amounts actually reported by employees. An employer or majority of employees may ask the IRS to apply a tip percentage of less than 8%, but no lower than 2%.

Reporting allocated tips. Your employer will show allocated tips in Box 8 of your Form W-2. However, this amount will not be included in Box 1 wages and you must add it to income yourself by reporting it on Line 7 of Form 1040. You also must compute Social Security and Medicare tax on the allocated tips on Form 4137 and enter the tax from Form 4137 on Line 57 of Form 1040. You may not use Form 1040A or Form 1040EZ.

26.8 Withholding on Gambling Winnings

Gambling winnings are generally reported by the payer to the IRS and to the winner on Form W-2G if the amount paid is $600 or more and at least 300 times the amount of the wager. The payer has the option of reducing the amount paid by the wager in applying the $600 test. Different reporting rules apply to winnings from poker tournaments, keno, bingo, and slot machines. Poker tournament winnings are reported on Form W-2G if they exceed $5,000, *reduced* by the wager or buy-in. Keno winnings are reported on Form W-2G if they are $1,500 or more, *reduced* by the wager. Winnings from bingo or slot machines of $1,200 or more, *not* reduced by the wager, are reported on Form W-2G.

Your winnings from gambling are subject to 25% withholding if your winnings minus the wager exceed:

1. $5,000 from lotteries, sweepstakes, and wagering pools (whether or not state-conducted), including poker tournaments, church raffles, *pari-mutuel* betting pools and on- and off-track racing pools; or
2. $5,000 from other wagering transactions apart from slot machines, bingo, or keno, if the proceeds are at least 300 times as large as the amount wagered, such as from wagers on horse races, dog races, or jai alai.

If your winnings exceed the $5,000 threshold, 25% withholding applies to your gross winnings less your wagers, and not just the amounts over $5,000. Any withholdings will be shown on Form W-2G.

The IRS requires you to tell the payers of gambling winnings if you are also receiving winnings from identical wagers; winnings from identical wagers must be added together to determine if withholding is required.

Caution

Backup Gambling Withholding

Winnings from bingo, keno, and slot machines are not subject to income tax withholding. However, if your slots or bingo winnings are $1,200 or more, keno winnings are $1,500 or more, or tournament poker winnings are $5,000 or more, and you do not provide a taxpayer identification number, the payer will withhold tax at the 28% backup withholding rate *(26.11)* on the winnings reduced, at the payer's option, by the wager.

If you have agreed to share your winnings with another person, give the payer a Form 5754. The payer will then prepare separate Forms W-2G for each of you.

26.9 FICA Withholdings

FICA withholdings are employee contributions for Social Security and Medicare coverage. Your employer is liable for the tax if he or she fails to make proper withholdings. The amount withheld is figured on your wages and is not affected by your marital status, number of exemptions, or the fact that you may be collecting Social Security benefits. On Form W-2, Social Security withholdings are shown in Box 4 and Medicare withholdings in Box 6.

Subject to FICA tax are your regular salary, commissions, bonuses, vacation pay, cash tips, group-term insurance coverage over $50,000, the first six months of sick pay, and contributions to cash or deferred (401(k)) pay plans or salary-reduction contributions to a simplified employee pension (SEP), SIMPLE IRA, or tax-sheltered annuity. Not subject to tax are the value of tax-free meals and lodgings *(3.12)*, and reimbursements for substantiated travel or entertainment expenses or for moving expenses.

Excess Social Security and Railroad Retirement withholding. If you have worked for more than one employer during 2010, attach all Copies B of Form W-2 to your return. Check to *see* that the total withheld in 2010 by your employers does not exceed your liability for Social Security taxes. The maximum 2010 liability for Social Security is $6,621.60, 6.2% on the first $106,800 of salary income. If too much was withheld, claim the excess as a payment on Line 69 of your 2010 Form 1040. On Form 1040A, the excess is included on the line for total tax payments; you cannot claim the excess on Form 1040-EZ.

Medicare tax is withheld at a rate of 1.45% on all salary and wage income.

Employees covered by the Railroad Retirement Tax Act (RRTA) receive Form W-2, which lists total wages paid and withholdings of income and Railroad Retirement taxes. Follow tax form instructions for claiming a credit for excess Railroad Retirement withholding.

If any one employer withheld too much Social Security or Railroad Retirement tax, you cannot claim the excess on your income tax return. You must ask that employer for a refund of the excess.

Wages you pay to your spouse or child. Wages you pay to your spouse for working in your business are subject to FICA tax and income tax withholding. Wages you pay to your child are subject to income tax withholding but if your child is under age 18 and your business is a sole proprietorship or a partnership in which the only partners are you and the child's other parent, the wages are exempt from FICA taxes. Wages you pay to your child under age 21 or to your spouse for domestic work or child care in your own home are exempt from FICA.

Filing Instruction

Uncollected Social Security and Medicare Taxes on Tips

If your employer is unable to collect enough money from your wages during the year to cover the Social Security or Medicare tax on the tips you reported, the uncollected amount is shown on your Form W-2 in Box 12 with Code A next to it for Social Security or Code B for Medicare. You must report the uncollected amount on Line 60 of Form 1040 (total tax) as an additional tax due; write "UT" and show the amount next to Line 60.

Planning Reminder

Wages Paid to Household Employees

See Chapter 38 for FICA withholding on wages paid to household employees.

26.10 Withholding on Retirement Distributions

Retirement distributions are subject to withholding taxes, but you may choose to avoid withholdings. The method of avoiding withholding varies with the type of payment.

Periodic payments. If you receive periodic payments in installments over more than one year, such as from a pension or an annuity, withholding is required unless you elect to avoid withholding on Form W-4P, or on a substitute form furnished by the payer. If you are a U.S. citizen or resident alien, withholding may not be avoided on pensions or other distributions paid outside the U.S. or U.S. possessions. Payment must be to your home address within the U.S. (or in a U.S. possession) to avoid withholding.

Unless you tell the payer otherwise, wage withholding tables are used to figure withholdings on periodic payments as if you were married and claiming three withholding exemptions. Withholding allowances may be claimed on Form W-4P for estimated itemized deductions, alimony payments, student loan interest, and deductible IRA contributions.

You may also request that the payer withhold a specific amount of additional tax for each payment.

Nonperiodic payments from IRAs and commercial annuities. Nonperiodic payments are subject to withholding at a flat 10% rate unless you elect to avoid withholding on Form W-4P (or substitute form). IRA distributions that are payable upon demand are considered nonperiodic and, thus, subject to the 10% withholding rule.

Planning Reminder

Rollover From Employer Plan Avoids Withholding

Your employer must withhold 20% from a distribution paid to you if the distribution was eligible for tax-free rollover *(7.8)*. Withholding does not apply if you have the employer make a direct rollover to a qualified plan or IRA.

Nonperiodic payments from qualified employer plans. Employers must withhold 20% from nonperiodic payments, such as lump-sum distributions that are eligible for tax-free rollover but which are paid directly to you. To avoid withholding you must direct your employer to make a direct rollover *(7.8)* of the funds to an IRA or to a qualified plan of your new employer. If you do not instruct your employer to make the direct transfer and elect to personally receive the distribution, 20% will be withheld before payment is made to you.

See *Chapter 7* for a further explanation and an Example showing the effects of the withholding rule where you receive the distribution and then decide to make a rollover yourself *(7.8)*.

26.11 Backup Withholding

Backup withholding is designed to pressure taxpayers to report interest and dividend income. You may be subject to backup withholding if you do not give your taxpayer identification number to parties paying you interest or dividend income, you give an incorrect number, or you ignore IRS notices stating that you have underreported interest or dividends. Your taxpayer identification number generally is your Social Security number or your employer identification number. The backup withholding rate is 28%.

Backup withholding will apply to fees of $600 or more (Form 1099-MISC) for work you do as an independent contractor, payments from brokers (Form 1099-B), royalty payments (Form 1099-MISC), and certain gambling winnings *(26.8)* if you do not give the payer your taxpayer identification number.

Civil and criminal penalties can be imposed if you provide false information to avoid backup withholding.

Chapter 27

Estimated Tax Payments

Income taxes are collected on a pay-as-you-go basis through withholding on wages and pensions, as well as quarterly estimated tax payments on other income. Where all or most of your income is from wages, pensions, and annuities, you will generally not have to pay estimated tax, because your estimated tax liability has been satisfied by withholding. But do not assume you are not required to pay simply because taxes have been withheld from your wages. Always check your estimated tax liability. Withholding may not cover your tax; the withholding tax rate may be below your actual tax rate when considering other income such as interest, dividends, business income, and capital gains.

Your estimated tax must also include liability for self-employment tax, alternative minimum tax (AMT), and FICA withholding tax for household employees.

If you expect your 2011 tax liability to be $1,000 or more after taking into account withholding taxes and credits, you should make quarterly estimated tax payments unless you expect the withholdings and credits to be at least 90% of your 2011 total tax, or, if less, 100% or 110% of your total tax for 2010. The 100% test applies if your 2010 adjusted gross income (AGI) was $150,000 or less, $75,000 or less if married filing separately in 2011. The 110% test applies if your 2010 AGI exceeded the $150,000 or $75,000 threshold.

Failure to pay a required estimated tax installment will subject you to a penalty based on the prevailing IRS interest rate applied to tax deficiences, unless the IRS waives the penalty.

27.1 Do You Owe an Estimated Tax Penalty for 2010?

When you have computed the exact amount of your 2010 tax liability on your 2010 return, you can determine whether you are subject to an estimated tax penalty. If you owe less than $1,000 on your 2010 return after taking into account withheld taxes, you are not subject to a penalty. If the tax owed after withholdings is $1,000 or more, you can now determine whether your 2010 withholdings plus estimated tax installments were at least 90% ($66\frac{2}{3}$% for farmers and fishermen) of your 2010 total tax. Total tax here means not only your 2010 regular income tax and alternative minimum tax (AMT) liability after credits, but also other taxes such as self-employment tax, household employment taxes, penalty taxes (such as penalties on early retirement plan distributions and on distributions from qualified tuition programs not used for education), and taxes from recaptured credits. If you met the 90% test, you are not subject to an estimated tax penalty for 2010.

Even if the 90% test was not met, you may be able to avoid a penalty if your 2010 withholdings and estimated tax installments were at least 100% of the total tax (*see* above) shown on your 2009 return. This exception requires that the 2009 return covered all 12 months. However, if your 2009 adjusted gross income exceeded $150,000 ($75,000 if you are married filing separately for 2010), your withholdings plus estimated tax installments for 2010 had to be at least 110% of your 2009 total tax (not 100%) to qualify for this prior-year liability exception.

Note that to *completely* avoid a penalty for 2010 under either the 90% current year exception or the 100%/110% prior-year exception, you must have paid at least 25% of the amount required under the applicable exception by each of the four payment dates. The penalty is figured separately for each payment period; *see* below.

Even if you owe $1,000 or more (after withholdings) on your 2010 return and you do not qualify for either the 90% current-year exception, or the 100%/110% prior-year exception, you are not subject to an estimated tax penalty for 2010 if you did not have to file a 2009 return or your 2009 total tax was zero. This exception applies only if you were a U.S. citizen or resident for all of 2009 and your 2009 tax year included 12 full months.

If you underestimated your 2010 liability because of an unexpected increase in income during 2010, or if you did not earn income evenly throughout 2010, such as where you operated a seasonal business, you may be able to lower or eliminate the penalty by using the *annualized income installment method*. Under this exception, you may avoid a penalty for an estimated tax installment by figuring the installment that would be due if the income (and deductions) earned before the date for the installment were *annualized*. Form 2210 and IRS Publication 505 have worksheets for applying the annualized income exception. The computation is complicated and its use may be discouraged by the complexity, despite the potential benefits.

Planning Reminder

Withholdings Cover Prior Underpayment

You have a choice in allocating withholdings from pay or other income that is subject to withholding: (1) You may treat your entire year's withholdings as having been withheld in equal amounts for each of the four payment periods or (2) you may allocate to each payment period the actual withholdings paid for that period. Also, if toward the end of the year you find that you have underestimated for an earlier period, ask your employer to withhold an extra amount that may be allocated equally over the four periods. This way, you may eliminate the underestimate for the earlier periods.

Penalties are figured separately for each payment period. Separate penalty determinations must be made for each of the four 2010 estimated tax payment periods, as of the applicable installment dates: April 15, June 15, and September 15 in 2010, and January 18, 2011. This means that if, after taking into account withholdings from your pay, you underpaid an installment, you may owe a penalty for that period even though you overpaid later installments to make up the difference. The penalty for each period, which is based on the prevailing IRS interest rate for deficiencies *(46.7)*, runs from the installment due date until the amount is paid or until the regular filing date for the final tax return, whichever is earlier.

Withholding payments are treated as if they were payments of estimated tax. In applying them, the total withholdings of the year are divided equally between each installment period unless you elect on Form 2210 to apply them to the periods in which they were actually withheld.

Figure the 2010 penalty for yourself on Form 2210 or let the IRS do it. In most cases you do not have to file Form 2210 to figure any estimated tax penalty for 2010; the IRS prefers to figure it and send you a bill if a penalty is due.

However, you must figure your penalty and file Form 2210 if (1) you request a partial waiver of your penalty (*see* below for waiver rules), (2) you use the annualized income method (Schedule AI of Form 2210) to reduce or eliminate your penalty, or (3) you elect to treat your withholdings as paid on the dates withheld rather than in equal amounts on the four installment dates.

In the following situations, the IRS requires you to file only page 1 of Form 2210 but not the rest of the form (Parts III and IV) on which the penalty computation is made: (1) you request a waiver for your entire penalty, or (2) you filed a joint return for either 2009 or 2010 (not both) and your required annual payment for 2010 was based on the 100% or 110% prior-year safe harbor. If you are requesting a waiver, attach a statement to page 1 of Form 2210 that explains the grounds for the request (*see* the waiver rules below). For situation (2), you are not required to figure your penalty, but you may use Part III or Part IV of Form 2210 as a worksheet to figure the penalty and enter it on your return, although the IRS does not want you to file Part III or Part IV, but only page 1 (Parts I and II).

If you use Part IV to figure the penalty under the regular method, an underpayment for any payment period reduces the payments made in the following period. That is, an underpayment of one period is carried over to succeeding periods on Form 2210. If you underpay for a period, any payment you make after that installment date will be applied first to the earlier underpayment. Thus, even if you make the required payment for a period, you could still be subject to a penalty for that period because your payment is applied to a prior underpayment.

If you *overpaid* for any period, the excess carries over to the next period. The excess cannot be used to make up for an underpayment of the prior period if the payments were made electronically, with Form 1040-ES vouchers or by credit card. However, withholdings are allocated equally over the year so that withholdings late in the year can reduce an underpayment for an earlier payment period.

Waiver of penalty for hardship, retirement, or disability. The IRS may waive the penalty if you can show you failed to pay the estimated tax because of casualty, disaster, or other unusual circumstances.

The IRS may also waive a penalty for a 2010 underpayment if in 2010 or 2009 you retired after reaching age 62 or became disabled, and you failed to make a payment due to reasonable cause and not due to willful neglect.

To apply for the waiver, attach an explanation to Form 2210 that documents the circumstances supporting your waiver request. For a waiver due to retirement or disability, show your retirement date and age or disability date. If an underpayment was due to a federally declared disaster, you do not have to request a waiver on Form 2210 because the IRS allows an automatic postponement following such a disaster. When you file your return, the IRS should identify your residence as being in a federally declared disaster area and if you still owe a penalty following the end of the disaster waiver period, the IRS will send you a bill. If you are requesting a waiver due to a disaster other than a federally declared disaster, other casualty, or unusual circumstance, attach documentation of the event, including police and insurance company reports, and an explanation as to how it prevented you from making estimated tax payments.

Farmers and fishermen. Farmers or fishermen who earned at least ⅔ of their 2009 or 2010 gross income from farming or fishing can use Form 2210-F to determine whether they owe an estimated penalty for 2010, but generally the form does not have to be filed because the IRS will figure any penalty; *see* the Form 2210-F instructions.

27.2 Planning Estimated Tax Payments for 2011

In planning your payments for 2011, you may not want to pay any more than is necessary to avoid a penalty. You can avoid a penalty for 2011 by planning payments in 2011 that meet the 90% current-year test or the 100%/110% prior-year safe harbor.

90% current-year test. If you expect your income, deductions, and tax credits for 2011 to be about the same as they were for 2010, and you will not have any additional liabilities for 2011that you did not have for 2010, such as for alternative minimum tax (AMT), self-employment tax, household employee taxes, penalty taxes, or recapture taxes, you can base your 2011 withholdings and quarterly estimated tax installments on 90% of your 2010 total tax.

If you expect your 2011 total tax to be lower than your 2010 total tax, such as where your income has dropped, you can base your 2011 withholdings and estimated tax installments on 90% of the estimated 2011 total tax.

You can use the 2011 Estimated Tax Worksheet in the instructions to Form 1040-ES for 2011 to figure the required annual payment under the 90% test, as well as under the prior-year safe harbor test discussed next.

Planning Reminder

Annualized Income Method

If your income typically fluctuates throughout the year, or if your income unexpectedly changes during the year, you may base installment payments on the annualized income method. This method allows you to avoid a penalty for installment periods during which less income is earned by reducing the required estimated tax payment for such periods. To figure your installment payments, use the Annualized Estimated Tax Worksheet in IRS Publication 505. If you base installment payments on the annualized method, you must file Form 2210 with your return to determine if you are subject to an estimated tax penalty.

Safe harbor for 2011 based on 2010 tax. If you are uncertain of the amount of your 2011 income and deductions, you can play it safe and avoid a possible penalty for 2011 by having 2011 withholdings and quarterly estimated tax installments equal to your 2010 total tax if your 2010 adjusted gross income is $150,000 or less ($75,000 or less if married filing separately for 2011), provided you filed a 2010 return covering a full 12 months. If your 2010 AGI exceeds the $150,000 (or $75,000) threshold, your payments for 2011 must be at least 110% of your 2010 tax.

If an accurate estimate for 2011 is possible, it is generally advantageous to base your estimated payments on the 90% test rather than the 100%/110% prior year test, as using this prior year test will probably result in an overestimation of your liability unless the 2011 tax turns out to be substantially larger than the 2010 tax.

You may use the worksheet and the tax rate schedule included in the 2011 Form 1040-ES to figure your estimated tax liability and the required annual payment to avoid a penalty under either the 90% current-year or the 100%/110% prior-year liability tests.

Making estimated tax payments. Reduce your 2011 estimated tax liability by expected withholdings from wages, pensions, and annuities. If after withholdings your estimated tax is $1,000 or more, you must make estimated tax payments unless the withholdings will cover at least 90% of your estimated 2011 liability or 100%/110% of your 2010 liability. If withholdings will not cover the amount required under the 90% or 100%/110% tests, you may pay the balance of the estimated tax with Form 1040-ES vouchers or by credit card. You may schedule electronic payments using the Electronic Federal Tax Payment System (EFTPS), or you can make estimated tax payments by direct debit from your checking or savings account if you electronically file your 2010 return. *See* the 2011 Form 1040-ES instructions for details on the payment options.

Planning Reminder

Credit Card or Electronic Payments

You may charge estimated tax payments using a Visa, MasterCard, American Express, or Discover Card. *See* the Form 1040-ES instructions. If you charge estimated tax payments, you do not have to file Form 1040-ES vouchers.

You may also make your payments electronically by authorizing withdrawals from your checking or savings account. You can schedule payments through EFTPS (Electronic Federal Tax Payment System) by enrolling online (www.eftps.gov) or by phone (1-800-316-6541). If you file your 2010 return electronically, your tax preparation software will allow you to schedule up to four 2011 estimated tax payments.

Crediting 2010 refund to 2011 estimated tax. If you are due a refund when you file your 2010 return, it may be credited to your 2011 estimated tax. You may also split up the amount due you. You may take part of the overpayment as a refund. The other part may be credited to your estimate of 2011 taxes. The IRS will credit the refund to the April installment of 2011 estimated tax unless you attach a statement to your return instructing the IRS to apply the refund to later installments.

Check your arithmetic before you apply an overpayment as a credit on your next year's estimate. If you apply too much, the amount credited may not be used to offset any additional tax due that the IRS determines you owe. For example, your 2010 return shows a $500 refund due, and you apply it towards your 2011 estimated tax. However, the IRS determines that you overpaid $200, not $500. You will be billed for the additional $300 tax, plus interest due; you may not offset the extra tax with the credited amount.

Farmers or fishermen. In figuring the required annual payment to avoid a penalty for 2011, a farmer or fisherman has to pay only 66⅔% of the 2011 estimated liability, rather than 90%. A penalty may also be avoided by paying 100% of the 2010 tax, provided a tax return covering a 12-month period was filed for 2010; the 110% test for higher-income taxpayers does not apply to a farmer or fisherman. To qualify as a farmer or fisherman under these rules, at least two-thirds of gross income for 2010 or 2011 must be from farming or fishing.

27.3 Dates for Paying Estimated Tax Installments for 2011

The four installment dates for 2011 estimated tax are: April 15, 2011; June 15, 2011; September 15, 2011; and January 17, 2012. Later installments may be used to amend earlier ones *(27.1)*. You do not have to file the January 17, 2012, voucher if you file your 2011 tax return and pay the balance of tax due by January 31, 2012.

If you use a fiscal year. A fiscal year is any year other than the calendar year. If you file using a fiscal year, your first estimated installment is due on or before the 15th day of the fourth month of your fiscal year. The second and third installments are due on or before the 15th day of the sixth and ninth months of your fiscal year with the final installment due by the 15th day of the first month of your next fiscal year.

Farmers and fishermen. Farmers only have to make one installment payment, generally by January 15 of the following year. The payment for 2011 must be made by January 17, 2012, or farmers may file their 2011 returns and pay the total tax due by March 1, 2012, instead of making an estimated tax payment. To qualify under these rules, a farmer must receive two-thirds of his or her 2010 or 2011 gross income from farming.

Fishermen who expect to receive at least two-thirds of their gross income from fishing pay estimated taxes as farmers do.

27.4 Estimates by Husband and Wife

A married couple may pay joint or separate estimated taxes. The nature of the estimated tax does not control the kind of final return you file.

Where a joint estimated tax is paid but separate tax returns are filed, you and your spouse can decide on how to divide the estimated payments between you. Either one of you can claim the whole amount, or you can agree to divide it in any proportion. If you cannot agree, the IRS will allocate the estimated taxes proportionally according to the percentage of total tax each spouse owes.

If separate estimated taxes are paid, overpayment by one spouse is not applied against an underpayment by the other when separate final returns are filed.

A joint estimated tax may be made by a husband and wife only if they are both citizens or residents of the United States. Both must have the same taxable year. A joint estimate may not be made by a couple who are divorced or legally separated under a decree. If a joint estimate is made and the spouses are divorced or legally separated later in that year, they may divide the joint payments between them under the above rule for spouses who file separately.

Prior-year safe harbor. If you filed separately for 2010 but expect to file a joint 2011 return, your 2010 total tax for purposes of determining the required 2011 annual payment under the prior-year safe harbor *(27.2)* is the total tax for both of you on the 2010 separate returns.

If you and your spouse filed jointly for 2010 but expect to file separately for 2011, you must figure your share of the 2010 joint return tax to apply the prior-year safe harbor. Figure the tax that each of you would have paid on separate returns for 2010 and then divide the tax on your separate return by the total tax for both separate returns. For example, if you would have paid tax of $7,000 on a separate 2010 return and your spouse would have paid $3,000 on a separate return, your 70% share ($7,000/$10,000) is the share of the 2010 joint return tax that you take into account in applying the prior-year safe harbor. Your spouse's share of the 2010 joint return tax is 30%.

If a joint estimated tax is made and one spouse dies, the estate does not continue to make installment payments. The surviving spouse is required to pay the remaining installments unless he or she amends the joint estimate. Amounts paid on the joint estimate may be divided as agreed upon by the spouse and the estate of the deceased. If they do not agree, the IRS will apportion the payments according to the percentage of the total tax owed by each spouse.

27.5 Adjusting Your Payments During the Year

If, during the year, your income, expenses, or exemptions change, refigure your estimated tax liability and adjust your payment schedule as shown in the following Examples. Increasing an installment payment cannot make up for an underpayment in a prior period; *see* Example 2 below. However, withholdings from pay, pensions, and IRA withdrawals can be allocated equally over all four periods and, thus, withholding increased at the end of the year may be applied to earlier periods.

If taxes paid in the previous installments total more than your revised estimate, you cannot obtain a refund at that time. You must wait until you file your final return showing that a refund is due.

EXAMPLES

1. Smith, who is self-employed, figures that to avoid a penalty for 2011 under the estimated tax rules discussed above, he must make estimated tax installments of $6,000. By April 15, 2011, he pays an installment of $1,500. In June, he amends his estimate, showing a tax of $3,000 instead of $6,000. He refigures the installment schedule by dividing $3,000 by 4, which gives a payment rate of $750 for each period. As he paid $1,500 in April, the $750 overpayment covers his June obligation. By September 15, 2011, he pays $750; by January 17, 2012, he pays $750.

2. In September 2011, Jones finds that his estimated 2011 tax liability should be $25,000 rather than his original estimate of $20,000. He paid $5,000 as his April and June installments ($10,000 total). Under the amended schedule, he should have paid $6,250 per period ($25,000 ÷ 4), $6,250 by April 15 and $6,250 by June 15. Thus, there is a $2,500 underpayment ($12,500 – 10,000) for the first two periods.

   To cover the underpayment of $2,500, which carries over to the third payment period (June 1 through August 31), Jones's installment by September 15 must be at least $8,750 ($6,250 + $2,500). If less than $8,750 is paid, there will be an underpayment for the third payment period, as payments in that period are applied first to the carried-over underpayment of $2,500. If at least $8,750 is paid by September 15, there is no third period underpayment to be carried over, so the required installment for the fourth period (September 1 through December 31), due by January 17, 2012, will be $6,250. Unless an exception *(27.1)* applies, the underpayments for the first two periods will be subject to a penalty.

Tax Planning

The chapters in this part will alert you to special tax situations. They will point out tax-saving opportunities and show you how to take advantage of tax-saving ideas and planning strategies.

Chapter 28

Tax Planning Overview

Tax planning is a year-round activity. By planning income and deduction strategies, you may be able to reduce your tax. You may realize capital gain income subject to lower capital gain rates, defer certain income to a later year in which you expect to pay a lower tax, and accelerate deductions to a higher tax year. Tax-free investments are available and, within limits, income splitting with family members may be possible.

This chapter illustrates basic tax-planning strategies. In subsequent chapters, tax-savings plans for homeowners, families, investors, and executives are discussed.

28.1 Tax-Saving Opportunities

The table below highlights some of the tax-saving opportunities discussed in this book.

Table 28-1 Tax-Saving Opportunities

Objective—	*Explanation—*
Realizing long-term capital gains	Long-term capital gains are taxed at lower rates than short-term gains and regular income. *See Chapter 5* for basic capital gain rules. *See Chapters 30* and *31* for discussions of special investment situations.
Earn qualifying dividends	Since 2003, qualified dividends *(4.2)* have been subject to the reduced tax rates for long-term capital gains. Legislation is needed to extend this treatment beyond 2010 but the extension is likely; *see* the *e-Supplement at jklasser.com* for an update.
Earning tax-free income	You can earn tax-free income by— 1. Investing in tax-exempt securities. However, before you invest, determine whether the tax-free return will exceed the after-tax return of taxed income *(30.12)*. 2. Taking a position in a company that pays tax-free fringe benefits, such as health and life insurance protection. For a complete discussion of tax-free fringe benefits, *see Chapter 3*. 3. Seeking tax-free education benefits with scholarship arrangements and educational IRAs; *see Chapter 33*. 4. Taking a position overseas to earn excludable foreign earned income; *see Chapter 36*. 5. Investing in Roth IRAs; *see Chapter 8*.
Deferring income	You can defer income to years when you will pay less tax through— 1. Deferred pay plans, which are discussed in *Chapter 2*. 2. Qualified retirement plans such as 401(k) plans *(Chapter 7)*, Keogh plans *(Chapter 41)*, and traditional IRA and Roth IRA plans *(Chapter 8)*. 3. The year-end planning techniques explained in this chapter *(28.2)*. 4. Transacting installment sales when you sell property; *see 5.21*. 5. Investing in U.S. Savings EE bonds or I-bonds *(4.28–4.29, 30.14–30.15)*.
Income splitting	Through income splitting you divide your income among several persons or taxpaying entities that will pay an aggregate tax lower than the tax that you would pay if you reported all of the income. Although the tax law limits income-splitting opportunities, certain business and family income planning through the use of trusts and custodian accounts can provide tax savings; *see* Chapters 24 and 39.
Tax-free exchanges	You can defer tax on appreciated property by transacting tax-free exchanges *(6.1, 31.3)*.
Buying a personal residence rather than renting	Homeowners are favored by the tax law. 1. Rather than paying rent, buy a home, condominium, or cooperative apartment. You may deduct interest and taxes. When you sell your home, you may avoid tax on gains of up to $250,000 if single and up to $500,000 if married filing jointly; *see Chapter 29*. 2. Homeowners can borrow on their home equity and deduct interest expenses *(15.3)*.
Take advantage of special personal tax breaks for education	The tax law provides several breaks for education expenses; *see Chapter 33*, which discusses scholarships, grants, tuition plans, savings bond tuition plans, education credits, Coverdell Education Savings Accounts, and student loan interest deduction.
Take advantage of personal tax credits	*See Chapter 25* for personal tax credits such as the child tax credit, dependent care credit, and adoption credit that can reduce your tax liability.

28.2 When To Defer Income and Accelerate Deductions

Your tax bracket may shift from year to year because of fluctuations in income or expenses. If you expect to pay less tax in the following year than in the current year, consider deferring income and accelerating deductible expenses and losses. Even if you expect your tax bracket to remain the same, you may want to accelerate deductions to reduce tax for the current year or defer income, if possible, to delay the payment of tax.

High-income taxpayers may be wary of deferring income beyond 2010 given the possibility that the top rates will be increased to raise revenue for the federal government.

In your year-end planning for 2010, take into account the following rules, which may affect your ability to defer income to 2011 or accelerate deductions to 2010.

Postponing income. You may not defer salary income by not cashing a paycheck or not taking salary that you have earned and that you can receive without restrictions. Under certain conditions, you may contract with your employer to defer the taxable receipt of current compensation to future years. To defer pay to a future period you must take some risk. You cannot have any control over your deferred pay account. If you are not confident of your employer's ability to pay in the future, you should not defer pay.

Accelerating deductions. In accelerating deductions, there are these limitations: You may not deduct prepaid interest and rent. Prepaid interest must be deducted over the period of the loan. Rentals must also be deducted over the rental period. You can generally deduct prepayments of state income tax, but prepayment should not be made if it would trigger AMT liability *(23.2)*. Annual subscriptions to professional journals and business magazines can be renewed before the end of the year. If the subscription is for more than a year, you may deduct only the first-year prepayment. The cost of the later subscription must be deducted in the later year. Business and investment expenses charged to credit card accounts are deductible in the year of charge, even though you do not pay your charge account bill until the next year. You can also realize losses by selling business or investment property that has lost value in the year you want to incur the loss.

Making an extra charitable donation at the end of the year also may provide an added deduction that may lower your tax. You may deduct a charitable gift made by check on the last day of the year, even if the check is not cashed until the new year begins. A credit card donation is deductible in the year of the charge. Charitable donations may be timed to give you the largest possible tax savings. If, toward the end of the year, you find that you need an extra deduction, you may make a deductible donation in late December. Doing so would be especially beneficial if you know that your tax bracket will be lower the following year; *see Chapter 14* for further planning details.

Also *see Chapter 13* for claiming the standard deduction and itemizing deductions in alternate years, and *Chapter 23* for planning steps when you may be subject to alternative minimum tax.

Deferring interest income to next year. As a general rule, you have to report interest credited to your savings account during the year, even if the account is a passbook account and you did not present the passbook to have the amount entered. However, there are opportunities to defer interest in the following ways:

1. Buy a savings certificate after June 30 with a maturity of one year or less. Interest is taxable in the next year when the certificate matures, provided that interest is specifically deferred until the following year by the terms of the certificate.
2. Buy Treasury bills that come due next year. 26-week bills bought after June 30 will mature in the next year.
3. Buy I bonds or Series EE bonds. These bonds may be cashed for their purchase price, plus the increase in redemption value due to accrued interest. You may defer the annual interest income until the year you cash the bond or the year the bond finally matures, whichever is earlier *(30.14–30.15)*.

Caution

Uncertainty Over 2011 Tax Rates

If you are in a position to defer income to 2011 and are in one of the top two rate brackets for ordinary income (33% and 35% for 2010), the possibility of higher rates in 2011 complicates the issue of whether to defer salary or business income towards the end of 2010. When this book went to press, it had not yet been decided whether all the 2010 rates would be extended to 2011 or if the top rates would be raised. Whether the 0% and 15% rates for long-term capital gains and qualified dividends *(5.3)* would be extended for all or only some taxpayers also had not been settled. *See* the *e-Supplement at jklasser.com* for a legislation update.

Planning Reminder

Deferring Business Income

If you are self-employed and are on the cash basis, you can defer income by delaying your billing at the end of the year or extending the time of collection. If you own a closely held corporation, you can time the payment of dividends and bonuses.

Planning Reminder

Year-End Securities Sales

If you have realized capital gains during the year and have paper losses, realizing losses can offset the gains plus up to $3,000 of other income. If you previously realized losses and have paper gains, you can selectively realize gains that can be offset by the losses. *See 30.1–30.2* for information on planning securities transactions.

Timing sales of property. A sale is generally taxable in the year title to the property passes to the buyer. Since you can control the year title passes, you can usually defer income realized on the sale to the year in which you will pay less tax. *See* the discussion of year-end sales of securities in *30.1*.

28.3 Tax Law Changes for Years After 2010

When this book went to press, the fate of dozens of tax provisions was yet to be determined, creating great uncertainty for 2011 tax planning. Unless Congress extends expiring provisions, key credit and deduction amounts will be scaled back. Also, as noted in *28.2*, Congress must decide whether to extend the 2010 tax rates on ordinary income as well as the preferential rates for long-term capital gains and qualified dividends to all taxpayers or to impose higher rates on high-income taxpayers. Check the *e-Supplement at jklasser.com* for an update on legislative developments.

Chapter 29

Tax Savings for Residence Sales

You may avoid tax on gain on the sale of a principal residence if you owned and used it for at least two years during the five-year period ending on the date of sale. If you are single, you may avoid tax on up to $250,000 of gain, $500,000 if you are married and file jointly. However, gain attributable to nonqualified use after 2008 is not excludable *(29.2)*.

If you used the residence for less than two years, you may avoid tax if you sold because of a change of job location, poor health or unforeseen circumstance *(29.4)*.

You may not deduct a loss on the sale of a personal residence. Losses on the sale of property devoted to personal use are nondeductible. However, there are circumstances under which you may claim a loss deduction on the sale of a residence *(29.9–29.10)*.

If you rent out a residential property and you or family members also use the residence during the year, rental expenses are subject to special restrictions *(9.7)*.

Filing Instruction

Reporting Home Sale Gain

If the entire gain on the sale of your principal residence is excludable from income under the rules discussed in this chapter *(29.1–29.7)*, you do not have to report the sale at all on your return. This is true even if you receive a Form 1099-S from the settlement agent showing a sales price exceeding the maximum $250,000/$500,000 exclusion. So long as your allowable exclusion equals or exceeds your gain, the sale does not have to be reported, regardless of the sales price.

If you have any gain that cannot be excluded, or you decide not to claim the exclusion for excludable gain, you must report the entire gain on Schedule D. If some of the gain is excludable, the exclusion is entered as a loss, reducing the reported gain. For example, if you have a gain of $650,000 and qualify for the maximum $500,000 exclusion on a joint return, the details of the sale would be reported on Line 8 of Schedule D. Directly below the $650,000 gain shown in column (f) of Line 8, you would subtract the $500,000 exclusion as if it were a loss; label it "Section 121 exclusion."

Planning Reminder

Form 1099-S

The settlement agent responsible for closing the sale of your principal residence must report the sale to the IRS on Form 1099-S if the sales price exceeded $250,000, or $500,000 if you are married filing jointly. If the price was $250,000/$500,000 or less and you provide a written, signed certification that the full amount of your gain qualifies for the exclusion, the settlement agent may rely on the certification and not file the Form 1099-S or may choose to file the form anyway. IRS Revenue Procedure 2007-12 has a sample certification form.

29.1 Avoiding Tax on Sale of Principal Residence

If you sell (or exchange) your principal residence at a gain *(29.5)*, up to $250,000 of the gain may be excluded from income if you owned and occupied it as a principal residence for an aggregate of at least two years in the five-year period ending on the date of sale and did not claim an exclusion on another sale within the prior two years. *See* the discussion of the two-out-of-five-year ownership and use tests in the following section *(29.2)*. If you are married filing jointly, you may be able to exclude up to $500,000 of gain *(29.3)*. Even if you do not meet the two-out-of-five-year ownership and use tests, you are entitled to a reduced maximum exclusion limit if the primary reason for your sale was a change in the place of employment, health reasons, or unforeseen circumstances *(29.4)*.

Caution: If you use a residence as a vacation home or rental property after 2008, an allocable part of your gain may not qualify for the exclusion, even if you meet the two-out-of-five-year ownership and use tests *(29.2)*.

Frequency of exclusion. If you meet the ownership and use tests for a principal residence *(29.2)*, you may claim the exclusion when you sell it although you previously claimed the exclusion for another residence, provided that the sales are more than two years apart. If you claim the exclusion on a sale and within two years of the first sale you sell another principal residence, an exclusion may not be claimed on the second sale even if you meet the ownership and use tests for that residence. There is an exception if the second sale was due to a change in employment, health reasons, or unforeseen circumstances. In that case, a prorated exclusion limit is allowed *(29.4)*.

Principal residence. A principal residence is not restricted to one-family houses but includes a mobile home, trailer, houseboat, and condominium apartment used as a principal residence. An investment in a retirement community does not qualify as a principal residence unless you receive equity in the property. In the case of a tenant-stockholder of a cooperative housing corporation, the residence ownership requirement applies to the ownership of the stock and the use requirement applies to the house or apartment that the stockholder occupies *(29.2)*.

Multiple homes. If you have more than one home, you may exclude gain only on the sale of your principal residence and only if you meet the ownership and use tests *(29.2)* for that residence. Your "principal residence" is determined on a year-to-year basis, based primarily on where you live most of the time. However, the IRS may also consider such factors as the primary residence of your family members, your place of employment, mailing address, the address listed on your tax returns, driver's license and automobile and voter registration, and the location of your bank.

Vacant land. Vacant land owned and used as part of a taxpayer's principal residence may qualify for the exclusion. The vacant land must be adjacent to the residence and the sale of the residence must be within two years before or after the sale of the land. Qualifying sales of land and residence are treated as one sale, so the $250,000 exclusion limit ($500,000 for qualifying joint filers) applies to the combined sales. If the sales occur in different years, the exclusion limit applies first to the residence sale.

Business or rental use. If part of your home was rented out or used for business, *see* the rules for deducting a loss where a residence is converted to rental property *(29.7)*.

Home destroyed or condemned. If your home is destroyed or condemned, any gain realized on the conversion may qualify for the exclusion. Any part of the gain that may not be excluded (because it exceeds the limit) may be postponed under the rules explained in *18.19*.

Sale of remainder interest. You may choose to exclude gain from the sale of a remainder interest in your home. If you do, you may not choose to exclude gain from your sale of any other interest in the home that you sell separately. Also, you may not exclude gain from the sale of a remainder interest to a related party. Related parties include your brothers and sisters, half-brothers and half-sisters, spouse, ancestors (parents, grandparents, etc.), and lineal descendents (children, grandchildren, etc.). Related parties also include certain corporations, partnerships, trusts, and exempt organizations.

Expatriates. You may not claim the exclusion if Section 877(a)(1) of the Internal Revenue Code applies to you. That section applies to U.S. citizens who have renounced their citizenship (and long-term residents who have ended their residency) if one of their principal purposes was to avoid U.S. taxes.

The exclusion is not mandatory. You do not have to apply the exclusion to a particular qualifying sale. For example, you are unable to sell a residence when you acquire a new residence. When you finally are able to find a buyer for the first home, you also decide to sell the second residence. Assume both sales may qualify for the exclusion, but the potential gain on the first house will be less than the potential gain on the sale of the second home. You will not want to apply the exclusion to the sale of the first home if doing so will prevent you from applying the exclusion to the second sale because of the rule allowing an exclusion for only one sale every two years.

Federal subsidy recapture. If your home was financed with the proceeds of a tax-exempt bond or a qualified mortgage credit certificate *(15.1)* and you sell or dispose of the home within nine years of the financing, you may have to recapture the federal subsidy received. Use Form 8828 to figure the amount of the recapture tax, which is reported on Form 1040 as a separate tax.

29.2 Meeting the Ownership and Use Tests

To qualify for the up-to-$250,000 exclusion, you must have owned and occupied a home as your principal residence for at least two years during the five-year period ending on the date of sale. The periods of ownership and use do not have to be continuous. The ownership and use tests may be met in different two-year periods, provided both tests are met during the five-year period ending on the date of sale. You qualify if you can show that you owned the home and lived in it as your principal residence for 24 full months or for 730 days (365 × 2) during the five-year period ending on the date of sale. ***However***, some of the gain on a sale after 2008 might not be excludable, even if the two-out-of-five-year ownership and use tests are met, if you use the residence after 2008 as a second home or rental property; *see* the discussion of the new law at the end of this section.

If you or your spouse serve on qualified official extended duty as a member of the uniformed services, Foreign Service of the United States, intelligence community, or Peace Corps, you can suspend the five-year test period for the years of qualified service; *see* below.

If you are a joint owner of the residence and file a separate return, the up-to-$250,000 exclusions applies to your share of the gain, assuming you meet the ownership and use tests.

If you are married and file a joint return, you may claim an exclusion of up to $500,000 if one of you meets the ownership test and both of you meet the use test *(29.3)*.

If the ownership and use tests are *not* met but the primary reason for the sale was a change in the place of employment, health reasons, or unforeseen circumstances, an exclusion is allowed under the reduced maximum exclusion rules *(29.4)*.

In counting the period of ownership and use of a residence that you bought as a replacement residence under the prior law rollover rules, you may include the ownership and use of all the prior residences bought under the rollover rules.

Even if the ownership and use tests are met, the exclusion is not allowed for a sale if within the two-year period ending on the date of sale, you sold another principal residence for which you claimed the exclusion. However, a reduced exclusion limit may be available *(29.4)*.

EXAMPLES

1. From 2001 through August 2010, Janet lived with her parents in a house that her parents owned. In September 2010, she bought this house from her parents. She continued to live there until December 15, 2010, when she sold it at a gain. Although Janet lived in the home for more than two years, she did not own it for at least two years. She may not exclude any part of her gain on the sale, unless she sold because of a change in her place of employment, health reasons, or unforeseen circumstances *(29.4)*.
2. John bought and moved into a house in January 2008. He lived in it as his principal residence continuously until October 1, 2009, when he went abroad for a one-year sabbatical leave. On October 1, 2010, he sold the house. He does not meet the two-year use test. Because his leave was not a short, temporary absence, he may not include the period of leave in his period of use in order to meet the two-year use test. He may avoid tax on gain if he sold because of a changed job location unforeseen circumstances, or poor health *(29.4)*.
3. Since 1991, Jonah lived in an apartment building that was changed to a condominium. He bought the apartment on December 1, 2006. In February 2008, he became ill and on April 14 of that year he moved into his son's home. On July 12, 2010, while still living there, he sold the apartment.

Filing Tip

Short Absences

Short temporary absences for vacations count as time you used the residence.

Court Decision

No Exclusion for Newly Constructed Residence

If a new house is built on the site of a former residence, the period of use of the old house does not count towards meeting the two-year use test for the new house. A couple wanted to remodel their home but, because of building code and permit restrictions, decided to demolish the old house and build a new one on the site. Once the new house was completed, they sold it for $1.1 million, which resulted in a $600,000 gain. On their joint return, they excluded $500,000 of the gain from their income. They had lived in the demolished home for a number of years but never lived in the newly constructed home.

The Tax Court agreed with the IRS that they did not qualify for the exclusion. The exclusion applies only if the dwelling sold was actually used by the taxpayer as a principal residence for the required two-out-of-five years before the sale. In this case, while the demolished home was used as a principal residence for the requisite period, the newly built home was not.

He may exclude gain on the sale because he met the ownership and use tests. The five-year period is from July 12, 2005, to July 12, 2010, the date of the sale of the apartment. He owned the apartment from December 1, 2006, to July 10, 2010 (over two years). He lived in the apartment from July 12, 2005 (the beginning of the five-year period) to April 14, 2008, a period of use of over two years.

4. In 2000, Carol bought a house and lived in it until January 31, 2007, when she moved and put it up for rent. The house was rented from February 1, 2007, until May 31, 2010. Carol moved back into the house on June 1, 2010, and lived there until she sold it on September 30, 2010. During the five-year period ending on the date of the sale (October 1, 2005 – September 30, 2010), Carol lived in the house for less than two years.

Five-year period—	*Home use (months)—*	*Rental use (months)—*
10/1/05–1/31/07	16	
2/1/07–5/31/10		40
6/1/10–9/30/10	4	
Total	20	40

Carol may not exclude any of the gain on the sale, unless she sold the house for health or employment reasons or due to unforeseen circumstances *(29.4)*.

Court Decision

Co-Owner Can Claim Full $250,000 Exclusion

A single taxpayer who sells her home at a gain after owning and using it for at least two of the five years preceding the date of sale can exclude up to $250,000 of gain from income. What if there are two co-owners: do they have to split the $250,000 exclusion? Yes, argued the IRS in a 2010 case, the $250,000 exclusion has to be shared, but the Tax Court allowed a full exclusion. The taxpayer owned a 50% interest in a home she used as her principal residence since February 1997. When the home was sold in 2005, her share of the gain was $264,644.50 (half of the $529,289 total gain). She excluded $250,000 of her gain on her 2005 return, but the IRS said she was only entitled to half of the full exclusion, or $125,000.

The Tax Court allowed the full $250,000 exclusion. The statute (Code Section 121) does not limit the exclusion for partial owners of a principal residence. In fact, an example in the IRS regulations specifically allows unmarried joint owners holding 50% interests in a home to each exclude up to the full $250,000 limit for their shares of the gain on a sale.

Military and Foreign Service personnel, intelligence officers, and Peace Corps workers can suspend five-year period. You may elect to suspend the running of the five-year ownership and use period while you or your spouse is on qualified official extended duty as a member of the uniformed services or Foreign Service of the United States. The suspension can be for up to 10 years. It is allowed for only one residence at a time. By making the election and disregarding up to 10 years of qualifying service, you can claim an exclusion where the two-year use test is met before you began the qualifying service and after your return; *see* the Example below. Qualified official extended duty means active duty for over 90 days or for an indefinite period with a branch of the U.S. Armed Forces at a duty station at least 50 miles from your principal residence or in Government-mandated quarters. Members of the Foreign Service, commissioned corps of the National Oceanic and Atmospheric Administration, and commissioned corps of the Public Health Service who meet the active duty tests also qualify.

Similarly, the five-year testing period is suspended for up to 10 years for intelligence community employees (specified national agencies and departments) and Peace Corps workers. Intelligence community employees who sold their residence after 2006 and before June 18, 2008 could suspend the five-year period only for periods of qualified extended duty at a duty station located outside the United States. However, for sales after June 17, 2008, the suspension rule applies if the extended duty station is located inside as well as outside the United States. The suspension rule for Peace Corps workers applies to Peace Corps employees, enrolled volunteers, or volunteer leaders for periods during which they are on qualified official extended duty outside the United States.

Law Alert

Exclusion for Heirs, Estates, and Revocable Trusts of Individuals Dying After 2009

A new law may allow the heirs and estates of a homeowner who died after 2009 to exclude from income gain on the sale of the decedent's home. An heir or estate can exclude up to $250,000 of gain if the decedent owned and used the home for two or more years and the sale is within three years of his or her death, thereby satisfying the requirement that the two-out-of-five-year test *(29.2)* be met in the five-year period ending on the date of sale. The exclusion is also allowed on a sale of the home by a trust established by the decedent if immediately before his or her death the trust was a qualified revocable trust.

EXAMPLE

Michael bought a home in Maryland in 1998 that he lived in for three years before moving to Brazil in November 2001 as a member of the Foreign Service of the United States. He serves there on qualified official extended duty for eight years, until the end of 2009. In January 2010, he sells the Maryland home at a gain. He did not use the home as his principal residence for two out of the five years preceding the sale and so does not qualify for an exclusion under the regular rule. However, Michael can exclude gain of up to $250,000 by electing to suspend the running of the five-year test period while he was abroad with the Foreign Service. Under the election, his eight years of service are disregarded and his three years of use from 1998—2001 are considered to be within the five-year period preceding the sale. He thus meets the two-out-of-five-year test and can claim the exclusion.

Cooperative apartments. If you sell your stock in a cooperative housing corporation, you meet the ownership and use tests if, during the five-year period ending on the date of sale, you:

1. Owned stock for at least two years, *and*
2. Used the house or apartment that the stock entitles you to occupy as your principal residence for at least two years.

Incapacitated homeowner. A homeowner who becomes physically or mentally incapable of self-care is deemed to use a residence as a principal residence during the time in which the individual owns the residence and resides in a licensed care facility. For this rule to apply, the homeowner must have owned and used the residence as a principal residence for an aggregate period of at least one year during the five years preceding the sale.

If you meet this disability exception, you still have to meet the two-out-of-five-year ownership test to claim the exclusion.

Previous home destroyed or condemned. For the ownership and use tests, you may add time you owned and lived in a previous home that was destroyed or condemned if any part of the basis of the current home sold depended on the basis of the destroyed or condemned home under the involuntary conversion rules *(18.19)*.

Caution

Residence Acquired in Like-Kind Exchange

A residence acquired in a like-kind exchange must be owned for at least five years before gain on its sale can qualify for the exclusion.

No Exclusion for Nonqualified Use After 2008

Even if the two-out-of-five-year test for an exclusion is met, gain attributable to "nonqualified" use after 2008 will not be eligible for the exclusion on a later sale. The primary intent of the rule is apparently to deny an exclusion for some of the gain realized by taxpayers who convert a vacation home or rented residence to their principal residence and live in it for a few years before selling. However, the law as written is broader, treating any period in 2009 or later for which the home is not used as a principal residence by you, your spouse, or former spouse as "nonqualified use." Nevertheless, given the post-2008 effective date and the exceptions to the nonqualified rule (particularly exception 1 shown below), the nonqualified rule is unlikely to apply for at least several years.

Exceptions to nonqualified use. There are exceptions that limit the impact of the nonqualified use rule. The law specifically exempts the following from the definition of post-2008 "nonqualified use": (1) the period after you or your spouse have moved out of the home, so long as it is within the five years ending on the date of sale, (2) temporary absences from the residence, not to exceed two years in total, due to a change in employment, health reasons (such as time in a hospital or nursing home), or other unforeseen circumstances to be specified by the IRS, and (3) periods of up to 10 years (in aggregate) during which you or your spouse are on qualified official extended duty (duty station at least 50 miles from residence) as a member of the uniformed services, as a Foreign Service officer, or as an employee of the intelligence community.

The IRS has not yet released guidelines on determining "nonqualified use," including any other possible exceptions. For example, it is not clear if home office use *(29.7)* after 2008 will be treated as nonqualified use, or whether short rental periods will be disregarded.

Figuring the excludable gain. To figure the exclusion on a sale where there is nonqualified use after 2008, the gain equal to post-May 6, 1997 depreciation is taken into account first. No exclusion is allowed for this depreciation amount; this is a long-standing rule is note changed by the nonqualified use calculation. *(29.7)*.

The portion of the remaining gain that is allocable to nonqualified use will not be eligible for the exclusion. The allocation is made by multiplying the gain by the following fraction:

$$\frac{\text{Total periods of nonqualified use after 2008}}{\text{Total period of ownership of the home}}$$

Here is an example from the Joint Committee on Taxation showing how the nonqualified use rule reduces the amount of gain that can be excluded: An individual buys a home on January 1, 2009, for $400,000, and uses it as rental property for two years, claiming $20,000 of depreciation deductions. On January 1, 2011, he converts the property to his principal residence. On January 1, 2013, he moves out and he sells the home for $700,000 on January 1, 2014. Gain on the sale is $320,000 ($700,000 – $380,000 basis ($400,000 – $20,000 depreciation)). The $20,000 of depreciation is recaptured as income, as under prior law. Of the remaining $300,000 gain, 40% is attributable to a nonqualified use; during the five years that the home was owned, it was used as rental property for two years ($^2/_5$ = 40%). Thus, $120,000 of the gain (40% × $300,000) does not qualify for the exclusion and is taxable. The $180,000 balance of the gain ($300,000 – $120,000 allocated to nonqualified use) is excluded from income, as it is less than the $250,000 exclusion limit.

Note that in the above example, the effect of the nonqualified use rule is to reduce the excludable gain by $70,000. Under the allocation formula, $120,000 of the $300,000 gain (after depreciation taken into account) is taxable, but the $50,000 of gain over the $250,000 exclusion limit ($300,000 – $250,000) would have been taxable even without the new law.

29.3 Home Sales by Married Persons

Where a married couple owned and lived in their principal residence for at least two years during the five-year period ending on the date of sale, they may claim an exclusion of up to $500,000 of gain on a joint return. Under the law, the up-to-$500,000 exclusion may be claimed on a joint return provided that during the five-year period ending on the date of sale: (1) *either* spouse owned the residence for at least two years, (2) *both* spouses lived in the house as *their* principal residence for at least two years, and (3) *neither* spouse is ineligible to claim the exclusion because an exclusion was previously claimed on a sale of a principal residence within the two-year period ending on the date of this sale. If Tests 1 and 3 are met but only one of you meets Test 2, your exclusion limit on a joint return is $250,000. However, even if the two-out-of-five-year use test is met, "nonqualified use" after 2008 may limit the exclusion you can claim; *see 29.2*.

Caution

Exclusion for Married Couple

For a recently married couple, the exclusion limit on a joint return is $250,000, not $500,000, where only one of the spouses has satisfied the ownership and use tests before a sale. Gain in excess of the $250,000 exclusion is reported on Schedule D.

EXAMPLES

1. You and your wife owned and occupied your principal residence for 10 years. In December 2010, you sell the house for a gain of $450,000. If you file jointly, none of the gain is taxable as the up-to-$500,000 exclusion applies.
2. As a widower, you used and owned your principal residence from June 2006 through the end of 2009. In January 2010 you remarried and you and your wife lived in the house for nine months. In October 2010, you sold the house and realized a gain of $350,000. You may claim an exclusion of $250,000 on your joint return; the balance of $100,000 is taxable. You meet the exclusion tests, but your wife does not. Thus, the exclusion is limited to $250,000.

Death of spouse before sale. If your spouse died before the date of sale, you are considered to have owned and used the property during any period of time when your spouse owned and used it as a principal home. This rule can enable you to satisfy the two-out-of-five-year ownership and use tests.

If you and your spouse met the ownership and use tests as of the date of your spouse's death, and you sell the residence in the year he or she dies, you may use the $500,000 exclusion limit, assuming you file a joint return for the year of your spouse's death. You are also entitled to use the $500,000 exclusion limit on a sale after 2007 that is within two years of your spouse's death, provided you and your spouse would have qualified for the $500,000 limit on a sale immediately before his or her death under Tests 1–3 at the beginning of this section.

Divorce. If a residence is transferred to a taxpayer incident to divorce, the time during which the taxpayer's spouse or former spouse owned the residence is added to the taxpayer's period of ownership. If pursuant to a divorce or separation a taxpayer moves out of a home that he or she owns or jointly owns with the other spouse (or former spouse), the taxpayer who has moved out is treated as having used the home for any period that he/she retains an ownership interest in the residence while the other spouse or former spouse continues to use it as a principal residence under the terms of the divorce or separation agreement.

Separate residences. Where a husband and wife own and live in separate residences, each spouse is entitled to a separate exclusion limit of $250,000 on the sale of his or her residence. If both residences are sold in the same year and each spouse met the ownership and use test for his or her separate residence, two exclusions may be claimed (up to $250,000 each), either on a joint return or on separate returns.

29.4 Reduced Maximum Exclusion

Generally, no exclusion is allowed on a sale of a principal residence if you owned or used the home for less than two of the five years preceding the sale *(29.2)*. Similarly, an exclusion is generally disallowed if within the two-year period ending on the date of sale, you sold another home at a gain that was wholly or partially excluded from your income.

However, even if a sale of a principal residence is made before meeting the ownership and use tests or it is within two years of a prior sale for which an exclusion was claimed, an exclusion is available if the primary reason for the sale is: (1) a change in the place of employment, (2) health, or (3) unforeseen circumstances. If the sale is for one of these qualifying reasons, you are entitled to a prorated portion of the regular $250,000 or $500,000 exclusion limit. The employment change, health problem, or unforeseen circumstance can be attributable to you or another "qualified individual," as defined below.

You automatically qualify for the reduced exclusion if your sale is within a safe harbor established by the IRS. If a safe harbor is not available, you may qualify by showing that the "facts and circumstances" of your situation establish that the primary reason for the sale was a change in the place of employment, health problem or unforeseen circumstances.

When you fall within a safe harbor or meet the primary reason test, you are allowed an allocable percentage of the regular $250,000 or $500,000 exclusion limit, depending on how much of the regular two-year ownership and use test was satisfied, or the time between this sale and a sale within the prior two years. For example, if you owned and lived in your home for 438 days before selling it to take a new job, you are entitled to 60% of the regular exclusion limit, which is based on 730 qualifying days ($^{438}/_{730}$ = 60%). Use Worksheet 29-1 to figure your reduced exclusion limit. Although the maximum exclusion is reduced, this may not disadvantage you. If the reduced exclusion limit equals or exceeds your gain, none of your gain is subject to tax.

IRS Alert

Amended Return to Claim Reduced Maximum Exclusion

If you reported gain on a sale that can be avoided under the reduced maximum exclusion rules for sales due to a change in place of employment, health, or unforeseen circumstances, a refund claim can be made on an amended return, provided the prior year is not closed by the statute of limitations *(47.2)*.

Qualified individual. In addition to yourself, the following persons are considered qualified individuals for purposes of qualifying for the reduced maximum exclusion: your spouse, a co-owner of the residence, or any person whose main home was your principal residence.

For purposes of the "health reasons" category, qualified individuals include not only the above individuals but also their family members: parents or step-parents, grandparents, children, stepchildren, adopted children, grandchildren, siblings (including step- or half-siblings), in-laws (mother/father, brother/sister, son/daughter), uncles, aunts, nephews, or nieces.

EXAMPLE

You bought and moved into your residence on April 1, 2009. In 2010, you move to a new job location in another state and sell your house at a gain of $50,000 on March 31, 2010. Since you owned and used your home for 365 days, your exclusion limit is reduced by 50%. You are single. Your reduced exclusion limit is $125,000 (50% of $250,000) and since the gain of $50,000 is totally covered by the exclusion it is not taxable.

Sale due to change in place of employment. The reduced exclusion limit applies if the primary reason for your sale is a change in the location of a qualified individual's employment; *see* the above definition of qualified individual. "Employment" includes working for the same employer at a different location or starting with a new employer. It also includes the commencement of self-employment or the continuation of self-employment at a new location.

The IRS provides a safe harbor based on distance. If a qualified individual's new place of employment is at least 50 miles farther from the sold home than the old place of employment was, the reduced exclusion limit is allowed so long as the change in employment occurred while you owned and used the home as your principal residence. If an unemployed qualified person obtains employment, the safe harbor applies if the sold home is at least 50 miles from the place of employment.

If the 50-mile safe harbor cannot be met, the facts and circumstances may indicate that a change in the place of employment was the primary reason for the sale, thereby allowing the reduced exclusion limit.

EXAMPLE

An emergency room physician buys a condominium in March 2009 that is five miles from the hospital where she works. In November 2010, she takes a new job at a hospital 51 miles away from her home. She sells her home in December 2010 and buys a townhouse that is four miles away from the new hospital. The sale does not qualify for the 50-mile safe harbor since the new hospital is only 46 miles further from the old home than the first hospital was. However, given the doctor's need to work unscheduled hours and to get to work quickly, the IRS allows the reduced exclusion limit; the facts show that her change in place of employment was the primary reason for the home sale.

Sale due to health problems. The reduced exclusion limit applies if a principal residence is sold primarily to obtain or facilitate the diagnosis, treatment, or mitigation of a qualified person's disease, illness or injury, or to obtain or provide medical or personal care for a qualified individual suffering from a disease, illness, or injury. A sale does not qualify if it is merely to improve general health. Note that for "health sales," the definition of qualified individual is broadened to include family members; *see* above.

A physician's recommendation of a change in residence for health reasons automatically qualifies under an IRS safe harbor.

EXAMPLES

1. One year after purchasing a home in Michigan, Smith is told by his doctor that moving to a warm, dry climate would mitigate his chronic asthma symptoms. Smith takes the advice, selling the house and moving to Arizona. The sale is within the doctor recommendation safe harbor and Smith may claim a reduced maximum exclusion for gain on the sale of the Michigan home.
2. In 2010, Mike and Kathy Anderson sell the house they bought in 2009 so they can move in with Kathy's father, who is chronically ill and unable to care for himself. The IRS allows the Andersons to claim a reduced maximum exclusion, as the primary reason for the sale is to provide care for Kathy's father, a qualified individual.

Sale due to unforeseen circumstances. A sale of a principal residence due to any of the following events fits within an IRS safe harbor for unforeseen circumstances and automatically qualifies for a reduced maximum exclusion:

(1) The involuntary conversion of the home;

(2) Damage to the residence from a natural or man-made disaster, war, or act of terrorism;

(3) Any of the following events involving a qualified individual (*see* above): death, divorce, or legal separation, becoming eligible for unemployment compensation, or change in employment or self-employment status that left the homeowner unable to pay housing costs and reasonable basic household expenses, or multiple births resulting from the same pregnancy.

Worksheet 29-1 Reduced Maximum Exclusion

Caution: *Complete this worksheet only if you qualify for a reduced maximum exclusion (under the rules at 29.4). Complete column (a).*			(a) **You**	(b) **Your Spouse**
1.	Maximum amount	**1.**	$250,000	$250,000
2a.	Enter the number of days (or months) that you used the property as a main home during the 5-year period* ending on the date of sale	**2a.**		
b.	Enter the number of days (or months) that you owned the property during the 5-year period* ending on the date of sale. If you used days on line 2a, you also must use days on this line and on lines 3 and 5. If you used months on line 2a, you also must use months on this line and on lines 3 and 5. (If married filing jointly and one spouse owned the property longer than the other spouse, both spouses are treated as owning the property for the longer period.)	**b.**		
c.	Enter the smaller of line 2a or 2b	**c.**		
3.	Have you (or your spouse, if filing jointly) excluded gain from the sale of another home during the 2-year period ending on the date of this sale? ☐ **No.** Skip line 3 and enter the number of days (or months) from line 2c on line 4. ☐ **Yes.** Enter the number of days (or months) between the date of the most recent sale of another home on which you excluded gain and the date of sale of this home	**3.**		
4.	Enter the smaller of line 2c or 3	**4.**		
5.	Divide the amount on line 4 by 730 days (or 24 months). Enter the result as a decimal (rounded to at least 3 places). But do not enter an amount greater than 1.000	**5.**		
6.	Multiply the amount on line 1 by the decimal amount on line 5	**6.**		
7.	**Reduced maximum exclusion.** Add the amounts in columns (a) and (b) of line 6. Enter it here and on Worksheet 29-3, Line 13	**7.**		

***If you were a member of the uniformed services or Foreign Service, an employee of the intelligence community, or an employee or volunteer of the Peace Corps during the time you owned the home, see 29.2 to determine your 5-year period.**

The IRS may expand the list of safe harbors in generally applicable revenue rulings or in private rulings requested by individual taxpayers.

Sales not covered by a safe harbor can qualify if the facts and circumstances indicate that the home was sold primarily because of an event that could not have been reasonably anticipated before the residence was purchased and occupied. The IRS in private letter rulings has been quite liberal in allowing the reduced maximum exclusion for unforeseen sales. However, an improvement in financial circumstances does *not* qualify under IRS regulations, even if the improvement is the result of unforeseen events, such as receiving a promotion and a large salary increase that would allow the purchase of a bigger home.

EXAMPLES

1. Three months after Jones buys a condominium as his principal residence, the condominium association replaces the roof and heating system and a few months later the monthly condominium fees are doubled. If Jones sells the condo because he cannot pay the higher fees and his monthly mortgage payment, the sale is considered to be due to unforeseen circumstances and Jones may claim a reduced maximum exclusion.
2. Tom and his fiancée, Alice, buy a house and live in it as their principal residence. The next year they break up and Tom moves out. The house is sold because Alice cannot afford to make the monthly payments alone. According to the IRS, the sale is due to unforeseen circumstances and Alice and Tom may each claim a reduced maximum exclusion.
3. A married couple purchased a home in a retirement community that had minimum age requirements for residents. Shortly after they moved in, their daughter lost her job and was in the process of getting a divorce. The daughter and her child wanted to move in but could not because of the community's age requirements. The couple sold the home and bought a new one in which their daughter and grandchild lived while the daughter looked for full-time employment. The IRS privately ruled that the sale of the retirement community home was due to unforeseen circumstances and the reduced maximum exclusion could be claimed.
4. A single mother bought a home and lived in it with her two daughters as their principal residence. One of the daughters was subjected to unruly behavior, verbal abuse, and sexual assault on the school bus. As a result, the daughter suffered from persistent fear and her school performance seriously declined. Her behavior was noticed by the school and brought to the mother's attention. She tried to work with the school district to resolve the problem, but when attempts failed, she sold her home and moved. The mother had not owned the home for two full years and asked the IRS whether she qualified for a partial exclusion. The IRS said yes. The primary reason for the sale prior to satisfying the two-year test was an unforeseen circumstance—the extreme bullying suffered by her daughter. Therefore, she can prorate the home sale exclusion for the part of the two years that she owned and lived in the home.

29.5 Figuring Gain or Loss

To figure the gain or loss on the sale of your principal residence, you must determine the *selling price*, the amount realized, and the *adjusted basis*. Worksheet 29-3 may be used to figure gain or loss on the sale of a principal residence.

Gain or loss. The difference between the amount realized and adjusted basis is your gain or loss. If the amount realized exceeds the adjusted basis, the difference is a gain that may be excluded *(29.1)*. If amount realized is less than adjusted basis, the difference is a loss. A loss on the sale of your main home may not be deducted *(29.8)*.

Foreclosure or repossession. If your home was foreclosed on or repossessed, you have a sale. *See Chapter 31*.

Selling price. This is the total amount received for your home. It includes money, all notes, mortgages, or other debts assumed by the buyer as part of the sale, and the fair market value of

Filing Tip

Form 1099-S

If you received Form 1099-S, Box 2 should show the gross proceeds from the sale of your home. However, Box 2 does not include the fair market value of any property other than cash or notes, or any services you received or will receive. For these, Box 4 will be checked. If the sales price of your home does not exceed $250,000 or $500,000 (if filing jointly) and you certify to the person responsible for closing the sale that your entire gain is excludable from your gross income, that person does not have to report the sale on Form 1099-S, but may choose to do so.

any other property or any services received. The selling price does not include receipts for personal property sold with your home. Personal property is property that is not a permanent part of the home, such as furniture, draperies, and lawn equipment.

If your employer pays you for a loss on the sale or for your selling expenses, do not include the payment as part of the selling price. Include the payment as wages on Line 7 of Form 1040. (Your employer includes the payment with the rest of your wages in Box 1 of your Form W-2.)

If you grant an option to buy your home and the option is exercised, add the amount received for the option to the selling price of your home. If the option is not exercised, you report the amount as ordinary income in the year the option expires. Report the amount on Line 21 of Form 1040.

Filing Tip

Jointly Owned Home

If you and your spouse sell your jointly owned home and file a joint return, you figure your gain or loss as one taxpayer. If you file separate returns, each of you must figure your own gain or loss according to your ownership interest in the home. Your ownership interest is determined by state law.

If you and a joint owner other than your spouse sell your jointly owned home, each of you must figure your own gain or loss according to your ownership interest in the home.

Amount realized. This is the selling price minus selling expenses, including commissions, advertising fees, legal fees, and loan charges paid by the seller (e.g., loan placement fees or "points").

Adjusted basis. This is the cost basis of your home increased by the cost of improvements and decreased by deducted casualty losses, if any *(29.6)*. Cost basis is generally what you paid for the residence. If you obtained possession through other means, such as a gift or inheritance, *see* the special basis rules for gifts and inheritances *(5.17)*.

Seller-paid points. If the person who sold you your residence paid points on your loan, you may have to reduce your basis in the home by the amount of the points. If you bought your residence after 1990 but before April 4, 1994, you reduce basis by the points only if you chose to deduct them as home mortgage interest in the year paid. If you bought the residence after April 3, 1994, you reduce basis by the points even if you did not deduct the points.

Settlement fees or closing costs. When buying your home, you may have to pay settlement fees or closing costs in addition to the contract price of the property. You may include in basis fees and closing costs that are for buying the home. You may not include in your basis the fees and costs of getting a mortgage loan. Settlement fees also do not include amounts placed in escrow for the future payment of items such as taxes and insurance.

Examples of the settlement fees or closing costs that you may include in the basis of your property are: (1) abstract fees (sometimes called abstract of title fees), (2) charges for installing utility services, (3) legal fees (including fees for the title search and preparing the sales contract and deed), (4) recording fees, (5) survey fees, (6) transfer taxes, (7) owner's title insurance, and (8) any amounts the seller owes that you agree to pay, such as certain real estate taxes, back interest, recording or mortgage fees, charges for improvements or repairs, and sales commissions.

Caution

Repairs

These maintain your home in good condition but do not add to its value or prolong its life. You do not add their cost to the basis of your property. Examples of repairs include repainting your house inside or outside, fixing gutters or floors, repairing leaks or plastering, and replacing broken window panes. Repairs tied to an improvement project may be capital improvements *(19.3)*.

Examples of settlement fees and closing costs *not* included in your basis are: (1) fire insurance premiums, (2) rent for occupancy of the home before closing, (3) charges for utilities or other services relating to occupancy of the home before closing, (4) any fee or cost that you deducted as a moving expense before 1994, (5) charges connected with getting a mortgage loan, such as mortgage insurance premiums (including VA funding fees), loan assumption fees, cost of a credit report, and fee for an appraisal required by a lender, and (6) fees for refinancing a mortgage.

Construction. If you contracted to have your residence built on land you own, your basis is the cost of the land plus the cost of building the home, including the cost of labor and materials, payments to a contractor, architect's fees, building permit charges, utility meter and connection charges, and legal fees directly connected with building the home.

Cooperative apartment. Your basis in the apartment is usually the cost of your stock in the co-op housing corporation, which may include your share of a mortgage on the apartment building.

29.6 Figuring Adjusted Basis

Adjusted basis in your home is cost basis *(29.5)* adjusted for items discussed below. *Worksheet 29-2* may be used to figure adjusted basis.

Increases to cost basis include: improvements with a useful life of more than one year, special assessments for local improvements, and amounts spent after a casualty to restore damaged property.

Decreases to cost basis include: gain you postponed from the sale of a previous home before May 7, 1997, deductible casualty losses not covered by insurance, insurance payments you received or expect to receive for casualty losses, payments you received for granting an easement or right-of-way, depreciation allowed or allowable if you used your home for business or rental purposes, any allowable tax credit after 2005 for a home energy improvement *(25.21)* that increases the basis of the home, residential energy credit (generally allowed from 1977 through 1987) claimed for the cost of energy improvements added to the basis of your home, adoption credit you claimed for improvements added to the basis of your home, nontaxable payments from an adoption assistance program of your employer that you used for improvements added to the basis of your home, first-time homebuyers credit (allowed to certain first-time buyers of a home in the District of Columbia), and an energy conservation subsidy excluded from your gross income because you received it (directly or indirectly) from a public utility after 1992 to buy or install any energy conservation measure. An an energy conservation measure is an installation or modification that is primarily designed either to reduce consumption of electricity or natural gas or to improve the management of energy demand for a home.

Improvements. Improvements add to the value of your home, prolong its useful life, or adapt it to new uses. You add the cost of improvements to the basis of your property.

Examples of improvements include: bedroom, bathroom, deck, garage, porch, and patio additions, landscaping, paving driveway, walkway, fencing, retaining wall, sprinkler system, swimming pool, storm windows and doors, new roof, wiring upgrades, satellite dish, security system, heating system, central air conditioning, furnace, duct work, central humidifier, filtration system, septic system, water heater, soft water system, built-in appliances, kitchen modernization, flooring, wall-to-wall carpeting, attic, walls, and pipes.

Adjusted basis does not include the cost of any improvements that are no longer part of the home.

EXAMPLE

You installed wall-to-wall carpeting in your home 15 years ago. In 2010, you replace that carpeting with new wall-to-wall carpeting. The cost of the old carpeting is no longer part of adjusted basis.

Record-keeping. Ordinarily, you must keep records for three years after the due date for filing your return for the tax year in which you sold your home. But you should keep home records as long as they are needed for tax purposes to prove adjusted basis. These include: (1) proof of the home's purchase price and purchase expenses, (2) receipts and other records for all improvements, additions, and other items that affect the home's adjusted basis, (3) any worksheets you used to figure the adjusted basis of the home you sold, the gain or loss on the sale, the exclusion, and the taxable gain, and (4) any Form 2119 that you filed to postpone gain from a home sale before May 7, 1997.

29.7 Personal and Business Use of a Home

If in 2010 you sold a home that was used for business or rental as well as residential purposes, you may be able to exclude part or all of any gain realized on the sale. The excludable amount depends on whether the non-residential and residential areas were part of the same dwelling unit, whether the ownership and use tests *(29.2)* were met, whether depreciation was allowable after May 6, 1997, and whether the non-residential use was before 2009 or after 2008.

Nonqualified use after 2008. Gain allocable to "nonqualified" use after 2008 is not excludable from income *(29.2)* even if the two-out-of-five-year test for that part of the property is met. The IRS has not yet indicated whether home office use after 2008 is considered nonqualified use. If, under the following rules, gain on the sale of a residence is allocable to a business or rental area separate from your dwelling unit and there was business or rental use after 2008, gain allocable to the post-2008 business/rental use will be considered "nonqualified use" and not eligible for an exclusion. However, there is an exception for business/rental use that occurs after you (and your spouse) have moved out if it occurs within the five-year period ending on the date of sale (exception 1, *29.2*).

Home office within your principal residence. The IRS takes the position that gain does not have to be allocated between the residential and business use portions of your home where both are within the same dwelling unit. This rule allows a home office to be considered residential property for purposes of the home sale exclusion. If the two-out-of-five-year ownership and use test *(29.2)* is met for the residential portion, you are also treated as meeting the two-year residential use test for the home office even if you used the area as a business office for your entire period of ownership. As a result, the gain on the entire residence is eligible for the exclusion, except for the gain equal to depreciation for periods after May 6, 1997. The gain equal to post–May 6, 1997, depreciation is never excludable; it must be reported on Schedule D (Form 1040) as unrecaptured Section 1250 gain *(5.3)*.

Planning Reminder

Gains Postponed Under Prior Law Rules

Gain on a previous home sale that you postponed under the prior law rollover rules reduces the basis of your current home if your current home was a qualifying replacement residence for the previous home. Postponed gains on several earlier sales may have to be taken into account under the basis reduction rule. The basis reduction will increase the gain on the sale of your current home.

Law Alert

Nonqualified Use After 2008 May Limit Exclusion

With certain exceptions, any period after 2008 that a home is not used as your principal residence is considered a period of "nonqualified use," and gain allocable to the nonqualified use is taxable, even if the two-year residential use test for an exclusion is otherwise met *(29.2)*.

Worksheet 29-2 Adjusted Basis of Home Sold

Caution: *See 29.6 before you use this worksheet.*

1.	Enter the purchase price of the home sold. (If you filed Form 2119 when you originally acquired that home to postpone gain on the sale of a previous home before May 7, 1997, enter the adjusted basis of the new home from that Form 2119.)			**1.** ______
2.	Seller-paid points for home bought after 1990 (see 29.5). Do not include any seller-paid points you already subtracted to arrive at the amount entered on line 1			**2.** ______
3.	Subtract line 2 from line 1			**3.** ______
4.	Settlement fees or closing costs (see 29.5). If line 1 includes the adjusted basis of the new home from Form 2119, skip lines 4a–4g and 5; go to line 6.			
	a.	Abstract and recording fees	**4a.** ______	
	b.	Legal fees (including fees for title search and preparing documents)	**4b.** ______	
	c.	Survey fees	**4c.** ______	
	d.	Title insurance	**4d.** ______	
	e.	Transfer or stamp taxes	**4e.** ______	
	f.	Amounts that the seller owed that you agreed to pay (back taxes or interest, recording or mortgage fees, and sales commissions)	**4f.** ______	
	g.	Other	**4g.** ______	
5.	Add lines 4a through 4g			**5.** ______
6.	Cost of additions and improvements. Do not include any additions and improvements included on line 1			**6.** ______
7.	Special tax assessments paid for local improvements, such as streets and sidewalks			**7.** ______
8.	Other increases to basis			**8.** ______
9.	Add lines 3, 5, 6, 7, and 8			**9.** ______
10.	Depreciation allowed or allowable, related to the business use or rental of the home		**10.** ______	
11.	Other decreases to basis (see 29.6)		**11.** ______	
12.	Add lines 10 and 11			**12.** ______
13.	**Adjusted basis of home sold**. Subtract line 12 from line 9. Enter here and on Worksheet 29-3, line 4			**13.** ______

Worksheet 29-3 Gain (or Loss), Exclusion, and Taxable Gain

Part 1. Gain or (Loss) on Sale

1.	Selling price of home	**1.** ______
2.	Selling expenses (including commissions, advertising and legal fees, and seller-paid loan charges)	**2.** ______
3.	Subtract line 2 from line 1. This is the amount realized	**3.** ______
4.	Adjusted basis of home sold (from Worksheet 29-2, line 13)	**4.** ______
5.	**Gain or (loss)** on the sale. Subtract line 4 from line 3. If this is a loss, stop here	**5.** ______

Part 2. Exclusion and Taxable Gain

6.	Enter any depreciation allowed or allowable on the property for periods after May 6, 1997. If none, enter -0-	**6.** ______
7.	Subtract line 6 from line 5. If the result is less than zero, enter -0-	**7.** ______
8.	Aggregate number of days of nonqualified use after 12/31/2008	**8.** ______
9.	Number of days taxpayer owned the property	**9.** ______
10.	Divide the amount on line 8 by the amount on line 9. Enter the result as a decimal (rounded to at least 3 places). But do not enter an amount greater than 1.00	**10.** ______
11.	Gain allocated to nonqualified use. (Line 7 multiplied by line 10)	**11.** ______
12.	Gain eligible for exclusion. Subtract line 11 from line 7.	**12.** ______
13.	If you qualify to exclude gain on the sale, enter your maximum exclusion (see 29.2 – 29.4). If you qualify for a reduced maximum exclusion, enter the amount from Worksheet 29-1, line 7. If you do not qualify to exclude gain, enter -0-	**13.** ______
14.	**Exclusion**. Enter the smaller of line 12 or line 13	**14.** ______
15.	**Taxable gain**. Subtract line 14 from line 5. Report your taxable gain on Line 1 or 8 of Schedule D depending on how long you owned the residence. The exclusion from Line 14 above is entered on the Schedule D line directly below the line on which the gain is reported; label it "Section121 exclusion" and enter it as a loss in column (f). Use Form 6252 if reporting the gain on the installment sale method (5.21); enter the exclusion from Line 14 above on Line 15 of Form 6252.	**15.** ______
16.	Enter the **smaller** of line 6 or line 15. Enter this amount on line 12 of the Unrecaptured Section 1250 Gain Worksheet in the instructions for Schedule D (Form 1040)	**16.** ______

The IRS has not given any indication that its favorable position for home offices has been adversely affected by the rule barring an exclusion for post-2008 nonqualified use *(29.2)*. If a home office were considered nonqualified use, gain allocable to the period of home office use (after 2008) would not be excludable from income, but the IRS had not adopted this position as of the time this book went to press. *See* the *e-Supplement* at *jklasser.com* and IRS Publication 523 for an update, if any.

EXAMPLE

1. Alice buys a house in 2005 and uses part of it as a law office until mid-2008. Depreciation deductions for the office space totaling $2,000 are claimed for 2005 through 2008. The home is sold in 2010. Assume that gain on the sale is $13,000. Since the office and residential area were in the same dwelling unit, Alice does not have to allocate gain to the office. She may exclude $11,000 of the $13,000 gain from her 2010 income. The $2,000 of gain equal to depreciation cannot be excluded. Alice reports her $13,000 gain on Line 8 of Schedule D (long-term gains and losses) and just below it, the $11,000 exclusion is shown as a loss. The $2,000 gain attributable to the depreciation is unrecaptured Section 1250 gain, which Alice enters on the Unrecaptured Section 1250 Gain Worksheet in the Schedule D instructions *(5.3)*.

Depreciation allowed or allowable. Under IRS rules, you must reduce your basis *(29.6)* in the home for purposes of figuring gain on a sale by any depreciation you were entitled to deduct, even if you did not deduct it. Furthermore, you cannot exclude the gain equal to the depreciation allowed or allowable for periods after May 6, 1997. This means that if you were entitled to take depreciation deductions for periods after May 6, 1997, but did not do so, the gain equal to the allowable depreciation is generally not excludable. However, if you have records showing that you claimed less depreciation than was allowable, the IRS will reduce the excludable gain only by the claimed (allowed) depreciation.

Business or rental area separate from your dwelling unit. If you sell property that was partly your home and partly business or rental property separate from your dwelling unit, and the business/rental use of the separate part exceeded three years during the five years before the sale, the gain allocable to the separate part is not eligible for an exclusion (since the two-year use test *(29.2)* has not been met) and must be reported as taxable income on Form 4797. This could be the case if you lived in one apartment and rented out other apartments in the same building, you rented out an unattached garage or building elsewhere on your property, your apartment was upstairs from your business, you operated a business from a barn or other structure separate from your business, or your home was located on a working farm. *See* IRS Publication 523 for reporting details.

29.8 No Loss Allowed on Personal Residence

A loss on the sale of your principal residence is not deductible. If part of your principal residence was used for business in the year of sale, treat the sale as if two pieces of property were sold. Report the business part on Form 4797. A loss is deductible only on the business part.

Second home or vacation home. If you sell at a loss a second home or vacation home (not your principal residence) that was used entirely for personal purposes, you report the loss transaction on Schedule D, even though the loss is not deductible. Instead of entering the loss amount in column (f) of Schedule D, enter "0." If in the year of sale part of the home was rented out or used for business, allocate the sale between the personal part and the rental or business part; report the personal part on Schedule D and the rental or business part on Form 4797.

29.9 Loss on Residence Converted to Rental Property

You are not allowed to deduct a loss on the sale of your personal residence. If you convert the house from personal use to rental use you may claim a loss on a sale if the value has declined below the basis fixed for the residence as rental property.

To determine if you have a loss for tax purposes, you need to know the conversion date basis. This is the *lower* of (1) your adjusted basis *(29.6)* for the house at the time of conversion or (2) the fair market value at the time of conversion. *Add* to the lower amount the cost of capital improvements made after the conversion, and *subtract* depreciation and casualty loss deductions claimed

Filing Tip

Loss Allowed

If you sell a house that has been converted from personal to rental use, and the sales price is less than the conversion date basis, a loss on the sale is deductible *(29.9)*.

after the conversion. To deduct a loss, you have to be able to show that this basis exceeds the sales price. For example, if you paid $200,000 for your home and convert it to rental property when the value has declined to $150,000, your conversion date basis for the rental property is $150,000. If the property continues to decline in value, and you sell for $125,000 after having deducted $10,000 for depreciation, you may claim a loss of $15,000 ($140,000 – $125,000). Your loss deduction will not reflect the $50,000 loss occurring before the conversion.

EXAMPLE

In 1988, Adams bought a house in Fort Worth, Texas. He paid $124,000, put in capital improvements, and lived there until he was forced to put it on the market when he lost his job. In 1989, he listed the house with a broker for $145,000. After receiving no offers, he decided to lease the house through 1990. By October of 1990 Adams owed $4,551 in property taxes and was three months behind on his mortgage payments. Fearing foreclosure, he sold the house for $130,000.

For purposes of figuring a loss, Adams assumed that the fair market value at the time of conversion was equal to the $145,000 list price. The adjusted basis of the house was $141,026. As this was less than the estimated fair market value of $145,000, he used the $141,026 adjusted basis to figure a loss of $11,026 ($130,000 – $141,026). The IRS claimed the fair market value at the time of conversion was equal to the actual sale price of $130,000. Since basis for the converted property is the lesser of fair market value ($130,000) or adjusted basis ($141,026), Adams had no loss on the sale.

However, the Tax Court allowed a $5,000 loss by fixing the fair market value at the time of conversion at $135,000. It held that Adams sold at a lower price because of his weak financial position of which the buyer took advantage. The court figured the $135,000 as follows: $129,000 fair market value in 1988 (based on an appraisal report, which both parties agree was correct), plus $6,000 of appreciation attributable to the capital improvements made to the property after it was converted.

Caution

Temporary Rental Before Sale

A rental loss may be barred on a temporary rental before sale. The IRS and Tax Court held that where a principal residence was rented for several months while being offered for sale, the rental did not convert the home to rental property. Deductions for rental expenses were limited to rental income; no loss could be claimed. A federal appeals court disagreed and allowed a rental loss deduction; also *see* 9.7.

Partially rented home. If you rented part of your home for over three years during the five years preceding the sale, you must allocate the basis and amount realized between the portion used as your home and the rented portion *(29.7)*. A loss on a sale is allowable on the rented portion, which is reported on Form 4797.

Profit-making purposes. Renting a residence is a changeover from personal to profit-making purposes. If the house is merely put up for rent or is rented for several months, the IRS may not recognize the house as rental property and may disallow the loss deduction. However, the Tax Court has approved a loss deduction where a house was rented on a 90-day lease with an option to buy. The court set down the following two tests for determining when a house is converted to rental property: (1) the rental charge returns a profit and (2) the lease prevents you from using or reoccupying the house during the lease period. Under the Tax Court approach, you have a conversion to rental property if you have a lease that gives possession of the house to the tenant during the lease period and if the rent, after deducting taxes, interest, insurance, repairs, depreciation, and other charges, returns you a profit.

Loss allowed on house bought for resale. A loss deduction may also be allowed where you acquired the house as an investment with the intention of selling it at a profit, even though you occupied it incidentally as a residence prior to sale. For example, an owner bought a house with the intention of selling it. He lived in it for six years, but during that period it was for sale. He was allowed to deduct the loss on its sale by proving he lived in it to protect it from vandalism and to keep it in good condition so that it would attract possible buyers.

In another case, an architect and builder built a house and offered it for sale through an agent and advertisements. He had a home and no intention to occupy the new house. On a realtor's advice, he moved into the house to make it more saleable. Ten months later, he sold the house at a loss of $4,065 and promptly moved out. The loss was allowed on proof that his main purpose in building and occupying the house was to realize a profit by a sale; the residential use was incidental.

Gain on rented residence. You have a gain on the sale of rental property if you sell for more than your adjusted basis at the time of conversion, plus subsequent capital improvements, and minus depreciation and casualty loss deductions. The sale is subject to the rules in *Chapter 44* for depreciable property.

29.10 Loss on Residence Acquired by Gift or Inheritance

You may deduct a loss on the sale of a house received as an inheritance or gift if you personally did not use it and offered it for sale or rental immediately or within a few weeks after acquisition.

Planning Reminder

Inherited Residence

If you inherit a residence in which you do not intend to live, it may be advisable to put it up for rent to allow for an ordinary loss deduction on a later sale. If you merely try to sell, and you finally do so at a loss, you are limited to a capital loss.

EXAMPLES

1. A couple owned a winter vacation home in Florida. When the husband died, his wife immediately put the house up for sale and never lived in it. It was sold at a loss. The IRS disallowed her capital loss deduction, claiming it was personal and nondeductible. The wife argued that her case was no different from the case of an heir inheriting and selling a home, since at the death of her husband her interest in the property was increased. The Tax Court agreed with her reasoning and allowed the capital loss deduction.
2. A widow inherited a house owned by her late husband and rented out by his estate. Shortly after getting title to the house, she sold it at a loss that she deducted as an ordinary loss. The IRS limited her to a capital loss deduction. The Tax Court agreed. She could not show any business activity. She did not negotiate the lease with the tenant who was in the house when she received title. She never arranged any maintenance or repairs for the building. Moreover, she sold the property shortly after receiving title, which indicates she viewed the house as investment, not rental, property.
3. An inherited residence was rented out by the owner to her brother for $500 a month when the fair market rental value was $700 to $750 per month. When she sold the residence at a loss, the IRS disallowed the loss, and the Tax Court agreed. The below-market rental was treated as evidence that she held the property for personal purposes, not as rental property or as investment property held for appreciation in value.

Chapter 30

Tax Rules for Investors in Securities

You have the opportunity to control the taxable year in which to realize gains and losses. Gains and losses are realized when you sell, and if there are no market pressures, you can time sales to your advantage.

If you sell securities at a gain before the end of 2010, and you held the securities more than one year, you can benefit from the 0% or 15% rate for long-term capital gains. The capital gain rates for 2011 were unsettled when this book went to press *(5.3)*.

The $3,000 limitation ($1,500 if married filing separately) on deducting capital losses from other types of income is a substantial restriction. If you have capital losses exceeding the $3,000 (or $1,500) limit, it is advisable to realize capital gains income that can be offset by the losses.

30.1 Planning Year-End Securities Transactions

First establish your current gain and loss position for the year. List gains and losses already realized from completed transactions. Then review the records of earlier years to find any carryover capital losses. Include nonbusiness bad debts as short-term capital losses. Then review your paper gains and losses and determine what losses might now be realized to offset realized gains or what gains might be realized to be offset by realized losses.

If you have already realized net capital losses exceeding $3,000 ($1,500 if married filing separately), you may want to realize capital gains that will be absorbed by the excess loss. Remember, only up to $3,000 (or $1,500) of capital losses exceeding net capital gain may be deducted from other income such as salary, interest, and dividends.

Planning for losses. Realizing losses may pose a problem if you believe the security is due to increase in value sometime in the near future. Although the wash-sale rule *(30.6)* prevents you from taking the loss if you buy 30 days before or after the sale, the following possibilities are open to you.

- If you believe the security will go up, but not immediately, you can sell now, realize your loss, wait 31 days, and then recover your position by repurchasing before the expected rise.
- You can hedge by repurchasing similar securities immediately after the sale provided they are not substantially identical. They can be in the same industry and of the same quality without being considered substantially identical. Check with your broker to *see* if you can use a loss and still maintain your position. Some brokerage firms maintain recommended "switch" lists and suggest a practice of "doubling up"—that is, buying the stock of the same company and then 31 days later selling the original shares. Doubling up has disadvantages: It requires additional funds for the purchase of the second lot, exposes you to additional risks should the stock price fall, and the new shares take a new holding period.

Planning Reminder

December 31 Deadline for 2010 Gains and Losses

If you want to realize gains on publicly traded securities, you have until December 31, 2010, to transact the sale. Gain is reported in 2010, although cash is not received until the settlement date in 2011. If you do not want to realize the gain in 2010, delay the trade date until 2011.

Losses are also realized as of the trade date; a loss on a sale made by December 31, 2010, is reported on your 2010 return.

EXAMPLE

You own 100 shares of Steel Co. stock that cost you $10,000. In November 2010, the stock is selling at $6,000 ($60 a share × 100 shares). You would like to realize the $4,000 loss but, at the same time, you want to hold on to the investment. You buy 100 shares at a market price of $60 a share (total investment $6,000) and 31 days later sell your original 100 shares, realizing the loss of $4,000. You retain your investment in the new lot.

30.2 Earmarking Stock Lots

Keep a record of all your stock transactions, especially when you buy the stock of one company at varying prices. By keeping a record of each stock lot, you may control the amount of gain or loss on a sale of a part of your holdings. If you do not make an adequate identification, the IRS will treat the shares you bought first as the shares being sold under a first-in, first-out (FIFO) rule. You may not average the cost of stock lots; averaging is allowed only for mutual-fund shares *(32.10)*.

If your stock is held by your broker, the IRS considers that an adequate identification is made if you give instructions to your broker about which particular shares are to be sold, and you receive a written confirmation of your instructions from the broker or transfer agent within a reasonable time.

EXAMPLE

Over a three-year period, you bought the following shares of Acme Steel stock: In 1997, 100 shares at $77 per share; in 1998, 200 shares at $84 per share; and in 1999, 100 shares at $105 per share. When the stock is selling at $90, you plan to sell 100 shares. You may use the cost of your 1999 lot and get a $1,500 loss if, for example, you want to offset some gains or other income you have already earned this year. Or you may get capital gains by selling the 1997 lot or part of the 1998 lot.

You must clearly identify the lot you want to sell. Say you want a loss and sell the 1999 lot. Unless you identify it as the lot sold, the IRS will hold that you sold the 1997 lot under the "first-in, first-out" rule. This rule assumes that, when you have a number of identical items that you bought at different times, your sale of any of them is automatically the sale of the first you bought. So the cost of your first purchase is what you match against your selling price to find your gain or loss. Here is what to do to counteract the first-in, first-out rule: If you have stock certificates registered in your name, show that you delivered the 1999 stock certificates. If the broker is holding the stock, specifically identify the 1999 lot in your selling instructions and get a written confirmation.

On the sale of mutual-fund shares, you generally have the option of using an average cost basis *(32.10)*.

Table 30-1 How To Identify Securities

If your securities are—	*Identify them by—*
Registered in your own name	The number, your name, and any other identification that they bear.
In a margin account registered in a "street" name	A specified block or security bought on a designated day at a particular price. A mere intention to sell a particular share without informing the broker is without significance.
New certificates received for old in a recapitalization	Record the new certificate with the lowest number as being in exchange for the old certificate with the lowest number. Do this until all the new certificates are matched with all the old.
Shares exchanged for shares in a reorganization	Allocate each of the new certificates to each of the old in your records. Where the exchange involves several blocks of stock and there is no specific identification, the IRS says you must average your costs.
Shares received in a stock split	Match the new certificates with the old ones surrendered. Identifying the securities being sold as the "highest cost" or "lowest cost" stock is insufficient. You have to match at the time of the split-up.
Stock dividends	The lot of stock on which you received the dividend. The new stock is part of the old lot. But if you receive one certificate for more than one lot, you may have to apply the first-in, first-out rule when you sell.
Acquired by exercise of non-taxed stock rights	The number, or other identification, of the lot you receive by exercising the rights. Each lot you so acquire is considered a separate lot received on the date of subscription.

30.3 Sale of Stock Dividends

A sale of stock originally received as a dividend is treated as any other sale of stock. The holding period of a *taxable* stock dividend *(4.8)* begins on the date of distribution. The holding period of a *tax-free* stock dividend or stock received in a *split (4.6)* starts from the time you acquired the original stock.

EXAMPLE

You bought 100 shares of X Co. stock on December 3, 1998. On August 10, 2010, you receive 10 shares of X Co. stock as a tax-free stock dividend. On December 14, 2010, you sell the 10 shares at a profit. You report the sale as long-term capital gain because the holding period of the 10 shares goes back to your original purchase date of December 3, 1998, not August 10, 2010.

Basis of tax-free dividend in the same class of stock. Assume you receive a common stock dividend on common stock. You divide the original cost by the total number of old shares and new shares to find the new basis per share.

EXAMPLE

You bought 100 shares of common stock for $1,000, so that each share has a basis of $10. You receive 100 shares of common stock as a tax-free stock dividend. The basis of your 200 shares remains $1,000. The new cost basis of each share is now $5 ($1,000 ÷ 200 shares). You sell 50 shares for $560. Your profit is $310 ($560 – $250).

Basis of tax-free dividend in a different class of stock. Assume you receive preferred stock dividends on common stock. You divide the basis of the old shares over the two classes in the ratio of their values at the time the stock dividend was distributed.

EXAMPLE

You bought 100 shares of common stock for $1,000. You receive a tax-free dividend of 10 shares of preferred stock. On the date of distribution, the market value of the common stock is $9 a share and that of the preferred stock is $30. That makes the market value of your common stock $900 and your preferred stock $300. So you allocate 75% ($900 ÷ $1,200) of your $1,000 original cost, or $750, to your common stock and 25% ($300 ÷ $1,200) of your cost to the preferred stock.

Basis of taxable stock dividend. The basis of a taxable stock dividend *(4.6)* is its fair market value at the time of the distribution. Its holding period begins on the date of distribution. The basis of the old stock remains unchanged.

EXAMPLE

You bought 1,000 shares of stock for $10,000. The company gives you a choice of a cash dividend or stock (one share for every hundred held). You elect the stock. On the date of the distribution, its market value was $15 a share. The basis of the new stock is $150 (10 × $15), the amount of the taxable dividend. The basis of the old stock remains $10,000.

30.4 Stock Rights

The tax consequences of the receipt of stock rights are discussed at *4.6*. The following is an explanation of how to treat the sale, exercise, or expiration of nontaxable stock rights. The basis of taxable rights is their fair market value at the time of distribution.

Expiration of nontaxable distributed stock rights. When you allow nontaxable rights to expire, you do not have a deductible loss; you have no basis in the rights.

Sale of nontaxable distributed stock rights. If you sell stock rights distributed on your stock, you treat the sale as the sale of a capital asset. The holding period begins from the date you acquired the original stock on which the rights were distributed.

Purchased rights. If you buy stock rights, your holding period starts the day after the date of the purchase. Your basis for the rights is the price paid; this basis is used in computing your capital gain or loss on the sale.

If you allow purchased rights to expire without sale or exercise, you realize a capital loss. The rights are treated as having been sold on the day of expiration. When purchased rights become worthless during the year prior to the year they lapse, you have a capital loss that is treated as having occurred on the last day of the year in which they became worthless.

Figuring the basis of nontaxable stock rights. Whether rights received by you as a stockholder have a basis depends on their fair market value when distributed. If the market value of rights is less than 15% of the market value of your old stock, the basis of your rights is zero, unless you elect to allocate the basis between the rights and your original stock. You make the election on your tax return for the year the rights are received by attaching to your return a statement that you are electing to divide basis. Keep a copy of the election and the return.

If the market value of the rights is 15% or more of the market value of your old stock, you must divide the basis of the stock between the old stock and the rights, according to their respective values on the date of distribution.

No basis adjustment is required for stock rights that become worthless during the year of issue.

Planning Reminder

Exercise of Stock Rights

You realize no taxable income on the exercise of stock rights. Capital gain or loss on the new stock is recognized when you later sell the stock. The holding period of the new stock begins on the date you exercised the rights. Your basis for the new stock is the subscription price you paid plus your basis for the rights exercised.

30.5 Short Sales of Stock

A short sale is a sale of stock borrowed from a broker. The short sale is closed when you replace the borrowed stock by buying substantially identical stock and delivering it to the broker or by delivering stock that you held at the time of the short sale. One objective of a short sale is to profit from an anticipated drop in the market price of the stock; another objective may be to use the short sale as a hedge.

Tax rules applied to short sales are designed to prevent you from:

- Postponing gain to a later year when you sell short while holding an appreciated position in the same or substantially identical stock. This type of short sale is called "a sale against the box."
- Converting short-term gains to long-term gains.
- Converting long-term losses to short-term losses.

Year in which gain on short sale is realized. Generally, you report gain on a short sale in the year in which you close the short sale by delivering replacement stock. However, if you execute a short sale while holding an appreciated position in the same stock (short sale against the box) or substantially identical stock is acquired to close an appreciated short position, the short sale or acquisition of substantially identical stock is treated as a constructive sale of an appreciated financial position *(30.8)* and you must report the transaction in the year of the constructive sale, even though delivery of replacement stock is made in a later year; *see* Examples 2 and 3 below. There is this exception to the constructive sale rule: The short sale is reported in the year of delivery of the replacement stock if you close the short sale before the end of the 30th day of the next year and continue to hold a similar position in the stock for at least 60 days after the closing of the short sale.

If the stock sold short becomes worthless before you close the short sale, you recognize taxable gain in the year the shares became worthless.

EXAMPLES

1. On May 4, 2010, you buy 100 shares of Auto Corp. stock for $1,000. On September 14, 2010, you borrow 100 shares of Auto Corp. from your broker and sell them short for $1,600. You make no subsequent transactions involving Auto Corp. stock. The short sale is treated as a constructive sale of an appreciated financial position because a sale of your Auto Corp. stock on September 14, the date of the short sale, would have resulted in a gain. You have a $600 short-term capital gain from the constructive sale and you have a new holding period for your Auto Corp. stock that begins on September 14, 2010.
2. In January 2010, you buy 100 shares of Steel Co. stock for $1,000 (100 x $10). In November 2010 when the stock is selling at $50, you execute a short sale of 100 shares (100 x $50 = $5,000). In February 2011, you deliver your shares to close the short sale. The tax law treats the short sale as a constructive sale of an appreciated financial position because a sale of your Steel Co. stock on the date of the short sale would have resulted in a gain. You report the gain of $4,000 ($5,000 – $1,000) in 2010, the year of the short sale, not in 2011 when you close the sale. To shift tax reporting to 2011, you would have had to close the short sale by the 30th of January and obtain similar stock, which you would have had to hold for at least 60 days after the closing of the short sale. Also *see* Example 3 and *30.8* for further details on constructive sales.
3. A taxpayer who does not own any shares of XYZ stock directs his broker in January of Year 1 to sell short borrowed XYZ shares. On December 31 of Year 1, when the value of XYZ shares has decreased, the taxpayer directs the broker to close the short sale by purchasing XYZ shares in a "regular-way" sale, with actual delivery of the shares taking place at the beginning of Year 2. The IRS ruled that the short position is an appreciated financial position as of December 31, given the decrease in the stock price since the short sale. The purchase of replacement shares on December 31 is a constructive sale of the appreciated position. Gain is taxable in Year 1, not in Year 2 when the shares were delivered.

Short-term or long-term gain or loss. Whether you have short-term or long-term capital gain or loss generally depends on your holding period for the property delivered to the broker to close the short sale. Furthermore, you must apply Rules 1 and 2 below if you answer "yes" to either of the following questions:

1. When you sold short, did you or your spouse hold for one year or less securities substantially identical to the securities sold short? (Substantially identical securities are described at *30.6*.)
2. After the short sale, did you or your spouse acquire substantially identical securities on or before the date of the closing of the short sale?

Rule 1. Gain realized on the closing of the short sale is short term. The gain is short term regardless of the period of time you have held the securities as of the closing date of the short sale.

Rule 2. The beginning date of the holding period of substantially identical stock is suspended. The holding period of substantially identical securities owned or bought under the facts of question (1) or (2) does not begin until the date of the closing of the short sale (or the date of the sale, gift, or other disposition of the securities, whichever date occurs first). But note that this rule applies only to the number of securities that do not exceed the quantity sold short.

Losses. A loss on a short sale is not deductible until shares closing the short sale are delivered to the broker. You may not realize a short-term loss on the closing of a short sale if you held substantially identical securities long term (that is, for more than a year) on the date of the short sale. The loss is long term even if the securities used to close the sale were held for one year or less. This rule prevents you from creating short-term losses when you held the covering stock long term. Loss deductions on short sales may be disallowed under the wash-sale rules in *30.6*.

EXAMPLES

1. On February 2, 2010, the stock of Oil Co., which you do not own, is selling at $90 per share. You expect the price to fall over the next year and sell short 500 shares borrowed from your broker for $45,000 (500 x $ 90). However, 13 months later, on March 10, 2011, after the price has risen to $110, you close the short sale by buying 500 shares of Oil Co. stock ($500 x $110 = $55,000 cost) and immediately delivering them to your broker. Your loss of $10,000 ($55,000 – $45,000) is treated as a short-term capital loss because your holding period for the delivered stock is less than one day.
2. On February 10, 2010, you buy 100 shares of Tech Corp. stock for $1,000. On July 13, 2010, you sell short 100 shares of Tech Corp. for $1,600. You close the short sale on November 16, 2010, by buying 100 shares for $1,800 and delivering them to your broker. On the short sale, you realize a $200 short-term capital loss.

   On February 22, 2011, you sell for $1,900 your original lot of Tech Corp. stock bought on February 10, 2010. Although you have held these shares for more than one year, the $1,900 gain realized on the sale is treated as a short-term capital gain under Rule 2 above. Rule 2 applies because on the date of the short sale, the February 10 shares were held short term (one year or less). Under Rule 2, the holding period of the February 10 lot is considered to begin on November 16, 2010, the date the short sale was closed.

Planning Reminder

Puts

The acquisition of a *put* (an option to sell) is treated as a short sale if you hold substantially identical securities short term at the time you buy the put. If you have held the underlying stock for one year or less at the time you buy the put, any gain on the exercise, sale, or expiration of the put is a short-term capital gain. The same is true if you buy the underlying stock after you buy the put but before its exercise, sale, or expiration. Your holding period for the underlying stock begins on the earliest of: (1) the date you dispose of the stock; (2) the date you exercise the put; (3) the date you sell the put; or (4) the date the put expires. However, the short-sale rules do not apply if on the same day you buy a put and stock that is identified as covered by the put. If you do not exercise the put that is identified with the stock, add its cost to the basis of the stock.

Expenses of short sales. Before you buy stock to close out a short sale, you pay the broker for dividends paid on stock you have sold short. If you itemize deductions, you may treat your payment as investment interest *(15.10)*, provided the short sale is held open at least 46 days, or more than a year in the case of extraordinary dividends. If the 46-day (or one-year) test is not met, the payment is generally not deductible and is added to basis; in counting the short-sale period, do not count any period during which you have an option to buy or are obligated to buy substantially identical securities, or are protected from the risk of loss from the short sale by a substantially similar position.

Under an exception to the 46-day test, if you receive compensation from the lender of the stock for the use of collateral and you report the compensation as ordinary income, your payment for dividends is deductible to the extent of the compensation; only the excess of your payment over the compensation is disallowed. This exception does not apply to payments with respect to extraordinary dividends.

An extraordinary dividend is generally a dividend that equals or exceeds the amount realized on the short sale by 10% for any common stock or by 5% for any preferred stock dividends. For purposes of this test, dividends on stock received within an 85-day period are aggregated; a one-year aggregation period applies if dividends exceed 20% of the adjusted basis in the stock.

Arbitrage transactions. Special holding period rules apply to short sales involved in identified arbitrage transactions in convertible securities and stock into which the securities are convertible. These rules can be found in Treasury regulations to Internal Revenue Code Section 1233.

30.6 Wash Sales

The objective of the wash-sale rule is to disallow a loss deduction where you recover your market position in a security within a short period of time after the sale. Under the wash-sale rule, which applies to investors and traders (but not dealers), your loss deduction is barred if within 30 days of the sale you buy *substantially identical* stock or securities, or a "put" or "call" option on such securities. The wash-sale period is 61 days—running from 30 days before to 30 days after the date of sale. The end of a taxable year during this 61-day period does not affect the wash-sale rule. The loss is still denied. If you sell at a loss and your spouse buys substantially identical stock within this period, the loss is also barred.

The wash-sale rule does not apply to gains. It also does not apply to acquisitions by gift, inheritance, or tax-free exchange.

Caution

Wash Sale Rule Applies If Replacement Bought in IRA

The IRS has ruled that a loss on the sale of stock is disallowed by the wash sale rule if within 30 days before or after the sale replacement shares are bought through a traditional IRA or Roth IRA.

Planning Reminder

Tax Advantage of Wash-Sale Rule

Sometimes the wash-sale rule can work to your advantage. Assume that during December you are negotiating a sale of real estate that will bring you a large capital gain. You want to offset a part of that gain by selling certain securities at a loss. You are unsure just when the gain transaction will go through. It may be on the last day of the year, at which point it may be too late to sell the loss securities before the end of the same year.

You can do this: Sell the loss securities during the last week of December. If the profitable deal goes through before the end of the year, you need not do anything further. If it does not, buy back the loss securities early in January. The December sale will be a wash sale and the loss disallowed. When the profitable real estate sale occurs next year, you can sell the loss securities again. This time the loss will be allowed and will offset the gain.

EXAMPLES

1. You bought common stock of Appliance Co. for $10,000 in 1993. On June 23, 2010, you sold the stock for $8,000, incurring a $2,000 loss. A week later, you repurchased the same number of shares of Appliance stock for $9,000. Your loss of $2,000 on the sale is disallowed because of the wash-sale rule. The basis of the new lot becomes $11,000, equal to the cost of the new shares ($9,000) plus the disallowed loss ($2,000).
2. Assume the same facts as in Example 1, except that you repurchase the stock for $7,000. The basis of the new lot is $9,000, the cost of the new shares ($7,000) plus the disallowed loss ($2,000).
3. Assume that in February 2011 you sell the new lot of stock acquired in Example 1 above for $9,000 and do not run afoul of the wash-sale rule. On the sale, you realize a loss of $2,000 ($11,000 basis – $9,000 sales price).

Buying replacement shares through IRA. The IRS has ruled that buying replacement shares in a traditional IRA or Roth IRA triggers the wash-sale rule. Some commentators had suggested that the wash-sale rule should not apply because the seller and the IRA, although "related," are different entities for tax purposes. The IRS disagrees. Although the IRA is a separate tax-exempt trust, the seller of the loss shares is treated as acquiring the replacement shares through the IRA.

There is an additional penalty for using an IRA to acquire replacement shares. The increase to basis that generally applies when a loss is disallowed by the wash-sale rule does not apply here. That is, your basis in the shares held in the IRA is not increased by the disallowed loss on the original sale and the loss is permanently disallowed. In other wash sales, the basis increase preserves for future use the economic value of the disallowed loss by allowing gain to be reduced, or loss to be increased, on a later sale of the replacement shares.

Loss on the sale of part of a stock lot bought less than 30 days ago. If you buy stock and then, within 30 days, sell some of those shares, a loss on the sale is deductible; the wash-sale disallowance rule does not apply.

EXAMPLE

You buy 200 shares of stock. Within 30 days, you sell 100 shares at a loss. The loss is not disallowed by the wash-sale rule. The wash-sale rule does not apply to a loss sustained in a bona fide sale made to reduce your market position. It does apply when you sustain a loss for tax purposes with the intent of recovering your position in the security within a short period. Thus if, after selling the 100 shares, you repurchase 100 shares of the same stock within 30 days after the sale, the loss is disallowed.

Oral sale-repurchase agreement. The wash-sale rule applies to an oral sale-repurchase agreement between business associates.

Defining "substantially identical." What is substantially identical stock or securities? Buying and selling General Motors stock is dealing in an identical security. Selling General Motors and buying Chrysler stock is not dealing in substantially identical securities.

Bonds of the same obligor are substantially identical if they carry the same rate of interest; that they have different issue dates and interest payment dates will not remove them from the wash-sale provisions. Different maturity dates will have no effect, unless the difference is economically significant. Where there is a long time span between the purchase date and the maturity date, a difference of several years between maturity dates may be considered insignificant. A difference of three years between maturity dates was held to be insignificant where the maturity dates of the bonds, measured from the time of purchase, were 45 and 48 years away. There was no significant difference where the maturity dates differed by less than one year, and the remaining life, measured from the time of purchase, was more than 15 years.

The wash-sale rules do not apply if you buy bonds of the same company with substantially different interest rates, buy bonds of a different company, or buy substantially identical bonds outside of the wash-sale period.

Planning Reminder

Basis Adjusted for New Stock

Although the loss deduction is barred if the wash-sale rule applies, the economic loss is not forfeited for tax purposes. The loss might be realized at a later date when the repurchased stock is sold, because after the disallowance of the loss, the cost basis of the new lot is increased by the disallowed loss. However, the basis increase is not allowed by the IRS if the shares are purchased by your IRA rather than by you individually.

Warrants. A warrant falls within the wash-sale rule if it is an option to buy substantially identical stock. Consequently, a loss on the sale of common stocks of a corporation is disallowed when warrants for the common stock of the same corporation are bought within the period 30 days before or after the sale. But if the timing is reversed—that is, you sell warrants at a loss and simultaneously buy common stock of the same corporation—the wash-sale rules may or may not apply depending on whether the warrants are substantially identical to the purchased stock. This is determined by comparing the relative values of the stock and warrants. The wash-sale rule will apply only if the relative values and price changes are so similar that the warrants become fully convertible securities.

Repurchasing fewer shares. If the number of shares of stock reacquired in a wash sale is less than the amount sold, only a proportionate part of the loss is disallowed.

EXAMPLE

You bought 100 shares of Stock A for $10,000. On December 13, 2010, you sell the lot for $8,000, incurring a loss of $2,000. On January 10, 2011, you repurchase 75 shares of Stock A for $6,000. Three-quarters (75/100) of your loss is disallowed, or $1,500 (3/4 of $2,000). You deduct the remaining loss of $500 on your return for 2010. The basis of the new shares is $7,500 ($6,000 cost *plus* $1,500 disallowed loss).

Holding period of new stock. After a wash sale, the holding period of the new stock includes the holding period of the old lots. If you sold more than one old lot in wash sales, you add the holding periods of all the old lots to the holding period of the new lot. You do this even if your holding periods overlapped as you purchased another lot before you sold the first. You do not count the periods between the sale and purchase when you have no stock.

Losses on short sales. Losses incurred on short sales are subject to the wash-sale rules. A loss on the closing of a short sale is denied if you sell the stock or enter into a second short sale within the period beginning 30 days before and ending 30 days after the closing of the short sale.

30.7 Convertible Stocks and Bonds

You realize no gain or loss when you convert a bond into stock, or preferred stock into common stock of the same corporation, provided the conversion privilege was allowed by the bond or preferred stock certificate.

Holding period. Stock acquired through the conversion of bonds or preferred stock takes the same holding period as the securities exchanged. However, where the new stock is acquired partly for cash and partly by tax-free exchange, each new share of stock has a split holding period. The portion of each new share allocable to the ownership of the converted bonds (or preferred stock) includes the holding period of the bonds (or preferred stock). The portion of the new stock allocable to the cash purchase takes a holding period beginning with the day after acquisition of the stock.

Basis. Securities acquired through the conversion of bonds or preferred stock into common take the same basis as the securities exchanged. Where there is a partial cash payment, the basis of the portion of the stock attributable to the cash is the amount of cash paid; *see* Examples 1 and 2 below.

If you paid a premium for a convertible bond, you may not amortize the amount of the premium that is attributable to the conversion feature.

EXAMPLES

1. On January 5, you paid $100 for a bond of A Co. Your holding period for the bond begins on January 6 *(5.9)*. The bond provides that the holder may receive one share of A Co. common stock upon surrender of the bond and the payment of $50. On October 19, you convert the bond to stock on payment of $50. For tax purposes, you realize no gain or loss upon the conversion regardless of whether the fair market value of the stock is more or less than $150 on the date of the conversion. The basis and holding period for the stock is as follows: $100 basis for the portion attributed to the ownership of the bond with the holding period beginning January 6; and $50 basis attributed to the cash payment with the holding period for this portion beginning October 20.
2. Same facts as in the above Example, but you acquired the bond on January 5 through the exercise of rights on that date. Since the holding period for the bond includes the date of exercise of the rights *(5.10)*, the portion of the stock allocable to the bond takes a holding period beginning on January 5.

30.8 Constructive Sales of Appreciated Financial Positions

One aspect of a constructive sale of an appreciated financial position was discussed in *30.5*, dealing with short sales. The constructive sale rules apply not only to short sales of stock but also to other transactions such as an appreciated financial position in a partnership interest or certain debt obligations.

You have made a constructive sale of an appreciated financial position if you:

1. Enter into a short sale of the same or substantially identical property,
2. Enter into an offsetting notional principal contract relating to the same or substantially identical property,
3. Enter into a futures or forward contract to deliver the same or substantially identical property, *or*
4. Acquire the same or substantially identical property (if the appreciated financial position is a short sale, an offsetting notional principal contract, or a futures or forward contract).

Caution

Constructive Sales of Appreciated Position

If you are subject to the constructive sale rules, you will have to report income as if you had made a sale although you still hold the position.

You are also treated as having made a constructive sale of an appreciated financial position if a person related to you enters into any of the above transactions.

A contract for sale of any stock, debt instrument, or partnership interest that is not a marketable security is not a constructive sale if it settles within one year of the date you enter into it.

Tax treatment. If you are considered to have transacted a constructive sale, you must report as taxable income gain on the financial position as if the position was sold at its fair market value on the date of the constructive sale. The property held by you receives a new holding period starting on the date of the constructive sale and its basis is the fair market value at that date. Thus, under the constructive sale rule you are also treated as immediately repurchasing the position as of the date of the constructive sale.

Closing a short sale to avoid a constructive sale. You may avoid the constructive sale rule if:

1. You close the transaction before the end of the 30th day after the end of your tax year,
2. You hold the appreciated financial position throughout the 60-day period beginning on the date you close the transaction,
3. Your risk of loss is not reduced at any time during that 60-day period by holding certain other positions.

If a closed transaction is reestablished in a substantially similar position during the 60-day period beginning on the date the first transaction was closed, this exception still applies if the reestablished position is closed before the end of the 30th day after the end of your tax year in which the first transaction was closed and, after that closing, tests (2) and (3) apply.

EXAMPLE

On October 6, 2010, you buy 100 shares of Oil Co. for $60 a share. On December 8, 2010, you sell short 100 shares of Oil Co. for $80 a share. On January 10, 2011, you buy for $75 a share 100 shares of Oil Co. to close the short sale. You hold the October lot for over 60 days after January 10, 2011. The December 2010 short sale is not treated as a constructive sale in 2010. You realized a loss of $5 per share when you closed the short position.

An appreciated financial position. You have an appreciated financial position interest in stock, a partnership interest, or a debt instrument (including a futures or forward contract, a short sale, or an option) if disposing of the interest would result in a gain.

An appreciated financial position does not include any position that is marked to market, including Section 1256 contracts. It also does not include any position in a debt instrument if:

1. The debt unconditionally entitles the holder to receive a specified principal amount,
2. The interest payments on the debt (or other similar amounts) are payable at a fixed rate or a variable rate described in Section 1.860G-1(a)(3) of the Regulations, *and*
3. The debt is not convertible, either directly or indirectly, into stock of the issuer (or any related person).

For the constructive sale rules, an interest in an actively traded trust is treated as stock unless substantially all of the value of the property held by the trust is debt that qualifies for the debt exception above.

A transaction treated as a constructive sale of an appreciated financial position is not treated as a constructive sale of any other appreciated financial position, as long as you continue to hold the original position. However, if you hold another appreciated financial position and dispose of the original position before closing the transaction that resulted in the constructive sale, you are treated as if, at the same time, you constructively sold the other appreciated financial position.

30.9 Straddle Losses

Tax accounting rules generally match losses against unrealized gains in offsetting straddle positions. Straddle rules apply to commodities and to stock options used in straddle positions. Straddle positions include actively traded stock if at least one of the offsetting positions is: (1) a position on that stock or substantially similar or related property, or (2) the stock is in a corporation formed or used to take positions in personal property that offset positions taken by any shareholder. True *hedging* transactions are not subject to the straddle tax rules.

A call option is not treated as part of a straddle position if it is considered a qualified covered call option. A *qualified covered call option* is an option that a stockholder who is not a dealer grants on stock traded on a national securities exchange. Furthermore, the option must be granted more than 30 days before its expiration date and must not be "deep-in-the-money." A "deep-in-the-money" option is an option with a strike or exercise price that is below the lowest qualified benchmark. The rules for determining these values are discussed in IRS Publication 550. A covered call option will not qualify if gain on the sale of the stock to be purchased by the option is reported in a year after the year in which the option is closed, and the stock is not held for 30 days or more after the date on which the option is closed. In such a case, the option is subject to the straddle loss deferral rules. The same loss deferment rule applies where the stock is sold at a loss, and gain on the related option held less than 30 days is reported in the next year.

Loss on a qualified covered call option with a strike price less than its applicable stock price is treated as long-term capital loss if loss realized on the sale of the stock would be long term. The holding period for stock subject to the option does not include any period during which the taxpayer is the grantor of the option.

Filing Tip

Carryback Election

If for 2010 you have a net loss on Section 1256 contracts, the loss may be carried back for three years under special rules. To carry back the net loss, you must make the election on Form 6781, file Form 1045 or an amended return (Form 1040X), and attach an amended Form 6781 for the applicable year. Follow the instructions to Form 6781.

Tax rules for straddles. The following paragraphs give a brief overview of the straddle rules, and if you have transacted straddles or are considering such transactions, we suggest that you *see* IRS Publication 550 and consult with an experienced tax practitioner.

Generally, a realized loss on a position that is part of a straddle is deductible on Form 6781 to the extent that it exceeds the unrecognized gains in offsetting positions as of the close of the taxable year. Any part of a loss that is not deductible is carried forward to the next year and subject to the same limitation. However, you may not deduct any loss from an identified position that was established in an identified straddle after October 21, 2004. Instead, you must increase the basis of the offsetting positions in the identified straddle that have unrecognized gain by the amount of the unallowed loss; *see* the Form 6781 instructions.

Filing Instruction

Form 6781

You use Form 6781 for reporting gains and losses on straddle positions and on Section 1256 contracts that are open at the end of the year but treated as sold under the marked-to-market rules.

Straddle positions of related persons (such as a spouse or child) or controlled flow-through entities (such as a partnership or an S corporation) are considered in determining whether offsetting positions are held.

The loss deferral rule does *not* apply to positions in a regulated futures contract or other Section 1256 contract subject to the marked-to-market system explained later in this section.

The loss deferral rule also does not apply to businesses that must hedge in order to protect their supplies of inventory or financial capital. Hedging transactions are subject to ordinary income or loss treatment. Hedging transactions entered into by syndicates do not qualify for the exception and are subject to the loss deferral rule if more than 35% of losses for a taxable year are allocable to limited partners or entrepreneurs. Furthermore, hedging losses of limited partners or limited entrepreneurs are generally limited to their taxable income from the business to which the hedging transaction relates.

Conversion transactions. On certain so-called "conversion transactions," discussed at *30.10*, gain realized on the disposition of certain positions is treated as ordinary income instead of capital gain.

Marked-to-market rules for gain or loss on regulated futures contracts and other Section 1256 contracts. Gain or loss on regulated futures contracts is reported annually under the marked-to-market accounting system of regulated commodity exchanges. To settle margin requirements, regulated exchanges determine a party's account for futures contracts on a daily basis. Each regulated futures contract is treated as if sold at fair market value on the last day of the taxable year. Any capital gain or loss is arbitrarily allocated: 40% is short term and 60% is long term. Use Form 6781 to figure gains and losses on Section 1256 contracts that are open at the end of the year or that were closed out during the year. These amounts are then transferred from Form 6781 to Schedule D.

Under the law, a regulated futures contract is considered a Section 1256 contract. Other Section 1256 contracts subject to the marked-to-market rules are foreign currency contracts, dealer equity options, and non-equity options.

Filing Instruction

Marked-to-Market Rules

Non-equity options and dealer equity options, which include options based on regulated stock indexes and interest rate futures, are taxed like regulated futures contracts. This means that they are reported annually under the marked-to-market accounting system. You treat all such options held at the end of the year as if they were disposed of at year-end for a price equal to fair market value. Any gain or loss is arbitrarily taxed as if it were 60% long term and 40% short term. It is advisable to ask your broker whether the specific options you hold come within this special rule.

You use Form 6781 to report 60/40% gains, which are then transferred to Schedule D.

Table 30-2 Key to Option Terms

Item—	*Explanation—*
Call option	An option contract that gives the holder the right to buy a specified number of shares of the underlying stock at the given exercise price on or before the option expiration date.
Put option	An option contract that gives the holder the right to sell a specified number of shares of the underlying stock at the given exercise price on or before the option expiration date.
Strike price/exercise price	The stated price per share for which the underlying stock may be bought (in the case of a call) or sold (in the case of a put) by the option holder upon exercise of the option contract.
At-the-money	An option is at-the-money if the exercise price of the option is equal to the market price of the underlying security.
In-the-money	A call option is in-the-money if the exercise price is less than the market price of the underlying security. A put option is in-the-money if the exercise price is greater than the market price of the underlying security.
Out-of-the-money	A call option is out-of-the-money if the exercise price is greater than the market price of the underlying security. A put option is out-of-the-money if the strike price is less than the market price of the underlying security.
Premium	The price of the option contract determined in the competitive marketplace, which the buyer of the option pays to the option writer.
Intrinsic value	The amount by which the option is in-the-money.
Time value (premium-intrinsic value)	The portion of the premium that is attributable to the amount of time remaining until the option's expiration date and to the fact that the underlying components that determine the value of the option may change during that time.
Secondary market	A market that provides for the purchase or sale of previously sold or bought options through closing transactions.
Expiration date	The expiration date is the last day on which an option may be exercised.
Writer	The seller of an option contract.

The marked-to-market rules do not apply to true hedging transactions executed in the normal course of business to reduce risks and that result in ordinary income or loss. Syndicates may generally not take advantage of this hedging exception if more than 35% of their losses during a taxable year are allocable to limited partners or entrepreneurs. Further, the ability of entrepreneurs or limited partners to deduct losses from hedging transactions is generally limited to taxable income from the business to which the hedging transaction relates.

Mixed straddle contracts. If you have a mixed straddle in which at least one but not all of the positions is a Section 1256 contract, the marked-to-market rules generally apply but you may elect to avoid this treatment and apply the regular straddle tax rules. The election, made on Form 6781, is irrevocable unless the IRS allows a revocation. Furthermore, the IRS allows an election to offset gains and losses from positions that are part of mixed straddles if you separately identify each mixed straddle or establish mixed straddle accounts for a class of activities for which gain and loss will be recognized and offset on a periodic basis.

Wash sales. Rules similar to wash-sale rules apply to losses arising from sales of shares that make up a straddle if within a 30-day period you acquire substantially identical shares; *see* IRS Publication 550 for further details.

Contract cancellations. Investors buying forward contracts for currency or securities may not realize ordinary loss by cancelling the unprofitable contract of the hedge transaction. Loss realized on a cancellation of the contract is treated as a capital loss.

Cash-and-carry transactions. You may not deduct carrying costs for any period during which the commodity or stock or option is part of a balanced position. The costs must be capitalized and added to basis. The rule does not apply to hedging straddles. Capitalized items are reduced by dividends on stock included in a straddle, market discounts, and acquisition discounts. These reductions, however, are limited to so much of the dividends and discounts as is included in income.

30.10 Capital Gain Restricted on Conversion Transactions

A "conversion transaction" is a transaction generally involving two or more positions taken with regard to the same or similar property. The investor is in the economic position of a lender who expects to receive income while undertaking no significant risks other than those of a lender. Where substantially all of your expected return is in the nature of interest on a loan from the following types of transactions, some or all of the income earned on the transaction is treated as ordinary income rather than capital gain:

- You acquire property and also agree to sell the property or substantially identical property for a determined price;
- You take offsetting positions on a straddle transaction; or
- You invest in a transaction marketed or sold as producing capital gain but your expected return is in the nature of interest on a loan.

Option dealers and commodity dealers are generally exempt from the new limitations.

Amount treated as ordinary income. In a conversion transaction, the amount of ordinary income is limited to an "applicable imputed income amount." This is generally the amount of interest that would have accrued on the net investment in the conversion transaction for the period ending on the date of disposition. To figure the interest element, 120% of the applicable federal rate, compounded semiannually, is used. The applicable rate is the federal short-term, mid-term, or long-term rate, depending on the term of the transaction. If the term is indefinite, the federal short-term rate is used. The federal rates are determined monthly and published in the Internal Revenue Bulletin.

Filing Tip

Reporting Conversion Transactions

You report conversion transactions on Form 6781. The ordinary income element is not reported as interest income, but as an ordinary gain on Form 4797.

30.11 Puts and Calls and Index Options

You may buy options to buy and sell stock. On the stock exchange, these options are named *calls* and *puts*. A call gives you the right to require the seller of the option to sell you stock during the option period at a fixed price, called the exercise or strike price. A put gives you the right to require the seller of the option to buy stock you own at a fixed price during the option period. *See* the chart on the following page for an explanation of different option terms.

The option price depends on the value of the stock, the length of the option period, the volatility of the stock, and the demand and supply for options for the particular stock.

Puts may be treated as short sales. Be careful in using puts when you own stock covered by the put. If you have held the stock short term, the purchase of the put is a short sale. The exercise or expiration of the put will then be treated as the closing of the short sale. Short-sale rules, however, do not apply (1) when you hold stock long term, and (2) when you buy a put and the related stock on the same day and identify the stock with the put *(30.5)*.

Planning Reminder

Speculate With Puts and Calls

Puts and calls allow you to speculate at the expense of a small investment—a call, for expected price rises, and a put, for expected price declines. They may also be used to protect paper profits or fix the amount of your losses on securities you own.

You do not have to exercise a put or call to realize your profit. You may sell the option to realize your profit. If you exercise a call, the cost of the call is added to the cost of the stock purchased. If you exercise a put, you reduce the selling price of stock sold by the cost of the put. If you do not exercise a call or put, you realize a capital loss.

Buyers of options. If you buy an option, the tax treatment of your investment in the option depends on what you do with it.

1. If you sell it, you realize short-term or long-term capital gain or loss, depending upon how long you held the option.
2. If you allow the option to expire without exercise, you incur a short-term or long-term capital loss, depending on the holding period of the option. The expiration date is treated as the date the option is disposed of.
3. If you exercise a call and buy the stock, you add the cost of the call to the basis of the stock. If you exercise a put, the cost of the put reduces your amount realized when figuring gain or loss on the sale of the underlying stock.

Grantors of options. If you write an option through the exchange, you do not treat the premium received for writing the option as income at the time of receipt. You do not realize profit or loss until the option transaction is closed. This may occur when the option expires or is exercised or when you "buy in" on the exchange an option similar to the one you gave to end your obligation to deliver the stock. Here are the rules for these events:

1. If the option is not exercised, you report the premium as short-term capital gain in the year the option expires.
2. If the option is exercised, you add the premium to the sales proceeds of the stock to determine gain or loss on the sale of the stock. Gain or loss is short term or long term depending upon the holding period of the stock.
3. If you "buy in" an equivalent option in a closing transaction, you realize profit or loss for the difference between the premium of the option you sold and the cost of the closing option. The profit or loss is treated as short-term capital gain or loss. However, a loss on a covered call that has a stated price below the stock price may be long-term capital loss if, at the time of the loss, long-term gain would be realized on the sale of the stock. Furthermore, the holding period of such stock is suspended during the period in which the option is open. Finally, year-end losses from covered call options are not deductible, unless the stock is held uncovered for more than 30 days following the date on which the option is closed.

Using a call as leverage. You expect a stock to appreciate in value but you do not have sufficient capital for a further investment. Instead of investing your limited amount of capital in an outright purchase, you might buy a call covering such stock. With a call, the same amount of capital allows you to speculate in many more shares than you could if you purchased stock outright. If the stock rises in value, your call also increases in value.

30.12 Investing in Tax-Exempts

Interest on state and local obligations is not subject to federal income tax. It is also exempt from the tax of the state in which the obligations are issued. In comparing the interest return of a tax-exempt with that of a taxable bond, you figure the taxable return that is equivalent to the tax-free yield of the tax-exempt. This amount depends on your tax bracket. For example, a municipal bond of $5,000 yielding 3% is the equivalent of a taxable yield of 4.167% subject to the tax rate of 28%.

You can compare the value of tax-exempt interest to taxable interest for your tax bracket by using this formula:

$$\frac{\text{Tax-exempt interest rate}}{\text{1 minus your tax bracket}}$$

The denominator of the above fraction is:

0.85 if your tax bracket is 15%
0.75 if your tax bracket is 25%
0.72 if your tax bracket is 28%
0.67 if your tax bracket is 33%
0.65 if your tax bracket is 35%

EXAMPLE

You are deciding between a tax-exempt bond and a taxable bond. You want to find which will give you more income after taxes. You have a choice between a tax-exempt bond paying 3.25% and a taxable bond paying 4%. Your tax bracket is 25%.

You find that the tax-exempt bond is a better buy in your tax bracket as it is the equivalent of a taxable bond paying 4.33%.

$$\text{Taxable Equivalent Rate (T)} = \frac{0.0325}{0.75\ (1.00 - 0.25)}$$

$$T = .0433, \text{ or } 4.33\%$$

Tax law restrictions. Most state and municipal bonds that are issued before July 1, 1983, except for housing issues, are in the form of bearer bonds; the owners are not identified, and interest coupons are cashed as they come due. However, state and municipal bonds issued after June 30, 1983, with a maturity of more than one year, as well as obligations of the federal government and its agencies, are in registered form. Principal and interest are transferable only through an entry on the books of the issuer.

In buying state or local bonds, check the prospectus for the issue date and tax status of the bond. The tax law treats bonds issued after August 7, 1986, as follows:

1. "Public-purpose" bonds. These include bonds issued directly by state or local governments or their agencies to meet essential government functions, such as highway construction and school financing. These bonds are generally tax exempt.
2. "Qualified private activity" bonds. Interest on private activity bonds is taxable unless the bond is a qualified bond. Qualified bonds generally finance housing, student loans, or redevelopment, or they benefit tax-exempt organizations. Interest on qualified private activity bonds issued after August 7, 1986, although tax free for regular income tax purposes, is a tax preference item for purposes of computing alternative minimum tax *(23.3)* unless an exception applies. Because of the AMT, these private activity bonds may pay slightly higher interest than public-purpose bonds.

   Several types of bonds have been excluded from private activity bond treatment so the interest is not treated as an AMT preference item, including qualified Section 501(c) (3) bonds, New York Liberty bonds, Gulf Opportunity Zone bonds, Midwestern disaster area bonds, and qualified housing bonds issued after July 30, 2008. In addition, any bonds issued in 2009 and 2010 that would otherwise be considered private activity bonds are not treated as private activity bonds, so the interest on the 2009/2010 bonds is not a tax preference item.

   Your broker can help you identify bonds subject to and exempt from AMT preference item treatment.
3. "Taxable" municipals. These are bonds issued for nonqualifying private purposes. They are subject to federal income tax, but may be exempt from state and local taxes in the states in which they are issued.

30.13 Ordinary Loss for Small Business Stock (Section 1244)

Shareholders of qualifying "small" corporations may claim within limits an ordinary loss, rather than a capital loss, on the sale or worthlessness of Section 1244 stock. An ordinary loss up to $50,000, or $100,000 on a joint return, may be claimed on Form 4797. On a joint return, the $100,000 limit applies even if only one spouse has a Section 1244 loss. Losses in excess of these limits are deductible as capital losses. Any gains on Section 1244 stock are reported as capital gain on Schedule D.

An ordinary loss may be claimed only by the original owner of the stock. If a partnership sells Section 1244 stock at a loss, an ordinary loss deduction may be claimed by individuals who were partners when the stock was issued. If a partnership distributes the Section 1244 stock to the partners, the partners may not claim an ordinary loss on their disposition of the stock.

If an S corporation sells Section 1244 stock at a loss, S corporation shareholders may not claim an ordinary loss deduction. The IRS with Tax Court approval limits shareholders' deductions to capital losses (which are deductible only against capital gains plus $3,000 ($1,500 if married filing separately) *(5.4)*.

Planning Reminder

Municipal Bond Funds

Instead of purchasing tax-exempts directly, you may consider investing in municipal bond funds. The funds invest in various municipal bonds and, thus, offer the safety of diversity. The value of fund shares will fluctuate with the bond markets. Also, an investment in the fund may be as small as $1,000 compared with the typical $5,000 municipal bond. Check on fees and other restrictions in municipal bond funds.

Filing Instruction

Interest Subject to AMT

Interest on qualified private activity bonds issued after August 7, 1986, is tax free for regular tax purposes but may be a tax preference item for alternative minimum tax (AMT) purposes *(23.3)*.

Planning Reminder

Record-Keeping for Section 1244 Stock

You must keep records that distinguish between Section 1244 stock and other stock interests. Your records must show that the corporation qualified as a small business corporation when the stock was issued, you are the original holder of the Section 1244 stock, and it was issued for money or property. Stock issued for services does not qualify. In addition, the records should also show the amount paid for the stock, information relating to any property transferred for the stock, any tax-free stock dividends issued on the stock, and the corporation's gross receipts data for the most recent five-year period.

Failure to keep these records will be grounds for disallowing a loss that is claimed on Section 1244 stock.

To qualify as Section 1244 stock:

1. The corporation's equity may not exceed $1,000,000 at the time the stock is issued, including amounts received for the stock to be issued. Thus, if the corporation already has $600,000 equity from stock previously issued, it may not issue more than $400,000 worth of additional stock.

   If the $1,000,000 equity limit is exceeded, the corporation follows an IRS procedure for designating which shares qualify as Section 1244 stock.

   Preferred stock issued after July 18, 1984, may qualify for Section 1244 loss treatment, as well as common stock.
2. The stock must be issued for money or property (other than stock and securities).
3. The corporation for the five years preceding your loss must generally have derived more than half of its gross receipts from business operations and not from passive income such as rents, royalties, dividends, interest, annuities, or gains from the sales or exchanges of stock or securities. The five-year requirement is waived if the corporation's deductions (other than for dividends received or net operating losses) exceed gross income. If the corporation has not been in existence for the five years before your loss, then generally the period for which the corporation has been in existence is examined for the gross receipts test.

Caution

Timing Redemptions of Older EE Bonds

In the year you cash in a savings bond you could lose interest by cashing it in too soon. Interest accrues only twice a year on EE bonds issued prior to May 1, 1997. The accrual months depend on the month of issue. If you cash pre–May 1997 bonds before the accrual month that applies to your bond, you will lose interest *(30.14)*.

Caution

All E Bonds Have Reached Final Maturity

The last outstanding E bonds reached their 30-year final maturity by June 2010 and are no longer earning additional interest. If you are still holding any E bonds, you can redeem them for their value as of the final maturity date.

30.14 Series EE and E Bonds

Savings bond purchases give you an opportunity to defer tax; *see* below. EE bonds must be held 12 months from the issue date before they can be redeemed. Bonds cashed in any time before five years are subject to a three-month interest penalty; *see* the Example below.

Series EE savings bonds with an issue date on or after May 1, 2005, earn a fixed rate of interest. Interest accrues monthly and is compounded semiannually. EE bonds issued from May 1997 through April 2005 continue to earn market-based interest rates set at 90% of the average five-year Treasury securities yields for the preceding six months; these rates change every May 1 and November 1. EE bonds issued before May 1997 earn various rates depending on the date of issue.

EXAMPLE

You purchased series EE bonds in March 2009. If you cash them 24 months later, in March 2011, you get your original investment back plus 21 months of interest (instead of 24 months of interest) because of the three-month penalty for redemptions within the first five years of ownership.

Deferring tax on savings bond interest. Unless you report the interest annually, Series EE bond interest is deferred *(4.29)* until the year you redeem the bond or it reaches final maturity. When you redeem the bond, the accumulated interest is taxable on your federal return but not taxable on your state and local income tax return. If in the year of redemption you use the proceeds to pay for higher education or vocational school costs, the accumulated interest may be tax free for federal tax purposes *(33.4)*.

Interest accrual dates for Series EE savings bonds. For EE bonds issued after April 1997, interest accrues on the first day of every month. For EE bonds issued before May 1, 1997, interest generally accrues on the first day of the issue month and the sixth month after the issue month. For example, if you own an EE bond issued in August 1995, interest accrues every August 1 (month of issue) and every February 1 (six months after the August issue month). An exception may apply for EE bonds issued March 1993 through April 1995. The twice-a-year accrual rule just discussed applies unless monthly increases are needed to guarantee a 4% return.

When you cash a bond, you receive the value of the bond as of the last date that interest was added. If you cash a bond in between accrual months, you will not receive interest for the partial period. For example, if interest accrues in February and August, and you cash a bond in during July, you would earn interest only through February. By waiting until August 1 to cash the bond, you would earn another six months of interest.

Final maturity for savings bonds. Do not neglect the final maturity date for older bonds. After the final maturity date, no further interest will accrue. No E bonds are still accruing interest. The last issued E bonds, those from June 1980, reached final maturity after 30 years in June 2010 and thus they as well as all older E bonds have ceased earning interest.

EE bonds issued in 1980 (the first year available) reached final maturity in 2010, 30 years after issue, after which no further interest will accrue. EE bonds issued in 1981 will stop earning interest in 2011 after the month in which 30-year final maturity is reached.

Table 30-3 Savings Bond Maturity Dates

Bond	*Issue Date*	*Final Maturity*
Series E	May 1941–November 1965	40 years after issue
	December 1965–June 1980	30 years after issue
Series EE	January 1980 or later	30 years after issue
Savings notes (Freedom Shares)	May 1967–October 1970	30 years after issue
H bonds	February 1957–December 1979	30 years after issue
HH bonds	January 1980–August 2004	20 years after issue

Accrual dates for Series HH bonds. Taxable interest on HH bonds obtained before Setember 1, 2004 in exchange for savings bonds or savings notes accrues semiannually at a fixed rate. A fixed interest rate applies for the first 10 years you hold an HH bond and the rate is then reset for the next 10 years until final maturity 20 years after the date of issue. For HH bonds issued or entering an extended maturity period after 2002, the rate is 1.5% per year. Interest on HH bonds issued from March 1993 through December 2002 will retain their 4% rate until they enter extended maturity after the first 10 years, and will then earn 1.5% per year.

30.15 I Bonds

Treasury "I bonds" provide a return that rises and falls with inflation. I bonds may be purchased from most banks, credit unions, or savings institutions or online from Treasury Direct at www.treasurydirect.gov. They earn interest for 30 years. Interest is added to a bond monthly and paid when the bond is redeemed.

I bonds are not redeemable within the first 12 months. You forfeit three months of interest if an I bond is redeemed within the first five years, the same rule as for EE bonds *(30.14)*.

Rates. Interest on an I bond is determined by two rates. One rate, set by the Treasury Department, remains constant for the life of the bond. The second rate is a variable inflation rate announced each May and November by the Treasury Department to reflect changes reported by the Bureau of Labor Statistics in the Consumer Price Index. If deflation sets in, a decline in the Consumer Price Index does not reduce the redemption value of the bond, even if the deflation rate exceeds the fixed rate.

Income tax reporting. Investors may defer paying federal income taxes on I bond interest, which is automatically reinvested and added to the principal. Deferral applies to the fixed rate interest as well as the variable inflation rate interest. You may defer federal tax on the interest until you redeem the bond or the bond reaches maturity in 30 years. You may report the interest each year as it accrues instead of deferring the interest. I bond interest is exempt from state and local income taxes.

If an I bond is redeemed to pay for college tuition or other college fees, all or part of the interest may be excludable from income under the rules discussed in *33.4*.

30.16 Trader, Dealer, or Investor?

The tax law recognizes three types of individuals who may sell and buy securities. They are:

Investor. You are an investor if you buy and sell securities for long-term capital gains and to earn dividends and interest.

Trader. You may be a trader if you buy and sell securities to profit from daily market movements in the prices of securities and not from dividends, interest, or capital appreciation. Your buy and sell orders must be frequent, continuous, and substantial. There are at present no clearcut tests to determine the amount of sales volume that qualifies a person as a trader. The term "trader" is not defined in the Internal Revenue Code or Treasury regulations. The IRS has not issued rulings for determining trader status. The Tax Court has held that sporadic trading does not qualify; *see* the Examples below.

Dealer. You are a dealer if you hold an inventory of securities to sell to others. Dealers report their profits and losses as business income and losses under special tax rules not discussed in this book.

EXAMPLES

1. After he retired, Holsinger began buying and selling stocks. In 2001, he made 289 trades over 63 days, and had losses of almost $179,000, which he reported as ordinary losses. In 2002, he made 372 trades over 110 days, and reported trading losses of just over $11,000 as an ordinary loss.

   The Tax Court held that Holsinger was an investor, not a trader. His trading losses were capital losses, and as such they could be deducted only to the extent of capital gains and then $3,000 of ordinary income. The Court held that the level of Holsinger's trading activities was not substantial enough to constitute a business. In addition, his trades were not aimed at catching the swings in daily market movements and profiting from these short-term changes, as evidenced by the fact that a significant amount of his positions were held more than 31 days. Since Holsinger failed to establish that he was in business as a trader, he could not make a mark-to-market election.
2. While holding a full-time job as a computer chip engineer in 1999, Chen made 323 transactions, 94 percent of which occurred in February, March, and April; he did no trading in June or August through December. Most of the securities were held for less than a month. He had losses of nearly $85,000, which he reported as ordinary losses.

   The Tax Court held that Chen was not a trader in securities and was limited to deducting $3,000 of his net 1999 loss against ordinary income. To be considered a trader, the purchases and sales of securities must amount to a trade or business. There is no exact number of trades or other clear standard used to make this determination. Rather, it is based on the taxpayer's intent, the nature of the income derived from trading, and the frequency, extent, and regularity of the transactions. During three months of the year, Chen bought and sold with frequency, but he failed to achieve trader status because, overall, his activities were not frequent, regular, and continuous. In prior cases, trader status has been found where such activities usually were frequent, regular, and continuous for a period of more than a single year. Because Chen could not claim trader status, he was ineligible to make a mark-to-market election.

Tax treatment of traders. The tax rules applied to traders are a hybrid of tax rules applied to investors and business persons, as discussed in the following paragraphs.

Reporting trader gains and losses. Unless a trader previously made a mark-to-market election, gains and losses are reported as capital gains and losses on Schedule D. As almost all or substantially all of a trader's sales are short-term, such gains are reported as short-term gains and losses as short-term losses. A net profit from Schedule D is *not* subject to self-employment tax *(45.1)*. Substantial losses subject to capital loss treatment are a tax disadvantage because capital losses in excess of capital gains are deductible only up to $3,000 of ordinary income in one tax year. True, carryover capital losses may offset capital gains in the next year, but your inability to deduct them immediately may subject you to paying a tax liability that might have been reduced or eliminated if the losses had been deductible for the year of the sale. If you are concerned about incurring substantial short-term capital losses that would be limited by capital loss treatment, you may consider a mark-to-market election *(30.17)*, which would allow you to treat your security gains and losses as ordinary income and loss.

Deducting trader expenses. Although a trader does not sell to customers but for his or her own account, a trader is considered to be in business. Expenses such as subscriptions and margin interest may be deducted as ordinary business losses on Schedule C of Form 1040. Home office expenses are deductible if the office is regularly and exclusively used as the principal place of conducting the trading business *(40.12)*; the deduction is computed on Form 8829 and entered on Schedule C.

An investor, on the other hand, may deduct margin interest only as an itemized deduction to the extent of net investment income *(15.10)*. Other investment expenses are allowed only as miscellaneous itemized deductions and only to the extent that, when added to other miscellaneous costs such as fees for tax preparation, they exceed 2% of adjusted gross income *(19.1)*. An investor may not deduct home office expenses since investment activities, no matter how extensive, are not considered a business; *see* the *Moller* decision discussed in *40.16*.

30.17 Mark-to-Market Election for Traders

A trader in securities may elect to have his gains and losses treated as ordinary gains and losses by making a mark-to-market election. As explained below, it is too late to make an election for 2010. In the absence of an election, gains and losses of a trader are treated as capital gains and losses on Schedule D.

If the mark-to-market election is made, you report trading gains and losses on closed transactions plus unrealized gains and losses on securities held in your trading business at the end of your taxable year as ordinary gains and losses on Form 4797. Trader profits are *not* subject to self-employment tax *(45.1)*, whether or not the mark-to-market election is made. The unrealized gain or loss on a security that is reported on Form 4797 increases or reduces the basis of the security. For example, if you report an unrealized gain of $50 on stock with a cost of $100, you increase the basis of the stock to $150. If you later sell the stock for $90, you report a loss of $60 in the year of the sale. The requirement to report unrealized gains and losses at the end of the year and to adjust basis of shares is a change in accounting method that requires you to file Form 3115 with the IRS National Office and report required adjustments; *see* IRS Publication 550 for details.

Once the mark-to-market election is made, it applies to all future years unless the IRS agrees to a revocation.

Making the election is not proof that you are actually a trader in securities. If you are audited by the IRS, you must be able to prove that your activities are such that you are in the business of making money by buying and selling over short periods of time. As mentioned in *30.16*, there are no hard and fast rules that specify how many daily or short-term trades qualify you as a trader.

When to make the mark-to-market election. The IRS requires you to make the election by the due date (without extensions) of the tax return for the year prior to the year for which the election is to be effective. Under this prior year tax return rule, it is too late to make an election for 2010, as this had to be done by April 15, 2010, the due date for your 2009 return.

A regulation gives the IRS authority to grant an extension of time to file the mark-to-market election if the taxpayer has acted reasonably and in good faith and allowing relief does not prejudice the interests of the government. However, the IRS has refused to allow such extensions, claiming that a late election invariably results in prejudice to the interests of the government.

The Tax Court has supported the IRS in cases where the taxpayers, in filing their elections several years late, were relying on hindsight to try to gain a tax advantage from ordinary loss treatment.

The Ninth Circuit Court of Appeals has also refused to allow a late election where the taxpayer was relying on hindsight to try to gain a tax advantage. On his 1999 return, Acar reported over $950,000 in losses from trading securities, treating them as capital losses. In early 2002, he filed an amended return and tried to make a retroactive mark-to-market election beginning with 1999 so he could treat his 1999 losses as ordinary losses and claim a refund. The IRS disallowed the late election and a federal district court and the Ninth Circuit affirmed. Allowing the late election would give Acar an advantage that was not available on April 15, 1999, the due date for making the election for 1999 under Revenue Procedure 99-17. When the late election was made, Acar knew that he had incurred losses and, with that hindsight, was trying to convert what had been capital losses on his original return into ordinary losses. It does not matter that any advantage from a late election for 1999 could be outweighed if Acar in later years realized trading gains that under the irrevocable election would have to be treated as ordinary rather than capital gains. That a taxpayer might come to regret an election in later years does not mean that hindsight was not used to gain an advantage at the time of the retroactive election.

In another case, the Tax Court was more sympathetic, allowing an extension to a taxpayer who filed his election for 2000 on July 21, 2000, three months after the IRS deadline of April 17, 2000. He had left his law practice and became a trader in January 2000. The accountant who prepared his 1999 return did not know about the mark-to-mark election but a friend told him about it in June 2000 and in July the taxpayer hired a law firm, which filed the election for him and asked the IRS to allow the extension. The taxpayer did not conduct any trading activities between the date he should have filed the election and the date he actually filed it. Over IRS objection, the

Tax Court allowed the late election on the grounds that the taxpayer had acted reasonably and in good faith by promptly employing the law firm after learning about the availability of the election. Since the taxpayer did not realize any further gains or losses between the date he should have filed the election and when he actually did so, the Court held that the interests of the government were not prejudiced.

How to make the mark-to-market election. An election for 2011 must be made by April 15, 2011, on a statement attached to your original 2010 return or on a request for an extension to file that return. The statement should specify that effective for the taxable year starting January 1, 2011, you are electing to report gains and losses from your trading business under the mark-to-market rules of Section 475(f). However, in the case of a new taxpayer, a different rule applies. A new taxpayer is defined as a taxpayer for which no federal tax return was required to be filed for the taxable year immediately preceding the election year. A new taxpayer, such as a newly organized partnership, would make the election by placing a statement of election in its books and records no later than two months and 15 days after the first day of the election year. A copy of the statement also must be attached to the original tax return filed for the election year.

One of the conditions of the election is that you must clearly distinguish between securities held for investment and trading purposes. The election applies only to the securities held in your trading business, not to the securities held for investment. Holding investment securities in a separate account is advisable.

An election may not be revoked in a later year except with IRS permission.

In light of the accounting requirements and the overall effect of reporting unrealized gains and losses, before making the election you should consult a professional experienced in the use of mark-to-market accounting.

See IRS Revenue Procedure 99-17 for details on making the mark-to-market election.

Chapter 31

Tax Savings for Investors in Real Estate

Real estate investors may take advantage of the following tax benefits:

- Sale of investment property may be taxed at capital gain rates.
- Depreciation can provide a source of temporary tax-free income *(31.1)*.
- Rental income can be used to offset passive losses *Chapter 10*.
- Tax-free exchanges make it possible to defer tax on exchanges of real estate held for investment *(31.3)*.

Losses on real estate transactions may be subject to the following disadvantages:

- Rental losses may not be deductible from other income such as salary, interest, and dividends unless you qualify as a real estate professional or for the special $25,000 rental loss allowance *Chapter 10*.
- Compromises of mortgage liability may subject you to tax *(31.10)*.

A foreclosure or repossession is treated as a sale on which you realize gain or loss. In addition, if you are personally liable on the loan and the amount of debt cancelled in the foreclosure exceeds the fair market value of the transferred property, you will owe tax on cancellation of debt income unless an exception is available *(31.9)*.

31.1 Investing in Real Estate Ventures

A real estate investment should provide a current income return and an appreciation in the value of the original investment. As an additional incentive, a real estate investment may in the early years of the investment return income subject to little or no tax. That may happen when depreciation and other expense deductions reduce taxable income without reducing the amount of cash available for distribution. This tax savings is temporary and limited by the terms and the amount of the mortgage debt on the property. Payments allocated to amortization of mortgage principal reduce the amount of cash available to investors without an offsetting tax deduction. Thus, the amount of tax-free return depends on the extent to which depreciation deductions exceed the amortization payments.

To provide a higher return of tax-free income, at least during the early years of its operations, a venture must obtain a constant payment mortgage that provides for the payment of fixed annual amounts that are allocated to continually decreasing amounts of interest and increasing amounts of amortization payments. Consequently, in the early years, a tax-free return of income is high while the amortization payments are low, but as the amortization payments increase, nontaxable income decreases. When this tax-free return has been substantially reduced, a partnership must refinance the mortgage to reduce the amortization payments and once again increase the tax-free return; *see* Examples 1 and 2 below.

The tax-free return is based on the assumption that the building does not actually depreciate at as fast a rate as the tax depreciation rate. If the building is depreciating physically at a faster rate, the so-called tax-free return on investment does not exist. Distributions to investors (over and above current income return) that are labeled tax-free distributions are, in fact, a return of the investor's own capital.

Caution

Management Fees

The promoter may be taking a real estate commission by having a commission paid to a company that he or she controls. A reliable promoter should disclose this fact and be willing to collect the commission only after the investors have recovered their capital. Also check the reasonableness of prepaid management fees and loan fees and whether or not the sale of property to the syndicate is from a corporation in which the syndicator has an interest. If there is such a sale, check its terms, price, interest rates, and whether there is any prepaid interest that may conceal a cash profit payout to the syndicator.

EXAMPLES

1. A limited partnership of 100 investors owns a building that returns an annual income of $100,000 after a deduction of operating expenses, but before a depreciation deduction of $80,000. Thus, taxable income is $20,000 ($100,000 – $80,000). Assuming that there is no mortgage on the building, all of the $100,000 is available for distribution. (Since the depreciation requires no cash outlay, it does not reduce the cash available for distribution.) Each investor receives $1,000. Taxable income being $20,000, only 20% ($20,000 ÷ $100,000) of the distribution is taxable. Thus, each investor reports as income only $200 of his or her $1,000 distribution; $800 is tax free.

2. Same facts as in Example 1, except that the building is mortgaged, and an annual amortization payment of $40,000 is being made. Consequently, only $60,000 is available for distribution, of which $20,000 is taxable. Each investor receives $600, of which 1/3 ($20,000 ÷ $60,000), or $200, is taxed, and $400 is tax free. In other words, the $60,000 distribution is tax free to the extent that the depreciation deduction of $80,000 exceeds the amortization of $40,000—namely $40,000. If the amortization payment were increased to $50,000, only $30,000 of the distribution would be tax free ($80,000 – $50,000).

Real estate investment trusts (REITs). The tax treatment of real estate investment trusts resembles that of open-end mutual funds. Distributions generally are reported to the investors on Form 1099-DIV as dividend income. However, distributions generally do not qualify for the reduced tax rate on qualified dividends *(4.1)*. A distribution qualifies for the reduced rate only to the extent it represents previously taxed undistributed income or qualifying dividends received by the REIT (from stock investments) that are passed through to the investors. Capital gain distributions reported on Form 1099-DIV must be reported as long-term capital gains regardless of how long the REIT shares have been held *(4.4)*. If the trust operates at a loss, the loss may not be passed on to the investors.

REMICs. A real estate mortgage investment company (REMIC) holds a fixed pool of mortgages. Investors are treated as holding a regular or residual interest. A REMIC is not a taxable entity for federal income tax purposes. It is generally treated as a partnership, with the residual interest holders as partners.

Investors with regular REMIC interests are treated as holding debt obligations. Interest income is reported to them by the REMIC on Form 1099-INT and original issue discount (OID) on Form 1099-OID.

The net income of the REMIC, after payments to regular interest holders, is passed through to the holders of residual interests. A residual interest holder's share of the REMIC's taxable income or loss is reported by the REMIC to the interest holder each quarter on Schedule Q of Form 1066, and the investor reports his or her total share of the year in Part IV of Schedule E.

31.2 Sales of Subdivided Land—Dealer or Investor?

An investor faces a degree of uncertainty in determining the tax treatment of sales of subdivided realty. In some situations, investor status may be preferred, and in others, dealer status.

Capital gain on sale. Investor status allows capital gain treatment. Capital losses may offset the gains. For capital gain, an investor generally has to show that his or her activities were not those of a dealer but were steps taken in a liquidation of the investment. To convince an IRS agent or a court of investment activity, this type of evidence may present a favorable argument for capital gain treatment:

- The property was bought as an investment, to build a residence, or received as a gift or inheritance.
- No substantial improvements were added to the tract.
- The property was subdivided to liquidate the investment.
- Sales came through unsolicited offers. There was no advertising or agents.
- Sales were infrequent.
- There were no previous activities as a real estate dealer.
- The seller was in a business unrelated to real estate.
- The property was held for a long period of time.
- Sales proceeds were invested in other investment property.

Planning Reminder

Installment Sales

The distinction between an investor and dealer is significant if land is sold on the installment basis. Investor status is preferable if you want to elect the installment method. Dealers may not elect installment sale treatment *(5.21)*.

Section 1237 capital gain opportunity. Section 1237 is a limited tax provision that provides a capital gain opportunity for subdivided lots only if arbitrary holding period rules and restrictions on substantial improvements are complied with. For example, the lots must generally be held at least five years before sale unless they were inherited. If the lots were previously held for sale to customers, or if other lots are so held in the year of sale, Section 1237 does not apply. Furthermore, substantial improvements must not have been made to the lots. According to the IRS, a disqualifying substantial improvement is one that increases the value of the property by more than 10%. The IRS considers buildings, hard surface roads, or utilities, such as sewers, water, gas, or electric lines, as substantial improvements.

Interest expense deductions. The distinction between an investor in land and a dealer is also important in the case of interest expenses. Dealer status is preferable here. Interest expenses incurred by an investor are subject to investment interest deduction limitations; *see Chapter 15*. On the other hand, interest expenses of a dealer in the course of business activities are fully deductible; *see* the Morley Example below.

Passive activity. Income from sales of lots is not considered passive activity income. Thus, losses from sales of land may offset salary and other investment income. If you hold rental property and also sell land, make sure that your accounts distinguish between and separate each type of income. This way income and losses from land sales will not be commingled with rent income subject to the passive activity restrictions discussed in *Chapter 10*. Your activity in real property development counts towards qualifying you as a real estate professional who may deduct rental losses from non-passive income if material participation tests are met *(10.3)*.

EXAMPLE

Morley was interested in buying farm acreage to resell at a profit. Two and a half million dollars was set as the purchase price. To swing the deal, Morley borrowed $600,000. A short time later, his attempts to resell the property failed, and he allowed the property to be foreclosed. While he held the property he incurred interest costs of over $400,000, which he deducted. The IRS held the interest was not fully deductible. It claimed the interest was investment interest subject to investment interest restrictions. That is, the debt was incurred to purchase and carry investment property. The IRS position was based on the so-called "one-bite" rule, which holds that a taxpayer who engages in only one venture may not under any circumstances be held to be in a business as to that venture. Morley argued that he bought the property not as an investment property but as business property for immediate resale.

The Tax Court sided with Morley, holding that he held the acreage as ordinary business property. The court rejected the "one-bite" rule. The fact that he had not previously sold business property did not mean that he could not prove that he held acreage for resale. Here, he intended promptly to resell it, and the facts supported his intention.

Planning Reminder

Exchanging a Building for Land

A tax-free exchange may be advantageous in the case of land. Land is not depreciable, but it may be exchanged for a depreciable rental building. The exchange is tax free and depreciation may be claimed on the building. However, be aware of a possible tax trap if you exchange rental property for land and the building was subject to depreciation recapture: The recapture provisions override the tax-free exchange rules. The "recapture element" will be taxable as ordinary income.

31.3 Exchanging Real Estate Without Tax

You may trade real estate held for investment for other investment real estate and incur no immediate tax. The potential tax on the gain is postponed to the time you sell the new property for more than your basis. A tax-free exchange may also defer a potential tax due on gain from depreciation recapture and might be considered where the depreciable basis of a building has been substantially written off. Here, the building may be exchanged for other property that will give larger tax deductions.

Fully tax-free exchanges. To transact a fully tax-free exchange, you must satisfy these conditions:

- The property traded must be solely for property of a "like kind." The words *like kind* are liberally interpreted. They refer to the nature or character of the property, not its grade, quality, or use. Some examples of like-kind exchanges are: farm or ranch for city property; unimproved land for improved real estate; rental house for a store building; and fee in business property for 30-year or more leasehold in the same type of property *(6.1)*. However, you may *not* make a tax-free exchange of U.S. real estate for real estate in foreign countries.
- The property exchanged must have been held for productive use in your business or for investment and traded for property to be held for productive use in business or investment. Therefore, trades of property used, or to be used, for personal purposes, such as exchanging a residence for rental property, cannot receive tax-free treatment. However, if you rent out your vacation home and meet the conditions of an IRS safe harbor *(6.1)*, the residence is treated as investment property rather than personal-use property, so it can be part of a like-kind exchange for other investment property.

  If you trade your principal residence for another principal residence, gain may be tax free under the home sale exclusion rules *(29.2)*.
- The trade must generally occur within a 180-day period, and property identification must occur within 45 days of the first transfer *(6.4)*.

A real estate dealer cannot transact a tax-free exchange of property held for sale to customers. Also, an exchange is not tax free if the property received is held for immediate resale.

Tax-free exchanges between related parties are subject to tax if either party disposes of the exchanged property within a two-year period *(6.6)*.

Disadvantage of tax-free exchange. Although the postponement of tax from a tax-free exchange is equivalent to an interest-free loan from the government equal to the amount you would have owed in taxes had you sold the property, this tax advantage is offset by a disadvantage in the case of an exchange of depreciable real estate. You must carry over the basis of the old property to the new property; *see* the following Example.

EXAMPLE

You have property with a basis of $25,000, now valued at $50,000, that you exchange for another property worth $50,000. Your basis for depreciation for the new property is $25,000.

If—instead of making an exchange—you sell the old property and use the proceeds to buy similarly valued property, the tax basis for depreciation would be $50,000, giving you larger depreciation deductions than you would get in the exchange transaction. If increased depreciation deductions are desirable, then it may pay to sell the property and purchase new property. Tax may be spread by transacting an installment sale.

Planning Reminder

Loss Deduction

A tax-free exchange is not desirable if the transaction will result in a loss, since you may not deduct a loss in a tax-free exchange. To ensure the loss deduction, first sell the property and then buy new property with the proceeds.

Project the tax consequences of a sale and an exchange and choose the one giving the greater overall tax benefits. You may find it preferable to sell the property and purchase new property on which MACRS may be claimed.

Partially tax-free exchanges. To be completely tax-free, the exchange must be solely an exchange of like-kind properties. If you receive "boot," such as cash or property that is not of like kind, gain is taxed up to the amount of the boot.

If you trade mortgaged property, the mortgage released is treated as boot *(6.3)*. When there are mortgages on both properties, the mortgages are netted. The party giving up the larger mortgage and getting the smaller mortgage treats the excess as boot. Taxable boot cannot exceed the amount of your gain. *See* the Example below and also the Example in 6.3, which illustrates how to report an exchange on Form 8824.

EXAMPLE

You own a small office building with a fair market value of $170,000, and an adjusted basis of $150,000. There is a $130,000 mortgage on the building. You exchange it for Low's building valued at $155,000, having a $120,000 mortgage, and for $5,000 in cash. You compute your gain in this way:

What you received		
Present value of Low's property		$155,000
Cash		5,000
Mortgage released on building you traded		130,000
Total received		$290,000
Less:		
Adjusted basis of building traded	$150,000	
Mortgage assumed by you	120,000	270,000
Actual gain on the exchange		$20,000

However, your actual gain of $20,000 is taxed only up to the amount of boot, $15,000.

Figuring boot		
Cash received		$5,000
Mortgage released on building traded	$130,000	
Less: Mortgage assumed on Low's property	120,000	10,000
Gain taxed to the extent of boot		$15,000

31.4 Timing Your Real Property Sales

Generally, a taxable transaction occurs in the year in which title or possession to property passes to the buyer. By controlling the year title and possession pass, you may select the year in which to report profit or loss. For example, you intend to sell property this year, but you estimate that reporting the sale next year will incur less in taxes. You can postpone the transfer of title and possession to next year. Alternatively, you can transact an installment sale, giving title and possession this year but delaying the receipt of all or most of the sale proceeds until next year *(5.21)*.

31.5 Cancellation of a Lease

Payments received by the tenant on the cancellation of a business lease held long term are treated as proceeds received in a Section 1231 transaction *(44.8)*. Payments received by the tenant on cancellation of a lease on a personal residence or apartment are treated as proceeds of a capital asset transaction. Gain is long-term capital gain if the lease was held long term; losses are not deductible.

Payments received by a landlord from a tenant for cancelling a lease or modifying lease terms are reported as rental income when received *(9.1)*.

Cancellation of a distributor's agreement is treated as a sale if you made a substantial capital investment in the distributorship. For example, you own facilities for storage, transporting, processing, or dealing with the physical product covered by the franchise. If you have an office mainly for clerical work, or where you handle just a small part of the goods covered by the franchise, the cancellation is not treated as a sale. Your gain or loss is ordinary income or loss. If the cancellation is treated as a sale, the sale is subject to Section 1231 treatment *(44.8)*.

31.6 Sale of an Option

The tax treatment of the sale of an option depends on the tax classification of the property to which the option relates.

If the option is for the purchase of property that would be a capital asset in your hands, profit on the sale of the option is treated as capital gain. A loss is treated as a capital loss if the property subject to the option was investment property; if the property was personal property, the loss is not deductible. Whether the gain or loss is long term or short term depends on your holding period.

EXAMPLES

1. You pay $500 for an option to purchase a house. After holding the option for five months, you sell the option for $750. Your profit of $250 is short-term capital gain.
2. The same facts as in Example 1 above, except that you sell the option for $300. The loss is not deductible because the option is related to a sale of a personal residence.

If the option is for a "Section 1231 asset" *(44.8)*, gain or loss on the sale of the option is combined with other Section 1231 asset transactions to determine if there is capital gain or ordinary loss.

If the option relates to an ordinary income asset in your hands, then gain or loss would be ordinary income or loss.

If you fail to exercise an option and allow it to lapse, the option is considered to have been sold on the expiration date. Gain or loss is computed according to the rules just discussed.

The party granting the option realizes ordinary income on its expiration, regardless of the nature of the underlying property. If the option is exercised, the option payment is added to the selling price of the property when figuring gain or loss.

31.7 Granting of an Easement

Planning Reminder

Basis Allocation

In reviewing an easement, the IRS will generally try to find grounds for allocating part of a property owner's basis to easement proceeds, especially where the allocation will result in a taxable gain. In opposition, a property owner will generally argue that the easement affects the entire property or that it is impossible to make an allocation because of the nature of the easement or the particular nature of the property. If he or she can sustain that argument, the proceeds for granting the easement reduce the basis of the entire property; *see* the Examples in *31.7*.

Granting an easement presents a practical problem of determining whether all or part of the basis of the property is allocable to the easement proceeds. This requires an opinion as to whether the easement affects the entire property or just a part of the property. There is no hard and fast rule to determine whether an easement affects all or part of the property. The issue is factual. For example, an easement for electric lines will generally affect only the area over which the lines are suspended and for which the right of way is granted. In such a case, an allocation may be required; *see* Example 1 below. If the entire property is affected, no allocation is required and the proceeds reduce the basis of the property. If only part of the property is affected, then the proceeds are applied to the cost allocated to the area affected by the easement. If the proceeds exceed the amount allocated to basis, a gain is realized. Capital gain treatment generally applies to grants of easements. The granting of a perpetual easement that requires you to give up all or substantially all of a beneficial use of the area affected by the easement is treated as a sale. The contribution to a government body of a scenic easement in perpetuity is a charitable contribution *(14.10)*, not a sale.

Condemnation. If you realize a gain on a grant of an easement under a condemnation or threat of condemnation, you may defer tax by investing in replacement property *(18.19)*.

EXAMPLES

1. The owner of a 600-acre farm was paid $5,000 by a power company for the right to put up poles and power lines. The right of way covered 20 acres along one boundary that the owner continued to farm. The cost basis of the farm was $60,000, or $100 an acre. The IRS ruled that he had to allocate the basis. At $100 an acre, the allocated basis for the 20 acres was $2,000. Thus, a gain of $3,000 was realized ($5,000 – $2,000).

2. The owner of a tract of unimproved land gave a state highway department a perpetual easement affecting only part of the land. He wanted to treat the payment as a reduction of the basis of the entire tract and so report no gain. The IRS ruled that he had to allocate basis to the portion affected by the road.
3. The owner of farmland gave a transmission company a 50-foot right of way for an underground pipeline that did not interfere with farming. During construction, the right of way was 150 feet. The owner received payments for damages covering loss of rental income during construction and for the 50-foot permanent right of way. The IRS ruled that the damage payment was taxable as ordinary income; the payment for the right of way was a taxable gain to the extent that it exceeded the basis allocated to the acreage within the 50-foot strip.

Release of a restrictive covenant. A payment received for a release of a restrictive covenant is treated as a capital gain if the release involves property held for investment.

EXAMPLE

You sell several acres of land held for investment to a construction company subject to a covenant that restricts construction to residential dwellings. Later, the company wants to erect structures other than individual homes and pays you for the release of the restrictive covenant in the deed. You realize capital gain on receipt of the payment. The restrictive covenant is a property interest and a capital asset in your hands.

31.8 Special Tax Credits for Real Estate Investments

To encourage certain real estate investments, the tax law offers the following tax credits:

Low-income housing credit. Qualifying investors are allowed to claim a tax credit in annual installments over 10 years for qualifying newly constructed low-income housing and also to certain existing structures that are substantially rehabilitated. The amount of the credit depends on whether the building is new and whether federal subsidies are received. To claim the credit, you, as the building owner, must receive a certification from an authorized housing credit agency. The agency allocates a credit to you on Form 8609, which you use to claim the credit on Form 8586. You must attach to your return Form 8586, and, in some cases, also Form 8609 and Schedule A, Form 8609.

Rehabilitation credit for pre-1936 buildings or certified historic structures. On Form 3468, you may claim a 10% tax credit for rehabilitating pre-1936 buildings or a 20% credit for rehabilitating certified historic structures. For both types of rehabilitation credits, you must generally incur rehabilitation expenses of $5,000 or your adjusted basis in the building, whichever is greater.

For purposes of figuring depreciation deductions, you must reduce basis by the full amount of either rehabilitation credit.

Both rehabilitation credits are subject to recapture if you dispose of the property within five years after it was placed in service or you change use of the property within the five-year period so it no longer qualifies for the credit; *see* Form 4255 for recapture details.

Midwestern disaster area and Gulf Opportunity Zone buildings. A higher credit rate is allowed on Form 3468 for pre-1936 buildings and certified historic structures in the Midwestern disaster area and the Gulf Opportunity Zone. In both areas, the credit percentage for a pre-1936 building is increased from 10% to 13% and for a certified historic structure the percentage is increased from 20% to 26%.

Certified historic structure. A certified historic structure may be used for residential or nonresidential purposes. The National Park Service must certify that a planned rehabilitation is in keeping with the building's historic status designation for the credit to be available.

In one case, a developer who rehabilitated a certified historic structure and donated a conservation easement to a historic society in the same year was required to base the credit computation on the rehabilitation expenses minus the charitable deduction claimed. If the donation had been made in a later year, a portion of the original credit claimed would be subject to recapture.

Court Decision

Rehabilitating Pre-1936 Building

In one case, the IRS and Tax Court interpreted the 75% external wall test for pre-1936 buildings as requiring that at least 75% of the existing external walls be retained in the same place, thereby denying the credit for a pre-1936 building that was relocated and then renovated. However, a federal appeals court disagreed, holding that there is no relocation restriction; the credit is allowed provided at least 75% of the external walls are retained as such after the renovation.

Filing Instruction

Donating Easement After Claiming Rehabilitation Credit

The charitable deduction for a historic building easement *(14.10)* must be reduced if a rehabilitation credit was claimed for the building in the five years preceding the donation.

Pre-1936 buildings. The 10% credit for pre-1936 buildings applies only to nonresidential property. A substantial portion of the building's original structure must be retained after the rehabilitation. At least 75% of the external walls must be intact, with at least 50% kept as external walls. At least 75% of the existing internal structural framework must be kept in place.

Tax credit limitations. Tax credits for low-income housing and rehabilitating historic or pre-1936 buildings may be limited by passive activity restrictions on Form 8582-CR *(Chapter 10)* and by tax liability limits for the general business credit *(Chapter 40)*.

31.9 Foreclosures, Repossessions, Short Sales, and Voluntary Conveyances to Creditors

If you are unable to meet payments on a debt secured by property, the creditor may foreclose on the loan or repossess the property. A foreclosure sale or repossession, including a voluntary return by you of the property to the creditor, is treated as a sale of the property on which you must figure gain or loss. Similarly, if the lender agrees to a "short sale" for less than the outstanding mortgage balance in which it accepts the sales proceeds in satisfaction of the mortgage, you must figure gain or loss. A loss on a principal residence or other personal real estate is not deductible. If you were personally liable on the debt, then in addition to realizing gain or loss on the transfer, you also have debt forgiveness income from the cancellation of the debt to the extent the cancelled debt exceeds the value of the property, unless an exception *(11.8)* applies. For example, if you were insolvent at the time of the debt discharge, the debt forgiveness is not taxable, and in the case of a principal residence, a special exception for up to $2 million of forgiven debt is generally allowed; *see 11.8*.

Caution

Form 1099-A Notifies IRS

If your mortgaged property is foreclosed or repossessed, and the bank or other lender reacquires it, or if the lender knows that you have abandoned the property, you should receive from the lender Form 1099-A, which indicates the foreclosure bid price, the amount of your debt, and whether you were personally liable. The IRS may compare its copy of Form 1099-A with your return to check whether you have reported income from the foreclosure or abandonment.

If the lender also cancels your debt of $600 or more, you may instead receive Form 1099-C, on which the information about the foreclosure or repossession will be included.

Figuring gain or loss and income from cancellation of debt on a foreclosure, short sale, or repossession. You have gain or loss equal to the difference between your adjusted basis *(5.20)* in the property and the amount realized on the foreclosure, short sale, or repossession. The amount realized depends on whether or not you are personally liable for the debt that secures the property, as discussed below. Note that if the property was your home or other personal-use property and a loss is realized on the foreclosure or repossession, the loss is nondeductible. If the property was your principal residence and you realize a gain on a foreclosure, short sale, or repossession, you may be able to exclude from income up to $250,000 of the gain, or $500,000 on a joint return, under the home sale exclusion rules *(29.1)*.

In addition to realizing gain or loss on the transfer of the property to the lender, you may also have to report income from the cancellation of the debt if you are personally liable for the debt *(11.8)*.

Amount realized if you are not personally liable (nonrecourse debt). If you are not personally liable on the debt secured by the property, the amount realized on the foreclosure, short sale, or repossession includes, in addition to any sale proceeds you receive, the full amount of the debt that is canceled as part of the transfer to the lender, even if the fair market value of the property is less than the cancelled debt.

You do not realize income from the cancellation of nonrecourse debt upon a foreclosure, short sale, or repossession. However, if in lieu of foreclosure (or repossession) the lender offers a discount for early repayment or agrees to a loan modification ("workout") in which the principal balance of the loan is reduced, the debt reduction results in income from the cancellation of debt even where you are not personally liable on the loan *(31.10)*.

Filing Instruction

Reporting a Foreclosure or Voluntary Conveyance

You generally report a foreclosure sale or voluntary conveyance to a creditor on Schedule D if the property was held for personal or investment purposes. However, if the property was your principal residence and you have a gain, the foreclosure or voluntary conveyance does not have to be reported on Schedule D (or anywhere else) if you can exclude all of it under the home sale exclusion rules *(29.1)*.

Foreclosures and reconveyances of business assets are reported on Form 4797.

If income from cancellation of indebtness is realized and it is not excludable under the rules discussed at *11.8*, you report the taxable amount on Line 21, Form 1040.

Amount realized if you are personally liable (recourse debt). If you are personally liable on the debt secured by the property, the amount realized includes the smaller of the cancelled debt or the fair market value of the property transferred to the lender. This is in addition to any sale proceeds received.

Where the cancelled debt exceeds the fair market value of the property, the excess must be reported as ordinary income from the cancellation of debt, unless the law allows it to be excluded. If debt secured by your principal residence is cancelled in a mortgage restructuring or foreclosure, you do not have to report the cancelled debt if you are eligible for the exclusion for qualified principal residence indebtedness *(11.8)*. Other exclusions that may be available are the exclusions for insolvency, bankruptcy, or qualified farm debt, discussed in *11.8*, or the exclusion for qualified business real estate debt discussed in *31.10*.

EXAMPLES

1. Jones could not meet the mortgage payments on a vacation home that cost him $185,000. He had paid cash of $20,000 and taken a mortgage loan of $165,000 on which he was personally liable. In 2010, when the remaining balance of the loan was $162,000, he defaulted, and the bank accepted his voluntary conveyance of the unit, cancelling the loan. Similar units at the time were selling for $150,000. On the transaction, Jones incurred a loss of $35,000: the difference between his adjusted basis of $185,000 and the fair market value of the unit of $150,000. The loss is not deductible because the unit was held for personal purposes. Jones also recognizes income on the cancellation of the loan because the amount of the debt ($162,000) exceeded the fair market value of the unit ($150,000) by $12,000. This amount is taxable, unless Jones can show he was insolvent at the time of the transfer to the bank; *see 11.8*.

   Note: If the property had been Jones's principal residence, the exclusion for qualified principal residence indebtedness *(11.8)* would be available and he would not have to report the $12,000 income from the debt cancellation as income on his return.

2. Brown invested in a vacant lot. He put down cash of $10,000 and assumed a mortgage of $20,000. When he could not make payments on the mortgage, the bank foreclosed. The net proceeds from the foreclosure sale were $32,000. Brown received $12,000 and realized a capital gain of $2,000 (the difference between his adjusted basis of $30,000 and the amount realized of $32,000). There is no income from cancellation of indebtedness because the debt was less than the value of the property.

31.10 Restructuring Mortgage Debt

Rather than foreclose on a mortgage, a lender (mortgagee) may be willing to restructure the mortgage debt by cancelling either all or part of the debt. As a borrower (mortgagor), do not overlook the tax consequences of the new debt arrangement. If the lender agrees to a "workout," under which part of your loan principal is reduced as part of a loan modification, or if you pay off the loan early in return for a "discount" that reduces the debt, the reduction or discount is canceled debt, reportable as ordinary income (cancellation of debt income) unless an exception applies. This is true whether or not you are personally liable for the debt. You may be able to avoid the ordinary income by taking advantage of one of the exclusions in the law, such as the exclusion for qualified principal residence indebtedness or the exclusions for insolvency, bankruptcy, qualified business real estate debt (*see* below), or qualified farm debt. Details of these exclusions are discussed in *11.8*. The Jones example below illustrates the IRS approach to figuring insolvency upon a reduction of a nonrecourse debt.

In the case of partnership property, tax consequences of the restructuring of a third-party loan are determined at the partner level. This means that if you are a partner and are solvent *(11.8)* you may not avoid tax on the transaction, even if the partnership is insolvent.

Caution

Form 1099-C

If your lender agrees to a "workout" that reduces the principal balance of your loan, the cancelled debt will be reported on Form 1099-C in Box 2. This amount must be included in your income unless one of the exclusion rules *(11.8)* applies.

EXAMPLE

In 2008, Jones borrowed $1,000,000 from Chester and signed a note payable for $1,000,000. Jones was not personally liable (nonrecourse) on the note, which was secured by an office building valued at $1,000,000 that he bought from Baker with the proceeds of Chester's loan. In 2010, when the value of the building declined to $800,000, Chester agreed to reduce the principal of the loan to $825,000. At the time, Jones held other assets valued at $100,000 and owed another person $50,000. In 2010, Jones realizes income of $175,000 on the reduction of the debt, but he can avoid tax to the extent he is insolvent.

To determine the extent of Jones's insolvency, the IRS compares Jones's assets and liabilities immediately before the discharge. According to the IRS, his assets total $900,000: the building valued at $800,000 plus other assets of $100,000. His liabilities total $1,025,000: the debt of $50,000 plus the liability on the note, which the IRS considers to be $975,000, equal to the $800,000 value of the building and the $175,000 discharged debt. The difference between the assets of $900,000 and liabilities of $1,025,000 is $125,000, the amount by which Jones is insolvent. As Jones is insolvent by $125,000, only $50,000 of the $175,000 discharged debt is treated as taxable income.

Jones must claim the insolvency exception on Form 982 by checking the box on Line 1b and entering the excludable $125,000 on Line 2. In Part II of Form 982, Jones must reduce his "tax attributes," such as the basis of his property. The $50,000 debt cancellation that is not excludable under the insolvency rule must be reported as ordinary income on Line 21 of Form 1040 ("Other income").

Restructuring debt on business real estate. A solvent taxpayer may avoid tax on a restructuring of qualifying business real estate debt *(11.8)* by electing to reduce the basis of depreciable real property by the amount of the tax-free debt discharge. The election to reduce basis is made on Form 982.

EXAMPLE

Grant, who is solvent, owns a building worth $150,000 used in his business. It is subject to a first mortgage of $110,000 and a second mortgage of $90,000. Grant's basis in the building is $120,000. On July 12, 2010, the second mortgagee agrees to reduce the second mortgage to $30,000. This results in debt discharge of $60,000 ($90,000 – $30,000). The $60,000 is considered debt discharge income. But Grant may elect to exclude $50,000. He reports the remaining $10,000 of discharged debt as taxable income. The exclusion limit is the excess of the pre-discharge mortgage balance over the fair market value of the building, reduced by the other mortgage *(11.8)*, calculated as follows:

2nd mortgage before discharge	$90,000
Less: Fair market value of building reduced by first mortgage ($150,000 – $110,000)	40,000
Excludable amount	$50,000

On Form 982, Grant may elect to exclude $50,000 from income because the basis of the building is sufficient to absorb a basis reduction of $50,000.

31.11 Abandonments

On an abandonment of business or investment real estate, you may claim an ordinary loss for the property's adjusted basis (when abandoned) on Form 4797. However, if the abandoned property is later foreclosed or repossessed, you may realize a gain or loss under the rules for foreclosures or voluntary conveyances to creditors *(31.9)*. For example, if an abandonment loss for mortgaged property is claimed in 2009 but in 2010 the property is foreclosed upon or repossessed by the lender, all or part of the cancelled debt will be treated as an amount realized by you on a sale in 2010. The amount realized depends on whether you were personally liable and the value of the property *(31.9)*. If personally liable, you may also realize ordinary income from cancellation of the debt *(31.9)*.

A loss is *not* deductible on the abandonment of property held for personal use. If the lender forecloses on the loan or repossesses the property, gain or loss (nondeductible loss) must be figured, and ordinary income from cancellation of debt may be realized *(31.9)*.

Abandoning a partnership interest. Where real estate values have sharply declined, partnerships may be holding realty subject to mortgage debt that exceeds the current value of the property. Some investors in such partnerships have claimed that they can abandon their partnership interests and claim abandonment losses. In one case, an investor in a partnership holding land in Houston, Texas, argued that he abandoned his partnership interest by making an abandonment declaration at a meeting of partners, and also declaring that he would make no further payments. He offered his interest to the others, who refused his offer. The IRS held that he failed to prove abandonment of his partnership interest or that the partnership abandoned the land. The Tax Court sided with the IRS, emphasizing his failure to show that the partnership abandoned the land. However, the appeals court for the Fifth Circuit reversed and allowed the abandonment loss. It held that the emphasis should be on the partner's actions, not the actions of the partnership. Although neither state law nor the IRS regulations described how a partnership interest is to be abandoned, the appeals court held that the partner's acts and declaration were sufficient to effect an abandonment of his partnership interest. The appeals court also held that the loss on the partnership interest could have been sustained on the basis of the worthlessness of his interest. The partnership was insolvent beyond hope of rehabilitation: (1) the partnership's only asset was land with a fair market value less than the mortgage debt; (2) the partnership had no source of income; and (3) the partners refused to contribute more funds to keep the partnership afloat.

In a subsequent case, the Tax Court held that a doctor had abandoned a movie production partnership interest when he refused to advance any more money or to participate in the venture because he disapproved of the content of the film being produced and feared it might jeopardize his position at a hospital operated by a religious organization. Also, the limited partners had voted to dissolve.

31.12 Seller's Repossession After Buyer's Default on Mortgage

When you, as a seller, repossess realty on the buyer's default of a debt that the realty secures, you may realize gain or loss. (If the realty was a personal residence, the loss is not deductible.) A debt is secured by real property whenever you have the right to take title or possession or both in the event the buyer defaults on his or her obligation under the contract.

Figuring gain on the repossession. Gain on the repossession is the excess of: (1) payments received on the original sales contract prior to and on the repossession, including payments made by the buyer for your benefit to another party, over (2) the amount of taxable gain previously reported prior to the repossession.

Gain computed under these two steps may not be fully taxable. Taxable gain is limited to the amount of original profit less gain on the sale already reported as income for periods prior to the repossession and less your repossession costs.

The limitation on gain does not apply if the selling price cannot be computed at the time of sale as, for example, where the selling price is stated as a percentage of the profits to be realized from the development of the property sold.

These repossession gain rules do not apply if you repurchase the property by paying the buyer a sum in addition to the discharge of the debt, unless the repurchase and payment was provided for in the original sale contract, or the buyer has defaulted on his or her obligation, or default is imminent.

In such cases, gain or loss on the repossession, and basis in the repossessed property, must be determined under the different rules for personal property; *see* IRS Publication 537 for details.

Caution

Character of Gain

The gain limitation rules *(31.12)* do not affect the character of the gain. Thus, if you repossess property as a dealer, the gain is subject to ordinary income rates. If you, as an investor, repossess a tract originally held long term whose gain was reported on the installment method, the gain is capital gain.

EXAMPLE

Assume you sell land for $25,000. You take a $5,000 down payment plus a $20,000 mortgage, secured by the property, from the buyer, with principal payable at the rate of $4,000 annually plus 9% interest. The adjusted basis of the land was $20,000 and you elected to report the transaction on the installment basis. Your gross profit percentage is 20% ($5,000 profit divided by $25,000 selling price). In the year of sale, you include $1,000 in your income on the installment basis (20% of $5,000 down payment). The next year you reported profit of $800 (20% of $4,000 annual installment). In the third year, the buyer defaults, and you repossess the property. Your repossession costs are $500. The amount of gain on repossession is computed as follows:

1. Compute gain:

Amount of money received	
($5,000 *plus* $4,000)	$9,000
Less: Amount of gain taxed in prior years ($1,000 *plus* $800)	1,800
Gain	$7,200

2. Compute limit on taxable gain:

Original profit		$5,000
Less:		
Gain reported as income	$1,800	
Repossession costs	500	2,300
Taxable gain on repossession		$2,700

The basis of repossessed property. This is the adjusted basis of the debt (face value of the debt less the unreported profits) secured by the property, figured as of the date of repossession, increased by (1) the taxable gain on repossession *and* (2) the legal fees and other repossession costs you paid.

EXAMPLE

Same facts as in the previous Example. The basis of the repossessed property is computed as follows:

1.	Face value of debt ($20,000 note less $4,000 payment)		$16,000
2.	*Less:* Unreported profit (20% of the $16,000 still due on the note)		3,200
3.	Adjusted basis at date of repossession		$12,800
4.	*Plus:* Gain on repossession	$2,700	
	Repossession costs	500	3,200
5.	Basis of repossessed property		$16,000

If you treated the debt as having become worthless or partially worthless before repossession, you are considered to receive, upon the repossession of the property securing the debt, an amount equal to the amount of the debt treated as worthless. You report as income the amount of any prior bad debt deduction and increase the basis of the debt by an amount equal to the amount reported as income.

If your debt is not fully discharged as a result of the repossession, the basis of the undischarged debt is zero. No loss may be claimed if the obligations subsequently become worthless. This rule applies to undischarged debts on the original obligation of the purchaser, a substituted obligation of the purchaser, a deficiency judgment entered in a court of law into which the purchaser's obligation was merged, and any other obligations arising from the transaction.

Principal residence. Special rules apply to repossessions and resales of a principal residence if you excluded all or part of the gain on your original sale of the residence *(29.1)*, and you resell it within a year after you repossess it.

The original sale and resale is treated as one transaction. You refigure the amount realized on the sale. You combine the selling price of the resale with the selling price of the original sale. From this total, you subtract selling expenses for both sales, the part of the original installment obligation that remains unpaid at the time of repossession, and repossession costs. The net is the amount realized on the combined sale-resale. Subtracting basis in the home from the amount realized gives the gain on the combined sale-resale before taking into account the exclusion rules. *See* Treasury Regulation Section 1.1038-2 for further details.

31.13 Foreclosure on Mortgages Other Than Purchase Money

If you, as a mortgagee (lender), bid in on a foreclosure sale to pay off a mortgage that is *not a purchase money mortgage,* your actual financial loss is the difference between the unpaid mortgage debt and the value of the property. For tax purposes, however, you may realize a capital gain or loss and a bad debt loss that are reportable *in the year of the foreclosure sale.*

Your bid is treated as consisting of two distinct transactions:

1. The repayment of your loan. To determine whether this results in a bad debt, the bid price is matched against the face amount of the mortgage.
2. A taxable exchange of your mortgage note for the foreclosed property, which may result in a capital gain or loss. This is determined by matching the bid price against the fair market value of the property.

EXAMPLES

1. *Mortgagee's bid less than market value.* You hold a $40,000 mortgage on property having a fair market value of $30,000. You bid on the property at the foreclosure sale at $28,000. The expenses of the sale are $2,000, reducing the bid price to $26,000. The mortgagor is insolvent, so you have a bad debt loss of $14,000 ($40,000 – $26,000). You also have a $4,000 capital gain (the fair market value of the property of $30,000 – $26,000).

Planning Reminder

Voluntary Conveyance

Instead of forcing you to foreclose, the mortgagor may voluntarily convey the property to you in consideration for your cancelling the mortgage debt. Your loss is the amount by which the mortgage debt plus accrued interest exceeds the fair market value of the property. If, however, the fair market value exceeds the mortgage debt plus accrued interest, the difference is taxable gain. The gain or loss is reportable in the year you receive the property. Your basis in the property is its fair market value when you receive it.

2. *Mortgagee's bid equal to market value.* Suppose your bid was $32,000, and you had $2,000 in expenses. The difference between the net bid price of $30,000 and the mortgage of $40,000 is $10,000. As the mortgagor is insolvent, there is a bad debt loss of $10,000. Since the net bid price equals the fair market value, there is neither capital gain nor loss.
3. *Mortgagee's bid greater than market value.* Suppose your bid was $36,000 and you had $2,000 in expenses. Your bad debt deduction is $6,000—the difference between the mortgage debt of $40,000 and the net bid price of $34,000. You also had a capital loss of $4,000 (the difference between the net bid price of $34,000 and the fair market value of $30,000).

Where the bid price equals the mortgage debt plus unreported but accrued interest, you report the interest as income. But where the accrued interest has been reported, the unpaid amount is added to the collection expenses.

31.14 Foreclosure Sale to Third Party

When a third party buys the property in a foreclosure, the mortgagee receives the purchase price to apply against the mortgage debt. If it is less than the debt, the mortgagee may proceed against the mortgagor for the difference. Foreclosure expenses are treated as offsets against the foreclosure proceeds and increase the bad debt loss.

You deduct your loss as a bad debt. The law distinguishes between two types of bad debt deductions: business bad debts and nonbusiness bad debts. A business bad debt is fully deductible. A nonbusiness bad debt is a short-term capital loss that can be offset only against capital gains, plus a limited amount of ordinary income *(5.33)*. In addition, you may deduct a partially worthless business bad debt, but you may not deduct a partially worthless nonbusiness bad debt. Remember this distinction if you are thinking of forgiving part of the mortgage debt as a settlement. If the debt is a nonbusiness bad debt, you will not be able to take a deduction until the entire debt proves to be worthless. But whether you are deducting a business or a nonbusiness bad debt, your deduction will be allowed only if you show the debt to be uncollectible—for example, because a deficiency judgment is worthless or because the mortgagor is declared bankrupt.

Planning Reminder

Keep Records

Preserve evidence of the property's fair market value. At a later date, the IRS may claim that the property was worth more than your bid and may tax you for the difference. Furthermore, be prepared to prove the worthlessness of the debt in order to support the bad debt deduction.

EXAMPLE

You hold a $30,000 note and mortgage that are in default. You foreclose, and a third party buys the property for $20,000. Foreclosure expenses amount to $2,000. The deficiency is uncollectible. Your $12,000 loss is figured as follows:

Unpaid mortgage debt		$30,000
Foreclosure proceeds	$20,000	
Less: Expenses	2,000	
Net proceeds		18,000
Bad debt loss		$12,000

31.15 Transferring Mortgaged Realty

Mortgaging realty that has appreciated in value is one way of realizing cash on the appreciation without current tax consequences. The receipt of cash by mortgaging the property is not taxed; tax will generally be imposed only when the property is sold. However, there is a possible tax where the mortgage exceeds the adjusted basis of the property and the property is given away or transferred to a controlled corporation. Where the property is transferred to a controlled corporation, the excess is taxable gain. Further, if the IRS successfully charges that the transfer is part of a tax avoidance scheme, the taxable gain may be as high as the amount of the mortgage liability.

Charitable donations. The IRS holds that a donation of mortgaged property to a charity is a part-sale, part-gift, and the donor has taxable gain to the extent the mortgage liability exceeds the portion of the donor's basis allocable to the sale part of the transaction *(14.6)*.

Chapter 32

Tax Rules for Investors in Mutual Funds

As a mutual-fund shareholder, you may receive several types of distributions, such as ordinary dividends, capital gain distributions, exempt-interest dividends, and return of capital distributions. The rules for reporting the different types of distributions are discussed in this chapter.

The tax law provides different methods of identifying the particular shares being sold when you sell a portion of your mutual fund holdings and of determining the cost basis of those shares. You may be able to use these methods to obtain a preferred tax result on the sale.

32.1 Timing of Your Investment Can Affect Your Taxes

You may buy a tax liability if you invest in a mutual fund that has already realized significant capital gains during the year. For example, if a fund is about to make a large year-end capital gain distribution and you invest shortly before that, you will in effect have to pay tax on the return of your recently invested money.

You will be eligible to receive a forthcoming dividend or capital gain distribution if you are a shareholder of record on the "record date" set by the fund. On the "ex-dividend date," the net asset value per share will be reduced by the distribution amount per share. If you buy before the record date, the higher cost for your shares will be offset by the distributions you receive, but you will have to pay tax on the distributions. On the other hand, because you paid the higher pre-distribution price, your higher basis will reduce any capital gain on a later sale, or increase any capital loss.

If you want to limit your current tax and forego the basis increase, postpone your investment until after the record date for distributions. By that time, the value per share that determines the price will have been reduced by the distribution. Before investing, you may be able to find out from the fund when distributions for the year are expected; call the fund or check the fund's website for an estimate of projected distributions.

32.2 Reinvestment Plans

A mutual fund will allow you to reinvest dividends and capital gain distributions from the fund in new fund shares instead of receiving cash. You report such distributions as if you received them in cash. Form 1099-DIV sent to you by a fund reports the gross amount of taxable distributions that you must report on your return *(32.3)*.

Keep track of reinvested distributions. If you reinvest your mutual-fund distributions instead of taking them in cash, keep a record of the distributions and of the shares purchased with the reinvestment. The reinvested distributions are considered your cost basis for the acquired shares. You need a record of reinvestments to figure your cost when you sell your shares; *see* below *(32.7)* for calculating gain on the sale of mutual-fund shares.

Reinvested distribution can trigger wash sale. If you redeem fund shares at a loss within 30 days before or after a dividend distribution is reinvested into your account, a "wash sale" results, and the portion of the loss allocable to the reinvestment is not deductible *(30.6)*. The allocable loss is disallowed even though the wash sale was inadvertently caused by the reinvestment. The disallowed loss is actually deferred, as it is added to the cost basis of the replacement shares and will affect the computation of gain or loss on a later sale.

32.3 Mutual-Fund Distributions Reported on Form 1099-DIV

Mutual-fund distributions are reported to you and the IRS by the fund on Form 1099-DIV or substitute statement. Distributions that you reinvested to acquire additional shares are reported and taxed in the same way as distributions that are actually paid out to you.

Types of distributions. The Form 1099-DIV (or substitute statement) from your fund for 2010 may show several kinds of distributions. Distributions that you reinvested *(32.2)* instead of receiving in cash are included on the Form 1099-DIV.

- ***Ordinary dividends***—are the most common type of dividend, payable out of the fund's earnings and profits. They are shown in Box 1a of Form 1099-DIV. Short-term capital gain distributions are reported as ordinary dividends.
- ***Qualified dividends***—shown in Box 1b, are your share of the ordinary dividends (Box 1a) that are qualified dividends *(4.2)* from the fund's investments in U.S. corporations and qualified foreign corporations. For 2010, this amount is eligible to be taxed at the 15% or zero capital gain rate, but only if you held your fund shares for at least 61 days during the 121-day period beginning 60 days before the ex-dividend date *(4.2)*.

  Caution: For 2011, the tax status of dividends was unclear when this book went to press. Unless Congress acts, the law that allows many dividends to be treated as qualified dividends eligible for capital gain treatment will not apply after 2010 and thus all dividends for 2011 will be taxed as ordinary income. However, Congress is expected to extend qualified dividend treatment; *see* the *e-Supplement* at *jklasser.com* for a legislation update.

Filing Tip

Reduced Rate for 2010 Qualified Dividends

Box 1b of Form 1099-DIV shows your qualified dividends, the portion of the amount in Box 1a (total ordinary dividends) that is eligible for the 15% or 0% capital gain rate.

- ***Capital gain distributions***—shown in Box 2a of Form 1099-DIV, are your share of the net long-term capital gains realized by the fund on sales of securities in its portfolio. These are taxable to you as long-term capital gain *(5.3)* regardless of how long you have owned your fund shares.

  If the fund retained long-term capital gains and paid tax on them, your share will be reported to you on Form 2439, rather than Form 1099-DIV *(32.6)*.
- ***Return of capital (nontaxable) distributions***—shown in Box 3 of Form 1099-DIV, are a return of your investment that reduce your basis in your shares and are not taxed until basis has been reduced to zero.

See 32.7 for details on how to report these distributions on your tax return.

Year-end dividends. Mutual funds sometimes declare dividends at the end of a calendar year but do not pay them until January of the following year. If the dividend is declared in October, November, or December, and paid in the following January, the fund will report the distribution as taxable in the year it is declared.

32.4 Tax-Exempt Bond Funds

Dividends from a bond fund that represent tax-exempt interest earned by the fund are not subject to regular income tax, but capital gain distributions are taxable. The exempt-interest dividends are shown by the fund in Box 8 of Form 1099-INT. You report exempt-interest dividends along with your other tax-exempt interest on Line 8b of Form 1040 or of Form 1040A. The amount on Line 8b is not taxable, but if you receive Social Security benefits, the amount may affect the amount of taxable benefits *(34.3)*. If part of the exempt-interest dividends are attributable to private activity bonds, that amount may be a preference item subject to alternative minimum tax (AMT) *(23.3)*. The amount subject to AMT is shown in Box 9 of Form 1099-INT.

Capital gain distributions are shown on Form 1099-DIV and must be reported on your return; *see Table 32-1*.

When you redeem your shares in a tax-exempt bond fund or exchange the fund shares for other shares in a different fund, you realize taxable capital gain or deductible loss.

If you received exempt-interest dividends on mutual-fund shares held for six months or less and sold those shares at a loss, the amount of your loss is reduced by the exempt-interest dividend. To reflect this adjustment, you increase the sales price reported on Line 1 in column (d) of Schedule D by the loss not allowed. Report the balance as a short-term capital loss.

EXAMPLE

In January 2010, you bought a mutual-fund share for $40. In February 2010, the mutual fund paid a $5 dividend from tax-exempt interest, which is not taxable to you. In March 2010, you sold the share for $34. If it were not for the tax-exempt dividend, your loss would be $6 ($40 – 34). However, you may deduct only $1, the part of the loss that exceeds the exempt-interest dividend ($6 – 5). On Schedule D in column (d), increase the sales price from $34 to $39 (the $5 nondeductible loss). You may deduct $1 as a short-term capital loss.

32.5 Fund Expenses

If you own shares in a *publicly offered* mutual fund, you do not pay tax on your share of the fund expenses. There should be no entry in Box 5 of your Form 1099-DIV. However, expenses of a *non–publicly offered* fund are included in Box 5 of Form 1099-DIV and must be reported as a taxable dividend, even though the amount has not actually been distributed to you. This amount is included as a fully taxable ordinary dividend in Box 1 of Form 1099-DIV. An offsetting deduction may be claimed on Schedule A as a miscellaneous itemized deduction, subject to the 2% adjusted gross income floor *(19.1)*.

Filing Tip

Undistributed Capital Gains From REITs

The reporting and credit rules for mutual funds *(32.6)* also apply if you own shares in a REIT that has retained its long-term capital gains.

32.6 Tax Credits From Mutual Funds

Undistributed capital gains. Some mutual funds retain their long-term capital gains and pay capital gains tax on those amounts. Even though not actually received by you, you include as a capital gain distribution on your return the amount of the undistributed capital gain allocated to you by the fund. If the mutual fund paid a tax on the undistributed capital gain, you are entitled to a tax credit.

Table 32-1 Reporting Mutual-Fund Distributions

Type of Distribution	*Shown by the Fund in*	*How To Report*
Ordinary dividends and short-term capital gain distributions.	Box 1a, Form 1099-DIV	Box 1a of Form 1099-DIV shows taxable ordinary dividends. The total includes ordinary dividends and short-term capital gain distributions, which are taxed as ordinary income, and also qualified dividends, if any, which are taxable at the 15% or 0% capital gain rate. The Box 1a total must be entered on Line 9a of Form 1040 or 1040A. If your total ordinary dividends from all sources exceed $1,500 or if you received as a nominee ordinary dividends on behalf of another taxpayer, you must itemize the ordinary dividends on Line 5, Schedule B of Form 1040, (Line 5, Schedule 1 of Form 1040A).
Qualified dividends (eligible for 15% or 0% capital gain rate if you held shares at least 61 days during the 121-day period beginning 60 days before the ex-dividend date).	Box 1b, Form 1099-DIV	Box 1b shows the portion of the Box 1a amount that is eligible for the 15% or 0% capital gain rate. Report these qualified dividends on Line 9b of Form 1040 or 1040A. Unless you have 28% rate gains or unrecaptured Section 1250 gains that have to be reported on the "Schedule D Tax Worksheet" in the Schedule D instructions, you may use the "Qualified Dividends and Capital Gain Tax Worksheet'" in the Form 1040 or Form 1040A instructions to figure your regular tax liability using the capital gain rates.
Capital gain distributions. (This represents your share of net long-term gains realized by a fund on sales made from its portfolio.)	Boxes 2a–2d, Form 1099-DIV	Box 2a of Form 1099-DIV shows your total capital gain distributions. If your only capital gains are capital gain distributions, you do not have capital losses, and no amount is shown in Boxes 2b–2d of all your Forms 1099-DIV, you generally do not have to complete Schedule D (Form 1040) and may report the capital gain distributions from Box 2a directly on Line 13 of Form 1040 or Line 10 of Form 1040A. In that case, you use the Qualified Dividends and Capital Gain Tax Worksheet in the Form 1040 or 1040A instructions to figure your tax using the capital gain rates. If Schedule D is required, the total capital gain distributions from Box 2a must be reported on Line 13 of Schedule D and the rest of Schedule D completed. Box 2b shows the part of Box 2a that is unrecaptured Section 1250 gain from the sale of depreciable buildings. Box 2c shows the part of Box 2a that is Section 1202 gain eligible for a 50% or 60% exclusion. Box 2d shows the amount of Box 2a that is 28% rate gain from sales of collectibles. If you have an amount in Box 2b, 2c, or 2d, you must complete Schedule D.
Return of capital distributions (nontaxable)	Box 3, Form 1099-DIV	A return of capital distribution is not taxable income. However, if your basis for your shares has been reduced to zero by return of capital gain distributions, report additional nontaxable distributions as either long-term or short-term capital gain on Schedule D of Form 1040, depending on how long you held the shares.
Exempt-interest dividends	Box 8, Form 1099-INT	Report along with other tax-exempt interest on Line 8b of Form 1040 or Form 1040A. The portion of the exempt-interest dividends that is attributable to private activity bonds subject to AMT *(23.3)* is shown in Box 9 of Form 1099-INT.
Undistributed capital gains	Undistributed gains shown on Form 2439, Box 1a Tax paid by fund shown on Form 2439, Box 2	Box 1 of Form 2439 shows your total share of undistributed long-term capital gains. The undistributed gains are reported on Line 11 of Schedule D. To get a tax credit for the tax paid by the fund, enter the tax on Line 69 of Form 1040. Increase the basis of your mutual-fund shares by the excess of the undistributed gains included on Schedule D over the tax credit claimed on Line 71 of Form 1040.
Fund expenses from non–publicly offered funds	Box 5, Form 1099-DIV	If you itemize deductions on Form 1040, the expenses are deductible as miscellaneous expenses, subject to the 2% adjusted gross income floor *(19.1)*.
Foreign taxes	Box 6, Form 1099-DIV. Box 7 shows the country imposing the tax.	The foreign taxes may be claimed as a tax credit on Form 1116 or as an itemized deduction on Schedule A of Form 1040 *(36.14)*.
Federal income tax withheld	Box 4, Form 1099-DIV. Box 4 Form 1099-INT.	If you are subject to back-up withholding, the amount of federal income tax withheld should be included on Line 61 of Form 1040 (Line 38 of Form 1040A).

To claim the credit, check the Form 2439 sent to you by your fund, which lists your share of undistributed capital gain and the amount of tax paid on it by the fund. Enter your share of the tax the fund paid on this gain on Line 71 of Form 1040, and check the box for Form 2439. Attach Copy B of Form 2439 to your return to support your tax credit. Increase the basis of your shares by the excess of the undistributed capital gain over the amount of tax paid by the mutual fund, as reported on Form 2439.

Foreign tax credit or deduction. You may be able to claim a foreign tax credit (on Form 1116) or a deduction on Schedule A for your share of the fund's foreign taxes. In Box 6 of Form 1099-DIV, the fund will report your share of the foreign taxes paid by the fund, and in Box 7, the name of the foreign country. The fund should give you instructions for claiming the foreign tax credit or deduction *(36.14)*.

32.7 How To Report Mutual Fund Distributions

You cannot report mutual fund distributions on Form 1040EZ. Further, you must file Form 1040 and cannot use Form 1040A if you must report an undistributed capital gain on Schedule D or you must report a return of capital distribution on Schedule D because your basis in your fund shares has been reduced to zero.

Check *Table 32-1* above for details on reporting distributions on your return.

32.8 Redemptions and Exchanges of Fund Shares

When you ask the fund to redeem all or part of your shares, you have transacted a sale subject to capital gain or loss rules explained in *Chapter 5*. Exchanges of shares of one fund for shares of another fund within the same fund "family" are treated as sales. If you owned the shares for more than one year, your gain or loss is long term; if you held them for a year or less, your gain or loss is short term. However, if you received a capital gain distribution before selling shares held six months or less at a loss, your loss must be reported as a long-term capital loss to the extent of the capital gain distribution attributable to the sold shares. Any excess loss is reported as a short-term capital loss. This restriction does not apply to dispositions under periodic redemption plans.

Caution

Wash-Sale Loss Disallowance

A loss on the redemption of fund shares is disallowed to the extent that within 30 days before or after the sale, you buy shares in the same fund. The wash-sale rule *(30.6)* is triggered even when the acquisition of new shares occurs automatically (within the 61-day period) under a dividend reinvestment plan.

EXAMPLE

In June 2010, you bought mutual-fund shares for $1,000. In August, you received a capital gain distribution of $50, and you sold the shares for $850 in September. Instead of reporting a $150 short-term capital loss ($1,000 cost – $850 proceeds), you must report a long-term capital loss of $50, the amount of the capital gain distribution; the remaining $100 of the loss is a short-term capital loss.

Identifying the shares you sell. Determining which mutual-funds shares are being sold is necessary to figure your gain or loss and whether the gain or loss is short term or long term *(32.9)*.

Holding period of fund shares. You determine your holding period by using the trade dates. The trade date is the date on which you contract to buy or redeem the mutual-fund shares. Do not confuse the trade date with the settlement date, which is the date by which the mutual-fund shares must be delivered and payment must be made. Most mutual funds will show the trade date on your purchase and redemption confirmation statements.

Your holding period starts on the day after the day you bought the shares. (The day you bought the shares is the trade date.) This same date of each succeeding month is the start of a new month regardless of the number of days in the month before. The day you dispose of the shares (trade date) is also part of your holding period.

Planning Reminder

Keeping Track of Cost Basis

Keep confirmation statements for purchases of shares as well as a record of distributions that are automatically reinvested in your account. These will show the cost basis for your shares. Your basis is increased by amounts reported to you by the fund on Form 2439, representing the difference between your share of undistributed capital gains that you were required to report as income and your share of the tax paid by the fund on undistributed gains. Your basis is reduced by nontaxable dividends that are a return of your investment. Keep copies of Form 2439 and information returns showing nontaxable dividends.

32.9 Basis of Redeemed Shares

To figure gain or loss, you need to know the basis per share. Generally, your basis is the purchase price of the shares, including shares acquired by reinvesting distributions back into the fund, plus commission or load charges.

Load charges. Basis does not include load charges (acquisition fees) on the purchase of mutual-fund shares if you held the shares for 90 days or less and then exchanged them for shares in a different fund in the same family of funds at a reduced load charge.

EXAMPLE

You pay a $200 load charge on purchasing shares for $10,000 in Fund A. Within 90 days, you exchange the Fund A shares for Fund B shares. Because Fund A and Fund B are in the same family of funds, the $200 load charge that would otherwise be due on the purchase of the Fund B shares is waived. For purposes of figuring your gain or loss on the exchange of Fund A shares, your basis is $10,000, not $10,200. The disallowed $200 is added to the basis of the new Fund B shares, provided those shares are held more than 90 days. If the waived load charge on Fund B shares had been $100, basis for the original Fund A shares would be increased by $100, the excess of the original $200 load charge over the amount waived on the reinvestment.

Planning Reminder

Specific Identification Method

When you redeem part of your shares, the specific identification method of identifying the shares sold provides you the most flexibility. However, note the paperwork requirements for this method in Examples 1 and 2 in this section *(32.9)*.

Identifying the sold shares. If your shares in a mutual fund were acquired at different times, you need to know the basis of the particular shares you are selling in order to determine gain or loss. There are several methods of identifying which shares you are selling:

- ***Specific Identification Method***—allows you to select exactly which shares are being sold, enabling you to determine your gain or loss and achieve a desired tax result (*see* Examples 1 and 2 below and *Table 32-2*). You may not use this method if you have used the averaging cost basis method on a prior sale from the same fund.
- ***Average Cost Basis Method***—averages your cost for all shares in the fund (*see* Example 3 below). Once you elect to use average basis, you must continue to do so for all accounts in the same fund; *see Table 32-2* for averaging details.
- ***First-in, first-out (FIFO) Method***—applies if you do not specifically identify the shares or elect the averaging method (*see* Examples 1 and 2 below).

See Table 32-2 for details on these identification methods.

EXAMPLES

1. In 1996, you bought 100 shares of a mutual fund for $10 a share. In 1999, you bought another 200 shares for $11 a share, and in 2000, another 500 shares for $15 a share. In 2010 you sell 130 shares at $20 a share, but do not specifically identify the shares being sold. Under the IRS FIFO method, you are treated as having first sold the original 100 shares from 1996, then 30 of the shares bought in 1999. Your basis for the sold shares is $1,330:

100 shares from 1996 costing $10 each	$1,000
30 shares from 1999 costing $11 each	330
	$1,330

   Your taxable gain is $1,270 ($2,600 sales price less $1,330 basis). Had you specifically designated shares from the most recent lot, which cost you more, you would have reduced the taxable gain. For example, if you had given the fund written instructions to sell 130 of the 500 shares that you bought in 2000 at $15 per share and the fund acknowledged in writing your instructions, your basis on the sale under the specific identification method would be $1,950 (130 × $15) instead of $1,330. Gain would be reduced from $1,270 to $650 ($2,600 sales price less $1,950 basis).

2. Hall sold by phone part of his holdings in two mutual funds acquired over a number of years without specifying the particular shares being sold. On his return, Hall claimed a net long-term capital loss of about $2,400 using a LIFO method (last-in, first-out). However, using the FIFO method, the IRS held that he had a long-term capital gain of $163,000. In the Tax Court, Hall argued that the specific identification rule applies only to stock certificates, not noncertificate shares left on deposit with a mutual fund. The court disagreed. Without specific identification, the IRS FIFO method is reasonable. If good records are kept, you can select the specific shares being sold at the time of sale. You cannot wait until you file your return to allot specific sales to gain a tax advantage.

   What if you give written instructions to a mutual fund that specific shares should be sold, but the fund does not acknowledge your specification in its written confirmation? Regulations require such a written confirmation within a reasonable time after the sale.

3. You bought 160 shares of the XYZ Mutual Fund on February 4, 2003, for $4,000. On August 5, 2003, you bought another 240 shares for $4,800. You obtained an additional 10 shares on December 16, 2003, when you reinvested a $300 dividend. On December 18, 2004, you obtained an additional 20 shares when you reinvested a $750 dividend. This was your last investment in the fund. You sell 200 shares of the fund on September 27, 2010, for $8,000.

   Using the single-category average basis method, your average basis is $22.91 per share. Your total cost basis for all 430 shares is $9,850. Dividing $9,850 by 430 gives you an average basis per share of $22.91. Thus, your basis for the 200 sold shares is $4,582 (200 × $22.91 = $4,582).

   Under the average-basis method, the shares you acquired first are the shares deemed to be sold for purposes of determining your capital gain holding period. Thus, you are deemed to have sold the 160 shares bought on February 4, 2003, and 40 of the 240 shares bought on August 5, 2003. The sold shares were held long term on the sale date of September 27, 2010. You have a $3,418 long-term capital gain on the sale: $8,000 proceeds less $4,582 basis figured under the average-basis method.

Planning Reminder

Shares Received as Gift

To determine your original basis of mutual-fund shares you acquired by gift, you must know the donor's adjusted basis, the date of the gift, the fair market value of the shares at the time of the gift, and whether any gift tax was paid on the shares (5.17).

32.10 Comparison of Basis Methods

Your choice of basis method can have a significant effect on the computation of capital gains and losses when you sell a portion of your shares in a mutual fund (32.9). The following example compares the single-category averaging method to the specific identification and FIFO methods.

Transaction history. Assume that on February 8, 1993, you made an initial investment of $4,500 for 375 shares in ABC Mutual Fund at $12 per share. Under the dividend reinvestment plan, you reinvested a $400 dividend, received in December 1993, for an additional 40 shares at $10 per share. On June 10, 1994, you bought 350 shares at $15 per share. In December 1994 you reinvested your dividend, this time for 25 shares at $12 per share. On September 14, 1995, you bought 200 shares at $16 per share. On August 17, 2006, you bought 200 shares at $25 per share. You did not reinvest your dividends received after 2004 and did not buy any more shares after August 17, 2006.

Now assume that you are planning to redeem some of your shares in 2011 and are trying to decide which of the three basis computation methods would provide the best tax result. To use the specific identification method, you must identify at the time of the sale the shares you want redeemed and get a written confirmation from the fund that it received your instructions. If you do not do this, you will have to use the FIFO method or averaging method to figure your gain or loss.

You decide to redeem 200 shares on October 18, 2011, when shares are selling at $20 per share. The table below shows your transaction history and following that is a comparison of how the three basis methods would work given these facts.

Transaction History

Date	*Action*	*Share Price*	*No. of Shares*	*Shares Owned*
2/8/1993	Invest $4,500	$12	375	375
12/20/1993	Reinvest $400 dividend	$10	40	415
6/10/1994	Invest $5,250	$15	350	765
12/14/1994	Reinvest $300 dividend	$12	25	790
9/14/1995	Invest $3,200	$16	200	990
8/17/2006	Invest $5,000	$25	200	1,190
10/18/2011	Redeem $4,000	$20	200	990

Specific identification method. If you identify the shares you sold, you can use the adjusted basis of those shares to figure your gain or loss. You must specify the particular shares to be redeemed at the time of the sale, and must receive a written confirmation of your specification within a reasonable time. Depending on your situation, you may want to either maximize or minimize your gain or loss on the sale.

Assume you want to realize a loss that can be used to offset other gains. You would specify the 200 shares purchased at $25 per share on August 17, 2006, as the shares sold. Since the sales price on October 18, 2011 was $20 per share, the loss would be $5 per share, for an overall long-term capital loss of $1,000 ($4,000–$5,000).

On the other hand, assume that you do not need the loss and want to realize a gain but to minimize it. You would specify the 200 shares bought at $16 per share on September 14, 1995, as the shares sold. Since the shares were sold for $20 per share, the gain would be $4 per share, for an overall $800 long-term capital gain ($4,000 – $3,200).

FIFO (first-in, first-out). If you do not identify which shares you sold or choose the averaging method, you must use the basis of the shares you acquired first as the basis of the shares sold. Therefore, the oldest shares still available, the February 8, 1993, shares, are considered sold first. Thus, the basis of the 200 shares sold would be $12 per share. Your long-term capital gain is $1,600 ($4,000 – $2,400).

Average cost. The ABC Mutual Fund may provide you with your average basis (under the single-category method) when you make the redemption. If it does not, you may compute the average basis for all shares owned at the time of disposition, regardless of how long you owned them, including shares acquired with reinvested dividends. The basis and gain is computed as follows: You total the number of shares owned prior to the sale, 1,190, and total your investment in these shares, which is $18,650. You divide $18,650 by 1,190, which gives an average cost of $15.67 per share and a total cost of $3,134 for the 200 redeemed shares. Your gain is $866 ($4,000 – $3,134). For holding period purposes, the shares sold are considered to be from the earliest lot in 1993, so your gain is long-term capital gain.

Conclusion. Given this transaction history and preferred gain or loss objective, the specific identification method is advantageous. It allows you to realize a loss if that is your preferred tax result, or to realize the lowest capital gain if that is your preferred tax result.

Caution

Get Written Confirmation for Specific Identification Method

If you want to take advantage of the specific identification method, make sure the fund sends you a written confirmation of your selling instructions.

The specific identification method allows you to designate specific shares as the shares sold, allowing you to minimize a gain on the sale or to select shares that, because of their basis, would give you a loss.

Table 32-2 Identifying Mutual-Fund Shares When You Sell

Method—	*Tax Effect—*
Specific identification of shares sold	If you sell some of your shares that have been left on deposit with an agent for the fund, and you identify the specific lot of shares being sold in your sell order, you can fix profit or loss on the sale, depending on the cost of the shares selected. *See* Example 1 in *32.9*. You should give the fund written instructions to sell shares that you bought on a particular date and at a particular price. Ask the fund for a written confirmation that acknowledges your instructions. The IRS requires that written confirmation of your instruction to sell particular shares be received within a reasonable time after the sale. The fund does not actually have to sell specific shares, just provide written confirmation that you instructed it to do so.
FIFO (First-in, first-out)	If you do not specifically identify the sold shares as just discussed, and you do not elect to average cost basis as discussed below, the IRS requires you to compute gain or loss as if shares were sold in the order that you acquired them. If the earliest acquired shares are treated as sold, taxable gain on a current sale will generally be higher than if the specific identification method was used, assuming that your least expensive shares were bought first; *see* Example 1 in *32.9*.
Averaging your basis	You may elect to average the cost of shares acquired at different times and prices. The election applies to mutual-fund shares held by an agent, usually a bank, in an account kept for the periodic acquisition or redemption of shares in the particular fund. You still need records of your total basis, but averaging avoids the difficult task of identifying the exact shares being sold. Many funds ease the record-keeping burden by providing to shareholders who have redeemed shares a statement showing their average cost basis under the single-category method. *See* Example 3 in *32.9*. The single-category method is easier to apply than the double-category method, as explained below. To elect either averaging method, attach a note to your return specifying the chosen method. Once you have elected one of the averaging methods, you must continue to apply the same method for all sales or exchanges of shares in all of your accounts that are in the same fund. However, you may use the specific identification method or the FIFO method, or the other averaging method for shares in other funds in the same "family" of funds. For example, if you own shares in the XYZ Co. growth fund and also in the XYZ Co. bond fund, you may use an averaging method for the bond fund shares and the specific identification method for the growth fund shares. You can use the average cost basis for sales of shares in one mutual-fund family, and use the specific identification method for sales of shares of other fund families. ***Single-category averaging.*** You figure the average cost per share by dividing your total basis for all shares in the account by the number of shares. For example, if you bought 100 shares of a fund in 2003 at $20 per share and another 100 shares in 2004 at $30 per share, your average basis per share is $25 ($5,000 total cost ÷ 200 shares). If you sell 50 shares in 2010 for $35 a share, your basis for the sold shares is $1,250 (50 × $25 average basis) and your gain on the sale is $500 ($1,750 sales proceeds less $1,250 basis). For holding period purposes, you are treated as having sold shares in the order you acquired them (first-in, first-out). ***Double-category averaging.*** You have to separate your account shares into a long-term category for shares held more than one year and a short-term category for shares held one year or less. You figure the average cost per share in each category by dividing the total basis for all shares in that category by the number of shares in that category. You may specify to the agent handling share transactions the category from which you are selling. If you do not so specify, the long-term shares are deemed to have been sold first. If the number of shares sold exceeds the number in the long-term class, the excess shares are charged to the short-term class.

Chapter 33

Educational Tax Benefits

The tax law provides several tax benefits for people attending school. If you can take advantage of them, you are in effect receiving a government subsidy that lowers the cost of education.

The following benefit provisions can provide substantial tax savings, but are hedged with restrictions that may bar or limit their availability: The American Opportunity Tax Credit, the Lifetime Learning credit, a student loan interest deduction, and a deferral of taxes on interest earned on contributions to state-sponsored college tuition programs and Coverdell ESAs. An above-the-line deduction for higher education tuition and fees may be available if your income is too high to claim an American Opportunity or Lifetime Learning credit, provided the deduction is extended to 2010 by Congress *(33.13)*.

33.1 Scholarships and Grants

Scholarships and fellowships of a degree candidate are tax free to the extent that the grants pay for tuition and course-related fees, books, supplies, and equipment that are required for courses. Amounts for room, board, and incidental expenses are taxable. If you are not a candidate for a degree (*see* the degree test below), your entire grant is taxable.

Generally, you must pay tax on grants or tuition reductions that pay for teaching or other services required as a condition of receiving the grant. This is true even if all degree candidates are required to perform the services. Thus, if you are a graduate student and receive a stipend for teaching, those payments are taxable, subject to withholding, and reported by the school on Form W-2. Similarly, no tax-free exclusion is allowed for federal grants where the recipient agrees to do future work with the federal government. However, a grant or tuition reduction that represents payment for teaching, research, or other services is not taxable if it is paid under the National Health Services Corps Scholarship Program or the Armed Forces Health Professions Scholarship and Financial Assistance Program.

Degree test. Scholarships given to students attending a primary or secondary school, or to those pursuing a degree at a college or university, meet the degree test. Also qualifying are full-time or part-time scholarships for study at an educational institution that (1) provides an educational program acceptable for full-time credit towards a higher degree or offers a program of training to prepare students for gainful employment in a recognized occupation and (2) is authorized under federal or state law to provide such a program and is accredited by a nationally recognized accreditation agency.

Caution

Graduate Teaching and Research Assistants

If you must teach, do research, or provide other services to obtain a tuition reduction for graduate studies, a tuition reduction from the school is tax free if it is in addition to regular pay for the services. If the tuition reduction is your compensation, it is taxable, unless it is paid under the National Health Services Corps Scholarship Program or the Armed Forces Health Professions Scholarship and Financial Assistance Program.

33.2 Tuition Reductions for College Employees

Free or partially free tuition for *undergraduate* studies provided to a faculty member or school employee is generally not taxable. The tuition reduction may be for education at his or her own school or at another school. Tuition benefits may be taxable to highly compensated employees if the tuition plan discriminates in their favor. Tuition reductions that represent compensation for services are taxable unless paid under the National Health Services Corps Scholarship Program or the Armed Forces Health Professions Scholarship and Financial Assistance Program.

Tax-free tuition benefits may also be provided to the employee's spouse, dependent child, a former employee who retired or left on disability, a widow or widower of an individual who died while employed by the school, or a widow or widower of a retired or disabled employee.

A child under the age of 25 qualifies for a tax-free tuition reduction if both parents have died and one of the parents qualified for tax-free tuition benefits. If the child is age 25 or over, tuition reductions are taxed even if both parents are deceased.

33.3 How Fulbright Awards Are Taxed

Fulbright awards for teaching, lecturing, or research are taxable unless you can claim the foreign earned income exclusion to avoid tax on the grant *(Chapter 36)*. If you do not qualify for the exclusion, your overseas stay is temporary, and you intend to return to your regular teaching position in the United States, you may deduct the cost of your travel, meals, and lodgings overseas.

33.4 United States Savings Bond Tuition Plans

Consider the use of Series EE bonds *(30.14)* or I bonds *(30.15)* to fund part of a college savings program. You can defer the interest income until final maturity (30 years) or report the interest annually. At redemption, the interest is not subject to state or local tax. For bonds purchased in your child's name, having your child report the interest annually may be advisable where it can be offset by the child's standard deduction or itemized deductions. To the extent interest is offset each year, it escapes tax *(4.29)*.

Interest exclusion may be available if you redeem EE bonds issued in your own name after 1989 or I bonds. If you purchased EE bonds in your own name or jointly with your spouse after 1989 and have been deferring the reporting of interest income, you may be able to exclude accumulated interest from federal tax in the year you redeem the bonds if in that year you pay tuition and enrollment education fees or you contribute to a Coverdell ESA *(33.11)* or qualified tuition program *(33.5)*. The interest exclusion rule also applies to redemptions of I bonds. The exclusion, claimed on Form 8815, is subject to several limitations as discussed in the following paragraphs.

Who qualifies for the exclusion. You must have been age 24 or over before the month in which the bonds were purchased, and the bonds must have been issued solely in your name or in the joint names of you and your spouse. You may not claim the exclusion for bonds bought in your child's name or owned jointly with your child. In the year the bonds are redeemed you must pay tuition and enrollment fees or contribute to a Coverdell ESA or qualified tuition plan for yourself, your spouse, or your dependents for whom you claim an exemption on your return. Thus, grandparents may not claim the exclusion if they buy savings bonds to fund the college education of grandchildren unless the children are dependents of the grandparents in the year the bonds are cashed. Tuition and fees must be for a college, university, or vocational school that meets federal financial aid standards. Room and board are not eligible expenses. Married persons filing separately are not eligible for the exclusion.

Excludable amount and phaseout rule. The tax-free amount of EE or I bond interest is figured on Form 8815. The amount of the exclusion depends on the amount of qualified higher educational expenses you pay and your modified adjusted gross income (MAGI) in the year of redemption. However, no exclusion is allowed to a married person who files separately, regardless of income or amount of expenses.

On Form 8815, qualified expenses must be reduced by the amount of any nontaxable scholarship or fellowship grant, tax-free employer-provided educational assistance, educational expenses taken into account when figuring a Hope or lifetime learning credit *(33.7)*, and educational expenses taken into account when figuring the tax-free portion of a distribution from a qualified tuition plan *(33.6)* or a Coverdell ESA *(33.11)*.

If after the required reductions qualified expenses equal or exceed the redemption proceeds, 100% of the interest is potentially excludable, subject to the phaseout based on MAGI. If the redemption amount exceeds the amount of educational expenses (after any required reduction), the excludable amount is based on the ratio of expenses to the redemption amount and the phaseout computation.

A full interest exclusion is allowed only to persons with MAGI below a phaseout threshold. For 2010, the MAGI phaseout ranges are $105,100 to $135,100 for married persons filing jointly and qualifying widow(er)s, and $70,100 to $85,100 for single persons and heads of household. For purposes of applying the phaseout, MAGI is generally your regular adjusted gross income plus the interest on the redeemed EE or I bonds, student loan interest *(33.14)*, or tuition and fees *(33.13)* that you deduct, and foreign income items and employer-provided adoption assistance that you excluded from income. *See* the Form 8815 instructions.

EXAMPLE

In November 2010, you redeem an I bond that you bought in September 2001 for $10,000 (face value). You receive $16,600, including $10,000 principal and $6,600 interest. In 2010, your qualified higher education expenses total $19,250. After taking into account $4,000 of expenses used to figure an American Opportunity credit *(33.8)*, you show $15,250 of qualified higher education expenses on Form 8815. The excludable percentage of interest is 91.87% ($15,250 education expenses divided by $16,660 redemption proceeds). Thus, $6,063 (91.87% x $6,600) of the interest is potentially excludable from income, subject to the phaseout rules.

Assume that you are married filing jointly and have MAGI of $117,867 for 2010. On Form 8815, you divide your excess MAGI of $12,767 ($117,867 – 105,100 threshold) by the $30,000 phaseout range to get a phaseout percentage of 42.56%. Thus, 42.56% of the potential $6,063 exclusion, or $2,580, is phased out. The exclusion is limited to $3,483 ($6,063 – $2,580).

33.5 Contributing to a Qualified Tuition Program (Section 529 Plan)

Qualified tuition programs (QTPs), also known as Section 529 plans, allow you to either prepay a designated beneficiary's future qualified higher education expenses or to establish a savings plan from which such expenses can be paid. States can sponsor savings plans and prepayment plans. Private colleges, universities, and vocational schools can set up prepayment plans only. Qualified higher education costs include tuition, fees, books, supplies, and eligible room and board costs. Distributions are generally tax free to the extent of qualified higher education expenses *(33.6)*.

In a prepayment plan, a parent or other relative can purchase tuition credits or certificates as a prepayment of a child's future college costs. Where the child will not start college for many years, prepaying tuition according to a set schedule can avoid higher inflation-based tuition costs down the road. In a state-sponsored savings plan, annual contributions are made to an account for the benefit of the designated beneficiary, earnings accumulate tax-free, and withdrawals can later be made to pay the beneficiary's qualified higher education costs.

Contribution details and other plan terms including investment options can vary greatly from plan to plan. If you are considering an investment, you should contact the state or educational institution maintaining the plan for details.

Contributions are not deductible for federal tax purposes. However, a state income tax deduction may be available to residents who contribute to a state-sponsored QTP.

You may contribute to both a QTP and a Coverdell ESA *(33.11)* in the same year on behalf of the same beneficiary.

Gift tax consequences. A contribution to a qualified tuition program is treated as a completed gift of a present interest passed from the contributor to the beneficiary at the time of contribution. Contributions are eligible for the annual gift tax exclusion, which applies separately to each individual to whom you make gifts during a year. For 2010, the per-donee exclusion is $13,000, but if you are married and your spouse elects to split the gift, the exclusion is $26,000. If your gift exceeds the annual exclusion, a special gift tax rule allows you to elect on Form 709 (annual gift tax and generation-skipping transfer tax return) to treat contributions of up to five times the annual exclusion as if they were made over five years. Thus, for 2010, you can elect to treat contributions of up to $65,000 (five times the $13,000 exclusion) as if the contributions were made ratably over five years, and this is doubled to $130,000 if your spouse elects to split gifts. If the election is made, you have to report as a 2010 gift on Form 709 only 20% of the contribution up to the $65,000/$130,000 limit, allowing that amount to be offset by the annual exclusion, plus the amount of any contribution exceeding the $65,000/$130,000 limit.

33.6 Distributions From Qualified Tuition Programs (Section 529 Plans)

The portion of a QTP distribution that is allocable to a recovery of contributions to the plan (basis) is not taxable. This is true whether the plan is a state QTP or a private educational institution QTP. A beneficiary who receives a distribution of earnings from a state or private QTP to pay college costs does not have to include the earnings in income if the total distribution does not exceed "adjusted qualified higher education expenses" for the year, as discussed below.

On Form 1099-Q, which you should receive from the plan paying the distribution, the gross distribution in Box 1 is divided between earnings in Box 2 and the return of investment (or basis) in Box 3.

Qualified higher education expenses. For purposes of figuring if part of a distribution from a QTP is taxable (*see* below), qualified higher education costs are tuition, fees, books, supplies, and equipment required for enrollment or attendance at an eligible educational institution, which is any college, university, vocational school, or other postsecondary school eligible to participate in federal student aid programs. The purchase of a computer, Internet access, and software in 2009 or 2010 (but not non-educational sports, games or hobby software) that will be used while the student is enrolled at an eligible educational institution is also treated as a qualified higher education expense.

Reasonable room and board costs for a designated beneficiary who is at least a half-time student also qualify. The limit that is considered reasonable for room and board expenses is the *greater* of the room and board allowance determined by the eligible institution for federal financial aid purposes or the actual amount charged for a student residing in housing that is owned and operated by the eligible educational institution. In the case of a special needs beneficiary, the definition of qualifying expenses includes all expenses that are necessary for that person's enrollment or attendance at an eligible institution.

Figuring the taxable portion of a distribution from a QTP. Whether or not a distribution of earnings from a QTP is taxable depends on whether the distribution exceeds adjusted qualified higher education expenses. The qualified higher education expenses paid during the year must be reduced by any tax-free assistance such as scholarships, Pell grants, veterans' assistance, and employer-paid expenses. If an American Opportunity or lifetime learning credit is claimed for the year of the distribution, the expenses taken into account in determining the credit also reduce qualified higher education expenses. If after the reductions the resulting adjusted qualified higher education expenses equal or exceed the total QTP distribution, the entire distribution is tax free. If after the reductions the resulting adjusted qualified higher education costs are less than the total QTP distribution, part of the earnings (shown in Box 2 of Form 1099-Q) is taxable. The Example below illustrates the computation of the taxable amount.

If earnings are taxable, a 10% "additional tax" may also be due, but there are exceptions for distributions that are taxable merely because qualified expenses had to be reduced by tax-free education assistance or expenses taken into account in figuring an American Opportunity or lifetime learning credit. The additional tax is figured on Form 5329.

EXAMPLE

In 2003, Marta's parents opened a savings QTP maintained by their state government. Over the years they contributed $18,000 to the account. The total balance in the account is $27,000 in June 2010 when a $3,600 distribution from the plan is made to Marta. In the summer of 2010, Marta enrolled in college and had $8,500 of qualified higher education expenses for the rest of the year. Marta was awarded a $3,000 scholarship. On their 2010 return, Marta's parents claimed an American Opportunity credit of $2,500 (the maximum credit per student for 2010 *(33.8)*.

Before Marta can determine the taxable portion of her withdrawal, she must reduce her total qualified higher education expenses. Note that the reduction for the American Opportunity credit is $4,000, as $4,000 of expenses are taken into account in figuring a $2,500 credit *(33.8)*.

Total qualified higher education expenses	$8,500
Less: Tax-free scholarship	–3,000
Less: Expenses taken into account in figuring American Opportunity credit	–4,000
Equals: Adjusted qualified higher education expenses (AQEE)	$1,500

Since Marta's adjusted qualified expenses of $1,500 are less than the $3,600 QTP distribution, she must pay tax on the part of the distributed earnings that is not allocable to the expenses. She received a Form 1099-Q that showed that $2,400 of the QTP distribution was a recovery of basis and $1,200 was earnings. Marta figures the taxable part of distributed earnings as follows:

1. The tax-free portion of the earnings is $500: $1,200 distributed earnings × $1,500 (AQEE)/ $3,600 distribution.
2. The balance of the earnings, or $700 ($1,200 – $500), is taxable. Marta must report it as "other income" on Line 21 of Form 1040.

Coordination with Coverdell ESA distributions. If distributions from both a QTP and a Coverdell ESA *(33.11)* are received in the same year and the total distributions exceed the adjusted qualified higher education expenses, the expenses must be allocated between the distributions. Assume that in the above example Marta had withdrawn $3,000 from her QTP and $600 from her Coverdell ESA instead of taking the entire amount from her QTP. Marta would allocate $1,250 of the expenses to the QTP distribution ($3,000 QTP / $3,600 total distribution × $1,500 expenses = $1,250), and $250 of the expenses to the ESA ($600 ESA/$3,600 distribution × $1,500 expenses = $250). She would then figure the taxable portion of earnings from each distribution based on the allocable $1,250 or $250 of expenses.

Contributor's loss on QTP investment. If the entire account is distributed and the total investment in the account has not been recovered, the contributor may be able to claim a loss. However, the loss is a miscellaneous itemized deduction subject to the 2% of AGI floor on Schedule A, Form 1040.

33.7 Education Tax Credits

For 2010, there are two tax credits for higher education tuition and qualified fees: The American Opportunity credit and the lifetime learning credit. Both credits are figured on Form 8863. You may not claim both credits for the same student for the same year.

The American Opportunity credit is an enhanced version of the pre-2009 Hope credit that applies only for 2009 and 2010 unless Congress extends it beyond 2010 with new legislation. An extension of the American Opportunity credit to at least 2011 was considered likely but had not yet occurred when this book went to press. *See* the *e-Supplement at jklasser.com* for a legislation update.

The maximum 2010 American Opportunity credit is $2,500 per eligible student for qualified expenses in the first four years of post-secondary education. 40% of the credit is generally refundable, meaning that it is allowed even if it exceeds your tax liability. *See 33.8* for details on the American Opportunity credit.

Unlike the American Opportunity credit, the Lifetime Learning credit may be claimed for higher education costs beyond the fourth year of post-secondary education and for non-degree courses that enable the student to acquire or improve job skills. Only tuition and fees/expenses required for enrollment or attendance qualify. The maximum Lifetime Learning credit is $2,000 annually, regardless of how many students you pay expenses for. *See 33.9* for details on the Lifetime Learning credit.

Both the American Opportunity and Lifetime Learning credits are subject to a phaseout based on income, but the phaseout range is more favorable for the American Opportunity credit; *see 33.10*.

Some of the qualification rules for the American Opportunity and Lifetime Learning credits are the same and these are discussed below.

The American Opportunity credit is discussed further at *33.8* and the Lifetime Learning credit at *33.9*.

Law Alert

Law Needed to Extend American Opportunity Credit to 2011

The American Opportunity credit, which increased the benefits of the prior law Hope credit for 2009 and 2010, had not yet been extended to years after 2010 when this book went to press, although an extension is likely. *See* the *e-Supplement at jklasser.com* for an update.

Rules Applicable to Both the American Opportunity Credit and Lifetime Learning Credit

Married persons filing separately are not eligible. If you are married at the end of the year, you must file jointly to claim either the American Opportunity credit or the Lifetime Learning credit.

Borrowed funds used to pay expenses. You can claim either the American Opportunity credit or the Lifetime Learning credit for eligible expenses paid with loan proceeds. If loan proceeds are sent directly to the educational institution, they are not considered paid until the institution credits the student's account.

Prepaid expenses. Your American Opportunity or Lifetime Learning credit for 2010 is based on qualified expenses you paid in 2010 for academic periods beginning in 2010, as well as 2010 payments of qualified expenses for academic periods beginning in the first three months of 2011. If you made a payment in 2010 for academic periods beginning after March 2011, the payment is not eligible for a 2010 credit or a 2011 credit.

Qualified expenses for eligible students at eligible educational institutions. To claim an American Opportunity credit or a Lifetime Learning credit you must pay qualified expenses for yourself, your spouse, or dependents claimed as exemptions on your return. The expenses must be for courses at eligible educational institutions. Specific student eligibility requirements for the American Opportunity credit are discussed at *33.8*. An eligible educational institution is any accredited public, nonprofit, or proprietary college, university, vocational school, or other postsecondary institution eligible to participate in the student aid programs administered by the U.S. Department of Education.

For both credits, qualified expenses include tuition, student activity fees that are required of all students for enrollment or attendance, and course-related books, supplies, and equipment that must be purchased from the educational institution as a condition of enrollment or attendance. Other required course materials, such as books or equipment bought privately, qualify for the American Opportunity credit but not the Lifetime Learning credit. Expenses for sports or hobby-related courses that are not part of the student's degree program do not qualify for the American Opportunity credit but such non-degree courses qualify for the Lifetime Learning credit if they help the student acquire or improve job skills. Room and board, insurance, medical expenses, transportation, and other personal expenses are not qualified expenses for either credit.

For purposes of figuring either credit, qualified expenses must be reduced by tax-free scholarships, Pell grants, Veteran's educational assistance or employer-provided educational assistance *(3.7)*. On Form 1098-T, the educational institution may report to the enrolled student the amount of qualified expenses received during the year, as well as any scholarships, grants, reimbursements or adjustments to expenses that could reduce the allowable credit.

Who can claim a credit for expenses paid by your child or by a third party? A dependent's expenses are treated as the expenses of the taxpayer claiming an exemption *(21.1)* for the dependent. For example, if your child is an eligible student and pays qualified expenses, and you claim an exemption for your child as a dependent on your tax return, only you can claim a credit for his or her expenses. Because you claim the child as your dependent, his or her payment of qualifying expenses is treated as your payment.

If a third party, such as the child's grandparent, pays tuition and related expenses for the child directly to a college, the student is treated as receiving the payment from the other person and making the payment to the school. If you claim a dependency exemption for your child, you treat the expenses as your own and may base a credit on the expenses. If the grandparent meets the support test for the child and claims the dependency exemption, the grandparent could use the expenses to claim a credit. The child can claim a credit based on the payment only if no one claims him or her as a dependent.

Qualified expenses paid directly to a school for a dependent under a court-approved divorce decree are also treated as paid by the dependent.

If you are eligible to claim the exemption for your child but do *not* do so, your child can claim a credit for qualifying expenses he or she pays as well as qualifying expenses that you paid.

Double benefits not allowed. You may not claim an American Opportunity credit and the Lifetime Learning credit for the same student for the same year. If you claim either credit, you may not claim the above-the-line tuition and fees deduction *(33.13)* for the same student for the same year.

You may be able to receive a tax-free distribution from either a Coverdell ESA or a state qualified tuition program (QTP) in the same year that you claim an American Opportunity credit or lifetime learning credit. The expenses taken into account as the basis of an American Opportunity or lifetime learning credit reduce eligible expenses for purposes of figuring the tax-free part of an ESA or state QTP distribution.

Phaseout of credits. Under phaseout rules based on modified adjusted gross income (MAGI), both credits can be reduced or eliminated. However, more taxpayers are eligible for the American Opportunity credit, which has a higher phaseout range than the Lifetime Learning credit; see *33.10*.

Recapture of credit. If you claim a credit and after you file your return for that year you receive tax-free educational assistance for the prior year or receive a refund of an expense used to figure the prior-year credit, you have to refigure the original credit. If the refund or assistance would have reduced the original credit, the amount of the reduction must be added to your tax liability for the year you receive the refund or assistance; *see* the Form 8863 instructions.

33.8 American Opportunity Credit

For 2010, you may claim an American Opportunity credit on Form 8863 for up to $2,500 of qualified tuition and fees paid for each eligible student in the first four years of college or other post-secondary institution.

An eligible student must meet the following requirements: (1) be enrolled in one of the first four years of postsecondary education, (2) be enrolled in a program that leads to a degree, certificate, or other recognized educational credential, (3) be taking at least one-half of the normal full-time workload for his or her course of study for at least one academic period beginning during the calendar year, and (4) not have any felony conviction for possessing or distributing a controlled substance.

The American Opportunity credit for 2010 is 100% of the first $2,000 of tuition, student-activity fees that are required as a condition of enrollment or attendance, and books, supplies, and equipment needed for courses. The books, supplies, and equipment qualify for the credit whether or not they had to be purchased from the educational institution.

The credit, however, phases out over a MAGI range of $80,000–$90,000 if you are single, head of household, or qualifying widow(er), or $160,000–$180,000 if married filing jointly. *See* the phaseout example at *33.10*.

The credit for 2010 is allowed to offset regular tax plus AMT liability and if the credit exceeds your liability, part of the credit is refundable, as discussed in the next paragraph.

Partially refundable credit. If the allowable American Opportunity credit, after application of the phaseout rule, exceeds your regular tax plus AMT liability, reduced by certain other credits (as shown on Form 8863), 40% of the credit is refundable, meaning that you receive it although it exceeds what you owe. Example 1 in *33.10* illustrates how the refundable portion is figured. The rest of the allowable credit is allowed to the extent of the regular tax and AMT liabilities. For example, assume that your otherwise allowable credit for 2010 is $2,500, but your regular tax plus AMT liabilities total $1,300. Your refundable credit is $1,000, 40% of the otherwise allowable credit. The $1,500 balance is limited to your total liability of $1,300. Your total credit is $2,300, $1,000 of which is refundable.

However, none of the credit is refundable if the taxpayer claiming the credit *(33.7)* is a child with investment income subject to the kiddie tax *(24.2)*.

33.9 Lifetime Learning Credit

For academic expenses paid during 2010, you may claim on Form 8863 a Lifetime Learning credit of up to $2,000 for the total qualified expenses paid for yourself, your spouse, or your dependents enrolled in eligible educational institutions *(33.7)* during the year, subject to the income phaseout *(33.10)*. In addition to tuition, qualified expenses include student activity fees and course-related books, supplies, and equipment that must be paid to the educational institution as a condition of enrollment or attendance.

In contrast to the American Opportunity credit, the Lifetime Learning credit does not have a degree requirement or a workload requirement. The credit may be claimed for one or more courses at an eligible educational institution that are either part of a post-secondary degree program or part of a nondegree program taken to acquire or improve job skills. The Lifetime Learning credit is not limited to students in the first four years of postsecondary education, as is the American Opportunity credit. There is no limit on the number of years for which the Lifetime Learning credit can be claimed.

The Lifetime Learning credit for 2010 is 20% of the first $10,000 paid in 2010 for qualified expenses for *all* eligible students in the family. Thus, the maximum Lifetime Learning credit you may claim for 2010 is $2,000 (20% of $10,000), subject to the income-based phaseout *(33.10)*. Under current law, both the credit percentage (20%) and the expense limit ($10,000) are fixed and not eligible for an inflation adjustment.

For students within the first four years of post-secondary education in 2010, both the Lifetime Learning credit and the American Opportunity credit are potentially available, but the American Opportunity credit is more advantageous. The Lifetime Learning credit is limited to $2,000 regardless of the number of students, whereas the American Opportunity credit is up to $2,500 per eligible student *(33.8)*. In addition, a more favorable phaseout range *(33.10)* applies to the American Opportunity credit.

33.10 Income Phaseout of Education Credits

Both the American Opportunity credit and the Lifetime Learning credit are subject to a phaseout on Form 8863 when your modified adjusted gross income (MAGI) is within a specified range. However, the phaseout range for the Lifetime Learning credit is substantially lower.

The Lifetime Learning credit is phased out if MAGI is between $50,000 and $60,000 and you file as single, head of household, or qualifying widow(er), or between $100,000 and $120,000 on a joint return. No credit is allowed once MAGI reaches $60,000, or $120,000 on a joint return.

The American Opportunity credit is phased out if MAGI is between $80,000 and $90,000 and you file as single, head of household, or qualifying widow(er), or between $160,000 and $180,000 if married filing jointly. No credit is allowed once MAGI reaches $90,000, or $180,000 on a joint return.

For most taxpayers, modified adjusted gross income is adjusted gross income (AGI) unless they have tax-free income earned abroad or from certain U.S. territories or possessions. If so, adjusted gross income is increased by such amounts.

EXAMPLES

1. Ron and Jackie are married and file jointly. In 2010, they pay $7,000 in qualifying college tuition and fees for their son Leo, and $8,500 for their daughter Ally. They claim both children as dependents on their 2010 joint return. Their MAGI for 2010 is $163,000. A tentative American Opportunity credit of $5,000, $2,500 for each child *(33.8)*, is allowed on Form 8863 prior to application of the phaseout rule. After the phaseout computation is made, their American Opportunity credit is reduced to $4,250. Their excess MAGI of $3,000 ($163,000 MAGI – $160,000 phaseout threshold on joint return) is 15% of the $20,000 phaseout range, so 15% of the tentative $5,000 credit, or $750, is phased out. The other 85%, or $4,250, is allowed under the phaseout rule. Of the $4,250, 40%, or $1,700, is a refundable credit, which Ron and Jackie enter on Line 66 of their Form 1040 (in the "Payments" section). The $2,550 credit balance ($4,250 – 1,700) is allowed as a nonrefundable credit on Line 49 of their Form 1040, assuming it is less than their tax liability, as reduced by certain other credits.
2. John, unmarried, pays $6,400 in qualified tuition and fees in 2010 for courses to improve his job skills. His MAGI for 2010 is $52,000. His tentative Lifetime Learning credit *(33.9)* before taking into account the phaseout is $1,280 (20% of $6,400). After applying the phaseout rule on Form 8863, John is allowed a Lifetime Learning credit of $1,024. His excess MAGI of $2,000 ($52,000 MAGI – $50,000 phaseout threshold for single filer) is 20% of the $10,000 phaseout range, so 20% of the tentative $1,280 credit, or $256, is phased out. The other 85%, or $1,024, is allowed as a nonrefundable credit, assuming it is less than his tax liability, as reduced by certain other credits.

Parent's option to forego child's exemption to let child claim credit. Your child may claim a credit if you are eligible to claim him or her as a dependent but do not do so *(33.7)*. If you are not allowed a credit for your dependent child's expenses because of the MAGI phaseout, and your child has tax liability against which the credit may be claimed, you can forego claiming the child as a dependency exemption on your return, which would allow the credit to be claimed on the child's return. Consider which of the child's credit or your dependency exemption would provide the larger tax savings.

33.11 Contributing to a Coverdell Education Savings Account (ESA)

A Coverdell Education Savings Account, or ESA, is a trust or custodial account set up specifically for the purpose of paying the qualified education expenses of the designated beneficiary of the account. A contribution cannot be made for a beneficiary after he or she reaches age 18 unless the beneficiary is a special needs beneficiary, as discussed below. Contributions must be in cash. Coverdell Education Savings Accounts were formerly known as Education IRAs.

Contribution deadline. The deadline for making a contribution for any year is the due date of your return for that year (not including extensions). You can make a contribution to a Coverdell ESA up until April 15, 2011, and designate it as a contribution for 2010.

Contribution limit for 2010. The maximum cash contribution that any individual (including the designated beneficiary) can make for a designated beneficiary for 2010 is $2,000. The $2,000 limit is generally reduced if your 2010 modified adjusted gross income (MAGI) is between $95,000 and $110,000, or if you are married filing jointly, between $190,000 and $220,000. For most individuals, MAGI is the same as adjusted gross income (AGI), but if the foreign earned income exclusion or an exclusion of income from Puerto Rico or American Samoa is claimed, the exclusion is added back to AGI. You may not contribute to a beneficiary's Coverdell ESA for 2010 if your MAGI is $110,000 or more, or $220,000 or more if filing a joint return.

If more than one Coverdell ESA has been set up for a beneficiary, the total 2010 contribution limit for all of the accounts is $2,000, regardless of how many persons contribute.

Law Alert

Possible Cutback in ESA Benefits for 2011

Unless Congress extends to 2011 the Coverdell ESA rules that were in effect for 2010, much less favorable rules will apply in 2011. The contribution limit per designated beneficiary would be reduced to $500, and a less favorable phaseout rule would apply to married persons filing jointly. Only withdrawals for higher education expenses would be considered qualified expenses for distribution purposes. *See* the *e-Supplement at jklasser.com* for an update on the rules for 2011.

A 6% excise tax applies to Coverdell ESA contributions that exceed $2,000 for 2010 for any beneficiary. The penalty is imposed on the beneficiary (Form 5329). The excise tax does not apply if the excess contributions (and any earnings) are withdrawn before the first day of the sixth month (June 1) of the following year. The withdrawn earnings are taxable for the year in which you made the excess contribution.

Caution: For 2011 and later years, the contribution limit will be reduced to $500 per beneficiary unless legislation extending the $2,000 limit is extended. *See* the *e-Supplement at jklasser.com* for an update.

Special needs beneficiary. For 2010, contributions to a Coverdell ESA for a special needs beneficiary may be made even if he or she is over age 18.

33.12 Distributions From Coverdell ESAs

Caution: As noted in the Law Alert at *33.11*, less favorable tax rules will apply to ESA distributions after 2010 unless Congress extends the 2010 rules to later years. Without the extension, elementary and secondary school expenses through grade 12 will not be qualified expenses. In addition, the rule allowing an ESA of a special needs beneficiary to continue past age 30 will no longer apply. *See* the *e-Supplement* at *jklasser.com* for an update on the post-2010 rules.

Tax treatment of 2010 ESA distributions. A designated beneficiary of a Coverdell ESA is not taxed on withdrawals made during 2010 that do not exceed qualified education expenses. If the total withdrawals in 2010 exceed the qualified education expenses (*see* below), a portion of the withdrawals is taxable to the beneficiary. The taxable portion is the amount of the excess withdrawal allocable to earnings; *see* the Example below and the worksheet in IRS Publication 970.

Filing Tip

Coordination With Education Credits

An American Opportunity credit or Lifetime Learning credit may be claimed for 2010 even if you exclude from 2010 income a Coverdell ESA distribution, as long as the distribution does not cover the same expenses for which a credit is claimed.

Qualified education expenses for 2010. In addition to qualified higher education expenses (as defined at *33.6* for QTPs), qualified expenses for 2010 ESA distribution purposes include contributions to a QTP *(33.5)* on behalf of the ESA beneficiary. Also qualifying are elementary and secondary education expenses, kindergarten through grade 12. The elementary or secondary school may be a public, private, or religious school. Eligible expenses for elementary and secondary school students include tuition, fees, academic tutoring, special services for special needs beneficiaries, books, supplies, computers and peripheral equipment, Internet access, and software. Software designed for sports or hobbies must be predominately educational in nature. Qualified expenses also include room and board, uniforms, transportation, and supplementary items and services including extended day programs required or provided by the school.

Coordination with 2010 education credits. If an American Opportunity credit or Lifetime Learning credit is claimed for 2010, qualified expenses for purposes of figuring whether a 2010 Coverdell ESA distribution is tax free must be reduced by the expenses taken into account when figuring the credit.

Figuring tax free and taxable part of a 2010 distribution. If the adjusted qualified expenses of the beneficiary equal or exceed the distribution, the entire distribution is tax free. If a distribution exceeds adjusted qualified education expenses, then part of the earnings included in the distribution is taxable. To determine the amount of adjusted qualified educational expenses, reduce the total qualified education expenses (defined above) by any tax-free educational assistance such as excludable scholarships, Pell grants, veteran's educational assistance or employer-provided educational assistance. Any expenses taken into account when figuring an American Opportunity credit or Lifetime Learning credit further reduce qualified expenses. The balance of qualifying expenses after subtracting tax-free educational assistance and credit-related expenses is the beneficiary's adjusted qualified educational expenses. The following Example shows how the taxable portion of the distribution is determined when the total distribution exceeds the adjusted qualified education expenses.

EXAMPLE

In 2010, Bianca Jane had $6,200 of qualified higher education expenses, her first year in college. She paid her college expenses from a variety of sources: a partial scholarship (excluded from gross income) of $1,500, a $1,000 Coverdell ESA withdrawal, a $1,500 gift from her parents, and $2,200 of earnings from a part-time job.

Of her $6,200 of qualified expenses, $4,300 was tuition and required fees that also qualified for an American Opportunity credit. Bianca Jane's parents claimed the maximum $2,500 American Opportunity credit on their 2010 tax return *(33.8)*.

Before Bianca Jane can determine the taxable portion of her ESA withdrawal, she must reduce her total qualified higher education expenses. Note that the reduction for the American Opportunity credit is $4,000, as $4,000 of expenses are taken into account in figuring a $2,500 credit *(33.8)*.

Total qualified higher education expenses	$6,200
Less: Tax-free education benefits	–1,500
Less: Expenses taken into account in figuring American Opportunity credit	–4,000
Equals: Adjusted qualified higher education expenses	$700

Since Bianca Jane's adjusted qualified education expenses of $700 are less than the $1,000 Coverdell ESA withdrawal, part of the withdrawal will be taxable. The balance in Bianca Jane's account before the $1,000 withdrawal was $2,800, to which $2,500 had been contributed. The Form 1099-Q sent to Bianca Jane shows that $893 of the $1,000 withdrawal is allocable to contributions (basis) and $107 to earnings. She must include $32 of the $107 earnings in her income, figured as follows:

1. The tax-free portion of the earnings used for qualified expenses is $75: $107 earnings x ($700 expenses / $1,000 distribution).
2. The balance of the earnings, or $32, ($107 - $75) is taxable, and must be reported as "other income" on Line 21 of Form 1040.

If Form 1099-Q had not provided Bianca with the breakdown between earnings and basis, she would need to rely on records showing her unrecovered contributions (basis) in order to figure the taxable part of the distribution. For example, Bianca's records show that total contributions to her account (none of which have previously been distributed) were $2,500. Dividing the $2,500 contributions by the $2,800 account balance and multiplying the result by the $1,000 distribution gives the $893 basis portion of the distribution ($1,000 x $2,500/$2,800 = $893). The balance of the distribution, or $107 ($1,000 – $893), is the earnings portion of the distribution.

Law Alert

Additional Tax Exception for Service Academy Appointees

If a designated beneficiary is appointed to the U.S. Military Academy, Naval Academy, Air Force Academy, Coast Guard Academy, or Merchant Marine Academy, a distribution is not subject to the 10% additional tax to the extent of the costs of "advanced education" at such academy (as defined by Section 2005(d)(3) of Title 10, United States Code.

Additional tax on taxable distributions. Generally, a taxable distribution is subject to a 10% additional tax, which is figured on Form 5329. However, the 10% additional tax does not apply to distributions that are: (1) made to a beneficiary (or to the estate of the designated beneficiary) on or after the death of the designated beneficiary, (2) made because the designated beneficiary is disabled, (3) made because the designated beneficiary received a tax-free scholarship or educational assistance allowance that equals or exceeds the distribution, or (4) taxable only because the qualified ESA education expenses were reduced by expenses used in figuring an American Opportunity or Lifetime Learning credit.

The 10% additional tax also does not apply to the withdrawal of an excess contribution (and allocable earnings *(33.11)* before June 1 of the following year.

Age 30 duration rule. If there are assets remaining in a Coverdell ESA when the designated beneficiary reaches age 30, the beneficiary must withdraw the assets within 30 days, unless he or she is a special needs beneficiary. The duration of the account can be extended by changing the designated beneficiary or rolling over the account to a member of the beneficiary's family who is under age 30; *see* below.

Rollovers and other transfers. Withdrawn assets may be rolled over tax free from one Coverdell ESA to another for the benefit of the same beneficiary or a member of the beneficiary's family if the recipient is under age 30. For example, if a beneficiary still has money in his or her account upon graduation from college, the Coverdell ESA can be rolled over tax free to the Coverdell ESA of a younger sibling. The withdrawal is considered rolled over if it is paid to another Coverdell ESA within 60 days. Only one rollover per Coverdell ESA is allowed during the 12-month period ending on the date of the payment or withdrawal. For rollover purposes, members of the beneficiary's family include the beneficiary's spouse, child, grandchild, stepchild, brother, sister (and a sibling's son or daughter), half-sister, half-brother, stepbrother, stepsister, father, mother (and siblings of parents), grandfather, grandmother, stepfather, stepmother, in-laws, and the spouses of any of the above.

The designated beneficiary can be changed to a member of the beneficiary's family (included in the above list) with no tax consequences if the new beneficiary is under age 30. The new beneficiary will have to withdraw the account balance no later than 30 days after reaching age 30, unless he or she is a special needs beneficiary.

If the beneficiary dies before age 30, the account balance generally must be distributed to the beneficiary's estate within 30 days of the date of death. However, if the Coverdell ESA is transferred to a surviving spouse or other family member (defined above) who is under age 30, the account may be maintained until he or she reaches age 30. The age 30 limitation will not apply if the new beneficiary is a special needs beneficiary.

33.13 Tuition and Fees Deduction

Caution:** The deduction for tuition and fees expired at the end of 2009, and although an extension of the deduction to 2010 is expected, Congress had not yet passed the extension legislation when this book went to press. The following discussion assumes that the extension will be enacted and that the deduction will be available on 2010 returns. Check the* *e-Supplement at jklasser.com* ***for an update on the expected extension legislation.

Depending on your income, you may be able to deduct up to $2,000 or $4,000 of qualifying higher education tuition and fees paid during 2010 on your 2010 return. The deduction is figured on Form 8917 and claimed directly from gross income on Form 1040, whether or not you itemize, or on Form 1040A.

You may *not* claim the deduction for expenses of a dependent for whom an American Opportunity credit or Lifetime Learning credit is claimed. You may *not* claim the credit for some of an eligible student's expenses and the deduction for the balance. If you qualify for both, you must choose between the credit and the deduction. A credit generally provides a larger tax savings, but the credit is phased out at a lower income level *(33.10)*. If your income is too high to claim a credit or most of the credit is phased out because of your income *(33.10)*, you may be able to take advantage of the deduction.

Filing Tip

Credit or Deduction?

If you have qualifying education expenses 2010, check to determine whether or not you can claim either the American Opportunity or Lifetime Learning credit. A credit produces a dollar-for-dollar reduction of your tax liability, while a deduction only reduces your taxable income. Claim the credit if it provides you with a larger tax benefit. You may not claim a credit and tuition and fees deduction for the same student in the same year.

Deduction amount based on income. If your modified adjusted gross income (MAGI) for 2010 does not exceed $65,000 or $130,000 if you are filing jointly, your maximum tuition and fees deduction is $4,000. If MAGI is more than $65,000 or $130,000, but not more than $80,000 or $160,000 if filing jointly, your maximum tuition and fees deduction is $2,000. No deduction is allowed if MAGI exceeds $80,000 or $160,000.

For purposes of the deduction, MAGI is generally the same as the AGI shown on your return, figured without taking into account the deduction for domestic production activities. You must add back to AGI any exclusion for foreign earned income or income from Puerto Rico or American Samoa, or the foreign housing exclusion or deduction.

Ineligible taxpayers. You may not claim the deduction if you are married filing separately. You are also ineligible if you may be claimed as a dependent on another taxpayer's return, whether or not you are actually so claimed.

Qualified higher education expenses. Expenses eligible for the deduction are the same as those qualifying for the Lifetime Learning credit. That is, the deduction is limited to tuition and enrollment fees paid to an eligible educational institution for yourself, your spouse or your dependents and student activity fees and course-related books that must be paid to the school *(33.9)*. You can claim your dependent's eligible expenses if you paid them and you claim an exemption for the dependent. You cannot claim the deduction for expenses paid by the dependent or by a third party on behalf of the dependent, even if you claim the exemption. Eligible expenses paid in 2010 for an academic period starting in the first three months of 2011 are deductible for 2010. Eligible educational institutions include any college, university, vocational school, or other post-secondary institution eligible to participate in the financial aid programs of the Department of Education.

Deduction affected by excludable education benefits. Expenses eligible for the deduction are reduced by tax-free scholarships *(33.1)* and other tax-free educational assistance. If you receive tax-free interest from an EE or I savings bond used for tuition *(33.4)*, the excludable interest reduces the expenses eligible for the deduction. A tax-free distribution of earnings from a Coverdell ESA *(33.12)* or a QTP *(33.6)* reduces the deduction-eligible expenses.

Recapture of deduction. If after you file your return on which the deduction was claimed you receive tax-free educational assistance for that year or receive a refund of an expense used to figure the deduction, you may have to repay (recapture) all or part of the original deduction. You recapture the deduction to the extent it gave you a tax benefit by reducing your tax. Refigure the original deduction by reducing it by the refunded amount and also refigure tax liability for that year. To the extent of the increase in tax liability, you must include the refunded amount in your income for the year you receive it.

33.14 Student Loan Interest Deduction

If you paid interest on a qualified student loan in 2010, you may be able to claim an above-the-line (directly from gross income) deduction of up to $2,500. Eligibility for the deduction is phased out if you have 2010 modified adjusted gross income (MAGI, *see* below) between $60,000 and $75,000, or between $120,000 and $150,000 if married filing a joint return. On a joint return, the deduction limit remains $2,500 even if you and your spouse each pay interest on a qualified student loan. If you are claimed as a dependent by another taxpayer, or you are married filing separately, you may not claim the deduction regardless of your income. The deduction is claimed on Line 33 of Form 1040 or Line 18 of Form 1040A. A worksheet in the form instructions may be used to figure your student loan interest deduction.

Caution: Unless Congress extends the 2010 rules beyond 2010, less favorable deduction rules will apply for 2011. The deduction will be allowed only for interest payments within the first 60 months for which interest was required. In addition, the phaseout will apply to lower incomes, and voluntary payments of interest during a period of loan forbearance will not be deductible. *See* the *e-Supplement at jklasser.com* for an update on the post-2010 deduction rules.

Qualified loans and expenses. A qualified student loan is one taken out to pay qualified higher education expenses for you, your spouse, or a person who was your dependent when you took out the loan. The education expenses must be paid or incurred within a reasonable time before or after the loan was taken out, and the funds obtained must be used toward education furnished while the student is enrolled at least half-time in a program leading to a degree or other recognized educational credential at an eligible educational institution. Eligible institutions are colleges, universities, vocational schools, and other post-secondary educational institutions eligible to participate in Department of Education student aid programs. Graduate school programs are included. Also included are medical internships or residency programs leading to a degree or certificate from an educational institution or hospital offering postgraduate training.

Qualified higher education expenses include tuition, fees, room and board (within qualified limits *(33.6)*), books, equipment, and other necessary expenses such as transportation. These costs must be reduced by:

1. Nontaxable employer-provided educational assistance benefits.
2. Nontaxable Coverdell ESA or QTP distributions.
3. U.S. Savings Bond interest excluded from income because it is used to pay higher education expenses.
4. Qualified tax-free scholarships.
5. Veterans' educational assistance benefits.

Loan origination fees and capitalized interest (unpaid interest that accrues and is added to the balance of the loan) can be counted as interest. In general, a payment, regardless of its label, is treated first as a payment of interest to the extent that accrued interest remains unpaid, second as a payment of any loan origination fees or capitalized interest, until such amounts are reduced to zero, and third as a payment of principal.

Voluntary interest payments are deductible. For 2010, you can deduct voluntary interest payments, such as when you have been granted a repayment deferment.

Dependents and married persons filing separately are ineligible. You may not claim a student loan interest deduction during any year in which someone claims you as a dependent. However, you may deduct interest payments made in a later year when you are no longer claimed as a dependent.

You may not claim a student loan interest deduction for any year in which you are married and file a separate tax return.

Other restrictions. A revolving line of credit is not a qualified loan unless you agree to use the funds solely to pay education costs.

You may not deduct interest paid on a loan from a relative as educational loan interest *(5.6)*.

You may not deduct interest on a loan from a qualified employer plan.

Caution

Deduction Lost for Student Dependent's Loan

If your parent or someone else claims you as a dependent on his or her return, you may not deduct interest on your return for student loan interest you paid. Furthermore, the person who claims you as a dependent may not deduct the interest where you are the borrower legally obligated to repay the loan.

You may not claim a student loan interest deduction for any amount you may deduct under any other tax law provision, for example home mortgage interest. You also cannot use the deduction if you use part of the borrowed money for purposes other than education, for instance to make improvements to your house.

Phaseout. The interest deduction is reduced or eliminated if your modified adjusted gross income (MAGI) exceeds phaseout limits. The reduction applies to your deduction for 2010 if MAGI is more than $60,000, or more than $120,000 on a joint return. If MAGI is $75,000 or more, or $150,000 or more on a joint return, you may not claim any deduction for 2010; the deduction is completely phased out. MAGI is the same as the adjusted gross income shown on your return (disregarding student loan interest) unless you claim a deduction for tuition and fees *(33.13)*, the exclusion for foreign earned income *(Chapter 36)*, the domestic production activities deduction *(40.23)*, or certain other items of foreign income or expenses were excluded or deducted from your income. Such items generally must be added back to adjusted gross income.

If your MAGI is within the phaseout range, figure the reduction to the 2010 deduction by multiplying your deductible interest (up to the $2,500 limit) by a fraction, the numerator of which is your MAGI minus $60,000, or $120,000 if married filing jointly, and the denominator of which is $15,000, or $30,000 if married filing jointly.

The student loan deduction worksheet in the Form 1040 or Form 1040A instructions can be used to figure the phaseout reduction and the amount of your deduction.

EXAMPLES

1. In 2010 you paid $900 interest on a qualified student loan. Your MAGI is $125,000 on a joint return. Your deduction is reduced by $150. You can deduct $750 ($900 – $150).

   $900 × $125,000 – $120,000/$30,000 = $150 reduction

2. The same facts as in Example 1, except you paid $2,600 interest. The maximum deduction of $2,500 is reduced by $417. You can deduct $2,083 ($2,500 – $417).

   $2,500 × $125,000 – $120,000/$30,000 = $417 reduction

Filing Tip

Deducting Unreimbursed Employee Educational Costs

Unreimbursed employee education costs, such as for travel, tuition, books, fees, and meals, are deductible only if you claim itemized deductions. You generally must report your expenses on Form 2106 or in some cases Form 2106-EZ *(19.3)* before entering the deductible amount on Line 21 of Schedule A, where they and other miscellaneous itemized deductions are subject to the 2% AGI floor.

Filing Tip

Lifetime Learning Credit or Tuition and Fees Deduction

If you have qualifying work-related education costs, you should determine whether you can claim the Lifetime Learning credit *(33.9)*. Also check to see if you are eligible for the above-the-line deduction for tuition and fees *(33.13)*. These tax breaks may be more valuable to you than a business or job expense deduction.

33.15 Types of Deductible Work-Related Costs

If you improve your job or professional skills by attending continuing education or refresher classes, advanced academic courses, or vocational training, you may be able to treat your expenses as a business expense deduction. As a self-employed business owner or professional, allowable expenses are deductible on Schedule C and reduce income subject to self-employment tax *(45.1)* as well as income tax liability. However, as an employee, the tax benefit of an unreimbursed educational expense deduction is limited because the expenses are miscellaneous itemized deductions, which, together with any other miscellaneous expenses, are deductible on Schedule A only to the extent that the total exceeds 2% of your adjusted gross income; *see 19.1*.

Keep in mind that tuition and fees (but not transportation and usually not books or supplies) for work-related educational courses may also qualify for the lifetime learning credit *(33.9)* or the tuition and fees deduction *(33.13)*. The lifetime learning credit, by reducing tax liability rather than taxable income, is more valuable than a deduction for education costs. However, you may be unable to claim the credit because your income exceeds the phaseout limit for the credit *(33.10)*. The tuition and fees deduction is an above-the-line deduction available even if you claim itemized deductions. If you are an employee and are within the income range for the tuition and fees deduction *(33.13)*, it is preferable to an itemized job expense on Schedule A that may be limited or eliminated by the 2% floor.

To deduct education costs on Schedule C (self-employed) or Schedule A (employee subject to the 2% AGI floor), you must show that the following conditions are met:

1. You are employed or self-employed;
2. You already meet the minimum requirements of your job, business, or profession;
3. The course maintains or improves your job or professional skills, or you are required by your employer or by law to take the course to keep your present salary or position; *and*

4. The course does *not* lead to qualification for a new profession or business. The cost of courses preparing you for a new profession is not deductible, even if you take them to improve your skills or to meet your employer's requirements. This rule prevents the deduction of law school costs. Furthermore, the cost of a bar review course or CPA review course is not deductible because it leads to a new profession as an attorney or CPA. If courses lead to qualification for a new business or profession, no deduction is allowed even if you keep your current position.

If your courses meet the above requirements you may deduct the following education costs on Schedule C if self-employed or on Schedule A subject to the 2% AGI floor if the courses are related to your job:

1. Tuition, textbooks, fees, equipment, and other aids required by the courses.
2. Local transportation costs *(33.17)*.
3. Travel to and from a school away from home, and lodging and 50% of meals while at school away from home *(33.17)*. The IRS will not disallow traveling expenses to attend a school away from home or in a foreign country merely because you could have taken the course in a local school. But it may disallow your board and lodging and expenses at the school if your stay lasts longer than a year.

Further details of the deduction requirements are provided in *33.16*.

33.16 Work-Related Tests for Education Costs

Educational costs are not deductible on Schedule C (self-employed) or Schedule A (employee) if you are unemployed or inactive in a business or profession. The cost of "brush-up" courses taken in anticipation of resuming work is also not deductible.

You are not considered unemployed when you take courses during a temporary leave of absence lasting one year or less.

Course must not meet minimum standards. You may not deduct the cost of courses taken to meet the minimum requirements of your job. The minimum requirements of a position are based on a review of your employer's standards, the laws and regulations of the state you live in, and the standards of your profession or business. That you are presently employed does not in itself prove that you have met the minimum standards for your job.

If minimum standards change after you enter a job or profession, courses you take to meet the new standards are deductible.

Teachers. The minimum educational requirements are those that existed when you were hired. If your employer set no tests fixing a minimum educational level, you meet the minimum requirements when you become a member of the faculty. Whether you are a faculty member depends on the custom of your employer. You are ordinarily considered a faculty member if: (1) you have tenure, or your service is counted toward tenure; (2) the institution is contributing toward a retirement plan based on your employment (other than Social Security or a similar program); or (3) you have a vote in faculty affairs.

That you are already employed as a teacher, with all the responsibilities of a teacher, may not establish that you have met the minimum educational requirements. A school system that requires a bachelor's degree before granting a permanent teaching certificate may grant temporary or provisional certificates after a person has completed a number of college credits. Renewal of the provisional certificate may be conditioned on the teacher's continuing education for a bachelor's degree. In this case, the IRS will disallow a deduction for the educational costs. The minimum requirements are not met until the teacher has the degree.

Course must maintain or improve job skills. To be deductible, the education must maintain or improve your current job skills. That you are established in your position and that persons in similar positions usually pursue such education indicates that the courses are taken to maintain and improve job skills. However, the IRS may not allow a deduction for a general education course that is a prerequisite for a job-related course.

If the courses lead to a change of position or promotion within the same occupation, a deduction for their cost will usually be allowed if your new duties involve the same general type of work. If, as a consequence of taking a job-related course, you receive a substantial advancement and the IRS

Planning Reminder

Teacher's Job Change

Elementary and secondary school teachers may deduct the cost of courses taken to make any of the following job changes: (1) elementary to secondary school classroom teacher; (2) classroom teacher in one subject (such as mathematics) to classroom teacher in another subject (such as English or history); (3) classroom teacher to guidance counselor; or (4) classroom teacher to principal. These are not considered a change to a new business.

questions the deduction of the course costs, be prepared to prove that you took the course primarily to maintain or improve skills of your existing job. However, if the course leads to qualification for a new profession, the IRS will disallow a deduction even if the course also improves current job skills.

Courses must not lead to qualification for a new profession. If a course improves your current job skills but leads to qualification for a new profession, the course is not deductible, even if you have no intention of entering that business or profession. For example, a deduction is not allowed for the cost of law school or medical school courses since they prepare you for a new profession. This is true even if you do not intend to practice medicine or law. The IRS with Tax Court approval has also held that a deduction is not allowed for the cost of college courses that are part of a degree program, such as a bachelor of arts or science degree.

If you are practicing your profession, the cost of courses leading to a specialty within that profession is deductible. For example, a practicing attorney may deduct the cost of a master's of law degree program (LLM).

EXAMPLES

1. Allemeier was originally hired as a sales representative by a manufacturer of orthodontic appliances. An outstanding employee, he quickly advanced in the company and was given greater responsibilities, including sales strategizing and conducting seminars. While he was encouraged in his decision to pursue an MBA, the corporation neither required such a degree for advancement nor reimbursed employees for the expense. Allemeier was promoted to several higher positions before obtaining the MBA. The Tax Court determined that Allemeier's MBA did not lead to a new trade or business and therefore his tuition payments were deductible. The MBA merely enhanced the skills he already used on the job, specifically, giving him a better understanding of financials, cost analyses, marketing, and advertising. His job requirements did not significantly change after he obtained the MBA.
2. A practicing dentist returned to school full time to study orthodontics while continuing his practice on a part-time basis. When he finished his training, he limited his work to orthodontics. The IRS ruled he could deduct the cost of his studies. His post-graduate schooling improved his professional skills as a dentist. It did not qualify him for a new profession.
3. A practicing psychiatrist may deduct the cost of attending an accredited psychoanalytic institute to qualify to practice psychoanalysis. A social worker has also been allowed a deduction for the cost of learning psychoanalysis. In one case, the Tax Court allowed a psychiatrist to deduct the cost of personal therapy sessions conducted through telephone conversations and tape cassettes. The court was convinced that the therapy improved his job skills by eliminating psychological blind spots that prevented him from understanding his patients' problems.
4. A licensed practical nurse may not deduct the costs of a college program that qualifies him or her as a "physician's assistant," which is a new business. Physicians' assistants and practical nurses are subject to different registration and certification requirements under state law, and, more importantly, the physician's assistant may perform duties, such as physical examinations and minor surgery, which go beyond practical nursing duties.
5. Edward, a self-employed golf instructor without an undergraduate degree, earned an associate's degree in business from the Golf Academy of the South. The IRS and Tax Court disallowed his deduction for tuition and fees. It does not matter that the courses may have improved his skills as a golf instructor. No deduction was allowed because completing the associate's program was a first step in acquiring a basic undergraduate degree that would qualify Edward for a variety of trades or businesses other than that of a golf instructor.

Caution

Are MBA Courses Deductible?

The cost of MBA courses is deductible if the courses enhance the skills required in your current position, are not a minimum job requirement, and do not qualify you for a new business. If an MBA degree is required to obtain a promotion to a new position, the MBA is a minimum job requirement and no deduction will be allowed. For a deduction, the courses must be related to your existing job responsibilities and not lead to qualification for a new business. The Tax Court has allowed deductions for MBA expenses where individuals with some managerial or administrative experience took the courses to improve skills needed for their existing jobs.

In one case, a college graduate who took a summer job before starting MBA courses was not allowed a deduction because he had not yet established himself in a business or employment; the summer position was just a temporary stage between schooling.

If your employer reimburses you for MBA courses that qualify for a deduction, the reimbursement is a tax-free working condition fringe benefit; *(3.6)*.

Further education required by employer or law. If, to retain your present job or rate of pay, your employer requires you to obtain further education, you may deduct the cost of the courses. The fact that you also qualified for a raise in pay or a substantial advancement in your position after completing the courses should not bar the deduction.

The employer's requirement must be for a bona fide business reason, not merely to benefit you. Only the minimum courses necessary for the retention of your job or rate of pay are considered by the IRS as taken to meet your employer's requirement. You must show any courses beyond your employer's minimum requirements were taken to maintain or improve your job skills.

33.17 Local Transportation and Travel Away From Home To Take Courses

If your courses meet the requirements in the preceding two sections *(33.15, 33.16)*, costs of local transportation and travel away from home may be included in the business/job expense deduction.

Local transportation expenses. If your courses qualify for a deduction under *33.16*, you may deduct transportation costs of going from your job directly to school. Transportation costs include the actual costs of bus, subway, cab, or other fares, as well as the costs of using your car. According to the IRS, the return trip from school to home is also deductible if you are regularly employed and going to school on a *temporary* basis. According to the IRS, you are going to school on a temporary basis if your courses are realistically expected to last for one year or less and actually do last no more than one year. This is the same one-year test for determining whether you can deduct the cost of commuting to a "temporary" work location *(20.2)* or living costs while away from home on a "temporary" assignment *(20.9)*. The IRS position is illustrated in the following Examples.

EXAMPLES

1. You regularly work in Camden, New Jersey, and every night for three weeks you drive from home to attend a refresher course. The course is considered temporary. You may deduct the round-trip transportation costs between home and school. The deduction is allowed regardless of how far you travel.

   If you went directly from your job to the school, you may deduct transportation from work to school, and from school to home.

2. On six consecutive Saturdays, which are nonworkdays for you, you drive from home to attend a qualifying course. This is considered a temporary course. You are allowed a deduction for round-trip transportation between home and school, even though you are traveling on a nonworkday.

3. You regularly work in Camden, New Jersey, and after work you drive from home to take classes twice a week for 15 months. The IRS does not consider the course to be temporary. You may deduct the cost of going directly from work to school, but the costs of going between home and school are nondeductible.

Using your car. If you use your own car for transportation to school, you may deduct your actual expenses or use the standard business mileage rate to figure the deductible amount. The standard mileage rate for 2010 is 50 cents per mile. Regardless of the method you use, you may deduct parking fees and tolls.

Travel and living expenses away from home. "Away from home" has a special tax meaning *(20.6)*. You are not away from home unless you are away overnight. If you are away from home to attend a qualifying course, you may deduct the cost of travel to and from the site of the course, plus lodging and 50% of meals while you are there.

Expenses of sightseeing, social visiting, and entertaining while taking the courses are not deductible. If personal reasons are your main purpose in going to the vicinity of the school, such as to take a vacation, you may deduct only the cost of the courses and your living expenses while attending school. You may not deduct the rest of your travel costs.

To determine the purpose of your trip, an IRS agent will pay close attention to the amount of time devoted to personal activities relative to the time devoted to the courses.

Is travel itself a form of education? A teacher generally may not deduct the cost of an "educational" trip to another state or country as a job expense. Although a trip may have educational value in that the teacher learns about people, culture, or places related to the courses that he or she teaches, the IRS position is that a specific statute, Code Section 274(m)(2), bars a deduction for travel that is a form of education. There may be exceptions where specific research can only be accomplished at a particular location, but a trip for "general" educational purposes does not qualify according to the IRS.

The Tax Court took a different view of the statute in a decision that opens the door to a deduction for teachers who travel overseas to take highly organized courses with regular lectures, a structured syllabus, tours to historically and culturally relevant sites, and extensive reading assignments. The Court allowed a California high-school English teacher and department chair to deduct $5,334 for her airfare, lodging, meals, and tuition for an 18-day trip to Greece in 1995. She was also allowed to deduct $7,705 for a two-week trip to Southeast Asia in 1996. In Greece, she took a course on Greek myths and legends and on the Asian trip, a course on Buddhist and Hindu traditions. Her school required neither course. For the Tax Court, the key to the deduction was the organized nature of the courses, which were sponsored by the Berkeley extension program, taught by university professors, and qualified for undergraduate credit, although the teacher was not taking the courses for credit. The regular lectures, tours, and readings were focused educational activities, not the type of mere educational travel that Congress intended to make nondeductible. After holding that a deduction was not barred by Section 274(m)(2), the Court still had to find that the courses had the primary purpose of maintaining or improving the teacher's skills, but it had little difficulty in doing so. The courses improved her teaching skills and helped her to develop curriculum. The courses on Asian traditions also helped her relate better to the predominantly Asian student population in her school. She spent most of her time attending courses and related programs and had minimal free time.

Chapter 34

Special Tax Rules for Senior Citizens

All of your Social Security benefits are tax free if your "provisional income," explained in *34.3*, is $25,000 or less if you are single, or $32,000 or less if you are married and file a joint return. No more than 50% of your benefits are subject to tax if you file a joint return and your provisional income is over $32,000 but no more than $44,000, or if you are single and your provisional income is over $25,000 but no more than $34,000. When provisional income exceeds $34,000 or $44,000 (depending on your filing status), more than 50%, but no more than 85%, of your benefits are subject to tax. If you are married and filing separately, and did not live apart for the whole year, you must apply the 85% rate without considering the base amounts. If you are married filing separately and you lived apart the entire year, are a head of household, or are a qualifying widow(er), use the $25,000 and $34,000 base amounts for single persons.

If you are receiving Social Security benefits but continue to earn wages or self-employed income, you must pay FICA taxes or self-employment tax on that income regardless of your age.

If you are on Medicare, be sure you understand the impact of adjusted gross income on your premiums *(34.12)*.

34.1 Senior Citizens Get Certain Filing Breaks

The following special tax rules favor senior citizens:

- ***Higher filing thresholds.*** If you are single and age 65 or older on or before January 1, 2011, you do not have to file a 2010 return unless your gross income is $10,750 or over. This is $1,400 more than for younger taxpayers. If you are married and you and your spouse are both age 65 or older, a joint return does not have to be filed unless your gross income is $20,900 or over, or $19,800 or over if only one of you is age 65 or older; *see* the chart on page 3 for further details.
- ***Higher standard deduction.*** If you are age 65 or older on or before January 1, 2011, you receive an additional standard deduction allowance if you do not itemize deductions. If you are single you get an additional $1,400 on your 2010 return, or 1,100 if you are married or a qualifying widow(er) *(13.4)*. Your 2010 standard deduction is $7,100 if you are single. If married filing jointly, it is $12,500 if one of you is age 65 or over, or $13,600 if both of you are *(13.4)*.
- ***Tax credit if age 65 or older.*** This is a limited tax credit for taxpayers age 65 or older who receive little or no Social Security or Railroad Retirement benefits. The credit may also be available to persons under age 65 who are totally disabled *(34.7)*. For example, if you are single, or married but only you are eligible, and receive more than $416 each month from Social Security, you may not claim the credit. If you are married and both you and your spouse are eligible for the credit and file a joint return, you may not claim the credit if you receive more than $625 each month from Social Security.
- ***Social Security benefits may be exempt from tax.*** The taxable portion of Social Security benefits may vary from year to year because it depends on an amount called "provisional income" *(34.3)*. If you are married and file jointly, none of your net Social Security benefits are taxable in 2010 if your provisional income is not more than a base amount of $32,000. The base amount is $25,000 if your filing status is single, head of household, qualifying widow(er), or you are married filing separately and did not live with your spouse at any time during 2010. Married persons who file separately and live together at any time during the year are not allowed any base amount; see *34.3* for computing taxable Social Security benefits.

34.2 Social Security Benefits Subject to Tax

If you received or repaid Social Security benefits in 2010, you will receive Form SSA-1099 from the Social Security Administration, showing the total benefits paid to you and any benefits you repaid to the government in 2010. Box 3 of Form 1099-SSA shows the total benefits paid to you in 2010. This may include, in addition to Social Security retirement benefits, survivor and disability benefits, which are subject to the same tax rules as retirement benefits, but not Supplemental Social Security (SSI), which is not taxable. Included in the Box 3 total are amounts withheld from your benefits for Medicare premiums, workers' compensation offset, or attorneys' fees for handling your Social Security claim; these and other withholdings are itemized in the "description" section below Box 3.

The *net benefit* shown in Box 5 of Form SSA-1099 (benefits paid less benefits repaid) is the benefit amount used to determine the taxable portion of your benefits (if any) *(34.3)*. Keep Form SSA-1099 for your records; do not attach it to your return.

Planning Reminder

Voluntary Withholding on Social Security Benefits

You can use your Social Security benefits to meet your estimated and final tax liability by electing on Form W-4V to have tax withheld from benefits at a 7%, 10%, 15%, or 25% rate.

Railroad Retirement benefits. The portion of your Tier 1 Railroad Retirement benefits that is equivalent to Social Security retirement benefits is subject to the computation for determining taxable benefits *(34.3)*. If any part of your 2010 Tier 1 benefits is equivalent to Social Security benefits, you will receive Form RRB-1099 from the government. The *net* Social Security Equivalent Benefit shown on Form RRB-1099 is the amount used to determine taxable benefits *(34.3)*. Other Tier 1 Railroad Retirement benefits, as well as Tier 2 benefits, are treated as pension income and not as Social Security benefits for tax purposes.

Benefits paid on behalf of child or incompetent. If a child is entitled to Social Security benefits, such as after the death of a parent, the benefit is considered to be the child's regardless of who actually receives the payment. Whether the child's benefit is subject to tax will depend on the amount of the child's income.

Medicare premiums deducted from benefits. The Medicare premiums deducted from your benefits are included in the total for benefits paid in Box 3 of Form SSA-1099. This includes premiums for Medicare Parts B, C and D. The premiums do not reduce the net benefits in Box 5 used to figure taxable benefits *(34.3)*.

Workers' compensation. If you are receiving Social Security disability payments and workers' compensation for the same disability, your Social Security benefits may be reduced by the workers' compensation. For example, you are entitled to Social Security disability benefits of $5,000 a year. After receiving a $1,000 workers' compensation award, your disability benefits are reduced to $4,000. For purposes of the computation steps to determine taxability of benefits *(34.3)*, you treat the full $5,000 as Social Security benefits.

Net benefits. The net benefit shown in Box 5 of Form SSA-1099 is the amount used to determine the taxable portion of your benefits. If Box 5 shows a negative amount (a figure in parentheses), none of your benefits are taxable. If the negative amount is related to Social Security benefits included in gross income in a prior year, you may be entitled to a deduction or a credit; *see* IRS Publication 915 for further instructions on how to figure the deduction or credit when your repayments exceed your gross benefits.

Taxable Social Security benefits are not considered earnings and therefore may not be the basis of an IRA contribution *(8.2)*, earned income credit *(25.10)*, or foreign earned income exclusion *(36.2)*.

Nonresident aliens. Unless provided otherwise by tax treaty, 85% of a nonresident alien's Social Security benefits will be subject to the 30% withholding tax imposed on U.S. source income that is not connected with a U.S. trade or business. *See* IRS Publication 915 for further details.

Worksheet 34-1 Figuring Your Taxable Benefits

(Form IRS Publication 915; see Example 2 on page 578)

Before you begin:

- If you are married filing separately and you lived apart from your spouse for all of 2010, enter "D" to the right of the word "benefits" on Form 1040, line 20a, or Form 1040A, line 14a.
- Do not use this worksheet if you repaid benefits in 2010 and your total repayments (box 4 of Forms SSA-1099 and RRB-1099) were more than your gross benefits for 2010 (box 3 of Forms SSA-1099 and RRB-1099). None of your benefits are taxable for 2010.

1. Enter the total amount from box 5 of ALL your Forms SSA-1099 and RRB-1099. Also enter this amount on Form 1040, line 20a, or Form 1040A, line 14a . . . 1. 15,000
2. Enter one-half of line 1 . . . 2. 7,500
3. Combine the amounts from:
   Form 1040: Lines 7, 8a, 9a, 10 through 14, 15b, 16b, 17 through 19, and 21
   Form 1040A: Lines 7, 8a, 9a, 10, 11b, 12b, and 13 . . . 3. 20,000
4. Enter the amount, if any, from Form 1040 or 1040A, line 8b . . . 4. 10,000
5. *Form 1040 filers:* Enter the total of any exclusions/adjustments for:
   - Qualified U.S. savings bond interest (Form 8815, line 14)
   - Adoption benefits (Form 8839, line 26)
   - Foreign earned income or housing (Form 2555, lines 45 and 50, or Form 2555-EZ, line 18), and
   - Certain income of bona fide residents of American Samoa (Form 4563, line 15) or Puerto Rico

   Form 1040A filers: Enter the total of any exclusions for:
   - Qualified U.S. savings bond interest (Form 8815, line 14)
   - Adoption benefits (Form 8839, line 26) . . . 5. -0-
6. Combine lines 2, 3, 4, and 5 . . . 6. 37,500
7. *Form 1040 filers:* Enter the amounts from Form 1040, lines 23 through 32, and any write-in adjustments you entered on the dotted line next to line 36. *Form 1040A filers:* Enter the amounts from Form 1040A, lines 16 and 17 . . . 7. -0-
8. Is the amount on line 7 less than the amount on line 6?
   No. (STOP) None of your social security benefits are taxable. Enter -0- on Form 1040, line 20b, or Form 1040A, line 14b.
   Yes. Subtract line 7 from line 6 . . . 8. 37,500
9. If you are:
   - Married filing jointly, enter $32,000
   - Single, head of household, qualifying widow(er), or married filing separately and you **lived apart** from your spouse for all of 2010, enter $25,000 . . . 9. 32,000

   Note. If you are married filing separately and you lived with your spouse at any time in 2010, skip lines 9 through 16; multiply line 8 by 85% (.85) and enter the result on line 17. Then go to line 18.
10. Is the amount on line 9 less than the amount on line 8?
    No. (STOP) None of your benefits are taxable. Enter -0- on Form 1040, line 20b, or on Form 1040A, line 14b. If you are married filing separately and you **lived apart** from your spouse for all of 2010, be sure you entered "D" to the right of the word "benefits" on Form 1040, line 20a, or on Form 1040A, line 14a.
    Yes. Subtract line 9 from line 8 . . . 10. 5,500
11. Enter $12,000 if married filing jointly; $9,000 if single, head of household, qualifying widow(er), or married filing separately and you **lived apart** from your spouse for all of 2010 . . . 11. 12,000
12. Subtract line 11 from line 10. If zero or less, enter -0- . . . 12. -0-
13. Enter the **smaller** of line 10 or line 11 . . . 13. 5,500
14. Enter one-half of line 13 . . . 14. 2,750
15. Enter the **smaller** of line 2 or line 14 . . . 15. 2,750
16. Multiply line 12 by 85% (.85). If line 12 is zero, enter -0- . . . 16. -0-
17. Add lines 15 and 16 . . . 17. 2,750
18. Multiply line 1 by 85% (.85) . . . 18. 12,750
19. **Taxable benefits.** Enter the **smaller** of line 17 or line 18. Also enter this amount on Form 1040, line 20b, or Form 1040A, line 14b . . . 19. 2,750

34.3 Computing Taxable Social Security Benefits

The taxable portion of your 2010 benefits depends on your *provisional income* and your filing status. Part of your net Social Security benefits (Box 5 of Form SSA-1099) will be subject to tax if your *provisional income* exceeds a base amount of $25,000 or $32,000. The *base amount* is $25,000 if your filing status is single, head of household, qualifying widow(er), or married filing separately and you lived apart from your spouse for all of 2010. The base amount is $32,000 if you are married filing jointly. You are not entitled to any base amount if you are married filing separately and you lived with your spouse at any time during 2010; *see* the Caution in this section.

To figure provisional income, you will have to increase the total income shown on your return by tax-exempt interest *(4.24)*, by 50% of your net Social Security benefits, and by certain tax-free fringe benefits and exclusions, before subtracting adjustments to income other than the student loan interest deduction *(33.14)*, the tuition and fees deduction *(33.13)*, and the domestic production activities deduction *(40.23)*. By completing Lines 1–8 of *Worksheet 34-1*, you arrive at provisional income, shown on Line 8.

Caution

Married Filing Separately

If you are married filing separately and during 2010 you lived with your spouse at any time, you must include in your taxable income the lesser of (1) 85% of your net Social Security benefits shown on Line 1 of *Worksheet 34-1* or (2) 85% of the provisional income shown on Line 8 of *Worksheet 34-1*.

EXAMPLES

1. Frank Adams, who is single, has 2010 earnings of $15,000 from a part-time job, $1,000 of interest income, and $1,200 of dividends. He also receives $10,800 of net Social Security benefits (Box 5 of Form SSA-1099). Completing Worksheet 34-1, Frank's provisional income on Line 8 is $22,600 ($15,000 + 1,000 + 1,200 + 5,400 (50% of the $10,800 net Social Security benefits). Since $22,600 does not exceed the $25,000 base amount on Line 9 of the worksheet, none of Frank's Social Security benefits are taxable.
2. Sam and Fran Baker receive in 2010 net Social Security benefits (Box 5 of Form SSA-1099) of $15,000. Their taxable interest, dividends, and capital gains are $20,000, and tax-exempt interest is $10,000. They file a joint return. Their provisional income from Line 8 of Worksheet 34-1 is $37,500 ($20,000 + 10,000 + 50% of the $15,000 net Social Security benefits). Since $37,500 exceeds the $32,000 base amount on Line 9 of the worksheet, part of their Social Security benefits will be taxed. By completing the rest of Worksheet 34-1, Sam and Fran figure that $2,750 of their benefits are subject to tax.

IRA contributions. Do *not* use *Worksheet 34-1* if you are an active participant in an employer retirement plan and you plan to make deductible IRA contributions *(8.4)*. You must use the worksheets printed in IRS Publication 590. With the worksheets, you first determine the amount of Social Security benefits that would be subject to tax, assuming you did not claim any IRA deduction. That amount is then used to figure the allowable IRA deduction, taking into account any limitations under the phase-out rules *(8.4)*, and, finally, the allowable IRA deduction is used to compute the taxable portion of your Social Security benefits.

If you are not covered by an employer retirement plan, you may use the worksheet to figure the taxable portion of your Social Security benefits.

34.4 Election for Lump-Sum Social Security Benefit Payment

If in 2010 you receive a lump-sum payment of benefits covering prior years, you have a choice as to how to determine the taxable portion of the benefits: (1) You may treat the entire payment as a 2010 benefit taxable under the rules in the preceding section *(34.3) or* (2) you may allocate the benefits between 2010 and the earlier years. Choose the method that provides the lowest required increase to income in the current year. For example, if you receive a 2010 lump-sum payment that includes benefits for 2009, you may find that an allocation of benefits is advantageous where your income over the two-year period has fluctuated and benefits allocated to 2009 would be subject to a lower taxable percentage than in 2010.

When you elect to allocate benefits to a prior year, you do not amend the return for that year. You compute the increase in income (if any) that would have resulted if the Social Security benefits had been received in that year. You then add that amount to the income of the current year.

See IRS Publication 915 for instructions and worksheets for making the allocation and figuring the amount to be reported on your return.

34.5 Retiring on Social Security Benefits

Retirement benefits are not paid automatically. You should file for Social Security retirement benefits three months before you want to start receiving benefits. The age for receiving full Social Security benefits, traditionally 65, has been slowly increasing; *see* the second Law Alert on this page. Reduced benefits may be elected if you are at least age 62. Even though your full Social Security retirement age is over 65, you should register with the Social Security Administration four months before the month in which you turn age 65 to ensure Medicare coverage.

If you are at least age 62 and elect reduced benefits, the reduction depends on the number of months between the start date and your full Social Security retirement age. For example, if you were born in 1947 and elect benefits at age 62 in 2010, the benefit reduction is 25%.

If you delay benefits beyond full Social Security retirement age, your potential Social Security benefit increases for each year you delay retirement. The yearly increase is 7% for those born in 1939 or 1940, 7.5% for those born in 1941 or 1942, and 8% for those born in 1943 or later. The increase for delaying benefits no longer applies once you reach age 70.

Law Alert

Zero Increase Projected for 2011 Social Security Benefits

When this book went to press, it appeared very likely that there would not be a cost-of-living benefit increase in 2011 for Social Security recipients, which would make it two straight years without an increase. If there is no increase in benefits, most existing Medicare Part B enrollees will not face an increase in Part B premiums for 2011 *(34.12)*.

Benefits before reaching full retirement age may be reduced because of earnings. If you are under full retirement age and are receiving benefits, $1 of benefits will be deducted for each $2 earned above an annual limit. In 2010, the limit is $14,160 (the 2011 limit will be listed in the *e-Supplement at jklasser.com*). For the year you reach full retirement age, $1 of benefits is deducted for each $3 earned over a different limit, which for 2010 is $37,680, but only earnings before the month you reach full retirement age are counted. Starting with the month in which you reach full retirement age, you are entitled to full benefits with no limit on how much you may earn.

There is also a favorable rule for the first year of retirement. A full benefit may be received for any month in which your earnings do not exceed $^1/_{12}$ of the annual limit, even if the yearly limit is exceeded.

Regardless of your age, you may receive any amount of income from sources other than work—for example, private pensions or investments—without affecting the amount of Social Security retirement benefits.

EXAMPLES

1. Jones retires and begins receiving reduced Social Security benefits in January 2010 at age 62. He is entitled to receive $600 a month ($7,200 annually). He works and earns $21,920, which is $7,760 over the $14,160 limit for 2010. Under the regular benefit reduction rule, Jones would lose $3,880 of benefits ($1 for every $2 over $14,160). However, since this is his first year of retirement, a full benefit would be paid for any month in which earnings were $1,180 ($^1/_{12}$ of $14,160) or less.
2. Smith, who began receiving benefits before 2010, reaches full retirement age of 66 in August 2010. He is entitled to monthly benefits of $600. He was fully employed during the year, earning $39,240 before August and $22,500 for the remainder of the year.The benefit reduction applies to his pre-August benefits. He earned $1,560 over the $37,680 limit and loses $520 of benefits ($1 for every $3 earned over $37,680). Starting in August, he begins to receive his full benefits regardless of the amount of his earnings.

Law Alert

Social Security Retirement Age

The retirement age for receiving full Social Security benefits is gradually increasing, as shown below.

Birth year—	*Full Social Security retirement age—*
Before 1938	65
1938	65 and 2 months
1939	65 and 4 months
1940	65 and 6 months
1941	65 and 8 months
1942	65 and 10 months
1943–1954	66
1955	66 and 2 months
1956	66 and 4 months
1957	66 and 6 months
1958	66 and 8 months
1959	66 and 10 months
1960 and after	67

So long as you continue to work, you pay Social Security taxes on your earnings, regardless of your age.

Request an estimate of benefits and copy of earnings record. You can get an estimate of retirement benefits by sending for Form SSA-7004. After mailing in a completed Form SSA-7004, you will receive a Personal Earnings and Benefit Estimate Statement, showing your earnings history, Social Security tax payments, and an estimate of your retirement, disability, and survivor's benefits.

Form SSA-7004 is available at your local Social Security office. You can also request the form from the Social Security Administration by calling 1-800-772-1213 or obtain it from the Social Security Administration website at www.ssa.gov.

34.6 How Tax on Social Security Reduces Your Earnings

There is an added tax cost of earning income if the earnings will subject your Social Security benefits to tax. Therefore, if your benefits are not currently exposed to tax, you have to figure *not only* the tax on the extra income *but also* the amount of Social Security benefits subjected to tax by those earnings. If the additional earnings will put you over the base amount *(34.3)*, then you will not only have to pay tax on the additional earnings but also on the Social Security benefits that will be subject to tax.

EXAMPLES

1. You are over full Social Security retirement age *(34.5)* and you and your spouse receive net Social Security benefits of $8,000. You file jointly. You have pension income of $27,000 and $800 in tax-exempt interest. Your provisional income *(34.3)* is $31,800. No part of your Social Security benefits is taxable because your provisional income of $31,800 does not exceed the $32,000 base amount for married persons filing jointly.
2. Same facts as in Example 1, except that you take a part-time job paying $7,000. This increases your provisional income to $38,800 and subjects $3,400 of Social Security benefits to tax.

Provisional income	$38,800
Less: Base amount	32,000
Excess	$6,800
50% of excess taxable *(34.3)*	$3,400

The $7,000 of additional earnings increases your taxable income by $10,400, which is the $7,000 of earnings plus the $3,400 of Social Security benefits made taxable because of the increase in provisional income.

When earnings result in forfeiture of Social Security benefits. If you receive reduced Social Security benefits before full Social Security retirement age, it is possible under the current tax structure to earn extra income and yet have only a small gain or even lose money when considering the increased tax on the earnings and on Social Security benefits, and also the forfeiture of benefits when earnings exceed the annual retirement earnings test; *see 34.5*.

Therefore, before taking on work to earn extra income, you should compute the tax cost of the extra earnings and the loss of benefits. As a rule of thumb, you may figure the extra tax cost by multiplying the earnings by your top federal tax bracket and also by the FICA tax rate of 7.65% (Social Security and Medicare withholdings) and by your top rate for state or local taxes. But be aware that this composite rate ignores the effect of the increased tax from crossing the thresholds for taxing up to 50% or 85% of Social Security benefits. Therefore, in such cases, the tax cost will be greater than the estimated composite tax rate. For greater accuracy, figure your tax position as if you were preparing two tax returns: one that does not include the extra income and the other that does include the extra income. The tax difference is the extra income tax cost of earning the extra pay. Add to this cost the FICA tax on the extra earnings and any additional state or local taxes. Then figure the amount of benefits that will be forfeited. This will give you a net gain or in some cases a net loss. If you have a tax consultant, it may be advisable to ask the consultant to make the computations.

34.7 Claiming the Credit for the Elderly and Disabled

You may qualify for a tax credit for 2010 if your income is quite low and you meet one of the following conditions:

- Your 65th birthday is on or before January 1, 2011; *or*
- You were under age 65 at the end of 2010, you retired before the end of 2010 because of permanent and total disability, and you received taxable disability income in 2010 from your former employer's disability plan. Disability income is taxable wages or payments in lieu of wages paid to you while you are absent from work because of permanent and total disability. Qualifying disability income does not include payments received after reaching mandatory retirement age.

You will not be able to claim a credit if your Social Security benefits or adjusted gross income is too high, or if you have no tax liability *(34.9)*.

Disabled. You are considered permanently and totally disabled if you are unable to engage in any substantial gainful activity by reason of any medically determinable physical or mental impairment that can be expected to result in death or that has lasted or can be expected to last for a continuous period of not less than 12 months.

For the first year you claim the credit, you need a physician's certification of your disability. For later years, new certifications are generally not required.

Nonresident aliens. You may not claim the credit if you are a nonresident alien at any time during 2010, unless you are married to a citizen or resident and you have elected to be treated as a resident *(1.5)*.

Amount of credit. The amount of the credit is 15% times the base amount after reductions. The base amount for the credit is generally $7,500, $5,000, or $3,750 *(34.8)*. The base amount is reduced by nontaxable Social Security and other tax-free pensions, as well as by adjusted gross income exceeding specific limits *(34.9)*.

The credit is not refundable. That is, it is allowed only up to your tax liability *(34.9)*.

How to claim the credit. You claim the credit on Schedule R if you file Form 1040 or Form 1040A. You may not claim the credit on Form 1040EZ.

Married couples. A married couple may claim the credit only if they file a joint return. However, if a husband and wife live apart at all times during the taxable year and file separately, the credit may be claimed on a separate return.

Law Alert

Lack of Inflation Adjustment Weakens Credit

Since 1983, the base amounts *(34.8)* and AGI phase-out thresholds *(34.9)* for figuring the credit for the elderly or disabled have remained the same while inflation adjustments and tax law changes have reduced tax liability. Since the credit cannot exceed tax liability, the number of taxpayers able to claim the credit has dropped drastically and continues to decline annually.

34.8 Base Amount for the Elderly or Disabled Credit

The law specifies an initial base amount for figuring the credit. This base amount is reduced by certain tax-free benefits and excess adjusted gross income before applying the 15% credit amount and the tax liability limitation, if any *(34.9)*.

The initial base amount is:

- $5,000, if you are single, head of household, or are a qualifying widow(er).
- $5,000, if you file a joint return and only one spouse is eligible for the credit.
- $7,500, if you file a joint return and both spouses are eligible for the credit. The credit is figured solely on this base; a separate computation is not made for each spouse.
- $3,750, if you are married and file a separate return. The credit may be claimed on a separate return only if you and your spouse have lived apart at all times during the year.

Base amount if disabled. If you are under age 65 and permanently and totally disabled, the base amount for figuring the credit is the *lower* of your 2010 taxable disability income or the initial base amount for your filing status shown above. For example, if you are single, under age 65, permanently and totally disabled, and received taxable disability income of $4,800, you figure the credit on $4,800, which is less than the base of $5,000 for single persons.

Joint return and both spouses qualify for the credit. If one spouse is age 65 or over and one spouse is under age 65 and receives disability income, the initial base amount is the lesser of (1) $7,500 or (2) $5,000 *plus* the disability income of the spouse under age 65. If both spouses are under age 65 and disabled, the initial base amount is the total of their disability income, not exceeding $7,500.

Caution

Low Social Security Benefits Required for Credit

The tax credit for the elderly or disabled is not available to an unmarried individual who receives $5,000 or more of nontaxable Social Security benefits or nontaxable federal pensions such as from the Veterans Administration. The $5,000 limit also applies if you are married filing jointly and only one spouse qualifies for the credit. The limit is $7,500 if you file a joint return and both spouses qualify for the credit.

34.9 Reduction of the Base Amount and Liability Limitation for the Credit

The $3,750, $5,000, or $7,500 credit base amount *(34.8)* is reduced by nontaxable pensions and Social Security, and also by "excess" adjusted gross income, figured as follows:

Nontaxable Social Security and pensions. The base amount is reduced by:

- Social Security and Railroad Retirement benefits that are *not taxable (34.3); and*
- Tax-free pension, annuity, or disability income paid under a law administered by the Veterans Administration (but not military disability pensions) or under other federal laws.

The base amount is not reduced by military disability pensions received for active service in the armed forces of any country, disability pensions for active service in the National Oceanic and Atmospheric Administration or Public Health Service, certain disability annuities paid under the Foreign Service Act of 1980, and workers' compensation benefits. However, if Social Security benefits are reduced by workers' compensation benefits, the amount of workers' compensation benefits is treated as Social Security benefits that reduce the base.

Excess adjusted gross income. You reduce the base amount by one-half of adjusted gross income (AGI) exceeding: $7,500 if you are single, head of household, or a qualified widow(er); $10,000 if you are married filing a joint return; or $5,000 if you are married, live apart from your spouse for the entire year, and file a separate return. Applying these income floors, the credit is no longer available to a single person when AGI reaches $17,500, $20,000 on a joint return where one spouse is eligible for the credit, $25,000 on a joint return where both spouses are eligible for the credit, and $12,500 where a married person files separately.

15% credit limited by tax liability. After reducing the credit base amount as just discussed for nontaxable Social Security and pensions and excess AGI, the remaining credit base is multiplied by 15%. This is the maximum credit but where this amount exceeds tax liability, the credit is limited to the lesser liability, as in the following Examples.

EXAMPLES

1. John Andrews is 58 years old and single. In 2007, he retired on permanent and total disability. In 2010, he receives a taxable disability pension of $10,000, nontaxable Social Security disability benefits of $2,500, and taxable interest of $100. Adjusted gross income (AGI) is $10,100 ($10,000 + $100). His taxable income after claiming the standard deduction ($5,700) and personal exemption ($3,650) is only $750. As shown below, the credit formula would allow a credit of $180, but the credit cannot exceed John's 2010 tax liability, which is $76 (based on taxable income of $750).

Initial base amount *(34.8)*	$5,000
Less: nontaxable Social Security disability	2,500
Less: 50% of AGI over $7,500 (50% of ($10,100 *minus* $7,500))	1,300
Credit base amount	$1,200
Credit (15% of credit base amount)	$180
Tax liability limitation	$76

2. William White, age 53, retired in 2006 on permanent and total disability. In 2010, he received a taxable disability pension of $6,300 and nontaxable Social Security disability benefits of $2,500. He files a joint return with his wife, Helen, age 49, who had wages of $9,546 and a taxable disability pension of $3,000 from a job from which she retired in 2010 on account of permanent and total disability. Their adjusted gross income (AGI) for 2010 is $18,846 ($6,300 + $9,546 + $3,000). Their taxable income (after the $11,400 standard deduction and $7,300 personal exemptions) is only $146 and their tax liability is just $14. Thus, the $87 credit allowed under the credit formula is limited to $14.

Initial base amount on joint return, two eligible spouses *(34.8)*	$7,500
Less: Nontaxable Social Security	2,500
Less: 50% of AGI over $10,000 (50% of ($18,846 – $10,000))	4,423
Credit base amount	$577
Credit (15% of credit base amount)	$87
Tax liability limitation	$14

34.10 Tax Effects of Moving to a Continuing Care Facility

Senior citizens who move into "continuing care" or "life-care" facilities pay large upfront entrance fees upon admittance, as well as monthly fees thereafter in return for a residence, meals, and lifetime health care, including long-term skilled nursing care, should that become necessary. The payments raise several tax issues discussed in this and the following section *(34.11)*.

Portion of monthly fees deductible as medical expense. Part of the monthly fees to a life-care community are allocable to health care, which you may deduct as an itemized medical expense subject to the 7.5% floor *(17.1)*. Continuing care facilities generally send a statement to the residents specifying the portion of their monthly service fees that went towards health care.

The IRS and Tax Court have approved the use of a "percentage method" for allocating the community's medical expenses among the residents. In general, the annual medical expenses of the community are divided by total operating expenses to get the medical care allocation percentage. In a particular case, the IRS could contest how the allocation is figured or how the allocated amount is divided among the residents.

For example, in a 2004 case (Baker, 122 TC 143), the IRS contested a couple's medical expense deduction for a portion of the monthly service fees paid for their two-bedroom duplex apartment, categorized as an "independent living unit" (ILU). Using a percentage method computation supplied by the resident council of their continuing care retirement community, the Bakers deducted $6,557 of their 1997 monthly service fees and $9,891 of their 1998 monthly fees as medical expenses. The IRS initially allowed a deduction for $4,488 of the 1997 fees and $5,142 of the 1998 fees using a different percentage method. Then, when the Bakers appealed to the Tax Court, the IRS argued that the deductible part of the service fees should be figured using an "actuarial method," which would increase the Bakers' two-year deduction by a few hundred dollars over what the examining agent had allowed.

However, the Tax Court refused to require use of the actuarial method, which requires projections of longevity and lifetime utilization of health-care services, and is so complicated that the IRS could not fully explain the method to the Court. The Court held that the percentage method is appropriate, noting that the IRS has approved use of the percentage method in rulings since 1967. However, in applying the percentage method to determine the Bakers' deductions, the Court had to resolve disputes over how certain expenses should be treated and how the allocated medical care percentage, once determined, should be split among the residents. For example, the Court held that the community's interest expenses, depreciation and amortization allowances should be included in both the numerator and denominator when dividing medical costs by operating costs to determine the medical care allocation percentage.

The Court calculated that 27.93% of the community's 1997 total costs and 30.07% of the 1998 costs were allocable to medical care. The Court then held that the Bakers could not simply multiply these percentages by the fees they paid to get their deductions. The same medical expense amount must be allocated to each ILU resident by multiplying the allocation percentage by a weighted average of the service fees paid each year by the ILU residents. The weighted average annual service fee for 1997 paid by the ILU residents was $13,902, which when multiplied by the allocation percentage of 27.93%, gave a medical care allocation of $3,883 per resident. For 1998, the weighted average annual service fee for ILU residents was $14,093, which when multiplied by the allocation percentage of 30.07%, gave a medical care allocation of $4,238 per resident. On their joint returns, the Bakers could treat double the per resident amounts as medical expenses; that is, $7,766 for 1997 and $8,476 for 1998.

Caution

Charitable Contribution Deductions

Payments made to a tax-exempt organization that operates a life-care community are generally not deductible charitable contributions because you are receiving services in exchange. If you donate amounts over and above your regular monthly fees and do not receive any extra benefit as a result, you may deduct the excess payment as a charitable contribution *(14.3)*.

Portion of nonrefundable entrance fee deductible as medical expense. What about the upfront payments required by life-care communities? If an entrance fee or founder's fee for lifetime care is nonrefundable, part may be treated as a medical expense *(17.1)* if you can prove what part of the lump sum is allocable to future medical coverage. The IRS recognizes that a deduction may be based on a showing that the life-care facility historically allocates a specified percentage of the fee to future medical care. With such proof there is a current obligation to pay and the allocable amount is treated as a deductible medical expense when the lump sum is paid. The same rules apply if the life-care or founder's fee is paid monthly rather than as a lump sum.

Separate sponsorship gift. In one case, an individual was allowed by the Tax Court and an appeals court to claim a charitable contribution deduction for a "sponsorship gift" paid to a life-care retirement facility where she and her husband were residents. The sponsorship gift was entirely separate from her entrance fee; it was not required for admission and did not entitle her to reduced monthly payments. She did not receive any extra benefit from her gift and was not entitled to a refund of any part of it.

34.11 Imputed Interest on Refundable Entrance Fees

You must pay a lump-sum entrance fee when you enter a continuing care community. Depending on the type of plan, a portion of this fee may be refundable, if you move from the community, or become payable to your heirs upon your death. Before 2006, the refundable portion of the entrance fee was considered to be a loan and subject to imputed interest rules. However, this tax treatment of the refundable entrance fee has been permanently repealed.

34.12 Part B Premiums for 2011 Affected by Social Security

At the time this book went to press, the Medicare Part B monthly premiums for 2011 had not yet been announced. The premiums are tied to what happens to Social Security benefits. Assuming there is no cost-of-living increase for Social Security benefits in 2011 (which appeared likely when this book went to press), a "hold-harmless" provision in the law will protect most Medicare B enrollees from a premium increase in 2011. If there is no benefit increase, the "hold harmless" provision will apply to Part B enrollees whose 2010 Part B premiums were withheld from their monthly 2010 Social Security benefits, provided their modified adjusted gross income (MAGI) for 2009 (two years before the 2011 benefit year) was below a threshold amount. For 2010 premium purposes, the MAGI threshold, based on 2008 income, was $85,000, or $170,000 for married persons filing jointly for 2008, and it is not clear if these amounts will be increased for 2011.

The "hold harmless" rule would not apply to enrollees first becoming eligible in 2011 for Part B or to enrollees who in 2010 paid Part B premiums directly to Medicare because they did not receive Social Security benefits in 2010. Such individuals will pay higher 2011 Part B premiums than those held harmless. Still higher Part B premiums will be paid in 2011 by enrollees with 2009 MAGI exceeding the applicable MAGI floor because of the income surcharge. There are four levels of surcharge for most enrollees, with an accelerated two-level surcharge for enrollees who were married and filed separately for 2009.

See the *e-Supplement at jklasser.com* for a table showing the 2011 premium amounts, including the income surcharges based on 2009 filing status.

Chapter 35

Members of the Armed Forces

Special tax benefits are provided to Armed Forces personnel. A major tax-free benefit is the combat pay exclusion. Under this exclusion, members of the Armed Forces, including active duty reservists, may exclude from gross income all compensation for active service received for any month in which they served in a combat zone or were hospitalized as a result of any wound, injury, or disease incurred while serving in a combat zone. Commissioned officers are allowed an exclusion equal to the highest rate of basic pay at the top pay level for enlisted personnel, plus any hostile fire/imminent danger pay received for the month.

Other pay benefits may be tax free, and you may be able to get filing extensions and time extensions for home residence replacements. A list of tax-free benefits may be found in *35.2*. Filing extensions are discussed in *35.5*.

Combat zones include Iraq and neighboring areas in the "Arabian Peninsula," Afghanistan and the Balkans *(35.4)*.

35.1 Taxable Armed Forces Pay and Benefits

Armed Forces personnel report as taxable pay the following items:

- Basic pay for active duty, attendance at a designated service school, back wages, drills, reserve training, and training duty.
- Special pay for hazardous duty, hostile fire or imminent danger, aviation career incentives, diving duty, foreign duty (for serving outside the 48 contiguous states and the District of Columbia), medical and dental officers, nuclear-qualified officers, and special duty assignments.
- Enlistment and reenlistment bonuses.
- Payments for accrued leave, and personal money allowances paid to high-ranking officers.
- Student loan repayment from programs such as the Department of Defense Educational Loan Repayment Program when year's service is not attributable to a combat zone.

Caution

Community Property

If you are married and your domicile (permanent home to which you intend to return) is in one of the following states, your military pay is subject to community property laws of that state: Arizona, California, Idaho, Louisiana, Nevada, New Mexico, Texas, Washington, and Wisconsin. *See 1.6* for community property reporting rules.

State income tax withholding. A state that makes a withholding agreement with the Secretary of the Treasury may subject members of the Armed Forces regularly stationed within that state to its payroll withholding provisions. National Guard members and reservists are not considered to be members of the Armed Forces for purposes of this section.

Where and when to file. Mail your return to the Internal Revenue Service Center for the place you are stationed. For example, you are stationed in Arizona but have a permanent home address in Missouri; you send your return to the Service Center for Arizona. For filing extensions on entering the service *(35.7)*.

35.2 Tax-Free Armed Forces Benefits

The following benefits are not subject to tax:

- Combat pay *(35.4)*.
- Living allowances for BAH (Basic Allowance for Housing). You may deduct mortgage interest and real estate taxes on your home even if you pay these expenses with BAH funds.
- BAS (Basic Allowance for Subsistence) living allowances.
- Housing and cost-of-living allowances abroad, whether paid by the U.S. Government or by a foreign government.
- VHA (Variable Housing Allowance).
- Family allowances for educational expenses for dependents, emergencies, evacuation to a place of safety, and separation.
- Death allowances for burial services, death gratuity payments to eligible survivors, and travel of dependents to burial site.
- Dislocation allowance, intended to partially reimburse expenses such as lease forfeitures, temporary living charges in hotels, and other expenses incurred in relocating a household.
- Temporary lodging expense allowance intended to partially offset the added living expenses of temporary lodging within the United States for up to 10 days and up to 60 days abroad.
- A moving-in housing allowance, intended to defray costs, such as for rental agent fees, home-security improvements, and supplemental heating equipment, associated with occupying leased space outside the United States.
- Travel allowances for annual round trip for dependent students, leave between consecutive overseas tours, reassignment in a dependent-restricted status, and transportation for you or your dependents during ship overhaul or inactivation.
- Defense counseling payments.
- ROTC educational and subsistence allowances.
- Survivor and retirement protection plan premium payments.
- Uniform allowances paid to officers and uniforms furnished to enlisted personnel.

Caution

Withholding on Differential Wages Paid to Workers Joining Military

Employees who enlist or are called up to active military service for over 30 days may receive "differential wages" from their former employer to cover some or all of the difference between their military pay and the wages that were being received prior to joining the military. The differential wages are taxable and cannot be excluded as combat pay *(35.4)*. Income tax must be withheld from the differential wages, but not FICA tax (Social Security and Medicare).

- Medical or hospital treatment provided by the United States in government hospitals.
- Pay forfeited on order of a court martial.
- Education, training, or subsistence allowances paid under any law administered by the Department of Veterans Affairs (VA). However, deductible education costs must be reduced by the VA allowance.
- Adjustments in pay to compensate for losses resulting from inflated foreign currency.
- Payments to former prisoners of war from the U.S. Government in compensation for inhumane treatment suffered at the hands of an enemy government.
- Benefits under Servicemembers' Group Life Insurance.
- Dividends on GI insurance. These are a tax-free return of premiums paid.
- Interest on dividends left on deposit with the Department of Veterans Affairs (VA).

Other tax breaks for military personnel and their families. The Heroes Earnings Assistance and Relief Tax Act of 2008 (HEART) extended certain tax breaks and provided some new ones to individuals in the military or to surviving family members.

Combat pay election for earned income credit. The election to treat nontaxable combat pay *(35.4)* as earned income for purposes of the earned income tax credit *(25.11)* has been made permanent.

Distributions to reservists. Reservists called to active duty for at least 180 days are not subject to the general 10% penalty for distributions before age 59½ from retirement plans and IRAs. They also are allowed in some cases to make withdrawals of unused benefits from a health flexible spending account. These rules are discussed further at *35.8*.

State and local bonuses are tax free. Some states and municipalities pay bonuses to active or former military personnel or their dependents because of service in a combat zone. Such payments are excludable from gross income under the new law. If such payments were reported as income in prior years, an amended return can be filed if the statute of limitations (usually three years from the return's due date) has not yet expired *(47.2)*.

Extended statute of limitations for disability determinations. Usually, a taxpayer must file for a refund claim *(47.2)* within three years of the due date of the return on which the income was reported. Payments from the government based on a service-connected disability are tax free, while payments based on length of service are taxable. The Department of Veterans Affairs may take a long time to make a disability determination, with the result that taxpayers may include the payments as income. Then, when they receive a favorable determination, they can file an amended return to receive a tax refund. The HEART Act gives taxpayers until one year after the date of a disability determination to file a refund claim if this date is later than the three-year period of limitation.

Death benefits. Beneficiaries who receive military death gratuities or payments from the Servicemembers' Group Life Insurance (SGLI) program can roll these amounts over to a Roth IRA or Coverdell education savings account (ESA) within one year of receipt. The usual limits on contribution amounts and income limitations for Roth IRAs *(8.20)* and Coverdell ESAs *(33.11)* do not apply to these rollovers.

Veterans not taxed on payments from Compensated Work Therapy program. In response to a 2007 Tax Court decision that held that payments made by the U.S. Department of Veterans Affairs (VA) to disabled veterans under the Compensated Work Therapy (CWT) program are tax-free veterans' benefits, the IRS reversed position and announced that it no longer treats CWT payments as taxable pay for services. Under the CWT program, the VA provides vocational rehabilitation services to veterans who have been unable to work and support themselves. The VA contracts with private industry and government agencies to provide these veterans with therapeutic work that emphasizes work skills training.

CWT recipients who paid tax on CWT payments in prior years can file for a refund if the deadline for filing an amended return has not passed. Since Form 1040X generally must be filed within three years of filing the original return *(47.2)*, the filing deadline for a refund claim for 2007 is generally April 15, 2011.

Disability retirement pay. Your disability retirement pay may be tax free if you are a former member of the Armed Forces of any country, the Foreign Service, the Coast Guard, the National Oceanic and Atmospheric Administration, or the Public Health Service. Tax-free treatment of disability retirement pay is retroactive to the date of the application for benefits. But Social Security disability payments made on account of a combat-related injury are taxable to the same extent as Social Security retirement payments *(34.3)*.

35.3 Deductions for Armed Forces Personnel

Members of the Armed Forces may deduct the items listed below as miscellaneous itemized deductions subject to the 2% adjusted gross income (AGI) floor *(19.1)*:

- Board and lodging costs over those paid to you by the government while on temporary duty away from your home base.
- Costs of rank insignia, collar devices, gold braids, etc., and the cost of altering rank insignia when promoted or demoted.
- Contributions to a "Company" fund made according to Service regulations. But personal contributions made to stimulate interest and morale in a unit are not deductible.
- Court martial legal expenses in successfully defending against the charge of conduct unbecoming an officer.
- Dues to professional societies. But you may not deduct dues for officers' and noncommissioned officers' clubs.
- Expense of obtaining increased retirement pay.
- Out-of-pocket moving expenses for service-connected moves. The 50-mile test and the 39-week test generally required to deduct moving expenses do not have to be met *(12.3)*.
- Subscriptions to professional journals.
- Transportation, food, and lodging expenses while on official travel status. But you are taxed on mileage and *per diem* subsistence allowance.
- Uniforms. The cost and cleaning of uniforms are deductible if: (1) they must be worn on duty; (2) they cannot under military regulations be worn off duty; and (3) the cost exceeds any tax-free clothing allowance.

Filing Tip

Away From Home Base

If your ship or squadron is away from your "home" port or base, you may be able to deduct travel expenses while away. However, you are not considered "away from home" if you are at your *permanent* duty station or you are a naval officer assigned to permanent duty aboard a ship; *see* also *20.6*.

35.4 Tax-Free Pay for Service in Combat Zone

If your grade is below commissioned officer and you serve in a designated combat zone during any part of a month, all of your qualifying military pay (*see* below) for that month is excluded from your taxable income. You may also exclude military pay earned during any part of a month that you are hospitalized as a result of wounds, disease, or injury incurred in a combat zone. The exclusion for military pay while hospitalized does not apply to any month that begins more than two years after the end of combat activities in that combat zone. Your hospitalization does not have to be in the combat zone.

Filing Tip

Who Qualifies for Exclusion?

Members of the U.S. Armed Forces qualifying for the exclusion include commissioned officers and enlisted personnel in all regular and reserve units under control of the Secretaries of Defense, Army, Navy, and Air Force, and the Coast Guard. Members of the U.S. Merchant Marines or the American Red Cross are not included.

Officers. If you are a commissioned officer, you may exclude up to the highest rate of basic pay at the highest pay grade that enlisted personnel receive per month plus any hostile fire/imminent danger pay received for each month during any part of which you served in a combat zone or were hospitalized as a result of the combat zone service.

If you are a commissioned warrant officer, you are considered an enlisted person.

What is included as tax-free pay? The following pay received as a member of the U.S. Armed Forces qualifies for tax-free treatment: (1) active duty pay earned in any month you served in a combat zone; (2) imminent danger / hostile fire pay; (3) a reenlistment bonus if the voluntary extension or reenlistment occurs in a month you served in a combat zone; (4) pay for accrued leave earned in any month you served in a combat zone (the Department of Defense must determine that the unused leave was earned during that period); (5) pay received for duties as a member of the Armed Forces in clubs, messes, post and station theaters, and other nonappropriated fund activities. The pay must be earned in a month you served in a combat zone; (6) awards for suggestions, inventions, or scientific achievements you are entitled to because of a submission you made in a month you served in a combat zone; and (7) student loan repayments earned for military service.

For each month of combat zone service during the year, 1/12 of the repayment for that year is considered tax-free combat zone pay.

Service in the combat zone includes any periods you are absent from duty because of sickness, wounds, or leave. If, as a result of serving in a combat zone, you become a prisoner of war or missing in action, you are considered to be serving in the combat zone as long as you keep that status for military pay purposes.

Retirement pay and pensions do not qualify for the combat zone exclusion. According to a Fourth Circuit Court of Appeals decision, a Navy severance pay package was taxable although the recipient became entitled to the payment while on active duty in the Persian Gulf. The court differentiated the package, which was provided in order to entice the man to leave the service, from a reenlistment bonus provided as compensation for active service.

Law Alert

IRA Contributions Based on Tax-Free Combat Pay

The "Heroes Earned Retirement Opportunities Act of 2008" allows members of the armed services serving in a combat zone to contribute to either a traditional IRA *(8.2)* or a Roth IRA *(8.20)* based on their tax-free combat pay.

Combat zones. A combat zone is any area the President of the United States designates by Executive Order as an area in which the U.S. Armed Forces are or have engaged in combat. An area becomes and ceases to be a combat zone on the dates designated by the President. At the time this book went to press, the following designations were still in place. For any changes, *see* IRS Publication 3 and tax form instructions.

The following Arabian Peninsula Areas (including airspace) have been designated combat zones since January 17, 1991: the total land areas of Iraq, Kuwait, Saudi Arabia, Oman, Bahrain, Qatar, and the United Arab Emirates; the Persian Gulf; the Red Sea; the Gulf of Oman; the part of the Arabian Sea that is north of 10 degrees north latitude and west of 68 degrees east longitude; and the Gulf of Aden.

Afghanistan, including the airspace above, was designated a combat zone beginning September 19, 2001.

Effective March 24, 1999, the Kosovo area was designated a combat zone including: the Federal Republic of Yugoslavia (Serbia/Montenegro), Albania, the Ionian Sea north of the 39th parallel, and the Adriatic Sea. Airspace above these areas is also part of the zone.

Qualifying service outside a combat zone considered combat zone service. Military service outside a combat zone is considered to be performed in a combat zone if: (1) the service is designated by the Defense Department to be in direct support of military operations in the combat zone, and (2) the service qualifies you for special military pay for duty subject to hostile fire or imminent danger. Military pay received for this service will qualify for the pay exclusion if the other requirements are met.

Nonqualifying service. The following military service does not qualify as service in a combat zone: (1) presence in a combat zone while on leave from a duty station located outside the combat zone; (2) passage over or through a combat zone during a trip between two points that are outside a combat zone; and (3) presence in a combat zone solely for your personal convenience. Such service will not qualify you for the pay exclusion.

Hospitalized while serving in a combat zone. If you are hospitalized while serving in a combat zone for a wound, disease, or injury, it will be presumed to have been incurred while serving in the combat zone unless there is clear evidence to the contrary.

EXAMPLES

1. You are hospitalized for a specific disease after serving in a combat zone for three weeks, and the disease for which you are hospitalized has an incubation period of two to four weeks. The disease is presumed to have been incurred while you were serving in the combat zone. On the other hand, if the incubation period of the disease is one year, the disease would not have been incurred while you were serving in the combat zone.
2. You were hospitalized for a specific disease three weeks after you left the combat zone. The incubation period of the disease is from two to four weeks. The disease is considered to have been incurred while serving in the combat zone.

Form W-2. The wages shown in Box 1 of your Form W-2 should not include combat pay. Retirement pay is not combat pay.

35.5 Tax Deadlines Extended for Combat Zone or Contingency Operation Service

You are allowed an extension of at least 180 days (*see* below) to take care of tax matters if you are a member of the Armed Forces who served in a combat zone or in a contingency operation. The extension applies to filing tax returns, paying taxes, filing a Tax Court petition, filing refund claims, and making an IRA contribution. The time allowed for the IRS to begin an audit or take collection actions is also extended. *See* IRS Publication 3 for details on the extension rules.

Filing Tip

Spouses of Combat Zone Personnel

If your spouse serves in a combat zone or contingency operation, you are generally entitled to the same deadline extension as he or she is. However, any extra extension for your spouse's hospitalization within the United States is not available to you. Further, a spouse's extension does not apply to any year beginning more than two years after the area ceases to be a combat zone or the operation ceases to be a contingency operation.

Support personnel. The deadline extension also applies if you are serving in a combat zone or contingency operation in support of the Armed Forces. This includes Red Cross personnel, accredited correspondents, and civilian personnel acting under the direction of the Armed Forces in support of those forces.

Extension is a minimum of 180 days. Your deadline for taking actions with the IRS is extended for at least 180 days after the later of: (1) the last day you are in a combat zone or serving in a contingency operation (or the last day the area qualifies as a combat zone or the operation qualifies as a contingency operation), or (2) the last day of any continuous qualified hospitalization for injury from service in the combat zone or contingency operation. Hospitalization may be outside the United States, or up to five years of hospitalization in the United States.

Time in a missing status (missing in action or prisoner of war) counts as time in a combat zone or contingency operation.

In addition to the 180 days, a filing deadline is also extended by the number of days you had left to file with the IRS when you entered a combat zone or began serving in a contingency operation. If you entered the combat zone or began contingency operation service before the time to file began, the deadline is extended by the entire filing time.

35.6 Tax Forgiveness for Combat Zone or Terrorist or Military Action Deaths

If a member of the Armed Forces is killed in a combat zone or dies from wounds or disease incurred while actively serving in a combat zone, any income tax liability for the year of death and any earlier year in which he or she actively served in a combat zone is waived. In addition, the service member's estate is entitled to a refund for income tax paid while serving there.

If a member of the Armed Forces was a resident of a community property state and his or her spouse reported half of the military pay on a separate return, the spouse may get a refund of taxes paid on his or her share of the combat zone pay.

Forgiveness benefits apply to an Armed Forces member serving outside the zone if service: (1) was in direct support of military operations there, and (2) qualified the member for special military pay for duty subject to hostile fire or imminent danger.

Caution

Training Exercises

Tax forgiveness for personnel killed in a "military action" does *not* apply to a U.S. civilian or military employee who dies as a result of a training exercise.

Missing status. The date of death for a member of the Armed Forces who was in a missing status (missing in action or prisoner of war) is the date his or her name is removed from missing status for military pay purposes. This is true even if death occurred earlier.

Tax forgiveness for civilian or military personnel killed in terroristic or military action. Tax liability is waived for civilian or military U.S. government employees killed in terroristic or military actions, even if the President has not designated the area as a combat zone. Tax liability is waived for the period beginning with the taxable year before the year in which the injuries were incurred and ending with the year of death. Refund claims for prior years must generally be filed on Form 1040X by the later of three years from the time the original return was filed or two years from the time the tax was paid. However, if death occurred in a combat zone, the filing period is extended by the time served in the combat zone, plus the period of continuous hospitalization outside the U.S., plus an additional 180 days. The individual must also be a U.S. government employee both on the date of injury and date of death.

How tax forgiveness is claimed. If the individual died in a combat zone or in a terroristic or military action, you file as the individual's representative: (1) Form 1040 if a U.S. individual income tax return (Form 1040, 1040A, or 1040EZ) has not been filed for the tax year. Form W-2,

Wage and Tax Statement, must accompany the return. (2) Form 1040X if a U.S. individual income tax return has been filed. A separate Form 1040X must be filed for each year in question.

Check with your local IRS office for the address of the IRS office to which the return is filed.

An attachment should accompany any return or claim and should include a computation of the decedent's tax liability before any amount is forgiven and the amount that is to be forgiven.

The following documents must also accompany all returns and claims for refund: (1) Form 1310, Statement of Person Claiming Refund Due a Deceased Taxpayer; and (2) a certification from the Department of Defense. Department of State certification is required if the decedent was a civilian employee of an agency other than the Department of Defense.

35.7 Extension To Pay Your Tax When Entering the Service

If you are unable to pay your tax when you enter the Armed Forces, you may get an extension until 180 days after entering the military *and* you actually apply for the extension after receiving a notice from the IRS asking for payment.

The extension does not cover your spouse, who must file a separate return and pay the tax due. But you and your spouse may file a joint return before the postponement period expires even though your spouse filed a separate return for that particular year. No interest is charged on this postponement of your tax.

Automatic extension of time to file your return. If you are on duty outside the U.S. or Puerto Rico on April 15, 2011, you get an automatic two-month extension to file your 2010 return; *see* page 6.

Interest charged on back taxes. If you do not show hardship qualifying you for the above interest-free payment extension, the IRS may reduce its interest rate on the deficiency if your service affected your ability to pay. The maximum interest rate the IRS may charge for taxes incurred prior to your entry into active service is 6%. This reduced rate applies only to interest charged during the period of your active duty.

35.8 Tax Information for Reservists

Transportation costs to reservist meetings generally are not deductible. A possible exception is the cost of traveling from your regular job location to a meeting held on a regular workday or traveling from home to a meeting outside the metropolitan area where you live and normally work. The cost would be deductible, subject to the 2% adjusted gross income (AGI) floor for miscellaneous itemized deductions *(19.1)*.

If you travel overnight more than 100 miles away from your tax home *(20.6)* to a meeting or training camp, you may claim an above-the-line deduction *(12.2)* for transportation, lodging, and meals (subject to the 50% reduction for meals) attributable to those trips; *see* the Filing Tip in this section.

If you are called for active duty away from your tax home, you may deduct travel expenses provided you keep your regular job while on active duty, return to it after you are released, and pay for those expenses at the military post. To the extent they exceed BAH (housing) and BAS (subsistence) allowances, the expenses are deductible only as a miscellaneous itemized deduction subject to the 2% AGI floor.

Deferring tax payments and reduction of IRS interest rate. If you owed a tax deficiency to the IRS before being called to active duty, the IRS may defer payment, without interest, if your ability to pay has been severely impaired by your call-up *(35.7)*. If you are not allowed a deferment, the IRS generally will reduce its interest charge to 6% on the taxes you owed before your call-up.

Penalty-free withdrawals from retirement plans. If you are called to active military duty for over 179 days, or indefinitely, distributions received during the active duty period are not subject to the 10% early distribution penalty. This applies to distributions from a traditional IRA and distributions attributable to elective deferrals you made to a 401(k) or 403(b) plan.

Furthermore, no tax (as well as no penalty) is due on a qualified reservist distribution if it is recontributed to the plan within two years after the end of the active duty period.

These rules apply to individuals called to active duty after September 11, 2001. If the statute of limitations period has not expired, a refund claim may be made on a timely amended return *(47.2)* for a penalty paid on a qualified distribution or for tax paid on a recontributed distribution.

Filing Tip

Overnight Travel to National Guard and Reserve Meetings

National Guard and Reserve members who travel over 100 miles and stay overnight to attend Guard or Reserve meetings may claim an above-the-line deduction from gross income for their meals, lodging, and incidental expenses that do not exceed the federal *per diem* rate, plus the standard mileage rate for driving costs and parking fees and tolls. The expenses are reported on Form 2106 and the amount attributable to the over-100-mile-away trips is entered on Line 24 of Form 1040 as an above-the-line deduction from gross income *(12.2)*. Other travel costs from Form 2106 are allowed only as miscellaneous itemized deductions, subject to the 2% of AGI floor.

Law Alert

Penalty-Free Withdrawals From Retirement Plans

Individuals who are called to active duty for over 179 days may withdraw IRA or qualified plan funds before age $59^1/_2$ without penalty *(35.8)*.

Distributions of unused balance from health flexible spending arrangement (HFSA). If you contribute to a health flexible spending arrangement *(3.15)*, but before you can use up your HFSA balance to reimburse your medical expenses you are called to active military duty for over 179 days, or indefinitely, you can withdraw the funds and use them for any purpose if your employer allows "qualified reservist distributions" and you withdraw the balance by the regular plan deadline for receiving reimbursements. If your employer allows employees to obtain reimbursements of medical expenses within a 2½-month grace period after the end of the plan year *(3.15)*, you have the same deadline to receive a distribution of your HFSA balance, but it does not have to be used to pay medical expenses.

Uniform costs of reservists. The cost and upkeep of uniforms is deductible only if you are prohibited from wearing them when off duty; *see 19.6*. A deduction allowed under this test must be reduced by any uniform allowance you receive, and the unreimbursed cost is subject to the 2% adjusted gross income (AGI) floor for miscellaneous itemized deductions.

Chapter 36

How To Treat Foreign Earned Income

There is a tax incentive for working abroad—in 2010 up to $91,500 of income earned abroad may escape U.S. income taxes and you may be entitled to an exclusion or deduction for certain housing costs. In measuring the economic value of this tax savings, consider the extra cost of living abroad. In some areas, the high cost of living and currency exchange rates will erode your tax savings.

The exclusion does not apply to investment income or to any other earned income that does not meet the exclusion tests.

To claim a foreign income exclusion you must satisfy a foreign residence or physical presence test *(36.5)*.

Employees of the U.S. government may not claim an exclusion based on the government pay earned abroad.

36.1 Claiming the Foreign Earned Income Exclusion

If your tax home is in a foreign country and you meet either the foreign residence test or physical presence test *(36.3)*, you may exclude up to $91,500 of foreign earned income earned in 2010. You must file a U.S. return if your gross income *exceeds* the filing threshold for your personal status, even though all or part of your foreign earned income may be tax free. For years after 2010, the maximum $91,500 exclusion may be increased by an inflation adjustment. The exclusion is not automatic; you must elect it. You elect the foreign earned income exclusion on Form 2555, which you attach to Form 1040. The housing cost exclusion *(36.4)* is also elected on Form 2555.

You may file simplified Form 2555-EZ if your 2010 foreign wages are $91,500 or less, you do not have self-employment income, and you do not claim the foreign housing exclusion, housing deduction, business expenses, or moving expenses.

A separate exclusion is allowed for the value of meals and lodging received by employees living in qualified camps; *see 36.8*.

If you claim the foreign income exclusion of $91,500, you may not:

- Claim business deductions allocable to the excluded income;
- Make a deductible traditional IRA contribution, or a Roth IRA contribution, based on the excluded income; *or*
- Claim foreign taxes paid on excluded income as a credit or deduction.

In deciding whether to claim the exclusion, compare the overall tax (1) with the exclusion and (2) without the exclusion but with the full foreign tax credit and allocable deductions. Choose whichever gives you the lower tax; *see 36.3* and *36.6*.

Keep in mind that if you claim the exclusion, any taxable income not subject to the earned income and housing exclusions will be taxed at the same rates that would have applied had no exclusions been allowed. To apply this "stacking" rule, you must figure your regular tax liability using the Foreign Earned Income Tax Worksheet in the instructions to Form 1040. Also, to figure AMT liability, use the Foreign Earned Income Tax Worksheet in the instructions to Form 6251.

Election applies until revoked. Once you elect the exclusion, that election remains in effect for all future years unless you revoke it. If you revoke the election, you cannot elect the exclusion again during the next five years without IRS consent. A revocation is made in a statement attached to your return for the year you want it to take effect. The foreign earned income exclusion and the housing cost exclusion must be revoked separately.

The IRS may consent to a reinstatement of the exclusion following a revocation under the following circumstances: you return for a period of time to the United States, you move to another foreign country with different tax rates, you change employers, or there has been substantial change in the tax law of the foreign country of residence or physical presence.

Caution

Claiming Foreign Tax Credit Revokes Prior Election

If you have been claiming the exclusion and decide that it would be advantageous this year to forego the exclusion and instead claim the foreign tax credit for foreign earned income, be aware that claiming the credit is treated by the IRS as a revocation of the prior exclusion election. You may not claim an exclusion for the next five years unless the IRS allows you to reelect the exclusion.

Claiming a foreign tax credit also may revoke a prior election to claim the housing cost exclusion. Depending on the foreign earned income in the year the credit is claimed, the credit may be considered a revocation of a prior earned income exclusion election and also a prior housing cost exclusion election, or as a revocation of only one of the elections.

A good faith error in calculating foreign earned income that leads to claiming a foreign credit will not be treated as a revocation of prior elections.

EXAMPLE

A U.S. citizen living abroad asked the IRS if the declaration of a tax holiday by a foreign country in 1999 was a substantial change of law. Prior to 1996, while working abroad he had claimed the foreign income exclusion. But in 1996 and 1997, he revoked the election and claimed a foreign tax credit for taxes paid on his foreign earnings. In 1999, he wanted to resume claiming the income exclusion due to the declaration of a tax holiday in the country in which he was employed. The IRS ruled that he can claim the exclusion. The declaration of a tax holiday is considered a substantial change of law because he went from being taxed to being exempt from tax.

36.2 What Is Foreign Earned Income?

For exclusion purposes, foreign earned income includes salaries, wages, commissions, professional fees, and bonuses for personal services performed while your tax home is in a foreign country and you meet either the foreign residence test or the physical presence test; *see 36.3*. Earned income also includes allowances from your employer for housing or other expenses, as well as the value of housing or a car provided by the employer. It may also include business profits, royalties, and rents, provided this income is tied to the performance of services. Earned income does not include pension or annuity income, payments for nonqualified employee trusts or nonqualified annuities, dividends, interest, capital gains, gambling winnings, alimony, or the value of tax-free meals or lodging under the rules in *3.12*.

Foreign earned income does not include amounts earned in countries subject to U.S. government travel restrictions.

Courts have agreed with the IRS that income earned in Antarctica, in international waters, and in international airspace is not earned in a foreign country and thus cannot qualify for the exclusion.

Foreign earned income eligible for the exclusion must be received no later than the taxable year after the year in which you perform the services. Pay is excludable in the year of receipt if you did not use the full exclusion in the year of the services.

U.S. government pay ineligible. If you are an employee of the U.S. government or its agencies, you may *not* exclude any part of your pay from your government employer. Courts have agreed with the IRS that U.S. government workers were U.S. employees even though they were paid from sources other than Congressionally appropriated funds. If you are not an employee of the U.S. government or any of its agencies, your pay is excludable even if paid by a government source. You are not considered a U.S. government employee if you work for a private employer that has contracted with the government, provided you are under the employer's control and supervision, you are paid by the employer, and no U.S. government agency would be liable for your salary if your employer defaulted.

Under a special law, tax liability is waived for a civilian or military employee of the U.S. government killed in a military action overseas; *see 35.6*.

Profits from sole proprietorship or partnership. If your business consists solely of services (no capital investment), 100% of gross income is considered earned income. If services and capital are both income-producing factors, the value of your personal services, but no more than 30% of your share of the net profit, is considered earned income. Net profit is reduced by the deduction for 50% of self-employment tax *(12.2)* before figuring your 30% share.

If you do not contribute any services to a business (for example, you are a "silent partner"), your share of the net profits is *not* earned income.

If you do not have a net profit, the portion of your gross profit that represents a reasonable allowance for personal services is considered earned income.

EXAMPLES

1. A U.S. citizen resides in England. He invests in an English partnership that sells manufactured goods outside the U.S. He performs no services for the business. His share of net profits does not qualify as earned income.
2. Same facts as in Example 1, except he devotes his full time to the partnership business. Then up to 30% of his share of the net profits may qualify as earned income. Thus, if his share of profits is $50,000, earned income is $15,000 (30% of $50,000), assuming the value of his services is at least $15,000.
3. You and another person are consultants, operating as a partnership in Europe. Since capital is not an income-producing element, the entire gross income of the business is earned income.

The partnership agreement generally determines the tax status of partnership income in a U.S. partnership with a foreign branch. Thus, if the partnership agreement allocates foreign earnings to partners abroad, the allocation will be recognized unless it lacks substantial economic effect.

Fringe benefits. The value of fringe benefits, such as the right to use company property and facilities, is added to your compensation when figuring the amount of your earned income.

Royalties. Royalties from articles or books are earned income if you receive them for transferring all of your rights to your work, or you have contracted to write the articles or book for an amount in cash plus a royalty on sales.

Royalties from the leasing of oil and mineral lands and from patents are not earned income.

Reimbursement of employee expenses. Do not include reimbursement of expenses as earned income to the extent they equal expenses that you adequately accounted for to your employer; *see 20.31*. If your expenses exceed reimbursements, the excess is allocated according to the rules in *36.6*. If reimbursements exceed expenses, the excess is treated as earned income.

Straight commission salespersons or other employees who arrange with their employers, for withholding purposes, to consider a percentage of their commissions as attributable to their expenses treat such amounts as earned income.

Caution

Rental Income

Rental income is generally not earned income. However, if you perform personal services, for example as an owner-manager of a hotel or rooming house in a foreign country, then up to 30% of your net rents may be earned income.

Reimbursed moving expenses. Reimbursements of moving expenses are not reported as income if you adequately account to your employer for the expenses; *see 12.8*.

A reimbursement is taxable if received under a non-accountable plan or for moving expenses that are not deductible *(12.3)* or that you deducted in an earlier year. However, for purposes of claiming the earned income exclusion, the reimbursement may be considered to have been earned in a year other than the year of receipt. This is important because an exclusion is allowed only for the year income is earned. If the move is from the U.S. to a foreign country, the reimbursement is considered foreign earned income in the year of the move if you qualify under the foreign residence or physical presence test for at least 120 days during that tax year. Reimbursement of moving expenses from one foreign country to another is considered foreign earned income in the year of the move, if you qualify under the residency or physical presence test at the new location for at least 120 days during the tax year. If you do not meet one of these tests in the year of the move, the reimbursements are earned income that must be allocated between the year of the move and the following tax year.

A taxable reimbursement for a move back to the U.S. is considered income from U.S. sources if you continue to work for the same employer. If you move back to the U.S. and take a job with a new employer or if you retire and move back to the U.S. and your old employer reimburses your moving expenses under a prior written agreement or company policy, the reimbursement is considered to be for past services in the foreign country and qualifies as foreign earned income eligible for the exclusion. The reimbursement is considered earned in the year of the move if you qualified under the residency or physical presence test *(36.5)* for at least 120 days during the tax year. Otherwise, the reimbursement is allocated between the year of the move and the year preceding the move. *See* IRS Publication 54 for details.

36.3 Qualifying for the Foreign Earned Income Exclusion

You may elect the exclusion for foreign earned income only if your tax home is in a foreign country *and* you meet either the foreign residence test or the foreign physical presence test of 330 days. The foreign residence and physical presence tests are discussed in *36.5*. Tax home is discussed at *20.6–20.8*. If your tax home is in the U.S., you may not claim the exclusion but may claim the foreign tax credit and your living expenses while away from home if you meet the rules in *20.9* for temporary assignments that are expected to last, and actually do last, for one year or less. U.S. government employees may not claim either the earned income exclusion or housing exclusion based on government pay.

Caution

Countries Subject to Travel Restrictions

You may not claim the foreign earned income exclusion, or the housing exclusion or deduction, if you work in a country subject to U.S. government travel restrictions. You are not treated as a bona fide resident of, or as present in, a country subject to the travel ban. *See* Form 2555 for countries on the restricted list.

Exclusion prorated on a daily basis. If you qualify under the foreign residence or physical presence test for only part of 2010, the $91,500 exclusion limit is reduced on a daily basis.

EXAMPLES

1. You were a resident of France from February 20, 2008, until July 1, 2010. On July 2, 2010, you returned to the U.S. Since your period of foreign residency included all of 2009, thereby satisfying the foreign residence test, you may claim a prorated exclusion for 2010. As you were abroad for 182 of the 365 days in 2010 (January 1 through July 1), you can exclude earnings up to $ 45,625, or 182/365 of the $91,500 maximum exclusion. If you earned more than $45,625, the exclusion is limited to $45,625.
2. You worked in France from June 1, 2009, through September 30, 2010. Your only days outside France were a 15-day vacation to the U.S. in December 2009. You do not qualify for an exclusion under the foreign residence test because you were not abroad for a full taxable year; you were not abroad for either the full year of 2009 or 2010. However, you do qualify under the physical presence test; you were physically present abroad for at least 330 full days during a 12-month period. The 12-month period giving you the largest 2010 exclusion is the 12-month period starting October 21, 2009, and ending October 20, 2010. *See 36.5* for figuring the 12-month period. Since you were abroad for at least 330 full days during that 12-month period, you may claim an exclusion. In 2010, you were abroad for 293 days within the 12-month period (January 1 to October 20, 2010, is 293 days). Thus, you exclude earnings up to $73,451 ($91,500 x 293/365). Earnings exceeding $73,451 are not excludable.

If you are married and you and your spouse each have foreign earned income and meet the foreign residence or physical presence test, you may each claim a separate exclusion. If your permanent home is in a community property state, your earned income is not considered community property for purposes of the exclusion.

Foreign earnings from a prior year. Foreign income earned in a prior year but paid in 2010 does not qualify for the 2010 exclusion. However, if the income was attributable to foreign services performed in 2009, the pay is tax free in 2010 to the extent that you did not use the full 2009 exclusion of $91,400. Under another exception, payments received in 2010 for 2009 services are treated as 2010 income if the payment was within a normal payroll period of 16 days or less that included the last day of 2009. If the services were performed before 2009, no exclusion is available to shelter the pay.

Income for services performed in the U.S. does not qualify for the exclusion, even though it is paid to you while you are abroad.

Foreign tax credit. Foreign taxes paid on tax-free foreign earned income do not qualify for a credit or deduction. But if your foreign pay for 2010 exceeds $91,500, you may claim a foreign tax credit or deduction for the foreign taxes allocated to taxable income. The instructions to Forms 2555 and 1116 and IRS Publication 514 provide details for making the computation.

36.4 How To Treat Housing Costs

The housing costs of employees and self-employed persons are treated differently by the tax law. Employees get a housing exclusion; self-employed persons get a deduction from taxable foreign earned income. If you live in a special camp provided by your employer, all housing costs are excluded; *see 36.8.*

Exclusion for employer-financed housing costs. The housing exclusion is the excess of the employer-financed reasonable housing expenses (see below) over a "base housing amount." The base housing amount is 16% of the maximum foreign earned income exclusion multiplied by the number of qualifying days of foreign residence or presence for the year. Thus, for 2010, the base housing amount is $14,640 ($91,500 maximum foreign earned income exclusion × 16%) if you qualify under the foreign residence or physical presence test for the entire year. If you qualify under the residence or presence test for only part of the year, the $14,640 maximum base amount is prorated on a daily basis, so $40.11 is allowed for each qualifying day in 2010.

Filing Tip

Claiming the Housing Exclusion

On Form 2555, you figure the housing exclusion before the foreign income exclusion. The income exclusion is limited to the excess of foreign earned income over the housing exclusion.

In figuring housing expenses in excess of the base housing amount, there is a limit on the expenses that can be taken into account. Generally, the housing expenses cannot exceed 30% of the maximum earned income exclusion, prorated as applicable by the number of qualifying days of foreign residence or presence for the year. Thus, for 2010, the limit on housing expenses is generally $27,450 (30% × $91,500), or $75.21 per day, and the maximum housing exclusion is generally $12,810 ($27,450 – $14,640 maximum base amount). However, the expense limit, and thus the exclusion, may be significantly more than this if you are working in a high cost locality. The IRS can raise the annual limit for housing expenses in expensive foreign areas. The adjusted limits will be provided in a table included in the instructions to Form 2555.

On Form 2555, your foreign earned income exclusion is limited to the excess of your foreign earned income (including employer-financed housing costs) over your housing exclusion.

Reasonable housing expenses. Include rent, utilities other than telephone costs, insurance, parking, furniture rentals, and repairs for yourself, your spouse, and dependents living with you. The following expenses do not qualify: cost of purchasing a home, furniture, or accessories; home improvements; payments of mortgage principal; domestic labor; and depreciation on a home or on improvements to leased housing. Furthermore, interest and taxes that are otherwise deductible do not qualify for the exclusion.

You may include the costs of a separate household that you maintain outside the U.S. for your spouse and dependents because living conditions at your foreign home are adverse.

Self-employed persons. On Form 2555, self-employed individuals may claim a limited deduction for housing costs exceeding the base housing amount. You may claim this deduction only to the extent it offsets taxable foreign earned income. The deduction is claimed as an "adjustment to income" on Line 36 of Form 1040, even if you do not itemize deductions.

Where you may not deduct expenses because you do not have taxable foreign earned income, expenses may be carried forward one year and deducted in the next year to the extent of taxable foreign earned income.

If you are an employee and self-employed during the same year. Housing expenses above the base amount are partly excludable and partly deductible. For example, if half of your foreign earned income is from services as an employee, half of the excess housing expenses over the base amount are excludable. The remaining excess housing costs are deductible to the extent of taxable foreign earned income. Follow the instructions to Form 2555.

Countries ineligible for tax benefits. Housing expenses incurred in a country subject to a U.S. government travel restriction are not eligible for the tax benefits explained in this section. *See* Form 2555 instructions for a list of countries to which travel restrictions apply.

36.5 Meeting the Foreign Residence or Physical Presence Test

Planning Reminder

Claiming Exemption From Withholding for Excludable Income

You can file Form 673 with your U.S. employer to claim an exemption from withholding on wages to the extent of your expected foreign earned income exclusion and foreign housing exclusion. You must certify, under penalty of perjury, that you have good reason to believe that you will qualify under the foreign residence or physical presence test and also must certify your estimated foreign housing costs.

To qualify for the foreign earned income exclusion, you must be either a U.S. citizen (or U.S. resident entitled to tax treaty benefits) meeting the foreign residence test or a U.S. citizen or resident meeting the physical presence test in a foreign country. The following areas are not considered foreign countries: Puerto Rico, Virgin Islands, Guam, Commonwealth of the Northern Mariana Islands, American Samoa, or the Antarctic region. The Tax Court has held that income earned in international airspace (by a flight attendant, for example) or in international waters (by a ship officer, for example) is not earned in a foreign country and thus does not qualify for the foreign earned income exclusion.

Waiver of time test. If war or civil unrest prevented you from meeting the foreign residence or physical presence test, you may claim the exclusion for the period you actually were a resident or physically present abroad. Foreign locations and the time periods that qualify for the waiver of the residency and physical presence tests are listed in the instructions to Form 2555.

If, by the due date of your 2010 return (April 15, 2011), you have not yet satisfied the foreign residence or physical presence test, but you expect to meet either test after the filing date, you may either file on the due date and report your earnings or ask for a filing extension under the rules at *36.7*.

Foreign residence test. You must be a U.S. citizen who is a bona fide resident of a foreign country for an uninterrupted period that includes one full tax year; a full tax year is from January 1 through December 31 for individuals who file on a calendar-year basis. A U.S. resident alien who is a citizen or national of a country with which the U.S. has an income tax treaty and meets the full-year foreign residence test also qualifies. Business or vacation trips to the U.S. or another country will not disqualify you from satisfying the foreign residence test. If you are abroad more than one year but less than two, the entire period qualifies if it includes one full tax year.

EXAMPLE

You are a bona fide foreign resident from September 30, 2009, to March 25, 2011. The period includes your entire 2010 tax year. Therefore, up to $91,500 of your 2010 earnings is excludable. Your overseas earnings in 2009 and 2011 qualify for a proportionate part of the maximum exclusion allowed for those years.

Caution

Residence or Domicile?

Residence does not have the same meaning as *domicile*. Your domicile is a permanent place of abode; it is the place to which you eventually plan to return wherever you go. You may have a residence in a place other than your domicile. Thus, you may go, say, to Amsterdam, and take up residence there and still intend to return to your domicile in the U.S. But your leaving your domicile does not, by itself, establish a bona fide residence in a new place. You must intend to make a new place your residence.

To prove you are a foreign resident, you must show your intention to be a resident of the foreign country. Evidence tending to confirm your intention to stay in a foreign country includes: (1) your family accompanies you; (2) you buy a house or rent an apartment rather than a hotel room; (3) you participate in the foreign community activities; (4) you can speak the foreign language; (5) you have a permanent foreign address; (6) you join clubs there; or (7) you open charge accounts in stores in the foreign country.

You will not qualify if you take inconsistent positions toward your foreign residency. That is, you will *not* be treated as a bona fide resident of a foreign country if you have earned income from sources within that country, filed a statement with the authorities of that country that you are not a resident there, and have been held not subject to the income tax of that country. However, this rule does not prevent you from qualifying under the physical presence test.

If you cannot prove that you are a resident, check to determine if your stay qualifies under the physical presence test.

Physical presence test. To qualify under this test, you must show you were on foreign soil 330 days (about 11 months) during a 12-month period. Whether you were a resident or a transient is of no importance. You have to show you were physically present in a foreign country or countries for 330 full days during any 12-consecutive-month period. The 330 qualifying days do not have to be consecutive. The 12-month period may begin with any day. There is no requirement that it begin with your first full day abroad. It may begin before or after arrival in a foreign country and may end before or after departure from a foreign country. A *full day* is from midnight to midnight (24 consecutive hours). You must spend each of the 330 days on foreign soil. In departing from U.S. soil to go directly to the foreign country, or in returning directly to the U.S. from a foreign country, the time you spend on or over international waters does not count toward the 330-day total.

EXAMPLES

1. On August 9, you fly from New York City to London. You arrive there at 10 a.m. August 10. Your first full qualifying day toward the 330-day period is August 11. You may count in your 330-day period:
   - Time spent traveling between foreign countries.
   - Time spent on a vacation in foreign countries. There is no requirement that the 330 days must be spent on a job.
   - Time spent in a foreign country while employed by the U.S. government counts towards the 330-day test, even though pay from the government does not qualify for the earned income exclusion.
   - Time in foreign countries, territorial waters, or travel in the air over a foreign country. However, you will lose qualifying days if any part of such travel is on or over international waters and takes 24 hours or more, or any part of such travel is within the U.S. or its possessions.
2. You depart from Naples, Italy, by ship on June 10 at 6:00 p.m. and arrive at Haifa, Israel, at 7:00 a.m. on June 14. The trip exceeded 24 hours and passed through international waters. Therefore, you lose as qualifying days June 10, 11, 12, 13, and 14. Assuming you remain in Haifa, Israel, the next qualifying day is June 15.

Choosing the 12-month period. You qualify under the physical presence test if you were on foreign soil 330 days during any period of 12 consecutive months. Since there may be several 12-month periods during which you meet the 330-day test, you should choose the 12-month period allowing you the largest possible exclusion if you qualify under the physical presence test for only part of 2010.

EXAMPLE

You worked in France from June 1, 2009, through September 30, 2010, and the next day you left the country. During this period, you left France only for a 15-day vacation to the U.S. during December 2009. You earned $93,500 for your work in France during 2010. Your maximum 2010 exclusion is figured as follows:

1. Start with your last full day, September 30, 2010, and count back 330 full days during which you were abroad. Not counting the vacation days, the 330th day is October 21, 2009. This is the first day of your 12-month period.
2. From October 21, 2009, count forward 12 months to October 20, 2010, which is the last day of your 12-month period.
3. Count the number of days in 2010 that fall within the 12-month period ending October 20, 2010. Here, the number of qualifying days is 293, from January 1 through October 20, 2010.
4. The maximum 2010 exclusion is $91,500 × $^{293}/_{365}$, or $73,451. You may exclude $73,451, the lesser of the maximum exclusion or your actual earnings of $93,500.

36.6 Claiming Deductions

You may not deduct expenses that are allocable to the foreign earned income and housing exclusions. If you elect the earned income exclusion, you deduct expenses as follows:

Personal or nonbusiness deductions, such as medical expenses, mortgage interest, and real estate taxes paid on a personal residence, are deductible if you itemize deductions. Business expenses that are attributable to earning excludable income are not deductible. Dependency exemptions are fully deductible; *see* Example 1 below.

If your foreign earnings exceed the exclusion ceiling, you allocate expenses between taxable and excludable income and deduct the amount allocated to taxable earned income; *see* Example 2 below.

EXAMPLES

1. You were a resident of Denmark and elect to exclude your wages of $70,000 from income. You also incurred unreimbursed travel expenses of $2,000. You may not deduct the travel expenses, since the amount is attributable to the earning of tax-free income.
2. You earn wages of $114,375 in Germany and satisfy the physical presence test. Your unreimbursed travel expenses for 2010 are $5,000, after reducing meals and entertainment by 50%. If you elect the $91,500 exclusion (80% of your foreign earnings), 20% of the travel expenses, or $1,000, attributable to the taxable 20% of earnings, may be claimed as a miscellaneous itemized deduction on Schedule A (Form 1040) subject to the 2% AGI floor.

If your job expenses are reimbursed and the expenses are adequately accounted for to your employer *(20.30)*, the reimbursements are not reported as income on your Form W-2. If the reimbursement is less than expenses, the excess expenses are allocated as in Example 2 above.

You may have to allocate state income taxes paid on your income.

If either you or your spouse elects the earned income or housing exclusion, you may not claim an IRA deduction based on excluded income.

If you were reimbursed by your employer under a non-accountable plan, or if the reimbursement is for expenses that you deducted in an earlier year, the reimbursement is considered earned income in the year of receipt and is added to other earned income before taking the exclusion and making the allocation. *See 36.2* for allocating reimbursements between the year of the move and the following year for purposes of claiming the exclusion.

If, after working in a foreign country, your employer transfers you back to the U.S. or you move back to the U.S. to take a different job, your moving expenses are deductible under the general rules discussed in *12.3*. If your residence and principal place of work was outside the U.S. and you retire and move back to the U.S., your moving expenses are also deductible, except that you do not have to meet the 39-week test for employees or the 78-week test for the self-employed and partners.

Filing Tip

Overseas Moving Expenses

These expenses are generally treated as related to your foreign earnings. Thus, if you move to a foreign country and exclude your income, you may not deduct your moving expenses. If your earned income exceeds the exclusion limit, you allocate moving expenses between your tax-free and taxable earned income.

Survivors of workers abroad returning to U.S. If you are the spouse or dependent of a worker who died while his or her principal place of work was outside the U.S., you may deduct your moving expenses back to the U.S. For the costs to be deductible, the move must begin within six months of the worker's death. The requirements for deducting moving expenses apply, except for the 39-week test for employees or the 78-week test for the self-employed and partners.

Compulsory home leave. Foreign service officers stationed abroad must periodically return to the U.S. to reorient themselves to American ways of life. Because the home leave is compulsory, foreign service officers may deduct their travel expenses; travel expenses of the officer's family are not deductible.

Filing Tip

Extension of Time To File

If you are living and working abroad on April 15, 2011, you have an automatic extension to June 15, 2011. For an additional four months, file Form 4868 by June 15, 2011, and pay the estimated tax to limit interest and late payment penalties. For a longer extension, in anticipation of owing no tax on your foreign income, you may file Form 2350 either with the Internal Revenue Service Center in Austin, TX 73301-0215, or with a local IRS representative. File Form 2350 before the due date for filing your 2010 return, which is June 15, 2011, if you are abroad and are on a calendar year. Generally, you will be granted an extension for a period ending 30 days after the date you reasonably expect to qualify for the foreign earned income exclusion.

36.7 Exclusion Not Established When Your Return Is Due

When your 2010 return is due, you may not have been abroad long enough to qualify for the exclusion. If you expect to qualify under either the residence or physical presence test after the due date for your 2010 return, you may either (1) ask for an extension of time for filing your return on Form 2350 until after you qualify under either rule or (2) file your return on the due date, reporting the foreign income on the return, pay the full tax, and then file for a refund when you qualify.

If you will have tax to pay even after qualifying for the exclusion—for example, your earned income exceeds the exclusion—you may file for an extension to file but you will owe interest on the tax due. To avoid interest charges on the tax, you may take one of the following steps:

1. File a timely return and pay the total tax due without the application of the exclusion. When you do qualify, make sure you file a timely *(47.2)* refund claim; *or*

2. Pay the estimated tax liability when you apply for the extension to file on Form 2350. If the extension is granted, the payment is applied to the tax shown on your return when you file.

36.8 Tax-Free Meals and Lodging for Workers in Camps

If you must live in a camp provided by your employer, you may exclude from income *(3.13)* the value of the lodging and meals furnished to you if the camp is (1) provided because you work in a remote area where satisfactory housing is not available; (2) located as near as is practical to the worksite; and (3) a common area not open to the public normally accommodating at least 10 employees.

You also may qualify for the earned income exclusion; *see 36.1*.

36.9 Virgin Islands, Samoa, Guam, and Northern Marianas

The Virgin Islands, Guam, American Samoa, and the Commonwealth of the Northern Mariana Islands have their own independent tax departments. Therefore, contact the particular tax authority for the proper treatment of your income and obtain a copy of IRS Publication 570, *Tax Guide for Individuals With Income From U.S. Possessions,* which provides phone, mail, and internet contact information.

Possession exclusion. A possession exclusion applies to bona fide residents of American Samoa for the entire year. On Form 4563, such residents may exclude for U.S. tax purposes their income from sources in American Samoa and income effectively connected with a business in these possessions. The exclusion applies to amounts earned for services as an employee of the American Samoan government or its agencies but does not apply to pay as an employee, whether civilian or military, of the U.S. government or its agencies.

Caution

Form 8898 To Report Change of Residence

You generally must file Form 8898 for a tax year in which you have worldwide income of over $75,000 and in which you become or cease to be a bona fide resident of a U.S. possession. A $1,000 penalty may be imposed for failure to file a required Form 8898.

36.10 Earnings in Puerto Rico

If you are a U.S. citizen who is also a resident of Puerto Rico for the entire year, you generally report all of your income on your Puerto Rico tax return. Where you report income from U.S. sources on the Puerto Rico tax return, a credit against the Puerto Rico tax may be claimed for income taxes paid to the United States.

If you are not a resident of Puerto Rico, you report on a Puerto Rico return only income from Puerto Rican sources. Wages earned for services performed in Puerto Rico for the U.S. government or for private employers are treated as income from Puerto Rican sources.

U.S. tax returns. As a U.S. citizen, you must file a U.S. tax return reporting income from all sources. But if you are a bona fide resident of Puerto Rico for an entire tax year, you do not report on a U.S. tax return any income earned in Puerto Rico during your residence there, except amounts received for services performed in Puerto Rico as an employee of the U.S. government. Similar rules apply if you have been a bona fide resident of Puerto Rico for at least two years before changing your residence from Puerto Rico. On a U.S. tax return, you may not deduct expenses or claim tax credits allocable to the excludable income. Personal exemptions are fully deductible.

If you are not a bona fide resident of Puerto Rico for the entire tax year, or were not a bona fide resident for two years prior to the tax year, you report on your U.S. tax return all income you earned in Puerto Rico, as well as all income from other sources. If you are required to report income earned in Puerto Rico on your U.S. tax return, you may claim a credit for income tax paid to Puerto Rico. You figure the credit on Form 1116.

See IRS Publication 570, *Tax Guide for Individuals With Income from U.S. Possessions,* for further information on filing U.S. and Puerto Rican tax returns.

Planning Reminder

Information for Puerto Rico Filing

Information on Puerto Rico tax returns may be obtained at www.hacienda.gobierno.pr. The phone number is 787-721-2020, extension 3611. Written requests may be sent to the Departamento de Hacienda, Negociado de Asistencia Contributiva, P.O. Box 9024140, San Juan, Puerto Rico, 00902-4140.

36.11 Tax Treaties With Foreign Countries

Tax treaties between the United States and foreign countries modify some of the rules discussed in this chapter. The purpose of the treaties is to avoid double taxation. Consult your tax advisor about the effect of these treaties on your income. IRS Publications 54 and 901 have information about the tax treaties the U.S. maintains with foreign countries.

36.12 Exchange Rates and Blocked Currency

Income reported on your federal income tax return must be stated in U.S. dollars. Where you are paid in foreign currency, you report your pay in U.S. dollars on the basis of the exchange rates prevailing at the time the income is actually or constructively received. You use the rate that most closely reflects the value of the foreign currency—the official rate, the open market rate, or any other relevant rate. Be prepared to justify the rate you use.

Fulbright grants. If 70% or more of a Fulbright grant is paid in nonconvertible foreign currency, U.S. tax may be paid in the foreign currency. *See* IRS Publication 54 for details.

Blocked currency. A citizen or resident alien may be paid in a foreign currency that cannot be converted into American dollars and removed from the foreign country. If your income is in blocked currency, you may elect to defer the reporting of that income until: (1) the currency becomes convertible into dollars, (2) you actually convert it into dollars, or (3) you use it for personal expenses. Purchase of a business or investment in the foreign country is not the kind of use that is treated as a conversion. (4) You make a gift of it or leave it in your will. (5) You are a resident alien and you give up your U.S. residence.

If you use this method to defer the income, you may not deduct the expenses of earning it until you report it. You must continue to use this method after you choose it. You may only change with permission of the IRS.

You do not defer the reporting of capital losses incurred in a country having a blocked currency.

There may be these disadvantages in deferring income:

- Many years' income may accumulate and all be taxed in one year.
- You have no control over the year in which the blocked income becomes taxable. You usually cannot control the events that cause the income to become unblocked.

You choose to defer income in blocked currency by filing a tentative tax return reporting your blocked taxable income and explaining that you are deferring the payment of income tax because your income is not in dollars or in property or currency that is readily convertible into dollars. You must attach to your tentative return a regular return, reporting any unblocked taxable income received during the year or taxable income that became unblocked during the year. When the currency finally becomes unblocked or convertible into a currency or property convertible to dollars, you pay tax on the earnings at the rate prevailing in the year the currency became unblocked or convertible. On the tentative return, note at the top: "Report of Deferrable Foreign Income, pursuant to Revenue Ruling 74-351." File separate returns for each country from which blocked currency is received. The election must be made by the due date for filing a return for the year in which an election is sought.

36.13 Reporting Foreign Bank Accounts

If you have a financial interest in, or signature or other authority over, a foreign bank account, a foreign securities account, or any other foreign financial account, you must report this fact on Form TDF 90-22.1 (Report of Foreign Bank and Financial Accounts, or FBAR) if the aggregate value of the accounts at any time during the year exceeds $10,000. The FBAR does not have to be filed if the accounts were with a U.S. military banking facility operated by a U.S. financial institution. If you file Form 1040, there is a checkbox on Schedule B to indicate that you had an interest in a foreign account during the year. Form TDF 90-22.1 is not filed with your income tax return. The form must be filed with the Department of the Treasury by June 30 of the year following the year in which you had this financial interest. The FBAR for 2010 must be reported by June 30, 2011.

IRS steps up scrutiny of foreign accounts. The IRS has been tightening enforcement of the FBAR reporting requirements as part of its crackdown on taxpayers who have failed to report income from foreign accounts. Penalties for failure to file an FBAR can be severe. The civil penalty for a non-willful violation can be up to $10,000 and for a willful failure the civil penalty can be up to the greater of $100,000 or 50% of the total balance of the foreign account. Criminal penalties can be up to $500,000.

36.14 Foreign Tax Credit

You may claim an itemized deduction for qualified foreign taxes or you may claim a foreign tax credit. You must file Form 1116 to compute your credit unless the *de minimis* exception applies; *see* below. You may not claim a foreign tax credit or deduction for taxes paid on income not subject to U.S. tax. If all of your foreign earned income is excluded, none of the foreign taxes paid on such income may be taken as a credit or deduction on your U.S. return. If you exclude only part of

Filing Tip

Choosing Credit or Deduction

If you qualify for a credit or deduction, you will generally receive a larger tax reduction by claiming a tax credit rather than a deduction. A deduction is only a partial offset against your tax, whereas a credit is deducted in full from your tax. Also, taking a deduction may bar you from carrying back an excess credit from a later year. However, a deduction may give you a larger tax saving if the foreign tax is levied at a high rate and the proportion of foreign income to U.S. income is small. Compute your tax under both methods and choose the one providing the larger tax reduction.

your foreign pay, you determine which foreign taxes are attributable to excluded income and thus barred as foreign tax credits by applying the fractional computation provided in the instructions to Form 1116 and IRS Publication 514.

In one tax year, you may not elect to deduct some foreign taxes and claim others as a credit. One method must be applied to all taxes paid or accrued during the tax year. If you are a cash-basis taxpayer, you may claim a credit for accrued foreign taxes, but you must consistently follow this method once elected.

Exemption from limit for *de minimis* foreign taxes. If you have $300 or less of creditable foreign taxes, $600 if married filing jointly, you may elect to be exempt from the overall limitation on the credit, provided that your only foreign source income is qualified passive income. If the election is made, a foreign tax credit may be claimed directly on Line 47 of Form 1040 without filing Form 1116. *See* the instructions to Form 1116 for rules on making this election.

Credit disallowed. The credit may *not* be claimed if:

- You are a nonresident alien. However, under certain circumstances, if you are a bona fide resident for an entire taxable year in Puerto Rico you may be able to claim the credit. Also, a nonresident alien engaged in a U.S. trade or business may claim a credit if he or she receives income *effectively connected* to that business.
- You are a citizen of a U.S. possession (except Puerto Rico) but not a U.S. citizen or resident.

No credit is allowed for taxes imposed by a country designated by the government as engaging in terroristic activities; *see* IRS Publication 514 for a list of these countries.

Taxes qualifying for the credit. The credit is allowed only for foreign income tax, excess profits taxes, and similar taxes in the nature of an income tax. It is not allowed for any taxes paid to foreign countries on sales, gross receipts, production, the privilege to do business, personal property, or export of capital. But it may apply to a:

- Tax similar to a U.S. tax on income.
- Tax paid by a domestic taxpayer in lieu of the tax upon income, which would otherwise be imposed by any foreign country or by any U.S. possession.
- Tax of a foreign country imposing income tax, where for reasons growing out of the administrative difficulties of determining net income or basis within that country, the tax is measured by gross income, sales, and number of units produced.
- Pension, unemployment, or disability funds of a foreign country; certain foreign social security taxes do not qualify.

Reporting foreign income on your return. You report the gross amount of your foreign income in terms of United States currency. You also attach a schedule showing how you figured the foreign income in United States currency.

Limit on credit. Your 2010 credit for foreign income taxes paid or accrued is subject to a limitation on Form 1116 unless you qualify for and elect the exemption for *de minimis* taxes discussed above. The limitation is your total U.S. regular tax liability multiplied by a fraction: the numerator is your net foreign source taxable income (after required adjustments), and the denominator is your total taxable income from all sources. To determine the limit, you must separate your foreign source income into either the passive income category or the general income category. If you have both categories of foreign source income, you must figure the credit limit for each category on a separate Form 1116. If you have income from activities in sanctioned countries, or certain income re-sourced by treaty as foreign source income, or you paid taxes on a foreign source lump-sum distribution from a pension plan, a separate Form 1116 must be used to figure the limit for these categories as well. Only one Form 1116 is filed. The credits for the separate categories are combined on Part IV of the Form 1116 with the largest credit. *See* IRS Publication 514 and the instructions to Form 1116 for the details on these computations.

Carryback and carryover of excess foreign tax credit. If you are unable to claim all of the qualified foreign taxes paid or accrued during the year because of the limit on the credit, the balance may be carried back one year and then carried forward 10 years. For further details, *see* IRS Publication 514 and the instructions to Form 1116.

Chapter 37

Planning Alimony and Marital Settlements

See also:

Alimony payments that meet tax law tests in this chapter are deductible if you pay them, and taxable if you receive them. Payments are not deductible by the payer unless taxable to the recipient.

You claim a deduction for deductible alimony that you pay on Line 31a of Form 1040. You deduct the payments even if you claim the standard deduction rather than itemizing deductions. You must enter the Social Security number of your ex-spouse. Otherwise, your deduction may be disallowed and you may have to pay a $50 penalty. If you pay deductible alimony to more than one ex-spouse, enter the Social Security number of one of them and provide similar information for the others on a separate statement attached to your return.

If you receive taxable alimony, report the payments on Line 11 of Form 1040. You must give your ex-spouse your Social Security number and could be subject to a $50 penalty if you fail to do so.

Transfers of property between spouses during marriage, as well as transfers incident to divorce, are generally treated as tax-free exchanges. The transferor-spouse does not realize gain or loss and the transferee takes the transferor's basis in the property *(6.7)*.

37.1 Planning Alimony Agreements

You can arrange beforehand the way in which the costs of a divorce are to be borne. You may specifically state in the decree or agreement that the alimony is neither taxable to the payee-spouse (under IRC Section 71) nor deductible by the payer-spouse (under IRC Section 215). Such a statement effectively disqualifies payments that otherwise would be taxable to the payee-spouse and deductible by the payer-spouse. A copy of the agreement that contains the statement must be attached to the tax return of the payee-spouse for each year the statement is applicable.

The first step in planning the after-tax consequences of alimony is convincing a couple that they may have a common financial interest; the second is projecting future tax consequences.

For example, assume that the husband is to make payments to the wife. If tax planning is approached from the viewpoint of each spouse separately, the tax deduction is an advantage for the husband; tax-free income is an advantage for the wife. However, both advantages cannot be achieved, and the couple must face the reality of the tax law, which allows the husband to deduct payments only if they are taxed as alimony to the wife. The husband and wife must compromise by setting amounts and tax consequences that balance their interests.

One approach is to view both spouses as a single economic tax unit. If this is done and the husband will be in a higher tax bracket during the payout period than the wife, an agreement should generally provide for taxable and deductible alimony. The tax savings provided by the deduction can conserve more of the husband's assets while providing funds required by the wife. The final amount of alimony to be paid depends on the spouses' tax brackets. Where their tax brackets are the same and are not likely to differ over the term of the agreement, there may be no advantage in making an agreement for taxable and deductible alimony when viewing the two parties as a unit.

If you agree that one spouse is to pay deductible alimony and the other spouse is to report the alimony as income, these rules must be met:

- The alimony must be paid under a decree of divorce or legal separation agreement or decree of support *(37.2)*.
- The agreement must provide for cash payments *(37.3)*. A noncash property settlement is not alimony. There is no minimum payout period for annual cash alimony payments of $15,000 or less. One payment of $15,000 can qualify as deductible and taxable alimony. There is also no minimum payout period for annual alimony payments exceeding $15,000. However, recapture of alimony deductions claimed in the first or second year may occur where annual payments of over $15,000 are scheduled and paid, but in the second or third year a reduced payment is made. To avoid recapture of deductions for payments over $15,000, carefully plan schedules of declining payments within the rules discussed at *37.7*.
- In providing for the support of children, a specific allocation to their support or the setting of certain contingencies disqualifies payments as deductible and alimony as taxable *(37.5)*.
- Divorced and legally separated parties must not live in the same household when payments are made. If they live in the same household, alimony payments are not deductible or taxable. However, there are these exceptions: A spouse who makes payments while preparing to leave the common residence may deduct payments made within one month before the departure. Also, where you are separated under a written agreement, but not legally separated under a decree of divorce or separate maintenance, you may deduct alimony payments even if you both are members of the same household.
- The payer spouse's liability to pay alimony must end on the death of the payee spouse. The alimony agreement does not have to state expressly that payments end on death if liability ends under state law *(37.4)*.

Filing Instruction

Reporting Alimony

If you paid alimony in 2010 meeting the deductible tests, claim your deduction on Line 31a of Form 1040, and enter the recipient's Social Security number. If you receive qualifying alimony payments, report them on Line 11 of Form 1040.

37.2 Decree or Agreement Required

Alimony, to be deductible and taxable, must be required by one of the following: (1) a decree of divorce or legal separation; (2) a written separation agreement; or (3) a decree of support. Voluntary payments are not deductible or taxable.

Divorced or legally separated. The obligation to pay alimony must be imposed by the decree of divorce or separate maintenance or a written agreement incident to the divorce or separation.

Alimony paid under a Mexican divorce decree qualifies. Payments under a Mexican or state decree declared invalid by another jurisdiction do not qualify according to the IRS. Two appeals courts have rejected the IRS position.

Planning Reminder

Property Transfers

A property transfer to a former spouse that is incident to a divorce is generally treated as a tax-free exchange *(6.7)*.

Table 37-1 Key to Alimony and Marital Settlement Issues

Item—	*Comments—*
Alimony	The same rules determine whether alimony is deductible and taxable. For example, if a husband makes deductible alimony payments to his ex-wife, the payments are taxable to her. He may not deduct payments that are not taxable to her. If you are currently planning an alimony agreement, consider the tax consequences to both spouses. If the spouse likely to make the payments is in a significantly higher tax bracket than the recipient spouse, and keep in mind that in the next few years the top rate may be increased above the current top rate of 35%, there may be a significant tax savings for you as a couple in negotiating an agreement that qualifies the payments as alimony deductible by the payer and taxable to the recipient *(37.1)*. ***Note***: Prior tax rules that apply to pre-1985 agreements are not discussed in this chapter. If you have a problem involving a payment of alimony under a pre-1985 agreement, refer to the 2004 revision of IRS Publication 504.
Child support agreements	A payment fixed as payable for the support of your child does not qualify as deductible or taxable alimony *(37.5)*.
Property settlements	Transfers of property between spouses that are incident to a divorce are treated as tax-free exchanges. There is no recognition of gain or loss. Future tax consequences should be considered by the spouse receiving appreciated property. When the property is sold, that spouse will be taxed on the appreciation *(6.7)*. If this is so, that spouse may want to bargain for larger alimony payments or additional property to compensate for the projected future tax.
Alimony to non-resident alien	If you pay alimony payments to a nonresident alien, and you are a U.S. citizen or resident, you must withhold 30% on each payment for income tax purposes, unless a tax treaty provides for an exemption from withholding or a withholding rate lower than 30%. *See* IRS Publications 504 and 515 for more information.
Exemptions for children	Exemptions for children of a divorced couple are governed by the rules explained in *21.7*. Further, where a spouse is in the income range requiring the phaseout or disallowance of personal exemptions *(21.12)*, there may be no advantage in providing the exemption to that spouse. The exemption should be given to the spouse who may claim a full deduction for the exemption.
Annuity or endowment policy	Funds for payments of alimony may be provided through the purchase of an annuity or endowment policy. You may not deduct payments made under the policies assigned or purchased for your spouse. For example, to meet an alimony obligation of $500 a month, you buy your spouse a commercial annuity contract. The full $500 a month received by him or her is taxable. You may not deduct these payments.
Trust to pay alimony	To meet your alimony obligations, you may transfer income-producing property to a trust that is to pay the income to your spouse. You may not deduct payments made by the trust. You are not taxable on the income earned by the trust, even though it meets your alimony obligations. This tax treatment is the equivalent of receiving a tax deduction for paying alimony. If you receive alimony from a trust, ask the trustee how to report such income. Tax treatment may depend on whether the trust was created before 1985 or after 1984. If the trust was set up after 1984, as a beneficiary you generally report trust income under the general trust reporting rules in *Chapter 11*. These general trust rules may not apply to certain alimony trusts created before 1985 that were subject to the prior alimony rules. Distributions from such trusts may be treated as taxable alimony regardless of whether the distributions are from income or principal. In any event, the trustee should provide you with the necessary tax information.
Retirement plans	A state court can allocate your interest in a qualified retirement plan to a former spouse in a qualified domestic relations order. The benefits are taxed to your former spouse when they are paid to her or him. Benefits paid to another beneficiary, such as a child, are taxable to you *(7.12)*. If you are required to transfer your traditional IRA to your former spouse by the terms of a decree or instrument incident to the decree, the transfer is tax free if a trustee-to-trustee transfer is made to an IRA in your former spouse's name, or if the name on your IRA is changed to your spouse's name.
Voluntary payments in excess of required alimony	Voluntary payments in excess of required alimony are not deductible or taxable as alimony. Amending the decrees retroactively to cover an increase does not qualify the increase as deductible and taxable alimony. The increase has to be approved by the court before the increased payments are made.
Avoiding or limiting liability for previously filed joint returns	Even though you are no longer married, you remain liable for the tax on a previously filed joint return unless you qualify for innocent spouse or equitable relief *(1.7–1.9)*.

Support payments ordered by a court in a wife's home state qualify as alimony, even though not provided for by an *ex parte* divorce decree obtained by the husband in another state. Similarly, payments qualified when a state court increased support originally ordered before the husband obtained an uncontested Mexican divorce.

Payments made under a separation approved by a Roman Catholic ecclesiastical board do not qualify.

When a decree of divorce or separate maintenance fails to mention alimony, payments qualify as long as they are made under a written agreement considered "incident to" the decree.

Payments made under an agreement amended after a divorce or legal separation may also qualify, if the amendment is considered "incident" to the divorce or separation. For example, the IRS agrees that a written amendment changing the amount of alimony payments is incident to the divorce where the legal obligation to support under the original agreement survived the divorce. However, payments under an amended agreement did not qualify where the original agreement settled all rights between the husband and wife and made no provision for future support. The legal obligation to support the wife did not survive the divorce and could not be revived by the new agreement.

Annulments. Payments made under an annulment decree qualify as deductible (and taxable) alimony.

Separated from spouse. Where a husband and wife are separated and living apart, alimony is deductible by the payer-spouse and taxable to the payee-spouse provided it is paid under either a written separation agreement or decree of support.

A decree of support. Any court decree or order requiring support payments qualifies, including alimony *pendente lite* (temporary alimony while the action is pending) and an interlocutory (not final) divorce decree.

In certain community property states, payments under a decree of alimony *pendente lite* which do not exceed the wife's interest in community income are neither deductible by the husband nor taxable to the wife; payments exceeding the wife's interest are taxable to her and deductible by the husband.

37.3 Cash Payments Required

Only payments of cash, checks, and money orders payable on demand qualify as taxable and deductible alimony. Your cash payment to a third party for a spouse qualifies if made under the terms of a divorce decree or separation instrument. For example, as required by your divorce decree, you pay your former spouse's mortgage payments and real estate taxes on a home he or she owns, as well as his or her medical costs and tuition expenses. Assuming the other alimony tests *(37.1)* are met, you may deduct the payments as alimony and your former spouse must report them as alimony received. Your former spouse may deduct the real estate taxes, mortgage interest, medical and tuition costs as if he or she had paid them directly, subject to the regular deduction limits.

You may not deduct payments to maintain property owned by you but used by your spouse. For example, you pay the mortgage expenses, real estate taxes, and insurance premiums for a house that you own and in which your former spouse lives. You may not deduct those payments as alimony even if they are required by a decree or agreement.

Providing services or transferring or providing property does not qualify. For example, you may not deduct as alimony your note, the assignment of a third party note, or an annuity contract.

Premiums paid for term or whole life insurance on your life made under a divorce or separation instrument qualify as deductible alimony to the extent your former spouse owns the policy.

37.4 Payments Must Stop at Death

Liability for a payment must end on the death of the payee-spouse. If all the payments must continue after the death of the payee-spouse, none of the payments, whether made before or after the payee's death, qualify as taxable (to payee-spouse) or deductible (by payer-spouse) alimony. If some payments must continue after the payee's death, that amount is not alimony regardless of when paid.

The divorce decree or separation agreement does not have to specifically state that payments end at death, if under state law the liability to pay ends on the death of the payee-spouse.

To the extent that one or more payments are to begin, increase in amount, or accelerate after the death of the payee-spouse, such payments may be treated as a substitute for continuing payments after the death of the payee-spouse. Such substitute payments will be denied alimony treatment.

Planning Reminder

Payments to a Third Party

Cash payments to a third party may be deducted as alimony if they are under the terms of a divorce decree or separation instrument. You may also deduct as alimony payments made to a third party at the written request of the payee spouse. For example, your former wife asks you to make a cash donation to a charitable organization instead of paying alimony installments to her. Her request must be in writing and state that both she and you intend the payment to be treated as alimony. You must receive the written request before you file your return for the taxable year in which the payment was made. Your former wife may deduct the payment as a charitable contribution if she claims itemized deductions.

EXAMPLES

1. Under the terms of a divorce decree, Smith is obligated to make annual alimony payments of $30,000, terminating on the earlier of the end of six years or the death of Mrs. Smith. She also is to keep custody of their two minor children. The decree also provides that if on her death the children are still minors, Smith is to pay annually $10,000 to a trust each year. The trust income and corpus are to be used for the children until the youngest child reaches the age of majority. Under these facts, Smith's possible liability to make annual $10,000 payments to the trust is treated as a substitute for $10,000 of the $30,000 annual payments. $10,000 of each of the $30,000 annual payments does not qualify as alimony.
2. Same facts as in Example 1, but the alimony is to end on the earlier of the expiration of 15 years or the death of Mrs. Smith. Further, if Mrs. Smith dies before the end of the 15-year period, Smith will pay her estate the difference between the total amount that he would have paid had she survived and the amount actually paid. For example, if she dies at the end of the tenth year, he will pay her estate $150,000 ($450,000 – $300,000). Under these facts, his liability to make a lump-sum payment to the estate is a substitute for the full amount of each of the annual $30,000 payments. Accordingly, none of the annual $30,000 payments qualify as alimony.

Attorneys' fees. Under the laws of many states, a court award of attorneys' fees remains enforceable after the death of the payee-spouse, thereby disqualifying a payer's alimony deduction for the payment and making it nontaxable to the payee-spouse. For example, a husband who was ordered by an Oklahoma court to pay his wife $154,000 for her attorneys' fees prior to the entry of a final divorce decree was unable to deduct his payment. The Tax Court and the Tenth Circuit Court of Appeals agreed with the IRS that under Oklahoma law, the husband's liability to pay the attorneys' fees would not have ended, as a hypothetical matter, had the wife died before the final decree was entered. The policy reason for the state law is to assure that attorneys get paid for their services, which will enable indigent clients to retain counsel in divorce actions.

In this situation, the payer can obtain a deduction if the attorneys' fees remain the liability of the payee-spouse and the court decree increases the amount of cash alimony to cover the fees, rather than having them paid separately. The cash alimony would be taxable to the payee-spouse. The payee-spouse's payment of the fees to the attorneys may be deductible, but only as a miscellaneous expense subject to the 2% of AGI floor.

37.5 Child Support Payments Are Not Alimony

A payment that is specifically designated as child support in the divorce or separation instrument *(37.2)* is not deductible by the payer or taxable as alimony to the payee.

Even if there is not a specific allocation to child support, a payment will be presumed by the IRS to be payable for child support if it is to be reduced on the happening of a contingency relating to the child, such as: the child reaches a specific age or income level, or the child leaves school, marries, leaves the parent's household, or begins to work.

If a divorce or separation instrument requires both alimony and child support payments, and child support payments for a prior year were missed, or current-year child support payments are less than the required amount, an expected alimony deduction for current-year payments can be lost because the payments are applied first to the child support obligations, including any arrearage. For example, a taxpayer paid $17,963 to his ex-wife in 2004. His total child support obligation in 2004 for his two children was $23,147, of which $12,000 was for 2004 child support, $5,125 for past-due child support, and $6,022 to reimburse his ex-wife for her payment of health insurance premiums and medical expenses for the children that he was obligated to pay. Since his total payments in 2004 of $17,963 were less than the total child support owed for 2004, the Tax Court held that all of the payments were allocable to the child support and not deductible as alimony.

Tax refund diversion for delinquent child support. The IRS can give your tax refund to a state that is paying support to your child if you fail to make support payments. The IRS will not notify you of the diversion until it is made to the state. However, the state agency must provide prior notice of the proposed offset and procedures for contesting it.

Caution

Alimony Reductions Tied to Child's Age

If a reduction in your payments is not specifically tied to your child's reaching majority age but the scheduled date for the reduction is within six months before or after your child reaches age 18 or 21 (or other age of majority under local law), the IRS holds that the reduction is tied to the child's age. The reduction amount will be treated as child support unless you can prove that the reduction is for some other purpose. The IRS makes the same presumption if you have more than one child and your alimony payments are to be reduced at least twice and each reduction is within one year of a different child's reaching a particular age between ages 18 and 24; *see* the Example in *37.5*.

EXAMPLE

On July 1, 2010, Thomas and Tina are divorced when their children, John (born July 15, 1995), and Jane (born September 23, 1997), are ages 14 and 12. Under the divorce decree, Thomas is to make monthly alimony payments of $2,000. The monthly payments are to be reduced to $1,500 on January 1, 2016, and to $1,000 on January 1, 2020. On January 1, 2016, the date of the first reduction, John will be 20 years, 5 months, and 17 days old. On January 1, 2020, the date of the second reduction, Jane will be 22 years, 3 months, and 9 days old. As each reduction is to occur not more than one year before or after each child reaches the age of 21 years and four months, the IRS will presume that the reductions are associated with the happening of a contingency relating to the children. The two reductions total $1,000 per month and are treated as the amount fixed for the support of the children. Thus, $1,000 of the $2,000 monthly payment does not qualify as alimony. To avoid this result, Thomas must prove that the reductions were not related to the support of the children.

37.6 No Minimum Payment Period for Alimony

There is no minimum payment period, but a recapture rule applies where payments fall by more than $15,000 within the first three years *(37.7)*.

37.7 3rd Year Recapture If Alimony Drops by More Than $15,000

The recapture rules are designed to prevent the so-called "front loading" of property settlement payments disguised as alimony. However, the rules apply even where no property settlement was intended if you come within their terms. For example, the recapture rules may be triggered where several scheduled payments in the first year are missed and paid in the second year. Here are the rules: Deductible payments made in the first year or second year may be recaptured (that is, reported as income) in the third year where payments within the first three years decline by more than $15,000. The three years are called "post-separation years." The first post-separation year is the first calendar year in which you pay alimony under a decree of divorce or separation agreement. The period does not begin with the year of the decree or agreement if no payments are made. Recapture does not apply to temporary support payments made before the final decree or agreement. The second and third post-separation years are the next two calendar years after the first post-separation year whether or not payments are made during those years.

Payments made in the second post-separation year are recaptured if the payments exceed the payments made in the third post-separation year by more than $15,000. Payments made in the first post-separation year are recaptured if they exceed the average payments made in the second post-separation year and the third post-separation year by more than $15,000. The Examples below illustrate how to make these computations.

When recapture does not apply. Recapture is not triggered if payments in both the first and second post-separation years do not exceed $15,000. Recapture also does not apply to:

- Payments made under a continuing liability to pay for at least three years a fixed part of your income from a business or property or from a job or self-employed business or profession, *or*
- Payments that end because of your death or the death of your former spouse or the remarriage of your former spouse at any time before the end of the third post-separation year.

The steps of recapture are:

Step 1. Recapture for the second-year payment is computed first. This is the excess, if any, of the second-year payment over the third-year payment, *minus* $15,000.

Step 2. Recapture for the first-year payment is computed next. There is recapture if the first-year payment exceeds by more than $15,000 the average payment made in the second and third years. In figuring the average payment, reduce the second-year payment by any recapture amount for the second year figured under Step 1.

Filing Tip

Reporting Recapture on Your Return

The payer-spouse reports the recaptured amount as income in the third year and the payee-spouse claims a deduction for the same amount. The payer reports the recaptured amount on Form 1040, Line 11 (alimony received); cross out "received" and write "recapture" along with the payee-spouse's Social Security number.

The payee-spouse deducts the recaptured amount on Form 1040, Line 31a (alimony paid). He or she crosses out the word "paid" and writes "recapture," and also enters on that line the payer-spouse's Social Security number.

EXAMPLES

1. In 2008, Jones obtains a divorce and pays deductible alimony of $50,000. His wife reports $50,000 as income. In 2009 and 2010, he makes no payments. On his 2010 return, $35,000 of the first year 2008 deduction is recaptured ($50,000 – $15,000) and reported as income by Jones. His ex-spouse deducts the recaptured $35,000 on her 2010 return.
2. In 2008, Smith makes his first alimony payment of $50,000; in 2009 he pays $20,000 and in 2010 he pays nothing. On his 2010 return, $32,500 is recaptured as follows:

Recapture of second-year payment:		
Payment in 2nd year		$20,000
Less: 3rd-year payment	$0	
Less: Allowance	15,000	15,000
Recapture for second year		$ 5,000
Recapture of first-year payment:		
Average calculation:		
Payment over the 2nd and 3rd years	$20,000	
Less: recapture in the 2nd year	$ 5,000	
	$15,000	
Average ($15,000 ÷ 2)	$ 7,500	
Payment in first year		$50,000
Less: Average	$ 7,500	
Less: Allowance	15,000	22,500
Recapture for first year		$27,500
Total recaptured in 2010:		
For second year		$ 5,000
For first year		$27,500
Total:		$32,500

37.8 Legal Fees of Marital Settlements

If you are receiving taxed alimony, you may deduct part of your legal fees. Ask your attorney to divide his or her fees into charges for arranging: (1) the divorce or separation and (2) details of the alimony payments.

You may be able to deduct the legal fees allocated to (2), but you may not deduct the fee attributed to the divorce or separation negotiation. However, the deduction is subject to the 2% adjusted gross income (AGI) floor on miscellaneous itemized deductions *(19.1)* and if you are subject to alternative minimum tax, the deduction is not allowed for AMT purposes *(23.2)*. If the alimony is not taxed to you, you may not deduct any part of the fee. However, part of a fee allocated to a property settlement may be added to the basis of the property.

If you are paying deductible alimony, you may not deduct legal fees paid for arranging a divorce or for resisting your spouse's demands for alimony. Furthermore, you may not deduct legal fees incurred in resisting your spouse's claims to income-producing property the loss of which would affect your earnings. That part of your legal fee that is identified as being paid for tax advice is allowed as a miscellaneous itemized deduction subject to the 2% AGI floor *(19.1)*, but no deduction is allowed for AMT purposes. The following types of proof may support the miscellaneous itemized deduction:

- The fee is charged by a firm that limits its practice to state and federal tax matters and is engaged to advise on the consequences of a property settlement involving the transfer of property in exchange for other property and the release of the other spouse's marital rights in the property.
- The fee is charged by a firm engaged in general practice that assigns tax problems, such as the tax consequences of creating an alimony trust, to its special tax department. On the bill, an allocation is made for tax advice based on time, complexity of the case, and the amount of tax involved.
- An attorney handles the divorce for a fixed fee and also gives advice on the right to claim exemptions for the children following the divorce. The bill allocates part of the fee to the tax advice, based on time, and fees customarily charged in the locality for similar services.

Caution

Spouse's Legal Fees

You may not deduct your payment of your spouse's legal fees as a miscellaneous itemized deduction, even if the fees are only for tax advice. Furthermore, a payment of your spouse's legal fees will not qualify as deductible alimony even if paid under court order if liability for the payment might survive the payee-spouse's death under state law *(37.4)*.

Chapter 38

Household Employment Taxes ("Nanny Tax")

If you employ someone to care for your children or a disabled or elderly dependent in your home, clean your residence, cook, or provide other personal services in or around your home, you may be obligated to pay and withhold Social Security and Medicare (FICA) taxes and also to pay federal unemployment (FUTA) taxes.

The reporting requirements for FICA and FUTA are discussed in *38.2* and *38.4*.

38.1 Who Is a Household Employee?

If you hired someone to do household work and you were able to control what work he or she did and how it was done, you had a household employee. Such a worker is your employee regardless of whether the work is full or part time or whether you hired the worker through an agency or from a list provided by an agency or association. Also, it does not matter if the wages were paid for work done on an hourly, daily, weekly, or per-job basis.

Workers who are not your employees. Workers you hire through an agency are not your employees if the agency is responsible for who does the work and how it is done. If you use a placement agency that exercises control over what work is done and how it is done, the worker is not your employee. Self-employed workers are also not your employees; in addition to maintaining control over how their work is done, self-employed workers usually provide their own tools and offer services to the general public.

Notable exceptions to the household employee definition. You do not have to file a Schedule H and report payments if the employee was your spouse, your parent, your child who was under age 21, or an individual under age 18 if providing household services was not his or her principal occupation. However, you must treat your parent as your household employee if he or she takes care of your child in your home and (1) the child is either under age 18 or has a physical or mental condition that requires personal care by a adult for at least four continuous weeks in a calendar quarter, and (2) you are divorced and not remarried, widowed, or are living with a spouse whose physical or mental condition prevents him or her from caring for your child for at least four continuous weeks in a calendar quarter.

Verifying employment status. It is unlawful to employ an alien who cannot legally work in the United States. If you hire a household employee to work for you on a regular basis, you and the employee must each complete part of the U.S. Citizenship and Immigration Services (USCIS) Form I-9, Employment Eligibility Verification. You must verify that the employee is either a U.S. citizen or an alien who can legally work in the U.S. and you must keep Form I-9 for your records. The form and a USCIS Handbook for Employers can be obtained at www.uscis.gov/portal/site/uscis or by calling 1-800-870-3676. For answers to other questions about the employment eligibility verification process or other immigration-related matters, contact the USCIS Office of Business Liaison at 1-800-357-2099.

Employee's Social Security number. You are required to get each employee's name and Social Security number and enter them on Form W-2. This applies to both resident and nonresident alien employees. You may not accept an individual taxpayer identification number (ITIN) in place of an SSN. An ITIN is only available to resident and nonresident aliens who are ineligible to work in the U.S. and need identification for tax purposes. You may verify up to 10 names and numbers by calling the Social Security Administration at 1-800-772-6270, or online at www.ssa.gov/bso/bsowelcome.

38.2 Social Security and Medicare (FICA) Taxes for Household Employees

Income tax withholding is not required for a household employee *(38.3)*, but generally you must withhold Social Security and Medicare (FICA) taxes from the employee's cash wages and also pay an equal amount yourself, unless the wages are below an annual threshold, which for 2010 was $1,700. You report and pay the FICA taxes on Schedule H, which you must attach to your Form 1040; *see 38.3*.

Once payments to a non-exempt employee *(38.1)* equal or exceed $1,700, the entire amount, including the first $1,700, is subject to FICA taxes. The $1,700 threshold may be increased for 2011 by an inflation adjustment.

Caution

W-2 Distribution Deadline

Even if you request an extension to file copies of Form W-2 with the Social Security Administration, you must still furnish Form W-2 for 2010 to each employee by January 31, 2011.

Tax rates. As an employer, you are liable for FICA taxes at the rate of 6.2% for Social Security and 1.45% for Medicare on wages up to the annual Social Security wage base, which for 2010 is $106,800. Your household employee owes the same amount, which you are responsible for paying. You must either withhold your employee's share from his or her wages or pay it from your own funds. If wages exceed the annual Social Security wage base, you and the employee each owe Medicare tax of 1.45% on the entire excess with no ceiling.

If you do not withhold the employee's share of FICA taxes, you are liable for the full amount. If you pay the employee's share of FICA taxes from your own funds instead of deducting it from wages, you must treat your payments as additional wages when you report the employee's wages on Form W-2, but the payment is not considered wages for Social Security, Medicare, or FUTA tax purposes; *see* the Example in *38.3*

Estimated taxes. You may need to increase the federal income tax withheld from your pay or pay estimated taxes to avoid an estimated tax penalty *(27.1)* based on your household employment taxes. However, you will not be penalized for failure to pay estimated taxes if you will not have federal income tax withheld from wages, pensions, or any other payments you receive and your income taxes, excluding your household employment taxes, would not be enough to require payment of estimated taxes.

Reporting options for self-employed persons who have regular business employees as well as household employees. Self-employed persons who have business employees in addition to household employees may use one of the following reporting options:

1. Report FICA and FUTA taxes and any income tax withholding for household employees annually on Schedule H, and report FICA taxes and any income tax withholding for other employees quarterly on Form 941 and FUTA taxes annually on Form 940 (or 940-EZ); or
2. Report FICA taxes and any income tax withholding for *all* employees (household employees as well as other employees) quarterly on Form 941 and report FUTA taxes annually on Form 940 or Form 940-EZ.

Small employers whose annual liability for Social Security, Medicare, and withheld federal income tax is $1,000 or less may be notified by the IRS that they must file Form 944 to report and pay the taxes only once a year, instead of quarterly on Form 941, but an employer receiving such notification may request a change to Form 941 filing; *see* the Form 944 instructions.

Employers of household employees must also give copies of Form W-2 (Wage and Tax Statement) to each employee and to the Social Security Administration, as discussed in *38.3*.

38.3 Filing Schedule H To Report Household Employment Taxes

You must file Schedule H with your 2010 Form 1040 if you paid any one household employee cash wages of $1,700 or more in 2010, or withheld federal income tax during 2010 for a household employee, or paid cash wages totaling $1,000 or more in any calendar quarter during 2009 or 2010 to all household employees. On Schedule H, you report the Social Security and Medicare taxes *(38.2)*, federal income taxes withheld, if any (*see* below), and federal unemployment taxes *(38.4)* for your household employees. Total household employment taxes from Schedule H are entered as an "Additional tax" on Line 59 (check box b) of your Form 1040.

If you get an extension to file your return, file Schedule H with the return by the extended due date. If you are not required to file a 2010 tax return, you may file Schedule H by itself by the filing deadline, April 15, 2011. The completed Schedule H should be mailed to the same address that you would use for filing a return, along with a check or money order for the total household employment taxes due.

Withholding federal income taxes. Income tax withholding is not required for a household employee, but if the employee requests withholding and you agree, the employee must furnish you with a complete Form W-4, Withholding Allowance Certificate. *See* Publication 926, Household Employer's Guide, and Publication 15 (Circular E), Employer's Tax Guide.

The earned income credit (EIC). Copy B of Form W-2 has a notice about the EIC. If you do not give Copy B (or a substitute with similar EIC information) to your household employee by January 31, 2011, you must provide equivalent EIC notice on Notice 797 or your own written equivalent statement by the January 31 deadline. If you agreed to withhold federal income taxes from the employee's 2010 wages, but the wages were under $1,700 so Form W-2 is not required, the notice should be given to the employee by February 7, 2011.

SCHEDULE H (Form 1040)
Department of the Treasury Internal Revenue Service (99)

Household Employment Taxes

(For Social Security, Medicare, Withheld Income, and Federal Unemployment (FUTA) Taxes)

▶ Attach to Form 1040, 1040NR, 1040-SS, or 1041.
▶ See separate instructions.

OMB No. 1545-1971
2010
Attachment Sequence No. **44**

Name of employer: Nancy Nixon

Social security number: X1X-00-0011

Employer identification number: 0 X 0 1 0 0 X 1 X

A Did you pay **any one** household employee cash wages of $1,700 or more in 2010? (If any household employee was your spouse, your child under age 21, your parent, or anyone under age 18, see the line A instructions on page H-4 before you answer this question.)

☑ **Yes.** Skip lines B and C and go to line 1.
☐ **No.** Go to line B.

B Did you withhold federal income tax during 2010 for any household employee?

☐ **Yes.** Skip line C and go to line 5.
☐ **No.** Go to line C.

C Did you pay **total** cash wages of $1,000 or more in **any** calendar **quarter** of 2009 or 2010 to **all** household employees? (**Do not** count cash wages paid in 2009 or 2010 to your spouse, your child under age 21, or your parent.)

☐ **No. Stop.** Do not file this schedule.
☐ **Yes.** Skip lines 1-9 and go to line 10 on the back. (Calendar year taxpayers having no household employees in 2010 **do not** have to complete this form for 2010.)

Part I **Social Security, Medicare, and Federal Income Taxes**

Line	Description			Line	Amount	
1	Total cash wages subject to social security taxes (see page H-4)	1	2,200			
2	Social security taxes. Multiply line 1 by 12.4% (.124)			2	272	80
3	Total cash wages subject to Medicare taxes (see page H-4)	3	2,200			
4	Medicare taxes. Multiply line 3 by 2.9% (.029)			4	63	80
5	Federal income tax withheld, if any			5		
6	**Total social security, Medicare, and federal income taxes.** Add lines 2, 4, and 5			6	336	60
7	Advance earned income credit (EIC) payments, if any			7		
8	**Net taxes** (subtract line 7 from line 6)			8	336	60

9 Did you pay **total** cash wages of $1,000 or more in **any** calendar **quarter** of 2009 or 2010 to **all** household employees? (**Do not** count cash wages paid in 2009 or 2010 to your spouse, your child under age 21, or your parent.)

☑ **No. Stop.** Include the amount from line 8 above on Form 1040, line 59, and check box **b** on that line. If you are not required to file Form 1040, see the line 9 instructions on page H-4.

☐ **Yes.** Go to line 10 on the back.

For Privacy Act and Paperwork Reduction Act Notice, see page H-7 of the instructions. Cat. No. 12187K **Schedule H (Form 1040) 2010**

Fringe benefits. All or part of the value of certain fringe benefits are specifically excluded from taxable income. If you provide a household employee with lodging or meals on your premises, the benefits will not be taxable if furnished for your convenience as a condition of employment. You may also provide tax free transportation assistance to an employee. The tax-free limit for transit passes you give to your household employee, or reimbursements you give for mass transit costs, is $230 per month for 2010. The $230 monthly tax-free limit also applies to reimbursements you provide for your employee's parking costs near your home or near a mass transit location from which your employee commutes to your home.

EXAMPLE

On March 2, 2010, Nancy Nixon hired Eleanor Edwards to clean her house every Wednesday. She paid Eleanor $50 every Wednesday and did not withhold Eleanor's share of Social Security and Medicare (FICA) taxes from her wages. Instead, Nancy will pay Eleanor's share of Social Security and Medicare taxes out of pocket when she files Schedule H with her 2010 Form 1040. Nancy also did not withhold any federal income taxes because Eleanor did not give her a W-4 or in any other way request that income taxes be withheld. Eleanor didn't receive any advance earned income credit payments.

Eleanor worked for a total of 44 Wednesdays and received $2,200 (44 x $50) in total compensation from Nancy.

Eleanor's total cash wages	$2,200 ($50 x 44 weeks)	

Eleanor's share of employment taxes paid by Nancy:

Social security tax	$136.40	($2,200 x 6.2%)
Medicare tax	$31.90	($2,200 x 1.45%)

Wages included in Box 1 of Eleanor's Form W-2 and Nancy's Form W-3:

Cash wages	$2,200.00
Eleanor's share of Social Security tax paid by Nancy	136.40
Eleanor's share of Medicare tax paid by Nancy	31.90
Total wages	$2,368.30

Nancy will report Eleanor's total wages of $2,368.30 in Box 1 of Eleanor's Form W-2. The total includes Nancy's payment of Eleanor's share of Social Security and Medicare (FICA) taxes. However, only the cash wages of $2,200 are reported as Social Security and Medicare wages in Boxes 3 and 5 of Eleanor's Form W-2. When Nancy computes her liability for Social Security and Medicare taxes on Schedule H, she pays the combined employer/employee rate of 12.4% for Social Security on Eleanor's total cash wages and also the combined employer/employee Medicare rate of 2.9% on the total cash wages.

Employer identification number (EIN). If you are a household employer, you will need an employer identification number (EIN) and you may have to pay employment taxes. You can obtain an EIN by completing Form SS-4, Application for an Employer Identification Number. The number can be obtained immediately by phone, over the Internet, or in four weeks if you apply by mail. If you are still waiting for your number, do not use your Social Security number as a substitute. Instead, enter "Applied For" and the date you applied for the EIN in the space provided for the number.

Caution

Check State Requirements for Employers

You may have to register and pay state unemployment tax for a household employee. Contact your state unemployment tax agency; IRS Publication 926 has contact information. You should also contact the state labor department to determine if you need to carry workers' compensation insurance or pay other state employment taxes.

Forms W-2 and W-3. You need an EIN in order to properly file the necessary W-2 and W-3 forms. You must file a Form W-2 for each household employee to whom you paid $1,700 or more of cash wages in 2010 that are subject to Social Security and Medicare taxes. If the wages were not subject to those taxes but you withheld income taxes, you must file Form W-2 for the employee. Furnish copies B, C, and 2 of Form W-2 to your household employee by January 31, 2011.

If you file one or more Forms W-2, you must also file a Form W-3, Transmittal of Wage and Tax Statement. You must send Copy A of all Forms W-2 and W-3 to the Social Security Administration (SSA) by February 28, 2011 (March 31 if you file electronically).

38.4 Federal Unemployment Taxes (FUTA) for Household Employees

As an employer, you are also liable for FUTA (federal unemployment taxes) for 2010 if you pay cash wages of $1,000 or more for household services during any calendar quarter of 2010 or if you did so in any quarter of 2009. Your employee is not liable for FUTA. You must pay it with your own funds. You do not pay FUTA on wages paid to your spouse, your parents, or your children under age 21.

The FUTA rate for 2010 is 6.2% of the first $7,000 of cash wages paid to each household employee. However, there is a credit of up to 5.4% for state unemployment taxes that reduces FUTA liability, resulting in a net tax of 0.8%. Only employers that pay all the required state unemployment fund contributions for 2010 by April 15, 2011, will receive the entire credit; the credit for payments made after April 15, 2011, is limited to 90% of the pre-deadline credit.

For wages paid to a household employee in 2010, you will generally report FUTA on Schedule H, which you attach to your Form 1040. If you have regular business employees, *see* 38.2 for more reporting options.

Caution

Reduced Credit for Some States

If you are in a state that owes money to the federal unemployment fund, your FUTA credit for state unemployment taxes is reduced on Schedule H.

Chapter 39

Gift and Estate Tax Planning

Gift planning can be an important part of estate planning. This chapter provides an overview of the federal gift tax and estate tax. Developing an estate plan for your assets requires professional assistance, but the basic guidelines in this chapter can help you begin to estimate your potential estate and start thinking about property transfers that may reduce or avoid the estate tax.

Relatively small gifts can completely avoid gift tax *(39.2)* because of the annual gift tax exclusion, which for 2009 was $13,000 per donee. Gifts to a spouse and certain gifts to pay educational or medical expenses also are not subject to the gift tax.

Gift tax *(39.4)* generally does not have to be paid even on very substantial taxable gifts because the tax is offset by a tax credit that effectively exempts up to $1 million of lifetime taxable gifts from the tax.

For 2010, there is no estate tax. The 2001 Economic Growth and Tax Relief Reconciliation Act repealed the estate tax for estates of individuals dying in 2010 only and Congress allowed the repeal to take effect. The fate of the estate tax for years after 2010 had not been determined when this book went to press *(39.7)*.

Planning Reminder

Annual Gift Tax Exclusion

The annual exclusion exempts from gift tax the first $13,000 of gifts of present interests to each donee during 2010. If your spouse consents on Form 709 to split your gifts, the exclusion for each donee doubles to $26,000. Any change to the exclusion amount for gifts made after 2010 will be reported in the *e-Supplement at jklasser.com*.

If you make gifts of present interests in trust for more than one beneficiary, each beneficiary is treated separately for purposes of the annual exclusion. Also, if you give a present interest in property to more than one person as joint tenants, the annual exclusion can be claimed for each donee.

39.1 Gifts of Appreciated Property

Making a gift of appreciated property to a family member in advance of an anticipated sale can reduce the income tax liability for the family as a whole. By making a gift of interests in the property to several family members, it is possible to spread the profit and the tax among a number of taxpayers in the lowest tax bracket. Depending on the value of the property, you may or may not have to file a gift tax return *(39.2)*.

However, the tax benefit of making gifts of property to younger family members has been cut back by the expansion of the "kiddie tax." The kiddie tax *(24.2)* now covers most 18-year-olds and college students age 19 to 23.

Do not make a gift of investment property such as stock that has decreased in value if you want a deduction for the loss. Once you give the property away, the loss deduction is gone forever. Neither you nor your donee can ever take advantage of it. The better way is first to sell the property, get a loss deduction, and then make a gift of the proceeds.

Warning: The IRS may claim that the gift was never completed if, after sale by the donee, you control the sales proceeds or have the use of them.

39.2 Gift Tax Basics

When you consider making gifts of cash or property, you must consider possible gift tax liability. However, it is possible to make substantial gifts without incurring gift tax liability because of exclusions allowed by the tax law. Even where a gift is technically subject to the gift tax, liability computed on Form 709 can generally be avoided by applying the lifetime credit, which effectively exempts up to $1 million of gifts from the tax *(39.4)*.

The annual exclusion and other tax-free gifts. Gift tax liability may be avoided by making gifts that do not exceed the annual exclusion. The annual exclusion applies separately to each donee to whom you make gifts during a calendar year. For 2010, the per-donee exclusion is $13,000, or $26,000 if your spouse consents on Form 709 to "split" the gifts. The annual exclusion is allowed only for cash gifts or gifts of present interests in property; gifts of future interests do not qualify. For 2011, the amount of the annual exclusion may be increased above $13,000 by a cost-of-living adjustment; *see* the *e-Supplement at jklasser.com.*

Gifts to your spouse are completely tax free under the gift tax marital deduction if your spouse is a U.S. citizen at the time of the gift. For gifts to a spouse who is not a U.S. citizen, there is an annual exclusion; for 2010 gifts, the exclusion is $134,000, provided that the $121,000 excess over the basic $13,000 annual exclusion otherwise qualifies for the marital deduction.

There is an unlimited gift tax exclusion for payments of another person's tuition or medical expenses, if you make the payment directly to the educational organization or care provider. The medical and educational exclusions are allowed without regard to the relationship between you and the donee for whom you are making the payments. The exclusion for directly paid educational expenses applies only to tuition, not to room and board, books, or supplies.

Contributions to a qualified tuition program (QTP; *see 33.5*) on behalf of a designated beneficiary do not qualify for the educational exclusion, but do qualify for an enhanced annual exclusion. You can elect to treat a QTP contribution over the basic annual exclusion as if it were made ratably over a five-year period, but only up to five times the annual exclusion. For example, a QTP contribution made in 2010 of up to $65,000 may be treated as if $^1/_5$, or $13,000, had been contributed in 2010 and in each of the next four years. Thus, the entire gift up to $65,000 can avoid gift tax and if your spouse consents to split the gift on Form 709 *(39.3)* the exclusion increases to $130,000. If you make QTP contributions for more than one person in the same year, you can make the special QTP election for each of them.

Taxable gifts. If you make a gift that exceeds the allowable annual exclusion and which is not otherwise exempt from the gift tax, you must report the gift on Form 709 *(39.3)*. *Table 39-1* shows the tax rates applicable to taxable gifts made in 2010. The top rate, which for 2009 was 45%, is reduced for 2010 gifts to 35%, the top individual income tax rate for 2010. The top rate for 2011 is scheduled to remain the same as the top individual income tax rate, but whether this is the same or more than 35% will depend on whether the "Bush" tax cuts are extended beyond 2010, which had not been determined when this book went to press. However, regardless of the top income rate, Congress could decide to align the top gift tax with the top estate tax rate included in the estate tax reform legislation for estates of individuals dying after 2010. *See* the *e-Supplement at jklasser.com* for an update on the post-2010 rates.

Basis for property received as gift. The basis for appreciated property received as a gift is generally the same as the donor's basis. If gift tax was paid by the donor, basis is increased. The basis computation is explained in *5.17*.

Table 39-1 Tax Rates for Gifts Made in 2010

If taxable amount is: over—	*But not over—*	*The tax is—*	*Plus %—*	*Of the amount over—*
$0	$10,000	$0	18	$0
10,000	20,000	1,800	20	10,000
20,000	40,000	3,800	22	20,000
40,000	60,000	8,200	24	40,000
60,000	80,000	13,000	26	60,000
80,000	100,000	18,200	28	80,000
100,000	150,000	23,800	30	100,000
150,000	250,000	38,800	32	150,000
250,000	500,000	70,800	34	250,000
500,000		155,800	35	500,000

39.3 Filing a Gift Tax Return

A gift tax return generally must be filed on Form 709 for a gift made during 2010 to an individual other than your spouse if it exceeds $13,000 or is a gift of a future interest (regardless of value). A return does not have to be filed for gifts qualifying for the tuition or medical expense exclusion discussed in *39.2*.

Married couples who consent to split gifts of over $13,000 in 2010 to any one person must report the gifts to the IRS on Form 709. No gift tax is due under the annual exclusion if the "split" gift is $26,000 or less.

Form 709 for 2010 generally must be filed by April 15, 2011. If you get a filing extension (Form 4868) for your income tax return, the extension also applies to the gift tax return. If you do not request an extension for your income tax return, you can use Form 8892 to request a filing extension for your gift tax return.

Caution

Gift Disclosure Starts Running of Statute of Limitations

To begin the running of the statute of limitations on gift valuation, the gift must be adequately disclosed on Form 709 filed for the year of the gift. Follow the disclosure instructions for Schedule A of Form 709. Given this statute of limitations consideration, even donors of property valued at under the annual exclusion ($13,000 for 2010) may want to report the gift on Form 709 in order to start the clock running on how long the IRS has to challenge valuation of the gift.

EXAMPLES

1. On July 14, 2010, Randall Johnson makes a gift of publicly traded stock to his son, Philip. He gives Philip 1,000 shares of stock valued at $20,000 ($20 per share). His cost basis for the 1,000 shares was $15,000. On Randall's Form 709, Randall's wife, Claire, consents to split the gift, thereby doubling the $13,000 annual exclusion for the gift. Neither Randall nor Claire made any other gifts during 2010. As a result of the gift splitting, Randall's share of the gift is reduced to $10,000 and is offset by the annual exclusion. No gift tax is due.
2. Same facts as in Example 1 except that the value of the stock given to Philip was $40,000 instead of $20,000. After Claire consents to split Randall's gift, there is a taxable gift of $14,000 ($40,000 – $26,000 annual exclusion), of which half, or $7,000, is attributed to each of them. They each must file their own Form 709. Assuming that this is the first taxable gift for both Randall and Claire, they will each figure a gift tax of $1,260 on their $7,000 gift *(Table 39-1)*. However, no tax is due because it is offset by a $1,260 credit. Randall and Claire each have a lifetime credit of $345,800 for gift tax purposes *(39.4)*, which effectively exempts $1 million of lifetime taxable gifts from tax. The $1,260 credit used this year reduces the remaining lifetime credit for each of them to $344,540 ($345,800 – $1,260). They each have a remaining lifetime exemption of $993,000.

39.4 Gift Tax Credit

On Form 709, any gift tax that you otherwise would owe is eliminated or reduced by a tax credit. The credit against taxable gifts for 2002 through 2010 is $345,000, effectively exempting $1 million of otherwise taxable gifts from the gift tax. Any part of the $345,000 credit that was used to offset gift tax in prior years reduces the credit available for 2010.

Although the $345,000 credit (and equivalent $1 million exemption) are scheduled to remain in effect after 2010, this may change if Congress enacts estate tax reform legislation that provides a unified credit that applies to both the gift tax and a restored estate tax; *see* the *e-Supplement at jklasser.com* for an update..

Law Alert

Lifetime Gift Tax Credit and Exemption

For 2002 and later years, a $345,800 lifetime credit is allowed, providing a lifetime exemption for $1 million of taxable gifts. If taxable gifts are made in one year, the amount of the credit used to offset the gift tax for that year reduces the credit available for use against gift tax in later years. The $345,800 credit and the $1 million exemption are fixed by law.

39.5 Custodial Accounts for Minors

A minor generally lacks the ability to manage property. You could create a formal trust, but this step may be costly. A practical alternative may be a custodial account under the Uniform Gifts to Minors Act (UGMA), or the Uniform Transfers to Minors Act (UTMA), which has replaced the UGMA in practically every state.

Custodial accounts set up in a bank, mutual fund, or brokerage firm can achieve income splitting; the tax consequences discussed below generally apply to such accounts. Trust accounts that are considered revocable under state law are ineffective in splitting income.

Although custodial accounts may be opened anywhere in the United States, the rules governing the accounts may vary from state to state. The differences between the laws of the states generally do not affect federal tax consequences.

There are limitations placed on the custodian. Proceeds from the sale of an investment or income from an investment may not be used to buy additional securities on margin. While a custodian should prudently seek reasonable income and capital preservation, he or she generally is not liable for losses unless they result from bad faith, intentional wrongdoing, or gross negligence.

When the minor reaches majority age (depending on state law), property in the custodial account is turned over to him or her. No formal accounting is required. The child, now an adult, may sign a simple release freeing the custodian from any liability. But on reaching majority, the child may request a formal accounting if there are any doubts as to the propriety of the custodian's actions while acting as custodian. For this reason, and also for tax record-keeping purposes, a separate bank account should be opened in which proceeds from sales of investments and investment income are deposited pending reinvestment on behalf of the child. Such an account will furnish a convenient record of sales proceeds, investment income, and reinvestment of the same.

Income tax treatment of custodian account. Income from a custodian account is generally taxable to the child. However, if the "kiddie tax" applies *(24.2)*, taxable income from a custodial account in excess of the annual "kiddie" tax floor ($1,900 in 2010) is taxed at the parent's tax rate.

If a parent is the donor of the custodial property or the custodian of the account and income from the account is used to discharge the parent's legal obligation to support the child, the account income is taxed to the parent.

Planning Reminder

Custodial Securities Account

Purchase of securities through custodial accounts provides a practical method for making a gift of securities to a minor child, eliminating the need for a trust. The mechanics of opening a custodial account are simple. An adult opens a stock brokerage account for a minor child and registers the securities in the name of a custodian for the benefit of the child. The custodian may be a parent, a child's guardian, grandparent, brother, sister, uncle, or aunt. In some states, the custodian may be any adult or a bank or trust company. The custodian has the right to sell securities in the account and collect sales proceeds and investment income, and use them for the child's benefit or reinvestment. Tax treatment of custodial accounts is discussed in *39.5*.

Gift tax treatment of custodial account. When setting up a custodial account, you may have to pay a gift tax. A transfer of cash or securities to a custodial account is a gift. But you are not subject to a gift tax if you properly plan the cash contributions or purchase of securities for your children's accounts. You may make gifts that are shielded from gift tax by the annual exclusion. The exclusion applies each year to each person to whom you make a gift. If your spouse consents to join with you in the gift, the annual exclusion is doubled. For gifts in 2010, the per-donee exclusion is $13,000, $26,000 if your spouse consents to split the gift.

If the custodial account is set up at the end of December, another tax-free transfer of up to the annual exclusion may be made in the first days of January of the following year. Assuming the annual exclusion in each year is $13,000, a total of $52,000 can be shifted within the two-month period with spousal consent.

Even if gifts exceeding the annual exclusion are made, gift tax liability may be offset by the unified credit applied to gift and estate taxes.

Estate tax treatment of custodial account. Assuming the estate tax is restored for years after 2010, the value of a custodial account will be taxed in your estate if you die while acting as custodian of an account before your child reaches his or her majority. However, you may avoid the problem by naming someone other than yourself as custodian. If you should decide to act as custodian, taking the risk that the account will be taxed in your estate, remember that no estate tax is incurred if the tax on your estate is offset by the estate tax credit.

If you act as custodian and decide to terminate the custodianship, care should be taken to formally close the account. Otherwise, if you die while retaining power over the account, the IRS may try to tax the account in your estate.

39.6 Trusts in Family Planning

You establish a trust by transferring legal title to property to a trustee who manages the property for one or more beneficiaries. As the one who sets up the trust, you are called the grantor or settlor of the trust. The trustee may be one or more individuals or an institution such as a bank or a trust company.

You can create a trust during your lifetime or by your will. A trust created during your lifetime is called an *inter vivos* trust; one established in your will is a testamentary trust. An *inter vivos* trust can be revocable or irrevocable. An irrevocable trust does not allow for changes of heart; it requires a complete surrender of property. By conveying property irrevocably to a trust, you may relieve yourself of tax on the income from the trust principal. Furthermore, the property in trust usually is not subject to estate tax, although it may be subject to gift tax. A trust should be made irrevocable only if you are certain you will not need the trust property in a financial emergency.

Planning Reminder

Revocable Trusts

In a revocable trust, you retain control over the property by reserving the right to revoke the trust. As such, it is considered an incomplete gift and offers no present income tax savings. Furthermore, the trust property will be included as part of your estate. But a revocable trust minimizes delay in passing property to beneficiaries if you die while the trust is in force. When you transfer property to a trust, the property is generally not subject to probate, administration expenses, delays attendant on distributions of estates, or claims of creditors. The interests of trust beneficiaries are generally more secure than those of heirs under a will because a will may be denied probate if found invalid.

Trust income. Where a child is a trust beneficiary, the child reports distributable net trust income as taxable income. Distributable net income may be subject to the "kiddie tax" *(24.2)*. Income that is accumulated for the benefit of a minor child is generally not taxable and, thus, not subject to the kiddie tax.

Grantor trusts. The grantor of a grantor trust is taxed on the income of the trust. A trust is treated as a grantor trust where the grantor has a reversionary interest (at the time of the transfer) of more than 5% of the value of the property transferred to the trust. Under an exception, a grantor is not treated as having a reversionary interest if that interest can take effect only upon the death before age 21 of a beneficiary who is a lineal descendant of the grantor. The beneficiary must have the entire present interest in the trust or trust portion for this exception to apply.

Given the highly compressed tax brackets for trust income, a grantor may intentionally retain an interest in the trust property so that he or she will be taxed under the grantor trust rules. By setting up such a "defective" grantor trust, trust income may be subject to lower tax at the grantor's tax bracket than under the trust rate schedule.

39.7 No Estate Tax for Estates of Individuals Dying in 2010

Congressional inaction allowed the estate tax to be repealed for estates of individuals dying in 2010, as had been scheduled under the 2001 Economic Growth and Tax Relief Act. The generation-skipping tax was also repealed for 2010 transfers.

Basis of property inherited from individuals dying in 2010. Prior law allowed a step-up in basis, up to fair market value on the date of death, for assets inherited from individuals dying before 2010 *(5.17)*. However, the law repealing the estate tax for 2010 imposes a modified carryover basis rule for heirs who inherit property from individuals dying in 2010. A step-up in basis is allowed only for up to $1.3 million of assets inherited from an individual dying in 2010, as designated by the executor of the estate, plus an additional $3 million for assets passing to a surviving spouse. For larger amounts, the heir's basis is the decedent's basis (carryover basis) for the property.

When this book went to press, the IRS had not yet released the form to be used by executors for allocating the $1.3 and $3 million amounts eligible for a stepped-up basis where the fair market value of property in the estate exceeds $1.3 million. The basis allocation information provided to the IRS will have to be given to the heirs who receive property within 30 days of the filing of the form. It is likely that when Congress agrees on estate tax legislation for years after 2010, it will allow stepped-up basis and include an option for executors of estates of individuals dying in 2010 to file a return under the post-2010 rules in order to obtain a full step-up in basis for the heirs.

See the *e-Supplement at jklasser.com* for an update on the basis rules.

Legislation expected for estate tax after 2010. When this book went to press, Congress had not yet agreed on an estate tax reform package for years after 2010. Without such new legislation, the estate tax will return in 2011 with only a $1 million exemption, compared to the $3.5 million exemption that applied for estates of individuals dying in 2009, and a top tax rate of 55%, compared to the 45% top rate that applied for 2009. The Administration has favored a permanent extension of the 2009 rules, but when this book went to press, it appeared more likely that Congress would agree to a phased-in increase to the $3.5 million exemption as well as a phased-in in reduction of the top estate tax rate. As noted above, any legislation is likely to provide executors of estates of individuals dying in 2010 with an option to apply the 2010 rules (no estate tax but modified carryover basis for heirs) or the rules as enacted in the new legislation, which will provide stepped-up basis for heirs. *See* the *e-Supplement at jklasser.com* for a legislation update.

39.8 Planning for a Restored Estate Tax

There will be a federal estate tax for years after 2010, although the rules were not set when this book went to press *(39.7)*. The following sections provide some general guidelines to help you begin to plan for your estate with the assistance of an experienced estate tax professional.

What is the estate tax? The estate you built up may not be entirely yours to give away. The federal government and, in most cases, at least one state government stand ready to claim their shares.

The federal estate tax is a tax on the act of transferring property at death. It is not a tax on the right of the beneficiary to receive the property; the estate and the estate alone pays the tax, although the property passing to individual beneficiaries may be diminished by the tax.

Understand what the word estate means in estate tax law so that you do not underestimate the value of your taxable estate. The estate includes not only your real estate (foreign and domestic), bank deposits, securities, and personal property such as art objects, but can also include insurance, your interest in trusts or jointly held property, and certain interests you have in other estates.

Planning Reminder

Life Insurance

If you are buying a new policy with yourself as the insured, and you want to keep the proceeds out of your gross estate, set up an irrevocable trust to buy the policy or have the individual beneficiary buy the policy. For example, a daughter applies for a $1 million policy on her father's life and is the policy owner under the terms of the policy. If the father pays the premiums, his payments are treated as gifts, but the proceeds paid at his death are not subject to estate tax because he never had ownership rights in the policy.

If you have an existing policy, you may assign your ownership rights, such as the right to change beneficiaries, the right to surrender or cancel the policy, the right to assign it, and the right to borrow against it, but the assignment must occur more than three years before death to exclude the proceeds from your estate.

39.9 Take Inventory of Your Potential Estate

The first step in estate tax planning follows a simple business practice of taking inventory of everything you own. Listing your belongings takes thought, time, and a surprising amount of work. On your list you should include records of purchases, fire and theft insurance inventories, bankbooks, brokers' statements, etc. You should also include your cash, real estate (here and abroad), securities, mortgages, rights in property, trust accounts, personal effects, collections, and art works. Life insurance is includible if: (1) it is payable to your estate; (2) it is payable to others and you have kept "incidents of ownership" such as the right to change beneficiaries, surrender or assign the policy, or pledge it for a loan; or (3) you assign the policy and die within three years.

If you own property jointly with your spouse, your estate includes only one-half its value.

If you had appraisals made of specially treasured items or collections, or property of substantial value, file such appraisals with your estate papers and then enter the value on your inventory.

Retirement benefits. The taxable estate generally includes benefits payable at your death from any of the following retirement plans: pension plan, profit-sharing plan, Keogh plan, individual retirement account, or annuity. However, the value of an annuity from an IRA or employer plan that is payable to a beneficiary other than your estate may qualify for a full or partial exclusion if IRA distributions began before 1985 or you separated from service before 1985; no exclusion is allowed to the extent of your own nondeductible contributions to the plan.

A full exclusion is allowed for IRA funds if you began taking distributions from the account before 1983 under a schedule that irrevocably set the form of benefits. If IRA distributions began in 1983 or 1984 and you irrevocably elected the form of benefits before July 18, 1984, a $100,000 exclusion is allowed.

If you began receiving distributions from an employer plan before 1983 under a schedule that irrevocably set the form of benefits, a full estate tax exclusion is allowed. If you separated from service in 1983 or 1984, a $100,000 exclusion is allowed if the form of benefits is not changed before death; this is true even if distributions did not begin until after 1984.

39.10 Valuing Your Potential Estate

When you have completed your inventory, assign to each asset what you consider to be its fair market value. This may be difficult to do for some assets. Resist the tendency to overvalue articles that arouse feelings of pride or sentiment and undervalue some articles of great intrinsic worth. For purposes of your initial estimate, it is better to err on the side of overvaluation. You can list ordinary personal effects at nominal value.

If you have a family business, your idea of its value and that of the IRS may vary greatly. Estate plans have been upset by the higher value placed on such a business by the IRS. You can protect your estate by anticipating and solving this problem with your business associates and counselors.

If your business is owned by a closely held corporation, and there is no ready or open market in which the stock can be valued, get some factual basis for a figure that will be reported on the estate tax return. One of the ways to do this is by arranging a buy-sell agreement with a potential purchaser. This agreement must fix the value of the stock. Generally, an agreement that binds both the estate and the purchaser and restricts lifetime sales of the stock will effectively fix the value of the stock for estate tax purposes. Another way would be to make a gift of some shares to a family member and have value established in gift tax proceedings.

If a substantial part of your estate is real estate used in farming or a closely held business, your executor may be able to elect, with the consent of heirs having an interest in the property, to value the property on the basis of its farming or business use, rather than its highest and best use.

Caution

Trusts Includible in Estate

There are some assets that you might not ordinarily consider as part of your estate. Nevertheless, include in your inventory any trust arrangements created by you in which you have: (1) a life estate (the income or other use of property for life); (2) income that is to be used to pay your legal obligations (support of a child, for example); (3) the right to change the beneficiary or his or her interest (a power of appointment); (4) the right to revoke a trust transfer or gift; and (5) a reversionary interest (the possibility that the property can come back to you).

39.11 Estimating Potential Estate Tax Liability

Before 2010, a single unified rate schedule applied to a decedent's estate and all post-1976 lifetime gifts *over* the annual gift tax exclusion. This unified rate computation is likely to be continued in the estate tax reform legislation that Congress will pass for years after 2010. Under the unified gift and estate tax rate, the overall tax on your property holdings is theoretically the same whether or not you make lifetime gifts. In actual cases, however, lifetime gifts may reduce the potential overall tax because of the annual gift tax exclusion *(39.2)*. When Congress passes new estate tax legislation and the post-2010 exemptions and rates are known *(39.7)* it will be possible to estimate what the estate tax could be for your estate. The revised Form 706 (United States Estate (and Generation-Skipping Transfer) Tax Return) for 2011 could be used to make an estimate. On the Form 706 and related schedules, you itemize the values of the property that are includible in the estate. The total is called the *gross estate.* From the gross estate you subtract certain deductions. For example, administration expenses for the estate and charitable bequests are deductible. An unlimited marital deduction is allowed for bequests to a surviving spouse who is a U.S. citizen. The net amount after deductions is your taxable estate. A unified credit (the amount of which will be set by Congress) is subtracted from the tax calculated on the taxable estate and other credits further reduce the federal estate tax on your estate. Computation of the gross estate and the estate tax liability will be more complicated if you have made taxable gifts (over the annual gift tax exclusion).

Caution

Get Expert Advice

Estate tax planning is not a do-it-yourself activity. You should contact experienced counsel for help in developing a plan for your future estate that will accomplish your tax and personal objectives.

39.12 Reducing or Eliminating a Potential Estate Tax

After Congress passes estate tax legislation for years after 2010 *(39.7)*, it will be possible to project whether your estate might be subject to estate tax. If estate tax is a possibility, there are general approaches that you can take to eliminate a potential estate tax. You can make direct lifetime gifts. Any appreciation on the property transferred will be removed from your estate. Furthermore, each gift, to the extent of the annual per donee exclusion ($13,000 in 2010), reduces your gross estate *(39.2)*. Life insurance can be assigned to avoid estate tax, provided the assignment takes place more than three years before death *(39.8)*. You can provide in your will for bequests that will qualify for the marital and charitable deductions.

The marital deduction. A married person may greatly reduce or eliminate estate tax by using the marital deduction. Property passing to a spouse is generally free from estate or gift tax because of an unlimited marital deduction.

Weigh carefully the tax consequences of leaving your spouse all of your property. For maximum tax savings, you may want to give your spouse only enough property to reduce your taxable estate to the exclusion floor *(39.11)*. The unified credit amount will then eliminate tax on that amount at the time of your death. By leaving your spouse less than the maximum deductible amount, you may be able to reduce the estate tax at the time of his or her death.

Planning Reminder

Marital Deduction

To qualify for the marital deduction, the property must generally be given to the spouse outright or by other arrangements that are the legal equivalent of outright ownership. There is an exception for income interests in charitable remainder annuity or unitrusts and certain other qualified terminable interest property (QTIP) for which the executor makes an election.

Life insurance proceeds may qualify as marital deduction property. Name your spouse the unconditional beneficiary of the proceeds with unrestricted control over any unpaid proceeds. If your spouse is not given this control or general power of appointment, and there is no requirement that proceeds remaining on your spouse's death be payable to his or her estate, the insurance proceeds will not qualify for the marital deduction.

What should be done if you believe your spouse cannot manage property? You will not want to give complete and personal control. The law permits you to put the property in certain trust arrangements that are considered equivalent to complete ownership. Your attorney can explain how you can protect your spouse's interest and qualify the trust property for the marital deduction.

Marital deduction restrictions for noncitizen spouses. A marital deduction may not be claimed for property passing outright to a surviving spouse who is not a U.S. citizen. However, the marital deduction is allowed if the surviving spouse's interest is in a qualifying domestic trust (QDOT). At least one trustee must be an individual U.S. citizen or domestic corporation with power to withhold estate tax due from distributions of trust corpus. The trust must maintain sufficient assets as required by IRS regulations. For the marital deduction to apply, the executor must make an irrevocable election on the decedent's estate tax return. On Form 706-QDT, estate tax will apply to certain distributions of trust corpus made prior to the surviving spouse's death, and to the value of the QDOT property remaining at the surviving spouse's death. You should consult an experienced tax practitioner to set up a QDOT trust and plan for distribution provisions.

The estate of a nonresident alien is subject to estate tax only to the extent that the estate is located in the United States. A marital deduction may be claimed by the estate of a nonresident alien for property passing to a surviving spouse who is a U.S. citizen. If the surviving spouse is not a U.S. citizen, then the transferred interest must be in the form of a QDOT.

Periodically review your estate plan. No estate plan is ever really final. Economic conditions and inflation constantly change values. For this reason, your plan must be reviewed periodically as changes occur in your family and business, as when a birth or death occurs; when you receive a substantial increase or decrease in income; when you enter a new business venture or resign from an old one; or when you sell, retire from, or bring new persons into business. A member of your family may no longer need any part of your estate, while others may need more. Material changes may occur in the health or life expectancy of one of your beneficiaries. Furthermore, your planning will be affected by legislative developments.

PART 6

Business Tax Planning

In this part, you will learn how to report your income from a business or profession, and how to reduce your tax liability by claiming expense deductions. Pay special attention to—

- Reporting rules for income and expenses on Schedule C *(Chapter 40)*.
- Restrictions on deducting home office expenses. Your deduction may be limited by a restrictive income test *(Chapter 40)*.
- The increased deduction for qualified domestic production activities income *(Chapter 40)*.
- Keogh, SEP, and SIMPLE retirement plan rules if you are self-employed. These plans offer tax deductions for contributions and tax-free accumulation of income within the plan.
- Health savings accounts and other medical plans *(Chapter 41)*.
- First-year expensing and depreciation write-offs for business assets *(Chapter 42)*.
- The IRS mileage allowance as an alternative to claiming operating expenses and depreciation for your business automobile *(Chapter 43)*.
- Computing and paying self-employment tax on self-employment earnings from a business or profession *(Chapter 45)*.

Chapter 40

Income or Loss From Your Business or Profession

As a self-employed person, you report income and expenses from your business or profession separately from your other income, such as income from wages. On Schedule C, you report your business income and itemize your expenses. Any net profit is subject to self-employment tax, as well as regular tax. A net profit can also be the basis of deductible contributions to a SEP or Keogh retirement plan, as discussed in *Chapter 41*.

If you work out of your home, you may deduct home office expenses.

If you claim a loss on Schedule C, be prepared to show that you regularly and substantially participate in the business. Otherwise, your loss may be considered a passive loss deductible only from passive income, as discussed in *Chapter 10*.

If you have a business loss that exceeds your other income, you may carry back the loss and claim a refund. For a loss in a tax year ending in 2010, the carryback period is generally two years *(40.18)*.

If you have no employees and business expenses of $5,000 or less, you may be able to file a simplified schedule called Schedule C-EZ *(40.6)*.

40.1 Forms of Doing Business

The legal form of your business determines the way you report business income and loss, the taxes you pay, the ability of the business to accumulate capital, and the extent of your personal liability. It is beyond the scope of this book to discuss the pros and cons of each form. The decision should be made with the services of a professional experienced in both the legal and tax consequences of doing business in a particular form as it applies to your current and future business prospects.

If you are going into business alone, your choices are: operating as a sole proprietor, incorporating, and forming a limited liability company (LLC). If you are going to operate with associates, you may choose to operate as a partnership, a corporation, or an LLC. If you are concerned with limiting your personal liability, your choice is between a corporation or an LLC. An LLC gives you the advantage of limited liability without having to incorporate.

As a sole proprietor, you report business profit or loss on your personal tax return, as explained in this chapter. If you are a partner, you report your share of partnership profit and loss as explained in *Chapter 11*. If you incorporate, the corporation pays tax on business income. You are taxable on salaries and dividends paid to you by the corporation. You may avoid this double corporate tax by making an S corporation election, which allows you to report corporate income and loss *(11.14)*.

If you operate through an LLC with no co-owners, you report income and loss as a sole proprietor. If you operate an LLC with associates, the LLC reports as a partnership and you report your share of income and loss. However, under check-the-box rules, the LLC may elect on Form 8832 to report as an association taxable as a corporation.

Filing Tip

Schedule F for Farming Business

If you are self-employed and your business involves farming, you report on Schedule F instead of Schedule C. However, much of the information contained in Chapters 40 through 45 applies to you as well.

Filing Tip

Did You Suffer a Loss?

Business persons and professionals with a 2010 net operating loss may get a refund of taxes paid in two prior tax years (more in some cases). If the loss is not fully eliminated by the income of the two prior years, the balance of the loss may be used to reduce your business income for up to 20 of the following years *(40.18)*.

40.2 Reporting Self-Employed Income

You file a separate Schedule C along with Form 1040 if you are a sole proprietor of a business or a professional in your own practice. If you do freelance work as an independent contractor, you are self-employed and use Schedule C. If you are an employee with a sideline business, report the self-employment income and expenses from that business on Schedule C. Do not file Schedule C if your business is operated through a partnership or corporation. *See* the guide to Schedule C in *40.6*.

On Schedule C, you deduct your allowable business expenses from your business income. Net business profit (or loss) figured on Schedule C is entered on Line 12, Page 1 of Form 1040. Thus, business profit (or loss) is added to (or subtracted from) nonbusiness income on Form 1040 to compute adjusted gross income. This procedure gives you the chance to deduct your business expenses, whether you claim itemized deductions or nonbusiness deductions on Schedule A, such as charitable contributions, taxes, and medical expenses, or you claim the standard deduction where it exceeds your allowable itemized deductions *(13.2)*.

You may be able to file a simplified schedule, Schedule C-EZ, if your income and expenses are below certain limits *(40.6)*.

Passive loss restrictions. Pay special attention to the passive loss restrictions discussed in *Chapter 10*. Generally, if you do not regularly and substantially participate in your business, losses are considered passive and are deductible only against other passive income.

Recordkeeping. You are required to keep books and records for your business activities, tracking your income and expenses carefully so you can report them accurately on your return. You enter this information according to your method of accounting *(40.3)*.

The tax law does not determine the way in which you must keep these records; today most self-employed taxpayers use computer-based recordkeeping systems.

Tax ID number. As a sole proprietor, you usually do not need a separate tax ID number for Schedule C; you can use your Social Security number as your tax ID number. However, you must obtain an employer identification number if you have any employees and/or maintain a qualified retirement plan (you may also need one to open a business bank account). You can obtain your employer identification number online at www.irs.gov/businesses/small/index.html (click on "Employer ID Numbers (EINs)."

Filing Tip

Husband and Wife Owners Can File on Schedule C

Instead of having to file a partnership return, a husband and wife who are the sole owners of a business, who both materially participate in the business, and who file a joint return can elect to file as sole proprietors on Schedule C. If the election is made, each spouse reports his or her respective share of the income and expenses on Schedule C; follow the 2010 instructions to Schedule C for reporting the respective shares.

If the election is made, each spouse's share of the net profit is considered to be his or her self-employment earnings for purposes of figuring self-employment tax *(45.1)* and for crediting Social Security and Medicare benefits.

Table 40-1 Key to Reporting Business and Professional Income and Loss

Item—	*Comments—*
Tax return to file	If you are self-employed, prepare Schedule C to report business or professional income. If your business expenses are $5,000 or less, and you have no employees, you may be able to file a simplified Schedule C-EZ *(40.6)*. If you are a farmer, use Schedule F. You attach Schedule C and/or F to Form 1040. If you operate as a partnership, use Form 1065; if you operate as a corporation, use Form 1120S or Form 1120.
Method of reporting income	The cash or accrual accounting rules determine when you report income and expenses. You must use the accrual basis if you sell a product that must be inventoried unless a safe harbor exception applies. The cash-basis and accrual-basis methods are discussed at 40.3.
Tax reporting year	There are two general tax reporting years: calendar years that end on December 31 and fiscal years that end on the last day of any month other than December. Your taxable year must be the same for both your business and nonbusiness income. Most business income must be reported on a calendar-year basis. If, as a self-employed person, you report your business income on a fiscal-year basis, you must also report your nonbusiness income on a fiscal-year basis. Use of a fiscal year is restricted for partnerships and S corporations.
Office in home	To claim home office expenses as a self-employed person, you must use the home area exclusively and on a regular basis either as a place of business to meet or deal with patients, clients, or customers in the normal course of your business or as your principal place of business. Form 8829 must be used to compute the deduction *(40.12)*.
Social Security coverage	If you have self-employment income, you may have to pay self-employment tax, which goes to financing Social Security and Medicare benefits; *see* Chapter 45.
Passive participation in a business	If you do not regularly, continuously, and substantially participate in the business, your business income or loss is subject to passive activity restrictions. A loss is deductible only against other passive activity income. The passive activity restrictions are discussed in detail in Chapter 10.
Self-employed Keogh plan	You may set up a retirement plan based on business or professional income. Individuals who are self-employed may contribute to a self-employed retirement plan, according to the rules in *Chapter 41*.
Health insurance	You may deduct 100% of premiums paid for health insurance coverage for yourself, spouse, and dependents. This deduction is claimed directly from gross income on Line 29 of Form 1040. You may also take advantage of a health savings account plan as explained in *Chapter 41*.
Depreciation	Under the increased first-year expensing deduction, you generally may deduct up to $250,000 for equipment placed in service in 2010 *(42.3)*. Depreciation rules for assets not deducted under first-year expensing are in *Chapter 42*. Cars and trucks are subject to special depreciation limits; *see Chapter 43*.
Net operating losses	A loss incurred in your profession or business is deducted from other income reported on Form 1040. If the loss (plus any casualty loss) exceeds income, the excess may generally be first carried back two years, and then forward 20 years until it is used up. A loss carried back to a prior year reduces income of that year and entitles you to a refund. A loss applied to a later year reduces income for that year. In some cases a three-year or five-year carryback applies *(40.18)*. You may elect to carry forward your loss for 20 years, foregoing the carryback *(40.22)*.
Sideline business	You report business income of a sideline business following the rules that apply to full-time business. For example, if you are self-employed, you report business income on Schedule C or C-EZ. You may also have to pay self-employment tax on this income; *see* Chapter 45. You may also set up a self-employment retirement plan based on such income; *see* Chapter 41. If you incur losses over several years, the hobby loss rules *(40.10)* may limit your loss deduction.
Domestic production activities deduction	If your business makes something in the U.S., you may be eligible for a 9% deduction, which effectively reduces the tax rate you would otherwise pay on this income *(40.23)*.

40.3 Accounting Methods for Reporting Business Income

Business income is reported on either the accrual or cash basis. If you have more than one business, you may have a different accounting method for each business.

Inventories. Unless a cash method safe harbor (discussed below) applies, the IRS requires inventories at the beginning and end of every taxable year in which the production, purchase, or sale of merchandise is an income-producing factor. If you must keep inventories, you must use the accrual basis.

Cash method. You report income items in the taxable year in which they are received; you deduct all expenses in the taxable year in which they are paid. Under the cash method, income is also reported if it is "constructively" received. You have "constructively" received income when an amount is credited to your account, subject to your control, or set apart for you and may be drawn by you at any time. For example, in 2010 you receive a check in payment of services, but you do not cash it until 2011. You have constructively received the income in 2010, and it is taxable in 2010.

On the cash basis, you deduct expenses in the year of payment. Expenses paid by credit card are deducted in the year they are charged. Expenses paid through a "pay by phone" account with a bank are deducted in the year the bank sends the check. This date is reported by the bank on its monthly statement.

IRS Alert

Cash Method Safe Harbor

Qualifying businesses with average annual gross receipts of $10 million are eligible to use a cash method safe harbor. Those who are ineligible may qualify under a $1 million safe harbor.

Advance payments. Generally, no immediate deduction can be claimed for advance rent or premium covering charges of a later year. However, under a "12-month rule," you can claim an immediate deduction for prepayments that create rights or benefits that do not extend beyond the earlier of: (1) 12 months after the first date on which the taxpayer realizes rights or benefits attributable to the expenditure, or (2) the end of the taxable year following the taxable year in which the payment is made. However, prepayments of rent remain nondeductible for accrual-method taxpayers under the economic performance rules.

Planning Reminder

Advantage of Cash-Basis Accounting

The cash basis has this advantage over other accounting methods: You may defer reporting income by postponing the receipt of income. But make certain that you avoid the constructive receipt rule. For example, if 2010 is a high income year or you might drop to a lower tax bracket in 2011, you might delay mailing some of your customers' bills so they do not receive them until 2011. You may also postpone the payment of presently due expenses to a year in which the deduction gives you a greater tax savings.

Cash method of accounting limited. The following may not use the cash method: a regular C corporation, a partnership with a C corporation as a partner, a tax shelter, or a tax-exempt trust with unrelated business income. Exceptions: A farming or tree-raising business may use the cash method even if it operates as a C corporation or a partnership with a C corporation as a partner. The cash method may also be used by personal service corporations in the fields of medicine, law, engineering, accounting, architecture, performing arts, actuarial science, or consulting. To qualify, substantially all of the stock must be owned directly or indirectly (through partnerships, S corporations, or personal service corporations) by employees.

If the production, purchase, or sale of merchandise is *not* an income-producing factor, the cash method may be used by a C corporation or a partnership with a C corporation as a partner if the average annual gross receipts over the prior three-year period were $5 million or less.

Cash method safe harbors. Business owners with average annual gross receipts of $10 million or less may be able to use the cash method if they qualify under the rules of Revenue Procedure 2002-28. For those who do not qualify for the $10 million safe harbor, such as retailers, wholesalers, and manufacturers, a $1 million safe harbor may be available under Revenue Procedure 2001-10. If either safe harbor applies, the cash method can be used even if the business owner would otherwise have to account for inventories under the accrual method. A qualifying taxpayer may not deduct items purchased for resale to customers or used as raw materials for producing finished goods until the year the items are provided to customers if that is later than the year the items were purchased. A qualifying small business that wants to apply the safe harbor guidelines must file for an accounting method change as explained in the instructions to Form 3115.

$10 million safe harbor. The taxpayer's average annual gross receipts must be $10 million or less for the three taxable years ending with *each* prior taxable year ending on or after December 31, 2000. If the test is not met, the cash method cannot be used for 2010 or any later year. If the business has not been in existence for three prior taxable years, including the period of any predecessor, the average is figured for the years it has been in existence.

The cash method safe harbor applies to service businesses, custom manufacturers, and any other taxpayer whose principal activity is not specifically ineligible under Revenue Procedure 2002-28. If a taxpayer's principal business activity is any of the following, Revenue Procedure 2002-28 bars the cash method safe harbor for that activity: retail or wholesale sales, manufacturing (other than eligible custom manufacturers), publishing, sound recording, or mining. The "principal" activity is the activity that produced the largest percentage of gross receipts in the prior year or the largest average percentage over the three prior years.

Where the taxpayer's principal activity is not in the prohibited group, the taxpayer may use the cash method for *all* of its businesses. Where the principal activity is in the prohibited group, the cash method safe harbor may not be used for *that* activity but it may be used for a separate secondary activity that does not fall within the ineligible group if a complete and separate set of books is maintained for it. For example, a plumbing contractor satisfies the prior-year principal activity test if in the prior year 60% of its gross receipts were from plumbing installations and 40% were from selling plumbing equipment at its retail store. Plumbing installation is a construction activity that is not within the prohibited group. The taxpayer may use the cash method for both the plumbing installation and retail businesses, subject to the timing rule for items purchased for resale and raw materials used to produce finished goods. If the principal activity had been retail sales, the cash method could not be used for that ineligible activity. However, if the taxpayer treats the two activities as separate businesses, each with it own complete set of books, the cash method could be used for the installation business assuming the $10 million gross receipts test is met.

$1 million safe harbor. This safe harbor applies to business owners whose average annual gross receipts are $1 million or less for the three taxable years ending with *each prior* taxable year ending on or after December 17, 1998. *See* IRS Publication 538 and Revenue Procedure 2001-10 for details.

Planning Reminder

Advantage of Accrual-Method Accounting

The accrual method has this advantage over the cash basis: It generally gives a more even and balanced financial report.

Accrual method. On the accrual method, report income that has been earned, whether or not received, unless your right to collect the income is unsure because a substantial contingency may prevent payment; *see* the Example below.

EXAMPLE

You report business income as a calendar-year accrual taxpayer. You sell several products on December 27, 2010, and bill the customer in January 2011. You report the sales income on your 2010 Schedule C, even though payment is not made until 2011. Under the accrual method, you are considered to earn the income when the products are sold and delivered to the customer.

Where you are prepaid for services to be performed in a later year, the IRS allows you to defer the prepayment until the next taxable year. Deferral cannot extend beyond the year following the year of payment even if the term of the agreement is for a longer period. *See* the following Examples and Revenue Procedure 2004-34 for further details.

EXAMPLES

1. In November 2010, you receive full payment under a one-year contract requiring you to provide 48 music lessons. In 2010 you give eight lessons, and report one-sixth ($^{8}/_{48}$) of the payment as income. In 2011, the remaining five-sixths of the payment must be reported, even if you do not actually give the required number of lessons by the end of 2011.
2. Assume in Example 1 that the contract is for two years, and eight lessons are provided in 2010, 48 lessons in 2011, and 40 lessons in 2012. You must report one-twelfth ($^{8}/_{96}$) of the 2010 payment as income for 2010 and the remaining eleven-twelfths of the payment as income for 2011.

Filing Tip

Changing Your Accounting Method

Generally, you must obtain the consent of the Internal Revenue Service prior to any change in accounting method. Apply for consent by filing Form 3115 as early as possible during the tax year for which you wish to make the change.

Expenses under the accrual method are deductible in the year your liability for payment is fixed, even though payment is made in a later year. To prevent manipulation of expense deductions, there are tax law tests for fixing the timing of accrual method expense deductions. The tests generally require that *economic performance* must occur before a deduction may be claimed, but there are exceptions, such as for "recurring expenses." These rules are discussed in IRS Publication 538.

Expenses owed by an accrual-method business owner to a related cash-basis taxpayer. A business expense owed to your spouse, brother, sister, parent, child, grandparent, or grandchild who reports on the cash basis may not be deducted by you until you make the payment and the relative includes it as income. The same rule applies to amounts owed to a controlled corporation (more than 50% ownership) and other related entities.

Long-term contracts. Section 460 of the Internal Revenue Code has a special percentage of completion method of accounting for long-term construction contractors.

Capitalize costs of business property you produce or buy for resale. A complicated statute (Code Section 263A) generally requires manufacturers and builders to capitalize certain indirect costs (such as administrative costs, interest expenses, storage fees, and insurance), as well as direct production expenses, by including them in inventory costs; *see* IRS Publication 538, Form 3115, and the regulations to Code Section 263A.

Non-accrual experience method (NAE) for deferring service income. Taxpayers using the accrual method who either provide services in the fields of health, law, accounting, actuarial science, engineering, architecture, performing arts, or consulting, or who meet a $5 million annual gross receipts test, can use the non-accrual experience method (NAE). If you qualify, you do not have to accrue amounts that on the basis of your experience will not be collected. However, if interest or a penalty is charged for a failure to make a timely payment for the services, income is reported when the amount is billed. Furthermore, if discounts for early payments are offered, the full amount of the bill must be accrued; the discount for early payment is treated as an adjustment to income in the year payment is made.

Regulation Section 1.448-2T allows four safe harbor NAE methods.

40.4 Tax Reporting Year for Self-Employed

Your taxable year must be the same for both your business and nonbusiness income. If you report your business income on a fiscal year basis, you must also report your nonbusiness income on a fiscal year basis.

Generally, you report the tax consequences of transactions that have occurred during a 12-month period. If the period ends on December 31, it is called a *calendar year*. If it ends on the last day of any month other than December, it is called a *fiscal year*. A reporting period, technically called a *taxable year*, can never be longer than 12 months unless you report on a 52-to-53-week fiscal year basis, details of which can be found in IRS Publication 538. A reporting period may be less than 12 months whenever you start or end your business in the middle of your regular taxable year, or change your taxable year.

To change from a calendar year to fiscal year reporting for self-employment income, you must ask the IRS for permission by filing Form 1128. Support your request with a business reason such as that the use of the fiscal year coincides with your business cycle. To use a fiscal year basis, you must keep your books and records following that fiscal year period.

Fiscal year restrictions. Restrictions on fiscal years for partnerships, personal service corporations, and S corporations are discussed in *11.11* and IRS Publication 538.

40.5 Reporting Certain Payments and Receipts to the IRS

In certain situations, you are required to report payments and receipts to the IRS. If you fail to comply with this reporting, you can be penalized.

Payments to independent contractors. If you pay independent contractors, freelancers or subcontractors a total of $600 or more within the year, you must report all payments to the IRS and the contractors on Form 1099-MISC. Furnish the contractor with the form by January 31, 2011, for the 2010 payments. You must file the form with the IRS by February 28, 2011 (March 31, 2011, if you file the form electronically).

The penalty for not filing or filing late depends on the extent of tardiness. For example, the penalty is only $15 per information return if you miss the due date but then file correctly within 30 days. The maximum penalty can go as high as $25,000 for a small business, which includes a self-employed individual with average annual gross receipts for three years of $5 million or less.

Receipts of cash payments over $10,000. If you are paid more than $10,000 in cash in one or more related transactions in the course of your business, you must report the transaction to the IRS. "Cash" includes currency, cashier's checks, money orders, bank drafts, and traveler's checks having a face amount of $10,000 or less received in a transaction used to avoid this reporting requirement. File Form 8300 with the IRS no later than the 15th day after the date the cash was received.

Caution

New Reporting Requirements for Merchant Transactions

Starting in 2011, banks and credit card processors will report to the IRS all credit card and electronic payments (including PayPal) of merchants. Exempt from reporting are "small" merchants (those with no more than $20,000 in total payments involving 200 or fewer transactions).

For example, if you receive a $12,000 cash payment on May 1, 2011, you must report it by May 15, 2011. If the deadline falls on a Saturday, Sunday, or legal holiday, file by the next business day.

You have until January 31 of the year following the year of the transaction to give a written statement to the party that paid you. In the example above, this means giving the statement to the party that paid you on May 1, 2011 by January 31, 2012.

There can be civil and even criminal penalties for not filing this return.

Pension distributions to employees. If your business maintains a qualified retirement plan and makes distributions from the plan to you or any employee, you must report the distributions to the IRS on Form 1099-R and furnish a copy to the recipient.

Furnish each contractor with a Form 1099-R by January 31, 2011, for 2010 payments. You must file the form with the IRS by February 28, 2011 (March 31, 2011, if you file the form electronically).

The penalty is $25 per day for late filing, up to a maximum of $15,000.

Retirement plans. If you maintain a qualified retirement plan (other than a SEP or SIMPLE-IRA), you must file an annual information return with the Department of Labor unless your plan is exempt.

No return is required if you (or you and your spouse) are the only participant(s) and plan assets at the end of 2010 do not exceed $250,000.

File Form 5500-EZ if you (or you and your spouse) are the only participant(s). If your plan covers employees, file Form 5500. The form is an IRS form, but it is filed with the Employee Benefits Security Administration of the U.S. Department of Labor. The due date for the form is the last day of the seventh month after the close of the plan year (e.g., August 1, 2011, for 2010 calendar-year plans because July 31 is on a Sunday).

The late filing penalty is $25 per day (up to $15,000).

Small cash transactions. If you are in a business, such as a convenience store, liquor store, or gas station, that sells or redeems money orders or traveler's checks in excess of $1,000 per customer per day or issues your own value cards, the government asks that you report any suspicious transactions that exceed $2,000. While this filing isn't mandatory (there is no penalty for nonfiling), the Treasury Department asks that you report when someone provides false or expired identification, buys multiple money orders in even hundred-dollar denominations or in unusual quantities, attempts to bribe or threaten you or your employee, or does anything else suspicious.

File Form TD F 90-22.56 with the Treasury Department within 30 days of the suspicious activity. Under federal law, you are protected from civil liability so the person you report cannot sue for damages.

Wages to employees. If you have any employees, including your spouse or child, you must report wages for the year to the Social Security Administration and the employee. Furnish the employee with Form W-2 by January 31 of the year following the year in which the wages were paid (January 31, 2011, for 2010 wages). File all W-2 forms for 2010 with the Social Security Administration by February 28, 2011 (March 31, 2011, if you file them electronically).

40.6 Filing Schedule C

In this section are explanations of how a sole proprietor reports income and expenses on Schedule C, a sample of which is on page 635. If you have more than one sole proprietorship, use a separate Schedule C for each business.

Schedule C-EZ. This simple form is designed for persons on the cash basis who do not have a net business loss and have:

- Business expenses of $5,000 or less;
- No inventory at any time during the year;
- Only one sole proprietorship;
- No employees;
- No home office expense deduction;
- No prior year suspended passive activity losses from this business; and
- No depreciation to be reported on Form 4562.

Filing Tip

Husband and Wife Owners Can File on Schedule C

Instead of having to file a partnership return, a husband and wife who are the sole owners of a business, who both materially participate in the business, and who file a joint return can elect to file as sole proprietors on Schedule C. If the election is made, each spouse reports his or her respective share of the income and expenses on Schedule C; follow the 2010 instructions to Schedule C for reporting the respective shares.

If the election is made, each spouse's share of the net profit is considered to be his or her self-employment earnings for purposes of figuring self-employment tax *(45.1)* and for crediting Social Security and Medicare benefits.

Law Alert

Health Insurance Premiums

As a sole proprietor, you do not deduct health insurance premiums on Schedule C. Instead, you deduct 100% of health insurance costs for yourself, your spouse, and your dependents on Line 29, Form 1040. However, this rule may be changed for 2010; *see* the *e-Supplement at jklasser.com* for an update.

Claim health savings account contributions on Line 25 of Form 1040 *(41.12)*.

Filing Tip

Security Trader's Operating Expenses

A security trader may deduct expenses of trading on Schedule C; for further details *(30.16)*.

Statutory employees. Statutory employees report income and expenses on Schedule C. Thus, expenses may be deducted in full on Schedule C rather than as a miscellaneous itemized deduction *(19.1)*, subject to the 2% adjusted gross income (AGI) floor on Schedule A. Statutory employees are full-time life insurance salespersons, agent or commission drivers distributing certain foods and beverages, pieceworkers, and full-time traveling or city salespersons who solicit on behalf of and transmit to their principals orders from wholesalers and retailers for merchandise for resale or for supplies.

The term *full time* refers to an exclusive or principal business activity for a single company or person and not to the time spent on the job. If your principal activity is soliciting orders for one company, but you also solicit incidental orders for another company, you are a full-time salesperson for the primary company. Solicitations of orders are considered incidental to a principal business activity if you devote 20% or less of your time to the solicitation activity. A city or traveling salesperson is presumed to meet the principal business activity test in a calendar year in which he or she devotes 80% or more of working time to soliciting orders for one principal.

IRS regulations give this example: A salesperson's principal activity is getting orders from retail pharmacies for a wholesale drug company called Que Company. He occasionally takes orders for two other companies. He is a statutory employee only for Que Company.

If you are a statutory employee, your company checks Box 13 on Form W-2, identifying you as a statutory employee. Although a statutory employee may treat job expenses as business expenses, the employer withholds FICA (Social Security and Medicare) taxes on wages and commissions.

You must check a box on Line 1 of Schedule C (or C-EZ) to indicate statutory employee status. If you also have self-employment earnings from another business, you must report the self-employment earnings and statutory employee income on separate Schedules C. If both types of income are earned in the same business, allocate the expenses between the two activities on the separate schedules.

Gross receipts or sales on Schedule C (Line 1). If you do not produce or sell goods, but provide only services, you do not determine cost of goods sold, but report only your receipts from services on Line 1.

Do not report as receipts on Schedule C the following items:

- Gains or losses on the sale of property used in your business or profession. These transactions are reported on Schedule D and Form 4797.
- Dividends from stock held in the ordinary course of your business. These are reported as dividends from stocks that are held for investment.

Deductions on Schedule C. You can usually deduct most expenses incurred in your business, although there may be limits on the amount or timing of deductions. The basic requirement for deductibility is that expenses must be ordinary and necessary to your business. An ordinary expense is one that is common and accepted in your business; a necessary expense is one that is helpful and appropriate to your business.

Deductible business expenses are claimed in Part II; the descriptive breakdown of items is generally self-explanatory. However, note these points:

Car and truck expenses (Line 9): In the year you place a car in service, you may choose between the IRS mileage allowance and deducting actual expenses, plus depreciation. You must also attach Form 4562 to support a depreciation deduction; *see Chapter 43*.

Depreciation (Line 13): Enter here the amount of your annual depreciation deduction. A complete discussion of depreciation may be found in *Chapter 42*. You must figure your depreciation deduction on Form 4562 for assets placed in service in 2010, or for cars, computers, or other "listed property," regardless of when the assets were placed in service.

Employee benefit programs including health insurance (Line 14): Enter your cost for the following programs you provide for your employees: accident or health plans; long-term care insurance coverage; wage continuation; self-insured medical reimbursement plans; educational assistance programs; supplemental unemployment benefits; and prepaid legal expenses. Retirement plan contributions, such as to pension and profit-sharing plans, are reported separately on Line 19.

Insurance other than health insurance (Line 15): Insurance policy premiums for the protection of your business, such as accident, burglary, embezzlement, marine risks, plate glass, public liability, workers' compensation, fire, storm, or theft, and indemnity bonds upon employees, are deductible. State unemployment insurance payments are deducted here or as taxes if they are considered taxes under state law.

SCHEDULE C (Form 1040)

Department of the Treasury
Internal Revenue Service (99)

Profit or Loss From Business

(Sole Proprietorship)

▶ Partnerships, joint ventures, etc., generally must file Form 1065 or 1065-B.
▶ Attach to Form 1040, 1040NR, or 1041. ▶ See Instructions for Schedule C (Form 1040).

OMB No. 1545-0074
2010
Attachment Sequence No. **09**

Name of proprietor | **Social security number (SSN)**

A Principal business or profession, including product or service (see page C-2 of the instructions) | **B Enter code from pages C-9, 10, & 11** ▶

C Business name. If no separate business name, leave blank. | **D Employer ID number (EIN), if any**

E Business address (including suite or room no.) ▶
City, town or post office, state, and ZIP code

F Accounting method: (1) ☐ Cash (2) ☐ Accrual (3) ☐ Other (specify) ▶

G Did you "materially participate" in the operation of this business during 2010? If "No," see page C-3 for limit on losses ☐ Yes ☐ No

H If you started or acquired this business during 2010, check here ▶ ☐

Part I Income

1	Gross receipts or sales. **Caution.** See page C-4 and check the box if: • This income was reported to you on Form W-2 and the "Statutory employee" box on that form was checked, or • You are a member of a qualified joint venture reporting only rental real estate income not subject to self-employment tax. Also see page C-3 for limit on losses. ▶ ☐	1	
2	Returns and allowances	2	
3	Subtract line 2 from line 1	3	
4	Cost of goods sold (from line 42 on page 2)	4	
5	**Gross profit.** Subtract line 4 from line 3	5	
6	Other income, including federal and state gasoline or fuel tax credit or refund (see page C-4)	6	
7	**Gross income.** Add lines 5 and 6 ▶	7	

Part II Expenses. Enter expenses for business use of your home **only** on line 30.

8	Advertising	8		18	Office expense	18	
9	Car and truck expenses (see page C-4)	9		19	Pension and profit-sharing plans	19	
10	Commissions and fees	10		20	Rent or lease (see page C-6):		
11	Contract labor (see page C-4)	11		a	Vehicles, machinery, and equipment	20a	
12	Depletion	12		b	Other business property	20b	
13	Depreciation and section 179 expense deduction (not included in Part III) (see page C-5)	13		21	Repairs and maintenance	21	
				22	Supplies (not included in Part III)	22	
				23	Taxes and licenses	23	
				24	Travel, meals, and entertainment:		
				a	Travel	24a	
14	Employee benefit programs (other than on line 19)	14		b	Deductible meals and entertainment (see page C-6)	24b	
15	Insurance (other than health)	15		25	Utilities	25	
16	Interest:			26	Wages (less employment credits)	26	
a	Mortgage (paid to banks, etc.)	16a		27	Other expenses (from line 48 on page 2)	27	
b	Other	16b					
17	Legal and professional services	17					

28	**Total expenses** before expenses for business use of home. Add lines 8 through 27 ▶	28	
29	Tentative profit or (loss). Subtract line 28 from line 7	29	
30	Expenses for business use of your home. Attach **Form 8829**	30	
31	**Net profit or (loss).** Subtract line 30 from line 29. • If a profit, enter on both **Form 1040, line 12,** and **Schedule SE, line 2,** or on **Form 1040NR, line 13** (if you checked the box on line 1, see page C-7). Estates and trusts, enter on **Form 1041, line 3.** • If a loss, you **must** go to line 32.	31	
32	If you have a loss, check the box that describes your investment in this activity (see page C-7). • If you checked 32a, enter the loss on both **Form 1040, line 12,** and **Schedule SE, line 2,** or on **Form 1040NR, line 13** (if you checked the box on line 1, see the line 31 instructions on page C-7). Estates and trusts, enter on **Form 1041, line 3.** • If you checked 32b, you **must** attach **Form 6198.** Your loss may be limited.	32a ☐ All investment is at risk. 32b ☐ Some investment is not at risk.	

For Paperwork Reduction Act Notice, see your tax return instructions. Cat. No. 11334P **Schedule C (Form 1040) 2010**

Caution

Interest on Business Tax Deficiency

Interest on a tax deficiency based on business income reporting is not a deductible business expense; interest on a tax deficiency is always nondeductible personal interest.

Premiums paid on an insurance policy on the life of an employee or one financially interested in a business, for the purpose of protecting you from loss in the event of the death of the insured, are not deductible.

Under a "12-month" rule, prepaid premiums can be deducted in the year paid if the coverage term does not extend more than 12 months beyond the first date coverage is received, and also does not extend beyond the taxable year following the year in which the premium is paid.

Premiums for disability insurance to cover loss of earnings when out ill or injured are nondeductible personal expenses. But you may deduct premiums covering business overhead expenses.

Interest (Line 16): Include interest on business debts, but prepaid interest that applies to future years is not deductible.

Deductible interest on an insurance loan is limited if you borrow against a life insurance policy covering yourself as an employee or the life of any other employee, officer, or other person financially interested in your business. Interest on such a loan is deductible only if the policy covers an officer or 20% owner (no more than five such "key persons" can be counted) and the loan is no more than $50,000 per person. If you own policies covering the same employees (or other persons) in more than one business, the $50,000 limit applies on an aggregate basis to all the policies. The interest deduction limit applies even if a sole proprietor borrows against a policy on his or her own life and uses the proceeds in a business; interest is not deductible to the extent the loan exceeds $50,000.

Pension and profit-sharing plans (Line 19): Keogh plan or SEP contributions made for your employees are entered here; contributions made for your account are entered directly on Form 1040 as an adjustment to income. In addition, you may have to file an information return by the last day of the seventh month following the end of the plan year *(41.8)*.

Filing Tip

Tax Advice and Tax Preparation Costs

On Line 17 of Schedule C, you deduct the portion of tax preparation costs allocable to preparing Schedule C and related tax forms. Also deduct on Line 17 fees for tax advice related to the business.

Rent on business property (Line 20): Rent paid for the use of lofts, buildings, trucks, and other equipment is deductible. Prepaid rents can be deducted by cash-method taxpayers in the year of payment if the rent term does not extend more than 12 months beyond the first day of the lease and also not beyond the end of the taxable year following the taxable year in which the prepayment is made. However, the economic performance rules prevent accrual-method taxpayers from deducting prepaid rent; economic performance occurs only ratably over the lease term.

Taxes on leased property that you pay to the lessor are deductible as additional rent.

Repairs (Line 21): The cost of repairs and maintenance is deductible provided they do not materially add to the value of the property or appreciably prolong its life. Expenses of replacements that arrest deterioration and appreciably increase the value of the property are capitalized and their cost recovered through depreciation.

Caution

Employment Tax Responsibilities

If you have employees, you must comply with employment tax responsibilities, such as collecting and paying to the government income tax withholding from employee wages. For details, *see* IRS Publication 15, Circular E, Employer's Tax Guide.

Taxes (Line 23): Deduct real estate and personal property taxes on business assets here. Also deduct your share of Social Security and Medicare taxes paid on behalf of employees and payments of federal unemployment tax. Federal highway use tax is deductible. Federal import duties and excise and stamp taxes normally not deductible as itemized deductions are deductible as business taxes if incurred by the business. Taxes on business property, such as an *ad valorem tax*, must be deducted here; they are not to be treated as itemized deductions. However, the IRS holds that you may not deduct state income taxes on business income as a business expense. Its reasoning: Income taxes are personal taxes even when paid on business income. As such, you may deduct state income tax only as an itemized deduction on Schedule A. The Tax Court supports the IRS rule on the grounds that it reflects Congressional intent toward the treatment of state income taxes in figuring taxable income.

For purposes of computing a net operating loss, state income tax on business income is treated as a business deduction.

If you pay or accrue sales tax on the purchase of nondepreciable business property, the sales tax is a deductible business expense. If the property is depreciable, add the sales tax to the cost basis for purposes of computing depreciation deductions.

Travel, meals, and entertainment (Line 24): Travel expenses on overnight business trips while "away from home" *(20.5)* are claimed on Line 24a. Total meals and entertainment expenses, reduced by 50%, are claimed on Line 24b. The 50% limit for meals and entertainment is increased to 75% for transportation industry workers subject to the Department of Transportation hours of service limits.

Self-employed persons may use the IRS meal allowance rates *(20.4)*, instead of claiming actual expenses. Record-keeping requirements for travel and entertainment expenses are discussed in *Chapter 20 (20.26–20.28)*.

Utilities (Line 25): Deduct utilities such as gas, electric, and telephone expenses incurred in your business. However, if you have a home office *(40.12)*, you may *not* deduct the base rate (including taxes) of the first phone line into your home *(19.14)*.

Wages (Line 26): You do not deduct wages paid to yourself. You may deduct reasonable wages paid to family members who work for you. If you have an employee who works in your office and also in your home, such as a domestic worker, you deduct that part of the salary allocated to the work in your office. If you claim an empowerment zone or Indian employment tax credit, the wage deduction is reduced by the credit.

Other expenses (Line 27): In Part V of Schedule C, you list deductible expenses not reported in Part II, such as amortizable business start-up costs *(40.11)*, business-related education *(33.15)*, subscriptions, and postage, and enter the total on Line 27.

Filing Tip

Deduction for Commercial Buildings

Owners and leaseholders of commercial buildings that are certified to meet certain energy-efficiency standards can qualify for a deduction of up to $1.80 per square foot.

40.7 Deductions for Professionals

The following expenses incurred by self-employed professionals in the course of their work are generally allowed as deductions from income when figuring profit (or loss) from their professional practices on Schedule C:

- Dues to professional societies.
- Operating expenses and repairs of car used on professional calls.
- Supplies.
- Subscriptions to professional journals.
- Rent for office space.
- Cost of fuel, light, water, and telephone used in the office.
- Salaries of assistants.
- Malpractice insurance *(40.6)*.
- Cost of books, information services, professional instruments, and equipment with a useful life of one year or less. Professional libraries are depreciable if their value decreases with time. Depreciation rules are discussed in *42.1*.
- Fees paid to a tax preparer for preparing Schedule C and related business forms.

Professionals as employees. Professionals who are not in their own practice may not deduct professional expenses on Schedule C. Salaried professionals may deduct professional expenses only as miscellaneous itemized deductions on Schedule A, subject to the 2% adjusted gross income (AGI) floor *(19.1)*. However, "statutory" employees may use Schedule C *(40.6)*.

The cost of preparing for a profession. You may not deduct the cost of a professional education *(33.16)*.

The IRS does not allow a deduction for the cost of a license to practice. However, the Tax Court has allowed attorneys to amortize over their life expectancy bar admission fees paid to state authorities.

Payment of clients' expenses. An attorney may follow a practice of paying his or her clients' expenses in pending cases. The IRS will disallow a deduction claimed for these payments on the grounds that the expenses are those of the client, not the attorney. The courts agree with the IRS position where there is a net fee agreement. In a net fee agreement, expenses first reduce the recovery before the attorney takes a fee. However, where the attorney is paid under a gross fee agreement, an appeals court has reversed a Tax Court decision that disallowed the deduction of the attorney's payment of client expenses. Under a gross fee agreement, the attorney's fee is based on the gross award; the prior payment of expenses does not enter into the fee agreement and so is not reimbursed. Because he would not be reimbursed, an attorney claimed his payment of client expenses was deductible. An appeals court accepted this argument and allowed the deduction. The court allowed the deduction although California law disapproved of the practice of paying client expenses without a right of reimbursement. The court believed that there is no ethical difficulty with the practice and other jurisdictions approve of it. It is necessary for and it is the practice of personal injury firms to pay the costs of many of their clients.

If you are not allowed a current deduction for payment of clients' expenses, you may deduct your advance as a bad debt if the claim is worthless in another year *(40.6)*.

Caution

Doctor's Malpractice Insurance

A self-employed doctor may deduct the premium costs of malpractice insurance. However, a doctor who is not self-employed but employed by someone else, say a hospital, may deduct the premium costs only as a miscellaneous itemized deduction subject to the 2% of adjusted gross income floor. Whether malpractice premiums paid to a physician-owned carrier are deductible depends on how the carrier is organized. If there is a sufficient number of policyholders who are not economically related and none of whom owns a controlling interest in the insuring company, a deduction is allowed provided the premiums are reasonable and are based on sound actuarial principles.

In one case, physicians set up a physician-owned carrier that was required by state insurance authorities to set up a surplus fund. The physicians contributed to the fund and received nontransferable certificates that were redeemable only if they retired, moved out of the state, or died. The IRS and Tax Court held the contributions to the fund were nondeductible capital expenses.

In another case, a professional corporation of anesthesiologists set up a trust to pay malpractice claims, up to specified limits. The IRS and Tax Court disallowed deductions for the trust contributions on the grounds that the PC remained potentially liable. Malpractice claims within the policy limits might exceed trust funds and the PC would be liable for the difference. Since risk of loss was not shifted to the trust, the trust was not a true insurance arrangement.

An attorney might deduct a payment to a client reimbursing the client for a bad investment recommended by the attorney. A court upheld the deduction on the grounds that the reimbursement was required to protect the reputation of an established law practice. However, no deduction is allowed when malpractice insurance reimbursement is available but the attorney fails to make a claim.

Daily business lunches with associates have been held to lack business purpose. Courts agree with the IRS that professionals do not need to have lunch together every day to talk shop. The cost of the meals is therefore not deductible.

EXAMPLES

1. A law partnership deducted the meal costs of the staff attorneys who lunched every day at the same restaurant to discuss cases and court assignments. The deductions were disallowed as personal expenses. The Tax Court and an appeals court agreed with the IRS that daily lunches are not necessary. Co-workers generally do not need luncheons to provide social lubrication for business talk, as is true with clients.
2. A physician held luncheon meetings three or four times a week with other physicians. He argued that the purpose of the luncheons was to generate referrals. A court held that such frequent luncheons became a routine personal event not tied to specific business. The cost of the meals was not deductible.
3. A medical professional corporation (PC) deducted the cost of meals taken by its physician-stockholders at a hospital cafeteria. It argued that the doctors discussed patients and met other doctors who made referrals to them. The Tax Court agreed with the IRS that the meal costs were not deductible; doctors ate in the cafeteria for their personal convenience. Furthermore, the meal costs were taxed to the doctors as dividends. The court noted that the PC might have been able to claim a deduction had it treated the meal costs as taxable pay; however, the PC refused to take this position, unsuccessfully gambling that it could claim the costs as business deductions.

Caution

Penalties and Fines

Penalties or fines paid to a government agency because of a violation of any law are not deductible. You may deduct penalties imposed by a business contract for late performance or nonperformance.

40.8 Nondeductible Expense Items

Capital expenditures may not be deducted. Generally, the cost of acquiring an asset or of prolonging its life is a capital expenditure that must be amortized over its expected life. If the useful life of an item is less than a year, its cost, including sales tax on the purchase, is deductible. Otherwise, you generally may recover your cost only through depreciation except to the extent first-year expensing applies *(42.3)*. IRS regulations provide safe harbors, including a "12-month" rule, for expenditures relating to intangible assets or benefits *(40.3)*.

EXAMPLE

A new roof is installed on your office building. If the roof increases the life of the building, its cost is a capital expenditure recovered by depreciation deductions. The cost of repairing a leak in the roof is a deductible operating expense. In several decisions, the Tax Court has allowed a deduction for the cost of a major roof renovation or replacement on evidence that the work was not designed to increase the value of the building but to prevent leaks and keep the property in working condition.

Expenses while you are not in business. You are not allowed to deduct business expenses incurred during the time you are not engaged in your business or profession.

EXAMPLE

A lawyer continued to maintain his office while he was employed by the government. During that time he did no private law work. He only kept the office to have it ready at such time as he quit the government job and returned to practice. His costs of keeping up his office while he was working for the government were not deductible.

Bribes and kickbacks. Bribes and kickbacks are not deductible if they are illegal under a federal or a generally enforced state law that subjects the payer to a criminal penalty or provides for the loss of license or privilege to engage in business. A kickback, even if not illegal, is not deductible by a physician or other person who has furnished items or services that are payable under the Medicare or Medicaid programs. A kickback includes payments for referral of a client, patient, or customer.

In one case, the IRS, with support from the Tax Court and a federal appeals court, disallowed a deduction for legal kickbacks paid by a subcontractor. The courts held that the kickbacks were not a "necessary" business expense because the contractor had obtained nearly all of its other contracts without paying kickbacks, including contracts from the same general contractor bribed here.

40.9 How Authors and Artists May Write Off Expenses

Self-employed authors, artists, photographers, and other qualifying creative professionals may write off business expenses as they are paid. The law (Code Section 263A) that requires expenses to be amortized over the period income is received does not apply to freelancers who personally create literary manuscripts, musical or dance scores, paintings, pictures, sculptures, drawings, cartoons, graphic designs, original print editions, photographs, or photographic negatives or transparencies. Furthermore, expenses of a personal service corporation do not have to be amortized if they directly relate to expenses of a qualifying author, artist, or photographer who owns (or whose relatives own) substantially all of the corporation's stock.

Current deductions are *not* allowed for expenses relating to motion picture films, videotapes, printing, photographic plates, or similar items.

An author or artist with expenses exceeding income may be barred by the IRS from claiming a loss under a profit motive test; in that case, the profit-presumption rule *(40.10)* may allow a deduction of the loss.

40.10 Deducting Expenses of a Sideline Business or Hobby

There is a one-way tax rule for hobbies: Income from a hobby is taxable as "other income" on Form 1040; expenses are deductible only to the extent you report hobby income, and the deduction is limited on Schedule A by the 2% adjusted gross income (AGI) floor for miscellaneous itemized deductions. Hobby losses are considered nondeductible personal losses. A profitable sale of a hobby collection or activity held long term is taxable as capital gain; losses are not deductible.

Planning Reminder

Hobby or Sideline Business

The question of whether an activity, such as dog breeding or collecting and selling coins and stamps, is a hobby or sideline business arises when losses are incurred. As long as you show a profit, you may deduct the expenses of the activity. But when expenses exceed income and your return is examined, an agent may allow expenses only up to the amount of your income and disallow the remaining expenses that make up your loss. At this point, to claim the loss, you may be able to take advantage of a "profit presumption" *(40.10)*, or you may have to prove that you are engaged in the activity to make a profit.

How to deduct hobby expenses. If the profit presumption discussed later does not apply and the activity is held *not* to be engaged in for profit, business operating expenses and depreciation are deductible only as miscellaneous itemized deductions and only up to the extent of income from the activity; a deduction for expenses exceeding the income is disallowed.

A special sequence is followed in determining which expenses are deductible from income. Deducted first on Schedule A are amounts allowable without regard to whether the activity is a business engaged in for profit, such as mortgage interest and state and local taxes, as well as casualty losses (after applying the dollar and percentage casualty floors *(18.12)*). These amounts are deductible in full on the appropriate lines of Schedule A without regard to income from the activity. However, they reduce gross income from the activity for purposes of figuring whether other deductions may be claimed. If after deducting these amounts from gross income there is any income remaining, "business" operating expenses such as wages, utilities, insurance premiums, interest, advertising, repairs, and maintenance may be claimed. Then deduct depreciation and excess casualty losses not allowed in the first step to the extent of remaining income. The "business" expenses, depreciation, and excess casualty losses are allowed only as miscellaneous itemized deductions subject to the 2% AGI floor *(19.1)*. Thus, even if the expenses offset income from the activity, none of the expenses will be deductible unless your total miscellaneous expenses (including those from the activity) exceed 2% of your adjusted gross income.

Presumption of profit-seeking motive. You are *presumed to be* engaged in an activity for profit if you can show a profit in at least three of the last five years, including the current year. If the activity is horse breeding, training, racing, or showing, the profit presumption applies if you show profits in two of the last seven (including current) years. The presumption does not necessarily mean that losses will automatically be allowed; the IRS may try to rebut the presumption. You would then have to prove a profit motive by showing these types of facts: You spend considerable time in the activity; you keep businesslike records; you have a written business plan showing how you plan to make a profit; you relied on expert advice; you expect the assets to appreciate in value; and losses are common in the start-up phase of your type of business.

Election postpones determination of profit presumption. If you have losses in the first few years of an activity and the IRS tries to disallow them as hobby losses, you have this option: You may make an election on Form 5213 to postpone the determination of whether the above profit presumption applies. The postponement is until after the end of the fourth taxable year (sixth year for a horse breeding, training, showing, or racing activity) following the first year of the activity. For example, if you enter a farming activity in 2010, you can elect to postpone the profit motive determination until after the end of 2014. Then, if you have realized profits in at least three of the five years (2010–2014), the profit presumption applies. When you make the election on Form 5213, you agree to waive the statute of limitations for all activity-related items in the taxable years involved. The waiver generally gives the IRS an additional two years after the filing due date for the last year in the presumption period to issue deficiencies related to the activity.

To make the election, you must file Form 5213 within three years of the due date of the return for the year you started the activity. If before the end of this three-year period you receive a deficiency notice from the IRS disallowing a loss from the activity and you have not yet made the election, you can still do so within 60 days of receiving the notice. These election rules apply to individuals, partnerships, and S corporations. An election by a partnership or S corporation is binding on all partners or S corporation shareholders holding interests during the presumption period.

40.11 Deducting Expenses of Looking for a New Business

When you are planning to invest in a business, you may incur preliminary expenses for traveling to look at the property and for legal or accounting advice. Expenses incurred during a general search or preliminary investigation of a business are not deductible, including expenses related to the decision whether or not to enter a transaction. However, when you go beyond a general search and actually go into business, you may elect to deduct or amortize your start-up costs.

Law Alert

Greater Deduction for Start-Up Costs

For a business begun in 2010, up to $10,000 of eligible start-up expenses is allowed as a 2010 deduction. This is double the amount allowed for earlier years.

Deductible or amortizable start-up costs. If you began your business in 2010, up to $10,000 of eligible start-up expenses is allowed as a 2010 deduction under the Small Business Jobs Act of 2010 (signed into law on September 27, 2010). After 2010, the limit is scheduled to drop to $5,000, the pre-2010 limit. The $10,000 limit for 2010 is reduced by the amount of start-up costs exceeding $60,000. Start-up costs over the first-year deduction limit may be amortized over 15 years. An election to amortize is made by claiming the deduction on Form 4562, and it is then entered in Part V ("Other Expenses") of Schedule C.

Eligible costs include investigating and setting up the business, such as expenses of surveying potential markets, products, labor supply, and transportation facilities; travel and other expenses incurred in lining up prospective distributors, suppliers, or customers; salaries or fees paid to consultants or attorneys, and fees for similar professional services. The business may be one you acquire from someone else or a new business you create.

Organizational costs for a partnership or corporation. Costs incident to the creation of a partnership or corporation are also deductible or amortizable under the rules for start-up costs discussed above. For a partnership, qualifying expenses include legal fees for negotiating and preparing a partnership agreement, and management, consulting, or accounting fees in setting up the partnership. No deduction or amortization is allowed for syndication costs of issuing and marketing partnership interests such as brokerage and registration fees, fees of an underwriter, and costs of preparing a prospectus.

For a corporation, qualifying expenses include the cost of organizational meetings, incorporation fees, and accounting and legal fees for drafting corporate documents. Costs of selling stock or securities, such as commissions, do not qualify.

An election to amortize is made on Part VI of Form 4562 for the first year the partnership or corporation is in business. The election on Form 4562 and the required statement must be filed no later than the return due date, including extensions, for the year in which the business begins.

Nonqualifying expenses. Deductible and amortizable expenses are restricted to expenses incurred in investigating the acquisition or creation of an active business, and setting up such an active business. They do not include taxes or interest. Research and experimental costs are not start-up costs, but are separately deductible or amortizable; *see* IRS Publication 535 and Code Section 174. For rental activities to qualify as an active business, there must be significant furnishing of services incident to the rentals. For example, the operation of an apartment complex, an office building, or a shopping center would generally be considered an active business.

If you do not elect to deduct or amortize qualifying start-up costs, you treat the expenses as follows:

- Costs connected with the acquisition of capital assets are capitalized and depreciated; *and*
- Costs related to assets with unlimited or indeterminable useful lives are recovered only on the future sale or liquidation of the business.

If the acquisition fails. Where you have gone beyond a general search and have focused on the acquisition of a particular business, but the acquisition falls through, you may deduct the expenses as a capital loss.

Caution

Nonqualifying Costs

You may *not* deduct or amortize the expenses incurred in acquiring or selling securities or partnership interests such as securities registration expenses or underwriters' commissions.

EXAMPLES

1. In search of a business, you place newspaper advertisements and travel to investigate various prospective ventures. You pay for audits to evaluate the potential of some of the ventures. You then decide to purchase a specific business and hire a law firm to draft necessary documents. However, you change your mind and later abandon your plan to acquire the business. According to the IRS, you may not deduct the related expenses for advertisements, travel, and audits. These are considered investigatory. You may deduct the expense of hiring the law firm.
2. Domenie left his job to invest in a business. He advertised and was contacted by a party who wished to sell. He agreed to buy, hired an attorney, transferred funds to finance the business, and worked a month with the company manager to familiarize himself with the business. Discovering misrepresentations, he refused to buy the company and deducted over $5,000 for expenses, including travel and legal fees. The IRS disallowed the deduction as incurred in a business search. The Tax Court disagreed. Domenie thought he had found a business and acted as such in transferring funds and drawing legal papers for a takeover.

Job-hunting costs. You may deduct the expenses of looking for a new job under certain circumstances *(19.7)*.

40.12 Home Office Deduction

If you operate your business from your home, using a room or other space as an office or area to assemble or prepare items for sale, you may be able to deduct expenses such as utilities, insurance, repairs, and depreciation allocated to your business use of the area. Collectively, these expenses are deducted as a single write-off, called the home office deduction.

Filing Tip

Using a Home Office for Administrative Tasks

A home office deduction may be claimed if you regularly and exclusively use part of your home as the only place for conducting the administrative or management activities of your business, or if only minimal administrative work is done outside your home. The home area qualifies as your principal place of business even if you spend most of your working time providing services at outside locations.

Exclusive and regular use. To deduct home office expenses, you must prove that you use the home area *exclusively* and *on a regular basis* either as:

1. ***A place of business to meet or deal with patients, clients, or customers in the normal course of your business (incidental or occasional meetings do not meet this test),*** *or*
2. ***Your principal place of business.*** Your home office will qualify as your principal place of business if you spend most of your working time there and most of your business income is attributable to your activities there.

Administrative (record-keeping) activity. A home office meets the principal place of business test (Test 2) if: (1) you use it regularly and exclusively for administrative or management activities of your business and (2) you have no other fixed location where you do a substantial amount of such administrative work. Self-employed persons are the beneficiaries of this administrative/management rule. Employees usually may not take advantage of the rule because of the application of the convenience-of-the-employer test to an employee's use of a home office; *see* the Example at *19.13*. Examples of administrative and management activities include billing customers, clients, or patients; keeping books and records; ordering supplies; setting up appointments; forwarding orders; and writing reports.

According to the IRS, performance of management or administrative activities under the following conditions do not disqualify a home office as a principal place of business:

- You have a company send out your bills from its place of business (*see* Example 1 below).
- You do administrative or management activities at times from a hotel or automobile (*see* Example 2 below).

- You occasionally conduct minimal administrative or management activities at a fixed location outside your home.
- You have suitable space to do administrative or management work outside your home but choose to use your home office for such activities (*see* Example 3 below).

Caution

Principal Place of Business Test

The tests for deducting office expenses will generally not present problems where the home area is the principal place of business or professional activity. For example, you are a doctor and *see* most of your patients at an office set aside in your home. A tax dispute may arise where you have a principal place of business elsewhere and use a part of your home for occasional work or administrative paperwork. Occasional use is not sufficient. If your deduction is questioned, you must prove that the area is used regularly and exclusively to meet with customers, clients, or patients or that the home office is the only place where administrative/management activities for the business are conducted. Have evidence that you have actual office facilities. Furnish the room as an office—with a desk, files, and a phone used only for business calls. Also keep a record of work done and business visitors.

Filing Instruction

Form 8829

You must report deductible 2010 home office expenses on Form 8829. Part I is used for showing the space allocated to business use *(40.14)*; Part II for reporting deductible expenses allocated to business use *(40.14)*; Part III for figuring depreciation on the business area *(40.13)*; and Part IV for carryover to 2011 of expenses not allowed in 2010 because of income limitations applied in Part II *(40.15)*. A sample copy of Form 8829 is on page 647.

EXAMPLES

1. A self-employed plumber does all of his repair and installation services outside of his home where he has a small office used to phone customers, order supplies, and keep his books. However, he uses a local bookkeeping service to bill his customers. He has no other fixed location for doing his administrative work. That he uses an outside billing service does not disqualify his home office as a principal place of business.
2. A self-employed sales representative for several products uses a home office to set up appointments and write up orders. When she is out of town, she writes up such orders from a hotel room. The occasional use of a hotel room to write up orders does not disqualify the home office as a principal place of business that otherwise meets the new tests.
3. A self-employed anesthesiologist spends most of his professional time at three local hospitals. One of the hospitals provides him with a small shared office where he could do administrative and management work; however, he does not use this space. He uses his home as an office to: contact patients, surgeons, and hospitals regarding schedules; prepare presentations; keep billing records and patient logs; and read medical journals and books. His use of the home office for administrative activities satisfies the principal place of business test. His choice to use his home office instead of the one provided by one hospital does not disqualify his home office as the principal place of business.

If you work at home and also outside of your home at other locations and you do not meet the administrative/management rule, deductions of home office expenses should be supported by evidence that your activities at home are relatively more important or time consuming than those outside your home.

Exclusive and regular business use of home area required. If you use a room, such as a den, both for business and family purposes, be prepared to show that a specific section of the den is used *exclusively* as office space. For example, a real estate operator was not allowed to deduct the cost of a home office, on evidence that he also used the office area for nonbusiness purposes. A partition or other physical separation of the office area is helpful but not required.

Under the regular basis test, expenses attributable to incidental or occasional trade or business use are not deductible, even if the room is used for no other purpose but business.

Even if you meet these tests, your deduction for allocable office expenses may be substantially limited or barred by a restrictive rule that limits deductions to the income from the office activity. This computation is made on Form 8829 *(40.15)*.

Multiple business use of home office. If you use a home office for more than one business, make sure that the home office tests are met for all businesses before you claim deductions. If one business use qualifies and another use does not, the IRS will disallow deductions even for the qualifying use, *see* the following paragraph.

Employee with sideline business. Employees who use a home office for their job and for a sideline business also should be aware of this problem. Most employees are unable to show that their home office is the principal place of their work *(19.13)*. Claiming an unallowable deduction for employee home office use will jeopardize the deduction for sideline business use. This happened to Hamacher, who as a self-employed actor earned $24,600 over a two-year period from an Atlanta theater and a few radio and television commercials. He also earned $18,000 each year as the administrator of an acting school at the theater. For his job as administrator, Hamacher shared an office at the theater with other employees. He had access to this office during nonbusiness hours. He also used one of the six rooms in his apartment for an office. Because of interruptions at the theater, he used the home office to work on the school curriculum and select plays for the theater. In connection with his acting business, he used the home office to receive phone calls, to prepare for auditions, and rehearse for acting roles.

The IRS disallowed his deduction for both self-employment and employee purposes because Hamacher's office use as an employee did not qualify. The Tax Court agreed. A single-office space may be used for different business activities, but all of the uses must qualify for a deduction. Here, Hamacher's use of the home office as an employee did not qualify. He had suitable office space at the theater. He was not expected or required to do work at home. As the employee use of the home office did not qualify, the Tax Court did not have to determine if the sideline business use qualified. Even if it had qualified, no allocation of expenses between the two uses would have been made. By requiring that a home office be used "exclusively" as a principal place of business or place for seeing clients, patients, or customers, the law imposes an all-or-nothing test.

Filing Tip

If You Rent Your Home

If you rent rather than own your home, and you meet the home office tests *(40.12)*, enter the rent you paid during the year on Column (b) of Line 21 (Other Expenses) of Form 8829.

Separate structure. If in your business you use a separate structure not attached to your home, such as a studio adjacent but unattached to your home, the expenses are generally deductible if you satisfy the exclusive use and regular basis tests discussed earlier. A separate structure does not have to qualify as your principal place of business or a place for meeting patients, clients, or customers. However, an income limitation *(40.15)* applies. In one case, a taxpayer argued that an office located in a separate building in his backyard was not subject to the exclusive and regular business use tests and the gross income limitation. However, the IRS and Tax Court held that it was. The office building was "appurtenant" to the home and thus part of it, based on these facts: The office building was 12 feet away from the house and within the same fenced-in residential area; it did not have a separate address; it was included in the same title and subject to the same mortgage as the house; and all taxes, utilities, and insurance were paid as a unit for both buildings.

Day-care services. The exclusive-use test does not have to be met for business use of a home to provide day-care services for children and handicapped persons, or persons age 65 or older, provided certain state licensing requirements are met. If part of your home is *regularly* but not exclusively used to provide day-care services, you may deduct an allocable part of your home expenses. You allocate expenses by multiplying the total costs by two fractions: (1) The total square footage in the home that is available for day-care use throughout each business day and regularly so used, divided by the total square footage for the home. (2) The total hours of business operation divided by the total number of hours in the year (8,784 in 2010).

If the area is exclusively used for day-care services, only fraction (1) applies.

EXAMPLE

In 2010, Alice Jones operates a day-care center at home from 7 a.m. to 6 p.m., five days a week for 50 weeks, for a total of 2,750 business-use hours during the year. Her family uses the area the rest of the time. Annual home expenses total $10,000 ($5,000 for interest and taxes; $4,000 for electricity, gas, water, trash collection, maintenance, and insurance; and $1,000 for depreciation). The total floor area of the home is 2,000 square feet; 1,500 square feet are used for day-care purposes. Alice multiplies her $10,000 of expenses by 75%, the part of the home used for day-care purposes (1,500 square feet ÷ 2,000 square feet), and also by 31.31%, the percentage of business-use time (2,750 hours ÷ 8,784 hours). Thus, she may deduct $2,348: $10,000 × 75% × 31.31%. The full $2,348 is deductible only if net income generated from the day-care facility is at least that much.

In one case, the Tax Court held that utility rooms, such as a laundry and storage room and garage, may be counted as part of the day-care business area. The IRS had argued that because the children were not allowed in these areas, the space could not be considered as used for business. The Tax Court disagreed. The laundry room was used to wash the children's clothes; the storage room and garage were used to store play items and equipment. Thus, the space was considered as used for child care even though the rooms were off limits to the children.

Storage space and inventory. If your home is the only location of a business selling products, you may deduct expenses allocated to space regularly used for inventory storage, including product samples, if the space is separately identifiable and suitable for storage.

40.13 What Home Office Expenses Are Deductible?

For a qualifying home office *(40.12)*, deductible costs may include real estate taxes, mortgage interest, operating expenses (such as home insurance premiums and utility costs), and depreciation allocated to the area used for business. The deduction figured on Form 8829 may not exceed the net income derived from the business *(40.15)*.

The deduction from Form 8829 is entered on Line 30 of Schedule C.

Expenses that affect only the business part of your home, such as repairs or painting of the home office only, are entered on Form 8829 as "direct" expenses. Expenses for running the entire home, including mortgage interest, taxes, utilities, and insurance, are deductible as "indirect" expenses to the extent of your business-use percentage *(40.14)*.

Household expenses and repairs that do not benefit the office space are not deductible. However, a pro rata share of the cost of painting the outside of a house or repairing a roof is deductible. Costs of lawn care and landscaping are not deductible.

If you install a security system for all your home's windows and doors, the portion of your monthly maintenance fee that is allocable to the office area is a deductible operating expense. Furthermore, the business portion of your cost for the system is depreciable. Thus, if the office takes up 20% of your home *(40.14)* you may deduct, subject to an income limitation *(40.15)*, 20% of the maintenance fee and a depreciation deduction for 20% of the cost.

Filing Instruction

When To Figure Depreciation on a Home Office Using 27.5 Year Recovery

While depreciation of a home office usually is figured using a 39-year recovery period, a 27.5 year recovery period can be used by an on-site landlord of a building in which at least one dwelling unit is rented out and 80% or more of the gross rental income is rental income from dwelling units within the building. In applying the 80% test, the rental value of the entire landlord's unit is treated as gross rental income and the rental value of the landlord's residential space (but not the home office) is treated as rental income from a dwelling unit.

For example, where a landlord lived in one unit of his eight-unit building and used a room in his unit for a home office, the IRS allowed the home office to be depreciated over 27.5 years as residential rental property.

Figuring depreciation. Even though a home is a residence, depreciation on a home office usually is figured as if it were commercial property using a 39-year recovery period (*see Table 40-2*). For depreciation purposes, the cost basis of the house is the lower of the fair market value of the house at the time you started to use a part of it for business or its adjusted basis, exclusive of the land. Only that part of the cost basis allocated to the office is depreciable. Form 8829 has a special section, Part III, for making this computation.

EXAMPLE

In April 2010, you start to use one room in your single family house exclusively and on a regular basis to meet with clients. This room is 10% of the square footage of your home. In 1993, you bought the property for $100,000, of which $90,000 was allocated to the house. The house has a fair market value of $185,000 in April 2010. You compute depreciation on the cost basis of $90,000, which is lower than the value. You multiply $90,000 by 10% (business-use percentage), which gives you $9,000 as the depreciable basis of the business part of the house. As you started business use in the fourth month of 2010, you multiply the depreciable basis of $9,000 by 1.819%. This percentage is listed for the fourth month in *Table 40-2*. Your depreciation deduction is $163.71 (9,000 × 1.819%).

40.14 Allocating Expenses to Business Use

Allocate to home office use qualifying operating expenses *(40.13)* as follows: If the rooms are not equal or approximately equal in size, compare the number of square feet of space used for business with the total number of square feet in the home and then apply the resulting percentage to the total deductible expenses.

If all rooms in your home are approximately the same size, you may base the allocation on a comparison of the number of rooms used as an office to the total number of rooms.

EXAMPLE

A doctor rents a apartment using three rooms for his office and seven rooms for his residence. The rooms are not equal in size. The apartment has 2,000 square feet; the office has 600. He allocates 30% ($^{600}/_{2,000}$) of the following expenses to his office:

	Total	*Office*	*Residence*
Rent	$7,200	$2,160	$5,040
Light	600	180	420
Heat	1,000	300	700
Wages of domestic	2,000	600	1,400
	$10,800	$3,240	$7,560

The $3,240 of office expenses are deductible as indirect interest expenses on Form 8829, subject to an income limitation *(40.15)*.

Table 40-2 Nonresidential Real Property (39 years—Property placed in service after May 12, 1993)

Use the column for the month of taxable year placed in service.

Year	1	2	3	4	5	6	7	8	9	10	11	12
1	2.461%	2.247%	2.033%	1.819%	1.605%	1.391%	1.177%	0.963%	0.749%	0.535%	0.321%	0.107%
2–39	2.564	2.564	2.564	2.564	2.564	2.564	2.564	2.564	2.564	2.564	2.564	2.564
40	0.107	0.321	0.535	0.749	0.963	1.177	1.391	1.605	1.819	2.033	2.247	2.461

40.15 Business Income May Limit Home Office Deductions

Even if your home business use satisfies the deduction tests *(40.12)*, deductions for the business portion *(40.14)* of utilities, maintenance, and insurance costs, as well as depreciation or rent deductions, may not exceed net business income after reducing the tentative profit from Schedule C by allocable mortgage interest, real estate taxes, and casualty deductions. To make sure that deductible expenses do not exceed income, the IRS requires you to use Form 8829. If you do not realize income during the year, no deduction is allowed. For example, you are a full-time writer and use an office in your home. You do not sell any of your work this year or receive any advances or royalties. Therefore, you may not claim a home office deduction for this year. *See also* the rules for writers and artists earlier in this chapter *(40.9)*.

Part II of Form 8829 limits the deduction of home office expenses to net income derived from office use. You start with the tentative profit from Schedule C. If you sold your home during the year, increase the tentative profit by any net gain (or decrease tentative profit by any net loss) that is allocable to the office area and reported on Schedule D or Form 4797. The following expenses are listed first in Part II of Form 8829 for purposes of applying the income limit: Casualty losses affecting the residence, deductible mortgage interest, and real estate taxes. If there is income remaining after these expenses are subtracted from the Schedule C tentative profit, then home insurance premiums, repair and maintenance expenses for the residence, utility expenses, and rent are claimed against the remaining income. Depreciation is taken into account last, in Part III of Form 8829.

Business expenses not related to the home are deducted on the appropriate lines of Schedule C. For example, a salary paid to a secretary is deducted on Line 26 of Schedule C; the cost of depreciable business equipment used in your home is deducted on Line 13 of Schedule C.

The amount of real estate taxes, mortgage interest, or casualty losses not allocated to home office use may be claimed as itemized deductions on Schedule A.

Planning Reminder

Carryover Allowed

Expenses disallowed because of the income limitation may be carried forward and treated as home office expenses in a later tax year (Part IV, Form 8829). The carryover as well as the expenses of the later year are subject to the income limitation of that year. For example, tentative profit for 2010 on Line 29 of Schedule C is $1,000. Expenses allocated to the home office are $2,000. Only $1,000 of the expenses are deductible; $1,000 is carried over to 2011.

EXAMPLE

Samuel Brown does sideline business consulting from a home office in his single-family house that he uses exclusively for business for all of 2010. His income in 2010 from consulting services is $12,400. He paid $7,600 for a photocopy machine and a computer, and had office telephone expenses of $600 and office supply costs of $800.

In addition, his home costs are:

Mortgage interest	$10,000
Real estate taxes	4,000
Insurance	1,200
Utilities	1,800

His office space took up 20% of the area of his home, and he figured depreciation allocated to business use of $1,200.

On Schedule C he claims first-year expensing *(42.3)* for the copier and the computer, and also deducts the office phone costs and supplies. This gives a tentative profit of $3,400 ($12,400 – $9,000) on Line 29, Schedule C.

In Part I of Form 8829, he lists the total area of the home and the area used for business, showing 20% business use.

In Part II, he enters the home costs listed above. We have taken only the relevant lines of the Form 8829 as an illustration. Samuel Brown's Form 8829 is on page 653.

Form 8829 Line—			
8.	Tentative profit from Schedule C, Line 29		$3,400
10b.	Mortgage interest	$10,000	
11b.	Real estate taxes	4,000	
12b.	Total	$14,000	
13 & 14.	Business portion of Line 12		2,800
15.	Remaining tentative profit		600
17b.	Insurance	1,200	
20b.	Utilities	1,800	
22b.	Total	3,000	
23, 25, & 26.	Business portion of Line 21		600
27.	Remaining tentative profit		0

No depreciation is deductible because there is no remaining business income and excess home office expenses may not generate a loss deduction. The depreciation is carried over to 2011. Home office expenses of $3,400 from Lines 14 and 26 are deducted on Line 30, Schedule C.

Planning Reminder

Substantiating the Sideline Business

In claiming home office expenses of a sideline business, it is important to be ready to prove that you are actually in business *(40.10)*. In the case cited in the Example in *40.16*, the Tax Court held that the doctor's personal efforts in managing the six units for tenants were sufficiently systematic and continuous to put him in the rental real estate business. In some cases, the rental of even a single piece of real property may be a business if additional services are provided such as cleaning or maid service.

40.16 Home Office for Sideline Business

You may have an occupation and also run a sideline business from an office in your home. The home office expenses are deductible on Form 8829 if the office is a principal place of operating the sideline business or a place to meet with clients, customers, or patients. *See* the deduction tests *(40.12)* and the income limit computation *(40.15)* for home office deductions. Managing rental property may qualify as a business.

EXAMPLE

A doctor was employed full time by a hospital. He also owned six rental properties that he personally managed. He sought new tenants, supplied furnishings, and cleaned and prepared the units for tenants. He used one bedroom in his two-bedroom home exclusively as an office to manage the properties. The room was furnished with a desk, bookcase, filing cabinet, calculators, and answering service; furnishings and other materials for preparing rental units for tenants were stored there. According to the Tax Court, the doctor's efforts in managing the rental properties constituted a business; he could deduct expenses allocable to the home office.

Managing your own securities portfolio. Investors managing their own securities portfolios may find it difficult to convince a court that investment management is a business activity. According to Congressional committee reports, a home office deduction should be denied to an investor who uses a home office to read financial periodicals and reports, clip bond coupons, and perform similar activities. In one case, the Claims Court allowed a deduction to Moller, who spent about 40 hours a week at a home office managing a substantial stock portfolio. The Claims Court held these activities amounted to a business. However, an appeals court reversed the decision. According to the appeals court, the test is whether or not a person is a trader. A trader is in a business; an investor is not. A trader buys and sells frequently to catch daily market swings. An investor buys securities for capital appreciation and income without regard to daily market developments. Therefore, to be a trader, one's activities must be directed to short-term trading, not the long-term holding of investments. Here, Moller was an investor; he was primarily interested in the long-term growth potential of stock. He did not earn his income from the short-term turnovers of stocks. He had no significant trading profits. His interest and dividend income was 98% of his income. *See* the discussion of trader expenses in *30.16*.

Form **8829** | **Expenses for Business Use of Your Home** | OMB No. 1545-0074

Department of the Treasury
Internal Revenue Service (99)

▶ File only with Schedule C (Form 1040). Use a separate Form 8829 for each home you used for business during the year.

▶ See separate instructions.

2010 Attachment Sequence No. **66**

Name(s) of proprietor(s): Samuel Brown | Your social security number: X1X0111111

Part I Part of Your Home Used for Business

Line	Description		(a)	(b)		Amount
1	Area used regularly and exclusively for business, regularly for daycare, or for storage of inventory or product samples (see instructions)				1	500 sq. ft.
2	Total area of home				2	2,500 sq. ft.
3	Divide line 1 by line 2. Enter the result as a percentage				3	20 %
	For daycare facilities not used exclusively for business, go to line 4. All others go to line 7.					
4	Multiply days used for daycare during year by hours used per day	4	hr.			
5	Total hours available for use during the year (365 days x 24 hours) (see instructions)	5	8,760 hr.			
6	Divide line 4 by line 5. Enter the result as a decimal amount	6	.			
7	Business percentage. For daycare facilities not used exclusively for business, multiply line 6 by line 3 (enter the result as a percentage). All others, enter the amount from line 3 ▶				7	20 %

Part II Figure Your Allowable Deduction

Line	Description		(a) Direct expenses	(b) Indirect expenses		Amount
8	Enter the amount from Schedule C, line 29, **plus** any net gain or (loss) derived from the business use of your home and shown on Schedule D or Form 4797. If more than one place of business, see instructions				8	3,400
	See instructions for columns (a) and (b) before completing lines 9–21.					
9	Casualty losses (see instructions)	9				
10	Deductible mortgage interest (see instructions)	10		10,000		
11	Real estate taxes (see instructions)	11		4,000		
12	Add lines 9, 10, and 11	12		14,000		
13	Multiply line 12, column (b) by line 7	13		2,800		
14	Add line 12, column (a) and line 13				14	2,800
15	Subtract line 14 from line 8. If zero or less, enter -0-				15	600
16	Excess mortgage interest (see instructions)	16				
17	Insurance	17		1,200		
18	Rent	18				
19	Repairs and maintenance	19				
20	Utilities	20		1,800		
21	Other expenses (see instructions)	21				
22	Add lines 16 through 21	22		3,000		
23	Multiply line 22, column (b) by line 7	23		600		
24	Carryover of operating expenses from 2009 Form 8829, line 42	24				
25	Add line 22 column (a), line 23, and line 24				25	600
26	Allowable operating expenses. Enter the **smaller** of line 15 or line 25				26	600
27	Limit on excess casualty losses and depreciation. Subtract line 26 from line 15				27	-0-
28	Excess casualty losses (see instructions)	28				
29	Depreciation of your home from line 41 below	29		1,200		
30	Carryover of excess casualty losses and depreciation from 2009 Form 8829, line 43	30				
31	Add lines 28 through 30				31	1,200
32	Allowable excess casualty losses and depreciation. Enter the **smaller** of line 27 or line 31				32	-0-
33	Add lines 14, 26, and 32				33	3,400
34	Casualty loss portion, if any, from lines 14 and 32. Carry amount to **Form 4684** (see instructions)				34	
35	**Allowable expenses for business use of your home.** Subtract line 34 from line 33. Enter here and on Schedule C, line 30. If your home was used for more than one business, see instructions ▶				35	3,400

Part III Depreciation of Your Home

Line	Description		Amount
36	Enter the **smaller** of your home's adjusted basis or its fair market value (see instructions)	36	238,975
37	Value of land included on line 36	37	50,000
38	Basis of building. Subtract line 37 from line 36	38	188,975
39	Business basis of building. Multiply line 38 by line 7	39	37,795
40	Depreciation percentage (see instructions)	40	3.175 %
41	Depreciation allowable (see instructions). Multiply line 39 by line 40. Enter here and on line 29 above	41	1,200

Part IV Carryover of Unallowed Expenses to 2011

Line	Description		Amount
42	Operating expenses. Subtract line 26 from line 25. If less than zero, enter -0-	42	-0-
43	Excess casualty losses and depreciation. Subtract line 32 from line 31. If less than zero, enter -0-	43	1,200

For Paperwork Reduction Act Notice, see your tax return instructions. Cat. No. 13232M Form **8829** (2010)

40.17 Depreciation of Office in Cooperative Apartment

If your home office meets the tests discussed in *40.12*, you may deduct depreciation on your stock interest in the cooperative. The basis for depreciation may be your share of the cooperative corporation's basis for the building or an amount computed from the price you paid for the stock. The method you use depends on whether you are the first or a later owner of the stock.

You are the first owner. In figuring your depreciation, you start with the cooperative's depreciable basis of the building. You then take your share of depreciation according to the percentage of stock interest you own. The cooperative can provide the details needed for the computation.

If space in the building is rented to commercial tenants who do not have stock interests in the corporation, the total allowable depreciation is reduced by the amount allocated to the space used by the commercial tenants.

You are a later owner of the cooperative's stock. When you buy stock from a prior owner, your depreciable basis is determined by the price of your stock and your share of the co-op's outstanding mortgage, reduced by amounts allocable to land and to commercial space.

Law Alert

Longer Carryback Period

Congress may lengthen the carryback period for 2010 net operating losses; *see* the *e-Supplement at jklasser.com* for an update.

40.18 Net Operating Losses (NOLs)

A loss incurred in your profession or unincorporated business is deducted from other income reported on Form 1040. If the loss exceeds your other income, you may have a net operating loss (NOL). An NOL can be used to offset income in other years. More specifically, you can usually carry the NOL back for two years and then forward for up to 20 years. A three-year carryback is allowed for an NOL attributable to casualty or theft losses, and for a qualified small business NOL attributable to a Presidentially declared disaster. A farming net operating loss may be carried back five years. *See* the instructions to Form 1045 for further details. A loss carried back to a prior year reduces income of that year and entitles you to a refund. A loss applied to a later year reduces income for that year. You may elect to carry forward your 2010 loss for 20 years, foregoing the carryback *(40.22)*.

The rules below apply not only to self-employed individuals, farmers, and professionals, but also to individuals whose casualty losses exceed income, stockholders in S corporations, and partners whose partnerships have suffered losses. Each partner claims his or her share of the partnership loss.

Carryover of loss from prior year to 2010. If you had a net operating loss in an earlier year that is being carried forward to 2010, the loss carryover is reported as a minus figure on Line 21 of Form 1040. You must attach a detailed statement showing how you figured the carryover.

Net operating losses from tax years beginning on or before August 5, 1997, expire after 15 carryforward years.

Change in marital status. If you incur a net operating loss while single but are married filing jointly in a carryback or carryforward year, the loss may be used only to offset your own income on the joint return.

If the net operating loss was claimed on a joint return and in the carryback or carryforward year you are not filing jointly with the same spouse, only your allocable share of the original loss may be claimed; *see* IRS Publication 536.

Passive activity limitation. Losses subject to passive activity rules of *Chapter 10* are not deductible as net operating losses. However, losses of rental operations coming within the $25,000 allowance *(10.2)* may be treated as net operating loss if the loss exceeds passive and other income.

40.19 Your Net Operating Loss

A net operating loss is generally the excess of deductible business expenses over business income. The net operating loss may also include the following losses and deductions:

- Casualty and theft losses, even if the property was used for personal purposes; *see Chapter 18*.
- Expenses of moving to a new job location; *see Chapter 12*.
- Deductible job expenses such as travel expenses, work clothes, costs, and union dues *(19.3)*.
- Your share of a partnership or S corporation operating loss.
- Loss on the sale of small business investment company (SBIC) stock.
- Loss incurred on Section 1244 stock.

Filing Instruction

Adjustment for Capital Losses

A net nonbusiness capital loss may not be included in a net operating loss. If nonbusiness capital losses exceed nonbusiness capital gains, the excess is an adjustment that reduces your loss on Schedule A of Form 1045. In figuring your loss, you may take into account business capital losses only up to the total of business capital gains plus any nonbusiness capital gains remaining after the adjustment for nonbusiness deductions.

An operating loss may *not* include:

- Net operating loss carryback or carryover from any year.
- Capital losses that exceed capital gain.
- Excess of nonbusiness deductions over nonbusiness income plus nonbusiness net capital gain.
- Deductions for personal exemptions.
- A self-employed person's contribution to a Keogh plan.
- An IRA deduction.

Income from other sources may eliminate or reduce your net operating loss.

EXAMPLE

You are self-employed and incur a business loss of $10,000. Your spouse earns a salary of $10,000. When you file a joint return, your business loss will be eliminated by your spouse's salary. Similarly, if you also had salary from another position, the salary would reduce your business loss.

40.20 How To Report a Net Operating Loss

You compute your net operating loss deduction on Schedule A of Form 1045, but this form need not be attached to your return. You start with adjusted gross income and personal deductions shown on your tax return. As these figures include items not allowed for net operating loss purposes, you follow the line-by-line steps of Schedule A (Form 1045) to eliminate them. That is, you reduce the loss by the nonallowed items such as deductions for personal exemptions, net capital loss, and nonbusiness deductions exceeding nonbusiness income. The Example at the end of this section illustrates the steps in the schedule.

Adjustment for nonbusiness deductions. Nonbusiness deductions that exceed nonbusiness income may not be included in a net operating loss deduction. Nonbusiness deductions include deductions for IRA and Keogh plans and itemized deductions such as charitable contributions, interest expense, state taxes, and medical expenses. Do not include in this non-allowed group deductible casualty and theft losses, which for net operating loss purposes are treated as business losses. If you do not claim itemized deductions in the year of the loss, you must treat the standard deduction as a nonbusiness deduction.

Nonbusiness income is income that is *not* from a trade or business—such as dividends, interest, and annuity income. The excess of nonbusiness capital gains over nonbusiness capital losses is also treated as part of nonbusiness income that offsets nonbusiness deductions.

EXAMPLE

Income from dividends and interest is $6,000 and nonbusiness deductions are $6,500. The excess deduction of $500 is an adjustment that reduces your loss on Form 1045.

At-risk loss limitations. The loss used to figure your net operating loss deduction is subject to the at-risk rules *(10.17)*. If part of your investment is in nonrecourse loans or is otherwise not at risk, you must compute your deductible loss on Form 6198, which you attach to Form 1040. The deductible loss from Form 6198 is reflected in the income and deduction figures you enter on the Form 1045 schedule to compute your net operating loss deduction.

EXAMPLE

You are single and in 2010 you have a salary of $3,000, interest of $1,200, a net business loss of $10,000 (income of $50,000 and expenses of $60,000), itemized Schedule A deductions of $5,900, and a net nonbusiness capital gain of $1,000. After the required addbacks and adjustments are made, your net operating loss is $7,000. The following computation approximates the steps of the computation on Schedule A, Form 1045.

Salary		$3,000
Interest		1,200
Capital gain income		1,000
Business loss		($10,000)
Adjusted gross income		($4,800)
Add: Exemption and itemized deductions		(9,550)
		($14,350)
Adjustments:		
Exemption	$3,650	
Excess nonbusiness deduction*	3,700	7,350
Net operating loss		($7,000)

**The excess nonbusiness expenses deduction was figured as follows:*

Itemized deductions		$5,900
Net capital gain income	$1,000	
Interest income	1,200	2,200
Excess		$3,700

Reporting NOLs. NOLs carried forward from prior years are reported on Line 21 of Form 1040 as "other income." The NOL is entered as a negative amount. When amending prior returns to account for an NOL carryback, the NOL is entered as a negative amount.

Planning Reminder

Advantage of Relinquishing the Carryback

You will generally make the election to relinquish the carryback if you expect greater tax savings by carrying the loss forward. You might also make the election if you are concerned you might be audited for earlier years if you carry back a loss for a refund. You make the election by attaching a statement to this effect to your return for the year of the loss, which must be filed by the due date plus extensions. The IRS refuses to allow a late election and received court approval for its position.

40.21 How To Carry Back Your Net Operating Loss

As discussed in *40.18*, a new law allows a carryback period for a 2010 net operating loss (NOL) of up to two years in most cases. When you carry back the loss, you recompute your tax for the earlier year on Form 1045. After recomputing the tax on Form 1045, your refund is the difference between the tax originally paid and the lower tax figured after taking the net operating loss deduction. *See* the instructions to Form 1045 and also IRS Publication 536 for details of the recomputation calculation.

Use Form 1045 as a "quick refund" claim. The IRS will usually allow or reject your claim within 90 days from the time you file Form 1045. Do not attach Form 1045 to your 2010 Form 1040. File Form 1045 separately, together with a copy of your return. Generally, Form 1045 may be filed within 12 months after the end of the NOL year. If the IRS allows the refund, it may still determine later that the refund was excessive and assess additional tax.

Although using Form 1045 is the quickest way to obtain the refund, you may instead file an amended return on Form 1040X to claim the refund. You have three years after the due date (including extensions) of your 2010 tax return to file Form 1040X.

Caution

Domestic Production Activities Deduction and NOLs

The domestic production activities deduction *(40.23)* cannot create or increase an NOL carryback or carryforward (with very limited exceptions).

40.22 Election To Carry Forward Losses

Instead of carrying back your 2010 net operating loss *(40.21)*, you may elect to forego the carryback. Instead, you just carry forward losses. The carryforward period remains 20 years under the election. The election is irrevocable. It applies for both regular tax and alternative minimum tax purposes.

If you are carrying forward a net operating loss from an earlier year to 2010, report the loss carryover as a minus figure on Line 21 of Form 1040 and attach a statement explaining how the carryover was computed.

40.23 Overview of the Domestic Production Activities Deduction

The domestic production activities deduction (also referred to as the "manufacturer's deduction") encourages manufacturing and other production activities in the United States. The deduction is a fixed percentage of income from qualified production activities or adjusted gross income, whichever is lower.

The percentage for 2010 is 9%.

Reporting the deduction. The deduction is figured on Form 8903. It is entered on Line 35 of Form 1040.

40.24 Qualified Production Activities

The law takes a broad view of the type of activities that can qualify for the domestic production activities deduction. These include not only traditional manufacturing, but also:

- Selling, leasing, or licensing items manufactured, produced, grown, or extracted in the U.S.
- Selling, leasing, or licensing films produced in the U.S.
- Construction in the U.S. Construction includes both erection and substantial renovation of residential and commercial buildings.
- Engineering and architectural services relating to a construction project performed in the U.S.
- Software developed in the U.S., regardless of whether it is to be purchased off the shelf or downloaded from the Internet. The term "software" includes video games. But, with some minor exceptions, the term does not include fees for online use of software, fees for customer support, and fees for playing computer games online.

Safe harbor. The deduction is limited to activities in whole or "significant part" in the U.S. Under a safe harbor, a taxpayer is treated as having manufactured, produced, grown, or extracted property in "significant part" within the U.S. if direct labor and overhead costs incurred within the

U.S. account for at least 20% of the total cost of the property. But even if you cannot meet this safe harbor, you may rely on the facts and circumstances to demonstrate that a significant part of the activities are in the U.S.

The following activities are specifically *not* qualified production activities:

- Cosmetic activities related to construction, such as painting
- Leasing or licensing to a related party
- The sale of food or beverages prepared at a retail establishment. However, if a business both manufactures food and sells it at a restaurant or take-out store, income and expenses can be allocated so that those related to manufacture and wholesale distribution qualify for the deduction. Thus, in the so-called "Starbucks" situation, roasting and packaging coffee beans could qualify, but selling the beans or brewed coffee at their stores would not.

40.25 Figuring the Deduction

To figure the domestic production activities deduction, start with domestic production gross receipts. If there are gross receipts from domestic and foreign production, you must make an allocation of gross receipts based on any reasonable method to determine qualified production activities income (QPAI).

Reduce this amount by all of the following (based on your books and records if possible, or on any reasonable method):

- The cost of goods sold that is allocable to domestic gross receipts
- Other deductions, expenses, and losses that are directly allocable to domestic gross receipts
- An appropriate share of other deductions, expenses and losses that are not directly allocable to domestic gross receipts or another class of income

Limitations. The deduction for 6% of qualified production activities income cannot exceed adjusted gross income for sole proprietors and owners of partnerships, limited liability companies, or S corporations (a taxable income limitation applies for C corporations).

The deduction also cannot exceed 50% of W-2 wages paid during the year to employees. W-2 wages include both taxable compensation and elective deferrals (e.g., employee contributions to 401(k) plans). It appears that *all* wages of a business, not just those related to domestic production, are taken into account for purposes of the 50%-of-W-2-wages limitation. There are three methods provided for determining W-2 income. One method looks to the lesser of the amounts in Box 1 or Box 5 of Form W-2, while the other methods are more complex; *see* the instructions to Form 8903.

Partnerships and S corporations. The deduction is applied at the owner, not the entity, level. This means that the business must allocate on the owner's Schedule K-1 gross receipts, cost of goods sold, and related expenses from qualified production activities to the owners, who then claim the deduction on their personal returns.

Caution

Wage Limitation

For S corporations, only wages allocable to a shareholder (and not the shareholder's personal wages) are taken into account for the limitation on the domestic production activities deduction. For both partnerships and S corporations, wages for the W-2 limit include only amounts paid to determine qualified production activity income.

40.26 Business Credits

You may be eligible to reduce your tax liability by credits related to your business. Unlike personal credits, however, many business-related credits are subject to a special limitation, called the general business credit. The general business credit is not a separate credit; it is a compilation of one or more separate business-related credits that are specifically included by law within the general business credit. The reason for grouping the credits as one is to impose an overall limitation, explained below. The *general business credit* includes the following credits:

- The investment credit on Form 3468, consisting of the rehabilitation property credit *(see 31.8)*, the energy credit, and the reforestation credit;
- The research credit on Form 6765;*
- The low-income housing credit on Form 8586 *(31.8)*;
- The disabled access credit on Form 8826;
- The renewable electricity production credit on Form 8835;
- The credit for small employer pension plan startup costs on Form 8881;
- The credit for employer-provided child-care facilities and services on Form 8882;
- The Indian employment credit on Form 8845;*

Planning Reminder

Employment-Related Credits

The work opportunity credit for hiring certain disadvantaged workers (Form 5884), the employer credit for FICA on tips of certain employees (Form 8846), and the empowerment zone and renewal community employment credit (Form 8844) are not part of the general business credit.

Filing Tip

Hybrid or Plug-in Vehicle

If you buy a hybrid or plug-in electric vehicle, only the portion of the applicable credit related to business driving is part of the general business credit. For example, in 2010 you buy a hybrid vehicle for which there is a $2,000 credit. You use the car 60% for business and 40% for personal driving. Only $1,200 (60% of $2,000) is part of the general business credit.

Planning Reminder

Small Business Health Care Credit

If you pay at least half the cost of coverage for your staff and meet certain eligibility tests, you can claim a tax credit for your payments. *See 41.14*.

Planning Reminder

Fuel-Related Credits

For a qualified business use, a refundable credit may be claimed for *gasoline or special fuels*. For example, a credit applies for fuel used in non-highway vehicles (other than motorboats), including generators, compressors, fork-lift trucks, and bulldozers. A credit may also be claimed for aviation fuel used for farming or commercial aviation. Different credit rates apply depending on the type of fuel. You must claim the credit on a timely filed income tax return, including extensions. You compute the credit on Form 4136, which you attach to Form 1040. For further details, *see* IRS Publication 378; farmers should *see* IRS Publication 225.

- The orphan drug credit on Form 8820;
- The credit for employer-paid Social Security and Medicare taxes on certain tips received by employees of food and beverage establishments on Form 8846;
- The credit for contributions to certain community development corporations on Form 8847;
- The new markets credit on Form 8874;*
- The railroad track maintenance credit on Form 8900;
- The biodiesel and renewable fuels credit on Form 8864;
- The low sulfur diesel fuel production on Form 8896;
- The nonconventional source fuel credit on Form 8907;
- The energy efficient home credit on Form 8908;
- The energy efficient appliance credit on Form 8909;
- The alternative motor vehicle fuel credit on Form 8910;
- The alternative fuel vehicle refueling property credit on Form 8911;
- The agricultural chemicals security credit for providing security (Form 8931);
- The credit for employer differential wage payments to activated military personnel (Form 8932);*
- The distilled spirits credit on Form 8906;
- The carbon dioxide sequestration credit on Form 8923; and
- The qualified plug-in electric drive motor vehicle credit on Form 8936 (for the portion of an electric vehicle used for business).

*These credits expired at the end of 2009 but Congress may extend them for 2010; *see* the *e-Supplement at jklasser.com* for an update.

Computing the general business credit. You compute each credit separately. If you claim only one credit, that credit is considered your *general business credit* for 2010. The credit is subject to a limitation based on tax liability that is figured on the form used to compute that particular credit. You then enter the allowable credit as your general business credit on Form 1040.

If you claim more than one credit, each of the credits is first computed separately. Most of the credits are then listed on Form 3800 but some of the credits, which have special tax liability limitations, are not entered on Form 3800. For the credits entered on Form 3800, you must figure an overall tax liability limitation. You must compute tentative alternative minimum tax (AMT) on Form 6251 even if the complete computation on Form 6251 shows that you do not have an actual AMT liability for the year. Your limit for the general business credit on Form 3800 is your regular tax liability (after tax credits other than the general business credit), *plus* actual AMT liability from Form 6251 (if any), *minus* whichever of the following is larger: either (1) tentative AMT from Form 6251 or (2) 25% of your regular income tax liability (after other credits) over $25,000.

Keep separate records of each of the component credits making up the general business credit. The credits are considered to be used up in a specific order; *see* the instructions to Form 3800.

Under prior law, general business credits in excess of the liability limitation could be carried back one year and then forward for up to 20 years. However, for the 2010 taxable year only, the Small Business Jobs Act of 2010 (signed into law on September 27, 2010) increases the carryback period to five years and the carryforward period to 25 years. The extended periods are allowed for sole proprietors, partnerships and corporations whose stock is not publicly traded, so long as the average gross receipts for the prior three years did not exceed $50 million. *See* the Form 3800 instructions for further new law details.

If you have business credits from a passive activity under the rules discussed in *Chapter 10*, you must figure the credits on Form 8582-CR; generally, the credits are limited to the tax liability from passive activities.

40.27 Filing Schedule F

The designation "farm" includes stock, dairy, poultry, fruit, and truck farms, plantations, ranches, and all lands used for farming operations. A fish farm where fish are specially fed and raised, and not just caught, is a farm. So too are animal breeding farms, such as mink, fox, and chinchilla farms.

A farmer who is a sole proprietor files Schedule F along with his or her Form 1040. This schedule is similar to Schedule C for sole proprietors other than farmers; it reports income and expenses related to farming activities.

The same rules for accounting, the reporting period, and for income and expenses to Schedule C apply for farmers filing Schedule F. However, there are some key exceptions designed to provide special breaks for farmers. Since most farmers report on the cash basis and use a calendar year for tax reporting, the following information is limited to these farmers.

Special income treatment. Certain types of farm-related income enjoy special tax treatment:

- Sales of livestock (including poultry) and produce can receive Section 1231 treatment. If crops are sold on a deferred payment contract, report the income when payment is received.
- Sales of livestock caused by drought, flood, or other weather conditions can be reported in the following year if you can show that the sale would not have occurred but for the weather condition and you are eligible for federal assistance because of the weather condition.
- Rents, including crop shares, are treated as rental income, rather than as farm income, and are not part of farm net income or loss.

Filing Tip

Figuring Tax on Farm Income

Farmers and commercial fisherman can use income averaging to figure the tax on their business income *(22.6)*.

40.28 Farming Expenses

Certain types of expenses related to farmers enjoy special tax treatment. Here are some key rules unique to farmers:

Depreciation. There are special recovery periods for certain farm animals and equipment, including farm buildings and agricultural structures (*see* IRS Publication 225).

Prepaid farm supplies. While cash method farmers usually can deduct expenses in the year they are paid, prepaid farm supplies must be deducted ratably over the period in which they are used. However, there is a special exception that allows them to be deducted in the year of payment if they do not exceed 50% of other deductible farm expenses (including depreciation and amortization); any prepaid expenses in excess of this limit are deductible in the following year.

Livestock feed. While the cost of feed usually is deductible in the year it is consumed, it can be deducted in the year of payment if:

1. The expense is a payment for the purchase of food (and not a deposit).
2. The prepayment has a business, and not merely a tax avoidance, purpose.
3. The deduction of feed costs does not result in a material distortion of income.

Breeding fees. A cash basis farmer can deduct breeding fees as a business expense; an accrual method farmer must capitalize the fees and allocate them to the cost basis of the calf, foal, or other animal to which they relate.

Fertilizer and lime. You can deduct the cost of fertilizer and lime in the year of payment *or* you can capitalize the cost and deduct a part of it each year in which the benefit lasts as long as the benefit lasts more than one year.

Soil and water conservation expenses. Usually, these expenses must be capitalized. However, you can elect to deduct them within limits (the deduction cannot be more than 25% of gross income from farming).

Reforestation expenses. You can deduct up to $5,000 ($10,000 if married filing jointly). Costs in excess of this dollar limit can be amortized over 84 months.

Excess farm losses. Starting in 2010, if you receive any direct or counter-cyclical payments under Title I of the Food, Conservation, and Energy Act of 2008 or Commodity Credit loans, your ability to use farm losses to offset non-farming business income is limited. The limit is $300,000 in losses or net farm income over the last five years, whichever is greater. Losses limited in the current year by this rule can be carried forward to subsequent years.

Filing Tip

Farm-Related Net Operating Losses

When expenses exceed farm income, a net operating loss may result. Unlike most business net operating losses that have a two-year carryback, farm net operating losses can be carried back for five years *(40.21)*.

Chapter 41

Retirement and Medical Plans for Self-Employed

Self-employed persons and partners can take advantage of tax-sheltered Keogh retirement plans or simplified employee pension plans (SEPs).

Advantages flow from: (1) tax deductions allowed for contributions to the plan (a form of forced savings); (2) tax-free accumulations of income earned on assets held by the plan; and (3) in some cases, special averaging for lump-sum benefits paid from a Keogh plan on retirement.

If you have employees, you must consider the cost of covering them when setting up your plan.

If you do not have any other retirement plan and have no more than 100 employees, you may set up a salary-reduction SIMPLE plan.

Self-employed persons can also pay for their health coverage on a more advantageous basis than other individuals. They can also use special health-related plans to further lower out-of-pocket medical costs while obtaining tax breaks. If you pay a certain amount for coverage of employees, you may be entitled to a tax credit *(41.4)*.

41.1 Overview of Retirement and Medical Plans

Self-employed individuals can shelter income and obtain desired retirement savings and health coverage using various plans. While the plans are tied to being in business, the deductions for them are not business write-offs. Instead, deductions for the self-employed person's own coverage are claimed directly on page 1 of Form 1040. For example, a self-employed person's deductions for contributions to his or her own account in a Keogh retirement plan *(41.2)*, SEP *(41.3)*, or SIMPLE IRA *(41.9)* are claimed on Line 28 of Form 1040. If the plans also cover employees of the self-employed person, deductions related to employees are claimed on Schedule C.

Self-employed individuals who obtain their own health insurance can deduct the premiums from gross income, rather than as an itemized medical expense *(12.2)*. They may be able to cut the high cost of health coverage by using a high-deductible health plan, combined with a health savings account (HSA) *(41.10)*. Contributions to the HSA are also deductible from gross income *(41.11)*. Alternatively, self-employed individuals who have previously set up Archer MSAs can continue to use these tax-advantaged accounts to pay for medical costs not covered by insurance *(41.13)*.

41.2 Choosing a Keogh Plan

You may set up a self-employed retirement plan called a *Keogh plan* if you have net earnings (gross business or professional income less allowable business deductions) from your sole proprietorship or partnership for which the plan is established. If you are an inactive owner, such as a limited partner, you do not qualify to set up a Keogh plan—unless you receive guaranteed payments for services that are treated as earnings from self-employment.

Set-up deadline. To deduct contributions for a tax year, your *Keogh plan* must be adopted by the last day of that year (December 31 if you report on a calendar year basis). If it is, contributions can be made up to the due date of your return for that year, plus extensions.

Partnership plans. An individual partner or partners, although self-employed, may not set up a Keogh plan. The plan must be established by the partnership. Partnership deductions for contributions to an individual partner's account are reported on the partner's Schedule K-1 (Form 1065) and deducted by the partner as an adjustment to income on Line 28 of Form 1040.

Including employees in your plan. You must include in your plan all employees who have reached age 21 with at least one year of service. An employee may be required to complete two years of service before participating if your plan provides for full and immediate vesting after no more than two years. You generally are not required to cover seasonal or part-time employees who work less than 1,000 hours during a 12-month period.

A minimum coverage rule requires that a defined benefit plan must include at least 40% of all employees, or 50 employees if that is less.

Your plan may not exclude employees who are over a certain age.

A plan may not discriminate in favor of officers or other highly compensated personnel. Benefits must be for the employees and their beneficiaries, and their plan rights may not be subject to forfeiture. A plan may not allow any of its funds to be diverted for purposes other than pension benefits. Contributions made on your behalf may not exceed the ratio of contributions made on behalf of employees.

There are two types of Keogh plans: defined-benefit plans and defined-contribution plans, and different rules apply to each. A defined-benefit plan provides in advance for a specific retirement benefit funded by quarterly contributions based on an IRS formula and actuarial assumptions. A defined-contribution plan does not fix a specific retirement benefit, but rather sets the amount of annual contributions so that the amount of retirement benefits depends on contributions and income earned on those contributions. If contributions are geared to profits, the plan is a profit-sharing plan. A plan that requires fixed contributions regardless of profits is a money-purchase plan. If you have a profit-sharing plan, a 401(k) plan arrangement can be included to allow you (and other participants) to make elective deferral contributions of before-tax compensation to the plan.

A defined-benefit plan may prove costly if you have older employees who also must be provided with proportionate defined benefits. Furthermore, a defined-benefit plan requires you to contribute to their accounts even if you do not have profits. For 2010, the benefit limit was the lesser of (a) 100%

Planning Reminder

Employees Who Are Self-Employed on the Side

If you are an employee-member of a company retirement plan, you may set up a Keogh plan if you carry on a self-employed enterprise or profession on the side. For example, you are employed by a company that has a qualified 401(k) plan to which you make salary deferrals. At the same time, you have a sideline consulting business. You may set up a Keogh plan based on your consultant earnings. Each plan is independent of the other. As an alternative to a Keogh plan, you may contribute to a simplified employee pension plan (SEP), *(41.3)*, or a SIMPLE IRA *41.9*.

Planning Reminder

One-Person 401(k) Plan

If you have no employees other than your spouse, you may want to consider a "one-person" 401(k) plan, which allows you to contribute more than a Keogh plan. For example, for 2010, elective deferrals of up to $16,500 could be made, or $22,000 if age 50 or older during the year. In addition to the deferrals, a contribution of up to 20% of net earnings (reduced by 50% of self-employment tax liability *(41.4)* can be made to your account, subject to the overall limit, which for 2010 is $49,000. You can add a Roth 401(k) option to your plan, allowing after-tax contributions to produce tax-free returns. The income limitation on eligibility to contribute to a Roth IRA does *not* apply to a Roth 401(k). *See* the *e-Supplement at jklasser.com* for the 2011 overall limit.

Planning Reminder

Small Employer Credit for Retirement Plan Startup Costs

Employers with 100 or fewer employees that do not have a qualified retirement plan generally may claim a tax credit on Form 8881 for administrative costs of setting up a pension plan, profit-sharing plan, 401(k) plan, SEP, or SIMPLE plan. *At least one non-highly-compensated employee must be covered.* The maximum credit is $500, 50% of the first $1,000 of startup costs. The credit is allowed for costs incurred in the year in which the plan takes effect and in the next two years.

of the participant's average compensation for the three consecutive years of highest compensation as an active participant or (b) $195,000. This dollar limit is reduced if benefits begin before age 62 and increased if benefits begin after age 65. The $195,000 limit is subject to cost-of-living increases; *see* the *e-Supplement at jklasser.com* for the 2011 limit.

For defined contribution plans, the 2010 limit on annual contributions and other additions (excluding earnings) was the lesser of 100% of compensation or $49,000. For years after 2010, the $49,000 limit may be adjusted for inflation; *see* the *e-Supplement at jklasser.com*.

Starting in 2010, small employers (with 500 or fewer employees) can opt for a hybrid retirement plan, called a DB(k). It combines a 401(k)-like account with a small-employer-funded pension. Because the IRS had not issued guidance early enough for financial institutions to create these plans for 2010, they will likely become more available after 2010.

41.3 Choosing a SEP

Under a SEP (simplified employee pension plan), you may contribute to a special type of IRA more than is allowed under the regular IRA rules. Contributions do not have to be made every year. When you do make contributions, they must be based on a written allocation formula and must not discriminate in favor of yourself, other owners with more than a 5% interest, or highly compensated employees. Coverage requirements for employees are in *8.15*. A salary-reduction arrangement for employees may be provided under a qualifying SEP established before 1997 or under a SIMPLE IRA plan established after 1996 *(8.17)*.

The deadline for both setting up and contributing to a SEP is the due date for your return, *including extensions*. Thus, if you have not set up a Keogh plan by the end of the taxable year *(41.1)*, you may still make a deductible retirement contribution for the year by contributing to a SEP by the due date of your return.

41.4 Deductible Keogh or SEP Contributions

Caution

Deadline for Setting Up Keogh Plan or SEP

You must formally set up a Keogh plan in writing on or before the end of the taxable year in which you want the plan to be effective. For example, if you want to make a contribution for 2010, your plan must be set up on or before December 31, 2010, if you report on a calendar year basis. If a profit-sharing Keogh plan is established by the end of 2010, you have up until the due date for filing your 2010 return, plus the extension, to make a deductible contribution within the limits discussed in this section.

If you miss the deadline for setting up a Keogh plan, you may contribute to a simplified employee pension plan (SEP) set up by the filing deadline for Form 1040, including extensions *(41.4)*.

The deductible limit for a Keogh plan depends on whether you have a defined-contribution plan (profit-sharing or money-purchase pension plan) or a defined-benefit plan. A SEP is treated as a profit-sharing plan subject to the defined-contribution plan deduction limits explained below.

If you have a defined-benefit plan, you generally may deduct contributions needed to produce the accrued benefits provided for by the plan, including any unfunded current liability. This is a complicated calculation requiring actuarial computations that call for the services of a pension expert.

Deductible contribution to a defined-contribution Keogh Plan or a SEP. Before figuring the deductible contribution you can make for 2010 to a profit-sharing Keogh or SEP account, or to a money-purchase pension plan, you must first figure your self-employment tax liability on Schedule SE and the 50% deduction for self-employment tax to be claimed on Line 27 of Form 1040. In computing your deductible plan contribution, your net profit from Line 31 of Schedule C, Line 3 of Schedule C-EZ, or Line 36 of Schedule F is *reduced* by the deduction for 50% of self-employment tax; *see* the Example below.

As a self-employed person, you are not allowed to figure the deductible contribution for yourself by applying the contribution rate stated in your plan. The rate must be reduced, as required by law, to reflect the reduction of net earnings by the deductible contribution itself. If your plan rate is a whole number, the reduced percentage is shown in the Rate Table for Self-Employed on Page 658. If the plan rate is fractional, the reduced percentage is figured using the Fractional Rate Worksheet for Self-Employed on page 658.

Figuring your maximum deductible contribution. After figuring your net earnings and reducing that amount by 50% of your self-employment tax liability, you multiply the balance by the reduced rate from the Rate Table or Fractional Rate Worksheet for Self-Employed on page 665. This is generally your maximum deductible contribution to a profit-sharing Keogh plan or SEP. However, the maximum deductible contribution cannot exceed the annual limit on additions to a defined contribution plan. The annual limit for 2010 is the lesser of (1) $49,000, or (2) $245,000 (maximum compensation that can be taken into account) multiplied by the stated plan contribution rate, not the reduced rate. *See* the Deduction Worksheet for Self-Employed on the next page, which takes you through the steps of figuring your deductible contribution.

If elective deferrals were made during the year, extra steps are required to compute the maximum deductible contribution; *see* Step 9 of the the Deduction Worksheet for Self-Employed shown below.

Deduction Worksheet for Self-Employed

Step 1 Enter your net profit from line 31, Schedule C (Form 1040); line 3, Schedule C-EZ (Form 1040); line 36, Schedule F (Form 1040); or line 14*, Schedule K-1 (Form 1065) . . . . *General partners should reduce this amount by the same additional expenses subtracted from line 14 to determine the amount on line 1 or 2 of Schedule SE	**147,000**
Step 2 Enter your deduction for self-employment tax from line 27, Form 1040	**8,590**
Step 3 Net earnings from self-employment. Subtract step 2 from step 1	**138,410**
Step 4 Enter your rate from the *Rate Table for Self-Employed* or *Fractional Rate Worksheet for Self-Employed*.	**.20**
Step 5 Multiply step 3 by step 4	**27,682**
Step 6 Multiply $245,000 by your plan contribution rate (not the reduced rate)	**61,250**
Step 7 Enter the **smaller** of step 5 or step 6	**27,682**
Step 8 Contribution dollar limit . . . . • **If you made any elective deferrals, go to step 9.** • **Otherwise, skip steps 9 through 18 and enter the smaller of step 7 or step 8 on step 19.**	$49,000
Step 9 Enter your elective deferrals made during 2010. Do not enter more than $16,500	______
Step 10 Subtract step 9 from step 8	______
Step 11 Subtract step 9 from step 3 . . . . ______	
Step 12 Enter one-half of step 11	______
Step 13 Enter the **smallest** of step 7, 10, or 12	______
Step 14 Subtract step 13 from step 3	______
Step 15 Enter the **smaller** of step 9 or step 14 . . . . • **If you made catch-up contributions, go to step 16.** • **Otherwise, skip steps 16 through 18 and go to step 19.**	______
Step 16 Subtract step 15 from step 14	______
Step 17 Enter your catch-up contributions, if any. Do not enter more than $5,500	______
Step 18 Enter the **smaller** of step 16 or step 17	______
Step 19 Add steps 13, 15, and 18. This is your ***maximum deductible contribution***	27,682
Step 20 Enter your total contributions for 2010 . . .	______
Step 21 Enter the smaller of step 19 or step 20. This is your ***deduction*** . . . . **Next:** Enter your deduction on line 28, Form 1040.	______ ______

EXAMPLE

You are a sole proprietor with no employees and have a profit-sharing plan that provides for a 25% contribution rate. Your net self-employment earnings for 2010 from Line 31 of Schedule C are $147,000. On Schedule SE, you figure your self-employment tax liability of $17,180, and you claim a 50% deduction for self-employment taxes of $8,590 (½ of $17,180 self-employment tax from Schedule SE) on Line 27 of Form 1040. By completing the Deduction Worksheet for Self-Employed on page 657, you figure your maximum deductible profit-sharing contribution for 2010 is $27,682.

Table 41-1 Rate Table for Self-Employed

If plan rate is—	*Self-employed person's reduced rate is—*
1 %	.009901
2	.019608
3	.029126
4	.038462
5	.047619
6	.056604
7	.065421
8	.074074
9	.082569
10	.090909
11	.099099
12	.107143
13	.115044
14	.122807
15	.130435
16	.137931
17	.145299
18	.152542
19	.159664
20	.166667
21	.173554
22	.180328
23	.186992
24	.193548
25*	.200000*

* *The maximum deductible percentage for contributions (other than elective deferrals) to your own profit-sharing Keogh, money-purchase Keogh, or SEP is 20% and for your employees, 25%.*

Fractional Rate Worksheet for Self-Employed

If the plan rate is fractional and thus not listed in the table above, figure your deductible percentage this way:

1. Write the plan rate as a decimal. For example, if the plan rate is 10.5%, write .105 as the decimal amount. ______
2. Add 1 to the decimal rate. For example, if the rate is .105, the result is 1.105. ______
3. Divide Step 1 by Step 2. This gives you the deductible percentage. If the plan rate is .105, the deductible percentage is .0950 (.105 ÷ 1.105). ______

Contributions for your employees. The deduction complications that apply to your own contributions do not apply to contributions for employees. You make contributions for your employees at the rate specified in your plan, based upon their compensation, subject to the annual limit discussed above. Thus, if your plan contribution rate is 25%, you would contribute 25% of your employees' pay to the plan, even though your own contribution rate is reduced to 20% under the Rate Table for Self Employed shown above. You deduct contributions for employees when figuring your net earnings from self-employment on Schedule C or Schedule F before figuring your own deductible contribution using the steps shown in the Example above.

Contributions allowed after age 70½. You may continue to make contributions for yourself to a Keogh plan or SEP as long as you have self-employment income. However, you must begin to receive required minimum distributions from a SEP by April 1 of the year following the year in which you reach age 70½ *(8.15)*. This age 70½ required distribution beginning date also applies to a Keogh plan if you are a more-than-5% owner of the business *(7.13)*.

Excess contributions. Contributions to a plan exceeding the deduction ceiling may be carried over and deducted in later years subject to the ceiling for those years. However, if contributions exceed the deductible amount, you are generally subject to a 10% penalty on nondeductible contributions that are not returned by the end of your tax year. The penalty is computed on Form 5330, which must be filed with the IRS by the end of the seventh month following the end of the tax year.

41.5 How To Claim the Keogh or SEP Deduction

Contributions made to your Keogh or SEP account as a self-employed person are deducted as an adjustment to gross income on Line 28 of Form 1040. A deduction for a contribution made for your benefit may not be part of a net operating loss.

Contributions for your employees are entered as deductions on Schedule C (or Schedule F) for purposes of computing profit or loss from your business. Trustees' fees not provided for by contributions are deductible in addition to the maximum contribution deduction.

Deductible Keogh plan contributions may generally be made at any time up to the due date of your return, including any extension of time. However, the plan itself must be set up before the close of the taxable year for which the deduction is sought. If you miss the December 31 deadline for setting up a Keogh plan, you have at least up to April 15, 2011 to set up a SEP for 2010. If you have a filing extension, you have until the extended due date to set up a SEP and make your contribution.

41.6 How To Qualify a Keogh Plan or SEP Plan

You may set up a Keogh plan and contribute to it without advance approval. But since advance approval is advisable, you may, in a determination letter, ask the IRS to review your plan. Approval requirements depend on whether you set up your own administered plan or join a master plan administered by a bank, insurance company, mutual fund, or a prototype plan sponsored by a trade or professional association. If you start your own individually designed plan, you pay the IRS a fee and request a determination letter; *see* IRS Publication 560.

If you join a master or prototype plan, the sponsoring organization applies to the IRS for approval of its plan. You should then be given a copy of the approved plan and copies of any subsequent amendments.

To set up a SEP with a bank, broker, or other financial institution, you do not need IRS approval. If you do not maintain any other qualified retirement plan and other tests are met, a model SEP may be adopted using Form 5305-SEP.

41.7 Annual Keogh Plan Return

Partial relief from one burdensome IRS paperwork requirement may be available if your pension or profit-sharing Keogh plan covers only yourself, or you and your spouse, or you and your business partners and the spouses of the partners. Such plans are treated as one-participant plans by the IRS.

If a one-participant Keogh plan meets minimum coverage requirements, does not cover a business that leases employees, and is not part of a controlled group or affiliated service group, an annual information return for the plan may be filed on Form 5500-EZ instead of the more extensive Form 5500.

Planning Reminder

Small Employer Credit for Retirement Plan Startup Costs

Employers with 100 or fewer employees that do not have a qualified retirement plan generally may claim a tax credit on Form 8881 for administrative costs of setting up a pension plan, profit-sharing plan, 401(k) plan, SEP, or SIMPLE plan. *At least one non-highly-compensated employee must be covered.* The maximum credit is $500, 50% of the first $1,000 of startup costs. The credit is allowed for costs incurred in the year in which the plan takes effect and in the next two years.

Caution

Prohibited Transactions

As an owner-employee (owning more than 10% of the business), your dealings with the Keogh trust are subject to restrictions. You are generally subject to penalties if you buy property from or sell property to the trust; or charge any fees for services you render to the trust. These restrictions also apply to any member of your immediate family and any corporation in which you own more than half the voting stock, either directly or indirectly.

Under an exception for small one-participant plans, Form 5500-EZ does not have to be filed if the value of plan assets at the end of the year is not more than $250,000. The exception applies if you have two or more one-participant plans that together have not exceeded the $250,000 asset threshold. All one-participant plans must file a Form 5500-EZ for their final plan year even if the plan assets have always been below $250,000.

The filing deadline for Form 5500-EZ or Form 5500 is the last day of the seventh month after the end of the plan year unless an extension is obtained; *see* the form instructions. Forms 5500 and 5500-EZ are not filed with the IRS; *see* the form instructions for the mailing address and the electronic filing alternative.

41.8 How Keogh Plan Distributions Are Taxed

Distributions from a Keogh plan generally may not be received without penalty before age 59½ unless you are disabled or meet the other exceptions listed in *7.15*. After 2010, you are a more-than-5% owner you must begin to receive minimum required distributions by April 1 of the year following the year in which you reach age 70½; penalties may apply if an insufficient distribution is received *(7.13)*.

A lump-sum and other eligible distributions *(7.7)* may be rolled over tax free to another employer plan or IRA. For participants born before January 2, 1936, 10-year averaging may be available *(7.2)*. Pension distributions from a Keogh are taxed under the annuity rules discussed in *7.25*, but for purposes of figuring your cost investment, include only nondeductible voluntary contributions; deductible contributions made on your behalf are not part of your investment.

If you receive amounts in excess of the benefits provided for you under the plan formula and you own more than a 5% interest in the employer, the excess benefit is subject to a 10% penalty. The penalty also applies if you were a more-than-5% owner at any time during the five plan years preceding the plan year that ends within the year of an excess distribution.

Other rules discussed in *7.1 – 7.16* apply to Keogh plans as well as qualified corporate plans.

After the death of a Keogh plan owner, distributions to beneficiaries may be spread over the periods discussed at *7.14* provided the plan covers more than one person. Distributions to a surviving spouse can be rolled over to that spouse's IRA. The plan may provide that distributions to non-spouse beneficiaries can be rolled over directly to an IRA, enabling them to spread distributions over their life expectancy.

SEP distributions. Distributions from a SEP are subject to the IRA rules at *7.8*.

41.9 SIMPLE IRA Plans

If you do not maintain any other retirement plan and have 100 or fewer employees, you may set up a salary-reduction type of plan for yourself and your employees. The SIMPLE IRA contribution rules are discussed at *8.17*. A SIMPLE plan may also be made as part of a 401(k) plan *(7.17)*.

Under a SIMPLE IRA for 2010, you may contribute to your own account $11,500 of net earnings plus an additional $2,500 if age 50 or over by the end of the year. You may also make a "matching" contribution of up to 3% of your net earnings.

If you have employees, they generally could make elective salary-reduction contributions for 2010 up to $11,500 (plus $2,500 if age 50 or over). You must make a 3% matching contribution unless you choose to make a 2% non-elective contribution.

See Chapter 8 for further details on SIMPLE IRAs *(8.17 – 8.18)*.

41.10 Health Savings Account (HSA) Basics

Health savings accounts (HSAs) can be used by individuals covered by a high-deductible health plan (HDHP) to save for health-care costs on a tax-free basis in an IRA-like account. HSAs are intended to supplant Archer MSAs; *see* the discussion of Archer MSA rules later in this Chapter *(41.13)*.

The HSA provides a tax-sheltered account for paying routine medical expenses that fall below the deductible set by the HDHP. To contribute to an HSA, you must not be enrolled in Medicare Part A or Part B and you must not be a dependent of another taxpayer.

A qualifying HDHP must have a minimum annual deductible and a maximum annual limit on out-of-pocket costs (*see* below). For 2010, the minimum annual HDHP deductible was $1,200 for self-only coverage and $2,400 for family coverage (it will be the same for 2011). The limit on out-of-pocket costs for 2010 was $5,950 for self-only coverage and $11,900 for family coverage (which will be the same for 2011). The limit applies to co-payments, deductibles, and other payments but not premiums.

Generally, contributions to an HSA are not allowed if the taxpayer has coverage under any health plan that does not meet the "high deductible" requirement of an HDHP, but there are exceptions. A plan that otherwise satisfies HDHP rules may provide preventive care benefits without a deductible or with a deductible below the minimum annual deductible. Benefits may also be provided under certain types of "permitted" coverage and insurance before the deductible of the HDHP is satisfied. Permitted coverage includes coverage for vision, dental or long-term care, accidents, and disability. Permitted insurance includes *per diem* insurance while hospitalized, insurance for a specific disease or illness (such as cancer, diabetes, asthma, or heart failure), and insurance relating to workers' compensation liability, tort liability, or liabilities relating to owning or using a car or other property.

HSA contributions and distributions. Taxpayers who are eligible under the above tests can make a deductible annual contribution to an HSA plus an additional contribution of $1,000 if age 55 or older by the end of the year. The allowable contribution is deductible "above the line" from gross income on Line 25 of Form 1040. Contribution limits are discussed further below *(41.11)*. Earnings accumulate tax free within an HSA, as with an IRA.

Distributions from an HSA are not taxable to the extent used to pay qualified medical expenses of the account owner, his or her spouse, or dependents *(41.12)*.

Note: *HSA contributions and distributions are reported on Form 8889. See the instructions to Form 8889 for further details not covered in 41.11 and 41.12.*

1040 *Filing Instruction*

Report HSA Contributions and Distributions on Form 8889

Report your HSA contributions on Form 8889 and follow the instructions to figure any limitations on the amount you may deduct. Also use Form 8889 to report an HSA distribution and figure the amount, if any, that is taxable. Form 8889 must be attached to your Form 1040.

41.11 Limits on Deductible HSA Contributions

If you are an eligible individual *(41.10)*, you can set up an HSA with an insurance company, bank, or other financial institution that has been approved by the IRS for this purpose. HSA contributions are reported to the IRS on Form 5498-SA.

The full contribution limit for 2010 (*see* below) is available regardless of when during the year you became eligible *(41.10)* for an HSA, so long as you were eligible on December 1, 2010; you are treated as if you were enrolled in the December 1 plan for the entire year. Contributions can be made up until the due date for filing your tax return (without extensions). Thus, HSA contributions for 2010 can be made through April 15, 2011.

For 2010, the maximum deductible contribution limit for an individual with self-only HDHP coverage is $3,050. For an individual with family coverage, the maximum deductible contribution for 2010 is $6,150. If a married couple has family HDHP coverage and both spouses are eligible for an HSA, they can decide between themselves how to allocate HSA contributions.

The contribution limit is increased for an account owner who is at least age 55 by the end of the year and who has not enrolled in Medicare. The "catch-up" contribution limit is $1,000. Starting with the month that an individual enrolls in Medicare Part A or B (generally at age 65), no further contributions, including catch-up contributions, can be made to his or her HSA.

The $3,050 and $6,150 caps are subject to cost-of-living increases, but they will remain unchanged for 2011.

You may have more than one HSA, but the above maximum annual contribution limit applies to the aggregate contributions to all of the HSAs.

If you are an employee eligible to contribute and your employer contributes to an HSA on your behalf, employer contributions within the limit are excludable from your income *(3.2)*. If your employer's contribution is below the applicable limit, you may contribute to your HSA but the totals of all the contributions cannot exceed the applicable limit.

Contributions exceeding your applicable HSA limit are not deductible and are subject to a 6% excise tax. Contributions by an employer to an employee's HSA in excess of the limit are includible in the employee's income and subject to the excise tax. However, the excise tax can be avoided by a timely withdrawal of the excess contribution and any allocable income. The withdrawal deadline is generally the filing due date including extensions, or April 15, 2011, for an excess 2010 contribution. However, if you timely file without making the withdrawal, you may do so by October 15, 2011. On a timely withdrawal, the income is taxed in the year withdrawn but the excise tax does not apply and the distribution of the excess contribution is not taxed. *See* the instructions to Form 5329 for further details.

Use Form 8889 to report your HSA contributions and figure your deduction. You must report your HSA contributions for 2010 and apply the deduction limits on Form 8889, which must be attached to Form 1040. The deduction from Form 8889 is entered on Line 25 of Form 1040, where it is deductible above the line from gross income.

Caution

IRS Can Levy on HSAs

The IRS can levy on an HSA to recover taxed owed. If the HSA owner is under age 65, there is a 10% penalty (there is no exception from this penalty for an involuntary distribution such as an IRS levy). Starting in 2011, the penalty doubles to 20%.

41.12 Distributions From HSAs

Distributions from an HSA used exclusively to pay or reimburse qualified medical expenses of the account owner, his or her spouse, or dependents are not taxable. Distributions used for anything other than qualified medical expenses are taxable. Taxable distributions are also subject to a penalty unless the distribution is made after the account owner becomes disabled, reaches age 65, or dies.

Distributions need not be taken in the year in which the expense is incurred to be tax free; they can be taken in the following year or in any later year. This may be necessary if there are insufficient funds to cover the expense at the time it is incurred. For example, an HSA account holder who incurs a $1,500 medical expense on December 1, 2010, can wait until 2011 (or later) when the account balance exceeds $1,500. The distribution is tax free so long as records are kept to show that the distribution was used to reimburse qualified medical expenses that were not covered by insurance or otherwise reimbursed and not claimed in a prior year as an itemized deduction. The HSA must have been set up prior to the incurrence of the expense.

For tax-free distribution purposes, a "qualified medical expense" is generally a non-reimbursed payment for medical care that would otherwise be eligible for an itemized deduction *(17.2)*. Qualified medical expenses for 2010 also include over-the-counter medications; starting in 2011, over-the-counter medications do not qualify as tax-free distributions without a doctor's prescription. However, health-care premiums generally do not qualify for HSA purposes, but there are exceptions. An HSA can pay for premiums for long-term-care insurance, COBRA health-care continuation coverage, health coverage while an individual is receiving unemployment compensation, and for individuals over age 65, Medicare Part A, B, or D, Medicare HMO, and the employee share of premiums for employer-sponsored health insurance including retiree health insurance. HSA distributions used to pay or reimburse long-term-care premiums are tax free only to the extent of the age-based deductible limit for such premiums *(17.5)*. For example, if a person age 41 uses HSA funds to pay long-term-care premiums of $1,800 in 2010, only $620 (the deductible limit for those age 41 through 50 in 2010) is tax free. The balance is taxable and subject to a 10% penalty for withdrawal of funds prior to age 65.

A qualified medical expense may be for the care of the account owner, his or her spouse, or dependents, without regard to whether they are eligible to make HSA contributions. In the case of a married couple where both spouses have HSAs, one spouse may use a distribution from his or her HSA to pay or reimburse the qualified medical costs of the other spouse. However, both HSAs may not reimburse the same expense.

If an HSA account holder mistakenly takes a distribution such as to reimburse an expense he or she reasonably but mistakenly believes is a qualified medical expense, the funds can be repaid to the HSA in order to avoid tax on the withdrawn amount, assuming the plan accepts a return of mistaken distributions. The funds must be returned by April 15 of the year following the first year that the account holder knew or should have known of the mistake.

Inherited HSAs. If the beneficiary of an HSA is the surviving spouse of the deceased account owner, the surviving spouse becomes the owner of the account and will be subject to tax only on distributions that are not used for qualified medical expenses. If the beneficiary is not the surviving spouse, the account ceases to be an HSA as of the date of the owner's death and the date-of-death value of the HSA assets must be included in the beneficiary's income. The beneficiary (other than the decedent's estate) may reduce the taxable amount by any HSA payments for the decedent's medical expenses made within one year after death. A beneficiary is not subject to the penalty for taxable distributions.

Report HSA distributions on Form 8889. You must report an HSA distribution on Part II of Form 8889, which must be attached to Form 1040. A taxable distribution, if any, from Form 8889 is reported on Line 21 of Form 1040 ("Other income"). On the dotted line next to Line 21 enter "HSA" and the amount. If there is a taxable distribution and no exception to the penalty is available, the 10% penalty is entered on Form 8889 and reported on Line 60 of Form 1040 ("Total tax"). On the dotted line next to Line 60, enter "HSA" and the amount. The HSA custodian or trustee will report the distribution to the IRS on Form 1099-SA.

41.13 Archer MSAs

Archer MSAs (medical savings accounts) have largely been replaced by health savings accounts (HSAs) *(12.9)*. The law authorizing the establishment of new Archer MSAs has expired. However, taxpayers who set up Archer MSAs before 2008 can continue to fund them.

An Archer MSA can be rolled over to an HSA. Contributions may not be made to an Archer MSA or to an HSA after you become entitled to Medicare benefits.

For 2010, a high-deductible health plan for self-only coverage must have a deductible of at least $2,000 and no more than $3,000. For family coverage, the deductible must be at least $4,050 and no more than $6,050. The high-deductible plan must limit out-of-pocket costs (other than premiums) for 2010 to $4,050 for self-only coverage and $7,400 for family coverage. You generally may not have any other coverage in addition to the high-deductible plan, but separate policies are allowed for disability, vision or dental care, long-term care, accidental injuries, specific diseases or illnesses, fixed payments during hospitalization, workers' compensation liability, tort liability, and liabilities arising from the ownership or use of property.

Caution

Employer Contribution to Spouse's MSA

If you and your spouse are covered under a high-deductible health plan with family coverage, employer contributions to either of your Archer MSAs bar both of you from making Archer MSA contributions for that year. If you each have self-only coverage under a high-deductible health plan, employer contributions to one of your Archer MSAs do not prevent the other from making MSA contributions.

Deductible contribution limit. If you are self-employed, the maximum deductible contribution for 2010 is 65% of the annual policy deductible if you have self-only coverage under a high-deductible plan, and 75% of the annual policy deductible if you have family coverage. To deduct the maximum amount, you must have the policy for the entire year. Otherwise one-twelfth of the limit may be deducted for each full month of coverage. The deduction may not exceed your self-employment income from the business through which you have the high-deductible insurance.

If you are an employee of an MSA-participating employer and your employer makes any contributions to your Archer MSA, you are barred from making a deductible contribution; also *see* the Caution on employer contributions to a spouse's Archer MSA. Your employer's contribution to your Archer MSA is not taxable to you if it is within the 65%/75% limit discussed above *(3.2)*.

Report contributions to your Archer MSA on Form 8853, which must be attached to your Form 1040. The deductible contribution shown on Form 8853 is entered on Line 36 of Form 1040; write "MSA" next to the entry.

Planning Reminder

MSA Contribution Deadline

You have until April 15, 2011, to make a deductible contribution to an Archer MSA for 2010.

Distributions from Archer MSA. You can take a distribution from your Archer MSA to pay for medical expenses that are not reimbursable under your high-deductible plan. For distribution rules, *see 41.12*.

41.14 Small Business Health Tax Credit

If you pay at least half of the premiums for your staff and you meet eligibility requirements, you can claim a tax credit of 35 percent of your payments on Form 8941. The credit is highly complex.

Caution

No Credit for Self-Employed Premiums

You cannot take a tax credit for premiums you pay to cover yourself, spouse, and dependent.

Eligibility. You must meet these three tests:

1. You have fewer than 25 full-time equivalent employees (FTEs) for the tax year. Add up the hours per year (but not more than 2,080 hours per employee) that employees (other than owners, relatives, and seasonal workers) work and divide by 2,080 to find the number of full-time equivalents.
2. The average annual wages of its employees for the year is less than $50,000 per FTE.
3. You must pay the premiums under a "qualifying arrangement."

Credit amount. A full credit applies if you have no more than 10 FTEs with average wages of $25,000 per FTE. The credit phases out for those with 10 to 25 FTEs and with wages of $25,000 to $50,000.

The credit is based on the lesser of actual payments or the average premium for the small group market in a state (2010 average premiums are listed in Rev. Rul. 2010-13).

Check the *e-Supplement at jklasser.com* for further details on the credit.

Chapter 42

Claiming Depreciation Deductions

There are several methods of claiming expense deductions for your purchases in 2010 of equipment, fixtures, autos, and trucks used in your business:

- First-year expensing (Section 179 deduction), which allows a deduction of up to $500,000 in 2010 (42.3) Bonus depreciation, which allows an additional first-year deduction to eligible property placed in service during 2010 *(42.21)*.
- Regular depreciation, which allows a prorated deduction over a period of years. Most business equipment is depreciable under MACRS (modified accelerated cost recovery system) over a six-year period. MACRS applies to new and used property. The objective of MACRS is to provide rapid depreciation and to eliminate disputes over useful life, salvage value, and depreciation methods. Useful life and depreciation methods are fixed by law; salvage value is treated as zero. If you do not want to use MACRS accelerated rates, you may elect the straight-line method.

Capital investments in buildings are depreciable using the straight-line method; residential buildings are depreciated over 27.5 years; nonresidential real property placed in service after May 12, 1993, is depreciated over 39 years *(42.13)*. Specific annual rates for each class of property are provided by IRS tables.

Land is not depreciable.

42.1 What Property May Be Depreciated?

Depreciation deductions may be claimed only for property used in your business or other income-producing activity. If the primary purpose of the property is to produce income but it fails to yield any income, the property may still be depreciated.

Depreciation may not be claimed on property held for personal purposes such as a personal residence or pleasure car. If property, such as a car, is used both for business and pleasure, only the business portion may be depreciated.

EXAMPLES

1. An anesthesiologist suspended his practice indefinitely because of malpractice premium rate increases. He continued to maintain his professional competence by taking courses and keeping up his equipment. The IRS ruled that he could not take depreciation on his equipment. Since he was no longer practicing, the depreciation did not relate to a current trade or business.
2. An electrician spent $1,325 on a trailer to carry his tools and protective clothing. Based on a useful life of three years less salvage value of $25, annual depreciation deductions came to $433. However, the IRS claimed that he could not claim depreciation during the months he was unemployed and the trailer was not used. The Tax Court disagreed. Depreciation is allowed as long as the asset is held for use in a trade or business, even though the asset is idle or its use is temporarily suspended due to business conditions.

Nondepreciable assets. Not all assets used in your business or for the production of income may be depreciable. Land is not depreciable, but the cost of landscaping business property may be depreciated if the landscaping is so closely associated with a building that it would have to be destroyed if the building were replaced. Qualifying trees and bushes are depreciable over 15 years.

Property held primarily for sale to customers or property includible in inventory is not depreciable, regardless of its useful life.

Amortization for business intangibles. The cost of goodwill, going concern value, and other intangibles including covenants not to compete, information bases, customer lists, franchises, licenses, and trademarks is amortizable over a 15-year period.

The amortization rule generally applies to property acquired after August 10, 1993 *(42.18)*.

Residences. For depreciation of rented residences, *see* 9.5. For depreciation of a home office, *see* *40.13*. For depreciation of a sublet cooperative apartment or one used in business, *see* *40.17*.

Farm property. Farmland is not depreciable; farm machinery and buildings are. Livestock acquired for work, breeding, or dairy purposes and not included in inventory may also be depreciated. For a detailed explanation of the highly technical rules for depreciating farm property and livestock, *see* IRS Publication 225, Farmer's Tax Guide.

Dispute over importance of useful life. According to the Tax Court, under ACRS (1981–86) and current MACRS law, useful life is irrelevant for claiming depreciation if you can show that an asset is subject to exhaustion, wear and tear, or obsolescence. Thus, in the case of antique musical instruments played by professional musicians, depreciation is allowable because of wear and tear, even though the instruments have an indeterminable useful life. Two federal appeals courts have agreed, allowing professional violinists to deduct ACRS depreciation for their instruments.

In a case involving exotic cars that were not used for transportation but for exhibition, MACRS depreciation was allowed because the owner showed that they were subject to obsolescence. The autos were purchased solely for exhibition. The three state-of-the-art autos were a 1987 Lotus Pantera costing $63,000, a Lotus Espirit costing $48,000, and a Ferrari Testarossa costing $290,453. Over a four-year period, the owner deducted depreciation of over $298,000 while reporting gross income from exhibition fees of $96,630. The IRS disallowed the depreciation because the cars had no determinable useful life. The Tax Court allowed the depreciation because such cars are subject to obsolescence in the car-show business when new models appear with newer designs and high-tech features. One witness testified this could occur in some cases within a year.

The Tax Court warned that such exotic cars should not be confused with museum pieces. If they had been museum pieces, such as antique cars, no depreciation would have been allowed. In the

Caution

Corrections to Prior Year Returns

If you did not deduct the correct amount of depreciation for a prior year, you may be able to make a correction by filing an amended return. However, if you did not deduct the correct amount of depreciation for two or more consecutive years, you must request an accounting method change; *see* IRS Publication 946 for details. Adjustments to basis for unclaimed depreciation taken in prior years is discussed in *5.20*.

case of art objects and antiques used as business assets, the useful life requirement remains relevant because such assets are not subject to exhaustion, wear or tear, or obsolescence.

The IRS may continue to dispute and litigate cases in which depreciation is claimed on assets with indeterminable useful lives. For example, in a private ruling, the IRS did not allow a developer to depreciate street improvements that had been turned over to a city. The improvements were an intangible asset that improved the developer's access to its real estate projects, but this asset had an unlimited life. There was no determinable useful life because the city had agreed to maintain and replace the improvements as necessary, and there was no evidence that the city would ever assess the developer for replacement costs.

Basis for depreciation. Generally, the basis of the property on which you figure depreciation is its adjusted basis, which usually is its cost. To determine basis when property is acquired other than by purchase, *see 5.16* through *5.20*.

If you convert property from personal to business use, the basis for depreciation purposes is the lower of its adjusted basis or its fair market value at the time of the conversion.

EXAMPLE

In 2008, you buy a computer for $2,400 for personal use. In 2010, when it is worth $800, you convert the computer to business use. The basis for depreciation is $800, the fair market value of the computer, which is lower than its adjusted basis of $2,400.

42.2 Claiming Depreciation on Your Tax Return

If you report business or professional self-employed income, use Form 4562 for assets placed in service during 2010 and enter the total deduction on Line 13, Schedule C. For claiming depreciation on "listed property" such as cars, computers, and cellular phones, you use Form 4562, regardless of the year placed in service. *See* the explanation of listed propery in this chapter *(42.10)*. If your only depreciation deduction is for pre-2010 assets, none of which is listed property, you do not need to use Form 4562; figure the deduction on your own worksheet, and enter it on Line 13, Schedule C.

If you are an employee claiming auto expenses, you must use Form 2106 to claim depreciation on an automobile used for business purposes.

If you claim a home office deduction, you must use Form 8829 to claim depreciation on the portion of your home used for business.

If you report rental income on Schedule E, you must use Form 4562 for claiming depreciation on buildings placed in service in 2010. For buildings placed in service before 2010, enter the depreciation deduction directly on Schedule E. If you have a rental loss on Schedule E, your deduction for depreciation and other expenses may have to be included on Form 8582 to figure net passive activity income or loss; *see Chapter 10*.

42.3 First-Year Expensing Deduction

The Small Business Jobs Act of 2010 (signed into law on September 27, 2010) increased the limit on first-year expensing for 2010 to $500,000 (from $250,000). The $500,000 limit will also apply for 2011. Up to $250,000 of the $500,000 limit may be applied to the combined cost of qualified leasehold improvement *(42.15)* property, qualified restaurant property, and qualified retail improvement property.

The $500,000 limit is phased out if the cost of qualifying property placed in service during the year exceeds $2 million.

Law Alert

Doubling of Expensing Limit for 2010 and 2011

The Small Business Jobs Act of 2010 (signed into law on September 27, 2010) increased the limit on first-year expensing for 2010 to $500,000 from $250,000. The $500,000 limit will also apply for 2011. In both years, up to $250,000 of the cost of qualified leasehold, restaurant and retail improvements is eligible for first-year expensing. The $500,000 limit will be phased out if the cost of qualifying property placed in service during the year exceeds $2 million.

Costs eligible for expensing. You may elect first-year expensing for tangible personal property bought for business use, such as machinery, equipment, or a car, truck or computer, provided the property is acquired from a non-related party. Expensing is not allowed for property held for investment.

For 2010 and 2011, expensing may also be elected for up to $250,000 of the cost of qualified leasehold, restaurant and retail improvements. Other interior improvements to buildings, and air conditioning and heating units, do not qualify. Refrigerators and furnishings used in operating an apartment building also do not qualify.

To elect the expensing deduction for up to $500,000 of the cost of qualifying property for 2010, the qualifying property must have been purchased and placed in service in 2010. You may not elect first-year expensing for property purchased before 2010, even if 2010 is the first year you use it for business. For example, if you bought a computer for family use in 2009 and in 2010 you converted it to business use, expensing is not allowed on your 2010 return. For equipment placed in service in 2010 by a business in an "enterprise zone" the deduction may be as high as $535,000. For an automobile placed in service in 2010, the maximum expensing deduction is $11,060 and for certain SUVs the expensing limit is $25,000 *(43.4)*.

The portion of cost not eligible for first-year expensing may be recovered by depreciation under the regular MACRS rules *(42.4–42.5)*. The first-year expensing deduction is technically called the "Section 179 deduction."

Electing first-year expensing. You make the election simply by reporting on Form 4562 the assets for which the election applies. You are permitted to make an election or revoke an election (or change the amount of an election or the assets for which the election applies) on a timely filed amended return. You do not need IRS consent. A revocation, once made, is irrevocable.

Partial business use. If you use the equipment for both business and personal use, business use must exceed 50% in the year the equipment is first placed into service to claim a first-year expensing deduction. The expensing deduction may be claimed for the cost allocated to business use up to the $500,000 limit; the 2010 limit is $11,060 for cars placed in service during 2010 *(43.4)*.

To elect first-year expensing for "listed property" such as a computer or car *(42.10)*, business use in the first year you use it must exceed 50%. If it does, you show the amount eligible for expensing in the section for "Listed Property" on Form 4562 and then transfer the amount to the part of Form 4562 where the expensing election is claimed.

Figuring the deduction. The maximum expensing deduction in 2010 is $500,000 of the cost of qualifying property and $11,060 for a car *(43.4)*. For business use of less than 100% (but more than 50%), the expensing deduction is limited to the business portion of the cost. As discussed below, the $500,000 limit may have to be reduced because your taxable income is lower than $500,000, eligible purchases exceed $2 million, or you are married filing separately.

If you qualify for the full $500,000 limit, you do not have to claim the entire amount. If in 2010 you place in service more than one item of property, you may allocate the $500,000 deduction between the items. If you placed in service only one item of qualifying property that cost less than $500,000, your deduction is limited to that cost.

If you acquire property in a trade-in, the cost eligible for expensing is limited to the cash you paid. You may not include the adjusted basis of the property traded in, although your basis for the new property includes that amount.

Effect on regular depreciation. If the cost basis of the property exceeds the first-year expensing limit, you compute depreciation on the cost of the property less the amount of the first-year deduction.

EXAMPLE

In 2010, you placed in service a $165,000 semi-truck and $360,000 of machinery. You elect to deduct as a first-year expense $165,000 for the truck and $335,000 of the machinery, a total of $500,000, the maximum first-year deduction. The $165,000 deduction has completely recovered the cost of the truck. The cost of the machinery is reduced by $335,000, giving a depreciable basis of $25,000 ($360,000 – $335,000).

Limit reduced if taxable income is lower. Your expensing deduction may not exceed net income from all your active businesses; *see* the Caution on this page.

Limit reduced if qualifying purchases exceed threshold. If the total cost of qualifying property placed in service during 2010 is over $2 million, the $500,000 expensing limit is reduced dollar for dollar by the cost of qualifying property exceeding $2 million. For example, if you place in service machinery costing $2,100,000, the $500,000 limit is reduced by $100,000. The reduced limit of $400,000 is shown on Form 4562 on the line labeled "Dollar limitation for tax year." If the total cost is $2,500,000 or more, no first-year expensing deduction is allowed.

Limit reduced if married filing separately. If you and your spouse file separate returns, the 2010 expensing limit for both of you is $500,000. Unless you agree to a different allocation, you are each allowed only one-half of the limit or $250,000. The $2 million cost threshold also

Law Alert

Leasehold, Restaurant and Retail Improvements

Qualified leasehold improvements, qualified restaurant property, and qualified retail improvements *(42.15)* placed in service before January 1, 2010, were treated as 15-year MACRS property. However, for 2010 and 2011, such improvements qualify for first-year expensing, but only up to a cost limit of $250,000.

Caution

Losses and Low Income May Limit Deduction

The expensing deduction may not exceed the net taxable income from all businesses that you actively conduct. Net income from active businesses is figured without regard to expensing, the deduction for 50% of self-employment liability, or any net operating loss carryback or carryforward. You may include wage or salary income as active business income and if you are married filing jointly, also include your spouse's net taxable income.

If you have an overall net loss from all actively conducted businesses, you may not claim an expensing deduction for 2010. If net income is less than the cost of qualifying assets, expensing is limited to the income. However, the cost over the income limit is carried forward to 2011 on Form 4562 provided you complete the expensing section of Form 4562 for 2010. You do not get a carryover unless the deduction is claimed on the return for the first year the property is placed in service. An expensing deduction cannot be used to create or increase a net operating loss.

Filing Instruction

Higher Expensing Limits

The expensing limit and the reduction threshold are increased for property in an enterprise zone or renewal community business and property in certain federal disaster areas; *see* the Form 4562 instructions.

applies to both of you as a unit. For example, if you place in service qualifying property costing $900,000 and your spouse places $1,200,000 of property in service, the total cost of $2,100,000 reduces the $500,000 limit by $100,000 to $400,000. The reduced limit for each of you on separate returns is $200,000.

Partners and S corporation stockholders. For property bought by a partnership or an S corporation, the $250,000 limit and taxable income limit applies to the business, as well as the owners as individual taxpayers. The partnership or S corporation determines its expensing deduction subject to the limits and allocates the deduction, if any, among the partners or shareholders. The allocated deduction may not exceed the net taxable income of the partnership or S corporation from actively conducted businesses.

An individual partner's expensing deduction may not exceed $500,000, regardless of how many partnership interests he or she has. However, the partner must reduce the basis of each partnership interest by the full allocable share of each partnership's expensing deduction, even if that amount is not deductible because of the $500,000 limit.

Disqualified acquisitions from related parties. Property does not qualify for the expense election if:

1. It is acquired from a spouse, ancestor, or lineal descendant, or from non–family-related parties subject to the loss disallowance rule *(5.6)*. For purposes of the expensing election, a corporation is controlled by you and thus subject to the loss disallowance rule *(5.6)* if 50% or more of the stock is owned by you, your spouse, your ancestors, or your descendants.
2. The property is acquired by a member of the same controlled group (using a 50% control test).
3. The basis of the property is determined in whole or in part (a) by reference to the adjusted basis of the property of the person from whom you acquired it or (b) under the stepped-up basis rules for inherited property.

Recapture of expensing deduction. Recapture of the first-year expensing deduction may occur on a disposition of the asset or if business use falls to 50% or less. If business use falls to 50% or less after the year the property is placed in service but before the end of the depreciable recovery period *(42.4, 42.10)*, you must "recapture" the benefit from the first-year expensing deduction. The amount recaptured is the excess of the expensing deduction over the amount of depreciation that would have been claimed (through the year of recapture) without expensing *(42.10)*. Recaptured amounts are reported as ordinary income on Form 4797.

When you sell or dispose of the property, the first-year expensing deduction is treated as depreciation for purposes of the recapture rules *(44.3)* that treat gain as ordinary income to the extent of depreciation claimed.

Planning Reminder

Year-End Purchases

Equipment placed in service on the last day of the 2010 taxable year may qualify for the entire first-year expensing limit. You do not have to prorate the limit for the amount of time you held the property.

42.4 MACRS Recovery Periods

Depreciable assets other than buildings fall within a three-, five-, seven-, 10-, 15-, or 20-year recovery period under the general depreciation system (GDS).

Straight-line recovery for buildings is claimed over a period of 27.5 years for residential rental property or 39 years for nonresidential real property *(42.13)*.

Note: The actual write-off period of depreciation for an asset is one year longer than the class life because of the convention rules *(42.5–42.7)*.

Three-year property. This class includes property with a class life of four years or less, other than cars and light-duty trucks, which are in the five-year class.

This class includes: special handling devices for the manufacture of food and beverages; special tools and devices for the manufacture of rubber products; special tools for the manufacture of finished plastic products, fabricated metal products, or motor vehicles; and breeding hogs. By law, racehorses of any age and other horses more than 12 years old when placed in service are also in the three-year class.

Five-year property. This class includes property with a class life of more than four years and less than 10 years such as computers *(42.10)*, typewriters, copiers, duplicating equipment, heavy general-purpose trucks, trailers, cargo containers, and trailer-mounted containers. Also included by law in the five-year class are cars, light-duty trucks (actual unloaded weight less than 13,000 pounds), taxis, buses, computer-based telephone central office switching equipment, computer-related peripheral equipment, semiconductor manufacturing equipment, and property used in

Planning Reminder

Recovery Periods

The depreciation recovery periods for different types of assets are generally fixed by law according to the rules on this page.

research and experimentation. These leasehold improvements eligible for a five-year recovery period must be depreciated using the straight-line method.

Seven-year property. This class includes any property with a class life of 10 years or more but less than 16 years. This is also a catch-all category for assets with no class life that have not been assigned by law to another class. Included in the seven-year class are: office furniture and fixtures, such as desks, safes, and files; cellular phones; fax machines; refrigerators; dishwashers; and machines used to produce jewelry, musical instruments, toys, and sporting goods.

Ten-year property. This includes property with a class life of 16 years or more and less than 20 years, such as vessels, barges, tugs, and water transportation equipment, and assets used in petroleum refining or in the manufacture of tobacco products and certain food products. The 10-year class also includes single-purpose agricultural and horticultural structures, and trees or vines bearing fruit or nuts.

Fifteen-year property. This includes land improvements such as fences, sidewalks, docks, shrubbery, roads, and bridges. It also includes other property with a class life of 20 years or more but less than 25 years, such as municipal sewage plants and telephone distribution plants. Gas station convenience stores are in the 15-year class if the property is no more than 1,400 square feet, or at least 50% of the floor space is devoted to selling petroleum products, or at least 50% of revenues are from petroleum sales. The owner of the gas station property does not have to be the operator of businesses on the property.

Twenty-year property. This class includes property with a class life of 25 years or more, such as farm buildings and municipal sewers, except that residential and nonresidential real estate is excluded *(42.13)*.

42.5 MACRS Rates

The MACRS rate under the general depreciation system depends on the recovery period *(42.4)* for the property and whether the half-year or mid-quarter convention applies. The 200% declining balance rate applies to three-year property, five-year property, and seven-year property. *See 42.8* for the 150% declining balance rate election. These rates are adjusted for the convention rules explained below. When the 200% declining balance rate provides a lower annual deduction than the straight-line rate, the 200% declining balance rate is replaced by the straight-line rate. The rates in the tables at the end of this section incorporate the applicable convention and the change from the 200% declining balance rate to a straight-line recovery. MACRS straight-line rates are discussed later in this Chapter *(42.9)*.

Conventions. Under the half-year convention, all property acquired during the year, regardless of when acquired during the year, is treated as acquired in the middle of the year. As a result, only one-half of the full first-year depreciation is deductible and in the year after the last class life year, the balance of the depreciation is written off. Furthermore, in the year property is sold, only half of the full depreciation for that year is deductible *(42.6)*.

The half-year convention applies unless the total cost bases of depreciable assets placed in service during the last three months of the taxable year exceed 40% of the total bases of all property placed in service during the entire year. If this 40% test applies, you must use a mid-quarter convention to figure your annual depreciation deduction *(42.7)*.

Buildings are depreciated using a mid-month convention *(42.13)*.

Depreciation tables. The following table provides year-by-year rates for property in the three, five-, and seven-year classes. The rates incorporate the adjustment for the half-year or mid-quarter convention and the switch from the 200% declining balance rate to the straight-line method. Use the rate shown in the table under the convention for your asset. The rate is applied to original basis, minus any first-year expensing deduction *(42.3)* and bonus depreciation you claimed for eligible property placed in service before 2010. After applying the rate from the table to the basis, you claim the deduction on Form 4562, Part III, Section B, labeled "General Depreciation System" (GDS).

You use the tables for the entire recovery period unless you claim a deductible casualty loss that reduces your basis in the property. For the year of the casualty loss and later years, depreciation must be based on the adjusted basis of the property at the end of the year. The tables may no longer be used; *see* IRS Publication 946 for further details.

Table 42-1 MACRS Depreciation Rates

Year	Half-Year Convention	Mid-Quarter Convention: 1st (Quarter)	2nd (Quarter)	3rd (Quarter)	4th (Quarter)
			3-Year Property		
1	33.33%	58.33%	41.67%	25.00%	8.33%
2	44.45	27.78	38.89	50.00	61.11
3	14.81	12.35	14.14	16.67	20.37
4	7.41	1.54	5.30	8.33	10.19
			5-Year Property		
1	20.00%	35.00%	25.00%	15.00%	5.00%
2	32.00	26.00	30.00	34.00	38.00
3	19.20	15.60	18.00	20.40	22.80
4	11.52	11.01	11.37	12.24	13.68
5	11.52	11.01	11.37	11.30	10.94
6	5.76	1.38	4.26	7.06	9.58
			7-Year Property		
1	14.29%	25.00%	17.85%	10.71%	3.57%
2	24.49	21.43	23.47	25.51	27.55
3	17.49	15.31	16.76	18.22	19.68
4	12.49	10.93	11.97	13.02	14.06
5	8.93	8.75	8.87	9.30	10.04
6	8.92	8.74	8.87	8.85	8.73
7	8.93	8.75	8.87	8.86	8.73
8	4.46	1.09	3.33	5.53	7.64

EXAMPLE

During June 2010, you place in business service a used machine costing $20,000. It is your only acquisition in 2010. (Assume you do not elect to expense the cost.) The machine is five-year property and is subject to the half-year convention. The depreciation rate for the first year is 20% (*see* the table above for five-year property). Your 2010 depreciation deduction is $4,000 ($20,000 × 20%). If you hold the machine for the entire six-year recovery period, your total deduction for all years will equal your $20,000 cost.

Summary of Deductions

Year	*Deduction*
1 (2010)	$4,000
2 (2011)	6,400
3 (2012)	3,840
4 (2013)	2,304
5 (2014)	2,304
6 (2015)	1,152
Total	$20,000

42.6 Half-Year Convention for MACRS

The half-year convention treats all business equipment placed in service during a tax year as placed in service in the midpoint of that tax year. The same rule applies in the year in which the property is disposed of. The effect of this rule is as follows: A half-year of depreciation is allowed in the first year property is placed in service, regardless of when the property is placed in service during the tax year. For each of the remaining years of the recovery period, a full year of depreciation is claimed. If you hold the property for the entire recovery period, a half-year of depreciation is claimed for the year following the end of the recovery period. If you dispose of the property before the end of the recovery period, a half-year of depreciation is allowable for the year of disposition.

See the Table of MACRS Depreciation Rates *(42.5)* for year-by-year rates under the half-year convention. Apply the rate from the table to the original basis, minus any first-year expensing *(42.3)* deduction and bonus depreciation claimed. The Example in *42.5* shows the year-by-year deduction computation for five-year property under the half-year convention.

If you dispose of property before the end of its recovery period *(42.5)*, your deduction for the year of disposition is one-half of the deduction that would be allowed for the full year using the rate shown in the table. For example, if you sell the machine in the Example in *42.5* in year three, the deduction is $1,920 (½ of $3,840).

Planning Reminder

Half-Year Convention

The half-year convention applies unless the total cost basis of depreciable assets placed in service during the last three months of the year exceeds 40% of the total basis of all property placed in service during the year.

Under the half-year convention, all assets placed in service during the year are treated as placed in service at the midpoint of the year.

42.7 Last Quarter Placements—Mid-Quarter Convention

A mid-quarter convention generally applies if the total cost basis of business equipment placed in service during the last three months of the tax year exceeds 40% of the total basis of all the property placed in service during the year. In applying the 40% rule, you do not count residential rental property, nonresidential realty, and assets that were placed in service and disposed of during the same year.

Under the mid-quarter convention, the first-year depreciation allowance for all property (other than nonresidential real property and residential rental property) placed in service during the year is based on the number of quarters that the asset was in service. Property placed in service at any time during a quarter is treated as having been placed in service in the middle of the quarter. The mid-quarter convention also applies to sales and disposals of property. The disposal is treated as occurring in the midpoint of the quarter.

EXAMPLE

During August 2010, you place in service office furniture costing $1,000, and in October, a computer costing $5,000. You are on the calendar year. The total basis of all property placed in service in 2010 is $6,000. As the $5,000 basis of the computer placed in service in the last quarter exceeds 40% of the total basis of all property placed in service during 2010, you must use the mid-quarter convention for the furniture and the computer. The office furniture, which is seven-year property, and the computer, which is five-year property, are depreciated using MACRS and a mid-quarter convention.

You first multiply the $1,000 basis of the furniture by 10.71%—the seven-year property mid-quarter convention rate for the third quarter *(see Table 42-1)*. The depreciation deduction is $107. You then multiply the $5,000 basis of the computer by 5%—the five-year property mid-quarter convention rate for the fourth quarter *(see Table 42-1)*. The deduction is $250. Total depreciation is $357.

If you dispose of property before the end of its recovery period *(42.5)*, your deduction for the year is figured by multiplying a full year of depreciation by the percentage listed in the following chart for the quarter in which you disposed of the property.

Quarter	*Percentage*
First	12.5%
Second	37.5%
Third	62.5%
Fourth	87.5%

EXAMPLE

On November 1, 2007, you placed in service a machine costing $10,000 with a five-year recovery period. You used the mid-quarter convention because it was the only item placed in service during the year. In May 2010, you sell the machine.

To determine depreciation for 2010, first figure the deduction for the full year *(see Table 42-1)*. This is $1,368 (13.68% (rate for fourth year, fourth quarter) of $10,000). Since May, the month of disposition, is in the second quarter of the year, you multiply $1,368 by 37.5% to figure your depreciation deduction for 2010 of $513.

42.8 150% Rate Election

Instead of using the 200% declining balance rate for property in the three-, five-, seven-, and 10-year classes, you may elect a 150% declining balance rate. You may prefer the 150% rate when you are subject to the alternative minimum tax (AMT). For AMT purposes, you must use the 150% rate and adjust your taxable income if the 200% rate was used for regular tax purposes *(23.2)*. If for regular tax purposes you elect to apply the 150% rate, use the same recovery period *(42.4)* you would have used if you had claimed the 200% declining balance rate. Thus, the recovery period is five years for cars and computers and seven years for office furniture and fixtures. If the half-year convention applies, the first-year rate for the five-year class is 15%, and 10.71% for the seven-year class; *see* the table below. Apply the rate from the table to your original basis, minus any first-year expensing deduction and bonus depreciation claimed. If you are subject to the mid-quarter convention, *see* IRS Publication 946 for the tables showing mid-quarter convention rates.

The election to use the 150% rate must be made for all property within a given class placed in service in the same year. The election is irrevocable.

For property placed in service before 1999, the 150% rate is applied over the ADS *(42.9)* recovery periods, which in some cases are different from the GDS recovery periods.

Table 42-2 Half-Year Convention—150% Rate

	Recovery Period	
Year—	*5-Year—*	*7-Year—*
1	15.00%	10.71%
2	25.50	19.13
3	17.85	15.03
4	16.66	12.25
5	16.66	12.25
6	8.33	12.25
7		12.25
8		6.13

Filing Tip

Should You Elect Straight-Line Recovery?

Accelerated rates of MACRS merely give you an opportunity to advance the time of taking your deduction. This may be a decided advantage where the higher deductions in the first few years will provide you with cash for working capital or for investments in other income-producing sources. That is, by accelerating the deductions, you defer the payment of taxes that would be due if you claimed smaller depreciation deductions, using more conservative straight-line rates. The tax deferral lasts until the rapid method provides lower depreciation deductions than would the more conservative method. You are generally more likely to benefit from accelerated MACRS in an ongoing business.

If you are starting a new business in which you expect losses or low income at the start, accelerated MACRS may waste depreciation deductions that could be used in later years when your income increases. Therefore, before deciding to use accelerated MACRS rates, consider your income prospects.

42.9 Straight-Line Depreciation

You may not want an accelerated rate and may prefer to write off depreciation at an even pace. There are two straight-line methods. You may make an irrevocable election to use the straight-line method over the regular MACRS recovery period *(42.4)* under the general depreciation system (GDS). Alternatively, you may elect straight-line recovery over the designated recovery period for the class life under the alternative depreciation system (ADS). For some assets, such as cars, the GDS and ADS recovery periods are the same (five years for a car). In most cases, the ADS recovery period is longer than the GDS recovery period. For example, the recovery period for office furniture and fixtures is seven years under GDS and 10 years under ADS.

Half-year and quarter-year conventions apply to both straight-line methods *(42.6, 42.7)* . A mid-month convention applies under the straight-line rule for buildings *(42.13)*.

Straight-line over regular recovery period (GDS). You make this election on Form 4562, Part III, Section B, labeled "General Depreciation System" (GDS). To elect this method for one asset, you must also use it for all other assets in the same class that are placed in service during the year. The straight-line election is irrevocable.

Straight-line under the alternative depreciation system (ADS). Under the alternative depreciation system (ADS), the straight-line recovery period is generally the same as the "class life" of the asset as determined by the IRS; the ADS recovery periods are shown in IRS Publication 946. The ADS recovery period for cars, light trucks, and computers is five years, the same as under the GDS. For business office furniture and fixtures, the ADS straight-line recovery period is 10 years. The ADS recovery period for personal property with no class life is 12 years. For nonresidential real and residential rental property, you may elect ADS straight-line recovery over 40 years. *See* IRS Publication 946 for other ADS class lives.

Except for real estate, the ADS election applies to all property within the same class placed in service during the taxable year. For real estate, the election to use the alternative depreciation method may be made on a property-by-property basis. The election is irrevocable. The deduction is claimed on Form 4562, Part III, Section C, labeled "Alternative Depreciation System" (ADS).

Straight-line rate table. The table below shows straight-line rates for five-year, seven-year, and 10-year property under the half-year convention. As discussed earlier, the recovery period depends on whether the GDS or ADS straight-line method is used. If you are subject to the mid-quarter convention *(42.7)*, *see* IRS Publication 946 for tables showing the applicable rates.

Table 42-3 Half-Year Convention—Straight-Line Rate

	Recovery Period		
Year—	*5-Year—*	*7-Year—*	*10-Year—*
1	10.00%	7.14%	5.00%
2	20.00	14.29	10.00
3	20.00	14.29	10.00
4	20.00	14.28	10.00
5	20.00	14.29	10.00
6	10.00	14.28	10.00
7		14.29	10.00
8		7.14	10.00
9			10.00
10			10.00
11			5.00

AMT depreciation. There is no AMT adjustment for depreciation if for regular tax purposes straight-line depreciation is claimed on tangible personal property placed in service after 1998. Similarly, for real estate placed in service after 1998, the straight-line depreciation deduction claimed for regular tax purposes does not have to be refigured for AMT. If for regular tax purposes straight-line depreciation is claimed for tangible personal property placed in service before 1999, then for AMT purposes straight-line depreciation is figured over the property's class life under the alternative depreciation system (ADS). For real property placed in service before 1999, regular tax straight-line depreciation is refigured for AMT purposes using the straight-line method over 40 years.

Mandatory straight-line depreciation. You are required to use the alternative depreciation system for automobiles *(43.3)* and certain computers *(42.10)* used 50% or less for business.

Alternative MACRS depreciation must also be used for:

- Figuring earnings and profits;
- Tangible property which, during the taxable year, is used predominantly outside the United States;
- Tax-exempt use property;
- Tax-exempt bond financed property; *and*
- Imported property covered by an executive order.

42.10 Computers and Other Listed Property

"Listed property" is a term applied to certain equipment that may be used for personal and business purposes. For such property, the law allows first-year expensing *(42.3)* or accelerated MACRS *(42.5)* deductions only if business use exceeds 50%. For business use of 50% or less, you must use ADS straight-line depreciation *(42.9)*. Deductions for listed property are claimed on Part V of Form 4562. If the more-than-50%-business-use test is met in the first year and first-year expensing or accelerated MACRS is claimed, but business use of listed property falls to 50% or less during the ADS straight-line recovery period *(42.9)*, you must "recapture" first-year expensing and accelerated MACRS deductions; *see* Example 2 below.

Law Alert

Delisting of Cell Phones

The Small Business Jobs Act of 2010 (9/27/10) removes cell phones from the category of "listed property" effective for 2010 and later years.

What is "listed property"? Listed property includes passenger autos and other transportation vehicles *(43.4)*, computers and peripheral equipment, boats, airplanes, and any photographic, sound, or video recording equipment that could be used for entertainment or recreational purposes. However, exceptions remove some items from the listed property category for many businesses. Listed property does not include (1) any computer or peripheral equipment that you own or lease that is used exclusively at a regular business establishment, and (2) photographic, phonographic, communications, or video equipment used exclusively and regularly in your business or regular business establishment. A home office that meets certain requirements *(40.12)* is considered a regular business establishment.

Cell phones were treated as listed property under prior law but starting in 2010 they are no longer subject to the listed property restrictions.

Caution

Depreciation Restrictions for a Computer

If you use a home computer for business but not in a qualified home office *(40.12)*, it must be used more than 50% of the time for business to claim a first-year expensing deduction. If used 50% or less for business, straight-line depreciation over the ADS recovery period is required.

EXAMPLES

1. You buy a computer in 2010 and use it exclusively in your regular business office. The computer is not listed property. You may claim either first-year expensing *(42.3)* or accelerated MACRS depreciation *(42.5)* for your investment on Form 4562. If business use falls to 50% or less after 2010, the only deduction subject to recapture is the first-year deduction *(42.3)*.
2. You have no regular business establishment and use a computer bought in 2010 as a freelance consultant. The computer is listed property and you may claim MACRS and/or first-year expensing only if you use the computer more than 50% for business. If business use does not exceed 50%, you may only claim ADS straight-line depreciation *(42.9)*. Your deductions are claimed in the section for "Listed Property" on Form 4562.

Deductions subject to recapture. If business use exceeds 50% in the first year but in a later year drops to 50% or less, MACRS and any first-year expensing deduction are subject to "recapture." In the year in which business use drops to 50% or less, you recapture the excess of (1) the MACRS and first-year expensing deductions claimed in prior years over (2) the deductions that would have been allowed using ADS straight-line depreciation *(42.9)*. For the rest of the recovery period, you continue to use the alternative straight-line rate.

Recapture is figured on Form 4797. The recapture computation follows the steps shown in *43.10* for recapture of excess depreciation on an automobile.

Planning Reminder

Computer Software

Software purchased "off the shelf" and used for business or investment purposes qualifies for first-year expensing in 2003–2010. If not expensed, it is depreciable over a three-year period provided it has a useful life exceeding one year. If the useful life does not exceed one year, the cost is immediately deductible. Also *see 42.19*.

Investor's use of a computer. For an investor who uses a home computer for managing an investment portfolio, the computer is treated as listed property. Unless the computer is also used for business, and the computer time spent on business work exceeds 50% of the total, only straight-line depreciation may be claimed; neither first-year expensing nor accelerated MACRS is allowed. Although the investment use is disregarded for purposes of the more-than-50%-business-use test, the investment use is combined with the business use for purposes of determining the percentage of depreciable cost. Depreciable investment use must relate to managing investments that produce taxable income. *See* the Examples below.

EXAMPLES

1. In 2010, Jane Adams buys a computer; she uses it 10% of the time for personal purposes, 50% of the time to manage her stock investments and 40% in a part-time research business. The more-than-50%-business-use test is not met for claiming first-year expensing or accelerated MACRS deductions. She must use ADS straight-line depreciation over five years *(42.9)*; her depreciable basis is 90% of cost.

2. Assume that Jane used the computer 60% of the time for business and 30% for investment. As business use exceeds 50%, she may claim first-year expensing *(42.3)*. If she instead claims accelerated MACRS, the MACRS rate is applied to 90% of her cost.

Leasing a computer or cellular phone. You may deduct the portion of your lease payments attributable to business use. However, if business use is 50% or less for any year, you must report as income an amount based on the fair market value of the unit, the percentage of business plus investment use, and percentages from two IRS tables shown in Publication 946.

42.11 Assets in Service Before 1987

Assets placed in service before 1987 were depreciated under a different recovery system called ACRS. Most of the assets have already been fully depreciated, although some assets, such as certain real estate placed in service before 1987, continue to be governed by these rules *(42.16)*.

42.12 Straight-Line Recovery for Assets in Service Before 1987

You may still be able to claim straight-line deductions for five-year ACRS property if a recovery period of 25 years was elected. For 10-year property, an election could have been made for straight-line depreciation over 25 or 35 years.

If you made the straight-line election, the straight-line rate to be used on your 2010 return is as follows:

Recovery Period—	*Rate—*
25 years	4.000%
35 years	2.857%

Because of the half-year convention, only 50% of the above percentages was allowed in the year the property was placed in service. If the property is held for the entire elected recovery period, another half-year of depreciation is allowed for the year following the end of the recovery period. If property is disposed of prior to the end of the recovery period, no cost recovery is allowable in the year of disposition. *See* IRS Publication 534 for further details.

42.13 MACRS for Real Estate Placed in Service After 1986

The recovery period for residential rental property placed in service after December 31, 1986, is 27.5 years. The recovery period for nonresidential real property is either 39 years or 31.5 years, depending on when the property was placed in service.

The method of recovery for nonresidential or residential property is the straight-line method using a mid-month convention. *See* the next page for rate tables for each class of property.

For nonresidential real property placed in service after December 31, 1986, but before May 13, 1993, the depreciation recovery period is 31.5 years.

For nonresidential real property placed in service after May 12, 1993, the recovery period is 39 years. Under a transition rule, the 31.5-year recovery period rather than the 39-year recovery period applies to a building placed in service before 1994 if before May 13, 1993, you had entered into a binding, written contract to buy or build it, or if, before that date, you had begun construction. The transition rule also applies if you obtained the contract or property from someone else who satisfied the pre–May 13, 1993, contract or construction requirement, provided he or she never put the building in service and you did so before 1994.

Residential rental property subject to the 27.5 year recovery period is defined as a rental building or structure for which 80% or more of the gross rental income for the tax year is rental income from dwelling units. If you occupy any part of the building, the gross rental income includes the fair rental value of the part you occupy.

A dwelling unit is a house or an apartment used to provide living accommodations in a building or structure, but not a unit in a hotel, motel, inn, or other establishment where more than one-half of the units are used on a transient basis.

Filing Tip

Additions and Improvements

The MACRS class for an addition or improvement is generally determined by the MACRS class of the property to which the addition or improvement is made. For example, if you put an addition on a rental home that you are depreciating over 27.5 years, the addition is depreciated as 27.5-year residential rental property. The period for figuring depreciation begins on the date that the addition or improvement is placed in service, or, if later, the date that the property to which the addition or improvement was made is placed in service.

Mid-month convention. Under a mid-month convention, all residential rental property and nonresidential real property placed in service or disposed of during any month is treated as placed in service or disposed of at the midpoint of that month. You may determine the first-year deduction for your property by applying the percentage from *Table 42-4* to the original depreciable basis. In later years, use the same column of the table to figure your deduction. If the property is disposed of before the end of the recovery period, the deduction for the year of disposition is figured by prorating the full-year deduction for the months the property was in service, treating the month of dispostion as one-half of a month of use.

EXAMPLES

1. In February 2010, you buy an apartment building for $100,000 and place it in service. You use the calendar year. *Table 42-4* below gives a first-year depreciation rate of 3.182% for 27.5-year residential rental property placed in service during February. Applying this rate, you get a deduction of $3,182.

   For 2011, the rate will be 3.636%, for a deduction of $3,636.

2. Assume that you sell the apartment building in Example 1 on March 7, 2012. A full year of depreciation for 2012 is $3,636 (3.636% × $100,000). You are treated as using the property for *2.5* months in 2012, so your deduction is $757.50 ($3,636 ÷ 12 × 2.5).

Additions or improvements to property. The depreciation deduction for any additions to, or improvement of, any property is figured in the same way as the deduction for the property would be figured if the property had been placed in service at the same time as the addition or improvement.

Table 42-4 MACRS Real Estate Depreciation

Residential Rental Property (27.5 years; *see* 42.13)

Use the column for the month of taxable year placed in service.

Month	*1*	*2*	*3*	*4*	*5*	*6*	*7*	*8*	*9*	*10*	*11*	*12*
Year												
1	3.485%	3.182%	2.879%	2.576%	2.273%	1.970%	1.667%	1.364%	1.061%	0.758%	0.455%	0.152%
2–9	3.636	3.636	3.636	3.636	3.636	3.636	3.636	3.636	3.636	3.636	3.636	3.636
10	3.637	3.637	3.637	3.637	3.637	3.637	3.636	3.636	3.636	3.636	3.636	3.636
11	3.636	3.636	3.636	3.636	3.636	3.636	3.637	3.637	3.637	3.637	3.637	3.637
12	3.637	3.637	3.637	3.637	3.637	3.637	3.636	3.636	3.636	3.636	3.636	3.636
13	3.636	3.636	3.636	3.636	3.636	3.636	3.637	3.637	3.637	3.637	3.637	3.637
14	3.637	3.637	3.637	3.637	3.637	3.637	3.636	3.636	3.636	3.636	3.636	3.636
15	3.636	3.636	3.636	3.636	3.636	3.636	3.637	3.637	3.637	3.637	3.637	3.637
16	3.637	3.637	3.637	3.637	3.637	3.637	3.636	3.636	3.636	3.636	3.636	3.636
17	3.636	3.636	3.636	3.636	3.636	3.636	3.637	3.637	3.637	3.637	3.637	3.637
18	3.637	3.637	3.637	3.637	3.637	3.637	3.636	3.636	3.636	3.636	3.636	3.636
19	3.636	3.636	3.636	3.636	3.636	3.636	3.637	3.637	3.637	3.637	3.637	3.637
20	3.637	3.637	3.637	3.637	3.637	3.637	3.636	3.636	3.636	3.636	3.636	3.636
21	3.636	3.636	3.636	3.636	3.636	3.636	3.637	3.637	3.637	3.637	3.637	3.637

Nonresidential Real Property (39 years—placed in service on or after May 13, 1993; *see 42.13*)
Use the column for the month of taxable year placed in service.

Year / Month	1	2	3	4	5	6	7	8	9	10	11	12
1	2.461%	2.247%	2.033%	1.819%	1.605%	1.391%	1.177%	0.963%	0.749%	0.535%	0.321%	0.107%
2–39	2.564	2.564	2.564	2.564	2.564	2.564	2.564	2.564	2.564	2.564	2.564	2.564
40	0.107	0.321	0.535	0.749	0.963	1.177	1.391	1.605	1.819	2.033	2.247	2.461

Nonresidential Real Property (31.5 years—placed in service before May 13, 1993; *see 42.13*)
Use the column for the month of taxable year placed in service

Year / Month	1	2	3	4	5	6	7	8	9	10	11	12
12	3.175	3.174	3.175	3.174	3.175	3.174	3.175	3.174	3.175	3.174	3.175	3.174
13	3.174	3.175	3.174	3.175	3.174	3.175	3.174	3.175	3.174	3.175	3.174	3.175
14	3.175	3.174	3.175	3.174	3.175	3.174	3.175	3.174	3.175	3.174	3.175	3.174
15	3.174	3.175	3.174	3.175	3.174	3.175	3.174	3.175	3.174	3.175	3.174	3.175
16	3.175	3.174	3.175	3.174	3.175	3.174	3.175	3.174	3.175	3.174	3.175	3.174
17	3.174	3.175	3.174	3.175	3.174	3.175	3.174	3.175	3.174	3.175	3.174	3.175
18	3.175	3.174	3.175	3.174	3.175	3.174	3.175	3.174	3.175	3.174	3.175	3.174
19	3.174	3.175	3.174	3.175	3.174	3.175	3.174	3.175	3.174	3.175	3.174	3.175
20	3.175	3.174	3.175	3.174	3.175	3.174	3.175	3.174	3.175	3.174	3.175	3.174
21	3.174	3.175	3.174	3.175	3.174	3.175	3.174	3.175	3.174	3.175	3.174	3.175

42.14 Demolishing a Building

When you buy improved property, the purchase price is allocated between the land and the building; only the building may be depreciated. The land may not *(42.1)*. If you later demolish the building, you may not deduct the cost of the demolition or the undepreciated basis of the building as a loss in the year of demolition. Expenses or losses in connection with the demolition of any structure, including certified historic structures, are not deductible. They must be capitalized and added to the basis of the land on which the structure is located.

Major rehabilitation. Where you are considering a major rehabilitation of a building that involves some demolition of the building, IRS guidelines may allow you to deduct the costs of demolition and a removal of part of the structure. Under the IRS rules, the costs of structural modification may avoid capitalization if 75% or more of the existing external walls are retained as internal or external walls and 75% or more of the existing internal framework is also retained. For certified historic structures, the modification must also be part of a certified rehabilitation.

42.15 Leasehold Improvements

For qualified leasehold improvements, qualified restaurant property, and qualified retail improvement property placed in service in 2010, up to $250,000 of cost ($250,000 combined for all three types) may be deducted in 2010 under first-year expensing *(42.3)*. The same expensing limit will apply for 2011.

Qualified leasehold, restaurant, and retail improvements placed in service before 2010 are depreciated under MACRS over a 15-year period. Other leasehold improvements are depreciated under the MACRS rates for buildings shown at *42.13*. The term of the lease is ignored under MACRS. If the lease term is shorter than the MACRS life and you do not retain the improvements at the end of the term, the remaining undepreciated basis is a deductible loss.

Law Alert

First-Year Expensing for Qualified Improvements

In each of 2010 and 2011, up to $250,000 of the cost of qualified leasehold improvements, qualified restaurant property, and qualified retail improvement property placed in service during the year may be deducted under first-year expensing *(42.3)*.

Planning Reminder

Abandonment of Leasehold Improvements

Upon the termination of a lease, the adjusted basis of a lessee's leasehold improvements that are abandoned may be claimed as a loss. For dispositions after June 12, 1996, a lessor may follow the rule applied to lessees if the improvements are irrevocably disposed of or abandoned at the termination of the lease. The lessor may recognize loss for the remaining adjusted basis of the improvements.

Qualified improvements eligible for first-year expensing. A qualified leasehold improvement must be made to an interior part of a building that is nonresidential realty. Leasehold, restaurant and retail improvements must be placed in service more than three years after the date that the building was first placed in service. For restaurant improvements, more than 50% of the building's square footage must be devoted to the preparation of meals and seating for on-premise consumption of prepared meals. For retail improvements, the portion of the building must be open to the general public and used in the retail trade or business of selling tangible personal property to the general public.

The total cost of qualified leasehold, restaurant, and retail improvements that is eligible for expensing in each of 2010 and 2011 is $250,000. *See* the Form 4562 instructions for further details.

42.16 Depreciating Real Estate Placed in Service After 1980 and Before 1987

The ACRS recovery period of almost all buildings placed in service before 1987 has already ended. Some pre-1987 buildings are still being depreciated over a 35-year or 45-year period if the straight-line election discussed in the next paragraph was made.

Election to use straight-line depreciation. For 15-year, 18-year, or 19-year real property, you may have elected to use the straight-line method over 35 or 45 years. An election of the straight-line method for real property had to be made on a property-by-property basis, by the return due date, plus extensions, for the year the property was placed in service.

Rate of recovery. The rate of recovery is listed in Treasury tables that are available in IRS Publication 534.

Substantial improvements. Substantial improvements made after 1986 to an ACRS building are depreciable under MACRS *(42.13)*, not ACRS.

Recapture. See *44.1* for recapture rules on the sale of ACRS property.

42.17 When MACRS Is Not Allowed

If you place in service personal property that you previously used or that was previously owned by a related taxpayer before 1987, you may not be able to apply MACRS rules. This anti-churning restriction is designed to discourage asset transfers between related persons to take advantage of MACRS deductions that exceed the deductions allowed before 1987 under ACRS. The anti-churning restriction does not apply to personal property if, for the first full taxable year of service, the deduction allowable under ACRS would be greater than the deduction allowable under MACRS.

The anti-churning rule also does not bar MACRS rules for real estate acquired after 1986, unless you lease back the real estate to a related party who owned it before 1987.

Special rules also apply to the transfer of property in certain tax-free corporate or partnership transactions where the property was used before 1987. If you receive property in a tax-free exchange, you may have to use the method used by the transferor in computing the ACRS deduction for that part of basis that does not exceed what was the transferor's basis in the property. To the extent that basis exceeds the transferor's, the MACRS rules may apply; for example, when you paid boot in addition to transferring property.

Where property is disposed of and reacquired, the depreciation deduction is computed as if the disposition had not occurred.

42.18 Amortizing Goodwill and Other Intangibles (Section 197)

The costs of intangibles coming within Section 197 are amortized over a 15-year period. The 15-year period applies regardless of the actual useful life of "Section 197 intangibles" acquired after August 10, 1993 (or after July 25, 1991, if elected), and held in connection with a business or income-producing activity.

Generally, the amount subject to amortization is cost. Annual amortization is reported on Form 4562. The 15-year period starts with the month the intangible was acquired.

A "Section 197 intangible" is: (1) goodwill; (2) going-concern value; (3) workforce in place; (4) information base; (5) know-how, but *see* exceptions below; (6) any customer-based intangible; (7) any supplier-based intangible; (8) any license, permit, or other right granted by a governmental unit or agency; (9) any covenant not to compete made in the acquisition of a business; and (10) any franchise, trademark, or trade name.

Goodwill. Goodwill is the value of a business attributable to the expectancy of continued customer patronage, due to the name or reputation of a business or any other factor.

Franchises, trademarks, and trade names. A franchise (excluding sports franchises), trademark, or trade name is a Section 197 intangible. Amounts, whether fixed or contingent, paid on the transfer of a trademark, trade name, or franchise are chargeable to capital account and must be ratably amortized over a 15-year period. The renewal of a franchise, trademark, or trade name is treated as an acquisition of the franchise, trademark, or trade name. Renewal costs are amortized over 15 years beginning in the month of renewal.

Know-how. A patent, copyright, formula, process, design, pattern, format, or similar item may be a Section 197 intangible. However, the following interests are not Section 197 intangibles unless acquired as part of the acquisition of a business: patents, copyrights, and interests in films, sound recordings, videotapes, books, or other similar property.

Customer-based intangibles. Customer-based intangibles include the portion of an acquired trade or business attributable to a customer base, circulation base, undeveloped market or market growth, insurance in force, investment management contracts, or other relationships with customers that involve the future provision of goods or services.

Supplier-based intangibles. The portion of the purchase price of an acquired business attributable to a favorable relationship with persons who provide distribution services, such as favorable shelf or display space at a retail outlet, the existence of a favorable credit rating, or the existence of favorable supply contracts, are Section 197 intangibles.

Going-concern value. This is the additional value that attaches to property because it is an integral part of a going concern. This includes the value attributable to the ability of a trade or business to continue to operate and generate sales without interruption in spite of a change in ownership.

Workforce in place. The portion of the purchase price of an acquired business attributable to a highly skilled workforce is amortizable over 15 years. Similarly, the cost of acquiring an existing employment contract is amortizable over 15 years.

Information base. This includes the cost of acquiring customer lists; subscription lists; insurance expirations; patient or client files; lists of newspaper, magazine, radio, or television advertisers; business books and records; and operating systems. The intangible value of technical manuals, training manuals or programs, data files, and accounting or inventory control systems is also a Section 197 intangible.

Self-created intangibles. A Section 197 intangible created by a taxpayer is generally not amortizable, unless created in connection with a transaction that involves the acquisition of assets of a business. However, this deduction bar for self-created intangibles does not apply to the following: (1) any license, permit, or other right granted by a governmental unit or agency; (2) a covenant not to compete entered into on the acquisition of a business; or (3) any franchise, trademark, or trade name. For example, the 15-year amortization period may apply to the capitalized costs of registering or developing a trademark or trade name.

A person who contracts for or renews a contract for the use of a Section 197 intangible may not be considered to have created that intangible. For example, a licensee who contracts for the use of know-how may amortize capitalized costs over 15 years.

The following intangible assets are not Section 197 intangibles. (1) interests in a corporation, partnership, trust, or estate; (2) interests under certain financial contracts; (3) interests in land; (4) certain computer software *(42.19)*; (5) certain separately acquired rights and interests; (6) interests under existing leases of tangible property; (7) interests under existing indebtedness; (8) sports franchises; (9) certain residential mortgage servicing rights; and (10) certain corporate transaction costs.

Planning Reminder

Covenants Not To Compete

A covenant not to compete is a Section 197 intangible if paid for in connection with the acquisition of a business. Excessive compensation or rental paid to a former owner of a business for continuing to perform services or provide the use of property is considered an amount paid for a covenant not to compete if the services or property benefits the trade or business. But an amount paid under a covenant not to compete that actually represents additional consideration for corporate stock is not a Section 197 intangible and must be added to the basis of the acquired stock.

Loss limitations. A person who disposes of an amortizable Section 197 intangible at a loss and at the same time retains other Section 197 intangibles acquired in the same transaction may not deduct the loss. The disallowed loss is added to the basis of the retained Section 197 intangibles. The same rule applies if a Section 197 intangible is abandoned or becomes worthless and other Section 197 intangibles acquired in the same transaction are kept. The basis of the remaining intangibles is increased by the disallowed loss.

You may not treat a covenant not to compete as worthless any earlier than the disposition or worthlessness of the entire interest in a business.

Anti-churning rule. No deduction is allowed for goodwill, going-concern value, or any other Section 197 intangibles acquired by a taxpayer after August 10, 1993, if:

1. The taxpayer or a related person held or used the intangible at any time on or after July 25, 1991, and on or before August 10, 1993;
2. The taxpayer acquired the intangible from a person who held it at any time on or after July 25, 1991, and on or before August 10, 1993, and, as part of the transaction, the user of the intangible does not change; or
3. The taxpayer grants the right to use the intangible to a person or a related person who held or used the intangible at any time on or after July 25, 1991, and on or before August 10, 1993.

See IRS Publication 535 for the definition of "related persons" and exceptions to the anti-churning rule.

Dispositions. An amortizable Section 197 intangible is not a capital asset. It is treated as depreciable property, and if held for more than one year, it will generally qualify as a Section 1231 asset *(44.1)*. Amortization claimed on a Section 197 intangible is subject to recapture under Section 1245 and gain on its sale to certain related persons is subject to ordinary income treatment under Section 1239.

Planning Reminder

Computer Software Not Subject to Amortization

Computer software is *not* a Section 197 intangible *(42.18)* if it: (1) is readily available to the general public; (2) is not subject to an exclusive license; and (3) has not been substantially changed. If these three tests are met, software purchased in 2003–2010 is eligible for first-year expensing *(42.3)*, or it may be depreciated over 36 months *(42.19)*. Computer software falling outside of this exception is considered a Section 197 intangible subject to 15-year amortization if it is acquired in the acquisition of a business.

42.19 Deducting the Cost of Computer Software

The cost of software installed in a computer that you buy and use in your business is not deducted separately, unless the software cost is separately stated. In most cases, the cost of software bundled with a computer is not separately stated. The cost of the computer including such software is depreciable *(42.10)*.

If you buy software for business use, such as a database or spreadsheet program, the treatment of the cost depends on your use of the program. If you use it for a year or less, such as an annual tax program, you may deduct the cost as a business expense for that year. If the useful life in your business exceeds a year, and the software meets the three tests in the Planning Reminder on this page, it is considered off-the-shelf software eligible for first-year expensing if bought in 2003–2010 *(42.3)*. Alternatively, you may depreciate the cost over 36 months.

Software acquired in the acquisition of a business is eligible for first-year expensing *(42.3)* or depreciable over 36 months if it meets the three tests listed in the Planning Reminder on this page; otherwise, 15-year amortization applies.

42.20 Amortizing Song Rights

Expenses paid or incurred with respect to musical compositions and rights to musical compositions placed in service in 2006–2010 can be amortized over five years. This would include, for example, advances made by song publishers to composers. If elected, the five-year amortization period begins with the month in which the compositions or rights are placed in service. *See* the Form 4562 instructions for details on the election.

42.21 Bonus Depreciation

Bonus depreciation is an additional first-year depreciation allowance equal to 50% of the adjusted basis of eligible property. The Small Business Jobs Act of 2010 (signed into law on September 27, 2010) extended bonus depreciation to eligible property placed in service during 2010. It was also allowed for eligible property placed in service in 2008 and 2009.

Bonus depreciation (also called a Section 168(k) allowance and a special depreciation allowance) can be claimed in addition to any first-year expensing. In figuring "adjusted basis" for purposes of bonus depreciation, any expensing deduction is taken into account first. Bonus depreciation is fully deductible for alternative minimum tax purposes *(23.2)*; no adjustment is required.

Bonus depreciation can be combined with first-year expensing to produce substantial write-offs for the year that eligible property is placed in service. First-year expensing is taken into account first; then you figure bonus depreciation on the cost of the property minus the first-year expensing allowance.

EXAMPLE

In July 2010 you place in service equipment costing $600,000. You elect to expense $500,000 of the cost. Your bonus depreciation deduction is $50,000, or $100,000 basis ($600,000 – $500,000) x 50%. You can depreciate the remaining adjusted basis of the equipment ($50,000) over the property's recovery period. If the equipment is five-year property, the depreciation allowance for 2010 is $10,000 ($50,000 x 20%). The total deductions for this equipment in 2010 equal $560,000 ($500,000 + $50,000 + 10,000).

Bonus depreciation allows the first-year dollar limit on write-offs for vehicles weighing less than 6,000 pounds to be increased by a fixed dollar amount reflecting bonus depreciation, provided business use exceeds 50%. This increases the total dollar limit for such vehicles placed in service during 2010 to $11,060 ($8,000 bonus depreciation plus $3,060 regular dollar limit) *(43.4)*.

Eligible property. Bonus depreciation can be claimed for any property with a recovery period of 20 years or less, computer software (other than a Section 197 intangible *(42.18)*, buildings that replace or rehabilitate property damaged, destroyed, or condemned as a result of a federally declared disaster, and qualified leasehold improvements. Qualified leasehold improvements are improvements made more than three years after the building is placed in service to an interior portion of a nonresidential building pursuant to a lease by the lessee, sublessee, or lessor; the interior of the building is occupied exclusively by the lessee or sublessee.

You must be the original user of the property. Property does *not* qualify if you entered into a written binding contract to acquire it before January 1, 2008. Property placed in service after December 31, 2010 is not eligible for the 50% allowance. Bonus depreciation cannot be claimed for property that must be depreciated under ADS *(42.9)*. For example, it may not be used for listed property used 50% or less for business since such property must be depreciated under ADS.

Claiming bonus depreciation. You report bonus depreciation in Part II of Form 4562 labeled "Special Depreciation Allowance, unless the property is a computer or other "listed property" *(42.10)*. For listed property, use Part V of Form 4562.

Election out of bonus depreciation. Unlike regular depreciation, you are not required to use bonus depreciation and have the option of electing out of its use. If eligible for 50% bonus depreciation, you can elect *not* to use it. If you fail to make an election not to claim bonus depreciation, then you are deemed to have claimed it (even though you did not) and must reduce the basis of the property by the amount of bonus depreciation that could have been claimed.

The election out is made on a per-asset-class basis. Thus, for example, you can opt out of bonus depreciation for all five-year property while claiming it for seven-year property. To make the election out of claiming bonus depreciation, attach a statement to your return specifying the class of property for which the election not to claim additional depreciation is being made.

Chapter 43

Deducting Car and Truck Expenses

The costs of buying and operating a car, truck, or van for business are deductible under rules hedged with restrictions. Depreciation deductions for most cars, trucks, and vans are subject to annual ceilings. For new cars placed in service in 2010 that are used over 50% for business, the first-year depreciation limit is $11,060, the regular $3,060 limit plus a bonus allowance of $8,000 *(43.4)*. For most new light trucks and vans, the 2010 limit is $11,160 if the $8,000 bonus is allowed or $3,160 if it is not *(43.4)*. The limits are reduced for personal use. If a vehicle placed in service in 2010 is used 50% or less for business, depreciation must be based on the straight-line method and the maximum deduction is reduced by personal use *(43.4)*.

To avoid accounting for actual vehicle expenses and depreciation, you may claim an IRS mileage allowance. For 2010, the allowance is 50 cents per mile. Keep a record of business trip mileage.

If you are self-employed, you deduct your vehicle expenses on Schedule C or Schedule C-EZ if eligible *(40.6)*. Use Form 4562 to compute depreciation if you claim actual operating costs instead of the IRS mileage allowance. If you are an employee, use Form 2106 to claim unreimbursed vehicle expenses, which are deductible only to the extent that together with other miscellaneous itemized deductions they exceed 2% of your adjusted gross income.

If you bought a hybrid or electric vehicle in 2010 for business and/or personal use, you may be eligible for a tax credit *(25.21)*.

Also see:

43.1 Standard Mileage Rate

If you start to use your car for business in 2010, you have a choice of either deducting the actual operating costs of your car during business trips or deducting a flat IRS allowance. For 2010, the rate is 50 cents per mile. The mileage allowance also applies to business trips in a van or pickup or panel truck as if it were a car.

If you placed a car, van, pick-up, or panel truck in service before 2010 and have always used the IRS mileage allowance, you may apply the cents-per-mile rate to your 2010 business mileage or deduct your actual operating costs plus straight-line depreciation over the remaining estimated useful life of the vehicle (assuming the vehicle is not considered fully depreciated).

The rate may not be used to deduct the costs of a vehicle used for nonbusiness income-producing activities such as looking after investment property.

Allowance must be elected for the first year. The choice of the allowance must be made in the first year you place the vehicle in service for business travel. If you do not use the allowance in the year you first use the vehicle for business, you may not use the allowance for that vehicle in any other year. Thus, if you bought a car for business in 2009 and on your 2009 return you deducted actual operating costs plus depreciation, you may not use the mileage allowance on your 2010 return or in any later year.

Allowance takes the place of fixed operating costs plus depreciation. If you claim the allowance, you cannot deduct your actual outlays for expenses such as gasoline (including state and local taxes), oil, repairs, license tags, or insurance, nor can you deduct depreciation or lease payments. Parking fees and tolls during business trips are deductible in addition to the mileage allowance. The IRS will not disallow a deduction based on the allowance even though it exceeds your actual vehicle costs. If you use more than one automobile in your business travel and elect the allowance, total the business mileage traveled in both cars.

EXAMPLES

1. You buy a car in 2010 and drive it on business trips. You keep a record of your business mileage. You traveled 32,000 miles during the year. You may deduct $16,000 (32,000 x 50 cents). In addition to the $16,000 allowance, you may deduct your expenses for tolls and parking.
2. You use one car primarily for business and occasionally your spouse's car for business trips. In 2010, you drove your car on business trips 10,000 miles and your spouse's car 2,000 miles. Total business mileage is 12,000 miles for purposes of the cents-per-mile allowance.

Records. You may decide to use the allowance if you do not keep accurate records of operating costs. However, you must keep a record of your business trips, dates, customers or clients visited, business purpose of the trips, your total mileage during the year, and the number of miles traveled on business. An IRS agent may attempt to verify mileage by asking for repair bills near the beginning and end of the year if the bills note mileage readings.

Mileage allowance for leased vehicle. The IRS mileage allowance is also available for leased cars, vans, and pick-up or panel trucks, but it must be used for the entire lease period or not at all. For example, if in 2010 you leased a car for business purposes and you claim the cents-per-mile allowance, you will also have to use it for the remainder of the lease period, including renewals.

Interest on a vehicle loan and taxes. The deduction rules are discussed in the following section *(43.2)*.

Mileage allowance disallowed. You may not claim the cents-per-mile allowance if:

- You have depreciated your vehicle using the ACRS or MACRS method, including straight-line MACRS, or you claimed first-year expensing or first-year bonus depreciation.
- You use in your business five or more vehicles simultaneously, such as in a fleet operation.
- You use your vehicle for hire—that is, you use it as a taxicab, carrying passengers for a fare.

Employer reimbursements. If your employer reimburses your vehicle costs at a rate lower than the IRS allowance, you may use the IRS rate to deduct the excess over your employer's reimbursement; *see* Example 3 at *20.33*.

Planning Reminder

First-Year Election Affects Later Years

In deciding whether to elect the allowance in the first year, consider not only whether you will get a bigger first-year deduction using the allowance, or deducting actual operating costs plus depreciation, but also project your mileage, operating expenses, and depreciation expenses over the years you expect to use the vehicle. If in the first year you elect to deduct actual costs, including MACRS or straight-line MACRS depreciation, you may not use the IRS auto allowance for *that vehicle* in a later year. On the other hand, claiming the IRS allowance in the first year you put a vehicle in service forfeits your privilege to use MACRS and first-year expensing. If you switch from the allowance to deducting actual expenses in later years, you may claim straight-line depreciation over the remaining estimated useful life of the vehicle if the vehicle is not considered fully depreciated.

IRS allowance includes depreciation. When you use the IRS mileage allowance, you may not claim a separate depreciation deduction. The IRS mileage allowance includes an estimate for depreciation. For purposes of figuring gain or loss on a disposition, you must reduce the basis of the vehicle by the following depreciation amounts: 17 cents per mile in 2005 and 2006, 19 cents per mile in 2007, 21 cents per mile in 2008 and 2009, and 23 cents per mile in 2010 (other rates apply for earlier years).

Depreciation when switching from allowance to actual costs. If you use the IRS mileage allowance in the first year, you may switch to the actual-cost method in a later year, but depreciation must be based on the straight-line method over the remaining estimated useful life. However, no depreciation may be claimed if basis has been reduced to zero under the annual cents-per-mile reduction rule in the preceding paragraph.

Table 43-1 Deducting Car and Truck Expenses

Item—	*Tax Rule—*
IRS mileage allowance	You may avoid the trouble of keeping a record of actual vehicle expenses and calculating depreciation by electing the IRS mileage allowance for a car, van, or pick-up or panel truck. However, to claim the allowance, you must be ready to prove business use of the vehicle and keep a record of your mileage. The allowance may give you a larger deduction than your actual outlays plus depreciation. You must elect the allowance in the first year you use the vehicle for business. If you do not, you may not use the allowance for that vehicle in any other year If your actual operating costs plus depreciation exceed the allowance for the first year you place the vehicle in business service, you may claim your actual operating expenses and depreciation, but doing so will forfeit your right to elect the allowance for that vehicle in any later year.
Depreciation	If you claim actual operating expenses, such as gasoline, repairs, and insurance costs, you may also claim depreciation. There is a cap on the annual depreciation deduction. For a car placed in service in 2010, the 2010 depreciation limit is $3,060, and for a light truck or van the limit is $3,160. For vehicles placed in service in 2010, the first- year depreciation limit for cars is generally $3,060, but for a new car used over 50% for business the limit is increased by an $8,000 bonus allowance. For light trucks and vans placed in service in 2010, the $3,160 limit is increased by the $8,000 bonus if the vehicle is new and used over 50% for business. These limits must be reduced for personal use *(43.4)*. Electing first-year expensing does not increase the limit (as reduced by personal use). The total of the first-year expensing and depreciation cannot exceed the applicable limit *(43.4)*. Electing first-year expensing or depreciation for a car or truck placed in service in 2010 prevents you from using the IRS mileage allowance *(43.1)* for that car in later years. For a cars and trucks placed in business service in 2010 that are used 50% or less for business, you must use straight-line depreciation subject to the applicable ceiling *(43.6)*. If business use is initially over 50% but declines to 50% or less in a later year, prior year depreciation deductions, including first-year expensing, must be recaptured as income to the extent they exceeded straight-line deductions *(43.10)*. For a vehicle placed in service before 2010, *see* Tables 43-2 and 43-3 for the maximum depreciation you can claim for 2010.
Vehicle used for business and personal driving	You may deduct only the amount allocated to business mileage. For example, total mileage is 20,000 in 2010 and your business mileage is 15,000. You may claim only 75% of your deductible costs (15,000 ÷ 20,000).
Tax return reporting	If you are an *employee*, you claim actual vehicle expenses or the IRS allowance on Form 2106. Form 2106 requires you to list mileage for business, commuting, and other personal trips. If your vehicle costs are not reimbursed by your employer, you must deduct them as miscellaneous deductions subject to the 2% AGI floor on Schedule A. If you are *self-employed*, you deduct business costs on Schedule C and use Form 4562 to compute depreciation if you claim actual operating costs. Costs deducted on Schedule C are not limited by the 2% adjusted gross income (AGI) floor.

43.2 Expense Allocations

If you do not claim the IRS mileage allowance, you may deduct car, truck, or van expenses on business trips such as the cost of gas and oil (including state and local taxes), repairs, parking, and tolls.

If you use your vehicle exclusively for business, all of your operating expenses are deductible. However, if you are an employee, the deduction is limited by the 2% adjusted gross income (AGI) floor *(19.1)*.

Apportioning vehicle expenses between business and personal use. For a vehicle used for business and personal purposes, deduct only the depreciation and expenses allocated to your business use of the vehicle *(43.3–43.5)*.

The business portion of vehicle expenses is determined by the percentage of mileage driven on business trips during the year.

EXAMPLE

In 2010, you drove your car 15,000 miles. Of this, 12,000 miles was on business trips. The percentage of business use is 80%:

$$\frac{\text{business mileage}}{\text{total mileage}} = \frac{12{,}000}{15{,}000} = 80\%$$

Your actual car expenses (gas, oil, repairs, etc.) for the year were $1,000, of which $800 ($1,000 × 80%) is deductible. If you are an employee, the $800 is only deductible as a miscellaneous itemized deduction subject to the 2% AGI floor *(19.1)*.

Interest on vehicle loan. If you are an *employee*, all of the interest is considered personal interest and is not deductible even if you use the vehicle 100% of the time for your job. If you are *self-employed*, the allocated business percentage of the interest is fully deductible on Schedule C; the personal percentage is not deductible.

Taxes paid on your car. The business portion of sales taxes paid on your vehicle is not deductible whether you are an employee or self-employed; the tax is added to the basis of the vehicle for depreciation purposes *(43.3)*.

State and local personal property taxes are deductible as itemized deductions on Schedule A if you are an employee. If you are self-employed, deduct the business portion of the personal property taxes on Schedule C and the personal percentage on Schedule A if you itemize.

Leased vehicle. If you lease a car, truck, or van for business use and do not claim the IRS mileage allowance *(43.1)*, you deduct the lease payments plus other costs of operating the vehicle. If the vehicle is also used for personal driving, the lease payments must be allocated between business and personal mileage. The rules requiring the reporting of extra income attributable to the lease are discussed later in this chapter *(43.12)*.

43.3 Depreciation Restrictions on Cars, Trucks, and Vans

The law contains restrictions on so-called "listed property" that limit and, in some cases, deny depreciation deductions for a business car, truck, or van. Employees may be unable to claim any deduction at all under an employer convenience test. Employees meeting that test and self-employed individuals must determine if they can use accelerated MACRS rates or must use straight-line rates. Finally, regardless of which depreciation method is used, the annual deduction may not exceed a ceiling set by law for passenger cars and certain light trucks and vans; details on the annual ceilings are in the following section *(43.4)*.

Employee must satisfy employer convenience test. If you are an employee and use your own vehicle for work, you must be ready to prove that you use it for the *convenience of your employer* who requires you to use it in your job. If you do not meet this employer convenience test, you may not claim depreciation or first-year expensing. A letter from your employer stating you need the vehicle for business will not meet this test.

The facts and circumstances of your use of the vehicle may show that it is a condition of employment. For example, an inspector for a construction company uses his automobile to visit construction sites over a scattered area. The company reimburses him for his expenses. According to the IRS, the inspector's use of the car is for the convenience of the company and is a condition of the job. However, if a company car were available to the inspector, the use of his own car would not meet the condition of employment and convenience of the employer tests.

Caution

Recapture of MACRS Deductions

If you meet the more-than-50% test in the year the car or other vehicle is placed in service, which entitles you to claim first-year expensing or accelerated MACRS, but business use falls to 50% or less in a later year, the recapture rules *(43.10)* apply.

More-than-50%-business-use test for claiming expensing or accelerated MACRS depreciation. Automobiles and other vehicles used to transport persons or goods are considered "listed property" *(42.10)*, whether you are an employee or are self-employed, but there are exceptions for ambulances, hearses, and trucks or vans that are qualified non-personal-use vehicles *(43.4)*. Unless the vehicle is excepted from the listed property rules, you may claim first-year expensing or accelerated MACRS *(43.5)* for a vehicle placed in service during 2010 only if you use it in 2010 more than 50% of the time for business. The annual ceiling, if applicable *(43.4)*, applies to the total of first-year expensing and MACRS depreciation.

If business use is *50% or less* in the year the vehicle is placed in service, first-year expensing and accelerated MACRS are barred; depreciation must be claimed over a six-year period under the straight-line method. Technically, the recovery period is five years but the period is extended to six years because, in the first year, a convention rule limits the deductible percentage. *See Tables 43-6* and *43-7 (43.6)*. The straight-line method must also be used in future years, even if business use in those years exceeds 50%.

If a vehicle is used for both business and investment purposes, only business use is considered in determining whether you meet the more-than-50%-business-use test and therefore qualify for MACRS. However, investment use is added to business use in determining your actual deduction.

EXAMPLE

Brown buys an automobile for $30,000 and places it in service in 2010. He uses it 40% for business and 20% for investment activity. Because he does not use his car more than 50% in his business, he may not claim first-year expensing or accelerated MACRS. He figures depreciation using the straight-line method *(43.6)*. The business use allocation rate for depreciation is 60% (40% for business use plus 20% investment use).

Do your employees use the vehicle? In certain cases, an employer who provides a vehicle to employees as part of their compensation may be unable to count the employee's use as qualified business use, thereby preventing the employer from meeting the more-than-50%-business-use test for claiming MACRS. An employer is allowed to treat the employee's use as qualified business use only if: (1) the employee is not a relative and does not own more than 5% of the business and (2) the employer treats the fair market value of the employee's personal use of the vehicle as wage income and withholds tax on that amount. If such income is reported, all of the employee's use, including personal use, may be counted by an employer as qualified business use.

If an employee owning more than a 5% interest is allowed use of a company-owned vehicle as part of his or her compensation, the employer may not count that use as qualified business use, even if the personal use is reported as income. The same strict rule applies if the vehicle is provided to a person who is related to the employer.

43.4 Annual Ceilings on Depreciation

Annual ceilings limit the amount of depreciation you may deduct for passenger cars and certain light trucks and vans. The ceilings apply both to self-employed individuals and employees. As a result of the ceilings, the actual write-off period for your car may be several years longer than the minimum recovery period of six years *(43.5)*.

Law Alert

Extension of Bonus Depreciation

Bonus first-year depreciation is allowed for certain vehicles placed in service in 2010 under the Small Business Jobs Act of 2010. The depreciation ceiling for 2010 is increased to $11,060 for cars and $11,160 for light trucks and vans provided the vehicle was purchased new and used over 50% for business in 2010 *(43.4)*.

Passenger cars. The ceiling on depreciation for a car placed in service in 2010 is generally $3,060, reduced by personal use. However, bonus depreciation allows an $8,000 increase in the first-year deduction for new vehicles used over 50% for business. For purposes of the annual depreciation ceilings, a car is any four-wheeled vehicle that is manufactured primarily for use on public thoroughfares and that is weight-rated by the manufacturer at 6,000 pounds or less when unloaded (without passengers or cargo). However, these vehicles are excluded from the car category and are thus exempt from the annual depreciation limits: (1) an ambulance, hearse, or combination ambulance-hearse used directly in a business, and (2) a vehicle such as a taxi cab used directly in the business of transporting persons or property for compensation or hire.

Year-by-year limits for cars placed in service in 2010 and prior years can be found in *Table 43-2*.

EXAMPLE

Theodore bought a used car on March 4, 2010, for $20,000 and for the rest of the year used it 75% for business.

Theodore does not claim a Section 179 deduction (first-year expensing) for the car. Bonus depreciation is not available because the car was used when purchased. His depreciable unadjusted basis is $15,000 ($20,000 x 75%). The MACRS deduction *(43.5)* using the 200% declining balance method and the half-year convention is $3,000 ($15,000 x .20). However, Theodore's depreciation deduction is limited to $2,295 ($3,060 limit for a car placed in service in 2010 x 75% business use).

Even if Theodore had claimed first-year expensing, the deduction could not exceed the $2,295 limit.

Light trucks, vans, and SUVs. A light truck, van, minivan, or SUV (sport utility vehicle) built on a truck chassis that is weight-rated by the manufacturer at 6,000 pounds or less when fully loaded (gross vehicle weight rating) is generally subject to annual depreciation ceilings.

However, the depreciation limits do not apply to trucks and vans that are qualified non-personal-use vehicles. These include moving vans, flatbed trucks, and delivery trucks with seating only for the driver (or driver seat plus folding jump seat). Also included are specially modified trucks and vans that are unlikely to be used more than a minimal amount for personal purposes. An example would be a van that has been painted to display advertising or the company's name and which has permanent shelving for carrying merchandise or equipment.

Where an exception does not apply, the deduction limits for light trucks, vans, and SUVs are slightly higher than those for cars. For trucks and vans placed in service in 2010, the 2010 limit is generally $3,160. However, bonus depreciation increases the 2010 limit for a new light truck or van used over 50% for business to $11,160. The applicable limit must be reduced for personal use. *Table 43-3* shows the year-by-year limits for trucks and vans.

Heavy trucks, vans, and SUVs. Trucks, vans, and SUVs built on a truck chassis that are weight-rated by the manufacturer at more than 6,000 pounds gross vehicle weight are not subject to the annual depreciation ceilings. However, first-year expensing *(42.3)* for the vehicle may be limited to $25,000 rather than the general expensing limit, which for 2010 is $250,000, although legislation pending when this book went to press would increase the limit to $500,000 *(42.3)*. The vehicle must be used more than 50% for business to qualify for first-year expensing. If first-year expensing is not or cannot be elected *(42.3)*, a full depreciation deduction using the MACRS rate *(43.5)* is allowed with no dollar limit.

The $25,000 limit on first-year expensing applies to SUVs rated at more than 6,000 pounds but not more than 14,000 pounds gross vehicle weight. For purposes of the $25,000 expensing limit, an SUV means any four-wheeled vehicle primarily designed or which can be used to carry passengers over public thoroughfares. Trucks and vans as well as SUVs can be covered by this definition, but the law allows certain exceptions. Exceptions are allowed for vehicles with seating for more than nine passengers behind the driver, for pickup trucks with an interior cargo bed at least six feet long that is an open area or is enclosed by a cap and not readily accessible to passengers, and cargo vans without rear seating and with no body sections protruding more than 30 inches ahead of the windshield. For these excepted vehicles, the $25,000 limit on first-year expensing does not apply.

43.5 MACRS Rates for Cars, Trucks, and Vans

Business autos, trucks, and vans are technically in a five-year MACRS class *(42.4)*, but because of the half-year or mid-quarter convention and the annual deduction ceilings *(43.3)*, the minimum depreciation period is six years.

Accelerated MACRS rate allowed only if business use in the first year exceeds 50%. To use accelerated MACRS rates, you must meet the more-than-50%-business-use test *(43.3)* in the year the vehicle is placed in business service. Generally, the accelerated MACRS rate is based on the 200% declining balance method, but a 150% declining balance rate may be elected, which may be advantageous when you are subject to the alternative minimum tax *(23.2)*.

If you meet the more-than-50%-business-use test, figure your first-year deduction using the rate from either *Table 43-4* (half-year convention) or *Table 43-5* (mid-quarter convention). The MACRS rates from the appropriate table will be used for each year of the recovery period unless business

Filing Tip

Claiming First-Year Expensing or Depreciation for Your Car

First-year expensing or depreciation (under the 200% or 150% declining balance method, or the straight-line method) is claimed on Form 4562 and then entered on Schedule C of Form 1040 if you are self employed. If you are an employee, use Form 2106 to calculate your deduction, which along with your other unreimbursed job expenses is subject to the 2% AGI floor *(19.3)* for miscellaneous itemized deductions on Schedule A of Form 1040.

Law Alert

Limit on Write-Off for SUVs

Congress may close the loophole for the increased write-off limit on heavy SUVs; *see* the *e-Supplement at jklasser.com*.

Filing Tip

Capital Improvements

A capital improvement to a business vehicle is depreciable under MACRS in the year the improvement is made. The MACRS deductions for the improvement and the vehicle are considered as a unit for purposes of applying the limits on the annual MACRS depreciation deduction.

use for a year falls to 50% or less. However, the deduction figured under the MACRS table may be claimed only to the extent that it does not exceed the annual depreciation ceiling *(43.4)* shown in *Table 43-2* or *Table 43-3*; *see* the Bill Johnston Example on page 690. *See* below for details on using the MACRS tables.

If you do not meet the more-than-50%-business-use test in the year the vehicle is placed in service, you must compute your depreciation deductions using the straight-line rates shown in *43.6*, subject to the annual limit; *see 43.4* and *Table 43-2* or *Table 43-3*.

Deduction for year of disposition. If you dispose of your vehicle before the end of the six-year MACRS recovery period, a partial-year deduction is allowed for the year of disposition under the half-year or mid-quarter convention *(43.7)*.

Use of vehicle after end of recovery period. If you continue to use the vehicle for business after the end of the recovery period, and the annual deduction ceilings prevented you from deducting your full unadjusted basis during the recovery period, you generally may deduct depreciation in the succeeding years up to the annual ceiling *(43.8)*.

Business use falls to 50% or less after the first year. What if business use exceeds 50% in the year the vehicle is placed in service but in a later year within the recovery period business use drops to 50% or lower? In that case, the right to use accelerated MACRS (200% or 150% declining balance method) terminates. You must use the straight-line method and recapture the benefit of the accelerated deductions claimed for the prior years *(43.10)* for the recapture rule.

Straight-line election for vehicle if business use exceeds 50%. If business use of your vehicle exceeds 50%, you may elect to write off your cost under the straight-line method *(43.6)* instead of using the regular MACRS 200% declining balance method. The straight-line deduction is limited by the annual ceilings shown on page 698. By electing straight-line depreciation, you avoid the recapture of excess MACRS deductions if business use drops to 50% or less in a later year *(43.10)*. If the election is made, you must also use the straight-line method for all other five-year property placed in service during the same year as the vehicle.

Electing 150% declining balance method. Depreciation rates under the half-year and mid-quarter conventions are generally based on the 200% declining balance method. You may instead make an irrevocable election to apply the 150% declining balance method. The 150% method may be advantageous when you are subject to the alternative minimum tax. For alternative minimum tax (AMT) purposes *(23.2)*, vehicle depreciation is based on the 150% declining balance method unless you use the straight-line method for regular tax purposes. If you are subject to AMT and use the 150% declining balance method instead of the 200% declining balance method for regular tax purposes, you do not have to report an AMT adjustment on Form 6251.

An election to use the 150% declining balance method is irrevocable and must be applied to all depreciable assets placed in service in the same year, except for nonresidential real and residential rental property.

MACRS Tables Applying the Half-Year Convention or Mid-Quarter Convention if Business Use Exceeds 50%

For the year you place the vehicle in service and the year (within the recovery period) you dispose of the property, you may not claim a full year's worth of depreciation. The deduction is limited by either the half-year convention or the mid-quarter convention, depending on the month in which the vehicle was placed in service and the other business assets, if any, placed in service during that year.

The applicable convention determines the rate table you will use to figure your depreciation deduction for the entire six-year recovery period, assuming that your business use each year exceeds 50%. The half-year and mid-quarter convention tables shown below reflect the 200% or 150% declining balance method, with a switch to the straight-line method when that method provides a larger deduction; the switch to straight line is built into the tables.

Rate applied to unadjusted basis. For each year in the recovery period, the rate from the applicable table is applied against the business use percentage of your unadjusted basis for the vehicle. Investment use may be added to the business use percentage, but keep in mind that the MACRS table below may be used only if business use by itself exceeds 50% *(43.3)*.

Unadjusted basis is your cost minus any first-year expensing deduction as well as any special first-year bonus depreciation for a vehicle placed into service after September 10, 2001, and before January 1, 2005, and during 2008 and 2009. The basis reduction for bonus depreciation applies if you were eligible for the special allowance (vehicle purchased new and used over 50% for business) even if you did not claim it, unless on your return you "elected out" of the special allowance for the vehicle and all other five-year property placed in service during the same year. The deduction figured under the table rate may be claimed to the extent that it does not exceed the annual depreciation ceiling *(43.4)*; *see* the Bill Johnston Example on the next page.

Basis for vehicle converted from personal to business use. The basis for depreciation is the lower of the market value of the vehicle at the time of conversion or its adjusted basis, which is your original cost plus any substantial improvements and minus any deductible casualty losses or diesel fuel tax credit claimed for the vehicle. In most cases, the value of the vehicle will be lower than adjusted basis, and thus the value will be your depreciable basis. For a vehicle converted to business use in 2010, the MACRS rate is applied to basis allocated to business travel. Unless you have mileage records for the entire year, you should base your business-use percentage on driving after the conversion. For example, in April 2010, you started to use your car for business and in the last nine months of the year you drove 10,000 miles, 8,000 of which were for business. This business percentage of 80% is multiplied by the fraction $^{9}/_{12}$ (months used for business divided by 12) to give you a business-use percentage for the year of 60% ($^{9}/_{12}$ of 80%).

Table 43-2 Maximum Depreciation Deduction for Cars (Must Be Reduced for Personal Use)

Date Placed In Service	*1st Year*	*2nd Year*	*3rd Year*	*4th and Later Years*
2010	$ 3,060[1]	$ 4,900	$ 2,950	$ 1,775
2008 or 2009	10,960[2]	4,800	2,850	1,775
2007	3,060	4,900	2,850	1,775
2006	2,960	4,800	2,850	1,775

[1] *$11,060 if bonus depreciation applies* (see *the* Law Alert *on this page).*

[2] *$2,960 if the car does not qualify for the special bonus allowance or if you elect not to claim any allowance.*

Law Alert

Extension of Bonus Depreciation

Bonus first-year depreciation is allowed for certain vehicles placed in service in 2010 under the Small Business Jobs Act of 2010. The depreciation ceiling for 2010 is increased to $11,060 for cars and $11,160 for light trucks and vans provided the vehicle was purchased new and used over 50% for business in 2010.

Table 43-3 Maximum Depreciation Deduction for Trucks and Vans (Must Be Reduced for Personal Use)

Date Placed In Service	*1st Year*	*2nd Year*	*3rd Year*	*4th and Later Years*
2010	$ 3,160[1]	$ 5,100	$ 3,050	$ 1,875
2009	11,160[2]	4,900	2,950	1,775
2008	11,160[3]	5,100	3,050	1,875
2007	3,260	5,200	3,150	1,875
2006	3,260	5,200	3,150	1,875

[1] *$11,160 if bonus depreciation applies* (see *the* Law Alert *on this page).*

[2] *$3,060 if the vehicle does not qualify for the special bonus allowance or if you elect not to claim the allowance.*

[3] *$3,160 if the vehicle does not qualify for the special bonus allowance or if you elect not to claim the allowance.*

Determining whether the half-year convention or mid-quarter convention applies. If you bought a vehicle for use in your business in 2010, and it was the only business equipment placed in service during the year, then the half-year convention applies, unless you bought the vehicle in the last quarter of 2010 (October, November, or December). Under the half-year convention, the vehicle is treated as if it were placed in service in the middle of the year. Use the table below to determine your deduction under the half-year convention.

If the only business equipment bought in 2010 was a vehicle bought in the last quarter (October, November, or December), the mid-quarter convention applies. Under the table for mid-quarter convention rates on page 691, a 5% rate applies for fourth-quarter property under the 200% declining balance method, subject to the deduction ceiling in 2010 *(43.4)*.

If you bought other business equipment in addition to the vehicle, you must consider the total cost basis of property placed in service during the last quarter of 2010. If the total bases of such acquisitions (other than realty) exceed 40% of the total bases of all property placed in service during the year, then a mid-quarter rate applies to *all* of the property (other than realty). The mid-quarter rate for each asset then depends on the quarter the asset was placed in service. If the 40% test is not met, then the half-year convention applies to all the property acquisitions. As shown in the mid-quarter convention table on page 691, mid-quarter rates for each year of the recovery period depend on the quarter the property is placed in service.

Caution

Basis Reduction for Bonus Depreciation Unless You Elect Out

If you were eligible for the special first-year depreciation allowance for a vehicle placed in service after September 10, 2001, and before January 1, 2005 or during 2008 or 2009, you must reduce depreciable basis by the amount of the available allowance even if you did not claim it, unless you specifically elected not to claim the allowance on a statement attached to your return.

Deduction from table cannot exceed annual ceiling. If the deduction figured under the half-year or mid-quarter convention MACRS table (*Table 43-4 or 43-5*) exceeds the annual deduction ceiling *(43.4)*, your deduction is limited to the annual ceiling, reduced by the percentage of your personal use. Keep in mind that if you were eligible for the special first-year depreciation allowance (bonus depreciation) for a vehicle placed in service after September 10, 2001, and before January 1, 2005 and during 2008 or 2009, basis for MACRS purposes is reduced by the special allowance unless you elected on your return not to claim it.

Table 43-4 MACRS Deduction: Half-Year Convention

Year—	*200% Rate*	*150% Rate*
1	20.00%	15.00%
2	32.00	25.50
3	19.20	17.85
4	11.52	16.66
5	11.52	16.66
6	5.76	8.33

EXAMPLE

On May 1, 2006, Bill Johnston placed in service a new car he used 100% for business. The car cost $20,000. He did not claim first-year expensing (there was no bonus depreciation in 2006). Here is Bill's depreciation schedule using the 200% declining balance rate, assuming the car is kept for the period shown below and is used 100% for business trips:

Year	***Deduction from rate table***	***Annual ceiling (43.4)***	***Allowable deduction***
2006	$4,000 (20% × $20,000)	$ 2,960	$ 2,960
2007	6,400 (32% × $20,000)	4,800	4,800
2008	3,840 (19.20% × $20,000)	2,850	2,850
2009	2,304 (11.52% × $20,000)	1,775	1,775
2010	2,304 (11.52% × $20,000)	1,775	1,775
2011*	1,152 (5.76% × $20,000)	1,775	1,152
2012		1,775	1,775
2013		1,775	1,775
2014		515	515

** Note that for the first five years (2006–2010), the allowable deduction is limited to the annual ceiling but in year six (2011), the deduction is based on the MACRS rate table because $1,152 (5.76% × $20,000) is less than the $1,775 annual ceiling.*

Table 43-5 MACRS Deduction: Mid-Quarter Convention

Year—	Placed in service in— First Quarter		Second Quarter		Third Quarter		Fourth Quarter	
	200% Rate	150% Rate	200% Rate	150% Rate	200% Rate	150% Rate	200% Rate	150% Rate
1	35.00%	26.25%	25.00%	18.75%	15.00%	11.25%	5.00%	3.75%
2	26.00	22.13	30.00	24.38	34.00	26.63	38.00	28.88
3	15.60	16.52	18.00	17.06	20.40	18.64	22.80	20.21
4	11.01	16.52	11.37	16.76	12.24	16.56	13.68	16.40
5	11.01	16.52	11.37	16.76	11.30	16.57	10.94	16.41
6	1.38	2.06	4.26	6.29	7.06	10.35	9.58	14.35

43.6 Straight-Line Method

You may not use first-year expensing (Section 179 deduction) or accelerated MACRS *(43.5)* if your business use of your car, truck, or van is 50% or less in the year you place it in service. Mandatory straight-line recovery rates for business use of 50% or less using the half-year or mid-quarter convention are shown below. These straight-line rates are also used if your business use exceeds 50% and you elect straight-line recovery instead of the regular MACRS method. *See* the preceding section *(43.5)* for determining whether the half-year or mid-quarter convention applies.

For each year of the six-year recovery period, apply the straight-line rate from the applicable table against your unadjusted basis, which is the business part of your cost minus any first-year expensing deduction or special depreciation allowance *(43.5)*. The deduction from the table is allowed only to the extent that it does not exceed the annual deduction ceiling *(43.4)*.

If business use initially exceeds 50% and accelerated MACRS is claimed but business use drops to 50% or less before the end of the six-year recovery period, a recapture rule applies a straight-line computation retroactively *(43.10)*.

Table 43-6 Straight-Line Half-Year Convention*

Straight-line year—	Half-year convention rate—
1	10%
2	20
3	20
4	20
5	20
6	10

**The deduction may not exceed the annual deduction ceiling (43.4).*

EXAMPLE

In April 2010, you place in service an automobile which cost $24,000 (assuming you opt out of the bonus allowance). You used it 40% for business. The depreciable basis is $9,600 (40% of $24,000). The depreciation deduction in 2010 is $960 (10% of $9,600) if the half-year convention applies. It is less than the annual deduction ceiling of $1,224 (40% of the $3,060 first-year ceiling for 2010) *(43.4)*.

Table 43-7 Straight-Line Mid-Quarter Convention*

	Placed in service in—			
Year	*First Quarter*	*Second Quarter*	*Third Quarter*	*Fourth Quarter*
1	17.50%	12.50%	7.50%	2.50%
2	20.00	20.00	20.00	20.00
3	20.00	20.00	20.00	20.00
4	20.00	20.00	20.00	20.00
5	20.00	20.00	20.00	20.00
6	2.50	7.50	12.50	17.50

**The deduction may not exceed the annual deduction ceiling (43.4).*

EXAMPLE

In 2010, you place in service a car costing $15,000 used 40% for business. Assume the mid-quarter convention applies. Depending on the applicable quarter, the deduction is listed below, figured on a basis of $6,000 ($15,000 x 40%). The first-year ceiling at 40% business use is $1,224 ($3,060 x 40%). The ceiling does not apply because the mid-quarter rates provide a lower deduction.

Quarter	*Deduction*
1	$1,050 ($6,000 x 17.5%)
2	750 ($6,000 x 12.5%)
3	450 ($6,000 x 7.5%)
4	150 ($6,000 x 2.5%)

43.7 Depreciation for Year Vehicle Is Disposed Of

If you dispose of your car, truck, or van before the end of the six-year recovery period, you are allowed a partial depreciation deduction for the year of disposition. The deduction depends on the depreciation method and convention being used.

If you were depreciating the vehicle under the half-year convention *(43.5)*, you may claim for the year of disposition 50% of the deduction that would be allowed for the full year under the 200% or 150% declining balance method, or the straight-line method.

If you were depreciating the vehicle under the mid-quarter convention *(43.5)*, your deduction for the year of disposition depends on the month of disposition. You deduct 87.5% of the full-year mid-quarter convention deduction *(43.5)* if the disposition occurred in October–December. If the disposition is in July–September, 62.5% of the full year's deduction is allowed. Your deduction is 37.5% of the full-year deduction if the disposition is in April–June, or 12.5% of the full-year deduction if the disposition is in January–March.

EXAMPLE

In December 2006, you bought a used car costing $20,000 that you used exclusively for business until you sold it in April 2010. You depreciated the car under the mid-quarter convention.

For 2010, the year of disposition, the full-year deduction would be $1,775. The $1,775 annual ceiling (fifth-year ceiling for cars placed in service in 2006) is less than the $2,188 deduction (10.94% x $20,000) allowed under the fourth quarter 200% rate mid-quarter convention table *(43.5)*. Since the car was disposed of in April, you may deduct 37.5% of $1,775, or $666, on your 2010 return.

43.8 Depreciation After Recovery Period Ends

If your business use of a car, truck, or van during the recovery period is 100% and your deductions are limited by the annual ceilings *(43.4)*, any remaining basis that was not deducted because of the ceilings may be depreciated in the years after the end of the recovery period.

If the vehicle was used less than 100% for business, any unrecovered basis may be deductible, but to determine unrecovered basis, original basis must be reduced by the depreciation that would have been allowed had the vehicle been used 100% for business.

EXAMPLE

In January 2004 you bought a used car costing $28,600 that you used 100% for business every year from 2004 through 2009. You elected not to claim first-year expensing and elected out of bonus depreciation. Your depreciation deductions for the six-year recovery period under the 200% declining balance method were limited because of the annual deduction ceilings *(43.4)*. For 2004 through 2008, you deducted the annual ceiling amounts. For 2008, your deduction was based on the MACRS half-year convention rate table *(43.5)* because this amount was less than the annual ceiling. Total depreciation deductions for 2004–2009 were $16,107, as shown below (assuming that the bonus depreciation was not used).

Year	*200% rate deduction*	*Annual ceiling*	*Allowable deduction*
2004	$5,720 (20% x $28,600)	$2,960	$2,960
2005	9,152 (32% x $28,600)	4,800	4,800
2006	5,491 (19.20% x $28,600)	2,850	2,850
2007	3,295 (11.52% x $28,600)	1,675	1,675
2008	3,295 (11.52% x $28,600)	1,675	1,675
2009	1,647 (5.76% x $28,600)	1,675	1,647

At the beginning of 2010, your unrecovered basis in the car is $12,993 (the original basis of $28,600 minus the $15,607 of depreciation deductions allowed from 2004 through 2009). If you continue to use the car 100% for business in 2010 and later years, you can deduct $1,675 in 2010 and also in later years until the $12,993 of unrecovered basis is used up. In years of partial business use, the deduction will be limited to $1,675 multiplied by the business-use percentage.

If you had *not* used the car for business 100% of the time in all prior years, your unrecovered basis would still be $12,993. That is because for purposes of figuring unrecovered basis, you must reduce original basis by the depreciation that would have been allowed based on 100% business use.

43.9 Trade-in of Business Vehicle

No gain or loss is recognized when you trade in your old car, truck, or van for a new one where you opt to treat the disposition as tax free (different rules apply if you do not make this election, as explained in IRS Publication 946). However, the trade-in affects the basis of the new vehicle for purposes of depreciation. The basis adjustment depends on whether the car you traded in was used solely or partially for business.

Old vehicle used entirely for business. The basis of the new vehicle acquired in the trade-in is the adjusted basis of the old vehicle (its cost reduced by depreciation deductions), plus any cash you had to pay.

EXAMPLE

You trade in your 2004 car used exclusively for business to acquire a new car this year that costs $20,000. The adjusted basis of the 2004 car is $3,000 and you pay $17,000 cash. Your basis in the new car is $20,000 ($3,000 adjusted basis of the trade-in car plus $17,000 cash).

If you claimed first-year expensing, or bonus depreciation, you must make additional adjustments to basis (*see* IRS Publication 463).

Caution

Trade-in Adjustment

The trade-in adjustment is *not* used for determining gain or loss on the disposition of the new car when it is later sold. It is used solely for depreciation purposes.

Old vehicle used partially for business. There is a special "trade-in adjustment" for cars, trucks, or vans used for both personal and business use. This adjustment reduces the basis of the new vehicle (but not below zero) by the amount of depreciation you would have claimed if you had used the old vehicle entirely for business. To figure the basis of the new vehicle, including the trade-in adjustment, start with the adjusted basis of the old vehicle (*see* above). Add any cash you pay to acquire the new vehicle. Then subtract the excess, if any, of the depreciation you could have claimed had you used the old vehicle entirely for business over your actual depreciation for the old vehicle (the trade-in adjustment). *See* the examples in IRS Publication 463.

43.10 Recapture of Deductions on Business Car, Truck, or Van

If you use your car, truck, or van more than 50% for business in the year you place it in service, you may use MACRS accelerated rates *(43.5)*. If business use drops to 50% or less in the second, third, fourth, fifth, or sixth year, earlier MACRS deductions must be recaptured and reported as ordinary income. In the year in which business use drops to 50% or less, you must recapture excess depreciation for all prior years. Excess depreciation is the difference between: (1) the MACRS deductions allowed in previous years, including the first-year expensing deduction and bonus first-year depreciation allowance *(43.4)*, if any, and (2) the amount of depreciation that would have been allowed if you claimed straight-line depreciation *(43.6)* based on a six-year recovery period.

The recapture rules do not apply if you elected straight-line recovery instead of applying accelerated MACRS rates.

Recapture is reported on Form 4797, which must be attached to Form 1040. Under the listed property rules, the 50%-business-use test and recapture rule apply to cars, trucks, vans, boats, airplanes, motorcycles, and other vehicles used to transport persons or goods, but there are exceptions for ambulances, hearses, and other trucks and vans that are considered qualified non-personal-use vehicles *(43.4)*.

Any recaptured amount increases the basis of the property. To compute depreciation for the year in which business use drops to 50% or less and for later years within the six-year straight-line recovery period, you apply the straight-line rates *(43.6)*.

EXAMPLE

On June 25, 2006, you bought a car for $11,000 that you used exclusively for business in 2006, 2007, 2008, and 2009.The half-year convention applied to your MACRS deductions *(43.5)*. The deductions figured under the half-year convention table ($2,200 for 2006, $3,520 for 2007, $2,112 for 2008, and $1,267 for 2009) applied as they were less than the annual ceilings for those years ($2,960, $4,800, $2,850, and $1,775, respectively). During 2010, you used the car 40% for business and 60% for personal purposes. As you did not meet the more-than-50%-business-use test in 2009, excess depreciation of $1,399 is recaptured and reported on Form 4797 for 2010:

Total MACRS depreciation claimed (2006–2009)	$9,099	
Total straight-line depreciation *(43.6)* allowable:		
2006—10% of $11,000	$1,100	
2007—20% of $11,000	2,200	
2008—20% of $11,000	2,200	
2009—20% of $11,000	2,200	7,700
Excess depreciation recaptured		$1,399

Your 2010 depreciation deduction is $880 ($11,000 × 20% straight-line rate in fifth year × 40% business use).

The amount of recaptured depreciation increases the adjusted basis for purposes of computing gain or loss on a disposition of the automobile.

43.11 Keeping Records of Business Use

Keep a log or diary or similar record of the business use of a car. Record the purpose of the business trips and mileage covered for business travel. In the record book or electronic record, also note the odometer reading for the beginning and end of the taxable year. You need this data to prove business use. If you do not keep written records of business mileage and your return is examined, you will have to convince an IRS agent of your business mileage through oral testimony. Without written evidence, you may be unable to convince an IRS agent that you use the car for business travel or that you meet the business-use tests for claiming MACRS. You may also be subject to general negligence penalties for claiming deductions that you cannot prove you incurred.

Mileage records are not required for vehicles that are unlikely to be used for personal purposes, such as delivery trucks with seating only for the driver.

Employees using company cars are not required to keep mileage records if (1) a written company policy allows them to use the car for commuting and no other personal driving other than personal errands while commuting home or (2) a written company policy bars all personal driving except for minor stops, such as for lunch, between business travel. Owners, directors, and officers of the company generally do not qualify for exception (1).

43.12 Leased Business Vehicles: Deductions and Income

If you lease rather than purchase a car, truck, or van for business use, you may deduct the lease charges as a business expense deduction if you use the vehicle exclusively for business. If you also use the vehicle for personal driving, you may deduct only the lease payments allocated to business travel. Also keep a record of business use; *see 43.11*.

Added income. If in 2010 you lease a vehicle for 30 days or more, you may have to report as income an amount based on an IRS table. This income rule applies if you deduct the business portion of your lease payments plus other operating costs; it does not apply if you claim the standard mileage allowance *(43.1)*. On Schedule C (if self-employed) or Form 2106 (if an employee), the income inclusion amount reduces your deduction for lease payments so that it equals the amount that would be deductible as depreciation if you had bought the vehicle outright. The income amount is reduced where you leased the vehicle for less than the entire year or business use is less than 100%.

The lease tables, which are in IRS Publication 463, show income amounts for each year of the lease. Publication 463 also has tables showing income amounts for vehicles leased before 2010.

Caution

Leased Vehicle

If in 2010 you leased a car, truck, or van for at least 30 days and you deduct the lease charges as a business expense *(43.12)*, you generally must reduce the deduction by an "income inclusion amount" based on an IRS table. If you claim the standard mileage allowance *(43.1)*, the income inclusion rule does not apply. *See* IRS Publication 463 for details.

Chapter 44

Sales of Business Property

On the sale of business assets, the tax treatment depends on the type of asset sold.

Inventory items: Profits are taxable as ordinary income; losses are fully deductible. Sales of merchandise are reported on Schedule C if you are self-employed or Schedule F if you are a farmer.

Depreciable property, such as buildings, machinery, and equipment: If you sell at a gain, the gain is taxable as ordinary income to the extent depreciation is recaptured *(44.1–44.2)*. Any remaining gain may be treated as capital gain or ordinary income, depending on the Section 1231 computation *(44.8)*. Losses may be deductible as ordinary losses *(44.8)*. Sales are reported on Form 4797. Depreciable business equipment subject to recapture is described as a Section 1245 asset. Depreciable livestock is also a Section 1245 asset. Depreciable realty is generally described as a Section 1250 asset.

Land: If used in your business, capital gain or ordinary income may be realized under the rules of Section 1231 *(44.8)*. If land owned by your business is held for investment, gain or loss is subject to capital gain treatment. Schedule D is used to report the sale of capital assets.

See also:

29.7 Personal and Business Use of a Home
29.9 Loss on Residence Converted to Rental Property
40.27 Filing Schedule F (farm income)

44.1 Depreciation Recaptured as Ordinary Income on Sale of Personal Property

On Form 4797, you report gain or loss on the sale of depreciable property. Gain realized on the sale of depreciable *personal property* (Section 1245 property) is treated as ordinary income to the extent the gain is attributed to depreciation deductions that reduced basis. In other words, the depreciation deductions are "recaptured" as ordinary income. If gain exceeds the amount of depreciation subject to recapture, the excess may be capital gain under Section 1231 *(44.8)*.

Gain on the sale of real estate placed in service before 1987 may be subject to depreciation recapture *(44.2)*.

Gain subject to recapture for Section 1245 property is limited to the lower of (1) the amount of gain on the sale (amount realized less adjusted basis) or (2) the depreciation allowed or allowable while you held the property. Generally, the depreciation deduction taken into account for each year is the amount allowed or allowable, whichever is greater. However, for purposes of figuring what portion of the gain is treated as ordinary income under the recapture rules (but not for purposes of figuring gain or loss), the depreciation taken into account for any year will be the amount actually "allowed" on your prior returns under a proper depreciation method, rather than the amount "allowable," if the allowed deduction is smaller and you can prove its amount.

The adjusted basis of personal property depreciable under ACRS, such as business equipment and machinery, is fixed as of the beginning of the year of disposition. However, property depreciated under MACRS is subject to the convention rules so that partial depreciation under the applicable convention is allowed in the year of sale; this year of sale depreciation reduces adjusted basis.

Caution

Dispositions Other Than Sales

Recapture rules affect gifts, charitable donations, and inheritances of depreciable property *(44.4)*, as well as like-kind exchanges and involuntary conversions *(44.5)*.

EXAMPLE

In March 2008, you bought and placed in service a light truck (five-year property) at a cost of $10,000. You used the truck 100% for business. You deducted depreciation under the half-year convention of $2,000 for 2008 and $3,200 for 2009; *see* the MACRS rates in 42.5. In January 2010, you sold the truck for $6,000. For 2010, you are allowed an MACRS deduction of one-half of the full year deduction, or $960 (19.20% x $10,000 ÷ 2). Your adjusted basis is $3,840 ($10,000 cost – $6,160 total depreciation). Your gain on the sale is $2,160 ($6,000 proceeds – $3,840 adjusted basis). You must recapture the entire $2,160 gain as ordinary income, as it is less than the $6,160 depreciation.

44.2 Depreciation Recaptured as Ordinary Income on Sale of Real Estate

All or part of gain on the sale of depreciable real property may be attributable to depreciation deductions that reduced the basis of the property. On Form 4797, gain attributable to depreciation on Section 1250 realty placed in service before 1987 is subject to recapture as ordinary income unless straight-line depreciation was used. The amount of depreciation recapture depends on when the building was placed in service and whether it was residential or nonresidential; *see* below.

There is no ordinary income recapture for residential rental and nonresidential real property placed in service after 1986 because such properties are depreciated using the straight-line MACRS method *(42.13)*. However, the 30% or 50% bonus depreciation that had been allowed on qualifying New York Liberty Zone real property and 50% bonus depreciation on GO Zone property is subject to recapture on Form 4797. Similarly, 50% bonus depreciation claimed for qualifying property placed in service in 2008 or 2009 (and 2010 if bonus depreciation is extended *(42.21)*) will be subject to recapture.

To the extent depreciation is not subject to ordinary income recapture, the gain on the sale is subject to the Section 1231 netting rules *(44.8)*. If there is a net Section 1231 gain, the gain attributed to the depreciation is entered on the Unrecaptured Section 1250 Gain Worksheet in the Schedule D (Form 1040) instructions. The unrecaptured Section 1250 gain from that worksheet is subject to a top rate of 25% on the Schedule D Tax Worksheet included in the Schedule D instructions.

Recaptured depreciation. Ordinary income recapture may apply to Section 1250 realty placed in service before 1987. Section 1250 property includes buildings and structural components, except for elevators and escalators or other tangible property used as an integral part of manufacturing, production, or extraction, or of furnishing transportation, electrical energy, water, gas, sewage disposal services, or communications. Property may initially be Section 1250 property and then, on a change of use, become Section 1245 property *(44.1)*. Such property may not be reconverted to Section 1250 property.

Depreciation claimed on realty during the years 1964 through 1969. Depreciation claimed during this period is not recaptured.

Depreciation claimed after 1969 for realty placed in service before 1981. For nonresidential realty, 100 percent of the depreciation claimed after 1969 in excess of straight-line recovery is subject to recapture but not in excess of the actual gain.

For residential rental property, there is no recapture of excess depreciation (over straight-line) claimed after 1969 and before 1976. Real property is considered residential rental property if 80% or more of gross income is from dwelling units. One hundred percent of the excess depreciation claimed after 1975 is subject to recapture. Part III of Form 4797 is used to compute the amount of depreciation recapture that is to be reported as ordinary income.

Depreciation claimed on realty placed in service after 1980 and before 1987. For real property placed in service after 1980 and before 1987 that was subject to ACRS, adjusted basis for computing gain or loss is the adjusted basis at the start of the year reduced by the ACRS deduction allowed for the number of months the realty is in service in the year of disposition *(42.16)*. The recapture rules distinguish between residential and nonresidential property.

If the prescribed accelerated method is used to recover the cost of *nonresidential* property, all gain on the disposition of the realty is recaptured as ordinary income to the extent of recovery allowances previously taken. Thus, nonresidential realty will be treated in the same way as personal property *(44.1)* for purposes of recapture if the accelerated recovery allowance was claimed. If the straight-line method was elected, there is no recapture; all gain is subject to the netting rules of Section 1231 *(44.8)*.

If accelerated cost recovery is used for a *nonresidential* building and straight-line depreciation is used for a substantial improvement to that building that you are allowed to depreciate separately *(42.16)*, all gain on a disposition of the entire building is treated as ordinary income to the extent of the accelerated cost recovery claimed. Remaining gain is subject to the rules for Section 1231 assets *(44.8)*.

For *residential* real estate, 100% of the excess depreciation claimed is subject to recapture. That is, there is ordinary income recapture to the extent the depreciation allowed under the prescribed accelerated method exceeds the recovery that would have been allowable if the straight-line method over the ACRS recovery period had been used. If the straight-line method was elected, there is no recapture. All gain is subject to Section 1231 netting *(44.8)*.

For *low-income rental housing*, the percentage of excess depreciation (over straight-line) subject to recapture is 100% minus 1% for each full month the property was held over 100 months, so that there is no recapture of cost recovery deductions for property held at least 200 months (16 years and 8 months). If you dispose of low-income housing with separate improvements, or with units placed in service at different times, the amount of excess depreciation must be computed separately for each element. *See* IRS Publication 544 for details on the recapture rules for low-income housing.

44.3 Recapture of First-Year Expensing

On Form 4797, the first-year expensing deduction (Section 179 deduction *(42.3)*) is treated as depreciation for purposes of recapture. When expensed property is sold or exchanged, gain is ordinary income to the extent of the first-year expense deduction plus ACRS or MACRS deductions and bonus depreciation *(42.20)*, if any *(44.1)*. If the entire cost of the property was expensed, adjusted basis will generally be reduced to zero, gain on a sale or exchange will equal the sales price (less expenses), and the entire gain will be recaptured as ordinary income.

Expensing deductions are also subject to recapture if property placed in service after 1986 is not used more than 50% of the time for business in any year before the end of the recovery period. The amount recaptured is the excess of the first-year *expensing* deduction over the amount of depreciation that would have been claimed in prior years and in the recapture year without expensing.

Caution

Installment Sale

If you sell property on the installment basis, the first-year expensing deduction claimed for the property in a prior year is recaptured in the year of sale on Form 4797. An installment sale does not defer recapture of the first-year deduction *(44.6)*.

Automobiles and other "listed property." If the more-than-50%-business-use test for a business automobile or other "listed property" such as certain computers *(42.10)* is not met in a year after the auto or other "listed property" is placed in service and before the end of the recovery period, any first-year expensing deduction is subject to recapture on Form 4797; *see* the Example at *43.10*.

44.4 Gifts and Inheritances of Depreciable Property

Gifts and charitable donations of depreciable property may be affected by the recapture rules. On the gift of depreciable property, the ordinary income potential of the depreciation carries over into the hands of the donee. When the donee later sells the property at a profit, he or she will realize ordinary income *(44.1)*. A person receiving a gift of low-income housing property includes in the holding period the period for which the donor held the property for purposes of applying the 200-month phaseout of recapture rule *(44.2)*.

On the donation of depreciable property, the amount of the contribution deduction is reduced by the amount that would be taxed as ordinary income had the donor sold the equipment at its fair market value.

The transfer of depreciable property to an heir through inheritance is not a taxable event for recapture purposes. The ordinary income potential does not carry over to the heir because his or her basis is usually fixed as of the date of the decedent's death.

Important: A gift of depreciable property subject to a mortgage may be taxed to the extent that the liability exceeds the basis of the property *(14.6, 31.15)*.

44.5 Involuntary Conversions and Tax-Free Exchanges

Involuntary conversions. Gain may be taxed as ordinary income in either of the following two cases: (1) you do not buy qualified replacement property or (2) you buy a qualified replacement, but the cost of the replacement is less than the amount realized on the conversion *(18.23)*. The amount taxable as ordinary income may not exceed the amount of gain that is normally taxed under involuntary conversion rules when the replacement cost is less than the amount realized on the conversion. Also, the amount of ordinary income is increased by the value of any nondepreciable property that is bought as qualified replacement property, such as the purchase of 80% or more of stock in a company that owns property similar to the converted property.

Distributions by a partnership to a partner. A distribution of depreciable property by a partnership to a partner does not result in ordinary income to the distributee at the time of the distribution. But the partner assumes the ordinary income potential of the depreciation deduction taken by the partnership on the property. When he or she later disposes of the property, ordinary income may be realized.

Caution

Tax-Free Exchanges

Ordinary income generally is not realized on a tax-free exchange or trade-in of the same type of property (unless some gain is taxed because the exchange is accompanied by "boot" *(6.3)* such as money). The ordinary income potential is assumed in the basis of the new property. However, where depreciable realty acquired before 1987 is exchanged for land, the amount of any depreciation recapture is immediately taxable in the year of the exchange.

44.6 Installment Sale of Depreciable Property

All depreciation recapture income (including the first-year expensing deduction) is fully taxable in the year of sale, without regard to the time of payment. Recapture is figured on Form 4797. On Form 6252, the gain in excess of the recapture income is reported under the installment method *(5.21)*.

44.7 Sale of a Proprietorship

The sale of a sole proprietorship is not considered as the sale of a business unit but as sales of individual business assets. Each sale is reported separately on your tax return.

A purchase of a business involves the purchase of various individual business assets of the business. To force buyers and sellers to follow the same allocation rules, current law requires both the buyer and the seller to allocate the purchase price of a business among the transferred assets using a residual method formula. Allocations are based on the proportion of sales price to an asset's fair market value and they are made in a specific order set out on Form 8594.

44.8 Property Used in a Business (Section 1231 Assets)

Form 4797 is used to report the sale or exchange of Section 1231 assets. The following properties used in a business are considered "Section 1231 assets":

- Depreciable assets such as buildings, machinery, and other equipment held more than one year. Depreciable rental property and royalty property fits in this category if held more than one year.
- Land (including growing crops and water rights underlying farmland) held more than one year.
- Timber, coal, or domestic iron ore subject to special capital gain treatment.
- Leaseholds held more than one year.
- An unharvested crop on farmlands, if the crop and land are sold, exchanged, or involuntarily converted at the same time and to the same person and the land has been held more than one year. Such property is not included here if you retain an option to reacquire the land.
- Cattle and horses held for draft, breeding, dairy, or sporting purposes for at least 24 months.
- Livestock (other than cattle and horses) held for draft, breeding, dairy, or sporting purposes for at least 12 months. Poultry is not treated as livestock for purposes of Section 1231.

Caution

Capital Gain or Ordinary Loss

Profitable sales and involuntary conversions of Section 1231 assets are generally treated as capital gain, except for profits on equipment *(44.1)* and real estate allocated to recaptured depreciation *(44.2)*, and losses are deducted as ordinary loss. However, the exact tax result depends on the net profit and loss realized for all sales of such property made during the tax year. Under the netting rules *(44.8)*, the net result of these sales determines the tax treatment of each individual sale. In making the computation on Form 4797, you must also consider losses and gains from casualty, theft, and other involuntary conversions involving business and investment property held more than one year. Follow the Form 4797 instructions.

Section 1231 netting. On Form 4797, you combine all losses and gains, except gains allocated to depreciation recapture, from:

- The sale of Section 1231 assets (from the list at the beginning of this section).
- The involuntary conversion of Section 1231 assets and capital assets held for more than one year for business or investment purposes. You include casualty and theft losses incurred on business or investment property held for more than one year. However, there is an exception if losses exceed gains from casualties or thefts in one taxable year.

Involuntary conversions of capital assets held for personal purposes are not subject to a Section 1231 computation but are subject to a separate computation; *see 18.25*.

Result of netting. A net gain on Section 1231 assets from Form 4797 is entered on Schedule D as a long-term capital gain unless the recapture rule (*see* the second Caution on this page) for net ordinary losses applies. A net loss on Section 1231 assets is combined on Form 4797 with ordinary income from depreciation recapture *(44.1)* and with ordinary gains and losses from the sale of business property that does not qualify for Section 1231 netting.

Installment sale. Gain realized on the installment sale of business or income-producing property held for more than a year may be capital gain one year and ordinary income another year. Actual treatment in each year depends on the net result of all sales, including installment payments received in that year *(44.6)*.

Losses exceed gains from casualties or thefts. On Form 4684, you must compute the net financial result from all involuntary conversions arising from fire, storm, or other casualty or theft of assets used in your business and capital assets held for business or income-producing purposes and held more than one year. The purpose of the computation is to determine whether these involuntary conversions enter into the above Section 1231 computation. If the net result is a gain, all of the assets enter into the Section 1231 computation. If the net result is a loss, then these assets do not enter into the computation; the losses are deducted separately as casualty losses, and the gains reported separately as ordinary income. If you incur only losses, the losses similarly do not enter into the Section 1231 computation.

Caution

Recapture of Net Ordinary Losses

Net Section 1231 gain is not treated as capital gain but as ordinary income to the extent of net Section 1231 losses realized in the five most recent prior taxable years. Losses are recaptured in chronological order on Form 4797. Losses that have already been "recaptured" under this rule in prior years are not taken into account.

EXAMPLE

You suffer an uninsured fire loss of $2,000 on business equipment and gain of $1,000 on other insured investment property damaged by a storm. All of the property was held more than one year. Because loss exceeds gain, neither transaction enters into a Section 1231 computation. The gain is reported as ordinary income and the loss is deducted as an ordinary loss. The effect is a net $1,000 loss deduction. If the figures were reversed, that is, if the gain were $2,000 and the loss $1,000, both assets would enter into the Section 1231 computation. If only the fire loss occurred, the loss would be treated as a casualty loss and would not enter into the Section 1231 computation.

44.9 Sale of Property Used for Business and Personal Purposes

One sale will be reported as two separate sales for tax purposes when you sell a car or any other equipment used for business and personal purposes, or in some cases where a sold residence *(29.7)* was used partly as a residence and partly as a place of business or to produce rent income.

You allocate the sales price and the basis of the property between the business portion and the personal portion. The allocation is based on use. For example, with a car, the allocation is based on mileage used in business and personal driving.

EXAMPLE

Two partners bought an airplane for about $54,000. They used approximately 75% of its flying time for personal flights and 25% for business flights. After using the plane for eight years, they sold it for about $35,000. Depreciation taken on the business part of the plane amounted to $13,000. The partners figured they incurred a loss of $6,000 on the sale. The IRS, allocating the proceeds and basis between business and personal use, claimed they realized a profit of $8,250 on the business part of the plane and a nondeductible loss of $14,250 on the personal part. The allocation was as follows:

		IRS Position	
	Partners' claim	*Business (25%)*	*Personal (75%)*
Original cost	$54,000	$13,500	$40,500
Depreciation	13,000	13,000	
Adjusted basis	41,000	500	40,500
Selling price	35,000	8,750	26,250
Gain (Nondeductible loss)	($6,000)	$8,250	($14,250)

The partners argued that the IRS could not split the sale into two separate sales. They sold only one airplane and therefore there was only one sale. A federal district court and appeals court disagreed and held that the IRS method of allocation is practical and fair.

44.10 Should You Trade in Business Equipment?

The purchase of new business equipment is often partially financed by trading in old equipment. For tax purposes, a trade-in may not be a good decision. If the market value of the equipment is below its adjusted basis, it may be preferable to sell the equipment to realize an immediate deductible loss. You may not deduct a loss on a trade-in. However, if you do trade, the potential deduction reflected in the cost basis of the old equipment is not forfeited. The undepreciated basis of the old property becomes part of the basis of the new property and may be depreciated. Therefore, in deciding whether to trade or sell where a loss may be realized, determine whether you will get a greater tax reduction by taking an immediate loss on a sale or by claiming larger depreciation deductions.

If the fair market value of the old equipment exceeds its adjusted basis, you have a potential gain. To defer tax on this gain, you may want to trade the equipment in for new equipment. Your decision to sell or trade will generally be based on a comparison between (1) tax imposed on an immediate sale and larger depreciation deductions taken on the cost basis of the new property, and (2) the tax consequences of a trade-in in which the tax is deferred but reduced depreciation deductions are taken on a lower cost basis of the property. In making this comparison, you will have to estimate your future income and tax rates. Also pay attention to the possibility that gain on a sale may be taxed as ordinary income under the depreciation recapture rules *(44.1)*.

The tax consequences of a trade-in may not be avoided by first selling the used property to the dealer who sells you the new property. The IRS will disregard the sale made to the same dealer from whom you purchase the new equipment. The two transactions will be treated as one trade-in.

44.11 Corporate Liquidation

Liquidation of a corporation and distribution of its assets for your stock is generally subject to capital gain or loss treatment. For example, on a corporate liquidation, you receive property worth $10,000 from the corporation. Assume the basis of your shares, which you have held long term, is $6,000. You have realized a long-term gain of $4,000.

If you incur legal expenses in pressing payment of a claim, you treat the fee as a capital expense, according to the IRS. The Tax Court and an appeals court hold that the fee is deductible as an expense incurred to earn income; the deduction is subject to the 2% adjusted gross income (AGI) floor *(19.1)*.

If you recover a judgment against the liquidator of a corporation for misuse of corporate funds, the judgment is considered part of the amount you received on liquidation and gives you capital gain, not ordinary income.

If you paid a corporate debt after liquidation, the payment reduces the gain realized on the corporate liquidation in the earlier year; thus, in effect, it is a capital loss.

If the corporation distributes liquidating payments over a period of years, gain is not reported until the distributions exceed the adjusted basis of your stock.

Chapter 45

Figuring Self-Employment Tax

Self-employment tax provides funds for Social Security and Medicare benefits. The self-employment tax is calculated on Schedule SE. You are required to prepare Schedule SE if you have self-employment net earnings of $400 or more in 2010, but you will not incur the tax unless your net self-employment earnings exceed $433.13. The tax is added to your income tax liability. When preparing your estimated tax liability, you must also include an estimate of self-employment tax; *see Chapter 27*.

On Schedule SE, self-employment income is reduced by a deduction reflected in the decimal of .9235 listed on the form. You also deduct 50% of the self-employment tax on Line 27 of Form 1040.

For 2010, the self-employment tax of 15.3% consists of the following two rates: 12.4% for Social Security and 2.9% for Medicare. After multiplying the net earnings by .9235, the combined 15.3% rate applies to a taxable earnings base of $106,800 or less; the 2.9% rate applies to all taxable earnings exceeding $106,800.

You are required to pay self-employment tax on self-employment income even after you retire and receive Social Security benefits.

45.1 What Is Self-Employment Income?

On Schedule SE, you generally figure self-employment tax on the net profit from your business or profession whether you participate in its activities full or part time. Net profit is generally the amount shown on Line 31 of Schedule C (or Line 3 of Schedule C-EZ) if you are a sole proprietor. If you are a partner, net earnings subject to self-employment tax are taken from Box 14, Schedule K-1, of Form 1065. If you are a farmer, net farm profit is shown on Line 36, Schedule F.

If you have more than one self-employed operation, your net profit from all the operations is combined. A loss in one self-employed business will reduce the income from another business. You file separate Schedules C for each operation and one Schedule SE showing the combined income (less losses, if any).

For self-employment tax purposes, net earnings are not reduced by deductible contributions to your own SEP or Keogh plan *(41.4)*. For years before 2010, net earnings also could not be reduced by the above-the-line deduction claimed by a self-employed person for health insurance premiums *(12.2)*. However, the Small Business Jobs Act of 2010 allows the income tax deduction for health insurance premiums (from Line 29 of Form 1040) to be taken into account as a reduction to net earnings in figuring the self-employment tax due for 2010. The IRS has implemented the law change on Line 3 of Schedule SE (in both Sections A and B), where the net profit from Schedule C, Schedule K-1, or Schedule F is reduced by the deduction for health insurance premiums. See the sample Short Schedule SE on page 706 and the Long Schedule on page 707 for the reduction on Line 3.

If you and your spouse are the only members of a business that you jointly own and operate, you each materially participate in the business, and you file a joint return, you can make a joint election to file as sole proprietors on Schedule C ("qualified joint venture election"). You make the joint venture election by filing separate Schedule Cs or C-EZs on which you each report your respective share (according to respective ownership interests) of the business income, gains, losses, deductions, and credits. If you make the election, each of you must file a separate Schedule SE to figure self-employment tax on your share of the joint venture income.

Law Alert

Deduction for Health Insurance Premiums Reduces Net Earnings

In calculating net earnings from self-employment for 2010 on Schedule SE, the income tax deduction *(12.2)* for health insurance premiums (claimed on Line 29, Form 1040) is subtracted from the net profit from your business. The Small Business Jobs Act of 2010 (signed into law 9/27/10) allows the reduction only for the 2010 tax year.

Caution

Freelancer Fees

Fees you earn for freelance work as an independent contractor are business earnings reportable on Schedule C, and if you have a net profit, they are subject to self-employment tax on Schedule SE.

Married couples. Where you and your spouse *each* have self-employment income, each spouse must figure separate self-employment income on a separate schedule. Each pays the tax on the separate self-employment income. Both schedules are attached to the joint return.

If you live in a community property state, business income is not treated as community property for self-employment tax purposes. The spouse who is actually carrying on the business is subject to self-employment tax on the earnings.

Exceptions. The following types of income or items are *not* included as self-employment income on Schedule SE:

1. **Rent from real estate is generally not self-employment income.** However, self-employment tax applies to the business income of a real estate dealer or income in a rental business where substantial services are rendered to the occupant, as in the leasing of—
   - Rooms in a hotel or in a boarding house.
   - Apartments, but only if extra services for the occupants' convenience, such as maid service or changing linens, are provided.
   - Cabins or cabanas in tourist camps where you provide maid services, linens, utensils, and swimming, boating, fishing, and other facilities, for which you do not charge separately.
   - Farmland in which the landlord materially participates in the actual production of the farm or in the management of production. For purposes of "material participation," the activities of a landlord's agent are not counted, only the landlord's actual participation.
2. **Capital gains are not self-employment income.** Self-employment income does not include gains from the sale of property unless it is inventory or held for sale to customers in the ordinary course of business. Thus, traders in securities *(30.16)* who buy and sell securities for their own account do not treat net gains or losses from the sales as self-employment income or loss. Dealers in commodities and options are subject to self-employment tax *see Table 45.1.*

Filing Tip

Real Estate Investor

The owner of one office building who holds it for investment (rather than for sale in the ordinary course of business) is not a real estate dealer, but a real estate investor. If the only tenant services provided are heat, light, water, and trash collection, report the rental income and expenses on Schedule E. The activity is not a Schedule C business subject to self-employment tax.

3. **Dividends and interest.** Generally, dividends and interest are not self-employment income. However, dividends earned by a dealer in securities and interest on accounts receivable are treated as self-employment income if the securities are not being held for investment. A dealer is one who buys stock as inventory to sell to customers.
4. **Conservation reserve payments received by retirees and disabled farmers receiving Social Security benefits.** This applies to payments received after December 31, 2007.

Net operating loss deduction. A loss carryover from past years does not reduce business income for self-employment tax purposes. Similarly, the personal exemption may not be used to reduce self-employment income.

Filing Tip

Trader in Securities

If you are a trader in securities *(30.16)*, gains or losses from your trading business are not subject to self-employment tax.

Statutory employees. Wages of a statutory employee, such as a full-time life insurance salesperson *(40.6)*, are not subject to self-employment tax, as Social Security and Medicare tax have been withheld.

Farmers. Cash or a payment in kind under the "Payment-in-Kind" program is considered earned income subject to self-employment tax.

Business interruption proceeds. The IRS and the Tax Court disagree over whether business interruption insurance proceeds must be reported as earnings subject to self-employment tax. The Tax Court held that insurance payments made to a grocer as compensation for lost earnings due to a fire were not subject to self-employment tax because the payment was not for actual services. The IRS refuses to follow the decision, holding that such payments represented income that would have been earned had business operations not been interrupted.

45.2 Partners Pay Self-Employment Tax

A general partner includes his or her share of partnership income or loss in net earnings from self-employment, including guaranteed payments. If your personal tax year is different from the partnership's tax year, you include your share of partnership income or loss for the partnership tax year ending within 2010.

A limited partner is not subject to self-employment tax on his or her share of partnership income except for guaranteed payments for services performed, which are subject to the tax.

If a general partner dies within the partnership's tax year, self-employment income includes his or her distributive share of the income earned by the partnership through the end of the month in which the death occurs. This is true even though his or her heirs or estate succeeds to the partnership rights. For this purpose, partnership income for the year is considered to be earned ratably each month.

Retirement payments from partnership. Retirement payments you receive from your partnership are *not* subject to self-employment tax if the following conditions are met:

1. The payments are made under a qualified written plan providing for periodic payments on retirement of partners with payments to continue until death.
2. You rendered no services in any business conducted by the partnership during the tax year of the partnership ending within or with your tax year.
3. By the end of the partnership's tax year, your share in the partnership's capital has been paid to you in full, and there is no obligation from the other partners to you other than with respect to the retirement payments under the plan.

Limited liability company (LLC) members. Are LLC members treated as general or limited partners for purposes of self-employment tax? The matter is not completely settled, but it appears that members owe self-employment tax when they perform services for their business, participate in management activities, and are not mere investors.

45.3 Schedule SE

Schedule SE has an introductory "road map" designed to lead you to either the short or long version of Schedule SE. Once you pass through the road map, the preparation of either the short or long schedule for 2010 is not difficult. On both schedules, you reduce your net profit by your income tax deduction for health insurance premiums (Line 29, Form 1040) and multiply the reduced amount by .9235 to get your net earnings from self-employment. In other words, only 92.35% of the net earnings is subject to self-employment tax. The .9235 adjustment is the equivalent of a 7.65% reduction to net earnings, which, along with the income tax deduction for 50% of self-employment tax on Line 27 of Form 1040, attempts to place self-employed individuals on the same level as employees subject to FICA taxes.

Filing Tip

50% Deduction

After you figure your self-employment tax on Schedule SE, deduct one-half of it on Line 27 of Form 1040.

The .9235 adjustment is made on Line 4 of either the short or long Schedule SE. For example, assume you can use the Short Schedule SE. If your net profit from Line 31 of Schedule C is $120,000 and you claim an income tax deduction for health insurance premiums of $6,000 (Line 29, Form 1040), your net earnings from self-employment, shown on Line 3 of the sample Short Schedule SE below, are $114,000. On Line 4, you multiply the $114,000 by .9235, and the result, $105,279, is the amount subject to the self-employment tax on Line 5.

After the .9235 adjustment is made, net earnings are subject to the 12.4% and 2.9% rates, assuming the resulting net earnings are $400 or more. For 2010, the 12.4% Social Security rate applies to the first $106,800 of net earnings and the 2.9% Medicare rate applies to all of the net earnings.

Note: Health insurance deduction. As discussed in *45.1*, it was likely when this book went to press that legislation would be enacted to allow the income tax deduction for health insurance premiums as a reduction to 2010 net earnings from self-employment. If the legislation is enacted, the IRS could change the Short Schedule SE and the Long Schedule SE, as shown in the worksheets below and on the next page. *See* the *e-Supplement at jklasser.com* for any changes to the Schedule SE.

Worksheet—Short Schedule SE

Section A—Short Schedule SE. Caution. Read above to see if you can use Short Schedule SE.

1a	Net farm profit or (loss) from Schedule F, line 36, and farm partnerships, Schedule K-1 (Form 1065), box 14, code A			1a	
b	If you received social security retirement or disability benefits, enter the amount of Conservation Reserve Program payments included on Schedule F, line 6b, or listed on Schedule K-1 (Form 1065), box 20, code Y			1b	( )
2	Net profit or (loss) from Schedule C, line 31; Schedule C-EZ, line 3; Schedule K-1 (Form 1065), box 14, code A (other than farming); and Schedule K-1 (Form 1065-B), box 9, code J1. Ministers and members of religious orders, see page SE-1 for types of income to report on this line. See page SE-3 for other income to report			2	120,000
3	Combine lines 1a, 1b, and 2. Subtract from that total the amount on Form 1040, line 29, or Form 1040NR, line 29, and enter the result (see page SE-3)			3	114,000
4	Multiply line 3 by 92.35% (.9235). If less than $400, you do not owe self-employment tax; **do not** file this schedule unless you have an amount on line 1b ▶			4	105,279
	Note. If line 4 is less than $400 due to Conservation Reserve Program payments on line 1b, see page SE-3.				
5	**Self-employment tax.** If the amount on line 4 is: • $106,800 or less, multiply line 4 by 15.3% (.153). Enter the result here and on **Form 1040, line 56,** or **Form 1040NR, line 54** • More than $106,800, multiply line 4 by 2.9% (.029). Then, add $13,243.20 to the result. Enter the total here and on **Form 1040, line 56,** or **Form 1040NR, line 54**			5	16,108
6	**Deduction for one-half of self-employment tax.** Multiply line 5 by 50% (.50). Enter the result here and on **Form 1040, line 27,** or **Form 1040NR, line 27**	6	8,054		

45.4 How Wages Affect Self-Employment Tax

If you have both a net profit from self-employment and also wage and/or tip income subject to FICA taxes (Social Security and Medicare), the amount of such FICA earnings may affect your self-employment tax liability.

If your 2010 FICA wages or tips were $106,800 or over, your net self-employment earnings (after the .9235 adjustment) are subject only to the 2.9% Medicare rate. If the total of your 2010 FICA wages (and tips) plus net profit was $106,800 or less, all of your net earnings are subject to the 12.4% Social Security rate and the 2.9% Medicare rate. If the total of your 2010 FICA wages and tips plus net earnings was over the $106,800 limit for the 12.4% Social Security rate, the 12.4% rate applies to the lesser of your net self-employment earnings shown on Line 6 of the Long Schedule SE (after the .9235 adjustment), or the excess of $106,800 over the FICA wages and tips shown on Line 9. The 2.9% Medicare rate applies to the entire amount of net self-employment earnings. *See* the following Example and the filled-in long Schedule SE worksheet below.

Caution

Foreign earned income

Even though you can exclude from gross income your foreign earned income of up to $91,500 in 2010, you are subject to self-employment tax on all of your earnings.

EXAMPLE

You earn a salary of $38,100 in 2010 and have a net profit from Schedule C of $73,000. You deduct health insurance premiums of $8,000 on Line 29 of Form 1040. Your net earnings from self-employment on Line 6 of the Long Schedule SE are $60,028 ($73,000 – $8,000 = $65,000 x .9235). The Line 9 amount is $68,700, the excess of the $106,800 maximum Social Security tax base over the $38,100 in wages. The 12.4% Social Security rate applies to the lesser amount, the net earnings of $60,028. The 2.9% Medicare rate also applies to the entire net earnings.

12.4% x $60,028	$ 7,443
2.9% x $60,028	+ 1,741
	9,184

Your self-employment tax liability is $9,184. One-half of that, or $4,592, is deductible on Line 27 of Form 1040.

Worksheet—Long Schedule SE

Part I Self-Employment Tax

Note. If your only income subject to self-employment tax is **church employee income,** see page SE-3 for specific instructions. Also see page SE-1 for the definition of church employee income.

A	If you are a minister, member of a religious order, or Christian Science practitioner **and** you filed Form 4361, but you had $400 or more of **other** net earnings from self-employment, check here and continue with Part I . . . . ▶ ☐				
1a	Net farm profit or (loss) from Schedule F, line 36, and farm partnerships, Schedule K-1 (Form 1065), box 14, code A. **Note.** Skip lines 1a and 1b if you use the farm optional method (see page SE-4)			1a	
b	If you received social security retirement or disability benefits, enter the amount of Conservation Reserve Program payments included on Schedule F, line 6b, or listed on Schedule K-1 (Form 1065), box 20, code Y			1b	( )
2	Net profit or (loss) from Schedule C, line 31; Schedule C-EZ, line 3; Schedule K-1 (Form 1065), box 14, code A (other than farming); and Schedule K-1 (Form 1065-B), box 9, code J1. Ministers and members of religious orders, see page SE-1 for types of income to report on this line. See page SE-3 for other income to report. **Note.** Skip this line if you use the nonfarm optional method (see page SE-4)			2	73,000
3	Combine lines 1a, 1b, and 2. Subtract from that total the amount on Form 1040, line 29, or Form 1040NR, line 29, and enter the result (see page SE-3)			3	65,000
4a	If line 3 is more than zero, multiply line 3 by 92.35% (.9235). Otherwise, enter amount from line 3 **Note.** If line 4a is less than $400 due to Conservation Reserve Program payments on line 1b, see page SE-3.			4a	60,028
b	If you elect one or both of the optional methods, enter the total of lines 15 and 17 here . .			4b	
c	Combine lines 4a and 4b. If less than $400, **stop**; you do not owe self-employment tax. **Exception.** If less than $400 and you had **church employee income,** enter -0- and continue ▶			4c	60,028
5a	Enter your **church employee income** from Form W-2. See page SE-1 for definition of church employee income.	5a			
b	Multiply line 5a by 92.35% (.9235). If less than $100, enter -0-			5b	
6	Add lines 4c and 5b			6	60,028
7	Maximum amount of combined wages and self-employment earnings subject to social security tax or the 6.2% portion of the 7.65% railroad retirement (tier 1) tax for 2010			7	106,800 00
8a	Total social security wages and tips (total of boxes 3 and 7 on Form(s) W-2) and railroad retirement (tier 1) compensation. If $106,800 or more, skip lines 8b through 10, and go to line 11	8a	38,100		
b	Unreported tips subject to social security tax (from Form 4137, line 10)	8b			
c	Wages subject to social security tax (from Form 8919, line 10)	8c			
d	Add lines 8a, 8b, and 8c			8d	38,100
9	Subtract line 8d from line 7. If zero or less, enter -0- here and on line 10 and go to line 11 . ▶			9	68,700
10	Multiply the **smaller** of line 6 or line 9 by 12.4% (.124)			10	7,443
11	Multiply line 6 by 2.9% (.029)			11	1,741
12	**Self-employment tax.** Add lines 10 and 11. Enter here and on **Form 1040, line 56,** or **Form 1040NR, line 54**			12	9,184
13	**Deduction for one-half of self-employment tax.** Multiply line 12 by 50% (.50). Enter the result here and on **Form 1040, line 27, or Form 1040NR, line 27** .	13	4,592		

45.5 Optional Method If 2010 Was a Low-Income or Loss Year

The law provides a small increased tax base for Social Security coverage if you have a low net profit or loss. The increased tax base is called the optional method and is figured in Part II of Section B of Schedule SE. One optional method is for nonfarm self-employment and another for farm income. You may not use the optional method to report an amount less than your actual net earnings from self-employment.

Nonfarm method. You may use the nonfarm optional method for 2010 if you meet all the following tests:

Test 1. Your net earnings (profit) from nonfarm self-employment on Line 31 of Schedule C, Line 3 of Schedule C-EZ, or Line 15a of Schedule K-1 (Form 1065) are less than $4,851.

Test 2. Your net nonfarm profits are less than 72.189% of your gross nonfarm income.

Test 3. You had net earnings from self-employment of $400 or more in at least two of the following years: 2007, 2008, and 2009.

Test 4. You have not previously used this method for more than four years. There is a five-year lifetime limit for use of the nonfarm optional base. The years do not have to be consecutive.

Filing Tip

Optional Method

Electing the optional method to increase the base for Social Security coverage may also increase earned income for dependent care and earned income credit purposes.

If your net profit from all nonfarm trades or businesses is $4,851 or less and less than 72.189% of gross nonfarm income, you may report two-thirds of the gross income from your nonfarm business as net earnings from self-employment.

EXAMPLES

1. Brown had net earnings from self-employment of $800 in 2008 and $900 in 2009 and so meets Test 3 above. In 2010, she has gross nonfarm self-employment income of $6,200 and net nonfarm self-employment earnings of $4,000. Net earnings from self-employment of $4,000 are less than $4,851 (Test 1 above) and also less than $4,476 (72.189% x $6,200) (Test 2). Brown may figure self-employment tax on $4,133 (2/3 of $6,200).
2. Same facts as in Example 1, but Brown has a net self-employment loss of $700. She may elect to report $4,133 (2/3 of $6,200) as net earnings under the optional method.
3. Smith had gross nonfarm income of $1,000 and net nonfarm self-employment earnings of $800. He may not use the optional method because net earnings of $800 are not less than 72.189% of $1,000 gross income, or $722.
4. Jones has gross nonfarm income of $525 and net nonfarm self-employment earnings of $175. Jones may not use the optional method because two-thirds of his gross income, or $350, is less than the minimum income of $400 required to be subject to the self-employment tax.

Optional farm method. If you have farming income (other than as a limited partner) you may use the farm optional method to figure your net earnings from farm self-employment.

You can use the nonfarm optional method only if your gross farm income was not more than $6,720 or your net farm profits were less than $4,851.

You may report the smaller of two-thirds of your gross income or $4,480 as your net earnings from farm self-employment.

Farm income includes income from cultivating the soil or harvesting any agricultural commodities. It also includes income from the operation of a livestock, dairy, poultry, bee, fish, fruit, or truck farm, or plantation, ranch, nursery, range, orchard, or oyster bed, as well as income in the form of crop shares if you materially participate in production or management of production.

45.6 Self-Employment Tax Rules for Certain Positions

Table 45-1 Self-Employed or Employee?

If you are—	*Tax rule—*
Babysitter	Where you perform services in your own home and determine the nature and manner of the services to be performed, you are considered to have self-employment income. However, where services are performed in the parent's home according to instructions by the parents, you are an employee of the parents and do not have self-employment earnings. Exception: Grandparents who provide care only for their own grandchildren (in their home or in the grandchildren's home).
Clergy	If you are an ordained minister, priest, or rabbi, a member of a religious order who has not taken a vow of poverty, or a Christian Science practitioner, you are subject to self-employment tax, unless you elect not to be covered on the grounds of conscientious or religious objection to Social Security benefits. An application for exemption from Social Security coverage must be filed on Form 4361 by the due date, including extensions, of your income tax return for the second taxable year for which you have net earnings from services of $400 or more. An exemption, once granted, is irrevocable. Self-employment tax does not apply to the rental value of any parsonage or parsonage allowance provided after retirement. Other retirement benefits from a church plan are also exempted.
Consultant	The IRS generally takes the position that income earned by a consultant is subject to self-employment tax. The IRS has also held that a retired executive hired as a consultant by his former firm received self-employment income, even though he was subject to an agreement prohibiting him from giving advice to competing companies. According to the IRS, consulting for one firm is a business; it makes no difference that you act as a consultant only with your former company. The IRS has also imposed self-employment tax on consulting fees, although no services were performed for them. The courts have generally approved the IRS position.
Dealer in commodities and options	Registered options dealers and commodities dealers are subject to self-employment tax on net gains from trading in Section 1256 contracts, which include regulated futures contracts, foreign currency contracts, dealer equity options, and non-equity options. Self-employment tax also applies to net gains from trading property related to such contracts, like stock used to hedge options.
Director	You are taxed as a self-employed person if you are not an employee of the company. Fees for attendance at meetings are self-employment income. If the fees are not received until after the year you provide the services, you treat the fees as self-employment earnings in the year they are received.
Employee of foreign government or international organization	If you are a U.S. citizen and you work in the United States for a foreign government or its wholly owned instrumentality, or an international organization, you pay self-employment tax if Social Security and Medicare taxes are not withheld from your pay.
Executor or guardian	If you are a professional fiduciary, you will always be treated as having self-employment income, regardless of the assets held by the estate. But if you serve as a nonprofessional executor or administrator for the estate of a deceased friend or relative, you will not be treated as having self-employment income unless all of the following tests are met: (1) the estate includes a business; (2) you actively participate in the operation of the business; and (3) all or part of your fee is related to your operation of the business. The IRS applied similar business tests to deny self-employment treatment for a guardian who was appointed by a court to care for a disabled cousin. The guardian negotiated sales of the cousin's property and invested the proceeds, but these activities were not extensive enough to be considered management of a business.
Former insurance salespersons	Termination payments by a former insurance salesperson may be exempt from self-employment tax. They must be received from an insurance company after the termination of a services agreement. No services may be performed for the company after the agreement ends and before the end of the tax year. The payments must be conditioned on the salesperson's entering into a covenant not to compete with the company for at least one year after termination. The amount of the payment must be primarily based on policies sold by (or credited to) the salesperson during the last year of the services agreement or on the period for which such policies remain in force after the termination.
Lecturer	You are not taxed as a self-employed person if you give only occasional lectures. If, however, you seek lecture engagements and get them with reasonable regularity, your lecture fees are treated as self-employment income.

Table 45-1 Self-Employed or Employee? (continued)

If you are—	Tax rule—
Nonresident alien	You do not pay Social Security tax on your self-employment income derived from a trade, business, or profession. This is so even though you pay income tax. Your exemption from self-employment tax is not influenced by the fact that your business in the United States is carried on by an agent, employee, or partnership of which you are a member. However, if you live in Puerto Rico, the Virgin Islands, American Samoa, the Commonwealth of the Northern Mariana Islands, or Guam, you are not considered a nonresident alien and are subject to self-employment tax.
Nurse	If you are a registered nurse or licensed practical nurse who is hired directly by clients for private nursing services, you are considered self-employed. You are an employee if hired directly by a hospital or a private physician and work for a salary following a strict routine during fixed hours, or if you provide primarily domestic services in the home of a client. Where registered or licensed practical nurses are assigned nursing jobs by an agency that pays them, the IRS, in several rulings, has treated such nurses as employees of the agency. Nurses' aides, domestics, and other unlicensed individuals who classify themselves as practical nurses are treated by the IRS as employees, regardless of whether they work for a medical institution, a private physician, or a private household.
Real estate agent or door-to-door salesperson	Licensed real estate agents are considered self-employed if they have a contract specifying that they are not to be treated as employees and if substantially all of their pay is related to sales rather than number of hours worked. The same rule also applies to door-to-door salespeople with similar contracts who work on a commission basis selling products in homes or other non-retail establishments.
Technical service contractor	Consulting engineers and computer technicians who receive assignments from technical service agencies are generally treated as employees and do not pay self-employment tax. The IRS distinguishes between (1) technicians who in three-party arrangements are assigned clients by a technical services agency and (2) those who directly enter into contracts with clients. Employee status covers only technicians in Group 1. Technical specialists who contract directly with clients may be classified as independent contractors by showing that they have been consistently treated as independent contractors by the client, and that other workers in similar positions have also been treated as independent contractors. Thus, they may treat their income as self-employment income. Firms that are treated as employers of technical specialists are responsible for withholding and payroll taxes.
Traders in securities	Gains and losses from a trading business are not subject to self-employment tax.
Writer	Royalties from writing books are self-employment income to a writer. Royalties on books by a professor employed by a university may also be self-employment income despite employment as a professor.

PART 7

Filing Your Return and What Happens After You File

This part is designed to help you —

- Organize your tax data. Whether you plan to prepare your own tax return or have someone else prepare it, you must first gather and organize your tax information.

  In *Chapter 46*, you will find record-keeping guides for income items and expense deductions.
- Understand how the IRS reviews your return and initiates audit procedures, including information on how the IRS matches your return with reports of distributions to you from banks, corporations, and government agencies.
- Avoid penalties for underpaying your tax. You may avoid penalties for positions taken on your tax return by making certain disclosures, obtaining authoritative support for your position, or showing reasonable cause for a tax underpayment *(46.8)*.
- Understand the factors that might lead to an audit. Your chances of being selected for an examination depend on your income, profession, deductions claimed, and even where you live *(48.1)*.
- Prepare for an audit. Advance preparations and knowing your rights can help support your position *(48.4)*.
- Dispute adverse IRS determinations. You can appeal within the IRS and go to court if you disagree with the IRS audit results. If you win, you may receive attorneys' fees and other expenses *(48.8)*.
- File a timely refund claim if you have overpaid your tax *(47.2)*.
- File an amended return if you omitted income or claimed excessive deductions on your original return *(47.8)*.

Chapter 46

Filing Your Return

Whether you prepare your return yourself or retain a professional preparer, you must first collect and organize your tax records. You cannot prepare your return unless you get your personal tax data in order. Good records will help you figure your income and deductions and will serve as a written record to present to the IRS in the event that you are audited.

Review income statements from banks, employers, brokers, and governmental agencies on their respective Forms 1099. Check for miscalculations, additions, and omissions.

Survey *Chapters 12–21* of this book for deductions you can claim directly from gross income and itemized deductions you can claim on Schedule A of Form 1040.

Reviewing your tax return from prior years will help refresh your memory as to how you handled income and expenses in prior years. This review will also remind you of deductions, carryover losses, and other items you might otherwise have overlooked that you might be eligible for. If your prior year returns were prepared by a professional, he or she can probably provide you with a copy of your returns if you do not have them. Otherwise, you may obtain copies of prior year tax returns by filing Form 4506 with the IRS and paying a fee.

In this chapter you will find a checklist of steps to take when preparing and checking your return. If you need an extension to file, *see 46.3*.

46.1 Keeping Tax Records

To maximize tax-savings opportunities, you must keep good records throughout the year. Good record-keeping makes it easier to prepare your return, reduces errors, and provides a defense to any challenge from the IRS.

- Make a habit of jotting down deductible items as they come along.
- Keep a calender or diary of expenses to record deductible items.
- Keep a file of bills and receipts. This will remind you of deductible items and provide you with supporting evidence to present to the IRS if audited.
- Use your credit card receipts, online account statements, and checkbook stubs as a record. If you own a business, you must keep a complete set of account books for it.

IRA records. If you have made nondeductible contributions to a traditional IRA, keep a record of both your nondeductible and deductible contributions. This will help you when you withdraw IRA money to figure the tax-free and taxed parts of the withdrawal *(8.9)*. Also keep records of contributions and conversions to Roth IRAs *(8.20–8.21)*. For these purposes, you should keep copies of Form 8606 and Form 5498 *(8.8)*.

IRS Alert

Getting a Copy of an Old Tax Return

You can obtain a copy of a prior year tax return from the IRS by filing Form 4506 and paying a $57 fee per return. Copies of Forms 1040, 1040A, and 1040EZ are generally available for seven years from filing before they are destroyed.

You can use Form 4506-T to order free of charge a transcript of tax return information that provides line entries from tax returns for the three prior years and a transcript of data from Forms W-2 and 1099 for up to 10 years in some cases.

Reinvested mutual-fund distributions. Keep annual statements that record the amount of mutual-fund distributions that you have reinvested in additional fund shares. The reinvested amounts are part of your cost basis in the fund. Unless your fund keeps track of basis for you, you need to know your basis when computing gain or loss on the redemption of fund shares *(32.10)*.

Passive losses. If you have losses that are suspended and carried forward to future years under the passive loss restrictions *(10.13)*, keep the worksheets to Form 8582 as a record of the carry-forward losses.

Home mortgage interest. Keep your bank statements and cancelled checks. If a loan secured by a first or second home is used to make substantial home improvements, keep records of the improvement costs to support your home interest deduction *(15.5)*.

How long should you keep your records? Your records should be kept for a minimum of three years after the year to which they are applicable, since the IRS generally has three years from the date your return is filed to audit your return. Some authorities advise keeping them for six years, since in some cases where income has not been reported, the IRS may go back as far as six years to question a tax return. In cases of suspected tax fraud, there is no time limitation at all.

Keep records of transactions relating to the *basis* of property for as long as they are important in figuring the basis of the original or replacement property. For example, records of the purchase of rental property or improvements thereto must be held as long as you own the property.

As mentioned above, if you have made any nondeductible IRA contributions, records of IRA contributions and distributions must be kept until all funds have been withdrawn. Similarly, you should save mutual-fund confirmations or other records showing reinvested dividends and cash purchases of shares; these are part of your cost basis and will reduce taxable gain when you sell shares in the fund.

46.2 Getting Ready To File Your Return

You must collect your tax records before you can start the preparation of your return. Even if you employ a tax professional to prepare your return, organizing your tax data is essential. Once you have compiled all your return information and your records are complete, decide whether to use Form 1040EZ, 1040A, or 1040 with the aid of the checklist at the front of this book on page 7. After you have decided which return to file, review the form to familiarize yourself with its details.

If you have access to the Internet, you may obtain forms from the IRS website at www.irs.gov. You can obtain forms by phone from the IRS by calling (800) 829-3676.

Planning Reminder

Keep Copies

Photocopy your signed return and keep the copy along with copies of Form W-2 and other income statements, receipts, cancelled checks, and other items to substantiate your deductions.

Checking for possible errors. After you have completed your return, put it aside and postpone checking your completed return for several hours or even a day so that you can review it in a fresh state of mind. *See* below for common errors that might delay a refund or result in a tax deficiency and interest costs.

If mailing your return. If you are mailing your return to the IRS, first check it to ensure the following:

- Your arithmetic is correct.
- Your Social Security number, and that of your spouse if you are filing jointly, is recorded correctly on each form and schedule.
- You have filled in the proper boxes that state your filing status and exemption claims, and reported the Social Security number of each dependent *(21.11)*.
- You have claimed the full standard deduction you are entitled to if you are age 65 or older, or blind *(13.4)*.
- You have used the Tax Table, Tax Computation Worksheet, or special capital gain or foreign earned income worksheet applicable to your tax status. If you do not have net capital gain or qualified dividends, use the Tax Table if your taxable income is less than $100,000, or the Tax Computation Worksheet if your taxable income is $100,000 or more. *See 22.4* if you have net capital gain or qualified dividends. *See 22.5* if you claimed the foreign earned income exclusion or foreign housing exclusion.
- You have put the refund due you or your tax payable on the correct line.
- If you owe tax and are paying by check, your check should be made out to the "United States Treasury" for the correct amount due and your Social Security number should be on the check. The IRS encourages, but does not require, that you send payment voucher Form 1040-V along with your Form 1040 payment.
- You have signed your return and, if you are filing a joint return, your spouse has also signed *(1.4)*.
- You have attached the correct copy of your Form W-2 and all appropriate forms and schedules to your return.
- If you have elected to have your refund directly deposited into your personal account, verify that you have provided the IRS with the correct routing information on Line 74 of Form 1040, Line 46 of Form 1040A, or Line 12 of Form 1040EZ.
- You have correctly addressed the envelope and affixed proper postage.
- You use certified or registered mail or an IRS-specified private delivery service to prove that your return was postmarked on or before the filing date.

Planning Reminder

Get Timely Postmark for Last Minute Mailing

Last minute filers may use specified services from *DHL*, *Federal Express*, and *UPS* as well as the *U.S. Postal Service*. If using the U.S. Postal Service, send the return certified (or registered) mail and keep the postmark receipt. If you use a private delivery service, keep a copy of the mailing label or obtain a receipt to verify a timely postmark. If your return is postmarked before or at any time on the filing due date (April 15, 2011, for 2010 returns), it is considered timely filed under a "timely-mailing-is-timely-filing" rule, even if the IRS receives it after the due date.

The timely mailing rule also applies if you obtain a filing extension and are mailing your return on or before the extended due date.

A timely foreign postmark for a return filed from abroad will also be accepted by the IRS as proof of a timely filing.

46.3 Applying for an Extension

If you cannot file your return on time, apply by the due date of the return for an extension of time to file. Send the extension request on Form 4868 to the Internal Revenue Service office with which you file your return.

Automatic filing extension. You may get an extension without waiting for the IRS to act on your request. You receive an automatic six-month extension for your 2010 return if you file Form 4868 by April 15, 2011. The extension gives you until October 15, 2011 to file your return. A late *filing* penalty will not be imposed if you fail to submit a payment with Form 4868 provided you make a good faith estimate of your liability based upon available information at the time of filing. However, although the extension will be allowed without a payment, you will be subject to interest charges and possible penalties (discussed below) on 2010 taxes due after April 15, 2011.

You may file Form 4868 electronically using tax preparation software or your tax preparer may file it electronically for you. You may use a credit card or debit card to make a tax payment. Payment is made through a service provider that handles the credit card transaction and charges you a fee. Fees vary between the service providers and are based on the amount of tax charged. When you pay by credit card, you get a confirmation number that you should keep for your records. *See* the Form 4868 instructions for the phone numbers and web addresses of the service providers.

When you file your return within the extension period, you enter on the appropriate line of the return any tax payment that you sent with your extension request, and include the balance of the unpaid tax, if any.

While the extension is automatically obtained by a proper filing on Form 4868, the IRS may terminate the extension by mailing you a notice at least 10 days prior to the termination date designated in the notice.

Planning Reminder

You Can Get a Six-Month Filing Extension

You can get an automatic six-month extension to file your 2010 return by filing Form 4868 by April 15, 2011. The extension is for filing only and does not extend the time to pay your taxes for 2010.

Interest and penalty for late payment. You have to pay interest on any 2010 tax not paid by April 15, 2011, even if you obtain a filing extension. In addition, if the tax paid with Form 4868, plus withholdings and estimated tax payments for 2010, is less than 90% of the amount due, you will be subject to a late-payment penalty (usually one-half of 1% of the unpaid tax per month)—unless you can show reasonable cause.

Abroad on April 15, 2011. You do not get an automatic extension for filing and paying your tax merely because you are out of the country on the filing due date. If you plan to be traveling abroad on April 15, 2011, and want to get a filing extension, you must submit a claim for the automatic six-month filing extension on Form 4868 or use a credit or debit card (*see* above) to make a payment with an extension request.

The only exception is for U.S. citizens or residents who live and have their main place of business outside the U.S. or Puerto Rico, or military personnel stationed outside the U.S. or Puerto Rico, on April 15, 2011. If you qualify, you are allowed an automatic two-month extension without having to request it, until June 15, 2011, to file your return and also pay any tax due. However, the IRS will charge interest from the original April 15 due date on any unpaid tax. If you cannot file within the two-month extension period, you can obtain an additional four-month extension by filing Form 4868 by June 15, 2011. This additional four-month extension is for filing only and not payment. In addition to interest, a late payment penalty may be imposed (*see* above) on any tax not paid by June 15, 2011.

If you are eligible for the two-month extension but expect to qualify for the foreign earned income exclusion *(36.3)* under the foreign residence or presence test after June 15, 2011, you can request on Form 2350 an extension until after the expected qualification date; *see 36.7*.

Installment arrangements. If you cannot pay the tax due for 2010 by the October 15, 2011, extension date, you should file your return and attach Form 9465 to request an installment arrangement; *see 46.5*.

46.4 Getting Your Refund

If you show an overpayment of tax on your 2010 return, you can have a refund check mailed to you or have the IRS directly deposit the refund into as many as three bank, brokerage, or mutual-fund accounts; *see* below. For a direct deposit you must provide the IRS with the correct routing information for your account. On Form 1040 and 1040A, you can apply all or part of your refund to your 2011 estimated tax; this is an irrevocable election.

Filing Tip

New Savings Bond Option for Refund

You can elect on Form 8888 to use your refund to buy Series I Savings Bonds. *See* the Form 8888 instructions.

Direct-deposit refund option. If you want the IRS to directly deposit your refund into only one account, just give the IRS the appropriate routing and account numbers on the refund line of your return. If you want the refund to be directly deposited into two or three accounts, File Form 8888 with your Form 1040, 1040A, or 1040EZ. You can have the refund directly deposited into a checking or savings account, or even to an IRA *(8.1)*, or health savings account *(12.9)*. If you want the deposit to go into an IRA, you must establish the IRA before you request direct deposit. Make sure that you notify the IRA trustee if you want the deposit to count as an IRA contribution for 2010 (rather than for 2011 when the deposit is made). To count as a 2010 IRA contribution, the direct deposit must actually be made to the IRA by the April 15, 2011 due date for your return (extensions are disregarded).

If you file Form 8379 (*see* below) for a refund as an injured spouse, you cannot use Form 8888.

Caution

Direct Deposit of Joint Refund

If you are due a refund on a joint return, your financial institution may reject a request to have a direct deposit of the joint refund made to an individual account or IRA. If the direct deposit is rejected, the IRS will mail you a refund check.

Checking refund status by phone or online. You can call the IRS to check on the status of an expected refund. When you call the IRS automated phone service, you must provide the Social Security number shown on the return (or the first Social Security number if you filed a joint return), filing status, and the amount of the refund.

The IRS automated refund information phone number is 1-800-829-4477, or you may call the IRS at 1-800-829-1954.

You can also check refund status online at www.irs.gov. The information needed to access the system is identical to that required by the phone system. Online, you can learn if the IRS has received the return, if the refund was processed, and when the direct deposit was made or the date the check was sent.

Form 8379: Injured spouse may get refund that was withheld to pay spouse's debts. If you showed a refund due on a joint return filed with a spouse who owed child or spousal support, federal student loans, or state income tax, the Treasury Department's Financial

Management Service (FMS) may have withheld payment of the refund to cover the obligations. If your spouse owed federal taxes, the refund may have been offset by the IRS. If you are not liable for the past-due payments, and your tax payments (withholdings or estimated tax installments) or refundable credits exceed your income reported on the joint return, you may file Form 8379 to get back your share of the refund.

Penalty for filing excessive refund claim. A 20% penalty can apply to an excessive claim for refund or credit on an original return or on an amended *(47.9)*. The penalty is 20% of the "excessive" amount, the excess of the refund or credit claimed over the amount allowed, unless there is a reasonable basis for the amount claimed.

The penalty does not apply to claims relating to the earned income credit *(25.10)*. It also does not apply to any portion of the excess that is subject to the accuracy-related penalties (including the penalty for understatements due to reportable or listed transactions), or the fraud penalty *(48.6)*.

Planning Reminder

Interest Not Paid on Most Refunds

If your 2010 return is filed on or before the April 15, 2011, filing deadline, the IRS does not have to pay interest if the refund is issued before May 31, 2011, which is 46 days after the April 15 filing due date. If the return is filed after April 15, 2011, with or without an extension, no interest is due on refunds issued within 45 days after the actual filing date. If the overpayment is not refunded within 45 days, interest is paid from the date the tax was overpaid up to a date determined by the IRS that can be as much as 30 days before the date of the refund check.

46.5 Paying Taxes Due

If you owe tax on a return that you are mailing to the IRS, you may pay by check, money order, or credit card. Payments can also be made by direct debit from your account, either by phone or online using the IRS's Electronic Federal Tax Payment System (EFTPS).

If paying by check or money order, make it payable to the "United States Treasury." Write your Social Security number on the check or money order. The IRS encourages you to send Form 1040-V along with your payment, but the form is not required.

A credit card or debit card payment can be made by phone or over the Internet with a service provider that handles the transaction for the IRS. The service provider will impose a fee based on the amount you are paying. The tax form instruction booklet includes the toll-free number and website addresses of the service providers.

IRS online or phone option for making payments. The IRS's Electronic Federal Tax Payment System (EFTPS) accepts online tax payments from individual as well as business taxpayers. You may use EFTPS to pay the balance due on your individual tax return or to pay estimated tax installments.

Payments are made by direct debit from an account that you designate when you enroll with EFTPS. Individual tax payments may be scheduled up to 365 days in advance and business taxes up to 120 days in advance. You can enroll online at www.eftps.gov.

Payments via EFTPS can also be made by phone after you enroll with EFTPS and set up a direct debit arrangement. Call 1-800-316-6541 for enrollment information.

Payments by electronic filers. If you file electronically, you may pay taxes by authorizing a direct debit from your checking or savings account, or by using a credit card. Check with the companies that process credit card payments for the fee that will be imposed.

Installment agreements. If you cannot pay the full amount due on your return when you file, but will be able to pay the full amount within 120 days, you may ask the IRS for a short-term extension by calling 1-800-829-1040 or by applying online at www.irs.gov. The IRS will not charge a fee for a 120-day extension, but interest will be charged and a late payment penalty *(46.9)* might be imposed.

If you need more than 120 days, you can request an installment agreement on Form 9465 or can request a payment agreement online at www.irs.gov by using the pull-down menu under "I need to…", and select "Set up a Payment Plan." Even if the IRS agrees to an installment arrangement, you will be charged interest and may have to pay a late payment penalty *(46.9)* on any tax not paid by the due date.

If you owe $10,000 or less and agree to pay the full amount owed within three years, your request for an installment agreement cannot be turned down, provided that for the previous five years, you (and your spouse if currently filing jointly) timely filed and paid the taxes due and did not have an installment agreement during that period. You must timely file and pay any taxes due while the agreement is in effect. In other cases, where you owe $25,000 or less in combined tax, interest and penalties, and agree to pay the total within 60 months, the IRS will generally agree to an installment plan.

The IRS may approve a request to make installment payments for less than the full amount you owe, but only after a thorough review of your financial circumstances and after you have sold assets and used home equity to reduce the tax bill. If agreed to, the IRS will reevaluate a partial payment plan every two years.

The IRS will usually inform you within 30 days if your proposed payment plan is accepted. If it is, you will have to pay a processing fee. Generally, the fee is $105, but the fee drops to $52 if payments are made by direct debit from your bank account. The user fee is $43 for individuals whose income does not exceed 250% of the poverty guidelines updated annually by the U.S. Department of Health and Human Services. When you apply for an installment agreement, whether on Form 9465, online (at IRS.gov), by phone, or face-to-face with an IRS employee, the IRS will automatically review the income information from your return to determine eligibility for the reduced fee. If the IRS approves a monthly installment plan without granting a reduced user fee and you think you qualify, you can request the reduced fee by filing Form 13844 with the IRS within 30 days of receiving the IRS's acceptance notice.

If you are using an installment agreement to pay the tax due on a timely filed return (including extensions), the late payment penalty is reduced by half from .5% to .25% per month.

Offer in Compromise. If your financial circumstances are dire and you believe you will be unable to pay what you owe even with an installment agreement, you may make an offer to pay off part of your unpaid balance using Form 656 (Offer in Compromise), as discussed in *48.9*.

46.6 Electronic Filing

Filing Tip

Free E-Filing

Go to www.irs.gov to find a description of the free tax preparation and electronic filing services offered by companies that have partnered with the IRS and determine whether you meet the eligibility criteria.

Electronic filing involves the transmission of your tax return to the IRS from the computer of a tax preparer, tax preparation software program, or online tax preparation service. To file electronically, you must use an authorized service; you cannot electronically file directly with the IRS. You may be eligible for free tax preparation and electronic filing services from commercial tax software companies that have joined with the IRS to form the Free File Alliance. At the IRS website, www.irs.gov, the free services provided by the companies are described and links are provided to their websites. Each company sets its own eligibility criteria, which generally are based on adjusted gross income, but your age, state residency, or military status may also be factors.

Electronic filing offers a faster refund—a check mailed within three weeks or a direct deposit to your bank account in one to two weeks. You authorize a direct deposit to a financial institution that was designated in the electronic portion of your return. On the electronic portion of the return, you provide the savings or checking account number and the "routing transit number" of your bank. The routing transit number is the electronic mailing address of your bank that directs the refund to the correct account. The number is on your checks or other account statements. Before naming a bank, first ask if it accepts direct deposits and what its conditions are for receiving a deposit.

If you must pay a fee for electronic filing, you must decide whether the faster refund is worth the fee. Keep in mind that even without electronic filing, you may instruct the IRS to directly deposit your refund to an account that you designate on your return *(46.4)*.

If you file electronically and owe taxes, you may be able to pay by credit card or by direct debit from your checking or savings account.

Refund anticipation loans. An electronic filing service may offer a refund anticipation loan to a taxpayer who wants to receive an expected refund even sooner than the three weeks or so offered by electronic filing. The loans are received from lenders affiliated with the electronic filing service. This service is strictly an agreement between you and the filing service; the IRS is not a party to the arrangement. Before agreeing to such a loan, consider the high additional cost and whether it is worthwhile in light of the short refund payment period.

46.7 Notify the IRS of Address Changes

If the IRS does not have your current address, payment of a refund due you may be delayed. If you owe taxes, the IRS may enforce a deficiency notice sent to the address on your most recently filed tax return, even if you never receive the IRS notice.

To avoid these problems, you can call the IRS to update your address at 1-800-829-1040. You also may file Form 8822 with the IRS to provide notice of an address change, or send a signed written statement to the IRS Service Center covering your old residence. The statement should state the new and old address, your full name, and your Social Security or employer identification number.

If you and your spouse separate after filing a joint return, you should each notify the IRS of your current address.

If after you move you receive an IRS correspondence that has been forwarded by the Post Office, you may correct the address shown on the letter and mail it back to the IRS. Your correction is considered notice of an address change.

46.8 Interest on Tax Underpayments

You may be charged interest by the IRS if you have underpaid the tax due. The interest rate, which equals the federal short-term rate plus 3%, is determined every quarter. Interest begins to accrue from the due date of the return. Interest is compounded daily except for estimated tax penalties. If you relied on IRS assistance in preparing a return, and taxes are owed because of a mathematical or clerical error, interest does not begin to accrue until 30 days from a formal demand by the IRS for the payment of additional taxes.

IRS interest rates on taxes owed are as follows:

Interest Rate on Underpayments

From—	To—	Underpayment Rate—
4/1/2009	12/31/2010	4%
1/1/2009	3/31/2009	5
10/1/2008	12/31/2008	6
7/1/2008	9/30/2008	5
4/1/2008	6/30/2008	6
1/1/2008	3/31/2008	7

Law Alert

Making a Deposit To Suspend Interest

So long as the IRS has not yet assessed an underpayment of income tax (or gift, estate, or generation-skipping tax), you can make a cash deposit in order to suspend the running of interest on a potential underpayment. If you are later found to owe tax and the IRS uses the deposit to pay it, you will not be charged interest. The running of interest is suspended on the date the IRS receives the deposit, not later when the liability is assessed or the deposit is actually applied to the liability. If the dispute is resolved in your favor, the deposit is returned to you and you are paid interest. You may also request the return of all or part of the deposit at any time before the IRS has used it to pay tax, unless the IRS determines that collection of tax is in jeopardy. You are paid interest on a returned deposit that was attributable to a disputable tax. Revenue Procedure 2005-18 has guidelines for making and recouping deposits.

46.9 Tax Penalties for Late Filing and Late Payment

Late filing. If your return is filed late without reasonable cause, the IRS may impose a penalty of 5% of the net tax due for each month the return is late, with a maximum penalty of 25%. If the return is more than 60 days late, there is a minimum penalty, equal to the smaller of $135 ($100 for returns required to be filed before 2009) and 100% of the tax due. In one case, the IRS tried to impose the minimum penalty on a taxpayer who did not owe any tax because her withholdings exceeded her liability. However, the Tax Court held that the minimum penalty does not apply unless tax is underpaid. The IRS has agreed to follow the decision.

If failure to file is fraudulent, the monthly penalty is 15% of the net tax due, with a maximum penalty of 75%.

If you are subject to penalties for both late payment and late filing, the 0.5% penalty for late payment (but not the 1% penalty) offsets the penalty for late filing during the period that the penalties run concurrently.

Late payments. If you are late in paying your taxes, a monthly penalty of 0.5% (½ of 1%) is imposed on the net amount of tax due and not paid by the due date. The maximum penalty is 25% of the tax due. The penalty is in addition to the regular interest charge. This penalty does not apply to the estimated tax *(27.1)*. The late payment penalty does not apply if you can show that the failure to pay is due to reasonable cause and not to willful neglect.

A special reasonable cause rule applies if you obtain a filing extension. If by the original due date you paid at least 90% of your total tax liability through withholdings, estimated tax installments, or payment with your extension request, reasonable cause is presumed and the penalty does not apply for the period covered by the extension.

Unless reasonable cause is shown, the 0.5% monthly penalty also applies for failure to pay a tax deficiency within 21 calendar days of the date of notice and demand for payment if the tax due is less than $100,000. If the tax is $100,000 or more, the penalty-free payment period is 10 business days.

The monthly penalty may be doubled to 1%, if, after repeated requests to pay and a notice of levy, you do not pay. The increased penalty applies starting in the month that begins after the earlier of the following IRS notices: (1) a notice that the IRS will levy upon your assets within 10 days unless payment is made or (2) a notice demanding immediate payment where the IRS believes collection of the tax is in jeopardy. If the tax is not paid after such a demand for immediate payment, the IRS may levy upon your assets without waiting 10 days.

Table 46-1 Income Record Keeper

Type of income	*Records Needed*	*Report on*
Wages and salaries	Form W-2. Your employer must send your 2010 Form W-2 by January 31, 2011. Attach Copy B to your federal return. Keep Copy C for your records. If you worked for more than one employer during 2010, attach all Copy B forms to your return.	Form 1040EZ, Line 1 Form 1040A, Line 7 Form 1040, Line 7
Tip income	Form 4070 or other record showing your monthly reports of cash tips of $20 or more. Form W-2. Also *see 26.7* for reporting FICA taxes on unreported tips.	Form 1040EZ, Line 1 Form 1040A, Line 7 Form 1040, Line 7
Interest income	Form 1099-INT Form 1099-OID Deposit slips of interest received on money you loaned to others	Form 1040EZ, Line 2 ($1,500 or less) Form 1040A, Line 8(a); Schedule B, Part I (over $1,500) Form 1040, Line 8(a); Schedule B, Part I (over $1,500)
Dividend income	Form 1099-DIV Company statements of dividend payments, especially if stock dividends have been paid	Form 1040A, Line 9a for total ordinary dividends, Line 9b for qualified dividends eligible for long-term capital gain treatment; Schedule B, Part II (ordinary dividends over $1,500) Form 1040, Line 9a for total ordinary dividends, Line 9b for qualified dividends eligible for long-term capital gain treatment; Schedule B, Part II (ordinary dividends over $1,500)
Taxable refund of state and local income tax	Form 1099-G	Form 1040, Line 10
Alimony received	Deposit slips of alimony received and ex-spouse's Social Security number Copy of divorce or separation decree or agreements	Form 1040, Line 11 if taxable
Business income or loss	Business accounting records, deposit slips Business checkbook, deposit slips, invoice receipts, cancelled checks, bank statements Form 1099-MISC	Form 1040, Line 12; Schedule C or C-EZ; Form 8582 if passive activity rules apply; *see Chapter 10*
Sale of stocks and bonds	Form 1099-B and broker confirmation statements	Schedule D Form 1040, Line 13
Sale of personal residence	Closing papers, records of purchase, improvements; *see 29.6.*	If taxable gain is realized, Schedule D
Sale of real estate	Closing statement, records of cost and improvements Records of depreciation	Form 4797 Schedule D Form 1040, Line 13
IRA distributions	Form 1099-R	Form 1040A, Line 11 Form 1040, Line 15
Pensions and annuities	Form 1099-R if you receive annuity payments or lump-sum distributions	Form 1040A, Line 12 Form 1040, Line 16
Commercial annuity income	Form 1099-R	Form 1040A, Line 12 Form 1040, Line 16

Table 46-1 Income Record Keeper (continued)

Type of income	*Records Needed*	*Report on*
Rent income	Account records, checkbook, cancelled checks, and receipts	Schedule E Form 1040, Line 17 Form 8582 if passive activity rules apply
Royalty income	Form 1099-MISC	Schedule E Form 1040, Line 17
Partnership income	Schedule K-1, Form 1065	Schedule E Form 1040, Line 17
Beneficiary of trust or estate	Schedule K-1, Form 1041	Schedule E Form 1040, Line 17
S corporation	Schedule K-1, Form 1120S	Schedule E Form 1040, Line 17
Unemployment compensation	Form 1099-G	Form 1040A, Line 13 Form 1040, Line 19
Social Security benefits	Form SSA-1099	Form 1040A, Line 14 Form 1040, Line 20
Gambling income	Form W-2G, diary or other record showing wins and losses, losing tickets	Form 1040, Line 21
Other income	Form 1099-MISC, records of amounts received, date received	Form 1040, Line 21
"Kiddie" tax on income of a child	Child's Forms 1099-INT, 1099-DIV, and 1099-OID	Form 1040, Line 44 Form 8615 if income is reported on child's return Form 8814 if parent elects to report child's income on Form 1040

Table 46-2 Deduction Record Keeper

Type of deduction	Records Needed	Report on
Exemptions for dependents	Records of support contribution for food, lodging, medical expenses, such as cancelled checks, diary entries. Birth certificates in case age of a child is questioned. School attendance record if student status is questioned. Form 8332 allowing noncustodial parent to claim the exemption. This form must also be attached to return by noncustodial parent claiming exemption; *see* 21.7. Forms 2120 if dependent's support is shared; *see* 21.6.	Form 1040A, Line 6(c) Form 1040, Line 6(c)
Educator expenses	Records of expenses/purchase and business use	Form 1040A, Line 16 Form 1040, Line 23
IRA deductible contribution	Trustee's statements of contribution, copy of plan	Form 1040A, Line 17 Form 1040, Line 32
Student loan interest deduction	Bank statement showing interest paid	Form 1040A, Line 18 Form 1040, Line 33
Tuition and fees deduction	Student's name and taxpayer identification number, cancelled checks and statements of tuition and enrollment fees. For dependents, records of support contributions.	Form 8917 Form 1040A, Line 19 Form 1040, Line 34
Health savings account deduction	Trustee's statements and Form 5498-SA, showing contributions	Form 1040, Line 25 Form 8889
Moving expenses	Cancelled checks or receipts for expenses incurred, diary or log	Form 1040, Line 26 Form 3903
One-half of self-employment tax	Schedule SE, Form 1040	Form 1040, Line 27
Self-employed health insurance premium	Cancelled check of payment, copy of contract, insurance statement	Form 1040, Line 29
Keogh, SEP, or SIMPLE contribution for yourself	Trustee statement, copy of plan	Form 1040, Line 28
Penalty on early withdrawal of savings	Form 1099-INT	Form 1040, Line 30
Alimony deduction	Cancelled checks, copy of divorce or separation decree, written separation agreement, ex-spouse's Social Security number	Form 1040, Line 31
Domestic production activities deduction	Business records, Forms W-2	Form 1040, Line 35 Form 8903
Employee expenses	Diary logs, receipts, copy of accounting to employer	Form 2106 Schedule A, Line 21
Home office expenses	Records of expenses, business use, and allocation	Form 8829 if self-employed; Schedule C, Line 30 Form 2106 if an employee; Schedule A, Line 21
Medical and dental expenses	Cancelled checks, statements, prescriptions; log of travel expenses and lodging costs	Form 1040 Schedule A, Lines 1–4

Table 46-2 Deduction Record Keeper (continued)

Type of deduction	*Records Needed*	*Report on*
Taxes—state and local income, general sales, personal property, real estate	Form W-2 for withholding of income tax Cancelled checks Credit card receipts showing sales tax Bank statements of property taxes paid by bank (mortgages) Form 1099-DIV for foreign tax Form 1099-INT or tax receipt for foreign tax withheld at source	Form 1040, Line 40 Schedule A, Lines 5–9
Mortgage interest	Bank statement showing interest paid Form 1098	Form 1040 Schedule A, Lines 10 and 11
Points	Copy of bank statements, canceled checks	Form 1040 Schedule A, Lines 10 and 12
Qualified mortgage insurance premiums	Bank mortgage statements; cancelled checks	Form 1040; Schedule A, Line 13
Cash donations	Cancelled checks, receipt from charity	Form 1040; Schedule A, Line 16
Volunteer expenses for charitable organizations	Log of travel, cancelled checks showing purpose	Form 1040 Schedule A, Line 16
Property donation	Description of property, records of fair market value and cost. Receipt from organization. A bank statement or written receipt from organization to substantiate all cash donations. Cancelled check is not sufficient. If car is valued at over $500, a written acknowledgment showing gross proceeds if the organization sold the car. If in excess of $5,000, qualified appraisal report and statement from organization	Form 1040 Schedule A, Line 17
Casualty and theft losses	*See 18.8*. For thefts, statements from witnesses, police records, or a newspaper account of the crime might help.	Form 1040 Schedule A, Line 20 Form 4684
Gambling losses	Losing tickets or receipts, diary showing daily wagers, wins, and losses	Form 1040 Schedule A, Line 28
Union dues	Wage statements showing withholding for dues or cancelled checks	Form 1040 Schedule A, Line 21
Unreimbursed travel and entertainment expenses	Diary log and receipts kept according to the rules of *20.26*	Form 2106 Form 1040; Schedule A, Line 21
Unreimbursed auto expenses if you are employed	Statement from employer requiring use of car Mileage log Receipts of expenses if actual costs are claimed Cost records of auto if depreciation is claimed	Form 2106 Form 1040 Schedule A, Line 21
Investment expenses	Cancelled checks	Form 1040; Schedule A, Line 23
Safe deposit box fee	Bank statements	Form 1040; Schedule A, Line 23
Tax preparation fees	Cancelled checks	Form 1040; Schedule A, Line 23

Table 46-3 Tax Credit Record Keeper

Type of credit	*Records Needed*	*Report on*
Earned income credit	Form W-2 if an employee, Schedule SE if self-employed, to show earnings	Form 1040 EZ, Line 9 Form 1040A, Line 41a; Schedule EIC Form 1040, Line 64; Schedule EIC
Advance payment of earned income credit	Form W-2, Box 9	Form 1040A, Line 36 Form 1040, Line 59
Child and dependent care expenses	Cancelled checks for amounts paid to care for child	Form 1040A, Line 29; Form 2441 Form 1040, Line 48; Form 2441
Credit for the elderly or the disabled	Physician's statement of condition	Form 1040A, Line 30; Schedule R Form 1040, Line 53; Schedule R
Child tax credit and additional child tax credit	Records of support contribution Birth certificates in case age of a child is questioned School attendance record if student status is questioned	Form 1040A, Line 33 and Line 42 Form 1040, Line 51 and Line 65 Form 8812
Education credits	Student's name and taxpayer identification number Cancelled checks and statements of tuition and enrollment fees For dependents, records for support contributions	Form 1040A, Line 31 and Line 43 Form 1040, Line 49 and Line 66 Form 8863
Adoption credit	Adopted child's name, date of birth, and taxpayer identification number Adoption papers showing the date the adoption became final	Form 1040, Line 71 Form 8839
Residential energy credit	Certification—if provided by manufacturer—and proof of purchase	Form 1040 Line 52; Form 5695
Hybrid car credit	Certification from manufacturer	Form 1040 Line 53; Form 8910
Foreign tax credit	Form 1099-DIV; foreign tax returns or statements	Form 1116 Form 1040, Line 47
Nonrefundable credit for prior year alternative minimum tax	Copy of prior year's Form 6251	Form 1040, Line 53 Form 8801
Refundable credit for prior year alternative minimum tax	Copy of Form 6251 for 2008	Form 1040, Line 71 Form 8801
Credit for federal taxes withheld	Form 1099 Form W-2 Form W-4V	Form 1040EZ, Line 7 Form 1040A, Line 38 Form 1040, Line 61
Credit for estimated tax payments	Cancelled checks and copy of Form 1040-ES	Form 1040A, Line 39 Form 1040, Line 62
First-time homebuyer credit	Record of home purchase	Form 1040, Line 67 Form 5405
Saver's credit	Record of retirement plan contributions	Form 1040A, Line 32 Form 1040, Line 50 Form 8880
Making Work Pay credit	Form W-2 if an employee, Schedule SE if self-employed, to show earnings	Form 1040EZ, Line 8 Form 1040A, Line 40 Form 1040, Line 63 Schedule M (Form 1040 and 1040A)

Chapter 47

Filing Refund Claims, and Amended Returns

File a refund claim on Form 1040X if you want to take advantage of a retroactive change in the law, if you have overpaid your tax because you failed to take allowable deductions or credits, or overstated your income. You may use Form 1040X to correct your return if you underreported your income or improperly claimed deductions.

File a refund claim on time. The time limits discussed in *47.2* must be strictly observed; otherwise, even if you file a valid refund claim, it will be denied because of late filing.

You do not have to file a refund claim if you have overpaid your tax due to excessive withholding of taxes on your wages or salary, or if you have overpaid your estimated tax. You get a refund on these overpayments by filing your tax return and requesting a refund for these amounts. You must file your return within three years from the time the tax was paid to get the refund *(47.2)*.

For a refund of an overpayment of FICA taxes, *see 26.10* for how to claim a refund on your tax return. If you are not required to file a tax return, you file a refund claim on Form 843.

If you are entitled to a refund due to the earned income credit for certain low-income working families, you must file your tax return to get your refund, even though your income and filing status would not otherwise require that a return be filed. *See Chapter 25*.

47.1 Filing An Amended Return

You should file Form 1040X (Amended U.S. Individual Income Tax Return) to revise a previously filed return, either to claim a refund (*see* below) or to report additional tax owed *(47.8)*.

As a refund claim, Form 1040X can be filed if you overpaid your tax on your original return, such as where you failed to take allowable deductions or credits or overstated your income. You generally can use Form 1040X to change your filing status, such as where you were entitled to head of household status but filed as a single taxpayer. You can change your filing status from married filing separately to married filing jointly, but you cannot switch from a joint return to separate returns after the due date for the return.

You do not have to file a refund claim if you have overpaid your tax due to excessive withholding of taxes on your wages or salary, or if you have overpaid your estimated tax. You will receive a refund on those overpayments by filing your tax return and requesting a refund at that time *(46.4)*.

Claiming an unwarrented refund can be costly. There is a 20% penalty for an excessive claim for refund or credit *(47.9)*.

47.2 When To File a Refund Claim

Caution

Time Limits Must Be Observed

Failure to file a timely refund claim is fatal, regardless of its merits. Even if you expect that your claim will have to be pursued in court, you must still file a timely refund claim with the IRS. Mailing a refund claim so that it is postmarked by the due date (including extensions) qualifies as a timely filing if you use the U.S. Postal Service. The timely mailing rule also applies to refund claims that are timely deposited with private delivery services that have been designated by the IRS.

You may file a refund claim on Form 1040X within three years from the time your return was filed, or within two years from the time you paid your tax, whichever is later. However, a refund claim on a late-filed return may be barred under a three-year "look back" rule; *see* below. A return filed before its due date is treated as having been filed on the due date. The filing deadlines are suspended while you are financially disabled.

A refund claim based on a bad debt or worthless securities may be made within seven years of the due date of the return for the year in which the debt or security became worthless.

The time for filing refund claims based on carrybacks of net operating losses or general business credits is within three years of the due date (including extensions) of the return for the year the loss or credit arose.

If you filed an agreement giving the IRS an extended period of time in which to assess a tax against you, you are allowed an additional period in which to file a claim for refund. The claim, up to certain amounts, may be filed through the extension period and for six months afterwards.

Refund claim for withholdings and estimated tax on late-filed original return. A refund for withheld income taxes or estimated tax installments can be lost if you delay filing your original return too long. The Supreme Court agrees with the IRS that the withholdings and estimated tax are considered to be paid on the original due date of the return. To obtain a refund of these taxes, you must file the return within three years of the due date, or within three years plus any extension period if a filing extension was obtained for the year the taxes were withheld or paid. If the return is filed after the end of this three-year (plus extension) "look-back" period, the withholdings and estimated taxes cannot be refunded. For example, if taxes were withheld from your 2007 wages and you are due a refund but have not yet filed your 2007 return, you must do so by April 15, 2011, to obtain a refund of the withholdings. If you had obtained an extension until October 15, 2008, to file your 2007 return, the deadline for filing the refund claim for the 2007 taxes would be October 15, 2011. Where such a refund is claimed on an original return mailed and postmarked (U.S. Postal Service) on or slightly before the last day of the "three years plus extension" period, the IRS at one time argued that the timely mailing/timely filing rule did not apply. But following a contrary appeals decision, the IRS now allows a refund in this situation. The IRS treats refund claims included on delinquent original returns as filed on the date of mailing for purposes of applying the "three years plus extension" look-back rule.

Planning Reminder

Disability Suspends Limitation

The limitations period for filing a refund claim is suspended during any period in which a person is unable to manage his or her financial affairs due to a physical or mental impairment that has lasted or is expected to last for at least one year or to result in death. The suspension does not apply during a period in which a guardian is authorized to handle the individual's financial affairs.

Armed Forces service members and veterans. In determining the time limits within which a refund claim may be filed, you disregard intervening periods of service in a combat zone or in a contingency operation, plus periods of continuous hospitalization outside the United States as a result of combat zone injury, and the next 180 days thereafter *(35.5)*.

Claiming refund for deceased taxpayer. If you are a surviving spouse filing an amended joint return to claim a refund for you and your deceased spouse, you only need to file Form 1040X. A court-appointed personal representative must attach Form 1310 to Form 1040X to claim the refund.

47.3 Joint Refund Claims

If a joint return was filed for a year in which a refund is due, both spouses are entitled to recover jointly and both must file a joint refund claim. Where separate returns were filed, each spouse is a separate taxpayer and may not file a claim to recover a refund based on the other spouse's return, except if that spouse becomes the fiduciary when one spouse becomes incompetent or dies. If you are divorced and incur a net operating loss or credit that may be carried back to a year in which you were married, you may file a refund claim with your signature alone and the refund check will be made out only to you; *see 40.18*.

47.4 Stating the Reasons for Refund Claim

On Line C of Form 1040X, you tell the IRS why you are claiming a refund. Where appropriate, you should attach a statement explaining:

- All the facts that support the claim. Attach all supporting documents and tax forms supporting your claim.
- All the grounds for the claim. If you are uncertain about the exact legal grounds, alternate and even inconsistent grounds may be given. For example: "The loss was incurred from an embezzlement; if not, from a bad debt." To protect against understating the amount of the claim, you might preface the claim with this phrase: "The following or such greater amounts as may be legally refunded."

If your refund claim is denied by the IRS, it may become the basis of a court suit. If you have not stated all the grounds, you may not be allowed to argue them in court.

47.5 Quick Refund Claims

Form 1045 may be used for filing refunds due to carrybacks from net operating losses, and the general business credit. Form 1045 also may be used for a quick refund based on a repayment exceeding $3,000 of income reported in an earlier year. Form 1045 generally must be filed within 12 months after the end of the year in which the loss, credit, or repayment claim arose; *see* the Form 1045 instructions for earlier deadlines in certain carryback cases. The IRS will generally process your claim within 90 days, or if later, 90 days after the end of the month in which your return is due. Payment of quick refund claims is not a final settlement of your return; the IRS may still audit and then disallow the refund claim. Note that the filing of a quick refund, if rejected, may not be the basis of a suit for refund; a regular refund claim must be filed.

47.6 Interest Paid on Refund Claims

If a refund claim is filed within the time limits in *47.2* and the IRS pays the refund within 45 days, interest is paid from the date of overpayment to the date the claim was filed. If the refund is not made within the 45-day period, interest is paid from the date of overpayment to a date set by the IRS that is not more than 30 days before the date of the refund check.

The IRS does not have to pay interest on overpayments resulting from net operating loss carrybacks or business credit carrybacks if a refund is paid within 45 days of the filing of the refund claim. If a refund claim based on a loss or credit carryback is filed and subsequently a quick refund claim is filed on Form 1045 for the same refund, the 45-day period starts to run on the date Form 1045 is filed.

Interest rates applied to overpayments are as follows:

Amounts outstanding between—	*Overpayment rate is—*
4/1/2009 - 12/31/2010	4%
1/1/2009 - 3/31/2009	5
10/1/2008 - 12/31/2008	6
7/1/2008 - 9/30/2008	5
4/1/2008 - 6/30/2008	6
1/1/2008 - 3/31/2008	7

47.7 Refunds Withheld To Cover Debts

The IRS may withhold all or part of your refund if you owe federal taxes. The Treasury Department's Financial Management Service may withhold all or part of your refund if you owe child or spousal support or federal non-tax debts such as student loans or state income taxes. If you file a joint return with a spouse who owes child support or federal debts, you may be able to obtain your share of a refund due on the joint return by filing Form 8379 *(46.4)*.

Caution

Refund Offset for Overdue State Taxes

If you owe state income taxes, the state can refer the debt to the Treasury Department's Financial Management Service (FMS). The FMS will offset your federal tax refund by the state tax if your address on the return is within the state seeking the offset. The state must give you written notice that the debt is being referred to the FMS and provide an opportunity for disputing the liability.

47.8 Amended Returns Showing Additional Tax

If, after filing your 2010 return, you find that you did not report some income or claimed excessive deductions, you should file an amended return on Form 1040X to limit interest charges and possible tax penalties.

If you filed early and then file an amended return by the filing due date (including any extensions) that shows additional tax due, you will not be charged interest or penalties based on the original return; the amended return is considered a substitute for the original.

You must pay the additional tax due as shown on Form 1040X. Even if you expect a refund on your original return, the IRS will not reduce the refund check to cover the additional tax. You must pay it and you will receive the original refund separately.

47.9 Penalty for Filing Excessive Refund Claim

A 20% penalty can apply to an excessive claim for refund or credit on any income tax return filed after May 25, 2007, whether on an original return *(46.4)* or amended return. The penalty is 20% of the "excessive" amount, the excess of the refund or credit claimed over the amount allowed.

There are exceptions. The penalty does not apply if the claim has a reasonable basis. It does not apply to claims relating to the Earned Income Credit *(25.10)* or to any portion of the excess that is subject to the accuracy-related penalties (including the penalty for understatements due to reportable or listed transactions), or the fraud penalty, discussed at *48.6*.

Here is an example of the penalty computation. Assume that a taxpayer mailed her 2009 Form 1040 to the IRS on March 9, 2010, and includes a $400 check to cover the tax due. On June 10, 2011, she files an amended return and claims a $2,000 refund based on an increase in itemized deductions. The IRS reduces the refund to $1,000. If there is no reasonable basis for the $1,000 difference, the IRS will assess a penalty of $200 (20% of the $1,000 excess).

Chapter 48

If the IRS Examines Your Return

Because the IRS is unable to examine every return, it follows a policy of examining returns which, upon preliminary inspection, indicate the largest possible source of potential tax deficiency.

Returns are rated for audit according to a mathematical formula called the discriminant function system (DIF). Various weights are assigned to separate items on each tax return, thus permitting the ranking of returns for the greatest potential error.

This chapter discusses what may trigger an audit and how you can handle an audit if your return is selected for examination.

48.1 Odds of Being Audited

The odds are low that your return will be picked for an audit. However, the number has been increasing, particularly with respect to high-income taxpayers.

Audit odds vary depending on your income, profession, type of return, type of transactions reported, and where you live. Individual returns are classified by all income items on the return without regard to losses. Professional or business income reported on Schedule C and farm income reported on Schedule F is classified by total gross receipts, and corporate returns are classified by total assets.

Your return may command special IRS scrutiny because of your profession, the type of transactions reported, or the deductions claimed. The chances of being audited are greater under the following circumstances:

- Your information reported on the tax return does not match information received from third-party documentation, such as Forms 1099 and W-2.
- Your itemized deductions exceed IRS targets.
- You claim tax-shelter losses.
- You report complex investment or business transactions without clear explanations.
- You receive cash payments in your work that the IRS thinks are easy to conceal, such as cash fees received by doctors or tips received by cab drivers and waiters.
- Business expenses are large in relation to income.
- Cash contributions to charity are large in relation to income.
- You are a shareholder of a closely held corporation whose return has been examined.
- A prior audit resulted in a tax deficiency.
- An informer gives the IRS grounds to believe that you are omitting income from your return.

Caution

IRS Increasing Audits

In recent years, the IRS has increased audits of high-income taxpayers, Schedule C filers, S corporations, partnerships, corporations, and abusive tax shelters.

Itemized deductions. If your itemized deductions exceed target ranges set by the IRS, the chances of being audited increase. The IRS does not publicize its audit criteria for excessive deductions, but it does release statistics showing the average amount of deductions claimed according to reported income. Here are IRS figures based on deductions claimed on 2008 returns filed through September 2009.

Table 48-1 Average Itemized Deductions for 2008

AGI (thousands)	*Medical*	*Taxes*	*Interest*	*Charitable*
$ 15 – <30	$ 7,074	$ 3,146	$ 9,245	$ 2,024
30 – <50	6,153	3,830	9,055	2,189
50 – <100	7,102	6,050	10,659	2,693
100 – <200	9,269	10,798	13,734	3,757
200 – <250	21,554	18,164	18,570	5,895
250 and over	37,143	50,267	27,865	20,930

Taxpayer Bill of Rights. As a taxpayer, you have the right to be treated fairly, professionally, promptly, and courteously by the IRS and its employees. Because of many complaints of abuse in the past, Congress has passed several statutes, collectively referred to as the Taxpayer Bill of Rights, to protect taxpayers from mistreatment by IRS personnel.

One aim of the Taxpayer Bill of Rights is to have the IRS inform you of the effect of the tax action it is taking and how you can proceed and protect your rights. *See* IRS Publication 1, *Your Rights as a Taxpayer*. Thus, when the IRS starts an action against you, you should ask for an explanation of the procedural rules affecting your case, if these are not already included in the documents sent to you. For example, before the IRS may enforce a tax lien by seizing property by levy, the IRS must provide you with a notice of your right to a hearing before an appeals officer, an explanation of the levy procedures, the availability of administrative appeals and the appeals procedures, the alternatives to the proposed levy such as an installment agreement, and the rules for obtaining the release of a lien. *See* IRS Publication 556, *Examination of Returns, Appeal Rights, and Claims for Refund;* IRS Publication 594, *The IRS Collection Process;* and IRS Publication 5, *Your Appeal Rights and How to Prepare a Protest if You Don't Agree.*

Planning Reminder

Taxpayer Rights Web Page

For IRS publications outlining taxpayer rights, notices, examinations of tax returns, appeal rights, and collection procedures, go to the "Individuals" page of the IRS website, www.irs.gov, and click on the link for "Taxpayer Rights." From there, you can link to the "Taxpayer Advocate" page. The Taxpayer Advocate Service may help you resolve a problem that could not be settled through normal IRS channels.

Taxpayer Advocate. The function of the Taxpayer Advocate Service is to assist taxpayers in resolving problems with the IRS, identify areas in which taxpayers have problems dealing with the IRS, propose changes in administrative practices of the IRS, and identify potential legislative changes that may mitigate the problems. From the Taxpayer Advocate Service, you can receive assistance if you have unsuccessfully tried to resolve your problem with the IRS and have not had your calls or letters returned. You will be assigned a personal advocate who is in the best position to try to resolve your problem. If you face a significant hardship because of an impending IRS action or lack of IRS response to your problem, you may apply for a Taxpayer Assistance Order on Form 911. Contact the Taxpayer Advocate Service by calling 1-877-777-4778, or you may write to the Advocate at the IRS office that last contacted you. Publication 1546, *The Taxpayer Advocate Service of the IRS,* has a state-by-state list of addresses and phone numbers for Advocate offices. At www.irs.gov, you can access the state-by-state list by going to the Taxpayer Advocate Service page and clicking on the link to the "Contact Your Advocate!" page.

48.2 When the IRS Can Assess Additional Taxes

Three-year statute of limitations. The IRS has three years after the date on which your return is filed to assess additional taxes. When you file a return before the due date, however, the three-year period starts from the due date, generally April 15.

Where the due date of a return falls on a Saturday, Sunday, or legal holiday, the due date is postponed to the next business day.

EXAMPLES

1. You filed your 2010 return on February 8, 2011. The last day on which the IRS can make an assessment on your 2010 return is April 15, 2014.
2. You filed your 2008 return on May 18, 2009. The IRS has until May 18, 2012, to assess a deficiency.

Caution

No Limitation Period for Fraud

There is no limitation on when tax may be assessed where a false or fraudulent return is filed with intent to evade tax, or where no return is filed.

Amended returns. If you file an amended return shortly before the three-year limitations period is about to expire and the return shows that you owe additional tax, the IRS has 60 days from the date it receives the return to assess the additional tax, even though the regular limitations period would expire before the 60-day period.

Six-year statute. When you fail to report an item of gross income which is more than 25% of the gross income reported on your return, the IRS has six years after the return is filed to assess additional taxes. An item that is adequately disclosed is not considered an omission.

IRS request for audit extension. If the IRS cannot complete an audit within three years, it may request that you sign Form 872 to extend the time for assessing the tax. However, where an individual was "scared" into signing such an agreement, it was held invalid. *See* the following Example.

EXAMPLE

Robertson, a plumber, won $30,000 in a sweepstakes. An IRS agent asked him to sign an extension agreement. Robertson never had any prior dealings with the IRS, he did not know that his return was under examination, and he was not in touch with the lawyer who prepared the return on which his sweepstakes winnings were averaged.

Robertson wanted to *see* his lawyer before signing Form 872, but the agent pressed hard for the signature, phoning him and his wife at home and at work 20 times in a week. The agent did not tell him the amount of additional tax that might be involved, or explain that if he refused to sign he would have an opportunity before the IRS and the courts to contest any additional tax. Instead, the agent's comments gave him the impression that his home could be confiscated if he refused to sign. Robertson signed and the IRS later increased his tax.

Robertson argued that the agreement was not valid. He signed under duress. The Tax Court agreed. He convinced the court that he really believed he could lose his house and property if he did not comply. No adequate explanation of the real consequences of refusal to sign was made, although Robertson asked. Since he signed Form 872 under duress, the IRS could not increase his tax after the three-year period.

48.3 Audit Overview

When you file, the IRS checks your return for computational accuracy and clerical errors, such as a missing signature or missing or inaccurate Social Security numbers. To check whether you have omitted income from your return, the IRS will match your return against the Forms W-2 and Forms 1099 it receives from employers, brokers, payers of interest and dividends, and others who have filed information returns reporting payments to you.

If an error is found, or you have not submitted required attachments, you will probably be advised by mail of the corrections and of additional tax due, or you may be asked to provide additional information to substantiate tax deductions or credits. If you disagree with an IRS assessment of additional tax, you may request an interview or submit additional information. If you file early for 2010, are advised of an error, and the correction is made before April 15, 2011, interest is not charged.

If your refund is selected for a more thorough review, you will be notified by mail. This may not happen for a year or two; *see 48.2*.

Types of audits. An examination may be held by correspondence, at a local IRS office, or at the taxpayer's place of business, office, or home. An examination at an IRS office is called a desk or office examination; an examination at a place of business or home is called a field examination. When you are contacted by the IRS, you should receive an explanation of the examination process.

In a correspondence audit, the IRS sends you a letter asking for additional information about an item on your return. For example, the IRS may ask you to document a claimed deduction for charitable contributions or medical expenses. If the IRS is not satisfied with your response, you may be called in for an office audit. The IRS also notifies you by letter of mathematical or clerical errors you have made on your return, or if you have failed to report income, such as interest or dividends, that are shown by payers on information returns and matched to taxpayer returns by IRS computers.

The complexity of the transactions reported on a return generally determines whether a return will be reviewed at an office or field examination.

Most audits of individual returns, except for the self-employed, are conducted at IRS offices. An office audit usually covers only a few specific issues which the IRS specifies in its notice to you. For example, the examining agent may only be interested in seeing proof for travel expense deductions or educational expenses.

Field audits generally involve business returns; they are more extensive and time-consuming than office audits and are handled by more experienced IRS agents. For self-employed individuals, most examinations are field audits at their place of business. It is advisable to have a tax professional go over the potential weak spots in your return and represent you at the examination.

Filing Tip

Authorize Someone To Discuss Return Processing Problems

Generally, a person authorized to practice before the IRS may discuss your tax return issues with the IRS only if you sign a power of attorney on Form 2848. However, just above the signature section of your 2010 Form 1040, 1040A, or 1040EZ, you may consent to contacts between the IRS and your designee to resolve return processing issues such as mathematical errors, missing return information, or questions about refunds or payments. The designee can be a friend or relative and need not be a tax professional. A power of attorney will still be needed to handle an audit, underreported income issues, appeals within the IRS, and collection notices.

48.4 Preparing for the Audit

After an office audit is scheduled, the first thing to do is look over your return. Refresh your memory. Examine the items the IRS questioned in its notice of audit, and organize your records accordingly. Also check the rest of your return and gather proof for items you are unsure of. At this point, you should take a broad view of your return to anticipate problems you may encounter. Before the actual examination begins, consider possible settlement terms. Assume that the agent will assess additional tax, but establish the range you will consider reasonable. You can always change your mind, but giving some thought beforehand to possible settlement terms will help you later when settlements are actually discussed.

You may authorize an attorney, CPA, enrolled agent, or other individual recognized to practice before the IRS to represent you at the examination without your being there. To do so, give your representative authorization on Form 2848. An attorney or other representative authorized on Form 2848 can perform any acts that you could, including entering into a binding settlement agreement.

If you attend the audit, take only the records related to the items questioned in the IRS notice. Do not volunteer extra records; if the agent sees them, it might suggest new areas for investigation.

If you are concerned that there may be a problem of fraud, *see* a qualified attorney before you come into contact with an IRS official. The attorney can put your actions in perspective and help protect your legal rights. Besides, what you tell an attorney is privileged information; he or she cannot divulge or be forced to divulge data you have provided, other than data used to prepare your tax return.

Planning Reminder

Audit Scheduling

Make sure that the examination is scheduled far enough in advance for you to get ready. Do not let the IRS hurry you into an examination until you are prepared. In some localities, particularly rural areas, the IRS may give short notice in scheduling a field audit. An agent may even appear at your home or place of business and try to begin the audit immediately. Resist this pressure and reschedule the meeting at your convenience.

A field audit of your business return is likely to involve a comprehensive examination and requires careful preparation. Together with your tax adviser, go over your return for potential areas of weakness. For example, the agent is likely to question deductions you have claimed for business travel. If you are an incorporated professional, the corporation's deductions for expenses of company-owned cars or planes will probably be reviewed. The agent may suspect that a portion of these business deductions are actually nondeductible personal travel costs; be prepared to substantiate the business portion of your total mileage and operating expenses.

Under the Taxpayer Bill of Rights *(48.1)*, the IRS is generally required to hold an office audit at the office located nearest to your home. The IRS generally may not conduct a field audit at the site of a small business if the audit would essentially require the shutting down of the business, unless a direct visit is necessary to determine inventory or verify assets.

48.5 Handling the Audit

If you have authorized someone to represent you at the examination, your representative may appear at the examination without you. If the IRS wants to question you, it must issue you an administrative summons. If you are present and questioned, you may stop the examination to consult with counsel, unless the examination is pursuant to an administrative summons.

Audits conducted at an IRS office may conclude quickly because they usually involve only a few specific issues. In some cases, the audit may take less than an hour. The key to handling the audit is advance preparation. When you arrive at the IRS office, be prepared to produce your records quickly. Records should be organized by topic so that you do not waste time leafing through pages for a receipt or other document.

If the agent decides to question an item not mentioned in the notice of audit, refuse politely but firmly to answer the questions. Tell the agent that you must first review your records. If the agent insists on pursuing the matter, another meeting will have to be scheduled. The agent might decide it is not worth the time and drop the issue.

Common sense rules of courtesy should be your guide in your contacts with the agent. Avoid personality clashes; they can only interfere with a speedy and fair resolution of the examination. However, be firm in your approach and, if the agent appears to be unreasonable in his or her approach, make it clear that—if necessary—you will go all the way to court to win your point. A vacillating approach may weaken your position in reaching a settlement.

If the IRS has scheduled a field audit, ask that the examination be held at your representative's office. If you have not retained professional help and the examination takes place on your business premises, do not allow the agent free run of the area: Provide the agent with a comfortable work area for examining your records. If possible, the workplace should be isolated so that the agent can concentrate on the examination without being distracted by office operations that might spark questions. Tell your employees not to answer questions about your business or engage in small talk with the agent. As with an office audit, help speed along the field examination by having prepared your records so that requested information can be quickly produced.

Recording the examination. You have the right to make an audio recording of any interview with an IRS official. Video recordings are not permitted. No later than 10 calendar days before the interview, give written notice to the agent conducting the interview that you will make a recording. Later requests are at the discretion of the IRS. You must pay for all recording expenses and supply the equipment. The IRS may also make a recording of the interview, upon giving notice of at least 10 calendar days. However, IRS notice is not necessary if you have already submitted a request to make a recording. You have the right to obtain a transcript, at your own expense, of any recording made by the IRS. Generally, a request for a copy must be received by the IRS agent within 30 calendar days after the recording, although later requests may be honored.

48.6 Tax Penalties for Inaccurate Returns

A 20% "accuracy-related" penalty generally applies to the portion of any tax underpayment attributable to any of the following: (1) negligence or disregard of IRS rules and regulations; (2) substantial understatement of tax liability; (3) overvaluation of property; or (4) undervaluation of property on a gift tax or estate tax return. There is no stacking of penalties. Only one 20% penalty can be imposed on a portion of an underpayment, even if that portion is attributable to more than one of the above types of prohibited conduct. These penalties may be avoided by showing that you acted in good faith and with reasonable cause in underpaying the tax. Reliance on a tax preparer may constitute reasonable cause and good faith, but the reliance on the preparer must be reasonable. The Tax Court has held that reliance on a preparer is not reasonable if the taxpayer does not provide the preparer with the documents necessary to make a professional conclusion, or if the preparer lacks sufficient expertise to justify reliance. A stricter reasonable cause exception applies to the penalty for overvaluing charitable donations, discussed below.

Penalties apply to taxpayers who fail to disclose participation in "reportable" transactions and to taxpayers who understate tax liability on "listed" transactions or on other reportable transactions with a significant tax avoidance purpose.

Penalties also may be imposed for filing an erroneous refund claim or a frivolous return.

Negligence or disregard of IRS rules or regulations. The 20% penalty applies to the portion of the underpayment attributable to negligence. Negligence is defined as failing to make a reasonable attempt to comply with the law. Failure to report income shown on an information return, such as interest or dividends, is considered strong evidence of negligence.

The 20% penalty may also apply if you take a position on a return which is contrary to IRS revenue rulings, notices, or regulations. This penalty for disregarding IRS rules or regulations may be avoided if you have a reasonable basis for your position and you disclose that position on Form 8275 or on Form 8275-R in the case of a good faith position contrary to a regulation. Thus, disclosure will not avoid a penalty for a position that does not have a reasonable basis.

Substantial understatement of tax. If you understate tax liability on a return by the greater of $5,000 or 10% of the proper tax, you may be subject to a penalty equal to 20% of the underpayment attributable to the understatement.

The penalty may be avoided if you have a reasonable basis for your position and you disclose the position to the IRS on Form 8275, or on Form 8275-R in the case of a position that is contrary to an IRS regulation.

The penalty also may be avoided if you can show that your position was supported by "substantial authority" such as statutes, court decisions, final, temporary, or proposed IRS regulations, IRS revenue rulings and procedures, and press releases or notices published by the IRS in the weekly Internal Revenue Bulletin. You may also rely on IRS private letter rulings and technical advice memoranda, as well as IRS actions on decisions and general counsel memoranda. However, according to the IRS, such rulings and internal IRS memoranda that are more than 10 years old should be accorded very little weight. Congressional committee reports and the tax law explanations prepared by Congress's Joint Committee on Taxation, known as the "Blue Book," may be relied on as authority for your position.

However, the exceptions for disclosed positions (with a reasonable basis) and substantial authority do *not* apply to items attributable to a tax shelter, which for this purpose means any arrangement that has tax avoidance or evasion as a significant purpose. An understatement of tax due to tax shelter positions may be subject to the understatement penalty for "reportable" transactions discussed below.

Caution

Too Good to Be True

If you claim a deduction, credit, or exclusion on your return that would seem to a reasonable person to be "too good to be true" under the circumstances, the IRS is likely to consider you negligent unless you show you made an attempt to verify the correctness of the position.

Overvaluing property value or basis. If the claimed value of property donated to charity is 150% or more of the correct value, resulting in a tax underpayment exceeding $5,000, a penalty equal to 20% of the underpayment applies, and the penalty is doubled to 40% if the overvaluation is 200% or more. A reasonable cause exception to the 20% penalty is available if you relied on a qualified appraisal and you investigated the value of the property in good faith *(14.16)*. The same penalty thresholds and rates apply where the basis of depreciable property has been inflated.

Undervaluation on gift or estate tax return. If the value of property reported on a gift tax or estate tax return is 65% or less of the correct value, and the resulting tax underpayment from the undervaluation exceeds $5,000, the penalty is 20% of the underpayment. The penalty doubles to 40% of the underpayment if the claimed value of the property is 40% or less of the correct value.

Penalties relating to reportable transactions. A penalty may be imposed on individuals and business entities who fail to adequately disclose a "reportable" transaction on Form 8886. Under prior law, the failure-to-disclose penalty was a fixed dollar amount that was higher for "listed" transactions than for other reportable transactions. The Small Business Jobs Act of 2010 (9/27/10) changes the penalty to 75% of the tax reduction claimed on the return as a result of the transaction, but not to exceed $100,000 for individuals ($200,000 for corporations) in the case of a listed transaction and $10,000 ($50,000 for corporations) for other reportable transactions. There is also a minimum $5,000 per transaction penalty ($10,000 for corporations), whether a listed or reportable transaction is involved. The new law retroactively applies to penalties assessed after December 31, 2006.

Law Alert

Failure To Disclose Reportable Transactions

In response to complaints that the fixed-dollar penalty for failure to disclose reportable transactions could be excessive in light of the tax benefit received, the Small Business Jobs Act of 2010 changes the penalty to 75% of the tax benefit, subject to a minimum and maximum amount.

A special "accuracy-related" penalty may also be imposed for understating tax liability attributable to a listed transaction or to any reportable transaction (other than a listed transaction) with a significant tax avoidance purpose. The penalty is generally 20% of the understatement if the transaction was adequately disclosed on Form 8886. There is an exception for reasonable cause, but to qualify, stringent requirements must be met; *see* Code Section 6664(d). If the transaction was not adequately disclosed, the penalty increases to 30% of the understatement and there is no reasonable cause exception.

Fraud penalty. A 75% penalty applies to the portion of any tax underpayment due to fraud. If the IRS establishes that any part of an underpayment is due to fraud, the entire underpayment will be attributed to fraud, unless you prove otherwise.

Interest on penalties. A higher interest cost is imposed on individuals subject to the following penalties: failure to file a timely return, negligence or fraud, overvaluation of property, undervaluation of gift or estate tax property, substantial understatement of tax liability, or understatements attributable to reportable transactions. Interest starts to run from the due date of the return (including extensions) until the date the penalty is paid. For other penalties, interest is imposed only if the penalty is not paid within 21 calendar days of an IRS demand for payment if the penalty is less than $100,000. The interest-free period is 10 business days after the IRS demand for payment if the penalty is $100,000 or more.

Penalty for filing excessive refund claim. A 20% penalty can apply to an excessive claim for refund or credit on any income tax return filed after May 25, 2007, whether on an original *(46.4)* or amended return *(47.9)*. The penalty is 20% of the "excessive" amount, the excess of the refund or credit claimed over the amount allowed, unless there is a reasonable basis for the amount claimed. The penalty does not apply to claims relating to the Earned Income Credit *(25.10)*. It also does not apply to any portion of the excess that is subject to the accuracy-related penalties (including the penalty for understatements due to reportable or listed transactions), or the fraud penalty.

Penalty for frivolous tax return or submission. In addition to any other penalty, there is a $5,000 penalty for filing a frivolous tax return. A $5,000 penalty also applies to frivolous submissions, including requests for a collection due process hearing or an application for an installment agreement, offer-in-compromise, or Taxpayer Assistance Order based on a frivolous position. In Notice 2008-14, the IRS lists positions it considers frivolous. The IRS will periodically revise the list.

Acting on wrong IRS advice. A penalty will not be imposed if you reasonably rely on erroneous advice provided in writing by IRS officials in response to your specific written request. It is necessary for you to show that you provided accurate information when asking for advice.

48.7 Agreeing to the Audit Changes

After the audit, the agent will discuss proposed changes either with you or your representative.

If you agree with the agent's proposed changes, you will be asked to sign a Form 870, which, when signed, permits an immediate assessment of a deficiency plus penalties and interest, if due. The Form 870 is called "Waiver of Restrictions on Assessment and Collection of Deficiency in Tax and Acceptance of Overassessment."

If you believe that you have done as well or better than expected regarding the proposed deficiency, you can bring the case to a close by signing the Form 870, but the agent's supervisor must also approve the assessment.

By signing the form, you limit the amount of interest charges added to the deficiency. A signed Form 870 does not prevent the IRS from reopening the case to assess an additional deficiency. If on review the deficiency is increased, you will receive a revised Form 870. You can refuse to sign the form. The signed first form has the effect of stopping the interest on the original deficiency. As a matter of practice, however, waivers of acceptances ordinarily result in closing of the case.

It is possible, although unlikely, that upon examining your return, the agent will determine that you are due a refund. In this situation, a signed Form 870 is considered a valid refund claim. You should file a protective refund claim even if you sign the Form 870 acknowledging the overpayment. Generally, the agent will process the refund, but if he or she fails to do so or the review staff puts it aside for some reason and the limitations period expires, the refund will be lost. The refund claim will protect you from such a mishap.

Caution

Waiving Your Right To Appeal

Before deciding whether to sign the Form 870, consider that, by signing, you are giving up your right of appeal to both the IRS Office of Appeals and the Tax Court. However, you may still file a refund suit in a federal district court or in the Court of Federal Claims unless you have agreed not to do so on the Form 870.

The payment of tax before the deficiency notice (90-day letter) is mailed is, in effect, a waiver of the restrictions on assessment and collection. If the payment satisfies your entire tax liability for that year, you cannot appeal to the Tax Court. You must sue for a refund in either federal district court or the Court of Federal Claims.

48.8 Disputing the Audit Changes

If you disagree with the agent and the examination takes place in an IRS office, you may ask for an immediate meeting with a supervisor to argue your side of the dispute. If an agreement is not reached at this meeting or the audit is at your office or home, the agent prepares a report of the proposed adjustments. You will receive a 30-day letter in which you are given the opportunity to request a conference. You may decide not to ask for a conference and await a formal notice of deficiency (90-day letter).

Appeals conference. If your examination was conducted as an office audit or by correspondence, or the disputed amount does not exceed $25,000, you do not have to prepare a written protest for a conference with the IRS Appeals Office. The written protest is a detailed presentation of your reasons for disagreeing with the agent's report. Even where a formal written protest is not required, you must provide a brief written statement indicating your reasons for disagreeing with the agent when you request an appeals conference. *See* IRS Publication 5, "Appeal Rights and Preparation of Protests for Unagreed Cases."

At the conference you may appear for yourself or be represented by an attorney or other agent, and you may bring witnesses. The conference is held in an informal manner and you are given ample opportunity to present your case.

If you cannot reach a settlement, you will receive a Notice of Deficiency, commonly called a 90-day letter. In it, you are notified that at the end of 90 days from the date it was mailed, the government will assess the additional tax.

Interest abatement. An IRS delay in completing an audit increases the interest that you have to pay when a deficiency notice is eventually issued. You may ask the IRS on Form 843 for an abatement of interest charges that are attributable to unreasonable errors or delays by IRS employees in performing a ministerial or managerial act.

A ministerial act is defined as a procedural or mechanical act that does not involve the exercise of an IRS employee's discretion or judgment, such as the transfer of a taxpayer's case to a different IRS office after the transfer is approved by a group manager. A managerial act refers to the exercise of discretion or judgment by an IRS employee in managing personnel. Misplacing the taxpayer's case file is also a managerial act. General IRS administrative decisions, such as prioritizing the order of processing returns, or decisions on applying the tax law, that result in delay, are not ministerial or management acts for which interest abatement is available.

If you make a request on Form 843 for an abatement of interest and the IRS rejects your claim, you can petition the Tax Court within 180 days to review whether the IRS abused its discretion, provided that your net worth does not exceed $2 million ($7 million for businesses). The same net worth limit applies to recoveries of administrative and litigation costs; *see 48.10*. The Tax Court has exclusive jurisdiction to review the denial of the interest abatement request; an appeal of the IRS decision cannot be brought in a federal district court or the U.S. Court of Claims.

Caution

Penalty for Frivolous Tax Court Action

If you bring a case to the Tax Court that the Court concludes is frivolous or brought primarily for delay, or you unreasonably failed to pursue IRS administrative remedies, the Tax Court may impose a penalty of up to $25,000. Furthermore, if you appeal a Tax Court decision and the federal appeals court or the Supreme Court finds that the appeal was frivolous or brought primarily for delay, the Court may impose a penalty.

Going to court. When you receive a 90-day letter, if you are still convinced that your position is correct, you may take your case to one of three courts. You may within 90 days file a petition with the Tax Court without having to pay the tax. The Tax Court has a small tax case procedure for deficiencies of $50,000 or less. Such cases are handled expeditiously and informally. Cases may be heard by appointed special trial judges. A small claim case may be discontinued at any time before a decision, but the decision when made is final. No appeal may be taken by you or the IRS.

Instead of petitioning the Tax Court, you may pay the additional tax, file a refund claim for it, and—after the refund claim is denied—sue for a refund in a federal district court or the U.S. Court of Federal Claims.

Generally, the decision to litigate should be considered by an experienced tax practitioner.

48.9 Offer in Compromise

If you are unable to pay a tax debt in full, you may be able to make an offer in compromise (OIC), but it should be considered a last resort. An OIC is an agreement between a taxpayer and the IRS in which the IRS accepts less than full payment of the outstanding tax liabilities as settlement of the tax debt.

However, the number of accepted offers has declined steadily according to the National Taxpayer Advocate, who believes that taxpayers are deterred from applying by the burdensome disclosure and other application requirements.

There is a $150 application fee that the IRS will keep unless the offer cannot be processed. In particular, the requirement to submit a nonrefundable payment with the offer on Form 656 has been criticized as a major reason for reducing access to the OIC program. An up-front payment equal to 20% of a lump-sum offer must be made with Form 656, with the balance payable in five or fewer installments. A taxpayer applying for a periodic payment OIC must submit the first proposed payment with Form 656 and regular payments must be made while the IRS considers the application. These upfront payments are not refundable even if the taxpayer withdraws the offer prior to IRS acceptance or the IRS rejects the offer. The only exception to the application fee and upfront payment requirements is for low-income individuals who certify that their income is below poverty guidelines. The IRS as well as the Treasury Department and Taxpayer Advocate have called for legislation to eliminate mandatory upfront payments and proposals have been made in Congress to do so; *see* the *e-Supplement* for an update if any.

Grounds for an Offer in Compromise. The IRS has authority to settle or "compromise" for one of the following reasons: Doubt as to liability, doubt as to collectibility, and effective tax administration. Doubt as to liability means that doubt exists concerning the correctness of the IRS's tax assessment. Doubt as to collectibility means that you may never be able to pay the full amount of tax owed. Even where there is no doubt that you owe the tax and you could manage full repayment, you can apply for an OIC on "effective tax administration" grounds if there are exceptional circumstances under which collection of the full tax would cause you economic hardship or would be unfair and inequitable.

Applying for an Offer in Compromise on Form 656. You must submit an OIC on Form 656. The IRS will consider the OIC only after other payment options have been exhausted, including an installment agreement. You must make an upfront payment when you submit the OIC on Form 656, as discussed above. Form 656-B, the OIC booklet, includes an explanation of the OIC program and instructions for completing the form. The booklet also includes financial disclosure statements that must be attached to support an OIC based on doubt as to collectibility or effective tax administration. Wage earners and self-employed individuals must use Form 433-A, while partnerships and corporations use Form 433-B. In some cases, the IRS may request Form 433-A from corporate officers or individual partners. Form 656-B is available online at www.irs.gov or can be obtained by calling 1-800-829-3676.

If your offer is rejected, you will be given an opportunity to appeal the decision and to amend the offer.

Law Alert

Proposals To Eliminate Upfront Payment Requirement

With the support of the Administration and the National Taxpayer Advocate, proposals have been made in Congress to repeal the 2006 law requiring nonrefundable payments to be made with the OIC application. Any legislative developments will be reported in the *e-Supplement*.

Application fee. A $150 application fee must be paid with Form 656 unless you certify on Form 656-A that your total monthly income is at or below federal poverty guidelines. The OIC Application Fee and Payment Worksheet in the Form 656-B booklet is used to determine eligibility for the exception.

Compliance conditions. If the IRS accepts an OIC, you must pay the agreed-to amount in accordance with the acceptance agreement and must timely file and pay all required taxes for a period of five years from the acceptance date, or until the accepted amount is paid in full, whichever is longer. You may also be asked as part of the agreement to pay a percentage of your future earnings to the IRS. A failure to comply with the agreement causes default of the OIC and the reinstatement of the original liability.

48.10 Recovering Costs of a Tax Dispute

In a tax dispute, you may believe that the IRS has taken an unreasonable position, forcing you to incur legal fees and other expenses to win your case. Generally, you may recover all or part of—

1. Reasonable administrative costs of proceedings within the IRS, and
2. Reasonable litigation costs in a court proceeding.

A judgment for reasonable litigation costs will *not* be awarded in any court proceeding if you did not exhaust all IRS administrative remedies. A refusal by the taxpayer to agree to an extension of time for a tax assessment is not a bar to an award, but unreasonably delaying the proceedings is.

You may *not* recover costs if your net worth at the time the action begins exceeds $2 million. The $2 million net worth limit applies separately to each spouse in determining whether a married couple filing jointly is entitled to recover legal fees. No recovery is allowed to sole proprietors, partnerships, and corporations if their net worth exceeds $7 million or they have more than 500 employees.

To receive an award, you must "substantially prevail" as to the key issues in the case or the amount of tax involved. If you do, you will be entitled to a recovery unless the IRS proves that it was "substantially justified" in maintaining the position that it did. You may be treated as the prevailing party if a court determines that your liability is equal to or less than an amount that you offered in settlement. The offer must be considered a qualified offer made during a period that begins on the date of the first letter of proposed deficiency allowing for an IRS administrative appeal and ends 30 days before the date first set for trial.

The Tax Court and other courts have interpreted "substantially justified" to be a reasonableness standard. The IRS is presumed not to be "substantially justified" if it does not follow its own published regulations, revenue rulings, procedures, notices, announcements, or a private ruling issued to the taxpayer. The IRS may try to rebut the presumption. A court may also consider whether an IRS position has been rejected by federal courts of appeal of other circuits in determining whether the IRS position was substantially justified.

Reasonable administrative costs include IRS fees, reasonable fees for witnesses and experts, and attorneys' fees subject to the annual limit; *see* below. The IRS determines the amount of such an award, which may include costs incurred from the date the IRS sent its first letter of a proposed deficiency allowing you to ask for an administrative appeal. For an award of administrative costs, you must file an application with the IRS before the 91st day after the date on which the IRS mailed you its final decision. To appeal a denial of your application, you must petition the Tax Court within 90 days from the date the IRS mailed the denial.

Planning Reminder

Recovering Attorneys' Fees

Attorneys' fees include the fees paid by a taxpayer for the services of anyone who is authorized to practice before the Tax Court or IRS.

Reasonable litigation costs include reasonable court costs, fees of witnesses and experts, and attorneys' fees. Fees of witnesses may not exceed the rate paid by the U.S. government. For attorneys' fees incurred in 2010 or 2009, the limit is $180 per hour. For attorneys' fees incurred in 2007–2008, the limit was $170 per hour, for 2006 it was $160 per hour, and for 2003–2005 it was $150 per hour. The court may also increase the award for attorneys' fees to account for special factors, such as the difficulty of the issues and the availability of local tax expertise. However, an attorney's general expertise in tax law or experience in tax litigation is not in itself a special factor warranting a higher fee award.

You may *not* recover attorneys' fees if you represent yourself *(pro se)*. However, you are still entitled to recover fees for witnesses and experts. If you represent a prevailing taxpayer on a *pro bono* basis or for a nominal fee, a court may award you or your employer reasonable attorneys' fees.

48.11 Suing the IRS for Unauthorized Collection

If an IRS employee or officer recklessly, intentionally, or negligently disregards the law or IRS regulations when taking a collection action, you may sue the IRS in federal district court for actual economic damages resulting from the IRS employee's misconduct, plus certain costs of bringing the action. The lawsuit must be filed within two years of the date your right to sue accrued.

For negligent IRS collection activities, you may sue for damages of up to $100,000, and for reckless or intentional misconduct, the maximum damage award is $1 million. Administrative remedies must be exhausted to obtain an award.

According to IRS regulations, actual economic damages that may be recovered are monetary losses you suffer as a direct result of the IRS's action. For example, a business may lose loyal customers and suffer an actual cash loss if the IRS's action damages the business's reputation. Other actual expenses could include the cost of renting a house or a car if the IRS puts a lien on or seizes your property, or loss of income due to the garnishment of your paycheck. Damages from the IRS for loss of reputation, inconvenience, or emotional distress are allowed only to the extent that they result in such actual monetary loss.

The IRS defines "costs of action" that you may recover as (1) fees of the clerk and marshall; (2) fees of the court reporter; (3) fees and disbursements for printing and witnesses; (4) copying fees; (5) docket fees; and (6) compensation for court-appointed experts and interpreters.

Litigation costs and administrative proceeding costs are not treated as "costs of the action." However, if the IRS denies your administrative claim for damages and you successfully sue in federal district court, you are considered a "prevailing party" and may recover attorneys' fees, related litigation expenses, and administrative costs before the IRS as discussed in *48.10*.

Caution

Penalty for Frivolous Action

If you bring an action in federal district court for unauthorized collection activities that the court considers to be frivolous, it may impose a penalty of up to $10,000.

Planning Reminder

IRS Failure To Release Lien

A suit for damages may also be brought in federal district court against the IRS if IRS employees improperly fail to release a lien on your property. Before you sue, you must file an administrative claim for damages. The lawsuit must be filed within two years after your claim arose. You may sue for actual economic damages plus costs of the action; the types of damages that may be recovered are similar to those discussed for suing the IRS for unauthorized collection actions.

2010 Draft Forms, Tables, and Worksheets

In the following pages, you will find draft tax forms, worksheets and tables from the IRS that are subject to change. The final versions will be available from the IRS website: www.irs.gov.

Use the Tax Table starting on page 755 to look up your regular tax liability if your taxable income is less than $100,000. If your taxable income is $100,000 or more, use the Tax Computation Worksheet on page 767.

If you have net capital gain or qualified dividends, do not use the Tax Table or the Tax Computation Worksheet. Depending on the nature of your capital gain income, figure your regular tax liability on the Qualified Dividends and Capital Gains Tax Worksheet, or the Schedule D Tax Worksheet; *see 22.4*.

If you claim the foreign earned income exclusion or housing exclusion on Form 2555 or Form 2555-EZ, you must use the Foreign Earned Income Tax Worksheet in the Form 1040 instructions to figure your regular income tax.

Caution: The forms, tables, and worksheets in this section are based on IRS drafts that are subject to change in light of late-breaking legislation and other developments. Final versions, as well as tax forms suitable for filing, can be downloaded from the IRS website: www.irs.gov.

Form **1040** Department of the Treasury—Internal Revenue Service

U.S. Individual Income Tax Return 2010

(99) IRS Use Only—Do not write or staple in this space.

For the year Jan. 1–Dec. 31, 2010, or other tax year beginning , 2010, ending , 20 — OMB No. 1545-0074

Name, Address, and SSN

See separate instructions.

PRINT CLEARLY

Your first name and initial	Last name	**Your social security number**
If a joint return, spouse's first name and initial	Last name	**Spouse's social security number**
Home address (number and street). If you have a P.O. box, see instructions.	Apt. no.	▲ Make sure the SSN(s) above and on line 6c are correct.
City, town or post office, state, and ZIP code. If you have a foreign address, see instructions.		Checking a box below will not change your tax or refund.

Presidential Election Campaign ▶ Check here if you, or your spouse if filing jointly, want $3 to go to this fund . . . . . ▶ ☐ **You** ☐ **Spouse**

Filing Status

Check only one box.

1 ☐ Single
2 ☐ Married filing jointly (even if only one had income)
3 ☐ Married filing separately. Enter spouse's SSN above and full name here. ▶
4 ☐ Head of household (with qualifying person). (See instructions.) If the qualifying person is a child but not your dependent, enter this child's name here. ▶
5 ☐ Qualifying widow(er) with dependent child

Exemptions

6a ☐ **Yourself.** If someone can claim you as a dependent, **do not** check box 6a . . . . .
b ☐ **Spouse** . . . . .

Boxes checked on 6a and 6b

c **Dependents:**

(1) First name Last name	(2) Dependent's social security number	(3) Dependent's relationship to you	(4) ✓ if child under age 17 qualifying for child tax credit (see page 17)
			☐
			☐
			☐
			☐

No. of children on 6c who:
• lived with you
• did not live with you due to divorce or separation (see instructions)
Dependents on 6c not entered above

If more than four dependents, see instructions and check here ▶ ☐

d Total number of exemptions claimed . . . . . **Add numbers on lines above ▶**

Income

Attach Form(s) W-2 here. Also attach Forms W-2G and 1099-R if tax was withheld.

If you did not get a W-2, see page 22.

Enclose, but do not attach, any payment. Also, please use **Form 1040-V.**

7	Wages, salaries, tips, etc. Attach Form(s) W-2		7
8a	**Taxable** interest. Attach Schedule B if required		8a
b	**Tax-exempt** interest. **Do not** include on line 8a	8b	
9a	Ordinary dividends. Attach Schedule B if required		9a
b	Qualified dividends	9b	
10	Taxable refunds, credits, or offsets of state and local income taxes		10
11	Alimony received		11
12	Business income or (loss). Attach Schedule C or C-EZ		12
13	Capital gain or (loss). Attach Schedule D if required. If not required, check here ▶ ☐		13
14	Other gains or (losses). Attach Form 4797		14
15a	IRA distributions	15a	b Taxable amount 15b
16a	Pensions and annuities	16a	b Taxable amount 16b
17	Rental real estate, royalties, partnerships, S corporations, trusts, etc. Attach Schedule E		17
18	Farm income or (loss). Attach Schedule F		18
19	Unemployment compensation		19
20a	Social security benefits	20a	b Taxable amount 20b
21	Other income. List type and amount		21
22	Combine the amounts in the far right column for lines 7 through 21. This is your **total income** ▶		22

Adjusted Gross Income

23	Educator expenses. CAUTION: See instructions	23	
24	Certain business expenses of reservists, performing artists, and fee-basis government officials. Attach Form 2106 or 2106-EZ	24	
25	Health savings account deduction. Attach Form 8889	25	
26	Moving expenses. Attach Form 3903	26	
27	One-half of self-employment tax. Attach Schedule SE	27	
28	Self-employed SEP, SIMPLE, and qualified plans	28	
29	Self-employed health insurance deduction	29	
30	Penalty on early withdrawal of savings	30	
31a	Alimony paid **b** Recipient's SSN ▶	31a	
32	IRA deduction	32	
33	Student loan interest deduction	33	
34	Tuition and fees. CAUTION: See instructions	34	
35	Domestic production activities deduction. Attach Form 8903	35	
36	Add lines 23 through 31a and 32 through 35		36
37	Subtract line 36 from line 22. This is your **adjusted gross income** ▶		37

For Disclosure, Privacy Act, and Paperwork Reduction Act Notice, see separate instructions. Cat. No. 11320B Form **1040** (2010)

Tax and Credits	38	Amount from line 37 (adjusted gross income)		38
	39a	Check if: ☐ **You** were born before January 2, 1946, ☐ Blind. ☐ **Spouse** was born before January 2, 1946, ☐ Blind. } **Total boxes checked ▶ 39a** ☐		
	b	If your spouse itemizes on a separate return or you were a dual-status alien, check here ▶ 39b ☐		
	40	**Itemized deductions** (from Schedule A) **or** your **standard deduction** (see instructions)		40
	41	Subtract line 40 from line 38		41
	42	**Exemptions.** Multiply $3,650 by the number on line 6d		42
	43	**Taxable income.** Subtract line 42 from line 41. If line 42 is more than line 41, enter -0-		43
	44	**Tax** (see instructions). Check if any tax is from: **a** ☐ Form(s) 8814 **b** ☐ Form 4972		44
	45	**Alternative minimum tax** (see instructions). Attach Form 6251		45
	46	Add lines 44 and 45 ▶		46
	47	Foreign tax credit. Attach Form 1116 if required	47	
	48	Credit for child and dependent care expenses. Attach Form 2441	48	
	49	Education credits from Form 8863, line 23	49	
	50	Retirement savings contributions credit. Attach Form 8880	50	
	51	Child tax credit (see instructions)	51	
	52	Residential energy credits. Attach Form 5695	52	
	53	Other credits from Form: **a** ☐ 3800 **b** ☐ 8801 **c** ☐	53	
	54	Add lines 47 through 53. These are your **total credits**		54
	55	Subtract line 54 from line 46. If line 54 is more than line 46, enter -0- ▶		55
Other Taxes	56	Self-employment tax. Attach Schedule SE		56
	57	Unreported social security and Medicare tax from Form: **a** ☐ 4137 **b** ☐ 8919		57
	58	Additional tax on IRAs, other qualified retirement plans, etc. Attach Form 5329 if required		58
	59	**a** ☐ Form(s) W-2, box 9 **b** ☐ Schedule H **c** ☐ Form 5405, line 16		59
	60	Add lines 55 through 59. This is your **total tax** ▶		60
Payments	61	Federal income tax withheld from Forms W-2 and 1099	61	
	62	2010 estimated tax payments and amount applied from 2009 return	62	
If you have a qualifying child, attach Schedule EIC.	63	Making work pay credit. Attach Schedule M	63	
	64a	**Earned income credit (EIC)**	64a	
	b	Nontaxable combat pay election 64b		
	65	Additional child tax credit. Attach Form 8812	65	
	66	American opportunity credit from Form 8863, line 14	66	
	67	First-time homebuyer credit from Form 5405, line 10	67	
	68	Amount paid with request for extension to file	68	
	69	Excess social security and tier 1 RRTA tax withheld	69	
	70	Credit for federal tax on fuels. Attach Form 4136	70	
	71	Credits from Form: **a** ☐ 2439 **b** ☐ 8839 **c** ☐ 8801 **d** ☐ 8885	71	
	72	Add lines 61, 62, 63, 64a, and 65 through 71. These are your **total payments** ▶		72
Refund	73	If line 72 is more than line 60, subtract line 60 from line 72. This is the amount you **overpaid**		73
	74a	Amount of line 73 you want **refunded to you.** If Form 8888 is attached, check here ▶ ☐		74a
Direct deposit? See instructions.	▶ b	Routing number ▶ **c** Type: ☐ Checking ☐ Savings		
	▶ d	Account number		
	75	Amount of line 73 you want **applied to your 2011 estimated tax** ▶	75	
Amount You Owe	76	Subtract line 72 from line 60. For details on how to pay, see instructions ▶		76
	77	Estimated tax penalty (see instructions)	77	

Third Party Designee

Do you want to allow another person to discuss this return with the IRS (see instructions)? ☐ **Yes.** Complete below. ☐ **No**

Designee's name ▶ | Phone no. ▶ | Personal identification number (PIN) ▶

Sign Here

Joint return? See page 15. Keep a copy for your records.

Under penalties of perjury, I declare that I have examined this return and accompanying schedules and statements, and to the best of my knowledge and belief, they are true, correct, and complete. Declaration of preparer (other than taxpayer) is based on all information of which preparer has any knowledge.

Your signature	Date	Your occupation	Daytime phone number
Spouse's signature. If a joint return, **both** must sign.	Date	Spouse's occupation	

Paid Preparer Use Only

Print/Type preparer's name	Preparer's signature	Date	Check ☐ if self-employed	PTIN
Firm's name ▶			Firm's EIN ▶	
Firm's address ▶			Phone no.	

Form **1040** (2010)

SCHEDULE A (Form 1040)

Department of the Treasury Internal Revenue Service (99)

Itemized Deductions

▶ Attach to Form 1040. ▶ See Instructions for Schedule A (Form 1040).

OMB No. 1545-0074

2010

Attachment Sequence No. **07**

Name(s) shown on Form 1040 | **Your social security number**

Medical and Dental Expenses		**Caution.** Do not include expenses reimbursed or paid by others.			
	1	Medical and dental expenses (see page A-1)	1		
	2	Enter amount from Form 1040, line 38 | 2 |			
	3	Multiply line 2 by 7.5% (.075)	3		
	4	Subtract line 3 from line 1. If line 3 is more than line 1, enter -0-		4	
Taxes You Paid (See page A-2.)	5	State and local income taxes	5		
	6	Real estate taxes (see page A-3)	6		
	7	New motor vehicle taxes from line 11 of the worksheet on back (for certain vehicles purchased in 2009)	7		
	8	Other taxes. List type and amount ▶	8		
	9	Add lines 5 through 8		9	
Interest You Paid (See page A-4.) **Note.** Your mortgage interest deduction may be limited (see page A-4).	10	Home mortgage interest and points reported to you on Form 1098	10		
	11	Home mortgage interest not reported to you on Form 1098. If paid to the person from whom you bought the home, see page A-4 and show that person's name, identifying no., and address ▶	11		
	12	Points not reported to you on Form 1098. See page A-4 for special rules	12		
	13	Mortgage insurance premiums (see page A-4)	13		
	14	Investment interest. Attach Form 4952 if required. (See page A-5.)	14		
	15	Add lines 10 through 14		15	
Gifts to Charity If you made a gift and got a benefit for it, see page A-6.	16	Gifts by cash or check. If you made any gift of $250 or more, see page A-6	16		
	17	Other than by cash or check. If any gift of $250 or more, see page A-6. You **must** attach Form 8283 if over $500	17		
	18	Carryover from prior year	18		
	19	Add lines 16 through 18		19	
Casualty and Theft Losses	20	Casualty or theft loss(es). Attach Form 4684. (See page A-7.)		20	
Job Expenses and Certain Miscellaneous Deductions (See page A-7.)	21	Unreimbursed employee expenses—job travel, union dues, job education, etc. Attach Form 2106 or 2106-EZ if required. (See page A-7.) ▶	21		
	22	Tax preparation fees	22		
	23	Other expenses—investment, safe deposit box, etc. List type and amount ▶	23		
	24	Add lines 21 through 23	24		
	25	Enter amount from Form 1040, line 38 | 25 |			
	26	Multiply line 25 by 2% (.02)	26		
	27	Subtract line 26 from line 24. If line 26 is more than line 24, enter -0-		27	
Other Miscellaneous Deductions	28	Other—from list on page A-8. List type and amount ▶		28	
Total Itemized Deductions	29	Add the amounts in the far right column for lines 4 through 28. Also, enter this amount on Form 1040, line 40		29	
	30	If you elect to itemize deductions even though they are less than your standard deduction, check here ▶ ☐			

For Paperwork Reduction Act Notice, see Form 1040 instructions. Cat. No. 17145C **Schedule A (Form 1040) 2010**

Worksheet for Line 7—New motor vehicle taxes

Use this worksheet to figure the amount to enter on line 7.

(Attach to Form 1040.)

Before you begin: ✓ You cannot take this deduction if the amount on Form 1040, line 38, is equal to or greater than $135,000 ($260,000 if married filing jointly).

✓ See the instructions for line 7 on page A-3.

1 Enter the state and local sales and excise taxes you paid in 2010 for the purchase of any new motor vehicle(s) **after** February 16, 2009, and **before** January 1, 2010 (see page A-3)	1		
2 Enter the purchase price **(before taxes)** of the new motor vehicle(s)	2		
3 Is the amount on line 2 more than $49,500? ☐ **No.** Enter the amount from line 1. ☐ **Yes.** Figure the **portion** of the tax from line 1 that is attributable to the first $49,500 of the purchase price of each new motor vehicle and enter it here (see page A-3).		3	
4 Enter the amount from Form 1040, line 38	4		
5 Enter the total of any— • Amounts from Form 2555, lines 45 and 50; Form 2555-EZ, line 18; and Form 4563, line 15, and • Exclusion of income from Puerto Rico	5		
6 Add lines 4 and 5	6		
7 Enter $125,000 ($250,000 if married filing jointly)	7		
8 Is the amount on line 6 more than the amount on line 7? ☐ **No.** Enter the amount from line 3 above on Schedule A, line 7. **Do not** complete the rest of this worksheet. ☐ **Yes.** Subtract line 7 from line 6	8		
9 Divide the amount on line 8 by $10,000. Enter the result as a decimal (rounded to at least three places). If the result is 1.000 or more, enter 1.000	9	.	
10 Multiply line 3 by line 9		10	
11 **Deduction for new motor vehicle taxes.** Subtract line 10 from line 3. Enter the result here and on Schedule A, line 7		11	

Schedule A (Form 1040) 2010

SCHEDULE B
(Form 1040A or 1040)

Department of the Treasury
Internal Revenue Service (99)

Interest and Ordinary Dividends

▶ Attach to Form 1040A or 1040. ▶ See instructions on back.

OMB No. 1545-0074

2010

Attachment Sequence No. **08**

Name(s) shown on return | **Your social security number**

Part I Interest

(See instructions on back and the instructions for Form 1040A, or Form 1040, line 8a.)

Note. If you received a Form 1099-INT, Form 1099-OID, or substitute statement from a brokerage firm, list the firm's name as the payer and enter the total interest shown on that form.

			Amount
1	List name of payer. If any interest is from a seller-financed mortgage and the buyer used the property as a personal residence, see instructions on back and list this interest first. Also, show that buyer's social security number and address ▶	1	
2	Add the amounts on line 1	2	
3	Excludable interest on series EE and I U.S. savings bonds issued after 1989. Attach Form 8815	3	
4	Subtract line 3 from line 2. Enter the result here and on Form 1040A, or Form 1040, line 8a . . . . ▶	4	

Note. If line 4 is over $1,500, you must complete Part III.

Part II Ordinary Dividends

(See instructions on back and the instructions for Form 1040A, or Form 1040, line 9a.)

Note. If you received a Form 1099-DIV or substitute statement from a brokerage firm, list the firm's name as the payer and enter the ordinary dividends shown on that form.

			Amount
5	List name of payer ▶	5	
6	Add the amounts on line 5. Enter the total here and on Form 1040A, or Form 1040, line 9a . . . . ▶	6	

Note. If line 6 is over $1,500, you must complete Part III.

Part III Foreign Accounts and Trusts

(See instructions on back.)

	You must complete this part if you **(a)** had over $1,500 of taxable interest or ordinary dividends; **(b)** had a foreign account; or **(c)** received a distribution from, or were a grantor of, or a transferor to, a foreign trust.	**Yes**	**No**
7a	At any time during 2010, did you have an interest in or a signature or other authority over a financial account in a foreign country, such as a bank account, securities account, or other financial account? See instructions on back for exceptions and filing requirements for Form TD F 90-22.1		
b	If "Yes," enter the name of the foreign country ▶		
8	During 2010, did you receive a distribution from, or were you the grantor of, or transferor to, a foreign trust? If "Yes," you may have to file Form 3520. See instructions on back		

For Paperwork Reduction Act Notice, see your tax return instructions. Cat. No. 17146N **Schedule B (Form 1040A or 1040) 2010**

General Instructions

Section references are to the Internal Revenue Code unless otherwise noted.

Purpose of Form

Use Schedule B if any of the following applies.

- You had over $1,500 of taxable interest or ordinary dividends.
- You received interest from a seller-financed mortgage and the buyer used the property as a personal residence.
- You have accrued interest from a bond.
- You are reporting original issue discount (OID) in an amount less than the amount shown on Form 1099-OID.
- You are reducing your interest income on a bond by the amount of amortizable bond premium.
- You are claiming the exclusion of interest from series EE or I U.S. savings bonds issued after 1989.
- You received interest or ordinary dividends as a nominee.
- You had a financial interest in, or signature authority (or other authority that is comparable to signature authority) over, a financial account in a foreign country or you received a distribution from, or were a grantor of, or transferor to, a foreign trust. Part III of the schedule has questions about foreign accounts and trusts.

Specific Instructions

TIP *You can list more than one payer on each entry space for lines 1 and 5, but be sure to clearly show the amount paid next to the payer's name. Add the separate amounts paid by the payers listed on an entry space and enter the total in the "Amount" column. If you still need more space, attach separate statements that are the same size as the printed schedule. Use the same format as lines 1 and 5, but show your totals on Schedule B. Be sure to put your name and social security number (SSN) on the statements and attach them at the end of your return.*

Part I. Interest

Line 1. Report on line 1 all of your taxable interest. Taxable interest should be shown on your Forms 1099-INT, Forms 1099-OID, or substitute statements. Include interest from series EE, H, HH, and I U.S. savings bonds. List each payer's name and show the amount. Do not report on this line any tax-exempt interest from box 8 or box 9 of Form 1099-INT. Instead, report the amount from box 8 on line 8b of Form 1040A or 1040. If an amount is shown in box 9 of Form 1099-INT, you generally must report it on line 12 of Form 6251. See the Instructions for Form 6251 for more details.

Seller-financed mortgages. If you sold your home or other property and the buyer used the property as a personal residence, list first any interest the buyer paid you on a mortgage or other form of seller financing. Be sure to show the buyer's name, address, and SSN. You must also let the buyer know your SSN. If you do not show the buyer's name, address, and SSN, or let the buyer know your SSN, you may have to pay a $50 penalty.

Nominees. If you received a Form 1099-INT that includes interest you received as a nominee (that is, in your name, but the interest actually belongs to someone else), report the total on line 1. Do this even if you later distributed some or all of this income to others. Under your last entry on line 1, put a subtotal of all interest listed on line 1. Below this subtotal, enter "Nominee Distribution" and show the total interest you received as a nominee. Subtract this amount from the subtotal and enter the result on line 2.

TIP *If you received interest as a nominee, you must give the actual owner a Form 1099-INT unless the owner is your spouse. You must also file a Form 1096 and a Form 1099-INT with the IRS. For more details, see the* General Instructions for Certain Information Returns (Forms 1098, 1099, 3921, 3922, 5498, and W-2G) *and the* Instructions for Forms 1099-INT and 1099-OID.

Accrued interest. When you buy bonds between interest payment dates and pay accrued interest to the seller, this interest is taxable to the seller. If you received a Form 1099 for interest as a purchaser of a bond with accrued interest, follow the rules earlier under *Nominees* to see how to report the accrued interest. But identify the amount to be subtracted as "Accrued Interest."

Original issue discount (OID). If you are reporting OID in an amount less than the amount shown on Form 1099-OID, follow the rules earlier under *Nominees* to see how to report the OID. But identify the amount to be subtracted as "OID Adjustment."

Amortizable bond premium. If you are reducing your interest income on a bond by the amount of amortizable bond premium, follow the rules earlier under *Nominees* to see how to report the interest. But identify the amount to be subtracted as "ABP Adjustment."

Line 3. If, during 2010, you cashed series EE or I U.S. savings bonds issued after 1989 and you paid qualified higher education expenses for yourself, your spouse, or your dependents, you may be able to exclude part or all of the interest on those bonds. See Form 8815 for details.

Part II. Ordinary Dividends

TIP *You may have to file Form 5471 if, in 2010, you were an officer or director of a foreign corporation. You may also have to file Form 5471 if, in 2010, you owned 10% or more of the total (a) value of a foreign corporation's stock, or (b) combined voting power of all classes of a foreign corporation's stock with voting rights. For details, see Form 5471 and its instructions.*

Line 5. Report on line 5 all of your ordinary dividends. This amount should be shown in box 1a of your Forms 1099-DIV or substitute statements. List each payer's name and show the amount.

Nominees. If you received a Form 1099-DIV that includes ordinary dividends you received as a nominee (that is, in your name, but the ordinary dividends actually belong to someone else), report the total on line 5. Do this even if you later distributed some or all of this income to others. Under your last entry on line 5, put a subtotal of all ordinary dividends listed on line 5. Below this subtotal, enter "Nominee Distribution" and show the total ordinary dividends you received as a nominee. Subtract this amount from the subtotal and enter the result on line 6.

TIP *If you received dividends as a nominee, you must give the actual owner a Form 1099-DIV unless the owner is your spouse. You must also file a Form 1096 and a Form 1099-DIV with the IRS. For more details, see the* General Instructions for Certain Information Returns (Forms 1098, 1099, 3921, 3922, 5498, and W-2G) *and the* Instructions for Form 1099-DIV.

Part III. Foreign Accounts and Trusts

Line 7a. Check the "Yes" box on line 7a if either (1) or (2) below applies.

1. You own more than 50% of the stock in any corporation that owns one or more foreign bank accounts.

2. At any time during 2010 you had a financial interest in, or signature authority (or other authority that is comparable to signature authority) over, a financial account in a foreign country (such as a bank account, securities account, or other financial account).

TIP *For line 7a, item (2) does not apply to foreign securities held in a U.S. securities account.*

Exceptions. Check the "No" box if any of the following applies to you.

- The combined value of the accounts was $10,000 or less during the whole year.
- The accounts were with a U.S. military banking facility operated by a U.S. financial institution.
- You were an officer or employee of a commercial bank that is supervised by the Comptroller of the Currency, the Board of Governors of the Federal Reserve System, or the Federal Deposit Insurance Corporation; the account was in your employer's name; and you did not have a personal financial interest in the account.
- You were an officer or employee of a domestic corporation with securities listed on national securities exchanges or with assets of more than $10 million and 500 or more shareholders of record; the account was in your employer's name; you did not have a personal financial interest in the account; and the corporation's chief financial officer has given you written notice that the corporation has filed a current report that includes the account.

See Form TD F 90-22.1 to find out if you are considered to have a financial interest in or signature authority (or other authority that is comparable to signature authority) over, a financial account in a foreign country (such as a bank account, securities account, or other financial account). You can get Form TD F 90-22.1 by visiting the IRS website at *www.irs.gov/pub/irs-pdf/f90221.pdf.*

If you checked the "Yes" box on line 7a, file Form TD F 90-22.1 by June 30, 2011, with the Department of the Treasury at the address shown on that form. Do not attach it to your tax return.

CAUTION *If you are required to file Form TD F 90-22.1 but do not do so, you may have to pay a penalty of up to $10,000 (more in some cases).*

Line 7b. If you checked the "Yes" box on line 7a, enter the name of the foreign country or countries in the space provided on line 7b. Attach a separate statement if you need more space.

Line 8. If you received a distribution from a foreign trust, you must provide additional information. For this purpose, a loan of cash or marketable securities generally is considered to be a distribution. See Form 3520 for details.

If you were the grantor of, or transferor to, a foreign trust that existed during 2010, you may have to file Form 3520.

Do not attach Form 3520 to Form 1040. Instead, file it at the address shown in its instructions.

If you were treated as the owner of a foreign trust under the grantor trust rules, you are also responsible for ensuring that the foreign trust files Form 3520-A. Form 3520-A is due on March 15, 2011, for a calendar year trust. See the Instructions for Form 3520-A for more details.

SCHEDULE C (Form 1040)

Department of the Treasury Internal Revenue Service (99)

Profit or Loss From Business

(Sole Proprietorship)

▶ Partnerships, joint ventures, etc., generally must file Form 1065 or 1065-B.

▶ Attach to Form 1040, 1040NR, or 1041. ▶ See Instructions for Schedule C (Form 1040).

OMB No. 1545-0074

2010

Attachment Sequence No. **09**

Name of proprietor | **Social security number (SSN)**

A Principal business or profession, including product or service (see page C-2 of the instructions) | **B Enter code from pages C-9, 10, & 11** ▶

C Business name. If no separate business name, leave blank. | **D Employer ID number (EIN), if any**

E Business address (including suite or room no.) ▶

City, town or post office, state, and ZIP code

F Accounting method: **(1)** ☐ Cash **(2)** ☐ Accrual **(3)** ☐ Other (specify) ▶

G Did you "materially participate" in the operation of this business during 2010? If "No," see page C-3 for limit on losses ☐ **Yes** ☐ **No**

H If you started or acquired this business during 2010, check here . . . ▶ ☐

Part I Income

1	Gross receipts or sales. **Caution.** See page C-4 and check the box if: • This income was reported to you on Form W-2 and the "Statutory employee" box on that form was checked, or • You are a member of a qualified joint venture reporting only rental real estate income not subject to self-employment tax. Also see page C-3 for limit on losses. . . ▶ ☐	1	
2	Returns and allowances . . .	2	
3	Subtract line 2 from line 1 . . .	3	
4	Cost of goods sold (from line 42 on page 2) . . .	4	
5	**Gross profit.** Subtract line 4 from line 3 . . .	5	
6	Other income, including federal and state gasoline or fuel tax credit or refund (see page C-4) . . .	6	
7	**Gross income.** Add lines 5 and 6 . . . ▶	7	

Part II Expenses. Enter expenses for business use of your home **only** on line 30.

8	Advertising . . .	8		18	Office expense . . .	18	
9	Car and truck expenses (see page C-4) . . .	9		19	Pension and profit-sharing plans .	19	
10	Commissions and fees .	10		20	Rent or lease (see page C-6):		
11	Contract labor (see page C-4)	11		a	Vehicles, machinery, and equipment	20a	
12	Depletion . . .	12		b	Other business property . . .	20b	
13	Depreciation and section 179 expense deduction (not included in Part III) (see page C-5) . . .	13		21	Repairs and maintenance . . .	21	
				22	Supplies (not included in Part III) .	22	
				23	Taxes and licenses . . .	23	
				24	Travel, meals, and entertainment:		
				a	Travel . . .	24a	
14	Employee benefit programs (other than on line 19) . .	14		b	Deductible meals and entertainment (see page C-6) . .	24b	
15	Insurance (other than health)	15		25	Utilities . . .	25	
16	Interest:			26	Wages (less employment credits) .	26	
a	Mortgage (paid to banks, etc.)	16a		27	Other expenses (from line 48 on page 2) . . .	27	
b	Other . . .	16b					
17	Legal and professional services . . .	17					

28	**Total expenses** before expenses for business use of home. Add lines 8 through 27 . . . ▶	28	
29	Tentative profit or (loss). Subtract line 28 from line 7 . . .	29	
30	Expenses for business use of your home. Attach **Form 8829** . . .	30	
31	**Net profit or (loss).** Subtract line 30 from line 29. • If a profit, enter on both **Form 1040, line 12,** and **Schedule SE, line 2,** or on **Form 1040NR, line 13** (if you checked the box on line 1, see page C-7). Estates and trusts, enter on **Form 1041, line 3.** • If a loss, you **must** go to line 32.	31	
32	If you have a loss, check the box that describes your investment in this activity (see page C-7). • If you checked 32a, enter the loss on both **Form 1040, line 12,** and **Schedule SE, line 2,** or on **Form 1040NR, line 13** (if you checked the box on line 1, see the line 31 instructions on page C-7). Estates and trusts, enter on **Form 1041, line 3.** • If you checked 32b, you **must** attach **Form 6198.** Your loss may be limited.		**32a** ☐ All investment is at risk. **32b** ☐ Some investment is not at risk.

For Paperwork Reduction Act Notice, see your tax return instructions. Cat. No. 11334P **Schedule C (Form 1040) 2010**

Part III Cost of Goods Sold (see page C-8)

33 Method(s) used to value closing inventory: a ☐ Cost b ☐ Lower of cost or market c ☐ Other (attach explanation)

34 Was there any change in determining quantities, costs, or valuations between opening and closing inventory? If "Yes," attach explanation . . . ☐ Yes ☐ No

35	Inventory at beginning of year. If different from last year's closing inventory, attach explanation	35	
36	Purchases less cost of items withdrawn for personal use	36	
37	Cost of labor. Do not include any amounts paid to yourself	37	
38	Materials and supplies	38	
39	Other costs	39	
40	Add lines 35 through 39	40	
41	Inventory at end of year	41	
42	**Cost of goods sold.** Subtract line 41 from line 40. Enter the result here and on page 1, line 4	42	

Part IV Information on Your Vehicle.

Complete this part **only** if you are claiming car or truck expenses on line 9 and are not required to file Form 4562 for this business. See the instructions for line 13 on page C-5 to find out if you must file Form 4562.

43 When did you place your vehicle in service for business purposes? (month, day, year) ▶ ___ / ___ / ___

44 Of the total number of miles you drove your vehicle during 2010, enter the number of miles you used your vehicle for:

a Business ________ b Commuting (see instructions) ________ c Other ________

45 Was your vehicle available for personal use during off-duty hours? . . . ☐ Yes ☐ No

46 Do you (or your spouse) have another vehicle available for personal use? . . . ☐ Yes ☐ No

47a Do you have evidence to support your deduction? . . . ☐ Yes ☐ No

b If "Yes," is the evidence written? . . . ☐ Yes ☐ No

Part V Other Expenses.

List below business expenses not included on lines 8–26 or line 30.

48 **Total other expenses.** Enter here and on page 1, line 27	48	

Schedule C (Form 1040) 2010

SCHEDULE D (Form 1040)

Department of the Treasury
Internal Revenue Service (99)

Capital Gains and Losses

► Attach to Form 1040 or Form 1040NR. ► See Instructions for Schedule D (Form 1040).
► Use Schedule D-1 to list additional transactions for lines 1 and 8.

OMB No. 1545-0074

2010

Attachment Sequence No. 12

Name(s) shown on return | Your social security number

Part I Short-Term Capital Gains and Losses—Assets Held One Year or Less

	(a) Description of property (Example: 100 sh. XYZ Co.)	(b) Date acquired (Mo., day, yr.)	(c) Date sold (Mo., day, yr.)	(d) Sales price (see page D-7 of the instructions)	(e) Cost or other basis (see page D-7 of the instructions)	(f) Gain or (loss) Subtract (e) from (d)
1						

2	Enter your short-term totals, if any, from Schedule D-1, line 2	2	
3	**Total short-term sales price amounts.** Add lines 1 and 2 in column (d)	3	
4	Short-term gain from Form 6252 and short-term gain or (loss) from Forms 4684, 6781, and 8824 .	4	
5	Net short-term gain or (loss) from partnerships, S corporations, estates, and trusts from Schedule(s) K-1	5	
6	Short-term capital loss carryover. Enter the amount, if any, from line 10 of your **Capital Loss Carryover Worksheet** on page D-7 of the instructions	6	( )
7	**Net short-term capital gain or (loss).** Combine lines 1 through 6 in column (f)	7	

Part II Long-Term Capital Gains and Losses—Assets Held More Than One Year

	(a) Description of property (Example: 100 sh. XYZ Co.)	(b) Date acquired (Mo., day, yr.)	(c) Date sold (Mo., day, yr.)	(d) Sales price (see page D-7 of the instructions)	(e) Cost or other basis (see page D-7 of the instructions)	(f) Gain or (loss) Subtract (e) from (d)
8						

9	Enter your long-term totals, if any, from Schedule D-1, line 9	9	
10	**Total long-term sales price amounts.** Add lines 8 and 9 in column (d).	10	
11	Gain from Form 4797, Part I; long-term gain from Forms 2439 and 6252; and long-term gain or (loss) from Forms 4684, 6781, and 8824	11	
12	Net long-term gain or (loss) from partnerships, S corporations, estates, and trusts from Schedule(s) K-1	12	
13	Capital gain distributions. See page D-2 of the instructions	13	
14	Long-term capital loss carryover. Enter the amount, if any, from line 15 of your **Capital Loss Carryover Worksheet** on page D-7 of the instructions	14	( )
15	**Net long-term capital gain or (loss).** Combine lines 8 through 14 in column (f). Then go to Part III on the back	15	

For Paperwork Reduction Act Notice, see your tax return instructions. Cat. No. 11338H **Schedule D (Form 1040) 2010**

Part III **Summary**

16 Combine lines 7 and 15 and enter the result **16**

- If line 16 is a **gain**, enter the amount from line 16 on Form 1040, line 13, or Form 1040NR, line 14. Then go to line 17 below.
- If line 16 is a **loss**, skip lines 17 through 20 below. Then go to line 21. Also be sure to complete line 22.
- If line 16 is **zero**, skip lines 17 through 21 below and enter -0- on Form 1040, line 13, or Form 1040NR, line 14. Then go to line 22.

17 Are lines 15 and 16 **both** gains?

☐ **Yes.** Go to line 18.

☐ **No.** Skip lines 18 through 21, and go to line 22.

18 Enter the amount, if any, from line 7 of the **28% Rate Gain Worksheet** on page D-8 of the instructions . . . . ▶ **18**

19 Enter the amount, if any, from line 18 of the **Unrecaptured Section 1250 Gain Worksheet** on page D-9 of the instructions . . . . ▶ **19**

20 Are lines 18 and 19 **both** zero or blank?

☐ **Yes.** Complete Form 1040 through line 43, or Form 1040NR through line 41. Then complete the **Qualified Dividends and Capital Gain Tax Worksheet** on page 39 of the Instructions for Form 1040 (or in the Instructions for Form 1040NR). **Do not** complete lines 21 and 22 below.

☐ **No.** Complete Form 1040 through line 43, or Form 1040NR through line 41. Then complete the **Schedule D Tax Worksheet** on page D-10 of the instructions. **Do not** complete lines 21 and 22 below.

21 If line 16 is a loss, enter here and on Form 1040, line 13, or Form 1040NR, line 14, the **smaller** of:

- The loss on line 16 or
- ($3,000), or if married filing separately, ($1,500)

. . . . **21** (   )

Note. When figuring which amount is smaller, treat both amounts as positive numbers.

22 Do you have qualified dividends on Form 1040, line 9b, or Form 1040NR, line 10b?

☐ **Yes.** Complete Form 1040 through line 43, or Form 1040NR through line 41. Then complete the **Qualified Dividends and Capital Gain Tax Worksheet** on page 39 of the Instructions for Form 1040 (or in the Instructions for Form 1040NR).

☐ **No.** Complete the rest of Form 1040 or Form 1040NR.

Schedule D (Form 1040) 2010

SCHEDULE SE (Form 1040) Department of the Treasury Internal Revenue Service (99)	**Self-Employment Tax** ▶ Attach to Form 1040 or Form 1040NR. ▶ See Instructions for Schedule SE (Form 1040).	OMB No. 1545-0074 **2010** Attachment Sequence No. **17**

Name of person with **self-employment** income (as shown on Form 1040)	Social security number of person with **self-employment** income ▶	

Before you begin: To determine if you must file Schedule SE, see the instructions on page SE-1.

May I Use Short Schedule SE or Must I Use Long Schedule SE?

Note. Use this flowchart **only if** you must file Schedule SE. If unsure, see *Who Must File Schedule SE,* on page SE-1.

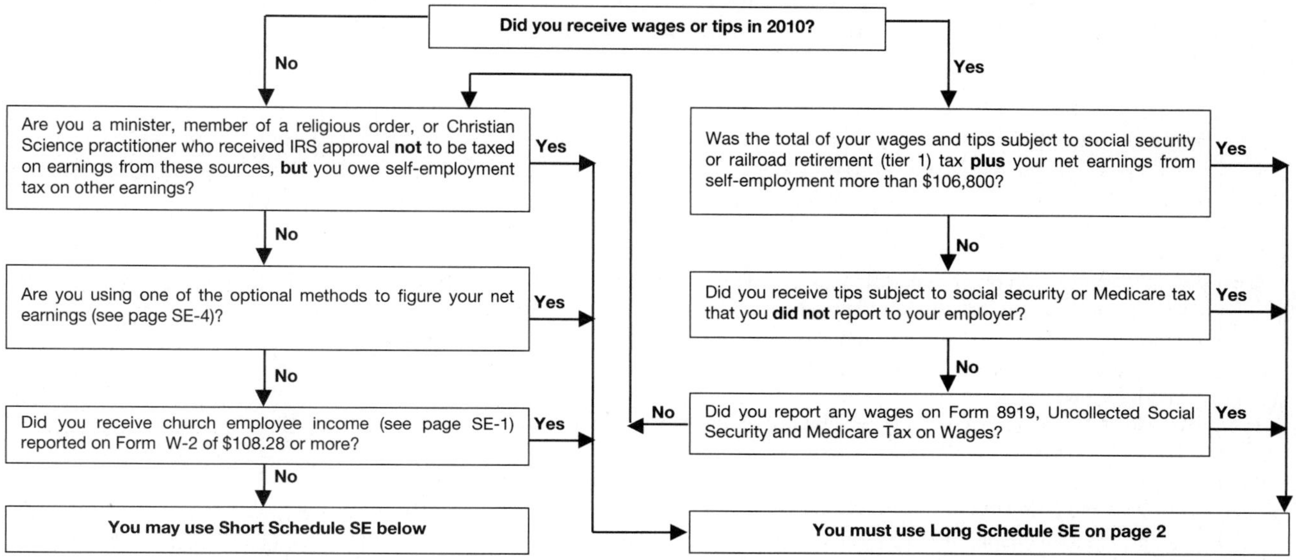

Section A—Short Schedule SE. Caution. Read above to see if you can use Short Schedule SE.

1a	Net farm profit or (loss) from Schedule F, line 36, and farm partnerships, Schedule K-1 (Form 1065), box 14, code A	**1a**	
b	If you received social security retirement or disability benefits, enter the amount of Conservation Reserve Program payments included on Schedule F, line 6b, or listed on Schedule K-1 (Form 1065), box 20, code Y	**1b**	( )
2	Net profit or (loss) from Schedule C, line 31; Schedule C-EZ, line 3; Schedule K-1 (Form 1065), box 14, code A (other than farming); and Schedule K-1 (Form 1065-B), box 9, code J1. Ministers and members of religious orders, see page SE-1 for types of income to report on this line. See page SE-3 for other income to report	**2**	
3	Combine lines 1a, 1b, and 2. Subtract from that total the amount on Form 1040, line 29, or Form 1040NR, line 29, and enter the result (see page SE-3)	**3**	
4	Multiply line 3 by 92.35% (.9235). If less than $400, you do not owe self-employment tax; **do not** file this schedule unless you have an amount on line 1b . . . . . ▶	**4**	
	Note. If line 4 is less than $400 due to Conservation Reserve Program payments on line 1b, see page SE-3.		
5	**Self-employment tax.** If the amount on line 4 is: • $106,800 or less, multiply line 4 by 15.3% (.153). Enter the result here and on **Form 1040, line 56,** or **Form 1040NR, line 54** • More than $106,800, multiply line 4 by 2.9% (.029). Then, add $13,243.20 to the result. Enter the total here and on **Form 1040, line 56,** or **Form 1040NR, line 54**	**5**	
6	**Deduction for one-half of self-employment tax.** Multiply line 5 by 50% (.50). Enter the result here and on **Form 1040, line 27,** or **Form 1040NR, line 27** **6**		

For Paperwork Reduction Act Notice, see your tax return instructions. Cat. No. 11358Z **Schedule SE (Form 1040) 2010**

Name of person with **self-employment** income (as shown on Form 1040)	Social security number of person with **self-employment** income ▶

Section B—Long Schedule SE

Part I Self-Employment Tax

Note. If your only income subject to self-employment tax is **church employee income,** see page SE-3 for specific instructions. Also see page SE-1 for the definition of church employee income.

A	If you are a minister, member of a religious order, or Christian Science practitioner **and** you filed Form 4361, but you had $400 or more of **other** net earnings from self-employment, check here and continue with Part I . . . . . . ▶ ☐			
1a	Net farm profit or (loss) from Schedule F, line 36, and farm partnerships, Schedule K-1 (Form 1065), box 14, code A. **Note.** Skip lines 1a and 1b if you use the farm optional method (see page SE-4)	**1a**		
b	If you received social security retirement or disability benefits, enter the amount of Conservation Reserve Program payments included on Schedule F, line 6b, or listed on Schedule K-1 (Form 1065), box 20, code Y	**1b**	( )	
2	Net profit or (loss) from Schedule C, line 31; Schedule C-EZ, line 3; Schedule K-1 (Form 1065), box 14, code A (other than farming); and Schedule K-1 (Form 1065-B), box 9, code J1. Ministers and members of religious orders, see page SE-1 for types of income to report on this line. See page SE-3 for other income to report. **Note.** Skip this line if you use the nonfarm optional method (see page SE-4)	**2**		
3	Combine lines 1a, 1b, and 2. Subtract from that total the amount on Form 1040, line 29, or Form 1040NR, line 29, and enter the result (see page SE-3)	**3**		
4a	If line 3 is more than zero, multiply line 3 by 92.35% (.9235). Otherwise, enter amount from line 3	**4a**		
	Note. If line 4a is less than $400 due to Conservation Reserve Program payments on line 1b, see page SE-3.			
b	If you elect one or both of the optional methods, enter the total of lines 15 and 17 here	**4b**		
c	Combine lines 4a and 4b. If less than $400, **stop**; you do not owe self-employment tax. **Exception.** If less than $400 and you had **church employee income,** enter -0- and continue ▶	**4c**		
5a	Enter your **church employee income** from Form W-2. See page SE-1 for definition of church employee income. **5a**			
b	Multiply line 5a by 92.35% (.9235). If less than $100, enter -0-	**5b**		
6	Add lines 4c and 5b	**6**		
7	Maximum amount of combined wages and self-employment earnings subject to social security tax or the 6.2% portion of the 7.65% railroad retirement (tier 1) tax for 2010	**7**	106,800	00
8a	Total social security wages and tips (total of boxes 3 and 7 on Form(s) W-2) and railroad retirement (tier 1) compensation. If $106,800 or more, skip lines 8b through 10, and go to line 11 **8a**			
b	Unreported tips subject to social security tax (from Form 4137, line 10) **8b**			
c	Wages subject to social security tax (from Form 8919, line 10) **8c**			
d	Add lines 8a, 8b, and 8c	**8d**		
9	Subtract line 8d from line 7. If zero or less, enter -0- here and on line 10 and go to line 11 . ▶	**9**		
10	Multiply the **smaller** of line 6 or line 9 by 12.4% (.124)	**10**		
11	Multiply line 6 by 2.9% (.029)	**11**		
12	**Self-employment tax.** Add lines 10 and 11. Enter here and on **Form 1040, line 56,** or **Form 1040NR, line 54**	**12**		
13	**Deduction for one-half of self-employment tax.** Multiply line 12 by 50% (.50). Enter the result here and on **Form 1040, line 27, or Form 1040NR, line 27** . **13**			

Part II Optional Methods To Figure Net Earnings (see page SE-4)

Farm Optional Method. You may use this method **only** if **(a)** your gross farm income[1] was not more than $6,720, **or (b)** your net farm profits[2] were less than $4,851.

14	Maximum income for optional methods	**14**	4,480	00
15	Enter the **smaller** of: two-thirds (2/3) of gross farm income[1] (not less than zero) **or** $4,480. Also include this amount on line 4b above	**15**		

Nonfarm Optional Method. You may use this method **only** if **(a)** your net nonfarm profits[3] were less than $4,851 and also less than 72.189% of your gross nonfarm income,[4] **and (b)** you had net earnings from self-employment of at least $400 in 2 of the prior 3 years. **Caution.** You may use this method no more than five times.

16	Subtract line 15 from line 14	**16**		
17	Enter the **smaller** of: two-thirds (2/3) of gross nonfarm income[4] (not less than zero) **or** the amount on line 16. Also include this amount on line 4b above	**17**		

[1] From Sch. F, line 11, and Sch. K-1 (Form 1065), box 14, code B.

[2] From Sch. F, line 36, and Sch. K-1 (Form 1065), box 14, code A—minus the amount you would have entered on line 1b had you not used the optional method.

[3] From Sch. C, line 31; Sch. C-EZ, line 3; Sch. K-1 (Form 1065), box 14, code A; and Sch. K-1 (Form 1065-B), box 9, code J1.

[4] From Sch. C, line 7; Sch. C-EZ, line 1; Sch. K-1 (Form 1065), box 14, code C; and Sch. K-1 (Form 1065-B), box 9, code J2.

Schedule SE (Form 1040) 2010

2010 Tax Table

See the instructions for line 44 on page 35 to see if you must use the Tax Table below to figure your tax.

Example. Mr. and Mrs. Brown are filing a joint return. Their taxable income on Form 1040, line 43, is $25,300. First, they find the $25,300–25,350 taxable income line. Next, they find the column for married filing jointly and read down the column. The amount shown where the taxable income line and filing status column meet is $2,961. This is the tax amount they should enter on Form 1040, line 44.

Sample Table

At least	But less than	Single	Married filing jointly *	Married filing sepa-rately	Head of a house-hold
		Your tax is—			
25,200	**25,250**	3,365	2,946	3,365	3,186
25,250	**25,300**	3,373	2,954	3,373	3,194
25,300	**25,350**	3,380	(2,961)	3,380	3,201
25,350	**25,400**	3,388	2,969	3,388	3,209

If line 43 (taxable income) is—		And you are—			
At least	But less than	Single	Married filing jointly *	Married filing sepa-rately	Head of a house-hold
		Your tax is—			
0	**5**	0	0	0	0
5	**15**	1	1	1	1
15	**25**	2	2	2	2
25	**50**	4	4	4	4
50	**75**	6	6	6	6
75	**100**	9	9	9	9
100	**125**	11	11	11	11
125	**150**	14	14	14	14
150	**175**	16	16	16	16
175	**200**	19	19	19	19
200	**225**	21	21	21	21
225	**250**	24	24	24	24
250	**275**	26	26	26	26
275	**300**	29	29	29	29
300	**325**	31	31	31	31
325	**350**	34	34	34	34
350	**375**	36	36	36	36
375	**400**	39	39	39	39
400	**425**	41	41	41	41
425	**450**	44	44	44	44
450	**475**	46	46	46	46
475	**500**	49	49	49	49
500	**525**	51	51	51	51
525	**550**	54	54	54	54
550	**575**	56	56	56	56
575	**600**	59	59	59	59
600	**625**	61	61	61	61
625	**650**	64	64	64	64
650	**675**	66	66	66	66
675	**700**	69	69	69	69
700	**725**	71	71	71	71
725	**750**	74	74	74	74
750	**775**	76	76	76	76
775	**800**	79	79	79	79
800	**825**	81	81	81	81
825	**850**	84	84	84	84
850	**875**	86	86	86	86
875	**900**	89	89	89	89
900	**925**	91	91	91	91
925	**950**	94	94	94	94
950	**975**	96	96	96	96
975	**1,000**	99	99	99	99
1,000					
1,000	**1,025**	101	101	101	101
1,025	**1,050**	104	104	104	104
1,050	**1,075**	106	106	106	106
1,075	**1,100**	109	109	109	109
1,100	**1,125**	111	111	111	111
1,125	**1,150**	114	114	114	114
1,150	**1,175**	116	116	116	116
1,175	**1,200**	119	119	119	119
1,200	**1,225**	121	121	121	121
1,225	**1,250**	124	124	124	124
1,250	**1,275**	126	126	126	126
1,275	**1,300**	129	129	129	129

If line 43 (taxable income) is—		And you are—			
At least	But less than	Single	Married filing jointly *	Married filing sepa-rately	Head of a house-hold
		Your tax is—			
1,300	**1,325**	131	131	131	131
1,325	**1,350**	134	134	134	134
1,350	**1,375**	136	136	136	136
1,375	**1,400**	139	139	139	139
1,400	**1,425**	141	141	141	141
1,425	**1,450**	144	144	144	144
1,450	**1,475**	146	146	146	146
1,475	**1,500**	149	149	149	149
1,500	**1,525**	151	151	151	151
1,525	**1,550**	154	154	154	154
1,550	**1,575**	156	156	156	156
1,575	**1,600**	159	159	159	159
1,600	**1,625**	161	161	161	161
1,625	**1,650**	164	164	164	164
1,650	**1,675**	166	166	166	166
1,675	**1,700**	169	169	169	169
1,700	**1,725**	171	171	171	171
1,725	**1,750**	174	174	174	174
1,750	**1,775**	176	176	176	176
1,775	**1,800**	179	179	179	179
1,800	**1,825**	181	181	181	181
1,825	**1,850**	184	184	184	184
1,850	**1,875**	186	186	186	186
1,875	**1,900**	189	189	189	189
1,900	**1,925**	191	191	191	191
1,925	**1,950**	194	194	194	194
1,950	**1,975**	196	196	196	196
1,975	**2,000**	199	199	199	199
2,000					
2,000	**2,025**	201	201	201	201
2,025	**2,050**	204	204	204	204
2,050	**2,075**	206	206	206	206
2,075	**2,100**	209	209	209	209
2,100	**2,125**	211	211	211	211
2,125	**2,150**	214	214	214	214
2,150	**2,175**	216	216	216	216
2,175	**2,200**	219	219	219	219
2,200	**2,225**	221	221	221	221
2,225	**2,250**	224	224	224	224
2,250	**2,275**	226	226	226	226
2,275	**2,300**	229	229	229	229
2,300	**2,325**	231	231	231	231
2,325	**2,350**	234	234	234	234
2,350	**2,375**	236	236	236	236
2,375	**2,400**	239	239	239	239
2,400	**2,425**	241	241	241	241
2,425	**2,450**	244	244	244	244
2,450	**2,475**	246	246	246	246
2,475	**2,500**	249	249	249	249
2,500	**2,525**	251	251	251	251
2,525	**2,550**	254	254	254	254
2,550	**2,575**	256	256	256	256
2,575	**2,600**	259	259	259	259
2,600	**2,625**	261	261	261	261
2,625	**2,650**	264	264	264	264
2,650	**2,675**	266	266	266	266
2,675	**2,700**	269	269	269	269

If line 43 (taxable income) is—		And you are—			
At least	But less than	Single	Married filing jointly *	Married filing sepa-rately	Head of a house-hold
		Your tax is—			
2,700	**2,725**	271	271	271	271
2,725	**2,750**	274	274	274	274
2,750	**2,775**	276	276	276	276
2,775	**2,800**	279	279	279	279
2,800	**2,825**	281	281	281	281
2,825	**2,850**	284	284	284	284
2,850	**2,875**	286	286	286	286
2,875	**2,900**	289	289	289	289
2,900	**2,925**	291	291	291	291
2,925	**2,950**	294	294	294	294
2,950	**2,975**	296	296	296	296
2,975	**3,000**	299	299	299	299
3,000					
3,000	**3,050**	303	303	303	303
3,050	**3,100**	308	308	308	308
3,100	**3,150**	313	313	313	313
3,150	**3,200**	318	318	318	318
3,200	**3,250**	323	323	323	323
3,250	**3,300**	328	328	328	328
3,300	**3,350**	333	333	333	333
3,350	**3,400**	338	338	338	338
3,400	**3,450**	343	343	343	343
3,450	**3,500**	348	348	348	348
3,500	**3,550**	353	353	353	353
3,550	**3,600**	358	358	358	358
3,600	**3,650**	363	363	363	363
3,650	**3,700**	368	368	368	368
3,700	**3,750**	373	373	373	373
3,750	**3,800**	378	378	378	378
3,800	**3,850**	383	383	383	383
3,850	**3,900**	388	388	388	388
3,900	**3,950**	393	393	393	393
3,950	**4,000**	398	398	398	398
4,000					
4,000	**4,050**	403	403	403	403
4,050	**4,100**	408	408	408	408
4,100	**4,150**	413	413	413	413
4,150	**4,200**	418	418	418	418
4,200	**4,250**	423	423	423	423
4,250	**4,300**	428	428	428	428
4,300	**4,350**	433	433	433	433
4,350	**4,400**	438	438	438	438
4,400	**4,450**	443	443	443	443
4,450	**4,500**	448	448	448	448
4,500	**4,550**	453	453	453	453
4,550	**4,600**	458	458	458	458
4,600	**4,650**	463	463	463	463
4,650	**4,700**	468	468	468	468
4,700	**4,750**	473	473	473	473
4,750	**4,800**	478	478	478	478
4,800	**4,850**	483	483	483	483
4,850	**4,900**	488	488	488	488
4,900	**4,950**	493	493	493	493
4,950	**5,000**	498	498	498	498

* This column must also be used by a qualifying widow(er).

(Continued on next page)

If line 43 (taxable income) is—		And you are—			
At least	But less than	Single	Married filing jointly *	Married filing sepa-rately	Head of a house-hold
		Your tax is—			
5,000					
5,000	5,050	503	503	503	503
5,050	5,100	508	508	508	508
5,100	5,150	513	513	513	513
5,150	5,200	518	518	518	518
5,200	5,250	523	523	523	523
5,250	5,300	528	528	528	528
5,300	5,350	533	533	533	533
5,350	5,400	538	538	538	538
5,400	5,450	543	543	543	543
5,450	5,500	548	548	548	548
5,500	5,550	553	553	553	553
5,550	5,600	558	558	558	558
5,600	5,650	563	563	563	563
5,650	5,700	568	568	568	568
5,700	5,750	573	573	573	573
5,750	5,800	578	578	578	578
5,800	5,850	583	583	583	583
5,850	5,900	588	588	588	588
5,900	5,950	593	593	593	593
5,950	6,000	598	598	598	598
6,000					
6,000	6,050	603	603	603	603
6,050	6,100	608	608	608	608
6,100	6,150	613	613	613	613
6,150	6,200	618	618	618	618
6,200	6,250	623	623	623	623
6,250	6,300	628	628	628	628
6,300	6,350	633	633	633	633
6,350	6,400	638	638	638	638
6,400	6,450	643	643	643	643
6,450	6,500	648	648	648	648
6,500	6,550	653	653	653	653
6,550	6,600	658	658	658	658
6,600	6,650	663	663	663	663
6,650	6,700	668	668	668	668
6,700	6,750	673	673	673	673
6,750	6,800	678	678	678	678
6,800	6,850	683	683	683	683
6,850	6,900	688	688	688	688
6,900	6,950	693	693	693	693
6,950	7,000	698	698	698	698
7,000					
7,000	7,050	703	703	703	703
7,050	7,100	708	708	708	708
7,100	7,150	713	713	713	713
7,150	7,200	718	718	718	718
7,200	7,250	723	723	723	723
7,250	7,300	728	728	728	728
7,300	7,350	733	733	733	733
7,350	7,400	738	738	738	738
7,400	7,450	743	743	743	743
7,450	7,500	748	748	748	748
7,500	7,550	753	753	753	753
7,550	7,600	758	758	758	758
7,600	7,650	763	763	763	763
7,650	7,700	768	768	768	768
7,700	7,750	773	773	773	773
7,750	7,800	778	778	778	778
7,800	7,850	783	783	783	783
7,850	7,900	788	788	788	788
7,900	7,950	793	793	793	793
7,950	8,000	798	798	798	798
8,000					
8,000	8,050	803	803	803	803
8,050	8,100	808	808	808	808
8,100	8,150	813	813	813	813
8,150	8,200	818	818	818	818
8,200	8,250	823	823	823	823
8,250	8,300	828	828	828	828
8,300	8,350	833	833	833	833
8,350	8,400	838	838	838	838
8,400	8,450	845	843	845	843
8,450	8,500	853	848	853	848
8,500	8,550	860	853	860	853
8,550	8,600	868	858	868	858
8,600	8,650	875	863	875	863
8,650	8,700	883	868	883	868
8,700	8,750	890	873	890	873
8,750	8,800	898	878	898	878
8,800	8,850	905	883	905	883
8,850	8,900	913	888	913	888
8,900	8,950	920	893	920	893
8,950	9,000	928	898	928	898
9,000					
9,000	9,050	935	903	935	903
9,050	9,100	943	908	943	908
9,100	9,150	950	913	950	913
9,150	9,200	958	918	958	918
9,200	9,250	965	923	965	923
9,250	9,300	973	928	973	928
9,300	9,350	980	933	980	933
9,350	9,400	988	938	988	938
9,400	9,450	995	943	995	943
9,450	9,500	1,003	948	1,003	948
9,500	9,550	1,010	953	1,010	953
9,550	9,600	1,018	958	1,018	958
9,600	9,650	1,025	963	1,025	963
9,650	9,700	1,033	968	1,033	968
9,700	9,750	1,040	973	1,040	973
9,750	9,800	1,048	978	1,048	978
9,800	9,850	1,055	983	1,055	983
9,850	9,900	1,063	988	1,063	988
9,900	9,950	1,070	993	1,070	993
9,950	10,000	1,078	998	1,078	998
10,000					
10,000	10,050	1,085	1,003	1,085	1,003
10,050	10,100	1,093	1,008	1,093	1,008
10,100	10,150	1,100	1,013	1,100	1,013
10,150	10,200	1,108	1,018	1,108	1,018
10,200	10,250	1,115	1,023	1,115	1,023
10,250	10,300	1,123	1,028	1,123	1,028
10,300	10,350	1,130	1,033	1,130	1,033
10,350	10,400	1,138	1,038	1,138	1,038
10,400	10,450	1,145	1,043	1,145	1,043
10,450	10,500	1,153	1,048	1,153	1,048
10,500	10,550	1,160	1,053	1,160	1,053
10,550	10,600	1,168	1,058	1,168	1,058
10,600	10,650	1,175	1,063	1,175	1,063
10,650	10,700	1,183	1,068	1,183	1,068
10,700	10,750	1,190	1,073	1,190	1,073
10,750	10,800	1,198	1,078	1,198	1,078
10,800	10,850	1,205	1,083	1,205	1,083
10,850	10,900	1,213	1,088	1,213	1,088
10,900	10,950	1,220	1,093	1,220	1,093
10,950	11,000	1,228	1,098	1,228	1,098
11,000					
11,000	11,050	1,235	1,103	1,235	1,103
11,050	11,100	1,243	1,108	1,243	1,108
11,100	11,150	1,250	1,113	1,250	1,113
11,150	11,200	1,258	1,118	1,258	1,118
11,200	11,250	1,265	1,123	1,265	1,123
11,250	11,300	1,273	1,128	1,273	1,128
11,300	11,350	1,280	1,133	1,280	1,133
11,350	11,400	1,288	1,138	1,288	1,138
11,400	11,450	1,295	1,143	1,295	1,143
11,450	11,500	1,303	1,148	1,303	1,148
11,500	11,550	1,310	1,153	1,310	1,153
11,550	11,600	1,318	1,158	1,318	1,158
11,600	11,650	1,325	1,163	1,325	1,163
11,650	11,700	1,333	1,168	1,333	1,168
11,700	11,750	1,340	1,173	1,340	1,173
11,750	11,800	1,348	1,178	1,348	1,178
11,800	11,850	1,355	1,183	1,355	1,183
11,850	11,900	1,363	1,188	1,363	1,188
11,900	11,950	1,370	1,193	1,370	1,193
11,950	12,000	1,378	1,198	1,378	1,199
12,000					
12,000	12,050	1,385	1,203	1,385	1,206
12,050	12,100	1,393	1,208	1,393	1,214
12,100	12,150	1,400	1,213	1,400	1,221
12,150	12,200	1,408	1,218	1,408	1,229
12,200	12,250	1,415	1,223	1,415	1,236
12,250	12,300	1,423	1,228	1,423	1,244
12,300	12,350	1,430	1,233	1,430	1,251
12,350	12,400	1,438	1,238	1,438	1,259
12,400	12,450	1,445	1,243	1,445	1,266
12,450	12,500	1,453	1,248	1,453	1,274
12,500	12,550	1,460	1,253	1,460	1,281
12,550	12,600	1,468	1,258	1,468	1,289
12,600	12,650	1,475	1,263	1,475	1,296
12,650	12,700	1,483	1,268	1,483	1,304
12,700	12,750	1,490	1,273	1,490	1,311
12,750	12,800	1,498	1,278	1,498	1,319
12,800	12,850	1,505	1,283	1,505	1,326
12,850	12,900	1,513	1,288	1,513	1,334
12,900	12,950	1,520	1,293	1,520	1,341
12,950	13,000	1,528	1,298	1,528	1,349
13,000					
13,000	13,050	1,535	1,303	1,535	1,356
13,050	13,100	1,543	1,308	1,543	1,364
13,100	13,150	1,550	1,313	1,550	1,371
13,150	13,200	1,558	1,318	1,558	1,379
13,200	13,250	1,565	1,323	1,565	1,386
13,250	13,300	1,573	1,328	1,573	1,394
13,300	13,350	1,580	1,333	1,580	1,401
13,350	13,400	1,588	1,338	1,588	1,409
13,400	13,450	1,595	1,343	1,595	1,416
13,450	13,500	1,603	1,348	1,603	1,424
13,500	13,550	1,610	1,353	1,610	1,431
13,550	13,600	1,618	1,358	1,618	1,439
13,600	13,650	1,625	1,363	1,625	1,446
13,650	13,700	1,633	1,368	1,633	1,454
13,700	13,750	1,640	1,373	1,640	1,461
13,750	13,800	1,648	1,378	1,648	1,469
13,800	13,850	1,655	1,383	1,655	1,476
13,850	13,900	1,663	1,388	1,663	1,484
13,900	13,950	1,670	1,393	1,670	1,491
13,950	14,000	1,678	1,398	1,678	1,499

* This column must also be used by a qualifying widow(er).

(Continued on next page)

2010 Tax Table–*Continued*

If line 43 (taxable income) is—		And you are—			
At least	But less than	Single	Married filing jointly *	Married filing separately	Head of a household
		Your tax is—			
14,000					
14,000	**14,050**	1,685	1,403	1,685	1,506
14,050	**14,100**	1,693	1,408	1,693	1,514
14,100	**14,150**	1,700	1,413	1,700	1,521
14,150	**14,200**	1,708	1,418	1,708	1,529
14,200	**14,250**	1,715	1,423	1,715	1,536
14,250	**14,300**	1,723	1,428	1,723	1,544
14,300	**14,350**	1,730	1,433	1,730	1,551
14,350	**14,400**	1,738	1,438	1,738	1,559
14,400	**14,450**	1,745	1,443	1,745	1,566
14,450	**14,500**	1,753	1,448	1,753	1,574
14,500	**14,550**	1,760	1,453	1,760	1,581
14,550	**14,600**	1,768	1,458	1,768	1,589
14,600	**14,650**	1,775	1,463	1,775	1,596
14,650	**14,700**	1,783	1,468	1,783	1,604
14,700	**14,750**	1,790	1,473	1,790	1,611
14,750	**14,800**	1,798	1,478	1,798	1,619
14,800	**14,850**	1,805	1,483	1,805	1,626
14,850	**14,900**	1,813	1,488	1,813	1,634
14,900	**14,950**	1,820	1,493	1,820	1,641
14,950	**15,000**	1,828	1,498	1,828	1,649
15,000					
15,000	**15,050**	1,835	1,503	1,835	1,656
15,050	**15,100**	1,843	1,508	1,843	1,664
15,100	**15,150**	1,850	1,513	1,850	1,671
15,150	**15,200**	1,858	1,518	1,858	1,679
15,200	**15,250**	1,865	1,523	1,865	1,686
15,250	**15,300**	1,873	1,528	1,873	1,694
15,300	**15,350**	1,880	1,533	1,880	1,701
15,350	**15,400**	1,888	1,538	1,888	1,709
15,400	**15,450**	1,895	1,543	1,895	1,716
15,450	**15,500**	1,903	1,548	1,903	1,724
15,500	**15,550**	1,910	1,553	1,910	1,731
15,550	**15,600**	1,918	1,558	1,918	1,739
15,600	**15,650**	1,925	1,563	1,925	1,746
15,650	**15,700**	1,933	1,568	1,933	1,754
15,700	**15,750**	1,940	1,573	1,940	1,761
15,750	**15,800**	1,948	1,578	1,948	1,769
15,800	**15,850**	1,955	1,583	1,955	1,776
15,850	**15,900**	1,963	1,588	1,963	1,784
15,900	**15,950**	1,970	1,593	1,970	1,791
15,950	**16,000**	1,978	1,598	1,978	1,799
16,000					
16,000	**16,050**	1,985	1,603	1,985	1,806
16,050	**16,100**	1,993	1,608	1,993	1,814
16,100	**16,150**	2,000	1,613	2,000	1,821
16,150	**16,200**	2,008	1,618	2,008	1,829
16,200	**16,250**	2,015	1,623	2,015	1,836
16,250	**16,300**	2,023	1,628	2,023	1,844
16,300	**16,350**	2,030	1,633	2,030	1,851
16,350	**16,400**	2,038	1,638	2,038	1,859
16,400	**16,450**	2,045	1,643	2,045	1,866
16,450	**16,500**	2,053	1,648	2,053	1,874
16,500	**16,550**	2,060	1,653	2,060	1,881
16,550	**16,600**	2,068	1,658	2,068	1,889
16,600	**16,650**	2,075	1,663	2,075	1,896
16,650	**16,700**	2,083	1,668	2,083	1,904
16,700	**16,750**	2,090	1,673	2,090	1,911
16,750	**16,800**	2,098	1,679	2,098	1,919
16,800	**16,850**	2,105	1,686	2,105	1,926
16,850	**16,900**	2,113	1,694	2,113	1,934
16,900	**16,950**	2,120	1,701	2,120	1,941
16,950	**17,000**	2,128	1,709	2,128	1,949

If line 43 (taxable income) is—		And you are—			
At least	But less than	Single	Married filing jointly *	Married filing separately	Head of a household
		Your tax is—			
17,000					
17,000	**17,050**	2,135	1,716	2,135	1,956
17,050	**17,100**	2,143	1,724	2,143	1,964
17,100	**17,150**	2,150	1,731	2,150	1,971
17,150	**17,200**	2,158	1,739	2,158	1,979
17,200	**17,250**	2,165	1,746	2,165	1,986
17,250	**17,300**	2,173	1,754	2,173	1,994
17,300	**17,350**	2,180	1,761	2,180	2,001
17,350	**17,400**	2,188	1,769	2,188	2,009
17,400	**17,450**	2,195	1,776	2,195	2,016
17,450	**17,500**	2,203	1,784	2,203	2,024
17,500	**17,550**	2,210	1,791	2,210	2,031
17,550	**17,600**	2,218	1,799	2,218	2,039
17,600	**17,650**	2,225	1,806	2,225	2,046
17,650	**17,700**	2,233	1,814	2,233	2,054
17,700	**17,750**	2,240	1,821	2,240	2,061
17,750	**17,800**	2,248	1,829	2,248	2,069
17,800	**17,850**	2,255	1,836	2,255	2,076
17,850	**17,900**	2,263	1,844	2,263	2,084
17,900	**17,950**	2,270	1,851	2,270	2,091
17,950	**18,000**	2,278	1,859	2,278	2,099
18,000					
18,000	**18,050**	2,285	1,866	2,285	2,106
18,050	**18,100**	2,293	1,874	2,293	2,114
18,100	**18,150**	2,300	1,881	2,300	2,121
18,150	**18,200**	2,308	1,889	2,308	2,129
18,200	**18,250**	2,315	1,896	2,315	2,136
18,250	**18,300**	2,323	1,904	2,323	2,144
18,300	**18,350**	2,330	1,911	2,330	2,151
18,350	**18,400**	2,338	1,919	2,338	2,159
18,400	**18,450**	2,345	1,926	2,345	2,166
18,450	**18,500**	2,353	1,934	2,353	2,174
18,500	**18,550**	2,360	1,941	2,360	2,181
18,550	**18,600**	2,368	1,949	2,368	2,189
18,600	**18,650**	2,375	1,956	2,375	2,196
18,650	**18,700**	2,383	1,964	2,383	2,204
18,700	**18,750**	2,390	1,971	2,390	2,211
18,750	**18,800**	2,398	1,979	2,398	2,219
18,800	**18,850**	2,405	1,986	2,405	2,226
18,850	**18,900**	2,413	1,994	2,413	2,234
18,900	**18,950**	2,420	2,001	2,420	2,241
18,950	**19,000**	2,428	2,009	2,428	2,249
19,000					
19,000	**19,050**	2,435	2,016	2,435	2,256
19,050	**19,100**	2,443	2,024	2,443	2,264
19,100	**19,150**	2,450	2,031	2,450	2,271
19,150	**19,200**	2,458	2,039	2,458	2,279
19,200	**19,250**	2,465	2,046	2,465	2,286
19,250	**19,300**	2,473	2,054	2,473	2,294
19,300	**19,350**	2,480	2,061	2,480	2,301
19,350	**19,400**	2,488	2,069	2,488	2,309
19,400	**19,450**	2,495	2,076	2,495	2,316
19,450	**19,500**	2,503	2,084	2,503	2,324
19,500	**19,550**	2,510	2,091	2,510	2,331
19,550	**19,600**	2,518	2,099	2,518	2,339
19,600	**19,650**	2,525	2,106	2,525	2,346
19,650	**19,700**	2,533	2,114	2,533	2,354
19,700	**19,750**	2,540	2,121	2,540	2,361
19,750	**19,800**	2,548	2,129	2,548	2,369
19,800	**19,850**	2,555	2,136	2,555	2,376
19,850	**19,900**	2,563	2,144	2,563	2,384
19,900	**19,950**	2,570	2,151	2,570	2,391
19,950	**20,000**	2,578	2,159	2,578	2,399

If line 43 (taxable income) is—		And you are—			
At least	But less than	Single	Married filing jointly *	Married filing separately	Head of a household
		Your tax is—			
20,000					
20,000	**20,050**	2,585	2,166	2,585	2,406
20,050	**20,100**	2,593	2,174	2,593	2,414
20,100	**20,150**	2,600	2,181	2,600	2,421
20,150	**20,200**	2,608	2,189	2,608	2,429
20,200	**20,250**	2,615	2,196	2,615	2,436
20,250	**20,300**	2,623	2,204	2,623	2,444
20,300	**20,350**	2,630	2,211	2,630	2,451
20,350	**20,400**	2,638	2,219	2,638	2,459
20,400	**20,450**	2,645	2,226	2,645	2,466
20,450	**20,500**	2,653	2,234	2,653	2,474
20,500	**20,550**	2,660	2,241	2,660	2,481
20,550	**20,600**	2,668	2,249	2,668	2,489
20,600	**20,650**	2,675	2,256	2,675	2,496
20,650	**20,700**	2,683	2,264	2,683	2,504
20,700	**20,750**	2,690	2,271	2,690	2,511
20,750	**20,800**	2,698	2,279	2,698	2,519
20,800	**20,850**	2,705	2,286	2,705	2,526
20,850	**20,900**	2,713	2,294	2,713	2,534
20,900	**20,950**	2,720	2,301	2,720	2,541
20,950	**21,000**	2,728	2,309	2,728	2,549
21,000					
21,000	**21,050**	2,735	2,316	2,735	2,556
21,050	**21,100**	2,743	2,324	2,743	2,564
21,100	**21,150**	2,750	2,331	2,750	2,571
21,150	**21,200**	2,758	2,339	2,758	2,579
21,200	**21,250**	2,765	2,346	2,765	2,586
21,250	**21,300**	2,773	2,354	2,773	2,594
21,300	**21,350**	2,780	2,361	2,780	2,601
21,350	**21,400**	2,788	2,369	2,788	2,609
21,400	**21,450**	2,795	2,376	2,795	2,616
21,450	**21,500**	2,803	2,384	2,803	2,624
21,500	**21,550**	2,810	2,391	2,810	2,631
21,550	**21,600**	2,818	2,399	2,818	2,639
21,600	**21,650**	2,825	2,406	2,825	2,646
21,650	**21,700**	2,833	2,414	2,833	2,654
21,700	**21,750**	2,840	2,421	2,840	2,661
21,750	**21,800**	2,848	2,429	2,848	2,669
21,800	**21,850**	2,855	2,436	2,855	2,676
21,850	**21,900**	2,863	2,444	2,863	2,684
21,900	**21,950**	2,870	2,451	2,870	2,691
21,950	**22,000**	2,878	2,459	2,878	2,699
22,000					
22,000	**22,050**	2,885	2,466	2,885	2,706
22,050	**22,100**	2,893	2,474	2,893	2,714
22,100	**22,150**	2,900	2,481	2,900	2,721
22,150	**22,200**	2,908	2,489	2,908	2,729
22,200	**22,250**	2,915	2,496	2,915	2,736
22,250	**22,300**	2,923	2,504	2,923	2,744
22,300	**22,350**	2,930	2,511	2,930	2,751
22,350	**22,400**	2,938	2,519	2,938	2,759
22,400	**22,450**	2,945	2,526	2,945	2,766
22,450	**22,500**	2,953	2,534	2,953	2,774
22,500	**22,550**	2,960	2,541	2,960	2,781
22,550	**22,600**	2,968	2,549	2,968	2,789
22,600	**22,650**	2,975	2,556	2,975	2,796
22,650	**22,700**	2,983	2,564	2,983	2,804
22,700	**22,750**	2,990	2,571	2,990	2,811
22,750	**22,800**	2,998	2,579	2,998	2,819
22,800	**22,850**	3,005	2,586	3,005	2,826
22,850	**22,900**	3,013	2,594	3,013	2,834
22,900	**22,950**	3,020	2,601	3,020	2,841
22,950	**23,000**	3,028	2,609	3,028	2,849

* This column must also be used by a qualifying widow(er).

(Continued on next page)

If line 43 (taxable income) is— At least	But less than	And you are— Single	Married filing jointly *	Married filing separately	Head of a household
		Your tax is—			
23,000					
23,000	**23,050**	3,035	2,616	3,035	2,856
23,050	**23,100**	3,043	2,624	3,043	2,864
23,100	**23,150**	3,050	2,631	3,050	2,871
23,150	**23,200**	3,058	2,639	3,058	2,879
23,200	**23,250**	3,065	2,646	3,065	2,886
23,250	**23,300**	3,073	2,654	3,073	2,894
23,300	**23,350**	3,080	2,661	3,080	2,901
23,350	**23,400**	3,088	2,669	3,088	2,909
23,400	**23,450**	3,095	2,676	3,095	2,916
23,450	**23,500**	3,103	2,684	3,103	2,924
23,500	**23,550**	3,110	2,691	3,110	2,931
23,550	**23,600**	3,118	2,699	3,118	2,939
23,600	**23,650**	3,125	2,706	3,125	2,946
23,650	**23,700**	3,133	2,714	3,133	2,954
23,700	**23,750**	3,140	2,721	3,140	2,961
23,750	**23,800**	3,148	2,729	3,148	2,969
23,800	**23,850**	3,155	2,736	3,155	2,976
23,850	**23,900**	3,163	2,744	3,163	2,984
23,900	**23,950**	3,170	2,751	3,170	2,991
23,950	**24,000**	3,178	2,759	3,178	2,999
24,000					
24,000	**24,050**	3,185	2,766	3,185	3,006
24,050	**24,100**	3,193	2,774	3,193	3,014
24,100	**24,150**	3,200	2,781	3,200	3,021
24,150	**24,200**	3,208	2,789	3,208	3,029
24,200	**24,250**	3,215	2,796	3,215	3,036
24,250	**24,300**	3,223	2,804	3,223	3,044
24,300	**24,350**	3,230	2,811	3,230	3,051
24,350	**24,400**	3,238	2,819	3,238	3,059
24,400	**24,450**	3,245	2,826	3,245	3,066
24,450	**24,500**	3,253	2,834	3,253	3,074
24,500	**24,550**	3,260	2,841	3,260	3,081
24,550	**24,600**	3,268	2,849	3,268	3,089
24,600	**24,650**	3,275	2,856	3,275	3,096
24,650	**24,700**	3,283	2,864	3,283	3,104
24,700	**24,750**	3,290	2,871	3,290	3,111
24,750	**24,800**	3,298	2,879	3,298	3,119
24,800	**24,850**	3,305	2,886	3,305	3,126
24,850	**24,900**	3,313	2,894	3,313	3,134
24,900	**24,950**	3,320	2,901	3,320	3,141
24,950	**25,000**	3,328	2,909	3,328	3,149
25,000					
25,000	**25,050**	3,335	2,916	3,335	3,156
25,050	**25,100**	3,343	2,924	3,343	3,164
25,100	**25,150**	3,350	2,931	3,350	3,171
25,150	**25,200**	3,358	2,939	3,358	3,179
25,200	**25,250**	3,365	2,946	3,365	3,186
25,250	**25,300**	3,373	2,954	3,373	3,194
25,300	**25,350**	3,380	2,961	3,380	3,201
25,350	**25,400**	3,388	2,969	3,388	3,209
25,400	**25,450**	3,395	2,976	3,395	3,216
25,450	**25,500**	3,403	2,984	3,403	3,224
25,500	**25,550**	3,410	2,991	3,410	3,231
25,550	**25,600**	3,418	2,999	3,418	3,239
25,600	**25,650**	3,425	3,006	3,425	3,246
25,650	**25,700**	3,433	3,014	3,433	3,254
25,700	**25,750**	3,440	3,021	3,440	3,261
25,750	**25,800**	3,448	3,029	3,448	3,269
25,800	**25,850**	3,455	3,036	3,455	3,276
25,850	**25,900**	3,463	3,044	3,463	3,284
25,900	**25,950**	3,470	3,051	3,470	3,291
25,950	**26,000**	3,478	3,059	3,478	3,299

If line 43 (taxable income) is— At least	But less than	And you are— Single	Married filing jointly *	Married filing separately	Head of a household
		Your tax is—			
26,000					
26,000	**26,050**	3,485	3,066	3,485	3,306
26,050	**26,100**	3,493	3,074	3,493	3,314
26,100	**26,150**	3,500	3,081	3,500	3,321
26,150	**26,200**	3,508	3,089	3,508	3,329
26,200	**26,250**	3,515	3,096	3,515	3,336
26,250	**26,300**	3,523	3,104	3,523	3,344
26,300	**26,350**	3,530	3,111	3,530	3,351
26,350	**26,400**	3,538	3,119	3,538	3,359
26,400	**26,450**	3,545	3,126	3,545	3,366
26,450	**26,500**	3,553	3,134	3,553	3,374
26,500	**26,550**	3,560	3,141	3,560	3,381
26,550	**26,600**	3,568	3,149	3,568	3,389
26,600	**26,650**	3,575	3,156	3,575	3,396
26,650	**26,700**	3,583	3,164	3,583	3,404
26,700	**26,750**	3,590	3,171	3,590	3,411
26,750	**26,800**	3,598	3,179	3,598	3,419
26,800	**26,850**	3,605	3,186	3,605	3,426
26,850	**26,900**	3,613	3,194	3,613	3,434
26,900	**26,950**	3,620	3,201	3,620	3,441
26,950	**27,000**	3,628	3,209	3,628	3,449
27,000					
27,000	**27,050**	3,635	3,216	3,635	3,456
27,050	**27,100**	3,643	3,224	3,643	3,464
27,100	**27,150**	3,650	3,231	3,650	3,471
27,150	**27,200**	3,658	3,239	3,658	3,479
27,200	**27,250**	3,665	3,246	3,665	3,486
27,250	**27,300**	3,673	3,254	3,673	3,494
27,300	**27,350**	3,680	3,261	3,680	3,501
27,350	**27,400**	3,688	3,269	3,688	3,509
27,400	**27,450**	3,695	3,276	3,695	3,516
27,450	**27,500**	3,703	3,284	3,703	3,524
27,500	**27,550**	3,710	3,291	3,710	3,531
27,550	**27,600**	3,718	3,299	3,718	3,539
27,600	**27,650**	3,725	3,306	3,725	3,546
27,650	**27,700**	3,733	3,314	3,733	3,554
27,700	**27,750**	3,740	3,321	3,740	3,561
27,750	**27,800**	3,748	3,329	3,748	3,569
27,800	**27,850**	3,755	3,336	3,755	3,576
27,850	**27,900**	3,763	3,344	3,763	3,584
27,900	**27,950**	3,770	3,351	3,770	3,591
27,950	**28,000**	3,778	3,359	3,778	3,599
28,000					
28,000	**28,050**	3,785	3,366	3,785	3,606
28,050	**28,100**	3,793	3,374	3,793	3,614
28,100	**28,150**	3,800	3,381	3,800	3,621
28,150	**28,200**	3,808	3,389	3,808	3,629
28,200	**28,250**	3,815	3,396	3,815	3,636
28,250	**28,300**	3,823	3,404	3,823	3,644
28,300	**28,350**	3,830	3,411	3,830	3,651
28,350	**28,400**	3,838	3,419	3,838	3,659
28,400	**28,450**	3,845	3,426	3,845	3,666
28,450	**28,500**	3,853	3,434	3,853	3,674
28,500	**28,550**	3,860	3,441	3,860	3,681
28,550	**28,600**	3,868	3,449	3,868	3,689
28,600	**28,650**	3,875	3,456	3,875	3,696
28,650	**28,700**	3,883	3,464	3,883	3,704
28,700	**28,750**	3,890	3,471	3,890	3,711
28,750	**28,800**	3,898	3,479	3,898	3,719
28,800	**28,850**	3,905	3,486	3,905	3,726
28,850	**28,900**	3,913	3,494	3,913	3,734
28,900	**28,950**	3,920	3,501	3,920	3,741
28,950	**29,000**	3,928	3,509	3,928	3,749

If line 43 (taxable income) is— At least	But less than	And you are— Single	Married filing jointly *	Married filing separately	Head of a household
		Your tax is—			
29,000					
29,000	**29,050**	3,935	3,516	3,935	3,756
29,050	**29,100**	3,943	3,524	3,943	3,764
29,100	**29,150**	3,950	3,531	3,950	3,771
29,150	**29,200**	3,958	3,539	3,958	3,779
29,200	**29,250**	3,965	3,546	3,965	3,786
29,250	**29,300**	3,973	3,554	3,973	3,794
29,300	**29,350**	3,980	3,561	3,980	3,801
29,350	**29,400**	3,988	3,569	3,988	3,809
29,400	**29,450**	3,995	3,576	3,995	3,816
29,450	**29,500**	4,003	3,584	4,003	3,824
29,500	**29,550**	4,010	3,591	4,010	3,831
29,550	**29,600**	4,018	3,599	4,018	3,839
29,600	**29,650**	4,025	3,606	4,025	3,846
29,650	**29,700**	4,033	3,614	4,033	3,854
29,700	**29,750**	4,040	3,621	4,040	3,861
29,750	**29,800**	4,048	3,629	4,048	3,869
29,800	**29,850**	4,055	3,636	4,055	3,876
29,850	**29,900**	4,063	3,644	4,063	3,884
29,900	**29,950**	4,070	3,651	4,070	3,891
29,950	**30,000**	4,078	3,659	4,078	3,899
30,000					
30,000	**30,050**	4,085	3,666	4,085	3,906
30,050	**30,100**	4,093	3,674	4,093	3,914
30,100	**30,150**	4,100	3,681	4,100	3,921
30,150	**30,200**	4,108	3,689	4,108	3,929
30,200	**30,250**	4,115	3,696	4,115	3,936
30,250	**30,300**	4,123	3,704	4,123	3,944
30,300	**30,350**	4,130	3,711	4,130	3,951
30,350	**30,400**	4,138	3,719	4,138	3,959
30,400	**30,450**	4,145	3,726	4,145	3,966
30,450	**30,500**	4,153	3,734	4,153	3,974
30,500	**30,550**	4,160	3,741	4,160	3,981
30,550	**30,600**	4,168	3,749	4,168	3,989
30,600	**30,650**	4,175	3,756	4,175	3,996
30,650	**30,700**	4,183	3,764	4,183	4,004
30,700	**30,750**	4,190	3,771	4,190	4,011
30,750	**30,800**	4,198	3,779	4,198	4,019
30,800	**30,850**	4,205	3,786	4,205	4,026
30,850	**30,900**	4,213	3,794	4,213	4,034
30,900	**30,950**	4,220	3,801	4,220	4,041
30,950	**31,000**	4,228	3,809	4,228	4,049
31,000					
31,000	**31,050**	4,235	3,816	4,235	4,056
31,050	**31,100**	4,243	3,824	4,243	4,064
31,100	**31,150**	4,250	3,831	4,250	4,071
31,150	**31,200**	4,258	3,839	4,258	4,079
31,200	**31,250**	4,265	3,846	4,265	4,086
31,250	**31,300**	4,273	3,854	4,273	4,094
31,300	**31,350**	4,280	3,861	4,280	4,101
31,350	**31,400**	4,288	3,869	4,288	4,109
31,400	**31,450**	4,295	3,876	4,295	4,116
31,450	**31,500**	4,303	3,884	4,303	4,124
31,500	**31,550**	4,310	3,891	4,310	4,131
31,550	**31,600**	4,318	3,899	4,318	4,139
31,600	**31,650**	4,325	3,906	4,325	4,146
31,650	**31,700**	4,333	3,914	4,333	4,154
31,700	**31,750**	4,340	3,921	4,340	4,161
31,750	**31,800**	4,348	3,929	4,348	4,169
31,800	**31,850**	4,355	3,936	4,355	4,176
31,850	**31,900**	4,363	3,944	4,363	4,184
31,900	**31,950**	4,370	3,951	4,370	4,191
31,950	**32,000**	4,378	3,959	4,378	4,199

* This column must also be used by a qualifying widow(er).

(Continued on next page)

2010 Tax Table–*Continued*

If line 43 (taxable income) is—		And you are—			
At least	But less than	Single	Married filing jointly *	Married filing separately	Head of a household
		Your tax is—			
32,000					
32,000	**32,050**	4,385	3,966	4,385	4,206
32,050	**32,100**	4,393	3,974	4,393	4,214
32,100	**32,150**	4,400	3,981	4,400	4,221
32,150	**32,200**	4,408	3,989	4,408	4,229
32,200	**32,250**	4,415	3,996	4,415	4,236
32,250	**32,300**	4,423	4,004	4,423	4,244
32,300	**32,350**	4,430	4,011	4,430	4,251
32,350	**32,400**	4,438	4,019	4,438	4,259
32,400	**32,450**	4,445	4,026	4,445	4,266
32,450	**32,500**	4,453	4,034	4,453	4,274
32,500	**32,550**	4,460	4,041	4,460	4,281
32,550	**32,600**	4,468	4,049	4,468	4,289
32,600	**32,650**	4,475	4,056	4,475	4,296
32,650	**32,700**	4,483	4,064	4,483	4,304
32,700	**32,750**	4,490	4,071	4,490	4,311
32,750	**32,800**	4,498	4,079	4,498	4,319
32,800	**32,850**	4,505	4,086	4,505	4,326
32,850	**32,900**	4,513	4,094	4,513	4,334
32,900	**32,950**	4,520	4,101	4,520	4,341
32,950	**33,000**	4,528	4,109	4,528	4,349
33,000					
33,000	**33,050**	4,535	4,116	4,535	4,356
33,050	**33,100**	4,543	4,124	4,543	4,364
33,100	**33,150**	4,550	4,131	4,550	4,371
33,150	**33,200**	4,558	4,139	4,558	4,379
33,200	**33,250**	4,565	4,146	4,565	4,386
33,250	**33,300**	4,573	4,154	4,573	4,394
33,300	**33,350**	4,580	4,161	4,580	4,401
33,350	**33,400**	4,588	4,169	4,588	4,409
33,400	**33,450**	4,595	4,176	4,595	4,416
33,450	**33,500**	4,603	4,184	4,603	4,424
33,500	**33,550**	4,610	4,191	4,610	4,431
33,550	**33,600**	4,618	4,199	4,618	4,439
33,600	**33,650**	4,625	4,206	4,625	4,446
33,650	**33,700**	4,633	4,214	4,633	4,454
33,700	**33,750**	4,640	4,221	4,640	4,461
33,750	**33,800**	4,648	4,229	4,648	4,469
33,800	**33,850**	4,655	4,236	4,655	4,476
33,850	**33,900**	4,663	4,244	4,663	4,484
33,900	**33,950**	4,670	4,251	4,670	4,491
33,950	**34,000**	4,678	4,259	4,678	4,499
34,000					
34,000	**34,050**	4,688	4,266	4,688	4,506
34,050	**34,100**	4,700	4,274	4,700	4,514
34,100	**34,150**	4,713	4,281	4,713	4,521
34,150	**34,200**	4,725	4,289	4,725	4,529
34,200	**34,250**	4,738	4,296	4,738	4,536
34,250	**34,300**	4,750	4,304	4,750	4,544
34,300	**34,350**	4,763	4,311	4,763	4,551
34,350	**34,400**	4,775	4,319	4,775	4,559
34,400	**34,450**	4,788	4,326	4,788	4,566
34,450	**34,500**	4,800	4,334	4,800	4,574
34,500	**34,550**	4,813	4,341	4,813	4,581
34,550	**34,600**	4,825	4,349	4,825	4,589
34,600	**34,650**	4,838	4,356	4,838	4,596
34,650	**34,700**	4,850	4,364	4,850	4,604
34,700	**34,750**	4,863	4,371	4,863	4,611
34,750	**34,800**	4,875	4,379	4,875	4,619
34,800	**34,850**	4,888	4,386	4,888	4,626
34,850	**34,900**	4,900	4,394	4,900	4,634
34,900	**34,950**	4,913	4,401	4,913	4,641
34,950	**35,000**	4,925	4,409	4,925	4,649

If line 43 (taxable income) is—		And you are—			
At least	But less than	Single	Married filing jointly *	Married filing separately	Head of a household
		Your tax is—			
35,000					
35,000	**35,050**	4,938	4,416	4,938	4,656
35,050	**35,100**	4,950	4,424	4,950	4,664
35,100	**35,150**	4,963	4,431	4,963	4,671
35,150	**35,200**	4,975	4,439	4,975	4,679
35,200	**35,250**	4,988	4,446	4,988	4,686
35,250	**35,300**	5,000	4,454	5,000	4,694
35,300	**35,350**	5,013	4,461	5,013	4,701
35,350	**35,400**	5,025	4,469	5,025	4,709
35,400	**35,450**	5,038	4,476	5,038	4,716
35,450	**35,500**	5,050	4,484	5,050	4,724
35,500	**35,550**	5,063	4,491	5,063	4,731
35,550	**35,600**	5,075	4,499	5,075	4,739
35,600	**35,650**	5,088	4,506	5,088	4,746
35,650	**35,700**	5,100	4,514	5,100	4,754
35,700	**35,750**	5,113	4,521	5,113	4,761
35,750	**35,800**	5,125	4,529	5,125	4,769
35,800	**35,850**	5,138	4,536	5,138	4,776
35,850	**35,900**	5,150	4,544	5,150	4,784
35,900	**35,950**	5,163	4,551	5,163	4,791
35,950	**36,000**	5,175	4,559	5,175	4,799
36,000					
36,000	**36,050**	5,188	4,566	5,188	4,806
36,050	**36,100**	5,200	4,574	5,200	4,814
36,100	**36,150**	5,213	4,581	5,213	4,821
36,150	**36,200**	5,225	4,589	5,225	4,829
36,200	**36,250**	5,238	4,596	5,238	4,836
36,250	**36,300**	5,250	4,604	5,250	4,844
36,300	**36,350**	5,263	4,611	5,263	4,851
36,350	**36,400**	5,275	4,619	5,275	4,859
36,400	**36,450**	5,288	4,626	5,288	4,866
36,450	**36,500**	5,300	4,634	5,300	4,874
36,500	**36,550**	5,313	4,641	5,313	4,881
36,550	**36,600**	5,325	4,649	5,325	4,889
36,600	**36,650**	5,338	4,656	5,338	4,896
36,650	**36,700**	5,350	4,664	5,350	4,904
36,700	**36,750**	5,363	4,671	5,363	4,911
36,750	**36,800**	5,375	4,679	5,375	4,919
36,800	**36,850**	5,388	4,686	5,388	4,926
36,850	**36,900**	5,400	4,694	5,400	4,934
36,900	**36,950**	5,413	4,701	5,413	4,941
36,950	**37,000**	5,425	4,709	5,425	4,949
37,000					
37,000	**37,050**	5,438	4,716	5,438	4,956
37,050	**37,100**	5,450	4,724	5,450	4,964
37,100	**37,150**	5,463	4,731	5,463	4,971
37,150	**37,200**	5,475	4,739	5,475	4,979
37,200	**37,250**	5,488	4,746	5,488	4,986
37,250	**37,300**	5,500	4,754	5,500	4,994
37,300	**37,350**	5,513	4,761	5,513	5,001
37,350	**37,400**	5,525	4,769	5,525	5,009
37,400	**37,450**	5,538	4,776	5,538	5,016
37,450	**37,500**	5,550	4,784	5,550	5,024
37,500	**37,550**	5,563	4,791	5,563	5,031
37,550	**37,600**	5,575	4,799	5,575	5,039
37,600	**37,650**	5,588	4,806	5,588	5,046
37,650	**37,700**	5,600	4,814	5,600	5,054
37,700	**37,750**	5,613	4,821	5,613	5,061
37,750	**37,800**	5,625	4,829	5,625	5,069
37,800	**37,850**	5,638	4,836	5,638	5,076
37,850	**37,900**	5,650	4,844	5,650	5,084
37,900	**37,950**	5,663	4,851	5,663	5,091
37,950	**38,000**	5,675	4,859	5,675	5,099

If line 43 (taxable income) is—		And you are—			
At least	But less than	Single	Married filing jointly *	Married filing separately	Head of a household
		Your tax is—			
38,000					
38,000	**38,050**	5,688	4,866	5,688	5,106
38,050	**38,100**	5,700	4,874	5,700	5,114
38,100	**38,150**	5,713	4,881	5,713	5,121
38,150	**38,200**	5,725	4,889	5,725	5,129
38,200	**38,250**	5,738	4,896	5,738	5,136
38,250	**38,300**	5,750	4,904	5,750	5,144
38,300	**38,350**	5,763	4,911	5,763	5,151
38,350	**38,400**	5,775	4,919	5,775	5,159
38,400	**38,450**	5,788	4,926	5,788	5,166
38,450	**38,500**	5,800	4,934	5,800	5,174
38,500	**38,550**	5,813	4,941	5,813	5,181
38,550	**38,600**	5,825	4,949	5,825	5,189
38,600	**38,650**	5,838	4,956	5,838	5,196
38,650	**38,700**	5,850	4,964	5,850	5,204
38,700	**38,750**	5,863	4,971	5,863	5,211
38,750	**38,800**	5,875	4,979	5,875	5,219
38,800	**38,850**	5,888	4,986	5,888	5,226
38,850	**38,900**	5,900	4,994	5,900	5,234
38,900	**38,950**	5,913	5,001	5,913	5,241
38,950	**39,000**	5,925	5,009	5,925	5,249
39,000					
39,000	**39,050**	5,938	5,016	5,938	5,256
39,050	**39,100**	5,950	5,024	5,950	5,264
39,100	**39,150**	5,963	5,031	5,963	5,271
39,150	**39,200**	5,975	5,039	5,975	5,279
39,200	**39,250**	5,988	5,046	5,988	5,286
39,250	**39,300**	6,000	5,054	6,000	5,294
39,300	**39,350**	6,013	5,061	6,013	5,301
39,350	**39,400**	6,025	5,069	6,025	5,309
39,400	**39,450**	6,038	5,076	6,038	5,316
39,450	**39,500**	6,050	5,084	6,050	5,324
39,500	**39,550**	6,063	5,091	6,063	5,331
39,550	**39,600**	6,075	5,099	6,075	5,339
39,600	**39,650**	6,088	5,106	6,088	5,346
39,650	**39,700**	6,100	5,114	6,100	5,354
39,700	**39,750**	6,113	5,121	6,113	5,361
39,750	**39,800**	6,125	5,129	6,125	5,369
39,800	**39,850**	6,138	5,136	6,138	5,376
39,850	**39,900**	6,150	5,144	6,150	5,384
39,900	**39,950**	6,163	5,151	6,163	5,391
39,950	**40,000**	6,175	5,159	6,175	5,399
40,000					
40,000	**40,050**	6,188	5,166	6,188	5,406
40,050	**40,100**	6,200	5,174	6,200	5,414
40,100	**40,150**	6,213	5,181	6,213	5,421
40,150	**40,200**	6,225	5,189	6,225	5,429
40,200	**40,250**	6,238	5,196	6,238	5,436
40,250	**40,300**	6,250	5,204	6,250	5,444
40,300	**40,350**	6,263	5,211	6,263	5,451
40,350	**40,400**	6,275	5,219	6,275	5,459
40,400	**40,450**	6,288	5,226	6,288	5,466
40,450	**40,500**	6,300	5,234	6,300	5,474
40,500	**40,550**	6,313	5,241	6,313	5,481
40,550	**40,600**	6,325	5,249	6,325	5,489
40,600	**40,650**	6,338	5,256	6,338	5,496
40,650	**40,700**	6,350	5,264	6,350	5,504
40,700	**40,750**	6,363	5,271	6,363	5,511
40,750	**40,800**	6,375	5,279	6,375	5,519
40,800	**40,850**	6,388	5,286	6,388	5,526
40,850	**40,900**	6,400	5,294	6,400	5,534
40,900	**40,950**	6,413	5,301	6,413	5,541
40,950	**41,000**	6,425	5,309	6,425	5,549

* This column must also be used by a qualifying widow(er).

(Continued on next page)

If line 43 (taxable income) is—		And you are—			
At least	But less than	Single	Married filing jointly *	Married filing sepa-rately	Head of a house-hold
		Your tax is—			
41,000					
41,000	41,050	6,438	5,316	6,438	5,556
41,050	41,100	6,450	5,324	6,450	5,564
41,100	41,150	6,463	5,331	6,463	5,571
41,150	41,200	6,475	5,339	6,475	5,579
41,200	41,250	6,488	5,346	6,488	5,586
41,250	41,300	6,500	5,354	6,500	5,594
41,300	41,350	6,513	5,361	6,513	5,601
41,350	41,400	6,525	5,369	6,525	5,609
41,400	41,450	6,538	5,376	6,538	5,616
41,450	41,500	6,550	5,384	6,550	5,624
41,500	41,550	6,563	5,391	6,563	5,631
41,550	41,600	6,575	5,399	6,575	5,639
41,600	41,650	6,588	5,406	6,588	5,646
41,650	41,700	6,600	5,414	6,600	5,654
41,700	41,750	6,613	5,421	6,613	5,661
41,750	41,800	6,625	5,429	6,625	5,669
41,800	41,850	6,638	5,436	6,638	5,676
41,850	41,900	6,650	5,444	6,650	5,684
41,900	41,950	6,663	5,451	6,663	5,691
41,950	42,000	6,675	5,459	6,675	5,699
42,000					
42,000	42,050	6,688	5,466	6,688	5,706
42,050	42,100	6,700	5,474	6,700	5,714
42,100	42,150	6,713	5,481	6,713	5,721
42,150	42,200	6,725	5,489	6,725	5,729
42,200	42,250	6,738	5,496	6,738	5,736
42,250	42,300	6,750	5,504	6,750	5,744
42,300	42,350	6,763	5,511	6,763	5,751
42,350	42,400	6,775	5,519	6,775	5,759
42,400	42,450	6,788	5,526	6,788	5,766
42,450	42,500	6,800	5,534	6,800	5,774
42,500	42,550	6,813	5,541	6,813	5,781
42,550	42,600	6,825	5,549	6,825	5,789
42,600	42,650	6,838	5,556	6,838	5,796
42,650	42,700	6,850	5,564	6,850	5,804
42,700	42,750	6,863	5,571	6,863	5,811
42,750	42,800	6,875	5,579	6,875	5,819
42,800	42,850	6,888	5,586	6,888	5,826
42,850	42,900	6,900	5,594	6,900	5,834
42,900	42,950	6,913	5,601	6,913	5,841
42,950	43,000	6,925	5,609	6,925	5,849
43,000					
43,000	43,050	6,938	5,616	6,938	5,856
43,050	43,100	6,950	5,624	6,950	5,864
43,100	43,150	6,963	5,631	6,963	5,871
43,150	43,200	6,975	5,639	6,975	5,879
43,200	43,250	6,988	5,646	6,988	5,886
43,250	43,300	7,000	5,654	7,000	5,894
43,300	43,350	7,013	5,661	7,013	5,901
43,350	43,400	7,025	5,669	7,025	5,909
43,400	43,450	7,038	5,676	7,038	5,916
43,450	43,500	7,050	5,684	7,050	5,924
43,500	43,550	7,063	5,691	7,063	5,931
43,550	43,600	7,075	5,699	7,075	5,939
43,600	43,650	7,088	5,706	7,088	5,946
43,650	43,700	7,100	5,714	7,100	5,954
43,700	43,750	7,113	5,721	7,113	5,961
43,750	43,800	7,125	5,729	7,125	5,969
43,800	43,850	7,138	5,736	7,138	5,976
43,850	43,900	7,150	5,744	7,150	5,984
43,900	43,950	7,163	5,751	7,163	5,991
43,950	44,000	7,175	5,759	7,175	5,999

If line 43 (taxable income) is—		And you are—			
At least	But less than	Single	Married filing jointly *	Married filing sepa-rately	Head of a house-hold
		Your tax is—			
44,000					
44,000	44,050	7,188	5,766	7,188	6,006
44,050	44,100	7,200	5,774	7,200	6,014
44,100	44,150	7,213	5,781	7,213	6,021
44,150	44,200	7,225	5,789	7,225	6,029
44,200	44,250	7,238	5,796	7,238	6,036
44,250	44,300	7,250	5,804	7,250	6,044
44,300	44,350	7,263	5,811	7,263	6,051
44,350	44,400	7,275	5,819	7,275	6,059
44,400	44,450	7,288	5,826	7,288	6,066
44,450	44,500	7,300	5,834	7,300	6,074
44,500	44,550	7,313	5,841	7,313	6,081
44,550	44,600	7,325	5,849	7,325	6,089
44,600	44,650	7,338	5,856	7,338	6,096
44,650	44,700	7,350	5,864	7,350	6,104
44,700	44,750	7,363	5,871	7,363	6,111
44,750	44,800	7,375	5,879	7,375	6,119
44,800	44,850	7,388	5,886	7,388	6,126
44,850	44,900	7,400	5,894	7,400	6,134
44,900	44,950	7,413	5,901	7,413	6,141
44,950	45,000	7,425	5,909	7,425	6,149
45,000					
45,000	45,050	7,438	5,916	7,438	6,156
45,050	45,100	7,450	5,924	7,450	6,164
45,100	45,150	7,463	5,931	7,463	6,171
45,150	45,200	7,475	5,939	7,475	6,179
45,200	45,250	7,488	5,946	7,488	6,186
45,250	45,300	7,500	5,954	7,500	6,194
45,300	45,350	7,513	5,961	7,513	6,201
45,350	45,400	7,525	5,969	7,525	6,209
45,400	45,450	7,538	5,976	7,538	6,216
45,450	45,500	7,550	5,984	7,550	6,224
45,500	45,550	7,563	5,991	7,563	6,231
45,550	45,600	7,575	5,999	7,575	6,241
45,600	45,650	7,588	6,006	7,588	6,254
45,650	45,700	7,600	6,014	7,600	6,266
45,700	45,750	7,613	6,021	7,613	6,279
45,750	45,800	7,625	6,029	7,625	6,291
45,800	45,850	7,638	6,036	7,638	6,304
45,850	45,900	7,650	6,044	7,650	6,316
45,900	45,950	7,663	6,051	7,663	6,329
45,950	46,000	7,675	6,059	7,675	6,341
46,000					
46,000	46,050	7,688	6,066	7,688	6,354
46,050	46,100	7,700	6,074	7,700	6,366
46,100	46,150	7,713	6,081	7,713	6,379
46,150	46,200	7,725	6,089	7,725	6,391
46,200	46,250	7,738	6,096	7,738	6,404
46,250	46,300	7,750	6,104	7,750	6,416
46,300	46,350	7,763	6,111	7,763	6,429
46,350	46,400	7,775	6,119	7,775	6,441
46,400	46,450	7,788	6,126	7,788	6,454
46,450	46,500	7,800	6,134	7,800	6,466
46,500	46,550	7,813	6,141	7,813	6,479
46,550	46,600	7,825	6,149	7,825	6,491
46,600	46,650	7,838	6,156	7,838	6,504
46,650	46,700	7,850	6,164	7,850	6,516
46,700	46,750	7,863	6,171	7,863	6,529
46,750	46,800	7,875	6,179	7,875	6,541
46,800	46,850	7,888	6,186	7,888	6,554
46,850	46,900	7,900	6,194	7,900	6,566
46,900	46,950	7,913	6,201	7,913	6,579
46,950	47,000	7,925	6,209	7,925	6,591

If line 43 (taxable income) is—		And you are—			
At least	But less than	Single	Married filing jointly *	Married filing sepa-rately	Head of a house-hold
		Your tax is—			
47,000					
47,000	47,050	7,938	6,216	7,938	6,604
47,050	47,100	7,950	6,224	7,950	6,616
47,100	47,150	7,963	6,231	7,963	6,629
47,150	47,200	7,975	6,239	7,975	6,641
47,200	47,250	7,988	6,246	7,988	6,654
47,250	47,300	8,000	6,254	8,000	6,666
47,300	47,350	8,013	6,261	8,013	6,679
47,350	47,400	8,025	6,269	8,025	6,691
47,400	47,450	8,038	6,276	8,038	6,704
47,450	47,500	8,050	6,284	8,050	6,716
47,500	47,550	8,063	6,291	8,063	6,729
47,550	47,600	8,075	6,299	8,075	6,741
47,600	47,650	8,088	6,306	8,088	6,754
47,650	47,700	8,100	6,314	8,100	6,766
47,700	47,750	8,113	6,321	8,113	6,779
47,750	47,800	8,125	6,329	8,125	6,791
47,800	47,850	8,138	6,336	8,138	6,804
47,850	47,900	8,150	6,344	8,150	6,816
47,900	47,950	8,163	6,351	8,163	6,829
47,950	48,000	8,175	6,359	8,175	6,841
48,000					
48,000	48,050	8,188	6,366	8,188	6,854
48,050	48,100	8,200	6,374	8,200	6,866
48,100	48,150	8,213	6,381	8,213	6,879
48,150	48,200	8,225	6,389	8,225	6,891
48,200	48,250	8,238	6,396	8,238	6,904
48,250	48,300	8,250	6,404	8,250	6,916
48,300	48,350	8,263	6,411	8,263	6,929
48,350	48,400	8,275	6,419	8,275	6,941
48,400	48,450	8,288	6,426	8,288	6,954
48,450	48,500	8,300	6,434	8,300	6,966
48,500	48,550	8,313	6,441	8,313	6,979
48,550	48,600	8,325	6,449	8,325	6,991
48,600	48,650	8,338	6,456	8,338	7,004
48,650	48,700	8,350	6,464	8,350	7,016
48,700	48,750	8,363	6,471	8,363	7,029
48,750	48,800	8,375	6,479	8,375	7,041
48,800	48,850	8,388	6,486	8,388	7,054
48,850	48,900	8,400	6,494	8,400	7,066
48,900	48,950	8,413	6,501	8,413	7,079
48,950	49,000	8,425	6,509	8,425	7,091
49,000					
49,000	49,050	8,438	6,516	8,438	7,104
49,050	49,100	8,450	6,524	8,450	7,116
49,100	49,150	8,463	6,531	8,463	7,129
49,150	49,200	8,475	6,539	8,475	7,141
49,200	49,250	8,488	6,546	8,488	7,154
49,250	49,300	8,500	6,554	8,500	7,166
49,300	49,350	8,513	6,561	8,513	7,179
49,350	49,400	8,525	6,569	8,525	7,191
49,400	49,450	8,538	6,576	8,538	7,204
49,450	49,500	8,550	6,584	8,550	7,216
49,500	49,550	8,563	6,591	8,563	7,229
49,550	49,600	8,575	6,599	8,575	7,241
49,600	49,650	8,588	6,606	8,588	7,254
49,650	49,700	8,600	6,614	8,600	7,266
49,700	49,750	8,613	6,621	8,613	7,279
49,750	49,800	8,625	6,629	8,625	7,291
49,800	49,850	8,638	6,636	8,638	7,304
49,850	49,900	8,650	6,644	8,650	7,316
49,900	49,950	8,663	6,651	8,663	7,329
49,950	50,000	8,675	6,659	8,675	7,341

* This column must also be used by a qualifying widow(er).

(Continued on next page)

2010 Tax Table–*Continued*

If line 43 (taxable income) is—		And you are—			
At least	But less than	Single	Married filing jointly *	Married filing separately	Head of a household
		Your tax is—			
50,000					
50,000	**50,050**	8,688	6,666	8,688	7,354
50,050	**50,100**	8,700	6,674	8,700	7,366
50,100	**50,150**	8,713	6,681	8,713	7,379
50,150	**50,200**	8,725	6,689	8,725	7,391
50,200	**50,250**	8,738	6,696	8,738	7,404
50,250	**50,300**	8,750	6,704	8,750	7,416
50,300	**50,350**	8,763	6,711	8,763	7,429
50,350	**50,400**	8,775	6,719	8,775	7,441
50,400	**50,450**	8,788	6,726	8,788	7,454
50,450	**50,500**	8,800	6,734	8,800	7,466
50,500	**50,550**	8,813	6,741	8,813	7,479
50,550	**50,600**	8,825	6,749	8,825	7,491
50,600	**50,650**	8,838	6,756	8,838	7,504
50,650	**50,700**	8,850	6,764	8,850	7,516
50,700	**50,750**	8,863	6,771	8,863	7,529
50,750	**50,800**	8,875	6,779	8,875	7,541
50,800	**50,850**	8,888	6,786	8,888	7,554
50,850	**50,900**	8,900	6,794	8,900	7,566
50,900	**50,950**	8,913	6,801	8,913	7,579
50,950	**51,000**	8,925	6,809	8,925	7,591
51,000					
51,000	**51,050**	8,938	6,816	8,938	7,604
51,050	**51,100**	8,950	6,824	8,950	7,616
51,100	**51,150**	8,963	6,831	8,963	7,629
51,150	**51,200**	8,975	6,839	8,975	7,641
51,200	**51,250**	8,988	6,846	8,988	7,654
51,250	**51,300**	9,000	6,854	9,000	7,666
51,300	**51,350**	9,013	6,861	9,013	7,679
51,350	**51,400**	9,025	6,869	9,025	7,691
51,400	**51,450**	9,038	6,876	9,038	7,704
51,450	**51,500**	9,050	6,884	9,050	7,716
51,500	**51,550**	9,063	6,891	9,063	7,729
51,550	**51,600**	9,075	6,899	9,075	7,741
51,600	**51,650**	9,088	6,906	9,088	7,754
51,650	**51,700**	9,100	6,914	9,100	7,766
51,700	**51,750**	9,113	6,921	9,113	7,779
51,750	**51,800**	9,125	6,929	9,125	7,791
51,800	**51,850**	9,138	6,936	9,138	7,804
51,850	**51,900**	9,150	6,944	9,150	7,816
51,900	**51,950**	9,163	6,951	9,163	7,829
51,950	**52,000**	9,175	6,959	9,175	7,841
52,000					
52,000	**52,050**	9,188	6,966	9,188	7,854
52,050	**52,100**	9,200	6,974	9,200	7,866
52,100	**52,150**	9,213	6,981	9,213	7,879
52,150	**52,200**	9,225	6,989	9,225	7,891
52,200	**52,250**	9,238	6,996	9,238	7,904
52,250	**52,300**	9,250	7,004	9,250	7,916
52,300	**52,350**	9,263	7,011	9,263	7,929
52,350	**52,400**	9,275	7,019	9,275	7,941
52,400	**52,450**	9,288	7,026	9,288	7,954
52,450	**52,500**	9,300	7,034	9,300	7,966
52,500	**52,550**	9,313	7,041	9,313	7,979
52,550	**52,600**	9,325	7,049	9,325	7,991
52,600	**52,650**	9,338	7,056	9,338	8,004
52,650	**52,700**	9,350	7,064	9,350	8,016
52,700	**52,750**	9,363	7,071	9,363	8,029
52,750	**52,800**	9,375	7,079	9,375	8,041
52,800	**52,850**	9,388	7,086	9,388	8,054
52,850	**52,900**	9,400	7,094	9,400	8,066
52,900	**52,950**	9,413	7,101	9,413	8,079
52,950	**53,000**	9,425	7,109	9,425	8,091

If line 43 (taxable income) is—		And you are—			
At least	But less than	Single	Married filing jointly *	Married filing separately	Head of a household
		Your tax is—			
53,000					
53,000	**53,050**	9,438	7,116	9,438	8,104
53,050	**53,100**	9,450	7,124	9,450	8,116
53,100	**53,150**	9,463	7,131	9,463	8,129
53,150	**53,200**	9,475	7,139	9,475	8,141
53,200	**53,250**	9,488	7,146	9,488	8,154
53,250	**53,300**	9,500	7,154	9,500	8,166
53,300	**53,350**	9,513	7,161	9,513	8,179
53,350	**53,400**	9,525	7,169	9,525	8,191
53,400	**53,450**	9,538	7,176	9,538	8,204
53,450	**53,500**	9,550	7,184	9,550	8,216
53,500	**53,550**	9,563	7,191	9,563	8,229
53,550	**53,600**	9,575	7,199	9,575	8,241
53,600	**53,650**	9,588	7,206	9,588	8,254
53,650	**53,700**	9,600	7,214	9,600	8,266
53,700	**53,750**	9,613	7,221	9,613	8,279
53,750	**53,800**	9,625	7,229	9,625	8,291
53,800	**53,850**	9,638	7,236	9,638	8,304
53,850	**53,900**	9,650	7,244	9,650	8,316
53,900	**53,950**	9,663	7,251	9,663	8,329
53,950	**54,000**	9,675	7,259	9,675	8,341
54,000					
54,000	**54,050**	9,688	7,266	9,688	8,354
54,050	**54,100**	9,700	7,274	9,700	8,366
54,100	**54,150**	9,713	7,281	9,713	8,379
54,150	**54,200**	9,725	7,289	9,725	8,391
54,200	**54,250**	9,738	7,296	9,738	8,404
54,250	**54,300**	9,750	7,304	9,750	8,416
54,300	**54,350**	9,763	7,311	9,763	8,429
54,350	**54,400**	9,775	7,319	9,775	8,441
54,400	**54,450**	9,788	7,326	9,788	8,454
54,450	**54,500**	9,800	7,334	9,800	8,466
54,500	**54,550**	9,813	7,341	9,813	8,479
54,550	**54,600**	9,825	7,349	9,825	8,491
54,600	**54,650**	9,838	7,356	9,838	8,504
54,650	**54,700**	9,850	7,364	9,850	8,516
54,700	**54,750**	9,863	7,371	9,863	8,529
54,750	**54,800**	9,875	7,379	9,875	8,541
54,800	**54,850**	9,888	7,386	9,888	8,554
54,850	**54,900**	9,900	7,394	9,900	8,566
54,900	**54,950**	9,913	7,401	9,913	8,579
54,950	**55,000**	9,925	7,409	9,925	8,591
55,000					
55,000	**55,050**	9,938	7,416	9,938	8,604
55,050	**55,100**	9,950	7,424	9,950	8,616
55,100	**55,150**	9,963	7,431	9,963	8,629
55,150	**55,200**	9,975	7,439	9,975	8,641
55,200	**55,250**	9,988	7,446	9,988	8,654
55,250	**55,300**	10,000	7,454	10,000	8,666
55,300	**55,350**	10,013	7,461	10,013	8,679
55,350	**55,400**	10,025	7,469	10,025	8,691
55,400	**55,450**	10,038	7,476	10,038	8,704
55,450	**55,500**	10,050	7,484	10,050	8,716
55,500	**55,550**	10,063	7,491	10,063	8,729
55,550	**55,600**	10,075	7,499	10,075	8,741
55,600	**55,650**	10,088	7,506	10,088	8,754
55,650	**55,700**	10,100	7,514	10,100	8,766
55,700	**55,750**	10,113	7,521	10,113	8,779
55,750	**55,800**	10,125	7,529	10,125	8,791
55,800	**55,850**	10,138	7,536	10,138	8,804
55,850	**55,900**	10,150	7,544	10,150	8,816
55,900	**55,950**	10,163	7,551	10,163	8,829
55,950	**56,000**	10,175	7,559	10,175	8,841

If line 43 (taxable income) is—		And you are—			
At least	But less than	Single	Married filing jointly *	Married filing separately	Head of a household
		Your tax is—			
56,000					
56,000	**56,050**	10,188	7,566	10,188	8,854
56,050	**56,100**	10,200	7,574	10,200	8,866
56,100	**56,150**	10,213	7,581	10,213	8,879
56,150	**56,200**	10,225	7,589	10,225	8,891
56,200	**56,250**	10,238	7,596	10,238	8,904
56,250	**56,300**	10,250	7,604	10,250	8,916
56,300	**56,350**	10,263	7,611	10,263	8,929
56,350	**56,400**	10,275	7,619	10,275	8,941
56,400	**56,450**	10,288	7,626	10,288	8,954
56,450	**56,500**	10,300	7,634	10,300	8,966
56,500	**56,550**	10,313	7,641	10,313	8,979
56,550	**56,600**	10,325	7,649	10,325	8,991
56,600	**56,650**	10,338	7,656	10,338	9,004
56,650	**56,700**	10,350	7,664	10,350	9,016
56,700	**56,750**	10,363	7,671	10,363	9,029
56,750	**56,800**	10,375	7,679	10,375	9,041
56,800	**56,850**	10,388	7,686	10,388	9,054
56,850	**56,900**	10,400	7,694	10,400	9,066
56,900	**56,950**	10,413	7,701	10,413	9,079
56,950	**57,000**	10,425	7,709	10,425	9,091
57,000					
57,000	**57,050**	10,438	7,716	10,438	9,104
57,050	**57,100**	10,450	7,724	10,450	9,116
57,100	**57,150**	10,463	7,731	10,463	9,129
57,150	**57,200**	10,475	7,739	10,475	9,141
57,200	**57,250**	10,488	7,746	10,488	9,154
57,250	**57,300**	10,500	7,754	10,500	9,166
57,300	**57,350**	10,513	7,761	10,513	9,179
57,350	**57,400**	10,525	7,769	10,525	9,191
57,400	**57,450**	10,538	7,776	10,538	9,204
57,450	**57,500**	10,550	7,784	10,550	9,216
57,500	**57,550**	10,563	7,791	10,563	9,229
57,550	**57,600**	10,575	7,799	10,575	9,241
57,600	**57,650**	10,588	7,806	10,588	9,254
57,650	**57,700**	10,600	7,814	10,600	9,266
57,700	**57,750**	10,613	7,821	10,613	9,279
57,750	**57,800**	10,625	7,829	10,625	9,291
57,800	**57,850**	10,638	7,836	10,638	9,304
57,850	**57,900**	10,650	7,844	10,650	9,316
57,900	**57,950**	10,663	7,851	10,663	9,329
57,950	**58,000**	10,675	7,859	10,675	9,341
58,000					
58,000	**58,050**	10,688	7,866	10,688	9,354
58,050	**58,100**	10,700	7,874	10,700	9,366
58,100	**58,150**	10,713	7,881	10,713	9,379
58,150	**58,200**	10,725	7,889	10,725	9,391
58,200	**58,250**	10,738	7,896	10,738	9,404
58,250	**58,300**	10,750	7,904	10,750	9,416
58,300	**58,350**	10,763	7,911	10,763	9,429
58,350	**58,400**	10,775	7,919	10,775	9,441
58,400	**58,450**	10,788	7,926	10,788	9,454
58,450	**58,500**	10,800	7,934	10,800	9,466
58,500	**58,550**	10,813	7,941	10,813	9,479
58,550	**58,600**	10,825	7,949	10,825	9,491
58,600	**58,650**	10,838	7,956	10,838	9,504
58,650	**58,700**	10,850	7,964	10,850	9,516
58,700	**58,750**	10,863	7,971	10,863	9,529
58,750	**58,800**	10,875	7,979	10,875	9,541
58,800	**58,850**	10,888	7,986	10,888	9,554
58,850	**58,900**	10,900	7,994	10,900	9,566
58,900	**58,950**	10,913	8,001	10,913	9,579
58,950	**59,000**	10,925	8,009	10,925	9,591

* This column must also be used by a qualifying widow(er).

(Continued on next page)

If line 43 (taxable income) is—		And you are—			
At least	But less than	Single	Married filing jointly *	Married filing separately	Head of a household
		Your tax is—			
59,000					
59,000	**59,050**	10,938	8,016	10,938	9,604
59,050	**59,100**	10,950	8,024	10,950	9,616
59,100	**59,150**	10,963	8,031	10,963	9,629
59,150	**59,200**	10,975	8,039	10,975	9,641
59,200	**59,250**	10,988	8,046	10,988	9,654
59,250	**59,300**	11,000	8,054	11,000	9,666
59,300	**59,350**	11,013	8,061	11,013	9,679
59,350	**59,400**	11,025	8,069	11,025	9,691
59,400	**59,450**	11,038	8,076	11,038	9,704
59,450	**59,500**	11,050	8,084	11,050	9,716
59,500	**59,550**	11,063	8,091	11,063	9,729
59,550	**59,600**	11,075	8,099	11,075	9,741
59,600	**59,650**	11,088	8,106	11,088	9,754
59,650	**59,700**	11,100	8,114	11,100	9,766
59,700	**59,750**	11,113	8,121	11,113	9,779
59,750	**59,800**	11,125	8,129	11,125	9,791
59,800	**59,850**	11,138	8,136	11,138	9,804
59,850	**59,900**	11,150	8,144	11,150	9,816
59,900	**59,950**	11,163	8,151	11,163	9,829
59,950	**60,000**	11,175	8,159	11,175	9,841
60,000					
60,000	**60,050**	11,188	8,166	11,188	9,854
60,050	**60,100**	11,200	8,174	11,200	9,866
60,100	**60,150**	11,213	8,181	11,213	9,879
60,150	**60,200**	11,225	8,189	11,225	9,891
60,200	**60,250**	11,238	8,196	11,238	9,904
60,250	**60,300**	11,250	8,204	11,250	9,916
60,300	**60,350**	11,263	8,211	11,263	9,929
60,350	**60,400**	11,275	8,219	11,275	9,941
60,400	**60,450**	11,288	8,226	11,288	9,954
60,450	**60,500**	11,300	8,234	11,300	9,966
60,500	**60,550**	11,313	8,241	11,313	9,979
60,550	**60,600**	11,325	8,249	11,325	9,991
60,600	**60,650**	11,338	8,256	11,338	10,004
60,650	**60,700**	11,350	8,264	11,350	10,016
60,700	**60,750**	11,363	8,271	11,363	10,029
60,750	**60,800**	11,375	8,279	11,375	10,041
60,800	**60,850**	11,388	8,286	11,388	10,054
60,850	**60,900**	11,400	8,294	11,400	10,066
60,900	**60,950**	11,413	8,301	11,413	10,079
60,950	**61,000**	11,425	8,309	11,425	10,091
61,000					
61,000	**61,050**	11,438	8,316	11,438	10,104
61,050	**61,100**	11,450	8,324	11,450	10,116
61,100	**61,150**	11,463	8,331	11,463	10,129
61,150	**61,200**	11,475	8,339	11,475	10,141
61,200	**61,250**	11,488	8,346	11,488	10,154
61,250	**61,300**	11,500	8,354	11,500	10,166
61,300	**61,350**	11,513	8,361	11,513	10,179
61,350	**61,400**	11,525	8,369	11,525	10,191
61,400	**61,450**	11,538	8,376	11,538	10,204
61,450	**61,500**	11,550	8,384	11,550	10,216
61,500	**61,550**	11,563	8,391	11,563	10,229
61,550	**61,600**	11,575	8,399	11,575	10,241
61,600	**61,650**	11,588	8,406	11,588	10,254
61,650	**61,700**	11,600	8,414	11,600	10,266
61,700	**61,750**	11,613	8,421	11,613	10,279
61,750	**61,800**	11,625	8,429	11,625	10,291
61,800	**61,850**	11,638	8,436	11,638	10,304
61,850	**61,900**	11,650	8,444	11,650	10,316
61,900	**61,950**	11,663	8,451	11,663	10,329
61,950	**62,000**	11,675	8,459	11,675	10,341

If line 43 (taxable income) is—		And you are—			
At least	But less than	Single	Married filing jointly *	Married filing separately	Head of a household
		Your tax is—			
62,000					
62,000	**62,050**	11,688	8,466	11,688	10,354
62,050	**62,100**	11,700	8,474	11,700	10,366
62,100	**62,150**	11,713	8,481	11,713	10,379
62,150	**62,200**	11,725	8,489	11,725	10,391
62,200	**62,250**	11,738	8,496	11,738	10,404
62,250	**62,300**	11,750	8,504	11,750	10,416
62,300	**62,350**	11,763	8,511	11,763	10,429
62,350	**62,400**	11,775	8,519	11,775	10,441
62,400	**62,450**	11,788	8,526	11,788	10,454
62,450	**62,500**	11,800	8,534	11,800	10,466
62,500	**62,550**	11,813	8,541	11,813	10,479
62,550	**62,600**	11,825	8,549	11,825	10,491
62,600	**62,650**	11,838	8,556	11,838	10,504
62,650	**62,700**	11,850	8,564	11,850	10,516
62,700	**62,750**	11,863	8,571	11,863	10,529
62,750	**62,800**	11,875	8,579	11,875	10,541
62,800	**62,850**	11,888	8,586	11,888	10,554
62,850	**62,900**	11,900	8,594	11,900	10,566
62,900	**62,950**	11,913	8,601	11,913	10,579
62,950	**63,000**	11,925	8,609	11,925	10,591
63,000					
63,000	**63,050**	11,938	8,616	11,938	10,604
63,050	**63,100**	11,950	8,624	11,950	10,616
63,100	**63,150**	11,963	8,631	11,963	10,629
63,150	**63,200**	11,975	8,639	11,975	10,641
63,200	**63,250**	11,988	8,646	11,988	10,654
63,250	**63,300**	12,000	8,654	12,000	10,666
63,300	**63,350**	12,013	8,661	12,013	10,679
63,350	**63,400**	12,025	8,669	12,025	10,691
63,400	**63,450**	12,038	8,676	12,038	10,704
63,450	**63,500**	12,050	8,684	12,050	10,716
63,500	**63,550**	12,063	8,691	12,063	10,729
63,550	**63,600**	12,075	8,699	12,075	10,741
63,600	**63,650**	12,088	8,706	12,088	10,754
63,650	**63,700**	12,100	8,714	12,100	10,766
63,700	**63,750**	12,113	8,721	12,113	10,779
63,750	**63,800**	12,125	8,729	12,125	10,791
63,800	**63,850**	12,138	8,736	12,138	10,804
63,850	**63,900**	12,150	8,744	12,150	10,816
63,900	**63,950**	12,163	8,751	12,163	10,829
63,950	**64,000**	12,175	8,759	12,175	10,841
64,000					
64,000	**64,050**	12,188	8,766	12,188	10,854
64,050	**64,100**	12,200	8,774	12,200	10,866
64,100	**64,150**	12,213	8,781	12,213	10,879
64,150	**64,200**	12,225	8,789	12,225	10,891
64,200	**64,250**	12,238	8,796	12,238	10,904
64,250	**64,300**	12,250	8,804	12,250	10,916
64,300	**64,350**	12,263	8,811	12,263	10,929
64,350	**64,400**	12,275	8,819	12,275	10,941
64,400	**64,450**	12,288	8,826	12,288	10,954
64,450	**64,500**	12,300	8,834	12,300	10,966
64,500	**64,550**	12,313	8,841	12,313	10,979
64,550	**64,600**	12,325	8,849	12,325	10,991
64,600	**64,650**	12,338	8,856	12,338	11,004
64,650	**64,700**	12,350	8,864	12,350	11,016
64,700	**64,750**	12,363	8,871	12,363	11,029
64,750	**64,800**	12,375	8,879	12,375	11,041
64,800	**64,850**	12,388	8,886	12,388	11,054
64,850	**64,900**	12,400	8,894	12,400	11,066
64,900	**64,950**	12,413	8,901	12,413	11,079
64,950	**65,000**	12,425	8,909	12,425	11,091

If line 43 (taxable income) is—		And you are—			
At least	But less than	Single	Married filing jointly *	Married filing separately	Head of a household
		Your tax is—			
65,000					
65,000	**65,050**	12,438	8,916	12,438	11,104
65,050	**65,100**	12,450	8,924	12,450	11,116
65,100	**65,150**	12,463	8,931	12,463	11,129
65,150	**65,200**	12,475	8,939	12,475	11,141
65,200	**65,250**	12,488	8,946	12,488	11,154
65,250	**65,300**	12,500	8,954	12,500	11,166
65,300	**65,350**	12,513	8,961	12,513	11,179
65,350	**65,400**	12,525	8,969	12,525	11,191
65,400	**65,450**	12,538	8,976	12,538	11,204
65,450	**65,500**	12,550	8,984	12,550	11,216
65,500	**65,550**	12,563	8,991	12,563	11,229
65,550	**65,600**	12,575	8,999	12,575	11,241
65,600	**65,650**	12,588	9,006	12,588	11,254
65,650	**65,700**	12,600	9,014	12,600	11,266
65,700	**65,750**	12,613	9,021	12,613	11,279
65,750	**65,800**	12,625	9,029	12,625	11,291
65,800	**65,850**	12,638	9,036	12,638	11,304
65,850	**65,900**	12,650	9,044	12,650	11,316
65,900	**65,950**	12,663	9,051	12,663	11,329
65,950	**66,000**	12,675	9,059	12,675	11,341
66,000					
66,000	**66,050**	12,688	9,066	12,688	11,354
66,050	**66,100**	12,700	9,074	12,700	11,366
66,100	**66,150**	12,713	9,081	12,713	11,379
66,150	**66,200**	12,725	9,089	12,725	11,391
66,200	**66,250**	12,738	9,096	12,738	11,404
66,250	**66,300**	12,750	9,104	12,750	11,416
66,300	**66,350**	12,763	9,111	12,763	11,429
66,350	**66,400**	12,775	9,119	12,775	11,441
66,400	**66,450**	12,788	9,126	12,788	11,454
66,450	**66,500**	12,800	9,134	12,800	11,466
66,500	**66,550**	12,813	9,141	12,813	11,479
66,550	**66,600**	12,825	9,149	12,825	11,491
66,600	**66,650**	12,838	9,156	12,838	11,504
66,650	**66,700**	12,850	9,164	12,850	11,516
66,700	**66,750**	12,863	9,171	12,863	11,529
66,750	**66,800**	12,875	9,179	12,875	11,541
66,800	**66,850**	12,888	9,186	12,888	11,554
66,850	**66,900**	12,900	9,194	12,900	11,566
66,900	**66,950**	12,913	9,201	12,913	11,579
66,950	**67,000**	12,925	9,209	12,925	11,591
67,000					
67,000	**67,050**	12,938	9,216	12,938	11,604
67,050	**67,100**	12,950	9,224	12,950	11,616
67,100	**67,150**	12,963	9,231	12,963	11,629
67,150	**67,200**	12,975	9,239	12,975	11,641
67,200	**67,250**	12,988	9,246	12,988	11,654
67,250	**67,300**	13,000	9,254	13,000	11,666
67,300	**67,350**	13,013	9,261	13,013	11,679
67,350	**67,400**	13,025	9,269	13,025	11,691
67,400	**67,450**	13,038	9,276	13,038	11,704
67,450	**67,500**	13,050	9,284	13,050	11,716
67,500	**67,550**	13,063	9,291	13,063	11,729
67,550	**67,600**	13,075	9,299	13,075	11,741
67,600	**67,650**	13,088	9,306	13,088	11,754
67,650	**67,700**	13,100	9,314	13,100	11,766
67,700	**67,750**	13,113	9,321	13,113	11,779
67,750	**67,800**	13,125	9,329	13,125	11,791
67,800	**67,850**	13,138	9,336	13,138	11,804
67,850	**67,900**	13,150	9,344	13,150	11,816
67,900	**67,950**	13,163	9,351	13,163	11,829
67,950	**68,000**	13,175	9,359	13,175	11,841

* This column must also be used by a qualifying widow(er).

(Continued on next page)

2010 Tax Table–*Continued*

If line 43 (taxable income) is—		And you are—			
At least	But less than	Single	Married filing jointly *	Married filing separately	Head of a household
		Your tax is—			
68,000					
68,000	**68,050**	13,188	9,369	13,188	11,854
68,050	**68,100**	13,200	9,381	13,200	11,866
68,100	**68,150**	13,213	9,394	13,213	11,879
68,150	**68,200**	13,225	9,406	13,225	11,891
68,200	**68,250**	13,238	9,419	13,238	11,904
68,250	**68,300**	13,250	9,431	13,250	11,916
68,300	**68,350**	13,263	9,444	13,263	11,929
68,350	**68,400**	13,275	9,456	13,275	11,941
68,400	**68,450**	13,288	9,469	13,288	11,954
68,450	**68,500**	13,300	9,481	13,300	11,966
68,500	**68,550**	13,313	9,494	13,313	11,979
68,550	**68,600**	13,325	9,506	13,325	11,991
68,600	**68,650**	13,338	9,519	13,338	12,004
68,650	**68,700**	13,350	9,531	13,351	12,016
68,700	**68,750**	13,363	9,544	13,365	12,029
68,750	**68,800**	13,375	9,556	13,379	12,041
68,800	**68,850**	13,388	9,569	13,393	12,054
68,850	**68,900**	13,400	9,581	13,407	12,066
68,900	**68,950**	13,413	9,594	13,421	12,079
68,950	**69,000**	13,425	9,606	13,435	12,091
69,000					
69,000	**69,050**	13,438	9,619	13,449	12,104
69,050	**69,100**	13,450	9,631	13,463	12,116
69,100	**69,150**	13,463	9,644	13,477	12,129
69,150	**69,200**	13,475	9,656	13,491	12,141
69,200	**69,250**	13,488	9,669	13,505	12,154
69,250	**69,300**	13,500	9,681	13,519	12,166
69,300	**69,350**	13,513	9,694	13,533	12,179
69,350	**69,400**	13,525	9,706	13,547	12,191
69,400	**69,450**	13,538	9,719	13,561	12,204
69,450	**69,500**	13,550	9,731	13,575	12,216
69,500	**69,550**	13,563	9,744	13,589	12,229
69,550	**69,600**	13,575	9,756	13,603	12,241
69,600	**69,650**	13,588	9,769	13,617	12,254
69,650	**69,700**	13,600	9,781	13,631	12,266
69,700	**69,750**	13,613	9,794	13,645	12,279
69,750	**69,800**	13,625	9,806	13,659	12,291
69,800	**69,850**	13,638	9,819	13,673	12,304
69,850	**69,900**	13,650	9,831	13,687	12,316
69,900	**69,950**	13,663	9,844	13,701	12,329
69,950	**70,000**	13,675	9,856	13,715	12,341
70,000					
70,000	**70,050**	13,688	9,869	13,729	12,354
70,050	**70,100**	13,700	9,881	13,743	12,366
70,100	**70,150**	13,713	9,894	13,757	12,379
70,150	**70,200**	13,725	9,906	13,771	12,391
70,200	**70,250**	13,738	9,919	13,785	12,404
70,250	**70,300**	13,750	9,931	13,799	12,416
70,300	**70,350**	13,763	9,944	13,813	12,429
70,350	**70,400**	13,775	9,956	13,827	12,441
70,400	**70,450**	13,788	9,969	13,841	12,454
70,450	**70,500**	13,800	9,981	13,855	12,466
70,500	**70,550**	13,813	9,994	13,869	12,479
70,550	**70,600**	13,825	10,006	13,883	12,491
70,600	**70,650**	13,838	10,019	13,897	12,504
70,650	**70,700**	13,850	10,031	13,911	12,516
70,700	**70,750**	13,863	10,044	13,925	12,529
70,750	**70,800**	13,875	10,056	13,939	12,541
70,800	**70,850**	13,888	10,069	13,953	12,554
70,850	**70,900**	13,900	10,081	13,967	12,566
70,900	**70,950**	13,913	10,094	13,981	12,579
70,950	**71,000**	13,925	10,106	13,995	12,591

If line 43 (taxable income) is—		And you are—			
At least	But less than	Single	Married filing jointly *	Married filing separately	Head of a household
		Your tax is—			
71,000					
71,000	**71,050**	13,938	10,119	14,009	12,604
71,050	**71,100**	13,950	10,131	14,023	12,616
71,100	**71,150**	13,963	10,144	14,037	12,629
71,150	**71,200**	13,975	10,156	14,051	12,641
71,200	**71,250**	13,988	10,169	14,065	12,654
71,250	**71,300**	14,000	10,181	14,079	12,666
71,300	**71,350**	14,013	10,194	14,093	12,679
71,350	**71,400**	14,025	10,206	14,107	12,691
71,400	**71,450**	14,038	10,219	14,121	12,704
71,450	**71,500**	14,050	10,231	14,135	12,716
71,500	**71,550**	14,063	10,244	14,149	12,729
71,550	**71,600**	14,075	10,256	14,163	12,741
71,600	**71,650**	14,088	10,269	14,177	12,754
71,650	**71,700**	14,100	10,281	14,191	12,766
71,700	**71,750**	14,113	10,294	14,205	12,779
71,750	**71,800**	14,125	10,306	14,219	12,791
71,800	**71,850**	14,138	10,319	14,233	12,804
71,850	**71,900**	14,150	10,331	14,247	12,816
71,900	**71,950**	14,163	10,344	14,261	12,829
71,950	**72,000**	14,175	10,356	14,275	12,841
72,000					
72,000	**72,050**	14,188	10,369	14,289	12,854
72,050	**72,100**	14,200	10,381	14,303	12,866
72,100	**72,150**	14,213	10,394	14,317	12,879
72,150	**72,200**	14,225	10,406	14,331	12,891
72,200	**72,250**	14,238	10,419	14,345	12,904
72,250	**72,300**	14,250	10,431	14,359	12,916
72,300	**72,350**	14,263	10,444	14,373	12,929
72,350	**72,400**	14,275	10,456	14,387	12,941
72,400	**72,450**	14,288	10,469	14,401	12,954
72,450	**72,500**	14,300	10,481	14,415	12,966
72,500	**72,550**	14,313	10,494	14,429	12,979
72,550	**72,600**	14,325	10,506	14,443	12,991
72,600	**72,650**	14,338	10,519	14,457	13,004
72,650	**72,700**	14,350	10,531	14,471	13,016
72,700	**72,750**	14,363	10,544	14,485	13,029
72,750	**72,800**	14,375	10,556	14,499	13,041
72,800	**72,850**	14,388	10,569	14,513	13,054
72,850	**72,900**	14,400	10,581	14,527	13,066
72,900	**72,950**	14,413	10,594	14,541	13,079
72,950	**73,000**	14,425	10,606	14,555	13,091
73,000					
73,000	**73,050**	14,438	10,619	14,569	13,104
73,050	**73,100**	14,450	10,631	14,583	13,116
73,100	**73,150**	14,463	10,644	14,597	13,129
73,150	**73,200**	14,475	10,656	14,611	13,141
73,200	**73,250**	14,488	10,669	14,625	13,154
73,250	**73,300**	14,500	10,681	14,639	13,166
73,300	**73,350**	14,513	10,694	14,653	13,179
73,350	**73,400**	14,525	10,706	14,667	13,191
73,400	**73,450**	14,538	10,719	14,681	13,204
73,450	**73,500**	14,550	10,731	14,695	13,216
73,500	**73,550**	14,563	10,744	14,709	13,229
73,550	**73,600**	14,575	10,756	14,723	13,241
73,600	**73,650**	14,588	10,769	14,737	13,254
73,650	**73,700**	14,600	10,781	14,751	13,266
73,700	**73,750**	14,613	10,794	14,765	13,279
73,750	**73,800**	14,625	10,806	14,779	13,291
73,800	**73,850**	14,638	10,819	14,793	13,304
73,850	**73,900**	14,650	10,831	14,807	13,316
73,900	**73,950**	14,663	10,844	14,821	13,329
73,950	**74,000**	14,675	10,856	14,835	13,341

If line 43 (taxable income) is—		And you are—			
At least	But less than	Single	Married filing jointly *	Married filing separately	Head of a household
		Your tax is—			
74,000					
74,000	**74,050**	14,688	10,869	14,849	13,354
74,050	**74,100**	14,700	10,881	14,863	13,366
74,100	**74,150**	14,713	10,894	14,877	13,379
74,150	**74,200**	14,725	10,906	14,891	13,391
74,200	**74,250**	14,738	10,919	14,905	13,404
74,250	**74,300**	14,750	10,931	14,919	13,416
74,300	**74,350**	14,763	10,944	14,933	13,429
74,350	**74,400**	14,775	10,956	14,947	13,441
74,400	**74,450**	14,788	10,969	14,961	13,454
74,450	**74,500**	14,800	10,981	14,975	13,466
74,500	**74,550**	14,813	10,994	14,989	13,479
74,550	**74,600**	14,825	11,006	15,003	13,491
74,600	**74,650**	14,838	11,019	15,017	13,504
74,650	**74,700**	14,850	11,031	15,031	13,516
74,700	**74,750**	14,863	11,044	15,045	13,529
74,750	**74,800**	14,875	11,056	15,059	13,541
74,800	**74,850**	14,888	11,069	15,073	13,554
74,850	**74,900**	14,900	11,081	15,087	13,566
74,900	**74,950**	14,913	11,094	15,101	13,579
74,950	**75,000**	14,925	11,106	15,115	13,591
75,000					
75,000	**75,050**	14,938	11,119	15,129	13,604
75,050	**75,100**	14,950	11,131	15,143	13,616
75,100	**75,150**	14,963	11,144	15,157	13,629
75,150	**75,200**	14,975	11,156	15,171	13,641
75,200	**75,250**	14,988	11,169	15,185	13,654
75,250	**75,300**	15,000	11,181	15,199	13,666
75,300	**75,350**	15,013	11,194	15,213	13,679
75,350	**75,400**	15,025	11,206	15,227	13,691
75,400	**75,450**	15,038	11,219	15,241	13,704
75,450	**75,500**	15,050	11,231	15,255	13,716
75,500	**75,550**	15,063	11,244	15,269	13,729
75,550	**75,600**	15,075	11,256	15,283	13,741
75,600	**75,650**	15,088	11,269	15,297	13,754
75,650	**75,700**	15,100	11,281	15,311	13,766
75,700	**75,750**	15,113	11,294	15,325	13,779
75,750	**75,800**	15,125	11,306	15,339	13,791
75,800	**75,850**	15,138	11,319	15,353	13,804
75,850	**75,900**	15,150	11,331	15,367	13,816
75,900	**75,950**	15,163	11,344	15,381	13,829
75,950	**76,000**	15,175	11,356	15,395	13,841
76,000					
76,000	**76,050**	15,188	11,369	15,409	13,854
76,050	**76,100**	15,200	11,381	15,423	13,866
76,100	**76,150**	15,213	11,394	15,437	13,879
76,150	**76,200**	15,225	11,406	15,451	13,891
76,200	**76,250**	15,238	11,419	15,465	13,904
76,250	**76,300**	15,250	11,431	15,479	13,916
76,300	**76,350**	15,263	11,444	15,493	13,929
76,350	**76,400**	15,275	11,456	15,507	13,941
76,400	**76,450**	15,288	11,469	15,521	13,954
76,450	**76,500**	15,300	11,481	15,535	13,966
76,500	**76,550**	15,313	11,494	15,549	13,979
76,550	**76,600**	15,325	11,506	15,563	13,991
76,600	**76,650**	15,338	11,519	15,577	14,004
76,650	**76,700**	15,350	11,531	15,591	14,016
76,700	**76,750**	15,363	11,544	15,605	14,029
76,750	**76,800**	15,375	11,556	15,619	14,041
76,800	**76,850**	15,388	11,569	15,633	14,054
76,850	**76,900**	15,400	11,581	15,647	14,066
76,900	**76,950**	15,413	11,594	15,661	14,079
76,950	**77,000**	15,425	11,606	15,675	14,091

* This column must also be used by a qualifying widow(er).

(Continued on next page)

If line 43 (taxable income) is— At least	But less than	And you are— Single	Married filing jointly *	Married filing separately	Head of a household
		Your tax is—			
77,000					
77,000	**77,050**	15,438	11,619	15,689	14,104
77,050	**77,100**	15,450	11,631	15,703	14,116
77,100	**77,150**	15,463	11,644	15,717	14,129
77,150	**77,200**	15,475	11,656	15,731	14,141
77,200	**77,250**	15,488	11,669	15,745	14,154
77,250	**77,300**	15,500	11,681	15,759	14,166
77,300	**77,350**	15,513	11,694	15,773	14,179
77,350	**77,400**	15,525	11,706	15,787	14,191
77,400	**77,450**	15,538	11,719	15,801	14,204
77,450	**77,500**	15,550	11,731	15,815	14,216
77,500	**77,550**	15,563	11,744	15,829	14,229
77,550	**77,600**	15,575	11,756	15,843	14,241
77,600	**77,650**	15,588	11,769	15,857	14,254
77,650	**77,700**	15,600	11,781	15,871	14,266
77,700	**77,750**	15,613	11,794	15,885	14,279
77,750	**77,800**	15,625	11,806	15,899	14,291
77,800	**77,850**	15,638	11,819	15,913	14,304
77,850	**77,900**	15,650	11,831	15,927	14,316
77,900	**77,950**	15,663	11,844	15,941	14,329
77,950	**78,000**	15,675	11,856	15,955	14,341
78,000					
78,000	**78,050**	15,688	11,869	15,969	14,354
78,050	**78,100**	15,700	11,881	15,983	14,366
78,100	**78,150**	15,713	11,894	15,997	14,379
78,150	**78,200**	15,725	11,906	16,011	14,391
78,200	**78,250**	15,738	11,919	16,025	14,404
78,250	**78,300**	15,750	11,931	16,039	14,416
78,300	**78,350**	15,763	11,944	16,053	14,429
78,350	**78,400**	15,775	11,956	16,067	14,441
78,400	**78,450**	15,788	11,969	16,081	14,454
78,450	**78,500**	15,800	11,981	16,095	14,466
78,500	**78,550**	15,813	11,994	16,109	14,479
78,550	**78,600**	15,825	12,006	16,123	14,491
78,600	**78,650**	15,838	12,019	16,137	14,504
78,650	**78,700**	15,850	12,031	16,151	14,516
78,700	**78,750**	15,863	12,044	16,165	14,529
78,750	**78,800**	15,875	12,056	16,179	14,541
78,800	**78,850**	15,888	12,069	16,193	14,554
78,850	**78,900**	15,900	12,081	16,207	14,566
78,900	**78,950**	15,913	12,094	16,221	14,579
78,950	**79,000**	15,925	12,106	16,235	14,591
79,000					
79,000	**79,050**	15,938	12,119	16,249	14,604
79,050	**79,100**	15,950	12,131	16,263	14,616
79,100	**79,150**	15,963	12,144	16,277	14,629
79,150	**79,200**	15,975	12,156	16,291	14,641
79,200	**79,250**	15,988	12,169	16,305	14,654
79,250	**79,300**	16,000	12,181	16,319	14,666
79,300	**79,350**	16,013	12,194	16,333	14,679
79,350	**79,400**	16,025	12,206	16,347	14,691
79,400	**79,450**	16,038	12,219	16,361	14,704
79,450	**79,500**	16,050	12,231	16,375	14,716
79,500	**79,550**	16,063	12,244	16,389	14,729
79,550	**79,600**	16,075	12,256	16,403	14,741
79,600	**79,650**	16,088	12,269	16,417	14,754
79,650	**79,700**	16,100	12,281	16,431	14,766
79,700	**79,750**	16,113	12,294	16,445	14,779
79,750	**79,800**	16,125	12,306	16,459	14,791
79,800	**79,850**	16,138	12,319	16,473	14,804
79,850	**79,900**	16,150	12,331	16,487	14,816
79,900	**79,950**	16,163	12,344	16,501	14,829
79,950	**80,000**	16,175	12,356	16,515	14,841

If line 43 (taxable income) is— At least	But less than	And you are— Single	Married filing jointly *	Married filing separately	Head of a household
		Your tax is—			
80,000					
80,000	**80,050**	16,188	12,369	16,529	14,854
80,050	**80,100**	16,200	12,381	16,543	14,866
80,100	**80,150**	16,213	12,394	16,557	14,879
80,150	**80,200**	16,225	12,406	16,571	14,891
80,200	**80,250**	16,238	12,419	16,585	14,904
80,250	**80,300**	16,250	12,431	16,599	14,916
80,300	**80,350**	16,263	12,444	16,613	14,929
80,350	**80,400**	16,275	12,456	16,627	14,941
80,400	**80,450**	16,288	12,469	16,641	14,954
80,450	**80,500**	16,300	12,481	16,655	14,966
80,500	**80,550**	16,313	12,494	16,669	14,979
80,550	**80,600**	16,325	12,506	16,683	14,991
80,600	**80,650**	16,338	12,519	16,697	15,004
80,650	**80,700**	16,350	12,531	16,711	15,016
80,700	**80,750**	16,363	12,544	16,725	15,029
80,750	**80,800**	16,375	12,556	16,739	15,041
80,800	**80,850**	16,388	12,569	16,753	15,054
80,850	**80,900**	16,400	12,581	16,767	15,066
80,900	**80,950**	16,413	12,594	16,781	15,079
80,950	**81,000**	16,425	12,606	16,795	15,091
81,000					
81,000	**81,050**	16,438	12,619	16,809	15,104
81,050	**81,100**	16,450	12,631	16,823	15,116
81,100	**81,150**	16,463	12,644	16,837	15,129
81,150	**81,200**	16,475	12,656	16,851	15,141
81,200	**81,250**	16,488	12,669	16,865	15,154
81,250	**81,300**	16,500	12,681	16,879	15,166
81,300	**81,350**	16,513	12,694	16,893	15,179
81,350	**81,400**	16,525	12,706	16,907	15,191
81,400	**81,450**	16,538	12,719	16,921	15,204
81,450	**81,500**	16,550	12,731	16,935	15,216
81,500	**81,550**	16,563	12,744	16,949	15,229
81,550	**81,600**	16,575	12,756	16,963	15,241
81,600	**81,650**	16,588	12,769	16,977	15,254
81,650	**81,700**	16,600	12,781	16,991	15,266
81,700	**81,750**	16,613	12,794	17,005	15,279
81,750	**81,800**	16,625	12,806	17,019	15,291
81,800	**81,850**	16,638	12,819	17,033	15,304
81,850	**81,900**	16,650	12,831	17,047	15,316
81,900	**81,950**	16,663	12,844	17,061	15,329
81,950	**82,000**	16,675	12,856	17,075	15,341
82,000					
82,000	**82,050**	16,688	12,869	17,089	15,354
82,050	**82,100**	16,700	12,881	17,103	15,366
82,100	**82,150**	16,713	12,894	17,117	15,379
82,150	**82,200**	16,725	12,906	17,131	15,391
82,200	**82,250**	16,738	12,919	17,145	15,404
82,250	**82,300**	16,750	12,931	17,159	15,416
82,300	**82,350**	16,763	12,944	17,173	15,429
82,350	**82,400**	16,775	12,956	17,187	15,441
82,400	**82,450**	16,788	12,969	17,201	15,454
82,450	**82,500**	16,802	12,981	17,215	15,466
82,500	**82,550**	16,816	12,994	17,229	15,479
82,550	**82,600**	16,830	13,006	17,243	15,491
82,600	**82,650**	16,844	13,019	17,257	15,504
82,650	**82,700**	16,858	13,031	17,271	15,516
82,700	**82,750**	16,872	13,044	17,285	15,529
82,750	**82,800**	16,886	13,056	17,299	15,541
82,800	**82,850**	16,900	13,069	17,313	15,554
82,850	**82,900**	16,914	13,081	17,327	15,566
82,900	**82,950**	16,928	13,094	17,341	15,579
82,950	**83,000**	16,942	13,106	17,355	15,591

If line 43 (taxable income) is— At least	But less than	And you are— Single	Married filing jointly *	Married filing separately	Head of a household
		Your tax is—			
83,000					
83,000	**83,050**	16,956	13,119	17,369	15,604
83,050	**83,100**	16,970	13,131	17,383	15,616
83,100	**83,150**	16,984	13,144	17,397	15,629
83,150	**83,200**	16,998	13,156	17,411	15,641
83,200	**83,250**	17,012	13,169	17,425	15,654
83,250	**83,300**	17,026	13,181	17,439	15,666
83,300	**83,350**	17,040	13,194	17,453	15,679
83,350	**83,400**	17,054	13,206	17,467	15,691
83,400	**83,450**	17,068	13,219	17,481	15,704
83,450	**83,500**	17,082	13,231	17,495	15,716
83,500	**83,550**	17,096	13,244	17,509	15,729
83,550	**83,600**	17,110	13,256	17,523	15,741
83,600	**83,650**	17,124	13,269	17,537	15,754
83,650	**83,700**	17,138	13,281	17,551	15,766
83,700	**83,750**	17,152	13,294	17,565	15,779
83,750	**83,800**	17,166	13,306	17,579	15,791
83,800	**83,850**	17,180	13,319	17,593	15,804
83,850	**83,900**	17,194	13,331	17,607	15,816
83,900	**83,950**	17,208	13,344	17,621	15,829
83,950	**84,000**	17,222	13,356	17,635	15,841
84,000					
84,000	**84,050**	17,236	13,369	17,649	15,854
84,050	**84,100**	17,250	13,381	17,663	15,866
84,100	**84,150**	17,264	13,394	17,677	15,879
84,150	**84,200**	17,278	13,406	17,691	15,891
84,200	**84,250**	17,292	13,419	17,705	15,904
84,250	**84,300**	17,306	13,431	17,719	15,916
84,300	**84,350**	17,320	13,444	17,733	15,929
84,350	**84,400**	17,334	13,456	17,747	15,941
84,400	**84,450**	17,348	13,469	17,761	15,954
84,450	**84,500**	17,362	13,481	17,775	15,966
84,500	**84,550**	17,376	13,494	17,789	15,979
84,550	**84,600**	17,390	13,506	17,803	15,991
84,600	**84,650**	17,404	13,519	17,817	16,004
84,650	**84,700**	17,418	13,531	17,831	16,016
84,700	**84,750**	17,432	13,544	17,845	16,029
84,750	**84,800**	17,446	13,556	17,859	16,041
84,800	**84,850**	17,460	13,569	17,873	16,054
84,850	**84,900**	17,474	13,581	17,887	16,066
84,900	**84,950**	17,488	13,594	17,901	16,079
84,950	**85,000**	17,502	13,606	17,915	16,091
85,000					
85,000	**85,050**	17,516	13,619	17,929	16,104
85,050	**85,100**	17,530	13,631	17,943	16,116
85,100	**85,150**	17,544	13,644	17,957	16,129
85,150	**85,200**	17,558	13,656	17,971	16,141
85,200	**85,250**	17,572	13,669	17,985	16,154
85,250	**85,300**	17,586	13,681	17,999	16,166
85,300	**85,350**	17,600	13,694	18,013	16,179
85,350	**85,400**	17,614	13,706	18,027	16,191
85,400	**85,450**	17,628	13,719	18,041	16,204
85,450	**85,500**	17,642	13,731	18,055	16,216
85,500	**85,550**	17,656	13,744	18,069	16,229
85,550	**85,600**	17,670	13,756	18,083	16,241
85,600	**85,650**	17,684	13,769	18,097	16,254
85,650	**85,700**	17,698	13,781	18,111	16,266
85,700	**85,750**	17,712	13,794	18,125	16,279
85,750	**85,800**	17,726	13,806	18,139	16,291
85,800	**85,850**	17,740	13,819	18,153	16,304
85,850	**85,900**	17,754	13,831	18,167	16,316
85,900	**85,950**	17,768	13,844	18,181	16,329
85,950	**86,000**	17,782	13,856	18,195	16,341

* This column must also be used by a qualifying widow(er).

(Continued on next page)

2010 Tax Table—*Continued*

If line 43 (taxable income) is—		And you are—			
At least	But less than	Single	Married filing jointly *	Married filing sepa-rately	Head of a house-hold
		Your tax is—			
86,000					
86,000	**86,050**	17,796	13,869	18,209	16,354
86,050	**86,100**	17,810	13,881	18,223	16,366
86,100	**86,150**	17,824	13,894	18,237	16,379
86,150	**86,200**	17,838	13,906	18,251	16,391
86,200	**86,250**	17,852	13,919	18,265	16,404
86,250	**86,300**	17,866	13,931	18,279	16,416
86,300	**86,350**	17,880	13,944	18,293	16,429
86,350	**86,400**	17,894	13,956	18,307	16,441
86,400	**86,450**	17,908	13,969	18,321	16,454
86,450	**86,500**	17,922	13,981	18,335	16,466
86,500	**86,550**	17,936	13,994	18,349	16,479
86,550	**86,600**	17,950	14,006	18,363	16,491
86,600	**86,650**	17,964	14,019	18,377	16,504
86,650	**86,700**	17,978	14,031	18,391	16,516
86,700	**86,750**	17,992	14,044	18,405	16,529
86,750	**86,800**	18,006	14,056	18,419	16,541
86,800	**86,850**	18,020	14,069	18,433	16,554
86,850	**86,900**	18,034	14,081	18,447	16,566
86,900	**86,950**	18,048	14,094	18,461	16,579
86,950	**87,000**	18,062	14,106	18,475	16,591
87,000					
87,000	**87,050**	18,076	14,119	18,489	16,604
87,050	**87,100**	18,090	14,131	18,503	16,616
87,100	**87,150**	18,104	14,144	18,517	16,629
87,150	**87,200**	18,118	14,156	18,531	16,641
87,200	**87,250**	18,132	14,169	18,545	16,654
87,250	**87,300**	18,146	14,181	18,559	16,666
87,300	**87,350**	18,160	14,194	18,573	16,679
87,350	**87,400**	18,174	14,206	18,587	16,691
87,400	**87,450**	18,188	14,219	18,601	16,704
87,450	**87,500**	18,202	14,231	18,615	16,716
87,500	**87,550**	18,216	14,244	18,629	16,729
87,550	**87,600**	18,230	14,256	18,643	16,741
87,600	**87,650**	18,244	14,269	18,657	16,754
87,650	**87,700**	18,258	14,281	18,671	16,766
87,700	**87,750**	18,272	14,294	18,685	16,779
87,750	**87,800**	18,286	14,306	18,699	16,791
87,800	**87,850**	18,300	14,319	18,713	16,804
87,850	**87,900**	18,314	14,331	18,727	16,816
87,900	**87,950**	18,328	14,344	18,741	16,829
87,950	**88,000**	18,342	14,356	18,755	16,841
88,000					
88,000	**88,050**	18,356	14,369	18,769	16,854
88,050	**88,100**	18,370	14,381	18,783	16,866
88,100	**88,150**	18,384	14,394	18,797	16,879
88,150	**88,200**	18,398	14,406	18,811	16,891
88,200	**88,250**	18,412	14,419	18,825	16,904
88,250	**88,300**	18,426	14,431	18,839	16,916
88,300	**88,350**	18,440	14,444	18,853	16,929
88,350	**88,400**	18,454	14,456	18,867	16,941
88,400	**88,450**	18,468	14,469	18,881	16,954
88,450	**88,500**	18,482	14,481	18,895	16,966
88,500	**88,550**	18,496	14,494	18,909	16,979
88,550	**88,600**	18,510	14,506	18,923	16,991
88,600	**88,650**	18,524	14,519	18,937	17,004
88,650	**88,700**	18,538	14,531	18,951	17,016
88,700	**88,750**	18,552	14,544	18,965	17,029
88,750	**88,800**	18,566	14,556	18,979	17,041
88,800	**88,850**	18,580	14,569	18,993	17,054
88,850	**88,900**	18,594	14,581	19,007	17,066
88,900	**88,950**	18,608	14,594	19,021	17,079
88,950	**89,000**	18,622	14,606	19,035	17,091

If line 43 (taxable income) is—		And you are—			
At least	But less than	Single	Married filing jointly *	Married filing sepa-rately	Head of a house-hold
		Your tax is—			
89,000					
89,000	**89,050**	18,636	14,619	19,049	17,104
89,050	**89,100**	18,650	14,631	19,063	17,116
89,100	**89,150**	18,664	14,644	19,077	17,129
89,150	**89,200**	18,678	14,656	19,091	17,141
89,200	**89,250**	18,692	14,669	19,105	17,154
89,250	**89,300**	18,706	14,681	19,119	17,166
89,300	**89,350**	18,720	14,694	19,133	17,179
89,350	**89,400**	18,734	14,706	19,147	17,191
89,400	**89,450**	18,748	14,719	19,161	17,204
89,450	**89,500**	18,762	14,731	19,175	17,216
89,500	**89,550**	18,776	14,744	19,189	17,229
89,550	**89,600**	18,790	14,756	19,203	17,241
89,600	**89,650**	18,804	14,769	19,217	17,254
89,650	**89,700**	18,818	14,781	19,231	17,266
89,700	**89,750**	18,832	14,794	19,245	17,279
89,750	**89,800**	18,846	14,806	19,259	17,291
89,800	**89,850**	18,860	14,819	19,273	17,304
89,850	**89,900**	18,874	14,831	19,287	17,316
89,900	**89,950**	18,888	14,844	19,301	17,329
89,950	**90,000**	18,902	14,856	19,315	17,341
90,000					
90,000	**90,050**	18,916	14,869	19,329	17,354
90,050	**90,100**	18,930	14,881	19,343	17,366
90,100	**90,150**	18,944	14,894	19,357	17,379
90,150	**90,200**	18,958	14,906	19,371	17,391
90,200	**90,250**	18,972	14,919	19,385	17,404
90,250	**90,300**	18,986	14,931	19,399	17,416
90,300	**90,350**	19,000	14,944	19,413	17,429
90,350	**90,400**	19,014	14,956	19,427	17,441
90,400	**90,450**	19,028	14,969	19,441	17,454
90,450	**90,500**	19,042	14,981	19,455	17,466
90,500	**90,550**	19,056	14,994	19,469	17,479
90,550	**90,600**	19,070	15,006	19,483	17,491
90,600	**90,650**	19,084	15,019	19,497	17,504
90,650	**90,700**	19,098	15,031	19,511	17,516
90,700	**90,750**	19,112	15,044	19,525	17,529
90,750	**90,800**	19,126	15,056	19,539	17,541
90,800	**90,850**	19,140	15,069	19,553	17,554
90,850	**90,900**	19,154	15,081	19,567	17,566
90,900	**90,950**	19,168	15,094	19,581	17,579
90,950	**91,000**	19,182	15,106	19,595	17,591
91,000					
91,000	**91,050**	19,196	15,119	19,609	17,604
91,050	**91,100**	19,210	15,131	19,623	17,616
91,100	**91,150**	19,224	15,144	19,637	17,629
91,150	**91,200**	19,238	15,156	19,651	17,641
91,200	**91,250**	19,252	15,169	19,665	17,654
91,250	**91,300**	19,266	15,181	19,679	17,666
91,300	**91,350**	19,280	15,194	19,693	17,679
91,350	**91,400**	19,294	15,206	19,707	17,691
91,400	**91,450**	19,308	15,219	19,721	17,704
91,450	**91,500**	19,322	15,231	19,735	17,716
91,500	**91,550**	19,336	15,244	19,749	17,729
91,550	**91,600**	19,350	15,256	19,763	17,741
91,600	**91,650**	19,364	15,269	19,777	17,754
91,650	**91,700**	19,378	15,281	19,791	17,766
91,700	**91,750**	19,392	15,294	19,805	17,779
91,750	**91,800**	19,406	15,306	19,819	17,791
91,800	**91,850**	19,420	15,319	19,833	17,804
91,850	**91,900**	19,434	15,331	19,847	17,816
91,900	**91,950**	19,448	15,344	19,861	17,829
91,950	**92,000**	19,462	15,356	19,875	17,841

If line 43 (taxable income) is—		And you are—			
At least	But less than	Single	Married filing jointly *	Married filing sepa-rately	Head of a house-hold
		Your tax is—			
92,000					
92,000	**92,050**	19,476	15,369	19,889	17,854
92,050	**92,100**	19,490	15,381	19,903	17,866
92,100	**92,150**	19,504	15,394	19,917	17,879
92,150	**92,200**	19,518	15,406	19,931	17,891
92,200	**92,250**	19,532	15,419	19,945	17,904
92,250	**92,300**	19,546	15,431	19,959	17,916
92,300	**92,350**	19,560	15,444	19,973	17,929
92,350	**92,400**	19,574	15,456	19,987	17,941
92,400	**92,450**	19,588	15,469	20,001	17,954
92,450	**92,500**	19,602	15,481	20,015	17,966
92,500	**92,550**	19,616	15,494	20,029	17,979
92,550	**92,600**	19,630	15,506	20,043	17,991
92,600	**92,650**	19,644	15,519	20,057	18,004
92,650	**92,700**	19,658	15,531	20,071	18,016
92,700	**92,750**	19,672	15,544	20,085	18,029
92,750	**92,800**	19,686	15,556	20,099	18,041
92,800	**92,850**	19,700	15,569	20,113	18,054
92,850	**92,900**	19,714	15,581	20,127	18,066
92,900	**92,950**	19,728	15,594	20,141	18,079
92,950	**93,000**	19,742	15,606	20,155	18,091
93,000					
93,000	**93,050**	19,756	15,619	20,169	18,104
93,050	**93,100**	19,770	15,631	20,183	18,116
93,100	**93,150**	19,784	15,644	20,197	18,129
93,150	**93,200**	19,798	15,656	20,211	18,141
93,200	**93,250**	19,812	15,669	20,225	18,154
93,250	**93,300**	19,826	15,681	20,239	18,166
93,300	**93,350**	19,840	15,694	20,253	18,179
93,350	**93,400**	19,854	15,706	20,267	18,191
93,400	**93,450**	19,868	15,719	20,281	18,204
93,450	**93,500**	19,882	15,731	20,295	18,216
93,500	**93,550**	19,896	15,744	20,309	18,229
93,550	**93,600**	19,910	15,756	20,323	18,241
93,600	**93,650**	19,924	15,769	20,337	18,254
93,650	**93,700**	19,938	15,781	20,351	18,266
93,700	**93,750**	19,952	15,794	20,365	18,279
93,750	**93,800**	19,966	15,806	20,379	18,291
93,800	**93,850**	19,980	15,819	20,393	18,304
93,850	**93,900**	19,994	15,831	20,407	18,316
93,900	**93,950**	20,008	15,844	20,421	18,329
93,950	**94,000**	20,022	15,856	20,435	18,341
94,000					
94,000	**94,050**	20,036	15,869	20,449	18,354
94,050	**94,100**	20,050	15,881	20,463	18,366
94,100	**94,150**	20,064	15,894	20,477	18,379
94,150	**94,200**	20,078	15,906	20,491	18,391
94,200	**94,250**	20,092	15,919	20,505	18,404
94,250	**94,300**	20,106	15,931	20,519	18,416
94,300	**94,350**	20,120	15,944	20,533	18,429
94,350	**94,400**	20,134	15,956	20,547	18,441
94,400	**94,450**	20,148	15,969	20,561	18,454
94,450	**94,500**	20,162	15,981	20,575	18,466
94,500	**94,550**	20,176	15,994	20,589	18,479
94,550	**94,600**	20,190	16,006	20,603	18,491
94,600	**94,650**	20,204	16,019	20,617	18,504
94,650	**94,700**	20,218	16,031	20,631	18,516
94,700	**94,750**	20,232	16,044	20,645	18,529
94,750	**94,800**	20,246	16,056	20,659	18,541
94,800	**94,850**	20,260	16,069	20,673	18,554
94,850	**94,900**	20,274	16,081	20,687	18,566
94,900	**94,950**	20,288	16,094	20,701	18,579
94,950	**95,000**	20,302	16,106	20,715	18,591

* This column must also be used by a qualifying widow(er).

(Continued on next page)

2010 Tax Table–*Continued*

If line 43 (taxable income) is—		And you are—			
At least	But less than	Single	Married filing jointly *	Married filing sepa-rately	Head of a house-hold
		Your tax is—			
95,000					
95,000	**95,050**	20,316	16,119	20,729	18,604
95,050	**95,100**	20,330	16,131	20,743	18,616
95,100	**95,150**	20,344	16,144	20,757	18,629
95,150	**95,200**	20,358	16,156	20,771	18,641
95,200	**95,250**	20,372	16,169	20,785	18,654
95,250	**95,300**	20,386	16,181	20,799	18,666
95,300	**95,350**	20,400	16,194	20,813	18,679
95,350	**95,400**	20,414	16,206	20,827	18,691
95,400	**95,450**	20,428	16,219	20,841	18,704
95,450	**95,500**	20,442	16,231	20,855	18,716
95,500	**95,550**	20,456	16,244	20,869	18,729
95,550	**95,600**	20,470	16,256	20,883	18,741
95,600	**95,650**	20,484	16,269	20,897	18,754
95,650	**95,700**	20,498	16,281	20,911	18,766
95,700	**95,750**	20,512	16,294	20,925	18,779
95,750	**95,800**	20,526	16,306	20,939	18,791
95,800	**95,850**	20,540	16,319	20,953	18,804
95,850	**95,900**	20,554	16,331	20,967	18,816
95,900	**95,950**	20,568	16,344	20,981	18,829
95,950	**96,000**	20,582	16,356	20,995	18,841
96,000					
96,000	**96,050**	20,596	16,369	21,009	18,854
96,050	**96,100**	20,610	16,381	21,023	18,866
96,100	**96,150**	20,624	16,394	21,037	18,879
96,150	**96,200**	20,638	16,406	21,051	18,891
96,200	**96,250**	20,652	16,419	21,065	18,904
96,250	**96,300**	20,666	16,431	21,079	18,916
96,300	**96,350**	20,680	16,444	21,093	18,929
96,350	**96,400**	20,694	16,456	21,107	18,941
96,400	**96,450**	20,708	16,469	21,121	18,954
96,450	**96,500**	20,722	16,481	21,135	18,966
96,500	**96,550**	20,736	16,494	21,149	18,979
96,550	**96,600**	20,750	16,506	21,163	18,991
96,600	**96,650**	20,764	16,519	21,177	19,004
96,650	**96,700**	20,778	16,531	21,191	19,016
96,700	**96,750**	20,792	16,544	21,205	19,029
96,750	**96,800**	20,806	16,556	21,219	19,041
96,800	**96,850**	20,820	16,569	21,233	19,054
96,850	**96,900**	20,834	16,581	21,247	19,066
96,900	**96,950**	20,848	16,594	21,261	19,079
96,950	**97,000**	20,862	16,606	21,275	19,091
97,000					
97,000	**97,050**	20,876	16,619	21,289	19,104
97,050	**97,100**	20,890	16,631	21,303	19,116
97,100	**97,150**	20,904	16,644	21,317	19,129
97,150	**97,200**	20,918	16,656	21,331	19,141
97,200	**97,250**	20,932	16,669	21,345	19,154
97,250	**97,300**	20,946	16,681	21,359	19,166
97,300	**97,350**	20,960	16,694	21,373	19,179
97,350	**97,400**	20,974	16,706	21,387	19,191
97,400	**97,450**	20,988	16,719	21,401	19,204
97,450	**97,500**	21,002	16,731	21,415	19,216
97,500	**97,550**	21,016	16,744	21,429	19,229
97,550	**97,600**	21,030	16,756	21,443	19,241
97,600	**97,650**	21,044	16,769	21,457	19,254
97,650	**97,700**	21,058	16,781	21,471	19,266
97,700	**97,750**	21,072	16,794	21,485	19,279
97,750	**97,800**	21,086	16,806	21,499	19,291
97,800	**97,850**	21,100	16,819	21,513	19,304
97,850	**97,900**	21,114	16,831	21,527	19,316
97,900	**97,950**	21,128	16,844	21,541	19,329
97,950	**98,000**	21,142	16,856	21,555	19,341
98,000					
98,000	**98,050**	21,156	16,869	21,569	19,354
98,050	**98,100**	21,170	16,881	21,583	19,366
98,100	**98,150**	21,184	16,894	21,597	19,379
98,150	**98,200**	21,198	16,906	21,611	19,391
98,200	**98,250**	21,212	16,919	21,625	19,404
98,250	**98,300**	21,226	16,931	21,639	19,416
98,300	**98,350**	21,240	16,944	21,653	19,429
98,350	**98,400**	21,254	16,956	21,667	19,441
98,400	**98,450**	21,268	16,969	21,681	19,454
98,450	**98,500**	21,282	16,981	21,695	19,466
98,500	**98,550**	21,296	16,994	21,709	19,479
98,550	**98,600**	21,310	17,006	21,723	19,491
98,600	**98,650**	21,324	17,019	21,737	19,504
98,650	**98,700**	21,338	17,031	21,751	19,516
98,700	**98,750**	21,352	17,044	21,765	19,529
98,750	**98,800**	21,366	17,056	21,779	19,541
98,800	**98,850**	21,380	17,069	21,793	19,554
98,850	**98,900**	21,394	17,081	21,807	19,566
98,900	**98,950**	21,408	17,094	21,821	19,579
98,950	**99,000**	21,422	17,106	21,835	19,591
99,000					
99,000	**99,050**	21,436	17,119	21,849	19,604
99,050	**99,100**	21,450	17,131	21,863	19,616
99,100	**99,150**	21,464	17,144	21,877	19,629
99,150	**99,200**	21,478	17,156	21,891	19,641
99,200	**99,250**	21,492	17,169	21,905	19,654
99,250	**99,300**	21,506	17,181	21,919	19,666
99,300	**99,350**	21,520	17,194	21,933	19,679
99,350	**99,400**	21,534	17,206	21,947	19,691
99,400	**99,450**	21,548	17,219	21,961	19,704
99,450	**99,500**	21,562	17,231	21,975	19,716
99,500	**99,550**	21,576	17,244	21,989	19,729
99,550	**99,600**	21,590	17,256	22,003	19,741
99,600	**99,650**	21,604	17,269	22,017	19,754
99,650	**99,700**	21,618	17,281	22,031	19,766
99,700	**99,750**	21,632	17,294	22,045	19,779
99,750	**99,800**	21,646	17,306	22,059	19,791
99,800	**99,850**	21,660	17,319	22,073	19,804
99,850	**99,900**	21,674	17,331	22,087	19,816
99,900	**99,950**	21,688	17,344	22,101	19,829
99,950	**100,000**	21,702	17,356	22,115	19,841

$100,000 or over — use the Tax Computation Worksheet

* This column must also be used by a qualifying widow(er)

2010 Tax Computation Worksheet—Line 44

CAUTION *See the instructions for line 44 on page 35 to see if you must use the worksheet below to figure your tax.*

Note. If you are required to use this worksheet to figure the tax on an amount from another form or worksheet, such as the Qualified Dividends and Capital Gain Tax Worksheet, the Schedule D Tax Worksheet, Schedule J, Form 8615, or the Foreign Earned Income Tax Worksheet, enter the amount from that form or worksheet in column (a) of the row that applies to the amount you are looking up. Enter the result on the appropriate line of the form or worksheet that you are completing.

Section A—Use if your filing status is **Single.** Complete the row below that applies to you.

Taxable income. If line 43 is—	**(a)** Enter the amount from line 43	**(b)** Multiplication amount	**(c)** Multiply (a) by (b)	**(d)** Subtraction amount	**Tax.** Subtract (d) from (c). Enter the result here and on Form 1040, line 44
At least $100,000 but not over $171,850	$	× 28% (.28)	$	$ 6,290.75	$
Over $171,850 but not over $373,650	$	× 33% (.33)	$	$ 14,883.25	$
Over $373,650	$	× 35% (.35)	$	$22,356.25	$

Section B—Use if your filing status is **Married filing jointly** or **Qualifying widow(er).** Complete the row below that applies to you.

Taxable income. If line 43 is—	**(a)** Enter the amount from line 43	**(b)** Multiplication amount	**(c)** Multiply (a) by (b)	**(d)** Subtraction amount	**Tax.** Subtract (d) from (c). Enter the result here and on Form 1040, line 44
At least $100,000 but not over $137,300	$	× 25% (.25)	$	$ 7,637.50	$
Over $137,300 but not over $209,250	$	× 28% (.28)	$	$ 11,756.50	$
Over $209,250 but not over $373,650	$	× 33% (.33)	$	$ 22,219.00	$
Over $373,650	$	× 35% (.35)	$	$ 29,692.00	$

Section C—Use if your filing status is **Married filing separately.** Complete the row below that applies to you.

Taxable income. If line 43 is—	**(a)** Enter the amount from line 43	**(b)** Multiplication amount	**(c)** Multiply (a) by (b)	**(d)** Subtraction amount	**Tax.** Subtract (d) from (c). Enter the result here and on Form 1040, line 44
At least $100,000 but not over $104,625	$	× 28% (.28)	$	$ 5,878.25	$
Over $104,625 but not over $186,825	$	× 33% (.33)	$	$ 11,109.50	$
Over $186,825	$	× 35% (.35)	$	$ 14,846.00	$

Section D—Use if your filing status is **Head of household.** Complete the row below that applies to you.

Taxable income. If line 43 is—	**(a)** Enter the amount from line 43	**(b)** Multiplication amount	**(c)** Multiply (a) by (b)	**(d)** Subtraction amount	**Tax.** Subtract (d) from (c). Enter the result here and on Form 1040, line 44
At least $100,000 but not over $117,650	$	× 25% (.25)	$	$ 5,152.50	$
Over $117,650 but not over $190,550	$	× 28% (.28)	$	$ 8,682.00	$
Over $190,550 but not over $373,650	$	× 33% (.33)	$	$ 18,209.50	$
Over $373,650	$	× 35% (.35)	$	$ 25,682.50	$

IRA Deduction Worksheet—Line 32

Keep for Your Records

If you were age 70½ or older at the end of 2010, you cannot deduct any contributions made to your traditional IRA or treat them as nondeductible contributions. ***Do not*** *complete this worksheet for anyone age 70½ or older at the end of 2010. If you are married filing jointly and only one spouse was under age 70½ at the end of 2010, complete this worksheet only for that spouse.*

Before you begin:

√ Be sure you have read the list on page 29. You may not be eligible to use this worksheet.

√ Figure any write-in adjustments to be entered on the dotted line next to line 36 (see the instructions for line 36 on page 33).

√ If you are married filing separately and you lived apart from your spouse for all of 2010, enter "D" on the dotted line next to Form 1040, line 32. If you do not, you may get a math error notice from the IRS.

		Your IRA	Spouse's IRA
1a.	Were you covered by a retirement plan (see page 29)?	**1a.** ☐ Yes ☐ No	
b.	If married filing jointly, was your spouse covered by a retirement plan?		**1b.** ☐ Yes ☐ No
	Next. If you checked "No" on line 1a (and "No" on line 1b if married filing jointly), skip lines 2 through 6, enter the applicable amount below on line 7a (and line 7b if applicable), and go to line 8. • $5,000, if under age 50 at the end of 2010. • $6,000, if age 50 or older but under age 70½ at the end of 2010. Otherwise, go to line 2.		
2.	Enter the amount shown below that applies to you. • Single, head of household, or married filing separately and you **lived apart** from your spouse for all of 2010, enter $66,000 • Qualifying widow(er), enter $109,000 • Married filing jointly, enter $109,000 in both columns. But if you checked "No" on either line 1a or 1b, enter $177,000 for the person who was not covered by a plan • Married filing separately and you lived with your spouse at any time in 2010, enter $10,000	**2a.** ________	**2b.** ________
3.	Enter the amount from Form 1040, line 22 . . . . **3.** ________		
4.	Enter the total of the amounts from Form 1040, lines 23 through 31a, plus any write-in adjustments you entered on the dotted line next to line 36 . . . . **4.** ________		
5.	Subtract line 4 from line 3. If married filing jointly, enter the result in both columns	**5a.** ________	**5b.** ________
6.	Is the amount on line 5 less than the amount on line 2? ☐ **No.** STOP None of your IRA contributions are deductible. For details on nondeductible IRA contributions, see Form 8606. ☐ **Yes.** Subtract line 5 from line 2 in each column. Follow the instruction below that applies to you. • If single, head of household, or married filing separately, and the result is $10,000 or more, enter the applicable amount below on line 7 for that column and go to line 8. **i.** $5,000, if under age 50 at the end of 2010. **ii.** $6,000, if age 50 or older but under age 70½ at the end of 2010. Otherwise, go to line 7. • If married filing jointly or qualifying widow(er), and the result is $20,000 or more ($10,000 or more in the column for the IRA of a person who was not covered by a retirement plan), enter the applicable amount below on line 7 for that column and go to line 8. **i.** $5,000, if under age 50 at the end of 2010. **ii.** $6,000 if age 50 or older but under age 70½ at the end of 2010. Otherwise, go to line 7.	**6a.** ________	**6b.** ________

IRA Deduction Worksheet—*Continued from page 30*

		Your IRA	Spouse's IRA
7.	Multiply lines 6a and 6b by the percentage below that applies to you. If the result is not a multiple of $10, increase it to the next multiple of $10 (for example, increase $490.30 to $500). If the result is $200 or more, enter the result. But if it is less than $200, enter $200. • Single, head of household, or married filing separately, multiply by 50% (.50) (or by 60% (.60) in the column for the IRA of a person who is age 50 or older at the end of 2010) • Married filing jointly or qualifying widow(er), multiply by 25% (.25) (or by 30% (.30) in the column for the IRA of a person who is age 50 or older at the end of 2010). But if you checked "No" on either line 1a or 1b, then in the column for the IRA of the person who was not covered by a retirement plan, multiply by 50% (.50) (or by 60% (.60) if age 50 or older at the end of 2010)	**7a.**	**7b.**
8.	Enter the total of your (and your spouse's if filing jointly): • Wages, salaries, tips, etc. Generally, this is the amount reported in box 1 of Form W-2. See page 29 for exceptions • Alimony and separate maintenance payments reported on Form 1040, line 11 • Nontaxable combat pay. This amount should be reported in box 12 of Form W-2 with code Q **8.**		
9.	Enter the earned income you (and your spouse if filing jointly) received as a self-employed individual or a partner. Generally, this is your (and your spouse's if filing jointly) net earnings from self-employment if your personal services were a material income-producing factor, minus any deductions on Form 1040, lines 27 and 28. If zero or less, enter -0-. For more details, see Pub. 590 . . . . **9.**		
10.	Add lines 8 and 9 . . . . **10.**		
	CAUTION *If married filing jointly and line 10 is less than $10,000 ($11,000 if one spouse is age 50 or older at the end of 2010; $12,000 if both spouses are age 50 or older at the end of 2010),* ***stop here*** *and see Pub. 590 to figure your IRA deduction.*		
11.	Enter traditional IRA contributions made, or that will be made by April 18, 2011, for 2010 to your IRA on line 11a and to your spouse's IRA on line 11b	**11a.**	**11b.**
12.	On line 12a, enter the **smallest** of line 7a, 10, or 11a. On line 12b, enter the **smallest** of line 7b, 10, or 11b. This is the most you can deduct. Add the amounts on lines 12a and 12b and enter the total on Form 1040, line 32. Or, if you want, you can deduct a smaller amount and treat the rest as a nondeductible contribution (see Form 8606)	**12a.**	**12b.**

Worksheet A—Earned Income Credit (EIC)—Lines 64a and 64b

Keep for Your Records

Before you begin: √ Be sure you are using the correct worksheet. Use this worksheet only if you answered "No" to Step 5, question 3, on page 50. Otherwise, use Worksheet B that begins on page 53.

Part 1

All Filers Using Worksheet A

1. Enter your earned income from Step 5 on page 50. [1]

2. Look up the amount on line 1 above in the EIC Table on pages 55–71 to find the credit. Be sure you use the correct column for your filing status and the number of children you have. Enter the credit here. [2]

   If line 2 is zero, STOP You cannot take the credit. Enter "No" on the dotted line next to line 64a.

3. Enter the amount from Form 1040, line 38. [3]

4. Are the amounts on lines 3 and 1 the same?

   ☐ **Yes.** Skip line 5; enter the amount from line 2 on line 6.

   ☐ **No.** Go to line 5.

Part 2

Filers Who Answered "No" on Line 4

5. If you have:
   - No qualifying children, is the amount on line 3 less than $7,500 ($12,500 if married filing jointly)?
   - 1 or more qualifying children, is the amount on line 3 less than $16,450 ($21,500 if married filing jointly)?

   ☐ **Yes.** Leave line 5 blank; enter the amount from line 2 on line 6.

   ☐ **No.** Look up the amount on line 3 in the EIC Table on pages 55–71 to find the credit. Be sure you use the correct column for your filing status and the number of children you have. Enter the credit here. [5]

   Look at the amounts on lines 5 and 2. Then, enter the **smaller** amount on line 6.

Part 3

Your Earned Income Credit

6. **This is your earned income credit.** [6]

   Enter this amount on Form 1040, line 64a.

Reminder—

√ If you have a qualifying child, complete and attach Schedule EIC.

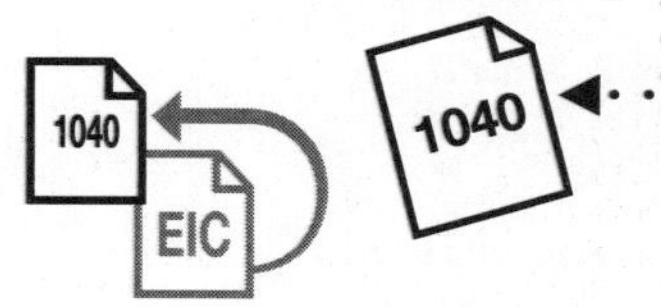

CAUTION *If your EIC for a year after 1996 was reduced or disallowed, see page 50 to find out if you must file Form 8862 to take the credit for 2010.*

Worksheet B—Earned Income Credit (EIC)—Lines 64a and 64b

Keep for Your Records

Use this worksheet if you answered "Yes" to Step 5, question 3, on page 50.

√ Complete the parts below (Parts 1 through 3) that apply to you. Then, continue to Part 4.

√ If you are married filing a joint return, include your spouse's amounts, if any, with yours to figure the amounts to enter in Parts 1 through 3.

Part 1

Self-Employed, Members of the Clergy, and People With Church Employee Income Filing Schedule SE

1a.	Enter the amount from Schedule SE, Section A, line 3, or Section B, line 3, whichever applies.		1a
b.	Enter any amount from Schedule SE, Section B, line 4b, and line 5a.	+	1b
c.	Combine lines 1a and 1b.	=	1c
d.	Enter the amount from Schedule SE, Section A, line 6, or Section B, line 13, whichever applies.	−	1d
e.	Subtract line 1d from 1c.	=	1e

Part 2

Self-Employed NOT Required To File Schedule SE

For example, your net earnings from self-employment were less than $400.

2. Do not include on these lines any statutory employee income, any net profit from services performed as a notary public, any amount exempt from self-employment tax as the result of the filing and approval of Form 4029 or Form 4361, any income or loss from a qualified joint venture reporting only rental real estate income not subject to self-employment tax or any other amounts exempt from self-employment tax.

a.	Enter any net farm profit or (loss) from Schedule F, line 36, and from farm partnerships, Schedule K-1 (Form 1065), box 14, code A*.		2a
b.	Enter any net profit or (loss) from Schedule C, line 31; Schedule C-EZ, line 3; Schedule K-1 (Form 1065), box 14, code A (other than farming); and Schedule K-1 (Form 1065-B), box 9, code J1*.	+	2b
c.	Combine lines 2a and 2b.	=	2c

**Reduce any Schedule K-1 amounts by any partnership section 179 expense deduction claimed, unreimbursed partnership expenses claimed, and depletion claimed on oil and gas properties. If you have any Schedule K-1 amounts, complete the appropriate line(s) of Schedule SE, Section A. Enter your name and social security number on Schedule SE and attach it to your return.*

Part 3

Statutory Employees Filing Schedule C or C-EZ

3.	Enter the amount from Schedule C, line 1, or Schedule C-EZ, line 1, that you are filing as a statutory employee.	3

Part 4

All Filers Using Worksheet B

Note. If line 4b includes income on which you should have paid self-employment tax but did not, we may reduce your credit by the amount of self-employment tax not paid.

4a.	Enter your earned income from Step 5 on page 50.	4a
b.	Combine lines 1e, 2c, 3, and 4a. **This is your total earned income.**	4b

If line 4b is zero or less, STOP You cannot take the credit. Enter "No" on the dotted line next to line 64a.

5. If you have:

- 3 or more qualifying children, is line 4b less than $43,352 ($48,362 if married filing jointly)?
- 2 qualifying children, is line 4b less than $40,363 ($45,373 if married filing jointly)?
- 1 qualifying child, is line 4b less than $35,535 ($40,545 if married filing jointly)?
- No qualifying children, is line 4b less than $13,460 ($18,470 if married filing jointly)?

☐ **Yes.** If you want the IRS to figure your credit, see page 50. If you want to figure the credit yourself, enter the amount from line 4b on line 6 (page 54).

☐ **No.** STOP You cannot take the credit. Enter "No" on the dotted line next to line 64a.

Part 5

All Filers Using Worksheet B

6. Enter your total earned income from Part 4, line 4b, on page 53. **6** ______

7. Look up the amount on line 6 above in the EIC Table on pages 55–71 to find the credit. Be sure you use the correct column for your filing status and the number of children you have. Enter the credit here. **7** ______

If line 7 is zero, STOP You cannot take the credit. Enter "No" on the dotted line next to line 64a.

8. Enter the amount from Form 1040, line 38. **8** ______

9. Are the amounts on lines 8 and 6 the same?

☐ **Yes.** Skip line 10; enter the amount from line 7 on line 11.

☐ **No.** Go to line 10.

Part 6

Filers Who Answered "No" on Line 9

10. If you have:

- No qualifying children, is the amount on line 8 less than $7,500 ($12,500 if married filing jointly)?
- 1 or more qualifying children, is the amount on line 8 less than $16,450 ($21,500 if married filing jointly)?

☐ **Yes.** Leave line 10 blank; enter the amount from line 7 on line 11.

☐ **No.** Look up the amount on line 8 in the EIC Table on pages 55–71 to find the credit. Be sure you use the correct column for your filing status and the number of children you have. Enter the credit here. **10** ______
Look at the amounts on lines 10 and 7.
Then, enter the **smaller** amount on line 11.

Part 7

Your Earned Income Credit

11. **This is your earned income credit.** **11** ______

Enter this amount on Form 1040, line 64a.

Reminder—

√ If you have a qualifying child, complete and attach Schedule EIC.

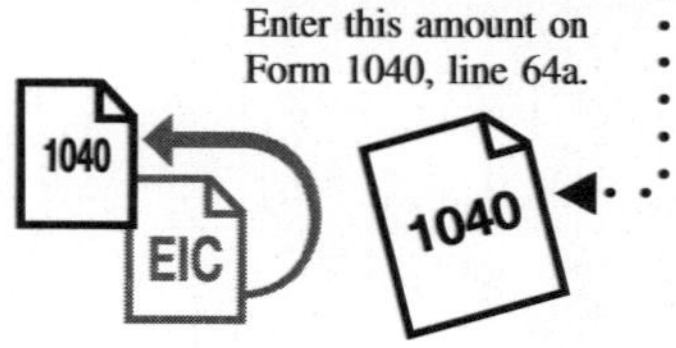

CAUTION *If your EIC for a year after 1996 was reduced or disallowed, see page 50 to find out if you must file Form 8862 to take the credit for 2010.*

2010 Earned Income Credit (EIC) Table

Caution. This is **not** a tax table.

1. To find your credit, read down the "At least - But less than" columns and find the line that includes the amount you were told to look up from your EIC Worksheet.

2. Then, go to the column that includes your filing status and the number of qualifying children you have. Enter the credit from that column on your EIC Worksheet.

Example. If your filing status is single, you have one qualifying child, and the amount you are looking up from your EIC Worksheet is $2,455, you would enter $842.

If the amount you are looking up from the worksheet is—		And your filing status is— Single, head of household, or qualifying widow(er) and you have—			
		No children	One child	Two children	Three children
At least	But less than	Your credit is—			
2,400	2,450	186	825	970	1,091
2,450	2,500	189	842	990	1,114

If the amount you are looking up from the worksheet is–		And your filing status is– Single, head of household, or qualifying widow(er) and you have–				Married filing jointly and you have–			
		No Children	One Child	Two Children	Three Children	No Children	One Child	Two Children	Three Children
At least	But less than	Your credit is–				Your credit is–			
$1	$50	$2	$9	$10	$11	$2	$9	$10	$11
50	100	6	26	30	34	6	26	30	34
100	150	10	43	50	56	10	43	50	56
150	200	13	60	70	79	13	60	70	79
200	250	17	77	90	101	17	77	90	101
250	300	21	94	110	124	21	94	110	124
300	350	25	111	130	146	25	111	130	146
350	400	29	128	150	169	29	128	150	169
400	450	33	145	170	191	33	145	170	191
450	500	36	162	190	214	36	162	190	214
500	550	40	179	210	236	40	179	210	236
550	600	44	196	230	259	44	196	230	259
600	650	48	213	250	281	48	213	250	281
650	700	52	230	270	304	52	230	270	304
700	750	55	247	290	326	55	247	290	326
750	800	59	264	310	349	59	264	310	349
800	850	63	281	330	371	63	281	330	371
850	900	67	298	350	394	67	298	350	394
900	950	71	315	370	416	71	315	370	416
950	1,000	75	332	390	439	75	332	390	439
1,000	1,050	78	349	410	461	78	349	410	461
1,050	1,100	82	366	430	484	82	366	430	484
1,100	1,150	86	383	450	506	86	383	450	506
1,150	1,200	90	400	470	529	90	400	470	529
1,200	1,250	94	417	490	551	94	417	490	551
1,250	1,300	98	434	510	574	98	434	510	574
1,300	1,350	101	451	530	596	101	451	530	596
1,350	1,400	105	468	550	619	105	468	550	619
1,400	1,450	109	485	570	641	109	485	570	641
1,450	1,500	113	502	590	664	113	502	590	664
1,500	1,550	117	519	610	686	117	519	610	686
1,550	1,600	120	536	630	709	120	536	630	709
1,600	1,650	124	553	650	731	124	553	650	731
1,650	1,700	128	570	670	754	128	570	670	754
1,700	1,750	132	587	690	776	132	587	690	776
1,750	1,800	136	604	710	799	136	604	710	799
1,800	1,850	140	621	730	821	140	621	730	821
1,850	1,900	143	638	750	844	143	638	750	844
1,900	1,950	147	655	770	866	147	655	770	866
1,950	2,000	151	672	790	889	151	672	790	889
2,000	2,050	155	689	810	911	155	689	810	911
2,050	2,100	159	706	830	934	159	706	830	934
2,100	2,150	163	723	850	956	163	723	850	956
2,150	2,200	166	740	870	979	166	740	870	979
2,200	2,250	170	757	890	1,001	170	757	890	1,001
2,250	2,300	174	774	910	1,024	174	774	910	1,024
2,300	2,350	178	791	930	1,046	178	791	930	1,046
2,350	2,400	182	808	950	1,069	182	808	950	1,069
2,400	2,450	186	825	970	1,091	186	825	970	1,091
2,450	2,500	189	842	990	1,114	189	842	990	1,114

(Continued on next page)

2010 Earned Income Credit (EIC) Table–*Continued* (**Caution.** This is **not** a tax table.)

If the amount you are looking up from the worksheet is–		And your filing status is–							
		Single, head of household, or qualifying widow(er) and you have–				Married filing jointly and you have–			
At least	But less than	No Children	One Child	Two Children	Three Children	No Children	One Child	Two Children	Three Children
		Your credit is–				Your credit is–			
2,500	**2,550**	193	859	1,010	1,136	193	859	1,010	1,136
2,550	**2,600**	197	876	1,030	1,159	197	876	1,030	1,159
2,600	**2,650**	201	893	1,050	1,181	201	893	1,050	1,181
2,650	**2,700**	205	910	1,070	1,204	205	910	1,070	1,204
2,700	**2,750**	208	927	1,090	1,226	208	927	1,090	1,226
2,750	**2,800**	212	944	1,110	1,249	212	944	1,110	1,249
2,800	**2,850**	216	961	1,130	1,271	216	961	1,130	1,271
2,850	**2,900**	220	978	1,150	1,294	220	978	1,150	1,294
2,900	**2,950**	224	995	1,170	1,316	224	995	1,170	1,316
2,950	**3,000**	228	1,012	1,190	1,339	228	1,012	1,190	1,339
3,000	**3,050**	231	1,029	1,210	1,361	231	1,029	1,210	1,361
3,050	**3,100**	235	1,046	1,230	1,384	235	1,046	1,230	1,384
3,100	**3,150**	239	1,063	1,250	1,406	239	1,063	1,250	1,406
3,150	**3,200**	243	1,080	1,270	1,429	243	1,080	1,270	1,429
3,200	**3,250**	247	1,097	1,290	1,451	247	1,097	1,290	1,451
3,250	**3,300**	251	1,114	1,310	1,474	251	1,114	1,310	1,474
3,300	**3,350**	254	1,131	1,330	1,496	254	1,131	1,330	1,496
3,350	**3,400**	258	1,148	1,350	1,519	258	1,148	1,350	1,519
3,400	**3,450**	262	1,165	1,370	1,541	262	1,165	1,370	1,541
3,450	**3,500**	266	1,182	1,390	1,564	266	1,182	1,390	1,564
3,500	**3,550**	270	1,199	1,410	1,586	270	1,199	1,410	1,586
3,550	**3,600**	273	1,216	1,430	1,609	273	1,216	1,430	1,609
3,600	**3,650**	277	1,233	1,450	1,631	277	1,233	1,450	1,631
3,650	**3,700**	281	1,250	1,470	1,654	281	1,250	1,470	1,654
3,700	**3,750**	285	1,267	1,490	1,676	285	1,267	1,490	1,676
3,750	**3,800**	289	1,284	1,510	1,699	289	1,284	1,510	1,699
3,800	**3,850**	293	1,301	1,530	1,721	293	1,301	1,530	1,721
3,850	**3,900**	296	1,318	1,550	1,744	296	1,318	1,550	1,744
3,900	**3,950**	300	1,335	1,570	1,766	300	1,335	1,570	1,766
3,950	**4,000**	304	1,352	1,590	1,789	304	1,352	1,590	1,789
4,000	**4,050**	308	1,369	1,610	1,811	308	1,369	1,610	1,811
4,050	**4,100**	312	1,386	1,630	1,834	312	1,386	1,630	1,834
4,100	**4,150**	316	1,403	1,650	1,856	316	1,403	1,650	1,856
4,150	**4,200**	319	1,420	1,670	1,879	319	1,420	1,670	1,879
4,200	**4,250**	323	1,437	1,690	1,901	323	1,437	1,690	1,901
4,250	**4,300**	327	1,454	1,710	1,924	327	1,454	1,710	1,924
4,300	**4,350**	331	1,471	1,730	1,946	331	1,471	1,730	1,946
4,350	**4,400**	335	1,488	1,750	1,969	335	1,488	1,750	1,969
4,400	**4,450**	339	1,505	1,770	1,991	339	1,505	1,770	1,991
4,450	**4,500**	342	1,522	1,790	2,014	342	1,522	1,790	2,014
4,500	**4,550**	346	1,539	1,810	2,036	346	1,539	1,810	2,036
4,550	**4,600**	350	1,556	1,830	2,059	350	1,556	1,830	2,059
4,600	**4,650**	354	1,573	1,850	2,081	354	1,573	1,850	2,081
4,650	**4,700**	358	1,590	1,870	2,104	358	1,590	1,870	2,104
4,700	**4,750**	361	1,607	1,890	2,126	361	1,607	1,890	2,126
4,750	**4,800**	365	1,624	1,910	2,149	365	1,624	1,910	2,149
4,800	**4,850**	369	1,641	1,930	2,171	369	1,641	1,930	2,171
4,850	**4,900**	373	1,658	1,950	2,194	373	1,658	1,950	2,194
4,900	**4,950**	377	1,675	1,970	2,216	377	1,675	1,970	2,216
4,950	**5,000**	381	1,692	1,990	2,239	381	1,692	1,990	2,239
5,000	**5,050**	384	1,709	2,010	2,261	384	1,709	2,010	2,261
5,050	**5,100**	388	1,726	2,030	2,284	388	1,726	2,030	2,284
5,100	**5,150**	392	1,743	2,050	2,306	392	1,743	2,050	2,306
5,150	**5,200**	396	1,760	2,070	2,329	396	1,760	2,070	2,329
5,200	**5,250**	400	1,777	2,090	2,351	400	1,777	2,090	2,351
5,250	**5,300**	404	1,794	2,110	2,374	404	1,794	2,110	2,374
5,300	**5,350**	407	1,811	2,130	2,396	407	1,811	2,130	2,396
5,350	**5,400**	411	1,828	2,150	2,419	411	1,828	2,150	2,419
5,400	**5,450**	415	1,845	2,170	2,441	415	1,845	2,170	2,441
5,450	**5,500**	419	1,862	2,190	2,464	419	1,862	2,190	2,464

(Continued on next page)

2010 Earned Income Credit (EIC) Table—*Continued* (**Caution.** This is **not** a tax table.)

If the amount you are looking up from the worksheet is—		And your filing status is— Single, head of household, or qualifying widow(er) and you have—				Married filing jointly and you have—			
At least	But less than	No Children	One Child	Two Children	Three Children	No Children	One Child	Two Children	Three Children
		Your credit is—				Your credit is—			
5,500	5,550	423	1,879	2,210	2,486	423	1,879	2,210	2,486
5,550	5,600	426	1,896	2,230	2,509	426	1,896	2,230	2,509
5,600	5,650	430	1,913	2,250	2,531	430	1,913	2,250	2,531
5,650	5,700	434	1,930	2,270	2,554	434	1,930	2,270	2,554
5,700	5,750	438	1,947	2,290	2,576	438	1,947	2,290	2,576
5,750	5,800	442	1,964	2,310	2,599	442	1,964	2,310	2,599
5,800	5,850	446	1,981	2,330	2,621	446	1,981	2,330	2,621
5,850	5,900	449	1,998	2,350	2,644	449	1,998	2,350	2,644
5,900	5,950	453	2,015	2,370	2,666	453	2,015	2,370	2,666
5,950	6,000	457	2,032	2,390	2,689	457	2,032	2,390	2,689
6,000	6,050	457	2,049	2,410	2,711	457	2,049	2,410	2,711
6,050	6,100	457	2,066	2,430	2,734	457	2,066	2,430	2,734
6,100	6,150	457	2,083	2,450	2,756	457	2,083	2,450	2,756
6,150	6,200	457	2,100	2,470	2,779	457	2,100	2,470	2,779
6,200	6,250	457	2,117	2,490	2,801	457	2,117	2,490	2,801
6,250	6,300	457	2,134	2,510	2,824	457	2,134	2,510	2,824
6,300	6,350	457	2,151	2,530	2,846	457	2,151	2,530	2,846
6,350	6,400	457	2,168	2,550	2,869	457	2,168	2,550	2,869
6,400	6,450	457	2,185	2,570	2,891	457	2,185	2,570	2,891
6,450	6,500	457	2,202	2,590	2,914	457	2,202	2,590	2,914
6,500	6,550	457	2,219	2,610	2,936	457	2,219	2,610	2,936
6,550	6,600	457	2,236	2,630	2,959	457	2,236	2,630	2,959
6,600	6,650	457	2,253	2,650	2,981	457	2,253	2,650	2,981
6,650	6,700	457	2,270	2,670	3,004	457	2,270	2,670	3,004
6,700	6,750	457	2,287	2,690	3,026	457	2,287	2,690	3,026
6,750	6,800	457	2,304	2,710	3,049	457	2,304	2,710	3,049
6,800	6,850	457	2,321	2,730	3,071	457	2,321	2,730	3,071
6,850	6,900	457	2,338	2,750	3,094	457	2,338	2,750	3,094
6,900	6,950	457	2,355	2,770	3,116	457	2,355	2,770	3,116
6,950	7,000	457	2,372	2,790	3,139	457	2,372	2,790	3,139
7,000	7,050	457	2,389	2,810	3,161	457	2,389	2,810	3,161
7,050	7,100	457	2,406	2,830	3,184	457	2,406	2,830	3,184
7,100	7,150	457	2,423	2,850	3,206	457	2,423	2,850	3,206
7,150	7,200	457	2,440	2,870	3,229	457	2,440	2,870	3,229
7,200	7,250	457	2,457	2,890	3,251	457	2,457	2,890	3,251
7,250	7,300	457	2,474	2,910	3,274	457	2,474	2,910	3,274
7,300	7,350	457	2,491	2,930	3,296	457	2,491	2,930	3,296
7,350	7,400	457	2,508	2,950	3,319	457	2,508	2,950	3,319
7,400	7,450	457	2,525	2,970	3,341	457	2,525	2,970	3,341
7,450	7,500	457	2,542	2,990	3,364	457	2,542	2,990	3,364
7,500	7,550	454	2,559	3,010	3,386	457	2,559	3,010	3,386
7,550	7,600	450	2,576	3,030	3,409	457	2,576	3,030	3,409
7,600	7,650	446	2,593	3,050	3,431	457	2,593	3,050	3,431
7,650	7,700	443	2,610	3,070	3,454	457	2,610	3,070	3,454
7,700	7,750	439	2,627	3,090	3,476	457	2,627	3,090	3,476
7,750	7,800	435	2,644	3,110	3,499	457	2,644	3,110	3,499
7,800	7,850	431	2,661	3,130	3,521	457	2,661	3,130	3,521
7,850	7,900	427	2,678	3,150	3,544	457	2,678	3,150	3,544
7,900	7,950	423	2,695	3,170	3,566	457	2,695	3,170	3,566
7,950	8,000	420	2,712	3,190	3,589	457	2,712	3,190	3,589
8,000	8,050	416	2,729	3,210	3,611	457	2,729	3,210	3,611
8,050	8,100	412	2,746	3,230	3,634	457	2,746	3,230	3,634
8,100	8,150	408	2,763	3,250	3,656	457	2,763	3,250	3,656
8,150	8,200	404	2,780	3,270	3,679	457	2,780	3,270	3,679
8,200	8,250	400	2,797	3,290	3,701	457	2,797	3,290	3,701
8,250	8,300	397	2,814	3,310	3,724	457	2,814	3,310	3,724
8,300	8,350	393	2,831	3,330	3,746	457	2,831	3,330	3,746
8,350	8,400	389	2,848	3,350	3,769	457	2,848	3,350	3,769
8,400	8,450	385	2,865	3,370	3,791	457	2,865	3,370	3,791
8,450	8,500	381	2,882	3,390	3,814	457	2,882	3,390	3,814

(Continued on next page)

2010 Earned Income Credit (EIC) Table–*Continued* (**Caution.** This is **not** a tax table.)

If the amount you are looking up from the worksheet is–		And your filing status is– Single, head of household, or qualifying widow(er) and you have–				Married filing jointly and you have–			
At least	But less than	No Children	One Child	Two Children	Three Children	No Children	One Child	Two Children	Three Children
		Your credit is–				Your credit is–			
8,500	**8,550**	378	2,899	3,410	3,836	457	2,899	3,410	3,836
8,550	**8,600**	374	2,916	3,430	3,859	457	2,916	3,430	3,859
8,600	**8,650**	370	2,933	3,450	3,881	457	2,933	3,450	3,881
8,650	**8,700**	366	2,950	3,470	3,904	457	2,950	3,470	3,904
8,700	**8,750**	362	2,967	3,490	3,926	457	2,967	3,490	3,926
8,750	**8,800**	358	2,984	3,510	3,949	457	2,984	3,510	3,949
8,800	**8,850**	355	3,001	3,530	3,971	457	3,001	3,530	3,971
8,850	**8,900**	351	3,018	3,550	3,994	457	3,018	3,550	3,994
8,900	**8,950**	347	3,035	3,570	4,016	457	3,035	3,570	4,016
8,950	**9,000**	343	3,050	3,590	4,039	457	3,050	3,590	4,039
9,000	**9,050**	339	3,050	3,610	4,061	457	3,050	3,610	4,061
9,050	**9,100**	335	3,050	3,630	4,084	457	3,050	3,630	4,084
9,100	**9,150**	332	3,050	3,650	4,106	457	3,050	3,650	4,106
9,150	**9,200**	328	3,050	3,670	4,129	457	3,050	3,670	4,129
9,200	**9,250**	324	3,050	3,690	4,151	457	3,050	3,690	4,151
9,250	**9,300**	320	3,050	3,710	4,174	457	3,050	3,710	4,174
9,300	**9,350**	316	3,050	3,730	4,196	457	3,050	3,730	4,196
9,350	**9,400**	313	3,050	3,750	4,219	457	3,050	3,750	4,219
9,400	**9,450**	309	3,050	3,770	4,241	457	3,050	3,770	4,241
9,450	**9,500**	305	3,050	3,790	4,264	457	3,050	3,790	4,264
9,500	**9,550**	301	3,050	3,810	4,286	457	3,050	3,810	4,286
9,550	**9,600**	297	3,050	3,830	4,309	457	3,050	3,830	4,309
9,600	**9,650**	293	3,050	3,850	4,331	457	3,050	3,850	4,331
9,650	**9,700**	290	3,050	3,870	4,354	457	3,050	3,870	4,354
9,700	**9,750**	286	3,050	3,890	4,376	457	3,050	3,890	4,376
9,750	**9,800**	282	3,050	3,910	4,399	457	3,050	3,910	4,399
9,800	**9,850**	278	3,050	3,930	4,421	457	3,050	3,930	4,421
9,850	**9,900**	274	3,050	3,950	4,444	457	3,050	3,950	4,444
9,900	**9,950**	270	3,050	3,970	4,466	457	3,050	3,970	4,466
9,950	**10,000**	267	3,050	3,990	4,489	457	3,050	3,990	4,489
10,000	**10,050**	263	3,050	4,010	4,511	457	3,050	4,010	4,511
10,050	**10,100**	259	3,050	4,030	4,534	457	3,050	4,030	4,534
10,100	**10,150**	255	3,050	4,050	4,556	457	3,050	4,050	4,556
10,150	**10,200**	251	3,050	4,070	4,579	457	3,050	4,070	4,579
10,200	**10,250**	247	3,050	4,090	4,601	457	3,050	4,090	4,601
10,250	**10,300**	244	3,050	4,110	4,624	457	3,050	4,110	4,624
10,300	**10,350**	240	3,050	4,130	4,646	457	3,050	4,130	4,646
10,350	**10,400**	236	3,050	4,150	4,669	457	3,050	4,150	4,669
10,400	**10,450**	232	3,050	4,170	4,691	457	3,050	4,170	4,691
10,450	**10,500**	228	3,050	4,190	4,714	457	3,050	4,190	4,714
10,500	**10,550**	225	3,050	4,210	4,736	457	3,050	4,210	4,736
10,550	**10,600**	221	3,050	4,230	4,759	457	3,050	4,230	4,759
10,600	**10,650**	217	3,050	4,250	4,781	457	3,050	4,250	4,781
10,650	**10,700**	213	3,050	4,270	4,804	457	3,050	4,270	4,804
10,700	**10,750**	209	3,050	4,290	4,826	457	3,050	4,290	4,826
10,750	**10,800**	205	3,050	4,310	4,849	457	3,050	4,310	4,849
10,800	**10,850**	202	3,050	4,330	4,871	457	3,050	4,330	4,871
10,850	**10,900**	198	3,050	4,350	4,894	457	3,050	4,350	4,894
10,900	**10,950**	194	3,050	4,370	4,916	457	3,050	4,370	4,916
10,950	**11,000**	190	3,050	4,390	4,939	457	3,050	4,390	4,939
11,000	**11,050**	186	3,050	4,410	4,961	457	3,050	4,410	4,961
11,050	**11,100**	182	3,050	4,430	4,984	457	3,050	4,430	4,984
11,100	**11,150**	179	3,050	4,450	5,006	457	3,050	4,450	5,006
11,150	**11,200**	175	3,050	4,470	5,029	457	3,050	4,470	5,029
11,200	**11,250**	171	3,050	4,490	5,051	457	3,050	4,490	5,051
11,250	**11,300**	167	3,050	4,510	5,074	457	3,050	4,510	5,074
11,300	**11,350**	163	3,050	4,530	5,096	457	3,050	4,530	5,096
11,350	**11,400**	160	3,050	4,550	5,119	457	3,050	4,550	5,119
11,400	**11,450**	156	3,050	4,570	5,141	457	3,050	4,570	5,141
11,450	**11,500**	152	3,050	4,590	5,164	457	3,050	4,590	5,164

(Continued on next page)

2010 Earned Income Credit (EIC) Table–*Continued* (**Caution.** This is **not** a tax table.)

If the amount you are looking up from the worksheet is–		And your filing status is– Single, head of household, or qualifying widow(er) and you have–				Married filing jointly and you have–			
		No Children	One Child	Two Children	Three Children	No Children	One Child	Two Children	Three Children
At least	But less than	Your credit is–				Your credit is–			
11,500	11,550	148	3,050	4,610	5,186	457	3,050	4,610	5,186
11,550	11,600	144	3,050	4,630	5,209	457	3,050	4,630	5,209
11,600	11,650	140	3,050	4,650	5,231	457	3,050	4,650	5,231
11,650	11,700	137	3,050	4,670	5,254	457	3,050	4,670	5,254
11,700	11,750	133	3,050	4,690	5,276	457	3,050	4,690	5,276
11,750	11,800	129	3,050	4,710	5,299	457	3,050	4,710	5,299
11,800	11,850	125	3,050	4,730	5,321	457	3,050	4,730	5,321
11,850	11,900	121	3,050	4,750	5,344	457	3,050	4,750	5,344
11,900	11,950	117	3,050	4,770	5,366	457	3,050	4,770	5,366
11,950	12,000	114	3,050	4,790	5,389	457	3,050	4,790	5,389
12,000	12,050	110	3,050	4,810	5,411	457	3,050	4,810	5,411
12,050	12,100	106	3,050	4,830	5,434	457	3,050	4,830	5,434
12,100	12,150	102	3,050	4,850	5,456	457	3,050	4,850	5,456
12,150	12,200	98	3,050	4,870	5,479	457	3,050	4,870	5,479
12,200	12,250	94	3,050	4,890	5,501	457	3,050	4,890	5,501
12,250	12,300	91	3,050	4,910	5,524	457	3,050	4,910	5,524
12,300	12,350	87	3,050	4,930	5,546	457	3,050	4,930	5,546
12,350	12,400	83	3,050	4,950	5,569	457	3,050	4,950	5,569
12,400	12,450	79	3,050	4,970	5,591	457	3,050	4,970	5,591
12,450	12,500	75	3,050	4,990	5,614	457	3,050	4,990	5,614
12,500	12,550	72	3,050	5,010	5,636	455	3,050	5,010	5,636
12,550	12,600	68	3,050	5,036	5,666	451	3,050	5,036	5,666
12,600	12,650	64	3,050	5,036	5,666	447	3,050	5,036	5,666
12,650	12,700	60	3,050	5,036	5,666	443	3,050	5,036	5,666
12,700	12,750	56	3,050	5,036	5,666	439	3,050	5,036	5,666
12,750	12,800	52	3,050	5,036	5,666	436	3,050	5,036	5,666
12,800	12,850	49	3,050	5,036	5,666	432	3,050	5,036	5,666
12,850	12,900	45	3,050	5,036	5,666	428	3,050	5,036	5,666
12,900	12,950	41	3,050	5,036	5,666	424	3,050	5,036	5,666
12,950	13,000	37	3,050	5,036	5,666	420	3,050	5,036	5,666
13,000	13,050	33	3,050	5,036	5,666	417	3,050	5,036	5,666
13,050	13,100	29	3,050	5,036	5,666	413	3,050	5,036	5,666
13,100	13,150	26	3,050	5,036	5,666	409	3,050	5,036	5,666
13,150	13,200	22	3,050	5,036	5,666	405	3,050	5,036	5,666
13,200	13,250	18	3,050	5,036	5,666	401	3,050	5,036	5,666
13,250	13,300	14	3,050	5,036	5,666	397	3,050	5,036	5,666
13,300	13,350	10	3,050	5,036	5,666	394	3,050	5,036	5,666
13,350	13,400	7	3,050	5,036	5,666	390	3,050	5,036	5,666
13,400	13,450	3	3,050	5,036	5,666	386	3,050	5,036	5,666
13,450	13,500	0	3,050	5,036	5,666	382	3,050	5,036	5,666
13,500	13,550	0	3,050	5,036	5,666	378	3,050	5,036	5,666
13,550	13,600	0	3,050	5,036	5,666	374	3,050	5,036	5,666
13,600	13,650	0	3,050	5,036	5,666	371	3,050	5,036	5,666
13,650	13,700	0	3,050	5,036	5,666	367	3,050	5,036	5,666
13,700	13,750	0	3,050	5,036	5,666	363	3,050	5,036	5,666
13,750	13,800	0	3,050	5,036	5,666	359	3,050	5,036	5,666
13,800	13,850	0	3,050	5,036	5,666	355	3,050	5,036	5,666
13,850	13,900	0	3,050	5,036	5,666	352	3,050	5,036	5,666
13,900	13,950	0	3,050	5,036	5,666	348	3,050	5,036	5,666
13,950	14,000	0	3,050	5,036	5,666	344	3,050	5,036	5,666
14,000	14,050	0	3,050	5,036	5,666	340	3,050	5,036	5,666
14,050	14,100	0	3,050	5,036	5,666	336	3,050	5,036	5,666
14,100	14,150	0	3,050	5,036	5,666	332	3,050	5,036	5,666
14,150	14,200	0	3,050	5,036	5,666	329	3,050	5,036	5,666
14,200	14,250	0	3,050	5,036	5,666	325	3,050	5,036	5,666
14,250	14,300	0	3,050	5,036	5,666	321	3,050	5,036	5,666
14,300	14,350	0	3,050	5,036	5,666	317	3,050	5,036	5,666
14,350	14,400	0	3,050	5,036	5,666	313	3,050	5,036	5,666
14,400	14,450	0	3,050	5,036	5,666	309	3,050	5,036	5,666
14,450	14,500	0	3,050	5,036	5,666	306	3,050	5,036	5,666

(Continued on next page)

2010 Earned Income Credit (EIC) Table—*Continued* (**Caution.** This is **not** a tax table.)

If the amount you are looking up from the worksheet is—		And your filing status is— Single, head of household, or qualifying widow(er) and you have—				Married filing jointly and you have—			
At least	But less than	No Children	One Child	Two Children	Three Children	No Children	One Child	Two Children	Three Children
		Your credit is—				Your credit is—			
14,500	14,550	0	3,050	5,036	5,666	302	3,050	5,036	5,666
14,550	14,600	0	3,050	5,036	5,666	298	3,050	5,036	5,666
14,600	14,650	0	3,050	5,036	5,666	294	3,050	5,036	5,666
14,650	14,700	0	3,050	5,036	5,666	290	3,050	5,036	5,666
14,700	14,750	0	3,050	5,036	5,666	286	3,050	5,036	5,666
14,750	14,800	0	3,050	5,036	5,666	283	3,050	5,036	5,666
14,800	14,850	0	3,050	5,036	5,666	279	3,050	5,036	5,666
14,850	14,900	0	3,050	5,036	5,666	275	3,050	5,036	5,666
14,900	14,950	0	3,050	5,036	5,666	271	3,050	5,036	5,666
14,950	15,000	0	3,050	5,036	5,666	267	3,050	5,036	5,666
15,000	15,050	0	3,050	5,036	5,666	264	3,050	5,036	5,666
15,050	15,100	0	3,050	5,036	5,666	260	3,050	5,036	5,666
15,100	15,150	0	3,050	5,036	5,666	256	3,050	5,036	5,666
15,150	15,200	0	3,050	5,036	5,666	252	3,050	5,036	5,666
15,200	15,250	0	3,050	5,036	5,666	248	3,050	5,036	5,666
15,250	15,300	0	3,050	5,036	5,666	244	3,050	5,036	5,666
15,300	15,350	0	3,050	5,036	5,666	241	3,050	5,036	5,666
15,350	15,400	0	3,050	5,036	5,666	237	3,050	5,036	5,666
15,400	15,450	0	3,050	5,036	5,666	233	3,050	5,036	5,666
15,450	15,500	0	3,050	5,036	5,666	229	3,050	5,036	5,666
15,500	15,550	0	3,050	5,036	5,666	225	3,050	5,036	5,666
15,550	15,600	0	3,050	5,036	5,666	221	3,050	5,036	5,666
15,600	15,650	0	3,050	5,036	5,666	218	3,050	5,036	5,666
15,650	15,700	0	3,050	5,036	5,666	214	3,050	5,036	5,666
15,700	15,750	0	3,050	5,036	5,666	210	3,050	5,036	5,666
15,750	15,800	0	3,050	5,036	5,666	206	3,050	5,036	5,666
15,800	15,850	0	3,050	5,036	5,666	202	3,050	5,036	5,666
15,850	15,900	0	3,050	5,036	5,666	199	3,050	5,036	5,666
15,900	15,950	0	3,050	5,036	5,666	195	3,050	5,036	5,666
15,950	16,000	0	3,050	5,036	5,666	191	3,050	5,036	5,666
16,000	16,050	0	3,050	5,036	5,666	187	3,050	5,036	5,666
16,050	16,100	0	3,050	5,036	5,666	183	3,050	5,036	5,666
16,100	16,150	0	3,050	5,036	5,666	179	3,050	5,036	5,666
16,150	16,200	0	3,050	5,036	5,666	176	3,050	5,036	5,666
16,200	16,250	0	3,050	5,036	5,666	172	3,050	5,036	5,666
16,250	16,300	0	3,050	5,036	5,666	168	3,050	5,036	5,666
16,300	16,350	0	3,050	5,036	5,666	164	3,050	5,036	5,666
16,350	16,400	0	3,050	5,036	5,666	160	3,050	5,036	5,666
16,400	16,450	0	3,050	5,036	5,666	156	3,050	5,036	5,666
16,450	16,500	0	3,046	5,031	5,660	153	3,050	5,036	5,666
16,500	16,550	0	3,038	5,020	5,650	149	3,050	5,036	5,666
16,550	16,600	0	3,030	5,010	5,639	145	3,050	5,036	5,666
16,600	16,650	0	3,022	4,999	5,629	141	3,050	5,036	5,666
16,650	16,700	0	3,014	4,989	5,618	137	3,050	5,036	5,666
16,700	16,750	0	3,006	4,978	5,608	133	3,050	5,036	5,666
16,750	16,800	0	2,998	4,968	5,597	130	3,050	5,036	5,666
16,800	16,850	0	2,990	4,957	5,587	126	3,050	5,036	5,666
16,850	16,900	0	2,982	4,946	5,576	122	3,050	5,036	5,666
16,900	16,950	0	2,974	4,936	5,565	118	3,050	5,036	5,666
16,950	17,000	0	2,966	4,925	5,555	114	3,050	5,036	5,666
17,000	17,050	0	2,958	4,915	5,544	111	3,050	5,036	5,666
17,050	17,100	0	2,950	4,904	5,534	107	3,050	5,036	5,666
17,100	17,150	0	2,942	4,894	5,523	103	3,050	5,036	5,666
17,150	17,200	0	2,934	4,883	5,513	99	3,050	5,036	5,666
17,200	17,250	0	2,926	4,873	5,502	95	3,050	5,036	5,666
17,250	17,300	0	2,918	4,862	5,492	91	3,050	5,036	5,666
17,300	17,350	0	2,910	4,852	5,481	88	3,050	5,036	5,666
17,350	17,400	0	2,902	4,841	5,471	84	3,050	5,036	5,666
17,400	17,450	0	2,894	4,831	5,460	80	3,050	5,036	5,666
17,450	17,500	0	2,886	4,820	5,450	76	3,050	5,036	5,666

(Continued on next page)

2010 Earned Income Credit (EIC) Table–*Continued* (**Caution.** This is **not** a tax table.)

If the amount you are looking up from the worksheet is–		And your filing status is–							
		Single, head of household, or qualifying widow(er) and you have–				Married filing jointly and you have–			
		No Children	One Child	Two Children	Three Children	No Children	One Child	Two Children	Three Children
At least	But less than	Your credit is–				Your credit is–			
17,500	**17,550**	0	2,878	4,810	5,439	72	3,050	5,036	5,666
17,550	**17,600**	0	2,870	4,799	5,429	68	3,050	5,036	5,666
17,600	**17,650**	0	2,862	4,789	5,418	65	3,050	5,036	5,666
17,650	**17,700**	0	2,854	4,778	5,408	61	3,050	5,036	5,666
17,700	**17,750**	0	2,846	4,767	5,397	57	3,050	5,036	5,666
17,750	**17,800**	0	2,838	4,757	5,386	53	3,050	5,036	5,666
17,800	**17,850**	0	2,830	4,746	5,376	49	3,050	5,036	5,666
17,850	**17,900**	0	2,822	4,736	5,365	46	3,050	5,036	5,666
17,900	**17,950**	0	2,814	4,725	5,355	42	3,050	5,036	5,666
17,950	**18,000**	0	2,806	4,715	5,344	38	3,050	5,036	5,666
18,000	**18,050**	0	2,798	4,704	5,334	34	3,050	5,036	5,666
18,050	**18,100**	0	2,790	4,694	5,323	30	3,050	5,036	5,666
18,100	**18,150**	0	2,782	4,683	5,313	26	3,050	5,036	5,666
18,150	**18,200**	0	2,774	4,673	5,302	23	3,050	5,036	5,666
18,200	**18,250**	0	2,766	4,662	5,292	19	3,050	5,036	5,666
18,250	**18,300**	0	2,758	4,652	5,281	15	3,050	5,036	5,666
18,300	**18,350**	0	2,750	4,641	5,271	11	3,050	5,036	5,666
18,350	**18,400**	0	2,742	4,631	5,260	7	3,050	5,036	5,666
18,400	**18,450**	0	2,734	4,620	5,250	3	3,050	5,036	5,666
18,450	**18,500**	0	2,726	4,610	5,239	*	3,050	5,036	5,666
18,500	**18,550**	0	2,718	4,599	5,229	0	3,050	5,036	5,666
18,550	**18,600**	0	2,710	4,588	5,218	0	3,050	5,036	5,666
18,600	**18,650**	0	2,702	4,578	5,207	0	3,050	5,036	5,666
18,650	**18,700**	0	2,694	4,567	5,197	0	3,050	5,036	5,666
18,700	**18,750**	0	2,686	4,557	5,186	0	3,050	5,036	5,666
18,750	**18,800**	0	2,678	4,546	5,176	0	3,050	5,036	5,666
18,800	**18,850**	0	2,670	4,536	5,165	0	3,050	5,036	5,666
18,850	**18,900**	0	2,662	4,525	5,155	0	3,050	5,036	5,666
18,900	**18,950**	0	2,654	4,515	5,144	0	3,050	5,036	5,666
18,950	**19,000**	0	2,646	4,504	5,134	0	3,050	5,036	5,666
19,000	**19,050**	0	2,638	4,494	5,123	0	3,050	5,036	5,666
19,050	**19,100**	0	2,630	4,483	5,113	0	3,050	5,036	5,666
19,100	**19,150**	0	2,622	4,473	5,102	0	3,050	5,036	5,666
19,150	**19,200**	0	2,614	4,462	5,092	0	3,050	5,036	5,666
19,200	**19,250**	0	2,606	4,452	5,081	0	3,050	5,036	5,666
19,250	**19,300**	0	2,598	4,441	5,071	0	3,050	5,036	5,666
19,300	**19,350**	0	2,590	4,431	5,060	0	3,050	5,036	5,666
19,350	**19,400**	0	2,582	4,420	5,049	0	3,050	5,036	5,666
19,400	**19,450**	0	2,574	4,409	5,039	0	3,050	5,036	5,666
19,450	**19,500**	0	2,566	4,399	5,028	0	3,050	5,036	5,666
19,500	**19,550**	0	2,558	4,388	5,018	0	3,050	5,036	5,666
19,550	**19,600**	0	2,550	4,378	5,007	0	3,050	5,036	5,666
19,600	**19,650**	0	2,542	4,367	4,997	0	3,050	5,036	5,666
19,650	**19,700**	0	2,534	4,357	4,986	0	3,050	5,036	5,666
19,700	**19,750**	0	2,526	4,346	4,976	0	3,050	5,036	5,666
19,750	**19,800**	0	2,518	4,336	4,965	0	3,050	5,036	5,666
19,800	**19,850**	0	2,510	4,325	4,955	0	3,050	5,036	5,666
19,850	**19,900**	0	2,502	4,315	4,944	0	3,050	5,036	5,666
19,900	**19,950**	0	2,494	4,304	4,934	0	3,050	5,036	5,666
19,950	**20,000**	0	2,487	4,294	4,923	0	3,050	5,036	5,666
20,000	**20,050**	0	2,479	4,283	4,913	0	3,050	5,036	5,666
20,050	**20,100**	0	2,471	4,273	4,902	0	3,050	5,036	5,666
20,100	**20,150**	0	2,463	4,262	4,892	0	3,050	5,036	5,666
20,150	**20,200**	0	2,455	4,252	4,881	0	3,050	5,036	5,666
20,200	**20,250**	0	2,447	4,241	4,870	0	3,050	5,036	5,666

*If the amount you are looking up from the worksheet is at least $18,450 but less than $18,470, your credit is $1. Otherwise, you cannot take the credit.

(Continued on next page)

2010 Earned Income Credit (EIC) Table–*Continued* (**Caution.** This is **not** a tax table.)

If the amount you are looking up from the worksheet is–		And your filing status is– Single, head of household, or qualifying widow(er) and you have–				Married filing jointly and you have–			
At least	But less than	No Children	One Child	Two Children	Three Children	No Children	One Child	Two Children	Three Children
		Your credit is–				Your credit is–			
20,250	**20,300**	0	2,439	4,230	4,860	0	3,050	5,036	5,666
20,300	**20,350**	0	2,431	4,220	4,849	0	3,050	5,036	5,666
20,350	**20,400**	0	2,423	4,209	4,839	0	3,050	5,036	5,666
20,400	**20,450**	0	2,415	4,199	4,828	0	3,050	5,036	5,666
20,450	**20,500**	0	2,407	4,188	4,818	0	3,050	5,036	5,666
20,500	**20,550**	0	2,399	4,178	4,807	0	3,050	5,036	5,666
20,550	**20,600**	0	2,391	4,167	4,797	0	3,050	5,036	5,666
20,600	**20,650**	0	2,383	4,157	4,786	0	3,050	5,036	5,666
20,650	**20,700**	0	2,375	4,146	4,776	0	3,050	5,036	5,666
20,700	**20,750**	0	2,367	4,136	4,765	0	3,050	5,036	5,666
20,750	**20,800**	0	2,359	4,125	4,755	0	3,050	5,036	5,666
20,800	**20,850**	0	2,351	4,115	4,744	0	3,050	5,036	5,666
20,850	**20,900**	0	2,343	4,104	4,734	0	3,050	5,036	5,666
20,900	**20,950**	0	2,335	4,094	4,723	0	3,050	5,036	5,666
20,950	**21,000**	0	2,327	4,083	4,713	0	3,050	5,036	5,666
21,000	**21,050**	0	2,319	4,073	4,702	0	3,050	5,036	5,666
21,050	**21,100**	0	2,311	4,062	4,691	0	3,050	5,036	5,666
21,100	**21,150**	0	2,303	4,051	4,681	0	3,050	5,036	5,666
21,150	**21,200**	0	2,295	4,041	4,670	0	3,050	5,036	5,666
21,200	**21,250**	0	2,287	4,030	4,660	0	3,050	5,036	5,666
21,250	**21,300**	0	2,279	4,020	4,649	0	3,050	5,036	5,666
21,300	**21,350**	0	2,271	4,009	4,639	0	3,050	5,036	5,666
21,350	**21,400**	0	2,263	3,999	4,628	0	3,050	5,036	5,666
21,400	**21,450**	0	2,255	3,988	4,618	0	3,050	5,036	5,666
21,450	**21,500**	0	2,247	3,978	4,607	0	3,050	5,036	5,666
21,500	**21,550**	0	2,239	3,967	4,597	0	3,039	5,022	5,652
21,550	**21,600**	0	2,231	3,957	4,586	0	3,031	5,012	5,641
21,600	**21,650**	0	2,223	3,946	4,576	0	3,023	5,001	5,631
21,650	**21,700**	0	2,215	3,936	4,565	0	3,015	4,991	5,620
21,700	**21,750**	0	2,207	3,925	4,555	0	3,007	4,980	5,610
21,750	**21,800**	0	2,199	3,915	4,544	0	2,999	4,970	5,599
21,800	**21,850**	0	2,191	3,904	4,534	0	2,991	4,959	5,589
21,850	**21,900**	0	2,183	3,893	4,523	0	2,983	4,949	5,578
21,900	**21,950**	0	2,175	3,883	4,512	0	2,975	4,938	5,568
21,950	**22,000**	0	2,167	3,872	4,502	0	2,968	4,928	5,557
22,000	**22,050**	0	2,159	3,862	4,491	0	2,960	4,917	5,547
22,050	**22,100**	0	2,151	3,851	4,481	0	2,952	4,906	5,536
22,100	**22,150**	0	2,143	3,841	4,470	0	2,944	4,896	5,525
22,150	**22,200**	0	2,135	3,830	4,460	0	2,936	4,885	5,515
22,200	**22,250**	0	2,127	3,820	4,449	0	2,928	4,875	5,504
22,250	**22,300**	0	2,119	3,809	4,439	0	2,920	4,864	5,494
22,300	**22,350**	0	2,111	3,799	4,428	0	2,912	4,854	5,483
22,350	**22,400**	0	2,103	3,788	4,418	0	2,904	4,843	5,473
22,400	**22,450**	0	2,095	3,778	4,407	0	2,896	4,833	5,462
22,450	**22,500**	0	2,087	3,767	4,397	0	2,888	4,822	5,452
22,500	**22,550**	0	2,079	3,757	4,386	0	2,880	4,812	5,441
22,550	**22,600**	0	2,071	3,746	4,376	0	2,872	4,801	5,431
22,600	**22,650**	0	2,063	3,736	4,365	0	2,864	4,791	5,420
22,650	**22,700**	0	2,055	3,725	4,355	0	2,856	4,780	5,410
22,700	**22,750**	0	2,047	3,714	4,344	0	2,848	4,770	5,399
22,750	**22,800**	0	2,039	3,704	4,333	0	2,840	4,759	5,389
22,800	**22,850**	0	2,031	3,693	4,323	0	2,832	4,749	5,378
22,850	**22,900**	0	2,023	3,683	4,312	0	2,824	4,738	5,368
22,900	**22,950**	0	2,015	3,672	4,302	0	2,816	4,727	5,357
22,950	**23,000**	0	2,007	3,662	4,291	0	2,808	4,717	5,346
23,000	**23,050**	0	1,999	3,651	4,281	0	2,800	4,706	5,336
23,050	**23,100**	0	1,991	3,641	4,270	0	2,792	4,696	5,325
23,100	**23,150**	0	1,983	3,630	4,260	0	2,784	4,685	5,315
23,150	**23,200**	0	1,975	3,620	4,249	0	2,776	4,675	5,304
23,200	**23,250**	0	1,967	3,609	4,239	0	2,768	4,664	5,294

(Continued on next page)

2010 Earned Income Credit (EIC) Table–*Continued* **(Caution.** This is **not** a tax table.)

If the amount you are looking up from the worksheet is–		And your filing status is– Single, head of household, or qualifying widow(er) and you have–				Married filing jointly and you have–			
At least	But less than	No Children	One Child	Two Children	Three Children	No Children	One Child	Two Children	Three Children
		Your credit is–				Your credit is–			
23,250	23,300	0	1,959	3,599	4,228	0	2,760	4,654	5,283
23,300	23,350	0	1,951	3,588	4,218	0	2,752	4,643	5,273
23,350	23,400	0	1,943	3,578	4,207	0	2,744	4,633	5,262
23,400	23,450	0	1,935	3,567	4,197	0	2,736	4,622	5,252
23,450	23,500	0	1,927	3,557	4,186	0	2,728	4,612	5,241
23,500	23,550	0	1,919	3,546	4,176	0	2,720	4,601	5,231
23,550	23,600	0	1,911	3,535	4,165	0	2,712	4,591	5,220
23,600	23,650	0	1,903	3,525	4,154	0	2,704	4,580	5,210
23,650	23,700	0	1,895	3,514	4,144	0	2,696	4,570	5,199
23,700	23,750	0	1,887	3,504	4,133	0	2,688	4,559	5,188
23,750	23,800	0	1,879	3,493	4,123	0	2,680	4,548	5,178
23,800	23,850	0	1,871	3,483	4,112	0	2,672	4,538	5,167
23,850	23,900	0	1,863	3,472	4,102	0	2,664	4,527	5,157
23,900	23,950	0	1,855	3,462	4,091	0	2,656	4,517	5,146
23,950	24,000	0	1,847	3,451	4,081	0	2,648	4,506	5,136
24,000	24,050	0	1,839	3,441	4,070	0	2,640	4,496	5,125
24,050	24,100	0	1,831	3,430	4,060	0	2,632	4,485	5,115
24,100	24,150	0	1,823	3,420	4,049	0	2,624	4,475	5,104
24,150	24,200	0	1,815	3,409	4,039	0	2,616	4,464	5,094
24,200	24,250	0	1,807	3,399	4,028	0	2,608	4,454	5,083
24,250	24,300	0	1,799	3,388	4,018	0	2,600	4,443	5,073
24,300	24,350	0	1,791	3,378	4,007	0	2,592	4,433	5,062
24,350	24,400	0	1,783	3,367	3,996	0	2,584	4,422	5,052
24,400	24,450	0	1,775	3,356	3,986	0	2,576	4,412	5,041
24,450	24,500	0	1,767	3,346	3,975	0	2,568	4,401	5,031
24,500	24,550	0	1,759	3,335	3,965	0	2,560	4,391	5,020
24,550	24,600	0	1,751	3,325	3,954	0	2,552	4,380	5,009
24,600	24,650	0	1,743	3,314	3,944	0	2,544	4,369	4,999
24,650	24,700	0	1,735	3,304	3,933	0	2,536	4,359	4,988
24,700	24,750	0	1,727	3,293	3,923	0	2,528	4,348	4,978
24,750	24,800	0	1,719	3,283	3,912	0	2,520	4,338	4,967
24,800	24,850	0	1,711	3,272	3,902	0	2,512	4,327	4,957
24,850	24,900	0	1,703	3,262	3,891	0	2,504	4,317	4,946
24,900	24,950	0	1,695	3,251	3,881	0	2,496	4,306	4,936
24,950	25,000	0	1,688	3,241	3,870	0	2,488	4,296	4,925
25,000	25,050	0	1,680	3,230	3,860	0	2,480	4,285	4,915
25,050	25,100	0	1,672	3,220	3,849	0	2,472	4,275	4,904
25,100	25,150	0	1,664	3,209	3,839	0	2,464	4,264	4,894
25,150	25,200	0	1,656	3,199	3,828	0	2,456	4,254	4,883
25,200	25,250	0	1,648	3,188	3,817	0	2,448	4,243	4,873
25,250	25,300	0	1,640	3,177	3,807	0	2,440	4,233	4,862
25,300	25,350	0	1,632	3,167	3,796	0	2,432	4,222	4,852
25,350	25,400	0	1,624	3,156	3,786	0	2,424	4,212	4,841
25,400	25,450	0	1,616	3,146	3,775	0	2,416	4,201	4,830
25,450	25,500	0	1,608	3,135	3,765	0	2,408	4,190	4,820
25,500	25,550	0	1,600	3,125	3,754	0	2,400	4,180	4,809
25,550	25,600	0	1,592	3,114	3,744	0	2,392	4,169	4,799
25,600	25,650	0	1,584	3,104	3,733	0	2,384	4,159	4,788
25,650	25,700	0	1,576	3,093	3,723	0	2,376	4,148	4,778
25,700	25,750	0	1,568	3,083	3,712	0	2,368	4,138	4,767
25,750	25,800	0	1,560	3,072	3,702	0	2,360	4,127	4,757
25,800	25,850	0	1,552	3,062	3,691	0	2,352	4,117	4,746
25,850	25,900	0	1,544	3,051	3,681	0	2,344	4,106	4,736
25,900	25,950	0	1,536	3,041	3,670	0	2,336	4,096	4,725
25,950	26,000	0	1,528	3,030	3,660	0	2,328	4,085	4,715
26,000	26,050	0	1,520	3,020	3,649	0	2,320	4,075	4,704
26,050	26,100	0	1,512	3,009	3,638	0	2,312	4,064	4,694
26,100	26,150	0	1,504	2,998	3,628	0	2,304	4,054	4,683
26,150	26,200	0	1,496	2,988	3,617	0	2,296	4,043	4,673
26,200	26,250	0	1,488	2,977	3,607	0	2,288	4,032	4,662

(Continued on next page)

2010 Earned Income Credit (EIC) Table—*Continued* (**Caution.** This is **not** a tax table.)

If the amount you are looking up from the worksheet is–		And your filing status is–							
		Single, head of household, or qualifying widow(er) and you have–				Married filing jointly and you have–			
At least	But less than	No Children	One Child	Two Children	Three Children	No Children	One Child	Two Children	Three Children
		Your credit is–				Your credit is–			
26,250	**26,300**	0	1,480	2,967	3,596	0	2,280	4,022	4,651
26,300	**26,350**	0	1,472	2,956	3,586	0	2,272	4,011	4,641
26,350	**26,400**	0	1,464	2,946	3,575	0	2,264	4,001	4,630
26,400	**26,450**	0	1,456	2,935	3,565	0	2,256	3,990	4,620
26,450	**26,500**	0	1,448	2,925	3,554	0	2,248	3,980	4,609
26,500	**26,550**	0	1,440	2,914	3,544	0	2,240	3,969	4,599
26,550	**26,600**	0	1,432	2,904	3,533	0	2,232	3,959	4,588
26,600	**26,650**	0	1,424	2,893	3,523	0	2,224	3,948	4,578
26,650	**26,700**	0	1,416	2,883	3,512	0	2,216	3,938	4,567
26,700	**26,750**	0	1,408	2,872	3,502	0	2,208	3,927	4,557
26,750	**26,800**	0	1,400	2,862	3,491	0	2,200	3,917	4,546
26,800	**26,850**	0	1,392	2,851	3,481	0	2,192	3,906	4,536
26,850	**26,900**	0	1,384	2,840	3,470	0	2,184	3,896	4,525
26,900	**26,950**	0	1,376	2,830	3,459	0	2,176	3,885	4,515
26,950	**27,000**	0	1,368	2,819	3,449	0	2,169	3,875	4,504
27,000	**27,050**	0	1,360	2,809	3,438	0	2,161	3,864	4,494
27,050	**27,100**	0	1,352	2,798	3,428	0	2,153	3,853	4,483
27,100	**27,150**	0	1,344	2,788	3,417	0	2,145	3,843	4,472
27,150	**27,200**	0	1,336	2,777	3,407	0	2,137	3,832	4,462
27,200	**27,250**	0	1,328	2,767	3,396	0	2,129	3,822	4,451
27,250	**27,300**	0	1,320	2,756	3,386	0	2,121	3,811	4,441
27,300	**27,350**	0	1,312	2,746	3,375	0	2,113	3,801	4,430
27,350	**27,400**	0	1,304	2,735	3,365	0	2,105	3,790	4,420
27,400	**27,450**	0	1,296	2,725	3,354	0	2,097	3,780	4,409
27,450	**27,500**	0	1,288	2,714	3,344	0	2,089	3,769	4,399
27,500	**27,550**	0	1,280	2,704	3,333	0	2,081	3,759	4,388
27,550	**27,600**	0	1,272	2,693	3,323	0	2,073	3,748	4,378
27,600	**27,650**	0	1,264	2,683	3,312	0	2,065	3,738	4,367
27,650	**27,700**	0	1,256	2,672	3,302	0	2,057	3,727	4,357
27,700	**27,750**	0	1,248	2,661	3,291	0	2,049	3,717	4,346
27,750	**27,800**	0	1,240	2,651	3,280	0	2,041	3,706	4,336
27,800	**27,850**	0	1,232	2,640	3,270	0	2,033	3,696	4,325
27,850	**27,900**	0	1,224	2,630	3,259	0	2,025	3,685	4,315
27,900	**27,950**	0	1,216	2,619	3,249	0	2,017	3,674	4,304
27,950	**28,000**	0	1,208	2,609	3,238	0	2,009	3,664	4,293
28,000	**28,050**	0	1,200	2,598	3,228	0	2,001	3,653	4,283
28,050	**28,100**	0	1,192	2,588	3,217	0	1,993	3,643	4,272
28,100	**28,150**	0	1,184	2,577	3,207	0	1,985	3,632	4,262
28,150	**28,200**	0	1,176	2,567	3,196	0	1,977	3,622	4,251
28,200	**28,250**	0	1,168	2,556	3,186	0	1,969	3,611	4,241
28,250	**28,300**	0	1,160	2,546	3,175	0	1,961	3,601	4,230
28,300	**28,350**	0	1,152	2,535	3,165	0	1,953	3,590	4,220
28,350	**28,400**	0	1,144	2,525	3,154	0	1,945	3,580	4,209
28,400	**28,450**	0	1,136	2,514	3,144	0	1,937	3,569	4,199
28,450	**28,500**	0	1,128	2,504	3,133	0	1,929	3,559	4,188
28,500	**28,550**	0	1,120	2,493	3,123	0	1,921	3,548	4,178
28,550	**28,600**	0	1,112	2,482	3,112	0	1,913	3,538	4,167
28,600	**28,650**	0	1,104	2,472	3,101	0	1,905	3,527	4,157
28,650	**28,700**	0	1,096	2,461	3,091	0	1,897	3,517	4,146
28,700	**28,750**	0	1,088	2,451	3,080	0	1,889	3,506	4,135
28,750	**28,800**	0	1,080	2,440	3,070	0	1,881	3,495	4,125
28,800	**28,850**	0	1,072	2,430	3,059	0	1,873	3,485	4,114
28,850	**28,900**	0	1,064	2,419	3,049	0	1,865	3,474	4,104
28,900	**28,950**	0	1,056	2,409	3,038	0	1,857	3,464	4,093
28,950	**29,000**	0	1,048	2,398	3,028	0	1,849	3,453	4,083
29,000	**29,050**	0	1,040	2,388	3,017	0	1,841	3,443	4,072
29,050	**29,100**	0	1,032	2,377	3,007	0	1,833	3,432	4,062
29,100	**29,150**	0	1,024	2,367	2,996	0	1,825	3,422	4,051
29,150	**29,200**	0	1,016	2,356	2,986	0	1,817	3,411	4,041
29,200	**29,250**	0	1,008	2,346	2,975	0	1,809	3,401	4,030

(Continued on next page)

2010 Earned Income Credit (EIC) Table—*Continued* (**Caution.** This is **not** a tax table.)

If the amount you are looking up from the worksheet is–		And your filing status is– Single, head of household, or qualifying widow(er) and you have–				Married filing jointly and you have–			
At least	But less than	No Children	One Child	Two Children	Three Children	No Children	One Child	Two Children	Three Children
		Your credit is–				Your credit is–			
29,250	29,300	0	1,000	2,335	2,965	0	1,801	3,390	4,020
29,300	29,350	0	992	2,325	2,954	0	1,793	3,380	4,009
29,350	29,400	0	984	2,314	2,943	0	1,785	3,369	3,999
29,400	29,450	0	976	2,303	2,933	0	1,777	3,359	3,988
29,450	29,500	0	968	2,293	2,922	0	1,769	3,348	3,978
29,500	29,550	0	960	2,282	2,912	0	1,761	3,338	3,967
29,550	29,600	0	952	2,272	2,901	0	1,753	3,327	3,956
29,600	29,650	0	944	2,261	2,891	0	1,745	3,316	3,946
29,650	29,700	0	936	2,251	2,880	0	1,737	3,306	3,935
29,700	29,750	0	928	2,240	2,870	0	1,729	3,295	3,925
29,750	29,800	0	920	2,230	2,859	0	1,721	3,285	3,914
29,800	29,850	0	912	2,219	2,849	0	1,713	3,274	3,904
29,850	29,900	0	904	2,209	2,838	0	1,705	3,264	3,893
29,900	29,950	0	896	2,198	2,828	0	1,697	3,253	3,883
29,950	30,000	0	889	2,188	2,817	0	1,689	3,243	3,872
30,000	30,050	0	881	2,177	2,807	0	1,681	3,232	3,862
30,050	30,100	0	873	2,167	2,796	0	1,673	3,222	3,851
30,100	30,150	0	865	2,156	2,786	0	1,665	3,211	3,841
30,150	30,200	0	857	2,146	2,775	0	1,657	3,201	3,830
30,200	30,250	0	849	2,135	2,764	0	1,649	3,190	3,820
30,250	30,300	0	841	2,124	2,754	0	1,641	3,180	3,809
30,300	30,350	0	833	2,114	2,743	0	1,633	3,169	3,799
30,350	30,400	0	825	2,103	2,733	0	1,625	3,159	3,788
30,400	30,450	0	817	2,093	2,722	0	1,617	3,148	3,777
30,450	30,500	0	809	2,082	2,712	0	1,609	3,137	3,767
30,500	30,550	0	801	2,072	2,701	0	1,601	3,127	3,756
30,550	30,600	0	793	2,061	2,691	0	1,593	3,116	3,746
30,600	30,650	0	785	2,051	2,680	0	1,585	3,106	3,735
30,650	30,700	0	777	2,040	2,670	0	1,577	3,095	3,725
30,700	30,750	0	769	2,030	2,659	0	1,569	3,085	3,714
30,750	30,800	0	761	2,019	2,649	0	1,561	3,074	3,704
30,800	30,850	0	753	2,009	2,638	0	1,553	3,064	3,693
30,850	30,900	0	745	1,998	2,628	0	1,545	3,053	3,683
30,900	30,950	0	737	1,988	2,617	0	1,537	3,043	3,672
30,950	31,000	0	729	1,977	2,607	0	1,529	3,032	3,662
31,000	31,050	0	721	1,967	2,596	0	1,521	3,022	3,651
31,050	31,100	0	713	1,956	2,585	0	1,513	3,011	3,641
31,100	31,150	0	705	1,945	2,575	0	1,505	3,001	3,630
31,150	31,200	0	697	1,935	2,564	0	1,497	2,990	3,620
31,200	31,250	0	689	1,924	2,554	0	1,489	2,979	3,609
31,250	31,300	0	681	1,914	2,543	0	1,481	2,969	3,598
31,300	31,350	0	673	1,903	2,533	0	1,473	2,958	3,588
31,350	31,400	0	665	1,893	2,522	0	1,465	2,948	3,577
31,400	31,450	0	657	1,882	2,512	0	1,457	2,937	3,567
31,450	31,500	0	649	1,872	2,501	0	1,449	2,927	3,556
31,500	31,550	0	641	1,861	2,491	0	1,441	2,916	3,546
31,550	31,600	0	633	1,851	2,480	0	1,433	2,906	3,535
31,600	31,650	0	625	1,840	2,470	0	1,425	2,895	3,525
31,650	31,700	0	617	1,830	2,459	0	1,417	2,885	3,514
31,700	31,750	0	609	1,819	2,449	0	1,409	2,874	3,504
31,750	31,800	0	601	1,809	2,438	0	1,401	2,864	3,493
31,800	31,850	0	593	1,798	2,428	0	1,393	2,853	3,483
31,850	31,900	0	585	1,787	2,417	0	1,385	2,843	3,472
31,900	31,950	0	577	1,777	2,406	0	1,377	2,832	3,462
31,950	32,000	0	569	1,766	2,396	0	1,370	2,822	3,451
32,000	32,050	0	561	1,756	2,385	0	1,362	2,811	3,441
32,050	32,100	0	553	1,745	2,375	0	1,354	2,800	3,430
32,100	32,150	0	545	1,735	2,364	0	1,346	2,790	3,419
32,150	32,200	0	537	1,724	2,354	0	1,338	2,779	3,409
32,200	32,250	0	529	1,714	2,343	0	1,330	2,769	3,398

(Continued on next page)

2010 Earned Income Credit (EIC) Table–*Continued* (**Caution.** This is **not** a tax table.)

If the amount you are looking up from the worksheet is–		And your filing status is–							
		Single, head of household, or qualifying widow(er) and you have–				Married filing jointly and you have–			
At least	But less than	No Children	One Child	Two Children	Three Children	No Children	One Child	Two Children	Three Children
		Your credit is–				Your credit is–			
32,250	**32,300**	0	521	1,703	2,333	0	1,322	2,758	3,388
32,300	**32,350**	0	513	1,693	2,322	0	1,314	2,748	3,377
32,350	**32,400**	0	505	1,682	2,312	0	1,306	2,737	3,367
32,400	**32,450**	0	497	1,672	2,301	0	1,298	2,727	3,356
32,450	**32,500**	0	489	1,661	2,291	0	1,290	2,716	3,346
32,500	**32,550**	0	481	1,651	2,280	0	1,282	2,706	3,335
32,550	**32,600**	0	473	1,640	2,270	0	1,274	2,695	3,325
32,600	**32,650**	0	465	1,630	2,259	0	1,266	2,685	3,314
32,650	**32,700**	0	457	1,619	2,249	0	1,258	2,674	3,304
32,700	**32,750**	0	449	1,608	2,238	0	1,250	2,664	3,293
32,750	**32,800**	0	441	1,598	2,227	0	1,242	2,653	3,283
32,800	**32,850**	0	433	1,587	2,217	0	1,234	2,643	3,272
32,850	**32,900**	0	425	1,577	2,206	0	1,226	2,632	3,262
32,900	**32,950**	0	417	1,566	2,196	0	1,218	2,621	3,251
32,950	**33,000**	0	409	1,556	2,185	0	1,210	2,611	3,240
33,000	**33,050**	0	401	1,545	2,175	0	1,202	2,600	3,230
33,050	**33,100**	0	393	1,535	2,164	0	1,194	2,590	3,219
33,100	**33,150**	0	385	1,524	2,154	0	1,186	2,579	3,209
33,150	**33,200**	0	377	1,514	2,143	0	1,178	2,569	3,198
33,200	**33,250**	0	369	1,503	2,133	0	1,170	2,558	3,188
33,250	**33,300**	0	361	1,493	2,122	0	1,162	2,548	3,177
33,300	**33,350**	0	353	1,482	2,112	0	1,154	2,537	3,167
33,350	**33,400**	0	345	1,472	2,101	0	1,146	2,527	3,156
33,400	**33,450**	0	337	1,461	2,091	0	1,138	2,516	3,146
33,450	**33,500**	0	329	1,451	2,080	0	1,130	2,506	3,135
33,500	**33,550**	0	321	1,440	2,070	0	1,122	2,495	3,125
33,550	**33,600**	0	313	1,429	2,059	0	1,114	2,485	3,114
33,600	**33,650**	0	305	1,419	2,048	0	1,106	2,474	3,104
33,650	**33,700**	0	297	1,408	2,038	0	1,098	2,464	3,093
33,700	**33,750**	0	289	1,398	2,027	0	1,090	2,453	3,082
33,750	**33,800**	0	281	1,387	2,017	0	1,082	2,442	3,072
33,800	**33,850**	0	273	1,377	2,006	0	1,074	2,432	3,061
33,850	**33,900**	0	265	1,366	1,996	0	1,066	2,421	3,051
33,900	**33,950**	0	257	1,356	1,985	0	1,058	2,411	3,040
33,950	**34,000**	0	249	1,345	1,975	0	1,050	2,400	3,030
34,000	**34,050**	0	241	1,335	1,964	0	1,042	2,390	3,019
34,050	**34,100**	0	233	1,324	1,954	0	1,034	2,379	3,009
34,100	**34,150**	0	225	1,314	1,943	0	1,026	2,369	2,998
34,150	**34,200**	0	217	1,303	1,933	0	1,018	2,358	2,988
34,200	**34,250**	0	209	1,293	1,922	0	1,010	2,348	2,977
34,250	**34,300**	0	201	1,282	1,912	0	1,002	2,337	2,967
34,300	**34,350**	0	193	1,272	1,901	0	994	2,327	2,956
34,350	**34,400**	0	185	1,261	1,890	0	986	2,316	2,946
34,400	**34,450**	0	177	1,250	1,880	0	978	2,306	2,935
34,450	**34,500**	0	169	1,240	1,869	0	970	2,295	2,925
34,500	**34,550**	0	161	1,229	1,859	0	962	2,285	2,914
34,550	**34,600**	0	153	1,219	1,848	0	954	2,274	2,903
34,600	**34,650**	0	145	1,208	1,838	0	946	2,263	2,893
34,650	**34,700**	0	137	1,198	1,827	0	938	2,253	2,882
34,700	**34,750**	0	129	1,187	1,817	0	930	2,242	2,872
34,750	**34,800**	0	121	1,177	1,806	0	922	2,232	2,861
34,800	**34,850**	0	113	1,166	1,796	0	914	2,221	2,851
34,850	**34,900**	0	105	1,156	1,785	0	906	2,211	2,840
34,900	**34,950**	0	97	1,145	1,775	0	898	2,200	2,830
34,950	**35,000**	0	90	1,135	1,764	0	890	2,190	2,819
35,000	**35,050**	0	82	1,124	1,754	0	882	2,179	2,809
35,050	**35,100**	0	74	1,114	1,743	0	874	2,169	2,798
35,100	**35,150**	0	66	1,103	1,733	0	866	2,158	2,788
35,150	**35,200**	0	58	1,093	1,722	0	858	2,148	2,777
35,200	**35,250**	0	50	1,082	1,711	0	850	2,137	2,767

(Continued on next page)

2010 Earned Income Credit (EIC) Table—*Continued* (**Caution.** This is **not** a tax table.)

If the amount you are looking up from the worksheet is–		And your filing status is– Single, head of household, or qualifying widow(er) and you have–				Married filing jointly and you have–			
At least	But less than	No Children	One Child	Two Children	Three Children	No Children	One Child	Two Children	Three Children
		Your credit is–				Your credit is–			
35,250	35,300	0	42	1,071	1,701	0	842	2,127	2,756
35,300	35,350	0	34	1,061	1,690	0	834	2,116	2,746
35,350	35,400	0	26	1,050	1,680	0	826	2,106	2,735
35,400	35,450	0	18	1,040	1,669	0	818	2,095	2,724
35,450	35,500	0	10	1,029	1,659	0	810	2,084	2,714
35,500	35,550	0	*	1,019	1,648	0	802	2,074	2,703
35,550	35,600	0	0	1,008	1,638	0	794	2,063	2,693
35,600	35,650	0	0	998	1,627	0	786	2,053	2,682
35,650	35,700	0	0	987	1,617	0	778	2,042	2,672
35,700	35,750	0	0	977	1,606	0	770	2,032	2,661
35,750	35,800	0	0	966	1,596	0	762	2,021	2,651
35,800	35,850	0	0	956	1,585	0	754	2,011	2,640
35,850	35,900	0	0	945	1,575	0	746	2,000	2,630
35,900	35,950	0	0	935	1,564	0	738	1,990	2,619
35,950	36,000	0	0	924	1,554	0	730	1,979	2,609
36,000	36,050	0	0	914	1,543	0	722	1,969	2,598
36,050	36,100	0	0	903	1,532	0	714	1,958	2,588
36,100	36,150	0	0	892	1,522	0	706	1,948	2,577
36,150	36,200	0	0	882	1,511	0	698	1,937	2,567
36,200	36,250	0	0	871	1,501	0	690	1,926	2,556
36,250	36,300	0	0	861	1,490	0	682	1,916	2,545
36,300	36,350	0	0	850	1,480	0	674	1,905	2,535
36,350	36,400	0	0	840	1,469	0	666	1,895	2,524
36,400	36,450	0	0	829	1,459	0	658	1,884	2,514
36,450	36,500	0	0	819	1,448	0	650	1,874	2,503
36,500	36,550	0	0	808	1,438	0	642	1,863	2,493
36,550	36,600	0	0	798	1,427	0	634	1,853	2,482
36,600	36,650	0	0	787	1,417	0	626	1,842	2,472
36,650	36,700	0	0	777	1,406	0	618	1,832	2,461
36,700	36,750	0	0	766	1,396	0	610	1,821	2,451
36,750	36,800	0	0	756	1,385	0	602	1,811	2,440
36,800	36,850	0	0	745	1,375	0	594	1,800	2,430
36,850	36,900	0	0	734	1,364	0	586	1,790	2,419
36,900	36,950	0	0	724	1,353	0	578	1,779	2,409
36,950	37,000	0	0	713	1,343	0	571	1,769	2,398
37,000	37,050	0	0	703	1,332	0	563	1,758	2,388
37,050	37,100	0	0	692	1,322	0	555	1,747	2,377
37,100	37,150	0	0	682	1,311	0	547	1,737	2,366
37,150	37,200	0	0	671	1,301	0	539	1,726	2,356
37,200	37,250	0	0	661	1,290	0	531	1,716	2,345
37,250	37,300	0	0	650	1,280	0	523	1,705	2,335
37,300	37,350	0	0	640	1,269	0	515	1,695	2,324
37,350	37,400	0	0	629	1,259	0	507	1,684	2,314
37,400	37,450	0	0	619	1,248	0	499	1,674	2,303
37,450	37,500	0	0	608	1,238	0	491	1,663	2,293
37,500	37,550	0	0	598	1,227	0	483	1,653	2,282
37,550	37,600	0	0	587	1,217	0	475	1,642	2,272
37,600	37,650	0	0	577	1,206	0	467	1,632	2,261
37,650	37,700	0	0	566	1,196	0	459	1,621	2,251
37,700	37,750	0	0	555	1,185	0	451	1,611	2,240
37,750	37,800	0	0	545	1,174	0	443	1,600	2,230
37,800	37,850	0	0	534	1,164	0	435	1,590	2,219
37,850	37,900	0	0	524	1,153	0	427	1,579	2,209
37,900	37,950	0	0	513	1,143	0	419	1,568	2,198
37,950	38,000	0	0	503	1,132	0	411	1,558	2,187

*If the amount you are looking up from the worksheet is at least $35,500 but less than $35,535, your credit is $3. Otherwise, you cannot take the credit.

(Continued on next page)

2010 Earned Income Credit (EIC) Table–*Continued* (**Caution.** This is **not** a tax table.)

If the amount you are looking up from the worksheet is–		And your filing status is– Single, head of household, or qualifying widow(er) and you have–				Married filing jointly and you have–			
At least	But less than	No Children	One Child	Two Children	Three Children	No Children	One Child	Two Children	Three Children
		Your credit is–				Your credit is–			
38,000	**38,050**	0	0	492	1,122	0	403	1,547	2,177
38,050	**38,100**	0	0	482	1,111	0	395	1,537	2,166
38,100	**38,150**	0	0	471	1,101	0	387	1,526	2,156
38,150	**38,200**	0	0	461	1,090	0	379	1,516	2,145
38,200	**38,250**	0	0	450	1,080	0	371	1,505	2,135
38,250	**38,300**	0	0	440	1,069	0	363	1,495	2,124
38,300	**38,350**	0	0	429	1,059	0	355	1,484	2,114
38,350	**38,400**	0	0	419	1,048	0	347	1,474	2,103
38,400	**38,450**	0	0	408	1,038	0	339	1,463	2,093
38,450	**38,500**	0	0	398	1,027	0	331	1,453	2,082
38,500	**38,550**	0	0	387	1,017	0	323	1,442	2,072
38,550	**38,600**	0	0	376	1,006	0	315	1,432	2,061
38,600	**38,650**	0	0	366	995	0	307	1,421	2,051
38,650	**38,700**	0	0	355	985	0	299	1,411	2,040
38,700	**38,750**	0	0	345	974	0	291	1,400	2,029
38,750	**38,800**	0	0	334	964	0	283	1,389	2,019
38,800	**38,850**	0	0	324	953	0	275	1,379	2,008
38,850	**38,900**	0	0	313	943	0	267	1,368	1,998
38,900	**38,950**	0	0	303	932	0	259	1,358	1,987
38,950	**39,000**	0	0	292	922	0	251	1,347	1,977
39,000	**39,050**	0	0	282	911	0	243	1,337	1,966
39,050	**39,100**	0	0	271	901	0	235	1,326	1,956
39,100	**39,150**	0	0	261	890	0	227	1,316	1,945
39,150	**39,200**	0	0	250	880	0	219	1,305	1,935
39,200	**39,250**	0	0	240	869	0	211	1,295	1,924
39,250	**39,300**	0	0	229	859	0	203	1,284	1,914
39,300	**39,350**	0	0	219	848	0	195	1,274	1,903
39,350	**39,400**	0	0	208	837	0	187	1,263	1,893
39,400	**39,450**	0	0	197	827	0	179	1,253	1,882
39,450	**39,500**	0	0	187	816	0	171	1,242	1,872
39,500	**39,550**	0	0	176	806	0	163	1,232	1,861
39,550	**39,600**	0	0	166	795	0	155	1,221	1,850
39,600	**39,650**	0	0	155	785	0	147	1,210	1,840
39,650	**39,700**	0	0	145	774	0	139	1,200	1,829
39,700	**39,750**	0	0	134	764	0	131	1,189	1,819
39,750	**39,800**	0	0	124	753	0	123	1,179	1,808
39,800	**39,850**	0	0	113	743	0	115	1,168	1,798
39,850	**39,900**	0	0	103	732	0	107	1,158	1,787
39,900	**39,950**	0	0	92	722	0	99	1,147	1,777
39,950	**40,000**	0	0	82	711	0	91	1,137	1,766
40,000	**40,050**	0	0	71	701	0	83	1,126	1,756
40,050	**40,100**	0	0	61	690	0	75	1,116	1,745
40,100	**40,150**	0	0	50	680	0	67	1,105	1,735
40,150	**40,200**	0	0	40	669	0	59	1,095	1,724
40,200	**40,250**	0	0	29	658	0	51	1,084	1,714
40,250	**40,300**	0	0	18	648	0	43	1,074	1,703
40,300	**40,350**	0	0	8	637	0	35	1,063	1,693
40,350	**40,400**	0	0	*	627	0	27	1,053	1,682
40,400	**40,450**	0	0	0	616	0	19	1,042	1,671
40,450	**40,500**	0	0	0	606	0	11	1,031	1,661
40,500	**40,550**	0	0	0	595	0	**	1,021	1,650
40,550	**40,600**	0	0	0	585	0	0	1,010	1,640
40,600	**40,650**	0	0	0	574	0	0	1,000	1,629
40,650	**40,700**	0	0	0	564	0	0	989	1,619
40,700	**40,750**	0	0	0	553	0	0	979	1,608

*If the amount you are looking up from the worksheet is at least $40,350 but less than $40,363, your credit is $1. Otherwise, you cannot take the credit.
**If the amount you are looking up from the worksheet is at least $40,500 but less than $40,545, your credit is $4. Otherwise, you cannot take the credit.

(Continued on next page)

2010 Earned Income Credit (EIC) Table—*Continued* (**Caution.** This is **not** a tax table.)

If the amount you are looking up from the worksheet is–		And your filing status is–							
		Single, head of household, or qualifying widow(er) and you have–				Married filing jointly and you have–			
At least	But less than	No Children	One Child	Two Children	Three Children	No Children	One Child	Two Children	Three Children
		Your credit is–				Your credit is–			
40,750	40,800	0	0	0	543	0	0	968	1,598
40,800	40,850	0	0	0	532	0	0	958	1,587
40,850	40,900	0	0	0	522	0	0	947	1,577
40,900	40,950	0	0	0	511	0	0	937	1,566
40,950	41,000	0	0	0	501	0	0	926	1,556
41,000	41,050	0	0	0	490	0	0	916	1,545
41,050	41,100	0	0	0	479	0	0	905	1,535
41,100	41,150	0	0	0	469	0	0	895	1,524
41,150	41,200	0	0	0	458	0	0	884	1,514
41,200	41,250	0	0	0	448	0	0	873	1,503
41,250	41,300	0	0	0	437	0	0	863	1,492
41,300	41,350	0	0	0	427	0	0	852	1,482
41,350	41,400	0	0	0	416	0	0	842	1,471
41,400	41,450	0	0	0	406	0	0	831	1,461
41,450	41,500	0	0	0	395	0	0	821	1,450
41,500	41,550	0	0	0	385	0	0	810	1,440
41,550	41,600	0	0	0	374	0	0	800	1,429
41,600	41,650	0	0	0	364	0	0	789	1,419
41,650	41,700	0	0	0	353	0	0	779	1,408
41,700	41,750	0	0	0	343	0	0	768	1,398
41,750	41,800	0	0	0	332	0	0	758	1,387
41,800	41,850	0	0	0	322	0	0	747	1,377
41,850	41,900	0	0	0	311	0	0	737	1,366
41,900	41,950	0	0	0	300	0	0	726	1,356
41,950	42,000	0	0	0	290	0	0	716	1,345
42,000	42,050	0	0	0	279	0	0	705	1,335
42,050	42,100	0	0	0	269	0	0	694	1,324
42,100	42,150	0	0	0	258	0	0	684	1,313
42,150	42,200	0	0	0	248	0	0	673	1,303
42,200	42,250	0	0	0	237	0	0	663	1,292
42,250	42,300	0	0	0	227	0	0	652	1,282
42,300	42,350	0	0	0	216	0	0	642	1,271
42,350	42,400	0	0	0	206	0	0	631	1,261
42,400	42,450	0	0	0	195	0	0	621	1,250
42,450	42,500	0	0	0	185	0	0	610	1,240
42,500	42,550	0	0	0	174	0	0	600	1,229
42,550	42,600	0	0	0	164	0	0	589	1,219
42,600	42,650	0	0	0	153	0	0	579	1,208
42,650	42,700	0	0	0	143	0	0	568	1,198
42,700	42,750	0	0	0	132	0	0	558	1,187
42,750	42,800	0	0	0	121	0	0	547	1,177
42,800	42,850	0	0	0	111	0	0	537	1,166
42,850	42,900	0	0	0	100	0	0	526	1,156
42,900	42,950	0	0	0	90	0	0	515	1,145
42,950	43,000	0	0	0	79	0	0	505	1,134
43,000	43,050	0	0	0	69	0	0	494	1,124
43,050	43,100	0	0	0	58	0	0	484	1,113
43,100	43,150	0	0	0	48	0	0	473	1,103
43,150	43,200	0	0	0	37	0	0	463	1,092
43,200	43,250	0	0	0	27	0	0	452	1,082
43,250	43,300	0	0	0	16	0	0	442	1,071
43,300	43,350	0	0	0	6	0	0	431	1,061
43,350	43,400	0	0	0	0	0	0	421	1,050
43,400	43,450	0	0	0	0	0	0	410	1,040
43,450	43,500	0	0	0	0	0	0	400	1,029
43,500	43,550	0	0	0	0	0	0	389	1,019
43,550	43,600	0	0	0	0	0	0	379	1,008
43,600	43,650	0	0	0	0	0	0	368	998
43,650	43,700	0	0	0	0	0	0	358	987
43,700	43,750	0	0	0	0	0	0	347	976

(Continued on next page)

2010 Earned Income Credit (EIC) Table–*Continued* (**Caution.** This is **not** a tax table.)

If the amount you are looking up from the worksheet is–		And your filing status is–							
		Single, head of household, or qualifying widow(er) and you have–				Married filing jointly and you have–			
		No Children	One Child	Two Children	Three Children	No Children	One Child	Two Children	Three Children
At least	But less than	Your credit is–				Your credit is–			
43,750	**43,800**	0	0	0	0	0	0	336	966
43,800	**43,850**	0	0	0	0	0	0	326	955
43,850	**43,900**	0	0	0	0	0	0	315	945
43,900	**43,950**	0	0	0	0	0	0	305	934
43,950	**44,000**	0	0	0	0	0	0	294	924
44,000	**44,050**	0	0	0	0	0	0	284	913
44,050	**44,100**	0	0	0	0	0	0	273	903
44,100	**44,150**	0	0	0	0	0	0	263	892
44,150	**44,200**	0	0	0	0	0	0	252	882
44,200	**44,250**	0	0	0	0	0	0	242	871
44,250	**44,300**	0	0	0	0	0	0	231	861
44,300	**44,350**	0	0	0	0	0	0	221	850
44,350	**44,400**	0	0	0	0	0	0	210	840
44,400	**44,450**	0	0	0	0	0	0	200	829
44,450	**44,500**	0	0	0	0	0	0	189	819
44,500	**44,550**	0	0	0	0	0	0	179	808
44,550	**44,600**	0	0	0	0	0	0	168	797
44,600	**44,650**	0	0	0	0	0	0	157	787
44,650	**44,700**	0	0	0	0	0	0	147	776
44,700	**44,750**	0	0	0	0	0	0	136	766
44,750	**44,800**	0	0	0	0	0	0	126	755
44,800	**44,850**	0	0	0	0	0	0	115	745
44,850	**44,900**	0	0	0	0	0	0	105	734
44,900	**44,950**	0	0	0	0	0	0	94	724
44,950	**45,000**	0	0	0	0	0	0	84	713
45,000	**45,050**	0	0	0	0	0	0	73	703
45,050	**45,100**	0	0	0	0	0	0	63	692
45,100	**45,150**	0	0	0	0	0	0	52	682
45,150	**45,200**	0	0	0	0	0	0	42	671
45,200	**45,250**	0	0	0	0	0	0	31	661
45,250	**45,300**	0	0	0	0	0	0	21	650
45,300	**45,350**	0	0	0	0	0	0	10	640
45,350	**45,400**	0	0	0	0	0	0	*	629
45,400	**45,450**	0	0	0	0	0	0	0	618
45,450	**45,500**	0	0	0	0	0	0	0	608
45,500	**45,550**	0	0	0	0	0	0	0	597
45,550	**45,600**	0	0	0	0	0	0	0	587
45,600	**45,650**	0	0	0	0	0	0	0	576
45,650	**45,700**	0	0	0	0	0	0	0	566
45,700	**45,750**	0	0	0	0	0	0	0	555
45,750	**45,800**	0	0	0	0	0	0	0	545
45,800	**45,850**	0	0	0	0	0	0	0	534
45,850	**45,900**	0	0	0	0	0	0	0	524
45,900	**45,950**	0	0	0	0	0	0	0	513
45,950	**46,000**	0	0	0	0	0	0	0	503
46,000	**46,050**	0	0	0	0	0	0	0	492
46,050	**46,100**	0	0	0	0	0	0	0	482
46,100	**46,150**	0	0	0	0	0	0	0	471
46,150	**46,200**	0	0	0	0	0	0	0	461
46,200	**46,250**	0	0	0	0	0	0	0	450
46,250	**46,300**	0	0	0	0	0	0	0	439
46,300	**46,350**	0	0	0	0	0	0	0	429
46,350	**46,400**	0	0	0	0	0	0	0	418
46,400	**46,450**	0	0	0	0	0	0	0	408
46,450	**46,500**	0	0	0	0	0	0	0	397

*If the amount you are looking up from the worksheet is at least $45,350 but less than $45,373, your credit is $2. Otherwise, you cannot take the credit.

(Continued on next page)

2010 Earned Income Credit (EIC) Table–*Continued* (**Caution.** This is **not** a tax table.)

If the amount you are looking up from the worksheet is–		And your filing status is–							
		Single, head of household, or qualifying widow(er) and you have–				Married filing jointly and you have–			
At least	But less than	No Children	One Child	Two Children	Three Children	No Children	One Child	Two Children	Three Children
		Your credit is–				Your credit is–			
46,500	**46,550**	0	0	0	0	0	0	0	387
46,550	**46,600**	0	0	0	0	0	0	0	376
46,600	**46,650**	0	0	0	0	0	0	0	366
46,650	**46,700**	0	0	0	0	0	0	0	355
46,700	**46,750**	0	0	0	0	0	0	0	345
46,750	**46,800**	0	0	0	0	0	0	0	334
46,800	**46,850**	0	0	0	0	0	0	0	324
46,850	**46,900**	0	0	0	0	0	0	0	313
46,900	**46,950**	0	0	0	0	0	0	0	303
46,950	**47,000**	0	0	0	0	0	0	0	292
47,000	**47,050**	0	0	0	0	0	0	0	282
47,050	**47,100**	0	0	0	0	0	0	0	271
47,100	**47,150**	0	0	0	0	0	0	0	260
47,150	**47,200**	0	0	0	0	0	0	0	250
47,200	**47,250**	0	0	0	0	0	0	0	239
47,250	**47,300**	0	0	0	0	0	0	0	229
47,300	**47,350**	0	0	0	0	0	0	0	218
47,350	**47,400**	0	0	0	0	0	0	0	208
47,400	**47,450**	0	0	0	0	0	0	0	197
47,450	**47,500**	0	0	0	0	0	0	0	187
47,500	**47,550**	0	0	0	0	0	0	0	176
47,550	**47,600**	0	0	0	0	0	0	0	166
47,600	**47,650**	0	0	0	0	0	0	0	155
47,650	**47,700**	0	0	0	0	0	0	0	145
47,700	**47,750**	0	0	0	0	0	0	0	134
47,750	**47,800**	0	0	0	0	0	0	0	124
47,800	**47,850**	0	0	0	0	0	0	0	113
47,850	**47,900**	0	0	0	0	0	0	0	103
47,900	**47,950**	0	0	0	0	0	0	0	92
47,950	**48,000**	0	0	0	0	0	0	0	81
48,000	**48,050**	0	0	0	0	0	0	0	71
48,050	**48,100**	0	0	0	0	0	0	0	60
48,100	**48,150**	0	0	0	0	0	0	0	50
48,150	**48,200**	0	0	0	0	0	0	0	39
48,200	**48,250**	0	0	0	0	0	0	0	29
48,250	**48,300**	0	0	0	0	0	0	0	18
48,300	**48,350**	0	0	0	0	0	0	0	8
48,350	**48,362**	0	0	0	0	0	0	0	1

VOLUME II

Professional Tax Practice

PART 9

Tax Law Authorities

The federal income tax law is based on statutes passed by Congress. The statutes are organized into a Code, which is currently cited as the Internal Revenue Code of 1986.

Ideally, there should be no need for legal sources other than the Code, and this is true where a statute as passed by Congress is so clear and specific that no one doubts its application. However, where the wording of a statute in the Code is general and may be interpreted in several ways, you must seek interpretations that may help you resolve a tax question or support your point of view in a tax dispute. Authoritative interpretations are made by the Treasury and the Internal Revenue Service in regulations and rulings and by federal courts in specific decisions. The relative authoritativeness of these sources is discussed in this part.

LEGISLATIVE AUTHORITIES

Internal Revenue Code

The 1986 Tax Act redesignated the Internal Revenue Code as the Internal Revenue Code of 1986. The prior designation date was 1954.

The title of the Code remains fixed with the date 1986, although sections of the Code may be amended every year. Structurally, the Code is divided into:

Subtitles (for example, Subtitle A: Income Taxes; Subtitle B: Estate and Gift Taxes, etc.);
Chapters (for example, Chapter I of Subtitle A: Normal Taxes and Surtaxes);
Subchapters (for example, Subchapter A of Chapter 1: Determination of Tax Liability);
Parts (for example, Part I of Subchapter A: Tax on Individuals); and
Sections (for example, Section I of Part 1: Tax Imposed).

Sections run consecutively in the Code from Section 1 up to Section 9834. However, in the sequence, many numbers are missing to allow for further expansion. Each section itself is then broken down as follows:

Lettered subsections: (a), (b), (c), etc.
Numbered paragraphs: (1), (2), (3), etc.
Capital-lettered subparagraphs: (A), (B), (C), etc.
Roman-numbered sub-subparagraphs: (i), (ii), (iii), etc.

Congressional Committee Reports

The legislative history of a Code section may be found in the reports of the Congressional committee that wrote the section. Under the Constitution, tax bills originate in the House of Representatives, although in practice, the Senate has sometimes considered tax legislation before the House. In recent years, the House and Senate increasingly have moved tax bills towards enactment without following the traditional practice of having the House Ways and Means Committee and the Senate Finance Committee release formal written reports explaining the provisions in their respective Committee bills, prior to consideration by the full House and Senate. Where there are no formal Committee reports, each Committee typically prepares a bill summary, and the Joint Committee on Taxation issues a description of the provisions in the respective House and Senate bills.

Where the House and Senate approve different versions of a bill, the traditional means of settling the differences between the two versions is for House and Senate leaders to appoint a Conference Committee that prepares a compromise measure and a Conference Committee report that explains it. If the House and Senate both pass the compromise bill, it is sent to the President and becomes law after the President signs it. In recent years, House and Senate Conferees have often met informally, and at times there has been no Conference Report. The Joint Committee on Taxation typically releases an explanation of the Conference Agreement, commonly called the "Blue Book." The Joint Committee explanation cannot be cited as the official Conference Committee Report, but it may be given deference by a reviewing court if it supports an official House, Senate, or Conference report, or is not contradicted by an official report.

House, Senate, and Conference Committee reports are available online from the Library of Congress website (http://thomas.loc.gov) and from the Government Printing Office (http://www.gpo.gov). The Joint Committee on Taxation website (http://www.house.gov/jct) has the Joint Committee explanations as well as links to the House Ways and Means Committee website (http://waysandmeans.house.gov) and the Senate Finance Committee website (http://www.senate.gov/~finance).

ADMINISTRATIVE AUTHORITIES

Treasury Regulations

Regulations authorized by the Internal Revenue Code have the force and effect of law and may be relied upon as authority. Failure to comply with such a regulation can result in a negligence penalty.

The validity of a regulation can be questioned. Courts are not bound by regulations and can overrule them if they are unreasonable and plainly inconsistent with the Code.

Once a regulation has interpreted a Code provision, passage of a similar law with the exact wording is regarded by the courts as evidence that Congress is satisfied with the regulation and, thus, the regulation generally will not be overruled. If a regulation is disapproved by a court, the IRS can continue to enforce the regulation unless the regulation is reversed by the Supreme Court.

New regulations are generally first announced as proposed regulations. During a stated time limit, tax professionals and taxpayers are allowed to suggest changes or additions. Often, the IRS will hold special hearings to discuss the proposals, and then, after reviewing the suggestions, will issue final regulations as Treasury Decisions (TDs), which include a general explanation of the regulations and are published in the Federal Register and in the IRS Internal Revenue Bulletin. The IRS also issues some regulations as temporary regulations, which generally are effective upon publication and remain in effect until replaced by final regulations. Temporary regulations must be simultaneously issued as proposed regulations and may remain in effect for no more than three years after the date of issuance. Temporary regulations, like final regulations, are issued as Treasury Decisions (TDs). Tax services for professionals provide the text of proposed, temporary, and final regulations to their subscribers.

Each section of the regulations is preceded by the section, subsection, or paragraph of the Internal Revenue Code that it interprets. The sections of the regulations are distinguished from sections of the Code by the Arabic numeral 1, followed by a decimal point (1.) before the corresponding provision of the Internal Revenue Code. This designation is then followed by a dash (-) and a number further identifying a section of the regulation. With these numbers you can find regulations interpreting a Code provision. Thus, the regulation explaining IRC Section 301 is designated 1.301, and a section of that regulation is identified as 1.301-1.

Revenue Rulings

Revenue Rulings make up a large body of IRS interpretations of the tax law. They are generally official replies by the IRS National Office to specific problems raised by taxpayers. They are published to provide guidance in cases having similar facts to those presented in the rulings.

Revenue Rulings are published weekly in the Internal Revenue Bulletin. Every half-year, these rulings are republished in a book, called the Cumulative Bulletin, which is available to the public from the Government Printing Office. The weekly bulletins are available online from the "Businesses" page of the IRS website, *www.irs.gov.*

See below for references to Revenue Rulings appearing in the Internal Revenue Bulletin and the Cumulative Bulletin.

In the Weekly Internal Revenue Bulletin

Rev. Rul. 2010-21, 2010-39 IRB 388 means that the particular ruling is the 21st ruling for 2010, it appears in the 39th weekly bulletin for that year, and can be found on page 388 of that bulletin.

In the Cumulative Bulletin

Rev. Rul. 94-43, 1994-2 CB 198—means that the ruling appears in the second semiannual Cumulative Bulletin for 1994 and, in that book, can be found on page 198.

Other IRS Rulings and Releases

After Revenue Rulings, there are several other IRS releases and rulings that are helpful in determining IRS policy.

Revenue procedures. These describe internal practices and procedures within the IRS and filing procedures for taxpayers. They are published in the Internal Revenue Bulletin. References to them are prefixed by the abbreviation "Rev. Proc." For example, Rev. Proc. 2010-36, 2010-42 IRB 439, means that the revenue procedure is the 36th procedure for 2010, it appears in the 42nd weekly bulletin for the year, and can be found on page 439 of that bulletin.

Notices and announcements. These describe current IRS policy toward a specific issue. They are primarily intended to provide IRS guidance on new tax law developments. They may contain the advance text of Revenue Rulings. Announcements and Notices are published in the Internal Revenue Bulletin.

Letter rulings. These include private rulings, determination letters, and technical advice memoranda. Such rulings are not officially published and may not be cited as a precedent by any other taxpayer. However, they may be helpful, as they reflect the IRS's policy and interpretation of the law. In one case, the Supreme Court noted that private letter rulings are evidence of an IRS position, although they have no authoritative force. Virtually all letter rulings are open to public inspection after all information that could identify the taxpayer involved has been deleted.

General counsel memoranda, actions on decisions, technical memoranda. These are internal IRS documents that provide reasons for rulings, regulations, and acquiescences or nonacquiescences to court decisions. General Counsel Memoranda (GCMs) are legal opinions on proposed revenue rulings, private rulings, and technical advice memoranda. Actions on Decisions (AODs) recommend whether or not to appeal adverse court decisions. Technical Memoranda (TMs) indicate the legal and policy basis for proposed Treasury regulations. The documents are released by the IRS after deletions are made to remove identifying information.

JUDICIAL AUTHORITIES

A taxpayer who receives a notice of deficiency can appeal to the Tax Court without actually paying the deficiency. Alternatively, the deficiency can be paid and a claim for a refund filed with the IRS; if the refund claim is denied, a refund suit can be brought in Federal District Court. A refund suit may also be brought in the U.S. Court of Federal Claims. Appeals from these courts are heard by a Federal Court of Appeals.

Court Decisions

The authority of court decisions varies. When using court decisions, keep these points in mind:

- The IRS is not bound to follow a court decision in any case apart from the case in which the decision has been handed down. The only exception to this rule is a decision of the Supreme Court.
- Court decisions are not of equal weight. A decision of the Tax Court has substantially greater significance than a decision rendered by a Federal District Court and often by a Federal Court of Appeals, primarily because the Tax Court hears cases all over the nation and will apply its decisions on a nationwide basis.

  Federal District Courts are local federal courts and a Court of Appeals hears appeals only on a regional basis. So whereas one decision of the Tax Court will generally be applied throughout the United States, there may be several conflicting interpretations between district courts in various localities and Courts of Appeals in the various geographical regions. For example, a district court in California is not bound to follow a decision handed down by a district court in New York. And a Court of Appeals for one region is not bound to follow a decision of a Court of Appeals for another region. On the other hand, the precedent of a Tax Court decision rendered in New York is generally controlling authority in a Tax Court hearing held anywhere else in the United States. However, the Tax Court generally will follow a decision of the Court of Appeals to which the current case is appealable if that prior decision is squarely on point.

U.S. Tax Court

The Tax Court is a special court for taxpayers who appeal tax deficiencies imposed by the IRS for income, estate, or gift taxes. It is independent of the IRS and the Treasury department; its members are judges, and its decisions are subject to the same judicial review as that of any other federal court. They can be appealed at a Court of Appeals and then to the Supreme Court.

Between the years 1924 and 1942, the Court was known as the Board of Tax Appeals. In 1942, it received the present name of Tax Court. Cases decided by the Court before 1942 are referred to, for example, as 20 BTA 45 and cases afterwards as 30 TC 43. (The first number of the citation designates the volume of the particular series of court decisions; the second number designates the page within the volume in which the case can be found.)

The IRS is not bound by a Tax Court decision except in the particular case in which the decision has been rendered. It can continue to litigate the same issue in other cases before the Tax Court and in other courts. However, in a tax dispute with a taxpayer involving the same issue that the Court decided against the government, the IRS may be more inclined to negotiate a settlement than have the taxpayer bring a case before the Tax Court for another unfavorable decision against its position.

There are three types of Tax Court decisions:

Regular decisions. These are officially reported by the Tax Court and published in the United States Tax Court Reports by the U.S. Government Printing Office. Regular decisions are available on the Tax Court website, www.ustaxcourt.gov. They are also available from private tax publishers and online services. In Part 10 of this book, we reference regular decisions to the CCH Tax Court Reporter if a citation to the official reporter was not available.

Memorandum decisions. These are not reported by the Tax Court in official volumes, but are available on the Tax Court website, www.ustaxcourt.gov, and from private tax publishers and online services. In Part 10, memorandum decisions are referenced to the CCH Inc. series, Tax Court Memorandum Decisions, cited "TCM," where such a citation is available. Otherwise, citations are to decision number, such as TC Memo 2010-147.

What is the court test for reporting a case as either a regular decision or as a memorandum decision? The Court says a memorandum decision involves no question of law, but merely facts that the Court believes are limited to a number of cases. If a memorandum decision does involve a question of law, the question is usually one that has been decided previously by the Tax Court and followed by the Court of Appeals. However, taxpayers can and do appeal memorandum decisions to the Court of Appeals as they can regular decisions.

Although these are considered by the Court as minor decisions, they are further examples of Tax Court policy toward a particular tax issue. Furthermore, memorandum decisions are often appealed and the decision of the appeals court in these cases may become important authority.

Current Tax Court policy in issues disputed by two or more Courts of Appeals is to follow the opinion of the Court to which the appeal may be taken, if that Court has ruled on the issue.

Summary opinions. These are cases decided under the Tax Court's small tax case procedure for deficiencies of $50,000 or less (IRC §7463). Such cases are handled expeditiously and informally. It is available at the option of the taxpayer if the Court concurs. Cases may be heard by appointed special trial judges. A small claim case can be discontinued at any time before a decision, but the decision, when made, is final. No appeal can be taken. A decision does not have precedential value. Summary opinions are available on the Tax Court website, *www.ustaxcourt.gov,* and from private tax publishers and online services.

IRS response to decision. The IRS may announce its acceptance of or disagreement with a Tax Court holding against a position held by the IRS in an officially reported decision. No policy statements are made for memorandum decisions. These announcements are made in the weekly Internal Revenue Bulletin, as acquiescences or nonacquiescences. The IRS cautions that an acquiescence of a particular decision merely signifies its acceptance of the Court's conclusion. It does not necessarily mean that it has accepted or approved of the Court's reasons for the conclusion, and it advises its officials to apply the rule of acquiesced cases only to cases that have substantially the same facts and circumstances as the acquiesced case. An acquiescence or nonacquiescence of a reported case can be recognized by the abbreviation (*Acq.*) or (*Nonacq.*) at the end of the case citation. However, if you are going to rely on an acquiesced case, try to find the exact terms of the IRS approval from the weekly Internal Revenue Bulletin or Cumulative Bulletin. Sometimes an acquiescence is limited only to one particular issue of a case. Finally, the IRS is free to withdraw an acquiescence or non-acquiescence.

Federal District Court

There is at least one Federal District Court for each state, with the more populous states having two or more district courts. A Federal District Court can hear only tax cases in which a taxpayer sues for a refund after his or her claim has been denied by the IRS.

Not all district court decisions are rendered in written form. But where they are in writing, they may be handed down as an Opinion, Findings of Fact and Conclusions of Law, or both. Generally, a district court opinion is not strong authority, primarily because of the local nature of a district court. However, a well-reasoned district court decision may be accepted by other courts and even the IRS, and in the absence of any other authority on a particular issue, a decision of a district court may prove helpful as presenting at least one published view of the problem.

District court decisions are referred in this book to their place in the Federal Supplement Series published by the West Publishing Company. For example, take the case Seymour Gale, 768 F. Supp. 1305 (N.D. IL. (1991)). Seymour Gale is the name of the case; 768 refers to the volume of the Federal Supplement Series, 1305 to the page within that volume, N.D. IL. to the Northern District of Illinois, and 1991 to the year of decision. District court decisions not cited to the Federal Supplement Series are cited to the U.S. Tax Cases published by Commerce Clearing House. These citations are explained in the section on Court of Appeals decisions below.

U.S. Court of Federal Claims

The only tax cases heard by the U.S. Court of Federal Claims (formerly called the U.S. Claims Court) are those involving refunds of taxes. Decisions by the U.S. Court of Federal Claims on income tax questions have not had an important effect on the development of the income tax law. However, a favorable decision of the Court of Federal Claims on a particular issue that you may be disputing with the IRS may encourage you to choose that court to hear your case. And a well-reasoned decision rendered by the Court of Federal Claims may be followed by the other courts. Appeals from the Court of Federal Claims decisions are heard by the Court of Appeals for the Federal Circuit.

Court of Federal Claims decisions are referred in this book to their place in the Federal Claims Reporter published by West Publishing Company. If citations to the Federal Claims Reporter are not available, Court of Federal Claims decisions are cited to the U.S. Tax Cases published by Commerce Clearing House.

Court of Appeals Decisions

There are 12 Courts of Appeals that hear appeals taken either by taxpayers or the government from decisions rendered by the Tax Court or Federal District Court. Eleven of these are regional courts that hear cases arising within their regions, which are technically called "circuits"; the twelfth hears cases arising within the District of Columbia. The circuits and the states within each circuit are listed in the table on the next page.

Appeals of tax refund decisions from the U.S. Court of Federal Claims are heard by a separate appeals court, the U.S. Court of Appeals for the Federal Circuit.

Court of Appeals decisions make up an important part of federal tax law. But the effectiveness of a particular decision may vary because of these factors:

- The IRS is not bound to follow any precedent set by an appeals court decision. The IRS will sometimes announce its decision to follow or not to follow a Court of Appeals decision.
- The Tax Court does not consider itself bound to follow any precedent set by an appeals court decision. The Tax Court view is that its nationwide jurisdiction cannot be restricted by the rules of the 12 different appeals courts. However, it will generally follow an appeals court decision in the circuit to which the case before it may be appealed.
- A Court of Appeals of one region is not bound to follow the precedent of a Court of Appeals in another region. Consequently, a decision of a particular appeals court is far stronger for taxpayers who can bring their appeals before that court than for taxpayers who must appeal to other appeals courts. A court will generally follow its own precedents unless it is overruled or later decides its original position was wrong.

Court of Appeals decisions are referred in this book to their place in the Federal Series reports published by the West Publishing Company. The first series is cited as "F.," the second series as "F.2d," and the third as "F.3d." For example, take the citation Albertson's, Inc., 12 F.3d 1529 (9th Cir. (1994)). Albertson's, Inc., is the name of the taxpayer, 12 refers to the volume of the third series of the Federal Series reports, 1529 to the page within that volume, 9th Cir. refers to the circuit appeals court, and 1994 is the year of the decision.

In some instances, citations are not available for the Federal Series. For example, Cathy M. Lantz, 2010-1 USTC ¶50,446 (7th Cir. 2010), may be found in U.S. Tax Cases published by Commerce Clearing House. These reports contain tax decisions from all levels of federal courts except the Tax Court. Except for years prior to 1934, two Commerce Clearing House volumes appear for each year. 2010-1 refers to the first volume of 2010; ¶50,446 is the paragraph at which the case is located.

Appeals court decisions may also be obtained from online services.

Supreme Court Decisions

Supreme Court decisions are the only decisions that the Internal Revenue Service and lower courts are required to follow. They have the same force as the Code and remain in force until Congress specifically changes the Court's interpretation or unless the Supreme Court in a later decision reverses its own position. Tax cases come before the Supreme Court when either a taxpayer or the government files a petition for a Writ of Certiorari, asking the Court to review the decision of a U.S. Court of Appeals. However, the Supreme Court limits its review of tax disputes generally to cases where there is a conflict of decisions among several U.S. Courts of Appeals on a specific interpretation of a tax law.

An example of a reference to a Supreme Court decision is: Harold Davis, 495 U.S. 472 (1990).

Harold Davis is the name of the taxpayer involved in the case; 495 refers to the official volume in which the case can be found; U.S. designates the official Supreme Court volumes; 472 refers to the page within a volume; and 1990 refers to the year of the decision. The case can also be found in volumes published by private publishers that are released before the official Supreme Court volumes. For example, unofficial Supreme Court decisions may be found in the Supreme Court Reporter, put out by West Publishing Company, or in U.S. Tax Cases, published by Commerce Clearing House. An example of a U.S. Tax Cases citation is: U.S. v. Sandra L. Craft, 2002-1 USTC ¶50,361.

States Within Court of Appeals Regions

FIRST CIRCUIT
Maine
Massachusetts
New Hampshire
Rhode Island
Puerto Rico

SECOND CIRCUIT
Connecticut
New York
Vermont

THIRD CIRUIT
Delaware
New Jersey
Pennsylvania
Virgin Islands

FOURTH CIRCUIT
Maryland
North Carolina
South Carolina
Virginia
West Virginia

FIFTH CIRCUIT
Canal Zone
Louisiana
Mississippi
Texas

SIXTH CIRCUIT
Kentucky
Michigan
Ohio
Tennessee

SEVENTH CIRCUIT
Illinois
Indiana
Wisconsin

EIGHTH CIRCUIT
Arkansas
Iowa
Minnesota
Missouri
Nebraska
North Dakota
South Dakota

NINTH CIRCUIT
Alaska
Arizona
California
Hawaii
Idaho
Montana
Nevada
Oregon
Washington
Guam

TENTH CIRCUIT
Colorado
Kansas
New Mexico
Oklahoma
Utah
Wyoming

ELEVENTH CIRCUIT
Alabama
Florida
Georgia

CIRCUIT FOR THE DISTRICT OF COLUMBIA
Washington, D.C.

Part 10

Citations of Authority

Part 10 contains the citations of authority for the text and material in Parts 1–7. You may use the Chapter Contents starting on page v or the Index starting on page 961 to locate the tax topic you are interested in researching. After locating the topic, authority for the discussion can be found by locating the same number in this part. Regardless of where you find the number of your topic—from the text, the index, or the checklists—you will find the citation of authority under that number in this part. The tax information in the text of Parts 1–7 is identified further by the use of italics under the identical number in this Part 10. For example, if you are interested in the tax law authorities for the discussion of tax-free employer accident and health plans at *3.1* on page 52, these may be found under *3.1* in Part 10 on page 810.

The references to law reviews, tax journal articles, and private letter rulings in this section are not cited as authority for any position taken in Your Income Tax. They are provided as a reference for your further study of the topics under which they are cited.

Key to Citations

Authority	*Example*	*Page*
Internal Revenue Code of 1986	IRC §305(b)(2)	783
Treasury Regulation	Reg. §1.305-1	783
U.S. Tax Court		784
Regular decision, in official court reporter	DeWayne Bond, 100 TC 32 (1993)	
Regular decision, not in official court reporter	Scott E. Rubenstein, 134 TC No. 13 (2010)	
Memorandum opinion, in Tax Court Memorandum Decisions	Douglas Kemmerer, 66 TCM 550 (1993)	
Memorandum opinion, not in Tax Court Memorandum Decisions	Matthias Heller, TC Memo 2010-147	
Summary opinion (the asterisk indicates that it may not be treated as precedent for any other case)	*Laura A. Brady, TC Summary Opinion 2010-107	
Reversed or affirmed	George S. Nalle, III, 997 F.2d 1134 (5th Cir. 1993), rev'g 99 TC 187 (1992)	
Board of Tax Appeals (predecessor to U.S. Tax Court)		784
Regular opinion	Steven Smith, 30 BTA 49	
Memorandum opinion	A.F.C. Oil Co., BTA Memo. Dec. 10, 958-F (1939)	
IRS Acquiescence	Jones, 12 TC 49 (Acq.)	785
IRS Non-acquiescence	Smith, 13 TC 62 (Nonacq.)	
Federal District Court		785
Decision in Federal Supplement	Chester J. Maleszewski, 827 F. Supp. 1553 (D.C. FL 1993)	
Decision not in Federal Supplement	James Hendrix, 2010-2 USTC ¶50,541 (D.C. OH 2010)	
U.S. Claims Court (renamed U.S. Court of Federal Claims, October 29, 1992)	Anthony Stack, 25 Ct. Cl. 634 (1992)	785
U.S. Court of Federal Claims		
Opinion, in Federal Claims Reporter	Robert P. Kliethermes, 27 Fed. Cl. 111 (1992)	
Recent opinion, not in Federal Claims Reporter	Cencast Services, L.P., 2010-2 USTC ¶50,599 (Ct. Fed. Claims, 2010)	
U.S. Court of Appeals		785
Opinion, in Federal Reporter	Mickey L. Worden, 2 F.3d 359 (10th Cir. 1993)	
Recent opinion, not in Federal Reporter	Cathy Marie Lantz, 2010-1 USTC ¶50,446 (7th Cir. 2010)	
U.S. Supreme Court		786
Opinion, in official court reporter	Harvey F. Euge, 444 U.S. 707 (1980)	
Recent opinion, not in official court reporter	Michael J. Knight, 2008-1 USTC ¶50,132 (Sup. Ct. 2008)	

Revenue Rulings, Treasury Decisions, Releases, and Abbreviations		**783**
Revenue Ruling found in Cumulative Bulletin	Rev. Rul. 94-44,1994-2 CB 190	
Revenue Ruling found in Internal Revenue Bulletin	Rev. Rul. 2010-21, 2010-39 IRB 388	
Announcement found in Internal Revenue Bulletin	Announcement 2010-89, 2010-46 IRB 669	
Internal Revenue News Release	News Release IR-2010-112	
Notice found in the Cumulative Bulletin	Notice 93-12, 1993-1 CB 298	
Notice found in the Internal Revenue Bulletin	Notice 2010-69, 2010-44 IRB 576	
Private Letter Ruling (the asterisk indicates that it may not be cited as authority)	* Letter Ruling 9530005 (pre-1999), 201027015 (post-1998)	
Revenue Procedure found in Cumulative Bulletin	Rev. Proc. 93-26, 1993-1 CB 504	
Revenue Procedure found in Internal Revenue Bulletin	Rev. Proc. 2010-42, 2010-46 IRB 459	
Treasury Decision found in Internal Revenue Bulletin	T.D. 9501, 2010-46 IRB 651	
Treasury Decision found in Federal Register	T.D. 9501, 75 F.R. 60309	

Law Reviews and Periodicals

Articles are cited according to their title, author, and periodical title. The number before the periodical title is the volume number, and the number following is the page number, which is then followed by the year of publication.

Filing Basics

Filing Tests

Income limits

IRC §6012

IRC §6017 (self-employed)

Filing for dependents

IRC §6012(a)(1)(c)

Joint returns

IRC §6013

File jointly even though spouse had no earnings

IRC §6013(a)

Reg. §1.6013-1(a)(1)

Determination of marital status

IRC §7703

Qualifying widow(er)

IRC §2(a)

Reg. §1.2-2

Spouse missing in action

IRC §2(a)(3)

Head of household

IRC §2(b)

Self-employment income

IRC §6017

Married, living apart

IRC §2(c)

IRC §7703(b)

Different tax years bar joint return

IRC §6013(a)(2)

Reg. §1.6013-1(c)

Different tax years before marriage

Frank E. Bertucci, 146 F. Supp. 949 (Ct. Cl. 1957)

Dependent

IRC §6012(a)(1)(C)(iv)

Nonresident alien

IRC §6012(a)(2)(C)(i)(ii)

Tax year of less than 12 months because of accounting period change

IRC §6012(a)(2)(C)(ii)

IRC §63(c)(6)(c)(1)

Gross income

IRC §61

Where To File

IRC §6091

Reg. §1.6091-2

Armed Forces

* IRS Publication 3

Filing Deadlines

April 15 due date for individuals

IRC §6072(a)

Reg. §1.6072-1

Due date falls on weekend or holiday

IRC §7503

Patriots' day

News Release IR-2006-37

Notice 2006-23, 2006-11 IRB 594

Timely mailing is timely filing

IRC §7502

Reg. §301.7502-1

Automatic six-month extension

Reg. §1.6081-4T

Citizens/residents with tax home outside or in military outside U.S. and Puerto Rico

Reg. §1.6081-5(a)(5) and (6) (automatic two-month extension)

Reg. §1.6081-4T and -5T (may file for additional four-month extension)

Postage meter date ignored

Irving Fishman, 51 TC 869 (1969), aff'd per curiam, 420 F.2d 491 (2d Cir. 1970)

Combat zone

IRC §7508

IRC §112

Spouse traveling outside U.S.

Rev. Rul. 82-161, 1982-2 CB 379

Note: *Paragraph numbers refer to Parts 1 through 7. Items marked* are research aids, not citations of authority;* see *"Key to Citations" on page 801*

1 Filing Status

1.1 Which Filing Status Should You Use?

* IRS Publication 501

Joint returns

IRC §6013

Qualifying widow(er)

IRC §2(a)

Reg. §1.2-2

Head of household

IRC §2(b)

Unmarried individuals

IRC §1(c)

1.2 Tax Rates Based on Filing Status

IRC §1

1.3 Filing Separately Instead of Jointly

IRC §1(d)

Non-community-property states; joint accounts

Rev. Rul. 59-66, 1959-1 CB 60

Three years to elect joint return after separate returns

Reg. §1.6013-2

Alternative minimum tax exemption

IRC §55(d)

Standard deduction restriction

IRC §63(c)(6)(A)

Reduction of itemized deductions

IRC §68

Phaseout of exemptions on separate return

IRC §151(d)(3)(B)

IRC §151(d)(3)(C)(iv)

1.4 Filing a Joint Return

* "Joint Tax Returns Offer Distinct Advantages—Generally," Steven C. Thompson and Randall K. Serrett, 68 Tax Strategies 158 (March 2002)

Unmarried couple can't file joint return

*Gabriel Mora, TC Summary Opinion 2010-60

Joint return with new spouse denied when state law invalidates prior Mexican divorce

A. Gersten, 267 F.2d 195 (9th Cir. 1957), aff'g in part 28 TC 756 (1957)

H.K. Lee, 64 TC 552, aff'd, 550 F.2d 1201 (9th Cir. 1977)

Interlocutory divorce decree

William F. Holcomb, 237 F.2d 502 (9th Cir. 1956)

J. R. Calhoun, Jr., 27 TC 115 (1956) (Acq.)

Joyce P. Lane, 26 TC 405 (1956) (Acq.)

Rev. Rul. 57-368, 1957-2 CB 896

Joint return with new spouse allowed although prior divorce decree declared invalid by state law

Harold E. Wondsel, 350 F.2d 339 (2d Cir. 1965), cert. denied, 383 U.S. 935

Herman Borax Est., 349 F.2d 666 (2d Cir. 1965), rev'g 40 TC 1001 (1963), cert. denied, 383 U.S. 935

Rev. Rul. 67-442, 1967-2 CB 65 (IRS will not follow Wondsel or Borax decisions)

No consent to file joint return disallowed

*Laura A. Brady, TC Summary Opinion 2010-107

Each spouse liable for tax

IRC §6013(d)(3)

Reg. §1.6013-4(b)

Vaughn C. Payne, 247 F.2d 481 (8th Cir. 1957), cert. denied, 355 U.S. 923

W. L. Kann, 210 F.2d 247 (3d Cir. 1954), cert. denied, 347 U.S. 967

Myrna S. Howell, 175 F.2d 240 (6th Cir. 1949)

Alma Helfrich, 25 TC 404 (1955) (Acq.)

Virginia M. Wilkins, 19 TC 752 (1953) (Acq.)

Eva M. Manton, 11 TC 831 (1948) (Acq.)

William W. Kellet, 5 TC 608 (1945) (Acq.)

Spouse relieved of joint return liability

IRC §6015

Notice 98-61, 1998-51 IRB 13

Divorce or legal separation

IRC §143(a)(2)

IRC §6013(d)

Reg. §1.6013-4(a)

Kenneth T. Sullivan, 256 F.2d 664 (4th Cir. 1958), aff'g 29 TC 71 (1957)

Executor disaffirms

IRC §6013(a)(3)

Reg. §1.6013-1(d)(5)

Dependent's joint return used as refund claim

Rev. Rul. 54-567, 1954-2 CB 108, affirmed by Rev. Rul. 65-34, 1965-1 CB 86

Sign as spouse's agent

Reg. §1.6013-1(a)(2)

Reg. §1.6012-1(a)(5)

Sick spouse

Rev. Rul. 70-216, 1970-1 CB 265

Intended joint return

Walter M. Ferguson, Jr., 14 TC 846 (1950) (Acq.)

Alfred E. Whitehouse Est., 14 TCM 501 (1955)

John Young, 11 TCM 239 (1952)

Jeremy H. Peirce, 43 TCM 400 (1982)

Frank Boyle, 67 TCM 294 (1994)

One spouse agreed to have other spouse handle tax matters

Muriel Heim, 251 F.2d 44 (8th Cir. 1958)

Myrna S. Howell, 10 TC 859 (1948), aff'd, 175 F.2d 240 (6th Cir. 1949)

Answers indicate intent

W. L. Kann, 210 F.2d 247 (3d Cir. 1954), cert. denied, 347 U.S. 967

Explain spouse's failure

Joyce P. Lane, 26 TC 405 (1956) (Acq.)

May elect joint return after separate return was filed

IRC §6013(b)(2)

After joint return filed may not elect separate returns after due date

Reg. §1.6013-1(a)(1)

Matthew L. Ladden, 38 TC 530 (1962) (Acq.)

Thomas J. Leger, 29 TCM 101 (1970)

IRS settlement with bankrupt husband does not protect wife

Carolyn S. Kroh, 98 TC 29 (1992)

1.5 Nonresident Alien Spouse

Nonresident alien spouse generally bars joint return

IRC §6013(a)(1)

Note: *Paragraph numbers refer to Parts 1 through 7. Items marked * are research aids, not citations of authority;* see *"Key to Citations" on page 801*

Reg. §1.6013-1(b)

Claim nonresident alien spouse as exemption

IRC §151

Reg. §1.151-1

Joint return under election

IRC §6013(g)

Special election where nonresident alien spouse becomes a resident during the year

IRC §6013(h)

1.6 Community Property Rules

* IRS Publication 555

Community property rules do not apply where couple does not elect joint return

IRC §879

One-half vested interest

Aimee D. Bagur, 66 TC 817 (1976), rem'd, 603 F.2d 491 (5th Cir. 1979)

Community rules inapplicable to certain separated couples

IRC §66(a)

Community property rules for earned income disregarded—spouse not notified of income

IRC §66(b)

Community property rules disregarded—innocent spouse

IRC §66(c)

California registered domestic partners must split income

*Chief Counsel Memorandum 201021050

Spouse receiving temporary alimony

Charlotte J. Kimes, 55 TC 774 (1971)

Renunciation of interest

Anne G. Mitchell, 403 U.S. 190 (1971)

Self-employment tax for spouses

Rev. Rul. 82-39, 1982-1 CB 119

Intention to move to a community property state

George D. Hampton, Jr., 38 TC 131 (1962)

Dependency exemption on joint return

Thomas R. Jones, 38 TCM 599 (1977)

1.7 Innocent Spouse Rules

IRC §6015(b) (basic innocent spouse relief)

IRC §6015(c) (separate liability relief)

IRC §6015(f) (equitable relief)

Reg. §§ 1.6015-1 through 1.6015-9 (final regulations, T.D. 9003, 7/17/02)

* IRS Publication 971

Innocent spouse election

IRC §6015(b)

Reg. §1.6015-2

Tax Court appeal

IRC §6015(e)

Shielding of battered spouse who files for relief

IRS News Release IR-2001-23

Appeals rights for nonrequesting spouses

Rev. Proc. 2003-19, 2003-5 IRB 371

Knowledge or reason to know standard

IRC §6015(b)(1)(C)

Reg. §1.6015-2(c) (reason to know)

Reg. §1.6015-3(c)(2) (actual knowledge)

Kathryn Cheshire, 282 F.3d 326 (5th Cir. 2002), aff'g 115 TC 183 (2000) (knowledge of omitted income bars relief)

Knowledge of omitted income bars innocent spouse relief

*Joe Stewart, TC Summary Opinion 2010-31

Lack of knowledge standard — Pre-1998 Act

Bokum II, 94 TC 126 (1990), aff'd, 922 F.2d 1132 (1993)

Gwen Erdahl, 58 TCM 1532 (1990), rev'd and

rem'd, 930 F.2d 585 (8th Cir. 1991)

Patricia A. Price, 887 F.2d 959 (9th Cir. 1989)

Janet Bliss, 59 F. 3d 374 (2d Cir., 1995), aff'g 66

TCM 522 (1993) (attorney's knowledge imputed to spouse)

Lucille E. Kistner, 18 F.3d 1521 (11th Cir. 1994)

1.8 Separate Liability Election for Former Spouses

IRC §6015(c)

* IRS Publication 971

Innocent spouse can recover attorneys' fees

Barbara A. Owen, TC Memo 2005-115

Helen E. Foy, TC Memo 2005-116

Separate liability election

IRC §6015(c)

Reg. §1.6015-3

Spouse's knowledge of omitted income

IRC §6015(c)

Reg. §1.6015-3(c)(2)(A)

Kathryn Cheshire, 282 F.3d 326 (5th Cir. 2002), aff'g 115 TC 183 (2000) (knowledge of omitted income bars relief)

Herbert L. Mitchell, 2002-2 USTC ¶50,475 (D.C. Cir. 2002) (follows Fifth Circuit's knowledge test analysis in Cheshire above)

Fredie Lynn Charlton, 114 TC 333 (2000) (relief where spouse does not know amount of omitted income)

Spouse's knowledge of erroneous deduction

Reg. §1.6015-3(c)(2)(B)

Isaac Baranowicz, TC Memo 2003-274

Patricia M. Mora, 117 TC 279 (2002)

Kathy A. King, 116 TC 198 (2001)

Tax Court appeal

IRC §6015(e)

Relief denied under tax benefit rule

Patricia M. Mora, 117 TC 279 (2002)

1.9 Equitable Relief

Equitable relief

IRC §6015(f)

Reg. §1.6015-4

Rev. Proc. 2003-61, 2003-32 IRB 296 (criteria for relief)

Two-year rule thrown out

Cathy Marie Lantz, 132 TC No. 8 (2009)

Appellate court upholds two-year rule

Cathy Marie Lantz, 2010-1 USTC ¶50,446 (7th Cir. 2010)rev'g 132 TC No. 8 (2009)

Tax Court remains opposed to two-year rule

Audrey Marie Hall, 135 TC No. 19 (2010)

Relief where other spouse fails to remit tax payment

Note: *Paragraph numbers refer to Parts 1 through 7. Items marked * are research aids, not citations of authority;* see *"Key to Citations" on page 801*

Mitchell S. Wiest, TC Memo 2003-91

No relief for spouse with reason to know of income omission

Michael B. Butler, 114 TC 276 (2000)

Equitable relief granted for former spouse's theft of tax money

Robby Goodale Gilbert, TC Summary Opinion 2007-16

Equitable relief denied to financially inexperienced spouse

Nancy A. Sjodin, TC Memo 2004-205

1.10 Death of Your Spouse in 2010

Joint return for decedent and survivor

IRC §6013(a)(3)

Reg. §1.6013-1(d)-3, -4

Remarriage

Reg. §1.6013-1(d)(2)

Change in accounting period

IRC §6013(a)(2)

IRC §443(a)(1)

Reg. §1.6013-1(d)(2)

Nonresident alien

IRC §6013(a)(1) and (g)(4)(B)

Reg. §1.6013-1(b)

Disaffirmance by executor

Reg. §1.6013-1(d)(5) and (6)

Co-executrix could not disaffirm

Frank J. Floyd Est., 51-2 USTC ¶9415 (Orphans' Ct., Del. County, Pa. 1951)

Treat as late return

Reg. §1.6013-1(d)(5) and (6)

Signing

IRC §6061

Reg. §1.6061-1

Reg. §1.6012-2(b)(1)

Reg. §1.6013-1(a)(2)

Privilege of treating survivor's return as joint return

IRC §2

Reg. §1.2-2

Reg. §1.6013-1(e)

Survivor bound to joint return liability

Maxine Ruzich, 47 TC 380 (1967)

1.11 Qualifying Widow(er)

Status If Your Spouse Died in 2009 or 2008

Qualifying widows or widowers

IRC §2(a)(1)(B)

1.12 Qualifying as Head of Household

Head of household defined

IRC §2(b)

Qualifying children for tax years starting after 2004

IRC §2(b)(1)(A)(i)

Special rule for parents

IRC §2(b)(1)(B)

Reg. §1.2-2(c)(2)

Maintaining household

IRC §2(b)(1)

IRC §1.2-2(c) and (d)

Interlocutory decree

Carole F. Brown, 31 TCM 194 (1972)

Support order pendente lite as interlocutory decree

Walter G. Brusey, 41 TCM 1223 (1981)

Separated spouse must live apart for last six months

Laurel Hopkins, 63 TCM 3113 (1992)

Status denied when children change residence after separation agreement

Fred J. Stanback, Jr., 77-1 USTC ¶9181 (D.N.C. 1977)

Parent in rest home

Rev. Rul. 70-279, 1970-1 CB 1

Taxpayer must reside in same home as dependent for substantial period

John C. Muse, 434 F.2d 349 (4th Cir. 1970)

Levon P. Biolchin, 433 F.2d 301 (7th Cir. 1970)

Relative resides in your household

IRC §2(b)(1)

Reg. §1.2-2(b)

Same residence for taxpayer and dependent

Reg. §1.2-2(c)

Rev. Rul. 72-43, 1972-1 CB 4

Sharon Stanford, 69 TCM 78 (1995)

Husband living in separate residence not head of household

W. E. Grace, 51 TC 685 (1969), aff'd per curiam, 421 F.2d 165 (5th Cir. 170)

James A. Petrie, IV, 70 TCM 1566 (1995)

Old-age home

Rev. Rul. 57-307, 1957-2 CB 12

John Robinson, 51 TC 520 (1968) (Acq.), vacated and rem'd, 442 F.2d 873 (9th Cir. 1970)

Nonresident alien not a dependent

Rev. Rul. 55-711, 1955-2 CB 13, amplified by Rev. Rul. 74-370, 1974-2 CB 7

Two-family house

Jean F. Fleming Est., 33 TMC 619 (1974)

Mother is head of household for child living in different states

Clair Smith, 332 F.2d 671 (9th Cir. 1964)

Rev. Rul. 72-43, 1972-1 CB 4 (IRS nonacq. to Smith)

Can still get dependency credit

Katherine Atchison, 17 TCM 718 (1958)

Same person can qualify only once

Reg. §1.2-2(b)(2)

Illegitimate child

Rev. Rul. 54-498, 1954-2 CB 107

Can move household

Reg. §1.2-2(c)

Dependent confined in hospital

Reg. §1.2-2(c)

Abbie D. Reardon, 158 F. Supp. 745 (D.S. Dak. 1958)

Father's absence because of marital dispute

Walter Petlow, 34 TCM 51 (1975)

Probably never return

Harold K. Brehmer, 191 F. Supp. 421 (D. Minn. 1961)

Walter J. Hein, 28 TC 826 (1957) (Acq.)

Rev. Rul. 66-28, 1966-1 CB 31

Pay more than one-half of household costs

IRC §2(b)

Reg. §1.2-2(d)

Figuring household costs

Donald G. Teeling, 42 TC 671 (1964)

Note: *Paragraph numbers refer to Parts 1 through 7. Items marked * are research aids, not citations of authority; see* *"Key to Citations" on page 801*

(Acq.)

Need not be head of family

Rev. Rul. 57-415, 1957-2 CB 13

Custody decree has no effect where son in boarding school

Allan L. Blair, 63 TC 214 (1974) (Acq.), aff'd, 538 F.2d 155 (7th Cir. 1976)

Mother keeps separate house for mentally ill son

Lillie B. McDonald, 61 TCM 2764 (1991)

1.13 Filing for Your Child

Minor's earnings and deductions

IRC §73
Reg. §1.73-1

Filing requirement for dependent child

IRC §6012(a)(1)(C)
IRC §63(c)(5)
Reg. §1.73-1
Reg. §1.6012-1(a)(4)

Signing return

Rev. Rul. 82-206, 1982-2 CB 356

Social Security number of dependent

IRC §6109(e)
IRC §6724(d)(3)(D)
IRC §6723 ($50 penalty)

Exemptions for dependent children

IRC §151(e)
Reg. §1.151-1
Reg. §1.151-2
Reg. §1.151-3

Deduction for pay to minor

Zeno J. Pucci, 10 TCM 529 (1951)
Samuel Rottenberg, 20 BTA 589 (Acq.)
Rev. Rul. 73-393, 1973-2 CB 33

Salary to young children

Nathaniel A. Denman, 48 TC 439 (1967)

Filing for Social Security self-employment tax

IRC §1401
IRC §1402
IRC §6017

Parental responsibility

IRC §6201(c)

Minors under age 18

IRC §1(g)

Child must pay penalties for parents' failure to file

Skye Bassett, 100 TC 41 (1993)

1.14 Return for Deceased

* IRS Publication 559

Responsibility for filing

IRC §6012(b)
Reg. §1.6012-3(b)(1)
Reg. §1.6012-1(a)(2)(ii)

How reported

IRC §443
Reg. §1.443-1(a)(2)
IRC §451(b)

U.S. Savings Bonds—jointly owned

Rev. Rul. 58-435, 1958-2 CB 370, distinguished by Rev. Rul. 68-145, 1968-1 CB 203

Community property

R. D. Merrill, 211 F.2d 297 (9th Cir. 1954)
Hunt Henderson Est., 155 F.2d 310 (5th Cir. 1946)
Stella W. Bishop, 152 F.2d 389 (9th Cir. 1946)
Rev. Rul. 55-726, 1955-2 CB 24

Income received after death

IRC §691
Reg. §1.691(a)-1

Income accrued

IRC §451(b)
Reg. §1.451-1(b)

Returns

IRC §6012(b)(1) and (4)
Reg. §1.6012-3

Deduction for estate tax

IRC §691(b)
Reg. §1.691(a)-4
Reg. §1.691(c)-1

Marital status

IRC §143
Reg. §1.143-1

Exemptions

IRC §153
Reg. §1.153-1

No estimated tax for years ending before 2 years after decedent's death

IRC §6654(1)(2)

Due date

IRC §6072
Reg. §1.6071-1(b)
Reg. §1.6072-1(b)

Refund

Reg. §301.6402-2

Death before return filed for previous year

Reg. §1.6013-1(d)(3)

Request for prompt assessment

IRC §6501(d)

1.15 Return for an Incompetent Person

Guardian files

IRC §6012(b)(2)
Reg. §1.6012-3(b)(3)
Rev. Rul. 55-387, 1955-1 CB 131

Incompetency bars joint return

David Herman, 38 TCM 119, aff'd in unpublished opinion (3d Cir. Dec. 13, 1979)

Spouse may file

Rev. Rul. 55-387, 1955-1 CB 131 (joint return for missing spouse)
Rev. Rul. 56-22, 1956-1 CB 558, modified by Rev. Rul. 58-267, 1958-1 CB 327 (return for incompetent spouse)

1.16 How a Nonresident Alien Is Taxed

IRC §871
* IRS Publication 519

Resident taxed as U.S. citizen

Reg. §1.871-1
Prop. Reg. §1.871-1(a)

Nonresident subject to 30% tax

IRC §871(a)

Capital gains

IRC §871(a)(2)

Doing business

IRC §871(b)

1.17 How a Resident Alien Is Taxed

* IRS Publication 519

Note: *Paragraph numbers refer to Parts 1 through 7. Items marked * are research aids, not citations of authority;* see *"Key to Citations" on page 801*

Same as U.S. citizen

Reg. §1.871-1

Prop. Reg. §1.871-1(a)

Work for foreign government

IRC §893

Reg. §1.893-1

Joint return

IRC §6013(a)(1)

IRC §6013(g) and (h)

1.18 Who Is a Resident Alien?

* IRS Publication 519

IRC §7701(b)

Foreign students

U.S. Treasury Doc. No. 5588

Rev. Rul. 54-87, 1954-1 CB 155, amplified by Rev. Rul. 67-159, 1967-1 CB 280

1.19 When an Alien Leaves the United States

* IRS Publication 519

1.20 Expatriation Tax

IRC §877 (expatriation before June 17, 2008)

IRC §877 (expatriation on or after June 17, 2008)

Notification and reporting requirements

IRC §7701(n)

IRC §6039G

Notice 2005-36, 2005-19 IRB 1007 (Form 8854 required)

* IRS Publication 519

2 Wages, Salary, and Other Compensation

2.1 Salary and Wage Income

IRC §61

Reg. §1.61-2

Mose Duberstein, 363 U.S. 278 (1960)

Lloyd M. Joshel, 296 F.2d 645 (10th Cir. 1962), aff'g 19 TCM 1349 (1960)

Thomas L. Johnson, 48 TC 636 (1967) (Acq.)

Hugh A. Brimm, 27 TCM 1148 (1968)

Abe A. Danish, 19 TCM 1349 (1960)

Reasonableness of CEO's compensation

Menard, Inc. and John R. Menard, Jr., 2009-1 USTC ¶50,270 (7th Cir. 2009)

City's moral obligation to disabled employee

Rev. Rul. 73-346, 1973-2 CB 24

Payments to parent of disabled child not tax-free foster care

*Chief Counsel Memorandum 2010-007

Gift of stock

Rev. Rul. 69-140, 1969-1 CB 46

Employee gifts and awards

IRC §274(b)

Ann. 82-7, 1982-3 IRB 48

NASA employee taxed

Robert Jones, 79 TC 1008 (1982)

Taxable severance pay sent by certified mail

Rev. Rul. 76-3, 1976-1 CB 114

Employee waiver does not make severance payment tax-free

Albert Taggi, 35 F.3d 93 (1994)

Chris Galligan, U.S. Dist. Ct. (E. Dist. of Pa. 1994)

Fees paid to controlled company

Terry Hardtke, 71 TCM 3220 (1996)

Contingent fee transfer

Richard Kochansky, 92 F.3d 357 (9th Cir. 1996)

Tip sharing

Kathleen Brown, 72 TCM 59 (1996)

Fee income held by a professional corporation

Carnation Y.L. Correa, D.C. Cir. (10/13/96)

Employee exclusion for donation to major disaster leave-sharing program

Notice 2006-59, 2006-28 IRB 60

Veteran not taxed on payments from compensated work therapy program

Roosevelt Wallace, 128 TC No. 11 (2007)

2.2 Constructive Receipt of Year-End Paychecks

Employee not taxed on check received until following year

Beatrice Davis, 37 TCM 42 (1978)

Check received after bank closes on last day of year

C. F. Kahler, 18 TC 31 (1952)

Refused back pay check delivered by courier taxable when delivered

Diane Visco, TC Memo 2000-77

2.3 Pay Received in Property Is Taxed

Reg. §1.61-1(a)

Reg. §1.61-2(d)(2)

Employer's note

Reg. §1.61-2(d)(4)

Samuel Segel, 24 TCM 1131 (1965)

Paul M. Potter, 5 TCM 116 (1946)

Debt cancelled by employer

Fred E. Werner, 21 TCM 1435 (1962)

Prize points

Rev. Rul. 70-331, 1970-1 CB 14

Frequent flyer miles

Philip Charley, 91 F.3d 72 (9th Cir. 1996)

* Letter Ruling 9340007

2.4 Commissions Taxable When Credited

Unearned commissions taxable when credited to account

Mary Rosenberg, 295 F. Supp. 820 (E.D. Mo. 1969), aff'd per curiam, 422 F.2d 341 (8th Cir. 1970)

Ada E. Sivley, 75 F.2d 916 (9th Cir. 1935)

C. E. Shockley, 6 TCM 1092 (1947)

Unearned commissions—income in year of advance despite repayment obligation

Rev. Rul. 79-311, 1979-2 CB 25

Rev. Proc. 83-4, 1983-1 CB 577

George Blood Enterprises, Inc., 35 TCM 436 (1976)

* Letter Ruling 9519002

Unearned commissions—no repayment required

James v. United States, 366 U.S. 213 (1961)

James J. Gales, 77 TCM 1316 (1999)

Write-off of advances

Rev. Rul. 69-465, 1969-2 CB 27

Repayment of commission when customer defaults

Note: *Paragraph numbers refer to Parts 1 through 7. Items marked * are research aids, not citations of authority;* see *"Key to Citations" on page 801*

Rev. Rul. 72-78, 1972-1 CB 45

Commission on own purchase taxable

Kenneth W. Daehler, 281 F.2d 823 (5th Cir. 1960), rev'g 31 TC 722 (1959) (Nonacq.)

Sol Minzer, 279 F.2d 338 (5th Cir. 1960), rev'g 31 TC 1130 (1959) (Nonacq.)

J. E. Ostheimer, 264 F.2d 789 (3d Cir. 1959), cert. denied, 361 U.S. 818

Jack Williams, 64 TC 1085 (1975)

Commissions waived on policies sold to friends still taxed

Charles O. Mensik, 37 TC 703 (1962), aff'd, 328 F.2d 147 (7th Cir. 1964), cert. denied, 379 U.S. 827

Agent not taxed on rebated commissions

Mickey L. Worden, 2 F.3d 359 (10th Cir. 1993), rev'g 64 TCM 408 (1992)

Agent taxed on illegal rebate of commission

James Alex, 70 TC 322 (1978)

2.5 Unemployment Benefits

IRC §85

Partial exclusion for 2009 benefits

IRC §85(c)

Contribution from unemployment benefits

Donald Russell, 71 TCM 3184 (1996)

2.6 Strike Pay Benefits and Penalties

Emergency benefits funded by federal government

Rev. Rul. 73-154, 1973-1 CB 40

Supplemental payments

News Release IR-156, May 29, 1956

Unemployment benefits from union fund

Halsey L. Williams, 37 TC 1099 (1962) (Acq.)

Strike benefits

Richard Osborne, 69 TCM 1895 (1995) (pilot's strike benefits taxable)

Allen Kaiser, 363 U.S. 299 (1960), aff'g 262 F.2d 367 (7th Cir. 1959)

James W. Godwin, 65-1 USTC ¶9121 (D. Tenn. 1965)

William A. Brown, 47 TC 399 (1967) (Acq.), aff'd per curiam, 398 F.2d 832 (6th Cir. 1968), cert. denied, 393 U.S. 1065

John N. Hagar, 43 TC 468 (1965)

Rev. Rul. 58-139, 1958-1 CB 14, modified by Rev. Rul. 61-136, 1961-2 CB 20

Rev. Rul. 57-1, 1957-1 CB 15

Pay penalty

Rev. Rul. 72-130, 1976-1 CB 16

2.7 Nonqualified Deferred Compensation

* "Deferred Compensation Revolution—Tough Transition to a Statutory System," Joni L. Andrioff, 83 Taxes 65 (May 2005)

Deferrals to nonqualified plans

IRC §409A

Final Regulations: TD 9321, 2007-19 IRB 1123

Notice 2007-86, 2007-46 IRB 990 (transition relief generally extended through 2008), modifying Notice 2006-79, 2006-43 IRB 763

Divorce transfer of deferred compensation

Rev. Rul. 2002-22, 2002-19 IRB 849

Notice 2002-31, 2002-19 IRB 908

State or local government deferred pay plan

IRC §457

Qualified cash or deferred arrangement

IRC §401

IRC §401(k)

Model rabbi trust

Rev. Proc. 92-64, 1992-2 CB 214

2.8 Did You Return Wages Received in a Prior Year?

IRC §1341

Reg. §1.1341-1

Return of embezzled funds — no claim of right computation

Rev. Rul. 65-254, 1965-2 CB 50

Return of unreasonable salary under agreement deductible

Rev. Rul. 69-115, 1969-1 CB 50

Author lacked unrestricted right to advanced royalties

Stewart H. Holbrook, 194 F. Supp. 252 (U.S. Dist. Ct. Ore. 1961)

No deduction where repayment not required

John G. Pahl, 67 TC 286 (1976)

Repayment of supplemental unemployment benefits—above-the-line deduction

IRC §62(a)(12)

Restitution payments may be deductible

Jess Kraft, et ux., 114 S. Ct. 467, cert. denied, 991 F.2d 292 (6th Cir. 1993)

Hedge agreement allows Section 1341 recalculation

Eugene Van Cleave, 718 F.2d 193 (6th Cir. 1983)

Escrow payment for contested liability deductible

Warnock Davies, 101 TC 282 (1993)

2.9 Waiver of Executor's and Trustee's Commissions

George M. Breidert, 50 TC 844 (1968) (Acq.)

Rev. Rul. 66-167, 1966-1 CB 20

Rev. Rul. 64-225, 1964-2 CB 15

Rev. Rul. 56-472, 1956-2 CB 21

2.10 Life Insurance Benefits

Final split-dollar insurance regulations

T.D. 9092, 2003-46 IRB 1055 (effective for split-dollar arrangements entered into or materially modified by September 17, 2003 and not materially modified thereafter)

Notice 2002-8, 2002-4 IRB 398 (guidance for split-dollar arrangements entered into before September 18, 2003)

* "The Effects of Notice 2002-8 on Split-Dollar Life Insurance Arrangements and Business Planning," Jeffrey J. Bryant and Richard Alltizer, 80 Taxes 25 (July 2002)

Effect of Sect. 409A deferred compensation rules on split-dollar insurance

Notice 2007-34, 2007-17 IRB 996

Assignment of group policy

Rev. Rul. 76-490, 1976-2 CB 300

Rev. Rul. 68-334, 1968-1 CB 403

Permanent and paid-up insurance—taxed to employee

Reg. §1.61-2(d)(2)

* Letter Ruling 9604001

Frank D. Yuengling, 69 F.2d 971 (3d Cir. 1934)

W. F. Parker, 38 BTA 989

Note: *Paragraph numbers refer to Parts 1 through 7. Items marked * are research aids, not citations of authority;* see *"Key to Citations" on page 801*

Rev. Rul. 56-400, 1956-2 CB 116

Rev. Rul. 78-420, 1978-2 CB 67

Rev. Rul. 64-328, 1964-2 CB 11, amplified by Rev. Rul. 66-110, 1966-1 CB 112

2.11 Educational Benefits for Employees' Children

Grants by private foundations

Rev. Proc. 76-47, 1976-2 CB 670, amplified by Rev. Proc. 77-32, 1977-2 CB 541

* Letter Ruling 9018068 (scholarship plan approved)

Educational benefit trusts

Rev. Rul. 75-448, 1975-2 CB 55

Richard T. Armantrout, 67 TC 996 (1977), aff'd per curiam, 570 F.2d 210 (7th Cir. 1978)

Grant-Jacoby, Inc., 73 TC 700 (1980)

John C. Saunders, 720 F.2d 871 (5th Cir. 1983), aff'g 45 TCM 82 (1982)

Reg. §1.677(b)-1(f)

2.12 Sick Pay Is Taxable

IRC §61

Tax-free benefits from private insurance

IRC §104(a)(3)

2.13 Workers' Compensation Is Tax Free

Workers' compensation

IRC §104(a)(1)

Reg. §1.104-1(b)

Given to employer

Rev. Rul. 56-83, 1956-1 CB 79

N.Y.C. teacher under Board of Ed. regulations

Madeline G. Dyer, 71 TC 560 (1979) (Acq. in result only)

N.Y.C. retirees may exclude job-related disability pay

Rev. Rul. 83-91, 1983-1 CB 38

Civil Service Retirement Act payments not workers' compensation

Daniel S. Haar, 78 TC 864 (1982), aff'd per curiam, 709 F.2d 1207 (8th Cir. 1983)

Policeman's sick leave under labor contract not workers' compensation

William Rutter, 48 TCM 1269 (1984), aff'd per curiam, 760 F.2d 466 (2d Cir. 1985)

Los Angeles Sheriff's sick leave elected under workers' compensation statute is tax free

Donald Givens, 90 TC 1145 (1988) (Nonacq.; 89-1 CB 1)

Policeman's disability amounts under state law not affected by PBA contract

James Fotis, 57 TCM 697 (1989)

Judge's medical disability tax free although same amount as regular retirement

Raymond J. Byrne, TC Memo 2002-319

New York City law change allows tax-free sick leave for police and firefighters

Local Law 87, 12/29/88

Local Law 78, 10/25/89

2.14 Disability Pensions

Military disability generally taxable

IRC §104(a)(4)

IRC §104(b)

Combat-related injuries

IRC §104(b)(2)(C)

IRC §104(b)(3)

Injuries from terroristic or military actions

IRC §104(a)(5)

Social Security disability benefits taxable

William D. Reimels, 123 TC 243 aff'd 2006-1 USTC ¶50,147 (2d Cir. 2006) (Vietnam veteran)

Will L. Thomas, TC Memo 2001-120

2.15 Stock Appreciation Rights (SARs)

SARs subject to post-2004 nonqualified deferred compensation regulations

Prop. Reg. §1.409A-1(b)(5)

Notice 2005-1, 2005-2 IRB 274 (initial guidance preceding proposed regulations to IRC §409A

Pre-AJCA 2004: No tax on receipt of SARs

Rev. Rul. 80-300, 1980-2 CB 165

Pre-AJCA 2004: Tax on expiration of SARs

* Letter Ruling 8120103

Pre-AJCA 2004: No constructive receipt on SAR tied to stock option

Rev. Rul. 82-121, 1982-1 CB 79

2.16 Stock Options

* "Incentive Stock Options Prop. Regs. Contain Subtle Changes," Barry L. Salkin, 71 Practical Tax Strategies 132 (September 2003)

* "Tax-Efficient Strategies for Exercising Compensatory Stock Options," Sidney R. Finkel and Kelly G. Besaw, 71 Practical Tax Strategies 15 (July 2003)

Qualified statutory stock options

IRC §421

Incentive stock options

IRC §422

Temp. Reg. §14a.422A-1

Employee stock purchase plans

IRC §423

Nonqualified stock options

IRC §83

Reg. §1.83-7

Pagel, Inc., 91 TC 200 (1988) (upholding Reg. §1.83-7)

Mandatory W-2 reporting on exercising nonqualified option

Announcement 2002-108; 2002-49 IRB 952

Divorce transfer of nonqualified options

Rev. Rul. 2004-60, 2004-24 IRB 1051

Rev. Rul. 2002-22, 2002-19 IRB 849

Notice 2002-31, 2002-19 IRB 908

2.17 Restricted Stock

Sale treated as option

Reg. §1.83-3(a)(2)

Restricted stock

IRC §83(c)

Executive cannot deduct loss on sale of restricted stock to key employees

Henry C. Tilford, Jr., 75 TC 134 (1980), rev'd, 705 F.2d 828 (6th Cir. 1983)

Section 83(b) election—electing tax on unrestricted value within 30 days

IRC §83(b)

Revoking Section 83(b) election

Rev. Proc. 2006-31, 2006-27 IRB 32

Attorney taxed on income remitted to firm

* Letter Ruling 9514008

Lapsed restrictions disregarded

Note: *Paragraph numbers refer to Parts 1 through 7. Items marked * are research aids, not citations of authority; see "Key to Citations" on page 801*

IRC §422A(e)(10)

3 Fringe Benefits

3.1 Tax-Free Health and Accident Coverage Under Employer Plans

Temporary COBRA premium reduction (through 5/31/10) after involuntary termination

Section 3001(a)(1)(A) of the American Recovery and Reinvestment Act of 2009 (65% subsidy), as extended by Continuing Extension Act of 2010, P.L. 111-157, 4/15/10

Section 3001(b) of the American Recovery and Reinvestment Act of 2009 (recapture of subsidy)

Employer-paid premiums not taxable

IRC §106(a)

Rev. Rul. 82-196, 1982-2 CB 53 (retired employee not taxed and deceased employee's survivors not taxed)

Rev. Rul. 85-121, 1985-2 CB 57 (laid-off employee not taxed)

* Letter Ruling 9409006

Rugby Productions, 100 TC 35 (1993)

Notice 94-103, 1994-51 IRB 10

Employee taxed on employer's reimbursement of premiums financed by pre-tax salary reduction

Rev. Rul. 2002-3, 2002-3 IRB 316, amplified by Rev. Rul. 2002-80, 2002-49 IRB 925

Employee taxed on "advance reimbursement" or "loan" intended to offset salary reduction

Rev. Rul. 2002-80, 2002-49 IRB 925, amplifying Rev. Rul. 2002-3, 2002-3 IRB 316

New dependent definition doesn't affect medical exclusion

Notice 2004-79, 2004-49 IRB 898

Employee taxed on coverage for domestic partner

* Letter Ruling 9717018

* Letter Ruling 9603011

* Letter Ruling 200108010

Long-term-care coverage

IRC §7702(B) (generally tax-free)

IRC §106(c) (taxable if provided through FSA)

Archer MSA coverage not taxed to employee

IRC §106(b) (contributions up to deductible limit of IRC §220(b)(1))

Access and portability rules for group health plans

IRC §4980D (daily penalties on employers)

IRC §9801 (pre-existing condition exclusions)

IRC §9802 (health status discrimination prohibited)

IRC §9811 (mothers and newborns)

IRC §9812 (mental health benefits)

Continuing coverage required (COBRA)

IRC §4980B

Rev. Rul. 96-8, 1996-1 CB 286

COBRA coverage for spouse dropped before divorce

Rev. Rul. 2002-88, 2002-52 IRB 995

3.2 Health Savings Accounts (HSAs) and Archer MSAs

HSA and HDHP inflation adjustments for 2010/2011

Rev. Proc. 2010-22, 2010-23 IRB 747 (for 2011)

Rev. Proc. 2009-29, 2009-22 IRB 1050 (for 2010)

Employer contributions to employee's health savings accounts (HSAs)

IRC §106(d) (contributions up to deductible limit of IRC §223(b))

Notice 2004-2, 2004-2 IRB 269

IRS guidelines for HSAs

Notice 2004-50, 2004-33 IRB 196 (Q&A)

Rev. Rul. 2004-38, 2004-15 IRB 717 (prescription drug coverage)

Rev. Proc. 2004-22, 2004-15 IRB 727 (transition for prescription drugs)

Notice 2004-23, 2004-15 IRB 725 (preventive care)

Notice 2004-25, 2004-15 IRB 727 (transition for 2004 expenses)

Notice 2004-43, 2004-27 IRB 10 (state law mandates)

High-deductible health plan

IRC §223(c)(2)

Rev. Proc. 2006-53, 2006-48 IRB 996 (for 2007)

HSA catch-up contribution limit

IRC §223(b)(3) (limits increasing through 2009)

Limited use of FSA and HRA with HSAs

Rev. Rul. 2004-45, 2004-22 IRB 971

HSA contributions during FSA grace period

Notice 2005-86; 2005-49 IRB 1075

HSA relief for plans disqualified by state law ending in 2006

Notice 2005-83, 2005-49 IRB 1075

Medicare Advantage MSA

IRC §138

Employer contribution limit to Archer MSA

IRC §106(b) (contributions up to deductible limit of IRC §220(b)(1))

3.3 Reimbursements and Other Tax-Free Payments From Employer Health and Accident Plans

Specific reimbursements of medical expenses

IRC §105(b)

Reg. §1.105-2

Rev. Rul. 63-181, 1963-2 CB 74

Reimbursement of dependent's expenses

IRC §105(b)

Health reimbursement arrangements

Rev. Rul. 2002-41, 2002-28 IRB 75

Notice 2002-45, 2002-28 IRB 93

Direct transfer from HRA to HSA

IRC §106(e)

Limited use of FSA and HRA with HSAs

Rev. Rul. 2004-45, 2004-22 IRB 971

Cash option renders HRA taxable

Rev. Rul. 2005-24, 2005-16 IRB 892

Reimbursements taxed if beneficiaries could receive unreimbursed amounts

Rev. Rul. 2006-36, 2006-36 IRB 353

Medical costs reimbursed with debit, credit, or stored value cards

Notice 2006-69, 2006-31 IRB 107 Rev. Rul. 2003-43, 2003-21 IRB 935 (debit card)

Sole proprietor reimbursement plan covering spouse

Note: *Paragraph numbers refer to Parts 1 through 7. Items marked* * *are research aids, not citations of authority;* see *"Key to Citations" on page 801*

Darwin J. Albers, TC Memo 2007-144 (spouse was bona fide employee but plan was not bona fide)

*Peter Speltz, TC Summary Opinion 2006-25 (spouse is bona fide employee)

Richard Haeder, TC Memo 2001-17 (spouse not a bona fide employee)

* James A. Poyda, TC Summary Opinion 2001-91 (spouse not a bona fide employee)

Self-insured medical reimbursement plans

IRC §105(h)

Reg. §1.105-11

Highly compensated under medical self-insured plans

IRC §105(h)(5)

IRC §401(k)(12)

Physicals may be given to executives only

Reg. §1.105-11(g)(1)

Permanent loss of use of part of body

IRC §105(c)

Reg. §1.105-3

Benefit must be based on injury

Randall Beisler, 814 F.2d 1304 (9th Cir. 1987)

Kenneth Rosen, 829 F.2d 506 (4th Cir. 1987)

Hypertension not loss of body function

Frank S. Watts, 82-1 USTC ¶9226 (D. Cal. 1982), aff'd, 83-1 USTC ¶9286 (9th Cir. 1983)

Pilot's heart attack not loss of body function

Oscar J. Hines, 72 TC 715 (1979)

Surgeon's nerve damage is loss of body function

Jon L. Stolte, TC Memo 1999-271

Taxable benefits under employer-paid coverage

IRC §105(a)

Reg. §1.105-1

Tax-free benefits under private policy

IRC §104(a)(3)

Reg. §1.104-1(d)

Disability payments from profit-sharing plan taxed

George H. Gordon, 88 TC 630 (1987)

Michael J. Berman, 58 TCM 919 (1989)

Close corporations

Alan B. Larkin, 48 TC 629 (1967), aff'd, 394 F.2d 494 (1st Cir. 1968)

Arthur R. Seidel, 30 TCM 1021 (1971)

Sanders & Sons, Inc., 26 TCM 671 (1967)

3.4 Group-Term Life Insurance Premiums

IRC §79

Reg. §1.79-0 through 3

Temp. Reg. §1.79-4T

IRS rate table

Temp. Reg. §1.79-3(d)(2)

Assignment of policy

Rev. Rul. 73-174, 1973-1 CB 43

Combination policies

Reg. §1.79-1(b)

Former employees

IRC §79(e)

Retire on disability

IRC §79(b)(1)

Key employees taxed under discriminatory plans

IRC §79(d)

Temp. Reg. §1.79-4T, question 6

Key employees defined

IRC §416(i)

IRC §79(d)(6) (includes retirees)

Separate discriminatory testing of active and retired employees

Reg. §1.79-4T, questions 7 and 8

Group-term insurance for dependents

Notice 89-110, 1989-49 IRB 17

3.5 Dependent Care Assistance

Dependent care services

IRC §129

Identify employer provider of child care on return

IRC §129(e)(9)

3.6 Adoption Benefits

Exclusion for employer benefits

IRC §137

* IRS Publication 968

Safe harbor for determining finality of foreign adoptions

Rev. Proc. 2005-31, 2005-26, IRB 1374

Announcement 2005-45, 2005-26 IRB 1377

3.7 Education Assistance Plans

Education assistance exclusion

IRC §127

Tuition reductions

IRC §117(c) and (d)

* Letter Ruling 9040045 (faculty and staff)

Daniel Wolpaw, 47 F.3d 787 (6th Cir. 1995)

Working condition benefit

IRC §132(h)(9)

3.8 Company Cars, Parking, and Transit Passes

IRC §132(a)(3)

Valuation of benefits

Reg. §1.61-21

Excludable non-personal-use vehicles

Temp. Reg. §1.274-5T(k)

Chauffeur bodyguard

Reg. §1.132-5(m)

100% inclusion rule for cars

Reg. §1.274-6T(c)

Transit passes, parking benefits, and bicycle commuting reimbursements

IRC §132(f)

Reg. §1.132-9

Parking at non-temporary location

IRS Legal Memorandum 200105007

3.9 Working Condition Fringe Benefits

IRC §132(d)

Reg. §1.132-5

* "Tax Consequences of Employer-Provided Computers," John C. Zimmerman, 78 Taxes 43 (October 2000)

IRS considering options for employee cell phone use

Notice 2009-46, 2009-23 IRB 1068

Job-placement assistance

Rev. Rul. 92-69, 1992-2 CB 51

Employee personal use of company

Note: *Paragraph numbers refer to Parts 1 through 7. Items marked * are research aids, not citations of authority;* see *"Key to Citations" on page 801*

airplane

IRC §274(e)(2) (overturning Sutherland decision below)

Sutherland Lumber-Southwest Inc., 255 F.3d 495 (8th Cir. 2001) (Acq.)

S Corp owners may deduct personally used plane

* Chief Counsel Advice 200344008

Unused commuting salary reductions cannot be refunded

Chief Counsel Information Letter 2003-0244

Financial counseling

* Letter Ruling 199929043

Mandatory employer-provided tax-preparation services

IRS Field Service Advice 200137039

Appeals court finds business purpose for fishing trips

Townsend Industries, Inc., Eighth Circuit, 9/15/03

3.10 *De Minimis* Fringe Benefits

IRC §132(e)

Reg. §1.132-6

Occasional overtime meal money or cab fare

Reg. §1.132-6(d)(2)(i)

Commuting under unsafe circumstances

Reg. §1.132-6(d)(2)(iii) (outside normal hours)

Reg. §1.61-21(k) ($1.50 valuation rule for hourly employees)

3.11 Employer-Provided Retirement Advice

IRC §132(m)

3.12 Employee Achievement Awards

IRC §74(c)

Taxable amount

Prop. Reg. §1.74-2

3.13 Employer-Furnished Meals or Lodging

Meals and lodging

IRC §119

Reg. §1.119-1

Maschmeyer's Nursery, Inc., 71 TMC 2188 (1996)

Boyd Gaming Corp., 117 F.3d 1096 (9th Cir. 1999)

Meals treated as furnished for employer's convenience

IRC §119(b)(4)

Remote camp in foreign country

James A. Nielson, TC Summary Opinion 2007-53

IRC §119(c)(2)

Company cafeteria

Reg. §1.119-1(d)

Hotel manager or executive

Charles N. Anderson, 371 F.2d 59 (6th Cir. 1967), cert. denied, 387 U.S. 906

Jack B. Lindeman, 60 TC 609 (1973) (Acq.)

Atlanta Biltmore Hotel Corp., 22 TCM 1266 (1963), mod'd and aff'd, 349 F.2d 677 (5th Cir. 1965)

Adolph Coors Co., 27 TCM 1351 (1968)

State civil service employee

Reg. §1.119-1(d)

No exclusion for purchases at commissary

Michael A. Tougher, Jr., 51 TC 737 (1969), aff'd per curiam, 441 F.2d 1148 (9th Cir. 1971), cert. denied, 404 U.S. 856

Executive luncheon

Carlton R. Mabley, 24 TCM 1794 (1965)

Casino employees

Boyd Gaming Corp., 117 F.3d 1096 (9th Cir. 1999)

Waitress's day off

Reg. §1.119-1(d)

Restaurant employees

Reg. §1.119-1(d)

Emergency

Reg. §1.119-1(a)(2)(ii)(a)

Reg. §1.119-1(d)

Bank teller

Reg. §1.119-1(f)

School superintendent one block away

Virgil L. Erdelt, 715 F. Supp. 278 (D.C. N. Dak. 1989), aff'd, 909 F.2d 510 (8th Cir. 1990), IRS Action on Decision 1992-001

Short meal period

Reg. §1.119-1(a)(2)(ii)(A) and (d)

* Letter Ruling 9602001

Lodging off premises

Charles Anderson, 371 F.2d 59 (6th Cir. 1967), rev'g 42 TC 410 (1964), cert. denied, 387 U.S. 906

Gordon S. Dole, 351 F.2d 308 (1st Cir. 1965), aff'g per curiam 43 TC 697 (1964) (Acq.)

Harold T. Giesinger, 66 TC 6 (1976) (Acq.)

Jack B. Lindeman, 60 TC 609 (1973) (Acq.)

College president taxed on lodging four miles away

Richard D. Winchell, 564 F. Supp. 131 (D. C. Neb. 1983), aff'd without opinion, 725 F.2d 689 (8th Cir. 1983)

* Letter Ruling 9404005

Faculty housing

IRC §119(d)

Lodging for dorm parents and evening house is tax free

* Letter Ruling 9404005

Hospital lodging not a condition of employment where others live in apartments

* Letter Ruling 8938014

Employer gives cash allowance

Reg. §1.119-1

Employer deducts fixed amount from pay

IRC §119(b)

Reg. §1.119-1(a)(3)(ii)

Melvin J. Boykin, 260 F.2d 249 (8th Cir. 1958)

Rev. Rul. 59-307, 1959-2 CB 48

Utilities

Charles R. Considine, 68 TC 52 (1977)

Rev. Rul. 68-579, 1968-2 CB 61

Workers in remote area

Reg. §1.119-1(d)

William L. Olkjer, 32 TC 464 (1959) (Acq.)

Farm supervision

M. Caratan, 442 F.2d 606 (9th Cir. 1971)

Note: *Paragraph numbers refer to Parts 1 through 7. Items marked * are research aids, not citations of authority; see "Key to Citations" on page 801*

Other employees

Lloyd N. Farnham, 6 TCM 1049 (1947)

Special Ruling, December 3, 1950

Insufficient eating facilities

Reg. §1.119-1(a)(2)(ii)(c)

Park employee

Robert L. Coyner, 344 F.2d 736 (3d Cir. 1965)

Partnerships

C.C. Wilson 376 F.2d 280 (Court of Claims 1967) (reimbursed food taxed)

Ann L. Armstrong, 394 F.2d 661 (5th Cir. 1968) (meals and lodging excludable)

Unprepared food

Walter Jacob, 493 F.2d 1294 (3d Cir. 1974)

Michael A. Tougher, Jr., 441 F.2d 1148 (9th Cir. 1971), cert. denied, 404 U.S. 856

Hotel partnership deductions

George A. Papineau, 16 TC 130 (1952) (Nonacq.)

Peace Corps volunteer

IRC §912

VISTA volunteer

Carol Goldstein, 73 TC 164 (1979)

3.14 Minister's Rental or Housing Allowance

IRC §107

Constitutionality of minister's tax-free benefits

Freedom From Religion Foundation, U.S. District Court for the Eastern District of California, 5/21/2010

Tax free allowance limited to fair rental value of house

IRC §107(2), as amended by the Clergy Housing Allowance Clarification Act of 2002, effectively reversing the holding in Richard D. Warren, 114 TC 343 (2000)

Services performed by minister

Reg. §1.1402(c)-5

Minister's expenses allocable to tax-free allowance not deductible

* Johnny J. Young, TC Summary Opinion 2005-76

Exclusion allowed for ordained executive directors of parochial schools

Rev. Rul. 62-171, 1962-2 CB 39

No deduction for ordained minister working for a nonreligious organization

Rev. Rul. 68-68, 1968-1 CB 51

Not allowed for unordained ministers

Rev. Rul. 59-270, 1959-2 CB 44

Unordained educational director

Robert D. Lawrence, 50 TC 494 (1968)

Cantors

Abraham A. Salkov, 46 TC 190 (1966) (Nonacq.)

Max Silverman, 253 F.2d 849 (8th Cir. 1958)

Rev. Rul. 78-301, 1978-2 CB 103

Traveling evangelist

Rev. Rul. 64-326, 1964-2 CB 37

Retired minister

Rev. Rul. 63-156, 1963-2 CB 79

Widow not entitled to exclusion

Rev. Rul. 72-249, 1972-1 CB 36

Anti-communist crusade

James D. Colbert, 61 TC 449 (1974)

Priest living as layman

Francis E. Kelley, 62 TC 131 (1974)

Not allowed for unordained executive of tax-exempt nonreligious organization

W. Astor Kirk, 425 F.2d 492 (D.C. Cir. 1970), cert. denied, 400 U.S. 853

Civilian chaplain at VA hospital

Rev. Rul. 72-462, 1972-2 CB 76

Administrator of nonreligious old-age home

Jesse A. Toavs, 67 TC 897 (1977)

Rev. Rul. 72-606, 1972-2 CB 78

No exclusion for rabbi as director of interreligious affairs

Marc H. Tanenbaum, 58 TC 1 (1972)

Exclusion for rabbi as UJA director

Melvin Libman, 44 TCM 371 (1982)

Minister teaching at church-related college

* Letter Ruling 9144047

3.15 Cafeteria Plans Provide Choice of Benefits

IRC §125

Reg. §1.125-3 (effect of Family and Medical Leave Act)

Reg. §1.125-4 (permitted election changes)

Prop. Reg. §1.125-2 (general questions and answers)

Key employees

IRC §125(b)(2)

3.16 Flexible Spending Arrangements

* "IRS Ruling Stretches Usefulness of Flexible Spending Accounts," Daniel N. Rashke, 72 Practical Tax Strategies 17 (January 2004)

IRC §125

Prop. Reg. §1.125-2 (general questions and answers)

Health plan flexible spending arrangements

Reg. §1.125-3 (effect of Family and Medical Leave Act)

Reg. §1.125-4 (permitted election changes)

Rev. Rul. 2003-102, 2003-38 IRB 559 (over-the-counter medications are reimbursable)

Prop. Reg. §1.125-2

Rev. Proc. 2004-22, 2004-15 IRB 727 (transition for prescription drugs)

One-time FSA-to-HSA transfer

IRC §106(e)

Employer option to extend use-it-or-lose-it deadline

Notice 2005-42, 2005-23 IRB 1204

Medical costs reimbursed with debit, credit, or stored value cards

Notice 2006-69, 2006-31 IRB 107

Cost of doctor-prescribed herb can be reimbursed by FSA

* Chief Counsel Letter, INFO 2010-0080

3.17 Company Services Provided at No Additional Cost

IRC §132(b)

Reg. §1.132-2

Highly compensated employees

IRC §132(j)(6) (defined)

Note: *Paragraph numbers refer to Parts 1 through 7. Items marked * are research aids, not citations of authority;* see *"Key to Citations" on page 801*

IRC §132(j)(1) (non-discrimination rule)

Line of business limitation

Reg. §1.132-4

Temp. Reg. §54.4977-1T (1985 election)

3.18 Discounts on Company Products or Services

IRC §132(c)

Reg. §1.132-3

* Letter Ruling 9328016

3.19 Volunteer Fir

fighter and Emergency Medical Responder Benefits

IRC §139B

*IRS Publication 15-B

4 Dividend and Interest Income

4.1 Reporting Dividends and Mutual-Fund Distributions

* IRS Publication 564

Ordinary dividend portion

IRC §854(b)(2)

Reg. §1.854-2

Rev. Rul. 77-149, 1977-1 CB 82

Long-term capital gain

IRC §852(b)(3)(B)

Exempt-interest dividend

IRC §852(b)(5)(B)

Undistributed capital gain

IRC §852(b)(3)(D)

Deferred annuities

Rev. Rul. 81-220, 1981-2 CB 175

Rev. Rul. 82-54, 1982-1 CB 11

Dividend declared in October, November, or December paid by following February

IRC §852(b)(7)

4.2 Qualified Corporate Dividends Taxed at Favorable Capital Gain Rates

IRC §301

IRC §305

Qualified dividends taxed at capital gain rates

IRC §1(h)(11)

* "Not All Dividends Qualify for the Reduced Tax Rate," James G.S. Yang, 72 Practical Tax Strategies 171 (March 2004)

* "New Dividend Planning Strategies for Shareholders and Corporations," Andrew R. Lee, 71 Practical Tax Strategies 204 (October 2003)

Qualified dividends from foreign corporations

Notice 2003-71, 2003-43 IRB 922 (readily tradable on securities market in U.S.)

Notice 2003-69, 2003-42 IRB 851 (qualifying tax treaties)

4.3 Dividends From A Partnership, S Corporation, Estate, or Trust

Partners

IRC §702(a)(5)

IRC §702(b)

S corporations

IRC §1368(c)(2)

Trusts

IRC §652(b)

4.4 Real Estate Investment Trust (REIT) Dividends

IRC §857

Shares held six months or less

IRC §857(b)(7)

Dividend declared in October, November, or December

IRC §857(b)(8)

4.5 Taxable Dividends of Earnings and Profits

IRC §301

Definition of dividend

IRC §316

Dividend reinvestment plan

Rev. Rul. 79-42, 179-1 CB 130

Rev. Rul. 78-375, 1978-2 CB 130

Rev. Rul. 77-749, 1977-1 CB 82

Rev. Rul. 76-33, 1976-1 CB 87

4.6 Stock Dividends on Common Stock

Stock dividends and rights

IRC §305

Reg. §1.305-1

Reg. §1.61-9(b)

Cash in lieu of fractional share

Reg. §1.305-3(c)

Shareholder approved sale plan

Rev. Rul. 69-15, 1969-1 CB 95

Rev. Rul. 69-202, 1967-1 CB 576

Elective dividend taxable

IRC §305(b)(1)

Reg. §1.305-2

4.7 Dividends Paid in Property

Dividend in kind

Reg. §1.61-9(b)

IRC §301

Reg. §1.301-1

IRC §317(a)

Reg. §1.317-1

Corporate benefits

James B. Munson, 40 TCM 173 (1980)

B. Morgan Heglin Inc., 38 TCM 255 (1979)

Richard F. Tyson, 38 TCM 557 (1979)

Company payments for shareholder are loans

Bradley K. Morrison, TC Memo 2005-53

4.8 Taxable Stock Dividends

IRC §305

Option to redeem stock dividend

Rev. Rul. 76-258, 1976-2 CB 95

Constructive dividends

Roy J. Champayne, 26 TC 634 (1956) (Acq.)

Charles Dreifus Co., 140 F. Supp. 499 (E.D. Pa. 1956)

4.9 Who Reports the Dividends

Dividends on stock sold

Reg. §1.61-9(c)

4.10 Year Dividends Are Reported

IRC §451(a)

Reg. §1.451-1

Note: *Paragraph numbers refer to Parts 1 through 7. Items marked * are research aids, not citations of authority; see "Key to Citations" on page 801*

Reg. §1.301-1(b)

Dividend payable 12/31

Sewell Lee Avery, 292 U.S. 210 (1934)

George E. Rex, 3 TCM 1260 (1944)

Harkness, 31 BTA 1100 (Acq.)

A. S. Eldridge, 30 BTA 1322, aff'd, 79 F.2d 629 (9th Cir. 1935)

Dividend checks mailed by savings and loan association

Maurice Fox, 218 F.2d 347 (3d Cir. 1955), aff'g 20 TC 1094 (1953) (Acq.)

Reasonable action could get dividend

Frank W. Kunze, 203 F.2d 957 (2d Cir. 1953), aff'g 19 TC 29 (1952)

Dividends received year after year declared

F. H. Mason, 275 U.S. 175 (1927)

Dividend taxed to seller retaining life income rights to stock

Willard S. Heminway, 44 TC 96 (1965) (Acq.)

4.11 Distribution Not Out of Earnings: Return of Capital

IRC §301(c)(2) and (3)

IRC §316(a)

"Dividends" on paid-up life insurance

Reg. §1.72-11(b)

4.12 Reporting Interest on Your Tax Return

* IRS Publication 550

Summary of interest income rules

IRC §61(a)(4)

Reg. §1.61-7(a)

Year received

Reg. §1.446-1(c)(1)(i)

U.S. obligations

IRC §103

Interest available

Reg. §1.451-2

Tax sale certificates

Charles H. Wiltsie, 3 F. Supp. 743 (Ct. Cl. 1933), cert. denied, 291 U.S. 664

Open accounts without specific agreement

Kurtz Bros., 42 BTA 561

Usurious interest

Reg. §1.61-7(a)

Discount on notes

Reg. §1.61-7(a)

Reg. §1.61-7(c)

Interest received in form of property

Reg. §1.61-1

Autos, boats received for long-term deposits

I.R. News Release 1032, April 14, 1970

Coupons from tax-exempt bonds

H. Gates Lloyd, 154 F.2d 643 (3d Cir. 1946), cert. denied, 329 U.S. 717

Rev. Rul. 55-73, 1955-1 CB 236

Note with accrued interest

Missouri State Life Insurance Co., 78 F.2d 778 (8th Cir. 1935)

Pontiac Commercial and Savings Bank, 41 F.2d 602 (6th Cir. 1930)

Wrap-around annuities

Rev. Rul. 80-274, 1980-2 CB 27

Saving certificates, deferred interest plans

Reg. §1.232

Rev. Rul. 73-220, 1973-1 CB 297

Deferred interest as original issue discount

I.R. News Release 1215, March 13, 1972

Six-month certificates

Prop. Reg. §1.451-2(a)(2)

Prop. Reg. §1.232-3(b)

Rev. Rul. 80-157, 1980-1 CB 186

Interest penalty bars constructive receipt on CD of one year or less

Reg. §1.451-2

Serviceman's interest

Rev. Rul. 67-450, 1967-2 CB 174

Interest on loan arrangement

Rev. Rul. 81-148, 1981-1 CB 207

4.13 Interest on Frozen Accounts Not Taxed

IRC §451(g)

IRC §165(1)

4.14 Interest Income on Debts Owed to You

Interest uncollectible

Corn Exchange Bank, 37 F.2d 34 (2d Cir. 1930)

Atlantic Coast Line RR Co., 31 BTA 730 (Acq.), aff'd, 81 F.2d 309 (4th Cir. 1936), cert. denied, 298 U.S. 656

Four restrictions on withdrawal of interest not considered substantial; bonus interest; closing agreements

Reg. §1.451-2(a)

Rev. Proc. 64-24, 1964-1 CB 693

Agreement with debtor

Annie B. Smith, 12 TCM 131 (1953)

W. H. Hughes, 11 TCM 797 (1952)

Rev. Rul. 63-57, 1963-1 CB 103

Debtor gives new note

George J. Mellinger, 21 F. Supp. 964 (Ct. Cl. 1938)

Interest in advance

Reg. §1.61-7(a)

Obligations given away

Ida S. Austin, 161 F.2d 666 (6th Cir. 1947), cert. denied, 332 U.S. 767

4.15 Reporting Interest on Bonds Bought or Sold

Redemption

Special Ruling, February 7, 1949

Included in sales price

Reg. §1.61-7(d)

Included in purchase price

Reg. §1.61-7(c)

Tax-free covenant bond

IRC §32(2)

Guarantor pays interest

Rev. Rul. 54-563, 1954-2 CB 50

Accrued interest in reorganization exchange

IRC §354(a)(2)(B)

Flat price

Reg. §1.61-7(c)

4.16 Forfeiture of Interest on Premature Withdrawals

IRC §62(a)(9)

Deductible amount on Form 1099-INT

Rev. Rul. 75-20, 1975-1 CB 29

Rev. Rul. 73-511, 1973-2 CB 402, clarified by Rev. Rul. 75-21, 1975-1 CB 367

Forfeited principal

Note: *Paragraph numbers refer to Parts 1 through 7. Items marked* * *are research aids, not citations of authority; see* *"Key to Citations" on page 801*

Rev. Rul. 82-27, 1982-1 CB 32

4.17 Amortization of Bond Premium

Election

IRC §171

Reg. §1.171-1

Reg. §1.171-3

Premium treated as offset to interest

IRC §171(e)

Computing amortization

IRC §171(b)(3)

Rev. Rul. 82-10, 1982-1 CB 46

Elect on return

IRC §171(c)(2)

Reg. §1.171-3(a)

Straight-line method

Reg. §1.171-2(f)

Yield-to-maturity method

IRC §171(b)(3)

Effect on other bonds

Reg. §1.171-3(a)

Sale and purchase of similar bonds

Rev. Rul. 55-353, 1955-1 CB 381

Premium amortization reduces OID

IRC §1272(a)(7)

Allocate premium for conversions

Reg. §1.171-2(c)

4.18 Discount on Bonds

IRC §1271 (retirement or sale of debt instruments)

IRC §1272 (current income treatment of OID)

IRC §1273 (what is OID)

IRC §1281 (short-term debt)

4.19 Reporting Original Issue Discount on Your Return

* IRS Publication 1212

4.20 Reporting Income on Market Discount Bonds

IRC §1276

Deferral of interest deduction

IRC §1277

Deferral of interest does not apply to tax-exempt obligations

IRC §1278(a)(1)(C)

Election to currently report discount

IRC §1278(b)

Partial principal payments

IRC §1276(a)(3)

4.21 Discount on Short-Term Obligations

Current inclusion required

IRC §1281

Tax-exempts excluded from inclusion rule

IRC §1283(a)(1)(B)

Deferred interest deduction

IRC §1282

4.22 Stripped Coupon Bonds and Stock

IRC §1286

Zero coupon bond (OID reported annually)

IRC §1272

Market discount bonds

IRC §1276

OID treatment for stripped preferred stock

IRC §305(e)

* IRS Publication 1212

4.23 Sale or Retirement of Bonds and Notes

IRC §1271

IRC §1272

* IRS Publication 550

* IRS Publication 1212

Registered form

IRC §1287

Retirement defined

Donald S. McClain, 311 U.S. 527 (1941)

Unearned original issue discount is capital gain

Ted Bolnick, 44 TC 245 (1965) (Acq.)

4.24 State and City Interest Generally Tax Exempt

* IRS Publication 550

State, city obligations

IRC §103(a)

Reg. §1.103-1

Rhode Island Hospital Trust Co., 8 BTA 555, vacated and remanded, 29 F.2d 339 (1st Cir. 1929)

Agreement of purchase and sale

Newlin Machinery Corp., 28 TC 837 (1957) (Acq.)

Sale of municipal certificates of indebtedness to municipality

Palm Beach Trust Co., 9 TC 1060 (1947), aff'd per curiam, 174 F.2d 527 (D.C. Cir. 1949), cert. denied, 338 U.S. 825

Qualified private activity bonds not taxed

IRC §141(e)

AMT exception for 2009/2010 private activity bonds

IRC §47(a)(5)(C)(vi)

4.25 Taxable State and City Interest

IRC §103(e)

Qualified private activity bonds not taxed

IRC §141(e)

Community open account purchases

Kurtz Bros., 42 BTA 561

Volunteer fire companies

Seagrave Corp., 38 TC 247 (1962)

Tax sale certificates

Charles H. Wiltsie, 3 F. Supp. 743 (Ct. Cl. 1933), cert. denied, 291 U.S. 664

Municipal bond in open market

Rev. Rul. 57-49, 1957-1 CB 62

Rev. Rul. 60-210, 1960-1 CB 38, modified by Rev. Rul. 60-376, 1960-2 CB 38

4.26 Tax-Exempt Bonds Bought at a Discount

IRC §1288

Bond bought at discount

Rev. Rul. 73-112, 1973-1 CB 47

Rev. Rul. 57-49, 1957-1 CB 62

Rev. Rul. 60-210, 1960-1 CB 38

Redeemed old bond at premium

Rev. Rul. 72-587, 1972-2 CB 74

District Bond Co., 1 TC 837 (1943)

Note: *Paragraph numbers refer to Parts 1 through 7. Items marked* * *are research aids, not citations of authority;* see *"Key to Citations" on page 801*

Redemption of bonds issued after June 8, 1980

Rev. Rul. 80-143, 1980-1 CB 89, modifying Rev. Rul. 72-587, 1972-2 CB 74

Market discount rules do not apply to tax-exempt bonds

IRC §1278

Stripped tax-exempt obligations

IRC §1286(d)

4.27 Treasury Bills, Notes, and Bonds

Taxable interest

Reg. §1.61-7

Taxed at maturity

IRC §454(b)

Gain on sale of short-term obligations (ratable share of discount)

IRC §1271(a)(3)(D)

Acquisition discount currently taxed to accrual-basis taxpayers and dealers

IRC §1281

Interest deduction limitation

IRC §1281

IRC §1282

4.28 Interest on United States Savings Bonds

* IRS Publication 550

Annual increase in value

IRC §454

Reg. §1.454-1(c) (taxed in year of redemption or final maturity)

Election to report interest annually on timely return

Rev. Rul. 55-655, 1955-2 CB 253

Change in taxpayer's reporting method

Rev. Proc. 89-46, 1989-2 CB 597

4.29 Deferring United States Savings Bond Interest

* IRS Publication 550

Changing from annual reporting to deferral

Rev. Proc. 2002-9, 2002-3 IRB 327

Postpone tax during extended maturity period

IRC §454(c)

Reg. §1.454-1

Change form of registration of E bond

IRC §454(c)

Reg. §1.454-1

Rev. Rul. 55-278, 1955-1 CB 471

Rev. Rul. 54-327, 1954-2 CB 50

Correction of error in registration

Rev. Rul. 70-428, 1970-2 CB 5

Co-owners

Rev. Rul. 54-143, 1954-1 CB 12

Rev. Rul. 55-278, 1955-1 CB 471

Rev. Rul. 58-435, 1958-2 CB 370, distinguished by Rev. Rul. 68-145, 1968-1 CB 203

Transfer to charity

* Letter Ruling 8010082

Bonds transferred by gift without reissue

Edward G. Chandler, 410 U.S. 257 (1973), rev'g 460 F.2d 1281 (9th Cir. 1972)

Mae Elliott Est., 57 TC 152 (1971), aff'd per curiam, 474 F.2d 1008 (5th Cir. 1973)

Lyla C. Curry Est., 409 F.2d 671 (6th Cir. 1969)

Alice H. Silverman, 259 F.2d 731 (3d Cir. 1958)

Helen K. Chambless, 1970 WL 319 (DCSC) (1970)

Death of owner

Rev. Rul. 64-104, 1964-1 CB 223, distinguished by Rev. Rul. 68-145, 1968-1 CB 203

Election on decedent's return

Rev. Rul. 68-145, 1968-1 CB 203

4.30 Minimum Interest Rules

IRC §7872 (loans)

IRC §1274 and §483 (seller financing)

4.31 Interest-Free or Below-Market-Interest Loans

IRC §7872

Prop. Reg. §1.7872-1 through §1.7872-14

Blended rate for gift loan

Rev. Rul. 2009-20, 2009-31 IRB 167 (blended rate for 2009)

Rev. Rul. 86-17, 1986-1 CB 377 (IRS authorizes blended rate)

$10,000 gift loan exception

IRC §7872 (c)(2)

Prop. Reg. §1.7872-8(b)

$100,000 gift loan exception

IRC §7872(d)

Prop. Reg. §1.7872-8(c)

4.32 Minimum Interest on Seller-Financed Sales

IRC §1274

IRC §1275

IRC §483

Reg. §1.1274-1 through §1.1274.7

Reg. §1.483-1 through §1.483-5

* IRS Publication 537

General rate required

IRC §1274A

Definitions and special rules

IRC §1275

Minimum interest rules not applicable to buyer of personal-use property

IRC §1275(b)

Which AFR rate applies to sales

Reg. §1.1274-6(e)

Reg. §1.483-4(d)

Timing of reporting under §483

Reg. §1.483-2(a)(ii)

Cash method election

IRC §1274A(C)

Rev. Rul. 2008-52, 2008-49 IRB 1233 (amount for 2009 and prior years)

6% rate for land sales between related parties

IRC §483(e)

9% safe harbor

IRC §1274A(b)

Reg. §1.1274A-1

Inflation adjustment to seller-financed amount for safe harbor

IRC §1274A(d)(2)

Rev. Rul. 2008-52, 2008-49 IRB 1233 (amount for 2009 and prior years)

5 Reporting Property Sales

5.1 General Tax Rules for

Note: *Paragraph numbers refer to Parts 1 through 7. Items marked * are research aids, not citations of authority;* see *"Key to Citations" on page 801*

Property Sales

IRC §1(h)

* IRS Publication 544

5.2 How Property Sales Are Classified and Taxed

IRC §1(h)

IRC §1221(capital asset defined)

IRC §1222 (short-term, long-term, net capital gain defined)

* IRS Publication 544

* "Single Sale Generates Multiple Types of Capital Gains," Joe Walsh, 67 Practical Tax Strategies 1 (July 2001)

Self-created musical works

IRC §1221(b)(3)

5.3 Capital Gains Rates and Holding Periods

IRC §1(h)

IRC §1222 (long-term, short-term net capital gain defined)

IRC §1223 (holding period)

Zero rate starting in 2008

IRC §1(h)(1)(B)

5.4 Capital Losses and Carryovers

IRC §1211

IRC §1212

IRC §1222(10)

Reg. §1.1222-1

Carryover loss if taxable income is negative

IRC §1212(b)(2)(B)

Loss must be considered even if no tax benefit is realized

Rev. Rul. 76-177, 1976-1 CB 224

Not deductible as a business expense

Frank Lester, 70 TMC 77 (1995)

5.5 Capital Losses of Married Couples

One capital loss deduction on joint return

John E. Ross, 37 TC 445 (1961)

Reg. §1.1211-1(d)

Reg. §1.1211-1(c)

Surviving spouse may not use deceased spouse's loss carryover

* Letter Ruling 8510053

5.6 Losses May Be Disallowed on Sales to Related Persons

* "Related-Party Sales Can Produce Unexpected Tax Results," Monica Brown Gianni, 59 Taxation for Accountants 23 (July 1997)

Nondeductible losses

IRC §267

Reg. §1.267(a)-1(a)

Bona fide

Reg. §1.267(a)-1(c)

Nathan Blum, 5 TC 702 (1945)

Stock exchange

John P. McWilliams, 331 U.S. 694 (1947)

John B. Shethar, 28 TC 1222 (1957)

Foreclose mortgage

Thomas Zacek, 8 TC 1056 (1947)

Pledgee's sale

Charles E. Cooney, 1 TCM 55 (1942)

Members of family

IRC §267(b)(1) and (c)(4)

Reg. §1.267(c)-1(a)(4)

Nominee

Charles J. Stamler, 45 BTA 37

O. Phil Nordling, 166 F.2d 703 (9th Cir. 1948), cert. denied, 337 U.S. 938

Wife's relative

J. Henry DeBoer, 194 F.2d 989 (2d Cir. 1952), (Nonacq.)

Son-in-law

Fervel Topek, 9 TC 763 (1947)

* Letter Ruling 9017008

Family hostility may not be considered

David L. Miller, 75 TC 182 (1980)

Withdrawal from joint ventures and partnerships

T. N. Mauritz, 205 F.2d 135 (5th Cir. 1953)

Fritz Busche, 229 F.2d 437 (5th Cir. 1956)

Henry V. B. Smith, 5 TC 323 (1945)

Controlled corporation

IRC §267

Reg. §1.267(b)-1

Reg. §1.267(c)-1

Other losses disallowed

IRC §267

Reg. §1.267(b)-1

Partnership and controlling persons

IRC §707(b)(1)(A)

Related party's profitable resale

IRC §267(d)

5.7 Deferring or Excluding Gain on Small Business Stock Investment

IRC §1045 (rollover of gain from small business stock)

IRC §1202 (exclusion of gain)

IRC §1397B (rollover of empowerment zone asset gain)

* IRS Publication 550

Increased exclusion

IRC §1202(a)(3)75% for stock acquired after 2/17/09 and before 9/28/10

IRC §1202(a)(4) **100%** for stock acquired after 9/27/10 and before 1/1/11

5.8 Sample Entries of Capital Asset Sales on Schedule D

* IRS Publication 544

Reporting capital gains and losses

IRC §1(h)

IRC §1222

* IRS Publication 544

Short-term and long-term transactions

IRC §1222

Capital losses

IRC §1211(b) and 1212(b)

IRC §62(a)(3)

5.9 Counting the Months in Your Holding Period

Long- and short-term capital gain or loss

IRC §1222

IRC §1223

Reg. §1.1222-1

Reg. §1.1223-1(a)

Exclude day asset acquired

Lewis Caspe, 694 F. 2d 1116 (8th Cir. 1982), aff'g 80-1 USTC ¶9201 (D.C. IA. 1980)

Holding period rules

IRC §1222

Note: *Paragraph numbers refer to Parts 1 through 7. Items marked* are research aids, not citations of authority;* see *"Key to Citations" on page 801*

Futures transactions

IRC §1222

5.10 Holding Period for Securities

Stock exchange transactions

Rev. Rul. 72-381, 1972-2 CB 233

Rev. Rul. 70-598, 1970-2 CB 168

Installment sale not allowed for publicly traded stock

IRC §453(k)(2)

Stock subscriptions

Mayme C. Sommers, Admtrx., 63 F.2d 551 (10th Cir. 1933)

William J. Wineberg, 20 TCM 1715 (1961), aff'd, 326 F.2d 157 (9th Cir. 1964)

Exercise of rights

IRC §1223(5)(6)

Reg. §1.1223-1(f)

Rev. Rul. 56-572, 1956-2, CB 182

Different lots

Reg. §1.1223-1(i)

Employee stock option

John H. Rolfe, 58 TC 361 (1972), aff'd per curiam, 488 F.2d 1092 (9th Cir. 1974)

Commodity satisfaction of futures contract

IRC §1223(8)

Reg. §1.1223-1(h)

"When issued" transactions

I.T. 3721, 1945 CB 164, as modified by Rev. Rul. 57-29, 1957-1 CB 519

Wash sales

IRC §1223(4)

Reg. §1.1223-1(d)

5.11 Holding Period for Real Estate

Rev. Rul. 54-607, 1954-2 CB 177

New construction

M. A. Paul, 206 F.2d 763 (3d Cir. 1953)

Fred Draper, 32 TC 545 (1959) (Acq.)

Portion of building constructed within long-term holding period

Rev. Rul. 75-524, 1975-2 CB 342

5.12 Holding Period: Gifts, Inheritances, and Other Property

Gift after 1920

IRC §1223(2)

Reg. §1.1223-1(b)

Donee's sale at loss

Rev. Rul. 59-86, 1959-1 CB 209

Automatic holding period of over one year for property acquired from decedent

IRC §1223(11)

Property purchased by executors

Marjorie K. Campbell, 313 U.S. 15 (1941)

Richard Van Nest Gambrill, 313 U.S. 11 (1941)

Distribution in kind from partnership

IRC §735(b)

Reg. §1.735-1

Involuntary conversion

IRC §1223(1)(A)

Reg. §1.1223-1(a)

5.13 Calculating Gain or Loss

Gain or loss

IRC §1001

Reg. §1.1001-1 (amount realized)

5.14 Amount Realized Is the Total Selling Price

Selling price

Reg. §1.1001

IRC §1001

Mortgage included in price

Beulah B. Crane, 331 U.S. 1 (1947)

Property valued at less than mortgage

John F. Tufts, 456 U.S. 960 (1983)

Legal fee—cost of sale

Fred W. Gunn, 49 TC 38 (1967)

5.15 Finding Your Cost

Unadjusted basis

IRC §1012

Reg. §1.1012-1

Improvements

IRC §1016

Reg. §1.016-2

Adjusted basis

IRC §1011

Reg. §1.1011-1

Improvements not covered by note

Glenda P. McCormick, 99-1 USTC ¶50,380

5.16 Unadjusted Basis of Your Property

* IRS Publication 551

Basis is cash cost

IRC §1012

Reg. §1.1012-1

Property subject to mortgage

Beulah B. Crane, 331 U.S. 1 (1947)

Adjusted cost after depreciation allowed

IRC §1016

Reg. §1.1016-3

Rendering services

Reg. §1.61-2

W. H. Weaver, 25 TC 1067 (1956)

Lawrence S. Vadner, 14 TCM 866 (1955)

Taxable exchange of property

Philadelphia Park Amusement Co., 126 F. Supp. 184 (Ct. Cl. 1954)

Rev. Rul. 56-100, 1956-1 CB 624

Tax-free exchange of property

IRC §1031

Reg. §1.1031(d)-1

Life estate or remainder interest

Reg. §1.1014-5

Sale of life estate—zero basis

IRC §1001(e)

Property subject to lease

Harriet M. Bryant Trust, 11 TC 374 (1948) (Acq.)

Distribution to settle claim

Rev. Rul. 55-117, 1955-1 CB 233

Compulsory or involuntary conversion

IRC §1033(b)

Distribution on orders of SEC

IRC §1081

Reg. §1.1081

Prenuptial agreement

Doris Farid-es-Sultaneh, 160 F.2d 812 (2d Cir. 1947), rev'g 6 TC 652 (1946)

Note: *Paragraph numbers refer to Parts 1 through 7. Items marked * are research aids, not citations of authority;* see *"Key to Citations" on page 801*

Basis of new residence after home sale deferral

IRC §1034(e)

Reg. §1.1034-1

Property purchased prior to March 1, 1913

IRC §1053

Reg. §1.1053-1

Dividends in property

IRC §301

Reg. §1.301-1

5.17 Basis of Property You Inherited or Received as a Gift

* "Basis of Property Acquired by Gifts," Katherine D. Black and Jeffrey N. Barnes, 82 Taxes 41 (November 2004)

IRC §1014

Reg. §1.1014-1

Reg. §1.1014-2

Foreign property

Rev. Rul. 84-139, 1984-2 CB 168

Gift tax paid increases basis

IRC §1015(d)(6)

Gift after December 31, 1920

IRC §1015

Reg. §1.1015-1

Gift in trust before January 1, 1921

IRC §1015(c)

Reg. §1.1015-3

Inheritance of property transferred to decedent within one year of death

IRC §1014(e)

Estate tax value questioned

Sam F. McIntosh, 26 TCM 1164 (1967)

Right to buy deceased's property

J. Gordon Mack, 3 TC 390 (1944), aff'd 148 F.2d 62 (3d Cir. 1945), cert. denied, 326 U.S. 719

Distributions from trust

IRC §1015

Reg. §1.1015-2

IRC §643(e)

Distribution from trust before June 2, 1984

Reg. §1.661(a)-2(f)

5.18 Joint Tenancy Basis Rules for Surviving Tenants

IRC §1014

Reg. §1.1014-2

IRC §2040(b)

* IRS Publication 551

* IRS Publication 559

Spousal joint tenancies created before 1977

M. Lee Gallenstein, 975 F.2d 286 (6th Cir. 1992)

Joy B. Patten, 116 F.3d 1029 (4th Cir. 1997)

Therese Hahn, 110 TC 1040 (1998) (Acq.)

5.19 Allocating Cost Among Several Assets

Apportionment of cost

Frederick Leake, 140 F.2d 451 (6th Cir. 1944), cert. denied, 323 U.S. 722

Nathan Blum, 5 TC 702 (1945)

Johnson Lumber Corp., 12 TC 348 (1949) (Acq.)

Fairfield Plaza, Inc., 39 TC 706 (1963) (Acq.)

Apportion land

McDonald, BTA Memo, P-H 41,409

Harlan E. McGregor, 14 TCM 897 (1955)

Sale of stock first bought

Reg. §1.1012-1(c)

A. F. Mack, 31 BTA 1149

5.20 How To Find Adjusted Basis

Improvements and betterments to property

IRC §1016

Reg. §1.1016-2

Edgar S. Appleby Est., 123 F.2d 700 (2d Cir. 1941)

Improvements covered by note not included in basis

John W. Owen, 34 F. Supp. 2d 1071 (W.D. Tenn. 1998)

Commissions on security sales

Adolph B. Spreckles, 315 U.S. 626 (1942)

Carrying charges

IRC §1016

Reg. §1.1016-2

Personal residence

Isaiah Megibow, 218 F.2d 687 (3d Cir. 1955)

Purchaser's share of real estate tax

IRC §164(d)

Reg. §1.164-6

Unharvested crops

IRC §1016(a)(11)

Reg. §1.1016-5(g)

Demolition cost

Reg. §1.165-3

Edgar S. Appleby Est., 123 F.2d 700 (2d Cir. 1941)

Deduction from basis

IRC §1016

Reg. §1.1016-1 through 8

Return of capital

IRC §1010(a)(4)

Reg. §1.1016-5(a)(1-2)

Casualty loss

IRC §1016(a)(1)

Pasquale Colabella, 17 TCM 704 (1958)

Wrap fees cannot be added to basis of securities

*Chief Counsel Advice 200721015

Depletion allowances

IRC §1016(a)(2)

Reg. §1.1016-3 and 4

Depreciation, amortization, obsolescence

IRC §1016(a)(2)

Reg. §1.1016-3 and 4

Rev. Proc. 97-37, 1997-33 IRB 18 (adjustment for unclaimed depreciation in a closed year)

5.21 Tax Advantage of Installment Sales

IRC §453

* IRS Publication 537

Depreciation recapture

IRC §453(i)

Not applicable to year-end sale of securities

IRC §453(k)(2)

Farmer who does not inventory

Temp. Reg. §15A.453-1(b)(4)

Not applicable to sale of inventory

Note: *Paragraph numbers refer to Parts 1 through 7. Items marked * are research aids, not citations of authority;* see *"Key to Citations" on page 801*

Andrew A. Monaghan, 40 TC 680 (1963) (Acq.)

IRC §453(6)(2)(B)

Crispo Gallery Inc., 2nd Cir. (6/13/96)

Not applicable to building contractor

Rev. Rul. 73-438, 1973-2 CB 156

Dealers

IRC §453(b)(2)

Timeshares and residential lots

IRC §453(1)(2) and (1)(3)

5.22 Figuring the Taxable Part of Installment Payments

Selling price

Temp. Reg. §15A.453-1(b)(2)(ii)

Contract price

Temp. Reg. §15A.453-1(b)(2)(iii)

Payments received

Temp. Reg. §15A.453-1(b)(3)

Gross profit

Temp. Reg. §15A.453-1(b)(2)(v)

Wraparound mortgages

Temp. Reg. §15A.453-1(b)(3)(ii)

Tax Court rejects IRS wraparound regs.

Professional Equities, Inc., 89 TC 165 (1987) (Acq.)

Pledges of installment obligations

IRC §453A(d)

5.23 Electing Not To Report on the Installment Method

IRC §453(d)

Reg. §15A.453-1(d)

Late election out barred for change in capital gain law

Rev. Rul. 90-46, 90-1 CB 107

Switch to installment method denied after n.o.l. reduced

* Letter Ruling 8338004

Switch to installment method allowed after accountant's mistake

* Letter Ruling 201027025
* Letter Ruling 200814013
* Letter Ruling 200323009
* Letter Ruling 8943039
* Letter Ruling 9141013

5.24 Restriction on Installment Sales to Relatives

IRC §453(e) and (g)

Two-year cutoff for property

IRC §453

Related party

IRC §453(f)(1)

IRC §318(a)

IRC §267(b)

Depreciable property

IRC §1239(b)

Controlled entity

IRC §453(g)

5.25 Contingent Payment Sales

Temp. Reg. §15A.453-1(c)

5.26 Using Escrow and Other Security Arrangements

Edward Grannemann, 649 F. Supp. 949 (E.D. Mo. 1987)

Marion H. McArdle, 11 TC 961 (1948) (Acq.)

Rev. Rul. 73-451, 1973-2 CB 158

Escrow lacks binding condition

J. Robert Rhodes, 243 F. Supp. 894 (D.S.C. 1965)

Everett Pozzi, 49 TC 119 (1968)

J. Earl Oden, 56 TC 569 (1971)

Escrow under court order

Nannie C. Harris, 477 F.2d 812 (4th Cir. 1973), rev'g 56 TC 1165 (1971) (Nonacq.)

Substitution of escrow for unpaid notes or deed of trust

Rev. Rul. 77-294, 1977-2 CB 173, revoking Rev. Rul. 68-246, 1968-1 CB 198

Certificate of deposit as security

Ulysses G. Trivett, Jr., 36 TCM 675 (1977) (disqualified installment sale allowed)

C. J. Porterfield, 73 TC 91 (1979) (installment sale allowed)

5.27 Minimum Interest on Deferred Payment Sales

IRC §483

Reg. §1.483

Exceptions and limitations

IRC §483(d)

5.28 Dispositions of Installment Notes

IRC §453B

Receipt of notes in Section 331 corporate liquidation

IRC §453(h)

Exchange of investment realty

Phil Blatt, 67 TCM 2125 (1994)

Transfer at death

IRC §453B(c)

IRC §691(a)(4)

Reg. §1.691(a)-5

5.29 Repossession of Personal Property Sold on Installment

IRC §453

5.30 Boot in Like-Kind Exchange Payable in Installments

IRC §453(f)(6)

5.31 "Interest" Tax on Sales Over $150,000 Plus $5 Million Debt

Interest tax

IRC §453(c)

Pledge rule

IRC §453A(d)

Dealers

IRC §453(1)

5.32 Worthless Securities

* "Worthless Stock and Debt Losses," Jerred G. Blanchard, Jr. and David C. Garlock, 83 Taxes 205 (March 2005)

IRC §165(a)

IRC §165(g)

Reg. §1.165-5

Partial worthlessness not allowed

Edwin Leo Coyle, 142 F.2d 580 (7th Cir. 1944)

Harry C. Howard, 20 BTA 207, aff'd, 56 F.2d 781 (6th Cir. 1932), cert. denied, 287 U.S. 619

Abandoned securities treated as worthless

Prop. Reg. Sec. 1.165-5(i)

Note: *Paragraph numbers refer to Parts 1 through 7. Items marked* are research aids, not citations of authority; see "Key to Citations" on page 801*

Statute of limitation

IRC §6511(d)(1)

Sale for nominal amount after worthlessness

J. Graham Brown, 94 F.2d 101 (6th Cir. 1938)

Frank C. Rand, 116 F.2d 929 (8th Cir. 1941), cert. denied, 313 U.S. 594

Insolvency

Alice G. K. Kleburg, 2 TC 1024 (1943)

Arthur C. Ansley, 217 F.2d 252 (3d Cir. 1954)

Potential value in stock despite insolvency

Paul Osborne, 70 TMC 243 (1995)

Norman Nelson, 131 F.2d 301 (8th Cir. 1942)

Business continued

Lola G. Bullard, 146 F.2d 386 (2d Cir. 1945)

George P. Snow, 90 F. Supp. 37 (E.D.N.Y. 1950)

Bankruptcy

Joseph A. Jeffrey, 62 F.2d 661 (6th Cir. 1933)

Dennis H. Long, 145 F.2d 234 (6th Cir. 1944)

In re Harrington, 1 F.2d 749 (D.C. Cir. 1924)

Court advice on claiming bad debt deduction

Minnie K. Young, 123 F.2d 597 (2d Cir. 1941)

Payments on note issued for stock

W. P. Tams, Jr., 33 F. Supp. 764 (D. W. Va. 1940)

Small business investment company

IRC §1242

Loss on short sale of SBIC stock

Rev. Rul. 63-65, 1963-1 CB 142

Political party debt

IRC §271

5.33 Tax Consequences of Bad Debts

Business bad debt

IRC §166

Reg. §1.166-1

* IRS Publication 548

* IRS Publication 535

Debt worthless after termination of business

IRC §166(d)(2)(A)

Reg. §1.166-5

Sell merchandise on credit

Reg. §1.166-6

No deduction for unpaid account receivable

Lawrence Washburn, 61 TCM 2529 (1991)

Business of investing or making loans

Allerton Cushman, 148 F. Supp. 880 (D. Ariz. 1956)

L. Washburn, 51 F.2d 949 (8th Cir. 1931)

Hyman R. Minkoff, 15 TCM 1404 (1956)

Morris H. Cone Estate, 13 TCM 512 (1954)

Sell your business

Reg. §1.166-5(d)(6)

Promoter

Vincent C. Campbell, 11 TC 510 (1948) (Acq.)

Loan to maintain business reputation

Wilfred J. Funk, 35 TC 42 (1960) (Acq.)

Stuart Bart, 21 TC 880 (1954) (Acq.)

Loan to insure merchandise delivery

Robert Haverty Est., 12 TCM 1295 (1953)

J. T. Dorminey, 26 TC 940 (1956) (Acq.)

Loan to controlled corporation to further business

Lawrence M. Weil Est., 29 TC 366 (1957) (Acq.)

Nonbusiness debt

IRC §166(d)

IRC §1211

Reg. §1.166-5

Reg. §1.1211-1

Guarantors

Reg. §1.166-9

Reg. §1.1211-1

Personal advances

Gifford A. Cochran, 14 TCM 206 (1955)

Attorney's loan to client

Robert H. McNeil, 251 F.2d 863 (4th Cir. 1958)

Payment of another's taxes

Albert Gersten, 28 TC 756 (1957) (Acq.), aff'd in part, rev'd in part on other issues, 267 F.2d 195 (9th Cir. 1959)

Payment of joint tax by spouse

Frank R. Haynes, 27 TCM 1531 (1968)

Loss of deposit

Rev. Rul. 69-457, 1969-2 CB 32

Dominant motive test

Edna Generes, 405 U.S. 93 (1972)

Loan by shareholder-employees to protect job

Edna Generes, 405 U.S. 93 (1972), rev'g 427 F.2d 279 (5th Cir. 1970)

Kenneth W. Graves, TC Memo 2004-140

Harry Litwin, 983 F.2d 997 (10th Cir. 1993)

Donald C. Niblock, Jr., 417 F.2d 1185 (7th Cir. 1969)

James O. Gould, 64 TC 132 (1975)

Odee Smith, 55 TC 260 (1970), vacated and rem'd per curiam, 457 F.2d 797 (5th Cir. 1972), on rem'd 60 TC 316 (1973) (Acq.)

Lawrence J. Doerfler, 36 TCM 789 (1977)

William G. Young, 33 TCM 397 (1974)

Loans to corporations

Charles Kadlec, 71 TCM 2399 (1996) (closely held corporation)

Donald C. Van Pelt, 191 F.2d 861 (6th Cir. 1951)

Janet McBride, 23 TC 926 (1955) (Acq.)

Weldon D. Smith, 17 TC 135 (1951), rev'd, 203 F.2d 310 (2d Cir. 1953), cert. denied, 346 U.S. 816

Sam Schaltzer, 13 TC 43 (1949) (Acq.), aff'd per curiam, 183 F.2d 70 (9th Cir. 1950), cert. denied, 340 U.S. 911

Rev. Rul. 60-48, 1960-1 CB 112

Unpaid stockholder loans to corporation

A. J. Whipple, 373 U.S. 193 (1963) (nonbusiness bad debt for payment to protect investment)

Stockholder loan to key employee deductible

Charles W. Carter, 39 TCM 456 (1979)

5.34 Four Rules To Prove a Bad Debt Deduction

Advances to insolvent corporation

Note: *Paragraph numbers refer to Parts 1 through 7. Items marked * are research aids, not citations of authority;* see *"Key to Citations" on page 801*

W. F. Young, Inc., 120 F.2d 159 (1st Cir. 1941)

Advances repaid only if profit is shown

Lucia C. Ewing, 20 TC 216 (1953), aff'd, 213 F.2d 438 (2d Cir. 1954)

Usurious loan

William K. Harriman, 26 TCM 941 (1967)

Usurious loan as a business loss

Herbert E. Tharp, 31 TCM 22 (1972)

Debtor-creditor relationship

Kentucky Rock Asphalt Co., 108 F.2d 779 (6th Cir. 1940)

W. M. Robertson, 7 TCM 62 (1948)

Loan included in income

IRC §166

Reg. §1.166-1

Consulting engineer

Jack Shapiro, 20 TCM 579 (1961)

Worthless during year

IRC §166

Reg. §1.166-1

Bankruptcy by court order

Reg. §1.166-2(c)

Final liquidation dividend

Leedom & Worrall Co., 10 BTA 825

First National Bank of Los Angeles, 6 BTA 850 (Acq.)

Corporation liquidation resolution

Pantex Oil Corp., 8 TCM 1079 (1949)

Disappearance of debtor

Fridolin Pabst, 36 F.2d 614 (D.C. Cir. 1930)

Debtor's refusal to pay

Philip C. Hughes, 10 TCM 204 (1951)

Revocation of corporate charter

Leila S. Kirby, 35 BTA 578 (Acq. and nonacq.), aff'd in part, rev'd in part, 102 F.2d 115 (5th Cir. 1939)

Cancelled debt

Nathan Fink, 29 TC 1119 (1958) (Acq.)

No hope of later value

American Trust Co., 31 F.2d 47 (9th Cir. 1939), aff'g 10 BTA 490

Alemite Die Casting & Manufacturing Co., 1 BTA 548

Debt worthless before due

Clarence Bonynge, 117 F.2d 157 (2d Cir. 1941)

Statute of limitations has run

Ralph H. Cross, 54 F.2d 781 (9th Cir. 1932)

Leo Stein, 4 BTA 1016

Statute ran before death

Clara Burdette, 69 F.2d 410 (9th Cir. 1934)

Debt guaranteed by collateral

John Hubble, 42 TCM 1537 (1981)

Release an endorser

Reg. §1.166-8

Eleanor A. Bradford, 22 TC 1057 (1954), rev'd, 233 F.2d 935 (6th Cir. 1956)

Breach of contract

Zelma T. Kyle, 242 F.2d 825 (2d Cir. 1957)

Less than full payment

Edgar H. Gleason, Jr., 62 TCM 600 (1991)

Embezzled funds

Reg.§ 1.165-8

5.35 Family Bad Debts

Reg. §1.166-1

* "Shore up Potential Deduction for Intrafamily Loan," Terri Guiterrez, 65 Tax Strategies 275 (November 2000)

Defaulted support payment

Carolyn Perry, 92 TC 470 (1989) (reaffirms Swenson)

Dale Swenson, 43 TC 897 (1965)

Shirley S. Imeson, 487 F.2d 319 (9th Cir. 1973), aff'g per curiam 28 TCM 899 (1969), cert. denied, 418 U.S. 917

Rev. Rul. 93-27, 1993 CB 32 (IRS rejects Ninth Circuit's possible deduction arguments)

M. J. Williford, 34 TCM 354 (1975)

Loans to family

Loy Bowman, 69 TCM 286 (1995)

Myer B. Barr, 77 TCM 1370 (1999)

6 Tax-Free Exchanges of Property

6.1 Trades of Like-Kind Property

IRC §1031

* IRS Publication 544

* "Rollover—Better Than Section 1031, But Why Stop There?," Martin J. McMahon Jr. 92 Tax Notes 1111 (August 20, 2001)

"Undivided Interests and Section 1031 Exchanges," Burgess J.W. Raby and William L. Raby, 90 Tax Notes 649 (January 29, 2001)

Personal use safe harbor for tax deferred exchange

Rev. Proc. 2008-16, 2008-10 IRB 547

Exchange solely for like-kind property

IRC §1031(a)

Reg. §1.1031(a)-1

Wittig, 70 TCM 824 (withdrawn 11/9/95)

Must be used in trade or business or for investment

IRC §1031(a)

Reg. §1.1031(a)-1

Depreciable equipment on which there is potential gain

IRC §1245(b)(3)

Farm for city property

L. M. Dyke, 1 BTA Memo 32-157

E. R. Braley, 14 BTA 1153 (Acq.)

Farms exchanged

Rev. Rul. 59-229, 1959-2 CB 180

Exchange of ownership interest in realty for 30-year leasehold

Reg. §1.1031(a)-1(c)

Rev. Rul. 78-72, 1978-1 CB 258

Land for water rights

Rev. Rul. 55-749, 1955-2 CB 295, distinguished by Rev. Rul. 67-255, 1967-2 CB 270

Exchange of partnership interests

IRC §1031(a)(2)(D)

Rollin E. Meyers, Sr., Est., 503 F.2d 556 (9th Cir. 1974), aff'g per curiam, 58 TC 311 (1972) (Nonacq.)

Reg. §1.1031(a)-1(a) and (e)

Tax-free oil lease for ranch

Rev. Rul. 68-331, 1968-1 CB 352

Taxable oil lease for ranch

William Fleming, 356 U.S. 260 (1958),

Note: *Paragraph numbers refer to Parts 1 through 7. Items marked * are research aids, not citations of authority;* see *"Key to Citations" on page 801*

rev'g 241 F.2d 78 (5th Cir. 1957)

Timber rights

Oregon Lumber Co., 20 TC 192 (1953) (Acq.)

Exchange of cattle of different sexes

IRC §1031(e)

Exception — residence for other residence

IRC §1034

Reg. §1.1034-1

Ethel Black, 35 TC 90 (1960)

U.S. and foreign real estate not "like kind"

IRC §1031(h)

Personal property used predominately in the U.S.

IRC §1031(h)(i)

Joint tenancy and tenancy in common

Rev. Rul. 46-437, 1956-2 CB 507

Other exchanges

IRC §1002

Reg. §1.1002-1

6.2 Personal Property Held for Business or Investment

Like-class test for depreciable tangible personal property

Reg. §1.1031(a)-2

Rev. Proc. 87-56, 1987-2 CB 674

General asset classes

Reg. §1.1031(a)-2(b)(2)

Product classes

Temp. Reg. §1.1031(a)-2T (NAICS codes)

Multiple property exchanges

Reg. §1.1031(j)-1

Trading in an SUV for a car

* Letter Ruling 200450005

6.3 Receipt of Cash and Other Property—"Boot"

* "Many Transaction Costs Can Reduce Boot in Like-Kind Exchanges," Craig W. Murel and Richard L. Panich, 74 Journal of Taxation 320 (May 1991)

Boot is taxed

IRC §1031(b)

Reg. §1.1031(b)-1

No loss recognized if boot given

IRC §1031(c) and (d)

Reg. §1.1031(c)-1 and (d)-1

Mortgage release is boot

Reg. §1031(d)-2

Beulah B. Crane, 331 U.S. 1 (1947)

Wittig, 70 TCM 824 (withdrawn 11/9/95)

Basis of property received

Reg. §1.1031(d)-2

Exclusion plus gain deferral on exchange of residence

Rev. Proc. 2005-14, 2005-7 IRB 528

6.4 Time Limits for Deferred Exchanges

Time limits

IRC §1031(a)(3)

Reg. §1.1031(k)-1(b)

Identifying replacement property

Reg. §1.1031(k)-1(c) and (d)

Safe harbors for security arrangements

Reg. §1.1031(k)-1(g)

Direct deed transfer

Rev. Rul. 90-34, 1990-1 CB 154

6.5 Qualified Exchange Accommodation Arrangements (QEAAs) for Reverse Exchanges

* "New Safe Harbor Promotes Reverse Exchanges," Bradley T. Borden, 66 Practical Tax Strategies 68 (February 2001)
* "Guidance from the IRS on Making Reverse-Starker Exchanges," Jeffrey J. Bryant and Richard L. Allitzer, 79 Taxes 2 (February 2001)

Escrow accounts—final regs

T.D. 9413, 73 F.R. 39614

Safe-harbor tests for reverse exchanges

Rev. Proc. 2000-37, 2000-40 IRB 308

Restriction on "parking" safe harbor

Rev. Proc. 2004-51, 2004-33 IRB 294

6.6 Exchanges Between Related Parties

IRC §1031(f)

Two-year freeze on exchange with related party

IRC §1031(f)

Prearranged plans

IRC §1031(f)(4)

6.7 Property Transfers Between Spouses and Ex-Spouses

IRC §1041

Temp. Reg. §1.041-IT

* "Code Sec. 1041 and Constructive Dividend Decisional Law: Irreconcilable Differences," Tina Steward Quinn and Rebecca C. Carr, 80 Taxes 37 (September 2002)
* "Interest Paid to an Ex-Spouse Incident to Divorce — Yes, It Can Be Deductible," Richard P. Algeo, 89 Journal of Taxation 310 (November 1998)

Final regulations: divorce-related stock redemptions

Reg. §1.1041-2 (tax-free treatment for transferor conditional on constructive distribution for non-transferor)

Divorce-related stock redemption is tax free

Joann C. Arnes, 981 F.2d 456 (9th Cir. 1993)

John A. Arnes, 102 TC 20 (1994)

Carol M. Read, 114 TC 14 (2000)

Linda Craven, 215 F.3d 1201 (11th Cir. 2000)

Divorce-related stock redemption is taxable

Gloria T. Blatt, 102 TC 5 (1994)

* Letter Ruling 9427009

Divorce transfer of nonqualified options

Rev. Rul. 2004-60, 2004-24 IRB 1051

Rev. Rul. 2002-22, 2002-19 IRB 849

Readjustment of property settlement

Louise F. Young, 2001-1 USTC ¶50,244 (4th Cir. 2001)

Cash paid for house transfer in property settlement

Michael J. Godlewski, 90 TC 200 (1988)

Nonresident spouses

IRC §1041(a)

Transfer of savings bonds

Rev. Rul. 87-112, 1987-2 CB 207

Gain realized on transfer in trust

IRC §1041(e)

Note: *Paragraph numbers refer to Parts 1 through 7. Items marked * are research aids, not citations of authority;* see *"Key to Citations" on page 801*

Temp. Reg. §1.1041-1T

Divorce-related exchange of marital rights is tax free

* Letter Ruling 200442003

Tax-free transfer for relinquishment of community property right to retirement pay

Hazel E. Balding, 98 TC 368 (1992)

Divorced wife taxed on sale of business

Vincent Yonadi, 21 F.3d 1292 (1994)

6.8 Tax-Free Exchanges of Stock in Same Corporation

Tax-free exchange of stock for stock in same company

IRC §1036

Reg. §1.1036-1

Recapitalization is a type of reorganization

IRC §368(a)(1)(E)

Reg. §1.368-2(e)

Stock dividends and stock rights

IRC §305(a)

6.9 Joint Ownership Interests

Exchange of tenants in common

Rev. Rul. 73-476, 1973-2 CB 300

Joint tenancy and tenancy in common

Rev. Rul. 56-437, 1956-2 CB 507

Boot not offset by assumption of liability

Rev. Rul. 79-44, 1979-1 CB 265

6.10 Setting up Closely Held Corporations

IRC §351

Securities as boot

IRC §351(a)

6.11 Exchanges of Coins and Bullion

IRC §1031

Mexican pesos for Austrian coronas

Rev. Rul. 76-214, 1976-1 CB 218

Silver bullion for gold bullion not tax free

Rev. Rul. 82-166, 1982-2 CB 190

U.S. gold coins for S. African Krugerrands

Rev. Rul. 79-413, 1979-2 CB 309

Swiss francs for U.S. double eagle coins not like-kind exchange

California Fed. Life Ins. Co., 76 TC 107 (1981), aff'd, 680 F.2d 85 (9th Cir. 1982)

6.12 Tax-Free Exchanges of Insurance Policies

Tax-free exchanges

IRC §1035

Reg. §1.1035-1

Tax-free exchange of policy from financially troubled insurer

Rev. Proc. 92-44, 1992-1 CB 875, amplified by Rev. Proc. 92-44A

Partial tax-free exchange of annuity contracts

Dona Conway, 111 TC 350 (1998), Acq. 1999-2 CB xvi

Tax-free exchange of key executive policy

Rev. Rul. 90-109, 1990-2 CB 191

Endorsement of annuity check for another annuity is taxable

Rev. Rul. 2007-24, 2007-21 IRB 1282

7 Retirement and Annuity Income

7.1 Retirement Distributions on Form 1099-R

* IRS Publication 575

Tax-favored withdrawals for Hurricanes Katrina, Rita, and Wilma victims

IRC §1400Q(a)

Notice 2005-92, 2005-51 IRB 1165

* IRS Publication 4492

Companies may not limit ex-employees' investments

Rev. Rul. 96-47, 1996-2 CB 35

State's ability to tax pension income limited

P.L. 104-95 (1/10/96)

Waiver of pension benefits taxable

Alfred Gallade, 106 TC 20 (1996)

7.2 Lump-Sum Distributions

Sections 1122(h)(3) and (5) of the Tax Reform Act of 1986 (P.L. 99-514)

* IRS Publication 575

Qualified plans

IRC §401

Computation of averaging

Reg. §1.402(e)-2(d)

Five-year participation test for 10-year averaging

Reg. §1.402(e)-2(e)(3)

Averaging barred by post-2001 rollover to same plan

Section 641(f)(3) of EGTRRA 2001

7.3 Lump-Sum Options If You Were Born Before January 2, 1936

20% withholding rate

IRC §3405(c)

Irrevocability of rollover election

Temp. Reg. §1.402(a)(5)-1T (Q&A-4)

Lump-sum treatment denied on retroactive revocation of plan qualification

John V. Fazi, 102 TC 31 (1994) (Tax Court will no longer follow its Baetens decision and will follow appeals courts)

Curtis B. Woodson, 73 TC 779 (1980), rev'd, 651 F.2d 1094 (5th Cir. 1981)

Theodore L. Baetens, 82 TC 152 (1984), rev'd, 777 F.2d 1160 (6th Cir. 1985)

Donald L. Benbow, 82 TC 941 (1984), rev'd, 774 F.2d 740 (7th Cir. 1985)

Partial lump-sum treatment on retroactive plan disqualification

Harold D. Greenwald, 366 F.2d 538 (2d Cir. 1982)

Making a partial rollover bars averaging

Sanford O. Barnes, Jr., 67 TCM 2341 (1994)

7.4 Averaging on Form 4972

Averaging election must apply to all eligible lump sums received in same year

Robert O. Fowler, 98 TC 503 (1992)

10-year averaging if born before 1936

P.L. 99-514 (1986 Tax Reform Act), Act Section 1122(h)(3) and (h)(5)

One lifetime election for averaging

IRC §402(e)(4)(B)

Taxable portion

IRC §402(a)(1)

Note: *Paragraph numbers refer to Parts 1 through 7. Items marked * are research aids, not citations of authority; see "Key to Citations" on page 801*

Prop. Reg. §1.402(a)-1(a)(9)(b)
IRC §402(e)(4)(D)
Prop. Reg. §1.402(c)-2(d)(2)

Community property

Prop. Reg. §1.402(e)-2(e)(2)

7.5 Capital Gain Treatment for Pre-1974 Participation

Electing 20% capital gain treatment if born before 1936

P.L. 99-415 (1986 Tax Reform Act), Act Section 1122(h)(3) and (h)(6)

7.6 Lump-Sum Payments Received by Beneficiary

IRC §402(e)(4)(A)(i)
Richard Gunnison, 461 F.2d 496 (7th Cir. 1972), aff'g 54 TC 1766 (1970)
Robert A. Stefanowski Est., 63 TC 386 (1974)

Five-year participation of employee not required

Prop. Reg. §1.402(e)-2(e)(3)

Beneficiary does not have to meet age test but deceased employee does

Mary E. Cebula, 101 TC 5 (1993)

Capital gain treatment

Prop. Reg. §1.403(a)-2(b)
Prop. Reg. §1.402(e)-2(d)

Up-to-$5,000 death benefit exclusion

IRC §101(b)

Distribution to trust or estate

Reg. §1.402(c)-3
Reg. §1.402(e)-2(e)(6)

7.7 Tax-Free Rollovers From Qualified Plans

* IRS Publication 575

Rollover of distributions

IRC §402(c)

Plan may allow immediate distributions of segregated rollovers

Rev. Rul. 2004-12, 2004-7 IRB 478

20% withholding if plan does not make direct rollover

IRC §3405(c)

Tax-sheltered annuity rollover

IRC §403(b)(8)
IRC §408(d)(3)(A)(iii)

Employer required to explain options

IRC §402(f)
Reg. §1.402(f)-1
Notice 2002-3, 2002-2 IRB 289 (IRS model notice)

Rollover treatment disallowed for minimum required distributions

IRC §402(c)(4)(B)
IRC §408(d)(3)(E)

Hardship distributions from 401(k) or 403(b) plan cannot be rolled over

IRC §402(c)(4)(c)
IRC §403(b)(8)(B)

Distribution under qualified domestic relations order (QDRO) to spouse or ex-spouse may be rolled over

IRC §402(e)(1)

7.8 Direct Rollover or Personal Rollover

* IRS Publication 575

20% withholding if plan does not make direct rollover

IRC §3405(c)

Taxable rollover to Roth IRA

IRC §408A(e)

Conduit IRAs

IRC §408(d)(3)(A)(ii)

Plan may allow immediate distributions of segregated rollovers

Rev. Rul. 2004-12, 2004-7 IRB 478

Commingled IRA funds prevent conduit rollover treatment

* Letter Ruling 9604028

Waiver on equitable grounds of 60-day rollover deadline

Rev. Proc. 2003-16, 2003-4 IRB 359

Distribution of life insurance

Rev. Rul. 81-275, 1981-2 CB 75

Extension of 60-day period for frozen assets

IRC §402(c)(7)

Rollover by surviving spouse

IRC §402(c)(9)
Section 641(f)(3) of EGTRRA 2001 (averaging barred for amounts rolled over by surviving spouse after 2001 to same plan)

Nonspouse beneficiary may make rollover to inherited IRA

IRC §402(c)(11)(A), as amended by the Worker, Retiree, and Employer Recovery Act of 2008

Diversification of rollover permitted

Rev. Rul. 79-265, 1979-2 CB 186

7.9 Rollover of Proceeds From Sale of Property

Rollover of sales proceeds

IRC §402(a)(6)(D)

Designation of cash

IRC §402(a)(6)(D)(iii)(II)

Designation of employee contributions

IRC §402(a)(6)(D)(iii)(I)

Allocation methods

IR-2086, February 6, 1979

7.10 Distribution of Employer Stock or Other Securities

* IRS Publication 575

Unrealized appreciation due to employee's contributions

IRC §402(e)(4)
Reg. §1.402(a)-1(b)
Reg. §1.402(a)-1(a)(9)(B)

Unrealized appreciation due to employer's contributions

IRC §402(e)(4)
Reg. §1.402(a)-1(b)
Reg. §1.402(a)-1(a)(9)(B)
Reg. §1.401(e)-2(d)(2)

Waiving tax-free treatment

IRC §402(e)(4)(B)

Shares valued below your cost

Rev. Rul. 71-251, 1971-1 CB 129, amplified by Rev. Rul. 72-15, 1972-1 CB 114

Worthless shares

Rev. Rul. 72-328, 1972-8 CB 224

Holding period

Reg. §1.402(a)-1(b)

Holding period for post-distribution appreciation

Rev. Rul. 81-122, 1981-1 CB 202

Note: *Paragraph numbers refer to Parts 1 through 7. Items marked * are research aids, not citations of authority;* see *"Key to Citations" on page 801*

Distribution other than lump sum

Reg. §1.402(a)-1(b)(3)
Reg. §1.402(a)-1(a)(9)(b)

Unrealized appreciation affects pro rata recovery for non-lump sum

Notice 89-25, 1989-1 CB 662

NUA attributable to employee contributions immediately taxed on rollover of partial distributions

IRC §402(a)(5)(D)(iv)

Electing to include NUA in income

Notice 89-25, 1989-1 CB 662

7.11 Survivor Annuity for Spouse

IRC §401(a)(1)

Survivor annuity requirements

IRC §417
Reg. §1.417(e)-1
Reg. §1.401(a)-1(a) and §1.401(a)-

20 questions and answers

Notice 94-23, 1994-1 CB 340

Involuntary cashouts

IRC §417(e)

7.12 Court Distributions to Former Spouse Under a QDRO

QDRO defined

IRC §414(p)

Averaging

IRC §402(d)(4)(J)

Spouse treated as payee

IRC §402(e)(1)
Marcia Fraser, 56 F.3d 722 (6th Cir. 1995)

Rollover

IRC §402(e)(1)(B)

Husband taxed on QDRO distribution

Robert L. Karem, 100 TC 34 (1993)

7.13 When Retirement Benefits Must Begin

Reg. §§ 1.401(a)(9)-1 through (a)(9)-9 (final regulations T.D. 8987, 2002-19 IRB 852)
* IRS Publication 575

Required minimum distributions suspended for 2009

IRC §401(a)(9)(H), added by the Worker, Retiree, and Employer Recovery Act of 2008

IRS extends period for rolling over 2009 RMD

News Release IR-2009-85
Notice 2009-82, 2009-41 IRB 491

Premature distributions

IRC §72(t)

Required beginning date

IRC §401(a)(9)(C)

All employees subject to 5% owner rule

Reg. §1.401(a)(9)-2 (Q&A-2(e))

Required beginning date for 403(b) annuities

IRC §403(b)(10)

Distribution methods

IRC §401(a)(9)(A) and (B)
Reg. §1.401(a)(9)-1, 5 and -9

Penalty for not receiving minimum distributions

IRC §4974(a)

Governmental and church plans

IRC §401(a)(9)(C)

No RMD required for active partner

* Letter Ruling 200524032

7.14 Payouts to Beneficiaries

Reg. §1.401(a)(9)-4, -5, -8, and -9
* IRS Publication 575
* "Planning Strategies for Distributions from Retirement Plans," Bradley T. Borden and Gregory S. Stieg, 69 Tax Strategies 273 (November 2002)

Determining designated beneficiaries

Reg. §1.401(a)(9)-4

Distribution period for beneficiaries

Reg. §1.401(a)(9)-5 (Q&A-5)

Single life expectancy table for beneficiary

Reg. §1.401(a)(9)-9 (Q&A-1)

Ex-spouse beneficiary gets 401(k) benefits

Donna Rae Egelhoff, U.S. Supreme Court, 3/21/01

Nonspouse beneficiary may make rollover to inherited IRA

IRC §402(c)(11)

7.15 Penalty for Distributions Before Age 59½

IRC §72(t)
* "Revised Rules for Penalty-Free Early Periodic Retirement Payments," Caroline K. Craig and Richard B. Toolson, 70 Practical Tax Strategies 86 (February 2003)

Penalty exceptions

IRC §72(t)(2)

Penalty exception for qualified reservists

IRC §72(t)(2)(G), as added by PPA 2006

Penalty exception for qualified public safety employees

IRC §72(t)(10)

Penalty exception for Hurricane Katrina, Rita, and Wilma victims

IRC §1400Q(a)(1)

Long-term depression requiring hospitalization qualifies for disability exception

* Mary L. Coleman-Stephens, TC Summary Opinion 2003-91

No penalty exception for financial hardship

Eugene Dollander, TC Memo 2009-187

7.16 Restrictions on Loans From Company Plans

IRC §72(p)
Reg. §1.72(p)-1

Higher loan limit for Midwestern disaster area victims

IRC 1400Q, applied to Midwestern disaster area by Act Section 702(a)(1)(D) of the Emergency Economic Stabilization Act of 2008
*IRS Publication 4492-B

Higher loan limit for Hurricane Katrina, Rita, or Wilma victims

IRC §1400Q(c)

50% security cap

Labor Dept. Reg. 2550.408(b)-1

Demand loan taxed

Thomas Gray Estate, 70 TCM 556 (1995)

Balloon loan taxed

Clayton W. Plotkin, TC Memo 2001-71

Note: *Paragraph numbers refer to Parts 1 through 7. Items marked * are research aids, not citations of authority; see "Key to Citations" on page 801*

Unpaid loan at separation from service

Notice 93-3, 1993-3 IRB 11

*Letter Ruling 200617037 (rollover of outstanding loan balance avoids taxable distribution)

Spousal consent

IRC §417(a)(4)

Interest deduction limitations

IRC §72(p)(3)

Residence used as loan collateral

* Letter Ruling 8933018

7.17 Tax Benefits of 401(k) Plans

* "401(k) Plans Are Not All They Are 'Cracked Up' To Be," Philip R. Fink, 69 Tax Strategies 214 (October 2002)

Automatic 401(k) enrollment

IRC §401(k)(13) (nondiscrimination tests)

Preapproved plan amendments for automatic enrollment

Notice 2009-65, 2009-39 IRB 413

Automatic annual increase of employee contributions

Rev. Rul. 2009-30, 2009-39 IRB 391

Plan qualification requirement: Plan must limit deferrals to 402(g) ceiling

IRC §401(a)(30)

Qualified cash or deferred arrangements

IRC §401(k)

Reg. §1.401(k)-1

Roth 401(k) option

IRC §402A

Reg. §1.401(k)-1(f) (Treasury Decision 9237, 12/30/05)

Prop. Reg. §§ 1.402 A-1, A-2 and A-10 (distributions)

Notice 2006-44, 2006-20 IRB 889 (IRS sample plan amendment)

IRS approves automatic 401(k) plan coverage

Revenue Ruling 98-30, 1998-25 IRB 8

Nondiscrimination rules

IRC §401(k)(3)

SIMPLE 401(k) satisfies nondiscrimination tests

IRC §401(k)(11)

Tax-exempt organizations may set up 401(k) plans

IRC §401(k)(4)(B)

Employees not taxed on contribution of excess vacation pay to 401(k) plan

* Letter Ruling 200311043

Partnership plans

Reg. §1.401(k)-1(a)(6)

Rev. Proc. 91-47, 1991-2 CB 757

7.18 Limit on Salary-Reduction Deferrals

Annual limit

IRC §402(g)(1)

News Release IR-2009-94 (limits for 2010)

"Catch-up" contributions if age 50 or older

IRC §414(v)

One-time election

Reg. §1.401(k)-1(a)(3)(iv)

Nondiscrimination rules

IRC §401(k)(3)

IRC §401(k)(12)

7.19 Withdrawals From 401(k) Plans Restricted

IRC §401(k)(2)(B)

Hardship tests

Reg. §1.401(k)-1(d)(2)

Qualified reservist distributions

IRC §401(k)(2)(B)(i)(V)

Hardship distributions ineligible for rollover

IRC §402(c)(4)

IRS may not levy 401(k) account until employee retires

IRS Legal Memorandum 200032004

7.20 Designated Roth Contributions to 401(k) Plans

Roth 401(k) option

IRC §402A

Reg. §1.401(k)-1(f)

Reg. §§ 1.402A-1, A-2 and A-10 (distributions)

Notice 2006-44, 2006-20 IRB 889 (IRS sample plan amendment)

Rollover from 401(k) to Roth 401(k)

IRC §402A(c)(4), as added by the Small Business Jobs Act of 2010, P.L. 111-240, 9/27/10

7.21 Annuities for Employees of Tax-Exempts and Schools (403(b) Plans)

IRC §403(b)

* IRS Publication 571

* "Code Sec. 403(b): Changes and Simplification After 2001," Robert T. Sullens, William J. Cenker and Matthew J. Verleny, 80 Taxes 29 (August 2002)

Penalty exception for qualified reservists

IRC §72(t)(2)(G)

Up-to-$3,000 annual exclusion for health insurance premiums of public safety officers

IRC §402(1)

Employer may automatically enroll employees in 403(b) plan

Rev. Rul. 2000-35, 2000-31 IRB 138

Salary-reduction limit

IRC §402(g)(3)(c)

IRC §401(a)(30) (plan qualification requirement)

One-time election

IRC §402(g)(3)

Increased salary-reduction limit for 15-year employees

IRC §402(g)(7)

Rollovers

IRC §403(b)(8)

Direct trustee-to-trustee transfer

Prop. Reg. §1.403(b)-10(b) (would repeal Rev. Rul. 90-24, which allowed transfer outside the plan)

Rev. Rul. 90-24, 1990-1 CB 97

Contribution limit for year of separation from service

IRC §415(c)(4)(A)

7.22 Government and Exempt Organization Deferred Pay Plans

Federal thrift plans

IRC §7701(j)

Note: *Paragraph numbers refer to Parts 1 through 7. Items marked * are research aids, not citations of authority;* see *"Key to Citations" on page 801*

Section 457 plan elective deferrals

IRC §457(e)(15)(A)

Up-to-$3,000 annual exclusion for health insurance premiums of public safety officers

IRC §402(1)

Employer may automatically enroll employees in Section 457 plan

Rev. Rul. 2000-33, 2000-31 IRB 142

Section 457 plan distributions

IRC §457(d)

Rollover options

IRC §457(e)(16)

Averaging for qualified plan distribution barred by post-2001 rollover from governmental 457 plan

Section 641(f)(3)

Unforeseen emergency: Section 457 plan withdrawals

Reg. §1.457-2(h)(4)

7.23 Figuring the Taxable Part of Your Annuity

* IRS Publication 575

What is an annuity?

IRC §72

Payments before annuity starting date

IRC §72(e)

Penalty for pre-59½ withdrawals from deferred annuity

IRC §72(q)

* Letter Ruling 200113022 (substantially equal payments exception to penalty)

Switch in pre-59½ payments schedule for owners of nonqualified annuities

Notice 2004-15, 2004-9 IRB 526

Unisex actuarial tables

Reg. §1.72-9

Pre–July 1986 investment and post–June 1986 investment

Reg. §1.72-6(d)(8)

Annuity exclusion limited to investment

IRC §72(b)(2)

Investment

IRC §72(c)(1)

Reg. §1.72-6

Expected return

IRC §72(c)(3)

Reg. §1.72-5

Deduction on final return for unrecovered investment

IRC §72(b)(3) and (4)

Refund feature

IRC §72(c)(2)

Reg. §1.72-7

Exclusion ratio

IRC §72(b)

Reg. §1.72-4

Total receipts for year

Reg. §1.72-4

Single annuity

Reg. §1.72-5(a)

Reg. §1.72-9, Table I or Table V

Temporary annuity

Reg. §1.72-9, Table IV or Table VIII

Reg. §1.72-5(a)(3)

One annuitant-stepped down annuity

Reg. §1.72-9, Tables I and IV, or Tables V and VIII

Reg. §1.72-5(a)(4)

One annuitant-stepped up annuity

Reg. §1.72-9, Tables I and IV, or Tables V and VIII

Reg. §1.72-5(a)(5)

Uniform joint and survivor annuities

Reg. §1.72-5(b)

Reg. §1.72-9, Table II or VI

Variable joint and survivor annuities

Reg. §1.72-9, Tables I, II, and IIA, or Tables V, VI, and VIA

7.24 Life Expectancy Tables

Reg. §1.72-6

* IRS Publication 939

Unisex actuarial tables

Reg. §1.72-9, Tables V, VI, VIA, VII, and VIII

7.25 When You Convert Your Endowment Policy

IRC §72(e) and (h)

Interest option

Henry L. Blum, 150 F.2d 471 (2nd Cir. 1945)

Sale of endowment contract

Percy W. Phillips, 30 TC 866 (1958) (Nonacq.), rev'd, 275 F.2d 33 (4th Cir. 1960)

Bolling Jones, 39 TC 404 (1962)

Sale of an annuity contract

Andrew Wineman Est., 163 F. Supp. 865 (Ct. Cl. 1958), cert. denied, 359 U.S. 943

First Nat'l Bank of Kansas City, 20 TCM 1411 (1961), aff'd, 309 F.2d 587 (8th Cir. 1962)

Harry Roff, 36 TC 818 (1961), aff'd, 304 F.2d 450 (3d Cir. 1962)

Sale of insurance policies

Gertrude H. Crocker Est., 37 TC 605 (1962)

7.26 Reporting Employee Annuities

IRC §72(d)

* IRS Publications 575 and 721

7.27 Simplified Method for Calculating Taxable Employee Annuity

IRC §72(d)(1)(B)

* IRS Publications 575 and 721

7.28 Employee's Cost in Annuity

Amounts paid

IRC §72(b) and (e)

IRC §403

Reg. §1.403(a)

Reg. §1.72-8

Employer's payments

Reg. §1.72-8

Taxpayer's inflation adjustment not allowed

Kenneth L. Nordtvedt, 116 TC 165 (2001), aff'd unpublished opinion, 2001-2 USTC ¶50, 772

7.29 Withdrawals Before Annuity Starting Date

IRC §72(e)(8)

Notice 87-13, 1987-1 CB 432

Employee contributions (and interest allocable) treated as separate contract

IRC §72(d)

Note: *Paragraph numbers refer to Parts 1 through 7. Items marked * are research aids, not citations of authority;* see *"Key to Citations" on page 801*

IRC §414(k) (defined benefit plans)

Notice 87-13, 1987-1 CB 432 (Q & A 14)

Plans existing on May 5, 1986

IRC §72(e)(8)(D)

8 IRAs

8.1 Starting a Traditional IRA

* IRS Publication 590

Individual retirement account

IRC §408(a)

Reg. §1.408-2

Individual retirement annuity

IRC §408(b)

Reg. §1.408-3

Loss on surrender of IRA annuity nondeductible

Rev. Rul. 80-268, 1980-2 CB 141

Flexible premiums

IRC §408(b)(2)

Prop. Reg. §1.408-3(b)(6)

Endowment contract issued after November 6, 1978

Reg. §1.408-3(e)

Broker restrictions

Special Ruling, August 24, 1983

Tax treatment of distribution

IRC §408(d)

Reg. §1.408-4

Diversification of investment permitted

Rev. Rul. 79-265, 1979-2 CB 186

Collectibles investments restricted

IRC §408(m)(3)

Bullion investment allowed if in trustee's possession

IRC §408(m)(3)

* Letter Ruling 200217059

Time for making contributions

IRC §219(f)(3)

Bankruptcy protection for IRAs

Public Law 109-8, 4/20/05

Rousey v. Jacoway, Supreme Court, 4/4/05

8.2 Traditional IRA

Contributions Must Be Based on Earnings

IRC §219

* IRS Publication 590

Limit on deductible contributions

IRC §219(b)(5)(A)

IRC §219(b)(5)(B) (catch-up contributions if age 50 or older)

Retirement plan limits for 2010

News Release IR-2009-94

No contribution if age 70½

IRC §219(d)(1)

Time for making contribution

IRC §219(f)(3)

Higher contribution limit for 401(k) participants of certain bankrupt companies

IRC §219(b)(5)(C)

Compensatory damages for mismanaged IRA may be redeposited

* Letter Ruling 200852034

* Letter Ruling 200850054

Compensation defined

Reg. §1.219-1(c)(1)

Unemployment benefits

Donald G. Russell, 71 TCM 3184 (1996)

Earned income

IRC §219

IRC §401(c)(2)

IRC §1402(a)

IRA contributions based on tax-free combat pay

IRC §219(f)(7)

Qualified reservist repayments

IRC §72(t)(2)(G)(ii)

Trader activities not earned income

Robert Miller, 77 TC 97 (1981)

Self-employment losses do not offset wages

Rev. Rul. 79-286, 1979-2 CB 121

Aggregating businesses

IRC §1402(a)

Reg. §1.1402(a)-2(c)

Endowment contract

IRC §219(d)(3)

Reg. §1.408-3(e)

Payment of fees

Rev. Rul. 84-146, 1984-2 CB 61

8.3 Contributions to a Traditional IRA If You Are Married

* IRS Publication 590

Deduction phase-out range for married couples filing jointly

IRC §219(g)(3)(B)(i) (both active participants)

IRC §219(g)(7) (non-participant spouse)

Married couples filing separately

IRC §219(g)(3)(B)(iii) (living together)

IRC §219(g)(4) (living apart all year)

Deductions for nonworking or low-earning spouse

IRC §219(c)

Working for spouse without receiving payment of wages

* Letter Ruling 8707004

8.4 IRA Deduction Restrictions for Active Participants in Employer Plan

IRC §219(g)

* IRS Publication 590

Deduction limitations

IRC §219(c) (compensation of spouses)

IRC §219(g) (active participants)

Active plan participation blocks IRA deduction

Ted T. Starnes, TC Summary Opinion, 2008-148

Phaseout thresholds

Notice 2008-102, 2008-45 IRB 1106 (for 2009).

News Release IR-2009-94 (for 2010)

No IRA deduction in year of joining or leaving plan

Sara Wartes, 65 TCM 2058 (1993)

John Wade, TC Memo 2001-114

8.5 Active Participation in Employer Plan

IRC §219(g)(5)

Notice 87-16, 1987-1 CB 446

Active participation rule for 401(k)

Note: *Paragraph numbers refer to Parts 1 through 7. Items marked * are research aids, not citations of authority;* see *"Key to Citations" on page 801*

Jeffrey W. Baumann, 70 TCM 61 (1995)

* Letter Ruling 8919064

Active plan participation blocks IRA deduction

Ted T. Starnes, TC Summary Opinion, 2008-148

8.6 Nondeductible Contributions to Traditional IRAs

IRC §408(o)

Penalties relating to nondeductible contributions

IRC §6693(b)

8.7 Penalty for Excess Contributions to Traditional IRAs

Excess contributions

IRC §4973

Prop. Reg. §54.4973-1

IRC §408(d)(4): contributions returned before due date

IRC §408(d)(5): contributions withdrawn after due date

Reg. §1.408-1(c)(1)

Compensatory damages for mismanaged IRA may be redeposited

* Letter Ruling 200852034

* Letter Ruling 200850054

Excess contributions treated as made in subsequent years

IRC §219(f)(6)

8.8 Taxable Distributions From Traditional IRAs

IRC §408(d)(1)

Pre-59½ penalty

IRC §72(t)

Tax-free transfer from IRA to charity if age 70½ or older

IRC §408(d)(8)

Qualified hurricane distributions

IRC §1400Q(a)

IRS levy of IRA is taxable distribution

M.E. Schroeder, 78 TCM 566 (1999)

Former spouse's garnishment of IRA for child support treated as distribution

Mark J. Vorwald, TC Memo 1997-15

Custodian's check to company for stock not a taxable distribution

Robert Ancira, 119 TC 135 (2002)

8.9 Partially Tax-Free Traditional IRA Distributions Allocable to Nondeductible Contributions

Figuring tax if nondeductible contributions have been made

IRC §408(d)(2)

Notice 87-16, 1987-1 CB 446 (loss allowed for unrecovered basis)

8.10 Tax-Free Rollovers and Direct Transfers to Traditional IRAs

IRC §408(d)(3)

* IRS Publication 590

Direct transfer of account between trustees is not rollover

Rev. Rul. 78-406, 1978-2 CB 157

Rollover within 60 days not taxed

IRC §408(d)(3)(A)

60-day loan

* Letter Ruling 901007

IRS discretion to waive 60-day rollover deadline in hardship cases

IRC §408(d)(3)(I)

Rev. Proc. 2003-16, 2003-4 IRB 359 (IRS guidelines for granting waiver)

* Letter Ruling 200327064 (IRS grants waiver when investment manager misappropriates funds)

* Letter Ruling 200422053 (IRS denies waivers for unemployed taxpayer's short-term loan)

* Letter Ruling 200634064 (IRS allows extension after online mixup)

* Letter Ruling 200921040 (extension allowed after failure to redeposit funds due to Parkinson's disease and memory loss)

* Letter Ruling 200921037 (extension allowed where medical condition impairs taxpayer's ability to manage financial affairs)

* Letter Ruling 200921038 (extension allowed where financial advisor fails to follow taxpayer's instructions)

* Letter Ruling 200914071 (extension denied financial institution fails to inform taxpayer of 60-day rollover period)

Rollover deadline extended where financial advisor misappropriates funds

* Letter Ruling 200922056

* Letter Ruling 200922057

* Letter Ruling 200922058

* Letter Ruling 200922059

* Letter Ruling 200922060

Extension denied where taxpayer believes rollover period to be 90 days

* Letter Ruling 200907049

* Letter Ruling 200919071

Extension granted for passive activity loss election

* Letter Ruling 201031008

* Letter Ruling 201031009

60-day period extended for frozen deposits

IRC §408(d)(3)(F)

* Letter Ruling 199933038

120-day rollover period for failed first home acquisition

IRC §72(t)(8)(E)

* Letter Ruling 200423033

Rollover treatment disallowed for minimum required distribution

IRC §408(d)(3)(E)

Stock bought with IRA distribution—no tax-free rollover

Albert Lemishaw, 110 TC 26 (1998)

Withdrawals following bank failure

Alan Aronson, 98 TC 283 (1992)

Beneficiary can authorize trustee-to-trustee transfer

* Letter Ruling 8716058

8.11 Transfer of Traditional IRA to Spouse at Divorce or Death

Transfer because of divorce

IRC §408(d)(6)

IRA transfer to ex-spouse

Stephen R. Jones, TC Memo 2000-19 (payment to spouse from closed-out account is taxable distribution)

QDRO

IRC §402(e)(1)(B)

IRC §402(d)(4)(J)

Rollover by surviving spouse

Note: *Paragraph numbers refer to Parts 1 through 7. Items marked* are research aids, not citations of authority;* see *"Key to Citations" on page 801*

IRC §408(d)(3)(C)(ii)

IRC §408(a)(6)

8.12 Penalty for Traditional IRA Withdrawals Before Age 59½

IRC §72(t)

* IRS Publication 590

* "Revised Rules for Penalty-Free Early Periodic Retirement Payments," Caroline K. Craig and Richard B. Toolson, 70 Practical Tax Strategies 86 (February 2003)

Exception for substantially equal payments

IRC §72(t)(2)(A)(iv) and (t)(4)

Rev. Rul. 2002-62, 2002-42 IRB 710 (IRS allows one-time switch from fixed payment method to required minimum distribution method)

Interest charges added to penalty for adjusting annuity-type schedule

* Letter Ruling 9401040

Divorce may modify annuitized distribution schedule

* Letter Rulings 200052039 and 200050046

* Letter Ruling 200503036 (broker's error permits corrective distributions)

Pre-59½ withdrawals allowed for medical expenses

IRC §72(t)(2)(B)

Unemployed medical insurance exception

IRC §72(t)(2)(D)(iii)

Penalty-free qualified reservist distributions

IRC §72 (t)(2)(G)

Penalty exception for Hurricane Katrina, Rita, and Wilma victims

IRC §1400Q(a)(1)

Penalty exception for higher education expenses

IRC §72(t)(2)(E)

Watch timing of IRA withdrawals for education expenses

Roger F. Duronio, TC Memo 2007-90

Linda Louise Lodder-Beckert, TC Memo 2005-162

* Malia K. Ambata, TC Summary Opinion 2005-93

Computer not "qualified" college expense

* James M. Gorski, TC Summary Opinion 2005-112

Withdrawals for high school subject to penalty

David Brian Nolan, TC Memo 2007-306

Penalty exception for first-time homebuyer expenses

IRC §72(t)(2)(F)

* Jeffrey Thomas Olup, TC Summary Opinion 2005-183 (both spouses must meet first-time test)

* Vincent A. Suarez Jr., TC Summary Opinion 2005-71 (homeowner not eligible for penalty exception)

Disability exception

IRC §72(t)(2)(A)(iii)

Depression may be exception

Robert Dwyer, 106 TC 18 (1996) (no exception for stockholder who continues to work)

*Mary L. Coleman-Stephens, TC Summary Opinion 2003-91 (exception allowed for long-term depression preventing employment)

* Beverly Johnson, TC Summary Opinion 2006-62 (no exception for short-term depression)

* Brian P. Keeley, TC Summary Opinion 2003-53 (no exception for short-term depression)

No penalty for IRS levy of plan account

IRC §72(t)(2)(A)(vii)

No penalty exception for withdrawals to pay child support

* James K. Moyer, TC Summary Opinion 2006-189

8.13 Mandatory Distributions From a Traditional IRA After Age 70½

IRC §408(a)(6)

Reg. §§ 1.408-8, 1.401(a)(9)-1 through -9 (final regulations, T.D. 8987, 2002-19 IRB 852)

* "Apply Tax Planning Ideas to Improve Retirement Distributions," Sandra Brown Sherman, Brad M. Kaplan, and Heidi Hansen, 71 Practical Tax Strategies 27 (July 2003)

* "Minimum Distribution Rules Redux," a CCH Interview With Seymour Goldberg, 80 Taxes 43 (August 2002)

Required minimum distributions suspended for 2009

IRC §401(a)(9)(H), added by the Worker, Retiree, and Employer Recovery Act of 2008

IRS extends period for rolling over 2009 RMD

News Release IR-2009-85

Notice 2009-82, 2009-41 IRB 491

Insufficient distribution penalty

IRC §4974(b)

Distributions don't have to be from each account

Notice 88-38 1988-15 IRB 9

Waiver of penalty

Reg. §54.4974-2 (Q&A-7)

8.14 Inherited Traditional IRAs

IRC §408(a)(6)

Reg. §§ 1.408-8, 1.401(a)(9)-4, -5, -8, and -9

* IRS Publication 590

* "Planning Strategies for Distributions from Retirement Plans," Bradley T. Borden and Gregory S. Stieg, 69 Tax Strategies 273 (November 2002)

* "Final Regs. Give Dramatic Benefits to Beneficiaries of Inherited IRAs," Howard M. Esterces, 69 Tax Strategies 4 (July 2002)

Distribution period for beneficiaries

Reg. §1.401(a)(9)-5 (Q&A-5)

Required minimum distributions suspended for 2009

IRC §401(a)(9)(H), added by the Worker, Retiree, and Employer Recovery Act of 2008

Single life expectancy table

Reg. §1.401(a)(9)-9 (Q&A-1)

Required distributions to trust beneficiaries

* Letter Ruling 200329048

Trust named as IRA beneficiary in will not a designated beneficiary

* Letter Ruling 200849019

Qualified disclaimer after taking RMD

Rev. Rul. 2005-36, 2005-26 IRB 1368

8.15 SEP Basics

IRC §219(b)(2)

IRC §404(h)

IRC §408(j), (k), and (l)

Reg. §1.219-1(d)(4) and -3

Note: *Paragraph numbers refer to Parts 1 through 7. Items marked * are research aids, not citations of authority;* see *"Key to Citations" on page 801*

Reg. §1.404(h)-1

Reg. §1.408-7 through 9

* IRS Publication 590

Overall tax-free SEP contribution limit

IRC §402(h)(2)

Employer retirement plan limits for 2007

News Release IR-2006-162

Salary-reduction SEP

IRC §408(k)(6)

Elective salary-reduction limit

IRC §402(g)(1)

Employer's deductible limit

IRC §404(h)(1)(c)

8.16 Salary-Reduction SEP Set Up Before 1997

* IRS Publications 560 and 590

SEP

IRC §408(k)(6)

SIMPLE

IRC §408(p)

8.17 Who Is Eligible for a SIMPLE IRA?

IRC §408(p)

SIMPLE salary-reduction limit

IRC §408 (p) (2) (E)

Automatic enrollment for SIMPLE IRAs

Notice 2009-66, 2009-39 IRB 418

Notice 2009-67, 2009-39 IRB 420

8.18 SIMPLE IRA Contributions and Distributions

IRC §408(p)

* IRS Publications 560 and 590

SIMPLE salary-reduction limit

IRC §408(p)(2)(E)

Retirement plan limits for 2010

News Release IR-2009-94

Penalty for distributions before age 59½

IRC §72(t)(6)

Rollover from SIMPLE to other plans

IRC §408 (d)(3)(G)

8.19 Roth IRA Advantages

IRC §408A

* IRS Publication 590

Roth IRA guidelines

Reg. §1.408A-1 through A-9

Direct rollover from employer plan to Roth IRA after 2007

IRC §408A(e)

8.20 Annual Contributions to a Roth IRA

* IRS Publication 590

Annual contributions to Roth IRA

IRC §408A(c)(2) (limit keyed to deductible IRA limit)

IRC §408A(c)(3) (phaseout of contribution limit)

Reg. §1.408A-3

Excess contributions to Roth IRA

IRC §4973(f)

Roth IRA contributions based on tax- free combat pay

IRC §219(f)(7)

8.21 Converting a Traditional IRA to a Roth IRA

* "Tax Rate Predictions Affect Roth vs. Traditional IRA Choice," George W. Kutner, Lloyd D. Doney, and James P. Trebby, 66 Practical Tax Strategies 19 (January 2001)

Conversion to Roth IRA

IRC §408A(c)(3)(B) ($100,000 MAGI limit for conversions before 2010)

IRC §408A(d)(3) (tax on conversion)

Reg. §1.408A-4 (Q&A)

Two-year ratable income inclusion for conversion made in 2010

IRC §408A(d)(3)(A)(iii)

IRC §408A(d)(3)(E)

RMD excluded from $100,000 MAGI test

IRC §408A(c)(3)(C)(i)(II)

Annuity conversion to Roth IRA must be valued at fair market value

Rev. Proc. 2006-13, 2006-3 IRB 315

Temp. Reg. §1.408A-4T

Rollover from qualified retirement plan to Roth IRA

Notice 2009-75, 2009-39 IRB 436

8.22 Recharacterizations and Reconversions

* IRS Publication 590

Undoing a conversion with recharacterization

IRC §408A(d)(6)

Reg. §1.408A-5

Recharacterization deadline

Reg. §1.408A-5 (Q&A-6) (filing due date)

Extension of deadline for late recharacterization

* Letter Rulings 200315027, 200317028, 200213030, 200116053, 200116057, and 200116059

Extension to recharacterize Roth IRA after IRS audit

* Letter Ruling 200533025

Delay required before reconverting

Reg. §1.408A-5 (Q&A-9)

8.23 Distributions From a Roth IRA

IRC §408A(d)

Reg. §1.408A-6

* IRS Publication 590

* "Optimize Early — and Penalty-Free — IRA Distributions," G.E. Whittenburg, William A. Raabe, and Martha Doran, 65 Tax Strategies 4 (July 2000)

* "IRA Planning: When Does What Went In Have To Come Out?" Walter Katz, 64 Tax Strategies 153 (March 2000)

8.24 Distributions to Roth IRA Beneficiaries

Reg. §1.408A-6 (Q&A-7) (five-year period for determining taxability)

Reg. §1.408A-6 (Q&A-11) (Roth IRA owner's death before end of five-year period)

Reg. §1.408A-6 (Q&A-14) (required minimum distributions under either five-year method or life expectancy method following rules of Reg. §1.401(a)(9)-3)

* IRS Publication 590

Required minimum distributions suspended for 2009

IRC §401(a)(9)(H), added by Worker, Retiree, and Employer Recovery Act of 2008

Note: *Paragraph numbers refer to Parts 1 through 7. Items marked * are research aids, not citations of authority;* see *"Key to Citations" on page 801*

9 Income From Rents and Royalties

9.1 Reporting Rental Income and Expenses

IRC §61(a)(5) and (6)

IRC §469

Reg. §1.61-8

* IRS Publications 527 and 925

Rents received

Reg. §1.61-8

Cash basis

Morris-Poston Coal Co., 42 F.2d 620 (6th Cir. 1930)

Andrew J. Pembroke, 23 BTA 1176, aff'd 70 F.2d 850 (D.C. Cir. 1935)

Jas. M. Butler, 18 BTA 718 (Acq.)

Accrual basis

Suffolk & Berks, 40 BTA 1121 (Acq.)

American Fork & Hoe Co., 33 BTA 1139

Oregon Terminals Co., 29 BTA 1332 (Nonacq.)

Advance rentals or bonuses

Reg. §1.61-8(b)

Hyde Park Realty, Inc., 211 F.2d 462 (2d Cir. 1954), aff'g 20 TC 43 (1953)

Chateau Frontenac, 147 F.2d 856 (6th Cir. 1945)

Clinton Hotel Realty Corp., 128 F.2d 968 (5th Cir. 1945)

Beach D. Lyon, 97 F.2d 70 (9th Cir. 1938)

Edward A. Renwick, 87 F.2d 123 (7th Cir. 1937)

R. L. Harcum, 164 F. Supp. 650 (E.D. Vir. 1958)

John Mantell, 17 TC 1143 (1952) (Acq.)

Advances transferred to new landlord

Hyde Park Realty, Inc., 211 F.2d 462 (2d Cir. 1954), aff'g 20 TC 43 (1953)

Security for performance

Astor Holding Co., 135 F.2d 47 (5th Cir. 1943)

Clinton Hotel Realty Corp., 128 F.2d 968 (5th Cir. 1942)

R. L. Harcum, 164 F. Supp. 650 (E.D. Vir. 1958)

Andrew J. Pembroke, 70 F.2d 850 (D.C. Cir. 1935)

John Mantell, 17 TC 1143 (1952) (Acq.)

Taxes, interest, etc. as rent

Reg. §1.61-8(c)

Insurance proceeds

John S. Mellinger, 228 F.2d 688 (5th Cir. 1956)

Oppenheim's Inc., 90 F. Supp. 107 (D. Mich. 1960)

Cancelled lease

Reg. §1.61-8(b)

Walter M. Hort, 313 U.S. 28 (1941)

Amortizing lease cancellation cost over term of old lease

Handlery Hotels, Inc., 663 F.2d 892 (9th Cir. 1981)

Improvement by tenant

IRC §109

Reg. §1.109-1

Personal holding companies

Char-Lil Corporation, 2000-2 USTC ¶50,827 (10th Cir. 2000), aff'g TC Memo 1998-457

9.2 Checklist of Rental Deductions

* IRS Publication 527

Maintenance expenses

IRC §212

Reg. §1.212-1

Salaries and wages

IRC §212

Reg. §1.212-1

Travel expenses

E. M. Goodson, 5 TCM 648 (1946)

Legal expenses

Arthur T. Galt, 19 TC 892 (1953), aff'd in part, rev'd in part, 216 F.2d 41 (7th Cir. 1954), cert. denied, 348 U.S. 951

Louis F. Tucker, Sr., 9 TCM 956 (1950)

E. M. Godson, 5 TCM 648 (1946)

Interest on mortgages

IRC §163(c)

Reg. §1.163-1

Commissions to secure rental

Mary C. Young, 59 F.2d 691 (9th Cir. 1953), cert. denied, 287 U.S. 652, on remand, 14 TCM 869 (1955)

John Griffiths, 70 F.2d 946 (8th Cir. 1934)

Louis A. Meyran, 63 F.2d 986 (3d Cir. 1933)

Central Bank Block Assn., 57 F.2d 5 (5th Cir. 1932)

Commissions to acquire property

IRC §263

Reg. §1.263(a)-1 and 2

Abandonment loss

Reg. §1.167(a)-8

Belridge Oil Co., 11 BTA 127

I. G. Zumwalt, 25 BTA 566

Rev. Rul. 54-581, 1954-2 CB 112

Insurance premiums

Reg. §1.162-1

Year deductible

Reg. §1.461-1(a)(1)

Rev. Rul. 70-413, 1970-2 CB 103

Inherited lease

Mary Y. Moore, 207 F.2d 265 (9th Cir. 1953), cert. denied, 347 U.S. 942, on remand, 14 TCM 869 (1955)

Release from mortgage

Rev. Rul. 57-198, 1957-1 CB 94

Rent for less than fair value

Nicath Realty (Hummel), 25 TCM 1260 (1966)

Cost of cancelling a lease

Handlery Hotels, Inc., 663 F.2d 892 (9th Cir. 1981)

Tenant in common

Elmer B. Boyd Est., 28 TC 564 (1957)

Payment of full tax by co-tenant deductible

Lulu Lung Powell, 26 TCM 161 (1967)

No deduction for co-tenant without proof of payment

Donald Peters, 29 TCM 1441 (1970)

9.3 Distinguishing Between a Repair and an Improvement

Capital improvements

IRC §263

Reg. §1.263(a)-1 and -2

Painting

Michael Markovits, 11 TCM 823 (1952)

Charles H. Cohen, 7 TCM 681 (1948)

Jones Hollow Ware Co., 12 BTA 48 (Acq.)

Note: *Paragraph numbers refer to Parts 1 through 7. Items marked * are research aids, not citations of authority;* see *"Key to Citations" on page 801*

Leedom & Worrall Co., 10 BTA 825

Replacing roof-covering materials to prevent leaks is deductible repair

* Thomas J. Northen, Jr., TC Summary Opinion 2003-113
* Nevia Campbell, TC Summary Opinion 2002-117

Oberman Manufacturing Co., 47 TC 471 (1967)

General improvement program

Home News Publishing Co., 18 BTA 1008

Cowell, 18 BTA 997

Repairs and improvements unconnected

W. A. Stoeltzing, 266 F.2d 374 (3d Cir. 1959), aff'g 17 TCM 567 (1958)

Major hotel allowed deduction for maintenance during improvement plan

Jerome Moss, 831 F.2d 833 (9th Cir. 1987)

9.4 Reporting Rents From a Multi-Unit Residence

* IRS Publication 527

Three-way allocation

Rev. Rul. 76-287, 1976-2 CB 80

Rental of condo during slack market

Edward W. Andrews, 931 F.2d 132 (1st Cir., 1991)

9.5 Depreciation on Converting a Home to Rental Property

* IRS Publication 527

Take depreciation

IRC §167(a)

Reg. §1.212-1(h)

Recapture of pre-MACRS depreciation

IRC §1250(d)(7)

Reg. §1.1250-3(g)

27½-year recovery

IRC §168(c)(1)

Lower of adjusted basis or value at conversion

Reg. §1.167(g)-1

J. Russell Parsons, 227 F.2d 437 (3d Cir. 1956)

Louise Biesek, 22 TCM 464 (1963)

Basis when you sell

Reg. §1.165-9(b)

Tindle and Union Trust Co., 276 U.S. 582 (1928)

Mary Louise Bok, 46 BTA 678 (Acq.), aff'd, 132 F.2d 365 (3d Cir. 1942)

Bert P. Newron, 11 TC 512 (1948) (Acq.)

Alan H. Colcord, 9 TCM 729 (1950)

Need of appraisal

Sam Perry Robinson, 19 TCM 1374 (1960)

Depreciation on vacant residence

Hulet P. Smith, 26 TCM 149 (1967), aff'd, 397 F.2d 804 (9th Cir. 1968)

George W. Mitchell, 47 TC 120 (1966) (Nonacq.)

Frank A. Newcombe, 54 TC 1298 (1970)

James J. Sherlock, 31 TCM 383 (1972)

Edward G. Lowry, Jr., 384 F. Supp. 257 (D. N.H. 1974)

9.6 Renting a Residence to a Relative

IRC §280A(d)(2)(A)

IRC §280A(d)(3)

* IRS Publication 527

Son's rental of Florida condo to parents

Cedric R. Kotowicz, 62 TCM 1229 (1991)

Renting inherited home to relatives

Ronald P. Barranti, 76 TCM 957 (1998)

9.7 Personal Use and Rental of a Residence During the Year

IRC §280A(d)

Personally used (14-day/10%) residence exempt from passive activity rules

IRC §469(j)(10)

14-day or 10% personal-use tests

IRC §280A(d)(1)

No deductions for rental of home space to employer

IRC §280A(c)(6)

Rental for less than 15 days

IRC §280A(g)

No deductions for short-term rentals

Charles M. Akers, TC Memo 2010-85

"Mini motor home" as vacation home

Ronald L. Haberkorn, 75 TC 259 (1980)

Time spent on repairs not personal use

Robert J. Twohey, 66 TCM 1394 (1993)

B&B's mixed-use areas ineligible for hotel exception

Charles E. Anderson, TC Memo 2006-33

9.8 Counting Personal-Use Days and Rental Days for a Residence

IRC §280A(d)

Personal-use day defined

IRC §280A(d)(2)

Income limitation on deductions

IRC §280A(c)(5)

Shared-equity financing agreement

IRC §280A(d)(3)(C)

Prop. Reg. §1.280A-1(e)(3)

Son's rental of Florida condo to parents

Cedric R. Kotowicz, 62 TCM 1229 (1991)

Rental of personal residence

IRC §280A(d)(4)

Stephen Bolaris, 776 F.2d 1428 (9th Cir. 1985), rev'g 81 TC 840 (1983)

Rental pool arrangements

Prop. Reg. §1.280A-3(e)

Richard S. Fine, 493 F. Supp. 540 (D. Ill. 1980), aff'd, 647 F.2d 763 (7th Cir. 1981)

Kenneth G. Byers, Jr., 82 TC 919

Rental guarantee on Florida condo

Mehdi Razavi, 96-1 USTC ¶50,060 (6th Cir. 1996)

9.9 Allocating Expenses of a Residence to Rental Days

* IRS Publication 527

IRS allocation method

Prop. Reg. §1.280A-3(d)(3)

Allocation method

Dorance D. Bolton, 77 TC 104 (1981), aff'd, 694 F.2d 556 (9th Cir. 1982)

Edith McKinney, 732 F.2d 414 (10th Cir. 1983), cert. denied (1984)

Interest expense

IRC §163(h)

Note: *Paragraph numbers refer to Parts 1 through 7. Items marked * are research aids, not citations of authority; see "Key to Citations" on page 801*

IRC §469(j)(7)

9.10 Rentals Lacking Profit Motive

IRC §280A

IRC §183

Profit motive

IRC §183

Terence D. Clancy, 37 TCM 400 (1978)

Marvin Eisenstein, 37 TCM 441 (1978)

Truett E. Allen, 72 TC 28 (1979) (Acq.)

Lester W. Lindow, 37 TCM 1257 (1978)

Richard H. Nelson, 37 TCM 1204 (1978)

Mark M. Vandeyacht, 62 TCM 2606 (1994)

Showing profit motive defeats hobby loss rule

* John E. Morrissey, TC Summary Opinion 2005-86

Failure to charge fair rental value

Lawrence E. Colbert, 63 TCM 1818 (1992)

Mobile home not rented for profit

James E. Wittstruck, 645 F.2d 618 (8th Cir. 1981), aff'g per curiam 39 TCM 1168 (1980)

Temporary rental preceding sale

Stephen Bolaris, 776 F.2d 1428 (9th Cir. 1985), rev'g 81 TC 840 (1983)

9.11 Reporting Royalty Income

License fees for use of patented article

Reg. §1.61-8(a)

Renting fees

Reg. §1.61-8(a)

Author's royalties

Reg. §1.61-8(a)

Rev. Rul. 60-31, 1960-1 CB 174, modified by Rev. Rul. 64-279, 1964-2 CB 121 and Rev. Rul. 70-435, 1970-2 CB 100

Works of art, etc.

Reg. §1.61-8(a)

Partial sale of rights

Reg. §1.61-8(a)

Lessee's payment of taxes

Wallin Coal Corp., 71 F.2d 521 (4th Cir. 1934)

Rev. Rul. 64-91, 1964-1 CB (Part I) 219

Royalty taxed as ordinary income

IRC §61(a)(6)

Reg. §1.61-8(a)

Royalty taxed as ordinary income

IRC §61(a)(6)

Reg, §1.61-8(a)

Depletion allowed

IRC §611

Reg. §1.611

Bonus payment

Reg. §1.612-3(a)(3)

Reg. §1.613-2(c)(5)

H. H. Weinert Est., 294 F.2d 740 (5th Cir. 1961)

Ann. 76-34, 1976-12 IRB 28

Rev. Rul. 73-537, 1973-2 CB 197

Percentage depletion allowed on advanced royalty

Fred Engle, 677 F.2d 564 (7th Cir. 1982), aff'd, 464 U.S. 206 (1984)

Ann. 84-59 1984-23 IRB 58

Local law

Henry Harmel, 287 U.S. 103 (1932)

Delay rental

Reg. §1.612-3(c)

Overriding royalty

Reg. §1.613-2 and 3(b)

E. G. Palmer v. Bender, 287 U.S. 551 (1933)

West Prod. Co., 121 F.2d 9 (5th Cir. 1941), cert. denied, 314 U.S. 682

H. R. Cullen, 118 F.2d 651 (5th Cir. 1941)

Production payments treated as loans

IRC §636

Oil payments

J. Steve Anderson, 310 U.S. 404 (1940)

Caldwell Oil Corp., 141 F.2d 559 (5th Cir. 1944)

Mamie S. Hammonds, 106 F.2d 420 (10th Cir. 1939)

Roy H. Laird, 97 F.2d 730 (5th Cir. 1938)

William Fleming, 82 F.2d 328 (5th Cir. 1936)

Chester Addison Jones, 82 F.2d 329 (5th Cir. 1936)

Elliott Petroleum Corp., 82 F.2d 193 (9th Cir. 1936)

Proof of oil payment

J. A. Morgan, 321 F.2d 781 (5th Cir. 1963), on remand, 245 F. Supp. 388 (D. Miss. 1965)

Both oil payment and overriding royalty

J. Steve Anderson, 310 U.S. 404 (1940)

E. G. Palmer v. Bender, 287 U.S. 551 (1933)

H. R. Cullen, 118 F.2d 651 (5th Cir. 1941), rev'g 41 BTA 1042

Marrs McLean, 120 F.2d 942 (5th Cir. 1941), cert. denied, 314 U.S. 670

Fred T. Hogan, 1 TCM 208 (1942), aff'd, 141 F.2d 92 (5th Cir. 1944), cert. denied, 323 U.S. 710

Net profits

Kirby Petroleum Co., 326 U.S. 599 (1946)

Thomas A. O'Donnell, 303 U.S. 370 (1938)

Carried interest

Abercrombie Co., 162 F.2d 338 (5th Cir. 1947), aff'g 7 TC 120 (1946) (Nonacq.)

Donald McMurray, 60 F.2d 843 (10th Cir. 1935), cert. denied, 287 U.S. 664

Carved-out oil payments

P. G. Lake, Inc., 356 U.S. 260 (1958)

Murphy J. Foster, 324 F.2d 702 (5th Cir. 1963)

9.12 Production Costs of Books and Creative Properties

IRC §263A

Exemption for freelance authors, artists, and playwrights

IRC §263A(h)

9.13 Deducting the Cost of Patents or Copyrights

Patent and copyright

Reg. §1.167(a)-6(a)

Depreciation deduction

Associated Partners, Inc., 4 TC 979 (1945)

Rev. Rul. 67-136, 1967-1 CB 58

Inherited

IRC §1014

John L. Whitehurst, 12 BTA 1416 (Nonacq.)

Note: *Paragraph numbers refer to Parts 1 through 7. Items marked * are research aids, not citations of authority;* see *"Key to Citations" on page 801*

Worthless interest

Robert S. Davis, 241 F.2d 701 (7th Cir. 1958)

James Petroleum Corp., 238 F.2d 678 (2d Cir. 1956), cert. denied, 353 U.S. 910

9.14 Intangible Drilling Costs

IRC §263(c)

Recapture of intangible drilling costs

IRC §1254

Prop. Reg. §1.1254

90-day "spudding"

IRC §461(i)(2)(A)

9.15 Depletion Deduction

* IRS Publication 535

IRC §611 through §613

Reg. §1.611-1

Reg. §1.612-1

Reg. §1.613-1 and 2

9.16 Oil and Gas Percentage Depletion

* IRS Publication 535

Percentage depletion for gas and oil wells

IRC §613A

No depletion for lease bonuses

IRC §613A(d)(5)

Prop. Reg. §1.613A-3(j)

Depletable gas quantity

Reg. §1.613A-5

Small-producer 75,000 barrel limit

IRC §613A(d)(4)

Retail sales less than $5 million

IRC §613A(d)(2)

Limit of 100% of taxable income from the property

IRC §613(a)

Limit of 65% of taxable income from all sources

IRC §613A(d)(1)

Higher rate for marginal production

IRC §613A(c)(6)

IRC §613A(c)(6)(H) (suspension of taxable income limit)

10 Loss Restrictions: Passive Activities and At-Risk Limits

10.1 Rental Activities

IRC §469 (c)(2)

Reg §1.469-4

Exceptions from rental activity category

Reg §1.469-1T(e)(3)

Exception for rental of personal residence

IRC §469(j)(10)

Exception for extraordinary personal services

Assaf F. Al Assaf and Rehab Assaf, TC Memo 2005-14

Material participation tests not met for seven-days-or-less rentals

Theodore Chapin, 71 TCM 2027 (1996)

Arnold Mordkin, 71 TCM 2796 (1996)

Loss on short-term resort rental

George Pohoski, 75 TCM 1574 (1998)

No deductions for short-term rentals

Charles M. Akers, TC Memo 2010-85

Rental losses from LLC can't offset wages from C corp

Carlos A. Senra, TC Memo 2009-79

10.2 Rental Real Estate Loss Allowance of up to $25,000

IRC §469(i)

Phaseout of allowance

IRC §469(i)(3)(A)

Phaseout of low-income housing and rehabilitation credits

IRC §469(i)(3)(B)

Estates

IRC §469(i)(4)

10.3 Real Estate Professionals

IRC §469(c)(7)

Reg. §1.469-9

Employee's services not counted

Antonio Pungot, TC Memo 2000-60

"On call" time not counted for real estate professional test

James F. Moss, TC No. 18 (9/20/10)

Specific election to aggregate required

Matti Kosonen, TC Memo 2000-107

Extension for aggregation election

* Letter Ruling 200044025

10.4 Participation May Avoid Passive Loss Restrictions

Material participation

IRC §469 (h)

Active participation

IRC §469 (i)

Passive loss rule avoided by attorney-landlord

Assaf F. Al Assaf and Rehab Assaf, TC Memo 2005-14

10.5 Classifying Business Activities as One or Several

Identifying and aggregating passive activities

Reg. §1.469-4

William A. Goshorn, 66 TCM 1499 (1993)

10.6 Material Participation Tests for Business

IRC §469(h)

Temp. Reg. §1.469-5T

Limited partner

IRC §469(h)(2)

LLC/LLP members not automatically passive investors

Paul D. Garnett, 132 TC No. 19

Managing member of LLC avoids passive loss treatment

Lee E. Newell, TC Memo 2010-23

LLC owners can materially participate in activities

James R. Thompson, 2009-2 USTC ¶50,501 (Fed. Cl. 2009)

IRS concedes LLC interest not presumptively passive

Action On Decision Memorandum (acquiescence to *Thompson* decision result)

Material participation test—not met

Joseph Machado, 70 TCM 1165 (1995)

Note: *Paragraph numbers refer to Parts 1 through 7. Items marked * are research aids, not citations of authority;* see *"Key to Citations" on page 801*

Charles M. Akers, TC Memo 2010-85

10.7 Tax Credits of Passive Activities Limited

IRC §469(a)(1)(B)
IRC §469(d)(2)

Phaseout of low-income and rehabilitation credit

IRC §469(i)(3)(B)

Basis adjustment for suspended credits

IRC §469(j)(9)

10.8 Determining Passive or Nonpassive Income and Loss

IRC §469(e)(1)

* "Generating Income by Doing Business With Yourself," Burgess J.W. Raby and William L. Raby, 91 Tax Notes 957 (May 7, 2001)

Compensation for personal services

IRC §469(e)(3)

Self-charged interest

Reg. §1.469-7, as amended by T.D. 9013, 2002-38 IRB 542

Self-charged management fees

David H. Hillman, 263 F.3d 338 (4th Cir. 2001), rev'g 114 TC 103 (2000) (no offset for self-charged management fees)

David H. Hillman, 118 TC 323 (2002) (alternative argument fails to avoid effect of Fourth Circuit decision cited above)

Covenant not to compete

William Schaefer, 105 TC 16 (1996)

10.9 Passive Income Recharacterized as Nonpassive Income

Significant participation

Temp. Reg. §1.469-2T(f)(2)
Temp. Reg. §1.469-5T(c)

Net interest income from passive equity-financed lending

Temp. Reg. §1.469-2T(f)(4)

Incidental rental of property by development activity

Reg. §1.469-2(f)(5)(i)

Rental property with an insubstantial depreciable basis

Reg. §1.469-2(f)(6)
Shirley M. Wiseman, 69 TCM 3144 (1994)

Property rented to business in which you materially participate (self-rentals)

Reg. §1.469-2(f)(6)

Gary Beecher, 2007-1 USTC ¶50,379 (9th Cir. 2007) (upholds constitutionality of self-rental rule)

Thomas P. Krukowski, 279 F.3d 547 (7th Cir. 2002), aff'g 114 TC 366 (2000) (upholds validity of recharacterization regulation)

Tony R. Carlos, 123 TC 275 (2004) (self-rental rule disallows loss offset despite grouping)

Licensing of intangible property
Temp. Reg. §1.469-2T(f)(7)

10.10 Working Interests in Oil and Gas Wells

IRC §469(c)(3)
Reg. §1.469-2(c)(6)
Temp. Reg. §1.469-1T(e)(4)

Working oil and gas interests outside of passive activity restrictions

IRC §469(c)(3)

10.11 Partners and Members of LLCs and LLPs

LLC/LLP members not automatically passive investors

Paul D. Garnett, 132 TC No. 19

Managing member of LLC avoids passive loss treatment

Lee E. Newell, TC Memo 2010-23

LLC owners can materially participate in activities

James R. Thompson, 2009-2 USTC ¶50,501 (Fed. Cl. 2009)

IRS concedes LLC interest not presumptively passive

Action On Decision Memorandum (acquiescence to *Thompson* decision result)

Retired partners

IRC §469(h)(3)

Limited partners

IRC §469(h)(2)
Temp. Reg. §1.469-5T(e)

Publicly traded partnerships

IRC §469(k)
Notice 88-75, 1988-2 CB 386

Publicly traded partnerships treated as corporations

IRC §7704

Allocation on disposition

Temp. Reg. §1.469-2T(e)(3)(ii)

10.12 Form 8582

* IRS Publication 925

10.13 Suspended Losses Allowed on Disposition of Your Interest

IRC §469(g)

Carryover

IRC §469(b)

Gifts

IRC §469(j)(6)

Installment sales

IRC §469(g)(3)

10.14 Suspended Tax Credits

Basis election for suspended credits

IRC §469(i)(9)

10.15 Personal Service and Closely Held Corporations

Closely held corporations

IRC §469 (j)(1)

Personal service corporations

IRC §469(j)(2)

Material participation tests

IRC §469(h)(4)

Full-time manager or employees

IRC §465(c)(7)(C)

Passive losses offset net active income

IRC §469(e)(2)

10.16 Sales of Property and of Passive Activity Interests

IRC §469(g)
Temp. Reg. §1.469-2T(c)

Installment sale

Note: *Paragraph numbers refer to Parts 1 through 7. Items marked * are research aids, not citations of authority;* see *"Key to Citations" on page 801*

IRC §469(g)(3)

Substantially appreciated property formerly used in nonpassive activity

Reg. §1.469-2(c)(2)(iii)

Property used in more than one activity in a 12-month period preceding disposition

Temp. Reg. §1.469-2T(c)(2)(ii)

Partnership and S corporation interests

Temp. Reg. §1.469-2T(e)(3)

Gain from 2001 "deemed sale" offset by suspended losses

Section 414(a)(2) of JCWAA 2002 (technical correction to Section 311(e) of Taxpayer Relief Act of 1997

Notice 2002-29, 2002-17 IRB 797

10.17 At-Risk Limits

IRC §465

Prop. Reg. §1.465-1 through §95

Activities subject to at-risk rules

IRC §465(c)

Arnold Berger, 67 TCM 3144 (1994)

Active corporation

IRC §465(c)(7)(B)

Aggregation of partnership or S corporation activities until further notice

Notice 89-39, 1989-1 CB 681

10.18 What Is At Risk?

IRC §465(b)

* "Borrowed Funds Do Not Always Increase Amounts At Risk," Joseph R. Oliver, 48 Taxation for Accountants 348 (June 1992)

Special at-risk rule for real estate

IRC §465(b)(6)

Lender's capital interest in loan after May 3, 2004

Reg. §1.465-8

Personal liability note to general partner not at risk

Rev. Rul. 80-327, 1980-2 CB 23

10.19 Amounts Not At Risk

Borrowing from relatives

IRC §465(b)(3)(A)

Dispositions of interest in property used in at-risk activity

Prop. Reg. §1.465-68

Recourse not convertible to nonrecourse

Rev. Rul. 81-283, 1981-2 CB 115

TV film investment

Rev. Rul. 78-413, 1978-2 CB 167

Gold mine venture

Rev. Rul. 80-72, 1980-I CB 109

Prop. Reg. §1.465-41

Ernest J. Saviano, 80 TC 955 (1983)

Potential cash call

John Callahan, 98 TC 22 (1992)

Jerry Pritchett, et al., 85 TC 580 (1985), rev'd, 527 F.2d 644 (9th Cir. 1987)

10.20 At-Risk Investment in Several Activities

Aggregation for actively managed businesses

IRC §465(c)(2)(B)(ii)

IRC §465(c)(3)(B)

Aggregation allowed for partnership or S corporation leasing of Section 1245 property

IRC §465(c)(2)(B)

10.21 Carryover of Disallowed Losses

IRC §465(a)(2)

10.22 Recapture of Losses Where At Risk Is Less Than Zero

IRC §465(e)

IRC §61

11 Other Income

11.1 Prizes and Awards

IRC §74(a)

Prizes and awards

IRC §74

Reg. §1.74-1

Civic achievement award

Rev. Rul. 65-161, 1965-1 CB 38

Pulitzer prize

Reg. §1.74-1

Rev. Rul. 54-110, 1954-1 CB 28

Government award

Francis M. Rogallo, 474 F.2d 1 (4th Cir. 1974), rev'g 341 F. Supp. 998 (D. Va. 1972)

Door prize

Reg. §1.74-1

Essay contest

Arsham Amirkian, 197 F.2d 442 (4th Cir. 1952)

Herbert Stein, 14 TC 494 (1950)

Frederick V. Waugh, 9 TCM 309 (1950)

Lottery ticket

* Letter Ruling 9217004

Award under Incentive Awards Act

Hobart M. Griggs, 314 F. Supp. 515 (Ct. Cl. 1963)

Prize from employer

Reg. §1.74-1

NASA award taxable

Robert Jones, 79 TC 1008 (1982)

Manufacturer's trip prize to dealer

Bell Electric Co., 45 TC 158 (1965) (Acq.)

Prize of car to football player

Paul Hornung, 47 TC 428 (1967) (Acq.)

Radio or TV contest

Reg. §1.74-1(b)

Prize of merchandise

Reg. §1.74-1(a)(2)

Vacation trip

Nathan L. Wade, 55 TCM 413 (1988)

Steamship ticket

Reginald Turner, 13 TCM 462 (1954)

Car prize

Lawrence W. McCoy, 38 TC 841 (1962) (Acq. 1963-1 CB 4)

Script award

Rev. Rul. 70-331, 1970-1 CB 14

Taxable scholarship to Miss America

Rev. Rul. 68-20, 1968-1 CB 55

Treasure you find

Rev. Rul. 53-61, 1953-1 CB 17

Transfer to charity or governmental unit

IRC §74(b)

Note: *Paragraph numbers refer to Parts 1 through 7. Items marked * are research aids, not citations of authority;* see *"Key to Citations" on page 801*

Rev. Proc. 87-54, 1987-2 CB 669

Employee achievement

IRC §74(c)

11.2 Lottery and Sweepstake Winnings

Lump sum received for future lottery payments

George Lattera, 437 F.3d 399 (3rd Cir. 2006)

Peter U. Boehme, TC Memo 2003-81

James F. Davis, 119 TC No. 1 (2002)

US v. J. Michael Maginnis, 2002-2 USTC ¶50,494 (D.C. Or. 2002)

Lottery prize held by parents as custodians

Joseph Anastasio, 67 TC 814 (1977)

Prize taxed when received not won

Roy V. Thomas, 99-1 USTC ¶50,451

Raffle winnings

Diane M. Solomon, 25 TC 936 (1956)

H. Collings Downes, 30 TC 396 (1958)

Sweepstake winnings divided among family members

Henry Braunstein, 21 TCM 1132 (1962)

Couple's joint ownership agreement

* Letter Ruling 9217004

Ticket bought for foreign uncle

Alfonso Diaz, 58 TC 560 (1972) (Acq.)

Sweepstake winnings held by court

Rev. Rul. 67-203, 1967-1 CB 105

Agreement to share winnings

Samuel L. Huntington, 35 BTA 835 (Acq.)

Agreement to pool winnings

Christian H. Droge, 35 BTA 829 (Acq.)

Lump-sum option ignored if installments received

IRC §451(h)

11.3 Gambling Winnings and Losses

IRC §67(b)(3) (losses not subject to 2% floor)

IRC §165(d) (losses allowed only to extent of gains)

Reg. §1.165-10

* "Offsetting Gambling Gains With Losses Not Always Possible," Burgess J.W. Raby and William L. Raby, 90 Tax Notes 1515 (March 12, 2001)

* "Wagering War With the Service: Winning Gambling Deductions," Nancy B. Nichols and Diane A. Riordan, 60 Taxation for Accountants 279 (May 1998)

Professional gambler may deduct loss as business expense

Anthony J. Ditunno, 80 TC 362 (1983)

Poker tournament losses in excess of winnings not deductible

George E. Tschetschot, TC Memo 2007-38 (2007)

Full-time gambler is in business

Robert P. Groetzinger, 107 S. Ct. 980 (1987)

Gains and losses of casual slot machine gamblers

*Chief Counsel Advice 2009-011

Casual slot machine players can't net wins and losses

George D. Shollenberger, TC Memo 2009-306

David J. Crawford, TC Memo 2010-54

Diary supported loss deduction

Leon Faulkner, 40 TCM 1 (1980)

Tickets with sequential numbers supported loss deduction

Theodore L. Wolkomir, 40 TCM 1078 (1980)

Game-show contestant is not in business

Stanley Whitten, 70 TCM 1064 (1995)

"Comps" offset by gambling losses

Robert Libutti, 71 TCM 2343 (1996)

Casino debt

David Zarin, 90-2 USTC ¶50,530 (3rd Cir. 1990)

11.4 Gifts and Inheritances

* "Deduction Offsets 'Double Tax' On Inherited Income," Craig J. Langstraat and Amber M. Cagle, 67 Practical Tax Strategies 86 (August 2001)

Gifts and inheritances exempt

IRC §102

Reg. §1.102-1

Incompetent's gift taxable

Carl Elmer Henry Bader, 23 TC 813 (1973)

No fixed rule to determine taxability of gifts

Mose Duberstein, 363 U.S. 278 (1960)

Will compromise

Munro L. Lyeth v. Hoey, 305 U.S. 188 (1938)

Sale of expected inheritance

Rev. Rul. 70-60, 1970-1 CB 11

Bequest to executor

Frederick L. Merriam, 263 U.S. 179

Bequest to attorney

Lee S. Jones, 23 TCM 235 (1964)

Victor R. Wolder, 493 F.2d 608 (2d Cir. 1974), aff'g 58 TC 974 (1972) (Nonacq.), cert. denied, 419 U.S. 828

Campaign contributions—when taxable

Rev. Rul. 68-19, 1968-1 CB 42

When beneficiary is taxed

IRC §652

When grantor is taxed

IRC §671

Adoption assistance from charity tax free

*Chief Counsel Information Letter 2006-0027

Hush money not a gift

* Milton D. Peebles, TC Summary Opinion 2006-61

11.5 Refunds of State and Local Income Tax Deductions

IRC §111

* IRS Publication 525

Prior law recovery exclusion

Reg. §1.111-1

11.6 Other Recovered Deductions

IRC §111

Refund of adjustable rate mortgage interest

Rev. Rul. 92-91, 1992-2 CB 49

Donated property returned

Sidney W. Rosen, 611 F.2d 942 (1st Cir. 1979)

Reimbursement of loss absorbed by $100

Note: *Paragraph numbers refer to Parts 1 through 7. Items marked * are research aids, not citations of authority;* see *"Key to Citations" on page 801*

floor not taxable

Rev. Rul. 80-65, 1980-1 CB 183

Debt forgiveness of accrual-basis debtor with carryover

IRC §111(c)

Annuity beneficiaries get IRD deduction

Rev. Rul. 2005-30, 2005-20 IRB 1015

11.7 How Legal Damages Are Taxed

IRC §104(a)(2)

* "Supreme Court Rules on the Taxation of Contingent Attorney Fees," James A. Doering, 83 Taxes 41 (August 2005)
* "The Demise of Cotnam and the Impact of the Jobs Act on the Income Tax Treatment of Contingent Legal Fees," Amy Youngblood Avitable, 83 Taxes 37 (June 2005)
* "What Litigation Recoveries Are Excludable as 'Physical'?," Robert W. Wood, 90 Tax Notes 936 (February 12, 2001)
* "Why Every Settlement Agreement Should Address Tax Consequences," Robert W. Wood, 92 Tax Notes 405 (July 16, 2001)

Compensatory damages received on account of physical injury or sickness after August 20, 1996

IRC §104(a)(2)

* Letter Ruling 200041022 (emotional damages allocable to physical assault may not be taxed)

Tax on damages for emotional distress and injury to professional reputation not unconstitutional

Marrita Murphy, 2007-2, USTC ¶50,531 (Dist. Ct. D.C. 2007), aff'd 2006-2 USTC ¶50,476 (D.C. Cir. 2006), vacating 2005-1 USTC ¶50,237 (Dist. Ct., D.C. 2005)

No exclusion for punitive-only damages

Linda R. Benavides, 2007-2, USTC ¶50,638 (5th Cir. 2007)

Damages for emotional distress are usually taxable

Nancy J. Vincent, TC Memo 2005-95

Partially tax-free settlement for discharged employee with MS

Julie Leigh Domeny, TC Memo 2010-9

Settlement for false imprisonment taxable

Daniel J. and Brenda J. Stadnyk, Sixth Circuit, 2/26/10

Employer discrimination settlement payment for emotional damages taxable

Justin W. Hansen, TC Memo 2009-87

Punitive damages received after August 20, 1996

IRC §104(a)(2)

IRC §104(c)

Holocaust reparations tax free after 1999

Public Law 107-358 (2002)

Supreme Court requires contingency fee to be included in gross income

John W. Banks II, 2005-1 USTC ¶50,155 (Sup. Ct. 2005)

Attorney fees under fee-shifting statute included in gross income

Nancy J. Vincent, TC Memo 2005-95 (issue not resolved by Supreme Court in Banks)

Contingent attorney fee must be included in gross income: pre–Supreme Court decision in Banks

David A. Raymond, 2004-1 USTC ¶50,124 (2d Cir. 2004)

Nancy J. Hukkanen-Campbell, 2002-USTC ¶50,351 (10th Cir. 2002)

Eldon R. Kenseth, 259 F.3d 881 (7th Cir. 2001)

Louise F. Young, 240 F.3d 369 (4th Cir. 2001)

Ivor F. Benci-Woodward, 219 F.3d 941 (9th Cir. 2000)

Franklin P. Coady, 213 F.3d 1187 (9th Cir. 2000)

Jack Baylin, 43 F.3d 1451 (Fed. Cir. 1995)

Contingent attorney fee excluded from gross income: pre–Supreme Court decision in Banks

Sigitas Banaitis, 2003-2 USTC ¶50,638 (9th Cir. 2003)

John W. Banks II, 2003-2 USTC ¶50,675 (6th Cir. 2003)

Mattie Foster, 249 F.3d 1275 (11th Cir. 2001)

Sudhir P. Srivastava, 220 F.3d 353 (5th Cir. 2000)

Estate of Arthur L. Clarks, 202 F.3d 854 (6th Cir. 2000)

Ethel W. Cotnam, 263 F.2d 119 (5th Cir. 1959

Above-the-line deduction for attorney fees in discrimination cases

IRC §62(a)(20)

IRC §62(e) (unlawful discrimination defined)

Loss of profit

Phoenix Coal Co., 231 F.2d 420 (2d Cir. 1956)

D. T. Longino Est., 32 TC 904 (1959)

Loss of wages

Bill McKay, 5th Cir. (4/10/96)

Personal injuries: pre-1996 Small Business Job Protection Act

IRC §104(a)(2)

Erich E. Schleier, 115 S.Ct. 2159 (1995)

Rev. Rul. 74-77, 1974-1 CB 33

Punitive damages for personal injuries: pre-1996 Small Business Job Protection Act

Ernest Horton, 33 F.3d 625 (6th Cir. 1994), aff'd, 100 TC 8 (1993)

Kelly M. O'Gilvie, 92-2 USTC ¶50, 567 (Dist. Ct., Ks. 1992)

Elizabeth A. Reese, Fed. Cl., 8/29/93

Bonnie Miller, 914 F.2d 586 (4th Cir. 1990), rev'g 93 TC 29 (1989)

Maurie Starrels, 304 F.2d 574 (9th Cir. 1962)

Rev. Rul. 84-108, 1984-2 CB 32, revoking Rev. Rul. 75-45, 1975-1 CB 47

A. P. Burford, 642 F. Supp. 635 (D.C. Ala. 1986), rejecting Rev. Rul. 84-108, 1984-2 CB 32

Glenshaw Glass Co., 348 U.S. 426 (1955)

Ray Wesson, 48 F.3d 894 (5th Cir. 1995)

Estate of Chester Moore, 53 F.2d 712 (5th Cir. 1995)

Slander or libel—state law governs

James E. Threlkeld, 87 TC 1294 (1986), aff'd 848 F.2d 81 (6th Cir. 1988)

Paul F. Roemer, Jr., 79 TC 398 (1982), rev'd 716 F.2d 693 (9th Cir. 1983) (Nonacq.) Rev. Rul. 85-143, 1985-2 CB 55

Defamation legal costs nondeductible to extent of tax-free damages

Wade E. Church, 80 TC 1104 (1983)

Taxes avoided on assigned damages

* Letter Ruling 200107019

Breach of promise to marry

Note: *Paragraph numbers refer to Parts 1 through 7. Items marked* * *are research aids, not citations of authority;* see *"Key to Citations" on page 801*

Lyde McDonald, 9 BTA 1340 (Acq.)

Alienation of affection

C. A. Hawkins, 6 BTA 1023 (Acq.)

Rev. Rul. 74-77, 1974-1 CB 33

Support of children

IRC §71(b)

Reg. §1.71-1

Business reputation

Mason Knuckles, 23 TCM 182 (1964), aff'd 349 F.2d 610 (10th Cir. 1965)

Paul Draper, 26 TC 201 (1956) (Acq.)

Prejudgement interest includible in gross income

Chad Anthony Chamberlain et al., 2005-1 USTC ¶50,194 (Fifth Cir. 2005)

Charles Francisco, 267 F.3d 303 (2001)

Joseph Rozpad, 154 F.3d 1 (1st Cir. 1998)

John Brabson, 73 F.3d 1040 (10th Cir., 1996)

Goodwill

Farmers and Merchants Bank of Catlettsburg, Kentucky, 59 F.2d 912 (6th Cir. 1932)

William Basle, 16 TCM 745 (1957), aff'd per curiam, 256 F.2d 381 (3d Cir. 1958)

Embezzlement forgiven

Rev. Rul. 61-185, 1961-2 CB 9

Extortion

James Rutkin, 343 U.S. 130 (1952), aff'g 189 F.2d 431 (3d Cir. 1951)

James J. Moran, 236 F.2d 361 (2d Cir. 1956), cert. denied, 352 U.S. 909

Swindlers

James A. Akers, 167 F.2d 718 (5th Cir. 1948), cert. denied, 335 U.S. 823

Attorney receives payment

Thomas H. Hannaford, 19 TCM 409 (1960)

11.8 Cancellation of Debts You Owe

Car repossession

* Timothy W. Fuller, TC Summary Opinion 2009-91

Cancelled debts

Reg. §1.61-12

Exclusion for discharge of qualified principal residence indebtedness

IRC 108(a)(1)(E)

IRC 108(h)

Debts cancelled as result of Hurricane Katrina

Act Section 401 of the Katrina Emergency Relief Act of 2005

Exclusion for cancellation of health professional's student loan

IRC §108(f)(4), as amended by the Affordable Care Act, 2/23/10

Exclusion for certain discharged debt

IRC §108

Reduction of tax attributes

IRC §108(b)

Reduce basis of depreciable property

IRC §108(b)(5)

IRC §108(c)

IRC §1017

S corp's discharged debt

IRC §108(d)(7)(A), overriding David A. Gitlitz, 121 S. Ct. 701 (2001)

Appreciated asset transferred to pay off debt taxable

James Gehl, 102 TC 37 (1994)

Loan cancelled by foundations

IRC §108(f)

Price adjustment not taxed

IRC §108(e)(5)

Student loan cancelled

IRC §108(f)

Credit card insurance is discharge of indebtedness

* Khen T. Huynh, TC Summary Opinion, 2001-131

* Gerald A. Bunker, TC Summary Opinion 2005-36

Income results from credit card settlement

Robert F. Melvin, TC Memo 2009-199

Income from debt forgiveness not avoided by divorce decree

Paul Neal Jensen, TC Memo 2010-77

Debtor taxed on reduction of nonrecourse mortgage debt

Rev. Rul. 91-31, 1991-1 CB19

Rev. Rul. 92-53,1992-2 CB 48 (effect of debt reduction on solvency)

Prepayment of mortgage at discount

Rev. Rul. 82-202, 1982-2 CB 35

Debt discharge income despite Agriculture Department's recapture rule

Dennis Jelle, 116 TC 63 (2001)

Insolvency of debtor

IRC §108(a)(1)(B)

George Aberl, 78 F.3d 241 (6th Cir., 1996)

Creditor-exempt assets included when determining insolvency

Roderick E. Carlson, 116 TC 87 (2001)

Insolvency determined at partnership level

IRC §108(d)(6)

Pre-1980 cases: Estate of Michael Newman, 934 F.2d 426 (2d Cir. 1991), rev'g 59 TCM 543 (1990)

D.B. Merkel, 99-2 USTC ¶50,848

Farm indebtedness

IRC §108(g)

Proceedings under Bankruptcy Act

Reg. §1.61-12

Reg. §1.1016-7

In re: James Bruner, 55 F.3d 195 (5th Cir. 1995)

In re: Bernice Haas, 48 F.2d 1153 (11th Cir. 1995)

Business real estate debt

IRC §108(8)(1)(D)

IRC §108(c)

Financial institution reporting of discharged debt

Reg. §1.6050P-1

Voluntary forgiveness by creditor

American Dental Co., 318 U.S. 322 (1943)

Creditor intended a gift

New York Creditmen's Adjustment Bureau, Inc., 110 F. Supp. 214 (S.D.N.Y. 1953)

Identify debt cancelled

Lewis F. Jacobson, 336 U.S. 28 (1949)

Adjust purchase price

Des Moines Improvement Co., 7 BTA 279 (Nonacq.)

Sobel, Inc., 40 BTA 1263 (Nonacq.)

Note: *Paragraph numbers refer to Parts 1 through 7. Items marked * are research aids, not citations of authority;* see *"Key to Citations" on page 801*

Decline in value of property

Kalman Hirsch, 115 F.2d 656 (7th Cir. 1940)

Borrow money

Manual A. Frank, 44 F. Supp. 729 (D. Pa. 1942), aff'd, 131 F.2d 864 (3d Cir.)

No legal obligation

Kern Co., 1 TC 249 (1942) (Acq.)

Hotel Astoria, Inc., 42 BTA 759 (Acq.)

Fulton Gold Corp., 31 BTA 519

Partial cancellation of indebtedness

Gehring Publishing Co., Inc., 1 TC 345 (1942) (Acq.)

Unauthorized sale of pledged stock is discharge of indebtedness

Regina A. Poczatek, 71 TC 371 (1978)

Inventory

Rev. Rul. 76-86, 1976-1 CB 37

11.9 Schedule K-1

* IRS Publications 541 (partnership) and 559 (estate)

11.10 How Partners Report Partnership Profit and Loss

* IRS Publication 541

Final check-the-box regulations

Reg. §301.7701-1 through 301.7701-3

Partnership not taxed

IRC §701

Reg. §1.701-1

What is a partnership?

IRC §761

Reg. §1.761-1

Health insurance premiums

IRC §162(l)

Salary from partnership guaranteed

IRC §707(c)

Reg. §1.707-1(c)

Special allocations

IRC §704(b)

Substantial economic effect

Reg. §1.704-1(b)(2)

Mary Ogden, 84 TC 871 (1985)

Allocations to partners upon property contributions made after December 20, 1993

Reg. §1.704-3

No advance ruling of partnership provisions re substantial economic effect

Rev. Proc. 79-14, 1979-1 CB 496

Change of partnership interests during the year

IRC §706(d)

Passive loss limitations

IRC §469

IRS may allow unincorporated businesses to choose partnership of corporate taxation

Notice 95-14, 1995-14 IRB 7 (check-the-box initiative)

Failure to file information return

IRC §6698

Sales to controlled partnership

IRC §1239(b) and (c)

Partner reports

IRC §702

Reg. §1.702-1

Transferring partnership interests

IRC §6050K

Reg. §1.6050K-1

Composite 25 transfer rule

Reg. §1.6050K-1(a)(3)

Substantially appreciated inventory

IRC §751(d)(1)

Assignment of outside referral fees to partnership

Stephen B. Schneer, 97 TC 643 (1991)

Retroactive allocations

IRC §706(d)

Net operating loss

Reg. §1.702-2

Credits deductible

IRC §702(b)

Reg. §1.702-2

Partner's distributive share

Temp. Reg. §1.704-IT

P.L. 103-465 12/8/94

Partnership distribution of contributed property within two years

IRC §707(a)(2)(B)

Reg. §1.707-3 through §1.707-9

Recognition of gain by partner on distribution of contributed property

IRC §732

11.11 When a Partner Reports Income or Loss

When a partnership reports income or loss

IRC §706

Reg. §1.706-1

Harry W. Lehman, 19 TC 659 (1953)

Fiscal year limitations

IRC §706(b)(1)

Fiscal year election

IRC §444

Temp. Reg. §1.444-1T

Limitations on electable fiscal years

Temp. Reg. §1.444-1T(b)(3)

Required payment

IRC §7519

Refund of required payments

IRC §7519(c)

Announcement 90-112, 1990-40 IRB 37

11.12 Partnership Loss Limitations

IRC §704

Reg. §1.704-1

F. A. Falconer, 40 TC 1011 (1963) (Acq.)

Limitation on losses

IRC §704(d)

IRC §465

Partners may not increase basis by accrued partnership liabilities

Rev. Rul. 88-77, 1988-2 CB 128

11.13 Unified Tax Audits of Partnerships

IRC §§ 6221-6231

11.14 Stockholder Reporting of S Corporation Income and Loss

IRC §1361 through 1379

* "Take Steps to Maximize Shareholder Basis in S Corporations," Lorence L. Bravenec and Edward L. Bravenec, 67 Practical Tax Strategies 210 (October 2001)

Note: *Paragraph numbers refer to Parts 1 through 7. Items marked * are research aids, not citations of authority;* see *"Key to Citations" on page 801*

Pass-through of income and losses

IRC §1366

Distributions

IRC §1368

IRC §1366(d)(1)(A)

Income must be included in return

IRC §1367(b)

Health insurance premiums

IRC §162(l)

IRC §1362(d)(3)

IRC §1366(f)(3)

IRC §1375

Relative treated as 2% S corporation shareholder

Richard E. and Mary Ann Hurst, 124 TC 16 (2005)

IRS previews family S corp guidance

Notice 2005-91, 2005-51 IRB 1164

Allocation for new and old shareholder

IRC §1377(a)

Family allocation

IRC §1366(e)

Appreciated property distribution

IRC §1363(d)

IRC §1362(a)

IRC §1362(b)

Effect of election on corporation

IRC §1363(e)

Invalid elections may be corrected

IRC §1362(b)(5) and 1362(f)

Built-in gains tax

IRC §1374

Rev. Rul. 86-141, 1986-2 CB 151

IRC §1362(d)

Inadvertent terminations

IRC §1362(f)

Treatment of termination year

IRC §1362(e)

Re-election following termination

IRC §1362(g)

IRC §1372

Waiver of tax

IRC §1375(d)

IRC §1374

IRS may approve invalid elections

IRC §1362(b)(5)

IRC §1362(f)

Agreement to terminate year

IRC §1377

Audit rules

IRC §§ 6241-6245 repealed (corporate level audit procedures)

IRC §6037(c) (shareholder must report consistently with S Corporation return)

Retroactive re-election

IRC §1362(g)

Adjustments before the loss limitation

IRC §1366(d)(1)(A)

IRC §1368(d)

Income in respect of a decedent

IRC §1367(b)(4)

11.15 How Beneficiaries Report Estate or Trust Income

IRC §652

Reg. §1.652(a) and (b)

* IRS Publication 559

Depreciation and depletion

IRC §167(g)

IRC §611(b)(3)

Net operating losses

IRC §642(d)

Reg. §1.642(h)-1

George W. Balkwill, 25 BTA 1147, aff'd, 77 F.2d 569 (6th Cir. 1935), cert. denied, 296 U.S. 609

George C. Reeves, 15 TCM 394 (1956)

When to report

IRC §652

Reg. §1.652(a)-1

Multiple trusts

IRC §643(f)

Consistent reporting by beneficiaries

IRC §6034A(c)

IRC §6048(d)

11.16 Reporting Income in Respect of a Decedent (IRD)

* IRS Publication 559

Attorneys' fees

IRC §2053(a)

Reg. §20.2053-3(c)

Administration expenses

IRC §2053(b)

Reg. §20.2053-3(a)

Capital gain reduction

IRC §691(c)(4)

Lump-sum distributions

IRC §691(c)(5)

Valuation of short sale closed after death

* Letter Ruling 9436017

11.17 Deduction for Estate Tax Attributable to IRD

* IRS Publication 559

* "Deduction for Inherited Income Raises Complex Computations," Ted D. Englebrecht and Michael L. Bandy, 68 Tax Strategies 150 (March 2002)

Deduction for estate tax paid

IRC §691(c)

Reg. §1.691(c)-1

No double deduction

IRC §2053

IRC §2054

Annuity beneficiaries get IRD deduction

Rev. Rul. 2005-30, 2005-20 IRB 1015

11.18 How Life Insurance Proceeds Are Taxed to a Beneficiary

IRC §101

IRC §7702

Reg. §1.101-1 to §1.101-4

Flexible premium policies issued before 1985

IRC §101(f)

Life insurance contract defined: policy issued after 1984

IRC §7702

Spouse's exclusion for interest: deaths before 12/23/86

IRC §101(d)(1)(B), prior to amendment by Tax Reform Act of 1986

Reg. §1.101-4(a)

Taxable interest on installment payments

IRC §101(c)

Reg. §1.101-3

No exclusion for combined insurance-

Note: *Paragraph numbers refer to Parts 1 through 7. Items marked * are research aids, not citations of authority;* see *"Key to Citations" on page 801*

annuity pre-1986 Tax Act

Rev. Rul. 65-57, 1965-1 CB 56

Remarriage does not affect interest exclusion pre-1986 Tax Act

Rev. Rul. 72-164, 1972-1 CB 28

Estate tax on life insurance

IRC §2042

Reg. §20.2042-1(c)

Policy transferred within three years of death included in taxable estate

IRC §2035

* Letter Ruling 9533001

Modified endowment contracts

IRC §7702A

IRC §72(e)(10)

IRC §72(v) (premature withdrawal penalty)

11.19 A Policy With a Family Income Rider

Reg. §1.101-4(h)

11.20 Selling or Surrendering Life Insurance Policy

Tax results of selling or surrendering policy

Rev. Rul. 2009-13, 2009-21 IRB 1029

Endowment policies paid because of death

Reg. §1.101-1(a)

Gain on surrender of policy

Reg. §1.72-11(d)

William W. Bodine, 103 F.2d 982 (3d Cir. 1939), cert. denied, 308 U.S. 576

Frank Hawkins, 3 TCM 1135 (1944), rev'd on other issue, 152 F.2d 221 (5th Cir. 1946)

Surrender of policy for cash—loss

Standard Brewing Co., 6 BTA 980

London Shoe Co., Inc., 80 F.2d 230 (2d Cir. 1935), cert. denied, 298 U.S. 663

Policy transferred for valuable consideration

IRC §101(b)

Reg. §1.101-1(b)

Sale of policy to viatical company is income

* Letter Ruling 9443020

12 Deductions Allowed in Figuring Adjusted Gross Income

12.1 Figuring Adjusted Gross Income (AGI)

* "Avoiding Taxes by Avoiding Deductions," Nicole E. Ballard, Cherie J. O'Neil, and Donald P. Samelson, 82 Taxes 45 (May 2004)

Gross income

IRC §61

Adjusted gross income

IRC §62

Reg. §1.62-1

Taxable income

IRC §63

Interest on rental property

Isaac R. Wharton, 207 F. 2d 526 (5th Cir. 1953)

12.2 Claiming Deductions From Gross Income

IRC §62

Reg. §1.62-1

Educator expenses

IRC §62(a)(2)(D)

IRC §62(d)

Self-employed health insurance deduction

IRC §162(l)

Health insurance for self-employed not a Schedule C deduction

*Chief Counsel Advice 200623001

Tuition and fees

IRC §222

Health savings account deduction

IRC §223

HSA inflation adjustments

Rev. Proc. 2010-22, 2010-23 IRB 747 (for 2011)

Rev. Proc. 2009-29, 2009-22 IRB 1050 (for 2010)

Rev. Proc. 2008-29, 2008-22 IRB 1039 (for 2009)

Reservists and National Guard Members

IRC §62(a)(2)(E)

IRC §162(p) (deemed away from home)

Attorneys' fees in unlawful discrimination cases

IRC §§ 62(a)(20) and 62(e)

Performing artists

IRC §62(a)(2)(B)

IRC §62(b)

State and local officials

IRC §62(a)(2)(C)

Domestic production activities deduction

IRC §199

12.3 What Moving Costs Are Deductible?

IRC §217(b)

* IRS Publication 521

Mileage rates

Announcement 2008-63, 2008-28 IRB 114 (special dual rates for 2008)

Rev. Proc. 2008-72, 2008-50 IRB 1286 (mileage rates for 2009)

Rev. Proc. 2009-54, 2009-51 IRB 930 (mileage rates for 2010)

Direct expenses

Reg. §1.217-2(b)(3), (4)

Cost of moving a pet deductible

Rev. Rul. 66-305, 1966-2 CB 102

Cost of moving car deductible

Rev. Rul. 65-309, 1965-2 CB 77

Depreciation not allowed

Rev. Rul. 70-656, 1970-2 CB 67

Cost of moving a boat nondeductible

William E. Aksomitas, 50 TC 679 (1968)

Cost of moving boat deductible

John R. Fogg, 89 TC 310 (1987)

Delay of family's move due to child's completing education

Rev. Rul. 78-200, 1978-1 CB 77

Reg. §1.217-2(a)(3)

* Letter Ruling 8346039

Furniture purchased en route

Rev. Rul. 70-625, 1970-2 CB 67

12.4 The Distance Test

IRC §217(c)(1)(A) and (B)

Reg. §1.217-2(a)(3)

* IRS Publication 521

Moving overseas

Note: *Paragraph numbers refer to Parts 1 through 7. Items marked * are research aids, not citations of authority;* see *"Key to Citations" on page 801*

Jon F. Hartung, 484 F.2d 953 (9th Cir. 1973), rev'g per curiam 55 TC 1 (1970)

Richard L. Markus, 486 F.2d 1314 (D.C. Cir. 1973), rev'g 30 TCM 1346 (1971)

William Hughes, 65 TC 566 (1975)

Armed services

Rev. Rul. 76-2, 1976-1 CB 82

Rev. Rul. 50-520, 1970-2 CB 66

Alien's moving expenses

Rev. Rul. 69-425, 1969-2 CB 16

Rev. Rul. 68-308, 1968-1 CB 336

12.5 The 39-Week Test for Employees

IRC §217 (c)(2)(A)

Reg. §1.217-2(c)(4)

Time test inapplicable in certain cases

Reg. §1.217-2(d)

Seasonal employee

Reg. §1.217-2(c)(4)(iv)(A)

Rev. Rul. 68-42, 1968-1 CB 94

No deduction for employee initiating transfer

Rev. Rul. 88-47, 1988-1 CB 111

12.6 The 78-Week Test for the Self-Employed and Partners

IRC §217(c)(2)(B)

Reg. §1.217-2(c)(4) and (f)(1)(2)

12.7 Claiming Deductible Moving Expenses

Deductible from gross income

IRC §62 (a)(15)

12.8 Reimbursements of Moving Expenses

Reimbursements of expenses are excludable from gross income

IRC §132(a)(6)

IRC §132(g)

Reimbursement on sale of home

Harris W. Bradley, 324 F.2d 610 (4th Cir.), aff'g 39 TC 652 (1963)

Seth E. Keener, Jr., 59 TC 302 (1972)

Willis B. Ferebee, 39 TC 801 (1963)

Otto S. Schairer, 9 TC 549 (1947)

Deduct moving expenses in computing net operating loss

Rev. Rul. 72-195, 1971-1 CB 95

Members of the military

IRC §217(g)

13 Claiming the Standard Deduction or Itemized Deductions

IRC §63 (standard deduction)

13.1 Claiming the Standard Deduction

* IRS Publication 501

When to itemize

IRC §63(e)

Changing an election

IRC §63(e)(3)

Average itemized deductions for 2007

IRS Statistics of Income Bulletin, Spring 2009

Taxable income

IRC §63(b)

Standard deduction

IRC §63(c)

Additional standard deduction for real estate taxes

IRC §63(c)(1)(C)

IRC §63(c)(7)

Additional standard deduction for net disaster losses

IRC §63(c)(1)(D)

IRC §63(c)(8)

IRC §165(h)(3)(B)

Additional standard deduction for state and local sales and excise taxes on purchase of qualified motor vehicle

IRC §164(a)(6)

IRC §164(b)(6)

Nonresident alien

IRC §63(c)(6)(B)

Estate or trust

IRC §63(c)(6)(D)

Short tax year

IRC §63(c)(6)(C)

13.2 Husbands and Wives Filing Separate Returns

IRC §63(c)(6)(A)

Claiming itemized deductions when you are living apart from your spouse

IRC §63(g)

IRC §7703(b) (considered unmarried)

Head of household status when living apart from your spouse

IRC §7703(b) (considered unmarried)

IRC §2(b)(1) (maintain home for qualifying child or relative)

13.3 Additional Standard Deduction for Real Estate Taxes, Motor Vehicle Taxes, and Net Disaster Loss

Additional standard deduction for real estate taxes

IRC §63(c)(1)(C)

IRC §63(c)(7)

Additional standard deduction for net disaster losses

IRC §63(c)(1)(D)

IRC §63(c)(8)

IRC §165(h)(3)(B)

Additional standard deduction for sales or excise taxes on new vehicle purchased from 2/17/09 through 12/31/09

IRC §164(a)(6)

IRC §164(b)(6)

13.4 Standard Deduction If 65 or Older or Blind

IRC §63(c)(3)

Age

IRC §63(f)(1)

Blindness

IRC §63(f)(2)

IRC §63(f)(4)

13.5 Standard Deduction for Dependents

* IRS Publication 501

IRC §63(c)(5)

Dependent's standard deduction not reduced by business loss

* Allyson C. Briggs, TC Summary Opinion 2004-22

13.6 Prepaying or Postponing Itemized Expenses

Note: *Paragraph numbers refer to Parts 1 through 7. Items marked* are research aids, not citations of authority;* see *"Key to Citations" on page 801*

13.7 No Phaseout of Itemized Deductions for 2010

IRC §68

Phaseout of reduction in 2006–2009

IRC §68(f)

14 Charitable Contribution Deductions

14.1 Deductible Contributions

IRC §170

IRC §501

IRC §508

* IRS Publication 526

* "An Array of Rules Govern Charitable Contributions," M. Jill Lockwood and Leslie B. Fletcher, 72 Practical Tax Strategies 87 (February 2004)

Substantiation requirement for property contributions exceeding $500

IRC §170(f)(11), as amended by PPA 2006

* IRS Publication 526

Substantiation requirement for charitablecontributions of $250 or more

IRC §170(f)(8), superseded for cash donations after 2006 by IRC §170(f)(17)

Reg. §1.170A-13(f)

* IRS Publication 526

All cash donations after 2006 must be substantiated by bank record or receipt from charity

IRC §170(f)(17)

Contribution by check

Reg. §1.170A-1(b)

Elie B. Witt Est., 160 F. Supp. 521 (D. Fla. 1956)

Estelle Broussard, 16 TC 23 (1951)

Modie J. Spiegel Est., 12 TC 524 (1949) (Acq.)

Rev. Rul. 54-465, 1954-2 CB 93

Direct distribution from IRA not deductible donation

IRC §408(d)(8(E)

Year-end mailing

Stanley G. Reedy, 42 TCM 1401 (1981)

Contribution of note

Sheldon B. Gurenj, 66 TC 118 (1976)

Norman Petty, 40 TC 521 (1963)

Credit cards

Rev. Rul. 78-38, 1978-1 CB 67

* Letter Ruling 9623035

Voluntary payroll deduction

Rev. Rul. 54-549, 1954-2 CB 94

Fund-raising agency

Rev. Rul. 55-192, 1955-1 CB 294; amplified by Rev. Rul. 86-25, 1986-1 CB 202

Religious

IRC §170(c)(2)(B)

IRC §501(c)(3)

Clarence Morey, 205 F. Supp. 918 (S.D. Cal. 1962)

Saint Germain Foundation, 26 TC 648 (1956) (Acq.)

Charitable

IRC §170(c)(2)(B)

IRC §501(c)(3)

IRC §509(a)

T. J. Moss Tie Co., 18 TC 188 (1952) (Nonacq.)

Isabel Peters, 21 TC 55 (1953) (Acq.)

William Waller, 39 TC 665 (1963) (Acq.)

Lorain Avenue Clinic, 31 TC 141 (1958)

Scientific, literary, and educational

IRC §170(c)(2)(B)

IRC §501(c)(3)

IRC §509(a)

Science and Research Foundation, Inc., 181 F. Supp. 526 (S.D. Ill. 1960)

Rev. Rul. 67-291, 1967-2 CB 184

Rev. Rul. 67-292, 1967-2 CB 184

Rev. Rul. 93-73, 1993-2 CB 75

Prevention of cruelty to children or animals

IRC §170(c)(2)(B)

IRC §501(c)(3)

John A. Mustard, Exr., 155 F. Supp. 325 (Ct. Cl. 1957)

Amateur athletic associations

IRC §170(c)(2)(B)

IRC §501(c)(3)

Domestic nonprofit veterans organizations

IRC §170(c)(3)

Rev. Rul. 57-327, 1957-2 CB 155

Rev. Rul. 59-151, 1959-1 CB 53

Domestic fraternal group

IRC §170(c)(4)

IRC §501(c)(8)

Nonprofit cemetery and burial companies

IRC §170(c)(5)

IRC §501(c)(13)

Rev. Rul. 58-190, 1958-1 CB 15

Foreign charities

IRC §170(c)(2)(A)

IRC §1.170-2(a)(1)

Dora A. Welti, 1 TC 905 (1943)

Louise K. Herter, 20 TCM 78 (1953)

Rev. Rul. 63-252, 1963-2 CB 101, amplified by Rev. Rul. 66-79, 1966-1 CB 48

Rev. Rul. 69-80, 1969-1 CB 65

Legal fees to preserve donation

Anne Archbold, 444 F.2d 1120 (Ct. Cl. 1971)

Organizations qualifying for deductible donations

IRC §170(c)

Rev. Rul. 54-243, 1954-1 CB 92

* IRS Publication 78 Cumulative List (online only)

United States, state, city, etc.

IRC §170(b)(1)(a)

IRC §170(c)(1)

Rev. Rul. 56-126, 1956-1 CB 56

Social Security system

Rev. Rul. 82-169, 1982-2 CB 72

Indian tribes

Rev. Rul. 74-179, 1974-1 CB 279

Land donated to municipality

Mary W. Toole (D. Fla. 1963), 63-1 USTC ¶9267 (D. Fla. 1963)

Citizens and Southern Nat'l Bank of S.C., 243 F. Supp. 900 (D.S. Car. 1965)

14.2 Nondeductible Contributions

Disclosure of nondeductibility by political fund-raisers

IRC §6113

Lobbying

IRC §170(c)

Note: *Paragraph numbers refer to Parts 1 through 7. Items marked* * *are research aids, not citations of authority;* see *"Key to Citations" on page 801*

IRC §501(c)(3)

IRC §501(h)

Alan B. Kuper, 332 F.2d 562 (3d Cir. 1964), aff'g 22 TCM 1208 (1963), cert. denied, 379 U.S. 920

Murray Seasongood, 227 F.2d 907 (6th Cir. 1956)

McClintock-Trunkey Co., 19 TC 297 (1952), rev'd on another issue, 217 F.2d 329 (9th Cir. 1955)

Mosby Hotel Co., 13 TCM 996 (1954)

Rev. Rul. 62-71, 1962-1 CB 85

Organization benefitting restricted groups

IRC §170(c)

Boston Safe Deposit & Trust Co., 30 BTA 679

Colonial Trust Co., Exr., 19 BTA 174 (Acq.)

Montgomery, 63 Ct. Cl. 588

Bar association donations

Rev. Rul. 77-232, 1977-2 CB 71, clarified by Rev. Rul. 78-129, 1978-1 CB 67

No deduction if bar association rates judicial candidates

Association of Bar of City of NY, 858 F.2d 876 (2d Cir. 1988), cert. denied, 109 S. Ct. 1768, rev'g 89 TC 599 (1987)

Communist organizations

IRC §170(k)

Sec. 11(a), Internal Security Act of 1950 (64 Stat. 996; 50 U.S.C. 790)

Reg. §1.501(e)-1

Benefit private individual

IRC §170(c)

IRC §501(c)(3)

Emanuel Kolkey, 27 TC 37 (1956) (Acq.), aff'd, 254 F.2d 51 (7th Cir. 1958)

Saint Germain Foundation, 26 TC 648 (1956) (Acq.)

Mark B. Lloyd, 29 TCM 453 (1970)

Purchase of church building bond

Rev. Rul. 75-112, 1975-1 CB 274

Rev. Rul. 58-262, 1958-1 CB 143

Blood donations

Rev. Rul. 162, 1953-2 CB 127

Foreign governments

R. Hess, 30 TCM 1043 (1971) (State of Israel)

Son's payment for mother's apartment

Ernest S. & Janet M. Klapperbach, 52 TCM 437 (1986)

Donation of services

Reg. §1.170A-1(g)

Rev. Rul. 67-236, 1967-2 CB 103

Rev. Rul. 57-462, 1957-2 CB 157

William W. Grant, 84 TC 809 (1985)

Value of use of property

IRC §170(f)(3)(A)

Reg. §1.170A-7(d)

No deduction for donated vacation home time

Rev. Rul. 89-51, 1989-1 CB 89

No deduction for payments to support Mormon missionary

Harold Davis, 110 S. Ct. 2014 (1990)

14.3 Contributions That Provide You With Benefits

* IRS Publication 526

Token benefits

Rev. Proc. 90-12, 1990-1 CB 471, amplified by Rev. Proc. 92-49, 1992-1 CB 987

Value in return for contribution

Katherine Channing, 67 F.2d 98 (1st Cir.), cert. denied, 291 U.S. 686

Morris N. Scharf, 32 TCM 124 (1973)

Albin J. Strandquist, 29 TCM 38 (1970)

Rev. Rul. 67-246, 1967-2 CB 104 distinguished by Rev. Rul. 74-348, 1974-2 CB 80

Rev. Rul. 58-303, 1958-1 CB 61

Tuition

Harold De Jong, 309 F.2d 373 (9th Cir. 1962), aff'g 36 TC 896 (1961)

Rev. Rul. 71-112, 1971-1 CB 93

Jacob Oppewal, 30 TCM 1177 (1971), aff'd, 468 F.2d 1000 (1st Cir. 1972)

Jewish day school courses not deductible despite IRS concession on Scientology courses

Michael Sklar, 2009-1 USTC §50,106 (9th Cir. 2008)

Michael Sklar, 279 F.3d 697 (9th Cir. 2002)

No deduction for Church of Scientology trainings

Robert L. Hernandez, 490 U.S. 680 (1989)

Rest home

O. J. Wardwell Est., 35 TC 443 (1960), rev'd, 301 F.2d 632 (8th Cir. 1962)

Deduction allowed for retirement community sponsorship gift

Ruth Dowell, 553 F.2d 1233 (10th Cir. 1977)

Deductible dues

Eunice A. Horne, 16 TCM 953 (1957)

Rev. Rul. 54-565, 1954-2 CB 95, modified by Rev. Rul. 68-432, 1968-2 CB 104

Rev. Rul. 55-192, 1955-1 CB 294, amplified by Rev. Rul. 86-25, 1986-1 CB 202

Benefit tickets

Rev. Rul. 74-348, 1974-2 CB 80

No deduction for regular price tickets even if not used

Charles F. Urbauer, 63 TCM 2492 (1992)

Athletic stadium tickets

IRC §170(m)

Membership benefits

Reg. §1.170 A-13 (f)(8)(i)(B)

14.4 Unreimbursed Expenses of Volunteer Workers

Out-of-pocket costs deductible

Reg. §1.170 A-1 (g)

Written acknowledgment of services required for expenses of $250 or more

Reg. §1.170 A-13 (f)(10)

Mileage rate for unreimbursed charitable volunteersIRC §170(i)***Higher mileage rate for Midwestern disaster relief***

Act Section 702(e)(2) of the Emergency Economic Stabilization Act of 2008

Travel expenses

Francois Louis, 25 TCM 1047 (1966)

Rev. Rul. 59-160, 1959-1 CB 59

Rev. Rul. 58-279, 1958-1 CB 145

Rev. Rul. 58-240, 1958-1 CB 141, clarified by Rev. Rul. 71-135, 1971-1 CB 94

Rev. Rul. 57-327, 1957-2 CB 155

Rev. Rul. 55-4, 1955-1 CB 291

No deduction for value of donated services

Reg. §1.170A-1(g)

Note: *Paragraph numbers refer to Parts 1 through 7. Items marked * are research aids, not citations of authority;* see *"Key to Citations" on page 801*

William W. Grant, 84 TC 809 (1985)

Per diem allowances

Rev. Rul. 74-433, 1974-2 CB 92

Rev. Rul. 67-30, 1967-1 CB 9

Uniform costs

Rev. Rul. 56-508, 1956-2 CB 126

Delegate

Harris W. Seed, 57 TC 265 (1971)

John R. Wood, 57 TC 220 (1971), aff'd per curiam, 462 F.2d 691 (5th Cir. 1972)

Rev. Rul. 58-240, 1958-1 CB 141, clarified by Rev. Rul. 71-135, 1971-1 CB 94

* Letter Ruling 8242042

Services authorized

Russell Doty, Jr., 62 TC 587 (1974)

Travis Smith, 60 TC 988 (1973) (Acq.)

Replacing engine while doing volunteer work

Rev. Rul. 59-239, 1959-2 CB 100

Noncompensated minister deducts car expenses

Rev. Rul. 69-645, 1969-2 CB 37

CAP volunteer

Larry A. Miller, 34 TCM 1207 (1975)

Repairs attributable to charitable services deductible

John Orr, 343 F.2d 553 (5th Cir. 1965)

Rev. Rul. 58-279, 1958-1 CB 145

Babysitting costs

Rev. Rul. 73-597, 1973-2 CB 69

Foster care costs

Rev. Rul. 77-280, 1977-2 CB 14

Kingman Babcock, 71 TCM 2257 (1996)

No deduction for travel unless elements of personal pleasure absent

IRC §170(j)

Notice 87-23, 1987-1 CB 467, modified by Rev. Proc. 90-15, 1990-1 CB 476

14.5 Support of a Student in Your Home

IRC §170(g)

Reg. §1.170A-2

14.6 What Kind of Property Are You Donating?

**** IRS Publication 526***

* "Structuring Charitable Gifts of Property in Lieu of Demolition or Condemnation," Bruce W. McCain and Paul J. Lee, 78 Taxes 31 (October 2000)

Gift of property

IRC §170

Rev. Rul. 55-410, 1955-1 CB 297

Magnolia Development Corp., 19 TCM 934 (1960)

Stock donation to private foundation

IRC §170(e)(5)(D)(ii)

* Letter Ruling 200112002 (applying family aggregation rules)

No deduction if voting rights retained

Rev. Rul. 81-282, 1981-2 CB 78

Delivery of stock gift

Jack W. Londen, 45 TC 106 (1965)

Fair market value of property

Philip Kaplan, 43 TC 663 (1965) (Acq.)

Daniel S. McGuire, 44 TC 801 (1965) (Acq.)

Morris Schapiro, 27 TCM 205 (1968)

Alexia DuPont O. De Bie Est., 56 TC 876 (1971) (Acq.)

Lucky Stores, Inc., 105 TC 28 (1996)

Guidelines for valuations

Rev. Rul. 66-49, 1966-1 CB 36, amplified by Rev. Rul. 72-366, 1972-2 CB 91

Ordinary income property

IRC §170(e)(1)(A)

Reg. §1.170A-4(b)(1)

Leonard Greene, 13 F.3d 577 (2nd Cir. 1994)

Congressman's papers

James H. Morrison, 71 TC 683 (1979), aff'd per curiam, 611 F.2d 98 (5th Cir. 1980)

No charitable deduction for McVeigh trial papers

Sherrel and Leslie Stephen Jones, 2009-1 USTC ¶50,316 (10th Cir. 2009)

Partnership property

Rev. Rul. 96-11, 1996-4 IRB 28

Deduction limits for tangible personal property

IRC §170(e)(1)(B)

Reg. §1.170A-4(b)(3)(ii)(b) (reasonably anticipate related use)

Recapture of deduction without certification of exempt-use

IRC §170(e)(7), for contributions after 9/1/06

Donating used car

IRC §170(f)(12) (for vehicles valued at over $500)

Notice 2005-44, 2005-25 IRB 1287

* IRS Publication 526

Partial interests

IRC §170(f)(3)(A) and (B)

Reg. §1.170A-7

Future interests in tangible personal property

IRC §170(a)(3)

Election to reduce appreciation

IRC §170(b)(1)(C)(iii)

Reg. §1.170A-8(d)(2)

Rev. Rul. 74-53, 1974-1 CB 60

Capital gain property donated to private foundation

IRC §170(b)(1)(D)

IRC §170(e)

Fair market value deduction for gift of publicly traded stock to private foundation

IRC §170(e)(5)

* Letter Ruling 200322005 (American Depositary Receipts)

John C. Todd, 118 TC No. 19 (2002)

Trust interests

IRC §170(f)(2)

Prepaid interest

IRC §170(f)(5)

Reg. §1.170A-3

Donation of remainder interests

IRC §664

Reg. §1.664-4

Gift of mortgaged property

Rev. Rul. 81-163, 1981-1 CB 433

Winston Guest, 77 TC 9 (1981) (Acq.)

Leo Ebben et al.,783 F.2d 906 (9th Cir. 1986)

Bargain sale

IRC §170(e)(2)

IRC §1011(b)

Note: *Paragraph numbers refer to Parts 1 through 7. Items marked* are research aids, not citations of authority;* see *"Key to Citations" on page 801*

Reg. §1.170A-4(c)(2)

Leonard Greene, 13 F.3d 577 (2nd Cir. 1994)

Gift of depreciable mortgaged property

Aaron Levine Est., 634 F.2d 12 (2d Cir. 1980)

Teofilo Evangelista, 629 F.2d 1218 (7th Cir. 1980)

Donating intellectual property to charity

Code Sections 170(e)(1)(B)(iii) and 170(m) (allowable deduction)

Notice 2005-41, 2005-23 IRB 1203 (donor notification)

T.D. 9206, 2005-25 IRB 1283 (donee reporting regulations)

14.7 Cars, Clothing, and Other Property Valued Below Cost

* Publication 526

* "New Rules for Donating Autos and the Sales Tax Deduction for Building Materials—A Reprise," Gary L. Maydew, 83 Taxes 41 (November 2005)

Used vehicles, boats, airplanes

IRC §170(f)(12)

Notice 2005-44, 2005-25 IRB 1287

* IRS Publication 526

Used clothing and household items

IRC §170 (f)(16)

Deduction limited to cost

LaVar Withers, 69 TC 900 (1978)

14.8 Bargain Sales of Appreciated Property

IRC §170(e)(2)

IRC §1011(b)

Reg. §1.170A-4(c)(2)

Reg. §1.1011-2

Appreciation reduction for contributed portion only

Estate of Pauline Bullard, 87 TC 261 (1986)

Basis allocation applies even if annual ceiling bars deduction

Warner W. Hodgdon, 98 TC 31 (1992)

Bargain sale under installment agreement

Kenneth L. Musgrave, TC Memo 2000-285

14.9 Art Objects

Art not used for tax-exempt purposes

IRC §170(e)(1)(B)(i)

Recapture of tax benefit on donated property not used for exempt purposes

IRC §170(e)(7)

Restrictions on contributions of fractional interests

IRC §170(o)

IRS statement of value

Rev. Proc. 96-15, 1996-3 IRB 41

Appraising contributions of art works

Adolph Posner, 35 TCM 943 (1976)

Edwin F. Gordon, 35 TCM 1227 (1976)

Appraisal fee an itemized expense

Rev. Rul. 67-461, 1967-1 CB 125

Family's allocation of portion of collection

Gifford M. Mast, 56 TCM 1523 (1989)

Deduction allowed despite lack of possession

James Winokur, 90 TC 733 (1988) (Acq.)

14.10 Interests in Real Estate

Fractional transfers

IRC §170(f)(3)(B)(ii)

Rev. Rul. 58-261, 1958-1 CB 143

Remainder interests

IRC §170(f)(4)

Prop. Reg. §1.170A-12

Option on realty

Rev. Rul. 82-197, 1982-2 CB 72

Farms or residences

IRC §170(f)(3)(B)(i)

Rev. Rul. 76-357, 1976-2 CB 285

Restrictions on contributions of facade easements on certified historic structures

IRC §170(h)(4)(B) and (C)

Mortgage bars charitable deduction for façade easement

Gordon Kaufman, 134 TC No. 9

Deduction allowed for facade easement

Dorothy Jean Simmonds, TC Memo 2009-208

No deduction for home donated to fire department

James Hendrix, DC Ohio, 2010-2 USTC ¶50,541

Vacation use retained

Rev. Rul. 75-420, 1975-2 CB 78

Right to use of property

IRC §170(f)(3)(A)

Reg. §1.170A-7(d)

Charles M. Petgers, 35 TCM 770 (1976)

Partial interests donated for qualified conservation purposes

IRC §170(h)

Charles F. Glass, 2007-2 USTC ¶50,111 (6th Cir. 2006)

No deduction for airspace over historic building

J. Maurice Herman, TC Memo 2009-205

Waiver of grazing permit not a charitable donation

Otto Bischel, 2006-1 USTC ¶50,216 (DC, NV)

Donating use of vacation home

Rev. Rul. 89-51, 1989-1 CB 89

14.11 Life Insurance

Deductible if irrevocably assigned

Eppa Hunton, IV, 1 TC 821 (1943) (Acq.)

Premiums deductible if beneficiary a charity

Mortimer C. Adler, 5 BTA 1063

Rev. Rul. 58-372, 1958-2 CB 99

Charity's insurable interest

* Letter Ruling 9147040, revoking Letter Ruling 9110016

Contribution of cash surrender value not deductible

Rev. Rul. 76-143, 1976-1 CB 63

Rev. Rul. 76-1, 1976-1 CB 57

Split-dollar insurance

IRS Notice 99-36, 1999-26 IRB

14.12 Business Inventory

Corporate inventory

Reg. §1.170A-4(e)

Gifts at fair market value

Note: *Paragraph numbers refer to Parts 1 through 7. Items marked * are research aids, not citations of authority;* see *"Key to Citations" on page 801*

IRC §170(e)

Charles N. Prothro, 209 F.2d 331 (5th Cir. 1954)

David C. Whitge, 104 F. Supp. 213 (D. Kan. 1952)

Rev. Rul. 55-138, 1955-1 CB 223

Crops

Clyde G. Tatum, 46 TC 736 (1966), aff'd, 400 F.2d 242 (5th Cir. 1968)

Certain corporate contributions for care of ill, needy, or infants

IRC §170(e)(3)

14.13 Donations Through Trusts

Income interests

IRC §170(f)(2)(B)

IRC §671

Abusive charitable lead trust transactions

Treasury Decision 8923, 1/5/01

Charitable remainder trusts

IRC §170(f)(2)(A)

IRC §170(f)(3)(B)

IRC §170(f)(4)

IRC §170(f)(7)

IRC §664

Treasury Decision 8926 (abusive remainder trust transactions)

Life income plans

IRC §170(f)(2)(A)

IRC §642(c)(5)

IRC §664

IRS valuation tables

Notice 89-60, 1989-1 CB 700

14.14 Records Needed To Substantiate Your Contributions

* IRS Publication 526

Appraisals and documentation requirements

IRC §170(f)(11)

Definition of qualified appraisal and qualifed appraiser revised

IRC §170(f)(11)(E)

Acknowledgement requirement for vehicles, boats, or airplanes valued at over $500

IRC §170(f)(12)

Notice 2005-44, 2005-25 IRB 1287

Substantiation for cash donations after 2006

IRC §170(f)(17) (bank record or receipt from charity regardless of amount)

Charitable contributions by payroll deductions

Notice 2006-11, 2006-51 IRB 1127

Charity disclosure statement for donations exceeding $75

IRC §6115

Contribution by check

Reg. §1.170A-1(b)

Elie B. Witt Est., 160 F. Supp. 521 (D. Fla. 1956)

Estelle Broussard, 16 TC 23 (1951)

Modie J. Spiegel Est., 12 TC 524 (1949) (Acq.)

Rev. Rul. 54-465, 1954-2 CB 93

14.15 Form 8283 and Written Appraisal Requirements

Appraisals and documentation requirements

IRC §170(f)(11)

* IRS Publication 526

Definition of qualified appraisal and qualifed appraiser revised

IRC §170(f)(11)(E)

Penalty for overvaluation

IRC §6662(e)(1)(A) (20% penalty)

IRC §6662(h)(2)(A) (40% penalty)

14.16 Penalty for Substantial Overvaluation of Property

20% penalty

IRC §6662 (e)(1)(A)

40% penalty

IRC §6662 (h)(2)(A)

Penalty and displinary action imposed on apprasiers for substantial or gross overvaluation

IRC §6695A

Reasonable cause reliance on appraisal

Reg. §1.6664.4 (g)

Professional appraiser subject to penalty

IRC §6701

14.17 Ceiling on Charitable Contributions

* IRS Publication 506

Cash contributions in 2008 for Midwestern relief

IRC 1400S(a)(4), applied to the Midwestern disaster area by Act Section 702(d)(12) of the Emergency Economic Stabilization Act of 2008

Direct distribution from IRA not deductible donation

IRC §408(d)(8(E)

Higher deduction ceiling for qualified conservation contributions

IRC §170(b)(1)(E)

Organizations qualifying for 50% ceiling

IRC §170(b)(1)(A)

Reg. §1.170A-9

30% limit for capital gain property

IRC §170(b)(1)(C)

30% limit for non-operating foundations

IRC 170(b)(1)(B)

20% limit for certain capital gain property

IRC §170(b)(1)(D)

Donations by corporations

IRC §170(b)(2)

Order of taking deductions

IRC §170(b)(1)(C) and (D)

Reg. §1.170A-8(f)

14.18 Carryover for Excess Donations

Individuals

IRC §170(d)(1)

Sidney Rimmer, 69 TCM 2620 (1995)

Corporations

IRC §170(d)(2)

Donations to foundations

IRC §170(b)(1)(B)

IRC §170(b)(1)(D)

14.19 Election To Reduce Property Gift Appreciation

Reduction for appreciation

IRC §170(e)(1)

Electing 50% ceiling

IRC §170(b)(1)(C)(iii)

Reg. §1.170A-8(d)(2)

Note: *Paragraph numbers refer to Parts 1 through 7. Items marked * are research aids, not citations of authority;* see *"Key to Citations"* on *page 801*

Election is irreversible

Orin Woodbury, 900 F.2d 1457 (10th Cir. 1990)

15 Itemized Deduction for Interest Expenses

15.1 Home Mortgage Interest

* IRS Publication 530

* IRS Publication 936

Residential mortgage interest

IRC §163(h)(2)(D)

IRC §163(h)(3)

Temp. Reg. §1.163-10T

Unmarried owners allocate $1 million acquisition debt limit between them

Chief Counsel Memorandum 200911007

Two-residence test

IRC §163(h)(4)(A)

Home mortgage certificates

IRC §25

Temp. Reg. §1.25-1T through 8T

Qualified residence

H. Roger Lawler, 69 TCM 1699 (1995)

15.2 Home Acquisition Loans

Interest deduction for $100,000 of home purchase loan over $1 million

Chief Counsel Memorandum 200940030

Acquisition indebtedness limits

IRC §163(h)(3)(B)

Beneficial owner can deduct interest on brother's mortgage

Paul Trans Dang, TC Memo 1999-233

Saffet Uslu, TC Memo 1997-551

Seller's debt

Wendell Belden, 70 TCM 274 (1995)

Refinancing

IRC §163(h)(3)(B)(i)

IRC §163(h)(3)(D)(iii) and (iv)

Passive activity interest

IRC §469

Married — separate returns

IRC §163(h)(4)(A)(ii)

Cooperatives

IRC §163(h)(4)(B)

Destroyed house rebuilt

Rev. Rul 96-32, 1996-25 IRB 4

15.3 Home Equity Loans

Home equity indebtedness limits

IRC §163(h)(3)(C)

Interest deduction for $100,000 of home purchase loan over $1 million

Chief Counsel Memorandum 200940030

15.4 Home Construction Loans

Residence under construction

Temp. Reg. §1.163-10T(p)(5)

Notice 88-74, 1988-2 CB 385

15.5 Home Improvement Loans

Residence under improvement

IRC §163(h)(3)(B)(i)(I)

15.6 Mortgage Insurance Premiums and Other Payment Rules

Joint obligor can deduct payment from own funds

Austin B. Ewell, Jr., TC Memo 1996-253

Barbara S. Finney, 35 TCM 1504 (1976)

Penalty for prepaying mortgage

Rev. Rul. 57-198, 1957-1 CB 94

Deduction for payments of mortgage insurance premiums

IRC §163(h)(3)(E)

Mortgage assistance payments under §235 of the National Housing Act not deductible

Reg. §1.163-1(d)

Rev. Rul. 75-271, 1975-2 CB 23

Delinquency charges not deductible

Robert G. West, 61 TCM 1694 (1991)

Graduated payment mortgages

* Letter Ruling 8031087

Reverse mortgage loan

Rev. Rul. 80-248, 1980-2 CB 164

Zero interest mortgages

Rev. Rul. 82-124, 1982-1 CB 89

Shared appreciation mortgage

Rev. Rul. 83-51, 1983-1 CB 48

H.U.D. interest reduction payments

Rev. Rul. 76-75, 1976-1 CB 14

Alvin V. Graff, 74 TC 743 (1980)

15.7 Interest on Refinanced Loans

Refinancing

IRC §163(h)(3)(B)(i)

IRC §163(h)(3)(D)(iii) and (iv)

James R. Huntsman, 91 TC (1988), rev'd by 905 F.2d 1182 (8th Cir. 1990)

Rev. Rul. 87-22, 1987-1 CB 146 (points)

David A. Kelly, 62 TCM 401 (1991) (Huntsman exception inapplicable)

15.8 "Points"

* IRS Publication 530

* IRS Publication 936

"Points" treated as prepaid interest

IRC §461(g)

IRS position on deducting points

Rev. Proc. 94-27, 1994-1 CB 613

Seller-paid points

Rev. Proc. 94-27, 1994-1 CB 613

Amortize points starting in second year

* Letter Ruling 199905033

VA and FHA loan origination fees deductible as points

Rev. Proc. 92-12A, 1992-1 CB 664

Loan fees amortized

Karl Von Muff, 46 TCM 1185 (1983)

Richard Goodwin, 75 TC 424 (1981)

Rev. Rul. 81-161, 1981-1 CB 313

Rev. Rul. 81-160, 1981-1 CB 312

Loan fees: prior law

Robert E. Stewart, 41 TCM 318 (1980)

Points withheld from principal not deductible

Roger A. Schubel, 77 TC 701 (1981)

Refinancing

James R. Huntsman, 91 TC (1988), rev'd by 905 F.2d 1182 (8th Cir. 1990)

Rev. Rul. 87-22, 1987-1 CB 146

Rev. Proc. 87-15, 1987-1 CB 624

Note: *Paragraph numbers refer to Parts 1 through 7. Items marked * are research aids, not citations of authority; see "Key to Citations" on page 801*

David A. Kelly, 62 TCM 401 (1991) (Huntsman exception inapplicable)

15.9 Cooperative and Condominium Apartments

* IRS Publication 936

Cooperative apartments

IRC §163(h)(4)(B)

IRC §216

Reg. §1.216-1(c) and (d)

Rev. Rul. 73-15, 1973-1 CB 141

Rev. Rul. 59-257, 1959-2 CB 101

Rev. Rul. 53-120, 1953-2 CB 130

Holdover tenants do not jeopardize deductions to co-op owners

Rev. Rul. 80-299, 1980-2 CB 82

Condominiums

Rev. Rul. 64-31, 1964-1 (Pt. 1) CB 300

Raymond J. Wachter, 75-1 USTC ¶9172 (D. Wash. 1975)

15.10 Investment Interest Limitations

* IRS Publication 550

Investment interest

IRC §163(d)(3)

IRC §163(h)(2)(B)

Rev. Rul. 95-16, 1995-1 CB 9

Warren Halle, 83 F.3d 649 (4th Cir. 1996)

Passive activity interest

IRC §469

Net capital gain and qualified dividends excluded from investment income unless election made

IRC §163(d)(4)(B)

Capital loss carryover reduces investment income

* William Lenehan III, TC Summary Opinion 2002-124

Carryforward of disallowed interest

IRC §163(d)(2)

15.11 Debts To Carry Tax-Exempt Obligations

Frank Batten, 322 F. Supp. 629 (E. D. Vir. 1971)

Amedeo Louis Marionenzi, 32 TCM 681 (1973), aff'd per curiam, 490 F.2d 92 (1st Cir. 1974)

Interest on borrowings to carry tax-exempt obligations

IRC §265

Reg. §1.265-2

Constance M. Bishop, 41 TC 154 (1963), aff'd, 342 F.2d 757 (6th Cir. 1965)

Rev. Proc. 72-18, 1972-1 CB 740, clarified by Rev. Proc. 74-8, 1974-1 CB 419

Interest on joint venture mortgage

Max R. Israelson, 367 F. Supp. 1104 (D. Md. 1974), aff'd per curiam, 75-1 USTC (4th Cir. 1975)

Interest on loan to carry mutual-fund shares paying exempt-interest dividends

IRC §265(a)(4)

Short sales

IRC §265(a)(5)

15.12 Earmarking Use of Loan Proceeds

Prop. Reg. §1.163-8T

Expenses within 30 days of depositing loan in account

Notice 89-35, 1989-1 CB 675

Pre-existing debt

Warren Halle, 83 F.3d 649 (4th Cir. 1996)

15.13 Year To Claim an Interest Deduction

Promissory note is not payment of interest

Francis R. Hart, 54 F.2d 848 (1st Cir. 1932)

Increasing of loan

Julius I. Peyser, 1 TCM 807 (1943)

Fred W. Leadbetter, 39 BTA 629 (Nonacq.)

Life insurance loan

L. B. Hirsch, 42 BTA 566 (Acq.), aff'd, 124 F.2d 24 (9th Cir. 1941)

Arthur A. Beaudry, 1 TCM 838 (1943), modified and rem'd, 150 F.2d 20 (2d Cir. 1945), on remand, 5 TCM 61 (1946)

J. Simpson Dean, 35 TC 1083 (1961) (Nonacq.)

Margin account with broker

Rev. Rul. 70-221, 1970-1 CB 33

Contested note or obligation

Allegheny Steel Co., 18 F. Supp. 398 (Ct. Cl. 1937)

Shellabarger Grain Products Co., 2 TC 75 (1943) (Acq.), aff'd in part, rev'd in part, 146 F.2d 177 (7th Cir. 1944)

Partial payment of loan

McConway & Torley Corp., 2 TC 593 (1943)

Theodore R. Plunkett, 41 BTA 700 (Acq.), aff'd on other grounds, 118 F.2d 644 (1st Cir. 1941)

Paul N. Bowen Est., 2 TC 783 (1973)

George R. Newhouse, 59 TC 783 (1973)

John B. Ferenc, 33 TCM 136 (1974)

Full settlement of debt

William J. Petit, 8 TC 228 (1947) (Acq.)

Warner Co., 11 TC 419 (1948), aff'd per curiam, 181 F.2d 599 (3d Cir. 1950)

Using borrowed funds to pay interest

News Release IR-83-93, July 6, 1983

Barry L. Battelstein, 631 F.2d 1182 (5th Cir. 1980), cert. denied

Donald L. Wilkerson, 655 F.2d 980 (9th Cir. 1981)

Note that is renewed

S. E. Thomason, 33 BTA 576

David J. Secunda, 36 TCM 763 (1977)

Interest paid with a loan from lender

Charles Davison, 107 TC 4 (1996)

15.14 Prepaid Interest

IRC §461(g)

16 Deductions for Taxes

16.1 Deductible Taxes

IRC §164

Election to deduct general state and local sales taxes

IRC §164(b)(5)

16.2 Nondeductible Taxes

IRC §164

Reg. §1.164-1

Nondeductible taxes

IRC §275

Transfer taxes on securities sale reduce amount realized

Note: *Paragraph numbers refer to Parts 1 through 7. Items marked * are research aids, not citations of authority; see "Key to Citations" on page 801*

Announcement 88-54, 1988-13 IRB 35

IRC §164(a)

Transfer taxes

Rev. Rul. 65-313, 1965-2 CB 47

Federal minimum tax not deductible

Rev. Rul. 77-396, 1977-2 CB 86

Cash basis

IRC §461

IRC §1.461-1(a)(1)

Joseph Shalleck, 1 TCM 292 (1942)

Borrowed funds

In re Barry L. Battelstein, 77-2 USTC ¶9516 (S.D. Tex. 1977)

Payment by bank

Frank J. Hradesky, 65 TC 87 (1975), aff'd per curiam, 540 F.2d 821 (5th Cir. 1976)

Rev. Rul. 78-103, 1978-1 CB 58

Water bills

Benjamin Mahler, 119 F.2d 869 (2d Cir. 1941), aff'g on the point BTA Memo., P-H 39,468, cert. denied, 314 U.S. 660

Rufus K. Steel, 7 TCM 558 (1948)

Assessments not deductible as taxes

Rev. Rul. 77-29, 1977-2 CB 538

Rev. Rul. 76-495, 1976-2 CB 43

Parking meter charges

Rev. Rul. 73-91, 1973-1 CB 71

Sewer fees

Louis M. Roth, 17 TC 1450 (1952) (Acq.)

Postage

Reg. §1.164-2

Turnpike or thruway tolls

Donald L. Cox, 41 TC 161 (1963)

16.3 State and Local Income Taxes or General Sales Taxes

* "New Rules for Donating Autos and the Sales Tax Deduction for Building Materials—A Reprise," Gary L. Maydew, 83 Taxes 41 (November 2005)

State and local income taxes

IRC §164(a)(3)

Deduction for sales or excise taxes on new vehicle purchased from 2/17/09 through 12/31/09

IRC §164(a)(6)

IRC §164(b)(6)

Election to deduct general state and local sales taxes

IRC §164(b)(5)

State tax paid before end of year

Rev. Rul. 74-140, 1974-1 CB 50

Rev. Rul. 82-208, 1982-2 CB 58

Accrual taxpayer contested liability

IRC §461(f)

Alabama unemployment tax deductible

Rev. Rul. 75-156, 1975-1 CB 66

Sales tax deduction on home purchase disallowed

Jason Dewey, TC Summary Opinion 2010-38

Carl D. Naso, TC Summary Opinion 2010-39

Rhode Island disability deductible

James R. McGowan, 67 TC 599 (1976)

News Release IR-1742 (1/28/77)

California disability deductible

Anthony Trujillo, 68 TC 56 (1977)

IR-1967, March 10, 1978

New York and New Jersey disability deductible

News Release IR-1967, March 10, 1978

16.4 Deducting Real Estate Taxes

Payments to bank escrow account deductible when disbursed to tax authorities

Rev. Rul. 78-103, 1978-1 CB 58

Buyer of foreclosed property

* Letter Ruling 8207030

Beneficial owner

Paul Trans Dang, TC Memo 1999-233

Husband for his wife

William A. Colston, 59 F.2d 867 (D.C. Cir. 1932), aff'g 21 BTA 396, cert. denied, 287 U.S. 640

Charles F. Dean Est., 1 BTA 27

Mortgage required husband to pay

Eugene W. Small, 27 BTA 1219

Condominium apartment owner

Rev. Rul. 64-31, 1964-1 (Pt. 1) CB 300

Cooperative apartment owner

IRC §216

Life tenant

Cornelia C. F. Horsford, 2 TC 826 (1943) (Acq.)

Jointly and severally liable for tax

Rev. Rul. 72-79, 1972-1 CB 51

Tenancy by the entirety

Thomas D. Conroy, 17 TCM 21 (1958)

F. C. Nicodemus, Jr., 26 BTA 125 (Acq.)

Rev. Rul. 71-268, 1971-1 CB 58

Tenant in common

Lulu Lung Powell, 26 TCM 161 (1967)

Joseph James, 70 TCM 1420 (1995)

Mortgagee

John Hancock Mutual Life Ins. Co., 10 BTA 736 (Acq.)

Lucy S. Schiffelin Est., 44 BTA 137 (Acq.)

Tax on others' property

Albion D. T. Libby, 133 F.2d 203 (3d Cir. 1943), aff'g BTA Memo. P-H 42,252

J. Raymond Batcheller, 5 TCM 746 (1946)

Solomon N. Scale, 9 TCM 48 (1950)

Gordon W. Bonnette Est., 9 TCM 158 (1950)

Eugene W. Small, 27 BTA 1219 (1971)

Virginia N. Cramer, 55 TC 1125 (1971) (Acq.)

Gregory E. Macdonald, 35 TCM 346 (1976)

Have interest in property

Alfred J. Grosso, BTA Memo. P-H 41,581

A. J. Gilbert, 11 TCM 457 (1952)

Protection of beneficial interest

Rev. Rul. 67-21, 1967-1 CB 45

Trust for life of another

Herman A. Harper, 4 TCM 1097 (1945)

Robert C. Ligget, 4 TCM 598 (1945)

John H. Hord, 95 F.2d 179 (6th Cir. 1944), rev'g 33 BTA 342

Realty owned by parent

J. Raymond Batcheller, 5 TCM 746 (1946)

Note: *Paragraph numbers refer to Parts 1 through 7. Items marked* are research aids, not citations of authority;* see *"Key to Citations" on page 801*

Stockholder property interest

Fred N. Acker, 258 F.2d 568 (6th Cir. 1958), aff'd, 361 U.S. 87 (1959)

16.5 Assessments

Homeowner's association fees not deductible

Rev. Rul. 76-495, 1976-2 CB 43

Charges for local benefits

IRC §164(c)(1)

Reg. §1.164-4

16.6 Tenants' Payment of Taxes

Deductible

Hawaii real property tax law:

Rev. Rul. 64-327, 1964-2 CB 56

California real property tax law:

Rev. Rul. 68-84, 1968-1 CB 71

Not deductible

Tax surcharge

Rev. Rul. 75-301, 1975-2 CB 66

U.K. rates tax:

Maynard Waxenberg, 62 TC 594 (1974); Rev. Rul. 73-600, 1973-2 CB 47

Maryland-Prince George's County renters: Rev. Rul. 75-558, 1975-2 CB 67

New York: Rev. Rul. 79-180, 1979-1 CB 95

16.7 Allocating Taxes When You Sell or Buy Realty

IRC §164(d)

Reg. §1.164-6

Form 1099-S

IRC §6045(e)

Accrual-basis deduction

IRC §164(d)(2)(B)

Reg. §1.164-6(d)(6)

IRC §461(c) (ratable election)

Seller on cash basis

Reg. §1.164-6(d)(1)

Buyer's payment of seller's back taxes capitalized

Al S. Reinhardt, 75 TC 47 (1980)

16.8 Automobile License Fees

Reg. §1.164-3(c)

Rev. Rul. 74-454, 1974-2 CB 57

16.9 Taxes Deductible as Business Expenses

IRC §162

IRC §212

Reg §1.263A-2(a)

16.10 Foreign Taxes

IRC §164(a)(3)

17 Medical and Dental Expense Deductions

17.1 Medical Expenses Must Exceed 7.5% of AGI

IRC §213(a)

* IRS Publication 502

Loan as payment

William J. Granan, 55 TC 753 (1971)

Rev. Rul. 78-173, 1978-1 CB 73

Credit card charge

Rev. Rul. 78-39, 1978-1 CB 73

17.2 Allowable Medical Care Costs

* IRS Publication 502

* "Nursing Home Expenditures and Special Schools—When Are They Deductible as Medical Expenses?" Gary L. Maydew, 78 Taxes 45 (August 2000)

IRC §213

Reg. §1.213-1

* IRS Publication 502

Sex reassignment surgery is deductible medical expense

Rhiannon G. O'Donnabhain, 134 TC No. 4 (2010)

Prescribed drugs

IRC §213(b)

IRC §213(d)(3)

IRS position on special foods

Rev. Rul. 55-261, 1955-1 CB 307

Extra cost of health food

Theron G. Randolph, 67 TC 481 (1976)

Leona Von Kalb, 37 TCM 1511 (1978)

Warren L. Becher, 53 TCM 683 (1987) (taxpayer appeal pending)

Nonrefundable advance payment for lifetime care of disabled dependent

* IRS Publication 502

Rev. Rul. 75-303, 1975-2 CB 87, as clarified by Rev. Rul. 93-72, 1993-2 CB 77

Medical treatments

Reg. §1.213-1(e)(1)(ii)

Rev. Rul. 55-261, 1955-1 CB 307

Premiums

Reg. §1.213-1(e)(1)(i)

Premiums allocable to lost wages, loss of life or limbs

Reg. §1.213-1(e)(4)

Medicare by persons not automatically covered

Rev. Rul. 79-175, 1979-1 CB 117

Smoking cessation costs

Rev. Rul. 99-28, 1999-1CB 1269

Weight loss program for obesity or other specific disease deductible

Rev. Rul. 2002-19, 2002-16 IRB 778

Rev. Rul. 79-151, 1979-1 CB 116

Breast reconstruction and vision correction

Rev. Rul. 2003-57, 2003-22 IRB 959

Childbirth classes

* Letter Ruling 8919009

Chiropractor (lic.)

Rev. Rul. 55-261, 1955-1 CB 307

Christian Science practitioner

Rev. Rul. 55-261, 1955-1 CB 307

Dermatologist

Rev. Rul. 55-261, 1955-1 CB 307

Obstetrical services

Reg. §1.213-1(e)(1)(ii)

Osteopath (lic.)

Rev. Rul. 55-261, 1955-1 CB 307

Nurse

Reg. §1.213-1(e)(1)(ii)

Jacob Hentz, Jr., Est., 12 TCM 368 (1953)

George B. Wendell, 12 TC 161 (1949)

Rev. Rul. 58-339, 1958-2 CB 106

Rev. Rul. 55-261, 1955-1 CB 307

Psychiatrist

Rev. Rul. 53-143, 1953-2 CB 129, modified by Rev. Rul. 63-91, 1963-1 CB 54

Note: *Paragraph numbers refer to Parts 1 through 7. Items marked * are research aids, not citations of authority;* see *"Key to Citations" on page 801*

Rev. Rul. 55-261, 1955-1 CB 307

Rev. Rul. 56-263, 1956-1 CB 135

Payments to unlicensed practitioners

Rev. Rul. 63-91, 1963-1 CB 54

Dental services

Reg. §1.213-1(e)(1)(ii)

Equipment and supplies

Reg. §1.213-1(e)(1)(ii)

Crutches, bandages and blood sugar test kits

Rev. Rul. 2003-58, 2003-22 IRB 959

Auto devices for handicapped

Rev. Rul. 66-80, 1966-1 CB 57

Modifications to van

David Henderson, TC Memo 2001-321

Elevator

Edna G. Hollander, 219 F.2d 934 (3d Cir. 1955), rev'g 22 TC 646 (1954)

James E. Berry, 174 F. Supp. 748 (D. Okla. 1958)

W. A. Post, 150 F. Supp. 299 (D. Ala. 1956)

W. E. Snellings, 149 F. Supp. 825 (E.D. Vir. 1956)

Rev. Rul. 59-411, 1959-2 CB 100

Laetrile

Rev. Rul. 78-325, 1978-2 CB 124

Contact lens replacement insurance protection

Rev. Rul. 74-429, 1974-2 CB 83

Fluoridation unit

Rev. Rul. 64-267, 1964-2 CB 69

Invalid chair

Rev. Rul. 58-155, 1958-1 CB 156

Rev. Rul. 66-80, 1966-1 CB 57

Rev. Rul. 67-76, 1967-1 CB 70

Wig

Rev. Rul. 62-189, 1962-2 CB 88

Elastic hosiery

Bessie Cohen, 10 TCM 29 (1951)

Lodging

* Letter Ruling 8516025

Special home construction costs deductible upon completion

Laurence S. Zipkin, 2000-2 USTC ¶50,863 (D.C. Minn. 2000)

Hospital services

Reg. §1.213-1(e)(1)(ii)

Rev. Rul. 55-261, 1955-1 CB 307

Alcoholic's inpatient care

Rev. Rul. 72-325, 1973-1 CB 75

Birth control pills

Rev. Rul. 73-200, 1973-1 CB 140

Clarinet lessons

Rev. Rul. 62-210, 1962-2 CB 89

Navajo sings

Raymond H. Tso, 40 TCM 1277 (1980)

Health institute

Rev. Rul. 55-261, 1955-1 CB 307

Drug center costs

Rev. Rul. 72-226, 1972-1 CB 96

Legal fees

Carl A. Gerstacker, 414 F.2d 448 (6th Cir. 1969)

Rev. Rul. 71-281, 1971-1 CB 121

Nurses' board and wages

Reg. §1.213-1(e)(1)(ii)

Federal Insurance Contributions Act

Rev. Rul. 57-489, 1957-2 CB 207

Remedial reading

Rev. Rul. 69-607, 1969-2 CB 40

Seeing-eye dog

Rev. Rul. 55-261, 1955-1 CB 307

Vasectomy

Rev. Rul. 73-201, 1973-1 CB 140

Sterilization

Rev. Rul. 73-603, 1973-2 CB 76

Egg donation costs

* Letter Ruling 200318017

Tuition fee

Rev. Rul. 54-457, 1954-2 CB 100

Wages of guide

Rev. Rul. 64-173, 1964-1 (Pt. 1) CB 121

Organ transplant costs

Rev. Rul. 68-452, 1968-2 CB 111

Telephone-teletype

Rev. Rul. 71-48, 1971-1 CB 99, amplified by Rev. Rul. 73-53, 1973-1 CB 139

Television adapter for closed caption service

Rev. Rul. 80-340, 1980-2 CB 81

Braille book

Rev. Rul. 75-318, 1975-2 CB 88

17.3 Nondeductible Medical Expenses

Reg. §1.213-1

Cosmetic surgery

RC §213(d)(9)

Sex change operation not deductible

*Chief Counsel Advice 200603025

Sex reassignment surgery is deductible medical expense

Rhiannon G. O'Donnabhain, 134 TC No. 4 (2010)

Payroll withholding to cover Medicare A not deductible

Rev. Rul. 66-216, 1966-2 CB 100

Car insurance premiums not deductible

Rev. Rul. 73-483, 1973-2 CB 75

Infant formula not deductible

*Letter Ruling 200941003

Toothpaste

Reg. §1.213-1(e)(2)

Antiseptic diaper service and maternity clothes

Rev. Rul. 55-261, 1955-1 CB 307

Male cannot deduct in vitro fertilization expenses

William Magdalin, First Circuit, 12/17/09

Monument

Carolyn W. Libby Est., 14 TCM 699 (1955)

No deduction for advance payment of services to be performed next year

R.M. Rose, 435 F.2d 149 (5th Cir. 1970)

Anticipated expenses not deductible

W.B. Andrews, 37 TCM 744 (1978)

Illegal operations, etc.

Reg. §1.213-1(e)(1)(ii)

Divorced wife

IRC §213(a)

Note: *Paragraph numbers refer to Parts 1 through 7. Items marked * are research aids, not citations of authority;* see *"Key to Citations" on page 801*

Cost of oil furnace

Reg. §1.213-1(e)(1)(ii)

Special hospital room

Reg. §1.213-1(e)(i)(iv)

Specially designed car

Rev. Rul. 55-261, 1955-1 CB 307

Rev. Rul. 58-8, 1958-1 CB 154, amplified by Rev. Rul. 67-76, 1967-1 CB 70

Special food or beverages

Rev. Rul. 55-261, 1955-1 CB 307

Leo R. Cohn, 38 TC 387 (1962) (Nonacq.)

John R. Newman, 902 F.2d 159 (2nd Cir. 1990)

T. G. Randolph, 67 TC 481 (1976)

Organically grown food

Warren Becher, 53 TCM 683 (1987)

Bottled water

Rev. Rul. 56-19, 1956-1 CB 135

Health programs

Rev. Rul. 57-130, 1957-1 CB 108

Domestic help

Rev. Rul. 58-339, 1958-2 CB 106

Athletic club

Rev. Rul. 55-261, 1955-1 CB 307

Health spa

Jill Ford Murray, 43 TCM 1377 (1982)

Healthy child to boarding school

Samuel Ochs, 17 TC 130 (1951), aff'd, 195 F.2d 692 (2d Cir. 1952), cert. denied, 344 U.S. 827

Tuition for problem child

Gordon Pascal, 15 TCM 434 (1956)

Transportation costs

James Donnelly, 28 TC 1278 (1957), aff'd, 262 F.2d 411 (2d Cir. 1959)

Rev. Rul. 55-261, 1955-1 CB 307

Toiletries and sundries

Reg. §1.213-1(e)(2)

O. G. Russell, 12 TCM 1276 (1953)

Hotel costs

Reg. §1.213-1(e)(1)(iv)

Loren Wilks, 27 TCM 1086 (1968)

Living costs of outpatient

Harlin H. Lucas, 25 TCM 1312 (1966)

Look for new place to live

Gunnar E. Erickson, 13 TCM 1045 (1954)

Change of environment trip

Rev. Rul. 56-474, 1956-2 CB 157

Dance lessons

John J. Thoene, 33 TC 62 (1959)

Irving A. Adler, 22 TCM 965 (1963), aff'd, 330 F.2d 91 (9th Cir. 1964)

Rose France, 49 TCM 508 (1980), aff'd, 82-1 USTC 9225 (6th Cir. 1982)

Fallout shelter

Fred H. Daniels, 41 TC 324 (1963)

Travel to golf course

Leon S. Altman, 53 TC 487 (1969)

Scientology fees

Donald H. Brown, 62 TC 551 (1974), aff'd per curiam, 523 F.2d 365 (8th Cir. 1975)

Rev. Rul. 78-190, 1978-1 CB 74

Divorce costs

Joel H. Jacobs, 62 TC 813 (1974)

Marriage counseling fee

Rev. Rul. 75-319, 1975-2 CB 88

Hotel room for sex therapy

Rev. Rul. 75-187, 1975-1 CB 92

Veterinary fees

L. J. Schoen, 34 TCM 736 (1975)

Babysitter expenses

Rev. Rul. 78-266, 1978-2 CB 123

Tattooing and ear piercing

Rev. Rul. 82-111, 1982-1 CB 48

Moving from airport noise

Luke W. Findlay, Jr., 44 TCM 123 (1982)

17.4 Reimbursements Reduce Deductible Expenses

Reimbursements reduce deduction

IRC §213(a)

Reg. §1.213-1(g)

Failure to make claim

* Letter Ruling 8102010

Loss of earnings, etc.

Reg. §1.213-1(e)(4)(i)

Excess reimbursements

Rev. Rul. 69-154, 1969-1 CB 46

Injury awards treated as medical cost reimbursements

Benjamin D. Morgan, 55 TC 376 (1970)

Daniel T. Cooney, 30 TCM 845 (1971)

17.5 Premiums of Medical Care Policies

IRC §213(d)(1)(C)

Policy for loss of life, limb, or sight—premium not deductible

Reg. §1.213-1(e)(4)

No deduction for policy guaranteeing specific amount for hospitalization

Rev. Rul. 68-451, 1968-2 CB 111

Self-employed health insurance deduction

IRC §162(l)(1)

* Letter Ruling 9409006

17.6 Expenses of Your Spouse

Deduction allowed

IRC §213(a)

Reg. §1.213-1(a)(3)

Status at the time medical expense is incurred or paid

Reg. §1.213-1(e)(3)

17.7 Expenses of Your Dependents

* IRS Publication 502

Dependents

IRC §213(a), as amended by WFTRA 2004

IRC §213(d)(5) (divorced or separated parents)

Must contribute half of support

IRC §152

Reg. §1.152-1 and 2

Not related at time of bill

Rev. Rul. 57-310, 1957-2 CB 206

Parent's welfare payments used to pay medical bills

Robert W. Hodge, 44 TC 186 (1965)

Adopted children

Benny L. Kilpatrick, 68 TC 469 (1977)

Rev. Rul. 60-255, 1960-2 CB 105

Note: *Paragraph numbers refer to Parts 1 through 7. Items marked * are research aids, not citations of authority; see "Key to Citations" on page 801*

Multiple support

IRC §152(c)

Reg. §1.152-3

Loring P. Litchfield, 330 F.2d 509 (1st Cir. 1964)

17.8 Decedent's Medical Expenses

IRC §213(d)

Reg. §1.213-1(d)

Rev. Rul. 77-357, 1977-2 CB 328

17.9 Travel Costs May Be Medical Deductions

Medical deduction for traveling expenses

IRC §213(d)(1)(B)

Reg. §1.213-1(e)(1)(iv)

Optional standard mileage rate

Announcement 2008-63, 2008-28 IRB 114 (special dual rates for 2008)

Rev. Proc. 2008-72, 2008-50 IRB 1286 (rate for 2009)

Rev. Proc. 2009-54, 2009-51 IRB 930 (rate for 2010)

Trip to medical conference deductible

Rev. Rul. 2000-24, 2000-19 IRB 963

Relieve specific chronic ailments

Rev. Rul. 58-110, 1958-1 CB 155

Rev. Rul. 55-261, 1955-1 CB 307

Sally L. Bilder, 369 U.S. 499 (1963), rev'g 289 F.2d 291 (3d Cir. 1961)

Taxi fare

Rev. Rul. 98-63, 1998-52 IRB

Out-of-pocket auto expenses

Maurice S. Gordon, 37 TC 986 (1962)

Lodging — $50 daily allowance

IRC §213(d)(2)

* Letter Ruling 8516025

Transportation to Florida deductible but not $50 lodging allowance

Earlene Polyak, 94 TC 20 (1990)

Hotel costs for convalescent

Daniel S. W. Kelly, 440 F.2d 307 (7th Cir. 1971), rev'g 28 TCM 1208 (1969)

Nurse's fare

Rev. Rul. 58-110, 1958-1 CB 155

Parent's trip prescribed

Martin J. Lichterman, 37 TC 586 (1961) (Acq.) (to take child to school — deductible)

Rev. Rul. 58-533, 1958-2 CB 108 (to visit child—deductible)

Robert Rose, 52 TC 21 (1969) (taking child on trip for health reason — deductible)

* Letter Ruling 7813004 (picking up mentally disturbed son—transportation plus overnight food and lodging — deductible)

Visit specialist

Bertha M. Rodgers, 25 TC 254 (1955) (Acq.), aff'd, 241 F.2d 552 (8th Cir. 1957)

Treatment in distant city

Reg. §1.213-1(e)(1)(iv), contra:

Stanley D. Winderman, 32 TC 1197 (1959) (Acq.) (airfare to see trusted doctor deductible)

Escape bad climate

Reg. §1.213-1(e)(1)(iv)

L. Keever Stringham, 12 TC 580 (1949) (Acq.), aff'd, 183 F.2d 579 (6th Cir. 1950)

Rev. Rul. 53-261, 1955-1 CB 307

Alcoholics Anonymous

Rev. Rul. 63-273, 1963-2 CB 112

Disabled veteran's commuting

Sanford H. Weinzimer, 17 TCM 712 (1958)

Wife's trip to provide nursing care deductible

Daniel S. W. Kelly, 28 TCM 1208 (1969), rev'd on other grounds, 440 F.2d 307 (7th Cir. 1971)

Travel costs of kidney transplant donor or prospective donor

Rev. Rul. 73-189, 1973-1 CB 139

Driving as therapy

Michael R. Bordas, 29 TCM 458 (1970)

General improvement

Reg. §1.213-1(e)(1)(iv)

Margherita Diamond Est., 22 TCM 1073 (1963)

Annual trips south are personal expenses

Bertha M. Rodgers, 241 F.2d 552 (8th Cir. 1957), aff'g 25 TC 254 (1955) (Acq.)

Meals en route

Morris C. Montgomery, 428 F.2d 243 (6th Cir. 1970), aff'g 51 TC 410 (1968)

Meals and lodging (pre-1984 decisions)

Reg. §1.213-1(e)(1)(iv)

Max Carasso, 34 TC 1139 (1960), aff'd, 292 F.2d 367 (2d Cir. 1961), cert. denied, 369 U.S. 874

Sally L. Bilder, 369 U.S. 499 (1963), rev'g 289 F.2d 291 (3d Cir. 1961)

Extra cost of salt-free food

Leo Cohn, 38 TC 387 (1962) (Nonacq.)

Leo Cohn, 240 F. Supp. 786 (D. Ind. 1965)

Meals and lodging in transit deductible

Morris C. Montgomery, 428 F.2d 243 (6th Cir. 1970), aff'g 51 TC 410 (1968)

Spiritual aid

Vincent P. Ring, 23 TC 950 (1955)

Climate more suitable to ill wife's condition

Lawrence Prem, 21 TCM 873 (1962)

Moving household furnishings

C. Earle Phares, 21 TCM 1446 (1962)

Auto for leg condition

Benjamin Ginsberg, 237 F. Supp. 968 (S.D.N.Y. 1965)

Special vehicle

Rev. Rul. 55-261, 1955-1 CB 307

Rev. Rul. 66-80, 1966-1 CB 57

Rev. Rul. 70-606, 1970-2 CB 66

Convalescence cruise

Margherita Diamond Est., 22 TCM 1073 (1963)

Transporting invalid child to public school

Rev. Rul. 65-255, 1965-2 CB 76

Loss on sale of car

Robert K. Weary, 510 F.2d 435 (10th Cir. 1975), cert. denied, 423 U.S. 838

Patient on medical seminar cruise

Rev. Rul. 76-79, 1976-1 CB 70

17.10 Schooling for the Mentally or Physically Disabled

* "Nursing Home Expenditures and Special Schools — When Are They Deductible as Medical Expenses?" Gary L. Maydew, 78 Taxes 45 (August 2000)

Note: *Paragraph numbers refer to Parts 1 through 7. Items marked * are research aids, not citations of authority;* see *"Key to Citations" on page 801*

* "Deductibility of Private School Costs for Disabled Children," Claudia L. Kelley, John P. Geary and DeAnna Leeper Maxwell, 76 Taxes 39 (July 1998)

Reg. §1.213-1(e)(1)(v)

Rev. Rul. 55-261, 1955-1 CB 307

Special education tuition for child's learning disability is deductible

* Letter Ruling 200521003

Private school with psychologists

C. Fink Fischer, 50 TC 164 (1968) (Acq.)

Hobart J. Hendrick, 35 TC 1223 (1960) (Acq.)

Boarding school recommended by therapist

John A. Dreifus, 36 TCM 368 (1977)

Hyperactive child in regular boarding school

Ernest M. Newkirk, 611 F.2d 373 (6th Cir. 1979)

Deduction for child's behavior therapy at school

Charles F. Urbauer, 63 TCM 2492 (1992)

Private military academy

H. Grant Atkinson, Jr., 44 TC 39 (1965) (Acq.)

Edward S. Enck, 26 TCM 314 (1967)

Rolland T. Olson, 23 TCM 2008 (1964)

Everett F. Glaze, 20 TCM 1276 (1961)

School in Arizona

Martin J. Lichterman, 37 TC 586 (1961) (Acq.)

Cost of college for deaf child (deductible)

Reuben A. Baer Est., 26 TCM 170 (1967)

Blind student at regular school

Arnold P. Grunwald, 51 TC 108 (F.2d 1968)

Halfway house

* Letter Ruling 7714016

Special public school class for retarded: cost of tuition and travel

Rev. Rul. 70-285, 1970-1 CB 52

Cost of remedial reading school

Paul H. Ripple, 54 TC 1442 (1970)

Cost of private school for epileptic

DeVora R. Shidler, 30 TCM 529 (1971)

17.11 Nursing Homes

* IRS Publication 502

* "Nursing Home Expenditures and Special Schools — When Are They Deductible as Medical Expenses?" Gary L. Maydew, 78 Taxes 45 (August 2000)

* "Tax Deductions Can Lighten the Cost of Assisted Living Arrangements," Jay A. Soled, 64 Tax Strategies 233 (April 2000)

Reg. §1.213-1(e)(1)(v)

Apartment rent

Sidney J. Ungar, 22 TCM 766 (1963)

17.12 Nurses' Wages

Daughter acting as nurse

Myrtle P. Dodge Est., 20 TCM 811 (1961)

Working parents

Maurice Levy, Jr., 20 TCM 1534 (1961)

Domestic

John Frier, 30 TCM 345 (1971)

Rev. Rul. 58-339, 1958-2 CB 106

Allocation of medical and household services

Rev. Rul. 76-106, 1976-1 CB 71

Clerk's salary

Sidney J. Ungar, 22 TCM 766 (1963)

Nonprofessional therapy

Rev. Rul. 70-170, 1970-1 CB 51

Relative providing care

Walter D. Bye, 31 TCM 238 (1972)

17.13 Home Improvements as Medical Expenses

Reg. §1.213-1(e)(1)(iii)

John Riach, 302 F.2d 374 (9th Cir. 1962)

Raymon Gerard, 37 TC 826 (1962) (Acq.)

Karlis A. Pols, 24 TCM 1140 (1965)

Air conditioning device

Rev. Rul. 55-261, 1955 CB 307

Removal of lead-based paint

Rev. Rul. 79-66, 1979-1 CB 114

Special bathroom in rented house

Rev. Rul. 70-395, 1970-2 CB 65

Swimming pool of osteoarthritis patient

Rev. Rul. 83-33, 1983-1 CB 70

Least expensive construction

Collins H. Ferris, 36 TCM 765 (1977), rev'd, 582 F.2d 1112 (7th Cir. 1978)

Buying house with pool

Paul A. Lerew, 44 TCM 918 (1982)

Pool of emphysema patient

Herbert Cherry, 46 TCM 1033 (1983)

Pool as personal convenience

C. W. Haines, 71 TC 257 (1979)

Operating costs

Reg. §1.213(e)(iii)

Handicap exception for ramps, etc.

Conference Committee Report to P.L. 99-514, Act Sec. 133, 1986-3 (vol. 4) CB 22

Rev. Rul. 87-106, 1987-2 CB 67

Modifications to van

David Henderson, TC Memo 2001-321

Special home construction costs deductible upon completion

Laurence S. Zipkin, 2002-2 USTC ¶50,863 (D.C. Minn. 2000)

17.14 Costs Deductible as Business Expenses

Medical checkup for job

Rev. Rul. 58-382, 1958-2 CB 59

Throat specialist fee

Rev. Rul. 71-45, 1971-1 CB 51

Services for physically handicapped

Rev. Rul. 75-317, 1975-2 CB 57

Psychoanalysis for social worker

Harry H. Voigt, 74 TC 82 (1980) (Nonacq.)

Therapy for psychiatrist

Kenneth Porter, 52 TCM 615 (1986)

17.15 Long-Term-Care Premiums and Service

Long-term-care premiums

IRC §213(d)(1)(D)

IRC §213(d)(10)

Rev. Proc. 2009-50, 2009-45 IRB 617 (deductible amounts for 2010)

Long-term care services

Note: *Paragraph numbers refer to Parts 1 through 7. Items marked * are research aids, not citations of authority; see "Key to Citations" on page 801*

IRC §213(d)(1)(C)

IRC §7702B(c) (definition of qualified long-term care services)

Exclusion for payments from qualified contracts

IRC §7702 B(a)(2)

IRC §7702 B(d)(2) (per diem limit)

17.16 Life Insurance Used by Chronically Ill or Terminally Ill Persons

Terminally ill: tax-free accelerated benefits

IRC §101(g)(1)(A)

IRC §101(g)(4)(A)

Chronically ill: tax-free accelerated benefits

IRC §101(g)(1)(B)

IRC §101(g)(3)

IRC §101(g)(4)(B)

Viatical settlements

IRC §101(g)(2)

18 Casualty and Theft Losses and Involuntary Conversions

18.1 Sudden Event Test for Casualty Losses

IRC §165(c)(3)

* "Casualty and Theft Losses Can Provide Significant Tax Deductions," Edward E. Milam and Donald H. Jones, Jr., 80 Taxes 45 (October 2002)

Great Lakes high water level

Rev. Rul. 76-134, 1976-1 CB 54

Repair of Chinese drywall is deductible casualty loss

Rev. Proc. 2010-36, 2010-42 IRB 439

Intoxicated driver allowed casualty loss deduction

Justin M. Rohrs, TC Summary Opinion 2009-190

Water damage to wallpaper

Rupert Stuart, 20 TCM 938 (1961)

Termites

E. G. Kilroe, 32 TC 1304 (1959) (Nonacq.)

Alan M. Winsor, 18 TCM 383 (1959), aff'd, 278 F.2d 634 (1st Cir. 1960)

Rev. Rul. 63-232, 1963-2 CB 97

Foreseeable damage

Jack R. Farber, 57 TC 714 (1972) (Acq.)

Harry Heyn, 46 TC 714 (1966) (Acq.)

Car towed away and destroyed

Abraham Hananel, 62 TCM 439 (1991)

Ring destroyed by disposal unit

William H. Carpenter, 25 TCM 965 (1966)

Ring destroyed by closing of door

John P. White, 48 TC 430 (1967) (Acq.)

Diamond unexplainedly lost

Theodore R. Kielts, 42 TCM 238 (1981)

Sinking ship from failure of pump

William D. Shields, 54 TCM 711 (1987)

Fire loss, damage, destruction

IRC §165

Reg. §1.165-7

Judgment paid by tenant

Rev. Rul. 73-41, 1973-1 CB 74

Automobile

Tracy V. Buckwalter, 20 BTA 1005, aff'd, 61 F.2d 571 (6th Cir. 1932)

Furniture and home

E. C. O'Rear, 80 F.2d 473 (6th Cir. 1935)

W. B. Brooks, 12 BTA 31, aff'd, 35 F.2d 178 (4th Cir. 1929)

* Francis N. Leonard, TC Summary Opinion 2005-114

Hurricane

Alfred M. Hickman, 207 F.2d 460 (4th Cir. 1953)

Willard T. Burkett, 10 TCM 948 (1951)

Tornado

Richard E. Stein, 14 TCM 191 (1955)

Heavy rains

Clarence E. Stewart, 12 TCM 921 (1953)

Lightning

S. F. Horn, 18 TCM 177 (1959)

Floods

W. M. Ferguson, 59 F.2d 893 (10th Cir. 1933)

E. T. Hutchings, 41-2 USTC ¶9673 (D. Ky. 1941)

Storms

Webb, 1 BTA 759

Robert B. Honeyman, Jr., BTA Memo. P-H 39,021

Landslides

W. K. Stowers, 169 F. Supp. 246 (D. Mass. 1959)

Smog

Rev. Rul. 71-560, 1971-2 CB 126

Drought

Jack M. Short, 55 TCM 54 (1988) (deduction claimed too late)

Frank Buttram, 87 F. Supp. 322 (D. Okl. 1943)

Rev. Rul. 66-303, 1966-2 CB 55

Rev. Rul. 54-85 1954-1 CB 58

Norman H. Ruecker, 41 TCM 1587 (1981)

Dust storms

R. F. Barry, 175 F. Supp. 308 (D. Okl. 1959)

Poor construction

Irving J. Hayutin, 31 TCM 509 (1972), aff'd, 508 F.2d 462 (10th Cir. 1975)

Shipwreck

IRC §165(c)(3)

Edward H. R. Green, 19 BTA 904

Sinking of land

Harry Johnston Grant, 30 BTA 1028 (Acq.)

Tidal wave

M. A. Ferst, 129 F. Supp. 606 (D. Ga. 1955)

Rev. Rul. 76-134, 1976-1 CB 54

Disturbances below earth's surface

Harry Johnston Grant, 30 BTA 1028 (Acq.)

Ice pressure

Paul E. Jackson, 13 TCM 1175 (1954)

Seward City Mills, 44 BTA 173

Underground water

Delbert P. Hesler, 13 TCM 972 (1954)

Car falling through ice

Rev. Rul. 69-88, 1969-1 CB 58

Note: *Paragraph numbers refer to Parts 1 through 7. Items marked * are research aids, not citations of authority; see "Key to Citations" on page 801*

Ice damage

Sherman L. Whipple, 25 F.2d 520 (D. Mass. 1928)

Richard R. Hollington, 15 TCM 668 (1956)

Frederick H. Nash, 22 BTA 482 (Acq.)

Cave-ins

W. K. Stowers, 169 F. Supp. 246 (D. Miss. 1959)

Harry Johnston Grant, 30 BTA 1028 (Acq.)

Quarry blast

Ray Durden, 3 TC 1 (1944) (Acq.)

Severe winter blizzard

Emory M. Nourse, 73 F. Supp. 70 (D. Iowa 1947)

Vandals

Burrell E. Davis, 34 TC 586 (1960) (Acq.)

Rentals for temporary living quarters

Rev. Rul. 59-398, 1959-2 CB 76

Potential buyer's resistance

George W. Finkbohner Jr., 788 F.2d 723 (11th Cir. 1986)

Gerald Chamales, TC Memo 2000-33 (O.J. Simpson trial)

Michael N. Caan, 99-1 USTC ¶50,349 (C.D. Cal 1999) (O.J. Simpson trial)

Gordon Lund, 2000-1 USTC ¶50,234 (C.D. UT. 2000)

Harvey Pulvers, 48 TC 245 (1967), aff'd per curiam, 407 F.2d 838 (9th Cir. 1969)

Lewis F. Ford, 33 TCM 496 (1974)

Charles W. P. Kamanski, 29 TCM 1702 (1970), aff'd, 477 F.2d 452 (9th Cir. 1973)

Jointly owned property

J. H. Anderson, 7 TCM 811 (1948)

Life estate holder may deduct damage for wind storm

Katherine Bliss, 27 TC 770 (1957) (Acq.), rev'd, 256 F.2d 533 (2d Cir. 1958)

Latent effects not considered

Leonard J. Jenard, 20 TCM 346 (1961)

Decrease in value of land

Bessie Knapp, 23 TC 716 (1955) (Acq.)

Cost less depreciation

Edmund W. Cornelius, 56 TC 976 (1971) (Acq.)

Myron E. Cherry, 26 TCM 556 (1967)

Market value based on inventory

Loy L. Stone, 31 TCM 1042 (1972)

Damage to trees, shrubs, etc.

John M. Winters, Jr., 58-1 USTC ¶9205 (D. Okl. 1958), rev'd on other grounds, 261 F.2d 675 (10th Cir. 1959), cert. denied, 359 U.S. 943

Bessie Knapp, 23 TC 716 (1955) (Acq.)

Subsoil shrinkage during drought

Rev. Rul. 54-85, 1954-1 CB 58

Wreck caused by icy road

George L. Shearer, 16 F.2d 995 (2d Cir. 1927)

Collision caused by faulty driving

Reg. §1.165-7(a)(3)

Elwood J. Clark, 5 TCM 236 (1946), aff'd, 158 F.2d 851 (6th Cir. 1947)

Lawn damage caused by careless use of weed killer

Jack R. Farber, 57 TC 714 (1972) (Acq.)

Defending suit for damages

L. Oransky, 1 BTA 1239

Sonic boom

Rev. Rul. 60-329, 1960-2 CB 67

Property used by dependent

Thomas J. Draper, 15 TC 135 (1950)

Howard Scharf, 32 TCM 1281 (1973), rem'd per curiam, 535 F.2d 1250 (4th Cir. 1976)

High water levels

Rev. Rul. 75-134, 1975-1 CB 33

Preventative measures nondeductible

Cade L. Austin, 74 TC 1334 (1980)

Washing machine flood damage deduction

* Pamela S. Cooper, TC Summary Opinion 2003-168

18.2 When to Deduct a Casualty Loss

* IRS Publication 547

* "Tax Planning Guidelines for Casualty Loss Deductions," Edwin K. Cline and William B. Pollard, 78 Taxes 43 (April 2000)

Reimbursement expected

Reg. §1.165-1(d)

Arthur T. Davidson, 34 TCM 1010 (1975)

Year in which insurance company denies liability is not controlling

Louis Gale, 41 TC 269 (1963)

Flood loss deducted year claim settled

Earl Callan, 235 F.2d 190 (9th Cir. 1956)

Unseasonable blizzard

Emory M. Nourse, 73 F. Supp. 70 (D. Iowa 1947)

Hurricane damage

Willard T. Burkett, 10 TM 948 (1951)

Loss allowed in year of drought not later year of discovery

Alfred M. Cox, 24 TCM 23 (1965), aff'd per curiam, 354 F.2d 659 (3d Cir. 1966)

Swimming pool damages not deductible in later year

Donald H. Kunsman, 49 TC 62 (1967)

Subsequent recovery of insurance taxable

John E. Montgomery, 65 TC 511 (1975)

18.3 Disaster Losses

IRC §165(h)

Reg. §1.165-11

Early election may be revoked up to filing due date

Chester Matheson, 74 TC 834 (1980) (Acq. in results only)

Relocation or demolition of house

IRC §165(k)

Disaster relief funds used to buy mobile home not taxed

News Release SD-2004-13

IRS interest abatement

IRC §6404(h)

Sale of land after disaster

Rev. Rul. 96-32, 1996-25 IRB 5

Insurance reimbursements for unscheduled personal property are tax free

IRC §1033 (h)(1)(A)

Disaster relief not taxed

IRC §139

New law blocks tax on flood mitigation grants

Note: *Paragraph numbers refer to Parts 1 through 7. Items marked * are research aids, not citations of authority; see "Key to Citations" on page 801*

IRC §139(g), as added by the 2005 Disaster Mitigation Payments Act

18.4 Who May Deduct a Casualty Loss

Separate return

Robert M. Loewenstein, 27 TCM 1112 (1968)

Rev. Rul. 75-347, 1975-2 CB 70

No deduction for cost of repairing rented car

J. Gill, 34 TCM 10 (1975)

Corporate shareholder

Drew Jensen, 39 TCM 163 (1979)

18.5 Bank Deposit Losses

* "Deduction Choice for Uninsured Bank Deposit Loss," Bruce M. Bird and Gene Poindexter, 84 Taxation for Accountants 147 (March 1996)

Bad debt deduction

IRC §166

Foreign bank — no loss deduction

Joyce Aston, 109 TC 109 (1998)

IRC §166

Casualty and ordinary loss elections

IRC §165(1)

Clyde Fincher, 105 TC 11 (1995)

Election of ordinary loss or casualty loss

Notice 89-28, 1989-1 CB 667

18.6 Damage to Trees and Shrubs

Shrubbery

Reg. §1.165-7(b)(2)

Tree loss

David W. Murray, Jr., 20 TCM 7 (1962)

Dutch elm disease

Howard F. Burns, 285 F.2d 436 (6th Cir. 1961)

John Alan Appleman, 338 F.2d 729 (7th Cir. 1964), cert. denied, 380 U.S. 956

Arthur Coleman, 76 TC 580 (1981)

Lethal yellowing disease

John A. Maher, 76 TC 593 (1981), aff'd, 680 F.2d 91 (11th Cir. 1982)

Southern pine beetle

Paul W. Black, 36 TCM 1347 (1977)

Herbert Nelson, 27 TCM 158 (1968)

Rev. Rul. 79-174, 1979-1 CB 99

Cost of replacing trees

Rev. Rul. 68-29, 1968-1 CB 74

Cost of removing infested trees

Anthony B. Cristo, 44 TCM 1057 (1982)

Winter freeze in Florida

Ben R. Thebaut, Jr., 47 TCM 401 (1983)

Horse eats tree bark

Rev. Rul. 73-123, 1973-1 CB 76

Casualty losses for property

Reg. §1.165-7

18.7 Deducting Damage to Your Car

Damage to car deductible

Reg. §1.165-7(a)(3)

No deduction for litigation and settlement expenses

Alexandre R. Tarsey, 56 TC 44 (1971)

Using car on business

Forest Anderson, 81 F.2d 457 (10th Cir. 1936), rev'g 30 BTA 597

Accident between two locations of same business deductible as business expense

Harold Dancer, 73 TC 1103 (1980)

Accident occurring during trip between different jobs nondeductible as business expense

Julian D. Freedman, 35 TC 1179 (1961), aff'd, 301 F.2d 359 (5th Cir. 1962)

Accident costs while commuting nondeductible business expense

Eldon Hall, 41 TCM 282 (1981), aff'd in unpublished opinion (1st Cir. 1981)

Race car

* Letter Ruling 8227010

Deduction allowed only for uninsured losses

Emanuel Hollman, 38 TC 251 (1962)

Damage to engine—not deductible

Emil Wold, 22 TCM 732 (1963)

Lyle W. Mader, 25 TCM 917 (1966)

Towing costs are not deductible

Virginia M. Cramer, 55 TC 1125 (1971) (Acq.)

Car in child's name

Frank W. Oman, 30 TCM 767 (1971)

Failure to winterize car

Mohiuddin, TC Memo 1996-422

Damage to rented car

Robert M. Miller, 34 TCM 528 (1975)

18.8 Proving a Casualty Loss

* IRS Publication 547

Cleanup expenses

Ralph Walton, 20 TCM 653 (1961)

Appraisal upheld

Doyle E. Collup, 21 TCM 128 (1962)

Auto bluebook

Gus S. Caras, 23 TCM 1103 (1964)

Dealer's estimate of trade-in not evidence

Gus S. Caras, 23 TCM 1103 (1964)

Fire damage

John Pfalzgraf, 67 TC 784 (1977) (Acq.)

Inventories of property destroyed by fire sustained loss

Loy L. Stone, 31 TCM 1042 (1972)

18.9 Theft Losses

Reg. §1.165-8

State law determines if theft committed

Arthur C. Bromberg, Exr., 232 F.2d 107 (5th Cir. 1956)

Necessity of proving cost

Jane V. Elliott, 40 TC 304 (1963) (Acq.)

Stanley J. Prescott, 28 TCM 435 (1969)

Must prove property was stolen

Paul Bakewell, Jr., 23 TC 803 (1955)

Mary F. Allen, 16 TC 163 (1951)

John L. Seymour, 14 TC 1111 (1950)

Edna M. Oatis, 6 TCM 569 (1947)

Corporate misconduct doesn't support theft loss deduction

Notice 2004-27, 2004-16 IRB 782

* Ronald C. Singerman, TC Summary Opinion 2005-4

Theft losses allowed to victims of Madoff and other Ponzi schemes

Rev. Rul. 2009-9, 2009-14 IRB 735

Note: *Paragraph numbers refer to Parts 1 through 7. Items marked * are research aids, not citations of authority;* see *"Key to Citations" on page 801*

Rev. Rul. 2009-20, 2009-14 IRB 749 (optional safe harbor)

Theft of trees

Ella Gene Raberge, 20 TCM 1490 (1961)

Locked valuable pin in compartment

Warner L. Jones, 24 TC 525 (1955) (Acq.)

Report to police

James W. Thomas, 12 TCM 41 (1953)

Henrietta Sava-Goiu, 9 TCM 128 (1950)

Allowed even though not reported

Robert W. Jorg, 52 TC 288 (1969) (Acq.)

Frederick C. Moser, 18 TCM 116 (1959)

Year reported

Reg. §1.165-1(d)(3)

Reg. §1.165-8

Virginia M. Cramer, 55 TC 1125 (1971) (Acq.)

Deduction based on estimated recovery is premature

Aben E. Johnson, 2007-1 USTC ¶50,136 (Ct. Fed. Cl. 2006)

Cannot recover property

Henry Kraft Mercantile Co., 14 TCM 833 (1955)

Legal fee

Katherine Ander, 47 TC 592 (1967)

Appraisal value on stamp collection

Max P. Engel, 31 TCM 1223 (1972)

Building contractor absconded

Thomas Miller, 19 TC 1046 (1953) (Acq.)

Allen Hartley, 26 TCM 1281 (1977)

Contractor runs out of money

Otis B. Kent, 12 TCM 1491 (1953)

Additional money to correct defects

IRC §1016(a)(1)

Reg. §1.1016-2

Payments to subcontractor

Evelyn Nell Norton, 40 TC 500 (1963) (Acq.), aff'd, 333 F.2d 1005 (9th Cir. 1964)

Embezzlement losses

Mary O. Alsop, 34 TC 606 (1960), aff'd, 290 F.2d 726 (2d Cir. 1961)

Embezzlement not cause of bank depositor's loss

Rev. Rul. 77-383, 1977-2 CB 66

Worthless stock

Paul C. Vietzke, 37 TC 504 (1961) (Acq.)

Illegal sale of unregistered stock not a theft loss

Carroll J. Beilis, 61 TC 453 (1973), aff'd, 540 F.2d 448 (9th Cir. 1976)

Loss from tax avoidance scheme based on fraudulent statements of advisor

Perry A. Nichols et al., 43 TC 842 (1965) (Nonacq.)

Extortion and ransom payment

Rev. Rul. 72-112, 1972-1 CB 60

Expenses of recovering abducted child nondeductible

Ebrahim Otmishi, 41 TCM 237 (1980)

Fortune tellers

George John Kreiner, 60 TCM 1251 (1990)

Seizure of car by creditors

Robert V. Rafter, 489 F.2d 752 (2d Cir. 1974), cert. denied, 419 U.S. 826

Payment for forged divorce decree deductible

* Letter Ruling 8146030

Vandalism

Ann E. Lattimore, 353 F.2d 379 (9th Cir. 1966)

Charles Gutwirth, 40 TC 666 (1963) (Acq.)

Burrell E. Davis, 34 TC 586 (1960) (Acq.)

Riot damage

IRC §165(c)(3) and (e)

Perishable food discarded after civil disturbance

Rev. Rul. 69-354, 1969-1 CB 58

No deduction for confiscation by foreign government

William J. Powers, 36 TC 1191 (1961)

L.B.G. Farcasanu, 70-2 USTC ¶9753 (D.C. Cir. 1970)

H.W. Mongold, 43 TCM 117 (1981)

Swindled by friend

Nanette Holt Price, 94-1 USTC ¶50,160 (N.D. OK. 1994)

18.10 Proving a Theft Loss

* IRS Publication 547

Must prove property was stolen

Paul Bakewell, Jr., 23 TC 803 (1955)

Mary F. Allen, 16 TC 163 (1951)

John L. Seymour, 14 TC 1111 (1950)

Edna M. Oatis, 6 TCM 569 (1947)

Report to police

James W. Thomas, 12 TCM 41 (1953)

Henrietta Sava-Goiu, 9 TCM 128 (1950)

18.11 Nondeductible Losses

Termite damage

Umit Sahkul, 29 TCM 260 (170)

Rev. Rul. 63-232, 1963-2 CB 97

Carpet beetles

J. Peter Meersman, 370 F.2d 109 (6th Cir. 1967)

Dry rot

Rudolph Lewis Hoppe, 42 TC 820 (1964), aff'd, 354 F.2d 988 (9th Cir. 1966)

Worth Rowley, 38 TCM 1297 (1979), aff'd in unpublished opinion (D.C. Cir. 1981)

Personal injuries

Karl Stern, 199 F. Supp. 488 (D. Ohio 1954)

Legal expenses in defending suit

L. Oransky, 1 BTA 1239

Personal property wrongfully seized

Fred J. Hughes, 1 BTA 944

Temporary quarters

Rev. Rul. 59-398, 1959-2 CB 76

Personal property lost in storage or transit

W. W. Bercaw, 6 TCM 27 (1947), aff'd, 165 F.2d 521 (4th Cir. 1948)

Passenger's luggage lost

Mildred Bauman, 10 TCM 31 (1951)

Accidental loss of ring

Edgar F. Stevens, 6 TCM 805 (1947)

Joint property taken by wife

Grover Tyler, 13 TC 186 (1949) (Acq.)

Loss of dog

Waddell F. Smith, 10 TC 701 (1948)

Note: *Paragraph numbers refer to Parts 1 through 7. Items marked * are research aids, not citations of authority;* see *"Key to Citations" on page 801*

Damage to crop by insects

Rev. Rul. 57-599, 1957-2 CB 142

Excavation on adjoining property

Daniel F. Ebbert, 9 BTA 1402

Rust of understructure of house

Hugh M. Matheson Exr., 54 F.2d 537 (2d Cir. 1931), aff'g 18 BTA 674

Moth damage

Rev. Rul. 55-327, 1955-1 CB 25

Dry well

James I. Goski, 24 TCM 828 (1965)

Charles E. Springer, 16 TCM 1075 (1957)

Natural phenomena

Texas & Pacific Railway Co., 1 TCM 863 (1943)

Damage to library book

Luther Ely Smith, 3 TC 695 (1944) (Acq. in part, nonacq. in part)

Damage to watch

Williard Thompson, 15 TC 609 (1950), rev'd and rem'd on other grounds, 193 F.2d 586 (10th Cir. 1952)

Jack Ward, 11 TCM 340 (1952)

Drop in value of securities

Reg. §1.165-1(d)

Adams, 1 BTA 985

Chicago Railway Equipment Co., 4 BTA 452 (Acq.), aff'd and rev'd in part, 39 F.2d 378 (7th Cir. 1930), rev'd, 282 U.S. 295 (1931)

E. O. Walgren, 4 BTA 1066

W. P. Davis, 6 BTA 1267

Loss due to illness

Jones, BTA Memo. P-H 42,324

Loss of contingent interest

Lillian S. Procter, 19 TC 387 (1952)

Chinaware upset by pet

Robert M. Diggs, 18 TCM 443 (1959), aff'd, 281 F.2d 326 (2d Cir. 1960), cert. denied, 364 U.S. 908

J. Raymond Dyer, 35 TCM 456 (1961) (Acq.)

Temporary fluctuation

Clarence A. Peterson, 30 TC 660 (1958)

Fire deliberately set by owner

Biltmore Blackman, 88 TC 677 (1987)

18.12 Floors for Personal-Use Property Losses

$500 or $100 floor

IRC §165(h)(1)

Reg. §1.165-7(b)(4)

10% AGI floor

IRC §165(h)(2)

Federally declared losses in 2008/2009 exempt from 10% floor

IRC 165(h)(3)

Midwestern and Kansas disaster losses exempt from $100/10% floors

IRC 1400S(b)(1), applied to Midwestern disaster area by Act Sections 702(a)(1)(F) and 702(d)(13) of the Emergency Economic Stabilization Act of 2008

IRC 1400S(b)(1), applied to Kansas disaster area by Act Sections 15345(a)(9) and 15345(c)(7) of the Heartland, Habitat, Harvest, and Horticulture Act of 2008

18.13 Figuring Your Loss on Form 4684

IRC §165

Reg. §1.165-7

* "Casualty and Theft Losses Can Provide Significant Tax Deductions," Edward E. Milam and Donald H. Jones, Jr., 80 Taxes 45 (October 2002)

$500 or $100 floor

IRC §165(h)(1)

Reg. §1.165-7(b)(4)

10% adjusted gross income limit

Reg. §165(h)

Cost less depreciation method

E.W. Cornelius, 56 TC 976 (Acq. 1977-2 CBI)

Proof of cost

Donald Owens, 305 U.S. 468

Hal Millsap, Jr., 46 TC 751 (1966) (Acq.), aff'd 387 F.2d 420 (8th Cir. 1968)

Jay Beams, 67 TCM 3152 (1994)

Vitale, TC Memo 1999-272

Separate computation for each item

Rev. Rul. 66-50, 1966-1 CB 40

Community property damaged before divorce settlement

Armore L. Kamins, 54 TC 977 (1970)

Loss of records in fire no bar

John Pfalzgraf, Jr., 67 TC 784 (1977) (Acq.)

Appraisals for disaster relief

IRC §165(i)(4)

18.14 Personal and Business Use of Property

IRC §165

Reg. §1.165-7(b)(4)(iv)

* IRS Publication 547

18.15 Repairs May Be a "Measure of Loss"

Cost of repairs

Reg. §1.165-7(a)(2)(ii)

S. P. Keith, Jr., 52 TC 41 (1969) (Acq.)

Estimated repairs not measure of loss

Claire E. Lamphere, 70 TC 391 (1978) (Acq.)

Venancio A. Bagnol, 37 TCM 1038 (1978)

Repairs, though not made, may affect post-casualty value

Paul Abrams, 41 TCM 1459 (1981)

Loss of value exceeds repair costs

George E. Conner, 439 F.2d 974 (5th Cir. 1971)

Anne Marie Hagerty, 34 TCM 356 (1975)

18.16 Insurance Reimbursements

Reimbursements reduce loss

IRC §165(a)

Reg. §1.165-1(c)(4)

Voluntary payments from employer

Rev. Rul. 55-131 1953-2 CB 112, distinguished by Rev. Rul. 57-1, 1957-1 CB 15 and Rev. Rul. 64-329, 1964-2 CB 463

Disaster relief

Rev. Rul. 76-144, 1976-1 CB 17

Red Cross

Special Ruling, 5-11-52

Relocation Act payments

Paul J. Smith, 76 TC 459 (1981) (Acq.)

Adjuster's fee

Ben R. Stein, 31 TCM 663 (1971), aff'd

Note: *Paragraph numbers refer to Parts 1 through 7. Items marked* are research aids, not citations of authority;* see *"Key to Citations" on page 801*

and remanded in unpublished opinion (7th Cir. March 4, 1974)

Gifts from friends do not reduce loss

Rev. Rul. 64-329, 1964-2 CB 58

Insurance claim must be filed

IRC §165(h)(4)(E)

18.17 Excess Living Costs Paid by Insurance Are Not Taxable

IRC §123

Reg. §1.123-1

Taxable income determined at end of dislocation period

Rev. Rul. 93-43, 1993-2 CB 69

18.18 Do Your Casualty or Theft Losses Exceed Your Income?

Carryback of losses

IRC §172

Reg. §1.172-1

Reg. §1.172-3(b)

18.19 Defer Gain by Replacing Property

IRC §1033

* IRS Publication 547

Gain on business disaster grants

Rev. Rul. 2005-46, 2005-30 IRB 120

18.20 Involuntary Conversions Qualifying for Tax Deferral

What is an involuntary conversion?

IRC §1033

Reg. §1.1033(a)-1

* IRS Publication 544

* IRS Publication 547

Deferral on preemptive sale of property in urban redevelopment area

* Letter Ruling 200145001

Threat of condemnation by government employee

Frank O. Maixner, 33 TC 191 (1959) (Acq.)

Carson Estate Co., 22 TCM 425 (1963)

Sale under hazard mitigation program

IRC §1033 (k)

Voluntary sale

Harry G. Masser, 30 TC 741 (1958) (Acq.)

Rev. Rul. 59-361, 1959-2 CB 183

Rev. Rul. 63-221, 1963-2 CB 332

Chemical contamination of home

*Chief Counsel Information Letter 2005-0013

Condemnation as unfit for habitation

Rev. Rul. 57-314, 1957-2 CB 523

Threat of building code violation not sufficient

Thorpe Glass Mfg. Corp., 51 TC 300 (1968)

Deferral relief for salvaged trees

Willamette Industries Inc., 118 TC 126 (2002)

Farmers—irrigation project

Reg. §1.1033(d)-1

Cattle diseased

IRC §1033(d)

Reg. §1.1033(e)-1

Livestock sales due to drought

IRC §1033(e)

Reg. §1.1033(f)-1

Sale to private party after governmental threat of conversion

Creative Solutions, Inc., 320 F.2d 809 (5th Cir. 1963)

Identity of threatening authority not disclosed

Rev. Rul. 74-8, 1974-2 CB 200

Tax sale

Rev. Rul. 77-370, 1977-2 CB 306

Gain on involuntary conversion

IRC §1033

Reg. §1.1033(a)-1 and 2

Russel C. Smith, 59 TC 107 (1972)

Pesticide crop damage

* Letter Ruling 9615041

House destroyed by a tornado

Rev. Rul. 96-32, 1996-1 CB 177

Contested award

Conlorez Corp., 51 TC 467 (1968) (Acq.)

Harry D. Aldridge, 51 TC 475 (1968)

Casalina Co., 60 TC 694 (1973) (Acq.), aff'd per curiam, 511 F.2d 1162 (4th Cir. 1975)

18.21 How To Elect To Defer Tax

* IRS Publications 544 and 547

Dissolution of partnership not termination

Morton Fuchs, 80 TC 506 (1983)

18.22 Time Period for Buying Replacement Property

Five-year replacement period for property in Kansas or Midwestern disaster area

Section 405 of KETRA 2005 applied to Midwestern disaster area by Act Sections 702(a)(2) and 702(e)(5) of the Emergency Economic Stabilization Act of 2008

Section 405 of KETRA 2005 applied to Kansas disaster area by Act Sections 15345(a)(10) and 15345(d)(8) of the Heartland, Habitat, Harvest, and Horticulture Act of 2008

Five-year replacement period for property in Hurricane Katrina disaster area

Section 405 of KETRA 2005

Five-year replacement period for New York Liberty Zone property

IRC §1400 L (g), as added by JCWAA 2002

Three-year replacement for condemned realty

IRC §1033(g)(4)

Four-year replacement period for principal residence involuntarily converted by disaster

IRC §1033 (h)(1)(B)

Election irrevocable

John McShain, 65 TC 686 (1976)

No substitution of replacement property

Rev. Rul. 83-39, 1983-1 CB 190

Environmental Protection Agency order

Rev. Rul. 89-2, 1989-1 CB 259

Advance payment of award starts replacement period

Stewart & Co., 57 TC 122 (1971)

Estate makes replacement

John E. Morris Est., 55 TC 636 (1971), aff'd per curiam, 454 F.2d 208 (4th Cir. 1972)

Isaac Goodman Est., 199 F.2d 895 (3d Cir. 1952)

Rev. Rul. 64-161, 1964-1 (Pt. 1) CB 298

Note: *Paragraph numbers refer to Parts 1 through 7. Items marked * are research aids, not citations of authority; see "Key to Citations" on page 801*

Investment by widow

George W. Jayne Est., 61 TC 744 (1974)

Must report details of replacement

Reg. §1.1033(a)-2(c)(2)

File for refund

Reg. §1.1033(a)-2(c)(2)

18.23 Types of Qualifying Replacement Property

Like-kind test

IRC §1033(g)

Reg. §1.1031(a)-1(b)

Related use

Liant Record Inc., 303 F.2d 326 (2d Cir. 1963), on rem'd, 22 TCM 203 (1963)

Clifton Investment Co., 312 F.2d 719 (6th Cir. 1963), cert. denied, 373 U.S. 921

Loco Realty Co., 306 F.2d 207 (8th Cir. 1962)

Thomas McCaffrey Jr., 275 F.2d 27 (2d Cir. 1960), cert. denied

Arnold L. Santucci, 32 TCM 840 (1973)

Rev. Rul. 64-237, 1964-2 CB 319

Replacement of rental house by residence does not qualify

Rev. Rul. 76-84, 1976-1 CB 219

Contract to buy does not qualify

Herrick L. Johnston Est., 51 TC 290 (1968), aff'd, 430 F.2d 1019 (6th Cir. 1970)

Purchase of leasehold of at least 30 years

Rev. Rul. 68-392, 1968-2 CB 338

Improvements to retained land

Rev. Rul. 67-255, 1967-2 CB 270

Rev. Rul. 67-255, 1967-2 CB 270

* Letter Ruling 9117030

* Letter Ruling 9118007

A.S. Davis, 589 F.2d 446 (9th Cir. 1979)

Business or investment property damaged in disaster area

IRC §1033(h)(2)

18.24 Cost of Replacement Property Determines Postponed Gain

Replacement

IRC §1033(a)(2)

Reg. §1.1033(a)-2(b) and (c)

Rev. Rul. 70-466, 1970-2 CB 165, amplified by Rev. Rul. 76-84, 1976-1 CB 219

John E. Morris Est., 55 TC 636 (1971), aff'd per curiam, 454 F.2d 208 (4th Cir. 1972)

Replacement of livestock—environmental contamination

IRC §1033(f)

Buying a replacement from a relative

IRC §1033(i)

Payments to mortgagee

Reg. §1.1033(a)-2(c)(1)

Frank W. Babcock, 28 TC 781 (1957) (Nonacq.), aff'd, 259 F.2d 689 (9th Cir. 1958)

Fortee Properties, Inc., 211 F.2d 915 (2d Cir. 1954), cert. denied, 348 U.S. 826

Interest paid on condemnation award taxable

Dominick DeNaples, TC Memo 2010-171

Real property condemned

IRC §1033(g)

Insurance proceeds allocated

Rev. Rul. 70-501, 1970-2 CB 163

18.25 Special Assessments and Severance Damages

Special assessment

Rev. Rul. 68-37, 1967-1 CB 359

Allocation to purchase of nonadjacent property

Rev. Rul. 72-433, 1972-2 CB 470

John L. McKitrick, 373 F. Supp. 471 (D. Ohio 1974)

Severance damage gain deferred by like-kind investment

Rev. Rul. 83-49 1983-1 CB 191

IRS computation method

* IRS Publication 549

Must allocate or entire award is payment for condemnation

Seaside Improvement Co., 105 F.2d 990 (2d Cir. 1938), cert. denied, 308 U.S. 618

Marshall C. Allaben, 35 BTA 327

Allocation allowed although not fixed in award

L. A. Beeghly, 36 TC 111 (1961) (Acq. in result only)

Rev. Rul. 64-183, 1964-1 (Pt. 1) CB 297

18.26 Reporting Gains From Casualties

Casualty gains exceed casualty losses

IRC §165(h)(2)(B)

Involuntary conversion netting

IRC §1231(a)(3)(A)

IRC §1231(a)(4)(C)

19 Deducting Job Costs and Other Miscellaneous Expenses

19.1 2% AGI Floor Reduces Most Miscellaneous Expenses

IRC §67(a)

Temp. Reg. §1.67-1T

IRC §62(a)(2)(A)

* IRS Publication 529

19.2 Effect of 2% AGI Floor on Deductions

IRC §67

19.3 Checklist of Job Expenses Subject to the 2% AGI Floor

IRC §67

* IRS Publication 529

Adjunct professor subject to 2% floor

* George Beitel, TC Summary Opinion 2001-101

19.4 Job Expenses Not Subject to the 2% AGI Floor

* IRS Publication 529

Impairment-related work expense

IRC §67(d)

Performing artists

IRC §62(a)(2)(B)

IRC §62(b)

Educator expenses

IRC §62(a)(2)(D)

IRC §62(d)

Note: *Paragraph numbers refer to Parts 1 through 7. Items marked* * *are research aids, not citations of authority; see "Key to Citations" on page 801*

19.5 Dues and Subscriptions

Professional society

Henry P. Keith, 1 TCM 184 (1942), aff'd, 139 F.2d 596 (2d Cir. 1944)

Kenneth Blanchard, 12 TCM 550 (1953)

Trade association

Robert S. LeSage, 6 TCM 1263 (1947), aff'd in part and rev'd in part on other issues, 173 F.2d 826 (5th Cir. 1949)

Stock exchange

Charles E. Robertson, 1 BTA 501 (Acq.)

Community "booster" club

Security-First National Bank of Los Angeles, BTA Memo., February 27, 1934

Chamber of Commerce

Smith-Bridgman & Co., 16 TC 287 (1951) (Acq.)

Jeff Rubin, 13 TCM 1094 (1954)

Union membership

George A. Tatum, Jr., 10 TCM 602 (1951)

Rev. Rul. 54-190, 1954-1 CB 46

Union assessments for old-age fund

Rev. Rul. 54-190, 1954-1 CB 46

Service charge to non-union members

Rev. Rul. 68-82, 1968-1 CB 68

Union dues

Rev. Rul. 72-463, 1972-2 CB 93

Union building fund nondeductible

Carl Briggs, 75 TC 465 (1980), aff'd, 694 F.2d 614 (9th Cir. 1983)

Kenneth M. Ridder, 76 TC 867 (1981)

Union election costs

James P. Carey, 56 TC 477 (1971) (Acq.), aff'd per curiam, 460 F.2d 1259 (4th Cir. 1972), cert. denied, 409 U.S. 990

19.6 Uniforms and Work Clothes

Protective clothing

Oron R. Morgan, 80 F. Supp. 537 (D. Tex. 1948)

Louis M. Roth, 17 TC 1450 (1952) (Acq.)

Lewis F. Cooper, 12 TCM 471 (1953)

T. G. Frazier, Jr., 12 TCM 1129 (1953)

Overalls

Louis M. Roth, 17 TC 1450 (1952) (Acq.)

O. G. Russell, 12 TCM 1276 (1953)

Harder use than customary garments

Louis Drill, 8 TC 902 (1947)

Soiled after day's work

Louis M. Roth, 17 TC 1450 (1952) (Acq.)

Plumber

Vern W. Pratt, 11 TCM 335 (1952)

Sanitation inspector

C. W. Strickler, 11 TCM 252 (1952)

Machinist's helper

Carl E. Noe, 11 TCM 431 (1952)

Carpenter

E. M. Taylor, 11 TCM 651 (1952)

Roy J. Coffman, 16 TCM 353 (1957)

Telephone repairman

John Young, 11 TCM 239 (1952)

Allowance is taxable

Rev. Rul. 72-110, 1972-1 CB 24

Fashion expert's clothing deductible

Betsy L. Yeomans, 30 TC 757 (1958) (Acq.)

Boutique manager's clothes nondeductible

Barry Pevsner, 38 TCM 121 (1979), rev'd, 628 F.2d 467 (5th Cir. 1980)

Airline pilots' uniforms

Dean L. Phillips, 9 TCM 51 (1950)

Nurse

Helen K. Harsaghy, 2 TC 484 (1943) (Acq.)

State highway patrol officer

Marcus O. Benson, 146 F.2d 191 (9th Cir. 1945)

Bakery salesman

Bennie Blatt, 6 TCM 94 (1947)

Marshall J. Hammons, 12 TCM 1318 (1953)

Cement finisher

Williard Thompson, 15 TC 609 (1950) (Acq. in part, nonacq. in part), rev'd and rem'd on other grounds, 193 F.2d 586 (10th Cir. 1952)

Commercial fisherman

Rev. Rul. 55-235, 1955-1 CB 274

Dairy worker

Ben A. Puente, 10 TCM 735 (1951), aff'd without discussion, 199 F.2d 940 (9th Cir. 1952)

Factory foreman's white coat and safety shoes

Oron R. Morgan, 80 F. Supp. 537 (D. Tex. 1948)

Hospital attendant

Oliver W. Bryant, 11 TCM 430 (1952)

Musician's formal wear

Wilson J. Fisher, 23 TC 218 (1954) (Acq. in part), aff'd on other issue, 230 F.2d 79 (7th Cir. 1956)

Paint machine operator

T. G. Frazier, Jr., 12 TCM 1129 (1953)

Plumber's special shoes and gloves

Lewis F. Cooper, 12 TCM 471 (1953)

Railroad firefighter

O. G. Russell, 11 TCM 334 (1952)

O. G. Russell, 12 TCM 1276 (1953)

Painter

Rev. Rul. 57-143, 1957-1 CB 89

Tennis clothing nondeductible

Cecil Mella, 52 TCM 1216 (1986)

Women's slacks

Oron R. Morgan, 80 F. Supp. 537 (D. Tex. 1948)

Dirty clothes a hazard

Elwood J. Clark, 158 F.2d 851 (6th Cir. 1947), aff'g per curiam 5 TCM 236 (1946)

Clothes worn at work only

Oliver W. Bryant, 11 TCM 430 (1952)

19.7 Expenses of Looking for a New Job

Job search while temporarily unemployed

Rev. Rul. 75-120, 1975-1 CB 55, clarified by Rev. Rul. 77-16, 1977-1 CB 37

Personal trips not deductible as "job hunting" excursions

* Mark W. Franklin, TC Summary Opinion 2004-126

Driving costs of unemployed secretary

Note: *Paragraph numbers refer to Parts 1 through 7. Items marked * are research aids, not citations of authority; see "Key to Citations" on page 801*

Herman Campana, 60 TCM 289 (1990)

CPA forms partnership

Howard L. Cormutt, 45 TCM 515 (1983)

Remained at same position

Kenneth R. Kenfield, 54 TC 1197 (1970)

Reimbursement of fees

Rev. Rul. 66-41, 1966-1 CB 233, distinguished by Rev. Rul. 73-351, 1973-2 CB 323

Payment of fee by employer

Rev. Rul. 73-351, 1973-2 CB 323

Company interested in your services

Rev. Rul. 63-77, 1963-1 CB 177

Former customers entertained

Harold Haft, 40 TC 2 (1963) (Acq.)

19.8 Local Transportation Costs

* IRS Publication 463

Rural letter carriers

IRC §162(o)(2)

Commuting to temporary location deductible

Rev. Rul. 99-7, 1999-5 IRB 4

19.9 Unusual Job Expenses

Shoeshine costs

Robert C. Fryer, 33 TCM 122 (1974)

Lobbying

James M. Jordan, 60 TC 770 (1973) (Acq.)

Depreciation on furnishings

LeRoy Gillis, 32 TCM 429 (1973)

Cost of meal assessments

Robert E. Cooper, 67 TC 870 (1977) (Nonacq.)

Salesman's private plane

William F. Sherman, Jr., 44 TCM 1324 (1982)

Executive's purchase of blazers

Norman L. Jetty, 44 TCM 373 (1982)

Repayment of lay-off benefits

Rev. Rul. 82-178, 1982-2 CB 59

Job dismissal insurance

* Letter Ruling 8321074

Public officials

Rev. Rul. 84-110, 1984-2 CB 35

Musician's depreciation deduction

Richard L. Simon, 103 TC 15 (1994) (violin bow)

Brian P. Liddle, 103 TC 16 (1994) (Ruggeri bass viol)

Exotic dancer

Cynthia Hess, TC Memo 1994-79

19.10 Computers Bought for Work

IRC §280F(d)

* "Tax Consequences of Employer-Provided Computers," John C. Zimmerman, 78 Taxes 43 (October 2000)

Cell phones no longer listed property

IRC §280F(d)(4), as amended by Small Business Jobs Act of 2010, P.L. 111-240, 9/27/10

Convenience of employer and condition of employment tests

IRC §280F(d)(3)

Writing off cost of computer

IRC §280F(b)

IRC §280F(d)(4)

Employee deductions barred

Robert L. Bryant, 66 TCM 1594 (1993), aff'd by unreported 3d Circuit decision (September 15, 1994)

Rev. Rul. 86-129, 1986-2 CB 48 (aerospace engineer)

* Letter Ruling 8710009 (insurance agent)

* Letter Ruling 8615024 (nursing professor)

* Letter Ruling 8615071 (engineers)

Husband and wife allowed deduction

Thomas Cadwallader, 57 TCM 1030 (1989)

Telemarketing sales manager allowed deduction

Sherri Mulne, 72 TCM 111 (1996)

19.11 Calculators, Copiers, Fax Machines, and Typewriters

IRC §280F(b)

IRC §280F(d)(4)

Temp. Reg. §1.280F-6T(b)

Hand-held calculator deductible

Robert G. Galazin, 38 TCM 851 (1979)

19.12 Small Tools

Substantiation of tool costs

Donald F. McGraw, 35 TCM 1016 (1976)

Ion Z. Josan, 33 TCM 645 (1974)

Harlan White, 33 TCM 652 (1974)

Reimbursements

Rev. Rul. 75-497, 1975-2 CB 29

19.13 Employee Home Office Deductions

IRC §280A

* IRS Publication 587

* "Home Office Deduction for Employees: Interaction of the Principal Place of Business Test and the Convenience of the Employer Test," Ronald E. Flinn, 81 Taxes 35 (August 2003)

Administrative office deductions allowed

IRC §280A(c)(1), overturning result of Supreme Court's Soliman decision

Supreme Court sets principal place of business tests in Soliman case

Nader Soliman, 113 S. Ct. 701 (1993)

Rev. Rul. 94-24, 1994-1 CB 87 (IRS examples applying Soliman tests)

Notice 93-12, 1993-1 CB 298 (IRS response to Supreme Court's Soliman decision)

Violinist's home studio

Katia V. Popov, 2001-1 USTC ¶50,353 (9th Cir. 2001) (deduction allowed under Soliman)

Ernest Drucker, 715 F.2d (2d Cir. 1983), rev'g 79 TC 605 (1982) (no deduction under pre-Soliman tests)

Professor's home office

David J. Weissman, 751 F.2d 512 (2d Cir. 1985)

Anesthetist employed by hospital

Byron K. Anderson, 44 TCM 1305 (1982)

Phone calls as dealing with clients

John W. Green, 78 TC 428 (1982), rev'd, 707 F.2d 404 (9th Cir. 1983)

Max Frankel, 82 TC 318 (1984)

Teachers not allowed to deduct home office

Note: *Paragraph numbers refer to Parts 1 through 7. Items marked * are research aids, not citations of authority;* see *"Key to Citations" on page 801*

costs

* Letter Ruling 7734023

Professors with sideline writing/consulting business not allowed deduction

* Letter Rulings 8030024, 8030025

Separate structure appurtenant to house

Charles A. Scott, 84 TC 683 (1985)

No deduction for renting space to employer

IRC §280A(c)(6)

19.14 Telephone Costs

No deduction for main phone line

IRC §262(b)

Telephone calls and telegrams for business

Reg. §1.162-6

Leo R. Marshall, 8 TCM 508 (1949)

Installation of home phone for business

Charles J. Voigt, 8 TCM 662 (1949)

Robert A. Phillips, 8 TCM 587 (1949)

C. W. Strickler, 11 TCM 252 (1952)

O. G. Russell, 11 TCM 334 (1952)

Robert H. Lee, 19 TCM 317 (1960)

Taxpayer deducted all toll charges

Paul E. Jackson, 14 TCM 1175 (1955)

Businessman confined to home

Dan R. Hanna, Jr., 10 TCM 566 (1951)

Deduction allowed for telephone but not for home office

Charles E. Shepherd, 35 TCM 219 (1976), aff'd in unpublished opinion (7th Cir. April 22, 1977)

Allocation of business phone

Robert G. Galazin, 38 TCM 851 (1979)

19.15 Checklist of Deductible Investment Expenses

IRC §212

Reg. §1.212-1(b)

2% floor

IRC §67(a)

Fees to bank in dividend reinvestment plan

Rev. Rul. 75-548, 1975-2 CB 331

Expense of collecting tax-exempt income nondeductible

IRC §265(a)(1)

Reg. §1.265-1

Safe-deposit box for securities

Albina E. Bodell, 1 TCM 395 (1943)

W. N. Fry, 5 TC 1058 (1945)

Daniel S. W. Kelly, 23 TC 682 (1955) (Acq.), aff'd on other issue, 228 F.2d 512 (7th Cir. 1956)

Home safe

* Letter Ruling 8218077

Traveling to check investments deductible

E. M. Godson, 5 TCM 648 (1946)

Martha E. Henderson, 27 TCM 109 (1968)

Investor may not deduct travel to business sites

William R. Kinney, 66 TC 122 (1976)

Proxy fight expenses

R. Walter Graham, 326 F.2d 878 (4th Cir. 1964)

J. Raymond Dyer, 23 TCM 1208 (1964), aff'd, 352 F.2d 948 (8th Cir. 1965)

Rev. Rul. 64-236, 1964-2 CB 64

Trip to broker not deductible

Stanley S. Walters, 28 TCM 22 (1969)

Trip to investigate prospective investments not deductible

Doran S. Weinstein, 420 F.2d 700 (Ct. Cl. 1970)

Mutual-fund fees

Rev. Rul. 55-23, 1955-1 CB 275

Business advice to produce income

Reg. §1.212-1(g)

Andrew Jergens, 2 TCM 385 (1943)

Edward E. Bishop, 4 TC 862 (1945) (Acq.)

Amelia E. Collins, 3 TCM 223 (1944)

Elma M. Williams, 3 TC 200 (1944) (Acq.)

Raymond Fitzgerald, 15 TCM 1450 (1956)

Building improvements on replacement property

* Letter Ruling 9421001

Expenses of fiduciary

Reg. §1.212-1(j)

Incompetency fees

Elsie Weil Est., 13 TCM 653 (1954)

Reduce income-producing ability

Ann F. Day, 57-1 USTC ¶9270 (D. Ariz. 1957)

Gertrude Lytton-Smith, 57-1 USTC ¶9271 (D. Ariz. 1957)

Robert S. Howard, 32 TC 1284 (1959) (Acq.)

Capital expenditures

IRC §263

Reg. §1.263(a)-1 and 2

Reg. §1.212-1(n)

No deduction for investor while on trip for company

J. D. O'Connor, 13 TCM 623 (1959)

Director's deduction for investment club convention

Walter Gustin, 46 TCM 1505 (1983)

Deduction barred for general investment seminar

IRC §274(h)(7)

Trip to investigate rental property not deductible

Patrick L. O'Donnell, 62 TC 781 (1974), aff'd in unpublished decision (7th Cir. 1975)

Travel cost to stockholders' meetings nondeductible

Rev. Rul. 56-511, 1956-2 CB 170

Trip to present stockholder resolution deductible

* Letter Ruling 8220084

Office of investor

Joseph J. Imhoff, 29 TCM 966 (1970)

No deduction for investor's home office expenses

IRC §280A

Joseph Moller, 721 F.2d 810 (Fed. Cir. 1983)

19.16 Costs of Tax Return Preparation and Audits

IRC §212(3)

Reg. §1.212-1(1)

2% floor

IRC §67(a)

Fees allocable to Schedule C, E, or F

Rev. Rul. 92-29, 1992-1 CB 20

David Burleson, 68 TCM 288 (1994) ($55 fee allowed on Schedule C despite non-business income)

Mileage costs for trips to IRS audit

Note: *Paragraph numbers refer to Parts 1 through 7. Items marked * are research aids, not citations of authority;* see *"Key to Citations" on page 801*

deductible

Dieter Stussy, TC Memo 2003-232

Foreign tax

Philip T. Sharples, 533 F.2d 550 (Ct. Cl. 1976)

Legal fees deductible although underlying transaction is capital

Philip T. Sharples, 533 F.2d 550 (Ct. Cl. 1976)

Tax advice on real estate deal

James A. Collins, 54 TC 1656 (1970) (Acq.)

Tax deficiency imposed on business income

Clarence Wood, 37 TC 70 (1961) (Acq.)

Clyde E. Thomas, Sr., 41 TC 614 (1964)

Interest on business-related deficiency

James Redlark, 106 TC 2 (1996)

Criminal tax fraud charge

Michael Shapiro, 278 F.2d 556 (7th Cir. 1960)

Tax advice on future deals

Basil L. Kaufman, 227 F. Supp. 807 (D. Mo. 1964)

Tax books deductible

Donald W. Fausner, 30 TCM 1170 (1971), aff'd on other issue, 413 U.S. 838 (1973)

Legal fees for tax advice and tax return preparation

IRC §212(3)

Reg. §1.212-1(1)

Personal checking account fees nondeductible

Florence E. Callander, 75 TC 334 (1980)

NOW account fees nondeductible

Rev. Rul. 82-59, 1982-1 CB 47

Money-market account fee

* Letter Ruling 8345067

Credit card fee for tax payment

* Chief Counsel Memorandum POSTN-151134-08 (1/5/09)

Mandatory employer provided tax-preparation services

* IRS Field Service Advice 200137039

19.17 Deducting Legal Costs

IRC §162

IRC §212

Reg. §1.212-1(1)

* "Contingent Attorney's Fees Paid from Award: Deduction vs. Exclusion," L. Stephen Cash, Thomas Dickens, and Virginia Ward Vaughn, 69 Tax Strategies 222 (October 2002)

* "Circuits Disagree About Proper Treatment of Attorneys' Fees," Leonard G. Weld and Charles E. Price, 80 Taxes 23 (September 2002)

Suspension of license arose from personal activity

Kenneth A. Cameron, 79-2 USTC ¶9477 (9th Cir. 1979)

Employment-related legal costs

Walter F. Tellier, 383 U.S. 687 (1966)

Don Gilmore, 372 U.S. 39 (1963)

Stanley Waldheim, 25 TC 839 (1956) (Acq.), aff'd on other issue, 244 F.2d 1 (7th Cir. 1957)

M. S. Kaufman, 12 TC 1114 (1949) (Acq.)

Jean Nidetch, 37 TCM 1307 (1978)

Steve Sikey, 37 TCM 548 (1978)

Milton Margoles, 27 TCM 319 (1968)

Rev. Rul. 64-277, 1964-2 CB 55

Libel suits

James E. Threlkeld, 87 TC 1294 (1986), aff'd, 848 F.2d 81 (6th Cir. 1988)

Paul F. Roemer, Jr., 716 F.2d 693 (9th Cir. 1983), rev'g 79 TC 398

J. Raymond Dyer, 36 TC 456 (1961) (Acq.)

Paul Draper, 26 TC 201 (1956) (Acq.)

Rev. Rul. 58-418, 1958-2 CB 18, distinguished by Rev. Rul. 75-230, 1975-1 CB 93

Allocation of fees where compensatory and punitive damages received

Rev. Rul. 85-98, 1985-2 CB 51

Libel suit of public official

* Letter Ruling 8018077

Will contest

Reg. §1.212-1(k)

Charles E. Parker, 573 F.2d 42 (Ct. Cl. 1978)

Wrongful death actions

Lawrence E. DeWeese, 276 F. Supp. 901 (D. Ore. 1967)

Injury during a business trip remains personal

Thomas Stricker, 70 TCM 1192 (1995)

Title issues or disputes

Reg. §1.212-1(k)

Fred W. Woodward, 397 U.S. 572 (1970)

Hilton Hotels Corp., 397 U.S. 580 (1970)

Walter W. Cruttenden, 70 TC 191 (1978), aff'd, 644 F.2d 1368 (9th Cir. 1981) (deduction allowed)

Allocation of legal fees where dispute involves title and income

Reg. §1.212-1(k)

Daniel S. W. Kelly, 228 F.2d 512 (7th Cir. 1956), aff'g 23 TC 682 (1955) (Acq.)

Andrew J. Stormfeltz, 142 F.2d 982 (8th Cir. 1944)

Birdie Kimbrell, 80 F. Supp. 695 (D. Ill. 1948)

Joseph P. Morgan Est., 37 TC 31 (1961) (Acq.), aff'd in part, rev'd in part, 332 F.2d 144 (6th Cir. 1964)

E. W. Brown, Jr., 19 TC 87 (1952), aff'd in part, rev'd in part and rem'd, 215 F.2d 697 (5th Cir. 1954)

Agnes P. Coke, 17 TC 403 (1951) (Acq.), aff'd per curiam, 201 F.2d 742 (5th Cir. 1953)

William A. Falls, 7 TC 66 (1946) (Acq.)

Fees of defending criminal tax fraud charge deductible

Michael Shapiro, 278 F.2d 556 (7th Cir. 1960)

Rev. Rul. 68-662, 1968-2 CB 69

Defense of illegal business

John DiFronzo, 75 TCM 1693 (1998)

Ellis L. McDonald, U.S. Dist. Ct. Al., 12/23/98

Fee to reduce assessment

Rev. Rul. 70-62, 1970-1 CB 30

Estate planning fee

Sidney Merians, 60 TC 187 (1973) (Acq.)

Legal fees in divorce

Estate of Terence P. Melcher et al., TC Memo 2009-210

19.18 Contingent Fees Paid Out of Taxable Awards

Above-the-line deduction for attorney fees in discrimination cases

IRC §62(a)(20)

IRC §62(e) (unlawful discrimination

Note: *Paragraph numbers refer to Parts 1 through 7. Items marked* are research aids, not citations of authority;* see *"Key to Citations" on page 801*

defined)

Contingent fee portion of award taxable

John W. Banks II, 2005-1 USTC ¶50,155 (Sup. Ct. 2005)

20 Travel and Entertainment Expense Deductions

* IRS Publication 463

20.1 Deduction Guide for Travel and Transportation Expenses

Reg. §1.162-2

Temporary assignments of one year or less

IRC §162 (a)

Rev. Rul. 93-86, 1993-2 CB 71 (IRS's realistic expectation test)

20.2 Commuting Expenses

* IRS Publication 463

* "Potholes for Teleworkers: Transportation Deduction Rules Present a Hazard for Flexible Work Arrangements," William V. Vetter, 82 Taxes 25 (December 2004)

* "Telecommuters' and Deductible Local Transportation Expenses," Steven C. Dilley and Janet Trewin, 91 Tax Notes 630 (April 23, 2001)

Commutation not deductible

Reg. §1.162-2(e)

Reg. §1.262-1(b)(5)

Oran R. Morgan, 80 F. Supp. 537 (N.D. Tex. 1948)

Leo M. Verner, 39 TC 749 (1963) (Acq.)

Joseph M. Winn, 32 TC 220 (1959)

Clarence H. O'Donnell, 21 TCM 609 (1962)

Travel from union hall to job

Russell Anderson, 60 TC 834 (1973)

Commuting to a temporary location

Rev. Rul. 99-7, 1999-5 IRB 4

Projected time determines if assignment is temporary

* IRS Legal Memorandum 200018052

No deduction for ironworker with temporary assignments in other cities

Daniela Aldea, TC Memo 2000-136

How break affects temporary location status

* IRS Legal Memorandum 200026025

Common-sense definition of metropolitan area should be used

* Corey L. Wheir, TC Summary Opinion 2004-117

Commuting to temporary job—pre-1999 IRS policy

Rev. Rul. 94-47, 1994-2 CB 18, amplifying Rev. Rul. 90-23, 1990-1 CB 28

Robert Burleson, 68 TCM 288 (1994)

Lumberjack's commuting costs

Charles W. Walker, 101 TC 537 (1993)

Rev. Rul. 94-47, 1994-2 CB 18 (IRS will not follow Walker)

Robert M. Burleson, 68 TCM 288 (1994) (Tax Court holds that IRS may not apply Rev. Rul. 94-47 retroactively)

Police officers' commuting expenses deductible

John R. Pollei, 877 F.2d 838 (10th Cir. 1989)

Doctor's emergency calls to hospital

Margaret G. Sheldon, 50 TC 24 (1968)

Carrying tools to work

Rev. Rul. 75-380, 1975-2 CB 59

Commute to nuclear power plant

John C. Banekatis, 56 TCM 376 (1988)

Electrician's commute to power plant

Philip D. Williams, 60 TCM 627 (1990)

Deductible travel from office in home

Thomas C. St. John, 29 TCM 1045 (1970)

Joe J. Adams, 43 TCM 1203 (1982) (repairman)

Thomas L. Wicker, 51 TCM 225 (1986)

Robert Leitch, 58 TCM 343 (1989)

Julio Mazzotta, 57 TC 427 (1971)

Musician driving from home office to restaurant

Leroy Kahuku, 58 TCM 1247 (1990)

20.3 Overnight-Sleep Test Limits Deduction of Meal Costs

Local lodging necessary to participate in employer business meeting

Notice 2007-47, 2007-24 IRB 1393

Sleep or rest rule

Homer O. Correll, 389 U.S. 299 (1968), rev'g 369 F.2d 87 (6th Cir. 1966)

Nap in parked car

Frederick J. Barry, 54 TC 1210 (1970), and per curiam, 435 F.2d 91 1290 (1st Cir. 1971)

Railroad personnel

Rev. Rul. 75-170, 1975-1 CB 60

Ferryboat captain's meals and incidentals

Marc G. Bissonnette, 127 TC No. 10 (2006)

Truck drivers

Rev. Rul. 75-168, 1975-1 CB 58

Meal costs during overtime not deductible

D. S. Courtney, 32 TC 334 (1959)

W. K. Liang, 34 TCM 1298 (1975)

20.4 IRS Meal Allowance

* IRS Publications 463 and 1542

* "Using Per Diem Rates for Simpler Record Keeping Can be Complicated," Edmund D. Fenton, Jr., 80 Taxes 15 (June 2002)

Optional meal allowance based on federal meals and incidental expense rate

Rev. Proc. 2010-39, 2010-42 IRB 459 (business trips from October 1, 2010 to September 30, 2011)

Rev. Proc. 2009-47, 2009-42 IRB 524 (business trips from October 1, 2009 to September 30, 2010)

Incidental expenses only

Rev. Proc. 2004-60, 2004-42 IRB 682

Department of Transportation deduction limit

IRC §274(n)(3)

20.5 Business Trip Deductions

Reg. §1.162-2(a)

Local lodging necessary to participate in employer business meeting

Notice 2007-47, 2007-24 IRB 1393

Laundry, cab fare

Rev. Rul. 63-145, 1963-2 CB 86

Lavish or extravagant

Rev. Rul. 63-144, 1963-2 CB 129

Double the highest per diem for cruise ship costs

IRC §274(m)(1)

Note: *Paragraph numbers refer to Parts 1 through 7. Items marked * are research aids, not citations of authority;* see *"Key to Citations" on page 801*

Saturday-night stayover

* Letter Ruling 9237014

20.6 When Are You Away From Home?

Place of business as tax home

Raymond K. Yeates, 55 TCM 1077 (1988)

J. N. Flowers, 326 U.S. 465 (1946)

Lee E. Daly, 72 TC 190 (1979), rev'd 631 F.2d 351 (4th Cir. 1980), aff'g Tax Court and rev'g after hearing en banc, 662 F.2d 253 (4th Cir. 1981)

Ethel Merman case

Robert F. Six, 450 F.2d 66 (2d Cir. 1971)

Robert Rosenspan, 438 F.2d 905 (2d Cir. 1971), cert. denied, 404 U.S. 864

Residence is tax home

Charles W. Rambo, 69 TC 920 (1978) (Acq. in result only)

Edward M. McKarzel, 30 TCM 366 (1971)

Eli F. McOimsey, 30 TCM 521 (1971)

Rev. Rul. 71-247, 1971-1 CB 54

Army officer at permanent duty port

H. A. Stidger, 386 U.S. 287 (1967)

Unmarried person

Robert Rosenspan, 438 F.2d 905 (2d Cir. 1971), cert. denied, 404 U.S. 864

Irving M. Sapson, 49 TC 636 (1968) (Acq.)

Max W. Tugel, 20 TCM 693 (1961)

Curtis L. Ralston, 27 TCM 1312 (1968)

Rev. Rul. 773-529, 1973-2 CB 37

Arthur Crossland, 33 TCM 1278 (1974), aff'd, 535 F.2d 1240 (2nd Cir. 1976)

Multiple short jobs at same locale

Thomas J. Mitchell, TC Memo 1999-283

Living with boyfriend doesn't create tax home

Susan D. Thompson, TC Summary Opinion 2009-111

20.7 Fixing a Tax Home If You Work in Different Locations

Edward W. Andrews, 60 TCM 277 (1990), rev'd, 931 F.2d 132 (1st Cir. 1991)

Francis Markey, 491 F.2d 1249 (6th Cir. 1974), rev'g 31 TCM 766 (1972)

Joseph Sherman, 16 TC 332 (1951) (Acq.)

Chong, TC Memo 1996-232

S. M. R. O'Hara, 6 TC 841 (1946)

Richard E. Benson, 27 TCM 1555 (1968)

John H. Webster, 9 TCM 550 (1950)

W. Edward Winterhalter, 10 TCM 268 (1951)

Vincent Treanor, 10 TCM 336 (1951)

Rev. Rul. 55-604, 1955-2 CB 49

Rev. Rul. 63-82, 1963-1 CB 33

Thomas J. Mitchell, TC Memo 1999-283

Baseball players, coaches, pilots, etc. might have other business

Rev. Rul. 54-147, 1954-1 CB 51

Tracy Stright, 66 TCM 1490 (1993)

Special Ruling, December 29, 1953

Maury Wills, 411 F.2d 537 (9th Cir. 1969)

20.8 Tax Home of Married Couple Working in Different Cities

Robert A. Coerver, 297 F.2d 837 (3d Cir. 1962), aff'g 36 TC 252 (1951)

Arthur B. Hammond, 213 F.2d 43 (5th Cir. 1954)

Virginia Foote, 67 TC 1 (1976)

George P. Leyland, 34 TCM 1502 (1975)

Charles J. Hundt, 20 TCM 369 (1961)

20.9 Deducting Living Costs on Temporary Assignment

* IRS Publication 463

Temporary assignments—one year or less

IRC §162 (a)

Rev. Rul. 93-86, 1993-2 CB 71 (IRS's realistic expectation test)

Family at temporary post

Emil J. Michaels, 53 TC 269 (1969) (Acq.)

Federal crime investigations

IRC §162(a)

Engineer on 20-month job

Philip Rolbin, 29 TCM 848 (1970)

Retired Florida stenographer

Virginia C. Avery, 29 TCM 1187 (1970)

Student's summer job

Saterios Hantzis, 38 TCM 1169 (1979), rev'd, 638 F.2d 248 (1st Cir. 1981), cert. denied, 101 S. Ct. 3112

Court rejection of one-year test

David L. Cowger, 25 TCM 513 (1966)

Ronald Brown, 30 TCM 41 (1971)

Louis R. Frederick, 457 F. Supp. 1274 (D.N. Dak. 1978), aff'd, 603 F.2d 1292 (8th Cir. 1979)

Recurrent summer job

Franklin C. Dilley, 58 TC 276 (1972)

State judge traveling to other circuits

Frank Fisher, 24 TC 269 (1955) (Acq.)

State judge who must live in district

James A. Emmert, 146 F. Supp. 322 (S.D. Ind. 1955)

Employed for test period

Richard C. Lipps, 21 TCM 358 (1962)

Rev. Rul. 60-314, 1960-2 CB 48

Employment for part of a year

James R. Whitaker, 24 TC 750 (1955)

George R. Lanning, 34 TCM 1366 (1975)

F. J. McGinley, Jr., 15 TCM 641 (1956)

Linesman working out of Oakland, California

Max W. Tugel, 20 TCM 693 (1961)

Baseball player's expenses

Rev. Rul. 54-147, 1954-1 CB 51

Professional football player

Ronald C. Gardin, 64 TC 1079 (1975)

Temporary assignment

James E. Peurifoy, 358 U.S. 59 (1958)

Michael Kuris, 15 TCM 854 (1956)

Robert K. Denning, 14 TCM 838 (1955)

Rev. Rul. 60-189, 1960-1 CB 60

Temporary becomes permanent

Hansel H. Johnson, Jr., 77 TCM 1966 (1999)

Itinerant worker

George H. James, 308 F.2d 204 (9th Cir. 1962), aff'g 176 F. Supp. 270 (D. Nev. 1959)

One-year test disregarded

Michael L. Hanna, 63 TCM 2917 (1992)

Ronald Brown, 30 TCM 41 (1971)

20.10 Business-Vacation Trips Within the United States

* IRS Publication 463

Note: *Paragraph numbers refer to Parts 1 through 7. Items marked * are research aids, not citations of authority;* see *"Key to Citations" on page 801*

Reg. §1.274-4(e)(2)
IRC §274(c)(3)

Saturday night stayover deductible

* Letter Ruling 9237014

20.11 Business-Vacation Trips Outside the United States

IRC §274(c)

Control over trip, managing executive, related to employer

Reg. §1.274-4(f)(5)

Counting days outside U.S.

Reg. §1.274-4(c)

Allocation formula

Reg. §1.274-4(f)

No allocation necessary if not managing executive or self-employed

Reg. §1.274-4(f)(5)

20.12 Deducting Expenses of Business Conventions

* IRS Publication 463

Business or pleasure trip

Reg. §1.162-2(b)

Convention expenses

Reg. §1.162-2(d)
Rev. Rul. 63-266, 1963-2 CB 88

Connection with business

Rev. Rul. 59-316, 1959-2 CB 57, clarified by Rev. Rul. 63-266, 1963-2 CB 88

No deduction for investment seminars after 1986

IRC §274(h)

Lawyer's convention expenses

Wade H. Ellis, 50 F.2d 343 (D.C. Cir. 1931)

Legal secretary's convention expenses

Rita M. Callinan, 12 TCM 170 (1953)

Insurance agent

C. J. D. Rudolph, 291 F.2d 841 (5th Cir. 1961), aff'g 189 F. Supp. 2 (N.D. Tex. 1960), cert. dismissed, 370 U.S. 269 (1962)

Business convention in coastal resort

Rev. Rul. 56-168, 1956-1 CB 93
Reg. §1.162-2(b)(1)

Cruises

DeWitt N. Burnham, 17 TCM 240 (1958)
Reuben B. Hoover, 35 TC 566 (1961) (Acq.)

No deduction for Super Bowl weekend meetings

Danville Plywood Corp., 16 Cl. Ct. 584 (1989), aff'd, 899 F.2d 3 (Fed. Cir. 1990)

Fraternal organizations' conventions

Reg. §1.162-2(d)

20.13 Travel Expenses of a Spouse or Dependents

Deduction restrictions for costs incurred after 1993

IRC §274 (m)(3)

Spouse as employee

Madyo A. Poletti, 330 F.2d 818 (8th Cir. 1965)
IRS policy (pre-1993 travel costs)
Rev. Rul. 63-144, 1963-2 CB 129

Spouse's expenses on convention or business trip (pre-1993 travel)

Reg. §1.162-2(c)
William N. Clement, Sr., 331 F. Supp. 877 (E.D.N.C. 1971)
Donald W. Scarborough, 30 TCM 613 (1971)

Company convention policy

J. C. Thomas, 289 F.2d 108 (5th Cir. 1961), cert. denied, 368 U.S. 837

Spouse acting as nurse

Allenberg Cotton Co., 61-1 USTC ¶9131 (W. D. Tenn. 1961)
William E. Reisner, 34 TC 1122 (1960) (Acq.)
Preston R. Riely, 23 TCM 449 (1964)

Spouse acting as host or hostess

Pierre C. Warwick, 236 F. Supp. 761 (E.D. Va. 1964)
Ron Merritt, 21 TCM 1011 (1962)
Roy O. Disney, 267 F. Supp. 1 (C.D. Cal. 1967), aff'd, 413 F.2d 783 (9th Cir. 1969)
Bank of Stockton, 36 TCM 114 (1977)

Spouse of controlling stockholder

Bywater Sales and Service Co., 24 TCM 849 (1965)

Spouse of foreign service employee

Fraser Wilkins, 348 F. Supp. 1282 (D. Neb. 1972)

20.14 Restrictions on Foreign Conventions and Cruises

Reasonableness of foreign location

IRC §274(h)

North American area

Rev. Rul. 2003-109, 2003-42 IRB 839
Rev. Rul. 2007-28, 2007-18 IRB 1039

Cruise ship conventions

IRC §274(h)(2) ($2,000 limit)
IRC §274(h)(s) (recordkeeping)

20.15 50% Deduction Limit

Allowable entertainment costs

IRC §274(a)

50% deduction limit

IRC §274(n)(1)
Reg. §1.274(a)(3)
Reg. §1.274(m)(3)

20.16 The Restrictive Tests for Meals and Entertainment

IRC §274(a)
Senate Comm. Report on Pub. L. No. 87-834
Reg. §1.274(a)(3)
Reg. §1.274(m)(3)

Lavish and extravagant entertainment

IRC §274(k)
Reg. §1.274-1
Rev. Rul. 63-144, 1963-2 CB 129
Donald G. Harper, 23 TCM 461 (1964)

Entertainment defined

Reg. §1.274-2(b)(1)(ii)

Business associates

Reg. §1.274-2(b)(2)(iii)

Prospective investors

* Letter Ruling 9414040

20.17 Directly Related Dining and Entertainment

IRC §274(a)(1)
Reg. §1.274-2(a)

Directly related entertainment

Reg. §1.274-2(c)

Note: *Paragraph numbers refer to Parts 1 through 7. Items marked * are research aids, not citations of authority;* see *"Key to Citations" on page 801*

Rev. Rul. 63-144, 1963-2 CB 129

Annual party for associates deductible

Robert Moore, 96-2 USTC ¶50413 (Dist. Ct. Va. 1996)

Doctor's entertainment

Karl Wolf, 64-1 USTC (W.D. Mo. 1964)

Richard A. Sutter, 21 TC 170 (1953)

C. W. Lokey, 16 TCM 18 (1957)

Kenneth Branchard, 12 TCM 550 (1953)

Fishing trip had business purpose

Townsend Industries, Inc., 2003-2 USTC ¶50,666 (8th Cir. 2003)

Hunting trips for clients not deductible

* Letter Ruling 9608004

20.18 Goodwill Entertainment

IRC §274(a)(1)(A)

Reg. §1.274-2(a)(1)(ii)

Reg. §1.274-2(d)

Rev. Rul. 63-144, 1963-2 CB 129

No deduction for entertaining co-workers

Donald Scalley, 63 TCM 2238 (1992)

20.19 Home Entertaining

Reg. §1.274-2(f)(2)(i)(b)

Rev. Rul. 63-144, 1963-2 CB 129

20.20 Your Personal Share of Entertainment Costs

John D. Moss, Jr., 80 TC 1073 (1983), aff'd, 758 F.2d 211 (7th Cir. 1985)

Ray A. Smith, 33 TC 1059 (1960)

Richard A. Sutter, 21 TC 170 (1953)

James P. Fenstermaker, 37 TCM 898 (1978)

Rev. Rul. 63-144, 1963-2 CB 129

20.21 Entertainment Costs of Spouses

Directly related test

Reg. §1.274-2(d)(4)

Goodwill entertainment

Rev. Rul. 63-144, 1963-2 CB 129

Entertainment of out-of-town customer's spouse

Rev. Rul. 63-144, 1963-2 CB 129

20.22 Entertainment Facilities and Club Dues

IRC §274(a)(1)(B)

Luncheon club not facility

Reg. §1.274-2(e)(3)(ii)

Deduction for club dues barred

IRC §274 (a)(3)

Reg. §1.274-2 (a)(2)(iii) (IRS exception for civic or public service organizations and professional associations)

Value of company plane taxed to employees

Sutherland Lumber-Southwest, Inc., 255 F.3d 495 (8th Cir. 2001) (Acq.)

20.23 Restrictive Test Exception for Reimbursements

IRC §274(e)

Reg. §1.274-2(f)(2)(iv)

20.24 50% Cost Limitation on Meals and Entertainment

General 50% limitation

IRC §274 (n)(1)

Exceptions to 50% limit

IRC §274(n)(2)

Reg. §1.274-2(f)

Restaurants and nightclubs

IRC 274(e)(8)

Limited to face value of ticket

IRC §274(l)(1)(A)

Charitable sporting events

IRC §274(l)(1)(B)

De minimis rule for employee meals

IRC §274(n)(2)(B)

IRC §119(b)(4)

Employee reimbursement

IRC §62(a)(2)(A)

Transportation industry workers

IRC §274(n)(3)

Sky boxes

IRC §274(l)(2)

Free employee meals

Boyd Gaming Corp., 117 F.3d 1096 (9th Cir. 1999)

20.25 Business Gift Deductions Are Limited

IRC §274(b)

Reg. §1.274-3

Rev. Rul. 63-144, 1963-2 CB 129

Gift to secretary

Richard Steel, 28 TCM 1301 (1969), aff'd per curiam, 437 F.2d 71 (2d Cir. 1971)

Gifts to employees

IRC §102(c)

Employee achievement awards

IRC §274(j)

Prop. Reg. §1.274-8

20.26 Record-Keeping Requirements

IRC §274(d)

Reg. §1.274-5

Reg. §1.274-5T

* IRS Publication 463

What your records must show

Reg. §1.274-5(b)

Reg. §1.274-5(c)

Business purpose

Reg. §1.274-5(c)(2)(ii)(b)

Need of receipt with diary

William F. Sanford, 50 TC 823 (1968), aff'd per curiam, 412 F.2d 201 (2d Cir. 1969), cert. denied, 396 U.S. 841

Inadequate travel and entertainment records not a basis for negligence penalties

John Robinson, 51 TC 520 (1968) (Acq.), aff'd, 422 F.2d 873 (9th Cir. 1969)

Oral testimony accepted

Harry G. La Forge, 434 F.2d 370 (2d Cir. 1970)

Oral testimony ignored

Arthur Hughes, 451 F.2d 975 (2d Cir. 1972)

Norman E. Kennelly, 56 TC 936 (1971), aff'd, 456 F.2d 1335 (2nd Cir. 1972)

Lost records

Raymond W. Jackson, 34 TCM 1315 (1975)

Joe F. Gizzi, 65 TC 342 (1975)

Credit card statements

John Shea, 112 TC 183 (1999)

20.27 Proving Travel and Entertainment Expenses

Note: *Paragraph numbers refer to Parts 1 through 7. Items marked * are research aids, not citations of authority;* see *"Key to Citations" on page 801*

Reg. §1.274-5(c)
Reg. §1.274-5T
* IRS Publication 463

Diary

Reg. §1.274-5(c)(2)(iii)
Joseph L. Weinfeld, 20 TCM 70 (1961)
Warren Cummings, 20 TCM 1699 (1961)

Travel receipt threshold raised to $75

Notice 95-50, 1995-2 CB 333

Hotel bill not needed if per diem allowance received

Rev. Proc. 63-4, 1963-1 CB 494

Receipts

Reg. §1.274-5(c)(2)(iii)
Notice 95-50, 1992-2 CB 333

Sampling

Temp. Reg. §1.274-5T(c)(3)(ii)
* IRS Publication 463

Noting expense items

Reg. §1.274-5(c)
Reg. §1.274-5(c)(6)

Failure to show business purpose

Norman E. Kennelly, 56 TC 936 (1971), aff'd, 456 F.2d 1335 (2nd Cir. 1972)

Time limit for keeping records

Reg. §1.274-5(c)(2)(iv)

Credit cards

Reg. §1.274-5(e)(2)
Rev. Rul. 59-410 1959-2 CB 64

Excuses for inadequate records

Reg. §1.274-5(c)

Attorney required to keep travel and entertainment records

William Andress, Jr., 51 TC 863 (1969), aff'd per curiam, 423 F.2d 679 (5th Cir. 1970)

Loss of records

Lewis M. Bryan, 33 TCM 1188 (1974)

Bills but no other proof

Cam F. Dowell, Jr., 522 F.2d 708 (5th Cir. 1975), cert. denied, 26 U.S. 920

Loss due to eviction

Irvin A. Murray, 41 TCM 337 (1980)

Loss due to destruction by estranged wife

Matthew J. Canfield, 41 TCM 461 (1980)

Loss of records due to fire

Robert Inazo, 76 TCM 231

20.28 Reporting T&E Expenses If You Are Self-Employed

Diary and receipts

Rev. §1.274-5(c)

20.29 Employee Reporting of Unreimbursed T&E Expenses

2% floor

IRC §67

50% limit on meals and entertainment

IRC §274(n)(1)

20.30 Tax Treatment of Reimbursements

* IRS Publication 463

Accountable plan requirements

Reg. §1.62-2

Per diem arrangements

Rev. Proc. 93-21, 1993-1 CB 529

Reimbursements of club dues or spousal travel costs

Reg. §§ 1.132-5(s) and (t)
IRC §62(c)

20.31 What Is an Accountable Plan?

IRC §62(c)
Reg. §1.62-2(c)(2) and (c)(4)

Reimbursement given to avoid FICA

* Letter Ruling 9504002

Failure to get reimbursed

Earl M. Coplon, 18 TCM 166 (1959), aff'd, 277 F.2d 534 (6th Cir. 1960)
Marvin A. Heidt, 18 TCM 149 (1959), aff'd, 274 F.2d 25 (7th Cir. 1960)
Eugene J. Rogers, 18 TCM 866 (1959)
Jack C. Morgan, 24 TCM 644 (1965)

Frequent flyer allowance under accountable plans

* Letter Ruling 9547001

20.32 *Per Diem* Travel Allowance Under Accountable Plans

* IRS Publications 463 and 1542
* "Using Per Diem Rates for Simpler Record Keeping Can Be Complicated," Edmund D. Fenton, Jr., 80 Taxes 15 (June 2002)

High-low reimbursement method

Rev. Proc. 2010-39, 2010-42 IRB 459 (business trips from October 1, 2010 to September 30, 2011)
Rev. Proc. 2009-47. 2009-42 IRB 524 (business trips from October 1, 2009 to September 30, 2010)

20.33 Automobile Mileage Allowance

* IRS Publication 463

Mileage allowance for 2010

News Release IR-2009-111

Rev. Proc. 2009-54, 2009-51 IRB 930

Mileage allowance for 2009

News Release IR-2008-131
Rev. Proc. 2008-72, 2008-50 IRB 1286

20.34 Reimbursements Under Non-Accountable Plans

Reg. §1.62-2(c)(3) and (c)(5)
* Letter Ruling 9443025
* IRS Publication 463

21 Personal Exemptions

21.1 How Many Exemptions May You Claim?

IRC §151
IRC §152
* IRS Publication 501

Definition of qualifying child

IRC §152(c)

Definition of qualifying relative

IRC §152(d)

$500 exemption for housing Midwestern displaced person

Section 302 of KETRA 2005 applied to Midwestern disaster area by Act Sections 702(a)(2) and 702(e)(1) of the Emergency Economic Stabilization Act of 2008

Social Security numbers

IRC §151(e)

Note: *Paragraph numbers refer to Parts 1 through 7. Items marked* * *are research aids, not citations of authority; see "Key to Citations" on page 801*

Spouses' Social Security numbers on joint returns

News Release IR-2000-68

Dependent can't claim exemptions

IRC §151(d)(2) (exemption amount is zero)

IRC §152(b)(1) (dependent cannot claim any dependents)

21.2 Your Spouse as an Exemption

Taxpayer's and spouse's exemption

IRC §151(b)

Reg. §1.151-1(b) (on joint or separate returns)

Spouse not claimed as dependent

IRC §152(d)(2)(H)

Reg. §1.151-1(b)

Joel Dewsbury, 146 F. Supp. 467 (Ct. Cl. 1954)

Charles W. Jamieson, 23 TCM 2091 (1964), aff'd 353 F.2d 1 (7th Cir. 1965)

Determination of marital status

IRC §7703

Divorce or separation

IRC §143(a)

Interlocutory decree

Reg. §1.6013-4(a)

William G. Ostler, 237 F.2d 501 (9th Cir. 1956)

Alice H. Evans, 19 TC 1102 (1953) (Acq.), aff'd, 211 F.2d 378 (10th Cir. 1954)

Rev. Rul. 75-536, 1975-2 CB 462

Rev. Rul. 57-368, 1957-2 CB 896, revoking I.T. 3942, 1949-1 CB 69

21.3 Qualifying Children

IRC §152(c)

* IRS Publication 501

Qualifying child defined

IRC §152(c)

Descendants of child

IRC §152(c)(2)(A)

Sibling and sibling's descendants

IRC §152(c)(2)(B)

IRC §152(f)(4) (sibling by half-blood)

Adopted child

IRC §152(f)(1)(B)

Foster child

IRC §152(f)(1)(C)

Principal place of abode test

IRC §152(c)(1)(B)

IRC §152(f)(6) (kidnapped children)

Age or student test

IRC §152(c)(3)

IRC §152(f)(2) (full-time students)

Tie-breaker rules

IRC §152(c)(4)

Can't provide over half of own support

IRC §152(c)(1)(D)

Infants born during tax year

Reg. §1.152-1(b)

Unborn child does not qualify

Andrea L. Cassman, 31 Fed Cl. 121 (1994)

Dependency exemption for nieces

Oralia Pavia, TC Memo 2008-270

No exemption or credits for raising girlfriend's child

*Monty E. Stone, TC Summary Opinion 2009-194

21.4 Qualifying Relatives

IRC §152(d)

* IRS Publication 501

Relationship test

IRC §152(d)(2)

Can't be qualifying child

IRC §152(d)(1)(D)

Support test

IRC §152(d)(1)

Nephew, niece

IRC §152(d)(2)(E)

Oralia Pavia, TC Memo 2008-270

Uncle, aunt

IRC §152(d)(2)(F)

In-laws

IRC §152(d)(2)(G)

21.5 Meeting the Support Test for a Qualifying Relative

IRC §152(d)(1)(C)

* IRS Publication 501

Support includes board, lodging, etc., from all sources

Reg. §1.152-1(a)(2)

Scholarship for full-time student not counted as support

IRC §152(f)(5)

Cost of car and T.V. may be support items

Rev. Rul. 77-282, 1977-2 CB 52

Summer camp

Betty A. Shapiro, 54 TC 347 (1970) (Acq.)

Singing and drama lessons

Raymond McKay, 34 TC 1080 (1960)

Musical instrument

Virginia M. Cramer, 55 TC 1125 (1955) (Acq.)

Payment by insurance company

Rev. Rul. 64-223, 1964-2 CB 50

Social Security benefits used for own support

Reg. §1.152-1(a)(2)(ii)

Social Security to children

Rev. Rul. 74-543, 1974-2 CB 39

Rev. Rul. 74-115, 1974-1 CB 100

Rev. Rul. 57-344, 1957-2 CB 112

Medicare benefits not counted as support

Alfred H. Turecamo, 64 TC 720 (1975), aff'd, 554 F.2d 564 (2nd Cir. 1977) (Acq.)

Rev. Rul. 79-173, 1979-1 CB 86

Medicaid benefits not counted as support

Mary Archer, 73 TC 963 (1980)

Use of welfare payments

Rev. Rul. 71-468, 1971-2 CB 115

Norman Williams, 71 TCM 2423 (1996)

Eddie Carter, 55 TC 109 (1970) (Acq.)

Lodging fair rental value

Reg. §1.152-1(a)(2)(i)

* IRS Publication 501

Allocating Social Security benefits

Wilfred Abel, 21 TCM 1044 (1962)

21.6 Multiple Support Agreements

IRC §152(d)(3)

Reg. §1.152-3

* IRS Publication 501

Note: *Paragraph numbers refer to Parts 1 through 7. Items marked * are research aids, not citations of authority;* see *"Key to Citations" on page 801*

Must actually furnish support

John L. Donner, 25 TC 1043 (1956)

21.7 Special Rule for Divorced or Separated Parents

IRC §152(e)

T.D. 9408, 2008-33 IRB 323

* IRS Publication 501

Decree or agreement required

IRC §152(e)(2)

Parents who were never married to each other

IRC §152(e)(1)(A)(iii) (living apart for last six months of year)

Jeffrey R. King, 121 TC 245 (2003)

$600 support rule requirement for each child under pre-1985 agreement

IRC §152(e)(2)(B)

Pre-2005 rule: exemption waiver required for noncustodial parent to claim exemption

IRC §152(e), prior to amendment by the Working Families Tax Relief Act of 2004

Michael K. Boltinghouse, TC Memo 2002-134

* Jeffrey S. Lindquist, TC Summary Opinion 2003-80

Cheryl J. Miller, 114 TC 184 (2000)

21.8 The Dependent Must Meet a Citizen or Resident Test

IRC §152(b)(3)

* IRS Publication 501

Adopted child exception

IRC §152(b)(3)(B)

Child born abroad to nonresident alien and U.S. citizen qualifies

Rev. Rul. 71-44, 1971-1 CB 49

21.9 The Dependent Does Not File a Joint Return

IRC §152(b)(2)

* IRS Publication 501

Joint return for refund purposes not a tax return

William J. Martino, 71 TC 456 (1978) (Acq.)

Rev. Rul. 65-34, 1965-1 CB 86

Rev. Rul. 54-567, 1954-2 CB 108

21.10 Spouses' Names and Social Security Numbers on Joint Return

* IRS Publication 501

IRS will computer-match both Social Security numbers

News Release IR-2000-68, 10/5/00

21.11 Reporting Social Security Numbers of Dependents

Exemptions denied if Social Security number not reported

IRC §151(e)

Religious beliefs

John W. Miller, 114 TC 511 (2000)

21.12 Personal Exemptions Not Subject to Phaseout for 2010

IRC §151(d)(3)(F)no phaseout for 2010

* IRS Publication 501

Phaseout of reduction in 2006–2009

IRC §151(d)(3)(E)

22 Figuring Your Regular Income Tax Liability

22.1 Taxable Income and Regular Income Tax Liability

IRC §1

Figuring taxable income

IRC §63(a)

22.2 Using the Tax Table

IRC §3

22.3 Tax Computation Worksheet

Individual tax rates

IRC §1(i)

Inflation adjustment

IRC §1(f)

22.4 Tax Calculation if You Have Net Capital Gain or Qualified Dividends

IRC §1(h)

IRC §1222

* IRS Publication 544

22.5 Foreign Earned Income Tax Worksheet

IRC 911(f)

* Form 1040 Instructions

22.6 Income Averaging for Farmers and Fishermen

IRC §1301

Averaging extended to fishing business

IRC §1301(a) and (b)

AMT relief

IRC §55(c)(2)

22.7 Tax Credits

Personal tax credits

IRC §21 (dependent care)

IRC §22 (credit for the elderly)

IRC §23 (adoption expenses)

IRC §24 (child credit)

IRC §25 (qualified home mortgage certificates)

IRC §25A (HOPE and Lifetime Learning credits)

IRC §25B (qualified retirement savings)

IRC §35 (displaced workers' health insurance)

IRC §36 (first-time homebuyer credit)

IRC §36A (Making Work Pay credit)

IRC §1400C (District of Columbia first-time homebuyer credit)

IRC §6428 (2008 recovery rebate credit)

23 Alternative Minimum Tax (AMT)

23.1 Computing Alternative Minimum Tax on Form 6251

Figuring AMT liability

IRC §55

AMT exemption

IRC §55(d)

AMT not avoided by not claiming deductions

Naila M. Qureshi, 2006-2 USTC ¶50,564 (Fed. Cir. 2006)

23.2 Adjustments for AMT

Note: *Paragraph numbers refer to Parts 1 through 7. Items marked * are research aids, not citations of authority; see "Key to Citations" on page 801*

IRC §56

Deductions for state and local taxes and miscellaneous expenses disallowed

IRC §56(b)(1)(A)

J. Kenneth Alexander, 69 TCM 1792 (1995)

Exemptions and standard deduction

IRC §56(b)(1)(E)

Personal exemptions trigger AMT

David R. Klaassen, TC Memo 1998-241

AMT deduction for mortgage interest covers multiple refinancings

Rev. Rul. 2005-11, 2005-14 IRB 816

News Release IR-2005-31, 3/17/05

Incentive stock options

IRC §56(b)(3)

Abatement of pre-2008 ISO-related underpayments, interest, and penalties

IRC 53(f)(1)

Exercising stock options does not create an AMT NOL carryback

Evan Marcus, 129 TC No. 4 (2007)

Passive losses

IRC §58(b)

Farm and passive loss

IRC §58

23.3 Tax Preference Items

IRC §57

Exception for private activity bonds issued in 2009 and 2010

IRC §57(a)(5)(C)(vi)

Exclusion for gain on small business stock

IRC §57(a)(7)

23.4 Net Operating Losses

IRC §56(d)

23.5 Tax Credits Allowed Against AMT

Foreign tax credit

IRC §59(a)

*Nonrefundable credits may offset AMT*IRC §26(a)(2)

23.6 AMT Tax Credit From Regular Tax

IRC §53

Refundable AMT credit

IRC §53(e)

Liberalization of refundable credit for 2008 and later years

IRC 53(e)(2)

Increase in refundable credit for certain ISO-related interest and penalties

IRC 53(f)(2)

23.7 Avoiding AMT

IRC §55, 56, and 57

* "Reduce the Impact of the Alternative Minimum Tax," Daniel J. Lathrope, 64 Tax Strategies 196 (April 2000)

24 Computing the "Kiddie Tax" on Your Child's Investment Income

24.1 Filing Your Child's Return

"Kiddie" tax rules

IRC §1(g)

* IRS Publication 929

24.2 Children Subject to the "Kiddie Tax" for 2010

IRC §1(g)(2)

* IRS Publication 929

24.3 Computing "Kiddie Tax" on Child's Return

IRC §1(g)

24.4 Parent's Election To Report Child's Dividends and Interest

Parent's election to report child's income on own return

IRC §1(g)(7)

25 Personal Tax Credits Reduce Your Tax Liability

25.1 Overview of Personal Tax Credits

IRC §21 (dependent care)

IRC §22 (credit for the elderly)

IRC §23 (adoption expenses)

IRC §24 (child credit)

IRC §25 (qualified home mortgage certificates)

IRC §25A (Hope and Lifetime Learning credits)

IRC §25B (qualified retirement savings)

IRC §25D (solar water heaters, solar panels, fuel-cell property)

IRC §35 (displaced workers' health insurance)

IRC §36 (first-time homebuyer credit)

IRC §36(A) (Making Work Pay credit)

IRC §1400C (District of Columbia first-time homebuyer credit)

IRC §6428 (2008 recovery rebate credit)

25.2 Child Tax Credit for Children Under Age 17

IRC §24(a) ($1,000 credit extended through 2010)

IRC §24(d) (refundable portion of credit)

25.3 Figuring the Child Tax Credit

IRC §24

* IRS Publication 972

25.4 Qualifying for Child and Dependent Care Credit

IRC §21

* IRS Publication 503

Dependent care credit denied if Social Security number of dependent is omitted

IRC §21(e)(10)

Joint returns

IRC §21(e)(2)

No FICA for family

IRC §3121(b)

Paying babysitter's share of FICA qualifies for credit

Carolyn Perry, 92 TC 470 (1989)

Dependent care provider must be identified on return

IRC §21(e)(9)

25.5 Limits on the Dependent Care Credit

Note: *Paragraph numbers refer to Parts 1 through 7. Items marked * are research aids, not citations of authority; see "Key to Citations" on page 801*

Amount of the credit

IRC §21(a)

Eligible expenses limited to earned income

IRC §21(d)

Credit liberalized after 2002

IRC §21(a)(2) (maximum credit percentage and phase-out threshold)

IRC §21(c) (increased limit on qualifying expenses)

25.6 Earned Income Test for Dependent Care Credit

IRC §21(d)

Spouse is student or disabled

IRC §21(d)(2), as amended by JCWAA 2002

Supervised transportation included in price qualifies for credit

Edith W. Zoltan, 79 TC 490 (1982)

25.7 Credit Allowed for Care of Qualifying Persons

Qualifying dependents

IRC §21(b), as amended by WFTRA 2004 for tax years beginning after 2004

Reg. §1.44A-1(b)

Maintaining a household

IRC §21(e)(1)

Monthly proration of household costs

Reg. §1.44A-1(d)(4)

Two or more families

Reg. §1.44A-1(d)(2)

25.8 Expenses Qualifying for the Dependent Care Credit

IRC §21(b)(2)

Expenses qualifying for the dependent care credit

Prop. Reg. 1.21-1, -2, -3, -4

FICA tax

Rev. Rul. 74-176, 1974-1 CB 68

Least expensive alternative not required

Reg. §1.44A-1(c)(3)(ii)

Outside-the-home care

IRC §21(b)(2)(B)

No credit for overnight camp

IRC §21(b)(2)(A)

Summer camp

Edith W. Zoltan, 79 TC 490 (1982)

No deduction for travel to day-care center

Dorothy E. Warner, 69 TC 995 (1978)

Payments to relatives

IRC §21(e)(6)

Medical expense

Reg. §1.44A-4(b)

Allocation between qualifying/nonqualifying service

Reg. §1.44A-1(c)(6)

Allocation of expenses on daily basis

Reg. §1.44A-1(c)(1)(ii)

Airplane transportation of children to grandparents ineligible

Caroline Perry, 92 TC 470 (1989)

Employer dependent care reduces credit base

IRC §21(c)

Dependent care provider must be identified on return

IRC §21(e)(9)

25.9 Dependent Care Credit Rules for Separated Couples

Marital status

IRC §21(e)(3)

Spouse is not member of your household

IRC §21(e)(4)

Special rule if divorced or separated

IRC §21(e)(5)

Reg. §1.44A-1(b)(2)

25.10 Qualifying Tests for EIC

Higher EIC for some families in 2009 and 2010

IRC §32(b)(3)

Rev. Proc. 2009-21, 2009-16 IRB 860

Qualifying child

IRC §32(c)(3)

Oralia Pavia, TC Memo 2008-270 (nieces)

Eligible individual

IRC §32(c)(1)

Childless workers may qualify for the credit

IRC §32(b)(1)(A)

Social Security number of eligible taxpayer and spouse required

IRC §32(c)(1)(F)

Married must file jointly

IRC §32(d)

IRC §7703

25.11 Income Tests for Earned Income Credit (EIC)

IRC §32(c)(2)(B)

* IRS Publication 596

Inflation adjustments to earned income amount and phase-out threshold

IRC §32(j)

Rev. Proc. 2009-21, 2009-16 IRB 860 (inflation adjustments for 2009)

Earned income eligible for credit

IRC §32(c)(2)(A)(i)

Election to treat tax-free combat pay as earned income

IRC §32(c)(2)(B)(vi)

Union paid strike benefits

Rev. Rul. 78-191, 1978-1 CB 8

Military housing allowance

Michael C. Neff, Ct. Cl., 5/25/99

Denial of credit if excessive investment income

IRC §32(i)

Phaseout of credit

IRC §32(b)(2)

Credit determined by tables

IRC §32(f)

25.12 Look up EIC in Government Tables

* IRS Publication 596

25.13 Advance Payment of Earned Income Credit

IRC §32(g)

IRC §3507

Advance payment no longer available

Education Jobs and Medicaid Assistance Act of 2010 (P.L.111-226), repealing IRC §§3507 and 32(g)

25.14 Qualifying for the

Note: *Paragraph numbers refer to Parts 1 through 7. Items marked * are research aids, not citations of authority; see "Key to Citations" on page 801*

Adoption Credit

IRC §23

* IRS Publication 968

25.15 Claiming the Adoption Credit on Form 8839

IRC §23

* IRS Publication 968

Safe harbor for determining finality of foreign adoptions

Rev. Proc. 2005-31, 2005-26, IRB 1374

Announcement 2005-45, 2005-26 IRB 1377

Substantiating the adoption credit for 2010

Notice 2010-66, 2010-42 IRB 437 (substantiating 2010 credit)

Rev. Proc. 2010-31, 2010-40 IRB 413 (finality of Hague Convention adoption)

25.16 Eligibility for the Saver's Credit

IRC §25B (qualified retirement savings)

Credit brackets for 2010

Notice 2009-94, 2009-50 IRB 848

25.17 Figuring the Saver's Credit

IRC §25B(b) (gross income limitations inflation indexing)

IRC §25B(h) (credit made permanent)

IRA contributions based on tax-free combat pay

IRC §219(f)(7)

25.18 Health Coverage Credit

IRC §35 (displaced workers' health insurance)

Health coverage tax credit clarified

Notice 2005-50, 2005-27 IRB 14

25.19 Mortgage Interest Credit

IRC §25 (qualified home mortgage certificates)

25.20 District of Columbia First-Time Homebuyer Credit

IRC §1400C

25.21 Residential Energy Credits

Nonbusiness energy property

IRC §25C (insulation windows and other home improvements)

IRS procedures for manufacturer's certification

Notice 2009-53, 2009-25 IRB 1095

Residential energy efficiency property

IRC §25D (solar panels, solar water heaters, geothermal heat pumps, wind and fuel-cell property)

Credit for home energy property installed in 2010

*Office of Chief Counsel INFO Letters 2010-0201, 2010-0219, 2010-0222

Insulated vinyl siding not eligible for home energy credit

* Chief Counsel Letter, INFO 2009-0237

25.22 Credits for Hybrid and Other Alternative Fuel Vehicles and Plug-in Electric Vehicles

Guidance on tax credit certification

IRC §30B

Notice 2006-9, 2006-6 IRB 413

Credit for electric vehicle

IRC §30

* IRS Publication 535

Credit for plug-in electric vehicle

IRC §30, added by the American Recovery and Reinvestment Act of 2009 (plug-in electric vehicles)

IRC §30D, added by the Emergency Economic Stabilization Act of 2008

News Release IR-2009-45 (plug-in electric drive motor vehicle)

25.23 First-Time Homebuyer Credit

IRC §36, as amended by the Homebuyer Assistance and Improvement Act of 2010

Allocation of first-time homebuyer credit between unmarried purchasers

Notice 2009-12, 2009-6 IRB 446

No credit for beneficiary purchasing from estate

* Chief Counsel Letter, INFO 2010-0071

No credit for child purchasing from a parent

* Chief Counsel Letter, INFO 2010-0073

Three-year separation before divorce bars credit

* Chief Counsel Letter, INFO 2009-0135

Having co-signer doesn't block credit

* Chief Counsel Letter, INFO 2009-0101

* Chief Counsel Letter, INFO 2009-0171

25.24 Making Work Pay and Government Retiree Credit

IRC §36A

26 Tax Withholdings

26.1 Withholdings Should Cover Estimated Tax

* IRS Publication 505

Form W-2

IRC §6051

Social Security maximum

IRC §31(b)(1)

Reg. §1.31-2

Graduated withholding rates

IRC §3402

Voluntary Social Security withholding

IRC §3402(p)

Indicate marital status on exemption certificate

IRC §3402(f)(1)

Allowable exemption on Form W-4

Reg. §31.3402(f)(1)-1

26.2 Income Taxes Withheld on Wages

Wages

IRC §3401(a)

Reg. §31.3401(a)-1

Fringe benefits

Temp. Reg. §31.3401(a)

Bonuses and supplemental wages—third lowest rate

Section 13273 of the Revenue Reconciliation Act of 1993

* IRS Publication 505

Payments other than wages (annuities, supplemental unemployment benefits)

Note: *Paragraph numbers refer to Parts 1 through 7. Items marked * are research aids, not citations of authority;* see *"Key to Citations" on page 801*

IRC §3402(o)

Reg. §31.3402(o)-1

Withholding required for differential wages paid after 2008

IRC §3401(h), added by Heroes Earnings Assistance Tax Relief Act of 2008

Rev. Rul. 2009-11, 2009-18 IRB 896

Domestics

Reg. §31.3401(a)-3(b)

Agricultural workers

IRC §3401(a)(2)

Computer operators

* Letter Ruling 9534002

Ministers

Reg. §31.3401(A)(9)-1

Nonresident aliens

Reg. §31.3401(a)(6)-1

Public officials

Reg. §31.3401(a)-2(b)

Traveling advances

Reg. §31.3401(a)-1(b)(2)

Board, lodging, health benefits, etc.

Reg. §31.3401(a)(11)-1

Reg. §31.3401(a)-1(b)(9) and (10)

Foreign government pay

Reg. §31.3401(a)(5)-1

Foreign residents

Reg. §31.3401(a)(8)(A)-1

U.S. possessions

Reg. §31.3401(a)(8)(B)-1

No withholding on cancellation of employment contract

Rev. Rul. 58-301, 1958-1 CB 23, distinguished by Rev. Rul. 74-252, 1974-1 (withholding required on dismissal payments) CB 287 and Rev. Rul. 75-44, 1975-1 CB 15 (withholding on payment for relinquishment of seniority rights)

Terminated employee

IRC §6051(a)

Refund of employer overwithholding

Rev. Rul. 82-84, 1982-1 CB 208

26.3 Low Earners May Be Exempt From Withholding

IRC §3402(i) and (p)

* IRS Publication 505

Electronic filing of W-4

Reg. §31.3402 (f)(5)-1(c)

Voluntary withholding on Social Security and other federal benefits

IRC §3402(p)

26.4 Are You Withholding the Right Amount?

IRC §3402(n)

IRC §3402(m)

Reg. §31.3402(m)-1

W-4 verification requirement dropped

Treasury Decision T.D. 9196, 2005-19 IRB 1000

26.5 When To File a New Form W-4

IRC §3402(f)(2)

Change in number of exemptions

Reg. §31.3402(f)(2)-1(b) and (c)

When new withholding exemption takes effect

IRC §3402(f)(3)

Reg. §31.3402(f)(3)-1

26.6 Voluntary Withholding on Certain Government Payments

IRC §3402(p)(1) and (2), as amended by EGTRRA 2001

26.7 When Tips Are Subject to Withholding

* "IRS May Collect Employment Taxes on Aggregate Amount of Unreported Tip Income," Kelley Wolf, 78 Taxes 35 (June 2000)

Tax withheld on tips

IRC §3402(k)

Reg. §31.3402(k)

Written report

IRC §6053

FICA tax

IRC §3101

IRC §3102

Rev. Rul. 95-7, 1995-1 CB 185

Tip allocation rules

IRC §6053(c)

Reg. §31.6053-3

Supreme Court approves IRS estimation method to assess employer FICA tax on tips

Fior D'Italia, Inc., 2002-1 USTC ¶50,549 (Sup. Ct. 2002)

* "Fior D'Italia: Supreme Court Approves Aggregate Method on Tips," R. Dan Fesler and Larry Maples, 80 Taxes 53 (November 2002)

26.8 Withholding on Gambling Winnings

IRC §3402(q)(1)

26.9 FICA Withholdings

IRC §3121

Wage base for 2010 and 2011

Social Security Administration news release and fact sheet, 10/15/10

Rate of tax

IRC §3101 (employee)

IRC §3111 (employer)

Withholding required for differential wages paid after 2008

IRC §3401(h), added by Heroes Earnings Assistance Tax Relief Act of 2008

Rev. Rul. 2009-11, 2009-18 IRB 896

"Wages" same as for income tax

Rowan Companies, Inc., 81-1 USTC ¶9479 (S. Ct. 1981)

Responsible person for withholding

Edward Finley, 82 F.3d 966 (10th Cir., 1996)

Mary Phillips, 73 F.3d 939 (9th Cir., 1996)

Ellen L. Marino, U.S. Dist. Ct. Florida, 5/12/04

Rev. Rul. 2004-41, IRB 2004-18, 845

Responsible person must be given written IRS notice before penalty

IRC §6672(b)

CFO escapes liability for trust fund taxes

Jose D. Salzillo, 2005-1 USTC ¶50,324 (Fed. Cl. 2005)

Deferred pay plans

Rev. Rul. 78-263, 1978-2 CB 253

Prop. Reg. §31.3121(v)(2)-1,2

Prop. Reg. §31.3306(r)(2)-1

Note: *Paragraph numbers refer to Parts 1 through 7. Items marked * are research aids, not citations of authority;* see *"Key to Citations" on page 801*

Sick pay

IRC §3121(a)(2)
IRC §3231(e)

Spouse and children as employees

IRC §3121(b)(3)(A) and (B)

Back wages subject to FICA when paid

U.S. v. Cleveland Indians Baseball Co., 121 S. Ct. 1433 (2001)

Student employees

IRC §3121(b)(10)
Notice 2004-12, 2004-10 IRB 556 (proposed guidelines)

26.10 Withholding on Retirement Distributions

IRC §3405

Making Work Pay credit withholding tables affect pension withholdings

News Release IR-2009-50
Notice 1036-P, 5/14/09

Withholding on payments outside U.S.

IRC §3405(e)(13)

20% withholding from employer plans

IRC §3405(c)
Notice 93-3, 1993-1 CB 293

26.11 Backup Withholding

IRC §3406(a)(1), as amended by EGTRRA 2001

$50 penalty

IRC §6723 and §6724(d)(3)

27 Estimated Tax Payments

27.1 Do You Owe an Estimated Tax Penalty for 2010?

IRC §6654
* IRS Publication 505

$1,000 threshold

IRC §6654(e)(1)

90% or prior year safe harbor

IRC §6654(d)

Special 2009 safe harbor for 2008 small business owner

IRC §6654(d)(1)(D)

Late filers can use prior-year estimated tax safe harbor

Rev. Rul. 2003-23, 2003-8 IRB 511

Safe harbor percentage if adjusted gross income exceeds $150,000

IRC §6654(d)(1)(C)

No liability in prior tax year

IRC §6654(e)(2)
Rev. Rul. 57-185, 1957-1 CB 454
Rev. Rul. 58-369, 1958-2 CB 894
John A. Guglielmetti, 35 TC 668 (1961) (Acq.)

Penalty waiver for hardship, retirement, or disability

IRC §6654(e)(3)

Farmers and fishermen

IRC §6654(i)

27.2 Planning Estimated Tax Payments for 2011

* IRS Publication 505

$1,000 threshold

IRC §6654(e)(1)

90% or prior year safe harbor

IRC §6654(d)

Safe harbor percentage if adjusted gross income exceeds $150,000

IRC §6654(d)(1)(C)

Pay estimated taxes with credit cards

News Release IR 1999-87; Form 1040 instructions

Partners

Reg. §1.6654-2(d)(2)

Farmers and fishermen

IRC §6654(i)

27.3 Dates for Paying Estimated Tax Installments for 2011

* IRS Publication 505

Due dates for required installments

IRC §6654(c)

Return filed by January 31

IRC §6654(h)

27.4 Estimates by Husband and Wife

* IRS Publication 505
Reg. §1.6654-2

27.5 Adjusting Your Payments During the Year

* IRS Publication 505

Amending your estimate

IRC §6654(c)

28 Tax Planning Overview

28.1 Tax-Saving Opportunities

28.2 When To Defer Income and Accelerate Deductions

Tax shelter investments—passive loss limitations

IRC §469

Children under age 18

IRC §1(g)

28.3 Tax Law Changes for Years After 2010

29 Tax Savings for Residence Sales

IRC §121
* IRS Publication 523

29.1 Avoiding Tax on Sale of Principal Residence

IRC §121
Reg. §§ 1.121-1 through 1.121-4
* IRS Publication 523

Only one exclusion every two years

IRC §121(b)(3)

Exclusion plus gain deferral on exchange of residence

Rev. Proc. 2005-14, 2005-7 IRB 528

Change in employment, health, or unforeseen circumstances

Reg. §1.121-3
Rev. Rul. 82-26, 1982-1 CB 114

No exclusion for newly constructed house

David A. Gates, 135 TC No. 1 (2010)

Summer home does not qualify as principal residence under final

Note: *Paragraph numbers refer to Parts 1 through 7. Items marked * are research aids, not citations of authority;* see *"Key to Citations" on page 801*

regulations

James M. Guinan, 2003-1 USTC ¶50,475 (D.C., Dist. AZ 2003)

Part of house used for business

Reg. §1.121-1(e)

Multiple homes

Reg. §1.121-1(b)(2)

Vacant land

Reg. §1.121-1(b)(3)

Remainder interest

IRC §121(d)(8)

Expatriates

IRC §121(e)

Depreciation element

IRC §121(d)(6)
Reg. §121-1(d)

Casualty damage can result in sale treatment

Chief Counsel Advice (ILM) 200734021

29.2 Meeting the Ownership and Use Tests

IRC §121(a)
Reg. §§ 1.121-1 through 1.121-4
* IRS Publication 523

Post-2008 exclusion cut back for post-2008 nonqualified use

IRC 121(b)(5)

One sale every two years

IRC §121(b)(3)

Change in employment, health, or unforeseen circumstances

IRC §121(c)

Prior rollovers

IRC §121(g)

Five-year test period suspended for military personnel, Foreign Service personnel, and intelligence officers

IRC §121(d)(9)
Reg. §1.121-5
* ILM 200630015 (military exception)

No exclusion for newly constructed house

David A. Gates, 135 TC No. 1 (2010)

Co-owner can claim full $250,000 exclusion

*Sung Huey Mei Hsu, TC Summary Opinion, 2010-68

Cooperative apartment

Reg. §1.121-4(c)

Incapacitated owner

IRC §121(d)(7)

Five-year ownership test for home acquired in like-kind exchange

IRC §121(d)(10)[(11)]

29.3 Home Sales by Married Persons

IRC §121(b)(2)
IRC §121(d)(1)
* IRS Publication 523

Joint returns

IRC §121(b)(2)

Deceased spouse

IRC §121(d)(2)

Sale by surviving spouse within two years

IRC 121(b)(4)

Divorced couples

IRC §121(d)(3)
* Chief Counsel Information Letter 2005-0055 (home used by other spouse pursuant to divorce decree or separation)

29.4 Reduced Maximum Exclusion

IRC §121(c)
Reg. §1.121-3
* IRS Publication 523

IRS guidelines—change in employment, health, or unforeseen circumstances

Reg. §1.121-3

September 11 terrorist attacks

Notice 2002-60, 2002-36 IRB 482

Being run out of town allows reduced exclusion

* Letter Ruling 200403049

Policeman's job change allows reduced exclusion

* Letter Ruling 200504012

Child adoption allows reduced exclusion

* Letter Ruling 200613009

Partial exclusion allowed for early move from retirement community

* Letter Ruling 200601023

Taking in paralyzed mother-in-law allows reduced exclusion

* Letter Ruling 200626024

Assaults in neighborhood allow reduced exclusion

* Letter Ruling 200630004 (crime exception)
* Letter Ruling 200601009 (crime exception)

Settlement proceeds for airplane noise eligible for exclusion

* Letter Ruling 200702032

Need for larger home following birth of another child is unforeseen circumstance

* Letter Ruling 200745011

29.5 Figuring Gain or Loss

* IRS Publication 523

Gain or loss

IRC §1001
Reg. §1.1001-1 (amount realized)

Selling price

Reg. §1.1001
IRC §1001

Mortgage included in price

Beulah B. Crane, 331 U.S. 1 (1947)

Property valued at less than mortgage

John F. Tufts, 456 U.S. 960 (1983)

Reduce price by expenses

Seleths O. Thompson, 9 BTA 1342 (Acq.)
Samuel C. Chapin, 12 TC 235 (1949), aff'd, 180 F.2d 140 (8th Cir. 1950)

Legal fee—cost of sale

Fred W. Gunn, 49 TC 38 (1967)

29.6 Figuring Adjusted Basis

Unadjusted basis

IRC §1012
Reg. §1.1012-1
* IRS Publication 551

Improvements

IRC §1016
Reg. §1.016-2

Note: *Paragraph numbers refer to Parts 1 through 7. Items marked * are research aids, not citations of authority;* see *"Key to Citations" on page 801*

Adjusted basis

IRC §1011

Reg. §1.1011-1

Improvements not covered by note

Glenda P. McCormick, 99-1 USTC ¶50,380

Basis is cash cost

IRC §1012

Reg. §1.1012-1

Adjusted cost after depreciation allowed

IRC §1016

Reg. §1.1016-3

Tax-free exchange of property

IRC §1031

Reg. §1.1031(d)-1

Basis of new residence after home sale deferral

IRC §1034(e)

Reg. §1.1034-1

Property subject to lease

Harriet M. Bryant Trust, 11 TC 374 (1948) (Acq.)

Property subject to mortgage

Beulah B. Crane, 331 U.S. 1 (1947)

Compulsory or involuntary conversion

IRC §1033(b)

29.7 Personal and Business Use of a Home

Reg. §1.121-1(e)

* IRS Publication 523

Post-2008 exclusion cut back for post-2008 nonqualified use

IRC 121(b)(5)

Exclusion plus gain deferral on exchange of residence

Rev. Proc. 2005-14, 2005-7 IRB 528

29.8 No Loss Allowed on Personal Residence

Reg. §1.165-9(a)

29.9 Loss on Residence Converted to Rental Property

IRC §165(c)(2)

Reg. §1.165-9(b)

90-day lease returning a profit with option to buy

Paul H. Rechnitzer, 26 TCM 298 (1967)

Rental loss on temporary rental before sale

Stephen Bolaris, 776 F.2d 1428 (9th Cir. 1985), rev'g 81 TC 840 (1983)

Ronald S. Adams, 69 TCM 2297 (1995)

No loss unless move out

Peter Seletos, 254 F.2d 794 (8th Cir. 1958)

Loss on rented vacation home

James B. Murtaugh, 74 TCM 75 (1997)

Annual rent

Austin F. Stillman, 9 TCM 425 (1950)

Conversion to business property

Reg. §1.165-9(b)

Isolated rental

Charles A. Foehl, Jr., 20 TCM 418 (1961)

Intent to sell at profit, loss allowed

Lucille H. Gaunt, 69 F. Supp. 747 (W.D. Ky.)

Albert W. Bassett, 35 TCM 40 (1976)

Vandalism

Elbert S. Tillotson, 12 TCM 171 (1953)

Architect

Leonard Hyatt, 20 TCM 1635 (1961), supplemented by 20 TCM 1712 (1961), aff'd, 325 F.2d 715 (5th Cir. 1964), cert. denied, 379 U.S. 832

Listing for sale or rent

George D. Morgan, 76 F.2d 390 (5th Cir. 1935), cert. denied, 296 U.S. 601

Walden E. Sweet, 68-2 USTC ¶9656 (N.D. Cal. 1968)

James J. Sherlock, 31 TCM 383 (1972)

Rental to buyer

Henry B. Dawson, Jr., 31 TCM 5 (1972)

Expenses of rental attempt

Paul F. Stutz, 24 TCM 888 (1965)

Deducting expense of vacant building put up for sale

George W. Mitchell, 47 TC 120 (1966) (Nonacq.)

Limit on expense deductions where house used for personal purposes during the year

IRC §280a

Widow allowed capital loss not rental loss

Victoria Balsamo, 54 TCM 608 (1987)

Stock in co-op apartment

Rev. Rul. 60-76, 1960-1 CB 296

Cecil P. Stewart, 5 TCM 229 (1946)

William M. Calder, Jr., 16 TC 144 (1951) (Acq.)

Sale of partly rented house

Virginia V. Gary, BTA Memo., P-H 32,174, December 1, 1932 (capital gain on rental part; nondeductible loss on personal part)

29.10 Loss on Residence Acquired by Gift or Inheritance

Residence acquired by gift or inheritance

IRC §165(c)(2)

N. Stuart Campbell, 5 TC 272 (1945) (Acq.)

Maria Assmann Est., 16 TC 632 (1951)

Reed A. Watkins, 32 TCM 1260 (1973)

George W. Carnrick, 9 TC 756 (1947) (Acq.)

Pauline Miller Est., 26 TCM 229 (1967)

30 Tax Rules for Investors in Securities

30.1 Planning Year-End Securities Transactions

Capital gain holding period

IRC §1222

Capital loss deduction against ordinary income

IRC §1211(b)

Gain and loss recognized on trade date for year-end sale of publicly traded securities

IRC §453 (k)(2)

30.2 Earmarking Stock Lots

Registered in own name

Reg. §1.1012-1(c)(5)

James E. Davidson, 305 U.S. 44 (1938)

Margin account registered in "street" name

James L. Rankin, Exr., 295 U.S. 123 (1936)

Laura M. Curtis, 101 F.2d 40 (2d Cir. 1939)

Note: *Paragraph numbers refer to Parts 1 through 7. Items marked * are research aids, not citations of authority;* see *"Key to Citations" on page 801*

James L. Rankin, Exr. 84 F.2d 551 (3d Cir. 1936)

Recapitalization

Robert E. Ford, 33 BTA 1229 (Acq.)

Reorganization—identified

Amelia D. Bloch, 148 F.2d 452 (9th Cir. 1945)

Failure to show certificate numbers

Kluger Associates, 69 TC 925 (1978), aff'd, 617 F.2d 323 (2d Cir. 1980)

Reorganization—average cost

Christian W. Von Gunten, 76 F.2d 670 (6th Cir. 1935)

Harry M. Runkle, 39 BTA 458

Pio Crespi, 126 F.2d 699 (5th Cir. 1942)

Big Wolf Corp., 2 TC 751 (1943) (Acq.)

Split-up

Robert E. Ford, 33 BTA 1229 (Acq.)

Herbert H. Franklin, 37 BTA 471 (Acq.)

Solomon B. Kraus, 88 F.2d 616 (2d Cir. 1937)

Stock dividends

George Vawter, 83 F.2d 11 (10th Cir. 1936), cert. denied, 299 U.S. 578

Stock rights

Williams R. Perkins, 12 F. Supp. 481 (Ct. Cl. 1935), cert. denied, 297 U.S. 710

30.3 Sale of Stock Dividends

Holding period

IRC §1223

Reg. §1.1223-1

Public utility stock dividend

IRC §305(e)

30.4 Stock Rights

Stockholder rights expire

IRC §1223

IRC §307

Reg. §1.1223-1(e)

Reg. §1.307-1 and 2

Sidney Z. Mitchell, 18 BTA 994, aff'd, 48 F.2d 697 (2d Cir. 1931), cert. denied, 284 U.S. 646

Stock rights sold

IRC §1223(5)

Reg. §1.1223-1(e)

Stock rights exercised

IRC §1223(6)

Reg. §1.1223-1(f)

Rights purchased

IRC §1223

Reg. §1.1223-1

Figuring basis of stock rights

IRC §307

IRC §307(b)(1)(B) ("less than 15%" exception)

Reg. §1.307-1

Election

Reg. §1.307-2

30.5 Short Sales of Stock

* IRS Publication 550

Rev. Rul. 2002-44, 2002-28 IRB 84 (timing of gain or loss reporting)

Short sale closing

H. S. Richardson, 121 F.2d 1 (2d Cir. 1941), cert. denied, 314 U.S. 684

William P. Doyle, 286 F.2d 654 (7th Cir. 1961), rev'g 19 TCM 677 (1960)

* Letter Ruling 9436017

Appreciated financial position at year-end

IRC §1259

Rev. Rul. 2002-44, 2002-28 IRB 84

* "Tax Planning for Short-Sale Transactions," Rolf Auster, 60 Taxation for Accountants 90 (Feb. 1998)

Husband and wife

Reg. §1.1233-1(d)(3)

Special short-sale rules

IRC §1233(b)

Reg. §1.1233-1(c)(2)

Special rule on short-sale losses

IRC §1233(d)

Reg. §1.1233-1(c)(4)

Time of loss

Walter Hendricks, 29 TCM 36 (1970), aff'd, 423 F.2d 485 (4th Cir. 1970)

Payment in lieu of dividends: 46-day rule

IRC §263(b)

Puts (options to sell)

IRC §1233(c)

Reg. §1.1233-1(c)(3)

Expenses of short sales; stock dividends

Rev. Rul. 72-521, 1972-2 CB 178

Cash dividends paid on stock sold short

IRC §263(h)

1955 Production Exposition, Inc., 41 TC 85 (1963)

Main Line Distributors, Inc., 37 TC 1090 (1962), aff'd, 321 F.2d 562 (6th Cir. 1963)

Compensation for use of collateral

IRC §263(h)(5)

Extraordinary dividends

IRC §263(h)(2)

IRC §263(h)(3)

Arbitrage transactions

IRC §1233(f)

Reg. §1.1233-1(f)

Death before sale is closed

Rev. Rul. 73-524, 1973-2 CB 307

Wash sales

IRC §1091(e)

30.6 Wash Sales

Wash sales

IRC §1091

Reg. §1.1091-1 and 2

Rev. Rul. 2008-5, 2008-3, IRB 271 (replacement shares purchased in IRA)

Trader

Sol H. Morris, 38 BTA 265 (Acq.)

Richard S. Coulter, 32 BTA 617

IRC §1236

Reg. §1.471-5

Wilson, 76 F.2d 476 (10th Cir. 1935)

Walter Hirshon, 116 F. Supp. 135 (Ct. Cl. 1953)

L. B. Maytag, 32 TC 270 (1959)

Dealer

IRC §1091(a)

Donander Co., 29 BTA 312

Oral agreement

Estate of Maxwell J. Estroff, 47 TCM 234 (1983)

Substantially identical securities

Corn Products Refining Co., 215 F.2d 524 (2d Cir. 1954), aff'd, 350 U.S. 46 (1955)

Trenton Cotton Oil Co., 147 F.2d 33 (6th Cir. 1945), rehearing denied, 148 F.2d 208 (6th Cir. 1945)

Marie Hanlin, 197 F.2d 429 (3d Cir.

Note: *Paragraph numbers refer to Parts 1 through 7. Items marked * are research aids, not citations of authority;* see *"Key to Citations" on page 801*

1939)

Sicanoff Vegetable Oil Co., 27 TC 1056 (1957)

Rev. Rul. 76-346, 1976-1 CB 247

Rev. Rul. 58-210, 1958-1 CB 523

Rev. Rul. 58-211, 1958-1 CB 529

Maturity dates

Marie Hanlin et al., 108 F.2d 429 (3d Cir. 1939)

Rev. Rul. 76-346, 1976-1 CB 247

Rev. Rul. 58-211, 1958-1 CB 259

Interest rates differed

Rev. Rul. 76-346, 1976-1 CB 247

Rev. Rul. 60-195, 1960-1 CB 300

Issue date and interest payments of bonds not material

Marjorie K. Campbell, 39 BTA 916 (Acq.), aff'd, 112, F.2d 530 (2d Cir. 1940), rev'd, 313 U.S. 15 (1941)

Warrants

Rev. Rul. 56-406, 1956-2 CB 523

Contract to sell stock

Rev. Rul. 59-418, 1959-2 CB 184

Short sales

Reg. §1.1091-1(g)

William P. Doyle, 286 F.2d 654 (7th Cir. 1961), rev'g 19 TCM 677 (1960)

Foreign currencies are not "securities"

Rev. Rul. 74-218, 1974-1 CB 202

Commodity futures

IRC §1092(b)

* Letter Ruling 8241006

30.7 Convertible Stocks and Bonds

No gain or loss

Rev. Rul. 72-265, 1972-1 CB 222

Holding period

IRC §1223(1)

Split-holding period

Rev. Rul. 62-140, 1962-2 CB 181

Basis

IRC §358

30.8 Constructive Sales of Appreciated Financial Positions

IRC §1259

30.9 Straddle Losses

IRC §1092

IRC §1256

IRC §263(g)

Loss barred on identified straddle position

IRC §1092(a)(2)(A), for positions established after October 21, 2004

Carryback of net Section 1256 loss

IRC §1212(c)

Mixed straddle election to avoid marked-to-market rules

Temp. Reg. §1.1092(b)-3T and §4T

30.10 Capital Gain Restricted on Conversion Transactions

IRC §1258

30.11 Puts and Calls and Index Options

IRC §1234(b)

IRC §1256

Capital gain

IRC §1234

Reg. §1234-1

Convert to long-term profits

Rev. Rul. 58-384, 1958-2 CB 410

Marked-to-market rules

IRC §1256(a)

30.12 Investing in Tax-Exempts

IRC §103

Qualified private activity bonds

IRC §141(e)

AMT exception for private activity bonds issued in 2009 and 2010

IRC §57(a)(5)(C)(vi)

Tax preference item

IRC §57(a)(5)

30.13 Ordinary Loss for Small Business Stock (Section 1244)

IRC §1244

* IRS Publication 550

Record-keeping

Reg. §1.1244(e)-1(b)

30.14 Series EE and E Bonds

* IRS Publication 550

Reporting E and EE bond interest annually

IRC §454(c)

Reg. §1.454-1

Deduction for estate tax

Rev. Rul. 58-435, 1958-2 CB 370, distinguished by Rev. Rul. 68-145 1968-1 CB 203

Savings bond tuition plans

IRC §135

EE bonds issued after April 2005 pay fixed interest

Treasury Department Press Release, 4/4/05

30.15 I Bonds

* IRS Publication 550

Taxation of Series I bonds

31 CFR Sec 359.9 (b)(1)

30.16 Trader, Dealer, or Investor?

* IRS Publication 550

* "On-line Transactions Intensify Trader vs. Investor Question," Jack Robinson and Richard S. Mark, 66 Practical Tax Strategies 80 (February 2001)

Sporadic trading bars trader status

William G. Holsinger, TC Memo 2008-141

Frank Chen, TC Memo 2004-132

Securities investor denied trader status

Frederick R. Mayer, TC Memo 1994-209

Home office deduction denied to investor

Joseph Moller, 721 F.2d 810 (CA-Fed. Cir. 1983)

30.17 Mark-to-Market Election for Traders

IRC §475(f)

Election procedure

Rev. Proc. 99-17, 1999-7 IRB 52

* IRS Publication 550

Deadline for mark-to-market election

Kazim Z. Acar, 2008-2 USTC ¶50,564 (9th Circuit 2008) (IRS deadline applies)

Ronald A. Lehrer, TC Memo 2005-167 (IRS deadline applies)

Note: *Paragraph numbers refer to Parts 1 through 7. Items marked * are research aids, not citations of authority;* see *"Key to Citations" on page 801*

L.S. Vines, 126 TC 279 (2006) (extension allowed over IRS objection)

31 Tax Savings for Investors in Real Estate

31.1 Investing in Real Estate Ventures

Syndicates

Reg. §301.7701-1

Limited partnership not taxable as corporation

Phillip G. Larson, 66 TC 159 (1976) (Acq.)

Rev. Rul. 79-106, 1979-1 CB 448

IRS to study minimum capitalization requirement

Ann. 83-4, 1983-2 IRB 31

Publicly traded partnerships

IRC §7704

IRC §469

Real estate investment trusts

IRC §856

IRC §857

IRC §858

Reg. §1.856

Reg. §1.857

Reg. §1.858

REMICs

IRC §860A-860G

* IRS Publication 550

31.2 Sales of Subdivided Land—Dealer or Investor?

IRC §1237

Reg. §1.1237-1

Liquidation of business property—no capital gain

John W. Kelley, 18 TCM 329 (1959), aff'd, 281 F.2d 527 (9th Cir. 1959)

No sales effort

Robert E. Austin, 263 F.2d 460 (9th Cir. 1959)

William T. Minor, Jr., 18 TCM 14 (1959)

James G. Hoover, 32 TC 618 (1959) (Acq.)

Allen Moore, 30 TC 1306 (1958) (Acq.)

Sam E. Broadhead Est., 32 TCM 1047 (1973)

Robert L. Adams, 60 TC 996 (1973) (Acq.)

Substantial improvements bar Section 1237 treatment

Jesse W. English, 65 TCM 2160 (1993)

Dealers may not use installment method

IRC §453(b)(2)(A)

IRC §453(l)

Sale to controlled corporation

Ralph E. Gordy, 36 TC 855 (1961) (Acq.)

Real estate dealer

Richard H. Pritchett, 63 TC 149 (1974) (Acq.)

Effect of condemnation

Thomas K. McManus, 65 TC 197 (1975)

Tri S. Corp., 400 F.2d 862 (10th Cir. 1968) (capital gains allowed)

Theodore H. Case, 633 F.2d 1240 (6th Cir. 1980) (capital gains denied)

Developer allowed capital gains on sale to city

Est. of Eileen Knudsen, 40 TCM 510 (1980)

Oscar Fraley, 66 TCM 100 (1993)

Developer not allowed capital gain on land sale

Robert P. Walsh, 67 TCM 3134 (1994)

31.3 Exchanging Real Estate Without Tax

IRC §1031

"Like kind"

Reg. §1.1031(a)-1(b) and (c)

Rev. Rul. 59-229, 1959-2 CB 180

P. G. Lake, Inc., 356 U.S. 260 (1958)

Productive use in trade or business

IRC §1031

Reg. §1.1031(a)-1(a)

Personal-use safe harbor for tax deferred exchange

Rev. Proc. 2008-16, 2008-10 IRB 547

Time limits

IRC §1031(a)(3)

Reg. §1.1031(a)-3

"Parking" for a like-kind exchange is limited

Rev. Proc. 2004-51, 2004-33 IRB 294

Treasury Department News Release JS-1798, 7/20/04

Direct deed transfer

Rev. Rul. 90-34, 1990-1 CB 154

Two-year freeze on exchange with related party

IRC §1031(f)

Basis

IRC §1031(d)

Reg. §1.1031(d)-1 and -2

Dealer

IRC §1031

Reg. §1.1031(a)-1(a)

Luther A. Harr, 15 F. Supp. 1004 (D.D. Pa. 1936)

Resale

Ethel Black, 35 TC 90 (1960)

Exchanges of remainder and life interests

Rev. Rul. 72-601, 1972-2 CB 467

Boot

Reg. §1.1031(b)-1

Partially tax-free exchanges

IRC §1031(b)

Reg. §1.1031(b)-1

Receipt of cash contractually obligated to be applied against liabilities not boot

Earlene T. Barker, 74 TC 555 (1980)

Loss not recognized

IRC §1031(a)

Reg. §1.1031(a)-1

Planning tax-free exchange

Rev. Rul. 77-297, 1977-2 CB 304

99-year lease exchanged for fee interest is like-kind

Carl E. Koch, 71 TC 54 (1978) (Acq.)

Optional renewal periods added to initial lease terms

Century Electric, 192 F.2d 155 (8th Cir. 1951), cert. denied, 342 U.S. 954

No tax-free exchange treatment for vacation property

Barry E. Moore, TC Memo 2007-134

31.4 Timing Your Real Property Sales

Note: *Paragraph numbers refer to Parts 1 through 7. Items marked * are research aids, not citations of authority; see "Key to Citations" on page 801*

Installment sales

IRC §453

Tax in year of sale

Milton S. Yunker, 26 TC 161 (1956), rev'd on other issue, 256 F.2d 130 (6th Cir. 1958)

Title passes

Alfred M. Bedell, 30 F.2d 622 (2d Cir. 1929)

Completion of terms of contingent sale

E. F. Baertschi, 412 F.2d 494 (6th Cir. 1969), rev'g 49 TC 289 (1967)

Deliver deed and possession

William C. King, 10 BTA 308 (Acq.)

Big Western Oil & Gas Co., 9 BTA 427 (Acq.)

Possession this year, deed next year

J. T. Pittard, 5 BTA 929 (Acq.)

Standard Lumber Co., 28 BTA 352

Buyer in possession

Ted F. Merrill, 40 TC 66 (1963), and per curiam, 366 F.2d 771 (9th Cir. 1964)

Marshall E. Boykin, 344 F.2d 889 (5th Cir. 1965)

Property held in escrow

Arthur Long, 1 BTA 796

Harry C. Moir, 14 BTA 23 (Nonacq.), aff'd, 45 F.2d 356 (7th Cir. 1930)

Deed delivered

William F. Scruggs, 281 F.2d 900 (10th Cir. 1960)

Option to sell exercised next year

Samuel C. Chapin, 180 F.2d 140 (8th Cir. 1950)

Contract to sell

Rev. Rul. 69-93, 1969-1 CB 139

No fair market value

A. M. Nichols, 44 F.2d 157 (3d Cir. 1930)

Nina Ennis, 17 TC 465 (1951)

Purchase price held

George I. Bumbaugh, 10 BTA 672

R. M. Waggoner, 9 BTA 629 (Nonacq.)

Preston R. Bassett, 33 BTA 182, aff'd per curiam, 90 F.2d 1004 (2d Cir. 1950)

K. E. Merren, 18 BTA 156 (Acq.), aff'd, 51 F.2d 44 (5th Cir. 1931)

31.5 Cancellation of a Lease

IRC §1241

Reg. §1.1241-1

31.6 Sale of an Option

IRC §1234

Reg. §1.1234-1

31.7 Granting of an Easement

David Fasten, 71 TC 650 (1979) (Acq.)

Inaja Land Co. Ltd., 9 TC 727 (1947) (Acq.)

Rev. Rul. 59-121, 1959-1 CB 212, clarified by Rev. Rul. 68-291, 1968-1 CB 351

Rev. Rul. 72-433, 1972-2 CB 470

Rev. Rul. 73-161, 1973-1 CB 366

Rev. Rul. 72-255, 1972-1 CB 221

Restrictive covenant released

Rev. Rul. 70-203, 1970-1 CB 171

31.8 Special Tax Credits for Real Estate Investments

Low-income housing credit permanently extended

IRC §42

Rehabilitating old and historic buildings

IRC §47

Recapture of rehabilitation credits

IRC §50(a)(i)

Substantial rehabilitation test applies to entire building

Karl R. Alexander III, 97 TC 244 (1991)

Credit allowed for relocated building

George Nalle, 997 F.2d 1134 (5th Cir., 1993)

Effect of charitable deduction on credit

Rome I, Ltd, 96 TC 697 (1991)

Higher credit for Gulf Opportunity Zone property

IRC §1400N(h)

31.9 Foreclosures, Repossessions, and Voluntary Conveyances to Creditors

IRS Publication 4681

Sale or exchange requirement

IRC §1222

Exclusion for discharge of qualified principal residence indebtedness

IRC 108 (a)(1)(E)

IRC 108 (h)

Capital asset treatment for lapse, cancellation, abandonment, etc., of commodity options

IRC §1234A

Property pledged as collateral

Morgan W. Jopling, 46 BTA 262

Voluntary conveyance of mortgaged property

Rev. Rul. 78-164, 1978-1 CB 264

Eugene L. Freeland, 74 TC 970 (1980)

Transfer by insolvent taxpayer

Rev. Rul. 90-16, 1990-1 CB 12

Foreclosure proceeds less than outstanding mortgage

Joseph Aizawa, 99 TC 197 (1992), aff'd. without published opinion, 29 F. 3d 630 (9th Cir. 1994)

Foreclosure bid price more than fair market value

Richard Frazier, 111 TC 243 (1998)

Business lease as 1231 asset

Rev. Rul. 72-85, 1972-1 CB 234

31.10 Restructuring Mortgage Debt

IRC §61(a)(12)

Exclusion for discharge of qualified principal residence indebtedness

IRC 108(a)(1)(E)

IRC 108(h)

Tax-free debt reductions

IRC §108(a)

Restructuring nonrecourse debt

Rev. Rul. 91-31, 1991-1 CB 19

IRS computation of insolvency

Rev. Rul. 92-53, 1992-2 CB 48

Relief for discharge of business real estate debt

IRC §108(a)(1)(D)

IRC §108(c)

31.11 Abandonments

Abandonment treated as sale

Milledge L. Middleton, 77 TC 310

Note: *Paragraph numbers refer to Parts 1 through 7. Items marked * are research aids, not citations of authority;* see *"Key to Citations" on page 801*

(1981), aff'd, 693 F.2d 124 (11th Cir., 1982)

James W. Yarbro, 45 TCM 170 (1982), aff'd, 737 F.2d 479 (5th Cir. 1984)

Abandonment of partnership interest

John C. Echols, 93 TC 553 (1989), rev'd by 950 F.2d 209 (5th Cir. 1991)

Philip Citron, 97 TC 200 (1991)

31.12 Seller's Repossession After Buyer's Default on Mortgage

IRC §1038

Reg. §1.1038-1 through 3

End of holding period for depreciation recapture purposes where property foreclosed

IRC §1250(D)(10)

Personal residence

IRC §1038(e)

31.13 Foreclosure on Mortgages Other Than Purchase Money

You bid on property at foreclosure sale

Reg. §1.166-6(a)(1) and (b)(1)

Hadley Falls Trust Co., 110 F.2d 887 (1st Cir. 1940)

Unreported but accrued interest as income in foreclosure

Midland Mutual Life Ins. Co., 300 U.S. 216 (1937)

Bid price as fair market value

West Production Co., 121 F.2d 9 (5th Cir. 1941), cert. denied, 314 U.S. 682

Harold S. Weil, 111 F. Supp. 390 (D. La. 1953)

Must prove worthlessness of debt

Reg. §1.166-2

Property voluntarily conveyed in satisfaction of debt

Achilles H. Kohn, 197 F.2d 480 (2d Cir. 1952)

Nonrecourse debt is not protected by insolvency

Rev. Rul. 91-31, 1991-1 CB 19

Rev. Rul. 92-53, 1992-2 CB 48

James J. Gehl, 102 TC 37 (1994)

* Letter Ruling 9302001

Unreported but accrued interest as income in voluntary conveyance

Reserve Loan Life Ins. Co., 18 BTA 359 (Acq. and nonacq.)

Prudential Ins. Co. of America, 33 BTA 332 (Nonacq.)

Year deductible

Hadley Falls Trust Co., 110 F.2d 887 (1st Cir. 1940)

William C. Heinemann & Co., 40 BTA 1090

31.14 Foreclosure Sale to Third Party

* "Gain on Foreclosure Sales of Realty Need Not Be Recognized," Edward J. Schnee, 54 Taxation for Accountants 292 (May 1995)

Foreclosure expenses

Coeur d'Alene Hotel Inc., BTA Memo., Dec. 12,097-A

Bowles Lunch, Inc., 33 F. Supp. 235 (Ct. Cl. 1940)

Foreclosure sale at less than your mortgage

Reg. §1.166-6(a)(1)

Business bad debt is fully deductible

IRC §166(a)

Nonbusiness bad debt is a limited capital loss

IRC §166(d)

Partially worthless debts

IRC §166(a)(2) and (d)(1)(A)

Business and nonbusiness bad debt must be uncollectible

IRC §166(a)(1) and (d)

31.15 Transferring Mortgaged Realty

Corporation

IRC §351

IRC §357

F. W. Drybrough, 376 F.2d 350 (6th Cir. 1967)

Gifts

Est. of Aaron Levine, 634 F.2d 12 (2d Cir. 1980)

Teofilo Evangelista, 629 F. 2d 1218 (7th Cir. 1980)

32 Tax Rules for Investors in Mutual Funds

32.1 Timing of Your Investment Can Impact Your Taxes

* IRS Publication 564

Capital gain

IRC §852(b)(3)

IRC §854(a)

Deferred annuities

Rev. Rul. 81-220, 1981-2 CB 175

Rev. Rul. 82-54, 1982-1 CB 11

Dividend declared in October, November, or December paid by following February

IRC §852(b)(7)

32.2 Reinvestment Plans

* IRS Publication 564

32.3 Mutual-Fund Distributions Reported on Form 1099-DIV

* IRS Publication 564

Qualified dividends taxed at capital gain rates

IRC §1(h)(11)

IRC §854(b)(2) (notice to shareholder of qualified dividend amount)

Capital gain distributions

IRC §852(b)(3)(B)

32.4 Tax-Exempt Bond Funds

Exempt-interest dividend

IRC §852(b)(5)(B)

32.5 Fund Expenses

IRC §67(c)(2)

32.6 Tax Credits From Mutual Funds

Undistributed capital gains

IRC §852(b)(3)(D)

Foreign dividends

* IRS Publication 514

32.7 How To Report Mutual Fund Distributions

* IRS Publication 564

Note: *Paragraph numbers refer to Parts 1 through 7. Items marked * are research aids, not citations of authority;* see *"Key to Citations" on page 801*

Qualified dividends taxed at capital gain rates

IRC §1(h)(11)

IRC §854(b)(2) (notice to shareholder of qualified dividend amount)

Capital gain distributions

IRC §852(b)(3)(B)

32.8 Redemptions and Exchanges of Fund Shares

Mutual-fund loss when stock held six months or less

IRC §852(b)(4)

Reg. §1.852-4(d)

Sales charges

IRC §852(f)

32.9 Basis of Redeemed Shares

* IRS Publication 564

Specific identification of sold shares

Joseph Hall, 92 TC 64 (1989)

Averaging cost on sale of shares

Reg. §1.1012-1(e)(i)

FIFO method if no specific identification

Reg. §1.1012-1(c)

32.10 Comparison of Basis Methods

* IRS Publication 564

Specific identification of sold shares

Joseph Hall, 92 TC 64 (1989)

FIFO method if no specific identification

Reg. §1.1012-1(c)

Averaging cost on sale of shares

Reg. §1.1012-1(e)(i)

33 Educational Tax Benefits

* "Tax Savings Ease the Task of Saving for College Tuition," David Lavin, Myron S. Lubell, and Angela F. Moree, 72 Practical Tax Strategies 283 (May 2004)
* "New Tax Breaks Compete With Traditional Wealth-Transfer Strategies," Barbara A. Taylor and Joseph A. Cipparone, 68 Tax Strategies 141 (March 2002)
* "Educational Incentives Can Be Coordinated For Greater Tax Savings," Mark E. Reid and Philip J. Harmelink, 67 Practical Tax Strategies 272 (November 2001)
* IRS Publication 970

33.1 Scholarships and Grants

IRC §117

Prop. Reg. §1.117-6

* IRS Publication 970

Prior law: primary purpose test

Richard E. Johnson, 394 U.S. 741 (1969),

rev'g 396 F. 2d 258 (3rd Cir. 1969)

Reg. §1.117-4(c)

Elmer L. Reese, Jr., 373 F. 2d 742 (4th Cir. 1967), aff'g per curiam, 45 TC 407 (1966)

Breach of federal scholarship

John Hawronsky, 105 TC 8 (1995)

Test for fellowship awards

Marc Spiegelman, 102 TC 14 (1994)

33.2 Tuition Reductions for College Employees

IRC §117(d)

* IRS Publication 970

Teaching and research income taxable

IRC §117(c)

Graduate student teaching and research assistants

IRC §117(d)(5)

Tuition reduction for domestic partner taxed

* Letter Ruling 200137041

33.3 How Fulbright Awards are Taxed

Rev. Rul. 61-65, 1961-1 CB 17

Award paid by U.S. agency

Laurence P. Dowd, 37 TC 399 (1961) (Nonacq.)

Professor on sabbatical leave

Rev. Rul. 62-2, 1962-1 CB 9

33.4 United States Savings Bond Tuition Plans

IRC §135

33.5 Contributing to a Qualified Tuition Program (Section 529 Plan)

IRC §529

* IRS Publication 970
* "Code Sec. 529 Plans: Estate Planning's Holy Grail?" Stephen C. Hartnett, 5 Practical Estate Planning 19 (August–September 2003)
* "Qualified Tuition Programs: The Often-Overlooked Downside," Rolf Auster, 70 Practical Tax Strategies 336 (June 2003)
* "What Every CPA Needs To Know About Code Sec. 529 Plans," Mark E. Reid, Daphne Main, and Linda Nelsestuen, 80 Taxes 17 (September 2002)

Private college QTPs

IRC §529(b)(1)

33.6 Distributions From Qualified Tuition Programs (Section 529 Plans)

Tax-free QTP distributions

IRC §529(c)(3)(B)(i) and (ii)

IRC §529(c)(3)(B)(iii)

Computer equipment and Internet access

IRC §529(e)(3)(A)(iii) (special rule for 2009 and 2010)

Qualified room and board

IRC §529(e)(3)(B)

Grantor trust rule if legal obligation to provide college education

Reg. §1.677(b)-1(f)

IRS allows changes in investment options

Notice 2001-58, 2001-39 IRB 299

33.7 Education Tax Credits

IRC §25A(a)

* IRS Publication 970

Reg. §§ 1.25A-1 through 1.25A-5

* "Optimizing the Use of Deductions and Credits to Minimize the Cost of Higher Education," Debra Ertel McGilsky, 81 Taxes 27 (June 2003)

American Opportunity Tax Credit

IRC §25A(i)

Who claims credit for expenses paid by dependent

Reg. §§ 1.25A-1(f) and 1.25A-5(a) (taxpayer claiming exemption for dependent gets credit)

Note: *Paragraph numbers refer to Parts 1 through 7. Items marked * are research aids, not citations of authority;* see *"Key to Citations" on page 801*

Reg. §1.25A-5(b) (expenses paid by third party directly to college)

Dependent student eligible for Hope credit

Reg. §1.25A-1(f)(2), example 2

* IRS Legal Memorandum 200236001

Prepaid tuition allows credit only for year of payment

Jayesh B. Patel, TC Summary Opinion 2006-40

33.8 American Opportunity Credit

IRC §25A(i)

* IRS Publication 970

Students in Midwestern disaster area

IRC §25A(i)(7) (coordination with American Opportunity credit)

IRC §1400O, applied to Midwestern disaster area by Act Sections 702(a)(1)(B) and 702(d)(8) of the Emergency Economic Stabilization Act of 2008

Dependent student eligible for credit

Reg. §1.25A-1(f)(2), example 2

* IRS Legal Memorandum 200236001

33.9 Lifetime Learning Credit

IRC §25A(c)

Reg. §1.25A-4

Higher Lifetime Learning credit for students in Midwestern disaster area

IRC §1400 O, applied to Midwestern disaster area by Act Sections 702(a)(1)(B) and 702(d)(8) of the Emergency Economic Stabilization Act of 2008

33.10 Income Phaseout of Education Credits

IRC §25A(d)

Reg. §1.25A-1(c)

33.11 Contributing to a Coverdell Education Savings Account (ESA)

IRC §530

* IRS Publication 970

Contribution limit

IRC §530(b)(1)(A)(iii)

Phaseout of contribution limit

IRC §530(c)

33.12 Distributions From Coverdell ESAs

IRC §530(d)

* IRS Publication 970

Coordination with Hope and Lifetime Learning credits and QTPs

IRC §530(d)(2)(C)

Exception to additional tax for Service Academy appointees

IRC §530 (d)(4)(B)(iv)

33.13 Tuition and Fees Deduction

IRC §222

* IRS Publication 970

33.14 Student Loan Interest Deduction

IRC §221

* IRS Publication 970

Phaseout of deduction

IRC §221(b)(2)(B)

33.15 Types of Deductible Work-Related Costs

Reg. §1.162-5

* IRS Publication 508

2% floor for employees

IRC §67(a)

MBA costs can be deductible

Daniel R. Allemeier Jr., TC Memo 2005-207

33.16 Work-Related Tests for Education Costs

Reg. §1.162-5

* "Tax Consequences Associated with Obtaining an MBA Degree," Leonard Goodman and Jay A. Soled, 79 Taxes 43 (July 2001)

Minimum job requirements

Reg. §1.162-5(b)(2)

Eduardo Antuna, 36 TCM 1778 (1977)

David Cooper, 37 TCM 529 (1978)

Maintain or improve skills

1.162-5(c)(1)

Clark S. Marlor, 251 F.2d 615 (2d Cir. 1958)

Qualification for new business

Reg. §1.162-5(b)(3)

Teacher did not abandon profession

John C. Ford, 56 TC 1300 (1971), aff'd per curiam, 487 F.2d 1025 (9th Cir. 1973)

Prerequisites not deductible

Neal F. Krauss, 39 TCM 725 (1979)

MBA expenses deductible

Daniel R. Allemeier Jr., TC Memo 2005-207

Robert C. Beatty, 40 TCM 438 (1980)

Frank S. Blair, 41 TCM 289 (1980)

MBA expenses not deductible

Ross L. Link, 90 TC 460 (1988)

Ronald T. Smith, 41 TCM 1186 (1981)

Eduardo Antuna, 36 TCM 1778 (1977)

Nurse can deduct cost of MBA

*Lori A. Singleton-Clarke, TC Summary Opinion 2009-182

Undergraduate courses not deductible by accountant

Diane Zimmer, 64 TCM 1388 (1992)

Undergraduate courses not deductible by financial planner

Judith Meredith, 65 TCM 2876 (1993)

Associate degree classes not deductible by golf instructor

* Edward M. Fields, TC Summary Opinion, 2001-35

Undergraduate courses not deductible by office manager

Theresa M. Malek, 50 TCM 792 (1985)

Undergraduate college costs not deductible by policeman

James A. Carroll, 51 TC 213 (1968), aff'd, 418 F.2d 91 (7th Cir. 1969)

Industrial psychologist

Cosimo A. Carlucci, 37 TC 695 (1962) (Acq.)

Engineering aide to maintain skills

Ralph A. Fattore, 22 TCM 1093 (1963)

Attorney attending graduate courses

Albert C. Ruehmann, 30 TCM 675 (1971)

Charles B. Johnson, 332 F. Supp. 906 (D. La. 1971)

Larry R. Adamson, 32 TCM 484 (1973)

Unemployed teacher

Edward J. P. Zimmerman, 71 TC 367 (1978), aff'd, 79-2 USTC ¶9617 (2nd

Note: *Paragraph numbers refer to Parts 1 through 7. Items marked * are research aids, not citations of authority;* see *"Key to Citations" on page 801*

Cir. 1979)

Engineer not established in his profession

Barry Reisine, 29 TCM 1429 (1970)

Thomas W. Gallery, 57 TC 257 (1971)

Orthodontic course

Rev. Rul. 74-78, 1974-1 CB 44

CPA review course not deductible

Rev. Rul. 69-282, 1969-1 CB 55

William D. Glenn, 62 TC 270 (1974)

Private tutoring in management

Walter G. Lage, 52 TC 119 (1969) (Acq.)

Bar admission fee not deductible

Arthur E. Ryman, Jr., 51 TC 799 (1969)

William J. Brennan, 22 TCM 1222 (1963)

Broker license cost not deductible

Robert Kersey, 50 F.3d 15 (9th Cir. 1995)

Music therapy courses not deductible

Herbert Hewett, 71 TCM 2350 (1996)

Flying lessons of freelance news photographer

Alan Aaronson, 29 TCM 786 (1970)

Flight school for NASA engineer not deductible

Ronald Z. Thompson, TC Memo 2007-174

Law school

Reg. §1.162-5(b)(2) and (3)

Jeffrey S. Augen, 33 TCM 1022 (1974)

Robert J. Connelly, 72-1 USTC ¶9188 (1st Cir. 1972)

Charles M. Watkins, 59 TCM 467 (1990)

Tax law courses taken by lawyer

Joseph T. Booth, III, 35 TC 1144 (1961)

Business law teacher

Juanita Ardavany, 38 TCM 569 (1979)

Amortization of fees to state bar admission authorities

Joel Sharon, 591 F. 2d 1273 (9th Cir. 1978), aff'g 66 TC 515 (1976)

Costs to practice law in second state

Joseph J. Vetrick, 37 TCM 392 (1978), aff'd, 628 F.2d 885 (5th Cir. 1980)

Lawyer must practice profession

Albert C. Ruehmann, III, 30 TCM 675 (1971)

Richard M. Randick, 35 TCM 195 (1976)

Paul R. Wassenaar, 72 TC 1195 (1979)

David M. Kohen, 44 TCM 1518 (1982)

* Letter Ruling 9112003

Psychiatry courses

John S. Watson, 31 TC 1014 (1959) (Nonacq.)

Psychoanalytic courses

Ramon M. Greenberg, 367 F.2d 663 (1st Cir. 1966)

Psychiatrist's therapy by phone and cassette

Kenneth Porter, 51 TCM 481 (1986)

Cost of physician's assistant course

Matthew J. Reisinger, 71 TC 568 (1979)

Social worker denied deduction for education necessary for faculty position

Kenneth C. Davis, 65 TC 1014 (1976)

Teaching assistant denied deduction of graduate study costs

Arthur M. Jungreis, 55 TC 581 (1970)

Teaching assistant denied deduction for bachelor degree

George Baisr, 56 TCM 781 (1988)

Paraprofessional denied deduction for costs of becoming classroom teacher

Leonarda Diaz, 70 TC 1067 (1978), aff'd, 607 F.2d 995 (2d Cir. 1979)

33.17 Local Transportation and Travel Away From Home To Take Courses

IRC §274(m)(2)

* IRS Publication 970

English teacher's deduction for trips to Greece and Asia

Ann Jorgensen, TC Memo 2000-138

Professor's nondeductible educational travel

Theodore Keller, TC Memo 1996-300

Trip between work and school

Gerhard F. B. Boerner, 30 TCM 240 (1971)

Robert J. Burton, 30 TCM 243 (1971)

Employer reimbursement or direct payment of tuition

Rev. Rul. 76-71 1976-1 CB 308, distinguished by Rev. Rul. 76-352, 1976-2 CB 37

Stipend paid by employer is taxable

Rev. Rul. 76-65, 1976-1 CB 46, distinguished by Rev. Rul. 76-352, 1976-2 CB 37

Payment for substitute teacher fund

Rev. Rul. 76-286, 1976-2 CB 41

Payments from VA

Rev. Rul. 83-3 1983-1 CB 72

34 Special Tax Rules for Senior Citizens

34.1 Senior Citizens Get Certain Filing Breaks

Higher filing threshold

IRC §6012(a)(1)(B)

Higher standard deduction

IRC §63(f)

Credit for elderly

IRC §22

Threshold for Social Security benefits tax

IRC §86

34.2 Social Security Benefits Subject to Tax

* IRS Publication 915

IRC §86

Repayments

IRC §86(d)(2)

Benefits to child

House Ways and Means Committee Report to P.L. 98-21

Workers' compensation

IRC §86(d)(3)

Disability benefits taxed despite workers' compensation offset

John M. Mikalonis, TC Memo 2000-281

Nonresident alien

IRC §871(a)(3)

Gambling winnings make Social Security benefits partly taxable

* Leroy J. Klingaman, TC Summary Opinion 2005-36

Note: *Paragraph numbers refer to Parts 1 through 7. Items marked * are research aids, not citations of authority;* see *"Key to Citations" on page 801*

34.3 Computing Taxable Social Security Benefits

* IRS Publication 915

Base amount and adjusted base amount

IRC §86(c)

Effect of IRA deductions

Announcement 88-38, 1988-10 IRB 60

34.4 Election for Lump-Sum Social Security Benefit Payment

IRC §86(e)

34.5 Retiring on Social Security Benefits

42 USCA §1382

* "Social Security Benefit Delayed Is Generally Wealth Denied," Sidney J. Baxendale, 65 Tax Strategies 203 (October 2000)

34.6 How Tax on Social Security Reduces Your Earnings

IRC §86

34.7 Claiming the Credit for the Elderly and Disabled

IRC §22

* IRS Publication 524

Age 65 or retired on disability

IRC §22(b)

Nonresident alien ineligible

IRC §22(f)

Married couples

IRC §22(e)(1)

34.8 Base Amount for the Elderly or Disabled Credit

Initial base amount

IRC §22(c)

Disability income limit

IRC §22(c)(2)(B)

Disability income defined

IRC §22(c)(2)(B)(iii)

Permanent disability defined

IRC §22(e)(3)

34.9 Reduction of the Base Amount and Liability Limitation for the Credit

IRC §22(c)(3)(A) (Social Security and pensions)

IRC §22(d) (adjusted gross income)

* IRS Publication 524

34.10 Tax Effects of Moving to a Continuing Care Facility

* IRS Publication 502

Portion of monthly fees allocable to medical expenses

Delbert L. Baker, 122 TC 143 (2004)

Charitable deduction for sponsorship gift

Ruth Dowell, 553 F.2d 1233 (10th Cir. 1977)

No charitable deduction for donation that represents cost of apportionment

Ernest Klappenbach, 52 TCM 437 (1986)

Medical deduction for portion of entry fee to assisted living facility

John O. Finzer, Jr., 2007-2 USTC ¶50,591 (D.C. IL 2007)

Investment in community equivalent to home purchase

* Letter Ruling 8837022

Highland Farms, Inc., 106 TC 12 (1996)

34.11 Imputed Interest on Refundable Entrance Fees

Imputed interest exception for qualified continuing care facilities

IRC §7872(h)

34.12 Part B Premiums for 2011 Affected by Social Security

Section 811 of the Medicare Prescription Drug, Improvement and Modernization Act of 2003 (authorizing Part B premium surcharges)

Part B Premiums for 2011

Centers for Medicare and Medicaid Services Fact Sheet, 11/4/10

Part B Premiums for 2010

Centers for Medicare and Medicaid Services Fact Sheet, 10/16/09

35 Members of the Armed Forces

35.1 Taxable Armed Forces Pay and Benefits

* IRS Publication 3

Regular pay, leave pay, enlistment bonuses taxable

Rev. Rul. 55-249, 1955-1 CB 21

Withholding required for differential wages paid after 2008

IRC §3401(h), added by Heroes Earnings Assistance Tax Relief Act of 2008

Rev. Rul. 2009-11, 2009-18 IRB 896

35.2 Tax-Free Armed Forces Benefits

* IRS Publication 3

Tax-free combat pay

IRC §112

Exclusion for qualified military benefits

IRC §134

Exclusion for death gratuity payment

Section 1478(a) of Title 10, U.S. Code IRC §134(b)(3)(C)

Withholding required for differential wages paid after 2008

IRC §3401(h), added by Heroes Earnings Assistance Tax Relief Act of 2008

Rev. Rul. 2009-11, 2009-18 IRB 896

Subsistence allowance

Rev. Rul. 55-572, 1955-2 CB 45, distinguished by Rev. Rul. 63-64, 1963-1 CB 30

Subsistence payments

Veterans Administration Release, February 14, 1957

Allotments for dependents

Special Ruling, Jan. 10, 1946

Rev. Rul. 70-87, 1970-1 CB 29

Serviceman's Readjustment Act

Veterans Administration Release, February 14, 1957

Ephraim Banks, 17 TC 1386 (1952)

Family separation allowance

Clifford Jones, 60 Ct. Cl. 552

Rev. Rul. 70-281, 1970-1 CB 16

Moving and storage

IRC §217(g)

Note: *Paragraph numbers refer to Parts 1 through 7. Items marked * are research aids, not citations of authority;* see *"Key to Citations" on page 801*

Mustering out pay

IRC §113

Reg. §1.113-1

Naval attaché expense money

Rev. Rul. 77-351, 1977-2 CB 23

Retirement pay reduction to provide survivor annuity

IRC §122

Return to active duty

Special Ruling, January 24, 1945

Travel expenses—permanent duty station

W. W. Bercaw, 165 F.2d 521 (4th Cir. 1948)

Rev. Rul. 55-571, 1955-2 CB 44

Uniforms, uniform allowances

Reg. §1.61-2(b)

Medical and pension benefit from Veteran's Administration

Rev. Rul. 72-605, 1972-2 CB 35

Injuries or sickness

Career Compensation Act of 1949, Sec. 402

Pay forfeited on court martial order

Armed Forces Fed. Income Tax, '77 ed.

Former prisoners of war

Rev. Rul. 55-132, 1955-1 CB 213

Rev. Rul. 56-462, 1956-2 CB 20

Bonuses

Rev. Rul. 56-610, 1956-2 CB 25

State bonus

Rev. Rul. 68-158, 1968-1 CB 47

Gratuity

Rev. Rul. 55-330, 1955-1 CB 236

Dividends on GI insurance

Special Ruling, February 3, 1947

Interest on VA life insurance dividends

Rev. Rul. 91-14, 1991-1 CB 18 revoking

Rev. Rul. 57-441, 1957-2 CB 45

Disability retirement pay

IRC §104(a)(4)

IRC §104(b)

Career Compensation Act of 1949, Sec. 402

Zebulon L. Strickland, Jr., 540 F.2d 1196 (4th Cir. 1976)

Rev. Rul. 78-161, 1978-1 CB 31

Veteran not taxed on payments from compensated work program

Roosevelt Wallace, 128 TC No. 11 (2007)

Rev. Rul. 2007-69, 2007-49 IRB 1083 (IRS acquiesces to *Wallace* decision)

35.3 Deductions for Armed Forces Personnel

Board and lodging costs

Rev. Rul. 55-571, 1955-2 CB 44, modified by Rev. Rul. 67-438, 1967-2 CB 82

Cost of insignia

Charles A. Harris, 12 TCM 42 (1953)

Contributions to "Company" fund

Rev. Rul. 73-296, 1973-2 CB 67

Rev. Rul. 55-201, 1955-1 CB 269

B. O. Mahaffey, 1 TC 176 (1942), rev'd, 140 F.2d 879 (8th Cir. 1944)

Morris Investment Corp., 156 F.2d 748 (3d Cir. 1946), cert. denied, 329 U.S. 788

Jacob Kaplan, 21 TC 134 (1953) (Acq.)

William F. Krahl, 9 TC 862 (1947)

Court martial expenses

Lindsay C. Howard, 202 F.2d 28 (9th Cir. 1953), aff'g 16 TC 157 (1951) (Acq.)

Professional societies

Rev. Rul. 55-250, 1955-1 CB 270

Increased retirement pay

IRC §212

Professional journals

Charles A. Harris, 12 TCM 42 (1953)

No away from home expenses for those at permanent duty station

Howe Stidger, 386 U.S. 287 (1967)

Travel status and duty expenses

Rev. Rul. 67-438, 1967-2 CB 82, modifying Rev. Rul. 55-571, 1955-2 CB 44

Charles A. Harris, 12 TCM 42 (1953)

Temporary lodging allowance

Rev. Rul. 76-2, 1976-1 CB 82

Fatigues

Rev. Rul. 67-1 15, 1967-1 CB 30

35.4 Tax-Free Pay for Service in Combat Zone

Combat pay exclusion

IRC §112

Reg. §1.112-1

Civilian employees not eligible for combat zone exclusion

Chief Counsel Memorandum AM 2009-003

Officers

IRC §112(b)

Severance pay not included

Ralph P. Waterman, 179 F.3d 123 (4th Cir. 1999), aff'g 110 T.C. 103 (1998)

Operation Iraqi Freedom

Notice 2003-21, 2003-17 IRB 817 (question and answer guidance on combat zone relief)

Executive Order No. 12744, 56 Fed. Reg. 2663 (1/23/91), designating the "Arabian Peninsula Areas" as a combat zone, continues to be in effect

Afghanistan

Executive Order No. 132-39, 66 Fed. Reg. 241 (12/14/01) (area designated as combat zone)

Notice 2002-17, 2002-9 IRB 567 (question and answer guidance on combat zone relief)

IRA contributions based on tax-free combat pay

IRC §219(f)(7), as added by Public Law 109-227, 5/29/06

News Release IR-2006-129 (HERO Act)

"Missing" status

IRC §112(d)

Joint return election by spouse of person MIA

IRC §6013(f)(1)

Waiver of tax

Rev. Rul. 68-393, 1968-2 CB 292

Rev. Rul. 72-169, 1972-1 CB 43

Hospitalized serviceman

IRC §112(a)(2)

35.5 Tax Deadlines Extended for Combat Zone or Contingency Operation Service

Note: *Paragraph numbers refer to Parts 1 through 7. Items marked * are research aids, not citations of authority;* see *"Key to Citations" on page 801*

* IRS Publication 3

IRC §7508(a)

Filing extensions extended to contingency operations

IRC §7508(a)

Operation Iraqi Freedom

Notice 2003-21, 2003-17 IRB 817 (question and answer guidance on combat zone relief)

Executive Order No. 12744, 56 Fed. Reg. 2663 (1/23/91), designating the "Arabian Peninsula Areas" as a combat zone, continues to be in effect

Five-year test period for home sale exclusion suspended

IRC §121(d)(9)

Desert Shield personnel qualify for extension

IRC §7508(f)

Extensions available to spouse

IRC §7508(c)

35.6 Tax Forgiveness for Combat Zone or Terrorist or Military Action Deaths

Combat zone

IRC §692

Afghanistan

Executive Order No. 132-39, 66 Fed. Reg. 241 (12/14/01) (area designated as combat zone)

Notice 2002-17, 2002-9 IRB 567 (question and answer guidance on combat zone relief)

Terroristic or military actions

IRC §692(c)

MIAs

IRA §692(b)

Filing extension for refund claims if combat zone death

IRC §7508(b)

35.7 Extension To Pay Your Tax When Entering the Service

* IRS Publication 3

Rev. Proc. 57-25, 1957-2 CB 1092

Soldiers' and Sailors' Civil Relief Act of 1940, Sec. 513

T.D. 5279, 1943 CB 952, amended by T.D.'s 5293, 5429, 5444, 5959

35.8 Tax Information for Reservists

* IRS Publication 3

Above-the-line deduction for overnight travel costs of National Guard and Reserve members

IRC §162(p)

Penalty exception for qualified reservists

IRC §72(t)(2)(G)

Operation Iraqi Freedom

Notice 2003-21, 2003-17 IRB 817 (question and answer guidance on combat zone relief)

Executive Order No. 12744, 56 Fed. Reg. 2663 (1/23/91), designating the "Arabian Peninsula Areas" as a combat zone, continues to be in effect

Penalty exception for qualified reservists

IRC §72(t)(2)(G)

36 How To Treat Foreign Earned Income

36.1 Claiming the Foreign Earned Income Exclusion

* IRS Publication 54

Foreign earned income exclusion

IRC §911

Exclusion amount adjusted for inflation

IRC §911(b)(2)(D)(ii)

Must file return even if exclusion is available

Reg. §1.911-6

IRC §6012

Reg. §1.6012-1(a)(3)

William Faltesek, 92 TC 78 (1989)

Panama Canal Commission employees

1986 Tax Act Section 1232

36.2 What Is Foreign Earned Income?

IRC §911(b)

Reimbursed moving expenses

Rev. Rul. 75-84, 1975-1 CB 236, amplified by Rev. Rul. 76-162, 1976-1 CB 197

Clifford Dammers, 76 TC 835 (1981)

36.3 Qualifying for the Foreign Earned Income Exclusion

Taxation of expatriates

IRC §877

Foreign residence and foreign physical presence test

IRC §911(d)(1)

Foreign tax home

IRC §911(d)(1)

IRC §911(d)(3)

International airspace not a foreign country

William D. Rogers, TC Memo 2009-111

Exclusion allowed in year services performed

IRC §911(b)(2)(B)

Prorating exclusion on daily basis

IRC §911(b)(2)

Exclusion must be elected

IRC §911(a)

No foreign tax credit on excluded income

IRC §911(d)(6)

No exclusion for countries under U.S. travel ban

IRC §911(d)(8)

Workers paid with nonappropriated funds

David Matthews, 907 F.2d 1173 (DC Cir. 1990), aff'g 92 TC 351 (1989)

Professor on sabbatical does not have foreign tax home

Lynn W. Gelhar, 63 TCM 2466

36.4 How To Treat Housing Costs

Exclusion for employer-financed housing

IRC §911(c)

Qualifying housing expense

IRC §911(c)(2)

Adjusted limit on housing amount

IRC §911(c)(1)-(2)

Notice 2010-27, 2010-15 IRB 531 *Deduction for housing costs not paid for by employer*

IRC §911(c)(3)

36.5 Meeting the Foreign Residence or Physical Presence Test

Note: *Paragraph numbers refer to Parts 1 through 7. Items marked * are research aids, not citations of authority;* see *"Key to Citations" on page 801*

Bona fide residence test

IRC §911(d)(1)(A)

IRC §911(d)(5)

Waiver of time tests due to war or civil unrest

IRC §911(d)(4)

International airspace not a foreign country

William D. Rogers, TC Memo 2009-111

Physical presence test—330-day/12-month requirement

IRC §911(d)(1)(B)

Reinstatement of exclusion after tax holiday

* Letter Ruling 200025019

36.6 Claiming Deductions

No deduction for expenses attributable to excluded income

IRC §911(d)(6)

Deducting expenses of moving overseas

IRC §217(h)

Retirees and survivors of workers abroad returning to U.S.

IRC §217(i)

Deduction for compulsory home leave expenses

Rev. Rul. 82-2, 1982-1 CB 367

Bruce C. Stratton, 448 F.2d 1030 (9th Cir. 1971)

36.7 Exclusion Not Established When Your Return Is Due

IRS Form 2350

36.8 Tax-Free Meals and Lodging for Workers in Camps

IRC §119(c)

36.9 Virgin Islands, Samoa, Guam, and Northern Marianas

* IRS Publication 570

Guam, Samoa, N. Mariana Islands

IRC §931

Virgin Islands

IRC §932

IRC §934

U.S. or agencies

IRC §931(d)

Rev. Rul. 54-612, 1954-2 CB 169

36.10 Earnings in Puerto Rico

IRC §933

Reg. §1.933-1

Rev. Rul. 56-585, 1956-2 CB 166

Moving expenses allocable to tax-exempt income from Puerto Rico not deductible

Alberto Roque, 65 TC 920 (1976)

36.11 Tax Treaties With Foreign Countries

IRC §894

IRC §877 (taxation of expatriates)

Reg. §1.894-1

IRC §7852(d)

Notice 95-31, 1995-22 IRB 5

36.12 Exchange Rates and Blocked Currency

* IRS Publication 54

Foreign currency gains and losses

IRC §988

Euro conversion

TD 8776; Reg. Sec. §1.985-8T

36.13 Reporting Foreign Bank Accounts

Form TDF 90.22.1

36.14 Foreign Tax Credit

* IRS Publication 514

Foreign tax credit

IRC §901(a)

Reg. §1.901-1 and 2

Deduction in lieu of credit

IRC §164(a)

De minimis credit

IRC §904(j)

Overall limitation

IRC §904(a)

Separate credit limitation categories

IRC §904(d)

Recapture of overall foreign loss

IRC §904(f)

Capital gains

IRC §904(b)(2)

Carryback and carryover

IRC §904(c)

37 Planning Alimony and Marital Settlements

37.1 Planning Alimony Agreements

* "Factor Estate Planning Considerations Into Divorce Arrangements," John J. Scroggin, 70 Practical Tax Strategies 23 (January 2003)
* "Not All Payments to Ex-Spouse Are Deductible Alimony," Steven C. Colburn, 68 Practical Tax Strategies 222 (April 2002)

Alimony paid deductible from gross income

IRC §62(a)(10)

IRC §215

IRC §1.215-1

Alimony received included in gross income

IRC §71

Reg. §1.71

Deductible in year paid

Reg. §1.71-2

Lily R. Reighley, 17 TC 344 (1951)

No deduction if paid by another

Reg. §1.215-1(b)

Same household rule

IRC §71(b)(1)(c)

Bertram Coltman, Jr., 980 F.2d 1134 (7th Cir. 1992)

Payments under written separation agreement deductible despite common household

Thomas Benham, TC Memo 2000-165

Designate nonqualifying payments

IRC §71(b)(1)(B)

Temp. Reg. §1.71-1T (Q-9)

Husband not taxed on payments from transferred property

IRC §71(d)

Alimony payments to nonresident alien

* IRS Publication 504

Wife not taxed on tax-exempt interest from

Note: *Paragraph numbers refer to Parts 1 through 7. Items marked * are research aids, not citations of authority; see "Key to Citations" on page 801*

alimony trust

Mary C. Ellis, 416 F.2d 894 (6th Cir. 1969)

Alimony trusts

IRC §682

Voluntary payment

Natalia D. Murray, 174 F.2d 816 (2d Cir. 1949)

Benjamin B. Cox, 176 F.2d 226 (3d Cir. 1949), aff'g 10 TC 955 (1948)

Permanent alimony after remarriage

Allen Hoffman, 54 TC 1607 (1971), aff'd, 455 F.2d 161 (7th Cir. 1972)

Alfredo Mass, 81 TC 112 (1983)

Voluntary payments after court order denies temporary alimony

Sylvia E. Taylor, 55 TC 1134 (1971)

Payments from oil lease are alimony

Ronald Prater, 55 F.3d 527 (10th Cir. 1995)

Payments recommended by state domestic relations master are not deductible

Eugene E. Deyette, 36 TCM 1343 (1977)

Wife taxable on voluntary alimony

Rev. Rul. 81-8, 1981-1 CB 42

Excess payments are voluntary

George H. Moore, 449 F. Supp. 163 (D.D. Tex. 1978)

Gift tax on voluntary payments

Rev. Rul. 79-118, 1979-1 CB 315

Post-remarriage payments not alimony

Martha K. Brown, 415 F.2d 310 (4th Cir. 1969)

Allen Hoffman, 54 TC 1607 (1970) (Acq.), aff'd per curiam, 455 F.2d 161 (7th Cir. 1972)

Deduction for estate

Homer Laughlin Est., 167 F.2d 828 (9th Cir. 1948)

Daniel G. Reid Est., 15 TC 573 (1950), aff'd, 193 F.2d 625 (2d Cir. 1952)

37.2 Decree or Agreement Required

* IRS Publication 504

Decree required—Pre-1985 law

IRC §71(a)(1)

Reg. §1.71-1(b)(1)

Decree or separation agreement required—Post-1984 law

IRC §71(b)(1)(A)

IRC §71(b)(2)

State decree declared invalid by another state: IRS view disallowing alimony deduction

Rev. Rul. 67-442, 1967-2 CB 65

Harold K. Lee, 550 F.2d 1201 (9th Cir. 1977)

State decree declared invalid by another state

Harold E. Wondsel, 350 F.2d 339 (2d Cir. 1965), cert. denied, 383 U.S. 935

Est. of Herman Borax, 349 F.2d 666 (2d Cir. 1965)

George J. Feinberg, 198 F.2d 260 (3d Cir. 1952)

Local support order after out-of-state divorce

Rev. Rul. 70-61, 1970-1 CB 18

Local support order before Mexican decree

Rev. Rul. 71-390, 1971-2 CB 82

Roman Catholic ecclesiastical board

Harold L. Clark, 40 TC 57 (1965)

Sample clauses for alimony agreements

Rev. Proc. 82-53, 1982-2 CB 842

Amendment of written agreement after divorce or legal separation

Rev. Rul. 60-140, 1960-1 CB 31

Rev. Rul. 60-141, 1960-1 CB 33

Rev. Rul. 58-152, 1958-1 CB 32

Agreement not incident

Rev. Rul. 60-142, 1960-1 CB 34

Annulment

Andrew M. Newburger, 61 TC 457 (1974) (Acq.)

George F. Reisman, 49 TC 570 (1968) (Acq.)

Anne S. Laster, 48 TC 178 (1967) (Acq.)

Written separation agreement

Howard Bogard, 59 TC 97 (1972) (Acq.)

Oral modification not valid

Eugene H. Bishop, 46 TCM 15

Reference to agreement not sufficient

Welford E. Garner, Jr., 32 TCM 353 (1973)

Support decree

Rev. Rul. 59-248, 1959-2 CB 31

Support decree valid after divorce

Joanne S. Knobler, 59 TC 261 (1972)

Support decree not valid after divorce

Benjamin Wolman, 64 TC 883 (1975)

37.3 Cash Payments Required

IRC §71(b)(1)

Payments to third party

Temp. Reg. §1.71-1T (Q-6 to 7)

37.4 Payments Must Stop at Death

IRC §71(b)(1)(D)

McNeill Stokes, 68 TCM 705 (1994)

Richard E. Hoover, 102 F. 3d 846 (6th Cir. 1996)

No deduction for attorneys' fees

Thomas D. Berry, 2002-1 USTC ¶50,453 (10th Cir. 2002)

* Leonard Salesky, TC Summary Opinion 2006-162

Deduction allowed for unallocated support

* Michael Robert Peterson, TC Summary Opinion 2003-122 (no post-death obligation under New Jersey law)

No deduction for unallocated support

John H. Lovejoy, 2002-2 USTC ¶50,473 (10th Cir. 2002)

37.5 Child Support Payments Are Not Alimony

IRC §71(c)

Reg. §301.6402-5

Temp. Reg. §1.71-1T (Q-15, 16, 17, 18)

Payments allocable to unpaid child support not deductible

Gregory H. Haubrich, TC Memo 2008-299

Refund diversion for delinquent child support

IRC §6402(c)

Reg. §301.3402-5(b)

Federal Court must provide notice

Elinor Nelson, 731 F.2d 105 (2nd Cir. 1984)

Kenneth Marcello, 574 F. Supp. 586 (D.C., RI. 1984)

Note: *Paragraph numbers refer to Parts 1 through 7. Items marked * are research aids, not citations of authority;* see *"Key to Citations" on page 801*

Interest on overdue child support is taxable income

* Chief Counsel Memorandum 200444026

37.6 No Minimum Payment Period for Alimony

Pre-1987 agreements

IRC §71(f)(1)

Notice 87-9, 1987-1 CB 421

37.7 3rd Year Recapture If Alimony Drops by More Than $15,000

IRC §71(f)

Notice 87-9, 1987-1 CB 421

Exceptions

IRC §71(f)(5)

37.8 Legal Fees of Marital Settlements

* "Alimony and Risk of Death," Burgess J.W. Raby and William L. Raby, 96 Tax Notes 231 (July 8, 2002)

Deduction allowed for legal fees for arranging details of alimony

Reg. §1.262-1(7)

Barbara B. LeMond, 13 TC 670 (1949) (Acq.)

Ruth K. Wild, 42 TC 706 (1964) (Acq.)

Jimmie T. Jernigen, 34 TCM 615 (1975)

No deduction for wife—property rights in issue

Georgia Leary Neill, 42 TC 793 (1964)

Fee added to basis of property

Shirley H. W. George, 434 F.2d 1336 (Ct. Cl. 1971)

Wife's legal action to increase alimony

Elsie B. Gale, 13 TC 661 (1949) (Acq.)

Husband's legal expenses

Don Gilmore, 372 U.S. 39 (1963)

Talbot Patrick, 372 U.S. 53 (1963)

Fee allocated to tax advice

Rev. Rul. 72-545, 1972-2 CB 179

Gurnee Munn, Jr., 455 F.2d 1028 (Ct. Cl. 1972)

Husband may not deduct wife's legal fees

Thomas D. Berry, 2002-1 USTC ¶50,453 (10th Cir. 2002), aff'g TC Memo 2000 373

R. William Johnson, 30 TCM 580 (1971)

Jack Rose, 30 TCM 634 (1971), aff'd, 459 F.2d 28 (6th Cir. 1972), cert. denied, 409 U.S. 879

* Letter Ruling 9542001

38 Household Employment Taxes ("Nanny Tax")

38.1 Who is a Household "Employee"?

IRC §3121(d) (general definition of employee)

IRC §3121(b)(3)(B) (exceptions for relative)

IRC §3121(b)(21) (exception for part-time employee under age 18)

* IRS Publication 926

38.2 Social Security and Medicare (FICA) Taxes for Household Employees

* IRS Publication 926

FICA withholding under Social Security Domestic Employment Reform Act of 1994

IRC §3121(a)(7)(B) (exclusion for wages below annual threshold)

IRC §3121(x) (inflation adjustments to threshold)

IRC §3510 (payment with income tax return)

FICA exemption for parent, child, spouse

IRC §3121(b)(3)

38.3 Filing Schedule H To Report Household Employment Taxes

* IRS Publication 926

The Social Security Domestic Employment Reform Act of 1994 (P.L. 103-387, 10/22/94)

Annual employment tax filing for small employers

T.D. 9239, 2006-6 IRB 401

38.4 Federal Unemployment Taxes (FUTA) for Household Employees

* IRS Publication 926

FUTA on household wages over $1,000

IRC §3306(a)(3)

39 Gift and Estate Tax Planning

* IRS Publication 950

39.1 Gifts of Appreciated Property

Reduced capital gain rates provide gift-planning opportunities

IRC §1(h) (0% rate through 2008–2010)

Give appreciated property

W. G. Farrier Est., 15 TC 277 (1950) (Acq.)

Charles N. Prothro, 209 F.2d 331 (5th Cir. 1954)

Elsie Sorelle, 22 TC 459 (1954) (Acq.)

Marvin Berry, 11 TCM 301 (1952)

Emily J. Haley, 381 F. Supp. 3431 (M.D. Ga. 1974)

Rev. Rul. 55-531, 1955-2 CB 520, distinguished by Rev. Rul. 63-66, 1963-1 CB 13, as modified by Rev. Rul. 75-11, 1975-1 CB 27

Avoid claim that gift not completed

William R. Tracy, 70 F.2d 93 (6th Cir. 1934)

Rev. Rul. 58-337, 1958-2 CB 13

Richard G. Shafto, 246 F.2d 338 (4th Cir. 1957)

Jeannette W. FitzGibbon, 19 TC 78 (1952)

Get loss deduction by selling first

Reg. §1.165-1(b)

Private annuities—gain reported ratably over life expectancy

Rev. Rul. 69-74, 1969-1 CB 43

Gain immediately taxed on secured private annuity

Bell Est., 60 TC 469 (1973)

212 Corp., 70 TC 788 (1978)

Recovery of basis defers gain in private annuity

Esther LaFargue, 689 F.2d 845 (9th Cir. 1982)

No interest deduction for annuity payments

Rebecca Bell, 76 TC 233 (1981), aff'd per curiam, 668 F.2d 448 (8th Cir. 1982)

Note: *Paragraph numbers refer to Parts 1 through 7. Items marked * are research aids, not citations of authority;* see *"Key to Citations" on page 801*

39.2 Gift Tax Basics

IRC §2001(c) (gift tax rates)

IRC §2503 (taxable gifts)

IRC §2505 (unified credit)

IRC §2522 (charitable deduction)

* "Indirect Gifts Failed to Multiply Gift Tax Exclusion," Craig J. Langstraat and Amber M. Cagle, 66 Practical Tax Strategies 4 (April 2001)

Annual gift tax exclusion

IRC §2503(b)

Rev. Proc. 2008-66, 2008-45 IRB 1107 ($13,000 annual exclusion for 2009)

* Letter Ruling 9532001

Lifetime $1 million unified credit for gifts after 2001

IRC §2505(a)(1)

Marital deduction

IRC §2523

* Letter Ruling 9606008

Gifting employee stock options

* Letter Ruling 9514017

Exclusion for educational or medical expenses

IRC §2503(e)

Qualified tuition program contributions

IRC §529(c)(2)(B)

Pre-paid tuition

* Letter Ruling 199941013

Valuation of life insurance contracts

Reg. §25.2512-6

Gift tax exclusion for contingent trust beneficiaries

Est. of Maria Cristofani, 97 TC 74 (1991)

IRS Action on Decision 1992-09 (IRS does not concede Cristofani issue)

* Letter Ruling 9141008 (IRS denies exclusion for contingent trust interests)

Loans to relatives taxable

IRC §7872

Esther C. Dickman, 465 U.S. 330 (1984)

Elizabeth Miller, 71 TCM 1674 (1996)

Cannot assign income

Paul R. G. Horst, 311 U.S. 112 (1940)

Guy C. Earl, 281 U.S. 11 (1930)

Edward T. Blair, 300 U.S. 5 (1937)

Donees liable for gift tax

Kirkman O'Neal, II, 102 TC 28 (1994)

Art donations valued by IRS

Rev. Proc. 96-15, 1996-1 CB 627

Assignment of licensing agreement by inventor

Lewis R. Heim, 262 F.2d 887 (2d Cir. 1959)

"Incomplete" gifts made by personal check included

Robert Rosano, 2001-1 USTC ¶60,401 (2d Cir. 2001)

Power of attorney must explicitly authorize gifts

Estate of Silvia S. Swanson, Court of Appeals for the Federal Circuit, 5/25/01

39.3 Filing a Gift Tax Return

IRC §2503

* IRS Publication 950

39.4 Gift Tax Credit

IRC §2505

* IRS Publication 950

39.5 Custodial Accounts for Minors

Investment income of children under age 18

IRC §1(g)

Income taxed to child

Rev. Rul. 55-469, 1955-2 CB 519

Rev. Rul. 56-484, 1956-2 CB 23

Rev. Rul. 59-357, 1959-2 CB 212

Trust accounts ineffective to split interest income

Roy K. Heintz, 41 TCM 429 (1980)

Child remains dependent and exemption allowed

IRC §151(e)

Reg. §1.151-2

Gift tax

IRC §2501

IRC §2503

Reg. §25.2503-3

Reg. §25.2503-4

IRC §2505

IRC §2513

Rev. Rul. 56-86, 1956-1 CB 449

Trust for child under 21

IRC §2503(c)

Invalid custodian account

John Dubisky, 1994 USTC ¶13745 (N. Dist. of Ill.), rehearing denied (7th Cir. 1995)

Estate tax

IRC §2001

IRC §2010

Rev. Rul. 57-366, 1957-2 CB 618

No estate tax where securities purchased with jointly owned funds in which deceased custodian had no interest

Estate of Jack F. Chrysler, 361 F.2d 508 (2d Cir. 1966)

No estate tax on estate of deceased spouse who was custodian and agreed to gift splitting

Rev. Rul. 74-556, 1974-2 CB 300

No estate tax where custodian made gift of custodial securities before death

Antonia B. Vogel Est., 36 TCM 875 (1977)

39.6 Trusts in Family Planning

Repeal of 10-year trust rule

1986 Tax Reform Act Section 1402, amending IRC 673

Kiddie tax

IRC §1(g)

5% grantor trust rule

IRC §673(a)

Minor lineal descendants

IRC §673(b)

Grantor trusts: spouse's interest

IRC §672(e)

Tax rates for trusts and estates

IRC §1(e)

Rev. Proc. 96-59, 1996-2 CB 392 (1997 rates)

Division of income

T. N. Mauritz, 206 F.2d 135 (5th Cir. 1953)

Estelle Morris Trusts, 51 TC 20 (1968), aff'd per curiam, 427 F.2d 1361 (9th Cir. 1970)

Trust for spouse may be taxed to creator

IRC §677(a)

Note: *Paragraph numbers refer to Parts 1 through 7. Items marked * are research aids, not citations of authority;* see *"Key to Citations" on page 801*

"Apocalypse" family trust

Rev. Rul. 75-257, 1975-2 CB 251

Rev. Rul. 75-258, 1975-2 CB 503

Rev. Rul. 75-259, 1975-2 CB 361

Rev. Rul. 75-260, 1975-2 CB 376

Family trust for earned income is tax avoidance scheme

Richard L. Wesenberg, 69 TC 1005 (1978) (Nonacq.)

Family trust materials not deductible

Louis P. Contini, 76 TC 447 (1981) (Acq.)

Rev. Rul. 79-324, 1979-2 CB 119

Trust sale of appreciated property within two years

IRC §644

Escape estate tax

IRC §2038

Green Estate, 68 F.3d 151 (6th Cir. 1995) (identical trusts)

Gift tax

IRC §2511

Reg. §1.2511-1

Revocable trust—no tax savings

IRC §676

IRC §2038

Testamentary trust—estate tax

IRC §2037

Accumulation trust

IRC §665 through 667

Foreign trusts with U.S. beneficiaries

IRC §643

IRC §668

IRC §679

Generation-skipping transfers

IRC §§ 2601 through 2622

39.7 No Estate Tax for Estates of Individuals Dying in 2010

Repeal of estate tax for 2010

IRC §2210(a)

Sunset provision for EGTRRA would restore estate tax in 2011

Act Section 901(a)(2) of the Economic Growth and Tax Relief Reconciliation Act of 2001

39.8 Planning for a Restored Estate Tax

Repeal of estate tax for 2010

IRC §2210(a)

Sunset provision for EGTRRA would restore estate tax in 2011

Act Section 901(a)(2) of the Economic Growth and Tax Relief Reconciliation Act of 2001

Phasedown of maximum tax rate prior to repeal

IRC §2001(c)

39.9 Take Inventory of Your Potential Estate

* "New Disclaimer Regs. And Other Rules Affecting Jointly Owned Property, " Edward G. Fee, Jr., 25 Estate Planning 117 (March/April 1998)

Gross estate defined

IRC §2031

Property in which decedent had interest

IRC §2033

Transfers with retained life estate

IRC §2036

Failure to use safe harbor language for power of appointment not fatal

Est. of Norman H. Vissering, 990 F.2d 578 (10th Cir. 1993), rev'g and rem'g 96 TC 749 (1991)

Life insurance

IRC §2042

IRC §2035(d)(2) (gifts within three years of death)

IRS concedes policy is excluded from estate where insured held no incidents of ownership

IRS Action on Decision 1991-012

Estate of Eddie L. Headrick, 918 F.2d 1263 (6th Cir. 1990), aff'g 93 TC 171 (1989)

Estate of Joseph Leder, 893 F.2d 237 (10th Cir. 1989), aff'g 89 TC 235 (1987)

Estate of Frank Martin Perry, 927 F.2d 209 (5th Cir. 1991), aff'g 59 TCM 67 (1990)

Estate of Samuel Ard, Jr., 59 TCM 869 (1990)

Assignment of group-term policy

Rev. Rul. 84-147, 1984-2 CB 201

Son paid premiums

Morris R. Silverman Est., 61 TC 338 (1974) (Acq.), aff'd, 521 F.2d 574 (2d Cir. 1975)

Exclusion for certain retirement benefits

Rev. Rul. 92-22, 1992-1 CB 313

Temp. Reg. §20.2039-IT

"Incomplete gifts" made by personal check

Robert Rosano, 2001-1 USTC ¶60,401 (2d Cir. 2001)

Power of attorney must explicitly authorize gifts

Estate of Sylvia S. Swanson, Court of Appeals for the Federal Circuit, 05/25/01

39.10 Valuing Your Potential Estate

* "Post-Death Events and Claims Against Estates," William L. Raby and Burgess J. W. Raby, 91 Tax Notes 105 (April 2, 2001)

* "Valuation Discounts Are Available in an Estate Plan," James C. Cavanaugh, 55 Taxation for Accountants 31 (July 1995)

Special farming or business use valuation

IRC §2032A

Estate freeze restrictions

IRC §2036(c)

Notice 89-99, 1989-2 CB 422

IRS evaluation of art donations

Rev. Proc. 96-15, 1996-3 IRB 41

Value of pending lawsuit

Estate of Davis, 66 TCM 542 (1993)

Value of lottery winnings

* Letter Ruling 9616004

Estate of Paul C. Gribauskas, 342 F. 3d 85 (2d Cir. 2003)

Estate of Gladys J. Cook, 2003-2 USTC ¶60,471 (5th Cir. 2003)

39.11 Estimating Potential Estate Tax Liability

Repeal of estate tax for 2010

IRC §2210(a)

Sunset provision for EGTRRA would restore estate tax in 2011

Note: *Paragraph numbers refer to Parts 1 through 7. Items marked * are research aids, not citations of authority;* see *"Key to Citations" on page 801*

Act Section 901(a)(2) of the Economic Growth and Tax Relief Reconciliation Act of 2001

39.12 Reducing or Eliminating a Potential Estate Tax

Annual gift tax exclusion

IRC §2503(b)

Lifetime gift tax exclusion of $1 million

IRC §2505(a)(1)

Marital deduction

IRC §2056

Accumulation clause defeats QTIP marital deduction

Estate of Ellingson, 96 TC 34 (1991)

Son's disclaimer declared valid

Quinto DePaoli, Jr., 62 F.3d 1259 (10th Cir. 1995)

Marital deduction disallowed for property surrendered in family settlement

Harry D. Schroeder, 924 F.2d 1547 (10th Cir. 1991)

Disclaimer disallowed

Estate of Monroe, 104 TC 16 (1994)

Conditional bequest loses marital deduction

Edwin L. Bond, 104 TC 31 (1995)

40 Income or Loss From Your Business or Profession

40.1 Forms of Doing Business

"Check-the-Box Final Regs. Simplify Entity Classification," Scott E. Grimes, Marilyn K. Wiggan, and Steven A. Martin, 58 Taxation for Accountants 132 (March 1997)

Check-the-box election

Reg. §§301.7701-1 through 301.7701-3

* "Partnerships, S Corporations, and LLC's," Roger F. Pillow, et al., 86 Journal of Taxation 197 (April 1997)
* "LLCs Are Generally—But Not Always—The Right Choice," Arlene M. Hibschweiler and Marion Kopin, 58 Taxation for Accountants 159 (March 1997)

Changing a partnership to an LLC

Rev. Rul. 95-37, 1995-1 CB 150

Rev. Rul. 95-55, 1995-2 CB 313

Electing LLC status

News Release IR 95-29 (3/29/95)

Employment taxes

Legal Memorandum ILM 199922053

40.2 Reporting Self-Employed Income

* IRS Publication 334
* "Tax Tips for Starting Up a Sideline Business," Steven C. Thompson and Randy K. Serrett," 61 Taxation for Accountants 166 (Sept. 1998)

Election for husband and wife sole owners

IRC 761(f)

Health insurance deduction for self-employed

IRC §162(l)

Passive losses

IRC §469

40.3 Accounting Methods for Reporting Business Income

* IRS Publication 538
* "IRS Guidance Encourages Voluntary Accounting Method Change," Joe Walsh, 69 Tax Strategies 85 (August 2002)
* "IRS Approves Cash Method for More Small Businesses," Sharon Burnett, 68 Tax Strategies 340 (June 2002)

Permissible methods

IRC §446(c)

Reg. §1.446-1

Advance payments—12-month rule

Reg. §1.263(a)-4(f)

Cash method safe harbor if average gross receipts are $10 million or less

Rev. Proc. 2002-28, 2002-18 IRB 815

Change from cash to accrual method

IRC §446(e) and (f)

Rev. Proc. 67-10, 1967-1 CB 585, amplified by Rev. Proc. 72-52, 1972-2 CB 833

Limits on use of cash method

IRC §448

More than one business

IRC §446(d)

Constructive receipt

Reg. §1.451-2

Deductions—generally

IRC §461

Reg. §1.461-1(a)

3½ month test for services or goods

Reg. §1.461-4(d)(6)

Taxes

Reg. §1.461-4(g)(6)

8½ month test

Reg. §1.461-5(b)(ii)

Payment through "pay by phone" account

Rev. Rul. 80-335, 1980-2 CB 170

Cash-basis tax shelters

IRC §461(i)

All events test—economic performance test

IRC §461(h)

Reg. §1.461-4

Economic performance—recurring item exception

IRC §461(h)(3)

Prop. Reg. §1.461-5

Reporting accrual income from disputed shipments

Rev. Rul. 2003-10, 2003-3 IRB 288

Payment to related cash-basis taxpayer of salary and interest

IRC §267(a)(2)

Long-term contracts

IRC §460

Advance interest payments ("paid or accrued")

IRC §163

Advance tax payments ("paid or accrued")

IRC §164

Accrual-effect of contingency

Safety Car Heating Co., 297 U.S. 88 (1936)

Continental Tie & Lumber Co., 286 U.S. 290 (1932)

American Code Co., 280 U.S. 445 (1930)

Deferred payments for use of property or services

IRC §467

Note: *Paragraph numbers refer to Parts 1 through 7. Items marked * are research aids, not citations of authority;* see *"Key to Citations" on page 801*

Income not deferred by agent

Rev. Rul. 70-294, 1970-1 CB 13

Income deferred on wheat sale

Rev. Rul. 58-162, 1958-1 CB 234, distinguished by Rev. Rul. 70-294, 1970-1 CB 13

Non-accrual experience (NAE) method of deferring accrued income from services

IRC §448(d)(5)

Reg. §1.448-2T(b)

40.4 Tax Reporting Year for Self-Employed

Taxable year

IRC §441(b)

Reg. §1.441-1(b)

* IRS Publication 538

Calendar year

IRC §441(d)

Fiscal year

IRC §441(e)

Personal service corporation year

IRC §441(i)

Partnership year

IRC §706(b)

S corporation year

IRC §1378(b)

52–53 weeks

IRC §441(f)

Reg. §1.441-2

Period of less than 12 months

IRC §443

Reg. §1.443-1

Sole proprietor's tax year

Rev. Rul. 58-389, 1957-2 CB 298, modified by Rev. Rul. 77-293, 1977-2 CB 91

Change of accounting period

IRC §442

Reg. §1.442-1(b)

40.5 Reporting Certain Payments and Receipts to the IRS

IRC §6050 I

Reg. §1.6050 I-1

Reg. §1.6050 I-2

Attorneys must identify clients paying over $10,000

News Release IR-93-113 (intentional disregard penalties may be imposed)

Goldberger and Dubin, 935 F.2d 501 (2d Cir. 1991)

Richard H. Sindel, 53 F.3d 874 (8th Cir. 1995) (disclosure of client identity not required if it would reveal confidential communications)

Attorney not required to identify client paying over $10,000 where IRS does not follow summons procedure

Nancy Gertner, 65 F.3d 963 (1st Cir.,1995)

Failure to report business car over $10,000

Announcement 90-142, 1990-53 IRB 63

Cash equivalents under $10,000

Reg. §1.6050I-1(c)(1)(ii)

$3,000 cash log requirement dropped

Treasury Regulations Bank Secretary Act §103.29

News Release IR 95-37

Cash bail over $10,000

Reg. §1.6050 I-2

Penalty for not providing statement

IRC §6721

Annnouncement 94-113, 1994-37 IRB 37

40.6 Filing Schedule C

* IRS Publication 535

Election for husband and wife sole owners

IRC 761(f)

Deduction for qualified domestic production activities

IRC §199

Statutory employees

IRC §3121(d)(3)

Reg. §31.3121(d)-1(d)(3)(IV)

Business expenses—adjusted gross income

IRC §62

Business expenses—in general

IRC §162

Reg. §1.162-1

Deductible repair or capital improvement to tangible property

Prop. Regs. §1.263(a)-1 through (a)-3; 71 Federal Register 48590, 8/21/06

No business deduction for personal expenses

William J. Dunn, TC Memo 2010-198

Restitution for fraudulent billings is deductible business expense

Peter D. Cavaretta, TC Memo 2010-4

Unreasonable business expense

Palo Alto Town & Country Village, Inc., 32 TCM 1048 (1973), aff'd in part, rev'd in part and rem'd, 565 F.2d 1388 (9th Cir. 1978)

No depreciation for B&B's mixed-use areas

Charles E. Anderson, TC Memo 2006-33

Inventory losses

Reg. §1.165-7(a)(4)

Reg. §1.471-2(c)

National Home Products, 71 TC 501 (1979)

Bad debts

IRC §166

Family day-care providers may use standard meal allowance

Rev. Proc. 2003-22, 2003-10 IRB 577

Workers' compensation

Harvey R. Otten, 68 TCM 1342 (1994)

Insurance premiums

Reg. §1.162-1

Disability insurance

Marvin J. Blaess, 28 TC 710 (1957)

Rev. Rul. 58-480, 1958-2 CB 62

Termination payments

Robert E. Milligan, 38 F.3d 1094 (9th Cir. 1994)

Advance payments—IRS proposes 12-month rule for created intangibles

Prop. Reg. §1.263(a)-4(f)

Prepaid premiums

Waldheim Realty & Investment, 245 F.2d 823 (8th Cir. 1957)

Boylston Market Ass'n, 131 F.2d 966 (1st Cir. 1942)

Premiums for disability insurance

Rev. Rul. 55-331, 1955-1 CB 271, modified by Rev. Rul. 68-212, 1968-1

Note: *Paragraph numbers refer to Parts 1 through 7. Items marked * are research aids, not citations of authority;* see *"Key to Citations" on page 801*

CB 91

Health insurance for self-employed

IRC §162(1) (100% above-the-line deduction)

* Chief Counsel Advice 200623001

Premium for malpractice insurance

Rev. Rul. 60-365, 1960-2 CB 49

Non-practicing malpractice insurance

Merlin A. Steger, 113 TC No. 18

Malpractice premiums to physician-owned carrier

Rev. Rul. 80-120, 1980-1 CB 41

Physicians may not deduct cost of setting up insurance carrier

Carl Herman, et al., 84 TC 120 (1985)

Policies for business overhead expenses

Rev. Rul. 55-264, 1955-1 CB 11

Interest

IRC §163

Reg. §1.163-1

Interest deduction limited to $50,000 on employee life insurance

IRC §264(a)(4)

Interest on deferred pay accounts

Albertson's, Inc., 12 F.3d 1539 (9th Cir. 1994)

No deduction for interest owed on business tax deficiency

Edward A. Robinson II, 119 TC No. 4 (2002) (Tax Court sides with IRS and appeals courts in disallowing deduction)

David Miller, 65 F.3d 687 (8th Cir. 1995), aff'g 841 F. Supp. 305 (N.D. 1993) (interest never deductible)

Richard R. Allen, Sr., 99-1 USTC ¶50,470 (4th Cir. 1999)

Nick Kikalos, 99-2 USTC ¶50,823 (7th Cir. 1999)

Interest on funds used in personal affairs

Ebb. J. Ford, Jr., 29 TC 499 (1957)

Payments before title passes treated as interest

Warren Halle, 83 F.3d 649 (4th Cir. 1996)

Rents

Reg. §1.162-1

Reg. §1.162-11

Rev. Rul. 74-209 1974-1 CB 46

Advance rents

Martin J. Zaninovich, 616 F.2d 429 (9th Cir. 1980)

No deduction of prepaid rent without substantial business purpose

Howard Howe, TC Memo 2000-291

Repairs

Reg. §1.162-4

Louise Kingsley, 11 BTA 296 (Acq.)

Incidental repairs deductible

Indopco, Inc., 112 S. Ct. 1039 (1992), aff'g 918 F. 2d 426 (2nd Cir. 1991)

Rev. Rul. 94-12, 1994-1 CB 36

Taxes

IRC §164

Reg. §1.164

State income taxes not a business deduction

D.H. Tanner, 363 F.2d 36 (4th Cir. 1966)

State income taxes for net operating loss

Rev. Rul. 70-40, 1970-1 CB 50

Business property tax

E. W. Brown, Jr., 439 F.2d 1065 (5th Cir. 1954)

Salaries and wages

IRC §162(a)(1)

Reg. §1.162-7(a)

Legal fees

Rev. Rul. 74-392, 1974-2 CB 10

Rev. Rul. 71-470, 1971-2 CB 12

Deduction for legal fee of unsuccessful defense of criminal charge arising out of business

Walter F. Tellier, 383 U.S. 687 (1966)

Litigation expense of retired officer's rank

Rev. Rul. 72-169, 1972-1 CB 43

Expenses of discontinued business

Rev. Rul. 67-12, 1967-1 CB 29

Wages to your children deductible

Walt E. Eller, 77 TC 934 (1981)

James A. Moriarty, 48 TCM 59 (1984)

Cell phone expenses

* George W. Moss, TC Summary Opinion 2004-56

40.7 Deductions for Professionals

IRS list of deductible professional expenses

Reg. §1.162-6

Cost of establishing professional reputation

Miron Kroyt, 20 TCM 1665 (1961)

Amortization of bar admission costs

Joel A. Sharon, 66 TC 515 (1976), aff'd, 591 F.2d 1273 (9th Cir. 1978), cert. denied

Doctor may amortize patient's records

Los Angeles Central Animal Hospital, Inc., 58 TC 269 (1977) (Acq.)

Payment for hospital rights

S. M. Howard, 39 TC 833 (1963)

E. Vance Walters, 383 F.2d 922 (6th Cir. 1967)

Amortizing cost of right to practice in a hospital

Rev. Rul. 70-171, 1970-1 CB 55

Payment of client's expenses

Reginald G. Hearn, 36 TC 672 (1961), aff'd, 309 F.2d 431 (9th Cir. 1962), cert. denied, 373 U.S. 909

C. Doris Pepper, 36 TC 886 (1961) (Acq.)

Advances to client deductible/not deductible

Warren Burnett, 356 F.2d 755 (5th Cir. 1966), cert. denied, 385 U.S. 832

James Boccard, 95-1 USTC §50,284 (9th Cir. 1995)

Professionals not in own practice

Wesley J. Rogers, 20 TCM 1515 (1961)

No deduction if failed to make malpractice claim

Rev. Rul. 78-141, 1978-1 CB 380

Extracurricular teaching costs

Samuel F. Patterson, 30 TCM 1003 (1971), on remand from 436 F.2d 359 (9th Cir.), rev'g and rem'g 27 TCM 640 (1968)

Seymour Feinstein, 29 TCM 1338 (1970)

Earl T. Jefferson, 74-1 USTC ¶9205 (N.D. Ga. 1974)

Adjunct professor must itemize expenses

* George A. Beitel, TC Summary Opinion 2001-101

Note: *Paragraph numbers refer to Parts 1 through 7. Items marked * are research aids, not citations of authority;* see *"Key to Citations" on page 801*

Luncheon discussion

John D. Moss, Jr., 758 F.2d 211 (7th Cir. 1985), cert. denied, 474 U.S. 979 (1985)

Richard R. Hankenson, 47 TCM 1567 (1984)

Myron W. Mizell, et al., 55 TCM 169 (1988)

Asbestos removal from office building is ordinary business expense

Cinergy Corp., 55 Fed. Cl. 489 (2003)

40.8 Nondeductible Expense Items

Capital expenditures

IRC §263

Reg. §1.263(a)

Uniform capitalization rules

IRC §263A

Temp. Reg. Sec. §1.263A-1T

Bonuses paid to shareholder-employees partly nondeductible

Pediatric Surgical Associates, P.C., TC Memo 2001-81

New roof on building

George W. Ritter, 163 F.2d 1019 (6th Cir. 1947)

Oberman Mfg., 47 TC 471 (1967) (Acq.)

Thomas J. Locke, 8 BTA 534 (Acq.)

Georgia Car and Locomotive Co., 2 BTA 986 (Nonacq.)

Personal expenses paid with business funds

IRC §262

Reg. §1.262-1

Expenses while not in business

Henry G. Owen, 23 TC 377 (1955)

Deductible repair or capital improvement to tangible property

Prop. Regs. §1.263(a)-1 through (a)-3; 71 Federal Register 48590, 8/21/06

Payment of fines

IRC §162(f)

Hoover Motor Express Co., Inc., 356 U.S. 38 (1958)

Tank Truck Rentals, Inc., 356 U.S. 30 (1958)

Herbert Davis, 26 TC 49 (1956) (Acq.)

Harry Wiedetz, 2 TC 1262 (1943)

Kickback

IRC §162(c)

Reg. §1.162-1(c)

Subcontractor's legal kickback not deductible

Car-Ron Asphalt Paving Co., Inc., 758 F.2d 1132 (6th Cir. 1985), aff'g 46 TCM 1314 (1983)

Contributions to campaigns

IRC §162(e)

40.9 How Authors and Artists May Write Off Expenses

IRC §263A(h)

Notice 89-67, 1988-1 CB 55

* IRS Publication 538

40.10 Deducting Expenses of a Sideline Business or Hobby

IRC §183

* IRS Publication 535

* "The Tax Court's Interpretation of the Hobby Loss Factors—A Score Sheet with Analysis," Paul J. Brennan, 83 Taxes 33 (July 2005)

* "When Is a 'Hobby' a Business for Tax Purposes?" Gary L. Maydew, 59 Taxation for Accountants 90 (August 1997)

* "Hobby Activities Can Increase Tax Liability," Alan D. Campbell, 53 Taxation for Accountants 78 (August 1994)

Order of claiming hobby deductions

Reg. §1.183-1(b)

Election to postpone determination of profit presumption

Temp. Reg. §12.9

Waiver of statute of limitations—items affected

IRC §183(e)(4)

Determining presumption period

Rev. Rul. 78-22, 1978-1 CB 72

Presumption period ends with death

Rev. Rul. 79-204, 1979-2 CB 111

Manner business conducted

Robert Schwartz, TC Memo 2003-86

James Jasienski, 64 TCM 1369 (1992)

Robert Matlock, 63 TCM 3108 (1992)

Leonard F. Barcus, 32 TCM 660 (1973), aff'd, 492 F.2d 1237 (2d Cir. 1974)

C. West Churchman, 68 TC 696 (1977)

Lester R. Westphal, 68 TCM 1038 (1994)

Danny Eldridge, 70 TCM 380 (1995)

History of income/losses from activity

Warren T. Brown, 280 F. Supp. 854 (D.N. Mex., 1968)

Henry P. White, 23 TC 90 (1954), aff'd per curiam, 227 F.2d 779 (6th Cir. 1956), cert. denied, 351 U.S. 939

Leonard P. Sasso, 20 TCM 1068 (1961)

Charles D. Eggert, 16 TCM 1010 (1957)

Lawrence Hoyle, 68 TCM 1321 (1994)

Anthony Ranciato, 52 F.3d 23 (2nd Cir. 1995)

* John E. Morrissey, TC Summary Opinion 2005-86

Sideline charter boat

John R. Zwicky, 48 TCM 1025 (1984)

Douglas C. Heppe, 70 TCM 63 (1995)

Jet charter business not a hobby

Leonard Rabinowitz, TC Memo 2005-188

Horse activity not a hobby

Maria Trescott Helmick, TC Memo 2009-220

Consulting activity not a business

Estate of Roger E. Stangeland et al., TC Memo 2010-185

Elements of personal pleasure/recreation

Valentine Howell, 41 TC 13 (1963), aff'd per curiam, 332 F.2d 428 (3d Cir. 1964)

Charles H. Carter, 37 TCM 859 (1978)

Peter Hurd, 37 TCM 499 (1978)

Norman D. Demler, 25 TCM 620 (1966)

Tolbert Wilkinson, 71 TCM 1959 (1996)

Aspiring authors

Paul Snyder, 674 F.2d 1359 (10th Cir. 1982) (allowed)

Maurice Dreicer, 78 TC 642 (1982) (disallowed), aff'd in unpublished opinion (D.C. Cir. 2/22/83)

Partnerships subject to IRC §183

Rev. Rul. 77-320, 1977-2 CB 78

40.11 Deducting Expenses of Looking for a New Business

* IRS Publication 334

Deduction of up to $10,000 of eligible start-up expenses allowed for 2010

Note: *Paragraph numbers refer to Parts 1 through 7. Items marked * are research aids, not citations of authority;* see *"Key to Citations" on page 801*

IRC §195(b)(3), as added by the Small Business Jobs Act of 2010, P.L. 111-240, 9/27/10

Election to deduct business start-up costs

IRC §195(b)(1)

Election to deduct organization costs of corporation

IRC §248(a)

Election to deduct organization costs of partnership

IRC §709(b)

Partnership syndication costs not amortizable

Rev. Rul. 89-11, 1989-1 CB 179

Expenses of getting a savings and loan charter; loss deduction is allowed

Harris W. Seed, 52 TC 880 (1969) (Acq.)

Funds advanced for mining

Charles T. Parker, 1 TC 709 (1943) (Acq.)

Investigating new business which is not entered into

Frank B. Polachek, 22 TC 858 (1954)

Morton Frank, 20 TC 511 (1953)

Johan Domenie, 34 TCM 469 (1975)

Rev. Rul. 77-254, 1977-2 CB 63

Search for car agency not deductible

William E. Day, 15 TCM 1303 (1956)

40.12 Home Office Deduction

IRC §280A

Prop. Reg. §1.280A-1 through 3

* IRS Publication 587

Administrative office in home

IRC §280A(c)(1), overturning result of Supreme Court's decision in Soliman

Employee subject to "convenience of employer" test

IRC §280A(c)(1)

* "Home Office Deduction for Employees: Interaction of the Principal Place of Business Test and the Convenience of the Employer Test," Ronald E. Flinn, 81 Taxes 35 (August 2003)

Supreme Court sets principal place of business tests—prior to amendment of IRC §280A(c)(i)

Nader Soliman, 113 S. Ct. 701 (1993)

Rev. Rul. 94-24, 1994-1 CB 87 (IRS examples applying Soliman tests)

Principal place of business (before Supreme Court's Soliman decision)

Rudolph Baie, 74 TC 105 (1980) (road stand)

Ernest Drucker, 79 TC 605 (1982) (musician), rev'd 715 F.2d 67 (2d Cir. 1983)

David J. Weissman, 751 F.2d 512 (2d Cir. 1985) (college professor)

Stanley Pomerantz, 860 F.2d 960 (9th Cir. 1988) (emergency room physician)

Violinist's home practice area

Katia V. Popov, 2001-1 USTC ¶50,353 (9th Cir. 2001) (deduction allowed under Soliman)

Multiple use of home office

Alfred Hamacher, 94 TC 348 (1990)

Inventory storage and product samples

IRC §280A(c)(2)

Portion of room as office

* Jack Chien Ching Huang, TC Summary Opinion 2002-93 (part of bedroom studio qualifies for deduction)

George H. Weightman, 42 TCM 104 (1981) (allowed); 45 TCM 167 (1982) (disallowed for following year on other grounds)

Reg. §1.280A-2(g)(1) (no partition required—follows Weightman case)

Practicing medicine at home—no deduction

Joon Chong, 71 TCM 3035 (1996)

Backyard office is "appurtenant"

Charles A. Scott, 84 TC 683 (1985)

Art gallery in home

Joseph Cunningham, 71 TCM 2527 (1996)

Day-care in home

IRC §280A(c)(4)

Brian Uphus, 67 TCM 2229 (1994)

Rev. Rul. 92-3, 1992-1 CB 141

40.13 What Home Office Expenses Are Deductible?

* "Home-Office Tax Myths Discourage True Tax Savings," Rolf Auster, 64 Tax Strategies 283 (May 2000)

Lawn care not deductible

Tom E. Butz, 35 TCM 532 (1976)

Home security system

Rev. Rul. 86-148, 1986-2 CB 43

Depreciation

IRC §168(c) (residential rental or nonresidential real property)

* IRS Publication 587

On-site landlord's home office depreciation

* Chief Counsel Advice 200526002

40.14 Allocating Expenses to Business Use

Any reasonable method accepted

Rev. Rul. 62-180, 1962-2 CB 52

Joseph Cunningham, 71 TCM 2527 (1996)

40.15 Business Income May Limit Home Office Deductions

IRC §280A(c)(5)

Prop. Reg. §1.280A-2(i) and 2(iii)

* Letter Ruling 8347012

40.16 Home Office for Sideline Business

Doctor with rental properties

Edwin R. Curphey, 73 TC 766 (1980)

Investors carrying on business

Joseph Moller, 721 F.2d 810 (CA-Fed. Cir. 1983)

40.17 Depreciation of Office in Cooperative Apartment

IRC §216(c)

Reg. §1.216-2

40.18 Net Operating Losses (NOLs)

IRC §172

Reg. §1.172

* IRS Publication 536

Up to five-year carryback for 2009 or 2008 NOL

IRC §172(b)(1)(H), as amended by the Worker, Homeownership, and Business Assistance Act of 2009

Rev. Proc. 2009-52, 2009-49 IRB

Carryback election for 2008 NOL of small business

IRC §172(b)(1)(H), as amended by the American Recovery and Reinvestment Act of 2009

Note: *Paragraph numbers refer to Parts 1 through 7. Items marked * are research aids, not citations of authority;* see *"Key to Citations" on page 801*

Rev. Proc. 2009-19, 2009-14 IRB 747

Theft losses allowed to victims of Madoff and other Ponzi schemes

Rev. Rul. 2009-9, 2009-14 IRB 735

Rev. Rul. 2009-20, 2009-14 IRB 149

Five year carryback for GO-Zone losses

IRC §1400N(k)(1)(A)

Five-year averaging for farmers

IRC §172(b)(1)(G)

Accounting change

Rev. Proc. 85-16, 1985-1 CB 517

40.19 Your Net Operating Loss

IRC §172

* IRS Publication 536

40.20 How To Report a Net Operating Loss

IRC §172

* IRS Publication 536

40.21 How To Carry Back Your Net Operating Loss

IRC §172(b)(1)

* IRS Publication 536

Quick refund

IRC §6411(a)(1)

Effect of spouse's death on carryback

Rev. Rul. 65-140, 1965-1 CB 127

Widow active in business allowed late husband's carryover

Vivian Rose, 32 TCM 965 (1973)

40.22 Election To Carry Forward Losses

IRC §172(b)(3)(C)

Carryforward period

IRC §172(b)(1)(B)

Timely filed return

John H. Young, 83 TC 831 (1984)

Election to forego carryback must cite Section 172

M. Lane Powers, 43 F.3d 172 (5th Cir. 1995)

Election to forego carryback not allowed on amended return

Diesel Performance, Inc., TC Memo 1999-302

Irrevocability of election to forego carryback

* Letter Ruling 199937020

40.23 Overview of the Domestic Production Activities Deduction

IRC §199

Reg. §1.199-1

40.24 Qualified Production Activities

IRC §199

Reg. §1.199-1

40.25 Figuring the Deduction

IRC §199

Reg. §1.199-1

40.26 Business Credit

General business credit

IRC §38

Five-year carryback for 2010 small business credits

IRC §39(a)(4), as added by the Small Business Jobs Act of 2010, P.L. 111-240, 9/27/10

Small business health tax credit

IRC §45R

Notice 2010-44, 2010-22 IRB 717

Small employer credit for retirement plan startup costs

IRC §45E

Employer-provided child-care credit

IRC §45 F

Work opportunity credit

IRC §51

New York Liberty Zone Work Opportunity Credit

IRC §1400L, added by JCWAA 2002

Notice 2002-42, 2002-27 IRB 36

Investment credit

IRC §46 through 48

Investment credit transition property

IRC §49(e)

Rev. Rul. 87-113, 1987-2 CB 33

Investment credit carryovers

IRC §49(c) (35% reduction)

IRC §39(d)

Recapture of investment credit

IRC §47(a)(1)

Reg. §1.47-1

Investment credit recapture for automobiles and other listed property

Temp. Reg. §1.280F-3T

When recapture does not apply

IRC §47(b)

Rehabilitation investment credit

IRC §48(g)

IRC §46(b)(4)

Business energy credit

IRC §46(b)

Alcohol fuels credit

IRC §40

Research credit

IRC §41

Low-income housing credit

IRC §42

Disabled access credit

IRC §44

David B. Hubbard, TC Memo 2003-245 (credit for general use equipment accommodating disabled and non-disabled patients)

Welfare-to-work credit

IRC §51A

Empowerment zone employment credit

IRC §1396(a)

Indian employment credit

IRC §45A

Employer Social Security credit on tips

IRC §45B(a)

Community development corporations credit

Section 13311 of the 1993 Revenue Reconciliation Act

No disposition under Bankruptcy Act

IRC §1017(c)(2), as amended by §2(b) of the Bankruptcy Tax Act

Transfer from private practice to professional corporation requires recapture

Note: *Paragraph numbers refer to Parts 1 through 7. Items marked * are research aids, not citations of authority;* see *"Key to Citations" on page 801*

Rev. Rul. 76-514, 1976-2 CB 11

Diesel vehicles

IRC §6427(g)

Federal gasoline and oil tax credit

* IRS Publication 510

IRC §34

Alternative fuel production credit

IRC §29

Enhanced oil recovery credit

IRC §43

Renewable electricity production credit

IRC §45

40.27 Filing Schedule F

* IRS Publication 225

40.28 Farming Expenses

* IRS Publication 225

41 Retirement and Medical Plans for Self-Employed

IRC §45E (small employer credit for retirement plan startup costs)

* IRS Publication 560

41.1 Overview of Retirement and Medical Plans

IRC §45 E (small employer credit for retirement plan startup costs)

IRC §401(d)

IRC §401(c)

Reg. §1.401-11

* IRS Publication 560

Earnings from more than one trade or business

Reg. §1.401-10(b)(2)

Reg. §1.401-10(c)

Controlled businesses

Reg. §1.401-12(1), (2), and (3)

S corporation shareholder may not set up a Keogh plan

Antonio Durando, 70 F.3d 584 (9th Cir. 1995)

Including employees in the plan

IRC §410

Minimum participation requirement for defined benefit plan

IRC §401(a)(26)

Contributions based on compensation

IRC §1.401-10

IRC §1.401-11

41.2 Choosing a Keogh Plan

IRC §401

Reg. §401(e)

25% of compensation limit

IRC §402(h)(2)(A)

Integration with Social Security

IRC §401(1)

41.3 Choosing a SEP

SEP defined

IRC §408(k)

Overall limit on employer SEP contributions

IRC §402(h)(2)

Deduction limit for SEP contributions increased to 25%

IRC §404(h)(1)(C)

Deductible SEP contributions up to filing date plus extensions

IRC §404(h)(1)(B)

Prop. Reg. §1.408-7(b)

State Department worker may contribute to SEP

Lisa Beth Levine, TC Memo 2005-86

41.4 Deductible Keogh or SEP Contributions

* IRS Publication 560

Limit on annual additions to defined contribution plans

IRC §415(c)(1)

Employer retirement plan limits

Notice 2006-98, 2006-46 IRB 906 (limits for 2007)

Benefit limit for defined benefit plans

IRC §415(b)

Earned income reduced by deductible contributions

IRC §401(c)(2)(A)(v)

IRC §404(a)(8)

Compensation limit

IRC §401(a)(17)

Deductible Keogh contributions up to due date of return

IRC §404(a)(6)

Deduction limit for profit-sharing plans increased to 25%

IRC §404(a)(3)(A)(i)(I)

10% penalty for nondeductible contributions

IRC §4972

41.5 How To Claim the Keogh or SEP Deduction

IRC §404

Reg. §1.404(a)-I

* IRS Publication 560

Time for making contributions

Temp. Reg. §11.40(a)(6)-I

Keogh contributions do not reduce self-employment income

Seymour L. Gale, 91-2 USTC ¶50,356 (Dist. Ct., Ill. 1991)

Deductible Keogh contributions up to due date of return

IRC §404(a)(6)

41.6 How To Qualify a Keogh Plan or SEP Plan

IRC §401

IRC §404

IRC §405

Failure to set up written plan

Nelson H. Jones, 51 TC 651 (1969)

Correction of defects made more affordable

Rev. Proc. 94-16, 1994-1 CB 576

41.7 Annual Keogh Plan Return

* IRS Publication 560

Filing requirement for one-participant plans

§1103 of the Pension Protection Act of 2006

41.8 How Keogh Plan Distributions Are Taxed

* IRS Publication 560

Lump-sum averaging

Sections 1122(h)(3)-(6) of 1986 Tax Reform Act (P.L. 99-514)

Note: *Paragraph numbers refer to Parts 1 through 7. Items marked * are research aids, not citations of authority; see "Key to Citations" on page 801*

10% penalty for excess benefits under plan formula

IRC §72(m)(5)(A)

Disqualification of plan completely bars tax-free rollover

Reg. §1.402(a)-1(a)(i)

John U. Fazi, 102 TC 31 (1994)

41.9 SIMPLE IRA Plans

IRC §408(p)

* IRS Publication 560

Limit on elective deferrals

IRC §408(p)(2)(E)

IRC §414(v)(2)(B)(ii)

Employer retirement plan limits

Notice 2006-98, 2006-46 IRB 906 (limits for 2007)

41.10 Health Savings Account (HSA) Basics

IRC §223

* IRS Publication 969

* "Health Savings Account: A New Defined Contribution Health Plan," Barry L. Salkin, 72 Practical Tax Strategies 196 (April 2004)

Deductible limit

IRC §223

IRS guidelines for HSAs

Notice 2004-50, 2004-33 IRB 196 (Q&A)

Rev. Rul. 2004-38, 2004-15 IRB 717 (prescription drug coverage)

Rev. Proc. 2004-22, 2004-15 IRB 727 (transition for prescription drugs)

Notice 2004-23, 2004-15 IRB 725 (preventive care)

High-deductible health plan

IRC §223(c)(2)

Coverage may be in name of self-employed owner

* Chief Counsel Advice 200524001

Annually adjusted minimum HDHP deductible and out-of-pocket maximum, and HSA contribution limit

Rev. Proc. 2008-29, 2008-22 IRB 1039 (for 2009)

Rev. Proc. 2009-29, 2009-22 IRB 1050 (for 2010)

Rev. Proc. 2010-22, 2010-23 IRB 747 (for 2011)

HSA catch-up contribution limit

IRC §223(b)(3)

HSA contributions for spouses

Rev. Rul. 2005-25, 2005-18 IRB 971

41.11 Limits on Deductible HSA Contributions

IRC §223

* IRS Publication 969

HSA and HDHP inflation adjustments for 2010/2011

Rev. Proc. 2010-22, 2010-23 IRB 747 (for 2011)

Rev. Proc. 2009-29, 2009-22 IRB 1050 (for 2010)

41.12 Distributions From HSAs

IRC §223(f)

* IRS Publication 969

41.13 Archer MSAs

* IRS Publication 969

Archer MSA deductions

IRC §220

Employer contributions

IRC §106 (contributions up to deductible limit of IRC §220(b)(i))

IRS guidelines on Archer MSAs

Notice 96-53, 1996-51 IRB 5

41.14 Small Business Health Tax Credit

IRC §45R

Notice 2010-44, 2010-22 IRB 717

42 Claiming Depreciation Deductions

42.1 What Property May Be Depreciated?

IRC §168

* IRS Publication 946

Nonproducing property

Reg. §1.212-1(b)

George W. Mitchell, 47 TC 120 (1966) (Nonacq.)

Maurice H. Connell, 11 TCM 771 (1952)

Charles D. Gallagher, 39 TCM 291 (1979)

Depreciation on residence put up for sale

Hulet P. Smith, 26 TCM 149 (1967), aff'd per curiam, 397 F.2d 804 (9th Cir. 1968)

Depreciation not allowed on idle ranch residence held by business

John T. Steen, 61 TC 298 (1973), aff'd per curiam, 508 F.2d 268 (5th Cir. 1975)

Cohan rule no basis for depreciation deduction

Tyson Foods, Inc., TC Memo 2007-188

Car partly for business

IRC §280F

J. R. James, 2 BTA 1071 (Acq.)

Kenneth Branchard, 12 TCM 550 (1953)

Paul McWilliams, 9 TCM (1950)

W. H. Wilson, 5 TCM 592 (1946), aff'd, 161 F.2d 556 (4th Cir. 1947), cert. denied, 332 U.S. 769

Depreciation not allowed on equipment in suspended medical practice

Rev. Rul. 77-32, 1977-1 CB 38

Depreciation allowed on equipment while owner unemployed

Charles D. Gallagher, 39 TCM 291 (1979)

Land

Reg. §1.167(a)-2

Clarence D. Hawkins, 14 TCM 382 (1955), rev'd on another issue, 234 F.2d 359 (6th Cir. 1956)

Cost of education not depreciable

Nathaniel A. Denman, 48 TC 439 (1967) (Acq.)

Goodwill, customer lists, agreements not to compete, and other intangibles

IRC §197

Election to apply amortization of intangibles retroactively

Revenue Reconciliation Act of 1993, Act Sec. 13261(g)(2)-(3)

One year or less

W. H. Tompkins Co., 47 BTA 292

International Shoe Co., 38 BTA 81 (Acq.)

Rev. Rul. 59-249, 1959-2 CB 55

Note: *Paragraph numbers refer to Parts 1 through 7. Items marked * are research aids, not citations of authority;* see *"Key to Citations" on page 801*

Farm property

Reg. §1.167(a)(6)

When depreciation is claimed

Reg. §1.167(a)-10

Depreciation allowed on violin

Richard Simon, 68 F.3d 41 (2nd Cir., 1995), aff'g, 103 TC 15 (1994)

Brian P. Liddle, 65 F.3d 329 (3rd Cir. 1995), aff'g 103 TC 285 (1994)

Depreciation allowed on exotic cars

Bruce Selig, TC Memo 1995-519

Work of art not depreciable

Rev. Rul. 68-232, 1968-1 CB 79

Depreciating paintings in office

D. Joseph Judge, 35 TCM 1264 (1976)

Cannot accumulate depreciation

Fort Orange Paper Co., 1 BTA 1230 (Acq.)

First National Bank of Thompson, Iowa, 2 BTA 735

Morris & Bailey Steel Co., 9 BTA 205 (Acq.)

42.2 Claiming Depreciation on Your Tax Return

IRC §168

* IRS Publication 946

42.3 First-Year Expensing Deduction

IRC §179

* IRS Publication 946

Expensing limit increased for 2010 and 2011

IRC §179(b)(1), as amended by

Small Business Jobs Act of 2010, P.L. 111-240, 9/27/10

Off-the-shelf software eligible for expensing in 2010 and 2011

IRC §179(d)(1)(A)(ii)

Expensing leasehold restaurant and retail improvements in 2010 and 2011

IRC §179(f), as added by Small Business Jobs Act of 2010, P.L. 111-240, 9/27/10

Changing expensing elections without IRS consent in 2010 and 2011

IRC §179(c)(2)

Reduction of expensing limit for excess purchases

IRC §179(b)(2), as amended by Small Business Jobs Act of 2010, P.L. 111-240, 9/27/10

New York Liberty Zone property

IRC §1400L(f)

First-year expensing deduction for enterprise zones

IRC §1397A

Increased expensing limit for GO Zone property

IRC §1400N(e)

50% business-use test for automobiles, computers, and other listed property

IRC §280F(b)

IRC §280F(d)(4)

Temp. Reg. §1.280F-6T(b)

Timing of expensing deduction for equipment components

*Courtney A. Brown, TC Summary Opinion 2009-171

Expensed assets should have been depreciated

Alacare Home Health Services, TC Memo 2001-149

Furniture bought in year before business begins—no expensing deduction

Kenneth A. Baratelle, TC Memo 2000-359

Expensing election cannot be increased after audit

Sam H. Patton, 116 TC 206 (2001)

Rental fleet motor home qualifies for first-year expensing

Robert D. Shirley, TC Memo 2004-188

Partners with more than one expensing deduction

Rev. Rul. 89-7, 1989-1 CB 178

Recapture of deduction if business use drops

IRC §179(d)(10)

42.4 MACRS Recovery Periods

IRC §168(e)

* IRS Publication 946

42.5 MACRS Rates

IRC §168(b)

42.6 Half-Year Convention for MACRS

IRC §168(d)(1)

42.7 Last Quarter Placements—Mid-Quarter Convention

IRC §168(d)(3)

Disregard real estate and property disposed of during year

IRC §168(d)(3)(B)

42.8 150% Rate Election

IRC §168(b)(2)

42.9 Straight-Line Depreciation

IRC §168(g)

42.10 Computers and Other Listed Property

* IRS Publication 946

* "Tax Consequences of Employer-Provided Computers," John C. Zimmerman, 78 Taxes 43 (October 2000)

Writing off cost of computer

IRC §280F

Computer is "listed" property

IRC §280F(d)(4)

Cell phones no longer listed property

IRC §280F(d)(4), as amended by Small Business Jobs Act of 2010, P.L. 111-240, 9/27/10

Cell phone expenses

* George W. Moss, TC Summary Opinion 2004-56

Recapture of excess depreciation if business use is 50% or less

Reg. §1.280F-3T(d)

Income inclusion for leases

Reg. §1.280F-5T(f)(2)

* IRS Publication 946

Employee deductions barred

Rev. Rul. 86-129, 1986-2 CB 48

* Letter Ruling 8710009

* Letter Ruling 8615024

* Letter Ruling 8615071

Husband and wife allowed deduction

Thomas Cadwallader, 57 TCM 1031 (1989)

Note: *Paragraph numbers refer to Parts 1 through 7. Items marked* * *are research aids, not citations of authority;* see *"Key to Citations" on page 801*

42.11 Assets in Service Before 1987

IRC §168(c) prior to 1986 Tax Act

* IRS Publication 534

42.12 Straight-Line Recovery for Assets in Service Before 1987

IRC §168(b)(1)(A) prior to 1986 Tax Act

Depreciation of automobiles and home computers

IRC §280F

42.13 MACRS for Real Estate Placed in Service After 1986

* IRS Publication 946

Residential rental property and nonresidential real property defined

IRC §168(e)(2)

Recovery periods

IRC §168(c)

15-year recovery for qualified leasehold improvement property

IRC §168(e)(3)(E)(iv)

IRC §168(e)(6) (qualified property defined)

15-year recovery for qualified restaurant property

IRC §168(e)(3)(E)(v)

IRC §168(e)(7) (qualified property defined)

42.14 Demolishing a Building

Capitalization required

IRC §280B

Test for partial demolition costs

Rev. Proc. 95-27, 1995-1 CB 704

Pre-1984 decisions

Donald S. Levinson, 59 TC 676 (1973)

John A. Lemm, 32 TCM 515 (1973)

J. Alfred Rider, 30 TCM 188 (1971)

Yates Motor Co., 561 F.2d 15 (6th Cir. 1977), rev'g 34 TCM 1235 (1975)

Rossel M. Hightower, 463 F.2d 182 (5th Cir. 1972)

Mayer Feldman, 335 F.2d 264 (9th Cir. 1964)

Herman Landerman, 454 F.2d 338 (7th Cir. 1972), cert. denied, 406 U.S. 967

Thomas P. Foltz, 458 F.2d 600 (8th Cir. 1972)

Ivan Grossman, 74 TC 1147 (1980) (Nonacq.)

42.15 Leasehold Improvements

Expensing leasehold restaurant and retail improvements in 2010 and 2011

IRC §179(f), as added by Small Business Jobs Act of 2010, P.L. 111-240, 9/27/10

15-year recovery for qualified leasehold improvement and restaurant property before 2010

IRC §168(e)(3)(E)(iv) (leasehold improvements)

IRC §168(e)(3)(E)(v) (restaurant property)

IRC §168(e)(6) (qualified property defined)

Lessor's disposition or abandonment of improvements

IRC §168(i)(8)

Depreciation and amortization

Reg. §1.167(a)-4

Option to renew—pre-1987 improvements

IRC §178(a)

Reg. §1.178-1

42.16 Depreciating Real Estate Placed in Service After 1980 and Before 1987

* IRS Publication 534

(The following citations are to Code sections before 1986 Tax Act)

Recovery period

IRC §168(c)(2)(D)

Low-income housing

IRC §168(b)(4)

IRC §168(c)(2)(F)

Treasury tables

Notice 81-16, 1981-2 CB 545

Election to use straight-line depreciation

IRC §168(b)(3)

Rate of recovery

IRC §168(b)(2)

Separate depreciation for components not allowed

IRC §168(f)(1)

Components added after March 15, 1984

IRC §168(f)(1)(B)

IRC §168(g)(4)

42.17 When MACRS Is Not Allowed

IRC §168(f)

42.18 Amortizing Goodwill and Other Intangibles (Section 197)

IRC §197

* "Section 197 Noncompete Covenants and Corporate Stock Redemptions," Burgess J.W. Raby and William L. Raby, 91 Tax Notes 1573 (May 28, 2001)

* "Section 197 Complicates Planning for Retiring LLC Members," Matthew A. Melone, 58 Taxation for Accountants 292 (May 1997)

15-year amortization required for covenant not to compete

Recovery Group, Inc., TC Memo 2010-76

15-year amortization for non-compete agreement in business acquisition

Frontier Chevrolet Co., 116 TC 289 (2001), aff'g 2003-1 USTC ¶50,490 (9th Cir. 2003)

42.19 Deducting the Cost of Computer Software

IRC §167(f) (36-month rule)

IRC §197(e)(3)(B)

42.20 Amortizing Song Rights

IRC §167(g)(8)

42.21 Bonus Depreciation

IRC 168(k), as amended by Small Business Jobs Act of 2010, P.L. 111-240, 9/27/10

*IRS Publication 946

43 Deducting Car and Truck Expenses

* "Purchase vs. Lease: Updated Directions for Business Car Users," Sidney J. Baxendale, William D. Stout, and Richard M. Walter, 71 Practical Tax Strategies 282 (November 2003)

43.1 Standard Mileage Rate

Note: *Paragraph numbers refer to Parts 1 through 7. Items marked * are research aids, not citations of authority;* see *"Key to Citations" on page 801*

* IRS Publication 463

IRS mileage rates for 2010

News Release IR-2009-111

Rev. Proc. 2009-54, 2009-51 IRB 930

IRS mileage rates for 2009

News Release IR-2008-131

Rev. Proc. 2008-72, 2008-50 IRB 1286

Allowance for rural delivery mail carriers

IRC §162(o)(2)

Two cars used at one time

Carroll H. West, 63 TC 252 (1974)

Married couple's separately owned cars

* Letter Ruling 8343005

Diary record of business mileage

John E. Frankel, 27 TCM 817 (1968)

Allowance for driving to distant research library

* Richard Orin Berge, TC Summary Opinion 2006-29

Interest

IRC §163(h)(2)(A)

IRC §163(d)(6)

Useful life: prior law

Rev. Proc. 75-3, 1975-1 CB 643

60,000 miles as useful life: prior law

Rev. Proc. 81-54, 1981-2 CB 649

43.2 Expense Allocations

* "Purchase vs. Lease: Updated Directions for Business Car Users," Sidney J. Baxendale, William D. Stout, and Richard M. Walter, 71 Practical Tax Strategies 282 (November 2003)

Allocation based on mileage

Temp. Reg. Sec. 1.280F-6T(e)

* IRS Publication 463

Some car expenses capitalized

Doris Jones, 11 TCM 529 (1952)

Apportioning car expense between business and personal use

IRC §163(h)(2)(A)

Lawrence Au, 40 TC 264 (1963), aff'd per curiam, 330 F.2d 1008 (9th Cir. 1964), cert. denied, 379 U.S. 960

Clarence J. Sapp, 309 F.2d 143 (5th Cir. 1962), aff'g 36 TC 852 91 (1961) (Acq.)

43.3 Depreciation Restrictions on Cars, Trucks, and Vans

IRC §280F

IRC §168(k)

* IRS Publication 463

Rev. Proc. 2008-22, 2008-12 IRB 658 (depreciation limits for vehicles placed in service during 2008)

Employer convenience test

IRC §280F(d)(3)

More than 50% business-use test

Temp. Reg. §280F(b)

Temp. Reg. §1.280F-6T(d)(4)

Business-investment percentage

Temp. Reg. §1.280F-6T(d)(3)

Temp. Reg. §1.280F-2T(i)

Vehicles other than cars

IRC §280F(d)(4)

Temp. Reg. §1.280F-6T(b)

Vehicles exempted from more-than-50%-business-use test

Temp. Reg. §1.280F-6T(b)

Temp. Reg. §1.274-5T(k)

Transportation for hire

IRC §280F(d)(4)(C)

Employee use of company car

IRC §280F(d)(6)

Temp. Reg. §1.280F-6T(d)(2)

43.4 Annual Ceilings on Depreciation

IRC §280F(a)

* IRS Publication 463

Bonus depreciation increases first-year ceiling by $8,000 through 2010

IRC §168(k)(2)(F)

Annual limit on depreciation

IRC §280F(a)

Rev. Proc. 2010-18, 2010-9 IRB 427 (pre-bonus depreciation limits for cars placed in service during 2010)

Rev. Proc. 2009-24, 2009-17 IRB 885 (depreciation limits for cars placed in service during 2009)

Rev. Proc. 2008-22, 2008-12 IRB 658 (depreciation limits for cars placed in service during 2008)

* IRS Publication 463

Passenger automobile defined

IRC §280F(d)(5)

Light trucks and vans

Rev. Proc. 2010-18, 2010-9 IRB 427 (pre-bonus depreciation limits for light trucks and vans placed in service during 2010)

Rev. Proc. 2009-24, 2009-17 IRB 885 (depreciation limits for light trucks and vans placed in service during 2009)

Rev. Proc. 2008-22, 2008-12 IRB 658 (depreciation limit for light trucks and vans placed in service in 2008)

T.D. 9069, 2003-37 IRB 525 (qualified non-personal-use vehicles not considered passenger automobiles)

First-year expensing limitation for cars

IRC §280F(d)(1)

First-year expensing limit of $25,000 for SUVs

IRC §179(b)(6)

Personal-use percentage reduces ceiling

IRC §280F(a)(2)

Temp. Reg. §1.280F-2T(i)

43.5 MACRS Rates for Cars, Trucks, and Vans

* IRS Publication 463

IRC §168(e)(3)(B)(i)

IRC §168(b)

IRC §168(c)

Annual deduction limits

IRC §280F(a)

Conventions

IRC §168(d)

Basis reduction for personal use

Temp. Reg. §1.280F-2T(g)

43.6 Straight-Line Method

Mandatory straight-line recovery

IRC §280F(b)(2) and (b)(4)

Temp. Reg. §1.280F-3T(c) and (e)

Optional straight-line recovery if business use exceeds 50%

IRC §168(f)(2)(c)

Prop. Reg. §1.168-2(c)

43.7 Depreciation for Year Vehicle Is Disposed Of

* IRS Publication 463

Note: *Paragraph numbers refer to Parts 1 through 7. Items marked* * *are research aids, not citations of authority;* see *"Key to Citations" on page 801*

* IRS Publication 946

IRC §280F

IRC §168(d) (applicable convention)

43.8 Depreciation After Recovery Period Ends

* IRS Publication 463

Converting a pleasure car to business use

Prop. Reg. §1.168-2(j)(1)

Increase in business use after recovery period

Prop. Reg. §1.168-2(j)(2) (Pre-6/18/84 cars)

43.9 Trade-in of Business Vehicle

Reg. §1.168(i)-6

* IRS Publication 463

* New Regulation Provides Guidance on MACRS Depreciation and Code Sec. 280F Limitations of Passenger Automobiles Involved in a Code Sec. 1031 Exchange," J. David Mason, 83 Taxes 17 (June 2005)

43.10 Recapture of Deductions on Business Car, Truck, or Van

Business use drops to 50% or less

IRC §280F(b)(2)

IRC §280F(b)(3)

Temp. Reg. §1.280F-3T(c)(2)

43.11 Keeping Records of Business Use

* IRS Publication 463

Record-keeping requirements

IRC §274(d)

Temp. Reg. §1.274-5T

Vehicles exempted from record-keeping requirements

IRC §274(d)(4)

Temp. Reg. §1.274-5T(k)

Written company policy restricting personal use

Temp. Reg. §1.274-6T

Control employees, owners and highly compensated

Reg. §1.274-6T(a)(3)(i)(E)

Reg. §1.61-2T(f)(5) and (f)(6)

Poor mileage log prevents deduction for car expenses

*Willie J. Moore et ux., TC Summary Opinion 2010-102

43.12 Leased Business Vehicles: Deductions and Income

IRC §280F(c)

* IRS Publication 463

* "Purchase vs. Lease: Updated Directions for Business Car Users," Sidney J. Baxendale, William D. Stout, and Richard M. Walter, 71 Practical Tax Strategies 282 (November 2003)

Rev. Proc. 2008-22, 2008-12 IRB 658 (inclusion amount tables for cars and trucks/vans with lease term starting in 2008)

Rev. Proc. 2009-24, 2009-17 IRB 885 (inclusion amount tables for cars and trucks/vans with lease term starting in 2009)

Rev. Proc. 2010-18, 2010-9 IRB 427 (inclusion amount tables for cars and trucks/vans with lease term starting in 2010)

44 Sales of Business Property

44.1 Depreciation Recaptured as Ordinary Income on Sale of Personal Property

* IRS Publication 544

IRC §1245(a)

IRC §1250

44.2 Depreciation Recaptured as Ordinary Income on Sale of Real Estate

IRC §1250

25% tax rate for unrecaptured Section 1250 gain

IRC §1(h)(1)(D)

Computing excess over straight line

Reg. §1.1250(b)(1)

Holding period where property is foreclosed

IRC §1250 (d)(10)

Reg. §1.1250-1 through 5

Recapture for GO Zone property

IRC §1400N(d)(5)

Recapture for NY Liberty Zone property

IRC §1400L(f)(3)

44.3 Recapture of First-Year Expensing

* IRS Publication 544

IRC §179(d)(10)

44.4 Gifts and Inheritances of Depreciable Property

IRC §1245(a)

Tax not imposed at time of gift or inheritance

IRC §1245(b)(1), (2), and (3)

Reg. §1.1245-4

44.5 Involuntary Conversions and Tax-Free Exchanges

* IRS Publication 544

IRC §1245(b)(4)

IRC §1250(d)(4)

Reg. §1.704-4

Reg. §1.737-1-5 (gain/loss recognition on partnership distributions of contributed property)

44.6 Installment Sale of Depreciable Property

Reg. §1.1245-6(d)

Sales after June 6, 1984

IRC §453(i)

44.7 Sale of a Proprietorship

Amortization of goodwill, customer lists, agreements not to compete, and other intangibles

IRC §197

Individual proprietorship

IRC §1231

Reg. §1.1231-1

Aaron F. Williams, 152 F.2d 570 (2d Cir. 1946)

IRC §1060

Rev. Rul. 55-79, 1955-1 CB 370

44.8 Property Used in a Business (Section 1231 Assets)

IRC §1231

Reg. §1.1231-1 and 2

* IRS Publication 544

12 months for livestock

IRC §1231(b)(3)

Recapture of ordinary loss

IRC §1231(c)

Note: *Paragraph numbers refer to Parts 1 through 7. Items marked * are research aids, not citations of authority;* see *"Key to Citations" on page 801*

44.9 Sale of Property Used for Business and Personal Purposes

Sale of airplane

Hugh Sharp, Jr., 199 F. Supp. 743 (D. Del. 1961), aff'd, 303 F.2d 783 (3d Cir. 1962)

44.10 Should You Trade in Business Equipment?

Loss on trade-in

National Outdoor Advertising Bureau, Inc., 89 F.2d 878 (2d Cir. 1937), on remand, BTA Dec. 10,072-C, 6/24/38

Sale to dealer

Rev. Rul. 61-119, 1961-1 CB 395

Trade-ins of personal property

IRC §1031(d)

Reg. §1.1031(d)-1

Rev. Rul. 72-111, 1972-1 CB 56

44.11 Corporate Liquidation

IRC §331

Louis Greenspan, 229 F.2d 947 (8th Cir. 1956)

Susan J. Carter, 170 F.2d 911 (2d Cir. 1948)

L. M. Graves, 11 TCM 467 (1952)

Rev. Rul. 59-228, 1959-2 CB 89

Legal expenses of collecting claim

Otto C. Doering, Jr., 335 F.2d 738 (2d Cir. 1964)

45 Figuring Self-Employment Tax

45.1 What Is Self-Employment Income?

IRC §1402

IRC §6017

Reg. §1.6017-1(b)

Reg. §1.1402(a)-1

Reg. §1.1402(b)-1

Health insurance premiums for self-employed deductible from net profits for 2010

IRC §162(l)(4), as amended by the Small Business Jobs Act of 2010, P.L. 111-240, 9/27/10

Health insurance for self-employed not a schedule C deduction

* Chief Counsel Advice 200623001

Qualified joint venture election for husband and wife owners

IRC §761(f)

Husband and wife

IRC §6017

Grandparents' childcare income not subject to self-employment tax

* Derrolyn Steele, TC Summary Opinion 2009-45

Rents

Reg. §1.1402(a)-4

Capital gains and losses

Reg. §1.1402(a)-6

Dividends and interest

Reg. §1.1402(a)-5

Net operating loss carryover

IRC §1402(a)(4) and (5)

Business interruption insurance proceeds not self-employment income

Max G. Newberry, 76 TC 441 (1981)

Illegal employment

Rev. Rul. 60-77, 1960-1 CB 386

Employee can be independent contractor for Keogh purposes

James S. Reece, 63 TCM 3129 (1992)

Insurance agent subject to SE tax

Bruce Isom, 70 TCM 376 (1996)

Extended earnings

Herbert Gump, Federal Cir. (6/12/96)

Robert Schelbe, 71 TCM 3166 (1996)

45.2 Partners Pay Self-Employment Tax

IRC §701

Reg. §1.701-1

Reg. §1.702-1

Limited partner not subject to self-employment tax

IRC §1402(a)(13)

Partner dying during taxable year

Reg. §1.1402(f)-1

Retirement payments for partnerships

IRC §1402(a)(10)

Rev. Rul. 79-34, 1979-1 CB 285

Restricting partnership status of foreign consultant does not avoid self-employment tax

Atef A. Gamal-Eldin, 55 TCM 582 (1988), aff'd in unpublished opinion 876 F.2d 896 (9th Cir. 1989)

45.3 Schedule SE

7.65% deduction for self-employment tax computation

IRC §1402(a)(12)

Health insurance premiums for self-employed deductible from net profits for 2010

IRC §162(l)(4), as amended by the Small Business Jobs Act of 2010, P.L. 111-240, 9/27/10*Income tax deduction for 50% of self-employment tax*

IRC §164(f)

45.4 How Wages Affect Self-Employment Tax

Effect of wages on self-employment tax rates

IRC §1402(b)

Notice 2007-92, 2007-47 IRB 1036

Health insurance premiums for self-employed deductible from net profits for 2010

IRC §162(l)(4), as amended by the Small Business Jobs Act of 2010, P.L. 111-240, 9/27/10

Wage base for 2010 and 2011

Social Security Administration news release and fact sheet, 10/15/10

45.5 Optional Method If 2010 Was a Low-Income or Loss Year

IRC §1402(a)(15)

IRC §1402(l)

45.6 Self-Employment Tax Rules for Certain Positions

Self-employed

IRC §1401

IRC §1402

IRC §1403

Reg. §1.1401-1

Note: *Paragraph numbers refer to Parts 1 through 7. Items marked * are research aids, not citations of authority; see "Key to Citations" on page 801*

Reg. §1.1402(a)-1
Reg. §1.1402(b)-1
Reg. §1.1402(c)-1

Babysitter

Rev. Rul. 77-279, 1977-2 CB 12

Clergy

IRC §1402(e)
Temp. Reg. §1.1402(e)-5T
James B. Hall, 30 F.3d 1304 (10th Cir. 1994)

Ministers who elected out of Social Security coverage may re-elect coverage

Section 403 of P.L. 106-170 (1999)

Consulting

Rev. Rul. 82-210, 1982-2 CB 203
Grosswald v. Schweicker, 653 F.2d 58 (2d Cir. 1981)
Steffens v. United States, 707 F.2d 478 (11th Cir. 1983)
James M. Hornaday, 81 TC 830 (1983) (fees received without services)

Dealers in commodities and options

IRC §1402(i)

Independent contractor

Dan P. Butts, 49 F.3d 713 (11th Cir. 1995)

LLC members

Prop. Regs. §§ 1.1402 (a)-18
Rev. Proc. 95-10, 1995-1 CB 501

Insurance agent treated as independent contractor

Dan P. Butts, 49 F. 3d 713 (11th Cir. 1995)

Director's fees

IRC §1402(a)
Rev. Rul. 68-595, 1968-2 CB 378

Drivers

Boles Trucking, Inc., 8th Cir. (2/12/96)

Adult entertainers

303 West 42nd Street Enterprises, Inc., NY District Court (2/28/96)

Used car salesmen

Martin Springfield, 9th Cir. (7/3/96)

Employees of foreign government or international organization

Reg. §1.1402(c)-3(d)

Jessica M. Smart, 222 F. Supp. 65 (S.D.N.Y. 1963)

Fees as executor

Cresence E. Clarke, 27 TC 861 (1957)
Rev. Rul. 58-5, 1958-1 CB 322, distinguished by Rev. Rul. 72-86, 1972-1 CB 273

Nonprofessional executor or administrator

Rev. Rul. 58-5, 1958-1 CB 322, distinguished by Rev. Rul. 72-86, 1972-1 CB 273
Special Ruling, August 19, 1952
Special Ruling, March 5, 1952
Special Ruling, January 10, 1952
Special Ruling, March 20, 1957

Guardian for disabled cousin

* Letter Ruling 8845025

Trust beneficiaries not self-employed

Reg. §1.1402(a)-2(b)

Fee for occasional speech

Rev. Rul. 55-431, 1955-2 CB 312

PIK payments to farmers

Pub. L. No. 98-4
Announcement 83-43, 1983-10 IRB 29

Nonresident alien

IRC §1402(b)

Nurses: IRS traditional tests

Rev. Rul. 75-101, 1975-1 CB 318
Rev. Rul. 61-96, 1961-2 CB 155
* Letter Ruling 8845049

Nurses obtaining job through agency

Rev. Rul. 75-41, 1975-1 CB 323
Rev. Rul. 75-101, 1975-1 CB 318
* Letter Ruling 8913002
* Letter Ruling 8839073
* Letter Ruling 8904033
Hospital Resource Personnel, Inc., 68 F.3d 421 (11th Cir. 1995)

Payroll taxes withheld from practical nurse's wages

* Letter Ruling 9123005

Gambling income not subject to self-employment tax

Alfred A. Gentile, 6 TC 1 (1946)

Public official

IRC §1402(c)
Reg. §1.402(c)-2

Technical specialists

Section 1706 of 1986 Tax Reform Act
Rev. Rul. 87-41, 1987-1 CB 296

Writer

Rev. Rul. 68-498, 1968-2 CB 377
Rev. Rul. 79-390, 1972-2 CB 308
Rev. Rul. 55-385, 1955-1 CB 100 (professor's writing as self-employment income)

Real estate salesman and door-to-door salesman

IRC §3508(a)
Rev. Rul. 85-63, 1985-1 CB 292

46 Filing Your Return

46.1 Keeping Tax Records

* IRS Publication 552
"Reporting When the W-2, 1099, or K-1 is Wrong," Burgess J.W. Raby and William L. Raby, 92 Tax Notes 1577 (September 17, 2001)

46.2 Getting Ready To File Your Return

* IRS instructions to Forms 1040, 1040A, and 1040EZ

Timely mailing treated as timely filing

IRC §7502(a)
Prop. Reg. §301.7502-1(e)(1) (proposed 9/20/2004; only registered and certified mail considered prima facie evidence of delivery)

Foreign postmarks

Rev. Rul. 2002-23, 2002-18 IRB 811

46.3 Applying for an Extension

Extension of time to file return

IRC §6081
Reg. §1.6081-4

Automatic six-month filing extensions

Temp. Regs. §1.6081-4T (T.D. 9229, 70 Federal Register 67356, 11/7/05)

IRS may terminate on 10 days notice

Reg. §1.6081-4(c)

Extension of time to pay tax

IRC §6161
Reg. §1.616-1 (undue hardship required)
IRC §6601(b)(1) (interest on

Note: *Paragraph numbers refer to Parts 1 through 7. Items marked * are research aids, not citations of authority; see "Key to Citations" on page 801*

underpayment applies from original due date)

IRS-designated private delivery services

IRC §7502(f)

Notice 2004-83, 2004-52 IRB 1030 (list of designated private delivery services)

Filing and payment extension until June 15 for being out of the country

Reg. §1.6081-5

Temp. Reg. 1.6081-5T (T.D. 9229, 70 Federal Register 67356, 11/7/05)

Penalty for late payment—90% exception for taxpayer with automatic extension

IRC §6651(a)(2)

Reg. §301.6651-1(c)(3)

46.4 Getting Your Refund

* IRS Publication 17

* IRS Instructions to Forms 1040, 1040A, or 1040EZ

Offers in compromise

IRC §7122

46.5 Paying Taxes Due

Paying tax in installments

IRC §6159

Online payment agreement

News Release IR-2006-159

IRS offers split-refund option to direct depositors

News Release IR-2006-85

46.6 Electronic Filing

Free File fillable forms

News Release IR-2009-005

Calling the IRS about your refund

* IRS Instructions to Forms 1040, 1040A, or 1040EZ

46.7 Notify the IRS of Address Changes

Last known address rule for deficiency notices

Rev. Proc. 90-18, 1990-1 CB 491

Barbara Abeles, 91 TC 1019 (1988) (acq. 1989-31 IRB4)

Nancy J. Bayer, 98 TC 19 (1991)

46.8 Interest on Tax Underpayments

IRC §6601

IRC §6621

Interest rates on overpayments and underpayments through December 2010

Rev. Rul. 2010-21, 2010-39 IRB 388

Same interest rate for deficiencies and refunds

IRC §6621(a)

Quarterly interest rates based on short-term federal rate

Notice 88-59, 1988-1 CB 546

Quarterly rates after 1986

IRC §6621(b)

Interest runs from due date without extensions to date paid

IRC §6601(a)

IRC §6601(b)(1)

Deposit suspends interest accrual on potential underpayment

IRC §6603

Rev. Proc. 2005-18, 2005-13 IRB 798

Interest and dividend information disclosed to government agencies

IRC §6103(1)(7)

46.9 Tax Penalties for Late Filing and Late Payment

Monthly penalty for late filing

IRC §6651(a)(1)

No tax due, no late filing penalty

Christine Patronik-Holder, 100 TC 374 (1993) (acq. 1993-38 IRB 4)

Reasonable/not reasonable cause for failure to file

Elizabeth Gravett, 67 TCM 2651 (1994)

Douglas D. Kemmerer, 66 TCM 550 (1993)

Monthly penalty for late payment

IRC §6651(a)(2)

47 Filing Refund Claims, and Amended Returns

47.1 Filing an Amended Return

Filing for disabled persons

Rev. Proc. 99-21, 1997-17 IRB

47.2 When To File a Refund Claim

Refund for overpayment

IRC §6401

IRC §6402

Reg. §301.6401-1

Reg. §301.6402-2(c) and -3

Three-year and two-year rule for filing refund claim

IRC 6511(a)

Withholdings and estimated tax considered paid on original due date

David H. Baral, 120 S. Ct. 1006 (2000)

News Release IR-2000-09

Refunds of withholdings and estimated taxes on late-filed original return

Astrid E.A. Omohundro, 2002-2 USTC ¶50,590 (9th Cir. 2002) (siding with T.D. 8932 and Weisbart decision)

T. D. 8932, 2001-11 IRB 813, amending Reg. §301.7502-1(f) to reflect IRS acquiescence to Weisbart, 222 F.3d (2d Cir. 2000)

Emanuel Weisbart, 222 F.3d 93 (2d Cir. 2000) (Acq; 2000-48 IRB)

Faye Anastasoff, 235 F.3d 1054 (8th Cir. 2000), vacating original decision at 223 F.3d 898 (8th Cir. 2000)

Tax Court refunds for delinquent filers

IRC §6512 (b)(3) (allowing three-year lookback period barred under 1996 Supreme Court Lundy decision)

Robert Lundy, 116 S. Ct. 647 (1996)

Suspension of limitations period during period of disability

IRC §6511(h)(1) (reverses effect of Supreme Court's Brockamp decision in certain cases)

Marian Brockamp, 117 S. Ct. 849 (1997)

Financial disability standard not met

Matthias Haller, TC Memo 2010-147

Bad debt and worthless securities

IRC §6511(d)(1)

Divorce and net operating loss carryback

Rev. Rul. 75-368, 1975-2 CB 480

Net operating loss carryback

Note: *Paragraph numbers refer to Parts 1 through 7. Items marked * are research aids, not citations of authority;* see *"Key to Citations" on page 801*

IRC §6511(d)(2)

Credit against future estimated tax liability

IRC §6402(b)

Refund diversion for overdue child support

IRC §6402(c)

Refund withheld if debt owed federal agency

IRC §6402(d)

Extension for Armed Forces combat zone service

IRC §7508

Payment with request for extension of time to file

Troy W. Ott, 98-1 USTC ¶50,331 (9th Cir. 1998)

47.3 Joint Refund Claims

* IRS Publication 504

Carryback of net operating loss after divorce

Rev. Rul. 75-368, 1975-2 CB 480, modified by Rev. Rul. 80-6, 1980-1 CB 296

Refund withheld to pay spouse's past-due debts

IRC §6402(c)

IRC §6402(d)

Reg. §301.6402-5

Temp. Reg. §301.6402-6T

47.4 Stating the Reasons for Refund Claims

Reg. §301.6402-2(b)

Form 1040X

47.5 Quick Refund Claims

IRC §6411

Reg. §1.6411-1(a)

Tax-shelter refunds

Rev. Proc. 84-84, 1984-2 CB 782

47.6 Interest Paid on Refund Claims

IRC §6611

Interest rates on overpayments and underpayments through December 2010

Rev. Rul. 2010-21, 2010-39 IRB 388

Same interest rate for deficiencies and refunds

IRC §6621(a)

Interest from date of overpayment

Reg. §301.6611-1(a)

Interest to 30 days before date of refund check

IRC §6611(b)(2)

Interest on net operating loss carryback

IRC §6611(f)

Reg. §301.6611-1(e)

45-day rule for original returns

IRC §6611(e)(1)

45-day rule for refund claims after 1994

IRC §6611(e)(2)

47.7 Refunds Withheld To Cover Debts

Past-due child support

IRC §6402(c)

Debt owed to federal agency

IRC §6402(d)

Past-due state income tax

IRC §6402(e)

47.8 Amended Returns Showing Additional Tax

Reg. §301.6402-3(a)

47.9 Penalty for Filing Excessive Refund Claim

IRC §6676

48 If the IRS Examines Your Return

48.1 Odds of Being Audited

Average itemized deductions for 2008

IRS Statistics of Income Bulletin, Winter 2010

48.2 When the IRS Can Assess Additional Taxes

IRC §6501(a) through (e)

Reg. §301.6501(a)-1 through (h)-1

Leslie Robertson, 32 TCM 955 (1973)

Unidentified check is a deposit, not a tax payment

Robert B. Risman, 100 TC 13 (1993)

Amended return following fraudulent return does not start limitations period

Ernest Bodaracco, 464 U.S. 386 (1984)

IRS has 60 days to assess tax on amended return

IRC §6501(c)(7)

Seizure of state tax refunds

R.A. Ketcham, 99-2 USTC ¶50,796

Six-year limitations period for omitting 25% of gross income

IRC §6501(e)(1)(A)

Stephen G. Colestock, 102 TC 12 (1994) (six-year statute applies to all items on return)

Overstatement of basis does not trigger six-year limitations period

Salman Ranch Ltd., 573 F.3d 1362 (Fed. Cir. 2009)

Bakersfield Energy Partners, 568 F.3d 767 (9th Cir. 2009)

IRS temporary regulation applies six-year statute of limitations for overstated basis

Treasury Decision 9466, 2009-43 IRB 551

Intermountain Insurance Service of Vail, 134 TC 11 (2010) (refuses to retroactively apply TD 9466)

48.3 Audit Overview

* IRS Publication 556

Time and place for audits

Temp. Reg. §301.7605-1T

IRS reconstruction of income/deductions was improper

Ragnhild A. Westby, TC Memo 2004-179

48.4 Preparing for the Audit

* IRS Publication 1

* IRS Publication 556

* "Forewarned is Forearmed at IRS Audits," Richard A. Carpenter, 60 Taxation for Accountants 154 (March 1998)

Notice of deficiency

IRC §6212

Extension of confidentiality privilege to authorized practitioner

Note: *Paragraph numbers refer to Parts 1 through 7. Items marked * are research aids, not citations of authority; see "Key to Citations" on page 801*

IRC §7525

Work product

Monroe Adlman, 68 F.3d 1495 (2d Cir. 1995)

Time and place for audits

Temp. Reg. §301.7605-1T

Explanation of audit process

IRC §7521(b)

Valuation dispute leads to a battle for supporting documents

Bradford C. Bernardo, 104 TC 677 (1995)

48.5 Handling the Audit

* IRS Publication 1

* IRS Publication 556

Representative handling your case

IRC §7521(b)(2) and (c)

Time and place for audits

Temp. Reg. §301.7605-1T

Tips for handling the audit

Gene Erekson, 70 F.3d 1153 (10th Cir., 1995)

Recording IRS examination

IRC 7521(a)

Notice 89-51, 1989-1 CB 691

48.6 Tax Penalties for Inaccurate Returns

Accuracy-related penalties for negligence, substantial tax understatements, valuation errors

IRC §6662

Reg. §§ 1.6662-1 through 1.6662-7

Accuracy-related penalty for understatements attributable to reportable transactions

IRC §6662A

IRC §6664(d) (reasonable cause exception to penalty)

Penalty for failure to disclose reportable transactions

IRC §6707A, as amended by Small Business Jobs Act of 2010, P.L. 111-240, 9/27/10

To avoid negligence penalties, reasonable reliance

Herbert T. Cobey, Jr., 67 TCM 24 (1994)

Negligence or disregard of rules or regulations

IRC §6662(b)(1) and (c)

Reg. §1.6662-3

Reliance on preparer exception fails to avoid penalty

*Patricia A. Kelly, TC Summary Opinion 2010

Negligence penalty applies to entire underpayment: prior law

Asphalt Products Co. Inc., 482 U.S. 117 (1987)

Disclosure prevents penalties

Emmanuel Fellouzis, 95-1 USTC §50,287

Information returns

IRC §6721-6724

Reasonable cause exception for accuracy-related penalties

IRC §6664(c)

Reg. §1.6664-4

Reasonable basis required for disclosed position on return

IRC §6662(d)(2)(B)(ii)

Temp. Reg. §1.6662-7T

Reg. §1.6662-4

Proposed Regulation §1.6664-4

Substantial understatement of tax

IRC §6662(d)

Anthony J. Pasqualini, et al., 68 TCM 89 (1994)

Substantial understatement

William Woods II, 91 TC 11 (1988)

Substantial valuation misstatement

IRC §6662(e)

Reg. §1.6662-5

Fraud penalty

IRC §6663

Frivolous return penalty

IRC §6702

Martin Bradley, 817 F.2d 1400 (9th Cir. 1987)

Criminal fraud and false statements

IRC §7206

Criminal willful evasion

IRC §7201

Criminal penalty for willful failure to pay or file

IRC §7203

Failure to file partnership return

IRC §6698

Failure to report Social Security number of dependents

IRC §6724(d)(3)(D)

Bad check

IRC §6657

Reg. §301.6657-1

Interest on penalties

IRC §6601(e)(2)(A)

Higher interest on certain penalties

IRC §6601(e)(2)(B)

Reliance on erroneous written IRS advice

IRC §6404(f)

Undervaluation on gift or estate tax return

IRC §6662(g) (20% penalty)

IRC §6662(h)(2)(C) (40% penalty)

48.7 Agreeing to Audit Changes

Waiver of restrictions on assessment

IRC §6213(d)

48.8 Disputing the Audit Changes

* IRS Publication 5

* "An Expanded Appeals Mediation Program With a Restriction," Ken C. Jones and Adrian Fenton, 96 Tax Notes 1889 (September 30, 2002)

* "The 'Stat' Notice in the new Millennium—Shouldn't the Notice be User Friendly?" Anthony F. Newton, 91 Tax Notes 1139 (May 14, 2001)

* "Deficient Statutory Notices and the Burdens of Proof: A Reply to Mr. Newton," Leandra Lederman, 92 Tax Notes 117 (July 2, 2001)

Telephone conversation qualifies as hearing

Scott William Katz, 115 TC No. 26 (2000)

Petition to Tax Court

IRC §6213

IRC §741-7465

IRS failure to specify deadline for Tax Court petition

Note: *Paragraph numbers refer to Parts 1 through 7. Items marked* are research aids, not citations of authority;* see *"Key to Citations" on page 801*

Virgil B. Elings, 324 F.3d 1110 (9th Cir. 2003)

James Rochelle, 293 F.3d 740 (5th Cir. 2002), aff'g per curiam 116 TC 356 (2001)

Eric E. Smith, 275 F.3d 912 (10th Cir. 2001)

Small tax cases ($50,000 or less)

IRC §7463

Civil action for refund

IRC §7422

IRS provides mediation option

Rev. Proc. 2002-44, 2002-26 IRB 10

Supreme Court says IRS lien overrides tenancy by the entirety

U.S. v. Sandra L. Craft, 2002-1 USTC ¶50,361 (Sup. Ct. 2002)

Howard D. and Sheila A. Popky, Third Circuit, 5/17/05, affirming Pennsylvania District Court, 6/15/04

Lien on commissions

Jefferson-Pilot Life Insurance Co., 37 F.3d 1495 (4th Cir., 1994)

Penalty on taxpayer for frivolous Tax Court action

IRC §6673(a)(1)

Nis Family Trust, 115 TC No. 532 (2000)

Ronald W. Davenport, TC Memo 2009-248

Mary Lynn Collard, Fifth Circuit, 11/11/09

Penalty on attorney for Tax Court delay

IRC §6673(a)(2)

Nis Family Trust, 115 TC No. 532 (2000)

Appeals court penalty

IRC §7482(c)(4)

Federal district court penalizes attorney for frivolous tax-protestor arguments

Donald Zimmerman, District Court, Eastern District of California, 2001-1 USTC ¶50,107, adopting findings at ¶50,106

IRS can reopen an estate audit despite closing letter

IRC §6404(e)

Robert A. Strang, TC Memo 2001-104 (no interest abatement for IRS delay due to workload)

Estate of Bommer, 69 TCM 2541 (1995)

IRS may abate interest charges

IRC §6404(e)(i)(B)

Reg. §301.6404-2

48.9 Offer in Compromise

IRC §7122

Reg. §301.7122-1(c)(3) (economic hardship)

Partial payments required with submission

IRC §7122(c)

Notice 2006-68, 2006-31 IRB 105

Offers deemed accepted if not rejected within a certain period

IRC §7122(f)

48.10 Recovering Costs of a Tax Dispute

IRC §7430

Net worth limitation in recovery of legal fees

IRC §7430(c)(4)(D)

Expenses of administrative proceedings after Nov. 10, 1988

IRC 7430(c)(2) and (c)(7)

Exhausting administrative remedies

Reg. Sec. 301.7430-1

Substantially justified same as reasonableness test

Ronald Sokol, 92 TC 760 (1989)

Tax expertise does not support increased award

Walter J. Levy, 63 TCM 2927 (1992)

Robert T. Cozean, 109 TC 227 (1997)

Higher attorneys' fees not awarded for tax law competency

Caspian Consulting Group, Inc., TC Memo 2006-85

Winning the dispute does not guarantee legal fees

Benjamin Harrison, 69 TCM 1969 (1995)

Legal fees disallowed

Walker B. Fite, 67 TCM 2794 (1994) (IRS position held justified)

Laura E. Austin, TC Memo 1997-157

Legal fee award for excessive IRS penalties

David Heasley, 967 F.2d 116 (5th Cir. 1992), rev'g 61 TCM 2503 (1991)

Penalty for bringing frivolous suit against the IRS

IRC 6673(b)(1)

IRS concession no guarantee of award

Ronald Sokol, 92 TC 760 (1989)

Pre-1986 cases: IRS pre-litigation position considered

Comer Family Trust, 856 F.2d 775 (6th Cir. 1988)

Sylvia Sliva, 839 F.2d 602 (9th Cir. 1988)

David Kaufman, 758 F.2d 1 (1st Cir. 1985)

David Powell, 791 F.2d 385 (5th Cir. 1986)

Pre-1986 cases: Only IRS litigating position considered

Robert Baker, 83 TC 822 (1984), aff'd 787 F.2d 637 (D.C. Cir. 1986)

Eva Wickert, 842 F.2d 1005 (8th Cir. 1988)

Ewing and Thomas, P.A., 803 F.2d 613 (11th Cir. 1986)

Balanced Financial Management Inc., 769 F.2d 1440 (10th Cir. 1985)

Refund of third party's tax payment allowed

Lori Williams, 115 S. Ct. 1611 aff'g 24 F.3d 1143 (9th Cir. 1995)

48.11 Suing the IRS for Unauthorized Collection

IRC 7433

Reg. §301.7433-1

Suing the IRS for wrongfully failing to release

IRC 7432

Unauthorized IRS sales

Carole Marshall, 921 F. Supp. 641 (Dist. Ct. Minn. 1996)

Commissions paid to independent contractor subject to continuous wage levy

Jefferson-Pilot Life Insurance Co., 49 F.3d 1020 (4th Cir. 1995), aff'g 95-1 USTC §50,263 (1994)

Note: *Paragraph numbers refer to Parts 1 through 7. Items marked * are research aids, not citations of authority;* see *"Key to Citations" on page 801*

Part 11

Practice Before the IRS

Because the IRS is unable to examine every return, it follows a policy of examining returns that, upon preliminary inspection, indicate the largest possible source of potential tax deficiency.

Returns are rated for audit according to a mathematical formula called the *discriminant function system* (DIF). Various weights are assigned to separate items on each tax return, thus permitting the ranking of returns for the greatest potential error. The specific factors entering into the DIF formula are not disclosed by the IRS.

Taxpayers are advised of their right to be represented by a certified public accountant, attorney, or enrolled agent. Once the taxpayer has chosen a representative, the IRS may not interview the taxpayer alone, unless consent is given. Together with the first letter of proposed tax deficiency, the IRS must give the taxpayer a clear and complete explanation of the administrative process from examination and appeals to the collection of taxes.

HOW RETURNS ARE EXAMINED

Preliminary Examination

Correspondence notices are used to correct the following types of obvious errors spotted at IRS Service Centers: medical expenses under the 7.5% adjusted gross income limitation; personal casualty and theft losses under the 10% adjusted gross income limitation; auto mileage rates for business transportation in excess of the IRS mileage allowance; and income on Form W-2 or Form 1099 incorrectly reported on a tax return. Taxpayers are advised by mail of the corrections and of additional tax due. The taxpayer may request an interview or submit additional information if he or she disagrees. Where the correction is made and additional tax is paid before the due date for filing the return, the taxpayer may avoid interest charges.

Where an underpayment of tax results from a mathematical or clerical error, the IRS may use a summary assessment procedure. However, the IRS must give the taxpayer an explanation of the error, and time to file a request for the abatement of the assessment. The IRS must honor that request (IRC §6213(b)(2)). It must then follow the normal deficiency procedures. These procedures are followed for the following types of mathematical and clerical errors: (1) arithmetic errors (addition, subtraction, multiplication, or division); (2) errors in transferring amounts on the tax forms; (3) missing schedules or forms; (4) incorrect use of any Treasury table; and (5) entries that exceed statutory limitations. Summary procedures also apply to the omission of a correct Social Security number by a taxpayer claiming personal exemptions, the dependent care tax credit, child tax credit, higher education credits, or the earned income credit (IRC §6213 (g)(2)).

Where an arithmetic error is made by an IRS representative who is helping a taxpayer prepare a return, the IRS may abate any interest due on the underpayment of tax for any period ending on or before the 30th day following the date of notice and demand for payment of the deficiency (IRC §6404(d)).

Interest Abatement Due to IRS Delay

The IRS may abate interest charges attributable to IRS procedural or mechanical errors that unreasonably delay processing of a deficiency, such as delays resulting from the loss of records, IRS personnel transfers, or extended training, illness, or leave of IRS personnel (IRC §6404(e)(1)(A)). Interest is not eligible for abatement if delay is related to general administrative decisions including IRS work priorities, discretionary judgments, or decisions concerning the application of the tax laws. An abatement request is made on Form 843.

The Tax Court may review whether the IRS has abused its discretion in failing to abate interest if the taxpayer meets the net worth and size requirements for recovering attorneys' fees (IRC §6404(h)). An eligible taxpayer must file a petition and pay a $60 filing fee (unless hardship is shown); *see* Tax Court Rule 281 for petition details.

Types of Personal Examinations

A specific examination of a tax return may be by correspondence, at a local IRS office, or at the taxpayer's place of business, office, or home. An examination at an IRS office or by correspondence is called a desk or office examination; an examination at a place of business or home is called a field examination. The complexity of the transactions reported on a return generally determines whether a return will be subject to an office or field examination.

An office examination is initiated by a letter of notification listing the items to be examined. The agent will ordinarily not go beyond these items. However, the agent may, in his or her discretion, extend an office examination to other items. A field examination may involve a review of the entire return.

A correspondence examination is used to question simple individual returns; it is a type of office examination handled entirely through correspondence. The taxpayer is asked to explain a particular item or to send supporting evidence. A correspondence examination may end up as an interview type of office examination or a field examination. Whether it does or not will depend on how satisfactory the answers to correspondence are and whether or not the answers indicate problems not appearing on the face of the return. If you feel that it is impractical to handle the examination through correspondence or that it places you at a disadvantage, request an office examination conference. Practitioners generally feel that the absence of personal contact and discussion is a disadvantage.

You may request a transfer of a case from an office examination to a field examination. Requests for transfers have been granted in cases of voluminous records or physical incapacity. A request will be denied if it is clear that you have no legitimate reason for the transfer.

A field examination may be shifted to the office of the taxpayer's representative if he or she has the client's records and it is more convenient to hold the examination there.

An individual taxpayer may appear at an examination in his or her own behalf, and a corporation may be represented by an officer. The preparer of a tax return may, if authorized, represent the client before an agent in connection with the return although the preparer is not enrolled to practice before the IRS. An attorney, enrolled agent, or CPA may also represent a taxpayer before the IRS.

If you represent a taxpayer, file a power of attorney, IRS Form 2848. Ask the IRS to send you all correspondence involving the examination. In your correspondence with the IRS, always reference the IRS code symbols found on the IRS's letter to you. Before the examination, review not only the return in question but also the records of prior examinations of the client's return. The agent has reviewed these records and will use them as a starting point for the present examination.

Restrictions on IRS Examinations of Books

The IRS may not make more than one examination of a taxpayer's books of accounts for any taxable period unless the taxpayer requests otherwise, or the IRS, after investigation, notifies the taxpayer in writing that an additional inspection is necessary (IRC §7605(b)). However, this restriction does not bar the IRS from examining public records or bank accounts. Nor does it bar examination of the books of a third party, such as the taxpayer's corporation, unless the identities of the taxpayer and his or her corporation are so inextricable that the examination of the books of one constitutes an examination of the books of the other.

A taxpayer may protest a second examination by refusing to give the agent access to his books. The IRS may then issue a summons. If the taxpayer still refuses access, the IRS may seek enforcement of the summons in district court. The taxpayer then has the opportunity at a hearing in the district court to show that a second examination is unnecessary.

The IRS tries to avoid examining the same items appearing on a taxpayer's returns for more than one year, such as the treatment of installment sale payments. Thus, where the taxpayer's return was examined in either of the two years prior to the current examination for the same items, and that examination resulted in no change in tax liability, the IRS will suspend the current examination, upon the taxpayer's notifying the appointment clerk or the examiner, pending a review of its files to determine whether the examination should proceed. If the IRS decides to proceed with the examination, the taxpayer has no recourse.

The IRS may not conduct audits based on financial status or "economic reality" to determine if income was omitted from a return unless there is a reasonable likelihood that income has not been reported (IRC §7602(e)).

Handwriting samples. The Supreme Court has ruled that the IRS can compel a taxpayer to furnish handwriting samples in the same manner as it can demand other physical evidence (Harvey F. Euge, 444 U.S. 707 (1980)).

Administrative Appeal Procedures Applicable to an Examined Return

It is important to follow IRS administrative appeal procedures to lay a basis for recovering from the IRS litigation costs and for shifting the burden of proof in a later noncriminal court case. If the IRS takes an unreasonable position at an audit and the dispute goes to court, you may not recover an award for litigation costs unless you have exhausted administrative remedies within the IRS (IRC §7430(b)(1)).

Similarly, you may not shift the burden of proof to the IRS if you did not exhaust all adminstrative appeals. In tax litigation, there is a presumption in favor of the IRS's determination of tax liability. This requires a taxpayer to come forward with evidence to disprove the IRS's determinations by a "preponderance of the evidence." A taxpayer may in a court action shift the burden of proof to the IRS with respect to factual issues relevant in determining tax liability. However, before the burden is shifted, the taxpayer must show: (1) compliance with substantiation and record-keeping requirements imposed by the Code or IRS regulations; and(2) cooperation with reasonable requests by the IRS for meetings, information, and access to witnesses, as well as exhaustion of all IRS adminstrative appeals (IRC §7491).

How To Handle the Examination

Common sense rules of courtesy should be your guide in your contacts with the agent. Avoid personality clashes; they can only interfere with a speedy and fair resolution of the examination. However, be firm in your approach and, if the agent appears to be unreasonable, make it clear that, if necessary, you will go all the way to court to win your point. A vacillating approach may weaken your position in reaching a settlement.

Where a practitioner is handling the audit, the taxpayer should not be present during discussions with the agent. The taxpayer can add nothing to the discussion that the practitioner does not already know after becoming thoroughly acquainted with the return. The taxpayer may damage the case by volunteering information harmful to his or her position.

In a field audit, the agent will want to review original books and records. If the agent also wants supporting secondary records, ask him or her to give you a list of needs, which you can then present as a unit.

Original records should not be taken out of your client's office; give *copies* of relevant records to the agent. Do not volunteer data. The agent will ask for any needed information. Try to provide an adequate area to work in.

After the review and before the report is prepared, the agent will discuss his or her findings and recommendations. At this stage, disputes generally involve questions of fact. The agent will readily use discretion in compromising issues of fact where, for example, there are inadequate primary records but there is other convincing evidence that the taxpayer has made a valid claim. As for conflicting interpretations of law, the agent will abide by well-defined IRS policy. The agent will not lean to an interpretation conflicting with or not covered by IRS policy. Compromises involving open issues or conflicts between IRS and court positions are possible at a higher level conference in the Appeals office. Occasionally, a disputed point in an examination may be resolved by asking the IRS for technical advice.

In some instances, you may be asked by the agent to submit a legal memorandum. This may be a signal that the agent is not sure of the legal issues involved in your case and wants your help. You are not required to do this and may refuse where the memo might reveal more of your case than you would care to divulge. However, where the facts are not in dispute and you feel a clarification of the law might expedite the case, a memo may be advisable. Keep in mind that anything submitted to the agent becomes part of the record that will pass through the levels of IRS review.

Also be alert to the possibility that the agent may be developing a fraud issue, which may be evidenced by the appearance of another agent. If you suspect such a possibility, consider whether you should allow the agent to see further records that may be incriminating. Also consider contacting a practitioner experienced in tax fraud issues.

Your readiness to compromise will depend on the extent of the agent's examination and the amount of the proposed deficiency or refund. Sometimes an agent will pick up one point but fail to develop another that could lead to a substantial deficiency. Here, it may be tactically advisable to accept the proposal. Carrying the case beyond this point might lead to an opening of other items on the return.

If You Agree With the Examiner

When you agree to the agent's proposed changes, your client generally will be asked to sign a Form 4549, "Income Tax Examination Changes," and a Form 870, "Waiver of Restrictions on Assessment and Collection of Deficiency in Tax and Acceptance of Overassessment," or other appropriate agreement form. When signed, the agreement permits an immediate assessment of a deficiency.

The only advantage in signing is to stop the running of interest on the tax deficiency within 30 days after the date the waiver is filed. In an overassessment, that is, where a refund is due, a signed waiver is merely an acknowledgment of the overassessment.

A signed Form 870 does not prevent the IRS from reopening the case to assess an additional deficiency. If on review the deficiency is increased, you will receive a revised Form 870. Your client can refuse to sign the form. The signed first form has the effect of stopping the interest on the original deficiency. As a matter of practice, however, waivers or acceptances ordinarily result in a closing of the case.

If your client signs a Form 870 after a formal deficiency notice (90-day letter) has been mailed, his or her right to appeal to the Tax Court is retained. But if Form 870 is signed before a deficiency notice has been mailed, your client loses the right to appeal to the Tax Court. Although an appeal to the Tax Court may not be made, a suit for a refund may still be filed unless your client agrees on the form not to seek a refund.

The payment of a tax before the deficiency notice is mailed is, in effect, a waiver of the restrictions on assessment and collection. If the payment satisfies your client's entire tax liability for that year, an appeal cannot be made to the Tax Court. The taxpayer's only recourse is to sue for a refund in either the District Court or U.S. Court of Federal Claims.

If a refund is due and a Form 870 is signed, you may file a protective refund claim. Generally, an agent will process the refund, but if he or she fails to do so or the review staff puts it aside for some reason and the limitation period expires, the refund will be lost. The refund claim will protect your client from such a mishap.

An Agreed Case Is Always Reviewed

Once a Form 4549 and Form 870 are signed, the agent prepares the report, which is reviewed. While the agent's report is approved in most cases, do not assume that this review is a mere formality. Agreed cases receive closer review than unagreed cases. Once approved, an agreed case has, except for isolated cases, "reached the end of the line." A reviewer thus realizes that he or she has a greater responsibility in checking the agreed case than in an unagreed case where the facts and law may be reviewed several times as the case proceeds through administrative channels. The reviewer will check the following points:

Facts appearing in the agent's report and in the return filed by the taxpayer. The reviewer may find facts that the agent overlooked or emphasize facts that did not appear important to the agent.

Agent's interpretation and application of the Code's provisions to the facts in the case.

Agent's judgment. The taxpayer might not have substantiated all of the deductions claimed with primary evidence, but the agent allowed a portion of the deduction based on secondary evidence. The reviewer may question the judgment of the agent or believe that the agent was too lenient. The agent may try to justify his or her position, but if the reviewer and agent cannot agree, the chief reviewer will resolve the problem.

Other tax returns. Where an individual's return shows income from an estate, trust, or partnership, the reviewer will usually ask the agent to check the estate, trust, or partnership return, or to transfer the case to an agent who may be examining one of these returns.

Tax returns of prior tax years. The agent may be required to examine the facts on the prior returns. The inquiry may result in the development of new facts that may widen the scope of the audit. The number of ways in which a reviewer may develop new facts depends only on his or her ingenuity, experience, and zeal. Therefore, remember that even after an agreement is signed (Form 870), the agent may ask for additional facts, and confront you with new interpretations.

You will not be allowed to argue your case directly with the reviewer. But you may be sure that the agent will present your case in the best light if for no other reason than to justify his or her own judgment.

What To Do If You Disagree With the Agent

If you disagree with the agent at an office examination, the agent is required to explain the adjustments and available appeal rights. If you desire an immediate conference with the agent's supervisor, it will be granted if practicable. In most cases, mediation may be requested through the IRS's Fast Track Mediation process to help resolve the dispute. You may withdraw from mediation at any time and either party may reject the mediator's proposals; *see* IRS Publication 3605, *Fast Track Mediation—A Process for Prompt Resolution of Tax Issues*.

If no agreement can be reached, you will receive a copy of the examination report and a 30-day letter providing the following alternatives: (1) You can agree to the proposed adjustments and sign enclosed Forms 4549 and 870; (2) you can request an Appeals office conference by written protest or small case request; or (3) you may ignore the letter, in which case you will eventually receive a statutory notice of deficiency (90-day letter).

If you disagree with the agent at the field examination, he or she will prepare a complete examination report fully explaining the proposed adjustments. The agent will then send it to the review staff for a technical and procedural review. If the review staff agrees with the agent, you will receive a 30-day letter, as in the case of the office examination. The 30-day letter is accompanied by a copy of the examination report and a detailed explanation of the available appeal procedures, with a request that you inform the IRS of your choice of action. You have the following alternatives:

1. Sign a Form 4549 and a Form 870 (which preclude appeal to the Tax Court);
2. Request an Appeals office conference by written protest or small case request;
3. Ignore the 30-day letter and wait for the statutory notice of deficiency (90-day letter); or
4. Pay the tax and file a claim for refund.

A 30-day letter is not required by the Code and, if the IRS wants to, it may dispense with it and send you the 90-day letter. The 30-day letter is merely an additional attempt by the IRS to settle the case without going to trial. If necessary, you may get additional time to file your protest or a small case request. However, if the limitation period for the assessment of tax is running out on the tax year in question, you will get neither a 30-day letter nor an extension unless you sign a waiver extending the limitation period.

Should You Ask for a Conference?

The answer lies in the nature of your disagreement with the auditing agent. You may feel his or her authority to accept proposals for settlement is too limited. You may believe the agent has overemphasized certain facts, or disregarded or failed to give proper weight to other facts. Perhaps he or she has misinterpreted applicable tax law or misapplied it to your case. The agent may even have ignored law that supports your claim.

The very existence of the conference procedure is in itself a recognition that your objection to the agent's decision may be right. If the IRS were convinced that the auditing agent was always correct, there would be no purpose to the conferences.

It is usually advisable to take your case to the Appeals office. The chances of a settlement are favorable. Most cases are settled in conference. But before going ahead, consider these points:

1. When the IRS has an established policy regarding the disputed issue, taking a case further in the IRS usually gains nothing. All IRS personnel are bound by the same rules.
2. Interest continues to run. It does not stop unless you make a cash deposit.
3. The IRS will find out your position on all issues. If the case comes to trial, there can be no element of surprise.
4. The IRS can always find additional issues.

Appealing Your Case

You start an appeal by filing either a written protest or a small case request.

You can make a small case request if the total amount of the IRS's proposed change in tax, penalties, and interest for a tax year is $25,000 or less. You can use Form 12203 to make a small case request, or you can simply send in a letter asking for a review of the IRS's proposed changes, noting the changes to which you object and your reasons. However, *no* small case requests are allowed for tax disputes of any amount involving partnerships, S corporations, employee plans, and exempt organizations.

When the total in dispute for any tax year (tax, interest, and penalties) exceeds $25,000, you must file a formal written protest. There is no special form for the protest. The important thing is to include information and arguments that will present your case in the best light to the appeals officer.

Seven specific points must be included in the protest:

1. Taxpayer's name, address, and daytime telephone number.
2. Date and symbols on the 30-day letter transmitting the proposed adjustments.
3. Years covered and the amounts of tax liability in dispute for each year. List here only the amount of the proposed deficiency with which you disagree. This is often less than the entire proposed deficiency.
4. An itemized schedule of the agent's findings with which you disagree. Make sure you cover every item contested. Where more than one finding is involved, list each separately and number it.
5. A statements of the facts supporting your position for each of the items named in (4). Use separate numbered paragraphs for each issue; make sure the number of each paragraph corresponds with the number of the item in (4) that it covers.
6. A statement of the law on which you rely for each of the items listed in (4); use separate paragraphs, numbered to correspond with the items in (4).
7. A request for a hearing with the Appeals office. You must make such request in the protest. Otherwise, you will get no hearing and the case will be decided on the basis of what you submit as your protest.

The most important part of the protest is the presentation of your arguments. These you divide into three parts: (1) Give the arguments in summary form, numbered. (2) Provide a statement of facts covering the disputed items. (3) Develop each argument and support it by citations of authority.

Separate protests do not have to be filed if more than one tax year is involved. All the tax years covered in the 30-day letter may be covered in one protest.

An original and a copy of the protest must be filed.

Stress the equities of your case. A case that shows that a decision against you would be unfair may be stronger than one where you have the technicalities on your side.

Write the facts so that they can be understood. They should be clear and accurate. List them in the order in which they happened.

Do not omit the facts that seem to be against you. When explained, they may not be as detrimental to your case as they first appear.

Substantiate the facts with exhibits, affidavits, or any other proof.

Try to avoid unimportant facts that are not relevant to the issue. Make sure you understand the principles of law affecting any fact you state. Otherwise, the argument you will later make may be weak.

Discuss the issues in the order of their importance. Leave the least important for last. Say what and who is involved.

Write short descriptive headings before each issue. Repeat important facts if they help your argument.

Summarize your point and show how it applies to your case.

Sometimes a short quotation from a leading case is effective if you can relate the case to your facts.

Be sure that every case you cite stands for what you say it does.

Try to put yourself in the place of the conferee who is going to read the protest. Ask yourself what you would want to know in order to answer the questions, and then try to supply the information.

Take the time to write a well-organized, succinct, and interesting protest.

Consider the appearance of the letter. Give it eye appeal. Use side heads to break up solid pages of type. Sometimes graphs, photographs, charts, and other illustrations help make your point in an attractive manner.

How the protest is signed. The taxpayer must certify, under penalty of perjury, that the statements of facts in the protest are true. Add the following signed statement to the protest: "Under penalties of perjury, I declare that I have examined the statement of facts presented in this protest and in any accompanying schedules and, to the best of my knowledge and belief, it is true, correct, and complete."

If you as the taxpayer's representative submit the protest, a substitute declaration may be used, stating that you prepared the protest and indicating whether you personally know that the statements of facts are true and correct. A power of attorney should be attached to the protest, if not previously filed.

If, after reading a protest, a reviewer believes that there is a basis for settlement, he or she will refer the case back for settlement. For this reason, make sure that your protest presents your case well so that a reviewer can have a basis for such a decision.

How the Appeals Office Operates

In the Appeals office, your case is assigned to an appeals officer. After he or she becomes acquainted with your case, the officer sets the time of the conference. If it is inconvenient, you may ask for another date or time. An immediate hearing may be granted if you have some unusual reason for it. The hearing may be held in a regional appeals office, a local branch of the Service, or "on circuit" (appeals officers sometimes travel to outlying districts to save taxpayers the expense and time involved in a trip to a metropolitan area).

The Appeals office is separated functionally from the Examination Division. The major purpose of the separation is to provide an appellate procedure that, organizationally at least, will tend to produce free and unbiased opinions. An officer in the Appeals office is not responsible to the Revenue Agent and his or her supervisor. Thus, the officer is less likely to be unduly influenced by the conclusions reached in that office and more likely to reach decisions objectively. The officer does not need, and does not seek, the approval of the Revenue Agent or the agent's supervisor for any decisions made.

To ensure the independence of the Appeals process, the IRS by law must prohibit *ex parte* communications between Appeals employees and other IRS personnel to the extent that such communications appear to compromise Appeals' independence (Section 1001(a) of the IRS Restructuring Act of 1998, P.L.105-206).

When you protest the conclusions reached in the Examination Division, the entire case file is sent to the Appeals office, and the Examination Division's control over the case ceases.

A primary concern of the Appeals office is the status of the statute of limitations. If not much time is available, the case may not be transmitted to an Appeals office unless at least 120 days remain before the limitations period expires. As a condition to appellate review, a taxpayer may be asked to sign either a Form 872 (Consent to Extend the Time to Assess Tax) or a Form 872-A (Special Consent to Extend the Time to Assess Tax).

In the majority of cases, neither the agent nor any other representative of the Examination Division will attend your conference with the appeals officer. If, in a few situations, the agent does attend a conference, it will be at the invitation of the Appeals office and only for the purpose of establishing the facts. Since you are appealing from the recommendations of the agent, do not reargue the case with him or her. Your sole problem will be to convince the appeals officer. In all cases, however, you should remember that the officer has a copy of the agent's recommendations and confidential report, which you never see.

Cases that reach the Appeals office after the 90-day letter has been issued are known as "90-day cases." Conferences at this stage are not easily granted. You must generally show that you have not had a previous conference for reasons beyond your control, and there is a reasonable expectation that a settlement will be reached.

The settlement authority in the Appeals office is broader than in the Examination Division. The Appeals office may trade or split issues where substantial uncertainties exist either in law or in fact, or in both, as to the correct application of the law. They may also settle issues based on their judgment as to the hazards of litigation. The agents have no authority to consider litigation hazards. One explanation for the reluctance of district office personnel to close a case is that they realize there is another administrative step following theirs. If they have any doubts about the acceptability of a settlement proposal, they can resolve their doubts by recommending that the case be considered by the Appeals office. The appeals officer thinks in terms of the cost and possible result of extended litigation. Cases are generally settled on the "merit approach." That is, the merits of each issue are considered, regardless of the amount of tax involved. A second, less preferred method of settlement is on the basis of a flat sum or percentage of the dollars involved. This second method is limited in use and may not be used, for example, where an issue will recur in subsequent years or where the issue is present in other similar cases, unless they are all to be disposed of together upon the same basis.

Settlement authority of appeals officers may also depend on whether or not the issue is on an IRS appeals coordinated issue list. If the issue is on the list, the officer does not have independent settlement authority; he or she must submit the proposed settlement to a person within the regional office who is in charge of reviewing issues placed on the coordination list. If this person does not agree to the settlement, the appeals officer may present the dispute to an appeals director in the region for a decision. You will not be given the chance to argue your position at this stage because the appeal coordination list procedure is an internal administration measure through which the IRS attempts to provide a consistent national settlement policy on certain issues that involve large numbers of taxpayers.

How To Handle the Conference

The conference is held in an informal manner. No stenographic record is made. Testimony under oath is not taken. Your approach to the conference will vary, depending on whether your client wishes to settle, whether the issues in dispute are factual or legal, and how strong you feel your case is on a specific issue.

You can assume the conferee:

- **Has the agent's recitation of the facts, opinions, and recom-mendations**—all of which appear in a transmittal memo that you do not receive. He or she also has a record of the informal conference and copies of reports covering examinations of prior years.
- **Has read your protest** with your version of the facts and your arguments. He or she will read the cases you cite. When you cite a case, make sure that it is on point. If you cite it for the dicta incorporated in the opinion, indicate that fact. There is nothing more discouraging than wading through a case only to find that it is not on point. The appeals officer may well conclude that you do not understand the issue, that you think the conferee does not understand the issue, or that you believe the conferee is careless enough to accept citations without reading the cases. Such conclusions will affect you adversely.

- **Knows the strengths and weaknesses of your position** and what you would settle for. If your case is the type that should be settled, the appeals officer has thought of possible settlements. As a general proposition, an officer would rather settle cases than send them to the Tax Court. But rarely is he or she more anxious to settle than you are.

You may bring witnesses. However, do not plan on using witnesses unless they are absolutely necessary and you are sure they will not testify beyond your objectives. Instead, you may want to present their statements in affidavit form. Facts brought up for the first time will be referred back to the Examination Division for reconsideration.

Sufficient time is given to present your side of the case. Additional hearings are granted as needed.

An attorney may become aware that his or her client has no hope of winning but is stalling the date of actual payment of the deficiency by going through the various appellate procedures. This tactic violates IRS rules of practice and professional canons of ethics.

Does It Pay To Settle Your Tax Dispute With the IRS?

Here are some approaches followed by practitioners:

If you want rapid settlement of the dispute and cannot convince the IRS of your position, consider paying the deficiency—then suing for refund in the District Court or Court of Federal Claims. But first check the docket of the District Court where you will sue. Some District Courts are as overloaded as the Tax Court.

In a dispute involving a difference of opinion over the facts, accept a fair offer from the IRS. You may not do any better before the Tax Court. Where the IRS refuses to accept any settlement offer, you may take your case to court. You will have to wait for a hearing, but you stand a good chance of getting a better break.

In a complicated case or one involving a difficult point of law, the Tax Court is favored over the District Court. There is less risk of judicial misinterpretation of the tax law since the Tax Court judges are more familiar with the intricacies of the Code.

Where you have a question of fact and your position is appealing to the average person, pay the deficiency and then sue for a refund in the District Court where a jury will determine the facts. In the Tax Court, the facts are determined by judges who may be less sympathetic. You are not entitled to a jury trial in Tax Court. Your case is also decided by a judge if you pay the deficiency and sue for a refund in the Court of Federal Claims.

What Happens When You Propose a Settlement

Settlement proposals are generally made orally but more complicated proposals may be in writing. If your proposal is accepted, you are asked to sign either a Form 870 or 870-AD. Form 870 is signed for a settlement based on a complete agreement with the changes originally recommended by the agent. Where the IRS makes concessions in reaching a settlement in the Appeals office, a conditional consent, Form 870-AD, is signed. Form 870-AD contains pledges against reopening; the Form 870 does not. This means that once a Form 870-AD is executed, the IRS may not make an additional assessment. If Form 870 is executed, it acts as a waiver of restriction on assessment when received whereas Form 870-AD is not effective until it is signed by the Commissioner of Internal Revenue or his or her delegate.

Form 870-AD has been called an informal closing agreement. It is an agreement not to file a claim for refund, except for overassessments shown on the agreement form and amounts attributed to a net operating loss carryback deduction. Similarly, the IRS agrees not to assert further deficiencies for the year in question, except where there is fraud, malfeasance, concealment, or misrepresentation of a material fact, an important mathematical error, an excessive tentative allowance of a net operating loss carryback or investment credit carryback, or deficiencies determined at a partnership-level audit or S corporation–level audit.

The effect of an 870-AD is one-sided. The taxpayer agrees to an immediate assessment of the deficiency, whereas the IRS does not agree to pay an immediate refund as, for example, where the agreement covers two years, and one year involves an overassessment. It may, therefore, be advisable to file a protective claim for refund at the same time as the Form 870-AD is signed, or at least before the expiration of the refund period for the year in question. The refund claim should be accompanied by a letter explaining that the purpose of the claim is to protect the taxpayer against an unfavorable disposition of the waiver issue, and that the claim will be withdrawn upon the IRS's favorable action on the waiver.

Whether or not Form 870-AD is binding on the IRS and the taxpayer as a closing agreement has been litigated. The decisions present conflicting opinions on the issue.

Filing a Form 870-AD does not automatically stop the running of interest. Interest stops 30 days after the date the IRS accepts the form. In any event, the accumulation of interest can be avoided by prepaying the deficiency.

After Form 870-AD is signed, the appeals officer presents the report to a reviewing officer, such as an Associate Chief. If the official approves the proposed settlement, he or she will accept the agreement and the case is then ready for closing.

What if the settlement on review is rejected by the Associate Chief or other official? He or she will then discuss the case with the appeals officer. If the case remains unapproved, you may ask for a hearing before the reviewer who turned down the settlement.

What if you do not submit a settlement or the appeals officer rejects your proposal? The officer then prepares the report together with a proposed statutory notice of deficiency. This is sent to an Associate Chief or other official for review. If the official approves the report, the case is then reviewed by the Chief Appeals Officer. The statutory notice of deficiency is checked by the Regional Counsel. After final approval by both offices, a 90-day letter is then mailed to your client.

Cash Deposit Stops Interest Accrual on Potential Deficiency

An individual who faces a potentially large interest charge on a tax deficiency may cut off the accrual of interest by making a cash deposit against a potential deficiency. Under Code Section 6603, a taxpayer can make a deposit with the IRS in order to suspend the running of interest on a potential underpayment of income, gift, estate, or generation-skipping transfer tax that has not yet been assessed by the IRS.

Under IRS guidelines provided in Revenue Procedure 2005-18, 2005-13 IRB 798, a deposit is made by submitting a check or money order, accompanied by a written statement that designates the remittance as a Section 6603 deposit, specifies the type of tax (e.g., income tax) and the tax year or years, and describes the amount and nature of the "disputable" tax. Without the required designation and statement, a deposit will be treated as a tax payment and applied toward any outstanding tax liability, starting with the earliest year for which there is a liability.

If the IRS ultimately assesses tax on a proposed deficiency and a Section 6603 deposit is applied against the assessed liability, the suspension of the running of interest is effective as of the date that the IRS received the deposit, not when the liability is later assessed or the deposit is actually applied to the liability.

The taxpayer can request a return of a Section 6603 deposit at any time unless the money has been used to pay a tax or the IRS believes payment is in jeopardy. The request must be made in writing and include the date and amount of the original deposit, the type of tax to which the deposit was intended to apply, and the tax years involved. Interest is payable on a returned deposit to the extent it is attributable to a disputable tax. Interest is figured at the applicable federal short-term rate, compounded daily, from the date of deposit to a date that is no more than 30 days before the date of the check paying the return of the deposit.

What To Do After Receiving a 90-Day Letter

Before the IRS can assess a deficiency, it must send by registered or certified mail a statutory notice of deficiency (IRC §6212(a)). This notice is called a "90-day letter." It gives your client the chance, within 90 days from the date of its mailing, to file a petition to the Tax Court of the United States. If the notice is mailed to an address outside the United States, you are allowed 150 days. In the event the 90th or 150th day falls on a Saturday or Sunday, or on a legal holiday in the District of Columbia, you have until the next business day to file a petition with the Tax Court (IRC §6213(a)).

The IRS must specifically note on deficiency notices when the 90-day period ends (IRC §6213(a)).

Your client receives a 90-day letter at the end of the period allowed in the 30-day letter if he or she has not signed a Form 870 or filed a formal protest, or after an Appeals office conference. At the end of the 90 (or 150) days, the deficiency is assessed.

On receipt of the 90-day letter, you can do one of the following:

File a petition with the Tax Court. No assessment can be made until its decision (which includes all appeals) becomes final. For a timely Tax Court petition, the Tax Court must receive the petition no later than the 90th day after the IRS's mailing of the deficiency notice. A petition postmarked by the U.S. Post Office by the 90th day is considered timely even if received by the Tax Court after the 90th day.

A dated receipt from an IRS-approved private delivery service also qualifies under the "timely-mailing-is-timely-filing" rule. Specific services from the following companies have been approved: DHL Express, Federal Express, and United Parcel Service; *see* the current Form 1040 instructions for the list.

Do nothing and wait for the assessment of the deficiency. Sign the Form 870. This limits the interest on the deficiency. Your client can still take his or her case to the Tax Court, or pay the disputed deficiency and file a refund claim. When it is rejected, your client can sue for a refund in a Federal District Court or the U.S. Court of Federal Claims.

An assessment may only be made if a notice of deficiency is sent to the taxpayer's last known address. Generally, a taxpayer's address is the address shown on his most recently filed return.

For a deficiency involving a joint return, the 90-day letter is mailed as a single joint notice. So, where a husband and wife have separated, notify the IRS of their separate addresses to insure receipt of the notice. The IRS will then send a duplicate original of the joint notice to both the husband and wife.

The IRS may issue more than one 90-day letter for the same year before the earliest of the following events: (1) expiration of the assessment period; (2) execution of a final closing agreement or compromise; or (3) filing of a timely petition to the Tax Court.

When a 90-Day Letter Is Not Necessary

The 90-day letter is the only notice of deficiency that the law requires the IRS to send. Without it, you cannot petition the Tax Court to litigate your matter. However, there are situations in which the 90-day letter is not required and you have no recourse to the Tax Court.

1. A 90-day letter is not sent where a mathematical error has been made in your return. Taking an excessive credit on your tax liability for taxes withheld or for estimated taxes paid is considered a mathematical error.
2. A voluntary payment "paid as a tax or in respect of a tax" eliminates any deficiency, allowing the IRS to assess without the issuance of a 90-day letter.
3. An immediate assessment may be made without issuance of a 90-day letter whenever the IRS believes that assessment or collection will be jeopardized by delay. For example, if the IRS finds out that a taxpayer is leaving the country with all assets before paying his or her tax liability, it is not necessary to send a 90-day letter and then wait 90 days before assessment.
4. In the case of bankruptcy or receivership, an assessment may be made before a 90-day letter is sent.
5. If you sign a Form 870 before a 90-day letter is sent, you are not thereafter entitled to a 90-day letter.

Getting a Settlement After Filing a Petition With the Tax Court

You may still be able to get a settlement even after you have filed a petition in the Tax Court. If you have brought your case to the Tax Court without first appealing to the Appeals office for a conference to settle the dispute, you will be asked to discuss a settlement with the Appeals office.

Even if you have filed a Tax Court petition after an unsuccessful conference in the Appeals office, your case will still be referred back to the Appeals office for settlement unless the Counsel determines that there is little likelihood of a settlement. The Appeals office may enter into a binding settlement. If the case is returned to the Counsel's office, it determines whether to settle or proceed to trial.

AUDIT RULES FOR PARTNERSHIPS

The IRS determines the tax treatment of partnership items at the partnership level in a unified administrative proceeding rather than in separate proceedings with the individual partners. All partnerships with more than 10 partners are subject to the rules. Partnerships with 10 or fewer partners, all of whom are individuals, C corporations, or estates of deceased partners are exempt, but may elect to have the rules apply (IRC §6231(a)(1)(B)).

S corporations. S corporation shareholders are audited on a shareholder-by-shareholder basis. Shareholders must report S corporation items consistent with the treatment on the corporation's Form 1120S unless the shareholder identifies the inconsistency in a statement to the IRS (IRC §6037(c)).

Partnership Audit Procedures and Judicial Review

The IRS generally may not audit individual partners but must bring proceedings at the partnership level. The IRS must conduct an administrative proceeding to challenge the partnership's treatment of income, deductions, or credit items (IRC §6223). Notice of the proceeding is first given to a so-called "tax matters partner" (TMP). The TMP is a specially designated general partner or, in the absence of a designation, the general partner having the largest interest in partnership profits at the end of the taxable year involved (IRC §6231(a)(7)). Notice of the proceeding is given to the other partners (except for certain indirect partners) by the IRS and the TMP (IRC §6223). In partnerships with more than 100 partners, the IRS does not have to give separate notice to partners with less than a 1% interest, but a group of partners with an aggregate interest of at least 5% may designate one of such partners to receive notice from the IRS (IRC §6223(b)). All partners are entitled to participate in the partnership proceeding.

If the IRS enters into a settlement with some partners, similar settlement terms must be offered to all other partners (IRC §6224).

Within 90 days of the IRS final partnership administrative adjustment (FPAA), the TMP may petition the Tax Court for review. Other notice partners are given an additional 60 days to file a court petition if the TMP does not do so. An appeal from the FPAA may also be filed in a Federal District Court or the U.S. Court of Federal Claims if the petitioning partner first deposits with the IRS an amount equal to the tax that would be owed if the FPAA determination were sustained. A petition filed in the Tax Court takes precedence over petitions filed in other courts. The first Tax Court petition filed is heard; if other partners have also filed petitions, their cases will be dismissed. If no Tax Court petitions are filed, the first petition filed in a Federal District Court or the U.S. Court of Federal Claims takes precedence. Regardless of which petition takes precedence, all partners who hold an interest during the taxable year involved will be bound by the decision unless the statute of limitations with respect to that partner has run (IRC §6226).

Statute of Limitations Against Partners

To assess tax against a partner, the IRS must do so within three years following the later of the actual filing date or the due date for the partnership return (IRC §6229(a)). If the IRS and the TMP so agree, the limitation period may be extended for all partners. Extension agreements may also be made with each partner. If the partnership understates gross income by more than 25%, the limitations period increases to six years. If the partnership return is fraudulent, there is an unlimited limitation period for partners participating in the fraud and a six-year period for other partners. If the IRS mails notice of an FPAA to the TMP, the statute of limitations stops running until one year after a final court decision is made, or, if the FPAA is not appealed, the limitations period is extended until one year after the period for filing a petition for court review expires (IRC §6229(d)).

Refund Requests by Partners

Partners must make refund claims by filing a "request for administrative adjustment," or RAA (IRC §6227), on Form 8082. The RAA request must be filed within three years of the actual filing date of the partnership return or the due date for the return (without extensions), whichever is later. The IRS may decide to conduct a partnership proceeding in response to the refund request.

If an RAA on behalf of all the partners is filed by the TMP and the IRS has not allowed any part of it within six months of filing, the TMP may petition the Tax Court, a Federal District Court, or the U.S. Court of Federal Claims to uphold the claim. A court petition must be filed between six months and two years after the RAA was filed. It must also be filed before the IRS has notified the partners that it plans to conduct a partnership proceeding. If the IRS conducts a partnership proceeding and notice of an FPAA determination is given to the TMP, a subsequent court petition on the RAA is barred; the TMP must seek review of the FPAA. All partners may participate in a court proceeding related to an RAA (IRC §6228).

If an RAA is filed by a partner other than the TMP and the IRS does not allow any part of the request within six months, that partner may sue for a refund in a Federal District Court or the U.S. Court of Federal Claims; the suit must generally commence within two years of the filing of the RAA. Once a refund action is filed, the partner will not be bound by a subsequent FPAA or judicial review of an FPAA. If the partner is notified that the items in question are to be treated as nonpartnership items, the partner may sue for a refund within two years of the IRS notice (IRC §6228).

THE TIME LIMITS WITHIN WHICH THE IRS MUST ACT FOR ADDITIONAL TAXES

The Three-Year Rule

Generally, the IRS has three years after the date on which your tax return is filed to proceed against you (IRC §6501(a)). However, when you file a return before the due date, the period does not start from the filing date but from the day after the due date. To illustrate, instead of filing your last quarterly estimated tax payment on January 15, you file a final return on January 31. The limitation period on the final return begins the day after April 15, the date the final return is due, not on January 31, the date the return is filed.

To start the running of the statute of limitations, the IRS must receive your return. In any controversy concerning the statute, you must prove that you filed a return. If you fail to do this, there is no limit on the time during which the government may make an assessment against you. Similarly, filing a return containing insufficient information of your tax liability does not start the running of the statute.

What Is the Starting Date for the Limitation Period?

Amended return. The statute starts running when the original return was filed. For amended returns, the IRS has 60 days from the date of receipt to assess additional tax, even though the regular limitations period would expire before the end of the 60-day period (IRC §6501(c)(7)).

Incorrect return form. The statute starts running when you file (or from the due date if later), if the return has all of the information on which the correct tax liability can be figured.

Tax information on a form other than a return. The statute starts running when you file the information (or from the due date if later), if it contains the information on which your tax liability can be figured. If you claim you do not have to pay a tax, notify the IRS of your claim and the basis for it. A tentative return does not start the period running since it does not specifically state the items of gross income and deductions.

Improperly executed return. The statute starts running when the return is properly executed. Example: A corporate return must be signed by one of the corporation's officers. Filing a return signed by an unauthorized person does not start the running of the statute.

Sometimes, a taxpayer or a group of taxpayers may operate as a trust or as a partnership without knowing that the organization under the tax law is really a corporation, and so must file a corporate return rather than a trust or partnership return. Even though a partnership or trust return is filed, this filing can be treated as the filing of a corporate return for purposes of starting the statute. To obtain this result, the taxpayer or taxpayers must prove that the determination of the trust or partnership status was made in good faith.

A similar rule covers a situation where a taxpayer, in good faith, determines that it is an exempt organization. In such cases, the filing of a return for an exempt organization starts the statute—even though it is later held to be a taxable corporation for that tax year.

There are several exceptions to the general rule that the filing of a return starts the running of the statutory period:

- Where a false or fraudulent return is filed with intent to evade tax, tax may be assessed at any time (IRC §6501(c)(1)). The Supreme Court has held (Badaracco, 464 U.S. 386 (1984)) that a later filing of an amended nonfraudulent return does not start the running of the three-year period of limitations.
- Where a willful attempt in any manner is made to defeat or evade the tax, tax may be assessed at any time (IRC §6501(c)(2)).
- Where a return is executed by the IRS (IRC §6501(b)(3)), the statute does not run with the making of the return.
- Where no return is filed (IRC §6501(c)(3)), the tax may be assessed at any time, but the subsequent filing of a nonfraudulent return starts the running of the three-year limitation period.

If More Than 25% of Gross Income Is Omitted

If you omit an amount that is more than 25% of the gross income shown on your return, the IRS may make an assessment within six years after the return is filed rather than three years (IRC §6501(e)(1)(A)). For example, on a 2008 return (filed on April 15, 2009), gross income of $50,000 was reported. But a $20,000 gain from the sale of a vacation home was omitted. In this case, the IRS has until April 15, 2015, to assess a deficiency on the 2008 return. The reason: The omitted $20,000 gain is more than 25% of the gross income reported on the return (25% of $50,000, or $12,500). However, if gross income is $100,000, the three-year statute applies rather than the six-year statute because the omission is not more than 25% of the reported gross income (25% of $100,000, or $25,000).

To apply the six-year statute, the IRS has the burden of proving that there is an omission and that it exceeds 25% of the reported gross income. If it fails to sustain its claim, the three-year statute applies. To be successful against such a claim, you must then show that the items were not omitted, for example, that the item was tax free or not taxable in the particular year, or that the IRS's valuation is incorrect. You cannot base your defense on a plea of an honest mistake or the use of an incorrect method of accounting, or that the omission was reduced to less than 25% by an amended return. The statute runs from the filing of the original return. It is not affected by the filing of an amended return.

In determining whether capital gains omitted from a return are "gross income" under the 25%-of-gross-income test, treat the gains as gross income, without regard to capital losses that may have been used to figure the net gain or loss shown on the return. Where you are in business, gross income means gross receipts, that is, the total amount received from the sale of goods or services unreduced by the cost of such goods or services. Gross income of a partner's share of partnership income means the partner's share of the partnership gross income, not partnership net income.

Tax Court refuses to retroactively apply temporary regulation that provides six-year limitations period for overstated basis. The IRS and the courts continue to battle over whether an overstatement of basis that reduces the gain on a sale of property is an 'omission" of gross income that can extend the IRS' time to audit a return. The IRS has long argued that a basis overstatement that reduces gain is an "omission", and if the omission exceeds 25% of gross income, the IRS' assessment period is extended from three to six years under Code Section 6501(e) (1), and the similar provision for partnerships in Section 6229(c) (2)).

The IRS position was rejected by the Ninth Circuit (affirming the Tax Court) and the Federal Circuit (Bakersfield Energy Partners, 568 F.3d767 (9th Cir. 2009); Salman Ranch Ltd, 573 F.3d 1362 (Fed. Cir. 2009)). These courts held that the IRS position was contrary to the Supreme Court's holding in Colony (357 U.S. 28 (1958)).

In response to the *Bakersfield* and *Salman Ranch* decisions, the IRS issued retroactive temporary regulations that reemphasized its position that an overstatement of basis can trigger the six-year assessment period. In announcing the regulations, the IRS said that they applied to all taxable years for which the "applicable" assessment period had not expired before September 24, 2009, the date of announcement (T.D. 9466, 2009-43 IRB 551).

Relying on the new regulations, the IRS asked the Tax Court to reconsider and vacate its decision in Intermountain (TC Memo 2009-195), in which the Tax Court reaffirmed its holding that the six-year assessment period was not triggered by basis overstatements. However, a majority of the Tax Court refused to retroactively apply the temporary regulations to the facts in Intermountain. In addition, the Tax Court majority held that the temporary regulations did not deserve judicial deference because they conflicted with the Supreme Court's holding in Colony. Under the Supreme Court's 2005 decision in Brand X, if an agency construction of a statute conflicts with a prior court decision, the later agency interpretation should be respected unless the court had held the statute to be ambiguous (Brand X, 545 U.S. 967 (2005)). That was not the case here, because the Supreme Court in Colony found the statute (the pre-1954 Code predecessor of Section 6501 (e) (1) (A)) and its legislative history to be unambiguous in applying the three-year limitations period to basis overstatements, thereby foreclosing the IRS' contrary interpretation in the temporary regulations (Intermountain Insurance Service of Vail LLC, 134 TC 11 (2010)).

The IRS is appealing the Intermountain decision and other decisions that reject its view that a six-year statute of limitations can apply to an overstatement of basis.

Adequate Disclosure. If you omit a questionable item from gross income, you may prevent an extension of the statute by adequately disclosing the facts of the omission. If the disclosure *adequately* tells the IRS of the nature and amount of the item omitted, that item will not be counted in determining whether there has been an omission of more than 25% of gross income.

The following are examples of adequate disclosure: (1) sales receipts were fully stated, but claimed deductions were excessive; (2) opening inventory was overstated, resulting in understated profits; (3) total income was revealed by a schedule attached to the return; and (4) total income was disclosed on the return, but was erroneously claimed as exempt.

There was not an adequate disclosure where the taxpayer liquidated his real estate corporation, attaching a statement of depreciation on the liquidation property, but failed to report gain realized on the liquidation.

When the Limitation Period May Be Reduced

To expedite the closings of income tax cases of estates and of liquidated corporations, the statutory period may be reduced to 18 months (IRC §6501(d)). After you have filed a return reporting income received by a decedent in his or her lifetime, an estate during administration, or a corporation being liquidated, send the Commissioner a letter specifically asking for a prompt assessment on the return in the following 18 months. Make this request after the return is filed, or it will not be effective. Send your letter in a separate envelope. Do not mail it with the return.

When the request is made for a corporation, you must notify the Commissioner that liquidation is contemplated within 18 months, begin the liquidation in good faith within that time, and complete the liquidation.

When you request a prompt assessment for an estate, also send evidence of your authority to act for the estate.

The receipt of the filing of the request for prompt assessment starts the 18-month period. The shortened limitation period will not apply if more than 25% of gross income is omitted from the return or if there is a fraudulent or willful attempt to evade tax.

Limitation Rules for Carryback

Net operating loss or capital loss carryback. A deficiency resulting from an erroneous carryback may be assessed within the statutory period of the loss year in which the carryback originated (IRC §6501(h)). For example, a net operating loss in 2009 carried back two years (IRC §172(b)(1)) to 2007 results in a refund of $5,000; in an audit of the 2009 return, the carryback is reduced and it is determined that the refund should have been $1,000. The IRS has until April 15, 2013, to recover $4,000 of the refund attributed to the carryback to 2007.

Foreign tax credit carryback. A deficiency resulting from an im-proper carryback of the foreign tax credit may be assessed within one year after the period for assessment for the year producing the excess foreign tax credit (IRC §6501(i)).

Investment credit or other general business credit carryback. A deficiency resulting from an erroneous carryback may be assessed within the statutory period of the year producing the credit (IRC §6501(j)).

Where a quick refund was elected, the IRS has an extended time to audit the year to which the carryback was made (except in the case of foreign tax credit). The IRS may assess within the statutory period for the year that produced the carryback a tax deficiency not to exceed the amount of the refund or credit arising from the carryback (IRC §6501(k)).

EXAMPLES

1. A calendar year corporation files a quick refund claim for 2006 based on an unused investment credit of $50,000 arising in 2008 and receives a refund of $50,000. In 2009, the IRS reduces the unused investment credit from $50,000 to $30,000. As the corporation filed its 2008 return on March 16, 2009, the period for assessing the excess $20,000 does not expire until March 19, 2010.
2. Same facts as in Example 1, but the IRS also finds that the corporation owes $40,000 of additional tax for 2006 because of its failure to report certain income for that year. On or before March 19, 2012, the IRS may assess a deficiency not in excess of $30,000.

Other Limitation Rules for Married Couples

Where separate returns were originally filed and later a joint return is filed, the period of limitations must extend to at least one year after the time the joint return was actually filed. The regular limitation periods are figured from the following filing dates, but if those periods would expire before one year after the joint return was filed, then the period is extended until the end of that one year (IRC §6013(b)(3) and (b)(4)).

Where both spouses previously filed separate returns, the regular limitation period begins on the last date that either spouse could have filed a separate return.

Where only one spouse filed a return because the other had gross income under the requirement for filing a return, the regular limitation period begins on the last date the spouse who filed could have filed his or her return.

Where only one spouse filed a return, even though the other had gross income requiring the filing of a return, the regular limitation period begins when they file the joint return.

Limitation Periods Where Recognition of Gain Is Deferred

Where an involuntary conversion has occurred, tax on the gain may be deferred by investing the proceeds in similar property. When tax is deferred, the three-year period starts when the IRS is notified that the property has been replaced or that no replacement has been or will be made (IRC §1033(a)(2)(C)).

If a replacement is made before the beginning of the last year in which any part of the gain is received on the conversion, then the limitation period for any year before that year (during which the election to replace was in effect) ends when the limitation period for the last year ends (IRC §1033(a)(2)(D)).

Warning: Failure to notify the IRS prevents the statute of limitation from closing.

Waiving the Limitation Period

If a return is being examined during a time close to the expiration of the statutory period for assessing deficiencies, the IRS may ask for a waiver of the statute of limitations on a Form 872. An IRS request that you agree to an extension of the limitations period for tax assessments must include a notice that you have the right to refuse an extension or limit an extension (IRC §6501(c)(4)(B)).

Should a Waiver Extending the Statute Be Signed?

A return is subject to a possible deficiency assessment for at least three years. An extension of the statute of limitations may be an advantage because the time to file refund claims is extended by the extension period plus six months. However, taxpayers generally regard an extension as a disadvantage. They assume the IRS, in making the request, has become suspicious of the return after a preliminary examination and a more thorough examination is likely to lead to a deficiency assessment.

It is advisable to agree to the consent if it is anticipated that disputed items may be amicably compromised.

If consent is refused, the statute of limitations binds both the taxpayer and the Commissioner. Neither party is obliged to agree to an extension.

What is the practical result of a refusal to consent? If the refusal comes:

- **Before the agent has had the opportunity to make an examination,** he or she can recommend the disallowance of every claimed deduction. A statutory notice of deficiency (90-day letter) can be sent on that basis. Since the refusal to an extension prevented any reasonable determination, the agent is forced to do this to protect the government's interest. The agent can, in appropriate cases, also recommend a jeopardy assessment. If a 90-day letter is issued without an audit, the IRS's action may be attacked as arbitrary.
- **Before the agent has completed the examination,** or before he or she has time to consider the merits of your position, the agent's recommendations will be based on the assumption that there is no merit to your position.
- **When your case is in the Appeals office** and before the appeals officer has an opportunity to consider the merits of your position, the agent's recommendations might be sustained.

In all of these situations, the case may have to go to court. There will be delay and expense. Give all these facts thought before you object to signing a Form 872.

You may stipulate on the Form 872 how long the statute of limitations is to be extended.

Form 872-A permits flexibility by extending the statute of limitations until 90 days after you are mailed a deficiency notice, or 90 days after you terminate or the IRS terminates the agreement (by filing Form 872-T).

When the Running of the Statute Is Suspended

The limitation period is automatically suspended in the following cases:

When a 90-day letter is sent, the period of limitations is automatically suspended for 150 days. (Technically, this includes the 90-day period during which the IRS cannot assess a deficiency, plus an additional 60 days.) However, if the period would have expired during the suspended period, the IRS cannot assess an additional deficiency after that time, though it can still assess the original deficiency (IRC §6503(a)(1)).

Note: Where a deficiency notice is sent to a corporation, the suspension covers not only the corporation but any other corporation with which it filed a consolidated return for the year covered by the notice (IRC §6503(a)(2)).

If you file a timely petition in the Tax Court, the limitation period is extended until the Tax Court decision (including all appeals) becomes final and for 60 days afterwards (IRC §6503(a)(1)).

Where a Title 11 bankruptcy case has commenced, a notice of deficiency may be mailed but assessment by the IRS is barred until 60 days after the termination of the case, or, if earlier, 60 days after the stay on assessment is lifted by the bankruptcy court (IRC §6503(h)).

Where assets are in the custody or control of a court, the period of limitation for collection after assessment is suspended for the period in which the assets are in the hands of the court and for six months thereafter (IRC §6503(b)).

When a taxpayer is out of the country for a continuous period of six months or more, the limitation period is suspended during the absence. The period of limitation does not expire until six months after he or she returns to the United States (IRC §6503(c)).

Where property of a third party is wrongfully seized by the government, the limitation period for collection after assessment is suspended. The suspension begins when the property is wrongfully seized or received and ends 30 days after the IRS determines the levy was wrongful and returns the property. If the third party goes to court, the suspension ends 30 days after entry of a final judgment that the levy was wrongful (IRC §6503(f)).

If the IRS is attempting to obtain records from a third party and a dispute over the records is not solved within six months after the IRS issues an administrative summons, the period is suspended until the issue is resolved. Further, if you intervene in a dispute between the IRS and the third-party record keeper, the limitation period is suspended from that date until the entire dispute is resolved (IRC §7609(e)).

Mitigating the Effect of the Limitation Period To Avoid Double Tax

Suppose income that should have been reported on a 2006 return is reported on a 2005 return. In March 2010, after the limitation period for filing a refund claim for 2005 has expired, the IRS asserts a deficiency on this item for 2006. You take the case to the Tax Court, but it upholds the government's position.

Can you get a refund for the tax paid on this item for 2005 even though the statute has run out on that year?

The answer is yes. In this and in certain other cases, the limitation period is lifted, not only to prevent double taxation of the taxpayer, but also to protect the government in cases where an item of income might otherwise escape taxation (IRC §1311).

EXAMPLES

1. Jones and his son were partners. Each was entitled to one-half of partnership profits. On his 2006 return, Jones Sr. included the entire partnership profits. In 2010, he filed a timely refund claim for that portion of tax he paid on his son's share for the year 2006. In 2011, a Federal District Court approves the claim. This allows the IRS to assess a deficiency against the son for that portion of the 2006 profits on which he did not pay tax.
2. Howe assigned his salary in 2005 to his wife. She reported it on her return for 2005. In 2008, the IRS assessed a deficiency against Howe for the omission of the salary in 2005. In 2010, the Tax Court upheld the IRS's position. Mrs. Howe was then entitled to a refund on the tax she paid on her husband's salary for 2006, even though the statute had expired for that year.

When a Closed Year May Be Reopened

Before the limitation period can be lifted, the taxpayer or the IRS must show there has been a final determination that requires an adjustment specifically covered by the relief statute. A final determination (IRC §1313(a)) may be a:

Closing agreement. It is considered final when the agreement is approved.

Decision of the Tax Court or other competent court. It is considered final at the end of the time allowed for taking an appeal if no appeal has been taken.

Final disposition of a refund claim. It is considered final as to:

- *Allowed items* either on the date of the allowance of the refund or the credit or on the date of mailing a notice of disallowance. The last situation arises when the allowed items are offset by other items.
- *Disallowed items* when time for filing a refund suit expires (unless a suit is started before that time). This rule covers items disallowed in whole or in part, or items that have reduced a refund.
- *Informal agreement signed by the taxpayer and the IRS (Form 2259).*

As pointed out above, a closed year may be reopened for an adjustment only in limited cases (IRC §1312). The law allows for a reopening in the following seven situations (an eighth situation involving affiliated companies is not discussed here). In the first five situations, there must have been an inconsistent position.

1. The determination includes in gross income an item that was erroneously included in the taxpayer's gross income or in the gross income of a related taxpayer in a tax year that is now closed (IRC §1312(1)).

Example: Smith, who keeps his books on the cash basis, included in his 2005 return an item of accrued rent. In 2010, after the limitation period for 2005 has expired, the IRS claims that the rent was received in 2006, and asserts a deficiency. It is upheld by the Tax Court. Smith can get a refund for tax paid on the rent on his 2005 return.

2. The determination allows a deduction or a credit that was erroneously allowed to the taxpayer or to a related taxpayer in a tax year now closed (IRC §1312(2)).

Example: Green, on his 2007 return, claimed and was allowed a deduction for the destruction of his house by a fire. The fire actually occurred in 2008. After the end of the period of limitations for the assessment of a deficiency for 2007, Green files a refund claim for 2008 based upon a deduction for the casualty loss in that year. The refund claim is allowed for 2008, and the IRS may make an assessment for the deduction taken for 2007.

3. The determination excludes from gross income an item on which the taxpayer paid a tax or that was included in a filed return (whether or not he paid a tax on it). However, in a closed year, the item was erroneously excluded or omitted from the taxpayer's gross income or from the gross income of a related taxpayer (IRC §1312(3)(A)).

Example: Brown, in 2007, received under a contract payments that were included in his 2007 return. In 2011, he filed a refund claim for 2007, asserting he was on the accrual basis, and since the payments had accrued in 2007, they should have been taxed then. The refund claim is allowed in 2012. An assessment may be made for 2007, even though the statute has run out on that year.

4. The determination involves the correction of a deduction or income item of an estate or a trust, or beneficiaries of either. An adjustment to the closed year is allowed where a determination requires the disallowance of an estate or trust deduction of an amount erroneously included in the income of a beneficiary or heir, or where a determination allows an estate or trust deduction for an amount that was erroneously omitted from income of a beneficiary or heir (IRC §1312(5)).

Example: A trustee claimed in a trust's return for 2006 a deduction for income distributed to the beneficiary. The beneficiary was taxed. In 2010, the IRS asserted a deficiency against the trust on the ground that the amount given to the beneficiary was corpus, not income. In 2011, the deficiency is sustained by the Tax Court. Even though the period for filing claims for a refund by the beneficiary for 2006 has expired, there still may be a refund.

5. The determination fixes the basis of property for any purpose, and the adjustment affects either an error made in the treatment of a transaction that the basis depends on or an error made in treating the transaction as one involving the basis in the first place (IRC §1312(7)). In applying this rule, the following two tests have to be met:
   a. This error has to be either an erroneous:
      - Inclusion in or omission from gross income;
      - Recognition or nonrecognition of gain or loss;
      - Deduction of an item that should have been charged to a capital account; or
      - Charge to a capital account that should have been deducted from income.
   b. Before any one of the above mistakes may be corrected in a closed year the taxpayer or the IRS must show that a determination was made in:
      The taxpayer's case; or
      A tax case of a party who received title to the property from the taxpayer after it was acquired in a transaction in which he or she treated improperly the basis of the property; or
      A tax case of a party who received title from the taxpayer by gift after erroneously treating a transaction that affected the basis of the donated property. Note that the improperly treated transaction does not have to be the one in which the taxpayer acquired the property. Compare this with the above rule in which the transaction is required to be the one in which the party acquired title.

Example: In 2005, Stone transferred property that had cost him $5,000 to A Co. in exchange for an original issue of stock worth $10,000. On his 2005 return, he treated the exchange as tax free.

In 2011, A Co. claims that gain should have been recognized and so the property should have a $10,000 basis. If its argument is sustained, there can be no adjustment in the 2005 tax of A Co. There was no erroneous inclusion in or omission from its gross income by A Co. or an erroneous recognition or nonrecognition of gain or loss. Nor was there an erroneous deduction of an item that should have been charged to a capital account or a charge to a capital account that should have been deducted from income. As for Stone, the determination on A Co.'s basis did not affect his tax. Nor does the determination relate to a transaction in which he acquired the property. It applies to the property A Co. acquired.

In 2011, Stone sells A Co. stock and claims that since gain should have been recognized on the exchange in 2005, the basis for figuring gain or loss should be $10,000. If his claim is allowed, an adjustment will be made to his 2005 tax. The basis for computing gain on the sale depends on the 2005 transactions. Here there was an erroneous nonrecognition of gain to Stone. He was the taxpayer for whom the determination was made.

Assume Stone does not sell the stock but gives it to his son, who later sells it and claims the $10,000 basis. A closing agreement sustains his claim. Stone's 2005 tax will be adjusted. The basis for computing gain or loss on the sale by his son depends on the 2005 transaction where there was an erroneous nonrecognition of gain. Stone is deemed the person who acquired title in the transaction and from whom his son derived title subsequent to the transaction.

6. The determination disallows a deduction or a credit that should have been allowed to, but was not allowed to, the taxpayer or to a related taxpayer in a tax year now closed (IRC §1312(4)).

Important: Here, a refund or a credit is allowed only if the deduction was not barred at the time the taxpayer first claimed it in writing, that is, where he or she files a return, a refund claim, or a petition to the Tax Court (IRC §1311(b)(2)(B)).

Example: Burns reports on the accrual basis. For 2006, he deducted an expense item that he paid in that year. (At the time he filed his 2006 return, the statute had not expired for 2005.) Later, the IRS claimed that the item should have been accrued in 2005. In 2010, the Tax Court disallowed the deduction for 2006. But Burns can get an adjustment for 2005 even though it is now a closed year. The reason: When he took the 2006 deduction, 2005 was still an open year. (**Note:** Suppose the liability should have been accrued in 2002 instead of 2005—Burns could not get an adjustment if a refund or credit for the year 2002 was already barred when he took the deduction by error for 2006.)

7. The determination rejects an IRS deficiency for an item of income that the taxpayer did not report or pay tax for, *but* holds that the income should have been reported in the taxpayer's gross income or in the gross income of a related taxpayer in a different tax year now closed (IRC §1312(3)(B)).

Important: Here, an adjustment is allowed only if a deficiency assessment was not barred at the time the IRS first claimed, either in a deficiency notice or before the Tax Court, that the item should be reported for the tax year to which the determination relates (IRC §1311(b)(2)(A)).

Example: Jones reports on the accrual basis. In 2005, he did some work for A Co. He got paid in 2005 and 2007. He did not report the 2006 payment in either year. In 2008, the IRS sent him a deficiency notice for 2005, claiming he should have reported all the payments then. Jones contested the deficiency notice on the basis that in 2005 he had no accruable right to the payments received in 2006. In 2011, the Tax Court agrees with him. But the IRS can assess a deficiency for 2006, even though it is now a closed year. The reason: A deficiency assessment for 2006 was not barred in 2008 when the deficiency notice for 2005 was sent.

Inconsistent Positions Requirement

In the first five situations previously discussed that allow the lifting of the statute of limitations, the taxpayer or the IRS must have maintained an inconsistent position in the determination (IRC §1311(b)(1)). This means that either party would benefit unfairly if the closed year was not reopened for an adjustment (either for a refund or an assessment of a deficiency). Here is how the rule works:

For an additional assessment: The taxpayer—not the IRS—must have maintained an inconsistent position.

Example: Adam, on his 2005 return, claimed and was allowed a deduction for a charitable contribution. In 2010, he filed a refund claim for the year 2006, claiming that the charitable contribution was made in 2006. The claim was later allowed. Adam maintained a position inconsistent with the allowance of the deduction for 2005 by filing a refund claim for 2006 based on the same deduction. So the Commissioner may assert an additional assessment for 2005.

For a refund or credit: The Commissioner—not the taxpayer—must have maintained an inconsistent position.

Example: Evans, in his 2006 return, erroneously included an item of income which should have been reported on his 2007 return. After the limitation period for 2006 has expired, the Commissioner asserts a deficiency for the year 2007 on this item. The Tax Court sustains the deficiency. Here, the Commissioner has maintained an inconsistent position. The Commissioner got Evans's tax for both 2006 and 2007. Evans may get a refund for the year 2006.

Related taxpayers. Where a taxpayer maintained an inconsistent position, a deficiency adjustment may not affect a related taxpayer unless his or her relationship to the taxpayer was maintained when the inconsistent position was taken in a return, in a refund claim, or in a Tax Court petition (IRC §1311(b)(3)). If a taxpayer does not hold an inconsistent position, then the relationship must be fixed at the time of the final determination. These rules do not apply to situation No. 7 above, which is not subject to the inconsistent position rule.

Only the following are considered "related taxpayers (IRC §1313(c))":

Husband and wife
Grantor and fiduciary
Grantor and beneficiary
Decedent and decedent's estate
Partners
Fiduciary and legatee, heir, or beneficiary
Members of an affiliated group of corporations

If the Statute Is Lifted

If there is an additional assessment for any of the adjustments described in the preceding pages, you will receive a statutory notice of deficiency (90-day letter). You can pay the deficiency and sue for a refund, or appeal to the Tax Court. The IRS must send a deficiency notice within one year from the date of the determination (IRC §1314(b)).

If entitled to a refund or credit, you must file a refund claim within one year from the date of the determination, unless the IRS makes the refund without a claim (IRC §1314(b)). If the claim is turned down, you can sue for a refund.

An informal agreement involving a closed year can be revoked or altered. When this happens, a later readjustment is treated in the same way as the original adjustment was treated.

Where the adjustment results in an additional assessment by the IRS, you will be charged with interest and penalties. Where the adjustment results in a refund to you, the IRS will pay interest. However, the adjustment that is made by lifting the statute of limitations is not affected by any item other than the one that is the subject of the adjustment.

FILING REFUND CLAIMS

The technical rules outlined in this chapter should be strictly observed. Often, refunds are denied because of a taxpayer's failure to comply with a technical rule. Moreover, the filing of a refund claim is the first step that must be taken before suing the government. Unless a proper claim has been filed, a suit will be dismissed.

But before you decide to file a refund claim, carefully review the return involved for accuracy. A refund claim opens the return to a thorough investigation in which the IRS may find errors that reduce or completely eliminate the refund claim, and may even lead to the assessment of a deficiency.

Some practitioners wait until the end of the limitation period to file refund claims. If the IRS, after the limitation period, finds a deficiency, it can use the deficiency only to offset the claimed refund.

If, in good faith, you accept an erroneous refund and the IRS later discovers its mistake, repay the refund promptly. Otherwise, you will be liable for interest.

File Timely Refund Claims

A refund claim for income taxes must meet a time limitation and a dollar limitation.

Time limitation for refund. A refund claim for income tax must be filed within three years from the time the return was filed or two years from the time the tax was paid, whichever period ends later (IRC §6511(a)). For purposes of determining the three-year period, a return that is filed before the original due date is deemed to have been filed on the due date. For example, a return due on April 15 but filed April 1 is deemed filed on April 15, the due date. However, where an extension for filing is obtained, a return filed before the extended due date is deemed to have been filed on the actual date of filing and not on the extended due date. For example, if your due date for filing is April 15 but you get an extension to October 15 and actually file the return on October 1, your return is deemed to have been filed on August 1.

Where the last day for filing falls on a Saturday, Sunday, or legal holiday, the return is treated as timely filed if the return is filed or postmarked on the next work day. A legal holiday includes a legal holiday in the District of Columbia, as well as a legal holiday in the state in which you have to file the claim (IRC §7503).

You may file a protective refund claim when a particular issue is being litigated by other taxpayers and you want to await the outcome. This type of claim is generally accompanied by a cover letter to the IRS explaining its nature. Filing the protective refund claim preserves your right to sue for a refund. A suit must be brought before the expiration of two years from the date that the notice of disallowance of your claim was mailed.

With agreement of the IRS, Form 907 may be used to extend the two-year period for filing suit. The two-year period may not be extended once it has run out.

File your refund claim with the IRS Service Center serving the district in which the tax was paid. Where circumstances have forced you to wait until the last minute to file a refund claim, make sure that you meet the filing deadline. If you timely mail the claim or obtain a timely electronic postmark, the claim is deemed to be timely filed even if it is not received by the IRS until after the filing deadline.

For an electronically filed claim, an electronic postmark means a record of the date and time (in the taxpayer's time zone) that an authorized electronic return transmitter receives the claim on its host system (Reg. §301.7502-1(d)). To be considered timely mailed, the document must be enclosed in an envelope that is properly addressed with postage prepaid and postmarked by the U.S. Postal Service on or before the last day of the statutory period (IRC §7502). To protect against the possibility that an envelope will not be postmarked on the day that it is deposited in the mail, or that the IRS will lose it, registered or certified mail should be used. Proof of registration or a certified mail receipt with evidence that the envelope was properly addressed is deemed to be "prima facie evidence" that the document was actually delivered to the IRS (Reg. §301.7502-1(e)).

Refund claim for bad debt or worthless security. A refund claim to deduct a bad debt or loss from worthlessness of a security may be filed within seven years from the due date (without extensions) of the return for the year of the loss (IRC §6511(d)(1)).

Disability suspends limitations period for refund claims. The statute of limitations is suspended for refund claims made during any period in which a person is unable to manage financial affairs because of a physical or mental impairment that may be expected to result in death or to last for a period of not less than 12 months (IRC §6511(h)). This rule does not apply, however, if a party is authorized to act on the disabled person's behalf in financial matters.

Dollar limitation for refund. Under a "look-back" rule, the amount of a refund may be limited. If the refund claim is filed within three years from the time the return was filed (thereby meeting the time limitation of Section 6511(a)), a refund is allowed for taxes paid within the three-year period, plus any extension of time for filing, preceding the filing of the refund claim (IRC §6511(b)(2)(A)). If the refund claim is not filed within three years of the filing of the return, a refund may not exceed the amount of tax paid within the two-year period preceding the filing of the claim (IRC §6511(b)(2)(B)). A taxpayer has no absolute right to the refund of an overpayment. The Commissioner may credit the amount of an overpayment against any tax liability of the taxpayer.

> **Example:** Smith's 2007 return is due on April 15, 2008. He obtains an extension for filing until October 15, 2008. His return is actually filed on October 9, 2008, and he remits a check with his return for a tax liability of $2,000. On October 6, 2011, Smith files a claim for a refund for $1,000 on his 2007 return. The claim is timely filed since he meets the time limitation (within three years of the actual date of filing, October 9, 2008) and the amount limitation (tax paid within the three years preceding the filing of the refund claim).

If no return was filed, the refund claim must be made within two years from the time the tax was paid, and the amount of the refund cannot be more than the tax paid during the two years immediately preceding the filing of the claim.

Refund of withheld taxes and estimated tax payments. All estimated taxes and taxes withheld by an employer are deemed to have been paid on the original due date of the return (IRC §6513(b); David H. Baral, 120 S. Ct. 1006 (2000)). For example, your 2007 return was due on April 15, 2008, but you received a six-month extension until October 15, 2008. You filed the return on October 7, 2008. Any estimated tax or withholding tax paid before April 15, 2008, is deemed paid on April 15, not October 7. Now suppose you file a claim for a refund of a portion of the estimated or withholding tax on July 14, 2011. The claim is timely, even though the estimated or withholding tax is deemed paid on April 15, 2008, or more than three years prior to the claim for refund. You meet the time limitation since the claim is filed within three years of the date the return was filed, October 7, 2008. Also, the refund is allowed under the dollar limitation since the refund claim is filed within three years, *plus any extensions of time for filing the return,* of the date of payment of estimated or withholding tax, April 15, 2008. The last day for filing a refund claim under the "three years plus extension" look-back period would be October 15, 2011 (three years from the April 15, 2008, payment date plus a six-month extension).

Where a refund is claimed on an original return mailed and postmarked (U.S. Postal Service) on or slightly before the last day of the "three years plus extension" period, the IRS will allow the refund claim. The Second Circuit held that the refund claim is treated as filed on the date of mailing under the timely mailing/timely filing rule of Code Section 7502 (Weisbart, 222 F.3d 93 (2d Cir. 2000). The IRS acquiesced (Action On Decision 2000-09) to *Weisbart* and amended the regulations (Reg. §301.7502-1(f)). The IRS treats refund claims included on delinquent original returns as filed on the date of mailing for purposes of applying the "three years plus extension" look-back rule of Section 6511(b)(2)(A). The Ninth Circuit overruled its prior position and now applies the same three-year rule as the IRS (Omohundro, 2002-USTC ¶50,590 (9th Cir. 2002), overturning its prior decision in *Miller,* 38 F.3d 473 (9th Cir. 1994)).

Extended assessment and refund period. When you agree with the IRS to extend the time during which it can assess your tax, you may file a refund claim during this extended period plus an additional six months afterwards (IRC §6511(c)(1)). A refund made during this time includes the refund you would have received if you had filed a claim at the time the extension was signed, plus the tax paid after the agreement was signed but before you filed your claim (IRC §6511(c)(2)). These extension period rules do not apply to refunds of estate taxes. Where your claim is filed more than six months after the end of the extended period, the refunded amount cannot be more than the tax paid during the two years before the filing of the claim (IRC §6511(c)(3)(B)).

> **Example:** A 2007 return, filed on April 15, 2008, is under audit. In January 2011, an agreement is made to extend the statutory period of assessment to July 5, 2012. But for this extension, the period during which a refund claim may be filed would have closed on April 15, 2011. With the extension, you now have until January 5, 2012, to file a refund claim on your 2007 return.

If you file a claim for a failure to take a bad debt deduction or worthless security deduction, you have seven years from the due date of your return. Here, all you get back is the tax related to the bad debt or worthless security deduction.

Refund lookback period for nonfilers. If no return is filed, a refund claim must be made within two years from when the tax was paid, and the amount of the refund cannot exceed the tax paid during the two years immediately preceding the filing of the claim (Reg. §301.6511(b)-1(b)(1)(iii)).

Under pre-1997 law, the Supreme Court held that if a refund claim was not filed as of the date of the deficiency notice, the Tax Court could only award a refund for taxes paid in the two years preceding the deficiency notice; the rule allowing a refund for taxes paid in the prior three-year period did not apply. Thus, if the IRS deficiency notice was mailed more than two years after the due date of the return, no refund at all could be obtained in the Tax Court for overwithheld taxes, which are deemed to have been paid on the return due date (Lundy, 116 S. Ct. 647 (1996)). Under current law, if a nonfiler receives an IRS deficiency notice in the third year after the return due date, a refund may be obtained in the Tax Court for a tax year ending after August 5, 1997, for taxes paid within the three years preceding the date of the deficiency notice (IRC §6512(b)(3)).

What Refund Form to Use

Refund claims should be filed on Form 1040X (for an individual who originally filed on Form 1040, Form 1040A, or Form 1040EZ) or on Form 1120X (for a corporation that filed Form 1120). Where an income tax form other than Form 1040, Form 1040A, Form 1040EZ, or Form 1120 was filed, a refund claim is generally made on an amended return. However, a partner must use Form 8082 to make a refund claim in the form of a request for administrative adjustment (RAA) of partnership items. Form 843 may be used for claiming refunds for estate, gift, and employment taxes or certain excise taxes.

To correct an error on a return filed before its due date, you can file a corrected return on or before its due date. This return is not considered an amended return. However, a corrected return filed after the due date is an amended return and acts as a refund claim.

Letters to the IRS are usually held by the courts as not satisfying the requirements for an adequate refund claim.

Overwithheld taxes. You need not file a formal claim for overpayment of personal income tax resulting from excessive withholding of taxes on wages or excessive estimated tax payments. In these two cases, a tax return requesting a refund of the overpayment acts as a claim for refund. But there is one exception. On the death of an individual who has overpaid tax, the administrator or executor of the estate files a refund claim on Form 1310.

Generally, refunds for excessive withholding or estimating of tax are made soon after a tax return is filed. However, a return may be subject to a "pre-refund" audit, especially where the income shown on the return is less than $10,000 or there are large deductions or many exemptions that require substantiation.

Preparing Your Refund Claim

The most important part of a refund claim is stating the "reasons" for the refund. A general claim where you just note an overpayment, without supporting facts and grounds, is not sufficient. If a claim is denied by the IRS, it may become the basis of a court suit. If you have not stated all the grounds, you may not be allowed to show them in court. The courts have limited taxpayers to the exact claim shown on the form. Make a full claim and show:

- All the facts that support the claim. You may attach to the form as much evidence as is helpful. Be sure your facts are simply and fully stated.
- All the grounds for the claim. You may hedge if you are uncertain about the exact grounds; alternate and even inconsistent grounds may be given. For example:

  The loss was incurred from an embezzlement; if not, it was incurred from a bad debt.

  The gain from the sale is entitled to capital gain treatment as the property sold was a capital asset; if not, it was depreciable property used in business.

  The loss was due to a loss on the acquisition of real estate and from a partial bad debt (where the claim arose from the extinguishing of a mortgage by a deed in lieu of a foreclosure).

While it is necessary to be complete and precise in specifying the facts and reasons for your claim, you are not required to present your evidence; you must merely inform the IRS of the basis for your claim.

To protect against your understating the amount of your claim, it may be advisable to preface the claim with this phrase: *"The following or such greater amounts as may be legally refunded."* However, neither this nor any other "protective clause" will allow you to support your refund claim on grounds other than those mentioned in the original claim or in amendments made before the period of limitations has expired.

A separate claim must be made for each year in which a refund is claimed. It must be made in duplicate and signed under oath by the taxpayer or the duly authorized agent. If an agent signs, he or she must attach to the claim evidence of authority. If the claim is based on a joint return, it must be signed by both spouses.

A refund claim filed before there is an overpayment is invalid, unless the IRS waives the defect.

When you file a petition to the Tax Court, thus giving that court jurisdiction over your case, you may no longer file a refund claim for any part of the tax for the taxable year in question.

Amending the Refund Claim

You may generally amend your refund claim before the occurrence of either of the following events: (1) expiration of the period for filing the original claim (generally two years after paying the tax or three years after filing the return, whichever is later), and (2) final action taken by the IRS on the refund claim. After the expiration of the time limitation, you may not raise new issues or grounds in an amended refund claim, even though the original claim was timely.

Regardless of the time limitations above, file your amended claim immediately upon discovering the need for the amendment. Make certain that your amended claim meets all the technical standards discussed in the previous paragraphs.

Filing an Informal Claim

There is no advantage in filing an informal claim for refund. An informal claim must meet the same requirements as a formal claim made on the official IRS form (Form 1040X, Form 1120X, or Form 843). Although some informal claims have been allowed, many more have been denied and have not been permitted to be the basis of refund suits. For example, you may not base a refund suit on an informal claim that is limited to a:

- Letter suggesting a change in tax computation;
- Request for a ruling stating the facts and grounds for a refund; or
- Sworn statement that states the facts and grounds for a refund but does not include a demand for one.

Refunds based on informal claims have been allowed where an informal claim was accompanied by a brief that gave the basis of the claim or where, as a result of a conference, letters and memoranda stating the taxpayer's position were filed and a general claim referring to these papers was later filed.

Getting a Partial Refund in a Contested Case

The IRS, in three situations, may allow partial refunds in cases where contested issues still remain to be settled.

1. Two or more refund issues where some issues are settled and others are still contested. Here, a refund may be allowed on the settled issues.

Example: You file a refund claim based on two issues. The first one, which would result in a $1,000 refund, is settled. The second one, which would result in a $500 refund, is contested. The IRS may give you a partial refund of $1,000.

2. Two or more issues where some issues will result in a refund and the others in a deficiency, but the overall netting results in a refund.

Example: A case involves a refund issue that is not contested and a deficiency issue that is contested. The allowance of the refund issue would result in a net overassessment of $5,000 after offsetting the deficiency issue. A $5,000 refund may be allowed, even though the contested issue is still pending.

3. Two or more years are under examination. In one year, there is a contested proposed deficiency. In the other year, there is an agreement on an overassessment that is greater than the proposed deficiency.

Example: For year 2010, the IRS proposes a deficiency of $4,000 that you contest. But for 2011, the IRS agrees that it owes you a refund of $7,000. A partial refund of not more than $3,000 may be made.

Note: The IRS will not give partial refunds in cases where there may be an overall deficiency, even though there is no dispute on the tax refunding issue.

If the refund differs from the amount you sought, you usually get a notice of adjustment explaining the difference before receiving the refund. But sometimes the refund is received without prior explanation. In that case, the IRS recommends this action: If the refund is smaller than you claimed, cash the check and write to your IRS Service Center asking why the refund was less than the amount claimed. If the refund exceeds your claim, return the check to the Service Center with a request for an explanation.

After a Refund Claim Is Filed

No matter how small a refund claim is, it is thoroughly scrutinized by the IRS.

The examination procedure is like the one used in examining your return. It provides for an agent's examination in a desk examination or in the field, and if the agent disputes your claim you may ask for a conference at a higher level.

If your claim is finally turned down, you are notified by certified or registered mail. A disallowed claim may not be amended. Sometimes the IRS will reconsider a denied claim. But this reopening cannot extend the time in which you can sue for a refund. Of course, you may file a new claim so long as the limitation period within which a claim may be filed has not expired, but it must be on new grounds.

A refund suit may not be filed in a federal District Court on the U.S. Court of Claims until six months after the date the refund claim is filed with the IRS, or, if earlier, the date of the IRS's denial of the claim. The deadline for commencing the court suit is two years from the date the IRS mails the notice of disallowance by certified or registered mail.

If a claim is allowed, you receive a Certificate of Overassessment. Check it for accuracy. The IRS does not have to pay interest for the period *after* the filing of the claim if the refund is paid by the 45th day after the claim is filed (IRC §6611(e)(2)). If the refund is not paid within the 45-day period, interest is calculated from the date of overpayment to a date preceding the date of the check by no more than 30 days (IRC §6611(b)(2)).

Before the check is mailed, the IRS investigates to see that no taxes are owed by the taxpayer for other years. If the taxpayer's record is clear, the check is mailed. If not, the check is held up until payment of the taxes, or it is credited against the outstanding balance.

Refunds in Excess of Two Million Dollars Checked by Congress

A tax refund or credit over $2,000,000 may not be made until 30 days after a report is made to Congress's Joint Committee on Taxation (IRC §6405). This provision of the law does not apply to refunds or credits resulting from tentative carryback adjustments. Where the refund claim is for the prior taxable year under the special disaster area loss election (IRC §165(i)), the IRS has discretion to allow the refund without regard to the 30-day rule, and to make a later report to the Joint Committee. These cases do not require greater documentation and are not subject to closer examination than regular cases. The right to appeal within the IRS is the same as in other cases. If a protest is not made and no Tax Court petition is filed, the report to the Joint Committee will be prepared by regional specialists in the Examination Division, called Joint Committee Coordinators. If a protest is made, the report is prepared either by an appeals officer or counsel attorney. The report contains:

The name of the person to whom the refund or credit is to be made;
The amount of the refund or credit;
A summary of the facts of the case; and
The decision of the Commissioner.

Quick Refund for Carryback of Loss or Unused Credit

You may file an application for a tentative carryback adjustment of prior years' taxes due to a carryback of net operating loss, unused general business credit, corporate capital loss, or a previously reported income item under claim of right. If accepted, you may receive a quick refund without extensive audit procedures (IRC §6411).

The application, on Form 1045 (Form 1139 for corporations), must be filed within 12 months from the end of the taxable year in which the loss or unused credit occurs. The IRS must act on your application within 90 days of filing or 90 days from the last day of the month in which your return is due, whichever is later. In the case of a quick refund based on a claim of right under IRC §1341(b)(1), the IRS must act within 90 days from the date on which the application is filed or the date of overpayment (the last day for the payment of tax for the year in which a deduction is allowed for the restoration of income held under a claim of right), whichever is later.

The IRS may refuse your application if there are computational errors or material omissions that cannot be corrected within the 90-day period. Further, quick refund claims attributable to questionable tax-shelter losses may be withheld by the IRS. If the IRS determines that a carried back net operating loss is "highly likely" the result of a gross misvaluation or false or fraudulent tax-shelter promotion (under IRC §6700), the IRS may reduce the refund to take into account the improper loss (see Revenue Ruling 84-175, 1984-2 CB 296).

The application does not act as a claim for refund. You may file a separate claim for refund before, at the same time, or after you file your application.

Even though the IRS allows the carryback adjustments according to your application and refunds prior taxes to you, it is not barred from later assessing a deficiency. The purpose of the quick refund procedure is to give you cash immediately when you most likely need it.

HOW TO ARRANGE CLOSING AGREEMENTS AND COMPROMISES

A closing agreement may be used to fix the final tax liability of a taxable period or to determine the tax consequences of specific items without settling the final tax liability of that period (IRC §7121).

A closing agreement is the only statutorily authorized method for entering into an agreement binding on both the service and a taxpayer. Section 7121 permits but does not require the IRS to enter into a closing agreement. As a result, the IRS has the discretion to decide whether and under what conditions a closing agreement is executed.

You may want a closing agreement, even though no tax is due for the period to which the agreement relates. You may enter into a series of agreements relating to the tax liability of a single period. To cover these and other situations, the IRS provides the following closing agreement forms:

Form 866, which covers liability for any past period.

Form 906, which closes specific items of tax liability for either past, current, or future periods (Reg §601.202(b)).

Procedures for entering into closing agreements are also detailed in IRS Revenue Procedure 68-16, 1968-1 CB 770, as modified by Revenue Procedure 94-67, 1994-2 CB 800.

Before entering into a closing agreement, make sure that you understand all of its consequences. After both you and the IRS sign, you cannot change your position. A closing agreement is final on the matter expressly stated in the agreement, unless there is a showing of fraud, malfeasance, or misrepresentation of a material fact. It cannot be modified, set aside, or disregarded in a later suit, action, or proceeding.

Why Use a Closing Agreement?

The main object of a closing agreement is to protect the individual against the reopening of an agreed matter at some later date by the IRS. It also stops an individual from suing or filing other claims for refund. A closing agreement also may be used to fix tax liability for a year barred or arguably barred by the statute of limitations.

You may want a closing agreement for recurring transactions. Cost, fair market value, or adjusted basis as of a given date in the past may be established.

Establishing tax liability may facilitate a transaction such as the sale of stock.

A corporation in the process of liquidation or dissolution may want an agreement to wind up its affairs.

In estate tax proceedings, a closing agreement can assure the fiduciary that the estate is closed for federal tax purposes.

When Is Form 866 Used?

Form 866, called Agreement as to Final Determination of Tax Liability, is used for tax periods ending before the agreement. It closes the total liability of the individual for those periods. It is used where the tax period for which the agreement is asked has ended, and tax liability for the period has been determined.

The total tax liability determined has to be separated into tax periods and types of taxes. Also, the exact section of the law under which each tax covered was imposed must be noted.

Whenever Form 866 is used, the tax liability stated for each period shown in the agreement has to be the total tax liability determined for each period, without any penalty or interest. But the government may want the closing agreement to include *ad valorem* penalties that have been incurred. Then the tax and penalty are described in the agreement. Three copies of Form 866 must be completed.

When Is Form 906 Used?

Closing agreements on specific items are made on Form 906. This is so whether they are related to past, current, or future periods. A closing agreement of a year ending after the agreement is always made on Form 906. It relates only to a specific item or items affecting tax liability. It cannot attempt to conclude total tax liability for any period. Specific items on past periods that it may cover are items such as:

Amount of gross income, deductions for losses, depreciation, or depletion;

Year for which an item of income is to be included in gross income;

Year for which an item of loss is to be deducted; and

Value of property on a specified date.

Combined Agreements

Neither Form 866 nor Form 906 is designed to determine both tax liability and tax consequences of specific items. Instead, a combined agreement may be used. The format is shown in Revenue Procedure 68-16, 1968-1 CB 770. The main reason for a combined agreement is that a determination of liability does not fix the amount of income or deductions taken into account in reaching liability. Later, you may be able to prove a net operating loss for the year liability was determined, even though the tax was based on facts showing taxable income. In such a case, while the tax liability has been fixed, the effect of transactions of that year on other years has not. If agreed, the problem may be avoided by a combined agreement determining taxable income for such year and any carryovers from the year.

How To Apply for Closing Agreements

To apply for a closing agreement, send your request to the Director with audit jurisdiction over the returns, or to the Appeals office if your request relates to a case pending before it.

A request is only an offer. It may be withdrawn any time before it is accepted. The closing agreement may be prepared by the taxpayer or the examining agent, but in most cases collaboration is preferable. The taxpayer executes the agreement first, but may withdraw prior to the signing on behalf of the Commissioner.

If it covers a joint return, both spouses have to sign. When an attorney or agent signs, he or she has to include papers proving the authority to sign. Specific instructions for the preparation of closing agreements are contained in Revenue Procedure 68-16, 1968-1 CB 770.

When preparing a closing agreement:

- Fill in the required number of forms. All copies have to be exactly the same. Avoid erasures or corrections; do not switch typewriters.
- Include a statement of how you want the liability fixed and your reasons.
- Use words describing the kind of tax liability involved, such as "Federal income tax."
- Mention all statutes, regulations, and decisions supporting your case, and show how they apply to your facts.
- Describe the taxes involved.
- Include anything else that will help the IRS decide the case.

When a closing agreement is submitted either on Form 866 or Form 906, the taxpayer is asked to sign a Form 870. This permits the immediate assessment and collection of the agreed deficiency. But it may be conditioned on the approval of the final closing agreement. The IRS will insert a paragraph stating this.

IRS Policy on Closing Agreements

The policy is to enter into a closing agreement in any case in which you can show:

- An advantage in having the case permanently closed, as, for example, where, in the settlement of disputed issues, you and the government have made mutual concessions.
- Good and sufficient reasons for desiring a closing agreement, and that the government will suffer no disadvantage if the agreement is entered into.
- The purpose is to mitigate the effect of the statute of limitations or to allow a deficiency dividend.
- Properly executed amended returns have been filed, after the expiration of the period in which assessments might have been made, and no fraud was involved.

A request for a closing agreement is reviewed much more closely than a request for a ruling. The very fact that the IRS is being asked to enter into a binding agreement often makes it suspicious of your motives. Because of the involved nature of the procedure connected with a closing agreement, the IRS is not anxious to use this form. It prefers the much simpler rulings procedure.

There is no assurance in the case of a closing agreement that the Commissioner will agree to it. But no application for a closing agreement can or will be rejected solely because it gives no apparent advantage to the IRS.

Offers in Compromise

The IRS may compromise any civil or criminal case (IRC §7122) unless the case has already been referred to the Department of Justice for prosecution or defense. Once the referral takes place, the Attorney General has the final authority to compromise.

An offer in compromise is a proposal by the taxpayer to pay a sum in full satisfaction of the unpaid tax liability, including interest, penalties, and other additions. When an offer has been accepted and the taxpayer has been notified by letter of the acceptance, the compromise is a legally enforceable contract between the IRS and the taxpayer. All questions of tax liability for the years in question are conclusively and finally settled. Neither the taxpayer nor the IRS may reopen the case except for the showing of falsification, concealment, or mutual mistake of a material fact.

The compromise of a tax liability may rest upon: (1) doubtful liability, (2) doubtful collectibility, or (3) economic hardship or exceptional circumstances. An offer in compromise will be accepted by the IRS if the amount offered reasonably reflects collection potential.

An offer in compromise is filed on Form 656, except for offers based on doubt as to liability, which must be submitted on Form 656-L.

A $150 application fee must accompany Form 656, except for qualifying low-income taxpayers. Low-income status is based on family size and monthly income criteria shown on a worksheet in the Form 656 booklet. Qualifying taxpayers must certify their eligibility for the fee-payment exception on Form 656-A.

When an offer is based on doubtful collectibility, economic hardship or exceptional circumstances, Form 656 must be accompanied by either Form 433-A (individuals) or Form 433-B (businesses), which are statements of financial condition.

Before rejecting a proposed offer, the IRS must provide for independent administrative review and if an offer is rejected, you must be notified of the right to appeal to the IRS Appeals office.

An offer is deemed to be accepted by the IRS if the IRS does not reject it within 24 months of the submission date, disregarding periods that tax liability is in dispute in a judicial proceeding (IRC §7122(f)).

Economic hardship or exceptional circumstances. Where there is no doubt as to liability or collectibility, the IRS may agree to a compromise to promote effective tax administration on the grounds of economic hardship or exceptional circumstances. The IRS will consider all the facts and circumstances, including the taxpayer's overall record of tax compliance, in considering the offer. An offer will not be accepted by the IRS if the taxpayer is involved in an open bankruptcy proceeding or if all required federal tax returns have not been filed.

The following are treated as economic hardship situations: (1) long-term illness or disability of the taxpayer or the taxpayer's dependent makes it likely that the taxpayer's financial resources will be exhausted, or (2) liquidation of the taxpayer's assets would prevent the taxpayer from meeting basic living expenses. An example of an exceptional circumstance may be erroneous advice from an IRS employee that results in additional tax liability and penalties (Reg. §301.7122-1(c)(3)).

Partial payments required. Upfront payments are required (IRC §7122(c)). For a lump-sum offer, which means offers to pay in five or fewer installments, the taxpayer must include with the offer an upfront payment of 20% of the offer amount. For periodic payment offers, the taxpayer must submit the first proposed installment with the application. The upfront payment is in addition to the regular user fee, but the fee will be credited to the outstanding tax liability.

The IRS will waive the partial payment requirement (as well as the $150 application fee) for low-income taxpayers who have certified their status on Form 656-A, and for taxpayers who have submitted an offer on Form 656-L based on doubt as to liability.

HOW TO GET THE IRS's OPINION ON A TAX PROBLEM

The IRS provides an invaluable service in giving, through letter rulings and determination letters, opinions on tax questions asked by taxpayers. Any taxpayer may ask for an opinion, and requesting one is often a necessary step in making business decisions. Not every tax problem may be satisfactorily resolved, and where an adverse tax holding might disrupt a planned transaction, requesting an IRS opinion before undertaking the proposed move is advisable. A fee must be paid to the IRS with your ruling request as discussed below.

An IRS opinion may also be requested for a closed transaction to determine how to report it on a tax return.

The IRS's discretion to rule on taxpayers' problems is broad. But as a matter of policy, it does not give opinions in certain areas and also distinguishes between the type of opinions that can be given by IRS personnel. A letter ruling is issued by the appropriate Office of Associate Chief Counsel in Washington and is in response to questions involving prospective transactions or completed transactions before a return is filed. A determination letter is issued by a Director in response to questions involving completed transactions. As for prospective transactions, determination letters are issued for determining the qualification of proposed pension or profit-sharing plans, or the exempt status of certain organizations. A determination letter is issued only if the questions presented can be specifically answered by clearly established rules in statutes, regulations, or IRS rulings and court decisions published in the Internal Revenue Bulletin.

Revenue rulings are generally modifications of letter rulings that have been selected because of their importance or interest for publication in the Internal Revenue Bulletin.

Procedures for requesting rulings and determination letters are detailed in Revenue Procedure 2010-1, 2010-1 IRB 1.

Should You Ask for an IRS Ruling?

Before requesting a ruling, it is advisable to carefully research the tax law applying to your problem. If your review shows that IRS policy is against your position, do not ask for a ruling. If you proceed without a ruling, there is always the chance that, if the transaction is examined, a settlement might be reached at that time.

Ask for a ruling if you have a fair chance of receiving a favorable ruling or have an alternative plan if you receive an unfavorable reply. Even if the request is turned down, at least you know that you will encounter possible litigation if you proceed with the transaction. This knowledge may also be important in planning and executing the transaction.

User Fee for Ruling

You must pay the IRS a fee for handling a ruling request. The amount of the fee depends on the specific type of ruling involved.

The user fee schedule can be found in Appendix A of Revenue Procedure 2010-1, 2010-1 IRB 1.

Getting Advice for Future Transactions

If your question involves a prospective transaction, then only the appropriate Office of Associate Chief Counsel in Washington has the authority to answer in a letter ruling. Unless the law or regulations specifically provide otherwise, the issuance of an answer is a matter that rests within the discretion of Associate Chief Counsel.

If the question is about the qualification of proposed pension, profit-sharing, or stock bonus plans, then a determination letter may be obtained under the rules in Revenue Procedure 2010-6, 2010-1 IRB 193.

Getting Advice on Closed Transactions

A problem concerning a completed transaction may be answered by the appropriate Office of Associate Chief Counsel in a ruling if no return has been filed, and the answer requires the interpretation of the tax laws.

If the answer to the question requires simply the routine application of established principles and policies, the appropriate IRS Director may answer in a determination letter.

In a particular case, it may be difficult to draw the line between a novel or routine problem. If you are not sure of your position, you can send your question to the appropriate Office of Associate Chief Counsel in Washington. The final decision on whether a question is routine or novel, simple or complex, rests with the IRS. If you send a question to an IRS Director on the theory that the matter is routine, he or she may decide that it is novel and refer the question to Associate Chief Counsel. You will be notified of the change.

You Cannot Get a Ruling for . . .

- Hypothetical transactions.
- Questions of fact involving: market value of property; reasonableness of compensation; accumulated earnings penalty.
- Matters involving a court decision adverse to IRS policy and the IRS has not decided whether to follow or litigate the issue.
- An issue that is identical to an issue involved in a return filed by the taxpayer for an earlier year and that issue is under examination or has been examined by an Area Director or has been considered by an Appeals office, and the statute of limitations has not yet expired.
- Questions involved in pending tax cases—if the government's position would be hurt by giving you a ruling.
- Tax avoidance schemes (you must have a legitimate business purpose in carrying out your transaction).
- Questions that the IRS thinks it cannot properly settle by rulings.

- An issue that is expected to be covered by imminent legislation.
- Questions on replacing involuntarily converted property, even though replacement has not been made, if a return has been filed for the year in which the property was converted. An Area Director can give a determination letter on this issue.

A listing of the areas for which the IRS will not issue rulings or determination letters is published from time to time in the Internal Revenue Bulletin. (*See* Section 6 of Revenue Procedure 2010-1, 2010-1 IRB 1 for a general discussion of no-ruling areas, and for a detailed list *see* Revenue Procedure 2010-3, 2010-1 IRB 110). The list is not all-inclusive since the IRS may decline to issue rulings or determination letters on other questions whenever warranted by the facts or circumstances of a particular case. Finally, when there has been new legislation, the IRS hesitates to rule on issues involving Code sections for which regulations have not been made final.

You cannot, by court action, force the IRS to give you a ruling or to apply a ruling in your favor.

Generally, rulings are not issued to business, trade, or industrial associations or to other similar groups relating to the application of the tax laws to members of the groups. However, rulings may be issued to such groups or associations relating to their own tax status or liability.

How To Request a Ruling

Your request must be in writing. The IRS does not issue rulings or determination letters upon oral requests. IRS employees ordinarily will not discuss a substantive tax issue prior to the receipt of a written request for a ruling. If they do, their oral opinions are not binding upon the IRS. This should not discourage an inquiry on whether the IRS will rule on a particular question or a discussion on the procedure for submitting a request for a ruling.

Conference before making a request. Sometimes, it is advisable to ask for a conference before you make your request for a ruling. There are advantages in having a conference before submitting your request. If you are uncertain whether you will get the ruling, the conference allows you to sound out the IRS without exposing the essential facts of the proposed transaction. In making a formal request for a ruling, you are required to supply the National Office with abundant materials and data, such as financial statements, minutes, and balance sheets. These are not returned if the ruling request is denied but are transmitted to the Area Director where they become part of your file.

If a conference is held, understand that what is said during the meeting is merely an aid. It does not bind the IRS. Before going to the conference, prepare your case well. Take with you the draft of your request for a ruling and any proposed contracts or other documents.

Making a request. To ensure that your request is in order so the IRS can respond quickly, complete the checklist in Appendix C of Revenue Procedure 2010-1, 2010-1 IRB 1, sign and date it, and attach it to the top of your request. The checklist highlights some of the following rules from Revenue Procedure 2010-1, 2010-1 IRB 1.

1. A declaration under penalties of perjury that the facts presented are true, correct, and complete must be signed by the person on whose behalf the request is made; *see* the declaration in Appendix B of Revenue Procedure 2009-1, 2009-1 IRB 1.
2. Send your letter ruling request to the appropriate Associate Chief Counsel at the following address:

   Internal Revenue Service, Attention: CC:PA:LPD:DRU, P.O. Box 7604, Ben Franklin Station, Washington D.C. 20044. If a private delivery service is used, the package should be sent to: Internal Revenue Service, Attention: CC:PA:LPD:DRU, Room 5336, 1111 Constitution Avenue, N.W., Washington, D.C. 20224.

For determination letters, send the request to the appropriate Director whose office has or will have audit jurisdiction, as shown in Appendix D of Revenue Procedure 2010-1, 2010-1 IRB 1.

Submit the original and two copies of the request if:

More than one issue is presented in the request.
A closing agreement is requested on the issue presented.

3. Do not submit alternative plans in requests for a ruling.
4. Be sure to include:

   Complete facts.
   Names, addresses, and taxpayer account numbers of all interested parties.
   Copies, not originals, of all pertinent documents. The copies should be attested to be the same as the originals. Do not send originals, as they become part of the IRS file and are not returned.

The balance sheet nearest the date of the transaction, if a corporate reorganization, distribution, or similar transaction is involved.
If documents are submitted, they must be accompanied by an analysis of their relevancy to the issue.

5. Give the business reason for the transaction (favorable rulings often depend upon the existence of a bona fide business reason for the transaction).
6. Give the grounds for your stand and your supporting authority and specify what ruling or rulings you want. If you want a particular determination, explain the basis for your contentions, together with a statement of relevant authorities. Even if you do not urge a particular determination, you must give your view of the tax result, supported by a statement of relevant authorities such as statutes and regulations. All requests must include a statement of whether the applicable law is uncertain and whether the issue is adequately addressed by relevant authorities.
7. The IRS encourages the disclosure of any legislation, regulations, revenue rulings, or revenue procedures contrary to the taxpayer's position. The IRS believes that disclosure will lead to more rapid action. Technically, the IRS encourages but does not require the statement of contrary authorities. However, if contrary authorities are not provided, the IRS wants the ruling request to include a statement that there are *no* contrary authorities. If the taxpayer does not take either action and refuses a subsequent request of the IRS to do so, the IRS may refuse to issue a ruling (Section 7.01(9) of Revenue Procedure 2010-1, 2010-

1 IRB 1). The IRS specifically requires that any relevant *pending* legislation be identified in the ruling request. The IRS must also be notified if legislation is introduced after the request is filed but before a ruling is issued (Section 7.01(10) of Revenue Procedure 2010-1, 2010-1 IRB 1).

8. If a conference on the issues is desired, ask for one in the ruling request or soon afterwards in writing.
9. Sign the request. If you are representing a taxpayer, include your power of attorney and if you are an enrolled agent, show evidence of enrollment. The ruling request is signed by the taxpayer or by an authorized representative who is (1) an attorney who has filed a written declaration that he or she is currently qualified as an attorney and is authorized to represent the taxpayer; (2) a certified public accountant who files with the IRS written declaration that he or she is currently qualified as a certified public accountant and is authorized to represent the taxpayer; (3) a person, other than an attorney or certified public accountant, enrolled to practice before the Service; or (4) any other person who has received a Letter of Authorization from the IRS Director of the Office of Professional Responsibility to represent the taxpayer in this particular matter.
10. Submit payment of user fee. Each ruling request must be accompanied by a check or money order, payable to the Internal Revenue Service, in the appropriate amount. For specific payment instructions, *see* Section 15 of Revenue Procedure 2010-1, 2010-1 IRB 1; user fees for employee plans and exempt organizations are in Section 6 of Revenue Procedure 2010-8, 2010-1 IRB 234.

Requests that do not comply with the above requirements will be acknowledged, and the requirements that have not been met will be pointed out. If the missing information is not supplied within 21 days, and an extension is not granted, the IRS will notify you in writing that the ruling request has been closed. If you supply the missing information after the closing letter is mailed, your request will be reopened and treated as a new request as of the date of the receipt of the information, but a new user fee must be paid (Section 8.05(3) of Revenue Procedure 2010-1, 2010-1 IRB 1).

The IRS has an alternate two-part procedure to expedite the processing of ruling requests for proposed transactions Section 7.02(3) of Revenue Procedure 2010-1, 2010-1 IRB 1. Under the procedure, you may submit, together with the detailed statement of facts, documents and other required information, a summary statement of the controlling facts that support your request. If the National Office finds your summary satisfactory, the ruling will be based on these facts. This procedure has the advantage of eliminating many of the facts that the reviewer must assess. In addition, it removes some of the subjectivity exercised by the reviewer in determining whether the transaction was carried out substantially as proposed and whether minor deviations are material. On the other hand, this procedure poses the problem of what is a sufficient statement of the facts.

Withdrawing your request. You may withdraw your request for a ruling or a determination letter at any time prior to the signing of the letter of reply. However, this may prove futile. The Office of Associate Chief Counsel may give its views on your request to the appropriate official with examination jurisdiction of the return. The information you submitted with your request will be considered in a later audit or examination of your return. Even though you withdraw your request, all correspondence and exhibits are retained by the IRS and are not returned to you.

Your Ruling Will Be Open to Public Inspection

Code §6110 requires the IRS to open to public inspection virtually all letter rulings, determination letters, and technical advice memoranda (called "written determinations") and related background files. Before your ruling is made public, it must be "sanitized" by deleting the following information:

1. Identifying details, such as names, addresses, Social Security numbers, and any other information that would identify any person (other than certain third parties who communicate with the IRS regarding the determination). Identifying details include information that would permit a person in the appropriate community (such as an industry or geographic location) to identify any person.
2. Information specifically authorized to be kept secret in the interest of national defense or foreign policy.
3. Information exempt from disclosure under other laws.
4. Trade secrets and privileged or confidential commercial or financial information.
5. Information the disclosure of which would constitute a clearly unwarranted invasion of personal privacy. This would include, for example, details not yet made public of a pending divorce or of medical treatment.
6. Information concerning the agency regulation of financial institutions.
7. Geological and geophysical information and data, including maps concerning wells.

Requesting deletions from written determination. When you request a determination letter, ruling, or technical advice memorandum, you must also submit a separate statement of proposed deletions (Section 7.01(11) of Revenue Procedure 2010-1, 2010-1 IRB 1). At the same time the letter ruling or determination letter on your case is issued, you will receive a notice that it will be disclosed to the public. You will also receive a copy of the text the IRS proposes to disclose on which is indicated the material the IRS proposes to delete, any substitutions, and any third-party communications. (In the case of a background file or written determination that is disclosed only on written request for disclosure, the disclosure notice will be mailed to you within a reasonable time after the IRS received its first request for disclosure.) You then have 20 days after the notice is mailed to submit a written statement identifying those items that you believe should be deleted but were not. You must also submit a copy of the proposed IRS text and indicate by brackets further deletions that you want the IRS to make. Generally, the IRS will not delete any material that you had not earlier proposed be deleted. The IRS will mail to you its final administrative conclusions regarding deletions within 20 days of receiving your response. The IRS will attempt to resolve the differences, but will not grant a conference specifically for that purpose. However, you may discuss issues involving deletions at any conference that has been otherwise scheduled with respect to the requested ruling or determination letter.

Court remedies when you and the IRS do not agree on deletions. If you are still not satisfied with the deletions proposed by the IRS, you may file a petition in the Tax Court (anonymously, if appropriate) within 60 days after the date on which the IRS mailed the disclosure notice (IRC §6110(f)(3)). You must have exhausted your remedies within the IRS prior to petitioning the Tax Court. If your request for deletions has not been responded to by the IRS within 50 days of the mailing of the disclosure notice, this is considered an exhaustion of administrative remedies allowing a filing of a petition in the Tax Court (Reg. §301.6110-5(b)(3)).

Within 15 days, the IRS will notify by registered or certified mail any other person identified by name and address in the written determination or background file that a petition has been filed in the Tax Court. Such person may intervene in the Tax Court action (anonymously, if appropriate) (IRC §6110(f)(4)(B)).

The Tax Court will make a decision as soon as possible on the extent of deletions and may close its proceedings on the issue to the public (IRC §6110(f)(5)).

When Written Determinations Are Open to Public Inspection

Generally, written determinations and background files will be open to public inspection not less than 75 days and not more than 90 days after the IRS mailed you the disclosure notice. If you sued in the Tax Court regarding deletions, the written determination or background file will be open to the public within 30 days after the court order becomes final, although the court may extend the 30-day period to give the IRS time to comply with its order (IRC §6110(g)).

Request for Delay of Disclosure

Where the transaction that is the subject of the written determination is not complete when the determination is issued, you may request that the IRS postpone disclosure until 15 days after the transaction is completed. However, disclosure generally must occur within 180 days after the IRS mailed you the disclosure notice (IRC §6110 (g)(3)). If the transaction is still not completed within the 180-day period, and disclosure would interfere with the transaction, you may again request a postponement until 15 days after the transaction. Overall, postponement may not exceed 360 days after the IRS mailing of the disclosure notice (IRC §6110 (g)(4); Reg. §301.6110-5(c)(2)(ii)(B)).

Your request for postponement must be in writing and state the date on which you expect to complete the transaction. To get the first postponement, send your request so that the IRS receives it within 60 days after the disclosure notice. To get the second postponement, send your request so that the IRS receives it within 15 days before the date you stated you expected to complete the transaction (Reg. §301.6110-5(c)(2)(ii)(C)).

You must notify the IRS when you complete the transaction if that happens earlier than you expected. The written determination will be open to public inspection 30 days after notice of completion or on the date originally scheduled for disclosure, whichever date is earlier (Reg. §301.6110-5(c)(2)(ii)(D)).

What To Do When the IRS Fails To Meet the Time Limitations or Fails To Make Deletions

Where the IRS fails to meet the time limitations, such as disclosing before 75 days after the disclosure notice was mailed to you or failing to postpone disclosure pursuant to your request, you may sue the government in the U.S. Court of Federal Claims. You or any other person identified in the determination may sue the government in the U.S. Court of Federal Claims if the IRS fails to make deletions as required by its own agreement or by court order. Where the court determines that any employee of the IRS intentionally or willfully failed to make a deletion or failed to act within the time limits, you may recover your actual damages (but not less than $1,000) plus costs and reasonable attorneys' fees for bringing the action (IRC §6110(j)).

How Soon May You Receive an Answer?

Letter rulings and determination letters are issued on a first-come-first-served basis. You may get a preference by showing a compelling need for a faster consideration (Section 7.02(4) of 2010-1, 2010-1 IRB 1). But the IRS will not assure you that your request will be processed within the time set by you. You may request that the IRS fax you or your representative a copy of the letter ruling, but the ruling is not considered "issued" until it is mailed (Section 7.02(5) of Revenue Procedure 2010-1, 2010-1 IRB 1).

To learn the status of a tax ruling, contact the representative indicated on the IRS acknowledgment of your request.

You May Get an Information Letter

Even though you request a ruling or a determination letter, you may receive an information letter. This is a statement issued either by the Office of Associate Chief Counsel or by a Director. It does no more than call attention to a well-established interpretation or principle of tax law without applying it to a specific set of facts. You may receive an information letter if your request seeks general information or does not meet all the requirements for a ruling or determination letter (Section 2.04 of Revenue Procedure 2010-1, 2010-1 IRB 1).

Can You Rely on a Letter Ruling?

You can usually rely on a letter ruling sent to you, although the IRS has the power to revoke the ruling retroactively. However, the IRS only under rare circumstances exercises this power. If the ruling is changed or revoked, the effect is almost always prospective. Be sure, in applying a ruling to the actual transaction, that the facts of the transaction are as you had stated them in your request and that the law has not changed in the meantime (Section 11.03 of Revenue Procedure 2010-1, 2010-1 IRB 1).

When preparing the return for the year in which the transaction involved takes place, attach a copy of the ruling or letter to the return. IRS personnel compare the facts reported on the return with the representations upon which the ruling was based. They do this to determine whether there has been a misstatement or omission of a material fact, or if the transaction upon which the ruling was based was actually carried out in a manner materially different from that represented.

When you receive a ruling, the IRS will generally audit the return reporting the transaction that is the subject of the ruling.

You are not justified in relying on a written determination issued to another taxpayer. The law specifically states that written determinations may not be used as precedent by either the IRS or taxpayers unless the IRS provides otherwise in regulatins (IRC §6110(k)(3)). The Supreme Court has stated that although the law bars the use of private rulings as precedents, they are nonetheless "evidence" of IRS views. The IRS may designate in a widely circulated official government publication (such as the Internal Revenue Bulletin) that a determination will be used as precedent.

You may not rely on a letter ruling issued to another taxpayer although the ruling may be helpful in discerning the IRS position on a particular issue.

You may rely on Revenue Rulings published in the Internal Revenue Bulletin in determining the rule applicable to your own case if the facts and circumstances of your transaction are substantially the same as in the published ruling.

Review and Revocation of Determination Letters

Determination letters involving income taxes are not generally reviewed by the Office of Associate Chief Counsel, as they merely repeat a position previously established in a regulation, ruling, or court decision published in the Internal Revenue Bulletin. If you believe a determination letter to be in error, you may ask the Director to reconsider the matter. You may also ask the Director to request technical advice from the National Office (Section 12.06 of Revenue Procedure 2010-1, 2010-1 IRB 1).

A Director may revoke a determination letter on re-examination of the issue or on an audit of the taxpayer's return. The revocation is automatically retroactive because the letter was issued for a completed transaction. Therefore, you did not rely upon the letter when entering into the transaction. The revocation of a determination letter on the status of pension and profit-sharing plans and exempt organizations, however, is generally prospective in effect.

How Letter Rulings Become Revenue Rulings

Revenue Rulings are generally revised letter rulings that the IRS believes have value as precedents or guides for taxpayers and IRS personnel. Although it is on the same subject matter, a Revenue Ruling differs from a letter ruling. When a letter ruling is edited for publication as a Revenue Ruling, the taxpayers' names and identifying facts are deleted. However, the ruling retains relevant facts with modifications to fit within the IRS's intention to propound a general rule. Finally, Revenue Rulings are subject to higher review, whereas many letter rulings are issued with no review above the branch level.

Requesting Technical Advice From the National Office

Generally, IRS field office personnel determine whether to request technical advice on an issue, but during an audit or conference, you may request that an issue on a closed transaction be referred to the Office of Associate Chief Counsel for technical advice. You may do this on the grounds that the issue has not been handled by the IRS in a uniform manner, or the issue, because of its complexity or unusualness, warrants consideration by the Associate Chief Counsel. Request for technical advice should be made as early as possible. If you wait until the case is in the Appeals office, the request for technical advice may be made before the Appeals office conference.

Your request for technical advice should be directed to the field office, either orally or in writing. The field office will notify you if it decides that your request for technical advice is unwarranted, and you may appeal the decision within 30 days of the notification by submitting to the field office a written statement of the reasons why the matter should be referred to the appropriate Office of Associate Chief Counsel. The statement should describe the pertinent facts and legal authorities and explain your position and the need for technical advice. The statement, along with the field office's statement of why technical advice is not needed, will be forwarded to the appropriate Compliance Director or territory manager for a decision. No conference will be held with you or your representative. If the Director proposes to deny the request, you will be sent a written explanation. You may not appeal a proposed denial, but at your request the Director will review the file and make a decision solely on the basis of the written record; no conference will be held. The reviewing Director will notify the field office of its decision within 45 days of receiving the information and then notify you (Section 5.04 of Revenue Procedure 2010-2, 2010-1 IRB 90).

If the field office intends to request technical advice, it will arrange a pre-submission conference to frame the issues and prepare the documents that must be included with the request. The pre-submission conference is generally conducted by telephone but may be conducted in person if the parties so choose (Section 6.07 of Revenue Procedure 2010-2, 2010-1 IRB 90).

The reply by the Associate Chief Counsel to the request for technical advice is called a Technical Advice Memorandum (TAM). You will be informed if the Associate Chief Counsel proposes to issue a TAM that is adverse to you, and a conference will be held, generally in person within 10 days unless you waive the right to the conference. Generally, you should attempt to provide all documents and arguments in writing well in advance of the conference, but if at the conference it appears that new information may be helpful, the new information should be provided 10 days after the conference. Extensions of the 10-day period must be requested in writing and are not typically granted (Section 9 of Revenue Procedure 2010-2, 2010-1 IRB 90).

A TAM contains: (1) a statement of the issues; (2) a statement of the facts pertinent to the issues; (3) the conclusions of the Associate Chief Counsel; (4) a discussion of the laws, regulations, rulings, and court decisions supporting the conclusions reached by the Associate Chief Counsel. The conclusions give direct answers, whenever possible, to the specific issues raised by the field office (Section 10.01 of Revenue Procedure 2010-2, 2010-1 IRB 90).

Accompanying the TAM is a notice under IRC §6110(f)(1) to disclose a TAM, including a copy of the version proposed to be open to public inspection. Before issuing the TAM, the Associate Chief Counsel will inform you if the IRS has decided to include in the TAM any of the material that you asked to be deleted. In that case, you have 10 days to submit further arguments supporting your proposed deletions (Section 10.03 of Revenue Procedure 2010-2, 2010-1 IRB 90).

After the Associate Chief Counsel provides a copy of the final TAM to the field office, the field office generally gives you a copy of the issued TAM, along with a copy of the version proposed to be open to public inspection (Section 10.07–10.10 of Revenue Procedure 2010-2, 2010-1 IRB 90). However, a copy of the TAM will not be given to you if your case involved a criminal or civil fraud investigation, or a jeopardy or termination assessment, until all of the proceedings in the investigation or assessment are complete (Section 10.13 of Revenue Procedure 2010-2, 2010-1 IRB 90).

Effect of technical advice. A technical advice memorandum represents the IRS's views of the law, applied to the facts of a specific case. Generally, a technical advice memorandum has the same effect as a ruling on a closed and completed transaction. It usually disposes of the matter in which it was requested and usually applies retroactively (Section 13 of Revenue Procedure 2010-2, 2010-1 IRB 90). But note: (1) Technical advice is not binding in a subsequent year, even though it is not revoked. (2) The IRS office handling your case may raise an issue in any taxable period, even though it has received technical advice concerning the same issue in another taxable period.

Technical advice memoranda often form the basis for revenue rulings.

Note: Other details on the furnishing of technical advice are in Revenue Procedure 2010-2, 2010-1 IRB 90.

How To Get Written Determinations Issued to Other Taxpayers

While you may not use letter rulings, determination letters, or technical advice memoranda issued to other taxpayers as precedent, they may be helpful as they reflect IRS policy and interpretation of the law. Written determinations are available in government reading rooms; background files are open to inspection only on written request.

Disclosure is not required of any technical advice memorandum (and its related background file) where the case involves civil fraud, criminal investigation, jeopardy, or termination assessment, until any action relating to the investigation or assessment is completed. Furthermore, a determination relating to IRS approval of the adoption or change in accounting method or period, qualified retirement plan funding method or plan year, or taxable year of a partner or partnership need not be open to public inspection, although the IRS must honor a written request for inspection.

Where You May Inspect Written Determinations

Some private publishing firms, such as Tax Analysts, Research Institute of America, and Commerce Clearing House, regularly publish rulings and technical advice memoranda.

Rulings and technical advice memoranda are available for inspection in the Freedom of Information Reading Room at the National Office (Reg. §301.6110-1(c)(1). The location of the National Reading Room is: 1111 Constitution Avenue, N.W., Room 1621, Washington D.C. Regional reading rooms have been eliminated (Reg. §601.702(b)(3)(ii)).

Actions To Obtain Additional Disclosure

You may seek disclosure of additional information on any written determination or background file open to public inspection. You must request the additional disclosure from the Internal Revenue Office that issued the written determination, specifying the deleted information that you believe should be disclosed and why. The IRS says it will not disclose names, addresses, or identifying numbers.

The IRS will notify all people identified by name and address in the determination or background file that additional disclosure is sought. If all agree to the additional disclosure within 20 days, the determination or background file will be revised to reflect the additional disclosure. If anyone objects, the IRS will deny your request (Reg. §301.6110-5(d)).

You may then file a petition in Tax Court or the District Court for the District of Columbia for the additional disclosure. The IRS will notify anyone identified by name and address in the determination or background file of the suit within 15 days by registered or certified mail, and such person may intervene in the suit (anonymously, if appropriate) (Reg. §301.6110-5(d)(2)-(5)).

CIRCULAR 230: WHO MAY PRACTICE BEFORE THE IRS

The requirements, privileges, and duties of persons qualified to practice before the IRS are described in Treasury Department Circular No. 230, which is available from the IRS website at www.irs.gov; go to the Tax Professionals page and select "Circular No. 230".

Proposed Circular 230 Amendments. The IRS has proposed major amendments to Circular 230 as part of its initiative to increase oversight of the tax return preparer industry. See below for the proposed regulated tax return preparer rules.

The proposed regulations clarify that a tax professional is engaged in "practice before the IRS" if he or she either prepares a return or files it; both acts are not required as some individuals had claimed (Proposed Reg. Section 10.2 (a) (4)).

The proposed regulations also provide that any individual who for compensation prepares or assists in the preparation of all or a substantial portion of a document pertaining to a taxpayer's liability for submission to the IRS is subject to the duties and restrictions and possible sanctions that apply to practitioners under Circular 230. Individuals who are not practitioners may not prepare or assist in the preparation of all or substantially all of a tax return or refund claim, or sign the return or refund claim (Proposed Reg. Section 10.8 (b).

The proposed regulations would generally take effect 60 days after the date that final regulations are published in the Federal Register. At the time this book went to press, the IRS was considering comments from the tax professional community. See the e-Supplement at jklasser.com for an update.

Proposed Circular 230 amendments for regulated tax return preparers. As part of its comprehensive "return preparer initiative", the IRS proposed a major revision to the Circular 230 regulations in August 2010 to govern the oversight of previously unregulated tax return preparers (REG-138637-07, 2010-44 IRB 581). Previously, Circular 230 did not apply to a tax preparer who was not an attorney, certified public accountant, enrolled agent, enrolled retirement plan agent, or enrolled actuary. The proposed regulations designate "registered tax return preparers" as a new class of practitioners authorized to practice before the IRS.

The proposed regulations do *not* change the Circular 230 rules for attorneys, certified public accountants and enrolled agents.

As discussed below, the authority of a registered tax return preparer to practice before the IRS is generally limited to preparing returns, refund claims and other documents for submission to the IRS after passing a written competency exam and obtaining a valid Preparer Tax Identification Number (PTIN).

PTIN required starting January 1, 2011. Under the final PTIN regulations issued on September 28, 2010 (T.D. 9501, 2010-46 IRB 651), anyone paid to prepare all or substantially all of a return must obtain a PTIN using the online application system at www.irs.gov/taxpros or by applying on Form W-12. The PTIN must be provided on all returns or refund claims filed after December 31, 2010. If a PTIN was obtained before September 28, 2010, the preparer must re-register using the new online system or Form W-12. The PTIN requirement applies to all paid preparers, including attorneys, certified public accountants, and enrolled agents. A $64.25 fee must be paid with the PTIN request.

IRS establishes the Return Preparer Office. The newly established Return Preparer Office is responsible for managing the PTIN registration system for paid preparers, as well as managing the competency testing and continuing education that will be required of all paid preparers. The IRS had not finalized the testing and annual continuing education requirements when this book went to press. To ease the transition to the new rules, the IRS announced that newly registered tax return preparers will not have to take continuing education courses in 2011. The testing requirements are expected to take effect in July 2011. See the e-Supplement at jklasser.com for an update, if any on the testing and continuing education requirements.

Office of Professional Responsibility (OPR). The Office of Professional Responsibility (OPR) enforces the Circular 230 standards of practice. OPR also administers the enrolled agent examination and applications to become an enrolled agent.

OPR may censure, suspend or disbar practitioners from practice before the IRS for willful violation of the Circular 230 rules or for reckless/grossly incompetent violations of the rules in Sections 10.34–10.37 covering tax return positions, tax shelter opinions and other written advice (Reg. §10.52 of Circular 230).

Proposed Regulations for Registered Tax Return Preparers

Proposed amendments to Circular 230 issued in August 2010 provide rules for registered tax return preparers (REG-138637-07, 2010-44 IRB 581). The proposals would generally take effect 60 days after the date that final regulations are published in the Federal Register.

The Return Preparer Office may designate an individual as a registered tax return preparer if he or she has a valid PTIN and passes a written minimum competency examination, provided the applicant has not engaged in disreputable conduct (Proposed Reg. Sections 10.3 (f), 10.4 (c)). The proposals do not provide details on the competency testing requirements, which are still being developed by the IRS. The IRS in the Preamble to the proposals states that initially there will be an examination covering wage and non-business income Form 1040 series returns, and another examination covering wage and small business income Form 1040 series returns.

A registered tax return preparer may prepare or assist in preparing all or substantially of a tax return or refund claim for which the preparer has passed the requisite competency examination, and may sign such returns. If the IRS questions a return signed by a registered tax return preparer, the registered tax return preparer may represent the taxpayer before revenue agents, customer service representatives or other IRS employees at the examination level. However, unless the IRS provides otherwise, a registered tax return preparer may not represent the taxpayer before appeals officers, IRS counsel or similar appeals level IRS officers (Proposed Reg. Section 10.3 (f) (2)).

A registered tax return preparer will be subject to the same Circular 230 obligations and restrictions as attorneys, certified public accountants, and enrolled agents (Proposed Reg. Section 10.3 (f) (3)).

Designation as a registered tax return preparer will be subject to periodic renewal. As a condition of renewal, continuing education requirements will have to be met. Under Proposed Regulation 10.6, a registered tax return preparer will have to complete at least 15 hours of continuing education during each registration year, including two hours of ethics, three hours of Federal tax law updates and 10 hours of Federal tax law topics.

Note: When this book went to press, the IRS was considering critical comments from tax professionals concerning the proposals for registered tax return preparers, including calls for exemptions from the testing and continuing education requirements for non-signing staff. IRS officials have indicated that exemptions may be provided for employees who work under the supervision of an accountant, attorney or enrolled agent.

To ease practitioners into the new program, the IRS announced that newly registered tax return preparers will not have to take continuing education courses in 2011. The testing requirements are expected to take effect in July 2011. See the e-Supplement at jklasser.com for an update, if any on the testing and continuing education requirements.

Attorneys, CPAs, Enrolled Agents, Enrolled Retirement Plan Agents, and Enrolled Actuaries File a Power of Attorney and Declaration

If you are an attorney in good standing, a certified public accountant, or enrolled agent, you may practice before the IRS by submitting a properly completed Form 2848 signed by your client, which serves as a power of attorney and as your declaration that you are currently qualified to practice under Circular 230 and that you are authorized to represent the taxpayer in the tax matters specified on Form 2848 (Reg. §10.3, Circular 230). The IRS will accept a power of attorney document other than Form 2848, but it cannot be processed for inclusion on the IRS's centralized computer database (CAF system) unless it is attached to a completed transmittal Form 2848.

Enrolled actuary. If you are enrolled as an actuary by the Joint Board for the Enrollment of Actuaries, you may practice before the IRS with respect to issues involving specified statutory provisions (such as those related to qualified employee plans). You must have a power of attorney and file a declaration attesting to your enrolled actuary status. Form 2848 can satisfy both requirements (Reg. §10.3(d), Circular 230).

Enrolled retirement plan agent. Individuals who pass a written examination and thereby demonstrate special competence in qualified retirement plan matters may practice before the IRS with respect to such issues as enrolled retirement agents (Reg. §§10.3(e), 10.4(b), Circular 230).

Enrolled Agents

Individuals other than attorneys and certified public accountants must demonstrate technical competence in tax matters before an application for enrollment to practice before the IRS may be filed (Reg. §§10.4(a), Circular 230). A special enrollment examination (SEE; *see* below) must be taken, except for certain former IRS employees who may apply for enrollment without examination, as discussed below.

Special Enrollment Examination (SEE). The test for individuals who want to become Enrolled Agents, the Special Enrollment Examination, is now administered by a private company, Thomson Prometric. An information bulletin on all aspects of the examination, including study materials, registration, scheduling, and fees, is at Thomson Prometric's website, *www.prometric.com/irs.*

Former IRS employees. You may be admitted to practice before the IRS without taking the SEE if you apply for enrollment within three years from the date you separated from service with the IRS. You generally must have had at least five years of continuous service with the IRS, and, during those five years, you must have been engaged in applying and interpreting the provisions of the Internal Revenue Code and regulations. The permission to practice may, at the discretion of the IRS, be limited to certain areas (Reg. §10.4(c), Circular 230).

Application for enrollment. After passing the SEE or if you are an eligible former IRS employee, you must apply for enrollment on Form 23 (Reg. §10.5(a) of Circular 230). A nonrefundable fee must be paid to the IRS with Form 23. In the process of evaluating your application, the IRS Office of Professional Responsibility (OPR) will conduct a background check that includes your record of tax compliance.

Upon receipt of a properly executed application, the Office of Professional Responsibility may grant you temporary recognition to practice pending a determination as to whether permanent enrollment should be granted (Reg. §10.5(d)).

If your application is denied, you will be informed of the reasons for the denial by the Director of the Office of Professional Responsibility. You may then, within 30 days after receipt of the notice of denial, file a written notice of appeal, together with supporting reasons, to the Secretary of the Treasury or the Secretary's delegate (Reg. §10.5(e), Circular 230).

Upon enrollment, you will be issued an enrollment card that is valid for three years before enrollment must be renewed.

Renewing enrollment. IRS rules require enrolled agents to renew enrollment status every three years on Form 8554. Tax-related courses must be completed as a requirement for renewal. A minimum of 16 hours of continuing education credit generally must be completed every year and a minimum of 72 hours during each three-year cycle (Reg. §10.6(e), Circular 230). Qualifying courses include tax or tax-related courses such as accounting or tax-preparation software. For enrolled retirement plan agents, courses must relate to qualified retirement plan matters. Writing articles or teaching courses are given credit toward the minimum education requirement (Reg. §10.6(f), Circular 230).

The Office of Professional Responsibility staggers renewals. The expiration date for enrolled agents depends on the last digit of the enrolled agent's Social Security number (Form 8554; Reg. §10.6(d), Circular 230). A user fee must be paid with Form 8554.

Changes to renewal periods and continuing education requirements are posted on the Enrolled Agents page of the IRS website at *www.irs.gov/taxpros/agents/index.html.*

Limited Practice in Special Cases

Even if you are not authorized to practice before the IRS, you may represent yourself or members of your immediate family provided you have their authorization. You may also represent a taxpayer in the following cases where you have authorization: (1) You represent your regular full-time employer or a partnership in which you are a partner or full-time employee. (2) You are an officer or regular full-time employee representing a corporation, trust, estate, association, or organized group. (3) You are a fiduciary or full-time employee, representing your trust, receivership, guardianship, or estate. (4) You are an officer or regular employee in the course of your official business, representing a governmental unit, agency, or authority. (5) You are serving as representative outside of the United States before personnel of the IRS (Reg. §10.7, Circular 230).

Under Proposed Regulation 10.8 (a), an individual who is not authorized to practice before the IRS and who prepares less than substantially all of a return or refund claim may appear as a witness for the taxpayer or furnish information requested by the IRS.

The Director of the Office of Professional Responsibility may also authorize any person to represent another without enrollment for the purpose of a particular matter.

Standards for Signing Returns and Advising Clients on Tax Return Positions

The practice standards under Section 10.34 of the Circular 230 regulations have historically been linked with the penalty standards for return preparers under Code Section 6694. Since the revision of the Section 6694 preparer penalties by the Emergency Economic Stabilization Act of 2008, the IRS has been considering whether new Section 10.34 guidelines should mirror the Section 6694 standards. The 2008 Act lowered the threshold for avoiding the first-tier penalty for undisclosed positions to "substantial authority" (Code Section 6694(a) (2) (A)), except in the case of positions related to a tax shelter or reportable transaction, which must meet a "more likely than not correct" test (Code Section 6694(a) (2) (C)). Further details on the preparer penalty rules are discussed below on page 938.

Proposed Section 10.34 standards. The IRS has proposed new Section 10.34 guidelines that generally are consistent with the penalty standards for tax return preparers in Code Section 6694 while also providing broader professional ethics standards. As proposed, the amendments will apply to returns and refund claims filed, or advice provided, 60 days after the date that final regulations are published in the Federal Register.

Signing returns. Under Proposed Regulation 10.34(a) (1) (i), a practitioner may not willfully, recklessly, or through gross incompetence sign a tax return or refund claim that he or she knows or reasonably should know contains a position that either (1) lacks a reasonable basis, (2) is unreasonable under the Code Section 6694 (a) (2) penalty rules, or (3) is a willful attempt by the practitioner to understate tax liability or intentionally disregard IRS rules under the penalty rules of Code Section 6694 (b) (2). The IRS will take into account a practitioner's pattern of conduct in determining whether the practitioner has acted willfully, recklessly or through gross incompetence.

Advice on tax return positions. The proposed standards for client advice mirror the above proposal for signing returns. Proposed Regulation 10.34(a) (1) (ii) provides that a practitioner may not willfully, recklessly, or through gross incompetence advise a client to take a position on a tax return that either (1) lacks a reasonable basis, (2) is unreasonable under the Code Section 6694 (a) (2) penalty rules, or (3) is a willful attempt by the practitioner to understate tax liability or intentionally disregard IRS rules under the penalty rules of Code Section 6694 (b) (2). Similarly, the practitioner may not willfully, recklessly, or through gross incompetence prepare a portion of a return that contains such a position.

Differences with preparer penalty standards. Note that the proposals subject a practitioner to discipline under Proposed Regulation 10.34 (a) only after willful, reckless, or grossly incompetent conduct, whereas a preparer penalty under Code Section 6694 may be imposed without such a showing. Thus, an assessment of a penalty under Code Section 6694 does not automatically lead to sanction under Section 10.34 (a). However, a practitioner may be subject to discipline under Proposed Regulation 10.34 (a) for a position taken on a return even if other positions on the return eliminate any tax understatement, whereas a preparer penalty must be abated (Code Section 6694 (d)) if there is a final determination that the taxpayer did not understate tax liability.

Covered Opinions and Other Written Advice

Detailed requirements must be met for so-called "covered" opinions under Regulation §10.35, Circular 230. The requirements spell out standards for making factual and legal assumptions and conclusions as to the likelihood that the taxpayer will prevail on the merits.

A covered opinion is any written (including electronic) advice concerning (1) transactions that are or are similar to tax avoidance or evasion transactions that have been identified as "listed" transactions by the IRS; (2) any arrangement that has as its principal purpose the avoidance or evasion of tax; or (3) any arrangement that has tax avoidance or evasion as a significant purpose where the written advice is a reliance opinion, a marketed opinion, subject to conditions of confidentiality, or subject to contractual protection.

A reliance opinion is written advice that concludes that there is a greater than 50% likelihood (more-likely-than-not test) that one or more significant federal tax issues would be resolved in the taxpayer's favor. The advice is excluded from the category of reliance opinions if there is a prominent disclaimer that the advice cannot be relied upon by the taxpayer as protection against IRS penalties. This disclaimer option is available only if the advice does not concern listed transactions or those with a principal purpose of avoiding/evading tax.

Although practitioners may be uncomfortable in informing clients that they may not rely on their advice for penalty protection, the high costs required to comply with the requirements of Section 10.35 for reliance opinions means that such opinions will be infrequently provided. As an alternative to providing such expensive opinions, practitioners have responded to the new regulations by routinely including the disclaimer language in written communications.

The same type of disclaimer can also be used to avoid marketed opinion treatment for advice that the practitioner knows (or has reason to know) will be used to promote an investment plan or arrangement.

Advice that limits disclosure to protect the confidentiality of the practitioner's tax strategies is treated as a covered opinion. A claim that a transaction is proprietary or exclusive is not treated as a limitation on disclosure if all of the recipients of the advice are told that there is no limitation on disclosure.

If the practitioner's fee is contingent on the taxpayer's realization of tax benefits, or if the fee is fully or partially refundable if all or some of the intended tax consequences addressed in the advice are not sustained, the advice is subject to the covered opinion requirements.

For further details on the covered opinion requirements, *see* Reg. §10.35.

Other written advice. Written advice that is not a covered opinion is subject to the requirements of Regulation 10.37. Advice must not be given if it is based on unreasonable factual or legal assumptions, if the practitioner does not take into account all relevant facts that he or she knows or should know, or the practitioner has unreasonably relied on statements, findings or agreements of the taxpayer or any other person. The advice also should not be given if in evaluating a tax issue, the practitioner takes into account the possibility that the issue will be settled or not raised on audit, or that the taxpayer's return will not be audited.

Advertising and Solicitation

Solicitation of employment in matters related to the IRS is prohibited if the solicitation violates a federal or state rule. Fee information may be communicated in professional lists, telephone directories, print media, radio and television, and certain mailings. In describing their professional designation, practitioners may not use the term "certified" or imply an employer/employee relationship with the IRS. Details on solicitation and advertising restrictions are in Regulation §10.30 of Circular 230.

Contingent Fees

A contingency fee may be charged for services rendered in connection with an IRS examination of, or challenge to, an original return, or an amended return or refund claim filed within 120 days of receiving from the IRS written notice of the examination or challenge. A contingency fee may also be charged in connection with reviews of interest and penalty assessments, and services connected with tax-related judicial proceedings (Reg. §10.27, Circular 230).

Sanctions

Any attorney, certified public accountant, enrolled agent, enrolled retirement plan agent, or enrolled actuary may be censured (publicly reprimanded), disbarred, or suspended from practice before the IRS for incompetence, willfully violating any of the practice regulations or engaging in "disreputable" conduct such as giving false or misleading information to the IRS, or by permitting a client to do so (Reg. §10.50, Circular 230). Under Proposed Regulation 10.51, sanctions may be imposed for willfully preparing or signing a return without having a valid PTIN.

A violation of the Section 10.34 rules on tax return positions, or the rules of Sections 10.35-10.37 on covered opinions and other written advice, are subject to sanction if the violation results from willfulness, recklessness, or gross incompetence (Reg. §10.52, Circular 230).

A monetary penalty may be imposed in addition to or in lieu of any suspension, censure, or disbarment. The amount may be up to the gross income derived (or to be derived) from the conduct giving rise to the penalty. A separate monetary penalty may be imposed on the employer of an offending practitioner, or firm on whose behalf the practitioner was acting, if the employer or firm knew or reasonably should have known of the practitioner's conduct (Reg. §10.50(c), Circular 230).

Further, Code Section 6701 allows a $1,000 penalty ($10,000 with respect to corporate returns) to be imposed on a representative who presents a return or other document (such as an affidavit) at an IRS examination knowing that it understates tax.

Practice by Former Government Employees

If you are a former government employee, you may not represent a client in a matter on which you previously worked as a government employee (Reg. §10.25(b)(2)). The matter may have involved a decision, a finding, a letter ruling, technical advice, or approval or disapproval of a contract. You are considered to have participated in a matter if you were substantially involved in making decisions, or if you prepared or reviewed documents (with or without the right to exercise a judgment of approval or disapproval), participated in conferences or investigations, or gave substantial advice.

Where you had official responsibilities for a particular matter within a period of one year before you left government service, you may not within two years after your government employment ended represent or assist in that matter any person who is or was a specific party to that matter (Reg. §10.25(b)(3)).

Within one year after leaving government service, you may not appear before, or communicate with the intent to influence, the IRS in a matter involving the publication, withdrawal, amendment, modification, or interpretation of a rule if you participated in its development or, within a period of one year prior to the termination of your government employment, you had official responsibility for the rule. However, you may appear on your own behalf or represent a client in a transaction involving the application or interpretation of the rule provided you do not use or disclose any confidential information you acquired in the development of the rule. A rule includes Treasury Regulations, whether issued or under preparation for issuance as Notices of Proposed Rule Making or as Treasury Decisions, and revenue rulings and revenue procedures published in the Internal Revenue Bulletin (Reg. §10.25(b)(4), Circular 230).

Firm representation. A firm of which you are a member may not represent or knowingly assist a person who was or is a specific party in any particular matter in which you participated as a government employee, unless the firm isolates you in such a way that you do not assist in the representation. Similarly, if you had official responsibility for the matter, no member of your firm may represent or knowingly assist a person who was or is a specific party in that matter, unless you are isolated in such a way that you do not assist in the representation. You and another member of your firm acting on behalf of your firm must sign a statement under oath that you will be isolated from participating in the transaction, and the statement must be provided by the firm, upon request, to the Director of the Office of Professional Responsibility (Reg. §10.25(c), Circular 230).

Tax Information Authorization

If you do not file a power of attorney, you have to file a tax information authorization in order to receive certain confidential tax information of your client, such as the tax return, and to receive certain information, such as the IRS's position towards his or her liability. The tax information authorization is signed by the taxpayer and specifies the particular authorization given. IRS Form 8821 may be used. The authorization only includes the right to receive information and does not allow you to represent the taxpayer before the IRS.

No tax information authorization is required where: (1) a power of attorney has already been filed for the same matter, or (2) the taxpayer is present, such as at a conference, when the information is divulged, or (3) the receipt of notices and other matters are not of a confidential nature.

TAX RETURN PREPARER PENALTIES

Preparers are subject to penalties for negligent or fraudulent preparation of returns and for violation of specific disclosure and record requirements. Therefore, the rules discussed in this chapter deserve careful consideration by all tax practitioners.

PTIN required starting January 1, 2011. Under final regulations issued on September 28, 2010 (T.D. 9501, 2010-46 IRB 651), all preparers who are compensated for preparing all or substantially all of a return must obtain a Preparer Tax Identification Number (PTIN) using the online application system at www.irs.gov/taxpros or by applying on Form W-12. The PTIN must be provided on all returns or refund claims filed after December 31, 2010. A paid preparer may no longer enter his or her Social Security number in lieu of a PTIN on a return filed after 2010.

The PTIN requirement applies to all paid preparers, including attorneys, certified public accountants, and enrolled agents. A $64.25 fee must be paid with the PTIN application.

A practitioner who obtained a PTIN before September 28, 2010 (effective date of the PTIN regulations) must re-register for a PTIN using the new online system or Form W-12. Generally, a prior PTIN holder will be reassigned his or her same number.

Who Is a Preparer?

Anyone who prepares or employs another to prepare all or a substantial part of any income tax return or refund claim for compensation is considered a tax return preparer (IRC §7701(a)(36)(A)).

A person may be considered a preparer regardless of educational qualifications or professional status (Reg. §301.7701-15(d)). But an IRS employee performing his or her official duties is not considered an income tax preparer (Reg. §301.7701-15(f)(1)).

You are not a preparer if you perform only the following services (Reg. §301.7701-15(f)):

- Merely type or reproduce returns; or
- Prepare a return or refund claim for your employer, an officer of your employer, a fellow employee, or a general partner in a partnership in which you are a general partner or an employee. An employee of a subsidiary corporation is also considered an employee of the parent corporation; or
- Prepare a return as fiduciary; or
- Prepare a claim for refund in response to a notice of deficiency issued to the taxpayer or a waiver of restriction after initiation of an audit of the taxpayer or another taxpayer, or a determination whether the audit of that other taxpayer affects the liability of the taxpayer for tax.
- Prepare a return for a friend, a relative, or neighbor with no implicit or explicit agreement for compensation, even though you receive a gift or return service or favor.

Signing and nonsigning preparers. Final regulations provide separate definitions for signing and nonsigning preparers. A signing preparer is the individual preparer with primary responsibility for the overall substantive accuracy of the return or refund claim (Reg. §301.7701-15 (b)(1)). A nonsigning preparer is a preparer other than a signing preparer who prepares all or a *substantial portion* (discussed below) of a return or refund claim with respect to events that have occurred at the time the advice is given. A preparer who provides written or oral advice to a taxpayer or other preparer is a nonsigning preparer where the advice leads to a position or entry that is a substantial portion of the return (Reg. §301.7701-15 (b)(2)). If you provide advice with respect to a proposed transaction but do not provide advice after it is completed, you are not considered a preparer because the advice was not rendered with respect to events that have occurred. Time spent on advice given after events occur may be ignored in determining whether a person is a nonsigning preparer if such time is less than 5% of the time spent providing advice on a position, but there is an anti-abuse exception to this rule (Reg. §301.7701-15 (b)(2)).

Substantial portion. Only a person who prepares all or a substantial portion of a return or refund claim is considered to be a preparer of the return or claim. You are considered the preparer of an entry on a return or refund claim if you rendered advice that is directly relevant to the determination of the existence, characterization, or amount of that entry (Reg. §301.7701-15 (b)(3)). Whether the entry is a substantial portion of the return or refund claim depends on whether you knew or reasonably should have known that the tax attributable to the schedule, entry or other portion is a substantial portion of the tax required to be shown on the return or refund claim. The IRS will take into account the size and complexity of the item relative to the taxpayer's gross income and the size of the understatement attributable to the item compared to the tax liability reported by the taxpayer.

A *de minimis* rule may apply to a person who otherwise would be considered a nonsigning preparer. A schedule, entry or other portion is not considered a substantial portion if it involves gross income, deductions, or amounts on which credits are based that are either (1) less than $10,000, or (2) less than $400,000 and also less than 20% of a taxpayer's adjusted gross income, or for non-individual taxpayers, 20% of the gross income shown on the return or refund claim. Where more than one schedule or other portion is involved, the amounts are aggregated (Reg. §301.7701-15(b)(3)(ii)).

Example:

You prepare for a taxpayer a Schedule B (Form 1040) that reports $4,000 in dividend income and also give advice about Schedule A that results in a claimed medical expense deduction of $5,000. You do not sign the return. You are not considered a nonsigning preparer under the *de minimis* rule because the total amount of the deductions are less than $10,000.

Even though entries on a return you prepare affect entries on the return of another taxpayer, you are not the preparer of the other return, unless the entries on the return you prepared are directly reflected on that other return and constitute a substantial portion of that return. For example, if you prepare a partnership return, you are not the preparer of a partner's return, unless the entries on the partnership return reportable on the partner's return constitute a *substantial portion* (as discussed above) of the return (Reg. §301.7701-15(b)(3)(iii)).

Preparer Penalties for Understatements of Taxpayer Liability

Section 6694 penalties. There is a "first-tier" penalty under Code Section 6694(a) for understatements due to unreasonable positions and a "second-tier" penalty for willful or reckless conduct under Code Section 6694(b). Effective for returns prepared after May 25, 2007, these penalties, previously applicable only to income tax return preparers, apply also to preparers of estate and gift tax, employment tax, and excise tax returns, and returns of exempt organizations.

If there is a signing preparer (discussed above) within a firm, he or she is generally considered the person primarily responsible for all of the positions on the return or refund claim giving rise to an understatement of liability, and thus is subject to a penalty under Section 6694. However, if the IRS concludes based on credible information that a nonsigning preparer (discussed above) within the same firm is primarily responsible for a position giving rise to an understatement, that nonsigning partner is subject to the Section 6694 penalty (Reg. §1.6694-1(b)(2)). If the IRS finds that both a signing and nonsigning preparer within a firm are responsible for a position giving rise to an understatement, the IRS will determine which of them is primarily responsible and the Section 6694 penalty will be assessed only against that primarily responsible preparer (Reg. §1.6694-1(b)(4)).

If preparers from different firms provide advice with respect to a position that gives rise to an understatement, and the IRS determines that both are primarily responsible for the position, both can be penalized (Reg. §1.6694-1(b)(1)). A firm that employs a preparer who is subject to a penalty under Section 6694 may also be subject to a penalty if the management participated in or knew about the conduct giving rise to the penalty or procedures for reviewing return positions were not provided or were willfully or recklessly disregarded (Regs. §§1.6694-2(a)(2) and 1.6694-3(a)(2)).

The maximum first-tier and second tier Section 6694 penalties are based on 50% of the compensation that the preparer receives or expects to receive with respect to the position on the return or refund claim that gave rise to the understatement (Reg. §1.6694-1(a)(1)). For purposes of calculating the penalties, only compensation for tax advice that is given with respect to events that have occurred at the time the advice is rendered and that relates to the position giving rise to the understatement is taken into account (Reg. §1.6694-1(f)(2)(ii)).

First-tier penalty. The amount of the first-tier penalty (Code Section 6694 (a)) is the greater of $1,000 or 50% of the return preparer's compensation (as discussed above). Under the Emergency Economic Stabilization Act of 2008 (P.L. 110-343, 10/3/08), the first-tier penalty applies to a preparer who knew or reasonably should have known of an "unreasonable" position to which an understatement of liability is due. An undisclosed position that is not attributable to a tax shelter or reportable transaction is unreasonable unless there was substantial authority for the position taken on the return (Code Section 6694(a)(2) (A)). A disclosed position that is not attributable to a tax shelter or reportable transaction is unreasonable unless there was a reasonable basis for it (Code Section 6694(a)(2) (B)). However, for positions relating to tax shelters and reportable transactions, whether or not disclosed, the penalty applies unless the preparer had a reasonable belief that the position would more likely than not be sustained on its merits (Code Section 6694(a)(2) (C)). There is an exception to the penalty if the preparer acted in good faith and can show reasonable cause for the understatement (Code Section 6694 (a) (3)). The 2008 Act amendments generally apply retroactively to returns prepared after May 25, 2007, but the provision for tax shelter and reportable transaction positions applies to returns prepared for taxable years ending after October 3, 2008.

Final regulations applicable to returns and refund claims filed after 2008 (T.D. 9436, 2009-3 IRB 268) did not provide substantive guidance with respect to the "substantial authority" standard but interim guidance was provided in Notice 2009-5 (2009-3 IRB 309). Under Notice 2009-5, the "substantial authority" rules of Section 6662 (accuracy-related penalty for taxpayers) apply for purposes of the Section 6694(a) preparer penalty until more formal guidance is released. Notice 2009-5 also provides interim compliance rules for tax shelter transactions. Until further guidance is issued, a position with respect to a tax shelter will not be deemed unreasonable if there was substantial authority for the position and the preparer advises the taxpayer in writing that if the position is deemed to have a significant purpose of tax avoidance or evasion, the taxpayer will be subject to a penalty under Section 6662 unless the taxpayer has a reasonable belief that the tax treatment was more likely than not correct. At the time this book went to press, the interim guidance in Notice 2009-5 was still in effect.

Second-tier penalty. The second-tier penalty of Code Section 6694(b) applies where an understatement of tax liability is willful, or due to reckless disregard of IRS rules. The second-tier penalty is the greater of $5,000 or 50% of the preparer's compensation (as discussed above). The penalty is reduced by the amount of any first-tier penalty (Code Section 6694(a)) paid with respect to the return.

Aiding and abetting understatements. In lieu of a penalty under section 6694(a) or 6694(b), the IRS may impose on a preparer a $1,000 penalty ($10,000 for corporate returns) for aiding and abetting the willful understatement of tax liability on a tax return or other document (IRC §6701).

The $1,000/$10,000 penalty may be imposed on a person who knows *or* has "reason to believe" that a return or document that he or she has helped prepare will be used in connection with tax matters. A supervisor who does not actually prepare a return or document is subject to the penalty if he or she orders or causes a subordinate to take actions subject to the penalty, or if the supervisor knows of such an act by a subordinate but does not attempt to prevent it.

Preparer Penalties for Not Meeting Disclosure and Record-Keeping Requirements

Under Code Section 6695, preparers may be penalized for failure to satisfy recordkeeping or disclosure requirements or not providing required information when preparing returns. The Section 6695 penalties, previously applicable only to income tax return preparers, to all other return preparers (estate and gift, employment and excise tax returns, and returns of exempt organizations), effective for returns prepared after May 25, 2007.

Failure to retain records on preparers. A person who employs one or more signing preparers must retain a record of the name, Social Security number, and place of work of each employed preparer (IRC §6060). The records must be retained for a three-year period following the close of the return period (defined as a 12-month period beginning on July 1 of each year), and the records must be made available for inspection upon request by the IRS (Reg. §1.6060-1(a)). There is a $50 penalty for each failure to retain and make available a proper record and $50 for each required item that is missing from the record. The maximum penalty for any return period is $25,000 (IRC §6695(e)). Showing reasonable cause may avoid the penalty.

Failure to sign returns. For a return or refund claim that is not electronically signed, a preparer considered to be a signing preparer must sign the return or claim after it is completed and before it is presented to the taxpayer for signature (Reg. §1.6695-1(b)(1)). If more than one person worked on the return, the person primarily responsible for the overall accuracy of the return (Reg. §301.7701-15(b)(1)) must sign the return in order to avoid a penalty.

The information on an electronically signed return must be provided to the taxpayer contemporaneously with furnishing Form 8879 (IRS e-file Signature Authorization)(Reg. §1.6695-1(b)(2)).

The penalty for failing to sign is $50 for each return unless reasonable cause is shown; the maximum penalty is $25,000 for returns filed during any calendar year (Reg. §1.6695-1(b)(3)). If the preparer required to sign is unavailable to sign the return, another preparer must so advise the client, review the entire preparation of the return or claim, and then sign it (Reg. §1.6695-1(b)(1)).

Failure to furnish identification number. A preparer considered to be a signing preparer (discussed above) is subject to a $50 penalty for not including an identification number on a return or refund claim unless reasonable cause is shown. The maximum penalty with respect to each calendar year is $25,000 (Reg. §1.6695-1(c)). As discussed earlier, final regulations require all paid preparers to obtain a PTIN and enter it on the returns or refund claims filed after December 31, 2010 (T.D. 9501, 2010-46 IRB 651). For returns filed before January 1, 2010, the identification number of a paid preparer is either the preparer's Social Security number or PTIN.

Failure to furnish client with copy of return or refund claim. A preparer considered to be a signing preparer (discussed above) must furnish a completed copy of the return or refund claim to the taxpayer no later than when it is presented to the taxpayer for signature (Reg. §1.6107-1 (a)(1)). The copy may be provided in any media, including electronic media, that is acceptable to both the taxpayer and the preparer (Reg. §1.6107-1 (a)(2)). Where two or more persons are considered preparers with respect to the same return, and there is an employment relationship between them, the employer is responsible for furnishing the copy; where there is a partnership relationship, the partnership must furnish the copy (Reg. §1.6107-1(c)).

Failure to furnish a copy results in a penalty of $50 for each failure, unless it can be shown that failure was due to reasonable cause and not due to willful neglect (Reg. §1.6695-1(a)(1)). There is a $25,000 maximum penalty per calendar year.

The preparer may request a receipt as proof of having satisfied this requirement (Reg. §1.6107-1(a)(1)).

Failure to retain copy or list. A signing preparer (see above) must keep for three years and make available for IRS inspection copies of all returns and refund claims he or she prepares or a list of the taxpayers for whom returns were prepared, including each name, taxpayer identification number, taxable year of the taxpayer for whom the return or refund claim was prepared, and the type of return or refund claim prepared (Reg. §1.6107-1(b)). A $50 penalty may be imposed for each failure, with a maximum penalty of $25,000 for each return period (Reg. §1.6695-1(d)).

Where there is an employment relationship or a partnership relationship between two or more preparers, the employer must retain the required records, and in the case of a partnership arrangement, the partnership must keep the records (Reg. §1.6107-1(c)).

If the preparer is a corporation or partnership that goes out of business before the end of the three-year period, the person who is responsible for winding up the affairs of the corporation or partnership under state law must retain the records until the three-year period ends. If state law does not specify who is responsible for winding up, the directors or general partners are subject to the record-retention rules. These individuals will be jointly and severally liable for the $50 penalty for each failure to retain records, up to the maximum penalty of $25,000 per return period (Reg. §1.6107-1(b)(2)).

Negotiation of refund checks prohibited. A preparer is subject to a $500 penalty for each endorsement or negotiation of a refund check resulting from a return that he or she prepared (IRC §6695(f)). However, the penalty does not apply to a preparer-bank where the full amount of the refund check is deposited to the taxpayer's account (Reg. §1.6695-1(f)(2)).

If the preparer obtains authorization from the taxpayer to affix the taxpayer's name to a refund check for the purpose of depositing it in the taxpayer's account, or in an account held jointly with anyone excluding the preparer, the penalty does not apply (Reg. §1.6695-1 (f) (1)).

Preparer Penalty Assessment Procedures

Penalties under IRC §6694(a) for understatements of tax or the penalties under IRC §6695 for failure to meet the disclosure and record-keeping requirements, must be assessed within three years after a return or refund claim is filed; no court proceeding for collection of the penalty without assessment may be begun after the three-year period. Penalties for willful or reckless understatements of tax liability under IRC §6694(b) may be assessed, or court proceedings for collection without assessment may begin, at any time (IRC §6696(d)(1)).

The IRS will issue a preparer a 30-day letter notifying the preparer of a proposed penalty and offering an opportunity to pursue administrative remedies prior to assessment of a penalty under Section 6694(a) or (b). If the preparer appeals an IRS penalty determination, the IRS cannot assess the penalties until after a final determination adverse to the taxpayer is made (Reg. §1.6694-4(a)(2)).

If a penalty for understatement of tax (either Section 6694(a) or (b)) is assessed and the preparer does not pursue an administrative remedy or pursues such a remedy but receives an adverse final administrative determination from the IRS, the preparer has two alternatives (Reg. §1.6694-4(a)(4)):

1. Pay the entire amount assessed and file a claim for refund of the amount paid not later than three years from the date the penalty is paid, which if denied may be appealed in court; or
2. Pay 15% or more of the penalty within 30 days of the IRS's statement of notice and demand for payment and file a claim for refund of the amount paid within the same 30-day period. Form 6118 is used to claim the refund.

If under alternative (2) a preparer timely pays at least 15% of the penalty and files a refund claim, the IRS has six months to act on the claim. During that period, the IRS may not seek collection of the remaining 85% of the penalty (Reg. §1.6694-4(a)(5)). If the IRS denies the refund claim, the preparer may bring an action for refund in a federal district court within 30 days of the date of denial. The action must be brought within the 30-day period to postpone or avoid collection measures by the IRS as to the remaining 85% of the penalty under the second alternative above. If the IRS does not deny a claim for refund by the end of six months after the claim is made, the preparer may bring an action in federal district court within 30 days after the expiration of the six-month period. If such an action is not brought, the IRS may pursue collection of the remaining 85% of the penalty (Reg. §1.6694-4(b)). If such an action is brought, the IRS may counterclaim for the balance of the penalty (Reg. §1.6694-4(a)(6)).

IRS May Seek Injunction Against Preparer

The IRS may seek an injunction in a federal district court to prohibit improper conduct by any tax return preparer (IRC §7407). An injunction may be sought regardless of whether penalties have been or may be assessed against the preparer. An injunction may be issued where the court finds that the preparer has:

- Engaged in conduct subject to the disclosure requirement penalties or the understatement of taxpayer liability penalties;
- Engaged in conduct subject to criminal penalties under the Internal Revenue Code;
- Misrepresented his or her eligibility to practice before the IRS or his or her experience or education as a tax return preparer;
- Guaranteed payment of any tax refund or the allowance of any tax credit; or
- Engaged in other fraudulent or deceptive conduct that interferes with administration of the tax laws.

A court may also enjoin the person from acting as a preparer if it finds that the person has repeatedly engaged in any of the above practices and an injunction prohibiting specified conduct would not be sufficient (IRC §7407(b)).

A

Accelerated cost recovery system (ACRS). A statutory method of depreciation allowing accelerated rates for most types of property used in business and income-producing activities during the years 1981 through 1986. It has been superseded by the modified accelerated cost recovery system (MACRS) for assets placed in service after 1986; *see* *42.4* and *42.11*.

Accelerated depreciation. Depreciation methods that allow faster write-offs than straight-line rates in the earlier periods of the useful life of an asset. For example, in the first few years of recovery, MACRS allows a 200% double declining balance write-off, twice the straight-line rate; *see* *42.5–42.8*.

Accountable reimbursement plan. An employer reimbursement or allowance arrangement that requires you to adequately substantiate business expenses to your employer, and to return any excess reimbursement; *see* *20.31*.

Accrual method of accounting. A business method of accounting requiring income to be reported when earned and expenses to be deducted when incurred. However, deductions generally may not be claimed until economic performance has occurred; *see* *40.3*.

Acquisition debt. Debt used to buy, build, or construct a principal residence or second home and that generally qualifies for a full interest expense deduction; *see* *15.2*.

Active participation. Test for determining deductibility of IRA deductions. Active participants in employer retirement plans are subject to IRA deduction phase-out rules if adjusted gross income exceeds certain thresholds; *see* *8.4*.

Adjusted basis. A statutory term describing the cost used to determine your profit or loss from a sale or exchange of property. It is generally your original cost, increased by capital improvements, and decreased by depreciation, depletion, and other capital write-offs; *see* *5.20*.

Adjusted gross income (AGI). Gross income less allowable adjustments, such as IRA, alimony, and Keogh deductions. AGI determines whether various tax benefits are phased out, such as personal exemptions, itemized deductions, and the rental loss allowance; *see* *12.1* and modified adjusted gross income (MAGI).

Alimony. Payments made to a separated or divorced spouse as required by a decree or agreement. Qualifying payments are deductible by the payor and taxable to the payee; *see* *Chapter 37*.

Alternative minimum tax (AMT). A tax triggered if certain tax benefits reduce your regular income tax below the tax computed on Form 6251 for AMT purposes; *see* *Chapter 23*.

Amended return. On Form 1040X, you may file an amended return within a three-year period to claim a refund or correct a mistake made on an original or previously amended return; *see* *Chapter 47*.

Amortizable bond premium. The additional amount paid over the face amount of an obligation that may be deducted under the rules in *4.17*.

Amortization of intangibles. Writing off an investment in intangible assets over the projected life of the assets; *see* *42.18*.

Amount realized. A statutory term used to figure your profit or loss on a sale or exchange. Generally, it is sales proceeds plus mortgages assumed or taken subject to, less transaction expenses, such as commissions and legal costs; *see* *5.14*.

Amount recognized. The amount of gain reportable and subject to tax. On certain tax-free exchanges of property, gain is not recognized in the year it is realized; *see* *6.1*.

Annualized rate. A rate for a period of less than a year computed as though for a full year.

Annuity. An annual payment of money by a company or individual to a person called the annuitant. Payment is for a fixed period or the life of the annuitant. Tax consequences depend on the type of contract and funding; *see* *7.23–7.29*.

Applicable federal rate. Interest rate fixed by the Treasury for determining imputed interest; *see* *4.30–4.32*.

Appreciation in value. Increase in value of property due to market conditions. When you sell appreciated property, you pay tax on the appreciation since the date of purchase. When you donate appreciated property held long term, you may generally deduct the appreciated value; *see* *14.6*.

Archer Medical Savings Account (MSA). A type of medical plan combining high deductible medical insurance protection with an IRA-type savings account fund to pay unreimbursed medical expenses; *see* *41.13*.

Assessment. The IRS action of fixing tax liability that sets in motion collection procedures, such as charging interest, imposing penalties, and, if necessary, seizing property; *see* *48.2*.

Assignment. The legal transfer of property, rights, or interest to another person called an assignee. You cannot avoid tax on income by assigning the income to another person.

At-risk rules. Rules limiting loss deductions to cash investments and personal liability notes. An exception for real estate treats certain nonrecourse commercial loans as amounts "at risk"; *see* *10.18*.

Audit. An IRS examination of your tax return, generally limited to a three-year period after you file; *see* *Chapter 48*.

Away from home. A tax requirement for deducting travel expenses on a business trip. Sleeping arrangements are required for at least one night before returning home; *see* *20.3* and *20.5–20.6*.

B

Balloon. A final payment on a loan in one lump sum.

Basis. Generally, the amount paid for property. You need to know your basis to figure gain or loss on a sale; *see* *5.16*.

Boot. Generally, the receipt of cash or its equivalent accompanying an exchange of property. In a tax-free exchange, boot is subject to immediate tax; *see* *6.3*.

C

Cancellation of debt. Release of a debt without consideration by a creditor. Cancellations of debt are generally taxable; *see 11.8.*

Capital. The excess of assets over liabilities.

Capital asset. Property subject to capital gain or loss treatment. Almost all assets you own are considered capital assets except for certain business assets or works you created; *see 5.2.*

Capital expenses. Costs that are not currently deductible and that are added to the basis of property. A capital expense generally increases the value of property. When added to depreciable property, the cost is deductible over the life of the asset.

Capital gain or loss. The difference between amount realized and adjusted basis on the sale or exchange of capital assets. Long-term capital gains are taxed favorably, as explained in *Chapter 5*. Capital losses are deducted first against capital gains, and then again up to $3,000 of other income; *see 5.1–5.5.*

Capital gain distribution. A mutual-fund distribution allocated to gains realized on the sale of fund portfolio assets. You report the distribution as long-term capital gain even if you held the fund shares short term; *see 32.4–32.5.*

Capital loss carryover. A capital loss that is not deductible because it exceeds the annual $3,000 capital loss ceiling. A carryover loss may be deducted from capital gains of later years plus up to $3,000 of ordinary income; *see 5.4.*

Capitalization. Adding a cost or expense to the basis of the property.

Carryback. A tax technique for receiving a refund of back taxes by applying a deduction or credit from a current tax year to a prior tax year. For example, a business net operating loss may be carried back for two years.

Carryforward. A tax technique of applying a loss or credit from a current year to a later year. For example, a business net operating loss may be carried forward 20 years instead of being carried back; *see 40.18.*

Cash method of accounting. Reporting income when actually or constructively received and deducting expenses when paid. Certain businesses may not use the cash method; *see 40.3.*

Casualty loss. Loss from an unforeseen and sudden event that is deductible, subject to a 10% income floor and an annual reduction (likely to be $500 for 2010) for personal losses; *see 18.1.*

Child and dependent care credit. A credit of up to 30% based on certain care expenses incurred to allow you to work; *see 25.4.*

Community income. Income earned by persons domiciled in community property states and treated as belonging equally to husband and wife; *see 1.6.*

Condemnation. The seizure of property by a public authority for a public purpose. Tax on gain realized on many conversions may be deferred; *see 18.19–18.20.*

Constructive receipt. A tax rule that taxes income that is not received by you but that you may draw upon; *see 2.2.*

Consumer interest. Interest incurred on personal debt and consumer credit. Consumer interest is not deductible.

Convention. Rule for determining MACRS depreciation in the year property is placed in service. Either a half-year convention or mid-quarter convention applies; *see 42.5–42.7.*

Coverdell Education Savings Account. A special account set up to fund education expenses of a student; *see 33.11–33.12.*

Credit. A tax credit directly reduces tax liability, as opposed to a deduction that reduces income subject to tax.

D

Declining balance method. A rapid depreciation method determined by a constant percentage based on useful life and applied to the adjusted basis of the property; *see 42.5 and 42.8.*

Deductions. Items directly reducing income. Personal deductions such as for mortgage interest, state and local taxes, and charitable contributions are allowed only if deductions are itemized on Schedule A, but deductions such as for alimony, capital losses, moving expenses to a new job location, business losses, student loan interest, and IRA and Keogh deductions are deducted from gross income even if itemized deductions are not claimed; *see Chapter 12.*

Deferred compensation. A portion of earnings withheld by an employer or put into a retirement plan for distribution to the employee at a later date. If certain legal requirements are met, the deferred amount is not taxable until actually paid, for example, after retirement; *see 2.7.*

Deficiency. The excess of the tax assessed by the IRS over the amount reported on your return; *see 48.8.*

Defined benefit plan. A retirement plan that pays fixed benefits based on actuarial projections; *see 41.2.*

Defined contribution plan. A retirement plan that pays benefits based on contributions to individual accounts, plus accumulated earnings. Contributions are generally based on a percentage of salary or earned income; *see 41.2.*

Dependent. A relative or household member for whom an exemption may be claimed; *see Chapter 21.*

Depletion. Deduction claimed for the use of mineral resources; *see 9.15.*

Depreciable property. A business or income-producing asset with a useful life exceeding one year; *see 42.1.*

Depreciation. Writing off the cost of depreciable property over a period of years, usually its class life or recovery period specified in the tax law; *see 42.4.*

Depreciation recapture. An amount of gain on the sale of certain depreciable property that is treated as ordinary income in the case of personal property. Recapture is computed on Form 4797; *see 44.1.* For recapture on the sale of realty, *see 44.2.*

Disaster losses. Casualty losses such as from a storm, in areas declared by the President to warrant federal assistance. An election may be made to deduct the loss in the year before the loss or the year of the loss; *see 18.3.*

Dividend. A distribution made by a corporation to its shareholders generally of company earnings or surplus. Most dividends are taxable but exceptions are explained in *Chapter 4.*

E

Earned income. Compensation for performing personal services. You must have earned income for a deductible IRA, *see 8.2*, or to claim the earned income credit, *see 25.10.*

Earned income credit. A credit allowed to taxpayers with earned income or adjusted gross income (AGI) below certain thresholds; *see 25.10.*

Education IRA. See Coverdell Education Savings Account and *33.11–33.12.*

Electronic Federal Tax Payment System (EFTPS). An online and phone tax payment system available 24 hours a day. For enrollment information, call 1-800-555-4477, or go to www.eftps.gov.

Estimated tax. Advance payment of current tax liability based either on wage withholdings or installment payments of your estimated tax liability. To avoid penalties, you generally must pay to the IRS either 90% of your final tax liability, or either 100% or 110% of the prior year's tax liability, depending on your adjusted gross income; *see Chapter 27.*

Exemption. A fixed deduction allowed to every taxpayer, except those who may be claimed as a dependent by another person. Extra exemption deductions are allowed for a spouse on a joint return and for each qualifying dependent. A deduction of $3,650 is allowed for each exemption claimed on 2010 returns: *see Chapter 21.*

F

Fair market value. What a willing buyer would pay to a willing seller when neither is under any compulsion to buy or sell.

Fiduciary. A person or corporation such as a trustee, executor, or guardian who manages property for another person.

First-year expensing (or Section 179 deduction). A deduction of the cost of business equipment in the year placed in service; *see 42.3* for limitations.

Fiscal year. A 12-month period ending on the last day of any month other than December. Partnerships, S corporations, and personal service corporations are limited in their choice of fiscal years and face special restrictions.

Flexible spending arrangement. A salary reduction plan that allows employees to pay for enhanced medical coverage or dependent care expenses on a tax-free basis; *see 3.16.*

Foreign earned income exclusion. In 2009, up to $91,400 of foreign earned income is exempt from tax if a foreign residence or physical presence test is met; *see 36.1–36.2.*

Foreign tax credit. A credit for income taxes paid to a foreign country or U.S. possession; *see 36.14.*

401(k) plan. A deferred pay plan, authorized by Section 401(k) of the Internal Revenue Code, under which a percentage of an employee's salary is withheld and placed in a savings account or the company's profit-sharing plan. Income accumulates on the deferred amount until withdrawn by the employee at age 59½ or when the employee retires or leaves the company; *see 7.17.*

G

Gift tax. Gifts in excess of an $13,000-per-donee annual exclusion are subject to gift tax, but the tax may be offset by a gift tax credit; *see 39.2.*

Grantor trust rules. Tax rules that tax the grantor of a trust on the trust income; *see 39.6.*

Gross income. The total amount of income received from all sources before exclusions and deductions.

Gross receipts. Total business receipts reported on Schedule C or Schedule C-EZ before deducting adjustments for returns and allowances and cost of goods sold; *see 40.6.*

Group-term life insurance. Employees are not taxed on up to $50,000 of group-term coverage; *see 3.4.*

H

Head of household. Generally, an unmarried person who maintains a household for dependents and is allowed to compute his or her tax based on head of household rates, which are more favorable than single person rates; *see 1.12.*

Health reimbursement arrangement (HRA). Employer established account that provides tax-free reimbursements to employees for deductibles and other expenses that could be taken as itemized deductions; *see 3.3.*

Health savings account. For calendar year 2009, taxpayers covered by an HDHP may contribute up to $3,000 ($5,950 for family coverage)plus $1,000 extra if age 55 or older;; *see 3.2* and *41.11.*

High deductible health plan (HDHP). For 2010, a high deductible health plan is a health plan with an annual deductible that is not less than $1,200 for self-only coverage or $2,400 for family coverage, and with annual out-of-pocket expenses that do not exceed $5,950 or $11,900, respectively.

Hobby loss. Hobby expenses are deductible only up to income from the activity; loss deductions are not allowed; *see 40.10.*

Holding period. The length of time that an asset is owned and that generally determines long- or short-term capital gain treatment; *see 5.3* and *5.9–5.12.*

Home equity debt. Debt secured by a principal residence or second home to the extent of the excess of fair market value over acquisition debt. An interest deduction is generally allowed for home equity debt up to $100,000 ($50,000 if married filing separately); *see 15.3.*

I

Imputed interest. Interest deemed earned on seller-financed sales or low-interest loans, where the parties' stated interest rate is below the applicable IRS federal rate; *see 4.31* and *4.32.*

Incentive stock option. Option meeting tax law tests that defers tax on the option transaction until the obtained stock is sold; *see 2.16.*

Inclusion amount for leased cars. Based on an IRS table, an amount that reduces a business deduction taken for payments on an auto leased for a minimum of 30 days; *see 43.12.*

Income in respect of a decedent. Income earned by a person before death but taxable to an estate or heir who receives it; *see 1.14* and *11.16.*

Independent contractor. One who controls his or her own work and reports as a self-employed person; *see* Chapters 40 and 45.

Individual retirement account (IRA). A retirement account to which up to $5,000 (or $6,000 if you are 50 or over) may be contributed for 2010, but deductions for the contribution are restricted if you are covered by a company retirement plan. Earnings accumulate tax free; *see Chapter 8.*

Installment sale. A sale of property that allows for tax deferment if at least one payment is received after the end of the tax year in which the sale occurs. The installment method does not apply to year-end sales of publicly traded securities. Dealers may not use the installment method. Investors with very large installment balances could face a special tax; *see 5.21.*

Intangible assets. Intangible assets that come within Section 197, such as goodwill, are amortizable over a 15-year period; *see 42.18.*

Inter vivos or lifetime trust. A trust created during the lifetime of the person who created the trust. If irrevocable, income on the trust principal is generally shifted to the trust beneficiaries; *see 39.6.*

Investment in the contract. The total cost investment in an annuity. When annuity payments are made, the portion allocable to the cost investment is tax free; *see 7.23* and *7.28.*

Investment interest. Interest on debt used to carry investments, but not including interest expense from a passive activity. Deductions are limited to net investment income; *see 15.10.*

Involuntary conversion. Forced disposition of property due to condemnation, theft, or casualty. Tax on gain from involuntary conversions may be deferred if replacement property is purchased; *see 18.19*.

Itemized deductions. Items, such as interest, state and local income and sales taxes, charitable contributions, and medical deductions, claimed on Schedule A of Form 1040. Itemized deductions are subtracted from adjusted gross income to arrive at taxable income; *see Chapter 13*.

J

Joint return. A return filed by a married couple reporting their combined income and deductions. Joint return status provides tax savings to many couples; *see 1.4*.

Joint tenants. Ownership of property by two persons. When one dies, the decedent's interest passes to the survivor; *see 5.18*.

K

Keogh plan. Retirement plan set up by a self-employed person, providing tax-deductible contributions, tax-free income accumulations until withdrawal, and favorable averaging for qualifying lump-sum distributions; *see Chapter 41*.

Kiddie tax. The tax on the investment income in excess of an anuual floor ($1,900 for 2010) of a child under age 18, and many children age 18–23. The tax is based on the parents' marginal tax rate and computed on Form 8615; *see 24.2*.

L

Legally separated. A husband and wife who are required to live apart from each other by the terms of a decree of separate maintenance. Payments under the decree are deductible by the payor and taxable to the payee as alimony; *see 37.2*.

Like-kind exchange. An exchange of similar assets used in a business or held for investment on which gain may be deferred; *see 6.1*.

Lump-sum distribution. Payments within one tax year of the entire amount due to a participant in a qualified retirement plan. Qualifying lump sums may be directly rolled over tax free, or, in some cases, are eligible for current tax under a favorable averaging method; *see 7.2*.

M

Marital deduction. An estate tax and gift tax deduction for assets passing to a spouse. It allows estate and gift transfers completely free of tax; *see 39.12*.

Market discount. The difference between face value of a bond and lower market price, attributable to rising interest rates. On a sale, gain on the bond is generally taxed as ordinary income to the extent of the discount; *see 4.20*.

Material participation tests. Rules for determining whether a person is active in a business activity for passive activity rule purposes. Unless the tests are met, passive loss limits apply; *see 10.6*.

Miscellaneous itemized deductions. Generally, itemized deductions for job and investment expenses subject to a 2% of adjusted gross income floor; *see Chapter 19*.

Modified ACRS (MACRS). Depreciation methods applied to assets placed in service after 1986.

Modified adjusted gross income (MAGI). This is generally adjusted gross income increased by certain items such as tax-free foreign earned income. MAGI usually is used to determine phaseouts of certain deductions and credits.

Mortgage interest. Fully deductible interest on up to two residences if acquisition debt secured by a home is $1 million or less, and home equity debt is $100,000 or less; *see 15.1*.

N

Net operating loss. A business loss that exceeds current income may be carried back against income of prior years and carried forward as a deduction from future income until eliminated. The carryback and carryforward periods are discussed in *40.18–40.22*.

Nonperiodic distributions. A 20% withholding rule applies to nonperiodic distributions, such as lump-sum distributions, paid directly to employees from an employer plan; *see 7.8* and *26.10*.

Nonrecourse financing. Debt on which a person is not personally liable. In case of nonpayment, the creditor must foreclose on property securing the debt. At-risk rules generally bar losses where there is nonrecourse financing, but an exception applies to certain nonrecourse financing for real estate; *see 10.18*.

O

Ordinary and necessary. A statutory requirement for the deductibility of a business expense.

Ordinary income. Income other than capital gains.

Ordinary loss. A loss other than a capital loss.

Original issue discount (OID). The difference between the face value of a bond and its original issue price. OID is reported on an annual basis as interest income; *see 4.19*.

P

Partnership. An unincorporated business or income-producing entity organized by two or more persons. A partnership is not subject to tax but passes through to the partners all income, deductions, and credits, according to the terms of the partnership agreement; *see 11.9–11.13*.

Passive activity loss rules. Rules that limit the deduction of losses from passive activities to income from other passive activities. Passive activities include investment rental operations or businesses in which you do not materially participate; *see 10.1*.

Patronage dividend. A taxable distribution made by a cooperative to its members or patrons.

Percentage depletion. A deduction method that applies a fixed percentage to the gross income generated by mineral property; *see 9.15*.

Personal interest. Tax term for interest on personal loans and consumer purchases. Such interest is not deductible.

Placed in service. The time when a depreciable asset is ready to be used. The date fixes the beginning of the depreciation period.

Points. Charges to the homeowner at the time of the loan. A point is equal to 1 percent. Depending on the type of loan, points may be currently deductible or amortized over the life of the loan; *see 15.8*.

Premature distributions. Withdrawals before age 59½ from qualified retirement plans are subject to penalties unless specific exceptions are met; *see 7.15* and *8.12*.

Principal residence. On a sale of a principal residence, you may avoid tax under the rules explained in *Chapter 29*.

Private letter ruling. A written determination issued to a taxpayer by the IRS that interprets and applies the tax laws to the taxpayer's specific set of facts. A letter ruling advises the taxpayer regarding the tax treatment that can be expected from the IRS in the circumstances specified by the ruling. It may not be used or cited as precedent by another taxpayer.

Probate estate. Property held in a decedent's name passing by will; *see* 39.7.

Profit-sharing plan. A defined contribution plan under which the amount contributed to the employees' accounts is based on a percentage of the employer's profits; *see* 8.5 and 41.2.

Provisional income. If your provisional income exceeds a base amount, part of your Social Security benefits may be subject to tax. To figure provisional income, *see* 34.3.

Q

Qualified charitable organization. A nonprofit philanthropic organization that is approved by the U.S. Treasury to receive charitable contribution deductions; *see* 14.1.

Qualified dividends. Dividends that are taxed at the long-term capital gain rate; *see* 4.2.

Qualified domestic relations order (QDRO). A specialized domestic relations court order that conforms to IRS regulations and provides instructions to pension plan administrators and IRA custodians as to how to pay benefits to a divorced spouse; *see* 7.12 and 8.11.

Qualified plan. A retirement plan that meets tax law tests and allows for tax deferment and tax-free accumulation of income until benefits are withdrawn. Pension, profit-sharing, stock bonus, employee stock ownership, and Keogh plans and IRAs may be qualified plans; *see* Chapters 7, 8, and 41.

Qualified tuition program (QTP). A state-sponsored college savings plan or prepayment plan, or a prepayment plan established by a private college; *see* 33.5.

Qualifying widow or widower. A filing status entitling the taxpayer with dependents to use joint tax rates for up to two tax years after the death of a spouse; *see* 1.11.

R

Real estate investment trust (REIT). An entity that invests primarily in real estate and mortgages and passes through income to investors; *see* 31.1.

Real estate professional. An individual who, because of his or her real estate activity, qualifies to deduct rental losses from nonpassive income; *see* 10.3.

Real property. Land and the buildings on land. Buildings are depreciable; *see* 42.13 and 42.16.

Recognized gain or loss. The amount of gain or loss to be reported on a tax return. Gain may not be recognized on certain exchanges of property; *see* 6.1.

Recovery property. Tangible depreciable property placed in service after 1980 and before 1987 and depreciable under ACRS; *see* 42.11 and 42.16.

Refundable tax credit. A credit that entitles you to a refund even if you owe no tax for the year.

Required Minimum Distributions (RMDs). Distributions that must be taken annually to avoid a 50% IRS penalty by a traditional IRA account holder starting with the year age 70½ is reached. For qualified plan participants the starting date may be delayed for employees working beyond age 70½. Minimum distribution rules also apply to beneficiaries of qualified plans, traditional IRAs, and Roth IRAs. *See* 7.13–7.14, 8.13–8.14, and 8.24.

Residence interest. Term for deductible mortgage interest on a principal residence and a second home; *see* 15.1–15.2.

Residential rental property. Real property in which 80% or more of the gross income is from dwelling units. Under MACRS, depreciation is claimed over 27.5 years under the straight-line method; *see* 42.13.

Retirement savers credit. Eligible taxpayers may claim a tax credit for 10%, 20%, or 50% of up to $2,000 of retirement plan contributions; *see* 25.16.

Return of capital. A distribution of your investment that is not subject to tax unless the distribution exceeds your investment; *see* 4.11.

Revenue ruling. A revenue ruling is the Commissioner's "official interpretation of the interpretation of the law" and generally is binding on revenue agents and other IRS officials. Taxpayers generally may rely on published revenue rulings in determining the tax treatment of their own transactions that arise out of similar facts and circumstances.

Revocable trust. A trust that may be changed or terminated by its creator or another person. Such trusts do not provide an income tax savings to the creator; *see* 39.6.

Rollover. A tax-free reinvestment of a distribution from a qualified retirement plan into an IRA or other qualified plan within 60 days; *see* 7.3, 7.8, and 8.10.

Roth IRA. A nondeductible contributory IRA that allows for tax-free accumulation of income. Qualifying distributions are completely tax free. *See* 8.19–8.24.

S

Salvage value. The estimated value of an asset at the end of its useful life. Salvage value is ignored by ACRS and MACRS rules.

S corporation. A corporation that elects S status in order to receive tax treatment similar to that of a partnership; *see* Chapter 11.

Section 179 deduction (or First-year expensing). A deduction allowed for investments in depreciable business equipment in the year the property is placed in service; *see* 42.3 for limitations.

Section 457 plan. Deferred compensation plan set up by a state or local government, or tax-exempt organization, which allows tax-free deferrals of salary; *see* 7.22.

Section 1231 property. Depreciable property used in a trade or business and held for more than a year. All Section 1231 gains and losses are netted; a net gain is treated as capital gain, a net loss as an ordinary loss; *see* 44.8.

Self-employed person. An individual who operates a business or profession as a proprietor or independent contractor and reports self-employment income on Schedule C; *see* Chapters 40 and 45.

Self-employment tax. Tax paid by self-employed persons to finance Social Security coverage. In 2010, there are two rates. A 12.4% rate applies to a taxable earnings base of 106,800 or less and a 2.9% rate applies to all net earnings; *see* Chapter 45.

Separate return. Return filed by a married person who does not file a joint return. Filing separately may save taxes where each spouse has separate deductions, but certain tax benefits require a joint return; *see* 1.3.

Short sale. Sale of borrowed securities made to freeze a paper profit or to gain from a declining market; *see* 30.5.

Short tax year. A tax year of less than 12 months. May occur with the startup of a business or change in accounting method.

Short-term capital gain or loss. Gain or loss on the sale or exchange of a capital asset held one year or less; *see 5.1, 5.2,* and *5.10*.

Simplified employee plan (SEP). IRA-type plan set up by an employer, rather than the employee. Salary-reduction contributions may be allowed to plans of small employers set up before 1997; *see 8.15–8.16*.

Standard deduction. A fixed deduction allowed to taxpayers who do not itemize deductions, based on filing status, plus certain additional amounts for qualifying individuals; *see 13.1*.

Standard mileage rate. A fixed rate allowed by the IRS for business auto expenses in place of deducting actual expenses; *see 43.1*.

Statutory employees. Certain employees, such as full-time life insurance salespersons, who may report income and deductions on Schedule C, rather than on Schedule A as miscellaneous itemized deductions; *see 40.6*.

Stock dividend. A distribution of additional shares of a corporation's stock to its shareholders; *see 4.6*.

Stock option. A right to buy stock at a fixed price.

Straddle. Taking an offsetting investment position to reduce the risk of loss in a similar investment; *see 30.9*.

Straight-line method. A method of depreciating the cost of a depreciable asset on a pro rata basis over its cost recovery period; *see 42.9, 42.12*.

T

Tangible personal property. Movable property, such as desks, computers, machinery, and autos, depreciable over a five-year or seven-year period; *see 42.4*.

Taxable income. Net income after claiming all deductions from gross income and adjusted gross income, such as IRA deductions, itemized deductions, or the standard deduction, and personal exemptions; *see 22.1*.

Tax attributes. When debts are cancelled in bankruptcy cases, the cancelled amount is excluded from gross income. Tax attributes are certain losses, credits, and property basis that must be reduced to the extent of the exclusion; *see 11.8*.

Tax deferral. Shifting income to a later year, such as where you defer taxable interest to the following year by purchasing a T-bill or savings certificate maturing after the end of the current year; *see Chapter 4*. Investments in qualified retirement plans provide tax deferral (*Chapters 7, 8,* and *41*).

Tax home. The area of your principal place of business or employment. You must be away from your tax home on a business trip to deduct travel expenses; *see 20.6–20.9*.

Tax identification number. For an individual, his or her Social Security number; for businesses, fiduciaries, and other non-individual taxpayers, the employer identification number.

Tax preference items. Items that may subject a taxpayer to the alternative minimum tax (AMT); *see 23.3*.

Tax-sheltered annuity. A type of retirement annuity offered to employees of charitable organizations and educational systems, generally funded by employee salary-reduction contributions; *see 7.20*.

Tax year. A period (generally 12 months) for reporting income and expenses; *see 40.4*.

Tenancy by the entireties. A joint tenancy in real property in the name of both husband and wife. On the death of one tenant, the survivor receives entire interest.

Tenants in common. Two or more persons who have undivided ownership rights in property. Upon death of a tenant, his or her share passes to his or her estate, rather than to the surviving tenants.

Testamentary trust. A trust established under a will.

Trust. An arrangement under which one person transfers legal ownership of assets to another person or corporation (the trustee) for the benefit of one or more third persons (beneficiaries).

U

Unrecaptured Section 1250 gain. Long-term gain realized on the sale of depreciable realty attributed to depreciation deductions and subject to a 25% capital gain rate; *see 5.3* and *44.2*.

Useful life. For property not depreciated under ACRS or MACRS, the estimate of time in which a depreciable asset will be used.

W

Wash sales. Sales on which losses are disallowed because you recover your market position within a 61-day period; *see 30.6*.

Withholding. An amount taken from income as a prepayment of an individual's tax liability for the year. In the case of wages, the employer withholds part of every wage payment. Backup withholding from dividend or interest income is required if you do not provide the payer with a correct taxpayer identification number. Withholding on pensions and IRAs is automatic unless you elect to waive withholding; *see Chapter 26*.

Note: References are to section numbers in Parts 1–8, followed by page numbers in boldface.

A

D

E

G

H

I

J

K

L

M

N

O

Q

R

S

T

U